D1156346

Every Day of the Civil War

Every Day of the Civil War

A Chronological Encyclopedia

BUD HANNINGS

McFarland & Company, Inc., Publishers

Jefferson, North Carolina, and London

LIBRARY OF CONGRESS CATALOGUING-IN-PUBLICATION DATA

Hannings, Bud.
Every day of the Civil War : a chronologial encyclopedia / Bud Hannings.
p.   cm.
Includes bibliographical references and index.

ISBN 978-0-7864-4464-9
illustrated case binding: 50# alkaline paper ∞

1. United States — History — Civil War, 1861–1865 — Chronology.
2. United States — History — Civil War, 1861–1865 — Encyclopedias.
I. Title.
E468.3.H35   2010
973.7 — dc22   2010016515

British Library cataloguing data are available

On the cover: Don Troiani, *Medal of Honor.*
Oil on canvas, 24½" × 30¾".

Manufactured in the United States of America

*McFarland & Company, Inc., Publishers
Box 611, Jefferson, North Carolina 28640
www.mcfarlandpub.com*

Contents

Preface

This book provides a day-by-day account of the American Civil War on land and at sea, with emphasis on minor skirmishes and individual units as well as major engagements. However, the scope and depth of the conflict is so immense that the work is not all-inclusive, due to the thousands of skirmishes on the ground and the innumerable encounters and clashes on the rivers and high seas, which include the exchanges between ground troops and the naval forces that patrolled the bays, rivers, sounds and creeks.

The book focuses on individuals as well as the battles, and it attempts to present the atmosphere of the conflict without embellishment or exaggeration in favor of either side. It is written in the present tense to keep a reader in closer touch with the arduous campaigns and the daily struggles of the combatants who tenaciously either defended their positions or attacked their objectives. It also chronicles the general officers, from the faint of heart to the bold and daring during their triumphant victories and their devastating defeats. Although the book provides a daily chronicle of the combat, it is written in narrative form to give the reader some continuity as they move from skirmish to skirmish.

The book also details the life span of about 600 vessels, both Union and Confederate, documenting, when available, the time of commissioning, various actions and engagements and time of decommissioning. It also documents, when possible, where vessels were acquired, whether by purchase or capture. And it documents the impetuous blockade runners who are captured or destroyed, along with the Confederate raiders that ravage U.S. shipping. The blockade runners throughout the war were relentless in their attempts to outwit the blockaders and in turn, the blockading squadrons maintained a permanent vigil on the Confederate-held ports to cripple the Confederate supply lines on the sea.

In addition, the book follows the general officers of both sides, documenting their careers, when information is available.

Military actions take a big part in the text; however, this work does not purport to focus on the political activity, other than primary decisions made by governments of the United States or the Confederate States of America.

Several reliable resources provided the basis for this work, including the Marine Corps Historical Division, the United States Naval Historical Division, the United States Army Historical Center, West Point, the Naval Academy and multiple volumes of the *Official Records of the War of the Rebellion.* Other primary sources included the Department of Interior (National Parks) and the National Archives, along with nineteenth century works and biographies, which are listed in the bibliography. In addition, visits to various battle sites and other prominent Civil War locations, primarily east of the Mississippi River, added to the depth of this work by enabling me to get a firsthand observation of the terrain and an opportunity to speak with onsite historians.

Because of the great amount of official factual records regarding the conflict, there was no great difficulty in compiling the information; however, at times, trying to distinguish vessels with identical names became a challenge. That obstacle was overcome thanks to the official histories of the ships made available by the United States Navy Historical Center and other reliable sources (listed in the bibliography). In addition, Internet searches through Comcast, Google and Yahoo provided access to many government records, regimental histories and other nineteenth century works.

I also attempted to include information on Medal of Honor awards with the corresponding action. When possible, the individual is named on the date and with the action as it occurred. To make the effort more comprehensive, an appendix is included that names each recipient and the date of the action, so a reader can go to the specific date to read about the action. Nonetheless, at times, details of the action are scant, making it impossible to detail precisely why the Medal of Honor was awarded.

At the outbreak of the war, while army and navy officers were choosing sides, the identical dilemma occurred in the United States Marine Corps. The Corps was essentially heavily splintered, as southerners hurried to join the Confederacy. Marines who remained loyal to the Union continued to serve and there is some documentation of their activity; however, without the assistance of the Marine Corps Historical Division, accurate details of their Civil War activity would have been absent from this work.

Essentially, the book provides a researcher, student of history or a general reader with a wide view of the conflict, in which every shot fired by an American was intended to kill another American. From the early seizure of U.S. government property during the latter part of 1860 until the final surrender of the Confederates during 1865, this book follows the individual units and exhibits the agony as well as the glory of the troops, regardless of the color of their uniform or the colors atop a mast.

Some say that only the victors write history; however, after the war, many on both sides penned works, and if one evaluates the more serious writings, it can be concluded that the various descriptions are in line with one another. Animosity began to fade away as the North and South began anew. By the outbreak of the Spanish-American War, a few of the former Confederate generals, those still able, fought as U.S. generals. General Robert E. Lee is known to have once said: "Give me Union infantry and Confederate cavalry and I'll lick anyone in the world."

General Lee's nemesis, General Ulysses S. Grant, later became president of the United States. General Lee retired his military uniform and became the president of Washington College in Lexington, Virginia (later named Washington and Lee University). General Lee kept a photograph of Pope Pius IX in his office out of apparent respect for the only foreign leader (Vatican) to acknowledge the Confederate States of America. Many years later, President Dwight D. Eisenhower kept a photograph of General Robert E. Lee in his office.

After the 1950s, the mutual respect of the opposing sides began to fade away and the flag of the Confederacy lost its luster; however, regardless of ongoing debates, it remains irrefutable that the legacy of both the Union and Confederate troops' actions on the battlefield had been honorable, heroic, inexhaustible and loyal to their respective causes.

THE CHRONOLOGY

1850

In Florida, Fort Harvie in Monroe County is fortified and greatly expanded to deal with the re-initiation of hostilities with the Seminoles. Forts in the region usually vary in size, but after renovations and expansion, the site is a complex containing about fifty structures. The fort is renamed in honor of Colonel (later brigadier general) Abraham C. Myers, who graduated from West Point during 1834. Myers never visited the fort. He became the son-in-law of General David E. Twiggs, who later surrenders all U.S. forces under him in Texas to the Confederates when the Civil War breaks out. His son-in-law, Colonel Myers, the great-grandson of Charleston's first rabbi, Moses Cohen, also chooses to serve with the Confederates. Myers, the quartermaster general at New Orleans, surrenders the supply station at New Orleans and resigns the service to fight with his fellow South Carolinians.

In Kansas, Fort Atkinson is established by Lt. Colonel Edwin Vose Sumner as another fort along the Santa Fe Trail, but unlike Forts Leavenworth and Marcy, it is in Indian Territory. Forts Leavenworth and Marcy, established during 1827 and 1846 respectively, are posted at opposite ends of the trail, the former along the Missouri River and the latter in New Mexico. Fort Atkinson, in the vicinity of Dodge City, causes Fort Mann, less than eight miles away, to become valueless. It is abandoned. Fort Leavenworth remains active until 1854. During 1855, Lt. Colonel Sumner is promoted to colonel and receives command of the 1st Cavalry. During the following year, Sumner becomes commanding officer of Fort Leavenworth, Kansas. Also, Fort Atkinson had been known by other names: Camp 57, Fort Sumner and Fort Sod.

January Government leaders engage in debate on the slavery issue, which later leads to legislation known as the Compromise of 1850. The United States is bulging with controversy over the slavery issue, with sentiments running feverishly high on both sides of the issue. At stake is the issue of the preservation of the Union. During heated Senate discussions, Senator Henry Clay of Kentucky presents a strong case for compromise intended to satisfy the states in the South, which prefer slavery at any cost, and the northern states, which wish to outlaw slavery period. Clay's speech calls for California to be admitted to the Union as a free state. He does not call for the abolition of slavery, merely the adoption of a more clearly defined fugitive slave law. Clay also presents suggestions for adjusting the Texas boundary and for the United States to assume the debts of Texas. Senator Clay is also attempting to have government established in the territories of New Mexico and Utah, but his speech makes no reference to the slavery issue concerning the two territories. Senator Clay's oratory prompts opposition from both sides of the issue, with debate occurring through May, when a Senate committee offers two bills of compromise. One is the Omnibus Bill with the Territories of New Mexico and Utah; the other forbids slave trade in the District of Columbia. Discussion continues through the summer, and finally, in early September, Congress reaches some conclusions based on the original resolutions of Senator Henry Clay, and a formal compromise is reached during September.

May   In Iowa, a contingent of the U.S. 6th Infantry Regiment led by Major Samuel Woods that had departed Fort Snelling, Minnesota, arrives aboard a steamboat, the *Highland Mary*, at Muscatine. Company E had been ordered to travel to Iowa and establish a fort and to support an operation designed to relocate the Mesquakie Indians. By November of this year, the U.S. Army establishes Fort Clarke near the Des Moines River at present-day Fort Dodge in Webster County.

During the following year, the fort's construction is completed and it is renamed Fort Dodge. Fort Dodge remains active during a turbulent period with Indians, and afterwards, during 1853, it is deactivated. At that time, the troops garrisoned there depart for Fort Ridgely, Minnesota. The abandoned fort is purchased by William Williams. One of the officers in charge of the construction is Major Lewis A. Armistead of Virginia. Armistead had attended West Point but did not graduate with the class of 1837. Nevertheless, he had served in the Mexican War as a lieutenant with the brevet of major. Armistead's connecting threads to the history of the U.S. stretch from Virginia to Maryland and beyond to Iowa and Pennsylvania. His uncle, Major Armistead, had commanded Fort McHenry during the War of 1812.

Armistead will resign from the U.S. Army during 1861 and join the Confederates. As a brigadier general he leads his brigade during Pickett's Charge at Gettysburg (July 1863).

June 3–12   In the South, government representatives from the Southern states meet in Nashville, Tennessee, to discuss state's rights and slavery. Secession is a topic, but moderate minds prevent any action on it.

July 9 (Tuesday) President Zachary Taylor, in office only slightly more than one and one-half years, succumbs. Vice President Millard Fillmore becomes the thirteenth president. He takes the oath of office the following day.

September After a brief period of mourning due to President Zachary Taylor's death, government begins to tackle the problems of the country, especially those regarding the U.S. territories and the issue of slavery. In early September, Congress makes New Mexico and Utah into U.S. territories.

September 9 (Monday) California is admitted to the union as the 31st state.

September 12 (Thursday) Congress passes the Fugitive Slave Act.

September 28 (Saturday) The U.S. Congress enacts legislation forbidding flogging (whipping) in the United States Navy.

October The USS *Saranac* is commissioned. The *Saranac* is a side-wheel steamer constructed at the navy yard in Kittery, Maine, and initially assigned duty on the Atlantic coast, but later it serves in the South Atlantic and the Mediterranean. Following an overhaul in Philadelphia during 1857, the *Saranac* is assigned to the Pacific Squadron. Although it remains in service during the Civil War, it does not participate directly in the States, but patrols to protect U.S. shipping in the Pacific. After the war it remains in service until 18 June 1875, when it is wrecked in the vicinity of Vancouver, British Columbia.

1853

March 4 (Friday) **In Washington, D.C.,** Franklin Pierce is inaugurated as fourteenth president of the United States.

In Missouri, Sterling Price becomes governor. Price, a veteran of the Mexican War who served as colonel of the 2nd Missouri Infantry, had also been a brigadier general of volunteers (1847) while acting as military governor of New Mexico. Price, who serves as governor until 1857, later joins the Confederacy; however, Missouri remains loyal to the Union.

May President Franklin Pierce, acting on the recommendation of Jefferson Davis, secretary of war, nominates James Gadsden as minister to Mexico. After confirmation he proceeds to Mexico City and during December successfully concludes a treaty which acquires new territory for the United States.

1854

May 26 (Friday) The territories of Kansas and Nebraska are established with the option of choosing or not choosing slavery. This will do much to continue the ongoing debate between northern and southern leaders. The establishment of these two territories by congressional action in essence repeals the Missouri Compromise Act of 1850.

May 30 (Tuesday) The Kansas-Nebraska Act is passed by Congress. It marks the Kansas Territory as a place for settlers and it affords the settlers the opportunity to decide by vote on whether Kansas will enter the union as a free state or a slave state. By summer, anti-slavery proponents establish a settlement in Kansas at Lawrence, initially known as Wakarusa. During October, the territorial governor, Andrew H. Reeder, arrives in Kansas. The area erupts in violence as pro-slavers and anti-slavers clash, with the pros supported by sympathizers in nearby Missouri.

1855

January 18 (Thursday) A contingent of U.S. dragoons (cavalry) led by Lt. Henry B. Davidson (West Point, 1853) based at Albuquerque, engages a band of Apaches along the Penasco River in New Mexico. Davidson will subsequently be transferred to Washington State, and by the following year, again he will be with the cavalry when it encounters more hostility from other Indians. He remains with the cavalry until he resigns his commission to join the Confederacy.

February The Brown brothers (sons of John Brown, the abolitionist) establish themselves in an area near Pottawatomie Creek and during autumn they are joined in Kansas by their father, who arrives from New York. Meanwhile, the pro-slavery forces and the anti-slavery forces continue to vie for domination in Kansas. By March, through the aid of Missourians in Kansas who are not eligible to vote, a legislature is formed and becomes known as the pro-slavery "Bogus Legislature."

March The First U.S. Cavalry Regiment is authorized by Congress through the efforts of Jefferson Davis. It is called the Second Cavalry and known as "Jeff Davis' Own." This detachment is formed for duty in Texas.

March 3 (Saturday) Camels arrive in the United States from Egypt for use in the deserts of the Southwest. This is done on the advice of secretary of war Jefferson Davis. The experiment does fairly well, but the idea does not get accepted for any permanent mode of transportation since the camels terrify the horses.

March 19 (Monday) **In New Mexico Territory,** the U.S. 8th Infantry Regiment, commanded by Colonel John Garland, establishes Fort Stanton near the Rio Bonito River at present-day Stanton, New Mexico. The fort is named during March in honor of Captain Henry W. Stanton, 1st U.S. Dragoons, killed by Apaches near the area of the post. It remains operational until it is deactivated during 1896. However, there are some interruptions including 1861, when the garrison abandons the fort to the Confederates. A plan by the troops to torch the fort fails when a rainstorm extinguishes the flames. Upon the departure of Fort Stanton, the worthwhile items left behind are procured by the settlers as well as some Indians and Mexicans. The fort is re-occupied by the Union during 1862.

March 30 (Friday) **In Kansas Territory,** elections in the new territory are marred when legions of armed men from Missouri cross into Kansas to vote for candidates who favor slavery. These Border Ruffians, as they are called, by casting their ballots in numbers more than 2,000, secure a pro-slavery legislature. The election results stand after acknowledgment by the federal governor of the territory, who accepts the results rather than face the possibility of increased violence between the Ruffians and the Free Staters.

July 28 (Sunday) The USS *Constellation II* is commissioned at the Norfolk Navy Yard. Shortly thereafter, it embarks for the Mediterranean and joins the squadron. It returns to the U.S. in June 1858 and is decommissioned at Boston on 13 August. Later, during June 1859, the vessel is recommissioned and becomes the flagship of the African Squadron.

December 7 (Friday) **In Kansas Territory,** pro-slavers from Missouri known as Border Ruffians and led by David Atchison lay siege upon Lawrence.

1856

February 11 (Monday)   In Kansas Territory, fighting between the Free Staters and the Border Ruffians is intensifying, prompting President Franklin Pierce to issue a stern warning to cease and desist all hostilities.

May 21 (Wednesday)   POTTAWATOMIE CREEK MASSACRE. Lawrence, Kansas Territory, is attacked by pro-slavers. Some damage is done, including the destruction of two newspapers that support Kansas as a free state. Within several days, a band under John Brown, the abolitionist, attacks and murders pro-slavers in the vicinity of Pottawatomie Creek. The incident takes the lives of five men.

June 2 (Monday)   BATTLE OF BLACK JACK Two groups of opposing factions, one pro-slavery (a contingent of Shannon's Sharpshooters) under Captain Pate and the other anti-slavery, under John Brown, engage each other outside of Lawrence near Palmyra in the southeastern sector of Douglas County, Kansas Territory. It is the first major clash between the two sides. Both sides sustain wounded, but the pro-slavers are defeated by John Brown's followers. From this encounter and other violent clashes that follow, Kansas becomes known in this period as "Bleeding Kansas." The territory is essentially lawless, with both sides participating in brutality and murder.

In the meantime, while a pro-slavery legislature is operating at Lecompton, another competing legislature (Free State) will convene during July at Topeka to raise the stakes. The turbulence continues and another anti-slavery leader, James Lane, often clashes with the pro-slavers. Lane actually establishes a route (Lane Trail) by which settlers can move into Kansas without passing through Missouri. In addition, he leads the anti-slave forces known as the "Jayhawkers."

August 10 (Sunday)   In Kansas Territory, pro-slavers and anti-slavers clash in the vicinity of Fort Franklin.

August 15 (Friday)   In Kansas Territory, abolitionists under John Brown engage pro-slavers near Fort Saunders, a fortification established by pro-slavers.

August 16 (Saturday)   In Kansas Territory, clashes occur between anti-slavers and pro-slavers near Fort Titus.

August 24–26   THE BATTLE OF OSAWATOMIE takes place when John Brown's followers engage pro-slavers near the Marais des Cygnes in Kansas Territory. Frederick Brown, a son of John Brown, is killed during the fighting.

September   In Kansas Territory, a band of Border Ruffians raid an area known as Grasshopper Falls (Valley Falls) in the vicinity of the town of Dunavant in Jefferson County. After this attack, the opposing side, a group of Jayhawkers under James Lane, attacks a contingent of the Ruffians near Hickory Point, also in Jefferson County.

September 20 (Saturday)   The sloop USS St. Mary's and the razee USS Independence, while operating in Central America off Panama, order contingents of Marines and sailors ashore to protect American citizens and their possessions.

October 23 (Thursday)   During a religious war in China, American citizens become endangered in Canton. A contingent of Marines and sailors from the USS Portsmouth moves ashore to guard the Americans. Later, reinforcements from the San Jacinto and Levant arrive to bolster the force. The trouble begins to escalate on November 16.

November 4 (Tuesday)   James Buchanan, a Democrat, defeats John Frémont for the presidency of the United States. Buchanan wins 14 slave states and four free states. Frémont wins 11 free states. One other free state was won by former President Millard Fillmore.

1857

In Kentucky, a former Mexican War veteran, John Hunt Morgan, establishes the Lexington Rifles. Subsequent to the outbreak of hostilities between the North and South, Morgan will side with the Confederacy.

In Virginia, an estate in the tranquil town of Alexandria becomes the home of Robert E. Lee, upon the demise of his wife's father. Lee had married Mary Ann Randolph Custis, a great-granddaughter of Martha Washington (by her first marriage), the wife of President George Washington. This estate on the banks of the Potomac River across from the capital becomes the paramount focus of the Union when hostilities finally break out. To the dismay of the Lee family, the property is confiscated during the first days of the conflict during 1861. In modern times the estate is better known as Arlington National Cemetery.

March 4 (Wednesday)   James Buchanan is inaugurated as the 15th president of the United States. His vice president is John C. Breckinridge (later Confederate general and Confederate secretary of war).

March 4–6   The U.S. Supreme Court rules in the Dread Scott case. It declares that Scott cannot sue in a federal court because he is a slave and not a citizen of the U.S. The court ruled against his premise that because he once resided in the Wisconsin Territory (which forbids slavery), he should be a free man.

May 21 (Thursday)   The USS Minnesota is commissioned. The Minnesota, attached to the East India Squadron, remains in service until it is decommissioned on 2 June 1859; however, at the outbreak of the Civil War, it is recommissioned on 2 May 1861. Also, the steam frigate USS Roanoke is commissioned this month. It is assigned to the Home Squadron and sees duty along the East coast and in the Caribbean until September 1857, when it is taken off active duty for repairs and remains out of service for nearly one year. During 1860, the vessel is again decommissioned until the outbreak of war. In June 1861, it is reactivated. During 1862, it is decommissioned, sent to New York and transformed into a triple turret ironclad.

July 20 (Monday)   In Texas, Comanches ambush a contingent of twenty men attached to the Second Cavalry, commanded by 1st Lieutenant John Bell Hood (West Point class of 1853), near Devil's River. The Second Cavalry is able to withstand the attack by more than 100 braves, killing 19 and wounding many more. The Cavalry loses two dead and five wounded. The 8th Cavalry from Fort Hudson arrives to reinforce Hood's troops and bring needed supplies. Hood subsequently joins the Confederacy and rises to the rank of lieutenant general.

July 24 (Friday)   In Utah Territory, Abraham Smoot arrives with the mail run from Independence, Missouri; however, he also brings discouraging news to the Mormons: the U.S. Army is heading to Utah to subdue the Mormons, known also at the time as the Saints (of the Kingdom of God). Preparations are soon initiated by the Mormon Church to prepare defenses and to impede the progress of the U.S. Army. Forces of Mormons are gathered under the direction of General Daniel Wells. The U.S. force ordered into Utah by President Buchanan is known as Johnston's Army named for Colonel (later Confederate general) Albert Sidney Johnston. The expeditionary force is to be led by General William S. Harney, but due to the turbulence in Kansas between the Free Staters and Border Ruffians, the command reverts to Johnston. He does not join the force until 11 September. In the meantime, the force remains under the temporary command of Colonel Edmund B. Alexander.

September   In Utah Territory, Colonel Albert Sidney Johnston arrives in Utah to assume command of the expeditionary force there. Prior to his arrival, the Mormons had succeeded in hampering the operation designed to bring about the end of the problems with the Mormons. The Mormon troops were harassing supply wagon trains and destroying anything thought to be useful to the U.S. troops. By November, Fort Bridger and Fort Supply are burned by the Mormons to prevent occupation by Johnston's Army.

September 1 (Tuesday)   In Utah Territory, a group of chiefs arrive in Salt Lake City to hold talks with Brigham Young and other Mormon leaders regarding the U.S. forces that have arrived in Utah to suppress the Mormon actions. Shortly thereafter, Indians aligned with a con-

tingent of Mormons attack a wagon train of settlers as they trudge forward to California. The settlers unsuccessfully attempt to purchase supplies from the Mormons at Cedar City, and afterwards they apparently seize some supplies without permission. The Mormons then incite the Indians to attack the train.

September 11 (Friday)   Mountain Meadows Massacre A group of settlers heading west from Arkansas, known as the Fancher party, is attacked by Indians while in camp during a pause along the tedious westward journey. The wagon train is large enough to supply some defenses and the men within the party withstand a four-day siege. All the while, no nearby Mormons come to their aid, but on the fourth day, a contingent of Mormons rides up to the camp under a white flag.

Following some conversation, the Mormons led by John D. Lee (Indian agent in Iron County) and others maliciously trick the settlers into relinquishing their weapons with the guarantee that the Mormons will get them to safety. Inexplicably, after disarming, the group composed of more than 100 people, including women and children, walk away from the safety of the wagons. Suddenly, the Mormons and the

Indians open fire. The Mormons kill the men while the Indians kill most of the women and children; however, some of the younger children are spared death. These are taken to Mormon homes, where they remain until returned to relatives who had not accompanied the train.

Despite the murders, Lee continues on as Indian agent without consequence. The U.S. government is unable to answer with justice, but the murders are not forgotten. About 1872, with pressure growing stronger, Lee relocates and afterward he is excommunicated from the Mormon Church because of his participation in the massacre, but no others in the church receive any penalty for their involvement.

The law finally catches up to John D. Lee during November 1874. He is captured at Lee's Ferry, Arizona, where he had established a ferry business. At this time, sentences are carried out without ten years of appeals. Lee is transported to Mountain Meadows where he had participated in the massacre and is executed there by a firing squad on 23 March 1877. He is survived by his wives, about nineteen of them, who bore him about sixty children. Lee is posthumously re-admitted in good standing to the Mormon Church during 1961.

1858

In Mexico, the Conservatives again seize power. President Ignacio Comonfort resigns during January. He departs for the United States. According to the mandate of the Mexican constitution, Benito Juarez, who had been selected to head the Supreme Court of Mexico, also became vice president of Mexico. With the absence of Comonfort, Benito Juarez is scheduled to succeed as regulated by the constitution. However, with the Conservatives in power, Juarez, as acting liberal president, moves from Mexico City to safer positions and later establishes his headquarters at Vera Cruz. Juarez had first concluded that the strength of the Conservative forces was too great to overcome. Felix Zuloaga and Manuel Robles Pezuela each serve as president under the Conservative regime during 1858. Zuloaga also serves during 1859. He will be succeeded by Miguel Miramon, who holds office from 1859 into 1860. This conflict continues into 1861 and beyond. Meanwhile, Europe takes advantage of the turmoil. Great Britain, France and Spain each demand payment of past debts, but the French extend the difficulties by initiating action to establish a French Empire. The French install Maximilian during 1864; the United States is unable to immediately react with armed forces because of the Civil War.

May 11 (Tuesday)   Minnesota is admitted to the union as the 32nd state.

May 19 (Wednesday)   The Marais des Cygnes Massacre Opposing pro- and anti-slave

forces engage each other at the Marais des Cygnes River in what becomes the final major confrontation of the "Bloody Kansas" period. The massacre of five men who support a free state of Kansas essentially is the last of lawlessness there.

June 16 (Wednesday)   Abraham Lincoln is endorsed by the Republican Party to run against incumbent Stephen Douglas for the U.S. Senate. During his acceptance speech, he states, "I believe this government cannot endure permanently half slave and half free." Douglas would engage in seven debates with Lincoln; although Lincoln loses the election, he becomes well known all over the country.

In Marine Corps activity, a contingent of twenty Marines is rushed to the jail in Washington, D.C., to quell a riot.

June 26 (Saturday)   *In Army activity,* Colonel Albert Sidney Johnston (later a Confederate general) arrives at Salt Lake City in the Utah Territory, dispatched there from Kansas to subdue the Mormons if their rebellious activities continue. Most Mormons depart the city, heading south. A federal military base is established for this expeditionary force at Camp Floyd. The difficulties with the Mormons are largely cleared up before the end of the year.

Alfred Cumming (West Point 1849) and Samuel W. Ferguson (West Point 1857) participate in this expedition. Cumming later joins the Confederacy as a lieutenant colonel, 10th Georgia Infantry. He is promoted to brigadier gen-

eral in late 1862. Ferguson also becomes a Confederate brigadier general. He resigns from the U.S. Army during March 1861 and joins the staff of General Pierre Beauregard in South Carolina.

President Abraham Lincoln and his son (Mottelay, *The Soldier in Our Civil War,* **1886).**

August 21 (Saturday) The USS *Dolphin*, while operating off Cuba, intercepts a slaver vessel, the *Echo*. During January 1859, the *Echo* is sold to a buyer in Charleston, South Carolina, and renamed the *Putnam*.

October The USS *Southern Star* (a wooden screw gunboat), built in Murfreesboro, North Carolina, this year, is chartered by the U. S. Navy. It participates in an expedition to Paraguay and afterward, following about three months off South America, returns to the States. Shortly thereafter, the vessel is renamed the USS *Crusader* and assigned to the West Indies to patrol for slave runners. Subsequent to the outbreak of war, it is assigned duty in the Gulf of Mexico. Later, following time out of service for repairs, it is assigned duty off South Carolina, then in September 1862, it is added to the North Atlantic Blockading Squadron.

December 16 (Thursday) In Kansas Territory, a group of abolitionists under John Brown raids Fort Scott. Following this raid, Brown initiates his movement along the Underground Railroad in an attempt to transport eleven slaves to safety. The group moves toward Harpers Ferry, Virginia (later West Virginia). By December of the following year, Brown's followers will attack the federal arsenal at Harpers Ferry.

1859

January 26 (Wednesday) The USS *Sumter* (*Sumpter*) and eighteen other U.S. warships arrive at Asuncion, Paraguay, to pay retribution for an attack made against the *Water Witch* in 1855. The government of Paraguay, not anxious to engage the fleet, offers an official apology and pays a sum of money, apparently in damages. The incident ends without violence. After returning to the States, five of the ships, including the *Sumter*, operate off Cuba, and they also cruise off Africa in search of slave traders. Subsequent to the outbreak of war, the *Sumter* is recalled and arrives back in the States on 15 September 1861.

May 12 (Thursday) The USS *Lancaster*, built in Philadelphia during 1857, is commissioned. Captain John Rudd receives command. The *Lancaster*, a sloop of war, embarks to join the Pacific Squadron on 27 July 1859. On the 29th, Flag Officer J.B.B. Montgomery makes it his flagship. The *Lancaster* remains in service for the duration of the Civil War; however, it remains in the west and only once comes in contact with Confederates (11 November 1863).

May 27 (Friday) The *Hartford*, launched at the Boston Navy Yard on 22 November 1858, is commissioned the USS *Hartford*. Captain Charles Lowndes receives command of the sloop of war. It is assigned to the East India Squadron under Flag Officer Cornelius K. Stribling (recently appointed commanding officer of the squadron). The *Hartford* departs for the Far East, and once there, Flag Officer Stribling officially makes the *Hartford* his flagship. Later, during 1861, as war erupts, the *Hartford* is ordered to return to the United States.

October 16–18 JOHN BROWN'S RAID The abolitionist John Brown leads his 22 man "Army of Liberation" on a raid against Harpers Ferry, Virginia, capturing the federal arsenal. A contingent of United States Marines is dispatched and Brown and the remaining survivors are captured. The Marines are led by Colonel Robert E. Lee, U.S. Army. Brown is convicted of treason and conspiracy. Subsequently, he is sentenced to death by hanging. Colonel Lewis Washington, the great-grand-nephew of George Washington, is among the hostages taken by Brown. During the Marine assault on the arsenal, Pvt. Luke Quinn is killed crashing through the door. It could be said that Quinn is the first serviceman to die in the Civil War.

November 21 (Monday) The USS *Constellation*, attached to the African Squadron, intercepts the *Delicia* and discovers it to be a slave runner operating without national colors.

November 29 (Tuesday) The *Mohican*, a steam sloop built at the Portsmouth Navy Yard during 1858 and launched in February of the following year, is acquired by the U.S. Navy. Commander S.W. Gordon receives command. The ship is assigned to the African Squadron.

December 2 (Friday) John Brown, recently seized at Harpers Ferry, Virginia, and tried and convicted of treason, dies by hanging in the public square of Charlestown, (West) Virginia. This is witnessed by many, including Edmund Ruffin, the South Carolina planter and intellectual who may have fired the first shot on Fort Sumter.

After John Brown's raid, a lawyer in Lynchburg named Samuel Garland, Jr., establishes the Lynchburg Home Guards (later the 11th Virginia Infantry Regiment). At the outbreak of hostilities Garland joins the Confederacy and becomes colonel of the 11th Virginia.

1860

January 9 (Monday) The USS *Mohican* departs from Portsmouth and remains with the African Squadron until August 1861. While with the squadron, the *Mohican* searches for pirates and slave runners. It arrives back in the United States at Boston during September 1861.

March 6 (Tuesday) While in the harbor at Anton Leyardo, Mexico, the USS *Saratoga* engages and defeats two Spanish ships, the steamers *Marquis of Havannah* and the *General Miramon*. Both vessels are captured at about midnight (6th–7th). The *Saratoga* (third *Saratoga*), initially commissioned on 4 January 1843, having been in and out of service multiple times, had been recommissioned on 6 September 1855 and assigned duty in the Caribbean and the Gulf of Mexico. Commander Thomas Turner received command of the vessel, a sloop of war.

April 28 (Saturday) The USS *Mohawk* (formerly the *Caledonia* under charter of the U.S. Navy), while operating off the east coast and in the West Indies against pirates and slave runners, encounters the *Wildflower*, a slave runner. The vessel is seized in the Old Bahama Canal and taken to Key West, Florida. More than 500 slaves are cramped in the vessel. At Key West, the slaves, for their protection and safety, are placed under the watch of a contingent of Marines attached to the *Mohawk*. Subsequently, the slaves are transported back to their native country. The *Mohawk*, a steamer, and another vessel, the steamer *Wyandotte* (formerly the SS *Western Port*), beginning in November 1860, operate from Key West. The ships play a pivotal part in maintaining the region and keeping it under U.S. control. In March 1861, the *Mohawk* departs the area for New York. The *Wyandotte* captures a slave runner, the *William*, off Cuba during May of this year and it too is taken to Key West.

November In New York, Edwin Denison is elected governor. Subsequently, newly elected President Abraham Lincoln appoints him major general in the Union Army (September 1861) to strengthen his authority. Governor Denison equips and mobilizes in excess of 225,000 men to aid the Union.

In Union general officer activity, William Tecumseh Sherman, in his memoir, reflected on the secession of the states: "Secession was treason." Sherman (West Point, 1840), born in Ohio, is at this time in Pineville, Louisiana, holding the position of superintendent of the Louisiana State Seminary of Learning and Military Academy. Quick-moving events regarding the imminent clash between the North and the South prompt his resignation the following January. Sherman re-enters the U.S. Army and later rises to the rank of lieutenant general during the conflict. Subsequently, he will attain the rank of full general and commander in chief of the army.

November 6 (Tuesday) Abraham Lincoln, a Republican, is elected president of the United States. Hannibal Hamlin becomes vice president. Through use of the telegraph, the results are quickly spread around the country. Lincoln receives 1,857,610 votes and 180 of the 183 electoral votes. One opponent, Stephen Douglas, receives 1,365,976 votes but falls short in the Electoral College, receiving only twelve votes, nine from the state of Missouri and three from New Jersey. John Cabell Breckinridge (later Confederate general) of Kentucky gathers 847,953 popular votes and 72 electoral votes. John Bell garnered 590,631 votes cast in the states of Kentucky, Tennessee and Virginia and 39 electoral votes.

Breckinridge, vice president under President Buchanan (1857–1861), will succeed John J. Crittenden in the U.S. Senate representing Kentucky during March 1861. However, by November of the same year, he abandons the Senate and the Union to join the Confederacy. The Senate chooses to expel Breckinridge during December 1861, but it seems quite apparent that the action is only symbolic, as Breckinridge by that time is a brigadier general in the Confederate Army.

November 7 (Wednesday) Major Robert Anderson (West Point, 1825) of the U.S. Army, is assigned the command at Charleston, South Carolina. He arrives in the city on 23 November, and within a few days, he contacts the War Department with a request for reinforcements. In related activity, Army Captain Truman (West Point, 1846) is placed under arrest while he is in charge of a detail transferring supplies from the federal arsenal in Charleston to Fort Moultrie. He will later be released and serve with gallantry in defense of Fort Sumter when war breaks out. Also, at Charleston, following the previous day's results in the election, the Stars and Stripes is lowered and replaced by the state flag, the Palmetto flag.

November 14 (Wednesday) In Georgia, Alexander Stephens, speaking to the state legislature, makes it clear Georgia should remain in the Union: "If the republic is to go down, let us be found at the last moment standing on the deck with the constitution of the United States waving over our heads…. I fear that if we evince passion and without sufficient cause shall take that step, a disruption of the ties that bind us to the union — that instead of becoming gods, we will become demons, and at no distant countenance cutting one another's throats."

Despite these strong feelings, Stephens, at the time a congressman, later, while a member of Georgia's secessionist convention, becomes vice president of the Confederacy on 9 February 1861.

November 21 (Wednesday) The USS *Constellation* seizes a bark, the *Cora*, which is transporting more than 700 slaves. Afterward, the slaves are transported to Monrovia, Liberia, and debarked there.

December 3 (Monday) In Washington, the 36th Congress convenes to initiate its second session.

December 4 (Tuesday) In Washington, D.C., President James Buchanan, long a supporter of Southern views and now of the belief that the North has caused the immediate problems, delivers his Message to Congress, but his position is awkward. He does not believe the individual states can secede on a whim or a matter of instant discontent: "In order to justify secession a constitutional remedy, it must be on the principle, that the federal government is a mere voluntary association of states, to be dissolved at pleasure by any one of the contracting parties. If this be so, the confederacy is a rope of sand, to be penetrated and dissolved by the first adverse wave of public opinion in any of the states…. [The Constitution] was intended to be perpetual, and not to be annulled at the pleasure of any one of the contracting parties." At this time, secession is inevitable, but some in Congress believe that the union might still be saved without bloodshed.

December 6 (Thursday) In Arkansas, a contingent of U.S. troops (Battery F, 2nd U.S. Artillery) under Lieutenants Anderson Merchant and St. Clair Dearing arrive by boat at Little Rock from Fort Smith. The commanding officer, Captain (later general) James Gilbert Totten had earlier departed to visit with his family in Little Rock, where his father is a doctor. The troops move from the steamboat landing to the empty Little Rock Barracks near the arsenal. Totten assumes command of the arsenal, replacing his step-brother, Captain William Fatherly. Prior to duty in Little Rock, Totten had participated in the effort to quell violence over slavery in "Bloody Kansas."

South Carolina, acting on the recent request of Governor William Henry Gist, elects delegates to prepare to secede from the Union. During the period following the election of Lincoln, he had urged the legislature to initiate action to prepare the militia for active duty and to begin stockpiling ammunition and arms for the inevitable struggle.

December 10 (Monday) In South Carolina, Francis W. Pickens becomes governor. Carrying on with the ideas of former Governor William Henry Gist, the move toward secession accelerates.

In Washington, D.C., the secretary of the treasury, Howell Cobb, apparently satisfied that he has contributed as much as possible to the cause of the Southern secession while serving under President James Buchanan, resigns his post to side with the South. Cobb will be appointed brigadier general during February 1861. Meanwhile, John A. Dix will succeed him as secretary of the treasury.

December 14 (Friday) In Washington, D.C., another of President Buchanan's cabinet, Secretary of State General Lewis Cass, resigns under protest because the president refuses to send reinforcements to augment Major Robert Anderson's garrison at Fort Sumter. Cass, formerly a senator representing the state of Michigan, had been a colonel under General William Hull during the War of 1812. Cass will be succeeded by Jeremiah Sullivan Black.

December 17 (Monday) In South Carolina at Columbia, amid an outbreak of smallpox, delegates convene to decide on secession. The assembly makes its decision on the 20th.

Also, a contingent of Texas Rangers, approximately 60 strong, in addition to settlers and scouts, pursue the Comanches under Chief Nawkohnee (also Necona or Nocone). The Ranger, led by Lawrence "Sul" Ross, are joined by a detachment of twenty-one men from the 2nd Cavalry. The Comanche village is crushed by the Americans; however, the chief and his braves are not in camp. The village, near Puanah, Texas, contains only women and children. During the raid a white woman and child are discovered and rescued. The woman turns out to be Cynthia Ann Parker, one of the children captured during the raid on Parker's Fort in 1836. She speaks no English and has become the wife of Nawkohnee. The chief and Cynthia Parker have had a child, Parker Quanah, who later leads the Comanches against settlers that reside on the Texas frontier.

Ross afterward resigns from the Texas Rangers, and during the summer of 1861, he enlists in the Confederate Army to serve in his brother Peter F. Ross's outfit, the Waco Company, which becomes part of the 6th Texas Cavalry.

December 18 (Tuesday) In Washington, D.C., the Senate attempts to deal with the ongoing crisis regarding the possible breakup of the United States. A senator from Kentucky, John J. Crittenden, moves to offer some measures of compromise to defuse the adversity. He proposes a restoration of the Missouri Compromise. Although it has some support, the measure by the end of the session will fail by a vote of twenty to nineteen.

December 20 (Thursday) In South Carolina, legislators make South Carolina the first state to secede from the Union. The resolution reads, in part: "We the people of the state of South Carolina, in Congress assembled, do declare and ordain, and it is hereby declared and ordained, that the ordinance adopted in convention by us in convention on the 23rd day of May in the year of Our Lord 1788, whereby the Constitution of the United States of America was ratified, and also all acts of the general assembly of this state ratifying the amendments to said Constitution are hereby repealed, and that the Union now subsisting between South Carolina and other states under the name of the United States of America, is hereby dissolved...." The convention also adopts, on the 24th, an Address to the People of the Slaveholding States and a Declaration of the Causes, which justify secession.

In Confederate general officer activity, U.S. Congressman Milledge L. Bonham at about this time resigns from Congress and is appointed major general and commander of the Army of South Carolina by Governor Francis Wilkinson Pickens. On or about April 19–23, 1861, he is appointed brigadier general in the Confederate Army. He will command a brigade attached to General P.G.T. Beauregard's army at Bull Run (First Manassas) during July of 1861.

In related activity, John Bratton (later brigadier general) shortly after secession joins the 6th South Carolina Regiment (state troops) as a private. Subsequently, the state forces are taken into the Confederate Army and Bratton again joins the service, still as a private. Following his enlistment, he quickly rises to the level of colonel.

Also, after the war begins, Micah Jenkins, co-founder of the King's Mountain Military School in Yorkville, S.C., joins the Confederacy and becomes colonel of the 5th South Carolina Regiment. Initially he sees action at 1st Manassas (Bull Run) in General David Rumph Jones' brigade, but subsequently he establishes the "Palmetto Sharpshooters," a regiment bonded together with troops that transfer from the 2nd, 5th and 9th South Carolina Infantry Regiments. He has the support of General James Longstreet and the concurrence of General Pierre G.T. Beauregard, the former suggesting that if Jenkins remains in command as a brigadier general, the men will stay "to a man." He retains command, but no promotion comes about until July 1862. D.R. Jones will be promoted to ensure that the command passes to Micah Jenkins.

William Henry T. Walker (West Point, 1837), a solid veteran of the Mexican War, resigns his commission in the U.S. Army. In May of the following year he is appointed to the rank of brigadier general in the Confederate Army. Many volunteer regiments begin to spring up across South Carolina; among these is the 18th, established by James M. Gadberry, who becomes its colonel. Later, William Henry Wallace, who joined the regiment as a private, becomes its lieutenant colonel and later brigadier general.

December 20 1860–June 8 1861 The Southern states secede in this order: (1) South Carolina, 12/20/1860; (2) Mississippi, 1/9/1861; (3) Florida, 1/10/1861; (4) Alabama, 1/11/1861; (5) Georgia, 1/19/1861; (6) Louisiana, 1/26/1861; (7) Texas, 2/1/1861; (8) Virginia, 4/17/1861; (9) Arkansas, 5/6/1861; (10) North Carolina, 5/20/1861; and (11) Tennessee, 6/8/1861.

The Confederacy also claims Kentucky and Missouri; however, both remain loyal to the Union. Nonetheless, the Confederate flag contains thirteen stars; eleven stars represent each of the Confederate states and two others represent Kentucky and Missouri. While the South is breaking away, Kansas enters the Union on January 29, 1861, and on February 28, 1861, Colorado becomes a U.S. territory. In addition, the Utah Territory is split into three: Dakota Territory, Nevada Territory and Utah Territory, on March 3, 1861.

December 24 (Monday) In Washington, D.C., the Navy orders the sloop of war USS *St. Louis,* attached to the squadron at Vera Cruz, to sail to Pensacola. The squadron, commanded by Commodore Pendergrast, also includes his flagship, the steamer *Powhatan,* the steam gunboat *Pocahontas,* and two ships of sail, the frigates *Sabine* and *Cumberland.* On 5 January orders are cut for the *Sabine* to move to Pensacola; however, the orders are not received by Pendergrast until 20 January and they stipulate that the *St. Louis* is not to sail. The two ships depart this day, but the delay in transit causes the vessels to arrive after Pensacola and its navy yard are taken by the Florida state forces.

In South Carolina, Governor Francis W. Pickens proclaims that South Carolina has "resumed her position among the nations of the world as a free, sovereign, and independent State."

December 25 (Tuesday) **In South Carolina,** at Fort Moultrie, Major Robert Anderson prepares to abandon the post and move to Fort Sumter, but the weather remains too nasty, compelling Anderson to suspend the evacuation until the following day.

December 26 (Wednesday) **In South Carolina,** federal troops stationed at Fort Moultrie prepare to move to Fort Sumter, the larger of the two forts protecting Charleston. Major Robert Anderson unfolds his operation methodically and cloaks it in secrecy. He orders the quartermaster — who is in charge of a small group of boats laden with supplies, provisions, ammunition and even household items — to depart for Fort Johnson, but the instructions direct him not to unload anything; rather, he is to await a signal, the firing of two guns, and at that time, to move to Fort Sumter. Meanwhile, following morning retreat, the troops still have no idea of Anderson's plans and only one officer is in Anderson's confidence.

At about sunset, the second in command,

Captain Doubleday, meets with Major Anderson, but Doubleday has not yet been informed of the plan. Captain Doubleday is told to be prepared to move out in twenty minutes. He also has to get his wife to safety with the other wives who were outside of the imperiled fort. Doubleday's company and those under Lt. R.K. Meade embark in two separate boats, with Anderson in the lead boat. The troops march to the boats without being detected. Nonetheless, Doubleday's boat encounters a Confederate patrol boat, the *General Clinch,* but the rebels detect no arms. In the twilight, the vessel appears innocent and passes itself off as a workmen's boat. Captain Doubleday's contingent is not entirely alone. There is still sufficient light that the movement is covered by the small detachment still at Fort Moultrie, and if the *General Clinch* had moved to intercept, it would have been fired upon. Major Anderson had taken the precaution to have two 32-pounders prepared to fire.

As the boats encroach Fort Sumter, only six men remain at Fort Moultrie: Captain Foster, the assistant surgeon, Mr. Moall, and four non-commissioned officers; however, another force under Captain Seymour is waiting for boats to return for his men. Captain Doubleday's contingent is the first to encounter the workmen when the troops reach Fort Sumter; however, the workmen, numbering about 150, after a small commotion, choose not to stand as obstacles in front of the fixed bayonets of Doubleday's command. In a flash, troops secure the main entrance to the fort and other sentries are posted at strategic points. The scheme unfolds flawlessly.

By 2000 hours, all is well at Fort Sumter, and it is under control of the Union. After securing the fort, boats are sent back to retrieve Seymour's command, leaving only Foster's contingent behind at Fort Moultrie. Meanwhile, Major Anderson, in a report to the adjutant-general, states that he had "just completed, by the blessing of God, the removal to this fort of all my garrison.... The step which I have taken was, in my opinion, necessary to prevent the ef-

Fort Moultrie (Mottelay, *The Soldier in Our Civil War,* 1886).

fusion of blood." At about the same time, the remaining two active guns at Fort Moultrie fire the signal. After hearing the sound of the guns, Lieutenant Hall moves from the west side of the bay "with the two lighters carrying the men's families and stores, and reached Sumter under sail."

Back at Fort Moultrie, the few troops there and some workmen load the items that initially could not be transferred to Fort Sumter. By about dawn on the 27th, the boats reach Sumter. However, ammunition and other supplies are still being transported to Fort Sumter. More than one month's supply of provisions has to be abandoned.

The guns are afterward spiked, but special attention is given to the artillery aimed toward Fort Sumter. The carriages are burned. The smoke that spirals upward from the cannon is easily spotted in Charleston, alerting the rebels that they had been fooled. Word had reached Charleston that Anderson was planning to take Sumter, but the rebels had not moved quickly. The Stars and Stripes that had flown over Fort Moultrie was prepared to be hoisted at Fort Sumter. At 11:45, the troops and about 150 workmen converge on the square at the flag staff. In conjunction with the flag raising ceremony, the chaplain says a prayer, giving thanks to God that they had safely reached Fort Sumter. The prayer included his hope that the flag would not ever be "dishonored, but soon float again over the whole country, a peaceful and prosperous nation." After the prayer, Major Anderson gets up off his knees as the troops present arms and the army band plays a rousing rendition of the "National Air," while the Stars and Stripes is hoisted to loud cheers. Nevertheless, Major Anderson is keenly aware that his forces are still imperiled.

Major Robert Anderson had urgently been requesting reinforcements to bolster his diminutive garrison, but to no avail. Anderson, a veteran of the Black Hawk, Florida (Seminole), and Mexican Wars, had assumed command of Castle Pinckney, Fort Moultrie and Fort Sumter

The revenue cutter *William Aiken* (or just *Aiken*) is seized in Charleston Harbor (Mottelay, *The Soldier in Our Civil War,* 1886).

during the previous November. Secretary of War John Buchanan Floyd, using his influence with President James Buchanan, has managed to ensure that no troops move to augment the fort. It is later reported that Floyd had, by the stroke of his pen, diverted more than 100,000 rifles from the arsenals at Springfield and Watervlet to locations in the South to provide the best weapons available should hostilities occur. This claim by Floyd is strongly contested by President Buchanan, who insists that Floyd had fabricated the story and that no weapons were stolen for the Confederacy. Another of Buchanan's cabinet members, Secretary of the Navy Isaac Toucey, will be censored by the House for his peculiar method of accepting an abundance of resignations of men supportive of the South, while the government is under attack.

December 27 (Thursday)   In South Carolina at Charleston, after the Rebels discover that the Union had abandoned Fort Moultrie, Governor Pickens dispatches his aide-de-camp, Colonel James J. Pettigrew (state militia), and another officer, Major Ellison Capers (later brigadier general), to meet with Major Anderson and demand that Fort Sumter be abandoned and that Anderson return to Fort Moultrie. The governor insists that there was an earlier agreement between his predecessor, Governor Gist, and President Buchanan that no military changes would occur at Charleston. Anderson declines, stating that he is not aware of any agreement, and he acted on his own authority to protect his command. Anderson also states in his response: "In this controversy between the North and the South, my sympathies are entirely with the South." However, he adds that he is ruled by his "sense of duty to his trust." After Anderson refuses the demands, he sends his compliments to the governor.

In related activity, a force of more than 100 men seizes Castle Pinckney in Charleston Harbor. The Union commander, Lt. R.K. Meade, and the small contingent, along with their families, are permitted to depart. The castle is later used as a prison for captured Union troops. Fort Moultrie is also occupied by state troops. Meanwhile, at Fort Moultrie, Major Anderson hoists Old Glory and prepares to defend the fort if it becomes necessary.

In Naval activity, the revenue cutter *William Aiken,* commanded by Captain Coste, U.S. Navy, is seized by the Confederates at Charleston. It and another vessel, the steam cutter *James Gray,* which is purchased by the Confederates, are the first two vessels to become part of the Confederate States' Navy. The USS *Aiken,* a first-class vessel of ninety tons, had been armed

with one 42-pounder pivot gun and manned by 30 men when seized.

December 28 (Friday)   In Washington, D.C., a small party composed of three commissioners (James H. Adams, Robert W. Barnwell and James L. Orr), recently sent by Governor Francis W. Pickens of South Carolina to confer with the president and Congress, meet with the president, but they are not recognized as official representatives of South Carolina. The president informs the three men that they are being received only as "private gentlemen" and "it was to Congress and to Congress alone that they must appeal." The president does, however, offer to have their proposals handed to Congress.

During the same meeting, the South Carolinians demand that Major Robert Anderson abandon Fort Sumter and remove all troops from the harbor before any negotiations can proceed. Buchanan patiently listens but makes no commitments. The southerners continue to press, particularly Barnwell, who repeatedly implies that there had been a "violation of faith." Barnwell more than a couple of times said, "But, Mr. President, your personal honor is involved in this matter, the faith you pledged has been violated and your personal honor requires you to issue the order" to withdraw to Fort Moultrie." By about the third time the president hears Barnwell's repetitious remarks, he interrupts: "Mr. Barnwell, you are pressing me too importunately; you don't give me time to say my prayers; I always say my prayers when required to act upon any great State affair." The commissioners make no headway in their quest for the "delivery of the forts and other real estate, for the apportionment of the public debt, and for a division of all the property of the United States" in South Carolina."

A meeting between the commissioners and the president had initially been scheduled for 27 December, but word of the unexpected activity at Charleston caused the meeting to be postponed. Secretary Floyd sent a telegram to Anderson and received a quick response. Major Anderson defended his action: "…Many things convinced me that the authorities of the State designed to proceed to a hostile act. Under this impression I could not hesitate that it was my solemn duty to move my command from a fort which we could not have held probably longer than forty-eight or sixty hours to this one where my power of resistance is increased to a very great degree." Meanwhile, President Buchanan had refrained from considering condemning Major Anderson for his actions until he was fully informed. Buchanan and his cabinet hastily met and the meetings continued for several days.

In South Carolina at Charleston, the customs house and the post office are taken over by the rebels. The American flag is replaced by the Palmetto flag and at the customs house and all of the federal workers quit.

In related activity, General Winfield Scott, holding a different opinion than that of Secretary of State Jeremiah S. Black, sends a request to Secretary of War John B. Floyd that Fort Sumter should be held and that the reinforcements should immediately be sent from Governor's Island, New York, aboard a merchant vessel rather than a warship. Meanwhile, the USS *Brooklyn* at Norfolk remains the preference of Secretary Black. The *Brooklyn* is scheduled to transport seasoned troops from Fort Monroe to bolster Major Anderson, while the merchant ship would carry fresh troops. On the 30th, General Scott bumps up the number of troops from 150 to 250, and his message is sent to the president.

Meanwhile, Secretary Floyd had resigned his post on the previous day. General Winfield Scott, born during 1786, the year prior to the adoption of the U.S. Constitution, is a brevet lieutenant general at the time of the outbreak of the war.

December 29 (Saturday) In Washington, D.C., the southern commissioners, in a joint letter to President James Buchanan, again demand the withdrawal of Major Robert Anderson's force from Charleston harbor. The cabinet again meets and the dissension continues for the duration of the meeting, with varying opinions of the president's response to the commissioners; however, the precise contents of the reply have never been publicized. The secretary of war, John B. Floyd, resigns from the cabinet.

He had used his powers of persuasion to maneuver President Buchanan into not reinforcing Fort Sumter; but his failed attempt to convince Buchanan to order Major Robert Anderson to abandon the fort and redeploy at Fort Moultrie convinces him that it is time to leave. President Buchanan had earlier, on the 23rd, requested Floyd's resignation. Floyd is also a former Governor of Virginia (1848–1852). He is succeeded on 18 January 1861 by a Kentuckian, Joseph Holt (later brigadier general).

Also, John Herbert, a cadet at West Point since 1857, quits to join the Confederate cause. He enters the Confederate Army as a second lieutenant in an artillery unit; however, later he receives a commission and joins the 14th Arkansas Regiment as a major (later brigadier general).

December 30 (Sunday) In South Carolina, the militia, led by Colonel John Cunningham (17th S.C. Infantry), captures the U.S. arsenal in Charleston, and the Confederates also prepare to occupy an abandoned post, Fort Johnson, but the latter is not occupied until early 1861.

In related activity, Governor Francis Pickens gives Commander T.T. Hunter (U.S. lighthouse inspector) permission to depart Charleston; however, Hunter is informed that he may not remove any U.S. property from the "buoy-shed."

December 31 (Monday) In Washington, D.C., the commissioners from South Carolina are informed that Major Robert Anderson had taken proper action and that no federal troops would be withdrawn from South Carolina. President James Buchanan states: "Fort Sumter will be defended against all hostile attacks from whatever quarter." Nevertheless, the president suspends immediate action to back up his decree, to allow time for the southern commissioners to respond to his reply to their correspondence. In his reply, the president refuses to acquiesce to the demands. A response from the southerners arrives on 2 January 1861. In the meantime, the president continues to prefer Secretary of State Jeremiah S. Black's blueprint to send the warship *Brooklyn* to Charleston.

In related activity, Acting Secretary of War Joseph Holt, successor to Secretary Floyd, confers with General Winfield Scott and directs Colonel Justin Dimick, the commanding officer at Fort Monroe, to assemble a contingent of four companies to reinforce Fort Sumter. The *Brooklyn* is prepared for the mission, but the warship's orders are later canceled and instead, the president agrees to Scott's plan. The merchant ship *Star of the West* gets the assignment and departs from New York on 5 January.

1861

In Iowa and Minnesota, after the outbreak of the Civil War, many of the troops stationed in this region are withdrawn to support the war effort, leaving the settlers at greater risk of danger from hostile Indians. By the following year, the Sioux rebel and soon thousands of settlers hurriedly depart the frontier.

Many Union-leaning families in Missouri seek safety in southern Iowa. Meanwhile, Confederate troops (irregulars from Missouri) initiate raids into the region of southern Iowa. In response, the governor, Samuel Kirkwood, establishes a Southern Border Brigade, similar to the Northern Border Patrol, which is to defend against the Indian raids. The Southern Border Brigade finds a dual purpose, to protect the borders against Confederates and to support Union forces.

In Maine, Fort McClary at Kittery in southern Maine, abandoned about 1846, is reactivated due to the Civil War. By 1863, the fort is in the process of being thoroughly re-fortified with double rows of cannon. The project is never totally completed and construction ceases temporarily during 1868. Work begins anew during 1874 and is further bolstered during 1898. However, the fort is never genuinely garrisoned during the period 1874–1898 except for awhile in 1898 when a contingent is dispatched from Fort Constitution.

In Utah Territory, the Mormons place their loyalty with the Union. By spring of the following year, the Mormon Church also forms units to defend the region as well as the routes that carry the U.S. mail. During August 1862, Union troops arrive to take over protection of the region.

January *In Union activity,* Henry Du Pont (West Point, 1833) is appointed major general, Delaware militia. He is the director of the Du Pont Powder Mills. Also, John Gross Barnard (West Point, 1833), former superintendent of West Point, is promoted to the rank of brigadier general. Barnard serves in the vicinity of Washington until 1864, when he transfers to General U.S. Grant's command. Barnard also receives four brevets major general prior to his retirement in 1881.

In Confederate general officer activity, Captain William Montgomery Gardner (West Point, 1846) resigns from the U.S. Army and soon becomes a lieutenant colonel of the 8th Georgia, Confederate States of America. Gardner is promoted to brigadier general during November of this year, following a severe wound sustained at Bull Run (First Manassas) during June.

Lucius Jeremiah Gartrell establishes the 7th Georgia Infantry and becomes its colonel. He leads the regiment until the following year, when he resigns to become a member of the Confederate Congress as a representative of Georgia. He serves until 1864, when he re-enters the service of Confederate Army as a brigadier general. And, Paul Jones Semmes becomes colonel (later brigadier general) of the 2nd Georgia Infantry. Semmes will lead his regiment in Virginia under General Magruder.

January–March *In Confederate general officer activity,* emotions are running high all across the country as various military personnel begin to choose which side to throw their allegiance, as conflict between the North and South seems inevitable. One of these, Patrick R. Cleburne, who was born just outside of County Cork, Ireland, and arrived in America during 1849, chooses the Southern cause. From his home in Louisiana he joins the 1st Arkansas State Troops as a captain, and by the latter part of July, he serves with the 15th Arkansas Regiment as its colonel. By March of 1862, he is promoted to brigadier general at the age of 34, just prior to his birthday, St. Patrick's Day, March 17.

The 1st Arkansas Infantry had been organized by a former member of the U.S. Army (Mexican War), James Fleming Fagan, who is commissioned a brigadier general in the Confederacy during September 1862. Fagan's first wife was a sister of Confederate General William N.R. Beall. Subsequent to her death, Fagan marries Miss Rapley of Little Rock, Arkansas. Also, recently elected (1860) Senator Thomas Lanier Clingman of North Carolina resigns from the Senate and during March accepts an appointment as colonel of the 25th (formerly 15th) North Carolina Regiment. The next May he is promoted to brigadier general.

January 1 (Tuesday)   In South Carolina, Governor Francis W. Pickens directs that no vessels attached to the lighthouse establishment at Charleston would be granted permission to depart from Charleston. Commander T.T. Hunter, the U.S. inspector, however, having received permission to depart 31 December, is able to leave by an overland route.

In Union general officer activity, Thomas William Sweeny, a native of Ireland and a veteran of the Mexican War (1st New York Volunteers), is promoted to captain (later brigadier general) of the 2nd U.S. Infantry. He participates in Missouri as commander of the 90-day Missouri militia. In January 1862, he is appointed colonel of the 52nd Illinois Infantry Regiment.

January 2 (Wednesday)   In Washington, D.C., President James Buchanan receives the response from the southern commissioners, but it is handled unofficially. Nevertheless, it is less than diplomatic, and the two-day delay in taking action only increases the imperiled defenders at Fort Sumter. President Buchanan, after reading the communication, and realizing there would be no peaceful solution, stated: "It is now all over, and reinforcements must be sent," but still, it would be a few days before the reinforcements embarked.

In South Carolina, a telegram from Senator Louis Tresevant Wigfall at Washington is received in Charleston. The message urges that action be taken: "Holt succeeds Floyd. It means war. Cut off all supplies from Anderson and take Sumter soon as possible." Joseph Holt, acting secretary of war, is officially appointed on 18 January. The South Carolina militia occupies Fort Johnson across the water from Fort Sumter in Charleston, South Carolina.

January 3 (Thursday)   In Washington, D.C., the three commissioners from South Carolina, having failed to convince President Buchanan and Congress to agree to the demands, depart the capital and return to South Carolina. Senator John J. Crittenden of Kentucky submits a proposal to re-institute the Missouri Compromise.

In Georgia, Fort Pulaski on the Savannah River, garrisoned only by a skeleton force, is seized by Georgia state troops commanded by General Alexander R. Lawton. Lawton is appointed brigadier general in the Provisional Confederate Army during the following April. General Lawton's career in the field for the Confederacy is cut short following a wound sustained during fighting at Sharpsburg (Antietam) during 1862.

In South Carolina, a company of militia known as the Gist Rifles (named in honor of Governor William H. Gist) is taken into state service. It moves to Camp Hampton and becomes Company D, Hampton Legion Infantry Battalion, led by Colonel (later general) Wade Hampton. The infantry battalion later becomes Hampton's Legion. After the First Battle of Manassas (First Bull Run), the battalion, which at this time is composed of artillery, infantry and cavalry, is separated.

January 4 (Friday)   At the request of President James Buchanan, this day is observed as a day of "fasting, humiliation, and prayer, to receive the guidance and protection of Almighty God." The request is honored by many across the nation.

In Alabama, Governor Andrew Moore directs state troops to seize the federal arsenal at Mount Vernon. The arsenal, established during 1829, is regained by the Union during 1865.

January 5 (Saturday)   In Washington, D.C., orders are issued directing the frigate *Macedonian* at Portsmouth, New Hampshire, to depart for Pensacola, Florida. In other activity, southern senators pass resolutions that call for the secession of their respective states. Those attending were: Clement Claiborne Clay (Alabama, resigns 21 January); Robert W. Johnson (Arkansas, resigns 3 March); Stephen Mallory (Florida, resigns 21 January); David Levy Yulee (Florida, resigns 21 January); Alfred Iverson, Jr. (Georgia, resigns 28 January); Robert A. Toombs (Georgia, resigns 4 February); Judah P. Benjamin (Louisiana, resigns 4 February); John Slidell (Louisiana, resigns 4 February); Jefferson Davis (Mississippi, resigns 21 January 1861); Albert G. Brown (Mississippi, resigns 12 January); John Hemphill (Texas, expelled from Senate during July 1861) and Louis T. Wigfall (Texas, resigns 23 March). It is also decided to hold a convention by 16 February at Montgomery, Alabama, for the purpose of establishing a confederacy. In the meantime, the senators remain in Congress to further their aims by stalling and interfering with legislation in progress that could help the incoming administration of Abraham Lincoln. These actions are in direct conflict with the senators' sworn oath to protect and defend the Constitution.

In Alabama, state militia seizes control of Fort Morgan, established during 1853, on Dauphin Island in Mobile Bay. The post had not yet been completed, but the Confederates finish the project. The Confederates seize another fort in the bay, Fort Morgan, established at Mobile Point during 1818. Subsequently, during 1864, Admiral David Farragut regains the forts. This is done in order to follow the course of the southern states and as a defensive move to protect Mobile.

In New York, at 1700, the merchant steamer *Star of the West,* chartered by the government, departs New York and pauses at Staten Island to pick up the reinforcements. Initially army recruits are scheduled for the mission, but instead,

Marines move aboard. The vessel carries a contingent of 250 enlisted men and four officers, with Lt. Charles R. Woods, 9th U.S. Infantry, in command. The mission, undertaken with secrecy, had been exposed prior to the ship's departure. The vessel's movement was published in a New York newspaper during the afternoon. Several days later, on 8 January, another newspaper, the *Constitution,* which operated in Washington, D.C., also publicized the ship's movements. Taking advantage of the notification in the press, the secretary of the interior, Jacob Thompson, on this day sends a telegraph to Charleston to alert the rebels. Senator Louis Tresevant Wigfall, another sympathizer, also telegraphed word of the ship's movements to the Confederates in Charleston. Meanwhile, Lt. Colonel Lorenzo Thomas, the assistant adjutant general (General Winfield Scott's staff) sends a letter to Major Robert Anderson at Fort Sumter to advise him of the plans, but the message is not treated as a priority.

In other activity, a detachment of forty Marines, commanded by Captain Algernon S. Taylor, moves from the Washington Navy Yard to Fort Washington in Maryland to bolster its defense.

January 6 (Sunday)   In Florida, the state militia seizes the federal arsenal at Apalachicola in another move to gain control of the South. The Federal government had not actually strengthened any of its arsenals in an effort to forestall the conflict, apparently convinced that to fortify the arsenals would have ignited the breakaway.

January 7 (Monday)   In Washington, D.C., the recent actions of Major Robert Anderson in Charleston are supported by a majority in the House, which passes a resolution that commends his actions, calling them "bold and patriotic." The resolution passed by a vote of 124 to 53. Also, orders are sent to the USS *Brooklyn* directing it to depart to support the *Star of the West;* however, the orders are not received until 9 January. Consequently, the *Brooklyn* arrives at Charleston on the 12th, too late to be of any assistance.

In Florida, state troops take possession of Fort Marion, formerly the French post Fort Castillo San Marcos. The United States assumed control of the fort during 1821 and renamed it in honor of Francis Marion, the Swamp Fox of the American Revolution, during 1825. The Confederates also seize the St. Francis Barracks. The Union forces are too few in number to raise opposition. Another post, unmanned Fort Clinch at Fernandina on Amelia Island (initially Isle de Mar), established during 1847, is seized by the Confederates. The fort is regained by the Union during March 1862.

Also, Senator David Levy Yulee, representing Florida, in a letter to a constituent in Tallahassee, explains how it is necessary for he and those of like mind to remain in Congress rather than give Lincoln an opportunity to come into office with proper bills passed to give him the means to neutralize the impending rebellion: "If we

Major General Robert Anderson (Johnson, *Campfire and Battlefield: History of the Conflicts and Campaigns*, 1894).

left here force, loan, and volunteer bills might be passed which would put Mr. Lincoln in immediate condition for hostilities; whereas by remaining in our places until the 4th of March, it is thought we can keep the hands of Mr. Buchanan tied and disable the republicans from effecting any legislation...." Senator Yulee resigns from the Senate on 21 January 1861, to join the Confederacy. Union troops, upon seizing Fernandina, Florida during March of 1862, discover this correspondence, which underscores the fashion in which Southern sympathizers had been conspiring in Congress to bring success to the South.

In North Carolina, Fort Johnston in the vicinity of Smithville is seized by civilians of Smithville.

In Virginia, the subject of secession comes to the forefront of the legislature. It calls for a special session to consider seceding from the Union.

January 8 (Tuesday)   In Washington, D.C., President James Buchanan delivers a message to Congress detailing the state of the nation. He makes it clear that in his opinion, "The fact cannot be disguised that we are in the midst of a great revolution." Buchanan attempts to seek concessions for the South to forestall armed conflict and to preserve the Union. The president attaches to his message alarming notes from citizens of South Carolina, who demand that he condemn the actions of Major Robert Anderson, who took control of Fort Sumter, or face serious consequences. He dismisses the

threat and refuses to admonish Anderson. Buchanan then tells Congress, "Whatever the result may be, I shall carry to my grave the consciousness that I at least meant well for my country."

The secretary of the interior, Jacob Thompson, in office since 6 March 1857, resigns from the cabinet. Thompson also sends a telegram to Charleston to inform the Confederates that the Union reinforcements are en route. Thompson is succeeded by Moses Kelly, who finishes out the term as acting secretary and is succeeded by Caleb Smith on 5 March 1861, during the Lincoln administration.

In Florida, a Union contingent, commanded by Lt. Adam Slemmer, repels an assault launched by secessionists against Fort Pickens. The Union also repulses a minor attack against Fort Barrancas, Florida.

Lt. Adam J. Slemmer, Commander of Fort Pickens (Mottelay, *The Soldier in Our Civil War*, 1886).

In South Carolina, a U.S. light vessel at Rattlesnake Shoals in the vicinity of Charleston harbor is reported to have sailed. The Lighthouse Board is notified of the movement. The board is also informed that three U.S. tenders in the harbor had been seized by state forces.

In Confederate general officer activity, Lucius B. Northrop (West Point, 1831) resigns his commission in the U.S. Army to join the Confederacy as a colonel (commissary general of the Confederacy) with the duty of distributing food to the troops and to Union prisoners, the latter responsibility not being too high on his list of priorities.

January 9 (Wednesday)   Mississippi secedes from the Union by a vote of 84 to 15. It is the second state to sever its ties. Mississippi will designate Jefferson Davis as the commander of

its army with a rank of major general. The state also authorizes the acquisition of arms to supply the army. In Mississippi at this time, there are few weapons and no manufacturing facilities with which to produce them.

In Virginia, orders arrive directing the USS *Brooklyn* to depart to support the merchant ship *Star of the West,* but the orders arrive two days after they were issued. Nevertheless, the warship departs on the same day that the *Star of the West* arrives at Charleston. The *Brooklyn* arrives at Charleston on the 12th, but after missing the merchant ship, in accordance with its orders, it does not move to pass the bar and instead returns to Virginia.

In South Carolina, the *Star of the West* arrives at Charleston about 0130. The Confederates, thanks to the press and telegrams, had been alerted. At Fort Sumter, Major Robert Anderson had also known the ship was en route after reading about it in a Charleston newspaper on the previous night. Anderson, however, hadn't believed what he read, because the article named the vessel as a merchant ship, not a warship. Consequently, Anderson did not take precautions to defend a relief ship. A letter, dated 5 January, had been sent by Colonel Lorenzo Thomas to Anderson, which authorized Anderson to take action "should a fire, likely to prove injurious, be opened upon any vessel bringing reinforcements or supplies, or upon tow boats within reach of your guns, they may be employed to silence such fire; and you may act in like manner in case a fire is opened upon Fort Sumter itself." Nonetheless, the letter had not yet arrived. At dawn, the *Star of the West,* commanded by Captain John McGowan, advances up the channel toward the waiting Confederate batteries. As the ship approaches Cummings Point on Morris Island, less than two miles from Fort Sumter, it comes under fire from a battery at Cummings Point. According to orders, the Stars and Stripes is hoisted to signal Fort Sumter and initiate the plan explained in Thomas' letter to Anderson. However, the guns at Sumter remain silent.

Meanwhile, the unarmed *Star of the West* continues to advance under fire, anticipating support fire, but instead, the crew spots imminent trouble: a steamer with an armed schooner in tow. The *Star of the West,* unable to defend itself, reverses course, and while still under fire from the shore, heads back to New York. The incident was documented by Captain Aber Doubleday:

> I saw a large steamer pass the bar and enter the Morris Island channel. It had the ordinary United States flag up; and as it evidently did not belong to the navy, I came to the conclusion it must be the *Star of the West....* Anderson himself was still in bed. When the vessel came opposite the new battery which had been built by the cadets, I saw a shot fired to bring her to. Soon after an immense United States garrison flag was run up at the fore.... I dashed down to Anderson's room.... He told me to have the long roll beaten, and to post the men on the parapet.... It took but a few

minutes for men and officers to form at the guns.... The battery was still firing, but the transport had passed by and was rapidly getting out of range. At the same time it was approaching within gunshot of Fort Moultrie. The latter immediately opened fire from one or two guns. Anderson would not allow us to return this fire; and the captain of the vessel, wholly discouraged by our failure to respond, turned about.... We had one or two guns bearing on Fort Moultrie; and as that was within easy range we could have kept down the fire there long enough to enable the steamer to come in.

While the guns on Fort Sumter remain silent, some officers, including Lt. Meade, advise Anderson not to fire. Meade insists that "fire should not be opened, as it would at once ... initiate civil war." Although Meade's advice is sincere, he would later leave the service and join the Confederates. Meanwhile, the *Star of the West* escapes damage, thanks in great part because the gunners were not experienced.

In Confederate general officer activity, Edmund Winston Pettus, the brother of John J. Pettus, governor of Mississippi, will join the Confederacy and subsequently become colonel (later brigadier general) of the 20th Alabama Regiment. Samuel Benton (later brigadier general), a participant in the secession convention of Mississippi, soon relinquishes his duties as a lawyer to join the 9th Mississippi Regiment (one year regiment) as a captain. Later, he is elected colonel of the 37th Mississippi Regiment, which is subsequently reorganized as the 34th Mississippi Regiment.

Winfield Scott Featherston will later become colonel (later brigadier general) of the 17th Mississippi Infantry, which will be attached during 1862 to the Army of Northern Virginia. And Claudius Wistar Sears (West Point, 1841) later joins the 17th Mississippi as a captain, but he will subsequently become colonel (later brigadier general) of the 46th Mississippi Regiment.

In Marine Corps activity, First Lieutenant Andrew J. Hays, leading a detachment of thirty Marines, departs the Washington Navy Yard en route to Fort McHenry, in Baltimore to help defend it.

January 10 (Thursday)   Florida secedes from the Union by a vote of 62 to 7; it is the third state to break away. Also, the federal navy yard at Pensacola surrenders to southern forces led by an insurgent naval officer, Captain Randolf, working in collusion with other officers at Pensacola who are sympathetic to the Confederate cause. Thirty-eight Marines commanded by Captain Josiah Watson are among the men who surrender. Lt. Adam J. Slemmer, an artillery officer attached to Fort McRee, and other troops, including soldiers from Fort Barrancas and a contingent of sailors and Marines attached to the USS *Wyandotte*, move to Fort Pickens to bolster it and defend it until reinforcements can arrive. At this time, Florida is not considered a primary concern for either the North or the South, as it is less populated and contains little

industry. Nevertheless, within a short while, it rises to a position of great importance to both sides, especially the South, subsequent to the Union victory at Vicksburg (1863). Florida raises about 15,000 troops for the South; however, the greatest number of these serve in other parts of the country, primarily in the Army of Tennessee and the Army of Northern Virginia.

In Louisiana, state troops take over Fort Jackson at Port Sulphur, about seventy miles below New Orleans, and at the same time Confederates seize nearby Fort St. Philip, which had been built by the Spanish on the opposite bank of the Mississippi. In addition, the federal arsenal at Baton Rouge, along with the barracks, is seized. The arsenal is regained during May of the following year.

In South Carolina at Fort Sumter, the tension continues to rise, particularly since the *Star of the West* failed to break through with provisions and supplies. On this day, Major Robert Anderson receives instructions from Washington that direct him to take only defensive steps.

In Confederate activity, Governor John Milton places Joseph Finegan, a native of Ireland, in charge of Florida's military affairs. The 1st Alabama Infantry commanded by Colonel (later brigadier general) Henry DeLamar Clayton will be based in Pensacola. DeLamar will subsequently establish the 39th Alabama Regiment. The 4th Alabama will join the forces at Pensacola and move to Virginia in time to participate at First Manassas (Bull Run) and the various other battles of the Army of Northern Virginia from Virginia to Gettysburg, Pennsylvania.

January 11 (Friday)   **In Washington, D.C.,** Philip Francis Thomas, recently appointed as secretary of the treasury in place of Howell Cobb, resigns. He is succeeded on the following day by John Dix. In Alabama, a vote to secede from the Union passes 61 to 39. Alabama is the fourth state to secede.

In Louisiana, state militia seizes the Marine Corps hospital in New Orleans. In addition, Fort St. Philip, below New Orleans, had recently been seized by state troops. The Union regains New Orleans during April 1862.

In New York, the *Star of the West*, having failed to reinforce Fort Sumter, enters the harbor. The officer in command of the reinforcements, Lt. Charles R. Woods, 9th U.S. Infantry, prepares a preliminary report for Colonel Lorenzo Thomas: "COLONEL: I have the honor to report that I reached this post at 8 o'clock this morning with my command, having been unable to reach Fort Sumter. I will make a detailed report without delay."

In South Carolina, the Confederates continue to work to strengthen their positions. At this time, they have few seasoned troops in Charleston that are familiar with artillery and their defenses are thin. Four hulks are deliberately sunk at the harbor's entrance to impede any U.S. vessels that attempt to enter. On this

day, Confederate representatives Judge Andrew G. McGrath, S.C. secretary of state, and David F. Jameson (Jamison), the S.C. secretary of war, arrive at Fort Sumter to demand surrender. In turn, Major Robert Anderson gathers his officers and discusses the ultimatum. Without dissent, the ultimatum is rejected. Meanwhile, McGrath continues to try to persuade Anderson to surrender, claiming that in Washington, there was nothing but chaos, and for their own welfare the post should capitulate. McGrath terminates his plea with: "May God Almighty enable you to come to a just decision."

In Confederate general officer activity, Zachariah Cantey Deas, a South Carolinian who had during his youth moved to Mississippi, establishes the 22nd Alabama Infantry Regiment by using some of his accumulated wealth as a cotton broker. Deas had also served in the U.S. Army during the Mexican War; however, his sympathies and his wealth are focused on the Confederacy. Deas later becomes a brigadier general (effective December 1862). Robert Emmett Rodes will enter the Confederate Army subsequent to the outbreak of hostilities and be appointed colonel of the 5th Alabama Regiment. Rodes will lead his regiment at First Manassas (Bull Run). John Tyler Morgan will be appointed lieutenant colonel of the 5th Alabama; however, he resigns in 1862 and establishes the 51st Alabama Partisan Rangers, of which he becomes colonel (later brigadier general).

January 12 (Saturday)   **In Washington, D.C.,** New York Senator William Henry Seward, in an address to the Senate, states: "I do not know what the Union would be worth, if saved by the use of the sword." Seward, formerly governor of New York (1832–1849), on 3 March 1861 resigns from the senate. He serves as secretary of war throughout the Lincoln administration and during the Andrew Johnson administration In other activity, Senator Albert G. Brown (Mississippi) resigns.

In Alabama, the U.S. customs collector at Mobile resigns to join the Confederacy. On 21 January, he informs Commander Handy that the state of Mississippi is taking control of the various lighthouses located within its boundaries.

In Florida, Fort McRee and Fort Barrancas at Pensacola are taken over by Florida state troops. Most of the stores at the forts had been disposed of by Lt. Adam J. Slemmer, but at the navy yard in Pensacola (seized on 10 January), the Confederates confiscate the stores. The U.S. arsenal at St. Augustine is seized and state troops also seize a coast survey vessel, the *F. W. Dana* (15 January). Confederate troops also seize the federal arsenal at Chattahoochee, Florida, at about this time.

In New York, the *Star of the West* arrives after failing to reach Fort Sumter. Lt. Charles R. Woods, commander of the relief force, prepares a report on the mission. Later, the ship is again contracted to sail to Texas and support the effort to evacuate troops there and transport them north.

In South Carolina, the Confederates issue an ultimatum to Fort Pickens, but it is ignored. Also, Colonel J.W. Hayne (South Carolina attorney general), the representative of Governor Francis Pickens, and Lt. Hall, representing Major Robert Anderson, depart Charleston for Washington. Hayne possesses yet another demand of the governor that Fort Sumter be surrendered. The two men arrive at the capital on the following day. Also, the USS *Brooklyn* arrives in the vicinity of Charleston, but it is too late to support the *Star of the West*. The *Brooklyn*, acting according orders, returns to Virginia.

January 13 (Sunday)   In Washington, D.C., a southern commissioner, Colonel J.W. Hayne, the representative of South Carolina Governor Francis Pickens, arrives in the capital to seek a solution for the ongoing crisis regarding occupation of Fort Sumter by U.S. troops.

In New York, Lt. Charles R. Woods completes a report on the mission to relieve Fort Sumter for Colonel Lorenzo Thomas:

My command consisted of two hundred men, recruits from the depot, fifty of whom were of the permanent party. My officers were First Lieut. W. A. Webb, Fifth Infantry; Second Lieut. C. W. Thomas, First Infantry, and Assist. Surg. P. G. S. Ten Broeck, Medical Department.... On Tuesday afternoon, 8th instant, arms and ammunition were issued to all the men. About midnight same evening we arrived off Charleston Harbor, and remained groping in the dark until nearly day, when we discovered the light on Fort Sumter, which told us where we were. The other coast light marking the approaches to the harbor had been extinguished, and the outer buoy marking the channel across the bar gone.... Before we were fired upon we had discovered a red palmetto flag flying, but could see nothing to indicate that there was a battery there.... We went into the harbor with the American ensign hoisted on the flagstaff, and as soon as the first shot was fired a full-sized garrison flag was displayed at our fore, but the one was no more respected than the other. We kept on, still under the fire of the battery, most of the balls passing over us, one just missing the machinery, another striking but a few feet from the rudder, while a ricochet shot struck us in the fore-chains, about two feet above the water line, and just below where the man was throwing the lead. An American flag Was flying at Fort Sumter, but we saw no flag at Fort Moultrie, and there were no guns fired from either of these fortifications.... Finding it impossible to take my command to Fort Sumter, I was obliged most reluctantly to turn about, and try to make my way out of the harbor before my retreat should be cut off by vessels then in sight, supposed to be the cutter Aiken, coming down the channel in tow of a steamer, with the evident purpose of cutting us off.

In other activity, Jefferson Davis, in a letter dated 13 January 1861, to Governor Francis Pickens of South Carolina, states: "I take it for granted that the time allowed to the garrison of Fort Sumter has been diligently employed by yourselves, so that before you could be driven out of your earthworks you will be able to capture the fort which commands them…"

On 20 January (one day before he resigns from the U.S. Senate), in regard to the *Star of the West*, Davis writes: "The occurrence of the *Star of the West* seems to me to put you in the best condition for delay, so long as the government permits that matter to rest where it is. Your friends here think you can well afford to stand still, so far as the presence of a garrison is concerned, and if things continue as they are for a month, we shall then be in a condition to speak with a voice which all must hear and heed."

January 14 (Monday)   In Washington, D.C., Marines begin preparations for defending the navy yard, including setting up artillery crews.

In Florida, Union forces occupy Fort Zachary Taylor, formerly Key West Barracks, in Key West. The Union controls the post for the duration of the war.

In Louisiana, Fort Pike on Lake Ponchartrain in the vicinity of New Orleans is taken over by state troops. It is regained by the Union during April 1862.

In Virginia, subsequent to action of the previous week, the legislature authorizes a convention for the purpose of considering secession from the Union.

January 15 (Tuesday)   The USS *Dana*, a schooner, is seized by Florida state troops.

January 16 (Wednesday)   In Washington, D.C., Senator Clement Claiborne Clay of Alabama urges the president to order Major Robert Anderson to abandon Fort Sumter. Meanwhile, other senators of similar thoughts continue to confuse things to permit the secession movement to continue. The representative of South Carolina remains in Washington, but the letter from the governor of South Carolina had not been delivered to President James Buchanan. The president rejects Clay's advice. At this time a truce is in place at Charleston. Clay states to President Buchanan that it could be extended until 4 March. Between this day and mid April, the debate continues, with Hayne demanding surrender on 1 February, and shortly afterward Secretary of War Joseph Holt informs Colonel Hayne that the fort will be retained by the U.S. All the while, information regarding Fort Sumter circulates, but much is erroneous and some is let out by Secretary of State William H. Seward (Lincoln administration) without knowledge of the president.

January 18 (Friday)   In Washington, D.C., Joseph Holt, a retired lawyer, commissioner of patents and postmaster general, is appointed as secretary of war by President James Buchanan. He succeeds John B. Floyd, who resigned during the previous December. Horatio King, assistant postmaster general during President Buchanan's administration, becomes acting postmaster general; on 12 February, he is appointed postmaster general.

In other activity, Secretary of the Treasury John Dix, dispatches a man from the treasury department to New Orleans with instructions to have the two cutters there prepared to sail to New York; however, difficulties occur when the commanding officer of the *Robert McClelland* later disregards the order.

In Florida, Fort Jefferson in the Tortugas (an island chain in the Gulf of Mexico off Key West) is garrisoned by Union forces.

In Louisiana, William Tecumseh Sherman, in a letter to Governor Thomas Overton Moore of Louisiana, states: "On no earthly account, will I do any act or think any thought hostile to the government of the United States."

January 19 (Saturday)   Georgia secedes from the Union by a vote of 208 to 89; it is the fifth state to secede.

In Virginia, the General Assembly passes resolutions calling for a way to find a peaceful solution to the crisis threatening the United States. A conference composed of representatives from thirty-one states will meet in Washington, D.C., on February 4; however, none of the states that have chosen secession will be in attendance of what becomes known as the Peace Conference.

January 20 (Sunday)   In Mississippi, seizure is anticipated by the U.S. forces at Fort Massachusetts, on Ship Island, initially established during 1859 to support the defense of New Orleans. When the Confederates take control it was essentially destroyed. The Union will retake the fort the following year and use it in the campaign to recapture New Orleans. The U.S. hospital along the Mississippi is also seized by state forces.

January 21 (Monday)   In Washington, D.C., Numerous senators voicing approval of the actions of the southern states withdraw after having made farewell speeches. One of these, Jefferson Davis, states: "I concur in the action of the people of Mississippi, believing it to be necessary and proper." Also, orders are issued that direct the USS *Brooklyn*, at Hampton Roads, to transport an artillery company, commanded by Captain Vogdes, from Fort Monroe, Virginia, to Fort Pickens at Pensacola. Captain Vogdes is to assume command upon his arrival at the fort.

By this time it is correctly thought in Washington that Fort Barrancas and Fort McRee had already been taken by the state forces; however, peculiarly, the order seems to only confuse the mission, as it states: "You are to understand that you are not to attempt any reoccupation or recapture involving hostile collision, but that you are to confine yourself strictly to the defensive."

In addition to Davis, other senators from the South resign: Clement Claiborne Clay (Alabama); Stephen Mallory (Florida); and David Levy Yulee (Florida). After giving his speech, Jefferson Davis prepares to depart for his home.

In Arizona, Fort Buchanan, formerly Camp Moore, established during 1856, is abandoned at about this time. The garrison moves to New Mexico to support the Union forces there.

January 22 (Tuesday) In *Marine activity,* the Marine Guard stationed at the Brooklyn Navy Yard in New York takes up arms in the event southern sympathizers move against the facility.

January 23 (Wednesday) In *Army activity,* Captain Pierre Gustave Toutant Beauregard (West Point, 1838), Corps of Engineers, is appointed superintendent of West Point. He succeeds Major Richard Delafield (West Point, 1818), Corps of Engineers, who has been superintendent since 1856; however, on 28 January, Major Delafield resumes his position, but he too will stay only a while, as hostilities with the South are looming. Delafield is succeeded by Major Alexander H. Bowman (West Point, 1825) on March 1, 1861. Delafield, already more than sixty years of age, will bolster the defenses in the vicinity of New York's Harbor and other vital spots in New York and northern New Jersey. Beauregard, from the state of Louisiana, had apparently voiced his strong opinions about his sympathy being with the Confederacy. Major Bowman will remain at West Point until 8 July 1864, when he retires as a lieutenant colonel. The authorities in Mississippi appoint Jefferson Davis as commander of the state forces.

January 24 (Thursday) In *Georgia,* the federal arsenal at Augusta is taken over by state troops pursuant to orders from the governor. Captain Arnold Elzey (Jones), who graduated West Point in 1837, is the officer in command of the facility, but his sympathies are conspicuously with the South and in April he resigns his commission, leaves the 2nd Artillery behind, and becomes a colonel in the Confederate 1st Maryland Infantry Regiment.

In Army activity, federal troops from Fort Monroe, Virginia, are sent to reinforce and defend Fort Pickens in Florida. This fort will not fall into Confederate hands. Fort Zachary Taylor in Key West remains in Union control as well. Both are important gulf bases and bolster the efforts to win the war. Second Lieutenant (later brigadier general) Richard Henry Jackson participates in the defense of Fort Pickens. He had enlisted in the army on 12 December 1851 as a private after arriving in the United States from Ireland. Subsequent to duty in Florida, he is ordered to the Department of the South. He participates in various actions and is for a time chief of artillery (X Corps).

In North Carolina, the Catawba Indians agree to serve with the Confederacy.

January 25 (Friday) In *Washington, D.C.,* former President John Tyler of Virginia, a member of the commissioners attending the Peace Conference, is informed that the USS *Brooklyn* had been sent to sea on the 21st. Tyler immediately inquires of President James Buchanan the purpose of the mission. Buchanan responds in a note that the *Brooklyn* is "on an errand of mercy and relief." The response also informs Tyler that the ship is not sailing toward Charleston. Nevertheless, the southern senators aren't convinced; they suspect the *Brooklyn* is

en route to retake Pensacola. The southerners locate Senator Stephen Mallory and charge him with making sure no action is taken by the *Brooklyn.* President Buchanan is assured that the Confederates will not move against Fort Pickens and in return, on the 29th, he issues orders for the *Brooklyn.*

In Louisiana, Confederate Captain Joseph E. Montgomery orders the *General M. Jeff Thompson* to be converted to a cottonclad ram. The ram, known as the *Jeff Thompson* after modifications, joins Montgomery's Mississippi River Defense Fleet. The modifications include a "4-inch oak sheath with a 1-inch iron covering on her bow, and ... double pine bulkheads filled with compressed cotton bales."

January 26 (Saturday) In *Georgia,* Fort Jackson, established during 1808 on the outskirts of Savannah, is seized by Georgia militia. The Confederates retain the post until it is abandoned during the final days of the war.

In Louisiana, the state secedes from the Union by a vote of 113 to 17. Louisiana is the sixth to break away.

In Confederate general officer activity, Daniel Weisiger Adams (later brigadier general) will soon become lieutenant colonel and then colonel of the 1st Louisiana Regulars. Also, Richard Taylor, the son of President Zachary Taylor, will be appointed colonel of the Confederate 9th Louisiana Regiment. Taylor (later lieutenant general) will initially lead his regiment at First Manassas (Bull Run) during July of this year. General Taylor is also the brother-in-law of Confederate President Jefferson Davis, who married one of Taylor's sisters.

January 28 (Monday) In *Washington, D.C.,* Senator Alfred Iverson, Jr., of Georgia, resigns. General David E. Twiggs is relieved of command of the Department of Texas, and he is succeeded by Colonel Carlos Waite. Nevertheless, Texas secedes from the Union on 1 February and appoints commissioners to confer with Twiggs regarding surrender of U.S. posts.

In Louisiana, Fort Macomb, formerly Fort Wood, established about ten miles from Fort Pike after the War of 1812, is seized by Louisiana state troops. Fort Pike had been seized on 14 January 1861. Both forts are recovered during the following year when New Orleans is regained.

January 29 (Tuesday) Kansas is admitted to the Union as the 34th state (free-state, no slaves).

In Washington, D.C., President Buchanan, based on assurances of southern senators, issues an order, signed by the secretary of war and by the secretary of the navy, and dispatched to the USS *Brooklyn:*

> In consequence of the assurances received from Mr. Mallory in a telegram of yesterday to Messrs. Slidell, Hunter, and Bigler ... that Fort Pickens would not be assaulted, and an offer of such an assurance to the same effect from Colonel Chase for the purpose of avoid-

ing a hostile collision, upon receiving satisfactory assurances from Mr. Mallory and Colonel Chase [commanding the Florida forces] that Fort Pickens will not be attacked and are instructed not to land the company on board the *Brooklyn* unless said fort shall be attacked or preparations shall be made for its attack. The provisions necessary for the supply of the fort you will land.... The commissioners of different States are to meet here on Monday, the 4th February, and it is important that during their session a collision of arms should be avoided ... our right ... to communicate with the Government by special messenger, and its right in the same manner to communicate with yourselves and them, will remain intact as the basis on which the present instruction is given."

Consequently, the naval vessels sent to the area were of no value in cutting off Confederate progress, and the failure to regain the navy yard at Pensacola afforded the Confederates an effortless task to transfer the guns at the yard (about 200) to bolster the defenses at Port Hudson and at Vicksburg.

In Louisiana, the revenue cutter USS *Robert McClelland,* commanded by Captain John G. Breshwood (Brushwood), surrenders to the Confederates. Breshwood had refused an order to leave New Orleans for New York. The secretary of the treasury, John Dix, moved to prevent capture of the vessel. He sent word to the second in command, S.B. Caldwell, to confine the captain; if he resisted, the order mandated that he be "as a mutineer." Dix also proclaims,: "If anyone attempts to haul down the American flag, shoot him on the spot." The order never reached the ship, but it would not have been obeyed. Brestwood and his second in command, Lt. Caldwell, joined the Confederacy and added the cutter to the Confederate service under the name CSS *Pickens.* The *Pickens* operates along the lower Mississippi during 1861 and early 1862.

In Confederate general officer activity, Felix H. Robertson, a cadet at West Point since 1857, resigns to join the Confederate cause. He rises to the rank of brigadier general (1864) following service in the artillery and field command in both Tennessee and Georgia.

January 31 (Thursday) In *Alabama,* the revenue cutter USS *Lewis Cass* surrenders at Mobile. Its commander, Captain J.J. Morrison, had chosen to join the Confederacy. The authorities in Alabama transfer the vessel to the Confederate States Navy about 2 February. Although Morrison joined the Confederacy, the crew remained loyal to the Union. After the surrender of the ship, the sailors made their way back to northern territory. Also, the tender *Alert,* attached to the lighthouse establishment, is also seized at Mobile.

In Louisiana, the USS *Washington,* a revenue schooner commanded by Captain Robert K. Hudgins, is seized by Louisiana state militia while the ship is at New Orleans undergoing repairs.

Late January   In Arkansas, a telegraph arrives in Little Rock presenting up-to-date information on the building crisis between the northern and southern states. Up until the arrival of the telegraph, Little Rock, like many other places, receives the news well after the fact. Within a short while, the Confederates in Arkansas move against the federal arsenal there.

February   Commander Josiah Tatnall, U.S. Navy, will resign his commission and accept a commission in the Confederacy as flag officer of the Navy in Georgia. During the following month, he is commissioned captain in the Confederate Navy.

February 1 (Friday)   Texas secedes from the Union against the opinion of Sam Houston. Although secession occurs, a referendum is held on 23 February and it, too, affirms secession.

February 2 (Saturday)   At about this time, in Mobile, Alabama, the recently captured USS *Lewis Cass* is transferred to the Confederate States Navy.

February 4 (Monday)   In Washington, D.C., a plan to reinforce the garrison at Fort Sumter, designed by Gustav Fox, a former naval officer, is presented to General Winfield Scott. Other plans had been considered, but not chosen. Fox's plan calls for anchoring

> three small men-of-war off the entrance to the Swash Channel as a safe base of operations against any naval attack from the enemy, the soldiers and provisions to be carried to the Charleston bar in the Collins steamer *Baltic,* all the provisions and munitions to be put in portable packages easily handled by one man, the *Baltic* to carry 300 extra sailors and a sufficient number of armed launches to land all the troops at Fort Sumter in one night. Three steam tugs of not more than 6 feet draft of water [were] to be used for carrying in the troops and provisions in case the weather should be too rough for boats. With the exception of the men-of-war and tugs, the whole expedition was to be complete on board the *Baltic,* and its success depended upon the possibility of running past batteries at night, which were distant from the center of the channel 1300 yards.

The plan, considered practical and feasible, gets approval from General Scott. However, shortly after Scott approves, Jefferson Davis gets elected (9 February) as president of the Confederate states and strategy in Washington changes. By 9 February, Fox is informed by General Scott that relief of Fort Sumter was doubtful.

In other activity, the following U.S. senators resign: Robert A. Toombs (Georgia), Judah P. Benjamin (Louisiana) and John Slidell (Louisiana).

In Montgomery, Alabama, representatives of the southern states, who have chosen not to attend the Peace Conference being initiated on this day in Washington, D.C., meet to map strategy for the establishment of a southern Confederacy. The states represented are Alabama, Georgia, Florida, Louisiana, Mississippi and South Carolina. The conference is chaired

by the former secretary of the treasury, Howell Cobb (later Confederate major general) of Georgia. His remarks concerning secession are less than ambiguous. He states, while giving his address, that the breakup of the Union is "a fact, an irrevocable fact; the separation is perfect, complete, and perpetual.... We will this day inaugurate for the south a new era of peace, security, and prosperity." The southern states draw up the "Provisional Constitution of the Confederate States of America." It will be unanimously adopted during the following month.

February 4–27   In Washington, D.C., a meeting convenes for the purpose of determining a way to maintain the Union and preserve peace. The 133 delegates are from twenty-one states, though none are from the nine states that have seceded from the Union. The Peace Conference is chaired by former President John Tyler. Following its conclusion on the 27th, a report is forwarded to Congress. The Senate discusses the options that are presented; however, no solution is found during these last remaining days of the congressional session.

February 6 (Wednesday)   In Arkansas, many Confederate supporters are now in Little Rock and more continue to flow into the town. They include the Yell Rifles, the Phillips County Guards, and militiamen, including the Jefferson Guards of Pine Bluff, the Southwestern Guards, and the LaGrange Cavalry. The Capitol Guards form an outer cordon around the militia camped on the State House grounds, but this action merely infuriates the camp. The governor, Henry M. Rector, demands the surrender of the U.S. arsenal. Former Governor John S. Roane, a general in the Arkansas State Militia, is dispatched to take command of the men gathered in Little Rock. General Thomas. D. Merrick, commander of the First Division, Arkansas Militia, delivers the ultimatum to Captain (later general) James G. Totten, the commander at the arsenal.

In Florida, Union reinforcements, transported by the USS *Brooklyn,* arrive to bolster Fort Pickens; however, due to earlier orders from Washington, the troops are only to land if the fort comes under attack.

February 7 (Thursday)   In Arkansas, Henry Rector receives a telegraph from Albert Pike and R.W. Johnson in Washington, D.C., pleading with the governor not to assault the federal arsenal and explaining that there are no grounds to seize it with force: "For God's sake do not complicate matters by an attack. It will be premature and do incalculable injury. We cannot justify it. The reasons that existed elsewhere for seizure do not exist with us." The governor receives a similar telegraph on the following day from T.C. Hindman.

In Confederate activity, the Choctaw Nation sides with the Confederacy. The Choctaw Indians had lived primarily in Mississippi and several other southern states until 1732, when they ceded their territory to Mississippi and relocated in present day Oklahoma.

February 8 (Friday)   In Alabama, the southern representatives gather in Montgomery to map out the blueprint of the Confederacy. They take decisive action and borrow the U.S. Constitution for its government, nearly in its entirety. But, it does inject a few southern-friendly items, designed to gain friends outside the South and across the ocean. The convention adopts a provision that opposes slave-trade and to ensure it doesn't anger Virginia, it adopts a provision that slaves may not be imported from any states beyond the Confederacy. On the following day, the Confederate representatives will select the president of the Confederate States of America.

In other activity, Pierre Gustave Toutant Beauregard, who was recently replaced as superintendent at West Point, resigns his commission.

In Arkansas, the federal arsenal at Little Rock is seized by the Confederacy. The sparse Union contingent is ordered to relinquish the arsenal or face attack; it complies. The arsenal is surrendered to Arkansas Governor Henry M. Rector. Subsequently, during September 1863, the Union regains the arsenal.

February 9 (Saturday)   In *Confederate activity,* Jefferson Davis is elected as first president of the Confederate States of America by unanimous decision. Davis' vice president, Alexander Stephens of Georgia, will take his oath of office in Montgomery on the 11th. Neither of the two men are considered extremists, which is expected to gain undecided states for the cause. Davis is informed of his presidency the following day, when he heads from Mississippi to Montgomery, Alabama, for his inauguration.

Confederate President Jefferson Davis (Johnson, *Campfire and Battlefield: History of the Conflicts and Campaigns,* **1894).**

President Davis' cabinet will be: Secretary of State Robert A. Toombs (Georgia); Secretary of Treasury Christopher Gustavus Memminger (South Carolina); Secretary of War LeRoy Pope Walker (Alabama); and Secretary of the Navy Stephen M. Mallory (Florida). Also, Judah Benjamin becomes attorney general and John Reagan is selected as postmaster general of the Confederacy. In the meantime, the federals continue preparations for the presidency of Abraham Lincoln, who is to be inaugurated on 4 March in the federal capital, Washington D.C., on the Potomac River.

February 10 (Sunday) In Mississippi, Jefferson Davis, while at his home (Brierfield Plantation) outside of Vicksburg, receives a telegram that informs him the has been elected president of the Confederacy. Davis, a former U.S. Army officer and at present, commander of the Mississippi state forces, was not expecting the news. He accepts the results of the election and makes preparations to depart for Montgomery, Alabama, for his inauguration. His reaction to the choice of the representatives of the southern states is "surprised and disappointed." Davis says he is "better adapted to command in the field, and Mississippi had given me the position which I preferred to any other-the highest rank in her army."

February 11 (Monday) In Illinois, Abraham Lincoln departs from his home in Springfield en route to Washington, D.C., for his inauguration as president of the United States. He expects to make several stops along the way before reaching the capital on 23 February. Just prior to departing, while at the railroad station, speaking to supporters, Lincoln said: "I now leave, not knowing when or whether ever I may return, with a task before me greater than that which rested upon Washington. Without the assistance of that Divine Being who ever attended him, I cannot succeed. With that assistance, I cannot fail. Trusting in Him who can go with me, and remain with you, and be everywhere for good, let us confidently hope that all will yet be well. To His care commending you, as I hope in your prayers you will commend me, I bid you an affectionate farewell."

In Mississippi, Jefferson Davis leaves his plantation en route to Montgomery, Alabama, for his inauguration as president of the Confederate States of America. During Davis' trek, while in Jackson, Mississippi, he encounters former chief justice William Lewis Sharkey, a sincere patriot of Mississippi, but also a Unionist. He inquires of Davis whether he expects war to erupt. Davis replies in the affirmative, that "there would be war, long and bloody, and that it behooved every one to put his house in order." While the two presidents-elect are traveling, at Montgomery, Alabama, the vice president of the Confederacy, Alexander Stephens, is sworn in. Formerly a U.S. congressman representing Georgia, Stephens makes no public statements and the ceremony is handled without fanfare.

February 12 (Tuesday) In Washington, D.C., Horatio King, acting postmaster general, is appointed postmaster general to fill out the term during the final part of President James Buchanan's administration. King, later during 1862 after acquiring a commission as captain, enters the army as assistant quartermaster (Volunteers) and he serves under General Silas Casey in the Army of the Potomac. Afterward, he serves under General Philip Sheridan. During the final stages of the war, on 31 March, he participates in skirmishing near Dinwiddie Court House. During 1897, his gallantry on that day was acknowledged. On 23 September, Horatio Collins King received the Medal of Honor, for his actions on 31 March, 1865.

In Arkansas, the U.S. arsenal at Napoleon is seized by state troops. Also, Texas secedes from the Union by a vote of 167 to 7. A public referendum succeeds on the 23rd. Texas is the seventh state to break from the Union.

In Indiana, President-elect Abraham Lincoln pauses in Indianapolis, and while speaking to the state legislature, he talks of the ongoing crisis in Charleston without specifically stating what his position would be after he takes office, yet implying that the U.S. action was correct. He said, "Would the marching of an army into South Carolina without the consent of her people, and with hostile intent toward them, be invasion? I certainly think it would; and it would be coercion also if the South Carolinians were forced to submit. But if the United States should merely hold and retake its own forts and other property, and collect the duties … or even withhold the mails from places where they were habitually violated, would any or all of these things be invasion or coercion?"

On this day, Lincoln also makes a speech in Cincinnati, Ohio. From today until 3 March, Lincoln will make more than twenty speeches while stopping in such places as Cleveland and Columbus in Ohio; Albany, Buffalo and New York City, in New York; Trenton, New Jersey; and Philadelphia, Harrisburg and Pittsburgh in Pennsylvania.

In Mississippi, Jefferson Davis, while in Jackson en route to Montgomery, Alabama, resigns his commission as major general of Mississippi state forces.

In Confederate general officer activity, many Texans flock to the Confederacy, including Allison Nelson, who raises the 10th Texas Infantry Regiment. Nelson is appointed colonel of the regiment and will subsequently take the unit to Arkansas to join with General Thomas Carmichael Hindman, who is appointed brigadier general of the Confederate Army during September of this year. In August, the 8th Texas Cavalry (Terry's Texas Rangers) is established by Benjamin Franklin Terry.

February 13 (Wednesday) In Washington, D.C., Abraham Lincoln is officially declared the president of the United States after the count of the electoral votes. The results: Lincoln, 180; John Bell, 39; John Breckinridge, 72; and Stephen Douglas, 12. Abraham Lincoln, the son of Thomas and Nancy Hanks Lincoln, was born in Kentucky (Hardin County) on 12 February 1809. His parents had two other children, Thomas and Sarah. Abraham married Mary Todd Lincoln during 1842 and they had four children: Robert Todd (born 1843); Edward Baker (born 1846, died young during 1850); William Wallace (born 1850, died young during 1862) and Thomas (Tad, born 1853, died in 1871).

One of Lincoln's first military appointments is that of Nathaniel Prentiss Banks, a former congressman and former governor of Massachusetts (resigned January 1861). Lincoln, to the astonishment of many army officers, is appointed as major general, despite no military service.

In Alabama, the Confederate Congress continues to discuss the situation with regard to the U.S. control within the boundaries of the Confederate States. It passes the following resolution: "That this Government takes under its charge the questions and difficulties now existing between the several States of this Confederacy and the Government of the United States relating to the occupation of the forts, arsenals, navy-yards, and other public establishments, and that the President of this Congress be directed to communicate this resolution to the governors of the States."

By passing the resolution, the Confederate Congress takes responsibility away from Charleston with regard to the plan of action against Fort Sumter and places responsibility solely with the Confederate Congress.

South Carolina Governor Francis Pickens is informed of the decision by telegraph and responds with a letter, written to the president of the Provisional Congress, Howell Cobb. It states:

> In the consideration of the question of Fort Sumter, I have not been insensible of those matters which are in their nature consequential, and have, I trust, weighed with all the care which befits the grave responsibilities of the case, the various circumstances which determine the time when this attack should be made. With the best lights which I could procure in guiding or assisting me, I am perfectly satisfied that the welfare of the new confederation, and the necessities of this state, require that Fort Sumter should be reduced before the close of the present administration at Washington. If an attack is delayed until after the inauguration of the incoming president of the United States, the troops now gathered in the capital may then be employed in attempting; that, which, previous to that time, they could not be spared to do. They dare not leave Washington now to do that which then will be a measure too inviting to be resisted. Mr. Lincoln can not do more for this State than Mr. Buchanan has done. Mr. Lincoln will not concede what Mr. Buchanan has refused. And Mr. Buchanan has placed his refusal upon grounds which determine his reply to six states as completely as to the same demand if made by a single state. If peace can be secured, it will be by the prompt use of the occasion when the forces of the United States are withheld from our harbor. If war can be

averted, it will be by making the capture of Fort Sumter a fact accomplished during the continuance of the present administration, and leaving to the incoming administration the question of an open declaration of war. Such a declaration, separated as it will be from any present act of hostilities during Mr. Lincoln's administration, may become to him a matter requiring consideration. That consideration will not be expected of him, if the attack on the fort is made during his administration, and becomes therefore, as to him, an act of present hostility. Mr. Buchanan can not resist, because he has not the power. Mr. Lincoln may not attack, because the cause of quarrel will have been, or may be considered by him, as past. Upon this line of policy have I acted, and upon the adherence to it may be found, I think, the most rational expectation of seeing that fort, which is even now a source of danger to the state, restored to the position of the state, without those consequences which I should most deeply deplore.

February 14 (Thursday)   In Montgomery, Alabama, the Confederate Congress passes a resolution giving authorization to the Committee on Naval Affairs to contact various U.S. naval officers regarding service in the Confederacy. The chairman of the committee, C.M. Conrad, without delay sends telegrams to targeted officers, one of whom was Commander Raphael Semmes, at present a member of the Lighthouse Board at the capital in Washington, D.C. Semmes receives the telegram while at home with his family. The message requests that he travel to Montgomery, Alabama, the temporary capital of the Confederacy, to confer with the Confederate Committee on Naval Affairs. At nearly the same time he opens the telegram he is preparing his answer. On the following day, Semmes offers his resignation and it is accepted. Simultaneously he offers his resignation from the Lighthouse Board.

February 15 (Friday)   In Washington, D.C., the Peace Conference continues, but without results.

In South Carolina, the rebels in Charleston maintain their intent to oust the federal troops from Fort Sumter.

In Union activity, the U.S. Navy accepts the resignation of Raphael Semmes, which he had submitted earlier in the day. He also submitted his resignation to the Lighthouse Board, but no response ever arrives. Semmes will arrive at Montgomery on the 18th and afterward will enter the Confederate States Navy with command of the CSS *Sumter,* initially built in Philadelphia as a steam merchant ship and named *Habana.* The Confederates purchase the vessel in New Orleans and transform it into a cruiser. During June, the ship is commissioned, and shortly thereafter, Semmes evades the Union naval blockade at the mouth of the Mississippi River and passes through the Gulf of Mexico into open seas.

February 16 (Saturday)   In Alabama, Jefferson Davis arrives at Montgomery from his home

in Mississippi. His wife, Varina Howell Davis, and their children do not arrive to join him until 1 March.

In Texas, the federal arsenal and barracks in San Antonio, Texas, is seized by the Confederacy. The arsenal is not regained until 1865.

In Confederate general officer activity, by this time, the ranks of the Confederate forces in Texas are rapidly expanding. Joseph Lewis Hogg, whose former Army service included participation in the Mexican War, is commissioned colonel (Texas troops) and initiates action upon authority of the governor to raise a force. During February 1862, Hogg is appointed brigadier general in the Confederate Army. Also, Matthew Duncan Ector, a Georgia attorney who had relocated Texas, enlists in the Confederate Army with the rank of private; however, shortly thereafter he is appointed colonel of the 14th Texas Cavalry. His command as part of General Hogg's brigade will move to Mississippi during spring of 1862, following the battle at Shiloh (Pittsburg Landing), Tennessee, in April. Ector also rises to the rank of brigadier general (August 1862). In addition, William Read Scurry (later brigadier general) is appointed lieutenant colonel of the 4th Texas Regiment.

February 18 (Monday)   In Montgomery, Alabama, Jefferson Davis is inaugurated president of the Confederate States; the ceremony takes place in the city that now serves as the capital of the Confederacy. He said in his speech: "We have entered upon a career of independence which must be inflexibly pursued through many years of controversy with our late associates of the northern states.... As a necessity, not a choice, we have resorted to the remedy of separation, and henceforth our energies must be directed to the conduct of our own affairs, and the perpetuity of the Confederacy which we have formed."

Confederate Vice President Alexander Stephens, who only a few short months ago had been pleading that Georgia remain loyal to the Constitution, now finds himself altering some of his views. While in Savannah making a speech later this month, Stephens explains that "our fathers [the founders of the country] held slavery to be wrong every way, socially, morally and politically.... Our new government is founded upon exactly the opposite ideas; its foundations are laid; its cornerstone rests upon the great truth that the Negro is not equal to the white man; that slavery, subordination to the superior race is his natural and normal condition. This, our new government, is the first in the history of the world based upon this great physical, philosophical and moral truth."

In Texas, General David E. Twiggs, U.S. Army, surrenders all federal bases and the troops under his command to the Texas state authorities, essentially giving the Confederates more then one million dollars worth of property, including arms, munitions, horses, wagons and mules. The Texas state troops that accept Twiggs' surrender in San Antonio are led by Colonel Ben

McCulloch. General Twiggs had been removed from command on 28 January 1861 and was succeeded by Colonel Carlos Waite. Colonel Waite (1st Infantry Regiment), at Camp Verde, Arizona, having part of his force in Texas and part in the Indian Territory, works get to the units (Companies A, G, H, I, and K) safely out of Texas. With orders to rendezvous near Indianola, the companies later arrive at Green Lake, but afterward, only three companies (A, H and I) make it out of Texas. The others are captured on 25 April 1861.

Also, Fort Belknap is one of the posts surrendered prior to the actual outbreak of the war. Another strategic post, Fort Davis, is abandoned due to Twiggs' orders. Confederate troops occupy Fort Davis (Jeff Davis County) during April of this year. Soon after, during May 1861, Twiggs is appointed to the rank of major general in the Confederacy. He is assigned command of the troops in Louisiana. In conjunction, Camp Cooper is abandoned on the 21st and at Fort Brown, Captain (later General) George Stoneman declines the order. He instead gathers the troops of the 2nd (later 5th) Cavalry, still loyal to the Union, and travels by ship to New York. Stoneman becomes a brigadier general during August 1861, and by March 1863, he rises to the rank of major general.

February 19 (Tuesday)   In Montgomery, Alabama, President Jefferson Davis' cabinet begins to be put in place (see also, **February 9, 1861**). While Davis' cabinet members are beginning to assume their duties, farther north in Washington, D.C., the opposite effect is occurring. The sympathies of many members of President James Buchanan's cabinet lie with the South and secession. Consequently, the pro-South members mischievously deal with government business and whenever possible, place obstacles in the way to assist the Southern cause.

In Washington, D.C., President James Buchanan and his cabinet face a jeopardized Fort Moultrie and the inability of its naval forces to assist against the insurrection. U.S. warships had been scattered far and wide, which makes it difficult if not nearly impossible to properly provide aid to the beleaguered forts that stretch across the South. All are thinly manned and unprepared to repulse a serious attack. At Fort Moultrie, S.C., it requires a minimum number of about 700 troops to properly operate and defend; however, the garrison stands only at about eighty troops, commanded by Major Robert Anderson.

In political activity, President-elect Abraham Lincoln arrives in New York City, having traveled through Indianapolis, Cincinnati, Columbus, Pittsburgh, Cleveland, Buffalo and Albany en route to Washington. The trip, expected to be reserved, is consumed with well wishers and the constant calls for him to speak to the people.

February 20 (Wednesday)   *In Confederate activity,* the Provisional Confederate Congress creates the Department of the Navy. Shortly afterward, Stephen M. Mallory, former U.S. senator from Florida, is selected as secretary of the Confederate States Navy. He is confirmed in early March by the Confederate Congress. Mallory remains in the position for the duration of the war; however, his selection brings about unexplained criticism. Mallory had been the chairman of the U.S. Naval Committee while in Congress and, with the birth of the Confederacy, he is faced with severe problems, primarily building and manning a navy that has no ships and a Confederacy that lacks materials to build them. Although large numbers of former U.S. naval officers are flocking to the Confederacy, there is a need to train fresh recruits. Mallory establishes a naval school at Richmond.

He is also faced with grave financial problems. The U.S. Naval blockade of southern ports curtails the export of the South's primary commodities; merchant ships that attempt to run the blockade risk destruction or capture. Nonetheless, the Confederate treasury has no funds to spend, making it difficult to purchase iron for shipbuilding. The price of iron jumps from about $25 a ton to about $1,300 per ton. From the latter part of June 1861 until 1 December 1862, Secretary Mallory enters into more than thirty separate contracts with companies in the south in the process of acquiring forty gunboats for the Confederacy, but he also consummates other contracts for the same purpose with suppliers outside the country.

In other activity, Stephen Dill Lee (West Point, 1854), a South Carolinian and a skilled artillery officer, resigns from the U.S. Army. He joins the Confederacy and becomes an aide-de-camp with the rank of captain to General Pierre Beauregard.

February 21 (Thursday) *In political activity,* President-elect Abraham Lincoln, en route to Washington, D.C., receives an assassination threat. Reluctantly, plans are changed. The main part continues as usual along the scheduled route, but Lincoln's route is switched. He is compelled to improvise and travel incognito through Baltimore to arrive in Washington without incident. The president, on the following day, after visiting the Pennsylvania Legislature in Harrisburg and the city of Philadelphia, travels after dark and arrives in Washington on Saturday morning February 23.

In Montgomery, Alabama, Confederate President Jefferson Davis sends two officers, Commander Semmes and Caleb Huse, on missions to procure arms for the Confederacy, with the former traveling to the northern states and the latter embarking for Europe.

In Texas, Camp Cooper, along the Clear Fork of the Brazos River, established during 1856, is abandoned by the Union.

February 22 (Friday) **In Pennsylvania,** while celebrating George Washington's birthday in Philadelphia, President Lincoln states: "There is no need for bloodshed and war." President Lincoln, after being asked, raises the Stars and Stripes over Independence Hall.

In Confederate activity, the Confederate Congress directs Pierre Beauregard to repair to Montgomery. The Congress afterward orders Beauregard to Charleston with instructions to report to Governor Francis Pickens. He arrives in Charleston on 3 March.

February 23 (Saturday) Abraham Lincoln, having evaded assassins by changing his route of travel, arrives unharmed at Willard's Hotel in Washington, D.C. at about 0600.

February 26 (Tuesday) In Texas, the Union abandons Camp Colorado, initially a temporary post that had been established during 1855 and later re-established in Coleman County north of the Colorado River. The Confederates hold the post for the duration of the war.

February 27 (Wednesday) In Washington, D.C., the Peace Commission, chaired by former President John Tyler, concludes on this day, without having any genuine success. The commission presents a proposition that calls for six amendments to the U.S. Constitution; however, the suggested amendments receive no consideration. Congress declines calling for a Constitutional Convention and the Crittenden amendment (restoration of the Missouri Compromise) fails to pass.

February 28 (Thursday) Colorado is established as a U.S. territory.

In Texas, Fort Chadbourne, established in Coke County in the vicinity of Oak Creek during 1852, is surrendered to Texas state troops led by Colonel Henry E. McCulloch. After the close of the war, U.S. troops reoccupy the post, but within a few years it is again abandoned.

March In Texas, the Union continues to abandon its forts, including Camp Wood, Camp Hudson, Forts Brown, Duncan, Clark, Inge, Lancaster, McIntosh, Mason and Fort Bliss, but troops in other posts also depart. The process continues during April.

In Confederate general officer activity, John Wesley Frazer (West Point, 1849) resigns his commission in the U.S. Army and joins the Confederacy as lieutenant colonel, 8th Alabama Infantry; however, Frazer leaves this position to assume the rank of colonel (later brigadier general), 28th Alabama. His regiment will operate in Kentucky.

March 1 (Friday) **In Washington, D.C.,** General David E. Twiggs, U.S. Army, is dishonorably discharged from the U.S. Army by order of Secretary of War Joseph Holt on March 1 due to charges of "treachery to the flag of the United States." He had surrendered all troops and property under his command in the state of Texas to Confederates. Twiggs, who had joined the Army during the War of 1812, had been about nine years old when President George Washington succumbed during 1799. And he had risen to the rank of major general during the Mexican War.

Some Union officers in Texas refuse to capitulate. One of these, Major Edmund Kirby Smith, 2nd Cavalry, informs the Confederate

Sul Ross (Texas Rangers) that Fort Colorado will be held. Nevertheless, on April 6, Major Smith has a different perspective.

In Union general officer activity, 2nd Lieutenant Eli Long (later major general), a cavalry officer, is promoted to the rank of 1st lieutenant. In August he transfers to the Department of the South and is attached to the 4th U.S. Cavalry; however, after the Battle of Murfreesboro, where he is wounded, he is appointed colonel of the 4th Ohio Cavalry, a volunteer regiment, which just prior to his appointment had been demoralized after surrendering to Confederate General John B. Hood. Long rebuilds the confidence of the men and rallies them into again being a formidable unit at Tullahoma and Chickamauga as well as during the Atlanta campaign.

In Confederate general officer activity, Captain Pierre Beauregard, who had resigned his commission the prior February, is appointed brigadier general in the Confederate Army. Also, Ambrose P. Hill (West Point, 1847) resigns form the U.S. Army to accept a position in the Confederacy. He is appointed colonel of the 13th Virginia Infantry.

Another future Confederate general, James Barbour Terrill, becomes major of the 13th Virginia and later colonel (May 1863). The 13th Regiment gains fame as a dependable and rigid unit throughout the various engagements in Virginia and Maryland up to and including Chancellorsville during May of 1863. Soon after, the regiment plays a key part at Gettysburg when Lee's Army moves into Pennsylvania.

March 2 (Saturday) The Utah Territory is split into three territories, adding Dakota and Nevada.

In Naval activity, the USS *Henry Dodge*, a revenue cutter commanded by 1st Lt. William P. Rogers, is confiscated in Galveston Bay by Texas authorities. Rogers switches allegiance to the Confederate States and remains as commander of the vessel, which is afterward transferred to the navy. The vessel remains in the region to bolster the defenses of the Texas coast, operating there until December of 1862, when it moves to Houston and comes under the jurisdiction of the quartermaster of the Confederate Army in the city.

March 3 (Sunday) **In Washington, D.C.,** Senator Robert W. Johnson (Arkansas) resigns. In other activity, U.S. General Winfield Scott mentions in a letter to the incoming secretary of state, William H. Seward, that "federal relief of Fort Sumter is not practical." Also, Washington is being prepared for the inauguration of Abraham Lincoln. Due to the recent threats against the president-elect, precautions are taken to ensure the inauguration ceremony is not interrupted by an assassin's bullet.

In South Carolina, Brigadier General Pierre G.T. Beauregard arrives at Charleston and assumes command. He confers with the governor and afterward begins inspecting the city's defenses.

In Confederate general officer activity, Captain Richard Heron Anderson, 2nd Dragoons, resigns his commission to join the Confederate cause. He becomes a major of infantry in the Confederacy, but during mid-July, he is promoted to brigadier general.

March 4 (Monday)   In Washington, D.C., Abraham Lincoln is inaugurated as the 16th president of the United States. He succeeds James Buchanan. Lincoln's vice president is Hannibal Hamlin of the state of Maine. John C. Breckinridge, the vice president under President James Buchanan, joins the Confederacy and becomes a major general. Subsequently he becomes the Confederate secretary of war.

During his inaugural address President Lincoln states: "No state on its own mere action, can get out of the Union, thus if war is to come, it will come over secession, not slavery." (Lincoln's philosophy was that the Union was perpetual.) He continues, "Intelligence, patriotism, Christianity and a firm reliance on Him [God] who has never yet forsaken this favored land, are still competent to adjust, in the best way, all our present difficulties. In your hands, my dissatisfied fellow countrymen, and not in mine, is the momentous issue of civil war. The government will not assail you. You can have no conflict without being yourselves the aggressors. You have no oath registered in Heaven to destroy the government; while I shall have the most solemn one to preserve protect and defend it." At the conclusion of the speech, Chief Justice Taney administers the oath of office to Lincoln.

Congress adjourns, following a most unusual session, consumed with speeches, many of which were delivered by members who were departing the Union to offer their services to the Confederacy. Some level antagonistic threats toward the laws of the nation, which they would not agree to abide by, and gave additional hints of the move to "trample the Union underfoot." The inauguration ceremony is surrounded by large numbers of troops to ensure that none of the many threats upon the life of President Lincoln would succeed.

In Montgomery, Alabama, Samuel Mallory, earlier named secretary of the Confederate States Navy, is confirmed by the Confederate Congress. After earlier being selected by President Davis, Mallory begins to assemble his department. Franklin Buchanan is appointed to the Bureau of Orders and Detail. Other appointments include George Minor to the Bureau of Ordnance and Hydrography and James A. Semple as paymaster to the Bureau of Provisions and Clothing. Mallory also appoints Doctor W.A. Spotswood to the Department of Medicine and Surgery.

Upon the return of Commander Raphael Semmes to Alabama after his northern venture, he is appointed to the Confederate Lighthouse Board, which is under the jurisdiction of the Confederate Treasury Department. Yet another selection is Edward M. Tidball, who is appointed as chief clerk of the Confederate Navy Department.

In other activity, the Confederates change the landscape. They raise the Stars and Bars over the capital in what becomes the initial unfurling of the flag of the Confederate States of America over the capitol. The flag is separate from the Confederate battle flag, which is later developed to distinguish it from the U.S. flag on the battlefield.

In Union general officer activity, Edwin Henry Stoughton (West Point, 1859), while on a leave of absence, subsequent to garrison duty in New York, resigns his commission; however, on 25 September, he is appointed colonel (later brigadier general) of the 4th Vermont Regiment. Afterward, the regiment is posted as part of the defenses of the capital during the winter of 1861–1862 and later participates in the Peninsular campaign.

March 5 (Tuesday)   In Washington D.C., in Congress, the Senate confirms the appointments to the cabinet of President Lincoln. The members are: secretary of state, William H. Seward (New York); secretary of the treasury, Salmon P. Chase (Ohio); secretary of war, Simon Cameron (Pennsylvania); secretary of the Navy, Gideon Welles (Connecticut); secretary of the interior, Caleb B. Smith (Indiana); postmaster general, Montgomery Blair (Maryland); and attorney general, Edward Bates (Maryland).

While the South is in the process of seizing federal property, particularly bases and supplies, the North and more so the West still believe that war is not imminent.

Also on this day, three Southern representatives, at the behest of the Confederate Congress, arrive in Washington in search of official recognition of their rank and mission of settling the differences separating the U.S. and the states that have seceded. They are permitted to remain in the capital; however, William H. Seward, the secretary of state, affords them no official communication. The Confederate representatives, selected by President Jefferson Davis on 27 February, are Martin J. Crawford, John Forsyth and A. B. Roman.

In South Carolina at Fort Sumter, the crisis continues and Major Robert Anderson has made it clear through repeated communications that in order to maintain control of the fort, reinforcements must be sent. He had also informed Washington that supplies were dwindling.

In Confederate general officer activity, General Pierre G.T. Beauregard assumes command of the Southern forces at Charleston, S.C. Former Lieutenant William Robertson Boggs (West Point, 1853) who had resigned his commission during the previous month to join the Confederacy, will be appointed captain (later brigadier general) and ordnance officer under Beauregard. Boggs, after a short stint in Charleston, transfers to the command of General Braxton Bragg in Florida, and from there he will move to Georgia (1862).

March 6 (Wednesday)   In Washington, D.C., the situation at Fort Sumter remains a top priority, but no solutions seem to be imminent. In one of Major Robert Anderson's recent messages, dated 28 February, he informed the administration that in addition to supplies and provisions, at least 20,000 reinforcements would be required to ensure Union control of the fort. President Abraham Lincoln's cabinet continues to work on the problem, but General Scott has already become convinced that reinforcements could not be sent for weeks. Major Anderson was informed on 28 February by the Department of War that Confederate commissioners were due to confer with the authorities; the message states that Secretary of War Joseph Holt (Buchanan's administration) "entertains the hope that nothing will occur now of a hostile character."

In South Carolina, General Pierre G.T. Beauregard is appointed commander of all forces (state and Confederate) in the state. His appointment had been a joint decision of the secretaries of the departments of war of both the Confederacy and the state of South Carolina (LeRoy Pope Walker and Andrew McGrath, respectively). The combined forces in South Carolina, at the time of Beauregard's appointment, number ten regiments and just under 9,000 troops.

March 7 (Thursday)   In Texas, Camp Verde, established during 1857 along the north bank of Verde Creek, is abandoned by the Union. The camp at one time was headquarters for the Camel Corps, established because of an idea of the secretary of war at the time, Jefferson Davis. Fort Ringgold (Ringgold Barracks) is also abandoned by the Union.

In Confederate general officer activity, former Lt. Colonel Braxton Bragg (West Point, 1837) who had left the Army in 1856, this day becomes a brigadier general in the Confederacy. Bragg will be dispatched from his home in

General Samuel Cooper (Mottelay, *The Soldier in Our Civil War,* **1886).**

Louisiana to command the area from Mobile, Alabama, to Pensacola, Florida. In less than one week, Bragg establishes his headquarters at Pensacola. He is promoted to major general during September.

Samuel Cooper (West Point, 1815) on this day is appointed brigadier general in the Confederacy. He resigned from the U.S. Army as adjutant general, a position he held since 1852. Cooper is promoted to full general during August of this year to rank from May. For the duration of the conflict, he reports only to President Jefferson Davis, who relies upon Cooper due to his skills regarding military procedures and organizational logistics rather than his field ability. He will spend no time in the field; however, the Confederacy gains immensely from his talents.

March 11 (Monday) **In New York,** the steamer USS *Mohawk*, having arrived from Key West, Florida, during early February, departs for an escort mission. It is to protect a supply ship, the *Empire City*, while it proceeds to Havana, Cuba. Once the supply ship safely concludes its voyage, the *Mohawk* sails to Indianola, Texas. From there after various stops, the *Mohawk* arrives at Pensacola during May, the month following the surrender of Fort Sumter.

In Montgomery, Alabama, the Confederate Congress adopts a Provisional Constitution protecting states' rights and slavery. Essentially, the Confederates' constitution in many ways parallels the U.S. Constitution. However, it does not become effective until the following year.

March 12 (Tuesday) **In Washington, D.C.,** the postmaster general, Montgomery Blair, aware of Gustavus Fox's relief plan for Fort Sumter, which had been set aside during the previous month, sends a telegram to Fox which requests that he repair to Washington. Fox responds in the affirmative and arrives in the capital from New York on the following day in an attempt to revive the effort to relieve the fort.

In Montgomery, Alabama, the Confederate Provisional Constitution, adopted on the previous day, is distributed to the various states for ratification. On this day, the Alabama Convention ratifies the document by a vote of 87 to 5.

In Texas, Fort McIntosh at Laredo is abandoned by the Union. Afterward, it is occupied by Confederate forces.

In Confederate Naval activity, in South Carolina the vessel *Lady Davis,* a warship acquired by Governor Francis W. Pickens at Richmond, is placed into the service of the Confederacy. The ship is commanded by Lieutenant Thomas B. Huger. In May its personnel will capture Pilot Boat 7 at Charleston and rename it the *Savannah* (a privateer).

March 13 (Wednesday) **In Washington, D.C.,** President Abraham Lincoln confers with Gustavus Fox, the latter having recently been summoned from New York by Montgomery Blair, the postmaster general, to again present his plan to relive the garrison at Fort Sumter at Charleston, South Carolina. After listening, the president and the others move to the office of General Winfield Scott.

As the discussion resumes, Scott offers his opinion that the defenses at Charleston during February were overcome, but at present, he insists that the Confederate batteries now in place would cause a rescue mission to fail. Consequently, Lincoln seeks additional counsel. He sends a message to each of his cabinet members seeking their input on the feasibility of the mission. The members file their respective opinions on 15 March.

In other activity, the USS *Powhatan*, the flagship of Commodore Pendergrast, arrives in New York after a long stay in the Gulf of Mexico at Vera Cruz. On the 27th, the *Powhatan* is placed out of service for repairs.

March 15 (Friday) **In Washington, D.C.,** President Lincoln's cabinet members return their reports to the president regarding their opinions on whether to launch the plan for the relief of Fort Sumter; the majority is against taking action. Only two members, Montgomery Blair (postmaster general) and Salmon Chase, the secretary of the treasury, support Gustavus Fox's plan. Those who oppose action are Edward Bates (attorney general); Simon Cameron (secretary of war), William H. Seward (secretary of state), Caleb B. Smith (secretary of the interior) and Gideon Welles (secretary of the navy).

Those in opposition voice various reasons, including finding themselves in agreement with General Scott's assessment that it is too late. Simon Cameron's response included: "As the abandonment of the fort in a few weeks, sooner or later, appears to be an inevitable necessity, it seems to me that the sooner it is done the better." Nevertheless, relief of the fort is not yet written off and discussions continue.

In Texas, Camp Wood, established in the vicinity of present-day Camp Wood in 1857, is abandoned by the Union. The following June, Texas Rangers occupy the post.

In Union activity, James William Forsyth (West Point, 1856) is promoted to the rank of 1st lieutenant (later brigadier general). Later on 24 October he is promoted to captain. He participates in the Peninsular campaign and the Maryland campaign. Subsequently, he becomes acting adjutant general on General Philip Sheridan's staff and later chief of staff. Forsyth receives the brevet rank of brigadier general after admirable service at several engagements, including Cedar Creek, Fisher's Hill and Winchester.

March 16 (Saturday) **In Montgomery, Alabama,** the present capital of the Confederacy, the Provisional Congress adjourns. On this day the Confederate government appoints three men as commissioners to England. They are William Lowndes Yancey, Pierre A. Rost and Ambrose Dudley Mann. The representatives are to seek help from England, including support to end the Union blockade of southern ports.

In Arizona, southern sympathizers proclaim that Arizona secedes from the Union. The Confederates attempt to control Arizona, but the Union prevails. Only one skirmish (15 April 1862) occurs between Union and Confederate troops in Arizona during the entire war.

In Georgia, the Confederate Provisional Constitution is ratified by a unanimous vote (260 votes in the affirmative). *In Army activity,* Robert E. Lee is promoted by General Winfield Scott to full colonel, commanding the First Cavalry, U.S. Army. President Lincoln signs the commission on March 28.

In Confederate general officer activity, Franklin Gardner (West Point, 1843), a veteran of the Mexican War, is appointed lieutenant colonel (later brigadier general) of infantry, Confederate Army. Gardner serves in Kentucky, Mississippi and Tennessee and rises through the ranks to become a major general in April of the following year.

William Stephen Walker, a veteran of the Mexican War, at present a captain in the 1st U.S. Cavalry, who resigned his commission on 1 May to join the Confederacy, is commissioned captain in the Regular Confederate Army. He is afterward promoted to colonel and named inspector general of the Department of South Carolina and Georgia.

March 17 (Sunday) **In Texas,** Camp Hudson, known also as Fort Hudson, established in June 1857 along the Chihuahua Trail (Kinner County, later Val Verde County), is abandoned by the Union. In October 1867, a contingent of the U.S. 9th Cavalry arrives to regarrison the post.

Fort Inge (initially called Camp Leona), established March 1849 just outside Uvalde along the Leona River, is abandoned by the Union. The garrison moves to Fort McKavett (Menard County). Union troops reoccupy the post during 1866. In addition, Fort Lancaster (Initially Camp Lancaster), established along Live Oak Creek near the Pecos River during 1855, is abandoned by the Union. U.S. Troops do not return to garrison the post until 1871.

March 19 (Tuesday) **In Washington, D.C.,** Gustavus Fox, pursuant to authorization from the president, departs Washington for Fort Sumter to investigate the situation and gather facts that could be helpful in the event the president authorizes a relief mission. Fox arrives in Charleston on the 21st and is escorted to meet Governor Francis W. Pickens by a former U.S. naval officer, now Confederate Captain Hartstene. Fox persuades the authorities to permit him to visit with Major Robert Anderson; however, he does not reach the fort until after dusk, making it difficult to scan the harbor area.

Major Anderson informs Fox that he agrees with the assessment of General Scott that time had run out. He also tells Fox that the sole solution would be to send an entire army and have it debark on Morris Island. Fox concurs with the impossibility of successfully entering the harbor; however, Fox, after not being able to observe an approaching boat in the darkness until he heard the movement of the oars as it neared the landing, believes a relief force could save the fort from being lost to the Confederates.

After completing the conversation, Fox departs without having made mention that a plan to send a relief force might occur. Major Anderson also informs Fox that his force would not be able to hold the fort beyond 15 April.

In Texas, the Union continues to abandon a post to get more troops to the east. Fort Clark, established during 1852 in the vicinity of Eagle Pass, surrenders to Texas state forces. The post is garrisoned by elements of the 2nd Texas Mounted Rifles until August of the following year; however, after the regiment departs, the post is maintained as a supply depot. Union troops reoccupy the post during December 1866.

March 20 (Wednesday)   In Texas, Fort Duncan, established during 1849 near Eagle Pass, is abandoned by the Union. The post, abandoned during 1859, was re-established by Lt. Colonel Robert E. Lee during March 1860. The Frontier Regiment (Texas troops) later occupy the post and refer to it as Rio Grande Station. U.S. forces return to the post during March 1868. Fort Brown in Brownsville is abandoned by the Union, but in 1863 the Union regains it.

March 21 (Thursday)   In Louisiana, the Confederate Provisional Constitution is ratified by a vote of 94 to 10.

In Confederate general officer activity, James Patrick Major (West Point, 1856) resigns his commission in the U.S. Cavalry. He joins the Confederacy and, subsequent to service on the staff of General Van Dorn, he participates in Missouri as a lieutenant colonel in a regiment composed of Missouri militia. Following his service in Missouri, he participates in the Red River Campaign, eventually rising to the rank of brigadier general during mid-1863. Also, 1st Lt. William Dorsey Pender (West Point, 1854) resigns his commission to join the Confederate Army. He is appointed colonel of the 3rd (subsequently 13th) North Carolina Regiment.

March 23 (Saturday)   In Washington, D.C., Senator Louis T. Wigfall (Texas) resigns. Shortly thereafter he is appointed as colonel in the South Carolina forces. Wigfall plays a part in the final moments of the siege of Fort Sumter.

In Texas, the Confederate Provisional Constitution is ratified by a vote of 126 to 2.

In Confederate general officer activity, Lafayette McLaws (West Point, 1842) resigns his commission as a U.S. Army officer to enter the Confederate Army. He is appointed colonel of the 10th Georgia Infantry, but is promoted to the rank of brigadier general during September. He is promoted to the rank of major general during May 1862.

March 25 (Monday)   In Washington, D.C., as President Abraham Lincoln has been doing for several weeks, he again confers with his advisers on the fate of Fort Sumter, South Car-

olina, and how to resolve the crisis. The meetings continue as the crisis deepens, but the president has gained confidence in the plan put forth by Gustavus Fox, particularly since he returned from Charleston.

In South Carolina, a party dispatched by President Lincoln confers with authorities in Charleston, but nothing substantial emerges, as both sides continue to gain the advantage amid a continuing flow of information, some factual and some erroneous.

March 26 (Tuesday)   In Mississippi, the Confederate Provisional Constitution is ratified by a vote of 78 to 7. Ratification by Mississippi as the fifth state makes the Confederate Constitution effective.

March 27 (Wednesday)   The USS *Powhatan,* at New York, is placed out of commission to allow the ship to undergo repairs. The ship's crew is transferred to the receiving ship and the officers are detached, with some heading to their respective homes on leave, while others are transferred to other ships. The deactivation complicates upcoming orders of 1 April.

March 28 (Thursday)   In Washington, D.C., at the request of President Lincoln, Gustavus Fox prepares another report, which is to formulate the organization of the relief mission. The report is to be distributed to the Department of the Navy and the War Department. By this time, despite the opposition of many in the president's cabinet, Fox has gained formidable strength from two naval officers, Commodore Silas H. Stringham and Commodore Charles Stewart. Both naval officers believe Fort Sumter can be reinforced, without it becoming a Herculean effort by, as perceived by Fox, using darkness for cover and rowing boats out to the fortress in the harbor. Complications develop when on this day General Winfield Scott forwards a message to the president that urges that Fort Sumter be evacuated, but Scott also calls for Fort Pickens at Pensacola to be abandoned.

Meanwhile, President Lincoln takes advantage of a state dinner being held this day. It is the first state dinner given by the president; once

Major General Lafayette McLaws (Johnson, ***Campfire and Battlefield: History of the Conflicts and Campaigns,*** **1894).**

his cabinet members arrive, each is shown the report of Fox. Afterward, they retire into a private room. Shortly thereafter, Gustavus Fox's plan receives approval, although no votes are taken. Consequently, General Scott's position is abandoned by the majority of cabinet members. A meeting is then set for the following day. After concluding the impromptu meeting, all retire to the dinner.

March 29 (Friday)   In Washington, D.C., President Lincoln holds a meeting that includes his entire cabinet to again discuss Fort Sumter. At the conclusion of the conference, only two cabinet members continued to oppose a relief force for Fort Sumter, William H. Seward, secretary of state, and Caleb Smith, secretary of the Interior.

President Lincoln this day issues an order for Secretary of the Navy Gideon Welles: "Sir: I desire that an expedition to move by sea be got ready to sail as early as the 6th of April next, the whole according to memorandum attached; and that you cooperate with the Secretary of War for that object." He also sends a message to the Navy Department: "The *Pocahontas,* at Norfolk, *Pawnee* at Washington, and revenue cutter *Harriet Lane* at New York, to be ready for sea with one month's stores. Three hundred seamen to be ready for leaving the receiving ship at New York." His message to the War Department states: "Two hundred men at New York, ready to leave garrison. One year's stores to be put in a portable form."

Although the plan is in motion, Seward has continued to communicate on his own with the southern commissioners informing them, without the knowledge of the president, that Fort Sumter is to be evacuated.

In Texas, the U.S. 2nd Cavalry abandons Fort Mason. The post was established during 1848 at Post Oak Hill near present day Mason, Texas. U.S. troops return to garrison the post on Christmas Eve, 1866.

March 30 (Saturday)   In Washington, D.C., pursuant to verbal orders from President Lincoln, Gustavus Fox departs for New York with instructions to make arrangements for the relief of Fort Sumter. The instructions caution Fox not to commit to any agreements. Fox, after not receiving written orders as expected, returns to Washington on 2 April.

March 31 (Sunday)   In South Carolina, at Fort Sumter, Major Robert Anderson reports that the garrison's supply of flour had been exhausted on the 29th. At this time, the Union troops are still able to acquire fruits and vegetables in Charleston, but with each passing hour, the situation becomes more dangerous as the Confederates and the Union continue to disagree on the fate of the fort.

In Texas, Fort Bliss in El Paso, established during 1848 in the vicinity of del Norte Pass near Mexico, surrenders to Confederate troops. Union troops under General James H. Carleton reoccupy the post after Confederates under General Henry Hopkins are compelled to abandon West Texas during 1862.

In Confederate general officer activity, First Lieutenant John Bordenave Villepigue (West Point, 1854) resigns from the U.S. Army. He joins the Confederacy as a captain of artillery and later climbs to the rank of brigadier general.

March–May   In the Dominican Republic, the country requests of Spain that it may again be part of the Spanish Empire. Spain, during May, seizing the advantage while the U.S. is concerned with its internal troubles, annexes the country. Protests arise in the United States, but due to preoccupation with the crisis in the southern states, no action is taken. Secretary of State William H. Seward reminds the Spaniards about the Monroe Doctrine. Later, due to the extreme harshness of Spanish rule, the Dominicans initiate a rebellion. The Spanish choose to depart the island voluntarily after the American Civil War.

April   William T. Sherman, recollecting in his book, said: "I thought and may have said, the national crisis has been brought about by the politicians, and as it was upon us, they might fight it out."

In Texas, the Union relinquishes Fort Quitman (on the 5th) and Fort Davis to the Confederates.

In Confederate general officer activity, Samuel Gibbs, French former West Point graduate (1846) from New Jersey, has relocated to Mississippi and is the state's chief of ordnance. Gibbs, a veteran of the Mexican War, is elevated to brigadier general in the Confederacy during October; following this promotion he rises to the rank of major general during August of the following year. Gibbs' artillery experience from West Point is of valuable service to the Confederacy. His tour of duty during the imminent conflict brings him to Richmond and the surrounding area, and later to North Carolina.

Archibald C. Godwin, former candidate for governor of Virginia, enters the Confederate service and is assigned responsibility for Libby Prison in Richmond. He receives a commission as major (later brigadier general). After Godwin's duty in Richmond, he is transferred to North Carolina and while there he forms the 57th North Carolina Infantry.

Also, U.S. Congressman Albert Gallatin Jenkins abandons his seat in Congress as Virginia representative, forms a company of cavalry composed of Virginians, and becomes colonel (later brigadier general) of the 8th Virginia Confederate Cavalry.

John McCausland, subsequent to the secession of Virginia, forms a contingent known as the "Rockledge Artillery," but shortly thereafter, McCausland establishes the 36th Virginia Infantry and receives a commission as colonel (later brigadier general) in the Confederate Army. He leads the 36th as part of General Floyd's Brigade operating in West Virginia and late in the year transfers with his command to Kentucky to join with General Albert S. Johnston.

Also, Thomas Lafayette Rosser, expected to be among this year's West Point graduating class, resigns from the academy to join the Confederacy. Initially Rosser is with the Washington Artillery of New Orleans, but subsequent to the First Battle of Bull Run (Manassas), he becomes colonel (later major general) of the 5th Virginia Cavalry.

Major Paymaster Robert Hall Chilton (West Point, 1837) resigns from the U.S. Army. Soon afterward he accepts a commission as lieutenant colonel in the Confederate Army. Following a stint in the Adjutant and Inspector General's Department (June 1861) and with General Joseph A. Johnston (August 1861), he becomes General Robert E. Lee's chief of staff (June 1862). Subsequent to serving under Lee, Chilton will see some field duty; however, he then gets assigned to Richmond for the duration. Chilton is promoted to brigadier general during autumn of 1862. Nonetheless, his promotion is not officially sanctioned by the Confederate Senate until early 1864.

In Union Naval activity, Secretary of the Navy Gideon Welles is diligently setting a pace for carrying out President Abraham Lincoln's directive to blockade the Southern seacoast. Welles confers with Captain Silas Stringham, whom he appoints as flag officer with responsibility to formulate plans for the blockade. Gideon Welles then prepares to move the naval academy to a safer location at Newport, Rhode Island, the same location used during the War of 1812. Welles later appoints Gustavus Fox to the post of assistant secretary of the Navy to assist with this astronomical task. Fox is a former naval officer who resigned from the service during 1856. He had been chief clerk of the Department of the Navy from May 1861 until his appointment during August 1861. Fox retains the post until May 1866.

April 1 (Monday)   In Washington, D.C., Secretary of State William H. Seward dispatches a message to Captain David D. Porter, U.S. Navy, requesting that he come to the secretary's home. Porter, after finishing dinner with his family, leaves to speak with the secretary. At the time he received the message, Porter had been preparing to leave the service, not to join the Confederacy; rather to travel to California to join the Pacific Mail Steamship Company. After arriving at Seward's residence, a discussion begins that centers around the possibility of a relief of Fort Pickens at Pensacola. Porter is asked to design a blueprint for the operation. Porter, apparently already aware of what Seward wants, has a copy of a plan he had already designed and discussed with Captain Montgomery Meigs (West Point, 1840), the latter attached to the engineers.

Meanwhile, Meigs arrives at the home of Seward and afterward, they depart to meet with President Lincoln to lay out the plan. The president concurs and the operation is put into motion. The *Powhatan* is selected as the ship to transport the relief force under the protection of the warships already in the region. Porter is chosen as commander, but Seward persuades the

Rear Admiral David D. Porter (*Memoir of Commodore David D. Porter,* 1875).

president to retain secrecy, including bypassing Secretary of the Navy Gideon Welles. Lincoln questions the secrecy with regard to Welles, but Seward and Porter get him to agree. President Lincoln issues the order without consulting Welles and the action is questionable, as Welles is both competent and loyal. Just as important, had Welles been informed and against the mission, the president without effort could have overruled him and still ordered the operation.

Nonetheless, the orders are prepared by Captain Porter. Captain Meigs makes a copy of the orders and they are signed by the president. However, as Lincoln orders the *Powhatan* to sea, it is not known that the *Powhatan* has already been assigned to the mission to relieve Fort Sumter. The order to Porter states: "You will proceed to New York, and with the least possible delay assume command of any naval steamer available. Proceed to Pensacola Harbor, and at any cost or risk prevent any expedition from the mainland reaching Fort Pickens or Santa Rosa [island]. You will exhibit this order to any naval officer at Pensacola, if you deem it necessary after you have established yourself within the harbor, and will request cooperation by the entrance of at least one other vessel. This order, its object, and your destination will be communicated to no person whatever until you reach the harbor of Pensacola."

The order creates a major problem for the Department of the Navy. The *Powhatan* was placed out of service on 27 March for repairs and its officers were detached. New orders are issued by the Navy Department, which transmits a telegram that countermands the original order to decommission the ship. The acting commandant, at New York, Captain Foote, despite the obstacles (See March 27) responds to the urgent telegram and commits to working around the clock to have the vessel ready to embark within four days. On 5 April, the

Powhatan is ordered by the Navy Department to participate in the relief of Fort Sumter.

Meanwhile, back at the meeting in the White House, other orders are issued. The second order concerns Captain Samuel Mercer of the *Powhatan*. It detaches him from command of the *Powhatan* due to undescribed circumstances "to place in command ... and for a special purpose, an officer who is duly informed and instructed in relation to the wishes of the Government."

A third order is issued to the commandant at the New York Navy Yard, who is directed as follows "to fit out the Powhatan without delay. Lieutenant Porter will relieve Captain Mercer in command of her. She is bound on secret service, and you will, under no circumstances, communicate to the Navy Department the fact that she is fitting out."

The president also signs a fourth order, which provides Captain Porter with "a commission of plenary powers." It states: "Lieutenant D. D. Porter will take command of the steamer Powhatan, or any other United States steamer ready for sea, which he may deem most fit for the service to which he has been assigned by confidential instructions of this date. All officers are commanded to afford him all such facilities as he may deem necessary for getting to sea as soon as possible. He will select the officers who are to accompany him." Quite peculiarly, some of the orders contain the following: "Recommended: Wm. H. Seward."

After the meeting with the president, Captain Porter and Captain Meigs leave for the headquarters of General Scott to discuss the role of the army in the expedition. Once at headquarters, Porter suddenly discovers that his expectations of commanding the expedition to relieve Fort Pickens by regaining the harbor at Pensacola are being derailed. Captain Porter is excluded from the meeting. He returns to his home, totally unaware of anything except his own orders, and he remains in the dark until the expeditionary force arrives at Pensacola.

Unknown to Porter, General Scott's orders place Colonel Harvey Brown in overall command of the operation. Scott's orders are buffered by a memorandum signed by President Lincoln, but the date on the memorandum is 1 April, the evening Porter was refused attendance at the meeting, which points to the fact that it was most probably prepared at Scott's headquarters the night before Lincoln affixed his signature. The order: "All officers of the Army and Navy, to whom this order may be exhibited, will aid by every means in their power the expedition under command of Col. Harvey Brown, supplying him with men and material and co-operating with him as he may desire." Meanwhile, Secretary of the Navy Gideon Welles still has no knowledge of the orders.

In South Carolina, a telegram sent by one of the southern commissioners, Martin J. Crawford, arrives from Washington with news that indicates that the Union is not planning to relieve Fort Sumter: "I am authorized to say that this government will not undertake to supply Sumter without notice to you. My opinion is that the President has not the courage to execute the order agreed upon in Cabinet for the evacuation of the fort, but that he intends to shift the responsibility upon Major Anderson by suffering him to be starved out." On this day, General Pierre G.T. Beauregard sends a telegram to Confederate Secretary of War LeRoy Pope Walker with the following message: "Batteries here ready to open Wednesday or Thursday. What instructions?"

April 2 (Tuesday)   In Washington D.C., Gustavus Fox returns from New York to attempt to get official orders from the president to continue the operation to relieve Fort Sumter. Two days later, he is able to get approval to resume the operation.

April 3 (Wednesday)   In South Carolina, following a period of debate in which some unsuccessfully attempt to prevent any free states from entering the Confederacy, the Provisional Constitution is ratified. The vote is 138 to 21.

In Naval activity, the American schooner SS *Rhoda H. Shannon*, operating out of Boston, while transporting a cargo of ice to Savannah, enters Charleston harbor accidentally and comes under fire by Confederate batteries. The merchant vessel's colors, the Stars and Stripes, instantly make it a target. At Fort Sumter, returning fire is discussed, and five of eight officers favor firing at the Confederate battery on Morris Island; however, Major Robert Anderson declines giving the order.

April 4 (Thursday)   In Washington, D.C., President Abraham Lincoln continues discussions with his cabinet and advisers regarding the dilemma faced by the federal defenders at Fort Sumter. In related activity, Gustavus Fox is told that messengers would be dispatched Charleston to inform the Confederates that an expedition to resupply the fort is being prepared. While meeting with the president, Fox attempts to explain the logistics involved and the short amount of time to bring the operation to fruition and reach Charleston in nine days. With written orders, signed by General Winfield Scott, Fox arrives back in New York on the following day.

In South Carolina, Major Anderson, who up to this point has not explained his reasons for not taking any offensive action, tells his officers that orders from Washington on 10 January and 23 February were to act only defensively.

Meanwhile, the South Carolina militia, already quite active, is awaiting orders. Major General Samuel McGowan (state militia) and Brigadier General Pierre Beauregard are poised to seize the Union fort if it does not heed the demand to surrender. McGowan will attain the rank of colonel, 14th South Carolina Infantry, the following year, and subsequent to the battle of Fredericksburg in December 1862, where he distinguishes himself as a fiery fighter, he is promoted to brigadier general.

In Virginia at Richmond, the State Convention rejects an ordinance of secession by about two to one.

April 5 (Friday)   In Washington, D.C., Union Secretary of the Navy Gideon Welles directs four U.S. vessels to the defense of Fort Sumter, South Carolina. The orders are issued to Captain Samuel Mercer and direct him "to protect them ... repelling by force, if necessary, all obstructions towards provisioning the fort and reinforcing it; for in case of resistance to the peaceable primary object of the expedition a reinforcement of the garrison will also be attempted." The orders also stipulate that if the authorities in Charleston permit access and allow the garrison to receive the provisions, the squadron is to "return north." One of the four designated vessels, the *Powhatan*, had already embarked for Fort Pickens, Florida, eliminating it from the squadron. The other vessels are the *Harriet Lane*, *Pawnee* and *Pocahontas*. Secretary Welles is unaware of President Lincoln's actions of 1 April, when at the urging of Secretary of State Seward, the president ordered the *Powhatan* to Florida.

In South Carolina, Major Robert Anderson is informed about a telegram from Confederate commissioner Crawford to the authorities in Charleston, dated 1 April, indicating that Washington was abandoning efforts to relieve the garrison. In disbelief, Anderson sends a telegram to Washington in hopes that Crawford had misinformation. In the same message, Anderson makes it clear that the fort is becoming untenable, stating: "Unless we receive supplies I shall be compelled to stay here without food, or to abandon this post very early next week." Captain (later brigadier general) Abner Doubleday, with regard to the grim situation, later notes: "At this time, the seeming indifference of the politicians to our fate made us feel like orphan children of the Republic, deserted by both the State and Federal administration."

In Texas, Fort Quitman, established in September 1858 near the Rio Grande River in Hud-

Fort Pickens, Santa Rosa Island, at Pensacola, Florida (Mottelay, *The Soldier in Our Civil War*, 1886).

speth County about eighty miles below El Paso, is abandoned by the Union. Afterward the obscure post is sporadically used by both Confederate and Union troops depending on who controls the area at the time. The Union reoccupies the post in January 1868 when a contingent of the U.S. 9th Cavalry arrives on New Year's Day.

April 5–15 THE EXPEDITION TO RELIEVE FORT SUMTER In New York, Gustavus Fox, the man named to command the expedition to relieve Fort Sumter, encounters a military obstacle when he arrives at the navy yard in New York. Fox presents the orders to Colonel H.L. Scott, coincidentally, the son-in-law of General Winfield Scott. The colonel is unimpressed with the idea of sending relief to Charleston and essentially displays his indifference by procrastinating, which wastes valuable time. Nevertheless, by the end of the day, Colonel Scott provides the volunteers, but they are not seasoned. He contracts the steamer *Baltic* and three tug boats, the *Freeborn, Uncle Ben* and the *Yankee*.

Four additional warships are assigned to the mission by Secretary of the Navy Gideon Welles, but one, the *Powhatan,* unknown to Welles, has been assigned to another mission. Fox, the commander of the mission, also remains unaware of the unavailability of the *Powhatan.* The others, the *Harriet Lane, Pocahontas* and the *Pawnee,* have their schedules of departure set and will depart from their respective ports. The *Harriet Lane,* commanded by Captain Faunce, departs New York on the 8th, while the *Pawnee,* commanded by Stephen Rowan, leaves Washington on the 8th. The *Pocahontas,* commanded by Captain Gillis, leaves Norfolk on the 9th. The warships are to rendezvous with Fox's convoy outside the Charleston bar.

Fox departs New York on the 9th aboard the *Baltic,* commanded by Captain Fletcher, and despite some bad weather the *Baltic* arrives at the rendezvous point during the early morning hours of 12 April. The *Harriet Lane* is there to greet the Baltic. About three hours later, at 0600, the *Pawnee* joins the group. It soon becomes apparent that the operation is about to

The Fort Sumter flag, carried to New York by Major Robert Anderson after the surrender of the fort during April 1861 (Mottelay, *The Soldier in Our Civil War,* 1886).

encounter problems. The *Powhatan* and the *Pocahontas* do not arrive, leaving the relief force without sufficient fire power to complete the mission. More difficulties occur when the three tug boats also fail to arrive at the rendezvous point. While the flotilla holds about ten miles east of the bar, the Confederate batteries have already been firing at Fort Sumter for about one and one half hours.

In the meantime, the relief force is of no value without the guns of the *Powhatan,* and to make the situation more intolerable, no tug boats arrive. Meanwhile, some merchant ships are in the area, giving the impression that an entire fleet is standing by. Since the break of dawn, the visible results of the shelling of Fort Sumter cause more agony for those who came to relieve the beleaguered garrison. Commander Rowan, after watching the bombardment, becomes aggravated because of not being able to help.

As time passes, the fort continues to be pulverized, but still no *Powhatan* and not a single tug boat arrives. Meanwhile, the seas remain rough and weather continues to deteriorate. One of the tug boats, the *Uncle Ben,* had advanced to North Carolina, but no farther as the high winds force the tug into port at Wilmington. Meanwhile, the *Yankee* encounters the same elements and its progress becomes extremely slow, while the third tug, the *Freeborn,* had never left the port of New York.

The nasty weather had no negative effect on the Confederate artillery, which continued to pour round after round into Fort Sumter. Nonetheless, the defenders remain undaunted. Return fire is overseen by Captain Abner Doubleday. At dusk, the Stars and Stripes still flies above the crumbling walls of the fort. Aboard the ships in the relief force, it is impossible to know what the defenders know, that they have sustained a continual bombardment, yet suffered no casualties. Darkness does not deter Fox, who continues to send signals in an attempt to make contact with the *Powhatan,* but still no contact. Meanwhile, the inability to support the defenders infuriates Commander Rowan. He requests a pilot to enable him to reach the fort to offer his services, but Fox rejects the idea.

While aboard the *Pawnee,* Fox is told by Commander Rowan that in a recent memorandum Captain Samuel Mercer had mentioned that he was detached from the *Powhatan.* It was not good news, but it did explain the absence of Captain Mercer. On the following morning, again the weather is deplorable, but a new factor emerges as an impenetrable fog hovers over the area. Nonetheless, the flotilla has no boats to carry supplies nor men to carry them. Fort Sumter continues to absorb unending barrages and the walls of the fort continue to crumble.

The *Baltic* attempts to advance using great caution, but the vessel hits Rattlesnake Shoal. Luckily, it sustains no damage. Still no tugboats arrive. At 1400 the *Pocahontas* arrives; however, without the *Powhatan,* the relief force remains powerless. A half hour later, at 1430, Major Anderson surrenders the garrison. Negotiations continue throughout the day and an official surrender agreed upon permits the Stars and Stripes at Fort Sumter to be saluted as it is brought down, and the garrison receives permission to march out with the colors unfurled. The ceremony occurs on the following day. Afterward, the garrison is transported by the *Isabel* to the *Baltic.* The defenders, the first of the Union troops to come under fire, sail north with their honor intact.

April 6 (Saturday) In Washington D.C., Secretary of the Navy Gideon Welles becomes aware of Secretary of State William H. Seward's activity with the president that bypassed the Department of the Navy and in the process complicated the efforts to relieve Fort Sumter. Welles is infuriated. He immediately moves to reverse the harm. Welles convinces the president of the necessity of the *Powhatan*'s participation in the mission to relieve Fort Sumter, but he is against the continued interference of Seward, who maintains that the ship is required at Pensacola.

Lincoln, now aware of the confusion in orders due to keeping the Navy Department in the dark, dismisses Seward's concerns. He countermands his earlier orders and directs that Captain Mercer, recently detached, be reattached as commander of the *Powhatan,* and he orders that the *Powhatan* be recalled and reassigned to the initial operation. A telegram is sent to the navy yard in New York instructing the commandant to cancel the earlier orders for the *Powhatan.* The telegram arrives in New York at 1500, one-half hour after the *Powhatan* departed for Florida. The commandant dispatches a fast-tug to intercept the flotilla. The *Powhatan,* accompanied by the transports *Atlantic* and *Illinois,* is intercepted at Sandy Hook, and the telegram, ordering him to transfer command to Captain Mercer, is delivered. The telegram, signed by Seward, states: "Give the *Powhatan* up to Captain Mercer. Seward." After reading the telegram, Captain Porter replied: "I received my orders from the president and shall proceed and execute them."

In South Carolina, another telegram is received. The message, signed "A Friend," was sent: "Positively determined not to withdraw Anderson. Supplies go immediately, supported by naval force under Stringham if their landing be resisted." It was subsequently discovered that the "Friend" was James E. Harvey, who had also been appointed as minister to Spain.

Robert S. Chew, attached to the Department of State, is sent by the president to Charleston to inform Governor Francis Pickens that Fort Sumter is to be re-supplied with provisions. The message to Pickens stipulates that if the Confederates do not interfere, no reinforcements will arrive. At this time, a former navy officer and future assistant secretary of the navy, Gustavus Fox, is preparing to leave New York with a relief force.

In Confederate general officer activity, in Texas, Major Edmund Kirby Smith (West Point, 1845), 2nd U.S. Cavalry, has a change of heart. During the previous month, Smith had ignored orders to surrender his command to the Confederates. At this time, he resigns his commission and enters the Confederate service, gaining the rank of lieutenant colonel. In June he is appointed brigadier general, and by October he becomes a major general.

Also, Stephen Dodson Ramseur (West Point, 1860) resigns his commission in the U.S. Army and later joins the Confederacy. He departs North Carolina to join in Alabama and then returns to his native state. Initially, Ramseur becomes a captain in Ellis' Light Artillery, a battery formed in North Carolina at Raleigh. After about eight weeks of training, Ramseur and the artillery battery moves to Yorktown, Virginia, to serve under General John B. Magruder as colonel (later brigadier general), 49th North Carolina Regiment, against the Union forces of General George B. McClellan.

April 7 (Sunday)   In Florida, additional Union reinforcements leave New York for Pensacola to bolster Fort Pickens.

In South Carolina, Confederate Brigadier General Pierre G.T. Beauregard directs a message to Major Robert Anderson that "no further communications between Fort Sumter and Charleston would be permitted by Confederate authorities." Beauregard cuts off all supplies to the beleaguered garrison at Fort Sumter. Until this prohibition, Anderson's force had been able to receive supplies from Charleston. In other activity, the Confederates initiate additional work on the batteries on Morris Island.

April 8 (Monday)   In South Carolina, messengers Robert Chew and Captain Theodore Talbott from Washington arrive at Charleston to inform the authorities of President Lincoln's intent to resupply Fort Sumter. The news is unsettling for the governor, Francis W. Pickens, when he learns that the government of the United States intends to deliver supplies to the garrison. This news arrives to the dismay of many southerners, who now want to level the fort.

A casemate at Fort Sumter in action during Confederate bombardment (Johnson, *Campfire and Battlefield: History of the Conflicts and Campaigns*, 1894).

By this time, South Carolina has greatly enlarged its militia forces and many new companies are steadily being formed. Major General Samuel McGowan (militia), a veteran of the Mexican War, prepares to lead a full brigade against the beleaguered force at Fort Sumter. Subsequently, McGowan is appointed colonel (later brigadier general) of the Confederate 14th South Carolina Infantry Regiment. By this day, another gun had been placed in position on Sullivan's Island, giving the Confederates there four guns. Gunboats and signal boats are also on patrol.

In Naval activity, the *Harriet Lane*, part of the relief force for Fort Sumter, departs New York, while the USS *Pawnee* leaves Washington this day. The *Pawnee*, a steam sloop built in Philadelphia, was commissioned during June 1860 and in autumn operated off Mexico.

April 9 (Tuesday)   In New York, part of the relief force under Gustavus Fox leaves New York en route to Fort Sumter. Other vessels depart from various ports at separate times.

In South Carolina, Confederate forces converge on Fort Sumter. Brigadier General Pierre G.T. Beauregard receives word from Confederate Secretary of War LeRoy Pope Walker to demand the surrender of Fort Sumter. General Beauregard delegates the mission to one of his aides, Louis Wigfall (later brigadier general). The matter becomes more important to the Confederates as the vessel *Harriet Lane*, which had departed New York on the previous day, arrives outside Charleston Harbor with the promised supplies for the besieged defenders under Major Robert Anderson. Nonetheless, the ship does not pass the bar. In Virginia, the *Pocahontas*, commanded by Captain Gillis, leaves Norfolk en route to join the relief force charged with resupplying Fort Sumter. (See also, **April 5–15 THE EXPEDITION TO RELIEVE FORT SUMTER.**)

April 10 (Wednesday)   The relief force under Gustavus Fox continues the voyage toward Fort Sumter. Unknown to Fox, part of the flotilla is running behind schedule, and one warship, the *Powhatan*, had been assigned to separate duty and does not participate in the mission (see also, **April 5–15 THE EXPEDITION TO RELIEVE FORT SUMTER**).

Meanwhile, at Charleston, General Beauregard's defenses have been bolstered and the Confederates continue to prepare to take the fort if it does not capitulate. By this time nearly sixty guns and just under twenty mortars are poised to strike the post.

In Naval activity, the *Water Witch*—a wooden-hulled side-wheel gunboat

built in 1851, commissioned the following year and decommissioned a second time during November 1860, is reactivated. During her earlier tours on active duty, the *Water Witch* participated in a mission that included warships, commanded by Flag Officer W.B. Shubrick, that sailed to South America on 17 September 1858 to demand an apology from Paraguay due to an incident that occurred during 1855.

The *Water Witch* arrives off Pensacola on 2 May 1861 to join the Gulf Blockading Squadron. Initially it is utilized to carry mail and deliver dispatches to the other ships in the squadron. It also makes mail runs to Havana, Cuba; however, the vessel also is assigned patrol duty at the mouth of the Mississippi River until the latter part of 1862.

April 11 (Thursday)   In South Carolina, the Confederates demand surrender of Fort Sumter. The party sent by General Pierre G.T. Beauregard to deliver the ultimatum includes Colonel James Chestnut (former U.S. senator), Captain (later brigadier general) Stephen Dill Lee, a West Point graduate (1854), and Lt. Colonel A.R. Chisolm. Major Robert Anderson rejects capitulation.

April 11–13   THE SIEGE OF FORT SUMTER Federal troops garrisoned at Fort Sumter under Major Robert Anderson face difficulties. At slightly past noon on 11 April, a boat flying a white flag departs Charleston, and at about 1530, it approaches the fortress. The three-man party, led by Confederate Colonel James Chestnut, formerly a U.S. senator, carries an ultimatum from General Pierre G.T. Beauregard. Anderson and his officers discuss the demand and conclude that they will not capitulate.

Meanwhile, the Confederates prepare for action. After receiving a message in Charleston on 4 April signed "A Friend," and in addition, having intercepted letters from Anderson intended for Washington, Beauregard is well informed about the conditions at the fort and the intent of Washington.

The Confederates continue naval patrols. On this day, an iron-clad floating battery arrives in the vicinity of the fort. Prior to returning to Charleston, Major Anderson inquired of the party whether Beauregard would initiate a bombardment without first notifying him. He received the following response from Colonel (later brigadier general) Chestnut: "I think not," then he added: "No, I can say to you that he will not, without giving you further notice."

Nonetheless, the ordeal does not end with the departure of the party, in part due to Anderson's remark that the garrison was close to starvation and that if the guns failed to dislodge his force, the lack of food would finish them. Anderson's remark is underscored and transmitted to Montgomery from Charleston. The authorities in Montgomery waste no time sending a reply: "Do not desire needlessly to bombard Fort Sumter. If Major Anderson will state the time at which, as indicated by him, he will evacuate, and agree that in the mean time he will not use his guns against us unless ours should be employed against Sumter, you are authorized thus to avoid the effusion of blood. If this or its equivalent be refused, reduce the fort as your judgment decides to be most practicable."

After receiving the new instructions, Beauregard dispatches another party to solicit surrender. Again the officers meet to consider their options, particularly their lack of food. After a long discussion, Anderson responds to the party: "I will, if provided with proper and necessary means of transportation, evacuate Fort Sumter by noon on the 15th instant … should I not receive prior to that time controlling instructions from my government or additional supplies."

The representatives of Beauregard, still led by Colonel Chestnut, after receiving Anderson's reply, confer. At 0320 on the morning of 12 April, the Confederates hand Anderson a succinct message as follows: "By authority of Brigadier General Beauregard, commanding the provisional forces of the Confederate States, we have the honor to notify you that he will open the fire of his batteries on Fort Sumter in one hour from this time."

Despite the pressure of a pending attack and the stress of responsibility for the garrison, Major Anderson remains focused on the task ahead of him: defending the post. The closing comments and the announcement that the batteries are about to storm the post ensures that Anderson will get no sleep and his officers will have an early reveille. Captain Abner Doubleday is the first to get rousted. At about 0400, Anderson enters Doubleday's quarters, but the room is pitch black and visibility is zero. Unable to see Doubleday, Anderson calls out his name and the groggy officer is informed that the fort will be attacked shortly. Doubleday, second in command, snaps into action and moves rapidly to rally the troops. The guards are ordered to leave their posts on the parapets. Others are directed to lock the entrances and all the troops are ordered to remain in the bomb-proofs until a roll of the drums signals them to report to their battle stations.

At 0430 on 12 April, upon orders from General Beauregard, a gun at Fort Johnson fires the signal shot which ignites the firestorm commencing the bombardment. Immediately thereafter the guns on Morris Island commence firing, followed by the other batteries. No conclusive evidence points to the individual on Morris Island who fired the first shot; however, the list is down to the probability of it being one of three men: Confederate Captain S. James, Confederate Lieutenant Henry S. Farley, or Edmund Ruffin, a Virginian who had long sought separation from the Union.

Although the bombardment is anticipated, the noise alone at the instant the guns open fire causes trepidation. The synchronized attack includes the guns on Sullivan's Island, including Cummings Point and the floating battery (one 9-inch, two 42-pounders, two 32-pounders and six 10-inch mortars); at Fort Moultrie (three 8-inch, two 32-pounders, six 24-pounders) and four guns in the new enfilade battery (two 32-pounders; two 24-pounders). On Morris Island the Confederates have deployed one 12-pounder

Blakely rifle, two 42-pounders, three 8-inch guns, and seven 10-inch mortars. At Fort Johnson, one 24-pounder and four 10-inch mortars are deployed, and yet more firepower, one 10-inch mortar, is deployed at Mount Pleasant.

The roaring noise of the twenty-seven guns and eighteen mortars, which sounds like amplified thunder, interrupts the tranquility of the night, while the catapulted shells, rimmed with multicolored fire, resemble arcing lightning bolts converging on the same spot: Fort Sumter. The ebony skies are suddenly illuminated as streams of fiery shells are propelled toward the silhouette of the fort, which is still partially veiled by the predawn darkness. Batteries, including those at Fort Johnson, Fort Moultrie, Cummings Point on Morris Island, Mount Pleasant and a formerly concealed battery on Sullivan's Island, proclaim the opening of hostilities.

The guns simultaneously pound the fort, creating a massive menacing thunderclap. The streams of multicolored flames create an eerie scene that seems to display deep scarlet and burnt orange projectiles exploding at every point along the walls. Although most of the troops remain in the bunkers, unable to observe the flaming streaks of fire, they are quite aware of the horrific results, particularly when the monstrous mortars rivet the fort and upon impact literally shake the ground. The defenders are rocked by relentless bombardments that continue to intensify as if in cadence with the approach of dawn.

While the Confederates pulverize the fort and huge chunks of the walls begin to collapse, none of the defenders or the workers who had remained at the fort as volunteers sustain any harm during the non-stop, two and one-half hour one-sided contest. Nevertheless, dawn brings no reprieve, but still, the troops remain in the bunkers, awaiting the signal to begin to return fire.

Neither Major Anderson nor Captain Doubleday is a stranger to adversity or the perils of combat, but nothing in their past compares to their present situation. Both are veterans of the Mexican War, but neither has faced such insurmountable odds, having under their command fewer than 100 troops and being faced with encirclement on their isolated island by no less than 6,000 Confederate troops. Nonetheless, their loyalty to the Union offsets the disadvantages and as dawn arrives, the garrison is able to focus on the task at hand, to preserve the fort or sacrifice their lives in the effort to defend the flag to the last man against men with whom they had only a short while before been friends and allied countrymen.

At 0700, Captain Doubleday initiates the order to return fire. The artillery under Doubleday totals fifty-nine guns and of those, the heaviest caliber, numbering twenty-seven, are concentrated in the upper tier of the fort, the most precarious location. On the second or middle tier, four 8-inch guns and one 10-inch gun, each mounted as a howitzer, are deployed, and on the lower tier, twenty-seven guns are deployed; twenty-three of the guns are 32-pounders and four are 42-pounders.

In accordance with the preparations for defending the post, the troops work in three groups, each working two hour shifts to ease the burden. Meanwhile, the workmen, numbering about 43, commit themselves as volunteers to bolster the garrison's strength. Although the troops had only a skimpy breakfast, their spirits remain high and their confidence in themselves skyrockets, as if the incessant barrages that are delivering shells in layers of destruction are energizing them. The guns on the lower tier begin to blast Fort Moultrie, Cummings Point and both batteries on Sullivan's Island, but the floating battery does not evade fire. Each of the targets is fired upon simultaneously. Fort Moultrie sustains damage, but the iron battery on Cummings Point remains unscathed, as its armor remains impenetrable.

The opposing guns refuse to be outdone and the contest continues to test the mettle of the men on both sides to determine which side will relent. Although the rebels have the dominating strength and more firepower, they do not possess more enthusiasm. The defenders become more defiant and the relief crews, not yet in action, become impatient to replace the first crew. They become oblivious to the danger and ignore the fact that parts of the walls are being transformed into pebbles with each succeeding shell that arrives. For any spectator observing from shore, it appears that the impregnable fortress is becoming a colossal pile of burning debris.

Major Anderson, having observed the increasing accuracy of the shore batteries, prohibits his men from manning the barbette guns on the parapets (open upper tier). In addition to the pernicious artillery bombardments, other dangers emerge when the barracks is set afire. While the fires are being fought, others are expeditiously attempting to remedy yet another problem: the supply of cartridge belts, about seven hundred, has been exhausted. Improvisation becomes the next priority and soon shirts are being sewed for new cartridge belts. Meanwhile, the beleaguered defenders attempt to get nourishment to maintain their strength, but there is no time to spare. In between returning fire, dodging incoming shells and dousing fires, the troops squeeze in a few seconds here and there, eating lunch while at their guns.

Later, the barracks again are afire, and before the day ends, they will be ablaze yet a third time. Meanwhile, the lack of cartridge belts compels Anderson to restrict fire. The troops that had become sewing champions work feverishly to sew additional cartridge belts, while the majority of the guns fall silent to permit six guns to maintain fire against Fort Moultrie and the two batteries on the western tip of Sullivan's Island. However, the guns on the lower tier lack the power to do great damage, particularly to the iron-clad batteries. The gunners also face another severe disadvantage. The guns are not equipped with breech-sights. Consequently, the gun crews are compelled to use a primitive method. They use notched sticks in place of the absent breech-sights. In the meantime, the Confederate batteries, unimpeded by shortages of any kind, continue to pummel Fort Sumter.

All the while, a relief force stands about ten miles east of the bar, still helpless, with no chance of passing the Confederate batteries without the USS *Powhatan*. Part of the relief force is lagging behind, and the most powerful ship, the *Powhatan*, had been reassigned, unknown to the commander of the improvised squadron, Gustavus Fox. Without the guns of the *Powhatan*, and with the absence of another vessel, the *Pocahontas*, as well as the three tug boats, the rescue effort is paralyzed by the combination of the strategically placed Confederate guns and the inclement weather.

After the guns of Fort Sumter cease fire for the night, the Confederate batteries maintain intermittent barrages about every fifteen minutes to keep pressure on the defenders and coerce them into surrendering. However, while their strength is being constantly further drained, and they have been moved beyond exhaustion, there is no exhibition of despair. By dusk, the results of the day-long bombardments appear to the naked eye to be catastrophic and they are; however, only in damage to the fortress. The Confederates fail to inflict any serious casualties. Each man at Fort Sumter who answered the call to arms during the predawn hours is alive to eat dinner, a remarkable feat.

During the remainder of the night, the troops frantically collect material, including bed sheets, to sew more cartridge belts. After a second restless night, dawn arrives in cadence with the resumption of the full-throttled bombardments, intended to reduce the already devastated walls of the fort. The Confederates' arsenal is bolstered by a recently acquired Blakely rifle (12-pounder) which arrives from Europe. The cannon and mortar fire again pack a double punch, with the former on horizontal paths and the latter descending vertically. A round from the Blakely rifle pounds the wall, penetrates and causes some shattering of the wall, and as the debris flies, a sergeant and three other troops are injured.

By about 0900, although the defenders remain in high spirits and have been returning fire, the situation takes a rapid turn. The Confederate shelling ignites a fire at the officers' quarters; however, fighting the fire is much more dangerous than it had been with the earlier fires at the barracks. The magazine is near the officers' quarters, and the danger of catastrophic explosion becomes quite possible as the fire intensifies and spreads. Every available man rushes to extricate the powder from the magazine before it can explode; however, despite the severity of the crisis, the guns remain in action. The emergency does not easily subside. Men risk their lives by entering the magazine, but all the while, the fire continues to spread.

About fifty barrels are removed from the magazine before the operation is halted due to the encroaching flames. Hurriedly the magazine is secured and the extricated powder is carried to the casemates. The ferocity of the raging fire becomes a more pernicious threat than the thousands of shells that have plastered the fort. What the Confederates have not been able to accomplish is within reach of the flames. The

officers' quarters have become a colossal fireball and the choking smoke, fueled by high winds, permeates the area and threatens to suffocate the troops.

With the possibility and probability that the powder in the casemates will blow, more desperate action is taken. Troops rush haphazardly, ignoring the ever-increasing danger, to get to the powder and remove it before a calamity occurs. The effort succeeds in getting all but five barrels out of harm's way by lobbing the explosive barrels into the water. Tragedy is avoided, but by now, in addition to the insufficient food supply, the garrison has seen beds and other items reduced to ashes, and now their ammunition has suddenly vanished.

As Major Anderson peers at the destruction, each turn of his head brings about more frustration. The garrison, stripped of all its defenses, still shows no signs of capitulating. Nevertheless, the Confederate batteries have shown no signs of lessening the incessant streams of shells. The fort itself resembles a shattered shell and with the passing of mere minutes, additional sections of the battered walls collapse. No section of the fort is spared devastation. Even the towers at the corners have been ravaged, and one of them had been a storage area holding an enormous supply of shells until incoming fire had ignited explosions and destroyed it.

Anderson's assessment contains no optimism. The fires, flying debris and skeleton walls are beyond description. Even the massive main gate is smoldering and the protective wall to the rear is destroyed, giving Anderson a clear view of the water approaches as he looks though a huge opening where the gates once stood. Although he sees no craft, it becomes obvious that any assault force would have little difficulty landing and entering the remnant fort. Nevertheless, the obvious was not the consensus of the garrison. The struggle continues, and if the Confederates anticipated that they had liquidated the spirit of the defending force, that idea is punctured at about 1300.

Confederate fire severs the flag staff and Old Glory tumbles, but similarly to the fighting spirit of her defenders, it quickly bounces back to its perch, although on an improvised staff. At about the same time the Stars and Stripes is rehoisted, a boat, flying a white flag and carrying two men, is spotted. The boat originated at Morris Island after Confederates there witnessed the sudden disappearance of Old Glory and interpreted it as surrender.

The Confederate party of two includes former U.S. senator Louis T. Wigfall, at present a colonel (South Carolina forces). After gaining entrance, the two men confer with Major Anderson. Colonel Wigfall, after inquiring about whether the fort was being surrendered, although unauthorized, speaks on behalf of General Beauregard. A tentative agreement is reached and Colonel Wigfall ascends to a parapet and waves an improvised white flag, his handkerchief.

Shortly thereafter, a new Confederate party arrives, including Colonel Chestnut, Colonel Roger A. Pryor and Colonel William Porcher

Miles. Afterward, more Confederates arrive and Anderson discovers that Colonel Wigfall's offer was not authorized by General Beauregard; rather he acted on his own. Negotiations continue for several hours, and at about 1900, an agreement is consummated. The garrison will salute the colors as the flag is taken down, and the pact permits the Union troops to retain their arms and baggage. The Confederates also agree to permit the troops to depart the fort with the colors unfurled as they march in cadence to their drums.

During the grueling two-day siege, the relief force under Gustavus Fox had been compelled to observe as non-participants. At the same time the Confederates took notice of the absence of the Stars and Stripes from its staff, those aboard the squadron also took note. They too, believing a surrender had occurred, sent a boat under a flag of truce to investigate. During the course of the negotiations, it is agreed that the *Baltic* will transport the garrison troops to New York.

On the following morning, Sunday, 14 April, the Union gathers at the flag staff for the final ceremony before retiring the colors. Despite the circumstances, the garrison remains in high spirits, aware of the bold and defiant stand in defense of the flag, and there are no emotions of failure or dishonor. As the ceremony gets underway, a 100-gun salute to the colors is planned, but after sustaining everything the Confederate threw at them without suffering any fatalities or serious injuries, one of the cannon fires prematurely and it results in the accidental death of one of the men, the mortal wounding of another, and four others suffer severe wounds. Nevertheless, a fifty-gun salute is fired. At 1600, the garrison forms in a column and with Major Anderson and Captain Doubleday at the head, the column (including the workmen who remained as volunteers) escorts the flag to the waiting vessel *Isabel*, which takes the troops out to the *Baltic*, where the men are greeted warmly and as heroes.

By dusk, the relief flotilla that had not completed its mission receives a consolation, having the honor of transporting the gallant defenders of Fort Sumter out of harm's way. Confederate Colonel Roswell S. Ripley occupies Fort Sumter with state militia.

April 12 (Friday) In Florida, the U.S. Navy lands troops, including more than 100 Marines commanded by 2nd Lieutenant John C. Cash, at Fort Pickens on Santa Rosa Island, bolstering its defenders and preventing the fort from being overtaken by the Confederacy. Fort Pickens will be a very important Gulf Coast fortification, giving the Union a base in the South. The vessels transporting the reinforcements and their artillery are the USS *Sabine* (Captain Adams); the frigate USS *Brooklyn* (Captain Walker), a steam sloop of war; the sloop of war *St. Louis*, carrying the commander of the operation, Commander Charles H. Poor; the gunboats *Crusader* and *Wyandotte*; and two supply vessels.

Within a few days, more reinforcements arrive aboard the steam transports *Atlantic* and

Illinois, which are escorted by the *Powhatan*, bringing the defending force to about 900 troops. Confusion complicates the mission. When the reinforcements arrive, under the authority of orders from General Winfield Scott, Captain Adams of the *Sabine* questions the authority, which essentially disrupted an ongoing truce. A messenger is sent to the capital, arriving there on 6 April. In turn, Lt. John Worden of the U.S. Navy, on the same night is sent to Pensacola to resolve the confusion. After receiving new directions from Worden upon his arrival on 10 April, the reinforcements schedule landings.

After completing his mission, Worden departs for Washington; however, he takes an overland route and the Confederates capture him while he is passing through Alabama. Worden is later released in time to participate in the epic sea battle between the CSS *Virginia* (formerly USS *Merrimack*) and the *Monitor* on 8 March 1862.

In South Carolina, the Confederates commence fire against Fort Sumter to ignite open hostilities between the North and the South. (See also, **April 11–13 THE SIEGE OF FORT SUMTER.**)

In Texas, Lt. (later brevet major general) Kenner Garrard is seized in San Antonio by Texans not yet enlisted in the Confederacy. He is exchanged on 27 August 1862.

April 13 (Saturday) In Washington, D.C., President Abraham Lincoln, still unaware of the ongoing battle at Fort Sumter, states: "I shall hold myself at liberty to repossess, if I can, places like Fort Sumter, if taken from federal control."

In related activity, three representatives of the Virginia Convention, during the previous month, visited the president and attempted to ask what plan of action Lincoln had in mind for the states that had seceded. He responds this day to the Virginia Convention, subsequent to being informed about the attack upon Fort Sumter, that he would "to the best of his ability, repel force with force."

In South Carolina, Fort Sumter capitulates. (See also, **April 11–13 THE SIEGE OF FORT SUMTER.**) Many future Confederate leaders participate during the siege of Fort Sumter, and they include Colonel (later brigadier general) Johnson Hagood, 1st South Carolina Regiment, who subsequently relocates in Virginia and with his regiment participates in the First Battle of Manassas (Bull Run). Another is Confederate Colonel (later brigadier general) Arthur M. Manigault, 10th South Carolina Regiment. He serves on the staff of General Pierre G.T. Beauregard and

oversees the establishment of batteries along the harbor at Charleston. Later, he receives command of the District of South Carolina and from there is transferred to Tennessee.

In Confederate general officer activity, Brigadier General Alexander Robert Lawton (West Point, 1841) is appointed brigadier general in the Confederate Provisional Army. His commission is confirmed by Congress on 28 August. General Lawton sustains a serious wound at Sharpsburg (Antietam) and afterward is appointed commanding officer of the quartermaster general's department during autumn 1863. He retains the post for the duration. After the war, General Lawton resumes his law practice. Later, during 1887, President Grover Cleveland appoints him as U.S. minister to Austria. General Lawton dies in New York City during July 1896 and is interred in Savannah, Georgia.

April 14 (Sunday) In Washington, D.C., President Lincoln and his cabinet meet. The chief executive through his proclamation of this day calls for 75,000 volunteers to serve for a period of three months to put down the insurrection. He explains that due to the excessive amount of combined strength of the states which have seceded, neither the normal judicial procedures nor the powers vested in the marshals by law are sufficient to end the crisis. The proclamation is publicized on the following day. Also, President Lincoln calls for Congress to convene at 12 noon on the 4th of July to take measures to terminate the insurrection.

In South Carolina at Fort Sumter, Union Major (later breveted major general) Robert Anderson and his men depart Fort Sumter, proceeding north by sea aboard the USS *Baltic* en route to New York. The Union troops suffer one man killed (Pvt. Hough) and three wounded by an accidental explosion during a

Left: Horses are lowered in the bay to swim to Santa Rosa Island, Florida. *Above:* Union reinforcements land on Santa Rosa Island (Mottelay, *The Soldier in Our Civil War*, 1886).

final salute to Old Glory. Many of the fort's civilians and families of the troops had departed during the previous December in anticipation of a Confederate assault. Confederate Colonel (later brigadier general) Roswell S. Ripley (West Point, 1823) occupies Fort Sumter with state militia. Ripley had served in the Mexican War and in the Florida Indian Wars (1849–1850) before resigning from the Army during 1853.

April 14–15 In California, a contingent of troops (Company B, 6th U.S. Infantry) commanded by 1st Lt. Joseph B. Collins (4th Infantry) engages a band of Indians that are part of a group involved in stealing stock. The engagement occurs at Van Dusen's Creek near the Mad River. Collins' report lists no army casualties and 15 to 20 Indians killed. On the 15th, Collins again attacks and Collins' force sustains one man seriously wounded after being hit in the back with an arrow. The Indians sustain five killed and three wounded.

April 15 (Monday) Hostilities begin; the North prepares to bolster its defenses and it intensifies efforts to gain the 75,000 volunteers that Lincoln has called for this day to serve for a period of ninety days. At this time, government leaders still think the country will quickly come together.

Not all of the governors exhibit enthusiasm. Governor Henry Massey Rector of Arkansas replies: "None will be furnished...." Missouri Governor Claiborne Fox Jackson claims that Lincoln's request for troops is "illegal, unconstitutional and revolutionary in its objects, inhuman and diabolical, and not to be complied with...." Governor Beriah Magoffin states that "Kentucky will furnish no troops for the wicked purpose of subduing her sister southern states." Governor John Willis Ellis of North Carolina says, "I can be no party to this wicked violation of the laws of the country, and to this war upon the liberties of a free people. You can get no troops from North Carolina." Lincoln also receives bad news from Tennessee Governor Isham Harris: "Tennessee will not furnish a single man for coercion, but 50,000 if necessary, for the defense of our rights or those of our southern brethren." Closer to the nation's capital, Governor John Letcher of Virginia refuses to provide troops: "You have chosen to inaugurate civil war; and having done so, we will meet it in a spirit as determined as the administration has exhibited toward the South." Two other nearby states, Maryland and Delaware, give ambiguous responses to try to remain in the middle and give no commitment.

In North Carolina, Fort Macon, established during 1826 as a defensive position at Bogue Point near Beaufort, is seized by the Confederates. During April of the following year, the fort is regained by Union troops.

In Union general officer activity, Richard Delafield (West Point, 1818) rushes to the Union cause. He lends his years of experience to recruiting New York volunteers and contributes to the supervision of the engineers' efforts in northern New Jersey and New York. Delafield

is appointed brigadier general the following month. Union Colonel Sullivan A. Meredith is another officer assigned to build up the Army. Sullivan is soon mustered in as colonel of the 10th Pennsylvania Infantry and assigned the task of training troops. Meredith (later brigadier general) will train and equip over 30,000 men during the initial stages of the war. Later, he organizes the 56th Pennsylvania Regiment and is appointed its colonel.

Also, Union Colonel Francis Engle Patterson (son of Brigadier General Robert Patterson), 17th Pennsylvania, a three-month regiment, is promoted to the rank of brigadier general, effective this date.

Lysander Cutler is appointed colonel of the 6th Wisconsin Regiment at about this time. Cutler's regiment becomes a component of the famed Iron Brigade. Lysander had been a teacher in Maine prior to the war and his combat experience had been only bullies in school. Cutler, aware that the students had flogged several teachers that preceded him, spent an unusual first day in the classroom. He flogged each of the known bullies and terminated any further difficulty in maintaining discipline in the class. Colonel Cutler participates at the Second Battle of Bull Run (Manassas) and sustains a wound. After his leg heals, he fights in the Battle of Fredericksburg, where he holds temporary command of a brigade (General Abner Doubleday's division).

George Francis McGinnis, a veteran of the Mexican war who served as a captain in the 2nd Ohio Volunteer Regiment, enlists in the army this day as a private (later brigadier general) in the 11th Indiana Regiment, commanded by Colonel Lew Wallace. However, within several days, McGinnis is appointed lieutenant colonel, and when the regiment's three-month enlistment terminates, McGinnis becomes its colonel upon re-mustering as a three-year regiment.

In Marine Corps activity, most of the United States Marines will serve aboard ships for the duration. However, some Marines choose to leave the corps and head south to serve with the Confederacy.

In Naval activity, the USS *Philadelphia* is taken into the federal service and at about this time assigned duty on the Potomac River. On occasion, it is utilized as a transport in the Chesapeake Bay. In December 1861 it is assigned patrol duty in the Atlantic; however, during August 1863, the vessel is transferred to the South Atlantic Blockading Squadron, where it remains until decommissioned at Washington, D.C., in August 1865. In September it is sold and under the original name and enters service as a commercial vessel. In 1869 it is renamed *Ironsides* and afterward continues in service until 29 August 1873, when it is lost off Hog Island, Virginia.

April 16 (Tuesday) In Florida, the relief force (the *Powhatan* and the transports *Atlantic* and *Illinois*) under the command of Colonel Harvey Brown arrives at Pensacola. The USS *Powhatan*, commanded by Captain David

Porter, ordered 1 April by the president, prepares to enter the harbor; however, Captain Montgomery Meigs, U.S. Army, had requested that the USS *Wyandotte* position itself where it would block the *Powhatan* from entering the harbor. The *Wyandotte* remains in the region until August, when it is ordered north to undergo required repairs. Curiously, on the following day, Colonel Brown contacts Confederate General Braxton Bragg and concocts an agreement that impedes any Union progress.

The screw gunboat *Wyandotte* had initially been built in Philadelphia during 1853 and named *Western Port*. It was purchased by the U.S. Navy and renamed *Wyandotte* when commissioned during September 1859. It remains off Florida until August, at which time it goes out of service to receive repairs. In December, the *Wyandotte* is assigned patrol duty off eastern Florida, Georgia and South Carolina. It heads north in December 1862 to join the Potomac Flotilla and remains in Virginia until decommissioned during June 1865. It is sold during August 1865.

In North Carolina, Fort Caswell and Fort Johnson are taken by the Confederates. Kentucky and North Carolina, by order of their respective governors, refuse to supply troops to the federal (Union) cause.

In Indian Territory (part of Oklahoma) at about this time, Fort Washita, established during April 1842 near Durant, is abandoned by the U.S. military. Lt. Colonel (later brigadier general) William H. Emory had assembled a force near the Red River for defensive purposes, but orders arrived to evacuate. The column moves to Fort Cobb and from there, both garrisons move to Fort Leavenworth, Kansas. Afterward, both posts are occupied by Confederates.

Other forts in the Indian Territory abandoned between this day and early May include Fort Arbuckle and Fort Davis. Colonel Emory (West Point, 1831) is credited with getting his entire command out of the Confederate territory without sustaining the loss of any of his men.

In Confederate general officer activity, one Kentucky contingent, the Lexington Rifles, established in Lexington several years ago by John Hunt Morgan, will later join the Confederacy and initially serve under General Simon Bolivar Buckner, who resigns his commission in the U.S. Army in August to accept a commission as brigadier general in the Confederacy the following month. Morgan's brother-in-law, Basil Wilson Duke, travels with the 17-man contingent when it departs Lexington. By the time it reaches Bowling Green, nearly two hundred riders have attached themselves to Morgan. The Lexington Rifles will become the foundation of the Confederate 2nd Kentucky Cavalry. Morgan and Duke both rise to the rank of brigadier general. Actually, there will be three Confederate generals in the family, as Lieutenant General Ambrose Powell Hill and Duke both marry sisters of John Hunt Morgan. Colonel John Echols is promoted to brigadier general to rank from this date.

In Naval activity, the U.S. Navy at about this time (April) charters a screw steam vessel, the *Dawn,* and during the following month, commissions it the USS *Dawn.* It is assigned to the Potomac flotilla as a gunboat. During the first several months in the service the crew seizes several vessels while on patrol. In October, 1861, the charter is canceled and the *Dawn* is purchased by the U.S. Navy. The *Dawn* moves to the navy yard in Washington, D.C., prior to departing for the South Atlantic Blockading Squadron in late April 1862.

April 17 (Wednesday)   In Montgomery, Alabama, Confederate President Jefferson Davis, in an effort to add incentive to aiding the Confederate cause, authorizes privateering. As in the days gone by, the waters along the southern coast, including the hidden inland lagoons and the mysterious bayous of Louisiana, are perfect for privateers. The U.S. Navy has previously outlawed this activity.

In Florida, Union Colonel Harvey Brown assumes command of Fort Pickens, Florida, succeeding Lt. Slemmer, who has been ordered to move to Fort Hamilton, New York, for the purpose of recruiting; however, prior to embarking, Slemmer is promoted to the rank of major, 16th Infantry Regiment (May 16). Colonel Brown sends a message to General Braxton Bragg, the Confederate commander in Pensacola, and essentially proclaims a truce.

At this time, the Confederate defenses are not suited to defend against a full-scale naval attack due to the poor condition of the batteries. Nonetheless, despite a strong naval force and a relief force, Pensacola receives a reprieve because of the truce initiated by Colonel Brown. The navy yard remains under Confederate domination until August of the following year.

In Missouri, Governor Claiborne Fox Jackson refuses to supply militia for the Union Army.

In Texas, the *Star of the West,* while in the process of evacuating U.S. forces, is seized off Indianola by Confederate troops out of Galveston. The transport is then taken to New Orleans, where arms and ammunition for Vicksburg are loaded. Following the mission, the Confederates self-destruct the vessel on the Tallahatchie River off Fort Pemberton to impede travel on the river by U.S. warships.

William Denison Whipple (West Point, 1851) the quartermaster (later brigadier general) at Indianola, is among the captured by the Texans; however, he escapes and makes his way back to the East.

In Virginia, by a vote of 88 to 55, Virginia secedes from the Union. It is the eighth state to do so. The recent proclamation by President Abraham Lincoln on 15 April calling for 75,000 volunteers had a reverse effect. Many Virginians, particularly in government, received the news essentially as a declaration of war against the southern states.

Virginia also passes an ordinance that directs the governor to "immediately invite all efficient and worthy Virginians and residents of Virginia in the army and navy of the United States to retire therefrom, and to enter the service of Virginia, assigning them to such rank as will not reverse the relative rank held by them in the United States service, and will at least be equivalent thereto." The Congress offers an identical invitation to those presently serving in the U.S. Revenue Service (forerunner of the Coast Guard). On 19 April, the state authorizes the appointment of a commander-in-chief, and with the position the appointee is to receive the rank of major general.

In yet other activity, Virginia also proclaims that the oath taken by Virginians to defend the U.S. Constitution is "declared inoperative and void, and of no effect, and the statutory provisions of the state which heretofore gave efficacy to that oath were repealed."

In Union general officer activity, Mahon Dickerson Manson, a veteran of the Mexican War era, is commissioned as captain of the 10th Indiana Regiment. Shortly thereafter, during the following May, he becomes colonel (later brigadier general) of the regiment.

April 18 (Thursday)   In Washington, D.C., a Union contingent dispatched from Pennsylvania arrives at the capital; however, it lacks weapons. More units follow, arriving from Massachusetts and from New York. Meanwhile, General Winfield Scott sets out to fortify Washington. He establishes a formidable ring around the capital.

In Arkansas, the Rebels take action in Pine Bluff by seizing the federal stores.

In New York, Major Robert Anderson and his command from captured Fort Sumter arrive in New York. While the ship is off Sandy Hook approaching New York Harbor, Major Anderson dispatches the following message to the war department:

> Off Sandy Hook, April 18th, 1861. Having defended Fort Sumter for thirty-four hours, until the quarters were entirely burned, the main gates destroyed by fire, the gorge wall seriously injured, the magazine surrounded by flames and its doors closed from the effects of the heat, four barrels and three cartridges of powder only being available, and no provisions but pork remaining, I accepted terms of evacuation offered by General Pierre G. T. Beauregard, being the same offered by him on the 11th inst., prior to the commencement of hostilities, and marched out of the fort, Sunday afternoon, the 14th inst., with colors flying

and drums beating, bringing away company and private property, and saluting my flag with fifty guns.

In Louisiana, at New Orleans, the CSS *Sumter,* commanded by Raphael Semmes, embarks on its initial cruise. At this time, the naval base is under the command of Commander L. Rousseau, but during the following July, he will be replaced.

In Tennessee, Governor Isham Harris refuses to supply troops for federal service.

In Virginia, a contingent of mounted riflemen commanded by Union Lt. Roger Jones destroys the federal arsenal at Harpers Ferry (later in West Virginia) to prevent its capture by Confederates. Following the reduction of the arsenal, Jones abandons the area and heads for Carlisle, Pennsylvania, to await orders from Lieutenant General Winfield Scott. In Richmond, the U.S. Post Office and the Customs House are seized.

In Confederate general officer activity, Robert Charles Tyler joins the Confederacy as a private (later brigadier general) in the 15th Tennessee Infantry. Subsequently he becomes a regimental quartermaster, but afterward, he commands the regiment at Belmont and at Shiloh, prior to becoming colonel of the regiment when it is reorganized at Corinth.

April 19 (Friday)   In Maryland at Baltimore, the 6th Massachusetts Regiment, commanded by Colonel Edward F. Jones, en route to the District of Columbia, stops at Baltimore. These troops, after being attacked by rioters carrying Confederate flags, lose four men: Luther C. Ladd, about seventeen years old, from Lowell; Addison O. Whitney, twenty-one years of age, of Lowell; Charles Taylor of Boston, each of these being killed immediately, and Sumner H.

Burning of the Gosport Navy Yard and (inset) burning of the U.S. arsenal at Harper's Ferry (Johnson, *Campfire and Battlefield: History of the Conflicts and Campaigns,* 1894).

Bodies of 6th Massachusetts soldiers killed at Baltimore are taken to Lowell (Mottelay, *The Soldier in Our Civil War*, 1886).

Flag Officer Silas H. Stringham (Mottelay, *The Soldier in Our Civil War*, 1886).

Needham of Lawrence, who is mortally wounded. Three others from the 6th Massachusetts are wounded. In addition, nine civilians are killed during the melee, when the soldiers are ordered to protect themselves by returning fire. The contingent fights its way to the railroad yard to join other Union troops. These men are the first casualties of the war. An additional 30 men are wounded after the initial confrontation. The 26th Pennsylvania Regiment, commanded by Captain Follansbee, is also in Baltimore during this incident, but it is unarmed and compelled to return to Philadelphia.

Five contingents from Pennsylvania had breezed through Baltimore prior to the southern sympathizers presenting these obstacles. They were the Allen Infantry Company, commanded by Thomas B. Yeager of Allentown; the Logan Guards, commanded by Captain Selheimer of Lewiston; the National Light Infantry, commanded by Captain E. McDonald of Pottsville; the Ringgold Light Artillery, commanded by Captain James McKnight of Reading; and the Washington Artillery Company, commanded by Captain James Wren of Pottsville. The troops from Pennsylvania and the 6th Massachusetts Regiment compose the initial defense ring around the capital until the route through Baltimore gets reopened.

In the meantime, the 7th Regiment out of New York is en route to Washington, aware of what befell the Massachusetts troops, but they continue the trip. Once in Philadelphia, the New Yorkers conclude that moving through Baltimore is not feasible. The regiment embarks by water aboard the USS *Boston*, which transports the troops to Annapolis. They arrive on the following day and join the troops under

General Butler and the 8th Massachusetts Regiment.

In Washington, D.C., southern sympathizers seize the federal steamer *St. Nicholas.*

In Ohio at Cincinnati, word of the attack against the 6th Massachusetts Regiment in Baltimore arrives by telegraph. The news sparks a spontaneous outbreak of patriotism. Colonel (later general) Robert Latimer McCook assembles his German regiment (9th Ohio), composed of more than 900 troops. The regiment, accompanied by several brass bands, parades through the streets, elevating the feelings of many and prompting enlistments. Nearly 800 men enlist in the Independent Guthrie Greys (6th Ohio).

On this same day, Major General William H. Lytle, commander of the 1st Division (Ohio Volunteer Militia) receives orders from headquarters at Columbus to establish a camp on the outskirts of Cincinnati. Lytle selects a site (Cincinnati Trotting Park) along the Cincinnati, Hamilton and Dayton Railroad less than ten miles from the city. The camp is named Camp Harrison. General Lytle, the next May, is appointed colonel of the 10th Ohio Regiment.

In Naval activity, President Abraham Lincoln orders a blockade of Confederate ports located in Alabama, Florida, Georgia, Louisiana, Mississippi and Texas. It will take some time to accomplish the mission. Lincoln will appoint Commodore Silas Horton Stringham commander of the Atlantic Naval Squadron, which will operate between Key West, Florida, to the south and stretch north to Cape Charles, Virginia, at the mouth of the Chesapeake Bay.

The 7th New York Regiment departs New York for Washington, D.C., on April 19, 1861 (Johnson, *Campfire and Battlefield: History of the Conflicts and Campaigns*, 1894).

Stringham's flagship will be the USS *Minnesota*, a forty-gun steam frigate and an accompanying fleet composed of 25 vessels with a complement of about 3,500 sailors and Marines to handle the operation designed to keep the Southern ports paralyzed.

Nevertheless, the United States Navy is suffering from the same ailment as the United States Army. It is called southern sympathy and sailors are beginning to move to fight for the Confederacy. The Marines are no exception; their ranks also thin quickly.

In Union activity, Thomas Turpin Crittenden is appointed captain of the 6th Indiana Regiment. On the 27th, he becomes colonel of the regiment.

April 20 (Saturday)   In Washington, D.C., a contingent of fifty Marines, commanded by Captain Hiram Paulding, leaves the Washington Navy Yard aboard the USS *Pawnee* for Norfolk, Virginia, to bolster the defenses at the Gosport Navy Yard. The *Pawnee* secures the USS *Cumberland* and tows it to a safe port. The Cumberland had originally been commissioned during November 1843. During 1855–1856, it was transformed into a slop of war and afterward was assigned as the flagship of the Africa Squadron (1857–1859) and the Home Squadron (1860). Meanwhile, the *Pawnee* patrols the Potomac River as part of the defensive measures taken to protect the capital.

In Missouri, Confederates seize control of the federal armory at Liberty.

In North Carolina, at about this time, the U.S. Branch Mint in Charlotte is seized.

In Ohio at Cincinnati, the Guthrie Greys (later 6th Ohio) converge on the parade ground (unoccupied Orphan Asylum lot) on Elm Street. At about 1500, the unit forms and marches to Camp Harrison outside the city. The contingent is accompanied by Menter's Brass Band. Other volunteers arrive at the camp by train; however, as the assembled troops continue to climb, reaching more than 1,600, many lack weapons. Nevertheless, training begins. Curiosity of the citizens causes the camp on the following day to be visited by large numbers of civilians who witness the entire force as it presents a dress parade at sunset. Late in the month, Brigadier General Joshua H. Bate (Ohio militia) assumes control of Camp Harrison.

In Virginia, Robert E. Lee resigns his United States Army commission. Lee says in a letter: "Save in the defense of my native state, I never desire again to draw my sword." Lee spends one day as a civilian, accepting the post of commander of Virginia's military and naval forces, bestowed upon him by Governor John Letcher. Robert E. Lee was not in favor of secession; however, he could not bear arms against his native Virginia. Lee becomes commander of the forces in Virginia. Once the Virginia troops switch their allegiance from the state service, Lee is confirmed as Confederate brigadier (14 May) in the regular service, and during June he achieves the full rank of general.

In other activity, Confederates strike and seize the navy yard in Norfolk. Union troops burn nine warships to prevent acquisition by southerners, but the move hurts the Union more than the rebels, as they lose the guns and the Confederates make good use of them. The Gosport Navy Yard is also torched. Approximately 3,000 cannon are captured along with a huge amount of supplies. Commodore C.S. McCauley simply does not get the vessels out of the port fast enough.

In addition, the Confederates seize a jewel of the American Revolution, the USS *United States,* which had been built during 1779 and remained in service in the navy until 1849, when it was moored at the Norfolk Navy Yard. Also, Horatio Gouverneur Wright (West Point, 1841) an engineer, is captured, but soon after released. He is appointed brigadier general during the following September.

After the Confederates seize the ship, it becomes the CSS *United States.* The vessel is used as a receiving ship until the following year. When the Union retakes Norfolk, the Confederates intentionally sink it during May 1862. Subsequently, the U.S. Navy is able to refloat the vintage vessel, but to no avail, as it is no longer capable of being repaired. Following close of hostilities, the U.S. Navy destroys the ship.

The Confederates subsequently raise one of the U.S. Navy's scuttled ironclads, the *Merrimack,* and turns it into one of their finest warships, the CSS *Virginia.* The Union also loses the USS *Pennsylvania,* which carries 130 guns and at this time is the largest ship in the U.S. fleet. Subsequent to the seizure, Commodore French Forest (formerly U.S. Navy) assumes command of the Norfolk Navy Yard. And Captain Arthur Sinclair (formerly U.S. Navy), now a captain of the Confederate Navy, will assume command of Fort Norfolk (21st). Initially, Confederate Captain Robert B. Pegram (appointed captain on 18th) is assigned command of Norfolk, but he is superseded by Forest.

In Union activity, John Adams Dix, recently appointed secretary of the treasury, while speaking in New York, delivers kind sentiments about former President James Buchanan, who many believe had acted inappropriately and indecisively prior to the outbreak of hostilities. Dix claims that if hostilities had been initiated in South Carolina against his administration as it now has been to the Lincoln Administration, "it would have been unanimously accepted." He infers that it was Buchanan's advisors, Floyd, Jacob Thompson and Cobb, who had been the problem. Dix, a veteran of the War of 1812, will be appointed major general of volunteers during the following month.

Major General John E. Wool, next in command under General Winfield Scott, general-in-chief of the U.S. Army, is at Troy, New York. As commander of the Eastern Department, General Wool focuses on assuming control of the troops moving into New York City for other destinations. From his headquarters, which will be established in the St. Nicholas Hotel, he gets

the troops dispatched, and he procures and expedites the shipment of arms into designated areas. New Jersey troops looking to find transportation will be placed aboard ships and transported to Annapolis via the Chesapeake.

Meanwhile, he seeks ways to accommodate about five thousand volunteers from Illinois; these are ordered to secure the arsenal at St. Louis, Missouri, and use its supply of about 21,000 stand of arms and more than 100,000 rounds of ammunition. General Wool also supplies six Ohio regiments with 3,000 muskets and ammunition, while providing additional Ohio units with 10,000 muskets and 400,000 rounds of ammunition. Indiana troops receive about 5,000 muskets, and New Jersey about 3,000 muskets. In Pennsylvania, General Robert Patterson receives 16,000 muskets, while Major General Sanford of New York gets 16,000. General Wool, while undertaking this complicated operation, is in ill health, but he disregards his condition to ensure that the Union is braced for any occurrence.

In Union general officer activity, Frederick S. Stumbaugh, a lawyer in Shippensburg, Pennsylvania, is commissioned colonel of the 2nd Pennsylvania Infantry; it includes Franklin County militia he had commanded prior to the outbreak of the war. The 2nd Regiment is a three-month unit; however, upon expiration of its enlistment term, Colonel Stumbaugh becomes colonel of the 77th Pennsylvania Regiment on 26 October. He participates at Shiloh and against Bragg when his Confederates invade Kentucky. Nonetheless, Stumbaugh is promoted to brigadier general on 29 November 1862. The senate takes no action and his commission is revoked on 22 January 1863. While in command of his regiment, General Stumbaugh had performed admirably. The records do not indicate why his commission was revoked. He resigns from the service on 15 May 1863 and resumes his law practice.

April 21 (Sunday)   In Virginia, Confederate brigadier general Philip St. George Cocke (Virginia state troops) is assigned duty that gives him responsibility for the Frontier Military District, which stretches along the Potomac River. He establishes headquarters in Alexandria.

In Naval activity, the sloop of war USS *Saratoga,* commanded by Commander (later rear admiral) Thomas Turner, while operating off Africa, intercepts and seizes a slave runner, the *Nightingale,* in the vicinity of Kabenda. The American warship rescues and frees the slaves onboard. Shortly thereafter, word of the outbreak of war reaches the *Saratoga.* It returns to the United States, arriving in August.

April 22 (Monday)   In Arkansas, governor, John Rector, declines supplying troops to support the federal government. The federal arsenal at Fayetteville is seized by Confederates.

In Florida, the Confederate Provisional Constitution is ratified by a unanimous vote (50 in the affirmative).

In Union activity, Robert Sanford Foster is appointed captain (later brevet major general) of the 11th Indiana Regiment. In June he is transferred to the 13th Indiana with the rank of major. Also, Gabriel Rene Paul (West Point, 1834), a veteran of the Mexican war, is commissioned major (later brigadier general) of the 8th Infantry. At the time he is stationed on the western frontier at Albuquerque. By December, he is appointed colonel of the 4th New Mexico Infantry Regiment.

In Confederate general officer activity, Brigadier General Joseph E. Johnston (West Point, 1829) resigns his U.S. commission and accepts a commission in the Confederacy as brigadier general during May. He will command at Harpers Ferry, and by August he is promoted to full general, following his efforts at Manassas (Bull Run). Also, James Dearing, a Virginian who entered the academy at West Point during 1858, resigns to head home and join the Confederacy. Dearing joins the Washington Artillery and receives the rank of lieutenant; in April 1864 he is promoted to brigadier general. In addition, 2nd Lt. Joseph Wheeler (West Point, 1859) resigns his commission to join the Confederacy as a first lieutenant. He becomes colonel (later major general) of the 19th Alabama Infantry in September.

In Confederate Naval officer activity, Captain Samuel Baron, Sr., resigns his commission in the U.S. Navy and accepts a commission as captain in the Virginia Navy effective April 23. Barron is promoted to captain, Confederate States Navy, during October, effective 26 March 1861.

In Naval activity, Lt. David Dixon Porter (later vice admiral) is promoted to the rank of commander. Confederate Captain M. Davis applies for a letter of marque at New Orleans for the *Landis* (also known as *Joseph Landis, I.C. Landis,* and *Landes*). The *Landis* is later acquired by the Confederacy at New Orleans for use as a tender to the CSS *Louisiana.*

April 23 (Tuesday)   In Texas, the Confederates seize federal officers and a contingent of Union infantry at San Antonio and retain them as prisoners of war. Robert E. Lee had been in command Department of Texas from 1857 through February 1861; however, he is back in Virginia at this time.

In Union general officer activity, Jacob Dolson Cox becomes a brigadier general of Ohio state forces and soon is appointed brigadier general of U.S. Volunteers by President Lincoln, effective May 1861. He serves in the West Virginia region under McClellan until August 1862.

In other activity, George B. McClellan (West Point, 1846), is appointed major general of Ohio Volunteers, becoming also commanding officer of all state troops. This appointment is short-lived, as within several weeks, McClellan is appointed by President Lincoln to the rank of major general, U.S. Regular Army, catapulting him to the second highest rank in the Army,

subordinate only to General Winfield Scott.

Also at about this time, Lincoln also appoints David Hunter as a brigadier general. Hunter (West Point, 1822) had been on duty at Fort Leavenworth until summoned east by Lincoln, who invited Hunter to ride with him on the inauguration train.

April 24 (Wednesday) In Texas, Confederates (Colonel Earl Van Dorn's command) capture a Union contingent at Saluria.

In Virginia, Confederate Brigadier Philip St. George Cocke (Virginia state troops)—while at his headquarters in Alexandria just outside of Washington, D.C., on the opposing bank of the Potomac River—becomes alarmed when he suddenly observes a huge federal force on the other side of the river. This poses a serious problem for Cocke, as he commands only several hundred state troops. General Robert E. Lee is informed of the situation and makes it clear that the Virginians are there defensively, and that if federal troops venture into Virginia, it would be construed as "an act of war."

In other activity, Confederate Major Thomas H. Williamson (engineers) and Lt. H.H. Lewis (Virginia state navy) inspect the terrain at Acquia Creek and determine that Cream Point is not suitable for a battery due to insufficient forces under Colonel Daniel Ruggles; however, Split Rock Bluff on the opposite bank is selected as a place that could be defended adequately by a small force. The Confederates erect a 13-gun battery, commanded by Captain William F. Lynch and a few other officers of the Virginia naval service. The battery also serves to distract the Union from Freestone Point and Matthias Point; however, it has drawbacks because the battery is vulnerable to an attack from the rear. Nonetheless, the Union realizes the battery threatens shipping on the Potomac.

In Union general officer activity, the 14th Ohio receives George Peabody Estey as its lieutenant colonel (later brigadier general). Estey is appointed colonel during November. His regiment joins the campaign to secure Western Virginia. Colonel Estey subsequently participates in Sherman's "March to the Sea," being wounded at Jonesboro, Georgia, while commanding a contingent of the XIV Corps during the latter part of August 1864.

In Naval activity, the CSS *Young America,* a tugboat, while attempting to guide the blockade runner *George M. Smith* into the James River, is intercepted and captured by the USS *Cumberland* at Hampton Roads, Virginia. The *Young America* is transformed into a tender for the Union, and the ammunition on the *George*

The federal arsenal in Fayetteville, Arkansas, is seized by Confederates (*Harper's Pictorial History of the Civil War,* 1896).

M. Smith fails to reach the Confederates. The *Young America* had been built during 1855 in New York City. En route to Washington, D.C., from Hampton Roads it encounters mechanical difficulties. Consequently, the USS *Resolute* tows it to the navy yard. Subsequent to receiving repairs, the *Young America* is attached to the North Atlantic Blockading Squadron.

April 25 (Thursday)   In Washington, D.C., the 8th Massachusetts Regiment and the New York 7th Regiment arrive from Annapolis.

In Illinois, U.S. Grant has been preparing the Illinois Volunteers by march and drill exercises at Galena, Illinois, while waiting for assignment. This day, the troops move to Springfield, where they are assigned as a contingent of the 11th Illinois Volunteer Infantry Regiment. This post at Springfield will be commanded by General Nathaniel Lyon (West Point, 1841), who succeeds Major W.H. Bell, the latter heading south to fight with the Confederacy. General Lyon will be commissioned on 17 May. Prior to his commission, Lyon had served on the Kansas frontier and afterward as commander of the arsenal in St. Louis.

In Texas, Fort Stockton (initially Camp Stockton), established during 1859 at Compton Springs, is abandoned by the U.S. Army. Afterward, Confederate troops occupy the post, evacuated by the U.S. 8th Infantry, but by August 1862 the post is regarrisoned by a elements of the 9th Colored Cavalry Regiment under Brigadier General Edward Hatch (West Point, 1845) Hatch, commissioned a captain in the 2nd Iowa Cavalry on 12 August 1861, will be commissioned brigadier general to rank from 28 September 1861.

Also, elements of the U.S. 1st Infantry Regiment that are attempting to move from Texas back to the north are intercepted while on transports at Saluria. Taken are Company G and K, along with the regimental band and the non-commissioned staff. Others, Companies A, H and I, safely depart Texas. After being caught, the troops are immediately paroled with the stipulation that they will not serve actively until exchanged. Following receiving paroles, the troops embark aboard the schooner *Horace* and arrive in New York on 31 May 1861.

In North Carolina, the tug *Uncle Ben* is seized by Confederates at Wilmington. The tugboat *Uncle Ben* (separate from the cotton-steamer *Uncle Ben*) operates in the vicinity of Wilmington into the summer of 1862, when the engine is transferred to the ironclad CSS *North Carolina*. Later in the summer, the hull of the *Uncle Ben* is sold and it becomes the privateer *Retribution* and afterward the *Etta*.

In Union general officer activity, Colonel John Cook musters into the 7th Illinois Regiment, which is the first Illinois regiment to be organized. Cook will fight gallantly at the siege of Fort Donelson, commanding a contingent of C.F. Smith's Division. Colonel Cook is promoted to brigadier general during March 1862. Lewis "Lew" Wallace, a veteran of the Mexican War (1st lieutenant, 1st Indiana Regiment) is commissioned colonel (later major general) of the 11th Indiana Regiment.

Thomas Algeo Rowley is commissioned colonel of the 13th Pennsylvania Regiment. The unit is a three-month regiment, but upon re-enlistment it becomes the 102nd Pennsylvania. Colonel Rawley is promoted to brigadier general (29 November) during 1862 and during the following year, he receives a court-martial and is apparently removed from command. Nonetheless, the secretary of war countermands the sentence and has him restored to duty. Afterward he is transferred to Pittsburgh, Pennsylvania, in command of the District of the Monongahela.

In Confederate general officer activity, George Burgwyn Anderson (West Point, 1852) resigns his commission in the Army to join the Confederacy as colonel of the 4th North Carolina Regiment. Also, Lunsford L. Lomax (West Point, 1856) resigns from the U.S. Cavalry to join the Confederacy. Initially, Lomax enters the state forces of Virginia, and subsequently becomes colonel (later major general) of the 11th

The steam tug *Uncle Ben* is seized by Confederates at Wilmington, North Carolina (Johnson, *Campfire and Battlefield: History of the Conflicts and Campaigns*, 1894).

Virginia Cavalry. Also, Captain Arnold Elzey (Jones), 2nd U.S. Artillery, resigns his commission to join the Confederacy. He is appointed colonel of the Confederate 1st Maryland Infantry Regiment. Elzey, a West Point graduate, class of 1837, participates at First Manassas (Bull Run) and is promoted to brigadier general for his actions at that battle.

April 26 (Friday)   In Missouri at St. Louis, Union Captain (later brigadier general) Nathaniel Lyon (West Point, 1841) and Colonel (later major general) Francis P. Blair take measures to transport arms and ammunition from St. Louis to Springfield. James Hughes Stokes (West Point, 1835), a classmate of General George Meade, is behind the success of the transfer. He succeeds in pulling off a ruse that distracts the southern sympathizers that have formed as a mob. With the arms out of St. Louis, the Confederates cannot gather them for their use. Following dusk, the arms are transferred to a steamboat that carries them to Alton, where Union-guarded trains move the arms (21,000 stand of arms, two cannon and 110,000 rounds of ammunition) to the arsenal at Springfield, Illinois. Once the arms are safely in Springfield, Governor Richard Yates oversees the distribution to ensure they go to troops loyal to the Union. Stokes (later brigadier general) is afterward employed by the state to procure arms, but he musters into the service during July of the next year.

In Confederate general officer activity, at about the time of the outbreak of war, some in Missouri join the Confederacy, and one of these men, Martin Edwin Green, abandons his business, leaving it to his brothers. Meanwhile, he establishes a contingent of cavalry composed of other Missourian southern sympathizers. The contingent, known as Green's Missouri Cavalry Regiment, later joins General Sterling Price's command. Colonel (later brigadier general) Lewis Henry Little from Maryland will join Price's force (Missouri Militia) as a colonel during the following month.

April 27 (Saturday)   In Washington, D.C., President Lincoln increases the scope of the naval blockade of southern ports which he had ordered on 17 April. The president orders all ports as far north as Virginia to be sealed by naval warships. Also, the president authorizes General Winfield Scott to lift the right of habeas corpus in the area stretching between Philadelphia and Washington, D.C., and later, on May 25, the suspension of the writ is also applied to the area beyond Philadelphia to New York.

General Scott had been born in Virginia during 1786, one year before the birth of the U.S. Constitution and about three years before George Washington was inaugurated as the first president of the United States. Scott served in the Army during the War of 1812 and during the Mexican War. When an inquiry was put to him about joining the southern cause, Scott responded: "I have served my country, under the flag of the Union for more than fifty years and so long as God permits me to live, I will defend that flag with my sword, even if my native state assails it."

In Maryland, the legislature convenes in Annapolis to attempt to coerce Union troops to remain out of Annapolis, claiming Maryland is a neutral state. This attempt, if successful, would totally isolate the capital from the states that had remained loyal to the Union. General Benjamin Franklin Butler, unimpressed with the action instigated by Governor Thomas Holliday Hicks, takes preventive action on May 5. During the following year, Governor Hicks is succeeded by Augustus Williamson Bradford, who serves until 1866.

In New York, the 6th New York Regiment (Wilson's Zouaves) is raised by Colonel William Wilson in New York City at Tammany Hall. Wilson, speaking to his regiment, drawn from the lower class neighborhoods of the city and alleged by some to be "rogues and criminals," informs them of the intent of their mission. While standing in the midst of his 1,200 troops, who have circled the room, he kneels down on one knee, using one hand to elevate Old Glory and the other to brandish his sword, as he begins to take an oath. In cadence with Wilson's motions, all in the room take the kneeling position and repeat, after him, the following oath: "To support the flag, and never flinch from its path through blood or death." Following this dramatic initiation, Wilson proclaims that the regiment will leave "but a monument of their bones in the streets" of Baltimore. Continuing, in response to cries of "death to the Plug Uglies [Pugly Uglies]," Wilson says: "Though I may be the first man slain, I have but one request to make. Let each of you, my followers, select his man and avenge my death."

The Plug Uglies had been involved with the disturbances that recently killed the Union troops in Baltimore. The regiment, this day, is transported to Staten Island for the purpose of later embarking for Baltimore, but after embarkation on June 13, they will discover that their destination has been changed.

In Ohio, General George B. McClellan, on behalf of the Department of Ohio, leases Camp Dennison, about fifteen miles outside Cincinnati. Soon after, units begin to arrive, including the 11th Ohio and five companies of the 3rd Ohio. The Cincinnati Brigade (Brigadier General Joshua H. Bates) is designated the 1st Ohio Brigade (5th, 6th, 9th and 10th Ohio Regiments). The 2nd Brigade (Brigadier General Jacob D. Cox) will be composed of the 4th, 7th, 8th and 11th Ohio Regiments, and the 3rd brigade (Brigadier General Newton Schleich) will be composed of the 3rd, 12th and 13th Ohio Regiments. The combined strength of the three brigades totals about 10,000 troops. General Joshua Bates will oversee the camp.

In Virginia, General Robert E. Lee orders Confederate Colonel Thomas J. Jackson to depart Fort Lee to take command of the forces at Harpers Ferry (later in West Virginia).

In Union general officer activity, Peter Joseph Osterhaus, a native of Prussia (later Coblenz, Germany), is commissioned major (later major general) in a Missouri battalion. During June 1862, he is promoted to brigadier general. In the meantime, he participates in various actions, including Pea Ridge (Elkhorn Tavern) in Arkansas. Also, James Blair Steedman is commissioned colonel of the 15th Ohio Regiment, a three-month unit. He participates at the Battle of Philippi, and afterward is ordered to the West, where he participates at various actions including Perryville and Murfreesboro.

In Confederate general officer activity, Union Captain (later Confederate major general) Samuel Jones, 1st Artillery, resigns his position and bears arms with the Confederates. Jones, a West Point graduate (1841), quickly lends his skills, participating with Beauregard at First Manassas (Bull Run) in command of Beauregard's artillery. During the following month, another of the many West Point alumni to defect to the Southern cause is Captain Thomas Jordan (graduated 1840). He throws his allegiance to the Rebels and is also with Beauregard at First Manassas. Jordan, who attended the military academy with General William T. Sherman, becomes a brigadier general during July of 1862 for his gallantry at Shiloh during April of the same year. He serves with both Beauregard and Bragg.

In Naval activity, President Abraham Lincoln instructs the navy to expand its blockade to include North Carolina and Virginia. At present, there are few Union vessels in American waters. The Confederates do not take the blockade seriously due to the vast amount of coastline involved. The southern coastline extends from the Chesapeake and stretches along the Carolinas to Savannah, Georgia, then beyond to Florida and on to Texas, with Louisiana tucked in the Gulf of Mexico, a distance calculated to be more than 3,000 miles. With the recent seizure of Norfolk, Virginia, the Union Navy has only four major warships, none immediately available. The seaworthy fleet is scattered around the globe.

April 28 (Sunday)   In Louisiana, the *William G. Hewes* (later USS *Malvern*), a civilian ship that operates between New Orleans and New York City as part of the fleet of Charles Morgan's Southern Steamship Company, is seized by order of Governor Thomas O. Moore. The *Hewes* is utilized as a blockade runner due to her agility and size, the latter making her capable of carrying nearly 1,500 bales of hay and having great speed and maneuverability. Nevertheless, the ship is not actually commissioned by the

Confederacy until 5 April 1862. At nearly the same time, the Union seizes New Orleans; however, the *Hewes* escapes capture and begins to operate out of the Carolinas under the name *Ella and Annie.*

April 29 (Monday)   In Alabama, Confederate President Jefferson Davis, speaking at the 2nd session of the Confederate Provisional Congress in Mobile, states: "We protest solemnly in the face of mankind, that we desire peace at any sacrifice, save that of honor and independence."

In Maryland, the state legislature decides to remain in the Union by a vote of 53 to 13.

In New York, the New York Zouaves Regiment, commanded by Colonel Elmer Ephriam Ellsworth, departs for Washington. During 1855 Ellsworth had moved to Chicago, Illinois, to become a law student. While there he, being strongly interested in the military, had joined a company and eventually became its captain. Once at its head, Ellsworth transformed the unit, modeling it after the French Zouaves who had fought in the Crimean War. Under his leadership, the unit known as the Chicago Zouave Cadets mandates that its members take a pledge to avoid cursing, a misdemeanor which causes immediate dismissal, and to abstain from liquor and tobacco. He also begins to work in the law office of Abraham Lincoln. By 1860, Ellsworth's Zouaves become very popular and they are asked to go on tour to exhibit their skills in drilling. He takes the Chicago Zouaves to New York and they perform to a crowd of about 8,000 people. Later in 1861, he is commissioned as a 2nd lieutenant in the Army, but he resigns and returns to New York to raise a regiment, the 11th New York Regiment (New York Zouaves), composed of 1,000 New York firemen.

Colonel Ephriam E. Ellsworth (Johnson, *Campfire and Battlefield: History of the Conflicts and Campaigns,* 1894).

In Virginia, General Robert E. Lee orders Colonel Andrew Talcott (West Point, 1818), an engineer who resigned from the Army during 1836, to lay the works at Burwell's Bay on the James River and then move to the mouth of the Appomattox River to prepare for Union attacks there.

In other activity, subsequent to acquiring intelligence on Union strength in Washington by Confederate lieutenants William L. Maury and William Taylor Smith, Colonel Daniel Ruggles is advised not to construct a battery above Acquia Creek. The two 8-inch guns at Alexandria are removed for use at Matthias Point, but they are later diverted to Acquia Creek.

In Union general officer activity, James Dada Morgan, a veteran of the Mexican War, is appointed lieutenant colonel of the 10th Illinois. On 20 May he becomes colonel of the regiment. Willis Arnold Gorman is commissioned colonel of the 1st Minnesota Infantry. During the Mexican War, Gorman had been a major in the 3rd Indiana. In addition, he served in Congress from Indiana from 1849 to 1853, when he was appointed governor of the Minnesota Territory by President Franklin Pierce.

April 30 (Tuesday)   In Indian Territory, federal troops begin to evacuate the forts in the Indian Territory, leaving it to Confederate control. The Confederates dispatch Colonel (later brigadier general) Albert Pike to negotiate treaties with the Indians and attempt to persuade them to assist the South.

In Union activity, Union General John E. Wool, having exceeded expectations of President Lincoln and General Winfield Scott regarding the arming and logistical movement of troops, is ordered to depart New York City, return to his headquarters in Troy, New York, and remain there while his health is in such poor condition. Wool, in recognition of his tremendous contribution, is recalled from retirement during August to receive another command.

In Confederate activity, 2nd Lt. Hylan B. Lyon (West Point, 1852), later Confederate brigadier general, resigns his commission to join the Confederacy.

May   *In Confederate general officer activity,* John Calvin Brown had earlier joined the Confederate Army as a private, but this month, he is promoted to colonel of the 3rd Tennessee Regiment. He becomes a major general in 1864. Also, former Major Alfred Holt Colquitt, U.S. Army, who served in the Mexican War and was also elected to Congress (as a representative from Georgia), is at this time elected colonel of the 6th Georgia Infantry. The 6th Georgia will deploy in Yorktown, Virginia, and remain in the garrison there until spring of the following year, when it is ordered to move out. The regiment participates in its first action at Yorktown during April 1862 and at Seven Pines and other contests in Virginia. During September 1862, Colquitt is promoted to brigadier general in the Confederate Army. Following its service in Virginia, the regiment moves south and will eventually bolt from Savannah to support the Confederates in East Florida under Brigadier General Finegan (1864).

Charles William Field (West Point, 1849) resigns his commission in the Army and is appointed colonel (later major general) of the Confederate 6th Virginia Cavalry. Major Richard Caswell Gatlin (West Point, 1832) resigns from the U.S. Army and becomes adjutant general of North Carolina as well as colonel (later brigadier general) in the Confederate Regular Army. Robert Hopkins Hatton joins the Confederacy as colonel (later brigadier general), 7th Tennessee Cavalry. Hatton had served in the U.S. Congress as a member of the "Know Nothing Party," which is staunchly anti–Catholic and anti-foreigner. Benjamin Grubb Humphreys (West Point, attendance 1825–1826) joins the Confederacy as an officer in the 21st Mississippi and becomes its colonel in November. His regiment is attached to the Army of Northern Virginia. Fitzhugh Lee, a graduate of West Point, class of 1856, resigns his teaching position at the military academy to join the Confederate cause. Lee has two uncles in the Confederacy, Samuel Cooper on his maternal side and Robert E. Lee on his paternal side. He enters the Confederate Army as a first lieutenant, but soon rises to brigadier general after a stint as lieutenant colonel of the 1st Virginia Cavalry.

Also, the former governor of Missouri, Sterling Price, is appointed major general of Missouri state troops by Governor Claiborne Fox Jackson. Although Missouri does not secede, Price will join the Confederacy, and during March 1862 he is appointed to the rank of major general. During the latter part of this year, Price establishes a camp for troops that want to serve in the Confederacy.

May 1 (Wednesday) In Massachusetts, a memorial service is held in Boston for the four Union soldiers killed during the recent Baltimore riots. The bodies are temporarily placed in the vaults of King Chapel. On May 6, the bodies of Luther C. Ladd and Addison O. Whitney are transferred to Lowell, Massachusetts, where a service is conducted at the "Hall" by the Reverend W.R. Clark of the Methodist Church. The remains of Charles Taylor and Sumner Needham are interred in Boston.

The State of Maryland authorizes on 5 March 1862 the sum of $7,000.00 to be given to the families of the soldiers who were killed during the riot (see also, **April 19 (Friday) In Maryland**).

In New York, Isaac Ferdinand Quinby (West Point, 1843), a classmate and close friend of Ulysses S. Grant, at about this time raises the "Rochester regiment," which is mustered into federal service as the 13th New York Regiment. Quinby is appointed colonel.

In New Hampshire, at about this time, Gilman Marston, a Harvard graduate and a lawyer, without military experience, begins to raise the 2nd New Hampshire Volunteer Regiment. Marston leads the regiment at First Bull Run (Manassas) as part of General Burnside's

brigade. Subsequently, Colonel Marston participates in the Peninsular Campaign. He is promoted to brigadier general on 29 November 1862 and participates as part of General J.B. Carr's brigade (General Sickles' division) at Fredericksburg in December 1862. Prior to the operations at Gettysburg, Marston is relieved from duty with the Army of the Potomac and directed to repair to Washington. He is sent to Maryland to establish a prison camp, which is afterward known as "Point Lookout Pen."

In Ohio, in response to an epidemic at Camp Dennison, the Sisters of Charity are called upon to rush to the camp to treat the troops. Five nuns are sent; Sisters Anthony and Sophia depart Cincinnati immediately and three others follow shortly thereafter. After the measles' epidemic subsides, they return to the convent at Cedar Grove, Ohio.

In Virginia, General Robert E. Lee directs Colonel Thomas J. Jackson to muster five regiments of infantry, one regiment of cavalry and two batteries of light artillery from counties surrounding Harpers Ferry, Virginia. Staunton's Light Artillery, commanded by Captain (later brigadier general) John Daniel Imboden, accompanies Jackson on this mission.

In Union general officer activity, Thomas Alfred Smyth, a native of Ireland who immigrated to the United States during 1854, raises a company of Irish volunteers at about this time. The unit, raised in Delaware, becomes part of the 24th Pennsylvania Regiment, a three-month regiment. Smyth becomes colonel of the 1st Delaware Regiment in February 1862. Also, John Converse Starkweather is commissioned colonel (later brigadier general) of the 1st Wisconsin Infantry at about this time.

In Confederate general officer activity, Edward Porter Alexander (West Point, 1857) resigns his commission in the U.S. Army to join the Confederacy. He is appointed captain of engineers and will serve with Pierre G.T. Beauregard at Manassas (Bull Run) and later become chief of artillery in General James Longstreet's Corps. Alexander is appointed brigadier general effective February 1864.

In Naval activity, a United States naval force begins the blockade of the mouth of the James River in Virginia. In other activity, at about this time (May 1861), a civilian vessel, the *Putnam* (formerly *Echo*) is commissioned by the Confederacy and renamed the *Jefferson Davis* (also *Jeff Davis*). In August 1861, the *Jefferson Davis* runs aground while attempting to enter the harbor at St. Augustine, Florida, and is lost. During its short-lived career, the *Jefferson Davis* had seized nine prizes, each a merchant ship.

In other activity, the *Albatross,* a wooden screw gunboat, is acquired by the U.S. Navy at about this time (July 1861) and commissioned during the following month. The Albatross had originally been constructed in Connecticut at Mystic during 1858 for use as a commercial steamship. It is attached to the North Atlantic Blockading Squadron and participates in block-

ade duty off North Carolina. During the following July, it captures two schooners, one of which is the *Enchantress,* which had earlier been seized by the Confederate privateer *Jefferson Davis.* The USS *Thomas Freeborn,* a side-wheel steam gunboat chartered by the U.S. Navy the previous April and purchased during May, is ordered to Hampton Roads.

May 2 (Thursday) *In Confederate general officer activity,* Raleigh Edward Colston is appointed colonel in the Confederate Army. He soon leaves for Norfolk, Virginia, to establish the 16th Virginia Infantry. During July, subsequent to the entry of Virginia into the Confederacy, the 16th Infantry enters the service of the Confederate Army. Colston will be promoted to brigadier general in late December.

In related activity, George Washington Custis Lee, the oldest son of Robert E. Lee, resigns his commission as a first lieutenant in the U.S. Army to join with the Confederates. Lee, like his father, is a graduate of West Point (1854). G.W.C. Lee will subsequently be promoted to the rank of major general (1863), but his service in the field will not occur until the latter part of the conflict; rather he will be assigned to the staff of President Jefferson Davis. William Henry Fitzhugh Lee, the middle son of Robert E. Lee, also decides to join the Confederacy. He had entered the Army during 1857, but remained only for about two years. W.H.F. Lee is assigned to the 9th Virginia Cavalry and quickly rises to the rank of colonel and subsequently to major general.

In Naval activity, the USS *Minnesota,* decommissioned on 2 June 1859, is recommissioned. Captain G. J. Van Brunt is appointed captain. The *Minnesota* will be attached to the Atlantic Blockading Squadron. It arrives at Hampton Roads on 13 May. In other activity, the USS *Massachusetts* (iron screw steamship) is acquired by the U.S. Navy at about this time (May) and is commissioned this month. Shortly thereafter it initiates patrol duty in the Mississippi Sound. Later it moves to the Gulf of Mexico, but during the early part of 1863, it goes out of service for repairs, and upon return to service it is utilized as a delivery vessel that carries supplies and men to various ports until 1863, when it is assigned to the South Atlantic Blockading Squadron.

May 3 (Friday) A British newspaper in London publishes President Abraham Lincoln's recent proclamation that ordered a blockade of southern ports.

In Washington, D.C., President Lincoln calls for 42,000 army volunteers and 18,000 seamen. Also, the president forms the Department of the Ohio, to be commanded by George McClellan (West Point, 1846), a retired army officer sent by the governor of Ohio with a force of volunteers to assist the people in West Virginia, who desire to remain in the Union. In addition, the U.S. Army is to be expanded by adding eight additional infantry regiments, one artillery regiment and one cavalry regiment. Volunteers are beginning to pour into the Union forces.

In Indiana, Governor Oliver P. Morton requested troops in proportional number to equal the president's request, about 4,000, but instead, 12,000 Indianians volunteer within eight days. In Indian Territory (Oklahoma), the garrison at Fort Arbuckle abandons the post and heads for Fort Leavenworth, Kansas, with Lt. Colonel William Emory's command, which during the previous month abandoned Fort Washita. Confederates soon after occupy the post. During 1865, elements of the 6th U.S. Infantry and 10th Cavalry regarrison the post.

In Ohio, William Haines Lytle, major general of militia, is appointed colonel of the 10th Ohio Regiment.

In Union general officer activity, Nathaniel James Jackson is appointed colonel of the 1st Maine Regiment, a three month unit; however, it is composed primarily of state militia and sees no action. Meanwhile, Colonel Jackson, after the regiment's enlistment expires, moves to the 5th Maine Regiment. During the fighting at Gaines' Mill, Colonel Jackson is severely wounded; however, he is back in the field and able to participate at South Mountain and at Antietam. Also, Captain John McArthur (Chicago Highlands Guards), later brigadier general, is appointed colonel of a 90-day regiment, the 12th Illinois Infantry. The regiment is re-mustered at the expiration of enlistment for three years.

In Confederate general officer activity, Brigadier General Albert S. Johnston, commanding officer, Department of the Pacific, resigns his commission. He returns to Texas and in August is appointed general (full rank) in the Confederate Regular Army. Also, 1st Lieutenant Henry Harrison Walker (West Point, 1853) resigns his commission and becomes a captain in the Confederate Army. Subsequently he is promoted to the rank of lieutenant colonel (later brigadier general), 40th Virginia Infantry.

In Naval activity, the U.S. Navy at about this time (May) acquires the *Montgomery,* a wooden screw steamship. Initially it is chartered, then soon placed in active service by commission. The Navy buys it in August. In the meantime, the *Montgomery* had been operating in the Gulf of Mexico and remains there through November 1861. Afterward, the vessel is moved to the

northern Gulf coast, and by early December, it begins to operate in the Mississippi Sound.

May 4 (Saturday) *In Union general officer activity,* Major General George B. McClellan, newly appointed commander of the Department of the Ohio, is making normal preparations for his position. McClellan selects Randolf B. Marcy (West Point, 1832) as his chief of staff. Marcy (McClellan's father-in-law) is appointed brigadier general during September 1861.

In Naval activity, the USS *Penguin* is acquired by the U.S. Navy at about this time (May) and commissioned as the gunboat USS *Penguin* the following month. Initially it is assigned duty with the Potomac Flotilla, and it also sees duty in North Carolina. During 1863, it is transferred to the West Gulf Blockading Squadron, where it remains until sold during August 1865.

May 5 (Sunday) **In Maryland,** Union Brigadier General Benjamin Franklin Butler dispatches a contingent of troops to a position less than ten miles from Baltimore, the Relay House, and he establishes positions there from where he can move into Baltimore to ensure that Maryland takes no action to halt the movement of Union troops through its land.

In Virginia, state militia troops under Brigadier General Philip St. George Cocke (J.E.B. Stuart's father-in-law), temporarily evacuate Alexandria, which is across the Potomac River from Washington, D.C. The contingent under Colonel A.S. Taylor is insufficient to repel a Union assault. The column—composed of two companies (150 troops) of fresh recruits, armed with old flint rifles and the Mount Vernon Guard (86 privates, armed with modern rifles and 52 without arms)—moves to Springfield and bivouacs along the Orange and Alexandria Railroad, less than ten miles from Alexandria. General Cocke (West Point, 1832) re-establishes headquarters at Culpeper. He is appointed brigadier general in the Provisional Confederate Army during October 1861.

Also, General Robert E. Lee issues Confederate General Order 10: "By order Major General Robert E. Lee: Troops mustered in will be by companies only Virginia volunteers."

In Confederate general officer activity, following the abandonment of Alexandria, Major

Montgomery D. Corse (state troops), Old Dominion Rifles, who had held the capacity of adjutant general, is attached to the 17th Virginia Regiment. He is promoted colonel, CSA, and participates in various battles, including Blackburn's Ford, 1st Manassas (Bull Run, 7/21/1862), 2nd Manassas (Bull Run, 8/30/1862), Seven Pines (5/31 to 6/1/1862), Seven Days' (6/6 to 7/1/1862), Sharpsburg (Antietam, 9/17/62), Yorktown (4/5 to 5/4/1862), and Williamsburg (5/5/1862). At these contests his courage is conspicuous and his stamina under fire is extraordinary, particularly when he leads his regimental survivors (56 troops) at Sharpsburg. Corse is promoted to brigadier general on November 1, 1862.

May 6 (Monday) **In Montgomery, Alabama,** Confederate President Jefferson Davis authorizes the declaration of war passed by the Confederate Congress, making the conflict official.

In Arkansas, the state secedes from the Union. It is the ninth to secede. Also, Captain Samuel D. Sturgis, U.S. Army, had been in command at Fort Smith, Arkansas, but he had refused to capitulate to the Confederates when the fort was recently seized. Instead, Sturgis, with his command, a contingent of the U.S. 1st Cavalry, had moved to Fort Leavenworth, Kansas. He becomes brigadier general on August 1, 1861.

In Michigan, the 1st Michigan Infantry Regiment is presented a flag at Detroit by ladies of the city to Colonel O.B. Willcox, who accepts it on behalf of the regiment. At about the same time, the ladies of Niles present a flag to Company E, 2nd Michigan, before it departs for Detroit to join the regiment. By the Battle of Fredericksburg (December 1862), the flag receives forty bullet holes. No longer fit for service, it is at that time returned to the donors, who preserve it. Eleven men who carry it or defend it first-hand in battle are either wounded or killed.

In Virginia, Robert E. Lee, in a letter to Colonel (also brigadier general of state troops) Philip St. George Cocke, the commanding officer at Culpeper Court House, states: "You are desired to post at Manassas Gap Junction, a force sufficient to defend against attack." Two guns recently evacuated from Alexandria are transported to Acquia Creek to defend the approaches to Fredericksburg from the Potomac River.

May 7 (Tuesday) **In South Carolina,** the steamer tug *James Gray,* constructed in Philadelphia during 1858 and purchased by Governor Francis W. Pickens during March of this year and renamed *Lady Davis,* is acquired by the Confederacy.

In Confederate general officer activity, Captain James McQueen McIntosh (West Point, 1849) resigns his commission in the U.S. Cavalry and accepts an appointment as captain (later brigadier general) in the Confederate cavalry, followed shortly thereafter by becoming colonel of the 2nd Arkansas.

New York troops, aboard sixteen transports, cross the Chesapeake Bay en route to Washington, D.C., via Annapolis, Maryland (Mottelay, *The Soldier in Our Civil War,* 1886).

In Naval activity, the wooden screw steamer *Reliance* is acquired by the U.S. Navy. The *Reliance* commissioned on the 13th and assigned to the Potomac Flotilla. Acting Lt. Jared P.K. Mygatt receives command of the gunboat.

May 8 (Wednesday) In Virginia (western), George Smith Patton joins the Confederate 1st Kanawha Regiment as captain of Company I (later Company H). The unit becomes known officially as the Kanawha Rifles. On 7 June he is promoted to lieutenant colonel of the regiment, which is commanded by General Henry Wise. Colonel Patton, a graduate of the Virginia Military Institute, is the grandfather of George S. Patton, Jr., who won fame during World War II, and the great-grandfather of Major General George S. Patton IV.

Colonel George S. Patton, while a cadet at VMI (courtesy the Patton family).

In Union general officer activity, Edward Moody McCook, a native of Ohio living in Colorado (Kansas Territory), heads for Washington at the outbreak of the war and on this day is commissioned a lieutenant in the U.S. Cavalry. Afterward, he serves with the 2nd Cavalry and by April of the following year, he commands the regiment with the rank of lieutenant colonel. Also, Robert Latimer McCook, a cousin of Edward Moody McCook, is commissioned colonel of the 9th Ohio Regiment. John McNeil, a captain in a Missouri volunteer company at the beginning of the war, is commissioned colonel of the 3rd Missouri Infantry on this day. He is mustered out during the following August; however, McNeil is commissioned colonel of the 2nd Missouri State Militia during August 1862. He is promoted to brigadier general to rank from 29 November 1862.

Joshua Thomas Owen, a native of Wales brought to the U.S. when he was about nine years old, is commissioned colonel of the 24th Pennsylvania Regiment. Colonel "Paddy" Owen, after the 24th, a 3-month regiment, musters out, becomes colonel of the 69th Pennsylvania Regiment. He participates at First Bull Run (Manassas) in command of the 24th. Afterward, he participates in various actions of the Army of the Potomac with the 69th. He is promoted to brigadier general on 20 November 1862; however, en route to Gettysburg, he is placed under arrest for not following orders (he fails to support an adjacent brigade at Cold Harbor). Consequently, his commission expires due to inaction by the senate. Nonetheless, General Owen escapes severe punishment. He is mustered out of the service about one month after the charges are placed against him by General Gibbon and he departs with an honorable discharge.

In Confederate general officer activity, George Earl Maney becomes colonel (later brigadier general) of the Confederate 11th Tennessee. Maney serves at various battles in Virginia under General Robert E. Lee and subsequently he is transferred to the Army of the Tennessee. Maney is assigned to Staunton, Virginia (General S. R. Anderson's brigade). His regiment serves in various battles, including Cheat Mountain, followed by service with General Thomas J. Jackson at Winchester before being transferred to Tennessee.

May 9 (Thursday) In Washington D.C., a fire breaks out in a liquor store next door to the Willard Hotel. It is quickly extinguished; however, within two hours, again the structure becomes engulfed with flames. Firefighters seem unable to gain control, but the New York Zouaves (composed of firemen) rush down the street led by Colonel Elmer Ephriam Ellsworth. The firemen try to tell Ellsworth that they will control the operation and Ellsworth responds: "Well. If you have more men here than I have, you can take it." Ellsworth, having relieved the one dissenting fireman of his trumpet, takes control of the operation, and his men beat out the fire, save the building, and in the process take many dangerous measures. One man's legs are held by two other troops as he dangles headfirst from the roof to reach a fire hose being lifted from the men in the street.

In New York, the 20th New York Regiment (Turner's Rifles), organized by Max Weber, is mustered into federal service. Weber, a native of Achern, Germany, had immigrated to the United States about 1848. He is appointed brigadier general on 28 April 1862. During the Battle of Antietam, he commands a brigade.

In Union general officer activity, William T. Sherman (West Point, 1840) is reappointed colonel (later full general) to the 13th U.S. Infantry in the Union Army. Also, John Wolcott Phelps (West Point, 1836) is appointed colonel of the 1st Vermont Regiment; however, on 9 August, he is appointed brigadier general to rank from 17 May. Initially, General Phelps is assigned to

support the defenses of Hampton Roads, but afterward, he is transferred to the Department of the Gulf. While in New Orleans, subsequent to a short command at Ship Island, he organizes the first unit of Negro troops; however, his action is not authorized by the Lincoln administration. Consequently, on 21 August 1862, Phelps resigns his commission. On that same day, the Confederate government proclaims Phelps an "outlaw" for attempting to form a Negro unit. When it is decided to include Negro troops, Phelps is offered an appointment as major general in command. He declines.

In Confederate general officer activity, Captain George Blake Cosby (West Point, 1852), 2nd U.S. Cavalry, resigns his commission to join the Confederacy. He is appointed captain (later general).

In Naval activity, in Maryland, Annapolis is viewed as a prime target and considered to be in a precarious position due to the conflict; is no longer seen as the proper place for the U.S. Naval Academy; therefore, the USS *Constitution* and the steamer *Baltic* are preparing to depart for Newport, Rhode Island, the location of the new naval academy. The steamer USS *Yankee* bombards a Confederate battery at Gloucester Point, Virginia.

Also, the Union Navy will begin a concentrated effort to accumulate as many new vessels as possible to strengthen the blockade of the South's ports. The tug *Jackson*, built in Cincinnati during 1849 and known as the *Yankee* (separate from the USS *Yankee*), is acquired by purchase at New Orleans by the Confederacy. Captain L. Rousseau transforms the vessel into a gunboat, the CSS *Jackson*.

May 10 (Friday) In Missouri, Union troops — numbering about 6,000 and led by Captain Nathaniel Lyon (later general), Colonel Francis Blair (former Congressman), Colonel Franz Sigel and others — encroach and surround Camp Jackson to foil a plot by two companies of state militia that are attempting the capture of St. Louis and the U.S. arsenal there to add to the stash of arms confiscated in Baton Rouge, Louisiana, and presently at Camp Jackson. The garrison, composed of state militia more than 600-strong commanded by Brigadier General Daniel Marsh Frost (West Point 1844), aware of the overwhelming strength facing it, surrenders without resistance.

Rufus Saxton (West Point, 1849), in command of an artillery unit at the St. Louis arsenal, supports Captain Lyons. Afterward, Saxton becomes quartermaster for Lyons and serves on the staff of General George McClellan. The 1st, 3rd and 4th Missouri, Reserve Corps, and the 3rd Missouri, U.S. Volunteers, participate in the seizure. General Daniel M. Frost is paroled and in March of the following year is appointed brigadier general in the Confederate Army.

Frost's chief of staff, John Stevens Bowen (West Point, 1853), later Confederate brigadier general, is also captured. Subsequent to his parole, Bowen establishes the Confederate 1st Missouri Infantry Regiment. Initially Bowen's regiment serves with General Leonidas Polk in Kentucky, but afterward, the 1st Missouri transfers to Tennessee, where it participates at the battle of Shiloh. (Pittsburg Landing) in April 1862.

In St. Louis, riots erupt, but the Union's 5th Missouri Regiment, U.S. Reserves, quashes them with a cost of four killed.

In Union general officer activity, Lt. Colonel Stephen Miller (later brigadier general) who mustered into the 1st Minnesota Infantry Regiment in late April, remains with the regiment, which is re-mustered for a three-year enlistment this day. He becomes colonel of the 7th Minnesota the following August. Meanwhile, he participates at Ball's Bluff (Leesburg) and in the Peninsular Campaign. Also, James Clay Rice is commissioned a lieutenant (later brigadier general) in the 39th New York on or about this day. He is appointed colonel of the 44th New York Regiment during April 1862.

In Confederate general officer activity, Brigadier General Benjamin Huger (West Point, 1825) takes command at Norfolk, Virginia, but his leadership is poor and he will evacuate the city without a fight during May 1862. Also, James Edward Rains, a lawyer who initially enlisted as a private in the 11th Tennessee at the beginning of hostilities, is commissioned colonel of the regiment on this day. Colonel Rains later participates at Cumberland Gap during the winter (1861–1862), but in June 1862, he is compelled to abandon the positions after being outflanked. Nevertheless, afterward, serving under General Carter Stevenson, Rains commands a brigade that opposes the Union in the Gap.

May 11 (Saturday)   In Missouri, at St. Louis, some unrest continues following the riots of the previous day; however, the Union forces maintain control.

In Union general officer activity, Charles Smith Hamilton (West Point, 1843) is appointed colonel of the 3rd Wisconsin Infantry. He holds the rank less than one week due to being promoted to brigadier general. General Hamilton commands a division in General Heintzelman's III Corps during the Peninsular Campaign until he is succeeded by General McClellan on 30 April. Difficulties emerge when McClellan declares Hamilton "unfit for command." Nevertheless, Hamilton is supported by General Philip Kearny. Hamilton is transferred to the western theater, and while there he performs admirably at such places as Iuka and Corinth. Also, Edward Harland is appointed as captain in the 5th Connecticut (Company D). During the following September, Harland is appointed colonel of the 8th Connecticut.

In Confederate general officer activity, Colonel Ben McCulloch (Texas state troops) is promoted to the rank of brigadier general in the Provisional Confederate Army. McCulloch had previously been a Texas Ranger who fought Indians, participated with Sam Houston against the Mexicans at San Jacinto during Texas' fight

for independence, and he also served with General Zachary Taylor during the Mexican War. His brother, Henry Eustace McCulloch, also joins the Confederacy. He will be appointed colonel of the 1st Texas Mounted Riflemen the following month. Also, Evander McNair, a veteran of the Mexican War who had fought as a member of the 1st Mississippi Rifles, will form a regiment later designated the 4th Arkansas Infantry and become its colonel (later brigadier general). The 4th Arkansas will serve under Ben McCulloch.

May 12 (Sunday)   In Florida, the USS *Mohawk* arrives at Pensacola.

In South Carolina, the USS *Niagara*—initially commissioned during April 1857 and having arrived back from a voyage to Japan the previous month—while operating off Charleston on blockade duty seizes a blockade runner, the *General Parkhill.*

In Maryland, Union troops (General Benjamin F. Butler's command) occupy a railroad depot (Baltimore and Ohio) at Relay House, slightly southwest of Baltimore. The troops' arrival is timely. They seize an unusual artillery piece known as Winans artillery gun, a rapid fire steam-powered cannon. The gun, created by Ross Winans, a prominent Southern sympathizer, is seized before the Confederates can transport it to Harpers Ferry in Western Virginia. General Butler dispatches a contingent of about 950 troops, including elements of the 6th Massachusetts (Colonel Edward F. Jones) and of the 8th New York Regiment (Lt. Colonel Waterbury), bolstered by a section of Major Cook's Battery to Baltimore.

Meanwhile, Butler's forces occupy Federal Hill. At about midnight (12th-13th) word arrives regarding riots in Baltimore. Butler discovers that arms have been carried to Snow Hill by secessionists, and he dispatches troops during the early morning hours of the 13th to seize the weapons there and at another location near the customs house. In addition, Butler places Ross Winans under arrest and sends him under escort to Fort McHenry. Butler dispatches other troops to seize gunpowder stored in Greenmount Cemetery.

May 13 (Monday)   In Maryland, General Benjamin F. Butler prepares to seize control of Baltimore. By this time, his force has occupied Annapolis and taken

control of the railroad running between Annapolis and the capital.

In New Mexico, Colonel W.H. Loring, the commander at Fort Fillmore, under suspicion of being a southern sympathizer, resigns from the U.S. Army. Loring had attempted to attach his troops in New Mexico to the Confederate cause; however, Lt. Colonel B.S. Roberts prevents it from happening. Loring had been in communication with Henry Hopkins Sibley; the latter on this day resigns from the service, although he is promoted to the rank of major.

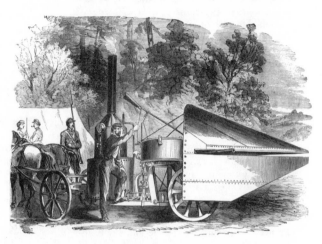

Union forces a capture steam gun at Relay House (Johnson, *Campfire and Battlefield: History of the Conflicts and Campaigns,* 1894).

The Bouquet Battery dominates the viaduct over the Patapsco River on the Baltimore and Ohio Railroad in the vicinity of the Relay House (Mottelay, *The Soldier in Our Civil War,* 1886).

Several days later, Sibley joins the Confederacy. On 20 May, Loring is appointed brigadier general in the Confederate Army. The great majority of men in New Mexico remain loyal to the Union; however, the Confederates gain strongholds, including La Messilla, where the Confederate colors are flown.

In Union general officer activity, Benjamin Stone Roberts (West Point, 1835), a veteran of the Mexican War, is promoted to major (later brigadier general) in his regiment, which is soon after renamed the 3rd U.S. Cavalry, pursuant to congressional action on 3 August. He participates in the operations against Confederate General Henry Hopkins Sibley in New Mexico. After the engagement at Valverde he receives the brevet of colonel, just prior to being ordered to return to the East. Upon his arrival, he becomes inspector general under General John Pope. While in that capacity, he is the individual who later presses charges against General Fitz John Porter as part of the group who seeks Porter's ouster from the service.

In Naval activity, the USS *Minnesota,* recently recommissioned, arrives at Hampton Roads. On the following day, the vessel departs and immediately seizes other vessels.

May 14 (Tuesday) England declares neutrality in the American Civil War. By mid–June, France, Spain and the Netherlands will also proclaim neutrality.

In Maryland, Union troops under General Benjamin Franklin Butler enter Baltimore and secure Federal Hill. Butler proclaims that he intends to maintain law and order. By occupying Baltimore, the route between Washington and all routes north are again open and accessible to moving Union Troops. Also, Governor Thomas H. Hicks issues an order calling for the service of four regiments to be deployed for the defense of Maryland and Washington.

In Virginia, Robert E. Lee, commander of the state forces, is appointed brigadier general in the Confederate service. During the following month, Lee is raised to the full rank of general.

In Union general officer activity, Colonel (later major general) Edward Richard Sprigg Canby (West Point, 1839) is appointed colonel of the 19th Infantry Regiment and assigned duty as commander of the Department of New Mexico with his Headquarters at Fort Defiance, New Mexico Territory (at this time, includes present day Arizona). Canby, for the past few years, has been assigned duty on the frontier, and before that he served on the West Coast. Canby also has experience against hostile Indians, including service against the Seminoles in Florida.

Joseph Bradford Carr (colonel, New York militia) is appointed colonel of volunteers. William Buel Franklin (West Point, 1843), a classmate of Ulysses S Grant, is commissioned colonel of the 12th U.S. Infantry Regiment. On 15 May he is commissioned brigadier general of volunteers. Also, Romeyn Beck Ayres (West Point, 1847) is promoted to captain (later brevet brigadier and brevet major general) of the 5th U.S. Artillery. In addition, Joseph Eldridge Hamblin is commissioned a 1st lieutenant (later brigadier general) in the 5th New York. At the same time he becomes adjutant of the regiment, which is also known as Duryee's Zouaves. He participates at Big Bethel (10 June) and afterward is sent to Baltimore and assigned to an engineering task; however, he is soon transferred to the 65th New York Regiment with the rank of major.

Samuel Peter Heintzelman (1826) is appointed colonel of the U.S. 17th Infantry Regiment. On the 17th, he is commissioned brigadier general, followed by promotion to major general to rank from 5 May 1862. Irvin McDowell (West Point, 1838), a veteran of the Mexican War, is appointed brigadier general in the U.S. Army. With more than twenty years in the army, he has no actual experience in the field in command of troops. However, he has taught tactics at West Point and as events unfold, some of his students become Confederate officers who use his strategy against him in the field. Captain Montgomery Cunningham Meigs (West Point, 1840) is appointed colonel of the 11th U.S. Infantry, and on the following day, he is appointed U.S. Army quartermaster general with the rank of brigadier general. William Henry Penrose, initially commissioned a second lieutenant of the 3rd U.S. Infantry during the initial days of the war, is promoted to first lieutenant. He remains with the regiment until 18 April 1863, when he is appointed colonel of the 15th New Jersey Volunteer Regiment.

In yet other activity, Andrew Porter (West Point, attendance), a veteran of the Mexican War on duty in Texas and other locations in the Southwest for about 14 years prior to the outbreak of the Civil War, is appointed colonel of the recently established 16th U.S. Infantry Regiment. However, he holds the rank only three days. He becomes a brigadier general on 17 May in an appointment made on 6 August. General Porter participates at First Manassas (Bull Run) in command of the 1st Brigade (General Hunter's division). Afterward, during the Peninsular Campaign, he is the provost marshal of the Army of the Potomac. General Porter then is relieved and sent to Pennsylvania to assist in recruiting and other duties, but his health continues to fail. He remains in the service until April 1864, but he sees no more field duty.

Charles Pomeroy Stone (West Point, 1845), the inspector general of the District of Columbia at the time of the outbreak of the war, is appointed colonel of the 14th U.S. Infantry, but on 6 August, he is again promoted, to brigadier general to rank from 14 May. William Rufus Terrill (West Point, 1853), the brother of Confederate General James Barbour Terrill, is commissioned captain (later brigadier general) of the 5th U.S. Artillery. Following command of an instruction camp in the vicinity of Louisville, Kentucky, he becomes chief of artillery of General Alexander McDowell McCook's 2nd Division. Captain Israel Vogdes (West Point, 1837) is promoted to major (later brigadier general). He participates in the defense of Fort Pickens, Florida.

Gouverneur Kemble Warren is appointed lieutenant colonel (later major general) of the 5th New York (Duryee's Zouaves). Warren becomes colonel of the regiment during the following August. Also, Louis Douglass Watkins is commissioned 1st lieutenant (later brigadier general) of the Regular Army and attached to the 5th U.S. Cavalry during the Peninsular Campaign. Prior to being commissioned, he had been a member of the 3rd Battalion, District of Columbia Infantry. Stephen Hinsdale Weed (West Point, 1854), a veteran of the Seminole Wars in Florida, is promoted to captain (later brigadier general) of the 5th U.S. Artillery.

In Naval activity, the USS *Minnesota,* on its first day at sea after leaving Hampton Roads, seizes three schooners, the *Delaware Farmer, Emily Ann* and *Mary Willis.* Also, on or about this day, the privateer CSS *Calhoun,* commanded by Captain J. Wilson, leaves New Orleans. Shortly after beginning the cruise, it seizes the bark *Ocean Eagle* (sources vary on exact date of capture), which was out of Portland, Maine, and transporting more than 3,000 casks of lime. The *Calhoun* tows the vessel to the Mississippi, assigns a prize crew and then resumes its cruise. Afterward, while on the same cruise, the *Calhoun,* with a crew of more than 100, seizes the vessel *Milan* with its cargo of salt. Next the *Calhoun* seizes another merchant ship, the schooner *Ella,* which is transporting a cargo of fruit. Also the blockade runner *North Carolina* is seized in Chesapeake Bay by Union vessels, including the USS *Quaker City.*

May 15 (Wednesday) **In Virginia,** General Robert E. Lee writes to Confederate Colonel (also brigadier general of state troops) Philip St. George Cocke: "I have to request that you fill up Colonel Garland and Colonel [William] Preston's regiments and send reinforcements when requested by Colonel Terrett at Manassas Junction and if Terrett is attacked, commit your whole force." Cocke is also responsible for gathering volunteers for the Confederate service.

In Union general officer activity, Major Robert Anderson (West Point, 1825), who had defended Fort Sumter, South Carolina, is appointed brigadier general by President Abraham Lincoln. In August, Anderson is dispatched to assume command the Department of the Cumberland. Also, George Archibald McCall (West Point, 1822) is appointed commissioned major general of Pennsylvania Volunteers. On the 17th McCall is commissioned brigadier general of U.S. Volunteers.

In Naval activity, the vessel *Music,* a side-wheel towboat, is commissioned as a Confederate privateer. The ship was built during 1857 in Jeffersonville, Indiana. The *Music,* commanded by Captain Thomas McClellan (also owner), operates in the defense of New Orleans. The *Music* later participates in activity on the Atchafalaya-Red River and is thought to have been one of the last Confederate vessels to operate there, but the naval records on the ship are unclear.

May 16 (Thursday)   In Ohio, at Camp Harrison, training continues as regiments prepare to move out when ordered. On this day 3,500 stand of arms are distributed and of those, the Guthrie Greys receive 853 muskets and some uniforms. On the following day, the Greys (6th Ohio) move to Camp Dennison, about fifteen miles outside Cincinnati, by marching through the city, accompanied by Mercer's Brass Band. Civilians line the streets to observe the spectacle.

In Union general officer activity, President Abraham Lincoln promotes Brigadier General Benjamin Franklin Butler to the rank of major general. He also appoints John Adams Dix to the rank of major general of Volunteers. General Dix had fought at the battle of Lundy's Lane (War of 1812) before he was fifteen. This appointment by Lincoln places Dix at the head of the list of volunteer officers, giving him seniority of rank. Dix is relegated to department duty at such backwaters as Suffolk, Virginia.

In Confederate activity, Major Henry Hopkins Sibley, who resigned from the U.S. Army on 13 May, is appointed colonel in the Confederate Army. Sibley is charged with bringing New Mexico into the Confederacy.

May 17 (Friday)   In Ohio, the 6th Ohio Regiment (Guthrie's Greys) arrives at Camp Dennison just after the arrival of the 10th Ohio Regiment. The site, located on the Little Miami, Columbus and Xenia Railroad fifteen miles outside Cincinnati, had been selected by General McClellan. Other units, the 5th and 9th Ohio, arrive on the following day.

In Union general officer activity, Ulysses Simpson Grant (West Point, 1843) and Benjamin Mayberry Prentiss both become brigadier generals in the Union Army. Grant, because of former Army rank, is senior officer. Also, Captain Nathaniel Lyon (West Point 1841), hero of the Mexican war (although he personally opposed the conflict) and a participant in the conflict against the Seminoles in Florida, is appointed brigadier general. Lt. Colonel Don Carlos Buell, stationed in California as adjutant Department of the Pacific, is also appointed brigadier general.

Also, James Cooper is appointed brigadier general by President Lincoln, effective this day. Lincoln authorizes Cooper to raise a brigade of Maryland troops. Philip Kearny, a veteran of the Mexican War and for a while in the French cavalry, who resigned his commission during 1851, is appointed a brigadier general 7 August, effective to rank from this day. Kearny had again served in the French military during the Italian War when he was in the Imperial Guard of Napoleon III. Colonel Erasmus Darwin Keyes (11th U.S. Infantry) is promoted to brigadier general during August 1861, to rank effective this day. He participates at First Manassas (Bull Run) prior to his promotion.

In other activity, John Alexander McClernand, a veteran of the Black Hawk War and a U.S. congressman, is appointed a brigadier general by President Lincoln. McClernand's only

military experience was gained when he was a private during the Black Hawk War. Nonetheless, his appointment, politically inspired, aids Lincoln in maintaining southern Illinois Democrats aligned with the Union. On this same day, John Frémont, who garnered 1,300,000 votes for president running behind the victor, President James Buchanan, who received 1,800,000 votes, is appointed brigadier general by President Lincoln, Buchanan's successor. Rufus King (West Point, 1833) is among the Union brigadier generals appointed by President Lincoln. King will organize the famed "Iron Brigade" (Wisconsin Regiments). Also, Colonel Joseph Jones Reynolds (West Point, 1843) commanding officer of the 10th Indiana (militia), is appointed brigadier general, effective 17 May. General Reynolds participates at Cheat Mountain in September but resigns form the service during January 1863, then returns to duty in September 1862.

In Confederate general officer activity, Captain John Porter McCown (West Point, 1840) resigns his commission in the U.S. Army. He is appointed colonel in the Tennessee Artillery Corps. McCown jumps rank to become a brigadier general the following October.

May 18 (Saturday)   *In Union general officer activity,* Colonel Joseph King Fenno Mansfield (West Point, 1822) is appointed brigadier general in the Regular service.

In Confederate general officer activity, Ambrose Ransom Wright is appointed colonel of the 3rd Georgia Infantry Regiment. He is promoted to brigadier general during June. Sterling Alexander M. Wood, who initially joined the Confederacy as a captain in the Florence Guards, is elected colonel (later brigadier general) of the 7th Alabama Infantry Regiment. Colonel Wood is assigned duty in Florida at Pensacola; however, in February of the following year, Wood is ordered to Kentucky.

May 18–19   In *Naval activity,* two Union vessels, the *Federal* and the *Monticello,* led by Commander Henry Eagle, engage Confederate shore batteries at Sewell's Point, Virginia, initiating the first Union offensive of the war. The defending Confederate units, commanded by Colonel Alfred Colquitt, 6th Georgia Infantry Regiment, include the City Light Guards, Wood's Rifles, a contingent of Light Artillery Blues, and a unit of the Norfolk Juniors. They exchange blows with the Union for nearly two hours. The Rebels fly the Georgia flag in place of the Confederate Colors. The Confederate fire finally compels the two federal steamers to withdraw. The Union sustains two wounded. The Confederate casualties are unavailable.

The USS *Monticello* had earlier this month been acquired (under charter) by the U.S. Navy. It is named *Star,* but only for a short while, less than a month. The Navy purchases the *Monticello* later this month.

Virginia is now under a reasonably tight sea blockade with the arrival of U.S. vessels that guard the mouth of the Rappahannock River.

The Union realizes the South will become dependent on Europe for supplies and wants to make it as difficult as possible for it to receive goods by sea.

May 19 (Sunday)   *In Union general officer activity,* Frederick (Friedrich) Salomon, a native of Prussia and one of four brothers who immigrated to the United States, is commissioned captain (later brigadier general) of the 5th Missouri, which is commanded by one of his younger brothers. Shortly after the 5th ends its three-month enlistment, he becomes colonel of the 9th Wisconsin on 26 November 1861. He is assigned duty in Arkansas and Missouri.

In Naval activity, the steamer USS *Freeborn,* while operating near Fort Washington on the Potomac, seizes two schooners, both of which are caught while transporting Confederate soldiers. The CSS *Lady Davis,* while operating off Savannah on a mission to locate the USS *Perry,* an armed brigantine, encounters a merchant ship, the *A.B. Thompson* (operating out of Maine), which it seizes and sails into Beaufort, South Carolina. Subsequently, the *Lady Davis* participates in the defense of Port Royal, South Carolina, on 7 November. Towards the latter part of 1862, the *Lady Davis* becomes a blockade runner that operates until Charleston falls in 1865. It is seized by the Union. Also, at about this time (May), the U.S. Navy acquires the *Phineas Sprague,* a screw steamship that had been built in Philadelphia during 1857. It is commissioned the USS *Flag* this month and assigned to the South Atlantic Blockading Squadron, where it serves on blockade duty in South Carolina, Georgia, and Florida for the duration of the war. The *Flag* participates in various operations, including the actions against Tybee Island (November 1861) and against Fernandina, Florida (March 1862). It is decommissioned in February 1865 and then sold in July 1865, when it begins service as a commercial steamship until 1876.

May 20 (Monday)   Acting under the authority of the United States government, U.S. marshals in the North move into the major telegraph offices and confiscate all telegrams in an attempt to discover the names of Southern sympathizers and spies to pinpoint them and prevent them from taking any further action against the Union.

In Montgomery, Alabama, the Confederate Provincial Congress selects the city of Richmond, Virginia, to be the new capital of the Confederacy. The government will transfer from Montgomery.

In North Carolina, the state secedes from the Union. It is the tenth state to do so. Zebulon Baird Vance, in anticipation of this vote, had resigned from the U.S. Congress during the previous March. By this time, Vance, a brother of Confederate General Robert Brank Vance, is a captain of the Rough and Ready Guards, a company he raised. The company is attached to the 26th North Carolina Infantry and Vance becomes colonel of the regiment. He participates at various actions, including New Bern (March) and Richmond (July); however, after thirteen months in command, he becomes governor of North Carolina and is reelected during 1864. After the war, Colonel Zebulon Vance is elected to the U.S. Senate during 1870, but he is refused his seat because he remains under parole. Later, during 1876, he is re-elected as governor, but his term is shortened when he is again elected to the U.S. Senate (1876), where he serves until his death on 14 April 1894.

In Union general officer activity, Pleasant Adam Hackleman is commissioned colonel (later brigadier general) of the 16th Indiana. The regiment enters federal service on the 22nd.

In Confederate general officer activity, William Wing Loring, formerly a colonel in the U.S. Army, becomes a brigadier general (later major general) in the Confederacy. Loring had lost one arm during the Battle of Chapultepec in the Mexican War. Also, at this time, Colonel John Magruder is assigned commander at Yorktown, Virginia. He becomes brigadier general during June. In October he is promoted to major general. In addition, Major (later brigadier general) James Monroe Goggin, 32nd Virginia Infantry, will serve under Magruder through the Peninsular Campaign and subsequently be assigned to General McLaws' division in the 1st Corps. Goggin had been accepted at the Military Academy at West Point during 1838, class of 1842, but he did not graduate.

Subsequent to the secession of North Carolina, William Ruffin Cox joins the 2nd North Carolina Infantry (state troops) and receives an appointment as major. He serves under Colonel C.C. Tew until his demise at Antietam (Sharpsburg). The regiment then comes under the command of Colonel W.P. Bynum until his resignation during March of 1863. At that point, Cox is promoted to colonel (later general). Also, Bryan Grimes, a widower and member of the State Secessionist Convention (Georgia), soon resigns his position and is appointed major (later brigadier general) in the 4th North Carolina Regiment, which at this time is led by colonel (later brigadier general) George Burgwyn Anderson (West Point, 1852). The regiment arrives in Virginia just after the battle at Manassas (Bull Run) during the following month.

In yet other activity, Armistead Lindsay Long (West Point, 1850), an artillery officer, becomes aide-de-camp to Brigadier General Edwin Sumner, his father-in-law. Nevertheless, the next month Long resigns from the army to accept a commission in the Confederate Army, initially under General Loring. Later he joins the staff of Robert E. Lee with the rank of colonel (later brigadier general).

May 21 (Tuesday) *In Union general officer activity,* Henry Warner Slocum (West Point, 1852) is appointed colonel of the 27th New York Regiment. Colonel Slocum had previously served in Florida against the Seminoles and for a while at Charleston prior to leaving the service to practice law. The regiment participates at First Manassas (Bull Run).

In Naval activity, the USS *Constellation* seizes a brigantine, the Triton. A party boards the ship and discovers no slaves; however, it becomes obvious that the ship is a slave runner. In August, the *Constellation,* attached to the African Squadron, is recalled.

May 22 (Wednesday) **In Maryland,** Union Major General Benjamin Franklin Butler departs Baltimore for duty at Fort Monroe, Virginia. Major General George Cadwalader (Pennsylvania state troops) will assume command of the city. Cadwalader, a veteran of the Mexican War, will be promoted to the rank of major general, U.S. Volunteers, the following year.

In Virginia, General Robert E. Lee writes to General Milledge L. Bonham (commanding officer, Manassas Junction): "The policy of the state is defensive, no attack or provocation for attack will therefore be given, but every attack resisted to the extent of your means."

In Western Virginia (later West Virginia), two enlisted men, Daniel Wilson and Bailey Brown of the Union 2nd Virginia Infantry, encounter Confederate pickets at Fetterman. The Confederates from Captain Robinson's company, 25th Virginia, order the two men to halt, but they continue walking. Brown fires at one of the pickets, Daniel W.S. Knight, and wounds him in the ear; however, Knight returns fire and Brown is slain. Brown had only been mustered into the company on 20 May and the company is not officially mustered until the 25th.

In Confederate general officer activity, Major General Charles Clark (Mississippi state troops), a veteran of the Mexican War, is appointed brigadier general in the Confederate Army, effective this date.

May 23 (Thursday) **In Virginia,** the Union begins to move its forces across the Potomac to secure Arlington. The Confederate colors had been conspicuously flying on the opposite bank in direct defiance of the Stars and Stripes, which remains in the sky over Washington. General Joseph King F. Mansfield intends to occupy the city and run down the Rebel flag. The crossing takes place beginning after dark and continues into the following morning. The New York Zouaves, commanded by Colonel Elmer Ephriam Ellsworth, arrives by ship during the early morning hours of the 24th. The regiment spots a Rebel flag atop the roof of the Marshall House, a hotel, and tears it down.

In other activity, Confederate Colonel Benjamin Huger (West Point, 1825) is assigned command of Norfolk. He is promoted to brigadier general during June; later during October he is promoted to major general.

In Confederate general officer activity, John B. Floyd, former governor of Virginia (1848–1852) and secretary of war under President Buchanan, is commissioned brigadier general. He participates under General Robert E. Lee during the campaign in West Virginia and afterward is transferred to Fort Donelson, Tennessee.

In Naval activity, Flag Officer Louis M. Goldsborough relieves Flag Officer Silas Stringham and assumes command of the North Atlantic Blockading Squadron. Stringham selects the USS *Minnesota* as his flagship.

May 24 (Friday) **In Virginia,** the Union Army, 6,000 strong, crosses the Potomac and occupies Arlington Heights and Alexandria. The units include the 5th, 7th, 11th, 12th, 25th and 28th New York Regiments and the 1st Michigan. The Union occupies the Arlington plantation owned by Robert E. Lee and his wife Mary. Mary's father was George Washington Parke Custis, grandson of Martha Washington (from her first marriage). The plantation is now known as Arlington National Cemetery. The sloop USS *Pawnee* participates in the occupation of Alexandria, and later this month and during early June, the *Pawnee* engages Confederate artillery batteries at Acquia Creek.

Colonel Elmer Ephriam Ellsworth, commander of the 11th New York Regiment, is shot and killed by a Southern sympathizer just after he removes a Confederate flag from the top of a hotel, the Marshall House, in Alexandria. James Jackson, the man who shoots Ellsworth, is the proprietor of the hotel. In the North,

Colonel Elmer Ephriam Ellsworth is killed at the Marshall House in Alexandria, Virginia, on May 24, 1861 (Mottelay, *The Soldier in Our Civil War*, 1886).

Left: The Marshall House in Alexandria, Virginia, is the scene of the death of Colonel Elmer Ephriam Ellsworth (Johnson, *Campfire and Battlefield: History of the Conflicts and Campaigns,* 1894). *Right:* The 1st Michigan Infantry Regiment and Ellsworth's Zouaves construct entrenchments at Alexandria, Virginia (Mottelay, *The Soldier in Our Civil War,* 1886).

Jackson is considered an assassin, but in the South he is given hero status. Pvt. Francis Brownell kills Jackson and receives the Medal of Honor; this is the first action to merit the Congressional Medal of Honor. The body of Colonel Ellsworth is removed to Washington and his funeral service is held in the White House. Following the ceremony, his remains are returned to Mechanicsville, New York, the residence of his parents, but along the route the party pauses in New York City, where a huge ceremony is given to honor his service to the country.

In other activity, a large Union force under the command of Major General George B. McClellan — including the 14th, 16th and 18th Ohio Regiments, the 1st Michigan, the 1st and 2nd Virginia Volunteers and a small contingent of artillery — advances towards Grafton (later part of West Virginia).

In Tennessee, volunteer companies (Confederate) composed of men from various counties (Coffee, DeKalb, Grundy, Putnam, Van Buren, Warren and White) depart from their assembly point at Estill Springs and move to Camp Trousdale, where the units are formed into the 16th Tennessee Regiment, commanded by Colonel John H. Savage, a former U.S. Army officer and veteran of the Mexican War. Camp Trousdale is located along the Louisville and Nashville Railroad (Sumner County) near the Kentucky state line. Thomas B. Murray is appointed lieutenant colonel of the regiment.

In Confederate activity, Brigadier General M.L. Bonham, commander at Manassas, Virginia, states in a letter to General Robert E. Lee: "If they attack us we will defend the place to the last." Lee replies: "Send an express to Colonel

Eppa Hunton [8th Virginia Infantry] at Leesburg to destroy all the bridges of the Loudon and Hampshire railroads as far down towards Alexandria as possible." Colonel Eppa Hunton is promoted to the rank of brigadier general during 1863.

May 25 (Saturday) *In Union general officer activity,* Israel Bush Richardson (West Point, 1841) has recently organized the 2nd Michigan Infantry Regiment. This day he is appointed colonel of the regiment and inducted into Union service. Richardson's contingent will fare well during the upcoming battle at Bull Run (Manassas). In June he is promoted to the rank of brigadier general. Richardson is a veteran of the Seminole Wars and of the Mexican War.

Also, Robert Cowdin (Coudin), colonel of the 2nd Massachusetts Militia Regiment, is mustered into federal service as colonel of the 1st Massachusetts Infantry Regiment. John McCauley Palmer is appointed colonel of the 14th Illinois Infantry. Leonard Fulton Ross, a veteran of the Mexican War, having served under Colonel Edward D. Baker as a lieutenant in the 4th Illinois Volunteer Regiment, is appointed colonel of the 17th Illinois to rank from this day. Afterward, he is assigned to duty in Missouri and Kentucky.

In Confederate general officer activity, William Henry Talbot Walker (West Point, 1837) is appointed brigadier general and initially assigned to Pensacola, Florida, and afterward in Northern Virginia; however, he does not receive a field command.

In Naval activity, the USS *Minnesota,* flagship of the Atlantic Blockading Squadron, seizes the bark *Winfred.* The tug *Gunnison* acquired by

the Confederacy is commissioned at Mobile, Alabama. It becomes the privateer *A.C. Gunnison* commanded by Captain P.G. Cook, who is also a part owner of the ship. During the following year, the *Gunnison* is taken over by the Confederate States Navy. In April 1865 it is handed over to the U.S. Navy. In other activity, the USS *Quaker City* seizes two blockade runners, the bark *Pioneer* in Hampton Roads, and off Cape Henry, it intercepts and seizes the bark *Winifred.*

May 26 (Sunday) **In Maryland,** Union soldiers place John Merryman, accused of participating in treasonable activity, under arrest. He attempts to convince Chief Justice Taney to provide him with a writ of habeas corpus (suspended by President Lincoln's order due to the war), and he quickly receives it to test the arrest, but to no avail. The judge sternly criticizes Lincoln, but the order stands.

In Naval activity, the USS *Brooklyn* blockades the port of New Orleans. An additional blockade is established at Mobile, Alabama.

In Confederate activity, General Robert E. Lee, in a letter to Governor Joseph E. Brown of Georgia, requests arms and ammunition for Georgia troops who had arrived in Virginia weaponless. General Lee explains the depletion of Confederate arms and the desperate need for help. Lee also, upon learning of the Union landing at Newport News, telegraphs Colonel Benjamin Huger, commander at Norfolk: "Telegraph the governor of North Carolina to divert troops heading for Norfolk and dispatch a sufficient force to Suffolk."

In another letter, Lee informs Confederate Colonel John B. Magruder, the commanding officer at Yorktown, that Union troops might move from Newport to Warwick Court House, then on to Yorktown. Lee then advises Magruder that Captains George B. Cosby and John B. Hood will instruct the cavalry.

In Confederate general officer activity, Captain (breveted major) Lewis Addison Armistead, U.S. 6th Infantry, resigns his commission and becomes a colonel in the Confederate Army, commanding the 57th Virginia Infantry. Armistead, who later becomes a brigadier general, had attended West Point (1834–1836) but did not graduate.

May 27 (Monday)   In Washington, D.C., Brigadier General Irvin McDowell (West Point, 1838) is appointed commander of the recently created Department of Washington. He will continue to mold this force, which will increase in size by early July to about 35,000 troops; however, many of these have enlisted for only a period of ninety days, at this time thought by the government sufficient to end the insurrection. McDowell, who was appointed brigadier on May 14, is promoted to the rank of major general the following March.

In Western Virginia (later West Virginia) along the Baltimore and Ohio Railroad in the region between Wheeling and Grafton at Glover's Gap, a contingent of Company A, 2nd Virginia Infantry (later 5th West Virginia Infantry), commanded by Lt. West, engages a contingent of Confederates under Captain Christian Roberts. Roberts is killed during the skirmish. The Union company claims that Roberts is the first "armed Confederate" fatality of the war. James Jackson, the hotel owner who killed Colonel Elmer E. Ellsworth and was afterward shot and killed in Baltimore was a civilian, not a Confederate soldier.

In Confederate Naval activity, the steamer CSS *William H. Webb,* which had departed New Orleans earlier this month, after being converted into a gunboat, arrives back in port. During the cruise, the gunboat seized three whale boats out of Massachusetts, the brigantine *Panama* and the schooners *John Adams* and *Mermaid.*

May 27–29   In Virginia, Union Major General Benjamin Franklin Butler's force (Department of Annapolis) advances on Newport News unopposed.

May 28 (Tuesday)   In Illinois, Union General Nathaniel Lyon directs the 4th Illinois Volunteers under Colonel Nicholas Schuttner to occupy Cairo, a strategic town at the confluence of the Ohio and Mississippi Rivers. Following its occupation, more reinforcements attached to the command of Brigadier General Benjamin M. Prentiss will arrive and establish military camps in the area. Prentiss, colonel of the 10th Illinois Infantry and a veteran of the Mexican War, had been promoted to the rank of brigadier general on May 17. Also, this influx of troops will bolster other Union forces just across the Mississippi River at Bird's Point (Charlestown), Missouri. The garrison will in-

crease in size to about 6,000 troops, but with detachments being dispatched to many different areas, it will be reduced to about 1,200 troops during July. Toward the latter part of July more troops arrive to rebuild its strength.

In Naval activity, the steamer USS *Union* initiates a blockade of Savannah, Georgia.

May 29 (Wednesday)   In Missouri, on or about this date, Union General William S. Harney, commander of the West, with his headquarters in St. Louis, is relieved of command due in great part to an alleged agreement with Confederate General Sterling Price (state troops) that Union troops would not interfere with his forces provided Price would not move against federal property. The government retires him during 1863. General Nathaniel Lyon (West Point, 1841) succeeds Harney.

Harney had carved out a gallant career, participating in Army actions against the Seminoles and Creeks, but subsequently, while serving as a lieutenant colonel of the 2nd Dragoons during the Mexican War, he apparently had not been able to remain in General Winfield Scott's favor and was relieved of command at Mexico City. At that point, politics entered into the situation and President Polk used his political weight to overrule Scott. Harney then continued his career, serving as commander of the Department of Oregon prior to his service in St. Louis. Although Harney is stripped of his command, in 1863 he is officially retired and breveted major general at the close of hostilities.

In Virginia, Union troops occupy Newport News.

In Naval activity, a Union naval contingent bombards Confederate batteries at Acquia Creek. The USS *Reliance* participates in this action, which continues into 1 June.

In Union activity, Captain (later brevet major general) Samuel Beatty is appointed colonel of the 19th Ohio Infantry Regiment.

May 30 (Thursday)   In Virginia, Union troops (Army of the Ohio) occupy Grafton (later part of West Virginia) to protect citizens and guard the Baltimore and Ohio Railroad line. Grafton is in the western portion of the state and inclined to remain loyal to the Union. The Confederacy claims it has the right to secede from the Union yet has no intention of allowing counties in western Virginia to secede from the Confederacy. The struggle for this part of Virginia will shortly intensify.

In Union general officer activity, Oliver Otis Howard (West Point, 1854) is commissioned colonel of the 3rd Maine Infantry at about this time (late May). Otis is a lieutenant of ordnance and a teacher at West Point. He resigns his regular commission on 7 June.

In Naval activity, the USS *Quaker City,* while on patrol in Chesapeake Bay, encounters and seizes a blockade runner, the schooner *Lynchburg,* which is transporting a cargo of coffee.

May 31 (Friday)   In Virginia, Confederate General Pierre G.T. Beauregard is given com-

mand of the Confederate Army of the Potomac in Northern Virginia, later designated First Corps, Army of the Potomac. Subsequently, it will be attached to the Department of Northern Virginia, commanded by General Joseph E. Johnston.

In Union general officer activity, James Madison Tuttle is commissioned lieutenant colonel (later brigadier general) of the 2nd Iowa Regiment. Upon the promotion of Colonel Samuel R. Curtis to brigadier general, he becomes colonel of the regiment on 6 September. He participates at Fort Donelson and afterward, he commands a brigade at Shiloh.

In Confederate general officer activity, Captain John Adams (West Point, 1846) resigns his commission to join the Confederacy. He becomes a captain and is assigned to command at Memphis, Tennessee. Subsequently he becomes brigadier general, effective December 1862.

In Naval activity, three U.S. gunboats, the *Thomas Freeborn* (flagship of Captain James H. Ward), the *Anacostia* and the *Resolute,* move into position and commence another bombardment of Confederate batteries at Acquia Creek, Virginia, about forty miles south of Washington, D.C., where the creek empties into the Potomac River. The Confederate batteries, commanded by Captain William F. Lynch, have been repositioned to hinder any attempt by U.S. vessels to bring men or supplies into the capital. The two sides trade shots for approximately two hours, and the Confederate batteries at the landing are put out of action, but the heavier guns firing from the heights are out of range. The Union vessels withdraw rather than risk great loss. The ships secure more firepower from their Potomac Flotilla (Flag Officer Silas Stringham) and reappear at Acquia Creek on the following day.

Late May   In Virginia, the Confederate 9th Alabama Infantry is established, and within a few weeks it moves from Richmond to the vicinity of Winchester. The 9th, like the 11th Alabama, is part of the brigade under General Edmund Kirby Smith. It moves out for Manassas (Bull Run); however, en route, a rail accident causes it to be delayed. Consequently, it misses the battle. The regiment moves to Yorktown, where the brigade is under the command of General John H. Forney (West Point, 1852) and afterwards, General Cadmus M. Wilcox (West Point, 1846), who assumes command during January of the following year. Edward Asbury O'Neal, a lawyer who joins the 9th Alabama at about this time, becomes colonel (later brigadier general) of the 26th Alabama during 1862.

June 1861   *In Confederate general officer activity,* Seth Maxwell Barton (West Point, 1849) resigns from the U.S. Army to join the Confederate cause. He is appointed lieutenant colonel, 3rd Arkansas Infantry, and becomes brigadier general in 1862. Also, Jeremy Francis Gilmer (West Point, 1839), a classmate of Union General Henry Halleck, resigns from the U.S. Army to join the Confederacy. He is appointed colonel and will be assigned to General Albert S. Johnston's command as chief engineer.

Also, William Whedbee Kirkland (West Point, attendance 1852) had resigned from the military academy and during 1855 switched uniforms and enlisted in the U.S. Marine Corps, serving there until 1860. Now, he again switches uniforms and joins the Confederacy as colonel (later brigadier general) of the 21st North Carolina Infantry.

In Naval activity, the *Henrietta,* a recently built private yacht (schooner) owned by James Gordon Bennett, Jr., and under loan to the Treasury Department's revenue marine, begins service at this time. Bennett serves as captain. The ship patrols off New York; in April 1762 it participates in the operation against Fernandina on Amelia Island, Florida.

June 1 (Saturday) England proclaims that neither the United States nor the Confederate States will be able to utilize British ports for their captured vessels. This action has little effect on the Union, but it is a severe blow to the Confederacy. The privateers must contend with the Union blockade of southern ports, and they had been expecting to bring their captured prizes to British territory. Essentially the dictate has no genuine effect on the U.S., because the Confederacy has no merchant marine to fall prey to the Union.

In New York, Morgan Henry Chrysler is appointed captain of the 30th New York. Initially, he enlisted as a private. Chrysler move rapidly through the ranks to become colonel of the 2nd New York Veteran Cavalry Regiment during 1863. The regiment remains in Washington during the winter of 1863–1864, and the following spring it moves to New Orleans.

In Virginia, the Union's Company B, 2nd Cavalry, composed of about 50 troops commanded by 2nd Lt. Charles H. Tompkins, engages Confederates, about 1,000 strong at Fairfax Courthouse. The Confederates sustain 25 killed or wounded and five captured. Tompkins' command sustains one killed, four wounded and one missing. Lt. Tompkins twice risks his life by galloping through the Confederate positions and while engaged, he snatches a carbine rifle from an enlisted trooper and kills the Confederate's captain. Lt. Tompkins becomes a recipient of the Medal of Honor for his heroism under fire, the first Union officer to be awarded the medal.

In other activity, a contingent composed of elements of a Michigan regiment and of Zouaves, commanded by Captains Brown and Roth respectively, skirmish with Confederates at Arlington Mills. The Union sustains one killed and one wounded. The Confederates suffer one wounded.

In Western (later West) Virginia, Isaac Hardin Duval enters the service as a major of the 1st West Virginia Infantry (three-month regiment), replaced during October 1861 by a three-year regiment. In September, Major

Duval is appointed colonel of the 9th West Virginia. Duval's service is confined primarily to West Virginia; however, the region is often consumed with combat. During the various skirmishes and engagements, Duval loses eleven horses that are shot from under him, and he sustains three wounds.

In Union general officer activity, John Dunlap Stevenson, a veteran of the Mexican War, is commissioned colonel of the 7th Missouri Regiment. He participates at the Battle of Shiloh and afterward he receives command at Jackson, Tennessee.

In Naval activity, ships attached to the Potomac Flotilla again return to Acquia Creek to quell Rebel batteries there. The three gunboats (*Freeborn, Anacostia* and *Resolute*) that bombarded the positions on the previous day are joined by the sloops of war *Pawnee* and *Yankee* to deliver a more potent package of cannon shot. As the five vessels commence firing, the Confederates instantaneously become the recipients of an unrelenting thunderclap that rips into the positions, including those in the heights, thanks to the longer-reaching guns of the sloops. Piece by piece, the defenses are blown apart by shell and fire as the wharf and railroad stations become consumed with flames. Twice, the Confederate batteries are quieted during the furious exchange, in which the five Union ships, combined, propel more than 700 rounds of fire. It is not determined whether the fires had been ignited by Union shells or by the Confederates while they were in the process of retiring. The USS *Anacostia* is manned primarily by volunteers of the New York 71st Regiment.

Also, the gunboat USS *Thomas Freeborn,* although struck by enemy fire, sustains only superficial damage, and the sloop *Pawnee,* which sustains nine hits, incurs some damage but no injuries.

In Union activity, Michael Kelley Lawler and his regiment, the 18th Illinois, is mustered into federal service at about this time. The regiment is mustered into service by Captain Ulysses S. Grant, a staff officer of the Illinois adjutant general. Colonel Lawler, a native of Ireland, is known for aggressive methods in retaining discipline in his regiment and his tactics bring about a court-martial; however, he is acquitted by General Henry Halleck. Lawler is promoted to brigadier general during spring of 1863, dating from 29 November 1862. Later at Vicksburg, he leads a charge that captures at least 1,100 Confederates.

June 2 (Sunday) By this date, about twenty percent of officers in the U.S. Navy have resigned to enter the service of the Confederacy. On the following day, the

U.S. Navy publishes lists of resignations and of the entire complement of officers. The lists detail that 821 southerners resigned and 850 southerners remained in the service of the U.S. Navy.

In other activity, the U.S. Navy acquires a civilian steamer, the *Eagle,* at about this time (June). It is commissioned during the latter part of July and utilized as a transport, carrying supplies and troops. Initially, it is sent to the Gulf of Mexico, but later is attached to the South Atlantic Blockading Squadron.

Henry Beebee Carrington (Yale 1845) at about this time (1861) is commissioned colonel in the U.S. Army. He participates in the West Virginia campaign. During the following year, Carrington is promoted to brigadier general and assigned recruitment duty in Indiana. Subsequent to the close of hostilities, he serves at Fort Phil Kearny (Dakota Territory).

June 3 (Monday) THE BATTLE OF PHILIPPI **In Western Virginia,** Union Major General George McClellan's troops decisively defeat the Confederates under Colonel Porterfield in a skirmish at Philippi, a strategic crossroads junction of the Baltimore and Ohio and the Northwestern Railways, near Rich Mountain. Two Union contingents, under the command of Brigadier General T.A. Morris, surprise the Rebels, commanded by Colonel George A. Porterfield. Union Colonel (later general) Benjamin Franklin Kelley's contingent — composed of his 1st (West) Virginia Regiment, the 9th Indiana Regiment under Colonel (later brigadier general) Robert Huston Milroy, and a detachment of the 16th Ohio under Colonel James Irvine (Irwine) — is to synchronize its attack with the other column, commanded by Colonel (later brigadier general) Ebenezer Dumont. The latter under Dumont is composed of the eight companies of his regiment, the 7th Indiana, four companies of the 6th Indiana commanded by Colonel (later brigadier general) Thomas T. Crittenden, a detachment of Barnett's Ohio Artillery commanded by Lt. Colonel Sturgis, and four companies of the 14th Ohio, led by Lt. Colonel (later brigadier general) James Blair Steedman.

Battle of Philippi, June 3, 1861 (Johnson, *Campfire and Battlefield: History of the Conflicts and Campaigns,* 1894).

A staff officer of General McClellan, Colonel Frederick W. Lander, rides with Dumont's column. The attack is scheduled to jump off at 0400 following about a twenty-mile march along the Beverly Turnpike. Kelley's column is scheduled to strike positions held by Confederate Colonel George Porterfield's force, while Dumont's command, from its positions in the hills above Philippi, commences firing to hammer the Rebels. Dumont's column, subsequent to a dreadful thirteen-mile march during a pesky rainstorm, reaches its designated positions at the appointed time, but no contact is made with Kelley, who has inadvertently taken a wrong road.

Rather than risk the Rebels escaping unscathed, Dumont orders the attack; however, as the troops are forming, the alarm is sounded by the Rebels when a woman spots the approaching Union troops and fires at Colonel Lander. Lacking the punching strength of Kelley, the lone contingent opens the assault, first by the accompanying cannon and then an impetuous charge. Union troops descend the heights streaming toward the Rebel lines and in the process secure the covered bridge that spans the river. Shortly thereafter, while the Rebels are in retreat, pulling out of Philippi, Kelley's force, although tardy due to the intentional actions of his guide, who led them down the wrong road, arrives and strikes at the flank rather than from the rear as planned.

Nevertheless, the Union's agility and the element of surprise forces the Confederates to hurriedly depart the town, but they return fire as best they can. The Rebel fire cuts Kelley down with what is thought to be a fatal wound to the chest, but he recovers and later becomes a brigadier general, the date being retroactive to May 17, 1861. The Confederates who evacuate the area head over the mountain and McClellan's Ohio boys start the process of securing West Virginia for the Union. Union participants are 1st West Virginia, 14th and 16th Ohio, and 7th and 9th Indiana regiments. The Union sustains two men wounded. Confederates sustain 16 wounded. Colonel Kelley, prior to the outbreak of the war, had been an agent of the Baltimore and Ohio Railroad. His subsequent service during the conflict is confined to the area of Virginia soon to be West Virginia and also in Maryland.

In Pennsylvania, Major General Robert Patterson assumes command of the U.S. Volunteer forces at Chambersburg. General Patterson, commissioned a 1st lieutenant during 1813, sees some duty in Virginia; however, he musters out of the service during July 1861.

In Naval activity, a Confederate privateer, the schooner CSS *Savannah,* commanded by Captain Thomas H. Baker, leaves Charleston to operate against the Union Naval forces and interrupt Union commerce. Also, at about this time (June), the U.S. Army acquires a civilian sidewheel towboat, the *Conestoga.* It is transformed into a "timberclad" gunboat and assigned to the Western Gunboat Flotilla.

June 4 (Tuesday) In Washington, D.C., General Winfield Scott instructs General Robert Patterson (father of Union General Francis E. Patterson) to increase the forces under his command to bolster his Army, which is composed of three-month volunteers. He is directed to add one battery of artillery and several companies of regulars (infantry).

In Michigan, a large group of women from Grand Rapids arrives at Cantonment Anderson to present a regimental flag to the 3rd Michigan Regiment. Another group of women arrives at Camp Williams just outside Adrian on the 21st to present the 4th Michigan Regiment with a flag. The other Michigan regiments also had regimental flags presented to them, and many are returned to the original donors following the termination of the respective regiment's service.

In Naval activity, the CSS *Savannah* captures the *Joseph,* which is transporting a cargo of sugar from Cuba to Philadelphia, Pennsylvania. The ship is taken to South Carolina. After dropping off the captured prize, the *Savannah* again departs, but soon it mistakes a Union warship, the brigadier USS *Perry,* for a commercial vessel. After launching an attack, the *Savannah* finds no escape route. It is captured while trying to break for safer waters. In other activity, the USS *Quaker City* captures the blockade runner *General Green* off Cape Henry.

In Confederate general officer activity, Henry Rootes Jackson, who had fought during the Mexican War as a colonel, is appointed brigadier general in the Provisional Confederate Army. General H.R. Jackson tosses his judicial robes (he is a Confederate judge) and gets fitted for the Confederate gray. He is assigned duty in Western Virginia under General Robert E. Lee; however, by the end of this year, Jackson resigns his commission.

June 5 (Wednesday) In Naval activity, the Union steamer *Harriet Lane* engages the Confederate batteries at Pig Point and at Hampton Roads, Virginia.

In Union general officer activity, Robert Cumming Schenck (former Congressman and minister to Brazil) is commissioned brigadier general (later major general), effective from 17 May. General Schenck participates at First Bull Run (Manassas) as a brigade commander and afterward serves in the Shenandoah Valley against Confederate General Thomas "Stonewall" Jackson. During the following year, he commands the 1st Division (General Sigel's I Corps).

The USS *Niagara,* while operating off Mobile, Alabama, participates in the seizure of a blockade runner, the schooner *Aid.* The *Niagara* continues operating in the Gulf of Mexico for about one year.

In Confederate general officer activity, Colonel Earl Van Dorn is appointed brigadier general. Van Dorn (West Point, 1842) is sent to Texas and commands there until September. Also, Theophilus H. Holmes (West Point,

1829), having recently resigned his commission in the U.S. Army, is appointed brigadier general in the Confederate Army. He rises through the ranks with great speed, becoming a major general during October of this year, and by October 1862 he is promoted to the rank of lieutenant general, Provisional Army of the Confederate States. Also, Henry Alexander Wise, a former U.S. congressman and diplomat (minister to Brazil), is appointed brigadier general in the Confederate Army. He commands a unit known as the Wise Legion. General Wise participates under General Robert E. Lee in West Virginia, followed by service in North Carolina with General Beauregard. Afterward, he is ordered to Charleston and from there to Florida, prior to being ordered during 1864 to return to Virginia and bolster the defenses of Petersburg. General Wise is the brother-in-law of Union General George Gordon Meade.

June 6 (Thursday) In Union general officer activity, Isaac Peace Rodman is commissioned captain (later brigadier general) of the 2nd Rhode Island Regiment. He later participates at Bull Run (Manassas).

In Confederate general officer activity, Robert Selden Garnett (West Point, 1841) who had resigned his commission as major in the U.S. 9th Infantry the previous April, is appointed brigadier general. He will command the forces in Northern Virginia. Garnett is the cousin of Confederate Brigadier General Richard Brooke Garnett (West Point, 1841). Former 1st Lieutenant Julius Adolph de Lagnel, who resigned his commission to join the Confederate cause, becomes Richard B. Garnett's chief artillery officer; however, the duty is not without complications, as his responsibility includes bolstering the defenses of the summit of Rich Mountain, despite having only one artillery piece. Also, John Crawford Vaughn, a veteran of the Mexican War (captain, 5th Tennessee) who was in Charleston when Fort Sumter came under attack, returns to Tennessee to raise a regiment. He is commissioned colonel of the 3rd Tennessee on this day at Lynchburg, Virginia. He is ordered to Harpers Ferry to report to General Joseph E. Johnston.

In Naval–Marine Corps activity, a detachment of sailors and U.S. Marines from the sloop USS *Pawnee* land at White House, Virginia, to protect a survey team.

June 7 (Friday) In Union general officer activity, Nathan Kimball, a veteran of the Mexican War (2nd Indiana Volunteers) is commissioned colonel (later brigadier general) of the 15th Indiana Regiment. The regiment participates at Cheat Mountain in September 1861.

In Union Naval Officer activity, Commander Thomas T. Craven is promoted to the rank of captain. He receives command of the USS *Brooklyn.*

June 8 (Saturday) Tennessee is the eleventh and final state to secede from the Union. Nevertheless, there remain strong Union loyalists in the eastern part of the state.

In Virginia, Union General Robert Patterson receives direction that clearly informs him he must act to secure victory against the Confederates and to act only when success is assured, as a stalemate battle would mean victory for the Rebels. Action is expected to occur near Harpers Ferry (later in West Virginia) and at Manassas Junction.

Since the outbreak of the war and in conjunction with the secession of the various states, the Confederate naval force, including seizures and purchase, by this time has ten vessels and fifteen guns. The vessels are the *McClelland* (five guns); *Lewis Cass* (one 68-pounder); *Aiken* (one 42-pounder); *Washington* (one 42-pounder); *Dodge* (one pivot gun); *James Gray* (one 42-pounder, acquired by purchase); *Bonito* (one gun, a captured slaver); *Nina* (one gun); *Everglade,* a steamer, and the *Fulton* (three 32-pounders, a captured U.S. war steamer). The *Fulton* was salvaged by the Confederates after it had been wrecked off Pensacola.

By this time, the Confederates control two of U.S. shipyards, in Pensacola, Florida, and Norfolk, Virginia. Nevertheless, the Union still has nine other productive navy yards: Brooklyn, Charlestown, Mare Island, Philadelphia, Portsmouth, Sackett's Harbor, and Kittery. In addition, the U.S. Naval forces blockade Pensacola and Norfolk, neutralizing Confederate productivity at both yards.

In Confederate general officer activity, subsequent to the secession of Tennessee this day, Benjamin J. Hill is appointed colonel of the 35th Tennessee Volunteers. Hill participates in various battles throughout Tennessee and Kentucky, including Murfreesboro, Chattanooga, Chickamauga, and Shiloh. Late in 1863, Hill becomes provost marshal, Army of Tennessee. Also, Carnot Posey, a veteran of the Mexican War, in which he served as a lieutenant in the 1st Mississippi Rifles, is elected colonel (later brigadier general) of the Confederate 16th Mississippi Regiment. Posey's unit, formed at Corinth, Mississippi, will head north to be attached to the Army of Northern Virginia. Also, Cadmus Marcellus Wilcox (West Point, 1846), a veteran of the Mexican War, resigns his commission in the U.S. Army. He is afterward appointed colonel of the 9th Alabama Infantry, which participates at First Manassas (Bull Run).

June 9 (Sunday)   In Virginia, at Fortress Monroe, after darkness falls, General Benjamin Franklin Butler unfolds an operation designed to surprise a contingent of Confederates that has been pulling off successful harassment raids against Union outposts that are thinly manned. These Confederates are operating out of Little Bethel less than ten miles north of Newport News. Butler orders contingents of the 1st Vermont and the 3rd Massachusetts Regiments, led by Lt. Colonel Washburn, to move from Newport News in coordination with another force, composed of three regiments and one artillery detachment, driving from Fortress Monroe to converge upon Little Bethel and stamp out the annoying Raiders. The vanguard out of Fortress Monroe, Colonel Abram Duryee's New York

Zouaves, moves out of Camp Hamilton about one hour before the other two regiments, giving it additional time to establish positions in the Confederates' rear to sever their escape route, while the regiments under Washburn are to strike at their front. The trailing regiments out of Monroe, the Albany Regiment, commanded by Colonel Townsend, and another New York Regiment, the New York Steuben (German and primarily German speaking regiment), commanded by Colonel Bendix, move out slightly afterward. They are scheduled to join at the crossroads that lead into Little Bethel from both Newport News and Hampton, positioning these reserves at a point from where they can pivot to bolster Lt. Colonel Washburn's force, which is to strike at the frontal positions of the Confederates.

During the night march, everything appears to be working perfectly, as the Union forces continue to arrive at their respective positions, but when the Albany Regiment nears its assigned position, the Steuben Regiment mistakes it for the enemy. A sudden and unexpected burst of friendly fire pounds the Albany Regiment, causing a chain reaction. The wild firing arouses the Confederates, but it also sends the wrong signal to the Zouaves under Duryee and the force out of Newport News under Washburn. Lt. Colonel Washburn, startled by the fire to his rear, pivots, assuming the enemy has discovered the assault force and initiated an attack, while Duryee, under the same impression, also speeds to the suspected scene of the fight to bolster the Union forces there.

Meanwhile, the Albany Regiment, having taken casualties, moves back to more tenable positions in the pitch dark night and returns fire, still unaware that friendly fire is striking both sides. Soon after, the speeding reinforcements arrive at the scene of the blind firefight and the pernicious mistake is uncovered. Meanwhile, the Confederates easily move out and rejoin the main force at Big Bethel (Bethel Church) on the highway between Hampton and Yorktown about twelve miles from Fortress Monroe.

Following the tragic mishap, the respective commanders, lacking any intelligence on either the size or precise locations of the Confederate positions at Big Bethel, conclude that an attack should be initiated to gain it. The force moves into Little Bethel, torches it and advances to the next objective, which is strongly defended by about 2,000 troops, including cavalry and artillery. Lacking sleep, the Union forces reinitiate the march and reach Big Bethel. The confrontation ignites during the early morning hours of the 10th.

In Naval activity, the steamer *R.R. Cuyler,* acquired by the U.S. Navy

during the previous May but not yet purchased (until August), arrives at Key West, Florida, from New York. Afterward, it is assigned blockade duty off Tampa, Florida.

June 10 (Monday)   France, following action of England, declares neutrality with regard to the conflict between the North and South.

BATTLE OF BIG BETHEL **In Virginia,** Union troops commanded by General Byron Root Pierce arrive at Bethel Church following a disastrous mistake on the previous night at Little Bethel. Confederates, commanded by Colonel (later lieutenant general) Daniel H. Hill, anticipating the arrival of the Union troops, have deployed skirmishing forces to the front of the perimeter, and in addition, Confederate guns are placed directly in the path of advance. As the Union forces encroach, a thunderous volley of cannon-shot hammers their columns. The Vermont and Massachusetts regiments, along with the German-speaking Steuben Regiment, head for a forest to the right of the road. The Albany Regiment under Townsend and the New York Zouaves move across open terrain in an attempt to reach an apple orchard which will afford them some cover. In the meantime, to attempt to neutralize the heavy fire, the accompanying artillery of Lt. Greble, three light field pieces, returns fire.

The infantry is unable to effectively counter the Confederate artillery. While the Union troops attempt to determine how to launch a successful attack, the Confederates under Colonel (appointed general this day) Daniel Harvey Hill (West Point, 1842) continue to pound the Union and wait somewhat comfortably in their positions on the left bank of the Black River. Their lines are augmented by a stream to their immediate front and concentrated earthworks on both sides of the approach road which dominates the bridge. The perimeter is further strengthened by a string of entrenchments that parallel a wooded swamp. The defending force of about 1,800 men includes a large contingent of Magruder's Virginia cavalry and the 1st North Carolina Regiment commanded by A.P. Hill. And the three pieces of Union artillery are matched by twenty heavy cannon and the Richmond Howitzer Battalion.

A burial party encounters heavy fire while carrying the body of Lieutenant Greble (2nd New York) from the field at Big Bethel (Mottelay, *The Soldier in Our Civil War*, 1886).

The Union troops can't easily see the strength, but they can sense the devastating potential of the firepower as the artillery bombards their positions without pause for about two hours. Despite the enfilade of fire and the lack of knowledge concerning the strength of the enemy, General Pierce, at about 1200, orders an assault to drive the Confederates from their superior positions.

On the signal, Duryee's Zouaves and Townsend's Albany Regiment drive forward from the left and right respectively, while the German (Steuben) Regiment, along with the 1st and 2nd New York Regiments commanded by Colonels William Allen and Joseph Carr, strike against the left flank, still against an enemy that remains concealed. Repeatedly, the Union troops charge into the inferno, encountering obstacle after obstacle, all the while being struck by sheets of fire. Ditches are impassible without the use of ladders, a stream is too deep to be forded without rafts and fire is impenetrable. The Union troops make some small progress, slowly penetrating the dogged resistance at the tip of the defenses and inching toward the rear of the entrenchment, but other factors cripple the attack. Colonel Duryee informs General Pierce that his regiment's ammunition is spent.

Meanwhile in the confusion of the battle, Colonel Frederick Townsend causes another tragic mistake as he inadvertently believes that a contingent of his force is Confederate, prompting him to pull back. Pierce, aware that Abram Duryee is out of ammunition, orders a withdrawal. While the cannon continue to jackhammer the Union forces, the three artillery pieces of Lieutenant Greble, holding position on naked ground since the initiation of the battle, continue to roar, throwing back as much return fire as possible to support the infantry. Greble's defiant stand takes a high toll on the artillerymen, including himself. An enemy shell strikes him in the head, killing him instantly. The artillery expends its ammunition, compelling the survivors to pull back. They retire in a disciplined withdrawal and bring their artillery back with them. Lt. Greble's body is carried off the field, along with nearly all of the other dead and wounded, the exceptions being two of the Zouaves and one officer, Major Theodore Winthrop, the military secretary of General Benjamin F. Butler.

Following the disengagement, the force returns to Fortress Monroe. A contingent of Zouaves from New York, carrying supplies to the front, is met by the withdrawing troops, their artillery laden with dead and wounded. The Union fatalities total 16 killed, 34 wounded and five missing. The Union forces of Butler and Pierce, although losing the first battle in the field, receive an abundance of praise for their valor; however the Union commanders, including Butler, quickly feel the wrath of the people and Congress. General Butler, who is nominated as major general shortly after this confrontation, nearly gets turned down, receiving the promotion by a mere two vote margin in the Senate.

The Confederates suffer one man dead and

seven injured. Confederate 2nd Lt. (later major general) Robert F. Hoke, Major (later brigadier general) James H. Lane and Lt. Colonel (later brigadier general) Matt Whitaker Ransom of the 1st North Carolina Infantry participate in this action. Hoke subsequently becomes colonel of the 21st North Carolina, Major Lane later becomes colonel of the 28th North Carolina, and Ransom becomes colonel of the 35th North Carolina Infantry. Following this action, General Daniel H. Hill's Regiment is dubbed the Bethel Regiment.

In Maryland, at Baltimore, Union Major General Nathaniel Prentiss Banks succeeds Major General George Cadwalader. Also, Union Colonel (later General) Lewis Wallace, while at his headquarters in Cumberland, receives information that the Confederates are amassing a huge force in the vicinity of Romney (later in West Virginia). He prepares to move his regiment, the 11th Indiana (Zouaves), to Romney, and on the following morning the force moves southeast toward its objective.

In Western Pennsylvania, Thomas L. Kane initiates action to raise a force from men living in Cameron, Elk, McKean, Potter and Tioga counties, a region in the mountainous area known as the "Wildcat" district. Kane and his other officers raise seven companies; the force becomes known as the Bucktail Regiment because a deer's tail is made part of each soldier's hat. The regiment moves to Lockhaven by rafts and from there travels by the railroad to Harrisburg and assemble at recently established Camp Curtain. In addition, Kane's command is joined by volunteer companies, one from Chester County, another from Perry, and yet another from the northern sector of the state, expanding the number to ten companies, the total required to complete a regiment. Afterward, the regiment officially becomes the 13th Regiment (a rifle sharpshooter regiment) attached to the Pennsylvania Reserve Corps.

The regiment enters federal service as the Pennsylvania 42nd Volunteer Infantry Regiment; however, it continues to be known as the Bucktail Regiment. In June 1861, the Bucktail Regiment and the 5th Pennsylvania Regiment receive orders to repair to Maryland to bolster the forces of General Lewis (Lew) Wallace in the Cumberland region. Wallace is also known as the author of *Ben Hur*.

In Union activity, Captain (later major general) Henry Eugene Davies, 5th New York, participates at the Battle of Big Bethel this day. In August he transfers to the 2nd New York Cavalry (Harris' Light Cavalry) with the rank of major. Subsequently, he

rises to brigadier general during September 1863. Also, Byron Root Pierce musters into the army as captain (later brevet major general) in the 3rd Michigan Regiment. He moves through the ranks and is appointed colonel during January 1863. Henry Dwight Terry is commissioned colonel (later brigadier general) of the 5th Michigan Infantry, a regiment recently raised by Terry. He is initially assigned duty with the defenses of the capital. Later, the regiment is attached to the III Corps and participates in the operations around Williamsburg and at Seven Pines (Fair Oaks).

In Confederate general officer activity, Union Brigadier General Edwin V. Sumner loses a member of his family to the Confederacy as well as a member of his staff because his son-in-law, Armistead L. Long (West Point, 1850), resigns from the U.S. Army to accept a commission as major (artillery) in the Confederate Army. Armistead is subsequently promoted to the rank of brigadier general. Brevet Major Edward Johnson (West Point, 1838) resigns from the Federal service. He accepts a colonelcy with the 12th Georgia Infantry and the following December is elevated to brigadier general.

In Naval activity, the blockade runner *Amy Warwick* is seized at Hampton Roads by U.S. vessels, including the USS *Quaker City*.

June 11 (Tuesday) **In Missouri,** Union Major General Nathaniel Lyon at St. Louis ignores a request from Governor Claiborne Jackson to disband all Missouri Home Guards.

In Virginia, the 11th Indiana Regiment (Zouaves), commanded by Colonel Lew Wallace, moves by train to New Creek Bridge, cutting off about 28 miles from the march to Romney. The trains arrive at about 2300. Once the troops debark, they are on the march, discounting any thoughts of a good night's sleep. The regiment covers the final length of the trek by

The Bucktail Regiment recruits in Philadelphia (Mottelay, *The Soldier in Our Civil War*, 1886).

marching through the night to arrive at about 0800 on the 12th. When they encroach the Confederate positions at Romney, they encounter Confederate scouts, who quickly make it back to their camp to signal the alarm.

In Union activity, John R. Kenly, a veteran of the Mexican War who served as a captain with the Baltimore "Eagle Artillery," is appointed (by President Lincoln) colonel of the 1st Maryland Infantry Regiment. Alexander Shaler (later brigadier general) is appointed colonel of the 65th New York Regiment (formerly known as the 1st U.S. Chasseurs). Shaler had earlier joined the Washington Grays, which became the 8th New York Regiment. He serves with the Army of the Potomac.

June 12 (Wednesday)   In Illinois, Major General Nathaniel Lyon, concerned that Confederates under General Gideon J. Pillow (Tennessee Provisional Army) will seize Cairo, takes steps to prevent it from occurring. He bolsters the defenses on Bird's Point, located on the opposite bank of the Mississippi River through the efforts of U.S. engineers commanded by Captain Henry Benham and Colonel Nicholas Schuttner. In addition, General Lyon dispatches a force under Colonel (later major general) Franz Sigel to protect the Pacific Railway.

In Maryland, Union Colonel George Henry Gordon (West Point, 1846) prepares his regiment, the 2nd Massachusetts, for battle against encroaching Rebels on the upper Potomac near Frederick. Gordon achieves the rank of brigadier general during June 1862, and participates at Cedar Mountain and Antietam and subsequently leads a division against Charleston during the siege in 1863.

In Western Virginia, the 11th Indiana Regiment, which had departed Maryland on the previous morning, closes upon a Confederate force composed of about 1,000 troops encamped at Romney. The Rebels receive little notice of the uninvited Yankees. The first wave

of the regiment encounters only minimal resistance, as the Confederates become disorganized and break for the opposite end of the town.

The Union force, moving at double-quick pace, observes the free flight of the defenders and picks up the pace. By about 0830, the Union troops enter Romney and pursue the Rebels as they zip through the town hopping over fences as they go. The Union officers, choosing not to high-jump the fences, dismount and join the foot chase. The Yankees who occupy the town relish some of the spoils, as the Rebels had fled just prior to consuming the breakfast, which had been ready to serve. Some of the Confederates are captured.

The Union sustains one man wounded. The Confederates sustain two killed and one man wounded. In the town, the Union soldiers discover about fifty women who had locked themselves in one of the houses, fearful of coming out while the Union troops hold the town, but after some negotiations, the women, after being persuaded that the Northern troops were not going to cause them any harm, emerge from the building.

This Union victory instills extra confidence into the Northern forces, which have often during these early days of the conflict come out on the short side of the skirmishes. Colonel Wallace, leading his regiment, departs the town at about 1100, arriving back at New Creek at about midnight on the 12th–13th. From there the trains move back to Cumberland, arriving at Camp McGinnis about 0800 on the 13th.

June 13 (Thursday)   In Missouri, Major General Nathaniel Lyon, commanding a force of about 2,000 troops, including a battery of artillery, departs St. Louis by steamboats en route to Jefferson City, from where the force will advance to attack the Confederate stronghold at Booneville.

In New York, the 6th New York Regiment ("Billy" Wilson Zouaves), commanded by Colonel William Wilson, leaves Staten Island for Baltimore, Maryland. The regiment receives from the Ladies' Soldiers' Relief Service a magnificent silk flag. They depart with the slogan "Death to the Plug Uglies of Baltimore," an apparent reference to the riot in that city that cost the lives of four men from the 6th Massachusetts Regiment the previous April. En route to Maryland, these troops are diverted to Florida. They arrive in Florida on June 16.

In Pennsylvania, at Chambersburg, General Robert Patterson receives information from headquarters that General Irvin McDowell will be striking Confederate positions at Manassas Junction, Virginia, based on the presumption that his (Patterson's) troops will be advancing into Virginia either on the 16th or 17th. In concert with this understanding, Patterson readies his command and then moves to Hagerstown, Maryland, reaching there on the 15th. From there, Patterson can bolt into Virginia.

In Union general officer activity, Fitz Henry Warren is commissioned colonel (later brigadier general) of the 1st Iowa Cavalry. He is initially assigned duty in middle and western Missouri to curtail Confederate sympathizers and in recruiting duty.

June 14 (Friday)   In Maryland, a Union force of District Volunteers, composed of about 200 troops led by Lt. Colonel Everett, skirmishes with a Confederate cavalry contingent composed of about 100 troops. The Union reports no casualties. The Confederates sustain two killed and one wounded.

In Missouri, Confederates abandon the town of Jefferson.

In Texas, Camp Wood, abandoned by the Union during the previous March, is occupied by a contingent of Texas Rangers.

In Virginia, Brigadier General Robert E. Lee is advanced to the rank of full general. He earlier held the position of commander-in-chief of state forces with the rank of major general. On 14 May, Lee was appointed brigadier general in the Confederate Army.

Confederate troops commanded by General Joseph E. Johnston begin to evacuate Harpers Ferry (later in West Virginia) in an attempt to avoid being cut off by Union Generals McClellan and Robert Patterson, who are closing upon the Rebels' positions.

In Union activity, George Day Wagner is appointed colonel of the 15th Indiana. Also, Stephen Augustus Hurlbut is appointed brigadier general by President Abraham Lincoln. During the following year, he is promoted to major general. John Pope (West Point, 1842), a veteran of the Mexican War, is appointed brigadier general effective 17 May. Also, Eliakim Parker Scammon (West Point, 1837) is appointed colonel (later brigadier general) of the 23rd Ohio Volunteer Infantry. He succeeds General William S. Rosecrans. He participates in various actions, including Carnifex Ferry (September 1861) in West Virginia. Colonel Scammon later commands a brigade.

Giles Alexander Smith, the brother of Union General Morgan L. Smith, a proprietor of a hotel in Bloomington, Illinois, is commissioned captain (later major general) of the 8th Missouri Infantry, commanded by his brother, Colonel Morgan L. Smith. In June 1862, upon his brother's promotion to brigadier general, he becomes colonel of the regiment.

June 15 (Saturday)   In Louisiana, the Confederate 8th Louisiana Regiment is established at Camp Moore. It will depart Louisiana and

The 11th Indiana Zouaves at Camp McGinnis following the battle at Romney, Western Virginia (Mottelay, *The Soldier in Our Civil War,* 1886).

arrive in Virginia, where it will be part of the 1st Louisiana Brigade. Francis R.T. Nicholls (West Point, 1855) will be elected lieutenant colonel (later brigadier general) of the regiment.

In Maryland, General Robert Patterson dispatches the bulk of his force across the Potomac River to a point in Virginia from which he can strike the rear of General Joseph E. Johnston's forces at Harper's Ferry, but in the meantime, Johnston had become aware of the potential for disaster and has removed his force from Harper's Ferry. He redeploys his force at Winchester, Virginia, slightly more than thirty miles south. This strategic move places his Confederates in position to pivot in several directions. Johnston can launch an assault to intercept Patterson if the Union initiates pursuit, or he can strike against Washington. Being in close proximity to Manassas, he can also move to augment Beauregard against General McDowell.

McDowell's offensive against Manassas does not occur, and in fact Patterson is not yet in Virginia. At this time, McDowell's force includes five divisions. The First Division, composed of four brigades, is commanded by General Daniel Tyler. The brigades and commanders are: 1st Brigade, Colonel Erasmas D. Keyes, 1st, 2nd and 3rd Connecticut Regiments augmented by Company B, 2nd U.S. Cavalry and a New York Battery commanded by Captain Varian; 2nd Brigade, Brigadier General R.C. Schenck, 1st and 2nd Ohio and 3rd New York Regiments, a light battery and a contingent of Company E, 3rd U.S. Artillery; 3rd Brigade, Colonel William T. Sherman, 13th, 69th and 79th New York Regiments, the 2nd Wisconsin Regiment, Company E, 3rd U.S. Artillery and one light battery of artillery; and 4th Brigade, Colonel I.B. Richardson), 2nd, 3rd Michigan, 1st Massachusetts and 12th New York Regiments.

The Second Division is commanded by Colonel David Hunter and has two brigades: 1st Brigade, Colonel Andrew Porter, 8th and 14th New York Regiments, one squadron of the 2nd U.S. Cavalry, one battalion of U.S. Regular infantry and a battery of the 5th U.S. Artillery; and 2nd Brigade, Colonel Ambrose E. Burnside, 2nd New Hampshire, 1st and 2nd Rhode Island, 71st New York and one battery of the 2nd Rhode Island Artillery. The Third Division, composed of three brigades, is commanded by Colonel Samuel P. Heintzelman: 1st Brigade, Colonel W.B. Franklin, the 1st Minnesota, 5th Massachusetts, 4th Pennsylvania, Company E, 2nd U.S. Cavalry and one light battery of Company I, 1st U.S. Artillery; 2nd Brigade, Colonel O.B. Wilcox, 1st Michigan, 11th New York, one light battery with Company D, 2nd U.S. Artillery; 3rd Brigade, Colonel O.O. Howard, 2nd, 4th, and 5th Maine Regiments and the 2nd Vermont Regiment.

The Fourth Division, commanded by General Theodore Runyon, is designated reserve for the upcoming action. It is composed of the 1st, 2nd, 3rd and 4th New Jersey Regiments, each a three-month militia regiment, and the 1st, 2nd and 3rd New Jersey Regiments, each a three-year volunteer regiment. The Fifth Division,

with two brigades, is commanded by Colonel Dixon S. Miles: 1st Division, Colonel Louis Blenker, 8th and 29th New York, the New York Garibaldi Guard and the 24th Pennsylvania Regiments; and 2nd Brigade, Colonel Thomas E. Davies, 16th, 18th, 31st and 32nd New York Regiments and one light battery of Company G, 2nd U.S. Artillery.

In Missouri, Major General Nathaniel Lyon's force, including contingents under Colonels Blair and Bornstein and Captain Lathrop, bolstered by Totten's artillery battery, arrives at Jefferson City. Lyon prepares to attack Colonel John S. Marmaduke's force at Booneville.

In Union activity, Hiram Gregory Berry is appointed colonel of the 4th Maine Volunteer Infantry. He is later, during the Peninsular Campaign, promoted to brigadier general, and during November 1862, he is raised to the rank of major general.

In Union general officer activity, Franklin Stillman is commissioned as major (later brigadier general) of the 4th Maine Infantry Regiment, which is organized this day at Rockland. In September he is promoted to lieutenant colonel. After the First Battle of Bull Run (Manassas), he is promoted to colonel of the 14th Maine, on 25 November. He is assigned duty in the Department of the Gulf.

In Naval activity, in New York, the USS *Iroquois* arrives in port. The *Iroquois,* operating in the Mediterranean, had been recalled due to the outbreak of the Civil War. It is ordered to sail to the Caribbean to search for blockade runners and southern privateers. During autumn, the *Iroquois* encounters the CSS *Sumter* at Martinique, but Captain Semmes, with the aid of French authorities, is able to evade capture by departing on 23 November without being detected.

In other activity, the captured Confederate vessel *Savannah* arrives in New York. It had been brought from off the coast of South Carolina by a crew selected from the USS *Minnesota* standing blockade duty there. Subsequently, the Confederate crew will arrive (in irons) transported by the USS *Harriet Lane,* a steamer. A controversy develops when it becomes known that the crew is subject to being tried as pirates rather than privateers; however, during February of the following year, it is decided that they shall be treated as prisoners of war. After being transferred to Fort Lafayette, they will be exchanged.

June 16 (Sunday)   In Florida, the 6th New York Regiment (Wilson's Zouaves) arrives at Pensacola and establishes camp about one mile east of Fort Pickens. Colonel William Wilson's regiment is less than disciplined. Their tricks and jokes create serious consequences later when Confederates attack during October. Confederate Colonel (later brigadier general) John King Jackson, 5th Georgia Infantry, participates in the action around Pensacola until he is transferred to Tennessee during the early part of the following year. Jackson, a lawyer,

was appointed colonel of the regiment during the previous month.

In Maryland, General Robert Patterson receives orders from General Winfield Scott to immediately dispatch every available regular troop to Washington, including infantry and cavalry, as well as the Rhode Island Regiment with its accompanying artillery battery. Patterson is also directed to restrain the remainder of his forces within the boundaries of Maryland, thus eliminating any opportunity to make an unwise move into Virginia, but Patterson does not quickly react for the demand to forward his troops to the capital, causing Scott to press the issue.

June 17 (Monday)   Spain and the Netherlands declare neutrality in the ongoing war in the United States.

In Maryland, Union and Confederates clash at Edwards Ferry. The Union (1st Pennsylvania Volunteers) sustains one killed and three or four wounded. The Confederates sustain 15 killed.

In Missouri, a skirmish between Union and Confederate soldiers occurs at Booneville. The Union contingents under Major General Lyon include Batteries H and I, 2nd Missouri, and the 1st Missouri Light Artillery. The Union suffers two dead and 19 wounded. The Confederates (General Price's command), commanded by Colonel John S. Marmaduke, suffer 14 dead and 20 wounded. Also, a Confederate contingent fires upon Union troops (Missouri Volunteers) led by Captains Price and David S. Stanley at Independence while they are under a flag of truce. In other activity, Union troops occupy Jefferson City.

In Virginia, Union Brigadier General Robert Patterson, having basically ignored General Winfield Scott's repeated order to dispatch troops to the capital, receives a third and more pressing demand to expedite the movement. Patterson, understanding the tone of the message, responds immediately. At Vienna, contingents of the 1st Ohio Regiment skirmish with Confederates. Union losses are five killed and six wounded. Confederate losses are six killed.

The federal government in Washington directs that the railroad lines between Alexandria and Leesburg, Virginia, must be guarded and kept open. A contingent of the 1st Ohio Regiment (Volunteers), commanded by Colonel Alexander McDowell McCook, composed of four companies (about 270 troops), departs Alexandria to set up a protective line, but they are unaware that about 2,000 Confederates have established a welcoming party. Brigadier General Robert C. Schenck accompanies the detachment. When the train approaches a point near Vienna, the troops, many of whom are aboard flat cars, come under heavy fire from either side of the tracks. The 1st South Carolina Regiment, holding concealed positions in the wooded hills, sprays the entire line of cars. The ambush fails to cause heavy casualties.

While the Confederates, led by Colonel (later General) Maxcy Gregg, 1st South Carolina Infantry, leisurely sweep the Union troops with a blanket of fire, the train's engineer decides to save himself. With quick motion, he disengages the engine and one passenger car from the train and rushes back toward Alexandria. The startled troops bolt from the cars and seek defensive positions in a nearby grove. The Confederates, rather than closing against and overcoming the stranded Union troops, retire to Fairfax Court House, permitting the Ohio remnants to collect their dead and wounded and march back to camp. The Union losses stand at five killed, six wounded and thirteen missing.

In West Virginia, Union Loyalists (in convention) vote to secede from Virginia and to form an independent state loyal to the Union.

In Union general officer activity, John Basil Turchin (Ivan Vasilovitch Turchinoff), a native of Russia and former colonel of the Imperial Guard and veteran of the Crimean War, is commissioned colonel (later brigadier general) of the 19th Illinois Regiment. Colonel Turchin, prior to immigrating to the United States, had also been responsible for the planning and construction of the coastal defenses of Finland.

In Confederate general officer activity, Barnard E. Bee (West Point, 1845), a former captain in the U.S. 10th Infantry until his resignation the previous March, is appointed brigadier general in the Confederate Army. Also, U.S. Major James Longstreet (West Point, 1842), having recently resigned his commission, is appointed brigadier general in the Confederate Army. And former Lt. Colonel John Bankhead Magruder (West Point, 1830) is appointed to the rank of brigadier general in the Provisional Confederate Army. At Lynchburg, Virginia, the 11th Alabama Regiment is enlisted into the Confederate Army. The regiment moves to the vicinity of Alexandria and from there to Yorktown, but it doesn't come under fire on the field until Seven Pines (May–June 1862), when it is under the command of Colonel Sydenham Moore.

Captain (later brigadier general) Young M. Moody leaves the 11th Alabama and forms the 43rd Alabama with Archibald Gracie, the latter becoming the regiment's colonel. William Joseph Hardee (West Point, 1838), formerly a lieutenant colonel and a veteran of the Mexican War, is appointed brigadier general in the Confederacy. Hardee has formed an Arkansas brigade and will maintain operations in Arkansas until the next spring. He is promoted to major general in October. Richard Stoddert Ewell (West Point, 1840), having resigned his commission the previous month, is appointed brigadier general in the Confederate Army. Ewell is promoted in January of the following year to major general.

David Rumph Jones (West Point, 1846) is named brigadier general in the Confederate Army. General Jones will lead a brigade at 1st Manassas (Bull Run) and will be promoted to major general, effective March 1862. Also, John Clifford Pemberton (West Point, 1837), who had resigned his commission in the U.S. Army

the previous April, is appointed brigadier general (later lieutenant general) in the Confederate Army, effective this date. Pemberton initially commands the Department of South Carolina, Georgia and Florida, but later he is assigned command of the Department of Mississippi and Eastern Louisiana. In yet other activity, Benjamin Huger (West Point, 1825), Thomas "Stonewall" Jackson, and Edmund Kirby Smith are appointed brigadier generals.

June 18 (Tuesday) **In Maryland,** a Union force encounters Confederate artillery at Conrad's Ferry. Following an exchange, both sides sustain casualties; however, the Union suffers heavily.

In Missouri, a skirmish occurs at Camp Cole between the Missouri Home Guards and Confederate forces. The Union suffers approximately 75 killed or wounded, and the Confederates have four dead and 20 wounded.

June 20 (Thursday) **In Western Virginia,** pro–Unionists unanimously elect Francis Harrison Pierpont as provisional governor of Virginia after having declared that the present Virginia elected officials abandoned the state by seceding from the Union. At a convention in Wheeling on the 13th, the Unionists denounced the Secession Convention and at that time Pierpont was a participant as a representative of Marion County. During 1863, West Virginia gains entrance to the Union as a state, and at that time Arthur Boreman succeeds Piermont, while the latter is made governor of the "restored state of Virginia," those sectors of the state controlled by the Union. During 1865, following the conclusion of the war, Pierpont becomes governor of the entire state of Virginia.

In Union activity, General Winfield Scott dispatches a message to General Robert Patterson, who is in Virginia, instructing him to forward his plan of operations for his command. Patterson responds to the general in chief on the following day.

In Naval activity, the USS *Reliance* engages Confederate batteries at Marlborough Point, Virginia. On patrol the following week, it engages a contingent of Confederates at Mathias Point.

June 21 (Friday) **In Tennessee,** the Confederate 16th Tennessee Regiment, pursuant to orders, departs by train for Haynesville in East Tennessee; after arriving, the regiment establishes a camp while awaiting further orders. Major General Samuel Read Anderson (militia) is in command of all Confederate troops in East Tennessee; however, on 9 July, he is appointed brigadier general in the Confederate service. Confederate Brigadier General Daniel Smith Donelson (militia) is in command of the Tennessee regiments, but he too is appointed brigadier general in the Confederate service on 9 July.

In Union activity, Brigadier General Robert Paterson, in response to a message on the previous day from General Winfield Scott, explains

in a message that he is aborting the plan to move upon Winchester, Virginia, and instead will transfer his supplies to Frederick, Maryland, while simultaneously occupying Maryland Heights with a brigade of infantry to support Colonel (later brigadier general) Abner Doubleday's artillery, which is to operate from Maryland Heights. Patterson also states that the remainder of his force will ford the river at Point of Rocks to join Colonel Charles P. Stone's command at Leesburg, Virginia. *In Confederate general officer activity,* John Henry Winder is appointed brigadier general in the Confederate Army. Winder is assigned duty in Richmond as provost marshal.

June 22 (Saturday) **In Washington, D.C.,** General Winfield Scott, having received a reply from General Robert Patterson on the previous day, dispatches a telegram to Patterson suggesting that he was pleased that by this time, Patterson's forces are crossing the river to strike against the enemy. However, the Union forces under Patterson remain in place. Confederate General Joseph E. Johnston holds Winchester, Virginia, with about 15,000 troops, while the force under Patterson numbers about 10,000. Paterson also has ten guns, but they are inoperable due to the lack of harnesses, necessary to move them.

June 23 (Sunday) *In Naval activity,* the USS *Massachusetts,* commanded by M. Smith and operating in the Gulf of Mexico, seizes four Confederate schooners, the *Basile, Freres, Olive Branch* and *Trois Freres.* In addition, a Mexican vessel, the schooner *Brilliant,* is also captured.

June 24 (Monday) **In Tennessee,** the legislature, having been informed of the Union threat against the Cumberland and Tennessee Rivers, informs the Confederate Congress and requests that four river steam boats (*Helman, Joseph Johnson, J. Woods,* and *B.M. Runyon*) at Nashville be purchased for the purpose of transforming them into ironclads to bolster the defenses against an invasion by a Union fleet. Afterward, the vessels are acquired and the project gets underway.

In Union general officer activity, Colonel William Starke Rosecrans (West Point 1842) is promoted to the rank of brigadier general (effective May 16, 1861); he also this day becomes colonel (State of Ohio) of the 23rd Ohio Infantry Regiment. Shortly after the outbreak of the war with the firing on Fort Sumter, Rosecrans became a staff officer with General McClellan.

In Naval activity, the Steamers *Monticello* and *Quaker City* come under Confederate fire while operating on the Rappahannock River.

June 25 (Tuesday) *In Confederate general officer activity,* Lt. Dabney H. Maury (West Point, 1846) is dismissed from the U.S. Army, subsequent to a determination that he was being disloyal. Soon after, he is appointed to the rank of colonel in the Confederate Army, and following service with Brigadier General Van Dorn, he is promoted to the rank of brigadier general (March 1862).

Leonidas Polk (West Point, 1827), at present a bishop in Louisiana, joins the Confederacy as a major general; during October 1862, Polk will be promoted to the rank of lieutenant general. At this time, General Polk receives command of Department No. 2. Polk forms the Army of Mississippi, which is eventually merged into the Army of Tennessee. Department No. 2 encompasses a huge amount of terrain including the Mississippi River defenses stretching between the Red River in Louisiana to Paducah, Kentucky, the latter at the Ohio River less than 150 miles from Nashville.

June 26 (Wednesday)   In Virginia at Patterson's Creek (Kelley's Island), elements of the 11th Indiana Regiment skirmish with a contingent of Confederates. The Union loses one killed and one wounded. The Confederate losses are seven killed and two wounded.

In West Virginia, the newly formed state government is recognized by President Lincoln (it officially becomes a state in June 1863).

In Union general officer activity, Nelson G. Williams is appointed colonel, 3rd Iowa Infantry. Williams will see duty at several skirmishes in Missouri and then be attached to General Stephen Augustus Hurlbut's command (4th Division under Grant) at Shiloh. During the vicious confrontation, Confederate shells pound Union positions and on one such barrage, Williams' horse is struck, falling on Colonel Williams, disabling him. Williams is appointed brigadier general at the end of November 1862, two days after ill health forces him to retire. Also, William Sooy Smith (West Point, 1853) is commissioned colonel (later brigadier general) of the 13th Ohio Infantry. In April 1862 he promoted to brigadier general.

In Naval activity, the USS *Quaker City* seizes the blockade runner *Sally Magee* at Hampton Roads.

June 27 (Thursday)   In Maryland at Baltimore, General Nathaniel Banks orders the arrest of the police marshal (Kane) and the disbanding of the police board. Banks is convinced

the marshal and the board members are conspiring with the enemy. Later in the month, Major General Nathaniel P. Banks is ordered to move to the Potomac and replace General Francis Patterson, who had been assigned with his 17th Pennsylvania Militia Regiment as river guards until ordered to move to Martinsburg, West Virginia.

In Virginia, Confederates under Colonel Daniel Ruggles successfully defend Matthias Point against a Union attack by the gunboats *Pawnee* and *Freeborn.* Union troops suffer one killed and three or four wounded. Captain John Williams (U.S. Navy) attached to the USS *Pawnee* during the attack on Confederate-held Mathias Point, while lying in the attack boat, states: "Men must die on this thwart sooner than leave a man behind." Commander James H. Ward is mortally wounded while using the bow gun on his flagship, the USS *Thomas Freeborn.* Ward is the first U.S. Navy officer killed in action during the Civil War.

June 28 (Friday)   In Maryland, General Robert Patterson, responding to a message on the previous day from General Winfield Scott, informs the general in chief that he has not moved across the Potomac to attack Winchester, Virginia, due to the strength of the enemy, and will only do so upon direct orders from Washington; no order to attack is forthcoming.

In Virginia, a contingent of the New Jersey Zouaves engages a group of Confederates. The Union sustains one killed and the Confederates sustain two killed.

In Union general officer activity, John White Geary, a veteran of the Mexican War, is appointed colonel (later brevet major general) of the 28th Pennsylvania Regiment. General Geary participates at Bolivar Heights and his command later seizes Leesburg (8 March 1862). Also, George Hector Tyndale is commissioned major (later brigadier general) of the 28th Pennsylvania Regiment.

In Naval activity, the Confederate privateer *Jefferson Davis,* a brig, formerly the slave-ship *Echo,* now commanded by Captain Louis M. Coxeter, leaves Charleston, South Carolina.

June 29 (Saturday)   In Maryland, supplies that include harnesses reach General Robert Patterson at his encampment. Patterson's artillery complement consists of only six smoothbore guns, but without the harnesses, they are of no value when the offensive commences.

In Union general officer activity, Thomas Howard Ruger (West Point, 1854) is commissioned lieutenant colonel (later brevet major

general) of the 3rd Wisconsin; on 1 September, he is appointed colonel of the regiment. He participates in action at Shenandoah and Cedar Mountain.

In Naval activity, Confederates attack and capture the steamer USS *St. Nicholas* on the Potomac River.

June 30 (Sunday)   In Virginia, a contingent of Confederate scouts engage pickets of the 4th Pennsylvania Regiment at Shuter's Hill. The Union suffers one killed and one wounded, while the Confederates sustain two killed and one wounded.

In Marine Corps activity, at this time, the United States Marine Corps stands at 2,386, including 48 officers and 2,338 enlisted men.

July   In *Confederate general officer activity,* Samuel Read Anderson is appointed brigadier general. He had recently been appointed major general of the Tennessee State forces. General S.R. Anderson is compelled to resign the following year due to bad health; however, late in 1864, President Jefferson Davis reappoints him as a brigadier general. Also, Confederate Colonel (later general) John R. Chambliss, 41st Virginia Infantry Regiment, becomes colonel of the 13th Virginia Cavalry. His contingent will serve in Virginia and during the Maryland Campaign. In November 1862, Chambliss' command will participate as a contingent of General William Henry Fitzhugh Lee's brigade. Initially, W.H.F. Lee is the commanding officer of the 9th Virginia Cavalry.

Also, the Confederate 13th Alabama Regiment is organized; Birkett Davenport Fry (West Point, attendance 1846) is appointed colonel. It participates in various clashes including: Chancellorsville (5/1 to 5/4/1862), Cold Harbor (6/1 to 6/12/1862), Gettysburg (7/1 to 7/3/1863), Malvern Hill (8/5/1862), Mechanicsville-Ellison's Mills (6/26/1862), Petersburg (6/1864 to 4/1865), Seven Pines (5/31 to 6/1/1862) Sharpsburg-Antietam (9/17/1862), South Mountain–Turner's Gap, Maryland (9/14/1862), Wilderness (5/5 to 5/7/1862), Yorktown (4/5 to 5/3/1862) and Appomattox Court House, Virginia. Elkanah Brackin Greer is appointed colonel (later brigadier general) 3rd Texas Cavalry.

July 1 (Monday)   In Missouri, a contingent of the Missouri Home Guards, commanded by Captain A.H.D. Cook, skirmishes a group of Confederate Mounted Guards at Farmington. The Union sustains no casualties. The Confederates suffer one killed.

In South Carolina, at about this time, men from across the state are rallying to the Confederacy and arriving at Columbia. Ten companies will be formed for each regiment, the first of these to be the 12th South Carolina. The 12th, led by Colonel G.M. Dunnovant, will later join with the 13th and 14th South Carolina regiments to form General Maxcy Gregg's Brigade. Colonel James J. Pettigrew (militia) will join the Hampton Legion, and within a short time he is elected colonel (later brigadier general) of the 12th South Carolina.

A Union reconnaissance column (General Nathaniel Banks' division) in the vicinity of Hyattsville, Maryland (Mottelay, *The Soldier in Our Civil War,* **1886).**

In Union activity, Thomas Egan, having joined the 40th New York Regiment, is appointed its lieutenant colonel on this day. The regiment is also known as the Mozart Regiment and the Constitution Guard.

In Naval activity, the blockade runner *Sally Mears,* a schooner, is encountered and captured by Union vessels, including the USS *Quaker City,* in the vicinity of Hampton Roads. At about this time (July) the tugboat *William G. Putnam* is acquired by the U.S. Navy. In August it is commissioned the *General Putnam* and will be assigned to the soon to be established North Atlantic Blockading Squadron. In November 1862, it will depart North Carolina and serve out of Hampton Roads and the surrounding region, including the Chesapeake Bay area, until later being ordered to the York and James Rivers to support ground forces and perform tug duties. After the war it moves to Washington, D.C., to be decommissioned during June 1865. It is transferred to the U.S. Treasury Department and renamed the *Putnam* and placed in the lighthouse service until 1885.

In other activity, the U.S. Navy acquires the *James Adger* (a wooden side-wheel steamship) at about this time (July) under charter. It is transformed into a gunboat at New York and commissioned the following August as the USS *James Adger* and ordered to join the search for two Confederate ministers (James Mason and John Slidell); however, the *Adger* fails to spot the prey. They are discovered and captured by another warship during early November. In December the *James Adger* is assigned to the South Atlantic Blockading Squadron. Also, the U.S. Navy acquires the *Mercedita,* a screw steamer, at about this time (July). It is transformed into a gunboat and commissioned the USS *Mercedita* in December and assigned to the Gulf Blockading Squadron.

July 2 (Tuesday)   In Maryland, the 1st Wisconsin and the 11th Pennsylvania Regiments, attached to a brigade commanded by Colonel George Henry Thomas, engage and defeat a Confederate force at Falling Waters (also called Haynesville or Martinsburg). The contest lasts more than six hours. The Union sustains eight killed and 15 wounded. The Confederates sustain 31 killed and about 50 wounded. Union Lt. Colonel John J. Abercrombie (later brigadier general) participates at this battle.

In Ohio, Brigadier General Jacob D. Cox, at Camp Dennison, is appointed by General McClellan to command a brigade composed of Ohio and Kentucky troops and repair to Point Pleasant, in Western Virginia.

In Virginia and West Virginia, Union troops under General Robert Patterson, en route to cut off the Confederates near Manassas, Virginia, defeat a Confederate force at Hoke's Run, West Virginia. Also, Confederate soldiers under the command of General Joseph E. Johnston withdraw from Martinsburg, Virginia, to avoid the approaching Union forces. The Rebels in Martinsburg lack adequate transportation and supplies, but Patterson's ninety-day volunteers,

nearing the end of their enlistment terms, exhibit more of a desire to depart for home than initiate an attack against the Confederates.

In Union general officer activity, Halbert Eleazer Paine, a cousin of Union General Eleazer Paine, is appointed colonel of the 4th Wisconsin Cavalry Regiment. Colonel Paine subsequently loses a leg at Port Hudson; however, he returns to service and is promoted brigadier general in April 1863 during the Vicksburg Campaign.

In Naval activity, the U.S. Navy at about this time acquires the *Louisiana,* a commercial steamship built during 1860 in Wilmington, Delaware. The vessel is transformed into a gunboat and commissioned the following July. The *Louisiana* is assigned to the North Atlantic Blockading Squadron and sees duty off the coasts of Virginia and North Carolina. The screw steamboat *Stars and Stripes,* constructed at Mystic, Connecticut, is acquired by the U.S. Navy at about this time. It is converted to a gunboat and in September commissioned the USS *Stars and Stripes* and assigned duty in the North Atlantic Blockading Squadron. It initially patrols along the Outer Banks of North Carolina and later extends to the Roanoke River and participates in the operations against New Bern. In September 1862 it is transferred to the East Gulf Blockading Squadron.

July 3 (Wednesday)   In New Mexico, Fort McLane is evacuated by the Union. New Mexico is included in the Western Department.

In Confederate general officer activity, Major William Whann Mackall, U.S. Army, resigns his commission to join the Confederacy. He is appointed lieutenant colonel (later brigadier general) and initially serves in the Adjutant General's Department.

In Naval activity, the CSS *Sumter,* while cruising off Cuba, seizes its first vessel, the bark *Golden Rocket* (operating out of Maine). The captured crew is taken aboard the *Sumter,* but the prize is afterward set afire. Subsequently, the *Sumter* seizes two brigantines, the *Cuba* and the *Machias.* Captain Raphael Semmes of the *Sumter* selects prize crews for the captured vessels, but aboard the *Cuba,* the original crew is able to overwhelm the Confederates under Midshipman Hudgins and regain control of the ship. The *Cuba* makes it to New York and the Confederates are turned over to the authorities there. They are to be tried as pirates but are later exchanged. Meanwhile, the *Sumter* arrives at Cienfuego with six prizes, but the Spanish prohibit Captain Semmes to await a decision of the Admiralty Court. The vessels are later returned to their owners. Semmes departs Cuba and sails toward Brazil.

July 4 (Thursday)   In West Virginia, Union troops under

General Robert Patterson begin their march into the Shenandoah Valley, engaging Confederates at Harper's Ferry in a brief skirmish.

In New York, Union troops at Newport stage a celebration in honor of the Fourth of July, including a parade marching to the music of a regimental band and a thirty-four gun salute rendered by a battery of the 1st New York Zouaves.

July 5 (Friday)   In Virginia, the 1st Company, 9th New York Regiment (Colonel Rush Hawkins), engages a Confederate contingent at Newport News. The skirmish costs the Union six wounded. The Confederates suffer three wounded.

Colonel Rush C. Hawkins, 9th New York Regiment (Mottelay, *The Soldier in Our Civil War,* 1886).

Recruiting for Colonel Hawkins' Zouaves (9th New York) (Mottelay, *The Soldier in Our Civil War,* 1886).

In Missouri, Union forces under General Franz Sigel, although better trained, are outnumbered three to one by Confederates under General James E. Rains and Sterling Price at Carthage (Dry Fork Creek and Brier Fork). The Union troops, including the 3rd and 5th Missouri and one battery of artillery, are attacked on both sides by southern cavalry. The Union troops quickly fall back. Union Casualties are 13 dead and 31 wounded. Confederates have about 30 dead, 125 wounded, and 45 prisoners.

In Union activity, General George McClellan, having been in command of all troops in and around Grafton, West Virginia, for about two weeks, prepares to move against the Confederates in Northern Virginia, now commanded by General Richard B. Garnett, who succeeded George Porterfield. At this time, Garnett is headquartered in Randolph County at Beverly on Laurel Hill, a huge ridge that runs parallel to the Allegheny Mountains. On the 6th, McClellan's forces initiate the move to eliminate the Confederates in northern Virginia.

July 6 (Saturday)   In Maryland, the 8th New York Regiment (Volunteers) engages a contingent of Confederates at Great Falls. The Union sustains two killed and the Confederates 12 killed.

In West Virginia, a large Union force under Major General George B. McClellan is gathering in the vicinity of Philippi. It includes Barnett's Cleveland Artillery, attached to the 6th Ohio (initially known as the Independent Guthrie Greys), the 1st, 6th, 8th, 9th, 10th and 13th Indiana, the 14th and 16th Ohio and Burdsall's Cavalry. Three separate commands, excluding the main body of McClellan's force, advances toward the Rebel positions. One contingent, led by General Thomas Armstrong Morris (West Point, 1834), advances toward Beverly. General Jacob Dolson Cox's force moves into the Kanawha Valley (West Virginia) to neutralize the Confederates under Confederate General Henry A. Wise. The third force, under General Charles E. Hill, marches to a point east of Philippi Western Union in Tucker County. Hill's mission is to intercept any Confederate forces attempting to escape by heading over the Allegheny Mountains.

In the meantime, General McClellan and the main body depart for Buckhannon (Middle Creek Fork). An advance unit, one company of the 3rd Ohio Regiment, arrives at Middle Creek Fork this day and a skirmish develops with Confederates there. Following the shootout, the Union sustains one killed and six wounded. The Rebels sustain seven killed. Another engagement occurs at Buckhannon when Confederates under General Henry A. Wise engage the 3rd and 4th Ohio Regiments under General Thomas A. Morris (Indiana volunteers). In this contest, the Union reports no casualties. The Confederates report 23 wounded and some captured.

In Union general officer activity, General John Frémont is appointed commander of the West with headquarters in St. Louis, Missouri; he has just returned from Europe, having been informed of his appointment as a major general (Regular Army) by President Lincoln, effective May 14, while there. Brigadier General Thomas Armstrong Morris (Indiana Volunteers), under McClellan, declines promotion to brigadier of U.S. Volunteers (1861) and major general of U.S. Volunteers (1862) respectively.

In Naval activity, the Confederate privateer *Jefferson Davis* seizes a brig, the *John Welsh,* commanded by Captain J.C. Field, which is en route from Trinidad to England with a cargo of sugar. The schooner *Enchantress* is also captured this day off Montauk, Long Island. Captain Louis M. Coxetter of the *Savannah* directs that the prize be taken to a southern port.

July 7 (Sunday)   In West Virginia, General George B. McClellan's force arrives at Buckhannon, having set out from the vicinity of Philippi on the previous day. His other contingents are also moving into position to strike against the Confederates under Brigadier General Richard B. Garnett, who is headquartered in Beverly, Virginia. McClellan's strategy is to have General Thomas A. Morris (Indiana Volunteers), at Laurel Hill in a small town named Bealington, to commence diversionary raids as a ruse to convince Garnett that he is being hit with the full force of the Union attack, giving the main body the element of surprise, with which it will strike the rear of the Rebels, which is well defended and includes several thousand troops under Lt. Colonel (later brigadier general) John Pegram (West Point 1854) that are deployed in the vicinity of Rich Mountain.

In Naval activity, the Confederate privateer *Savannah* captures a commercial vessel, the *S.J. Waring,* off Sandy Hook, New Jersey. The captured prize sails toward South Carolina, but the privateers permit some of the crew, including William Tillman, a colored cook, to remain aboard. Tillman and three others sail with the five-man Confederate crew. The CSS *George Page,* seized by the Confederates at Acquia Creek the previous May, engages the USS *Pocahontas* on the Potomac River. The *George Page* sustains damage. The *George Page,* built in Washington, D.C., during 1853 is thought to have been renamed the *City of Richmond* by the Confederates.

In Confederate general officer activity, William R. Peck joins the Confederate Army as a private in the 9th Louisiana Infantry serving under colonel (later brigadier general) Richard Taylor. Peck climbs through the ranks to become a brigadier general during the final year of the war, and his regiment accompanies the Army of Northern Virginia for the duration.

July 8 (Monday)   In Washington, D.C., Confederate Major Taylor arrives at Union lines to deliver letters to President Abraham Lincoln and General Winfield Scott from President Jefferson Davis and General Pierre G.T. Beauregard. He is escorted through the lines, but he is blindfolded. After delivering the messages, he returns to his line, still under a flag of truce.

In other activity, the U.S. Army engineers initiate the operation to establish a ring of defense around the capital. Within six months about 60 forts are completed and afterward, the total doubles. During the construction period, troops continue to arrive in Washington from all points. Other defensive measures are undertaken to protect Washington. One includes the erection of a bullet proof and movable barricade at Chain Bridge which links Maryland with Virginia. The chief engineer in charge of the project is Major John Gross Barnard (West Point 1833). The initial forts required near Alexandria, Virginia, include Fort Corcoran. Two support forts, Bennett and Haggerty, are both built in the vicinity of the aqueduct. Also, Fort Runyon, Fort Jackson and Fort Albany are built to protect the Long Bridge.

In New Mexico, Brigadier General Henry Sibley (West Point, 1838) takes command of all Confederate troops in the New Mexican Territory. The next February Sibley's command clashes with the Union at Valverde and Glorieta. Sibley had resigned from the U.S. Army during the previous May, and during June he had been commissioned a brigadier general in the Confederate Army. Confederate Captain (later brigadier general) William Polk Hardeman, 4th Texas Cavalry, participates in this activity.

In West Virginia, Union forces under George B. McClellan and Confederate forces under Robert S. Garnett skirmish near Bealington (Laurel Hill). One of the Union detachments, a scouting party of the Ninth Indiana led by Colonel Robert H. Milroy, is dubbed "The Tigers of the Bloody Ninth," in apparent recognition of their ferocity in the woods. It is reported that the Confederates call them "Swamp

Union guards at Fort Runyon inspect wagons prior to permitting them entrance into Washington, D.C., via the Long Bridge (Mottelay, *The Soldier in Our Civil War*, 1886).

Devils." While the opposing sides battle, a troop of Confederate Cavalry arrives and moves to turn the tide against the Union infantry; however, at about the same time, Union artillery moves up and pounds the woods with blistering fire that takes the steam out of the assault, neutralizing the horsemen. Another unit involved in this action is the 14th Ohio. Union losses during this action are two killed and six wounded. Confederate casualties are estimated to be about twenty killed and forty wounded.

Following the engagement, Milroy's main body arrives at Laurel Hill, where the woods are controlled by the Ohio Ninth Regiment. Also, other forces of McClellan, detachments of the main body at Buckhannon, encounter some Confederate units, but the activity is between small groups and no considerable force of Rebels is encountered until the 10th.

In Confederate general officer activity, former Captain Charles S. Winder (West Point, 1850) is appointed colonel (later brigadier general) of the 6th South Carolina Infantry Regiment. Also, Colonel Richard Caswell Gatlin (West Point, 1832) is appointed brigadier general. He is assigned to the Department of North Carolina as its commanding officer.

In Naval activity, Confederate General Benjamin Huger at Norfolk is informed that a Union vessel will approach to pick up a passenger. The USS *Adriatic,* commanded by Commodore Augustus Ludlow Case (fleet-captain of the North Atlantic blockading squadron), attempts to pick up the daughter of Colonel Segur, but Confederate batteries on Craney Island commence firing despite the ship's conspicuous display of a white flag of truce. The *Adriatic* then dispatches a boat and it too is fired upon. Finally, two Confederate officers, also in a boat, exchange conversation with the Union seamen about the passage of the colonel's daughter. The *Adriatic* holds in place for about four hours, but the passenger is never brought

to the ship, prompting the Union vessel to withdraw.

July 9 (Tuesday) **In Virginia,** a contingent of Union troops composed of two companies (unit unknown) led by Lt. Colonel Young engages a Confederate force at Vienna. Estimated casualties: Union, none; Confederates, about three or four wounded.

In West Virginia, in the vicinity of Rich Mountain near Wheat Hill, during an ongoing storm, a contingent of Confederates initiates a weak offensive against the 14th Ohio and 9th Indiana Regiments, but the defenders easily repel the assault.

In Union activity, the Union commanders, including division, brigade and staff at Martinsburg, Virginia, discuss strategy. Colonel Charles P. Stone of the 14th U.S. Infantry urges a move to Charlestown rather than an attack against Confederate positions at Manassas, particularly due to the condition and morale of many of the troops and the lack of equipment and transportation. Some of the ninety-day wonders lack even shoes. In turn, Brigadier General Robert Patterson dispatches a message to General Scott requesting orders to move to Charlestown, establish supply depots at Harpers Ferry and be prepared to move in cadence with the attack against Manassas. Scott responds on the 12th.

In Naval activity, the Confederate privateer *Jefferson Davis* seizes the *Mary Goodell* while it is en route from New York to South America. The vessel is released; however, the Confederates transfer the prisoners they had been detaining to the vessel. After release, the *Mary Goodell* sails into Portland, Maine. The *Jefferson Davis* this day also seizes the *Mary E. Thomson* en route to Montevideo. The Union, once informed of the success of the *Jefferson Davis,* dispatches warships to track and destroy the privateer, which is sailing by now toward South

America. The vessels involved that depart from separate ports during the coming days up to 13 July are the cutters *Jackson, Crawford* and *Varina,* followed by the *Henrietta, Morris, Caleb Cushing* and the *Vincennes.*

In Confederate general officer activity, the Confederacy is attempting to further bolster its position against the northern states. On this day, Major General Samuel R. Anderson (Tennessee State Militia), a veteran of the Mexican War, is appointed brigadier general in the Provisional Army of the Confederacy. He will participate in the Western Virginia and the Peninsular campaigns until his health fails. He resigns during spring 1862, but returns to service during 1864. Also, Major General Benjamin Franklin Cheatham (Tennessee State Militia) is appointed brigadier general in the Confederate Army. Cheatham will serve in the Western Theater.

Daniel S. Donelson (West Point, 1825), brigadier general in the Tennessee State Militia, is appointed brigadier general in the Confederate Army. Donelson, a nephew of President Andrew Jackson, serves under General W.W. Loring in Western Virginia as well as later serving in South Carolina and then in Mississippi. From the latter, he moves to Tennessee and leads a brigade at the Battle of Murfreesboro (General Cheatham's division) during December 1862. Major General Gideon J. Pillow (Tennessee state troops) is promoted to the rank of brigadier general (later major general) in the Confederate Army effective this date. General Pillow, a veteran of the Mexican War (twice wounded during the operation against Mexico City), had been named senior major general of Tennessee's provisional army earlier this year.

July 10 (Wednesday) **In Missouri,** the 16th Illinois and 3rd Iowa Regiments, bolstered by the Hannibal Home Guards, skirmish with a Confederate force at Monroe Station. The Union, commanded by Lt. Colonel Young, sus-

Left: **The USS *Adriatic,* under a flag of truce, comes under fire at Craney Island near Norfolk, Virginia, on July 8, 1861.** *Right:* **A contingent of the Ninth Indiana (known as the "Tigers of the Bloody Ninth") skirmishes with Confederates** (Mottelay, *The Soldier in Our Civil War,* 1886).

tains three killed. The Confederates sustain four killed, 20 wounded and about 75 captured.

In West Virginia, General George B. McClellan moves against the Confederates under Brigadier General Robert S. Garnett. McClellan dispatches a force under General Rosecrans, composed of the 8th, 10th and 13th Indiana and the 19th Ohio, along with an artillery battery, to assault the force led by Confederate Lt. Colonel John Pegram at Rich Mountain, while he leads the main body toward Laurel Hill. Rosecrans' force marches along a circuitous route that takes them through wooded mountainous terrain. By the time they arrive at the objective, the Confederates are fully prepared to defend their positions because a runner sent by McClellan to forward information is captured en route by Confederate troops, giving Pegram an advance signal of the imminent attack.

In related activity, Union contingents, the 9th Indiana and 14th Ohio, posted near Wheat Hill, having repulsed a minor assault on the previous day, find themselves in uncontested possession of the woods near the hill; however, later in the day, a skirmish erupts and the Union continues to hold the positions.

In Naval activity, the USS *Minnesota,* flagship of the Atlantic Blockading Squadron, seizes the bark *Mary Warick.*

In Confederate general officer activity, Colonels Daniel H. Hill, 1st North Carolina Infantry, and Jones Mitchell Withers (West Point, 1835), 3rd Alabama, are promoted to the rank of brigadier general. Withers, the recent mayor of Mobile, Alabama, is again promoted the following April. General Hill is promoted during March 1862 and again in July 1863.

July 11 (Thursday) BATTLE OF RICH MOUNTAIN Union troops from the 8th, 10th, and 13th Indiana and the 19th and 33rd Ohio Regiments engage Confederates under Lt. Colonel John Pegram (later brigadier general) at Rich Mountain, West Virginia (not yet a state). At dawn, General William Starke Rosecrans' brigade moves through the woods to pass around the Confederates to a position from where it can strike the rear. Although the terrain is unfamiliar, Rosecrans is guided by a young Union loyalist, David L. Hart. Hart's family farm is located on the crest of Rich Mountain, at present in the middle of the Confederate positions.

Rosecrans expects to surprise the Confederates but a runner earlier sent by McClellan to update Rosecrans had been captured, eliminating an unexpected assault. Nevertheless, Rosecrans' column continues its trek along a circuitous route, ignoring the rain as the afternoon begins to fade. Just as the column encroaches the turnpike in the vicinity of the Hart residence, it is Rosecrans' troops who receive the surprise, as Confederates are deployed and awaiting the approach of the column. A fierce but brief skirmish develops as the Union troops overwhelm the defenders and compel them to retreat hurriedly to rejoin the main body. The effortless rout gives the Union control of a strategic point which dominates the road lead-

ing from the mountain to Beverly and proves fatal for the Confederates under Lt. Colonel Pegram, leaving him with one option, abandon his untenable positions. However, a major obstacle impedes his retreat, an entire brigade, making it next to impossible for him to carry off his horse-drawn artillery.

After dark, Pegram orders the mountain abandoned, leaving the artillery for the Union forces. Pegram intends to flee from the mountain and head for Laurel Hill to hook up with General Garnett, but the combination of unfamiliarity with the terrain and the darkness of the night causes the troops to become lost as they stumble into Union lines. In addition, Pegram's abandonment of his positions jeopardizes Garnett's positions, leaving his rear unprotected. Garnett attempts to move to beat McClellan to Beverly; however, McClellan's troops control the area, forcing a fight at Carrick's Ford on the 13th.

Meanwhile, Garnett, aware of the results of Rich Mountain, is preparing to abandon his positions and retire toward Beverly, where his reserves are deployed intending to reach the town before McClellan. Afterward, with those forces and Pegram's command, Garnett intends to go through Huttonsville and the Cheat Mountain passes. Throughout the night, Union forces (9th Indiana and 14th Ohio) posted at Wheat Hill, continue to pick up muffled voices from the Confederate encampment, and they are able to hear some teamsters cursing, but no determination is made as to whether the commotion is due to the arrival of reinforcements or a general withdrawal.

At dawn on the 12th, sentinels of the 9th Indiana report the curious events that occurred during the night, but the thought of a Confederate withdrawal is initially discounted and the reports are thought to have been a ploy, suggesting an ambush or merely a feint. Nonetheless, by noon, the ambiguous intentions of General Garnett become clear when a messenger sent from General McClellan arrives at Wheat Hill and brings news of the victory at Rich Mountain.

The 9th Indiana, 14th Ohio and other units are ordered forward, and shortly thereafter, the vacant Confederate camp is occupied by Union forces. Meanwhile, General Garnett is in full retreat. It becomes obvious the camp was quickly abandoned; a large amount of items left behind include "tents thrown down and torn in pieces; tent poles, some half burned; camp-kettles, mess-pans, plates, spoons, knives and forks, and all the utensils common to camps; camp-stools, cots, and blankets; champagne baskets and bottles, flasks, decanters, flagons; hospital stores, bandages, lint, litters, and stretchers; seedy boots and shoes, old clothes, stockings; and an endless litter of papers, letters, boxes, barrels...." In addition, the Union confiscates "fifty barrels of flour, as many of hard biscuit, and a quantity of corn in the ear were found in one place; in another, whole bundles of stockings, pants, coats, and blankets."

By afternoon, the Union initiates pursuit and the two sides clash at Carrick's Ford on 13 July.

Captain Benham leads the vanguard. The pursuers, as well as the retreating Confederates, are equally plagued by a nasty rainstorm that continues throughout the night. Meanwhile, Lt. Colonel Este, 14th Ohio, remains in the area with a contingent of about 700 men to maintain control of the various camps. The two sides clash at Carrick's Ford on 13 April.

At Rich Mountain, the Union sustains 11 dead and 35 wounded. Confederates have 60 dead, 140 wounded and 100 captured. One captured officer is Julius A. de Lagnel, who with a detachment of a few infantry companies and sparse artillery, holds off the Union troops for a while, but the summit is eventually overwhelmed. De Lagnel is wounded while attempting to singlehandedly operate the solitary gun. Initially he escapes capture, but he is seized while attempting to sneak through Union lines to reach safety. Subsequent to his release, de Lagnel is appointed brigadier general during April of 1862, but he refuses the commission, choosing to remain a lieutenant colonel. He serves for the duration in the ordnance bureau and for some time he is assigned duty as an inspector of arsenals.

Union Colonel (later general) Joshua Woodrow Sill (West Point, 1853) participates in this battle with the 33rd Ohio Volunteers and becomes its commanding officer during August. Colonel Sill becomes a brigadier general during April 1862. In addition, the Confederate 25th Virginia Infantry (Taliaferro's Brigade) under Major A.G. Roger enters its initial battle during this action. It will remain in the Army of the Northwest until June of the following year. However, during November of this year, the 25th becomes part of General Edward Johnson's Brigade (General Thomas J. "Stonewall" Jackson's Division), Army of Northern Virginia, with which it serves until the close of hostilities. The "Augusta Lee Guards," formed by Robert Doak Lilley (later brigadier general), is attached to the regiment.

July 12 (Friday) **In Virginia,** a skirmish develops at Newport News between the 7th New York Infantry and a Confederate force. Casualties are unavailable; however, about 12 Confederates are captured. In other activity, Confederate General Robert B. Garnett continues to evade McClellan and move toward southern Virginia. Also, Union General Robert Patterson is ordered, as previously requested by him, to move to Charlestown. The dispatch also informs Patterson that the attack against the Confederates at Manassas is scheduled to jump off on 16 July.

Confederate General Robert S. Garnett, unable to make Beverly, attempts to take a different route toward points farther south in Virginia, but Union troops under Captain Benham are in heated pursuit. With few options, Garnett will choose to make his stand on the following day at Carrick's Ford.

In West Virginia, a skirmish between Union and Confederate troops occurs at Barboursville (Red House) in the Kanawha Valley. The Union contingent, attached to General Jacob D. Cox, is the 2nd Kentucky Volunteers, commanded by Lt. Colonel Neff, while the Confederates are under Lt. Colonel Pegram. The Union loses one killed. Confederates suffer 10 killed. While Cox's force is engaging the Rebels in the valley, he also repels an attack on the 17th.

The Union 4th and 9th Ohio Volunteer Regiments engage Confederates at Beverly, which is occupied this day by General McClellan's forces. The Union sustains 13 killed and about 40 wounded. The Confederates suffer more than 100 casualties. A force of about 600 Confederates under Lieutenant Colonel Pegram surrender at Beverly during the afternoon. Following the fighting at Rich Mountain (11th), Pegram's command, in an attempt to get to Laurel Hill, found itself confused in the mountains and inadvertently within Union lines. Pegram will later be released and return to duty, becoming a colonel in 1862 and a brigadier general effective November 1862.

July 13 (Saturday) BATTLE OF CARRICK'S FORD Union troops from the 14th Ohio (Colonel James Blair Steedman), the 7th (Colonel Ebenezer Dumont) and 9th Indiana (Colonel Robert Huston Milroy), under the command of Brigadier General Thomas A. Morris (West Point, 1834), engage Confederates under General Robert Selden Garnett at Carrick's Ford, Western Virginia. Union Captain (later general) Henry W. Benham's force, acting as vanguard for the main body under General Thomas A. Morris, having linked together on the previous night, picks up the chase and speeds toward the suspected positions of the fleeing Confederates. Although aware that the Confederates have been weakened due to their retreat from Laurel Hill, the Union is also on the brink of exhaustion, having marched nearly twenty miles and eaten only a minimal amount of food since the previous afternoon (12th).

The vanguard descends from the mountain and encroaches a Rebel camp near the Cheat River, but no troops are there, only the campfire intended to cook their breakfast. In pursuit of the retreating enemy, the column crosses the river at Kahler's, where the water, although flowing rapidly, is knee deep, but extremely cold. After completing the crossing, the column advances to yet another ford. In the meantime, it becomes apparent that action is close at hand. Small arms fire in the distance is heard and in a flash, the thunderous sounds of artillery bellow.

While at the second ford, a Confederate baggage train that had paused after the exhausting march over Cheat Mountain is spotted. Rather than mount an immediate assault, Benham decides to await the arrival of Steedman's 2nd Battalion and Dumont's regiment; however, premature firing of a rifle warns the resting Rebels of the Union approach, prompting them to hurriedly resume their retreat. A few rebels hold back acting as rear guards, but heavy fire commences and the resistance soon fades. Meanwhile, Barnett's artillery (Dumont's regiment) pounds the nearby woods in which six companies of Colonel James Ramsey's 1st Georgia Regiment remain isolated.

The effective fire clears the obstacles, permitting the column to advance, but in the meantime, the Georgians had been able to escape from their isolation by moving through the woods. Meanwhile, the Union advance approaches Carrick's Ford, which is now heavily fortified by the Confederates, giving the Rebels a distinct advantage due to the elevation more than fifty feet above the river bank on the opposite bank. Once the Union advances into range, the Confederates open fire. Small arms and artillery ring down upon Steedman's regiment. Once again, Barnett's artillery is called upon to neutralize the incoming fire.

Plans are executed to maneuver elements of the force to ford the river above the Rebels at a point from where an attack can be launched against their rear. Six companies of the 7th Indiana are directed to cross 300 yards up the river, but something causes a mistake in communications and the contingent doubles the distance before fording the river. The error impedes progress, costing time, but in less than twenty minutes, the plan is back on target. Nevertheless, a hill selected for ascent is deemed too steep. Consequently, the original six companies are bolstered by the remainder of the regiment.

While the artillery is continuing to bombard the Confederate positions, Dumont's regiment works its way down to positions alongside of the road near the Confederate positions. Meanwhile, Colonel Milroy's 9th Indiana arrives at the ford. All the while, the contest continues to come under a rain storm that has plagued the march almost without pause since the previous day.

As Dumont's regiment reaches the road, the ongoing incessant fire terminates, and at the same time, the Confederates initiate a hurried retreat with the 7th Indiana on their heels. Pursuit continues for about one-half mile before a new skirmish erupts. The Confederates maintain a fighting retreat; however, during the tenacious bout, Confederate General Robert Garnett, in the vicinity of James Carrick's house, sustains a mortal wound while he attempts to rally Colonel Taliaferro's 23rd Virginia Regiment. Except for one young soldier from Georgia, no other troops are nearby. The Virginians maintain their flight while the general and the Georgian go down together and alone.

The body of General Garnett and that of the soldier from Georgia, described as laying along the banks of the Cheat River with "back to the field and face to the foe," are recovered by Union troops. By 1400, the Union, too exhausted to continue pursuit, halt to take time to eat and get some rest. Although many of the rebels continue to retreat, they leave behind most of their baggage and about forty wagons, giving the force "a large amount of new clothing, camp equipage, and other stores; their Head-quarter papers and military chest; also, two stands of colors; also, a third flag, taken since, and one fine rifled piece of artillery."

According to the battle report of Captain Benham, the Confederates lose about twenty men killed and another fifty are taken prisoner.

His unit of cavalry sustains two killed and six wounded, with one of the latter being seriously wounded. In the meantime, just as the fighting was concluding, the 6th Indiana led by Colonel Thomas Turpin Crittenden arrives at Carrick's Ford; however, it is too late to participate in the fighting.

By about 1700, the storm ceases, but the troops remain soaked. Night positions are established and the troops receive a reprieve from combat, permitting them to spend a quiet night. Meanwhile, the Yankees anticipate that another Union force under General Hill will intercept and capture those who had escaped; however, the Rebels make it to the Shenandoah Valley.

On the following morning, burial detachments are assigned and those on both sides who did not survive are interred. One of the Confederates, the unknown Georgian who remained at the side of General Garnett, receives a separate burial. The Union inters him on the property of James Carrick and they erect a wooden plaque that states: "Name unknown. A brave fellow, who shared his general's fate, and fell fighting at his side, while his companions fled."

General Garnett's body is escorted to Rowlesburg by a detachment led by Major Gordon. Afterward, the general's remains and personal effects, including his sword, are taken to Washington D.C., and from there his remains are transported through Confederate lines to be given to his family at Richmond.

Meanwhile, at about 1300 on the 14th, the brigade begins its return to Laurel Hill. A contingent composed of Companies C and H (6th Ohio) remain at Carrick's Ford to guard the prisoners and the captured supplies. During this engagement, the Union loss is 13 killed and 40 wounded; Confederates lose 20 dead, 10 wounded and 50 captured. General Robert S. Garnett, a graduate of West Point (1841), becomes the first general officer killed during the conflict.

Following the defeat of the Confederates, Union Major General George B. McClellan, convinced the southern insurrection has been thwarted sends a dispatch to headquarters: "Our success is complete, and secession in this country is complete."

In related activity, General Robert E. Lee will succeed the late General Garnett and assume command of all Confederate forces in the State of Virginia. One Union officer, Henry Washington Benham (West Point, 1837), had led the vanguard of General T.A. Morris' column in pursuit of General Garnett during the chase from Laurel Hill. Benham, chief engineer of the Department of the Ohio, is breveted colonel in the Regular Army for his action at the time. However, he is unable to prove himself in the eyes of General Rosecrans (McClellan's successor) or General David Hunter.

In Washington, D.C., army headquarters dispatches a message to General Robert Patterson at Charlestown, with instructions and options based upon previous dispatches from Patterson regarding the situation of his force and the intelligence reports regarding the enemy force at Winchester, Virginia: "If not strong enough to beat the enemy early next week, make a demonstration so as to detain him in the valley or in Winchester." Patterson responds, informing General Scott that the opponent, General Joseph Johnston, is well positioned at Winchester and able to have his force doubled in size by the time Patterson would reach his positions. Continuing, Patterson, rather than inform Scott of what action he is going to take, requests further instructions from Washington; none arrive. Nonetheless, Patterson moves out on the 16th.

In Western Virginia, General McClellan occupies Huttonsville, which had been occupied by Confederates; however, prior to departing, the Confederates had burned the bridge that spans the Tygart's Valley River.

In Confederate activity, Major General Leonidas Polk at about this time is appointed commander of Department No. 2 (Mississippi River defenses from Red River to Paducah, Kentucky).

In Naval activity, the gunboat CSS *Oregon*, seized by the state of Louisiana during 1861 subsequent to operating as a blockade runner, along with the CSS *Arrow*, while operating in the vicinity of Ship Island, attempt to draw the USS *Massachusetts* into a trap from where Confederate shore batteries can effectively fire upon it, but the *Massachusetts* does not take the bait. In September 1861, the *Oregon* participates in evacuating personnel from Ship Island, Mississippi.

July 14 (Sunday)   In Western Virginia, General McClellan, at Huttonsville, sends a telegram to Washington, D.C., informing headquarters of the victory on the 13th at Carrick's Ford. General Joseph Reynolds' command, composed primarily of Ohio and Indiana regiments, will occupy Beverly, Elkwater and Huttonsville, with Reynolds establishing headquarters at Elkwater. Reynolds' force is also composed of the 2nd West Virginia Regiment and Daum's battery. Initially the force acts as a protective contingent for the safety of the civilians, but it also engages in clearing the area of Confederate guerrillas known as bushwackers.

In Naval activity, the U.S. Navy initiates the blockade of the port at Wilmington, North Carolina; however, only one ship, the USS *Daylight*, is assigned the task, leaving the Confederates opportunities to evade capture or destruction for the time being. The *Daylight*, a 682-ton screw steam gunboat, initially a commercial vessel, came under charter by the Navy during the previous May. It patrols off North Carolina and Virginia until the latter part of 1864. The *Daylight* participates in the seizure of four blockade runners during 1861.

The Navy acquires another vessel this month, the *Mississippi*, which is transformed into a warship and commissioned the USS *Connecticut* during the following month. The ship operates as a transport delivering troops and supplies to various places along the seacoast from Virginia to Texas in support of the Union naval block-

ade. It seizes several blockade runners during 1861 into 1862. Toward the latter part of 1862, it is reassigned as a convoy and tow ship operating out of Panama. In June 1863, the *Connecticut* is assigned to the North Atlantic Blockading Squadron. During its tour the vessel's crews seize or destroy six blockade runners. The *Connecticut* is decommissioned during August 1865 and afterward as a civilian ship is renamed the *South America*.

July 15 (Monday)   In West Virginia, General McClellan orders the 3rd and 9th Ohio Regiments and Loomis' Battery, bolstered by other troops, to advance to positions close to the crest of Cheat Mountain to fortify positions there. In the meantime, the Confederate Army of Northern Virginia has sustained a thrashing and has scattered. Most of the army's artillery and baggage has been seized by McClellan's forces. Nonetheless, the Confederates begin making their way across the mountains, where they trek across the tip of Maryland and enter Hardy County, Virginia, en route to join with General Joseph E. Johnston's force in the Shenandoah Valley. Once aware that the Union pursuit had ceased, the remnant army halts at Petersburg. Afterward, Colonel Ramsey leads the column to Monterey (Highland County), where it joins with the command of General H.R. Jackson.

In Confederate general officer activity, at about this time, the commander at Fort Wise, Colorado, drops an AWOL officer, James Deshler (West Point, 1854) from its ranks, a task which is not unusual, as various members of the armed forces are leaving to serve with the Confederacy. Deshler apparently had gone on permanent leave. Deshler (West Point, 1854) turns up as a captain of artillery in the Confederate Army.

July 15–17   In Missouri, the Union 8th Missouri Volunteer Regiment skirmishes with Confederates in the vicinity of Millville (Wentzville). The Union sustains seven killed and one wounded. The Confederates suffer seven killed.

July 16 (Tuesday)   In Washington, D.C., John A. Dahlgren, commandant of the Washington Navy Yard, is promoted to the rank of captain. Soon after his promotion, Dahlgren is appointed chief of Bureau of Ordnance.

In Virginia, approximately 35,000 Union troops in and around Washington, D.C., under the command of General Irvin McDowell (West Point 1838) advance to Fairfax Court House. Some depart Camp Princeton in Arlington. General Daniel Tyler's First Division advances along the Leesburg Road and by night enters and occupies Vienna, from which it will operate as the right wing. General David Hunter's Second Division moves along the most direct route to Fairfax, the Turnpike Road, acting as the center force, while General Samuel Heintzleman's Third Division advances along the Little River Turnpike.

Meanwhile, Colonel Dixon S. Miles' Fifth

Division, operating on the left wing of the force, marches along the old Braddock Road. Throngs of citizens raise cheers as McDowell's troops march through Washington heading for Manassas, where they expect to capture the railroad junction and move on toward Richmond to end the insurrection. Politicians and private citizens take refreshments and follow the troops to watch the upcoming battle. Washington is filled with excitement and the town is crammed with green troops and an overflow of wagons. People from the South also converge on Manassas.

General Robert Patterson, at Charlestown, moves toward Bunker Hill along the road to Winchester, Virginia. The advance pushes Johnston's pickets back into Winchester. This is the day that was scheduled for the attack against Manassas (Bull Run), per a previous message from General Scott to Patterson.

In Naval activity, a captured vessel, the *S.J. Waring*, is nearing Charleston guided by its small crew. However, there are some aboard who had been captured on July 7, including William Tillman, a colored cook. Tillman seizes control of the vessel while the captain and first mate are asleep. Tillman kills three with a hatchet and the others are subdued. Despite the lack of navigational skills, the new crew, with the help of the two surviving Confederates, returns the vessel north to New York under Captain Tillman.

In Union general officer activity, William Farrar Smith (West Point, 1845) is commissioned colonel of the 3rd Vermont Regiment. On 13 August, he is promoted to brigadier general. General Smith is assigned to command a division in the VI Corps. He leads it during the Peninsular campaign and during the Maryland campaign, prior to becoming commander of the corps by December 1862.

In Confederate general officer activity, Camille Armand Jules Marie Prince de Polignac, a Frenchman who served in the Crimean War as a lieutenant (4th Hussars), has joined the Confederate cause. He is appointed lieutenant colonel (later brigadier general). De Polignac rises through the ranks, becoming a brigadier general (later major general) in January 1863 assigned to duty in the Trans-Mississippi Department in command of a Texas brigade that fights primarily in Louisiana, including the Red River Campaign.

July 17 (Wednesday)   In Missouri, a Union force composed of about 400 troops (3rd Missouri Reserves) skirmishes with Confederates at Fulton. The Union sustains one killed and 15 wounded.

In Virginia, forces of General Irvin McDowell (Department of Washington) arrive at Fairfax Court House and discover it abandoned by the Confederates, who moved to Centreville. McDowell directs General Daniel Tyler to move to Georgetown about two miles down the Warrenton Turnpike; the First Division arrives there during the night and establishes bivouac. Tyler, on the following morning, dispatches a force that encroaches Confederate positions outside of Centreville. Meanwhile, Confederate General Pierre Gustave T. Beauregard requests aid in an effort to repulse the federal advance into Virginia. Beauregard is headquartered at Manassas with a force of about 22,000 men. His request is sped to Richmond and soon after, Joseph E. Johnston is directed to move from the Shenandoah (Winchester) with his 10,000 men to reinforce Beauregard. Johnston arrives on the 20th and 21st, many of his men hitting the battlefield immediately after leaving their troop trains, with scarcely enough time to load their weapons. In related activity, Union General Robert Patterson moves from Bunker Hill back to Charlestown, but makes no move against Johnston at Winchester.

In Western Virginia, Union troops—the 2nd Kentucky and the 12th and 21st Ohio Regiments, bolstered by the artillery of the 1st Ohio Battery under General Jacob D. Cox—repulse a Confederate attack led by General Henry A. Wise at Scarytown. Lt. Col. Neff captured. The Union loses 9 killed and 38 wounded. Confederate casualties are unknown. The Confederate forces include the Kanawha Rifles.

On the previous day, the Union had spotted a Confederate artillery piece near the mouth of the Poca River and skirmishes occurred. Initially, the Rebels held their ground; however, repeated advances finally forced the Confederates to retreat from their positions where the Little Scary Creek converges with the Poca. On this day, the Union initiates repeated charges to dislodge the Rebels from a bridge during a period of about three hours. In the final charge, Lt. Colonel Patton is wounded in the shoulder. Afterward, Captain Albert Jenkins assumes command of the 22nd Virginia. Jenkins observes the Union troops as they fall back. The Rebels claim victory. Afterward, Patton, due to his wound, is left at Charleston as an exchanged prisoner. He returns to the regiment in April 1862.

July 17–19 In Missouri, a Union force, composed of about 170 troops led by Major George Van Horne (Van Horne's Battalion), skirmishes with Confederates, the Cass County Home Guards, under Captain Duncan at Harrisonville and Parkersville. The Union sustains one killed and the Confederates suffer 14 killed.

July 18 (Thursday) In Virginia at Georgetown, Union General Daniel Tyler dispatches a contingent of his First Division toward Centreville. As they approach Mitchell's Ford as ordered on June 20, a Confederate brigade of South Carolina troops under Brigadier General Milledge L. Bonham, rather than engage the Union, pulls back to join Major General Pierre G.T. Beauregard.

In other activity, Union troops from General Irvin McDowell's command, the 4th Brigade (Colonel I.B. Richardson), First Division, engage Confederates at Blackburn's Ford, where Beauregard happens to be on this day with Longstreet's force, Bonham's brigade, contin-

gents of Evans' brigade, and some artillery and cavalry, the latter at Stone's Bridge. Portions of the 1st Massachusetts, 2nd and 3rd Michigan and 2nd U.S. Cavalry participate against the Confederates under the command of Brigadier General James Longstreet (West Point, 1842).

A turbulent skirmish develops; the Rebels fire artillery from concealed positions. Reinforcements move up and lead another attack against the Rebel positions, but to no avail. By about 1600, McDowell, aware that an attack against the left flank would also fail, orders a retreat to Centreville. The Union suffers 19 dead and 38 wounded. The Confederates sustain 16 dead and 53 wounded. General Beauregard remarks after hearing of the Confederate victory: "God be praised for your successful beginning."

In related activity, Union Brigadier General Robert Patterson, in Charlestown at about 0100, sends a telegram to General Winfield Scott detailing his intelligence regarding the enemy's condition at Winchester and that of his own forces, concluding with a question: "Should I attack?" But no reply is forthcoming. Patterson does not take the initiative to attack Winchester in support of General McDowell's ongoing offensive.

In Missouri, a contingent of the Union 1st Missouri Reserves led by Major Earl Van Horn skirmishes with a Confederate contingent led by Captain Duncan in a battle at Martinsburg that lasts several hours. The Union loses one killed and one wounded.

In Confederate general officer activity, Major Richard Heron Anderson (West Point, 1842) is appointed brigadier general.

July 19 (Friday) In Union activity, General Irwin McDowell's force at Centreville still expects to engage and vanquish the Confederates under Beauregard by capturing the Manassas Gap Railway, thereby severing their supplies. McDowell prepares to attack on the following day subsequent to the receipt of supplies.

In Confederate activity, the forces of Generals Thomas Jonathan Jackson (soon to be nicknamed Stonewall) and Joseph E. Johnston move through Thoroughfare Gap, Virginia, en route to reinforce Pierre Gustave T. Beauregard at Manassas. Also, Secretary of State and Congressman Robert A. Toombs is appointed brigadier general. Toombs will participate in various actions, including that rigorous encounter at Sharpsburg (Antietam Creek), a bloodbath for both sides, during September 1862.

July 20 (Saturday) In Washington, D.C., General Winfield Scott receives a message from General Robert Patterson informing him that the Confederates have abandoned Winchester, Virginia, and are heading southeast toward Manassas. Patterson's forces remain in Charlestown and make no move to intercept or pursue Johnston's columns. Patterson receives orders to move to Harper's Ferry and occupy it.

In related activity, General Irvin McDowell, lacking supplies and ammunition, is unable to

begin an attack. In conjunction, the enlistment of some of McDowell's force has expired and they are en route home. The 4th Pennsylvania and one artillery battery move to Washington, D.C., and from there to their homes in Pennsylvania, leaving McDowell with a force of about 28,000 troops, including infantry and cavalry, plus forty-nine cannon. In addition, the reserve force of about 5,000 troops under General Theodore Runyon remains available.

The Union offensive begins at 0200 on the following morning, supposedly allowing time to arrive at Stone's Bridge by 0400 to initiate a diversionary attack while the main body (Second and Third Divisions under David Hunter and Samuel P. Heintzleman, respectively) strikes at the rear of the Confederate lines. In the meantime, the 4th Brigade, Second Division, under Colonel (later major general) Israel Bush Richardson is to remain at Centreville on the far left standing in reserve, and the 1st Brigade, First Division, under Colonel (later brigadier general) Erasmus Darwin Keyes is to hold the road that leads to Manassas.

General Irvin McDowell remains convinced that General Robert Patterson is holding Johnston's force at Winchester, unaware that he has effortlessly moved out to join General Beauregard. Ironically, General Beauregard has himself been planning an offensive, also to be initiated on the 21st, but at a later hour.

In Confederate activity, General William Wing Loring at about this time assumes command of the Northwestern Army (West Virginia). Subsequently, he will be relieved of duty with General Jackson and transfer to southwestern Virginia and from there to the Vicksburg area.

July 21 (Sunday) FIRST BATTLE OF BULL RUN (MANASSAS) Roaring Union cannon announce the beginning of the battle in Virginia, as Union troops struggle forward against darkness on small, unfamiliar roads toward their objective. When the Union guns strike the Rebels under Colonel Nathan George Evans (West Point 1848) at Stone Bridge on the left flank of the Confederate positions, Evans, believing the attack to be the main event, calls for reinforcements. Meanwhile, the guns of the Fifth Artillery, in support of Daniel Tyler's First Division, maintain their fire. Evans, believing the main attack will strike his left flank, decides at 0830 to redeploy his force. He leaves four companies of Colonel John B.E. Sloan's 4th South Carolina Regiment to hold the bridge, taking the remainder of the regiment, five Companies of Major C.R. Wheat's Louisiana battalion and two guns of Latham's battery, to the Brentsville Road to intercept the expected assault. In addition, Colonel Philip George St. Cocke's 5th Brigade is deployed at Ball's Ford, and with the absence of Evans, the 5th Brigade holds the line near the Stone Bridge until just prior to the arrival of Colonel Arnold Elzey's reinforcements (1st Maryland Infantry).

Colonel (later general) Nathan Evans' decision to move proves to be a large plus for the Confederates, as by redeploying his force they

General Michael Corcoran (Johnson, *Campfire and Battlefield: History of the Conflicts and Campaigns*, 1894).

A family waves to Union troops advancing toward Manassas (Johnson, *Campfire and Battlefield: History of the Conflicts and Campaigns*, 1894).

stand as a solid line against the Yankees. Meanwhile, the 5th Brigade attacks on the left and performs extremely well. While the Union is maintaining the rear attack at Stone Bridge, Colonel Ambrose Burnside, following a tough journey on nasty roads, brings up his 2nd Brigade, Second Division, arriving at about 1000. Nevertheless, the Confederates hold the line for nearly one hour of incessant firing. The Confederates under Pierre G.T. Beauregard and Jackson had in the meantime realized that the assault against Stone Bridge is a diversionary tactic, and troops from Colonel Nathan Evans' command temporarily stifle the main Union advance, led by General Irvin McDowell.

Upon the arrival of Colonel William T. Sherman's 3rd Brigade, First Division, and shortly thereafter the tardy arrival of General Samuel P. Heintzelman's 3rd Division, the Union plunges forward as the Confederate lines begin to falter under the pressure. Contingents of Colonel Andrew Porter's 1st Brigade, Second Division, arrive to further bolster the Union.

Confederate reinforcements under Generals Bernard E. Bee and Francis S. Bartow rush to stem the tide, to no avail. By about 1200, the Confederates withdraw to a point south of Stone Bridge. Meanwhile, Colonel Ambrose Burnside's brigade has expended its full supply of ammunition. The 3rd Brigade, 3rd Division, led by Colonel Oliver O. Howard, remains in the fight. The 1st Brigade, First Division, under Erasmus Darwin Keyes, is to hold the road leading to Manassas. Keyes and the 3rd Brigade, First Division, under William T. Sherman, are still on the move. The southerners retreat in disarray to Henry House Hill where Jackson's brigade is holding firm, bolstered by thirteen guns widely distributed around the area.

With the influx of troops, Jackson is now bolstered by the brigades of Bartow, Bee and Nathan G. Evans. General Bee shouts, "There stands Jackson like a stone wall. Rally behind the Virginians." Bee's encouragement coupled with the arrival of Johnston and Beauregard permits time for the Confederates to pull their disorganized troops together.

The rejuvenated Rebels are zealously inspired by Jackson and prepared to drive the exhausted Yankees back to Washington. Near Henry House, atop the hill that dominates the terrain,

the New York Zouaves (late Colonel E.E. Ellsworth's Regiment), supported by artillery of Charles Griffin and James B. Ricketts, launch a charge to secure the hill, but they are intercepted by a defiantly bold Alabama regiment that has no intention of folding. The artillery is put out of action during the first barrage of fire, preventing any further advancement, and the batteries become jeopardized.

The Rebels then strike the flank of the Zouaves, while two detachments of the Confederate Black Horse Cavalry pound against their rear, prompting a quick displacement of the Zouaves. General Heintzleman directs the 1st Michigan and the 1st Minnesota Regiments to support the batteries, now naked, and retrieve the men, but neither can overcome the opposition to extricate either the guns or the artillerymen. Jackson repeatedly attempts to retrieve the guns, but without success, as the Zouaves and the New York 35th Regiment keep them at bay. Eventually, it is the Yankees who retrieve the guns.

While this action continues, Colonel William T. Sherman's brigade launches an assault to secure the Confederate batteries on the plateau that are hammering the Union attack, but following several attempts, the force of opposition compels Sherman to order a pull-back; during this heated battle, Colonel Michael Corcoran of the New York 69th Militia Regiment is wounded and captured. Colonel James Cameron, brother of the secretary of war and commanding officer, 79th New York Regiment, is also killed.

The devastation of the day spares neither side, as the Confederates also sustain horrible casualties. Generals Barnard E. Bee and Francis Bartow, leading the 4th Alabama and the 8th Georgia Regiments respectively, are both lost in the battle. The Confederates have also stymied the attempts of the 2nd Maine and the 3rd Connecticut under Colonels Charles D. Jameson and Chatfield, respectively, who attack to put eight guns entrenched at Robinson's buildings, but all attempts fail and the units are forced to retire.

By 1500, the Union force is nearly drained. The reserves, including by this time Burnside's brigade, which has been out of action since about noon, and Colonel Schenck's Brigade at Stone Bridge, are not called upon. And with the failure of Robert Patterson to corral Johnston at Winchester, the Confederates' ranks expand with the influx of reinforcements, including General Kirby Smith's command, the 6th N.C. Regiment commanded by Colonel Charles F. Fisher, and contingents of Colonel Arnold Elzey's brigade along with additional artillery. All of this Confederate strength faces Irvin McDowell's overtired 13,000 remaining troops, none of whom have bolted across Bull Run since 1200.

The Confederates, although equally exhausted from the grueling fighting, also have the advantage of defending positions. Beauregard orders an attack to penetrate McDowell's right flank and slice into his rear, hoping to finish the job before both sides are forced

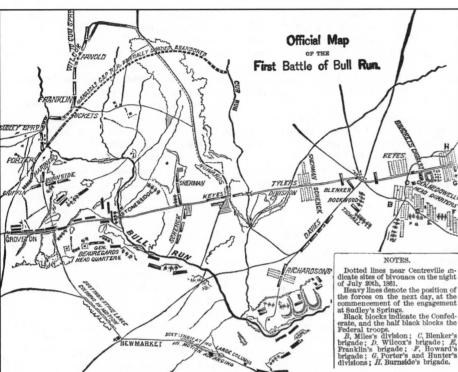

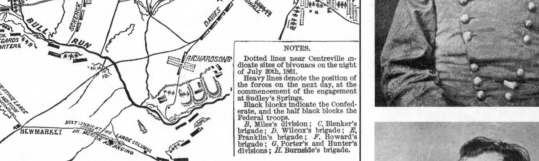

The First Battle of Manassas (Mottelay, *The Soldier in Our Civil War*, 1886).

through exhaustion to disengage. Colonel Elzey — leading the 10th, 13th and 28th Virginia, the 1st Maryland (his regiment), the 2nd and 8th South Carolina and the 3rd Tennessee — initiates a thunderous attack against the Union flank and soon recovers the plateau. In a synchronized maneuver, General Jubal A. Early, commanding the 24th Virginia Infantry, jack-hammers the rear, causing the seams of the Union lines, except for eight companies of regulars under Colonel George Sykes, to collapse.

General Jacob A. Cox's force of regulars covers the retreat, which to many seems totally undisciplined, but in fact, much has to do with the troops' lacking proper drilling. This does lead to chaos and disorder, especially as the civilians who had come to observe the contest are fleeing along the same roads so desperately needed by the Union troops. Nevertheless, Cox's troops hold the Rebels back until their positions become totally untenable.

While the Union troops are breaking for safety and the Confederates are in hot pursuit, all roads are leading toward Centreville and seemingly Confederate forces are blocking the routes at every point. Troops under Jubal Early, Jeb Stuart, Ellerbee Cash and Joseph Kershaw as well as John S. Preston, Wade Hampton (Gist Rifles/Hampton Legion) and James L. Kemper all join the chase, but it terminates as the Union makes it to Centreville Ridge. Beauregard con-

templates a continuance of the attack, but considering the condition of his own forces and the threatening skies, he aborts pursuit.

Meanwhile, General McDowell deploys a brigade at Cub Run on the Warrenton Road, and other contingents under Andrew Porter and Louis Blenker join it to intercept the Confederates if they continue the attack. At Centreville, it is decided to continue the retreat to Washington to protect the capital. The march commences prior to midnight and continues until the columns reach the capital during the early morning hours. Union Brigadier General Daniel Tyler (West Point, 1819), 1st Connecticut Infantry Regiment, in apparent reaction to his execution of orders during the contest, is mustered out of the army the following month.

Union losses at Bull Run amount to over 2,700 killed, wounded or missing. Battery D, 5th U.S. Artillery, loses every gun except one. Lt. Adelbert Ames (West Point, 1861) is seriously wounded while directing artillery fire. He refuses to leave the field and while atop a caisson he continues to direct the fire. He becomes a recipient of the Medal of Honor.

Also, Captain (later brigadier general) James B. Ricketts, in command of a battery, is wounded four separate times during the engagement and is captured then held until exchanged during January 1863. Also, Colonel Robert Cowdin (1st Massachusetts Infantry) is unscathed; however, his horse is shot from under

Top right: General Pierre G.T. Beauregard. *Middle:* General Thomas "Stonewall" Jackson (Johnson, *Campfire and Battlefield: History of the Conflicts and Campaigns,* 1894). *Bottom:* General Barnard Bee (Mottelay, *The Soldier in Our Civil War,* 1886).

him and killed during the fighting. Colonel Orlando Bolivar Willcox (1st Michigan Infantry), leading a brigade (General Heintzelman's division) is wounded after having led repeated charges, but he is also captured and held in captivity until August 1862. Colonel Willcox's conduct does not go unnoticed, but his heroism in the field is not officially recognized until thirty-four years after the battle, when he becomes a recipient of the Medal of Honor on 2 March 1895.

Colonel (later major general) Henry Warner Slocum (27th New York) is wounded. In addition, Brigadier General George W. Taylor is mortally wounded while attempting to reach the bridge that spans Bull Run. His brigade lacks artillery and is struck by Confederate Colonel Isaac Trimble's command, bolstered by two batteries. General Taylor dies in Alexandria on 1 September.

Confederate losses are over 1,900 killed, wounded, or missing, including Brigadier General Barnard Elliott Bee (West Point, 1845) and General Francis Bartow of the 7th Georgia Regiment. Bee is fatally wounded and succumbs on the following day at his headquarters. Confederate Colonel Clement H. Stevens, the brother-in-law of General Bee, is wounded during this action. Stevens will afterwards be elected colonel of the 24th South Carolina. Also, Confederate Lt. Colonel William Montgomery Gardner (West Point, 1846) is severely wounded. He remains on sick leave for about one year and afterward is unsuitable for field command. Nonetheless, he is promoted to brigadier general during the latter part of this year. Also, Colonel Charles F. Fisher, 6th North Carolina, is mortally wounded.

This first battle of Bull Run, witnessed by Confederate President Jefferson Davis, is a costly victory for the South. Many of the Union soldiers exhaust their ammunition during the contest and the defenses at Washington are fragile, but the Confederates fail to follow up their victory with pursuit. The Union quickly fortifies Washington to prepare it for an anticipated attack, which does not materialize.

During the federal retreat, Captain Richard Arnold (West Point, 1850 and later brigadier general) of the 5th Artillery loses all but one gun while covering the withdrawal. The surviving gun is saved by the heroic actions of Corporal Owen McGough, who becomes a recipient of the Medal of Honor for his gallantry under fire. Colonel (later brigadier general) Michael Corcoran, 69th New York Infantry, is wounded and captured. Corcoran, born in Ireland, has previously been subjected to a court-martial during 1860 for refusing a direct order to parade his command, known as the "Irish Legion," past the Prince of Wales, who was visiting the United States. Also, Union Colonel Oliver Otis Howard (West Point, 1854) sees his command (four regiments) retreat in disarray, but headquarters in Washington promotes him to brigadier general during early September for his actions at Bull Run.

Union General William T. Sherman observes: "It is easy to criticize a battle after it is over, but all now admit that none others, equally raw in war, could have done better than we did at Bull Run." A contingent of 365 Marines, including twelve officers, commanded by Major John C. Reynolds, participates as part of the Union Army's 1st Brigade.

In Confederate activity, after the first battle of Manassas (Bull Run), General Beauregard decides to change the Confederate flag because of confusion when the Yankees and Confederates fill the field. The Confederate flag consists of a red background with two crossed blue stripes containing 13 stars. Eleven of the stars represent the secessionist states and two are for states the Confederacy claims (Missouri and Kentucky). Also, Brigadier General Theophilus Hunter Holmes (West Point, 1829) commands a brigade at this battle and subsequently leads a division at the Seven Days' Battle. General Pierre Gustave T. Beauregard is second in command to General Johnston at Bull Run (Manassas), and due to his actions at this battle will be promoted to general of the Armies of the Confederate States, effective July 21. In addition, the Confederate 5th Brigade, composed of the 8th, 18th, 19th, 28th and 49th Virginia Regiments, commanded by Colonel (later General) Philip St. George Cocke, participates in this action.

The Confederate 1st Virginia led by Colonel Patrick T. Moore (Longstreet's brigade) participates in this action. Moore receives a serious wound in the head that terminates his field duty until the closing days of the conflict; however, he will continue to serve the Confederacy and be promoted to the rank of brigadier

general during 1864. Also, following the battle, Confederate General Milledge Luke Bonham's Brigade is abolished. Consequently, he loses his command. During January of the following year, Bonham, a veteran of the Seminole Wars and the Mexican War, resigns from the service to become a member of the First Regular Confederate Congress. After the war he returns to his law practice. Also, Confederate Lieutenant Colonel (later brigadier general) John Echols leads his 27th Virginia Regiment at this battle. Colonel Arnold Elzey performs to the great satisfaction of his superiors and shortly after the battle, he is promoted to brigadier general.

In related activity, the Confederate Hampton's Legion Infantry Battalion is soon split up; the artillery becomes Hart's/Hulsey's Horse Artillery and is attached to Jeb Stuart's cavalry; the cavalry becomes the foundation of the 2nd South Carolina Cavalry, while the infantry retains the name Hampton's Legion under the leadership of Colonel (later lieutenant general) Wade Hampton. Also, Confederate Captain John D. Imboden, commanding officer of Staunton's Light Artillery, subsequent to his service at this action, will begin to establish the 1st Virginia Partisan Rangers (later 62nd Virginia Mounted Infantry).

In related activity, the 25th Alabama participates in the fight at Manassas; one of its officers, 2nd Lt. George Doherty Johnston, is appointed to the rank of brigadier general in 1864. Also, Colonel Whedbee Kirkland's 21st North Carolina Infantry Regiment participates at this action. Following this battle, the 21st North Carolina accompanies General Thomas "Stonewall" Jackson during the campaign in the Valley (1862).

In Confederate general officer activity, Brigadier General Pierre G.T. Beauregard is promoted to full general in the Confederate Army, effective this date. Also, Colonel Jubal Anderson Early (West Point, 1837) is commissioned brigadier general effective this date. Captain William Richard Henry, a cavalryman, succeeds Early as colonel of the 24th Virginia. General Early is assigned to the Army of Northern Virginia. He will be promoted to major general during January 1863, and due to his exploits in the various campaigns, Early will attain the rank of lieutenant general effective May 1864.

Also, Major Samuel Jones, chief of artillery to General Beauregard, is later promoted to the rank of brigadier general effective this day. Jones is again promoted during March 1862 to the rank of major general. And Major William Henry C. Whiting (West Point, 1845) is promoted to the rank of brigadier general. Whiting will initially serve in Virginia in command of a division and later is ordered to North Carolina to bolster the defenses of Fort Fisher.

In Naval activity, the Confederate privateer *Jefferson Davis* captures the vessel *Alvarado,* a bark transporting a cargo of hides and wool, off Massachusetts. It is taken as a prize and put into the Confederate Navy. This *Alvarado* is separate from another vessel, the schooner *Alvarado* pur-

Southerners in Richmond celebrate victory at First Manassas with a 100-gun salute (Mottelay, *The Soldier in Our Civil War,* 1886).

chased in Philadelphia on 13 August 1861 for the purpose of being purposely sunk in the South as one of the ships known as the "Stone fleet." However, no records exist to verify or disclaim its fate.

In Union general officer activity, William High Keim and Robert Patterson, with the Pennsylvania Volunteers, a regiment that has been part of the Washington defenses, are mustered out of service. Nevertheless, Keim is appointed brigadier general of volunteers on 20 December 1861 and Patterson, at present a major general of militia, is appointed brigadier general of volunteers on 15 April 1862, effective from 11 April 1862. Keim later becomes ill with fever during the campaign against Williamsburg.

July 22 (Monday) In Washington, D.C., it is apparent that the southern insurrection will not be over in a short period of time. The conflict is to be a war of rebellion. President Abraham Lincoln calls for an army of 555,000 men to volunteer for a period of three years.

In other activity, the large casualties sustained by both sides at the battle on the previous day prompt improvisation to acquire available hospital space to treat the wounded. One such facility is the Union General Hospital in Georgetown, Washington, D.C., which had been formerly known as the Union Hotel. Union troops in these hospitals and those in the field are quickly learning that since their stay away from home is lasting much longer than anticipated, communication with and from their families becomes a priority. Express companies such as the Adams Express Company pop into existence to deliver parcels and mail to the soldiers, lifting their spirits.

In Arkansas, Confederate General William Joseph Hardee, also known as "Old Reliable," at about this time becomes commander of the Confederate forces in Arkansas.

In Missouri, troops attached to General Thomas Sweeny — the 1st Iowa Volunteers, 2nd Kansas Volunteers, the Stanley Dragoons (Captain David S.) and Captain James Totten's Battery — clash with Confederates at Forsyth in a skirmish that lasts about one hour. The Union sustains three wounded. The Confederates sustain five killed.

In West Virginia, Confederate General Loring arrives at Monterey and assumes command of the Army of the Northwest.

In Union general officer activity, Thomas Ogden Osborn is commissioned lieutenant colonel of the 39th Illinois Infantry Regiment at about this time. On 1 January he is appointed colonel of the regiment. Also, David Stuart, a lawyer and former Congressman, is commissioned lieutenant colonel (later brigadier general) of the 42nd Illinois Infantry Regiment. Also, Horatio Phillips Van Cleve (West Point, 1831), who left the army during 1836, is commissioned colonel (later brevet major general) of the 2nd Minnesota Infantry Regiment.

July 23 (Tuesday) In New Mexico, the Union abandons Fort Buchannan.

In Virginia, Union Troops garrisoned at Newport News are on alert and working diligently on strengthening the fortifications. There is some cause for alarm when the 1st New York Regiment of Zouaves hears artillery fire, but it is only the friendly fire from the guns of Duryee's regiment, which is practicing.

In Union activity, Brigadier General William S. Rosecrans at about this time becomes commander of the Department of the Ohio, succeeding Major General McClellan, who will assume command of the Army of the Potomac.

In Union general officer activity, John Eugene Smith, a native of Switzerland who arrived in the U.S. when he was a young boy, is commissioned colonel (later brigadier general) of the 45th Illinois Regiment. Colonel Smith, a jeweler and goldsmith, had no military experience prior to the outbreak of war. He participates in the operations against Fort Henry and Fort Donelson. In addition, he leads a brigade at the battle of Shiloh.

July 24 (Wednesday) In Missouri, the 5th Missouri (Reserves) engages Confederates at Blue Mills. The skirmish costs the unit one killed and 12 wounded. Confederate casualties are unavailable.

In West Virginia, Confederates under Brigadier General Henry A. Wise positioned on Tyler's Mountain are unable to repel an assault by Union forces under Brigadier General Jacob Cox. The Union forces the Confederates under General Wise to begin a withdrawal from the Kanawha Valley.

In Union general officer activity, Elliott Warren Rice (later brigadier general) joins the army as a private in the 7th Iowa Regiment. He rises in the ranks to become major on 30 August and becomes colonel of the regiment during April of the following year.

July 25 (Thursday) In Washington, D.C., Congress authorizes an expansion of the United States Marine Corps, increasing it to 93 officers and 3,074 enlisted men.

In other activity, Congress during this month passes legislation authorizing the postponement of the payment of all governmental foreign obligations, ostensibly to use every available dollar for the war effort. The payments are to resume after a period of two years. This particular legislation is not especially well received in Mexico, which is suffering through bankruptcy. Mexico's creditors, located in England, France and Spain, decide to take matters into their own hands in October.

In New Mexico, troops from Fort Fillmore commanded by Major Isaac Lynde engage Confederate forces from Texas commanded by Colonel John Baylor at Mesilla, where the Confederates claim the territorial capital. Baylor's force numbers fewer than 100 troops of the 2nd Texas Mounted Rifles; however, soon after the Union launches the attack, the Texans return fire from

formidable positions and the first wave (1st U.S. Mounted Rifles) is repelled rather quickly. As they return to the main body composed of about 400 infantry troops, the commander chooses to disengage. After firing a couple of rounds from the artillery, the Union is ordered back to the fort. Within a few days, Fort Fillmore is abandoned without a fight as Lynde attempts to make it to Fort Stanton. En route, the Confederates intercept the column and its artillery wagons. Again, Lynde offers no resistance; he surrenders the command. Major Lynde is afterward discharged (officially on 25 November, 1861 by order of General McClellan) from the U.S. Army for his actions; however, subsequent to the close of hostilities, during November 1866, he is placed on the list of retired officers.

In West Virginia, General Rosecrans issues Special Order No. 1, which defines his 4th Brigade as the 1st and 2nd Kentucky Regiments, 11th and 12th Ohio Regiments, U.S. Volunteer Infantry Regiments, the 19th and 21st Ohio Volunteer Militia Regiments, elements of the 18th and 22nd Ohio Volunteer Militia; the Ironton Cavalry Regiment and other miscellaneous troops. The 4th Brigade is then designated the "Brigade of the Kanawha." Rosecrans also appoints Brigadier General Jacob Cox as brigade commander. Cox's brigade will remain in the Kanawha Valley until the early part of September, and during the period, will find itself opposed by Confederates under Generals John Floyd and Henry Wise.

July 25–27 In Missouri, Home Guards and contingents of the Kansas Cavalry clash with Confederates in and around Harrisonville. Casualty figures are unavailable.

July 26 (Friday) In Missouri, a contingent of the Missouri Home Guard engages Confederates in the vicinity of Rolla Missouri (Lane's Prairie). The Union sustains three wounded. The Confederates sustain one killed and three wounded.

In New Mexico, skirmishes have been occurring near Fort Fillmore, with the federal troops only temporarily holding off the Confederates. This day, a Union force composed of the 7th U.S. Infantry, bolstered by a battery and a detachment of rifles, led by Major Isaac Lynde, engages a Confederate force of lesser size near Mesilla. The Union sustains three killed and six wounded. The Confederates sustain 11 killed and wounded. The following day, the Union is trounced.

In Union general officer activity, Eleazer A. Paine (West Point, 1839) is appointed colonel of the 9th Illinois Regiment. Paine, a friend of President Lincoln, is commissioned a brigadier general on 3 September 1861. He is also a cousin of Union General Halbert Eleazer Paine.

In Confederate general officer activity, General Felix Zollicoffer (commissioned brigadier general July 9, 1861), at about this time becomes commander in East Tennessee. In conjunction, Zollicoffer acquires a quartermaster, Alfred E.

Jackson, who joins the Confederacy with the rank of colonel and later rises to the rank of brigadier general.

July 27 (Saturday) In Indiana, Major General Thomas Morris, having returned to Indiana following his service in command of the state's ninety day regiments, is honorably discharged. Within several weeks, he is offered and accepts a commission as major general from President Lincoln. However, the commission is not forthcoming, supposedly due to opposition by General McClellan, Morris' commander during the recent campaign in West Virginia. The next year Morris is again offered a commission, initially as a brigadier general and afterward as a major general. Nonetheless, Morris declines, stating that "self-respect forbade the acceptance of any other commission than that originally tendered and then withheld without any assigned cause."

In New Mexico, Union forces under Major Isaac Lynde, who had repelled a Confederate assault on their positions at Fort Fillmore on the 25th, now abandon the fort. Confederates under Captain John Baylor seize the fort, capturing approximately 420 men. Portions of the U.S. Mounted Infantry and 7th U.S. Infantry participate at this battle. Major Lynde and Captain Alfred Gibbs (West Point, 1846) are among the captured. Gibbs will be exchanged the following year and again participate with the cavalry. He is promoted to the rank of brigadier general during October 1864. Lynde is also exchanged. He serves for the duration, but promotions are not forthcoming. Lynde, still at the rank of major, resigns from the army during 1866.

Second Lieutenant James S. Brisbin is wounded twice during the fight. Brisbin will become brigadier general during May of 1865. During his post–Civil War service, he will lead a battalion of General John Gibbon's command during the Little Big Horn campaign of 1876. In addition, another officer and veteran of the

The Union force under General Nathaniel Banks evacuates Hampton, Virginia, on the James River in the face of a large Confederate force advancing toward the town (Mottelay, *The Soldier in Our Civil War*, 1886).

Mexican War, Joseph Haydn Potter (West Point, 1843), is captured. Potter, later brigadier general, is exchanged during the following year and afterward appointed colonel of the 12th New Hampshire Regiment.

In Virginia, Major General Benjamin Franklin Butler, concerned that Confederates in force are moving against his positions at Hampton, orders a retirement and the destruction of some buildings, including the jail and Oddfellows hall, prior to departing.

In Union general officer activity, General George B. McClellan replaces General McDowell as commander of the Army of the Potomac. McClellan strives to turn his raw recruits into a skilled fighting force. His endeavor is successful. General John A. Dix succeeds Major General Nathaniel P. Banks as commander of the Department of Pennsylvania with headquarters in Baltimore. Banks receives command of the Department of the Shenandoah. In addition, Conrad Feger Jackson is appointed colonel of the 9th Pennsylvania Reserves, a three-month regiment.

July 28 (Sunday) In Missouri, Confederate forces occupy New Madrid. Also, a contingent of Confederates attacks the Union positions at Hickory Hill and encounter fierce resistance. Three companies of a regiment commanded by Colonel James Mulligan, bolstered by several companies of Home Guards, steadfastly hold their ground and repel the assault. Casualty figures are unavailable; however, the Union does seize some prisoners. In Tennessee, the 16th Tennessee Regiment, having departed Haynesville on the previous day, arrives at Bristol, Tennessee, but it remains there only until the following day. Orders arrive on the 28th directing the regiment to repair to Lynchburg, Virginia. Afterward, on 1 August, it moves to Staunton, where it remains until 3 August, when it receives orders to move to Charlottesville. Other Confederate regiments are also being shuffled. The 16th ends its point-to-point movement when it arrives at Huntersville on 8 August, when it becomes part of General Loring's brigade.

In Naval activity, the USS *St. Lawrence,* on patrol outside of Charleston, South Carolina, detects the Confederate privateer *Petrel* (formerly the revenue cutter *Aiken*). The *Petrel,* commanded by Captain William Perry, succeeds in slipping out of Charleston, but the vessel becomes imperiled when it encounters the USS *St. Lawrence,* which is poised to trap the prey. The *Petrel* mistakenly identifies the frigate *St. Lawrence* as a merchant ship when it

observes all of the latter's ports closed. The *Petrel* moves close and fires several shots, anticipating a quick seizure; however, the innocent looking frigate responds immediately and hurls a thunderclap of fire. At least one of the shells scores devastating results when it explodes in the hull, terminating the engagement instantly as the *Petrel* begins to sink. The *St. Lawrence* sends boats to rescue the crew, and all but four of the 36-man crew is brought to safety aboard the *St. Lawrence.* Nonetheless, the crew is not given a heroes' welcome; rather, their hands and legs are bound and they are transferred to the USS *Flag,* which lands them in Philadelphia 6 August. They are then held for trial in Moyamensing prison. The *Petrel* is separate from the *Petrel II* (formerly *Duchess*), a tinclad wooden steamer that joins the Union service (Mississippi Squadron) during December 1862.

July 29 (Monday) In Naval activity, the steamer USS *Freeborn,* supported by a contingent of Union troops, engages a Confederate force commanded by Colonel Ruggles at Matthias Point, Virginia. The Union sustains one casualty. The Confederates sustain about three or four casualties. In other activity, General John Pope (West Point, 1842) is appointed brigadier general on June 14, effective May 17. He assumes command of Union forces in Northern Missouri. He is the brother-in-law of General Manning F. Force. They married sisters.

July 30 (Tuesday) In Illinois, the Union reinforces the Garrison at Cairo in the face of a possible attack by Confederate forces under Generals Gideon Johnson Pillow and Jeff Thompson (Thompson's Raiders). The steam vessels *City of Alton, Empress, January, Jeanie Dean, Graham, Louisiana, War Eagle* and *Warsaw* arrive, transporting about 4,000 troops under General John Charles Frémont. With Cairo fortified, General Benjamin M. Prentiss will be directed to occupy Cape Girardeau, Ironton and Pine Knob, Missouri, which it is believed will become primary targets of the Confederates.

General Gideon J. Pillow had earlier been engaged in business dealing with Nathan B. Forrest and Robert V. Richardson; the latter serves with Pillow during the beginning stages of the war, but later, he establishes the 12th Tennessee Cavalry and is assigned duty with General Forrest. Also, Jeff Thompson is a former mayor of St. Louis, Missouri.

In Union activity, Isaac Stevens (West Point, 1839) is appointed colonel of the 79th New York Infantry, known as the Highlanders. Stevens succeeds Colonel James Cameron, who was killed at the First Battle of Manassas (Bull Run). At the time of this appointment, there is great turmoil in the regiment and the situation is escalating toward mutiny; however, Stevens, although of minor stature, about one inch taller than five feet, quells the trouble and gains respect from the troops.

July 31 (Wednesday) In Louisiana, Confederate Captain George N. Holland assumes command of the naval station at New Orleans. He succeeds Commander L. Rousseau.

In Missouri, one day after the offices of governor, lieutenant governor and secretary of state had been declared vacant, Hamilton Gamble is elected governor in place of Claiborne Jackson, a pro-Confederate governor.

In Confederate general officer activity, Lt. Colonel Gabriel J. Rains (West Point, 1827), 5th U.S. Infantry, resigns his commission with the intent to join the Confederacy. Rains is appointed brigadier general the following September.

August *In Confederate general officer activity,* Thomas Reade Rootes Cobb, brother of Confederate General Howell Cobb, is appointed colonel of "Cobb's Legion 28," which he founded after leaving the Confederate Provisional Congress. Thomas Cobb will be promoted to brigadier general during November 1862.

In Texas, the 8th Texas Cavalry (Terry's Texas Rangers) is formed this month, and the following month it becomes part of the Confederate Army.

August 1 (Thursday) Brazil declares neutrality in the ongoing civil war in the United States.

In Illinois, the federal arsenal at Springfield is hard pressed to supply the Union troops in the region with the needed weaponry. Alexander B. Dyer (West Point, 1837) is in charge of the armory. He will be appointed brigadier general during 1864 and become chief of ordnance, subsequent to the retirement of General James W. Ripley. Initially, he is based at the Springfield armory.

In Union activity, Joseph Tarr Copeland at about this time (August) is commissioned lieutenant colonel of the 1st Michigan Cavalry. Copeland's regiment participates in the Shenandoah Campaign. In August 1862, Copeland becomes colonel of the 5th Michigan Cavalry. Lewis Addison Grant is commissioned a major (later brevet major general) in the 5th Vermont Regiment at about this time. Also, Joseph Farmer Knipe is commissioned colonel of the 46th Pennsylvania Volunteer Infantry. He participates under General Nathaniel P. Banks in the Shenandoah Valley and the Battle of Cedar Mountain. Later he participates at Gettysburg.

Joseph Andrew Jackson Lightburn is commissioned colonel of the 4th West Virginia Infantry at about this time (August). He participates in various actions in West Virginia prior to being transferred to the Vicksburg region. Daniel Henry Rucker, a veteran of the Mexican War, attached to the Quartermaster's Department at the opening of hostilities, is promoted to major. He sees no field duty; however, he receives the brevet of major general of volunteers and in the Regular Army prior to the end of hostilities. In conjunction with the reorganization of the U.S. Army in 1866, General Rucker is appointed assistant quartermaster general with the rank of colonel. On 13 February 1882,

he is promoted to brigadier general; less than two weeks later, he retires.

In Confederate general officer activity, George Gibbs Dibrell (later brigadier general), who had previously joined the Confederate Army as a private, is elected lieutenant colonel of his regiment. Subsequently, during September 1862, he establishes the 8th (also known as 13th) Tennessee Cavalry. Also, Randall Lee Gibson, an aide to Governor Thomas Overton Moore of Louisiana, is appointed colonel (later brigadier general) of the 13th Louisiana Infantry. Gibson is a lawyer and has no military experience. The regiment participates at Shiloh and during the Kentucky campaign.

John Wilkins Whitfield, a veteran of the Mexican War, raises a company of cavalry in Texas at about this time (August). The company is known as Whitfield's Rifles. Subsequently, he becomes colonel (later brigadier general) of the 27th Texas, and afterward he commands Whitfield's Legion. Whitfield, born in Tennessee, had moved to Missouri during the early 1850s and for some time had been Indian agent in Arkansas and Missouri. Later, after some time in Kansas, he relocated to Texas.

In Naval activity, at about this time (August), the *Augusta,* a side wheel steamship built during 1852, is acquired by the U.S. Navy and transformed into a gunboat. Commissioned the USS *Augusta,* the vessel is retained by the navy until December 1868, when it is sold and renamed the *Magnolia.* The *Magnolia* afterward sails between New York and the southern states until lost in a storm on 30 September 1877.

Also at about this time, the U.S. Navy acquires the *DeSoto* (a wooden side-wheel steamship). The vessel, built in Brooklyn, New York, during 1859, is transformed into a gunboat and assigned duty in the Gulf Blockading Squadron. It initiates patrols as a blockade ship. During its service in the Gulf, its crews seize more than twenty blockade runners. During June 1864 it is taken out of service for repairs and remains inactive until the war comes to a conclusion. The *DeSoto* is recommissioned in August 1865 and remains in service until it is sold in 1868. This *DeSoto* is separate from the side-wheeled steamer taken by the Confederates during 1861, surrendered at Island No. 10, then renamed the USS *General Lyon.*

August 2 (Friday) **In Washington, D.C.,** Congress authorizes 500,000 additional troops and a sum of 5 million dollars with which to end the war. At this time the monthly rate of pay for colonels and lower rank is as follows: colonels, $218.00; lieutenant colonels, $194.00; major, $175.00; captain, $108.50; first lieutenant, $108.50; second lieutenant, $103.50; brevet second lieutenant $103.50; first or orderly sergeant, $29.00; other sergeants, $27.00; corporals, $22.00; privates, $20.00 and musicians, $21.00.

In Missouri, Union forces of General Nathaniel Lyon defeat Confederate forces (General McCulloch's command) under Colonel John Sappington Marmaduke (West Point, 1857) at Dug

Springs in a battle that lasts about three hours. The Union 1st Iowa and the 3rd Missouri Volunteer Regiments, supported by contingents of the Missouri Light Artillery, participate. Union losses are four killed and 37 wounded. Confederate losses are 40 killed and about 40 wounded.

In New Mexico, Confederate forces under Colonel Baylor assault Fort Stanton, forcing the Union troops to abandon their positions.

In Naval activity, the *Florida* (wooden sidewheeled steamship), operating as a civilian vessel since 1850, is acquired by the U.S. Navy at about this time (August). It is transformed into a gunboat, commissioned the USS *Florida* during the following October and assigned to the South Atlantic Blockading Squadron. Toward the latter part of the war, the *Florida* is utilized as a supply ship and to transport Confederate prisoners. It remains in active service until decommissioned during April 1867; it is sold in December 1888 and renamed the *Delphine* (merchant steamer). Later it is acquired by Haiti and used as a warship, named the *Republique,* until the mid–1870s.

August 3 (Saturday) *In Union general officer activity,* Colonel Erasmus D. Keyes (West Point, 1832) is appointed brigadier general of volunteers effective May 17. Keyes, who participated at First Manassas, will participate during the Peninsular campaign without distinction; in 1864 he resigns from the service following a disagreement with General John Dix. In addition, James Wolfe Ripley (uncle of Confederate General Roswell Ripley) is appointed brigadier general in Union Army. Ripley, a graduate of West Point (1814), assumes a position in the Ordnance Department. Edward Winslow Hincks is appointed colonel of the 19th Massachusetts Infantry. Prior to this appointment, Hincks had been an officer in a ninety-day regiment (Massachusetts militia) and resigns this day to accept the colonelcy. Also, Major George Douglas Ramsay (West Point, 1820) is promoted to lieutenant colonel (later brigadier general). Before the war, Colonel Ramsay had commanded about ten separate arsenals. On 10 June 1863, he is promoted to colonel. In a political debate that year, President Abraham Lincoln prefers Ramsay as a successor to General James W. Ripley (chief of ordnance), and Edwin Stanton (secretary of war) is pushing for Captain George T. Balch.

In other activity, Lt. Colonel Lorenzo Thomas (West Point, 1823; chief of staff to General Winfield Scott since 1855), a veteran of the Seminole Wars in Florida, and of the Mexican war, where he served as chief of staff to General William O. Butler, is appointed adjutant general and with it, he is appointed brigadier general. Nevertheless, he is unable to gain the confidence of Secretary of War Edwin Stanton. Consequently, during 1863, General Thomas is ousted from Washington and sent to the Military Division of the Mississippi, assigned duty with organizing colored regiments. He remains there for the duration of the war. He retires from the army in 1869.

In Naval activity, a Union gunboat, the steamer USS *South Carolina*, exchanges blows with Confederate batteries at Galveston, Texas. The *South Carolina* had been acquired by the U.S. Navy during May 1861 and commissioned the same month. During its first several months on patrol off the coast of Texas, it either seizes or destroys more than twelve vessels that attempt to run the blockade. Later in the year, operating off Louisiana, it captures a sloop and three schooners.

August 5 (Monday) In Washington, D.C., the enlistment time for the Union Army is changed from three months to two years.

In Maryland, the 28th New York Regiment (volunteers), commanded by Lt. Colonel Brown, engages a contingent of Confederate Cavalry led by Captain Mead at Point of Rocks. The Union sustains no casualties. The Confederates suffer three killed, two wounded and about seven captured.

In Missouri, the 21st Missouri Home Guards and the 21st Missouri Volunteers, commanded by Colonel David Moore, engage a Confederate force composed of more than 1,000 troops, commanded by Colonel (later brigadier general) Martin Edwin Green, at Athens. The fighting lasts for about one hour. The Union suffers three dead, eight wounded; the Confederates have 14 dead and 14 wounded.

In Union general officer activity, Henry Goddard Thomas is commissioned captain (later brigadier general) of the recently raised 11th U.S. Infantry Regiment. Thomas, a lawyer, had initially joined the army as a private in the 5th Maine Regiment the previous April. Captain Thomas for the duration of the war is primarily involved with organizing and recruiting Negro troops. He becomes colonel of the 79th U.S. Colored Infantry, followed by command of the 19th Colored Infantry during January 1864.

In Naval activity, the Confederate privateer *Jefferson Davis* seizes the vessel *Windward*, a schooner transporting a cargo of salt, off Turk

Island in the Bahamas. The vessel *Alvarado*, recently captured by the CSS *Jefferson Davis*, is spotted by the USS *Jamestown* off Florida. The *Jamestown* forces the vessel to shore in the vicinity of Fernandina. Afterward, the *Alvarado* is burned.

August 6 (Tuesday) In Missouri, Union General Nathaniel Lyon arrives at Springfield. The commands of General Thomas W. Sweeny, Colonel Franz Sigel and Major Samuel D. Sturgis fall under his authority, but combined, his force numbers only slightly more than 5,000 troops. Southern Missouri contains at this time about 20,000 Confederates.

In Union general officer activity, Frederick West Lander is commissioned as brigadier general, effective May 17, 1861. He has participated with McClellan's forces at the recent battles at Philippi and Rich Mountain, West Virginia. Following his promotion, Lander assumes command of a brigade in General Charles P. Stone's division. Also, Thomas West Sherman (West Point, 1836) is appointed brigadier general effective 17 May. General Sherman is a veteran of the Mexican War and of the frontiers. He receives command of the land forces designated to attack Port Royal, South Carolina. In April 1862, General Sherman receives command of a division of the Army of Ohio. He leads the division during the operations against Corinth. He is ordered to New Orleans in August 1862. In other activity, Colonel Charles P. Stone is promoted to brigadier general, effective 12 May. Colonel Ambrose Burnside is promoted to brigadier general.

In Naval activity, the Confederate privateer *Jefferson Davis* seizes the vessel *Santa Clara* while it is en route from Puerto Rico to New York. Captain Louis M. Coxetter of the *Jefferson Davis* transfers the prisoners he had captured the previous day on the *Windward* to the *Santa Clara* and releases it.

August 7 (Wednesday) In Virginia, Confederate troops under Brigadier General John Banks Magruder occupy and burn the town of Hampton near Fortress Monroe. Only five of the approximately 500 houses and the town's Episcopal church are spared the flames. The 20th New York Regiment (Volunteers), commanded by Colonel (later brigadier general) Max Weber, engages the Confederates at Hampton. The Union reports no casualties. The Confeder-

Review of Confederate troops in front of the Pulaski Monument in Savannah prior to moving north to Virginia (Mottelay, *The Soldier in Our Civil War*, 1886).

ates sustain three killed and six wounded. Weber, who was operating a hotel in New York at the time of the outbreak of the war, established the Turner Rifles, which was incorporated into Union service during May of this year and named the 20th New York Regiment.

In Union general officer activity, Franz Sigel (major, 5th New York Militia) is appointed brigadier general, effective on 17 May. Also, Colonel Fitz John Porter (West Point, 1845), recently commissioned colonel of the 15th U.S. Infantry, is appointed brigadier general, effective 17 May.

August 8 (Thursday) In Virginia, the 16th Tennessee Regiment arrives at Huntersville. It is attached to a brigade commanded by General D.S. Donelson and attached to General Loring's division. Other Confederate units at Huntersville include the 8th Tennessee Regiment, the 48th Virginia Regiment, one Georgia regiment, one battalion of cavalry and one artillery battery. At this time, General Loring's division is encamped at Valley Mountain, and he is preparing to launch an attack against Union lines at Cheat Mountain. Confederate Generals Floyd and Wise are deployed along the Charleston Road near the Gauley River in the Kanawha Valley. They are threatening General Rosecrans; however, the brigades at Huntersville are to be held in reserve. Union General Joseph Reynolds is also at Cheat Mountain facing the threat from Loring (General Robert E. Lee's command). Nevertheless, the 16th joins General Loring at Valley Mountain on 8 September.

In Virginia, a 100-man contingent of the 19th New York Regiment (Volunteers), led by Captain Kennedy, engages a Confederate force at Lovettsville. The Union sustains no casualties. The Confederates suffer one killed and about five wounded.

In Union general officer activity, Union Colonel Henry Hayes Lockwood is appointed brigadier general. General Lockwood, a West

The USS *South Carolina* bombards Confederate batteries at Galveston, Texas, on 5 August 1861 (Mottelay, *The Soldier in Our Civil War*, 1886).

Point graduate, has seen service during the Mexican War on the USS *United States*. The general sees field service at Gettysburg, commanding troops of Slocum's XII Corps, and again at the outskirts of Washington to defend against Jubal Early. Lockwood will return to the Naval Academy after the war to resume his career teaching midshipmen, and after his death he is interred at Annapolis, a most unusual resting place for a general.

In Confederate general officer activity, the Union captain of dragoons, Beverly H. Robertson, who had changed his allegiance previously and throws his sympathies and services to the South, is officially dismissed from the U.S. Army. Robertson (West Point, 1849), already having received a commission in the Confederacy as a captain, will become colonel, 4th Virginia Cavalry. He leads his command in the Shenandoah Valley campaign of 1862 and reaches the rank of brigadier general following the death of General Turner Ashby (early June 1862). Also, William H. Payne, who enlists in the Confederate Army as a private and member of the Black Horse Cavalry, becomes a major (later brigadier general) in the 4th Cavalry. Subsequently, he leads the regiment in various actions in Virginia, including Williamsburg.

August 9 (Friday)   In Missouri, Union General Nathaniel Lyon departs Springfield for Wilson's Creek to engage General Ben McCulloch's force, which includes the commands of Confederate General Sterling Price (Missouri Militia) and Colonel James Edward Rains. The columns arrive in position to attack by about dawn on the following day. Union General Nathan Lyon expects to use the element of surprise to neutralize the additional strength of the enemy. His force, composed of one brigade under Major Samuel D. Sturgis and another under Lt. Colonel George Andrews, will assault the frontal lines, while another force under Colonel Franz Sigel (later major general) simultaneously attacks the Confederates' rear. The latter under Sigel is composed of the 3rd and 5th Missouri Volunteers, one company of recruits, one company of dragoons, led by Lt. C.E. Farrand, and one battery of six guns. General Thomas W. Sweeny, singularly opposed to the attack, does not participate.

General Lyon's force is composed of Sturgis' brigade, comprising a battalion of regular infantry, commanded by Captain Joseph B. Plummer (West Point, 1841), one battalion of Missouri volunteers, commanded by Major Peter J. Osterhaus (a Prussian), a company of mounted Kansas volunteers, led by Captain Wood, one company of 1st U.S. Cavalry, commanded by Lt. Charles W. Canfield, and a battery of artillery, commanded by Captain James Totten. General Lyon's second brigade is commanded by Lt. Colonel Andrews, and is composed of the 1st Missouri Volunteers, one battalion of regulars commanded by Captain Frederick Steele (West Point, 1843) and a battery of artillery (four pieces) commanded by Captain James Totten. His third brigade, commanded by Colonel (later brigadier general) George

Washington Dietzler (Kansas state militia), comprises the 1st Iowa, the 1st and 2nd Kansas Volunteers and about two hundred Missouri Mounted Home Guards.

In Union general officer activity, Ormsby MacKnight Mitchel (West Point, 1829) an instructor at the military academy, is appointed brigadier general (later major general) in the Union Army by President Abraham Lincoln. He will soon assume command of the Department of the Ohio. Also, Colonel Louis (Ludwig) Blenker is appointed brigadier general of volunteers. Colonel Israel Bush Richardson (West Point, 1841), 2nd Michigan Infantry Regiment, is promoted to brigadier general. John James Peck (West Point, 1843) is appointed brigadier general. General Peck had left the army during 1853. Also, Colonel Darius N. Couch, 7th Massachusetts, is named brigadier general effective 17 May. General Couch participates in the Peninsular Campaign (spring 1862). He commands a division in General Keyes' IV Corps until illness prompts him to resign his commission (July 1862); however, General McClellan chooses not to send Couch's resignation to the War Department.

Also, James S. Wadsworth, who had served as a volunteer at First Bull Run (Manassas) with General Irvin McDowell, is appointed as brigadier general on the recommendation of McDowell; however, he has no military experience. During March, 1862, he is appointed military governor of Washington, D.C. Subsequently, General Wadsworth commands the 1st Division, I Corps. Alfred Napoleon Alexander Duffie, a Frenchman who resigned his commission in the French Army to serve in the U.S. Army, is commissioned captain in the 2nd New York Cavalry (Harris Light Cavalry). The following October he rises to major, and by July 1862, he is promoted to colonel of the 1st Rhode Island. Randolph Marcy, on the staff of his son-in-law, General George McClellan, is appointed as one of four inspectors general of the U.S. Army. With the appointment, he receives the rank of colonel.

John Henry Martindale (West Point, 1835) is appointed brigadier general. He runs into difficulty while participating in the Peninsular Campaign. He is investigated by a court of inquiry, instigated by General Fitz John Porter, on charges of declaring that he would surrender rather than leave his wounded behind after Malvern Hill. Nevertheless, Martindale is acquitted and afterward assigned to new duty: military governor of Washington, D.C. William Reading Montgomery (West Point, 1825), a veteran of the Mexican War (8th Infantry), is appointed brigadier general. General Montgomery, subsequent to the outbreak of hostilities, had organized the 1st New Jersey Volunteer Regiment and became its colonel. Nonetheless, he does not receive field command. General Montgomery commands at various places, including Annapolis and Philadelphia. His health deteriorates and he is compelled to resign during April 1864.

In yet other activity, George Webb Morell

Brigadier General Louis Blenker (Mottelay, *The Soldier in Our Civil War*, 1886).

(West Point, 1835) is appointed brigadier general of volunteers. Before the war Morell was a colonel and quartermaster with the New York militia, and after the eruption of war, he had served in Washington regarding defenses of the capital. General Morell participates in the Peninsular Campaign as a brigade commander in General Fitz John Porter's V Corps. Also, Colonel Henry Warner Slocum is promoted to brigadier general.

In Confederate general officer activity, Colonel Isaac Ridgeway Trimble (West Point, 1822) is appointed brigadier general; during January of the following year he is promoted to major general. Also, Colonel Daniel Ruggles (West Point, 1833) is commissioned brigadier general.

August 10 (Saturday)   THE BATTLE OF WILSON'S CREEK (SPRINGFIELD AND OAK HILL) At Wilson's Creek, Missouri, at about 0500, Union guns, the batteries of Captain James Totten (West Point, 1805) and Lt. John Van Deusen Du Bois (West Point, 1855), announce the presence of the Yankees; however, the Confederates, under General Ben McCulloch, themselves making preparations to assault the Union at Springfield, are up for the fight, reducing the element of surprise. Nevertheless, the Union makes progress against the Confederate Missouri Guards under Generals (state troops) John Bullock Clark Jr., J.H. McBride, William Y. Slack and Mosby Monroe Parsons. The Union Infantry, supported by the mounted horse guards, pushes the Rebels back beyond some hills. The 1st Iowa and 1st Missouri Regiments secure the ground, protected by the guns of Totten in the heights and those of DuBois to the rear, staring down toward the concealed Confederate batteries.

Meanwhile, Colonel Franz Sigel plows

against the rear and forcefully drives the Rebels into the woods. His 1,200 troops and six guns convince Confederate Colonel Ben Brown and Colonel Thomas J. Churchill (1st Arkansas Mounted Rifles) to seek more tenable positions. Sigel, like Lyon, continues to advance, but neither is aware of the other's progress. Many of the Rebels also wear blue uniforms, causing confusion on the field.

At General Lyon's positions, a large contingent of troops, thought surely to be Union, seem to be approaching the guns, but when they reach a point close to the line, like the pirates of old, the Rebels replace the Union colors with the Stars and Bars, revealing their identity. The ploy works perfectly, but only for awhile, as the effective fire of the Union's guns turn the force back, essentially saving the guns and the battalion of regular infantry, led by Captain Joseph Plummer (West Point, 1841).

In the meantime, to the rear, a similar experience befalls Franz Sigel as he notices that the intensity of the firing of the Union guns had slackened immensely, giving him the false impression that the Confederates had been beaten at the front. He continues the advance driving down Fayetteville Road and soon after, he is informed that friendly troops are approaching. Upon this seemingly good news, Sigel brings his columns to a halt to await what he expects to be the forces of Lyon. And then as the advancing columns of blue get within close range of Sigel's line, the Stars and Stripes vanishes and is replaced the Stars and Bars, followed by a enfilade of incoming fire. This new unexpected action, including a deadly continuing sheet of fire emerging from concealed artillery positions, causes horrendous problems for the Union. Lyon's line collapses as the troops scatter, and in an instant, their discipline vanishes.

The Confederate fire relentlessly rakes the Union column, kills the artillery's horses and collapses the flank. The successful ruse nearly costs Sigel his entire force. About 300 troops, including Sigel, manage to pull back, dragging one gun out of six with them and accomplishing that feat only by compelling some reluctant Confederate prisoners to pull the cannon from harm's way.

All the while, the forces of Lyon continue to hold their own against the Rebels, but still there is no word of Sigel's action in the rear. Suddenly the Confederate pressure bursts through the line to the left of Totten's battery. As the Rebels make progress, General Lyon alters his plans, transferring Major Frederick Steele's battalion of regulars to bolster the gap and rally the troops. Steele holds the line as his troops forge an impenetrable wall of fire. Both sides fight to a stalemate for about one hour.

General Lyon moves between the enfilade of fire to maintain morale and discipline, but a shot kills his horse and another shell wounds him in the leg, then yet another shot strikes him in the head. He somehow changes horses and rejoins the battle, ignoring his severe wounds to lead a cavalry charge to change the tide and bring the momentum back to his army.

The 1st Kansas and 1st Iowa Regiments, having lost their commanders, mount a bayonet charge, led by General Lyon. At about 0900, while ferociously engaged in the attack, he receives another wound, his third, but this last one is mortal and he is taken from the field. At this time, subsequent to about four constant hours of combat, the Union has been able to forestall defeat, and they have reclaimed and held the previously lost ground.

The command passes to Major Samuel Davis Sturgis, who still has no intelligence regarding Sigel's action in the rear. While information is sought, Major Sturgis is confronted by another ruse by the Confederates facing him. They slowly approach in blue uniforms presenting themselves as friendly troops, but as they encroach, the Stars and Stripes is again replaced with the Confederate colors when the assault begins. The Union lines meet the grueling attack and hold the ground, driving the Rebels back; however, the unrelenting pressure and the superior numbered Rebels regroup and mount yet another charge. This surge turns the tide. Sturgis, still unaware of Sigel's plight, has no alternative. He orders a retreat following six hours of incessant battle and begins the trudge to Springfield, joined by the survivors of Sigel's command as they retire, arriving back at Springfield at the conclusion of the nine-mile march at about 1700.

The Union suffers 223 killed, 721 wounded and 291 missing. The Confederates have 265 killed, 800 wounded and 30 missing. Union Brigadier General Nathaniel Lyon (West Point, 1841) is mortally wounded while charging Confederate positions during the engagement; his body remains on the field and is recovered by Confederates. Also, Colonel Robert Byington Mitchell (2nd Kansas Infantry) is severely wounded. Confederate General Sterling Price (Missouri Militia) ensures that General Lyon's body is returned to

Springfield; however, soon after, the Union troops under Colonel Sigel retire from Springfield and again General Lyon's remains are left behind. Confederates under General J. B. Clark prepare his remains for burial and deliver the body to Mrs. J.S. Phelps, who arranges internment. Later, General Lyon's body is removed and is buried at East Hartford, Connecticut.

Colonel (later brigadier general) George Washington Dietzler, 1st Kansas Volunteers, sustains a severe wound that incapacitates him for a prolonged period of time. Union Pvt. Nicholas Boquet, Company D, 1st Iowa Infantry, at great risk, saves a Union cannon from capture and after the ordeal is awarded the Congressional Medal of Honor for his bravery. The 1st Cherokee Mounted Rifles under Stand Watie (later brigadier general) participate at this battle.

In Missouri, a contingent of the Missouri Home Guards engages a group of Confederates at Potosi. The Union suffers one killed. The Confederates sustain two killed and three wounded. In other activity, a Union contingent skirmishes with Confederates at Charleston. The Union sustains one killed and six wounded, including Colonel Thomas E. Ransom. The Confederates sustain 40 killed.

In Union general officer activity, Union Captain Charles Champion Gilbert (West Point, 1846) is wounded. Gilbert is subsequently promoted to brigadier general during September 1862 and commands the 3rd Provisional Corps at Perryville in October 1862, where he will be chastised for not contributing his support to General Alexander McCook, then under heavy pressure from the Rebels. Major Samuel D. Sturgis (West Point, 1846), who assumed command after the demise of General Lyon, is appointed brigadier general during the following March, effective the date of the Battle of Wilson's Creek.

In Confederate general officer activity, Captain (or Major) Francis Marion Cockrell, leading a company of Missouri militia, participates in this battle. Cockrell is promoted to brigadier general during July 1863. In addition, Colonel (later brigadier general) Thomas Pleasant Dockery commands the 19th Arkansas Infantry at this action. The Confederate 3rd Texas Cavalry, led by Colonel (later brigadier general) Elkanah B. Greer, participates in this battle, as does the 3rd Texas Cavalry, led by Lt. Colonel (later brigadier general) Walter P. Lane. At this time, Major General Sterling Price (Missouri State Guard) retains his title, given to him previously by former Missouri Governor Claiborne Fox Jackson; Price does not receive his appointment in the Confederate Army until April of the following year.

August 11 (Sunday) In *Union general officer activity,* Julius Stahel, a Hungarian originally named Julius Szamvald, who immigrated to the United States in 1859 after living in London and Berlin, is commissioned colonel of the 8th New York. Stahel and General Louis Blenker

The Battle of Wilson's Creek (Johnson, *Campfire and Battlefield: History of the Conflicts and Campaigns*, 1894).

had raised the regiment initially known as the 1st German Rifles. Colonel Stahel succeeds Blenker as colonel of the regiment. Also, Brigadier General (Connecticut militia) Daniel Tyler (West Point, 1819), who was commissioned colonel of the 1st Connecticut Regiment, a 90-day unit, musters out of the service this day; however, the following March he is commissioned brigadier general of volunteers. He participates in the operations against Corinth as a brigade commander. Following other duty regarding an investigation of General Buell's campaign in Kentucky and Tennessee, he becomes commander at Harpers Ferry in West Virginia and later at Baltimore. Subsequently, he commands the District of Delaware, but sees no further command in the field.

In Confederate general officer activity, John Buchanan Floyd, who had resigned his position as secretary of war in December 1860, joined the Confederacy and was named brigadier general the previous May, assumes command of the forces in the Kanawha Valley (West Virginia).

August 12 (Monday) In Texas at Fort Davis, Apaches led by Chief Nicholas had raided the fort, held only by one company of the 2nd Texas Mounted Rifles, commanded by Lt. Reuben E. Mays. Lt. May and a 14-man detachment gave chase, following the trail into Big Bend country, but on this day the Apaches ambush the contingent and the entire detachment is slain. The unit's Mexican guide is able to escape.

In Naval activity, the USS *Quaker City* (side-wheel steamer under charter to the U.S. Navy), built in Philadelphia during 1859, is purchased by the U.S. Navy. It is commissioned the following December. The USS *Lexington*, a sidewheel steamer constructed in Pennsylvania at Pittsburgh and acquired by the War Department following conversion to a gunboat, joins the Western Flotilla at Cairo, Illinois.

August 13 (Tuesday) In Missouri, the Union is facing some turmoil in the city of St. Louis, prompting action against the riots. Martial law will be put into place on the following day.

In West Virginia, a contingent of the 4th West Virginia Volunteers, composed of one company led by Captain Dayton, engages a contingent of Confederates, estimated at about 200, at Grafton. The Union sustains no casualties. The Confederates sustain some wounded.

In West Virginia, Colonel E.B. Taylor is directed by General William Rosecrans to move his 7th Ohio Regiment to Cross Lanes about twenty miles above General Jacob Cox's lines at Gauley Bridge, from where the 7th can defend Carnifex Ferry. By about this time, the Confederate forces in the region number about 8,000 troops, including about 2,000 militia from Fayette, Mercer and Raleigh Counties, commanded by Confederate General Augustus A. Chapman (militia). The Union anticipates an attack against Gauley Bridge.

In Union general officer activity, Major George Stoneman (West Point, 1846) is appointed brigadier general of volunteers.

In Confederate general officer activity, a Union officer, Frank Crawford Armstrong, who recently took the field at Bull Run (Manassas) in Union Blue, this day resigns his commission and changes his allegiance to the Confederacy. Armstrong will serve with Generals James McQueen McIntosh and Ben McCullouch. Later he becomes colonel of the 3rd Louisiana Infantry. He will subsequently be appointed brigadier general effective 20 January 1863. Also, Colonel Thomas Moore Scott (12th Louisiana) is promoted to brigadier general.

August 14 (Wednesday) In Washington, D.C., the 79th New York Regiment, which had performed admirably at Bull Run (Manassas), tarnishes its glory this day by initiating a mutiny. After it is suppressed, the regiment is stripped of its colors by direct order of Major General George B. McClellan.

In Missouri, in response to riots of the previous day, General Frémont declares martial law in St. Louis.

In Union general officer activity, President Lincoln appoints James W. Denver brigadier general of Volunteers, giving him command of the federal troops in the state of Kansas. General Denver later participates at Corinth in William Sherman's command. Also, Calvin E. Pratt is officially appointed colonel of the 31st New York Infantry Regiment; Pratt and another man had previously organized the regiment, and it did participate at the Battle of Bull Run (Manassas).

August 15 (Thursday) In Washington, D.C., the Department of Kentucky is incorporated into the Department of the Cumberland, which now includes the states of Kentucky and Tennessee.

In Missouri, tensions remain high. General Frémont becomes concerned that threats from Confederates require additional forces. Consequently, he requests reinforcements.

In West Virginia, by about this time, General Joseph Reynolds' force at and around Elkwater stands at about 9,000 troops, composed of one battalion of the 2nd West Virginia (Colonel Moss); 13th Indiana (Colonel J.C. Sullivan); 14th Indiana (Colonel Nathan Kimball); 15th Indiana (Colonel G.D. Wagner); 17th Indiana (Colonel M.S. Hascall); 3rd Ohio (Colonel Beatty); 6th Ohio (Colonel Anderson); 24th Ohio (Colonel Ammen); Battery G (Captain Howe), 14th U.S. Artillery; Loomis Michigan Battery; and two guns of the West Virginia Battery under Captain Daum. General Reynolds'

The colors of the 79th New York Regiment are stripped due to a mutiny at Washington on 14 August 1861 (Mottelay, *The Soldier in Our Civil War*, 1886).

force is also bolstered by one company of Indiana cavalry, commanded by Captain Bracken. Reynolds' supply depots are located at Clarksburg and Grafton. The cavalry is utilized to maintain communication with the depots as well as headquarters.

General Reynolds initiates defensive measures intended to assure a superior force does not penetrate the breastworks. Some complications develop because the various units are not dressed identically and some of the regiments don grey uniforms, causing false identification. The problem is quickly worked out and those resembling Confederates are re-outfitted in Union blues. Nonetheless, the uniforms, because they resemble Confederate uniforms, also give the Union some advantages. Union spies pass freely into Confederate lines without discovery and while there they gather intelligence. Consequently, the Union is able to obtain knowledge of a pending attack, permitting Reynolds to prepare his defenses at Elkwater and Cheat Mountain.

In the meantime, the Confederates continue to build their forces at nearby Huntersville, where General William W. Loring commands about 8,000 troops (Army of the Northwest) in his force, composed of three regiments from Tennessee under Colonels George E. Maney (1st Tennessee Regiment), Robert H. Hatton (7th Tennessee Regiment) and John H. Savage (16th Tennessee Regiment). Other forces include the 48th Virginia Regiment (Colonel James H. Campbell); 9th Virginia Infantry (Lt. Colonel James Gilliam); 9th Virginia Cavalry (William Henry Fitzhugh Lee); Burk's Virginia infantry; and 6th North Carolina (later 16th North Carolina, Colonel Stephen Lee). In addition, the 12th Georgia Infantry Regiment (Colonel Edward Johnson) is deployed, as well as two artillery batteries (Anderson's Virginia Lee battery, on Allegheny Mountain) and a battery under Lindsay M. Shumaker (Shoemaker).

Other Confederate forces in the area include those under General Henry R. Jackson, headquartered at Greenbrier (Green Briar). The units, totaling about 6,000 troops, include: 1st Georgia (Colonel James N. Ramsey, posted between Allegheny Mountain and Monterey);12th Georgia (Colonel R. Johnston); three Virginia regiments, the 44th under Colonel William C. Scott, the 37th under Samuel V. Fulkerson and the 52nd Virginia (between Allegheny Mountain and Monterey), under Colonel John B. Baldwin; 3rd Arkansas Regiment (Colonel Albert Rust); two batteries under Anderson and Shumaker and Major George Jackson's 14th Virginia Cavalry. William Taliaferro's 23rd Virginia is posted at Monterey.

Other units in West Virginia include the 37th North Carolina (Colonel Charles C. Lee) and the 21st Virginia (Colonel William Gilham), both deployed along the road that runs between Huntersville and Valley Mountain. General Robert E. Lee, dispatched from Richmond, is to command the troops. Upon his arrival, Lee distributes the forces of Generals Loring and Henry R. Jackson at Big Springs, located on Valley Mountain. Not realizing that General Joseph Reynolds has become aware of the plan, Lee prepares to move against Clarksburg and Grafton.

In Union general officer activity, at about this time, Union General Robert Anderson (West Point, 1825) assumes command of the Department of the Cumberland. He will depart from New York, where he has been since the surrender of Fort Sumter, South Carolina. Anderson will resign in ill health during 1863. William Passmore Carlin (West Point, 1850) is appointed colonel of the 38th Illinois Infantry. Also, Charles Edward Hovey, a former school teacher, is commissioned as colonel of the 33rd Illinois Infantry Regiment. The regiment is assigned duty in Missouri.

In Confederate general officer activity, former Lt. Colonel George Bibb Crittenden (brother of Union General Thomas L. Crittenden), who recently resigned his commission in

General George B. Crittenden (Johnson, *Campfire and Battlefield: History of the Conflicts and Campaigns*, 1894).

General Albert Pike (Johnson, *Campfire and Battlefield: History of the Conflicts and Campaigns*, 1894).

the U.S. to side with the Confederate cause, is appointed brigadier general; then on November 9, Crittenden (West Point, 1832) is promoted to the rank of major general. Confederate Colonel Roswell S. Ripley (West Point, 1823), who had occupied Fort Sumter at the time of its fall, is promoted to the rank of brigadier general effective this date.

Also, Albert Pike is promoted to brigadier general in the Confederate Army, effective this date. Subsequently, Confederates under General Pike establish Fort Davis (in honor of Confederate President Jefferson Davis) in present-day Muskogee County and designate it Confederate military headquarters for the Indian Territory (Oklahoma). The fort is destroyed by a Union force (under Colonel W. A. Phillips) on 22 December 1862.

August 16 (Friday)   In Washington, D.C., President Lincoln, by proclamation, terminates all trade with states that have seceded from the Union.

August 17 (Saturday)   In *Union activity,* Major General John E. Wool is recalled from retirement. He will replace Major General Benjamin Franklin Butler at Fortress Monroe and assume command of the Department of Southeastern Virginia. Butler prepares to launch an attack against Hatteras Inlet, North Carolina. Also, the Departments of Northeast Virginia, Washington and the Shenandoah are incorporated into the Department of the Potomac.

In other activity, Colonel George Henry Thomas is appointed brigadier general. Thomas (West Point, 1840), a veteran of the Mexican War with fifteen years' experience in the artillery service, had declined an offer to become the chief of ordnance for the state forces of Virginia during the previous March. He will soon depart for Kentucky and assume command at Fort Dick Robinson in eastern Kentucky during Sep-

tember. Also, Egbert Ludovicus Viele (West Point, 1847) is appointed brigadier general of volunteers. He participates in the operations against Fort Pulaski (April 1862). After the seizure of Norfolk, Virginia, he becomes military commander of the city until October 1863, when he is ordered to Ohio. On 20 October, he resigns his commission.

In Missouri, a Union contingent of the 5th Missouri Reserves skirmishes with a group of Confederates at Brunswick. The Union sustains one killed and seven wounded. Confederate casualties are unavailable.

In Confederate activity, Colonel Paul Octave Hebert, commander, 1st Louisiana Artillery Regiment, is promoted to the rank of brigadier general. He transfers to Texas and assumes command of the Department of Texas on 18 September.

August 18 (Sunday)   In Maryland, about two companies of the 2nd Massachusetts Regiment skirmishes with a Confederate force estimated at more than 200 at Sandy Hook. The Union sustains no casualties. The Confederate casualties are estimated at two killed and five wounded.

In Virginia, a contingent of Union troops skirmishes with Confederates at Lady's Fork. The Union suffers two killed and two captured. The Confederates sustain two wounded. In other activity, a contingent of the Lincoln Cavalry (1st New York Cavalry) commanded by Lt. Gibson engages a contingent of Confederates at Pohick Church. The Union sustains one killed. Confederate casualties are unavailable.

August 19 (Monday)   In Missouri, Charlestown (Bird's Point) is the location of a battle between the 22nd Illinois, attached to General Frémont's command, and Confederate troops led by Colonel Hunter. The Union suffers one killed and six wounded; Confederates have 40 killed and about 17 captured. The Confederates in the region are becoming more confident following their actions at Wilson's Creek and Springfield, Missouri. Another skirmish breaks out at Commerce, Illinois; here, the Union captures a battery attached to Confederate Colonel Jeff Thompson's force (Thompson's Raiders).

In Union general officer activity, James Shields is appointed brigadier general.

In Naval–Marine Corps activity, the Union's Potomac Flotilla, searching for Confederate fortifications in Maryland, receives a detachment of 200 Marines from the Navy yard at Washington, D.C., to assist in its operation.

In Union general officer activity, Henry W. Halleck (West Point, 1839) is appointed major general. General Halleck had married Elizabeth Hamilton, a sister of General Schuyler Hamilton and the granddaughter of Alexander Hamilton. James Clifford Veatch, a lawyer and state legislator (1861–1862) from Indiana, is commissioned colonel of the 25th Indiana.

August 20 (Tuesday) In Illinois, Alfred Washington Ellet is commissioned as captain (59th Illinois Infantry). During spring of the following year he is appointed lieutenant colonel (later brigadier general) and aide-de-camp to his brother, Charles Ellet (Ellet's Fleet of Rams).

In Missouri, a 50-man contingent of the Centralia cavalry, commanded by Captain Robert D. Noleman, has a brief encounter with a contingent of Confederates in the vicinity of Fish Lake. The 15-minute incident gives the Union about 33 prisoners and 38 stacks of arms. In other activity, Confederate troops fire upon a train that is transporting Union troops in the vicinity of Lookout Station. The Union sustains one killed and six wounded.

In West Virginia, the 11th Ohio Volunteers skirmish with a contingent of Confederates commanded by Colonel St. George Croghan at Hawk's Nest. The Union sustains three killed, two wounded and one missing. Confederate casualties, if any, are unavailable. General William S. Rosecrans, at Clarksburg, subsequent to earlier proclamations by General McClellan and Virginia Governor John Letcher, issues a new proclamation calling for West Virginians to defend their rights and giving a reason for the Union presence:

The Confederates have determined at all hazards to destroy the government which for eighty years has defended our rights and given us a name among the nations. Contrary to your interests and your wishes they have brought war on your soil.... My mission among you is that of a fellow-citizen, charged by the government to expel the arbitrary force which dominated over you; to restore that law and order of which you have been robbed, and to maintain your right to govern yourselves under the Constitution and laws of the United States.... Citizens of western Virginia, your fate is mainly in your own hands. If you allow yourselves to be trampled underfoot by hordes of disturbers, plunderers, and murderers, your land will become a desolation. If you stand firm for law and order and maintain your rights, you may dwell together peacefully and happily as in former days.

In Union general officer activity, Benjamin Franklin Potts is commissioned captain (later brigadier general) of the 32nd Ohio.

In Confederate general officer activity, in North Carolina, at about this time, General Richard Gatlin (West Point 1832) assumes command of the Department of North Carolina. Gatlin is appointed brigadier general, Provisional Army, effective July 8, 1861. Also, William Nelson Rector Beall (West Point, 1844) resigns his position in the U.S. 1st Cavalry to join the Confederate cause. He is appointed captain in the Confederate Army; in 1862 he is promoted to brigadier general. Beall's sister marries Confederate General James F. Fagan (first wife).

August 21 (Wednesday) In Confederate general officer activity, at about this time,

General John Breckinridge Grayson (West Point, 1826) becomes commander of the Department of Middle and East Florida. Grayson had recently resigned his commission in the U.S. Army while stationed in the New Mexico Territory. He is appointed brigadier general, effective this date.

In Naval activity, the U.S. Navy receives the Hetzel, a side-wheel steamer, built at Baltimore for the U.S. Coast Survey. Upon transfer, Lt. H.K. Davenport receives command of the ship. The USS Hetzel is assigned to the North Atlantic Blockading Squadron. It arrives at Newport News on 18 November 1861. In other activity, the U.S. Navy acquires the Rescue. It is fitted out as a gunboat in Philadelphia and assigned to the Potomac Flotilla. Lt. H.S. Newcomb receives command of the vessel.

August 21–22 In Missouri, the Home Guards skirmish with Confederate units this day and again on the 22nd in the vicinity of Jonesboro. Casualties, if any, are unavailable.

August 22 In Union general officer activity, Galusha Pennypacker, not yet eighteen years old, is commissioned captain (later major general of volunteers) of the 97th Pennsylvania Regiment. During the following October, he is promoted to major and afterward is assigned to the Department of the South.

In Naval activity, the USS Lexington seizes a steamer, the W.B. Terry, at Paducah, Kentucky.

August 23 (Friday) In Arkansas, the Cherokee nation joins forces with the Confederacy. Their most concentrated effort will be at the Battle of Pea Ridge (March 6–8, 1862).

In New Mexico, a contingent of New Mexico Volunteers, commanded by Captain Hubbell, skirmishes with Confederates under Lt. Colonel Baylor at Fort Craig. The Confederates capture 10 Union troops.

In Naval activity, the steamers USS Release and Yankee engage Confederate batteries that are deployed at the Mouth of Potomac (Potomac Creek), Virginia. The exchange lasts for about forty minutes. Casualty information is unavailable.

August 24 (Saturday) In Washington, D.C., the Department of Pennsylvania is incorporated into the Department of the Potomac.

In Tennessee, the Confederates award contracts for the construction of two ironclads, the CSS Arkansas and the CSS Tennessee, with the stipulation that both be completed by 24 December this year. The Confederates are attempting to bolster their defenses along the Mississippi against Union warships.

August 25 (Sunday) In New Mexico, Union forces initiate an offensive against the Indians in the vicinity of Fort Stanton. The mission lasts until September 8. Casualty figures are unavailable.

In Texas, Union forces from Fort Bliss (El Paso) skirmish with a band of Indians. Casualties are unknown.

In Naval activity, the USS Saratoga, recently returned from duty off Africa, is decommissioned. The officers and crew are detached. The Saratoga is recommissioned on 24 June 1863.

August 26 (Monday) In West Virginia, the 7th Ohio Infantry, commanded by Colonel Erastus B. Tyler, battles with the Confederates at Cross Lanes in the vicinity of Summerville. The Confederate force, commanded by General John Floyd, estimated at more than 3,000 troops, attacks while the Union is eating breakfast and decisively defeats the force and compels it to scatter. The Union suffers five killed, 40 wounded, and 200 captured. The Confederates had been able to ford the Gauley River at Carnifex Ferry and strike with surprise. The Union afterward crosses the mountains headed for Elk River and from there to Charleston, while Floyd establishes positions, unaware that his encampment is an obstacle standing between General Rosecrans and General Jacob Cox.

In Union general officer activity, Emerson Opdycke is commissioned as a 1st lieutenant in the 41st Ohio Regiment, commanded by Colonel William B. Hazen (later major general). Opdycke participates at Shiloh, but resigns in September 1862. He does not leave the military; rather, he becomes involved in raising a new regiment, the 125th Ohio, of which he becomes lieutenant colonel on 1 October of this year and colonel on 14 January 1863. Following the Battle of Franklin, Tennessee (December 1864), he is breveted major general of volunteers. He does not receive the full rank of brigadier general until after the close of hostilities, on 26 July 1865. His regiment performed heroically at Chattanooga, while he commanded it as part of a larger command of about one-half of a brigade. Opdycke's force was among the first troops to reach the summit of Missionary Ridge. He also participated at Rocky Face and at Resaca. He sustained a severe wound at the latter.

In other activity, Lt. Colonel John Fulton Reynolds (West Point, 1841) (14th U.S. Infantry) is commissioned brigadier general. Prior to the war, Reynolds served in the Mexican War and afterward on the western frontier until September 1860, when he was appointed commandant of cadets at West Point. He also taught tactics at the academy.

In Naval activity, a federal fleet, commanded by Flag Officer Silas Stringham, departs Hampton Roads for Hatteras Inlet, North Carolina, to destroy the Confederate fortifications there. The armada, in addition to Stringham's flagship, the USS Minnesota (Captain G.A. Van Brunt), includes the frigate Wabash (Captain Samuel Mercer), the gunboat Monticello (Commander John P. Gillis), steam sloop Pawnee (Commander S.C. Rowan), the Harriet Lane (Captain John Faunce), the steam transports George Peabody (Lt. R.B. Lowery) and Adelaide

(Commander H.S. Stellwagen) and the tug *Fanny* (Lt. Pierce Crosby). The fleet is also bolstered by the sail frigate *Cumberland*, commanded by Captain John Marston, U.S. Navy, and the steam frigate *Susquehanna*, commanded by Captain J. Chanuncey, both of which are under orders to sail to the rear of the fleet. This naval force arrives in the vicinity of their objective, Fort Hatteras, on the following day. In other activity, Union gunboats, including the USS *R.R. Cuyler*, intercept and seize the vessel Finland while operating in Apalachicola Bay, Florida.

August 27 (Tuesday)   In Virginia, two companies of the 23rd New York Regiment encounter a Confederate force at Ball's Crossroads. The Union suffers one killed and two wounded.

In North Carolina, Flag Officer Silas Stringham's fleet arrives in the vicinity of Fort Hatteras. Union troops (including Marines) under the command of General Benjamin Franklin Butler, prepare to attack the Confederate positions on the following day. Butler, who had volunteered to lead the assault, is succeeded at Fortress Monroe by General John E. Wool. The units that participate in the action are the 9th New York (220 men), commanded by Colonel Rush C. Hawkins; the 20th New York (500 men), commanded by Colonel Max Weber;

The Union captures Fort Clark, North Carolina (Johnson, *Campfire and Battlefield: History of the Conflicts and Campaigns*, 1894).

about 100 troops of the Union Coast Guard, commanded by Captain Nixon; and nearly 60 troops of the 2nd U.S. Artillery, commanded by Lt. Frank Larned. A contingent of U.S. Marines also participates.

In West Virginia, the 5th West Virginia Volunteers, commanded by Captain Smith, engage a contingent of Confederates at Wayne Court House.

In Union general officer activity, John Franklin Miller is commissioned colonel (later brevet major general) of the 29th Indiana Infantry Regiment. Stephen Gano Burbridge (later brigadier general) is appointed colonel of the 26th Kentucky Infantry Regiment.

In Naval activity, Charles Wilkes, named commander of the steam frigate *USS San Jacinto* the previous May, arrives in Monrovia, Liberia, and assumes command of the vessel just prior to its departure for the United States. Wilkes, before this assignment, had participated in the destruction of the facilities at the navy yard in Norfolk to prevent its use by the Confederates.

August 27–28   In Virginia, two companies of the 23rd New York Volunteers, commanded by Colonel Henry C. Hoffman, skirmish with a large force of Confederates at Ball's Cross Roads; however, casualties remain low. The Union sustains one killed and one wounded. The Confederate casualties are unavailable.

August 28 (Wednesday)   In Missouri, Union Colonel Jefferson C. Davis, 22nd Indiana Regiment, delivers instructions to Brigadier General U.S. Grant directing him to go to St. Louis. Davis is to assume command of the troops in Jefferson City. Davis, who was at Fort Sumter when it was attacked by the Confederates in April 1861, had been appointed colonel of the regiment earlier this month. In December, Davis is commissioned brigadier general of volunteers.

In Union general officer activity, James Henry Van Alen is commissioned as colonel (later brigadier general) of the 3rd New York Cavalry, a regiment that he raised. The regiment is assigned duty at the capital and participates in the defenses of Washington.

August 28–29   ATTACK AGAINST FORTS HATTERAS AND CLARK Union warships had arrived off the coast in the vicinity of Fort Hatteras and Fort Clark, North Carolina, on the 27th. On the 28th at 0500, Flag Officer Louis M. Goldsborough (successor to Flag Officer Silas Stringham), aboard the USS *Minnesota*, orders the ships to open fire and take on the Confederate shore batteries. The

powerful show of naval fire continues the bombardment without pause until 0900. The steam frigates *Minnesota* and *Wabash,* supported by the sloops *Cumberland* and *Susquehanna,* commence firing. Marines from each of the ships' respective detachments join with the army force for the assault. Many of the troopers under General Benjamin Butler get stranded on a sandbar while landing, but Confederate Forts Hatteras and Clark haul down their colors. Fort Clark is abandoned and a contingent of Coast Guardsmen and other troops under Colonel Weber secure it.

Meanwhile, the USS *Monticello* advances onward toward Fort Hatteras, reaching a point about 600 yards from the objective when it comes under severe fire from the Confederate batteries. The artillery barrage inflicts some damage to the vessel. Rather than risk further harm or possible destruction of the ship, the *Monticello* pulls back, permitting the *Minnesota, Pawnee* and *Susquehanna* to ease up and provide a substantial amount of fire power to silence the guns on shore. Throughout the day, the naval guns bombard the Fort, while the southerners trade fire with the vessels and simultaneously pour fire into Union-held Fort Clark. By nightfall, exhaustion overwhelms both sides, mandating a pause in the fighting.

The incessant day-long barrages have inflicted a high toll on the Rebels within Fort Hatteras. The commander, Confederate Colonel William Martin, too tired to even stand, passes command to Flag Officer Samuel Barron, the naval officer in command of the Confederate ships in the area of Pamlico Sound. During the night of the 28th–29th, Confederate reinforcements arrive to bolster the beleaguered garrison.

Back at Fort Clark, the Union troops abandon their positions to seek safer positions out of the range of the Confederate artillery, but these troops also redeploy a battery of three guns, which, on the morning of the 29th, does much to deter additional reinforcements that approach on Confederate vessels. The guns, overseen by Coastguardsman Lt. Johnson, pinpoint the passageway and with a blanket of fire forbid passage, which eliminates any possibility of getting the reinforcements ashore.

At 1030, the Confederates hoist a white flag above the fort. Shortly thereafter, the garrison proposes to surrender the fort if afforded full honors of war, but Stringham and Butler decline. Having no genuine options, the beleaguered Confederates capitulate. Captain Samuel Barron of the Confederate States Navy (previously served in the U.S. Navy) boards the USS *Minnesota* and surrenders the fort. Confederate Brigadier General Richard C. Gatlin (West Point, 1832), commanding officer, Department of North Carolina, receives the blame for the loss and also for that of New Bern, North Carolina, during March of 1862. Captain Samuel Barron is paroled on September 25. After release, he is assigned duty in the Department of the Cumberland and Tennessee. During 1863 he is assigned command of the Confederate Naval forces in Europe.

The Union loses one killed and two wounded. Confederate losses are five killed, 51 wounded, 715 captured. U.S. Navy Seaman Benjamin Swearer, stationed on the USS *Pawnee,* is the first man to raise the Stars and Stripes over captured Fort Clark. Swearer, for his extraordinary heroism under fire in the face of the enemy, becomes a recipient of the Medal of Honor.

Early in the engagement, the aide-de camp of General Butler swims to shore against heavy seas to deliver information to Colonel Weber at Fort Clark, but while there he gathers an enormous amount of intelligence that alters Butler's plans. It had been the objective to destroy the forts; however, due to the new information, Butler returns to Washington and convinces General Scott to hold the forts. Scott orders Butler to proceed to New England to raise a voluminous force for use in North Carolina. During the latter part of September, the 20th Indiana Regiment, commanded by Colonel W.L. Brown, will arrive at Hatteras to bolster the forces already there.

August 28–30 In Virginia, a Union contingent commanded by Captain Dillman and Major Champlin skirmish with Confederates at Bailey's Corner (Cross Roads). Each side sustains three wounded.

August 29 (Thursday) In Missouri, General Ulysses S. Grant is assigned command of the District of Southeast Missouri (St. Louis, south and southern Illinois). Grant makes his headquarters in Cairo on 4 September. In other activity, the Missouri Home Guards engage a contingent of Confederates, estimated at more than 3,000 troops, at Lexington. The Union sustains one killed and six wounded. The estimated Confederate casualties are eight killed, 52 wounded and two captured.

In Naval activity, the USS *Quaker City* seizes the schooner *Fair Wind.*

August 30 (Friday) In Missouri, Union General John C. Frémont issues a decree calling for confiscation of Confederate property in that state. His proclamation (Emancipation Proclamation) also calls for freeing slaves in Missouri. President Lincoln countermands the

General John C. Frémont (Johnson, *Campfire and Battlefield: History of the Conflicts and Campaigns,* 1894).

order. Lincoln modifies the proclamation by stating that it applies only to slaves who are serving in the Confederate military.

In Union general officer activity, John Aaron Rawlins (later brigadier general) is commissioned as a captain and becomes aide-de-camp to Ulysses S. Grant, who at this time is a brigadier general. Rawlins remains a close friend and confidante to Grant. He continues to rise in the ranks and becomes brigadier general during August 1863.

In Naval activity, the USS *Hartford,* on duty in the Far East since 1859, is recalled due to the eruption of war. On this day, it and the USS *Dacotah* departs from the Strait of Sumda. The *Hartford* arrives in Philadelphia on 2 December and is fitted out for service in the war.

August 31 (Saturday) In Virginia, two companies of the 3rd New Jersey Regiment (Volunteers) engage Confederates at Munson's Hill.

The Union sustains two killed. The Confederates sustain two wounded. In other activity, at Hampton Roads, John LaMountain, aboard the USS *Fanny,* experiments by initiating the first flight in a balloon, launched from the deck of the ship. He ascends and from his location he is able to observe activity at the Confederate positions on Sewall's Point.

In Union general officer activity, Lt. Colonel John J. Abercrombie (West Point, 1822) is appointed brigadier general, Volunteers. Also, Union Lieutenant Colonel Silas Casey (West Point, 1826) is promoted to the rank of brigadier general. His primary field duty occurs at Seven Pines, where his command braces and opposes the heaviest portion of A.P. Hill's initial assault. Subsequently, Casey is stationed near Washington, D.C., where he commands a brigade. In addition, Lincoln also appoints Abram Duryee a brigadier general of volunteers, effective this day.

In other activity, George Gordon Meade (West Point, 1835) is appointed brigadier general. Meade, a veteran of the Mexican War, at the time of the outbreak of the Civil War is back on active duty with the rank of captain in the engineers. After a time on duty with the defenses of the capital, he joins General McClellan on the peninsula during the summer of 1862. John Sedgwick (West Point, 1837), a veteran of the Mexican War who became colonel of the 1st Cavalry upon the resignation of Robert E. Lee and William Hardee when they joined the Confederacy, is appointed brigadier general. Lt. Colonel Charles Ferguson Smith (West Point, 1825) is appointed brigadier general of volunteers and later, on 9 September, he is promoted to colonel of the 3rd U.S. Infantry (Regular Army). In other activity, Wager Swayne, the son of Chief Justice Noah Swayne, is commissioned major (later brigadier general) of the 43rd Ohio Regiment. He participates in various actions, including New Madrid and Island No. 10. Later, at the Battle of Corinth, he becomes a recipient of the Medal of Honor.

In Confederate general officer activity, General Albert Sidney Johnston (West Point, 1826) receives his appointment as full rank general in the Confederate Army, effective May 30, 1861.

September In Virginia, Union General William S. Rosecrans, successor to General George B. McClellan, has been steadily building his army. He learns that a large Confederate force is building in the area around Carnifex Ferry on the Gauley River close to Meadow Creek outside of Summerville, Nicholas County, in the western part of Virginia. The opposition, he is told, is led by Confederate General John B. Floyd, former U.S. secretary of war. Rosecrans takes decisive action to eliminate the threat. Meanwhile, Confederate General Henry A. Wise is to remain at Pickett's Mills to hold the rear against a possible assault by Union General J.D. Cox, presently at Hawk's Nest. Another Union force under General Joseph J. Reynolds is within striking distance of Confederate General Robert E. Lee's command at

Fort Clark and Fort Hatteras are secured by Union forces on 28–29 August (Johnson, *Campfire and Battlefield: History of the Conflicts and Campaigns,* 1894).

Cheat Mountain. Meanwhile, on 3 September, Rosecrans starts out on a march across dangerous mountains to intercept and engage Floyd; he arrives in the vicinity of Carnifex Ferry on the 9th.

In Confederate activity, Joseph H. Lewis becomes colonel (later brigadier general) of the Confederate 6th Kentucky Infantry. James Green Martin (West Point, 1840), who had recently resigned his commission to join the Confederate cause, becomes a major general (Georgia Militia). William Hugh Young forms a company of Texans for the Confederacy and as its captain, joins the 9th Texas Infantry Regiment. The regiment later moves to Tennessee and will participate at various battles, including Shiloh, Perryville and Murfreesboro, the latter during December 1862.

In Naval activity, the U.S. Navy acquires the *Ceres,* a side-wheel gunboat built in New York during 1856. The USS *Ceres* serves for the duration in the region covering North Carolina and southern Virginia as part of the blockading force. During July 1865, it is decommissioned. The Navy also acquires a civilian ferryboat, the *Nuestra Senora del Regla,* which was built in New York (1861). It is commissioned the USS *Commodore Hull* during the following November and goes into service as a 376-ton gunboat. The *Commodore Hull* operates primarily in the vicinity of the North Carolina sounds and nearby rivers.

September 1 (Sunday)   In Missouri, a 38-man contingent of the Missouri Home Guards engages a Confederate force estimated at more than 300 troops at Bennight's Mills (Bennett's Mills). The Union suffers three killed and six or eight wounded. Confederate casualties, if any, are unavailable.

In West Virginia, Boone's Courthouse is the site of another engagement between Confederate and Union soldiers. The 1st Kentucky Regiment (Volunteers) engages the Rebels, suffering six wounded. The Confederates suffer 30 dead. The biggest loser is the town itself, which is burned.

In Union general officer activity, Orlando Metcalfe Poe (West Point, 1856) is appointed colonel of the 2nd Michigan at about this time (September). He participates with his regiment during the first stages of the Peninsular Campaign; however he becomes ill and does not return to duty until Second Manassas. He also participates at Fredericksburg (December 1862) one month after he is appointed brigadier general on 29 November 1862. Also, Thomas Leonidas Crittenden, brother of Confederate General George B. Crittenden, is appointed brigadier general at about this time (September). Thomas is also a cousin of Union General Thomas T. Crittenden.

In other activity, John Cleveland Robinson is commissioned colonel of 1st Michigan Infantry. Robinson had attended West Point during 1835, but due to some violation of regulations, he was dismissed the following year. He was commissioned as second lieutenant in the U.S. 5th Infantry during 1839. At the outbreak of the war, Robinson had been in command at Fort McHenry in Baltimore. Also, Alexander Schimmelfennig, a native of Prussia, working for the War Department at the outbreak of hostilities is commissioned colonel of the 74th Pennsylvania Regiment at about this time (September). General Schimmelfennig is suspended from command in the field due to sickness and a mishap. He is injured when his horse falls, but he also contracts smallpox. However, he recovers in time to participate at Second Bull Run (Manassas).

Also, Gustavus Adolphus Smith, who entered the service soon after the fall of Fort Sumter and engaged in drilling recruits, is commissioned colonel of the 35th Illinois Infantry Regiment. Colonel Smith, prior to the war, had been a manufacturer of carriages; however, he had no military experience. Smith's regiment becomes known as "Gus Smith's Independent Regiment." In yet other activity, James Gallant Spears, a Tennessean and slave owner wanted for disloyalty to the Confederacy, had fled the state for Kentucky, where he helps organize the Union 1st Tennessee Infantry. He is commissioned lieutenant colonel (later brigadier general) of the regiment on this day.

In yet other activity, Robert Ogden Tyler (West Point, 1853) is commissioned colonel of the 4th Connecticut Regiment (later 1st Connecticut Heavy Artillery). Colonel Tyler participates in the Peninsular Campaign and the regiment loses only one gun during the entire campaign. Later, after being promoted to brigadier general on 29 November 1862, he participates at Fredericksburg. Subsequently, at Gettysburg, it is the 130 guns of General Tyler that decimates the charging Rebels (Pickett's Charge) in front of Cemetery Ridge.

In Confederate general officer activity, Thomas Fenwick Drayton (West Point, 1828) is appointed brigadier general in the Confederate Army. Drayton's brother, Percival, is a captain in the U.S. Navy and at about this time is in command of the gunboat USS *Pocahontas,* which will soon (October) leave Virginia for Hilton Head, South Carolina. General Drayton serves in the Army of Northern Virginia, but subsequent to the battle at Sharpsburg (Antietam), he apparently loses his field service, despite his close relationship with President Jefferson Davis. During the final two years of the conflict, General Drayton holds only minor commands in the Trans-Mississippi Department. Upon the cessation of hostilities, he engages in farming.

In Naval activity, the U.S. Navy acquires a civilian steamer, the *Saint Marys,* a side wheeled gunboat built in Wilmington, Delaware, during 1861. It is commissioned the USS *Hatteras* the following month and assigned duty off the coast of Florida, prior to being assigned to the Gulf of Mexico. The U.S. Navy also acquires the *Isaac Smith* (screw steam gunboat) at about this time (September). It is commissioned the following month and assigned to the South Atlantic Blockading Squadron. The USS *Norfolk Packet* is another of the Navy's acquisitions about this time. It is transformed into a mortar schooner and commissioned in February 1862. The *Norfolk Packet* is assigned duty on the lower Mississippi River. Later, during November 1862, it is transferred to the South Atlantic Blockading Squadron to patrol off Florida, Georgia and South Carolina for the duration of the war. After the war it is decommissioned during July 1865 and sold the following month.

Also, the USS *Para* is acquired by the U.S. Navy at about this time. After modifications, the vessel, built at Wilmington, Delaware, for civilian purposes, is transformed into a mortar schooner, commissioned in February 1862 and assigned duty with the mortar flotilla which operates along the Mississippi River. It remains with the squadron until early 1863. It is transferred to the South Atlantic Blockading Squadron and remains there until decommissioned during August 1865 and sold the following month. The timberclad gunboat USS *Tyler,* acquired by the U.S. for the Union Army's Western Gunboat Flotilla, acquired during the previous June, is commissioned at about this time (September). Initially assigned duty on the Mississippi River, it remains there and on its tributaries for the duration of the war, including when it is transferred to the U.S. Navy during October 1862.

September 2 (Monday)   In Florida, a small Union force under Lt. Shipley moves out of Fort Pickens and heads for the Warrington Navy Yard on the opposite side of the channel that leads into Pensacola. Once there, the detachment sets the facility afire, then safely returns to the fort.

In Missouri, Major General Sterling Price (Missouri Confederate Militia), having decided during the latter part of August to make an offensive move, has up to this point met no genuine opposition. This day at Dry Wood (Fort Scott), in the vicinity of the Kansas border, contingents of his force encounter a group of Union troops attached to the command of General James H. Lane. The superior numbered Confederate force pushes the Union contingent beyond Fort Scott. The 5th and 6th Kansas Regiments and one company of the 9th Kansas participate in the skirmishing. Union losses are four killed and nine wounded. In Dallas, the 11th Missouri Regiment (Volunteers) skirmishes a contingent of Confederates. Casualty figures, if any, are unavailable.

In West Virginia, three companies of Union Troops commanded by Colonel Crosman engage a contingent of Confederates at Worthington. The Union loses two killed. Confederate casualties, if any, are unavailable.

In Union activity, Abram Sanders Piatt, who raised a three-month regiment, the 13th Ohio, during the initial stage of the war, is on this day appointed colonel (later brigadier general) of the 34th Ohio Regiment. His regiment is ordered to West Virginia and Colonel Piatt is assigned duty in the mountains guarding the rear of General William S. Rosecrans' forces through the winter of 1871–1862.

Major General Sterling Price leaves elements at Fort Scott, Missouri, then heads for Warrenton. Word spreads that the Rebels are en route and the Union dispatches troops to Warrenton to collect, transport and hold the U.S. currency of the loyal residents to keep it from being seized by the Rebels and to protect the civilians if feasible from the encroaching enemy forces. Price arrives at Warrenton on the 11th and prepares immediately to strike the Union at Lexington, Missouri, on the following day.

Brigadier General James H. Lane, who will also participate in the upcoming battle at Lexington as a brigadier general of Volunteers, in December takes a seat in the Senate representing Kansas, remaining there until he becomes paralyzed by a stroke. Lane earlier had become a lawyer, but joined the Army as a private to fight in the Mexican War. His rank rose quickly and at Buena Vista, he led a brigade. Following service in the Mexican War, he became lieutenant general of Indiana and later a Congressman. During 1856 he was prevented from taking his seat in the Senate. Nevertheless, the Kansas State Legislature elects him to the Senate during 1861 and 1865. On 11 July January 1866, Lane, unable to perform his Senatorial duties due to health, commits suicide at his home in Leavenworth, Kansas.

In Union general officer activity, Justus McKinstry (West Point, 1838), a veteran of the Mexican War on duty in St. Louis as quartermaster of the Department of the West, is appointed brigadier general. General McKinstry for a short time commands a division under General Frémont; however, he returns to quartermaster duty, but simultaneously, he uses the department for his personal gain and his tactics include taking payoffs from contractors. His scheme is discovered when General Hunter launches an investigation. McKinstry is cashiered on 28 January 1863. George Crockett Strong (West Point, 1857), who had been based at several arsenals prior to the outbreak of the war and afterward on General McClellan's staff during the operations at Manassas, is transferred to General Benjamin F. Butler's staff. He receives the rank of major (later brigadier general) and becomes adjutant general of volunteers. While in Louisiana, after the seizure of New Orleans, Major Strong is hit repeatedly with sickness and compelled to take extended sick leave (June–September 1862 and later December 1862 to June 1863).

In Confederate general officer activity, at about this time, General Leonidas Polk assumes command of the forces in Arkansas and Mississippi. In other activity, Claudius C. Wilson is appointed colonel (later brigadier general) of the 25th Georgia Infantry, a regiment he earlier joined as captain.

September 3 (Tuesday) In Washington, D.C., a detachment of U.S. Marines stationed at the U.S. Navy Yard is dispatched to reinforce the Union-held garrison at Fort Ellsworth in Alexandria, Virginia. Skirmishing also develops at Mason's Island, Maryland.

In West Virginia, Confederate General Wise and Augustus Chapman complete their strategy to launch an attack against the lines of General Jacob Cox at Gauley's Bridge in the vicinity of Hawk's Nest. Also, General William S. Rosecrans initiates an exhausting march to reach Gauley Bridge along the Kanawha River to bolster General Cox. Rosecrans departs Clarksburg with three brigades, those of Colonels Benham, Robert Latimer McCook and Colonel Eliakim Parker Scammon.

In Union general officer activity, Daniel E. Sickles is commissioned as a brigadier general and becomes commander of the New York Excelsior Brigade. Colonel Lewis Wallace (11th Indiana) is appointed brigadier general. Another officer, Robert H. Milroy, is appointed brigadier general. Colonel Oliver Otis Howard is appointed as a brigadier general effective this date. Charles Davis Jameson is appointed brigadier general. Prior to his appointment, Jameson had commanded a Maine militia regiment and participated at First Manassas (Bull Run).

Also, Colonel Alexander McDowell McCook (West Point, 1852), commander of the 1st Ohio Volunteer Regiment, is appointed brigadier general and during the following year is promoted to major general. McCook had participated with his regiment at First Manassas (Bull Run). General McCook is the brother of Union Generals Daniel and Robert Latimer McCook, and he is a cousin of General Edward Moody McCook. Colonel Ebenezer Dumont is appointed brigadier general.

In Confederate general officer activity, Joseph Reid Anderson (West Point, 1836) is appointed brigadier general in the Confederate Army. Initially, he commands at Wilmington, North Carolina, but later he is transferred to Virginia (spring 1862).

September 3–5 In Maryland at Great Falls, a Union contingent led by 1st Lieutenant C.W. Squires, 1st Company, 1st Washington Artillery of New Orleans, departs Camp Orleans on the 3rd. On the following day at about 0700, the unit arrives at Great Falls on the Potomac. The unit includes part of a battery and cavalry. The rifled cannon and howitzers are deployed on the right bank (Maryland side) of the river on high ground. Elements of a South Carolina regiment are encamped on the opposite bank in Virginia. The artillery fire ceases about 0900 and afterward, the contingent resumes its march and arrives at Germantown, about 20 miles distant at about dusk. At that time, the unit is ordered to return to camp.

September 4 (Wednesday) In California, Union colonel (later general) Patrick E. Connor, who had served admirably during the Mexican War, is dispatched to assume the command of the Department of Utah, which includes present-day Nevada. The primary responsibility facing him is to keep the U.S. mail flowing. Connor will be forced to deal with many hostile Indian tribes, including the Cheyenne, Sioux, Brannocks and Arapaho, but his mission is successful. At the conclusion of hostilities, Connor will establish Fort Connor (renamed Fort Reno) on the Powder River in Wyoming.

In Maryland, the 7th and 8th Pennsylvania Infantry Regiments (Brigadier General George Archibald McCall's command), commanded by Colonel Harvey, encounter and skirmish with a group of Confederates at Great Falls. The Union sustains two killed. Confederate casualties are unavailable.

In Virginia, a contingent of the 13th Massachusetts Regiment (Volunteers) engages Confederate Home Guards at Beher's Mills. The Confederates sustain three killed, five wounded and 20 captured.

In Kentucky, Confederate troops under Major General Gideon Pillow, acting pursuant to recent orders from General Leonidas Polk, defy the neutrality of Kentucky and occupy the towns of Columbus and Hickman, both along the Mississippi River. This compels the Union to take quick action and secure Paducah. General Pillow, at the time of the incursion, is the senior major general in Tennessee.

In Missouri, the 3rd Iowa Volunteer Regiment, numbering about 1,100 troops led by Colonel (later brigadier general) Nelson Grosvenor Williams, encounters a larger Confederate force led by Colonel Martin Green in the vicinity of Shelbina. The activity between the two units lasts about one and one-half hours. Neither side sustains heavy casualties. One Union soldier is wounded.

In Confederate general officer activity, Colonel Henry Eustace McCulloch, commander of

Union artillery in action at Great Falls, Maryland, on 3 September 1861 (Mottelay, *The Soldier in Our Civil War,* 1886).

the 1st Texas Mounted Riflemen, is appointed commander of Confederate troops in Texas. He will replace General Earl Van Dorn, who is promoted to major general during the following September and assigned to duty in Virginia.

In Union general officer activity, Charles Henry Van Wyck (Congressman 1858 to March 1863 and a lawyer) is commissioned colonel of the 56th New York Infantry (known also as the Tenth Legion), a regiment that he raised. The regiment participates in the initial stages of the Peninsular Campaign. In December 1862 the regiment is transferred to South Carolina and remains in the vicinity for the duration of the war. Later, during September, 1865, Colonel Van Wyck is promoted to brigadier general. After departing the service he is again elected to Congress, followed by election to the U.S. Senate.

In Naval activity, the USS *Conestoga, Lexington* and the *Tyler* engage the gunboat CSS *Jackson,* which is bolstered by land batteries off Hickman, Kentucky. As the Union warships drift down within accurate range of the shore batteries, they reverse course. In other activity, the Confederate steamer *Elise* is seized by Union warships, including the USS *Quaker City.* Following this action, the *Quaker City* leaves area (Virginia) and sails north for repairs and to receive a navy crew.

September 5 (Thursday) Union troops under General Ulysses S. Grant move toward Paducah, Kentucky, located near the mouth of the Cumberland River and the convergence of the Ohio and Tennessee Rivers. During the night, two transports, including the *G.W. Graham,* protected by two gunboats, carry the 9th and 12th Illinois Regiments commanded by Major J.J. Phillips and Colonel (later brevet major general) John McArthur toward the objective. Four guns of the Chicago artillery accompany the infantry; this unit of General Charles Smith's artillery is commanded by Lieutenant Willard.

In Union general officer activity, William Plummer Benton, veteran of the Mexican War, is appointed colonel (later brevet major general) of the 13th Ohio Regiment. Thomas Church Haskell Smith, a lawyer, is commissioned lieutenant colonel (later brigadier general) of the 1st Ohio Cavalry. In July 1862, General John Pope places Smith on his staff as aide-de-camp. Smith, closely aligned to Pope, gives testimony at the court-martial of General Fitz John Porter that greatly injures Porter's case; however, later, when Porter is exonerated, Smith's testimony is proved to have been more fiction than fact and greatly exaggerated. Smith remains with Pope when he is replaced by General McClellan and sent to Minnesota.

September 6 (Friday) **In Kentucky,** Confederate troops under Major General Leonidas Polk, who had earlier moved into Columbus, prompt a Union reaction. Federal troops under General Ulysses S. Grant move into Paducah without opposition. Paducah provides the Union with a strategic position from which it can execute the River Campaigns. While the Union forces debark, the gunboats USS *Tyler* and USS *Conestoga,* commanded by Commodore C.R.P. Rodgers and Lt. S.L. Phelps respectively, and the *Lexington* are on scene. Grant's gathering of the gunboats which had spearheaded his move to seize Paducah and Smithland is his first use of the Navy. It counters the Confederate attempt to gain the state of Kentucky and greatly aids in keeping the state under Union domination. With naval support during the future campaigns, the Confederate strategy is foiled and eventually, the entire Mississippi comes under Union control. While Grant is securing Paducah, Confederate colonel (later brigadier general) Lloyd Tilghman, with a small contingent of men, is evacuating the town on the opposite side. Other Confederate troops were within 15 miles of Paducah, but they returned to Columbus, unaware that Grant's force is thin.

Union General Charles F. Smith (West Point, 1825) commands at Paducah. Also, the 9th Illinois Regiment deploys at the northern terminus of the Mobile and Ohio Railroad, while the 12th Illinois Regiment establishes its positions at the Marine Hospital. Some troops move to the post office, confiscating mail, while at the railroad depot, large amounts of supplies are seized. Meanwhile, a Union contingent composed of five companies, led by Captain J. J. Phillips and accompanied the guns, move about seven miles beyond the town to destroy a railroad bridge and trestle by the torch, meeting no opposition during the mission. Meanwhile, Commodore Rogers dispatches a force to seize the telegraph office and all correspondence therein. He discovers that Confederate vessels are anticipated, prompting him to dispatch the *Conestoga* to seek the prey. Shortly thereafter, the ship encounters an escaping vessel laden with tobacco and captures it.

In New Mexico Territory, Union and Confederate troops skirmish in the vicinity of Fort Craig. Casualty figures are unavailable.

September 7 (Saturday) **In Kentucky,** the 8th and 41st Illinois Regiments and the American Zouave Regiment arrive at Paducah to augment the forces already there. The Sisters of Charity of Nazareth have been volunteering their services to care for the sick and wounded, including Confederate captives. Twenty-three nuns, authorized by Bishop Martin John Spaulding, are manning hospitals in and around Louisville. Many of the wounded had never before seen a Catholic nun, causing severe skepticism as well as suspicion; however, through their selfless actions and professional care, the nuns earn respect as they tend to the wounds and even bathe the patients. The number of nuns (various orders) that sacrifice their lives during the conflict is uncertain, but it is known to be in the hundreds. One of the first is Sister Mary Lucy, a young nun working in Paducah who contracts typhoid from one of her patients and dies on 20 December 1861. The nuns as time goes on become known as "Angels of the Battlefield." Reaction by the troops upon the death of Sister Mary Lucy is unexpected. The soldiers form an escort at Central Hospital for her remains and afterward, the column marches with muffled drums to the wharf, where a gunboat is waiting to carry her remains to Uniontown, Kentucky, where she is interred at St. Vincent's Academy. All the while, the escort keeps a vigil. During the night, the troops stand around the coffin with lighted torches and remain with the coffin until Sister Mary Lucy is interred.

In Virginia, Union General William S. Rosecrans' force, en route from the Arlington-Washington area toward Carnifex Ferry, continues to move along treacherous Kreitz and Powell mountain ranges, which at times force the columns to move in single file and on their knees, something not usually occurring as troops move into battle. The Union force makes it to the pinnacle of the final range overlooking the objective on the 9th.

In West Virginia, three companies of the 4th Ohio Volunteer Regiment skirmish with Confederates in the vicinity of Petersburg. No casualties are reported.

In Union general officer activity, Colonel Willis A. Gorman is appointed brigadier general effective this day. General Gorman had participated at Ball's Bluff with his 1st Minnesota Regiment. Edward Needles Kirk is commissioned colonel (later brigadier general) of the 34th Illinois Infantry Regiment. Charles Mynn Thurston, a graduate of West Point and a veteran of the War of 1812, but with service in New York, is appointed brigadier general of volunteers. His primary responsibility is to protect the Baltimore and Ohio Railroad in the vicinity of Cumberland, Kentucky, a strategic link on the railroad. Nonetheless, General Thurston, convinced he is too old for the responsibility, resigns his commission on 17 April 1862. Thurston is also the mayor of Cumberland during 1861–1862.

In Naval activity, the USS *Conestoga,* operating in the vicinity of Paducah, Kentucky, intercepts and captures two Confederate vessels. Both, along with a ship seized on the previous day, are soon taken to Cairo, Illinois.

September 8 (Sunday) Union forces under General Ulysses S. Grant that had occupied Paducah, Kentucky, on the 6th continue to bolster their positions unhindered by Confederate opposition. General Charles Smith, commanding the city, directs his force to bolster the approaches to the town by constructing earthworks and other obstacles.

September 9 (Monday) **In Missouri,** the 13th Missouri Regiment, commanded by Colonel Everett Peabody, arrives at Lexington, having returned from Warrenton. Peabody's force brings with it about $100,000 belonging to loyalists in Warrenton to keep it from the fast encroaching forces of Sterling Price's Confederates, who are also en route to Lexington. Other Union troops are arriving at Lexington from Jefferson City, including Colonel James A. Mul-

General Ulysses S. Grant's forces occupy Paducah, Kentucky, on 8 September 1861 (Mottelay, *The Soldier in Our Civil War*, 1886).

Colonel James A. Mulligan (Johnson, *Campfire and Battlefield: History of the Conflicts and Campaigns*, 1894).

ligan's 23rd Illinois Regiment, attached to the Irish Brigade, about 500 Home Guards, the 1st Illinois Regiment (Cavalry), commanded by Colonel T.M. Marshall, and a contingent of the 8th Missouri Regiment under Colonel White to bolster the small force already there. In addition, some Kansas Volunteers led by General James Henry Lane participate.

In New York, some trouble develops at a recruiting camp as two commanders, each raising a separate regiment, find themselves involved with unexpected competition which causes some excitement and some casualties. Colonel Le Gendre, who is forming the New York Rifles' Regiment, learns that one of his companies is planning to move to a regiment of Colonel

Fardella. At this time, many recruiting camps are suffering losses by desertion, but this is an unusual set of circumstances. Le Gendre orders two of his officers to have the men restrained in their quarters. Meanwhile, another officer, Captain Cresto, is negotiating to have the men released to him so they can transfer to the other regiment. An accidental shot is fired and two men are killed and several are wounded. Finally it is settled and the whole regiment is sent to the front lines.

In Virginia at Carnifex Ferry, General William S. Rosecrans' overtired troops finally ascend to the crest of the last peak in the Powell Mountain Range, ending a tedious seventeen mile trek, and although weary, they realize the fight against the Confederates is imminent, particularly when shortly after arriving there at 1200, shots are exchanged between Confederate pickets from Carnifex Ferry and themselves. Rosecrans will be joined on the following day by Colonel Henry W. Benham's Brigade, composed of the 10th Ohio (Colonel William Haines Lytle), 12th Ohio (Colonel James Lowe), 13th Ohio (Colonel W.S. Smith) and two batteries of artillery under Captains James R. McMullen (McMullin) and William Schneider. Combined, the troops under Colonel Benham and Rosecrans swell the Union force to about 4,000 troops against about 2,000 defenders under Confederate General John B. Floyd.

In Union general officer activity, Nelson Appleton Miles is commissioned 1st lieutenant in the 22nd Massachusetts Infantry. He participates in the Peninsular Campaign and sustains a wound during the Battle of Seven Pines (May 1862). Subsequently, during June 1864, he is promoted to brigadier general. Also, Thomas Kilby Smith, a lawyer, is commissioned lieutenant colonel (later brigadier general) of the 54th Ohio Regiment.

In Confederate activity, the 14th South Carolina Regiment is established at Aiken. Initially the troops from various towns and rural areas had formed in the vicinity of Columbia at Lightknotwood Springs. James Jones is the first colonel. Abner M. Perrin, who joins the regiment as a captain, becomes its colonel in February 1863. Also, the 8th Texas Cavalry is mustered into the Confederate Army in Houston. Benjamin Franklin Terry becomes its colonel, and its second in command is Lt. Colonel Thomas S. Lubbock. Also, Thomas Harrison is elected as major (later brigadier general). The regiment is scheduled for service in Virginia, but is diverted to Kentucky by General Albert Sidney Johnston.

September 10 (Tuesday) In Virginia, a contingent of the 79th New York Infantry, commanded by Captain Ireland, skirmishes with a Confederate Cavalry Troop at Lewisville. The Union sustains one killed; the Confederates sustain four killed and two captured.

In Union general officer activity, Brigadier General George Henry Thomas (West Point, 1840) receives command of Fort Dick Robinson, East Kentucky.

In Naval activity, the USS *Lexington*, a gunboat commanded by Colonel Wagner, and the *Conestoga* are fired upon while operating in the vicinity of Lucas Bend, Missouri, by Confederate batteries supported by the CSS *Jackson* and contingents of Confederate cavalry. The CSS *Jackson* sustains damage to its wheel house and side, leaving it with only one engine. The *Jackson* retires.

September 10–11 THE BATTLE OF CARNIFEX FERRY At about 1500, Union General William Starke Rosecrans' forces attack the Confederates under General John Buchanan Floyd at Carnifex Ferry, Virginia. The Confederate force is composed of six regiments and about 15 or 16 pieces of artillery. It is a vicious and unrelenting contest that underscores the phrase "rally round the flag," and it spins chills in the spine whether blue or gray. The Union, determined to vanquish its foe, strikes like a tornado, and the Confederates return the favor by launching a typhoon of blistering fire. In a sense, this battle, like all others in this peculiar war of brother against brother, is pernicious and profane, while simultaneously being bold, heroic, proud and profound. Both sides exhibit equal talent ranging from the scared kid and the gentle farmer

Colonel John Lowe, killed at Carnifex Ferry on 10 September 1861 (Johnson, *Campfire and Battlefield: History of the Conflicts and Battlefield: History of the Conflicts and Campaigns*, 1894).

to the fearless horsemen and the stoic sharp-shooters, the difference in many cases being confined to the accents of the common language that separates the opposing regiments.

As the 4,000 Yankees form to assault the Rebel lines, Colonel Benham requests and receives the order to lead the attack with his brigade. The vanguard approaches a camp, but it is unoccupied, giving the impression that Floyd had begun a retreat, but shortly thereafter, it is determined that the Confederates had actually formed nearby in a stronghold. Colonel Lytle's 10th Ohio, the Irish Regiment, at the point, begins the charge. The troops advance at full speed to pound, pack and push the Rebels from the line, but in a short while, the units encounter a stiff wall of fire originating from a parapet battery, positioned just off the main road. The lightning-quick barrage momentarily stuns the attackers, as they are in the direct line of fire, but just as quickly, Union artillery under Captains McMullen and Schneider move up to assist and get the attack reinitiated.

The Union cannon spew shell after shell into the obstacle, keeping the Confederates' guns diverted while the Irish Regiment bolts forward and storms the center of the Confederate lines lying along a nearby hill. Here too, the defenders pour relentless fire into the advancing Yankees, who seemingly disregard the deadly fire as they drive relentlessly to penetrate the lines. The sounds are deafening as shot and shell continue to fly. The attacking regiment sustains hit after hit, some troops dropping in either gruesome pain or stark death, while others maintain the tenacious attack.

Nevertheless, the pressure fails to crack the solid line. The ruthless contest continues and the blood pours more profusely, layering the land with some crimson pride. The four companies of the brigade crash forward, listening to the rallying cry of Lytle: "Follow Tenth!" And they do, driving further against a solid ring of fire, following the Stars and Stripes, but the defiant defenders refuse to budge, choosing to stand steadfastly to defend their Stars and Bars. Colonel Lytle, in the midst of this savage attack, is struck, receiving a serious wound to his leg, and shortly thereafter, his horse, which also had sustained a wound, gives out. Under a riveting fire, troops feverishly rush to his aid and extract him from the field. Lytle, realizing his troops are too slight in numbers to break through, orders them to pull back and reform.

In the meantime, Lytle's color sergeant, Fitzgibbons, is soon struck and his flag-bearing hand is shattered. Rather than relinquish the colors, he places it in his left hand and conspicuously waves it from left to right to ensure that the Rebels understand there is life remaining in the Irish Regiment. All the while, shot and shell and choking smoke permeates the area. The bloody saga continues. A Confederate round finds its mark, striking Fitzgibbons in the head, killing him; the flag drops to the reddened earth, but immediately thereafter, it is swooped from the ground by Sergeant O'Connor, himself wounded. O'Connor raises the colors, waving them back-and-forth until finally his

wounds take a toll, and then, overcome by pain and sheer exhaustion, he too slumps to the earth, bringing Old Glory down with him.

The Confederates continue to rain fire upon the beleaguered Yankees, and their marksmen place a high priority on the flag bearers. Once O'Connor falls by the wayside, the Stars and Stripes is immediately plucked from him by Captain Stephen McGroarty, whose outfit has not yet been able to seek cover from the hurricanes of shot and shell. He proudly boasts the colors as the others take cover, but before he reaches safety, yet another Confederate sharpshooter sets his sights, clicks the trigger and places a bullet into the chest of McGroarty. This, the "Bloody Tenth," as it is dubbed, preserves the colors, its pride and its fighting spirit, while making preparations to reinitiate the agonizing assault.

All the while, the 12th and 13th Ohio Regiments are hammering against the right flank of the Confederate positions, engaging in an equally bloody and give-no-quarter contest, with both sides delivering earth-shattering fire upon the other. On the left flank, the Confederates are under assault by Colonel Robert L. McCook's Brigade. Nonetheless, the Rebels budge not an inch in submission to their cousins from the north. Rather, they remain well entrenched holding the advantageous ground and are taking little in the way of casualties.

In McCook's sector, from atop his horse, he rallies his own German Regiment, the 9th Ohio and the 3rd and 28th Ohio Regiments, repeatedly urging them as they advance, furiously waving his hat and yelling, "Forward my bully Dutch! We'll go over the entrenchments if every man dies on the other side." However, Rebel fire emerges from the entire line, preventing progress at every point. Union casualties climb, but still, the attackers struggle to advance. McCook attempts to inch forward, but to no avail.

Colonel John Lowe of the 12th Ohio, attacking on the right flank, also hits immovable opposition. While leading an assault, he is struck by a bullet to the head and killed. In the meantime, the beleaguered and outnumbered forces of Floyd continue to hold the impenetrable wall and draw yet another a crimson line outside the perimeter; however, the Union, although unable to pierce the lines with ground forces, is able to inflict some casualties on the Rebels, and by about dusk, due to the effective fire of the artillery, the guns of the Confederates are silenced. By this time, the 13th Ohio under Colonel William S. Smith has advanced to striking distance of Floyd's right flank, and he awaits orders to charge to sever the line and create a gap, but the order is not forthcoming.

Prior to jumping off, Rosecrans decides to postpone the assault until the following morning. As darkness overtakes the field and the sounds of battle subside, the Union takes pause to get some rest and prepare for the attack scheduled for the following day.

Within the Confederate lines, the outnumbered defenders make other plans. The Rebels, having apparently come close to exhausting

their supplies and expecting no reinforcements from General H. A. Wise at Pickett's Mills, evacuate Carnifex Ferry without detection by the Union. The forces of Floyd, abandoning their positions and large quantities of supplies, quietly slip away by crossing the Gauley River and moving to Dogwood Gap, at the intersection of the Charleston and Summersville Roads. From there, Floyd marches to Meadow Bluff, where he is later joined by the forces of Robert E. Lee.

General Rosecrans, after discovering that the Confederates had abandoned their defenses, decides to make camp at Cross Roads (or Lanes) with the main body, but he orders Colonel McCook to move his brigade out in pursuit of General Floyd. Rosecrans will then redeploy his force at New River to stare down Robert E. Lee on Big Sewell Mountain, as the Union continues to work to evict the Confederates from the western part of Virginia. When Rosecrans' troops occupy the abandoned camp of Floyd, they discover some Union wounded troops in a hospital. The troops, from Colonel Tyler's command, had been captured earlier on 26 August.

The Union suffers 16 dead and 102 wounded, including Colonel John W. Lowe of the 12th Ohio, who was killed. Lt. Colonel Carr Bailey White succeeds Colonel Lowe. The Confederate casualties are estimated at one killed and 10 wounded, with the latter including General Floyd. The Union 3rd Ohio, 9th Ohio (Colonel Robert L. McCook), 10th (Colonel William Haines Lytle), 12th (Colonel Lowe), 13th (Colonel W.S. Smith), 28th Ohio (Colonel A. Moore) and 47th Ohio participate at this battle.

September 10–14 THE BATTLE OF CHEAT MOUNTAIN General Robert E. Lee's plan to move against Clarksburg and Grafton, West Virginia, get underway. General Loring advances directly toward Cheat Mountain, while Lee marches toward Elkwater. After Loring seizes Cheat Mountain, he is to join with Lee at Elkwater and from there together the entire force expects to resume the march toward Clarksburg. Meanwhile, the Union force under General Joseph Reynolds, having intelligence on Lee's operation, is deeply entrenched at Cheat Mountain awaiting the arrival of the Confederate column.

On the morning of 10 September, the brigades of General Donelson and S.R. Anderson link, and the five regiments initiate their move from Valley Mountain against Cheat Mountain. General Loring, peculiarly dressed in civilian clothes, including a heavy velvet frock coat, ride up and down inspecting the line, and for the first time for many of the troops, it became known that General Loring had only one arm, having lost the other during an engagement at Molino Del Ary (Mexican War).

At dawn, while from the top of the mountain the sun beams brilliantly, the tranquil valley below is blanketed with fog. The advance moves quickly with two objectives and neither is expected to be a simple operation. Elements of Loring's division, under General Jackson, ad-

1861

81

vance toward the frontal positions of the Union lines on the Huttonsville Pike, while Donelson's brigade takes a circuitous route through the Tygart Valley, moving along Conley's Run, but as it nears the Union lines, the brigade is to pivot and move to Beckley's Run. From there, at a point opposite the Union lines, the brigade climbs a ridge to reach a point from which the Union is to be surprised by an attack against its rear defenses at Crouch's (Tygart's Valley, Randolph County).

The routes are equally difficult, as no roads exist though the wilderness and the primitive terrain is a non-stop series of dangers that threaten the success of the advances, about thirty miles where each succeeding step could cause the loss of life from falling into the gorges. None of the brigades are able to carry accompanying artillery. Nevertheless, the march continues without incident, but still the Confederates have no knowledge that spies have informed the Union of the pending attacks.

By about 1100 on the 11th, Donelson's brigade, having made more progress than it anticipated, reaches positions in the valley too distant to support Anderson's brigade. It finds itself in a precarious position amid the Union lines to the front and rear, but adding to the problem, mountains are to their left and right. Nonetheless, as the column creeps toward the advance outposts, the Confederates gain the needed surprise and eliminate them without giving notice of their presence to the main picket line. Shortly thereafter, the main pickets are taken by a contingent of the 16th Tennessee Regiment and still, surprise favors the brigade. Afterward, Colonel Savage of the 16th demands surrender of the entire company, under threat of death within five minutes if they refuse. The company surrenders and none escape to warn the main camp below their position. Consequently, the Confederates control the primary approach to the left flank of the Union positions, and from the same point they control the approach to their rear leading to Becky's Run.

By dusk on the 11th, a few Union pickets that attempted escape had been killed, more than fifty officers and men had been captured, and yet no alarm had been sounded. Afterward Colonel Fulton's regiment ascends the ridge under cover of darkness and deploys within a few hundred yards of the Union's rear lines. In the meantime, Colonel Savage's regiment halts for the night at the top of the hill. At about 2100, Colonel Savage, with all units in their assigned positions, finalizes preparations for an attack at dawn on the 12th. Early in the day, General Robert E. Lee, the overall commander, had been on scene to reconnoiter the area. During his time in the field, his chief engineer, Colonel Washington, encountered a Union ambush and died instantly when struck by about three shots; however, Washington's fate is unknown by Lee until after the contest.

General Loring remains along the Huttonsville Pike to the Union's front, while Donelson to the rear and H.R. Jackson in front of Cheat Mountain are positioned from where one can support the other. Meanwhile, following a night of inces-

sant rain, dawn breaks and the Confederates, having attempted to sleep with their arms, prepare to attack. The first order of business is to put their muskets in shape by working on their charges, flints and cartridges. Despite the torrential rains, the troops manage to keep their powder dry. The troops become impatient, awaiting the signal to attack. While awaiting the signal, the reasons for not executing the plan become known. The all-night rain storm had caused the Valley River to swell, making what usually would have been a simple maneuver — fording the river to launch the attack — an impossible chore. General Loring, on the opposite bank, is unable to cross. The snag prevents an assault against the front lines. Consequently, the entire operation becomes jeopardized.

Meanwhile, Henry R. Jackson's order to the 3rd Arkansas at the Greenbrier River, to take the Union stronghold at Cheat Mountain Pass along the Staunton-Parkersburg Road, had been aborted on the previous night (11th) after intelligence proved the position too well fortified to be seized. Jackson, after being made aware, ordered Colonel Rust to return to camp, Leaving Jackson atop the first summit of Cheat Mountain and the Union in control of the pass, located between the first and second summits of the mountain. The attack of the 3rd Arkansas was to be the signal for the remainder of the units to launch their respective assaults. Suddenly, the Confederate force, which had been on the brink of a full scale offensive, finds itself in precarious positioning and the entire operation on the edge of disaster.

A retreat is ordered by Lee. Donelson is directed to withdraw into the valley. By this time, the Union is on the move against the intruders. Elements of the Tennessee 16th Regiment, led by Captain H.H. Dillard, encounter fire as the detachment reaches the bottom of the hill. Fire is returned at about the same time as other Union troops speed to catch the advance guard; together the column ascends the hill. Meanwhile, the trailing Confederate force continues to descend, still under the concealment of the thick brush. The Union fire is scattered and does not inflict punishment, but it does cause some of the Confederates to taunt the Union by yelling that they are only shattering the trees with their marksmanship.

By this time, the exchange of fire is intensifying. The Confederates begin to toss away their blankets and other items to lessen their respective handicaps and the Union closes; there is some difficulty for both sides in determining friend from foe. Meanwhile, Colonel Savage of the Tennessee 16th bellows an order: "Charge the damned rascals and pack them off on your bayonets!" The men of the 16th bolted almost as quickly as Savage had given the order. The Union, not expecting an attack from the retreating Rebels, nor the "Rebel Yell," is pushed back with the Confederates in pursuit. During this short action of about ten minutes, while the Union retreats, some Union casualties occur. The 16th Confederate Tennessee Regiment loses one man (Private Alpha Martin) and several others wounded.

In the meantime, the main body of the Union force ascends the ridge to the positions just abandoned by the Confederates, preventing the latter from retrieving the items they had left. However, the baggage had been abandoned prior to the charge, not in conjunction with the retreat. Donelson's brigade continues the retreat, and at a point about eight miles distant it reaches the crest of yet another mountain. The brigade establishes night positions, and the following day (13th), resumes the march. On the 14th, the brigade repositions itself in the valley at about the same place it had seized the pickets on the 11th.

Also on 14 September, General Lee issues a new order: The forced reconnaissance of the enemy's position, both at Cheat Mountain pass and on Valley River, having been completed, and the character of the natural approaches and the nature of the artificial defenses exposed, the Army of the Northwest will resume its former position, and at such time and in such manner as General Loring shall direct, and continue its preparations for further operations. The commanding general experienced much gratification at the cheerfulness and alacrity displayed by the troops in this arduous operation. The promptitude with which they surmounted every difficulty, driving in and capturing the enemy's pickets on the fronts examined, and exhibiting that readiness for attack, gives assurance of victory when opportunity offers.

The Union units under General Joseph Jones Reynolds that participate include the 13th, 14th, 15th Indiana, the 3rd, 6th and 25th Ohio, and the 2nd West Virginia. Union casualties are nine killed, 12 wounded. Confederates sustain approximately 80 wounded. Colonel John A. Washington, CSA, is struck by a mortal blow during this engagement. Union Colonel John T. Wilder comes to the aid of Washington, who is a nephew of General Robert E. Lee. The young colonel dies while being comforted by Wilder. Colonel Wilder, under a white flag, personally returns the man's body to Confederate lines and receives the thanks of General Lee for his concern.

September 11 (Wednesday) In Missouri, Major General Sterling Price (Missouri Confederate Militia) arrives in Warrenton en route to attack Lexington and to attempt to confiscate the U.S. currency in the town, estimated to be about $800,000. The objective, defended by Colonel James A. Mulligan, lies on the south bank of the Missouri River about 120 miles west of Jefferson City and 300 miles above St. Louis. The town had been defended only by about one-half regiment of Home Guards until these reinforcements arrived, bringing the defender's numbers to about 2,400, still insufficient to hold the town unless more reinforcements arrive. Nevertheless, Mulligan, who had assumed command due to his seniority, sets to the task of establishing defensive positions. Price has much incentive to secure the town. In addition to capturing a position that is strategically located to give it dominance over the primary route to Kansas, the town's vaults now contain the money from Warrenton and an additional $800,000 in gold coin, a commodity that the Confederates badly need.

Mulligan's task is difficult. He establishes headquarters on Masonic Hill near the college building and establishes a line of breastworks around another building to the right of the college. His troops dig a huge ditch that spans a distance of eight feet in width, supported by pits that are encircled with mines, but he lacks much necessary supplies. The cavalry has no guns or rifles, and his two mortars have no shells. And the Union's six cannon have only sparse ammunition. Meanwhile, Price's contingents are preparing to place the clamps on Lexington on the following day. In conjunction, Jeb Stuart (James Ewell Brown Stuart, West Point, 1854) is promoted to Confederate brigadier general on September 24. His opponent, Isaac Ingall Stevens (West Point, 1839) becomes a brigadier on September 28.

In Virginia at Lewinsville, a large Union force—including the 19th Indiana, 65th New York Volunteers, 79th New York Militia and the 3rd Vermont Regiments—battle Confederates under Colonel James "Jeb" Stuart. The Union force, commanded by Colonel Isaac Stevens, sustains about three to six killed, eight or nine wounded and three captured. The Confederate estimated casualties are four killed.

In West Virginia, the 15th and 17th Indiana and the 3rd Ohio Regiments engage and defeat a contingent of Confederates at Elkwater. The Union sustains 6 killed and 4 wounded. The Confederate casualties are estimated at about 15 to 25 killed and less than 15 wounded. In other activity, General William S. Rosecrans initiates pursuit of the forces under General John B. Floyd (see also, **September 10–11 THE BATTLE OF CARNIFEX FERRY**).

September 11–17   In West Virginia, the 1st Brigade, Army of the Ohio (Rosecrans' command), commanded by Brigadier General Joseph Jones Reynolds (West Point, 1843), while operating in West Virginia, engages Confederates (Robert E. Lee's command) in the vicinity of Cheat Mountain at Elk Water, Cheat Mountain Pass, Cheat Summit and Point Mountain Turnpike (see also, **September 10–14 THE BATTLE OF CHEAT MOUNTAIN**).

September 12 (Thursday)   In West Virginia, Union and Confederate units skirmish at both Petersburg and Peytona. Specific units and casualties are unavailable.

In Missouri, three companies of the 1st Indiana Cavalry, commanded by Major John S. Gavitt, skirmish a Confederate unit at Black River. The Confederates sustain about five killed and five captured. Major Gavitt is subsequently killed in action during October 1861 at Fredericktown.

In Union general officer activity, George Crook (West Point, 1852), on duty on the West Coast at the outbreak of the war, is appointed

General Braxton Bragg (Mottelay, *The Soldier in Our Civil War***, 1886).**

colonel of the 36th Ohio. He is appointed brigadier general in August 1862. He participates in the Maryland campaign and later, he commands a cavalry division in the Army of the Cumberland.

In Confederate general officer activity, Brigadier General Braxton Bragg is appointed major general effective this date. He will lead the 2nd Corps (General Albert Sidney Johnston's command). Major James E. Slaughter serves on Bragg's staff, and by the following March he is promoted to brigadier general.

September 12–20   In Missouri at Lexington, Confederates under Major General Sterling Price (Missouri Confederate Militia) initiate the attack against Colonel James Mulligan's defenses in the new section of Lexington. Nine guns under Captains Churchill Clark and Emmett McDonald commence propelling strings of fire and steel toward the entrenchments on the left, considered to be the thinnest along the line. Clouds of gray smoke begin to hover above the field, and Colonel Oliver Anderson's house, being utilized as a hospital, sustains much of the pounding throughout the day. The Union receives a thunderous assault from four separate directions: Colonel Congreve Jackson from the extreme left, the main body at the center, and to the right, General Parsons (state troops) with Captain Guibor's Battery, as well as Confederate General Sterling's Price's contingent force staring straight into the Anderson

house. During the day, the Rebels force the Union to condense its lines and give some ground.

Toward evening the attacks subside, giving Mulligan some breathing room to further his defensive efforts while waiting for reinforcements from General Frémont. A detachment of eleven men, led by Lt. Rains from the Irish Brigade, volunteer to head for Jefferson City to get reinforcements. During the same time period (12th–17th), Major General Sterling Price continues to receive reinforcements, and his troops scatter far and wide in an attempt to discover any federal troops that are en route to rescue the besieged force at Lexington. The Rebels on this front succeed. They capture one arms-laden vessel carrying supplies, intercept a few contingents of Union troops heading toward Lexington, preventing their advance and capturing some, but more importantly, they seize the *Sunshine*. Upon boarding they discover the volunteers that had been dispatched to Jefferson City, severing this opportunity to get help.

In the meantime, General Price and his bulging force prepare to launch another assault against the hard-pressed defenders who have by now even had their water supply cut off. At his headquarters in the courthouse in New Lexington, Price gives the signal to attack on the morning of the 18th. At 0800, again the Confederate guns roar. The thunderclap pounds into the Union lines, hammering them relentlessly throughout the dreary day, which becomes more intolerable as nature seemingly sides with the Rebels. Soaking rains drench both sides, but it is the Union that receives the double cloud burst of iron and rain. The relentless bombardment continues through the night into the morning of the 20th. At this point, Price's force swells even more as about 2,700 troops (2nd Missouri Division) under Brigadier General Thomas Harris arrive.

Soon a strong assault is sprung and the Rebels overwhelm part of the Union line and seize the hills north of Lexington and the Anderson house (hospital). In total disregard of their slim

The siege of Lexington, Missouri, September 12–19, 1861 (Johnson, *Campfire and Battlefield: History of the Conflicts and Campaigns***, 1894).**

numbers, a group of eighty men of the Irish Brigade under Captain Michael Gleason charge and regain the Anderson house, but only for a time. Having lost thirty of their troop during the assault and Captain Gleason becoming wounded, they are more easily compelled to pull back. At about this time, General Price, realizing their water supply had been diminished, their casualties high and their ammunition either gone or nearly gone, senses blood and absolute victory from the beleaguered force. He requests immediate surrender; however, Colonel James A. Mulligan, defying and ignoring his untenable positions, possible still believing help is on the way, responds in unambiguous language: "If you want us, you must take us." To some in his command, this is a startling response.

The Missouri Home Guards, who have up to this point fought bravely and with honor, have become somewhat disheartened in part because no hope is in sight. They react differently and quickly raise a white flag, to the dismay of Mulligan who dispatches a detachment to pull it back down and in quick-time. Captain John W. McDermott's Detroit Jackson Guard removes the white flag and ignites a new and more powerful response from the Confederates. They initiate a ferocious assault that rips into the shredding ranks of the Union, pouring relentless fire into the lines, followed by attack after attack, staggering the gallant but overmatched defenders. The depth of penetration becomes deeper and deeper as the Union is simply overwhelmed by sheer force.

By 1400, the Rebels are nearly at arms' length of the remaining defending force and no reinforcements have arrived. The officers, including Mulligan, who has become wounded in the leg, conclude that further resistance would be futile and a decision is made to unfurl the white flag to end the storm of fire. The Union had attempted to hold out for reinforcements from General Frémont, who was expected to dispatch help either from his command or that of General John Pope at Jefferson City; however, none are dispatched. Frémont will, toward the end of the month, begin a move to prevent the forces of Confederate Generals Price (Missouri militia) and McCulloch from joining together in Arkansas; he will move a force of about 15,000 into Jefferson City.

The Union suffers 42 dead, 108 wounded and 1,624 missing. Colonel Benjamin W. Grover was mortally wounded on the 19th after a shell broke his thigh. He succumbs on 30 October. The Confederates suffer 25 dead and 75 wounded. The Confederates also sustain a very large number of casualties due to explosions in about six mines that had intentionally been ignited during the tenacious attacks. The Confederates, in addition to seizing the gold and money totaling about $900,000, also secure about 3,000 stand of arms, more than 700 horses and an enormous amount of equipment. Subsequent to his exchange, Colonel Mulligan receives the thanks of Congress, and his regiment, the 23rd Illinois (Mulligan's Irish Brigade, composed primarily of Catholic

troops) is authorized to place the word "Lexington" on their colors. The Confederates will evacuate Lexington toward the end of the month and move to Arkansas in an effort to join forces with Confederate General Ben McCulloch.

The 23rd Illinois, 8th, 25th and 27th Missouri Regiments, and the 13th and 14th Missouri Home Guards, supported by Van Horn's Missouri Cavalry and the 1st Illinois Cavalry, participate in the action. Also, Green's Missouri Cavalry Regiment), commanded by Colonel Martin E. Green, participates in this action.

September 13 (Friday)   In Florida, a group of about 100 troops, commanded by Lt. John H. Russell and attached to the USS *Colorado,* which has only recently arrived at Fort Pickens, springs a raid against the CSS *Judah.* The raiding party, using oars instead of sail, silently row to the target. In what amounts to only several minutes, the group boards the vessel, which is in port at the Warrington Navy Yard, Pensacola, being refitted as a Confederate privateer. The assault party dashing dare sets the vessel afire. Confederates react and the raiders sustain three killed and about ten wounded, but the mission, nonetheless, is a success.

In Missouri, a contingent of Home Guards commanded by Captain Eppstein skirmishes with a Confederate force at Boonville. The Union sustains one killed and four wounded. The estimated Confederate casualties are more than 10 killed and 20 or 30 wounded. Also, Union troops occupy St. Joseph's.

In West Virginia, the 2nd Virginia Regiment (later 5th West Virginia), which arrived at Elkwater on the previous day from its camp at Beverly, participates in evicting the Confederates (Robert E. Lee's command) from Cheat Mountain. The 2nd Virginia acts as vanguard while the 3rd Ohio leads the attack, which is under the overall command of General Joseph J. Reynolds. The charge moves over a foothill and the Rebels are dislodged after being hit while they are eating breakfast.

September 14 (Saturday)   In West Virginia, a Union contingent engages Confederates at Shepherdstown. The Union sustains four killed. The estimated Confederate casualties are none killed and more than 10 wounded.

In Union activity, Washington Lafayette Elliott, who initially joined the army as a lieutenant during 1846, on this day is appointed colonel of the 2nd Iowa Cavalry. Elliott entered West Point during 1841, but left the academy prior to graduation during 1844 to study medicine. Afterward, Elliott joins General John Pope and participates at Wilson's Creek and Island No. 10. Later, during the siege of Corinth, he commands a brigade of cavalry.

In Union general officer activity, Edward Otho Cresap Ord (West Point, 1839) is appointed brigadier general. Prior to the outbreak of war, he served in California during the Mexican War, and he was in California during 1859. He returned to the East Coast and participated

with Robert E. Lee, U.S. Army, in the operation against John Brown at Harpers Ferry; however at the start of hostilities, he had been back in California.

In Confederate general officer activity, Simon Bolivar Buckner (West Point, 1844) is appointed brigadier general in the Confederate Army. He had only recently, during the previous month, rejected an appointment as brigadier general in the Union Army. Buckner, at the outbreak of hostilities, had been adjutant general of Kentucky in command of the state guard, but his mission of trying to maintain the neutrality of the state had not been an easy one. As a Confederate, he will remain in Kentucky in command of the Central Division until the fall of Fort Henry during February of the following year.

In Naval activity, the USS *Colorado,* commanded by Lt. Russell, U.S. Navy, engages and destroys the Confederate privateer *Judah* while attacking a shipyard in Pensacola, Florida. A contingent of sailors and Marines under the command of Captain Edward M. Reynolds rows into the harbor, boards the privateer and sets it afire.

September 15 (Sunday)   In Virginia, a Union force composed of the 28th Pennsylvania and the 13th Massachusetts Volunteer Regiments and commanded by Colonel Geary engages and defeats a Confederate contingent at Pritchard's Mills (Damestown), Virginia. The Union sustains one killed. The Confederates sustain eight killed and about 75 wounded. In addition, the Confederates lose two guns.

In Confederate general officer activity, General Albert Sidney Johnston becomes commander of Department No. 2, succeeding Major General Leonidas Polk. In conjunction, General Polk is assigned duty as a corps commander.

In Naval activity, at about this time, the vessel Mount Vernon, built during 1859 and under contract with the U.S. Navy since the outbreak of the war, is acquired by the navy and commissioned as the USS *Mount Vernon* in September. The ship previously had been operating in the Gulf of Mexico and afterward in various blockade operations in the area around Chesapeake Bay. Later it moves to join the blockade operations off North Carolina and spends the remainder of the war in that region. During 1862 and 1863, the Mount Vernon destroys 12 blockade runners. Also, at about this time (September 1861), the U.S. Army acquires the *New Era,* a steam ferry, and attaches it to the Western Gunboat Flotilla. The ship retains its name and is transformed into a warship, a 355-ton "timberclad" gunboat. During November of this year, the *New Era* participates in an expedition on the Cumberland River. Subsequently, the *New Era* is renamed, becoming the USS *Essex.* This *New Era* is separate from the stern-wheel steamer USS *New Era,* which is acquired by the U.S. Navy during October 1862. The Navy also acquires the *Maria Denning,* but the exact date during 1861 is unknown. The side-wheel steamer had been built in Cincinnati in 1859. It serves as a transport along the western rivers and later, the USS *Maria Denning* is a receiving ship at Cairo, Illinois, from November of this year until April 1862. In December 1862, it is transferred to the U.S. Army and utilized also as a transport until April 1863 until it is decommissioned and returned to civilian use. It is destroyed by fire at Algiers, Louisiana, on 11 May 1866.

September 16 (Monday) **In Maryland,** a small contingent of the 34th New York Regiment encounters and engages about three companies of Confederate troops at Seneca Creek. The Union sustains two killed. Confederate casualties are unavailable.

In Union general officer activity, Horatio G. Wright (West Point, 1841) is appointed brigadier general. Alfred Thomas Archimedes Torbert (West Point, 1851) is appointed colonel of the 1st New Jersey Regiment. He succeeds General William R. Montgomery. On the 25th, Torbert is promoted to captain of the 5th U.S. Infantry (final full rank promotion while in the regular army). Ironically, Torbert had been nominated and confirmed as a first lieutenant of artillery in the Army of the Confederacy. He is promoted to the rank of brigadier general in November 1862. Also, William Nelson, a naval veteran of the Mexican War, is appointed brigadier general of volunteers. Prior to his appointment, Nelson had executed some tasks for the Union in Kentucky and when completed, he handed his findings to President Lincoln. Nelson had established Camp Dick Robinson in Garrard County, Kentucky, during the previous April; it is where the 1st Kentucky Volunteer Cavalry Regiment is raised. Camp Dick Robinson is relocated in Jessamine County on the Jessamine side of the river, considered to be a more strategic location from which to defend against a Confederate attack. The new camp is named Camp Nelson.

In Confederate general officer activity, Secretary of War Leroy Pope Walker resigns his cabinet position. He will receive an appointment as brigadier general on the 17th and move to Alabama, but once there, he fails to acquire a command in the field, prompting him to also quit this post. He resigns during March of 1862.

In Naval activity, the USS *Conestoga* defeats two Confederate vessels on the Cumberland River in Kentucky. Also, a Union naval force transports a contingent of troops from Hatteras, North Carolina, to spring an assault against Confederate-held Fort Ocracoke at Ocracoke Inlet, a strategic entrance to Pamlico Sound. The Expeditionary Force, commanded by Lt. James Y. Maxwell, transports 67 troops (naval brigade) under Lt. Rowe and Lt. Tillotson aboard the tug *Fanny* and an additional twenty-eight troops and one howitzer in tow aboard a launch of the gunboat *Pawnee*. The *Susquehanna* and the *Tempest* begin the journey; however, discovering their draft of water much too great, they return to Hatteras.

The objective is reached at 1100 and the troops land to assault, only to discover the fort abandoned and partially destroyed. The mission's purpose is to destroy rather than occupy the fort, and the troops complete the unfinished work of the Confederates, using both torch and manpower to knock the fortification out of action. The Expeditionary Force returns to Fort Hatteras on the following morning. With Forts Clark and Hatteras in hand and the elimination of Fort Ocracoke, the Confederates still hold two other primary targets that will hinder Union operations, Loggerhead (New) Inlet and Oregon Inlet, and both are north of Hatteras. Action against them begins on September 29.

September 17 (Tuesday) **In Mississippi,** Union forces capture Ship Island for use as a blockade port for the U.S. Navy. The Rebel forces evacuate, allowing the Union forces to use the island as a base for impending actions along the Gulf Coast. Union troops will occupy it in force during December of this year.

In Missouri, a skirmish lasting about one hour occurs between the Union 3rd Iowa Volunteers commanded by Lt. Colonel F. Scott and about 4,000 Confederate troops at Blue Mills Landing. The Union force, composed of about 500 troops, sustains 11 killed and 39 wounded. The Confederates sustain 10 killed and about 60 wounded. Also, at Morristown, Missouri, a skirmish develops between the 5th, 6th and 9th Kansas Cavalry, bolstered by the 1st Kansas Battery and a force of Confederates numbering about 400 troops. The Union force, commanded by Colonels James Montgomery and F. Smith, numbers about 600 troops. The Union sustains two killed and six wounded. The Confederates sustain seven killed. In other activity, the 19th Illinois Regiment suffers about 100 casualties, including killed and wounded, when a train transporting them on the Ohio and Mississippi Railroad has an accident.

September 18 (Wednesday) **In Kentucky,** Confederate troops commanded by General Felix Zollicoffer force Union Home Guard troops to evacuate Barboursville (also Red House, West Virginia), Kentucky. The Confederates occupy the town on the following day. Union losses are one dead, one wounded and one captured. Confederates count seven dead. Also, a Confederate force occupies Bowling Green.

In Union general officer activity, William Thomas Ward, a veteran of the Mexican War and former congressman, is appointed brigadier general of volunteers. Initially he serves Kentucky; in November 1862 he is assigned to the Army of the Tennessee and made post commander at Gallatin. Subsequently, he is transferred to the Army of the Cumberland in command of the 1st Division (General Oliver Howard's XI Corps).

In Union Naval officer activity, Captain Samuel F. Du Pont assumes command of the Union South Atlantic Blocking Squadron.

In Confederate general officer activity, General Simon Bolivar Buckner receives command of the Central Division of Kentucky.

In Naval activity, the gunboat USS *Rescue,* while on patrol in the vicinity of Mathias Point and Pope's Creek, intercepts and seizes the schooner *Harford,* which is transporting a contraband cargo, including tobacco and wheat.

September 19 (Thursday) **In Kentucky,** Union troops in Paducah begin construction of a pontoon bridge to span the Ohio River, using their ingenuity by linking a large amount of coal barges, which had been acquired in Cincinnati, Ohio, to provide strength. The bridge, which will stretch 6,000 feet from shore to shore, will be completed in four days. In other activity, a Union force composed of about 300 troops is engaged and defeated by a Confederate force commanded by Colonel C. Battle (General Zollicoffer's command) at Barboursville (also Red House, West Virginia), Kentucky. The Union suffers 12 killed and two captured. The Confederates sustain two killed and three wounded.

In Union activity, the Department of the Ohio is reorganized. General Ormsby MacKnight Mitchel assumes command; however, the department will soon be incorporated into the Army of the Cumberland, commanded by General Don Carlos Buell. Also, Joseph Warren Revere, a grandson of the Revolutionary War hero Paul Revere, is commissioned colonel (later brigadier general) of the 7th New Jersey Infantry Regiment. Revere had previously joined the U.S. Navy at about age sixteen and served for more than twenty years when he retired during 1850. Afterward, while residing in California, Revere had also served as a colonel in the Mexican Army. The regiment, attached to General Hooker's division (General Heintzelman's III Corps) participates in the Peninsular Campaign; however, Colonel Revere seems to have been engaged only at the Seven Days' Battle.

In yet other activity, John Blair Smith Todd (West Point, 1837) is appointed brigadier general. General Todd, a Kentuckian, is a veteran of the Mexican war and of frontier duty, but he also is a lawyer, supposedly related to President Lincoln by marriage. He becomes commander of the North Missouri District, but subsequently, during June 1862, he commands the 6th Division of the Army of the Tennessee. Nevertheless, General Todd, in conjunction with the Dakota Territory established the previous December, becomes a delegate to Congress, terminating his military service.

In Confederate general officer activity, Gustavus Woodson Smith is appointed major general in the Confederate Army this day. He will command the 2nd Corps of the Army of the Potomac (Army of Northern Virginia). In January 1863, he becomes disgruntled and resigns his commission when he is passed over for promotion to major general. Smith is subsequently appointed major general in the Georgia militia. Also, Confederate Brigadier General Earl Van Dorn (West Point, 1842) is promoted to the rank of major general. He is succeeded in command by Brigadier General Paul Octave Hebert (West Point, 1840). General Hebert, cousin of Confederate Brigadier General Louis Hebert, becomes commander of the Department of Texas and of the Subdistrict of Northern Louisiana. Colonel Henry Eustace McCulloch had recently (September 4) been placed in temporary charge of the Confederate troops in Texas.

September 20 (Friday)   In Kentucky, Union troops stationed at Paducah, Kentucky, continue to drill, sharpening their battle skills for the encounters which will come. General Ulysses S. Grant insists on readiness. By November, his command numbers approximately 20,000 enlisted men. Also, Mayfield is evacuated by the Confederates this day.

In Missouri, Union reinforcements anticipated by the defenders at Lexington do not arrive. The Confederates under Major General Sterling Price (Missouri Confederate Militia) capture the city. The city had been defended by slightly more than 2,500 troops of the Irish Brigade, Home Guards and the 8th Missouri Regiment, led by Colonel James Mulligan. The Union, following the action, which lasts about fifty-nine hours, sustains 42 killed, 108 wounded and about 1,600 to 2,000 captured or missing. The Confederates sustain 25 killed, 75 wounded and six captured. In addition, the Confederates seize about 3,000 stands of arms (see also, **September 12–20 In Missouri**).

In Union activity, Charles Cruft is appointed colonel of the 31st Indiana Infantry. He participates in the reduction of Fort Donelson while in command of a brigade (Lew Wallace's division).

September 21 (Saturday)   In Missouri, a Union force, composed of the 5th, 6th and 9th Kansas Cavalry Regiments, commanded by General John Q. Lane, engages and defeats a contingent of Confederates at Papinsville (Osceola). The Union sustains 17 killed. The Confederates sustain 40 killed and 100 captured.

In West Virginia, on the previous day, General Lee, subsequent to the setback at Cheat Mountain, had arrived at General Floyd's positions at Sewell Mountain. General Henry Alexander Wise, who was serving under Floyd, is relieved of his command and within about five days departs for Richmond. Subsequently, Wise will participate in the campaign in North Carolina, followed by serving in North and South Carolina. He also serves in Virginia defending Richmond. General Wise is the brother-in-law of Union General George Gordon Meade. In other activity, Strong Vincent, who entered the service during April in a Pennsylvania militia unit, is commissioned lieutenant colonel of the 83rd Pennsylvania Regiment. Later, on 27 June 1862, he becomes colonel of the regiment.

In Confederate activity, at about this time, General Robert E. Lee assumes command of all Confederate forces in the Kanawha Valley. Also,

Colonel Albert Gallatin Blanchard (West Point, 1829), 1st Louisiana Volunteers, is appointed brigadier general. Blanchard apparently sees no battlefield commands for the duration of the conflict. Colonel Thomas Carmichael Hindman, 2nd Arkansas Infantry, is promoted to brigadier general.

In Naval activity, the U.S. Navy acquires the tug *Shawsheen* (built during 1855 in New York), but no records exist regarding when it was commissioned. The ship is transferred to the South Atlantic Blockading Squadron with Acting Lt. Edmund R. Colhoun as its initial commanding officer. The *Shawsheen* arrives at Hampton Roads during early November, but it had sustained disabling damages, preventing it from continuing the voyage on its own power.

The USS *John L. Lockwood* is commissioned at Washington, D.C. The ship was constructed at Athens, New York, during 1854; on 1 September 1861 it was acquired by the U.S. Navy at New York City. Acting Master William F. North receives command of the ship, which is assigned to the North Atlantic Blockading Squadron. In other activity, the U.S. Navy purchases a wooden schooner, the *Rachael Seaman.* It is commissioned in Philadelphia on 16 November; Acting Master Quincey A. Hooper receives command. It sails for the Gulf of Mexico during early November to begin blockade duty.

September 22 (Sunday)   In Missouri, a Union contingent of the 7th Iowa Volunteers skirmishes with a Confederate force of about fifty troops at Elliott's Mills (Camp Crittenden). The Union suffers one killed and five wounded. Confederate casualties are unavailable.

In Union activity, Theopholus Toulmin Garrard, the cousin of Union general Kenner Garrard, is appointed colonel of the 7th Kentucky Infantry Regiment.

September 23 (Monday)   In West Virginia, the 4th and 8th Ohio Regiments (Volunteers) and Ringgold's Cavalry commanded by Colonels Parke and Cantwell engage a Confederate force of about 700 troops at Romney (Hanging Rock). The two sides maintain the skirmishing until the 25th. The Union, composed of slightly less than 1,000 men, sustains three killed and 50 wounded. The Confederates sustain about 35 killed.

In Texas at Galveston, several vessels, including the *Diana, Bayou City* and *Neptune No. 2,* are on the block for either charter or sale by the Houston Navigation Company. The *Bayou City* and the *Diana* become ram gunboats in the service of the Texas Marine Department. Both vessels are assigned duty as defenders on Galveston Bay. The *Diana* and the *Bayou City* remain in service as late as autumn of 1863. The ram *Diana* is separate from the side-wheel steamer ironclad *Diana* captured by the USS *Cayuga* at New Orleans on 27 May 1862 and retaken by the Confederates on 11 April 1863.

In Union general officer activity, Union Major Seth Williams (West Point, 1842) is appointed

brigadier general. General Williams becomes adjutant general of the Army of the Potomac, and subsequently General U.S. Grant appoints him inspector general. He sees no field command. In addition, he is breveted major general of volunteers during the summer of 1864 and remains in the service beyond the close of hostilities until his health fails, causing him to take a leave of absence in February 1866. He dies on 23 March from "congestion of the brain." Also, Major John Gross Barnard, 5th U.S. Artillery, is appointed brigadier general. General Barnard, chief engineer in charge of the defenses of Washington, later becomes chief engineer of the armies under General Grant. After the war, Barnard becomes colonel in the Corps of Engineers. Winfield Scott Hancock (West Point, 1844) is appointed brigadier general.

John Newton (West Point, 1842) is appointed brigadier general. Initially he is assigned duty involving the defenses of the capital, but by the following spring, he is attached to General Slocum's division (VI Corps) and given command of a brigade, which he leads during the Peninsular Campaign of General George McClellan. Subsequently, he participates in the Maryland campaign and at the Battle of Fredericksburg, the latter during December 1862. Innis Newton Palmer (West Point, 1846), a classmate of General George B. McClellan and Confederate General Thomas "Stonewall" Jackson, is appointed a brigadier general. Prior to the outbreak of war, General Palmer had served primarily on the western frontier; in 1855 he became a captain with the newly established 2nd U.S. Cavalry. During his time with the 2nd Cavalry he served under three men who join the Confederacy, Albert S. Johnston, Robert E. Lee and William J. Hardee, each a Confederate general.

Also, Stewart Van Vliet (West Point, 1840) is appointed brigadier general. General Vliet, a veteran of the Mexican War, at this time is chief quartermaster, Army of the Potomac. During July 1862, he is relieved at his own request and his commission expires (17 July). For the remainder of the hostilities, he is based in New York assigned to duty involving arranging for transportation and supplies. While there, he is reappointed brigadier general during November 1865, effective 13 March 1865. He retires during 1881. In yet other activity, Gabriel James Rains (West Point, 1827), who resigned from the U.S. Army on 31 July, is appointed brigadier general in the Provisional Confederate Army. Rains had been lieutenant colonel of the 5th U.S. Infantry. He is an explosives expert who introduces the anti-personnel mine used at Yorktown.

September 24 (Tuesday)   In West Virginia, General Cox informs General Rosecrans that most of his positions at Camp Sewell are concealed and that he expects the Confederates to withdraw from their positions near the Kanawha River.

In Union general officer activity, Ferdinand Van Derveer, a veteran of the Mexican War who served as first sergeant and afterward as captain

(1st Ohio Volunteers), is commissioned colonel of the 35th Ohio Regiment. Van Derveer remains with the regiment and participates at various actions, including Corinth, Perryville and Murfreesboro. Afterward, he commands a brigade at Chattanooga. During the Atlanta campaign he and the regiment muster out of the service; however, the following October he re-enters service and is commissioned brigadier general. Also, William Vandever, a lawyer, is commissioned colonel of the 9th Iowa Regiment. Colonel Vandever participates at the Battle of Pea Ridge (Elkhorn Tavern) during March 1862 and is promoted to brigadier general on 29 November 1862.

September 25 (Wednesday)   **In Kentucky,** Union troops occupy Smithland at the mouth of the Cumberland River about eighty miles from Paducah.

In New Mexico, a Union contingent of New Mexico Volunteers led by Captain John H. Minks engages a force of Confederates numbering more than 100 at Canada Alamosa. Nine Union troops are captured.

In Virginia, a contingent of Union gunboats engages Confederate batteries at Freestone Point.

In West Virginia, the Union 1st Kentucky Regiment and the 34th Ohio Volunteers, commanded by Colonel David A. Enyart, skirmish with a contingent of Confederates led by Colonel Davis at Chapmansville. The Union sustains four killed and nine wounded. The Confederates sustain 60 killed, 50 wounded and about 47 captured.

In Union general officer activity, Major Joseph Bennett Plummer is appointed colonel of the 11th Missouri Cavalry.

In Confederate general officer activity, Colonel Lafayette McLaws is appointed brigadier general (later major general).

In Naval activity, the steamers USS *Jacob Bell* and the *Seminole* attack Confederate positions at Freestone Point, Virginia. The *Jacob Bell,* built in New York City during 1842 for commercial use, was acquired by the U.S. Navy in August 1861. Its war service is primarily on the Potomac and Rappahannock Rivers until decommissioned during May 1865. On 6 November while en route to New York under tow, the *Jacob Bell* is lost at sea.

September 26 (Thursday)   **In Kentucky,** a contingent of Union Cavalry (Stewart's Cavalry) composed of 75 troopers led by Captain Stewart engages a Confederate force of fewer than 50 at Lucas Bend. The Union sustains no casualties. The Confederates suffer four wounded and five captured.

In Missouri, Union Cavalry (Stewart's Cavalry) engages a contingent of Confederates at Hunter's Farm. The Union sustains no casualties. The Confederates sustain 10 killed and four captured.

In New Mexico, Company C, U.S. 3rd Cavalry, commanded by Captain Robert M. Morris, engages and defeats a Confederate force at Fort Thorne in a skirmish that lasts slightly less than two hours. Casualties are unavailable.

In Texas, Commander W. Hunter, Confederate States Navy, the commanding officer of the Texas Marine Department, charters the vessel *Bayou City,* a mail runner, from the Houston Navigation Company. The ship, under jurisdiction of the state of Texas, is assigned duty in Galveston Bay and the Trinity River until October 1862, then is transferred to the Confederate War Department. Beginning in 1863, under the Marine Department, the *Bayou City* patrols along the coast of Texas for the duration of the war. Sometime in 1861, the *Mary Hill,* a transport (side-wheel steamer) built at Smithfield, Texas, was fitted out by the Confederates as a cottonclad gunboat. The *Mary Hill* remains in service along the Texas coast for the duration of the war, primarily operating between Galveston and Matagorda Bay.

September 27 (Friday)   **In Missouri,** a contingent of the Union 8th Illinois Infantry Regiment, composed of about 200 troops and commanded by former Illinois state senator Colonel Richard James Oglesby, engages a Confederate force at Norfolk. Casualty figures are unavailable. Oglesby, a veteran of the Mexican War, is promoted to brigadier general the following year, subsequent to the battles in Tennessee at Fort Donelson and Fort Henry.

In Virginia, a crack brigade, composed of two regiments, the 1st and 2nd U.S. Sharpshooters, engage in their first action with Confederates at Lewinsville. Two companies of the 1st Regiment, C and E, encounter and engage a Confederate foraging contingent. The regiments, commanded by Colonel Hiram Berdan, remain in their training camp near Washington, D.C., from September 1861 until the following March. In addition to being a specialized brigade, the troops also wear distinctive green uniforms. Colonel Berdan, a New York native, from the beginning had intended to raise a force of the most skilled marksmen in the North. He received authorization from the secretary of war to form the unit. Each man is required to pass a test that includes the ability to group ten successive shots within a 10-inch circle from a distance of two-hundred yards. The sharpshooters participate in many engagements and become renowned for their fighting ability. One of the most famous of the sharpshooters is Truman Head (1st Regiment), known more by the name California Joe. Another of the more familiar men of the brigade is Lorenzo

Barber (2nd Regiment), known as the "Fighting Parson." Colonel Berdan receives the brevet of brigadier general; however, following the Battle of Gettysburg his promotion to brigadier general is not forthcoming and he leaves the service. The 1st Regiment is mustered out of service in November 1864 and the 2nd Regiment closes its service during early 1865.

In Naval activity, the USS *Mohawk,* on duty with the African Squadron since early 1860, arrives at Boston. It is assigned to the South Atlantic Blockading Squadron.

September 28 (Saturday)   **In Michigan,** at Camp Lyon, the 1st Michigan is presented a flag from the people of Springwells. The flag, accepted by Colonel T.F. Brodhead on behalf of the regiment, is made of "blue silk, heavily fringed, with the national arms on each side, under which was emblazoned in gold letters, First Michigan Cavalry."

In Missouri, General John Frémont, on the march to intercept Confederate General Ster-

Brigader General Justus McKinstry (Mottelay, *The Soldier in Our Civil War,* 1886).

General Frémont's headquarters, Camp Lillie, at Jefferson, Missouri (Mottelay, *The Soldier in Our Civil War,* 1886).

1861

87

ling Price (Missouri Confederate Militia), establishes Camp Lillie at Jefferson City, the state capital. Subsequent to the recent actions of Confederate General Price in the area, General John Frémont moves with a force of about 15,000 Infantry troops, bolstered by about 500 cavalrymen, including the commands of Generals Alexander S. Asboth, David Hunter (West Point, 1822), John Pope (West Point, 1842), Justus McKinstry (West Point, 1838) and Franz Sigel. Meanwhile, General Sterling Price is preparing to evacuate Lexington and head for Arkansas.

In Virginia, the Confederates abandon Munson's Hill.

In Union general officer activity, Colonel George Wright (West Point, 1822) is promoted to the rank of brigadier general. Wright had been in command of the Department of Oregon; however, he is perceived as an expert regarding California and the Pacific Northwest and consequently as the war began he had been placed in command of the Department of the Pacific. He remains on the Pacific coast for the duration, essentially lacking troops during the entire war. Toward the close of hostilities, he was en route to assume command of the Department of the Columbia; however, he loses his life aboard the vessel *Brother Jonathan,* which is wrecked on 30 July 1865 off northern California. Also, John Porter Hatch (West Point, 1845) is appointed brigadier general. The following year, General Hatch commands the cavalry in General Nathaniel Banks' command during the campaign in the Shenandoah. William Henry French (West Point, 1837) is named brigadier general. He is promoted to major general in November 1862.

Colonel Isaac Stevens, 79th New York, is promoted to brigadier general. The men in his regiment, which recently reached the brink of mutiny, request transfer to serve in his brigade. William Thomas H. Brooks (West Point, 1841) is appointed brigadier general. Colonel Randolph Barnes Marcy (inspector general) is appointed brigadier general. However, Marcy, the father-in-law of General George McClellan, is not confirmed by the Senate. His commission expires on 4 March of the following year. Subsequently, he is assigned various inspection duties from July 1863 until the close of hostilities. Marcy, a graduate of West Point (1832), also serves at army headquarters in the capital and remains in the service beyond the close of the war. During 1878, he is appointed inspector general of the U.S. Army with the rank of brigadier general. General Marcy retires during 1881. His death occurs on 2 November 1887, about two years after the death of his son-in-law, George McClellan.

Edwin Denison Morgan, elected governor of New York during 1860, is appointed major general of volunteers by President Lincoln, who assigns him as commander of the Department of New York. David Sloane Stanley (West Point, 1852) is named brigadier general. Stanley had been stationed at Fort Washita in the Indian Territory (Oklahoma) at the outbreak of war.

He declined a commission in the Confederacy and instead led his command to Fort Leavenworth, Kansas, and participated in the operations in Missouri. General Stanley later sustains a broken leg that keeps him from the field for the winter of 1861–1862. George Sykes (West Point, 1842), a veteran of the Mexican War who commanded a brigade at First Manassas, is appointed brigadier general. General Sykes is promoted to major general on 29 November 1862. Also, Thomas Williams (West Point, 1837) is appointed brigadier general of volunteers. Williams, a veteran of the Florida Seminole Wars and the Mexican War, had been stationed at Fort Monroe at the opening of hostilities. He became major of the 5th Artillery on 14 May. General Williams is initially placed in command of inspector general of the Department of Virginia for a short while, but afterward he moves to Philadelphia in command of his old regiment, prior to participating in the Burnside expedition to North Carolina. He is ordered afterward to Louisiana to participate in the operations against New Orleans.

In Naval activity, the USS *Constellation,* having recently been recalled while on station with the African Squadron, arrives at the navy yard at Portsmouth, New Hampshire. Also, Colonel John Milton Brannan is appointed brigadier general. William Wallace Burns (West Point, 1847) is commissioned brigadier general. In yet other activity, William Kerley Strong is appointed brigadier general by President Lincoln. At the outbreak of the war, Strong had been in Egypt, but he moved to France to acquire arms for the Union cause. General Strong sees no field duty; rather he commands at various places, including the St. Louis Barracks, the District of Cairo, and New York (his home state). Later, he returns to St. Louis as president of an investigative commission examining the circumstances surrounding the evacuation of New Madrid. He resigns his commission while in command of the Department of Missouri on 20 December 1863. After returning to New York he devotes time to recruiting Negroes; however, shortly thereafter, he is thrown from his carriage, is paralyzed from the injuries and never recovers. He dies on 16 March 1867.

September 29 (Sunday) In Kentucky, at James Bayou Bridge, a force of about 100 Union troops engage a Confederate contingent of more than 200 troops. The Union sustains no casualties. The Confederates sustain five wounded and one captured.

In Maryland, another contest occurs at Berlin, about 130 miles from Washington in the vicinity of Ocean City.

In Virginia, skirmishes between Confederate units and Union forces occur at Falls Church, just across the Potomac River from Washington. The Union sustains no casualties. The Confederates suffer 10 killed and 20 wounded. Also, troops from the 69th Pennsylvania mistakenly fire upon the 71st Pennsylvania troops, killing nine and wounding about 23 at Munson's Hill.

In Naval activity, the steamers *USS Ceres* and USS *Putnam,* transporting the recently arrived 20th Indiana Regiment under Colonel William L. Brown, departs from Hatteras, North Carolina, this day to land at a point between Chicamacomico and Kinnakeet to reconnoiter Roanoke Island, which is south of Loggerhead Inlet. Due to a shallow depth, small boats are utilized to land the troops. The regiment is to await supplies, due on the 30th with the arrival of the tug *Fanny,* but the tug does not show at the appointed time.

September 30 (Monday) In Missouri, Major General Sterling Price (Missouri Confederate Militia) abandons Lexington and moves toward Arkansas. Some troops remain behind and Union prisoners are still in the city. A detachment of Union cavalry under Major Frank J. White will later arrive, gain the freedom of the troops and, in the process, capture many of the Confederates who had been guarding them. Major White then joins General Frémont at a town named Tipton shortly after 11 October.

In New Mexico, Union forces in New Mexico initiate a mission against Indians in the vicinity of Fort Robeldo. The mission is completed on October 7.

In Union general officer activity, Henry Bohlen is appointed colonel of the 75th Pennsylvania Volunteer Infantry Regiment.

In Confederate general officer activity, Lieutenant Colonel Adley Hogan Gladden, 1st Louisiana Regulars, is promoted to the rank of brigadier general. He transfers from Pensacola, Florida, to Mississippi, where he leads a brigade at Corinth.

October In Union activity, Union regiments are being strengthened to meet the Confederate threat. John Sanford Mason (West Point, 1847) is appointed colonel, 4th Ohio Infantry. Colonel Mason leads his regiment through the Western Virginia campaign during the fall and winter months of 1861–62, prior to becoming a brigadier general on 29 November 1862. He participates at the Battle of Fredericksburg, but the *Official Records* lists him as a colonel. During the following April he is relieved of field duty and assigned to recruiting. At the close of hostilities, he does receive brevets through the ranks of brigadier general in the Regular Army.

In Confederate general officer activity, Thomas E. Lloyd is appointed colonel of the 35th Georgia Infantry. He will become a brigadier general in November of the following year. Also, Nathan Bedford Forrest, a wealthy private in the 7th Tennessee Cavalry, had formed a battalion of cavalry using funds he had acquired from his plantation. At this time, he is chosen as lieutenant colonel. Later he becomes colonel of the 3rd Tennessee and is promoted to brigadier general during July 1862. Forrest had apparently acquired his fortune, despite the lack of a formal education, by planting, dealing in cattle and horses and selling real estate and slaves. Also, Jean Jacques Alfred A. Mouton

(West Point, 1850) is appointed colonel (later brigadier general) of the 18th Louisiana Infantry.

October 1 (Tuesday)   In Washington, D.C., President Abraham Lincoln appoints General Benjamin Franklin Butler commander of the Department of New England.

In Virginia, an eleven-man Union contingent led by Surgeon Cox skirmishes a Confederate contingent numbering slightly less than 100 troops at Edsall's Hill. The Union sustains one man killed and three captured. The Confederates sustain no casualties.

In West Virginia, the Union forces as well as the Confederates under Rosecrans and Floyd each get a reprieve as the autumn rains that had begun during early September finally cease; however, both sides have sustained problems ranging from logistics to sickness. The tedious task of transporting supplies to the vicinity of Sewell's Mountain from Rosecrans' supply base 60 miles distant has taken a huge toll on the horses and mules. Meanwhile, the Confederates have identical supply problems. The elements have caused a lack of aggressive activity by either side. By the 5th, Rosecrans begins to return to Gauley Bridge.

In Union activity, Major Charles Carroll Walcutt (Ohio state service) is commissioned major of the 46th Ohio Regiment. Also, at about this time (October), George Henry Chapman, formerly a midshipman, joins the 3rd Indiana Cavalry. He rises quickly through the ranks; he is made colonel of the regiment during 1863 and promoted to brigadier general the following year. In 1865, he receives the brevet rank of major general. His career is rather obscure; however, he participates in many engagements, including 2nd Manassas (Bull Run), Antietam (Sharpsburg), Chancellorsville, Gettysburg, and the Petersburg campaign.

Lovell Harrison Rousseau, who served as a captain (2nd Indiana Volunteer Regiment) in the Mexican War, is appointed brigadier general. In yet other activity, Colonel Adolph Wilhelm August Friedrich von Steinwehr (29th New York), a native of the Duchy of Brunswick who immigrated to the U.S. during 1847, is commissioned a brigadier general of volunteers. Also, Melancthon Smith Wade, born during 1802 and having held the rank of brigadier general of militia (Ohio), is commissioned brigadier general of volunteers. Initially he becomes the first commander of Camp Dennison, located along the Little Miami River northeast of Cincinnati. Nonetheless, due to his advancing age and declining health, General Wade does not get an opportunity to command in the field. He resigns his commission on 18 March 1862. General Wade's name does not find its way into even the index of the *Official Records.*

In Naval activity, the USS *Fanny,* a tender en route to deliver supplies to a reconnaissance expedition of the 20th Indiana Regiment at an island south of Loggerhead Inlet near Roanoke Island, is captured by the Confederates off Pam-

lico Sound, North Carolina. The *Fanny* becomes the CSS *Fanny.* In addition to the loss of the ship and supplies, about 30 men are captured. The Confederates meanwhile also prepare to mount an assault to destroy the Union 20th Indiana Regiment on the 4th. In other activity, the *Coeur de Lion* (side-wheel gunboat), which had been built in Coxsakie, New York, at about this time, is commissioned the USS *Coeur de Lion.* Just after the eruption of war the vessel had been on loan to the navy, apparently as a U.S. Lighthouse tender. The vessel serves for the duration on the Potomac, James and other tributaries of Chesapeake Bay. In June 1865 the *Coeur de Lion* is returned to the U.S. Lighthouse Board and remains in its service until it is sold during 1867 and renamed *Alice.* As a commercial vessel it remains operational until about 1873. Also, at about this time (October), the U. S. Navy acquires the *Ellen,* a civilian ferryboat built in New York City. It is transformed into a light draft gunboat and commissioned the USS *Ellen,* assigned to the South Atlantic Blockading Squadron. The *Ellen* later embarks from New York and arrives at Port Royal during November. Also, the USS *Seneca* is commissioned at about this time (October). It is assigned duty with the South Atlantic Blockading Squadron.

October 2 (Wednesday)   In *Union general officer activity,* Napoleon Jackson Tecumseh Dana is appointed colonel, 1st Minnesota. Dana (West Point, 1842) has prior service during the Mexican War and was severely wounded at Cerro Gordo, Mexico, where he remained on the field and was thought dead. Dana subsequently rises to the rank of major general.

In Naval activity, the U.S. Navy acquires the vessel *Commodore Barney,* an armed side wheel ferry built in New York during 1859. The *Commodore Barney* is commissioned this month and assigned to the North Atlantic Blockading Squadron in January 1862.

In Union general officer activity, Benjamin Henry Grierson is commissioned major (later major general). He becomes colonel of the regiment during the following April.

October 3 (Thursday)   In Louisiana, Governor Thomas O. Moore uses a ploy to try to prompt Europe to recognize the Confederate States of America. He issues an order prohibiting the delivery of cotton to New Orleans to prevent its exportation to Europe and proclaims it effective for the duration of the ongoing Union blockade. The South Atlantic Blockade Squadron under Captain Samuel Du Pont is maintaining the blockade.

In Virginia, a contingent of Union General John Newton's Brigade (Slocum's Division, VI Corps), led by Colonel (later general) Calvin Edward Pratt, skirmishes with some small Confederate units, but his force, numbering about 800, easily overcomes the opposition at Springfield Station. Newton, a graduate of West Point (1842), had only recently become brigadier general (September). In related activ-

ity, Union troops occupy Pohick Church near Springfield Station.

In West Virginia, a Union force composed of about 5,000 troops, led by General John Fulton Reynolds, engages and defeats a Confederate force of about 9,000 troops commanded by General R.E. Lee at Greenbrier, in a vicious contest that lasts about one hour. The Union seizes large amounts of supplies. Participating in this battle are the 24th, 25th and 32nd Ohio, the 7th, 9th, 13th Indiana and Battery G, 4th U.S. Artillery. The Union has 8 dead and 32 wounded; the Confederates count 100 killed and 75 wounded. The Confederate 25th Virginia Regiment (General Taliaferro's Brigade) participates in this action. The Union also overwhelms a Confederate contingent at the Greenbrier River in Virginia.

October 4 (Friday)   In Kentucky, Union and Confederate contingents skirmish at Buffalo Hill. The Union sustains twenty killed. The Confederates sustain about 50 killed. No unit affiliations are reported.

In Maryland, a Union force attached to the command of General Charles P. Stone skirmishes with a Confederate contingent at Edward's Ferry. No casualty figures are available.

General Charles P. Stone (Mottelay, *The Soldier in Our Civil War,* 1886).

In North Carolina, Confederate troops unsuccessfully attack federal troops near the recently captured Forts Hatteras and Clark. Colonel W.L. Brown's 20th Indiana Regiment, lacking supplies that were aboard the *Fanny,* captured on October 1, engages a Confederate force composed of about 2,500 troops from Roanoke Island. Following darkness, the Yankees retreat toward Hatteras Lighthouse, arriving there after dawn on the following morning; fortuitously, they encounter a friendly force of about 500 men (9th and 20th New York Volunteer Regiments) under Colonel Rush Hawkins that had been en route to reinforce Brown. Together, they head north to engage the Confederates, believed to be in pursuit of the 20th Regiment. The vessels USS *Monticello* and USS *Susquehanna* cruise offshore, shadowing the advance and holding their guns at the ready for the expected guests. About 15 miles north of the lighthouse, the Confederates are spotted. In an instant, the naval guns propel shells into their ranks, compelling the Confederates to scatter. The Rebels disperse into the woods and break for the vessels that had debarked them earlier in the day, but the Union gunboats continue to pour fire upon the infantry while simultaneously challenging the Confederate vessels. The Rebels continue to come under fire until dusk. Following the cessation of the bombardment, the *Monticello* heads back to Hatteras to protect the Union lines there.

In New Mexico Territory, a Confederate force of about 110 troops attacks a Union force that includes Captain Mink's Cavalry and U.S. Regulars at Alamosa. The Union repels the attack. The Confederates sustain 11 killed and about 30 wounded. No casualties are reported by the Union.

In Naval activity, the U.S. Navy authorizes the building of ironclad warships, which include the USS *Cairo,* USS *Cincinnati,* USS *Louisville* and USS *Pittsburg,* gunboats uniquely designed by Samuel Pook and built by James B. Eads of St. Louis. Also, the USS *South Carolina,* a steamer, captures two Confederate schooners in the vicinity of the South West Pass of Mississippi.

October 5 (Saturday)   In West Virginia, General William S. Rosecrans begins to withdraw from Big Sewell Mountain to return to Gauley Bridge. Upon arrival his deploys at various places: Cox's brigade camps at Gauley Bridge near Rosecrans' headquarters at Camp Gauley Mountain, Benham's brigade encamps about six miles out, Robert L. McCook's at ten miles out and Schhenck's brigade makes camp about ten miles outside Gauley Bridge.

In Union general officer activity, Charles Jackson Paine is commissioned a captain (later brigadier general) in the 22nd Massachusetts Infantry Regiment. Paine remains with the regiment through part of the winter 1861–1862 in Washington, D.C., as part of the defenses of the capital. However, during January 1862 he transfers with the rank of major to the 30th Massachusetts until the following March. Paine's great-grandfather had spent much time in the capital years before. He was Thomas Treat Paine, a signer of the Declaration of Independence. Subsequent to his service in the capital, Paine is transferred to the Department of the Gulf.

In Naval activity, the USS *Monticello,* a gunboat commanded by Lt. D. L. Braine, bolsters the attack by the 29th Indiana Volunteer Infantry against Confederates at Chicamicomico (Kinnakeet, Cape Hatteras), North Carolina. Action lasts about four hours; the Confederates lose about 28 killed. The Union reports no ca-

sualties. Also, the steamer *Monticello* engages and sinks a privateer, the *Louisiana* at Chincoteague Inlet, Virginia.

October 6 (Sunday)   The Confederate ship *Alert,* a blockade runner, is captured by the USS *Flag* off the coast of Charleston, South Carolina.

October 7 (Monday)   In Missouri, a Union force under General John Frémont departs St. Louis for Springfield, in an attempt to intercept Confederate General Sterling Price. Washington has been pressing without success for Frémont to initiate the advance. Frémont arrives at Tipton on the 11th.

Union troops (General Frémont's command) on a foraging mission in Missouri (Mottelay, *The Soldier in Our Civil War,* 1886).

In Confederate general officer activity, Brigadier General Thomas J. "Stonewall" Jackson, promoted to major general of the Confederate Army this day, proceeds to the Shenandoah Valley to assist in the protection of Richmond, the capital of the Confederacy. Jackson becomes a lieutenant general on October 10, 1862. In other activity, Mansfield Lovell (West Point, 1842) and Benjamin Huger are appointed to the rank of major general in the Confederacy. Lovell departs New York City for New Orleans (Department No. 1) to assume command there. Huger is in command of Norfolk, Virginia. Also, Brigadier General James Longstreet is promoted to the rank of major general.

In Naval activity, the USS *Conestoga* and the USS *Lexington* exchange fire with a Confederate battery at Lucas Bend, Missouri, and silence the guns. At the time, the *Conestoga* is providing support fire during a Union ground force. A Confederate vessel, the *Yankee,* sustains damage inflicted by the USS *Lexington.* Nonetheless, the Confederate guns at Columbus, Kentucky, preserve the *Yankee* and another steamer from further damage. During October the *Conestoga* is transferred to the U.S. Navy.

October 8 (Tuesday)   In Florida at Pensacola, a Confederate force of more than 1,000 troops is moving against the New York Zouaves' (6th New York Regiment) bivouac just outside Fort Pickens. The Rebels, aware that they cannot overpower the fort, intend at least to disrupt the Yankees from New York.

In Kentucky, a skirmish that lasts about twenty minutes erupts in Hillsborough between Union Home Guards, commanded by Lt. Sadler, and Confederates led by Captain Holliday. The Union sustains three killed and two wounded. The Confederates suffer 11 killed, 29 wounded and about 29 captured.

In Union activity, Union General William Tecumseh Sherman replaces General Robert

Anderson (the commander of Fort Sumter at the opening of the war) as commander of the Department of the Cumberland. Deteriorating health, particularly his nerves, following the trauma at Fort Sumter, forces Anderson's retirement and ends his active military service. General Sherman's headquarters will be at Louisville, Kentucky. In other activity, Charles A. Heckman, a sergeant in the Mexican War, is this day appointed lieutenant colonel of the 9th New Jersey Regiment. He serves under General Ambrose Burnside during the North Carolina expedition.

October 9 (Wednesday)   In Florida, Confederate forces, estimated to be between 1,000 and 1,400 strong, under the command of General Richard Heron Anderson, unsuccessfully attack federal shore batteries at Santa Rosa Island in Pensacola Bay. However, the 6th New York Regiment, famous for pulling jokes on the regular troops in Fort Pickens, receives help almost too late to halt the assault. Colonel Wilson's Zouaves, the 6th New York Regiment, had often teased the regulars, sometimes firing their weapons as if being attacked. In this instance, the fort disregards the initial firing by the Zouaves. In addition, the poorly disciplined Zouaves had been under strength due to desertions and from genuine causes such as sickness. Wilson has a force only of about 200 soldiers to meet the attack.

The Rebels are able to strike from the flank while the main body strikes the front, forcing the Zuoaves to give ground. The Rebels move into the camp and pluck it dry, then set the torch to destroy it. Nevertheless, the Zouaves are formidable fighters and, supported by the regulars from Fort Pickens, dole out a lot of punishment to the Confederates. Detachments under Majors Lewis G. Arnold and Vogdes, Captains Heildt and Robinson and Lieutenants D'Orville, Shipley and Zeeley lead the attacks to evict the Rebels and successfully push them back to their boats.

While the Confederates are evacuating the area, one of their vessels is pounded so strongly that it sinks, while all are still aboard. Following this skirmish, both sides accelerate their expansion programs, bringing in more troops. While Fort Pickens builds to about 1,300 troops, the Confederates holding Forts Barrancas and McRee increase their strength to about 6,000 troops under the command of General Braxton Bragg. The Union retains a naval blockade squadron composed of the USS *Niagara*, USS *Richmond* and USS *Montgomery*.

Union losses are estimated at 14 killed, 29 wounded and nine taken prisoner; Major (later general) Israel Vogdes is among the men captured. He is exchanged during August of the following year and promoted to brigadier general on 29 November 1862. Vogdes is ordered to South Carolina, where he becomes involved in designing and erecting defenses. At the close of the war, he commands the defenses in Norfolk and Portsmouth, Virginia, but he does not see field command. He receives the brevet rank of brigadier general in the Regular Army toward the close of hostilities and afterward commands a district in Florida. He retires during January 1881. Meanwhile, Major (later general) Lewis G. Arnold (West Point, 1837) takes command of Fort Pickens. The Confederates sustain between 350 and 400 killed, wounded or missing. Three of the prisoners taken by the Yankees are Confederate officers. Union participants are the 6th New York Regiment, Company A, 1st U.S. Artillery, Companies C and E, U.S. 3rd Infantry, and Company H, 2nd U.S. Artillery.

In Union activity, John Thomas Croxton (Yale, 1857) is appointed lieutenant colonel of the 4th Kentucky Mounted Infantry. During the following year he becomes colonel of the regiment. In July 1864 he is appointed brigadier general. General Croxton participates in various engagements, including Mill Springs (Logan's Cross Roads), Chickamauga, Atlanta and Nashville. At the close of hostilities, he assumes command of the military district of West Georgia, where he remains until his resignation during December 1865.

October 10 (Thursday) In Kentucky, a Confederate contingent attacks Union Pickets (4th Cavalry Regiment) at Paducah. Two Union troops are killed and two Confederates are captured.

In Naval activity, the steamer USS *Daylight* exchanges fire with Confederate batteries at Lynnhaven Bay, Virginia. Also, after receiving intelligence that a Confederate force is completing the fitting out of a schooner at Quantico Creek (also Dumfries Creek), the USS *Union* commanded by Lt. Harrell embarks from its position at Acquia Creek to destroy the vessel and scatter the Rebels. Also, the U.S. Navy acquires the *Whitehall*, a ferryboat that is transformed into a side-wheel gunboat. The *Whitehall* is commissioned shortly after being purchased at the New York Navy Yard. Acting Master Francis P. Allen receives command. The vessel is assigned to the South Atlantic Blockading Squadron.

October 11 (Friday) In Missouri, Union forces under General Frémont, in pursuit of Confederate General Sterling Price (Missouri Militia), arrive at Tipton. Frémont establishes camp on the fairgrounds.

In Virginia, the USS *Union*, commanded by Lt. Harrell, arrives at Quantico Creek from Acquia Creek during the early morning hours and discovers its target, a Confederate schooner. The detachment uses two boats and a launch to destroy it. Confederate ground troops, aided by the flames of the burning ship, pound the *Union* with fire, but it escapes damage and no casualties are sustained.

In Confederate general officer activity, Brigadier General Edmund Kirby Smith is promoted to major general. He will later serve in East Tennessee.

In Union general officer activity, Richard W. Johnson is appointed a brigadier general. Johnson, a Kentuckian, had graduated West Point with the class of 1849. He received the appointment through the efforts of his older brother, who himself serves in the war as a surgeon with the Confederacy. General Johnson is assigned to the Army of Ohio with brigade command in General Alexander McCook's division. Nonetheless, Johnson becomes ill, which delays his arrival and causes him to join the force after the battle at Shiloh. General Johnson, after his arrival, vows to capture Confederate General John B. Hunt.

Thomas John Wood (West Point, 1845) is commissioned brigadier general of volunteers. General Wood, who is a veteran of the Mexican War and who had extensive service on the Indian frontier with the 2nd Cavalry, had been on leave in Europe (1859–1861), but upon his return, he was involved in recruiting troops from Indiana into federal service.

In conjunction, Isaac Wistar, a captain in the regular service, is catapulted to colonel of the 2nd Cavalry due to the flood of cavalry officers heading south to join the Confederacy.

In Naval activity, the USS *Rescue*, working together with the USS *Union*, encounters and captures the *Martha Washington*, a schooner at Quantico Creek (Dumphries Creek) that is preparing to embark a contingent of Confederates; however, the two Union gunboats arrive prior to the Rebel troops. The Union troops seize the vessel and set it afire.

October 12 (Saturday) In Kentucky, a Confederate force composed of fewer than 150 troops attacks a Union force of less than 50 men, commanded by Captain S. Taylor, in Barren County. The Union suffers three killed and the Confederates sustain four killed.

A detachment from the USS *Union* destroys a Confederate schooner in Quantico Creek, Virginia (Mottelay, *The Soldier in Our Civil War*, 1886).

In Louisiana, the 79th New York Volunteers skirmish with Confederates at Bayle's Cross Roads; no casualties are reported. Also, a Confederate fleet, including the CSS *Pickens* (formerly USS *Robert McClelland*), engages a Union squadron — the *Preble, Richmond, Vincennes* and the *Water Witch*— at Head of the Passes.

In Missouri, Union forces, including cavalry and the 39th Indiana Volunteers, skirmish with Confederates at Cameron. The Union sustains one killed and four wounded. The Confederates sustain eight killed and five captured. A separate contingent of the 39th Indiana Volunteers under Captain Thomas Herring engages Confederate Cavalry at Upton's Hill, Kentucky. The Union sustains five wounded and the Confederates sustain three wounded.

In South Carolina, two Confederate commissioners, John Slidell and James Mason, representing the Confederacy to France and England respectively, break through the Union blockade at Charleston. The vessel transporting them, the *Theodora*, using inclement weather as a prop, eludes the Union warships and speeds towards the Caribbean to use Cuba as a jump-off point for reaching Europe.

In Virginia, a skirmish develops in Green River between a 40-man Union contingent and a Confederate force of about 300 troops; casualty figures are unavailable.

In Naval activity, the Confederate ironclad *Manassas* and other vessels, including the CSS *Jackson, Ivy* and *James L. Day* (Hollin's Mosquito Fleet), engage the USS *Preble, Richmond, Vincennes* and *Waterwitch* on the Mississippi River (Head of the Passes) in Louisiana. The Union vessels, although in jeopardy, particularly the *Richmond* and *Vincennes*, both of which are temporarily grounded, successfully withdraw. The CSS *Jackson*, which participates in the engagement, moves to New Orleans to bolster the defenses of Forts Jackson and St. Philip. The city surrenders during April 1862; however the CSS *Jackson*, commanded by Lt. F.B. Renshaw, escapes capture. Nevertheless, the

Jackson is destroyed by its crew after the city capitulates to prevent capture by Admiral Porter's fleet. Another vessel, the CSS *McRae*, formerly the Mexican vessel *Marquis de la Habana* (seized during 1860 by the U.S. Navy for suspected piracy) acquired by the Confederacy for the purpose of defending New Orleans, participates in the engagement. The USS *Vincennes*, originally commissioned during August 1826, following this action seizes the vessel *Empress* before the end of the year, but for the remainder of its service, it is used primarily on duty at Ship Island, Mississippi. After the war it is decommissioned during August 1865 and sold during October 1867.

October 13 (Sunday) In Missouri, following a tedious two-day march, General Frémont arrives at Haw Creek and Warsaw on the Osage River. Elements of Major Frank J. White's cavalry, the "Prairie Scouts," join him there, arriving from Lexington, where they freed Union prisoners and captured many of their Confederate guards. From here, Frémont will head for Springfield through Bolivar, but his progress is greatly impeded by bad weather that has caused the many streams to swell. The artillery will be the crossed on a flatboat and by utilizing a temporary bridge. General Frémont's Hussars and the other cavalry units will seek other points where the river is fordable and cross at those points. By the 23rd, his force arrives in Pomme de Terre. Also, a Union Cavalry force led by Lt. Tuft skirmishes with a contingent of Confederates at Beckwith's Farm. The Union sustains two killed and five wounded. The Confederates sustain five killed and three wounded. Other Union forces, including the 6th and 10th Missouri Cavalry, bolstered by a battalion of General John Frémont's Cavalry, encounter Confederates at Wet Glaize (Shanghai, Henrytown and Monday's Hollow). The engagement is brief, lasting less than ten minutes; however, the Union sustains one killed and about 20 wounded, while the Confederates lose 30 captured and more than 50 killed.

In Naval activity, the USS *Young America* departs the Navy yard at Washington, D.C., for Baltimore to receive additional repairs prior to joining the North Atlantic Blockading Squadron. It returns to Hampton Roads during late November.

October 14 (Monday) In Missouri, a Union contingent — including the 13th Illinois Volunteer Regiment and the 6th Missouri Cavalry — skirmishes with Confederates and captures about 40 Confederate troops around Linn Creek. Another skirmish develops at Underwood's Farm between a 26-man contingent of Captain Nolan's Centralia Cavalry, led by Lt. Tufts, and a Confederate force of about 100 troops. The Union suffers six casualties, including killed and wounded. The Confederates sustain four wounded.

In Union activity, Edward Ferrero, a lieutenant colonel (militia) at the time of the outbreak of war and a former dance instructor at West Point, is appointed colonel of the 51st New York Infantry Regiment. General Ferrero and the regiment participate in the North Carolina expedition under General Ambrose Burnside. Afterward, he participates at Second Manassas, Antietam (Sharpsburg) and Fredericksburg as commander of an IX Corps brigade.

In Confederate activity, Lt. Colonel Thomas Hart Taylor, 1st Kentucky Infantry Regiment, becomes colonel of the regiment. The following summer he is assigned duty under General Kirby Smith in East Tennessee after his one-year regiment is disbanded. Afterward, Taylor will be assigned duty in Vicksburg under General John Pemberton.

October 15 (Tuesday) In Missouri, Jeff Thompson's Raiders (2nd and 3rd Dragoons) successfully assault Union forces at Potasi. The Rebels also succeed in burning the Big River Bridge. The Union sustains one killed, between 6 and 20 wounded and 25 to 50 captured. Confederates have five dead and four wounded. Some contemporary reports of this incident list about 20 Confederates killed. Casualty figures sometimes differ due to the difficulty of keeping meticulous battle records.

In Virginia, a six-man contingent of the 1st New Jersey Volunteers, led by Lt. Tillou, engages a force of about twenty Confederates at Little River Turnpike. Each side sustains one man killed and the Confederates lose one man captured.

In Confederate general officer activity, Edward Lloyd Thomas, a veteran of the Mexican War (Georgia mounted volunteers, Newton County Independent Horse) is appointed colonel (later brigadier general) of the 35th Georgia Infantry.

In Naval activity, several Union warships depart from New York Harbor in search of the Confederate vessel *Nashville*, thought to be transporting the Confederate commissioners to Europe; however, the two men, Slidell and Mason, are instead aboard the *Theodora*, which is actually en route to Cuba. The *Theodora* slipped out of Charleston, South Carolina, on 12 October.

October 16 (Wednesday) In Missouri, Union troops, including contingents of the 1st Missouri Cavalry and the Irish Brigade, led by Major White, recapture Lexington from the Confederates. Skirmishing continues in the area until the 20th, with the Union sustaining some 50 killed and 100 wounded. Moreover, many Union troops are listed as missing. In other activity, a Union 15-man contingent of Major General John Frémont's Cavalry, commanded by Lt. Kirby, engages a Confederate force of about 45 troops at Linn Creek. The Confederates sustain five killed and one wounded. Also, Confederate forces clash with Union contingents at Warsaw; the units are not reported. The Union sustains no casualties, while the Confederates sustain five killed and one wounded, and they lose 10 stacks of arms.

In Virginia, a large contingent of about 600 troops of the 13th Massachusetts, 3rd Wisconsin and 28th Pennsylvania, while they are confiscating about 20,000 bushels of wheat, encounter Confederates under Colonel (later brigadier general) Nathan G. Evans at Bolivar Heights. In this skirmish, the Union force, commanded by Colonel (later major general) John White Geary, suffers four killed and seven wounded, but after almost six hours of fighting, the Confederates are driven off. The Confederates have 13 missing; other casualties are unavailable. The Union seizes four prisoners, while the Confederates capture two Union troops.

In Naval activity, the USS *Fort Henry*, while on a mission on the Apalachicola River, engages Confederates along the banks and calls for assistance. The USS *Sagamore* speeds to support the *Fort Henry* and the Confederates are forced to retire. Afterward, the Union vessels advance further and come upon a Rebel ship, the *G.L. Brockenborough*, which is stranded at the mouth of a creek near Apalachicola, Florida. The two men aboard, the master and one passenger, are seized, along with its cargo of 64 bales of cotton. The ship is refloated, taken to Key West and acquired by the U.S. Navy on 16 November 1862, then assigned to the East Gulf Blockading Squadron as a tender to the USS *Port Royal*, a sidewheeler, and the USS *Somerset*, formerly a ferryboat.

October 17–21 (Thursday) In Missouri, a Confederate contingent clashes with the Union at Fredericktown. The Union force, commanded by Colonel Alexander, is composed of the 11th Missouri and 17th, 20th, 21st, 33rd and 38th Illinois Regiments, bolstered by the 1st Indiana and the 8th Wisconsin Regiments. Company A of the 1st Missouri Artillery provides some extra power. The confrontation rages, with both sides pounding the other, but when the battle subsides, the Union prevails. The Union sustains six killed and about 60 wounded, while the Confederates sustain heavy casualties, including about 200 wounded. Confederate death casualties are unavailable. The two sides continue to skirmish for the next several days, until the 21st. The action includes fighting at Irontown and another large-scale clash at Fredericktown on the 20th between the Union forces of Colonel William P. Carlin and the Confederates under Colonel Gideon Thompson.

October 18 (Friday) In Virginia, following the engagement at Bull Run (Manassas), Union troops began to create a protective shield around Washington, to prevent it from coming under attack. The Blue Line stretches along the Maryland banks of the Potomac River from the capital to Harpers Ferry. Major General Nathaniel P. Banks' force holds the terrain from Darnesville to Williamsport in the vicinity of Williams' Ferry, while other troops under Generals Wilson F. Smith and George Arthur McCall are deployed at Chain Bridge, and yet other contingents under General Charles Stone's Brigade guard about four miles between Edward's Ferry and Conrad's Ferry, Virginia. Smaller forces under Colonels John W. Geary and Frederick W. Lander fill the remaining gap leading to Harper's Ferry. This day, General McClellan directs Brigadier General George McCall to move from his positions near Chain Bridge to Dranesville, occupy it and gather intelligence on the Confederate forces of Colonel Nathaniel G. Evans, which as it has been reported, just evacuated Leesburg. Stone's force dominates the road that leads to Leesburg, which is about forty miles from Harper's Ferry.

In Confederate general officer activity, Colonel Lloyd Tilghman (West Point, 1836) is promoted to the rank of brigadier general, effective this date.

October 19 (Saturday)   In Missouri, a contingent of the 18th Missouri Regiment (Volunteers), with slightly more than 200 troops commanded by Colonel Morgan L. Smith, engages a Confederate force at Big Hurricane Creek. The Union sustains two killed and 14 wounded. The Confederates suffer 14 killed and eight wounded.

In Virginia, Union Brigadier General George Archibald McCall's force, pursuant to orders of the previous day, completes the occupation of Drainsville (Fairfax County), about seventeen miles west of Washington. Union forces continue to dispatch reconnaissance missions in many directions to determine the strength the Confederates may have in and around Leesburg, which seemingly has been evacuated. No opposition is encountered; however, the evacuation by the Rebels is not confirmed. In other activity, General McClellan orders General Baker to move toward Leesburg, where Confederate Colonel Nathan G. "Shanks" Evans is deployed to investigate the activity there. Baker moves out with a force of about 3,000 troops; however, on the following day, McClellan attempts to countermand his order after deciding that Baker's encroachment might cause Evans to retire to sanctuary out of McClellan's reach. On the 20th, McClellan dispatches General Charles P. Stone, who is deployed on the Maryland side of the Potomac, to send a large contingent toward Leesburg in an attempt to corral Evans.

In Union general officer activity, Samuel Kosciuszko Zook is commissioned colonel (later brigadier general) of the 57th New York Regiment. Zook, initially from Pennsylvania, had relocated to New York. Prior to the war he had been lieutenant colonel of the 6th New York Militia, with which he served during the initial stages of the war; however, the regiment was mustered out of service on 31 July. During the First Bull Run campaign, he had been military governor of Annapolis.

In Naval activity, the CSS *Florida* (afterward *Selma*), a civilian steamer transformed into a gunboat in the Confederate service since the previous April and operating in the vicinity of New Orleans and Mobile Bay, clashes with the USS *Massachusetts.*

October 20 (Sunday)   In Virginia, Union Brigadier General Charles Pomeroy Stone receives a message from Major General George B.

McClellan advising him of Brigadier General George A. McCall's progress and the general's desire for Stone to keep vigil to see if the reinforced scouting detachments expose the Confederates. McClellan adds: "Perhaps a slight demonstration on your part would have the effect to move them." Stone is directed to ford the river at two separate places, Edward's Ferry and Ball's Bluff. Upon receipt of McClellan's message, Stone takes immediate action. At about 1200, Gorman's Brigade — the 7th Michigan, 1st Minnesota, the Putnam Rangers, two troops of the Van Alen Cavalry and a detachment of Captain Bunting's Rhode Island Battery — moves from its positions on the main road (leading to Leesburg) to Edward's Ferry. Colonel Charles Devens moves part of his regiment, the 15th Massachusetts, by ferry to Harrison's Island (Ball's Bluff).

Meanwhile, a battalion of Colonel W. Raymond Lee's 20th Massachusetts and some Rhode Island and New York Regiments are ordered by Stone to move to Conrad's Ferry. The 1st California Regiment commanded by Brigadier General Edward D. Baker and some other units, totaling about 3,000 troops, are held in reserve near both ferries in the event they are needed. Baker, who had just been promoted, had emigrated to the U.S. from England with his Quaker parents, who settled in Pennsylvania. His regiment, although referred to as the California Regiment, is composed primarily of Pennsylvanians. General Stone, on the following day, expects to make a wide sweep to flush out any Rebels still remaining in the area.

Meanwhile, a contingent of Confederates is spotted on a hill opposite Gorman's positions at Edward's Ferry. About 100 troops, utilizing three boats, cross the Potomac, while the remainder of the brigade feints a genuine crossing in force. The combination of some artillery barrages and the landing of the small party disperses the Rebels. At about 2200, a detachment of the 13th Massachusetts, led by Captain Chase Philbrick, dispatched at about dusk on a reconnaissance mission, returns to Harrison's Island, reporting to Colonel Charles Devens, Jr., 15th Massachusetts, that they had discovered a Confederate camp in the vicinity of Leesburg. The information is forwarded to General Stone, who orders Devens to launch a night raid and surprise the Rebels while they sleep. Colonel W. Raymond Lee is ordered to move his unit, the 20th Massachusetts, from Conrad's Ferry to Harrison's Island, and from there, dispatch a contingent to the bluff to cover Devens' contingent when it returns following the raid.

At about 0200 on the 21st, General Baker is directed to move his regiment to Conrad's Ferry and be in place by dawn to replace Colonel Lee's regiment. General George A. McCall is ordered to return to Chain Bridge. Meanwhile, Colonel Devens moves out during the early morning hours of the 21st, and at about sunrise, the force reaches the site where the Confederates' encampment is reported to be located; however, to his surprise, there are no enemy troops and no encampment. Devens requests new orders and remains in place. In the meantime, rein-

forcements under Lt. Colonel George H. Ward are dispatched toward Devens' position. Upon their arrival, Devens' force rises to about 650 troops.

October 21 (Monday)   BATTLE OF BALLS BLUFF (LEESBURG) Union forces led by Colonel Charles Devens, Jr., are outside Leesburg, Virginia, in the vicinity of Balls Bluff awaiting orders from General Charles P. Stone following an unsuccessful night expedition to discover a suspected Confederate encampment. At about 0700, Confederate infantry and cavalry are spotted moving along the road to Leesburg. Within an hour, Colonel Devens moves his force back toward the bluff; acting upon orders from General Stone, he waits in place for reinforcements. A contingent of Colonel James H. Van Alen's Cavalry advances to reinforce Devens, followed later by Colonel Napoleon J.T. Dana, who moves out and crosses at Edward's Ferry with a contingent of his 1st Minnesota under a potent steel umbrella compliments of a battery of artillery.

At about 1200, following some sporadic firing in the woods, the Confederates strike Devens' command using their riflemen, who from their positions in the woods rake the Yankees, while a unit of Confederate cavalry surges forward. The combined force of the cavalry and units of the 18th Mississippi and the 8th Virginia Regiments press the Union, which falls back to gain more tenable positions closer to Colonel Lee, who is on the bluff. Shortly afterward, Devens again pulls back, moving even closer to the bluff, halting on open ground. In the meantime, General Baker had arrived at the ferry by 1200 with punctuality, despite being informed of the move at 0200, but from there, his attempt to shift his force to Harrison's Island is difficult. And getting from the island to the opposite shore is even more demanding, due to the wild currents of the river, which by its unruliness handicaps the maneuver and delays the attempt to reinforce Devens.

Making matters worse, once across the river, General Edward D. Baker's troops of the 1st California Regiment and other units, including Cogswell's Tammany Regiment, must ascend a steep cliff to reach the embattled force. After overcoming the obstacles, Baker's force, numbering nearly 1,300 men, arrives at Devens' positions at about 1400. At about the same time, Cogswell's New Yorkers (Colonel Milton Cogswell, 42nd New York Regiment) are hitting the end of the ascent of the serpentine path. Baker assumes command of the entire force and he is empowered with the authority to choose whether to engage or extricate Devens and withdraw. However, there are really no options, as the heated battle is ongoing when he arrives, prompting him to stay and hold the ground, naked though it be. With at best very scant cover, the Union returns fire with equal tenacity, using its few guns to attempt to forestall disaster. Baker continually moves about his ranks to encourage his troops, but his actions make him a conspicuous target.

Confederate Colonel Nathaniel G. Evans,

who the Yankees initially thought had evacuated Leesburg, had in fact been in the area and with considerable strength, sufficiently strong to manhandle the Union forces. Inexplicably, but possibly due to the lack of proper communications, there are many Union troops within a reasonable distance who could be called upon to neutralize the Rebel strength, but they are not informed of the heavy concentration, nor are they requested.

Meanwhile, General Evans tightens the deadly ring of fire and launches an attack at about 1500, sending in the 17th Mississippi under Colonel (later general) Winfield Scott Featherston, the 18th Mississippi under Colonel E.R. Burt, the 13th Mississippi under Colonel (later general) William Barksdale, and the 8th Virginia commanded by Colonel (later general) Eppa Hunton, supported by cavalry commanded by Colonel Jenifer. Evans spares no effort directing his force to hammer the Union line from three separate directions. Like an ocean of gray waves, a scarlet sea of fire and a stream of riveting steel, the Rebels charge, delivering a triple-strength attack that simultaneously crashes full-force against the Union ranks, bending the line but not collapsing it. Union fire is heartily returned and the men, under an avalanche of shot and shell, attempt to advance. Baker, besieged but not deterred, continues to rally his troops and lead the advance, but the Confederate fire intensifies as the Blue and the Gray clash along the line in close-quartered fighting. The sounds of battle do little to soothe the soul as officers on both sides are yelling commands, while bugles blare amid the horrific sounds of the artillery.

At about this time, Baker, still suffering from a wound of a week prior that has forced him to operate with one arm slung in his shirt, receives a series of wounds. One agile Confederate moves in close and from point-blank range pumps five shots into General Baker, then makes a move to take his sword as a prize, while at the same time yet another Rebel shot strikes him in the head. He is then hit by additional fire, inflicting wounds to his side and leg, assuring an agonizing death. The Confederate who had struck the first of the fatal wounds moves to clasp Baker's sword, but Captain Louis Beirel, Company G, 1st California Regiment, snaps off a few rounds that slay him. Beirel retrieves the general's body and his sword and leaves the Rebel dead in his place.

Nevertheless, the death of one Confederate in trade for Baker does little for the Union cause. Lieutenants Frank S. French, (Battery 1) and Walter Bramhall (9th N.Y. State Militia) assume the responsibilities of command in support of Colonel Cogswell, who succeeds Baker, but soon after, both lieutenants sustain wounds that knock them out of action and drain the Union of its determination. Cogswell ponders a withdrawal, but with a mere glance toward the rushing, unwieldy current of the river, he concludes that such a move would undoubtedly cause great loss of life; therefore he decides to use the imminent darkness as a tool to support his men while they slice a route to Edward's Ferry.

Captain Louis Beirel (Mottelay, *The Soldier in Our Civil War*, 1886).

Cogswell is convinced that, given a little good fortune, he can link with Colonel Willis A. Gorman, stabilize the situation and beat back the attackers.

In the meantime, the Confederates show no signs of easing the pressure; rather, more doggedly they pound the lines. Along the left flank of the Union, all ammunition is expended, causing near panic, but troops from the right flank expeditiously move to meet the crisis. Meanwhile, the Confederate progress compels Cogswell to dispel the idea of going to Edward's Ferry and instead, risk the dangerous withdrawal to Harrison's Island or face complete destruction of his force. Colonel Charles Devens, Jr., leading the 15th Massachusetts Regiment, covers the withdrawal, but the Rebels are too close, too strong and too riled to be repelled. The retirement, only just underway, suddenly loses discipline and the retreat becomes a humiliating and devastating rout.

The race to the cliff and the clumsy descent by the retreating force provides easy targets for the Confederate riflemen. And then inexplicably, at the river bank, only one flatboat is available for the evacuation, causing it to quickly become overloaded with crammed troops, all yearning for Harrison's Island to escape the wrath of Evans' force. Burdened with an overload and struggling to overcome the wild currents, the boat is also being relentlessly pummeled by Confederate shells. Consequently, the heavy-laden bullet-riddled vessel sinks with all aboard, casting survivors into the raging waters. Those capable swim to shore, while others are caught in the swirling waters destined to succumb by drowning.

Meanwhile, General Charles P. Stone, unaware of Gorman's positions (sent back to Chain Bridge) and uninformed on the progress of Baker, had dispatched a telegram to General Banks requesting a brigade with which to cross the river. In the meantime, Devens prepares to dispatch his force, but soon after, he counter-

mands his order once the survivors begin arriving at Harrison's Island with the unfortunate news. Changing plans, Devens begins to reinforce the island to ensure that the Rebels cannot seize control of it. Reinforcements sent by Banks begin arriving about 0200 on the following morning (22nd), at about the same time that General Banks arrives.

This battle is the second loss to the Confederates in Virginia and is still surrounded by unanswered questions concerning the reason for such a tragic and unnecessary loss, considering that about 40,000 other troops under General George McClellan's command had been within range of rendering aid but had not been called upon. Some claim it was due to poor communications. Nonetheless, the questions linger regarding how and why the Union permitted such a small force of only 2,000 troops to be placed in such jeopardy. General Charles Pomeroy Stone (West Point, 1845) had been in command of the Union forces. Stone is later blamed by Congress for the defeat. He is arrested 8 February 1862 and confined at Forts Hamilton and Lafayette, but he is subsequently released (6 August 1862) without being charged with any wrongdoing. During 1863, he will be recalled and assigned to the Department of the Gulf with General Nathaniel Banks.

The Union suffers more than 400 killed, wounded, or captured. The Confederates sustain 36 killed, including Colonel E.R. Burt, 18th Mississippi Regiment, and 264 wounded. Union Major General Edward D. Baker, U.S. Volunteers, is killed at this battle. Colonel Devens, 15th Massachusetts, escapes by riding his horse, which manages to swim to Harrison's Island. Devens also enjoyed some luck during the fierce battle; a shot from a Rebel's rifle struck him, but the killing blow is foiled by a military button on his uniform, saving him from harm. Colonel Charles Devens will become a brigadier general during April 1862. General F.W. Lander is wounded during the skirmish. Also, Union Colonels Milton Cogswell and William R. Lee are captured.

The Confederate commander, Nathaniel C. Evans (West Point, 1848), is appointed brigadier general effective this day. In addition to this victory, Evans had commanded a gallant contingent of Rebels at Bull Run, which had aided him in receiving the appointment, but as the war progresses, he begins to disagree with his superiors. Nevertheless, Evans participates in other campaigns, including Second Manassas (Bull Run), South Mountain, Sharpsburg (Antietam) and Vicksburg. He participates in North Carolina in command of his brigade, known as the "Tramp Brigade." From about early 1863, General Evans loses favor with higher command. He is tried on charges of intoxication and disobedience and is acquitted, but he is still plucked from any primary command by General Pierre G.T. Beauregard. After the war he becomes a high school teacher in Midway, Alabama, until his death in November 1868.

In other activity, elements of the 3rd Massachusetts Regiment commanded by Captain Barnes engage a Confederate force at Young's Mills. Casualty figures, if any, are unavailable.

In Kentucky, Confederate troops attached to Brigadier General Felix Zollicoffer's force attacks Union forces at Crab Orchard (Camp Wild Cat, Wild Cat Mountain, Rockcastle Hills), but the Union troops there attached to the command of General Albin Francisco Schoepf twice repel them. Schoepf, of Austrian-Polish descent, had been appointed brigadier general on September 21. The 14th and 17th Ohio Regiments (Volunteers), 33rd Indiana Regiment, the 1st Kentucky Cavalry, 7th Kentucky Infantry, the 1st Tennessee and the 1st Ohio Battery participate in the action, the first confrontation between Union and Confederate troops in the state of Kentucky. Subsequent to this action, Colonel Theophilus Garrard (7th Kentucky) participates at the Battle of Richmond and afterward is attached to the staff of General Samuel P. Carter, followed by command of a brigade in General McClernand's XIII Corps' activity in Louisiana. Lt. Colonel James G. Spears (1st Tennessee) will later lead his regiment, more accurately a battalion, at Mill Springs the following January.

In Union general officer activity, Colonel Thomas Welsh, who initially entered the army as a private during the Mexican War, is appointed colonel of the 45th Pennsylvania Regiment. In 1862 he moves to South Carolina, but he arrives back with the Army of the Potomac prior to the battles at South Mountain and Antietam. Welsh is promoted to brigadier general on 29 November 1862; however, at the Battle of Fredericksburg, he continues to command the 45th Pennsylvania.

In Confederate general officer activity, Colonel James Trapier (West Point, 1838) is appointed brigadier general. He is assigned duty as commanding officer of the District of Middle and East Florida. Colonel (later lieutenant general) Richard Taylor, 9th Louisiana Infantry, is promoted to brigadier general. It will be Taylor, the son of former President Zachary Taylor, who opposes Union General Banks' advance

during the Red River Campaign. General John Breckinridge Grayson (West Point 1826), who fought during the Mexican War, including the battles at Contreras and Chapultepec, dies of natural causes. Colonel Nathan George Evans, promoted this day to brigadier general, is the brother-in-law of Captain (later brigadier general) Martin Witherspoon Gary. Captain Gary enters the Confederacy and joins Hampton's Legion. Colonel Cadmus Marcellus Wilcox, 9th Alabama Infantry Regiment, is promoted to the rank of brigadier general. Wilcox is assigned duty with the Army of Northern Virginia. Colonel Robert Emmett Rodes is promoted to brigadier general. Colonel Louis Trezevant Wigfall is appointed brigadier general by President Jefferson Davis.

In Naval activity, a U.S. fleet under the command of Commodore Samuel Du Pont leaves Annapolis, Maryland, for Hampton Roads, Virginia, from where it will later, on the 29th, head to South Carolina to attack Port Royal. It had earlier been decided that Port Royal would be the perfect location for the Union to dominate the area for future actions and provide a safe harbor which could double as a coaling station. Meanwhile, the Confederates toil to build up the defenses. Among these is Captain (later general) Stephen Elliott, Jr. He is promoted to brigadier general during May 1864.

In other activity, the CSS Nashville, a "brig rigged, passenger steamer" seized by the Confederates at Charleston in April, initiates its cruise as a blockade runner. It departs from England and becomes the first Confederate ship to fly the Confederate colors in English waters. The Nashville returns to Beaufort, North Carolina, during February 1862. Also, the USS Rescue, while on duty at Matthias Point, engages Confederate batteries.

October 22 (Tuesday) In Missouri, Union and Confederate contingents clash at Buffalo Mills. The specific units are not reported. Confederates sustain 17 killed.

In Virginia, a contingent of Van Alen's cavalry (raised by Colonel James Van Alen), commanded by Major Mix, initiates a reconnaissance mission that takes it into the vicinity of Goose Creek. Union General Nathaniel Banks arrives at Harrison's Island and assumes control of all Union forces, following the unexpected defeat of troops under General Charles Pomeroy Stone by Rebels under General Nathan George Evans. Also, Union General Benjamin Franklin Kelley assumes command of the Department of Harper's Ferry and Cumberland.

In Confederate activity, at about this time, the Department of Northern Virginia comes under the command of Major General Joseph Eggleston Johnston (West Point, 1829). General Pierre G.T. Beauregard receives command of the Potomac, Major General Theophilus Holmes, command of Aquia, and Major General Thomas Jonathan Jackson is assigned command of the Shenandoah Valley. Also, in Richmond, Virginia, Hood's Texas Brigade is organized and composed of the 1st, 4th and 5th Texas Infantry Regiments. The 1st Regiment is commanded by Colonel Louis T. Wigfall and Lt. Colonel Hugh McCleod, the 4th by Colonel John B. Hood and Lt. Colonel John Marshall, and the 5th by Colonel James Archer and Lt. Colonel Jerome B. Robertson. Late this year, the brigade expands with the addition of the 18th Georgia Infantry led by Colonel (later general) William Tatum Wofford. This brigade supplies the only Texas regiments that fight in the campaigns of the Eastern Theater. Following its establishment, the Texas Brigade finds little time for rest and relaxation, as it participates in more than twenty contests during 1862, followed by equally intense service for the duration, underscored by the fact that the unit sustains a casualty rate of about sixty percent.

October 23 (Wednesday) In Kentucky, Confederates and Union troops skirmish briskly at West Liberty. The Union troops, commanded by Colonel Harris, are Ohio contingents, including Loughlin's Cavalry, the 1st Ohio Cavalry, the 1st Ohio Artillery and the 2nd Ohio Regiment (Volunteers). The Union sustains two wounded. Confederates count 10 killed and five wounded. Also, a contingent of the 6th Indiana Regiment (Volunteers), commanded by Lt. Grayson, engages a Confederate force at Hodgesville. The Union sustains three wounded. The Confederate casualties are estimated at three killed and five wounded.

In Missouri, General John Frémont's force arrives at Pomme de Terre, about fifty miles north of Springfield. Once informed of a Confederate force at Springfield, Frémont directs Major Charles Zagonyi to prepare to take the Bodyguard Cavalry of Frémont and Major Frank White's Cavalry, the Prairie Scouts, to attack and secure the enemy encampment if it seems possible. Major Zagonyi departs on the 25th.

In Union general officer activity, William Grose is appointed colonel of the 36th Indiana Infantry Regiment. The regiment participates at the Battle of Shiloh.

In Confederate general officer activity, Samuel Gibbs French (West Point, 1849) is appointed brigadier general.

October 24 (Thursday) In Washington, D.C., after much thought and discussion, during a long series of Cabinet sessions regarding John Frémont, President Abraham Lincoln orders Major General David Hunter to replace Major General Frémont as commander of the Western Department (Army).

Union cavalry on a reconnaissance mission in the vicinity of Harper's Ferry, Western Virginia (Harper's Pictoral History of the Civil War, 1896).

In Kentucky, Confederates skirmish in Green County with pickets attached to General William Thomas Ward. The Union loses one man captured. The Confederates sustain two killed.

In Union general officer activity, Colonel (later brigadier general) James D. Fessenden is assigned to General David Hunter's staff. First Lieutenant James W. Forsyth (West Point, 1856) is promoted to captain, Ohio Volunteers. Forsyth sees action during the Peninsular Campaign with the Army of the Potomac and with General Sheridan at Winchester and Cedar Creek (1864), receiving the brevet of brigadier general toward the end of the war.

October 25 (Friday) BATTLE OF SPRING-FIELD At Pomme de Terre, Missouri, a force of Union cavalry (General John Frémont's command), composed of about 150 troops and commanded by Major Charles Zagonyi (Zagony), moves toward Springfield to engage a Confederate force of undetermined size. It moves to positions close to the objective and discovers the enemy strength to be about 2,000 troops. Another force, commanded by Major Frank White, is not moving quite so quickly due to White having become ill. Instead of pausing to await the trailing force, Zagonyi decides to launch the assault. Speaking to his men prior to the charge, he states: "Follow me and do like me.... The enemy is two thousand strong and we are but one hundred and fifty. It is possible no man will come back. If any of you would turn back, you can do so now."

In unison, the troops respond with resounding cheers as they initiate the charge, leaving none in their rear. In a flash the hooves of 150 horses begin the attack, building toward a full gallop as they race through a tiny brook, bolt over a low fence and burst upon a strong line of Confederate infantry, with nearby cavalry support on the left flank, riding under and through a hail of blazing fire that smashes into the cavalrymen and horses alike. Many fall as casualties to the fierce storm of shell, but the deter-

mined charge continues with the remainder still atop their horses defying the bullets. Still, devastating fire pounds the attackers and yet more fall, but the determination of the others intensifies as they continue to defy the odds.

Lt. Majthenyi receives the signal to hit the support cavalry. His contingent peels off and plows into the Rebels, splitting their ranks. Some Union horsemen pivot left while others swing right to shatter the opposing lines. The Confederates, apparently stunned by the impetuous nature of the assault, break their ranks and lose their discipline, giving the Union cavalry further advantage. As the Rebels scatter, Union reinforcements arrive and join the chase. Fifty horsemen under Captain McNaughton, the vanguard of Major Frank White's scouts, gallop forward with a second powerful charge that also crashes into the fleeing Rebels.

Bullets are flying and swords are slashing as the Union momentum propels them into the woods on the heels of the retreating troops. The momentum of the thrust carries the Union straight through the thicket and upon the streets of Springfield, now a center of total confusion. The Confederates make no stand to hold their ground. They abandon the streets to the Union and retire into the woods on the other side of town, but here, too, there is no reprieve, as the Yankees bolt right through Springfield and maintain a hearty pursuit until there seemed to be no further reason to continue the chase. The city is taken and held by this spectacular impetuous charge executed by 200 cavalrymen. The Union loses eighteen killed and thirty-seven wounded. The Confederates sustain 106 killed.

In Union activity, Captain Isaac Peace Rodman, 2nd Rhode Island Regiment, resigns his commission to accept appointment as colonel of the 4th Rhode Island, which he accepts on 30 October.

In Naval activity, the Union initiates the construction of another ironclad warship, which is later christened the *Monitor*, in New York at Greenpoint (Long Island). The vessel will be completed and in service by March of the following year and will play a pivotal part in a naval battle at Hampton Roads, Virginia, at that time.

October 26 (Saturday) In Kentucky, three companies of the 9th Illinois Volunteers, commanded by Major J.J. Phillips and supported by the USS *Conestoga*, a gunboat commanded by Lt. Commander S. L. Phelps, engage Confederates at Saratoga. The Union sustains about four wounded. The Confederates suffer eight killed.

In West Virginia, the 2nd Maryland Infantry Regiment commanded by Colonel Johns encounters a contingent of Confederates at South Branch Bridge. Subsequent to a skirmish, the Union sustains one killed and eight wounded. In other activity, a Union force under General Benjamin Franklin Kelley engages Confederates at Romney (Mill Creek) Mills. The skirmish lasts about two hours, but the Yankees prevail. The Union sustains two killed and 13 to 15 wounded. The Confederates suffer 20 killed, 15 wounded and about 50 captured. The 4th and 8th Ohio Regiments, 7th West Virginia Regiment (Volunteers), 2nd Regiment, Potomac Home Brigade, Maryland Volunteers and Ringgold's Cavalry Battalion participate in the fight.

In Confederate general officer activity, General William H. Carroll (Provisional Army of Tennessee), later colonel, 37th Tennessee Infantry (Confederate), is appointed brigadier general in the Confederate Army effective this day. Carroll, stationed in a border state, is dispatched to Knoxville to extinguish anti–Confederate sentiment. Soon after arrival, he imposes martial law.

In Naval activity, the *Isaac N. Seymour* (also *Seymour*, *I.N. Seymour*, and *J.N. Seymour*) built at Keyport, New Jersey, during 1860, is acquired by the U.S. Navy. It is assigned to the North Atlantic Blockading Squadron on 20 November and within several additional days is assigned duty at Hampton Roads.

October 27 (Sunday) In Missouri, Union troops spring an attack against Confederate positions in Plattsburg. The Confederates lose eight killed, and about 12 are captured. Specific units are not recorded. The Yankees also capture one gun. Also, at Spring Hill, one company of the 7th Missouri Cavalry clashes with Confederates. The encounter costs the unit five wounded. Confederate casualties, if any, are unavailable.

October 28 (Monday) In *Naval activity,* a Union steamer engages Confederate batteries at Budd's Ferry, Maryland. No casualties or damage is reported. In other activity, the USS *Resolute* is detached from the Potomac Flotilla, attached to the North Atlantic Blockading Squadron and assigned duty on the Rappahannock River.

October 29 (Tuesday) A large Union fleet commanded by Flag Officer Samuel Du Pont departs Hampton Roads, Virginia, heading south to Hilton Head, South Carolina, to capture Forts Beauregard and Walker. Du Pont's naval force of more than 75 ships includes supply vessels, coal vessels, transports, and warships. The bulk of its punitive power includes the steam frigate *Wabash*, Du Pont's flagship, commanded by C.R.P. Rodgers, and the gunboats *Augusta* (E.G. Parrot), *Bienville* (Charles Steedman), *Curlew* (Lt. P.G. Watmough), *Florida* (Captain J.R. Goldsborough), *Isaac H. Smith* (Captain J.W.A. Nicholson), *Mohican* (Commander L.W. Gordon), *Ottawa* (Lt. Commander R.H. Wyman), *Pawnee* (Lt. Comman-

General Frémont's body guard, commanded by Major Zagonyi, launches an attack in the vicinity of Springfield, Missouri, on 25 October 1861 (Johnson, *Campfire and Battlefield: History of the Conflicts and Campaigns,* 1894).

der T.H. Stevens), *Pocahontas* (Captain Percival Drayton), *Penguin* (Lt. F.A. Budd), *Pembina* (Lt. J.P. Bankhead), *R.B. Forbes* (Captain H.S. Newcomb), *Seminole* (Commander J.P. Gillis), *Seneca* (Lt. Daniel Ammen), and *Unadilla* (Lt. N. Collins). Later, the *Susquehanna* will join the fleet as it cruises past Charleston and the *Vandalia* will sail from Savannah to join. The naval force sails without incident, but on November 2, a violent storm arrives off Cape Hatteras (North Carolina) and threatens the mission and the fleet.

The USS *Bienville* had been acquired by the U.S. Navy during August 1861 and commissioned in October. Also, the USS *Ottawa,* commissioned earlier this month, is attached to the South Atlantic Blockading Squadron. It remains with the squadron for the duration of the war and patrols off Florida, Georgia and South Carolina until decommissioned in August 1865. It is sold during October of the same year. The USS *Pembina* is also commissioned at about this time (October). It joins the South Atlantic Blockading Squadron in time to participate in attack on Port Royal.

In Kentucky, a contingent of the 17th Kentucky Infantry Regiment, 26th Kentucky Infantry and the 3rd Kentucky Cavalry, commanded by Colonel Stephen Gano Burbridge, skirmishes with Confederates at Woodbury and Morgantown. Casualties are reported as minimal for the Union: one wounded. Confederate casualties are unknown.

In Union activity, Albert Lindley Lee is commissioned major (later brigadier general) of the 7th Kansas Cavalry.

In Confederate general officer activity, Colonel Hugh W. Mercer (West Point, 1828) is promoted to brigadier general. He will command at Savannah, Georgia, and lend support to the Confederates at Atlanta against Sherman during 1864. General Mercer is the grandson of General Hugh Mercer, who served with General George Washington during the American Revolution. Also, Brigadier General William H.T. Walker resigns his commission, but he is immediately appointed to the rank of major general in the Georgia militia. However, Walker will rejoin the Confederate Army during February 1863.

October 31 (Thursday)   Turbulence is brewing south of the border in Mexico. To discuss Mexico, which has defaulted on its loans to foreign creditors due to its financial crisis, a meeting is held in London (Treaty of London). This day, England, France and Spain decide to combine forces and commence a military expedition to compel Mexico to make good on its obligations. The armada reaches Mexico in December. Due to the ongoing internal conflict, the United States is unable to properly react to the crisis in Mexico at this time.

In Kentucky, a contingent of the Kentucky Home Guards and one company of Kentucky Volunteers, commanded by Captain Porter and Lt. Rogers, engage Confederates at Morgantown. Casualties are not reported.

In Union general officer activity, Francis Trowbridge Sherman (later brigadier general) is appointed lieutenant colonel of the 56th Illinois Regiment (known also as Mechanic Fusileers). Nonetheless, the regiment musters out during February 1862 and soon after, Sherman becomes major of the 12th Illinois Cavalry.

November   *In Confederate general officer activity,* Lt. Colonel Evander McIvor Law becomes colonel (later, brigadier general) of the 4th Alabama Regiment. During the following spring, Law takes his regiment into battle at Seven Pines, and later the regiment fights during the Seven Days' Retreat.

November 1 (Friday)   **In Washington, D.C.,** U.S. Major General George B. McClellan is appointed general-in-chief, replacing General Winfield Scott.

In Missouri, a Union contingent commanded by Lt. Colonel Morse engages a superior numbered Confederate force at Renick and succeeds in driving them off. Casualties are unreported and specific units are unknown.

In Virginia, Confederates under General Floyd make an unsuccessful attempt to capture General Rosecrans' force at Gauley.

In Illinois, General U.S. Grant dispatches a detachment under Colonel Richard Oglesby (8th Illinois Infantry), with orders to attack a reported enemy force of 3,000 men who are posted along the St. Francis River, about fifty miles outside of Cairo. Oglesby will subsequently be promoted to the rank of brigadier general.

In Union general officer activity, George Washington Cullum (West Point, 1833) is appointed brigadier general and assigned to the staff of General Halleck. Cullum in September 1864 leaves the staff to assume command of West Point, where he remains for two years. He retires during 1874 and marries General Halleck's widow, Elizabeth Hamilton Halleck, who is also a granddaughter of Alexander Hamilton. Also, Robert Kingston Scott, having earlier this year entered the 68th Ohio as a major, on this day is promoted to lieutenant colonel. During the following year, he is again promoted, attaining the rank of colonel during July. The regiment participates in the Vicksburg campaign as part of General John Logan's division in the XVII Corps. In addition to other actions, Colonel Scott participates as a brigade commander during the Atlanta campaign.

In Confederate general officer activity, Humphrey Marshall (West Point 1832), having accepted a commission as brigadier general in the Confederacy on October 30, is ordered to report to Eastern Kentucky. Subsequently, he will serve in West Virginia until he resigns his commission during June of 1862. Also, Clement Anselm Evans, a lawyer in Atlanta, Georgia, is commissioned major (later brigadier general) of the 31st Georgia Infantry at about this time (November). The following April he becomes colonel of the regiment. He is attached to the Army of Northern Virginia and remains active during each of the campaigns for the duration of the war.

November 2 (Saturday)   **In Missouri,** Major General John Frémont's forces are deployed in the vicinity of the Ozark Hills near Springfield, still in pursuit of General Sterling Price's Confederate force. But this day, the plan changes, as Frémont is informed that he is to be succeeded as commander of the Department of the West by General David Hunter, who is en route to the area. Frémont reluctantly accepts the orders, but initially he attempts to retain control of his army. The decision to relieve him of his command follows many conferences about his leadership and attitude held by President Lincoln and his cabinet. Frémont will remain in the army in a lesser capacity until he resigns during 1864.

In Naval activity, a large naval force commanded by Commodore Samuel Du Pont, while en route to seize Forts Beauregard and Walker at Hilton Head, sails into a tremendous storm, so treacherous that from the flagship, only one of the more than seventy vessels is visible. The fleet, in addition to its sailors and Marines, is also transporting the ground forces, composed of three brigades under General Thomas West Sherman. One of the vessels, the steamer *Governor*, is lost; members of the crew, including a Marine battalion of 300 men commanded by Major John C. Reynolds, is safely

During a ferocious storm on November 2, the USS *Sabine* rescues a battalion of Marines aboard the foundering USS *Governor* (Mottelay, *The Soldier in Our Civil War*, 1886).

During the Great Storm of November 2, the transports *Star of the South* and the *Peerless* collide (Mottelay, *The Soldier in Our Civil War*, 1886).

transferred to the frigate USS *Sabine*, commanded by Captain Ringgold; however, one corporal and six enlisted Marines are lost. Three other transports — the *Peerless*, which collides with the *Star of the South* while the latter is attempting to rescue it, and the *Osceola* and the *Union* — are driven to shore and into the hands of Confederate forces. All aboard are seized and imprisoned. Two gunboats, both on the brink of disaster, manage to lighten their loads by heaving several of their guns overboard to successfully avoid destruction and continue the mission. Two ferry boats and one steamer sustain enough damage to force them to abort the mission and return to Fortress Monroe, Virginia.

In other Naval activity, a fleet (Stone Fleet) of what could be considered "over the hill" vessels leave New Bedford, Massachusetts, heading south to be intentionally sunk with their granite cargoes. They reach Savannah during December, but at that time, they will be diverted back to Charleston. All vessels are purposely sunk by January 26, 1862, but the operation does not achieve much success.

In Confederate general officer activity, at about this time, John Cabell Breckinridge (former vice president under Buchanan and former U.S. senator) is appointed brigadier general in the Confederate Army. One member of Breckinridge's staff will be a Confederate congressman from Kentucky, George B. Hodge. He is a graduate of the naval academy (Annapolis), class of 1845, who joins the Confederate Army as a private and twice rises to the rank of brigadier general to lead a brigade of cavalry rather than a naval squadron.

November 3 (Sunday) Union forces initiate a mission into Lower Missouri in an effort to rid the area of the Confederates (2nd and 3rd Dragoons) under Colonel Jeff Thompson; the operation continues until the 11th.

In Union activity, General David Hunter arrives at General John Frémont's headquarters (Department of the West) at Springfield, Missouri, on Sunday night at about midnight (3rd–4th) to succeed General Frémont. Frémont and his staff in a short while return to St. Louis. General Hunter is expected to resume the pur-

suit of Sterling Price, but by mid–December, headquarters modifies its plans and directs Hunter to retire from Springfield and head toward St. Louis. During March of the following year, Frémont receives a new command. Also, Andrew Jackson Smith (West Point, 1838), commissioned colonel (later major general) of the 2nd U.S. Cavalry during the opening of hostilities, is commissioned chief of cavalry.

November 4 (Monday) In Missouri, Union troops commanded by colonel (later major general) Grenville Mellen Dodge (commander, 4th Missouri Infantry) occupy Houston. His force confiscates large amounts of enemy supplies and property as well as some prisoners.

In Confederate activity, dissension continues to cause friction between President Jefferson Davis and some of his generals following a string of differences of opinion between Beauregard and Davis that began immediately following Manassas. Politics, rumors and innuendos that shift blame regarding pursuit of the Union still simmers. Some say Davis did not permit pursuit and Davis claims the rumors are completely false. Davis, this day, attempts, by letters to Generals Robert E. Lee and Samuel Cooper, to gain information about the controversy that is still circulating. Meanwhile, the Confederacy is preparing to elect a permanent president within a few days. Davis, the provisional president, is seeking the presidency and the stories about the incompetence of his administration do not flatter his candidacy.

In Naval activity, the Union fleet under Commodore Samuel Du Pont, which had departed Annapolis on October 21, arrives off Port Royal, South Carolina, and will be joined there by additional vessels.

November 5 (Tuesday) In South Carolina, Confederate General Robert E. Lee departs Charleston for Richmond. While in Charleston, Lee has constructed impregnable works at Fort Pulaski. These defenses protect both Charleston, South Carolina, and Savannah, Georgia, from being captured by sea during the entire war. At about this time, General Lee receives command of the Department of South Carolina, Georgia and East Florida.

In Naval activity, Flag Officer Samuel Du Pont confers with officers of his fleet to make final preparations for the Union assault on Confederate Forts Beauregard and Walker at Hilton Head, South Carolina. A reconnaissance force supported by several gunboats, including the *Curlew, Isaac Smith, Ottawa* and *Seneca*, moves up the channel to gather intelligence on the Confederate defenses. Soon after, several of the

eight Confederate steamers attached to the command of Commodore Josiah Tatnall are encountered, and after a brief exchange, the Rebels retire. The Union then proceeds further and when it comes within range of the batteries at Hilton Head and Bay Point, the Confederates commence firing. The gunboats return fire. Following an exchange lasting about one hour, the ships withdraw to the fleet. In the meantime, it is decided to launch the assault on the following day, but strong winds force a postponement until the 7th. Forts Beauregard and Walker, the latter being the strongest, continue to strengthen their defenses in anticipation of the attack.

Fort Walker, defended by twenty-four guns, is commanded by General Thomas Fenwick Drayton (West Point, 1828), a classmate of Jefferson Davis who had just been appointed brigadier general on September 25. Among the Union officers is Drayton's brother, Captain Percival Drayton, commanding officer of the gunboat USS *Pocahontas*. The transport CSS *Resolute, Lady Davis* and the *Savannah*, commanded by Confederate flag officer J.P. Jones, oppose the Union fleet.

In Missouri, the 11th Illinois, under Colonel William Harvey L. Wallace, departs Bird's Point (Charlestown) to reinforce Colonel Richard J. Oglesby's expedition on the St. Francis River. On this day, Grant, commanding at Cairo, directs all available troops in the region to move in the direction of Columbus, Kentucky. He is certain that his force is too light to attack Columbus, the point from which he has learned that General Leonidas Polk was sending reinforcements to General Sterling Price. However, he believes that a feint against Columbus, and by attacking Belmont on the opposite bank of the Mississippi River, might suffice. Grant orders General Charles F. Smith to depart Paducah, Kentucky, and move south toward Mayfield and to a point near Columbus in two separate columns; he is also directed to dispatch a smaller unit to a town 12 miles north of Columbus, Ellicott's Mills. Meanwhile, Grant himself departs Cairo with about 3,000 men to converge on Columbus, Kentucky.

November 6 (Wednesday) In Missouri and Kentucky, General Grant's force reaches a point six miles outside of the Confederate-held Columbus, Kentucky. The troops are drawn from General John A. McClernand's brigade. The units include the 22nd Illinois (Colonel H. Dougherty), 27th Illinois (Colonel Napoleon B. Buford), 30th Illinois (Colonel Philip B. Fouke), 31st Illinois (Colonel John A. Logan), the 7th Iowa (Colonel J.G. Lauman) and one battery of Smith's Chicago Artillery, commanded by Captain Ezra Taylor. The force is further supplemented by three companies of cavalry, led by Captain J.J. Dollin and Lieutenant J.R. Catlin (Delano's Cavalry). Three steam transports, the *Bells, Memphis* and *Scott*, carry the troops, and they are protected by the gunboats *Lexington* and *Tyler*, commanded by captains Campbell and Walke respectively. The vessels, rather than debark the troops, stay off

Island Number 1 less than ten miles south of Cairo, Illinois, throughout the night as a ruse to trick the Rebels into thinking the attack would be launched against Columbus. Grant will set up pickets on the Kentucky side of the river. Also, a Union force, composed of detachments of the 4th and 5th Missouri Cavalry and Kowald's Missouri Battery, engages a large Confederate force at Little Santa Fe, Missouri. The Union sustains two killed, six wounded and some captured. Confederate casualties are unavailable.

In South Carolina, the Confederates continue to strengthen the defenses at Forts Beauregard and Walker. Fort Walker is held by three companies of the 9th (also 11th) South Carolina Regiment (Colonel William C. Hayward), four companies of the 12th South Carolina Regiment (Lt. Colonel Barnes), the 15th South Carolina (Colonel W.D. De Saussure), a contingent of Georgia Volunteers, two companies of Colonel John A. Wagner's South Carolina Artillery and one battery of artillery commanded by Captain Reed. Fort Beauregard at nearby Bay Point is commanded by Colonel R.G.M. Dunovant. It is guarded by twenty guns, supporting just under 650 men of the 12th S.C. Regiment and the Beaufort artillerymen. In addition, the Rebels maintain one other smaller fortification in the area and it is guarded by only six guns.

The Union ground forces are composed of Thomas W. Sherman's three brigades. The First Brigade, commanded by General Egbert L. Viele, comprises the 8th Maine Regiment (Colonel Lee Strickland), the 3rd New Hampshire (Colonel E.W. Fellows), 46th New York (Colonel Rudolph Rosa), 47th New York (Colonel Henry Moore) and 48th New York (Colonel James H. Perry) regiments. The Second Brigade, commanded by General Isaac I. Stevens, comprises the 8th Michigan (Colonel William Fenton), the 79th New York (Lt. Colonel William H. Nobles), the 50th Pennsylvania (Colonel B.C. Christ) and the Pennsylvania "Roundhead Volunteers" (Colonel David Leasure). The Third Brigade, commanded by General Horatio G. Wright, is composed of the 6th and 7th Connecticut led by Colonels James L. Chatfield and A. H. Terry, respectively, the 9th Maine (Colonel Richworth Rich) and the 4th New Hampshire (Colonel Thomas J. Whip). Also, the Union assault force is augmented by the 21st Massachusetts, a volunteer battalion of engineers from New York, and the 3rd Rhode Island Regiment, all of which remain unattached to a specific brigade.

In Virginia, Provisional President Jefferson Davis is elected as the president of the Confederacy; his provisional vice president, Alexander Stephens, also retains his position. The term is set for six years; however, it is obviously contingent upon the results of the conflict.

In Naval activity, the USS *Resolute* while on patrol on the Rappahannock River encounters a suspicious vessel, which is intercepted and seized. The schooner captured at Corrotman Creek is named *Ada* and is a Confederate ammunition storage vessel. In other activity, the USS *Whitehall* at Newport News departs for Hampton Roads subsequent to receiving repairs while en route to Port Royal, South Carolina. Nevertheless, it returns to Hampton Roads on the following day after encountering rough seas. By the following day, it is found to be unseaworthy. It is towed to South Carolina by the USS *Connecticut,* which departs on 12 November. The *Whitehall* is compelled to return to Hampton Roads on the 13th, and on the same day, it is ordered to Baltimore to undergo major repairs.

November 7 (Thursday) BATTLE OF PORT ROYAL Union Flag Officer Samuel F. Du Pont's Union Fleet, a massive array of ships that includes the vessels *Susquehanna, Wabash, Mohican, Pawnee, Seminole,* and the *Penguin,* attacks Forts Beauregard and Walker at Hilton Head, South Carolina. Union naval fire commences at about 1000 following a series of maneuvers that places the warships to the front of Fort Walker and simultaneously places a squadron in position to protect the rear in the event Josiah Tatnall's Confederate steamers, including the CSS *Sampson,* try to attack from the rear; however, the Confederate fleet is compelled to retire to Skull Island. Meanwhile, the Union naval barrage lobs shell after shell into the Confederate positions and in return, the Confederate shore batteries try to plaster the fleet. All the while, the Union ground forces remain aboard, acting as reluctant witnesses to the spectacular ex-

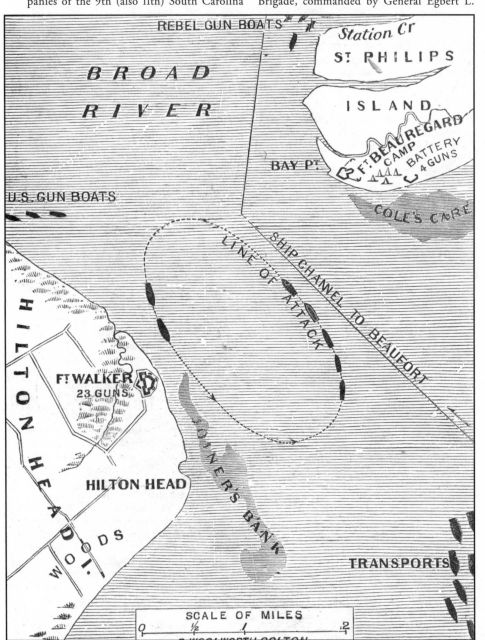

The naval battle of Port Royal, South Carolina, November 7, 1861 (Mottelay, *The Soldier in Our Civil War,* 1886).

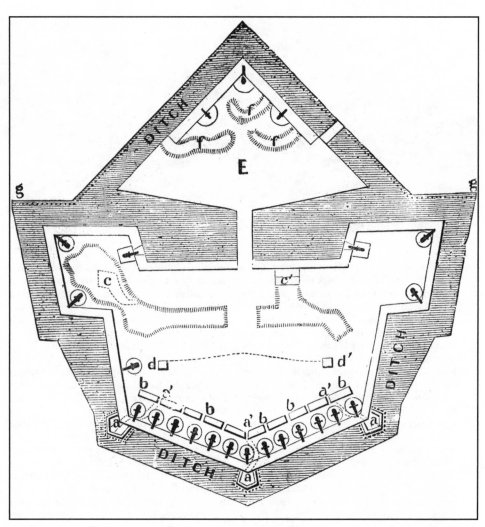

Above: Rear Admiral Samuel Du Pont. *Right:* Plan of Fort Walker, South Carolina (Mottelay, *The Soldier in Our Civil War*, 1886).

change. The Union ships maintain a pace of perpetual motion, moving around the forts as they fire deadly broadsides, perplexing the Confederates, who must strike the ships which have made themselves elusive moving targets. The Union armada makes several passes around the fortifications, but it maintains a focus on reducing the defenses to ruins.

At about 1200, the Union vessels increase the intensity by cruising closer to shore and from extremely close-range they propel devastating barrages that pummel the fortifications and inflict heavy casualties upon the Confederate ranks, while substantially damaging the forts. By about 1330, the incessant bombardment compels the Confederates to abandon their positions to seek safety from the pernicious fire. The defenders at Fort Walker break for Bluffton, while the troops at Fort Beauregard head for Cat, Port Royal and St. Helena Islands. Confederate General Roswell S. Ripley is among those who move to Port Royal. The battle, which lasts about four hours, had been a grueling test of endurance; however, the overpowering force of the fleet brings victory to the Union.

Both strategic forts fall to the Union, which will use the harbor as a base for blockading Southern ports. Fort Walker is renamed Fort

Welles and Fort Beauregard becomes Fort Seward. This is an excellent position for the Union, located between Charleston and Savannah.

A contingent of 650 Marines and sailors commanded by Major John C. Reynolds holds Forts Walker and Beauregard until General Thomas W. Sherman brings in Army reinforcements. The Confederates lose most of their guns and supplies to Union troops as they abandon their untenable positions. General Thomas W. Sherman commands the fort until his transfer to New Orleans during the following August. The Union sustains eight killed and 23 wounded. The Confederates suffer approximately 50 killed or wounded. Although the Confederate batteries inflict some damage to the fleet, no vessels

are lost. The vessels *Pawnee* (nine hits), *Bienville* (five hits) and the *Wabash* (34 hits) sustain damage. The *Augusta*, *Isaac Smith*, *Mohawk*, *Ottawa*, *Pembina*, *Unadilla* and *Seneca* also participate in the attack. The *Mohawk* sustains six hits, but only minor damage; however, it loses one man killed and seven wounded.

Blacksmith's shop (Mottelay, *The Soldier in Our Civil War*, 1886).

Left: A Union fleet bombards Fort Walker (Johnson, *Campfire and Battlefield: History of the Conflicts and Campaigns*, 1894). *Right:* A Union grave site of officers and enlisted men lost in the Battle of Port Royal, South Carolina (Mottelay, *The Soldier in Our Civil War*, 1886).

BATTLE OF BELMONT, In the vicinity of Belmont, Missouri, on the Mississippi River, General U.S. Grant's forces debark the transports at Hunter's Point, too far away for the guns of the Rebel batteries in Columbus, Kentucky, to deal them any harm. Once ashore, two companies of the 7th Iowa and three companies of the 22nd Illinois remain at Hunter's Point to protect the vessels, while the main body, two separate brigades, advances toward Belmont shadowed by the gunboats *Tyler* and *Lexington*. The vessels intentionally proceed slowly toward Columbus. General John A. McClernand's force is composed of the 27th, 30th and 31st Illinois Regiments, bolstered by Dollin's cavalry, Taylor's artillery battery, and Colonel H. Dougherty's brigade, which is composed of seven companies of his regiment, the 22nd Illinois, eight companies of the 7th Iowa Regiment and two companies of cavalry. The assault line is held in the center by Colonel Phillip B. Fouke and the left and right wings are commanded by Colonels Napoleon Bonaparte Buford and John A. Logan respectively.

The Rebel force facing this massive column is the command of Confederate General Gideon Johnson Pillow, composed of the 13th Arkansas (Colonel James Camp Tappan), 12th Tennessee (Colonel R.M. Russell), 13th Tennessee (Colonel John V. Wright), 21st Tennessee (Colonel Edward Pickett, Jr.) and 22nd Tennessee (Colonel Thomas J. Freeman) bolstered further by a battery of Beltzhoover's artillery commanded by Captain Watson and one battalion of cavalry commanded by Lt. Colonel Miller. Captain William Hicks Jackson (West Point, 1847) is seriously wounded while his artillery unit is engaged in this action. He recovers and will be promoted to the rank of colonel, 1st (later 7th) Tennessee Cavalry Regiment. The Confederates number about 4,400 troops. General Leonidas Polk, once aware of Grant's intent, had rushed several regiments to support Fort Pillow (Tennessee). As the Union closes to attack, the Confederates launch an assault to intercept and drive back the Union force; however, General Grant commits his entire line and soon after, the close-quartered struggle begins.

Union pressure lobs the Confederates back to their lines. Nonetheless, while Grant's brigades encroach the Confederate positions, they are simultaneously within the range of the guns at Columbus. Nevertheless, the attack presses forward despite the ferocious barrage of shot and shell that slams into its path, propelled from the opposite banks and from the fortifications to the front. When within reach of their objective, the troops forge ahead to begin scaling the barricades. From there, with drawn bayonets, the Yankees bolt toward the batteries, capturing both following a tenacious exchange.

While this battle rages, both General Grant and General McClernand have their horses shot from under them, but neither is seriously hurt and later, yet another horse under McClernand is also shot. Undeterred, McClernand, who is again thrown to the ground, jumps up, secures a captured gun and turns it on the enemy. Meanwhile, lacking the guns, the Confederates are compelled by the overwhelming thrust to hurriedly fall back to the river bank. With the Rebels evicted from their camp, Colonel (later general) Napoleon Bonaparte Buford's force, the first to enter the camp, unfurls Old Glory. The Union then sets fire to the camp and prepares to move back to its vessels, aware that the guns in Columbus would soon be upon them. The Union troops retire toward their point of landing and from there return to their base. Grant's troops receive no reprieve. Confederate General Polk had dispatched additional troops under General Benjamin Franklin Cheatham and Colonel Mark, who strike the Union at their flank and rear respectively. The Confederates fail to greatly impede the retirement, although for awhile, Grant's command is virtually surrounded while trying to get back to the ships. However, the attacks are beaten back. At about 1700, the troops arrive at the point of departure, where the vessels are waiting to take them away.

The supporting gunboats had engaged in some extracurricular activity during the six-hour battle, shelling the battery positions on Iron Banks in the vicinity of Columbus, trying to knock out some of the twenty-one guns there that had been lambasting Grant's assault force. Following this morning exercise, the *Lexington* and *Tyler* return to offer aid to the Union if needed. Essentially, due to the threat of the guns at Columbus, Grant is unable to capitalize on the victory against Generals Floyd, Pillow and Leonidas Polk. The Confederates are now given time to regroup while reinforcements are rushing to their aid.

When the Union forces depart from Belmont, they also transport two of the rebel guns and about 200 prisoners. General Grant, on the following day, mentions as part of the General Order: "It has been my fortune to have been in all the battles fought in Mexico by Generals Scott and Taylor, save Buena Vista, and I never saw one more hotly contested, or where troops behaved with more gallantry."

Major Elliott Warren Rice (7th Iowa), subsequent to the wounding of his colonel and the death of the regiment's lieutenant colonel, had assumed command of the regiment and he too is badly wounded. Rice is unable to participate in the operations against Fort Donelson due to remaining on crutches; however, he does participate Shiloh (6 April 1862).

Union losses are 498 casualties: 90 killed, 173 wounded and 235 missing; the 7th Iowa sustains the highest amount of casualties. Colonel Henry Dougherty of the 22nd Illinois sustains a terrible wound and is captured during the contest. Union Colonel Napoleon B. Buford, 27th Illinois (West Point, 1827), participates at this battle. Buford, the brother of Union General John Buford, is at the fight of Island Number 10 during April 1862 and will be appointed brigadier general of volunteers on the 15th. Also, Colonel (later brevet major general) sustains a severe wound.

Confederate losses total 963: 260 killed, 425 wounded and 278 missing; the losses include the death of Colonel John V. Wright, 13th Tennessee. Later, the 13th Tennessee will be led by Lt. Colonel (later brigadier general) Alfred J. Vaughan, Jr., when the regiment participates in the upcoming engagements of the Army of Tennessee. The Confederate 12th Louisiana Regiment, led by Colonel Thomas Moore Scott, is present during this action, but the regiment is not committed; it will later move to Island No. 10 near Fort Pillow. Also, the Confederate 15th Tennessee Regiment, commanded by Lt. Colonel (later brigadier general) Robert C. Tyler, participates at this action. Following the contest at Belmont, Tyler is promoted to the rank of colonel.

In Naval activity, the Confederate steamer *General Rusk* repels an attempt by U.S. Marines and sailors aboard the USS *Santee* to seize it. Nevertheless, the *Santee* then encounters and captures the Confederate vessel *Royal Yacht* in the Bolivar Channel near Galveston, Texas. The Union sustains one killed and eight wounded. The Confederates sustain three wounded. Also, the USS *Wabash* moves to Hilton Head, South Carolina, transporting a large assault force. Major John C. Reynolds, commanding a contingent of 650 Marines and sailors, lands and seizes Fort Beauregard at Bay Point, then holds it until army forces under General Thomas W. Sherman arrive to relieve them.

In other activity, the U.S. Navy acquires the *Marion* (side-wheel ferry boat) constructed at New York this year. It is commissioned the USS *Morse* on 9 November. Acting Master Peter Hays receives command of the gunboat and on the 20 it arrives at Hampton Roads as a member of the North Atlantic Blockading Squadron.

November 8 (Friday)   In Kentucky at Fort Anderson (Paducah), the commander, General C.F. Smith, aware of a lethal threat from Confederate warships, informs Washington that the Confederates are working to transform steamers into ironclads (contracts had also been awarded by the Confederates on 24 August in Memphis to construct the warships *Arkansas* and *Tennessee*). With regard to General Smith's observation, the Confederates are in the process of transforming four river steamboats (*Helman, Joseph Johnson, J. Woods* and *B.M. Runyon*) into ironclads. In East Kentucky, many pro-Unionists in the mountainous region become impatient while waiting for Union troops to arrive. Consequently, citizens there arm themselves and begin to press the Confederates. The Rebels under Zollicoffer find these mountaineers to be of firm resolve and their strength is sufficient enough to prompt General Zollicoffer to request reinforcements to suppress the Yankees and terminate their actions. The mountaineers wreck tracks, destroy railroad bridges and raid the more thinly guarded Rebel outposts.

In South Carolina, the Union dispatches a Reconnaissance force to operate in and around Hilton Head. On Sunday the 10th, the reconnoitering moves out further in a continuing effort to determine the strength of the Rebels.

In Missouri at Belmont, the Union and Confederates come to terms and allow each other to bury the dead. They also exchange captured troops.

In Confederate general officer activity, Alexander P. Stewart (West Point, 1842) had earlier joined the Confederacy and his duty had been augmenting the batteries at Belmont. On this day, he is appointed brigadier general in the Confederate Army. General Stewart rises through the ranks and becomes a lieutenant general during 1864.

In Naval activity, Union Marines and sailors stationed on the USS *San Jacinto* wait patiently off Cuba for the British vessel *Trent* to depart for

Union batteries at Paducah, Kentucky (Mottelay, *The Soldier in Our Civil War,* 1886).

England. The Union has information that two Confederate ministers are aboard. When the *Trent* leaves port and enters open waters, the *San Jacinto* intercepts and boards the ship, to the surprise of the English. Captain Charles Wilkes orders the forceful, if necessary, capture of both Confederate diplomats, James Mason and John Slidell. Once the Confederate diplomats are in custody, the British vessel is permitted to continue its journey unmolested, creating a problem for Washington, because the vessel is not seized. Captain Wilkes had been waiting north of Cuba to intercept the vessel, but he had not been acting on orders from Washington; however, the capture prevents the Confederates from reaching Europe and possibly convincing the European powers to side with the Confederacy in the war.

When word of the incident reaches England, there is a loud cry of retaliation, and soon England begins to place itself on a war footing by bolstering its Navy and dispatching troops to Canada. The incident causes anxiety in the United States, as the seizure of the two diplomats is against U.S. policy. Nevertheless, if the *San Jacinto* had also seized the *Trent* as a prize, it would not have violated U.S. policy. During the latter part of December, the U.S. makes amends. The families of both diplomats are not taken from the British vessel. They complete the voyage to Europe.

In other activity, the gunboat USS *Rescue* captures its second Confederate ammunition ship, the *Urbania,* while on patrol on the Rappahannock River. Subsequent to this action, the *Rescue,* on or about 15 November, is reassigned.

November 9 (Saturday)   In Washington, D.C., the Department of the Cumberland is redesignated the Department of the Ohio, which now includes Ohio, Michigan, and Indiana added to Kentucky and Tennessee.

In Arizona–New Mexico, at about this time, the Union Department of New Mexico is re-established. Colonel (later brigadier general) Edward Canby, commanding officer 19th Infantry Regiment at Fort Defiance, Arizona (New Mexico Territory), will command.

The USS *San Jacinto* intercepts the *Trent,* which is transporting Confederate ministers, on 8 November 1861 (Mottelay, *The Soldier in Our Civil War,* 1886).

In Kentucky, Union troops (General Buell's Department of the Ohio), including the 2nd, 21st and 33rd Ohio, plus the 16th Kentucky, commanded by Colonel (later general) Joshua Woodrow Sill, engage Confederates led by Colonel John Stuart Williams (Confederate 5th Kentucky Infantry) at Fry Mountain (also Ivy Mountain or Piketown), capturing 200 Confederates. The Union sustains four killed and 26 wounded. The Confederates sustain 18 killed and 45 wounded. Confederate Colonel John S. Williams, formerly of the 6th U.S. Infantry and 4th Kentucky Volunteers (Mexican War era), officially receives his commission in the Confederacy on November 16, 1861.

In Union general officer activity, Jeremiah Tilford Boyle is appointed brigadier general of volunteers. He participates as a brigade commander at the Battle of Shiloh (General Thomas L. Crittenden's division). During May of the following year, General Boyle becomes commander of the Union forces in Kentucky.

In Naval activity, troops attached to the USS *Seneca* seize Beaufort, South Carolina, and demolish its arsenal. The *Seneca* also seizes a Confederate vessel, the *City of Branford*, near Beaufort.

November 10 (Sunday)   In North Carolina, Union General Thomas Williams has been attempting to fortify the captured forts at Cape Hatteras in eastern North Carolina, but nature has taken her toll. The storms coming in off the Atlantic have scattered the defenses, but the Confederates have pulled back from the area. There is growing concern that thousands of Rebels are massing on the other side of the Pamlico with intentions of recapturing Fort Hatteras.

In South Carolina, a Union reconnaissance

Union troops destroy a Confederate arsenal at Beaufort, South Carolina, on 9 November 1861 (Mottelay, *The Soldier in Our Civil War*, 1886).

force departs Hilton Head for Braddock's Point, South Carolina.

In Tennessee, a large group of civilians loyal to the Union skirmish with a Confederate detachment of slightly more than 20 men at Taylor's Ford on the Watauga River. The civilians sustain about nine killed and seven wounded.

In Virginia, some residents of the town of Guyandotte have been accused of murdering several Union soldiers. The town is torched in retaliation. During the affair, the Union (recruits of the 9th West Virginia Volunteers) sustain seven killed, 20 wounded and some captured. The Confederates suffer two killed and 20 wounded. Also, the 11th Ohio Volunteers and 2nd Kentucky Cavalry commanded by General Jacob D. Cox and Colonel C. DeVilliers, respectively, engage Confederates (General H. A. Wise's command) at Gauley Bridge, West Virginia. The Rebels under Wise are forced to retreat. The Union sustains eight killed and 11 wounded. Confederate casualties, if any, are unavailable; however, the Union seizes a huge number of stands of arms.

November 11 (Monday)   In Missouri, a contingent of the 7th Kansas Cavalry, numbering about 110 troops commanded by Colonel Daniel Anthony, attacks an encampment of Confederate guerrillas led by Colonel Upton Hays at Little Blue. The Union sustains about seven killed and about seven to nine wounded. Confederate casualties, if any, are unavailable.

In Virginia, a Union contingent commanded by Colonel Weber skirmishes with Confederates at New Market Bridge.

In Union general officer activity, Charles G. Harker (West Point, 1858) is commissioned colonel (later brigadier general) of the 65th Ohio Regiment. Colonel Harker, an orphan at a young age, received his appointment due to Congressman N.T. Stratton of New Jersey. Harker serves under General Don Carlos Buell (Army of the Ohio). Later at Shiloh, Harker's regiment is attached to the brigade of Lt. Colonel James Garfield. Also, Isaac Jones Wistar, a lawyer who raised a company of volunteers in Philadelphia, which became part of the 76th Pennsylvania Regiment, known more so as the California Regiment, is commissioned as colonel of the regiment. He succeeds General Edward D. Baker (killed at Ball's Bluff during the previous month).

In Confederate general officer activity, Lt. Colonel Lucius M. Walker (West Point, 1850), 40th Tennessee Infantry Regiment, is

promoted to the rank of colonel (later brigadier general) and assigned command in Memphis, Tennessee. Also, Major General George B. Crittenden is assigned command of the District of the Cumberland Gap.

November 12 (Tuesday)   In North Carolina, the USS *Monticello* stops momentarily at Fort Clark at Cape Hatteras to inform troops of the Union's successes at Port Royal, South Carolina. Troops from the New York Zouaves are happy to hear of the good news and believe that the next step must be Charleston, South Carolina.

In Virginia, a reconnaissance detachment, composed of a contingent of the New York 1st Cavalry led by Captain Henry B. Todd, advances to Occoquan Creek and encounters a Confederate force. Following a skirmish, the Union, which is compelled to retire, sustains three killed, one wounded and three captured.

Also, the USS *Shawsheen*, disabled since arriving at Hampton Roads during the early part of the month, remains unable to join the South Atlantic Squadron on its own power. The USS *Connecticut* tows the *Shawsheen* and the *Whitehall* to get both vessels to South Carolina, but despite the urgent need for more vessels, both ships soon after they debark are compelled to return to Newport News for more repairs. At Newport News, the situation is also critical. Consequently the *Shawsheen* remains there rather than heading to New York for the repairs. While there, the *Shawsheen* participates with other vessels to protect the USS *Congress* and the *Cumberland*. The USS *Congress*, originally commissioned during May 1840, had served in the Mediterranean and the Pacific Squadron prior to the eruption of the war. The frigate was used in the Mexican War and afterward was a flagship in the Brazil Squadron. It was recalled to the United States at the outbreak of the war.

In Union general officer activity, Colonel Philip St. George Cooke (West Point, 1827), 2nd Dragoons, is promoted to brigadier general. His son, former 2nd Lt. John Rogers Cooke, has sided with the Confederacy and was earlier appointed colonel of the 27th North Carolina. John Rogers Cooke is subsequently (November 1862) promoted to brigadier general. John R. Cooke is also the brother-in-law of General Jeb Stuart. Also, Schuyler Hamilton, the grandson of Alexander Hamilton (West Point, 1841) who served during the Mexican War and was severely wounded twice, and who had re-entered the service as a private during April 1861, is commissioned as a brigadier general. Christopher Columbus Augur (West Point, 1843) is appointed brigadier general.

George Washington Morgan is appointed brigadier general of volunteers. General Morgan had entered West Point, but he departed prior to graduation. Afterward he served as colonel of the 2nd Ohio Regiment and the 15th U.S. Infantry during the Mexican War and received the brevet of brigadier general during 1847. Joshua Howell (Pennsylvania Militia) is mustered into federal service. He is appointed colonel (later brigadier general) of the 85th Pennsylvania Regiment. Initially, the regiment is assigned to the defenses of Washington, D.C. And afterward, it joins the expedition to North Carolina, followed by participation (1863) against Charleston. In yet other activity, Jesse Lee Reno (West Point, 1846) is appointed brigadier general. Reno had been stationed in Alabama prior to the outbreak of the war and was compelled to surrender the Mount Vernon arsenal to state forces during January. Colonel Julius Stahel (8th New York) is promoted to brigadier general.

In Confederate general officer activity, Colonel Richard Griffith, 12th Mississippi Regiment, a Pennsylvanian who had relocated to Mississippi and served in the Mexican War under Jefferson Davis, is commissioned brigadier general in the Confederate Army. He is assigned a brigade composed of three Mississippi Regiments (Army of Northern Virginia).

In Naval activity, the schooner *Beauregard,* a privateer recently commissioned (14 October) by Confederate President Davis while out on its sixth day on the high seas, is seized by the USS *W. G. Anderson,* a bark. Confederate Captain Gilbert Hays and his 23-man crew had not yet encountered any other vessels, nor fired its pivot gun. The ship is seized about 100 miles northeast of Abaco. The *Beauregard,* unable to match the firepower of the *Anderson's* six 32-ponders and one rifle-cannon, surrenders without a fight; however, the Confederates work expeditiously to destroy the ship's weapons, ammunition, rigging and sails before being boarded. In addition to Captain Hays and the 23-man crew, the officers aboard—1st Lt. John B. Davis, 2nd Lt. Joseph H. Stuart, and the purser, Archibald Lilly—are also captured. The Confederates are afterward taken to Key West, Florida, where they are imprisoned in the county jail.

In other activity, the USS *Samuel Rotan* (wooden, center-board schooner), acquired by the U.S. Navy during the previous September, is commissioned in Philadelphia. Acting Master John A. Rogers receives command. The *Samuel Rotan,* assigned to the Gulf Squadron, arrives at Fort Pickens, Florida, on the 16 December to begin blockade duty. The U.S. Navy acquires the *Wissahickon* (screw gunboat), which had been built this year in Philadelphia. It is commissioned on 25 November 1861. Lt. A.N. Smith receives command of the vessel, which is assigned to the West Gulf Blockading Squadron.

November 13 (Wednesday)   In West Virginia at Romney, a skirmish develops between Confederates and pickets of General Benjamin Franklin Kelley's command. Kelley is responsible for maintaining the free flow of the Baltimore and Ohio Railroad and preventing the Rebels from disrupting the rails and communications. The Union loses two killed. The Confederates lose about 12 captured.

In Naval activity, the CSS *Sumter* arrives at St. Pierre (Martinique), but the USS *Iroquois* also arrives and stands offshore. The *Sumter* remains trapped until the night of 23 November.

November 13–18   In Missouri, Union contingents are dispatched from Greenville to Doniphan on a scouting expedition that is completed on the 15th. In addition, another mission is initiated. A reconnaissance force travels through Texas and Wright Counties, completing their task on the 18th.

November 14 (Thursday)   A contingent of Union troops (commanded by Colonel Geary) attached to a Pennsylvania Regiment skirmish with a group of Confederates near the Virginia-Maryland border at Point of Rocks, Maryland. The Confederates sustain about three wounded. Also, at McCoy's Mill, a Union force composed of contingents of the 7th and 37th Ohio Regiments (Volunteers) supported by Schneider's Rifled Battery skirmishes with a Confederate unit. The Union reports no casualties. The Confederates sustain some wounded. The Union force is commanded by General Henry Washington Benham (West Point, 1837) assisted by Colonel William R. Creighton. The Confederates are attached to General John Buchanan Floyd's command. Before the end of the year, General Floyd is transferred to Kentucky to serve under General Albert S. Johnston. The Confederate 36th Virginia Infantry led by Colonel John McCausland is among the units that accompany Floyd to Kentucky.

In Confederate general officer activity, Lt. Colonel William Montgomery Gardner is promoted brigadier general, while still recuperating from a wound sustained at First Manassas (Bull Run). His leg wound keeps him from field duty; however, he does receive command of the District of Middle Florida. In 1864 he receives command of all Confederate military prisons east of the Mississippi River. Afterward, toward the closing days of the war, General Gardner commands the post at Richmond. In other activity, Richard Brooke Garnett (West Point, 1841), a cousin and classmate of Confederate General Robert Selden Garnett, is promoted brigadier general.

In Naval activity, there is minor activity off Cape Hatteras, North Carolina. Union gunboats are in the vicinity and a Confederate vessel moves in and out around the horizon, moving at one point close enough to send in a couple of rounds towards Camp Wool. The Zouaves return fire to acknowledge the visit. Also, the USS *Corwin,* while operating in Hatteras Inlet, repels an attack by the CSS *Curlew.*

November 15 (Friday)   In Virginia, the USS *San Jacinto* with its captives—James Mason, Confederate minister to England, and John Slidell, Confederate minister to France—enters the waters off Fort Monroe. Captain Wilkes and the crew initially receive a hero's welcome after the news of the capture spreads, but soon after, particularly when lawyers get involved, the Union's perspective changes. Arguing develops regarding the incident occurring in international waters and the element of foreign intervention emerges as part of the equation. Apprehension abounds as the lawyers and politicians refer to the possibility of England or France re-

taliating and joining the hostilities on the side of the Confederacy. Not surprisingly, the armed forces become the scapegoat, as if the world in Washington seemingly forgets that Union warships were dispatched for the purpose of intercepting the alleged vessel carrying the ministers. Nevertheless, the Confederate ministers are soon transferred to a Fort Warren, a military prison in Boston, Massachusetts. Neither the British nor the French enter the hostilities on the side of the Confederates, to the dismay of the Confederate government.

In Union general officer activity, General Don Carlos Buell (West Point, 1841) assumes command of the Department of the Ohio. He is under orders of Major General George B. McClellan to lead the Army of the Ohio to East Tennessee. His instructions mandate a route via Louisville and Knoxville, but he believes the route lacks proper roads and rails to transport about 50,000 troops. His force moves via the Cumberland and Tennessee Rivers toward Nashville. President Abraham Lincoln and General George McClellan remain opposed to the route; however, later it proves correct and timely with regard to coordinating with General Ulysses S. Grant's operations in that area.

In Confederate general officer activity, John Stuart "Cerro Gordo" Williams, a Kentuckian and former state legislator (1851–1853), is appointed colonel (later brigadier general) of the 5th Kentucky Infantry.

In Naval activity, the gunboat *Rescue* on or about this date is ordered to move to Hampton Roads from the Rappahannock River. It initiates duty there as a patrol ship, but it also engages as a tow ship. During October of the following year, it moves to Washington, D.C., for repairs and then sails to Port Royal, South Carolina, to patrol off Charleston. The *Rescue* returns to Baltimore in June 1864 and by September is reassigned to the Potomac Flotilla. The *Rescue* remains in service way beyond the close of hostilities, at Washington, D.C. It is used as a tug and a fireboat until 1889, when it is condemned and, later, on 25 March 1891, sold.

November 16 (Saturday)   In Virginia, a Confederate contingent operating in the vicinity of Doolan's Farm overwhelms and captures a Union detachment while it is on a foraging mission.

In Mississippi, Union and Confederate units each on foraging missions skirmish in Cass County. The supplies and wagons are seized by one side and then recaptured by the other. Initially, the Rebels prevail; however, the Yankees gain the advantage when they re-seize the food supplies. Both sides sustain casualties.

In Confederate general officer activity, Colonels Lawrence O'Bryan Branch, 33rd North Carolina Regiment, and William Mahone, 6th Virginia Infantry, are appointed to the rank of brigadier general effective this day.

In Naval activity, Confederate Naval Captain Duncan N. Ingraham is directed to report to

Charleston, South Carolina. He is to bolster the defenses of the harbor and to oversee the operation of the batteries, and to carry out any other subsequent order given him by Flag Officer Josiah Tatnall. Commander Tatnall had resigned from the U.S. Navy in February 1861, and the following month, he was placed in charge of the naval defenses covering the coasts of Georgia and South Carolina.

November 17 (Sunday) In Kentucky, a Union detachment engages and defeats a Confederate force led by Major (later colonel) Hiram Hawkins at Cypress Bridge. The Union sustains 10 killed and 15 wounded. Confederate casualties are unavailable.

In North Carolina, according to the diary of a Union trooper, Charles F. Johnson, the mail delivery works even on Sundays, as this day, the USS *Spaulding* moves into Camp Wool (Cape Hatteras) with mail for the troops. Also, at Roanoke Island, the Confederates continue to strengthen their defenses, including the installation of shore batteries. Approximately five Confederate vessels patrol the waters off Roanoke.

November 18 (Monday) In Kentucky, Confederate troops hold a meeting in Russellville and decide to establish a Confederate government in opposition to the government that remains loyal to the Union. Identical action had earlier occurred in Missouri, but both Kentucky and Missouri remain loyal to the Union for the duration.

In Missouri, a detachment of the 3rd Missouri Cavalry skirmishes with Confederates at Palmyra. The Union reports no casualties. The Confederates sustain three killed, five wounded and about five captured. Another clash between a Union contingent and Confederates occurs at Warrensburg; casualty figures are unavailable.

In North Carolina, at Cape Hatteras, a group of people sympathetic to the Union had denounced the secession of North Carolina (May 20 of this year) and these representatives from more than forty counties establish a provisional government. Nonetheless, the state remains with the Southern cause for the duration.

In Virginia, a contingent of the 14th New York State Militia on picket duty skirmishes with a detachment of Confederates at Falls Church. The Union sustains one wounded. In other activity, General Robert E. Lee says in a letter to Confederate Secretary of War Judah P. Benjamin: "The enemy having complete possession of the water and inland navigation, commands all the water and inland navigation, commands all the islands on this coast, and threatens both Savannah and Charleston.... We have no guns to resist their batteries and no resource but to prepare to meet them in the field." The Confederate Congress (provisional government of the Confederate States) convenes its fifth session in Richmond.

In Union general officer activity, Union Captain (later brigadier general) Thomas Casimer

Devin is appointed colonel of the 6th New York Cavalry. He participates in battles at Antietam, Chancellorsville and Fredericksburg. Devin sees action at Gettysburg in July 1863 and is active again at Crooked Run, Virginia, in 1864, where he is slightly wounded. Finally, in March 1865 he is appointed brigadier general.

In Naval activity, the gunboat USS *Connecticut,* commanded by Commander Maxwell Woodhull, while operating off the coast of Florida, seizes a blockade runner, the British schooner *Adeline.*

November 19 (Tuesday) In West Virginia, a detachment of the 1st West Virginia Cavalry encounters and engages a contingent of Confederates at Wirt Court House. The estimated Confederate casualties are one killed and about five wounded. No Union casualties are reported.

In Union activity, Union Major General Henry W. Halleck assumes command of the Department of Missouri, which includes Arkansas, Illinois and West Kentucky (east to the Cumberland River) and Missouri. Halleck supersedes General John Frémont. General David Hunter is in temporary command. Also, at about this time (November), the Department of Kansas is established in place of the Department of the West. Union General David Hunter (West Point, 1822) will command in Kansas; however, during March of the following year Hunter becomes commander of the Department of the South. In addition, the Department of Ohio is established; it will include Indiana, East Kentucky (west to the Cumberland River), Michigan, Ohio, and Tennessee. The department will be commanded by General Don Carlos Buell. He succeeds General William T. Sherman.

In Naval activity, the CSS *Nashville,* a side-wheel steamer, previously a passenger ship seized at Charleston and converted into an armed cruiser, encounters an American merchant ship in the English Channel, the *Harvey Birch,* which is en route from Havre, France, to New York. After it is intercepted and captured, the valuables and other items of interest to the Confederates are taken from the *Harvey Birch* and then it is set afire in the English Channel. The Rebels remove the crew and Captain Nelson and continue their voyage to Southampton to debark two passengers, Colonel John L. Peyton (North Carolina agent in England) and his wife, whom the Confederate secretary of war had ordered the *Nashville* to deliver to England.

November 19, 1861–January 1862 In the Indian Terri-

tory, Union forces initiate operations against hostile Indians. The mission continues until January 4 of the following year. The Confederate units in the Indian Territory have alliances with some Indians, but the Rebels too have clashes, as all are not aligned with the Confederacy. A group of Creeks, while attempting to make it from the Indian Territory to Kansas, will be encountered by Rebels, and southern aligned Creeks ignite a clash in the vicinity of Round Mountain on or about November 19.

November 20 (Wednesday) In California, Union forces initiate a mission of pursuit to intercept and seize a group conspicuously tied to the Confederacy known as the Showalter Party, led by Daniel Showalter. The Confederate leaning group is corralled and eighteen men, including the leader, are captured by the end of this month at a ranch southeast of Los Angeles.

In Missouri, a Union contingent engages a Confederate detachment at Butler. The estimated Confederate casualties are five killed and an equal amount wounded. Union and Confederate forces have been sporadically skirmishing in the vicinity of Butler since the beginning of October. They also clash in Little Santa Fe. Specific units are not recorded and casualty figures are unavailable.

In North Carolina, a contingent of four companies of New York Zouaves, commanded by Lieutenant George F. Colonel Betts, engages an equal number of Rebels near Fort Wool. The Zouaves open fire, then pull back, reversing direction to regroup behind the reserves, who are to hold the positions, but in the meantime, some reserves retreat, causing a rout of the Union.

The CSS *Nashville* destroys the U.S. merchant ship *Harvey Birch* in the British Channel on 19 November 1861 (Johnson, *Campfire and Battlefield: History of the Conflicts and Campaigns,* 1894).

November 21 (Thursday) **In Kentucky,** a contingent of General Don Carlos Buell's command (Department of the Ohio), led by Brigadier General George H. Thomas, prepares to depart Danville en route for East Tennessee.

In Missouri, Confederates raid and destroy a Union supply depot at Warsaw.

In Tennessee, Confederate Brigadier General Lloyd Tilghman (West Point, 1836) is ordered to inspect Fort Donelson along the Tennessee River and Fort Henry at the Cumberland River, both in strategic locations near the border with Kentucky. Tilghman will assume command of Fort Henry.

In Union general officer activity, Thomas Jefferson McKean (West Point, 1831) is appointed brigadier general effective this day. McKean had initially resigned from the army during 1834, and later he participated in the Seminole Wars (1837–1838) as adjutant of the 1st Pennsylvania Volunteers. Later, despite his credentials and experience, his application for a commission during the Mexican War was not forthcoming. Nonetheless, McKean joined as an enlisted man. At the outbreak of the Civil War, he was initially appointed as paymaster prior to his promotion to brigadier general. His duties are primarily non-field due to his age (over fifty); however, at the Battle of Corinth (October 1862), he commands a division. In autumn of 1864, while in the Department of the Gulf, he receives temporary command as chief of cavalry. He musters out of the army with the brevet of major general of volunteers in August 1865.

November 22 (Friday) **In Florida,** a contest between artillery and infantry commences. At about 1000, the guns of Fort Pickens target the Confederate positions, particularly the navy yard across the channel, in an attempt to strike the Confederate transports there. Later, the USS *Niagara* and *Richmond,* as well as Union shore batteries, bolster the firing power by targeting Forts McRee and Barrancas. The exchange continues for the duration of the day and neither side is able to claim victory, but by evening, the guns firing from the navy yard become silent, and at both Confederate-held forts, the incoming fire had been greatly decreased. The 1st U.S. Artillery (Batteries A, F, and L), the 2nd U.S. Artillery (Batteries C, H and K), Companies C and E of the 3rd U.S. Infantry and Companies G and I of the 6th New York Regiment (Volunteers) participate. The Union commanders are Colonel Harvey Brown and Flag Officer William W. McKean, the latter commanding the naval forces. The Confederates are attached to Major General Braxton Bragg's command.

In Confederate general officer activity, Brigadier General Albert Pike assumes command of the Department of the Indian Territory. Pike had been commissioned Confederate brigadier general during the previous August and assigned the task of forging an alliance with the Indians west of the Arkansas River.

In Naval activity, the steamers *A.J. View* and the *Henry Lewis* are snagged by Union gunboats, including the *R.R. Cuyler,* that are operating on the Mississippi River and its tributaries. The *R.R. Cuyler* also intercepts fiver other runners during December and participates in their capture. The vessels are the sloops *Advocate, Express,* and *Osceola,* along with the schooners *Delight* and *Olive.*

In Naval activity, the U.S. Navy acquires a side-wheel steam ferryboat, the *Westfield.* It is commissioned during the following month and assigned duty with the Mortar Flotilla of commander (later rear admiral) David D. Porter. It leaves for Key West, Florida, but arrives after Porter's flotilla had departed. Consequently it joins the flotilla on 18 March at the Passes of the Mississippi.

November 23 (Saturday) **In Florida,** the Confederates once again unsuccessfully assault Union-held Fort Pickens. The Union Naval vessels are unable to participate due to low tides. This activity more or less closes out exchanges between the opposing sides until January 1, 1862, when a Confederate steamer encroaches the navy yard at Pensacola.

In Union general officer activity, John Grubb Parke (West Point, 1849) is appointed brigadier general. He serves under General Burnside (North Carolina expedition). Also, General Parke had returned east from the Washington Territory during October 1861, following an assignment regarding surveying. Parke receives command of a brigade during the North Carolina expedition and is promoted to major general during August 1862. Neal Dow, a Quaker, is appointed colonel of the 13th Maine Infantry. The regiment participates in the campaign to seize New Orleans. While en route to join with General Benjamin Butler, the transport runs aground off North Carolina; however, the regiment and the other troops aboard the transport safely arrive at Ship Island.

In Naval activity, during the evening, after the French fire a gun to signal 2000, the CSS *Sumter*—trapped at St. Pierre, Martinique, since 13 November—moves to escape from the USS *Iroquois.* Another U.S. ship in the port sends the a signal of two lights to alert the *Iroquois* that the *Sumter* is sailing southward; however, Captain Raphael Semmes, aware of being under surveillance, spots the signal, then changes course and sails in a northerly direction, while the *Iroquois* moves southward. The privateer *Sumter* eludes capture, then departs St. Pierre. In other activity, in Virginia slightly after midnight, the USS *Shawsheen* and the USS *John L. Lockwood* launch a bombardment of a Confederate encampment along the Yorktown Road just outside Newport News.

November 24 (Sunday) **In Georgia,** Union troops begin to gain ground in the vicinity of Fort Pulaski, Georgia. Confederate batteries within the fort will also open fire on approaching Union ships within a few days. In other activity, Union forces occupy Tybee Island.

In Kentucky, Confederate Lt. Colonel Nathan Bedford Forrest initiates a series of missions into the state. These cavalry operations under Forrest continue until December 5.

In Missouri, a contingent of Missouri Home Guards skirmish with a Confederate force at Johnstown. No casualties are reported. Also, Union troops attached to the 21st Missouri Volunteers, commanded by Colonel David Moore, encounter and defeat a Confederate force at Lancaster. The contest lasts about one-half hour and both sides are nearly equally matched in numbers at about 400 to 450. The Union sustains two killed and one wounded. The estimated Confederate casualties are about 10 to 13 killed.

In Massachusetts, the USS *San Jacinto,* transporting the two captured Confederate ministers to England and France, arrives at Boston from Hampton Roads, Virginia. The two Ministers, James Mason and John Slidell, are imprisoned in Fort Warren at Boston Harbor. Meanwhile, their fate continues to be debated in Washington, D.C., and the incident, now referred to as the Trent Affair, continues to raise tensions between the United States and England, the latter still perturbed that the Yankees had boarded one of their vessels and seized the captives. All the while, Captain Wilkes and his crew remain heroes to some and scapegoats for others, as the lawyers and diplomats argue both sides of the capture. Eventually, the Union concludes that it is wiser to release the two men. An agreement between the United States and England will be reached the following month.

In Naval activity, the USS *John L. Lockwood* departs Hampton Roads, Virginia, for Baltimore for repairs. It remains out of service until recommissioned on 6 December.

November 25 (Monday) **In Georgia,** the crew of the USS *Seneca,* which had seized Big Tybee Island without incident on the previous day, establishes defenses and holds the island until the arrival of the blockading squadron. No opposition is encountered during the mission, giving the Union a strategic location at the entrance to the Savannah River. The next objective is Fort Pulaski on Cockspur Island, another strategic fortification that had been constructed during 1829–1831 to protect the Tybee roads and the Savannah River approach to the city of Savannah. Georgia state troops had seized the fort during January 1861 and handed it over to the Confederate government. A widely known lighthouse can be spotted from a distance of twelve miles, but the illumination here and at all other lighthouses taken by the Confederates have been extinguished to prevent any inadvertent aid to the U.S. Navy.

In South Carolina, the U.S. gunboats *Pawnee, Pembina, Unadilla* and *Vixen* arrive at St. Helena Sound. The warships initiate attacks against Confederate positions and remain in the area on the offensive until the 28 November. The gunboats return to this area of South Carolina during early December.

In Naval activity, the CSS *Sumter* seizes the *Montmorenci,* which is transporting a cargo of coal.

November 26 (Tuesday)   In Missouri, the 7th Kansas Cavalry clashes with Confederates at Independence (Little Blue). The Union estimate one killed and one wounded. The Confederates sustain two killed.

In Virginia, a skirmish develops between the 1st Pennsylvania Cavalry, commanded by Colonel (later general) George Dashiell Bayard, and a Confederate unit led by Captain Farley in Dranesville. The Union suffers two wounded. The Confederates sustain two killed and two captured. In other activity, a detachment of the 3rd Pennsylvania Cavalry commanded by Captain Bell, while on a reconnaissance mission, encounters and skirmishes with Confederates at Hunter's Mills. The Union sustains one killed and some captured.

In West Virginia, a convention for the loyal state of West Virginia (after secession from Virginia) convenes at Wheeling. The government adopts a constitution that mandates the state of West Virginia as part of the Union.

In South Carolina, a Confederate squadron, including the transport CSS *Resolute,* the *Sampson* and the *Savannah* under the command of Confederate Flag Officer J. Tattnall, attacks the Union fleet at the mouth of the Savannah River. Two days later, the *Resolute* and the *Sampson* succeed in delivering supplies to Fort Pulaski.

November 27 (Wednesday)   THE TRENT AFFAIR England receives word that one of its vessels, the *Trent,* had been intercepted and boarded by the crew of a Union warship, the *San Jacinto,* off Cuba and that while in international waters, the Yankees removed two Confederate diplomats. The British ire is raised and immediately, the English oratory begins to bellow. The British perceive the action as an insult to the English ensign. Suggestions of war are uttered. London's diplomats will hurriedly scribe messages to Washington, demanding the release of the Confederates; however, the letters make no reference about releasing the two, James Mason and John Slidell, to the Confederates, rather the captives are to be transferred to the British. Washington will, upon receipt of the request, take it under advisement. Meanwhile, the two diplomats remain in Boston, Massachusetts, well out of the reach of the Confederates. (See also, **November 30** and **December 4.**)

In Virginia, a detachment of the Lincoln Cavalry commanded by Captain William Boyd engages Confederates at Fairfax Court House. The Confederates sustain one wounded.

November 28 (Thursday)   In South Carolina, the Union receives authorization from headquarters in Washington, D.C., to confiscate all farm products in the vicinity of Port Royal and to use the slaves to assist in bolstering the defenses of the area. It is the policy of the Union to compensate slaves who work for the Union.

In Virginia, the Confederate government in Richmond claims Missouri as a state. The Confederacy claims both Missouri and Kentucky, although neither state secedes. The Confederate battle flag contains 13 stars, 11 representing the states that have seceded and two representing Kentucky and Missouri. Union Brigadier General Benjamin Mayberry Prentiss receives command of the Department of North Missouri and holds responsibility for keeping the rails of the St. Joseph Railroad open, and he is also to maintain telegraph operations in the region.

November 29 (Friday)   In Missouri, a contingent of the 1st Missouri Cavalry, commanded by Major Rosell M. Hough, engages Confederate forces at Black Walnut Creek (vicinity of Sadalai). The Union suffers 15 wounded; the Confederates sustain 17 dead. John McAllister Schofield (West Point, 1853), major in the 1st Missouri Cavalry, is promoted to brigadier general with responsibility for the entire complement of Missouri's Union militia.

In Virginia, Union contingents, commanded by Captain Drake DeKay, skirmish with the Confederate Prince Edward Cavalry at New Market Bridge.

In Naval activity, the gunboat USS *Rachael Seaman* arrives at Fort Pickens, Florida, from Philadelphia and reports for duty in the Gulf Blockading Squadron. It begins patrols in Mississippi Sound and vicinity until December, when it moves to support the blockade of Galveston, Texas. The USS *Whitehall,* plagued with problems in need of repair, is detached from the South Atlantic Blockading Squadron and attached to the North Atlantic Blockading Squadron.

**November 30 (Friday)   **The British reaction to the seizure of the vessel *Trent* by Union naval forces and the forceful abduction of the Confederate ministers to France (John Slidell) and England (James Mason) rises to a pinnacle. England's foreign secretary dispatches a message to Lord Lyons, British minister to the United States, to insist upon an apology and demand the return of the captives. Meanwhile, London places its Royal Navy on a war-footing, with the caveat that it is not to engage in hostilities with any Union forces. The political process continues as the British attempt to save face and the Union decides which course of action best suits its needs, while the Confederacy is essentially left to the part of spectator. Lord Lyons' instructions include orders to depart the United States with his entire delegation if a sufficient response is not forthcoming from Washington.

In Missouri, Union forces encounter and skirmish with Confederates at Grand River. Specific units are not recorded and casualties, if any, are unavailable.

In West Virginia, a Union contingent clashes with Confederate bushwackers at the Little Cacapon River. The Union sustains three wounded. Confederate casualty figures are unavailable.

In Naval activity, Captain Charles Wilkes is detached from the USS *San Jacinto* and transferred to Washington, D.C., assigned to the Board of Naval Examiners. He retains the post until summer of 1862.

December   In Missouri, Major General Sterling Price, commander of Missouri state troops, begins to gather men who wish to serve in the Confederate Army. These volunteers are sent to a new camp established by Price. Shortly thereafter, another officer in the Missouri militia who has already joined the Confederacy, Henry Little, is appointed commander of the camp. Price will remain in the militia until April of the following year.

In Confederate general officer activity, Hiram Bronson Granbury is elected major, 7th Texas Infantry, and by the latter part of the year, he becomes colonel (later brigadier general) of the regiment.

In Naval activity, the U.S. Navy commissions the USS *Southfield,* a 750 ton side-wheel ferry boat that had been built in Brooklyn, New York, during 1857. By February 1862, the *Southfield* is on duty in the North Carolina sounds.

**December 1 (Sunday)   **Union and Confederate contingents clash in separate skirmishes at Whippoorwill Creek, Kentucky; Morristown, Tennessee; and Shanghai, Missouri. Casualties are not recorded.

In Union general officer activity, Walter Chiles Whitaker, a veteran of the Mexican War (3rd Kentucky), is commissioned colonel (later brigadier general) of the 6th Kentucky Regiment at about this time (December). He is assigned to General Buell's Army of the Ohio and the regiment participates at Shiloh. It is not present at Perryville; however, during December 1862, the 6th Kentucky is in the field at Murfreesboro.

In Naval activity, Union gunboats operating in Kentucky appear off Fort Holt. The gunboat USS *Penguin* intercepts the blockade runner *Albion,* which apparently is running supplies between the Bahamas and the southern ports. The *Albion,* transporting a hefty cargo, including supplies and weapons, is cut off and captured off Charleston, South Carolina. The gunboat USS *Sciota* is commissioned at about this time (December). It is attached to the Gulf Blockading Squadron during the following month, and after leaving from Philadelphia, it arrives in time to participate in the operations against New Orleans and against Vicksburg (1862). In 1863 it is transferred to support the blockade against Galveston, Texas.

December 2 (Monday)   In Washington, D.C., Congress convenes (37th Session) and the agenda is full, as the politicians argue over the seizure of the British vessel *Trent,* while others trade shots over the way the Army is conducting its strategy in Virginia. The politicians debate whether the Army should be going on the offensive rather than preparing for the win-

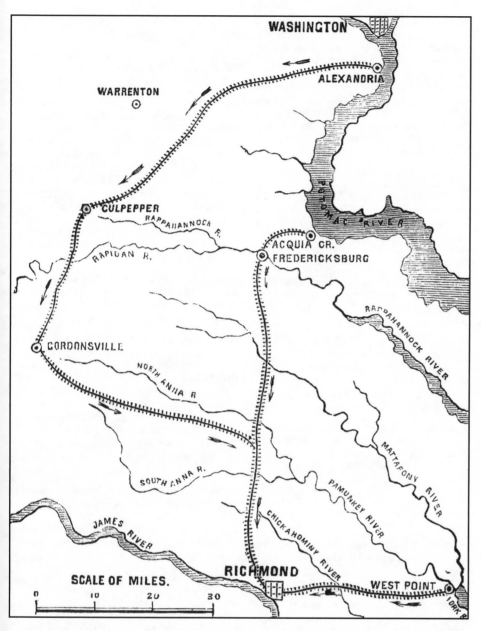

Routes leading to Richmond — This sketch illustrates the advantages, in point of distance, of the three proposed routes to Richmond. The first, abandoned by Burnside, assumes the basis of supply to be Alexandria. The second, proposed by him, assumes it to be at Acquia Creek. The third, that adopted by McClellan, places it at West Point (*Harper's Pictoral History of the Civil War*, 1896).

Subsequently, he will serve with General William T. Sherman during the siege of Corinth, Mississippi. The city of Denver, Colorado, which at the time of his governorship was included in the Kansas Territory, is named in honor of General Denver.

In Confederate general officer activity, Brigadier General Henry Rootes Jackson, having chosen to move to Georgia to accept an appointment as major general in command of state troops, resigns his commission in the Confederate Army. Jackson's divisional command in Georgia is short-lived due to the Conscript Act, which mandates that his state division be incorporated into the Confederate Army. Nonetheless, H.R. Jackson re-enters the Confederate Army during September of 1863, when he is again commissioned a brigadier general.

In Naval activity, Union gunboats, including the *Shawsheen* and *Hetzel,* come under attack by the CSS *Patrick Henry,* but the latter sustains the damage and is compelled to limp back to Norfolk. In early January 1863, the *Hetzel* arrives at Hatteras Inlet, North Carolina, for new duty. The U.S. Navy acquires a ferryboat, the *Clifton,* which was built in New York at Brooklyn during 1861. It is commissioned by early 1862 and assigned to the Mortar Flotilla (West Gulf Blockading Squadron). It participates during the campaign against New Orleans and in June 1862 against the Confederate positions at Vicksburg.

December 3 (Tuesday) In Washington, D.C., President Abraham Lincoln delivers his State of the Union message to Congress. He emphasizes the paramount importance of preserving the Union.

In Mississippi, Union troops under Major General Benjamin F. Butler land at Ship Island, from where they will prepare to embark for the Gulf Coast. Butler will arrive later, in March.

In Missouri, a unit of the 10th Missouri Cavalry, commanded by Major Thomas M. Bowen, engages and defeats a Confederate contingent commanded by Colonel Freeman at Salem. The Union sustains three to six killed, eight to 10 wounded and two captured. The Confederates sustain 16 killed, 20 wounded and about 10 captured. General John Pope assumes command of all Union troops in the area between the Missouri and Osage Rivers. His forces will later move against Madrid and Island No. 10, Tennessee.

In South Carolina, Robert E. Lee rejects a resolution passed by the citizens of Beaufort District asking Lee to impose martial law on the coast of South Carolina.

In Virginia, one squad of the 3rd Pennsylvania Cavalry, commanded by Captain Charles A. Bell, skirmishes with a detachment of Confederates at Vienna. The Confederates capture the Union detachment, including about four men who are wounded. The Confederates sustain about three killed.

ter. It is not known whether those complaining are concerned that the Confederates might interrupt their session, but since the initial session of Congress, the politicians, from their congressional chairs, have been second guessing the military and there is no sign that the practice will change.

Congress also raises concerns about the general military strategy of President Abraham Lincoln. In accordance with his advisors, he has set out a three-pronged plan, with a priority of holding the terrain standing between the capital and Richmond, the capital of the Confederacy, gaining domination of the Mississippi River to control the west and trying to pull Tennessee

back into the Union. Also, Union Major General Henry Halleck is given authority from Washington to abandon the writ of habeas corpus (compelling the arresting party to take the person to court and prove the validity of the arrest) within the territory overseen by the Department of the Missouri.

In Union general officer activity, Union Brigadier General James William Denver assumes command of all Union troops in Kansas. Denver had previously (1858) been governor of the Kansas Territory. During August of this year, President Lincoln had appointed him brigadier and assigned him to duty in Kansas.

In Union general officer activity, Thomas Greely Stevenson is commissioned colonel (later brigadier general) of the 24th Massachusetts Regiment, which includes a battalion initially raised by Stevenson. Stevenson's regiment is ordered to join General Burnside's Carolina expedition. Also, Charles John Stolbrand, a native of Sweden who immigrated to the U.S. in 1850, is appointed major of Battery De Kalb. Stolbrand serves at a multitude of campaigns, and during 1864, he commands a brigade; however, promotion escapes him. By the latter part of January 1865, disillusioned, he requests permission to be mustered out of the service. However, General Sherman is not anxious to see Stolbrand depart. Sherman asks Stolbrand to deliver a package of dispatches to President Lincoln in Washington while he is en route to Illinois. Unknown to Stolbrand, one of the dispatches is a personal letter to the president requesting a promotion for him. Lincoln promotes Stolbrand to brigadier general immediately upon finishing the letter. General Stolbrand serves for the duration, and during the final operations against Richmond he commands a brigade composed of three Illinois regiments. He musters out of the service in January 1866.

December 4 (Wednesday) The British have recently raised objections regarding the seizure of two Confederates aboard an English ship, and talk of the possibility of hostilities has been raging; however, this day, it seems as if England is softening its position. Queen Victoria declares the prohibition of exporting weapons and gunpowder, and materials pertinent to the manufacture of such items, to the United States. Consequently, the recent news of the British Navy being on war alert seems less than probable and the queen's proclamation cannot be viewed in a positive nature by Richmond. The Confederate hope of being recognized by England becomes more obscure.

In Washington, D.C., the Senate ousts Senator John Breckenridge of Kentucky; however, the move is symbolic, as Breckenridge has already relinquished his seat and become an officer in the Confederate Army.

In Kentucky, a Union reconnaissance contingent destroys the Bacon Creek Bridge.

In Missouri, at Dunksburg, civilians attack Confederates under Captain Wheatley. Confederates report 10 killed and about seven wounded. Civilian casualty figures are not reported.

In Virginia, a 30-man contingent of the 3rd New Jersey Volunteers, commanded by Colonel (later general) George William Taylor, skirmishes with Confederates at Annandale. Also, the 3rd New Jersey is attached to General Philip Kearny's New Jersey Brigade.

In Confederate general officer activity, Major General William Joseph Hardee (West Point, 1838) assumes command of the Confederate Central Army of Kentucky. Hardee had commanded a brigade of Arkansas regiments. He will later be called upon to serve under General (full rank) Albert S. Johnston.

In Naval activity, the USS *Montgomery,* a wooden screw steamship built during 1857 and commissioned in May 1861, engages the steamer CSS *Florida* and the CSS *Pamlico.* The *Montgomery* remains in the gulf during 1862, and during the tour, it seizes or destroys about six blockade runners. The *Florida* is renamed the CSS *Selma* the following July, and in February 1863 it is sunk in the vicinity of Mobile, but then is refloated. It participates in the Battle of Mobile Bay (early August 1864).

December 5 (Thursday) **In Washington, D.C.,** Congress continues in session and various bills have arisen that deal with the abolition of slavery; however, the discussions which garner the most consideration are the proposed bills that place emphasis on the slaves held by owners in the states that have seceded from the Union.

In Georgia, Union troops, Marines and sailors attached to the USS *Ottawa, Seneca* and the *Pembina* occupy and hold Wassah Island, Warsaw Sound.

In North Carolina, Confederate gunboats move in toward the Union forts at Hatteras to exchange fire with Union gunboats on Pamlico Sound. The Union craft do not venture out beyond the range of the shore batteries to engage the CSS *Fanny* and the other vessels.

In South Carolina, U.S. gunboats initiate an operation in St. Helena Sound. The warships *Pawnee, Pembina, Unadilla* and *Vixen* repeat their performance of the previous month. They operate in the area until December 9.

In Kentucky, a Union contingent reconnoiters in the vicinity of Russellville. The mission terminates on the 8th.

In Missouri, Union reconnaissance units operate in the vicinity of the Current Hills through the 9th.

December 6 (Friday) **In Maryland,** Confederate cavalry skirmishes with Union pickets at Dam No. 5. At Back Creek, Confederate infantry skirmishes with Union forces. Reinforcements are sent to bolster both Union contingents. However, on the following day, the Confederates begin to move in force toward Dam No. 5. In response, Captain Gilbert Robinson, Company D, 1st Virginia Regiment, moves to the dam with a 28-man contingent, and he dispatches a 10-man contingent under a first lieutenant to Fankell's Ferry. The skirmishing continues sporadically throughout the day, and for awhile, it ceases, but at about 2100, again the two sides exchange fire until about 0200 on the morning of the 8th.

In Missouri, a Union force commanded by Major Bowen occupies Salem and shortly thereafter his contingent is attacked by Confederates led by Colonel Freeman, but the Rebels are repelled. The two sides had previously clashed on the 3rd.

In South Carolina, the Union, having recently secured a position Hilton Head, initiates a mission to expand its base. Contingents are dispatched to Port Royal Ferry and Beaufort.

In Virginia, a Union foraging party moves to Gunnell's Farm in the vicinity of Dranesville.

In Naval activity, the USS *Whitehall* departs the Virginia Capes for Annapolis, Maryland, to deliver arms and supplies and afterward return to Hampton Roads. The USS *Augusta* seizes a blockade runner, the *Cheshire,* off Charleston; prior to the end of the year it snatches another runner, the *Island Belle.* The *Augusta,* following this activity, remains off Charleston until August, except for a short mission at Wassau Sound, Georgia. Following time out of service in Philadelphia receiving repairs, it departs for the Gulf of Mexico on escort duty for a convoy of army transports. It returns to Charleston during January 1863.

December 7 (Saturday) **In Missouri,** a contingent of an Illinois regiment engages a Confederate force commanded by Captain Sweeney at Glasgow. About 35 Rebels are captured.

In Naval activity, the USS *Santiago de Cuba,* commanded by Commodore Daniel B. Ridgely, while operating near the mouth of the Rio Grande River as part of the blockade mission against New Orleans, Louisiana, scores a hit when it halts a British vessel, the *Eugenia Smith* and relieves it of one agent of the Confederates, J.W. Zacharie. The politicians in Washington, D.C., already apprehensive about the Trent Affair, now have another reason to get their blood pressure up.

December 8 (Sunday) **In Georgia,** a contingent of Marines and sailors attached to the USS *Savannah* land and attack a Confederate-held fort on Tybee Island that guards Savannah, but the attack force is repulsed and compelled to return to the ship.

In Confederate Naval activity, the steamer CSS *Sumter,* commanded by Raphael Semmes, who resigned from the U.S. Navy the previous February, seizes a commercial whaling vessel, the *Eben Dodge,* in the Atlantic. The *Sumter* had been blockaded at Martinique during the previous November, but Semmes was able to evade the USS *Iroquois* and escape. From the latter part of November 1861 until January 1862, the *Sumter* captures six vessels, adding to the twelve captured earlier. Semmes, for his service against Union shipping, is promoted to captain the next August.

In Kentucky, a Union contingent clashes with Confederates at Fishing Creek near Somerset. Specific units are unreported.

In Missouri, General Henry Halleck issues General Orders No. 13: "Lieut.-Col. BERNARD G. FARRAR is hereby appointed Provost-Marshal General of this Department [of Missouri]. Capt. GEORGE E. LEIGHTON is Provost-Marshal of the City of St. Louis and its vicinity. All local Provost Marshals will be subject to the order of the Provost-Marshal General, who will receive his instruction direct from these headquarter."

In **Virginia,** General Robert E. Lee, in a rare moment of peace, writes to his daughter Annie: "I enclose some violets I plucked in the yard of a deserted house I occupy. I wish I could see you and give them in person."

In **West Virginia** at Dam 5, Chesapeake and Ohio Canal, the 13th Massachusetts Regiment supported by one Illinois regiment skirmishes with Confederates. No casualties are recorded. Also, Union and Confederate forces clash at Romney. No casualties are reported and specific units are unknown.

December 9 (Monday) In **Washington, D.C.,** Congress is uncomfortable with the way the military leaders are conducting the war with the South. Distressed due to some recent defeats at the hands of the Confederates, particularly the loss at Balls Bluff, Congress establishes the Joint Committee on the Conduct of the War. From their arm-chairs in the Senate, they call upon various generals and lesser ranked officers to appear before the committee and answer questions regarding the action in the field. Political considerations play a part in these hearings. Consequently, the results span the spectrum and include some good information, some sugar coating and some conspicuous finger pointing. In other activity, Garret Davis is elected to the Senate representing Kentucky in place of John Breckenridge, who has joined the Confederacy.

In **Arkansas,** a large contingent of Creek Indians (fighting for the Union) led by Opethleyholo, engages Confederates and pro-South Creeks under Colonel Douglas Hancock Cooper in a battle near Bushy Creek. The Indians sustain heavy casualties. However, the Confederates are unable to follow up the victory due to shortages of supplies.

Colonel Cooper, a veteran of the Mexican War (1st Mississippi Rifles), had been appointed U.S. agent to the Choctaw Nation in the Indian Territory by President Franklin Pierce. At the outbreak of hostilities, Cooper was commissioned colonel of the Confederate 1st Choctaw and Chickasaw Mounted Rifles.

In **Georgia and South Carolina,** many of the cotton fields on the plantations near the coastline are intentionally set afire to keep the cotton from being confiscated by the Union.

In **Missouri,** a Union contingent clashes with Confederates at Union Mills. Specific units are unreported.

In **the Indian Territory,** a Confederate force, including Indians, clashes with Creek Indians at Bird Creek (High Shoal) near Tulsey Town (present day Tulsa, Oklahoma). *In Naval activity,* a U.S. naval contingent engages Confederates at Freestone Point, Virginia.

December 11 (Wednesday) In **Missouri,** a contingent of the 2nd Illinois Cavalry, bolstered by Union Infantry, commanded by Lt. Colonel William C. Rhodes, skirmishes with Confederates at Bertrand. The Union captures some Confederates but loses one killed.

In **South Carolina,** an unexplained fire strikes Charleston, devastating a good portion of the city, including many landmarks close to the hearts of the Charlestonians, such as Institute Hall, where the secession ordinance was debated.

In **Virginia,** Confederates skirmish with Union pickets attached to the 12th Indiana Volunteer Regiment at Dam No. 4 along the Chesapeake and Ohio Canal at Potomac. The Union loses some captured. The Confederates sustain several killed.

In **West Virginia,** a skirmish between Union and Confederate forces also erupts at Greenbrier (Greenbriar) Bridge. Specific units are unreported.

In Naval activity, the Union steamers *Henry Andrews, Ottawa, Pembina* and *Seneca* maneuver in the vicinity of Ossabaw Sound, Georgia, in search of Confederates. The bark *Arthur,* built during 1855 at Amesburg, Massachusetts, and acquired by the U.S. Navy on 1 August 1861, is commissioned the USS *Arthur* this day at New York. Acting Volunteer Lieutenant John W. Kittredge receives command of the ship, which is assigned to the Gulf Blockading Squadron. The *Winona,* a side-wheel gunboat launched September 1861, is commissioned in New York and assigned to the Gulf Blockading Squadron; however, the squadron is shortly thereafter split into two, East and West. The *Winona* is attached to the West Gulf Squadron.

December 12 (Thursday) In **Kentucky,** a six-man contingent of the 6th Kentucky Regiment (Volunteers) skirmishes with a detachment of Confederates more than three times its size at Bagdad. The Union sustains one wounded. Confederate casualties, if any, are unavailable. Also, a Union contingent clashes with Confederates at Gradyville. Specific units are unreported.

In Naval and Marine Corps activity, Marines attached to the USS *Dale* are transferred to the USS *Isaac Smith,* from which they debark at Fenwick's Island Fort, North Carolina, to execute a reconnaissance mission. The force later burns several Confederate buildings at Mosquito Creek Junction, North Carolina, before returning to their ship. The USS *Dale,* a sloop of war originally commissioned during 1840, had captured two Confederate schooners up to this point during October–November of this year. Subsequent to this mission, it becomes a store ship for the duration, first at Port Royal and afterward at Key West, Florida. After the war it becomes a training ship at Annapolis, Maryland. Later it is transferred to the Washington Navy Yard as a store ship until 1895, when it is transferred to the Maryland State Naval Militia and renamed *Oriole* (1904). It is sold during December 1921.

In other activity, the blockade runner *Admiral* is captured off Savannah by the USS *Alabama,* commanded by Commander Edward Lanier. The USS *Alabama,* a wooden side-wheel steamer acquired by the U. S. Navy the

previous August and commissioned in September 1861, had been attached to the South Atlantic Blockading Squadron. It remains on blockade duty off Florida and Georgia until December 1862, when it cruises to the West Indies in search of Confederate raiders. It remains with the squadron for the duration of the war. It is decommissioned in Philadelphia in June 1865. This USS *Alabama* is separate from the *Alabama* built in 1819 and commissioned the USS *New Hampshire* on 28 October 1863.

December 13 (Friday) In **West Virginia,** Union troops under General Robert H. Milroy, including the 9th and 13th Indiana, 25th and 32nd Ohio Regiments and the 2nd West Virginia Regiment, engage Confederates under General Edward Johnson (West Point, 1838), promoted this day, at Buffalo Mountain. The engagement continues for nearly seven hours as the Union force, numbering nearly 1,800 troops, attempts to vanquish about 2,000 troops. The opposing sides bludgeon each other with riveting and incessant fire, but neither claims the field of victory. Both sides, one as exhausted as the other, disengage and retire. The Union attackers withdraw to Cheat Mountain while the Rebels move towards Staunton, Virginia. The Union counts 20 dead and 107 wounded. Confederates have 20 dead and 90 wounded. Confederate Captain (later brigadier general) James Deshler is twice wounded, being hit in both legs. Deshler will recover and afterwards is promoted to colonel and assigned to North Carolina, where he serves as chief of artillery under General Theopholis H. Holmes. The Confederate 25th Virginia Infantry Regiment (General Edward Johnson's Brigade, General Thomas J. Jackson's Division, Army of the Northwest), participates at this action.

In Union general officer activity, James Streshly Jackson, a veteran of the Mexican War who enlisted as a private, resigns from the U.S. Congress to accept the rank of colonel in the 3rd Kentucky Regiment. In July 1862, he is appointed brigadier general. Also, James Richard Slack, a former Indiana state senator (nine terms) is appointed colonel (later brigadier general) of the 47th Indiana Infantry Regiment. During the upcoming operations against Corinth and Island No. 10, he commands a brigade under General John Pope. Later he participates in the White River expedition and he commands a brigade in General Hovey's division of the XIII Corps. This service is followed by an assignment to the Department of the Gulf, where he remains for the duration of the war.

In Confederate general officer activity, Colonel Edward Johnson (West Point, 1838), a veteran of the Seminole Wars and the Mexican War, is promoted to brigadier general.

December 14 (Saturday) Prince Albert, the husband of Queen Victoria, succumbs in England. Meanwhile in Great Britain, the incident known as the Trent Affair continues to be unsettled. Prince Albert had favored a non-belligerent attitude towards the United States. The queen also exhibits no propensity to move towards open hostilities. Meanwhile, in Washington, President Lincoln and his advisors are working to find a solution favorable to both the United States and England, while the two captives, James Mason and John Slidell, remain in a prison in Massachusetts. The complex diplomatic problem will be solved by the end of this year.

In Confederate general officer activity, General Henry Hopkins Sibley (West Point, 1838) assumes command of the Confederate troops in the Upper Rio Grande region, New Mexico and Arizona. Also, Colonel Maxcy Gregg, 1st South Carolina Infantry, is promoted to the rank of brigadier general. Gregg participates in many of the battles fought by the Army of Northern Virginia during the following year, including the Peninsula Campaign, Cedar Mountain, 2nd Manassas, Sharpsburg (Antietam) and Fredericksburg.

In Naval activity, the *Quaker City*, acquired earlier this year by the U.S. Navy, is commissioned the USS *Quaker City*. James M. Frailey commands the ship. It is detached from the North Atlantic Blockading Squadron and ordered to join a search for the CSS *Sumter*.

December 15 (Sunday) In Virginia, Union reconnaissance contingents operate along the lower Potomac and maintain this mission in Virginia until the 17th.

In West Virginia, Union contingents initiate a mission that keeps them in the vicinity of Meadow Bluff until the 21st.

Confederate minister James Murray Mason (Mottelay, *The Soldier in Our Civil War,* 1886).

In Naval activity, the *Henry Brinker*, built in Brooklyn, New York, in 1861 and acquired by the U.S. Navy that October, is commissioned the USS *Henry Brinker* on this day soon after it arrives at Hampton Roads. Acting Master John E. Giddings receives command of the ship. The *Henry Brinker* arrives at Hatteras Inlet, North Carolina, on 10 January 1862 to join the North Atlantic Blockading Squadron.

December 16 (Monday) In South Carolina, at about this time, the Confederates abandon Rockville.

In Confederate general officer activity, General Robert E. Lee, in a letter to Confederate General States Rights Gist (South Carolina Militia), says that about 80 Union vessels had been counted in Port Royal on the 12th, but the Confederates should be able to halt the advance on Charleston. Gist is appointed brigadier general in the Confederate Army during March 1862. In other activity, on this day, another West Pointer, Henry C. Wayne, who had served his country during the conflict with Mexico, dons the Confederate Gray and becomes a brigadier general. General Wayne, who graduated in 1838, has a relatively short career with the regulars, resigning early the next year. He returns to Georgia and is deeply involved with the state militia for the balance of the war.

In Naval activity, the U.S. Navy acquires the *Hunchback*, a ferry boat built in New York City during 1852. The *Hunchback* moves to Hampton Roads, where it is commissioned on 3 January 1862. Command of the vessel is given to Acting Lt. Edmund R. Colhoun, and it is ordered to move to join the North Atlantic Blockading Squadron at Hatteras Inlet, North Carolina.

December 17 (Tuesday) A fleet of English, French and Spanish vessels debark troops to occupy Vera Cruz, Mexico, to strong-arm the Mexican government into making good on its obligations and to protect their respective interests. The foreign powers are aware of Mexico's financial crisis and equally aware that the United States is too preoccupied to intervene. England and Spain unwittingly have become ensnared into a French plot to actually take over the troubled Mexican government, transform the country into a Catholic monarchy and dominate it from France. As the English and Spanish become aware of the scheme of Napoleon III, they distance themselves from the mission, returning to their respective homelands April 8 of the following year. The French occupy Mexico City in June 1863 while the U.S. is still consumed with war.

In Kentucky, a contingent of the 32nd Indiana Regiment (Volunteers), composed of about four companies and commanded by Colonel August Willich, skirmishes with the Confederate 8th Texas Cavalry (Terry's Texas Rangers) led by Colonel Benjamin Franklin Terry at Rowlett's Station (also called Mumfordsville or Woodsonville). The Union sustains 10 killed and 22 wounded. The Confederates sustain 33 killed

and 50 wounded. Colonel Terry is killed during this action. Lt. Colonel Thomas S. Lubbock, suffering from an illness, receives command of the regiment; however, he succumbs from sickness within a few days. Captain (later brigadier general) John Austin Wharton is selected as colonel of the regiment. Some of the troops of the 8th Texas Cavalry have come down with measles and others have not acclimated to the cold weather, which has caused many of the troops to become ill.

Colonel Willich, a veteran of the Prussian Army, had recruited a large number of Germans, reportedly about 1,500 men, at the beginning of the war. He initially served with the 9th Indiana until he was appointed colonel of the 32nd Indiana Regiment. Willich trained his German troops to respond to bugle calls while drilling. He later participates in various actions including Shiloh, Perryville and Murfreesboro, where he is captured.

December 18 (Wednesday) In Washington, D.C., President Abraham Lincoln and his advisors continue to work on resolving the controversy concerning the two prominent captives, Confederate ministers James Mason and John Slidell. No solution is agreed upon despite more demands from the British through Lord Lyons. There have been loud cries from the English since the seizure and even some mild hints of hostilities, but the British seem less than eager to enter the conflict on the side of the Confederates. British news reporters are by this time on the scene and could escalate the crisis. The British remain insulted because their flag was impugned when the U.S. Navy boarded the British vessel *Trent* on the 18th of the previous month.

In Kentucky, Union reconnaissance contingents cover the terrain stretching between Somerset and Mill Springs.

In Missouri, Union troops attached to General John Pope's command—the 27th Ohio, 8th, 12th, 22nd, and 24th Indiana, 31st Kansas, 1st Iowa Cavalry, a detachment of the U.S. Cavalry and a portion of the 1st Missouri Light Artillery—engage and handily defeat a large Confederate force at Milford (Black Water Creek). The Union suffers two dead and eight wounded; 1,300 Confederates are captured. In addition, the Union seizes about 1,000 stacks of arms. Other Union contingents reconnoiter the area between Rolla and Houston.

In South Carolina, a Union contingent of the 8th Michigan Regiment, while operating on Chisholm's Island, seizes six pickets of the 14th South Carolina Regiment. The regiment is part of General Maxcy Gregg's brigade, which also includes the 12th and 13th South Carolina Regiments.

In Virginia, Union reconnaissance units initiate a mission that moves to the vicinity of Pohick Church.

In Confederate Naval activity, Secretary of the Navy Stephen Mallory authorizes a payment of one thousand dollars to the owners of the

Alonzo Child, a large side-wheel steamer. The payment is for a particular service rendered to the Confederacy, but it is unspecified. The ship, built in Indiana during 1857, had been operating on the Mississippi River prior to the war. In December 1862 its engines are removed and at some point installed on the CSS *Tennessee*. After the loss of engines, the *Alonzo Child* is used as a barge on the Yazoo River.

December 19 (Thursday)   In Maryland, a Union force composed of about six companies of a Pennsylvania Regiment, commanded by Colonel Gabriel DeKorponay, skirmish with Confederates at Point of Rocks in a contest that lasts only about a half hour. The outnumbered Confederates lose about 10 to 14 wounded. Union casualties, if any, are not reported.

In Virginia, following the battle at Balls Bluff the previous October, Confederates moved in and occupied Dranesville, which had been held by Union Brigadier General George A. McCall until ordered to withdraw to Chain Bridge. These Rebel troops have been causing problems along the Union lines in both Maryland and Virginia and plans have been laid to eliminate the threat. The attack, to be launched by forces under General E.O. Ord, is scheduled for the following day. Two other brigades — those of Generals J.F. Reynolds and George G. Meade — are to bolster the attack, joining Ord's forces at Difficult Creek. Ord's brigade is composed of the 6th, 9th, 10th and 12th Pennsylvania Regiments, one battery of guns commanded by Captain H. Easton, five companies of the Pennsylvania Cavalry and Colonel T.L. Kane's Bucktail Rifles. The Confederate force at Dranesville includes the 10th Alabama (Colonel John H. Forney), 1st Kentucky (Colonel Thomas H. Taylor), 6th South Carolina (Colonel Andrew Jackson Secrest) and the 11th Virginia Infantry (Colonel Samuel Garland, Jr.) regiments, plus a contingent of North Carolina Cavalry commanded by Major James Byron Gordon and a detachment of artillery.

In Naval activity, the CSS *Diana* tows the captured "metal life boat" *Francis* to San Jacinto, Texas, where it is to be refurbished and used by the CSS *General Rusk*. On 20 January 1862, the *Francis* transports the crew of the *General Rusk* from Galveston to Houston, Texas.

December 20 (Friday)   In Virginia, a Union brigade led by General Ord and supported by two additional brigades moves toward Dranesville to strike a force of Rebels under General Jeb Stuart. While en route, the Yankees are spotted by a large Confederate force with about two hundred wagons that had departed Dranesville on a foraging mission. At a point about two miles outside Dranesville, the Rebels initiate a charge and head into the vanguard, the Bucktail Rifles (42nd Pennsylvania Volunteer Regiment) artillery and some cavalry under Colonel Bayard. The 11th Virginia and the 6th South Carolina Infantry Regiments bore into the front of the columns using both surprise and force, which causes the Union to stagger under the crush of the assault, but reinforce-

ments are well within earshot of the blazing fire. Soon the 6th and 9th Pennsylvania Regiments are at the front lines and the Rebel momentum loses its spin. The combined counterforce of the vanguard and the reinforcements, bolstered by the effective fire of artillery, compel the Confederates to pull back to regroup. They form to strike the flank, but at about this time, General McCall reaches the hot point of the battle and discovers the dangerous position of his left flank.

Quickly, word is dispatched to Colonel McCalmont, who is able to alter his positions and prepare for the juggernaut. Soon after the attack is commenced, a blanket of fire strikes the Rebels as they emerge from the woods, and with its unrelenting ferocity, the attackers are forced to retire to the woods from which they came. Meanwhile, the Rebels are also striking the front and the rear of the Union lines, but to no avail, as the Union also repulses them. In one instance, Confederates begin to fire upon friendly forces when the 6th South Carolina Regiment is mistakenly thought to be a Union outfit by the 1st Kentucky Regiment; this incident causes a good deal of the Confederate casualties. All along the line, the contest ensues with tenacity, but the Confederates are unable to penetrate.

While both sides trade vicious shots and at times become involved with close-quartered fighting, another incident occurs that involves mistaken identity. The 1st Kentucky Regiment again faces a force of unknown identity and as it approaches, Colonel Taylor inquires: "Who are you?" He receives an enthusiastic response, "The Ninth!" Taylor, yells, "of what Ninth?" and in short order a donnybrook ensues as Colonel Jackson responds, "the Ninth Pennsylvania." Eventually, the Union fire gains the advantage and the Confederates break off as the lines falter.

The Rebels head for the woods, leaving behind some supplies and wounded. The Union loses seven killed and about sixty wounded. The Confederates sustain 43 killed, 143 wounded and some taken prisoner.

Colonel (later major general) John H. Forney is among the wounded. General McCall's forces haul off 22 wagon loads of corn and 16 loads of hay. Union contingents give chase to the Rebels, but having no success, they return to the scene of the skirmish. Subsequently, due to an inability to hold the ground because of strong Confederate forces at Centreville, the Union abandons Dranesville.

In Naval activity, the Union purposely sinks in Charleston Harbor some of the antiquated vessels in the "Stone Fleet" it had brought down from Massachusetts laden with cargoes of granite. The rest of the Stone Fleet, still afloat, will be sunk by mid–January of the following year. General Robert E. Lee informs Confederate Secretary of War Judah Benjamin that the Union has brought their Stone Fleet to Charleston Harbor and sunk between 13 and 17 vessels in the main channel.

In Union general officer activity, Colonel John McCauley Palmer is appointed brigadier general.

December 21 (Saturday)   In Missouri, a detachment of the 7th Missouri Cavalry, commanded by Major McKee, engages a Confederate force in a skirmish at Hudson. The Union force is outnumbered by about four to one, but manages to prevail. The Union sustains five wounded; however, some are captured. The Confederates sustain about 10 killed. In other activity, at about this time, Confederate General Henry Alexander Wise is ordered to report for duty in North Carolina. He will serve under General P.G.T. Beauregard. Subsequently he will serve in the defense of Charleston, South Carolina.

In Naval activity, the USS *Tahoma* is commissioned in Philadelphia. Lt. Commander John C. Howell receives command of the wooden-hulled gunboat, which is assigned duty with the East Gulf Blockading Squadron.

December 22 (Sunday)   In Virginia, a contingent composed of four companies of the 20th New York Volunteer Regiment, commanded by Colonel (later general) Max Weber, skirmishes with a Confederate contingent at New Market Bridge in a contest that lasts more than four hours. The Union sustains five or six wounded. The Confederates suffer 10 killed and about 20 wounded.

December 23 (Monday)   In Missouri, a skirmish develops at Dayton between Union and Confederate detachments. Specific units and casualties, if any, are unreported. In other activity, Colonel James Abraham Garfield (later President Garfield), commander of the 42nd Ohio Regiment, is ordered to report to Eastern Kentucky to serve in General Don Carlos Buell's Army of the Tennessee. Buell will give Garfield a brigade and dispatch him into the Sandy Valley, where he encounters Confederate General Humphrey Marshall (West Point, 1832) at Middle Creek, Kentucky, on 10 January 1862.

December 24 (Tuesday)   In Missouri, a Union contingent of the Missouri Home Guards skirmishes a detachment of Confederates at Wadesburg. The Union sustains two wounded. Confederate casualties are unreported.

In Virginia, a Union reconnaissance contingent initiates a mission that operates in the vicinity of Fairfax Court House and terminates on the following day.

In Confederate general officer activity, Colonel Raleigh Edward Colston (16th Virginia) is promoted to brigadier general.

In Naval activity, the recently commissioned USS *Arthur* embarks from New York en route to Key West, Florida, to join the Gulf Blockading Squadron. After arrival in Key West, it is sent to patrol the coast of Texas in an area stretching between Matagorda and Corpus Christi. The *Arthur* arrives on station off Matagorda on 25 January 1862. In other activity, Union gunboats, including the USS *Ellen*, exchange fire with Confederates on Tybee Island, Georgia. The *Ellen* participates in various operations that occur between Georgia and northern Florida until autumn 1862, when it is decommissioned and transformed into a "floating carpenter shop" based at Port Royal, South Carolina. The *Ellen* is sold after the war in September 1865.

December 25 (Wednesday)   In Maryland, a Union contingent clashes with Confederates at Fort Frederick. Specific units are unreported.

In West Virginia, Union and Confederate units clash at Cherry Run. Specific units are unreported.

In Union activity, Brigadier General Samuel R. Curtis (West Point, 1831) assumes command of the Federal Southwestern District of Missouri and immediately begins to run pro-Confederate troops out of the state. General Curtis will command the Union forces at Pea Ridge, Arkansas, during March 1862. Curtis was appointed brigadier general of volunteers effective 17 May 1861.

December 26 (Thursday)   THE TRENT AFFAIR In Washington, D.C., subsequent to a long string of cabinet meetings and a series of diplomatic sessions, President Lincoln concludes that the captive Confederate ministers should be released to the British, as they have been urging. Neither the British nor the Union has discussed releasing the diplomats to the Confederate government in Richmond. After the decision made this day, James Mason and John Slidell, previously seized by the Union while they were en route to Europe, are freed from their internment at Fort Warren, Massachusetts. They are put under the protection of the British. Secretary of State William H. Seward officially explains the U.S. position, stating that Captain Charles Wilkes, U.S. Navy, by permitting the *Trent*, a British vessel, to continue on its voyage rather than taking it as a prize, made the seizure illegal, mandating that the prisoners be released. The release of the prisoners essentially calms the tensions between the United States and England, averting war between them, which in all probability would drain the U.S. and open the door to southern independence and the demise of the Union.

Also, Seward's articulate reply serves another purpose. By his skilled use of the English language, he is also able to smooth the fiery tempers of the Americans who opposed the release, although it does little to quell the immense dislike of the British. The British had hinted at the possibility of war if the diplomats had not been released. To underscore their position, two British warships had recently been ordered to Canada to stand by in case of an outbreak of hostilities.

In Kentucky, a Confederate contingent skirmishes with pickets under Major Ousley at Camp Boyle. Casualties are unavailable.

In Missouri, General Halleck issues an order placing St. Louis under martial law; however the decree also extends to the railroads throughout the state.

In South Carolina, a detachment of Marines from the sloop USS *Dale* skirmish with Confederate troops on the South Edisto River.

In Union general officer activity, Jasper Adalmorn Maltby, a veteran of the Mexican War who served as a private in the 15th U.S. Infantry, is appointed lieutenant colonel of the 45th Illinois Infantry Regiment, placing him second in command to Colonel John E. Smith. Subsequently, Colonel Maltby participates in the operations against Forts Henry and Donelson in Tennessee. At the latter he sustains a severe leg wound.

In Confederate General Officer activity, General Philip St. George Cocke (West Point, 1832), who commanded a brigade under General Pierre Gustave T. Beauregard at Manassas (Bull Run), is suffering bad health; this day he commits suicide.

December 27 (Friday)   In Missouri, five companies of sharpshooters and six troops of cavalry under Colonel John M. Glover and Captain James T. Howland engage a Confederate force under Captain A.J. Johnson at Hallsville. The Union (General Benjamin M. Prentiss' command) sustains about two wounded. The Confederates sustain about five killed and some captured. Union General Benjamin M. Prentiss, assigned to keep communications open in the state of Missouri, has his hands full. The two sides clash on the following day at Mt. Zion.

In Naval activity, the *Norwich*, a wooden screw steamer acquired by the U.S. Navy during September 1861, is commissioned at New York. Lt. James M. Duncan receives command of the gunboat, which is assigned to the South Atlantic Blockading Squadron.

December 28 (Saturday)   In Kentucky, a Union force, the 3rd Kentucky Cavalry commanded by Major Murray, engages Confederates under Colonel Nathan Bedford Forrest at Sacramento. The Union suffers one killed and eight wounded. The Confederates sustain 30 killed and wounded. Also, a Union reconnaissance force moves through Kentucky en route to Camp Beauregard and Viola. The mission lasts until the end of the month.

In Missouri, the 3rd Missouri Cavalry bolstered by Birge's Sharpshooters (Prentiss' command) engage and defeat Confederates led by Colonel Caleb Dorsey at Mount Zion. The Confederates are compelled to scatter following this clash. The Union suffers five killed and 63 wounded. The Confederates sustain 25 killed and about 125 wounded.

In West Virginia, Union forces occupy Beckley (Raleigh Court House).

December 29 (Sunday)   In Missouri, Confederates led by Jeff Thompson (Thompson's Raiders) attack Commerce and attempt to destroy a Union steamer, the *City of Alton*, but they are repulsed.

In West Virginia, Union forces seize Suttonville (Braxton Court House). Nevertheless, skirmishing continues in Braxton County as well as in Clay and Webster Counties for several days, terminating on the 31st.

In Union general officer activity, Brigadier General Thomas Algeo Rowley, commander of the District of the Monongahela with headquarters at Pittsburgh, Pennsylvania, resigns his commission and returns to private life.

In Naval activity, the USS *John L. Lockwood* and the USS *Morse* engage several Confederate batteries at Sewell's Point, Virginia. Also, the CSS *Sea Bird* seizes a schooner and afterward launches an attack against an army steamer, but shortly thereafter it faces nine U.S. warships, including the USS *Whitehall* off Hampton Roads. The *Sea Bird*, following a clash that lasts about one half hour, is able to extricate itself and withdraw to a position from which it comes under the protection of Confederate batteries. The *Whitehall* and another gunboat, the *Morse*, provide cover fire while the gunboats retire.

December 30 (Monday)   In West Virginia, Union forces clash at several locations, including Braxton, Clay, and Webster Counties. These confrontations in some instances had carried over from the previous day as the Union and the Confederacy each attempt to dominate the region.

In Naval activity, the USS *Agassiz*, a United States Coast Survey ship, which was transferred to the U.S. Coast Guard shortly after war broke out, is ordered to cease duty as a receiving ship in New York and move to Sag Harbor (Long Island) to begin duty as a revenue cutter. In other activity, the USS *Rachael Seaman* arrived off the Texas coast to initiate patrols off Galveston.

December 31 (Tuesday) Acting on a report that Port Royal Island, South Carolina, is defended by about 8,000 troops, a Union Naval force—(Flag Officer Samuel Du Pont's command) commanded by C.R.P. Rodgers, including the gunboats *Ellen, Ottowa, Pembina, Penguin* and *Seneca* accompanied by four large boats of the *Wabash* and one ferry boat—sail to destroy the fortifications on the island. The ground forces led by General Isaac Stevens include the 8th Michigan, 47th, 48th and 79th New York Regiments and the 50th and 100th Pennsylvania Regiments. The flotilla spends New Year's Eve preparing to do battle on the following morning. The naval force divides itself with those vessels transporting the ground forces sailing along the Coosaw River, while others take Whale Creek, eventually converging at the ferry near the target.

In Union general officer activity, James Sidney Robinson, a newspaper editor prior to the war, is commissioned major (later brigadier general) of the 82nd Ohio Regiment. On 29 August, he becomes colonel of the regiment. Robinson participates in the Shenandoah and later at Gettysburg.

1862

In Iowa, subsequent to the Sioux uprising in neighboring Minnesota, settlers flee the region and very few troops are available due to the Civil War, which caused many to be recalled to support the war effort. Fewer than 100 troops (Sioux City Cavalry) are on the scene to protect the remaining settlements along the western and northern borders of Iowa from attack. To deal with the emergency, the governor of Iowa, Samuel Kirkwood, establishes the Northern Border Brigade, a forerunner of the Iowa National Guard, to counteract the threat. He also directs that a series of forts be built along the border with Minnesota. These cavalry units will be deployed at six separate locations, including Sioux City, Fort Dodge and Spirit Lake. And the forts (blockhouses) are established at Chain Lake, Cherokee, Correctionville, Estherville, Peterson and Spirit Lake.

In Minnesota, a Sioux uprising occurs in the southern part of the state, and before it is suppressed about 600 settlers lose their lives. In addition, about 100 women and children are taken captive by the Indians. Thousands of settlers scatter from the region.

In New Mexico, Fort Stanton, abandoned the previous year by the Union, is re-occupied. The troops there, including the New Mexican Volunteers led by Kit Carson, soon are engaged against the Mescalero Apaches. Through Carson's efforts many of the Apaches surrender and are subsequently detained at Fort Sumner, along

General Lewis "Lew" Wallace (Mottelay, *The Soldier in Our Civil War*, 1886).

with Navajos who are also confined at Fort Sumner. Carson had been appointed Indian Agent at Taos, New Mexico, during 1854, prior to the outbreak of the Civil War. In 1865, the Mescalero Apaches break away and head for the familiar territory in the Sierra Blanca Mountains from where they can operate at times with impunity. The hostilities with the Apaches do not permanently cease until the third surrender of Geronimo during 1886. Fort Stanton remains busy for the duration, but it does receive some other guests besides Apache prisoners, and they include William Bonney (Billy the Kid), who is for a while incarcerated there during the 1880s, and General Lewis Wallace, who had been appointed territorial governor of New Mexico. Wallace, the author of novels including *Ben Hur: A Tale of the Christ*, apparently worked on the *Ben Hur* manuscript while at the fort.

Also the U.S. Army establishes Fort Wingate, named in honor of Captain Benjamin Wingate, who had fallen in the fighting with Confederates at the Battle of Valverde. Fort Wingate is established during October at Ojo del Gallo, near present-day San Rafael, by a contingent of troops under Captain Rafael Chacon. The establishment of the fort had been ordered by General James Carleton and it is initially commanded by Lt. Colonel Jose Francisco Chaves. During the following year, 1863, the garrison participates in the operation to relocate the Navajos to Bosque Redondo, a journey of more than 200 miles that stretches from the fort to Fort Sumner at the Pecos River. The Navajos, nomadic by nature, will not adjust to the attempt to transform them into farmers. Consequently, the round-up proves to be a huge failure and the displacement is reversed, but too late to prevent the deaths of many Navajos, who succumb during the walk to the Pecos. In 1868, a decision is made by the government to relocate Fort Wingate to Ojo del Oso outside of Gallup, New Mexico. By 1882, the "Iron Horse" arrives in the region and afterwards, the fort becomes unnecessary. It is later used by the U.S. when the Wingate Ordnance Department is established there during 1918. The installation remains an ammunition depot until 1993.

January *In Confederate general officer activity,* Colonel John King Jackson, 5th Georgia Infantry, is promoted to the rank of brigadier general. Initially, Jackson will be sent to Grand Junction to expedite the organization of newly arriving troops required to halt the Yankee momentum at Shiloh; however by the time of the decisive encounter, Jackson will command the 3rd Brigade in the field. Following this action, he will accompany General John B. Hood's forces into Kentucky and from there he will participate in action in Tennessee and Georgia during the Atlanta campaign.

January 1 (Wednesday) In Washington, D.C., President Lincoln has eliminated the complications that developed regarding the seizure of two Confederate diplomats, but he is now preoccupied with a problem caused by the continuing illness of Major General George B. McClellan, and the armchair generals in the Senate who continue to question strategy. McClellan will recover from his bout with typhoid fever, but the relationship between him and the president will deteriorate.

In Florida, Union guns at Fort Pickens fire upon a Confederate vessel that is approaching the Rebel-held navy yard across the channel in the vicinity of Forts McRee and Barrancas. The Confederates, commanded by General Braxton Bragg, initiate return fire, and the exchange continues for most of the day with negligible results, but damage is sustained by the Pensacola Navy Yard when buildings catch fire, and in the village of Woolsey, there also is damage from fire. The Union forces under Colonel Harvey Brown sustain light casualties.

In Missouri, a Union reconnaissance contingent initiates a mission that operates in the areas of Morristown, Dayton and Rose Hill and last until 3 January.

In South Carolina, at Port Royal during the early morning hours, the 8th Michigan Regiment advances against Port Royal Island on the Coosaw River. When the Union column approaches the objective, it is suddenly greeted by a concealed Confederate battery and soon after, by the appearance of the 14th South Carolina Regiment. The Confederate infantry briskly advances in cadence with a chorus of a vociferous "Rebel yell" as it intercepts the landing force. The skirmish intensifies as the Yankees attempt to advance and the Rebels pour shells upon them. Union gunboats move in to neutralize the Confederate guns, while the 79th New York Regiment rushes to reinforce the assault. The ferocity of the Union ground forces combined with the strong and effective accuracy of the naval fire presses the Confederates to pull back. In the meantime, the 50th Pennsylvania Regiment, transported by some oversized boats, debarks and galvanizes the Union line to bring about victory. Subsequent to the eviction of the Confederates, the Union seizes the works and destroys the fortifications. Once the mission is completed, the troops return to Beaufort, South Carolina. The Union has one killed and two wounded. Confederate casualties are unavailable.

In Union general officer activity, David McMurtie Gregg (West Point, 1855) is appointed colonel (later brigadier general) of the 8th Pennsylvania Cavalry. Edward Henry Hobson, a veteran of the Mexican War, is appointed colonel of the 13th Kentucky Regiment. Colonel Hobson is promoted to brigadier general during April 1863, effective 29 November 1862. James Murrell Shackelford is appointed colonel of the Union 25th Regiment, a unit he recruited. Subsequently, he raises the 8th Kentucky Cavalry and becomes its colonel during September of the following year.

In Naval activity, the USS *C.P. Williams* is commissioned at about this time (January). The U.S. Navy had acquired it during September 1861. It is assigned to the Mortar Flotilla. As a mortar schooner, it participates in the operations against the forts at New Orleans in April 1862 and against Vicksburg in June–July 1863. The USS *Huron* (screw steam gunboat) is commissioned at about this time (January). The *Huron*, built in Massachusetts, is assigned to the South Atlantic Blockading Squadron, where it remains until 1864, when it is transferred to the

North Atlantic Blockading Squadron. The USS *Kanawha* (screw steam gunboat) is commissioned at about this time. It is assigned to the Gulf Squadron and operates in the Gulf of Mexico and vicinity. During February 1862, it serves off Mobile, Alabama, and prior to departing to patrol off the coast of Texas during spring of 1864, it seizes eighteen blockade runners, only one of which is not a sailing vessel. During May 1865, the *Kanawha* is ordered to sail north. It is decommissioned during July 1865, sold during June 1866, and afterward goes into service as a civilian vessel under the name *Mariano* until about 1878. Also, the ironclad USS *Mound City* (Cairo class river gunboat) is commissioned at about this time (May). It had been built specifically for the U.S. Army's Western Gunboat Flotilla.

January 2 (Thursday)   In Missouri, a Union reconnaissance force that had initiated a mission

on the previous day continues to operate in the terrain stretching between and near Morristown, Dayton and Rose Hill. The mission terminates on the following day when the force returns to Morristown. The trek includes some clashes with Confederates and the reduction of the town of Dayton.

In Naval activity, the USS *Shawsheen* receives orders to depart Newport News and move to Hatteras Inlet, North Carolina, to join the task force that is building for a planned attack and invasion of against Roanoke Island, the strategic location that dominates Albermarle Sound. The USS *Norwich* departs New York for Port Royal, South Carolina. Upon arrival, it is assigned blockade duty off Savannah, Georgia. The USS *Whitehall* leaves Hampton Roads for Hatteras Inlet, North Carolina, but once again, it experiences problems and becomes disabled. It is sent back to Hampton Roads. Flag Officer Louis M. Goldsborough later remarks that the *Whitehall* is "the worst sea boat of all the ferryboats with which I have had to do, and certainly the most unfortunate." The U.S. Navy commissions the USS *Vermont* at about this time (September). It is a ship of the line that was built in 1818; however, it was not launched until 1848. The *Vermont* is used primarily as a store ship for the South Atlantic Blockading Squadron. It operates out of Port Royal, South Carolina. Subsequent to service with the squadron it is transferred to New York, where it becomes a receiving ship on active duty until December 1901. It is sold in April of the following year.

January 3 (Friday)   In Virginia, Union forces occupy Big Bethel.

In West Virginia, a detachment of the 39th Illinois Volunteers commanded by Captain Samuel S. Linton skirmishes with Confederates at Bath. The Union sustains three wounded and some captured. The two sides again clash on the following day. Contingents of the 25th Ohio and 2nd West Virginia Regiments supported by the 1st Indiana Cavalry engage Confederates at Huntersville. The Union sustains one wounded. The Confederates suffer one killed and seven wounded. Confederates under General Thomas J. Jackson are operating in West Virginia in an attempt to destroy the dams along the Chesapeake and Ohio Canal and to rip up the rails of the Baltimore and Ohio Railroad to impede the Union during an offensive known as the Romney Campaign. General Jackson initiated the offensive on 1 January.

In Missouri, a contingent of the 10th Missouri Cavalry composed of four companies engages a Confederate force at Hunnewell.

In Naval activity, the USS *Western World,* acquired by the U.S. Navy on 21 September 1861 in New York, is commissioned, one day after receiving orders to depart for Port Royal, South Carolina, to join the South Atlantic Blockading Squadron.

January 4 (Saturday)   In Missouri, Union detachments clash with Confederates at Cal-

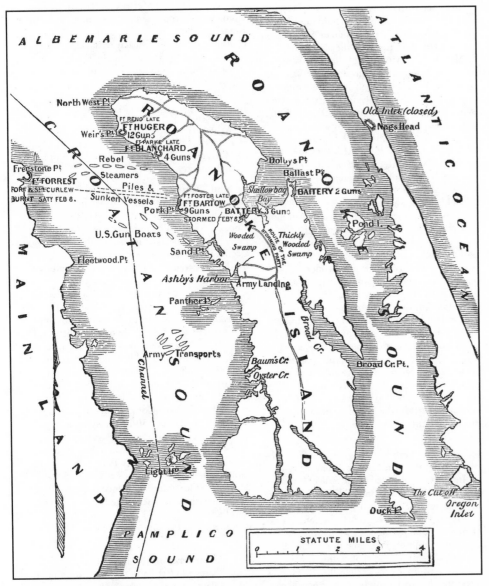

Map of Roanoke Island and its Confederate-held forts (Johnson, *Campfire and Battlefield: History of the Conflicts and Campaigns,* 1894).

General George McClellan's headquarters at Big Bethel (Mottelay, *The Soldier in Our Civil War*, 1886).

houn. The Union sustains 30 wounded. The Confederates sustain about 30 wounded.

In West Virginia, elements of the 39th Illinois, commanded by Captain James H. Hooker, skirmishes with Confederates at Great Cacapon Bridge, Alpine Depot, Slanes Cross Roads and Sir John's Run. The Union suffers two killed and two wounded. The estimated Confederate casualties are 30 wounded. Also, another contingent of the 39th Illinois Regiment, commanded by Captain Samuel S. Linton, again skirmishes with Confederates at Bath.

In Naval activity, the CSS *Sumter* arrives in port at Cadiz, Spain, but by the following day, Captain Semmes is informed by the Spanish authorities that he must make sail within 24 hours. Semmes insists his ship is in need of repairs and that he is carrying 43 prisoners he wants to turn over to the U.S. authorities there. The Spanish accept the prisoners and permit the *Sumter* to proceed to Carraca, less than ten miles from Cadiz, to make repairs. Nevertheless, on 17 January, Semmes is again ordered to depart Spanish waters. In other activity, the USS *Hetzel* arrives off Hatteras Inlet, North Carolina.

January 5 (Sunday) Confederates under General Thomas J. "Stonewall" Jackson are engaged by a Union contingent commanded by Brigadier General Frederick W. Lander at Hancock, Maryland. The Union holds its positions, then two days later moves out for Romney, Virginia. The Yankees under Lander successfully repel the Rebels. Jackson's force, which had Lander on the run from the vicinity of Bath, Virginia, reaches the Potomac but fails to cross it into Hancock; rather it uses artillery to launch a two-day bombardment.

January 6 (Monday) **In Kentucky and Tennessee,** Confederate forces under General Felix Zollicoffer have been crossing the Cumberland River from Tennessee and fortifying positions in the vicinity of Beach Grove and Mill Spring, Kentucky. Zollicoffer's superior, General Albert Sidney Johnston, had strongly urged that the troops remain in Tennessee with the river to their front. Later in the month when an expected Union force approaches, the decision by

Zollicoffer offers the Confederates few options regarding the battle. Other Confederate reinforcements under General George B. Crittenden arrive to bolster the forces under Zollicoffer. Crittenden will arrive later and assume overall command.

In Union general officer activity, Union Colonel Schuyler Hamilton, grandson of Alexander Hamilton and the brother-in-law of General Halleck, is named brigadier general, effective 12 November 1861. Hamilton becomes assistant chief of staff in the Department of Missouri, serving under General Henry Halleck.

In Confederate general officer activity, Colonel Henry Heth, 45th Virginia (West Point, 1847), is appointed brigadier general.

In Naval activity, the USS *Sumter*, back in the United States since the previous September, is ordered to sail for Port Royal, South Carolina, to join the South Atlantic Blockading Squadron. It arrives at Port Royal on 2 February and is assigned blockade duty off Charleston. The *Sumter* was originally built during 1853. As a merchant steamer (formerly the *Atlanta* and *Parker Vein*) it was chartered by the U.S. Navy during September 1858, then acquired by the Navy in May 1859 and renamed *Sumter* (*Sumpter*).

January 7 (Tuesday) **In West Virginia,** Union troops — including the 4th, 5th, 7th and 8th Ohio Regiments, the 14th Indiana Volunteers and the 1st West Virginia Cavalry — engage and defeat a contingent of Confederates in front of Romney at Blue Gap. The Union, led by Colonel Samuel Dunning, sustains no casualties. The Confederates suffer 15 dead and some captured. Also, the 2nd Virginia Infantry Regiment arrives at the foot of Cheat Mountain from Elkwater. On 5 April it moves toward Staunton.

In Kentucky, Union Colonel James A. Garfield (later president) departs Middle Creek to engage forces under Confederate General Humphrey Marshall at Paintsville. Garfield's force includes the 14th Kentucky and 42nd Ohio Regiments and about 300 cavalrymen of the 2nd Virginia Cavalry. Marshall, apparently warned of the Union approach, moves out of Paintville to avoid a skirmish and heads farther up the river. Garfield, after discovering that the town had been abandoned, occupies it and directs his cavalry to give chase. Later this day there is a slight skirmish when the cavalry encounters some Rebels about three miles outside of town at Jennie's Creek, but the engagement is of short duration with both sides sustaining light casualties. The Union 1st West Virginia Cavalry contingent, composed of four companies and commanded by Colonel W.M. Bolles, sustains three killed and one wounded. The Confederates sustain six killed and 14 wounded.

In Union general officer activity, General Ambrose Burnside assumes command of the newly created Department of North Carolina.

In Confederate general officer activity, Colonel Johnson Kelly Duncan (West Point, 1849), a Pennsylvanian who had been a resident of New Orleans when hostilities broke out, is promoted to brigadier general. Since joining the Confederate Army he has been focusing on bolstering the defenses along the coast of the strategic city, particularly Forts Jackson and St. Philip, in an effort to repulse the anticipated appearance of the Union naval forces. Confederate Colonel Sterling Alexander Martin Wood, 7th Alabama, is promoted to the rank of brigadier general. Wood, at Pensacola, Florida, will be assigned duty under General Albert S. Johnston in Kentucky. Brigadier General Henry Constantine Wayne, commissioned the previous December, resigns his commission. Nonetheless, Wayne, a West Point graduate (1838) and a veteran of the Mexican War, does not terminate his military career. He assumes command of the Georgia militia and serves in that capacity until September 1864, when he is relieved by Major General Gustavus Smith, also of the Georgia militia. After the war, General Wayne engages in the lumber business in Savannah (1866–1875). His death occurs in Savannah during March 1883.

January 8 (Wednesday) **In Kentucky,** Union Colonel James A. Garfield's force at Paintville is bolstered by the arrival of the 40th Ohio Infantry Regiment and another contingent of cavalry, increasing his force to nearly 2,500 troops, but still the Confederates under General Humphrey Marshall number about 3,000, including two Kentucky regiments, two Virginia regiments and two cavalry units, as well as four pieces of Artillery. In other activity, Union and Confederate units clash at Fishing Creek.

In Missouri, a Union force commanded by Colonel Nicholas Perczel, composed of the 10th Iowa Volunteer Regiment and contingents of the 11th, 20th and 22nd Illinois Regiments, skirmish with Confederates at Charlestown. The Union sustains eight killed and 16 wounded. Another heated skirmish develops at Silver Creek (also Sugar Creek or Roan's Tan Yard) when a Union contingent commanded by Majors W.G.M. Torrence and Garret H. Hubbard engages a Confederate force led by Colonel John A. Poindexter. The Union force — composed of contingents of the 1st and 2nd Missouri Regiments, the 4th Ohio and the 1st Iowa Cavalry — battle the rebels for about three-quarters of an hour; the Union prevails. It sustains five killed and six wounded. The Confederates sustain 80 wounded and some prisoners.

In West Virginia, a detachment of West Virginia cavalry, composed of one company, skirmishes with a Confederate unit at Dry Forks, Cheat River. Casualties are not reported.

January 9 (Thursday) **In Kentucky,** Union forces under Colonel James Garfield, having been in pursuit of Confederate General

Humphrey Marshall's forces for several days, finally discovers the positions of his main body in the vicinity of Preston. His force makes no offensive move, choosing to hold off until the early morning hours of the following day to launch the assault, due in great part to defenses that are well manned in the heights above the forks of Middle Creek.

In Missouri, the 1st Kansas Cavalry, commanded by Captain C.S. Merriman, engages a Confederate force commanded by Colonel Elliot at Columbus. The Confederates prevail. The Union sustains five killed.

In Confederate general officer activity, Captain John G. Walker — a veteran of the Mexican War who had recently resigned from the U.S. Army to join the Confederacy as a major in the cavalry and shortly thereafter, lieutenant colonel of the 8th Texas Cavalry — is this day appointed to the rank of brigadier general and will serve in the Army of Northern Virginia.

Major General John G. Walker (Johnson, *Campfire and Battlefield: History of the Conflicts and Campaigns,* **1894).**

January 10 (Friday) BATTLE OF PRESTONBURG Confederate troops under Brigadier General Humphrey Marshall (West Point, 1832) engage the Union forces commanded by General James Abram Garfield at Prestonburg, Kentucky (Big Sandy Valley). Well before dawn, the Union force moves out and advances up Abbot's Creek, arriving at Prestonburg at about 0800. Garfield then takes his time and meticulously deploys his troops and establishes positions for his artillery to maintain a focus upon all approaches to his positions. Soon after, one contingent of cavalry advances to draw out the Confederate positions, while another cavalry unit moves along the upper part of a hill. The mission succeeds, as troops of the 54th Virginia

under Colonel Trigg, entrenched at the Cross Roads, initiate fire to ignite the skirmish, which continues throughout the afternoon. Nearby Confederate artillery commences fire in an attempt to stymie the advancing cavalry and the trailing infantry.

Meanwhile, both the Yankees and the Rebels receive reinforcements, the former giving Garfield added incentive to take bolder steps. He encourages his force to advance to drive the Rebels back. The hills and ridges all along the line become engulfed in battle, with neither side ready to submit to the other. Then, at about 1600, an additional 700 Union troops under Colonel Sheldon arrive to provide Garfield with more punch as both sides are tiring. Garfield maintains the attack and in the process commits his entire reserve force. By dusk, the Union succeeds in pushing the Rebels from their positions all along the line, giving the Union control of the ground. Confederate General Marshall retires, moving through Abingdon and across the Clinch River into Virginia.

The Union remains at Preston for several days, retrieving supplies left behind by the Confederates. Afterward Garfield orders his forces back to Paintsville. Colonel Garfield will be appointed brigadier general, effective 11 January 1862. Garfield will be elected president of the United States during November of 1880; however, he is assassinated during his first year in office.

In Illinois, a Union force commanded by General John A. McClernand and composed of the 10th, 18th, 27th, 29th, 30th, 31st and 48th Infantry Regiments, bolstered by about nine companies of cavalry and two light artillery batteries, departs Cairo on a campaign into Kentucky, which continues until the 21st.

In West Virginia, Confederate Major General Thomas J. Jackson approaches Romney. Meanwhile, the Union abandons it. The Confederates occupy Romney and establish winter quarters.

In Confederate activity, Major General Earl Van Dorn assumes command of the Trans-Mississippi Department No. 2 (Army of the West). Van Dorn accepts the command offered by President Jefferson Davis. The command had been turned down by two others, Henry Heth and Braxton Bragg. Van Dorn will command the Confederates at the Battle of Elkhorn Tavern (Pea Ridge) during May of this year.

January 11 (Saturday) In Washington, D.C., Simon Cameron, the secretary of war, hands in his resignation. It is quickly accepted due to many accusations about the competency of Cameron as well as insinuations regarding

The U.S. fleet transporting the Burnside expeditionary force crosses the Hatteras bar (Johnson, *Campfire and Battlefield: History of the Conflicts and Campaigns,* 1894).

acts of fraud. Although there is great suspicion with various contracts, there is no hard evidence that the secretary himself is crooked.

In Union activity, Union General John M. Brannan assumes command of the Department of Key West, Florida. Later he serves under General W.S. Rosecrans at Tullahoma, Tennessee (July 1863).

In Naval activity, during the evening into the following early morning hours a fleet transporting an expeditionary force departs Fortress Monroe, Virginia, en route to Roanoke Island, North Carolina, which dominates two sounds that form a protective watery shield over a large portion of North Carolina and some of Virginia. The expedition is under the overall command of Brigadier General Ambrose Everett Burnside, while the fleet is commanded by Flag Officer Louis M. Goldsborough, commanding officer, North Atlantic Squadron. The flotilla includes twenty vessels with a combined total of fifty guns. They are: the *Brinker* (Acting Master Giddings), *Ceres* (Acting Master McDiarmid), *Commodore Barney* (Acting Master Renshaw), *Commodore Perry* (Acting Master Flusser), *Delaware* (Lt. Quackenbush), *General Putnam* (Acting Master Hotchkiss), *Granite* (Acting Master Boomer), *Hetzel* (Lt. Davenport), *Hunchback* (Lt. Calhoun), *Lockwood* (Acting Master Graves), *Louisiana* (Lt. Murray), *Morse* (Acting Master Peter Hayes or Hays), *Seymour* (Acting Master Wells), *Shawsheen* (Acting Master Woodward), *Southfield* (Acting Lt. Behm), *Stars and Stripes* (Lt. Worden), *Underwriter* (Lt. Leffers), *Valley City* (Lt. Chaplin), *Whitehead* (Acting Master French) and the *Whitehall* (Acting Master West).

The flotilla also includes about forty transports carrying three brigades with 15,000 to 16,000 ground troops and the gunboats *Pickett*, Burnside's flagship, *Chasseur, Hussar, Lancer, Pawnee, Pioneer, Ranger* and the *Vidette.* The expeditionary force encounters a heavy fog as it moves south, and although some of the vessels reach Hatteras safely, those unable to arrive during the afternoon get caught in a tremendous storm that wreaks havoc on the ships.

In other activity, the gunboat USS *Essex* (formerly USS *New Era*) engages Confederate gunboats in the vicinity of Lucas Bend, Missouri. The *Adolph Hugel*, a schooner built in Philadelphia during 1860 and purchased by Captain (later rear admiral) Samuel F. Du Pont on 21 September 1861, is commissioned the USS *Adolph Hugel* this day. Du Pont expects to utilize the ship in his pending attack against Port Royal, and then it is to join the South Atlantic Blockading Squadron. Nonetheless, delays occur while fitting it out as a warship. Consequently the *Adolph Hugel* misses the operation against Port Royal and is reassigned twice more prior to beginning active service. Also, the USS *Rachael Seaman* and the USS *Midnight* exchange fire with a Confederate battery at Pass Cavallo, Texas.

January 12 (Sunday)   In West Virginia, the 37th Ohio Volunteer Regiment, commanded by Colonel Siber, initiates a mission in the vicinity of Logan Court House and the Guyandotte Valley. The unit reports two men killed during the operation, which lasts until the 23rd. No Confederate casualties are reported.

In Naval activity, about 15,000 to 16,000 Union troops being transported from Fort Monroe, Virginia, to assault Confederate positions on Roanoke Island, North Carolina, are threatened, not by the enemy, rather by nature. The fleet carrying them is caught in a violent storm, considered the worst northwestern gales to ever strike the area. These troops, commanded by General Ambrose Burnside, are aboard forty transports, many of which have not yet reached Hatteras Inlet when the storm whips up and causes mass confusion. The weather becomes so nasty that it becomes impossible for any one vessel to communicate with another. Some are driven far out to sea by the force of the winds and others are pushed into shore. The tempest lasts more than two days, but loss of life and the damage to the fleet is much less than expected. (See also, **January 14, In *Naval activity*.**)

January 13 (Monday)   In Washington, D.C., President Abraham Lincoln selects a lawyer, Edwin Stanton, as secretary of war to replace Simon Cameron, who had recently resigned. The Senate acts quickly, confirming Stanton's appointment on the 15th.

In Florida, U.S. Marines on the USS *Hatteras* debark at Cedar Keys and raid Confederate positions. During the operation, Confederate supplies are destroyed.

In Naval activity, the USS *Adolph Hugel*, commanded by Acting Master Hollis B. Jencks, and the USS *George Maugham* depart Chester, Pennsylvania, en route to Hampton Roads, Virginia. From there, the *Adolph Hugel* and the *George Maugham* move to join the fleet under Admiral David D. Porter in the Mississippi Delta. The two vessels participate in the attack against Forts Jackson and Fort St. Philip (18

April) on opposite banks of the Mississippi as the defenders of the waterways leading to New Orleans.

January 14 (Tuesday)   In *Confederate general officer activity,* Brigadier General John Clifford Pemberton is promoted to the rank of major general. Colonel George E. Pickett (West Point, 1846) is appointed to the rank of brigadier general effective this date. Colonel John King Jackson (5th Georgia) is promoted to brigadier general. He is ordered to Grand Junction, Tennessee, where he engages in organizing troops expected to participate in the defense of Corinth and Shiloh.

In Naval activity, off the Atlantic coast, a Union fleet continues to get hammered by a fierce storm that had begun on the 12th. The transport *New York*, commanded by Captain Nye, had been shattered into pieces while nearby vessels could only watch in horror, unable to offer any assistance. The weather was so terrible and the waves so horrific that the crews of each vessel were tied to the rigging to prevent them from being tossed overboard. Some of the crew of the *New York* are rescued, but many drown. Other casualties of the storm are the *Louisiana*, *Pocahontas*, *Zouave* and a floating-battery, the *Grapeshot*, in tow by the *New Brunswick*, but all on board are rescued.

The *Cossack* and the *Hope* collide with each other, but both survive the accident and the storm with only slight damage and no loss of life.

Several men of the New Jersey 9th Regiment, including Colonel J.W. Allen and Surgeon Weller, attempting to render aid to some men ashore, are lost when their boat is overwhelmed by crashing waves. A naval officer of the transport *Ann E. Thomas*, named Taylor, is also on the ill-fated boat. Although the storm subsides, it has so disrupted the mission that the entire fleet will not arrive at Hatteras Inlet until the latter part of January. General Burnside, commanding the expedition, had not waited out the storm in his cabin. The entire time he was conspicuously present, hanging onto the rigging and trying to give orders and inspire his troops and the crews of the imperiled vessels as his ship, the diminutive *Pickett*, braved the waves and dashed from point to point among the fleet.

Also, Union gunboats move down the Mississippi River towards Columbus, Kentucky, and while on the reconnaissance mission, the vessels discover Confederate positions and initiate a bombardment of the camps. The USS *Iroquois* intercepts the British sloop *Rinaldo*. An inspection reveals that two Confederate ministers, James Mason and John Slidell, are aboard. Both had earlier been seized en route to Europe and were released from detainment in Massachusetts on 26 December 1861. Commodore Palmer, commanding officer of the *Iroquois*, does not arrest either. The British ship is permitted to continue its voyage to England.

January 15 (Wednesday)   In Kentucky, a Union force, including the 3rd U.S. Infantry (Regular) commanded by General Charles F.

Smith (West Point, 1825), departs Paducah on a reconnaissance mission to Fort Henry, Tennessee. The operation lasts until the 25th. Union warships are also moving along the Tennessee River toward Paducah.

In Louisiana, pursuant to orders from Confederate Secretary of War Judah Benjamin (issued 14th), General M. Lovell initiates action to seize ships owned by Charles Morgan's Southern S.S. Company. One of the seized vessels is the *Atlantic*; it becomes a blockade runner operating as the *Elizabeth* under British registration and is not taken into the Mississippi River Defense Force. General Lovell receives the CSS *Galveston* in its place. According to the Naval Historical Division records, it appears that the CSS *Galveston* soon after becomes the CSS *General Quitman*. The fourteen vessels seized also include the *Anglo-Norman*, initially built at Algiers, Louisiana, during 1850; at the time of confiscation it is in service as a towboat.

The *Anglo-Norman* is not among the ships listed as a vessel of the Mississippi Defense Fleet subsequent to the seizure of Forts Jackson and St. Philip during April 1862; however, on 1 May of 1862, it is among the vessels listed in the pending cases before arbitrators. Another of the ships taken is the *Arizona* (Hull No. 57, built in 1858). The *Arizona* is an iron paddle-steamer, but as a sea steamer, it is not well suited for river duty. The *Arizona* is transformed into a blockade runner operating between southern ports and the West Indies. Yet another seized vessel is the side-wheeler the *Hercules*. It is converted into a "cotton clad" ram and renamed the *Colonel Lovell*. The *Colonel Lovell* participates in the defense of Fort Pillow (May 1862) and at the naval battle at Memphis (June 1862). The *Grampus*, a stern-wheel steamer built during 1856 in Pennsylvania at McKeesport, is also seized and afterward used as a transport and gunboat. The *Grampus* operates on the Mississippi River. The Confederates also seize the *Magnolia*, but it too is not suited as a gunboat. It becomes a blockade runner.

Yet another of the seized ships is the *Orizaba*, which before mid–1861 had been seized by the Confederacy. The *Orizaba*, however, does not appear to have ever been armed as a gunboat. It operates as a blockade runner and is lost during 1865. The *Orizaba* is sometimes confused with another ship with the same name, but the latter, a large passenger liner, sailed to the West Coast during 1856 and did not return to the East Coast. The *Austin* (iron side-wheeler) built at Wilmington, Delaware, in 1859, also among the seized ships; is rated unsuitable as a gunboat and instead is transformed into a Confederate government owned blockade runner, commanded by Master's Mate Charles Fowler, Confederate States Navy. Also, the commercial ship *Florida*, a screw steam gunboat, is seized by the Confederates. It was originally built in Greenpoint, New York, in 1859. It is used as a blockade runner until captured during the following April, acquired by the U.S. Navy, and in December 1862 commissioned the USS *Hendrick Hudson*.

In Missouri, a Union force, composed of the 17th Illinois Regiment and the 7th Illinois Cavalry, initiates a mission to reconnoiter the Benton, Bloomfield and Dallas area. Majors F.M. Smith and Rawalt lead the force. No casualties are reported during the operation, which lasts until the 17th; however, the Union does seize about 57 Confederates.

January 16 (Thursday)   In Kentucky, Union contingents under General George H. Thomas continue their advance and begin to close upon the Cumberland River near Beach Grove.

In Naval activity, a Union naval force launches an attack against Cedar Keys, Florida. Some Confederates are captured. No casualty reports are available. However, the warships inflict damage to the dock area and disrupt the activity of the blockade runners; more than five of these vessels are destroyed by fire. The vessel Cincinnati, a stern-wheel gunboat built in St. Louis in 1861, is commissioned the USS Cincinnati at Mound City. It is assigned to duty with the U.S. Army with the Western Gunboat Flotilla commanded by Flag Officer A. H. Foote.

In other activity, the Penobscot, a gunboat launched on 19 November, arrives at the Boston Navy Yard this day. It is afterward commissioned and assigned to the North Atlantic Blockading Squadron. The USS Albatross, while operating off the coast of North Carolina, intercepts and seizes the York. In April 1862 it transfers to blockade duty off South Carolina; it seizes a schooner and a tug that year. Afterward, the Albatross sails to Boston for repairs and returns to duty during August to patrol off the coast of Texas. It moves up the Mississippi River to support operations against Baton Rouge in December 1862.

January 17 (Friday)   In Tennessee, United States Naval ships bombard Fort Henry on the Tennessee River. The bombardments continue until the 22nd. This naval force is transporting Union troops (General C.F. Smith's command) separately from another Union force under General John A. McClernand, which had departed Cairo, Illinois, on January 10th and is also moving towards Confederate positions in Kentucky.

In Confederate Naval activity, at Carraca, Spain, the authorities inform Captain Semmes of the privateer Sumter that he must make sail within six hours. The Confederates were not granted permission to take on coal and the vessel departs low on fuel. Nevertheless, Semmes sets a course for Gibraltar and safely arrives 19 January.

January 18 (Saturday) 1862   In Kentucky, at the headquarters of Confederate Generals George B. Crittenden and Felix Zollicoffer near the Cumberland River in the vicinity of Beech Grove and Mill Spring, plans are being made to commence an offensive against Union General George H. Thomas before the approaching Union forces can assault Confederate positions. The Rebels have learned that Thomas has divided his force and is forming to drive against their flank. A small contingent is at Somerset under the command of General Schoepf, while the main body under Thomas is heading southwest through Jamestown to hit the flank.

Crittenden realizes his strength is not sufficient to withstand an attack by the combined Union force. He orders an offensive to strike before the two Union contingents can be joined. Crittenden also faces another disadvantage due to the fact that Zollicoffer has transferred his forces to the Kentucky side of the Cumberland River, providing no flexibility to easily pull back if necessary.

Slightly after midnight (19th–20th) two Rebel brigades advance. One of these, commanded by General Zollicoffer, is composed of one Mississippi regiment and three Tennessee regiments supported by one battery of artillery (four guns) commanded by Captain Rutledge. The 2nd Brigade commanded by General William Henry Carroll comprises three Tennessee regiments and one battery of artillery (two guns) under Captain McClung. In addition, Zollicoffer has a reserve force composed of one Alabama regiment and two battalions of cavalry, bringing his total force to a strength of about 5,000 troops. The Confederate units include the 15th Mississippi, 17th, 19th, 20th, 25th, 28th and 29th Tennessee Regiments and the 16th Alabama Regiment.

General Thomas' force, numbering about 3,000 men, is composed of the 4th (Colonel S.S. Fry) and 12th Kentucky, 2nd Minnesota, 9th Ohio and 10th Indiana Regiments, supported by three batteries of artillery under Captains Kinney, Standart and Wetmore respectively, and a contingent of Kentucky cavalry commanded by Colonel Wolford.

In Virginia at Richmond, former President John Tyler (1841–1845), at this time a Confederate congressman, succumbs at 12:15 A.M. at the Exchange Hotel in Richmond. President Tyler, age 72, is the only president of the United States to hold office in the Confederacy. He had never run for president; rather he had been vice president under President William H. Harrison, who succumbed shortly after his inauguration. Tyler was the first vice president to succeed to office following the death of a president, and at that time it wasn't clear whether he was only to be acting president until a new election could be held. He settled the issue by having himself sworn in, to the dismay of some of his detractors.

January 19 (Sunday)   THE BATTLE OF LOGAN'S CROSSROADS (MILL SPRINGS, FISHING CREEK) Two Confederate forces under Generals Felix Zollicoffer and William H. Carroll break camp and just after midnight (18th–19th) initiate their march, pestered along the entire route by a light rain, to intercept and attack the advancing Union troops under General Henry Thomas in Kentucky. As the Confederates press ahead, they encounter a contingent of Colonel Wolford's Kentucky cavalry and effortlessly push them back. They retire to the positions of the 4th Kentucky and the 10th Indiana, commanded by Colonels Speed Smith Fry and Mahlon D. Manson, respectively.

The Confederates, eager to engage the approaching Union forces, pick up the pace and at about 0600 encroach the positions of the 4th Kentucky and 10th Indiana and at the signal commence the attack. The Union holds the line, but only momentarily, as the Confederate strength drives them back. They move from a hill and redeploy on another slope. Here too the Union is able to hold only for a short while, as they expend their entire ammunition supply, compelling them to relinquish the ground and sprint for the woods. In reaction, the Confederates, sensing the kill, execute a flanking movement to finish off the imperiled regiments, but at about this time, General Thomas is on scene and he spots what he believes to be an intent to crush the flank. While he directs the 9th Ohio (Colonel Robert Latimer McCook) and 2nd Minnesota (Colonel Horatio Phillips Van Cleve) to advance in support, the Confederates receive reinforcements from Brigadier William H. Carroll's brigade.

Still holding the momentum, the Confederates accelerate their efforts by initiating a thunderous charge. The force of the attack and the accompanying riveting fire staggers the Union line, nearly collapsing it, but just in time, the 12th Kentucky, led by Colonel W.A. Hoskins, hits the line and stabilizes the Union positions. Fire from both sides intensifies, and with the additional shelling by the opposing artillery, the battlefield is seemingly shrinking as the troops become intertwined in the struggle for victory.

A huge Confederate thrust forces some Union artillery to withdraw from its positions on a hill at about the same time General Zollicoffer arrives at the front of the Confederate

Battle of Logan's Crossroads in Kentucky, 19 January 1862 (Mottelay, The Soldier in Our Civil War, 1886).

Confederate General Felix Zollicoffer is killed at the Battle of Logan's Crossroads (Mottelay, *The Soldier in Our Civil War*, 1886).

lines. A Union officer, Colonel Speed Smith Fry of the 4th Kentucky Regiment, spots him and moves forward. A Confederate then fires and shoots Fry's horse from under him. Following this, Zollicoffer is shot and immediately killed when he inadvertently encroaches a Union vanguard. Zollicoffer's death incites the Rebels, who launch a massive charge that prompts a hectic hand-to-hand encounter that causes even more carnage.

Back at the Union line, Colonel Robert L. McCook, undergoing a full day of action, including earlier having his horse shot from under him in addition to receiving a leg wound, rapidly reacts to the Rebel charge. The regimental surgeon had insisted that McCook remain off the field, but he ignores the demand. Incensed, Colonel McCook clasps his pistol, moves to the point and begins to yell: "Take courage anew! Bayonets out! Charge! Charge!" His 9th Ohio Regiment, with bayonets drawn, lunges forward to execute a tenacious attack, which cracks the Rebel lines and forces a pull-back. Crittenden, who assumed command on the field following the death of Zollicoffer, works in vain to regroup and rally his Confederate force, but the effort is fruitless, as the 9th Ohio gives no quarter. The Union penetrates further, still badgering the Rebels, forcing a withdrawal to Beech Grove (Beach Grove). But there is no reprieve at Beech Grove. The unchallenged Union guns atop Moulden's Hill propel a steady stream of fire into the Rebel camp. The relentless bombardment continues until dark without losing effectiveness. Consequently, the Confederates remain pinned down, unable to ford the Cumberland River.

In the meantime, Brigadier General Albin F.

Schoepf's brigade, held up by surging streams, moves into the federal positions to bolster Thomas, and the 10th Ohio and 14th Kentucky Regiments also arrive. The added strength convinces Thomas to finish the job on the following morning. However, following dusk, the Confederates, under the overall command of General A.S. Johnston, withdraw to Nashville, arriving on 14 February, followed by Brigadier General Don Carlos Buell's army. Johnston is to sustain additional setbacks at Forts Donelson and Henry during February 1862. The body of General Felix Zollicoffer is not moved from within Union lines, but General Thomas ensures that his remains receive proper care; he is laid in a metal casket and transported by wagon to Munfordville and from there, following a Union salute of honor, Zollicoffer's remains are transferred under a flag of truce to Confederate Brigadier General Thomas Hindman's command. Zollicoffer is interred at Nashville, Tennessee.

On the morning of the 20th, Union forces secure the vacated Confederate fortifications, confiscating eight guns, 1,000 stand-of-arms, a large amount of ammunition and supplies and about 100 wagons. Later, when troops ford the river at White Oak Creek, more supplies and six additional guns are seized. This battle, fought by forces under Confederate General A.S. Johnston and Union General George H. Thomas, includes skirmishes at Mill Springs (Logan's Crossroads), Fishing Creek, Beech Grove and Somerset, Kentucky. The Union suffers 38 dead and 194 wounded; Confederates suffer 190 dead, 160 wounded and 89 captured. Confederate General George Bibb Crittenden (West Point, 1832) will resign his commission as major general during November. Nevertheless, he will remain in the service of the Confederacy for the duration.

Subsequent to the demise of Zollicoffer, his quartermaster, Major Alfred E. Jackson, is transferred to Knoxville, Tennessee, and is assigned duty as paymaster; however, he is promoted to the rank of brigadier general in 1863 and will see some duty in the field in Tennessee. Union Major General George Henry Thomas (West Point 1840), born in Virginia, has remained loyal to the Union, but his family retains allegiance to the Confederacy. Also, Confederate General William Henry Carroll participates at this battle. Soon after the contest, he runs into trouble with General Braxton Bragg and finds himself under arrest, accused of several charges, including intoxication and neglect of duty. Carroll resigns his commission in February 1863. Confederate General George Bibb Crittenden is held responsible for the loss

of his baggage trains and his artillery. He resigns his commission in October but continues to serve the Confederacy in other capacities for the duration. After the close of hostilities, he becomes a librarian of the state of Kentucky.

In Confederate activity, the CSS *Sumter,* commanded by Captain Semmes, essentially evicted from Carraca, Spain, by the Spanish on the 17th, arrives at the British port in Gibraltar. While there, Semmes receives money from James Mason, the Confederate minister in London. Afterward, Semmes attempts to purchase coal, but no suppliers will sell him the fuel. Semmes then dispatches two men to purchase the fuel at Cadiz, but en route aboard a French vessel they stop at Tangier. The two Confederates, Semmes' paymaster, Myers, and Thomas J. Tunstall, are detained by the authorities on a request made by the U.S. consul. Neither returns to Gibraltar. Both are placed in irons and transported to the United States. In the meantime, several Union warships, the USS *Tuscarora, Kearsarge* and *Chippewa* arrive to trap the *Sumter.* Captain Semmes, having insufficient fuel and facing the blockade, confers with James Mason, the Confederate minister in London, and it is decided to abandon the vessel. Semmes and the other officers depart for London in mid–April and the crew is discharged. A small ten-man detachment is left behind to maintain the *Sumter.* The *Chippewa* had been commissioned the previous month, following acquisition by the U.S. Navy.

January 20 (Monday)   In Kansas, one company of the 1st Missouri Cavalry, commanded by Union Captain Irving W. Fuller, initiates a mission in the vicinity of Atchison. The operation lasts until the 24th and results in the capture of some Confederates. One Confederate is reported killed. The Union reports no casualties.

In South Carolina, more of the "Stone Fleet" is intentionally sunk off Charleston to further block the entrance to the harbor.

In Virginia at Hampton Roads, Captain David G. Farragut receives orders from Secretary of the Navy Gideon Welles to depart for the Gulf of Mexico and meet with Flag Officer McKean to receive the command of the Western Gulf Squadron. Welles states: "There will be attached to your squadron, a fleet of bomb vessels, and enough steamers to manage them, all under the command of Commodore D. Porter, who will be directed to report to you."

In Naval activity, Union warships intercept a British blockade-runner, the schooner *Andracita* (also known as *J.W. Wilder*) off the Alabama coast and attempt to seize it. The vessel is driven toward shore, but intervention by Confederate ground fire prevents the Union from gaining the prize. The Gulf Blockading Squadron is split into two sections, which establishes the East Gulf Blockading Squadron (Flag Officer McKean) and the West Gulf Blockading Squadron (Rear Admiral David Farragut), with the *Water Witch* being attached to the East Gulf Blockading Squadron. It patrols the area off the gulf coasts of Alabama and Florida; however, in addition, it is still assigned to carrying mail. The *Samuel Rotan* is among the gunboats attached to the East Gulf. It becomes involved with taking a cargo of contraband to Philadelphia the following month, but returns to Florida in April 1862, where it remains in service until November 1862. It then moves to Philadelphia for repairs.

January 21 (Tuesday) **In Illinois,** General John A. McClernand's force, including the 10th, 18th, 27th, 29th, 30th, 31st and 48th Infantry Regiments, returns to Cairo, terminating an expedition into Kentucky that had begun on 10 January.

January 22 (Wednesday) *In Confederate activity,* Brigadier General Henry A. Wise receives command of Roanoke Island, North Carolina. Wise will later serve with Pierre Beauregard in the defense of Charleston, South Carolina.

In Missouri, a contingent of the 2nd Missouri Cavalry skirmishes with Confederates at Knob Noster. No casualties are reported. In other activity, one Battalion (Wright's Battalion) of Missouri Cavalry, commanded by Lt. Colonel Thomas C. Wright, occupies Lebanon.

January 23 (Thursday) **In Pennsylvania,** in response to a request from the state surgeon general, a party of four nuns (Sisters of Saint Joseph), including Mother Monica Pue, depart Philadelphia for Harrisburg to tend to the sick troops at Camp Curtain. Upon their arrival, they are not received cordially by some (not the doctors). The doctors refer to them as Sisters of Charity and Sisters of Mercy, two other orders, and the nuns attempt to identify themselves as Sisters of Saint Joseph without success. The surgeon general explains that it would be in vain to try to explain the different orders. The surgeon general, aware of the drastic changes in the hospitals, writes to the nuns' superior at Chestnut Hill in Philadelphia on 2 February: "I have found all the Sisters perfectly well, and with no complaints after their trial of the inconveniences and exposure attendant on military life. Already each hospital shows the blessing attendant on their presence. Every thing is now neat, orderly and comfortable." By 18 February, the troops at the camp are ordered to the front. The Sisters of St. Joseph leave the church hospital on the 27th and the depart Camp Curtain for home on 8 April. Soon after, a team of four nuns, including Mother Pue, are sent to Fortress Monroe, Virginia.

In Union activity, John Wilson Sprague is appointed colonel of the 63rd Ohio Regiment. Colonel Sprague participates at New Madrid, Missouri, and at Island No. 10 in Tennessee as part of General John Pope's command.

In Naval activity, the gunboat USS *Samuel Rotan,* while on blockade duty with the Gulf Squadron and on patrol in East Bay (Mississippi delta), intercepts and seizes the Confederate privateer *Calhoun* as it attempts to enter the Southwest Pass. The *Calhoun*'s cargo is a bo-

nanza for the *Samuel Rotan,* as it is transporting about 25 tons of gunpowder, along with chemicals, coffee and other items including rifles; in turn, it is a great loss for the Confederates. It is determined by the Union that the *Calhoun* is not suited (due to the inclement weather of the winter months) for the voyage north. Consequently, the cargo and associated papers are transferred to the *Rotan.* In mid–February, the cargo is carried north to Philadelphia by the *Rotan.*

January 24 (Friday) *In Union general officer activity,* Union Major Lewis Golding Arnold (West Point, 1837) is promoted to brigadier general, U.S. Volunteers. He had served at Fort Pickens at the outbreak of the Civil War. He will assume command of the Department of Florida in February.

In Confederate general officer activity, Brigadier General Richard S. Ewell is promoted to major general. He will rise to lieutenant general the next May, subsequent to the demise of General Thomas J. "Stonewall" Jackson. Confederate Colonel James McQueen McIntosh, 2nd Arkansas Mounted Rifles, is promoted to the rank of brigadier general. His brother, John Baillie McIntosh, who had graduated from the naval academy, remains loyal to the Union and rises to the rank of major general. Bushrod Rust Johnson (West Point, 1840), who joined the Confederacy with the rank of colonel of engineers, is also named brigadier general.

General Richard S. Ewell (Johnson, *Campfire and Battlefield: History of the Conflicts and Campaigns,* 1894).

January 25 **In Louisiana** at New Orleans, the *Little Rebel,* built at Belle Vernon, Pennsylvania, during 1859, having been acquired at New Orleans by the Confederacy, begins to undergo conversion to a cottonclad ram. The *Little Rebel* is attached to the Mississippi River De-

fense Fleet. Work also begins on the tugboat *Resolute,* which is to become a cottonclad gunboat ram; it too will be attached to the Mississippi River Defense Fleet. The *Resolute* is separate from another vessel, the tugboat *Resolute* built in Savannah during 1858. The latter *Resolute* serves as a towboat and also as a transport; however, it also acts as a receiving ship and a tender to the CSS *Savannah.* The transport *Resolute* serves primarily on the coastal and inland waters of Georgia and South Carolina. Also, the CSS *Warrior,* a civilian tugboat on the Mississippi prior to being acquired by the Confederacy, is also being converted into a side-wheel gunboat cottonclad ram. The officer in charge of the operation is Captain James E. Montgomery. The *Warrior* is to be refurbished with a "4-inch oak sheath with a one-inch iron covering on its bow, and by installing double pine bulkheads filled with compressed cotton bales to protect machinery and boilers." Captain J.A. Stevenson receives command of the *Warrior.*

In Naval activity, the USS *Arthur* arrives off Matagorda, Texas, to initiate duty as a blockade vessel. On its first day, the crew spots a schooner moving toward shore at a point slightly more than 15 miles northeast of the Pass Cavallo bar. Two cutters are sent to intercept the craft before it can be run aground. Meanwhile, the *Arthur* fires a warning shot, which prompts the schooner to halt. The ship is identified as the Confederate blockade runner *J.J. McNeil,* which is carrying a cargo of coffee and tobacco. The prize is sent to Ship Island, Mississippi, and from there it is sailed to New York.

January 26 (Sunday) *In Naval activity,* Union gunboats, including the *Ellen, Ottawa, Potomska, Seneca, Isaac H. Smith* and the *Western World,* supported by troops commanded by Brigadier General Horatio Wright, arrive in the vicinity of Wilmington Narrows, Georgia. The Union gunboats clash with Confederate gunboats on the 27th and the 28th. The Union Naval forces are commanded by Captain C.H. Davis. The Confederates are attached to Flag Officer Josiah Tatnall's command.

January 27 (Monday) **In Washington, D.C.,** President Lincoln issues General Order 1, directing a general land and sea movement against the Confederacy to commence on February 22 in an effort to motivate General McClellan and his Army of the Potomac.

In Confederate activity, General Pierre Beauregard departs the District of the Potomac for duty in the West. He travels to Columbus, Kentucky, and later serves with General Albert Sidney Johnston at Shiloh (April 1862). Brigadier General Jones Mitchell Withers assumes command of the Army of Mobile at Mobile, Alabama. Withers had recently been mayor of the city (1858–1861). Brigadier General Samuel Jones receives command of the Army of Pensacola (Florida). He succeeds General Braxton Bragg.

In Naval activity, the USS *Whitehall* yet again is found to be in poor condition, including its machinery as well as its hull. Despite the vessel's condition, in March it participates against the CSS *Virginia* at Newport News.

January 28 (Tuesday) **In Georgia,** Union troops maintain their sights on Fort Pulaski on Cockspur Island. Reconnaissance missions have been in progress to determine the best plan of attack and conclude that the gunboats at this time could not reach the Savannah River. Instead a blockade is planned. On this day, two separate reconnaissance contingents, one under the command of General H.G. Wright and Commander C.H. Davis, U.S. Navy, and another under Captain John Rodgers, USN, and General E.L. Viele, converge in the vicinity of Fort Pulaski and engage a Confederate force composed of five gunboats led by Commodore Josiah Tatnall. The Confederates are forced to disengage and retire.

In Kentucky, a contingent of Union cavalry, the 1st Ohio, commanded by Lt. Colonel T.C.A. Smith, engages Confederate cavalry led by Captain Morgan in the vicinity of Greensburg and Lebanon. The two groups also engage each other on February 2. The Confederates capture several of the Union troops.

In Missouri, Union General Halleck, who has previously ordered martial law in St. Louis, continues the orders and has them strengthened to make it difficult for the Southern sympathizers in Saint Louis. Southern sympathizers are liable for arrest if they disobey Halleck's law.

In North Carolina, the remainder of the storm-battered fleet transporting General Burnside's force arrives at Hatteras Inlet, North Carolina, but the preparations for the impending assault to seize Roanoke Island are behind schedule. It will take several more days before all is ready. Meanwhile, the three brigades and the warships are in place. The First Brigade, commanded by General John G. Foster (commissioned October 1861), is composed of the 10th Connecticut and 23rd, 24th, 25th and 26th Massachusetts Regiments. The Second Brigade, commanded by General Jessie L. Reno, comprises the 21st Massachusetts, 6th New Hampshire, 9th New Jersey, 51st New York and the 51st Pennsylvania Regiments. The Third Brigade, commanded by General John G. Parke, is composed of the 8th and 11th Connecticut, 53rd and 89th New York, and the 4th Rhode Island Regiments. In addition it includes one battalion of the 5th Rhode Island Regiment and one battery of Colonel Belzier's Rhode Island Artillery (six guns, 106 troops and 106 horses).

In Virginia, a contingent of the 37th New York Volunteers and the 1st New Jersey Cavalry engage a Confederate force at Occoquan Bridge. The Union sustains three killed and one wounded. Confederate casualties, if any, are unavailable.

In Confederate general officer activity, General Earl Van Dorn is appointed commander of the Trans-Mississippi Department, which encompasses the states of Arkansas, Missouri and part of Louisiana extending as far south as the Red River and the Indian Territory west of Arkansas.

In Naval activity, the USS *Hartford* departs from the Delaware Capes as the flagship of Flag Officer David G. Farragut (commanding officer of the recently established West Gulf Blockading Squadron). The USS *Western World* participates in a mission in which a Union flotilla sweeps the Savannah River (Georgia) and some of its tributaries. Other vessels that participate include the *Ellen, Isaac Smith, Ottawa, Potomska* and the *Seneca,* along with the transports *Boston, Cosmopolitan* and *Delaware.* Brigadier General Horatio G. Wright and a force of about 2,400 troops are aboard the transports. On this first day out, the warships engage and repel an attack by five Confederate warships. On the following day the mission is completed and the survey project is finished.

January 29 (Wednesday) **In Missouri,** a Union contingent of the 7th Missouri Mounted Infantry led by Captain William S. Oliver skirmishes with Confederates led by Quantrill at Blue Springs. The opposing units again clash in the same general area on February 3.

In Naval activity, the U.S. Navy commissions the USS *Miami,* a "double ender" side-wheel gunboat built at the Philadelphia Navy Yard. The *Miami* is dispatched to the Gulf of Mexico to participate in the operations against New Orleans. Afterward, it operates in the Gulf and along the Mississippi River until transferred to duty in the North Carolina Sounds.

January 30 (Thursday) Confederate ministers James Mason and John Slidell finally arrive in London, England, following a long journey that began during October of the previous year and was soon after interrupted when thy were captured at sea and detained in prison in Massachusetts until President Lincoln arranged for their release on December 26.

In Illinois, General Ulysses S. Grant at Cairo, who earlier this month had reconnoitered the

Confederate minister John Slidell (Mottelay, *The Soldier in Our Civil War,* 1886).

area around Confederate-held Fort Henry, Tennessee, and determined that it could be seized, receives permission this day from General Henry Halleck to assault and capture it.

In Naval activity, the USS *Monitor* is officially launched at Greenpoint, Long Island. The vessel is an ironclad and has arrived on the scene just in time to meet a Confederate threat off the shores of Virginia. The *Monitor* engages the CSS *Virginia* (formerly *USS Merrimack*) during March 1862. The schooner *Arletta,* built in Mystic, Connecticut, during 1860, is commissioned the USS *Arletta* at New York. Acting Master Thomas E. Smith receives command.

January 31 (Friday) England reiterates its position of neutrality during the American Civil War, much to the dismay of the Confederate states, which diligently sought their aid as well as Spain's. However, the restated position of neutrality does give the southern states recognition, which bolsters their resistance.

Washington, D.C., President Abraham Lincoln issues Special War Order No. 1, which is specifically designed to push General McClellan to get the Army of the Potomac on the offensive in Virginia. The order is a follow up to another order issued on January 27. It directs that the Army of the Potomac seize control of Manassas Junction.

In Marine Corps activity, a contingent of twenty seven enlisted Marines and one officer are ordered to serve aboard the USS *St. Louis,* the flagship of the armada that will support General Grant's assaults during February 1862 against Confederate-held Forts Donelson and Henry on the Cumberland and Tennessee Rivers respectively.

In Union activity, David Allen Russell (West Point, 1845) is appointed colonel of the 7th Massachusetts Infantry.

February 1 (Saturday) **In Illinois,** Union forces under General Ulysses S. Grant prepare to move up the Tennessee River from Cairo to capture Fort Henry, Tennessee, which is held by about 3,000 troops under the command of Confederate General Lloyd Tilghman. They depart the following day. Also, Joseph Dana Webster, a veteran of the Mexican War, is appointed colonel of the 1st Illinois Light Artillery; however, the batteries never serve together as a unit. Nonetheless, his rank as colonel permits him the proper rank to become chief of staff to General Grant. He handles the artillery at the Battle of Shiloh and later is appointed brigadier general of volunteers on 29 November 1862. During the Vicksburg campaign, General Webster becomes General Sherman's chief of staff. Subsequently, he also becomes chief of staff under General George H. Thomas. At the close of hostilities, he receives the brevet of major general of volunteers.

In Kentucky, a contingent of the 2nd Indiana Cavalry engages Confederates at Bowling Green. The Union reports no casualties. The Confederates suffer three killed and two wounded.

In Naval activity, the USS *Hatteras* engages the CSS *Mobile* in Atchafalaya Bay, Louisiana, but neither ship is destroyed or captured. From June 1862 to May 1863 the *Mobile* operates along the Yazoo River. In other activity, at about this time (May), the USS *Aroostook* (screw steam gunboat) is commissioned. Built at Kennebunk, Maine, it was commissioned in February 1862. It moves to Hampton Roads, but en route, during some nasty weather, it moves to assist the USS *Vermont* (early March), which sustains damage from the storm that cripples the vessel. However, in the process of administering help, the *Aroostook* also sustains damage. Nevertheless, it is able to reach its destination, subsequent to receiving repairs. Once on station, it initiates patrols and participates against Drewry's Bluff (15 May) and later with the Potomac Flotilla prior to being assigned to the Gulf of Mexico.

The USS *Varuna* is also commissioned this month. Also, the USS *Benton,* an ironclad gunboat, is acquired by the U.S. government and commissioned at about this time (February). The gunboat, prior to being modified for military purposes, had been a "catamaran snagboat" constructed at St. Louis, Missouri. The *Benton* was initially attached to the U.S. Army's Western gunboat flotilla, but in August 1862 is transferred to the U.S. Navy to serve with the Mississippi Squadron. The USS *Katahdin* is commissioned at about this time (February). It is assigned duty in the Gulf of Mexico and the lower Mississippi River. The USS *Kennebec* (screw steam gunboat) is also commissioned in February and assigned duty on the lower Mississippi River and the Gulf of Mexico.

February 2 (Sunday) In Illinois at Cairo, General Grant's army embarks for Paducah, Kentucky, from which it will assault Fort Henry, being carried by Naval ships under the command of Flag Officer Andrew Foote. The ground forces are aboard transport vessels accompanied by seven gunboats, the armored vessels USS *Cincinnati* (flagship of Commander Stembel), *Carondelet* (Commander Walke), *Essex* (Commander Porter), *St. Louis* (Commander Paulding), and the wooden vessels *Conestoga* (Lt. Phelps), *Lexington* (Lt. Shirk) and the *Tyler* (Lt. Givin). The flotilla arrives at its destination during the evening.

In Tennessee, a detachment of the Confederate 1st Tennessee Cavalry, commanded by Colonel (later brigadier general) Danville Leadbetter, skirmishes with a Union force in Morgan County. The Union sustains about six killed and one captured. Confederate casualties are unavailable.

In Union activity, Cadwalader C. Washburn is appointed colonel (later major general) of the 2nd Wisconsin Cavalry Regiment.

In Naval activity, the USS *John L. Lockwood* is ordered to move to Hatteras Inlet, North Carolina, to participate in the campaign to seize Roanoke Island.

February 3 (Monday) In Kentucky, during the early morning hours, the Union naval force

under Flag Officer Andrew H. Foote, which is transporting General Grant's Army, nudges toward Fort Henry. The ground forces debark at Bailey's Ferry and establish night positions in the high ground near the river to await the order to attack. Meanwhile, the gunboats advance to a point within about nine miles below the Confederate fort. Reconnaissance contingents are dispatched both by water and by land to ascertain the strength and positions of the Rebels. Following a gathering of intelligence, it is initially determined to launch the assault on the 5th at precisely 1100.

In Virginia, a contingent of the 3rd Michigan Infantry Regiment, composed of about 75 troops commanded by Captain Lowing, initiates a reconnaissance mission into the area around Occoquan Villagea. The Confederates sustain slight casualties. No Union casualties are reported.

In Union general officer activity, Captain John W. Davidson (West Point, 1845) is appointed brigadier general, U.S. Volunteers. Davidson sees field service during the Peninsular Campaign and is subsequently stationed in Missouri and Arkansas. Another Union appointment in February is that of Ethan Allen Hitchcock (West Point, 1817), who is named major general of Volunteers and is assigned the position of commissioner for the exchange of prisoners. After the war, during November 1865, he is appointed commissary general of prisoners. He musters out of the service during 1867.

Also, William Scott Ketchum (West Point, 1834) becomes a brigadier general in the Union Army. He remains in recruiting for the duration without seeing field duty. However, he becomes colonel of the 11th U.S. Infantry during 1864 and receives the brevets of brigadier and major general in the U.S. Army at the close of hostilities. He is mustered out of the volunteer service in 1866, but remains in the army at the adjutant general's headquarters in Washington, D.C. for about four years. After 15 March 1869 he remains unassigned until he voluntarily leaves the service during December 1870. About one month later he dies amid mysterious circumstances while visiting a boarding house in Baltimore on 26 January 1871. The owner of the house, Elizabeth G. Wharton, is tried for his murder (by poisoning him), but she is found not guilty during 1872.

February 4 (Tuesday) In Tennessee, Union forces poised at positions within striking distance of Fort Henry prepare to launch their assault on the following day; however, unexpectedly a storm moves into the area and causes complications for the ground forces. General Ulysses S. Grant's Army is composed of the divisions of General John A. McClernand and General C.F. Smith. The units of the combined force include the 7th, 8th, 9th, 11th, 12th 18th, 20th, 27th 28th 29th, 30th, 31st, 41st, 45th, and 48th Illinois Regiments. It also includes the 7th and 12th Iowa, the 8th and 30th Missouri and the 11th Indiana Regiments. To further bol-

ster the assault force, there is a large complement of cavalry and artillery.

In Virginia at Richmond, the Confederate government, pressed for troops, discusses the possibility of seeking the enlistment of free blacks into the Confederate Army.

In Naval activity, off North Carolina, the *Patuxent* moves about the giant Union fleet leaving instructions with each vessel, directing it to advance toward Roanoke Island beginning on the following morning. In other activity, the steamer CSS *Dunbar* along with the CSS *Lynn Boyd* depart Fort Henry (Tennessee) en route to Paris Landing to pick up two regiments. Two days later, when Fort Henry capitulates to the Union, the Confederates self-destruct the *Dunbar* on Cyprus Creek to prevent the Union fleet from capturing it. Also, the USS *Arletta* departs New York to join Admiral David G. Farragut's West Gulf Blockading Squadron. The Confederate vessels *Lynn Boyd* and *Dunbar* depart Fort Henry for Paris Landing to embark two regiments deployed there. Two days later when the fort surrenders to the Union, the *Lynn Boyd* and the *Dunbar,* both on the Tennessee River near the mouth of Duck River, are set afire to prevent capture by the Union.

February 5 (Wednesday) In Tennessee, General Grant issues orders to advance against Fort Henry, which is situated approximately eleven miles from Fort Donelson, but the plans go awry. The area has sustained a solid rainstorm during the night, creating severe handicaps for the ground forces. The streams swell and the ground goes beyond soggy, becoming deeply muddied. The assault is postponed until the following day.

In Naval activity, the Union fleet off North Carolina at Hatteras Inlet moves against Roanoke Island. Flag Officer Goldsborough forms the fleet in three separate columns under Commander Stephen Rowan. The columns are commanded by Lieutenants Reed Werden, Alexander Murray, and H.K. Davenport and utilizes the gunboats as the vanguard of the armada. The fleet, transporting a huge number of infantry, will dispatch a reconnaissance mission on the 6th to determine, if possible, the strength of the enemy and the most plausible sites to land the assault troops. The objective, Roanoke Island, is commanded by Confederate Brigadier General Henry A. Wise, but due to illness, he is being treated at Nag's Head. The command in his absence is under Colonel Shaw of the 8th North Carolina Regiment; however, Wise, despite his bad health, will be at Roanoke to engage the Union.

The defending force includes the 8th (Colonel Henry M. Shaw) and 31st (Colonel John V. Jordan) North Carolina Regiments and three companies of the 17th North Carolina Regiment (Major G.H. Hill). Another contingent of about 450 troops commanded by Colonel Anderson are at Roanoke, and the defenses are bolstered by forty shore guns and a meager naval force of eight vessels (eleven guns), commanded by Lt. W.F. Leach. In contrast, more than 25 gunboats, including the USS *Hetzel*, accompany the Union fleet.

February 6 (Thursday) SURRENDER OF FORT HENRY Union forces under General U.S. Grant move against Confederate-held Fort Henry in Tennessee. General C.F. Smith's division trudges toward Fort Hieman, while McClernand's division advances ever so slowly toward a position along the Dover Road between Forts Henry and Donelson. Meanwhile, the gunboats, unaffected by the unruly water, maneuver into position at Panther Island in the western channel and from there, out of harm's way of the long-range Confederate guns, commence a powerful bombardment that continues until about 1400. The fort's gunners return fire at an equally determined pace, but the commander, Confederate General Lloyd Tilghman, concludes that the situation is critical, and if given enough time, he is convinced that the Union will isolate his positions, making them untenable and leaving no escape route. Rather than risk a devastating defeat, Tilghman decides to evacuate his force and dispatch it to Fort Donelson. He, however, remains within the confines of the fort until the Union naval guns have nearly demolished the entire place, leaving only seven of the original seventeen guns under Captain Jesse Taylor operational.

Fort Henry, prior to the troops' departure to Fort Donelson, is defended by two brigades under Colonels A. Hieman and Joseph Drake. Heiman's force is composed of his regiment, the 10th Tennessee (Lt. Colonel McGavock), 27th Alabama (Colonel Hughes), 48th Tennessee (Colonel Voorhies), one battalion of cavalry under Lt. Colonel Gantt, and a battery of four guns under Captain Culbertson. Drake's brigade comprises his regiment, the 4th Mississippi, presently commanded by Major Adair, 15th Arkansas (Colonel Gee), 51st Tennessee (Colonel Browder), one battalion of Alabama troops led by Major Garvin, and a contingent of rangers commanded by Captain Melton. Drake's brigade is further augmented by two companies of cavalry commanded by Captains Milner and Padgett. Subsequent to the troops departing for Fort Donelson, Tilghman, having only about 100 troops still with him at the fort, surrenders to Flag Officer Andrew Foote, who dispatches Commander Stembel and Lt. Commander S.L. Phelps to unfurl Old Glory over the captured Fort Henry in the Mississippi Valley. General Tilghman is exchanged during autumn of this year.

The 15,000 troops under General Ulysses S. Grant do not arrive in time to fight; however, as it turns out, the navy in this instance did not require any assistance. Upon the arrival of Grant's ground troops, pursuit of the Rebels commences. Elements of the 4th Illinois Cavalry give chase, but their effort nets only a few troops and several pieces of light artillery. The Union sustains two killed and 38 wounded; of these, 29 occur when a boiler on the USS *Essex* explodes after being hit by a 32-pounder hurled from the fort. Of the two deaths, one is Lt. S.B. Brittan, Jr., of New York. He is instantly killed

while aboard the *Essex* as Captain Porter's aide when he is struck directly in the head by a 42-pound shot. The Confederates lose five dead and 11 wounded. Grant telegraphs General Halleck after the victory: "I shall take and destroy Fort Donelson on the 8th and return to Fort Henry."

Bad weather and orders from Halleck to fortify Fort Henry prevent Grant from moving against Fort Donelson until 12 February. The Rebels afford the Yankees extra shelter from the inclement weather by leaving about 8,000 tents behind when they evacuate. Grant, having arrived on the scene late at Fort Henry, causes him problems in the near future with Halleck; however, he is vindicated.

Fort Heiman, situated near Donelson, has been evacuated by the Confederates after a heavy naval bombardment. Union ground troops under General Charles Smith are slightly disappointed because Fort Heiman falls before their arrival. At Bowling Green, Kentucky, subsequent to the fall of Fort Henry, Confederate General Simon Bolivar Buckner transfers his force to Fort Donelson, Tennessee, which is about ten miles southeast of Fort Henry at Dover.

Following the capture of Fort Henry, Flag Officer Andrew Foote retires to Cairo to get needed repairs to his gunboats and to lay plans for the next operation. The *Cincinnati*, *Essex* and *St. Louis* depart, but Foote leaves the *Carondelet* and the older wooden gunboats, the *Conestoga*, *Lexington* and *Tyler* to bolster the Yankees that move against Fort Donelson. Under Lt. Commander S.L. Phelps, these vessels cruise up the Tennessee River.

The *Tyler* destroys a portion of the railway bridge of the Memphis and Ohio Valley Railway and the railroad system in the area, while the *Conestoga* and *Lexington* pursue a couple of Confederate transports. The Union warships close tightly, but before the transports can be captured, the Rebels set them afire and abandon them. The small Union flotilla continues as far as Florence, Alabama, prior to returning to Fort Henry. Also, the USS *Essex*, which sustains severe damage, departs for repairs. The commanding officer, William D. Porter, modifies the *Essex* by increasing its size and rearming it to make it a much more potent warship. The project is completed in time for the *Essex* to participate in the Vicksburg Campaign.

In Union general officer activity, James Scott Negley, a veteran of the Mexican War who entered service as a private, had been appointed brigadier general of militia (18th Division) in Pittsburgh, Pennsylvania, during 1861. On this day he is appointed brigadier general of volunteers, effective 1 October of the previous year. General Negley becomes commander at Nashville during autumn of this year, and following the Battle of Murfreesboro in late 1862, he is promoted to major general. Thomas Francis Meagher, a native of Ireland who initially joined the Union Army by forming a company of Zouaves which becomes part of the 69th New York Militia Regiment, is commissioned a

brigadier general this day by President Lincoln. He participated at the First Bull Run (Manassas). During the following year, he organizes the Irish Brigade in New York City. Also, at about this time, Thomas Hewson Neill (West Point, 1847), who was stationed on the frontier with the U.S. 5th Infantry at the outbreak of the war, is commissioned as colonel (later brevet major general) of the 23rd Pennsylvania. Neill had been on the staff of Major General Cadwalader just prior to his appointment.

February 6–10 (Thursday) In *Naval activity,* a group of Union vessels, the steamers *Conestoga*, *Lexington* and *Tyler* under Lt. Commander Phelps, initiate a mission that has them operating in the vicinity of Florence, Alabama. The operation lasts until the 10th. No casualties are reported; however, the Union force seizes a large cache of Confederate arms.

February 7 (Friday) In **Virginia,** a contingent of the Cameron Dragoons, composed of five companies commanded by Major J.L. Moss, engages a Confederate force at Flint Hill and Hunter's Mill. Both sides sustain minimum casualties.

In Naval activity, a Union squadron composed of the USS *Conestoga*, *Lexington* and *Tyler* capture the uncompleted iron-clad steamer CSS *Eastport* on the Tennessee River at Cerro Gordo. The vessel was initially built in Indiana at New Albany during 1852 and acquired by the Confederacy in January 1862. Although the warship had not yet been completed, the Union also confiscates all of the material not yet applied to complete the armament at Cairo. The ship becomes the USS *Eastport* and is attached to the U.S. Army's Western Gunboat Flotilla.

February 7–9 BATTLE OF ROANOKE ISLAND Off North Carolina, the U.S. fleet prepares to seize Roanoke Island. At about 1000 on the 7th, a signal is given by Flag Ship Officer Louis M. Goldsborough: "This day our country expects every man to do his duty." As the message is hoisted for the fleet to see, the gunboats, arranged in three columns, led by the USS *Stars and Stripes*, *Louisiana* and *Hetzel*, proceed to the positions from which they will pummel the objectives, beginning with Fort Bartow, defended by nine guns, located off Pork Point. While these vessels prepare to initiate the bombardment, the transports are maneuvering to debark the ground forces at Ashby's Harbor.

By about 1100, Fort Barlow becomes the recipient of an incessant barrage until diverted by the Confederate naval force under W.F. Lynch. Once the Confederate vessels attempt to intercept the Union fleet, the Confederate ships become the center of attention, as a large portion of the guns of the Union gunboats begin to target Lynch's flotilla. The overmatched Rebel fleet is forced to pull back. Its largest ship, the CSS *Curlew*, receives such terrible damage that it is forced to beach on the mainland near Fort Forrest. Meanwhile, the USS *Hunchback* exchanges blows with the fort from close range and sustains severe damage; however, the *Hunchback* remains in service and its guns greatly contribute to the effort to reduce the fort. Once the Union gunboats dismiss Lynch's interference, all guns are again turned on Fort Bartow. By 1300, it is reduced to shattered wreckage, its flagstaff severed, its buildings afire and its guns silent.

In the meantime, at Ashby's Harbor, a force of about 2,000 Confederates is in place to engage the Union landing force, but prior to the landing, the Union gunboats commence firing and the defenders withdraw. Despite the lack of resistance, the landing is not a smooth operation due to other obstacles. The water is too shallow to permit most of the small boats to reach shore. Consequently, while the area is being blanketed with a dreary rainstorm, most of the troops are forced to abandon their boats and trek through more than 100 feet of thick mud, about knee-high, to reach shore. The troops continue to land throughout the day. By about 2300 at least 11,000 men are ashore.

At 0700 on the following day (8th) three rigid columns move out, advancing toward the Confederate entrenchments in the interior of the island between Fort Bartow and Shallowbag Bay, the latter on Roanoke Sound on the Atlantic Ocean side of the island. The brigades under Generals John J. Foster, Jesse Lee Reno and John G. Parke move forward trudging through terrible terrain, primarily through swampland. All the while, the Confederates dispatch troops to intercept the Union, but they encounter identical elements. To add complications, while the troops establish a night perimeter, a rainstorm saturates the land and the troops, guaranteeing an uncomfortable and nearly sleepless night.

During the early morning hours of the ninth, the Union reinitiates the advance, and within a short while the two sides clash. Once contact is made, the Union guns of Midshipman B.F. Porter commence firing in support of the charging 23rd and 25th Massachusetts, both of which begin to sustain casualties under the ringing fire of Rebel sharpshooters, who from their concealed positions remain unscathed. At about the same time, troops of the 24th Massachusetts Regiment bolt forward and drive the Confederates from their entrenchments in the thick woods.

In the meantime, the Second and Third Brigades under Generals Jessie Reno and John G. Parke, respectively, are moving up from the rear to bolster General Foster's assault. To inject further power into the attack, the 10th Connecticut and the 26th Massachusetts Regiments quickly move to the front and come under severe fire from the determined Rebels, who refuse to budge from their earthworks. Equally undaunted, the Union presses ahead as the Second Brigade under Reno advances to the right of Foster's lines and immediately barges into Wise's Legion, igniting a heated skirmish that draws casualties from both antagonists; however, the Union eventually plunges forward and drives the defenders back, with their commander, Captain O. Jennings Wise, himself sustaining a wound.

The artillery of each side continues to pound

the opponent, causing more confusion on the field as each attempts to hammer the other into extinction. Ammunition supplies first become scarce and then are fully expended. Major E.A. Kimball of Colonel Hawkins' New York Zouaves Volunteers to lead a charge with bayonets drawn. The Union bugler sounds cease fire, and in a flash the signal to charge is given. The New York Zouaves (9th New York), positioned in the center, sprint forward yelling "Zou Zou Zou...," the peculiar battle cry itself sending unwelcome signals to the defenders. The Zouaves, trailed closely by the 10th Connecticut, are also flanked by Parke's Third Brigade facing the Confederates' right and Reno's Second Brigade moving toward the Rebels' left. With the unfolding momentum of the charging streams of blue uniforms pounding against the Confederate positions from both sides, the Rebels find their positions untenable and break for safer positions to escape the onslaught.

Union troops climb the parapets of a three-gun battery and discover that the defenders had so hurriedly departed that the guns had not been spiked. All the while other Union troops are spreading across the island. At the parapet, troops of the 21st Massachusetts and the 51st New York, the first to reach the position, unfurl Old Glory. Spontaneously, the jubilant troops raise a hearty cheer and contribute some enthusiastic clapping to celebrate this, their first victory. They then pursue the Rebels, who are racing toward the river to escape to Nag's Head across Roanoke Sound. To the north, General Foster encounters troops under Colonel Shaw, accompanied by a white flag of truce, to request terms. Foster without hesitation responds: "Unconditional;" more than 2,000 troops capitulate here.

In General Reno's sector, the troops under Colonel Jordan also surrender. Still remaining for the Union is one last obstacle. The badgered Fort Bartow had been re-occupied by some hard-line defenders and troops resume firing against the fleet. In a short while, Union troops move into the fort and silence the guns. Shortly thereafter, a signal is sent to the fleet: "The fort is ours!" The U.S. Marines, attached to the fleet, participate in the fight to seize the objective. The Union troops capture more than 2,500 Confederate soldiers. Fort Bartow is renamed Fort Foster. Fort Blanchard and Fort Huger in the northern part of the island are renamed Forts Parke and Reno respectively. Many of the prisoners are placed in makeshift stockades to the rear of Fort Reno (Fort Huger). The victory becomes a dangerous dagger in the heart of the South's domination of North Carolina by providing the Union with an anchor hold, while it also jeopardizes the Confederate supply line by severing Norfolk's supply line.

Other units that participate in the action in the battle for Roanoke Island are the 1st Regiment New York Zouaves, 21st, 23rd, 24th, 25th and 27th Massachusetts, the 10th Connecticut, the 9th, 51st, and 53rd New York, the 9th New Jersey, the 51st Pennsylvania, and the 4th and 5th Rhode Island. The Union suffers 35 dead and 200 wounded; the Union fleet sustains a

loss of six killed and 19 wounded. The Confederates sustain 16 dead, 39 wounded, and 2,527 captured. The Union forces are under the command of General Ambrose C. Burnside (West Point, 1847). Colonel Charles S. Russell (10th Connecticut) and Lt. Colonel Vigier de Monteuil (9th New York) are among the Union losses. Confederate Commander General Henry A. Wise is able to escape by boat to Nag's Head. His son, Captain O. Jennings Wise, wounded four times during the siege, is captured, but his wounds are mortal and he succumbs. Also, the Confederate fleet under Lt. W.F. Lynch moves up Albemarle Sound to Elizabeth City; prior to departing the Rebels set fire to the barracks at Red Point and they also torch the vessel CSS *Curlew*, which had earlier been damaged by naval fire. On the following day, Union gunboats will move to engage the Confederate flotilla. Participating Union vessels are the *Commodore Barney, Henry Brinker, Ceres, Chasseur, Delaware, Granite, Hetzel, Hunchback, Hussar, Lockwood, Louisiana, Morse, Commodore Perry, Picket, Pioneer, Putnam, I.N. Seymour, Shawseen, Southfield, Stars and Stripes, Underwriter, Valley City, Vidette* and *Whitehead*. The *Southfield* remains in the region through April and participates in the operations against New Bern (March 1862) and Beaufort (April) in North Carolina. Afterward, it moves to Virginia and operates along the James and York Rivers until the latter part of this year, before being ordered to return to the vicinity of North Carolina, where it participates in the attacks against Plymouth. The *Commodore Barney* later participates in the capture of New Bern (13–14 March) and afterward patrols various rivers in Virginia.

February 8 (Saturday)   In Virginia, a contingent of the 5th West Virginia Regiment skirmishes with a Confederate unit at Linn Creek. The Union sustains one killed and one wounded. The Confederates sustain eight killed and seven wounded.

In West Virginia, a contingent of the Confederate 45th Virginia Regiment, commanded by Lt. Colonel William E. Peters, skirmishes with a Union force at the Bluestone.

In Union general officer activity, Brigadier General Charles P. Stone, discredited due to the defeat at Ball's Bluff and a target of radicals in Congress, is arrested. Despite no charges at this time or in the future, he is jailed initially at Fort Lafayette and afterward at Fort Hamilton until 6 August; he receives neither an apology nor an explanation. Afterward, he remains without a command until the following year, when he is assigned to the Department of the Gulf. General Banks had requested that Stone be attached to his command.

In Naval activity, Union forces capture two Confederate ships, the *Muscle* and the *Sallie Wood*, off Chickasaw, Mississippi. While moving back downstream with the prizes, the *Muscle* sinks. The *Sallie Wood* (sometimes wrongly called *Sallie Ward*, however, makes the trip. It is taken into service with the U.S. Navy as a transport and as an ammunition ship, but is also at times used as a tugboat. Also, Union gunboats encroach Florence, Alabama. The Confederates there destroy the CSS *Sam Kirkman*, thought to be a cargo ship, to prevent its capture. The *Sam Kirkman* had been built in Paducah, Kentucky, during 1859.

February 9 (Sunday) **In Missouri,** a contingent of Union Cavalry commanded by Lt. Colonel Thomas C. Wright skirmishes with Confederates at Marshfield. The Union reports no casualties. The Confederates sustain slight casualties. Another clash occurs at Marshfield on 14 February.

In North Carolina, Union troops under General Ambrose Burnside are bivouacked around a farmhouse that General Burnside has chosen as his headquarters at Roanoke Island.

February 10 (Monday) **In *Naval activity,*** a U.S. fleet consisting of more than ten vessels, including the USS *Valley City, Hetzel, Morse, Commodore Perry* and the *Shaween,* departs Roanoke Island in pursuit of a small Confederate naval force (the Mosquito Fleet), reported to be in the vicinity of Croatan Sound in North Carolina. The Union fleet, once in range of the force at Elizabeth City, bombards Rebel fortifications, including a battery of four guns, and simultaneously engages the Confederate ships under Lt. William F. Lynch, which had earlier departed Roanoke Island during the Union assault. The contest that rages on the Pasquotank River lasts only about forty-five minutes, as it becomes obvious to the Rebels that their firepower is not sufficient to vanquish the Union fleet. Confederate Lt. Lynch directs the various crewmen to head their vessels toward shore and once there to set them afire to prevent them from falling into the hands of the Union. The CSS *Appomattox* (formerly the *Empire*), commanded by Lt. C.C. Simms, attempts to escape through the Dismal Swamp Canal, but its beam is too high, which prevents it from entering. The vessel is set on fire and explodes. The *Ellis* fails to be totally destroyed. It is salvaged by the Union and placed into the federal fleet. Lt. C.L. Franklin receives command of the USS *Ellis.* The Union loses two killed and six wounded during the battle.

Aboard the USS *Valley City* circumstances could have been devastating except for the courageous actions of one gunner, John Davis. The vessel becomes seriously damaged, but it is also susceptible to a fatal blow when fire spins out of control and heads toward open barrels of gunpowder. Davis plunges himself upon the barrel to protect it from explosion until others can extinguish the flames. Davis receives the Medal of Honor for his heroism under fire and in an extra show of appreciation, the secretary of the Navy promotes him to acting gunner and increases his yearly salary from $300.00 to $1,000.00. Union troops occupy Fort Cobb and Elizabeth City, the latter having been unsuccessfully set afire by the Rebels. Marine detachments of all vessels participate in the occupation of the Confederate held forts.

In South Carolina, a Union contingent (50th Pennsylvania Infantry Regiment) commanded by Captain Gordon Z. Dimock and Lt. Foot encounter and skirmish with Confederate pickets at Barnwell Island. No casualties are reported.

In Confederate general officer activity, Colonel James Patton Anderson is promoted to brigadier general.

February 11 (Tuesday) **In Kentucky,** the Confederates abandon Bowling Green. A division commanded by Union General Ormsby M. Mitchel, attached to the forces of General Don C. Buell, departs its positions at Bacon Creek in the vicinity of Munfordville and moves toward Bowling Green, arriving there on the 15th.

General Ormsby MacKnight Mitchel (Mottelay, *The Soldier in Our Civil War,* 1886).

In South Carolina, the 47th New York Infantry, commanded by Colonel H. Moore, secures Edisto Island. It will be occupied in force during April.

In Tennessee at Fort Henry, General Grant meets with his staff and it is decided that an attack will immediately be made to secure Fort Donelson, rather than delaying to await reinforcements. During the afternoon, contingents of General McClernand's Division depart, heading for the objective; however, the main body does not leave until the following day. Meanwhile, General Ulysses S. Grant is planning to commit a third division that will be brought to the area by Flag Officer Foote upon his return from Cairo. This Third Division is to be commanded by General Lew Wallace.

In Texas, Union operations commence in the vicinity of Aransas Pass and continue until the 13th.

In Naval activity, Union vessels commanded by Lt. A. Maury, upon orders from Commander Stephen C. Rowan, U.S. Navy, move to Edenton, North Carolina. In addition, the Union troops demolish one schooner and eight guns and seize two other schooners, each carrying a cargo of corn.

February 12 (Wednesday) **In Missouri,** Union troops under General S.R. Curtis are closing against Springfield, headquarters of Confederate Major General Sterling Price, who had thought his fortifications secure. Recent skirmishes had prompted Price to have a change of heart. Curtis' force, comprising the troops under Generals Franz Sigel and Alexander Sanborn Asboth and Colonels (later generals) Jefferson C. Davis and Eugene A. Carr, have been together since the latter part of the previous December. During the beginning of February these divisions had departed Rolla, where the railroad from St. Louis leading to Springfield ends. This day following dusk, Price's 4,000 troops abandon the city. The Union occupies the city on the following day.

In North Carolina, a Union naval force arrives at Edenton and it is seized.

In Tennessee, General U.S. Grant departs Fort Henry with approximately 15,000 men, reaching positions near Confederate-held Fort Donelson at noon. Union Generals Charles Smith and John A. McClernand flank Grant during the march. Union warships move up the Cumberland River to assist in the siege. The USS *Carondelet* and the steamer USS *Alps* arrive on the 13th, to be joined by the USS *St Louis, Louisville, Pittsburg, Tyler* and the *Ticonderoga.* Although the ground troops encounter no opposition en route, during the afternoon there are some small skirmishes with Confederate pick-

Major General Howell Cobb (Johnson, *Campfire and Battlefield: History of the Conflicts and Campaigns,* 1894).

ets, but they soon are pushed back. Fort Donelson is heavily defended by about 15,000 troops under General John B. Floyd, who succeeds General A.S. Johnston this day. The garrison includes the 3rd Tennessee and the 3rd, 10th, 18th, 26th, 30th, 32nd 41st, 42nd, 48th, 49th,

General Ulysses S. Grant (Mottelay, *The Soldier in Our Civil War*, 1886).

Rear Admiral Andrew Foote (Mottelay, *The Soldier in Our Civil War*, 1886).

50th, 51st, and 56th Virginia Regiments. In addition, it includes the 2nd and 8th Kentucky, the 7th Texas, 15th Arkansas, and the 27th Alabama Regiments. Two other contingents, Colin's and Gowan's infantry battalions, are also at Donelson, as well as Gantt's and Milton's cavalry battalions. About 700 artillerymen support the infantry and cavalry.

In Confederate general officer activity, George Wythe Randolph, a grandson of Thomas Jefferson, is appointed to the rank of brigadier general in the Confederate Army. Apparently convinced his position in the Confederate Cabinet is not being used to his ability, he resigns from the cabinet during November of this year. Subsequently, Randolph discovers that he has tuberculosis. He retains his commission until December of 1864. Randolph had established the Richmond Howitzers and had served in Virginia under General John B. Magruder during the early part of the conflict. Also, Howell Cobb (secretary of the treasury under President James Buchanan) is appointed brigadier general.

February 13 (Thursday) SIEGE OF FORT DONELSON Fort Donelson, reinforced by the Confederates who had safely escaped the Union net at Fort Henry, and by some others who have arrived from Bowling Green, Kentucky, with General Bolivar Buckner, brace for the Union assault force of 15,000, currently surrounding the outer works of the fort, which, similarly to Fort Henry, had been constructed only recently during summer of 1861. Fort Donelson, on the west bank of the Cumberland River, stands as a protector to the rear of Bowling Green, Kentucky, and as a deterrent to any Union troops heading for Nashville, Tennessee.

The massive Union line, having the guns of Major Cavender positioned directly opposite the Rebel lines, with Oglesby's brigade and McClernand's force holding the right and left respectively and McClernand's division propped in the center, extends for a distance of about four miles. While the Union is forming in place, the 66th Illinois Regiment is heavily involved with Confederates, pouring a steady stream of fire into a battery to keep it inactive or at least ineffective. More action follows, as at about noon, an attack is launched against the middle redoubt by the 17th Illinois (Major Smith), 48th Illinois (Colonel Haynie) and the 49th Illinois (Colonel Morrison), supported by McAllister's battery. The regiments progress for awhile and ascend the hill, but the Confederates, including the complete line of infantry and the guns,

commence firing and lay down an impenetrable wall of steel that jolts the attackers and forces them to drop back momentarily to regroup.

Meanwhile, the 45th Illinois hits the front in support, and it too joins the dogged advance under the cover fire of the batteries of Schwartz and Taylor. But the Rebels are immovable. Repeatedly the Union drives forward only to be thrown back, sustaining heavy casualties as they pound against the line for one hour of hellish combat. To the left, more tenacious fighting is occurring. The 25th Indiana and the 14th Iowa Regiments, while holding the 7th Iowa and the 66th Illinois in reserve, drive against another battery. The Confederate fire inflicts severe casualties, but the Yankees persevere, gaining yards at a time, finally securing more tenable positions. After dusk, the Rebel guns again pound the Union lines. Orders arrive directing them to return to their starting point.

In the meantime, the USS *Carondelet* arrives from Fort Henry and bombards enemy positions until return fire strikes the vessel and causes a massive explosion in the boiler room, rendering the vessel out of action. No crew members sustain injuries. While both sides begin settling in for the night, the artillery maintains activity, with the opponents blasting each other. More reinforcements arrive to aid the Union cause at about midnight. Flag Officer Andrew Foote's flotilla moves in position at about midnight (16th–17th) and debarks the Third Division. While the six gunboats shadow the transports, about 10,000 troops debark several miles below the objective. The force is composed of two brigades; one is under Colonel Charles Cruft, comprising the 31st Indiana (Colonel Osborn), 44th Indiana (Colonel Reed), 17th Kentucky (Colonel Jno. H. McHenry), and the 25th Kentucky (Colonel James Murrell Shackelford). The Second Brigade, commanded by Colonel John M. Thayer, is composed of the 1st Nebraska (Colonel William D. McCord), 58th Ohio (Colo-

The Union attack against Fort Donelson, Tennessee (Mottelay, *The Soldier in Our Civil War*, 1886).

nel James Blair Steedman or Steadman) and the 76th Ohio (Colonel C.R. Woods) Regiments. Later, Thayer will also receive the 46th (Colonel John A. Davis), 57th (Colonel William H. Baldwin) and 58th (Colonel William F. Lynch) Illinois Regiments. And the forces swell even more on the following day when General Wallace arrives to take command of his division: the 11th Indiana, the 8th Missouri Regiment and the Chicago Battery. Colonel Thomas Sweeny (52nd Illinois) is wounded.

In Washington, D.C., Congress authorizes construction of 21 Union iron-clad gunboats.

In Missouri, while Union forces had been seizing Forts Henry and Donelson in Tennessee, another army under General Samuel R. Curtis occupies Springfield, Missouri, evacuated by the Confederates during the previous night. Curtis immediately sets out to intercept and engage Confederate General Sterling Price's troops who are heading for Arkansas.

In Confederate general officer activity, Colonel James R. Chalmers, 8th Mississippi Infantry, is appointed brigadier general. The following month, he will participate with his regiment as part of Wither's command at Shiloh. General Jones M. Withers (West Point, 1835) will become a major general as a result of his actions at Shiloh. Colonel Joseph B. Kershaw, 2nd South Carolina, is promoted to the rank of brigadier general and will serve in the Army of Northern Virginia for the duration.

In Naval activity, Union vessels under the command of Lt. Jeffers move to destroy the Albemarle and Chesapeake Canal (North Carolina), but upon their arrival, they discover that the Confederates have already begun their task and are in the process of knocking the canal out of operation. The Rebels depart when the Union arrives, permitting the Union without incident to destroy two vessels that are in the river. In other activity, the USS *Arthur,* while operating in the vicinity of Aransas, Texas, exchanges fire with a contingent of Confederate cavalry.

Canal locks and boats are destroyed (Mottelay, *The Soldier in Our Civil War,* 1886).

February 14 (Friday)   In Washington, D.C., Congress authorizes the deletion of all persons bearing arms against the United States from the pension rolls, thus denying future payments to individuals so described.

In Kentucky, the 49th Indiana Volunteer Regiment and the 6th Kentucky Cavalry engage Confederates at Flat Lick Ford. The Confederates sustain four killed and four wounded.

In Missouri, a contingent of Union Cavalry attached to General S.R. Curtis' command skirmishes with Confederates of General Sterling Price at Crane Creek. No casualties are reported. Contingents of the 6th Missouri and the 3rd Illinois Cavalry, commanded by Captain Montgomery, attack a Confederate force at Marshfield. The Confederates sustain two killed, three wounded and several captured.

In Tennessee, a Union contingent composed of the 1st Battalion, Kentucky Cavalry, commanded by Lt. Colonel Munday, engages Confederates at Cumberland Gap. The Union reports no casualties. The estimated Confederate casualties stand at about five killed, two wounded and two captured. At about this time, General Ulysses S. Grant is assigned command of the District of West Tennessee.

In West Virginia, a Union force commanded by General Frederick Lander attacks and defeats a Confederate force at Bloomery Gap (Blooming Gap). The 8th Ohio, 7th West Virginia and the 1st West Virginia Cavalry participate. The 67th Virginia Volunteers and the Company A, 89th Virginia Volunteers also participate. The Union sustains two killed and five wounded. The Confederates suffer 13 killed and some captured. General Lander, subsequent to the victory, requests that he be relieved due to ill health. Nevertheless, no replacement arrives and he succumbs at Camp Chase, Paw Paw, Virginia, in early March.

In Naval activity, the USS *E.B. Hale* and the *Western World,* while on patrol on the Mud and Wright's Rivers, intercept and capture four Confederate vessels as they attempt to break through the blockade. The blockaders working in the area also thin out other Confederate activity on the Savannah River and afford security for a recently established Union battery at Venus Point. The *Western World* returns to Port Royal on 2 June.

February 14–16 THE BATTLE OF FORT DONELSON The Union for the past several days has been laying siege upon the Confederate held fort in Tennessee, and in return, the resistance has been resolute. With the arrival of reinforcements from Cairo and the return of the gun-

boats, General U.S. Grant had scheduled a massive offensive this day to crack the resistance and seize the objective; however, the belated arrival on the previous night of the Third Division, which had been compelled to march by a circuitous route to avoid the Rebel fortifications, mandates a postponement of the three-division attack and causes the fleet to proceed, lacking infantry and cavalry support. Nonetheless, artillery and Union sharpshooters lend aid as the gunboats break the day's silence during the afternoon at about 1500, sending "iron Valentines" toward the Confederate positions. The initial burst, fired by the USS *Carondelet,* bombards the batteries on the water, established to guard the passageway.

The USS *St. Louis, Louisville,* and *Pittsburg* will soon add their guns, and they will be further supported by the wooden gunboats *Conestoga, Lexington* and *Tyler.* Meanwhile, the Rebels, manning the battery, concentrate their fire on the advancing fleet, particularly the ironclads, but Foote withholds his fire until reaching a point only several hundred yards from the batteries. In unison the fleet's heavy guns pummel the shore batteries. The exchange intensifies, turning into a ferocious contest. One battery in an elevated position receives a devastating barrage, forcing its occupants to abandon it, and at about this time, Foote decides to break past the lines. In a flash, plans change. He spots the USS *Louisville* drifting near-dead in the water, and soon his flagship, the *St. Louis,* is nearly knocked out of action when its wheelhouse is struck by a shell that causes the death of the pilot and cripples the ship. After about one and one-half hours of incessant battle, the *Carondelet* and the *Pittsburg* retire, following the *St. Louis* and *Louisville,* which had already been compelled to withdraw. In short order the wooden gunboats also disengage and leave the area, terminating the river-to-shore battle, to the rousing cheers of the Rebels.

The enthusiasm is temporary. Union reinforcements pour into Lick Creek, tightening the stranglehold on the fort. The Rebels make a desperate attempt to break out, with some success, but communications become confused. The Confederates are erroneously ordered back to their fortifications. Grant seizes the opportunity, ordering an immediate counterattack, sealing the fate of the fort. At about 1700, Confederate General Floyd, convinced that the fort cannot withstand the Union siege without massive reinforcements, convenes a meeting with his staff and unanimously, they conclude that the best option other than absolute capitulation is to mount an offensive to break through the Union lines.

On the following morning (Saturday, the 15th) at 0500, about 10,000 troops led by Generals Gideon J. Pillow and Bushrod R. Johnson move out to punch a hole in the line and escape. The Rebels drive into McClernand's division, but they have advanced with little noise, giving them the advantage of surprise. The Union pickets are easily shoved back to camp, but here, too, there is great amazement at the boldness of the advance. McClernand's lines falter under the pressure, but Oglesby's brigade firmly holds its positions along the road, repelling the first attack and repulsing a cavalry charge against its right side.

Nonetheless, the Confederates continue to pour forward, while the Union lines fire round after round to stem the tide. The effort works well until all their ammunition is expended, forcing the brigade to retreat, with only the 31st Illinois, on the far left, still holding its ground. Its commander, Colonel John A. Logan, refuses to budge; his troops pump out a firestorm of shells that hammer the Confederates to their front, breaking their stride to halt the gushing horde of attackers. In the meantime, reinforcements speed to the shattered line, the first to arrive being the 11th and 20th Illinois Regiments, attached to Wallace's division, and they are closely trailed by about 3,500 additional troops also of Wallace's force.

The opposing sides continue to plaster each other, volley after volley, each tearing the opponent's line into bloodied earth. Continuing without pause, the Union and Confederates each gain a few yards, then relinquish them again. The see-saw struggle takes an exhausting toll on both sides, but still, at 2000, the clashing swords, piercing bayonets, rapid rifle fire and hurling cannon shots accomplish only stalemate, with neither victor nor vanquished. General McClernand remains concerned that the seemingly unending stream of advancing Confederates might still fold his beleaguered troops, to a man, on the brink of total exhaustion. He dispatches an urgent request to Wallace requesting immediate aid, but Wallace, under strict orders to hold the center at "all hazards," first requests permission from headquarters to redeploy some of his force to bolster McClernand.

In the meantime, McClernand apprehensively awaits the reinforcements; his flank is being turned by the Rebels. Another more urgent dispatch is sent explaining the deteriorating situation and again requesting immediate help. Wallace, unable to communicate with General Grant, who is offshore meeting with Flag Officer Andrew Foote, directs Colonel Charles Cruft to race to McClernand's support. En route, his command is sent too far to the right. Instead of encountering McClernand's troops, he is met by a contingent of Confederates who had just bolted from a ravine to the rear of Oglesby's line.

The rapidly advancing juggernaut plows into Cruft's brigade, driving it to the rear, and soon after, other troops under Wallace, McArthur and Oglesby also are pressed back. At about this time, General Wallace arrives with Colonel Thayer's brigade. It acts as a wedge and positions itself between the retiring Yankees and the moving tide of Rebels. In quick-time, some light artillery is dragged into position from which it can rivet the path of approach. Soon after, a wave of gray uniforms bashes into the 1st Nebraska Regiment, but the Nebraskans hold like a granite wall and then initiate a counterattack that pushes the Rebels back.

Meanwhile, General Grant orders a major offensive to vanquish the Rebels as they retire. The 8th Missouri and 11th Indiana lead the pack, with two Ohio Regiments close behind, held as reserve. In concert, one brigade under Cruft advances to strike the left flank, while another under Colonel Smith attacks the Confederates' right flank. Cruft's Brigade, earlier forced to pull back, now moves around the base of a hill to launch its assault. Cruft's force encounters brutal opposition, but it gains ground on the ridge and holds it throughout the night, while on the right, Smith plows against the Confederates with a stream of regiments. They advance in a thunderous charge led by the 2nd and 7th Iowa and the 25th Indiana and supported by the umbrella of Colonel Stone's Missouri battery, which launches a stunning barrage that sails into the Rebel lines with a ferocious roar. Other troops, including the 14th Iowa, the 56th Indiana and Berge's Sharpshooters, plow forward, encountering vicious and unyielding fire from the Confederate positions, but the Union troops disregard the devastating fire and continue the advance, all the while holding their fire until within close range, at which point their bayonets are drawn. With a sprint they lunge into the Rebel ranks, seizing the ground with steel. However, with darkness settling in over the bloodied field, the fighting subsides. Smith's Brigade holds in place for the night.

With the sounds of battle done, the Union prepares to reinitiate the attack in the morning. Meanwhile, the Confederates, Generals Floyd and Pillow, meet with the staff officers. After an extremely argumentative session, they decide to forego further fighting. Prior to dawn, Generals Floyd and Pillow escape to Nashville and Columbia, Tennessee, respectively, but they leave General Simon B. Buckner (West Point, 1844) the task of facing the Union. Adam Rankin Johnson, who has been a scout for General Floyd, accompanies him when he departs. Johnson, later known also as "Stovepipe" Johnson, is promoted to colonel in August.

A contingent of 700 cavalrymen, under Nathan B. Forrest, break away on the 16th by crossing Lick Creek without being caught. Just as the Union is ready to signal the attack on Sunday morning, the men notice that the Confederate colors have been replaced by white flags. General Buckner dispatches Major George B. Cosby to General Grant requesting surrender terms. Grant's response, carried back by Cosby: "No terms except unconditional and immediate surrender can be expected. I propose to move immediately upon your works." Buckner responds: "The distribution of the forces under my command, incident to an unexpected change of commanders, and the overwhelming force under your command, compel me, notwithstanding the brilliant success of the confederate arms yesterday, to accept the ungenerous and unchivalrous terms which you propose." This victory gives the Union control of the Cumberland River around Nashville. Once word of the victory reaches Washington, General Grant becomes the recipient of great praise for the accomplishment. On 17 February, he is promoted to the rank of major general.

The Union captures about 47 pieces of artillery and between 2,000 and 4,000 horses. The Confederates suffer approximately 231 killed, 1,007 wounded, and 13,829 captured. The Union sustains 446 dead, 735 wounded and 150 missing. Colonel Thomas E. Ransom, 11th Illinois, earlier wounded in Missouri at Charleston, is again wounded. The Confederate 36th Virginia Infantry led by Colonel John McCausland evades capture and makes it to Nashville, Tennessee. The 36th then moves to Chattanooga, Tennessee, until it moves back into Virginia, where it serves under General William Loring, John Echols and Samuel Jones, the latter assuming command of the Department of West Virginia in December 1862. Officer Norton P. Chipman is wounded twice during a bayonet charge. Chipman refuses to leave the field. He is afterward promoted to colonel, assigned to General Halleck's command and participates at Corinth prior to becoming chief of staff to General Samuel Curtis in Arkansas.

Confederate Colonels John Calvin Brown, 3rd Tennessee, William Edwin Baldwin, 14th Mississippi Infantry, John Gregg, 7th Texas Infantry, and Lt. Colonel Hiram B. Granbury, 7th Texas Infantry, are captured at Donelson. All three are exchanged; shortly thereafter, Baldwin, John C. Brown and John Gregg are promoted to the rank of brigadier general. Lt. Colonel Granbury rises to the rank of colonel. Confederate Colonel Roger W. Hanson, 2nd Kentucky Infantry, is captured; he too is later released and promoted to brigadier general. Colonel (later brigadier general) Joseph Benjamin Palmer, 18th Tennessee, is captured, but he will be released and later fight at Murfreesboro. Confederate Brigadier General Bushrod R. Johnson (West Point, 1840) is among the captured, but he escapes.

Confederate Colonel (later brigadier general) Gabriel C. Wharton, 51st Virginia Regiment, escapes. Wharton, later as a brigade commander, participates against the Union troops of General David Hunter as they retreat toward Harpers Ferry after the battle of New Market during May 1864. Confederate Lt. Colonel (later brigadier general) Hylan B. Lyon, 8th Kentucky Infantry, is among the captured; he is later exchanged (autumn 1864) and will serve in the division commanded by Brigadier General Tilghman (Army of West Tennessee). The Union troops under General Grant had certainly bottled up a sufficient number of high ranking Confederates at Donelson, but the exchange allows these officers to regain positions of leadership against the Union. Colonel William A. Quarles, 42nd Tennessee, had been captured. After his exchange, he becomes a brigadier general in July 1863 and participates as part of General Joseph E. Johnston's command until he is wounded at Franklin, Tennessee, and again captured.

Mid-February Confederate General Sterling Price leads his Missouri State Guard into Arkansas, where he joins Confederate Brigadier General Ben McCulloch. This combined force is then attached to Confederate Major General Earl Van Dorn, who begins his campaign with 16,000 men to capture St. Louis, Missouri, for the Confederacy.

February 15 (Saturday)   In Georgia, a small detachment of the 3rd Rhode Island Regiment, commanded by Captain Gould, encounters and skirmishes with Confederate gunboats in the vicinity of Venus Point. The exchange lasts about one hour. No casualty reports are available.

In Kentucky, Union General Ormsby M. Mitchel arrives at Bowling Green from Camp Madison. Mitchel's Division, following its departure from Camp Madison on the 13th, marches the final 42 miles in about 32 hours. His force occupies the city without incident, as the Confederates under General Simon Bolivar Buckner had evacuated subsequent to setting the town afire, causing about $500,000 in property damages. The two bridges that span the Barren River are also destroyed.

In Missouri, a Union detachment attached to General Samuel R. Curtis' command skirmishes with a Confederate contingent at Flat Creek. Casualty reports are unavailable.

February 16 (Sunday)   In Arkansas, a Union force — Wright's Battalion, Mississippi Cavalry, the 3rd Illinois Cavalry, the 1st Missouri Cavalry a contingent of artillery (Major Bowen's battery), commanded by Lt. Colonel Thomas C. Wright — engages a Confederate force at Pott's Hill. The Union sustains one killed. The estimated Confederate casualties are three wounded. Also, General S. R. Curtis's force, in pursuit of Confederate General Price, moves into Arkansas and begins to close the gap between them. A clash occurs on the following day at Sugar Creek.

In New Mexico, Confederates under General Henry H. Sibley arrive from Texas in the area near Fort Craig. The Rebels move to within one mile of the fort but then reverse back into the Val Verde (Green Valley). Union forces under General Canby later move out of the fort to engage the Confederates. A confrontation occurs on 21 February.

In Tennessee at Fort Donelson, captured this day by naval forces and ground troops under Flag Officer Andrew Foote and General Grant respectively, steps are taken to further pound the Confederates. Foote, during the evening, orders the vessel *St. Louis* to venture up the Tennessee River and bombard the Tennessee Iron Works, located about seven miles above Dover. The *St. Louis* sustained severe damages during the operation to reduce Fort Donelson; however it remains operable. The *St. Louis*, initially built as a 512-ton Cairo class ironclad for the Union Army's Western Gunboat Flotilla, was commissioned the previous January. Following service at Fort Pillow, Island No. 10 and Memphis, the vessel is transferred to the Navy and renamed the USS *Baron Dekalb* in September. (See also, **February 14–16 THE BATTLE OF FORT DONELSON.**)

February 17 (Monday)   In Arkansas, the 1st and 6th Missouri Regiments and the 3rd Illinois Cavalry engage Confederates at Sugar Creek. The Union sustains five killed and nine wounded. Confederate casualties, if any, are unavailable.

In Naval activity, Flag Officer Andrew Foote, still suffering badly from a wound sustained at the battle to seize Fort Donelson at Dover, Tennessee, leaves Cairo, Illinois, on a cruise up the Cumberland River with two gunboats, the USS *Cairo* and the *Conestoga*, to strike two Confederate-held forts located about fifty miles northwest of Nashville near Clarksville, Tennessee.

February 18 1862 (Tuesday)   In Arkansas, a contingent composed of Hussars (Benton's and Frémont's) and Captain Ebert's Artillery Battery, commanded by Brigadier General Alexander S. Asboth, encounters a Confederate force commanded by Colonel Rector in the vicinity of Bentonville. The Union lists no casualties. The Confederates sustain some wounded and lose more than 30 stands of arms.

In Missouri, the 2nd Ohio Cavalry engages Confederates at Independence. The Union sustains one killed and three wounded. The Confederates suffer four killed and five wounded. Also, a Union contingent of the 3rd Iowa Cavalry, commanded by Captain Mudgett, initiates a two-day reconnaissance mission in the vicinity of Mount Vernon. The operation lists no casualties; however, several Confederates are captured. A separate contingent of the 3rd Iowa Cavalry and the 6th Missouri Cavalry, commanded by Lt. Colonel Wood, clash with Confederates in the vicinity of West Plains. The Union reports no casualties. The estimated Confederate casualties are several killed and wounded and some captured.

In North Carolina, the USS *Hunchback* in support of army operations debarks troops along the Chowan River.

In Virginia at Richmond, following the termination of the Confederate Provisional Congress on the previous day, the First Congress of the Confederate States of America holds its initial session.

In Union general officer activity, Stephen Thomas, born during 1809, prior to the War of 1812, is commissioned colonel of the 8th Vermont Regiment. The regiment is specifically recruited to participate in General Benjamin Butler's expedition against New Orleans. Later, he is involved with the protection of the Opelousas Railroad. In 1863, he commands a brigade during the operations against Port Hudson, Louisiana. Afterward, he participates at Sabine Pass, Texas. During July 1864, Thomas and his regiment are ordered to move to Fort Monroe, Virginia.

February 19 (Wednesday)   In Naval activity, Union vessels of the Atlantic Squadron and their respective Marine Corps attachments depart Edenton, North Carolina to transport a Union force up the Chowan River to seize Winston, North Carolina. The extended trip causes the actual assault to occur on the following day. Another U.S. flotilla moves to Plymouth, North Carolina, on the Albemarle Sound, and upon approaching shore, Confederate fire originating on the bank greets them. Upon orders from Commander Stephen Rowan, the vessels return fire, which devastates the town.

In other activity, the USS *Brooklyn* and the USS *South Carolina* seize the blockade runner *Magnolia*. The prize is taken into the U.S. Navy on 22 July at New York. It undergoes major repairs and serves out the duration of the war. On 12 July 1865, it is sold at auction. The USS *Magnolia* is separate from the CSS *Magnolia*, a New Orleans sidewheeler (built in New Albany, Indiana, during 1859) which served the Confederate Navy as a transport in the western rivers until destroyed near Yazoo City in spring 1863.

In Tennessee, two Union gunboats commanded by Flag Officer Andrew H. Foote arrive at Clarksville and prepare to bombard the two Confederate-held forts that stand guard over the city. Foote discovers that both forts had been abandoned by the Confederates; his forces enter Clarksville on the following day. Prior to their departure, the Rebels burn the railway bridge that spans the Cumberland River.

In Missouri, elements of a Union force attached to General S.R. Curtis skirmish with Confederates under General Sterling Price at West Plains. The Union breaks the Confederate stand and Price reinitiates his movement heading for Fayetteville, Arkansas.

Confederate prisoners after the capture of Fort Donelson (Mottelay, *The Soldier in Our Civil War,* 1886).

February 20 (Thursday) In Washington, D.C., personal tragedy strikes President and Mrs. Lincoln. Their son Willie, ill from typhoid fever, succumbs this day at age 12. General William T. Sherman also has a young son named Willie, and during the following year at age 11, he dies from yellow fever.

In Georgia, Union Colonel Quincy A. Gillmore (West Point, 1849) assumes command of Tybee Island. He orders the construction of eleven bombproof batteries at a section of the island known as Goat Point. The selected area is within range of the guns at Fort Pulaski, mandating that the construction be undertaken only during the dark hours. It will take about six weeks to complete the project (April 9th), with the bulk of the toil being done by the 45th New York Regiment (Colonel Ross), 7th Connecticut (Colonel Alfred H. Terry) and a contingent of engineers commanded by Lt. Colonel James F. Hall.

In Tennessee, troops under Flag Officer Andrew Foote occupy Clarksville. Soon a formidable Union force led by General Charles F. Smith arrives and holds it. Foote will then return to Cairo, Illinois, to lay plans for an attack against Nashville, Tennessee.

In Naval activity, following an eighteen day voyage, Captain David Farragut arrives at Ship Island off Mississippi from Hampton Roads, Virginia. From here Farragut will continue his mission, heading for the Gulf of Mexico, from where he will attack New Orleans in coordination with General Butler's forces.

In Confederate activity, Brigadier General Louis T. Wigfall resigns the commission he has held since 1861. General Wigfall had served with Beauregard and with the 1st Texas Infantry (Hood's Texas Brigade). He then takes his seat in the Confederate Senate. While in the Senate, he becomes a nemesis of Jefferson Davis and of General Joseph E. Johnston. At the end of the conflict General Wigfall flees to England. In 1872, he returns to the U.S. He dies in Galveston, Texas, in February 1874. Also, Colonel John B. Hood is promoted to the rank of brigadier general during early March and is ap-

pointed commanding officer of the brigade. Hood will remain as leader for only about six months, but the brigade, composed of the original 1st, 4th and 5th Texas Infantry Regiments, and the recently acquired 18th Georgia Infantry, retains its indelible name, "Hood's Texas Brigade." It gains more strength during June of this year.

In Naval activity, the USS *Hartford* arrives at Ship Island, Mississippi, which Flag Officer David Farragut is using as a staging area for his pending attack to seize New Orleans. Ship Island is strategically located about midway between the mouth of the Mississippi River and Mobile Bay. Other warships and some Union army units are at Ship Island when Farragut arrives aboard the *Hartford,* his flagship. Farragut's forces will be further augmented with the arrival of David D. Porter's schooners (mortar flotilla) during mid–March. The schooners are towed to Ship Island by steam gunboats. In other activity, the USS *Seymour,* while participating in an expedition initiated to sever communication between Albemarle Sound and Norfolk, Virginia, strikes an abandoned anchor in Hatteras Inlet. Rescue operations begin, and it is refloated and returned to duty after being repaired the following May.

February 21 (Friday) In New Mexico, Confederates commanded by Colonel Henry Hopkins Sibley (West Point, 1838) clash with Union forces under Colonel (later General) Richard Canby near Fort Craig (Valverde, New Mexico). General Canby, leading his entire garrison (New Mexico militia), except for a contingent under Colonel Juan Cristobal Armijo, to protect the fort, fords the Rio Grande River at about 1000 to engage the Confederates on the east bank. The vanguard, McRae's battery, protected by infantry, is the first to hit the east bank, but with unexpected results. Sibley sends a contingent to engage, and the vanguard, including the infantry, is mauled by a tenacious charge. All in McRae's battery except for five men are killed and their escorting infantry detachment also sustains high casualties. Captain Alexander McRae is among the fatalities. During the initial part of the firestorm, the Confederates lose 27 troops, including Major Samuel Lockridge (5th Texas Cavalry). Lockridge is apparently struck with the fatal shot while the Union is in the process of crossing. After spotting a young boy acting as flag bearer, Lockridge was ordering his troops to spare the boy when he got hit with a fatal blow.

The engagement continues to intensify as each side pounds the other throughout the afternoon. Fire is incessant and troops are not the only casualties. The trees

are so frequently struck that the leaves and small branches are severed, leaving charred stubs. Toward the latter part of the day, Sibley orders an attack by four companies, each carrying only their handguns and lances, bolstered by four companies brandishing double-barreled shotguns.

Sibley's order calls for the right sector of the Union line to be struck first by those with handguns; after expending their ammunition, they are to stand aside and reload while the lancers drive ahead to finish the attack, but a mixup in orders causes the Confederates to split their force and instead attack at two separate points. The confusion becomes costly when the lancers charge without the added strength of the pistols and shotguns.

Two hundred and eighty lancers charge the entrenched infantry and of those, forty are not cut down. Meanwhile, the Rebels armed with shotguns fare much better, and the Union infantry that receives the deadly fire sustains high casualties. At about 1630, Union Major Robert H. Stapleton moves out under a flag of truce. He is met by Confederate Lieutenant Van Patten. The two sides agree to a three-day truce to allow time to bury their respective dead. At dusk, the Union returns to the fort.

The Union sustains Union 62 killed and 140 wounded. Captain George Nicholas Bascom (West Point, 1858), Captain Alexander McRae and Captain Benjamin Wingate are among the killed. The Confederates sustain 32 to 40 killed and about 150 wounded. Participants are the 1st New Mexico Cavalry, 2nd Colorado Cavalry, contingents of the 2nd and 5th New Mexico, and the 5th, 7th and 10th U.S. Infantry Regiments. In addition, Hall's and MacRae's batteries support the infantry and cavalry. Although Canby had been unable to defeat the Rebels under General Henry H. Sibley, the Confederates are not in a position of capitalizing on their victory. They lack sufficient supplies and will soon be forced to return to Texas.

Canby will be promoted to brigadier general in May and transferred to the Eastern Theater, where he will serve in New York until 1864. As a major general, effective May 1864, he will serve with General Nathaniel Prentiss Banks in the Red River Campaign. Also, the 5th Texas Cavalry led by Colonel (later general) Thomas Green participates at this action.

February 22 (Saturday) In Texas, Union and Confederate forces clash at Aransas Pass.

In Virginia, Jefferson Davis, previously the provisional president of the Confederacy, is on this day sworn in as the president of the Confederate States of America. Also, a Union contingent composed of troops of the 5th Pennsylvania Cavalry and the Cameron Dragoons, commanded by Colonel Max Friedman, initiates a mission into the vicinity of Flint Hill and Vienna. No casualty reports are available; however, it is reported that the Union captures several Confederates.

In Missouri, a large Union force commanded by Brigadier General John Pope departs St.

A Union fleet at Ship Island, Mississippi (Mottelay, *The Soldier in Our Civil War*, 1886).

Louis en route to engage the Rebels at New Madrid and nearby Island No. 10 in Tennessee, a strategic stronghold of the Confederates under General Pierre G.T. Beauregard and Brigadier General John P. McCown. Union General Henry W. Halleck, who intends to totally dominate the Mississippi River, had ordered the attack, realizing that only after the reduction of these fortifications could his open passage strategy occur.

In Texas, Union gunboats exchange fire with Confederates at Aransas Bay. No casualties are reported.

In Union activity, Union Brigadier General Lewis Golding Arnold (West Point, 1837) assumes command of the Department of Florida, succeeding Colonel Harvey Brown. Also, Hugh Thompson Reid is appointed colonel (later brigadier general) of the 15th Iowa Regiment. He participates at Shiloh and sustains a serious wound.

February 23 (Sunday) In Arkansas, Union General S.R. Curtis' force moves into Fayetteville. Some Rebels are captured, but the greater number of Price's force evacuates the town, setting part of it afire before departing. Price heads over the Boston Mountains.

In Missouri, a contingent of the Missouri Mountain Rangers, commanded by Captain John M. Richardson, initiates a reconnaissance mission to Pea Ridge Prairie, Missouri. The operation lasts until the following day and results in a skirmish with Confederates.

In South Carolina, a continent of the 8th Michigan Volunteer Regiment, commanded by Captain Ralph Ely, initiates a reconnaissance mission in the vicinity of the Bull River and Schooner Channel. The operation terminates on the 26th. No casualties are reported.

In Tennessee, Union troops attached to General Buell's army enter Nashville. The first unit to arrive is the 4th Ohio Cavalry, commanded by Colonel Kenner; it is a contingent of General Ormsby M. Mitchel's division. The remainder of the division will arrive later and establish positions at Edgefield across from Nashville. The CSS *James Woods* (also known as *James Wood*) is sunk by the Confederates prior to its completion as a gunboat, upon the approach of the Union forces at Nashville.

In Naval activity, six gunboats, including the USS *Morse* and the *Delaware*, depart Hatteras Inlet, North Carolina, on a reconnaissance mission on Croatan Sound. The squadron approaches Winton with the *Delaware* at the point and it is attacked by artillery and small arms fire. The *Delaware* and the other ships immediately return fire against the battery, and simultaneously elements of the 9th New York Zouaves debark and move against the town. The Zouaves enter the town and begin to destroy military stores and equipment.

February 24 (Monday) In Missouri, a Union force under Brigadier General John Pope, en route to New Madrid, reaches Commerce. A skirmish develops between the cavalry and Rebel guerrillas under Jeff Thompson. The Union captures three guns and several prisoners.

In Virginia, at Lewis' Chapel, Union Pickets (General Israel Bush Richardson's command) are attacked by Confederates. No casualties are reported. A detachment of the 37th New York Volunteer Regiment skirmishes with Confederates at Mason's Neck (Occoquan). The Union sustains two killed and one wounded. Confederate casualties, if any, are unavailable.

In West Virginia, Union troops under Major General Nathaniel P. Banks skirmish with a contingent of Confederates near Harpers Ferry, then move in and occupy the town.

In Confederate general officer activity, Peter B. Starke is commissioned colonel (later brigadier general) of the Confederate 28th Mississippi Cavalry. He is assigned to duty in Vicksburg, Mississippi. Colonel Starke is the brother of Confederate Colonel (later brigadier general) William E. Starke, 60th Virginia Infantry Regiment.

February 25 (Tuesday) In Missouri, a Union contingent composed of two companies of the 1st Indiana Cavalry, Captain Hawkin's company of Missouri Volunteers, and Captain Leeper's company (Missouri state militia), commanded by Major Clendenning, operating during a reconnaissance mission that initiated on the 23rd, skirmishes this day with a Confederate force at St. Francisville. The Union sustains slight casualties. Confederate casualties, if any, are unavailable.

In Tennessee, Union Major General Don Carlos Buell arrives at Edgefield, across from Nashville. One of his divisions, under Ormsby MacKnight Mitchel, is there to greet him. The city of Nashville surrenders on the following day. General William Nelson, sent by General Ulysses S. Grant, also joins Buell, then this combined force of 15,000 men will occupy Nashville. The Confederates evacuate the city, showing no signs of a fight. Buell also orders General Smith (at Clarksville) to bring his entire force to Nashville in case of a Confederate attack. General Nelson has previous service as a Naval officer and is the only Naval officer to acquire the full rank of major general during the war.

In related activity, Flag Officer Foote, aboard the *Conestoga*, also arrives this day at Nashville; the *Conestoga* runs guard for the transport vessels that carried the troops under General Nelson from Clarksville to Edgefield. In East Tennessee, Confederate General Edmund Kirby Smith is assigned command of the Department of East Tennessee. He assumes command the following month.

In Virginia, the 28th Pennsylvania Infantry Regiment, supported by artillery and commanded by Colonel Geary, begins operating in Loudon County and continues the operation until May 6.

In Naval activity, General Butler departs Hampton Roads, traveling aboard the USS *Mississippi*, for Ship Island, off the coast of the state of Mississippi. Butler's wife and his staff are aboard for what becomes a harrowing voyage. The vessel twice becomes damaged while passing around North Carolina, and it is compelled to pause at Port Royal for repairs before finally arriving at its destination on the 25 March. The USS *Mohican*, operating in conjunction with the USS *Bienville* as part of the South Atlantic Blockading Squadron and in conjunction with a pending attack against Fernandina, Florida, captures a blockade runner, the *Arroto*. Also, the USS *Monitor*, the first armor-turret gunboat, is commissioned. It soon leaves from New York for Hampton Roads and its arrival is timely. The CSS *Virginia*, an ironclad, is ravaging the Union fleet. The two sea monsters encounter each other during early April.

February 26 (Wednesday) In Missouri, a contingent of the 6th Missouri Cavalry, commanded by Captain Montgomery, clashes with Confederates (Texas Rangers) led by Major Lawrence Sullivan Ross (later general) at Keetsville (also Keytesville or Keittsville). Ross becomes colonel of the 6th Texas Cavalry during May of this year and subsequently becomes a brigadier general, effective December 1863. Major Ross had previously led the Texas Rangers during the successful rescue of Cynthia Ann Parker from the Comanches at Puanah, Texas, during 1860.

In Tennessee, at Edgefield, across from Nashville, Confederate Major R.B. Cheatham arrives to officially surrender the city of Nashville to General Don Carlos Buell. Union troops occupy the city on the 28th. The Confederates under General John Buchanan Floyd, who had only recently escaped from General Grant's forces at Fort Donelson, order the destruction of two bridges and two uncompleted gunboats before they depart.

In Confederate general officer activity, Brigadier General John Porter McCown (West Point, 1840) assumes command at New Madrid (Madrid Bend), Missouri. McCown, who had been appointed brigadier general the previous October, is promoted to major general effective 10 March 1862. Also, Colonels Ambrose P. Hill, 13th Virginia Infantry, and James J. Pettigrew, 12th South Carolina Infantry, are promoted to the rank of brigadier general. Hill is made a major general in May 1862. Colonel (later brigadier general) James Alexander Walker succeeds General Hill as commander of the 13th Virginia Infantry.

In Confederate Naval activity, the CSS *Nashville*, while returning from European waters, encounters a merchant ship, the schooner *Robert Gilfillan*. After it is seized, the vessel is burned. The *Nashville* afterward resumes its course. On the 28th, the *Nashville* evades a naval blockade and arrives at Beaufort, North Carolina. It later moves to South Carolina, but it does not again sail as part of the Confederate Navy. The *Nashville* is sold, and then later (5

November 1862), it changes owners and becomes a privateer, the *Rattlesnake.* In other activity, the USS *Young America* departs Hampton Roads for Currituck Inlet to rescue the crew and cargo of the USS *R.B. Forbes,* which was grounded 25 February.

February 27 (Thursday) In *Naval activity,* the USS *Monitor* departs New York Harbor for Hampton Roads, Virginia, arriving on March 8.

In Confederate general officer activity, Danville Leadbetter (West Point, 1836), who had earlier joined the Confederacy (1861) and was assigned duty as an engineer in Alabama, is promoted to the rank of brigadier general effective this date. Leadbetter will be assigned responsibility for supervising the defenses at such strategic places as Chattanooga and Knoxville in Tennessee and at Mobile, Alabama. Lt. Colonel William W. Mackall (West Point, 1837) is also promoted to brigadier general. Colonel Carter L. Stevenson (later major general) is promoted to the rank of brigadier general. At about this time, Goode Bryan (West Point 1834), a Georgian and captain in the Confederate Army (16th Georgia Regiment), achieves the rank of colonel. In August 1863 he is promoted to brigadier general.

February 28 (Friday) In South Carolina, a fleet commanded by Flag Officer Samuel Francis Du Pont arrives at Port Royal, and this day, the fleet, led by Du Pont's flagship, the USS *Wabash* (steam screw frigate), departs for Amelia Island en route to seize a formidable post, Confederate-held Fort Clinch, and the deep water port there. The rendezvous point is set at St. Andrew's Bay in Georgia. The Union is concentrating on eliminating more southern ports to squeeze the Confederacy, but also to bolster the naval blockade by acquiring more ports for the Atlantic Blockade Squadron. Fort Clinch defends the town of Fernandina. Other ships that participate in the attack include the USS *Alabama* (a wooden side-wheel steamer); *Bienville* (side wheel steamship, commissioned October 1861); *Flag* (screw steamer, formerly the *Phineas Sprague,* converted to warship); *Henrietta* (a private yacht on loan to the Coast Guard; the *Huron* (Unadilla class screw steam gunboat); *Isaac Smith* (Unadilla class screw steam gunboat); *James Adger* (wooden side wheel steamship converted into warship); *Keystone State* (side wheel steamship, formerly civilian steamer *Keystone State*); *Mohican; Ottawa* (Unadilla class screw steam gunboat); *Potomska* (wooden screw steamer rigged as a three masted schooner); *Penguin* (steamship, converted into screw steam gunboat); *Seminole; Seneca* and the *Susquehanna.* The force also includes the transports *Belvidere, Boston, Empire City, George's Creek, McClellan, Marion* and *Star of the South.* The fleet is further bolstered with a battalion (289 men) of Marines commanded by Major Reynolds, as well as 230 U.S. Marine guards and an army brigade led by Brigadier General Horatio Wright.

In Tennessee, General U.S. Grant arrives in Nashville to check the situation. After con-

firming that there is no Confederate threat to Nashville, the reinforcements under General C.F. Smith, who arrive by steamship this day, return to Clarksville. In the meantime, other troops spread out in the city. Old Glory is unfurled at the state capital and at city hall. Andrew Johnson, with the rank of brigadier general, is appointed to run the affairs of state as military governor; Johnson becomes president (17th) of the United States following the death of President Lincoln. Andrew Johnson, a North Carolinian, had been a senator at the outbreak of the war, but he remains loyal to the Union. Johnson's appointment is confirmed by the senate on 4 March 1862. Another senator, L.W. Powell of Kentucky, a state that remains loyal but is also claimed by the Confederacy, also remains in the Senate. The other senators from the southern states resign.

Flag Officer Andrew Foote, having participated at the fall of Forts Henry and Donelson as well as the occupation of Nashville, will soon return to Cairo to establish plans for the seizure of Columbus, Kentucky.

In Florida, Brigadier General Samuel Jones succeeds General Braxton Bragg as commander of the Department of Alabama and West Florida.

In Naval activity, the CSS *Nashville* arrives at Beaufort, North Carolina, following a cruise to England. While at sea, the *Nashville* was sold and turned into a blockade runner with a new name, the *Thomas L. Wragg.* The USS *Oneida* is commissioned this day. It had been built at the New York Navy Yard as a three-mast screw sloop and initially launched the previous month. Captain Samuel P. Lee receives command of the gunboat, which is assigned to the West Gulf Blockading Squadron.

March 1862 *In Confederate activity,* Colonel Thomas James Churchill is promoted to brigadier general, as is Colonel William Field (West Point, 1849). Field will lead a brigade and participate at various battles, including Seven Days' (6/26 to 7/1/1862), Cedar Mountain or Slaughter Mountain (8/9/1862) and Second Manassas or Second Bull Run (8/30/1862). Also, Brigadier General States Rights Gist of the South Carolina Militia, who previously served with General Barnard E. Bee, is appointed brigadier general in the Confederate Army. Gist had succeeded Bee in command upon his demise at First Manassas (Bull Run). General Gist is assigned to General Major General John Clifford Pemberton's command, the latter being recently promoted during the previous January. The Confederate 25th Virginia Infantry Regiment is attached to Colonel Elzey's brigade, General Ewell's division, Army of the Northwest, commanded by Brigadier General Edward Johnson.

March 1 (Saturday) In Arkansas, Union General Samuel R. Curtis, believing that reinforcements in strength had arrived to bolster Confederate General Sterling Price, decides to withdraw from Fayetteville. Initially he transfers his force, composed only of four divisions, to Sugar Creek, which is near Bentonville. From

there he moves to Mottsville, located south of Pea Ridge. His entire force, including infantry and cavalry, numbers about 10,500 troops, supported by 49 pieces of artillery and one mountain gun.

The Union force is composed of four divisions. The First Division, led by General Sigel, comprises three brigades, commanded by Colonels Peter J. Osterhaus, Nicholas Greuse and W.N. Coler. The Second Division, commanded by Colonel A.A. Asboth, comprises two brigades, commanded by Colonels Frederick Schaeffer and Joliet. The Third Division, commanded by Colonel Jefferson A. Davis, is composed of two brigades commanded by Colonels Benton and Julius White. The Fourth Division, commanded by Colonel Eugene A. Carr, has two brigades, commanded by Colonels Grenville M. Dodge and William Vandever. Other troops unattached to the division include a contingent of the 3rd Missouri Regiment, the 24th Missouri Regiment, the 3rd Iowa Cavalry, Bowen's Battery of Missouri Cavalry and an artillery battery commanded by Captain Stevens.

General Sterling Price had been reinforced by General Ben McCulluch's contingents, and soon afterward a large number of Indians, led by General Albert Pike, arrive, pushing Price's force, according to the estimates of General Samuel R. Curtis, at between 30,000 and 40,000 troops. The command of all Confederate forces is assumed by General Earl Van Dorn. The two opposing sides collide on March 6.

In Missouri, elements of the 7th Cavalry and the 10th Illinois Volunteers skirmish with Confederates at Sikestown. Casualties are unavailable.

In Tennessee, Confederate General James Trapier (commanding officer, Tallahassee, Florida) sends the 24th Mississippi Regiment under William Dowd to reinforce General A.E. Johnston in Tennessee and leaves behind only enough troops to defend the Apalachicola River on the route to Georgia.

In Confederate general officer activity, Colonels Robert Ransom, Jr., 1st North Carolina Cavalry (also 9th North Carolina Volunteers), and Charles Sidney Winder, 6th South Carolina Infantry, are promoted to the rank of brigadier general, effective this date. Winder is assigned command of a brigade composed of Virginia regiments.

In Naval activity, the USS *Marblehead* (screw steam gunboat) is commissioned at about this time (March). It is assigned to duty on the Pamunkey and York Rivers in Virginia in support of the Peninsular Campaign. Around June it is sent to the South Atlantic Blockading Squadron for duty off the coast of Georgia and South Carolina.

March 2 (Sunday) In Kentucky, sometime between this day and the following morning, the Confederates evacuate Columbus. They are able to also move most of their artillery. The Union is preparing to seize it, unaware of the abandonment by the Rebels.

In Missouri, some skirmishing occurs at New Madrid between Union forces and Jeff Thompson's raiders.

In New Mexico, the Union forces abandon Albuquerque under pressure from Confederate General H.H. Sibley.

In Tennessee, General U.S. Grant receives orders from General Halleck to leave a sparse garrison at Fort Donelson and return the balance of his force to Fort Henry. From this point, troops are directed against Eastport and Paris. Expeditions are also launched against Humboldt, Corinth and Jackson.

U.S. gunboats, including the USS *Lexington* and *Tyler,* move up the Tennessee River to assist General Grant's imminent assault on Confederate positions at Eastport, Mississippi. The gunboats support the 32nd Illinois Volunteer Regiment, under the command of Brigadier General George Washington Cullum (West Point, 1833), which clashes with a Confederate force led by Colonel Jean Jacques Mouton (West Point, 1850) at Pittsburg Landing (Shiloh). The Union, holding overwhelming firepower, sustains five killed and five wounded. The Confederates sustain 20 killed and about 200 wounded.

In Virginia, Union General Frederick West Lander succumbs of natural causes at Paw Paw while waiting to be relieved. He is succeeded by General James Shields.

In Union general officer activity, Colonel Andrew Jackson Smith, chief of cavalry under General Henry Halleck, is promoted to brigadier general.

March 3 (Monday)   In Florida, a Confederate defending force commanded by Colonel William McBlair abandons Amelia Island, which lies in northern Florida near Georgia. Union troops under General Horatio Gouverneur Wright occupy the island on the following day. Fort Clinch (Fernandina, Florida) is seized and the Union retains it for the duration of the war.

In Kentucky, the Union seizes unoccupied Columbus. The Confederates had abandoned it during the previous day and most probably during the early hours of this day. In advance of the main body, a reconnaissance force of about 250 cavalry troops (2nd Illinois) under Lt. Hogg occupies the fort there and unfurls Old Glory.

In Missouri, Union troops under Brigadier General John Pope and Confederate troops under General J.P. McCown skirmish at New Madrid. The Union 59th Indiana, 5th Iowa, 2nd Michigan, 39th and 63rd Ohio Infantry Regiments and the 7th Illinois Cavalry participate. Union casualties are one killed and three wounded. Pope, having arrived from St. Louis, discovers many more Confederate troops than had been expected, and they are supported by gunboats, commanded by Commodore George Nichols Hollins. Pope dispatches a message to headquarters at Cairo, Illinois, requesting the expeditious arrival of heavy artillery. The attempt to capture New Madrid continues until the 13th.

In New Mexico, Confederates under Captain A.S. Thurmond seize Cubero, which is defended by a contingent commanded by Captain Francisco Aragon.

In Virginia, Union forces under Colonels Erastus Tyler and Jeremiah C. Sullivan (General James Shields' division), bolstered by Colonel Nathan Kimball (14th Indiana), engage and defeat Confederate troops under General Stonewall Jackson at Kernstown. It is one of the few battles Jackson loses. The Union suffers 118 dead, 450 wounded, and 22 missing. Confederates sustain 80 dead, 375 wounded and 263 missing. Colonel Kimball is badly wounded during the skirmish; he again receives severe wounds in the struggle at Fredericksburg in December. Confederate General John Echols is also wounded. Echols, who had been promoted to colonel following his efforts at Manassas (Bull Run), was promoted to brigadier general effective the previous month.

In Confederate general officer activity, General Pierre Gustave Toutant Beauregard assumes command of the Southern Army in Mississippi. Also, Daniel Marsh Frost (West Point, 1844) is appointed brigadier general. Frost had been a brigadier general of Missouri militia and is a veteran of the Mexican War. He declines command of a brigade at Elkhorn Tavern (Pea Ridge) due to his perception that it is small. Consequently, he participates at the battle as a spectator. Afterward, he serves for a short while as inspector general under General Braxton Bragg; afterward he is transferred to Arkansas, where he serves under General Hindman.

In Naval activity, a contingent from the USS *Pawnee,* using boats, seizes the CSS *Darlington* in the vicinity of Fernandina, Florida. The *Darlington* is afterward taken into Union service and assigned duty between northern Florida and southern South Carolina. In September 1862, the *Darlington* is transferred to the Union Army, which utilizes the vessel as a transport. The *Darlington,* which had been a civilian steamer prior to the war (1849–1861), is sold in 1866. It operates as a civilian ship until 1874.

March 4 (Tuesday)   In Washington, D.C., former senator Andrew Johnson's recent appointment as military governor of Tennessee with the rank of brigadier general, effective this day, is confirmed by the U.S. Senate.

In Arkansas, Confederate General Van Dorn begins to depart Arkansas with 16,000 men to strike Missouri, but an obstacle must first be overcome. The Union forces of General Samuel R. Curtis stand between General Van Dorn and his objective. The two will clash in a major confrontation at Pea Ridge on March 7; however, in the meantime other skirmishes are fought.

In Florida, a battalion of Marines under Major John C. Reynolds occupies Ferandina.

In Georgia, a detachment of Marines and sailors attached to the sloop USS *Mohican* occupies Fort Clinch.

In Illinois, during the pre-dawn hours, an expeditionary force attached to Flag Officer Andrew Foote's fleet departs from Cairo to seize Columbus, Kentucky. The flotilla is composed of three transports, the USS *Aleck Scott, Illinois,* and *T.L. McGill,* assigned to carry about 2,000 troops, commanded by Brigadier General William Tecumseh Sherman. Sherman's command comprises the 27th Illinois and contingents of the 54th Ohio, 74th Ohio and the 55th Illinois Regiments. The troop ships are protected by the potent strength of six gunboats, the USS *Carondelet* (Captain Stembel), *Cincinnati* (Captain Davis), *Lexington* (Captain Thompson), *Louisville* (Lt. Paulding), *St. Louis* (Captain Walke) and *Pittsburg* (Lt. Kirk). In addition, the fleet is supported by four mortar boats, each of which carry deadly firepower.

The naval force arrives at its objective slightly after dawn and, to the surprise of the troops, they spot Old Glory in the distance atop the defending fort. Initially, it is thought that it might be a Confederate ruse. A contingent of the 27th Illinois, led by Colonel Napoleon B. Buford, debarks and cautiously approaches the fort. They are greeted by a detachment of the 2nd Illinois Cavalry, which coincidentally had been earlier dispatched from Paducah by General Sherman to execute a reconnaissance mission. Upon their arrival at Columbus on the previous day, the cavalrymen discovered the fort abandoned by the Rebels. Their commander, Lt. Hogg, convinced that his force of 250 could hold the fort, decided to unfurl the Stars and Stripes and await reinforcements. The fleet returns to Cairo, but about 2,000 infantrymen and 400 cavalry troops remain to garrison Columbus.

In New Mexico, Union forces evacuate Santa Fe. Also, Confederate Colonel Albert Rust, 3rd Arkansas Infantry, is promoted to brigadier general, effective this date.

In Tennessee, Union Major General Henry Halleck succeeds in causing Major General Ulysses S. Grant problems because of Grant's late arrival at the siege of Fort Donelson. General C.F. Smith takes command of Grant's troops, moving on the Mississippi Valley from Fort Henry.

In Missouri, a contingent of Union troops composed of slightly less than 100 troops commanded by Captains Ludlow and Heiden initiate a reconnaissance mission that covers Douglas, Laclede and Wright Counties and lasts until the 11th.

In Union general officer activity, Andrew Johnson (later 17th president of the U.S.) is commissioned a brigadier general of volunteers in conjunction with his appointment as military governor of Tennessee. He establishes his headquarters in Nashville, and due to the Union retaining control of the city for the duration, he is not compelled to change places. Nevertheless, during the national election of 1864, he becomes the vice presidential candidate on the ticket with President Lincoln. Also, Alfred Sully (West Point, 1841) a veteran of the Seminole

Wars in Florida and of the Mexican War, is commissioned colonel of the 1st Minnesota Regiment. Just prior to the outbreak of hostilities, he had been on frontier duty.

In Confederate general officer activity, Major General (effective 14 January 1862) John Clifford Pemberton becomes commander of the Department of South Carolina, Georgia and East Florida. He succeeds General Robert E. Lee. Also, Colonels Winfield Scott Featherston, Samuel Bell Maxey (West Point, 1846) and William Booth Taliaferro (formerly major general, Virginia militia) are promoted to the rank of brigadier general. Maxey is assigned to East Tennessee under General Joseph E. Johnston and remains there until the latter part of 1863. Taliaferro is assigned to the command of General Robert S. Garnett and subsequently with General Thomas J. Jackson. Also, General Hamilton Prioleau Bee (Texas Militia) is appointed brigadier general in the Confederate Army effective this date. He will assume command of Brownsville, Texas. General Bee will serve during the Red River Command (March–May 1864) and afterward, during the final months of the conflict, Bee commands a cavalry division in the Trans-Mississippi Department under General John A. Wharton and later an Infantry Brigade in the command of General Kirby Smith. Colonel Patrick Ronayne Cleburne (15th Arkansas) is promoted to brigadier general.

March 5 (Wednesday)   In Virginia, Union contingents attached to General Alpheus Starkey Williams skirmish with Confederates at Bunker Hill. Casualty reports are unavailable.

In Arkansas, during the evening hours, Confederate forces on the march toward Missouri from Arkansas are discovered in the vicinity of Cross Hollows, slightly more than ten miles from Sugar Creek, by scouts of General Franz Sigel (attached to General Samuel Curtis' force). The pickets get word to Sigel and he takes action to meet the threat. Sigel dispatches his cavalry to Osage Springs to secure the right flank and retains the 36th Illinois and contingents of the 2nd Missouri at Bentonville to hold the rear, while the remainder of his force heads for Sugar Creek to join the main body of Curtis's force.

In Tennessee, Union forces of General Charles Ferguson Smith (West Point, 1825) arrive at Savannah from Fort Henry. The force establishes positions around the town. U.S. gunboats and troop ships reinforce Smith's command. Also, Lt. Colonel James Gallant Spears (1st Tennessee) is promoted to brigadier general. General Spears afterward participates at various actions, including the seizure of Cumberland Gap and the later retreat from there. Later he participates at Murfreesboro, followed by command of a brigade during the relief of Knoxville.

In Confederate activity, Colonel James M. Hawes (West Point, 1845) is promoted to brigadier general. He assumes command of the cavalry (Western Department of the Confeder-

acy). Hawes will relinquish command at his own request after the battle at Shiloh to command a brigade under General Breckinridge. Subsequently, he serves in Arkansas under General Theophilus Holmes, followed by command at Galveston, Texas, beginning in 1864.

In Naval activity, a new Union vessel, the ironclad-warship *Monitor,* is ordered to depart the Continental Works at Greenpoint, New York, on its trial voyage and sail to Fortress Monroe, Virginia. The peculiar vessel with its two 11-inch Dahlgren guns arrives at its destination on the 8th. The commander, Lt. John L. Worden, reports to Flag Officer Marston and to General John Wool. The *Monitor,* ordered to Newport News, loads a cargo of ammunition and departs to the scene of an ongoing battle.

In other activity, the USS *Water Witch* encounters a Confederate blockade runner, the schooner *William Mallory.* The *Water Witch* initiates pursuit, but the blockade runner takes flight and the chase continues throughout the day, but after about five hours, the chase ends and the ship is seized. In April the *Water Witch* is ordered to receive repairs and remains out of service until the following September.

March 6 (Thursday)   In Illinois, Union Major General Henry Halleck informs General Grant that upon his return, Grant will be under arrest. General McClellan calls for Grant's "relief from duty for misbehavior." Other Union generals had also placed blame on Grant for his actions at Fort Henry, Tennessee.

In Virginia, the 63rd Pennsylvania Volunteer Regiment, commanded by Lt. Colonel A.S.M. Morgan, skirmishes with Confederates in the vicinity of Pohick Church. The Union sustains two killed and two wounded. In conjunction, a detachment of the 63rd skirmishes with another Confederate group at Occoquan. No casualties are reported.

In Confederate general officer activity, at about this time, General Pierre Beauregard assumes command of the Army of the Mississippi. Subsequently, he will serve under General Albert Sidney Johnston at Shiloh (April 1862). In other activity, Colonel George Hume Steuart, 1st Maryland Infantry Regiment, is promoted to the rank of brigadier general, effective this date. He is assigned command of a brigade of Virginians, but he also retains his regiment. Steuart leads the regiment as part of General Ewell's Division, Army of Northern Virginia. Lt. William Thomas Clark is promoted to captain (13th Iowa). He is promoted to brigadier general during May 1865 and commissioned a major general in November 1865.

March 6–8   BATTLE OF PEA RIDGE (ELKHORN) On the 6th, as a prelude to the imminent major clash between the Union troops (Army of the Southwest) under General Samuel R. Curtis and Confederates under General Sterling Price, a small powder keg explodes while General Sigel is en route in Arkansas from Bentonville to Sugar Creek to join the main Union force. Due to some confusion when orders had

been issued the previous night regarding the movement of Franz Sigel's force, a contingent of about 600 troops and their five pieces of artillery are inadvertently left behind and surrounded by a Louisiana regiment. Just as they are about to be overwhelmed, Sigel, utilizing his rear guard, fights his way back and rescues the besieged contingent and in the process, his troops repel attacks against both of his flanks and another to the rear. Once the unit is rescued, the Union fights its way back, again yard by yard. Reinforcements, a contingent of Curtis' force, arrives from Sugar Creek and the episode ends. The Union sustains 28 killed or wounded and slightly under fifty prisoners.

On the 7th, Confederate troops are discovered north of Curtis' encampment, advancing along the primary road in the vicinity of Elk Horn Tavern. Confederate Brigadier General Earl Van Dorn swings down from north of the Union positions to avoid what he considers a suicidal frontal attack and strikes from west of Pea Ridge and the Round Top. One contingent of Confederates, including Cherokee Indians (1st Cherokee Mounted Rifles) under General Albert Pike, moves to Curtis's extreme right to attract attention from Van Dorn, while two other groups under Generals Ben McCulloch and James McQueen McIntosh move against Curtis' right flank. In turn, Curtis modifies his lines to prevent a disaster. Generals Sigel and Alexander S. Asboth are rushed to the left, while Eugene A. Carr and Peter J. Osterhaus move to the right, with Jefferson C. Davis in the center creating a connected line extending for about three and one-half miles from Sugar Creek to Elk Horn Tavern. This strategy leaves a no-man's land as a buffer, a huge ravine, Cross Timber Hollow, which separates the two forces.

Nevertheless, the Confederates strike and they hit hard, slamming against the 24th Missouri's positions near Elk Horn Tavern. Nearly at the first sounds of fire, a relief force is dispatched by Colonel Carr. A contingent, commanded by Colonel Osterhaus, including the 22nd Indiana Infantry, the 1st Missouri Cavalry, a contingent of the 3rd Iowa Cavalry and Captain Peter Davidson's Peoria Battery, comprising three guns, speeds toward Leetown to engage what is expected to be a small force of Rebels. Charging toward the sounds of the guns, the cavalry arrives in timely fashion and chases the Rebels, giving the Missourians a reprieve, but the Confederates have not shown their full hand. While the trailing force under Osterhaus is arriving on the scene, thinking the matter settled, there is an unsettling rustle in the woods, which conceal a massive force.

With the blare of bugles, the thunder of hooves, the crackle of the rifles and the "Rebel Yell," waves of gray uniforms descend upon the Union, delivering a horrific blow that shatters the lines, plows the defenders back in disarray and threatens the entire force. The cunning trap had been sprung and the Confederates increase the pressure to finish the rout with the combined forces of McCulloch, McIntosh and Pike. The Union attempts to raise resistance, but the Rebel thrust has pushed it to the brink of a ter-

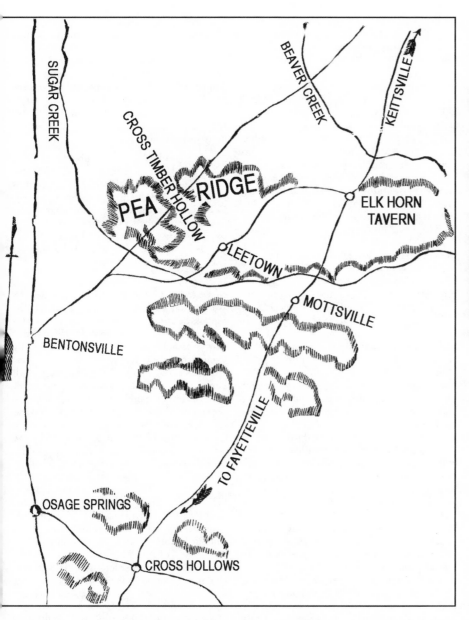

The area around Pea Ridge (Elkhorn Tavern), Arkansas (Mottelay, *The Soldier in Our Civil War*, 1886).

Major General Earl Van Dorn (Johnson, *Campfire and Battlefield: History of the Conflicts and Campaigns*, 1894).

has one antagonist gaining some ground, only to be bloodied as the other pushes it back. The struggle remains in a see-saw stalemate; however, the seemingly unending contingents of Confederate reinforcements begin to wear out the Union lines, weaken their determination and bring to the forefront the exhaustion which for awhile they had no time to contemplate. All the while, the invigorated Confederates press to totally crush the resistance. But, the 18th Indiana swoops upon the field like an unwelcome Midwest tornado and begins to clear the ground. The regiment with hearty enthusiasm and overflowing confidence rolls into the opposing forces, engaging both the Texans and the Indians, their tomahawks and knives no match for the deadly bayonets.

While the Indiana regiment moves like rolling thunder, the others pull up their boot straps, forget their misery and one more time, renew the attack. The inspired advance forces the Confederates to pull back, enabling the Union to regain lost ground and to recapture the two guns they had earlier abandoned. Wasting no time, the men pivot the regained guns upon the Rebels, who themselves now begin to feel the sting of exhaustion. The effective fire of the guns ensures a further withdrawal, and as the Confederates move back, the guns inflict gruesome punishment and grave casualties. But the Rebels, although battered, are not defeated. They begin to reform for yet another attack, only to be set upon by other forces under General Franz Sigel who arrive at a most inopportune time, particularly because the reinforcements include two hefty batteries. Before the Rebel charge can be executed, General Franz Sigel's well positioned guns propel incessant fire into their ranks, preventing the offensive from

rible disaster and in the process, it has lost much ground and two precious guns. Just as the Rebels are close to absolute victory, following their repeated pounding against the now shattered Union lines, fresh forces, led by General Jefferson C. Davis with Colonel Julius White's brigade, arrive to forestall calamity.

In the meantime, Confederate General Sterling Price has been hammering against General Carr's positions, propelling regiment after regiment in a resolute effort to crush the line and roll over the Union defenders. Carr requests reinforcements from General Curtis, but none are immediately sent, causing the crisis to worsen. At this time, one gun has been lost, Carr is wounded (three wounds) and the supply of ammunition reaches a dangerous level. With the Union lines faltering here and, unknown at the time to Carr, the situation at Osterhaus's posi-

tions equally terrible, the Confederates are on the verge of victory.

While the confidence of his troops is extremely low and sinking further, General Curtis finally dispatches some troops he can spare, his bodyguard cavalry and one gun. They sprint to the aid of Carr, and with great jubilation when they arrive, he rallies his troops: "One more struggle boys, and the day is ours! And then, with one arm in a sling, Carr leads his troops in a rejuvenated attack. Combined, the two forces advance, and with the effective use of their bayonets, they evict the Rebels and reclaim the ground they had earlier been compelled to relinquish.

Back at Osterhaus's lines, the welcome arrival of Colonel White's brigade transforms imminent defeat into a grand slugfest, with each side badgering the other during a brutal duel, which getting started and instead forcing a retreat toward General Price's positions near Elk Horn Tavern.

The Confederates count two of their generals, Ben McCulloch and James McIntosh, dead and a colonel captured. This turn of events devastates the Rebels, and they reel off in disarray towards Elkhorn Tavern. Following the grueling battle, darkness brings welcome relief to both sides. The stragglers from McCulloch and McIntosh's commands begin filling the Confederate ranks of Price to meet the federal counterattack in the morning, while the Union uses the pause to again redeploy its contingents. At dawn on Saturday (8th), Carr is holding the center, flanked by Sigel and Davis on the left and right respectively.

On the 8th, Union General Curtis' Artillery commences firing with thundering blasts just prior to a combined infantry and cavalry attack against the crumbling defenses of Van Horn. To the left, Siegel's troops are strongly supported by artillery as they drive up the hill facing them, while Davis's force on the right is turning the Rebel left and pushing it straight into the fire zone of the artillery. Shortly thereafter progress on all points is rapidly accelerating as the Confederates' two flanks become encircled, prompting the Yankees to fix bayonets and initiate another dogged charge. The Rebels heroically hold out for about two hours, but by this time, the pressure is too overwhelming and their ammunition is expended, forcing them to retreat, but in orderly fashion. General Van Dorn's force moves south and General Price's force heads toward Keitsville. Pursuit is mounted by Sigel's troops.

Union General Curtis had anticipated an attack from the south. The Rebel assault originating from the west nearly costs him his entire Army and Union control of Missouri; however, his early strategic moves to counter the assault had saved the day. During the battle, about one thousand Cherokees, commanded by Brigadier General Albert Pike and Colonel Douglas H. Cooper (later brigadier general), fight for the Confederates at Pea Ridge, successfully assaulting a three-gun Union battery. Union artillery in support of the beleaguered battery is zeroed in on the assaulting Cherokees with resounding success, causing the Indians to fall back to the

woods. The Missouri Guardsmen are not yet officially in the Confederacy, but they participate in the battle. Union Soldiers from Missouri, Iowa, Illinois, Indiana and Ohio (many of them Germans) are the major Union participants in the battle.

The Union suffers approximately 1,350 killed, wounded, or missing. The Confederates suffer approximately 5,200 killed, wounded, missing or captured. Confederate Brigadier General Ben McCulluch of Tennessee, who fought with Crockett in Texas, is killed by a bullet to the breast. Confederate Brigadier General James McIntosh (West Point, 1849 and brother of Union Major General John B. McIntosh) is killed leading a feverish cavalry charge. A shot pierces his heart. Confederate General William Y. Slack (state troops) is mortally wounded on the 7th at Elkhorn Tavern and succumbs to his wounds on the 21 March. General Slack is promoted posthumously to the rank of brigadier general in the Confederate Army during April 1862. Also, Confederate Colonel Louis Hebert, 3rd Louisiana Infantry, is captured and later exchanged; he is promoted to brigadier general during May 1862. Union Brigadier General Alexander Sandor Asboth (born in Hungary) and Acting Brigadier General Eugene A. Carr are wounded. General Carr (West Point 1850) is wounded three times while directing his men in combat. Carr's gallantry is rewarded by the Congressional Medal of Honor.

Union Brigadier General F.J. Herron is also awarded the Medal of Honor for his valor during this tenacious contest, but he does not receive it until thirty years later. General Herron, while in temporary command of the 9th Iowa, has his horse shot out from under him by a cannon ball, which at the same time breaks his ankle and causes him to be captured. Union Colonel Gustavus Smith receives an unexpected volley from the Confederates as he is supervising the guns of the 1st Iowa Battery. His horse is shot out from under him and while waiting for another, he takes multiple wounds. During that time, a bullet strikes his sword while it is in his hand, and another bullet severs his belt from his waist, while yet another shot strikes his shoulder. He takes yet another wound when he sustains a hit from a shell fragment that fractures his skull. He is literally carried from the

field and thought to have been fatally wounded. Nevertheless, he does survive and he is promoted to brigadier general of volunteers after his partial recovery from the wounds. Brigadier General Samuel R. Curtis (West Point, 1831) will be promoted to major general subsequent to the victory at Pea Ridge. Confederate Colonels (later generals) John Bullock Clark, Jr., Martin E. Green and Dandridge McRae participate at this battle.

March 7 (Friday)   In Missouri, the 4th Missouri Cavalry commanded by Captain Benjamin Ludlow skirmishes with Confederates at Fox Creek. The Union sustains five wounded. Confederate casualties, if any, are unavailable. Also, at Bob's Creek, a detachment the 1st Missouri Cavalry commanded by Captain Windmueller skirmishes with a Confederate unit. Each side sustains slight casualties.

In Virginia, the Union Army of the Potomac, commanded by General McClellan, departs Washington, leaving a large force to protect the capital, heading for Fortress Monroe. As McClellan penetrates deeper into Confederate territory, he encounters land mines devised by Confederate General Gabriel J. Rains (West Point, 1827) to impede Union progress. Both Union and Confederates argue the merits of these devices used under the surface, but before the end of the war they are in use by both sides. Also, a Union contingent that includes the 5th Connecticut Infantry, Cole's cavalry and some artillery (Matthew's battery), commanded by Captain Henry Cole, skirmishes with Confederates (7th Confederate Virginia Cavalry) led by Lt. Colonel (later general) Turner Ashby at Winchester (Kernstown). Estimated Union casualties are three killed and none wounded. Confederates have six killed and about seven wounded. Confederate Colonel (later brigadier general) William W. Kirkland is severely wounded during this action and will not be able to report to duty until the latter part of this year, when he arrives in Tennessee to become chief of staff to General Cleburne.

Also, at about this time and continuing through the 9th of March, Confederate forces evacuate Dumphries, Evansport, Manassas and Occoquan. Meanwhile, Union forces are advancing toward Manassas. Also, Union Colonel Thomas A. Davies (West Point, 1829), 16th New York, is appointed brigadier general, Volunteers. Davies' service takes him to the siege of Corinth, and subsequently he holds commands throughout Kentucky, Missouri, north Kansas, and Wisconsin.

In Union general officer activity, Colonel Eugene Asa Carr (West Point, 1850) is appointed brigadier general. General Carr commands a division of the XVI Corps during the Vicksburg Campaign and afterward serves in Arkansas. Near the end of the war, Carr receives the brevet of major general in the regular and volunteer service. In 1892 he is commissioned brigadier general.

In Confederate general officer activity, Colonel William Duncan Smith, 20th Georgia In-

Battle of Pea Ridge (Elkhorn Tavern) (Mottelay, *The Soldier in Our Civil War*, 1886).

The USS *Cumberland* is rammed by the CSS *Virginia* on 8 March 1862 (Johnson, *Campfire and Battlefield: History of the Conflicts and Campaigns*, 1894).

fantry, is promoted to the rank of brigadier general. Smith is transferred to South Carolina for duty in the command of General John C. Pemberton, District of South Carolina. General Smith is a graduate of West Point (1846) and a veteran of the Mexican War. In June, Pemberton will be promoted to the rank of major general and W.D. Smith will succeed him in command.

In Naval activity, Union gunboats bombard Confederate positions, particularly the batteries stretching from Liverpool Point to Boyd's Hole and Acquia Creek, Virginia.

March 8 (Saturday) In Virginia, Union forces under Colonel John White Geary occupy Leesburg.

In Tennessee, there is skirmishing around Nashville between the 1st Wisconsin Infantry supported by the 4th Ohio Cavalry and Confederate troops under Lt. Colonel John Hunt Morgan (appointed colonel of 2nd Confederate Kentucky Cavalry in April). Also, Confederate forces under General John Buchanan Floyd occupy Chattanooga.

In Virginia, this Saturday morning, a contingent of Colonel Andrew T. McReynolds' 1st New York (Lincoln) Cavalry, commanded by Lt. Harry B. Hidden, is dispatched to Burke's Station to guard the railroad there while a bridge is under repair. General Philip Kearny will arrive on the 10th.

In Confederate general officer activity, Colonel James Edwin Slaughter is promoted to the rank of brigadier general. He is assigned duty with General Albert Sidney Johnston.

In Naval–Marine Corps activity, a contingent of 25 Marines attached to both the USS *Mohican* and the steamer USS *Pocahontas* lands at Brunswick, Georgia, near the border with

Florida. While operating off Hampton Roads, the USS *Minnesota* observes three Confederate warships, the CSS *Jamestown*, *Patrick Henry*, and *Virginia* (formerly the USS *Merrimack*), the latter having been transformed into an ironclad, just as they are skirting around Sewell's Point. Flag Officer Goldsborough, aboard the USS *Minnesota*, anticipating that Newport News is their objective, directs Captain G.J. Van Brunt to initiate pursuit. As the *Minnesota* reaches a point slightly more than one mile outside Newport News, the ship grounds. In the meantime, the Confederates launch their attack, with the *Virginia* passing the USS *Congress* to plow into the USS *Cumberland*, and soon afterward it rams the USS *Congress*. In the meantime, all three Confederate vessels commence fire upon the *Minnesota*, inflicting casualties, including fatalities. The *Minnesota* remains grounded into the following day during the famous duel between the *Monitor* and the *Virginia* (*Merrimack*). Also, the CSS *Jamestown*, built during 1853 as a passenger steamer, had been seized by the state of Virginia in Richmond during 1861 and afterward transferred to the Confederate States Navy and as the *Thomas Jefferson*; however, the ship is usually referred to as the *Jamestown*. (See also, **March 8–9 BATTLE BETWEEN THE *MONITOR* AND THE *VIRGINIA* [*MERRIMACK*].)**

In Naval activity, the USS *Young America* tows the USS *Roanoke* to positions off Sewell's Point, from where it bombards Confederate batteries.

March 8–9 BATTLE BETWEEN THE *MONITOR* AND THE *VIRGINIA* [*MERRIMACK*] The Confederate ironclad *Virginia,* commanded by Flag Officer Franklin Buchanan, departs Norfolk, Virginia, with two smaller gunboats, the CSS *Patrick Henry* (six guns) and the CSS *Jamestown* (four guns). The CSS *Virginia* was formerly the USS *Merrimack* (sometimes spelled *Merrimac*), a frigate that had been sunk during April 1861 by the federals when they abandoned Norfolk. By about noon, the three Confederate vessels unexpectedly are spotted on the Elizabeth River closing against the Union ships at Hampton Roads. At this time, five men-of-war lay in the har-

bor, the *Roanoke* (flagship), a steam frigate, armed with 40 guns, the USS *Congress*, a sailing frigate (50 guns), the USS *Cumberland* (24 guns), USS *Minnesota* (40 guns) and the USS *St. Lawrence* (50 guns).

The Union fleet at Hampton Roads attempts to destroy this unique armor-plated Confederate ship. One small vessel, a gunboat, takes a shot with its solitary gun; the shell bounces off harmlessly. The *Virginia* then clunks through the water at a snail's pace to devastate the USS *Congress,* an older sailing vessel, certainly no match for this strange iron fortress of the sea. The USS *Cumberland*, with its Dahlgren guns, is a little prepared for the *Virginia,* but the contest is uneven from the beginning, with the Union vessel taking a thrashing, while the crew maintains return fire and struggles despite the odds as the *Virginia* continues to rake the *Cumberland* with incessant deadly fire. The *Virginia* closes on the *Cumberland* and crashes into the aged wooden warship, inflicting a fatal blow. Nonetheless, as the *Cumberland* begins to sink, the crew continues to return fire and the flag still flies: the crew refuses to strike the colors.

More than sixty men of the crew had been killed during the broadsides and by the time the *Cumberland* goes under, only about 150 of the 291-man crew are able to jump ship and attempt escape. The commander of the *Cumberland,* Captain William Radford, is absent on court-martial duty at Old Point and arrives back at Newport News at about the same time the *Cumberland* sinks. In the meantime, another vessel, the *Wilden,* dispatched from Newport News by General Joseph Mansfield, arrives in time to rescue some of the survivors from the water and others from small boats in which they had sought safety.

The Confederate ironclad maneuvers to finish off the stranded USS *Congress,* which has run aground while attempting to escape the fire of the *Virginia*. Confederate guns pour fire into the *Congress* until it is consumed by multiple fires, causing the crew to fight both the enemy and the raging blazes that have caught the sails and the body of the helpless ship. Cannon shot

The USS *Monitor* and the CSS *Virginia* engage near the Union fleet at Hampton Roads (Johnson, *Campfire and Battlefield: History of the Conflicts and Campaigns*, 1894).

keeps raking the vessel, finally forcing the colors to be struck. The confident Confederates attempt to board and seize the vanquished ship, but Union shore batteries and marksmen commence firing and succeed in preventing the *Congress* from being taken.

During the Union shelling, an irritated and infuriated Buchanan is wounded. The victorious *Virginia* pulls back to Hampton Roads without capturing the Union ship. During the long dark night, illuminated only by the burning timbers of the crumbled fleet, an explosion finishes the *Congress* and sends it to the depths. The remaining Union vessels are disabled and unable to aide the *Congress*. However, shortly after midnight (8th–9th) the Union ironclad *Monitor* arrives from Fortress Monroe and moves in close to the *Minnesota*, surely a target for the *Virginia* when dawn arrives.

At daybreak on the 9th, the overconfident *Virginia* ventures fearlessly towards its prey, the USS *Minnesota*, expecting to pulverize the Union ship in short order, but as the *Virginia* approaches the sitting duck (grounded on a sandbar), a sigh of astonishment is heard across the *Virginia* when a startled crew sights a weirdly shaped object moving into range and hoisting the Stars and Stripes.

The *Minnesota* has been unable to get back into action despite an all-night operation by tug boats to free it. Although unable to sail freely, its guns are operational. The battle rages for over four hours without a lull. A devastating shell (100-pound Armstrong) drills into the *Monitor*, striking at the turret and penetrating, but is does nothing to disable the vessel. Meanwhile, the *Virginia*, unsuccessful in its attempt to vanquish the *Monitor*, focuses its guns on the *Minnesota*, which had earlier received a shot that penetrated directly above the water line.

As the Confederate vessel approaches, the *Minnesota* fires off a full broadside, which does no apparent damage, but in turn the *Minnesota* is struck by a two-shot barrage, one of which ignites an explosion and sets a fire, while the other shell also strikes the *Minnesota* and passes straight through to hit a steam-tug, the *Dragon*, which is in the process of towing the crippled *Minnesota*. Before a third round can be fired into the *Minnesota*, the *Monitor*, which had temporarily disengaged to check for damages, re-enters the fight and positions itself to divert the *Virginia*. And by now, the *Virginia*, taking on water and fearful of a deadly blow that might penetrate the bruised armor, makes a move for Norfolk on the orders of its commander, Catesby Jones. The *Monitor*, its commander, Lieutenant John Worden, blinded by shell fire, is low on ammunition, unable to pursue the withdrawing vessel and its accompanying gunboats, which had essentially been only spectators at the contest.

The battered Union fleet has been saved, and the Stars and Stripes, hastily raised over the *Monitor* prior to the engagement, is still flying atop this new iron sea horse. This is the first sea battle ever fought between two armored warships. The Union vessel *Roanoke*, grounded about midway between Fortress Monroe and

Left: Lt. Harry B. Hidden (Mottelay, *The Soldier in Our Civil War*, 1886). *Right:* General Philip Kearny (*Harper's Pictoral History of the Civil War*, 1896).

Newport News, does not participate in the action. The Union casualties: three killed and sixteen wounded aboard the *Minnesota* and several men aboard the *Dragon*. The Confederates sustain seven killed and seventeen wounded, including Captain Buchanan and Lieutenant Minor among the latter. Aboard the *Monitor*, the only casualties were Lt. Worden and three other men who each suffered a concussion when the turret sustained a hit. On the previous day, the Union sustained 244 casualties, including killed, drowned and wounded. Also, during the two-day engagement, the USS *Minnesota* expended 282 shells and 247 solid shot. The USS *Monitor* fired 41 shots and sustained 22 hits. The CSS *Jamestown* was originally a merchant ship built during 1853. It was seized in Virginia during April 1861 for use by its navy and later handed over to the Confederacy and renamed the CSS *Thomas Jefferson*; however, it continued to be known as the CSS *Jamestown*.

March 9 (Sunday)   In Washington, D.C., the mood is much more favorable in the afternoon, as news of the battle between the *Virginia* and *Monitor* fills the conversations about town. The fears that Washington itself may fall victim to the shells of the *Virginia* are subdued, as the *Monitor* has calmed the waters and allowed continuance of the Union blockade. In addition, the impending advance of General George B. McClellan is less dangerous as he prepares to move toward Richmond against General Joseph Johnston.

In Missouri, a contingent of Union cavalry under Captain Windmueller clashes with Confederates at Big Creek. At Mountain Grove, a contingent of the 10th Missouri Cavalry led by Captain J.G. Rich skirmishes with Confederates. The Union sustains 10 killed and two wounded. Confederate casualties, if any, are unavailable.

In Tennessee, a contingent of the 1st Louisiana Cavalry, commanded by Captain Scott, skirmishes with Union forces at Granny White's Pike. Also, Confederate General Edmund Kirby Smith assumes command of the Department of East Tennessee.

In Virginia, General Philip Kearny arrives at Burke's Station, where repairs are being made at a bridge. While approaching the town, several Confederate scouts had been spotted, prompting Kearny to dispatch a 14-man troop of New York cavalry led by Lieutenant Harry B. Hidden to give chase. The contingent encounters a Rebel force composed of about 150 troops. The impetuous cavalrymen, disregarding the vast superiority of the Rebels, charge their positions and surprisingly drive many of the Rebels back; however, others stand resolutely and drill the tiny unit. Lt. Hidden, at the point, is struck in the shoulder with a shell that passes into his neck and kills him. Corporal Eugene Lewis assumes command and the skirmish continuing with some of the cavalrymen continuing the fight on the ground. Eventually, the Confederates retire. The cavalrymen return to their lines, bringing eleven prisoners with them. Subsequently, Lt. Hidden's body is returned to New York City and, escorted by several companies of the 22nd New York and 71st New York Regiments and a few members of his own regiment, the Lincoln Cavalry (1st New York), Lt. Hidden is buried following services at the Fourteenth Street Presbyterian Church.

In Confederate general officer activity, Colonel Charles William Field (West Point, 1849), commander of the 6th Virginia Cavalry, is promoted to brigadier general. He is assigned command of an infantry brigade that participates at various engagements, including Seven Days' Battles, Cedar Mountain and at Second Manassas.

In Naval activity, the Confederates destroy the CSS *George Page,* which has been operating in Virginia, to prevent its capture by the Union. Also, the USS *Young America* succeeds in refloating the USS *St. Lawrence* and maneuvers the *St. Lawrence* to a position from where it is able to fire against the CSS *Virginia.* (See also, **March 8–9** BATTLE BETWEEN THE *MONITOR* AND THE *VIRGINIA* [*MERRIMACK*].)

In Georgia on this day and the next, a squadron of United States ships, including the USS *Mohican,* a steam sloop of war, the sloop *Pocahontas* and schooner *Potomska* seize and occupy Brunswick, St. Simons, and Jekyll Islands, all of which had been abandoned by the Confederates.

March 10 (Monday)   In Missouri, a detachment of the 1st Iowa Cavalry, commanded by Lt. J.D. Jenkins, operating in Lafayette County, sees action against Confederates. Both sides sustain slight casualties.

In Virginia, the Confederates continue to bolster their force in Virginia to offset the Union advantage. They are converging on the Rappahannock River to engage General McClellan. In related activity, the 3rd Pennsylvania Cavalry under Colonel (later brigadier general) William W. Averell occupies Centreville. Also, contingent of the 1st New York Cavalry clashes with a band of Confederates at Burke's Station. The Union sustains one killed. The Confederates sustain three killed and five wounded.

In Union general officer activity, Walter Quintin Gresham is appointed colonel (later

brevet major general) of the 53rd Indiana. The regiment participates in the Vicksburg campaign as part of the XVII Corps.

In Confederate general officer activity, Brigadier Generals Benjamin Franklin Cheatham and John Porter McCown are promoted to the rank of major general effective this day. Colonel John Horace Forney (West Point, 1852), 10th Alabama Infantry, is promoted to brigadier general. Soon after, Forney is again promoted, becoming a major general during October. He is the brother of Captain (later general) William Henry Forney, who joined the regiment as captain of the 10th Alabama Infantry. Also, Brigadier General David Rumph Jones is promoted to major general.

In Naval activity, the USS *Minnesota,* damaged recently during the engagement at Newport News, through the work of the steamer *S.R. Spaulding,* several tug boats and the toil of the crew, which tosses many guns overboard, is refloated, permitting it to move to Fortress Monroe for repairs. The *Monitor,* which had engaged the CSS *Virginia* (*Merrimack*), moved to Hampton Roads following the battle. In other activity, the USS *Young America* rescues the crew of the USS *Whitehall,* which is destroyed by fire.

March 11 (Tuesday)   In Washington, D.C., General George B. McClellan is demoted by President Lincoln, who removes him as general-in-chief of the Union Army and places him in command of only the Army of the Potomac, which at this time is in Virginia. All commanders now come under the authority of Secretary of War Edwin Stanton until Lincoln decides on the next general-in-chief. President Lincoln issues an order concerning McClellan, stating: "General McClellan having personally taken the field at the head of the Army of the Potomac, until otherwise ordered, he is relieved from the command of the other Military De-

partments, he retaining the command of the Department of the Potomac."

In Florida, the USS *Wabash* arrives at St. Augustine and seizes Fort Marion and the St. Francis Barracks without encountering any resistance. The Confederates had seized the posts during January 1861.

In Tennessee, Union contingents of the 5th Iowa Cavalry and 1st Nebraska Cavalry supported by Battery K, 1st Missouri Artillery, commanded by Captain Croft, clash with Confederates at Paris.

In Virginia, Confederates under General Stonewall Jackson evacuate Winchester and move southward. Jackson's army, split into three brigades, departs to the cheers of the citizens, and from the soldiers the people could hear voices in the column saying, "We'll be back soon." Some in the town follow the column with intent of finding safety behind the new Confederate lines. Meanwhile, town documents are transferred and the wagon trains are dispatched to the Valley Turnpike, where they pause in two contingents, one at Kernstown and the other at Newtown. Orders arrive instructing the train to halt in place. Meanwhile, the Confederate 2nd Brigade under Colonel Burks reverses direction and begins to move northward to bolster Colonel Ashby. Colonel Turner Ashby (commander of Jackson's cavalry), whose forces had been engaging Union cavalry since the previous day, at about 1000, is suddenly faced with fresh Union cavalry. General Jackson had ordered Burk to support Ashby against the new threat. Upon the appearance of Burks, the Union infantry withdraws. Nearby, General Banks has two contingents deployed, one at Bunker Hill and another at Charlestown; however, the Union does not advance to engage Burks. Consequently, Burks is recalled and the evacuation of Winchester proceeds. The troops after abandoning Winchester establish night

Left: General John Pope's baggage train is snared by mud (Johnson, *Campfire and Battlefield: History of the Conflicts and Campaigns,* 1894). *Right:* Pursuit of Union troops (General Banks' command) through Winchester, Virginia, on 11 March 1862 (Mottelay, *The Soldier in Our Civil War,* 1886).

positions in the vicinity of the wagon trains. Meanwhile, the Union troops begin to occupy the town and the operation is completed by the following day.

In Union general officer activity, General Henry W. Halleck receives the command of all the Western armies (new Department of the Mississippi). Halleck, nicknamed "Old Brains," takes command of Buell's Army of the Ohio, Major General Sam Curtis' Army of the Southwest, C.F. Smith's (Grant's) Army of the Tennessee and Pope's Army of the Mississippi (Department of Kansas, Department of Missouri and part of the Department of Ohio). General John Frémont, who had transferred his command to General Hunter while in pursuit of General Sterling Price the previous November, receives command of the Mountain Department, which includes the territory lying between the Departments of the Potomac and the Mississippi. General David Hunter will become commander of the Department of the South. General Halleck is not loved by all. General George B. McClellan mentions frequently that he considers Halleck extremely stupid. In other activity, Colonel Joseph B. Plummer, commander at Cape Girardeau, Missouri, until this month, is appointed brigadier general to rank from 22 October 1861. He participates in the operations against New Madrid and Corinth.

In Confederate general officer activity, President Jefferson Davis removes Generals Gideon J. Pillow and John B. Floyd from command because of their actions at Fort Donelson on February 16. However, General Floyd is afterward appointed brigadier general of Virginia State Troops. Also, Colonel Lucius M. Walker (West Point, 1850) is promoted to the rank of brigadier general effective this date. Walker is in command at Memphis, Tennessee; however, he is stricken with an illness that causes him to miss the engagement at Shiloh the following month. Lt. Colonel Seth Maxwell Barton is appointed brigadier general in the Confederate Army. He had served with the forces of Stonewall Jackson during the Valley Campaign in Virginia the previous winter.

In Naval activity, the USS *Arletta* initiates duty as a blockade vessel off Mobile Bay. On 15 March it proceeds to Ship Island, Mississippi and once there is towed by the USS *Harriet Lane* to the Mississippi Delta, arriving at its destination on the river on the 18th.

In Naval activity, the USS *Constellation,* under orders to move to the Mediterranean, departs Portsmouth and arrives in the area on 19 April. It remains on station for two years and afterward, returns and joins with Admiral David D. Porter's fleet. With the terms of enlistment of most of the crew expiring, Admiral David G. Farragut on November 27 orders the *Constellation* to move to Hampton Roads. It arrives back at Fortress Monroe on Christmas Day. At the beginning of the new year, the crewmen whose enlistments had not yet expired are transferred to the USS *St. Lawrence.* Later as the war winds down, the *Constellation* is utilized as a receiving ship at Norfolk, then moves to Philadelphia also as a receiving ship and remains in service until 1869. It is recommissioned on 25 May 1871. After various types of service and periods in and out of service, it is decommissioned for the final time on 4 February 1955 and taken to Baltimore. On 2 July 1999, the *Constellation* is placed on display once again at the Inner Harbor at Baltimore.

March 12 (Wednesday)   An epidemic strikes Victoria, British Columbia, Canada, when the steamship *Brother Jonathan* arrives from San Francisco carrying people infected with smallpox. By this time, there is a vaccine, discovered during the 1790s. However, the available vaccine is doled out mostly to non–Indians. Consequently, more than 10,000 Indians (Northwest Coast tribes) succumb. Many Indians move to their former lands and transport the disease along with them, taking it as far north as Alaska.

In Arkansas, a Union contingent commanded by 1st Lieutenant Rose clashes with Confederates led by Captain William C. Quantrill at Aubrey. Quantrill initially fights as part of the Confederate Army; however, he initiates his own band of guerrillas and pillages various towns until his demise during 1865.

In Florida, Union troops occupy Jacksonville.

In Missouri, Union Brigadier General John Pope, encamped outside of New Madrid, receives the heavy artillery he had earlier requested from Cairo to give him added strength. The three eighty-pound guns and one mortar are placed into position during the evening to provide support for an attack against Fort Thomp-

son, to be initiated on the following morning. Another skirmish develops in the vicinity of Lebanon. The Union reports no casualties. The Confederates suffer 13 killed and five wounded. Also, a contingent of the 1st Iowa Cavalry skirmishes with a Confederate detachment at Lexington. The Union sustains one killed and one wounded. Confederates sustain nine killed and three wounded.

In North Carolina, a fleet of 13 warships and transports (carrying General Burnside's force) under Commander Stephen Rowan departs Hatteras Inlet and moves up the Neuse River toward New Bern and arrives there on the following day.

In Virginia, Union troops complete the occupation of Winchester, an operation that began on the previous day, just after the town was abandoned by the Confederates under General Jackson. The occupying force includes two infantry brigades, bolstered by a cavalry contingent and seven artillery pieces. The Union learns that Colonel Ashby's cavalry is still within reach, south of Winchester. Members of a contingent under Captain Cole mount their horses and advance toward the suspected positions, but the Rebels are not caught by surprise.

Just as Cole's troops begins to round a bend on the turnpike, they come under attack near Parkins' Mill (later Keckley's). The cavalry column is suddenly fired upon by the flanks in coordination with other fire originating to the immediate front of the column. The cavalry withdraws and returns to Winchester. During the brief exchange, two men are severely wounded, several others are shot from their horses and three others are killed. In addition, the Confederates gain just under ten horses and some pistols that had been lost by the Union during the fight. Afterward, Colonel Turner Ashby leads a contingent to the edge of Winchester, but no Union cavalry moves out to challenge him. General Jackson continues to execute a very slow march toward Strasburg, while General Banks remains in Winchester, rather than pursue the Confederates while he awaits new orders.

In Naval activity, seven U.S. gunboats in support of trailing transports move from Hatteras Inlet and sail toward Slocum's Creek on an expedition designed to gain control of New Bern (Newberne), North Carolina. The ground troops included on the mission are nearly in their entirety: the three brigades of Generals John G. Foster, Jesse Lee Reno and John G. Parke, which had secured Roanoke Island. In addition, the strike force includes three companies of U.S. Marines, a contingent of Coast Guardsmen and one battery of McCook's artillery. The Union fleet arrives at Slocum's Creek during the evening.

A 13-ship squadron, including the USS *Morse,* departs Hatteras Inlet en route for Brant Island on the Neuse River to provide support fire during a landing of ground troops who are participating in the campaign to seize New Bern. After the campaign, the *Morse* begins to

Union cavalry on the advance (Mottelay, *The Soldier in Our Civil War,* 1886).

patrol on the York River in Virginia until July, when it is assigned to the James River Flotilla.

March 13 (Thursday) In Arkansas, the 3rd Iowa Cavalry and the 6th Missouri Cavalry, commanded by Lt. Colonel Samuel Wood, engage a force of Confederates at Spring River. The Union sustains some casualties. Confederate casualties are unavailable.

In Missouri, Union Brigadier General John Pope's troops (Army of the Mississippi) launch a heavy bombardment against Confederate fortifications at New Madrid. The Confederates return fire throughout the day, but by evening, the Union fire silences three of the fort's guns, and several gunboats off Island No. 10 are damaged. In concert, the ground forces under Brigadier Generals Eleazer A. Paine (West Point, 1839) and John McCauley Palmer drive forward and force the pickets to retire. Meanwhile, other troops under General Joseph B. Plummer (West Point, 1841) move in and occupy Point Pleasant. Combined, these advances convince the Confederates that their positions are no longer tenable. After dusk and during a fierce thunderstorm, the Confederates evacuate their positions, giving Pope easy access to New Madrid, from where he will launch the assault on Confederate-held Island No. 10, on the Mississippi River several miles above the city. The Union occupies the city of New Madrid on the following morning. In conjunction, General David S. Stanley participates in the operations against New Madrid, and he will participate in the operations against Island No. 10.

In Virginia, the Union convenes a council of war at Fairfax Court House and decides that all troops not needed to hold Manassas Junction are to be landed at Fortress Monroe to ensure the safety of the capital. Fortress Monroe is scheduled to be the first base of operations for the campaign to seize Richmond, using an advance through Yorktown and West Point, the latter also to be used as a base of operations against the Rebel capital.

In Union general officer activity, John Morrison Oliver, who enlisted as a private with the 4th Michigan Infantry the previous April, is appointed colonel of the 15th Michigan Regiment. He had been commissioned a lieutenant soon after joining the 4th Michigan. Colonel Oliver (later brigadier general) participates at Shiloh and later commands a brigade at the Battle of Corinth.

In Confederate general officer activity, Colonel John Bordenave Villepigue is promoted to the rank of brigadier general effective this date. Villepigue is transferred from Florida to Mississippi to serve under General Braxton Bragg.

In Naval activity, Union forces aboard the steamers USS *Alice Price, New Brunswick, Patuxent* and *Pilot Boy,* attached to the command of General Ambrose Burnside, debark their respective transports and prepare to move against New Bern, North Carolina. Gunboats — including the USS *Delaware, Henry Brinker, Stars and Stripes, Hetzel, Decatur, Ohio, Perry* and the *St. Lawrence* — stand by in case of unexpected Confederate greetings. The brigades will advance toward New Bern on the following day. It is defended by Brigadier General Lawrence O. Branch, who has under his command eight infantry regiments, about 500 cavalrymen and eighteen artillery pieces. The defenders are deployed among five separate river fortifications.

March 13–14 In North Carolina, the 21st Massachusetts Regiment, as part of General Burnside's force, lands at the mouth of Slocum's Creek and advances along the south bank of the Neuse River en route to New Bern. After reaching a vast field, the regiment pauses to await General Reno and the remainder of the brigade. Shortly after suspending the march a contingent discovers some empty Confederate barracks, which had been under use by cavalry until a short time before the arrival of the Yankees. The abandonment of the barracks seems to have been due to the cannon fire originating on the gunboats prior to the landing. After-

General Ambrose Burnside (Johnson, *Campfire and Battlefield: History of the Conflicts and Campaigns,* 1894).

ward, the column approaches Croatan, and it too has been recently evacuated. The 21st Regiment raises its colors over the earthworks. Toward evening additional Confederate posts are discovered, but none are occupied; however, abandoned supplies are confiscated. Night positions are established and pickets (24th Massachusetts and 51st New York) are posted. Although no opposition is encountered, the troops become victims of a rainy night, which also causes problems for the small arms.

On the following morning, the area is blanketed by a deep fog. The rain had caused many of the contingent's muskets to become inoperable; however, the troops with the Enfield rifled muskets fix their bayonets and engage the enemy with their pointed steel. By about 0700, the brigade advances through the woods and

Left: Thieves are drummed out of Fortress Monroe, Virginia. *Right:* Captain John D. Frazer, 21st Massachusetts, captures his captors on 14 March 1862 (Mottelay, *The Soldier in Our Civil War,* 1886).

swampland with the 21st Massachusetts as vanguard. Confederate defenders are deployed across a road to the right side of the railroad tracks. A huge firestorm erupts as Confederate artillery initiates a bombardment of the advancing Union column, and the incessant streams of smoke from about 30 cannon add to the dismal fog, making it extremely difficult to clearly observe the battle, which begins to intensify. The only way of spotting the Confederate positions comes from the noise of the guns.

Meanwhile, the Confederates are bolstered with fresh reinforcements from New Bern. Nevertheless, the Union continues to inch its way forward. A heavy dose of fire from Company C, 21st Massachusetts, dislodges the Rebels from their rifle pits and prompts them to move to new positions in a ravine to the rear of a brickyard. At about this time, Sergeant Bates is ordered by General Jesse Reno to hoist the Stars and Stripes on one of the buildings within the Confederate lines. The regiment is jubilant when the colors are hoisted, but the mood soon turns somber when 1st Lt. F.A. Stearns of Company I is fatally wounded, the first man in the regiment to fall. Nonetheless, General Reno again orders the column to advance. Reno leads the force across the railroad tracks while under heavy fire, which costs the lives of 21 men within a matter of a few minutes.

General Reno becomes convinced that the Confederates by this time have been outflanked. He moves to bring up the remainder of the brigade, but the Confederates suddenly commit more firepower that diverts his attention and compels him to focus on the new threat to the immediate front of his brigade, the 16th and 86th North Carolina Regiments. The North Carolinians are entrenched behind solid positions and the railroad on their left flank is heavily fortified. The incessant fire forbids passage.

At this time, Lt. Colonel W. S. Clark, commanding officer of the 21st Massachusetts, faces a dilemma: retire or mount a charge. He chooses the latter and orders his command of about 200 men to launch a bayonet charge. The attack succeeds and the Rebels lose one gun, a six-pounder, which ironically had been manufactured in Massachusetts at Chicopee. The prize is later given to the regiment by General Burnside. In the meantime, Lt. Colonel Clark swings it around and uses it against the Rebels.

When the Confederates realize that Clark's command is not large, they decide to attack. The 7th, 35th and 37th North Carolina Regiments advance, but fortuitously, no volley precedes the charge and the troops with shouldered arms hesitate before lurching forward, giving the Yankees a reprieve. The Confederates charge, but they do not fire. Meanwhile, Clark orders a retreat to the railroad. By the time the Rebels reach a point from which they can fire upon the retreating force, most reach safety. Nevertheless, Clark's command sustains 41 casualties.

Once back at the railroad, Colonel Clark links with Colonel Isaac Rodman (4th Rhode Island) and shortly thereafter, Colonel Edward Harland (8th Connecticut) arrives. Both regi-

ments initiate a charge and the Confederates retire without firing a shot and regroup back at the ravine. During the day's fighting, Captain John D. Frazer, commander of Company H, 21st Massachusetts, is captured while leading a charge. He becomes wounded and drops his sword, but using his left arm he retrieves his saber and continues to lead the attack. During the retreat to the railroad he stumbles and falls into the water. The Rebels capture him, confiscate his sword and place him under a three-man guard. During the Union charge by the regiments under Colonels Rodman and Harland, the Confederates retreat, but Frazer's guards are unable to get their prisoner to speed up. Frazer, who still possesses his pistol, draws it and threatens to shoot his guards. Surprisingly, they surrender to him. Captain Frazer hands the three guards over to the 4th Rhode Island Regiment. The Confederate lieutenant who received Frazer's sword is also captured. Consequently, before the day's fighting ends, Frazer also gets his sword back.

Later, the Confederate prisoners, about 260 able bodied men, including 12 officers, are placed aboard the USS *Albany*. Also about 40 Confederate wounded troops are cared for by Confederate doctors and nurses. According to the report of Captain Frazer, casualties for the 13 participating regiments and one battery total 88 killed and 352 wounded.

March 14 (Friday) In North Carolina, Commander Stephen Rowan's naval force arrives off New Bern. The vessels, including the USS *Hunchback*, land troops under General Burnside, who launches an attack to seize the city. The Confederate shore batteries exchange fire with the naval force; however, the landing is successful. The invasion force, including U.S. Marines and sailors, attack the defending Confederates, commanded by General Lawrence Branch. The battle lasts throughout the day until eventually the Union is able to penetrate the defenses and force the Confederates to retire. Lt. Tillottson's naval battery, commanded by Lt. McCook, participates at this action. The Union seizes Fort Lane and Fort Ellis and captures more than 400 men, but the victory is costly. The Union loses nearly 100 killed and hundreds wounded. The Confederates evacuate the area, abandoning many supplies. The Union also seizes two steamboats.

With the loss of New Bern and the earlier loss of Fort Hatteras, Brigadier General Richard C. Gatlin is sacked within a week. Nevertheless, he remains in the Confederate service until September. Also, Confederate General Lawrence O'Bryan Branch is ordered to Virginia to be attached to General A.P. Hill's division. Confederate losses are ap-

proximately 170 killed or wounded and 413 captured. Also, the Union, after securing the area, operates from Fort Thompson. The rosin works, the railway bridge and the naval stores are destroyed.

In Missouri, Union forces prepare to reinitiate their attack to seize New Madrid, but it becomes unnecessary as information, delivered under a white flag of truce, arrives explaining that the Confederate troops have withdrawn. General John Pope's troops occupy the town, which is bulging with abandoned supplies. The Union confiscates 33 cannon, several thousand rifles, huge stores of ammunition and an abundant supply of horses, mules, wagons and tents.

In Tennessee, a Union contingent — including the 2nd East Tennessee, Company A, 1st East Tennessee, Company B, 49th Indiana and a detachment of the 1st Battery, Kentucky Cavalry — arrives in the vicinity of Big Creek Gap following a forced march that departed Boston, Kentucky, on the 7th. The force, commanded by Colonel J.P.T. Carter, clashes with Confederates, led by Lt. Colonel White. The Union loses one wounded. The estimated Confederate casualties are five killed, 15 wounded and about 15 captured. Also, elements of the 2nd Tennessee Volunteers, commanded by Colonel J.P.T. Carter, skirmish with Confederates in Jacksborough. The Union sustains one wounded. The Confederates lose one captured.

In Virginia, Union General Stoneman, commanding a brigade of cavalry and the 57th New York Volunteers, initiates a strong reconnaissance mission in the vicinity of Cedar Run. The operation lasts until the 16th. No casualties are reported.

In Confederate general officer activity, Colonel John Stevens Bowen (West Point, 1853), commanding officer of the 1st Missouri Infantry Regiment, is appointed brigadier general effective this day. Colonel Benjamin H. Helm (West Point, 1851), 1st Kentucky Cavalry, and Colonel Henry E. McCulloch, 1st Texas Mounted Rifles, are each promoted to brigadier general.

In Naval activity, the USS *Wamsutta*, a screw steamer acquired by the U.S. Navy on 20 Sep-

Lt. Tillottson's naval battery, commanded by Lieutenant McCook, at the Battle of New Bern, North Carolina (Mottelay, ***The Soldier in Our Civil War***, 1886).

tember 1861 in New York, is commissioned. Acting Volunteer Lieutenant William L. Stone receives command of the ship, which is assigned to the South Atlantic Blockading Squadron.

March 15 (Saturday) **In Missouri,** while Union Brigadier General John Pope is securing New Madrid, ten gunboats, commanded by Flag Officer Andrew Foote, arrive from Cairo, Illinois, and lay anchor at a spot about five miles from the next objective, Island No. 10, Tennessee. Separately, two steam transports, carrying the 16th and 47th Illinois Regiments and two batteries of light artillery, also arrive and join the fleet. In an effort to size up the Confederate strength, Foote dispatches reconnaissance detachments to gather intelligence. Upon their return, Foote learns that the objective resembles an invulnerable fortress, which most surely would withstand an attack by land. The island's defenses are shrewdly laid out with guns controlling all approaches, making the positions nearly invulnerable against an infantry assault. Nonetheless, Foote prepares to reduce the resistance, beginning on the following day.

In Union activity, at about this time, the 5th Minnesota Volunteer Regiment is organized; the regiment is complete by the end of April. Green Clay Smith is commissioned colonel of the 4th Kentucky Cavalry. It is thought that he originally enlisted in the service as a private, but it is not certain. Nevertheless, he is promoted to brigadier general as of 11 June 1862.

In Naval activity, the gunboats USS *Anacostia* and USS *Yankee* bombard Confederate batteries at Acquia Creek, Virginia.

March 16 (Sunday) **In Missouri,** Captain Kaiser skirmishes with Confederates at Marshall. Casualty reports are unavailable.

In Tennessee, General Beauregard, the commanding officer at Island No. 10, has diligently laid out his defensive works to discourage an assault. Seventy-five heavy guns are dispersed within 11 separate earthworks, and these are heavily supplemented by an additional 16 guns, strategically placed upon an armor-protected floating battery. Confederate gunboats with their complement of guns also stand nearby to lend their firepower to defend the island. Nonetheless, Union Flag Officer Foote is determined to destroy the defenses and seize the objective.

At 0830, the Union gunboats commence a colossal bombardment of Confederate positions at Island No. 10, the blocking stone which holds the key to Eastern Tennessee. The flagship USS *Benton* begins the festivities and is shortly thereafter followed by the other gunboats and the potent mortar boats. The interdiction fire is maintained for about eight hours, all the while receiving no return fire from the Confederates. The unrelenting barrages that hurl shell after shell pound the positions; however, they inflict no apparent damage. Meanwhile, the Union moves the 2nd Illinois Battery to the Missouri bank of the river, where it debarks at a point from which it can fire upon the Confederate gunboats.

At slightly before 1700, the guns are in action, and by dusk, the gunboats retire. The contest is resumed on the following day. As it becomes evident that the fleet alone cannot seize the objective, a suggestion by General Schuyler Hamilton gains prominence. He proposes that a canal be constructed to enable the Union to get its infantry and cavalry to the point of battle. The ambitious project under the leadership of Colonel J.W. Bissel and Lt. Henry B. Gall of the engineers is completed by April 5.

In Virginia, Union General George B. McClellan communicates with Secretary of War Edwin M. Stanton by letter to request that all troops in the area of Fortress Monroe be under his command, and that it occur with the merger of the Department of Virginia and the Department of the Potomac. McClellan suggests that General Joseph F. Mansfield take temporary command of Fortress Monroe. McClellan believes that this action will prove more expedient during the campaign to capture Richmond.

March 17 (Monday) **In Florida,** troops from the USS *Mohican* occupy St. Augustine.

In Kentucky, elements of the 22nd Kentucky, 40th and 42nd Ohio and the 1st Ohio Cavalry, commanded by Brigadier General James A. Garfield, engage Confederates commanded by Major Thomson at Pound Gap. The Union reports no losses. The Confederates have fewer than 10 wounded.

In Tennessee, General U.S. Grant is vindicated of all charges concerning his conduct at Fort Henry on February 6. He regains command of the Army of the Tennessee. General Charles F. Smith, Grant's temporary replacement, has become seriously ill and is jubilant at seeing Grant return. Smith does not recover from his illness. Grant remarks, "His [Smith's] personal courage was unquestioned, his judgment unsurpassed and his death a severe loss to our Western Army." After regaining command, Grant prepares to move against Pittsburg Landing on the Tennessee River, 22 miles northeast of Corinth, Mississippi, while he awaits Buell's Army. His forces arrive there on April 1.

Grant's Army of the Tennessee consists of five divisions: First Division, C.F. Smith (Lew Wallace, temporary commander); Second Division, John A. McClernand; Third Division, Lew Wallace; Fourth Division, William T. Sherman; and Fifth Division, Stephen A. Hurlbut. Reinforcements continue to pour into camp, which creates a new division under Benjamin M. Prentiss. Grant still awaits Buell before attacking Corinth.

In other activity, a Union contingent, including elements of the 4th Illinois Cavalry and the 5th Ohio Cav-

alry, commanded by Lt. Colonel Heath, engages Confederates at Black Jack Forest. The Union sustains four wounded. Confederate casualties are estimated at two wounded.

In Virginia, the Confederates move to fortify Richmond against a Union naval force that could navigate the James River to reach the capital. The site selected, Drewry's Bluff, had been named for Captain Augustus H. Drewry, a landowner in the area. The contingent that erects the defensive position is that of Captain Drewry's Southside Artillery. The men begin construction of their fortress in the sky that stands about 90 feet above the James and at a particularly dangerous bend in the river, giving the defenders sanctuary in the heights and excellent positioning for artillery domination of the river below. In addition to earthworks, the troops construct barracks and establish positions for three ominous seacoast guns, one 10-inch Columbiad and two eight-inch Columbiads. The fortification is named Fort Darling and stands less than ten miles from Richmond.

In Union general officer activity, Colonel William H. Emory is promoted to brigadier general. General Emory participates in the Peninsular Campaign under General McClellan. In 1864, he commands the XIX Corps in the Red River Campaign and the Shenandoah Campaign. In May 1865, General Emory receives the full rank of major general. Also, Colonel Orris Sanford Ferry (5th Connecticut) is named brigadier general. He participates in the Shenandoah Campaign as a brigade commander under General James Shields, and later he leads a brigade (General Keyes IX Corps) during the Peninsular Campaign. Afterward, he serves with the Army of the James in the IX Corps under General Butler. After the war General Ferry is elected to the U.S. Senate.

In Naval activity, in Tennessee at Island No. 10, Union gunboats are for awhile stymied as a dense fog remains until about 1100. Using some improvisation against this most formidable ob-

Union troops in camp outside of Corinth, Mississippi (Mottelay, *The Soldier in Our Civil War*, 1886).

stacle, the gunboats USS *Benton*, *Cincinnati* and *St. Louis* are linked together by lines and nudged forward to within close range of the Confederate batteries, which from the previous day still have not responded to the thunderous Union bombardments. Other unattached gunboats, the USS *Carondelet*, *Mound City* and *Pittsburg*, support the peculiar floating battery; combined they launch repeated volleys into the Rebel batteries. Unlike the previous day's activities, which had caused no damage, this enfilade demolishes two of the guns, while redistributing some of the earthworks and buildings by the accumulative power of the explosions.

In the meantime, the silent guns of the Confederates roar into action and the exchange continues until 1900, when the Union gunboats and the floating triple-ship battery retire. The Union vessels sustain some damage. The USS *Benton* sustains three hits and the USS *Cincinnati* one; however, neither gunship suffers any casualties. Another vessel, the USS *St. Louis*, during the initial phase of the fighting, loses two killed and two others severely wounded when the port-bow gun explodes. Island No. 10, nevertheless, remains potent, and the opposing Union forces exhibit no signs of easing the pressure.

March 18 (Tuesday)   In Arkansas, contingents of the 6th Missouri and 3rd Iowa Cavalry skirmish with Confederates at Salem. No casualty reports are available.

In Mississippi, the first contingents of the main body (approximately 44,000) of Confederate troops commanded by General A. Johnston occupy Corinth and prepare to strike Union lines at Shiloh.

In Tennessee, the Union again reinitiates its effort to reduce Island No. 10, action is slight. Of the ten gunboats in the vicinity, only the USS *Benton* commences firing and its participation is minimal. The bulk of the day's activity is handled by the mortar boats, which propel their devastating projectiles throughout the day and into the night in an effort to weaken the resistance and ostensibly to interrupt the Rebels' attempt to get some sleep. The bombardments commence at fifteen minute intervals, and to intensify the deafening attacks, six more mortar boats arrive prior to dawn. They too commence firing.

In Virginia, at Winchester, General Banks, pursuant to new orders, dispatches General Shields' force of about 11,000 troops to advance to Strasburg, where Confederate General Jackson's army is encamped. Banks also dispatches a contingent of his army to Manassas. On the 20th, Banks begins to withdraw to Manassas.

In other activity, Confederate President Jefferson Davis appoints Judah Benjamin as secretary of state. He succeeds Robert Mercer Taliaferro (former U.S. senator), who had left office during the previous month to become a member of the Senate of the Confederate States of America. Also, George W. Randolph is appointed Confederate secretary of war this day. Thomas Bragg, Confederate attorney general, resigns. He is replaced by Thomas H. Watts.

In Missouri, a contingent of the 1st Iowa Cavalry commanded by Captain Ankeny skirmishes a band of Confederates at Leesville. The Union sustains four wounded. The estimated Confederate casualties are two killed and one wounded. Also, a contingent of Missouri state militia, commanded by Lieutenants Christian and Jewell, initiates a reconnaissance mission in Johnson County. The operation lasts until the 23rd. The Union sustains one killed and one wounded. The estimated Confederate casualties are four killed. Another operation is launched as a contingent of the 5th Kansas Cavalry, commanded by Lt. Colonel Clayton, moves into the vicinity of Carthage and reconnoiters the area until the following day.

In Tennessee, Union Brigadier General Don Carlos Buell's 44,000 men (Army of Ohio) reach Columbia, Tennessee, which lies about eighty-five miles from Pittsburg Landing. At about this time, Confederate Colonel William Scott Dilworth (commander, 3rd Florida Infantry Regiment) is assigned command of the Department of Florida. He will succeed Brigadier General James H. Trapier (District of Eastern and Middle Florida). Apparently Trapier will travel to Alabama and later serve in South Carolina, but without distinction. His death occurs in December 1865.

In Confederate general officer activity, Brigadier General Samuel Jones is promoted to the rank of major general. He had succeeded General Bragg as commander of the Department of East Florida and Alabama the previous month. Like Bragg's, Jones' headquarters is at Pensacola. Subsequent to his duty in Florida, Jones is transferred to Corinth, Mississippi, where he will command a division under General Earl Van Dorn.

In Naval activity, in Tennessee, at Island No. 10, Flag Officer Andrew Foote's fleet, for the fourth consecutive day, commences fire upon the Confederate positions. Similarly to the previous day, the mortar boats handle the bulk of the bombardments, with the gunboats USS *Benton* and *Mound City* becoming involved only slightly. At about 1300, the Confederates receive a reprieve, as inclement weather moves in and causes a cancellation of any further combat activity. After this day there is little activity between the Union fleet and the Confederates until the 23rd. In other activity, Union blockade ships, including the USS *Sumter*, seize a British blockade runner, the *Emil St. Pierre*, off Charleston.

March 19 (Wednesday)   In *Union general officer activity,* Captain Daniel Phineas Woodbury (West Point, 1836) is appointed brigadier general of volunteers. At the outbreak of war he had been in North Carolina, married to a southerner, and he was solicited to abandon the Union for the Confederacy; however, he ignored the offers. He somehow acquired a pass from Jefferson Davis, which assured him of safe passage through Confederate lines, and arrived back in the north with his wife and children in time to participate at First Bull Run (Manassas).

Afterward, he participates in the Peninsular Campaign in command of a brigade of engineers. Subsequently, he participates at Fredericksburg in command of an operation that sets up pontoon bridges at the Rappahannock. He is afterward transferred to the Department of the Gulf, where he is struck by yellow fever. He dies on 15 August 1864 in Key West.

In Confederate general officer activity, General Richard Caswell Gatlin, commander of the Department of North Carolina, is relieved of command following the loss of Fort Hatteras and New Bern. General Gatlin resigns his commission the following September; however, he remains in another post he has held since 1861, that of adjutant general of North Carolina. After the war Gatlin engages in farming in Arkansas. His death occurs on 8 September 1896. Also, Brigadier General Samuel Jones is promoted to major general.

March 20 (Thursday)   In Missouri, a detachment of the Missouri state militia, commanded by Lieutenant McCabe, encounters and engages Confederates at McKay's Farm. The Union sustains one killed and one wounded.

In North Carolina, Union troops commanded by Colonel Thomas G. Stevenson and attached to the command of General Burnside depart New Bern and land at Washington, North Carolina, then gain it without incident.

In South Carolina, contingents of the 3rd New Hampshire Volunteers and the 3rd Rhode Island Volunteers commanded by Lt. Colonel Jackson initiate an operation in the vicinity of Bluffton. The mission continues until the 24th and includes skirmishes at Buckingham and Hunting Island.

In Virginia, General Thomas J. "Stonewall" Jackson's forces advance on Union positions near Strasburg and compel the Union troops in that area begin to withdraw. Meanwhile, General Banks, at Winchester, begins to withdraw toward Edward's Ferry, while General Shields, ordered to Strasburg on the 18th, is ordered to retire to Winchester to defend the southern approaches to Washington. On 22 March, the opposing armies collide at Kernstown (Winchester).

In Union general officer activity, Marsena Rudolph Patrick (West Point, 1835) is appointed brigadier general. General Patrick is a veteran of the Seminole Wars in Florida and of the Mexican War. General McClellan's recommendation had brought about his commission. He participates at Second Bull Run (Manassas) in command of a brigade (General Rufus King's division) and afterward, a division in General Joseph Hooker's corps, prior to his appointment to inspector marshal general of the armies involved in the campaign against Richmond. Colonel Isaac Ferdinand Quinby (13th New York) is commissioned brigadier general as of 17 March. He is assigned to the Department of the Mississippi.

In Confederate general officer activity, John S. Roane, former governor of Arkansas, is appointed brigadier general in the Confederate Army, effective this date. He is known to have opposed secession.

March 21 (Friday) In Tennessee, a large Union reconnaissance force — including contingents of the 1st East Tennessee, 7th Kentucky, 16th Ohio, 49th Indiana, bolstered by the 1st Kentucky Cavalry and one battery of the 9th Ohio, commanded by Colonel Samuel P. Carter — operates in the vicinity of Cumberland Gap until the following day. A brief skirmish occurs with Confederates. Casualties are unavailable.

In Union general officer activity, President Abraham Lincoln appoints James Craig to the rank of brigadier general, U.S. Volunteers, effective this date. Craig is dispatched to the western frontier for the purpose of protecting the U.S. mail. In November 1862, he receives command of the Department of Nebraska. He resigns his commission in May 1863; however, a year later in May 1864, he is appointed brigadier general of the Missouri State Militia, a post he retains until his resignation during January 1865. Also, Brigadier General Lewis Wallace is promoted to major general. Colonel John A. Logan, former Congressman who fought at Bull Run (Manassas) as a volunteer and afterward raised the 31st Illinois Regiment, is appointed brigadier general. Brigadier General Samuel R. Curtis is promoted to major general. Colonel Grenville Mellen Dodge (4th Iowa Infantry) is promoted to brigadier general effective this day. Colonel Speed Smith Fry (4th Kentucky) is named brigadier general. General Fry participates in the Stones River campaign (Battle of Murfreesboro), but afterward, he is assigned to garrison duty for the duration. He resigns from the service during August 1865; however, he does not receive the brevet rank of major general.

In other activity, Henry Moses Judah (West Point, 1843), who resigned his command as colonel of the 4th California Regiment in November 1861 to return east, is appointed a brigadier general. Prior to his appointment, he had been serving with the forces defending the capital. General Judah becomes acting inspector general of Grant's army at Shiloh. Subsequent to this duty, he commands a division under General Halleck during the Corinth operations. In winter 1862–1863, he is appointed inspector general of the Army of the Cumberland. General Judah, for a while during the summer of 1863, commands a division; however, his actions with regard to pursuit of Confederate General John Hunt Morgan, while his raiders threaten Ohio, fail to impress his superiors. For the remainder of the war, Judah is absent from all field duty and confined to administrative tasks. On 30 June 1862, Judah had been promoted to major of the 4th U.S. Infantry. He is mustered out of the service at the conclusion of the war and is assigned command of the garrison at Plattsburg Barracks in New York. While in command there, he dies on 14 January 1866.

In yet other activity, Brigadier General John A. McClernand is promoted to major general as of this day. Colonel Horatio Phillips Van Cleve (2nd Minnesota Infantry) is promoted to brigadier general. He participates at Murfreesboro, Tennessee, where he sustains a wound and at Chickamauga. William Harvey Lamb Wallace, a veteran of the Mexican War, is appointed brigadier general of volunteers. At the first stage of opening hostilities, General Wallace re-entered the army as colonel of the 11th Illinois Regiment, a 90-day unit.

In Naval activity, in Florida, the Union gunboats USS *Henry Andrew* and *Penguin* clash with Confederates at Mosquito Inlet. The Union sustains eight killed and eight wounded. A field report also lists two captured.

March 22 (Saturday) In Washington D.C., the Middle Military Department is established. It encompasses New Jersey, Pennsylvania, Delaware, the Eastern Shore of Maryland and the Eastern Shore of Virginia, as well as other counties in Maryland (Baltimore, Cecil, Harford, and Anne Arundel). General John Adam Dix is appointed commander. He retains the post until 9 June 1863.

In Missouri, contingents of the Union 2nd Kansas Regiment, commanded by Colonel Robert B. Mitchell, skirmishes with Confederates at Independence (Little Santa Fe). The Union sustains one killed and two wounded. Estimated Confederate casualties are seven killed and six captured.

In Union general officer activity, Brigadier Generals Don Carlos Buell, John Pope, Franz

General Don Carlos Buell (Mottelay, *The Soldier in Our Civil War,* 1886).

Sigel and Charles F. Smith are on this day promoted to the rank of major general. Colonel Jacob Gartner Lauman (commissioned colonel of the 7th Iowa Infantry during July 1861) is appointed brigadier general, effective this day in acknowledgment of his action during the operations against Fort Donelson. Colonel Robert Latimer McCook is promoted to brigadier general to rank from 21 March 1862. Richard James Oglesby is promoted to brigadier general. Oglesby, born in Kentucky during 1824, was orphaned at age nine. After losing his parents he was raised by relatives in Decatur, Illinois.

In Naval activity, at Island No. 10 in Tennessee, the Confederates maintain resolute control, despite remaining under siege by a large Union force, composed of a fleet under Flag Officer Andrew Foote and the Army of Mississippi under Major General John Pope. This day there is only some sporadic firing between the fleet and the Confederate batteries. The siege, which had begun on the 15th, still has seen no action between the opposing ground forces, and the Confederate positions still retain nearly all of the original 75 guns and the other 16 on a floating battery. The ten Union gunboats and accompanying mortar boats have been pounding the fortifications without cracking the determination of the defenders.

In Confederate Naval activity, the CSS *Florida,* initially named *Oreto* and built for the Confederacy in England, departs this day from Liverpool for Nassau to deliver the vessel to Confederates. John Lowe (master, Confederate, States Navy) is aboard. The captain and crew are English and they depart without weapons. The armaments are shipped separately aboard the steamer *Bahama.*

March 22–23 BATTLE OF KERNSTOWN (WINCHESTER) A force of Confederate cavalry under Colonel Turner Ashby raids Union pickets at Winchester, Virginia, but following a brief skirmish, it is driven back shortly after the alarm spreads; infantry, bolstered by artillery, join the fight and shower the intruders with shot and shell. During the action, Union General James Shields sustains a wound to the arm and another to his side, apparently caused by a shell from Chew's battery of Flying Artillery. Nevertheless, he remains in command and prepares for what he expects to be a major battle on the following day. Shields dispatches a brigade, commanded by Colonel Nathan Kimball, commander of the 14th Indiana Regiment, to Kernstown. Kimball is supported by Daum's Battery, and a reserve brigade under Colonel Jeremiah C. Sullivan (6th Indiana Regiment) is also available.

Confederate General Jackson had sent Colonel Ashby forward as a vanguard as part of his strategy to prevent any movement by General Banks that would position the Union on his left flank. Colonel Ashby, however, is inadvertently deceived by the numbers at Winchester. His report, dispatched to Jackson, indicates that Winchester is defended by only a small Union force; however, the erroneous information is caused because the greater part of Shields' division holds positions that are concealed by a group of hills. Nonetheless, based on the communication from Ashby, General Jackson initiates the advance and following an exhausting march, Jackson's main body, at about 1300, advances to Winchester and arrives on the following day.

On the 23rd, Colonel Kimball, in command due to General Shields' injuries, spots the Confederate forces to his front at Kernstown and discovers only Turner Ashby's cavalry, but there is a considerable force of Rebels in the nearby woods about one-half mile south of the town. Unknown to the Union, the Confederates, following a tedious two-day march, are near the point of exhaustion. General Jackson is well aware of the condition of his troops, but upon his arrival at about noon, he is also confident that his three brigades will perform. General Nathaniel Banks, thinking the strength of the Rebels is too light to attack, goes to Washington in response to a summons he had earlier received. Meanwhile, General Jackson, now aware of a larger Union force slightly west of Winchester, but still unaware of the forces concealed by the layer of the hills, discerns that he must attack or possibly face a bigger foe and defeat when Union reinforcements arrive.

Jackson splits his cavalry into two contingents, with those under Major Funsten ordered to cover the left flank. Colonel Ashby is given responsibility to contain the main body stretching east of the turnpike, and to block any retreat toward Winchester, while Jackson launches an attack against the western sector of the Union lines to gain the advantage by inflicting a stunning and decisive blow. The area to Kimball's front remains tranquil for the duration of the morning; however, at about noon, the Confederates under General Thomas J. Jackson commence an artillery attack that is immediately answered by Daum's Battery. Kimball's visible forces form a defensive line that stretches to the east side of the Valley Turnpike. On the west side of the positions, a strong contingent of infantry is deployed, bolstered by two batteries.

General Jackson launches the primary attack against Kimball's flank (west), but he is denied progress by the 8th Ohio and several companies of the 67th Ohio Regiment, which bolt to the Valley Turnpike and deploy on both sides, giving the Union troops sturdy positions from which they repulse the assault. Undaunted, Jackson pivots and strikes the right flank, drawing attention from the batteries. At about the same time, Jackson throws yet another force against the left flank. The flawless and overpowering maneuver jolts the Union. Daum's Battery is forced to pull back.

In the meantime, General Shields, still in bed due to his injuries of the previous day, is informed of the crisis. Instantly, he reacts by sending in Colonel Erastus B. Tyler's brigade in an effort to capture Jackson's batteries and force his left flank. At about 1500, the regiments form for the assault. At the signal, the 1st Virginia, 7th Indiana, 7th and 29th Ohio and the 110th Pennsylvania Regiments advance. The pace nat-

urally picks up to a full charge that is met head-on by the Confederates.

General Jackson had committed his final regiment when he observed the previously undiscovered brigade entering the fight. Kimball's troops cross the turnpike to engage the approaching Stonewall Brigade, while the concealed brigade closes against the 21st and 27th Virginia Regiments. Fulkerson's contingent is overwhelmed and more forces are advancing. Jackson, in an effort to save his outnumbered command, orders a withdrawal to enable him to reform at more tenable positions.

General Jackson arrives at the designated spot and directs General Robert Garnett to advance, but in the meantime, other Union units occupy the ground just abandoned and together a general advance moves at a quick pace toward Jackson's new line. At that point at about dusk, Jackson orders a full withdrawal. The column retires and moves toward Harrisonburg. Jackson's infantry bivouacs at Newtown to rest and Ashby's cavalry establishes night positions at Bartonville. The Union does not pursue the retreating column.

Other Union forces that participate in the battle include the 13th and 14th Indiana, the 84th Pennsylvania, the 5th and 62nd Ohio Regiments and contingents of the 8th and 67th Ohio Regiments. The Union sustains 103 dead, 440 wounded and 24 missing. Colonel William G. Murray of the 84th Pennsylvania Regiment is among the killed. The Confederates sustain 80 dead, 342 wounded and 269 captured. Confederate Colonel (later brigadier general) Francis R.T. Nicholls is severely wounded; he loses his left arm. Nonetheless, he returns to his command and will again be wounded at Chancellorsville in May 1863.

March 23 (Sunday)   In Florida, a Union contingent commanded by Captain Bird skirmishes with Confederates at Smyrna. The Union sustains about seven killed and three captured. The Confederates sustain some wounded.

In Missouri, a 200-man contingent of the 7th Illinois Cavalry commanded by Major Jonas Rawalt initiates a mission in the vicinity of Little River, where it encounters and engages a contingent of Confederates. The Union sustains two killed. The Confederates sustain two wounded and four captured. At Carthage, detachments of the 6th Kansas Cavalry skirmish with Confederates. No casualty figures are available.

In North Carolina, the forces of General Ambrose Burnside, which have seized Roanoke Island, New Bern and Washington, receive a new objective. Gunboats depart New Bern accompanying a brigade under General John G. Parke,

Union mortar bombarding Fort Macon, Georgia (Mottelay, *The Soldier in Our Civil War*, 1886).

which is en route to seize Morehead City. The forces secure the city and gain the terminus point of the Atlantic and North Carolina Railway. In related activity, a Union force composed of 13 regiments, supported by artillery and commanded by General John Grubb Parke, initiates an attack and siege against Confederate-held Fort Macon.

In Virginia, Union General Samuel P. Heintzelman's Corps, aboard ships, arrives near Fortress Monroe and debarks. Major General George McClellan will arrive during early April.

In Naval activity, in Tennessee at Island No. 10, on the Mississippi River, the Union gunboat USS *Mound City* moves into position and begins, for awhile, to fire upon Confederate batteries on the Kentucky shore opposite the island. Mortar boats join in the action to pick up the slack. They pour fire into the Rebel earthworks throughout the day, and by the end of the incessant fire, the battery on the Kentucky shoreline is put out of action. Following this day's action, the area remains relatively quiet until April 1. The Union fleet still maintains the siege, as the Confederate fortifications remain much too strong to risk a ground attack.

March 24 (Monday)   In North Carolina, Union troops, commanded by General John Parke (West Point, 1849) under General Ambrose Burnside, demand surrender of Confederate-controlled Fort Macon. The Confederates refuse the ultimatum and a siege is initiated.

In Virginia, after gathering all of his wounded, General Jackson moves out of Newtown and advances to Woodstock. The column, including wagons and ambulances, arrives without interruption; however, the Union does initiate pursuit. Union General Nathaniel Banks returns to Winchester from Washington. He had been kept informed of the previous day's fighting at Kernstown while in the capital, and his command had been ordered back to the Shenandoah Valley to ensure the Confederates are unable to break through toward either the capital or Harpers Ferry. This day, Banks takes personal command and dispatches a force in pursuit of General Thomas J. Jackson's retiring army. The Union advances toward Woodstock and establishes camp on Cedar Creek.

In Union general officer activity, Colonel Mahlon Dickerson Manson (10th Indiana) is promoted to brigadier general.

March 25 (Tuesday)   In North Carolina, Beaufort falls to Union troops under the command of General Ambrose Burnside; it is occupied without incident. The 4th Rhode Island and the 8th Connecticut Regiments remain there to hold it, while the other troops in General John G. Parke's Brigade are involved with the ongoing siege of Fort Macon. Major John H. Allen, 4th Rhode Island Regiment, is appointed provost marshal of Beaufort.

In Virginia, Union General Banks, en route to Woodstock, arrives at Strasburg and establishes camp there, but he dispatches troops toward Woodstock and the contingent encounters Confederate cavalry under Colonel Ashby and two regiments, the 42nd and 48th under Colonel Jesse Burks. Some skirmishing occurs and afterward, the Union pulls back to Tom's Brook and establishes a defensive line of pickets. The main body under Banks remains in place at Strasburg until 2 April. Meanwhile, General Stonewall Jackson departs Woodstock with the other brigades and establishes positions at Mt. Jackson.

In Naval activity, Marines aboard the USS *New London* participate in the sea battle against the Confederate vessels *Oregon* and *Pamlico* in the Gulf of Mexico at Pass Christian, Mississippi. The CSS *General Earl Van Dorn* (known also as *Van Dorn, Earl Van Dorn* and *General Van Dorn*) departs New Orleans under the jurisdiction of the Confederate Army en route to join the Mississippi River Defense fleet. It pauses at Memphis to complete its ironwork. Afterward, the *Van Dorn* moves to Fort Pillow, Tennessee.

March 26 (Wednesday)   In Missouri, a 25-man contingent of the Union 6th Missouri Regiment, commanded by Captain Ostermayer,

skirmishes with a Confederate force composed of about 40 troops at Gouge's Mill. The Union reports no casualties. The Confederates sustain one man killed. In other activity, a contingent of Missouri state militia, commanded by Major Emory S. Foster, skirmishes with Confederates led by Major Houx at Post Oak. The Union force, numbering about 60 troops, is outnumbered by the 200-man Confederate force. The Union sustains two killed and seven wounded and the Confederates sustain about five killed and 15 captured. Also, at Humansville, Companies A, B, D and E, commanded by Captains Stockton, Cosgrove, Gravely and Smith respectively, clash with a Confederate force estimated at about 400 troops. Union casualties are reported as 12 wounded. Confederates report 16 killed and 20 wounded as well as three captured.

In Naval and Marine Corps activity, the USS *Mercedita* and *Sagamore* sail to attack Confederate positions and vessels at Apalachicola in West Florida. Marines and sailors aboard both vessels participate in the action and occupy the town on April 3.

In Confederate general officer activity, Brigadier General Daniel H. Hill is promoted to the rank of major general. William Nelson Pendleton, who carries the title reverend as well as being a colonel, is promoted to brigadier general. Pendleton had been a minister in Lexington, Virginia, at Grace Church when hostilities erupted; he soon entered the artillery service (Rockbridge Artillery) of Virginia. His service remains with the Army of Northern Virginia and is essentially concentrated on the army's artillery. At this time, he serves on the staff of General Joseph E. Johnston. His primary responsibilities center on administrative duties and command of reserve ordnance. Pendleton's daughter marries Edwin Gray Lee, who also becomes a brigadier general in the Confederacy.

In Naval activity, the USS *Sebago* (double-ended sidewheel gunboat) is commissioned. Lt.

Edmund W. Henry receives command of the gunboat, which is attached to the North Atlantic Blockading Squadron. It embarks from Portsmouth, New Hampshire, on 6 April and arrives at Newport News on 11 April.

March 26–28   THE BATTLE OF APACHE CANYON (GLORIETTA PASS) In New Mexico, a column composed of the 1st Regiment Colorado Volunteers, bolstered by two small batteries and led by Colonel John B. Slough, recently departed Fort Union to rendezvous with a force under General Canby. On this day, a contingent of Slough's force, composed of about 200 cavalry and 180 infantry troops under Major Chivington, encounters a force of Sibley's Confederates about 15 miles east of Santa Fe at Johnson's Ranch in Apache Canyon. The two sides clash in a tenacious skirmish that erupts at about 1100 when the Confederate pickets are approached. The Confederates, under Major Charles Pyron, stand at about 350 troops, bolstered by some artillery. The gunners on each side are quickly put into action in the field of battle in a steep gorge shadowed on each side by sheer inclines. The ground itself is a collection of colossal boulders and undersized cedar trees adorning a primitive wagon path.

The thunderous sounds of the opposing sides' artillery reverberates throughout the canyon and infantry fire becomes incessant as the contest continues throughout most of the afternoon; however, the Union does not commit its entire force. Colonel Slough, informed that the Confederate baggage trains as well as the ammunition supplies are all located at Johnson's Ranch, had earlier dispatched Major John Chivington's command to the ranch. Chivington travels over the mountain and the Confederates fail to detect his movement.

Meanwhile, the Confederates in the canyon continue to raise fierce resistance, but the Union retaliatory action is equally tenacious. Nevertheless, by late afternoon, the Confederates disengage and retire haphazardly to Santa Fe. While Colonel Slough finishes up in the canyon,

Left: General Burnside is en route on the rails from New Bern to Beaufort, North Carolina. *Right:* General Ambrose Burnside's headquarters at New Bern (Mottelay, *The Soldier in Our Civil War,* 1886).

the Confederate supplies are intercepted and destroyed by Chivington's command. The Union, however, does not initiate pursuit. Colonel Slough, convinced his objective had been obtained, returns to Fort Union. Colonel Chivington retires to Pigeon Ranch. Also, General Canby departs Fort Craig for Albuquerque, a Confederate-held town, but Confederates arrive there in time to dissuade Canby from launching an attack. He returns to Fort Craig.

The loss of supplies at Apache Canyon inflicts a severe handicap on Sibley's campaign. After pondering the loss of nearly all of his equipment and baggage, combined with the later insertion of the "California Column," composed initially of the 1st California Cavalry, five companies commanded by Colonel Edward E. Eyre, the 1st California Infantry (Colonel James H. Carleton) and a light battery consisting of four brass field pieces commanded by 1st Lt. John B. Shinn (3rd U.S. Artillery), Colonel Sibley decides to abandon the campaign. The California Column is soon reinforced by the 5th California Infantry, commanded by Colonel George W. Bowie. Sibley's decision to abandon the campaign to secure the Indian Territory for the Confederacy ensures that it will remain under Union domination. The Confederates initiate their return to Texas about mid–April or early May. The Union sustains 32 killed, 75 wounded and 35 missing. The Confederates suffer 36 killed, 60 wounded and about 93 missing.

Union Colonel John R. Slough (later brigadier general) contributes greatly to the victory over Sibley, although he acted in direct opposition to Canby, the ranking officer in the region. The 7th Texas (Confederate) Cavalry participated with General Sibley during this campaign, in which they expected to hold the Indian Territory. Confederate Colonel William Steele (West Point, 1840), commanding the 7th Texas Cavalry Regiment, is promoted brigadier general in September.

March 27 (Thursday)   In Florida, Companies D and K, 6th New York Volunteers, supported by Company L, 1st Artillery, commanded by Captain Closson, initiate a reconnaissance mission in the vicinity of Santa Rosa Island. The operation continues until March 31.

In Tennessee, Confederate Tennessee infantry and cavalry contingents commanded by Colonel (later brigadier general) John C. Vaughn (3rd Tennessee Regiment) move into Morgan and Scott Counties. Some skirmishing occurs with Union forces. Union casualties stand at five killed and seven wounded. Confederate estimated casualties are about 15 killed and wounded.

In Virginia, Confederate cavalry attached to General Turner Ashby's command attacks a Union Camp in the vicinity of Strasburg. The Union sustains one killed and one wounded. Confederate casualties, if any, are unavailable.

March 28 (Friday)   In Georgia, a Union reconnaissance contingent, commanded by Major O.T. Beard, initiates an operation in the vicinity of the Mouth of the St. Augustine Creek.

In New Mexico, a battle erupts at Glorietta Ranch (Pigeon's Ranch). (See also, **March 26–28 THE BATTLE OF APACHE CANYON [GLORIETTA PASS].**)

In Tennessee, a Union force under Major General Don Carlos Buell departs Nashville en route to join General Grant at Pittsburg Landing, from where they are to launch a joint attack against the Confederates at Corinth, Mississippi. When Confederate General Beauregard learns of the imminent convergence of the two Union armies, he decides to depart Corinth and accomplish two things: prevent the forces of Grant and Buell from joining, and to attack and defeat Grant before Buell can arrive. It is thought by the Confederates that the army under Buell cannot arrive before April 7.

In Virginia, the 28th Pennsylvania Volunteer Regiment, commanded by Colonel John White Geary, skirmishes with Confederates at Middleburg.

March 29 (Saturday)   In Virginia, Confederate General Robert E. Lee dispatches General Cadmus M. Wilcox's brigade to reinforce General J.B. Magruder at Yorktown. Lee, in a letter to General Magruder, explains the possibility of an attack upon Norfolk instead of Yorktown.

In Confederate activity, the Confederate Armies of the Kentucky and of the Mississippi are joined as the Army of the Mississippi, commanded by General Albert S. Johnston, with General Pierre Gustave T. Beauregard becoming second in command. Generals Leonidas Polk (First Corps), Braxton Bragg (Second Corps), William J. Hardee (Third Corps) and George B. Crittenden (Reserve Corps) also hold command in the Army of the Mississippi.

March 30 (Sunday)   In Georgia, the Union 13th Georgia and the 46th New York Regiments, commanded by Colonel Rosa, clash with Confederates led by Captain Crawford at Wilmington and Whitemarsh Island. The Union sustains one killed. The Confederates sustain one wounded and some captured. The clashes occur until the following day.

In Mississippi, Confederate General Albert S. Johnston, quartered at Corinth, is reinforced by the commands under Beauregard, Bragg, Crittenden, Hardee and Polk. This combined Army is preparing to face the Union at Shiloh, Tennessee, on April 6. General William J. Hardee selects Colonel (later brigadier general) St. John R. Liddell as his confidant to relay messages between his headquarters and General Johnston, but here at Corinth, he will be assigned command of a brigade.

In Tennessee, Union forces — including the 27th Illinois Volunteer Regiment, 15th Wisconsin Volunteer Regiment, the 2nd Illinois Cavalry, Captain Hutchin's Cavalry and Sparrestrom's Artillery Battery — close on Union City. Fourteen Rebels are captured.

In Missouri, a unit of the 1st Iowa Cavalry skirmishes at Clinton. The Union sustains one wounded. The Confederates sustain about one killed and some wounded.

March 31 (Monday)   In Missouri, Union gunboats are closing at New Madrid Bend. At the time New Madrid is abandoned by the Confederates, the CSS *Kanawha Valley*, a hospital boat, is there, but it is destroyed by fire during the attack against Island No. 10. A Union contingent of the Missouri Cavalry, led by Colonel Peabody, skirmishes with Confederates at Pink Hill. The Union suffers three wounded. The Confederates sustain about six wounded.

In New Mexico, Colonel Canby departs Fort Craig en route to link with another force under Colonel Gabriel R. Paul. Colonel Paul's column departs Fort Union on 6 April, and afterward the combined forces pursue the retreating Confederates. A clash occurs at Peralta on 15 April.

In North Carolina, Union and Confederate contingents clash at Deep Gully. Units are not recorded and casualties are unavailable.

In Tennessee, Company I, 5th Ohio Cavalry, commanded by Lieutenant Murray, engages Confederates at Purdy Road. The Confederates seize three Union troops. Also, Union Captain Haw leads a contingent into the vicinity of Paris. The mission lasts until April 2.

In Confederate general officer activity, Brigadier General Leroy Walker, having been assigned garrison duty at Mobile and afterward at Montgomery, Alabama, and unable to get an

General Albert S. Johnston (Johnson, ***Campfire and Battlefield: History of the Conflicts and Campaigns,*** **1894).**

assignment in the field, resigns his commission. Nonetheless, General Walker, with the rank of colonel, presides over a Confederate military court in northern Alabama from 6 April until the end of the war. Afterward he resumes his law practice. He succumbs during August 1884.

April 1 (Tuesday)   In Mississippi, Confederates under General Albert S. Johnston depart Corinth for Shiloh, Tennessee, where they intend to attack General Grant's lines. At this time, Grant's army is completely in place at Pittsburg Landing (Shiloh) on the Tennessee River, about 20 miles northeast of Corinth. The Confederates are hampered by continuing delays, causing postponement of the assault until advance units of Johnston's cavalry can be pressed into service to harass Union lines. This cavalry activity solidifies Grant's suspicions that a Confederate offensive will soon occur.

In Tennessee at Island No. 10, the siege continues, and although it has been ongoing since February 16, the opposing ground forces have not yet encountered each other. Flag Officer Andrew Foote's fleet has been maintaining bombardments in an effort to lessen the resistance. Nonetheless, the Confederates provide no outward signs of capitulating. This day, all remains rather quiet until the evening, when the Union executes an enormously dangerous operation amid a wild hurricane that is ravaging the area. After acquiring a yawl (small two-masted boat) and an especially diligent crew from one of the gunboats, Colonel George W. Roberts, 42nd Illinois Regiment, with his detachment of 40 troops, is rowed to shore. The crew utilizes muffled oars to lessen the possibility of being detected, but with the elements being so nasty, no surprise is gained, because a sudden bolt of lightning exposes the boat to some sentinels. The guards, for a short while, begin firing in the darkness and then return to their lines. Without returning fire, the boat slips through the darkness and makes it to shore. The detachment without interference sprints to the battery and spikes each of the guns there. Shortly

thereafter, the Union troops re-board the yawl and return to the gunboats. The gunboats USS *Benton, Pittsburg, St. Louis, Cincinnati* and the *Mound City* had been just offshore in the event Colonel Roberts' unit became engulfed in more than they could handle.

In Missouri, a 50-man contingent of Missouri cavalry commanded by Captain Murphy skirmishes with Confederates at Little Sni River. The Union reports two wounded. The Confederate estimated casualties are five killed, six wounded and one captured. Also, an Advance Guard of the 38th Illinois Infantry Regiment, commanded by Colonel William P. Carlin, skirmishes with Confederates at Doniphan. The unit suffers one killed. Confederate casualties are unavailable.

In Virginia, Union General McClellan continues diverting 12 divisions of the Army of the Potomac to reinforce General John Ellis Wool's force at Fortress Monroe. The move is a continuation of the plan to strike the forces under Confederate General John Magruder at Yorktown.

In Union general officer activity, Colonel William Sooy Smith (13th Ohio Infantry) is appointed brigadier general at about this time. General Smith commands XIV Corps during the Vicksburg campaign; afterward he becomes chief of cavalry under General Grant and under General Sherman. James Alexander Williamson, following a short time with the 4th Iowa as adjutant, becomes lieutenant colonel of the regiment at about this time (April). In July, he becomes colonel of the regiment as successor to Colonel Grenville M. Dodge, the latter having been promoted to brigadier general the previous month. He participates in various actions, including Elkhorn Tavern, the Vicksburg Campaign and the Chattanooga Campaign, and toward the close of hostilities he becomes commander of the District of Missouri.

In Confederate general officer activity, Colonel Lewis Addison Armistead is appointed

brigadier general. He will serve under Brigadier (later major general) George E. Pickett and participate with his brigade during the Peninsular Campaign and at Gettysburg. Major (later brigadier general) William Gaston Lewis, 43rd North Carolina Regiment, is named lieutenant colonel at about this time (April). The 18th North Carolina (state troops) is reorganized. John Decatur Barry, a private (later general) in the regiment, is elected captain. The regiment will participate in such battles as Seven Days,' Cedar Mountain, Second Manassas, Sharpsburg (Antietam) and Gettysburg.

In Naval activity, the *Corwin,* a side-wheel gunboat built during 1849 in Philadelphia for the Coast Survey and in 1861 transferred to the U.S. Revenue Service, is attached to the North Atlantic Blockading Squadron. It operates as part of the squadron until mid–July.

April 2 (Wednesday)   In Missouri, a Union contingent commanded by Colonel Silas C. Toler initiates a reconnaissance mission that departs Cape Girardeau and operates in Dallas, Jackson and Whitewater. The mission terminates on the 4th. Meanwhile, Union Colonel (later General) William P. Carlin's main force arrives at Putnam's Ferry and engages Confederates there. The contingent includes the 21st and 38th Illinois Volunteer Infantry Regiments, the 5th Illinois Cavalry and Ohio Artillery. The Union reports no casualties. The Confederates sustain one wounded and four captured.

In Tennessee, at Island No. 10, the siege into its 18th day is no closer to conclusion. Still, there has been no contact between the land forces and the Union Fleet. The warships, although quiet this day, have up to this point catapulted thousands of rounds into the Confederate positions, but without gain.

In Virginia, Major General George B. McClellan arrives at Fortress Monroe. At this time about 58,000 troops and much artillery is on hand. On the following day, McClellan will move toward Yorktown. Confederate units have

Left: Union invasion and capture of Island No. 10 during a hurricane on 1 April 1862. *Right:* Thoroughfare Gap, a pass in the mountains on the Manassas Gap Railroad in the vicinity of Strasburg, Virginia (Mottelay, *The Soldier in Our Civil War*, 1886).

General George B. McClellan (Mottelay, *The Soldier in Our Civil War*, 1886).

A Union column en route to Yorktown, Virginia, crosses Howard's Bridge in the vicinity of Big Bethel (Mottelay, *The Soldier in Our Civil War*, 1886).

continued to move into the area to meet the threat. One of these is the 49th North Carolina, led by Colonel (later brigadier general) Stephen D. Ramseur. In other activity, the Union 28th Pennsylvania Volunteer Regiment occupies Thoroughfare Gap. General Banks, under orders from General McClellan to intercept General Jackson's force and drive him from the Shenandoah, makes little progress. Jackson remains in the vicinity of Mt. Jackson, however, Union pursuit following the fighting at Kernstown on the 22nd-23rd has been inactive except for some small units. On this day, Banks departs Strasburg and returns to Woodstock.

April 3 (Thursday) In Mississippi, a large Union force—including the 9th Connecticut and the 6th Massachusetts Regiments commanded by Major General Charles R. Lovell, while in operation in the vicinity of Biloxi and Pass Christian—encounters a Confederate force. However, no major action occurs. The Union had departed Ship Island and will return on the following day

In Tennessee, at Island No. 10 on the Mississippi River, the Union unequivocally concludes that the Union fleet by itself is insufficient to reduce the resistance. Major General John Pope had been of the belief that ground forces should have been in place to attack the rear of the Confederate batteries on the Kentucky side. During the evening (midnight 3rd-4th) another tremendous thunderstorm pummels the area. Using the storm to its advantage, the gunboat USS *Carondelet,* led by Commander Henry Walke, departs for New Madrid. As the vessel passes beyond the island but well within range of the Confederate guns, the storm generates enough lightning to illuminate the entire ship as if it were on parade. The batteries, using the lightning for illumination and as a target loca-

tor, commence firing. The highlighted vessel ignores the fire, declines to return the barrages and pushes on as fast as possible, somehow avoiding injury and damage during the enfilade, and safely reaches New Madrid. Also, a skirmish develops at Monterey when the 5th Ohio Cavalry, commanded by Colonel William H.H. Taylor, clashes with the Confederate 1st Alabama Cavalry, commanded by Colonel (later general) James H. Clanton. The Union reports one wounded and one Confederate captured.

In Virginia, the Army of the Potomac begins to move against the Rebels under Major General John B. Magruder at Yorktown. Two columns led by Generals Samuel P. Heintzelman and Erasmus Keyes advance with an intent to prevent the forces of General Joseph E. Johnston from reaching and reinforcing Magruder. Heintzelman's force is composed of the divisions of Generals Charles S. Hamilton and Fitz John Porter. General Keyes' contingent is composed of the divisions of Darius N. Couch and William F. Smith.

In Naval activity, the *Somerset* (wooden-hulled, side-wheel ferryboat), acquired by the U.S. Navy at Washington, D.C., on 4 March 1862, is commissioned the USS *Somerset* and assigned to the East Gulf Blockading Squadron. It arrives at Key West, Florida, on 27 April to begin service with the squadron.

April 4 (Friday) In Tennessee, Confederate cannon fire erupts and bombards the Union lines at Shiloh, while cavalry springs an evening attack on a Union picket post, capturing one officer and seven enlisted men. Union Colonel Ralph Buckland's regiment and troops attached to General William T. Sherman's command give chase, but the Rebel cavalry escapes. In the meantime, Confederate General Beauregard, apprehensive about an assault because of the loss of the element of surprise, is unsuccessful in his attempt to convince General Albert S. Johnston to

call off the attack against Grant. Meanwhile, a contingent composed of detachments of the 5th Ohio Cavalry and the 48th, 70th and 72nd Ohio Regiments, commanded by Lieutenant Charles Murray, skirmishes with Confederates at Adamsville (Crump's Landing). The Union reports losses as two wounded and three troops captured. Confederate losses are estimated at 20 wounded. Another skirmish erupts at Lawrenceburg when a contingent composed of the 26th Ohio and the 17th Indiana, bolstered by the 3rd Ohio Cavalry and commanded by General Milo S. Hascall, clashes with Confederates as it advances towards Shiloh. The Union reports no losses. The Confederates' estimated loss is two wounded. And yet another clash occurs in the vicinity of Pittsburg Landing (Shiloh). A Union contingent composed of a guard detachment of the 70th Ohio and Company B, 72nd Ohio Regiment, commanded by Lieutenant Herbert and Major L. Crockett respectively, skirmishes with a Confederate force that encroaches its lines. The Union casualties are estimated at eight wounded and 11 captured. The Confederate estimated casualties are two wounded and 10 captured.

In Virginia, the Union force under General Samuel Heintzelman, which had departed Fortress Monroe on the previous day, arrives at

General George McClellan's army between Big Bethel and Yorktown, Virginia (Johnson, *Campfire and Battlefield: History of the Conflicts and Campaigns,* 1894).

Three views of Battery No. 4 in front of Yorktown, Virginia (Johnson, *Campfire and Battlefield: History of the Conflicts and Campaigns*, 1894).

Big Bethel. The other column, which had moved out with General Erasmus D. Keyes, arrives at Warwick Court House. General George B. McClellan accompanies Heintzelman. The two forces converge in front of Yorktown on the following day. Meanwhile, Confederate General John B. Magruder had initially decided to make a stand near Big Bethel at Ship Island and Young's Mills, but the superiority of the Union forces has compelled him to alter his plan. A new line is established that stretches from Yorktown to Wayne's Mills on the Warwick River. About 20,000 Confederate troops are preparing for the assault. Two other Confederate divisions of the Army of Northern Virginia will arrive during the middle of April to boost the force to about 50,000 men. In contrast, about 10,000 men in Union General Louis Blenker's division have been diverted to support General John Frémont in the Shenandoah Valley, and General McClellan also loses McDowell's Corps, which is also needed to defend Washington; however, reinforcements still continue to pour into the area. McClellan will request and receive General Franklin's Division, which will be detached from McDowell's Corps.

In Confederate general officer activity, John Hunt Morgan is commissioned colonel (later brigadier general) of the 2nd Kentucky Cavalry.

In Naval activity, the USS *Carondelet,* commanded by Commander Henry Walke, had the previous night volunteered to run the batteries along Island No. 10, Tennessee. The ironclad, packed with hay for added protection, having

successfully completed the mission by reaching New Madrid, causes the crews of the other vessels to become confident that they too can challenge the guns. The southern fortress, with more than seventy-five guns and some gunboats, has shown no signs of buckling. The safe passage of the daring *Carondelet* ensures that more vessels will soon run the gauntlet to aid the ground troops and doom the Confederates on Island No. 10.

April 5 (Saturday)   In South Carolina, the Union 3rd New Hampshire Regiment commanded by Colonel Enoch Fellows occupies Edisto Island.

In Tennessee, Confederate General Albert S. Johnston's 40,000 man Army comes within two miles of U.S. Grant's lines at Shiloh (Pittsburg Landing). Johnston positions his men around a log house called Shiloh Church. Meanwhile, Grant is confident the Rebels will only use hit and run tactics. He does not believe they will capture either Pittsburg or Crump's Landing, Tennessee (Union transports and supplies are stationed at Crump's Landing).

At the siege of Island No. 10, the Union completes a canal that extends about twelve miles in length and fifty feet wide, the larger part of it stretching from a position opposite Island No. 8, straight through the swamps to a place opposite New Madrid. In the meantime, steamboats have arrived from Cairo. In addition, Union General John Pope has modified some barges, linking them together to create improvised floating batteries.

In Confederate general officer activity, Joseph Finegan, in charge of Florida's military affairs, is appointed brigadier general. He receives command of the District of Middle and East Florida.

In Naval activity, the USS *Port Royal* ("double-ender" side wheel steam gunboat) is commissioned at about this time (April). Initially it serves on the James River, but later in the year, it is transferred farther south to the North Carolina sounds prior to being transferred to the Gulf of Mexico, where it remains on duty beyond the end of the war. It is decommissioned during 1866 and sold the following month.

April 5–6   In Texas, the Confederate 13th Texas Infantry, based in the vicinity of San Luis Pass, encounters a peculiar vessel. At 1900, information arrives at headquarters of Confederate Colonel Joseph Bates (4th Texas Volunteers) that a steamer flying the British flag and the Confederate flag appeared off San Luis Pass at 1600. The vessel was actually from the blockading squadron commanded by Lt. Charles Hunter. The Confederate imposter had spotted a blockade running schooner in the harbor. Hunter fools the defenders and moves into the harbor and destroys the *Columbia,* and the Yankees seize a schooner. During the daring scheme, a small party of eight men, including Confederate Lt. O.W. Edwards, is drawn out to the imposter. They are seized and their boat is later used to innocently pass the batteries, move to the rear of the island and destroy the *Columbia.* The boat is also used to send the crew of the *Columbia* back to shore. By daylight on the 6th, reinforcements arrive, but the *Columbia* and its cargo of cotton is already in flames. At dawn on 6 April, the Confederate batteries exchange fire with the Union vessel, but Hunter returns to Farragut's fleet unscathed.

April 5–May 3   In Virginia, the Confederates under Major General John B. Magruder at Yorktown come under Federal siege. The Union Second, Third, and Fourth Corps, Army of the Potomac, participate. The Rebels, although outnumbered, hold the town until compelled to evacuate on 3 May. Colonel Isaac St. John, Magruder's chief engineer, contributes greatly to the Rebel ability to hold out. St. John becomes a brigadier general during February 1865 in the last days of the war.

April 6 (Sunday)   In Virginia, Union troops, including the 1st New York Light Artillery, engage Confederates at Warwick Courthouse. Confederate fire hits an ammunition chest, setting it afire and causing concern for the troops; but the actions of Sgt. David L. Smith extinguishes the fire, saving many lives. Smith becomes the recipient of a Medal of Honor for his actions.

In Tennessee, a three-company contingent of the Confederate 43rd Tennessee Regiment (General Kirby Smith's Command), commanded by Lt. Colonel Key, departs Greenville en route to the vicinity of Laurel Valley, North

Carolina. During the operation, the Union loses slightly more than 10 killed. The Confederates sustain two killed and one wounded.

In Missouri at New Madrid, the USS *Carondelet*, under orders from Major General John Pope, embarks on a reconnaissance mission to Point Pleasant, where Union Brigadier General Gordon Granger's force is deployed. The Union warship spots various earthworks and easily determines that they are manned and active due to some quick reaction to the sight of the vessel, which prompts heavy shore fire as the *Carondelet* passes by. Nevertheless, the *Carondelet*, except for some minor return fire, does not become diverted, rather it continues on the mission. During the return voyage to New Madrid, subsequent to passing a bothersome battery, the *Carondelet* delivers some devastating return fire, prompting the gunners to evacuate their positions. Shortly thereafter, a detachment under Captain Marshall moves ashore and spikes each gun in the battery. When the *Carondelet* returns to New Madrid, the *Pittsburg*, which has also succeeded in passing the guns at Island No. 10, is there to greet it. Major General John Pope then orders both gunboats to move to Tiptonville and clear the way for his troops to follow and land there to join with the troops arriving from the recently constructed canal. Both ships depart and the mission is accomplished: the batteries are silenced with effective fire as the ships advance. Commander Walke orders many of the guns, those posted below Watson's Landing, to be spiked.

In New Mexico, a large Union force, commanded by Colonel (later general) Edward Richard S. Canby, skirmishes with Confederates at Albuquerque. The Union reports no casualties. The Confederates sustain one wounded. Colonel Gabriel Paul departs Fort Union leading his column toward a link up with General Canby, who had departed Fort Craig on 31 May.

The combined forces then pursue the retreating forces of Confederate General H.H. Sibley.

In Confederate general officer activity, Joseph Finegan, who has been in charge of Confederate military affairs in Florida as a civilian, is this day promoted to brigadier general. His command will be the Department of Middle and East Florida. Brigadier General Jones Mitchell Withers, subsequent to his activity at Shiloh, is promoted to the rank of major general, effective this date.

April 6–7   BATTLE OF SHILOH The Confederate Army of the Mississippi, at about 0300, boldly and with total surprise launches a massive attack against Union lines at Shiloh, Tennessee. The Confederates, with General William J. Hardee's Third Corps in the center at the point, flanked on the left by Leonidas Polk's First Corps and on the right by Braxton Bragg's Second Corps, each begin moving into position on the Corinth Road, Owl Creek and Ridge Road respectively. The entire operation is concluded without detection by the Union, setting up a colossal ambush that awaits only the signal to launch the assault. It comes at precisely 0500 and the three solid lines push off. General Hardee's advance troops, trailed closely behind by the main body, smash into General Prentiss' picket lines, driving them back.

On the right, two brigades plow into General William T. Sherman's left flank near Shiloh Church and drive through, slamming directly into General Prentiss' main force. Both the strength and the depth of this attack catch the Union off guard, and to make the situation even more critical, many of the Union contingents have never seen battle. This Confederate juggernaut is their baptism under fire and they are being inundated, which compels them to retire in undisciplined fashion. Nearby, the 1st and 4th Brigades of Colonels John D. McDowell and Ralph Buckland, having only just set up

their lines, are also effortlessly driven back to Major General John A. McClernand's positions, losing a battery in the process.

McClernand's force is ordered up to provide support to Sherman's left flank, while General Stephen A. Hurlbut is speeding to bolster Prentiss. All the while the Rebels continue to strike blow after blow as they advance with a feeling of invincibility against the faltering Union lines. In addition to the sheer power of the ground assault, the Confederates under General Daniel Ruggles unleash their 62 cannon, the largest artillery force ever assembled on a North American battlefield.

By 0700, Sherman's entire line is being overwhelmed with a sea of gray and McClernand's

Colonel Everett Peabody, 13th Missouri (Mottelay, *The Soldier in Our Civil War*, 1886).

Left: The final stand of General Ulysses S. Grant at Pittsburg Landing on 6 April 1862 (Johnson, *Campfire and Battlefield: History of the Conflicts and Campaigns*, 1894). *Right:* The 44th Indiana is heavily engaged at Pittsburg Landing (Shiloh) while raging fires are moving toward their lines (Mottelay, *The Soldier in Our Civil War*, 1886).

left flank to the rear of Prentiss is engaged all along the line. But by now, with the shock wearing off and the hefty support of Taylor's Chicago Battery, Sherman's troops have dug in rigidly, and with the added inspiration of Sherman himself, who is moving all along the line, despite having sustained a wound to the hand, the Union force regains stability. Sherman's high visibility, although a sharp target for the Confederates, is a swaggering example of boldness to his troops.

In the meantime, General Grant is informed of the crisis in Sherman's sector. With some reformed units, he rushes there to stiffen the defensive line. As the whirlwind of shot and shell soars overhead and the bayonets clash with deadly results, more Confederates gush into the field of battle. At about 0900, Sherman's left flank, already under severe stress, receives another devastating blow as Hardee's Third Corps emerges from the woods, along with a strong contingent of Bragg's Second Corps. Simultaneously, Polk's First Corps stalks Sherman's rear. Meanwhile, the units under W.H.L. Wallace that Grant, prior to moving to aid Sherman, had ordered to reform are moving up from Crump's Landing.

The reinforcements form a new defensive line on a ridge to the front of Snake Creek and tightly hold the line there, halting a tenacious Rebel advance. However, more Confederate troops arrive and they pounce upon Colonel Everett Peabody's 1st Brigade, threatening to overwhelm it and crack right through Prentiss' lines to reach the river. General Hurlbut dispatches his 2nd Brigade to lend support, but he withholds the 1st and 3rd Brigades. The reinforcements are insufficient to halt the Confederates' progress. They continue to pour incessant fire and advance almost at will. Hurlbut speeds the remaining two brigades forward, but their arrival is too late to stem the tide.

During the course of the fighting, Colonel Nelson G. Williams, while leading a brigade (Hurlbut's division), becomes severely injured (temporarily paralyzed) when an artillery shell strikes his horse, causing it to fall upon him.

Other Union reinforcements, Prentiss's 2nd Brigade under Colonel Madison Miller and General W.H.L. Wallace's 2nd Brigade under General John McArthur (appointed brigadier general earlier this year), move to support a contingent of Sherman's force, David L. Stuart's brigade, which had inadvertently become positioned beyond a huge gap along the Hamburg Road and comes under tremendous pressure as the surging Rebels begin to encircle it. Both brigades, Miller's and MacArthur's, encounter large enemy forces and each is compelled to retire. And at Prentiss's positions, the situation is grave. The Confederates mass a huge line and with relentless fury, hammer the 1st Brigade under Colonel Peabody. Consequently, Peabody's brigade becomes totally isolated from the remainder of the main force, which severely weakens Prentiss, who with his few remaining regiments attempts to forestall disaster.

Meanwhile, Peabody, while leading the 25th Missouri, is lost during the early fighting, deep-

ening the predicament for Prentiss. The Union, pressed by the overwhelming strength of the Rebels, makes a hasty retreat toward the Tennessee River with the Rebels running up their backs. Once there, and commanding more tenable positions, they regroup and form a staunch line at Sunken Road, dubbed the "Hornet's Nest." Prentiss is able to fend off a series of devastating attacks, but following about three hours of incessant combat, coupled with the fact that he is encircled, Prentiss is compelled to surrender.

In the meantime, still more Confederate units slam into McClernand's main body along the Corinth and Pittsburg Landing Road, and yet others force Colonel David L. Stuart's brigade to retreat. It pulls back to positions that nearly are off the field of battle. All the while, as the Union attempts to regroup and repel the attacks, more and more Rebel contingents arrive to inflict even heavier punishment. By 1100, McClernand's lines are driven back to those of General Hurlbut, and within an hour, the Confederates occupy much of the terrain that had earlier in the day encamped the forces of McClernand, Prentiss, Sherman and Stuart. The Confederates also seize many cannon and a large number of prisoners, including about one-half of Captain Edward McAllister's and Major Adolph Schwartz's artillerymen.

Other Union outfits are able to buy some time at the expense of Prentiss' 6th Division by digging in at Pittsburg Landing and constructing a desperate final line of defense. The Union is being dealt such a serious blow that nearby there remains only two intact divisions, Wallace's Second and Hurlbut's Fourth, along with the shattered remnants of the other units of Prentiss's Sixth Division. W.H. Wallace expeditiously shifts his lines to fill a hole on Hurlbut's left flank, which also provides some protection to the supplies and the wagons.

The Union, despite losing about half of both McAllister's and Schwartz's batteries, still controls some additional firepower. Major Cavender is on hand with the batteries of Richardson, Stone and Webber. Nonetheless, the Confederates hold the momentum and expect to overwhelm the guns and drive the Union line back

to the river. However, the badly bruised Union forces are not quite ready to capitulate. Instead, they prepare to defend against another massive assault.

Three Rebel units, the divisions of Benjamin Franklin Cheatham and Jones M. Withers and the Reserve Corps under John C. Breckinridge, smash into the lines, and for the duration of the afternoon, the opposing sides bludgeon each other. The artillery batteries trade barrages and the field becomes layered with casualties. Destroyed equipment lies in flames, as the incessant artillery bombardments have set many areas of the woods afire. Some units, including the Union 44th Indiana, become heavily engaged while the blazes and smoke sweep violently in

Lt. Colonel Edward F.W. Ellis, 15th Illinois, killed at the Battle of Shiloh (Mottelay, *The Soldier in Our Civil War*, 1886).

Soldiers burn dead horses after the Battle of Shiloh (Mottelay, *The Soldier in Our Civil War*, 1886).

front of their lines. The raging fires create huge hovering clouds of thick choking smoke that further impede the contest. The Confederates launch repeated assaults, seemingly with Hurlbut's artillery as the primary objective, but the Peach Orchard is firmly held by the defenders and their guns rivet the Rebel columns.

In the meantime, other Confederates whack the right side of the front line, forcing a slight crack, while additional units pound the flanks, igniting a donnybrook. Hurlbut's command is pressed further and compelled to again pull back moving closer to the river. This retirement then causes the remnants of Sherman's and McClernand's divisions to head for more tenable positions in the same general area. General W.H.L. Wallace, while attempting to thwart the attacks of Polk's and Hardee's forces, is mortally wounded. Colonel J.M. Tuttle, commanding the 1st Brigade, succeeds him as commander of the division. He is promoted to brigadier general the following June.

By this time, at about 1700, the savage, close-quartered fighting has exhausted and disorganized both sides. At the river, after sustaining about 4,000 casualties, the Union troops are scattered along the high banks of the landing and along the lower banks near the transport vessels. Attempts are immediately made to reform and rally the troops, but initially, the effort is fruitless. Meanwhile, the Confederates, having already gained both the advantage and the momentum, are preparing to mount another solid attack to inflict total defeat and demoralize the Yankees. The Union, to avoid absolute disaster, must hold at all hazards until the arrival of General Buell's force that is en route.

During the late afternoon, the Union gets an unexpected reprieve. A detachment commanded by Colonel Joseph D. Webster, General Grant's chief of staff, places 53 guns on the high ground in support of the troops who are now compressed in a fragile half-moon position. The Confederates, unaware of the arrival

of the additional guns, complete the preparations for what is expected to be the final assault to crush the Union.

The Rebels, with an enormous amount of vitality, sound the attack, and the columns advance to the roaring guns of the artillery, but this time, it is the Confederates who receive the surprise. The tattered Union lines have finally regrouped and the Union guns greet the Rebels with a furious hurricane of fire, so heavy that the attack striking the right is quickly forced back. In the meantime, the Union gunboats, USS *Tyler* and *Lexington*, until now mere spectators, finally get their opportunity to propel pernicious salutations to the overwhelming numbers of Confederates. The interdiction fire is extraordinarily explosive and particularly deadly as the gunboats' 64-pound shot and 12-inch shells rock the slopes and create bedlam within the Rebel ranks, inflicting extremely heavy casualties.

At about this same time, early evening, the spirits of the beleaguered Union troops experience a huge lift with the arrival of Buell's advance guard, which moves in and covers Grant's left. The combined fire of the Union infantry, artillery and the gunboats secure the field and cut off a Confederate attempt to cross Dill Creek, prior to a subdued darkness, which temporarily silences the blazing gunfire which has raged ruthlessly throughout the day.

At about dusk, General Lewis Wallace's force, ordered up earlier in the morning, finally arrives and it is received with welcome arms, but Grant is also annoyed at the delay in arrival, attributed to some confusion. Wallace explains that he had indeed departed immediately upon receiving the order to move out. He informs Grant that he had advanced toward positions expected to be in the heat of the battle, but due to unanticipated Confederate gains, he had been off en route by about six miles. Once informed by Captain John Rawlins, Grant's adjutant general who had intercepted Wallace, who had been

inadvertently advancing to the Confederate rear, retraces his steps and although tardy, deploys in the proper positions to bolster the exhausted Yankees.

Although this day's battle concludes at about 2100, the gunboats USS *Lexington* and *Tyler*, using synchronized firing systems, pound Confederate shore positions at 15 minute intervals, allowing Buell's troops to move into Union lines undetected, setting the stage for a horrendous surprise for the Confederates, who still suspect that Grant's beleaguered lines are ready to be sliced into pieces. In addition, the Confederates, who have also sustained heavy casualties, have lost their commander-in-chief, General Albert S. Johnston. Command reverts to General Pierre Beauregard, who establishes headquarters at Shiloh Church. Neither side has an opportunity to receive much relaxation, as the bombardments are maintained throughout the night, causing the Rebels to constantly seek safer positions. In addition, both sides are forced to contend with a terrible storm that drenches the entire area.

On the 7th, prior to dawn, Grant, with the addition of Lew Wallace's division (Grant's army) and Buell's army, including Thomas L. Crittenden (Fifth Division), A. McCook (Second Division), and Nelson (Fourth Division), has 55,000 troops available to repulse whatever is thrown at his lines by the Confederates. The First Division under General George H. Thomas is too far to the rear to arrive in time and the Sixth Division under General T.J. Wood is only able to get one brigade to the scene of battle; however, Grant's other forces, which received a thrashing on the previous day, are anxious to redeem themselves. The Union line stretches from the Hamburg and Purdy Roads to Owl Creek, with Buell holding the left and General Lewis Wallace holding the right. The forces of McClernand, Hurlbut and Sherman, which had been engaged on the previous day, are stacked in the center.

In contrast, the Confederates have been compelled by the night-long bombardments to relinquish much of the ground they had secured. They now stand to the front of the encampments they held on the previous day. On the right, held by General Hardee, Chalmers' and Jackson's brigades, both attached to Withers' division, prepare to attack, and holding the center are the forces of Breckinridge and Polk. The far left is held by the remnants of Bragg's force.

On this day, it is the Union which initiates the action. Slightly before dawn, on the Union right, Lew Wallace's force commences a powerful bombardment that strikes Rebel positions in a thickly wooded ravine that lies opposite their positions. In concert with the booming artillery barrage, and following the silencing of one of the Confederate guns, Wallace orders an assault to penetrate the Confederate line defended by General Bragg. The Union advances and secures a hill, and anticipating a quick advance by Sherman, Wallace moves to turn the Confederate flank, expecting Sherman to move in and hold the gap; however, the Rebels strike

The Shiloh log chapel where the Battle of Shiloh ignited on 6 April 1862 (Mottelay, *The Soldier in Our Civil War*, 1886).

first, intending to collapse Wallace's right. Union artillery and the 8th Missouri Regiment neutralize the attempt and repel an assault, which includes Confederate cavalry. At about the same time, Colonel Morgan L. Smith's 1st Brigade is struck by a tenacious but unsuccessful infantry assault that advances under the fire of the guns of a Louisiana battery. Following these vicious engagements, Sherman arrives and both divisions move toward Shiloh Church, Beauregard's headquarters. The columns proceed without encountering any heavy resistance until they encroach the objective.

In the meantime, at about 0530, on the Union's right, General Nelson's Fourth Division advances, trailed by Crittenden's Fifth Division and Rousseau's 4th Brigade (McCook's Second Division). Soon after, they encounter and push back Confederate pickets attached to Forrest's cavalry, but as the advance broadens, resistance stiffens. Standing in the path of advance are contingents of three separate brigades, Chalmer's, Gladden's and Jackson's, bolstered by some unattached Tennessee and Alabama regiments and supporting artillery. The Yankees come under a severe assault that forces them to fall back toward the trailing division of Crittenden, but when they join, the line becomes galvanized. The Union turns the tables and strikes back with a disciplined advance under the umbrella security of hefty artillery. The power of the attack drives the Rebels back, permitting the Union to regain a battery that had earlier been lost.

Once the Rebels begin to retreat, fresh troops arrive to bolster them and permit the flight to end. By about 0800, the Confederates are able to launch a new offensive and the blood-soaked field becomes engulfed in close-quartered slaughter, with each side delivering punishing blows. Amid the wild fighting, the artillery, indifferent to man and beast, jolts the earth, causing high casualties among both; suddenly many of the opposing cavalrymen become horseless from the blazing fire of the cannon and rifles. Nonetheless, the Rebels once again press to smash a gap into the lines of the Union, now held by two divisions and Lovell H. Rousseau's 4th Brigade (McCook's Second Division), which just arrived on Crittenden's left. General Buell has also arrived with his brigade.

Crittenden's division arrives from Shiloh Church and moves into position on Breckinridge's line. All the while, the determined Confederates remain unaware of the added Union strength. They advance and whack the 19th Brigade under Colonel William B. Hazen and push it upon an open field and beyond. The troops desperately seek to reach better positions in the woods to Crittenden's left, but during the attempt to gain tenable positions, the unit gets caught in a devastating artillery crossfire. At the same time, Colonel Jacob Ammen's 10th Brigade, Fourth Division under Nelson, comes under extreme pressure. It is close to being turned, which would cause a collapse in the line, but reinforcements, Terrell's Battery (McCook's Division), arrive, bringing with them twenty-four pound howitzers. Ammen's brigade, bolstered by the artillery, commences a tremendous bombardment that slings sheets of fire toward the Rebel positions and repels the assault, but still there is neither victor nor vanquished.

The Confederates are stalled but not defeated. At about this time, more Union reinforcements begin to fill the ranks. Boyle's 11th Brigade (Crittenden's Fifth Division) sprints forward and deploys to the left of Nelson's Fourth Division. Once there, a colossal amount of support fire pours in from the batteries of Terrell, Mendenhall and Bartlett, giving Boyle's brigade some running room. It bolts forward and delivers a solid blow that staggers the Rebels. With unrelenting vengeance, the brigade doggedly drives ahead and the enormous pressure compels the Rebels to give more ground until eventually they are driven beyond their second and third batteries, both of which are quickly seized by the Union. And still more Union troops are speeding to the front lines. While Nelson is reversing the situation on his front, McCook's Second Division is also becoming stronger as large contingents of fresh troops at Savannah are being ferried across the river.

Colonel Edward N. Kirk's 5th Brigade and a contingent of the 6th Brigade, led by Colonel W.H. Gibson, deploy to cover Rousseau's right and rear respectively, and they are supported by the 32nd Indiana Regiment under Colonel August Willich and two other regiments of Hurlbut's command. The Confederates assault McCook's positions, but his additional strength gives him a large advantage and the determined Rebels are repulsed. McCook, not intent on holding his ground, orders an attack to whip and scatter the assault troops. The Union jumps off and plunges a deadly wedge into the line of the Rebel forces, compelling them to retire.

Meanwhile, the Union accelerates its attack and inflicts more punishment. The surging troops seize a Rebel battery and fold the right side of the Confederate line, providing Lovell H. Rousseau's 4th Brigade an opportunity to funnel through the gap and hook up with elements of Nelson's Fourth Division, which had been massing in the area where McClernand had been encamped on the previous day. A heated contest erupts as Rousseau's troops and the Rebels fight for control of the camp. When Rousseau bolted from his positions to advance, a gap in the line had been created. The Rebels spot the hole and take action to exploit the situation.

As the morning continues to fade into afternoon, Confederates swiftly move to drive a wedge into the gap between McCook and Crittenden to force McCook's left to turn and permit the Rebels to widen the hole, but the maneuver is detected. Colonel Willich's 32nd Indiana commences a nasty bayonet attack, while Kirk's 5th Brigade slides in behind Willich and fills the void created by the departure of Rousseau. In the meantime, the Confederates, although initially thwarted, again attempt to advance and drive a wedge between McCook and Crittenden.

The Rebels strike with enormous strength and plow full-force into the left side of the line, defended by Colonel W. H. Gibson's 49th Ohio. Repeatedly, the Rebels pounce upon the regiment and twice the Union is compelled to reform the front line to prevent penetration, which could jeopardize the entire line. While the Rebels are prevented from breaking through, Rousseau moves back to get re-supplied.

By about 1400, Rousseau's brigade arrives back at the line to reinitiate its attack. It is supported by McClernand's force on the right and by two of Hurlbut's regiments on the left. Soon after, with the added support of artillery originating from the remaining batteries of McAllister and Wood, the columns advance, but surprisingly, they encounter only slight resistance as they encroach some dense woods. Wallace's force, which had commenced its attack prior to dawn, has been battling the Rebels at Shiloh Church. While the Confederates are battling to maintain the edge at all points, the Union, as it nears the thicket, receives the signal to launch a general attack. Now, as the afternoon weighs heavily on both sides, the monstrous general assault of the Union raises the stakes, and the Confederates under Beauregard, supported by Generals Polk, Bragg and Breckinridge, must hold, or their cause is lost.

In Wallace's sector at Shiloh Church, the left flank has been twice jeopardized but never broken. However, the Rebels have succeeded in cracking Sherman's flank and creating a large gap. While Sherman's force regroups to launch an offensive to reclaim the terrain, the 23rd Indiana and the 1st Nebraska turn back a cavalry assault. Soon after, the 11th Indiana under Colonel Francis McGinnis, the 76th Ohio under Charles R. Woods and a contingent of McClernand's force hits the field, giving Wallace an abundance of firepower to hold tightly and launch an assault to demoralize the beleaguered Confederates. The Union advance forces the Confederates to surrender ground as they hurriedly abandon the field under orders of General Beauregard, who has concluded that lacking reinforcements, remaining on the field would merely cost more lives. Runners carrying urgent dispatches requesting reinforcements are sent to General Earl Van Dorn, but they can locate neither his positions nor his scouts.

Reluctantly, at about 1430, Beauregard leads his force toward Corinth. He leaves Breckinridge with his 12,000 troops that had been held in reserve to cover the retirement. Beauregard's specific orders: "This retreat must not be a rout. You hold the enemy back, if it requires the loss of your last man." Breckinridge responds: "Your orders shall be carried out to the letter." He deploys his troops on a nearby ridge to await the pursuing Union troops, but none arrive. After about a half hour, he withdraws to establish night positions about two miles from the blood soaked battlefield. By now, Union troops, freshly arrived as part of General Thomas J. Wood's Division, had begun pursuit; however, after reaching Lick Creek, the chase terminates. By 1600, all firing ends.

Despite the cessation of the guns, there is still

incessant misery. The area is hit by another grueling night of bad weather that includes a pesky drizzling rain and annoying hail. But even more discouraging is the task of burying the dead. Immediately following the conclusion of the battle, the dead on both sides are buried and the animals that had been killed are burned to eliminate health hazards. The Confederates, sustaining high casualties, nearly out of ammunition and without any hope of receiving reinforcements, march unchallenged to Corinth.

Grant's forces, badly hurt themselves, are forced to allow the Confederates to withdraw without pursuit. The arrival of Generals Don Carlos Buell, Lew Wallace, and William Nelson most certainly save the Union Army from defeat. Grant is also aided by ships, including the USS *Tyler* and *Lexington*. Additional reinforcements, a brigade (Thomas J. Wood's Division, General Don Carlos Buell's Army of the Cumberland) under General Milo Hascall, arrives on the 17th. It will participate at Corinth. General Hascall had been recently appointed brigadier general effective April 1862. Also, Colonel (later brigadier general) Edward N. Kirk is wounded while leading a brigade (McCook's 2nd Division). Later this year, Kirk's brigade will be transferred to General Sill's corps.

Confederate Colonel (later brigadier general) Alexander T. Hawthorn, 6th Arkansas Infantry, participates at this action. Also, Confederate Major John Kelly, commanding the 9th Arkansas Battalion, following his service with the 14th Arkansas Regiment, participates in this action and for his apparent conspicuous heroism he is promoted to the rank of colonel the following month. Kelly continues to serve with distinction in Tennessee, participating in such battles as Perryville, Murfreesboro and Chickamauga, the latter springing him to a promotion to brigadier general. The 8th Texas Cavalry (Terry's Texas Rangers), led by Colonel John Austin Wharton, also participates at this action; Wharton sustains a wound in the process.

Union casualties are 1,735 killed, 7,882 wounded and 3,956 captured. Confederate casualties total 1,728 killed, 8,012 wounded and 959 captured. Union General Harvey Lamb Wallace is mortally wounded while extricating his troops from an untenable position at the infamous "Hornet's Nest"; he dies on 10 April. General John McArthur receives command of Wallace's division. Alexander Chambers (West Point, 1853) is wounded twice while fighting with his command, the 16th Iowa. Chambers is appointed brigadier general in November 1863. Captain (later brigadier general) Francis Fessenden, 19th U.S. Infantry (younger brother of Union General James D. Fessenden), participating in his first battle, is also wounded. Colonel Everett Peabody (13th Missouri Volunteer infantry) is also killed (6th). Lt. Colonel Edward F.W. Ellis, 15th Illinois, is killed instantly when his regiment comes under heavy fire on Monday morning. Colonel Thomas E. Ransom is wounded, his third wound, but he refuses to leave the field. Later he is appointed chief of staff to General John McClernand.

Union Colonel Mason Brayman participates

at this battle. In September he is commissioned a brigadier general. He later receives the command of Bolivar, Tennessee, where he remains until June 1863. During 1865, Brayman commands at Natchez. Union Colonel Ralph P. Buckland participates at Shiloh, commanding a brigade under William T. Sherman. Buckland becomes brigadier general on November 29, 1862. Union Colonel Marcellus M. Crocker (later brigadier general) of the 13th Iowa, 6th Division, Army of the Tennessee, also participates. Major (later brevet major general) Charles Carroll Walcutt sustains a shoulder wound; however, doctors do not remove the bullet. It remains in his shoulder for the rest of his life. Afterward, Walcutt continues to serve with General William Sherman. Walcutt is promoted to colonel of his regiment, the 46th Ohio, on 16 October.

The mayor of Cincinnati had earlier requested that Sisters of Charity treat the sick and wounded troops of the Ohio regiments. With the archbishop's approval they had accepted. Their arrival after the Battle of Shiloh and Pittsburg Landing assures them of many patients. Upon their arrival, many civilian women offer to assist with the patients, but the sisters soon find themselves alone. A smallpox epidemic breaks out and the civilian women leave the hospital.

Confederate General Albert S. Johnston, commander-in-chief, is mortally wounded on the 6th when a Minié ball strikes him through a boot and severs a main artery. Johnston's chief of engineers, Colonel Jeremy Gilmer, is wounded. Confederate General Braxton Bragg (West Point, 1837) assumes command of the 2nd Corps after Johnston's death. Major General Braxton Bragg, after the demise of General A.S. Johnston, is promoted to the full rank of general in the Confederate Regular Army. Confederate Brigadier General Adley H. Gladden is mortally wounded, initially suffering the loss of an arm while leading his brigade of Alabama and Louisiana units. Gladden succumbs on 12 April. Following Gladden's death, Colonel Zachariah C. Deas takes temporary command of the brigade.

Confederate Colonel Zachariah C. Deas, commander of the 22nd Alabama, sustains a serious wound, but he will recover and join with General Braxton Bragg during the latter's invasion of Kentucky. Confederate Major (later brigadier general) James T. Holtzclaw, 18th Alabama Regiment, is severely wounded in the lung and it is thought to be a fatal blow, but he survives and returns to active duty within several months. Holtzclaw is soon promoted to colonel and becomes a brigadier general on 7 July 1864. Also, George W. Johnson, provisional governor of Kentucky, is killed during fighting on the 7th. Confederate Colonel Jean Jacques A. Mouton (West Point, 1850) is also severely wounded; however, he recovers. Mouton is appointed brigadier general on 16 April and later serves during the Red River Campaign.

Confederate Generals John Stevens Bowen (6th), Charles Clark (6th), and Thomas C. Hindman (6th) are wounded. Confederate Col-

onel William B. Bate is seriously wounded while leading his Confederate 2nd Tennessee Regiment. Confederate Colonel (later general) Daniel W. Wise, 1st Louisiana Regulars, loses sight in his right eye during the battle. Also, Lt. Colonel (later general) Henry Watkins Allen, 4th Louisiana Infantry Regiment, is wounded. Allen receives a devastating wound at Baton Rouge, Louisiana, in August. His leg is so badly wounded that he uses crutches for the rest of his life. Colonel Robert C. Tyler, 15th Tennessee Regiment, is wounded at this action. Colonel Alexander T. Hawthorn (6th Arkansas) participates.

Colonel (later brigadier general) Randall Lee Gibson commands the 13th Louisiana at this action. Confederate Major (later brigadier general) George D. Johnston and his 25th Alabama Regiment participate. The 25th Alabama serves in the Army of Tennessee in each of its engagements from here to Bentonville, North Carolina, in 1865. Confederate Major (later general) William Wirt Allen, 1st Alabama Cavalry Regiment, is promoted to colonel for his heroism during the fighting at Shiloh. The Confederate 12th Tennessee Cavalry, led by Colonel (later brigadier general) Robert V. Richardson, participates. Also, Confederate Brigadier General Daniel Ruggles, subsequent to this action, will be assigned duties in an administrative capacity rather than in the field; however, he does participate in some actions.

April 7 (Monday)   In Florida, the Confederate Marianna Dragoons, commanded by Captain R.S. Smith, engage Union forces at St. Andrew's Bay. The Union sustains some killed. Confederate casualties, if any, are unavailable.

In North Carolina, two companies of the New York 9th Infantry initiate a two-day mission into the vicinity of Elizabeth City. The contingent engages a Confederate force of about equal size. The Union reports no casualties. Confederates sustain one killed, one wounded and some captured. Also, a detachment of Confederate pickets led by Captain Boothe skirmishes with Union forces at Newport. The Union sustains one wounded and some captured. Confederate casualties are unavailable.

In Tennessee, Union troops land on Confederate-held Island No. 10 and prepare to capture the Confederate garrison defending the island. General John Pope's main force begins crossing the river at Watson's Landing. Pope is informed that the Confederates are beginning to evacuate their positions, heading for their only route of escape, Tiptonville, the exact spot that Pope's force (General Hamilton's command) is advancing toward. With this new intelligence available, once the troops hit shore, Pope orders them to Tiptonville, where they establish night positions. On the following morning, the forces of Generals Schyler Hamilton, Eleazer Paine and David S. Stanley move to vanquish the Confederates and end the siege.

In Naval activity, the USS *Mound City* captures the CSS *Red Rover* at Island No. 10. The following June, subsequent to repairs, the *Red*

Rover is utilized by the U.S. Army's Western Gunboat Flotilla as a hospital ship. It is acquired by the U.S. Navy in September and commissioned the USS *Red Rover* during December. For the duration, the *Red Rover* is utilized as a hospital ship in the Mississippi Squadron. The medical complement aboard the ship includes the first nurses to serve aboard a U.S. naval vessel. The nurses are Catholic nuns, including Mother Angela, from the Order of the Sisters of the Holy Cross. The sisters also treat the sick and wounded at Mound City and other hospitals. From the latter part of 1864 until November 1865, when the *Red Rover* is decommissioned, it is based at Mound City, Illinois.

The CSS *Admiral* is seized by the Union. The *Admiral*, a side-wheel river steamer used as a picket boat by the Confederates, is handed over to the Union Army. The *De Soto*, a side-wheel steamer seized by the Confederacy during 1861, carries Confederate officers who had surrendered at Island No. 10 and approaches a Union force to surrender. Union officers board the *De Soto* and accept the surrender. Afterward, the vessel is taken into the U.S. Navy as the USS *De Soto*; however, later, the ship is renamed the *General Lyon*. This *De Soto* is separate from a wooden side-wheeled steamship called *De Soto*, purchased by the U.S. Navy during 1861. The CSS *Grampus* is scrapped off Island No. 10 by the Confederates to prevent capture by the Union; however, the vessel is salvaged. This *Grampus* is a separate vessel from the USS *Grampus* (formerly the *Ion*), a receiving ship purchased by Rear Admiral David Porter at Cincinnati during July 1863. The CSS *John Simonds*, utilized by the Confederate Army as a support vessel, is also sunk off Island No. 10.

The CSS *Mars*, a side-wheel steamer built in Cincinnati during 1856 and subsequently acquired by the Confederates, is captured. It is taken into the U.S. Navy and used as a tender in the U.S. Mississippi Squadron until 1863, when it is released to the commercial service. After the war, on 8 July 1865, the merchant ship *Mars* strikes an obstacle and sinks off Cogswell Landing, Missouri. The CSS *Mohawk*, known as a watch boat, but possibly also a gunboat, is also sunk by the Union force subsequent to the battle for Island No. 10. The Union also captures the CSS *Ohio Belle*, a side-wheel steamer built in Cincinnati during 1855. After being acquired by the Confederacy, the *Ohio Belle* is used by the army as a watch boat patrolling the Mississippi. Subsequently, during 1864, the *Ohio Belle*, operating under the name *Alabama Belle*, becomes a transport for the Union Army. Following the close of hostilities, the *Alabama Belle* is dismantled during 1867.

The CSS *Oregon* is destroyed by the Confederates to prevent its capture. Also, another Confederate vessel, the CSS *Prince*, built in Cincinnati during 1859 and used as a transport by the Confederacy, is destroyed to prevent capture. And yet another transport, the CSS *Yazoo*, a side-wheel river streamer, is captured and afterward sunk. The *Yazoo* had been built at Jeffersonville, Indiana, during 1860.

In Union general officer activity, Major Elliott Warren Rice, a brother of General Samuel A. Rice, is promoted to colonel (7th Iowa). He participates at Corinth in October 1862 and continues duty in Tennessee. Later he participates in the Atlanta Campaign.

April 7–12   THE GREAT LOCOMOTIVE CHASE
In Tennessee, orders arrive at each of the three Ohio regiments of General Joshua Sill's brigade with instructions that one man from each company was to be selected for a special clandestine mission. The commanders of the respective companies gather to determine the intent of the mission and the skills required from the men to execute the mission. The mission is to commandeer a Confederate railroad train and burn bridges to disrupt the Confederate rail system. The plan, concocted by a civilian spy, James Andrews, had been tried earlier, but the mission conducted by men of the 2nd Ohio had failed. Nonetheless, it is to be once again attempted and again led by Andrews. Those who had volunteered earlier had barely escaped with their lives and decline to participate in a second raid.

The first priority remains getting men who can operate a train. The captains, aware of the requirement, begin to select the troops from their respective companies by asking for those familiar with operating a train to step forward. One of the engineers chosen, Wilson Brown, inquires of General Mitchel about the chances of success and receives this response: "That depends upon circumstances. If the enterprise can be carried out as planned by Mr. Andrews, I think the chances are very good indeed; but if any delay happens, the difficulty will be increased." Brown replies, "Why so, General?" Mitchel responds: "Because as the armies draw nearer, the roads will be more occupied with troops and stores moving back and forth, and these will be in your way. Your mission is very hazardous. It is not pleasant for me to send such a number of picked men into the enemy's power; but in war great risks must be run, and we are engaged in a war of right and wrong; armed treason must be met and conquered; and if you fall, you die in a glorious cause. I have great confidence in Mr. Andrews, your leader; I trust that the great ruler of the destinies of man will protect you all!"

The selected men, who did not know who the others were, each had to dress in civilian clothes and meet with Andrews. Then the 22 men, including three civilians, initiate a 200 mile journey deep into Confederate territory en route to seize a train at Big Shanty, Georgia, and afterward proceed to destroy the tracks between Chattanooga and Atlanta. If caught, each is subject to being hanged as a spy.

Andrews instructs the men to avoid troops of the Confederate Army, which is grabbing volunteers, and if approached the men are to inform the Rebels that they are Kentuckians attempting to get south to join a regiment and "escape the rule of the Yankees." He tells them they are to "break up in small squads of two, three, or four, and travel east into the Cumberland Mountains, then south to the Tennessee River. You can cross the river and take passage on the cars at Shell-Mound or some station between that and Chattanooga on the Memphis and Charleston." Most importantly, he tells them, "You must be at Chattanooga not later than Thursday afternoon [10th], and reach Marietta the same evening, ready to take passage northward on the train the next morning. I will be there with you, or before you, and will then tell you what to do…. "When we once meet at Marietta, we will stay together and either come through in a body or die together."

At Marietta on Saturday, 12 April, two of the men, Porter and Hawkins, were not awakened by the waiter because they did not pay him anything. Consequently, Andrews' unit is reduced to nineteen men. In a last-minute conference in the railroad hotel, Andrews cautions the men and explains: "When the train stops at Big Shanty for breakfast, keep your places till I tell you to go. Get seats near each other in the same car, and say nothing about the matter on the way up. If anything unexpected occurs, look to me for the word."

All board the train and enter the same car. Later, the train arrives at Big Shanty (later Kennesaw), and as the crowd is leaving, Andrews initiates the move. The engine is discovered empty. Andrews directs one of his men to uncouple the car at the beginning of the first baggage car, to the rear of three empty freight cars. Suddenly, the Confederate train is controlled by Union troops and the valve is shoved open, but unexpectedly, the switch had been thrown to quickly, creating a problem. Instead of roaring away, the wheels only begin to spin, but it lasts only a few seconds, too quick for the Confederates to react. Finally, after those seconds of desperation, the engine does roar, the wheels kick in and the theft had occurred so quickly that not a shot had been fired as Andrews' train speeds away heading back to Union lines.

All seems well initially; however, as the train speeds forward, the steam level drops, due to a failure to reopen the dampers (on the engine fires) that had been closed while the train had paused in Big Shanty. Hurriedly, some oil and some fresh wood eradicate the problem. During the short pause, the troops sever the telegraph lines to eliminate warnings being sent from Big Shanty to alert other Confederates of the insolent intruders. At the time the town has no telegraph; however, Andrews remains concerned that a portable battery might be available.

At Moon's Station, Andrews is able to acquire a tool to help expedite the operation to pull out the railroad spikes along the tracks. The workman hands over the bar without resistance, so no violence is necessary. Some dissatisfaction is noticed, however, as the train speeds through various stations without pausing to pick up passengers. Later, the train, the *General*, stops for water and fresh wood at Cassville. While stopped, Andrews explains that he had been sent by General Beauregard to acquire ammunition and rush it to him.

The *General* arrives at Kingston and must pull onto a side track to await the approach of the scheduled passenger train, but Andrews becomes impatient, as it is running late. Finally it arrives and the story regarding the ammunition for Beauregard again holds up, but Andrews also gains intelligence. The conductor of the passenger train details the capture of Huntsville by General Mitchel and that his forces are en route to Chattanooga, without any Confederate forces to intercept the columns. All the while, Andrews' men are in the boxcars, confined to silence and unaware of the reason for the delay.

Andrews insists that he must move out immediately and the conductor inquires, "What will you do about Mitchel at Huntsville?" Andrews, continuing his flawless ruse, replies: "I do not believe the story. Mitchel would not be fool enough to run down there, but if he is, Beauregard will soon sweep him out of the road. At any rate I have my orders." Meanwhile, back at Big Shanty, the "Conductor Fuller, Engineer Cain, and the foreman of the road machine shops, Mr. Anthony Murphy" take steps to get the train back. A horseman had sped to Marietta and sent a wire to Atlanta. While in Marietta, the runner acquires a train, which speeds to Big Shanty to load troops. Afterward, the train initiates the chase.

The holdup at Kingston allows the pursuers to close, and when the *General* finally moves out of Kingston, the Confederates are close behind. Nevertheless, as soon as the train is out of sight of the station, it pauses to permit one of the men to ascend a pole to cut the telegraph line to ensure no helpful message is forwarded about the ammunition train for General Beauregard. In addition, with knowledge of a pursuing train, more track is ripped up to impede progress.

Andrews reaches Adairsville and asked identical questions, he responds with the story of rushing ammunition to Beauregard. When asked what about the Yankees under Mitchel, Andrews responds by telling the men that Beauregard is nearly out of ammunition and he must continue, despite the advance of Mitchel toward Chattanooga. The story is bought and the *General* departs expeditiously, although the Confederate trains are off schedule due to the Union advance and Andrews has to worry about an oncoming train as the *General* heads toward Calhoun, less than ten miles distant. After a tense delay, Andrews is able to move out of the station, but close behind, the Confederates arrive at the station, and in a new engine, the *Texas*, they quickly pull out with the sounds of their whistle now being picked up by Andrews' party.

Andrews travels through Resaca, having no time to destroy a bridge nor pull up tracks. A few more close calls occur, but still the Rebels do not catch the *General* as it safely speeds through Dalton. About one mile beyond Dalton, the *General* halts to cut the wires, but a message had already been sent warning of the stolen train. By now a rain that has been falling throughout the race intensifies. The Yankees are down to one car and Andrews orders it set afire. The boxcar is set ablaze on one of the Chickamauga bridges, but the rain had soaked the

wood, so it does little damage and there is not sufficient time to move it to the next bridge. The *General* resumes its speed and passes through Ringgold.

Nevertheless, shortly afterward, Andrews issues an order to abandon the train, and for each man on his own to attempt to make it back to Union lines. Anderson had not had any military experience and the men, although shocked that he would order them to split up, obeyed the order. In that instant the chase was essentially over. But Andrews issues the order again and the men abandon the train at a point about five miles beyond Ringgold and less than 20 miles from Chattanooga. At the time, the train had sufficient fuel and was operating well, under the circumstances.

The entire band is eventually captured, including the two who missed the train at Marietta. Later, an escape is attempted by some, including Andrews, but he is later recaptured and given brutal punishment before being hanged. On 18 June, seven others are hanged. They are William Campbell, George D. Wilson, Marion A. Ross, Perry G. Shadrack, Samuel Slavens, and Samuel Robertson. The remaining 14 include Wilson W. Brown, William Knight, J.R. Porter, Martin J. Hawkins, Mark Wood, J.A. Wilson, John Wollam and D.A. Dorsey; they escape on 16 October 1862. The others, Jacob Parrott, Robert Buffum, William Bensinger, William Reddick, E.H. Mason and William Pittinger are exchanged on 18 March 1863. Each man becomes a recipient of the Medal of Honor for individual courage and valor above and beyond the call of duty. Initially, the six escapees receive the Medal, the first six awards presented. The others, except the civilians, receive the medal later, some posthumously.

At the hangings, the Confederates had not provided coffins. The Union troops were buried in a common grave, but after the war, the U.S. government moved quickly to extricate the remains of the Union heroes and have them reinterred in the National Cemetery at Chattanooga. On 11 April 1887, Andrews' remains are extricated and he is reinterred at Chattanooga with those of his detachment that had also been hanged.

April 8 (Tuesday) Surrender of Island No. 10 In Tennessee at Island No. 10, General Beauregard, having concluded at this time that the Union has completed the canal and had successfully run his batteries, realizes the island cannot be held much longer. However, his plans to evacuate are discovered by General Pope and the island is now in jeopardy. This morning General Schuyler Hamilton's force is moving along the shore of Reelfoot Lake in synchronization with the commands of General David S. Stanley, who is moving along the banks of the Mississippi, and General Eleazer Paine, who is driving straight up the road. The

Confederates faced with this force are compelled to halt their escape and head back toward the swamps. Meanwhile, on Island No. 10, a detachment bearing a white flag of truce approaches Admiral Foote.

The offer to surrender is accepted. A contingent of troops under Colonel Napoleon Bonaparte Buford occupies the island. The Confederate commander of Island No. 10 at the time of surrender is General William D. McCall, and the other nearby forces are under the command of Major General John P. McCown. General Beauregard, along with the larger part of the army, escapes toward Corinth, Mississippi. Lt. (later brigadier general) William Young Conn Humes, assigned to the island's artillery, is captured and later exchanged. After his release, Humes, who had graduated from the Virginia Military Institute, will be assigned to Colonel Joseph Wheeler's cavalry corps and serve as his chief of artillery.

This victory gives the Union control of the Mississippi River as far as Memphis, Tennessee. Following this action, General Pope begins to march toward Pittsburg Landing to join the other Union forces already there. In the vicinity of Shiloh, Confederate Colonel Nathan Bedford Forrest's troops act as rear guard, covering Beauregard's retreat to Corinth. Forrest's men repulse a Union attempt to catch the retreating Rebels. The Union detachment in pursuit, commanded by Brigadier General William T. Sherman, discontinues the chase and returns to Shiloh.

Confederate Captain William C. Humes is captured during the struggle. After a prisoner exchange, Humes is assigned to Colonel Wheeler's Cavalry, becoming brigadier general during November of 1863. Colonel (later brigadier general) Henry B. Davidson (West Point, 1853) is also seized. After his release, he too will join Wheeler's cavalry. Another Confederate, Brigadier General William W. Mackall (West Point, 1837), is captured and later exchanged. Mackall will become chief of staff to General Bragg during 1863 and to Joseph E. Johnston in 1864. Confederate Colonel (later brigadier general) Thomas M. Scott, 12th Louisiana, participates. Colonel (later general) Alpheus Baker is seized at Island No. 10. He is

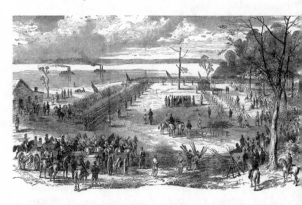

Confederates at Island No. 10 surrender on 8 April 1862 (Johnson, *Campfire and Battlefield: History of the Conflicts and Campaigns*, 1894).

later exchanged and will then serve at the defense of Vicksburg under General William Loring.

In Missouri, a Union contingent (unit unknown) skirmishes with Confederate guerrillas at Medicine Creek. The Union sustains one killed and two wounded. Confederate casualties, if any, are unavailable.

In Tennessee, General Ormsby M. Mitchel departs camp en route to seize Huntsville, but no one is aware of his destination. The move is coordinated with James Andrews, who is en route to Georgia to seize a Rebel train and destroy rail tracks while running the train toward Huntsville.

In New Mexico at Albuquerque, a skirmish erupts between Union and Confederate contingents.

In Virginia, General George B. McClellan, encamped about five miles outside of Yorktown, is conspicuously upset with President Lincoln, who the previous day instructed McClellan to "break the enemy lines at once." McClellan, in his biography, mentions that he was "tempted to tell Lincoln to come and do it himself."

In Union general officer activity, Robert Byington Mitchell, a veteran of the Mexican War who served as a lieutenant in the 2nd Ohio Regiment, is appointed brigadier general of volunteers effective this day. Mitchell joined the service shortly after the hostilities began when he was commissioned colonel of the 2nd Kansas Infantry. General Mitchell receives command of a brigade at Fort Riley, Kansas. He participates at the Battle of Perryville during October in command of General Gilbert's 9th Division. He also participates in the Chickamauga Campaign (chief of cavalry, Army of the Cumberland) prior to being transferred to the capital for duty regarding court-martials. Afterward, he receives command of various districts in Nebraska and Kansas. General Mitchell musters out of the army on 6 January 1866. On the same day he is nominated governor of the New Mexico Territory. He becomes governor on 6 June 1866 but resigns in 1869.

In Confederate general officer activity, Major General Sterling Price (Missouri state troops) resigns his command and accepts a commission in the Confederate Army with the rank of major general. Price's force will depart Missouri en route for Corinth. Initially the force is transported by ship to Memphis, and from there the troops board trains.

April 9 (Wednesday)   In California, the 2nd U.S. Cavalry Regiment skirmishes with Confederates at Owen's River. The Union loses one killed and two wounded. Confederate casualties, if any, are unavailable.

In Georgia, the ongoing work to build 11 bombproof batteries on Tybee Island is completed this day. The Union commanders of the batteries and their armaments are as follows: Captain Rodman Totten (four 10-inch mortars); Captain Roger McClellan (two 84-pound and two 64-pound James); Captain Seldeneck Sigel (five 30-pound Parrott and one 48-pound James); Captain Mason Scott (four 10-inch and four eight-inch Columbiads); Captain Sanford Halleck (two 13-inch mortars); Captain Francis Sherman (three 13-inch mortars); Sergeant Wilson Burnside (one 13-inch mortar); Captain Pelouze Lincoln (three 8-inch Columbiads); Captain Pelouze Lyon (four 10-inch Columbiads); Captain Palmer Grant (three 10-inch mortars); and Captain Skinner Stanton (three 10-inch mortars).

The Union Commander at Hilton Head, General David Hunter, who recently succeeded Brigadier General William T. Sherman, dispatches Lt. J.H. Wilson to deliver a surrender ultimatum to Colonel Charles H. Olmstead, the commander of Fort Pulaski. The demand is rejected, setting up an imminent attack.

In Florida, Union forces under Brigadier General Horatio G. Wright evacuate Jacksonville. In June he will serve as commander of a division at Secessionville, South Carolina.

In Mississippi, the 3rd Brigade, 5th Division (Army of the Tennessee), bolstered by the 4th Illinois Cavalry, engages and defeats a Confederate force in the vicinity of Corinth. The Union reports no casualties. The Confederates sustain 15 killed, about 25 wounded and about 200 captured.

In Missouri, Union Major General H.W. Halleck departs St. Louis for Pittsburg Landing, Tennessee. Once there, he begins to reorganize the armies. Also, a Union force composed of contingents of Companies A, B and C, Missouri Cavalry Militia, commanded by Captain William Flentz, skirmishes with Confederates led by Captain Jefferies at Jackson. Both sides sustain several killed and wounded. The Union loses one missing. The Confederates sustain one captured.

April 9–16   In Missouri, Union forces initiate an operation that includes scouting missions to the vicinity of Quincy, Little Niangua, and Hickory County, as well as a skirmish in between. In addition, the contingent scouts the area between Humansville and Montevallo in Vernon County. The Union sustains several killed and wounded. The Confederates sustain about two killed and one wounded.

April 10 (Thursday) In Florida, a Union contingent — led by Captain Baker and composed of elements of the 9th Maine Regiment bolstered by the 1st Florida Cavalry — engages Confederates commanded by Captain Footman at Fernandina. The Union sustains one killed and about six captured. Confederate casualties, if any, are unreported.

In Georgia on Tybee Island, subsequent to the Confederates' rejection of a surrender demand on the previous day, the Union batteries unleash a monstrous artillery assault beginning at 0800 with the two guns of Captain Sanford. The additional ten batteries follow with their barrages shortly thereafter, and the deafening enfilade continues without pause well into the following morning. The Confederate batteries return fire at an equally tenacious pace. By about 1300, the main flagstaff atop the fort is blown away. The Union batteries transfer the duties between units as the bombardments are conducted by three batteries at a time for a period of fifteen minutes each.

In Virginia, Confederate reinforcements land in the vicinity of Yorktown. Union Major General George McClellan, lacking heavy guns, does not order an attack. In addition, the weather is tremendously bad, making travel along the roads difficult. Some units, including the 9th Massachusetts, are encamped within several miles of Yorktown.

In Confederate general officer activity, General Mosby M. Parsons, commanding officer, 6th Division, Missouri State Guard, receives command of the entire Missouri State Guard. He is officially promoted to brigadier general in the Confederacy during November.

April 11 (Friday)   In Alabama, Union troops under Colonel John Turchin, the 3rd Division (General Ormsby MacKnight Mitchel's Command), Army of the Ohio, engage the Confederates at Huntsville. They capture about 200 Confederate soldiers and control the nearby Memphis and Charleston Railroad. General Mitchel, appointed brigadier on 9 August 1861, becomes a major general effective this date.

Camp of the 9th Massachusetts in the vicinity of Yorktown, Virginia, on 10 April 1862 (Mottelay, *The Soldier in Our Civil War,* **1886).**

Mitchel will dispatch some of his force into Alabama on reconnaissance missions, but he does not participate in any major battles while serving with General Buell. Mitchel is later transferred to the Department of the South. Also, a Union contingent (General William T. Sherman's Command), including General Fry's brigade and the 4th Illinois Cavalry, supported by the gunboats USS *Tyler* and *Lexington*, initiate a reconnaissance mission to Bear Creek. The two-day operation reports no casualties.

In Louisiana, the CSS *Little Rebel*, having completed a modification project to become a gunboat, departs for Tennessee to bolster the defenses of Fort Pillow.

In Georgia, Union forces commanded by Colonel Quincy Adams Gillmore (West Point, 1849) attack and capture Fort Pulaski. The fort guarding the entrance to Savannah had been doomed once Gilmore deployed mortars on nearby Tybee Island. The strongly defended Confederate-held fort had come under siege on the previous day. At dawn this day, it comes under heavy fire from the Union batteries, later augmented by a battery just completed on Long Island about two miles from Fort Pulaski. A nearby gunboat, the *Norwich,* firing from its location on Lazaretto Creek, also batters the Confederate positions. Some of the crew of the frigate USS *Wabash* move ashore to relieve a crew of gunners at Battery Sigel.

The two sides continue to exchange fire, but by about 1400, the signs of a Union victory become prevalent. The southeastern sector of the fort, which has taken the brunt of the two-day bombardment, has a huge gap in the wall. The magazine is now exposed and in imminent danger of exploding. The relentless bombardments have also silenced two strategic guns on Cockspur Island.

Sensing victory, the officers discuss landing an assault force, but they are convinced too many casualties would be sustained and the idea

Union battery in action at Yorktown, Virginia (Mottelay, *The Soldier in Our Civil War,* 1886)

is dropped. While a second offer to surrender is being prepared, the resolute defenders within the fort are lowering their colors, seemingly concluding that to continue the fight would only prolong the inevitable against the overwhelming strength of the Union firepower. After the white flag replaces the Confederate standard, Brigadier General Henry W. Benham and Colonel Quincy Adams Gillmore move to Goat Point and once there, accompanied by staff officers, they head for Fort Pulaski, where the party is joined by a messenger who had been dispatched from the USS *McClellan* by General Hunter, who observed the entire operation.

The fort is officially surrendered and with it about 360 prisoners, 47 guns and an abundance of supplies. The Stars and Stripes is quickly hoisted and the Union entourage departs before dusk. Colonel Alfred H. Terry will be named commander of the captured fort. Terry's 7th Connecticut Regiment, two companies of the 3rd Rhode Island Artillery and one company of New York Volunteer Engineers will fortify it. The 46th and 48th New York Regiments, the 5th and 7th Connecticut, the 8th Maine Volunteer Regiment, two companies of the New York Engineers (Volunteer), Company A, Union Corps of Engineers (Regular), bolstered by the U.S. 15th Infantry Regiment, and the steamer *Wabash* participate in this action.

In Missouri, Union and Confederate contingents clash at Little Blue River. Specific units are not listed. The Union reports no casualties. The Confederates sustain five killed.

In Tennessee, Union Major General Henry W. Halleck arrives at Pittsburg Landing (Shiloh) to

take command. Also, a Confederate contingent of about 200 troops of the 8th Tennessee Cavalry, commanded by Lt. Colonel Starnes, skirmishes with a Union contingent about three times its size in the vicinity of Wartrace. No Union casualties are reported. Estimated Confederate casualties are three killed and eight wounded.

In Virginia, Union General McClellan is informed that General Fitz John Porter has gone up in a balloon which strays and seems to land in enemy territory. McClellan prepares to dispatch a contingent to rescue the general, but he is pleasantly surprised to see him walk into headquarters. The balloon had passed over enemy territory and landed close to Union headquarters. McClellan reacts: "You may rest assured of one thing: you won't catch me in the confounded balloon, nor will I allow any other generals to go up in it."

Elements of the 12th New York and the 57th and 63rd Pennsylvania Volunteer Regiments, commanded by Colonel Campbell, skirmish with about 700 Confederates near Yorktown. The Union sustains two killed and eight wounded. No Confederate casualties are reported. Also, a Union contingent (pickets), commanded by Major Webster, including detachments of the 77th Ohio Volunteers and the 1st West Virginia Cavalry, come under attack at Monterey. The Union reports three wounded. Confederate casualties, if any, are unavailable.

In Union general officer activity, Cassius Marcellus Clay, who had formerly turned down a commission as major general, is commissioned as such. He retains the rank until 11 March 1863, but sees no active field service. Clay had also rejected an appointment as minister at Madrid, Spain, that President Lincoln offered. Nonetheless, he accepts a post as minister to Russia and serves there from 1863 until 1869. Upon the election of President U.S. Grant, his diplomatic service ends abruptly. Afterward, General Clay seems to turn against all levels of authority. At one point he fortifies his house against attack. Eventually, he is described as a lunatic.

In Confederate general officer activity, William N. Beall, a cavalry officer, is appointed

Fort Pulaski, Georgia, is under bombardment on 11 April 1862 (Johnson, *Campfire and Battlefield: History of the Conflicts and Campaigns,* 1894).

brigadier general effective this date. Also, Colonel Martin Luther Smith (West Point, 1842), of the 21st Louisiana Infantry Regiment and a New Yorker, is promoted to brigadier general as of this day. Smith will focus on stiffening the defenses at Louisiana and the harbor at New Orleans as well as Vicksburg, Mississippi. General Smith is promoted during November to the rank of major general. Also, Lt. Colonel Edward Cary Walthall, formerly of the 15th Mississippi Regiment, is appointed colonel (later brigadier general) of the 29th Mississippi. In other activity, Colonel Franklin Gardner is promoted to the rank of brigadier general effective this date. Gardner participates in General Braxton Bragg's raid into Kentucky. His brigade is attached to General Withers' division (General Leonidas Polk's corps). By the end of this year, Gardner is named major general.

In Naval activity, the CSS *Virginia* (*Merrimack*) moves into the vicinity of Hampton Roads by traveling along the Elizabeth River and catching the Union off guard. It captures three unprotected Union transports. Following the mission, the vessel clears out of the area, leaving no time for the *Monitor* to intercept it. Meanwhile, the CSS *Jamestown* (*Thomas Jefferson*) departs with the *Virginia,* but the former moves to the northern part of Hampton Roads and seizes three merchant ships. In other activity, the USS *Sebago* arrives at Newport News from Portsmouth, New Hampshire. It immediately joins the naval forces in support of General McClellan's offensive on the peninsula during a push to take Richmond.

April 12 (Saturday) **In Georgia,** a Union detachment steals a Confederate train at Big Shanty (see also, **April 7–12 THE GREAT LOCOMOTIVE CHASE**).

In Mississippi, the Confederate vanguard, Colonel Lewis H. Little's 1st Missouri Brigade, arrives at Corinth from Memphis, Tennessee. The unit establishes camp outside of Corinth at Rienzi, and later the brigade is joined by Major General Sterling Price. Colonel Little is promoted to the rank of brigadier general within a few days.

In South Carolina, Union Major General David Hunter, while at his headquarters in Hilton Head, issues an order directing that all slaves at Fort Pulaski and Cockspur Island are to be "confiscated and thenceforth free."

In Tennessee at Pittsburg Landing, Major General Henry W. Halleck reorganizes the armies, placing Brigadier General George H. Thomas in command of the right wing, Major General Don Carlos Buell in charge of the center, and General John Pope's Army of the Missouri in command of the left wing. Halleck designates his army the Grand Army of the Tennessee and names General Ulysses S. Grant second in command. Major General John A. McClernand will command the reserves. The total force comprises more than 100,000 troops, but it will not make a serious effort toward Corinth, Mississippi, until early May.

In Naval activity, the *Maratanza,* constructed in Massachusetts at the Boston Navy Yard, is commissioned. G.H. Scott receives command of the gunboat.

April 13 1862 (Sunday) In England, on or about this day, Confederate Captain Semmes, former commander of the CSS *Sumter,* departs England for America; but en route at Nassau, he is intercepted and informed that he is to return to England to assume command of the CSS *Alabama.* Before abandoning the CSS *Sumter* at Gibraltar, the *Sumter* had been on the high seas for about six months. During that time, the privateer had seized eighteen vessels; of those, eight were destroyed at sea by fire and the others, except the *Cuba,* which was recaptured, were either bonded or released.

In Alabama, Union troops occupy Decatur. Also, a Union detachment of cavalry commanded by Major Thielemann initiates a reconnaissance mission along the Corinth, Mississippi, and Purdy, Tennessee Road. No encounters with Confederate forces are recorded.

In North Carolina, a Union contingent of the 103rd New York Infantry Regiment, commanded by Colonel Baron Fred. W. Von Egloffstein, skirmishes a Confederate detachment of the 2nd North Carolina Volunteers commanded by Colonel William G. Robinson at Gillett's Farm. The Union casualties are listed as four killed and two wounded. The estimated Confederate casualties are two killed, seven wounded and three captured.

In Naval activity, the USS *Westfield* moves upriver to engage two Confederate vessels near Fort Jackson (New Orleans), but after firing two rounds, the Rebels quickly move to reach a point from which the vessel is protected by the fort's guns. The *Westfield,* however, moves closer to resume its fire. It effectively strikes the CSS *Defiance* and severs its shaft. The crew abandons the *Defiance* and sinks it.

April 13–22 **In New Mexico,** the Union initiates pursuit of the Confederates under General H.H. Sibley. On the 13th, a contingent under Colonel Paul links with General Canby's forces at Tijeras during the evening. The combined force moves out for Peralta on the 14th after being informed that the Confederates had departed Albuquerque. The Union column reaches Peralta prior to the arrival of the Confederates, and the latter have no knowledge of the Union's movement to intercept them. On the morning of the 15th, a Confederate wagon train composed of seven wagons and one artillery piece is intercepted outside off Peralta. After a struggle the train is seized. Six of the Confederate escort force are killed, three are wounded and 30 are captured. After securing the train, Colonel Paul, leading his column and three companies of cavalry, advances to the front of Peralta. A fierce firefight ensues, but Union prevails and Union troops clear the resistance, then occupy the bosque to the rear and front of Peralta. After securing the ground, the

force suspends further attempts to seize the stronghold, Peralta, in favor of food and rest, following a tedious three-day period in which some of the troops have had no rest and little or no food. Meanwhile, reconnaissance patrols scrutinize the terrain to select points from which the attack will be launched; however, during the night of the 15th–16th, the Confederates abandon Peralta, considered the second strongest position, behind Albuquerque, they had held in the region. The Confederates bolt to the right bank of the river but are unable to carry the wounded and sick. Consequently, they are left to the mercy of the Union with no medicine. Pursuit begins, and by the afternoon, the Union is close on the heels of the Rebels' rear guard, but still on the opposite side of the river. That night, the Confederates abandon 38 of their wagons before heading into the mountains. Nevertheless, after securing safety for the confiscated wagons, the pursuit resumes, but it halts for a day at Pohadera. Meanwhile, the Confederates move farther into the mountains, while the Union forces of General Canby arrive at Fort Craig on the 22nd. On the following day, General Canby sends a report to headquarters in Washington, D.C.

April 14 (Monday) **In Missouri,** elements of the 1st Kansas Cavalry skirmish with a contingent of Confederates at Diamond Grove. The Union sustains one wounded. Meanwhile, the 2nd Missouri Militia Cavalry skirmishes with a contingent of Confederates at Walkersville. The Union loses two killed and three wounded. Also, two companies of the 1st Iowa Cavalry skirmish with Confederates at Montevallo. The Union sustains two killed and six wounded. The Confederates suffer two killed and 10 wounded.

In North Carolina, a Union contingent skirmishes with Confederates at Pollocksville. The Union reports no casualties. Confederates estimate seven wounded.

In Tennessee, by this date, Flag Officer Andrew Foote, following the recent capture of Island No. 10, completes his preparations for seizing his next primary objective, Memphis, but two other obstacles, Fort Pillow and Fort Randolph, must first be taken. Foote now has mortars in place at Craighead Point just a few miles below Fort Pillow. However, a Confederate naval force composed of eight gunboats and four steam rams also protects the city. At this time, Union Major General John Pope's ground forces remain in Arkansas, temporarily unable to move due to the swollen waters, but it is expected that the river will soon return to its normal height. Meanwhile, only two regiments, commanded by Colonel Graham Fitch, return to Pittsburg Landing, essentially leaving Foote to maintain the operation by himself. Soon the bombardments begin. Nevertheless, the Confederate gunboats impede the operation and it is not until May that the land operation gets underway.

In Virginia, Major General George B. McClellan, still awaiting heavy guns before continuing the assault against Richmond, states: "I shall not quit the camps until I do so to continue the attack on Richmond."

In Union general officer activity, Cuvier Grover (West Point, 1850), captain of the 10th Infantry at Fort Union, New Mexico, at the outbreak of war, is appointed brigadier general. General Grover participates at the Second Battle of Manassas (Bull Run), and later after being transferred to the Department of the Gulf, Grover commands the 4th Division in General Banks' XIX Corps. Also, Amiel Weeks Whipple (West Point, 1841) is commissioned brigadier general. At the onset of the war, Whipple was a member of General Irvin McDowell's staff, operating as chief topographical engineer at First Bull Run (Manassas). Afterward, he commanded a brigade as part of the defenses of the capital. Subsequently, he participates at Fredericksburg and Chancellorsville.

In Confederate general officer activity, Brigadier Generals John Cabell Breckinridge and Thomas Hindman are appointed to the rank of major general effective this day. Hindman, commander of the Department of Arkansas, during the following month orders an arsenal established at Arkadelphia. Colonel William Preston, assigned to his brother-in-law's (General A.S. Johnston) staff until his recent demise, becomes brigadier general effective this day. Preston, whose last actual combat experience had been as a member of the 4th Kentucky Rifles during the Mexican War, brushes up his skills and prepares to participate in various battles in Mississippi and Tennessee, including the siege at Corinth (April 30 to May 30, 1862) and Murfreesboro (December 31, 1862, to January 2, 1863), respectively. Preston, subsequent to fighting at Chickamauga and Chattanooga as part of General Breckinridge's division, will be appointed as minister to Mexico representing the Confederacy, but his mission is never fulfilled, as he fails to reach the court of Maximilian. Instead he finishes the last days of the conflict in the Department of the Trans-Mississippi. Also, Thomas Jordan (West Point, 1844), former chief of staff to General Bragg, is promoted to brigadier general, effective this day, for his actions at the Battle of Shiloh. During the latter part of the war he receives command of the 3rd Military District of South Carolina. After the war, he resumes his writing career.

In Naval activity, the steamer USS *Pochahantas* maneuvers near Seabrook Island, Edisto River, South Carolina. A contingent of Marines and a unit of the 3rd New Hampshire Volunteers debark and initiate a reconnaissance mission. In other activity, the USS *Wamsutta* arrives in Port Royal, South Carolina, to join the South Atlantic Blockading Squadron. Shortly thereafter, it is assigned blockade duty in St. Simond's Sound, Georgia.

April 15 (Tuesday) In Arizona, a small unit of Confederates commanded by Captain Sherod Hunter is attacked at Picacho (Pechacho) Pass by the vanguard of Union Captain William P. Calloway. The brisk confrontation ends with three Union troops killed. The Rebels are forced to withdraw, as the main Union force, which exceeds 1,000 men, is advancing along the Gila River toward their positions, thus ending Arizona's only Civil War battle. Union Lieutenant James Barrett is killed. The Union sustains three killed and three wounded. Confederate casualties, if any, are unavailable.

In New Mexico, a Union detachment attached to Colonel (later brigadier general) Edward Canby skirmishes with Confederates at Peralta. Casualty figures, if any, are unavailable.

In Union general officer activity, Benjamin Alvord (West Point, 1833), who served in the 4th Infantry during the Seminole Wars and Mexican War, is promoted to brigadier general of volunteers. Alvord assumes command of the newly created Department of Oregon, where he remains in command until March 1865. Also, Colonel Charles Devens (15th Massachusetts Regiment) is appointed brigadier general. Rufus Saxton (West Point, 1849) is appointed brigadier general of volunteers. Saxton, formerly quartermaster for Generals Nathaniel Lyon and George McClellan, receives command of the defenses of Harper's Ferry. General Saxton's primary role for the duration of the war is enlisting Negroes, particularly former slaves, into the Union Army. After the war Saxton is breveted major general in the volunteers and breveted brigadier general in the Regular Army. Also, Captain George Lucas Hartsuff (West Point, 1852) is appointed brigadier general. Colonel Napoleon Bonaparte Buford (West Point, 1827), commander of the 27th Illinois Regiment, is appointed brigadier general. At the end of the war he is breveted major general. Buford is the half-brother of Union general John Buford and the cousin of Confederate General Abraham Buford. Francis Engle Patterson, the son of Major General Robert Patterson and the brother-in-law of General John Joseph Abercrombie, is appointed brigadier general. General Patterson, a veteran of the Mexican War, participates as a brigade commander at Williamsburg and at Seven Pines.

In yet other activity, Carl Schurz, a native of Prussia who arrived in the U.S. in 1852, is appointed brigadier general to rank from this date. Despite having no military experience, he receives command of a division under General John Frémont, who is operating in the Shenandoah Valley. Afterward, he participates at Second Manassas (Bull Run), and at the time, General Frémont is succeeded by General Sigel and the army is under General John Pope. Colonel James Henry Van Alen (3rd New York Cavalry) is promoted to brigadier general. During the Peninsular Campaign, Alen commands at Yorktown and at Gloucester. After being relieved during October 1862, he is appointed to a court of inquiry charged with investigating General Irvin McDowell's conduct at Second Bull Run (Manassas). Afterward, he serves as aide-de-camp to General Joseph Hooker.

April 16 (Wednesday) In Alabama, Union forces occupy Tuscumbia.

In Georgia, a contingent composed of detachments of the 8th Michigan Volunteer Regiment, bolstered by one battery of Rhode Island light artillery, commanded by Lt. Wilson, clashes with Confederates at Wilmington Island (Whitemarsh), Georgia. The Union sustains about 10 killed and 35 wounded. The Confederates suffer five killed and about seven wounded.

In Tennessee, Union cavalry clashes with Confederate pickets at Savannah. The Union reports no casualties. The Confederates sustain five killed and about 65 wounded.

In Virginia, a Confederate force routs a Union contingent attached to the command of General William F. Smith at Lee's Mills in the vicinity of Dam No. 1 on the Warwick River. Initially, a detachment of Vermont troops, supported by Colonel Romeyn B. Ayres' battery, ford the river. The artillery forces two Confederate regiments, one from Georgia and the other from North Carolina, to withdraw, but soon they are strongly reinforced. The Confederates rally and drive the Vermont troops back across the river. A second attack is launched, but again the Confederates push the Yankees back. During the retreat, 1st Sergeant Edward A. Holton, 6th Vermont Regiment, retrieves the colors from the fallen bearer while retreating under extremely heavy fire. Due to his extraordinary heroism, Holton is awarded the Medal of Honor. The 3rd, 4th and 6th Vermont Regiments participate, supported by Romeyn B. Ayres' battery and one other battery of the 5th U.S. Artillery. The Union sustains 35 killed and 120 wounded; the bulk of the casualties are incurred by the 3rd Vermont. The Confederates suffer 20 killed, about 75 wounded and 50 captured.

In Union general officer activity, Colonel Nathan Kimball (12th Indiana) is promoted to brigadier general.

In Confederate general officer activity, Colonel Lewis H. Little, a veteran of the Mexican War, is promoted to the rank of brigadier general. After fighting at the siege of Corinth, Mississippi, Lewis is assigned command of a division under General Bragg. Also, Confederate Colonel George Maney, due to his recent heroism on the field at Shiloh while leading a brigade (Cheatham's division), is appointed brigadier general effective this date. Maney, subsequent to duty in Virginia, had requested a transfer to Tennessee to bolster the forces there after the reduction of Forts Donelson and Henry. Confederate Colonel John Stuart Williams is promoted to the rank of brigadier general, effective this date. In autumn 1863 he is appointed commander of the Department of East Tennessee, but he requests relief of his command during November of that year. Subsequently, he is attached to General Wheeler's corps. After the close of hostilities, he returns to Kentucky and engages in farming; afterward, he serves again in the state legislature, followed by his election to the U.S. Senate. He dies during July 1898. Also, Colonel Jean Jacques Alfred Alexander Mouton (West Point, 1850) is promoted to brigadier general.

In Naval activity, the USS *Iroquois* arrives at Ship Island, Mississippi, to join Admiral Farragut's fleet and participate in the attack to regain New Orleans. Meanwhile, on this day, Admiral Farragut — aboard the USS *Arletta* and accompanied by some other schooners — arrives within firing distance of Fort Jackson. Confederate batteries commence fire, but the ships are out of range. The USS *Arletta* launches five rounds toward Fort Jackson and one explodes within the fort. Farragut accomplishes his mission — to test the range of his guns. Following an intense operation lasting about one month, Admiral Farragut had succeeded in getting all of his ships, except the USS *Colorado*, across the bar and into the river near the two formidable forts on opposite banks.

April 17 (Thursday)   In Virginia, Union troops under General William F. Smith are engaged by Confederates near Yorktown. General McClellan is informed that Union casualties reach nearly 200 killed or wounded. During the evening, Confederates attempt to cross the stream in front of Smith's lines, but they are repulsed on two occasions. In other activity, General Banks departs Strasburg and his forces seize New Market without incident. Meanwhile, General Stonewall Jackson, still in the vicinity of Mt. Jackson since the fighting at Kernstown on 22–23 March, is planning to again strike Banks' force, particularly because this belated move now threatens not only the southern units in the Shenandoah Valley, but also General Ewell's army, which is positioned east of the ridge.

In West Virginia, the 10th West Virginia Volunteer Regiment skirmishes with Confederates at Holly River. The Union sustains three wounded. The Confederates sustain two killed.

In Naval activity, Union naval forces under Admiral David Farragut and Commodore David D. Porter are off Ship Island, Mississippi, preparing an assault on New Orleans, Louisiana. The fleet moves to positions about four miles

from the forts that guard the entrance to New Orleans. The Confederates send some rafts, which are afire, toward the fleet, but boats from the USS *Arletta, Iroquois* and *Westfield* intercept them and nudge them toward shore, where they continue burning but cause no harm to the armada. The fleet includes: *Arletta,* Acting Master Thomas E. Smith (one 13-inch mortar, two 32-pounder smoothbores, two 12-pounder smoothbores); *Hartford,* Captain Wainwright (flagship, 28 guns); *Pensacola,* Captain Morris (24 guns); *Brooklyn,* Captain Craven (26 guns); and *Richmond,* Captain Alden (26 guns). The gunboats are: *Iroquois,* Commander De Camp (nine guns); *Oneida,* Commander S.P. Lee (10 guns); *Portsmouth,* Commander Rogers (17 guns); *Varuna,* Captain Boggs (12 guns); *Cayuga,* Lt. Harrison (five guns); *Winona,* Lt. Nichols (four guns); *Katahdin,* Lt. Preble (six guns); *Itasca,* Lt. Caldwell (five guns); *Kineo,* Lt. Ransom (five guns); *Wissahickon,* Lt. A.N. Smith (five guns); *Pinola,* Lt. Crosby (five guns); *Kennebec,* Lt. Russell (five guns); *Sciota,* Lt. Donelson (six guns); *Kittatinny,* Lt. Lamson (nine guns) and the *Westfield,* Captain Renshaw (six guns).

Additional vessels commanded by Lt. Harrell are the *Clinton, Jackson, Saxon* and *Miami.* Also, mortar boats supplement the fleet. They are: *Norfolk Packet, T.A. Ward, Horace Beales, Oliver H. Lee, C.P. Williams, William Bacon, Para, Orletta, Sidney C. Jones, M. Vassar, Jr., M.J. Carleton, Adolph Hugel, Orvetta, George Maugham, John Griffith, Sarah, Bruin, Henry James, Dan Smith, Raur* and the *Sea Foam.* In conjunction, Commodore David D. Porter is aboard the steamer *Harriet Lane* (his flagship), which is supported by the gunboat *Owasco* (five guns), commanded by Lieutenant Guest. The accompanying ground force, numbering about 9,000 troops, is aboard five transports. They are: *Mississippi,* transporting General Butler and his staff, the 26th and 31st Massachusetts Regiments commanded by Colonels Edward F. Jones and Oliver P. Gooding, and Charles Everett's 6th Massachusetts Battery; *Great Republic,* with General Thomas Williams with the 4th Wisconsin (Colonel Eleazer Paine), 6th Michigan (Colonel Frederick W. Curtenius) and 21st Indiana (Colonel James Winning McMillan) Regiments; *North America,* transporting the 30th Massachusetts (Colonel Nathan Augustus M. Dudley), one company of Durviage's Cavalry and one company of Red's Cavalry; *Matanzas,* transporting General Phelps with the 9th Connecticut Regiment (Colonel Thomas W. Cahill) and Captain Pythagoras E. Holcomb's Second Vermont Battery; and *Will Farley,* transporting the 12th Connecticut Regiment, commanded by Colonel Henry C. Deming.

April 18 (Friday)   In Louisiana, Confederate-held Fort Jackson takes action against the Union fleet that is preparing to attack. The fort's guns commence firing, but return fire is soon offered by the USS *Owasco* and the mortar boats, six of which are being closely observed by the troops in the fort. Fourteen other mortar boats are holding concealed positions along the shore and also propel cogent barrages toward the Rebel positions. Commodore David Porter camouflages the mortar boats with a thick coating of Mississippi mud and adds an assortment of tree branches to the masts and rigging. The exchange continues throughout the day. During the attack, the USS *Arletta,* assigned to the first division of schooners, catapults 96 shells into the two forts. The Union sustains one man killed and three wounded. Two mortar boats sustain some damage. Admiral David D. Porter's mortar ships continue to bombard the forts for six days.

In Virginia, the 2nd New York Cavalry (General Christopher Augur's command) clashes with Confederates at Falmouth and captures it. The Union sustains five killed and 16 wounded. The Confederates suffer 19 captured. In other activity, General Thomas "Stonewall" Jackson, still having his three brigades at Mt. Jackson, decides to initiate an offensive due to recent activity by General Banks' forces, which have occupied New Market. Jackson intends to seize control of Swift Run Gap through the Blue Ridge Mountains before the Union arrives to dominate the pass. Jackson takes a circuitous route. He leads the column back to the vicinity of Harrisonburg, skirts around it, then the column advances to Massanutton Mountain. The column ignores the roughness of the forced march and advances slightly more than thirty miles by the end of the day, stopping about five miles east of Harrisonburg.

In South Carolina, the Union steamer *Crusader,* in support of the 3rd New Hampshire and the 55th Pennsylvania Volunteer Regiments, commanded by Lt. Commander Rhind, clashes with Confederates at Edisto Island. The Union sustains three wounded. Confederate casualties are unavailable.

In Union general officer activity, the war is heating up in the east. By the end of May, Colonel Edward Canby is promoted to the rank of brigadier general and transferred from New Mexico to the Eastern Theater. Colonel Benjamin S. Roberts (West Point, 1835), attached to the 3rd Cavalry serving with Canby, is also promoted to brigadier general and sent east. General Roberts will participate at the 2nd Manassas (Bull Run) in the capacity of General Pope's chief of cavalry.

April 19 (Saturday)   In Arkansas at Talbot's Ferry, the Union 4th Iowa Cavalry encounters and skirmishes with a detachment of Confederates. The Union sustains one killed. The Confederates lose three killed.

In Louisiana, at New Orleans, the Union gunboats and mortar boats continue to bombard

General Thomas "Stonewall" Jackson's troops in prayer at camp (Johnson, *Campfire and Battlefield: History of the Conflicts and Campaigns,* 1894).

Confederate positions at Fort Jackson and in turn receive heavy fire from the Confederates. The mortar boat *M.J. Carleton* is sunk and one other is temporarily disabled. During the day's fighting, one man is killed and two others are wounded.

In North Carolina, Union and Confederate troops skirmish at Camden, South Mills. The Union's 6th New Hampshire, 9th and 89th New York, 21st Massachusetts and 51st Pennsylvania Regiments, commanded by General Jesse Reno, depart Beaufort on gunboats and move up the Pasquotank River to intercept a contingent of Confederates, commanded by Colonel Ambrose Ransom Wright (commander, 3rd Georgia Infantry Regiment) before it can depart for Norfolk. Reno's force is hoping to strike with surprise, but the Rebels have learned of the movement. Suddenly, when the Yankees reach a point about one and one-half miles from South Mills, the woods on the opposing banks come alive as Confederates, firing from concealed positions, bludgeon the Yankees with a blanket of grapeshot and canister shot. The Union, following the initial shock of the ambush, reacts, and with the support of one of the transports, the Rebels are driven away. Nonetheless, the mission is aborted. The Union losses stand at 12 killed and about 99 wounded. The Confederate losses are unavailable.

While General Reno had been on his mission, General Parke sets out on a reconnaissance mission to gather intelligence at Bogue Spit. Once there, with the quick work of the 4th and 5th Rhode Island Regiments, the Confederate pickets are driven back toward Fort Macon, and the Union is able to secure strategic positions on which to place their guns for the imminent attack to seize the fort.

In Virginia, the Confederates under Major General Thomas J. "Stonewall" Jackson leave the vicinity of Harrisonburg, cross over the Massanutton Mountain and then, after strengthening a bridge, the cross the south fork of the Shenandoah River and move toward Conrad's store east of the river. Afterward, Jackson secures the pass at Swift Run Gap. He establishes camp on the Elk Run. General Banks at New Market dispatches a contingent to pursue Jackson. The forces arrive at Luray and encounter the Rebels, who are in the process of destroying two bridges. The Union contingent is sufficiently strong enough to drive off the Confederates and save the bridges. General Banks is advised that the forces of Jackson had departed the area around Harrisonburg and positioned themselves on Banks' left flank.

The information causes concern for Banks, who becomes more passive when he concludes that Confederate General Ewell, deployed east of the ridge, is in position to reinforce Jackson. Banks ponders his situation and becomes more concerned as he concludes also that Jackson, once bolstered by reinforcements, could retrace his steps and sever the line of retreat. One option for Banks is to advance to Staunton; however, that plan is plagued with danger. If he fails to intercept General Frémont's force, his situation would become more precarious. Consequently, he declines moving south. Circumstances change shortly thereafter. General James Shields' division is detached from Banks and transferred to General McDowell. Banks is directed to move back to Strasburg.

Also, Major General Irvin McDowell will, within several days, be ordered to join McClellan in front of Richmond, but he is to deploy his force so that if necessary, he can dash to Washington if it becomes threatened by Confederates. Robert E. Lee is informed that Confederate General Charles W. Field (West Point, 1849) has evacuated Fredericksburg, making camp 14 miles south of the town. The Confederates burn the bridges across the Rappahannock as they withdraw.

April 20 (Sunday)   In Louisiana, naval gunfire from Admiral David Farragut's fleet bombards Confederate Forts Jackson and St. Philip, defended by 74 and 40 guns respectively. Fort Jackson, on the west side of the Mississippi River, also has a six-gun battery. Confederate Lt. Colonel (later brigadier general) Edward Higgins, 21st Louisiana Infantry, commands all the fortifications. The river defenses are under the command of General Johnson Kelly Dun-

can. The Confederates have stretched a giant iron chain across the river. The obstacle has been laid over eight hulks and extends from Fort Jackson to the opposing embankment. The city of New Orleans is also defended by gunboats: the iron-clad CSS *Louisiana* (a floating battery of 16 guns) CSS *Manassas* (an ironclad ram of one gun), CSS *Governor Moore* (three guns), *General Quitman* (two guns), *Stonewall Jackson* (two guns), *Warrior* (two guns), *Resolute* (two guns), *Defiance* (two guns), *McRae* (eight guns), *Galveston* (two guns), *Anglo-Norman* (two guns), *Breckinridge* (one gun), *Colonel Lovell* (one gun) and *Star* (one gun).

The Union, this day, concludes that the fleet must run the gauntlet and pass the forts. After

Rear Admiral David Farragut (Johnson, *Campfire and Battlefield: History of the Conflicts and Campaigns*, 1894).

Left: A Union squadron passes Forts Jackson and St. Philip outside New Orleans. (Johnson, *Campfire and Battlefield: History of the Conflicts and Campaigns*, 1894). *Right:* Confederate gunboats, rams and other vessels are burned as the Union fleet approaches New Orleans (Mottelay, *The Soldier in Our Civil War*, 1886).

1862

165

dark the gunboats USS *Itasca* and *Pinola*, bolstered by the *Iroquois*, *Kennebec* and *Winona*, depart to sever the chain and create a path to the main objective: New Orleans. It becomes a harrowing chore. The USS *Pinola* gets snagged by the wild current while it is in the process of lobbing a petard, an explosive device to be detonated by an electric spark. However, the conductor wire snaps before the spark can be transferred to the hulk. Meanwhile, crewmen from the *Itasca* do board one of the hulks and cut the chain, but in the process the *Itasca* gets pressed between the free moving hulk and the shore, placing the vessel in jeopardy. The *Pinola* speeds to the *Itasca*'s aid and pulls it free before it is swamped. Within a few days, the fleet safely passes the fort, heading for New Orleans. The CSS *Manassas* and *Louisiana* are destroyed.

In Confederate general officer activity, General Earl Van Dorn (West Point, 1842), who had resigned his commission as a major general (state troops) the previous January to join the Confederacy as a colonel, receives word that he is heading for Texas to assume command. He is commissioned brigadier general on 5 June.

In Union general officer activity, Major Henry Prince (West Point, 1835), a veteran of the Mexican War, on active duty in Washington at the outbreak of the war, is commissioned brigadier general. He is assigned to General Banks' corps and will command a brigade and afterward a division.

April 21 (Monday) In Tennessee, Union Major General John Pope's 30,000-man force arrives at Pittsburg Landing, increasing General Halleck's force to three armies for use against Confederate-held Corinth, Mississippi. The arrival of Pope brings the combined Union strength to more than 100,000 troops. Major General Halleck does not initiate action quickly enough, causing additional problems for the Union forces, as the Confederates are able to safely evacuate Corinth during the latter part of May.

In Virginia, Confederate General W.H. Taylor writes from Fredericksburg to General Charles W. Field: "Lee wishes you to prepare a firm front to the enemy" and "not to retire further than is positively necessary." In other activity, Confederate General Thomas "Stonewall" Jackson, at Massanutton Mountain on Union General Banks' flank, communicates with General Joseph E. Johnston on strategy modifications against Banks, but Johnston insists that no action be taken that could jeopardize the forces of General Ewell, the latter positioned east of the Blue Ridge, by preventing reinforcement if Ewell requires help. Johnston is of the belief that Fredericksburg will come under attack and suggests that Jackson and Ewell combine their forces to strike Banks. Only about 2,500 men under General Field hold Fredericksburg.

In Naval activity, the USS *Tyler* seizes the CSS *Alfred Robb* at Florence, Alabama. The vessel had been acquired by the Confederacy at an undetermined time during 1861, had been built at

Pittsburgh, Pennsylvania, and had operated primarily of the Ohio River before becoming a Confederate steamer. On or about this date, the CSS *Dunbar* is burned, and with the demise of both vessels, the Union gains total control of the Tennessee River. Lt. Gwinn, commander of the *Tyler*, renames the *Alfred Robb* the *Lady Foote*; however, Admiral Foote, not too happy with the vessel being named in honor of his wife, orders the original name restored. Also, due to the inability to safely take the prize to a federal court, the *Alfred Robb* is sailed to Cairo, Illinois, and attached to the Western Flotilla. The vessel, having bypassed an admiralty case hearing in court, begins its service during early June as a "tinclad" gunboat, the *Robb*.

In other activity, a contingent from the USS *Arthur*, led by Lt. Kittredge, moves ashore in three separate boats at Cedar Bayou, Texas, in search of the Confederate schooner *Burkhart*, which the *Arthur* had earlier pursued and lost. On the following day, Kittredge's force seizes three small sloops; however, a Confederate force numerically superior to Kittredge's diminutive detachment moves against the Yankees, forcing them to abandon their prizes as well as two of their three boats. Despite having only one boat, the party makes it back to the *Arthur* without sustaining any losses. Also, the ironclad USS *Galena*, commissioned on 21 April, arrives at Fortress Monroe from New York by tow. Commander Alfred Taylor, who arrives aboard the ironclad, is succeeded this day by Commander John Rogers. The *Galena* is assigned to the North Atlantic Blockading Squadron, commanded by Flag Officer L.M. Goldsborough.

April 22 (Tuesday) In South Carolina, Confederate Brigadier General Maxcy Gregg is directed to depart South Carolina to reinforce the troops in Virginia with his brigade, composed of the 12th, 13th and 14th South Carolina Regiments.

In Texas, Confederates seize several vessels (launches) in Aransas Bay.

In Virginia, Confederate artillery continues to fire against Major General McClellan's lines at Yorktown, but no damage is inflicted. During the morning, there is some activity between the Confederates and General W.F. Smith's troops, but the Rebels are repulsed.

April 23 (Wednesday) In Alabama, a Union contingent skirmishes with a Confederate detachment at Bridgeport. No casualties are reported.

In North Carolina at Bogue Spit, Union forces attached to Major General Ambrose Burnside's army are finishing work on the positions for the batteries at this recently captured terrain.

A battery of the 3rd New York Artillery, commanded by Lieutenants Flagler and Prouty, and a battery of 1st U.S. Regular Artillery, commanded by Captain Morris, will operate there. Confederate General Stonewall Jackson communicates by letter with General Robert E. Lee and discloses his plans to attack General Banks.

In New Mexico, Colonel B.S. Roberts sends a dispatch to General Lorenzo Thomas, adjutant general in Washington, D.C.:

I have the honor to report myself in command of the Central, Santa Fe and Northern Military Districts, Department of New Mexico, and that I have established and garrisoned the posts at Albuquerque and Santa Fe, recently occupied by Confederate troops of General Sibley's brigade. It will gratify you to know that the Texan troops are in retreat out of the country, having been compelled by our operations to abandon most of their supplies of all kinds and to take the mountain route behind the Socorro range to avoid the capture of their small remaining force of the 3,000 troops that invaded the Territory. They have abandoned their sick and wounded everywhere on their line of retreat, and are leaving in a state of demoralization and suffering that has few examples in any war. The long line of their retreat over Jornada and wastes of country without water and that furnish no supplies will render their march extremely difficult and aggravate the ordinary sufferings of a disorganized army under defeat.

Colonel Roberts adds that his animals are in poor condition and that he lacks sufficient supplies and cavalry, rendering pursuit of Sibley nearly impossible.

In West Virginia, the 3rd Maryland Regiment and the Potomac Guards, led by Colonel Downey, engage Confederates at Grasslick. The Union reports three killed. The Confederates lose some captured.

In Naval activity, outside New Orleans, Admiral David Farragut's fleet prepares to move against the city. The Union takes precautions to keep the vessels from sustaining too much damage. Large coils of iron chain cables are draped over the sides to cushion the ships against shells and protect the machinery. Other devices are improvised to fend off burning barges, and yet

The USS *Mississippi* fires upon a Confederate steamer (Mottelay, *The Soldier in Our Civil War*, 1886).

Captain Theodorus Bailey, U.S. Navy, commander of the USS *Cayuga* (Mottelay, *The Soldier in Our Civil War*, 1886).

An artist on the foretop of the USS *Mississippi* sketches the engagement between the Union fleet on the Mississippi River and Confederate forts and gunboats at New Orleans (Mottelay, *The Soldier in Our Civil War*, 1886).

other measures are taken to be instantly prepared to tow any vessels that become crippled. At about 2300, the *Itasca* moves to the point and verifies that the chain the Union had removed had not been replaced by the Rebels. Word is sent back signaling that the channel is open and clear. The fleet advances during the early morning hours of the following day. The vessels include: USS *Hartford, Richmond, Brooklyn, Cayuga, Pensacola, Portsmouth, Mississippi, Oneida, Katahdin, Varuna, Kineo, Wissahickon, J.P. Jackson, Sciota, Iroquois, Pinola, Itasca, Winona* and *Kennebec*. The *Harriet Lane, Owasco, Westfield, Clinton* and the *Miami* also participate.

The USS *John L. Lockwood*, along with the *Putnam* and *Whitehead*, establish a blockade at the mouth of the Chesapeake and Albemarle Canal in the vicinity of Elizabeth City, North Carolina. During the operation the warships sink one schooner and destroy some other obstacles. The *Lockwood* remains in the area (inland waterways) until 3 September 1863, when it heads north to Hampton Roads to receive required repairs. The following January, the *Lockwood* departs Norfolk on the 8th and arrives at New Bern on 14 January. In other activity, the USS *Sumter*, on duty off Charleston, returns to Port Royal to receive repairs. Once the repairs are completed, it departs for Wassaw Inlet, Georgia, on 29 April to initiate patrols. It returns to Charleston during May and remains on station until August.

April 24 (Thursday) CAPTURE OF NEW ORLEANS At about 0100, the Union fleet prepares to pass the two Confederate strong points, Forts Jackson and Philip, and move against New Orleans, Louisiana. At 0200, during a period of stark darkness caused by a deep ghostly fog, so thick that it causes the smoke from the steamers to hover upon the water, two tiny red lights are posted signaling the advance. By 0330, all vessels are underway in three slow-moving columns that cautiously cut their through the pea soup fog. Admiral David Farragut, on the left, heads the column in the USS *Hartford*, while the right column is led by Captain T. Bailey in the USS *Cayuga*. The center is led by Captain Henry H. Bell aboard the USS *Sciota*. In synchronization with the advance of the fleet, the mortar boats commence a gargantuan bombardment upon Fort Jackson and the nearby battery, the latter being si-

multaneously attacked by the gunboats *Harriet Lane, Owasco, Westfield, Clinton* and *Miami*.

The Confederate batteries at Fort Jackson initially hold their fire until the *Cayuga*, in the center column, comes within close range, whereupon the guns propel a thunderous barrage. The *Cayuga* returns fire only when it reaches a strategic point from which to strike Fort Philip. Meanwhile, the trailing vessels also come under fire but safely pass the forts, except for the *Portsmouth* and its tow, the *Jackson*, which drifts aimlessly downstream. Although the guns of Fort St. Philip fail to get the *Cayuga*, it faces more danger. Once it passes the fort, the Confederate flotilla under Captain Mitchell of the CSS *Louisiana* moves against it. The *Cayuga*, alone and with no help in the vicinity, battles the Rebels singlehandedly, trying to forestall disaster. The Confederates try to board, but the attempt is repelled. Other Rebel gunboats maneuver to ram the *Cayuga*, but again Captain Theodorus Bailey avoids disaster and in the process, although sustaining damage, the Yankees force three of the attacking gunboats to surrender. One other gunboat becomes grounded. Meanwhile, the *Varuna* comes up to extricate the *Cayuga*, permitting the damaged vessel to resume its part in the operation.

Suddenly, the *Varuna* becomes imperiled when Confederate warships close against it. Captain Charles S. Boggs, choosing not to be sacrificed, sails the *Varuna* directly into the center of the swarming gunboats and unleashes incessant broadsides from close quarters to break up the menacing attack. This permits the *Cayuga* to continue its advance, but shortly thereafter, yet another Rebel vessel, the *Governor Moore*, commanded by Captain Beverley Kennon, moves in close, opens up with a heavy barrage and rams the USS *Varuna*, inflicting damage, killing four and wounding nine crew members. In the midst of the tenacious confrontation, Captain Boggs orders his crew to concentrate their fire on the armor. Three-inch shells and incessant rifle fire pay dividends for Boggs, prompting the CSS *Governor Moore* to disengage and retire to repair the damage.

While the *Varuna* is checking casualties and damages, another Confederate vessel, the *Morgan*, which is lurking nearby, crashes into the USS *Varuna* twice, causing fatal damages, but prior to going down, the *Varuna* is able to fire some eight-inch shells into the attacking ship and force it to head for the beach, where the crew sets it afire. At about this same time, the USS *Oneida* and other Union warships move up and begin to rescue the crew of the sinking *Varuna*. The *Hartford* becomes imperiled when the CSS *Manassas* pushes a burning raft into it; however, in response, the *Hartford* quickly douses the flames and roars forward to unleash heavy broadsides into both defending forts. The USS *Pensacola, Richmond* and *Brooklyn* also pass the forts, with the *Pensacola* receiving heavy fire that causes casualties.

The *Brooklyn* also incurs damages when it gets snared by hulks and rafts intertwined with the chain barricade the Confederates constructed to impede progress of the fleet. The fire from Fort St. Philip inflicts the damage; however, the Brooklyn is also attacked by a Confederate ram and a steamer. As the steamer closes to a range of about sixty yards, the *Brooklyn* fires a broadside that succinctly terminates the threat of the steamer, which is knocked out of the contest. In addition, the ram *Warrior* is struck repeatedly by the guns of the *Brooklyn*, and the broadside of eleven shots causes a huge explosion. The *Warrior* is driven ashore just above Fort St. Philip, but shortly thereafter, the burning vessel is destroyed. Meanwhile, the *Brooklyn* becomes free of the obstacles and resumes its course up the river.

The *Richmond*, the slowest of the vessels, escapes unscathed. As the last part of the fleet begins to pass the forts, at about dawn on the 25th, the first section of the third column passes without harm, but the trailing *Kennebec* and *Winona* get caught by fire originating from both forts, and the *Itasca* takes such severe fire that it is compelled to withdraw.

Once the armada passes the forts, Farragut's fleet is intercepted by the ram CSS *Manassas*, apparently the only available Confederate warship. It is met by the USS *Mississippi*, which commences fire with effective broadsides. Soon after, the *Manassas* is boarded, but it is severely damaged and the Yankees set it afire. With the bulk of the fleet beyond the forts and closing on New Orleans, the ground forces are taken to Sable Island, slightly more than ten miles from New Orleans. From here, Lt. Weitzel of the U.S. Navy will use small boats and some marching through the muddy swamps to eventually, on Saturday, the 26th, reach the Quarantine grounds. U.S. Marines aboard the naval vessels participate, including manning secondary guns.

The cotton-clad ram *General Quitman* (which operated frequently with the *Governor Moore* and is often confused with it) is self-destructed by the Confederates. This vessel is separate from the transport *General Quitman* (according to the Navy Historical Center, "thought to be built in New Albany, Indiana, during 1859 and one of the last to escape from the city the 24th, evacuating upriver a good many ladies, some officers, and some ordnance stores.").

The CSS *McRae* sustains severe damage during the engagement, and its commanding officer, Lt. Thomas B. Huger, is among the fatalities. The *McRae* moves to New Orleans under a flag of truce on the 27th, but soon after arriving, it sinks. The CSS *Star*, a steam tug chartered by the Confederates during May 1861, while attached to the command of Commander J.K. Mitchell and being utilized as a telegraph station below Forts Jackson and St. Philip, is destroyed during the battle by fire from a Union gunboat. At about dusk, the USS *Arletta* and the other schooners in its division head down river to Southwest Pass, where they anchor. Afterward they return to sea duty and begin operations in the Gulf of Mexico on blockade duty, while waiting for Admiral Farragut and the deep-draft vessels to conclude the operations at New Orleans and return to initiate operations against Mobile.

In North Carolina, Union Major General Ambrose Burnside arrives at Bogue Spit in the vicinity of Confederate-held Fort Macon. Burnside observes the completion of the placement of the batteries and sets the time of the attack for the following day. The batteries comprise Lt. Flagler's four 10-inch mortars, Lt. Prouty's four eight-inch mortars and Captain Morris' three 30-pound Parrott guns. The U.S. gunboats (commanded by Commander Lockwood) *Barque, Chippewa, Daylight, Gemsbok* and *State of Georgia* also support the operation. The USS *Daylight* sustains damage inflicted by Confederate batteries; in October 1864, the *Daylight* moves to patrol the James River in Virginia and will remain in the area for the duration. It is decommissioned in May 1865 in New York.

In West Virginia, the Union 2nd Virginia Infantry is attacked at Beverly by a superior force and is compelled to withdraw to abandon the positions; however, the regiment returns to the town on 21 May.

April 25 (Friday)   In Louisiana at New Orleans, a U.S. naval bombardment initiated by Admiral David Farragut destroys the Confederate battery at Chalmette, the scene of the famous Battle of New Orleans during the War of 1812. The flotilla of nine vessels advances in the early morning hours, but the USS *Cayuga*, at the point, moves too far out in front and is the first to be attacked by the twenty guns at Chalmette. The trailing ships soon arrive, and their combined fire terminates the threat. The Rebels also send vessels laden with burning cotton and timbers toward the flotilla, but no damage is incurred. The fleet occupies New Orleans after the Confederates evacuate. A detachment of U.S. Marines unfurls the Stars and Stripes over the quarantine station. Confederate General Mansfield Lovell and the governor of Louisiana, Thomas O. Moore, had each ordered the destruction of property prior to evacuating. Lovell, who had succeeded General David E. Twiggs as commander of the Confederate Department of the South, also ensures that the Algiers Shipyard on the opposite bank of the Mississippi River is set afire. The not yet completed ironclad ram CSS *Mississippi* is also destroyed.

In North Carolina, the siege of Fort Macon terminates. U.S. Marine units aboard the steamers USS *Daylight, State of Georgia,* and *Chippewa* and the bark *Gemsbok* participate in the attack. The USS *Ellis* also participates. Following about one and one-half hours of combat, the rough seas force the gunboats to back off. At about 1600, a white flag is raised over Fort Macon and an offer to surrender proposed by the Union is accepted. Union troops under General Burnside occupy Fort Macon on the following day.

In Virginia, General Robert E. Lee responds to a letter from General Thomas Jackson, dated 23 April, and acknowledges Jackson's "forethought" regarding Lee using General Ewell's force if needed.

In Union general officer activity, Union Major General Charles F. Smith dies of dysentery and complications from an infection at Grant's headquarters in Savannah, Tennessee. Union General George Cadwalader, who had been a general during the Mexican War and is now major general of Pennsylvania state troops, is appointed a major general of U.S. Volunteers. He is relegated to garrison duty and special assignments. During the final portion of the war he is the commanding officer at Philadelphia. Union Brigadier General George Henry Thomas is promoted to the rank of major general effective this date. Major Samuel W. Crawford, who commanded a battery at Fort Sumter during April 1861, is named brigadier general.

William A. Hammond is appointed surgeon general of the U.S. Army and receives the rank of brigadier general. Subsequently, he begins to have differences with Secretary of War Edwin M. Stanton. Later, Hammond requests a court-martial, and despite a lack of solid evidence, the court-martial board finds him guilty of "ungentlemanly conduct." Hammond is dismissed from the service. Colonel John White Geary is commissioned brigadier general. Colonel Milo S. Hascall (17th Indiana) is promoted to brigadier general to rank from this day. Henry Walton Wessels (West Point, 1833), a veteran of the Seminole Wars in Florida and of the Mexican War, is appointed brigadier general of volunteers. At the outbreak of hostilities, he had been colonel of the 8th Kansas Infantry, posted along the border with Missouri; however, the previous month he was ordered to move east, where he was attached to the Army of the Potomac.

In Missouri, a detachment of Colonel Phillips' 1st Missouri Cavalry, commanded by Major Foster, skirmishes with Confederate guerrillas commanded by William Clark Quantrill. The Union sustains two killed and 11 wounded. The Confederates sustain about nine killed and some wounded.

April 25–26   In North Carolina, the USS *Daylight, State of Georgia, Chippewa,* and *Gemsbok* along with artillery had bombarded Fort Macon the previous day, forcing capitulation. The Confederates under Colonel Moses J. White officially surrender the fort on the 26th to Union General John G. Parke. The Union sustains one killed and 11 wounded; Confederates have seven killed, 18 wounded and 450 captured. The Union initiated the siege against Fort Macon on 23 March. (See also, **April 25 In North Carolina.**)

April 26 (Saturday)   In Kansas, a Union contingent of the 5th Kansas Cavalry skirmishes with Confederates at Turnback Creek. The Union sustains one killed. Confederate casualties are unavailable.

In Louisiana, although the Union has seized control of New Orleans, Lt. Colonel Edward Higgins, in command at Fort Jackson, refuses a surrender demand of Commodore David Porter. Higgins refuses to believe the city has fallen. The fort capitulates on the 28th.

Left: Confederates surrender Fort Macon, North Carolina, on 26 April 1862. *Right:* The 1st Massachusetts Regiment successfully attacks a Confederate redoubt outside of Yorktown (Mottelay, *The Soldier in Our Civil War*, 1886).

In Missouri, a contingent of the 1st Missouri Cavalry commanded by Colonel Hubbard engages a force of Indians at Neosho. The Union reports no casualties. The Indians sustain 30 wounded and about 60 captured.

In North Carolina, Confederate-held Fort Macon, commanded by Colonel Moses White, is recaptured by a Union contingent led by General Parke.

In Tennessee, a Union contingent of the 2nd Michigan Regiment skirmishes with Confederate pickets at Atkins' Mills. Also, a nine-man Confederate contingent led by Captain Ballentine initiates a scouting mission into the vicinity of Forked Deer River. The operation continues into the following day. No hostile encounters or casualties are reported.

In Virginia, a Union contingent of the 1st Massachusetts Volunteer Regiment, commanded by Lt. Colonel George D. Wells, engages about two companies of Confederates at a redoubt in front of Yorktown. Union casualties are estimated at four killed and 13–16 wounded. Confederate casualties are unavailable.

In Naval activity, the gunboat USS *Tahoma,* while on patrol duty off Sea Horse Key, Florida, spots a blockade runner, a schooner. The *Tahoma* gives pursuit. The schooner runs aground while in flight and afterward is destroyed.

In Union general officer activity, Colonel Leonard Fulton Ross (17th Illinois) is promoted to brigadier general. He does not participate at Shiloh; however, General Ross does participate during the operations against Corinth. Late in 1862 he receives command of a division under General Grant, and he commands the infantry during the Yazoo Pass expedition. Colonel Alfred Howe Terry (7th Connecticut) is appointed brigadier general (later major general).

April 27 (Sunday) In Louisiana, fresh Union troops commanded by General Benjamin Butler debark near New Orleans. These troops are to oversee the Union control of the city. Following the fall of New Orleans, Con-

federate Forts Livingston, Pike, Quitman and Wood come into Federal hands.

In North Carolina, a contingent of the 103rd New York Volunteer Regiment, commanded by Colonel Baron Frederick W. Von Egloffstein and composed of slightly more than 100 troops, skirmishes with a Confederate force of about 30 men at Haughton's Mills (Horton's Mills). The Union sustains one killed and six or seven wounded. The Confederates sustain about three killed, three wounded and three captured.

In Naval activity, the USS *Potomska* and USS *Wamsutta* operating on the Riceboro River engages a contingent of Confederate cavalry (dismounted) on Woodville Island, Louisiana. Confederate casualties are unknown; however, the Navy silences their weapons. During the mission, the presence of the warship prompted the Confederates to set a British vessel on fire to prevent its capture. The contest lasts for about forty minutes and the *Wamsutta* sustains some minor damage and two men wounded.

April 28 (Monday) In Alabama, a small contingent of the 10th Wisconsin Volunteers, led by Sergeants Makimson and Nelson, skirmishes with Confederates at Paint Rock Bridge. The Union suffers six wounded. The Confederates sustain six wounded.

In Louisiana, Union Commodore David D. Porter forces the surrender of Confederate Forts Jackson and St. Philip. The surrender terms are signed aboard the USS *Harriet Lane.* Commanders D.D. Porter and W.B. Renshaw sign on behalf of the Union. General Johnson K. Duncan and Lt. Colonel (later brigadier general) Edward Higgins sign on behalf of the Confederacy. The Confederate officers and the enlisted men are granted parole, but only the officers are permitted to retain their arms. Following his release, Duncan becomes chief of staff to General Braxton Bragg, but Duncan succumbs by fever in Knoxville, Tennessee, during mid–April 1862. Following the capitulation, the guns aboard the CSS *Louisiana,* a Confederate floating battery, are destroyed and the battery is set afire and allowed to pass into the cur-

rent to sink, but as it passes Fort Philip, it explodes and causes one death within the fort before heading for the bottom of the river.

The *Landis* and the *W. Burton* also fall into Union hands. The *Landis* afterward becomes a tug for the Union Army and operates in the Gulf of Mexico and on the Mississippi River for the duration of the war. Following the surrender of the city, Commodore Porter remains with Farragut and his Mississippi Flotilla operates between New Orleans and Vicksburg until July of this year, when Porter is appointed acting rear admiral and commander of the Mississippi Squadron as successor to Flag Officer Charles Davis.

In Tennessee at Bolivar, a Union detachment engages Confederates. Specific units are unknown and casualty figures are unavailable. A skirmish develops at Monterey when five companies of the 2nd Iowa Cavalry encounter and engage Confederates. The Union reports no casualties. The Confederates sustain five wounded and some captured. Also, elements of the 16th and 42nd Ohio Regiments and the 22nd Kentucky skirmish with Confederates at Cumberland Mountain. Casualty figures are unavailable.

In Virginia, General Thomas "Stonewall" Jackson informs General Robert E. Lee by letter that his forces stand at one day's march from Union General Banks' positions. Lee is also informed that Union General Louis Blenker stands at Winchester with a force of about 7,000 men. Jackson further states: "I propose to attack Banks if you will send me 5,000 more men.... Now, as it appears to me, is the golden opportunity for striking. Until I hear from you, I will watch an opportunity for striking some exposed point." Later, Lee replies that of the three plans he submitted, he was certain that Jackson would choose "the one that promised the most good to the cause in general." As circumstances change, Jackson moves toward Staunton to attack General Robert H. Milroy.

In Union general officer activity, Colonel John Cleveland Robinson (1st Michigan Infantry) is promoted to brigadier general effective this date. He participates under General McClellan during the Peninsular Campaign as a brigade commander. He also participates at Gettysburg and Spotsylvania. Major Truman Seymour is promoted to brigadier general. He receives command of a brigade in General McCall's division in the V Corps. Colonel Jeremiah Cutler Sullivan (13th Indiana), a midshipman before the war, is promoted to brigadier general. Daniel Ullman is commissioned colonel of the 78th New York Regiment (78th Highlanders). Colonel James Clifford Veatch is promoted to brigadier general.

Colonel John Curtis Caldwell is also named brigadier general. Caldwell is slightly wounded twice at Fredericksburg, where his command does less than well against the Confederates. Caldwell assumes command at Gettysburg (II Corps) after General Winfield S. Hancock is wounded, and he continues this duty until he is relieved in March 1864. In addition, Colonel John White Geary, 28th Pennsylvania Volunteer Regiment, is promoted to brigadier general. Geary had served in the Mexican War as lieutenant colonel of the 2nd Pennsylvania Infantry Regiment. Colonel James Henry Carleton is appointed brigadier general. He is assigned as commander of the Department of New Mexico. He succeeds General Edward R.S. Canby. Colonel Joseph R. West succeeds Carleton as commander of the 1st California Infantry Regiment. Carleton arrives in New Mexico at Santa Fe during September 1862. Andrew Atkinson Humphreys (West Point, 1831), an aide to General McClellan since the previous year, is appointed brigadier general. During September of this year, Humphreys receives command of a division in the V Corps. General Humphreys' division participates in the Maryland Campaign and at Fredericksburg, followed by Chancellorsville. Following his participation at Gettysburg, he is promoted to major general. Colonel William P. Benton (8th Indiana Infantry), Colonel Henry Bohlen (75th Pennsylvania), Colonel Quincy Adams Gillmore, Colonel Neal Dow (13th Maine) and Colonel Thomas Turpin Crittenden (6th Indiana) are promoted to brigadier general. Crittenden is the cousin of Confederate General George Crittenden and of Union General Thomas L. Crittenden.

In Confederate general officer activity, General John Horace Forney receives command of the Department of Alabama and West Florida.

In Naval activity, the vessel *Oreto* (CSS *Florida*), built in England for the Confederates, arrives at Nassau, but before it gets to sea under Captain J.K. Maffitt, complications develop. Although the vessel carries a British crew and flies the British ensign, the U.S. consul, aware that it is to become a Confederate warship, protests, and twice the British governor of the island orders the ship seized. Nevertheless, after all the papers are authenticated, the admiralty court orders its release. On 10 August the armaments are transferred to the vessel.

April 29 (Tuesday)   In Alabama, a Union force numbering about 1,000 troops attached to the 3rd Division, Army of the Ohio, commanded by Brigadier General Mitchel, skirmishes with a Confederate force estimated at about 600 at West Bridge (Bridgeport) in a contest that lasts about two hours. The Union casualty figures, if any, are unavailable. The Confederates sustain about 72 killed and wounded and about 350 captured.

In Louisiana, Union Major General Benjamin Franklin Butler now officially controls New Orleans. With the Stars and Stripes flying again, Butler appoints George F. Shepley as post commander. Shepley is promoted to brigadier general during July of 1862. Two hundred U.S. Marines, commanded by Captain John L. Broome, occupy the city and maintain it until army troops arrive on 1 May.

In Mississippi, Union Major General Henry W. Halleck makes preparations to assault Corinth, which is defended by Confederate General Pierre Gustave T. Beauregard. Also, Union forces (General Halleck's command) pursue Confederates to Guntown.

In Missouri, units of the 1st Iowa Cavalry and the 1st Missouri Artillery skirmish at Blackwater with a Confederate contingent, composed of about 65 men, led by Colonel Parker. The Union sustains one killed and two wounded. The estimated Confederate casualties are 5–10 killed, five wounded and five captured.

In North Carolina, a contingent of Confederate Cavalry skirmishes with Union troops at Batchelder's Creek. The Union sustains one killed and one missing.

In South Carolina, the Enfield Battalion and the Holcombe Legion, commanded by Confederate Colonel P. P. Stevens, engages Union forces on Edisto Island. The Union suffers two killed, three wounded and about 15–18 captured. The Confederates report no casualties.

In Tennessee, a Union force (Brigadier General Stanley's command), commanded by Colonel Elliott and Major Love, skirmishes with Confederates at Monterey. The Union sustains one killed and four wounded. Confederate casualties are unavailable, but some are taken prisoner. And at Cumberland Gap, a Union contingent under acting Brigadier General Samuel Powhatan Carter (formerly a lieutenant in the U.S. Navy) skirmishes with Confederates. The Union reports four wounded. Carter is promoted to brigadier general on 1 May. Following the campaign in Cumberland Gap, Carter will command a division of cavalry (XXIII Corps) during the fighting in East Tennessee and at the siege of Knoxville.

April 30 1862 (Wednesday)   In Tennessee, Union Major General Henry W. Halleck leaves Shiloh with the Army of the Ohio under Don Carlos Buell, the Army of the Mississippi under John Pope and the Army of the Tennessee under Ulysses S. Grant, heading for Corinth. Grant, although second in command under Halleck, is not utilized in this capacity. A contingent composed of one brigade of infantry and three bat-

talions of cavalry, led by Colonel Morgan L. Smith, advance to the vicinity of Purdy. Following a skirmish with a group of Confederates, the force successfully destroys part of the track of the Mobile and Ohio Railway and a nearby bridge, severing the route for supplies and reinforcements from Jackson, which otherwise would be able to reach Beauregard at Corinth. During the mission, the Union is able to seize and destroy a locomotive that had departed Corinth to offer support to some Rebel reinforcements en route from Memphis.

In Virginia, upon orders of General Robert E. Lee, units under Confederate Colonel W.E. Starke (1,000 men), Colonel J.L. Orr (2,000 men) and additional troops under General Maxcy Gregg in South Carolina are directed to move to reinforce General Field at Fredericksburg. Lee orders General Joseph R. Anderson to depart Richmond with his brigade to assume command in Fredericksburg. While Lee is preparing his strategy, Union General McClellan is busy preparing to seize Yorktown. McClellan's artillery is working well, and he anticipates a general assault in a few days. The weather is still terrible with the possibility of snow. The Union artillery has succeeded in chasing Confederate schooners from a wharf in range of the guns.

In Union general officer activity, James B. Ricketts, who as a captain commanded a battery at the First Battle of Bull Run (Manassas), is appointed brigadier general retroactive to 21 June 1861, the day of the battle. General Ricketts receives command of a division in General Irvin McDowell's corps. Colonel Isaac P. Rodman is promoted to brigadier general effective 28 April. Colonel Abram Sanders Piatt is also named brigadier general. He participates at Second Bull Run (Manassas), Maryland, and during December of this year at Fredericksburg.

May   *In Confederate general officer activity,* Captain George Pierce Doles of the "Baldwin Blues," a Georgia State Militia unit that had been brought into the 4th Georgia Infantry Regiment, is appointed colonel of the regiment. In November Doles will be promoted to brigadier general. Captain Bryan Grimes is promoted to the rank of lieutenant colonel. He is made a colonel in June and a brigadier general in 1864. Colonel Wade Hampton is promoted to the rank of brigadier general. During July 1862, he receives command of a brigade (Jeb Stuart's command). Captain (later brigadier general) Edward A. Perry, 2nd Florida Infantry, is promoted to the rank of colonel, with command of his regiment. On 28 August 1862, Perry is promoted to brigadier general. He later commands the Florida Brigade at Chancellorsville (May 1863).

May 1 (Thursday)   In Louisiana at New Orleans, Union Army troops arrive to relieve the Marines who have been maintaining order in the city. Major General Benjamin Franklin Butler dispatches some troops to the Algiers Ship Yard and orders the 31st Massachusetts and 10th Wisconsin Regiments, bolstered by the heavy guns of Everett's Battery, into the city. Marching to the music of "The Star Spangled Banner," they proceed to the customs house, where the artillery is deployed. Other Union outfits that participate are the 21st Indiana, 30th and 39th Massachusetts, 4th Wisconsin, 6th Michigan, 9th and 12th Connecticut, 5th and 6th Massachusetts Batteries and the 2nd Vermont Cavalry.

In Tennessee, a Confederate contingent led by Colonel John Hunt Morgan engages a Union wagon train at Pulaski. The Confederates capture a large number of prisoners.

In Virginia, Major General George B. McClellan is troubled that he is being pressured to prematurely attack Yorktown and that his political enemies are attempting to have him relieved of duty: "I am tired of public life; and even now when I am doing the best I can for my country in the field, I know that my enemies are pursuing me more remorselessly than ever."

In West Virginia, a Union contingent, Company C, 23rd Ohio Volunteers, commanded by Captain Stiles, skirmishes with Confederates at Clark's Hollow. Union casualties are listed as one killed and 21 wounded. Confederate casualties are unavailable. A contemporary casualty report lists Union casualties as four killed and 17 wounded and Confederate casualties as 16 killed and more than 50 wounded.

In Union general officer activity, Lt. Colonel (later brevet major general) Elias Smith Dennis becomes colonel of the 30th Illinois Regiment. Colonel Dennis had participated at Fort Donelson, and for his actions there he was recommended for promotion.

In Naval activity, a submarine is launched at Philadelphia. Later it is towed to the Philadelphia Navy Yard, where it is officially acquired by the U.S. Navy on 13 June. Later the tug *Fred Kopp* tows the vessel to Hampton Roads. After reaching Hampton Roads on the 23rd, the submarine begins to be called the *Alligator* and the name is used in official correspondence. Nevertheless, the *Alligator* does not see active service. On 18 March 1863, following modifications, the submarine goes through some maneuvers that are observed by President Lincoln. Afterward, it is towed to South Carolina by the USS *Sumter*.

A Union column crosses Pierre Bayou (Guernsey, *Harper's Pictoral History of the Civil War*, 1884).

to support the operations of Rear Admiral Samuel F. Du Pont against Charleston. In other activity, the USS *Somerset* departs Key West to initiate patrols off Cuba's coast. Several days later, on the 4th, it seizes a blockade runner, the *Circassian*, a screw steamer sailing under British colors at a point between Havana and Matanzas. The prize is towed to Key West and, following adjudication, is acquired by the U.S. Navy.

May 2 (Friday)   In Louisiana, at New Orleans, General Benjamin F. Butler takes up residence in the St. Charles Hotel, the former quarters of Confederate Major General Mansfield Lovell. He invites the mayor and some other city officials to meet with him at the hotel, but the mayor declines, insisting that he would meet only in City Hall. Butler then informs the mayor that his proposal is valueless, then he persuades the mayor to reconsider. Afterward, the mayor and others appear at the appointed time. While there, a crowd of Confederate sympathizers gathers around the hotel, which is now bolstered by more troops and cannon. General Thomas Williams sends a messenger to Butler informing him that the crowd is out of control and he is not certain that order can be maintained. The information does not seem to upset the mayor. Butler directs the messenger to inform Williams that the situation will end properly. His message: "Give my compliments to General Williams, and tell him, if he finds he cannot control the mob, to open upon them with artillery." The disorderly crowd is quickly calmed by the mayor, who terminates the problem. Also, General Butler reads his proclamation, which includes martial law, to some people at his quarters. The newspaper *True Delta* had refused to allow its type to be used to print the proclamation. Nonetheless, the troops use the newspaper's office and its type. The proclamation is issued on 6 May.

In North Carolina, a Union contingent skirmishes with Confederate pickets at Deep Gully. The Union sustains one killed and one wounded. Confederate casualties, if any, are unavailable.

In Virginia, Major General George B. McClellan is ready to reduce Yorktown. His force numbers more than 100,000 troops and he has eleven batteries that contain 111 supporting guns and mortars.

In Union general officer activity, Brigadier General Samuel P. Carter, appointed as a general officer on the previous day, prepares to assume his new responsibilities. He had been assigned to the War Department, but now sees field duty, primarily in Kentucky and Tennessee, his native state. Carter had graduated from Annapolis in 1846, but the ex-sailor now participates as a soldier at several

battles, including Fishing Creek and Cumberland Gap, Tennessee. Carter later serves as a cavalry commander at Knoxville and leads a division of infantry in Schofield's command during the Carolina campaign. Also, Captain John Gibbon (West Point, 1847), a veteran of the Mexican War and at present, chief artillery officer in General Irvin McDowell's division, is appointed as brigadier general. He receives command of the Iron Brigade. General Gibbon commands the brigade at the Battle of Second Manassas (Bull Run) and during the Maryland Campaign. In November 1862, he receives command of the 2nd Division (General John F. Reynolds' corps).

May 2–9   In Tennessee, Confederate General Patrick R. Cleburne leads a reconnaissance mission from Trenton into Paris and Dresden. The mission lasts until 9 May. A skirmish develops at Lockridge Mill. The Union force, at about 125-man strength, is outdone by the Confederate force estimated at more than 1,000 troops.

May 3 (Saturday)   In California at Fort Yuma, Brigadier General James H. Carleton, commander of the "California Column," sends a dispatch rider to Colonel Canby's headquarters in Santa Fe, New Mexico, to inform him that reinforcements are about to depart to reinforce Canby and support the drive to eliminate the Confederates from the territory. Carleton explains that his force will depart once he receives a reply from Canby. General Carleton also requests that the rider be given escort when he returns to get him past the hostile Apaches. The message states that Carleton's "forces of light artillery (Company A, Third Artillery) of two 12-pounder howitzers and two 6-pounder guns, and fifteen companies of infantry and five companies of cavalry, California Volunteers, [are] well armed and provided for, and the men are as fine material as any in the service." Carleton adds that he can add "another regiment or more of infantry" if necessary.

In Mississippi, in the vicinity of Corinth at Farmington, Union forces engage Confederates. Participants include the 10th, 16th, 22nd, 27th, 42nd and 51st Illinois, the 10th and 16th Michigan Infantry Regiments, the 2nd Michigan Cavalry, and Company C, 1st Illinois Artillery. The Union sustains two killed and 12 wounded. The Confederates sustain 30 killed and unknown wounded.

Union Major General John Pope orders Generals H.E. Paine and John McCauley Palmer to proceed toward a Confederate outpost at Farmington, outside of Corinth and manned by Colonel (later major general) John S. Marmaduke. Once the Union force arrives, a skirmish develops and the Union is able to drive the Rebels from their positions. Marmaduke returns to Corinth while the Union continues to advance toward Glendale to the east. The Union sustains two killed and 21 wounded. The Confederates sustain about 30 killed, 100 wounded and some captured. When the Union reaches Glendale, the rails are destroyed and two railroad trestle bridges are demolished. The 10th and 16th Michigan and 10th, 16th, 22nd, 42nd and 51st Illinois Regiments participate, supported by Yates' Illinois Sharpshooters (battalion), Hezcock's Ohio Battery and Houghtaling's Battery. The 2nd Michigan Cavalry also participates.

In Virginia at Yorktown, during the afternoon, Confederate batteries commence firing at the positions of Union Brigadier General Samuel P. Heintzelman, but actually the Confederate forces of Brigadier General John B. Magruder are quietly abandoning their positions. The artillery fire continues until about midnight. The Confederates holding Yorktown evacuate and move toward Richmond; however, prior to their departure, they scatter torpedoes (land mines) all over the area, causing considerable grief to the Union troops. Confederate Brigadier General Gabriel J. Rains, an explosive expert, had initiated the idea of planting the mines. Following this campaign, Rains transferred to Richmond, Charleston and other locations to further implement his specialty with mines to bolster Southern defenses. His last field command was at Seven Pines. Meanwhile, General George B. McClellan takes issue with reports that his Union troops had conducted themselves as a "horde of savages," using "fiend-like behavior." He defends the actions of his forces and retorts that the mine fields that had been created by the Rebels had in fact been intolerable. McClellan remarks: "It is the most murderous and barbarous thing I ever heard of." McClellan's troops occupy the city the following day.

The Confederate commanding officer in the region is General Joseph E. Johnston. The USS *Maratanza* participates in the seizure of Yorktown. Also, the Sisters of Saint Joseph continue to tend to wounded troops aboard the hospital ships *Whillden* and *Commodore* since their recent arrival at Fortress Monroe. A priest, Father Dillon (congregation of the Holy Cross), arrives to visit the troops aboard both hospital ships and provide the sacraments. On the 6th, the nuns are aboard the *Commodore* when it moves to Yorktown to pick up casualties.

In Union general officer activity, Brigadier General Edward O.C. Ord is promoted to the rank of major general.

In Confederate general officer activity, Major (later brigadier general) Allen Thomas, 29th Louisiana Infantry Regiment, is promoted to the rank of colonel.

In Naval activity, the USS *R.R. Cuyler,* operating out of Key West, Florida, seizes the schooner *Jane.* Prior to the end of the month, the *Cuyler* also seizes two additional blockade runners, the *Eugenie* and the *Isabel,* both schooners, off Mobile Bay.

May 4 (Sunday) **In Mississippi,** a three-company contingent of the 3rd Michigan Cavalry skirmishes with Confederates at Farmington Heights. The contest lasts for about one hour. The Union sustains one wounded. Confederate casualty figures, if any, are unavailable.

In Missouri, a Union contingent, including elements of the 5th Missouri Militia Cavalry and the 24th Missouri Volunteers, skirmishes with Confederates at the town of Licking. The Union sustains one killed and two wounded.

In Tennessee, a Union contingent skirmishes with a Confederate unit at Pulaski. Specific units and casualty figures are unavailable. In other activity, Confederates under John Hunt Morgan arrive in Lebanon and remain there for the night. Morgan stays at the home of the mayor.

In Virginia, the Army of the Potomac under Major General George B. McClellan occupies Yorktown. General Charles Jameson, "General of the Trenches," is the first to observe that Yorktown had been evacuated. This capture places McClellan's forces in position to move against Richmond. Also, Sergeant Robert J. Coffee, 4th Vermont Infantry, captures five men from the 8th Louisiana Regiment at Banks' Ford Road; he receives the Medal of Honor for his courage in the face of the enemy. General McClellan directs General Edwin V. Sumner to initiate pursuit. In turn, Sumner orders General Stoneman to take all available cavalry and horse artillery and pursue the Confederates toward Williamsburg. Four batteries of horse artillery, the 1st and 6th Cavalry, and Baker's Illinois Cavalry participate in the mission. The divisions of Generals Darius N. Couch, William F. Smith and Silas Casey follow, taking the Wynne's Mill Road. General Hooker's division also moves out to support Stoneman. Meanwhile, Generals Samuel P. Heintzelman and Philip Kearny hold back as reserves. The divisions of Generals Fitz John Porter, Israel B. Richardson and John Sedgwick remain in the vicinity of Yorktown, but later both divisions advance to West Point.

Meanwhile, General Stoneman's force encounters Confederate resistance at Fort Magruder and heavy skirmishing develops. The Yankees take casualties from intense enemy fire. Union Colonel Grierson makes several gallant cavalry charges, but the cost is high. General Hooker is detained by bad weather and Stoneman is forced to withdraw. By about 1700, W.F. Smith's division arrives and afterward, about midnight, Hooker arrives and his force deploys to the left of Smith. During the confrontation, Union General William H. Emory's (West Point, 1831) command is kept in reserve on the James River.

In other activity, a Union contingent, composed of elements of the 3rd Pennsylvania Regiment and the 1st and 6th U.S. Cavalry Regiments, skirmishes with a Confederate force at Cheesecake Church. Casualty figures are unavailable.

May 5 (Monday) BATTLE OF WILLIAMSBURG Contingents of the 3rd and 4th Army Corps, Army of the Potomac (General George B. McClellan), engage the Confederates near Williamsburg, Virginia. The Confederates, commanded by General Joseph E. Johnston, are held up in Fort Magruder, which has walls six feet high and nine feet thick. The Union is deployed with General George Stoneman holding the primary road supported by General William F. Smith to his right and Generals Joe Hooker at center and William Emory deployed to the left, guarding the road to Allen's Farm. At about 0700, troops attached to Hooker's command advance. The 1st Massachusetts and the 2nd New Hampshire Regiments move out on the left and right respectively, trailed by artillery, which establishes positions and commences firing upon the Confederate works. Soon after, the 11th Massachusetts and the 26th Pennsylvania move up on the left of the 2nd New Hampshire. Consequently, Fort Magruder is silenced and the Rebel rear guard scatters. As the Union advances it encounters a much stronger line of resistance, which turns out to be part of Longstreet's corps, including the Palmetto Brigade led by Colonel Micah Jenkins (General D.R. Jones' Brigade), which has arrived from Williamsburg. Heavy skirmishing develops as the 6th, 7th and 8th New Jersey Regiments engage the defenders, but the Confederates now outnumber the Yankees and the New Jersey Regiments begin to falter.

Meanwhile, General Cuvier Grover arrives with the 70th and 72nd New York Regiments, but still Hooker desperately needs more aid. At about noon he sends urgent requests for reinforcements, but except for General John James Peck's brigade, which repels an assault on Hooker's right, his command is compelled to hold on its own merits against the combined force of Generals James Longstreet, Roger Pryor, George Pickett and Samuel Gholson (Alabama state forces). Meanwhile, General Edwin Sumner is unable to dispatch Winfield Scott Hancock, as he had already been ordered to Queen's Creek to intercept a Confederate advance there.

An ongoing storm has so badly damaged the roads between Williamsburg and Yorktown that troops stationed further to the rear are unable to navigate the route. Hooker's able troops reach a critical point of only about 1,700 men and making his situation more grave, the Confederates have also captured some of his guns. The Confederates take the advantage of Hooker's problems and McClellan is informed that his presence is urgently needed at the battlefield. The Union forces are getting beat fairly conclusively, but McClellan arrives to rejuvenate the troops, who proceed to retake the offensive.

By about 1700, Philip Kearny's division arrives and shortly thereafter, two brigades of General Darius Couch move up. Kearny dispatches contingents of the 2nd Michigan and the 5th New Jersey Regiments to provide protection to Major Wainright's batteries, and he also directs two brigades, under Generals H.G. Berry and David B. Birney, to the left and right of the Williamsburg Road respectively, while simultaneously sending Colonel John Henry Ward's 38th New York and Colonel Edward J. Riley's 40th New York Regiments to seize the rifle pits that are anchoring the Rebels' center. Following a bloody contest, the Yankees reduce the obstacle by nightfall, but at high cost, including about one-half of the officers of the 38th New York Regiment.

In the meantime, tremendously bitter fighting erupts as Union General Winfield Scott Hancock attacks the Rebel positions at Cub Dam Creek. Confederate General Joseph E. Johnston, aware that Hancock is positioning his troops to collapse the left, rushes the 24th Virginia and the 15th North Carolina Regiments under Brigadier General Jubal Early and Colonel William MacRae, respectively, to drive the Yankees back. Hancock, holding a much smaller force and aware that no reinforcements are en route, pulls back and redeploys near the dam to await the Confederate thrust. At about this time, Jubal Early becomes wounded, leaving MacRae to lead the assault.

As the two Confederate Regiments encroach his lines, Hancock peers forward, assesses the danger and, despite the odds, he orders a bayonet attack. The Union advances with fixed bayonets and solidly punctures the lines of the Rebels. At close quarters, Hooker's troops use their bayonets effectively and begin to overwhelm the superior attack force. The Confederates bravely defend their positions and defiantly hold their ground in expectation of reinforcements, but none arrive. Eventually the ferocious Union attack compels the Rebels to retire toward Williamsburg, giving Hancock a decisive victory. General W.F. Smith arrives with reinforcements and the Union settles down for the night. Hancock sustains the loss of only 31 men from his command. Hancock's contingents consist of the 5th Wisconsin, 6th Maine, 49th Pennsylvania, 7th Maine, and Davidson's Brigade (the 30th New York). General George McClellan says of Hancock's actions at Cub Dam Creek: "This was one of the most brilliant engagements of the war."

Colonel Robert Cowdin, 1st Massachusetts Regiment, displays heroic service during the battle, prompting General Hooker to recommend him for promotion to brigadier general. Union General Joseph Hooker's brigade suffers high casualties in the engagement. Confederate Lieutenant Colonel William C. Wickham, leading the 4th Virginia Cavalry, is wounded during this confrontation. Following the battle between Hancock and the Confederates at the dam, Hancock states: "The 15th North Carolina and 24th Virginia deserve to have the word 'immortal' inscribed on their banners."

The Union sustains 456 killed, 1,400 wounded, 372 missing. The Confederates sustain 1,000 killed, wounded or captured. Confederate Colonel (later general) Samuel Garland, Jr., 11th Virginia Infantry Regiment, is wounded, but he recovers and later this month he is promoted to the rank of brigadier general. Garland also sustains other problems, as his wife (Elizabeth C. Meem) succumbs during this month and their only child, also named Samuel, dies in August. Confederate Major William H. Fitzhugh Payne, 4th Virginia Cavalry, is wounded and captured. Subsequent to his release, Payne is assigned to the 2nd North Carolina Cavalry as a lieutenant colonel.

In Virginia, Union General William B. Franklin is ordered by General McClellan to depart his positions along the Posquotin River and move to West Point to join the forces of Generals Israel B. Richardson, John Sedgwick and Fitz John Porter; General Franklin arrives at his destination on the following day.

In Kentucky, a one-company contingent of the 5th Iowa Cavalry skirmishes with Confederates led by Jeff Thompson at Dresden. No casualty figures are available.

In Tennessee, the 1st, 4th, and 5th Kentucky Cavalry Regiments and a detachment of the 7th Pennsylvania Cavalry under General Ebenezer Dumont engage Confederates led by Colonels J.H. Morgan and General Sterling A.W. Wood at Lebanon. The Union cavalry, on the advance from Murfreesboro, strikes Morgan's positions at about dawn and catches the Confederates off-guard. A tenacious contest continues for about one and one-half hours when the Rebels come under attack at their encampment near the town square and Cumberland University. Morgan and most of his force are able to break out and head eastward, but some continue the fight by reforming at the Odd Fellows Hall; nonetheless, their fate is sealed. The Union captures about sixty of Morgan's cavalrymen. The Union sustains six killed and 25 wounded. Union Colonel (later brigadier general) Green C. Smith (4th Kentucky Cavalry) participates. Colonel Morgan is appointed brigadier general during the following month. The Confederate 3rd Virginia Infantry, commanded by Colonel Roger Atkinson Pryor, also participates at this battle. Shortly thereafter, Pryor is appointed brigadier general effective 14 April 1862.

In Confederate general officer activity, Brigadier General David R. Jones is promoted to major general effective 10 March 1862. Colonel Micah Jenkins will assume command of his brigade and will be promoted to brigadier general in July.

In Naval activity, the CSS *Jamestown* (*Thomas Jefferson*) and the CSS *Patrick Henry* move to Norfolk, and on the following night they pass the Union batteries at Newport News, along with the CSS *Richmond*, CSS *Hampton* and some boats; however, a second attempt to reach Norfolk fails. The *Diana*, which was seized by the USS *Cayuga* on 27 April a few days after it escaped gunboats at New Orleans, becomes a U.S. transport and is assigned duty with the Union warships operating in the vicinity of Berwick Bay, Louisiana.

May 6 (Tuesday) In Louisiana, Major General Benjamin Franklin Butler proclaims martial law in New Orleans. The proclamation stipulates that all Confederate flags are to be removed from view and all people who had previously raised arms against the United States are to lay down their arms. It stipulates that if a Union soldier is killed, the perpetrator would be tried for murder.

In Virginia, General George B. McClellan's Army of the Potomac is waking up to the sounds of another dreary, miserable day. The Confederates suffer the same elements, as the rain makes the night sleepless for most of them. McClellan decides to send for additional reinforcements after being informed that the opposition being encountered is not a rear action; rather a concentrated Rebel force that had attempted to get out of the area prior to the arrival of the Federals. The Confederates evacuate Williamsburg during the night and move beyond the Chickahominy River. Union forces occupy the town and encounter large amounts of Confederate wounded. McClellan allows eighteen Confederate surgeons of General Joseph E. Johnston's command to enter the town to tend the wounded. Union Colonel William W. Averell (West Point, 1855) is dispatched with a cavalry force to intercept the Confederate rear guard, but muddy roads and nasty elements impede travel. Averell is suspends the chase and returns to his camp at Williamsburg. Essentially, Union activity remains dormant until the 8th.

Also, a contingent of the 5th New York Cavalry, en route from New Market to Williamsburg, encounters and skirmishes with Confederates in the vicinity of Harrisburg. The Union reports one killed and one captured. The Confederates sustain about 10 killed and six captured. Confederate Colonel George Burgwyn Anderson will be promoted to brigadier general effective June 9 for his gallantry during the fighting around Williamsburg. He will command a brigade at Malvern Hill.

In Naval activity, the USS *Commodore*, a hospital ship, and other vessels move down the James River to Yorktown to board casualties. From about 1700 straight into the following morning until 0200, wounded, Union and Confederates, are brought on board. Saint Joseph nuns are aboard to tend to the wounded who lay in row after row along the decks of the steamers.

Captain (later brevet major general) Newton Martin Curtis is severely wounded during the fighting at West Point. His subsequent service is confined primarily to "departmental duty." However, he does recuperate sufficiently to participate in the attacks against Fort Fisher, North Carolina, during December 1864 and January 1865 as a brigade commander (General Ames' division). His extraordinary heroism at Petersburg makes him the recipient of the Medal of Honor during the latter part of the war.

May 7 (Wednesday) In North Carolina, Company C, 9th New York Volunteers, departs Roanoke Island for Gatesville. The Union force is commanded by Captain Parsen and Captain Woodward, U.S. Navy. The contingent encounters Confederates, but the Union reports no casualties. The Confederates suffer one killed. The mission lasts until the following day.

In Virginia, Confederates attached to General Joseph Johnston's rear guard attack Union troops under General Franklin at West Point (Elthan's Landing). The Confederates, commanded by Major General William Henry C.

Whiting, are first engaged by the 16th, 31st and 32nd New York Regiments as well as the 95th and 96th Pennsylvania Regiments, supported by the 5th Maine Regiment and the 1st Massachusetts Artillery and Battery D, 2nd U.S. Artillery. The skirmish lasts for four hours, but once artillery is unloaded from the gunboats, the Rebels are forced to continue their retreat. The Union loses 49 dead, 104 wounded, 41 missing and some captured. A contemporary casualty list estimates the Confederate losses at eight killed and 32 wounded. This skirmish passes control of an important road junction to the Union. Other Union contingents are subsequently debarked, giving the Union a stronghold on what is to become a base of operations against Richmond. Hood's Texas Brigade participates in this action.

The 13th Indiana Volunteers, commanded by Colonel (later brigadier general) Robert Sanford Foster, skirmish with Confederates at Somerville Heights. The Union sustains seven wounded and 24 missing. The Confederates sustain seven captured.

May 8 (Thursday) BATTLE OF BULL PASTURE Confederate General Stonewall Jackson, who moved his forces from Harrisonburg, Virginia, to positions on the opposite side of the Shenandoah River during the middle of the previous month, has recently been strongly reinforced by Major General Richard S. Ewell's division and two brigades of General Edward Johnson's division. The Confederate strategy has been for Jackson to maintain vigilance on General Banks' forces at Harrisonburg, while General Robert E. Lee concentrates on cutting the communications between Winchester and Alexandria.

In the meantime, Jackson is informed that General Frémont is moving contingents of his force, specifically, General Robert H. Milroy's command, from Romney to Staunton, causing a drastic change in plans. General Jackson, in keeping with the tone of the master blueprint, leaves Major General Ewell to shadow Banks, while he speeds five brigades under General Edward Johnson toward Staunton to intercept General Milroy. Jackson is to join Johnson later. In the meantime, Johnson's brigades greatly outnumber Milroy, compelling the latter to retire to the Pasture Mountains (McDowell), and here he is joined by one of General Robert C. Schenck's brigades. At about this time, General Jackson decides that he will also move to support Edward Johnson.

By the morning of the 8th, it is apparent that the Union faces a problem, as Johnson is now reinforced by Jackson and a huge mass of Confederates are staring down from a ridge that dominates the Union Camp. In a determined effort to clear the high ground, Milroy dispatches the 3rd Virginia, 25th, 32nd, 75th and 82nd Ohio Regiments, one six-pounder of the 12th Ohio Battery and others who join in later. The effort to evict Jackson is valiant but unsuccessful.

The two sides relentlessly pummel each other with staggering blows, but the Confederates

hold the ridge as darkness settles over the area. At this time, Milroy pulls out of what he considers extremely untenable positions and prepares to retire to Franklin, Virginia. Union participants are the 25th, 32nd, 75th and 82nd Ohio; 3rd West Virginia; 1st West Virginia Cavalry; 1st Connecticut Cavalry and the 1st Indiana. Jackson's troops force the Union attackers to retreat. The Union suffers 28 dead and 225 wounded. The Confederates sustain 100 killed and 200 wounded. General Edward Johnson is among the wounded.

General Jackson initially sets out to pursue the Yankees, but reaching Franklin, he is informed that Banks is preparing to depart Harrisonburg. Jackson then decides to move to New Market, Virginia, to join with Major General Richard S. Ewell, thereby placing Confederate strength against Banks at about 20,000 troops. The Rebels move against Port Royal (Front Royal) and launch an attack on May 23.

In Alabama, a skirmish develops between Union and Confederate detachments at Athens. Specific units and casualty figures are unavailable; however, Colonel Turchin's command does seize Athens this month. The vanguard of Turchin's command, the 18th Ohio, comes under fire by citizens of Athens, and they also throw stones. Turchin becomes infuriated and encourages and condones the actions of his troops who pillage the town. Afterward, Turchin is court-martialed and relieved of command. Another charge lodged against him is that his wife accompanies him in the field. Nevertheless, Mrs. Turchin persuades President Lincoln to countermand the order and restore her husband to duty with the rank of brigadier general (July 1862).

In Arkansas, Confederate troops, including the 10th Texas Infantry, skirmish with a contingent of Federal troops near White River (DeVall's Bluff). Confederate Colonel Allison Nelson, later a brigadier general, participates at this minor confrontation. The Texas regiment under Nelson is attached to Confederate Major General Thomas C. Hindman's command of the Trans-Mississippi Department.

In Louisiana, a landing party from the USS Iroquois, commanded by Commander Porter, goes ashore at Baton Rouge. The city surrenders to Porter.

In Mississippi, detachments of the 7th Illinois Cavalry commanded by Lt. Colonel Minty and Major Applington skirmish with Confederates at Glendale in the vicinity of Corinth. The Union sustains one killed and four wounded. The Confederates suffer 30 killed and wounded.

In Naval activity, U.S. naval vessels, commanded

by Captain James L. Lardner, including the steamers USS *Susquehanna, San Jacinto, St. Lawrence, Mount Vernon,* and the sloops USS *Dakota* and *Seminole,* bombard Sewell's Point, Virginia. The Confederates at first do not return fire, but when they do, the Union calculates that only seventeen of their guns are operational. The *Monitor* is also involved with the bombardment, but a battle with the CSS *Virginia (Merrimack)* does not occur. The *Virginia* moves out of Norfolk at about 1430 to engage the Union flotilla, but once it spots the *Monitor* it backs off and remains out of reach of the *Monitor*'s guns. At about 1700, the fleet is ordered to retire. Marines participate in this action, which relentlessly pounds the Confederate positions; within two days, Norfolk capitulates to U.S. Army forces. Confederate batteries on Craney Island exchange fire with Union warships and the Union fleet (Flag Officer Goldsborough's command) continues to bombard the island until 12 May.

In related action, the USS *Galena,* accompanied by the gunboats *Aroostook* and the *Port Royal,* move up the James River toward Richmond. The warships encounter resistance from Confederate battery (11 guns) at Rock Wharf during the morning, and afterward they engage another battery, composed of 12 guns, at Mother Tyne's Bluff slightly after the noon hour. Of the 23 Confederate guns, the warships silence all but one. The *Galena* takes on the final gun, while the gunboats run past the position. In the meantime, the *Galena* eliminates the final gun. The rising flames and smoke are easily visible from the decks of the ships.

In other activity, the USS *Potomska* and the *Wamsutta* arrive at Darien, Georgia, to confiscate lighthouse equipment thought to be stored there, but subsequent to a search executed on the 9th, no equipment is discovered. The two ships depart the same day. The *Wamsutta* remains in the area off Darien and patrols in Doboy Sound, Georgia.

May 9 (Friday) **In Alabama,** a skirmish develops in the vicinity of Elkton Station near Athens when Company E, 27th Indiana Regi-

Union fleet of Flag Officer Louis M. Goldsborough bombards Confederate forts on Craney Island (Mottelay, *The Soldier in Our Civil War*, 1886).

ment, commanded by Captain Connet, engages Confederates led by Colonel Woodward. The Union suffers five dead and 43 captured. The Confederates sustain 13 killed.

In Florida, Union troops approach Pensacola. The Southern troops, anticipating the Union advance, evacuate, giving the Union control of the area by May 12.

In Louisiana, a detachment of U.S. Marines from the USS *Iroquois* lands at Baton Rouge and re-captures the U.S. arsenal, and during the action, the Marines hoist Old Glory to the top of the staff.

In Mississippi, Confederates attack a Union contingent, commanded by Colonels James D. Morgan and Gilbert W. Cumming, at Farmington, which had been left there by General John Pope, while his main body continues to advance. The small contingent of Union troops evades capture of the entire outfit by retreating behind Seven Miles Creek, but the major Confederate force does inflict casualties and retake the town. The Union sustains about 16 killed and more than 100 wounded. In addition, about 13 troops are captured. Confederate casualty figures are unavailable. Also, Union and Confederate forces clash in the vicinity of Corinth with an advancing vanguard contingent of cavalry (General Alexander McCook's Division), commanded by Colonel Innes. Casualty figures are unavailable.

In North Carolina, Company A, 24th Massachusetts Regiment, commanded by Captain Walker, skirmishes with a Confederate unit at Washington. The Union reports no casualties. The Confederates suffer six wounded.

In South Carolina, Union General David Hunter, in command of the forces in Georgia, Florida and South Carolina, issues an order stipulating that in these states martial law exists and that "under Martial Law, slavery and Martial Law in a free society are altogether incompatible."

The U.S. 6th Cavalry clashes with Confederate cavalry under General J.E.B. Stuart (Mottelay, *The Soldier in Our Civil War,* 1886).

In Tennessee, a skirmish between Union forces and Confederates, including Texas Rangers led by Lt. Colonel Woodward, erupts at Elk River and lasts only about ten minutes. The Union loses about 15–17 captured. The Confederates sustain about five killed and seven wounded.

In Virginia, Union General George Stoneman of McClellan's command holds the junction of the West Point and New Kent Courthouse roads after skirmishes on the 7th. Two New Jersey regiments are left behind to hold New Kent Courthouse, while Captain Elon Farnsworth's 8th Illinois Cavalry advances to Cumberland. Also, General Wool leads a reconnaissance mission toward Sewell's Point. Treasury Secretary Salmon Chase and some engineers are with the group. It is decided to land about 5,000 troops at Ocean View on Willoughby's Beach. Meanwhile, to divert attention from the genuine intent of the Union, this afternoon the warships commence another bombardment of the Confederate batteries. Meanwhile, a Union force — composed of contingents of the 6th U.S. Cavalry, 98th Pennsylvania and the 2nd Rhode Island Volunteers — skirmish with Confederates at Slatersville. The Union sustains four killed and three wounded. The Confederates suffer 10 killed and 14 wounded.

In Union general officer activity, Colonel George William Taylor (3rd New Jersey), formerly a midshipman (1827–1831) and a veteran of the Mexican War (captain, 10th U.S. Infantry) is appointed brigadier general.

In Naval activity, Union warships, including the USS *Potomska,* initiate a reconnaissance mission in the vicinity of Darien. In other activity, Captain Charles Davis is appointed flag officer of the Mississippi Flotilla. He succeeds Flag Officer Andrew Foote.

May 10 (Saturday) BATTLE OF PLUM RUN BEND A Union fleet — commanded by Captain Charles H. Davis in place of Flag Officer Andrew Foote, who remains troubled by an old wound suffered at Fort Donelson — initiates an attack against Fort Pillow, Tennessee, and is met by a Confederate naval force (commanded by Captain Joseph E. Montgomery) composed of eight Confederate gunboats and four steam rams armed with cast iron rams, capable of inflicting great damage to the Union fleet. The Confederate fleet is composed of the gunboats CSS *General Bragg* (Captain W.H.H. Leonard); CSS *General Stirling Price* (First Officer J.E. Hawthorne); CSS *Sumter* (Captain W.W. Lamb); CSS *General Van Dorn* (Captain Isaac D. Fulkerson); *General Jeff Thompson* (Captain J.H. Burke); the *Colonel Lovell* (Captain J.C. Delancy); CSS

McRae; and the CSS *General Beauregard* (Captain J.H. Hunt).

The river duel becomes savage. The CSS *McRae* speeds around Craighead Point and blasts the mortar boat of Acting Master Gregory. While the opponents trade blistering shots, two Union gunboats, the *Mound City* and the *Cincinnati,* move in to quash the Rebel ram, but instead, the *McRae* pours devastating broadsides into the *Cincinnati,* while simultaneously ripping into its sides with the ramming device. The *Cincinnati* sustains large gaping holes in its sides. At this time, the *Mound City* closes to aid the *Cincinnati,* but before it can take on the *McRae,* the Confederate ram *Van Dorn* plows into the *Cincinnati* and at about the same time, yet another Confederate vessel, the *Sumter* begins to attack the *Mound City.* In the meantime, the *Mound City* has plastered the *McRae,* quieting its heavy bow gun, while simultaneously sending repeated broadsides against the three attacking vessels. Then suddenly, the *Sumter* whacks the *Mound City,* ramming with such force that it creates a huge hole in the bow.

Although badly battered and near extinction, the *Mound City* is saved as the *Benton* roars into action, and with the effective use of its fifty-pound Parrott guns, the *McRae* lowers its flag and the *Van Dorn* and the *Sumter* retire, the latter sustaining a major explosion caused by a shell that struck the boiler room. The current starts to carry the crippled *McRae* downstream. Following the culmination of the battle, the ships of both sides remain within striking distance of each other; however, there are no further confrontations until early the following month. Commander R.N. Stembel of the *Cincinnati* is seriously wounded during the action.

The Union fleet manages to beat the Rebels back, but little damage has been suffered by the Confederates. U.S. Marines participate in the battle, manning secondary guns. The fort remains under attack until its capitulation on 4 June, which gives the Union the doorstep to Memphis. The *Cincinnati,* having been sunk, is refloated and after receiving repairs, during the following October, it is transferred from the army's Western Gunboat Flotilla to the U.S. Navy. The *Cincinnati* was originally commissioned during January 1862 for use in the flotilla. The *Mound City,* similarly to the *Cincinnati,* had originally been commissioned during January 1862 for the U.S. Army's Western Gunboat Flotilla. After repairs, the *Mound City* returns to action the following month. Also, the CSS *General Bragg,* prior to being used by the Confederacy, had been the commercial steamer *Mexico,* built in New York during 1850. After serving as the USS *General Bragg* and being decommissioned on 24 July 1865 and sold the next month, it is renamed *Mexico* and remains active as a civilian vessel until sold to a foreign buyer during 1870.

In Arizona, General Carleton arrives in Tucson leading his California command. The column is en route to Santa Fe, where Carleton will assume command of the Department of New

The destruction of the CSS *Virginia* (formerly USS *Merrimack*) (Mottelay, *The Soldier in Our Civil War*, 1886).

Mexico. The column does not depart Tucson until 20 July.

In Minnesota, the 5th Minnesota Volunteer Regiment departs for Mississippi and once there is attached to the 2nd Brigade, 2nd Division, Army of the Mississippi. Some of its units, however, do not move with the regiment. Company D will move to Fort Abercrombie, Dakota Territory. Companies B and C will move to Fort Ridgely, Minnesota.

In Virginia, during the early morning hours, Union troops land on Ocean View on Willoughby Beach without incident. Generals John E. Wool, Egbert L. Viele and Joseph K. F. Mansfield take command and a contingent is dispatched to secure the bridge that spans Tanner's Creek to the rear of the Confederate battery at Sewell's Point. By the time the troops approach the objective, it is afire and they come under attack by Rebel artillery positioned on the opposite bank. Union artillery is sped forward, but the firing ceases and the march resumes without resistance. Later during the afternoon, General Wool's force reaches an abandoned Confederate camp, which still contains twenty-nine operable guns. By about 1700, the Union is within striking distance of Norfolk, but just prior to initiating an attack, the mayor of the city approaches, bearing a flag of truce. Wool accepts the surrender of the city and places General Viele in charge as its military governor. The troops enter Norfolk and Portsmouth, moving one step closer to Richmond. The Confederate troops commanded by Major General Benjamin Huger had abandoned the area the day before, destroying all guns before departing to prevent their capture. The Confederates also destroy the CSS *Virginia* and the CSS *Portsmouth* (an uncompleted gunboat) and torch the navy yard during the night of the 10th–11th. Nevertheless, the Union gains about 200 guns. The Confederates, compelled to self-destroy the *Virginia* to prevent capture, begin to have some concerns about threats against Rich-

mond without the presence of the *Virginia* on the James River. The Union 10th, 20th and 99th New York Regiments, the 1st Delaware, 58th Pennsylvania, 20th Indiana and the 16th Massachusetts participate. In addition, Battery D, 1st U.S. Artillery, and the 1st New York Mounted Rifles also participate in the capture of Norfolk and Portsmouth.

In other activity, Union forces skirmish with Confederates, including the 22nd Virginia, at Giles Court House (West Virginia). Lt. Colonel George S. Patton, recently back with the regiment since he was wounded and captured the previous July, is again wounded at this skirmish and yet again he is captured, but he is held for less than one month prior to being exchanged. After he returns on 25 May, he is promoted to colonel of the regiment. Subsequently, General John Echols becomes commander of the Confederate forces in West Virginia (1863). Colonel Patton frequently finds himself as brigade commander during prolonged absences of General Echols due to a combination of bad health and for political purposes. Patton participates in a string of raids (Jones and Imboden raid) during spring 1863, designed to disrupt the B&O Railroad "over hangs," while Patton leads his command around West Virginia and into Maryland.

May 11 (Sunday) In Virginia at Williamsburg, Union General George Stoneman dispatches Major Williams and six companies of cavalry to occupy the railroad facility at White House, and while guarding the area, he dispatches scouting parties to ensure knowledge of Confederate activity. Stoneman's troops are in desperate need of supplies, especially food.

In Kentucky, a Union train is seized by Confederates under Colonel John Hunt Morgan at Cave City.

In Missouri, a contingent of Confederates led by Colonel Phelan skirmishes with a Union detachment composed of six squadrons of the 1st Wisconsin Cavalry at Bloomfield. The Confederates sustain one killed and about 11 wounded.

May 12 (Monday) In Mississippi, a contingent of Union troops (Michigan Regiment), commanded by Captain J.W. Latimer, skirmishes with Confederates at Farmington. Casualty figures are unavailable.

In Naval activity, a Union fleet under Admiral David Farragut closes on Natchez, Mississippi. Farragut had recently seized Baton Rouge, Louisiana, and is en route to support the Union effort at Vicksburg. Natchez submits to Farragut's demand to surrender. Commander Porter of the USS *Iroquois* and the USS *Oneida* take control of the city on the following day. While moving toward Vicksburg, Farragut will encounter Confederate opposition at Ellis' Cliffs on 3 June and Grand Gulf on 9 June.

In other activity, the USS *Galena, Port Royal* and *Aroostook* are joined by the *Monitor* and *Naugatuck* as they move farther up the James River toward Richmond. By the following day, the squadron runs past Harrison's Bar and advances to City Point. The USS *Lioness*, subsequent to being fitted out at Pittsburgh (April 1862), Pennsylvania, departs New Albany for Cairo, Illinois. The *Lioness* was built in Philadelphia during 1857 and acquired by the U.S. Navy during 1862. The U.S. Navy, at about this time, (spring 1862) receives a gunboat, the USS *Naugatuck*, on loan from the Treasury Department. During an engagement against Confederate batteries at Drewry's Bluff, a few days later, it experiences a problem.

May 12–22 *In Naval activity,* the USS *Hunchback* initiates a reconnaissance mission that continues until the 22nd. While operating on the Chowan River in North Carolina the *Hunchback* reduces one Confederate battery and seizes four small ships. Following its return to base, it patrols the North Carolina sounds.

May 13 (Tuesday) In Alabama, Union forces, including the 1st Wisconsin and 38th

Natchez, Mississippi (*Harper's Pictorial History of the Civil War,* 1896).

Indiana Volunteer Regiments and Union cavalry, commanded by Colonel John C. Starkweather, occupy Rogersville. Four Confederate troops are captured. The occupation continues into the following day and includes a skirmish at Lamb's Ferry.

In South Carolina, martial law is implemented in Charleston. In other activity, during the early morning hours at about 0400, the Confederates are about to lose one of their vessels, the sidewheel steamer *Planter*. The ship, attached to the engineer department at Charleston, is utilized by General Ripley as a transport and an armed dispatch. While the ship's captain, C.J. Relyea, is ashore, the pilot, Robert Smalls, a Negro slave, inconspicuously lets the ship slide away from the dock. With its colors flying, Smalls eases the ship through the harbor, passing the forts without interference, and in fact, Smalls makes it a point to carry out the natural method of blowing the whistle in salute at the passing of each fort. Smalls, at great risk, moves past the final fort and after reaching a safe distance, well out of range of the Confederate guns, he lowers the Confederate colors hoists a white flag.

Smalls' daring plan endangers more than himself. His motive is to gain freedom for others too. Aboard the vessel with Smalls is a group that includes five women, three children and seven other men, all of whom would pay severely if the scheme fails. However, it succeeds flawlessly. The *Planter*, boasting its white flag of surrender, actually becomes a bonus for the Union when Smalls delivers it to the USS *Onward*. Smalls informs the officers that the Confederates have abandoned their defenses along the Stono River.

On the following day, the *Planter* is taken to Port Royal and turned over to Admiral Du Pont, who is greatly appreciative of the newest entry to his fleet, adding its armaments and four guns that are aboard to his arsenal. Smalls is retained by Du Pont to serve as pilot aboard the USS *Planter*. Union appreciation for Smalls' bold action goes beyond a pat on the back and a handshake. His feat is transmitted to Washington and on 30 May 1862, both Houses of Congress by special legislation award Smalls and his crew one-half of the value of the ship and its cargo.

In the meantime, Admiral Du Pont has attached the ship to fleet and assigned Acting Master Philemon Dickenson as its commander. Dickenson sails to North Edisto and once there is relieved by Acting Master Lloyd Phoenix. The *Planter* then takes its place within the South Atlantic Blockading Squadron.

In Tennessee, at Monterey, a Union force (Colonel Morgan Lewis Smith's brigade) skirmishes with Confederates. The Union sustains two wounded. The Confederates suffer two killed and three wounded. Colonel Smith had been commanding officer of the 8th Missouri Infantry until the attack against Fort Donelson, at which time he became a brigade commander. He is promoted to brigadier general in July.

In West Virginia, a Union contingent (Brigadier General Benjamin Franklin Kelley's command) skirmishes with Confederates at Reedy. No casualty figures are available.

In Confederate general officer activity, Colonel Richard Waterhouse begins his first day as colonel of the 19th Texas Infantry Regiment, a regiment he was instrumental in raising. Colonel Waterhouse and his regiment are assigned to the Trans-Mississippi Department and will serve with Generals Thomas Hindman and Theopolis H. Holmes. During 1864, Waterhouse will be transferred to Louisiana.

In Naval activity, the USS *Iroquois* and the USS *Oneida* seize control of Natchez, Mississippi, placing another strategic southern city under Union control. In other activity, the CSS *Corypheus*, actually a yacht built in New York during 1859 and seized in New Orleans during 1861, is captured by a cutter from the USS *Calhoun* at Bayou Bonfuca, Louisiana. The ship is sailed to Key West and soon is acquired by the U.S. Navy and commissioned the USS *Corypheus*.

May 14 (Wednesday)   In Virginia, Union General George B. McClellan telegraphs Secretary of War Edwin Stanton expressing his opinion that the Rebels are massing at Richmond. McClellan requests additional reinforcements to show excessive force, but no immediate response to his message arrives. McClellan notifies Stanton that his force has been badly depleted by casualties, sickness and a large amount of garrison forces, which prevent his fielding 80,000 men against Richmond. He further states: "I ask for every man the War Department can spare me. I will fight the enemy, whatever their force may be, with whatever force I may have; and I firmly believe that we shall beat them but our triumph should be made decisive and complete." Stanton responds on the 18th, stating that General McDowell will "march upon that city [Richmond] by the shortest route, keeping himself always in position to save the capital from all possible attack." McDowell is ordered to maneuver so that his left wing will communicate with the right wing of McClellan's force.

In Mississippi, a skirmish between Union and Confederate troops occurs along the Memphis and Charleston Railroad in the vicinity of Corinth.

In Tennessee, Union and Confederate troops clash near Fayetteville. Specific units are unavailable.

In Union general officer activity, Colonel Erastus B. Tyler, 7th Ohio Volunteer Regiment, is promoted to brigadier general. During the following August, General Tyler receives command of a division and he participates at the Battle of Antietam, but his command is held in reserve.

In Naval activity, the USS *Galena*, in the vicinity of City Point, Virginia, encounters Confederate sharpshooters scattered about the banks that ambush the warship. However, the guns of the *Galena* compel the Rebels to retire.

May 15 (Thursday) THE BATTLE OF DREWRY'S BLUFF Confederate batteries at Fort Darling, one of the formidable defensive positions charged with protecting the Confederate capital at Richmond, comes under attack by a Union naval squadron composed of the gunboats *Aroostook*, *Galena* (ironclad), *Monitor* (Lt. William N. Jerrers), *Naugatuck* and the *Port Royal*. The naval force is commanded by Lt. Commander Watson Smith. Fort Darling, also headquarters for the Confederate Naval Academy, is prepared to meet the threat. Confederate ground troops are deployed along the banks of the James River, and high up on the bluff, the Confederates had recently installed three gargantuan seacoast guns, one 10-inch Columbiad and two 8-inch Columbiads. The position is bolstered by six other heavy guns that are deployed slightly upriver. Other impediments have also been used to prevent easy passage for Union vessels. Confederate Commander Ebenezer Farrand, charged with overseeing the construction project, arranges for a number of

Four of the nine slaves who captured the Confederate steamer *Planter* on 13 May 1862 (Mottelay, *The Soldier in Our Civil War*, 1886).

vessels, including the CSS *Jamestown* (*Thomas Jefferson*) to be intentionally sunk to create some concealed obstacles immediately under the bluff.

There had been some fear in Richmond, following the recent destruction of the CSS *Virginia*, that the capital would be vulnerable to an attack by water. Separately, the Union had come to the identical conclusion. Commander Rogers' fleet gets an early start and by about 0700, the Union vessels approach Fort Darling, which towers above the river. At 0715, the ironclad *Galena* commences fire and shortly thereafter, the Rebel guns respond, raking the *Galena* with a blanket of shot and shell that pounds the *Galena* and begins to expose its vulnerability due to its thinly coated armor. The other guns along the river also begin their barrages, creating thunderous bombardment that delivers incessant waves of fire that inflicts damage to the fleet. The gunboats return relentless fire, but from less than advantageous positions, and the fire power from the fleets is unable to catapult the shells high enough to reduce the obstacles on the bluff about ninety feet above the river. Meanwhile, the *Monitor* has problems adapting to the shallow water and its guns are not able to perform at one hundred percent.

The Confederates, however, have not created a perfect storm and they too experience problems. At the instant the 10-inch Columbiad fires its first round, the recoil is so powerful that it literally disables the carriage, rendering the gun out of action for the greater part of the contest. Another of the guns deployed outside of Fort Darling becomes immobilized when its casemate collapses. Nevertheless, neither side is willing to acquiesce as the tenacious artillery exchange continues for more than four grueling hours. At that time, 1130, Commander Rogers, aware that the fleet's supply of ammunition is nearly expended, orders the gunboats to retire. The Confederates, although not able to destroy the squadron, do deter the Union from being anxious to again move up the James River to attack Richmond. The fort remains unscathed until 1864.

Subsequent to the clash, the area remains tranquil. The Confederates however, continue to fortify the bluff and surrounding area to increase the defenses to defend Richmond from attack, either by land or sea. Captain Sydney Smith Lee is placed in command of the fort and under his leadership, the defenses are bolstered and expanded. Within the fort itself, the troops also construct barracks, officers' quarters and a chapel. The post also contains the Confederate Naval Academy and includes the Confederate Marine Corps Camp of Instruction.

The formidable U.S. fleet had withstood the layers of fire without sustaining the loss of any vessels; however, the Confederate fire had inflicted severe damage, particularly to the *Galena*, which had been hit repeatedly by artillery rounds and by shots from the ground troops posted along the river. The *Galena* sustains 12 men killed and 15 wounded. Nevertheless, the battered warship remains in action and maintains its patrols along the James River, en-

gaging enemy shore batteries and at times giving support to General McClellan's campaign. In September 1862, the *Galena* shifts from its positions on the James and moves to Hampton Roads, from where it operates until May 1863. Total Union casualties amount to at least 14 killed and 13 wounded. The Confederates sustain seven killed and eight wounded. Corporal John F. Mackie, serving on the USS *Galena*, becomes the first U.S. Marine to receive the Medal of Honor due to his actions above and beyond the call of duty during the engagement.

Following the engagement at the bluff, the gunboat USS *Aroostook* participates during General McClellan's campaign on the peninsula and afterward is transferred to duty in the Gulf of Mexico, where it sees action against blockade runners. In November 1863, the *Aroostook* operates off Texas and captures several additional blockade runners before heading north during September 1865 to be decommissioned in Philadelphia, only to be recommissioned during 1866, sent to the Far East as part of the Asiatic Squadron until September 1869, then decommissioned at Hong Kong and sold. During the engagement, the *Naugatuck's* rifled gun explodes and it is disarmed, unable to make a substantial contribution. Shortly after this action, the *Naugatuck* is returned to the Treasury Department's Revenue Cutter service. It becomes the USRC *E.A. Stevens* and remains as a revenue cutter until sold during 1890, when it becomes the merchant ship *Argus*.

In Arkansas, a contingent of the 3rd Illinois Cavalry, commanded by Lt. Smith, skirmishes with Confederates at Batesville No casualties are noted; however, it is reported that the Union captures three Rebels.

In Louisiana, General Benjamin Franklin Butler, disturbed by some actions of the citizens of New Orleans against Union soldiers who are under orders not to retaliate against the harassment, reacts after women continue to spit on his troops. He issues Order No. 28: "As the officers and soldiers of the United States have been subject to repeated insults from the women of New Orleans, in return for the most scrupulous non-interference and courtesy on our part, it is ordered that hereafter, when any female shall, by word, gesture, or movement, insult or show contempt for any officer or soldier of the United States, she shall be regarded and held liable to be treated as a woman of the town plying her avocation."

In Missouri, elements of the 1st Iowa Cavalry skirmishes with a Confederate contingent at Butler. The Union sustains three killed and one wounded. Confederate casualty figures are unavailable. Also, the 1st Wisconsin Cavalry clashes with Confederates at Chalk Bluffs. The Union sustains one killed and three wounded. Confederate casualty figures, if any, are unavailable.

In North Carolina, Confederates skirmish with a contingent of Union troops as they retreat near Trenton. The Union and Confederate units continue to clash until the following day, skir-

mishing also at Young's Cross Roads and Pollocksville. The Union 17th, 25th and 27th Massachusetts Volunteer Regiments, supported by Battery B, 3rd New York Artillery, and two contingents of U.S. cavalry participate in the operation. The Union sustains four wounded. The Confederates suffer about six killed and four wounded. And each side captures two prisoners.

In Virginia, General Thomas "Stonewall" Jackson's army is advancing toward Harrisonburg. Jackson makes camp at Lebanon Springs. At Linden, one company of Pennsylvania volunteers skirmishes with Confederates. The Union sustains one killed, three wounded and 14 missing. Confederate casualty figures are unavailable.

In West Virginia, at Princeton, the Kanawha Division (Union General Jacob Dolson Cox) skirmishes with Confederates. Cox remains with General McClellan's army until August, when he is transferred to General John Pope's Army of Virginia. Cox's division skirmishes also on May 16 and May 18. The Union sustains 30 killed and 70 wounded.

In Confederate general officer activity, the southern cause sees yet another West Pointer become a brigadier general in the Confederacy. Major General (North Carolina State Militia) James G. Martin, who served his country during the Mexican War as a major and lost an arm in the process, is appointed brigadier general effective this date. General Martin (West Point, 1840) has done a splendid job of recruiting and equipping the troops of his native state. His zeal and invigorating leadership rub off onto his men, and at the siege of Petersburg he displays the trademark of a true West Pointer, exhibiting fearlessness on the field against his brothers in blue. However, General Martin resigns during July of this year. In August, he re-enters the Army with his rank of brigadier general effective the same day as his first commission, May 15.

In Naval activity, the USS *Somerset*, while on blockade patrol duty in the vicinity of Cedar Keys and St. George's Sound, initiates a reconnaissance mission that leads to an encounter with a contingent of Confederate troops in the vicinity of Way Key, Florida. Subsequent to bombarding a Confederate post there, during the following month the *Somerset* returns to the area. In other activity, on or about this day, the USS *Sumter* lowers a boat and dispatches a detachment to the vicinity of Fort Pulaski, Georgia, on a reconnaissance mission to gather intelligence on Confederate gunboats, but the party is detected and captured when it inadvertently moves into St. Augustine Creek near Fort Jackson. Following this incident, the *Sumter* is ordered to Fernandina, Florida, to initiate blockade patrols there. It remains in the region until October, when it sails north for repairs. Afterward the *Sumter* is assigned to the North Atlantic Blockading Squadron on patrol duty out of Hampton Roads. In June 1863, it moves to the vicinity of Yorktown, Virginia, to support a search for the Confederate privateer *Clarence*.

May 16 (Friday) **In Virginia,** Major General George B. McClellan advances his headquarters to White House, about 20 miles from Richmond, but the roads remain terrible because of the abundance of rainfall. The weather finally clears on the 17th, allowing McClellan to prepare to advance, but the orders from John Stanton, the secretary of war, complicate his plans. In other activity, Confederate General Jackson's force, en route to Harrisonburg, remains at camp at Lebanon Springs to observe that day as proclaimed by President Davis as a day of fasting and prayer.

In Confederate general officer activity, Brigadier General Joseph Lewis Hogg passes away, suffering from dysentery, at Corinth, Mississippi.

May 17 (Saturday) **In Virginia,** General Irvin McDowell receives orders to advance in conjunction with General McClellan against Richmond, the capital of the Confederacy. Meanwhile, a Union force composed of elements of the 8th and 17th Infantry Regiments, a unit of rifles and a contingent of the U.S. 5th Artillery, commanded by Major Willard, initiates a reconnaissance mission along the Pamunkey River. In other activity, General Thomas "Stonewall" Jackson breaks camp at Lebanon Springs and resumes the march toward Harrisonburg.

During the advance, Colonel Grigsby, commander of the 27th Virginia, experiences problems when some of his troops initiate a mutiny due to the expiration of their 12-month enlistments. Grigsby refuses to permit the troops to depart. Consequently, they lay down their arms. Grigsby seeks instructions from Jackson. After being informed of the crisis, Jackson reacts, saying: "Why does Colonel Grigsby refer to me to learn how to deal with mutineers? He should shoot them where they stand." Shortly thereafter, the remainder of the regiment parades with the weapons loaded and the mutineers' two companies are offered two distinct propositions, "instant death or instant submission." The disgruntled troops, familiar with Grigsby, need no time to decide. They choose to surrender.

In other activity, General Ewell arrives to confer with General Jackson to inform him of the situation in the valley. Jackson is told that Union General Banks had moved to Strasburg and that Ashby's Confederate cavalry was engaged in creating obstacles (cutting trees down and moving boulders to block the mountain paths) to impede the progress of General Frémont. General Banks' force is isolated from General Frémont, prompting the Confederates to consider striking Banks.

Available forces of Ewell's and Jackson's armies (defined as divisions) are as follows. Jackson's Division: Stonewall Brigade, General Winder, 2nd, 4th, 5th, 27th and 33rd Virginia; Second Brigade, Colonel Campbell, 21st, 42nd and 48th Virginia and 1st Regulars (Irish); Third Brigade, Colonel Taliaferro, 10th, 23rd and 37th Virginia, Ashby's Cavalry, 7th Virginia, and several new companies and five batteries, 22 guns. Ewell's Division: First Brigade,

General Richard Taylor, 6th, 7th, 8th and 9th Louisiana, Wheat's Battalion of Louisiana Tigers; Second Brigade, General Trimble, 21st North Carolina, 21st Georgia, 15th Alabama, and 16th Mississippi; Third Brigade, General Elzey, 13th, 31st, and 25th Virginia and 12th Georgia; Fourth Brigade, General Edward Johnson, 44th, 52nd and 58th Virginia, 1st Maryland Cavalry (General G.H. Steuart), 2nd Virginia (Colonel Munford), 6th Virginia (Colonel Flournoy) and six batteries, 26 guns.

In Mississippi, brisk skirmishing in the vicinity of Corinth, at Russell's House, costs both sides casualties. However, the Rebels keep the city and will do so until the end of the month, when they evacuate. The Union force (General Morgan Lewis Smith's command) sustains 10 killed and 31 wounded. The Confederates suffer 12 killed.

In Union general officer activity, General John Ellis Wool — born February 1784, just weeks before King George III of England proclaimed that the treaty of peace signed between England and the United States during 1783 had been ratified — this day is commissioned brigadier general in the Regular Army effective 16 May. He had been commander of the Department of East and of the Pacific at the outbreak of hostilities. He will command the Department of Virginia until he retires on 1 August 1863.

In Confederate general officer activity, Colonel Thomas Lanier Clingman (25th North Carolina) is promoted to brigadier general.

May 18 (Sunday) **Washington, D.C.** President Abraham Lincoln authorizes General George B. McClellan to organize two provisional Army corps, the 5th and 6th Corps. The Army of the Potomac now consists of General Edwin V. Sumner's 2nd Corps, General Samuel P. Heintzelman's 3rd Corps, General Erasmus Keyes' 4th Corps, General Fitz John Porter's 5th Corps and General William Franklin's 6th Corps. McClellan changes his headquarters to White House, Virginia. McClellan is forced to divide his army to go along with the orders issued by Secretary of War Stanton concerning McDowell's advance on Richmond by land. McClellan must dispatch part of his force across the Chickahominy River, thus preventing his Union force from concentrating along the James River. The order for General Irvin McDowell's advance is soon cancelled, placing McClellan's split force into added jeopardy.

In Mississippi, General Pope moves back to Farmington and encounters no resistance; his force re-occupies the town, which Confederates had seized on May 9. In other activity, following the seizure of Baton Rouge, Louisiana, and Natchez, Mississippi, a naval force advances to Vicksburg where Commander S.P. Lee issues a demand to the Confederates to surrender. The Confederate commander replies with the following: "Mississippians don't know and refuse to learn, how to surrender to an enemy. If Commodore Farragut or Brigadier General Butler can teach them, let them come and try."

In Virginia, General Stonewall Jackson's Confederates continue to harass the Union in the Shenandoah Valley. However, the Yankees capture Suffolk, south of Norfolk. Also, a Union contingent led by Captain Forsyth moves toward Old Church. The reconnaissance mission continues into the following day.

In Union general officer activity, Union Brigadier General William H. Keim dies of natural causes at Harrisburg, Pennsylvania. He had become ill at around the time of the Battle of Williamsburg and the fever never relented.

In Naval activity, the USS *Shawsheen* and the USS *Hunchback,* operating in Potecase Creek, encounter, intercept and capture the schooner CSS *Smoot.* The Union is informed that the schooner had been involved in transporting supplies and troops for the Confederacy.

May 19 (Monday) **Washington, D.C.** Congress, which has recently forbidden slavery in Washington, D.C., now enacts legislation forbidding slavery in any of the U.S. territories.

In Arkansas, a Union contingent composed of troops of the 4th Missouri Cavalry and 3rd and 17th Missouri Volunteer Regiments, augmented by Battery B, 1st Missouri Light Artillery, commanded by Colonel John S. Coleman, engages Confederates at Searcy. The Union sustains 18 killed and 27 wounded. The Confederates sustain about 150 killed, wounded and missing.

In Mississippi, elements of the 3rd Battalion, 3rd Michigan Regiment, commanded by Major Gilbert Moyer, engages a Confederate force at Farmington. The Union sustains two wounded. The Confederates suffer three killed.

In North Carolina, a Union contingent clashes with a Confederate unit at Clinton. Specific units are unknown. The Union suffers five wounded. The Confederates sustain nine wounded.

In Tennessee, a Union force composed of the 34th and 47th Indiana Regiments, a contingent of the 54th Illinois Regiment, and the 2nd Illinois Cavalry, bolstered by the 2nd Illinois Artillery, advances down the Mississippi River toward Fort Pillow The operation, commanded by General Isaac F. Quinby, lasts until the 23rd.

In Virginia, Company I, 24th Georgia Infantry (Confederate), commanded by Captain Willis, skirmishes with Union contingents at City Point. After-battle reports indicate Union casualties as fewer than 10 killed and about nine captured. No Confederate casualty figures are available.

In Naval activity, Admiral David Farragut's fleet continues toward Vicksburg, Mississippi, another prime Confederate stronghold.

May 20 (Tuesday) **In Arizona,** the vanguard of General Carleton's force occupies Tucson. Colonel Joseph West (1st California Infantry) orders the Stars and Stripes hoisted. The Confederates had abandoned Tucson prior to the arrival of the Union and headed toward the Rio Grande. The town is taken without incident.

In **Virginia**, the 5th New York Cavalry, commanded by Brigadier General John Porter Hatch, skirmishes with Confederate Cavalry (General Turner Ashby's command) at Strasburg. It is reported that six Confederates are killed and about six are captured. The Union reports no casualties. Also, Confederate General Thomas J. "Stonewall" Jackson diverts General Richard S. Ewell and his crack troops to cut off the Union forces under General Nathaniel Banks, in an attempt to prevent Banks from reinforcing George McClellan. The opposing forces will confront each other at Port Royal on the 23rd. Confederate General Maxcy Gregg's brigade arrives in Richmond from South Carolina. It deploys at Milford Station but in less than two weeks the regiment moves to the vicinity of Fredericksburg and establishes camp at Summit Station.

In **New Mexico**, troops of the 3rd U.S. Cavalry commanded by Captain Joseph Green Tilford encounters a Confederate contingent composed of about 100 troops at Paraje. No casualty reports are available.

In **Tennessee**, a skirmish develops between Union and Confederate forces at Elk River. Specific units are not reported. Casualties, if any, are unreported.

In **Virginia**, General Thomas "Stonewall" Jackson arrives at New Market and joins Colonel Ashby, whom Jackson had dispatched there on the previous day.

In Union general officer activity, Lt. Colonel Thomas Maley Harris is appointed colonel of the 10th West Virginia Regiment.

May 21 (Wednesday)   In Mississippi, Union forces, including the 1st Kentucky Infantry, skirmish with Confederates at Corinth. The Union, commanded by Brigadier General John Sedgwick and bolstered by one battery of artillery, skirmishes with Confederates at Widow Serratt's Farm. Following a two-hour contest, the Union sustains three killed and 20–23 wounded. Confederate casualty figures are unavailable. Also, a contingent of the Union 2nd Division (Army of the Tennessee), commanded by General Thomas A. Davies, skirmishes with Confederates at Phillip's Creek. The Union sustains three wounded. Confederate casualty figures are unavailable.

In **Virginia**, General Stonewall Jackson departs New Market and advances northward the Valley Pike, from where he expects to launch a surprise attack against General Banks. General Richard Taylor's (son of President Zachary Taylor) force acts as vanguard as the column moves across the mountains toward Luray to establish night positions.

In Union general officer activity, Lewis Cass Hunt, the brother of Union General Henry Jackson Hunt, is appointed colonel of the 92nd New York Regiment. A graduate of West Point (1847), Hunt participates at the Battle of Seven Pines.

In Naval activity, the USS *Arletta,* operating in the Gulf of Mexico, encounters a blockade runner, which had most probably penetrated the blockade at Mobile Bay. The *Arletta* initiates pursuit; however, the runner disposes of its cargo of cotton and escapes capture.

May 22 (Thursday)   In Washington, D.C., the War Department establishes a Bureau of Colored Troops. By the end of the war, one hundred thousand Negroes are enrolled as U.S. Volunteers. Others serve in state units.

In **Mississippi,** one company of the 3rd Michigan Regiment, commanded by Lt. Caldwell, skirmishes with Confederates at Farmington. The Union pickets sustain one wounded.

In **Missouri,** a troop of the 3rd Iowa Cavalry clashes with Confederates at Florida, Missouri. The Union sustains two wounded. Confederate casualty figures are unavailable.

In **North Carolina,** Company I, 17th Massachusetts Regiment, skirmishes Confederates at Trenton Cross Roads in the vicinity of New Bern. The Union sustains three killed and eight wounded. Confederate casualty figures are unavailable.

In **South Carolina,** a Union detachment on a reconnaissance mission captures a group of Confederate pickets in the vicinity of Battery Island.

In **Virginia,** General George B. McClellan confers with General Irvin McDowell about a combined move against Richmond, but a stunning blow inflicted by the Confederates at Port Royal the following day changes everything. Jackson had traversed from Lebanon Sulphur Springs to the vicinity of Front Royal. The Confederate forces under Jackson that are in the vicinity of Front Royal (Port Royal) are the brigades commanded by Colonels Alexander W. Campbell, Samuel V. Fulkerson and Charles S. Winder, and General Richard Ewell's brigades commanded by Generals Arnold Elzey, Richard Taylor and Isaac R. Trimble. In addition, the Confederates are supported by Ashby's Cavalry, the 2nd and 6th Confederate Virginia Cavalry and the Brockenborough and 1st Maryland Batteries. Front Royal is defended by only about 1,400 Union troops under Colonel John R. Kenly.

In other activity, a contingent of the 6th Pennsylvania Cavalry commanded by Colonel Rush initiates a reconnaissance mission that leads to New Castle and Hanovertown ferries. The Union reports no casualties. The Confederates sustain some wounded. General Thomas "Stonewall" Jackson breaks camp at Luray and his army advances toward Front Royal, held by Union forces (Colonel Kenly's 1st Maryland Regiment) under General Banks, who arrived there to replace General Shields' command, which had earlier been ordered to move across the Blue Ridge to bolster General Irvin McDowell. Kenly's contingent of about 1,100 men is bolstered by some artillery. Kenly's command, charged with protecting two bridges, is deployed between the river and the town on low ground.

Meanwhile, the Confederates, by evening, suspend the advance about ten miles outside the town and establish night quarters. Up to this point, the Confederates remain undiscovered and in Washington, there is no intelligence that reveals Jackson's elusive force is composed of about 17,000 men, poised to strike Banks' flank.

May 23 (Friday)   In New Mexico, a forty-man detachment of the 3rd U.S. Cavalry commanded by Captain (later general) Joseph Green Tilford clashes with a Confederate contingent composed of about 200 troops near Fort Craig. The encounter, which lasts about three hours, leaves three Rebels wounded. No Union casualties are reported.

In **Virginia,** Confederate General Stonewall Jackson attacks Union forces under Generals Nathaniel Banks and John Porter Hatch, including contingents of the 1st Maryland, 29th Pennsylvania, 5th New York Cavalry and the 1st Pennsylvania Artillery at Front Royal (Port Royal). The diminutive Union force is not anticipating a major assault, but its commander, Colonel (later brigadier general) John R. Kenly, chooses to fight rather than run.

The Confederates spring from concealed positions in some woods and catch the pickets by surprise, then the Confederates enter the town. Colonel Kenly reacts as quickly as possible and utilizes his artillery to forestall disaster. Some time is bought by the effective artillery fire, but the momentum of the Rebels is too superior to be repelled. Kenly pulls back to Guard Hill and in the process the Union sets fire to a bridge; however, the Confederates extinguish it and continue pursuit.

In the meantime, the 6th Virginia Cavalry launches a charge against the hill and one of the riders is Jackson, who joins the charge as it fords the river and, after crossing to the north bank, pushes the Union from hill. From Guard Hill, Jackson dispatches the cavalry in pursuit of the Union, which retires to Cedarville. Jackson hangs back and follows later with the infantry and artillery. Despite being outnumbered and outgunned, Colonel Kenly again raises stiff resistance when attacked at Cedarville; however, Confederate fire knocks Kenly out of action. After he is wounded, the Rebel pressure collapses the resistance.

Colonel Ashby does not participate in the charge. At the time, he is with the 7th Virginia Cavalry at Buckton (Riverton), which is destroying railroad tracks and severing the telegraph lines in time to intercept a message being sent to General Banks, who still has no knowledge of the attack at Front Royal or of the presence of Jackson in the area. Ashby's cavalry engages about two companies at Buckton. The Union troops (3rd Wisconsin and the 27th Indiana) remain barricaded in a fortified log cabin. Casualties are sustained, about 12 killed, including the deaths of two of Ashby's veteran cavalry officers, Captain George F. Sheetz (Company F, 7th Virginia Cavalry) and Captain John Fletcher (Company A, 7th Virginia Cavalry). Nonetheless, the Confederates finally overcome the opposition. Some of the

Union troops attempt to escape by boarding two freight trains, but they are captured. Meanwhile, diversionary action by three cavalry companies (Ashby's command) in front of Banks' positions at Woodstock has convinced Banks that Jackson is advancing along the Valley Turnpike.

Other Confederates under Captain Sam Myers and Captain E.H. McDonald taunt the Union lines near Strasburg by insolently constructing breastworks in the heights within easy view of the Union troops and by constantly maneuvering around different spots, creating the illusion that their strength is greater than the actual force. Late in the day, General Banks breaks camp at Strasburg. General Jackson holds up at Cedarville.

The Confederates capture about 700 troops, including Colonel Kenly, who is wounded. The rout causes General Banks serious problems; however, the bold actions of Kenly's regiment saves Banks' army from destruction. The Union sustains probable loss of a regiment of infantry and two companies of cavalry, according to McClellan. The loss at Front Royal prompts President Lincoln to send a telegram to McClellan: "I have been compelled to suspend General Mcdowell's movements to join you. The enemy is making a desperate push upon Harper's Ferry and we are trying to throw General Frémont's force and part of McDowell's in the rear." General Banks, at Strasburg, is informed of the great loss of Kenly's command and he immediately concludes that Jackson is en route to sever his supply route and seize Winchester. Banks chooses to make a race for the prize, Winchester, setting out for it on the following morning. Winchester lies about half-way between Strasburg and Front Royal (Port Royal).

In other action, a heated skirmish erupts at Lewisburg between Confederates led by Colonel Henry Heth and the Union 36th and 44th Ohio Regiments, commanded by Colonel (later general) George Crook. The skirmish leaves 14 Union soldiers dead and 60 wounded. Confederates suffer 40 dead, 66 wounded and 100 captured. Meanwhile, Union troops led by Colonel (later major general) Woodbury clash with Confederates at Hogan's Run and Mechanicsville. The Union participants include the 4th Michigan and a troop of 2nd U.S. Cavalry. At Mechanicsville, the Union prevails and seizes a large number of prisoners. And at Hogan's Run (New Bridge), the Confederates, although again losing some captured, seem to prevail.

In Union general officer activity, Charles (Karl) Leopold Matthies, a native of Prussia, later Bydgoscz, Poland, is appointed lieutenant colonel of the 5th Iowa Regiment. Matthies had formerly joined the 1st Iowa on 14 May 1861 with the rank of captain. Colonel Matthies had participated at Island No. 10 and the siege of Corinth. Subsequent to his appointment as colonel he participates at Iuka (September 1862) and in the operations against Vicksburg. During the Vicksburg campaign, on 4 April, he is promoted to brigadier general to rank from 29 November 1862.

In Confederate general officer activity, Colonel Daniel Weisiger Adams (1st Louisiana Regulars) is promoted to brigadier general. He will lead the regiment at Perryville and Murfreesboro, Tennessee. Confederate Colonel Turner Ashby is promoted to brigadier general; Ashby has been in command of General Thomas J. (Stonewall) Jackson's cavalry. Also promoted to brigadier general are Lt. Colonel John Robert Jones, 33rd Virginia, Samuel Garland, Jr., and Colonel Wade Hampton. In July, Hampton receives command of a cavalry brigade (Jeb Stuart's cavalry corps).

May 23–24   In Virginia, General George B. McClellan's force and the Confederates under General Robert E. Lee are opposing each other at the Chickahominy River as the Rebels prepare to defend Richmond. This day, a Union contingent is directed by McClellan to advance several miles up the river to search for a good crossing. As the unit approaches Ellison's Mill, it spots a Confederate detachment burning a bridge. The vanguard, the Pennsylvania 6th Regiment, charges the bridge, disperses the Rebels and protects the crossing of three batteries, Wheeler's, Tidball's and Robinson's. Once across, the Union establishes positions in the high ground and soon becomes the target of Confederate artillery and an unsuccessful assault, permitting the Union to dig in deeper and remain there for the night.

On the following day, the Rebels again launch an assault, but Union artillery is rushed to the front and it meets the attack with devastating fire that rivets the Confederate lines, in support of a Union bayonet attack that completely breaks up the assault. Later in the day, a column (part of 1st Brigade, 4th Corps) led by Union General Henry M. Naglee moves toward Seven Pines and it too comes under a combined attack, including infantry, cavalry and artillery. The skirmish is determinedly fought by each side and the engagement also places the 8th Pennsylvania Cavalry against Confederate cavalry. The Union cavalry in this instance wins the contest, as the Rebels are forced to retire. Following the engagement, which lasts about two hours, the Confederates retire into a forest and from there they move toward Richmond. Pursuit is initiated, but after advancing only several miles, intelligence is gathered that shows a huge Confederate force is positioned near a railroad, prompting the chase to be terminated.

May 24 (Saturday)   In Tennessee, elements of the 9th Brigade, 3rd Division, Army of the Ohio commanded by Colonel (later brigadier general) William H. Lytle, skirmish with Confederates at Winchester and occupy the town.

In Virginia at Strasburg, Major General Nathaniel Banks during the morning hours prepares to depart for Winchester to secure it before it falls to the Confederates under General Thomas "Stonewall" Jackson. He takes the lead with his trains under the protection of a contingent of infantry and cavalry, commanded by Colonel Dudley Donnelly. Banks' rear is guarded by General John P. Hatch, and to his

General Nathaniel Banks (*Harper's Pictoral History of the Civil War*, 1896).

front, holding the center, is a force under Colonel George H. Gordon. En route, a contingent of Rebel cavalry attacks the train, but it is quickly ordered to the rear and the trailing infantry and cavalry race to the front to quickly beat off the attackers, who are pushed back toward Front Royal (Port Royal). The 28th New York and 46th Pennsylvania, under Colonels Edwin Franklin Brown and Joseph F. Knipe, bolstered by Cochran's battery, pursue the Confederates. Following the interruption, the advance continues and in the meantime a reconnaissance party moves out and returns with word that the route to Winchester is clear. When the main body passes Middleton, new intelligence arrives indicating that General Jackson has indeed beat Banks to Winchester. Consequently, Banks picks up the pace and the rush begins.

In a while, a contingent of Confederates (2nd Virginia) under General George H. Steuart strikes part of the column just as it reaches Newtown, but again, the Union repels the assault and drives off the attackers, thanks to the aggressive action of the 2nd Massachusetts, 27th Indiana and the 28th New York Regiments. The column reaches Winchester at about midnight (24th–25th) and immediately thereafter, Banks establishes night positions, from which he will be prepared to meet an anticipated early morning assault. Also, a confrontation occurs at New Bridge between Michigan troops led by Lt. George Custer and a contingent of Confederates. Lieutenant (later general) George Armstrong Custer distinguishes himself and receives congratulations from McClellan for his actions. The Confederates sustain 40 killed or wounded, in addition to 27 captured. The Union losses are slight. McClellan promotes Custer to his personal staff as aide-de-camp, a position he retains until McClellan is relieved of command of the Army of the Potomac. In related activity, a

125-man contingent led by Colonel Rush moves toward Hanover Court House. No encounters with Confederates are reported. Also, at Ellison's Mills, elements of two Union brigades, General George Stoneman's and General John W. Davidson's, clash with Confederates. The Union sustains two killed and four wounded. The Confederate casualty figures are unavailable.

In other activity, a five-company contingent of Michigan troops encounters Confederates in the vicinity of Cold Harbor. It is reported that the Union sustains about 10 killed. The estimated Confederate casualties are high and include some captured. Also, a contingent of the Union's First Brigade, 4th Corps (General Naglee's command), clashes with Confederates at Seven Pines. The Union sustains one killed and four wounded. Confederate casualty figures are unavailable. At Mechanicsville, a large Confederate force, estimated at well more than 1,000 troops, skirmishes with Union forces (General Davidson's command). The Union sustains two killed and one wounded. Confederate casualty figures are unavailable.

In Naval activity, the USS *Bienville,* while on patrol off the coasts of Georgia and Florida, captures a blockade runner, the *Stettin.* On the 27th, the *Bienville* seizes another blockade runner. In other activity, the USS *Amanda* and the brigantine *Bainbridge,* operating off Key West, Florida, intercept and seize the CSS *Swan,* a cargo boat. The vessel is later utilized by the Union army. The USS *Bainbridge* had been originally commissioned during December 1842. Prior to the outbreak of the war, it was attached to the Home Squadron and afterward with the Brazil and African squadrons.

May 25 (Sunday) BATTLE OF WINCHESTER Confederates under Generals Stonewall Jackson and Richard S. Ewell advance launch a predawn attack from opposing sides against General Nathaniel Banks' positions. The Confederate line stretches from the Valley Turnpike to Pritchard Hill when the signal to attack is given. The force advances in columns and some resistance is met on the Middle Road where it passes a ridge on or near the "Beutell property." Some casualties are sustained by the Confederates, but the Union contingent there pulls back to high ground in the vicinity of Hahn's stone mill to the southwest. The Union offers stiff resistance, but the line withdraws with discipline to a fortified line on the ridge that extends from Abrams Creek toward Winchester. In the meantime, Ewell's force, composed only of one brigade, Trimble's, which is bolstered by seven guns, had been on the Valley Turnpike just outside of Winchester during the previous night and is pressing forward to link with Jackson. Ewell's force maneuvers to swing though a cemetery and hit Banks' rear. The reserve units under Taliaferro and Elzey are advancing from the turnpike to deploy to the left of Jackson's Stonewall Brigade, the latter encountering stiff opposition at the ridge extending toward Winchester from Abrams Creek, while another brigade (formerly John-

son's) under Colonel W.C. Scott ascends a steep hill above an old wool factory.

Trimble's brigade advances along the Front Royal Road, unaware that Colonel Donnelly's First Brigade is entrenched to their front along west of the Rouss (Hollingsworth) Spring. One of Donnelly's regiments remains concealed behind a stone fence at a point where the road curves toward the spring. Just as the column under Trimble reaches the point in the road where it swerves, the column is unexpectedly stunned when the concealed regiment suddenly arises from behind the wall and commences fire from close range, raking the column. The blanket of fire takes out about eighty Confederates and compels the column to pull back. Nevertheless, after reforming, Trimble's force again advances, undaunted by the setback, and their determination increases, forcing the Union at the wall to pull back to Cemetery Hill. At the same time, General Jackson's force is attacking all along the ridge, compelling the Union forces there to seek more tenable positions in the vicinity of F.A. Shryock's gardens; however, the gardens open the Union up to more punishing fire. By that time, General Ewell's artillery has a line on the positions and his gunners pour in waves of fire, wreaking havoc on the defenders. Trimble's infantry races to the area and the Union troops are captured.

General Ewell secures the prisoners and charges Trimble with guarding them while he leads his cavalry and artillery to Senseny Ridge, where the Union brigade is passing in retreat, but Ewell speeds to the flank and holds fast on the flank, seizing many of the troops in the vicinity of Shawnee Hollow. All the while, as Donnelly's brigade is taken out of the fight, General Jackson's forces on the ridge continue to pound the Union line held by General Gordon's Massachusetts regiments, which are bolstered by a substantial contingent of cavalry. The cavalry, in defense of the line, launches a charge against a portion of Taylor's Louisiana units, but the cavalry is intercepted by the 10th Virginia Regiment, which strikes the flank. Afterward, the Louisiana troops join with the 10th Virginia and with their combined strength, they plow into Gordon's brigade and create more havoc, forcing Gordon's command to relinquish the ground.

With the forces of Trimble and Gordon taken out of the fight, the Rebels still possess enough strength and momentum to drive straight into Winchester, with Banks lacking sufficient strength to repel Jackson's thrust. At about the same time that Gordon's brigade is shattered, General Elzey's brigade arrives on the summit to bolster the advance. Edged on by the scent of victory and the chants of the Rebel Yell, the Confederates plow forward, and as some of the Confederates had promised during the previous March, they deliver General Jackson back to Winchester.

General Banks, under the unstoppable pressure, abandons Winchester. General Jackson works to gain one more rally to pursue and finish off Banks' battered and shattered army, but his forces are exhausted and unable to initiate a full-scale pursuit. Jackson's reserve gives chase and Ashby's cavalry trails the retreating Union force; however, Ashby's horses are equally exhausted. Jackson's repetitive call to "Press on to the Potomac" for the time being is a river too far, leaving the federal capital for another campaign. The people in Winchester become jubilant while they observe the Union Blue in retreat and the Confederate Gray moving along the town's streets.

The Confederates advance only as far as the Carter farm (later Jackson farm). General George H. Steuart had been ordered to use his fresh regiment of cavalry to pursue the Yankees, but he refused Jackson's order on the grounds that it did not come from General Ewell. However, Steuart belatedly departs to join with Ashby's cavalry and joins in the pursuit. The cavalry is able to capture some prisoners, but Banks continues to retreat toward Martinsburg, while Union cavalry supported by artillery continue to raise ferocious resistance covering the retreat.

On the left, the Confederates are repelled and sustain severe casualties; however, the right stroke deals a heavy blow to the Union. The Rebels drive to turn the flank and in the meantime the center is also pounded by General John Porter Hatch's cavalry. The battle continues incessantly with both sides being bloodied, but the Confederates continually receive fresh troops. Banks' command desperately forestalls disaster for a while, but the overwhelming strength and stamina of the Confederates following about five hours of grueling combat forces him to pull back. The entire line begins to crumble under the never-ending pressure.

The trains are ordered to retire toward the Potomac, while the troops retreat through Winchester protected in the rear by the 2nd Massachusetts and the 3rd Wisconsin. Once safely beyond Winchester, Banks divides his command into three separate columns, each with a strong rear guard, that are to remain parallel as they make a fighting retreat toward Martinsburg, completing the twenty-three mile march during the afternoon. Following a pause at this place, the columns reinitiate the march heading for Williamsport and the Potomac, reaching it at about 1800. The entire force completes the crossing of the Potomac to the safety of Maryland by about noon on the following day.

Although Union casualties had been alarming, Banks' actions against a superior numbered force might have been much worse. The Union, thanks to having a pontoon bridge with them, is able to save all the guns, and of the approximately 500 wagons, only about 55 are lost. The Union troops that participated in this battle include the 1st Vermont Cavalry, the 1st Michigan Cavalry, 1st New York Artillery, 2nd Massachusetts and the 46th Pennsylvania. The Union records 38 dead, 155 wounded and 711 missing. Confederate casualties are unavailable; however, General Thomas "Stonewall" Jackson reports his casualties for 23 May to 31 May as 68 killed, 329 wounded and three missing. Jackson reports casualties at Cross Keys and Port Republic as 139 killed, 951 wounded, 60 missing. Jackson's totals differ from the *Official Records*, which for the identical period list Confederate casualties as 230 killed, 1,378 wounded and 232 missing, for a total of 1,878.

In Washington, D.C., President Abraham Lincoln conveys to General McClellan: "I think the time is near when you must either attack Richmond or give up the job and come to the defense of Washington. Let me hear from you instantly." McClellan responds: "Telegram received independent of it, the time is very near when I shall attack Richmond.... I have two corps across the Chickahominy, within six miles of Richmond; the others on this side at same distance, and ready to cross when the bridges are complete." Actually, it has been raining every day since the 22nd with the exception of this day, and the rains will continue with increasing intensity, including a severe storm on the 30th.

President Lincoln countermands the previous orders given to General Irvin McDowell, diverting him from Richmond and ordering him to speed 20,000 troops into the Shenandoah to relieve General Banks and check the progress of General Jackson. General Frémont is also rushing toward Harrisonburg, Virginia, to bolster McDowell. Frémont and McDowell intend to get to the rear of Jackson's force and intercept it.

In Union general officer activity, Philip Sheridan (West Point, 1853) is appointed colonel of the 2nd Michigan Cavalry. He will be promoted to brigadier general on 13 September and to major general during 1863, retroactive to the Battle of Murfreesboro on December 31.

In Marine Corps activity, a contingent of Marines commanded by Captain Charles G. McCawley reoccupies the Navy yard at Gosport, Norfolk.

In Naval activity, the gunboat USS *Kennebec*, commanded by Captain John H. Russell, exchanges fire with Confederates in the vicinity of Vicksburg, Mississippi, while on a reconnaissance mission.

A Confederate magazine in the vicinity of Fredericksburg, Virginia, explodes (Mottelay, *The Soldier in Our Civil War*, 1886).

May 26 (Monday)   Texas is incorporated in the Confederate Trans-Mississippi Department.

In Virginia, the unexpected advance by General Thomas J. "Stonewall" Jackson and the accompanying progress against General Banks has created apprehension in the capital, and it is thought by many that Washington is about to be attacked. Urgent requests have been sent out to the governors in the Union states requesting troops. President Abraham Lincoln has also taken precautions to order that the rails be kept open for the movement of supplies and ammunition as well as infantry and cavalry. In other activity, elements of the U.S. 1st Cavalry and McClellan's dragoons, commanded by Lt. Colonel Grierson, advances toward Hanover Court House. During the reconnaissance mission, no casualties are reported.

In Mississippi, a contingent of Union troops commanded by Cpt. DeKay encounters and clashes with a large Confederate cavalry force at Grand Gulf. The Union sustains one killed. Confederate casualty figures are unavailable.

In Missouri, Union and Confederate contingents (specific units not reported) skirmish at Big Creek. No casualty figures are available. Also, a contingent of the 1st Iowa Cavalry clashes with Confederates at Osceola. Casualty figures are unavailable.

In Confederate general officer activity, Colonel John Creed Moore, 2nd Texas Infantry Regiment, is promoted to the rank of brigadier general effective this date. He will participate in various actions in Mississippi, including Vicksburg.

In Naval activity, Lt. George H. Preble, commander of the USS *Katahdin*, in a letter, informs Admiral David Farragut that on the 24th two coal vessels, the *Althea* and the *Golden Lead*, were anchored less than ten miles above Natchez. On the 28th, while Farragut is moving up the Mississippi River aboard the USS *Hartford*, as it passes the *Althea*, it is pulled alongside and carried to Baton Rouge by the *Hartford*, which arrives at the city on the 28th.

May 27 (Tuesday) BATTLE OF HANOVER COURT HOUSE Union troops (Fifth Corps) under General Fitz John Porter commence a forced march, during yet another heavy rain storm, for Hanover Court House, Virginia. Porter's mission is to clear the area of Confederates to make way for a speedy advance by General Irvin McDowell, who is at Fredericksburg with about 40,000 troops. The task also includes the burning of particular bridges over the

Pamunkey River to help block General Thomas J. "Stonewall" Jackson's force, which is in northern Virginia and thought to be en route to Richmond. The assault force is spearheaded by Brigadier General W.H. Emory (West Point, 1831) leading the 5th and 6th Cavalry supported by a Horse Battery of the 2nd U.S. Artillery.

Following Emory is a division under Brigadier General George W. Morell. A provisional brigade commanded by Colonel G.K. Warren travels a different route along the Pamunkey River, and additional reinforcements join Emory. By about noon, after a tedious trek through the sloppy mud, the Union finds itself two miles from Hanover Court House staring at Confederate defenders deployed at the Hanover Court House Road. In a flash, gunfire erupts and a feverish skirmish erupts as advance elements of the Union force move cautiously against Confederate positions.

Reinforcements under General Daniel Butterfield, four regiments strong, change the pace of the contest. The Yankees escalate their movements and charge the Confederates, who are forced to begin withdrawal. At one point, the Yankees overrun a position, capturing one gun. The cavalry begins pursuit of the retreating Rebels, followed by infantry and artillery contingents. Another contingent of Yankees under General John Henry Martindale (West Point, 1835) presses toward the Rebels, who are holding at Ashland Road near Beake's Station on the Virginia Central Railroad, where they force a Confederate pull-back toward Ashland. Activity is fierce in the entire area.

A strong force of Union troops under Warren seizes a large number of Confederates on the Pamunkey. The Rebels regroup and attack the positions of Martindale who is moving up to rejoin the main command at Hanover Court House. All hell breaks loose as General Fitz John Porter orders his command at Hanover Court House to turn about and race to the rear to assist troops under attack. This maneuver, spearheaded by agile cavalry, quickly turns the situation into a victory for the Yankees who, by nightfall, have the Rebels in trouble. Yankees begin pouring in from all directions, simply overpowering the Confederates. James McQuade's brigade crashes from the woods, striking the Rebels from one direction, while Daniel Butterfield advances by the rails and through the woods, thoroughly routing the southerners. Confederate General Lawrence O.B. Branch and the remainder of his force retire to the woods, abandoning their encampment.

The day ends with the Union gaining terrain and equipment. One company of Captain James E. Harrison's 5th U.S. Cavalry captures equipment that can fully supply two full companies of infantry with weapons and ammunition. The Yankees also seize the rails, two railway trains and one 12-pound howitzer. The Union sustains a loss of 53 killed and 344 wounded during the confrontation. The Confederates suffer 200 killed and wounded and more than 700 captured. The Union 12th, 13th, 14th, 17th, 25th and 44th New York Regiments, the 62nd and 83rd Pennsylvania Regiments, the

16th Michigan, and the 9th and 22nd Massachusetts Regiments participate. In addition, the 2nd Maine Artillery, Battery F, 5th U.S. Artillery and the 1st U.S. Sharpshooters also participate. General George B. McClellan is quite happy with the victory, but still concerned with the Confederate threat, he subsequently backs up Porter with General George Sykes' division, which moves from New Bridge on the 28th to support the seizure of Hanover Court House against possible assault by a large Confederate force suspected of being near Ashland, Virginia.

In Arkansas, at Big Indian Creek in the vicinity of Searcy Landing, a six-man contingent of the Union 1st Missouri Cavalry engages a Confederate band of about 40 troops. The Union sustains three wounded. The Confederates sustain five killed and about 25 wounded. Also, a contingent of the 9th Illinois Cavalry commanded by Lt. Colonel Hiram F. Sickles and Captain Blakemore at Cache River Bridge skirmishes with a Rebel force. The Union reports no casualties. The Confederates sustain one killed and one captured.

In Georgia, a contingent of the 60th New York Infantry skirmishes with Confederates at New Hope. Corporal Follett Johnson receives the Medal of Honor for his heroic actions during this engagement. Colonel George S. Greene (West Point, 1823) had joined the regiment during the previous January, but upon his promotion to brigadier general on 28 April, he relinquishes command of the regiment.

In Mississippi, a contingent of the 2nd Division (General Buell's command), commanded by General Richard W. Johnson, clashes with Confederates at Bridge Creek in a contest that lasts only about thirty minutes. The Union lists no casualties. The Confederates suffer two killed. Admiral Farragut, after assessing the strength of the Confederates' guns defending Vicksburg, discerns that from their positions in the heights on a bluff they are capable of pummeling his fleet, while his naval guns are incapable of striking the batteries. The fleet retires; however, his schooners (mortar ships) remain in position to maintain a blockade below the town. In other activity, a contingent of the Army of the Ohio clashes with Confederates in the vicinity of Corinth. The Union sustains about 20–25 killed and wounded. The Confederates suffer 25–30 killed or wounded. The 5th Minnesota Volunteer Regiment participates in this skirmish.

In Missouri, Union and Confederate troops clash at Osceola. The 1st Iowa Cavalry sustains three killed and two wounded. Confederate casualties are unavailable.

In Naval activity, the USS *Bienville,* on patrol off the coasts of Georgia and Florida, seizes a blockade runner, the *Patras.*

May 28 (Wednesday)   In Mississippi, Lt. Isaac Brown, pursuant to orders of 26 May, assumes command of the CSS *Arkansas.* Shortly thereafter, the *Arkansas* moves to Yazoo City, where it can be readied for service. When com-

pleted, the *Arkansas* will be fitted with two 8-inch Columbiads (two forward bow ports), two 9-inch Dahlgren guns, two 6-inch rifled guns, and two 30-pounders. The vessel is also transformed into an ironclad; however, the quality of the iron is poor, having been iron from railroad tracks. However, it is also equipped with two new engines, both built in Memphis. Lt. Brown's crew is gathered from various sources, primarily from former crew members of sunken gunboats and about sixty volunteers attached to Colonel Jeff Thompson's raiders; however, none of Thompson's men (from Missouri) have any naval experience, nor experience with heavy guns.

In Virginia, Union Major General McClellan pays tribute to General Fitz John Porter: "Porter's actions of yesterday [at Hanover Court House] was truly a glorious victory; too much credit cannot be given to this magnificent division and its accomplished leader. The rout of the rebels was complete; not a defeat but a complete rout." Also, Union Major Williams, 6th U.S. Cavalry, takes a detachment and begins destroying bridges spanning the Pamunkey River and the railroad bridges that cross the South Anna. The following day, these Union cavalry troops destroy the Fredericksburg-Richmond Railroad bridge and the turnpike bridge, both of which span the South Anna. McClellan had ordered the destruction of these bridges following the unexpected success of Confederate General Thomas J. "Stonewall" Jackson in northern Virginia. In other activity, a Union force composed of elements of the Potomac Guards, 3rd Maryland Regiment, and the 3rd Indiana Cavalry engage Confederates at Wardensville. The Union reports no casualties. The Confederates sustain two killed and three wounded.

In Naval activity, the USS *Hartford,* Admiral Farragut's flagship, arrives at Baton Rouge with a coal ship, the *Althea,* in tow. Crew members of the *Hartford* immediately notice the absence of the Stars and Stripes that had been atop the arsenal when the *Hartford* earlier embarked. Admiral Farragut dispatches a party to deliver a written protest; however, prior to the boat reaching shore, a contingent of mounted Confederates open fire on the boat and three of the men, including two of the rowers and the *Hartford*'s chief engineer, James B. Kimble, are wounded. Admiral Farragut orders the crew to cut the *Althea* loose to clear the path for the guns. Records on the *Althea* fade after this incident; however, it later resurfaces in the records on 27 February 1863, when it delivers coal to various blockade vessels off the Texas coast. From May to November 1863, a schooner *Althea* is recorded as delivering supplies to blockade ships off Charleston. Afterward, there are no further details on the *Althea.*

May 28–30   In Virginia, the Confederates are maneuvering to flank the Union, which is moving too close to Richmond. Reinforcements have been arriving from all directions for a major stand to block Union entrance to the

heart of the Confederacy. The Union forces under General George B. McClellan are making adjustments to finalize plans for the assault against the Confederate capital. General Erasmus Keyes orders Silas Casey's division to advance along the Williamsburg Road to Fair Oaks just in front of Seven Pines. General Darius Couch's division is at the line in rifle pits, while six field guns and new rifle pits are being constructed to complement the picket line, which now extends from the Chickahominy River to White Oak Swamp. Union General Samuel P. Heintzelman is met by fierce opposition as he approaches the front, encouraging his deployment of two brigades of Philip Kearny's force near Savage's Station, poised to rush to General Casey if the situation warrants it. All the while, the Confederates are not resting lazily. They are closing in on Casey, the advance element of the 4th Corps.

In other activity, a Union force composed of elements of the Potomac Guards, 3rd Maryland Regiment, and the 3rd Indiana Cavalry engage Confederates at Wardensville. The Union reports no casualties. The Confederates sustain two killed and three wounded.

May 29 (Thursday)   In Mississippi, the Confederates evacuate Corinth in anticipation of a Union assault. While in the process of preparing for a possible evacuation, General Pierre Gustave T. Beauregard has for the past several weeks been transferring the wounded to safer positions, and he has been steadily removing all supplies. Prior to departing, the Rebels set much of the town afire and they detonate the magazines. The Rebels halt at a point about six miles outside of Corinth, expecting the Union to pursue, but no major chase commences. Union General Henry W. Halleck has been in the area for some time but no general assault is initiated, allowing the Confederates to get away. The Union will move in and occupy the city the following day.

In other activity, elements of the 2nd Iowa and the 2nd Michigan Regiments, commanded by Colonel W.L. Elliott, clash with Confederates at Booneville. The Union sustains no casualties. The Confederates suffer one killed and about nine captured. The two opponents again clash on the following day. The 5th Minnesota Volunteer Regiment participates in the battle for Corinth and the fighting at Booneville.

In South Carolina, elements of the 50th Pennsylvania, 79th New York and the 8th Michigan Volunteer Regiments, bolstered by the 1st Massachusetts Cavalry, skirmish with Confederates at Pocotaligo. The Union force, commanded by Colonel B.C. Christ, sustains two killed and nine wounded. Confederate casualty figures are unavailable.

In Virginia, Union General William H. Emory dispatches a contingent of the 5th Cavalry in an operation similar to that of his 6th Cavalry at the South Anna on the previous day. Capt. William P. Chambliss with his unit advances to Ashland, destroys the railroad bridge crossing Stoney Creek and drives Confederates from the town. General McClellan, realizing the positions are ultimately untenable, orders General George Stoneman to pull back from Ashland and Hanover Court House and rejoin the main body. McClellan realizes he cannot support them with reinforcements and that McDowell cannot reach them either.

Union troops numbering about 40,000 press forward, nearing Confederate positions at Harper's Ferry. Confederate General Thomas J. "Stonewall" Jackson, sensing that his army is dangerously positioned, takes measures to avoid entrapment by the closing Union forces of Generals Irvin McDowell and John Frémont. Jackson dispatches a force under General Richard S. Ewell toward Harper's Ferry, West Virginia, defended by General Rufus Saxton; however, it is only a diversion to cover his retirement from Winchester to Strasburg. Jackson's army departs on the following day. Also, in the vicinity of Seven Pines, a Union contingent clashes with a Confederate force composed of several hundred troops. The Union sustains two killed and two wounded. Confederate casualties are unreported.

May 30 (Friday) In Mississippi, Union forces under Generals Henry Halleck and Ulysses S. Grant occupy Corinth unopposed. General Pierre Gustave T. Beauregard has withdrawn, taking all supplies and wounded with him. Halleck immediately begins fortifying Corinth, but the extra precautions and defenses prove unnecessary, as they are never used. A contingent under General Gordon Granger departs Corinth in search of Rebels and discovers only some scattered stragglers in the vicinity of Guntown. Union General William S. Rosecrans had overmatched Confederate General Earl Van Dorn, who recently also sustained a loss at Pea Ridge, Arkansas. Subsequent to the loss of Corinth, Van Dorn (Army of Mississippi) is succeeded by General John C. Pemberton. Van Dorn receives command of Pemberton's cavalry force.

In related activity, Union Generals John Pope

and Don Carlos Buell begin pursuit of Beauregard's command, but after advancing 30 miles without serious contact, return to camp. Also, in Booneville, the 2nd Iowa and the 2nd Michigan Cavalry, commanded by Colonel W.L. Elliott, capture the town and about 2,000 Confederates. Battle reports indicate about 700 Confederates are captured.

In Virginia, Confederate General Thomas J. "Stonewall" Jackson abandons his positions in Winchester and heads for Strasburg. During the march, he orders the bridges burned to impede the Union forces. In addition, detachments are sent out in several directions to destroy other bridges that could possibly be used by pursuing Union troops. In other activity, the Confederates operating around Richmond dispatch reconnaissance contingents to gather intelligence on Union forces that threaten their positions. The detachment moves toward General Silas Casey's Division, which is deployed on both sides of the Williamsburg Road just beyond Seven Pines about six miles from the Confederate capital, but no hostilities occur. Casey's right is held by General Henry M. Naglee's brigade, composed of the 11th Maine (Lt. Colonel Baldwin), the 52nd (Colonel John C. Dodge) and 104th (Colonel W.W.H. Davis) Pennsylvania Regiments, the 56th (Colonel C.H. Van Wyck) and 104th (Colonel J.M. Brown) New York Regiments. The left is held by General Innis Palmer's brigade, which is composed of the 55th (Colonel J.S. Belknap), 81st (Lt. Colonel De Forest), 92nd (Lt. Colonel Anderson) and 98th (Lt. Colonel Durkee) New York Regiments. Naglee's center is held by General Henry W. Wessels' brigade: the 96th New York Regiment, and the 85th, 101st, and 103rd Pennsylvania Regiments commanded by Colonels J. Fairman, J.B. Howell, J.H. Wilson and T.F. Lehman, respectively. Innis Palmer's brigade stands to the immediate front of General Darius Couch's division (Keyes' corps), and is deployed at Seven Pines   stretching

from there to the far right at Fair Oaks Station. General Heintzelman's corps is deployed on the left and holds responsibility for protecting the approaches to White Oak Swamp.

The Confederates have selected Keyes' positions as a target and will launch an assault on the following day. General McClellan is again struck by unfavorable weather: a violent summer storm erupts, neutralizing the bulk of the work done on the defenses. The giant Union Army is hampered by fiendishly impassable roads, making their positions extremely vulnerable to an enemy attack, should one be mobilized. Confederate General Joseph Johnston perceives the situation correctly and readies an aggressive general assault to destroy the Army of the Potomac the following day, hoping to strike while McClellan is thus immobilized. On the following day, an aide-de-camp to General Johnston is captured by Union pickets but they are unable to force much information about Confederate intentions from him. General Erasmus Keyes, suspicious because of Johnston's reconnaissance officer being too close, implements extra caution, and within an hour after the capture, Keyes orders a general alarm sounded at 11 A.M. on the 31st. In other activity, a Union brigade and the 1st Rhode Island Cavalry occupy Front Royal. The Union sustains five killed and eight wounded. The Confederate casualty figures are unavailable, but 156 Rebels are captured.

In Naval activity, Admiral Farragut's fleet arrives back at New Orleans following an expedition that had advanced to Vicksburg. Upon his arrival, Farragut receives new orders that direct him to clear the river and join the Western Flotilla. The mortar schooners at Mobile are recalled to join in the expedition. Afterward, the operation begins, and by the 26th, the Union squadron is positioned slightly below Vicksburg.

Left: Union attack at Corinth (Johnson, *Campfire and Battlefield: History of the Conflicts and Campaigns,* 1894). **Right:** Union troops hoist the Stars and Stripes atop Corona Female College at Corinth (Mottelay, *The Soldier in Our Civil War,* 1886).

Left: Battle of Seven Pines (Fair Oaks). *Right:* Union troops at Grapevine Bridge during fighting at Seven Pines (Fair Oaks), Virginia, near Richmond (Johnson, *Campfire and Battlefield: History of the Conflicts and Campaigns*, 1894).

May 31 (Saturday) **In Arizona,** the light artillery battery commanded by Lt. Shinn, a contingent of the "California Column," commanded by Brigadier General James H. Carleton, arrives at Fort Barrett near the Pinal Indian villages. Shinn is expected to depart shortly for Tucson. The Californians had established the fort earlier this month and named it in honor of Lt. James Barrett, who was killed during a skirmish with Confederates at Picacho Pass on 15 April. Barrett had been attached to the vanguard of General Carleton's column, led by Colonel Joseph West (1st California Infantry). General Carleton arrives in Tucson during June. The Union will also reoccupy Fort Buchanan and rename it Fort Stanford, and the Californians will reoccupy Fort Breckenridge. The most recent post, Fort Barrett, is abandoned during June and in its place a new post (later Camp Lowell) is established near Tucson.

In Mississippi, one company of the 7th Illinois Cavalry, commanded by Major Rawalt, clashes with Confederates at Tuscumbia Creek. The Union sustains one killed and six wounded.

In Missouri, elements of the 10th Illinois Cavalry and the 14th Missouri Cavalry, commanded by Captain Richardson, skirmish with Confederates under Major George M. Wright and Captain J.T. Coffee at Neosho. The Union sustains two killed and three wounded. Confederate casualty figures are unavailable.

In North Carolina, the 3rd New York Cavalry, commanded by Lt. Allis, clashes with Confederates in the vicinity of Washington, along the Greenville Road. The Union reports one wounded. The Confederates suffer three killed and two wounded.

In Union general officer activity, Colonel Edward Canby is appointed brigadier general. Canby, who has commanded the Department of New Mexico, is now ordered east. He is replaced by General James Henry Carleton, who

remains commander of Department of New Mexico until 1866.

May 31–June 1 BATTLE OF SEVEN PINES (FAIR OAKS) The Confederates under General Joseph E. Johnston near Richmond, Virginia, attack General McClellan's Army of the Potomac, striking with the combined force of Generals D.H. Hill, Benjamin Huger, James Longstreet, and Gustavus Woodson Smith against Union General Silas Casey's line. The defiant Confederates move against Casey with swashbuckling strides. Casey sends out a regiment from Innis Palmer's brigade to assist the picket lines, but the Confederates crash right through, receiving little harm from the brigade. Union reinforcements under General John J. Peck speed to fill the void to the left of the Williamsburg Road in an attempt to contain the Confederate onslaught.

As the Union attempts to fortify its positions, the Confederates strike again, this time against the beleaguered positions of General Casey, and the assault comes from separate directions. An alarm is sent calling for reinforcements, but there is confusion and the messenger does not reach Generals Joseph Hooker and Philip Kearny until the desperate hour of 3 P.M. All the while, the command of Casey is getting badly thumped in a deadly confrontation between two opposing forces. Both refuse to give any quarter.

Heavy rains threaten the bridges recently constructed by the Union, further jeopardizing their positions. During early afternoon, Union General Edwin Sumner's Second Corps, consisting of Generals Israel B. Richardson's and John Sedgwick's Divisions, is rushed across the Chickahominy to bolster Heintzelman. The Confederates overpower the positions of General Casey and capture the redoubt, forcing the Yankees to retreat in the face of overpowering forces and regroup at positions held by General Darius Couch. During this incessant struggle, General Couch has fallen into serious compli-

General Joseph E. Johnston (Johnson, *Campfire and Battlefield: History of the Conflicts and Campaigns*, 1894).

cations himself, engaging a strong Confederate force that is heading toward the railroad at Fair Oaks Station. Couch is reinforced with extra men, but the added strength is not sufficient to offset the Confederate threat. Couch is pressed into retreat. His forces head towards the Grapevine Bridge, expressing confidence that he can join with General Sumner to hold the line at that point before Fair Oaks Station.

Federal reinforcements attached to Kearny's command finally arrive in the area to assist the beleaguered Union troops. Union General Hiram G. Berry quickly takes up positions in the woods and begins to flank the enemy from the left, pouring fire into their lines and taking some heat off the Union troops. General Charles D. Jameson, also of Kearny's command, drives into the woods and holds firm against several vehement Confederate assaults. After the fall of darkness, Jameson maneuvers his command out of his isolated position and arrives on Casey's left by the morning of the 1st.

The silence of night is jolted at 0500 on the 1st of June. The crackling of rifles and artillery erupts near General Richardson's positions when Confederate Cavalry is discovered at close range, prompting the cessation of yawning and the commencement of firing by Battery B, 1st New York, which rapidly reacts by pumping shells into the advancing Confederate cavalry. The Rebels drive forward and rout the Union line. This is surely to be another continuous day of battle. General Hooker races to the railroad with the 5th and 6th New Jersey Regiments. A brigade under General Daniel E. Sickles is close behind, but the Union artillery is completely immobilized because of the abominable mud. Nonetheless, the Union takes the offensive and crashes through the woods, fighting feverishly against determined Confederates under General Joseph E. Johnston, who are firmly resolved to hold. After a vicious one-hour duel, the Confederates are forced to back off from the pressure of the two New Jersey regiments and the support brigade under General David B. Birney.

A thrust with fixed bayonets ordered by General Hooker turns the tide. The Confederates are finally thrown back in disarray, leaving many wounded on the field in spaces filled by Union wounded at arms' touch. It is a bloody and tragic scene. Blood from the North and South flows together wasted in the muddy terrain. The battle culminates with neither side accomplishing anything. Each exhausted army retains the same positions it held before the confrontation began. Heavy casualties are sustained by both sides. The courage of the men on both sides is demonstrated by the following: during one of the assaults, Union Lt. William R. Shafter, Co. I, 7th Michigan, leads 22 men in a valiant charge across an open field. Eighteen of his men lay dead and he is also seriously wounded. Shafter, his horse shot out from under him, conceals his wounds and continues to fight. Also during the engagement, Lt. Colonel Thomas Wilberforce Egan (40th New York) orders the arrest of the commanding colonel for misconduct. Shortly thereafter, Egan is promoted to colonel. Another example of the level of courage on the field is demonstrated by the Confederate 4th North Carolina Infantry led by Lt. Colonel Bryan Grimes, who remains as the only officer unscathed at the battle's end, and of more than 500 troops, nearly 90 percent are either killed or wounded. Although Grimes is unhurt, it is reported that his horse is decapitated.

The 4th Alabama Regiment led by Colonel Evander McIvor Law and the 26th Alabama commanded by Colonel (later brigadier general) Edward A. O'Neal participate at this action. Confederate President Jefferson Davis places Robert E. Lee in command of the Army of Northern Virginia after General Johnston is wounded. Johnston is first replaced by his second in command, Gustavus W. Smith. Nonetheless, Smith suffers a nervous breakdown on June 1, causing Davis to give the command to Lee. General Smith resigns during January 1863 after he is bypassed for promotion.

Union casualties are 890 killed, 3,627 wounded, and 1,300 missing. Confederate casualties are 2,800 dead, 3,897 wounded, and 1,300 missing. Union Generals John Joseph Abercrombie, Oliver O. Howard and Henry W. Wessells are wounded. General Howard loses one leg. Colonel Henry S. Briggs, 10th Massachusetts, sustains wounds in both legs. Briggs becomes brigadier general in July 1862. In addition, Union Colonel Lewis C. Hunt (West Point, 1847) suffers a vicious wound. Hunt, a colonel with the 92nd New York, is the brother of General Henry J. Hunt. He becomes a brigadier general on 29 November 1862. He later is assigned special duty in Connecticut and afterward Kansas and Missouri, prior to assuming command of the New York defenses with the rank of major (Regular service, 14th Infantry during 1863) and the brevet rank of brigadier general (Regular service) at the end of the war. Subsequent to the close of hostilities, Hunt serves in various places, including his final post at Fort Union, where he dies on 6 September 1886, six days after he arrives there. Also, General Charles Devens, Jr., is among the wounded.

Confederate Brigadier General Robert H. Hatton is killed while leading his brigade; he had just recently been promoted to brigadier general. Confederate Brigadier General James Pettigrew is captured. Following his release, General Pettigrew is transferred to Petersburg, and from there he serves for a while in the Carolinas prior to returning to Virginia to join General A.P. Hill's Corps during the Pennsylvania Campaign (1863). Confederate Generals Joseph E. Johnston and Robert Emmett Rodes are wounded. Confederate Colonel Thomas E. Lloyd, 35th Georgia Infantry, participates at this battle and will subsequently perform with the Army of Northern Virginia in nearly every major battle between this date and the close of hostilities. Also, Confederate Colonel (later general) John Bratton is wounded and captured. After his release, he will continue his services in General John B. Hood's Division and will be is promoted to brigadier general (May 1864).

Confederate Captain James Conner (Connor) is promoted to colonel (22nd North Carolina Regiment) soon after this action. And, Confederate Colonel (later General) John Rogers Cooke (27th North Carolina Infantry), the brother-in-law of Confederate General Pierre Beauregard and the son of Union General Philip St. George Cooke, sustains a wound during this action. According to reports, he is repeatedly wounded in various clashes prior to being promoted during November 1862, and he proves to be a prominent officer for the duration under Robert E. Lee during the campaigns in Virginia and Maryland. Also, Confederate Colonel (later brigadier general) Birkett D. Fry, 13th Alabama Infantry, sustains a severe wound. Lt. Colonel (later brigadier general) Robert Daniel Johnston, 23rd North Carolina Regiment, is wounded.

June 1862   *In Confederate activity,* in South Carolina at John's Island, Colonel John Dunovant, 1st South Carolina Regulars, is tossed out of the regular service due to apparent chronic intoxication; however, he retains favor with Governor Francis Wilkinson Pickens, who reclaims him and appoints him colonel (later general) of the 5th South Carolina Cavalry. Also, Hood's Texas Brigade, Army of Northern Virginia, attaches eight companies of Hampton's Legion, a brigade that had originally contained artillery, cavalry and infantry until after the fighting at Manassas (Bull Run) the previous June. At this time, Hampton's Brigade, from South Carolina, is commanded by Colonel (later general) Martin Witherspoon Gary, subsequent to the wounding of Colonel Wade Hampton at 1st Manassas (Bull Run).

In Union activity, George Leonard Andrews (West Point, 1851) re-enters the army to become lieutenant colonel of the 2nd Massachusetts Regiment.

June 1 (Sunday)   In Mississippi, the Confederates led by General Pierre Gustave T. Beauregard continue to move towards Tulpelo after the abandonment of Corinth. General Sterling Price's force bivoucas in the vicinity of Baldwyn. Price remains there for nearly one week before pushing to Corinth. At Tupelo, General Beauregard becomes ill and the army will come under the command of General Braxton Bragg.

In South Carolina, on or about this date, General H.W. Benham, based at Port Royal, South Carolina, decides to launch an assault against James Island, defended by about 8000 Confederates at Fort Johnson under Colonel J.G. Lamar. Benham informs General Hunter, commanding officer, Department of the South, about the impending action and Hunter concurs. Fort Johnson is heavily defended to thwart a possible Union assault against the city of Charleston. The Union forces move by transports up the Stono River, and on the 4th of May the two sides encounter each other.

In Virginia, General Robert E. Lee, subsequent to the wounding of General Joseph E. Johnston on the previous day at Seven Pines, becomes commanding officer of the Confederate Army of Northern Virginia. Also, General Thomas "Stonewall" Jackson's forces reach Strasburg, but they pass right through the town and move toward Harrisonburg. Union Major General John C. Frémont's force moves out of the mountains and arrives there shortly after General Jackson passes through; however, no pursuit is initiated. On the following day, reinforcements arrive.

Following the battle at Seven Pines, elements of the Union 2nd Michigan Infantry Regiment, commanded by Major Louis Dillman, initiate a reconnaissance mission that spreads out beyond the Union lines and lasts into the following day. Also, the Union 8th West Virginia Regiment, 60th Ohio, bolstered by the 1st New Jersey Cavalry and the 1st Pennsylvania Cavalry, initiate operations along the Strasburg Staunton Road that continue through the next day. The contingent sustains two wounded. Confederate casualties, if any, are unavailable.

In Union activity, the Department of Virginia (Union) is incorporated into the command of Major General George B. McClellan. Union Major General John Wool is assigned to the Middle Department and Major General John Adams Dix assumes command of Fort Monroe, Virginia. General Wool assumes his new command on 9 June. Also, Colonel James Madison Tuttle is promoted to brigadier general. While in the service, General Tuttle twice runs for governor of Iowa, but fails during both attempts.

June 2 (Monday)   In Kentucky, Union Brigadier General Jeremiah T. Boyle, fresh from commanding a brigade in Thomas Leonidas Crittenden's Division (Buell's Corps), is preparing for his new command, which is to take charge of Union troops in Kentucky. Rebels under Braxton Bragg (primarily John Hunt Morgan's command) persistently attack the state Boyle is to protect. Boyle is best suited for "calling for reinforcements instead of fighting and his leadership is constantly under fire." Boyle remains in command until January 1864, when he resigns after being assigned to Knoxville.

In Mississippi, a 30-man contingent of the 42nd Illinois Regiment clashes with Confederates at Rienzi. The Confederates seize some prisoners. Other casualty figures are unavailable. Meanwhile, contingents of the 1st Ohio Cavalry, commanded by Lt. Colonel (later brigadier general) Thomas C.H. Smith, skirmish with Confederates at Blackland. The Union reports no casualties, and it reports the capture of one Confederate soldier. Confederate casualty figures are unavailable. Also, Union Colonel W.L. Elliott's brigade, augmented by Albert M. Powell's artillery battery, skirmishes with Confederates at Osborn's and Wolf's Creeks. Elliott's command sustains two killed and about eight wounded. The Confederates sustain about 30 killed and wounded.

In North Carolina, Mix's New York cavalry clashes with Confederates at Tranter's Creek. The Confederates seize several prisoners.

In Virginia, Union General George D. Bayard arrives at Strasburg to reinforce General John Frémont. The advance troops of General James Shields' cavalry are with the column. Without pausing for rest, following the long march, pursuit of Jackson is immediately undertaken. Soon the column encounters Jackson's rear guard. Some skirmishing develops as the chase continues into the following day, but once Jackson's force crosses the Mount Jackson Bridge, it is burned. The guns of Colonel Pilson's battery

begin shelling the Rebels as they cross the Shenandoah River. Miserable rains have been plaguing the area for the past several days. Lacking a bridge, the Union is forced to abandon the pursuit. Jackson advances to Harrisonburg, reaching it on the 5th.

In Naval activity, the USS *Agassiz* (Coast Guard revenue cutter) is ordered to depart Sag Harbor (Long Island) for New London. It remains on duty there until the latter part of the year, when it is transferred to a new duty station in North Carolina.

June 3 (Tuesday)   In South Carolina, contingents of the 28th Massachusetts and 100th Pennsylvania Regiments encounter and skirmish with Confederates at Legare's Point. The Union sustains five wounded. Confederate casualties are unavailable.

In Virginia, Union artillery (Colonel Pilson's battery) shells the rear guard of the Confederate army as it crosses the Shenandoah River. Also, a Union contingent commanded by Major Myer initiates a reconnaissance mission to the James River to make contact with a Union Fleet. It continues through June 7.

In Confederate general officer activity, Colonel Ambrose Ransom Wright, commanding officer, 3rd Georgia Infantry Regiment, is promoted to brigadier general. Also, Colonel James Jay Archer, 5th Texas Regiment, is appointed brigadier general. General Archer, a veteran of the Mexican War, had resigned from the U.S. Army during 1861 to join the Confederacy. He succeeds Robert Hatton as commander of the Tennessee brigade. Colonel James L. Kemper and Colonel William Dorsey Pender are promoted to the rank of brigadier general. Pender is assigned command of a brigade in Ambrose P. Hill's Division, Army of Northern Virginia.

In Naval activity, Admiral David Farragut leaves a small detachment at Ellis' Cliffs as the fleet departs for Vicksburg. Ships, including the schooner USS *Arletta,* under tow, depart New Orleans about two weeks later. Southern shore batteries at Grand Gulf fire upon the flotilla as the ships advance; however, return fire silences the artillery and the ships pass without harm.

June 3–5   In North Carolina, Union troops, including the 1st New York Marine Artillery, skirmish with Confederates at Tranter's Creek.

In Tennessee, Union Forces, after a relentless siege on Fort Pillow (Fort Wright), Tennessee, take the fort; however, its commander, Brigadier General John B. Villepigue, and the garrison, subsequent to finishing the destruction that had been begun by the Union, make it to safety. The Union forces are assisted by the

Union artillery (Colonel Pilson's battery) shells the rear guard of the Confederate column as it crosses the Shenandoah River (Mottelay, *The Soldier in Our Civil War,* 1886).

USS *Benton, Louisville, Cairo,* and other ships. The Confederates, by evacuating Fort Pillow, place Memphis in jeopardy.

June 4 (Wednesday)   In Alabama, skirmishes develop at Huntsville and Woodville. Specific units are unreported and casualty figures are unavailable.

In South Carolina, Union troops, recently arrived from Port Royal, are on James Island encamped at two separate locations, each about two miles from Confederate lines. The Union forces are commanded by Generals Isaac I. Stevens and Horatio G. Wright. The Confederates are commanded by Colonel T.G. Lamar. This day, during the morning, the Rebels spring a surprise raid and succeed in capturing twenty Union troops. During the afternoon, the Union initiates an assault against the Confederate positions and seizes a battery comprising four guns.

In Tennessee, at Jasper Sweden's Cove, Union and Confederate forces clash. The Union 79th Pennsylvania, 5th Kentucky Cavalry, 7th Pennsylvania Cavalry and the 1st Ohio Battery participate. The Union force, commanded by Brigadier General James S. Negley, sustains two killed and seven wounded. The Confederates, commanded by General Daniel W. Adams, sustain 20 killed and 20 wounded. Also, Union Captain Charles H. Davis, commanding the Naval forces outside Memphis, is informed that Forts Pillow and Randolph have been evacuated by the Confederates. Contingents are dispatched to occupy both locations. The abandonment of the forts occurs with the Confederate withdrawal from Corinth, Mississippi. The Confederate naval force under Commodore George N. Hollins pulls back from the vicinity of the forts and takes a position near the Arkansas shore in front of Memphis. Meanwhile, more Union vessels are en route to the area.

In Virginia, General Robert E. Lee telegraphs Confederate Major A.W. Harman at Staunton to "march down the valley and communicate with Jackson."

In Naval activity, the steamer CSS *Arrow,* a gunboat seized by the state of Louisiana the previous year and transferred to the Confederate Army, after escaping from New Orleans during the previous April, is set afire on the West Pearl River to prevent its capture by the Union. Another vessel, the tug *Arrow,* operated by the Virginia State Navy, had operated in the vicinity of Craney Island; however, there is no record of the tug *Arrow* ever being taken into the Confederate States Navy.

June 5 (Thursday)   In North Carolina, a Union force composed of the 24th Massachusetts, Company I, 3rd New York Cavalry and a unit of a Marine artillery battery, commanded by Lt. Colonel Osborn, engages a contingent of Confederates led by Colonel Singeltary at Tranter's Creek. The Union sustains seven killed and eleven wounded. Confederate casualties are unavailable. Also, Confederates attack Union scouts (24th Massachusetts Regiment) along Pactolus Road. Seven Union troops are reported killed. Confederate casualty figures are unavailable.

In Virginia, Confederate General Thomas J. "Stonewall" Jackson's force arrives at Harrisonburg from Strasburg. The Union pursuit had been delayed by one full day while a new bridge was built over the Shenandoah River. A rear guard, including the 2nd and 6th Virginia Cavalry and accompanying infantry, is left at Harrisonburg, but Jackson continues toward Port Republic on the north fork of the river. In the meantime, Union Major General John Frémont has reinitiated pursuit and General James Shields' Cavalry, on the eastern side of the river, is also giving chase. Also, at New Bridge, the 1st Maryland Light Artillery skirmishes with Confederates. The Union reports no casualties. The estimated Confederate casualties are two killed.

June 6 (Friday)   Naval Battle at Memphis, Tennessee A Union fleet, including gunboats, mortar boats and troop transports, commanded by Flag Officer Charles H. Davis, moves toward Memphis, which is lightly defended. Meanwhile, an order issued at 12:30

A.M. from General Beauregard places Brigadier General Jeff Thompson and Captain James Montgomery in joint command of the city's river defenses in anticipation of an attack. Davis' fleet is bolstered by the arrival of a separate fleet, composed of stern-wheel vessels, which had been constructed and commanded by Colonel Charles Ellet, Jr. The rams under Ellet are not part of the U.S. Navy and not under its jurisdiction. The fleet includes the *Lancaster, Monarch, Switzerland,* and *Queen of the West.* The ram *Lancaster,* a sidewheel steamer, had been purchased by Ellet for the War Department during the previous April. Ellet's fleet had been assembled to neutralize Confederate rams operating on the Mississippi River.

The Union fleet advances at the crack of dawn. Meanwhile, a Confederate flotilla under Captain James Montgomery moves out to defend the city and block passage of the armada; however, Montgomery's navy is not seasoned. Pilots had been transformed into officers and his fleet is outgunned, including weapons capable of firing from long range. The Confederates, aware of Davis's fleet, had no intelligence regarding Ellet's ram vessels, which had increased Davis' firepower, as well as the number of warships, the latter having jumped from five to nine, against Montgomery's eight vessels.

The Confederate gunboat *Little Rebel* is the first to challenge the approaching fleet. It swings into action and fires upon the point vessel, the *Cairo,* igniting a tenacious fast-moving one and one-half hour heated contest that involves incessant fire. Once fired upon, the *Little Rebel* becomes the center of attraction, Ellet's rams push forward to the front of Davis' gunboats to initiate the close-quartered battle. The *Queen of the West* engages the *Colonel Lovell* and heads directly for the vessel, then rams it to deliver an instant fatal blow. The *Colonel Lovell,* a wooden warship, is unable to withstand the crippling impact. The ship's timbers collapse and the vessel is inundated with water that renders it out of action. It starts to drift aimlessly and soon after sinks.

At about the same time, the *Queen of the West* becomes the recipient of Confederate retaliation. The *Beauregard* rams it with a powerful hit that inflicts severe damage that causes it to become unstable. It begins drifting toward the opposite shore, on the Arkansas bank of the river. All the while the guns of the other vessels continue to exchange fire. The Union fire inflicts more punishment upon the Confederate fleet. Both the *Little Rebel* and the *General Beauregard* sustain hits to their boilers, causing them to explode. The *Beauregard,* however, is

Colonel Charles Rivers Ellet (*Harper's Pictoral History of the Civil War,* 1896).

able to charge toward the ram USS *Monarch,* but misses the target and instead crashes into the Confederate vessel *Price,* which severs the wheelhouse of the latter and renders the ship disabled. It too is knocked out of the contest. The *Price* sinks by the Arkansas embankment of the river.

Meanwhile, the Union gunboats target the *Little Rebel,* which sustains a fatal hit when shells strike near the waterline and explode near the engines, leaving the men aboard little time to abandon the vessel, but the pilot is able to get it close to shore before it sinks. Captain Montgomery and Captain Fowler, both aboard the *Little Rebel,* make it to the Arkansas bank. All but about three crew members make it to the swamps and evade capture.

The remaining Confederate vessels, despite the insurmountable odds, continue to exchange fire as they simultaneously move downstream with the Union gunboats and Elliot's rams in hot pursuit. One of the remaining Confederate ships, the *Van Dorn,* laden with ammunition, disengages and speeds to Vicksburg rather than risk losing the cargo to the Union or the river. Meanwhile, the *Bragg* and the *Sumter* are both chased to shore, but an attempt to self-destroy the ships to prevent capture is unsuccessful. The *General Sumter* is afterward acquired by the U.S. Navy and commissioned the USS *Sumter.* In August the *Sumter* becomes stranded at Bayou Sara, Louisiana, and is abandoned. Also, the crew of another vessel, the CSS *Jeff Thompson,* is successful in destroying their ship to prevent its capture.

At the conclusion of the duel, the Confederates have lost every vessel except the *Earl Van Dorn* (Captain Isaac Fulkerson). The CSS *General Beauregard* (Captain J. Henry Hart) and *Colonel Lovell* (Captain James C. Dellaney) are sunk. The *General Sterling Price* (Capt. Thomas E. Henthorn) and the *Little Rebel* (Captain J.

General Frémont's division crosses a pontoon bridge at the Potomac River in pursuit of Confederate General Thomas "Stonewall" Jackson (Mottelay, *The Soldier in Our Civil War,* 1886).

White Fowler) are each run ashore and abandoned. The *General Bragg* (Captain W. H. H. Leonard) and the *Sumter* (Captain Wallace W. Lamb) are captured and the *Jeff Thompson* (Captain John Burk) runs ashore, burns and explodes, leaving remnants half submerged. The captured *General Bragg* is sent for repairs and commissioned the USS *General Bragg*. The *General Price* is salvaged and becomes the USS *General Price*. In addition, the *Little Rebel* is taken into Union service.

The Union, on or about this date, seizes a Rebel transport, the *New National*, and the transport *Victoria*, the latter having been built during 1858 at Elizabeth, Pennsylvania. The *Victoria* is separate from the steamer *Victoria* built at Mystic, Connecticut, in 1859. The steamer *Victoria* had been seized at New Orleans during January 1862 and afterward operated as a Confederate government blockade runner under the command of Captain Lambert. The blockade runner *Victoria* vanishes from the records after autumn of 1862; however, it does survive beyond the war and is lost during 1866.

The Union vessels that participate are the gunboats *Benton* (flagship, commanded by Lt. S.L. Phelps); *Cairo* (lieutenant commanding, N.C. Bryant); *St. Louis* (lieutenant commanding, Wilson McGunnegle); *Carondelet* (Commander Henry Walke); *Lioness* (Lt. Crandall); and *Louisville* (Commander B. Dove). Union Lt. Colonel Alfred W. Ellet and his brother Colonel Charles Ellet participate in this battle. Charles Ellet is mortally wounded and succumbs within a few days. Alfred becomes a brigadier general the following November. After the battle, the fleet moves into Memphis and two regiments led by Colonel G.N. Fitch occupy the city. Exact Confederate casualties are unknown. William Cable, the pilot of the *Colonel Lovell*, is killed during the battle.

The Union, later in the day, discovers and confiscates a few Confederate vessels in the harbor at Memphis. The ships include the *Victoria,* a side-wheel steamer built in Elizabeth, Pennsylvania, in 1858. The Confederate government had acquired it for use as a transport. The Union uses the *Victoria* primarily as a store-ship for Davis' flotilla until the organization (army, commanded by naval officers) is transferred to the U.S. Navy on 1 October. At that time the organization is renamed the Mississippi Squadron. Another transport, the *Kentucky,* is seized; however, the name *Kentucky* is in widespread use along the Mississippi and the U.S. Navy is unable to determine the origin of the vessel. The Union initiates action to transform it into a receiving ship at St. Louis; however, it is in poor condition. On 30 June the *Kentucky* is listed on a Navy report as having been returned to its owners. Also, the CSS *General Price,* now the USS *General Price,* was originally built at Cincinnati during 1861 as a towboat, the *Laurent Millaudon,* prior to serving as a ram in Confederate service.

In Kentucky, elements of the 9th Pennsylvania Cavalry led by Captain McCullough and Lt. Langsdorf clash with Confederates at Tompkinsville. The Union sustains one killed and four wounded. Confederate casualties are unavailable.

In Mississippi, a contingent of Union Cavalry (Colonel Sheridan's 2nd Michigan) initiates a reconnaissance mission at Boonesville that moves toward Baldwin. One trooper is wounded.

In Virginia, a Union reconnaissance force, composed of a detachment of the 1st New Jersey Cavalry under Colonel Percy Wyndham, encounters what is thought to be a small Confederate force in the vicinity of Harrisonburg. The Union engages the Rebels and pursues them into the nearby woods, where the Confederates have laid a cunning trap. Wyndham's troops suddenly find themselves encircled, and despite a gallant effort, they are unable to fight their way out of the woods. The Confederates take more than sixty prisoners, including Colonel Wyndham. In the meantime, other Union troops under General Bayard and Colonel Gustave Paul Cluseret arrive and encounter the Confederates as they are moving back with their prisoners.

A grueling skirmish breaks out and soon more Rebels, a brigade of General Stewart, arrives. The two sides club each other for several more hours until the Confederates are forced to retire into a nearby pine. Still the confrontation continues, as toward evening about 125 troops of Colonel Kane's Bucktail Rifles (42nd Pennsylvania Volunteer Regiment) enter the forest to seek their prey. Instead, the Rebels turn the Yankees into the prey and spring yet another ambush. Similarly to Wyndham's force, the Rebels close the clamps, but just before they become entirely encircled, the Bucktails fight their way out, despite being engaged by about four separate regiments. Following a vicious night fight and losing six men killed and 46 either wounded or missing, the Bucktails reach safety. The regimental commander, Colonel Thomas Kane, is among those missing; he is taken prisoner. On 7 September, Colonel Kane is appointed a brigadier general and assigned to the XII Corps, and afterward participates at the Battle of Chancellorsville in command of a brigade. Confederate General Turner Ashby, the commander of Jackson's cavalry, is killed during this action while heroically leading his troops. Ashby is buried in Lexington, Virginia, near his commander, Stonewall Jackson.

June 7 (Saturday) In Louisiana, subsequent to a court martial, Francis Mumford, convicted of taking the U.S. flag down from its staff at the U.S. mint and defacing it, along with other charges, including inciting trouble within the city of New Orleans, is executed by hanging following his arrest, trial and conviction as a traitor, by order of General Benjamin Butler. Mumford, originally from North Carolina, at the time of the Union occupation of New Orleans was a resident of the city. The incident leads to protests by General Robert E. Lee in communications with General Halleck. Confederate President Jefferson Davis issues a proclamation on 23 December 1862 declaring "that all commissioned officers in the command of said Benjamin F. Butler be declared not entitled to be considered as soldiers engaged in honorable warfare, but as robbers and criminals, deserving death; and that they and each of them be, whenever captured, reserved for execution."

In Tennessee, the 30th Illinois and 78th Ohio Regiments, commanded by Colonels Elias S. Dennis and Mortimer D. Leggett respectively, seize the town of Jackson. Meanwhile, a Union contingent (General James S. Negley's command), commanded by Colonel Henry A. Hambright, launches an attack against Confederate-held Chattanooga. The Yankees attack again on the following day. The Confederates, however, hold Chattanooga. In other activity, a contingent of the Confederate 2nd Tennessee Cavalry, commanded by Colonel Starnes, skirmishes with Union troops at Readyville. The Union sustains some killed and captured. Confederate casualty figures, if any, are unavailable. Leggett, a lawyer, was a civilian aide to his friend General George McClellan before being commissioned colonel of the 78th Ohio during January 1862.

In Virginia, three companies of the 4th New Jersey Volunteer Regiment, commanded by Lt. Colonel Hatch, begin moving beyond the east bank of the Chickahominy River on a reconnaissance mission. Another Union contingent, including the 85th and 92nd New York Volunteer Regiments, augmented by one company of cavalry commanded by Captain Gary, initiates a reconnaissance mission on the New Market Road. The Confederates are in retreat.

June 8 (Sunday) BATTLE OF CROSS KEYS General Jackson's main body, while his rear guard has been engaged with Union troops under General George D. Bayard outside of

Union forces under General Frémont move through the woods in pursuit of Confederates (Mottelay, *The Soldier in Our Civil War,* 1886).

Harrisonburg, Virginia, pushes on toward Port Republic with other Union troops on his heels. General John Frémont intercepts the retiring Confederate force. Frémont attacks the three rear-guard brigades, those of Generals George H. Steuart, Arnold Elzey and Isaac R. Trimble, before they can cross the north fork of the Shenandoah River. The Rebels hold positions along a ridge that overlooks Cross Keys (Union Church). The forces of Generals Julius Stahel (Stahl), Robert C. Schenck and Robert H. Milroy charge up the slopes against steadfast resistance, but still they advance while receiving a solid dose of shot and shell that inflicts heavy casualties.

Nevertheless, this assault, which had begun during the morning of what began as a tranquil Sunday, is maintained without pause throughout the afternoon. As the casualties continue to spiral to a dangerously high point, the Confederates still hold absolute control of the ridge. Finally, after more than 600 casualties, the Yankees disengage. In the meantime, General Thomas J. "Stonewall" Jackson reaches Port Republic, but at about the same time, a contingent of General James Shields' force, commanded by General Samuel S. Carroll, arrives at the fringes of the town. Some minor skirmishes occur, but the main clash occurs on the following morning.

The 1st and 27th Pennsylvania, 1st Ohio Battery, and the 2nd, 3rd, 5th and 8th West Virginia units participate. The Union has 67 killed, 361 wounded and 574 missing. Confederates have 88 dead, 535 wounded and 34 missing. Confederate Generals Arnold Elzey (West Point, 1837) and George Hume Steuart (1848) are wounded. General Elzey remains on sick leave for an extended time. The 1st Virginia Partisan Rangers (62nd Virginia Mounted Infantry) led by Captain (later brigadier general John D. Imboden participate at this action, as does the 25th Virginia Infantry (Ewell's Division). General Louis Blenker and Colonel Gustave Paul Cluseret also participate at the Battle of Cross Keys. Cluseret, due to his actions at this engagement, is promoted to brigadier general in October.

In Arizona at Tucson, General James H. Carleton, the military governor of the recently established Arizona Territory (formerly part of the New Mexico Territory), issues a proclamation declaring the territory as "all the country eastward from the Colorado river, which is now occupied by the forces of the United States, known as the 'Column from California.' And as the flag of the United States shall be carried by this column still further eastward, these limits will extend in that direction until they reach the furthest geographical boundary of the territory." Martial law is proclaimed, effective throughout the territory.

In South Carolina, a Union contingent commanded by Colonel J.H. Morrow, which includes eight Union gunboats and some ground forces, initiates a reconnaissance mission on James Island. The Union sustains two killed and about seven wounded. Confederate casualty figures, if any, are unavailable.

In Naval activity, Admiral Farragut's fleet, below Vicksburg, advances up the Mississippi and encounters heavy enemy fire from Confederate batteries. The ships' advance is covered by fire from the mortar schooners. While the gunboats and the mortar schooners exchange fire, the advance succeeds in passing the batteries, while sustaining only minor damage. On 30 June, Flag Officer Davis' Western Flotilla links with Farragut's force at a point above Vicksburg; however, the naval forces lack the strength in ground forces to seize Vicksburg. With regard to the offensive, Admiral Porter states: "Ships cannot crawl up hills 300 feet high, and it is that part of Vicksburg which must be taken by the Army." In other activity, the USS *Penobscot,* on patrol off Shallotte Inlet, North Carolina, spots a grounded schooner, the *Sereta.* The schooner is discovered to be abandoned. It is then destroyed.

June 9 (Monday) BATTLE OF PORT REPUBLIC Following the battle at Cross Keys on the previous day, General Thomas "Stonewall" Jackson marched his main body to Port Republic; however, one division (Richard S. Ewell's) had been directed to remain at the scene to impede any advance by Frémont against Jackson's new positions. Jackson, after arriving at Port Republic, prepares plans to strike the lines of Union General Shields at Lewis' farm, just outside Port Republic. Nonetheless, on this day, Union troops, about 3,000 strong, attached to Major General John Frémont, advance against about 6,000 Confederates under "Stonewall" Meanwhile, Ewell's command arrives to bolster Jackson. On the night of 8 June at about 2200, Colonel John D. Imboden receives a message from Jackson directing him to depart the area of Mount Crawford Cross Keys and repair to Port Republic with his cavalry battalion, four howitzers and his Parrott gun. At the time he received the message, Imboden had been deployed to protect Jackson's flank. His contingent arrives at Port Republic prior to dawn to further augment Jackson's strength.

Meanwhile, General Jackson, fully clothed and wearing his sword and boots, is awakened by Iboden. After a short, friendly discussion, Jackson accepts Iboden's congratulations on the victory of the previous day and replies: "Yes, God blessed our army again yesterday, and I hope with his protection and blessing we shall do still better to-day." Jackson then adds: "We move at dawn. Charles Winder [brigadier general commanding his old Stonewall brigade] will cross the river at daybreak and attack Shields on the Lewis farm [two miles below]. I shall support him with all

the other troops as fast as they can be put in line. General Richard Taylor will move through the woods on the side of the mountain with his Louisiana brigade, and rush upon their left flank by the time the action becomes general. By 10 o'clock we shall get them on the run."

General Winder's force launches the attack. Waves of Confederate troops pound against the flank, but the equally determined Yankees under Shields stand steadfastly, and the assault is repelled. Immediately thereafter, the Union launches a counterattack that drives the Confederates under Winder into the woods. Meanwhile, the contingent under General Richard Taylor has not yet emerged from the woods as expected, causing problems for the Confederates; however, Jackson is informed of the crisis as Union pressure builds against Winder. Jackson locates his former brigade, which had given some ground. As he rides into their position, rousing cheers greet him as he bellows: "The Stonewall brigade never retreats; follow me!" At about the same time, Taylor finally leads his force from the woods and shortly thereafter, the Confederates are back on the offensive.

The Rebels mount a dual assault that pounds the flank and the center, all the while under the effective support of artillery fire. The massive force of the assault pushes the Union forces back and in the process, due to the heavy losses of horses, only one of nine guns is removed from the field. While the Yankees retire, the cavalry of General Samuel S. Carroll protects the rear. Once General Erastus B. Tyler's forces cross the river, the bridge is set afire to delay Jackson. However, still the Confederates press the faltering Union units and pursuit begins as the Union retires to Harrisonburg.

Meanwhile, the thunderous sounds of the battle had prompted Union General John Frémont to quicken the pace of his force, which arrives to bolster Tyler. The Union retires to Harrisonburg, reaching it later this night. From there, Frémont moves to Mount Harrison and General James Shields moves out for New Market. Confederate General Stonewall Jackson es-

Frémont's dragoons cook in the camp kitchen (Mottelay, *The Soldier in Our Civil War,* 1886).

tablishes camp at Weyer's Cave, where he remains until the 17th. The Union loses 88 dead, 361 wounded and 574 missing. The Confederates sustain 87 dead, 535 wounded and 34 missing. The Union 7th, 29th, and 66th Ohio, the 84th and 110th Pennsylvania, the 7th Indiana, 1st West Virginia, and the 4th U.S. Artillery participate in this action. The 25th Virginia Infantry also participates. Also, General Robert E. Lee receives a telegram informing him of Jackson's victory at Port Republic. This good military news is offset when Lee receives word of the death of his grandson (daughter-in-law Charlotte's son).

In the 35 days since General Stonewall Jackson's arrival at Staunton, his forces fought four battles and emerged as the victor in each. In the process, his army marched from Staunton to McDowell, from there to Front Royal, then to Winchester and from there to Port Republic, covering just under 250 miles. The Battle of Port Republic culminates Jackson's Shenandoah Campaign. He departs Port Republic on 17 June.

In Maryland, Major General John E. Wool becomes commander of the Middle Military Department. He succeeds Major General John A. Dix. General Wool holds the post until 22 December of this year.

In Mississippi, Admiral David Farragut's fleet continues toward Vicksburg. This day, he encounters some Confederate activity in Gulfport. Farragut leaves a small force there and pushes on, arriving at Vicksburg on the 26th. In related activity, gunboats, including the USS *Itasca* and *Wissahickon*, exchange fire with Confederate batteries at Grand Gulf. Also, a Union force that includes the 2nd Iowa and the 2nd Michigan Cavalry, commanded by Colonel (later general) Philip Sheridan, reconnoiters the area around Baldwin.

In Tennessee, the CSS *General Pillow* (Gunboat No. 20), initially the Confederate steamer *B.M. Moore,* is captured by the USS *Pittsburg* on the Hatchee River in Tennessee. The *General Pillow* is transferred by the War Department to the U.S. Navy, where it serves with the light draft squadron that operates on the Cumberland and Tennessee Rivers. Subsequent to receiving repairs at Cairo, Illinois, the USS *General Pillow* departs on 23 August to join the Mississippi Squadron. In February 1863, the *General Pillow* returns to Cairo and is assigned duty as a guard for ammunition barges and mortar ships. During July 1865, it is decommissioned and afterward, on 26 November 1865, it is sold.

In Union general officer activity, Colonel Julius White is promoted to brigadier general. He had initially joined the service as colonel of the 37th Illinois Regiment (known also as the Frémont Rifles) during the early days of the war. Union General David Bell Birney, accused of disobeying an order during the battle of Seven Pines and acquitted at a court-martial, regains his command (a brigade in General Kearny's Division, III Corps); Birney will command in

a major contest again at Chantilly during September. Also, Major Charles Griffin is promoted to the rank of brigadier general, as is Colonel Stephen G, Burbridge (Volunteers). Griffin is assigned to the V Corps with command of a brigade. Afterward, he commands a division at Fredericksburg (December 1862).

In Confederate general officer activity, Colonel Beverly H. Robertson is promoted to the rank of brigadier general effective this date. He will serve under General Jeb Stuart in Virginia, followed by some service in North Carolina before arriving back in Virginia before the Army of Northern Virginia advances toward Pennsylvania.

June 10 (Tuesday)   In Mississippi, Union detachments of Generals John Pope and Don Carlos Buell return to Corinth. Although the Union has not caught the retreating forces of General Beauregard, the Confederates are pushed out of western Tennessee. On this day, Buell departs Corinth with the Army of the Ohio, taking the Memphis Charleston Railroad, heading for Chattanooga and Nashville.

In Tennessee, a skirmish develops between Union and Confederate troops at Winchester. Specific units are unreported. Also, the 42nd Ohio Volunteer Regiment commanded by Lt. Colonel Pardee clashes with Confederates at Roger's Gap and Wilson's Gap. Casualty figures are unavailable.

In South Carolina, Union troops at James Island attack Confederate positions in the vicinity of Secessionville and capture the earthworks there. In turn, the Confederates launch artillery shells into the Union lines of General Horatio G. Wright and against the accompanying gunboats. The gunboats are unable to return fire, as they are out of range. During the afternoon, the Rebels attack the Union lines, but they are in turn received by a vigorous bayonet attack. The Confederates bring up additional artillery and the Union is compelled to pull back. During the day's fighting, the Union sustains three killed and 13 wounded in addition to the 20 captured during the morning. The Confederates sustain 17 killed and 30 wounded. By day's end, the Confederates place the artillery to the front of General Isaac Stevens' Camp.

In Virginia, General McClellan's naval force is positioned at White House on the Pamunkey (former home of Martha Washington, which had been inherited by Rooney Lee, the son of Robert E. Lee). McClellan's troops are positioned east to northeast of Richmond with some warships close enough to give assistance. The Chickahominy separates General Fitz John Porter's Corps from the main Union force.

In Naval activity, following its return to Port Royal and a short mission to the St. Johns River in Florida to deliver supplies and provisions to blockaders on patrol, the *Western World* on this day departs Port Royal to begin patrols off Georgetown, South Carolina.

June 11 (Wednesday)   In the Arizona Territory, Acting Assistant Adjutant General Ben-

jamin C. Cutler is appointed secretary of state of the new territory. Three days earlier, General James H. Carleton, at Tucson, proclaimed martial law. In other activity, General Carleton sends another rider to reach General Canby in New Mexico with a message:

I had the honor to write to you on the 3d ultimo [3 May] from Fort Yuma, Cal., that I was on my way to Arizona, and desired to co-operate with you in driving the rebels from New Mexico. My messenger was unable to reach you via the Salinas Fork of the Gila on account of high water. I therefore dispatch another through Mexican territory. I am ordered to recapture all the works in New Mexico which had been surrendered to rebels. This I shall proceed to do, starting from here as soon as the rains have filled the natural tanks, say early in July. What number of troops can find subsistence, say at twenty days notice at Mesilla and Fort Bliss, in Texas? I can start from here with sixty days' supply for one battery of artillery, one regiment of infantry and five companies of cavalry. With this force I desire to co-operate with you. This will enable me to hold this country besides....

In Kentucky, a Union contingent, including Captain Blood's Mounted Provost Guards, plus the 13th Indiana Battery commanded by Captain Ben S. Nicklin, engage and defeat the Confederates at Monterey (Montgomery), Owen County, Kentucky. The Union has two dead; the Confederates have about 100 captured. A contemporary reports notes only about 25 Confederates captured.

In Virginia, Robert E. Lee orders Jeb Stuart to circumvent McClellan's Army of the Potomac, gaining his rear, and to destroy Union wagon trains. Lee also speeds reinforcements to Jackson to aid his opposition to McClellan. In a letter to Confederate Secretary of War George W. Randolph, Lee requests "that Randolf use his influence to prevent any mention of Confederate troop movements."

In Tennessee, elements of the 3rd, 5th and 6th Tennessee Volunteer Regiments, commanded by Brigadier James Gallant Spears, skirmish with Confederates at Big Creek Gap this day and the next. The Union reports no casualties. Confederate casualties are estimated at two killed and three captured.

In Union general officer activity, Union Colonel W.L. Elliott, who had commanded the first Union cavalry charge of the conflict at Corinth against the Mobile and Ohio Railroad, is appointed brigadier general, effective this day. Also, Albion Parris Howe (West Point, 1841), a veteran of the Mexican War, is named brigadier general effective this date. He participates as a brigade commander (IV Corps) and afterward commands the 2nd Division at Fredericksburg, Virginia. In autumn of 1863, after the fighting at Gettysburg, General Howe is stripped of field command. He receives command of the artillery depot and the Office of the Inspector of Artillery at the capital. He remains at the post until 1866. Despite the unexplained removal from the field, General Howe receives the brevets of brigadier general and major general in the Volunteers and the U.S. Army.

June 12 (Thursday)   In Arkansas, a contingent of the 9th Illinois Cavalry, commanded by Colonel Brackett, engages Confederates at Waddell's Farm in the vicinity of Village Creek. The Union sustains 12 wounded. The Confederates sustain 28 killed or wounded.

In South Carolina at James Island, Union General David Hunter returns to Port Royal, leaving General H.W. Benham in command of the two divisions under Generals H.G. Wright and Isaac Stevens. His instructions mandate that no assault be launched; rather the defenses are to be bolstered to repel any assault that might be launched by the Confederates.

In Virginia, Union troops occupy Mount Jackson.

June 12–13   In Virginia, General George Archibald McCall (West Point, 1822), a Philadelphian, arrives in Virginia to reinforce the Army of the Potomac. McCall's Division (Pennsylvania Reserves) will act as vanguard of General Porter's V Corps (McClellan's command) during the upcoming clash with Confederates at the Chickahominy.

In Union general officer activity, Zealous Bates Tower (West Point, 1841) is appointed brigadier general, his rank effective from 23 November 1861. Tower, a veteran of the Mexican War, performed his first service during this conflict as chief engineer at Fort Pickens, Florida. He participates at various actions in the North, including Second Manassas (Bull Run), Thoroughfare Gap and Cedar Mountain.

June 13 (Friday)   In South Carolina, a skirmish occurs on James Island. The Union sustains three killed and ten wounded. The Confederates suffer nineteen killed and six wounded.

In Virginia, at Old Church near Turnstall Station, a contingent of the U.S. 5th Cavalry clashes with units of Stuart's Confederate cavalry. The Union sustains no casualties. The Confederates sustain one killed. In conjunction, the Confederate cavalry, composed of the 1st, 4th and 9th Virginia Cavalry, Jeff Davis' Legion and four pieces of artillery participate. The Rebels also burn fourteen wagons and two schooners at Garlick's Landing on the Pamunkey River, and they capture 165 Union troops and 260 horses and mules, while harassing the Army of the Potomac.

June 14 (Saturday)   In Virginia, near Turnstall Station, Confederates fire into a railway train inflicting casualties. Four men are killed and eight others are wounded.

In Naval activity, the Union gunboat *Mound City* and the tug *Spitfire* combine to seize the *Clara Dolsen,* a side-wheel steamer, on the White River during the ongoing St. Charles expedition. The *Clara Dolsen* is not taken into U.S. service; however, it does participate in operations in Kentucky during July 1862. After-

ward it sails to Cairo, Illinois. Later, during April 1864, the *Clara Dolsen* is returned to its owners.

June 15 (Sunday) In Alabama at about this time, the state acquires the *Baltic,* a side-wheel ironclad ram. The vessel, built in Philadelphia during 1860 for use as a river towboat, is transformed into a warship and transferred to the Confederate States Navy. Nonetheless, the *Baltic* is deemed unseaworthy by the early part of 1863. The armor is removed and by July 1864 the *Baltic* is dismantled. In May 1865, the hull is seized in Alabama on the Tombigbee River by the Union and sold the following December.

In Arizona, General James H. Carleton, at Tucson, in an effort to get word to General Canby in New Mexico that the California Column is en route and close to arriving to reinforce him, sends riders on the mission. Expressman John Jones and Sergeant Wheeling (Company F, 1st California Infantry), escorted by a Mexican guide named Chaves, set out this day; however, the route takes the contingent through dangerous territory. On the third day out, the party is attacked by Apaches and in the struggle Wheeling and Chaves both are killed. Nonetheless, John Jones escapes death and capture. He resumes the trip and evades the Apaches; however, he is afterward intercepted and captured by Confederates near the Rio Grande River in the vicinity of Pichaco, New Mexico, close to La Messilla (later Messilla). The Confederates confiscate Jones' dispatches and Jones is taken to the headquarters of Colonel (later brigadier general) William Steele, a native New Yorker. Steele learns of the imminent arrival of Carleton's force and places Jones under confinement in a jail. Nonetheless, Jones is somehow able to smuggle word to General Canby of Carleton's imminent arrival at the Rio Grande.

General Frémont's headquarters at Mount Jackson (Mottelay, *The Soldier in Our Civil War,* 1886).

Canby has been awaiting the reinforcements; but it was thought that the arrival of the column was improbable.

In Tennessee, contingents of the Union 3rd, 5th and 6th Tennessee Volunteer Regiments, commanded by Colonel Leonidas C. Houk, engages Confederates at Big Creek Gap. Casualty figures are unavailable.

In Virginia, Confederate cavalry under General J.E.B. Stuart terminates its raids that began on June 13 and included clashes at Garlick's Landing, Hawes' Shop and Old Church (see also, **June 13 In Virginia**). It is reported that the Confederates capture a large amount of Union troops during this mission. Also, contingents of the 73rd New York Infantry skirmish with Confederates in the vicinity of Seven Pines.

In Naval activity, the USS *Somerset* returns to the area in the vicinity of Way Key, Florida, where it had engaged a Confederate battery during the previous month. A detachment from the ship lands and destroys the battery. On the following day, the *Somerset,* while operating on patrol near Cedar Keys, encounters and seizes a blockade runner, the schooner *Curlew.*

June 16 (Monday) BATTLE OF SECESSIONVILLE In South Carolina at James Island, the Union under General Isaac Stevens — with support from General H.G. Wright, who moves on his left with an additional 3,000 troops to provide protection to the flank — launches a pre-dawn assault against Confederates; how-

Battle of Secessionville, James Island, South Carolina (Johnson, *Campfire and Battlefield: History of the Conflicts and Campaigns,* 1894).

Lt. Colonel David Morrison (79th New York) crashes into the tower battery at James Island and enters the fort (Mottelay, *The Soldier in Our Civil War*, 1886).

ever, inadvertently the jump off time is delayed and the attack against Fort Johnson does not begin until after dawn. The Confederates effortlessly turn back nearly every attacking regiment. Only the 8th Michigan and 79th New York Regiments make it through the hurricane of shot and shell to reach the fortifications. Contingents of these two units, with the effective use of their bayonets, gain the parapet and drive the Rebels from the guns. One contingent, led by Lt. Colonel David Morrison (79th New York), breaks through the tower battery and enters the fort, but lacking sufficient strength, it is compelled to withdraw. Support troops under Colonel Robert Williams move to bolster Stevens, but complications develop as the column gets lost in the woods and comes under a severe unsuspected attack which catches the force in a cross fire.

The situation deteriorates and the Rebels have the Union trapped with little chance of escape. Nevertheless, the instinct for survival kicks in and the inevitable is forestalled. Contingents of two regiments, the 3rd New Hampshire and the 3rd Rhode Island, mount a desperate but tenacious bayonet attack led by Colonel Robert Williams which drives the Confederates from the woods, preventing the capture of the entire force. The regiments, despite having put the guns in the fort's towers out of the fight, are unable to storm the earthworks due to the lack of reinforcements.

Meanwhile, two Confederate Regiments arrive from Fort Johnson. By this time the Union, having faced a much smaller force, has sustained more than 700 casualties, and still the U.S. gunboats remain too far out to offer support. The attack is aborted and it is later determined that the strongly defended fort could not have been taken without an enormous amount of additional troops. Fort Johnson is protected not only by a large force, but it has a ditch to its front that contains about seven feet of water and a parapet of about seven feet high. The Confed-

erates commanded by General N. Evans also take heavy losses while repelling the Union assault by units of the 46th, 47th, and 79th New York, the 3rd Rhode Island, 45th and 97th Pennsylvania and the 1st Massachusetts.

Although Evans is in overall command, the action, including that of the Confederate cavalry, had primarily occurred at James Island (Fort Lamar), Secessionville, by a 500-man force commanded by Confederate Colonel J.G. Lamar Benjamin, which although outnumbered, holds off over 6,000 Union attackers. The Union sustains 85 killed, 472 wounded and 138 missing. The Confederates suffer 51 killed and 144 wounded. This Confederate victory prevents the Union from capturing Charleston, South Carolina, and forces it to withdraw. Confederate Brigadier General William Duncan Smith, commanding officer of the Department of South Carolina, also participates in this action; he leads an attack. General Smith is to succeed General John C. Pemberton; however, sudden illness strikes Smith and he succumbs during October.

First Sgt. Frederick Jackson of the 7th Connecticut Infantry receives the Medal of Honor for gallantry during this action. Union General Henry W. Benham is relieved of command after this unsuccessful assault and replaced by General David Hunter. Benham subsequently commands the engineering brigade of the Army of the Potomac. Benham's commission as brigadier general is also revoked, but President Lincoln countermands the revocation. Both General Stevens and General Horatio Wright had been opposed to this attack, due to their contention that the fort could not be taken with their available strength.

The Union 46th, 47th, and 79th New York, 3rd Rhode Island, 3rd New Hampshire, 45th, 97th and 100th Pennsylvania, 6th and 7th Connecticut, 8th Michigan and 28th Massachusetts Regiments participate. In addition, the 1st New York Engineers, 1st Connecticut Artillery, Battery E of the 3rd U.S. Artillery, Battery I of 3rd Rhode Island Artillery, and Company H, 1st Massachusetts Cavalry, are involved. After the Battle of Secessionville, General Wright is transferred to Department of the Ohio, where he remains until May of 1863, when he is ordered to depart Cincinnati for the East. He participates at Gettysburg in July 1863. General Wright is promoted to the rank of major general effective this day, but the Senate rejects the appointment on 12 March 1863.

In Arkansas, the Confederate transport *Mary Patterson* and two other vessels, the *Eliza G.* and

the *Maurepas*, are intentionally sunk along the White River in the vicinity of St. Charles to impede the progress of Union warships.

In Confederate general officer activity, Brigadier General Humphrey Marshall resigns his commission. However, several days later, he is reappointed a brigadier effective 30 October 1861, the date of his initial commission. He later serves in Kentucky with General Bragg, but he again resigns during June of the following year.

June 17 (Tuesday)   In Arizona at Tucson, General James H. Carleton designates Colonel Edward E. Eyre as commander of the vanguard that will depart Tucson on 21 June on the mission to repair to the New Mexico to link up with General Canby's forces. Carleton's order reads:

COLONEL: It is important that a forced reconnaissance be made in advance of the column [California Column] from the Rio Grande, and you are selected for this delicate and at the same time hazardous duty. You will take with you for this purpose a squadron of your regiment to be composed of all the effective officers and men of Companies B and C now here. For transportation you will have three mule teams. Take six aparejos in the wagons for packing purposes when necessary. Take, say, four days' pork, and dried beef and pemmican, and flour, coffee, sugar, salt, and vinegar for thirty days. Take 70 rounds of ammunition for the Sharp's carbines per man and 30 rounds per man of navy-revolver ammunition. You should have at least six pick-axes and 12 long handled shovels as intrenching tools. Acting Assistant Surgeon Kittredge will accompany you.

In Arkansas, Union gunboats and Confederate artillery duel at St. Charles, White River. Contingents of the 43rd and 46th Indiana Regiments supported by the gunboats *Lexington, Mound City, Conestoga* and *St. Louis* engage Confederates and subsequently occupy the fort. The Union forces are commanded by Flag Officer C.H. Davis and Colonel Graham Fitch. The Confederates suffer 155 killed and 144 wounded. The Union forces sustain over 100 killed and many wounded when a boiler aboard the USS *Mound City* explodes, but the vessel survives and later participates in operations along the Yazoo River, the Vicksburg Campaign and the Grand Gulf Campaign. In 1864, the *Mound City* participates in the Red River Campaign. Also, a skirmish develops at Smithville. The Union suffers two killed and four wounded. The Confederates sustain four wounded and fifteen captured.

In Missouri, at Warrensburg, the 7th Missouri Cavalry (Militia) skirmishes with Confederates and sustains two killed and two wounded. Confederate casualties are unavailable.

In Virginia, Union Major General John Pope replaces Major General John Frémont as commander of Frémont's Corps, Army of Virginia. Frémont resigns from the Army rather than serve under General John Pope, who assumes command of the Army of Virginia. Also, Confederate General Thomas J. "Stonewall" Jackson departs his positions at Weyer's Cave in the vicinity of Port Republic and moves toward Richmond to augment General Robert E. Lee. Jackson, however, directs part of his force to remain at Port Republic, including the cavalry under Brigadier General Beverly H. Robertson, Chew's battery and a small contingent under Colonel Imboden, while he advances toward Richmond. The Union does not detect Jackson's departure from the valley.

In Union general officer activity, Ranald Slidell Mackenzie graduates from West Point as a 2nd lieutenant (later brigadier general) and is assigned to the engineers. Mackenzie's father is the brother of the Confederate minister John Slidell, but he added Mackenzie to his name, apparently to honor his maternal uncle. Confederate general Pierre Beauregard, who for a short while was Mackenzie's commanding officer at West Point, is related to him through marriage. Beauregard married the sister of John Slidell's wife as his second wife.

June 18 (Wednesday) In Arkansas, a Union contingent skirmishes with a Confederate force at Smithville. The Union reports two killed and four wounded. The Confederates sustain four wounded and 15 captured. Specific units are not reported.

In Florida, Union and Confederate units clash at Tallahassee. Casualty figures and specific units are unavailable.

In Missouri, the 7th Missouri Cavalry (Militia) skirmishes with a contingent of Confederates at Warrensburg.

In Tennessee, Confederate troops assault Union positions at Cumberland Gap. The Union force, commanded by General George W. Morgan, is thrown back, causing the Yankees to withdraw toward the Ohio River. Colonel Joseph A. Cooper, 6th Tennessee, participates at this battle. Cooper (brigadier general, July 1864), before retreating, has his outfit reorganized with new equipment and sets out for Murfreesboro, where they engage in heavy skirmishing at the end of the year. Also, a Union contingent skirmishes with Confederates at Wilson's Gap. Casualty figures and specific units are unavailable.

In Virginia, 16th Massachusetts Regiment encounters and skirmishes with Confederate contingents, including the 2nd and 3rd South Carolina Regiments commanded by Colonel James D. Nance, on the Williamsburg Road. The Union sustains seven killed and 57 wounded. The Confederates sustain five killed and nine wounded. Also, a Union force commanded by Colonel Powell Wyman and composed of elements of the 16th Massachusetts Volunteer Regiment, bolstered by artillery (Captain Bramhall's battery), skirmishes with Confederates at Fair Oaks (Seven Pines). It is reported that the Union loses about 16 killed and 28 wounded. The Confederates sustain about 39 killed and 15 captured.

In other activity, Confederate General Robert E. Lee orders General Theophilus H. Holmes to move his force from Goldsboro, North Carolina, to Virginia to neutralize the Union threat of Union General Ambrose Burnside at Petersburg. Holmes arrives at Petersburg on the 21st, assuming command of the department between the James and Cape Fear Rivers.

June 19 (Thursday) In Minnesota, a Union force, including contingents of Company C, 5th Minnesota Volunteers, commanded by Lt. T.J. Sheehan, departs Fort Ripley for Fort Ridgely to join Company B, which had moved there in March. Sheehan's contingent arrives at Fort Ridgely on June 28.

In New York, the Sisters of Charity responds to another call to nurse wounded soldiers. A party of eleven nuns and a chaplain, Father Bruhl, a Hungarian, depart for Beaufort, North Carolina, on 16 July and upon their arrival, they are treated extremely well by the commander, General John Foster. They embark on the USS *Catawba,* which is also transporting about 500 horses for the cavalry. They arrive at Beaufort during a summer rainstorm and the nuns, each dressed in their black habits, were spotted as they debarked and walked toward the hospital. Some of the wounded troops observe the nine women in black and initially it was thought that they were nine widows, seeking the bodies of their husbands. Two of the nuns die while in Beaufort treating the wounded, and most of the others become seriously ill, but survive. Initially, the nuns are looked upon with skepticism and worse. The steward at the hospital later stated that he remained awake on stakeout observing the nuns in case they tried to "poison the patients, or do some other terrible thing, they being confessed emissaries of the Pope." The nuns took care of Union and Confederate soldiers and eventually, as in other locations, they earn great respect. Often they become attached to the troops, writing letters for them to their families and wrestling them out of periods of melancholy. One prominent Confederate, President Jefferson Davis, subsequent to the war while speaking with a group of the Catholic nuns (Sisters of Mercy), states: "Will you allow me, ladies, to speak a moment with you. I am proud to see you once more. I cannot forget your kindness to the sick and wounded in our darkest days, and I know not how to testify my gratitude and respect for every member of your noble order."

In Virginia, a Union contingent of the 20th Indiana Infantry Regiment skirmishes with Confederates along the Charles City Road. The Union reports three wounded. Confederate casualty figures are unavailable.

In Confederate general officer activity, Confederate Lt. Colonel Bryan Grimes, 4th North Carolina Infantry, is promoted to the rank of colonel. His regiment serves in the brigade of General George B. Anderson, the former commander of the regiment.

June 20 (Friday) In the Dakota Territory, Union contingents, including Company D, 5th Minnesota Volunteer Infantry, skirmish with Confederates at Fort Abercrombie.

In Virginia, Union and Confederate artillery units exchange blows at New Bridge. The Union participants include Battery B, 1st New York Light Artillery, and Battery I, 5th U.S. Artillery, commanded by Captain Adolph Voegelee and Captain S. Weed respectively. The Union sustains one wounded. The estimated Confederate casualty figures are two killed and four wounded. Also, at Gill's Bluff, Union and Confederate contingents clash. Specific units and casualty figures are unavailable.

June 21 (Saturday) In Arizona, Lt. Colonel Eyre, attached to General James H. Carleton's "California Column," departs Tucson leading a large reconnaissance force toward the Rio Grande to reinforce General Canby in New Mexico. The march is intensive and the column arrives at the river on 4 July.

In Louisiana, the Union initiates the advance to seize Vicksburg. The force is carried from Baton Rouge by vessels that are escorted by gunboats attached to Admiral David Farragut's command. The ground force is commanded by Brigadier General Thomas Williams.

In Mississippi, Confederate defenders at Vicksburg under General Earl Van Dorn, anticipating a Union assault, continue to fortify their positions around the city.

In South Carolina, a Union contingent composed of one company of the 51st Pennsylvania Volunteers, commanded by Lt. A.C. Rhind, U.S. Navy, and the gunboats *Crusader* and *Planter* clash with Confederates at Simon's Bluff. Casualty figures are unavailable.

In Tennessee, Union and Confederate forces clash at Battle Creek. The Union force, commanded by Colonel (later brigadier general) Joshua W. Sill, includes the 2nd and 33rd Ohio, 10th Wisconsin, 24th Illinois, 4th Kentucky Cavalry, 4th Ohio Cavalry and some artillery (Edgerton's Battery). The Union sustains four killed and three wounded. Confederate casualty figures are unavailable.

In Virginia, a Union contingent clashes with Confederate pickets at Fair Oaks Station. Specific units are not reported.

In Naval activity, in South Carolina, Lt. Rhind, aboard the gunboat USS *Crusader,* leads a mission that includes the transport USS *Planter.* The vessels attached to the Blockading Squadron advance to Simmons Bluff, Wadmelaw River. A contingent of the 55th Pennsylvania Regiment debarks and launches a surprise raid against a Confederate camp for troops (16th South Carolina Infantry) working on the Charleston and Savannah Railroad at Charleston. The Confederates in the camp, unprepared for a fight, retire without raising resistance. The Union destroys the camp and wastes no time getting back to the ships. No casualties occur on either side. The recently acquired *Planter* remains with the squadron for the rest of the summer, but the vessel had been constructed so it is only capable of using wood for fuel, a difficult situation. Consequently, Admiral Du Pont transfers the *Planter* to the Union Army at Fort Pulaski in Georgia. The *Planter* is lost on 1 July 1876; however, the cause has never been determined.

June 22 (Sunday)   In Louisiana, a Union contingent, the 8th Vermont Regiment, skirmishes with Confederate guerrillas at Raceland (Algiers). The Union sustains three killed and eight wounded.

In Virginia, the 3rd Battalion, 5th Pennsylvania Cavalry (Colonel Archibald Campbell's brigade) initiates a Reconnaissance Mission into Gloucester and Mathews Counties. Also, elements of the 8th Pennsylvania Cavalry led by Colonel (later general) Daniel McMurtie Gregg reconnoiter the region near White Oak Swamp. During the operation, which lasts until the following day, the Confederates capture one trooper.

June 23 (Monday)   In Missouri, the Union 7th Missouri Cavalry (militia) engages a contingent of Confederates at Raytown. The Union sustains one killed and one wounded. Confederate casualties are unavailable.

In Virginia, General Thomas "Stonewall" Jackson is directed to report to General Robert E. Lee's headquarters to attend a strategy conference on the subject of preserving Richmond from McClellan's army. Other officers in attendance include General Ambrose P. Hill, General Daniel Hill, and General James Longstreet. The meeting concludes with a decision to launch an attack on 26 June against the Union lines at Beaver Dam. In conjunction, Jackson is ordered to depart the Shenandoah Valley and prepare to advance along the ridge that separates the Pamunkey and the Chickahominy Rivers. Meanwhile, Daniel Hill is to deploy along the Mechanicsville Pike and prepare to cross the river at Mechanicsville Bridge, following Jackson's attacks to clear the way. Meanwhile, Ambrose Hill is to retain a portion of his division at Meadow Bridge, while the remainder is to cross the Chickahominy. Also, elements of the 11th Pennsylvania Cavalry commanded by Captain R.B. Ward reconnoiter the area near New Kent Court House.

In Confederate general officer activity, John Robert Jones (33rd Virginia) is promoted to brigadier general.

June 24 (Tuesday)   In North Carolina, a Union contingent of the 3rd New York Cavalry, commanded by Captain Jocknick departs Washington en route to Tranter's Creek.

In South Carolina, twenty Marine Sharpshooters attached to the steamers USS *James Adger, Albatross,* and *Keystone State* transfer to gunboats, the *Andrew* and *Hall,* and move up the Santee and Wahamau Rivers to raid Confederate positions.

In Virginia, by this date, General Fitz John Porter's forces posted north of the Chickahominy River have completed some well-planned defenses in anticipation of an attack by General Robert E. Lee or by General Thomas

"Stonewall" Jackson, who has moved into the area to defend Richmond. The Union establishes concealed artillery positions in the high ground slightly east of Beaver Dam Creek, and as a separate surprise, General Porter has ordered Generals John F. Reynolds' and Truman Seymour's brigades to inconspicuously remain there to engage the approaching Rebels. All but a few of the troops at Mechanicsville are dispatched to the front of Reynolds' command to sound the alarm. Once contact is made with the approaching Rebels, these picket troops are to speed back to Reynolds at Beaver Dam. Also nearby, Reynolds has the forces of Generals George A. McCall and George W. Morell to his right and rear respectively, each positioned to rally to his side at the first sounds of the guns. The Confederates move against the Union lines here on the 26th.

In Naval activity, the USS *Sumter,* while operating in the vicinity Smith Island, Virginia, collides with the USS *General Meigs* and sinks about seven miles off the island. The crew, however, is rescued by the crew of the USS *Jamestown* and carried to Newport News.

June 25 (Wednesday)   THE SEVEN DAYS' BATTLES (BATTLE OF OAK GROVE) Confederate General Thomas J. "Stonewall" Jackson arrives at Ashland, Virginia, from the Shenandoah Valley with a force of about 35,000 men. Union Major General George B. McClellan directs General Samuel P. Heintzelman to advance with his corps and a part of Generals Keyes' and Sumner's forces along the Williamsburg Road, creating an accidental clash at Oak Grove (King's Schoolhouse). Union Generals Joseph Hooker and Philip Kearny's Divisions, 3rd Corps, Army of the Potomac, participate. The Confederates are commanded by Brigadier General Ambrose R. Wright.

The divisions of Hooker and Kearny receive the brunt of the attacks and sustain the heaviest casualties. General Philip Kearny is the nephew of General Stephen Kearny, who served in the Mexican War. The 3rd and 4th Maine Regiments, 2nd New Hampshire, 1st, 7th, 10th, 11th, 16th and 19th Massachusetts Regiments, the 2nd Rhode Island, and the 1st, 2nd, 36th, 37th, 40th, 70th, 71st, 72nd 73rd, 74th, 87th and 101st New York Regiments participate. Also involved are the 5th and 17th New Jersey Regiments, 26th, 63rd and 105th Pennsylvania, 2nd, 3rd and 5th Michigan Regiments and the 20th Indiana Regiment, bolstered by the 2nd Battery, New Jersey Artillery, and the 4th U.S. Artillery. The Union sustains 51 dead, 401 wounded and 64 missing. The Confederates sustain 65 dead, 465 wounded and 11 missing.

The following day, General Robert E. Lee is headquartered at Mechanicsville Turnpike, Virginia, and another bloody battle erupts, with the Yankees pressing to reach Richmond, and the Rebels fighting to prevent the seizure of their capital. The Yankees advance to the woods along the Williamsburg Road and begin setting their attack against Old Tavern on the 26th.

In Arkansas, the 4th Iowa Cavalry skirmishes with Confederates at Little Red River. The

Union sustains two wounded. Confederate casualties are unavailable.

In Tennessee, the Union 56th Ohio Regiment skirmishes with Confederates at Germantown and sustains ten killed. Confederate casualties are unavailable.

In Naval activity, the USS *Western World,* accompanied by two other gunboats, the *Andrew* and the *E.B. Hale,* move onto the North Santee River, South Carolina, en route to reduce a strategic Confederate railroad bridge. While on the missions, detachments are debarked to set some plantations on fire and in the process the troops also gather about 400 slaves and take them aboard the ships.

June 25–July 1   THE SEVEN DAYS' BATTLES Confederates under General Robert E. Lee attempt a move to push back McClellan's Army, initiating a series of attacks, successfully stemming the Union advance on Richmond. Union forces withdraw to Harrison's Landing (Berkeley Plantation) on the James River. The engagements during the Seven Days' Battles include Mechanicsville, Cold Harbor (Gaines' Mills, the only firm Confederate victory), Peach Orchard, White Oak Farm, Glendale, Frazier's Farm, Savage's Station and others. Union losses total 15,849 killed, wounded or missing. Confederate losses were 20,614 killed, wounded or missing. Union Major General Edwin V. Sumner and General George Meade are wounded. Union Generals John Sedgwick and John J. Abercrombie (West Point, 1832) are also wounded during the battle. Confederate Brigadier General Richard Griffith (born in Philadelphia) is mortally wounded while leading four Mississippi Regiments (Magruder's Division) at Savage's Station on the 29th. Confederate Generals Joseph Reid Anderson (West Point, 1836), William D. Pender (West Point, 1854) and Winfield Scott Featherston are wounded. And Colonel Edward A. Perry, 2nd Florida Infantry, is wounded at Frazier's Farm. The Berkeley Plantation is where "Taps" is composed by Union General Daniel Butterfield one solemn night with Union troops on one side of the river and Confederates just across the bank, each recovering from the hazards of killing.

Also during the same period, Union General Stoneman initiates a mission to seek an destroy Confederate supply sources in the vicinity of White House Landing, Virginia.

June 26 (Thursday)   THE SEVEN DAYS' BATTLES (BATTLE OF MECHANICSVILLE, BEAVER DAM, ELLISON'S MILLS) A Confederate attack fails to get off during the morning hours as scheduled. The elements favor an attack; however, the forces of General Thomas "Stonewall" Jackson are behind schedule and the forces under Ambrose Hill, Daniel Hill and James Longstreet receive no communications from Jackson. By noon, Ambrose Hill, expected to advance behind Jackson, receives authorization to attack.

At about 1500, when General Ambrose P. Hill fords the Chickahominy at Meadow Bridge, the Confederates commence the assault unaware that more than 5,000 Union troops and supporting artillery under General John F. Reynolds hold dominating positions in the heights at Beaver Dam. General Fitz John Porter, the commanding officer of the Fifth Corps, is at the scene of the battle for the entire day. The Rebels are met with ravaging fire, but still they doggedly advance toward the creek. Despite the heavy casualties, the assault continues, but following the artillery and infantry fire, the attackers are engaged by contingents of Charles Griffin's brigade, which strikes from Reynolds' right, and by George A. McCall's forces, which strike from the left, forcing the Confederates to quickly retire from the creek and seek safer positions. The slug-fest terminates at about 2100. The Union sustains 52 casualties Confederates sustain about 4,000 casualties.

After the day's combat, Union Major General George B. McClellan is informed that General Thomas J. "Stonewall" Jackson had passed Beaver Dam and McClellan is already aware that General Robert E. Lee, in direct command of the entire operation to defend Richmond, is in the process of severing McClellan from his strong base of operations at White House. Consequently, McClellan decides to also have a plan to retire toward the James River if it becomes necessary. Union Colonel Rufus Ingalls, assistant quartermaster general, begins to move all the wounded and the stores and supplies to Savage's Station. Also, the Fifth Corps begins its redeployment. The operation, which includes moving even the heavy guns and the wagons, is completed by about dawn on the following day. The columns cross the New Bridge and deploy slightly east of Gaines' Mills between New Cool Arbor (Cold Harbor) and the Chickahominy River. At this new line, the Union Fifth Corps awaits the Confederate assault. Confederate Colonel (later major general) Thomas L. Rosser is wounded during this action; he is then assigned as colonel of the 5th Virginia Cavalry. Also, Colonel (later brigadier general) Calvin E. Pratt is wounded when a rifle ball strikes him

in the face. The rifle ball is not extracted for thirty years.

In Mississippi, Admiral David Farragut arrives at Vicksburg. The vanguard of his fleet, commanded by Commander S.P. Lee, had arrived earlier and demanded the surrender of the city; however, the military governor and the mayor of Vicksburg, James L. Antry and L. Lindsay, respectively, had refused the ultimatum. This day, in lieu of a surrender, Farragut's mortar boats and warships initiate a horrendous bombardment, which continues intermittently for two consecutive days. Nonetheless, the city remains for the most part unscathed.

In Virginia, the 8th Illinois Cavalry commanded by Colonel John F. Farnsworth clashes with Confederate cavalry and supporting artillery at Atlee's Station, Hanover Court House and Meadow Bridge, Virginia. Casualty figures are unavailable. Union and Confederate units skirmish at Hundley's Corner on the 26th and 27th. Specific units and casualty figures are unavailable.

In Naval activity, the rams USS *Monarch* and the USS *Lancaster,* under command of Colonel Charles C. Ellet, in pursuit of the *Van Dorn* since her escape after the naval battle at Memphis, arrive at a point on the Yazoo River just below Yazoo City and from there they set the CSS *General Earl Van Dorn* afire, set by the crew to prevent capture by the Union. The Confederates also destroy the CSS *Polk* and the CSS *Livingston.* According to Confederate logs, the ships were "oiled and tarred" in preparation of the arrival of the Union warships and upon first sight, the ships were set ablaze within sight of the battery at Liverpool.

June 27 (Friday)   THE SEVEN DAYS' BATTLES (BATTLE OF GAINES' MILLS, GAINES' FARM, NEW COOL ARBOR OR COLD HARBOR) In Virginia, the Union is newly deployed in a half-moon position from which they can guard the approaches to the bridges that span the Chickahominy. The left is held by George W. Morell's Division, while the right is held by George Sykes' Division, the latter composed of regular troops and Zouaves, who are stretched along a deep ravine. George A. McCall's force is posted behind Morell. Robertson's and Griffin's batteries are to Morell's right and left respectively and another battery, Tidball's, is posted to the rear near Truman Seymour's brigade. Contingents of the 1st and 5th U.S. Cavalry and the 6th Pennsylvania Cavalry, commanded by General Philip St. George Cooke, holds in the Chickahominy Valley just beyond Alexander's Bridge.

Major General George E. Pickett, CSA (Johnson, *Campfire and Battlefield: History of the Conflicts and Campaigns,* 1894).

Dawn breaks, but no attack is imminent. Nevertheless, the Union remains prepared. Then, at about 1400, the silence is shattered. Major General Ambrose Hill's heavy guns plaster the Union positions, but Union return fire is equally devastating and the Rebels are required to move their guns back. Meanwhile, with Confederate General Thomas J. "Stonewall" Jackson having not yet arrived, General Longstreet is directed to advance to support General Hill. His force mounts a feint against the Union left but makes no progress; however, it becomes clear that the heights must be taken by an attack. At about the time he prepares to launch the assault General Jackson arrives. Confederate General William H.C. Whiting's force sets up on James Longstreet's left to bolster the charge. Union General Fitz John Porter's corps is struck by the combined forces of Longstreet, Whiting and Hill.

The Rebels advance under severe fire and sustain heavy casualties, but they refuse to pause, pressing through the swamp and eventually pushing the Yankees into the woods. Meanwhile, General Richard S. Ewell's Division, on Jackson's right, and the trailing brigades of Jackson's corps join with those troops advancing under Hill to seize the heights. The Union troops pour out relentless fire, both rifle and artillery, from their commanding positions in the heights. Nevertheless, the Rebels claw their way forward and soon become embroiled in a fiercely contested close-quartered hand-to-hand battle. Unending Confederate troops reach the high ground, but despite urgent calls for reinforcements, none arrive. Still the under-strength Yankees maintain their ground, but casualties shred their line. Finally General Henry W. Slocum's Division arrives to help steady the

A Union fleet departs White House, Virginia, en route to the James River. Confederate ammunition and stores are burning in the background (Johnson, *Campfire and Battlefield: History of the Conflicts and Campaigns,* 1894).

Union positions, but by now, the lines are so badly mauled that Slocum has to widely stretch his troops, adding little momentum to the cause as the Rebels hammer them from all sides and continue to close the loop. The grueling contest for the heights still is not gained by the Rebels, as the Yankees cling to the frail hope that more help will arrive.

Suddenly, fresh troops appear, but the reinforcements are Confederate. By the time two Union brigades, those of Thomas F. Meagher and William H. French (Richardson's Command) arrive, the entire Rebel force, except some reserves, are committed to the field of battle. Both Longstreet and Whiting continue to pound General Morell's lines, which hold for awhile, but the intense pressure finally forces the Union positions here to fold. Simultaneously, the center is being penetrated. As the Union falls back, fortuitously, two brigades of Richardson's cross the river to join with Sykes' command to hold the Rebels, while the Union attempts to regroup at Alexander's Bridge. The stance holds its ground and by dusk, the fighting ceases for the day as the Confederates also retire.

Both sides suffer staggering losses. Following the day's action, the Union crosses the Chickahominy River, burning all bridges behind them, and redeploys at Savage's Station. The Union loses about 6,000 killed and wounded. Colonel Gouverneur Warren, while leading a brigade (Sykes' Division) sustains a wound; however, he recovers and participates at Second Manassas under General Fitz John Porter and afterward at Antietam and Gettysburg. The Confederates sustain about 9,000 killed and wounded. Confederate Brigadier General George E. Pickett is wounded at this action. Also, Confederate Lt. Colonel (later brigadier general) Henry H. Walker, 40th Virginia Infantry, sustains two wounds at this action. General Robert E. Lee writes to Jefferson Davis: "The enemy driven from his strong position at Beaver Dam Creek. I grieve to state that our loss in officers and men was great, we sleep in the field and shall renew the contest in the morning."

The contest at the Seven Days' Battles continues fiercely. Union General John F. Reynolds, covering a withdrawal of McClellan during the 27th, is captured and held until exchanged on August 8. Confederate General J.B. Magruder has completely fooled General McClellan and the Union about the extent of his force, which is considerably smaller than the Union believes, allowing the Rebels another edge. Also, recently promoted Confederate Colonel (later general) James Conner (Connor), 22nd North Carolina, sustains a serious wound in one leg and remains incapacitated for a couple of months; however, he does return to duty and remains with the regiment until he is promoted to brigadier general during June 1864. The Confederate 25th Virginia Infantry Regiment participates in this action (Ewell's Division). The brigade of Confederate General Maxcy Gregg had been splintered a few days prior to this action when the 14th South Carolina Regiment had been tagged with picket duty at Smith's Farm in the Chick-

ahominy Valley, but the 14th Regiment makes it back to the main body during the day's fighting.

In Arkansas, a contingent of the 3rd Iowa Cavalry clashes with Confederates at Waddel's Farm. The Union sustains four killed and four wounded. Confederate casualty figures are unavailable.

In Louisiana, elements of the 21st Indiana Volunteer Regiment, commanded by Lt. Colonel Keith, skirmish with a contingent of Confederates at Williams' bridge (Amite River). The Union loses two killed and four wounded. The Confederates sustain four killed and 11 captured.

In Mississippi, Confederate General Braxton Bragg dispatches a division under Sterling Price from Tupelo toward Chattanooga, Tennessee, to counter the impending Union threat there. General Bragg, with General Earl Van Dorn, moves towards Vicksburg, while Sterling Price is directed to harass General Grant at Corinth, applying just enough pressure to divert the Yankees with Grant from supporting General Don Carlos Buell at Chattanooga. Bragg has permitted modification of the plans by arranging possible support by Van Dorn for Price, provided no danger would come to Vicksburg. Nonetheless, when attempts are made by Price to join with Van Dorn for a combined move against Union forces in Tennessee, nothing is consummated while the month of August arrives and slips away.

The Union initiates a project to construct a canal on the peninsula ostensibly to turn the Mississippi River in front of Vicksburg to sever its primary water supply; however, the real purpose is to give the Union fleet a way to evade the Confederate defenses at Vicksburg. Nonetheless, the project (William's Canal), undertaken by several thousand men under General William Thomas, fails. Many of the men are struck by sickness and injuries, but others fall prey to exhaustion from the intense heat and all suffer from poor shelter from the elements. Despite the handicaps, the project continues. The Union dispatches detachments from plantation to plantation to gather Negroes to dig up roots and remove trees, but still nature outweighs man, and by 24 July, the project is terminated. In January, General Grant resumes the project and William's Canal becomes known as Grant's Canal. Grant's attempt fares no better. The elements continue to wreak havoc on the workers, and Confederate artillery at Vicksburg seals

the fate of the canal. Grant terminates the project by March 1863. The site is in the vicinity of the Vicksburg National Military Park and considered to be part of the park.

In Virginia, in the vicinity of Garnett's Farm, Confederate artillery slugs it out with Union artillery of General William F. Smith's Division. Other heavy fighting occurs at Gaines' Mill (Cold Harbor). The V Corps, supported by Meagher's and French's brigades, 1st Division, II Corps, battles Rebels under General Thomas Stonewall Jackson. One regiment, the 9th Massachusetts, composed of Irish troops, sustains a severe attack at its positions on Turkey Hill. The Confederates are repulsed, but 281 casualties are sustained, including the deaths of six line officers. Within several days, at Malvern Hill, the regiment again performs admirably; however, its commanding officer, Colonel Thomas Cass, sustains a fatal wound. Cass will be succeeded by Colonel Patrick Guiney.

In Naval activity, the USS Galena initiates a bombardment of City Point, Virginia. In conjunction with the attack, two boats move to shore and the landing force destroys the depots located there. Also, General McClellan goes aboard the *Galena*, and while aboard he is able to locate a new camp for his army. He selects terrain near Harrison's Landing. However, by 30 June, circumstances change and the Union is compelled to retire down the James River. The USS Tioga is commissioned at about this time (late June). Shortly thereafter it departs Massachusetts for Virginia. It is assigned duty on the James River and then along the Potomac. In August, it is sent to the West Indies, and from there it is transferred to the East Gulf Squadron during September 1863. The following year an epidemic of yellow fever strikes the crew. The *Tioga* is ordered to sail north. After-

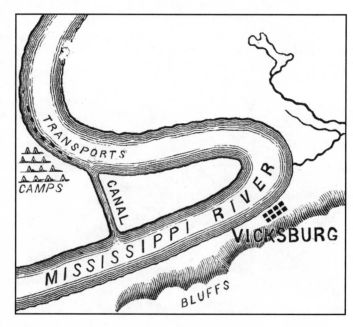

William's and Grant's Canal (*Harper's Pictoral History of the Civil War*, 1896).

ward, it is decommissioned and remains out of service until after the close of hostilities to receive a major overhaul. Once returned to service, it is assigned duty off New England and afterward in the Gulf of Mexico until decommissioned during June 1866 and sold four months later. The USS *Ellis*, operating near Winton, North Carolina, engages a contingent of Confederate cavalry.

June 28 (Saturday) THE SEVEN DAYS' BATTLES The Confederates again turn up the heat in the ongoing duel. General Richard S. Ewell's Division, supported by the Ninth Confederate Cavalry, crosses the Chickahominy in pursuit of the retreating Union forces under General George B. McClellan, who is establishing new headquarters in the vicinity of Savage's Station, Virginia. Union General W.F. Smith's Division (General Franklin's Sixth Corps) near Woodbury's Bridge at Golding's Farm becomes the recipient of a tremendous artillery bombardment, which forces the Union to evacuate the untenable positions. Early the next morning at about 0300, General McClellan departs Savage's Station heading for his new line of defense along the James River. Prior to his departure, McClellan had ordered his forces to abandon their positions and retire to the next line at the river. Also, Companies I and K, 8th Illinois Cavalry, commanded by Captain Elon Farnsworth, clash with Confederates at Dispatch Station, Virginia. No casualty figures are available. Also, a contingent of Union troops led by Captain J.C. Lee departs from Fort Monroe, Virginia, to establish contact with the Army of the Potomac. The mission, which lasts until July 4, costs the unit about eight men captured. Meanwhile, a contingent of Union General W.F. Smith's Command, composed of the 23rd and 49th New York Regiments augmented by the 3rd New York Artillery Battery, commanded by Captain Mott, skirmishes with Confederates at Garnett's Farm and Golding Mills, Virginia.

In Arkansas, elements of the 9th Illinois Cavalry, commanded by Colonel Albert G. Brackett, engage a contingent of Confederates at Village Creek.

Admiral Farragut's fleet at Vicksburg (Mottelay, *The Soldier in Our Civil War*, 1886).

In Naval activity, at 0300, Admiral David Farragut's fleet, including the schooner *Arletta*, initiates a bombardment of Vicksburg. The steamers USS *Brooklyn, Hartford* and *Richmond* and the gunboats USS *Sciota, Pinola, Wissahickon, Iroquois, Winona, Oneida* and *Kennebec* again bombard the Confederate batteries as they attempt to run past the obstacles to reach Vicksburg. However, one of the vessels, the USS *Clifton*, attached to the Mortar Squadron, sustains a hit in the boiler, which explodes and kills seven crew members. Nevertheless, it survives and later participates in the capture of Galveston (October 1862). During this action at Vicksburg, U.S. Marines participate, manning secondary guns. Farragut has been lambasting Vicksburg since the 26th, but the city still refuses to capitulate. Farragut concludes that it will be necessary to create a canal that will run across the narrow neck of the peninsula that lies opposite Vicksburg through which the Union can move transports to reach the opposite end of the Mississippi. In addition, he plans on linking his force with that of Commodore Charles H. Davis. The Confederate batteries are silenced and all but three of Farragut's vessels pass safely. Once beyond the batteries, Farragut encounters Lt. Colonel Alfred Ellet (who succeeded his brother, Charles R. Ellet, who recently was killed at Memphis) of the ram fleet, and shortly thereafter, he confers with Commodore Davis. Farragut and Davis decide to launch a reconnaissance expedition along the Yazoo River, while awaiting reinforcements that were recently requested from General Halleck for the main assault to seize Vicksburg.

The side-wheel steamer CSS *Capitol* burns at Liverpool, Mississippi. During the following month, the Confederates sink the hull on the Yazoo River as an obstacle to impede Union vessels. The ship machinery is transported to Selma, Alabama.

June 29 (Sunday) SEVEN DAYS' BATTLES (BATTLE OF SAVAGE'S STATION) Pursuant to orders of Major General George B. McClellan, the Union forces are moving back from the Chickahominy River to new positions at the James River. General W.F. Smith's Division is at the point, trailed by the contingents of Generals Samuel P. Heintzelman, Erasmus D. Keyes, William B. Franklin and Fitz John Porter. The divisions of Generals Joseph Hooker and Philip Kearny are protecting the rear. Meanwhile, the Confederates, having been informed of the general retreat, spring into action. The forces of Generals James Longstreet and Ambrose Hill ford the Chickahominy at New Bridge, using a bridge recently constructed by General Magruder's forces. In concert, while Longstreet is advancing down the Darbytown and Long Bridge Roads, General Stonewall Jackson's contingents cross the river at Grapevine Bridge and maneuver along the south side of the Chickahominy to strike at McClellan's rear. Other Confederate forces under Generals John B. Magruder and Benjamin Huger advance along the Charles City and Williamsburg Roads, respectively, to jolt the Union's flank and the rear simultaneously.

Despite the fact that the Union had gotten a good head start, Magruder manages to reach the vicinity of Savage's Station by about 0900. He immediately launches an assault against the right portion of General John Sedgwick's Division (Sumner's Second Corps). General Edwin Sumner designs a line of defense and orders the unit to deploy across the railroad tracks there. Meanwhile, Magruder is convinced that the Union is advancing, prompting him to halt and await reinforcements. Shortly thereafter, when two of Huger's brigades arrive, Magruder learns that the opposition is merely protecting the main body's retreat and orders an attack. General Jackson's force encounters difficulty getting to the battlefield due to the necessary repairs at the Grapevine Bridge; they arrive at Savage's Station on the following day, the 30th.

Supported by artillery, concealed in the woods, the Rebels emerge from the dense thicket and strike the positions of Generals William W. Burns, Winfield Scott Hancock and William T.H. Brooks. All the while the Union

Union gunboats at Vicksburg (Johnson, *Campfire and Battlefield: History of the Conflicts and Campaigns*, 1894).

artillery batteries commanded by Captains Rufus D. Pettit, Walter M. Bramhall and Thomas W. Osborn return fire equal to that which they are receiving. In coordination with the tumultuous bombardment, the Union Irish Brigade repeatedly charges the Confederate lines, essentially neutralizing the assault and preventing any severing of the lines by the Confederates. Eventually, the Confederates, having sustained about 400 casualties, retire to the woods. The Union, which had held off the Rebels, suffers about 800 casualties in the process.

Following the termination of the grueling fighting at Savage's Station, the Union, which is unable to evacuate its wounded, reinitiates its retreat toward the James River. The columns will cross the White Oak Swamp and creek by about 0800 the following morning. Union General William T.H. Brooks, while commanding a contingent of VI Corps troops (Army of Potomac) near Savage's Station, is wounded during the withdrawal of McClellan's troops to Harrison's Landing. General Brooks will be wounded again at Antietam. His health will be severely impaired as time goes on, but he still commands a division of the VI Corps at Fredericksburg and Chancellorsville. General Brooks attempts to continue service and ably leads a division of the X Corps at Cold Harbor and Petersburg. Poor health finally forces his retirement in July 1864.

Also, the 5th Vermont sustains 149 men killed or wounded. Lt. Colonel Lewis Addison Grant, 5th Vermont, participates in this action. Afterward he becomes colonel of the regiment and leads the Vermont Brigade during the Battle of Fredericksburg. Also, Confederate Colonel John D. Kennedy (2nd South Carolina Infantry) participates at this battle. Kennedy comes down with fever after the battle but rejoins his command and subsequently becomes brigadier general in December 1864.

In Virginia, Union cavalry led by General Darius N. Couch skirmishes with a contingent of Confederates at James River Road. In addition, elements of the 2nd and 6th Corps, Army of the Potomac, under Generals Edwin V. Sumner and William B. Franklin respectively, clash with Confederates along the Williamsburg Road. Also, a Union reconnaissance force (General Philip Kearny's Brigade) encounters and skirmishes with Confederates at Jordan's Ford. Casualty figures are unavailable.

In Naval activity, Flag Officer Charles Davis departs Memphis to join the fleet of David Farragut at Vicksburg. Also, the USS *Mohican,* on duty off the coast of South Carolina and Florida, is ordered north to receive repairs. It is decommissioned in Philadelphia in July and recommissioned on 17 October 1862.

June 30 (Monday) THE SEVEN DAYS' BATTLES (BATTLE OF WHITE OAK SWAMP, FRAZIER'S FARM, WHITE OAK FARM, GLENDALE OR CHARLES CITY) The ongoing fighting between the forces of McClellan and those of Jackson and Lee for the fate of Richmond, which had

begun on the 26th, once again erupts as the Union continues to withdraw to the James River. Union troops, with the Confederates on their heels, cross the White Oak Swamp and White Oak Creek and form a new defensive line at Willis Church. General Winfield Scott Hancock deploys to the right and General Fitz John Porter holds the left, while the middle is secured by the forces of Samuel P. Heintzelman and Edwin Sumner. Meanwhile, Confederate General Thomas "Stonewall" Jackson arrives at Savage's Station and discovers that the Union had abandoned it, apparently in a hurry, as more than 2,000 sick and wounded troops remain behind.

Jackson, leading the forces of Ambrose P. Hill and James Longstreet, gives pursuit. A second column composed of the forces of John B. Magruder and Benjamin Huger advances on Jackson's right along the Charles City Road to initiate an assault against the Union flank. The Confederates reach White Oak Creek, but their crossing is delayed, as the bridge has been destroyed by the Union. Efforts are undertaken to rebuild the bridge, but Union artillery forbids the action. Jackson then attempts to have his force ford the creek, but here, too, the effort fails due to effective Union fire originating from General W.F. Smith's infantry and the artillery batteries. However, some Confederates successfully cross.

Meanwhile, other Confederate forces under A.P. Hill and Longstreet reach Frazier's Farm (Glendale Farm or Nelson's Farm) and encounter the units of Union Generals Sumner and Hooker on the right, Kearny on the left, and to the front center, General George A. McCall. General James Longstreet, with Robert E. Lee and President Jefferson Davis accompanying him, concludes that the opposing force warrants a pause to await additional reinforcements. Later, about 1600, subsequent to the arrival of more units, Longstreet initiates the assault and bumps into friendly troops, General James Kemper's brigade, which is holding on Union Brigadier General George A. McCall's left.

The attack is met by Pennsylvania reserves led by Colonel S.G. Simmons. The Pennsylvanians offer resolute resistance, and following a fiercely contested skirmish, they launch an offensive and bulldoze the Confederates, compelling them to retire to the woods following a loss of about 250 killed and wounded. The Yankees seize another 200 as prisoners. Nevertheless, the Confederates strike back immediately after the arrival of more fresh troops. This offensive delivers a punishing blow to the Yankees and forces them to reel back after sustaining severe casualties.

The Confederates maintain a forceful thrust, preventing the Union troops from regaining their composure, but at about this time rein-

Battle of White Oak Swamp (Johnson, *Campfire and Battlefield: History of the Conflicts and Campaigns,* 1894).

forcements under General Joseph Hooker arrive to prop up the staggering line. Hooker's Division hangs tough against the pressing blows of Longstreet and Hill, and the entire line ignites into a furious conflagration as the Rebels valiantly and repeatedly pound against the Union lines, only to be repulsed by extreme tenacity. And then, an Alabama brigade drills a fine hole that soon cracks the line and permits the Rebels to pour through at a rapid pace, despite an incessant wave of devastating fire that hammers them at every step. Still, they advance, and with extraordinary impetuousness pounce upon and capture a battery on McCall's left, then seize a second battery.

With the loss of Cooper's and Randall's artillery, the Union faces a bleak afternoon, but the equally tenacious Irish Brigade is again called upon. Seemingly inexhaustible, the Irish charge, but iron resistance prevents them from making any progress. In a short while, the seesaw bloodbath again reverses. The forces of Heintzelman, Meade, and McCall join the Irish Brigade to crack the Confederate wall. The trailing forces of Hooker and Kearny join the battle, and the Confederates are compelled to pull out every remaining ounce of energy to forestall disaster. The Rebels steadfastly meet the threat and engage in fiercely contested hand-to-hand combat.

Meanwhile, the Irish Brigade, which earlier had been unable to recapture the lost batteries, has by this time reclaimed them, adding even more power to the attack. By dark, both sides have badly bloodied the other and bodies and severely wounded men are spread across the battlefield as the din of battle subsides, with neither gaining much more than they had when the combat began. The Confederates retire to the woods and the Union stands on the same ground that it had earlier surrendered. Just prior to dusk, Confederate General Maxcy Gregg's brigade that had been detached from General A.P. Hill's Division speeds to the left side of the Confederate line to augment Generals Winfield Scott Featherston, Roger A. Pryor and the others at that spot.

During this activity, the 14th South Carolina comes across General Featherston, who is badly wounded. The regiment continues to battle the Yankees at this area until well after dark, and they save Featherston from being captured by the Union. During the heated exchange that has been occurring during the Seven Days' Battles, Union General George A. McCall's command encounters the 47th Virginia at Frazier's Farm, Virginia. The Confederates capture McCall after he inadvertently rides into the 47th Virginia's lines while he is inspecting his own lines without any accompanying staff troops. The Confederates use their captive to gain the release of Confederate General Simon B. Buckner, who has been held by the Union since the fall of Fort Donelson in February. Subsequent to his parole at Libby Prison, General McCall is exchanged for Buckner on 18 August 1862. Buckner remains out of service on sick leave, and in March 1863 he resigns from the service. In the meantime, General Truman Seymour assumes command of McCall's Division.

General George Meade and Colonel S.G. Simmons (Pennsylvania Reserves) are wounded during the action. In related activity, Union forces successfully destroy a Confederate train abandoned at White Oak Swamp (Glendale), Virginia. Captain Martin T. McMahon (U.S. Volunteers) receives the Medal of Honor for his valor during this action. Colonel Edward W. Hincks (later brigadier general) is wounded. The Union sustains about 1,800 killed and wounded. The Confederates sustain slightly more than 2,000.

During the night Union forces again reiniti- ate the retreat toward the James River, moving to Malvern Hill. They dig in upon a high plateau that provides commanding positions from which to meet the next Confederate as- sault and places the troops near — for the first time since the Seven Days' Battles began — the Union gunboats. These tenable positions also include 60 well-placed cannon, which are set to focus their combined firepower upon the im- mediate front or to the left, whichever becomes the point of the anticipated attack.

The forces of George Sykes and George W. Morell deploy on the far left. Stretching from there are the forces of Darius N. Couch's divi- sion, composed of P. Kearny, J. Hooker, J. Sedg- wick, Israel B. Richardson, W.F. Smith, H.W. Slocum and S. Casey. The lines form a semi- loop with both flanks nudging against the James River. This day's battle (30th) is sometimes re- ferred to as the battle of the following: Charles City Cross Roads, Glendale, Nelson's Farm, Fra- zier's Farm, Turkey Bend, and New Market Cross Roads. The Confederate 25th Virginia Infantry participates in this action, attached to a brigade in General Richard S. Ewell's Division.

In Minnesota, Companies B and C, 5th Min- nesota Volunteer Regiment, and Renville's Rangers move from Fort Ridgely to the Sioux Agency at the Yellow Medicine River to ensure discipline and order during an annuity payment by the government to the Indians. Later, dur- ing mid–August, the Indians resort to violence.

In Virginia, Union contingents (General Dar- ius Couch's Command) skirmish with Confed- erates at New Market Road. Meanwhile Bat- tery K, 4th U.S. Artillery, clashes with Confederates at Brackett's Ford. Also, at Turkey Bridge, elements of General Fitz John Porter's command, led by Colonel Gouverneur Warren, clash with Confederates. Additional skirmishes erupt at Jones' Bridge, Luray and New Kent Court House. In other activity, at this time, the U.S. Marine Corps' active duty strength stands at 2,406; it includes 51 officers and 2,355 en- listed men.

In Union general officer activity, Union Col- onel William B. Campbell is appointed brigadier general. General Campbell (born in 1807), formerly the governor of Tennessee, will resign his commission in January 1863.

In Naval activity, while operating on the Gulf of Mexico, the USS *Quaker City* intercepts and seizes a blockade runner, the *Model.* The USS *Sebago,* following the defeat of General McClel- lan during the Seven Days' Battles, participates in escorting troop transports down the James River. Afterward it is transferred to the South Atlantic Blockading Squadron.

July 1862 *In Confederate general officer ac- tivity,* Confederate Colonel St. John Richard Liddell, born in Mississippi and residing in Louisiana at the outbreak of hostilities, is this day promoted to the rank of brigadier general in the Confederate Army. Liddell, initially an aide to General Hardee and later a brigade com- mander at Corinth, will serve in Tennessee at such battles as Chickamauga in September 1863 and Murfreesboro in December 1862.

July 1 (Tuesday) THE SEVEN DAYS' BATTLES (THE BATTLE OF MALVERN HILL) Following yet another day of brutal combat, the Confed- erates form to launch an assault to evict and de- feat McClellan's Army. These two opposing forces have been pummeling each other for five days, and although the Union is still in retreat, the Rebels have been unable to deliver a killing blow; they have inflicted only one clear win during the blood-filled saga. Al- though both sides have continued to forestall total exhaustion, neither is vac- cinated against the ongo- ing stress of incessant bat- tle. Rather than being immune, they seemingly ignore the pain and an- guish to bring victory to their cause. By 0900, and in spirited fashion, the Confederates spread out for the charge, still un- aware of the overwhelm- ing firepower of the Union artillery. The Confeder- ates commence firing, using some unfocused ar- tillery barrages to test the mettle of the Union lines,

but General Robert E. Lee realizes quickly that it will take yet another ground assault to seize the plateau.

Generals Magruder and Huger, holding the extreme positions on the right side of the line, stand next to the divisions of Stonewall Jackson, D.H. Hill, and H.C. Whiting, and contingents of Richard S. Ewell. At 1500, the Confederate guns fire in unison to knock out the Union bat- teries and give the infantry some safety when they initiate the charge. Once the signal is given by Huger's Division, the Rebels are to launch a full scale attack along the entire line, but inad- vertently, at 1800 a false signal prompts Confed- erates under General D.H. Hill to prematurely spring the attack. His force plows into the lines of Generals Darius Couch and John Fitz Porter, initiating a donnybrook, but the Confederates are out on a thin limb. Lacking reinforcements, they are able to hold only for a short while. The Rebels are overwhelmed and pushed back into the woods.

Meanwhile, other Confederates charge and then their entire line is in action. A series of brigades slams into the positions of the Union batteries, but they hold and return devastating fire. Magruder and Huger pound the Union left in concert with simultaneous assaults against the right and center by Barksdale, G.B. Ander- son, William Mahone and Ambrose R. Wright, but still the Union holds. The curtain of fire continues to gush upon the charging Confed- erates, who refuse to retire. While the Union ar- tillery fires cascades upon the Rebels, the in- fantry withholds its fire until the Confederates are well into close range, adding additional dev- astation to their ranks. The Rebels repeatedly exhibit fearlessness and boldness, but their armor is confined to their bloodied gray uni- forms. Still, they advance up the slope, but as they near the crest, they are met with a combi- nation of riveting fire and pointed bayonets. On each occasion a bayonet attack would force the Rebels to descend the slope. Nevertheless, the bold tenacity of the Union is equal to the threat, and all assaults are repulsed.

Battle of Malvern Hill (Johnson, ***Campfire and Battlefield: His-*** ***tory of the Conflicts and Campaigns,*** **1894).**

A slight pause in the battle follows as the Confederates regroup for yet another attack, with which they still intend to drive the Yankees into the James River. In the meantime, the Yankees accept the pause and rekindle their desire to hold their ground. To bolster their cause, reinforcements appear from the commands of Generals Meagher and Sickles, who had been dispatched from Generals Sumner and Heintzelman respectively. Following the lull, again the Confederates burst full speed toward the Union lines and encounter a tumultuous reception, this time not only from artillery and infantry fire, but also from Union gunboats hurling shells into their positions. Undeterred and oblivious to the hurricanes of fire, the Rebels drive forward through a blizzard of shot and shell in a series of overlapping lines that refuse to disengage. Nonetheless, the Confederate casualties continue to spiral upward and the Union fire relentlessly continues. Finally, the savage beating takes its toll and the Rebels are compelled to disengage and retire into the woods.

At about 2100, the guns are silenced, the bayonets sheathed and those on both sides who are among the survivors are able to ponder the devastating results of the fighting that has sent so many of their friends to their deaths in the battle that ends the Peninsula Campaign. Following the battle, the Union continues its retreat heading for Harrison's Landing, just a few miles farther down the James River, harassed along the way by Confederate cavalry until the gunboats move into action and convince the pursuers that further attacks would become too costly. Later, the Confederates move to Richmond.

The Union casualties are: General Fitz John Porter's Fifth Corps, 4,278 (620 killed, 2,460 wounded, 1,198 missing); General George Archibald McCall's Division, First Corps (attached to Porter's 5th Corps), 3,074 (253 killed, 1,240 wounded, 1,581 missing); General William Buel Franklin's Sixth Corps, 2,737 (245 killed, 1,313 wounded, 1,179 missing); General Edwin Vose Sumner's Second Corps, 2,111 (187 killed, 1,076 wounded, 848 missing); General Samuel Peter Heintzelman's Third Corps, 2,073 (189 killed, 1,051 wounded, 833 missing); General Erasmus Darwin Keyes' Fourth Corps, 777 (69 killed, 507 wounded, 201 missing); and cavalry and unattached troops, 249, for a total of 15,299 casualties. Major General E.V. Sumner and Brigadier Generals William Thomas H. Brooks (29th), William Wallace Burns and George Gordon Meade are wounded, the latter being wounded twice at about the same time.

Confederate casualties are: Generals John Bankhead Magruder, 1,783 (258 killed, 1,495 wounded, 30 missing); Benjamin Huger, 1,350 (187 killed, 803 wounded, 360 missing); General James Longstreet, 4,931 (763 killed, 3,929 wounded, 239 missing); General Ambrose P. Hill, 3,870 (619 killed, 3,251 wounded); General Thomas "Stonewall" Jackson, 5,446 (966 killed, 4,417 wounded, 63 missing); General Daniel H. Hill, 3,954 total casualties; General Theophilus Hunter Holmes, 2 killed and 52 wounded; and General James "Jeb" Stuart's cavalry and unattached troops (William Nelson Pendleton's artillery), 150.

Confederate General Richard Griffith, a Philadelphian, is killed (29th) and Brigadier Generals George B. Anderson and William D. Pender are wounded (29th). Brigadier General Winfield Scott Featherston also sustains a wound during the Seven Days' Battles. Featherston will serve out the remainder of the year with the Army of Northern Virginia and then request and receive permission to transfer to Vicksburg, Mississippi, where he will lead a brigade in General Loring's division. Also, Confederate Lt. Colonel (later general) William L. Brandon, 21st Mississippi Regiment, is badly wounded and must have one leg amputated. Brandon later rejoins the Army and subsequent to his service at Gettysburg (July 1863), is promoted to colonel. Colonel Stephen D. Ramseur, 49th North Carolina, sustains a wound while leading a charge and permanently loses the use of his right arm, which becomes paralyzed.

Confederate Colonel Evander McIvor Law and his 4th Alabama Regiment participate in this action. Colonel Law also participates in the upcoming contest at Sharpsburg (Antietam), and in October he is promoted to the rank of brigadier general. Confederate Colonel Clement Anselm Evans is wounded, sustaining one of five wounds he receives throughout the war. Evans recuperates and will receive command of a brigade at Fredericksburg, Virginia, in December 1862. The Confederate 25th Virginia Infantry Regiment (Ewell's Division) participates in this action. After the Seven Days' Battles, Confederate General John Bankhead Magruder is assigned command of the District of Texas, New Mexico and Arizona.

Union Brigadier General Fitz John Porter is later promoted to major general of volunteers for his actions at Malvern Hill. He also receives the brevet of brigadier general in the Regular Army.

In Washington, D.C., Congress forbids polygamy, the practice of having more than one wife at the same time. This law is directed against Mormons, some of whom condone the practice as part of their religion. Despite the prohibition, polygamy continues in the area (primarily Utah) to this day.

In Mississippi, Philip H. Sheridan, recently promoted to colonel, 2nd Michigan Cavalry, repulses a superior force at Booneville. Sheridan (West Point, 1853) is promoted to brigadier general after this victory. The 2nd Iowa Cavalry participates in this skirmish. The Union sustains 40–45 killed and wounded. The Confederates sustain about 65–75 killed and wounded.

In Tennessee, the 1st Ohio Cavalry skirmishes with Confederates at Russellville. Also, a contingent of the 57th Ohio Volunteer Regiment skirmishes with Confederate Cavalry at Morning Sun. The Union sustains four wounded. The Confederates sustain 11 killed and 26 wounded.

In Naval activity, in Georgia, the USS *Potomska,* while conducting a reconnaissance mission along the Great Ogeechee River, encounters and engages a Confederate battery. Afterward the *Potomska* moves to Philadelphia for required repairs, but returns to the area during September. After reaching Port Royal, the ship moves to assist in the blockade of St. Simons Sound and, afterward, Sapelo Sound. Also, the USS *John Paul Jones* is commissioned at about this time. From this month into summer of the following year, it is attached to the South Atlantic Blockading Squadron in South Carolina. During August 1864, it is decommissioned while undergoing repairs and returns to duty in April 1865 during the closing days of the war. Subsequent to the close of hostilities, the *John Paul Jones* remains in active service and pulls duty in the Gulf of Mexico until decommissioned during July 1867. This *John Paul Jones* is separate from the *John Paul Jr.*, a steam launch constructed during 1862–1863 and assigned as a tender to the gunboat USS *Seneca.* The *John Paul Jones Jr.* remains in service until June 1864 and afterward is sold on 17 August 1865.

July 2 (Wednesday) In Virginia, Union Captain (later brigadier general) Henry A. Barnum is wounded during General McClellan's retreat to Harrison's Landing. Barnum is presumed dead but he survives and is captured by Confederates at Malvern House and imprisoned in Richmond. Barnum will be exchanged, and he later fights at Chattanooga, Tennessee, and in the Atlanta campaign, being wounded during both. Also, a Confederate contingent skirmishes with a detachment of Union Cavalry at Malvern Hill. Casualty figures are unavailable. Another skirmish develops between Union and Confederate units at New Kent Court House. Specific units are not reported.

In Naval activity, the Mississippi flotilla, commanded by Flag Officer Charles Davis, arrives

Flag Officer Charles Davis (*Harper's Pictorial History of the Civil War,* 1896).

in the vicinity of Vicksburg and joins with the forces under Admiral Farragut, the latter having arrived a few days earlier. Davis' flotilla moves in late July to the mouth of the Yazoo River. During an expedition in Winyah Bay, South Carolina, Union warships intercept and seize a British blockade runner, the schooner *Volante*. Nonetheless, the Confederate fire combined with an inability to advance along slim bends in the river cause the mission to be aborted on the following day. In late October, the *Western World* sails north to New York for repairs. It leaves New York during February 1863 and sails to Hampton Roads to join the North Atlantic Blockading Squadron.

July 3 (Thursday)   In Arkansas, the 13th Illinois Cavalry skirmishes with Confederate guerrillas at Grand Haze.

In Virginia, the Army of the Potomac under Major General George B. McClellan completes its trek to Harrison's Landing following recent fighting at Malvern Hill. By the following day, McClellan dispatches a reconnaissance force that moves out along the Charles City Road. Also, the 14th Indiana, 7th West Virginia and the 4th and 8th Ohio Volunteer Regiments skirmish with Confederate units at Haxall's Landing (Elvington Heights). The Union suffers eight killed and 32 wounded. The Confederates sustain about 100 killed and wounded. Elements of the 4th and 8th Ohio, 14th Indiana and 7th West Virginia bolstered by Tibbal's Artillery Battery, commanded by General Nathan Kimball, skirmish with Confederates at Herring Creek on this day and the next.

In Union Naval general officer activity, Captain Henry K. Thatcher, initially commissioned as a midshipman during March 1823, is promoted to the rank of commodore. His tours of duty included the Mediterranean Squadron, the African Squadron and the Pacific Squadron. During 1860–1861, Thatcher had been stationed at the Boston Navy Yard. During 1862–1863, he commands the steam frigate USS *Constellation* (Mediterranean Squadron). In 1864, Commodore Thatcher receives command of the steam frigate USS *Colorado*. His ship participates in the attacks against Fort Fisher, North Carolina, during December 1864 and January 1865. Commodore Thatcher is promoted to rear admiral on 25 July 1866.

In Naval activity, the USS *Quaker City*, while operating off Hole-in-Wall, Virginia, intercepts and seizes a blockade runner, the *Lilla*, which is carrying a cargo of drugs. In other activity, the USS *Genesee* is commissioned. Commander William M. Macomb receives command of the ship, which is attached to the North Atlantic Blockading Squadron. On 6 July, the *Genesee* departs Boston en route to Hampton Roads, where it is assigned duty as escort for mail steamers on the James River.

July 4 (Friday)   In California, Camp Independence is established by elements of the 2nd California Cavalry under Lt. Colonel George S. Evans. The fort is constructed in the Owen

River Valley at Oak Creek in Inyo County and located several miles from Independence. The garrison had been charged with the protection of mining operations in the area during a time of turbulence with the Indians that reside in the region by the Sierra Nevada Mountains. The camp is never officially designated as a fort. Tension in the area subsides during 1864 when the Indians are corralled at the fort and forced to move to Fort Tejon; however, after the fort is abandoned during 1864, most of the Indians depart Fort Tejon and return to the area around Camp Independence. By December 1864, Nevada troops are ordered to repair to the camp. During March 1865, troops from Nevada reestablish the fort for the protection of the miners. It is permanently abandoned in July 1877.

In New Mexico, a relief column led by Lt. Colonel Eyre (California Column) that departed Tucson, Arizona, on 21 June arrives at the Rio Grande River in the vicinity of Fort Thorne, recently abandoned by the Confederates. Eyre's contingent occupies the fort, and shortly after his arrival, he is joined by elements of the 3rd U.S. Cavalry. Lt. Colonel Eyre moves to seize Fort Fillmore, New Mexico, and Fort Bliss in Texas (El Paso), but some confusion in orders hinders the operation. Eyre receives conflicting orders from Colonel Chivington and Colonel M. Howe, the latter the acting assistant adjutant general. Nevertheless, Eyre's arrival is timely and his presence prevents the lingering Confederates from destroying La Messilla and Las Cruces, New Mexico. The Confederates gain from the mixed orders received by Eyre, which prevent him from pouncing upon the Confederates under Colonel Steele; however, Eyre is able to rehoist the Stars and Stripes over Fort Thorne, Fort Fillmore, and Fort Bliss.

In Texas, Confederates launch an attack against Union warships off Velasco. No damages or casualty reports are available.

In Virginia, Confederates under General Richard S. Ewell skirmish with Union contingents at Westover.

In Union general officer activity, Brigadier General Darius N. Couch, who tendered his resignation due to illness and discovered that General McClellan had not forwarded it to the War Department, is promoted to major general effective this day. General Couch, under General Ambrose Burnside, participates at Antietam (Sharpsburg) during September 1862 and at Fredericksburg in December 1862. Subsequently, he serves at Chancellorsville (May 1863) under General Hooker.

Also, Brigadier General William Farrar Smith is promoted to major general. Complications develop after the debacle at Fredericksburg (December 1862) when Smith and General William B. Franklin write a letter (addressed to President Lincoln) of apparent condemnation of General Burnside's campaign plans. Smith is a friend and supporter of General McClellan. Smith is stripped of his command of the VI Corps and the Senate fails to confirm his nomination.

Consequently, his commission (major general) expires on 4 March 1863.

In Naval activity, the USS *Maratanza* captures the CSS *Teaser*, an armed tug that was acquired by the state of Virginia during April 1861 and transferred to the Confederate States Navy. The *Teaser* is commissioned the USS *Teaser*. It is attached to the Potomac Flotilla and operates in Virginia until decommissioned in June 1865. After the war it becomes the civilian tug *York River*. In other activity, the gunboat USS *Sonoma*, the first 1105-ton "double-ender" side wheel steam gunboat, is commissioned at about this time (July) at the Portsmouth Navy Yard in Kittery, Maine. It is ordered to patrol in the West Indies and in the western Atlantic in search of Confederate raiders that are attacking U.S. shipping. After receiving an overhaul, it is transferred to the South Atlantic Blockading Squadron during September 1863.

July 5 (Saturday)   In Virginia, Confederates led by Colonel (later general) Stephen Dill Lee bombard Union shipping along the James River. Lee, a West Point (1854) graduate, is skilled in artillery. Subsequent to his service during the Virginia campaigns, he is promoted to brigadier general (November 1862) and transferred to the western theater, where he will assist in the defense of Vicksburg (General John C. Pemberton's command). Also, detachments of the 1st Maine Cavalry skirmish with Confederates at Sperryville. Casualty figures are unavailable. The 1st Maine Cavalry, which is serving under various generals, will join as a whole unit during August under the command of Colonel Samuel H. Allen and will be assigned to General George D. Bayard's Brigade.

In Union general officer activity, this day, Brigadier General Israel Bush Richardson is promoted to major general, effective the previous day. Richardson will serve with General Hooker and will be involved with the battle at Sharpsburg (Antietam).

In Naval activity, the *Cimarron* (originally spelled Cimerone), a side-wheel double-ended steam gunboat launched on 3 March of this year in Bordentown, New Jersey, is commissioned the USS *Cimarron*. Commander Maxwell Woodhull receives command. The vessel later departs Philadelphia and arrives at Fortress Monroe on 8 July.

July 6 (Sunday)   In Arkansas, a contingent of the 24th Indiana Volunteer Regiment (Colonel Hovey's command), commanded by Colonel William T. Spicely, skirmishes with Confederates at Grand Prairie in the vicinity of Aberdeen. The Union sustains one killed and 21 wounded. The Confederates suffer about 84 casualties, including killed and wounded.

In North Carolina, Union General Ambrose Burnside departs North Carolina en route to Virginia to reinforce the Army of the Potomac. Brigadier General John Gray Foster assumes command of the Department of North Carolina. In autumn Foster will augment Burnside at Knoxville.

In Naval activity, Captain Charles Wilkes is appointed commander of the newly created James River Flotilla. During the following month, Wilkes is promoted to the rank of commodore. The flotilla is formed by ships of the Atlantic Blockading Squadron, commanded by Flag Officer Louis M. Goldsborough. Subsequent to this action, Goldsborough requests that he be relieved of command. His contention is that Richmond cannot be taken without the land forces of General McClellan. He is succeeded by Wilkes during early September. Nonetheless, soon after he requests to be relieved, Goldsborough is promoted to the rank of admiral. From September 1862 until the close of the war, Admiral Goldsborough works in Washington, D.C. with the Department of the Navy. Also, the USS *Galena* continues with the squadron until September, when it is assigned picket duty at Hampton Roads and Newport News, Virginia.

July 7 (Monday)   In Arkansas, the 11th Wisconsin, 33rd Illinois, 1st Missouri Light Artillery, 1st Indiana, and the 5th and 13th Illinois Cavalry under General Samuel R. Curtis engage and defeat Confederates under General Albert Rust at Bayou Cache (Hill's Plantation), Arkansas. The Union counts seven dead and 57 wounded. Confederates report 110 dead and 200 wounded. Troops under Curtis will, within a few days, occupy Helena at a point where Crowley's Ridge joins the Mississippi River. This gives the Union control of that port city about 70 miles below Memphis, Tennessee, and about 225 miles above Vicksburg, Mississippi, but it also gives the Union a vantage point for further penetration into Arkansas. Fort Curtis is established there.

In Virginia, elements of the 5th Pennsylvania Cavalry, commanded by Major Jacob P. Wilson, initiate a reconnaissance mission moving out from Yorktown. It is reported that about 10 troopers are captured by Confederates during the operation, which lasts until the 9th.

In Naval activity, the USS *Huntsville,* in cooperation with the *Quaker City,* seizes the steamer *Adela* in the vicinity of Great Abaco Island. The *Huntsville,* a wooden screw steamship, had been built during 1857 for civilian purposes, but during April 1861, it came under charter by the U.S. Navy and was commissioned the USS *Huntsville* in May. In August it officially became part of the Navy as one of its blockade gunboats along the east coast.

The *Adela,* an iron-hulled side-wheel steamer, had been operating put of Belfast, Ireland, and was en route from Bermuda to New Providence to take on a cargo of ordnance for the Confederacy when captured following a struggle. After ignoring repeated warning shots, the *Adela* sustains a damaging blow; the sixth round finally convinces the blockade runner to halt. A prize crew from the *Quaker City* boards the Adela, which is then towed to Key West, Florida. The *Adela* is acquired by the U.S. Navy on 23 May 1863 and assigned to blockade duty off the southern coast. In other activity, the USS

Tahoma, while operating off the Yucatan Peninsula, seizes a blockade runner, the schooner *Mose.* The *Mose,* carrying 115 bales of cotton, inadvertently sails up to the *Tahoma,* which is anchored.

July 8 (Tuesday)   In Virginia, the Army of Northern Virginia under Robert E. Lee reaches the defenses of Richmond, concluding its march from Malvern Hill.

In Naval activity, the recently commissioned gunboat *Cimarron* arrives at Fortress Monroe, Virginia. The *Cimarron,* attached to the James River Flotilla, operates in the area from 11 July until 4 September.

July 9 (Wednesday)   In Kentucky, Morgan's Raiders successfully pillage Tompkinsville, defended by elements of Pennsylvania Cavalry, commanded by Major Thomas J. Jordan. The Union loses four dead and six wounded. Confederate casualties are 10 killed or wounded.

In Naval activity, a squadron under Stephen C. Rowan, composed of the USS *Ceres, Commodore Perry, Shawsheen* and other vessels operating on the Roanoke River near Hamilton, North Carolina, receive heavy enemy fire from land-based troops. Nonetheless, the Union 9th New York Volunteer Regiment captures the town. The U.S. also seizes the CSS *Wilson,* a transport built in 1856 at Beaufort. The *Wilson* is transferred to the U.S. Army on 22 July.

July 9–15   Acting Volunteer Lieutenant John W. Kittredge, U.S. Navy, commanding officer of the bark USS *Arthur,* boards the tender USS *Corypheus,* which is able to operate in the shoal waters of Aransas Bay, Texas. As the *Corypheus* nears Lamar, a stranded schooner is spotted. Kittredge adds a second cutter to the mission and proceeds beyond the reefs, but the Confederates accelerate their activity and place the vessels back in an upright position prior to completing the job of caulking. Nonetheless, the schooner takes on water and begins to sink. Later the *Corypheus* gives chase after a schooner that had passed by. The ship is soon after located at anchor and it is the *Reindeer,* earlier captured by the General Butler. On the following day, the *Corypheus* arrives at the town of Aransas on San Jose Island and the crew captures the sloop *Belle Italia,* a small vessel. The *Belle Italia* after capture serves as another tender for the USS *Arthur;* however, the *Belle Italia,* which serves until at least through autumn of 1862, is not commissioned. None of the *Belle Italia's* logs have been preserved.

On the 12th, the *Arthur* seizes an armed schooner, the *Breaker,* at Aransas, and on the same day, while at Corpus Christi, Kittredge's force prompts the Rebels to destroy another armed schooner, the *Elma and Hannah,* by fire to prevent capture by the *Arthur.* On the 15th

President Lincoln and General McClellan review troops at Harrison's Landing, Virginia (Mottelay, *The Soldier in Our Civil War,* 1886).

the *Arthur* captures the steamer *A.B.* (also known as *A. Bee*), which is stranded in a narrow channel that leads into Nueces Bay in the vicinity of Corpus Christi. The steamer, however, despite strong efforts, is not refloated. Consequently, Kittredge orders the *A.B.* to be destroyed by fire.

July 10 (Thursday)   In Arkansas, a contingent of the 1st Wisconsin Cavalry commanded by Captain Allen skirmishes with Confederates at Scatterville. Casualty figures are unavailable.

In Union Naval general officer activity, Captain Thomas T. Craven, commanding officer of the USS *Brooklyn,* is promoted to commodore. He receives command of the steam frigate USS *Niagara.* In 1864, Commodore Craven is assigned special duty in European waters. He operates off Europe during 1864–1865. On 10 October 1866, Craven is promoted to the rank of rear admiral and appointed commandant of the U.S. Navy Yard, Mare Island, California, until 1869, when he is named commander of the North Pacific Squadron.

July 11 (Friday)   In Washington, D.C., President Abraham Lincoln appoints General Henry W. Halleck general-in-chief of the Union Army, as recommended by General Winfield Scott. Halleck departs for Washington, leaving General Thomas in command of that portion of the Grand Army of Tennessee still in Corinth. General Grant is again appointed to the command of his old army. Grant's jurisdiction, however, is enlarged.

In Kentucky, a contingent of the 33rd Ohio Regiment, commanded by Lt. Colonel Moore, skirmishes with Confederates at New Hope.

In Missouri, a Union contingent of the 1st Iowa Cavalry and Missouri militia clash with Confederate guerrillas at Pleasant Hill. The Union sustains 10 killed and 19 wounded. The Confederates suffer six killed and five wounded.

In Virginia, Union troops under Colonel Childs depart Harrison's Landing on a reconnaissance mission that takes them beyond Charles City Court House. The Union reports no casualties. The Confederates sustain one killed and three captured. At Williamsburg, Union and Confederate pickets skirmish. Specific units are not reported. The Confederates sustain three killed.

July 12 (Saturday) In Washington, D.C., Congress authorizes its Congressional Medal of Honor, America's highest decoration.

In Kentucky, Confederates commanded by John H. Morgan strike at Union positions in the vicinity of Lebanon. The Union forces, commanded by Colonel A.Y. Johnson, include elements of the Lebanon Home Guards and the 28th Kentucky Volunteer Regiment (Brigadier General Ebenezer Dumont's command). The Union sustains two killed and about 65 captured.

In Virginia, a Union contingent composed of elements of the 1st Maryland, 1st Vermont, 1st West Virginia and the 5th New York Cavalry, commanded by General Hatch, engages Confederate cavalry at Culpeper. The Union reports no casualties. The Confederates sustain one killed and five wounded.

In Confederate general officer activity, Brigadier General Benjamin Huger is relieved from duty after the Confederate Congress ruled that he lacks sufficient leadership skills. He is transferred to ordnance and becomes inspector of artillery, where he better utilizes the skills he had learned at West Point. Brigadier General Albert Pike resigns his commission; however, the Confederate government does not officially acknowledge the resignation until early November. Pike had not fared well with the Confederates, who distrusted him. Later he is indicted by the United States government for treason. Nevertheless, Pike is able to resume a normal life in retirement at Memphis, Tennessee.

July 13 (Sunday) In Tennessee, Confederates handily defeat Union forces at Murfreesboro. The Union defenders under General Thomas T. Crittenden (cousin of Confederate General George B. Crittenden and Union General Thomas L. Crittenden) are startled, taken off guard and captured by Confederates commanded by Nathan B. Forrest. Initially, Forrest had intended to free some local civilians being held in the town jail; however, he uses some heavy bravado while implying his force is stronger than it actually is and the bluff is successful. The garrison capitulates to his demand for surrender. Union forces participating include the 9th Michigan, 3rd Pennsylvania, 4th Kentucky, 3rd Minnesota, 7th Pennsylvania Cavalry, and 1st Kentucky Battery. The Union suffers 33 dead, 62 wounded, and 800 missing or captured. This occurs one day after Crittenden assumes command in the area, and he is unfamiliar with the defenses of the town. Nevertheless, the incident does not enhance his career. He resigns his commission during the following year. The Confederates sustain 50 dead and 100 wounded. Captain (later major general, Volunteers) Christopher Columbus Andrews (3rd Minnesota) is among the captured.

In Virginia, a contingent of the 1st Maryland Cavalry, commanded by Major later Brig. General Deems, skirmishes with Confederates at Fairfax. Casualty figures are unavailable.

In Naval activity, the USS *Corwin* is detached from the North Atlantic Blockading Squadron and reassigned duty at Hampton Roads and the immediate region to engage in surveying along the Potomac River.

July 14 (Monday) In Arkansas, elements of the 4th Iowa Cavalry skirmish with Confederates at Batesville.

In Virginia, Union General John Pope dispatches a message to the troops of the Army of Virginia, of which he has just assumed command. He delivers his ideas regarding future actions and past mistakes and includes his empathy for their concerns. In regards to rumors and innuendo that has been spreading around the encampments about holding defensive positions, he states: "The strongest position a soldier should desire to occupy is one from which he can most easily advance against the enemy…."

In Naval activity, Union vessels *Carondelet* and *Tyler,* acting upon orders of Commodore Farragut, are near the confluence of the Yazoo and Mississippi Rivers on a mission that entails surveying the Yazoo and to discover the location of a supposed monster-sized iron-plated Confederate ram, the *Arkansas.* This night, they anchor at the mouth of the Yazoo about fifteen miles above Vicksburg, Mississippi. Two deserters from the *Arkansas* board the USS *Essex* and inform the captain that the *Arkansas* is scheduled to attack the fleet, either during the night or by the following morning. The intelligence catches the Union by surprise because the Confederates near Vicksburg do not possess the means to have built an ironclad. On the following morning, two vessels advance up the river and the intelligence proves correct. The fleet encounters the CSS *Arkansas.*

In Confederate general officer activity, Brigadier General Richard Heron Anderson (West Point, 1842) is appointed major general effective this date. Anderson, a veteran of the Mexican War, had resigned his captain's commission to join the Confederacy on 3 March 1861.

In Naval activity, Lt. Macomb, the commander of the steamship USS *Genesee,* pens a letter to Commodore Wilkes, commander of the James River Flotilla, acknowledging receipt of orders from the Navy Department given to him by Wilkes. Subsequently, Wilkes becomes accused of "gross negligence of duty" on various charges, including an accusation by the secretary of the navy that Wilkes never

gave Macomb the orders. The possession of Macomb's letter becomes evidence during the trial. Macomb was to be suspended from duty. On 5 August, Wilkes is censured by the Navy Department. The matter is settled in September and Wilkes is named commander of the West India Squadron. In other activity, the USS *R.R. Cuyler* seizes the *Kate Dale,* a steamer. Afterward the *Cuyler* is ordered to join the massive search for the CSS *Tallahassee.*

July 15 (Tuesday) The Battle Between the CSS *Arkansas* and the Union Fleet Just after dawn, Confederate Commander Brown begins to move down the Yazoo River near Vicksburg toward the Union fleet, while at about the same time, several Union vessels, acting upon intelligence gained on the previous night, are advancing up the river, moving three abreast. The 13-gun *Carondelet* holds the center, flanked by the ironclad *Queen of the West* and the gunboat *Tyler.* After spotting the Union vessels, Brown speaks to the officers: "Gentlemen, in seeking the combat as we now do, we must win or perish. Should I fall, whoever succeeds to the command will do so with the resolution to go through the enemy's fleet, or go to the bottom. Should they carry us by boarding, the *Arkansas* must be blown up, on no account must she fall into the hands of the enemy. Go to your guns!"

Meanwhile, the Union squadron sees the oncoming CSS *Arkansas,* which suddenly propels a series of rounds at the *Tyler.* The *Tyler* swivels, turns its guns on the *Arkansas,* and scores several direct hits; however, they bounce harmlessly off the armored vessel. In the meantime, the *Arkansas* strikes a devastating blow which kills or wounds about 25 of the *Tyler's* crew. The *Carondelet* moves up and its commander, Captain Henry Walke, instructs Captain William L. Gwinn (*Tyler*) to head back down the river to warn the fleet, while the *Carondelet* attempts to engage the *Arkansas.*

Without pause, the *Carondelet* moves into position and repeatedly pounds the *Arkansas,* but still the armor buffers the shock and no damage is sustained; but the *Arkansas* has also been pounding the *Carondelet* and it sustains damage. Captain Walke concludes that it is nec-

The CSS *Arkansas* engages the Union fleet at Vicksburg, Mississippi (*Harper's Pictoral History of the Civil War,* 1896).

essary to board and seize the Confederate ship. However, as the troops board the *Arkansas*, to their surprise, there is no resistance. The crew of the *Arkansas* has bottled itself up in a secure iron-proof shell, and from there the crew uses loopholes to pour shot and shell as well as hot water and steam upon the *Carondelet*. Consequently, the *Carondelet* reacts by using the same tactics and executes similar action, creating a peculiar sea duel.

During the confrontation, the two vessels become separated as the grapples become loosened and the *Arkansas* slips away by drifting down the river towards the Union fleet. The *Arkansas* first encounters Gunboat No. 6, which greets the Rebels with a round from its Dahlgren gun. The staggering shot penetrates the armor, but the *Arkansas* continues moving and delivers a pounding broadside to the gunboat. Without missing a beat, the *Arkansas* passes the *Louisville*, and then it is in position to whack the entire fleet. The *Arkansas* hammers the transports and gunboats as it travels. The exchange of fire is extraordinary, and the streams of shot and shell create a maze of smoke that permeates the area, transforming the early daylight into a scene of drab gray and pitch black. The skies become an ominous collection of color spots as shells are fired and upon impact explode thunderously amid and above the thick blankets of choking smoke.

The *Arkansas* moves through the walls of fire originating from the entire Union fleet and passes the *Hartford*, *Iroquois*, and *Richmond*, all the while pursued by the *Benton*, *Louisville* and *Cincinnati*. Soon after, the *Essex* commences firing. Its guns strike two solid hits that pass through the armor, one of which hits below the water line and causes a leak. Meanwhile, the *Arkansas* continues to be the object of relentless small arms fire as it continues to singlehandedly battle the fleet.

Soon after, the *Arkansas* is struck by a 100-pound shell, fired from the *Richmond*, that passes straight through the vessel. Nonetheless, the *Arkansas* maintains its course, seemingly invulnerable to the typhoon of fire. A close call arises when the ram *Lancaster* moves to crash directly into the *Arkansas*, but instead, the *Arkansas* cranks off a round that bowls over the steam-pipe, knocking the *Lancaster* out of action and saving the *Arkansas* from possible destruction or capture. The *Arkansas*, following this escapade, evades further harm as it scurries farther down the river and reaches the protection of the Confederate batteries. Union pursuit terminates when the vessels close against the *Arkansas* and receive fire from the batteries at Vicksburg.

The crew of the *Arkansas* does sustain casualties during the exchange with the *Carondelet*. The chief pilot, John Hodges, is struck while at the wheel and sustains a mortal wound. Another, the Yazoo River pilot J.H. Shacklett, is hit and disabled. In addition, Lt. Commander Isaac Brown sustains a small bruise, but afterward, a Minié ball inflicts a superficial wound as it scrapes his left temple and causes him to tumble through the hatchway onto the gun deck, where he is temporarily knocked unconscious. While being carried to the cockpit, Brown regains consciousness and again takes command. He then sustains some other minor wounds, to his hand and to his shoulder, but he continues to direct the action. Another member of the crew picks an inopportune time to become curious. Just as the man places his head out of a port, a gun is being "run in for loading." The man is decapitated by a cannon ball.

In Arizona, contingents of the 2nd California Cavalry engage Confederates at Apache Pass. The Union sustains one wounded. Confederate casualty figures are unavailable.

In Arkansas, a Union contingent of about 600 troops including cavalry, led by Major W.H. Miller, clashes with a Confederate force nearly three times its size at Fayetteville. The Union captures about 150 Confederates.

In Tennessee, a contingent of cavalry skirmishes with Confederates at Decatur. The Union sustains four wounded. Confederate casualty figures are unavailable.

In Union general officer activity, Daniel McCook, Jr., the brother of Union Generals Alexander and Robert Latimer McCook and the cousin of Union General Edward Moody McCook, is commissioned colonel of the 52nd Ohio Regiment. Prior to the war, McCook had been a law partner of Union Generals William T. Sherman and Thomas Ewing.

In Confederate general officer activity, Confederate Major General David E. Twiggs dies of natural causes at age 72. Twiggs surrendered the Department of Texas to Colonel Ben McCulloch (later Confederate general) during the early stages of the war.

July 16 (Wednesday)   In Virginia, a contingent of the 5th U.S. Cavalry, commanded by Captain Harrison, departs Westover on a reconnaissance mission.

In Union general officer activity, Captain Jacob Ammen (West Point, 1831) is promoted to the rank of brigadier general of Volunteers. Ammen's service for the duration is primarily the command of garrisons and courts-martial rather than field service. He resigns from the service during January 1865. Brigadier General Edwin Vose Sumner, appointed brigadier in conjunction with the dismissal of General Twiggs the previous year, is promoted to major general effective 5 May. General Sumner, born in 1797, had first joined the army during 1819.

Colonel Cadwallader C. Washburn is appointed brigadier general. Lt. Colonel Francis Jay Herron (9th Iowa) is commissioned brigadier general. Benjamin Stone Roberts, inspector general under General John Pope, is promoted to brigadier general effective this day. He apparently sees no field duty during the war; however, he had been aligned with officers opposed to Generals Fitz John Porter and George B. McClellan. Nonetheless, toward the close of hostilities, Roberts receives the brevets of brigadier general of the Regular Army and major general

of volunteers. After the war, he is appointed lieutenant colonel of a regiment. In 1868, he is assigned as professor of military science at Yale. He retires during 1870. Afterward, also being a lawyer he begins to prosecute claims against the United States. Colonel Joshua Sill (West Point 1853) is appointed Brigadier General.

Colonel Fitz Henry Warren is promoted to brigadier general. Toward the latter part of the year, he becomes commander at Houston, Missouri. In September 1863 he is transferred to the Department of the Gulf and from there he later moves to Texas. Colonel Charles Croft (31st Indiana) is appointed brigadier general this day. General Croft participates at the Battle of Richmond, Kentucky, and later he commands a brigade at Murfreesboro and at Chickamauga. During the Battle of Nashville, he commands the "provisional division," composed of nearly all Negro troops formed from various corps.

In Naval activity, Flag Officer Charles Davis, commander of the Mississippi Flotilla, is promoted to the rank of commodore (rear admiral). In autumn, Commodore Davis is ordered to Washington, D.C., to assume the duties of the chief of the Bureau of Navigation (Navy Department). Also, Commander Stephen Rowan is promoted to the rank of captain. He is later rewarded for "distinguished gallantry" and promoted to commodore effective this same date. Commodore Rowan participates in the capture of New Bern, North Carolina, and in the naval activity off Charleston, including the attacks against Forts Wagner, Gregg and Moultrie. After the war he is promoted to the rank of rear admiral on 25 July 1866 and given command of the Norfolk Navy Yard, followed by an assignment in 1868 as commander of the Asiatic Squadron.

In other activity, Commander (later rear admiral) Thomas Turner is promoted to the rank of captain. Also, Captain William B. Shubrick, a veteran of the War of 1812 and the Mexican War who commanded the Brazil Squadron and the Paraguay Expedition of 1859, is commissioned as a rear admiral on this day. He serves also as chairman of the Lighthouse Board from 1860 to 1869. Captain Joseph Smith, a veteran of the War of 1812 and the Mexican War, presently the chief of the Bureau of Yards, is promoted to the rank of rear admiral. Admiral Smith remains in his post until 1869, when poor health compels him to resign. Also, Flag Officer Stringham, a veteran of the War of 1812, the Mexican War and an active officer in the ongoing conflict, is named rear admiral. At his own request, he was relieved of command (North Atlantic Blockading Squadron) the previous September. He is assigned special duty during 1862 and 1863, and in 1864, he receives command of a Navy yard, a post he retains until after the war.

Another Union naval officer, Captain Samuel L. Breeze, also a veteran of the War of 1812 and the Mexican War, is promoted to the rank of rear admiral. At the time of the outbreak of war, Admiral Breeze had been commandant of the New York Navy Yard. During 1862, he is a lighthouse inspector, and afterward he is assigned special duty in New York. Promotion to rear admiral is also granted to Captain Hiram Paulding, a veteran of the War of 1812. During the Mexican War, Paulding had been commander of the East Indies Squadron; from 1853 through 1858, he was commandant of the Washington Navy Yard. At the time of the outbreak of war, Paulding had been in Washington on special duty. After his promotion, Admiral Paulding is ordered to assume command of the New York Navy Yard. He retains the post until 1865, when he is relieved from duty. He becomes governor of the Naval Asylum from 1867 to 1869, then is port admiral at Boston.

Captain Thomas Crabbe, commissioned a midshipman during 1815, is promoted to commodore. On 25 July 1866, he is promoted to rear admiral. Captain John B. Montgomery, commander of the Pacific Squadron (1860–1861), is also named commodore. During 1862–1863, Montgomery serves as commandant of the Boston Navy Yard, and then is commandant of the Washington Navy Yard in 1864–1865. On 25 July 1866, he is named rear admiral and afterward serves as commandant of the naval station at Sackett's Harbor in New York (1867–1869). Captain Cornelius K. Stribling is also named commodore. Stribling was first commissioned as a midshipman in June 1812. His assignments during the war include serving as commandant of the Philadelphia Navy Yard (1863) and as commanding officer of the Eastern Gulf Blockading Squadron in 1865. Subsequently, on 25 July 1866, he is promoted to rear admiral. Promotion to commodore is also granted to Captain Joshua R. Sands, initially commissioned as a midshipman in June 1812. During the 1850s, he served as captain aboard the USS *Susquehanna*, and during 1860, he commanded the Brazilian Squadron. Commodore Sands serves as a lighthouse inspector from 1862 until 1866. At that time, on 25 July, he is promoted to rear admiral.

Also, Captain Charles H. Bell, initially commissioned as a midshipman during June 1812, is elevated to the rank commodore. Captain Bell served under Commodore Chauncey during the War of 1812 and with Commodore Chauncey's Mediterranean Squadron, followed by service in the West India Squadron, the Pacific Squadron and the Brazil Squadron. During 1856–1858, he commanded the USS *Constellation*. During 1860, Bell had been appointed commandant of the Norfolk Navy Yard. As commodore, he commands the Pacific Squadron until 1864, followed by special duty at the James River in 1865. Commodore Bell is promoted to rear admiral on 25 July 1866. The rank of commodore is also assigned to Levin M. Powell, initially commissioned as a midshipman in March 1817. His service included the Mediterranean Squadron (1829–1830) and West India Squadron (1836–1837). Other tours included coast survey duty, patrols off Africa and the Potomac Blockading Squadron. Subsequent to his promotion, Commodore Powell serves as a lighthouse inspector until 1866. He is promoted to rear admiral during 1869.

Promotion to commodore is also given to Captain Charles Wilkes, who was responsible for capturing Confederate ministers Mason and Slidell. He is active during the war and in 1864 he receives a court-martial. On 25 July 1866, Commodore Wilkes is promoted to rear admiral. Captain Andrew H. Harwood, initially commissioned as a midshipman during January 1818, also becomes a commodore on this date. Prior to the war, Captain Harwood served with the Mediterranean Squadron on several different tours of duty between 1833 and 1855. In 1861, Harwood had been chief of the Bureau of Ordnance. After his promotion he is named commandant of the Washington Navy Yard (during 1862–1863) and afterward serves as a lighthouse inspector. Later, during 1869, he is promoted to rear admiral. Another seaman who was commissioned a midshipman in January 1818, Captain Theodorus Bailey, is made a commodore. Previously he served with the Pacific Squadron and the East India Squadron. During the Mexican War, Bailey commanded the store ship *Lexington* and participated in naval actions. Subsequently, Captain Bailey served as commander with the Western Blockading Squadron (1861–1862). He was second in command during Admiral Farragut's campaign to seize New Orleans. At this time, Commodore Bailey's health is poor; however, he refuses to leave sea duty and requests an active command. During autumn of this year, he is appointed commander of the Eastern Gulf Blockading Squadron. Bailey focuses on the blockade runners operating along the coast of Florida. In 1865, Commodore Bailey is assigned as commandant of the Portsmouth Navy Yard, where he serves into 1867. Meanwhile, he is promoted to rear admiral on 25 July 1866.

Captain James L. Lardner is another given the rank of commodore; he was commissioned a midshipman during July 1820. He served in the Pacific Squadron in 1827–1830 and with the Mediterranean Squadron during 1834–1835. Later he again served with the Pacific Squadron and at Philadelphia, prior to duty off the coast of Africa during 1853. Subsequent to becoming commodore, Lardner is assigned as commander of the Eastern Gulf Blockading Squadron. He is appointed commander of the West India Squadron during 1864. During the final year of the war, Commodore Lardner is assigned on special duty. On 25 July 1866, he is promoted to the rank of rear admiral.

July 17 (Thursday) In Washington, D.C., Congress authorizes President Abraham Lincoln to create national cemeteries "for the soldiers who shall die in the service of the country." Battlefield cemeteries are established in Antietam, Chattanooga, Gettysburg, Knoxville and Stone's River. In other activity, General McClellan telegraphs a message to President Lincoln requesting reinforcements to renew his offensive, and he strongly urges no withdrawal from the area. McClellan rests blame for the failure at the Seven Days' Battles on the doorsteps of the capitol for lack of the government's giving him adequate forces to win. Mc-

Clellan, on the 28th of June, after the devastating loss at Savage's Station, says in a telegram to Secretary of War Edwin Stanton: "I know that a few thousand more men would have changed this battle from a defeat to victory. As it is the government must not and cannot hold me responsible for the result.... I have seen too many dead and wounded comrades to feel otherwise than that the government has not sustained this army. If I save this army now [Army of the Potomac], I tell you plainly that I owe no thanks to you or to any other persons in Washington. You [Washington] have done your best to sacrifice this army." Also this day, President Lincoln signs the Second Confiscation Act, which gives freedom to those slaves who arrive in areas under Union jurisdiction.

In Kentucky, Morgan's Raiders engage Union forces at Cynthiana and capture the town. Among the participants for the Union are the 18th Kentucky, 7th Kentucky Cavalry and the Kentucky Home Guards (Bracken, Cincinnati, Cynthiana and Newport County Home Guards). The Union suffers 17 killed and 34 wounded. The Confederates sustain eight killed and 29 wounded.

In Naval activity, 28 Marines board the steamer USS *Grey Cloud,* which sails to join the USS *New London;* both vessels embark on a mission to seek and destroy Confederate vessels suspected of transporting cotton in the vicinity of Pascagoula, Mississippi.

In Union general officer activity, Colonel Conrad Feger Jackson (9th Pennsylvania Reserve Regiment, also known as the 38th Pennsylvania Infantry) is promoted to brigadier general, effective this day. On 30 August, General Jackson becomes ill and is compelled to retire from the service, but in December he returns and participates at Fredericksburg. Colonel James Blair Steedman and Colonel James Dada Morgan are promoted to brigadier general effective this date. General Morgan serves in Alabama during the Chickamauga and Chattanooga campaigns, then afterward, he commands a brigade during the Atlanta Campaign. For a while he also commands Jefferson C. Davis' division. Colonel Henry Dwight Terry is another officer promoted to brigadier general this day. He participates against Confederate General James Longstreet at Suffolk, Virginia, and during the following year he participates at Gettysburg, then returns to the Army of the Potomac. Promotion to brigadier general is also granted to Colonel John B. Turchin and Colonel August Willich. Brigadier General Thomas L. Crittenden is promoted to major general.

In Confederate general officer activity, Major General D. H. Hill is assigned command of the Department of North Carolina.

July 18 (Friday) In Washington, D.C., General George B. McClellan is still attempting to reinforce his Army of the Potomac to insure the safety of Washington and to cause the fall of Richmond. He telegraphs President Lincoln for the third time in a week requesting Washing-

Major General John Gray Foster (Mottelay, *The Soldier in Our Civil War*, 1886).

ton's solution to the problem. On the 17th he had requested that General Ambrose Burnside's troops in North Carolina be brought up to start a new offensive to take Richmond, but no response arrived. Burnside will later be sent, and upon his departure, General J.G. Foster will succeed him as commander of the Department of North Carolina.

In Indiana, a small Confederate guerrilla contingent led by Colonel (actually appointed August 1862) Adam Rankin Johnson rides into the Union held town of Newburgh and successfully captures it. Using a deteriorating wagon with two old stovepipes tied to the running gear, the men load the wagon with supplies and ammunition and then escape across the Ohio River, transporting all of their contraband in the process. The operation goes off without a hitch and the partisan rangers under Johnson, soon to be tagged "Stovepipe," accomplish the mission without any use of firearms.

In Missouri, a 400-man Union contingent — composed of elements of the 2nd Missouri Cavalry and the 9th and 11th Missouri State Militia and commanded by Major Clopper — skirmishes with a Confederate force (about 600 troops) at Memphis. The Union sustains 13 killed, 35 wounded and some missing. The Confederates sustain 23 killed.

In Union general officer activity, John Gray Foster, appointed brigadier general the previous October, is promoted to major general. General Foster participates in the move to relieve General Burnside at Knoxville, Tennessee, during 1863, but after being injured while in command of the Department of the Ohio when his horse falls upon him, he resumes duty as commander of the Department of the South and later the Department of Florida. In March 1865, General Foster is breveted major general in the Regular Army. Also, Colonel George Foster Shepley, 12th Maine Cavalry, is promoted to brigadier general effective this day. Shepley, subsequent to

Union occupation of Richmond during April 1865, is appointed military governor of Richmond, but only for a short while. He resigns his commission during July 1865 to resume his law practice in Maine.

Other appointments to brigadier general include Major Alfred Pleasonton (West Point, 1844), 2nd Cavalry, who commands a cavalry division during the Maryland campaign and later at Fredericksburg and Chancellorsville, and Colonel Frederick (Friedrich) Salomon, who is assigned to Kansas and receives command of a brigade. Salomon participates in various actions including the Battle of Jenkins' Ferry and receives the brevet of major general on 13 March 1865. Colonel George Foster Shepley, commander of the post at New Orleans, is also appointed brigadier general. In 1864 he is assigned to the District of Eastern Virginia and afterward becomes chief of staff to General Godfrey Weitzel. For a short while after the fall of Richmond, he becomes military governor of the city until he musters out of the service during July 1865. In yet other activity, Brigadier General Horatio Gouverneur Wright is promoted to major general of volunteers to rank from this day. Nonetheless, the Senate declines the appointment in March 1863.

July 19 (Saturday) *In Union general officer activity,* Colonel James Streshly Jackson, 3rd Kentucky Cavalry, is promoted to the rank of brigadier general. Jackson is assigned as commander of cavalry in General William Nelson's Army of Kentucky and later transferred to the Army of Ohio. He participates in the Battle of Perryville on 8 October 1862. Brigadier General William Nelson is promoted to major general. He is transferred to Nashville, and from there he is sent to Kentucky to intercept forces under Confederate Generals Braxton Bragg and E. Kirby Smith.

In Confederate general officer activity, General Joseph Reid Anderson resigns his commission to focus his efforts on overseeing the operations at the Tredegar Iron Works in Richmond, Virginia, that are intended to further the Confederate cause. Anderson had been superintendent of the iron works during the 1840s. The operations there continue until Richmond is evacuated in 1865.

July 20 (Sunday) **In Arizona,** General James Carleton initiates his march to Santa Fe, New Mexico. The vanguard departs Tucson on this day.

In Arkansas, elements of the 13th Illinois Cavalry clash with Confederates at Pittman's Ferry.

In Tennessee, Confederate guerrillas skirmish with a contingent of the 2nd Kentucky Volunteer Regiment at Nashville.

In Virginia, a Union contingent led by Colonel Brodhead skirmishes with Confederates at Orange Court House. Casualty figures are unavailable. Also, one squadron of the 8th Pennsylvania Cavalry, commanded by Captain P. Keenan, skirmishes with Confederate pickets at Turkey Island Bridge.

July 21 (Monday) **In Arizona** at Tucson, General Carleton issues General Order No. 11: "All of the Territory of Arizona west of a meridian line running through what is known as Apache Pass, on the Butterfield Mail Route, hence to Mesilla, will constitute a military district, to be known as the District of Western Arizona, the headquarters of which shall be Tucson, Arizona. Major David Ferguson First California Volunteer Cavalry is hereby placed in command of this district, as well as of the post and town of Tucson...."

In Tennessee, General William Tecumseh Sherman's brigade arrives near Memphis and will deploy in and around Fort Pickering on the 22nd. General Sherman assumes command at Memphis on the following day.

In Confederate activity, Colonel Nathan Bedford Forrest, who received command of a cavalry brigade (Army of the Tennessee) the previous month, is promoted to the rank of brigadier general. He receives a new command and will ride to cut and disrupt General Ulysses S. Grant's supply lines and communications in the western sector of Tennessee during the latter part of this year. Colonel Martin E. Green and Colonel Thomas Green, 5th Texas Cavalry, are each promoted to brigadier general. T.G. Green is the brother-in-law of Confederate General James Patrick Major, who is also promoted to the rank of brigadier general this day, along with Colonel Johnson Hagood.

In Naval activity, the USS *Huntsville*, while operating as part of the blockading squadron along the east coast, seizes the vessel *Reliance*. Also, the USS *Sallie Wood*, formerly the CSS *Sallie Wood*, comes under severe fire from Confederate batteries on Argyle Landing and from Island No. 82. While attempting to avoid disaster, the ship sustains a hit to its steam drum and is immobilized by the damage. The *Sallie Wood* runs aground on Island No. 82. The Confederates afterward burn the vessel.

July 22 (Tuesday) **In Georgia,** Union Colonel John W. Sprague, commanding a small force of the 63rd Ohio Infantry, engages and repulses a superior Confederate force at Decatur, preventing Rebels from seizing Union trains in the area.

In Virginia, a contingent of Union Cavalry encounters a five-man Confederate force at Westover. The Union, led by Captain Taylor, sustains the loss of one man. In other activity, Union Major General John Adams Dix assumes command of the Seventh Army Corps, Department of Virginia. General Dix (later governor of New York) is essentially assigned to department duty due to his age.

In Confederate general officer activity, Colonel Micah Jenkins is promoted to the rank of brigadier general.

In Naval activity, the Union vessel *Dolly Webb*, a gunboat with five artillery pieces and a 200-man complement, is described by Lt. George Preble as "a towboat altered." The *Dolly*, as she is sometimes called, is only mentioned in the official records twice. Rear Admiral David Farragut, above Vicksburg, receives orders to return to New Orleans. He departs on 24 July and arrives back at New Orleans on the 28th. Shortly thereafter, the USS *Hartford* (Farragut's flagship) leaves New Orleans for Pensacola for repairs.

July 23 (Wednesday)   In Washington, D.C., Major General Henry W. Halleck, rising on the success of the victories of some of his subordinates, is appointed commander-in-chief of the Union armies.

In Arizona, General James H. Carleton departs Tucson en route for the Rio Grande Apache Pass; along the route remains dangerous ground due to the hostility of the Apache Indians (Chiricahua). Carleton orders his force to establish a post there to counteract the Apaches. The post is named Fort Bowie and the garrison is charged with guarding the water in that area.

In Missouri, a contingent of the 3rd Iowa Cavalry, led by Major H.C. Caldwell, skirmishes with Confederates at the town of Florida. The Union sustains 22 wounded (a contemporary report lists Union casualties as 26 killed and wounded). The Confederates sustain three killed. Also, a contingent of the 7th Missouri Cavalry clashes with Confederates at Columbus.

In Virginia, a contingent of the 2nd New York Cavalry and 3rd Indiana Cavalry, commanded by Lt. Colonel Hugh J. Kilpatrick, skirmishes with Confederates at North Anna River. No casualty figures are available. Kilpatrick, an 1861 graduate of West Point, becomes colonel of the regiment the following December.

July 24 (Thursday)   In Alabama, Company E, 31st Ohio Volunteer Regiment, led by Captain M.B.W. Harman, skirmishes with Confederates at Trinity. The Union sustains two killed and 11 wounded. The Confederates suffer 12 killed and 30 wounded.

In Mississippi, Union and Confederate forces clash at Coldwater. Specific units are not reported.

In Missouri, elements of the 3rd Iowa Cavalry clash with Confederates at Bott's Farm. Other units of the 3rd Iowa skirmish with Confederates at Santa Fe.

In New York, Martin Van Buren, the eighth president of the United States, dies at his farm (Lindenwald) in Kinderhook.

In Confederate general officer activity, Lt. Colonel Fitzhugh Lee, 1st Virginia Cavalry, is promoted to the rank of brigadier general.

In Naval activity, the USS *Quaker City* seizes a blockade runner, the *Orion*, at Champeche Bank south of Key West, Florida.

July 25 (Friday)   In Alabama, Confederates clash with a Union contingent composed of two companies of Kentucky volunteers and two companies of the 1st Iowa Cavalry at Courtland

Bridge. The Confederates seize a large number of Union troops.

In Louisiana at New Orleans, General Benjamin Franklin Butler proclaims that all property belonging to well known Confederate officials, including civilian and military, will be confiscated. The proclamation also states that all other lesser known Confederate sympathizers must pledge allegiance to the Union by September 23 of this year or face the confiscation of their property.

In Missouri, the 3rd Iowa Cavalry again clashes with Confederates at Santa Fe. Meanwhile, at Big Piney, three companies of the 3rd Missouri Cavalry, bolstered by Battery L, 2nd Missouri Artillery, commanded by Captain George D. Bradway, engage Confederates under Colonel William O. Coleman. The Union reports no casualties. The Confederates sustain five killed (a contemporary report lists eight Confederates killed, 12 wounded and 17 missing).

In Tennessee, a contingent of Union cavalry, commanded by Major Wallace, skirmishes with Confederates led by Captain Faulkner at Brownsville. Casualty figures are unavailable.

In Virginia, a Union contingent (General Gibbon's command) on a reconnaissance mission skirmishes with Confederates at Orange Court House. The Confederates sustain five killed.

In Union general officer activity, Brigadier General John J. Peck is promoted to major general, effective 4 July. Prior to promotion, Peck had commanded the 2nd Division in General Keyes' IV Corps. Also, Brigadier General George Webb Morell is promoted to major general of volunteers, to rank from 4 July. General Morell, aligned with General Fitz John Porter, sees his career fade away after his testimony at Porter's court-martial. He does participate at Antietam (Sharpsburg); however, afterward he sees no field command. He resigns from the service in December 1864. Brigadier General Henry Warner Slocum is promoted to major general effective 4 July.

In Confederate general officer activity, Colonel Harry T. Hays, 7th Louisiana, having recovered from a wound sustained at the battle of Port Republic, is promoted to brigadier general. Hays remains with the Army of Northern Virginia, but subsequently, he is transferred to the Trans-Mississippi Department. Jeb (James Ewell Brown) Stuart is promoted to the rank of major general. He receives command of the cavalry division (later corps) of the Confederate Army of Northern Virginia, a post he retains until his death (11 May 1864). Brigadier General James Green Martin resigns his commission; however, soon after on 11 August, he is reappointed to rank of his first appointment (15 May 1862). He receives command of the Department of North Carolina until the summer of 1864, when he is ordered to Petersburg, Virginia.

In Naval activity, the USS *Sebago* departs from Hampton Roads en route to Charleston to join the South Atlantic Blockading Squadron. It ar-

rives off Charleston on 29 July and initiates blockade duty.

July 26 (Saturday)   In Mississippi, Confederate Major General John C. Breckinridge (Van Dorn's command), at Vicksburg, will move against Union-held Baton Rouge, Louisiana. Trains of the New Orleans and Jacksonville Railroad transport the force to Tangapaho (Tangipahoa), Louisiana, a journey of about 125 miles, but still slightly more than 60 miles from Baton Rouge. General Van Dorn will notify Breckinridge when the CSS *Arkansas* and two other vessels will be available to support the assault.

In Missouri, a small contingent of Missouri Militia composed of about one company skirmishes with a large Confederate force at Paten. The Union sustains three wounded. The Confederates sustain about 25 killed and wounded. Meanwhile, a contingent composed of the 3rd and 12th Missouri Militia, commanded by Captain Bradway, skirmishes with Confederates led by Colonel Coleman at Greenville. The Union reports no casualties. The estimated Confederate casualties are five killed and about 12 wounded.

In Virginia, with General John Pope now heading the Army of Virginia, orders are dispatched to General Jacob Dolson Cox in Western Virginia directing him to move out and cross the Rappahannock River to create a threat to the Confederate lines at Gordonsville, the strategic link to the southern entrances to the Shenandoah Valley. Meanwhile, General McClellan is concentrating on preventing the Confederates from focusing their full force upon Pope. He soon initiates a series of raids that manage to temporarily keep Robert E. Lee's forces on the defensive. One of these raids causes General Hooker's force to tangle with a Confederate contingent at Malvern Hill, the scene heavy fighting on July 1.

In West Virginia, a skirmish erupts at Buckhannon. Specific units are not recorded.

In North Carolina, elements of the 9th New Jersey and the 3rd New York Cavalry depart Newport on a reconnaissance mission through the 29th. The unit skirmishes with Confederates at Young's Cross Roads. The Union sustains seven wounded. The Confederates suffer four killed and 13 wounded.

July 27 (Sunday)   In Virginia, Confederate Brigadier General Maxcy Gregg's Brigade (12th, 13th and 14th South Carolina Regiments), part of General Ambrose P. Hill's Division, is assigned to General Thomas J. Jackson's command. Hill's Division had only been assigned to Longstreet's command a few days earlier. General Hill's Division moves out by overland route via Richmond and board trains for Gordonsville.

In Missouri, a contingent of the 2nd Iowa Cavalry clashes with a Confederate unit at Brown Springs. Casualty figures are unavailable.

July 28 (Monday) In Louisiana, Admiral David Farragut departs Baton Rouge, leaving General Thomas Williams in command there.

In North Carolina, a Union force — Companies D, G and H, 27th Massachusetts Regiment, Company C, New York Artillery and Company G, New York Cavalry, commanded by Captain Sanford — departs Batchelder's Creek on a reconnaissance mission along the Neuse River Road. The Union reports no casualties. Confederates sustain two killed and 10 captured. In Missouri, a Union contingent, commanded by Colonel Guitar and composed of elements of the 3rd Iowa Cavalry, 2nd Missouri Cavalry, 9th Missouri Volunteer Regiment and the 3rd Indiana Battery, clashes with Confederates led by J.C. Porter and Cobb at Moore's Mills. The Union suffers 19 killed and 21 wounded. The Confederates sustain 30 killed, about 100 wounded and one captured. A contemporary source lists Confederate casualties at about 75 killed and wounded.

In Virginia, Union General McClellan telegraphs General Halleck, emphasizing the desperate need for reinforcements to initiate an attack against Richmond: "Here is the defense of Washington ... I should be reinforced at once so I can advance. Retreat would be disastrous to the army and the cause." A Union reconnaissance force led by Captain Duncan departs Harrison's Landing en route to St. Mary's Church.

In the Indian Territory, elements of the 1st, 2nd and 3rd Kansas Indian Territory Home Guards, bolstered by the 1st Kansas Battery, commanded by Colonel William Phillips, skirmish with Confederates led by Colonel Thomas H. Taylor at Bayou Bernard. Casualty figures are unavailable. One contemporary lists Confederate casualties as high.

In Confederate general officer activity, Brigadier General Richard Taylor is promoted to the rank of major general.

In Naval activity, the USS *Cimarron,* operating on the James River, engages Confederate ground troops at Harrison's Landing, Virginia.

July 29 (Tuesday) In Kentucky, elements of the 18th Kentucky Regiment and Kentucky Home Guards led by Captain J.J. Evans and Major Bracht engage Confederates at Mount Sterling. The Union reports no casualties. The Confederate casualties are estimated as high. Meanwhile, Confederate guerrillas, commanded by Colonel Richard M. Gano, attack defending Union contingents (Russellville Home Guards and 70th Indiana Volunteer Regiment) at Russellville, and they capture the town. The Union sustains one wounded. Confederate casualties, if any, are unavailable.

In Missouri, two companies of the 13th Missouri Volunteer Regiment skirmish with Confederates at Arrow Rock (Bollinger's Mills). The Union reports no casualties. The Confederates sustain 10 killed.

In Tennessee, a company of the 15th Illinois Cavalry skirmishes with a detachment of Confederates near Brownsville. Each side sustains four killed and six wounded.

July 30 (Wednesday) In Kentucky, a Union force composed of the 9th Pennsylvania Cavalry, commanded by Lt. Colonel James, skirmishes with Confederates at Paris. The Union reports no casualties. The Confederates sustain 27 killed and 39 wounded.

In Naval activity, a Union naval force (gunboats) departs from Harrison's Landing, Virginia, heading towards Jones' Ford along the Chickahominy River. Also, the USS *Arletta* and other vessels of Admiral Farragut's flotilla arrive at Hampton Roads from New Orleans to support the Union operations in Virginia, where its advance had been halted by General Lee at Harrison's Landing. General Benjamin F. Butler had requested 12 schooners from Porter; however, he arrives with the whole flotilla to bolster the James River Flotilla. The USS *Arletta* moves to Norfolk for repairs and then is towed on 9 August by the USS *Satellite* to positions near the Claremont Plantation. It remains in the area for about one month to support General George McClellan's forces while they withdraw to northern Virginia to bolster the defenses at Washington, D.C.

July 31 (Thursday) In Mississippi, William Anderson Pile, commissioned as chaplain (later brevet major general) of the 1st Missouri Light Artillery on 12 June 1861, has taken on different duties. On this day he is Captain William Pile in command of Battery I during the operations at Corinth. Within a month, he is promoted to lieutenant colonel of the 33rd Missouri Infantry, which becomes known as the Merchants' Regiment. During the following month, on the 23rd, he is appointed colonel of the regiment. Colonel Pile is assigned duty in Arkansas, and his regiment is charged primarily with garrison duty.

In Virginia, Confederates attack Union positions and shipping in the vicinity of Shirley and Harrison's Landing, including Coggins Point. The clashes continue into the following day. The Union sustains 10 killed and 12 wounded. The Confederates sustain one killed and nine wounded.

In Union general officer activity, James Hughes Stokes (West Point, 1835, later brigadier general) musters into Federal service as a volunteer commander of a battery. Later, he participates at the actions in the West, stretching from Perryville to Chattanooga. Stokes commands an artillery division at Missionary Ridge (November 1863). During February 1864, he is removed from the line and assigned duty in the quartermaster department (Military Division of the Mississippi) as an inspector with the rank of lieutenant colonel.

In Naval activity, the USS *Magnolia* seizes a blockade runner, the *Memphis.* It is a steam merchant ship built in Dunbar, Scotland. The U.S. Navy acquires the *Memphis* from the prize

court in New York, then in October it is commissioned the USS *Memphis* and assigned blockade duty off Charleston, South Carolina. Another gunboat that arrives at about this time is the USS *Conemaugh,* commissioned at the Portsmouth Navy Yard in Kittery, Maine, this month. The *Conemaugh* remains off the Carolinas into 1863. After repairs, it is attached to the West Gulf Blockading Squadron in February 1864. The Navy also purchases the vessel *Satellite,* a 217-ton tug built in 1854. It is commissioned in September and attached to the Potomac Flotilla. The *Satellite* operates against Confederate forces on shore in Virginia for the remainder of the year. Later it operates in support of General McClellan's Peninsular Campaign, and it transfers back to the Potomac Flotilla during August 1862. In other activity, the USS *Adolph Huger,* one of 12 mortar ships recalled from Admiral David Porter's squadron by Secretary of the Navy Gideon Welles to support efforts in Virginia, arrives at Hampton Roads. The ship is in poor condition. Instead of moving to the James River, the *Adolph Huger* is sent to Baltimore for repairs. The USS *Cimarron* engages Confederate-held Fort Powhatan (Prince George's County) In Virginia.

August In Utah, Union troops, including cavalry under Major Edward McGarry and volunteers from California (3rd California Infantry) led by Colonel Patrick E. Connor, arrive at Salt Lake City. Colonel Connor is appointed commander of the Department of Utah, which at this time includes Nevada. Colonel Connor, rather than occupying Fort Crittenden (formerly Camp Floyd), which had been abandoned the previous year, establishes Fort Douglas, which he names in honor of Stephen Douglas. The garrison attempts to maintain order within the Mormon population and simultaneously deal with the Shoshone Indians in the Bear River Valley. By the following year, the campaigns here against the Indians intensify.

In Naval activity, the U.S. Navy acquires the USS *Signal* (Tinclad No. 8), built in West Virginia during 1862. The vessel, built for commercial purposes, is a 190-ton stern-wheel tinclad river gunboat, and after modifications, it is commissioned with a few months. The *Signal* participates in the Yazoo River operations during November and December 1862 and devotes much of its time clearing the river of mines.

August 1 (Friday) In Virginia, a Union reconnaissance force (Bayard's Cavalry Brigade) skirmishes with Confederates at Orange Court House. Casualty figures are unavailable.

In Missouri, Confederate guerrillas, commanded by Captain Joseph C. Porter, assault a 73-man contingent of the 11th Missouri (state militia), commanded by Captain Lair, at Newark. The skirmish lasts about two hours and terminates with a Union surrender (60-men). Union losses other than those captured are four killed and four wounded. The Confederates lose about 75, including killed and wounded.

In Naval activity, the USS *Penobscot,* while on patrol in the vicinity of New Inlet, North Carolina, seizes a blockade runner, the sloop *Lizzie.* In other activity, the *Housatonic,* a sloop of war built in Massachusetts and commissioned at about this time (August), is assigned to the South Atlantic Blockading Squadron. It arrives off Charleston in September. The U.S. Navy acquires the vessel *Saint Clair* at about this time (August). The *Saint Clair,* transformed into a tinclad river gunboat (Tinclad No. 19), is commissioned the USS *Saint Clair* in September and assigned to duty on the Cumberland River and on the Green and Ohio Rivers. The *Saint Clair* also participates in the relief of Fort Donelson, Tennessee, the following February.

In Union general officer activity, Colonel Michael Corcoran is exchanged. He had been captured at the Battle of Bull Run (Manassas) in July 1861. Colonel Corcoran at about this time (August) is promoted to brigadier general, effective 21 July 1861, the date of the battle.

August 2 (Saturday)   In Mississippi, a contingent of the 11th Wisconsin Volunteer Regiment skirmishes with Confederates in Coahoma County. The Union sustains five wounded. Confederate casualty figures are unavailable. Another clash occurs at Austin, where a Union contingent of the 8th Indiana Volunteer Regiment skirmishes with Confederates. Casualty figures are unavailable.

In Missouri, a 75-man detachment of the 14th Missouri Militia, commanded by Captain Birch, skirmishes with Confederates at Ozark (Forsythe). The Union sustains one wounded. The Confederates suffer three killed and seven wounded. Also, four companies of the Union 1st Iowa Cavalry skirmish with Confederates at Clear Creek.

In Virginia, Union Major Generals George B. McClellan and John Pope are diligently involved with the seizure of Confederate-held Orange Court House and Malvern Hill. This day, a reconnaissance force departs Harrison's Landing en route to reoccupy Malvern Hill. The mission lasts until the 8th. Also, elements of the 5th New York Cavalry and the 1st Vermont Cavalry (General Samuel W. Crawford's command) skirmish with Confederates at Orange Court House. The Union sustains four killed and 12 wounded. The Confederates sustain 11 killed and 52 captured.

August 3 (Sunday)   In Arkansas, elements of the 1st Wisconsin Cavalry skirmish with Confederates at Jonesboro. The Union sustains four killed, two wounded and 21 missing. Also, a contingent of the 1st Wisconsin Cavalry clashes with Confederates at Lauguelle Ferry. The Union sustains 17 killed and 38 wounded. Confederate casualty figures are unavailable.

In Missouri, the 6th Missouri Cavalry skirmishes with Confederates at Chariton Bridge. Casualties are Union, two wounded; Confederates, 11 killed and 14 wounded.

In Virginia, Union General Henry W. Halleck orders General George B. McClellan to depart

the peninsula and join John Pope at Fredericksburg. General Pope is then in charge of all Union troops in the East except those under McClellan's command. In other activity, a Union reconnaissance force composed of the 5th U.S. Cavalry and 3rd Pennsylvania Cavalry under Colonel (later general) William W. Averell's command, operating on the south side of the James River, skirmishes with Confederates at Sycamore Church, in the vicinity of Petersburg, the rear door to Richmond. The Union sustains two wounded. The Confederates sustain six wounded and two captured.

In Naval activity, the USS *Santiago de Cuba,* a 1567-ton (burden) wooden side-wheel steamer operating off the Bahamas, intercepts and seizes the British steamship *Columbia,* an iron screw steamer trying to deliver arms to the Confederates. The *Santiago de Cuba* was initially built during 1856 as a merchant ship, but it was acquired by the U.S. Navy during September 1861 and converted into a cruiser. Prior to seizing the *Columbia,* the ship captured the schooner *Victoria* the previous December. The U.S. Navy also acquires the *Columbia* this August and transforms it into a gunboat, the USS *Columbia.* Union warships, including the USS *Henry Brinker,* initiate a reconnaissance mission on the Chowan River that lasts until the 23rd. Afterward the *Henry Brinker* resumes patrols from Hatteras Inlet, North Carolina.

August 4 (Monday)   In Washington, D.C., President Abraham Lincoln orders the induction of 300,000 additional men to serve for nine months.

In Missouri, a Union contingent led by Captain Birch clashes with contingent of Confederate guerrillas at White River. Casualty figures are unavailable.

In Tennessee, a Union contingent — including elements of the 4th Kentucky Regiment and the 7th Indiana Cavalry, commanded by Colonel George C. Wynkoop — skirmishes with Confederates at Sparta. Wynkoop's force numbers about 170 troops and the Confederates stand at about 700, as the two sides battle for about one hour. The Union lists one man wounded. Confederate casualties are unlisted; however, a contemporary source estimates 30 killed and 10 wounded during this Confederate victory.

In Virginia, General George B. McClellan telegraphs General Henry Halleck concerning his thoughts about abandoning the peninsula and joining Pope: "I am convinced that the order to withdraw this army [Army of the Potomac] to Acquia Creek will prove disastrous to our cause. I fear it will be a fatal blow." McClellan realizes that Acquia Creek is 75 miles from Richmond and the only way of reaching it will be on land. He continues his case, stating further: "Here directly on front of this army is the heart of the rebellion; it is here that all our resources should be collected to strike the blow which will determine the fate of the nation."

A Union reconnaissance force, composed of elements of the 5th U.S. Cavalry and the 3rd

Pennsylvania Cavalry (Colonel William W. Averell's command), led by Captain Wilkins, departs Coggins Point and moves out beyond Sycamore Church in the vicinity of Petersburg. The next day, the contingent skirmishes with Confederates at White Oak Swamp Bridge.

In Naval activity, the USS *Lodona,* a 861-ton (burden) iron screw gunboat, was originally the blockade running steamship of the same name. It was built at Hull, England, in 1862 and captured in Ossabaw Sound, South Carolina, on this day by the USS *Unadilla.* The Navy acquires the vessel the following September and converts it to a warship. The *Lodona* is commissioned in early January 1863. On the James River, the USS *Cimarron* exchanges fire with a Confederate battery at Swan's Point. During the following month, the *Cimarron* is transferred to the South Atlantic Blockading Squadron. Also, the USS *Wamsutta* departs Doboy Sound, Georgia, for Port Royal, South Carolina, to receive repairs. Shortly thereafter, it sails north to New York, where it is decommissioned on 3 December 1862. After repairs the *Wamsutta* is recommissioned on 2 February 1863 and returns to Port Royal.

August 4–5   In Louisiana, a Confederate force under General John Breckinridge arrives at positions near Baton Rouge in preparation for an imminent attack. Meanwhile, Breckinridge has recently been informed that the CSS *Arkansas* will arrive early on the following day to support the assault; however, it appears off Baton Rouge slightly before midnight. The commander, Lt. Isaac Brown, remains ill in Grenada. In his absence, the *Arkansas* is under the command of Lt. Stevens. Union General Thomas Williams, in anticipation of the attack, requests and receives the assistance of gunboats, including the USS *Kineo, Sumter, Katahdin* and *Cayuga,* all of which move into position near the waterfront. Meanwhile, Williams deploys the 6th Michigan and two guns across the Clay Cut and Cemetery Roads.

General Williams directs the 21st Indiana and four guns to establish positions to the right of Greenwell Springs Road and the rear of Magnolia Cemetery in some dense woods. And to the rear on the far right, he posts the 7th Vermont and the 30th Massachusetts Regiments, bolstered by Nim's Battery. General Williams' far left at Bayou Gros is held by the 4th Wisconsin Regiment and two guns of Manning's Battery; Manning's remaining four guns are spotted with the 9th Connecticut Regiment in the Government Cemetery. The 14th Maine Regiment stands on the left of Greenwell Springs Road and to the rear of the Bayou Sara Road.

General Breckinridge, using the advantage of fog and a superior force, assaults General Williams' Union positions at Baton Rouge, the state capital, located about 40 miles below the mouth of the Red River. The right wing under Breckinridge strikes during the early morning hours and power its way forward, hammering the 6th Michigan, 14th Maine and the 21st Indiana Regiments. The Union holds for a while, but eventually it is forced to pull back.

General Thomas Williams is killed on 4 August 1862 (*Harper's Pictoral History of the Civil War*, 1896).

Soon the 4th Wisconsin and the 30th Massachusetts speed to the fight and are later joined by the 7th Vermont. Artillery is also brought to bear upon the attacking Rebels in the grueling two-hour duel. Colonel George T. Roberts, commanding officer of the Vermonters, is mortally wounded (he dies two days later) and nearly all other officers, particularly those of the 21st Indiana, lie dead, prompting General Williams to take personal command in an effort to rally the Indiana troops. Williams yells: "Boys your field officers are all killed! I will lead you!" The spontaneous response is a rousing cheer that comes from the entire line. With Williams at the point, the Indianians charge into the wall of fire. Williams takes a shot to the heart which kills him instantly, but his "boys" keep advancing and drive the Confederates back.

Still, the Union is overmatched by the sheer numbers of the Confederates. A dogged close-quartered fight erupts and the hand-to-hand combat proves bloody for both sides. Colonel Thomas W. Cahill of the 9th Connecticut, sensing the overwhelming strength of the Confederates, directs the Union to disengage and retire from the field, while simultaneously requesting that the gunboats continue to lambaste the Confederates. The naval barrage compels the Confederates to retire. Confederate gunboats are supposed to support the attack, but that does not come about due to mechanical problems aboard the CSS *Arkansas*.

On the following day, Union vessels again pursue the *Arkansas*, commanded by Lieutenant Stevens. The Union loses 82 dead, 316 wounded and 34 missing. The Confederates lose 84 killed, 316 wounded and 78 missing. Confederate General Charles Clark is struck by a shell fragment that does severe permanent damage to his hip and compels him to resign from the service. He is elected governor of Mississippi and serves 1863–1865. Also, the USS *Essex* remains with the U.S. Army's Western Gunboat Flotilla until October and then is transferred to the U.S. Navy.

August 5 (Tuesday) **In Tennessee,** a small contingent of Don Carlos Buell's command is intercepted by a Confederate contingent led by Captain J.M. Hambrick near Winchester. The small unit, including General Robert L. McCook, has no chance of escape. However, the Union tries to turn the wagon and flee. During the encounter, McCook, who is in a wagon due to illness, is shot and the wound is fatal. He succumbs the next day. Also, Union troops holding Fort Donelson are able to repel a strong Confederate assault.

In Virginia, Union forces of General Joseph Hooker's division (Third Corps) and General Israel Bush Richardson's division (General Sumner's Second Corps), supported by cavalry, encounter and engage Confederate Brigadier General Wade Hampton's command at Malvern Hill along the James River. The Confederate positions are defended by the Fauquier Virginia Battery, led by Captain Stribling, and infantry regiments, including the 8th and 17th Georgia and elements of the 47th North Carolina, bolstered by two regiments of cavalry. At about dawn, the 8th Illinois Regiment, supported by the guns of Captain Henry M. Benson, attacks the Confederate battery. And close behind is Hooker's 1st Brigade, commanded by General Cuvier Grover (West Point, 1850). The assault force advances with lightning speed and the Confederates are compelled to retire; however, about 100 are seized as prisoners. The Union sustains three killed and 11 wounded.

In other activity, a Union reconnaissance force led by Captain Wilkins continues operating in the vicinity of Sycamore Church. A detachment led by Lt. Byrnes skirmishes with Confederates at White Oak Swamp Bridge. The Union sustains no casualties. The Confederates suffer 10 killed and 28 captured.

In Union general officer activity, Brevet 2nd Lieutenant Charles Hale Morgan (West Point, 1857) is appointed captain in the Regular Army. However, he is on sick leave and does not return to active duty until after the Battle of Antietam (Sharpsburg) in September. On 1 October, Morgan is appointed chief of artillery of the II Corps. He is promoted to lieutenant colonel of volunteers on 1 January 1863, and finally in May 1865, he is promoted to full brigadier general of volunteers. He serves for the duration with the Army of the Potomac.

August 6 (Wednesday) **In Arizona,** near the Miembrez River, General James H. Carleton, advised of some people who are near starvation, directs Colonel Joseph R. West to alleviate the problem:

COLONEL: I have been credibly informed that there are some 20 families of men, women, and children at the Pino Alto mines, some 40 miles from this camp, who are nearly perishing for want of food, the Indians having robbed them of what they had, and the secessionists having captured and appropriated to themselves a train of supplies which was on the way some time since to their relief. You will send Capt. E.D. Shirland, First California Volunteer Cavalry, and Lieut. D.C. Vestal, First California Volunteer Infantry, with a sufficient escort of cavalry and infantry, to the Pino Alto mines with some provisions for these starving people. Send them 5 beeves [ox or cow], 600 pounds, more or less, of pemmican [fine pounded beef mixed with fat], 3,000 pounds of flour, and 1,500 pounds of panoche [Mexican sugar]. These provisions will be given to the most needy. If it be not practicable to distribute them all at once, they will be left in the hands of some responsible man for this purpose....

Carleton also directs West to designate two officers to report on the conditions of the people at the mine and whether they have the capability of protecting themselves from further Indian raids.

In Kentucky, Confederates under General Kirby Smith, which had recently departed Knoxville, Tennessee, and entered Kentucky, skirmish with Union troops at Tazewell, just south of Cumberland Gap. The Union 16th and 42nd Ohio, the 14th and 22nd Kentucky and the 4th Wisconsin Battery, commanded by Colonel John F. DeCourcey, participate. The Union sustains three killed, 23 wounded and 50 missing. The Confederates sustain nine killed and 40 wounded. Kirby Smith's force is ahead of the remainder of Bragg's Army. The other two corps arrive in Kentucky in early September.

In Missouri, a Union contingent (Missouri militia) commanded by Colonel John McNeil, skirmishes with Confederate guerrillas under Colonel Joseph C. Porter at Kirksville. The Union sustains 20 killed and 60 wounded. The Confederates sustain 128 killed and about 200 wounded. Also, a detachment of the 3rd Wisconsin Cavalry, commanded by Major Montgomery, skirmishers with Confederate guerrillas at Montevallo. The Union sustains one wounded and three missing.

In Virginia, at Malvern Hill, Union General Joseph Hooker's Division skirmishes with Confederate pickets under General Nathan G. Evans's command. The Confederates capture four Union troops. Colonel William Gamble of the 8th Illinois Cavalry is wounded. He remains out of service until December, when he participates in the Battle of Fredericksburg. By early January 1863 he receives command of a brigade, and it participates at Gettysburg during July 1863. In other activity, a Union contingent of General Rufus King's division, commanded by Colonel Lysander Cutler, skirmishes with Confederates at Matapony (Thornburg). The Union sustains one killed, 12 wounded and about 72 missing. Confederate casualty information is unavailable.

In West Virginia, a contingent of the 4th West Virginia Volunteer Regiment clashes with a Confederate force at Beech Creek. The Union sustains three killed and eight wounded. The Confederates sustain one killed and 11 wounded.

In Union general officer activity, Joseph Hooker (West Point, 1837), a veteran of the Mexican War, is commissioned brigadier general of volunteers effective retroactively to May 1861. Hooker had attempted to re-enter the service during 1858, but his request received no action.

In Confederate general officer activity, Colonel William E. Starke, 60th Virginia Infantry, is promoted to the rank of brigadier general. Starke will command a division at Sharpsburg (Antietam). He is the brother of Union General Peter Burwell Starke.

In Naval activity, the CSS *Arkansas*, which had mechanical difficulties that prevented it from supporting Breckinridge's attack against Baton Rouge, Louisiana, still has problems that remain unsolvable by engineers. Meanwhile, the Union vessels *Essex*, *Cayuga* and *Sumter* resume their search in an attempt to discover and destroy the vessel. Later, the Union reports an engagement that destroys the *Arkansas* following a terrific barrage that causes the vessel to head for shore for abandonment and a subsequent explosion of its magazine. The Confederates claim that it had sustained no damage at Baton Rouge on the previous day, and because of engine trouble it is abandoned and permitted to drift downstream toward the *Essex*, which then destroys it. In a report dated 9 September 1862, Confederate General Earl Van Dorn maintains: "She was no trophy for the *Essex,* nor did she receive any injury at Baton Rouge from the hands of any of her adversaries...."

August 7 (Thursday) **In Arizona,** the detachment dispatched the day before to provide food to families at the Pino Alto Mines reports as ordered on the conditions. Captain E.D. Shirland states:

> We found about 30 Americans, French, Germans, &c.; two of the Germans with families; all the rest were Mexicans. Most of them were extremely poor and destitute, there being scarcely any ore at all in the mines. They had received some little assistance previous to our arrival, before which time they had been living on purslane and roots, and several had become insane from hunger.... All the people seemed to be loyally inclined, although several

Union warships destroy the CSS *Arkansas* (*Harper's Pictorial History of the Civil War*, 1896).

of them had belonged to the Arizona Rangers, a company formed for the purpose of fighting the Indians in the Territory. The Indians were represented as being extremely hostile and in the habit of committing depredations upon the settlers whenever they had anything to steal.

Although no Indians are presently in the area, the people there expect them to return, now that supplies have arrived. They request military protection.

In New Mexico, a detachment of California troops commanded by General Edward R. Canby skirmishes with Confederates under Colonel Henry Hopkins Sibley (West Point, 1838) at Fort Fillmore. The Confederates sustain one killed. In other activity, General Carleton arrives at Fort Thorne, located along the Rio Grande in the vicinity of Hatch and also near Santa Barbara. Carleton, once at the post, informs General Canby, the department commander, of his arrival.

In Tennessee, a contingent of the 2nd Illinois Cavalry clashes with a contingent of Confederates at Trenton. The Confederates sustain 30 killed and 20 wounded. The Union sustains no casualties.

In Virginia, General John Pope disperses his infantry at positions between Sperryville and Culpeper Court House, while dispatching his cavalry toward Gordonsville. His reconnaissance patrols spread out in many directions, and one of these contingents, led by General Samuel W. Crawford, encounters and drives away a Confederate force at Orange Court House. Following the eviction of the Rebels, the Yankees occupy the town.

In Union general officer activity, Union Captain Richard Busteed, who resigned from his position with the Chicago Light Artillery during October 1861, is appointed brigadier general. Busteed will serve at Fortress Monroe under General Erastus Keyes until President Abraham Lincoln appoints him a judge in Alabama during 1863.

In Missouri, Confederate guerrillas led by a Rebel officer named Coffin attack Union troops led by Major Montgomery in Dodd County. Casualty figures are unavailable.

August 8 (Friday) **In Arizona,** General Carleton dispatches an update on his progress and adds a request: "My command did not use tents in crossing the desert. I had a few (two to a company) when I left Tucson, but 13 of these were left to shelter the garrison at Fort Bowie, Apache Pass, Chiricahua Mountains. I have sent to Fort Yuma to have all the tents at that post repaired and sent on as soon as possible. Should I need them, can you lend me some? I left Tucson July 23; stopped one day at the Cienega de Sauz, and four

and a half at Ojo de la Vaea, and arrived here on the 7th (About three miles above Fort Thorn on the Arizona bank of the Rio Grande)."

In Missouri, elements of the 1st Missouri Cavalry (militia) skirmish with Confederates at Panther Creek. The Union sustains one killed and four wounded. Confederate casualty figures are unavailable. Other skirmishing erupts in the vicinity of Walnut Creek (Grand River).

In Virginia, Confederate Generals Thomas J. "Stonewall" Jackson and Richard S. Ewell, concerned about the Union takeover of Orange Court House, cross the Rapidan River at Burnett's Ford and drive out the units posted there. The Union reacts quickly. General Samuel W. Crawford is dispatched to meet the threat, and he will deploy in the vicinity of Cedar Mountain (Slaughter Mountain). Additional Union reinforcements move to bolster Crawford. General Banks' Corps speeds toward Burnett's Ford on the following morning.

In Naval activity, the USS *Wabash* and *New Ironsides* move to Morris Island, South Carolina. Once there, a contingent of troops, including ninety Marines, commanded by 1st Lieutenant H.B. Lowry, go ashore and establish positions for a series of guns. The *New Ironsides* had only recently (August 1862) been commissioned. It had been built during the previous year as an armored warship. In January 1863, it joins the South Atlantic Blockading Squadron and remains on duty there for about one year in support of the blockade of Charleston.

August 9 (Saturday) BATTLE OF CEDAR MOUNTAIN (SLAUGHTER MOUNTAIN) There is much maneuvering in Virginia, with both the Union and Confederates trying to gain the advantage. The forces of General Nathaniel Banks' corps is rushing to support that of General Samuel W. Crawford, who had arrived in the vicinity of Cedar Mountain on the previous day. This afternoon, contingents of General Stonewall Jackson's command discover the advancing columns. A decision is made by Jackson to engage the Union prior to the arrival of more reinforcements. Soon after, General Richard S. Ewell is directed to move forward and deploy two of his brigades west of Cedar Mountain, while sending the other brigade, under Jubal Early, to the Culpeper Road to link with a contingent of Jackson's command to establish a tight line along a ridge to the right. General Charles S. Winder is moving along the left side of the road leading "Jackson's Own." Winder's brigade is held back under the temporary command of Colonel Charles P. Roland. The artillery is supported by two brigades, Campbell's and Taliaferro's. Union artillery includes Knapp's battery (Pennsylvania Reserves).

The Confederates initiate the action at about 1600 when the artillery of one battery commences firing upon the positions of Generals Samuel Crawford and George H. Gordon. Not to be outdone, the Union begins to return fire, and in a short while, a giant bombardment gets underway, as nearly every available gun on both sides is propelling shells into the opposing lines. In the meantime, General C.S. Winder's command, trailed by General George H. Thomas' brigade, moves to the front toward some woods, the latter arriving on the field at about 1700, while the battle is nudging into high gear.

General Nathaniel Banks' columns, meanwhile, are closing on Crawford's positions, but it becomes apparent that the Confederate force in his path is greatly superior and their artillery holds dominating ground. With this in mind, Banks chooses to attack the heights to overrun the artillery. In short order, the signal is given and the attack is launched. The advance is pounded heavily by shot and shell, but the Union continues to press forward, ignoring the naked ground they must cross to reach the base of the mountain. As they reach the foundation, fresh Confederate forces move from the woods to intercept them and drive a portion of the troops back; however, many more press forward tenaciously and drive a wedge into the Rebel line. The gap is widened and the Confederate line falters, then collapses. But this situation is soon rectified as General Jackson rushes forward. He personally reforms the shattered line. In concert, Jackson brings in the forces of James J. Archer and William D. Pender, giving the Rebels two additional brigades to neutralize the Union advance.

Once the Union advance is halted, it takes only a short while for the surging Confederates to fold the entire Union line, forcing it to retreat. The Confederates give hot pursuit, but the Yankees reach a point that is a predefined line drawn by General John Pope, defended by Israel Richardson's division, and bolstered by some hefty artillery. The Confederates are struck by cascading shells as they trail Banks' forces and find themselves amid a hurricane of fire that forbids further advance. An artist, Edwin Forbes, describes the scene as the battle subsides: "The scene at night was very striking. It was past ten o'clock. There was a bright moonlight and a clear blue sky. We were on rising ground while the enemy's batteries were shelling us from the woods, our batteries replying, and one by one driving them further back.... I have taken my sketch just as McDowell's corps was marching on the field."

General Henry W. Halleck and President Lincoln continue to be at odds with the actions of General George B. McClellan. Telegrams have been burning the wires for several weeks, with directives from Washington and responses from McClellan. General McClellan is annoyed at the insinuations that he is not moving fast enough with evacuating the wounded on transports. McClellan responds continuously, claiming that Halleck is incorrect in his assumptions and that everything humanly possible is being done to facilitate execution of the orders.

The casualties are heavy on both sides. This is the beginning of the 2nd Bull Run Campaign (Manassas), which continues until September of 1862. The Union sustains 450 dead, 660 wounded and 290 missing. The Confederates suffer 229 killed, 1,047 wounded, and 31 missing. Confederate Brigadier General Charles S.

Winder (West Point, 1850) is killed at the battle. Union General Henry Prince is captured; he is not exchanged until December. Union Generals S.S. Carroll, J.W. Geary (twice) and Christopher C. Augur are wounded. Confederate General Charles William Field (West Point, 1849) participates at this battle. Union General George L. Andrews (West Point, 1851) also takes part, as does the 1st Maine Cavalry. The Maine cavalry, under Colonel Samuel Allen, heads for Fairfax Court House with General John Pope's other units, arriving there on September 3. Also, the Confederate 25th Virginia Infantry (General Early's Brigade, General Ewell's Division) participates. Colonel Daniel Ullman (78th New York) is captured during the retreat and held in Richmond until the following October, when he is paroled.

In Missouri, elements of the Missouri State Militia, commanded by Colonel John McNeil, clash with Confederates at Stockton. Casualty figures are unavailable.

In Union activity, Brigadier General Joseph B. Plummer, wounded at Wilson's Creek, dies today. Plummer participated in the enduring siege of Corinth, Mississippi, from April 30 to May 30.

In Union general officer activity, James Birdseye McPherson (West Point, 1853) is appointed brigadier general of volunteers. McPherson, who graduated West Point at age 20, was a lieutenant in the engineers the previous August. He participates at the Battle of Corinth and is promoted in October to major general of volunteers. He receives command of XII Corps by January 1863, followed by command of the Army of the Tennessee during March 1864. Also, Brigadier General Christopher C. Augur is promoted to major general. He will command General Nathaniel Banks' left wing during the campaign to seize Port Hudson. In October 1863, General Augur receives command of XII Corps and the Department of Washington. He is breveted as brigadier general and major general in the Regular Army. After the war he becomes colonel of the 12th Infantry Regiment, and later, during 1869, he is promoted to brigadier general in the Regular Army.

August 10 (Sunday)   In Louisiana, Union troops occupy Bayou Sara.

In Missouri, a contingent of Missouri State Cavalry, commanded by Colonel Smart, clashes with Confederates at Reelsville. Skirmishing continues in the area around Walnut Creek (Grand River) until the 13th. Casualty figures are unavailable.

In Texas, a contingent of Texans (loyal to the Union) skirmish with Confederates along the Nueces River near Fort Clark. Forty Texans are killed. The Confederates sustain eight killed and 14 wounded.

In Confederate Naval activity, the vessel *Oreto* rendezvous with a schooner that holds the armaments at Green Cay. After receiving the armaments (two 7-inch Blakely rifled guns and

four 6-inch Blakely rifled guns), the *Oreto,* a steam screw cruiser, is renamed the CSS *Florida.* Around this time an epidemic strikes the crew, composed only of eighteen men. Master J.K. Maffitt is one of its victims. In less than one week, the crew is reduced to about five men who are unaffected by yellow fever. Initially the ship moves to Cuba, but in early September Maffitt decides to head for Mobile, Alabama, where the vessel encounters the blockading squadron on the 4th. The *Florida* is separate from the CSS *Florida* that later became the CSS *Selma* and afterward the USS *Selma.*

August 11 (Monday)   In Arkansas, a contingent of Wisconsin cavalry skirmishes with Confederates at Helena. The Union sustains one killed and two wounded.

In Missouri, the 9th Missouri Militia Regiment and other units commanded by Colonel Guitar skirmish with Confederates led by Colonel John A. Poindexter at Grand River. The Union sustains about 100 casualties and about 200 captured. The Confederates sustain seven killed and about 27 captured. Also, elements of the 7th Missouri Cavalry commanded by Colonel John Buell engage a 750-man guerrilla force, commanded by Colonel John T. Hughes, at Independence. The Union sustains 14 killed, 18 wounded and about 312 missing. A contemporary source lists Union casualties as 26 killed and 30 wounded. Also, elements of the 1st Missouri and the 3rd Wisconsin Cavalry skirmish with Confederates at Taberville.

In New Mexico, General James H. Carleton's "California Column" crosses the Rio Grande almost 20 miles below Fort Thorne and arrives at Las Cruces en route to join with General Canby. The troops are greeted by four companies of U.S. infantry from Fort Craig and the forces under Lt. Colonel Eyre that had arrived earlier. General Canby, commander of the Department of New Mexico, informs General Carleton that an invasion of Texas from Las Cruces is not advisable; however, he leaves the decision to Carleton.

In Tennessee, a Union contingent of the 3rd Kentucky and 1st Tennessee Cavalry, numbering slightly more than 100 troops and commanded by Major McGowan, clashes with about 175 Confederates led by Major Anderson at Kinderhook. Also, a Union contingent (General James S. Negley's command) led by Major Kennedy clashes with Confederate guerrillas at Williamsport. Casualty figures are unavailable. Union troops attached to the 11th Illinois Cavalry skirmish with Confederate guerrillas at Salisbury and capture the town.

In Virginia, Union reinforcements arrive to augment General John Pope's force in the vicinity of Cedar Mountain. Other troops under General Franz Sigel had arrived on the day of the recent battle, but due to some apparent confusion with his orders and the route of march, his force did not arrive until dusk. Confederate General Thomas J. "Stonewall" Jackson, aware of the superior number of Yankees in the area, withdraws his force across the Rapidan River to more tenable positions. However, once Confederate reinforcements arrive, plans are then made by Jackson to strike the Pope's Army before it can be further reinforced by George McClellan's force.

In West Virginia, a skirmish develops at Wyoming Court House when a unit of the 37th Ohio Regiment clashes with a Confederate unit. The Union sustains two killed. Confederate casualty figures are unavailable.

August 12 (Tuesday)   In Tennessee, Morgan's raiders attack and occupy Gallatin. The occupation lasts less than 24 hours, as the Union recaptures it. The Union sustains 30 dead, 50 wounded and about 200 captured. The Confederates suffer six dead and 18 wounded. The Union 2nd Indiana Cavalry (41st Regiment Volunteers), 4th and 5th Kentucky Cavalry and the 6th Pennsylvania Cavalry participate.

In Union activity, Captain Charles Camp Doolittle (4th Michigan Infantry) is promoted to colonel of the 18th Michigan. He is assigned duty in Kentucky, but in 1863 he is transferred to Nashville, Tennessee, where he serves as provost guard until June 1864.

In Confederate general officer activity, Colonel William Barksdale (13th Mississippi), a veteran of the Mexican War as an enlisted man and officer, is promoted to brigadier general. Barksdale had been a U.S. Congressman (1852–1861) and at the outbreak of hostilities, he was appointed quartermaster general of Mississippi. General Barksdale's command participates at Second Manassas (Bull Run) and at Fredericksburg. At the latter, Barksdale's troops deploy in the cellars of various buildings to meet the Union threat as they cross the Rappahannock.

In Naval activity, the USS *Reliance,* attached to the Potomac Flotilla, while on patrol encounters and seizes the sloop *Blossom.* It lowers a boat and the detachment moves into Sturgeon Creek and captures another sloop, the *Painter,* in the vicinity of Alexandria, Virginia.

August 12–18   In Naval activity, the USS *Belle Italia, Sachem, Reindeer* and *Corypheus* navigate a manmade canal, enter Corpus Christi Bay off of the Texas shore, encounter the Confederate *Breaker* and force it to run ashore. The Confederates abandon the vessel after setting it afire; however, the Union troops extinguish the flames. The *Breaker,* formerly a pilot boat operating at Pass Cavallo, is refloated by the boarding party and seized as a prize. Meanwhile, other Confederates abandon the armed schooner *Elma* and the sloop *Hannah.* The mission continues and Lt. John W. Kittredge remains in the area for several more days. A contingent debarks on the 13th and issues an ultimatum for the Confederate military to abandon the area. The demand stipulates that civilians can remain and their property will not be harmed. Nevertheless, if the Confederates choose to resist, the Rebels are warned that "they must remove their women and children if they intended to make a stand." The Rebels choose to fight.

At about daybreak on the 15th, the Confederates commence firing; however, the gunboats immediately return effective fire that silences the Rebel guns. The Union bombardment stops and the Rebel guns resume firing. The gunboats initiate another bombardment that forces the Confederates to temporarily abandon their guns to seek safer positions. At dusk, Lt. Kittredge pulls back out of range of the Confederate artillery. Just before midnight, the Confederates set fire to the steamer *A.B.*, which is grounded in a small channel that links Corpus Christi to Nueces Bay. On the 18th, Kittredge positions his squadron from where another bombardment can be initiated. The *Belle Italia* provides support fire for a contingent of 30 troops that land to destroy the battery. The Confederates begin to pound the advancing Union force, but at about the same time, Rebel cavalry and infantry launch a counterattack, which is quickly halted by the incoming fire from the gunboats. Meanwhile, the landing force expends its ammunition and is compelled to head back to the squadron. After the contingent returns to the ships, the gunboats bombard the town. By this time, the squadron's ammunition supply nears exhaustion. Kittredge orders it to return to Aransas Bay to await the arrival of the USS *Arthur,* which had gone to New Orleans to replenish the squadron's ammunition.

August 13 (Wednesday)   In Arkansas, the Union scores a big success at Clarendon when elements of Colonel Alvin P. Hovey's Division (13th Corps, General Sam Curtis' command) engage Confederates (General Thomas Hindman's command). The Union sustains seven killed. The Confederates lose about 700 captured. Colonel Hovey is promoted to brigadier general during the fall (1862).

In Missouri, a Union contingent led by Colonel Oden Guitar engages a band of Confederate guerrillas under Colonel Poindexter at Yellow Creek. The Union captures a large number of Confederates.

In Tennessee, Union forces under Colonel Silas Miller retake Gallatin, which had been lost on the previous day. The 13th and 69th Ohio Regiments and the 11th Michigan Regiment participate.

In Union general officer activity, Captain Adin Ballou Underwood (2nd Massachusetts Infantry Regiment) is promoted to lieutenant colonel of the 33rd Massachusetts Regiment. Underwood will be named colonel of the regiment in April. His force participates at Chancellorsville, where it sustains only light casualties. Later, the regiment, attached to the XI Corps, participates at Gettysburg and Chattanooga.

August 14 (Thursday)   In Arkansas, a contingent of Union troops clash with Confederate guerrillas at Helena. Casualty figures and specific units are unavailable.

In Tennessee, two divisions dispatched by General Grant are rushing to join with and reinforce General Don Carlos Buell, whose force

is en route to Chattanooga, heading east to repair the Memphis-Chattanooga Railroad.

In North Carolina, a Union reconnaissance force — the 24th Massachusetts Marine Battery and the gunboats USS *Wilson,* and *Ellis,* bolstered by some infantry and one squadron of cavalry — departs Newport and moves toward Swansboro (Swannsborough). The expedition is commanded by Colonel (later general) Thomas G. Stevenson, commanding officer of the 24th Massachusetts, and Colonel (later general) Charles A. Heckman.

In Virginia, the Union Third and Fifth Army Corps depart Harrison's Landing moving toward Acquia Creek. The operation lasts until the following day. Also, Union cavalry operates through the 19th in the rear of Union forces (Army of the Potomac) between Harrison's Landing and Williamsburg.

August 15 (Friday)   In Arizona, Mesilla is designated the headquarters of the District of Arizona.

In New Mexico, General Carleton informs General Canby that on the following day, he is moving to Fort Bliss in Texas with Company B, 1st California Cavalry, and Company B, 2nd California Cavalry.

In Tennessee, one company of the 2nd Illinois Cavalry engages Confederates at Merryweather's Ferry. The Union sustains three killed and six wounded. The Confederates sustain 20 killed.

In Virginia, Union Major General McClellan departs Harrison's Landing and move to Acquia Creek, about 60 miles from Richmond, an order he reluctantly carries out. It can only be reached by marching overland. McClellan, with the tremendous support of Colonel McCleod Murphy, who oversees the construction of a pontoon bridge across the Chickahominy River about one mile from its confluence with the James River, permits McClellan to cross his entire force (infantry, cavalry and artillery) without the loss of a man by the 18th. Several gunboats under the command of Commodore Charles Wilkes stand nearby to provide additional security.

In Naval activity, the USS *Ellis* initiates an expedition to Swansboro, North Carolina, to destroy a Confederate battery and a salt works located here. The operation lasts through the 19th.

August 16 (Saturday)   In Louisiana, Union forces supported by gunboats depart Baton Rouge. Commodore David Porter's fleet initiates a series of probing reconnaissance missions. During the expedition, the Confederates raise opposition near Bayou Sara and Natchez, but receive heavy bombardments in return from Commodore Porter. Following this action, Porter returns to Port Hudson.

In Kentucky, Confederate guerrillas, led by Colonel Sam Johnson, attack and capture Hopkinsville.

In **Missouri,** a contingent of the Missouri cavalry (militia), composed of about 800 troops commanded by Major Foster, battles a Confederate force of several thousand troops led by Colonel John Coffee for about four hours at Lone Jack. The two sides had also clashed on the 11th and the 15th. In all the clashes, the Union sustains about 60 killed and 100 wounded. The Confederates suffer about 110 including killed and wounded.

In **New Mexico,** General James H. Carleton, leading three companies of his cavalry, departs Las Cruces and advances toward Fort Bliss in Franklin (El Paso), Texas. The cavalry seizes 25 sick and wounded Confederate troops and the column regains U.S. government supplies earlier seized by Confederates. The supplies are transported to La Mesilla (later Mesilla), where a supply depot had recently been established. Afterward, General Carleton continues to advance along the Rio Grande with the cavalry and penetrates nearly 100 miles into Texas.

In **Pennsylvania,** the 125th Regiment, mustered into Federal service on the 10th, is organized on this day. Colonel Jacob Higgins receives command. The regiment receives Springfield rifled muskets, and later that day the men board boxcars and are taken to Baltimore. From there they move to Washington, D.C.

In **Virginia,** Union Major General George B. McClellan leaves Harrison's Landing to join General John Pope near Alexandria. Prior to his departure, McClellan has safely transported nearly 10,000 sick and wounded to be cared for in safe Union territory. Also, at about this time, Confederate Brigadier General Maxcy Gregg's brigade, near Gordonsville, moves out and redeploys along the Rapidan River at Crenshaw's Farm.

In Naval activity, Union gunboats and accompanying U.S. Marines bombard Confederate positions through the 18th at Corpus Christi, Texas. The Union force is commanded by Lieutenant J. W. Kittredge, U.S. Navy, and the Confederates are led by Major Alfred M. Hobby. The Union reports no casualties. The Confederates sustain one killed.

August 17 (Sunday)   In Minnesota, Sioux Indians rebel over their treatment, including terrible living conditions. The Indians begin to massacre white settlers. U.S. soldiers are brought in to eradicate the rebellion. General Henry Hastings Sibley (cousin of Confederate General Henry Hopkins Sibley) is placed in charge of the troops. Sibley had been Minnesota's first governor after statehood, and he is respected by many of the Indians. He is able first to contain and then end the disturbances by the end of September.

In **Virginia,** a Confederate reconnaissance force of about 12 men (Jeff Davis' Legion) commanded by Lt. Frederick Waring initiates a mission in the vicinity of Forge Bridge.

August 18 (Monday)   In Louisiana, Union forces (58th and 76th Ohio Volunteer Regiments) attack Confederate fortifications near Milliken Bend, capturing 40 prisoners and the steamer *Fair Play*. In other activity, the Union prepares to abandon Baton Rouge. The evacuation is completed by 21 August. The Union does not reenter the city until the following December.

The *Fair Play*, a tinclad river gunboat, was initially a civilian vessel built during 1859 and taken into the Confederacy during the early days of the conflict as a transport. In September it is transferred to the U.S. Navy, commissioned the USS *Fair Play*, and transformed into a gunboat that will operate on the Cumberland, Ohio and Tennessee rivers during the war.

In **Minnesota,** the Dakotas move from Redwood Ferry to the Upper Agency and attack it, but it holds as the settlers gather at a storage house. In other activity, a contingent of troops (one company of the 5th Minnesota Volunteer Regiment) and some settlers under Captain John R. Marsh are ambushed at Redwood Ferry on the Minnesota River while they are en route to Fort Ridgely to sound the alarm about the Dakota hostilities. The initial fire kills more than ten troops and the remainder is unable to make use of the ferry. An attempt is made by the party to move downstream to find another crossing, but Indians await them here too. While under fire, the men begin to cross by swimming. The remainder of the troops escape, but Captain Marsh drowns trying to cross the river, leaving Sergeant John F. Bishop to lead fifteen able-bodied soldiers and five wounded men to Fort Ridgely.

In **Mississippi,** Union and Confederate units skirmish at Rienzi. Specific units and casualty figures are unavailable.

In **Tennessee,** the USS *Skylark* and *Sally* are destroyed by Confederate guerrillas at Duck Creek.

In **Virginia,** the second session of the Confederate Congress convenes in Richmond. President Davis updates the Congress regarding the situation in the various theaters and emphasizes the terrible conditions of the Confederates captured; however, his words in general are quite positive with regard to the cause and its opportunities for victory. Also, the 125th Pennsylvania Regiment arrives in the vicinity of Fort Richardson about seven miles from Washing-

Left: Union troops destroy a railroad (*Harper's Pictoral History of the Civil War*, 1896). *Right:* Union fleet of Flag Officer Louis M. Goldsborough bombards Confederate forts on Craney Island (Mottelay, *The Soldier in Our Civil War*, 1886).

ton. It establishes a camp which it names Camp Welles. The regiment is attached to General William Denison Whipple's command and is considered part of Washington's defenses. The regiment remains only a short while. By the 26th, it moves to Fort Bernard, a more sanitary location.

In Confederate general officer activity, Colonel Edward Dorr Tracy is promoted to the rank of brigadier general. He served in the 19th Alabama Regiment under Colonel (later general) Joseph Wheeler prior to being transferred to the command of John P. McCown's Division in East Tennessee. Tracy will be transferred during the following spring to Vicksburg, Mississippi.

August 19 (Tuesday)   In Minnesota, Dakota Indians launch an afternoon attack against New Ulm, a settlement established by Germans. The settlers hold off the attackers for about two hours, and at that time a rainstorm covers the area, essentially ending the assault as the Indians begin to retire. Some sporadic fighting continues. A new attack is launched on 22 August, but it too fails to destroy the settlement. Following the day-long battle of 22 August, the settlers evacuate the women and children under the protection of a large wagon train. The family members are transported to Mankato.

In Tennessee, six companies (71st Ohio Volunteers) of Union forces under the command of Colonel Rodney Mason surrender to Confederates without resistance at Clarksville. Later, Colonel Mason has the dubious honor of being one of the first Union officers to leave the field at the first sound of Confederate gunfire at Shiloh. Meanwhile, on this day, the Confederate force at Clarksville is composed of about 800 troops commanded by Colonel Woodward. The 71st Ohio Regiment's captives are later paroled. Subsequent to their exchange, the 71st will be reorganized and stationed around the railroads in Tennessee until it again participates in battle during the upcoming struggle for Nashville. Colonel H.K. McConnell will succeed Mason as commanding officer of the 71st Ohio.

In Union general officer activity, Colonel Orlando Bolivar Willcox, held captive since his capture at the First Battle of Bull Run (Manassas), is released, and on this day he is promoted to brigadier general of volunteers, effective 21 July 1861, the day of the battle.

August 20 (Wednesday)   In Kentucky, elements of the 2nd Illinois Cavalry, commanded by Captain F.F. Moore, attack a Confederate camp at White Oak. The Union sustains two wounded. The Confederates sustain four killed and 19 captured.

In Tennessee, a contingent of Confederate guerrillas, led by Colonel John H. Morgan, skirmishes with a detachment of the 50th Indiana Volunteer Regiment, which is deployed (unassigned) to guard the Nashville Chattanooga Railroad as part of the Army of Ohio. The contest takes place at Edgefield Junction. The Confederates sustain eight killed and 18 wounded.

In Missouri, contingents of the 1st Missouri Cavalry and the 13th Illinois Cavalry, commanded by Union Major Price, skirmish with Confederates at Union Mills. The Union sustains four killed and three wounded. The Confederates sustain one killed.

In Virginia, Confederates under General David R. Jones (Jackson's Corps) are preparing to take Thoroughfare Gap, a town which stands before Jackson's force, which is rushing to aid the Rebels at Manassas who are jeopardized by the Yankees. General Jackson speeds through the gap on the 27th, thanks to the victorious efforts of Jones' troops. Elements of Confederate General Maxcy Gregg's brigade skirmish with Union troops (John Pope's command) at the north bank of the Rapidan River as the brigade presses towards the Rappahannock River. Union contingents, including the 1st Maine Cavalry, skirmish with Confederates at Brandy Station as they make their way toward Fairfax Court House. The Confederates sustain three killed and 12 wounded. Also, General McClellan continues his advance to Acquia Creek.

In Union general officer activity, Brigadier General John G. Parke is promoted to major general, effective 18 July. William Ward Orme is commissioned colonel (later brigadier general) of the 94th Illinois Regiment, which is organized this day. Prior to the outbreak of war, Orme had been a lawyer in Washington, D.C., and a partner of one of President Lincoln's close friends, Leonard Swett. Brigadier General Jesse Lee Reno is promoted to major general to rank from 18 July.

August 20–22   In Minnesota, Companies B and C, 5th Minnesota Volunteer Regiment, and the Renville Rangers, commanded by Lt. T.J. Sheehan, engage and defeat a Sioux Indian force in the vicinity of Fort Ridgely. The Union sustains three killed and 13 wounded. Indian casualty figures are unavailable. In November, Company B will march to Fort Snelling, accompanying the captured Sioux, and subsequently rejoin the regiment (which had moved to Mississippi during the previous May) in the vicinity of Oxford, Mississippi. The contingent of Company C that had also been with Lt. Sheehan will depart Fort Ridgely during September to rejoin the regiment.

August 20–September 6   In the Dakota Territory, Indians prepare to assault Fort Abercrombie, commanded by Captain John Vanderhack; however, the activity outside the fort doesn't materialize for a while, buying time for the garrison to bolster the defenses. Nevertheless, the fort is encircled. On 3 September at about 0500, the fort is rocked by the assault just as the sun is slipping over the horizon, but the troops had remained at the ready. Return fire, including menacing artillery fire, is immediately commenced. The heated exchange lasts for about six hours, but for the Indians, including Dakota and Ojibwes, it has been at an expensive cost with at least several hundred casualties. Despite the whirlwind attack, the force within the garrison sustains only one man

killed, Private Edward D. Steel, and another man wounded. Although the Indians sustain grievous losses, they do not retire; they maintain a siege.

For a couple of days, there is a steady stream of incoming fire from the opposite bank of the river, but by 6 September, the fort is again struck by a powerful assault. Again, the Indians launch the strike at about dawn. Initially there is some enemy penetration, but it is short-lived. Nevertheless, the fort remains under incessant assault until about 1500, when the Indians disengage. The effective fire from the fort again inflicts high casualties upon the Indians, essentially terminating any further attacks. However, some long distance skirmishing continues.

August 21 (Thursday)   In Tennessee, two corps of Confederate General Braxton Bragg's army cross the Tennessee River at Harrison and move toward Pikeville, arriving there on the 30th. Also, two Union regiments, bolstered by cavalry (detachments of the 2nd Indiana, 4th and 5th Kentucky and the 7th Pennsylvania Cavalry), led by General Richard W. Johnson (West Point, 1849), engage Confederates under Colonel John Hunt Morgan outside of Gallatin. General Johnson, whose brother is a surgeon in the Confederacy, had vowed to capture Morgan; however at this battle, the Confederates vanquish Johnson's force and seize about seventy-five prisoners, including Johnson. General Johnson is exchanged during December 1862. He will subsequently assume command of the 12th Division, Army of the Cumberland.

In South Carolina, Union and Confederate contingents skirmish at Pinckney. The Union sustains three killed, three wounded and about 30 wounded. Confederate casualty figures are unavailable.

In Virginia, cavalry units attached to the Army of Virginia, bolstered by artillery, skirmish with Confederates along the Rappahannock River at Kelley's Ford.

In Union general officer activity, Henry L. Eustis (Harvard, 1838, and West Point, 1842) becomes colonel of the 10th Massachusetts. Eustis' health had been poor but he heeds the Union's call for help. Eustis will participate at Fredericksburg, Chancellorsville and Gettysburg, before becoming a brigadier general on 12 September 1863. Also, Edward Augustus Wild, a surgeon who was captain of the 1st Massachusetts Regiment, is commissioned colonel of the 35th Massachusetts.

August 22 (Friday)   In Kentucky, Confederate Colonel John S. Scott (1st Louisiana Cavalry) and Colonel James W. Starnes (4th Tennessee Cavalry) skirmishes with the 9th Pennsylvania Cavalry (General Green Clay Smith's command) at Crab Orchard.

In Tennessee, a group of Confederate guerrillas attack a Union train, defended by a contingent of the 42nd Illinois Volunteer Regiment, in the vicinity of Courtland. The Union sustains two wounded and two missing. The Confederates sustain about eight killed, but prevail.

In Texas, General James H. Carleton, in the vicinity of Fort Quitman, issues General Order No. 16, which includes:

> I. At 12 m. today Capt. John C. Cremony, with his company (B, of the Second California Volunteer Cavalry), will proceed to Fort Quitman and hoist over it the national colors, the old Stars and Stripes. By this act still another post comes under its rightful flag and once more becomes consecrated to the United States. II. Capt. Edmond D. Shirland, First California Volunteer Cavalry, will proceed without delay, yet by easy marches to Fort Davis Tex., and hoist over that post the national colors. If Captain Shirland finds any sick or wounded soldiers there he will make them prisoners of war, but put them upon their parole and let them proceed without delay to Texas. If they are unable to travel, Captain Shirland will report to these headquarters by express what they need in the way of surgical or medical attention.... If the fort is abandoned, Captain Shirland will retrace his steps and report in person to these headquarters.

In Virginia, General Henry W. Halleck telegraphs General George McClellan and instructs him to "leave such garrisons in Fortress Monroe, Yorktown, etc., as you may deem proper.... The forces of Burnside and Pope are hard pushed and require aid as rapidly as you can send it." The Third Army Corps departs Yorktown to reinforce Generals Ambrose Burnside and John Pope. Also, Union General Henry Bohlen is killed on the Rappahannock River in the vicinity of Remington. Bohlen's Brigade had been on a reconnaissance mission until driven back by a powerful force of Jackson's Army. General Bohlen, born in Germany, had organized the 75th Pennsylvania Volunteer Regiment. He is interred at Laurel Hill Cemetery in North Philadelphia. General Schimmelfennig assumes command of his 1st Brigade (General Schurz's division, General Sigel's corps). In other activity, at Catlett's Station, Confederate cavalry attack elements of the Parnell Legion (Maryland) and the 1st Pennsylvania Rifles. Casualty figures are unavailable.

In Union general officer activity, Colonel John Reese Kenly (1st Maryland), exchanged on 15 August, is promoted to brigadier general and given command of the Maryland Brigade, composed of the 4th, 6th, 7th and 8th Maryland Regiments. Subsequently, he commands the 3rd Division (I Corps) in autumn. Afterward, he commands the District of Delaware with headquarters at Wilmington, prior to taking command of the Eastern shore of Maryland, where he serves until the conclusion of the war. He receives the brevet of major general and leaves the service during August 1865.

August 23 (Saturday)   In Kentucky, a Union contingent of the 7th Kentucky Cavalry and the 3rd Tennessee Volunteer Regiment, commanded by Colonel Metcalf, skirmishes with Confederates at Big Hill. The Union sustains 10 dead and 40 wounded or missing. Confederates have 25 dead.

In Missouri, some skirmishing erupts at Hickory Grove and at Spring Creek. Casualty figures, if any, are unavailable.

In New York, a group of recruits in the Empire Brigade, commanded by General Spinola, start a riot; Captain David M. Cohen, leading a detachment of Marines, departs the Brooklyn Navy Yard and quickly terminates the trouble.

In Virginia, Union troops under General John Pope and Confederate Artillery from the Army of Northern Virginia under Robert E. Lee exchange fire for five hours along the Rappahannock. Skirmishes occur simultaneously in the same area at Clark's Mountain and Rapidan Station.

In Confederate general officer activity, Matthew Duncan Ector is promoted to brigadier general. Ector, a Georgia lawyer who relocated to Texas and served in the legislature there, joined the Confederacy as a private during 1861. Soon he became adjutant of General Hogg's brigade and was afterward appointed colonel of the 14th Texas Cavalry. Subsequently, General Ector participates at Chickamauga. During the Atlanta campaign, he sustains a wound that costs him his leg by amputation. Although his service in the field terminates, he is transferred to Mobile after recuperating and he plays a role in the defenses of Mobile until the city falls. After the war he returns to Texas and resumes his law career. Later he becomes chief judge on the Texas Court of Appeals, until his death on 29 October 1879. Also, elements of the Army of Virginia (General John Pope) skirmish with Confederates at Waterloo Bridge, Lee Springs, Freeman's Ford and Sulphur Springs through the 25th.

August 24 (Sunday)   The Sixth Army Corps departs from Fort Monroe, Virginia, to bolster the forces of Generals Ambrose Burnside and John Pope. Meanwhile, Confederate Brigadier General Maxcy Gregg's South Carolina Brigade, having recently arrived at the Rappahannock River, deploys in the high ground (Rappahannock Hills) to bolster the artillery already there. Gregg's command is greeted throughout the day by nearby Union artillery, and some casualties are sustained by the 13th and 14th S.C. Regiments. On the following day, Gregg's Brigade will depart the area heading toward Cobbler's Mountain, and from there it will bolt towards Manassas (Bull Run).

In Missouri, a contingent of the Union 12th Missouri (Militia) Cavalry, commanded by Major Bazel F. Lazear, engages Confederates under Colonel William Jeffries at Dallas. The Union sustains three killed and one wounded. In other activity, detachments of the Union 2nd and 6th Kansas Regiments led by Major Campbell skirmish with Confederate guerrillas under Quantrill at Coon Creek (Lamar). The Union sustains two killed and 22 wounded. Confederate casualties are unavailable.

In Union general officer activity, Lt. Colonel (later brigadier general) Stephen Miller (1st Minnesota) is appointed colonel of the recently

organized 7th Minnesota Regiment. The regiment had been formed primarily to deal with the Sioux, who are causing turbulence in the state.

In Naval activity, the CSS *Alabama* is commissioned. The *Alabama*, originally a merchant ship, departed England during April of this year and was transformed into a fighting ship when it was armed off the Bahamas. The commanding officer is Captain Raphael Semmes. The *Alabama* captures more than 24 vessels by the end of this year and most are destroyed. One of those spared is the mail carrier *Ariel*, which is seized during early December 1862.

In Naval activity, the *Corypheus,* a tender to the USS *Arthur,* seizes the *Water Witch,* a blockade runner operating out of Jamaica, when it attempts to penetrate the blockade and enter Aransas Bay to deliver its cargo, which includes gunpowder. The USS *Seymour,* while on patrol on the Neuse River, hits a bank and sinks (second time) at a point several miles above New Bern. At the time it is providing support during a landing by ground troops. However, the vessel again is saved, refloated and back in service following repairs in October.

August 25 (Monday)   In Florida, U.S. Marines prepare to reoccupy the navy yard at Pensacola.

In Missouri, a 130-man contingent of the 13th Illinois Cavalry, led by Major Lothar Lippert, skirmishes with a Confederate force numbering about 350 troops led by Colonel William Hicks Jackson at Bloomfield. The Confederates sustain 20 killed and wounded. The Union reports no casualties.

In Tennessee, contingents of the 71st Ohio and the 5th Iowa Cavalry, commanded by Colonel William Warren Lowe, engage Confederates led by Colonel Thomas G. Woodward in the vicinity of Fort Donelson and at Cumberland Iron Works. These units also skirmish again on the following day. The Union sustains 31 killed and wounded. The Confederates sustain 30 killed and wounded.

In Virginia, Union troops, including the 5th New York Cavalry, skirmish at Waterloo Bridge. Pvt. John Tribe assists in burning the bridge to prevent Confederate use of it. Tribe's actions play a significant role during this engagement, and for his heroism he becomes a recipient of the Medal of Honor.

In Union general officer activity, Colonel John Potts Slough (1st Colorado Infantry) is promoted to brigadier general. President Lincoln appoints him military governor of Alexandria, a post he retains until the close of hostilities. He resigns from the army on 24 August 1865. Afterward he is appointed chief justice of the New Mexico Territory. He develops problems there after a territorial legislator (Captain W.L. Ryerson) introduces a resolution that censures Slough for "unprofessional conduct." The conflict culminates on 15 December 1867 during an altercation between the men at a billiard parlor in the Fonda (Old Exchange Hotel) in

Santa Fe. General Slough receives a mortal wound and dies two days later.

August 25–26   In Minnesota, Union troops (units unspecified), commanded by Captain Flandrau, clash with Indians at New Ulm on the 25th and 26th. The Union sustains 10 killed and 50 wounded. Indian casualties are unreported.

In Virginia, General Robert E. Lee dispatches half his force, under General Thomas J "Stonewall" Jackson, to attempt to get Union General Pope to his rear. About 45,000 Union troops are deployed from the Station to Warrenton Springs. One of Pope's missions is to guard the approaches to the capital, as well as to keep the path open for reinforcements to reach him from Acquia Creek. However, by the circuitous route being taken by Jackson, Pope is inclined to extend his lines. He has requested more troops, but he can count only on the forces under Generals Philip Kearny and Joseph Hooker, both attached to Samuel Heintzelman's corps, and the force of John F. Reynolds of Fitz John Porter's corps, which has arrived at Warrenton. Within two days, Jackson's troops cover 54 miles, placing his force of 25,000 men at Bristoe Station, in position to split Pope from Washington. This plan has some drawbacks. Jackson finds himself in the middle of 100,000 Union soldiers with more on the way. After leading a small command behind Union lines, he continues to Manassas Junction and captures the Union supply base there on the 27th. On the 26th, Jackson and Longstreet push through Thoroughfare Gap, Virginia, to reinforce Confederates at Manassas, where the 2nd Battle of Bull Run (Manassas) occurs on the 30th. Confederates under Jackson's command destroy the railroad and bridge across Broad Run, severing Pope's supply line, which prompts the battle.

August 26 (Tuesday)   In Kentucky, a detachment of Union cavalry commanded by Lt. Colonel Porter skirmishes with Confederate guerrillas at Madisonville. Casualty figures are unavailable. Also, a Union contingent, the Kentucky Home Guards, skirmishes with Confederates at Harrodsburg and Danville. Casualty figures are unavailable.

In Mississippi, contingents of the 2nd Iowa Cavalry and the 7th Kansas Cavalry engage Confederates at Rienzi and Kossuth.

In New Mexico, at Santa Fe, General Canby issues General Special Order No. 153: "Brig. Gen. James H. Carleton, U.S. Army, will repair without delay to Santa Fe, for the purpose of relieving Brigadier General Canby in the command of the Department of New Mexico." General Carleton learns of the command change on 2 September.

In Tennessee, the Union sustains five killed and twelve wounded. Also, a 130-man contingent composed of about 130 troops, comprised of elements of the 71st Ohio Volunteer Regiment and the 5th Iowa Cavalry, commanded by Colonel William W. Lowe, skirmishes with about 500 Confederate troops at the Cumberland Iron

Works. The Union sustains two killed and 18 wounded. Confederate casualty figures are unavailable.

In Virginia, the Second Army Corps departs Fort Monroe to reinforce the Army of Virginia, which is facing the forces of Robert E. Lee and Thomas "Stonewall" Jackson.

In Naval activity, the USS *Young America* arrives at Nags Head, North Carolina, and rescues personnel on the vessel *Henry Adams,* which is grounded. The next month, the *Young America* moves to Baltimore for repairs.

August 27 (Wednesday)   In Alabama, elements of the 33rd Ohio Volunteer Regiment and a detachment of cavalry skirmish with Confederates at Fort McCook. Casualty figures are unavailable. In addition, Union forces evacuate their positions at Battle Creek.

In Texas, at Franklin (El Paso), General Carleton directs Colonel Joseph R. West to order Captain Roberts' Company E, 1st California Volunteer Infantry, and Company D (Captain Pishon), 1st California Volunteer Cavalry, to repair to Franklin. Upon arrival, Roberts' company is to remain and Pishon's company is to head for Fort Stockton to assume responsibility for Confederate prisoners there.

In Virginia at Manassas, Union General John Pope is prepared to move against the Confederates. At 1830, he directs General Fitz John Porter to advance to Bristoe Station with his entire corps at 0100 on the 28th, giving him time to arrive there by dawn. He instructs Porter to inform Banks to replace him at Warrenton Junction. If Banks is not at Warrenton, Porter is to keep one regiment and two pieces of artillery to hold that place until General Banks arrives, and then immediately move out to join the main body. Fitz John Porter must move ten miles, but much of it is over bad terrain, including many streams and swamps that hinder his 2,000 wagons. Nevertheless, he does arrive at Bristoe Station at about 0800.

Union General Irvin McDowell is directed at 2100 to move from his positions at dawn on the 28th, drive to Manassas Junction, and deploy his right flank at the Manassas Gap Railroad and his left flank to the east. General Jesse Reno is instructed to march upon Manassas Junction from his positions at Gainesville. And General Philip Kearny, stationed in the rear of Reno, is to advance to Bristoe. Meanwhile, Generals McDowell, Franz Sigel and John F. Reynolds are to attempt to intercept the forces of James Longstreet at Gainesville and from there proceed to Manassas Junction.

Confederate General Thomas J. "Stonewall" Jackson deduces that the Union is in the process of encircling his force. He takes steps to outmaneuver his foe. Jackson will feign an attack against Washington. He directs Generals Richard S. Ewell and Ambrose Hill to march northeast toward Washington, while his division, "Jackson's Own," commanded by General William Taliaferro, moves north. Ewell and Hill move to Centreville, but at that point he pivots

and moves away from Washington, heading north to converge with the main body of Jackson's Corps.

In Union activity, Lt. Kenner Garrard, upon official exchange, is appointed colonel of the 146th New York Regiment.

August 27–28   In Virginia, Union troops under General Joseph Hooker (Hooker's Division, 3rd Corps) defeat Confederates under General Ewell at Kettle Run. Union losses are about 300 killed or wounded. Confederate losses are about equal. Union troops, including the 11th and 12th Ohio and the 1st, 3rd, 4th New Jersey, clash with Confederates, led by General Fitzhugh Lee, at Bull Run Bridge. Union Brigadier General George W. Taylor's troops are being carried by train to defend the bridge at Bull Run, but an accident had disrupted the rails and Taylor is compelled to disembark from the train about one mile from the station. In addition, his force lacks artillery. Taylor's brigade engages a Confederate division led by General Isaac R. Trimble. The Union is at a tremendous disadvantage, and the lack of artillery makes the situation more grave. During the tenacious clash, the Confederates, possessing two batteries, compels the Union to retire toward Fredericksburg. General G.W. Taylor is mortally wounded during the battle. He succumbs on 1 September and his brigade is disbanded.

In other activity, shortly after 1:35 P.M., General McClellan receives a telegram stating that an entire brigade under George W. Taylor sent to Bull Run Bridge earlier this morning has been cut to pieces or captured. General Taylor succumbs from wounds on September 2. McClellan's troops are not involved, but John Pope's command is engaged at Groveton. In other activity, a contingent of the 1st U.S. Cavalry led by Lt. M. Harris defeats a Rebel force at Smithfield.

August 28 1862 (Thursday)   In Missouri, Union forces enter and occupy Hernando. Meanwhile, detachments of the 4th Missouri Militia Cavalry skirmish with Confederates in Howard County. Casualty figures are unavailable.

In Tennessee, the 23rd Kentucky Infantry Regiment (10th Brigade, Army of the Ohio), commanded by Colonel Marc Mundy, engages Confederate cavalry led by General Nathan Bedford Forrest at Readyville (Round Hill). The Union sustains ten wounded.

In Virginia, the Union forces of Generals Fitz John Porter and Philip Kearny arrive at Bristoe Station. General John Pope, subsequent to a conference with General Porter, departs for Manassas with Hooker's force. Generals Jesse Reno and Philip Kearny are to follow as soon as possible. At about noon, Kearny's troops encounter Jackson's rear guard at Manassas, but after a brief skirmish, the Rebels retire toward Sudley Springs Road. General Pope, convinced that Jackson is retreating toward Centreville, directs Kearny to move there, but he orders Mc-

Left: Thoroughfare Gap. *Right:* A monument on the Battlefield at Groveton, Virginia (*Harper's Pictoral History of the Civil War*, 1896).

Dowell to remain at Bristoe Station until orders arrive to move out. Pope arrives at Centreville during the afternoon. Assuming that Kearny has intercepted Jackson's main force, Pope directs Rufus King's division and McDowell's corps to hold the Warrenton Pike at all hazards, while he directs Kearny to drive from Centreville to engage Jackson's front, and he directs Porter to move to Centreville, which Pope believes will be the area for the battle. Pope orders a general advance to be initiated on the 29th.

Jackson has positioned his forces between Sudley Springs and Groveton, where he anxiously awaits the forces under James Longstreet. The positions are well established in dense woodlands with "Jackson's Own"—now commanded by General William E. Starke, bolstered by artillery—anchored on the right, while the center is held by General Edward P. Alexander with Ewell's division. The left is defended by General Ambrose P. Hill.

In other activity, elements of the 2nd West Virginia Cavalry, commanded by Lt. Montgomery, skirmish with Confederates at Shady Spring. Casualty figures are unavailable.

In Naval activity, Union gunboats commanded by Commodore Charles Wilkes bombard and destroy City Point along the James River in Virginia.

In Confederate general officer activity, Confederate Colonel Edward A. Perry, 2nd Florida Infantry Regiment, is promoted to the rank of brigadier general, effective this date. Shortly after his promotion, General Perry contracts typhoid fever, which keeps him from field duty until the Overland campaign of 1864.

August 28–29   In Virginia, the Union First Corps, under Major General Franz Sigel, and the Third Corps under Major General Irvin McDowell, bolstered by the commands of Generals Joseph Hooker and Philip Kearny, engage Confederate forces under General Thomas J. Jackson at Groveton and Gainesville. At about dusk on the 28th, a division (Rufus King's) of McDowell's corps encounters Confederates attached to Brigadier General William E. Starke in the vicinity of Groveton, igniting a battle

that lasts about four hours. Brigades of both General Abner Doubleday and John Gibbon participate. Doubleday, subsequent to the seizure of Fort Sumter, had been promoted to brigadier general and assigned to a brigade in General McDowell's corps.

Casualties are extremely high on both sides due to the effectiveness of artillery. The skirmish terminates at about 2100 when the Union pulls back to establish more tenable night positions. Confederate General William B. Taliaferro receives a serious wound during the day's action and Confederate Major General Richard S. Ewell loses one leg. After Taliaferro is wounded, Brigadier General William E. Starke assumes command of his division (Jackson's old division).

Meanwhile, Confederates under Major General David Rumph Jones clear a path at Thoroughfare Gap, permitting General James Longstreet an effortless advance, while his forces compel Brigadier General James B. Ricketts' force to retire toward Bristoe Station. General King, without orders, retreats from the Warrenton Turnpike and moves to Bristoe Station. In the meantime, General Longstreet, with the new flexibility, moves up and deploys on Jackson's left. Maxcy Gregg's brigade covers the far left of the Rebel lines, using the 14th South Carolina Regiment as the most extended unit to guard the left flank. To its immediate right stands the 12th South Carolina Regiment, followed by the 1st and 13th South Carolina Regiments, with some extra strength, Orr's Rifles, held in reserve. Union General Pope, subsequent to learning of King's retreat, orders Generals Heintzelman, Reno and Kearny, the latter bringing King's Division with him, to depart Centreville and move to Gainesville. He also directs Sigel and Reynolds to strike against General Thomas J. Jackson at Groveton.

At about 0600 on the 29th, General Franz Sigel's artillery commences firing upon Jackson's positions, followed by Infantry assaults by contingents of Generals Robert Milroy, Robert Schenck and Carl Schurz. The assaults push Jackson back, but only for awhile, as the Rebels dig in deeply at an abandoned railroad, from where they begin to pour devastating fire upon

the Union. Initially, the Union takes the bashing and continues to hold firmly, but Confederate reinforcements and additional artillery units arrive, which forces them to pull back.

General John Pope soon arrives and his force neutralizes the fresh Confederate reinforcements under Longstreet. Jackson's forces stand steadfastly, and to Jackson's right Longstreet is in position from the Warrenton Road stretching south beyond the Manassas Gap Railroad. His right is protected by General Stuart's Cavalry and a brigade under General Robertson. General Longstreet's infantry divisions are those of Generals D.R. Jones, J.L. Kemper and J.B. Hood. To Hood's left stands the Washington Artillery with three brigades under Cadmus Wilcox supporting it. The Confederates probe Pope's lines throughout the afternoon.

At about 1600 (29th), General Pope orders a

General Ambrose P. Hill (Mottelay, *The Soldier in Our Civil War*, 1886).

three-division assault, sending Hooker, Kearny and Reno against Jackson's center and left, while anticipating that the combined forces of McDowell and Fitz John Porter will turn Jackson's right. Hooker's force strikes the Rebels at the abandoned railroad; Cuvier Grover's brigade dashes forward and drives a wedge into the line, positioning itself between the forces of Confederate Generals Bryan M. Thomas and Maxcy Gregg. The penetration cuts Gregg off from the main body; however, only temporarily, as the 49th Georgia and the 40th South Carolina Regiments are called from their reserve positions. They are soon joined by the 8th Louisiana Brigade and Harry T. Hays' Louisiana brigade, as well as Jubal Early's brigade.

During this most tenacious fighting in Gregg's sector, an urgent message from General Ambrose P. Hill is delivered to General Gregg inquiring whether his South Carolina Brigade was capable of holding their ground. Gregg directs the courier to inform Hill: "Tell General Hill that my ammunition is exhausted, but that I will hold my position with the bayonet." Following a tenacious close-quartered contest, the Yankees are forced to fall back, but both sides experience grievous casualties.

Shortly thereafter, Union General Philip Kearny presses against General A.P. Hill's positions and makes progress against stiff opposition, but here too the Rebels move up fresh troops and compel the outnumbered Yankees to pull back. In the meantime, General Fitz John Porter meets with General Irvin McDowell to ascertain the feasibility of striking against the positions of Longstreet, but they decide that an attack would be fruitless. Rather, McDowell directs Porter to conceal his forces in the woods and prepare for either an attack or a defensive move.

By about 1200, Porter is alone in the woods as McDowell moves out toward Sudley Springs with his force and that of Rufus King's Division (8,000 troops), the latter bringing up the rear of the column. Later, at about 1700, while General Fitz John Porter remains in place, there are several minor skirmishes, and once during the afternoon he believes Franz Sigel is pulling back under Rebel pressure. Porter, with Longstreet's force to his front, ponders rushing to Sigel's aid, but decides against, it concluding that he had been mistaken. General John Porter Hatch (McDowell's Corps), commanding King's Division, arrives at Groveton and deploys near the positions of General Sigel. Shortly after Hatch's arrival McDowell orders him to send three of King's brigades against what is supposed to be, according to information provided by General Pope, Jackson's retreating army.

Hatch's force moves westward and when it reaches a point slightly beyond Groveton, he encounters Longstreet's force, which is advancing to attack. The encounter instigates a grueling battle that does not subside until dusk and costs the Union heavily. However, by holding his ground in the woods, General Porter is able to divert some of the forces of Longstreet. Had Porter instead marched to the positions of Sigel,

the situation might be even worse, as the route of advance had been terrible.

At about 2030, General Pope issues new orders for Porter, directing him to move to Groveton and to arrive there by 0800 on the following day. General Porter, with about 7,000 men, arrives during the early part of the morning, but confusion occurs in great part due to the rush to follow Pope's order and causes the brigades of Generals Charles Griffin and Abram Piatt to move to Centreville rather than Groveton.

During these two days, the Union sustains approximately 7,000 killed, wounded or missing, and the figures for the Confederates are about the same. The Confederates repulse all attacks, although the Union breaks the line temporarily on occasion. Confederate General James Longstreet arrives with reinforcements to aid Lee. Union General Pope — who disperses his entire army, except for two brigades at Bristoe Station defending the wagons, around Groveton — is totally unaware of Confederate reinforcements. Meanwhile, General Robert E. Lee reforms the Confederate lines. He reels in Jackson's units to prepare to launch an assault on the 30th. Longstreet's force on the left remains inconspicuous in the woods.

August 29 (Friday) In Missouri, a contingent of the 1st Wisconsin Cavalry skirmishes with Confederates at the Castor River and Bloomfield.

In Tennessee, two companies of the 18th Ohio and one company of the 9th Michigan skirmish with Confederates at Manchester. The Confederates lose 100 killed or wounded. The Union sustains no losses.

In Naval activity, the USS *Anglo-American* engages Confederate batteries at Port Hudson, Louisiana. In other activity, Commodore Wilkes (recently promoted to the rank of commodore) is detached from the James River Flotilla and named commander of the Potomac River Flotilla; however, the assignment lasts only until 8 September.

In Union general officer activity, Godfrey Weitzel (West Point, 1855), chief engineer with General Nathaniel Butler at New Orleans, is promoted to brigadier general.

In Confederate general officer activity, John Gregg, a lawyer from Alabama and representative in the Confederate Congress who raised the 7th Texas Cavalry, is promoted to brigadier general. Gregg and his regiment had been captured at Fort Donelson.

In Union Naval officer activity, Captain Joseph Lanman, commissioned during 1861 and former commandant of the Washington Navy Yard (1855–1856), is promoted to the rank of commodore. Lanman, commander of

the steam sloop USS *Saranac*, which operates as part of the Pacific Squadron, in 1863 becomes commander of the steam sloop USS *Lancaster,* also attached to the Pacific Squadron. In 1864, Commodore Craven receives command of the frigate USS *Minnesota,* with which he operates as part of the North Atlantic Blockading Squadron. The vessel also participates in the attacks against Fort Fisher, North Carolina, during December 1864 and January 1865, with Commodore Lanman in command of the 2nd Division of Admiral David D. Porter's fleet. The USS *Saranac* remains with the Pacific Squadron for its entire time in service, which terminates when it is wrecked and lost off Vancouver, British Columbia, on 18 June 1875.

August 30 (Saturday) THE SECOND BATTLE OF BULL RUN (MANASSAS) The day starts in silence. Union General John Pope assumes quiet means the Rebels have withdrawn and orders pursuit. The deeply entrenched Rebels have not moved and hold the line at Deep Cut, the unfinished railroad. Pope directs Fitz John Porter to drive along the Warrenton Road, where it is thought Jackson is in retreat. The forces of King and John F. Reynolds trail Porter. Meanwhile, Pope orders General James Ricketts to take the point and, followed by Heintzelman, drive along the Haymarket Road to strike Jackson's left. Pursuant to the new orders, John F. Reynolds, on Porter's left, takes positions to the rear of Porter, thereby exposing the Union's left flank to an assault by Longstreet. In the meantime, General King at Gainesville creates a problem when, without orders, he pulls back, which forces General Ricketts at Thoroughfare Gap to pull back with his division. Consequently, their responsibility of preventing Longstreet from linking with Jackson fails to halt Longstreet.

Fitz John Porter's Corps moves to strike Jackson, but Confederates under Longstreet pound his column as the troops approach the fringe of the woods at Groveton. Simultaneously, Longstreet hammers the exposed flank. Reynolds' absence threatens the entire line, but Sigel sends Generals Robert Schenck and

The 12th Massachusetts Regiment struggles with a wagon during a storm (Mottelay, *The Soldier in Our Civil War,* 1886).

Robert E. Lee (Mottelay, *The Soldier in Our Civil War*, 1886).

Robert Milroy to Bald Hill to fill the gap and meet the attack. Reynolds is also rushed to the scene, and he sets up on the left of Sigel's contingents. A contingent of James Ricketts' division and George Sykes' division of Porter's corps also joins Reynolds. Suddenly Bald Hill is full of Union troops. General Gouverneur Warren, who picked up the mistake of removing Reynolds, takes quick action and moves his own brigade to fill the void, but by buying time and preventing even more disaster, his brigade is heavily mauled by the advancing troops of General John B. Hood.

All the while, Fitz John Porter's corps, bolstered by King's division, drives against General Thomas J. Jackson at the abandoned railroad. Porter's troops launch three successive assaults, each being met by impenetrable fire, which inflicts severe casualties. Porter is compelled to pull back and reform with defensive night positions. Some contingents face Jackson, while other units, led by General Sykes, deploy at Henry House Hill to guard the Union's left wing. Meanwhile, valiant, desperate stands by the troops on Chinn Ridge and Henry Hill preserve the Union line. Darkness arrives to allow the Yankees to make a run for Washington. The Union's hasty retreat from Bull Run saves additional lives. Pope retreats across Bull Run and moves to Centreville to reform and prepare to meet the next Confederate threat. This Confederate victory bolsters the South's confidence, enough to entice them to prepare to invade the North.

While the Union fortifies the defenses of Washington, Robert E. Lee makes plans to drive into Maryland. The Army of Northern Virginia begins its advance towards Pennsylvania on September 2, and the vanguard of Lee's force arrives at Frederick City, Maryland, on the 8th. Union General Pope attempts to blame the disaster at

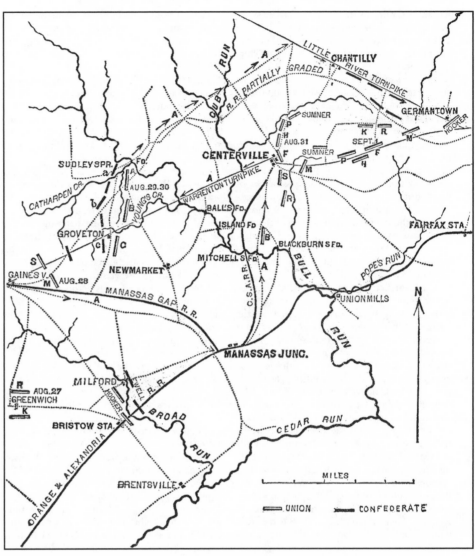

Second Battle of Bull Run (Johnson, *Campfire and Battlefield: History of the Conflicts and Campaigns*, 1894).

Manassas on General Fitz John Porter, but Pope is at fault due to his tactics. Porter receives a court-martial on charges of "disloyalty, disobedience and misconduct in the face of the enemy" brought by General Pope. Also, General Rufus King receives a reprimand for his actions regarding pulling back without orders. Inexplicably, King is assigned as one of the officers on the board for General Fitz John Porter's court-martial. General King does not get assigned to any further duty of substance. His health begins to fail due to epilepsy and he resigns during 1863. King is sent to Rome as an American minister, but Congress forces the mission to be closed by not authorizing funds. King dies in New York in 1876.

After this battle, General George McClellan is put back in charge of all troops in the East. Edwin Forbes, a sketch artist who accompanied the Union forces at this battle, notes in a letter to his publisher: "I have been at four battles where Jackson commanded the enemy's forces, and could not help remarking the similarity of

the ground chosen by him in his several actions. His position is such that he invariably leaves a dense wood on one of our flanks and open ground on the other, and by moving his whole force under cover of the wood, outflanks us."

The Union suffers 7,800, killed, wounded or missing. The 8th New Jersey Regiment sustains heavy casualties, including its officers, all either killed or wounded. General Abram Duryee sustains two wounds during the campaign of Second Manassas. He is wounded three additional times during the fighting at South Mountain and Antietam. Colonel (later brigadier general) Sullivan Meredith sustains a severe wound, but he recovers. He is promoted to brigadier general on 29 November; however, he continues to recuperate during July 1863. At that time, he is assigned duty at Fort Monroe. In 1864, he is transferred to St. Louis and does not see any further service in the field. Brigadier General Robert C. Schenck sustains a wound while commanding the 1st Division (I Corps). The injury to his arm is severe and causes the termination of service in the field. Nevertheless, he rises to the rank of major general of volunteers and is assigned command of the Middle Department, a post he holds until he resigns during December 1863. Brigadier General Zealous Bates Tower sustains a debilitating wound while leading his brigade (General Ricketts' division). His field service is terminated and he remains out of service on sick leave until July 1864, when he is appointed superintendent of the United States Military Academy at West Point. Later, he is ordered to Nashville to bolster the defenses of the city. He remains in Tennessee for the duration of the war. He receives the brevet of major general in the volunteers and the Regular Army toward the close of hostilities and remains in the service beyond the end of the war. He is promoted to lieutenant colonel of engineers during 1865 and makes colonel in January 1874. General Tower retires from the Army during 1883.

The Confederates sustain 3,700 killed, missing or wounded. The 14th South Carolina Regiment, having been heavily engaged on the 29th, sees little action this day as Union guns compel them to keep close to the ground. However, the 18th South Carolina Regiment sees its share of combat, and during the fighting, Colonel James M. Gadberry is killed. He is succeeded by Lt. Colonel William H. Wallace, who is promoted to colonel effective this date, and although he carries the rank, his nomination is not officially given to the Confederate Senate until 10 June 1864. In the meantime, he leads the regiment at Sharpsburg (Antietam) and afterward, he moves to South Carolina where he remains until his brigade (General Stephen Elliott's brigade) is ordered to Virginia to bolster the defenses at Petersburg. Confederate Brigadier General Charles W. Field is seriously wounded at this battle and forced from the field

Combat at the Second Battle of Bull Run (Johnson, *Campfire and Battlefield: History of the Conflicts and Campaigns*, 1894).

for a prolonged period of time. Nonetheless, he does regain his health and is promoted to major general during 1864. Confederate Brigadier General Micah Jenkins (Palmetto Brigade) is wounded, but upon his recovery he joins the 1st Corps, Army of Northern Virginia, during its time in Tennessee. Colonel (later brigadier general) Alexander Hays is seriously wounded. He is out of action for the Maryland campaign. Subsequent to recuperating, Hays is based in the capital and remains until June of the following year.

Confederate Colonel (later brigadier general) Jerome B. Robertson, 5th Texas Regiment, is wounded. Also, during the battle, the flag of Company K, 26th Pennsylvania, is first lost, and then recaptured by First Sergeant George W. Roosevelt. Subsequently, during the battle at Gettysburg, he captures a color bearer and the flag of the regiment, but he becomes seriously wounded during the clash. Roosevelt receives the Medal of Honor for his heroism under fire. The Confederate 25th Virginia Infantry participates in this action as part of General Early's brigade (Ewell's Division). The 12th Massachusetts Regiment, commanded by Colonel Fletcher Webster, participates at this battle. Colonel Webster, the son of Senator Daniel Webster, is killed during the battle.

In Kentucky, Union and Confederate troops clash (Battle of Richmond) fiercely at Richmond. The Confederates, led by Major General Edmund Kirby Smith (West Point, 1845), devastate a Union force under General William Nelson. The Union loses about 200 killed, 700 wounded and approximately 4,000 missing or captured. The Confederates lose about 250 killed and 500 wounded. In addition, the Yankees lose their trains, nine pieces of artillery and 10,000 stands of small arms. General Nelson sustains a slight wound. The Union participants are primarily troops from Indiana, including the 12th, 16th, 55th, 66th, 69th and 71st Regiments. The 6th and 7th Kentucky Cavalry, the 95th Ohio, 18th Kentucky regiments and Batteries D and G of the Michigan artillery also participate. Union General Mahon D. Manson is wounded and captured, but in December he is exchanged. General Manson is involved with operations in the vicinity of Lebanon, Kentucky, against Confederate General Pegram's incursions; afterward, he receives temporary command of the XXIII, prior to the Atlanta campaign. Confederates under Kirby Smith and Brax-

ton Bragg suffer fewer than 500 killed, wounded or missing.

Union Brigadier General John Buford (West Point, 1848), appointed July 27, is severely wounded while commanding a reserve cavalry brigade and left for dead on the battlefield as the Union forces retreat. Buford, however, survives and becomes commander of cavalry, Army of the Potomac, under both Generals McClellan and Burnside. Another Union cavalry commander, General Washington L. Elliott, is also wounded. He attended West Point for three years but withdrew to pursue a medical career in 1844. Union Colonel Solomon Meredith (appointed brigadier general, November 1862) is severely wounded, while participating in Doubleday's brigade; in addition, General Zealous B. Tower (West Point, 1841) receives a near-fatal blow that ends his battlefield service. He is relegated to the superintendent's position at West Point.

In Tennessee, Union forces, including the 20th and 29th Ohio Infantry, commanded by Colonel (later brigadier general) Mortimer D. Leggett, skirmish with Confederates led by General Frank C. Armstrong at Bolivar. The Union suffers five dead, 18 wounded, and 64 missing; Confederates sustain 100 dead or wounded. General Armstrong had participated at the First Battle of Manassas on the side of the Union; however, he resigned during August 1861 to join the Confederacy. He became colonel of the 3rd Louisiana Infantry before becoming commanding officer of the Confederate cavalry under General Sterling Price.

At McMinnville (Little Pond), Confederate cavalry under General Nathan Bedford Forrest strikes against General Don Carlos Buell's left, covered by General Thomas J. Wood's division, in a diversionary attack to allow Braxton Bragg to advance his main body northward. The Union troops, commanded by Colonel E.P. Fyffe (26th Ohio), rout the Rebel cavalry, but the victory is not quickly won. The 26th Ohio, 17th and 58th Indiana and the 8th Indiana Battery participate. Forrest's force sustains heavy casualties. He rejoins Bragg on September 5.

In Texas, at Fort Davis, Captain Edward. D. Shirland, Company C, 1st California Calvary, having arrived on the 28th and completed his investigation on the 29th, departs at dawn. While at the abandoned post, Captain Shirland has discovered one corpse; the man had a wound from a pistol and others from arrows. Shirland believes the man was a wounded Confederate left behind when the fort was abandoned. He takes copious notes prior to departing. While moving back to camp, the detachment pauses at Dead Man's Hole and departs from there at about 0900. After ten miles, the contingent is approached by an Indian on horseback carrying a white flag. A band of about five other Indians are behind him. Capt. Shirland attempts to hold a parley, but the Indians' flag is but a ruse, as another band of about 25 to 30 continue to maneuver around the column. Nevertheless, Captain Shirland becomes aware of the trap, particularly when he spots yet another group of Indians all on foot and fast approaching the area. Shirland orders a fighting maneuver to avoid encirclement and simultaneously outfight the Indians. The mounted Indians pursue, but Union fire quickly halts their progress, but those on foot also participate. Captain Shirland reports that the Indians leave four killed on the field. One is a leader of their horsemen and another is a leader of the band on foot. The Union detachment sustains two wounded but no fatalities; only one is wounded severely, by a strike to his shoulder. Capt. Shirland estimates enemy wounded at no less than 20. Subsequent to the clash, the column arrives at Eagle Springs at about 2300. On the following day, the detachment arrives back at the Rio Grande.

In Union general officer activity, James William Reilly is appointed colonel (later brigadier general) of the 104th Ohio Regiment. Initially he is based in various places in Kentucky; however, in summer 1863 the regiment moves to East Tennessee.

In Confederate general officer activity, Colonel John Calvin Brown (3rd Tennessee) is promoted to brigadier general to rank from this day.

August 31 (Sunday) **In Alabama,** a Union force of more than 1,000 troops engages a Confederate force numbering about 900 troops, commanded by Colonel Alexander McKinstry at Stephenson. The contest lasts about four hours and the Confederates prevail. Casualty figures are unavailable, except for a report that two Confederates are wounded. In other activity, Union forces (General Buell's command) holding Huntsville evacuate the city.

In Tennessee, at Medon Station, elements of the 45th Illinois and the 7th Missouri Regiments, commanded by Major Oliver, engage a large force of Confederates. The Union sustains three killed, 13 wounded and 43 missing. Confederate casualties are not available.

In Kentucky, at Yates Ford, the 94th Ohio Regiment skirmishes with Confederates. The Union sustains three killed and ten wounded.

In Virginia, General Robert E. Lee is injured when his horse, Traveler, is startled. Lee, although dismounted, takes a severe fall, damaging both his hands. In other activity, the Union forces under General John Pope at Centreville are joined by the corps of Generals William Buel Franklin and Edwin V. Sumner. These reinforcements arrive in time to prevent General Thomas J. "Stonewall" Jackson from initiating a flanking movement. Meanwhile, Jackson moves out with his division and that of Richard Ewell, heading across Sudley Ford and the Little River Turnpike. However, a bad storm approaches and prevents any further advance by the Rebels. Consequently, the attack is aborted. The nasty weather continues throughout the night into the following day, but Lee's forces trace the steps of Jackson and Richard Ewell, and by about noon on September 1, it becomes obvious that Washington is imperiled. Mean-

while, Fredericksburg is abandoned by the Union forces (General Ambrose Burnside's command).

In West Virginia, two companies of the 6th West Virginia Regiment skirmish with Confederates at Weston. Casualty figures are unavailable.

In Confederate general officer activity, Brigadier General Samuel Gibbs French is promoted to major general. He is initially assigned duty in Virginia and North Carolina, but later he is transferred to Mississippi, where he remains until May 1864, when he is transferred to the Army of Tennessee.

In Minnesota, a contingent of troops under Major Joseph R. Brown advances to Redwood Ferry on the Minnesota River, the site where Captain John R. Marsh's contingent had recently been ambushed. By the following day, the column retrieves more than forty bodies between the ferry and Birch Coulee. In the meantime, the Dakota, led by Gray Bird, are watching the movement and preparing for another ambush. It occurs on 3 September.

September 1862–April 1865 Robert E. Lee's Army is marching towards Antietam. As the Rebels pass through Frederick, Maryland, they find the townsmen have taken in their Union flags to avoid confrontation with the corps of Stonewall Jackson. One elderly lady, Barbara (Frietchie) Fritchie, refuses to haul down her flag, and when a Rebel trooper blasts it from its position, she defiantly places it out her window and defies the intruders. General Jackson prevents any of the troops from harming the lady Patriot, and the long lines of troops march through town, glancing up at Old Glory. Fritchie passes away during 1865.

Hetty M. McEwen, an elderly supporter of the Union whose husband had fought in the War of 1812, sees red as Tennessee is being torn from the Union. McEwen, who had six uncles who fought in the Revolution, four of whom were killed at the Battle of King's Mountain, does her part to fight the secessionists. She and her husband, Colonel Robert H. McEwen, make their own flag and defiantly hoist it in Nashville. Demands are made upon the elderly Patriots to take the flag down. They nail the flag to the staff and then nail the staff to the chimney. The Rebels attempt to take it down by force, but the shotgun of Hetty prompts Isham Harris and his followers to turn away. The flag is subsequently taken, but upon the return of Union troops after the fall of Fort Donelson, the flag is restored. A poem is written about Hetty's exploits.

Came the day when Fort Donelson Fell
and the Rebel reign was done;
And into Nashville, Buell then,
Marched with a hundred thousand men
With waving flags and rolling drums
Past the heroine's house he comes;
He checked his steed and bared his head
Soldiers! Salute that flag he said;
'And cheer boys cheer!— give three times three
For the bravest woman in Tennessee

Mrs. Booth, the widow of Major Booth, who was killed at the massacre at Fort Pillow, returns from Mound City with the flag that flew over the fort. She obtained the blood-filled banner from one of the survivors of the battle and presents it to the remnants of Major Booth's First Battalion, which is now part of the Sixth U.S. Heavy Artillery. Her inspirational words, in part: "I have given to my country all I had to give—my husband—such a gift! Next to my husband's cold remains, the dearest object left to me in the world, is that flag—the flag that waved in proud defiance over Fort Pillow! Soldiers! This flag I give to you, knowing that you will ever remember the last words of my noble husband, 'never surrender the flag to traitors!'"

During a march into Tennessee in spring of 1862, Union General Turchin becomes ill and his wife, Madame Turchin, assumes command of the regiment and directs them under fire in several skirmishes, with absolute obedience and respect from the troops. Madame Turchin is in the field during most of the regiment's battles, constantly assisting the wounded but always ready to lead if necessary. She dodges many bullets and shells but is never wounded during the war.

Bridget Divers, also known as Michigan Bridget, or as Sheridan's men referred to her, "The Irish Biddy," accompanies the First Michigan Cavalry, in which her husband is a private, from the beginning to the end of the war and is known for her courage and bravery. Frequently, Bridget Divers takes a wounded man from the field and then returns with his weapon to take his place on the line of fire. In at least two instances, it is Divers who rallies retreating troops and convinces them to return to the fight, helping to prevent defeat. In yet another distinct act of bravery, Divers learns that the colonel of the regiment is wounded and the captain killed. She takes the colonel to the hospital and returns to find that the captain has been left on the field. Divers, now without sleep for four days, grabs a horse and penetrates 15 hard miles, retrieves the body of the dead captain and returns his remains to City Point before rejoining the regiment.

Another heroine, Kady Brownell, the wife of an orderly sergeant of the First and subsequently the Fifth Rhode Island Infantry, practices daily with a sword and rifle, becoming an expert marksman who serves on the field in such places as First Bull Run, where she is the color bearer. She holds firm with the colors until her regiment and several others retreat. Although nearly captured by the Confederates, she makes it back to Union lines. Brownell participates with Burnside against New Bern and Roanoke Island and assists the wounded on both sides. She also prevents disaster by catching a mistake that would have had the Fifth Rhode Island fired upon by other Union troops.

During the heavy fighting at Gettysburg on 1 July, Union sharpshooters had held commanding positions at the Harmon house near Oak or Seminary Ridge. The Union troops had not received permission to occupy the house and when they withdraw toward nightfall, Confederates approach and instruct Amelia Harmon and her aunt, with whom she lived, to evacuate because the Rebels intend to torch the home. Harmon indignantly tells the Rebels that the Union had not received permission to be on her property and to please spare the house. The Rebels say no and Harmon pleads again, stating that her deceased mother was a Southerner and she should not be disgraced by Southerners burning the home. A Rebel whispers in her ear that if they would pay tribute to the Confederate flag, the house would be spared. Amelia responds: "Burn the house if you will! I will never do that while the Union which protects me and my friends, exists." The house is quickly burned to the ground and the two ladies are forced to make their way through the battlefields, with both armies firing as they run for their lives. Neither is harmed and both work feverishly with the wounded.

September 1 (Monday) BATTLE OF OX HILL (CHANTILLY, GERMANTOWN) General McDowell's corps, Army of Virginia, and Hooker and Kearny's divisions, Army of the Potomac, engage Confederates at Ox Hill, Virginia. The Little River Turnpike has for the past day or so funneled the troops of Confederate Generals Jackson, Ewell and Lee, positioning them near Germantown, from where they can commence a major push against General John Pope to finish him off and create a path straight into Washington. General John Pope realizes that Washington is in real danger. General Hooker's force moves across the turnpike and establishes positions near Germantown. To his left, spread out along the Centreville Road, are Generals McDowell, Franklin, Heintzelman, John Fitz Porter and Sumner. In addition, Generals Kearny and Reno hold positions at Ox Hill Heights. In the meantime, General Banks ar-

Major General Isaac Stevens (*Harper's Pictoral History of the Civil War*, 1896).

rives with the wagons from Bristoe Station. He is directed to take the wagons to Alexandria. All the while, the Confederates continue to advance.

At about 1700, contingents of General Thomas J. Jackson's force arrive to the front of General Reno's lines at Ox Hill. Confederate General Lawton, in command of General Richard Ewell's division, and General Hill are in the center and far right respectively. The Rebels engage the Union advance and another gruesome engagement begins. Confederate pressure begins to crack Reno's lines. General Isaac I. Stevens leads his Second Division (IX Corps) forward to support Reno, but the Rebel fire prevents progress and Stevens is killed. The lines quickly begin to falter and Reno's force reaches the brink of losing all discipline. However, before the entire line retreats, General Kearny's troops arrive. His vanguard is David B. Birney's Brigade, but close behind are the forces of McDowell and Hooker. At about the same time, another miserable storm arrives and drenches the area, making it nearly impossible to even use the ammunition, but Kearny is not to be deterred. He maintains order, deploys his troops and batteries and even takes personal command of one battery. Nevertheless, shortly thereafter, General Kearny spots a large and dangerous gap in the lines due to the retirement of General Stevens. He moves up to reconnoiter the area and inadvertently enters Confederate lines. Shortly thereafter he is slain by Rebel fire. General David B. Birney assumes command of his division.

Birney orders a bayonet attack. The 1st, 38th and 40th New York Volunteers, commanded by Colonel Thomas Egan, doggedly advance. The charge, bolstered by cold steel, breaks up the Confederate assault and compels them to withdraw. The bold assault terminates at dusk, ending the grueling day. The Union is badly bruised from the battle on the 30th at Bull Run, and the severe casualties inflicted upon them this day prevent any pursuit. General John Pope retires to the safety of Washington.

The Union has 1300 killed, wounded or missing. Confederates sustain 800 killed, wounded or missing. Major General Kearny and Brigadier General Isaac Stevens (West Point, 1839) are both killed on the Union side. Also, the Confederate 25th Virginia Infantry participates at this action as part of General Early's brigade (Ewell's division). And Confederate General Maxcy Gregg's brigade participates. Gregg's 14th South Carolina Regiment, led by Colonel William D. Simpson after the recent wounding of Colonel Samuel McGowan at Manassas (Bull Run), sustains about 26 casualties, including several killed.

In Kentucky, Confederate troops occupy Lexington. During their occupation a 12-man detachment moves to Nazareth and proceeds to the convent of the Sisters of Charity to seek help for their wounded. The nuns agree. A Confederate asks how many nuns can be spared and he receives the answer: "Six now and more later, if necessary." Immediately thereafter, the troops

accompanied by the nuns, attired in their habits and carrying only their rosaries and some books, set out for Lexington, a distance of about 60 miles. Later in this year, another group of the nuns of the Sisters of Nazareth are back in Lexington, tending to Union troops.

In Tennessee, a Confederate cavalry force composed of about 5,000 troops and commanded by General Armstrong strikes the Union at Britton's Lane. The Union force is commanded by Colonel Elias Dennis, includes the 20th and 30th Illinois Regiments and the 4th Illinois and Foster's Illinois Cavalry, bolstered by Battery A, 2nd Illinois Artillery, which firmly hold for the four-hour engagement. The Union sustains five killed and 52 missing. The Confederates sustain 179 killed and 100 wounded. This Confederate contingent is part of General Price's force, which has been ordered by General Bragg to head from Tupelo, Mississippi, to join Bragg in Kentucky. Price is also directed to disrupt General Rosecrans' forces as he moves to keep him penned in and unable to aid Buell.

General Grant concludes that the Confederates are getting progressively more aggressive, and he expects a move to cut his lines of communications. He directs Rosecrans to depart Tuscumbia, Alabama, using the Memphis and Charleston Railway and head for Corinth, and to bring with him part of General Daniel S. Stanley's division.

In Texas, General James H. Carleton at Franklin (El Paso) places the recently captured sick and wounded Confederate prisoners in wagons and with an escort (Company D, 1st California Volunteer Cavalry) transports them to San Antonio, which is held by the Confederates. Afterward, Carleton returns to Las Cruces, New Mexico, and from there, he departs for Santa Fe and arrives there on the 16th.

In Virginia, Union Brigadier General George William Taylor dies from wounds sustained on a special mission in the recent Bull Run campaign.

In Union general officer activity, James Meech Warner (West Point, 1860), in command of Fort Wise (later Fort Lyons), Colorado, until ordered east during the previous month, is commissioned colonel (later brigadier general) of the 11th Vermont Infantry Regiment. The regiment is initially assigned duty in Washington to bolster the defenses. It is transformed into a heavy artillery regiment, composed of about 2,000 troops divided among 12 companies; however, the 11th, including the Wilderness, is at times utilized as an infantry regiment.

In Confederate general officer activity, Colonel Junius Daniel (West Point, 1851), 14th North Carolina Infantry, is promoted to brigadier general, effective this date. General Daniel will serve for awhile in North Carolina, but during the coming winter, he and his brigade will be dispatched to the Army of Northern Virginia as part of the division of Brigadier General Robert E. Rodes (2nd Corps). Also, Colonel Alfred Holt Colquitt (6th

Georgia), a veteran of the Mexican war and a former U.S. Congressman, is promoted to brigadier general.

In Naval activity, at about this time (September) the USS *Indianola* is commissioned, despite being incomplete. The gunboat, built at Cincinnati, is hurried into service due to a threat against the city. The attack does not materialize, and by January 1863, the *Indianola* is prepared for duty. It is assigned to the Mississippi Squadron and participates in the operations against Confederate-held Vicksburg, Mississippi. In other activity, a side-wheel steamer called the *Aleck Scott,* utilized by the U.S. Army (1861–1862) as a quartermaster vessel, at about this time is renamed the *Lafayette* and is being modified as an ironclad. During the following month, it is transferred to the U.S. Navy and commissioned in February 1863. The *Lafayette* participates in the operations against Vicksburg and afterward operates primarily on the lower Mississippi until decommissioned during July 1865 and sold in March 1866.

September 2 (Tuesday) **In Kentucky,** a Union contingent, including the Kentucky 8th Cavalry, engages Confederate guerrillas under Colonel (later brigadier general) Adam R. Johnson at Morganville. Johnson had earlier fought at Fort Donelson, and after its fall, he began operating as a separate contingent, sometimes referred to as a ranger unit. He later picks up the nickname "Stovepipe." Meanwhile, Confederate cavalry units occupy Versailles.

In Minnesota (BATTLE OF BIRCH COULEE), a force of settlers under Major Joseph H. Brown in Minnesota is attacked at about dawn by a Dakota war party that had encircled the camp the previous night. Brown's force sustains casualties during the unexpected assault, but the Indians fail to break through. On the following morning reinforcements arrive from Fort Ridgely to lift the siege. Meanwhile, the Dakota depart.

In New Mexico, General James H. Carleton is informed that he is to relieve General Canby and assume command of the Department of New Mexico. General Carleton returns from Texas to Las Cruces. Once there, he transfers command of the Department of Arizona to Colonel Joseph R. West, but he retains command of the "California Column."

In North Carolina, a contingent including Company F, 9th New York, and the Union 1st North Carolina Volunteer Regiment skirmish with Confederates commanded by Colonel Garrett at Plymouth. The estimated Confederate casualties are 30 killed and 40 captured.

In Virginia, General John Pope's request to be relieved of command is accepted. President Lincoln and General Halleck inform General McClellan that he is to assume command of "all the fortifications of Washington and of all the troops for the defense of the capital." General Pope is transferred to the Department of the Northwest, where he is in command during the Sioux uprising in Minnesota. Also, President

Lincoln, while speaking with McClellan at the latter's residence in Washington, receives a request that General Nelson Miles withdraw from Harpers Ferry to join him (McClellan). The absence of Miles' 11,000 troops at Harpers Ferry, a position of no known strategic value, could do no harm, while the addition of the force to McClellan's Army would be valuable. Nevertheless, General Halleck determines that Miles should hold in place. Rather than move out of the town and control the heights, Miles follows Halleck's orders and later, the decision proves costly. In conjunction, the Union Army will be reformed. Generals Burnside, Porter, Franklin and Sumner retain command of their respective corps; however, General Hooker assumes command of General McDowell's army and General Mansfield receives command of General Banks' corps. Banks now commands the fortifications surrounding the capital.

The Confederate forces under General Robert E. Lee swell to about 70,000 troops as General A.P. Hill's force arrives. With the newest infusion of troops, Lee prepares to invade Maryland. In other activity, the Union 1st Minnesota Volunteer Regiment initiates a reconnaissance mission in the vicinity of Vienna. The contingent sustains one killed and six wounded.

In Union activity, Major John Ramsay receives command of the 8th New Jersey Volunteer Regiment, succeeding the temporary commander, Captain George Hoffman. The 8th Regiment, during the Second Battle of Manassas (Bull Run), lost by either death or injury all of its officers. Previous to this command, Ramsay had been attached to the 5th New Jersey Regiment. During the following month on the 21st, Ramsey is promoted to lieutenant colonel; on 1 April 1863, he is raised to the rank of colonel.

In Confederate general officer activity, Abraham Buford (West Point, 1841) is appointed brigadier general in the Confederate Army effective this day. Buford's cousin, Napoleon B. Buford, and his half-brother, John Buford, become generals in the Union Army. All three are from the state of Kentucky.

In Naval activity, the *Vanderbilt,* a wooden side-wheel steamship built as a commercial ship and chartered by the U.S. Army as a transport during the initial days of the war, is commissioned at about this time. The USS *Vanderbilt* had been transferred from the U.S. Army to the U.S. Navy in March, at which time work began to transform the ocean transport into a cruiser. By November it is at sea in search of the CSS *Alabama,* and the duty extends through all of 1863, but without success; however, it is able to seize three other vessels: the *Peterhoff,* February 1863; steamer *Gertrude,* April 1863; and the bark *Saxon* in October 1863. The cruise takes a toll on the *Vanderbilt* and it is placed out of commission for nearly all of 1864. It returns to service and is assigned duty in the North Atlantic. During November 1864 it moves south to North Carolina and participates in blockade duty off Wilmington, and then participates in the operations against Fort Fisher (December

1864–January 1865). Afterward it transports troops to the Gulf of Mexico and engages in other service such as towing vessels from that region to ports on the east coast. After the war, it becomes a receiving ship and remains in active service until May 1867. Then it remains inactive in California at Mare Island Navy Yard until sold during April 1873. The ship is renamed *Three Brothers,* and toward the latter part of the century it becomes a coal hulk at Gibraltar until 1929.

September 3 (Wednesday) **In the Dakota Territory,** Union detachments, including Company D, 5th Minnesota Volunteer Infantry Regiment, engage Sioux Indians at Fort Abercrombie. The fighting continues until the 6th. Fighting again breaks out here on September 23.

In Kentucky, Confederate troops commanded by General E. Kirby Smith occupy Frankfort. Also, Union cavalry commanded by Lt. Colonel Foster skirmishes with Confederate guerrillas at Slaughterhouse. The Confederates sustain three killed, two wounded and 25 captured. A contingent of the 8th Kentucky Cavalry under Colonel James M. Shackelford (later brigadier general) skirmishes with Confederates guerrillas under Colonel Adam R. Johnson at Greiger's Lake, in a fight that lasts about two hours. Colonel Shackelford receives a slight wound during the contest.

In Minnesota, Union contingents also engage Indians in a fight at Hutchinson. The Union again clashes with the Indians on the following day. Casualty figures are unavailable.

In Virginia, the 1st Maine Cavalry, commanded by Colonel Samuel Allen, arrives at Fairfax Court House after leaving Cedar Mountain on August 9. Following a meeting between Colonel Allen and General Reno, the 1st Maine Regiment departs for Washington, D.C., arriving there on the following day. Also, Winchester is abandoned by the Union forces deployed there.

In Union general officer activity, Joseph Holt (secretary of war under President Buchanan) is appointed judge advocate general of the army by President Lincoln. Holt receives the rank of colonel. On 22 June 1864, he is promoted to brigadier general. General Holt retires during 1875 and resides in Washington, D.C. He later goes blind and dies on 1 August 1894.

September 4 (Thursday) **In Washington, D.C.,** the 1st Maine Cavalry arrives and is attached to General Burnside's Corps. General Lee and his forces initiate their plan to invade Washington by crossing the Potomac and preparing the Maryland campaign. By the 7th, his forces will be encamped at Frederick, Maryland. This day, the Union evacuates Frederick.

In Kentucky, Generals Gordon Granger and Sheridan reach Louisville before Buell.

In Louisiana, a contingent of 60 Union soldiers from the 8th Vermont Infantry repulses a Confederate assault on a train in the vicinity of Boutte Station.

In Mississippi, upon receiving orders from Washington, Grant dispatches Brigadier General Gordon Granger's division from Corinth to reinforce Buell, who is still heading for Chattanooga.

In North Carolina, a contingent of Union soldiers, including the 1st New York Mounted Rifles, attack and capture 120 Confederate soldiers at Sandy Crossroads. Sgt. Frank W. Mills receives the Medal of Honor for bravery during this action.

In Tennessee, a detachment of the 6th Tennessee Volunteers skirmishes with Confederates at Big Creek Gap. Casualty figures are unavailable. In White County, Colonel George Dibrell organizes the 8th Tennessee Cavalry (also known as the 13th Tennessee Cavalry). This regiment is composed of partisan rangers and is not in any way affiliated with Smith's 8th Tennessee Cavalry (established during 1863 and designated the 4th Tennessee Cavalry). When the regiment was initially being formed by Colonel Charles Carroll, the Union captured him at Murfreesboro, prior to his muster report being dispatched to Richmond. The regiment is erroneously designated there as the 13th Tennessee Cavalry.

In Virginia, a contingent of New York Mounted Rifles, led by Colonel Joseph Wheeler, encounters and skirmishes with a group of Confederates at South Mills and captures about 100. In other activity, Confederate troops occupy Ravenswood.

In Union activity, Oliver Edwards, aide-de-camp to General Darius N. Couch, is appointed colonel of the 37th Massachusetts Regiment. Edwards' regiment afterward participates at Fredericksburg and Chancellorsville in Virginia, then at Gettysburg, Pennsylvania, the latter during July 1863. Edwards also serves in New York as part of the force that suppresses the rioters, prior to returning to the Army of the Potomac. Colonel Charles Gilbert is appointed brigadier general by President Lincoln. He is then named commander of the III Provisional Corps, Army of the Ohio. Major Francis Trowbridge (later brigadier general) is appointed colonel of the 88th Illinois Regiment, also known as the Second Board of Trade Regiment. He participates at the Battle of Murfreesboro and afterward receives command of a brigade in the XX Corps. Subsequently, he is attached to the IV Corps on the staff of General Oliver O. Howard.

In Naval activity, the CSS *Florida* arrives near Mobile, Alabama, and encounters several Union warships on patrol to block the port. The *Florida* hoists the British flag and initially, the ruse works. The *Florida* is permitted to advance across the bar, but as the Union orders the vessel to halt, the crew runs down the British colors and unfurls the Confederate flag. The sloop of war USS *Oneida* wastes no time in declaring its welcome. The *Oneida* commences fire from close range. The broadside is followed by other Union fire and the CSS *Florida* receives its bap-

tism under fire for nearly two hours. Nevertheless, the overmatched steamer manages to reach the safety of Fort Morgan's guns, slightly before 1830, which prevent the blockade squadron from totally destroying it. At that time, the *Oneida, Winona* and the *Rachael Seaman* abort the chase. Nonetheless, the barrages inflict severe damage to the rigging. One man is killed and seven others are wounded. Afterward, the ship is completely fitted out, and with a full crew obtained in Mobile, the *Florida* departs on 15 January 1863, in an attempt to again run through the blockade. The USS *Cayuga* also participates in this action.

September 5 (Friday) General Halleck, acting on a directive from Lincoln, dismantles General John Pope's Army of Virginia, placing it under General George McClellan's Army of the Potomac. Pope is ordered to another command in the Midwest (Minnesota). In other activity, General Braxton Bragg's Army enters Kentucky; one corps, that of Kirby Smith, has been in the state for awhile. Two brigades under General Buckner move toward Munfordville, which is defended by Colonel J.T. Wilder. Confederates capture and occupy Poolesville, Maryland. Meanwhile, another force, composed of Confederate cavalry, seizes Pikesville, Virginia.

In Union general officer activity, Colonel Charles E. Hovey is promoted to brigadier general to rank from this day; however, the Senate takes no action. Consequently, his commission expires on 4 March 1863. Prior to the expiration, Hovey participates in the capture of Arkansas Post.

In Union general officer activity, Lt. Colonel Gabriel Rene Paul (promoted to lieutenant colonel in April) is promoted to brigadier general. However, his commission expires on 4 March 1863 due to inaction by the Senate. Nevertheless, he is re-nominated on 18 April 1863 and afterward confirmed.

September 6 (Saturday) **In the Dakota Territory,** Fort Abercrombie is attacked by a band of Indians composed of about 300 braves. The attack is repulsed with a loss of one trooper killed and three wounded. Elements of the 5th Minnesota Volunteer Regiment under Lt. Sheehan participate.

In North Carolina, during the early morning hours Confederate cavalry launches a surprise attack against Union forces commanded by Colonel Edward Potter at Washington. Hand-to-hand fighting ensues, and some nearby gunboats, the USS *Pickett* and *Louisiana,* lend some greatly appreciated muscle. The Confederates are compelled to retire. The 3rd New York Cavalry and its light artillery, the 24th Massachusetts and the Union 1st North Carolina Regiments also participate. The Union is under the overall command of General J.G. Foster, who had succeeded General Ambrose Burnside. Foster's forces still in the Department of North Carolina remain dangerously low in numbers since the departure of Burnside, who has moved to support McClellan at Richmond, Virginia.

Reinforcements have been promised, but as of now, none have arrived.

In West Virginia, a contingent of Union troops under Major Hall skirmishes with Confederates under Colonel Stratton at Chapmanville. The Union sustains one killed and one wounded. At Martinsburg, a Confederate force of about 300 troops engages a Union force under General Julius White. The Union sustains about two killed and 10 wounded. The Confederates lose some captured. General White is new to the Virginia campaign, following his service in Arkansas and his promotion to brigadier general during June. At Cacapon Bridge, elements of the 1st New York Cavalry, under Colonel Andrew McReynolds, skirmish with Confederates led by Colonel (later general) John D. Imboden.

In Arkansas, a contingent of the 1st Missouri Cavalry skirmishes with Confederates at La Grange. Casualty figures are unavailable.

In Naval activity, the USS *Water Witch,* recently reactivated following repairs that began in April, is re-commissioned this day. The *Water Witch,* previously attached to the East Gulf Blockading Squadron, is ordered to South Carolina to join the South Atlantic Blockading Squadron, commanded by Rear Admiral Samuel F. Du Pont. The vessel arrives in Charleston on 18 September.

September 7 (Sunday) **In Kentucky,** Union forces seize Shepherdsville.

In Maryland, General Robert E. Lee's forces are across the Potomac at Frederick City. Lee had believed that his advance would prompt the Union forces at Harpers Ferry and at Martinsburg to evacuate, but it does not occur. Consequently, Lee intends to seize both. He directs General Jackson's corps and about one-half of Longstreet's corps to move against Martinsburg. Following its fall, the force is to drive to Harpers Ferry. Meanwhile, Lee keeps the remainder of Longstreet's corps, all of the available cavalry and General D.H. Hill's division. Confederate General McLaws is directed to attack and seize Maryland Heights, which is situated across from Harpers Ferry on the opposite bank of the Potomac, and he orders General John G. Walker to capture Loudon Heights, on the Shenandoah River at its convergence with the Potomac. Union General George B. McClellan initiates the movement of his forces, which now stand in Maryland slightly north of the capital. Using a formation of five separate lines to cover Baltimore and Washington, the Union marches toward Frederick City. General Burnside holds the right wing with his Ninth Corps, commanded by Reno and Hooker's corps (formerly McDowell's corps). The center is held by General Sumner with his Second Corps and Mansfield's Twelfth Corps (formerly Bank's Twelfth Corps). The far left is held by General Franklin with the Sixth Corps and General Darius Couch's division. General Porter's corps, except Sykes' force, stays in place in Washington; however, on the 12th, it will

Signal station at Maryland Heights (*Harper's Pictorial History of the Civil War*, 1896).

move and join the main body of the army near Turner's Gap on the 14th. In other activity, elements of the 3rd Indiana and the 8th Illinois Cavalry clash with Confederates at Poolesville. The Union sustains two killed and six wounded and the Confederates sustain three killed and six wounded.

In Mississippi, General Grant receives word that Confederate Generals Earl Van Dorn and Sterling Price are advancing, probably toward Corinth.

In Missouri, Clinton B. Fisk is appointed colonel of the 33rd Missouri Infantry. Within the month, Fisk is assigned to establish a brigade and is appointed brigadier general. His battlefield service is primarily in Missouri, where he and his troops are successful in repulsing Confederates under John S. Marmaduke, Sterling Price and Colonel Joseph O. Shelby.

In Tennessee, at Clarksville (Rickett's Hill), a Union contingent composed of elements of the 11th Illinois, 13th Wisconsin, 71st Ohio Regiments and the 5th Iowa Cavalry, bolstered by two batteries of artillery, commanded by Colonel William W. Lowe, engage Confederates and recapture the town. Casualty figures are unavailable.

In Union general officer activity, Colonel Joseph Bradford Carr, 2nd New York Infantry

Regiment, is promoted to brigadier general of volunteers. His commission expires on 4 March, 1863; however, he is re-nominated on 31 March of the same year. Nevertheless, by May, the Senate takes no action. Consequently, Carr is junior to his brigade commanders. General Carr will see action at Fredericksburg and Chancellorsville.

Colonel Gershom Mott (6th New Jersey) is appointed brigadier general of volunteers. Mott had been wounded at the Battle of Seven Pines, and later he becomes wounded at the Battle of Chancellorsville. Also, Colonel Nelson Taylor (72nd New York), a veteran of the Mexican War, is appointed brigadier general. He participates at various engagements, including Fredericksburg (December 1962). However, on 16 January 1863, his resignation is accepted by the War Department. He returns to New York to resume his law practice. He is elected to Congress and serves from 1865 to 1867.

In Naval activity, the USS *Cimarron* departs from Fortress Monroe, Virginia, to join the South Atlantic Blockading Squadron. It arrives in Port Royal, South Carolina, on the 13th. Also, a naval fleet under Commodore Porter clashes with Confederate shore batteries and inland artillery batteries in the vicinity of Port Hudson, Louisiana.

September 8 (Monday) In Kentucky, Confederate troops occupy Boyd's Station.

In Maryland, a Union contingent composed of elements of the 3rd Indiana Cavalry and the 8th Illinois Cavalry led by Major Chapman enter and occupy Poolesville. The Union sustains one killed and seven wounded. The estimated Confederate casualties are eight killed. Also, General Robert E. Lee, headquartered outside of Frederick, issues a proclamation to the citizens that cites what Lee perceives as the wrongs done to the citizens by the federal government: "The people of the South have long wished to aid you in throwing off this foreign yoke, to enable you again to enjoy the inalienable rights of freemen and restore the independence and sovereignty of your state." Neither the Confederate Army nor the proclamation is well received by the people of Maryland. The people had draped their windows, locked their doors and all business shops had closed in advance. Confederate recruiting offices are quickly opened, but there is no race to the doors. Confederate units from Maryland are few and far between, except for the Confederate 1st Maryland Regiment led by General Arnold Elzey. Many of the men from Maryland might well have already joined the Confederacy; however, the effort likely failed due to the loyalty of the state to the Union. About 50,000 men from Maryland join the Union Army.

In Naval activity, the secretary of the Navy appoints Charles Wilkes as commander of the

newly established West Indies Squadron by the following: "You have been selected to command a squadron for this purpose, to be composed of the steamers *Wachusett, Dacotah, Cimarron, Sonoma, Tioga, Octorara* and *Santiago de Cuba.*" Wilkes, appointed commodore the previous month, is promoted to the rank of acting rear admiral. Wilkes is also informed that "two or more armed vessels without any recognized national flag, and which are understood to be owned by rebels, are cruising in the West Indies with a view to deprecate on American commerce," and that "the Department has information that other vessels are destined for similar purposes in the same quarter, and it is therefore essential that prompt and vigorous measures be adopted for annihilating these lawless depredators by their capture, and, if necessary, destruction." Wilkes prepares to embark and rendezvous with the ships of the squadron off the Bahamas. He sails from Washington to Hampton Roads on 17 September, and on the 20th, he receives new orders.

September 9 (Tuesday) In Louisiana, at Des Allemands, elements of the 21st Indiana and the 4th Wisconsin Regiments skirmish with Confederate contingents. The Union lists no casualties. The Confederates sustain twelve killed.

In Maryland, Confederate troops occupy Middletown. At Nolansville, elements of the 3rd Indiana Cavalry and the 8th Illinois Cavalry Regiments skirmish with Confederates. Casualty figures are unavailable.

In Missouri, Union cavalry led by Colonel Burris clashes with Confederate guerrillas under William Clark Quantrill at Big Creek. Casualty figures are unavailable.

In Tennessee, a contingent of the 42nd Illinois Regiment, under Colonel George Bomford, skirmishes with Confederates at Columbia. The Union lists no casualties. The Confederates sustain 18 killed and 45 wounded.

In Virginia, Union troops repel an attack by Confederate forces at Williamsburg. The 5th Pennsylvania, led by Colonel Campbell, reacts quickly to the Confederate cavalry and artillery, and the assault ends within in one-half hour. The Rebels under Colonel Shingles abandon their positions. In other activity, the Rebels are also compelled to evacuate Fredericksburg.

In Union general officer activity, Captain William Rufus Terrill is promoted to brigadier general on the recommendation of General H.G. Wright, commanding officer of the Department of the Ohio.

September 10 (Wednesday) In Maryland, a contingent of the 6th U.S. Cavalry led by Captain Saunders clashes with a Confederate force composed of cavalry and artillery at Sugar Loaf Mountain. It is reported that the Confederates prevail; however, casualty figures are unavailable. Meanwhile, the Confederates (Robert E. Lee's command) evacuate Frederick.

In Mississippi, Confederate General Price's force arrives at San Jacinto. A Union force at

Iuka, when informed of the approaching Rebel cavalry, abandons the town. Also, in Cold Water, the 6th Illinois Cavalry engages and defeats a force of Confederates. The Union lists no casualties. The Confederates sustain four killed and 80 wounded.

In Ohio, fears of a Confederate attack nearly paralyze Cincinnati. The Ohioans deploy several thousand laborers in trenches to bolster the city's defenses. That same day, Pennsylvanians call for the defense of Pennsylvania, which is also anticipating a Confederate assault.

In West Virginia, a Union force composed of about 1,200 troops, including elements of the 34th and 37th Ohio and the 4th West Virginia Volunteer Regiments, commanded by Colonel Siber, engages a Confederate force of about 5,000 troops under General William W. Loring at Fayetteville. The Union sustains 13 dead, 80 wounded and 36 missing. Confederate casualty figures are unavailable.

In Union general officer activity, Colonel Edward Calvin Pratt is promoted to brigadier general, volunteers, full rank. Also, Colonel Edward Ferrero, 51st New York, is promoted to brigadier general effective this day. Nevertheless, he does not receive confirmation by the Senate and his commission expires in March 1863. On 6 May he is re-nominated. Also, Robert Brown Potter, a New York lawyer who joined the army as a private (51st New York Regiment) shortly after he outbreak of hostilities, is this day promoted to colonel. Potter participates at Fredericksburg in December 1862 and afterward is transferred to Ohio, where he is promoted to brigadier general the following March.

September 11 (Thursday)   In Kentucky, a contingent of Confederates under Brigadier General Richard Montgomery Gano occupy Maysville.

In West Virginia, a Union force — composed of elements of the 34th and 37th Ohio and the 4th West Virginia Regiments, which had on the previous day clashed with Confederates at Fayetteville — this day skirmishes with Confederates at Cotton Hill.

In Maryland, Union forces enter and occupy Newmarket, while a Confederate force under Colonel (later general) Thomas L. Rosser, commanding officer, 5th Virginia Cavalry Regiment, occupies Westminster. Colonel Rosser had been preparing for graduation at West Point, scheduled for two weeks later, when he resigned during April 1861 to serve with the Confederacy.

In Virginia, Union troops begin a retreat from Martinsburg and move toward Harpers Ferry, West Virginia, upon sight of approaching troops under General Thomas "Stonewall" Jackson. Union troops are ordered to depart Ganby, Virginia, and to destroy all government property before they evacuate the town. The Union also abandons its positions at Gauley.

In Missouri Confederate Guerrillas attack Union-held Bloomfield through the 13th. It is

defended by the 13th Illinois Volunteers, the 1st Wisconsin Cavalry, Missouri Militia and Battery E, 2nd Missouri Artillery. The Confederates capture the town.

September 12 (Friday)   In Kentucky, Confederate forces enter and occupy Frankfort.

In Maryland, advance contingents of the Union Army of the Potomac, including elements of the 1st Maine Cavalry, clash with Confederates at Frederick, where the bulk of the regiment has established its camp. The arrival of McClellan's army is met with wild enthusiasm. The city is decked out with U.S. flags flying from nearly every window and the previously closed shops have their doors wide open to welcome the troops. Company G, 1st Maine Cavalry, is with General Reno at South Mountain and Companies M and H are serving with General Fitz John Porter in the vicinity of Antietam. Inadvertently, General McClellan acquires a copy of Robert E. Lee's blueprint for the Confederate battle plan, which details the missions of Generals Thomas Jackson, James Longstreet and Lafayette McLaws, as well as the orders for General John J. Walker and Daniel Harvey Hill. McClellan's luck pinpoints the targets of Lee's generals. Jackson is heading for Martinsburg via Sharpsburg, from where he intends to bolt across the Potomac. Subsequent to his seizure of Martinsburg, Jackson is to speed to Harpers Ferry to support McLaws in the capture of it. Meanwhile, McLaws is to take the high ground overlooking the town and provide extra support for Walker. The rear guard duty is assigned to D.H. Hill's force, and Longstreet has been directed to halt in place at Boonesborough (Boonsboro). The plan also calls for a regrouping at Boonesborough or Hagerstown following the operation. The Confederates anticipate the abandonment of Martinsburg and Harpers Ferry upon the arrival of Lee's forces.

In Mississippi, most Union troops around Corinth, including Rosecrans' force, detailed to guarding the rails east of Corinth, are drawn in closer to the city to prepare for an advancing Confederate force.

In Missouri, Bloomfield, recently seized by the Confederates, is regained by a Union force led by Colonel Boyd.

In West Virginia, contingents of the 34th Ohio and the 4th West Virginia Volunteer Regiments skirmish and defeat a contingent of Confederates commanded by Colonel Lightfoot at Charlestown. The town is destroyed. Casualty figures are unavailable.

In Confederate general officer activity, Colonels James Fagan (1st Arkansas Infantry), Allison Nelson (10th Texas Infantry) and William Steele (7th Texas Cavalry) are promoted to the rank of brigadier general, effective this day. Fagan transfers to the Trans-Mississippi Department. Nelson is assigned to duty under General Theophilus Holmes; however, General Nelson had been struck the previous day with deadly fever and he succumbs in October. General Steele is assigned duty in the In-

dian Territory, and later, during 1864, he participates in the defense of Galveston, Texas. Confederate Lt. Colonel William Read Scurry and Colonel Francis Asbury Shoup (West Point, 1855) are promoted to brigadier general. Shoup commands a brigade of Louisianians during the defense of Vicksburg.

September 12–15   In Maryland, on the 13th, Confederate General John G. Walker's Division (Jackson's command) secures Loudon Heights without opposition, and Confederate General Lafayette McLaws (West Point, 1842) orders Generals Joseph B. Kershaw and William Barksdale to attack Maryland Heights. Confederates defeat a Union force led by Colonel Ford and secure the town by 4:30 P.M. on the 13th, sending the Union in retreat for Harpers Ferry.

In West Virginia, Union troops commanded by Colonel Dixon Miles are decisively defeated at Harpers Ferry by Confederates under Stonewall Jackson. The Confederates capture supplies and ammunition. The Union suffers 80 killed, 120 wounded and 11,583 captured. Jackson pushes towards Sharpsburg, Maryland, and allows Gen. A.P. Hill to accept the surrender. Confederates suffer 500 dead or wounded. Union General Julius White arrives from Martinsburg just prior to the Confederate threat and opts for discretion, because of unfamiliarity with men and country. He turns command to Colonel Miles, who does terribly. The loss of Harpers Ferry permits Jackson to roll into Antietam at full stride. Colonel White is afterward placed under arrest; however, following an inquiry, he is exonerated. Later, during January 1863, he is transferred to the Department of the Ohio and given command of a division (XXIII Corps) at Knoxville, where he remains until General Burnside is transferred back to the Army of the Potomac. White accompanies Burnside as his chief of staff (see also, **September 14–15 BAT-TLE OF HARPERS FERRY**). The Union 39th, 111th, 115th, 125th and 126th New York Militia, the 32nd, 60th and 87th Ohio, 9th Vermont, 65th Illinois, 15th Indiana, 1st and 3rd Maryland Home Brigades, 8th New York Cavalry and four batteries of artillery participate. Also, the Confederate 25th Virginia Infantry attached to General Early's Brigade (Ewell's Division) participates in this action.

September 13 (Saturday)   In Arkansas, Major (later brigadier general) George C. Strong, leading three companies of the 12th Maine Regiment and one company of the 26th Massachusetts Regiment, embarks aboard the USS *Ceres* en route to raid on a Confederate strongpoint at Ponchatoula, headquarters of Confederate Brigadier General (Missouri state troops) M. Jeff Thompson. Another contingent of 100 troops of the 13th Connecticut boards the USS *New London*. The contingent on the *New London* is to debark at Manchac Bridge and push any defenders there northward toward Ponchatoula. Unexpected difficulties emerge due to the vessels and the waterways, causing a delay in the operation.

Acquia Creek, Virginia, General Ambrose Burnside's base of supplies (*Harper's Pictoral History of the Civil War*, 1896).

In Maryland, Union and Confederate rearguard troops skirmish at Frederick City. The Union enters and occupies the city. General McClellan obtains an order given by General Robert E. Lee concerning his plans to take Sharpsburg and in quick succession, Martinsburg and Harpers Ferry. The Confederate order also spells out the present positions of Lee's forces and it makes it clear that no attacks will be launched against either Washington or Baltimore, provided McClellan is positioned between the two cities. The Confederate document is dated September 9.

McClellan and Lee have a mutual respect for each other. They are both graduates of West Point and served together during the Mexican War. McClellan takes precautions to check Lee without giving him an opportunity to strike a deadly blow. McClellan, in response to the recently gained intelligence, orders an advance to South Mountain. One force moves through Turner's Gap; Burnside takes the point, trailed by Sumner. Another force led by General Franklin advances through Crampton Gap, which is in front of Burkittsville and leads into Pleasant Valley. Union Cavalry under General Alfred Pleasonton is positioned near Turner's Gap, but the infantry does not arrive until the following morning.

In Mississippi, a Confederate force under General Sterling Price occupies Iuka. A small detachment of Union soldiers, commanded by Colonel R.C. Murphy, had earlier evacuated without a fight and fled to Corinth. General Rosecrans had paused at Iuka en route to Corinth to join Buell and left there, under the charge of Murphy, huge amounts of supplies. Murphy hastily departed without destroying them, prompting Rosecrans to later call for his arrest. Skirmishing continues in the area until the 19th. In other action, General Rosecrans receives additional reinforcements from both Bolivar and Jackson, giving him a total of about 17,000.

In Missouri, a Union contingent of the 3rd and 6th Missouri Cavalry skirmishes with Confederates at Newtonia. Casualty figures are unavailable.

In Union general officer activity, Colonel James Murrell Shackelford (formerly 25th Union Kentucky Regiment) becomes colonel of the 8th Kentucky Cavalry, which he had raised.

In Naval activity, the USS *Cimarron* arrives at Port Royal, South Carolina, and is attached to the South Atlantic Blockading Squadron. The *Cimarron* operates along the coastal and inland waters of Florida, Georgia and South Carolina.

September 14 (Sunday) BATTLE OF SOUTH MOUNTAIN (BOONSBORO GAP) Union cavalry contingents and troops of the 1st and 2nd Brigades of General Jacob Cox's division each conduct reconnaissance missions, and afterward, General Reno concludes that an attack should be launched against Confederate positions south of Turner's Gap, Maryland. The Union artillery batteries of McMullin and Simmons commence a huge bombardment to supply cover fire for the advance. Under the umbrella of the barrage, the contingents of Cox lead the way, trailed by Rodman, Wilcox and Sturgis. The Yankees ascend the slopes of South Mountain and soon encounter the forces of General Garland (General A.P. Hill's division). Both sides fight furiously as the Rebels attempt to retain the ground, but Garland is slain during the battle, forcing the Rebels to lose some momentum and get driven back.

In the meantime, General Longstreet at Hagerstown is ordered by Hill to speed to the scene. As the struggle for the mountain continues, Confederate reinforcements arrive at about the same time that the Union forces of Rodman, Sturgis and Willcox, which had been trailing Cox, arrive. Thirty thousand Rebels dominate the gap and the two summits when Hooker's First Corps arrives at 1400, guaranteeing yet another grim blood bath. Hooker sprints to strike the Confederate left at Hagerstown Road. He is trailed by General Meade, who has arrived from Kittoctan Creek. In addition, General James Ricketts is ordered to follow the turnpike in coordination with an advance by Reno's Ninth Corps. Reno will advance on the far left, while General John Hatch leads King's division in the center. All the while, the Confederates maintain incessant fire to repel the surging Union columns. Nevertheless, neither side relents, and the skirmishing erupts all along the line, creating a massive display of savage fury. The relentless fire that the Confederates pour upon the ascending Yankees is not sufficient to halt the attack and hold the positions. The Union reaches the crest, and only the dark of night is able to silence the guns and terminate the slaughter.

Union General Jesse Lee Reno (West Point,

Left: Battle of South Mountain (Mottelay, *The Soldier in Our Civil War*, 1886). *Above:* A view of Boonsboro and Turner's Gap from the west (*Harper's Pictoral History of the Civil War*, 1896).

1846) is killed while leading his troops; he is succeeded by Brigadier General (later major general) Jacob D. Cox. In addition, Union Brigadier General John P. Hatch and Colonel W. P. Wainright are both wounded. Subsequent to recuperation, General Hatch is confined to administrative duties for the duration of the war. General William Buel Franklin, who had been moving through Crampton's Gap, also succeeds in besting the Rebels under General McLaws. Franklin's force advances against three brigades commanded by Brigadier General Howell Cobb. Three divisions under General Henry W. Slocum pound the Confederate front, while General William F. Smith's force scales the left side of the mountain. Smith takes the mountain, but the charge costs 533 in killed and wounded. The Confederates abandon the crest and retire down the west side of the mountain; 400 are seized as prisoners and several hundred stands of arms are seized. The Confederates lose about 600 during this contest.

General Robert E. Lee, noting the dangerous positions he holds due to the Union threat from Turner's Gap and Crampton's Gap, decides to fall back to Sharpsburg. Major General Hooker's First Corps, 6th Corps under Major General William B. Franklin, and the Ninth Corps under Major General Jesse Reno (West Point, 1846) participate in this Union victory. The Union counts 443 dead and 1,806 wounded. Confederates have 500 killed, 2,343 wounded and 1,500 captured. Union Major General Jesse Lee Reno is killed and Confederate Brigadier General Samuel Garland is mortally wounded. Also, Major (later brigadier general) Rutherford B. Hayes (23rd Ohio) is wounded. Colonel Edward Augustus Wild is again seriously wounded. He loses one arm. Nonetheless, he recuperates, returns to service and becomes involved in raising Negro regiments that become known as "Wild's African Brigade," which he commands for the duration of the war. Confederate Colonel Iverson, 20th North Carolina Infantry and the son of U.S. Senator Alfred Iverson, will be promoted to the rank of brigadier general in November 1862 and will assume command of Garland's brigade.

This Union victory greatly alarms General Lee, particularly because his force now numbers only slightly more than forty thousand troops. Lee redeploys his force at the village of Sharpsburg with his flanks buffered by the Potomac River and the Antietam Creek, the latter flowing freely to the front with four separate stone bridges spanning it as well as a practical ford. The Confederates have all bridges except the northernmost span.

First Lieutenant G. Hooker, 4th Vermont Infantry, single-handedly accepts surrender of a Confederate regiment; he receives the Medal of Honor. Private James Allen, Company F, 16th New York, captures 14 Confederate soldiers of the 16th Georgia Infantry at South Mountain; Allen also becomes the recipient of the Medal of Honor. Company G, 1st Maine Cavalry, participates in this action in support of General Reno.

In Kentucky, Confederates who occupied Maysville on the 11th abandon it. A nearby Union contingent reoccupies the town without incident. In other activity, a Union force surrenders its fort at Bacon Creek to a Confederate contingent led by Colonel Morrison. The Union loses about 29 troops captured. The Rebels gain about fifty guns.

In Louisiana, elements of the 12th Maine, 26th Massachusetts and the 13th Connecticut Regiments, commanded by Major (later brigadier general) George Crockett Strong, move to raid a Confederate stronghold at Ponchatoula; however, the USS *New London*, transporting part of Strong's force, is unable to pass the bar to reach Manchac. The *Ceres*, transporting Major Strong, is too large to maneuver on the Tangipahoa River. Strong changes strategy and moves to Manchac Bridge and suspends the attack until the following morning.

In New Mexico at Albuquerque, orders from headquarters are dispatched to Colonel Joseph R. West, commander of the Department of Arizona, directing him to send a column to Fort Craig to relieve the garrison:

> The general commanding directs that you send for this purpose Lieut. Col. Edwin A. Rigg, First California Volunteer Infantry, with about 200 rank and file, so selected as not to take from your command more than three companies. Captain Fritz, First California Volunteer Cavalry will proceed to Tucson, as previously directed, with 25 wagons. If Wagon-master Veck has not already started for Peralta with 15 wagons, as directed, the general commanding orders that his train be increased to 35 wagons. If he has already started, send 20 additional wagons when Colonel Rigg goes to Fort Craig.... BEN. C. CUTLER, Acting Assistant Adjutant-General.

In Texas, the Confederates seize Lieutenant Kittredge of the U.S. Navy, his seven-man crew and their row boat at Flour Bluffs, about 12 miles from Corpus Christi, while the detachment is examining the entrance to Laguna Madre. Kittredge had initially been on a mission ordered by Admiral Farragut to attempt to win the freedom of the family of Judge Edmund Jackson Davis, a Texan who is loyal to the Union. The Union unit is caught by surprise by an overwhelming force of two companies accompanied by artillery. The squadron returns to Aransas Bay.

September 14–15 BATTLE OF HARPERS FERRY At Harpers Ferry, West Virginia, during the morning of the 14th, about 14,000 troops, including those which recently arrived from Martinsburg under General Julius White, face the approaching forces of Confederate General Thomas J. "Stonewall" Jackson, which are in the process of encircling the town. The commanding officer, Colonel D.S. Miles, has been ordered by McClellan to hold out until it is no longer possible and then attempt to reoccupy Maryland Heights, which had been abandoned on the 13th by a small force under Colonel Ford. Meanwhile, during the afternoon, Confederate

batteries, at Maryland Heights and Loudon Heights, across the Potomac and Shenandoah Rivers respectively, initiate a bombardment of the Union positions.

During the evening, Miles orders his cavalry, led by Colonel Davis, to depart Harpers Ferry, but he makes no attempt to reoccupy Maryland Heights, permitting Jackson's forces to effortlessly complete the encirclement with absolute domination of the heights. Meanwhile, Davis' cavalry moves toward Greencastle, Pennsylvania, arriving there on the following morning with some extra baggage, having captured fifty of General James Longstreet's wagon trains, each heavily laden with ammunition. By dawn on the following morning (15th), the terrain to the rear of Harpers Ferry is occupied by Confederates. A new battery arrives, and from the high ground, the guns catapult sheets of fire into the town. An attack by units including Maxcy Gregg's brigade prepares to advance, but suddenly a flag is spotted. Colonel Miles raises a white flag, but he is mortally wounded before the Rebels realize it had been a flag of surrender.

General White, who upon arriving at Harpers Ferry had relinquished command to Colonel Miles, surrenders the town along with 11,583 troops, 13,000 stands of arms, about 200 wagons, seventy-three Cannon, some ammunition and an abundance of supplies, including the town's manufacturing tools used to build firearms. However, the cavalry under Colonel Benjamin F. Davis refuses to surrender. It fights its way through the Confederate lines and in the process captures the baggage trains of General James Longstreet. Confederate General A.P. Hill's division will remain in Harpers Ferry to scrutinize the captured supplies and to gather intelligence from the captive Union troops. Nonetheless, Hill's division will participate at Sharpsburg (Antietam). Colonel Miles succumbs shortly after capitulation. There are unsubstantiated rumors that his actions had been due to disloyalty.

Colonel Thomas H. Ford, who had abandoned Maryland Heights, is dismissed from the Union service on the grounds of a "lack of military capacity as to disqualify him from a command in the service." The 12th New York State Militia, 39th, 111th, 115th, 125th, and 126th New York Regiments, the 32nd, and 67th Ohio Regiments, the 9th Vermont, and 65th Illinois Regiments participate. The 1st and 3rd Maryland Regiments, the 15th Indiana Regiment, Battery 5, New York Artillery, three batteries of the 8th New York Artillery, the 12th Illinois Cavalry and the 1st Maryland Cavalry also participate at this battle.

September 14–16 In Kentucky, the 18th U.S. Infantry; 28th and 23rd Kentucky; 17th, 50th, 60th, 67th, 68th, 74th, 78th and 89th Indiana; Conkles' Battery; and the 13th Indiana Artillery engage Confederates under General Duncan (Bragg's command) at Munfordville. The Confederates decisively defeat the Union forces under Colonel J.T. Wilder, capturing the city. The Union suffers 50 dead and 3,566 captured.

Battle of Mumfordsville (Johnson, *Campfire and Battlefield: History of the Conflicts and Campaigns*, 1894).

Confederates count 714 dead or wounded. General Buell, informed through captured documents, discovers that Bragg's target is Louisville, rather than Nashville, Tennessee. Buell on the following day moves to intercept the Confederates.

September 15 (Monday) In Louisiana, Major George C. Strong at Manchac Bridge dispatches one company under Captain Wintel to head south to further destroy the railroad on Manchac Island. Meanwhile, one company under Captain John Pickering remains behind to protect the vessel, while Captains Thornton and Farrington move against Ponchatoula, which stands at about ten miles distant. As the column encroaches the town, Confederates aboard a train spot the Yankee column, and they speed to the town to sound the alarm. The Rebels also send word to Camp Moore that reinforcements are needed. Strong had been about one mile outside the town when spotted, so although the element of surprise had been lost, Strong wastes no time in storming the town. Some resistance is immediately met and the barrage strikes Captain Thornton, inflicting a severe wound; however, the Rebels are driven back and out of the town. Major Strong in his after battle report mentions that Commander Buchwest (Gulf Blockading Squadron) had accompanied him on the mission and contributed valuable assistance.

In Maryland (ANTIETAM-SHARPSBURG), in accordance with orders of General Robert E. Lee, the forces of Generals Longstreet and A.P. Hill arrive at Sharpsburg. The forces of Generals Thomas "Stonewall" Jackson and John G. Walker arrive there on the following day. In conjunction, General McLaws is unable to ford the river at Harpers Ferry, causing him to move by way of Shepherdstown, which delays his arrival until the 17th, while the battle of Antietam is in progress. In the meantime, on this day, McClellan, once informed that Lee is retiring, orders a chase. Union cavalry initiate pursuit and later, they skirmish with Confederate troops at Boonsboro. In addition, opposing infantry and artillery duel on the Keedysville and Sharpsburg Road.

In Tennessee, Union General Don Carlos Buell departs Nashville for Louisville, Kentucky, to bolster it against attack by the Confederates under Braxton Bragg. Also, elements of the Missouri Militia, commanded by Colonel John McNeil, clash with a force of Confederate guerrillas under Porter at Shelbourne, Missouri.

In Union general officer activity, Major Henry Jackson Hunt is appointed brigadier general. Hunt, orphaned at ten years old and an 1839 graduate of West Point, had been in charge of the artillery defenses of the capital, and he participates at First Manassas (Bull Run) and at Antietam. He is also the brother of Union General Lewis C. Hunt.

In Confederate general officer activity, Colonel Joseph R. Davis (formerly lieutenant colonel of the 10th Mississippi Infantry) is promoted to brigadier general effective this day, but charges of nepotism impede the process. Hearings are held prior to the Confederate Senate approving the promotion. Davis, the nephew of President Jefferson Davis, is at this time is a staff officer in Richmond, Virginia; however, subsequent to the dismissal of the charges, he will command a brigade in the Army of Northern Virginia and participate in many of the primary battles yet to be fought. Davis' brigade will be with Robert E. Lee at Gettysburg, Petersburg, Richmond and Appomattox. Also, Colonel William Henry Fitzhugh Lee (Robert E. Lee's middle son) is promoted to the rank of brigadier general. He remains with General Beauregard's force.

September 16 (Tuesday) In Maryland at Sharpsburg, General Robert E. Lee prepares to engage General George B. McClellan. He disperses his forces in the heights and in the woods that stand between Antietam Creek and Sharpstown. Longstreet deploys on the right of Boonsboro Road, while D.H. Hill establishes positions on the left of the road. Jackson, supported by Stuart's Cavalry, holds the left on the road to Hagerstown. General John G. Walker, posted near Shaveley's Farm, defends Longstreet's right.

Following a reconnaissance mission by General McClellan, it is determined that one of the bridges is unprotected. McClellan chooses to attack over that span, the upper and northernmost bridge. His right wing will launch the assault.

General Joseph Hooker is directed to ford the Antietam Creek to launch an assault against the left side of the Confederate lines. Hooker's command, including

James Ricketts,' George Meade's and Abner Doubleday's forces, using one of four stone bridges, cross the creek at a point slightly below Pry's Mill in the vicinity of Keedysville. Some skirmishing develops as the Union advances to positions east of the road that winds into Hagerstown, where Hooker establishes night positions. Later, General Mansfield's Twelfth Corps arrives and establishes positions to Hooker's rear.

At the Confederate lines, during the night (16th–17th), reinforcements under General Alexander R. Lawton arrive; his two brigades (Ewell's command) relieve General Hood's forces. Lawton's left is covered by "Jackson's Own" and the remainder of Ewell's division. For the entire day, the opposing artillery units had serenaded each other with relentless volleys. Subsequent to the din of battle and the blanket of darkness, McClellan dispatches General Mansfield's force across Antietam Creek to bolster Hooker, and he directs General Sumner to prepare to move out during the predawn hours. While the Union adjusts its plan, Lee modifies his positions by ordering General Jackson to deploy on Lee's left, which places all of Lee's Army except for about two thousand troops in battle positions.

September 17 (Wednesday) BATTLE OF ANTIETAM (SHARPSBURG) Confederate General Lee's advancing Army is met by George McClellan at Antietam in what will be a tenacious, vicious, and near impossible day-long battle culminating with outrageous casualties on both sides. Soon after break of day, the battle commences as Pennsylvania reserves skirmish with the Confederates in a field. General Hooker soon joins the fray with his troops crashing into the vicious struggle near the diminutive Dunker Church, which stands on a road that runs north from Sharpsburg toward Hagerstown, Maryland. The usually quiet woods on either side of the road suddenly burst as the blue of Hooker plows into the gray of "Stonewall" Jackson, igniting a feverish one-hour slugfest at just about the crack of dawn.

A contingent of Union cavalry skirmishers on the advance in the Blue Ridge Mountains (Mottelay, *The Soldier in Our Civil War*, 1886).

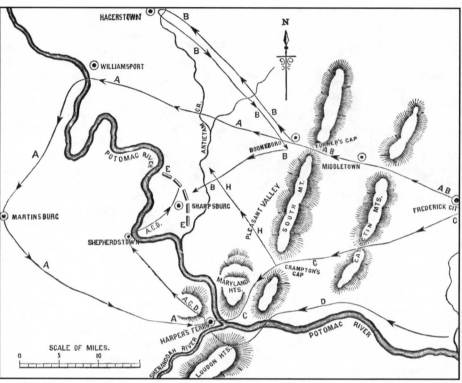

Above: General George Crook (Mottelay, *The Soldier in Our Civil War*, 1886). *Right:* Map of movements at Antietam, September 10–17 (*Harper's Pictoral History of the Civil War*, 1896).

Initially Meade's Pennsylvania reserves drive the Confederates from the field, but only temporarily, as determined Southern reinforcements keep pouring into the battle lines, prompting Hooker to call for General Joseph Mansfield's corps, which promptly advances and unleashes his forces, but shortly thereafter, while inspecting his positions, Mansfield is struck by a fatal blow. Despite the premature loss of their commanding officer, the troops maintain the advance. Colonel Joseph Knipe leads a brigade after the loss of General Mansfield. Union General George Hartsuff (West Point, 1852) is badly wounded and removed cautiously from the battlefield.

By about 0700, the bellowing sounds of the mighty guns have shattered the early morning silence. The terrain is jarred by an unfolding full-blown explosion of shot and shell and the blood-running-cold clash of rigid steel as the entrenched Rebels attempt to repel the charging Yankees. Mansfield's force gains the woods west of the road and hold it with steadfastness, underscored by great loss of blood. The thick woods provide superior cover for the Confederate sharpshooters, who fire round after round into the ranks of the Union. Many fall, but the attack continues against the wall of fire. At about this time, General Hooker is hit, and he sustains a severe wound that requires him to be carried from the field. Meanwhile, Sumner's corps is crossing Antietam Creek.

Elements of General Sumner's corps arrive by 9:00 A.M. and the troops immediately begin to form for battle; however, here too, the Confederate fire is constant. Sumner's forces drive forward and evict the Rebel divisions to their front and reach the area at Dunker Church. Sumner's progress creates an opportunity to

gain full advantage and inflict defeat upon Lee's Army. His corps begins to drive forward across the entire line; but again the Confederates get reinvigorated as two new divisions jump to the left side from the right and wind up in the center of a gap in Sumner's line.

Meanwhile, Sedgwick's 1st Division begins plowing into the woods west of the turnpike to support the beleaguered forces of General Samuel Crawford, while Union Generals Israel B. Richardson and William French drive toward Dunker Church. Sedgwick is able to push the Confederates back, but he penetrates too far and becomes isolated, as French's force on his left has outdistanced any chance of providing assistance. Nonetheless, at about this time, the fresh Confederate troops begin pressing the positions of General Greene's division, while simultaneously maneuvering on Sedgwick's left flank.

In the meantime, Doubleday's guns silence one Confederate battery and survive an attack by the 4th Alabama and 1st Texas Regiments. The Yankees are forced back, this time with Rebels in pursuit, until General Gorman's brigade holds firm, aided by a regiment of General Napoleon J.T. Dana's brigade, which begins pumping incessant fire into the Rebels and shatters their advance.

Shots are ringing from all directions and cries of battle echo through the smoke, which is sometimes thick enough to conceal a bleeding soldier lying helplessly on the field. With a thin lull in the ferocious contest, General Willis A. Gorman discovers that his command, still entangled in the woods, now faces a much larger Confederate force as more of the Union lines have again fallen back. Sedgwick has been compelled to pull back to the opposite side of the

clearing to the eastern part of the woods. The Confederates initiate an attack, and it is met by the roar of the guns of the Union batteries. The tumultuous thunderclap succeeds in halting the advance. The Confederate assault troops move back to escape the ring of fire and seek some protection among the rocks and the dense terrain beyond the turnpike. However, the battle continues to rage and the men continue to fall at an ungodly rate.

On this last fling with death, Union Generals Sedgwick and Dana are both seriously wounded and removed from the field. At around the same time, General Hooker receives a bad wound and is replaced on the field by General Meade. It is certainly not a general's day today, and the Confederates fare no better as the day evolves into a massive bloodbath, taking a heavy toll on the officers as well. Confederate Generals Lawrence O'Bryan Branch, George B. Anderson and William Starke are killed, the latter sustaining three wounds. Brigadier Generals Lawton and Ripley are among the seriously wounded. The tedious day wears on and both the cornfields and sunken road are ravaged by charging troops and pounding fusillades in a see-saw battle.

During one encounter, a group of Confederates attempt to outdistance the 5th New Hampshire as both seek to gain the advantage of a strategic piece of real estate, but the race ends with the Yankees reaching the ground first, and once there, they quickly get support from the 81st Pennsylvania Regiment. Shortly thereafter, the Confederates relinquish their claim. During the sprint, both sides are closely aligned and each continues a barrage of fire against the other as the race progresses.

General French pushes his troops to the left

and plows the Confederates back with the full force of three divisions, each moving directly against Roulette's Farm. The two sides continue to massacre each other as muskets and bayonets clash along the entire front. The reckless Confederates in death-defying movements advance into the fire originating from the guns of the 132nd Pennsylvania Volunteers and the U.S. 7th Virginians, who repulse the advance with a non-stop barrage of withering fire. And then the Union reinitiates its attack in similarly reckless fashion. This charge succeeds in capturing about 300 Confederates.

The attack continues as an attempt is immediately made to assist General William French (West Point, 1837), who has been under pressure and extremely heavy fire from the Rebels for about four devastating hours. The situation remains the same across the timber slaughterhouse throughout the entire day, with the Yankees and Confederates slugging it out to the death. The amount of ammunition expended during this conflict is still spoken about years later; when the trees are cut it creates a huge problem at the sawmill. The trees in the vicinity of Dunker Church are studded with so many shells that the saw blades are destroyed cutting the timber.

Slightly south and east of the church lies a treacherous sunken road named Bloody Lane, but rather than taking a straight path it veers off in several directions, essentially running on a parallel with the Confederate positions and at one point moving across their lines. The Confederates have established formidable defenses along it to whack any Union attack forces; however, when the assault is launched, the Confederates sustain heavier losses due to the precise firing of the Union batteries that are stretched out along the heights that stand east of Antietam Creek. The Union assault against the sunken road lacks the expected punch of General Burnside. He had received orders at about 0700 to prepare for attack; nonetheless, orders

are dispatched at about 0800 directing him to drive across the bridge on the Confederate right, but he does not receive the message until about 0900, delaying action, which now turns out to be a crucial error. Other troops under General Porter are available, but Porter is under orders to remain in reserve. All the while, units in the field are requesting support.

By about 1200, General William B. Franklin arrives from Crampton's Gap. His forces split up to support Generals Hooker and Sumner. In the meantime, Burnside's force has made its move to crash across the bridge at about 0900. Initially, General Crook's brigade dashes forward, but it inadvertently loses its way and emerges too far above the span and in the middle of a Confederate hurricane of fire that stalls the brigade. Undaunted, Burnside dispatches the 2nd Maryland and the 6th New York Regiments, but they too encounter an impenetrable wall of fire.

Confederate Brigadier General David Rumph Jones' defenders show no signs of relenting. Nonetheless, Burnside must take the bridge. Additional rolling firepower arrives as the third attempt to run the fiery gauntlet is about to start. Two guns are set up in a position from which they can level the playing field and decrease the resistance simultaneously. The task is given to Colonels Robert B. Potter of the 51st New York and John F. Hartranft of the 51st Pennsylvania.

Following the distinct sounds of the cannon, the two regiments initiate a charge, and to their delight and to the dismay of the defenders, the cannon assure success. The two guns deliver a walloping blow to the sunken road and soon the Yankees race to the west side of the creek and pounce upon the resistance. Shortly thereafter, General Crook's brigade is able to extricate itself from the untenable positions and rush to support the vanguard. The Confederates are driven back. While Burnside had been stymied at the bridge (sometimes referred to as Burn-

side's bridge), other forces had, after some difficulty, discovered a ford and made their way across the creek, but valuable time had been spent and the crossing had been extremely expensive. Burnside lost more than two hundred troops to the deadly but necessary excursion. The 51st New York sustains 87 killed and the 51st Pennsylvania suffers 120 lost during the operation.

The crossing is completed by about 1300; however, the Confederates refuse to fold their tents. Meanwhile, as Burnside moves to seize the guns and take the high ground, McClellan's right side is still engulfed in heavy fighting and time is slipping away, as is the possibility of vic-

Brigadier General Joseph K. Mansfield (*Harper's Pictoral History of the Civil War*, 1896).

Left: General Ambrose Burnside's forces surge across the bridge at Antietam Creek to strike Confederate positions. *Above:* Confederate cavalry drives stragglers back to their positions at Antietam (Mottelay, *The Soldier in Our Civil War*, 1886).

tory. Burnside continues to surge forward, but reducing the resistance is time consuming.

All the while, the reserves under General Porter remain in place. Throughout the day's bitter fighting, the Union has not amassed its full force to throw against the lesser forces of Robert E. Lee. Toward the latter part of the day, Burnside gains the heights and has silenced the Confederate guns, but by this time, the situation again changes. The contest on McClellan's right by now has subsided. General Lee pivots and uproots some of his forces there and redeploys them on his near-faltering left side to plug the line with more strength. He succeeds also in getting the last of his force in place as General A.P. Hill arrives from Harpers Ferry at about 1530 and immediately storms into the fight. Hill's two thousand troops, all with untapped stamina, encounter some opposition, but the 16th Connecticut, a fresh unit, collapses and leaves General Rodman's left vulnerable. Hill's force strikes Rodman's 4th Rhode Island just as it is approaching the Burnside Bridge and before Rodman can properly prepare for the onslaught. Soon after, Rodman sustains a fatal shot to his chest.

Hill's force joins with the others on Lee's imperiled right, and with a hearty yell, the Rebels charge and evict the forces of Union General Burnside. Continuing, the Rebels regain the lost battery. This is the final action of the blood-filled day. Both sides are over-exhausted from the grueling contest, which will go down in history as one of the bloodiest fights in the history of the United States.

Men had dropped from shot and shell as well as from the saber and the bayonet, leaving the ground piled high in some places with layers of bodies of the men in blue and the men in gray, each saturated with the others' blood. In many cases, it was their first and last battle. The horrid scene becomes less gruesome as the sun sets for the survivors, but they each receive an indelible vision of the horrors of war.

Killing's Cave, a place of safety on the Potomac near Sharpsburg during the fighting at Antietam (Mottelay, *The Soldier in Our Civil War*, 1886).

The Confederates will withdraw to Virginia and Washington is saved from attack; however, Robert E. Lee has not been eliminated or defeated. Lee's retirement is not challenged; however, a strong rear-guard — including the 28th North Carolina, led by Brigadier General James H. Lane, and Maxcy Gregg's brigade — will cover the operation, which commences late on the 18th into the pre-dawn hours of the 19th. Although McClellan's force increases on the 18th with the arrival of reinforcements, the Union launches no offensive. As the night sky arrives this evening (17th), it is perfectly clear that only veterans remain to remember their fallen friends. The battle's fury had left no green troops on the field. Neither side can claim a clear victory, but both sides gain a new respect and a different perspective about their enemy.

At about this time, General Sturgis' division has plowed across to support the Union's left side. Sturgis' troops have been heavily involved all day, but take the orders in good spirit, and advance with confidence and energy, successfully aiding in neutralizing the enemy as darkness settles in. Neither army changes positions from where it stands at battle's end. The Union holds the east woods and the Confederates remain in the west woods and the great cornfield. Confederate General James Longstreet subsequently writes of the battle: "We were so badly crushed at the close of the day 10,000 fresh troops could have come in and taken Lee's army and everything it had, but McClellan did not know it, and feared when Burnside was pressed back that Sharpsburg was a Confederate victory, and that he would have to retire."

On the following day General Robert E. Lee informs President Davis about the battle. Lee states that the arrival of General A.P. Hill in late afternoon has turned the tide. Lee states: "Between three and four o'clock P.M. General A. P. Hill with five of his brigades had reached the scene of action, drove the enemy immediately from the position they had taken and continued the contest until dark, restoring our right and maintaining our ground." Union General McClellan states: "Our soldiers slept that night conquerors on a field won by valor and covered with the dead and wounded of the enemy." McClellan further states: "Thirteen guns, 39 colors, upwards of 15,000 stands of small arms and more than 6,000 prisoners were the trophies which attest the success of our arms in the battles of South Mountain, Crampton's Gap and Antietam. Not a single gun or color was lost by our army during these battles."

The 125th Pennsylvania Regiment nearly loses its colors during a retreat from the woods when Color Sergeant George A. Simpson is struck and killed, along with five color

guards. Eugene Boblitz, Company H, retrieves the colors, but he, too, is severely wounded. The flag is taken by Sergeant Walter Greenland, who then hands the colors to Captain Wallace. Many in the regiment fall, but they refuse to abandon the flag. It was later reported by a Confederate officer that Captain Wallace "must have led a charmed life, as one hundred rifles were aimed at him without effect" while he was carrying the regimental colors.

General McClellan's estimate of the Confederates under Lee is 97,445, and he fixes his own force at 87,164. However, Lee claims his force at 37,000, and General Longstreet places the Confederate strength at Frederick at 61,000. Longstreet estimates Lee's force at Antietam to be 41,000. Nevertheless, within the Union force, the bulk of the fighting is handled by about 60,000 troops. The commands of General Couch, the division of General Andrew Humphreys and the division of General Morrell are not committed to the battle. In addition, only a part of General Sykes' division and Franklin's corps participates in the fighting. In contrast, except for two brigades of Confederate General A.P. Hill, Lee's entire army participates.

Union casualties for the day are 2,010 dead, 9,416 wounded and 1,043 missing. Confederates count 3,500 killed, 16,400 wounded and 600 missing. Union Brigadier General Joseph Mansfield (West Point, 1822) is mortally wounded and dies on the following day. General Alpheus Williams succeeds him as commander of the 12th Corps. Union Major General Israel B. Richardson and Union General Isaac Rodman are mortally wounded. Richardson becomes a victim of an artillery shell. He is carried off the field to McClellan's headquarters. He succumbs from his wounds on November 3. Rodman is struck in the chest and soon after removed from the field to a hospital. He succumbs on September 30. General Nathan Kimball is unscathed, but his brigade (French's division) sustains more than 600 killed or wounded.

Union Generals George L. Hartsuff, Samuel W. Crawford, Max Weber, John Sedgwick, Napoleon Jackson Tecumseh Dana and Joseph Hooker are wounded. General Weber literally loses the use of his right arm; however, he returns to duty in late 1863, with limited command at Washington and later at Harpers Ferry. Also, General James Ricketts has two horses shot, and the second one causes severe injuries to Ricketts when it falls. Afterward, Ricketts serves on the court-martial that hears the case of General Fitz John Porter, but he does not return to the field until March 1864, when he receives command of a division in General John Sedgwick's VI Corps. Also, Colonel Thomas H. Ruger (3rd Wisconsin), in command of a brigade, sustains a wound. He recovers and participates in the Maryland campaign (attached to XII Corps) and afterward at Chancellorsville and Gettysburg. In the meantime he is promoted to brigadier general effective 29 November 1862. Another officer, Lt. Colonel Hector Tyndale (later brigadier general), sustains two

Left: Union bivouac (12th Massachusetts) near Hyattsville, Maryland. *Right:* Union troops enter Falmouth, Virginia (Mottelay, *The Soldier in Our Civil War*, 1886).

wounds while leading his brigade and three horses are shot from under him.

Colonel Edward W. Hincks, previously wounded at Glendale, Virginia, is twice wounded during this action. During the following April, he is appointed brigadier general to rank from 29 November 1862. At the time of his promotion, he is still recuperating from his wounds. After returning to duty, he serves on a court-martial and he is assigned recruitment duty. He commands a Negro division (XVIII Corps) during the Petersburg campaign. After the close of hostilities, he resigns his commission during June 1865. During the following year he becomes colonel of the 40th Infantry and then is transferred to the 25th Infantry during 1869, where he remains until he retires in 1870 with the rank of colonel.

Confederate Brigadier Generals Lawrence Branch, George B. Anderson and William E. Starke are killed. Colonel Stephen D. Ramseur will succeed Anderson as brigade commander of four North Carolina regiments. Confederate Generals Roswell Ripley (West Point, 1843), Alexander R. Lawton (West Point, 1839), Robert A. Toombs, Ambrose Wright and Matt W. Ransom are wounded. In addition, Confederate Colonel (later general) Montgomery D. Corse sustains a serious wound while leading the remainder of his regiment, 56 troops of the 17th Virginia Infantry. Of these, 49 are killed or wounded, leaving only five privates and two officers, Major Arthur Herbert and Lt. Thomas Perry, still standing at battle's end. The brigade under Alexander Lawton begins the battle with about 1,150 troops and sustains more than 550 casualties. General Harry T. Hays' regiment sustains about 323 casualties after entering the combat with 550 men, and the 50th Georgia initiates its action with about 210 troops on the field; of these more than 125 troops are cut down in less than one-half hour. The Confederate 1st South Carolina, composed of 106 troops, loses all of its officers except one, and only fifteen enlisted men come out of the battle standing.

Colonel Birkett D. Fry, previously wounded at Seven Pines, sustains another wound; however, he recovers and will sustain a third wound

at Gettysburg. Also, the Confederate 25th Virginia Infantry (Jubal Early's brigade, Ewell's division) participates at this action. Confederate Major General John George Walker, subsequent to this action, is transferred to the Trans-Mississippi to participate in the Red River Campaign against General Banks. General Walker assumes command of a Texas division. Colonel (later brigadier general) Hugh B. Ewing participates at this battle. Afterward, he assumes command of a brigade (IX Corps), but his command is then transferred to Sherman's XV Corps.

The Union soldiers do not attempt to pursue the retreating Confederate forces, who withdraw to Virginia. The Union finds some solace in the fact they have turned the Confederates back to prevent an attack against Washington.

In Kentucky, elements of the 10th Kentucky Cavalry clash with Confederates at Florence. Casualty figures are unavailable. Meanwhile, Munfordville is surrendered by Union forces under Colonel Dunham.

In Maryland, Companies M and H, 1st Maine Cavalry, participate in the fighting at Antietam as part of General Fitz John Porter's command. The main body of the regiment is encamped at Frederick. Also, the 12th Massachusetts Regiment participates in the fighting at Antietam. The regiment formed in Boston during 1861 and is commanded by Colonel Coulter. It sustains the highest percentage of casualties among Union regiments. Coulter's report states:

> The Twelfth Massachusetts had killed and disabled eleven officers of fifteen taken into the field. The loss of this regiment, owing to its position, was by far the most severe in the brigade. Major Burbank commanded at the commencement of the action and was disabled early. He performed his whole duty while in the field. Captain Allen, who next assumed command, was also severely wounded. I cannot express too high an opinion of this officer. He has proved himself one of the most gallant officers in the brigade. The command of this regiment next devolved upon Capt. B.F. Cook, who commanded during the reminder of the action, and brought the regiment off the field.

In Pennsylvania, an accidental explosion at the Pittsburgh Arsenal during the afternoon kills 78 people. The cause of the explosion is never determined, but it is thought that a spark from either a barrel or a horseshoe ignited loose powder. Most of the workers at the arsenal are women and children.

In Virginia, Colonel Kilpatrick's cavalry brigade skirmishes with Confederate infantry at Goose Creek and along the Leesburg Road during a reconnaissance mission. At Falmouth, a contingent of Home Guards, commanded by Colonel Berry, clashes with Confederates. The Union sustains one wounded. The Confederates sustain two killed, four wounded and one captured.

In Tennessee, a contingent of the 52nd Indiana Volunteer Regiment, led by Lt. Griffin, skirmishes with Confederates led by Lt. Colonel Faukner at Durhamville. The Union force is estimated at about 150 troops. The number in the Confederate contingent is unavailable. The Union sustains one killed and 10 wounded. The Confederates sustain eight killed and 10 to 20 wounded. Also, the Union forces of General George W. Morgan evacuate Cumberland Gap. In conjunction, General Morgan afterward has problems with General Sherman. Morgan's performance during the Vicksburg campaign is rated unsatisfactory by Sherman. General Morgan resigns his commission prior to the fall of Vicksburg (July 1863).

In Union general officer activity, Brigadier General Schuyler Hamilton (grandson of Alexander Hamilton) is promoted to major general. General Hamilton had commanded a division (John Pope's Corps) during the previous spring in the campaign to gain Corinth, but he came down with malaria and remains on sick leave, causing complications with his promotion. Also, Brigadier General Joseph J. Reynolds, who resigned from the army in January following the death of his brother, is this day reappointed brigadier general. He is promoted to major general on 29 November. Also, Brigadier General Stephen A. Hurlbut is promoted to major general.

In Naval activity, the Union warships, including the USS *Cimarron,* engage Confederate batteries on the St. John's River in Florida. Afterward the *Cimarron* returns to Beaufort, South Carolina, and resumes operations there until January 1863, then sails north for repairs and remains in Philadelphia until April 1863.

September 18 (Thursday)   In Maryland, Confederate Brigadier General James H. Lane's 28th North Carolina covers the retreating Rebels with a rear guard action. McClellan receives reinforcements when about 18,000 troops under Generals Darius Couch and Andrew A. Humphreys arrive, but Robert E. Lee also becomes reinforced when troops arrive from Harpers Ferry. Nevertheless, neither side is in position to initiate an offensive. McClellan had anticipated more reinforcements, but orders from Washington had prevented them from arriving on the 17th.

In Mississippi, Union General Edward O. Ord (West Point, 1839) departs Corinth by rail, while General Rosecrans during inclement weather advances against Iuka from the east along Fulton Road. Late in the day Rosecrans reaches Jacinto. Grant temporarily remains at Burnsville in order to keep contact with both Union armies.

In New Mexico, General Carleton assumes command of the Department of New Mexico. He succeeds General Canby. Carleton's California troops, particularly in the southern sector of the department, are constantly focused on eliminating the hostile Apaches that are wreaking havoc in the region, unleashing incessant raids in Doña Ana County. The order states: "GENERAL ORDERS, HDQRS. DEPARTMENT OF NEW MEXICO, No. 83. *Santa Fe, N. Mex., September* 18, 1862. The undersigned hereby relinquishes the command of this department to Brig. Gen. T. H. Carleton, and is gratified in announcing as his successor an officer whose character, services, and experience in this country entitle him to the confidence of the people of New Mexico."

In Confederate general officer activity, William Edmondson Jones (West Point, 1848), who had earlier formed the Washington Mounted Rifles and joined the Confederate 1st (later 7th) Virginia Cavalry, is promoted to the rank of brigadier general effective this date.

In Naval activity, the USS *Water Witch* arrives in Charleston and is attached to the South Atlantic Blockading Squadron. It is assigned patrol duty and operates out of a station along the St. John's River in the northeastern sector of Florida.

September 19 (Friday)   In Maryland, General George McClellan learns that the Confederates have abandoned their positions and moved back across the Potomac. As the fog lifts, the information becomes well known. General Porter is sent in pursuit. The Union encounters and engages the Confederates in the vicinity of the Shepherdstown Ford and captures many of them. The Rebels have established positions on

the opposite bank. The brigades of Charles Griffin and James Barnes assault to seize the eight batteries that Robert E. Lee had established to guard the river approaches. Subsequent to a heated skirmish, four of the guns are seized, two of which had been captured by the Rebels at the First Battle of Bull Run in 1861. The Union loses 220 killed and wounded.

In Missouri, detachments of the 6th Kansas Cavalry clash with Confederates at Hickory Grove. Casualty figures are unavailable.

In Union general officer activity, Brigadier General Charles S. Hamilton is promoted to major general. His promotion is influenced by General U.S. Grant; however, while he played up to Grant, behind Grant's back he told a member of the U.S. Senate that Grant was a "drunk." Also, Colonel Gustavus "Gus" A. Smith is promoted to brigadier general to rank from this date. Smith is still recovering from wounds thought to have been fatal; this prevents him from resuming field duty. The Senate does not confirm the appointment and his commission expires on 4 March 1863. Colonel Francis Laurens Vinton (West Point, 1856) is appointed brigadier general of volunteers. Vinton was commissioned colonel of the 43rd New York Infantry the previous October. Due to inaction by the U.S. Senate, his commission expires on 4 March 1863. On 9 April, he is reappointed to rank from 13 March, and the Senate confirms the appointment; however, he resigns his commissions (Regular Army and volunteers) 5 May 1863, possibly because of poor health. He lives in New York before moving to Colorado, where he dies during October 1870.

In Confederate general officer activity, Colonel William Edwin Baldwin (14th Mississippi Infantry), captured at Fort Donelson and transferred to Fort Warren, Massachusetts, until released during August 1862, is promoted to brigadier general to rank from this day. He participates during the Vicksburg campaign and is yet again captured. Also, William Edmundson "Grumble" Jones (7th Virginia Cavalry) is promoted to brigadier general.

September 19–20   THE BATTLE OF IUKA Union forces under General William S. Rosecrans clash with Confederates under General Lewis H. Little (General Sterling Price's principal commander) at Iuka, Mississippi. Rosecrans marches twenty miles, but en route to Iuka, his cavalry skirmishes with a Confederate cavalry force at Barnett's Corner. During the latter part of the afternoon, about two miles from Iuka, his troops encounter a large contingent of Rebels who have established positions in the heights on an extremely densely wooded ridge. Orders arrive from General Grant to take the offensive. With Rosecrans holding the center, flanked on the left and right respectively by Generals David Stanley and Charles S. Hamilton, skirmishers are sent out to probe the Rebels, but it is soon determined that his artillery is unable to be brought into the battle except for one battery of the Eleventh Ohio. General Ord is directed to remain with General

Ross's troops about four miles outside of Iuka and upon the sound of Rosecrans' artillery to rush to the scene. However, the intruding hills and the direction of the winds prevent Ord from hearing the guns.

Meanwhile, General Price's artillery continues to hammer the Union positions, particularly the 11th and 26th Missouri and the 5th Iowa, deployed in support of the battery. Price detects what he believes is a weak link and orders a charge to seize the battery. The Rebels race forward and the Union, still being pounded by artillery, is unable to hold. The defenders spike two of the guns, but then the Confederates seize the battery, leaving the Union only four operable guns. Undaunted, the Union moves to regain the ground. The 48th Indiana, trailed by the 16th Ohio and the 4th Minnesota, commanded by Colonels Eddy, Chambers, and Le Gro respectively, initiate a furious bayonet charge that deeply bloodies the attacking Rebels and propels them backward, giving the Union the ground and the guns that had just been lost.

The Confederates remain equally determined, and with total disregard for their own casualties, again they charge. The Union is jolted back and the guns once more change hands. The Rebels, in addition to regaining the guns, also seize a large number of prisoners. The vicious contest ends at dusk. On the 20th, the Union enters Iuka against only minimal resistance. The Confederates retire toward Ripley. In conjunction, neither General Rosecrans nor General Stanley are able to give pursuit. The Union sustains 144 men killed and 598 wounded. The Confederates suffer 263 dead, 692 wounded and 561 captured. Union Colonel Eddy is killed and Colonel Boomer receives a serious wound. Also, Colonel Alexander Chambers, 16th Iowa Infantry, is wounded. Chambers, also wounded at Shiloh, will become a brigadier general later in the year.

Confederate Brigadier General Lewis H. Little is killed while sitting on his horse in conversation with Generals Price and Hebert and Colonel Whitfield. Colonel John Wilkins Whitfield is seriously wounded, but he recovers and will later participate under Van Dorn during spring of 1863 (he is actually commissioned brigadier general on May 9, 1863). Confederate fire almost destroys the 11th Battery, Ohio Light Artillery; nearly all the men and horses are killed or wounded. Bad communications, particularly the directive for Ord to listen for the guns before entering the battle, contribute to high casualties for the Union on the 19th. General Ord arrives at Iuka on the 20th at just about the time the Union is preparing to pursue Price. The 5th Minnesota Volunteer Regiment also participates in this action.

In Kentucky, a Union contingent composed of elements of the 14th Kentucky Cavalry and Spencer's (Indiana County) Home Guards, commanded by Colonel Netter, clashes with Confederate guerrillas led by Lt. Colonel Wood at Owensburg. On the 19th, the Union prevails; however, on the following day when the two sides again clash, the Confederates defeat the

Union. The Union sustains two killed and 18 wounded. Confederate casualty figures are unavailable.

September 20 (Saturday) In Maryland, Confederate forces occupy Williamsport; however, they quickly abandon it. Contingents of General Darius N. Couch's division (Army of the Potomac) regain control of the town.

In Mississippi, Union forces move into Iuka. General Rosecrans initiates pursuit of General Price's force, which is retiring toward Ripley. The Federals, upon entering the town, recover the six guns lost on the previous day. The Union cavalry does, on several occasions during the chase, encounter and engage rear-guard contingents, but only a few troops are captured. General Rosecrans will depart for Corinth. General Ord will remain at Bolivar. General Grant moves to Jackson.

In Virginia, a Union force composed of elements of Charles Griffin's and James Barnes' brigades (Fitz John Porter's 5th Corps) skirmishes with a Confederate force (A.P. Hill's division) at Blackford's Ford and Shepherd's Town (Sheppardstown). The Union troops are forced to retreat to terrain north of the Potomac River, but the Confederates also sustain many casualties, particularly during a daring charge by troops, including Maxcy Gregg's brigade. As the Confederates charge, the line is struck by an enfilade of devastating artillery fire. Afterward A.P. Hill's division establishes camp in the vicinity of Winchester and at Berryville, where his command remains until late November. The Union sustains 92 dead, 131 wounded and 103 missing. The Confederates suffer about 33 dead and 231 wounded, and of these, the 14th South Carolina Regiment sustains about 10 killed and 45 wounded.

Meanwhile, Robert E. Lee's army retreats under cover fire from General Pendleton's troops. The Union attacks at Blackford's Ford against the Brigades of Maxcy Gregg, William D. Pender (West Point, 1854) and James Archer, but the troops are driven back, allowing Lee to withdraw to Opequon. From there he moves toward Winchester to regroup.

In Naval activity, meanwhile, the ram USS *Queen of the West* and accompanying transports, laden with elements of the 33rd Illinois Regiment, commanded by Lt. Colonel Lippincott, engage Confederate guerrillas at Prentis and Bolivar, Mississippi. The Union sustains three killed and one wounded. Confederate casualty figures are unavailable. Also, elements of the 2nd Kansas Volunteers and 3rd Indiana Home Guards, commanded by Colonel John Ritchie, clash with and defeat Confederates at Shirley's Ford, Missouri. The Union reports no casualties. The estimated Confederate casualties are more than 50 killed and wounded.

A contingent of the 4th Iowa Cavalry clashes with Confederates at Helena, Arkansas. Casualty figures are unavailable. Also, Commodore Wilkes, at Hampton Roads, receives orders to proceed to Bermuda. Afterward, he departs with some of his squadron, the *Sonoma, Tioga*

and *Wachusett*, all of which are not in good condition. Upon his arrival in Bermuda, the squadron easily spots British vessels that are without question blockade runners. Wilkes leaves the *Sonoma* and *Tioga* to deal with the blockade runners, but Wilkes, aboard the *Wachusett*, moves to the Bahamas, where he is joined by the *Octorara*. After the linkup in the Providence Channel, the two ships head for Havana, where Wilkes establishes headquarters.

September 21 (Sunday) In Arkansas, the Union 1st Arkansas Cavalry, commanded by Captain Gilstray, battles Confederate troops at Cassville. The Union secures the town and captures about 19 Confederates.

In Kentucky, the Union regroups and attacks Munfordville, which had been lost to the Confederates on the 17th. Cavalry attached to Colonel Alexander McCook's command, led by Major Foster, occupies the town. Also, Confederate cavalry assaults Shepherdsville, which is defended by Colonel Robert S. Granger. The Union prevails. The Confederates sustain five killed and about 28 wounded. Colonel Granger had been captured early in the war while in Texas and was exchanged the previous August. Following his release, he was assigned duty in Kentucky. Granger is promoted to brigadier general of Kentucky Volunteers during October.

In New Mexico, General James H. Carleton, commander of New Mexico and of the California Column, relinquishes command of the latter. General Carleton is succeeded by Colonel Joseph R. West. With a strong recommendation of General Carleton, West is promoted to brigadier general on 25 October.

September 22 (Monday) In Washington, D.C., President Lincoln shares his Emancipation Proclamation with his cabinet. Lincoln's proclamation frees all slaves in the rebellious states. However, the proclamation does not free the slaves in the northern states nor in the non-rebellious border states.

In Virginia, elements of the 2nd Pennsylvania Cavalry and the 1st West Virginia Cavalry, commanded by Colonel Price, skirmishes with Confederates at Ashby's Gap. Casualty figures are unavailable.

In West Virginia, the Union re-occupies Harpers Ferry. General Sumner then begins work to connect it with the Potomac and Shenandoah by constructing pontoon bridges. The Union Army remains in the vicinity of Sharpsburg until the latter part of October, when it crosses the Potomac River and returns to Virginia.

In Missouri, Confederate guerrillas led by Captain Cunningham skirmish with a Union contingent commanded by Major Hunt at Sturgeon. Casualty figures are unavailable.

In Confederate general officer activity, Colonel John Crawford Vaughn is promoted to brigadier general.

In Naval activity, Commodore David Dixon Porter is informed that he is to command the Mississippi Squadron.

September 23 (Tuesday) BATTLE OF WOOD LAKE Elements of the 3rd, 6th, and 7th Minnesota Volunteer Regiments and the Renville Guards, commanded by Colonel Henry Hastings Sibley, engage and defeat a band of Dakota Indians under Chief Little Crow at Wood Lake, Minnesota. The fighting lasts about two hours. The Union sustains about four killed and 30 wounded. Chief Mankato is killed. By the following day, the Dakotas release their prisoners (more than 250). At this time, Camp Release is established to bring the families of the captives together. By 27 September, many of the released prisoners move to Fort Ridgely, but some remain at the camp to attend the trial of the Dakotas, which begins on 28 September. In conjunction, Colonel Sibley, the first governor of Minnesota as a state, is promoted to brigadier general during the latter part of this month; however, his commission is not confirmed by the Senate and it expires in March.

In Mississippi, a contingent of the 57th Ohio Volunteer Regiment clashes with Confederates at Wolf Creek Bridge. Casualty figures are unavailable.

In Virginia, a contingent of the 10th West Virginia Regiment, led by Major Withers, engages a Confederate contingent at Sutton. The Union prevails at the first skirmish; however, the two sides again clash and the Confederates win the second contest. Casualty figures are unavailable.

In the Dakota Territory, Union forces, including Company D, 5th Minnesota Volunteer Regiment at Fort Abercrombie, engage Sioux Indians through the 25th.

September 24 (Wednesday) In Washington, D.C., President Lincoln takes action to halt activity that is hindering the Union. He suspends the writ of habeas corpus for any and all who attempt to interfere with enlistments or evade the draft, and he includes anyone who provides support or comfort to the Rebels.

In South Carolina, Confederate General Pierre G.T. Beauregard assumes command of the Department of South Carolina and Georgia. Beauregard had earlier become ill and while on sick-leave, General Braxton Bragg succeeded him as commander of the Army of Tennessee. At this time, Beauregard is not especially in the favor of Confederate President Jefferson Davis.

In Texas, Union warships arrive near Fort Sabine, established by the Confederates the previous year at Sabine Pass. The ships bombard the post and inflict damage. The Confederates abandon the post. Nevertheless, by spring of 1863, the Confederates complete Fort Griffin in the same area to impede Union progress in the region.

In Naval activity, the USS *Rachael Seaman*, *Henry James* and the *Kensington* capture the Confederate Forts at Sabino Pass, Texas. The Union operation is commanded by Acting Master Crocker and continues into the next day.

September 25 (Thursday)   In Kentucky, Union General Buell arrives at Louisville, having traveled from Nashville, Tennessee. The city is defended by General William Nelson. Buell's army, with the addition of Nelson's command, stands at about 100,000 men. Buell has won the race, beating General Bragg's army to the city. The Confederates under Bragg are running behind schedule due to the destruction of a bridge that spans the Salt River at Bardstown.

In Florida, the Confederate-held navy yard at Pensacola is recaptured by U.S. Marines.

In Union general officer activity, Lt. Colonel George Washington Getty is promoted to the rank of brigadier general effective this day. Getty will command a division in the IX Corps at Fredericksburg in December.

In Naval activity, the USS *Kensington, Henry James* and *Rachael Seaman* combine to bombard a Confederate garrison at Sabine Pass, Texas, and the effective fire empties the fort. On the following day, troops are debarked and seize the abandoned fort; however, lacking ground forces, the naval force is unable to maintain control of the post.

September 26 (Friday)   In Mississippi, Union General William Rosecrans arrives at Corinth from Iuka. Shortly after his arrival he begins to bolster his defenses to prepare for an attack, which he believes will come from the northwest. Rosecrans uses the expertise of General Grant's chief engineer, Major Prime, to make the area as impregnable as possible, yet he is not certain that Corinth will be the target. While shoring up his defenses, Rosecrans also reels in the outposts at Burnsville, Iuka and Rienzi, while simultaneously, he repeatedly dispatches cavalry reconnaissance patrols to probe for any approaching enemy forces.

In Missouri, the 9th Missouri Militia Cavalry skirmishes with Confederates at Cambridge. Casualty figures are unavailable.

In Virginia, a 125-man contingent of Union cavalry, commanded by Colonel Nathaniel McLean, skirmishes with a large force of Confederates at Warrentown Junction. Casualty figures are unavailable.

In Union general officer activity, Colonel William Woods Averell is promoted to brigadier general. Also, Colonel Robert Cowdin is elevated to that rank. However, his commission expires on 4 March 1863 due to the Senate's inaction. On 30 March he is relieved from duty. Colonel Albert Sully (1st Minnesota) is promoted to brigadier general. He participates at Fredericksburg and in the Chancellorsville campaign, but afterward he is transferred back to the frontier as commander of the Department of Dakota. Also, Colonel Gouverneur Kemble Warren (5th New York) is promoted to brigadier general.

September 27 (Saturday)   In Kentucky, the Union gunboat *Belfast* and Kentucky Home Guards, commanded by Colonel J. Taylor Bradford, attack and capture Augusta, defended by Confederates led by Captain Duke. The Union sustains 12 killed and wounded. The Confederates sustain high casualties. It is sometimes reported that the gunboat *Kensington* participated in this action; however, at this time the *Kensington* is operating in the vicinity of Sabine Pass, Texas. Augusta had been seized earlier by a large cavalry force that had overcome fierce resistance by the Union defenders.

In West Virginia, elements of the 34th Ohio Regiment, commanded by Colonel Toland, assaults a Confederate encampment at Buffalo. The Confederates lose seven killed and about nine seized as prisoners.

September 28 (Sunday)   *In Confederate general officer activity,* Major General Theophilus Holmes, who previously replaced General Hindman as commander of the Confederate Trans-Mississippi Department, appoints General Allison Nelson as commanding officer of the 2nd Division (three brigades); however, Nelson is severely ill and will not assume the command. He dies of fever shortly thereafter. Also, General Van Dorn arrives at Ripley, Mississippi, joining with General Price. Van Dorn assumes overall command.

In Virginia, a contingent of the 1st New York Mounted Rifles Battalion (7th New York Cavalry Regiment), composed of three companies commanded by Colonel (later general) Charles Cleveland Dodge, skirmishes with Confederate infantry at Blackwater. Casualty figures are unavailable. Dodge became colonel of the unit the previous month. His cavalry regiment serves entirely in the vicinity of Suffolk under the command of General John J. Peck and the overall command of General John A. Dix. Also, a Union reconnaissance contingent, composed of about one brigade of cavalry commanded by Lt. Colonel Karge, initiates a mission that takes it from Centreville toward Warrenton. The mission succeeds in capturing more than 1600 Confederate prisoners.

September 29 (Monday)   In Kentucky, Union General Jefferson C. Davis, after an argument, shoots Union General William Nelson. The shooting occurs at the Gaft House in Louisville. No charges are filed and Davis resumes his normal duties in the Union Army. General Nelson had apparently had a previous run-in with Davis and accused him of insults, and on this day he had slapped General Davis in the face just moments before being shot. General Nelson had been a naval officer prior to serving in the Army, and he is the only naval officer in both the Union and the Confederacy to become a full-rank general during the Civil War. General Nelson is interred at Maysville.

In Union general officer activity, Colonel Alexander Hays (West Point, 1844), 63rd Pennsylvania Volunteer Regiment, is appointed brigadier general. Colonel Nathaniel James Jackson is also named brigadier general; his brigade is part of General Geary's division of the XII Corps. Jackson participates at Fredericksburg in December 1862, but afterward, he is in-jured in an accident. Upon recovery he moves to New York on temporary duty until 20 September 1864. Henry Hastings Sibley, first governor of the state of Minnesota, is also elevated to brigadier general. Nonetheless, the Senate takes no action and his commission expires on 4 March 1863. Afterward he is re-nominated and confirmed by the Senate. There is no documentation to verify that General Sibley, the cousin of Confederate General Henry Hopkins Sibley, ever faced an armed Confederate contingent, but he receives the brevet of major general on 25 November 1865 and is mustered out of the army on 30 April 1866.

September 30 (Tuesday)   In Kentucky, a Union contingent composed of elements of the 17th Kentucky Regiment and other units under Colonel Harrison skirmish with Confederates at Russellville. The Union reports no casualties. The estimated Confederate casualties are 35 killed and 10 captured. Also, Confederates occupy Grayson.

In Missouri, a Union force of about 4,000 troops — including elements of the 1st Brigade, Army of Kansas and the 4th Brigade, Missouri State Militia, commanded by Brigadier General Salomon — engages in a heated battle with Confederates led by Colonels Douglas H. Cooper (commanding officer, 1st Choctaw and Chickasaw Rifles) and Joseph Orville Shelby at Newtonia. The Union sustains 50 killed, 80 wounded and 115 missing. The Confederates sustain 220 killed and 280 wounded. Before the war, Cooper was agent to the Choctaw Nation

Brigadier General Isaac P. Rodman (Mottelay, *The Soldier in Our Civil War*, 1886).

in the Indian Territory; however, at the outbreak of war, he was persuaded by the Confederacy to secure the Indians' allegiance against the Union.

In Union general officer activity, General Isaac P. Rodman, wounded in the chest earlier this month at Antietam, succumbs in a field hospital.

In Naval activity, the USS *Kensington,* operating in the vicinity of Sabine Pass, Texas, seizes a British blockade runner, the *Velocity.* The *Velocity* is taken to Key West, Florida, and armed with two Dahlgrens, to be attached to the blockading force. However, in July of the following year, the *Velocity* is recaptured by the Confederates.

In Naval activity, the vessel *Terror,* a screw tugboat built at the request of the U.S. Army, is taken into the U.S. Navy and commissioned the USS *Ivy.* It is assigned to the Mississippi Squadron and participates in the operations leading to the seizure of Vicksburg in July 1863. During the operations against Fort Hindman, Arkansas, it serves as the flagship of Admiral David D. Porter. In other activity, the captured CSS *DeSoto* is transferred to the U.S. Navy. It is renamed the USS *General Lyon* in October 1862.

October The Confederate 3rd Arkansas Regiment is attached to Hood's Texas Brigade in place of the 18th Georgia Regiment and Hampton's Legion. The latter, having sustained heavy casualties at Antietam (Sharpsburg), becomes attached to the command of General Micah Jenkins' infantry brigade (Palmetto Sharpshooters). The 18th Georgia is attached to General Thomas R.R. Cobb's brigade and will fight at Fredericksburg. Cobb is promoted to brigadier general the following month.

In Pennsylvania, the Confederate cavalry under Jeb Stuart initiates raids. His cavalry continues to outmaneuver General McClellan's forces for the duration of the mission. Stuart's force seizes supplies, and when the contingent returns to Virginia during mid–October, the column has a large number of additional horses that had also been seized.

October 1 (Wednesday) **In Kentucky,** General Don Carlos Buell departs Louisville en route to Bardstown, where Confederate General Braxton Bragg's force is deployed. The army is composed of three corps. General Bragg will withdraw to Springfield, and he orders General Kirby Smith to abandon Frankfort and move to Perryville, where the two forces will converge. General Hardee's corps is directed to move to Perryville. Also, a Union contingent composed of elements of the 4th Indiana Cavalry, the 34th Illinois Regiment and the 77th Pennsylvania Volunteers, commanded by Colonel Kirk, skirmishes with Confederate cavalry at Floyd's Fork. No casualty figures are available. The 77th, including Captain Muller's artillery battery, had participated at various actions, including Shiloh, and the regiment is part of the resistance against Bragg's invasion of Kentucky.

General William Hardee (Johnson, *Campfire and Battlefield: History of the Conflicts and Campaigns,* 1894).

Meanwhile, Confederate forces abandon Shelbyville. In yet other activity, Confederate cavalry under John Hunt Morgan engage a contingent of the Carter County Home Guards at Olive Hill. Casualty figures are unavailable. Meanwhile, the Army of the Ohio continues to advance. At Mount Washington, Buell's force skirmishes with Confederates under General Kirby Smith. Casualty figures are unavailable.

In Mississippi, General Grant now understands Van Dorn's intentions to attack Corinth with his combined forces and those of Mansfield Lovell (West Point, 1842), Price, Bushrod R. Johnson (West Point, 1840) and John B. Villepiqigue. Also, Union Cavalry (Army of the Mississippi) skirmishes with Confederates at Baldwyn. Casualty figures are unavailable.

In Tennessee, the Union 1st Tennessee Cavalry, commanded by Colonel William Stokes, clashes with Confederate guerrillas under Colonel Bennett at Gallatin. Union casualties are unreported. Confederate estimated casualties are 40 wounded and 39 captured.

In Virginia, Union forces — including contingents of the 8th Illinois Cavalry, 8th Pennsylvania Cavalry and the 3rd Indiana Cavalry, bolstered by Pennington's battery — clash with Confederates commanded by General Wade Hampton at Shepherdstown and Martinsburg. The Union sustains 12 wounded and three captured. The Confederates suffer 60 killed and 10 captured.

In Union general officer activity, Union Captain

Charles H. Morgan (West Point, 1857) is promoted to chief of artillery, II Corps. He will subsequently be attached to General Winfield Scott Hancock and serve with him for the duration of the war. At Gettysburg, he will contribute greatly when Hancock assumes command after the death of General John F. Reynolds. In other activity, Colonel Lovell H. Rousseau, 3rd Kentucky Regiment, is appointed brigadier general. On 22 October, he is promoted to major general.

In Confederate general officer activity, Major General George Bibb Crittenden resigns his commission at about this time (October); however, he remains in the service in a lower capacity for the duration. After the war, he becomes the librarian of the state of Kentucky. He dies during November 1880.

In Naval activity, the U.S. Army relinquishes its Western Gunboat Flotilla to the U.S. Navy. The gunboats, including the USS *Eastport,* remain on duty, but the flotilla is renamed the Mississippi Squadron. The *Dahlia* (formerly *Firefly*), a screw tug acquired by the U.S. Army at St. Louis, Missouri, is among the vessels involved. It remains in service of the western rivers for the duration of the war. Afterward it operates as a civilian vessel until about 1872. In other activity, the USS *Water Witch, Cimarron,* and *Uncas* cruise up the St. Johns River in Florida to the vicinity of St. John's Bluff to investigate the Confederate batteries deployed in the high ground. The mission proves the Confederate guns are formidable, and after an exchange of fire, the gunboats retire due to the effective artillery fire. The *Intrepid,* a screw tug attached to the U.S. Army, is among the ships transferred to the Navy. Built in St. Louis during 1861, the vessel is renamed the USS *Fern.* While attached to the Mississippi Squadron, its service includes participation on the Yazoo River (March 1863) and the Red River (June 1865). The *Fern* is sold in August 1865. It then operates as a civilian tugboat until about 1877.

Troops of the 77th Pennsylvania (Captain Muller's battery) make fascines and gabions for breastworks (Mottelay, *The Soldier in Our Civil War,* 1886).

October 1–3   In Florida, a Confederate battery, earlier deployed at St. Johns Bluff in the vicinity of Jacksonville, had been established by General Finnegan to hinder any attempt by Union warships to advance along the St. Johns River; however, a Union flotilla arrives at the mouth of the river from Hilton Head, South Carolina, this day and debarks a land force at Mayport Mills. Another contingent debarks at Mount Pleasant Creek. Meanwhile, at the river, the fleet is joined by gunboats under Commander Charles Steedman. With the ground force at Pleasant Creek approaching the bluff from the rear and the other units at Mayport Mills making a frontal approach, Confederate Lt. Colonel Charles F. Hopkins realizes that his diminutive contingent is holding an untenable position. He orders the post abandoned after dark on 2 October.

On the 3rd, the gunboats arrive at the bluff without incident. The ground troops, about 1,500 men, are commanded by Union General John M. Brannan. The transports *Boston, Ben DeFord, Cosmopolitan* and *Neptune* participate in this action. Also, the USS *Cimarron, Water Witch* and the *Uncas* participate. The *Water Witch* remains in the region for several days after the unopposed landing and advances upriver to bombard and destroy Confederate positions and to sink river barges.

October 2 (Thursday)   In Florida, Union troops debark from a flotilla and move inland in the vicinity of St. John's Bluff to engage the Confederate batteries there; however, the Rebels abandon the positions (see also, October 1–3 In Florida).

In Union general officer activity, Robert Seaman Granger (West Point, 1838) is appointed brigadier general of volunteers. He had been captured during the early days of the war while stationed in Texas with the rank of major. He was exchanged in September. Afterward, he was appointed a brigadier of Kentucky volunteers. General Granger for the duration is confined to garrison duty. After the war he is breveted major general in the U.S. Army. Also, he becomes lieutenant colonel of the 11th Infantry Regiment. He retires during 1873. Francis Barretto Spinola, a lawyer, is appointed brigadier general. General Spinola, born on Long Island, was a city alderman before the war and a member of the state legislature, with six years in the House and four in the state Senate. Prior to his appointment, he had raised a brigade of four regiments. He participates in various actions in Virginia and North Carolina, then after the battle at Gettysburg, the command is called upon to support the Union's pursuit of the retreating Confederate Army during July 1863.

In Naval activity, the *Marmora* (Tinclad No. 2, a stern-wheel river gunboat) is commissioned at about this time (October). It is assigned duty with the Union forces operating against Vicksburg, Mississippi. It engages in mine clearing operations and other duties on the Yazoo River for the remainder of the year. During January 1863, it participates against Fort Hindman (Arkansas Post). The vessel then resumes patrol duty on the Little Red River and the White River for the duration of the war. During July 1865, it is decommissioned and sold the following month. Also, the USS *Iroquois* arrives in New York for repairs following service at Vicksburg and vicinity. The ship is decommissioned on 6 October. The officers are separated and the crew is reassigned. On 8 January 1863, the *Iroquois* is recommissioned.

October 3 (Friday)   In *Naval activity,* U.S. naval vessels, including the *Hunchback* and the *White Head,* commanded by Captain Flusser, bombard Confederate positions below Franklin, Virginia, while the *Commodore Perry* successfully bombards the fortifications. The ships are unable to advance to Franklin; however, the heated battle below the town continues for about three hours. The Confederates attempt to trap the ships by cutting trees to the rear of the flotilla, but once the plot is detected, the warships retire before the narrow river channel becomes blocked. The ships had been rushed from North Carolina at the request of the army commanders in conjunction with a large Confederate force gathering near Franklin. During the contest, the *White Head* is temporarily stranded while rounding a bend of the Black Water River, but is freed before Rebel guns can destroy it. Many Confederate artillery pieces are permanently silenced by this action. The Union sustains 19 killed and wounded. Also, a formidable naval force, including nine gunboats (Commodore Steedman) and Union ground troops occupy the fortifications on St. Johns Bluff, Florida.

In Union general officer activity, James Isham Gilbert is appointed colonel of the 27th Iowa Infantry. His first combat occurs the following year during the Red River campaign.

In Confederate general officer activity, Colonel William Brimage Bate, 2nd Tennessee Infantry, is appointed brigadier general. Bate had previously served in the U.S. Army during the Mexican War and had been a U.S. senator. Bate will participate at Chattanooga, Chickamauga, and the Tullahoma Campaigns in Tennessee, as well as the campaigns in Georgia and the defense of North Carolina, the latter at the close of hostilities.

October 3–4   THE BATTLE OF CORINTH Skirmishing occurs between Union and Confederate troops outside of Corinth, Mississippi. This encounter makes it clear that Corinth is the objective. A detachment that is moving along the Chewalla Road is intercepted by a strong Confederate force which pushes the Union contingent back to the Union lines. The Rebels are encroaching the positions of Colonel John M. Oliver's brigade. The forces of General Hamilton hold the right wing while Thomas McKean guards the left and the center is held by General Thomas A. Davies.

Confederate General Mansfield Lovell's division holds the right with the brigades of Generals John Stevens Bowen, Albert Rust Johnson and John B. Villepigue, each posted northwest of the town. General Price is deployed on the left with Generals Louis Herbert and Dabney H. Maury. The Confederates deployed northwest of the Memphis and Charleston and Mobile and Ohio Railroads make it difficult for Union reinforcements to reach Corinth. Grant directs General McPherson to rush from Jackson with reinforcements to aid Rosecrans, and Van Dorn fully expects to capture Union General Rosecrans before the arrival of any of his reinforcements.

At about 0800 on the 3rd, Lovell's force lunges forward injecting so much force that the Union troops on the hill are pushed off and driven back toward Forts Robinett, Williams and Phillips, where they regroup in a series of entrenchments. Soon another gushing wave of Rebels is upon them and the application of relentless fury is even more powerful, pushing back the entire center line held by General Davies. The seemingly never ending lines of Confederate attackers threaten the stability of the entire line, and apparently only the subtle arrival of darkness is able to bring the attack to an end. Following the day's grim combat, each side makes preparations to reinitiate the tenacious fight in the morning.

At dawn on the 4th, General Van Dorn's artillery commences firing, but heavy fire from Fort Williams soon knocks these guns out of action. Following this brief exchange, the Yankees and Rebels begin trading artillery and rifle shots until about 0930, when the Confederates sprint forward from their positions near the rail-

Union troops under General Stephen A. Hurlbut trudge through mud as they advance on Corinth, Mississippi (Johnson, *Campfire and Battlefield: History of the Conflicts and Campaigns,* 1894).

road and charge down the Bolivar Road toward Fort Powell. However, the Union lines patiently await their arrival, and once in range, the Yankees open up with an enfilade of fire that severs the lines and creates wide gaps in the formations. The vanguard, comprising Texans and Mississippians, doggedly presses forward, oblivious to the sheets of grape and canister that are pummeling them as they move. Layers of troops are mounting along the way, but still they drill forward and the pressure finally overwhelms the lines at the fort, which falls into Rebel hands.

As the Rebels hold Fort Powell, essentially the key to the city, other Confederates are crashing against the Union at Fort Robinett, and here too the Rebels are met by incessant deadly fire. However, here the Ohio brigade steadfastly holds and its fire is so horrific that the Rebels are compelled to retire to the woods to regroup. Soon after, again, the Rebels charge, their boldness carrying them once again into the fires of hell. This charge brings even more devastating results as scores and scores of men drop from their wounds. Others equally courageous and without fear move about their fallen buddies to drive a wedge through the fort. At the head of the charge, Colonel William P. Rogers, the Rebel colors in hand, leads the way, and his Texas Sharpshooters bolt over the ditches and ascend the parapet, expecting to storm the defenders. To their dismay, concealed behind the walls and in perfect position from which to fire at near point-blank range are both the Ohio troops under Colonel John W. Fuller and the 11th Missouri Regiment. Major Wager Swayne at about this time had rallied his troops and restored discipline in the 43rd Ohio. His actions above and beyond the call of duty cause him to become a recipient of the Medal of Honor.

Once the Confederates are in their sights, the Yankees emerge from their cover and in unison commence firing. Again the Rebels fall in great numbers, but their courage is unshaken. They continue to fiercely engage the Yankees in a savage close-quartered man-to-man donnybrook. The tenacity of the Rebels gains them possession of the guns, but before they can pivot them to turn the fire upon the defenders, a general charge is sounded and the Confederates who had only just entered the fort are struck with the remaining strength of every available man in the fort.

The Confederates, overwhelmed by the onslaught, retire in disarray, leaving everything behind as they attempt to make it back to the woods. This severe and pivotal setback at Fort Robinett clinches the day. General Van Dorn, realizing that he no longer has the ability to take the forts and facing the probability that Union reinforcements will arrive imminently, orders a general withdrawal from the battlefield. The Union, by repulsing Van Dorn in good fashion, literally prevents the Confederates from reinforcing General Bragg at Perryville. A large portion of Company E, 24th Missouri, becomes casualties during this tremendous skirmish. Confederate Brigadier General Albert Rust Johnson participates at this action; however, afterward, he is transferred to duty in Arkansas

and Louisiana for the duration. He loses everything during the war, prompting him to depart Virginia for Arkansas, where he engages in farming in El Dorado, outside of Little Rock, until his death on 4 April 1870.

The Union has 315 dead, 1,812 wounded and 232 missing or captured. For the Confederates, there are no reports, but according to Union General Rosecrans, they have 1,423 dead and 2,025 captured or wounded. It is later reported from the official Union records that the Confederates sustain 1,423 killed, 5,692 wounded and 2,248 missing. Union reinforcements under Generals McPherson and Hurlbut arrive, insuring success for Rosecrans. As the Rebels retreat, General Ord keeps pressing, causing the Rebels to take another route. Union General Ord is wounded during this action. Union General Pleasant A. Hackleman is killed and General Richard J. Oglesby seriously wounded. Colonel Thomas Sweeny (52nd Illinois), upon the death of General Hackleman, assumes command of Hackleman's brigade. Colonel Joseph Anthony Mower (11th Missouri), later a major general, is wounded and captured. Mower is able to escape, but the Confederates recapture him. Subsequently, he will participate in the Vicksburg campaign as a brigade commander.

Meanwhile, although Grant directs Rosecrans on two occasions to follow up the victory, General Rosecrans fails to pursue the Confederates; however, on the following morning, Sunday the 5th, General McPherson is ordered to give chase. The 5th Minnesota Volunteer Regiment also participates in this action. The 63rd Ohio under Colonel John Sprague sustains high casualties. About forty-five percent of the regiment is either killed or wounded and nine of the regiment's thirteen officers are among the casualties. Colonel (later brigadier general) Green Berry Raum participates at this action and leads his regiment, the 56th Illinois, in a successful bayonet attack.

October 4 (Saturday) In Kentucky, the Army of the Ohio continues to advance against the Confederates. A vanguard force, led by Major Foster, encounters and clashes with the rear guard of Major General Polk's command at Bardstown.

In Mississippi, General Grant directs General E.O.C. Ord to either attack the Confederate rear or intercept its retreat from Corinth. Ord, having his own force and that of General S.A. Hurlbut's command, will encounter General Van Dorn's retiring forces on the following day.

In West Virginia, elements of the Pennsylvania 54th Regiment clash with Confederates in the vicinity of Paw Paw Tunnel and Little Cacapon Bridge. In other activity, elements of the 1st New York Cavalry skirmish with Confederates in the vicinity of Romney. Earlier, on the 2nd, the New York contingent and elements of the 54th Pennsylvania Infantry Regiment had skirmished with Confederates in the same area.

In Union general officer activity, Colonel John M. Thayer is promoted to brigadier general.

Thayer, initially commissioned colonel of the 1st Nebraska Regiment (infantry converted to cavalry during 1863), participates at the capture of Fort Donelson and at Shiloh as brigade commander (Lew Wallace's division). Colonel John Henry Hobart Ward (38th New York), a veteran who enlisted in the army as a private during 1842, is appointed brigadier general. General Ward, who earlier participated at First Manassas (Bull Run) and during the Peninsular Campaign, later participates at Fredericksburg, Chancellorsville and Gettysburg. At the latter he is wounded, and subsequently, during the campaign in the Wilderness and Spotsylvania, he is again wounded. John Milton Thayer, prior to the war a brigadier general of Nebraska militia, is appointed brigadier general. At the outbreak of war, he had been commissioned colonel of the 1st Nebraska Regiment, initially an infantry regiment, but later converted into the 1st Nebraska Cavalry Regiment. The Senate takes no action and his commission expires on 4 March 1863; however, shortly thereafter, he is re-nominated and confirmed with his rank effective 13 March 1863. He participates in the Vicksburg campaign and in February 1864 receives command of the District of the Frontier.

In Confederate general officer activity, Brigadier General William Duncan Smith, having contracted yellow fever, dies on this day at Charleston. General Smith was a veteran of the Mexican War and a graduate of West Point (1846).

In Naval activity, the USS *Somerset* attacks the Confederate salt works located near the Fernanda Railroad terminus at Depot Key, Florida, and it again strikes on the 6th to destroy the facility. In other activity, the USS *Clifton, Harriet Lane, Henry James, Owasco,* and *Westfield* launch an attack against Galveston, Texas.

October 5 (Sunday) In Florida, Union forces occupy Jacksonville.

In Kentucky, a contingent of the 20th Kentucky Volunteer Regiment, led by Colonel Bruce, skirmishes with Confederates at Glasgow. Meanwhile, the 4th Indiana Cavalry clashes with Confederates at Madisonville. Casualty figures are unavailable for either.

In Mississippi, Union General Rosecrans finally takes up pursuit of the retreating Rebels who fled Corinth after the devastating defeat they sustained, but Rosecrans' troops, led by General McPherson, take the wrong road, allowing the Confederates to escape. When the Rebels cross the Hatchie River, they burn the Crown Bridge, which also holds up McPherson until he makes repairs; his force of three regiments renews the chase on the following day. Elements of the 5th Minnesota Volunteer Regiment participate in the pursuit. Meanwhile, President Lincoln congratulates Grant on the marvelous victory and Grant is inclined to suggest to General-in-chief Halleck an assault against Vicksburg.

Another Union force, under General Ord, intercepts Van Dorn at Pocahontas (Metamora) during the early morning hours as the Confederates attempt to continue their retreat to hook up with General Bragg. The front guard of Van Dorn's force is encountered and a ferocious battle erupts. Van Dorn's force, in retreat following the blood-bath at Corinth, lacks sufficient time to genuinely regroup, giving Ord's force greater advantage. The engagement referred to as the Battle of the Hatchie is won by the Union, forcing Van Dorn to again fall back subsequent to surrendering two batteries with a combined total of twelve guns and sustaining about 500 casualties. The next day, General McPherson's force, also in pursuit, reaches the destroyed bridge that postpones his progress.

October 6 (Monday)   In Kentucky, Confederate General Bragg is withdrawing toward Harrodsburg, with Union troops under General Buell in pursuit. They clash on the 8th at Perryville. In the meantime, the 3rd Corps, Army of the Ohio, maintains its advance towards Perryville and reaches Springfield and beyond to the vicinity of Texas, Kentucky.

In Mississippi, General McPherson, in pursuit of Confederates under Van Dorn, reaches Ripley, but he is ordered by Rosecrans to return to Corinth, as the forces of Van Dorn had in the meantime (5th) been intercepted and defeated by General Ord's command at Pocahontas (Metamora on the Big Hatchie River). Major General Edward O.C. Ord sustains a serious wound during the actions against the Confederates subsequent to their failed attack against Corinth. He remains on sick leave until the following June, when he participates in the operations against Vicksburg.

In Union general officer activity, Brigadier General Jacob Dolson Cox at about this time is promoted to major general, effective October 6. His commission expires the following March, but only temporarily, as he reverts again to major general during December 1864.

In Missouri, Confederate guerrillas led by Quantrill engage the Union 5th Missouri Cavalry (militia) at Liberty and Sibley's Landing. Casualty figures are unavailable.

In Virginia, elements of the U.S. 6th Cavalry, commanded by Colonel Robertson, skirmish with Confederates at Charleston. Casualty figures are unavailable.

In Naval activity, the USS *Tahoma,* accompanied by the USS *Somerset,* while off Sea Horse Key, Florida, bombard Confederate positions. After firing stops, a contingent of 111 troops in eight boats lands. The howitzers posted on two of the boats disrupt the Confederates and force them to scatter. Meanwhile, the Union landing party destroys 28 boilers and every building in the area. The operation disrupts the salt making operation and concludes without any casualties, nor the firing of any weapons. In other activity, the gunboat USS *Rachel Seaman,* while operating in Texas, seizes a blockade runner, the schooner *Dwarf,* at Sabine Pass.

October 7 (Tuesday)   In Arkansas, Confederate General Alison Nelson (West Point, 1855)

dies of natural causes while stationed in Arkansas under General Hindman's command. He had recruited the 10th Texas, an infantry regiment which participated against Union troops near White River, DeVall's Bluff, in May.

In Kentucky, during the latter part of the day, Union troops under General R.B. Mitchell (leading the center column of General Charles C. Gilbert) encounters the rear of General Bragg's army, but the Union, anticipating a major battle on the following day, does not initiate action. General Buell instead directs General Alexander McCook to move two divisions, those of Rousseau and James S. Jackson, forward on the Mackville Road to close up on his (Buell's) left. McCook's remaining division under General Sill had earlier been dispatched to Harrodsburg. The Union's right column, led by General Thomas L. Crittenden, is expected to arrive by way of Bardstown. General Philip Sheridan's division is positioned in the high ground overlooking Doctor's Creek. Also, the Confederates evacuate Lexington, Kentucky.

In Tennessee, Union Troops attached to General John McCauley Palmer's brigade engage Confederates under General James Patton Anderson at La Vergne just outside of Nashville. The Union sustains five killed and nine wounded. The Confederates suffer 80 killed and wounded and about 175 captured.

October 8 (Wednesday)   THE BATTLE OF PERRYVILLE (CHAPIN HILL) In this bloody battle in Kentucky, the 1st Corps Army of the Ohio, under Major General Alexander McDowell McCook (West Point, 1852), and a division under Brigadier General Sheridan (West Point, 1853), engage in a furious and tenacious skirmish with the Confederates commanded by General Braxton Bragg. During the early morning hours, while McCook's brigade (Sheridan's division) is advancing from its positions near Doctor's Creek to more tenable positions, Confederates spring an attack against the vanguard, the 85th Illinois, but it is closely trailed by the 2nd Michigan Cavalry, which helps meet the threat. The cavalry maintains the pressure against the Confederates until McCook's regiments hit the battlefield. Meanwhile, Confederate artillery opens up to afford cover fire for an attack to seize a hill in the center of the Union lines, the same hill Buell has determined to secure due to its strategic value. The coveted hill dominates Chaplin's Creek, the source of water for the troops and horses.

General McCook's contingents—the 85th Illinois, 52nd Ohio, 86th and 125th Illinois Regiments and the cavalry—reacting to the horrendous artillery barrage, quickly deploy in safer positions. The line forms to the left of General Gilbert's force, which is composed of General William Terrill's brigade (James Jackson's division), a fresh and untested unit, and the brigades of Colonels William H. Lytle and L.A. Harris, both of which are attached to General Rousseau's division. In addition, the brigades of Colonels Hall, Starkweather and Webster are held in reserve. The Confederates

field the divisions of Polk's corps and those of Generals Benjamin F. Cheatham, Simon B. Buckner and Robert Houston Anderson.

Slightly after the noon hour, Confederate General Cheatham initiates an artillery bombardment of Terrill's troops, and in concert an infantry assault is launched. The Union for a while holds, thanks in great part to the personal leadership of General James S. Jackson, who continuously rallies his men, but the untried line is pounded repeatedly until it folds and is pushed from the field, having sustained the loss of one battery, Captain Parsons,' and the life of Union General James S. Jackson. Union General William Terrill sustains a mortal wound and succumbs later in the day.

With Terrill's force nearly inoperable, Bragg strikes two of Rousseau's brigades, giving most of his attention to the far right defended by Lytle. The overwhelming force of the assault inflicts heavy casualties and drives Lytle's brigade to the rear, jeopardizing the positions of Generals Schoepf and Philip Sheridan (Gilbert's corps). However, it is later determined that Gilbert's failure to support General Alexander McCook's corps caused McCook to withdraw, and consequently, Gilbert's left flank had been exposed.

The Rebels, noticing the exposed positions following the retirement of Lytle, commence a tenacious charge to seize the hills to dislodge Sheridan and Schoepf. But Sheridan stands ready and his guns shred the assault troops as they attempt to ascend the coveted hill. Following a short-lived attack, the Rebels are pushed back to the bluffs by Carlin's brigade, which fortuitously had been positioned to Sheridan's right. Although the Confederates fail to crack Sheridan's lines, they are simultaneously hammering the left side of the Union lines. Generals Cheatham and Simon B. Buckner are drilling forward, making some progress. A Union reserve force under Starkweather intercepts a movement expected to flank Harris. Soon after, support from two other brigades, Hall's and Webster's, arrive on scene. At this line the raging fury continues for several hours, the pace so horrific that both the Union infantry and artillery units diminish their ammunition and have to pull back to get re-supplied.

In the meantime, as the Yankees withdraw from their positions near the Russell House, they are shadowed by advancing Rebels, who are about to take advantage and whip them before they can reach the ammunition supplies. At this time, fresh troops arrive and the Rebels no longer face empty weapons. Colonel Gooding with his men to the left and one of R.B. Mitchell's brigades, also under his command, stands on the right. Together they charge into the melee and initiate yet more grueling fighting. Both sides hammer each other with unrelenting determination. Cruel casualties are inflicted by both sides and the close-quartered bashing exhibits no mercy. Finally, at about dusk, the exhausted troops, Yankees and Rebels, disengage, but the Union does regain every yard that had earlier been surrendered.

The Union scores another victory and the

Confederates are forced to pull back farther. The Union, rather than pursuing Bragg, waits in place expecting reinforcements, the remainder of Crittenden's corps, before initiating another attack the following day. Meanwhile, Bragg's retreating army heads for Murfreesboro, Tennessee, where Bragg establishes winter quarters. Another Union army under Rosecrans pursues Bragg as far as Nashville.

The Union suffers 916 dead, 2,943 wounded and 489 missing. The Confederates suffer 2,500 killed, wounded or missing. Confederate General Daniel Weisiger Adams participates in the battle. Colonel Union Brigadier Generals James S. Jackson and William R. Terrill are both killed. General Terrill is hit in the thigh by a shell fragment while attempting to rally his troops at about 1600 and dies later that night in a field hospital. Colonel George Webster is killed and Colonel Michael Gooding is captured after having his horse shot from under him; of the 1,423 men in his brigade, 549 are reported as either killed or wounded. In Rousseau's division, the casualties soar to more than 2,000.

Confederate Brigadier General Sterling A. Wood is seriously wounded while leading a brigade in General Patrick R. Cleburne's division. Union Colonel William P. Carlin (West Point, 1850) serves admirably during the battle and will be appointed brigadier general this November. He will participate at the vicious struggle at Stones River and the balance of the Atlanta campaign, then command the 1st Division, III Corps, during the campaign in the Carolinas. Confederate Colonel (later general) John Calvin Brown is wounded. After the fighting around Perryville, Confederate General Buckner will move to Mobile, Alabama, to strengthen the defenses there. He remains at Mobile until spring of the following year. Confederate Brigadier General George Maney's brigade — composed of the 1st, 4th, 6th, 9th and 23rd, 49th and 50th Tennessee Infantry Regiments and the recently added 41st Georgia Regiment — played a principal part in this action. Subsequently, Maney's brigade will participate at many other battles, including Murfreesboro, Chattanooga and Chickamauga, before moving into Georgia to support the defense of Atlanta.

Also, General Charles Gilbert is admonished after the action for his failure to support General Alexander D. McCook. He is relieved of command. In addition, the Senate takes no action on his nomination as brigadier and it expires on 4 March 1863. General Gilbert is not reappointed. Nevertheless, he remains in the service, and during July 1863 he becomes major in the 19th Infantry, but he is restricted to a desk job for the duration of the war. He is promoted to lieutenant colonel during 1868, and in 1881 he is elevated to colonel. He retires during 1886. Also, Lt. Colonel (later brigadier general) Edward Moody McCook participates at this battle in command of a brigade composed of his 2nd Cavalry and several Kentucky regiments. General Albin Francisco Schoepf, like General Gilbert, pays heavily for his actions during the fighting. He is appointed commander of Fort

Delaware on the Delaware River in the vicinity of New Castle, Delaware, and southern New Jersey. He musters out of the service on 15 January 1866.

In Texas, Confederate-held Galveston surrenders to a Naval force commanded by Commodore W.B. Renshaw. A contingent of about 250 Union soldiers attached to the 42nd Massachusetts and commanded by Colonel Burrill are also with Renshaw. The gunboats *Westfield,* his flagship, the *Harriet Lane, Owasco, Clifton, Coryphaeus* and *Sachem* remain to support the diminutive force which holds the town. The Confederates will attempt to regain Galveston early next year.

In Tennessee, on or about this date, the newly formed Confederate 8th (also known as 13th) Tennessee Cavalry, led by Colonel George G. Dibrell, departs Sparta en route to Murfreesboro to serve with General Nathan B. Forrest. These Tennessee Volunteers, many of whom are farmers, will participate in an array of skirmishes and full-scale engagements from the region of West Tennessee into Virginia, the Carolinas and Georgia, providing enormous support to the Confederate infantry forces and artillery units. Its commanding officer, Colonel Dibrell, is remembered for his later boast: "Not a piece of artillery was ever lost when supported by the Eighth."

In Union general officer activity, Major Patrick Henry Jones, 37th New York Regiment, known as the "Irish Rifles," is appointed colonel of the 154th New York Regiment. The regiment is assigned to the XI Corps of General Oliver O. Howard. Jones' regiment misses the Battle of Fredericksburg (December 1862; however it is on line by the Battle of Chancellorsville (May 1863).

In Confederate general officer activity, Elkanah B. Greer is promoted to the rank of brigadier general. He is assigned to the Trans-Mississippi Department.

October 9 (Thursday)   In Kentucky, after the battle at Perryville on the previous day, General Bragg's force is now heading for Harrodsburg to be joined there by the forces of Generals Kirby Smith and Jones M. Withers. The wounded and sick troops remain behind at Harrodsburg, but the Army moves from there heading for Eastern Tennessee via Danville, Loudon and Powell's Gap. Unhindered by Union pursuit, the Confederates are able to confiscate supplies as they move. However, at Lawrenceburg (Dog Walk), a heated battle erupts when a force of about 3,000 Union troops, composed of elements of the 15th and 19th U.S. Infantry Regiments, the 1st and 49th Ohio Volunteer Regiments, Battery H, 5th U.S. Artillery and the 9th Kentucky Cavalry, commanded by Colonel Parrott, clash with an equally large force of Confederates (General Kirby Smith's command). The contest lasts for about five hours, but casualties are light. The Union sustains about six killed and 18 wounded. The Confederates suffer 18 killed and unknown wounded.

In Pennsylvania, Confederate general Jeb Stuart's raiders still engage in stealing Union horses and equipment around Chambersburg. Stuart has completely encircled General McClellan's Union Army of the Potomac to continue this endeavor.

In Virginia, a contingent of Union cavalry skirmishes and defeats a band of Confederates at Aldie, capturing about 40 troops.

In Confederate general officer activity, Major General James Longstreet is promoted to the rank of lieutenant general.

October 10 (Friday)   In Kentucky, Confederates under General Braxton Bragg are still in retreat and moving out of the state. As they pull out, the Union troops are becoming more firmly entrenched. Buell's main Army, under the command of General Thomas, is moving toward Nashville; he travels to Louisville. In other activity, Union troops (9th Kentucky Cavalry) under Lt. Colonel John Boyle seize Harrodsburg and capture its 1,600 defenders. Casualty figures are unavailable.

In Confederate general officer activity, Brigadier General Carter L. Stevenson is promoted to major general effective this date. Also, Brigadier General John Clifford Pemberton is promoted to the rank of lieutenant general as of this date. General Pemberton is assigned as commander of the Department of Mississippi and Eastern Louisiana and will be faced with the challenge of General Ulysses S. Grant at Vicksburg during the following year. He succeeds General Van Dorn, who had recently been defeated at Corinth. Van Dorn, after relinquishing command, assumes command of Pemberton's cavalry. Major General William Joseph Hardee, following the battle of Murfreesboro later this year, is promoted to lieutenant general effective this date.

Brigadier General Henry Heth (West Point, 1847) is promoted to the rank of major general, also effective this date; however, the Senate rejects the nomination. Heth does receive the promotion in 1864, effective retroactively to May 1863. Brigadier General George E. Pickett is promoted to the rank of major general. Major General Leonidas Polk, known also as the "Fighting Bishop," is promoted to the rank of lieutenant general, effective this date.

October 11 (Saturday)   In Arkansas, a Union contingent of the 4th Iowa Cavalry, led by Major Benjamin Rector, skirmishes with Confederates (Texas Rangers) led by Lt. Colonel Giddings at La Grange. The Union sustains three killed and nine wounded. The Confederates sustain nine captured.

In Maryland, elements of the 3rd and 4th Maine Regiments skirmish with Confederates in the vicinity of the mouth of the Monacy River.

In New Mexico, General Carleton orders an expedition against hostile Mescalero Apaches. The force, composed of Companies A and D, 1st California Cavalry, are dispatched to Dog

Canyon. The contingent is to coordinate with Colonel Christopher (Kit) Carson, who had been ordered to reoccupy Fort Stanton. Carson's force is composed of five companies of his 1st New Mexico Cavalry. The expedition succeeds and about 500 are captured.

In North Carolina, the Union gunboat USS *Maratanza* comes under attack by Confederates at the Cape Fear River. Casualty figures are unavailable.

In Virginia, Union cavalry commanded by Colonel Andrew McReynolds engage Confederates led by Captain Imboden at Cacapon Bridge. Casualty figures are unavailable. Also, a Union contingent (General Stahel's command) skirmishes with Confederates at Paris while executing a reconnaissance mission. The Union reports the capture of about 130 Confederates.

In Union general officer activity, James Bowen is appointed brigadier general. He is assigned as provost marshal general of the Department of the Gulf. He remains in the post at New Orleans until he resigns his commission on 27 July 1864. During the following year he receives the brevet rank of major general. John Henry Ketcham is appointed colonel of the 150th New York Regiment. The regiment is assigned duty at Baltimore, but it later participates in the Battle of Gettysburg (July 1863). Afterward, the regiment is attached to the XII Corps and it participates in the Atlanta campaign.

October 12 (Sunday)   In Kentucky, the Army of the Ohio maintains its advance in pursuit of Confederate General Braxton Bragg's army.

October 13 (Monday)   In Mississippi, the 4th Minnesota Infantry Regiment, having pursued Confederates from Corinth to Ripley and completing the operation on the previous day, prepares to join with General Grant's forces (Central Mississippi Campaign). Confederate General Van Dorn had been recently intercepted and defeated.

October 14 (Tuesday)   In Washington, D.C., President Lincoln is not particularly pleased with the way General McClellan is handling the Army of the Potomac. Lincoln wishes McClellan to take the offensive in Virginia. General McClellan sends a telegram to General Halleck requesting additional cavalry to handle the Rebel cavalry of Jeb Stuart that is still harassing the area. The telegram states: "With my small cavalry force, it is impossible for me to watch the line of the Potomac properly. This makes it necessary for me to weaken my line very much by extending the infantry to guard the enumerable fords." There is apparently growing tension among Halleck, Lincoln and McClellan, and it continues with another exchange of sarcastic telegrams on the 25th.

In Kentucky, the vanguard of Buell's Army of the Ohio clashes with General Bragg's rearguard at Stanford. The Union reports no casualties. The Confederates sustain one killed and 14 captured.

In Missouri, a skirmish develops between Union and Confederate contingents at Hazel Bottom. Casualty figures and specific units are unavailable.

In Confederate general officer activity, Lieutenant Colonel Francis R. Nicholls (West Point, 1855) is appointed brigadier general. General Nicholls has been badly damaged in this vicious brothers' war. He sacrifices an arm after injuries sustained at Winchester. The general, at that time, still lieutenant colonel of the 8th Louisiana, did not retire. He moves on to Chancellorsville, where incessant shooting and shelling inflicts another grievous wound, costing him part of his leg while leading his Louisiana brigade. General Nicholls serves only in non-combat roles from this point; he first receives duty at Lynchburg, and from there he transfers to the Department of the Trans-Mississippi. After the war, General Nicholls serves as governor of Louisiana in a disputed election, and in 1888, he is again elected governor. Subsequently, he serves on the state Supreme Court. He retires to his plantation during 1911, but he dies soon after on 1 January 1912.

Colonel Gustave Cluseret is promoted to brigadier general. General Cluseret, a Frenchman, is reportedly arrested during January 1863 (charges unknown). He resigns his commission in February 1863. General Rosecrans had earlier requested that Cluseret be transferred to his command, and he received this response from General Henry Halleck: "If you knew him better, you would not ask for him. You will regret the application as long as you live."

In Naval activity, the USS *Memphis* (former blockade runner *Memphis*), operating off Charleston, seizes the blockade runner *Ouachita*. Also, the USS *Ellis* receives orders to move to a position from where it can block Bogue Inlet, North Carolina. About one week later, the *Ellis* intercepts and captures the schooner *Adelaide*, which is transporting a cargo of cotton, tobacco and turpentine.

October 15 (Wednesday)   In Florida, a Union naval reconnaissance force (blockading force) bombards and devastates Apalachicola on the Apalachicola River.

In Illinois, Commodore David Dixon Porter arrives at Cairo to assume command of the Mississippi Squadron. He succeeds Commodore Charles Davis. Davis had been assigned as chief of Bureau of Navigation at the Navy Department in Washington, D.C.

In Virginia, one company of the 7th Pennsylvania Cavalry, commanded by Lt. Williams, skirmishes with Confederates at Carsville. Casualty figures are unavailable.

In Union general officer activity, Colonel Eliakim Parker Scammon (23rd Ohio Regiment) is appointed brigadier general. He is assigned command of the Kanawha District, a post he retains until February 1864.

In Naval activity, the recently captured *Victoria,* taken at Memphis the previous June and later acquired as a Union naval vessel, is renamed the *Abraham.* Acting Ensign William Wagner receives command of the river boat. The *Abraham* serves for the duration of the war, but not in a combat capacity. Also, the USS *Kensington* and the *Rachel Seaman,* operating in the vicinity of Taylor's Bayou, destroy a strategic Confederate railroad bridge, severing the possibility of the Confederates sending reinforcements to Sabine Pass, Texas. The two gunboats also destroy the schooners *Stonewall* and the *Lone Star* by fire, and a Confederate barracks is also reduced by fire.

October 16 (Thursday)   In Mississippi, General Grant is making preparations for an assault against the major Confederate stronghold at Vicksburg. Confederate General Bragg is continuing his retreat from Kentucky. The Union troops under General Buell have no great success in cutting off Bragg's escape. Nonetheless, the Army of the Ohio continues its operations in pursuit of the Confederates.

In Virginia, Charleston is occupied by Union General Winfield Scott Hancock's brigade. The Union sustains one killed and eight wounded. The Confederates sustain eight captured.

October 17 (Friday)   In Kentucky, a large Confederate force of several thousand troops under General John Hunt Morgan clashes with a Union contingent of the 3rd and 4th Ohio Cavalry at Lexington. The Union is overwhelmed and sustains four killed, 24 wounded and about 350 troops captured, essentially the entire command.

In Virginia, a detachment of Union Cavalry (General Julius Stahel's command) clashes with Confederates at Thoroughfare Gap. Initially, the Union prevails; however the two sides clash a second time and the Confederates prevail. The Union sustains three killed and 27 captured. The Confederate casualty figures are unavailable; however, 100 are captured. General Stahel, a Hungarian actually named Julius Szamvald, had commanded the 1st Division, Sigel's corps, during the battle at Second Manassas, subsequent to the wounding of General Robert C. Schenck; but at this time his command is in reserve.

In Naval activity, the USS *Water Witch,* following duty in Florida, returns to Charleston. It remains with the squadron until February 1863 and then requires repairs; however, the vessel is unable to embark on its own. It is towed to Virginia. After repairs the *Water Witch* arrives back at Port Royal on 14 June 1863.

October 18 (Saturday)   In Arkansas, Union elements under General Francis J. Herron skirmish with Confederates at Cross Hollow and Fayetteville on this day and again on the 24th, 27th and the 28th of this month.

In Kentucky, Confederate General John Hunt Morgan's raiders engage a detachment of the 4th Ohio Cavalry led by Captain Robey near Lexington. Casualty figures are unavailable.

In Arkansas, a contingent of the 43rd Indiana Volunteer Regiment clashes with Confederates at Helena. Casualty figures are unavailable.

In Virginia, a contingent of the 6th Ohio Cavalry skirmishes with a large Confederate force at Haymarket. The Confederates capture about 23 troops.

October 19 (Sunday)   In Kentucky, the army under Confederate General Braxton Bragg continues its retreat.

In Tennessee, Confederate cavalry led by Colonel Jeffries occupies the town of Commerce.

October 20 (Monday)   In Kentucky, skirmishing develops in several areas. Union wagon trains are assaulted and destroyed in the vicinity of Bardstown.

In Missouri, a contingent of the 10th Illinois Cavalry, led by Lt. Colonel Stuart, skirmishes with Confederates at Marshfield. The Union captures about 27 Confederate troops.

In Tennessee, Confederate troops under General Forrest engage Union troops under Colonel John F. Miller outside of Nashville. Elements of the 10th Missouri Militia Cavalry commanded by Major Woodson skirmish with Confederate guerrillas at Auxvois River. Casualty figures are unavailable.

In Virginia, Confederate General Lee is deeply saddened when his 23-year-old daughter Annie dies of a sudden illness.

In Confederate general officer activity, Lt. Colonel Robert Hall Chilton (West Point, 1837), chief of staff to General Robert E. Lee and inspector general of the Army of Northern Virginia, is promoted to brigadier general; however, his commission is not approved by the Confederate Senate until 20 February 1864. One month later he is relieved from field duty at his request and assigned to Richmond for the duration of the war as an inspector. After the war, he moves to Columbus, Georgia, where he dies during February 1879.

In Naval activity, Commodore Charles Wilkes, commander of the West India Squadron based at Havana, Cuba, informs the Department of the Navy that the vessels *Cimerone* (*Cimarron*), *Dacotah, Santiago de Cuba* and *Vanderbilt* had not yet arrived to join the squadron. The *Vanderbilt* had not initially been assigned to the squadron, but later it is dispatched on a mission to discover and capture or destroy the CSS *Alabama.*

October 20–22   In Tennessee, the 45th Ohio Mounted Infantry, the 1st, 11th and 12th Kentucky Cavalry and the 24th Indiana Battery engage Confederates at Philadelphia. The Union has 20 dead, 80 wounded and 354 missing; the Confederates report 15 dead, 82 wounded and 111 missing.

In Kentucky, Confederate Colonel Joseph Wheeler's cavalry captures Loudon. Colonel Wheeler will fight in later years as a U.S. general during the Spanish-American War (1898).

October 21 (Tuesday)   In the Indian Territory (Oklahoma), Indians loyal to the Union and Confederates, led by Colonel Leper, near the convergence of Pound Creek and the Washita River at present-day Fort Cobb (Caddo County). One Confederate is listed as killed.

In South Carolina, at Hilton Head, the 3rd Rhode Island, 3rd and 4th New Hampshire, 6th and 7th Connecticut, 47th, 55th, and 76th Pennsylvania Regiments, the 1st New York Engineers and the 1st Massachusetts Cavalry embark on gunboats and transports to strike Confederates in the vicinity of Pocotaligo (Yemassee) and at Coosawhatchie. The force, numbering about 5,000 troops commanded by General John M. Brannan, also includes Batteries D and M, 1st U.S. Artillery, and Battery E, 3rd U.S. Artillery. Skirmishes develop on the following day.

In Tennessee, a contingent of the 2nd Illinois Cavalry, commanded by Major John J. Mudd, skirmishes with Confederates at Woodville. Casualty figures are unavailable; however, it is reported that the Union captures a large number of Confederates.

In Virginia, a reconnaissance detail of General John Geary's brigade, operating near Lovettsville, captures about 75 Confederate troops.

October 22 (Wednesday)   In Arkansas, the Union 1st Division, commanded by General Blunt, engages a large Confederate force in the vicinity of Old Fort Wayne (Maysville). After the tenacious confrontation, which lasts about one hour, the Union compels the Confederates to retire from the area. The Union sustains five killed and nine wounded. The Confederates sustain about 50 killed. In another action, a contingent of Union cavalry commanded by Major Lazear skirmishes with a Confederate contingent of about 150 troops, led by Colonel Boone, at Van Buren. Casualty figures are unavailable.

In South Carolina, Union and Confederate forces engage at Pocotaligo (Yemassee) and Coosawhatchie. A Union contingent that had embarked from Hilton Head on the previous day advances toward the railway, but Confederate pickets encounter the Union and a heated engagement ignites. The Confederates (Beauregard's command) drive the Yankees back toward Pocotaligo. Unexpectedly, Confederate guns and riflemen, concealed in the swamps, commence firing. The Yankees aggressively return fire, but after a while, their ammunition supply becomes dangerously low, prompting General John M. Brannan to order the troops to board the vessels.

In the meantime, the other forces of Brannan, commanded by Colonel Barton, which had

Union troops repair a railroad bridge at Goose Creek that Confederates destroyed while in retreat (Mottelay, *The Soldier in Our Civil War,* 1886).

landed at Coosawhatchie, spots a Rebel train laden with reinforcements. The Union fires at the passing train, killing some Confederates, including their commanding officer, Major Harrison. Shortly afterward, more Confederates, bolstered by artillery, arrive and the Union is compelled to board the vessels and return to Hilton Head. The Union suffers 43 dead and 258 wounded; Confederates report 14 dead and 102 wounded. The USS *Wabash* participates in this battle.

In Tennessee, a 200-man contingent of the 83rd Illinois Volunteer Regiment, led by Major Blott, skirmishes with Confederate guerrillas in a battle that lasts about one hour at Waverly. The Union sustains one killed and two wounded. The Confederates sustain about 40 killed and wounded and 30 captured. Also, a reconnaissance detachment, composed of elements of the 55th Illinois Regiment commanded by Colonel David Stuart, skirmishes with a group of Confederates at Shelby Depot. The Confederates sustain eight killed.

In Virginia, a reconnaissance force skirmishes with Confederates at Hedgeville. The force is composed of two squadrons of the 4th Pennsylvania Cavalry led by Captain Duncan. The Union reports no casualties. The Confederates sustain 19 captured.

In Union general officer activity, Brigadier General Lovell Harrison Rousseau is promoted to major general effective 8 October. General Rousseau participates at various actions, including Shiloh and Perryville, then is transferred to Tennessee to command a division in the Army of the Cumberland.

In Naval activity, the USS *Mohican,* subsequent to receiving repairs at Philadelphia, joins the search for the CSS *Alabama* and the CSS *Florida.* It returns to Philadelphia on 14 April 1864. Shortly afterward it is decommissioned. Following repairs, it is reactivated on 7 October 1864. In other activity, the USS *Penobscot,* while on blockade duty near Cape Fear, encounters and seizes a British blockade runner, the brigantine *Robert Burns.*

October 23 (Thursday)   In the Indian Territory (Oklahoma), the Tonkawa tribe at the

Wichita Agency and several whites are attacked by a group of Delawares and Shawnees that had recently traveled into Oklahoma from Kansas. After dark, these Indians and some from other tribes attempt to encircle the agency. From inside the headquarters four white men wound one Indian and apparently kill another. The shooting prompts the Tonkawa to flee from the reservation. Meanwhile, the men in the agency are murdered. The Delaware and Shawnee pursue the Tonkawa and intercept them on the following day. The Tonkawa number at least several hundred, but they are no match for the warriors against them. The loss rises well above 100 Tonkawa.

In Kentucky, a large contingent of Colonel Edward M. McCook's cavalry skirmishes with Confederate cavalry at Big Hill. The Union reports no casualties. The Confederates sustain four killed.

In Union general officer activity, Emery Upton (West Point, 1861) is appointed colonel (later brigadier general) of the 121st New York Regiment. Major Charles Jackson Paine is appointed colonel of the 2nd Louisiana Colored Regiment. He participates in the operations against Port Hudson. Subsequently, Colonel Paine commands a brigade of the XIX Corps and later a cavalry brigade. He resigns his colonel's commission during March 1864 to accept a position on the staff of General Butler.

October 24 (Friday)   In Washington, D.C., President Abraham Lincoln places General William Rosecrans in command of the Department of Kentucky, replacing General Don Carlos Buell. This places all other Union contingents in the vicinity of Kentucky and Tennessee under Rosecrans' command. President Lincoln had become unhappy with the tardy progress of Buell following the battle at Perryville. General Buell is scrutinized for his actions by a military commission that is formed during November of this year; however, they are unable to come to any conclusions that place blame on Buell. Nonetheless, no new orders arrive, and Buell resigns his commission during May of 1864.

In Missouri, two battalions of the Missouri Militia Cavalry, led by Major Frank White, skirmish with Confederate guerrillas at Grand Prairie. The Union sustains three wounded. The estimated Confederate casualties are eight killed and 20 wounded.

In Kentucky, Confederate guerrillas led by John Hunt Morgan skirmish with a Union contingent (specific unit unidentified) at Morgantown. The Yankees capture about 16 Rebels.

In Tennessee, General William Starke Rosecrans focuses on the task of toughening up his forces to enable them to handle the forces of Confederate General Bragg, which are threatening Nashville. At this time, the Union forces are deployed in the vicinity of Bowling Green, Kentucky, Glasgow and Nashville. Rosecrans divides the force into three corps (Army of the Cumberland). In addition, the Union immedi-

ately begins working to repair the Louisville and Nashville Railroad, but the first trains are not able to reach Nashville until November 26. Meanwhile, fighting continues in Tennessee and Kentucky. With the departure of Rosecrans from Mississippi, General Charles Smith Hamilton is assigned command at Corinth.

In Virginia, skirmishing develops in the vicinity of Catlett's Station. A contingent of the 3rd West Virginia Cavalry, led by Captain Conger, captures two Confederates while on a reconnaissance mission. In early November, Union General Francis E. Patterson, acting on erroneous information concerning enemy strength in this region, withdraws all his troops from the area. General Patterson dies from an accidental discharge of his own weapon on 22 November.

In other activity, a skirmish erupts between a Union contingent of about 80 troops and a 150-man Confederate group at Manassas Junction. Casualty figures are unavailable and specific units are unreported. Meanwhile, elements of the 1st New York Mounted Rifles (7th New York Cavalry Regiment), 39th Illinois and the 62nd Ohio Volunteer Regiments, commanded by Brigadier General Orris S. Ferry, skirmish with Confederates at Blackwater. The Union sustains one killed. The Confederates suffer six killed.

In Naval activity, the CSS *DeSoto* is renamed the USS *General Lyon.* Master John R. Neeld receives command of the ship, which is attached to the Mississippi Squadron. In other activity, the USS *Seymour* receives orders to tow the USS *Minnehahato* to Plymouth, North Carolina. It returns to New Bern about five days later with the damaged USS *Whitehead* in tow.

October 25 (Saturday)   In Tennessee, U.S. Grant assumes command of the Department of Tennessee. On the following day, Grant, with added confidence since the victory at Iuka, Mississippi, requests authorization from General Halleck to assault Vicksburg. In the Eastern Theater, tension is heating up between McClellan and Washington. McClellan previously requested fresh horses for his tired mounts in addition to extra contingents of cavalrymen. Today, President Lincoln sends the following telegram to McClellan: "I have just received your dispatch about sore-tongued and fatigued horses. Will you pardon me for asking what the horses of your army have done since the battle of Antietam that fatigues anything?" McClellan responds: "Since the battle of Antietam, six regiments have made one trip of two hundred miles, marching fifty-five miles in one day while endeavoring to reach Stuart's cavalry.... General Pleasonton states in his official report that he with the remainder of the available cavalry marched seventy-eight miles in twenty-four hours.... Besides these, our cavalry has been scouting one hundred and fifty miles of riverfront since the battle of Antietam, engaging the enemy on every occasion afforded."

In Arkansas, a contingent of the 43rd Indiana Regiment, while executing a foraging mission, is attacked by a band of Confederate guerillas

in the vicinity of Helena. The Union sustains three killed and two wounded.

In Union general officer activity, General William S. Rosecrans assumes command of the Department of Kentucky. Colonel Joseph R. West, commander of the Department of Arizona and the California Column, is promoted to brigadier general. West had succeeded General Carleton as commander of the "Column" during the previous month. West, a veteran of the Mexican War, had been appointed lieutenant colonel early in the war.

October 26 (Sunday)   In Virginia, General McClellan's Army of the Potomac enters Virginia. Lincoln, annoyed at his lethargic pace, continues to push for a major offensive against the South. Lincoln is at least temporarily satisfied that McClellan has decided to take the offensive.

In Georgia, Union forces devastate the town of St. Mary's.

In Mississippi, General Grant initiates an assault upon Vicksburg. Contingents depart from both Bolivar and Corinth. Grant departs Jackson on the following day to take personal command of the operation.

In Naval activity, the USS *Clifton* and USS *Westfield* capture the city of Indianola, Texas.

In Union activity, Edmund Jackson Davis, who defected from the Confederacy in Texas during 1861 and formed the Union 1st Texas Cavalry, is appointed colonel. Colonel Davis establishes "political beachheads" in Mexico, opposite Brownsville, Texas, in Matamoros.

October 27 (Monday)   In Louisiana, a Union force commanded by Brigadier General Weitzel and composed of elements of the 8th New Hampshire Infantry, the 12th and 13th Connecticut Regiments, the 75th New York Volunteers, bolstered by the 1st Louisiana Cavalry and the 1st Maine Battery, clashes with Rebels led by Colonel McPheeters at Georgia Landing (Labadieville). The Union sustains 18 killed and 74 wounded. The Confederates sustain six killed, 15 wounded and about 208 captured.

In Missouri, elements of the 23rd Iowa, the 24th and 25th Missouri Volunteer Regiments, the 1st Missouri Militia and the 12th Missouri Cavalry, commanded by Colonel Lewis, engage Confederates at Putnam's Ferry. Casualty figures are unavailable; however, it is reported that about 40 Confederates are captured.

In Confederate general officer activity, Colonel Preston Smith, 154th Tennessee Regiment, is promoted to the rank of brigadier general. Brigadier General John Horace Forney, commissioned a brigadier general the previous March, is jumped up to major general this day; however, there is nothing in the record that explains the quick promotion. Subsequently, he participates in the defense of Vicksburg. Also, Colonel Preston Smith will command a brigade at Chickamauga (1863).

In Naval activity, the U.S. Navy acquires a stern-wheel steamer, the *New Era,* which had been built during 1862 and initially operated on the Ohio River. It is commissioned the following December. Acting Master Frank W.F. Flanner receives command of the ship. This *New Era* is separate from the steam ferry of the same name that had been transformed into an iron-clad river gunboat acquired by the U.S. Army during 1861 and renamed the USS *Essex.*

October 27–November 2 The march initiated by McClellan to move against the Confederates commences on the 26th after successful completion of the pontoon bridge at Berlin. By today, Lovettsville, Virginia, is congested with Union troops. On the 26th, two divisions of the 9th Corps cross together with a brigade of General Alfred Pleasonton's cavalry. Additional troops continue to flow across the Potomac from today until 2 November. As usual, McClellan is still plagued with extremely bad weather, hampering his intended offensive.

October 28 (Tuesday)   In Arkansas, a Union force of about 1,000 Cavalry troops (Army of the Frontier), commanded by Brigadier General Francis J. Herron, skirmishes with Confederate force commanded by Colonel Craven at Cross Hollows in a contest that lasts about one hour. The Union reports no casualties. The Confederates sustain eight wounded. Herron had been wounded and captured at Pea Ridge in March 1862.

In Kentucky, a contingent of the 7th Kentucky Volunteer Regiment skirmishes with Confederates at Williamsburg. Casualty figures are unavailable.

In Missouri, a contingent of the 2nd Illinois Artillery, commanded by Captain Rodgers, while en route to Clarkson clashes with Confederate guerrillas led by Colonel Clark. No Union casualties are reported. The Confederates sustain 12 killed and about 45 wounded.

In Naval activity, the blockade runner *Arizona* is seized by the USS *Montgomery* as it attempts to enter Mobile with a cargo of munitions and saltpeter. However, the *Arizona,* seized by the Confederacy during the previous January, is operating under the name *Caroline* (under provisional British registry) when it is captured. Subsequently, the *Arizona* is sold in Philadelphia during June 1863, and afterward, again named USS *Arizona,* the vessel is transferred to the West Gulf Blockading Squadron, the squadron which captured it.

October 29 (Wednesday)   In Missouri, a contingent of the 1st Kansas Colored Troops (79th U.S. Colored Troops), commanded by Colonel Seaman, skirmishes with Confederate guerrillas under Cockerill at Butler and at Osage. The Union sustains eight killed and 10 wounded. The Confederates suffer about 30 killed and wounded.

In Virginia, a Union contingent (reconnaissance force) led by Lt. Colonel Iswick skirmishes with Confederates in the vicinity of Pe-

tersburg. The Union reports no casualties. The Confederates lose about 16 captured. Also, Major Keenan leads a reconnaissance team from Purcellsville toward Aldie. Casualty reports are unavailable.

In Confederate general officer activity, Colonel Alfred Cumming is promoted to brigadier general. He is assigned to the forces under General Pemberton and participates in the defenses of Vicksburg.

October 30 (Thursday)   In South Carolina, Union General Ormsby MacKnight Mitchel (West Point, 1829), commander of the Department of the South and X Corps, dies at Beaufort from yellow fever. Mitchel has been in command of troops of the contingent of the Army of Ohio, which seized the Memphis and Charleston Railroad at Huntsville, Alabama, in April. He had only assumed command of the Department of the South in September.

In Virginia, a contingent of Union cavalry commanded by Colonel Wyndham skirmishes with Confederates at Thoroughfare Gap. Casualty figures are unavailable.

In Confederate general officer activity, Colonels William Stephen Walker and Joseph Wheeler are promoted to the rank of brigadier general. Walker continues serving in various sectors of South Carolina until April 1864, when he is transferred to North Carolina to assume command at Kinston. General Wheeler, chief of cavalry (Army of the Mississippi) since being appointed to the position in July, will continue in this position. Wheeler is promoted to major general in January 1863.

October 31 (Friday)   In Virginia, a Union contingent composed of elements of the 1st New Jersey Cavalry and 2nd New York Cavalry (General George D. Bayard's brigade) skirmishes with Confederate cavalry commanded by General Jeb Stuart at Aldie. In other activity, two batteries of Union artillery bombard Confederate positions in Franklin. Casualty figures are unavailable for either.

In Naval activity, the U.S. Navy acquires the *Romeo* (Gunboat No. 3). The wooden stern-wheel tinclad, after being commissioned on 11 December, is assigned to the Mississippi Squadron. Acting Ensign Robert B. Smith is appointed commanding officer.

In Union general officer activity, General Winfield Scott requests retirement, following more than fifty years in the service. General Scott dies while at West Point on 29 May 1866. He is interred at the academy in the Post Cemetery.

November 1 (Saturday)   In North Carolina, the Union Steamer USS *Northerner* and the gunboat USS *States of the North,* bolstered by a contingent of the 3rd New York Cavalry commanded by Major Garrard, moves along Pungo Creek. During the mission, about 25 Rebels are captured.

In Texas, the USS *Clifton* and the *Westfield* (gunboats) bombard Confederate-held Lavacca.

In Mississippi, the 5th Minnesota Volunteer Regiment remains in the state as part of the 2nd Brigade, 2nd Division, Army of the Mississippi; however, this month it will be transferred for duty with the 2nd Brigade, 8th Division, and participate as part of the left wing of the 13th Army Corps (old), Department of Tennessee, until the following month.

In Union general officer activity, Lt. Colonel Alfred Ellet is commissioned a brigadier general. Ellet had succeeded his brother Charles as commander of a ram fleet (Ellet's Marine Brigade).

In Virginia, Union General Alfred Pleasonton's cavalry (Army of the Potomac) skirmishes with Confederate General Jeb Stuart's cavalry at Philomont this day and the next. The Union sustains one killed and 14 wounded. The Confederates suffer three killed and 10 wounded.

In Confederate general officer activity, Colonel Jerome Bonaparte Robertson is promoted to the rank of brigadier general. His son Felix H. Robertson also becomes a brigadier general during 1864. The elder Robertson leads his Texas brigade at various battles in Virginia and Pennsylvania prior to serving in Tennessee. Lt. Colonel Young M. Moody, 43rd Alabama Regiment, is promoted to colonel and assigned command of the 43rd Regiment. Colonel James H. Lane, 24th North Carolina Regiment, is promoted to brigadier general effective this date. General Lane sustains three separate wounds during the conflict and participates in the service of the Army of Northern Virginia for the duration.

Colonel George Pierce Doles (4th Georgia) is promoted to brigadier general. Afterward, he participates at various actions, including Fredericksburg, Chancellorsville, the Wilderness, Spotsylvania and at Bethesda Church, the latter on 2 June 1864. Colonel George Thomas "Tige" Anderson is appointed brigadier general. Colonel Thomas Reade Rootes Cobb, the brother of Confederate General Howell Cobb, is also promoted to brigadier general effective this date. He will command a brigade at Fredericksburg in December. Confederate Colonel Montgomery D. Corse, 17th Virginia Infantry, is promoted to brigadier general. Corse, already widely known for his exploits in battle, receives command of General Pickett's old brigade in Pickett's division. In addition, Confederate Major Elisha Franklin Paxton is jumped to the rank of brigadier general, effective this date, thanks to the recommendation of his commanding officer, General Thomas J. Jackson. Paxton at this time is on Jackson's staff.

Major General John B. Hood has recently been assigned command of a division. In conjunction, General Jerome B. Robertson assumes command of Hunt's Texas Brigade, which is part of Hunt's new command. Brigadier General Evander McIvor Law's 4th Alabama will be part of Hood's force (Lt. General Longstreet's corps). Colonel Stephen Dodson Ramseur, 49th North Carolina Infantry Regiment, is promoted to the rank of brigadier general. He had been wounded during the Seven Days' Battle, and he will again sustain wounds at Chancellorsville (May 1863) and Spotsylvania (May 1864). After being elevated to the rank of major general during June of 1864, Ramseur will sustain yet a fourth wound at Cedar Creek (October 1864). Colonel Edward Lloyd Thomas is another promoted to brigadier general effective this date, as is Colonel John Rogers Cooke (27th North Carolina Infantry Regiment), the son of Union General Philip St. George Cooke. At the time of this promotion, Cooke has already sustained at least seven wounds. He remains in the field primarily in Virginia for the duration. After the war he engages in business in Richmond, Virginia, and becomes one of the founders of the Confederate Soldiers' Home there. General Cooke succumbs in Richmond on 10 April 1891.

John Brown Gordon, who entered the Confederacy as captain in a company known as the "Raccoon Roughs," is promoted to brigadier general. He had sustained a life threatening wound to his head at Sharpsburg (Antietam) in September. Subsequent to his promotion, he participates in the Wilderness campaign and accompanies General Jubal Early in the Shenandoah Valley. The rank of brigadier general is also assigned to Colonel Alfred Iverson (20th North Carolina), who participates at Chancellorsville and Gettysburg before being ordered to relieve General Henry R. Jackson, commanding state troops, at Rome, Georgia. In 1864 he commands a cavalry brigade in General William T. Martin's division (Wheeler's cavalry corps). General Iverson engages in business in Macon for a while after the war, but later he moves to Florida and operates as an orange grower. He dies in Atlanta, Georgia, on 31 March 1911. Also, Colonel Carnot Posey (16th Mississippi) is promoted to brigadier general.

November 2 (Sunday)   In Maryland, the 1st Maine Cavalry Regiment based at Frederick is relieved by fresh troops. The 1st Maine will be assigned in December to General Bayard's cavalry brigade at Falmouth, Virginia.

In Missouri, a Union reconnaissance force led by Colonel Joel Allen Dewey operates in the vicinity of Pittman's Ferry.

In Virginia, Union General McClellan's command, including the batteries of the Second Corps, Army of the Potomac, enter and occupy Snicker's Gap. The Confederates lose 10 men captured. In other activity, elements of the Union cavalry (Army of the Potomac) move toward Upperville. Meanwhile, other Union cavalry units move toward Bloomfield and Union. The Union sustains two killed and 10 wounded. The Confederates suffer three killed and 15 wounded (see also, **November 2–3**).

In Naval activity, the USS *Ossipee* (steam screw sloop) is commissioned at about this time. It sees some service in the Atlantic Ocean prior to being attached to the West Gulf Blockading Squadron during May of the following year. The *Ossipee* remains in the region for the duration. Subsequent to the close of hostilities it is attached to the Asiatic Squadron during 1866 and remains in the Far East until 1872. It is ac-

tive in the western Atlantic until 1884, then is again ordered back to the Pacific until 1887. The vessel is decommissioned during 1889 and sold in 1891. In other activity, a naval force that includes the USS *Hunchback* initiates a reconnaissance mission to Hamilton, North Carolina, that lasts through the 6th.

November 2–3   The Army of the Potomac has virtually completed crossing into Virginia. The 2nd Corps occupies Snicker's Gap. About 5,000 to 6,000 Confederates in the vicinity begin to initiate an assault to recapture the town, but after some sparse Union fire, they abort the attack. Snickersville is taken by the 5th Corps while the 6th Corps sets camp in the vicinity of Wheatland. General Pleasonton's cavalry pushes the Confederates out of Union, Virginia, as the 9th Corps advances to Bloomfield, Philomont and Union. The 1st Corps advances to Philomont on the 3rd, with the 2nd Corps advancing to Upperville, where Pleasonton's cavalry is pressed into action again to drive the Rebels away.

November 3 (Monday)   In Florida, Union contingents bombard Confederate-held Tampa.

In Louisiana, the Union gunboats USS *Calhoun, Diana, Estrella, Colonel Kinsman* and the *St. Mary,* bolstered with the 21st Indiana Volunteers, skirmish with Confederates bolstered by the CSS *J.A.* at Bayou Teche. The Union sustains one killed and three wounded, excluding casualties aboard the *Colonel Kinsman.* Confederate casualties are unavailable. The *Colonel Kinsman,* a sidewheel steamer, was seized by the Union when New Orleans fell in April; it was transformed into an army gunboat. In response to a request from General Benjamin F. Butler, Admiral David Porter supplied naval officers to command it and other army gunboats. Acting Volunteer Lieutenant George Wiggins had received command of the *Colonel Kinsman* the previous month. During this engagement, the *Colonel Kinsman* sustains more than fifty hits and suffers two killed and four wounded. The *Estrella* had been built in England during 1853 for use as a blockade runner; however, it was captured by the Union during 1862 and transferred from the U.S. Army to the U.S. Navy for use as a gunboat.

In North Carolina, elements of the 24th and 44th Massachusetts Regiments, 9th New Jersey Volunteers and artillery units from New Jersey and New York batteries skirmish with Confederates at Rawles' Mills. The Union sustains one killed. Confederate casualties are unavailable.

In Missouri, Confederate guerrillas led by Quantrill attack a Union escort force composed of detachments of the 5th and 6th Missouri Cavalry and led by Lt. Newby. The Union initially is beaten by the Rebels; however, following a second clash, the Union prevails. The Union re-

ports eight or ten killed and three or four wounded. The Confederate casualties are estimated at about six killed and 20 wounded.

In Naval activity, the USS *Penobscot,* on patrol near Shallotte Inlet, North Carolina, spots a British blockade runner called the *Pathfinder* and initiates pursuit. The *Pathfinder* runs aground. Afterward, the *Penobscot* destroys it. Also, at about this time (November), the U.S. Navy acquires the *Antietam,* a screw steam tugboat. It is commissioned the USS *Dandelion* the following month and assigned to the South Atlantic Blockading Squadron, where it remains on patrol duty off Florida, Georgia and South Carolina for the duration of the war.

November 4 (Tuesday)   In Mississippi, elements of General Grant's force occupy La Grange.

In Illinois, a contingent of U.S. Marines, composed of seventy-five enlisted men and three officers, occupies and garrisons the new naval station at Cairo.

In Virginia, Ashby's Gap is seized by the 2nd Corps, Army of the Potomac, while Union cavalry takes Piedmont.

In Confederate general officer activity, Captain William Robertson Boggs is appointed brigadier general in the Confederate Army. Boggs has recently been chief engineer for the

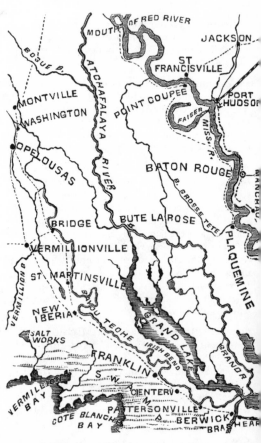

Bayou Teche (*Harper's Pictorial History of the Civil War,* 1896).

State of Georgia. He will transfer to the Trans-Mississippi Department with General Kirby Smith and become his chief of staff. Also, William G.M. Davis, a Virginian transplanted to Florida who had organized the Confederate 1st Florida Cavalry and was elected its colonel, is promoted to brigadier general. Davis also donated a large sum of money to the Confederate cause. His cavalry unit serves initially with the Department of Tennessee; however, he resigns his commission during May of the following year. Davis, also an attorney, spends most of his time during the war between Richmond, Virginia, and Wilmington, North Carolina, where he focuses on running the blockade between the United States and Nassau in the Bahamas.

Colonel Archibald Gracie, 43rd Alabama, is promoted to the rank of brigadier general, as is Colonel Evander McNair, effective this date. Colonel William George Mackey (1st Florida Cavalry), a lawyer and cotton speculator who raised his own cavalry regiment, is promoted brigadier general. He resigns his commission during May 1863. In the meantime, for a while he commands the Department of East Tennessee. Colonel James Edwards Rains is promoted to brigadier general. He is assigned to General John P. McCown's division (General Hardee's corps). Also, Thomas Hart Taylor, a veteran of the Mexican War (3rd Kentucky Infantry), named colonel of the 1st Kentucky Regiment in October 1861, is elevated to brigadier general. After the 1st Kentucky mustered out during the summer of 1862, Taylor transferred to East Tennessee in command of a brigade under General Kirby Smith. Nevertheless, General Taylor's nomination is not given to the Senate by President Jefferson Davis.

In Naval activity, the USS *Santiago de Cuba* arrives in Havana to join the West India Squadron under Commodore Charles Wilkes.

Commodore Charles Wilkes (Mottelay, *The Soldier in Our Civil War*, 1886).

At this time, Wilkes still only has four of the seven ships assigned to the squadron, and of those, none are fully capable of the tasks assigned them. Only two, the *Wachusett* and the *Santiago de Cuba,* have the capability of traveling faster than ten knots.

In other activity, the *Commodore McDonough,* a former ferryboat and acquired by the U.S. Navy, is commissioned at about this time (November) and assigned to the South Atlantic Blockading Squadron. The light draft gunboat departs for South Carolina to begin patrol duty along the coastal rivers as a blockade ship. After the surrender of Charleston, it joins other ships in the task of clearing obstacles from the harbor. In August it is towed north en route to New York; however, it founders on 23 August and is lost.

November 5 (Wednesday)   In Washington, D.C., Union General Ambrose E. Burnside is named as successor to General McClellan as head of the Army of the Potomac. Burnside reluctantly accepts the post. McClellan learns of this on the 7th. The impatience of Lincoln causes this change, and as the chain of events unfolds, it is clear the appointment of Burnside is a genuine military disaster.

In Kentucky, elements of the 8th Kentucky Cavalry, commanded by Major Halloway, skirmishes with Confederate guerrillas led by Colonel Fowler at Greenville Road. The Union reports no casualties. The estimated Confederate casualties are eight killed.

In Missouri, at Lamar, Confederate guerrillas under Quantrill engage and defeat a Union contingent composed of elements of the 8th Missouri Cavalry and the 8th Missouri Militia Cavalry. The guerrillas capture the town.

In Tennessee, at Nashville, a Union contingent—including the 16th and 51st Illinois, 69th Ohio, 14th Michigan and the 78th Pennsylvania Volunteer Regiments, bolstered by the 5th Tennessee Cavalry and the 7th Pennsylvania Cavalry—battles elements of a Confederate force of about 5,000 troops under Generals Nathan B. Forrest and John Hunt Morgan. The Union sustains 26 wounded. The Confederates lose about 23 captured. A contemporary report lists Union casualties at five killed and 19 wounded.

In Virginia, a brigade of the 9th Corps, Army of the Potomac, still under the command of McClellan, advances beyond the Manassas Railroad between Piedmont and Salem, and a skirmish between Confederate and Union cavalry (Averell's Union cavalry) develops at Manassas Gap. Also, a Union cavalry brigade (General Alfred Pleasonton's command) skirmishes with Confederate cavalry (General Stuart's command) at Barbee's Cross Roads and at Chester Gap. The Union sustains five killed and 10 wounded. The Confederates sustain 36 killed and some captured. Also, a cavalry brigade commanded by Colonel Perry Wyndham engages Confederate cavalry bolstered by artillery at New Baltimore, Salem and Thoroughfare

Gap. The Union occupies Salem. Casualty figures are unavailable.

In Confederate general officer activity, Colonels Dandridge McRae, 21st Arkansas Regiment, and James Camp Tappan, 13th Arkansas Regiment, are promoted to the rank of brigadier general effective this date. And General Mosby Monroe Parsons (Missouri State Guard) is appointed brigadier general in the Confederate Army. Parsons participates in various actions, including Elkhorn and the Red River Campaign in Louisiana. Tappan is assigned to duty in the Trans-Mississippi Department. The following spring, he commands a brigade in the command of General Sterling Price. Subsequently, Tappan will lead a division during the Red River Campaign.

In Confederate Naval activity, the *Thomas L. Wragg* (formerly *CSS Nashville* [I]) is commissioned as the privateer *Rattlesnake.* Also, Colonel Edwin Henry Stoughton, not yet 25 years old, is promoted to brigadier general following his leave of absence from July to November. He leads a brigade of Vermont regiments while posted along the outer perimeter of the capital defenses. In March 1863, he establishes headquarters at Fairfax Court House.

November 6 (Thursday)   In Kentucky, a Union force commanded by Captain Ambrose Powell skirmishes with Confederate guerrillas at Leatherwood, Kentucky. The Union reports no casualties. The Confederates lose about 7 killed. Also, elements of the 8th Kentucky Cavalry clash with Confederates at Garrettsburg. The Union reports no casualties. The Confederates sustain 17 killed and 85 wounded.

In Tennessee, Union Colonel Edward M. McCook's corps, following a two-day march, arrives at Edgefield en route to Nashville. In conjunction, General Sill's division reaches Nashville on the following day.

In Virginia, the Union 1st Corps moves to Warrenton, the 2nd to Rectortown, and the 5th to White Plains, while the 9th Corps is advancing to the Rappahannock in the vicinity of Waterloo. In addition, the Army of the Potomac has its other troops on the move. The 11th Corps extends from New Baltimore beyond Thoroughfare Gap to Hopewell's Gap. The Union cavalry attached to the Army of the Potomac also guards the rails and scouts for enemy contingents. On this day McClellan establishes his headquarters at Rectortown, which near Front Royal (Port Royal).

In Union general officer activity, General Charles Davis Jameson, who contracted camp fever after the battle of Seven Pines (Fair Oaks), dies on a steamboat en route to Bangor, Maine.

In Confederate general officer activity, promotions to lieutenant general are given to Generals Thomas J. "Stonewall" Jackson (effective 10 October) and James Longstreet (9 October). General Robert E. Lee's army is broken into two corps, four divisions each. Lee had become commanding officer of the Army of Northern

Virginia after General Joseph E. Johnston was injured in May at Seven Pines. Colonel Stephen Dill Lee (West Point, 1854) is promoted to brigadier general.

November 7 (Friday) **In Arkansas,** elements of the 3rd Indiana Home Guards clash with Confederates at Rheas Mills. Casualty figures are unavailable. Meanwhile, contingents of the 3rd and 4th Iowa and the 9th Illinois Cavalry, commanded by Captain Perkins, skirmish with Confederates at Mariana. The Union sustains three killed and 20 wounded. The Confederates suffer about 50 killed and wounded.

In Missouri, a Union contingent, composed of two companies of the 10th Illinois Regiment and two companies of Missouri Militia, commanded by Captain Barstow, clashes with Confederates led by Colonel Green at Big River Creek in a contest that lasts about five hours. The Confederates capture about 300 troops.

In Tennessee, Union forces under General Sill (vanguard of Rosecrans' force) arrive in Nashville and apparently in timely fashion, as Confederates under Generals Forrest and John H. Morgan have recently been raiding Union lines around Nashville. Upon the arrival of the reinforcements, the Rebels, numbering about 3,200 troops, retire in a southward direction. Forrest and Morgan's Cavalry are respectively operating as the left and right wing of Bragg's force.

In Virginia, Union General Pleasonton is directed to move his cavalry towards Washington and Sperryville and from there to Culpeper Court House. General McClellan is informed he is to be relieved of command and replaced by General Burnside. The directive further states that General Hunter is to assume command of the corps vacated by Burnside. President Lincoln also replaces General Fitz John Porter with General Hooker. Union General McClellan is officially fired by President Lincoln. The presidential order relieving McClellan of command is handed to him at 11:30 P.M. by General Burnside and Colonel Buckingham. McClellan, who is given no reason for his loss of command, notes: "They have made a great mistake. Alas for my poor country! I know in my heart she never had a truer servant." McClellan states in his farewell to his officers and men: "In you I have never found doubt or coldness. The battles you have fought under my command will proudly live in our country's history … we shall ever be comrades in supporting the Constitution of our country and the nationality of its people." McClellan, instructed to report to his home in Trenton, New Jersey, to await further orders, has a long wait. No orders are forthcoming. He is elected governor of New Jersey in 1878.

In other activity, Union Colonel Elias S. Dennis is appointed brigadier general (29th). Also, Confederate Colonel John Pegram is promoted to the rank of brigadier general effective this day.

In Naval activity, the USS *Potomska* provides an escort for an army transport, the *Darlington,* as it moves along the Sapelo River in Georgia.

November 8 (Saturday) **In Mississippi,** the Confederates, commanded by General John C. Pemberton, are entrenched at Tallahatchie, but the Confederates holding Holly Springs evacuate the town. Also, a Union reconnaissance contingent, composed of elements of the 7th Kansas Cavalry and the 2nd Iowa Cavalry, commanded by Colonel Albert Lee, while operating near Hudsonville, engage Confederates. The Union casualty figures are unreported. The Confederates sustain about 16 killed and 175 to 185 captured.

In Tennessee, Union General Nathaniel Banks replaces General Benjamin Butler as commander of the Department of the Gulf Army. Grant's Army, consisting of 30,000 men, occupies Grand Junction and LaGrange. Sherman is deployed on his right at Memphis, James B. McPherson (West Point, 1853) is on his left, and C S. Hamilton (West Point, 1843) is in the center.

In Virginia, elements of General Bayard's brigade (Army of the Potomac) skirmish with Confederates at Rappahannock Bridge. The Confederates lose about 13 captured.

In Confederate general officer activity, Brigadier General John George Walker is promoted to major general.

November 9 (Sunday) **In Louisiana,** Confederate General John Villepique (West Point, 1854), who previously served with the 2nd Dragoons in such places as Kansas, Nebraska, and Utah while in the U.S. Army and later was the commanding officer of Fort Pillow, dies of fever while in Port Hudson. Villepique ordered the Confederate defenses at Fort Pillow, Tennessee, to be blown up after he received orders to evacuate.

In Missouri, Union and Confederate contingents skirmish at Bastin Mountain. Specific units and casualty figures are unreported. Also, the 14th Kentucky Cavalry, commanded by Union Captain Morgan, skirmishes with Confederates while operating within Perry County. The Union reports no casualties. The Confederates sustain three killed.

In Virginia, General Burnside's troops score some early successes against the Confederates, as the stage is set for the upcoming battle at Fredericksburg, which commences on 11 December. Lincoln's directive to promote Burnside soon proves foolhardy, because Lee wins overwhelmingly over Burnside at Fredericksburg. The 1st Indiana Cavalry, commanded by Captain Dahlgren on a reconnaissance mission, clashes with Confederates near Fredericksburg. The Union sustains one killed and three missing. The Confederates suffer three killed and 39 captured. Meanwhile, a Union contingent composed of elements of the 1st New York Mounted Rifles (7th New York Cavalry), Ringgold's cavalry, the Washington Cavalry and the 23rd Illinois Volunteer Infantry Regiment, commanded by General Benjamin F. Kelley, skirmishes with Confederates at Moorefield. The Union sustains four wounded. The Con-

federates suffer 50 captured. Confederate casualty figures are unavailable.

In Naval activity, the Union gunboat USS *Mohawk* bombards Confederate-held St. Mary's, Florida. The USS *Hartford*, having been at Pensacola for repairs, arrives back at New Orleans. Meanwhile, Admiral Farragut intends to join the operations against Vicksburg, which at this time is becoming the objective of the Union Army. Farragut's fleet is to blockade the mouth of the Red River to cut off supplies for the Confederate Army. The Confederates anticipate a Union move against Port Hudson, Louisiana, and continue to fortify it.

November 10 (Monday) General Robert E. Lee is at Culpeper, Virginia, with Lt. General James Longstreet. Lee initiates troop movements to deploy for the anticipated battle. Lee is acutely aware Burnside's force exceeds 100,000, excluding some 100,000 support troops guarding Washington. Lee is also concerned about a Union supply depot at Acquia Creek capable of transporting Union troops toward either the James River or North Carolina. In other activity, Union cavalry led by Lt. Ash skirmishes with Confederate cavalry at Warrenton. Seven Confederates are captured. Meanwhile, other Union troops under Captain Gillmore initiate a reconnaissance mission that leads them through Greenbrier County.

In Tennessee, General Rosecrans arrives at Nashville. He begins to build up his supplies and initiates intensive drilling of the troops to prepare for an offensive against Confederate General Bragg. However, the Confederate cavalry reactivates its attacks and mounts repeated raids against the rail lines to harass the repair operations and disrupt communications.

In Kentucky, a Union reconnaissance force operates in the northwestern sector of the state.

In Union general officer activity, General Lewis Golding Arnold, who had previously commanded the Department of Florida until transferred to New Orleans during autumn, suffers a severe stroke. It is not fatal; however, he is unable to resume duty. He remains on the sick leave until he is retired during February of 1864. He succumbs on 22 September 1864. Also, Lt. Colonel George Leonard Andrews, 2nd Massachusetts Regiment, is appointed brigadier general of volunteers. Andrews will participated at Cedar Mountain and Antietam, and later he became chief of staff to General Nathaniel P. Banks.

November 11 (Tuesday) **In North Carolina,** Union pickets skirmish with Confederates at New Bern (Bachelor's Creek). Specific units are unreported. Casualty figures are unavailable.

In Tennessee, a contingent of Tennessee Home Guards, commanded by Captain Duncan, skirmishes with Confederates at Huntsville. Meanwhile, another Union contingent, composed of elements of the 1st Kentucky Cavalry and the 4th Michigan Cavalry, commanded by Captains Kennett and Wolford, skirmishes with Confederate cavalry (General John Hunt Morgan's command) at Lebanon. Union casualties, if any, are unreported. The estimated Confederate casualties are seven killed and 125 captured.

November 12 (Wednesday)   In Mississippi, General Grant receives word from Halleck that Grant is in charge of all troops sent his department and to fight as he pleased. This dispels a rumor that Generals Grant and McPherson are to have separate commands. In other activity, a Union contingent of cavalry, composed of elements of the 2nd Illinois, 3rd Michigan, 2nd Iowa and 7th Kansas Regiments, commanded by Major Mudd, skirmishes with Confederate cavalry, including the 1st (later 7th) Tennessee, commanded by Colonel William Hicks Jackson, at Lamar and Holly Springs. The Union reports no casualties. The estimated Confederate casualties are four wounded.

November 13 (Thursday)   In Kentucky, a Union contingent commanded by Colonel Shanks attacks a Confederate guerrilla encampment at Calhoun. Casualty figures are unavailable.

In Mississippi, U.S. Grant's cavalry enters Holly Springs, forcing the Confederates to pull out and head south of Tallahatchie.

November 13–15   In Tennessee, there are various troop movements by both sides. Bragg's Confederates leave Chattanooga, attempting to reinforce Breckinridge at Murfreesboro. Grant requests a meeting with Sherman at Columbus, Kentucky, and instructs him to bring two divisions. Sherman arrives on the 29th with three divisions, which are soon dispatched to destroy the Mississippi and Central railroads. The action is successful but no permanent damage is inflicted.

In Virginia, the Army of the Potomac under Burnside moves from Warrenton on the 15th toward Fredericksburg.

November 14 (Friday)   In Virginia, Union General Burnside reorganizes the Army of the Potomac.

In Union general officer activity, Andrew Jackson Hamilton, a Texan who remained loyal to the Union, is appointed brigadier general by President Lincoln, effective this day. Hamilton, a former Congressman, earlier this year had been called a traitor by fellow Texans and was compelled to flee to Mexico before making his way to Washington. Lincoln also appoints Hamilton as the governor of Texas. Nonetheless, Hamilton spends most of his time for the duration of the war in New Orleans.

November 15 (Saturday)   The Union Army of the Potomac is reorganized into three divisions by General Burnside after he succeeds General George McClellan as commander. The Right Grand Division is commanded by General Edwin V. Sumner and composed of Generals Darius N. Couch's Second Corps (formerly Sumner's corps) and General Willcox's Ninth Corps (formerly Burnside's corps). The Left Grand Division, commanded by General

William B. Franklin, is composed of General John F. Reynolds' First Corps (formerly Hooker's corps) and General W.F. Smith's Sixth Corps (formerly Franklin's corps). The Center Grand Division, commanded by General Joseph Hooker, comprises General George Stoneman's Third Corps (received from the Washington Garrison) and General Daniel Butterfield's Fifth Corps (formerly Fitz John Porter's corps). The 11th Corps, commanded by General Franz Sigel, is held as a reserve force. Sumner's force departs Warrenton this day and arrives at Falmouth, Virginia, on the 17th. Each of the other three divisions also begins to move out toward the latter part of the day.

In other activity, John Baillie McIntosh is appointed colonel (later brevet major general) of the 3rd Pennsylvania Cavalry. Colonel McIntosh, a veteran of the Mexican War who served as a midshipman on the USS *Saratoga*, initially entered the army with a commission as second lieutenant of the 2nd U.S. Cavalry. He joined with the Union just after his brother, Confederate Brigadier General James McIntosh, joined the Confederacy. The McIntosh brothers' great uncle was General Lachlan McIntosh of the American Revolutionary War who killed Button Gwinnett (signer of the Declaration of Independence) following a long feud that culminated soon after Gwinnett had Lachlan's brother, a Loyalist, arrested.

In Confederate general officer activity, Colonel John S. Marmaduke (West Point, 1857) is promoted to the rank of brigadier general, effective this date. General Marmaduke resigned his commission in the U.S. Army during 1861 and became a colonel in the Missouri militia, prior to becoming colonel of the 1st Arkansas Battalion and then colonel of the 3rd Confederate Infantry.

November 16 (Sunday)   In Tennessee, the vanguard of Union General Sill's brigade skirmishes with Confederate cavalry at Nashville. Casualty figures are unavailable.

In West Virginia, the 1st and 2nd Brigade (Sturgis' Division), the 9th Corps and some cavalry, commanded by General Sturgis, engages Confederates at Fayetteville and White Sulphur Springs (Little Washington). The Union sustains one killed and three wounded. Confederate casualty figures are unavailable.

November 17 (Monday)   In Virginia, General Burnside, his Army at 120,000, reaches Stafford Heights on the north bank of the Rappahannock, across from Fredericksburg. General Lee's Confederates arrive later and occupy the high ground before the Yankees can cross the river. The Union Army had been in the vicinity of Warrenton. The Yankees occupy the hills opposite Fredericksburg on the 20th and prepare to assault the town. Lee states in a telegram to Jefferson Davis: "I think Burnside is concentrating his whole army opposite Fredericksburg." Lee's intent is to force battle at Fredericksburg, but not for Fredericksburg, in order to preserve the culture and beauty of the picturesque town.

Elements of the 104th Pennsylvania Volunteer Regiment skirmish with Confederate cavalry at Gloucester. The Union sustains one killed and three wounded. The Confederates lose one captured. Confederate casualty figures, if any, are unavailable.

November 18 (Tuesday)   In North Carolina, a contingent of the 3rd New York Cavalry led by Lt. Colonel Simon Mix engages a Confederate force at Cove Creek.

In Tennessee, the 8th Kentucky Cavalry, commanded by Colonel Hawkins, skirmishes with Confederates at Rural Hills. The Union reports no casualties. The estimated Confederate casualties are about 16 killed.

In Virginia, a contingent of the Army of the Potomac, commanded by General Sumner, occupies Falmouth on the 17th and 18th.

In Confederate general officer activity, Colonel John Austin Wharton, 8th Texas Cavalry (Terry's Texas Rangers), is promoted to the rank of brigadier general effective this date.

In Naval activity, the U.S. Navy acquires the *Cricket*, a stern-wheel steamer built in Pittsburgh, Pennsylvania. It was purchased at Cairo, Illinois, and on 19 January 1863, it is commissioned the USS *Cricket*.

November 19 (Wednesday)   In Kentucky, the Harlan County State Guards skirmish with Confederate guerrillas at Wallen's Creek. Casualty figures are unavailable.

In Virginia, the Union and Confederate armies are making preparations for an imminent confrontation at Fredericksburg. Lee, having received intelligence that Union General Sumner's division of more than 30,000 troops are on the march toward Fredericksburg, dispatches two divisions from Culpeper to beat Sumner to the river and establish defenses. Confederate forces reach the Rappahannock at about 1500, but by then Union troops had already arrived and the Confederates observe the Union encamped at Stafford Heights overlooking Fredericksburg from the north side of the river. In other activity, elements of the New York Mounted Rifles, commanded by Colonel Dodge, attack Confederate positions at Blackwater. Casualty figures are unavailable.

In Union general officer activity, Brigadier General George Lucas Hartsuff is promoted to major general. General Hartsuff, previously wounded twice, receives command of the XXIII Corps.

November 20 (Thursday)   In Virginia, Confederate cavalry attacks Union pickets at Bull Run (Manassas). The Confederates capture three Union troops. In other activity, Confederate cavalry units occupy Warrenton, which had been abandoned by the Union on the 17th, and they also occupy Leesburg.

In Arkansas, a Union reconnaissance contingent operates in the vicinity of Van Buren and Fort Smith through the 23rd.

In Naval activity, the USS *Seneca* seizes a blockade runner, the *Annie Dees,* off Charleston, South Carolina. The U.S. Navy acquires the vessel on 9 December 1863. It is renamed the *Thunder* and assigned to the South Atlantic Blockading Squadron with duty as a tender ship. It is sold at Port Royal on 8 August 1865.

November 21 (Friday)   In Louisiana, a contingent of the 31st Massachusetts Regiment, commanded by Captain Darling, skirmishes with Confederates led by Captain Evans at Bayou Bontouca. The Union reports one wounded. The Confederates sustain four killed.

In Virginia, Union major general Edwin V. Sumner, whose troops had occupied Falmouth on the 17th, gives the citizens of Fredericksburg the option of surrender or evacuation. In a severe winter storm, the older citizens, women and children, take what they can carry and flee the city, but the weather prompts Burnside to delay action. The city is not burned. The Union remains on the north bank of the Rappahannock awaiting transportation to cross the river. In the meantime, the Confederates continue to bolster the defenses. By the end of the month, about 80,000 Rebels, split into two separate corps commanded by Lt. Generals Thomas J. "Stonewall" Jackson and James Longstreet, are deployed in a half-moon position around the town. Jackson's corps consists of the divisions of Generals A.P. Hill, D.H. Hill, R.S. Ewell and William B. Taliaferro. Longstreet's corps is composed of the divisions of Generals Lafayette McLaws, M.W. Ransom, R.H. Anderson, George E. Pickett and S.A.M. Wood. In other activity, Confederate forces occupy Salem.

In Union general officer activity, Captain Benjamin Franklin Potts (later brigadier general) is promoted to lieutenant colonel of the 32nd New York in conjunction with reorganization of the regiment. During the following month, on the 28th, he is appointed colonel of the regiment. He leads the regiment during the Vicksburg campaign. Afterward Colonel Potter participates, primarily as a brigade commander, in the Atlanta campaign, including the "March to the Sea."

November 22 (Saturday)   In Virginia, on this day, Union Brigadier General Francis E. Patterson is killed when his own pistol accidentally discharges. General Patterson had command of a brigade in General Hooker's division at Williamsburg and Seven Pines earlier in the year, and most recently his duties include responsibility for the Orange and Alexandria Railroad around Catlett's Station. He had made an untimely and premature withdrawal from his position, thinking a large Confederate force was approaching his area. This presumption was false, as there was no large concentration of Rebel forces at Warrenton. The matter is taken under investigation at the time of his death. Patterson is the brother-in-law of Union General Abercrombie and also son of American General Robert Patterson.

In other activity, a contingent of the 1st New York Cavalry Regiment, commanded by Captain Harkins, skirmishes with Confederates at Winchester. The Union reports no casualties. The estimated Confederate casualties are four killed. At this time, Confederate General A.P. Hill, whose encampments have been in and around Winchester for about eight weeks, is moving from the vicinity of Winchester en route to Fredericksburg. The forced march carries them about 175 miles in less than two weeks; they arrive in early December.

November 23 (Sunday)   In Arkansas, a Union reconnaissance detachment operating in the vicinity of Fort Smith and Van Buren (20th–23rd) returns to its positions at Fort Babcock. No casualty figures are available.

November 24 (Monday)   In Missouri, a 50-man contingent of the 3rd Missouri Cavalry and the 21st Iowa Volunteer Regiment is attacked by Confederate guerrillas while it guards a supply train in the vicinity of Beaver Creek. The Union sustains five killed and 12 wounded. The Confederates sustain about five killed and 11 wounded. At Greenfield, Union forces initiate an expedition into Jasper and Barton Counties through the 26th.

In Confederate general officer activity, General Joseph E. Johnston is appointed commander of the Confederate Army of the West.

In Naval activity, the *Blackhawk,* a tinclad river gunboat built in 1859 as a steamship for civilian use under the name *Uncle Sam* (later *Blackhawk*), is acquired by the U.S. Navy. It is commissioned early the next month. The USS *Ellis,* while on a mission to Jacksonville, North Carolina, had succeeded in capturing two vessels, but while returning to base, it becomes grounded. The commanding officer, Lt. W.B. Cushing, attempts to free it, but in vain. During the night, Cushing transfers the crew except for a small contingent and most of the equipment and supplies to one of the seized schooners. The schooners move down river while Cushing remains aboard the *Ellis.* Meanwhile, the Confederates prepare to attack.

On the following morning, the Confederates commence fire and Cushing decides not to surrender. He sets the *Ellis* ablaze in five separate places, but keeps the one gun poised to fire after it is detonated by the flames. Meanwhile, Cushing and his small detachment abandon the ship and safely reach the schooners. The *Ellis* is destroyed (25th) when the fire spreads to the magazine. The Confederates also attempt to cut off escape by sending cavalry to intercept the schooners at the mouth of the New River Inlet, but without success. Also, the USS *Reliance* seizes the longboat *New Moon* and confiscates its cargo.

November 25 (Tuesday)   In Arkansas, a contingent of the 3rd Kansas Indian Home Guard skirmishes with Confederates in the vicinity of Camp Babcock. Skirmishes also occur at Pittman's Ferry and Cane Hill. In other activity, a Union expedition is initiated that moves

to Yellville. The mission continues until the 29th.

In Missouri, a contingent of the Missouri Enrolled Militia, commanded by Captain Reeves, skirmishes with Confederates in Crawford County. The Union reports no casualties. The Confederates sustain two killed.

In Tennessee, Confederate cavalry seizes Henderson.

In Virginia, a contingent composed of New York Mounted Rifles led by Colonel Dodge engages Confederates (two artillery batteries) at Zuni. The Union sustains one wounded. No casualty figures for the Confederates are available.

Confederate General McLaws arrives at Fredericksburg during the period the Confederates are fortifying the city against a Union assault. General McLaws notes that upon orders of General Longstreet, he directed one of his brigades to occupy the city. He sends out pickets that patrol from the Falmouth dam to slightly below Deep Run Creek, essentially patrolling directly opposite Union patrols on the northern bank of the Rappahannock River. McLaws' troops stationed in the city initiate a construction project. They begin to dig rifle pits along the river bank across from Stratton Heights and simultaneously, they are given use of the basements of the houses in the city for the deployment of riflemen. However, the river defenses do not include artillery. The Confederates, aware of the Union artillery in the heights across the river, realize Union fire would quickly knock their cannon out of action. The entire operation progresses only from dusk to dawn, preventing the Union from detecting the operation.

November 26 (Wednesday)   In Arkansas, a Union force commanded by Brigadier General Cadwallader C. Washburn departs Helena on an expedition into Mississippi.

In Kansas, Brigadier General James G. Blount assumes command of the District of Kansas.

In Mississippi, the 7th Illinois Cavalry attacks a Confederate encampment at Summerville. The Union seizes 28 Confederates. In other activity, the Union evacuates Rienzi.

In Tennessee, the 5th Brigade (General Sill's Division), commanded by Colonel Joseph B. Dodge, skirmishes with Confederate cavalry (Bragg's command) led by Brigadier General Joseph Wheeler at Scrougesville.

In Virginia, Union Major William H. Powell, 2nd West Virginia Cavalry, leads a detachment of 20 men who succeed in capturing Sinking Creek and its 500 defenders without suffering any Union casualties. Also, a contingent of the 2nd West Virginia Cavalry, led by Colonel Paxton, clashes with Confederate cavalry at Cold Knob Mountain. The Union seizes 100 Confederate troops.

At about this time, General Lee concludes that Fredericksburg will be the scene of the confrontation. The Confederates inform the residents either this day or the 27th that they should evacuate the city. At about the same time, General Lee arrives in Fredericksburg from Culpeper.

In West Virginia, a Union reconnaissance force, led by General John W. Geary, departs Harpers Ferry moving towards Berryville, Virginia.

In Missouri, activity between the Union and Confederates ensues in Jackson and Lafayette Counties through the 29th.

November 27 (Thursday) In Missouri, elements of the 2nd Cavalry skirmish with Confederates at Carthage. Casualty figures are unavailable.

In Tennessee, Union forces under Colonel Edward N. Kirk (promoted to brigadier general effective 29 November) push a contingent of Brigadier General Joseph Wheeler's cavalry out of Lavergne. Also, other Union troops under General Sheridan compel Confederates (General John A. Wharton's command) to relinquish control of Nolensville.

In Virginia, General Robert E. Lee corresponds with General Thomas "Stonewall" Jackson, informing him of the large Union buildup at Acquia. Lee states his troops have located four war steamers, seven gunboats and other vessels, including fifteen vessels under sail, and in addition, tugboats guiding barges laden with Union supplies. Lee also informs Jackson that a contingent of Union cavalry had been spotted at Brentsville. Just after the arrival of Lee, the remainder of his forces arrive. General Jackson is directed to move from the Blue Ridge. Upon his arrival, Jackson informs Lee that it would be more advantageous to engage from behind the North Anna to permit pursuit, which could not be accomplished at the Rappahannock; however, Lee is not persuaded. Jackson predicts victory, but without the ability to pursue, it would be fruitless.

Meanwhile, in addition to the naval buildup, the Yankees are preparing the rails to transport troops. Nonetheless, Lee, aware of the magni-

tude of the threat, seems confident. He writes to Confederate President Davis stating that his army is in good health and prepared to give a good fight. He also informs Davis of the lack of flour and meat.

As the various Confederate forces arrive, the deployments are established, primarily upon a series of three hills near the river: Taylor's Hill (Anderson's division), then southward at Marye's Hill (Randsom's and McLaws' divisions), and Telegraph Hill (Pickett's division), the tallest of the trio. Telegraph Hill becomes known also as Lee's Hill due to it being where he posts himself for the greater part of the battle. In addition, others are deployed along Deep Run Creek (Hood's division), and at Hamilton's Crossing, about 30,000 troops under General Thomas J. "Stonewall" Jackson are deployed upon a small unnamed hill. The units at Jackson's positions are the divisions of A.P. Hill, Jubal Early and William B. Taliaferro. In addition, D.H. Hill's division is held in reserve.

The responsibility for giving the signal to start the Union attack is handed to the Washington Artillery posted on Marye's Hill. At the time of the attack, Lee's Confederates stand at about 65,000 troops, while the Union Army at Stafford Heights stands at more than 115,000 men.

In Union general officer activity, Colonel Nelson Grosvenor Williams (3rd Iowa), severely injured at the Battle of Shiloh, resigns his commission. However, Colonel Williams, prior to his poor health, had applied for promotion. Two days following his resignation, his promotion comes through on 29 November. Nevertheless, General Williams is out of the army. The Senate declines the appointment on 9 March 1863.

In Arkansas at Helena, a Union expeditionary force initiates a mission that operates between Helena and Grenada, Mississippi, through December 5.

November 28 (Friday) In Alabama, a contingent of the 2nd Division, Sixteenth Corps, engages Confederates at Little Bear Creek. Casualty figures are unavailable.

In Arkansas, a large Union force, commanded by General James Blunt, assaults Confederate lines at Cane Hill, Boston Mountains and Boonesboro. The Yankee force, composed of 5,000 men, scores a decisive blow against Confederate General John Marmaduke, forcing the Rebels to withdraw to the Boston Mountains. The Union sustains four killed and 36 wounded. The Confederates sustain about 75 killed and 300 wounded. General Blunt had scored a victory against Confederate General Douglas Cooper at Old Fort Wayne the previous October.

In Mississippi, the 1st Indiana Cavalry skirmishes with Confed-

erates at Cold Water River. Casualty figures are unavailable.

In Virginia, Union gunboats arrive at Port Royal during the night. General Robert E. Lee anticipates the gunboats being able to make passage to the Rappahannock River, but also believes the Union troops will not attempt to cross the river in front of Fredericksburg, choosing instead a site below the city, if a crossing is indeed to be made. In other activity, a contingent of the 3rd Pennsylvania Cavalry (pickets) skirmishes with Confederate cavalry at Hartwood Church. The Union sustains four killed and 9 wounded. Confederate casualties are unavailable.

In Union general officer activity, Brigadier General Washington L. Elliott receives temporary command of the Department of the Northwest. Subsequently, he participates at Chancellorsville and at Gettysburg, prior to becoming commander of the 1st Cavalry Division, Army of the Cumberland.

In Naval activity, the USS *Arletta,* having been on duty on the James River since the latter part of July, is reassigned to the North Atlantic Blockading Squadron. It arrives at Fort Monroe on 2 December.

November 29 (Saturday) In Maryland, a contingent of the Maryland Home Guards, commanded by Captain Mears, skirmishes with Confederate cavalry at Berlin.

In Mississippi, a Union cavalry force, the vanguard of General Grant's army, skirmishes (29th–30th) with Confederates at Waterford and Lumkin's Mills. The Union reports no casualties. The Confederates sustain six killed.

In Union general officer activity, Egbert Benson Brown, a brigadier general of the Missouri State Militia, is appointed brigadier general, U.S. Volunteers. He performs admirably in various skirmishes, including the defense of Springfield, Missouri, during January 7–8, 1863. He also opposes Sterling Price in autumn 1864. While commanding a contingent of cavalry in the skirmish at Westport on October 23, 1864, he is relieved of command and placed under arrest by General Pleasonton for disobeying orders to attack. No charges are filed. Charles Thomas Campbell, colonel of the 1st Pennsylvania Artillery, is also appointed brigadier general. Campbell was wounded three times during the Peninsular Campaign while serving with Kearny's III Corps and will be severely wounded again at Fredericksburg in December 1862. In addition, Lieutenant Colonel William Dwight (West Point attendance) is appointed brigadier general. He was seriously wounded at Williamsburg, Virginia, during June and left on the field for dead.

Colonel Charles K. Graham is also promoted to brigadier general today, along with Colonel James A. Hardie (West Point, 1843). Another Union officer promoted to brigadier general this day is Colonel Frank Wheaton, who is married to the daughter of Confederate General Samuel Cooper. General Wheaton is assigned to the VI

Confederates under Generals Wheeler and Wharton during a fighting withdrawal (Mottelay, *The Soldier in Our Civil War*, 1886).

Corps and serves gallantly from Fredericksburg until the fall of Petersburg. He afterward receives the brevets of major general in the Regular Army and in the volunteers. During 1866, he musters out of the volunteers and becomes lieutenant colonel of the 39th U.S. Infantry and colonel of the 2nd Infantry. He is promoted to major general during 1897 and dies in 1903. He is interred in Arlington National Cemetery. Also, Colonel Thomas Welsh is promoted to brigadier general. General Welsh repairs to Ohio to serve under General Ambrose Burnside, but his commission expires due to inaction of the Senate. He is re-commissioned in March.

Major Albert Lindley Lee, 7th Kansas Cavalry, is promoted to brigadier general during April of the following year, but his rank is retroactive to this day. Colonel Charles A. Heckman (promoted to colonel on 10 February 1862) is commissioned as a brigadier general. He serves with the Army of the James and assumes responsibility for the defenses of Norfolk and Portsmouth during the winter of 1863–1864. Colonel Daniel E. Sickles, Colonel James Barnes (18th Massachusetts), a graduate of West Point (1829), and Colonel Alfred T.A. Torbert (Volunteers) are promoted to brigadier general. General Torbert has been in command of infantry troops since he entered the service during 1861; however, during the campaign to seize Richmond, General Torbert, along with General David McMurtrie Gregg (also promoted to brigadier general effective this day), are assigned command of cavalry divisions under General Philip Sheridan in April 1864.

Other promotions include Colonel Nathaniel C. McLean, brigadier general; Brigadier General William Henry French, major general; Colonel David A. Russell, 7th Massachusetts Infantry, brigadier general; and Colonel Hugh B. Ewing, 30th Ohio Volunteers, brigadier general. Ewing attended West Point but dropped out just prior to graduation in 1848. He is the brother of Generals Charles and Thomas Ewing and the foster brother of William T. Sherman. Colonel John Beatty (3rd Ohio), Colonel Samuel Beatty (19th Ohio), and Robert Christie Buchanan are appointed brigadier general. Buchanan's commission expires on 4 March 1863. Afterward, he assumes command of Fort Delaware, followed by becoming colonel of the 1st U.S. Infantry. At the end of the war he is breveted brigadier and major general. Others named brigadier general are Colonel Stephen Gardner Champlin and Colonel Joseph Tarr Copeland, 5th Michigan Cavalry. Copeland receives command of a Michigan cavalry brigade. Just before the Battle of Gettysburg, General Copeland's brigade is turned over to General George Custer. Just after Gettysburg, Copeland receives command of the depot for drafted men at Annapolis. Later he commands a similar post at Pittsburgh, and he then is transferred to Illinois where he commands the military prison and post at Alton. He resigns from the service on 8 November 1865.

Colonel Marcellus Monroe Crocker (13th Iowa) is appointed brigadier general effective this date. He was in the Battle of Corinth, and after his promotion, he joins the Vicksburg campaign. Later, Crocker, suffering from tuberculosis, is relieved while he is en route to join with General Sherman in Georgia during May 1864. He offers his resignation the following June; however, it is declined. Instead he is ordered to New Mexico for his health. He recuperates but never returns to the field. He dies in Washington, D.C., on 26 August 1865.

Colonel Lysander Cutler (6th Wisconsin), Colonel Elias Smith Dennis (30th Illinois) and Colonel Edward N. Kirk are brigadier generals effective this date. Subsequent to the Vicksburg Campaign, General Dennis is transferred to New Orleans. Toward the end of the war, he receives the brevet rank of major general due to his actions during the campaign against Mobile. Afterward, General Dennis is temporarily placed in command (military governor) at Shreveport. He leaves the service during August 1865. Colonel John Franklin Farnsworth, commanding officer of the 8th Illinois Regiment and the uncle of General Elon Farnsworth, is promoted to brigadier general, effective this day. General Farnsworth, a former Congressman, participates in the Battle of Fredericksburg in December; however, the next March he resigns his commission to return to Congress. Brigadier General John F. Reynolds is promoted to major general effective this day. Colonel Theophilus Garrard is promoted to brigadier general. He is ordered to Arkansas to report to General Benjamin Prentiss' headquarters at Helena. Colonel Charles Kinnard Graham, a midshipman during the Mexican War, is appointed brigadier general. Brigadier General Winfield Scott Hancock, subsequent to the death of General Israel Richardson at Antietam, assumed command of the 1st Division, II Corps. He is promoted to major general effective this day. John Smith Phelps, who served in Congress for eighteen years and raised a regiment that participated at the Battle of Pea Ridge (Elk Horn Tavern) the previous year, is appointed brigadier general by President Lincoln, effective 19 July. President Lincoln had also appointed Phelps as military governor of Arkansas during July. Nonetheless, the Senate takes no action. General Phelps' commission expires on 4 March 1863. He returns to his law practice in Missouri and later is elected governor of Missouri. He dies on 20 November 1886.

Colonel John Eugene Smith (45th Illinois) is promoted to brigadier general. He participates in the operations against Vicksburg as a brigade commander (General Logan's division, General McPherson's XVII Corps). Brigadier General David Sloane Stanley is made major general. He receives the post of chief of cavalry of General Rosecrans' Army of the Cumberland and commands in that capacity from November to September of the following year, when he succeeds General Oliver Howard as commander of the IV Corps. Colonel David Stuart (55th Illinois) is also promoted to brigadier general; however, the Senate, takes no action and rejects his commission on 11 March 1863. General Sherman is disappointed with Stuart's departure from the service.

November 30 (Sunday)   In Arkansas, a Union contingent composed of elements of the 1st Iowa, 10th Illinois and 2nd Wisconsin Regiments, commanded by Colonel Wickerman, while operating in the vicinity of Yellville, encounters and skirmishes a contingent of Confederates. Casualty figures are unavailable; however, the Union seizes about 500 stands of arms.

In Mississippi, a reconnaissance force led by Union General Albert Lindley Lee skirmishes with Confederates at Abbeville. Casualty figures are unavailable.

In Virginia, a Union reconnaissance force, the 1st Cavalry Brigade (General Stahl's Division), while on a mission in the vicinity of Snicker's Ferry and Berryville, skirmish with Confederates. The Union casualty figures, if any, are unavailable. The estimated Confederate casualties are 45 killed and wounded and 40 captured.

In Missouri, a Union force departs Rolla on 30 November and advances to the Ozark Mountains. The mission continues until 6 December.

In Naval activity, the USS *Young America* and the USS *Zouave* combine to tow the vessel *Passaic,* a monitor, to Washington, D.C., for repairs.

December   In *Confederate activity,* Brigadier General Franklin Gardner is appointed to major general effective this month. His appointment is not officially confirmed until June 1864. Gardner will be transferred to Mississippi. Also, George Washington Gordon, drill master, 11th Tennessee Infantry, is promoted to the rank of colonel. Following a stint in East Tennessee, Gordon will participate at various battles and skirmishes, including Chattanooga, Chickamauga and Murfreesboro, Tennessee, and he will be in Georgia during the Atlanta Campaign prior to returning to Tennessee with General John B. Hood. Gordon is promoted to brigadier general in August 1864.

Major General Samuel Jones, following duty in Tennessee, is assigned command of the Department of Western Virginia. Colonel Edwin Gray Lee, 33rd Virginia Regiment, apparently suffering from poor health, hands in his resignation. Colonel Lee had served under General Stonewall Jackson beginning at Harpers Ferry and continuing until the battle of Fredericksburg this month. Lee is married to the daughter of Confederate General William Pendleton. He will re-enter the army during 1863. Colonel Lucius Eugene Polk, 15th Arkansas Infantry Regiment, is promoted to the rank of brigadier general effective this date. Polk, a nephew of Confederate Lt. General Leonidas Polk, will succeed General Patrick Cleburne as brigade commander. Cleburne is promoted to major general.

December 1 (Monday)   In Virginia, Union troops attached to the 2nd Division, 12th Corps, commanded by General Henry Slocum, engage Confederates at Charles Town and Berryville in minor skirmishes. The Union reports no casualties. The Confederate estimated casualties are five killed and 18 wounded. Also, a detachment of the Union 3rd Virginia Cavalry, led by Captain Cruger, captures Warrenton and seizes one Confederate soldier. The 5th Minnesota Volunteer Regiment, recently transferred to the 13th Corps, is later this month transferred to the 2nd Brigade, 8th Division, 16th Army Corps, Army of the Tennessee, and remains with it until April 1863.

In Missouri, a contingent of the 4th Missouri Cavalry, commanded by Major Kelly, skirmishes with Confederates at Horse Creek. The Union captures five Confederates.

December 2 (Tuesday)   In Mississippi, the Confederates abandon Abbeville. The Union is right on their heels, and a contingent of Union cavalry (General Grant's command) moves into the town and occupies it.

In Missouri, elements of the 3rd and 9th Missouri Cavalry, commanded by Colonel Glover, skirmish with Confederates at Ozark. The Union reports no casualties. The Confederates sustain four wounded and two captured.

In the Indian Territory (Oklahoma), a skirmish occurs at Saline.

In Virginia, Confederate Major Thomas M.R. Talcott returns from a surveillance detail and reports to General Robert E. Lee that all potential crossing points of the Rappahannock River are unfavorable for a pontoon bridge to be utilized against Fredericksburg. Also, elements of the Union 11th Pennsylvania Cavalry, commanded by Colonel Spear, skirmish with Confederate cavalry augmented by artillery at Franklin. The Union seizes about 20 Confederates and two guns, along with about twenty-five stand of arms. A 60-man contingent of the 8th Pennsylvania Cavalry led by Captain Wilson, on duty at King George Court House, is attacked by Confederate cavalry. The Confederates prevail; however, no casualty figures are available. Meanwhile, a Union force under General Geary departs Bolivar Heights on a reconnaissance mission that takes the unit to Charleston. A skirmish develops with Confederates. The Union casualty figures are unavailable. The estimated Confederate casualties are 70 killed and wounded and about 145 captured.

In Confederate general officer activity, William Thompson Martin, initially thought to be a strident supporter of the Union, is commissioned a brigadier general (later major general). Prior to his promotion, he had become colonel of the Jeff Davis' Legion, with which he participated with Jeb Stuart against General McClellan. He is ordered to the West, where he participates in the Tullahoma campaign and at Chickamauga before joining General Longstreet's command.

December 3 (Wednesday)   In Kentucky, elements of the 91st Indiana Infantry Regiment and the 15th Kentucky Cavalry Regiment, commanded by Major Henry, occupy Princeton.

In Mississippi, Grenada is seized and occupied by a large Union force commanded by General Alvin Hovey. The Confederates, prior to departing, take the time to destroy many railroad cars and locomotives to prevent their capture and use by the Yankees. In other activity, elements of the 1st Indiana Cavalry skirmish with Confederates at Oakland. Casualty figures are unavailable. Meanwhile, a contingent of the 2nd Cavalry Brigade (General Hatch's command) skirmishes with Confederate contingents at Oxford. The Union sustains about 20 killed and wounded. The Confederate casualty figures are unavailable; however, 92 are captured.

In Virginia, Confederate General Ambrose P. Hill's division, including Maxcy' Gregg's South Carolina brigade, arrives at Fredericksburg from Winchester, terminating a twelve-day march.

In Naval activity, the *Glide,* a stern-wheel tinclad built in Pennsylvania at Shousetown during 1862, is commissioned the USS *Glide.* The ship had been purchased by Rear Admiral D.D. Porter at Pittsburgh in November 1862. Acting Lt. Selim E. Woodworth receives command of the *Glide.* After being commissioned on 3 January 1863, the *Glide* departs to join the Mississippi Squadron.

December 4 (Thursday)   In Alabama, Union and Confederate contingents (specific units not identified) skirmish at Tuscumbia. The Union captures about 70 Confederates.

In Mississippi, the 1st and 2nd Cavalry Brigades skirmish with Confederates at Water Valley. Casualty figures are unavailable; however, the Union captures about 300 Confederates.

In Kentucky, the 39th Kentucky Volunteer Regiment skirmishes with Confederates at Wireman's Shoals. Casualty figures are unavailable.

In Minnesota, civilians launch an assault against Indian prisoners being held at Mankato.

In Virginia, Union troops under General Ambrose E. Burnside and Confederates under Robert E. Lee skirmish in several areas in the vicinity of Fredericksburg. The Union troops in Northwestern Virginia have begun withdrawing towards New Creek, leaving a meager force of about 200 at Beverly. Union troops under General John W. Geary seize Winchester. Lee reinforces his confidence and states in a letter to Jefferson Davis: "It [the army] was never in better health or in better condition for battle than now." Lee is concerned his army might need to be pulled back to defend Richmond with difficulty, for the area is again hit by snow. In related activity, six Union gunboats trade blows with Confederate batteries at Port Royal for about two hours.

In Arkansas, operations initiated by the Union at Cane Hill continue. A skirmish erupts at Reed's Mountain on December 5, the final day of the mission.

In the Indian Territory (Cherokee Country), Union forces initiate an expedition that continues for nine days.

In Confederate general officer activity, General Arnold Elzey (Jones) (West Point, 1837), having recently recuperated from a serious wound sustained at the Seven Days' Battle, is appointed major general. Elzey assumes command of the Department of Richmond; however, he does not resume further field duty until the latter part of the conflict, rather he focuses on organizing government civilians to bolster the city's defenses by forming a "local defense brigade." Subsequent to his stint in Richmond, Elzey transfers to the Army of Tennessee and is assigned command of its artillery.

In Naval activity, the USS *R.R. Cuyler* intercepts and searches the steamer *Armstrong.* The search uncovers contraband aboard the vessel. The *Armstrong* is afterward destroyed. Subsequent to the capture, the *Cuyler* resumes its mission to search for the CSS *Tallahassee.* The *Cuyler* after the mission returns to patrol duty and remains in service until hostilities are terminated.

December 5 (Friday)   In Arkansas, Confederates attack the Union positions defended by the 30th Iowa and the 29th Wisconsin Volunteer Regiments at Helena. The Union reports no casualties. The Confederates sustain eight killed and 30 wounded. Meanwhile, the 2nd Kansas Cavalry skirmishes with Confederates at Reed's Mountain. Casualty figures are unavailable.

In Georgia, the steamers USS *Ottawa, Seneca* and *Pembina* move to Wassah Island, Georgia, where a contingent of troops, including U.S. Marines, debark and occupy an abandoned Confederate fort. Afterward the *Pembina* is transferred to the Gulf Coast for the duration of the war. It participates in the operations against Mobile, and later, during September

Troops of the 41st Massachusetts Regiment, aboard the transport *North Star* on its hurricane deck, write letters to home while off Ship Island en route to New Orleans (Mottelay, *The Soldier in Our Civil War,* 1886).

1865, it is decommissioned. The vessel is sold during November, renamed the *Charles E. Gibson*, transformed into a schooner and placed in commercial service.

In Mississippi, Confederate troops assault the positions of the Union cavalry brigades (1st Brigade Brigadier General John Porter Hatch, 2nd Brigade Colonel Lee and 3rd Brigade, Colonel Mizner) of Grant's Army of the Tennessee at Coffeeville. The bitter skirmish, fought between about 2,000 Union cavalry troops and about 5,000 Confederate infantrymen, ceases after two strenuous hours with both sides suffering casualties. The battle costs the Union approximately 10 killed and 54 wounded. The Confederates lose seven killed and 43 wounded.

In New York, the recently organized 41st Massachusetts Infantry departs for New Orleans aboard the transport *North Star*. The vessel pauses at Ship Island and arrives in New Orleans on 15 December.

In Union activity, Lt. Colonel William Gamble is promoted to colonel of the 8th Illinois Cavalry.

December 6 (Saturday)   In Missouri, Union and Confederate forces clash at Parkersburg.

In Tennessee, elements of the 93rd Ohio Volunteer Regiment, commanded by Colonel C. Anderson, are attacked while protecting a Union foraging wagon train in the vicinity of Lebanon. The Union sustains one killed and three wounded. Confederate casualty figures, if any, are unavailable.

In Naval activity, the USS *New Uncle Sam*, acquired the previous month by the U.S. Navy, is commissioned, but on 13 December, it is renamed the USS *Blackhawk*. Lt. Commander K.R. Breese becomes the *Blackhawk's* commanding officer. The vessel becomes the flagship of Admiral David D. Porter (Mississippi Squadron) and later of Admiral Samuel P. Lee. The *Blackhawk* participates in operations against Vicksburg this month, and during the following month it takes part in the operations against Confederate-held Fort Hindman in Arkansas. Another vessel, the monitor *Montauk*, is acquired by the Navy this month. The *Montauk*, a Passaic class monitor built in New York, is commissioned this month. Commander John L. Worden receives command. The ship arrives at Port Royal in early January 1863 and joins the South Atlantic Blockading Squadron.

December 7 (Sunday)   In Arkansas, a large Confederate force, commanded by General Thomas Hindman, assaults a combined Union force, composed of the 1st, 2nd and 3rd Divisions (Army of the Frontier), commanded by Generals Blunt and Francis J. Herron, in the vicinity of Fayetteville (Prairie Grove). General Hindman had succeeded Brigadier General John Selden Roane as Confederate commander of the District of Arkansas. General Roane, subsequent to this action, spends the remainder of the war in Arkansas, Louisiana and Texas, but he is assigned primarily to garrison duty until

his parole during June 1865. The vicious battle concludes with both sides taking casualties, but the Union is unable to prevent the Confederates from pulling off the startling surprise raid. The Union suffers 167 killed, 798 wounded and 183 missing. The Confederates sustain 300 killed and 1,200 missing or wounded. Units participating in this battle include contingents of the 1st, 2nd, and 3rd Divisions, Army of the Frontier. Union General Herron had marched two divisions 125 miles in three days to assist in the battle. Confederate Generals Daniel M. Frost (West Point, 1844), James F. Fagan and John S. Roane participate. Frost, during the following year, begins to have personal problems at his home outside St. Louis, as the citizens there apparently take offense at his service with the Confederacy, although in Missouri, emotions run high on both sides of the conflict. Nevertheless, Frost's family is continuously harassed and compelled to abandon their home.

In Tennessee, Union troops (Dumont's Division) commanded by Colonel A.B. Moore, including the 106th, and 108th Ohio, the 104th Illinois, the 2nd Indiana Cavalry, and the 11th Kentucky Cavalry, engage Morgan's Raiders, who decisively defeat the Union at Hartsville. The loss is humiliating for the Union, with nearly 1,800 men captured, 55 killed and over 200 wounded. The Confederates lose approximately 21 killed and 114 wounded. Confederate General J.H. Morgan evens the score against General Dumont, who had repulsed him at Lebanon, Tennessee, earlier this year. General Dumont is compelled to take sick leave this month.

In Naval activity, the CSS *Alabama* seizes the mail steamer *Ariel* off Cuba. The ship, carrying more than 200 passengers, is released without harm. In other activity, the USS *Maratanza*, operating in the vicinity of Smith's Island, North Carolina, seizes a Confederate sloop, the *Ceres*.

December 8 (Monday)   In Mississippi, General Grant orders General William T. Sherman to return to Memphis to assume command of all Union troops in the area. Sherman is also instructed to leave a competent officer in charge. Grant states: "Leave a garrison of four infantry regiments, the siege guns and whatever cavalry may be there." Sherman then departs Columbus, Kentucky, on the naval ships of Flag Officer David D. Porter and sails toward Vicksburg.

December 9 (Tuesday)   In Arkansas, Union and Confederate forces skirmish at Mudtown.

In Tennessee, elements of the 35th Indiana, 51st Ohio, and the 8th and 21st Kentucky Volunteer Regiments, bolstered by the 7th Indiana Battery, serving as guards to a foraging wagon train, are attacked by Confederates at Dobbin's Ferry (La Vergne). The Union sustains five killed and 48 wounded. Confederate casualty figures are unavailable. Contingents of the 25th Illinois, 8th Kansas and the 81st Indiana Volunteer Regiments, augmented by the 8th Wisconsin Battery, commanded by Colonel Martin,

skirmish with a 400-man Confederate force at Brentsville. Casualty figures are unavailable.

In Virginia, at Fredericksburg on or about this night, General McLaws and General Barksdale are among the thousands of Confederates who were listening to some of their former favorite tunes, "Hail Columbia" and "The Star Spangled Banner," being played by Union bands at the terminus of the railroad bridge in the Union sector. The Confederates do not react, but after awhile, they retaliate with the first Confederate strike against the Union in what becomes the brief battle of the bands. The Confederate band blasts "Dixie," which is apparently greatly enjoyed by the Union. No return tunes are played to taunt the Rebels; rather the Yankees break out in loud applause and cheers, as do the Rebels. The musical duel ends in a draw; however, Generals McLaws and Barksdale remain skeptical. McLaws reinspects all of his lines and directs his forces to construct additional rifle pits near the river bank just in case the serenade is the prelude to the river crossing. He also assigns more guards to the bridge approaches.

In Missouri, a Union force initiates an expedition into Marion County, Arkansas, that lasts through the 15th. The column departs Ozark on this day.

December 10 (Wednesday)   In North Carolina, Confederates attack the Union garrison and naval facilities at Plymouth. The USS *Southfield* sustains severe damage during the engagement.

In Virginia, Union General Burnside makes final preparations for the assault against Fredericksburg. General Henry J. Hunt, Burnside's chief of artillery, has positioned twenty-nine batteries with a combined 147 guns atop the heights for the purpose of protecting the construction of the pontoon bridges that cross the river and to protect the crossings of the troops. In other activity, General Lee is again bereaved because one of his grandchildren has died. Also, eight Union gunboats clash with Confederate batteries at Port Royal in a contest that lasts for about three hours. The Union sustains one killed and three wounded. Confederate casualties are unavailable.

December 11 (Thursday)   In North Carolina, a Union force departs New Bern to attack Confederate positions at Goldsboro. It includes the brigades of General Wessels and Colonels Amory, Horace Lee, and Thomas G. Stevenson and the 3rd New York Cavalry, as well as some artillery (New York and Rhode Island batteries).

In Virginia, about one hour prior to sunrise, while most of Lee's Confederates are sleeping, the unit charged with remaining vigilant is alert, and in an instant or two, the entire defending force is awakened as cannon fire shatters the silence on the south bank of the Rappahannock. The tumultuous sounds originate with the Washington Artillery, which, from its positions on Marye's Heights, detects the Union movement at the river's edge. Without much

Left: Confederate sharpshooters at Fredericksburg (Johnson, *Campfire and Battlefield: History of the Conflicts and Campaigns*, 1894). *Right:* General William B. Franklin's division crosses the Rappahannock (*Harper's Pictoral History of the Civil War*, 1896).

discernment, the Confederates realize the signal has been given and the attack is unfolding. General Barksdale's Mississippi brigade on picket duty is the first to react.

Meanwhile, the Union forces under Burnside begin to place three bridges across the river at Fredericksburg. The operation had begun at about 0100 under a heavy fog. The operation is guarded by two of Hancock's units, the 56th and 57th New York Regiments. The Rebel fire from Barksdale's brigade makes it temporarily impossible to complete the laying of the bridges. Volunteers are requested to cross the ring of fire in open boats. The 7th Michigan, 19th and 20th Massachusetts and the 42nd New York Regiments heed the call and head for the opposing bank while a hurricane of fire is delivered by Mississippians deployed in rifle pits near the south bank. These sharpshooters from the 17th Mississippi pick off about three hundred men during the harrowing crossing, during which the Union is repeatedly repulsed.

At about 1300, the Union reverts to extraordinary action when the guns pummel the town. The descending fire from Stafford Heights rains down with devastating results, igniting fires and collapsing buildings. The whirlwind of fire crashes to the left, the right and in the center, with shot and shell seemingly descending as a blizzard of iron snow flakes, each separate and equally pernicious. However, the Mississippians in the rifle pits—commanded by Lt. Colonel John C. Fiser of the 17th Mississippi Regiment and composed of his regiment, ten sharpshooters attached to the 13th Mississippi Regiment and three companies of the 18th Mississippi (commanded by Lt. Colonel Luse)—are neither dislodged nor deterred from holding the bank. As if oblivious to the sheets of fire, Barksdale's brigade creates its own wall of impenetrable fire, erected by about 3,000 of Barksdale's command, none of whom abandon their positions until the order from General James Longstreet arrives directing Barksdale to withdraw. At the time Longstreet issues the order, he is prepared for the next phase.

While the Yankees hit the south bank and the Mississippi brigade withdraws, the efforts

related to the bridges continue and additional troops begin to cross the river. General Howard's division crosses in boats at about 1600 and a skirmish develops between his troops and the Confederate 8th Florida and the 18th and 19th Mississippi Regiments. The Yankees seize some of the defenders in the rifle pits who had not yet retired. Following the engagement, the Yankees occupy the town; however, the Rebels still control the high ground west of the city, and in addition, some of the troops, those deployed in the various basements of private homes, do not receive the order to retire and are captured. Nevertheless, most of the defenders make their way to the assembly point along Princess Anne Street and from there, General McLaws, believing the positions would become untenable by dawn of the 12th, directs General Barksdale to move to more defensible positions under Marye's Heights near a sunken wall along Telegraph Road. By about 1900, the exchanges of gun fire cease.

Without much resistance, General William B. Franklin moves to positions about one mile below Fredericksburg to a point where the Deep Run Creek converges with the Rappahannock, placing his force near Stonewall Jackson's corps. Meanwhile, Union General Sumner's division and a part of General Joseph Hooker's division are able to cross and move into the charred town.

Later this night, General Thomas R.R. Cobb receives orders to relieve General Barksdale's brigade. Cobb deploys three of his Georgia regiments and Phillips' Legion, which is also attached to his brigade, to the sunken wall along Telegraph Road at the base of Marye's Heights. Barksdale's brigade redeploys in Bernard's Woods at the rear of General McLaws' lines.

In Confederate general officer activity, Colonel John Hunt Morgan (2nd Kentucky Cavalry) is promoted to brigadier general.

December 12 (Friday)   In Alabama, a Union contingent led by Colonel Sweeney skirmishes with Confederates at Little Bear Creek. Casualty figures are unavailable. Also, a Union contingent (Colonel Sweeney's command) skir-

mishes with Confederates led by Colonel Philip Dale Roddey at Corinth. The Union reports one killed. Confederate casualties are 11 killed, about 30 wounded and 40 captured.

In Mississippi, the USS *Cairo* is sunk on the Yazoo River as it approaches a mine. Detonated by an electronic device, the mine sets off two explosions. The *Cairo,* commanded by Lieutenant Commander T.O. Selfridge, becomes the first vessel blown up by an electronic device.

In North Carolina, elements of the 3rd New York Cavalry, commanded by Captain Hall, clash with Confederates at Trenton. The Union captures 18 troops. A Union force—General Wessels' Brigade (General Peck's Division) and the 1st, 2nd and 3rd Brigades (1st Division, Department of North Carolina), commanded by General John Gray Foster—while on an expedition to Goldsboro clashes with Confederate units through the 18th. The Union sustains 90 killed and 478 wounded. The Confederates sustain about 739 killed and wounded.

In Tennessee, the advancing forces of Union General Stanley strike the Confederates at Franklin. Stanley's cavalry sustains one killed. The Confederates suffer five killed, 10 wounded and 12 captured.

In Virginia, General Lee presses for reinforcements to meet the Union threat at Fredericksburg. During Union preparations for the assault, Union General Henry J. Hunt oversees his artillery emplacements. General Hunt's artillery commences firing in the early morning of the 13th to initiate the attack, but his 147 guns cannot turn the tide and the Union suffers a most grievous loss. In other activity, the Union continues to move forces across the Rappahannock into Fredericksburg. Also, a Union brigade (General Terry's), while reconnoitering the area around Zuni, clashes with Confederate batteries. Terry's artillery exchanges blows with the Rebels for about three hours. Casualty figures are unavailable. Meanwhile, Confederate General A.P. Hill (General Thomas J. Jackson's Corps) moves from his encampment outside Fredericksburg and relieves Major General

John Bell Hood at Hamilton's Crossing. Hill's division, on the following day, will form the right side of the Confederate line at Fredericksburg.

In Naval activity, the USS *Shawsheen* and several other ships attached to Commodore Stephen Rowan's squadron initiate a mission along the Neuse River in North Carolina in support of an offensive by a Union Army force charged with destroying tracks and railroad bridges in the vicinity of Goldsboro. The flotilla experiences problems due to shallow waters and is compelled to abort the mission on its fourth day after advancing only about 15 miles.

December 13 (Saturday) BATTLE OF FREDERICKSBURG During the pre-dawn hours, all is tranquil atop the three Confederate-held hills around Fredericksburg, but the aura of battle hovers and the tension begins to build under the ominous, impenetrable fog that blankets the area and obscures vision, leaving the Confederates to wonder just when the imminent Union assault will begin. The Union holds an advantage by having use of the telegraph, which is introduced for the first time to a battlefield, permitting the Union to retain constant communications between headquarters and the forces in the field.

While awaiting the attack, Confederate General James Longstreet examines his lines, and while at his right, held by Hood's division, still, the Union force remains concealed by the mist, but their movement, although cautious, is heard on the opposite bank, alerting the defenders. General Hood anticipates that the assault would first strike his lines; however, Longstreet explains that his positions are not the objective due to the Union being aware that they would be placed in untenable positions and threatened by attack from three directions: Jackson from one position, Pickett and McLaws on the other, and a direct frontal attack by Hood himself.

At the same time, it is explained to Hood

that the forces of General William B. Franklin would strike General Jackson's lines. In the event that Franklin might penetrate, Longstreet directs Hood to redeploy on Jackson's right from where he, bolstered by Pickett, is to strike those attempting to reduce Jackson's lines. Prior to departing Hood's positions, Longstreet also informs Hood that his (Longstreet's) positions at Lee's Hill (Telegraph Hill) would come under assault; however he emphasizes that his positions are invulnerable and no assistance would be required to support him.

Soon after daybreak, General Burnside's artillery commences fire. The ground at Stafford Heights begins to bounce from the concussion of the fire from 147 guns deployed by General Henry J. Hunt, which simultaneously pour fire that descends upon Confederate positions while about 100,000 Yankees, still concealed along the north bank of the Rappahannock, are poised to advance across the river to cut their way through the pea-soup fog against the Confederates, who are equally blinded by the fog.

As time slowly passes, the elements of nature alter the situation for both sides when at about 1000, the sun appears and the fog just as suddenly dissipates, creating a clear view of the valley to both sides and revealing the massive force at the river's edge. The Confederates spot Franklin's force of about 40,000 men, composed of General George G. Meade's division, bolstered by General John Gibbon's division (John F. Reynolds' I Corps) to Meade's right and Abner Doubleday's force held in reserve. Other troops on the line include elements of General Joseph Hooker's, and all of the units stand near General Thomas "Stonewall" Jackson's lines, just as Longstreet had predicted.

From the ground, the sight is not overpowering, but from the heights, the scene exhibits the tremendous contrast as the Union is finely attired and their columns well formed under their respective colors, while on the opposite bank, the scene displays Jackson's less well

dressed force and the nearby forces of General Stuart's cavalry, the latter wearing conspicuous yellow butternut suits and having worn and tattered hats. Within the city itself, there is little visible evidence of troops; however, they are posted, only concealed by the battered houses.

Just as the dense fog evaporates, the Union Army begins its fateful charge against the Confederate positions of Stonewall Jackson, but his lines are prepared for the onslaught. General Franklin's force extends from the immediate front of Jackson toward Telegraph Hill, placing one end of the line nearly within reach of the Rebels' finest artillery, while the opposite end to the east enters an area covered by the horse artillery commanded by Major John Pelham and attached to General Jeb Stuart.

Initially, General Franklin's force, near Hamilton's Crossing, comes under a hurricane of fire from Pelham's guns, but after plastering the attackers, the advance begins to jeopardize Pelham's positions and he is ordered to retire. Afterward, Franklin accelerates the advance, unaware that Jackson had been inconspicuously awaiting his approach. In a flash, the Union is pummeled with streams of punishing fire that creates disorder among the ranks. The confusion temporarily impedes progress; however, despite the incessant fire, the line reforms and the advance resumes.

In the meantime, a hole in Jackson's line emerges between the forces of Lane and Archer and the Union capitalizes by funneling through it to imperil Jackson's lines by threatening General Gregg's brigade. During the tenacious fighting, complications arise for the Confederates at Gregg's positions, as the impact stuns the Confederates at about the same time Orr's rifles falter, but in quick time, other South Carolina contingents close ranks. During this relentless savage exchange, General Maxcy Gregg, at the head of Orr's Rifles, mistakes Union troops as Confederates from his ranks. He moves to get his force to cease fire to prevent friendly fire

Left: **Attack on Fredericksburg, December 1862.** *Right:* **Sunken wall at Marye's Heights** (Johnson, *Campfire and Battlefield: History of the Conflicts and Campaigns,* 1894).

Left: General James Longstreet, CSA. *Right:* Battle of Fredericksburg (Johnson, *Campfire and Battlefield: History of the Conflicts and Campaigns,* 1894).

from cutting down his troops. However, the mistake is fatal. The closing Union attackers cut loose with a new barrage. General Gregg is cut down with a mortal wound, a shot to his spine.

In the meantime, the positions of Lane and Archer both receive reinforcements that arrive in time to participate in a Confederate counterattack. The Union advance quickly becomes neutralized as the mounting pressure from the charging divisions of Early and Taliaferro plow into the Union attackers to ignite a more tenacious contest that finds both sides bludgeoning each other. The Union is at the time unable to counter the pressure and is compelled to pull back to positions behind the railroad station. Nevertheless, the withdrawal gives some solace, as the new line is beyond the reach of the Confederate guns.

The retreat and heated pursuit causes some of the Confederates to be distracted from the battle conditions, and as their adrenalin begins to increase they venture far beyond the realm of caution and find themselves within the reach of the Union force, which with far greater numbers begins to overwhelm the spearhead of the counterattack. Those Rebels begin a haphazard withdrawal.

At about the same time, a previously undiscovered Union brigade advances at Deep Run Creek and is detected. The Confederates expeditiously move to isolate it and terminate the threat. General William D. Pender and General Evander Law are quick to pounce upon the intruders. The Confederate brigades initiate an attack and the Union force at Deep Run Creek is shoved into retreat, giving the Confederates the upper hand on Lee's right and left.

Meanwhile, the Confederate guns atop Marye's Heights and Prospect Hill continue to pound the Union forces, and the defenses earlier constructed have the range of a plateau and the sunken road at the base of Telegraph Hill (Lee's Hill). The area appears quite innocent, as

does a stone wall along one side of Telegraph Road; however, the docile wall conceals deadly fire power. General T.R.R. Cobb and his Georgia brigade and a contingent of General Kershaw's brigade lurk silently, awaiting the Union blue columns. Two thousand five hundred riflemen await the signal to fire, while the Union advances closer to what is thought to be the weakest link in the Confederate chain and the path to total victory.

Slightly before noon, the Confederate artillery receives the order, Commence fire! Suddenly, every available gun on Prospect Hill and Marye's Heights begins a thunderous bombardment that rivets the streets in Fredericksburg and impacts with the effect of a sledgehammer. The Union hurriedly seeks safer positions, and under an umbrella of deadly fire the streets of the city are abandoned. The forces converge on Telegraph Road to the front of the stone wall; however, the unyielding Confederate fire continues to descend in waves.

Meanwhile, the Union continues to take casualties as artillery fire strikes from the left and right as well as from Telegraph Hill to their front. Despite the grievous losses already sustained, the Union forms for the charge amid a storm of fire. The signal to charge is given and the Yankees initiate the advance, intending to get out of the cauldron and to seize the heights. With extraordinary determination, the sea of blue advances. With each step, more troops fall, but the ranks close to fill in the gaps.

Still under a raging thunderclap of artillery fire, the troops encroach the stone wall, totally oblivious to yet another insurmountable Confederate obstacle. Just as the Union moves to a point within range of the infantry hidden behind the wall, the Rebels there arise and commence firing. The withering fire shreds the ranks nearly in an instant; however, the hovering clouds of smoke conceal the death and carnage for a short while.

Yet again, the Union forms to attack. During a fourth assault, General Cobb is wounded in the thigh, and due to a massive loss of blood, he dies within minutes. At the same time, General Kershaw arrives at the wall with the remainder of his brigade. Kershaw's arrival is just in time, as he assumes command before the Union launches a fifth assault, but it too is repelled. The Union, still determined to crack the lines, launches a sixth attack; however, the Confederates are not dislodged and the Union only increases its casualties in vain.

The arrival of darkness terminates the day's fighting and the Union blood bath. In some places, Union dead are layered three high in front of the sunken wall, and not one solitary Union soldier reaches it. Confederate small arms fire inflicts about 5,000 casualties, including killed and wounded, to the front of Marye's Heights, but when casualties from the artillery are counted, the numbers skyrocket further.

Neither side exhibits any lack of boldness or courage; however, at Fredericksburg, it had been the inanimate stone wall that had given the Confederates the impregnable positions that deprived the Union of any chance of victory. Grim silence replaces the incessant fire of the muskets and cannon and new sounds emerge from the eerie darkness, the cries of desperately wounded Union troops still stranded amid a field of death at the base of Marye's Hill.

The cries of anguish move great distances due to the night air and apparently touch the hearts and minds of the victors. In one instance, Confederate Sergeant Richard Kirkland (2nd South Carolina Infantry), so sensitive to the cries of wounded Union soldiers, carries water to them. A monument to Kirkland's noble gesture still stands at Sunken Road and Stone Wall. Sergeant Kirkland is remembered as "The angel of Marye's Heights." Confederate General James Longstreet, after assessing the aftermath of the battle, stated: "No troops could have displayed greater courage and resolution than was shown by those brought against Marye's Hill. But they miscalculated the wonderful strength of the line behind the stone fence."

Although the fighting had ended for the day and the Confederates had vanquished General Burnside, there is no restful night ahead for Robert E. Lee's victorious forces. During the night, a Union soldier accidentally finds himself within the Confederate lines and is captured. The trooper is carrying a message that details General Burnside's plans for the following day, and the Confederates confiscate it and forward the information to General Lee. Burnside's strategy to launch yet another attack at dawn is prematurely disclosed to the Rebels.

The Confederates react immediately. General Ransom's force, held in reserve throughout the day's fighting, is ordered to dig a line of rifle pits atop Marye's Heights. Lee directs other troops to deploy a series of guns on Taylor's Hill. The new defensive positions are manned and poised prior to dawn on the 14th for the next onslaught; however, the intercepted message was outdated when it was confiscated and written prior to the slaughter. After the huge losses, Burnside canceled the attack of the 14th. Nonetheless, Lee's forces remain alert, unaware of Burnside aborting the assault. Meanwhile, the Union remains in place during the 14th and 15th, without any serious offensive action, although some skirmishing continues during that time. After dusk on the 15th, the Union retires. General Lee's forces then redeploy along the Rappahannock, still celebrating what becomes General Lee's finest victory during the war.

General Burnside's devastating defeat at Fredericksburg would illuminate Lincoln's decision to place him in charge of the Army of the Potomac. Burnside accepts full blame for the defeat. Union casualties are 1,180 killed, 9,028 wounded and 2,145 missing. Union Brigadier General George D. Bayard (West Point, 1856) is killed. Brigadier General Conrad F. Jackson is hit in the head by a single shot which instantly kills him. General John Gibbon receives a severe wound that knocks him out of service for several months. Upon his return to duty, General Gibbon receives command of the 2nd Division in General Winfield S. Hancock's II Corps. In addition, Brigadier General Nathan Kimball sustains a wound; however, he recovers and will command a division (XVI Corps during the operations against Vicksburg. Another officer, Brigadier General Abram Sanders Piatt, while leading is brigade (General Whipple's III Corps) suffers a debilitating injury to his back when his horse falls.

The Confederates sustain more than 5,000 killed, wounded, or missing. Confederate Generals Maxcy Gregg and Thomas Reade Rootes Cobb are also killed; Cobb sustains a complicated wound that splinters his hip and apparently injures his thigh, causing him to bleed to death, ironically within sight of his mother's girlhood home. Colonel William Tatum Wofford assumes command of Cobb's brigade. With regard to the battle, General Robert E. Lee would remark: "I wish these people would go away and leave us alone." Lee also states: "It is well that war is so terrible, or we should grow too fond of it." Following the battle, Colonel Reuben Lindsay Walker (commander of the 14 guns on Prospect Hill) accompanies the command of Confederate Lieutenant General James Longstreet. In other related activity, Union General Francis L. Vinton (West Point, 1856) is severely wounded at this battle. Lt. Colonel (later major general) Adelbert Ames (20th Maine) participates.

Confederate Colonel (later brigadier general) Clement Anselm Evans commands a brigade.

Confederate Colonel (later brigadier general) Archibald Campbell Godwin leads the 57th North Carolina Infantry. The Confederate 25th Virginia Infantry (Early's brigade, Ewell's division) participates, as does Confederate Colonel Samuel McGowan. He is promoted to brigadier general effective January 17, 1863. He will assume command of the late General Gregg's brigade; in the meantime, Colonel D.H. Hamilton is in temporary command. Brigadier General William B. Taliaferro, subsequent to the fighting at Fredericksburg, is transferred to Charleston, where he serves under General Beauregard.

In Alabama, a Union contingent composed of two infantry regiments and one company of cavalry (specific units not reported) skirmishes with Confederates at Tuscumbia Creek. The Union sustains four killed and 14 wounded. The Confederates lose 70 captured. Confederate casualty figures are unavailable.

In North Carolina, Union General John Gray Foster's force, having advanced from New Bern on the 11th, nears Goldsboro. A Confederate contingent of about 2,000, commanded by General Nathan George "Shanks" Evans, intercepts the advancing columns at Southwest Creek, but the 9th New Jersey and 85th Pennsylvania lead a charge that breaks the resistance and permits the Union to quickly make progress, which pushes the Union to Kinston during the latter part of the day. The 9th New Jersey, 85th Pennsylvania Volunteer Regiment, the 3rd New York Cavalry and the 3rd New York Artillery participate in the action. Meanwhile, as General John G. Foster's column approaches Kinston, he learns that about 6,000 Rebels hold the town.

In Confederate general officer activity, Lt. Colonel Marcus Joseph Wright, 154th Tennessee, is promoted to the rank of brigadier general. Brigadier General Patrick Ronayne Cleburne is promoted to major general effective this date (his promotion is actually received on the 20th). Also, Colonel Zacharia Cantey Deas, 22nd Alabama Infantry, is promoted to brigadier general. Deas will receive command of a brigade composed of the 19th, 22nd, 25th, 39th, and 50th Alabama Regiments, the 17th Alabama Battalion Sharpshooters and Dent's Alabama Artillery. Also, Confederate Colonel Edward Cary Walthall, 29th Mississippi, is promoted to brigadier general effective this date. Walthall becomes ill and is unable to participate in the engagement at Murfreesboro, Tennessee. Colonel Lucius Eugene Polk, who entered Confederate service as a private (Yell Rifles) and rose to colonel of the 15th Arkansas Infantry, is promoted to brigadier general. He participates in various actions, including Murfreesboro, Chickamauga and Chattanooga, as well as the Atlanta campaign.

December 14 (Sunday)   In Kentucky, a 200-man Union contingent led by Captain Thornberry skirmishes with a Confederate force at Wireman's Shoals. The Union captures about 700 stands of arms. Casualty figures are unavailable.

In North Carolina, General John G. Foster's force attacks Kinston. Union General Henry Walton Wessels (West Point, 1833) leads the assault with his brigade (attached to Peck's division). At about 1030, the two forces clash at a strategic bridge. The Confederates, commanded by General Nathan George Evans, raise heavy resistance and the skirmish costs both sides in casualties. The 9th New Jersey and the 17th Massachusetts hold the point, but the New Jersey troops expend their ammunition and pull back to get re-supplied. Meanwhile, the Rebel artillery maintains its steady fire. Unable to crack the line, the Union decides to launch a flanking assault. The 23rd and 45th Massachusetts charge from the right, while the 3rd New York Cavalry lunges forward from the left, all in concert with Major Garrard's force, composed of infantry cavalry and artillery, driving up the center. Still the Rebels hold and the contest rages for about three hours before the Union is finally able to overwhelm the line. The Confederates abandon their positions and retire to Goldsboro. The Union sustains 40 killed and 120 wounded. The Confederates suffer 50 killed, 75 wounded and 400 captured. The Rebels lose a substantial amount of arms to the Yankees.

In Texas, a Union wagon train is seized by a band of Mexicans near Pine Brown Road. Casualty figures are unreported.

In Virginia, at Fredericksburg, the bewildered Union troops begin to prepare to make their way back across the Rappahannock; however, General Burnside does not order the retreat until the night of the 15th. Although the Confederates delivered a massive blow to the Yankees, the Confederates do not capitalize on the victory, because Lee's victorious, outnumbered troops do not re-attack, thereby permitting the Union to retreat. An attack against Burnside's vanquished army was deterred primarily because the Confederate positions had been designed for defensive purposes, and to launch an

Battle of Kinston, North Carolina (*Harper's Pictorial History of the Civil War*, 1896).

assault across the Rappahannock would expose Lee's forces to the huge artillery force of nearly 150 guns that dominated the heights and could shred Lee's forces similarly to the way his guns mauled the Union. Nonetheless, Lee does receive some criticism for not pursuing the Union.

In Naval activity, the *Juliet,* constructed at Brownsville, Pennsylvania, during 1862 and acquired by the U.S. Navy on 1 November 1862, is commissioned the USS *Juliet.* Prior to being commissioned it receives armor plating. Acting Volunteer Lieutenant Edward Shaw receives command of the *Juliet.* It is assigned to the Mississippi Squadron and dispatched to Mississippi to support operations against Vicksburg. In other activity, the USS *Winona* is attacked by a Confederate battery at Profit Island, Mississippi. At the time it is at anchor and unable to effectively return fire due to a lack of proper steam. The *Winona* retires.

December 15 (Monday) In Mississippi, Union troops en route to Vicksburg are intercepted by Confederates. General Nathan Forrest, who departed his headquarters several days earlier, impedes the progress of the Union advance.

In Missouri, a contingent of Union troops skirmishes with Confederates at Neosho.

In North Carolina, a contingent of Union troops under Major Garrard (General John G. Foster's command) initiates a reconnaissance mission toward Goldsboro and encounters a force of Confederates in the vicinity of Whitehall. A brief skirmish occurs, but it is on the following day that a major clash develops.

In Virginia, the Union takes advantage of a terrible thunderstorm. General Burnside abandons Fredericksburg. The troops begin to recross the Rappahannock, and by dawn on the 16th, the

Whitehall, North Carolina, 16 December 1862 (*Harper's Pictoral History of the Civil War*, 1896).

move is complete, including the transfer of the artillery. Burnside regroups in Stafford Heights. Subsequent to this setback, Burnside prepares to launch a new attack against Richmond, but he is informed by President Lincoln that no offensive is to be initiated without his (Lincoln's) consent.

December 16 (Tuesday) In Kentucky, Union cavalry (Wolford's cavalry) commanded by Captain Silas Adams strikes Confederate positions at New Haven and catches them off guard. The Union captures about 1,200 troops.

In Louisiana, at New Orleans, General Butler, pursuant to an order by President Lincoln of 9 November, is relieved by General Banks as commander of the Department of the Gulf. General Butler, in his final order, issued this day commends the troops in his command for their services for their country: "By steady at-

tention to the laws of health, you have stayed the pestilence, and, humble instruments in the hands of God, you have demonstrated the necessity that His creatures should obey His laws, and, reaping His blessing in the most unhealthy climate, you have preserved your ranks fuller than those of any other battalions of the same length of service. You have met double numbers of the enemy, and defeated him in the open field; but I need not further enlarge upon this topic. You were sent here to do that. I commend you to your commander. You are worthy of his love."

In North Carolina, a Union force—the 9th New Jersey, 17th, 23rd, 24th and 45th Massachusetts Volunteer Regiments, and the 3rd New York Cavalry supplemented by the 3rd and 23rd New York Batteries (General John G. Foster's command)—skirmishes with Confederates led by General Evans at Whitehall. The two sides blast each other with artillery barrages for about one hour. Following the exchange, the Confederates pull back to Goldsboro.

In Virginia, the Union completes its abandonment of Fredericksburg. Captain Romeyn Beck Ayres (West Point, 1847), Union artillery commander, must regroup his troops, who have done admirably despite losses. Ayres will become a brigadier general toward the end of the conflict, in 1865.

December 17 (Wednesday) In Louisiana, Union forces under General Nathaniel Banks reoccupy Baton Rouge, which had been abandoned in August.

In Mississippi, at Holly Springs, General Grant, acting on complaints from officers, including General William T. Sherman, issues a controversial order (No. 11): "The Jews as a class, violating every regulation of trade established by the Treasury Department and also department order, are hereby expelled from the department within twenty-four hours from the receipt of this order. Post commanders will see that all of this class of people be furnished passes and required to leave, and any one returning after

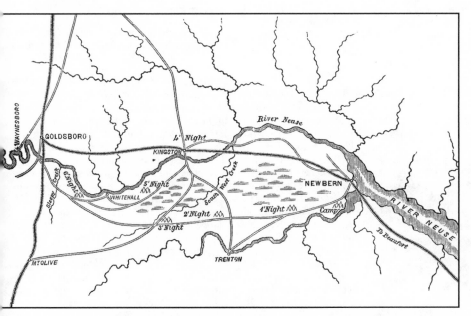

New Bern to Goldsboro (*Harper's Pictoral History of the Civil War*, 1896).

such notification will be arrested and held in confinement until an opportunity occurs of sending them out as prisoners, unless furnished with permit from headquarters. No passes will be given these people to visit headquarters for the purpose of making personal applications for trade permit."

On 10 November 1862, General Grant had issued an order to General Webster at Jackson, Tennessee: "Give orders to all conductors on the road that no Jews are to be permitted to travel on the railroad southward from any point. They may go north and be encouraged in it; but they are such an intolerable nuisance that the department must be purged of them." On this same day, General Grant writes to C.P. Wolcott, assistant secretary of war, stating:

I have long since believed that in spite of all vigilance that can be infused into post commanders, the specie regulations of the Treasury Department have been violated, and that mostly by Jews and other unprincipled traders. So well satisfied have I been of this that I instructed the commanding officer at Columbus to refuse all permits to Jews to come South, and I have frequently had them expelled from the department, but they come in with their carpet-sacks in spite of all that can be done to prevent it. The Jews seem to be a privileged class that can travel everywhere. They will land at any wood-yard on the river and make their way through the country. If not permitted to buy cotton themselves they will act as agents for someone else, who will be at a military post with a treasury permit to receive cotton and pay for it in treasury notes which the Jew will buy up at an agreed rate, paying gold. There is but one way that I know of to reach this cue: that is for the government to buy all the cotton at a fixed rate and send it to Cairo, Saint Louis, or some other point to be sold. Then all traders (they are a curse to the army) might be expelled.

Grant's orders essentially deal with the complaints about unscrupulous merchants, based on complaints of sales practices, not religious views. Nevertheless, on 4 January 1863, the order is revoked by General Halleck.

In North Carolina, General John G. Foster's expeditionary force advances to Goldsboro, defended by Confederates under General Gus-

tavus W. Smith, who is bolstered by reinforcements. The Union commences an artillery barrage, which is immediately responded to by a heavy dose of return fire. Nevertheless, the Union guns force a Rebel contingent at a bridge to fall back and permit the Union to advance. The bridge instantly becomes the center of attention as Rebel artillery plasters the area to keep it from falling into Union hands. The Union reacts by unleashing several attacks from separate points, and at one of these, troops ford the stream and position themselves within striking distance of the enemy positions. Despite the heavy fire, the Union is able to set the bridge afire; Lt. George W. Graham, 23rd New York Rocket Battery, is the first man to use the torch. In addition, the Union tears out the railroad tracks and destroys some rail cars, the depot and the water station. Following this heated contest, the Union returns to New Bern, arriving there on the 20th. This expedition costs the Union 90 killed and 354 wounded. The Union also captures slightly less than 500 prisoners.

In Virginia, following the Battle of Fredericksburg, Union and Confederate troops begin to establish winter quarters on opposite sides of the Rappahannock River. Confederate Brigadier General Montgomery D. Corse will be summoned to Fredericksburg from his winter camp to receive a new command. He is to lead a fresh brigade, composed of the 15th, 17th, 30th and 32nd Virginia Regiments. The 29th Virginia will later bolster the force. The brigade will also be in General Pickett's division; however, it will miss duty in Gettysburg, due to being posted at the time, July 1863, at Hanover Junction. Following the action in Pennsylvania, Corse's brigade will return to Virginia with Robert E. Lee.

In Missouri, a Union contingent departs Madrid and moves to Clarkton, executing a mission that lasts until the 21st.

In Naval activity, the *Florence*, a stern-wheel steamer built in Pittsburgh, Pennsylvania, during 1862, is acquired by the U.S. Navy. The *Florence* is transformed into a light draft gunboat and in February 1863 commissioned the USS *Curlew.*

December 18 (Thursday)   In Tennessee, Confederate cavalry under General Nathan B. Forrest clashes with Union troops heading for Vicksburg in a skirmish at Lexington. The Union participants include the 11th Illinois, 5th Ohio and the 1st and 2nd Tennessee Cavalry under Colonel Ingersoll. The Union sustains 7 killed, 10 wounded and 114 missing or captured. The Confederates suffer 7 killed and 28 wounded. The Confederates occupy the town.

Also, other contingents of the 11th Illinois and the 5th Ohio Cavalry Regiments supported by the 43rd and 61st Illinois Volunteer Infantry Regiments skirmish with Confederates at Jackson. Casualty figures are unavailable.

Meanwhile, General Grant receives orders from Washington to divide his command into four army corps with General John A. McClernand receiving a command and being directed to move down the Mississippi River. General McClernand, at Springfield, Illinois, is informed by dispatch of his new command. The corps and their commanders are: Thirteenth Corps, General John A. McClernand; Fifteenth Corps, General William T. Sherman; Sixteenth Corps, General Stephen A. Hurlbut; and Seventeenth Corps, General James B. McPherson. General McClernand, involved with others against General McClellan in the East, is also a critic of General Grant. During the Vicksburg campaign, McClernand provides the press with a letter praising his troops as "the heroes of the campaign." The incident prompts General Grant to send McClernand back to Illinois.

Confederate General Johnson Kelly Duncan (West Point, 1849), chief of staff to General Bragg, dies of fever in Knoxville. Duncan had been in charge of the Confederate batteries at Forts Jackson and St. Philip in Louisiana.

December 19 (Friday)   In Virginia, a Union wagon train guarded by elements of the 12th Army Corps, commanded by Colonel Rush, is attacked by Confederates in the vicinity of Occoquan. Casualty figures are unavailable.

In Naval activity, the *Florence Miller* (tinclad gunboat No. 1.), acquired by the U.S. Navy the previous month, is commissioned at Cairo, Illinois, this day as the USS *Rattler* (wooden sidewheel steamer). Acting Master Amos Longthorne receives command.

December 20 (Saturday)   In Arkansas, a skirmish develops at Cane Hill.

In Louisiana, a contingent of U.S. Marines, commanded by Captain McLane Tilton, moves into and garrisons Pilot Town.

In Mississippi, Confederates from General Van Dorn's command launch a surprise attack on Union lines at Holly Springs and capture over 1,000 Union troops of the 8th Wisconsin Regiment. Colonel Murphy, the commanding officer of the garrison, disgraces himself, although the men under his command are not at fault. The 2nd Illinois Cavalry, rather than capitulate, fights its way out of the area. Murphy is the same officer who evacuated Iuka, Mississippi, without a fight on 13 September 1862. All Union supplies are lost to the enemy and subsequently destroyed. Confederate Colonel William Hicks Jackson, subsequent to this action, is promoted to the rank of brigadier general, effective 29 December 1862. General Jackson remains in the area throughout the campaign for Vicksburg in command of a division of cavalry. Also, General Van Dorn's troops attack other Union garrisons without success.

Skirmish near Goldsboro, North Carolina (*Harper's Pictoral History of the Civil War*, 1896).

In **Tennessee,** Confederate General Nathan B. Forrest continues to launch raids to disrupt Union rail lines between Jackson, Tennessee, and Columbus, Kentucky. It is more than a week before General Grant is able to open communications between the two points. Also, a Union force, composed of elements of the 7th Tennessee Cavalry, the 122nd Illinois Volunteers, commanded by Colonel Fry, and some troops in sickbay are captured by Confederates under General Nathan B. Forrest at Trenton and Humboldt. The Union sustains one killed and 250 captured. The Confederates sustain 17 killed and 50 wounded.

In **Virginia,** a contingent of Union Cavalry commanded by Captain Vernon skirmishes with Confederate guerrillas at Halltown. The Union captures three Confederate troops.

December 21 (Sunday) In Arkansas, Confederate and Union forces clash at Van Buren. At Fayetteville, the Union initiates an expedition toward Huntsville which lasts until the 23rd.

In **Virginia,** the Confederate 6th North Carolina Infantry begins setting up winter quarters at Dumphries.

In **Mississippi,** General Sherman, who has recently arrived at Friar's Point from Memphis, is joined by Commodore Porter. The USS *Black Hawk* (flagship), *Conestoga* and *Marmora* accompany him, as do troops transported from Helena. Friar's Point is demolished prior to the force moving out. The *Marmora* had only been commissioned in October. Later it participates in the operations at Vicksburg, followed by operations on the Yazoo and White River until it is decommissioned during July 1865.

At Davis Mill, about Union 250 troops, including elements of the 25th Indiana Volunteers and the 5th Ohio Cavalry, commanded by Colonel Morgan, engage a large Confederate force (Van Dorn's command). The Union sustains three wounded. The Confederates sustain 22 killed, 50 wounded and 20 missing. The Union also seizes about 100 stands of arms.

In **Tennessee,** a Union contingent (General Horatio P. Van Cleve's division) skirmishes with a Confederate reconnaissance detachment in the vicinity of Nashville. Casualty figures are unavailable.

In **Virginia,** a contingent of the 1st New York Mounted Rifles, commanded by Lt. Colonel Onderdonk, is attacked by Confederates (General Roger Pryor's command) at Isle of Wight Court House. The Union sustains two wounded. During the previous month, General Pryor, who had led a brigade at the Seven Days' Battle and at 2nd Manassas (Bull Run), had relinquished his brigade and received a smaller brigade with duty in the area south of the James River; however, before spring his force is reassigned. Lacking a command, Pryor will resign during August 1863.

December 22 (Monday) In Maryland, Major General Robert C. Schenck is appointed

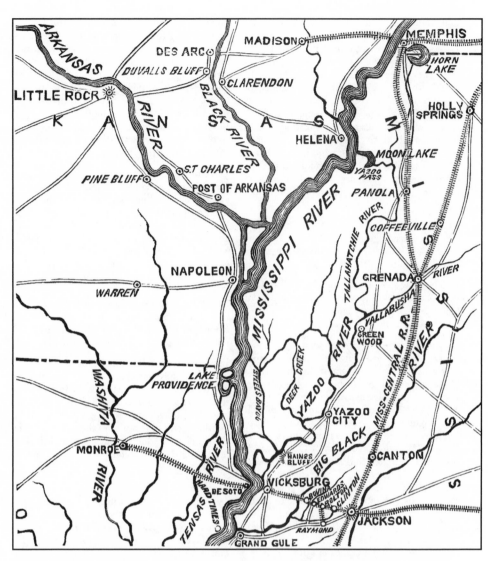

Operations along the Arkansas and Yazoo Rivers (*Harper's Pictorial History of the Civil War,* 1896).

commander of the Middle Military Department. He succeeds Major General John Wool and retains the post until 10 August 1863.

In **Mississippi,** the Union fleet under Commodore David D. Porter and the forces of General William T. Sherman depart Friar's Point. They sail to the mouth of the White River, and on the following day they reach Gaines' Landing. On the 24th, the fleet arrives at Milliken's Bend, and by the 25th, it is at the mouth of the Yazoo River.

In Naval activity, the U.S. Navy acquires a tinclad wooden steamer, the *Duchess,* at Cincinnati. The vessel is commissioned the USS *Petrel* (II) and assigned to the Mississippi Squadron. During the following spring, the *Petrel* participates in the operations against Haynes Bluff (30 April–1 May). Subsequently, the *Petrel* patrols along the Yazoo River and the Sunflower River in search of Confederate vessels. By summer, the *Petrel* switches operations and initiates patrols along the Black River, Quachita River,

Red River and the Tensas River. During the tour it seizes four Confederate vessels.

December 23 (Tuesday) In Arkansas, Union troops skirmish with a Confederate contingent along the Saint Francis Road in the vicinity of Helena.

In **Virginia,** Union forces occupy Winchester.

In **Mississippi,** a U.S. fleet, including the *Baron de Kalb, Juliet* and the *Romeo,* sails up the Yazoo River. The expedition destroys four stranded Confederate vessels, including the *Golden Age* and the *Scotland,* then returns on the 27th with a huge amount of captured supplies.

In **Tennessee,** Union reinforcements arrive at Jackson to relieve a trapped contingent of the 106th Illinois, saving them from destruction.

In **Missouri,** the Union initiates operations in Sugar Creek Hills and vicinity that last until the end of the year.

December 24 (Wednesday) In Kentucky, Morgan's Raiders clash with a contingent of the

2nd Michigan Cavalry (General Philip Sheridan's command) commanded by Captain Dickey at Glasgow (Munfordville). The Union suffers one dead and one wounded. Confederates count three killed and three wounded. In other activity, at Columbus, while Confederates threaten the garrison, the recently commissioned USS *New Era* arrives to support the garrison, and its presence prevents the Confederates from gaining the city. At this time, Columbus is a vital post for the Union and it is utilized as a base of supplies for the fleet and the troops operating against Vicksburg. After the threat diminishes, the *New Era* returns to Cairo, Illinois.

In Mississippi, a contingent of the 12th Michigan Volunteer Regiment skirmishes with Confederates at Middleburg. Casualty figures are unavailable.

In Virginia, a detachment of the 11th Pennsylvania Cavalry skirmishes with a contingent of Confederates (infantry and cavalry) at Joiner's Bridge. The Union captures four troops.

In Union general officer activity, James Hewett Ledlie, 3rd New York Artillery (formerly 19th New York Infantry), is appointed brigadier general. At the beginning of the war, Ledlie was commissioned major of the 19th New York, but he moved up the ranks to colonel. The Senate takes no action to confirm. Consequently, Ledlie's commission expires on 4 March 1863. Subsequently, on 27 October 1863, he is re-nominated and afterward confirmed. Initially, he commands an artillery brigade in the Carolinas, and afterward, he is attached to the Army of the Potomac and assigned to the IX Corps under General Ambrose Burnside. Also, Acting Colonel Edward Elmer Potter (Union 14th North Carolina), formerly chief commissary of General John G. Foster's brigade, is appointed brigadier general. He is assigned to various commands in the Department of the South. Colonel Thomas Greely Stevenson (24th Massachusetts) is appointed brigadier general;

however, the Senate does not confirm his appointment. After his commission expires on 4 March 1863, he is reappointed and confirmed on 9 April 1863 to rank from 14 March. He is assigned duty in the Department of the South and participates in the operations against Charleston. Later, he is attacked by malaria and remains on sick leave through the winter of 1863–1864. After recuperating, he moves north to serve under General Burnside in command of a division of the IX Corps.

December 25 (Thursday)   In Kentucky, Confederates under General John Hunt Morgan are active, spending much of their Christmas Day engaging the Union in separate skirmishes. Detachments of the 4th and 5th Indiana Cavalry commanded by Colonel Gray skirmish with Morgan's Confederates at Green's Chapel (Munfordville), where the Rebels sustain nine killed, 22 wounded and five captured. At Bear Wallow, a Union force composed of two battalions of the 12th Kentucky Cavalry, commanded by Colonel Shanks, engage Morgan's rear guard troops. At Bear Wallow, the Confederates sustain one killed, two wounded and 10 captured.

In Mississippi, following the loss of his supply depot at Holly Springs (captured 20 December), General Grant is forced to instruct his troops to forage and confiscate all food and supplies within a radius of fifteen miles. The Southerners, exuberant after the destruction of the supplies, are soon dismayed that their own food supplies will become a source of energy for the Yankees.

December 26 (Friday)   In Kentucky, Morgan's advance guard skirmishes with one company of the 2nd Michigan Regiment, commanded by Captain Dickey at Bacon Creek. The Union sustains 23 wounded. Also, elements of the 14th Kentucky Cavalry led by Major Stevens, while on a reconnaissance mission in Powell County, skirmishes with Confederate guerrillas. The Union seizes 12 Confederates.

In Minnesota, thirty-nine Sioux Indians are hanged in Mankato for their activity during the recent uprising that took the lives of 450 settlers. The executions were scheduled for December 19, but they were postponed by President Lincoln until this day.

In Tennessee, General Rosecrans' Union force, during a nasty, cold morning, advances from the vicinity of Nashville to strike General Bragg's Confederate force. Colonel Edward McCook, operating on the right wing, moves down the Nolensville Turnpike toward Triune, which is manned by Confederates under General Hardee, while the left wing under General Critten-

den advances along the Murfreesboro Road, which leads to Lavergne. Union General George H. Thomas splits his four divisions, having two move along the Franklin and Williamson Pikes, while the two remaining divisions hold at Nolensville to augment Colonel Edward M. McCook's troops.

In Mississippi, Union troops under General William T. Sherman push toward Vicksburg. The troops depart from the vicinity of the mouth of the Yazoo River aboard vessels attached to Commodore David D. Porter's fleet. Sherman's forces number more than 40,000, comprising four divisions.

December 26 1862–January 3 1863   The USS *Romeo* initiates a patrol along the Yazoo River and some of its tributaries in search of Rebel boats which are being used to launch torpedoes and to drop off new mines in areas previously cleared by U.S. While on the mission, the *Romeo* also engages Confederate shore batteries and some infantry units that are posted in rifle pits along the river banks. The region has been plagued with torrential rains, and by this day, the gunboats out on patrol as part of the operations against Vicksburg are ordered to withdraw.

December 27 (Saturday)   In California, the USS *Independence* arrives at Mare Island. A company of U.S. Marines, commanded by Major Addison Garland, debarks and establishes quarters there to garrison the base.

In Mississippi, a Union fleet attacks Confederate positions at Haines Bluff on the Yazoo River. Heavy fighting rages for one and one-half hours. Tremendous fire from Confederate shore batteries drives off the Union vessels. During the battle, Lt. Commander William Gwinn, in command of the USS *Benton*, is severely wounded. He succumbs on 3 January 1863 aboard a hospital ship on the Mississippi River.

In Kentucky, Morgan's Raiders successfully attack Union positions of the 9th Illinois Regiment at Elizabethtown, capturing the fort and some 500 defenders.

In Tennessee, the Union forces of Generals Thomas L. Crittenden and Alexander McCook depart Lavergne and Nolensville respectively, each en route to Triune.

In Virginia, Confederate General Fitzhugh Lee (nephew of Robert E. Lee) leaves Fredericksburg and captures Union supplies at Chopawansic, then moves north through Prince William County. Jeb Stuart's cavalry skirmishes with the Yankees in the vicinity of Dumfries. The engagement at Dumfries involves contingents of the 5th, 7th, and 66th Ohio Volunteers, the 6th Maine Battery and the 12th Illinois and 1st Maryland Cavalry, commanded by Colonel Candy. The Union sustains three killed and eight wounded and some captured. The Confederates sustain 25 killed and 40 wounded.

In Union general officer activity, William Hays (West Point, 1840) is appointed brigadier general.

Admiral Porter's fleet at the mouth of the Yazoo River (*Harper's Pictoral History of the Civil War*, 1896).

In Naval activity, the monitor USS *Nahant* is commissioned at about this time (late December). It is assigned to the South Atlantic Blockading Squadron and remains in service for the duration of the war.

December 28 (Sunday)   In Arkansas, Union forces (General Blunt's command) skirmish with Confederates at Van Buren (Dripping Springs), and the Union prevails and captures the town. Fighting at Van Buren also occurs on the following day.

In Kentucky, elements of the 6th Indiana Cavalry engage Confederates under General John Hunt Morgan at Muldraugh's Hill in a battle that continues for about 10 hours. Casualty figures are unavailable. Meanwhile, elements of the 6th and 10th Kentucky Cavalry, led by Major Foley, skirmish with Confederates at Elk Fork. The Union reports no casualties. The Confederates sustain 30 killed, 176 wounded and 51 captured.

In Louisiana, a contingent of Union cavalry skirmishes with Confederates at Clinton. The Union sustains one killed. Confederate casualty figures are unavailable.

In Mississippi, the 6th Missouri Regiment crosses Chickasaw Bayou and takes a defensive position while skirmishing with Confederates.

In Missouri, Union forces in New Madrid evacuate the town.

In Tennessee two separate Union forces, those of Generals Crittenden and Edward McCook, arrive at Triune and Stewart's Creek respectively, and at each location, the Confederates are compelled to pull back as the Union closes against General Bragg's main body.

In Virginia, a Union reconnaissance force under Colonel Alfred Gibbs (130th New York Infantry) skirmishes with Confederate cavalry in the vicinity of Suffolk. Casualty figures are unavailable. In August 1863, the unit is reorganized as a cavalry regiment and designated the 1st New York Dragoons, but it is also known as the 19th New York Cavalry. In other activity, elements of the 2nd and 17th Pennsylvania Cavalry skirmish with Confederates at Occoquan. Casualty figures are unavailable.

The 6th Missouri Regiment skirmishes at Chickasaw Bayou, Mississippi (*Harper's Pictoral History of the Civil War*, 1896).

December 28–29   In Mississippi, the Union Army of the Tennessee under William T. Sherman engages Confederates at Chickasaw Bayou (Chickasaw Bluffs). The Union suffers 191 dead, 982 wounded and 756 missing; the Confederates sustain 207 wounded. The Union divisions of Generals G.W. Morgan, Frederick Steele (commissioned on 3 March 1863, to rank from 29 November 1862), Morgan L. Smith and Andrew J. Smith participate. Colonel J.B. Wyman is killed while leading the 13th Illinois Regiment. Union Major General Morgan L. Smith is severely wounded and will not return to active service until October 1863. Smith assumes command of the 2nd Division, XV Corps, at Chattanooga in November of 1863. Also, Confederate colonel (later brigadier general) Allen Thomas of the 29th Louisiana Infantry Regiment is captured. General William T. Sherman, following the engagement and considering the serious casualties incurred, confers with Commodore David D. Porter. They make plans to launch a combined assault to gain possession of the Yazoo. Sherman has concluded that without the help of the Union Navy, his force cannot seize Haines Bluff. They schedule an assault for 1 January 1863.

December 29 (Monday)   In Tennessee, Union General Alexander McCook's corps reaches Riggs Cross Roads in coordination with the forces of Generals Crittenden and Thomas, both of which are moving along the Murfreesboro Turnpike. Misinformation regarding the evacuation of Murfreesboro by the Confederates under Bragg causes a premature move by the advancing troops. One of Crittenden's divisions, led by Colonel Charles G. Harker, is directed to cross Stones River and occupy the town. Captain Milton Russell, leading the 51st Indiana Infantry, is first to cross Stones River. In the face of heavy Confederate resistance, the assault commences successfully, throwing the Confederates back. Later the division encounters a large Confederate force under General

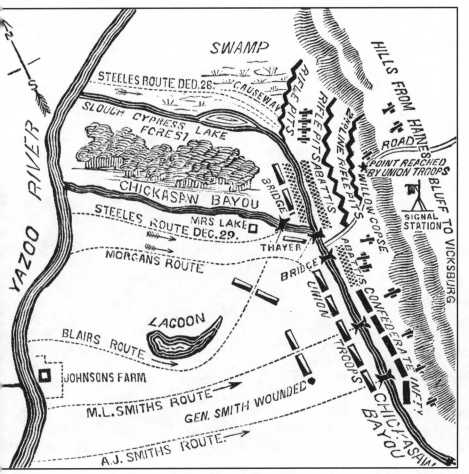

The Battle of Chickasaw Bayou (*Harper's Pictoral History of the Civil War*, 1896).

Breckinridge. By nightfall, the commanding officer, Colonel Charles G. Harker, is recalled.

In related activity, General Rosecrans arrives and establishes his headquarters in the vicinity of Stewart's Creek. Heated skirmishing with the Confederates will continue through the following day. The Union 3rd Kentucky Regiment encounters a Confederate contingent at Stewart's Creek and a skirmish develops there.

In Confederate general officer activity, Colonel William Hicks "Red" Jackson (7th Tennessee Cavalry, formerly 1st Tennessee) is promoted to brigadier general. He participates in the defense of Vicksburg and later receives command of the Army of the Mississippi's cavalry corps during the Atlanta campaign. He serves with General John B. Hood when the latter invades Tennessee. By February 1865, he commands all Tennessee cavalry attached to General Nathan B. Forrest's command.

Late December General Grant, stung by Confederate John Bedford Forrest's raids upon Union rail lines, decides to discontinue his thrust into the interior and returns his scattered command to Grand Junction and La Grange, Tennessee, from where he may use the Mississippi River for his supply route through Rebel territory.

December 30 (Tuesday)   In Arkansas, Union and Confederate contingents clash at La Grange. On 3 January another skirmish erupts.

In Tennessee, Union forces (General Jeremiah C. Sullivan's command), including the 18th, 106th, 119th, and 122nd Illinois, the 27th and 39th Iowa, the 7th Tennessee and the 7th Wisconsin Battery engage Confederates led by General Nathan Bedford Forrest at Parker's Crossroads (Red Mound). The Union counts 23 dead, 139 wounded and 58 missing. Confederates sustain 50 dead, 150 wounded and 300 missing. At day's end, the Union is well fortified along the west side of Stones River. General Thomas L. Crittenden's lines extend from the river bank across the Nashville and Chattanooga Railroad and the Nashville Turnpike to the center of General Thomas' lines (center point),

which stretch across the Wilkinson Turnpike. The far right of the Union lines stretches to the Franklin Road and includes Alexander McCook's three divisions, which have been transferred to Generals Sheridan, Davis and Johnson.

In contrast, the Confederates hold the line about two miles from Murfreesboro, with Breckinridge deployed on the far right across the northeastern bank of the river. General Polk's corps stretches out and defends the center, while General Hardee's command holds the left at the Franklin Road, directly opposite the forces of Union Generals Davis and Johnson. During the evening, the Union holds a conference and it is determined that on the following day, Crittenden will launch an assault against Breckinridge's lines, while the remaining Union forces are to neutralize the left and center of the Confederates lines. The strategy is expected to give Crittenden the opportunity to seize Murfreesboro from the rear. Union regimental bands do a musical battle with the Confederate bands on the opposing lines at Murfreesboro. "Hail Columbia" opposes the "Bonnie Blue Flag," then "Dixie" attempts to silence "Yankee Doodle." This melodic skirmish ends in a draw with "Tattoo" extinguishing the lights and music for the night.

In the meantime, the Confederates are also preparing to take the offensive. General Bragg, in an effort to sever the Union communications with Nashville, orders an attack scheduled for early the following morning against the Union left. In other activity, elements of the 2nd Brigade, 1st Division, General Thomas' corps, skirmishes with Confederates at Jefferson. The Union sustains 20 killed and 40 wounded. The Confederates suffer 15 killed and 50 wounded. Also, the 7th Ohio Cavalry and the 9th Pennsylvania Cavalry engage Confederates at Watauga Bridge and Carter's Station. The Union sustains one killed and two wounded. The Confederates sustain seven killed, 15 wounded and 273 captured or missing. General Sullivan remains in the West until September, when he is transferred back to

General Thomas L. Crittenden (Johnson, ***Campfire and Battlefield: History of the Conflicts and Campaigns,*** **1894).**

the Department of West Virginia, commanded by his father-in-law, General Benjamin F. Kelley.

In Naval activity, the USS *Rhode Island* rescues the crew of the sinking USS *Monitor* off Cape Hatteras, North Carolina. The *Monitor,* in tow by the steamer USS *Rhode Island,* had been en route to Beaufort, South Carolina. Twelve men are lost when the vessel goes down; those lost had been fearful of moving from the turret to the boats during the severe wind storm that had

Left: **Battle of Stones River (Murfreesboro), Tennessee.** ***Right:*** **Crew members are rescued as the USS** *Monitor* **is lost off Cape Hatteras, North Carolina, during a storm (Johnson,** ***Campfire and Battlefield: History of the Conflicts and Campaigns,*** **1894).**

struck the area. Commander John Bankhead is among the rescued; he departs the ship at about midnight (30th–31st). Afterward the USS *Rhode Island* is sent to the West Indies in search of Confederate raiders. Later it returns to the U.S. and resumes patrols along the East coast until April 1864, when it is placed out of commission for repairs until the following September. It participates in the operations against Fort Fisher at Wilmington, North Carolina, during December 1864 and January 1865. The *Rhode Island* remains in active service for the duration of the war and beyond. It is decommissioned in 1867. After being sold in October, it operates as a commercial vessel, the *Charleston*.

December 31 1862–January 2 1863 BATTLE OF MURFREESBORO (STONES RIVER) As dawn approaches in Tennessee, the music of the day is the sound of thundering cannon. As scheduled, prior to dawn, two Union divisions (Crittenden's corps), Van Cleve's followed by Wood's, ford the river and prepare to attack, but in the meantime, the Confederates attack the Union right, thwarting the Union's plans. Bragg's thrust strikes the far right of Alexander McCook's lines prior to the jump-off of General Van Cleve. The Confederates under Major General John P. McCown strike at one point, while Patrick R. Cleburne plows into General Jefferson C. Davis' positions. The Rebels push the Yankees into the Cedar Woods, nearly to the Nashville Pike, where they finally hold. Initially, in Davis' sector, the Rebels meet stiff resistance; however, reinforcements under General Polk arrive and the cavalry penetrates to the rear, costing the Yankees heavy casualties and the loss of the ammunition trains.

Meanwhile, General Sheridan, whose three brigades hold on higher ground, withstand three heated assaults and pour deadly fire into the attackers. Nevertheless, Rebel reinforcements under General Polk arrive to bolster the assault and the ground is overrun by the Confederates. Sheridan's troops, following the exhaustion of their ammunition, initiate a bayonet assault to forestall further Rebel progress as the division fades back toward the Nashville Pike. In the meantime, with the right side of the Union lines in jeopardy, the Confederates focus on the center held by General Thomas' force. Similarly to the actions of Sheridan, Thomas's troops repel repeated attacks until their ammunition is exhausted. Urgent calls for reinforcements are placed to meet what seemingly appears to be wave after wave of Confederate troops. Undaunted by the overwhelming odds, Thomas's troops also initiate a fierce bayonet attack that prevents a rout. By about this time, reserves under General Rousseau burst through the cedars to assist, and another contingent, regulars under Major Ring, advance to hold the ground that holds the path to the Union rear, which has been evacuated by Brigadier General James C. Negley.

The retreat by Negley had permitted the Rebels to reach positions from which they begin to pour devastating fire upon the Yankees, trapping them in a crossfire. Thomas orders a pull back to the Nashville Pike. During this ongoing Confederate offensive, Crittenden's forces had been recalled from the river bank and redeployed in positions from which they could engage the Confederates as they attempt to emerge from the cedars. General John McCauley Palmer's Division single-handedly holds the front, with its left wing (19th Brigade) under Colonel W.B. Hazen holding the terrain between the railroad and the Nashville Pike and its right wing and center held by Lt. Colonel Charles E. Cross and Colonel Charles Cruft posted in positions that stretch westward toward the woods.

All the while, the Confederates maintain a steady assault to collapse the Union defenses. At the river, Colonel Hazen's command encounters repeated attacks. With the river protecting his left flank, Hazen repels the pressurized Rebel waves, prevents the capture of his entire line and simultaneously, without detection by the Rebels, creates a new line which holds tightly while awaiting the arrival of reinforcements of Colonels Charles Cross and Charles Cruft. The dramatic actions of Hazen, who has only 1,200 troops, hold toughly and the Rebels are unable to crush the line here.

The Union for the second time this day extricates itself from disaster, but this ground under Hazen is held at extremely high cost, particularly to the 9th Indiana (Colonel W.H. Blake), 6th Kentucky (Colonel W.C. Whittaker), 41st Ohio (Colonel A. Wiley), 110th Illinois (Colonel T.S. Casey), and the 1st Ohio Battery (Colonel Cockerill). Hazen's boys brazenly defy the odds, and in addition to saving the day, they buy the precious time needed by General William S. Rosecrans to shore up his right defenses in time to be prepared for the anticipated Confederate attack there.

At about 1500, the Rebels gush forth from the cedars to strike the lines which they expect to quickly fall, but to their dismay, the Union had indeed been prepared. With Van Cleve's infantry and some nearby artillery posted in the high ground, the Rebels encounter an invincible enfilade of fire that shreds the ranks of the massive attack. So terrible and so unexpected, the Rebels hurriedly retire, but only for the purpose of regrouping. Despite the horrific fire that has just subjected them to high casualties, they mount yet another bold assault.

From their new jump-off point, the Confederates impetuously charge, still determined to overwhelm the defenses; however, the artillery in the heights near the railway commences firing. The thunderclap rings perniciously and the casualties begin to mount, soaring even higher than those inflicted in the earlier attack. Once again, the Rebels are driven back. Still, Bragg is determined that he will prevail. Although he is convinced that the iron wall on the Union right cannot be penetrated, Bragg regroups for another assault to be launched against the Union left, which is considered to be not yet fully manned. General Breckinridge, having fresh troops, dispatches some contingents across the river to the right of General Polk. From here, an advance is initiated against

Top: **Brigadier General Joshua W. Sill.** *Bottom:* **General Leonidas Polk** (Johnson, *Campfire and Battlefield: History of the Conflicts and Campaigns*, 1894).

the defiant troops under Colonel Hazen, who had earlier refused to surrender even one bloody yard and are now comfortably reinforced and well prepared for the imminent onslaught.

As the bugles blare, the Rebels advance straight into Hazen's lines, igniting a furious donnybrook, but with the effective fire of the Union artillery, the Confederates, following a heroic attempt to penetrate, are once again forced to fall back hurriedly. Bragg sends in a new wave of troops, but these too receive a heated reception and become entangled in an incessant barrage of Yankee fire that forces them to retire from the field by nightfall. The fighting subsides with both sides sustaining many casualties, but the two armies finish the day with neither side gaining victory and each side harassed by the elements of the cold, rainy night.

Union Colonel Hazen pulls back ever so

slightly and re-establishes his lines to the rear of his formerly invincible positions, and the Confederates maintain the ground they had gained during the initial stages of the fighting on the Union right. The cost to the Union during this one day of brutal combat has been about 7,000 casualties, including Rosecrans' chief of staff, Colonel J.P. Garesche, who had been struck in the head while at the side of Rosecrans, who was observing a late afternoon advance by Colonel Hazen's force. Rosecrans himself had nearly been killed; the shell which struck Garesche bounced off his head and also struck Rosecrans. Major Adam J. Slemmer sustains a severe wound that terminates his service in the field; however, he is able to remain in the service. The following April he is promoted to brigadier general.

General Sheridan's command loses about 1,800 troops, including more than seventy officers, and within the brigade, Lt. Colonel Shepherd, about 500 troops (Regulars) and more than 20 officers become casualties. In contrast, the Confederates also sustain severe casualties, suffering the loss of about 4,000 killed, wounded or missing. Following the day's battle, Rosecrans confers with his staff to prepare for the next step. It is ascertained that about 3,000 troops have been captured by the Rebels and that the Union has also lost about twenty percent of their artillery to the Confederates, including the units under Edgarton and Houghtaling, as well as a large number of artillery pieces within the commands of Brush and Goodspeed. Nonetheless, the Union decides to reinitiate the battle on the following morning.

The following day, 1 January, there are no New Year's Day celebrations. It is extremely quiet, with both sides poised for possible action, but no major skirmishes occur. During the latter part of the afternoon, Rosecrans is reinforced by the arrival of two brigades under W.H.T. Walker and J.C. Starkweather. With this new infusion and due to the wounding of General Van Cleve on the previous day, the troop deployment is modified. In the absence of Van Cleve, Colonel Beatty (19th Ohio) assumes temporary command of the Fifth Division.

Beatty crosses the river and brings one of General Palmer's brigades with him to reinforce the positions, which are established on the upper ford. General Palmer's remaining brigades are east of the railway near Rousseau's lines. Behind these positions stand the forces of Negley in reserve. McCook's command holds the far right positions. The Union stands ready, but it is Bragg who makes the first move, beginning with the establishment of artillery positions during the night (1st-2nd).

On 2 January, at 0800, Confederate artillery commences firing to initiate the contest. Four recently erected batteries blast the lines of Colonel Loomis Rousseau's division. This fire is quickly returned by Union guns, and soon after, even more Union artillery pinpoints the Confederate artillery emplacements, making the exchange uneven. The Confederate guns are silenced. For a short while, the battlefield remains tranquil, but during the eerie silence, the Confederates are forming for one more gallant assault, in an attempt to fold the Union left. Confederate General Bragg initiates a massive assault at 1500 by sending Breckinridge's entire brigade against Beatty's division.

The Rebel brigade is heavily bolstered by the combined cavalry units of General John Pegram and John Austin Wharton and by the artillery under Captain Robertson. The sudden thrust and lingering power of the assault press straight through the first line of defense as the Union, despite being braced for the assault, is unable to withstand the onslaught. While the lines retire, additional units rush up from the reserves to fortify the line, but still the Rebels push deeper. Beatty is compelled to pull back as the reinforcing Ohio and Kentucky regiments still cannot maintain the line. Beatty directs his command to ford the river to reach the safety of some sixty guns posted there along the opposing bank (McFadden's Ford). This reluctant maneuver saves the command from extinction and foils the well laid plans of the Confederates.

The artillery, already poised for fire, bellows its ferocious roar as the Confederates under Breckinridge charge toward the positions. The riveting fire continues for nearly one hour, but for the attackers, it is seemingly an eternity, as about one third of the Rebels are cut down. In the meantime, more reinforcements rush to the front to ensure the stability of the Union lines, as the Rebels remain undaunted. Three brigades and James St. Clair Morton's corps of engineers arrive and accelerate the tenacity of the contest. The dueling artillery delivers massive exchanges of fire that inflict colossal damage to the opposing sides.

While the shells continue to rain death and destruction, the Union is ordered to propel forward by initiating an attack along the entire line to break the spine of the Confederate thrust. The 78th Pennsylvania takes the point, trailed by the 18th, 21st and 74th Ohio Regiments. These units are further augmented by the 11th Michigan, 19th Illinois, and 37th Indiana Regiments. The vanguard under Colonel Stillwell pounds against the steadfast Rebels, and the trailing Union regiments hammer forward as well, but the equally persistent Confederates return substantial punishing fire that prevents the contest from going to the Union. The Rebels remain immovable, but at about this time, yet more Yankees throw their weight into the struggle.

The units under General Stanley's cavalry and the inexhaustible force under Colonel Hazen turn the tide as Bragg's right wing begins to falter. As these Confederate forces retire toward Lytle's Creek, other Confederates who had been steadily holding the center of the line also give way and trace the steps of Bragg's right wing. By dusk, the Rebels' lines are reforming directly in front of Murfreesboro. The Union, faced with uncertainty from the darkness and inclement weather, which has brought a terrible storm to the area, cancels any further action for the day. In preparation for yet another grueling battle, Crittenden's command moves across the river during the night of the 2nd-3rd. On the 3rd, the weather remains nasty and there is no major contact between the two sides. Nonetheless, the Union continues to fortify its positions and maintain preparations for an impending battle on the following day.

At dawn on Sunday, January 4, the Union discovers that the Confederates under Bragg had moved out, passing through Murfreesboro en route to Tullahoma and Shelbyville. Brigadier General Zachariah C. Deas' brigade, composed of the 19th, 22nd, 25th, 39th, and 50th Alabama Regiments, the 17th Alabama Battalion Sharpshooters and Dent's Alabama artillery, participate in this battle. In February, General Braxton Bragg accuses General McCown of alleged "disobedience of orders." A court-martial is convened during March and General McCown is convicted and sentenced to lose his pay for a period of six months with an attached loss of rank.

Total Union casualties amount to 13,000 men, killed, wounded or missing; the Confederates suffer 10,000. The difference in the battle is clearly the Union artillery. This indecisive engagement stalls Union troops from taking Chattanooga, a primary rail station for the Confederate supply lines. The Union force stands at 45,000: the Confederate force at about 38,000. Union Brigadier General Joshua W. Sill (West Point, 1853) is killed. General Sheridan will subsequently name Fort Sill in Oklahoma in honor of his classmate at West Point. Union Brigadier General Edward N. Kirk is mortally wounded (dies 7-21-63). General Thomas Wood sustains a wound, but he refuses to be taken from the field. Confederate Brigadier General James E. Rains is killed while charging a Union battery. Colonel Robert B. Vance assumes command of Rains' brigade, but soon falls ill from typhoid fever. Brigadier General Roger Weightman Hanson is mortally wounded on the 2nd, succumbing on the 4th. Confederate Generals Wirt Allen and Daniel Weisiger Adams (second time) are wounded. Union General John Beatty suffers no injuries; however, he has two horses shot from under him. Beatty resigns his commission during January 1864. Union Sergeant Joseph L. Follett, 1st Missouri Light Artillery, receives his second Medal of Honor for valor during this action. His first was for heroism at New River, Missouri, on March 3, 1862. First Lieutenant Henry Freeman, 18th U.S. Infantry, also receives the Medal of Honor for bravery at this battle. Confederate Colonel Thomas Harrison commands a company of the 8th Texas Cavalry (Terry's Rangers). He is promoted to brigadier general toward the latter part of the conflict. Harrison had assumed command of the 8th Cavalry upon the promotion of Colonel John A. Wharton in November. Also, Confederate Brigadier General George Earl Maney's brigade participates in this action. Confederate Colonel (later brigadier general) Joseph Benjamin Palmer, 18th Tennessee Regiment, sustains wounds.

December 31 1862–January 25 1863 Confederate General Marmaduke initiates an expedition into Missouri that continues until the 25 January.

1863

In New Mexico, a force under Colonel Kit Carson attacks the Navajo to seize them and force their relocation to Fort Sumner. By January 1864, the Navajos are desperate and essentially unable to withstand a major assault when Carson's troops prepare to attack the remaining position at Canyon de Chelly. Those Indians there are seized, but many are not at the camp and evade capture. Manuelito, who had attacked Fort Defiance to spark this conflict, remains on the loose for two more years. Another Navajo leader, Hoskinnini, holds out in the region west of Monument Valley for about four years. Those Navajo who are compelled to relocate suffer harsh conditions, lack of supplies and food, and in addition, they sustain raids by Comanche and Kiowa war parties while near Fort Sumner on the Pecos.

By 1866, General Carleton loses his command. He is succeeded by General George Washington Getty. With Carleton's removal plan a proven failure, the Navajos are finally permitted to go home during June of 1868. Also, Fort Bascom, named for Captain George Nicholas Bascom (West Point, 1858), killed the previous February at Valverde, is established north of the town of Tucumcari and remains operational until 1874. The troops have responsibility for protecting the region; however, in addition to threats from the Indians, the post also must deal with bands of renegades known as Comancheros, composed of both Americans and Mexicans who routinely engage in dealing with stolen cattle, often acquired by the Indians, and illegally obtained weapons provided to the Indians along with spirits to complicate the tasks of the U.S. Army.

Also, Fort McRae is established in the vicinity of Butte Lake. It remains active until 1876. Another post, Fort Cummings, is established by the U.S. Army in the vicinity of Deming, which is near the City of Rocks, actually a huge rock formation rather than a settlement or town. The fort joins other army installations on the frontier along the route to the West Coast. The garrison holds responsibility for protecting settlers from hostile Indians and to form a strong link in the region to prevent the Confederates from gaining domination. Fort Cummings is deactivated during 1885.

In Oregon, at about this time, Fort Stevens is established at Point Adams outside Hammand and west of Astoria near the mouth of the Columbia River. The fort, named in honor of General Isaac Stevens (also territorial governor of Washington), who had been killed during fighting at Chantilly, Virginia (1862), becomes the anchor fort there with two others, Forts Canby and Columbia, both in Washington. The forts come to be known as the Three Fort Harbor Defense System. Fort Stevens remains active until 1947.

In Rhode Island, the Union Army establishes Fort Greble on Dutch Island between Jamestown to the east and Saunderstown to the west. The fort is named in honor of a Civil War soldier, Lieutenant Colonel John Trout Greble (West Point, 1854), a veteran of the Indian Wars who was killed at Big Bethel, Virginia, on 10 June 1861 during the early days of the Civil War. The fort remains active until 1947. Prior to the establishment of the fort, the U.S. government had acquired some land on the island to erect a lighthouse to guide the vessels near Dutch Island harbor, and its first keeper was a veteran of the American Revolution, William Dennis, who remained at the position until his demise during 1843, while in his nineties. Dutch Island during the early 1600s had been the location of a trading post of the Dutch West India Company.

January *In Confederate general officer activity,* Major (later general) Robert Houston Anderson (West Point, 1857) is promoted to colonel, 5th Georgia Cavalry Regiment. General Milledge L. Bonham becomes a member of the First Regular Confederate Congress. He holds the post until January 1863, when he becomes governor of South Carolina and serves out his term, which lasts until December 1864. Lieutenant Dudley McIver DuBose is appointed colonel of the 15th Georgia Infantry Regiment. DuBose's regiment is part of the Army of Northern Virginia. In November 1864, Dubose will be promoted to brigadier general. He is the son-in-law of Confederate Brigadier General Robert Toombs. Brigadier General Gustavus Woodson Smith resigns his commission; however, he is appointed a major general in command of Georgia militia.

January 1 (Thursday) THE BATTLE OF GALVESTON Confederate troops commanded by General Magruder launch an assault to capture Galveston, Texas, at 0100. The Union forces,

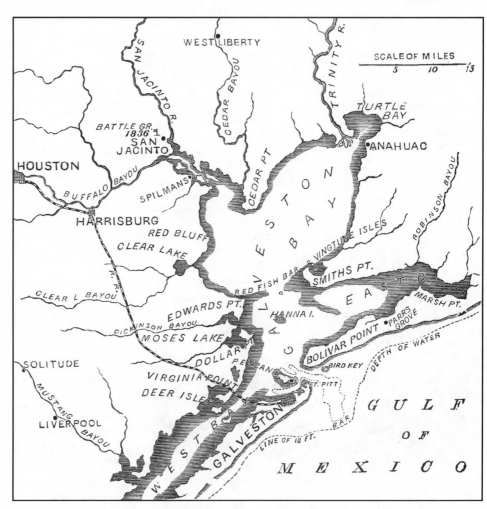

Map of Galveston Bay (*Harper's Pictorial History of the Civil War*, 1896).

commanded by Colonel Burrill, raise resistance, but while the assault force is being heavily engaged, General Magruder orders his battery, which has been speedily erected on nearby Pelican Island during the previous night, to pour fire upon the Union gunboats. The USS *Harriet Lane*, *Clifton* and *Westfield* silence the guns on Pelican Island, but the Confederates still are able to pound the Yankees. Meanwhile, four Confederate gunboats, including the *Bayou City* and the *Neptune*, arrive and the *Harriet Lane* is pounced upon. The *Harriet Lane*, commanded by Commander J.M. Wainwright, runs down the CSS *Neptune* and then takes on the *Bayou City*, knocking out its only gun, but the damaged vessel manages to ram the *Harriet Lane*, and the Rebels board it.

The crew of the *Harriet Lane* puts up a vicious fight, but following the bloody hand-to-hand struggle, the Rebels capture the ship; the crew is taken prisoner and Commander Wainwright is killed. During the struggle, the *Owasco* moves up to assist the *Harriet Lane*, but heavy fire forces it to pull back. In the meantime, the *Westfield* runs aground while firing upon Fort Point, a Union battery position which has been captured by the Rebels. The *Clifton* moves in to support the *Westfield*, but the situation is quickly deteriorating. By about 0800, the Confederates demand surrender, giving the Yankees only one hour to accept the offer.

It is decided that further resistance would be foolhardy considering their circumstances, facing a superior numbered force and being down to one effective warship, the *Owasco*. While negotiations are underway, the Rebel-held *Harriet Lane* moves to shore and captures the remaining troops of Colonel Burrill. The surviving sailors attempt to destroy the grounded *Westfield* by fire and then escape aboard the gunboats, but after coating the vessel with turpentine and preparing to abandon ship, a premature explosion occurs. The crew is safely aboard the *M.A. Bardman*, but Commodore Renshaw, Lt. Zimmerman and several other officers are instantly killed as the *Westfield* is blown into oblivion. Although the explosion had been set off too early, it had nonetheless been the signal for the surviving ships to escape. They depart with the

Confederates giving chase, but the Rebels fail to catch them.

Following the loss of Galveston, Commodore Farragut sends Commodore Bell aboard the *Brooklyn* (flagship) and six other vessels to reestablish the blockade of Galveston. Within several days, Confederate General Magruder declares that the port of Galveston is "open for trade to all friendly nations." General Magruder remains in Texas for the duration. At the end of hostilities, he enters Mexico and becomes a major general in the imperial forces. Subsequent to ousting the French under Maximilian, he returns to Texas, where he dies on 18 February 1871 at Houston.

Brigadier General William R. Scurry had commanded the Confederate land troops other than those with the warships. The CSS *Bayou City*, a Confederate Army gunboat, was built in Indiana during 1859, chartered in 1861 by the Texas Marine Department, and acquired by the Confederate Army during October 1862. The *Bayou City* remains in service and operates in the vicinity of Texas for the duration of the war. The *Neptune* sustains heavy damage after ramming the *Harriet Lane* and sinks within a few days.

In Washington, D.C., President Lincoln publishes the Emancipation Proclamation, which he had presented to his cabinet on September 22, 1862.

In South Carolina at Charleston, a contingent of thirty Marines, attached to the South Atlantic Squadron, land at Murrells Inlet and raid a Confederate schooner, sinking it.

In Mississippi, a previously scheduled attack against Haines Bluff by the combined forces of General Sherman and the fleet under Commodore Porter is aborted due to extremely heavy fog. General Sherman moves back to Milliken's Bend by the following day.

In Tennessee, a Union contingent composed of elements of the 10th Ohio Infantry and the 3rd Ohio Cavalry skirmish with Confederates at Stewart's Creek. Also, the 1st Michigan Engineers and Mechanics skirmish with Confederates at La Vergne. Casualty figures are unavailable.

In Naval activity, the USS Colonel *Kinsman*, an army gunboat, is transferred to the U.S. Navy. Also, the monitor USS *Patapsco* is commissioned at about this time (early January).

In Union general officer activity, Major General Edwin Denison Morgan, commander of the Department of New York, resigns his commission. General Morgan had been finishing his second term as governor when he was elected to the U.S. Senate. He takes his seat on 4 March of this year.

January 2 (Friday)   In Arkansas, a Union contingent skirmishes with Confederates at Cane Hill.

In Mississippi, General Sherman's force, having experienced difficulty with the weather on the previous day, by this time has abandoned the effort to seize Haines Bluff along the Yazoo River, north of Vicksburg. Union gunboats, including the USS *Juliet*, provide support during the withdrawal to the Mississippi River by following the transports and the other gunboats down the Yazoo.

In Tennessee, Union Colonel (later general) John Beatty, a participant at the Battle of Murfreesboro, has two horses shot from under him but escapes without injury. General Beatty later participates at the battles of Chickamauga and assists General Sherman when he heads for Knoxville to relieve General Burnside during November 1863. Also, Union General August von Willich is captured during the fighting at Murfreesboro. He will be exchanged and will join Alexander McCook's XX Corps at Chickamauga in September.

In Virginia, Confederate cavalry strikes Union positions defended by Major Herring at Dumfries.

In Union Naval officer activity, Captain Sylvanus W. Godon is promoted to the rank of commodore. He participates in the attacks against Fort Fisher during December 1864 and January 1865. After the war, on 25 July 1866, Commodore Godon is promoted to rear admiral of the South Atlantic Squadron, and during 1869, he is named commandant of the New York Navy Yard. In other activity, Commander Charles H. Poor is promoted to the rank of commodore. He assumes command of the USS *Saranac*, a sloop of war operating as part of the Pacific Squadron. During his tour aboard the *Saranac* (1864–1865), in one incident, Commodore Poor uses the power of his sailors and U.S. Marines to compel the authorities at Rio La Hache, Venezuela, to apologize for insulting the U.S. flag by having them hoist Old Glory and salute it. His actions are afterward approved by the Navy Department. In 1866, Commodore Poor is appointed as commander of the U.S. Naval Station at Mound City, Illinois. He is promoted to the rank of rear admiral on 20 September 1868 and made commandant of the Washington Navy Yard. During August of the following year, on the 19th, Admiral Poor assumes command of the North Atlantic Squadron.

January 3 (Saturday)   In Arkansas, elements of Colonel Cadwallader Washburn's cavalry regiment strikes the Confederate positions at La Grange. The Union reports no casualties. The estimated Confederate casualties are 10 killed and 12 captured.

In Tennessee, Union General William S. Rosecrans' troops occupy Murfreesboro, while Confederate General Bragg withdraws to Tullahoma, about 40 miles away. This retreat surrenders Confederate control of central Ten-

The USS *Harriet Lane* is seized in Galveston Bay (*Harper's Pictoral History of the Civil War*, 1896).

nessee, and the Confederates also sustain the loss of food production from the area. The Union fortifies the city and calls it Fortress Rosecrans for "Old Rosy." It is the largest earthen fortification built during the Civil War. This gigantic supply base aids the imminent Union attack on Chattanooga, and it helps to slice a wedge through the Confederacy. The Battle of Murfreesboro does much to devour the proud Army of Tennessee.

In West Virginia, a contingent of the 116th Ohio Volunteer Regiment skirmishes with Confederates at Morefield.

In Naval activity, the USS *New Era* departs Cairo en route to join the fleet that will move up the White River in Arkansas to attack Fort Hindman. It joins the fleet on the following day. The USS *Glide* departs Cairo, Illinois, en route to the lower Mississippi to join the Mississippi Squadron. After arriving, the *Glide* participates in the attack against Fort Hindman (Arkansas Post) on 11 January. In February 1863, the *Glide* returns to Cairo for repairs. The *Linden* (side-wheel steamer) acquired by the U.S. Navy during November 1862, is commissioned. Acting Master Thomas E. Smith receives command.

January 4 (Sunday)   In Washington, D.C., in response to an order issued on 17 December by General U.S. Grant at Holly Springs, Mississippi, General Halleck revokes the order: "A paper purporting to be General Orders, No. 11, signed by you December 17, has been presented here. By Its terms it expels all Jews from your department. If such an order has been issued, it will be Immediately revoked" (see also, **December 17** [1862], **In Mississippi**).

In Missouri, a Union scouting detachment departs Ozark for Dubuque, Arkansas. The mission lasts until 6 January.

In North Carolina, General G.W. Smith receives a letter from General Robert E. Lee stating, in part: "I would recommend that you collect a force at Goldsboro, adequate to oppose the enemy. Take the field in person and endeavor to get our troops from North Carolina for her defense. Wilmington should be defended at all hazards."

In Mississippi, General John A. McClernand arrives at Milliken's Bend from Cairo, Illinois. He assumes command of the Army of the Tennessee and begins to divide the army into two corps: the 15th, commanded by General Sherman and composed of the divisions of Generals Frederick Steele and David Stuart, and the 13th under General George W. Morgan, composed of the divisions of Generals P.J. Osterhaus (formerly G.W. Morgan's Division) and A.J. Smith. Afterward, General McClernand leads his force toward Arkansas Post, Arkansas.

In Tennessee, some activity occurs between the Union under Rosecrans and Bragg's Confederates, the latter involved in retiring from the Murfreesboro area.

In Arkansas, the Union initiates an offensive to seize Fort Hindman (Arkansas Post) on the 4th and culminates the operation on the 11th. The fleet under Admiral David D. Porter is transporting troops from General William T. Sherman and a contingent of U.S. Marines. The USS *Romeo* participates and then returns to its operations on the Yazoo on 6 February.

In Naval activity, the USS *Quaker City* captures the blockade runner *Mercury* off Charleston.

January 5 (Monday)   In Tennessee, a contingent of Union cavalry, attached to the Army of the Cumberland, skirmishes with Confederates at Middleton. Casualty figures are unavailable.

In West Virginia, a contingent of Union troops commanded by Captain McNeill is attacked by a Confederate force in Hardy County. Casualty figures are unavailable.

In North Carolina, a contingent of advance guards (General John G. Foster's command) skirmishes with Confederate pickets at Kinston.

In Union general officer activity, General Abram Duryee (wounded in battle five times), following command changes, including the reassignment of his division's regiments and a new corps commander (John Gibbon), resigns his commission. During the closing days of the war, he receives the rank of brevet major general.

January 6 (Tuesday)   In Tennessee, a band of Confederate guerrillas (cavalry) led by Captain J.H. McGehee capture the USS *Jacob Musselman,* a steam transport, on the Mississippi opposite Memphis. The guerrillas at this time are charged with harassing Union shipping on the Mississippi River. The transport is taken to Bradley's Landing and destroyed. At Murfreesboro, in what appears to be a reaction to a recent declaration of Confederate President Jefferson Davis that Union officers would no longer be paroled, Union General Rosecrans issues an order forbidding the parole of Confederate officers.

In Virginia, General Robert E. Lee writes to Confederate President Davis congratulating him upon his safe return from the Western Theater: "I attribute the great victory of General Bragg [Murfreesboro] to the courage diffused by your cheering words and presence."

In Naval activity, the USS *Pocahontas,* operating in the Gulf of Mexico, spots a merchant ship moving toward the entrance of Mobile Bay. The *Pocahontas,* during the morning, moves to intercept the blockade runner before it can come under the protection of the guns at Fort Morgan, one of the defending forts of New Orleans and less than ten miles distant. The runner increases its speed, but in turn, the *Pocahontas* also accelerates and begins to close at about dusk. The *Pocahontas* fires a warning shot, which prompts the ship to hoist the British colors; however, it makes no attempt to halt. At about 2300, the *Pocahontas* again closes to within range of the guns, then again opens fire.

At the time, the two ships have reached a point about 30 miles from Cape San Blas, Florida. The blockade runner *Antona* finally halts after two rounds are fired. The *Antona,* an iron-hulled screw steamer built at Glasgow, Scotland, is carrying a cargo of gunpowder, small arms and other items, including tea and brandy, which it had taken aboard at Havana, Cuba, prior to departing for Mobile on 1 January 1863. The *Antona* is taken back to the blockading squadron off Mobile and from to Philadelphia, where it is commissioned during March 1863.

January 7 (Wednesday)   In Virginia, a reconnaissance team (elements of the 1st New York Cavalry), led by Lt. Colonel Von Schickfuss, departs Winchester for Woodstock.

In Naval activity, the USS *Lodona,* assigned to Rear Admiral Samuel F. Du Pont's South Atlantic Squadron, departs Philadelphia for Port Royal, South Carolina. During the voyage, the *Lodona* pauses at Hampton Roads and at Fort Monroe in Virginia. The USS *Weehawken* is in tow. Both vessels arrive in Port Royal on 5 February.

In Missouri, a contingent of Union troops, including convalescents and citizens of Springfield, are confronted by Confederate troops under Generals Price and Marmaduke on this day and the next. The town is not captured by the Rebels, who are forced to move onward. Union General Egbert B. Brown is wounded. One of his arms is amputated. The Union sustains 14 killed and 144 wounded. The Confederates suffer 40 killed and about 200 wounded or missing.

January 8 (Thursday)   In Arkansas, Union gunboats bombard Confederate Fort Hindman on the Arkansas River, prior to the assault on the 11th by soldiers and U.S. Marines. Grant at first opposes the attack, to be launched by General John A. McClernand, until he realizes what mischief 5,000 to 6,000 defenders could do behind Union lines. The Union initiates a scouting operation. The detachment departs Elk Horn for Berryville and concludes the mission on the 10th.

In Tennessee, a contingent of the 2nd Illinois Cavalry commanded by Captain Moore attacks Confederates under Lt. Colonel Dawson at Ripley. The Union sustains three wounded. The Confederates sustain about eight killed, 20 wounded and some captured.

In Confederate general officer activity, at about this time, Confederate Major General Mansfield Lovell loses his command. He had been at New Orleans and subsequently absolved of responsibility of its loss. He had participated in the battle of Corinth in October 1862. Nevertheless, he receives no new command, and in 1864 the requests of his service by two generals is rejected. Lovell will be recalled to duty during the latter part of the war; however, the hostilities end before he reaches the headquarters of General Robert E. Lee. In other activity, Confederate Colonel James Cantey is appointed brigadier general, effective this date. General

Cantey suffers from ill health which impairs his performance.

In Naval activity, the USS *Iroquois,* out of commission for repairs since the previous October, is recommissioned. The ship, now commanded by Commander Henry Rolando, successor to Commander Palmer, leaves New York during the latter part of the month to escort the *Weehawken* to Newport News, Virginia. Afterward, the *Iroquois* heads south to join the Blockading Squadron off North Carolina. In other activity, the USS *Tahoma,* while on patrol in Tampa Bay, seizes a blockade runner, the Silas Henry, which is transporting a cargo of cotton.

January 9 (Friday)   In Virginia, a Union contingent — consisting of artillery, infantry and cavalry units — fords the Rappahannock River at several spots between Beverly and Kelly's Fords and attacks Confederate positions. The duel lasts well into the day, but the Confederates finally drive the Union back across the river at about 1700.

In Arkansas, a Union contingent departs Huntsville in Madison Country and makes an expedition to Buffalo River that lasts through the 12th.

January 10 (Saturday)   In Arkansas, Union troops commanded by General John A. McClernand take positions around Confederate Fort Hindman. Union warships are offshore pummeling Confederate positions and neutralizing the Confederate artillery.

In Mexico at Yukatan on Majores Island, the U.S. Marine guard attached to the USS *Wachusett,* composed of eighteen men, assumes control of the CSS *Virginia,* a captured ironclad steamer; the Marines sail the vessel to Key West, Florida, where it is to be destroyed.

In Missouri, a Union contingent clashes with Confederates at Carrollton.

In Virginia, a contingent of Union cavalry, commanded by General Schimmelfennig, skirmishes with Confederate cavalry under General Wade Hampton at Catlett's Station. Casualty figures are unavailable. General Robert E. Lee writes to Confederate Secretary of War James A. Seddon about the shortage of men and the frequent inability to finish off the Union because of lopsided forces. General Lee pleads for help from the Confederate states: "They must put forth their full strength at once. Let them hear the appeal of their defenders for help and drive into the ranks from very shame, those who will not heed the dictates of honor and of patriotism. Let the state authorities take the matter in hand, and see that no man able to bear arms be allowed to evade his duty."

January 11 (Sunday)   In Arkansas, Union gunboats — including the USS *Cincinnati,* USS *Baron De Kalb* (formerly *Louisville,* renamed *Baron De Kalb* during September 1862 after being transferred to the Navy from the Gulf Western Squadron), the *Signal* and Admiral David Porter's flagship, the *Blackhawk* (formerly *New Uncle Sam*) — bombard Confederate Fort

Hindman at Arkansas Post, while General McClernand's troops, including General William T. Sherman's corps, simultaneously attack on land. Naval records state the USS *Ivy* was Porter's flagship during this operation. The *Ivy* participates heavily in the engagement and at one time assists in extinguishing fires aboard the *Cincinnati* and the *Louisville.* During the battle, Rebels raise the white flag. General Sherman enters the fort to find Confederate General Thomas J. Churchill in conversation with Union Admiral David D. Porter. After some confusion with Confederate infantry is rectified, the fort surrenders. The 5,000 captured Confederates under General Churchill are transported to St. Louis. General Churchill, upon his release, will rejoin the Confederate Army and serve during the Red River Campaign, including the Battle of Sabine Cross Roads. Confederate Colonel James Deshler is also captured. Subsequent to his release, he is promoted to brigadier general (July 1863) and transferred to the Army of Tennessee, where he serves in General Patrick Ronayne Cleburne's division. Union Colonel Cyrus Bussey, 3rd Iowa Cavalry, participates at this battle. He fought at Pea Ridge in March 1862 and later, he leads a division of cavalry at Vicksburg. Colonel Bussey is promoted to brigadier general on 5 January 1864. Brigadier General Charles E. Hovey is wounded. General Sherman later states that Hovey continued to command his brigade. It is reported that a shell passed through both of his arms, compelling him to resign (May 1863), and he does vanish from the Official Records. However, on 13 March 1865, in line with the "omnibus brevet promotions," Hovey is promoted to major general. General Hovey is a distant cousin of Union General Alvin P. Hovey.

Admiral Porter orders the USS *New Era,* which had participated in the campaign, to receive the wounded men from the USS *Cincinnati* and the *Baron De Kalb* and transport them to a hospital ship at the mouth of the White River. After delivering the troops to safety, the *New Era* moves to Island No. 10 in Tennessee to relieve the USS *Carondelet.* Secretary of the Navy Gideon Welles notes in a memorandum regarding the USS *Ivy:* "The officers and crew behaved with great coolness, though under a brisk fire of musketry." The naval attack, directed from *Ivy,* resulted in Sherman's capture of the fort, a severe blow to the Confederate cause in the West.

In Missouri, a Union force composed of elements of the 21st Iowa and 99th Illinois Infantry Regiments supported by the 3rd Iowa and 3rd Missouri Cavalry Regiments and artillery (Battery I, 2nd Missouri Battery), commanded by Colonel Lewis Merrill, engages Confederates under General Marmaduke in a day-long battle at Hartsville (Wood's Fork or Wood's Creek). The Union sustains seven killed, 64 wounded, five captured and two missing. The Confederates sustain about 150 killed and wounded and more than 100 captured.

In Tennessee, Confederates capture the steamer *Grampus* on the Mississippi opposite Memphis.

Commodore Homer Blake (*Harper's Pictorial History of the Civil War,* 1896).

In Naval action, the Confederate privateer *Alabama,* commanded by Captain Raphael Semmes, approaches the blockade squadron of Commodore Henry Bell off Galveston, Texas. The vessel approaches from the southeast, but it is using a ruse, pretending to be a British vessel. When the USS *Hatteras* closes and requests identification, the *Alabama* responds that it is the HMS *Spitfire.* As Captain Homer C. Blake of the USS *Hatteras* informs the ship that he is sending a boat, the imposter moves up and unfurls its Confederate colors and delivers a deadly blow to the unsuspecting *Hatteras.* The Union gunners return fire, but too late, as the *Hatteras* begins to sink and the crew is forced to surrender.

The USS *Agassiz,* which departed New London, Connecticut, on 23 December, arrives at New Bern, North Carolina. The *Agassiz* (a Coast Guard revenue cutter) will operate in the North Carolina sounds to provide support to the Navy and for various Union army operations in the region. The USS *Katahdin* had also joined the warships off Galveston by this time. It remains in the vicinity for the duration of the war and at that time is sent north. It is decommissioned in New York during July 1865 and renamed *Juno.*

January 12 (Monday)   In Arkansas, General John A. McClernand withdraws his entire force from Fort Hindman to return to Napoleon, situated at the mouth of the Arkansas River. Grant receives subsequent requests from both General Sherman and Admiral Porter to speed to Napoleon to see for himself the inadequacies of McClernand, and they request that Grant assume personal command of the troops. Grant receives permission from his superiors to replace McClernand if necessary. General Grant and Admiral Porter had conferred in Cairo, Illinois, during December 1862 and the meeting ended with each respecting the other's problems. Cooperation between the two for the duration remains quite strong. In other activity, a detachment of the 2nd Wisconsin Cavalry skirmishes with Confederates at Lick Creek. Casualty figures are unavailable.

January 13 (Tuesday) **In Arkansas,** a Union flotilla, composed of light steamers commanded by General Gorman and Lt. Walker, moves up the White River on an expedition. The force demolishes the towns of Des Arc and Duval's Bluff before joining McClernand at Napoleon. The mission concludes on 19 January.

In Missouri, Union and Confederate contingents skirmish at Carthage.

In Tennessee, the Confederates capture the Union gunboat *Sidel,* commanded by Lt. Van Dorn, along the Cumberland River. The *Sidel* is operating under jurisdiction of the Army rather than the Navy and Van Dorn is an army lieutenant. The vessel surrenders without a fight. The loss of the ship ignites an investigation at the Department of the Navy; however, Commodore Porter is able to explain that the vessel had not been a Navy ship.

In Union general officer activity, Colonel Daniel Ullman (78th New York Regiment) is promoted to brigadier general. He is ordered to New Orleans with instructions to organize five Negro regiments. Later he commands at Port Hudson and afterward at Morganza, Louisiana. William Birney, brother of General David Birney, is appointed major of the 4th New Jersey regiment. During the following year (May '63) he becomes a brigadier general.

January 14 (Wednesday) **In Louisiana,** a Union force led by Commodore Buchanan and General Weitzel engage Confederates under Colonel Gary at Bayou Teche. Union troops, including the 8th Vermont, 12th Connecticut, 75th New York, and the gunboats USS *Calhoun, Diana, Colonel Kinsman* and *Estrella* participate. The Union sustains 10 dead and 27 wounded; the Confederates sustain 15 killed and some captured. Union Commodore Buchanan is killed by a fatal wound to the thigh while aboard the *Calhoun,* conspicuously directing the vessel amid the enemy torpedoes. The Confederate gunboat CSS *J.A. Cotton,* commanded by E.W. Fuller, had taken a thrashing during the day. Commander Fuller sustains a broken arm, but he manages to steer the wheel with his feet to back the gunboat up the bayou following the death of his pilots. The *J.A. Cotton* is too wide to be turned in the slim channel. It is spotted the following day in flames as it drifts down the bayou. The Confederates had abandoned it after applying the torch. In addition, the USS *Colonel Kinsman* sustains damage. The Union gunboat USS *Queen of the West* is seized by Confederates on the Red River.

In Confederate activity, the Confederate Southwestern Army is established under the command of General E. Kirby Smith.

In Naval activity, the USS *Columbia,* attached to the North Atlantic Blockading Squadron since its capture in November, runs aground at Masonboro.

January 15 (Thursday) **In Arkansas,** Union forces enter Mound City and set it afire. In other

General E. Kirby Smith (Johnson, *Campfire and Battlefield: History of the Conflicts and Campaigns,* 1894).

activity, Confederates launch an attack against the 2nd Wisconsin Cavalry at Helena and along the Clarendon Road. The Union reports no casualties. The Confederates suffer about seven killed and wounded and nearly 20 captured.

In New York, Colonel Nicholas Day succeeds Colonel Charles S. Turnbull as commanding officer of the recently organized (mustered in on 6 September 1862) 131st New York Regiment, which is part of the Metropolitan Brigade.

In Confederate general officer activity, Major General David R. Jones (West Point, 1846), having retired from active service because of ill health, dies of heart failure. General Jones had been involved since the beginning of the war. He participated at the Rebel seizure of Fort Sumter, with Beauregard, at 1st Manassas (Bull Run), Thoroughfare Gap, 2nd Manassas (Bull Run) and Antietam.

In Naval activity, the CSS *Florida* awaits darkness, then departs from Mobile and successfully evades capture. One of the ships on patrol, the gunboat USS *R.R. Cuyler,* initiates pursuit, but the *Florida,* commanded by Lt. James Newland Maffitt, outruns it and sails to Cuba. On the 25th, the *Florida* arrives at Nassau along with three prizes. A U.S. squadron commanded by Captain Wilkes is involved in a search to locate the *Florida.* The squadron commander discovers that it had arrived at Nassau and acquired fuel, leaving him to believe that the next stop would have to be the French port at Martinique, because neutrality laws prohibit the *Florida* from refueling at a British port for three

months. Consequently, Wilkes sends one of his warships toward Martinique; however, the *Florida* instead refuels in Barbados on 24 February. The USS *Alabama, Oneida, R.R. Cuyler,* and *San Jacinto* join the squadron at various times during January and February of this year. The USS *Juniata* and the USS *Rhode Island* have not yet joined the squadron.

January 16 (Friday) **In Arkansas,** the Union gunboat USS *Baron DeKalb,* commanded by Lt. John G. Walker, and elements of the 24th Indiana Volunteer Regiment (General Gorman's command) operate in the vicinity of Duvall's Bluff and Des Arcs. The Union reports no casualties. The Confederates lose seven captured. In addition, the Union seizes two guns and about 200 stands of arms.

In Kansas, pursuant to General Order No. 14 (War Department), Fort Scott is re-established as a permanent post.

January 17 (Saturday) **In Washington, D.C.,** Congress authorizes $100,000,000 in U.S. notes to guarantee pay for the Union soldiers.

In Arkansas, General Grant arrives at Napoleon to confer with other officers on General McClernand's ability to command. Grant orders McClernand's entire army to Young's Point and Milliken's Bend, Louisiana, on the 20th. General Stephen A. Hurlbut's 16th Corps remains behind to insure control of the area for the Union.

In North Carolina, Union troops occupy the town of Des Arc. Also, elements of the 3rd New York Cavalry skirmish with Confederates at Pollocksville and North East River. Casualty figures are unavailable.

In New Mexico Territory, Union soldiers under Brigadier General Joseph R. West's command, operating in the vicinity of Pinos Altos, engage Apaches under Chief Mangus Coloradas (father-in-law of Cochise). Coloradas is captured, and later that night, he is shot and killed, supposedly for trying to escape. Subsequently, General West commands the District of Arizona, but later he participates as a divisional commander during the Red River campaign. Afterward, for a while he joins in the operations against General Sterling Price (late 1864); however, toward the close of the war, he commands all the cavalry units in the Department of the Gulf. General West is breveted major general of volunteers on the day he musters out of the army, 1 January 1866.

In Confederate general officer activity, Brigadier General Daniel S. Donelson is assigned command of the Department of East Tennessee to succeed General Edmund Kirby Smith, the latter having recently received command of the Trans-Mississippi Department. Donelson had led the 1st Brigade, General Cheatham's division, at the recent battle of Murfreesboro, Tennessee. General Marcus Joseph Wright will assume command of Donelson's brigade. Colonel Robert F. Hoke, 21st

North Carolina Infantry Regiment, is promoted to the rank of brigadier general, effective this date. Hoke's promotion is due to his exemplary service in the Army of Northern Virginia during the period covering May 1862 through the action at Chancellorsville (May 1863). Colonel William Tatum Wofford, 18th Georgia Infantry, is promoted to the rank of brigadier general effective this date. Wofford had taken command of General Cobb's brigade upon the demise of the latter at Fredericksburg, Virginia, in December. Wofford continues to serve in the Army of Northern Virginia, participating at various battles, including Chancellorsville and the Pennsylvania Campaign that follows it. Also, Colonel Samuel McGowan is made brigadier general effective this date. McGowan had also been a major general of South Carolina militia during 1861. His promotion is in conjunction with the death of General Maxcy Gregg in December. In yet other activity, Henry Lewis Benning is appointed brigadier general effective this day. He will be attached to the 1st Corps and serve with General Hood's division for the duration of the conflict.

January 18 (Sunday)   In the Indian Territory (Cherokee Country), a skirmish develops.

January 19 (Monday)   In Virginia, General Robert E. Lee informs Confederate President Jefferson Davis that Union forces under Major General Henry W. Slocum (West Point, 1852) are crossing the Wolf Run Shoals, for either Dumfries or Fredericksburg. In other activity, an 18-man detachment of the 5th Pennsylvania Cavalry led by Lieutenant Vezin reconnoiters the area near Burnt Ordinary and encounters Confederate cavalry numbering about 75 troops. Casualty figures are unavailable. Also, the Army of the Potomac, essentially immobilized since the Battle of Fredericksburg in December, is about to again cross the Rappahannock, but the weather continues to deteriorate as General Burnside make his final preparation to regain Fredericksburg.

January 20 (Tuesday)   In Massachusetts, Governor John Andrew calls for the enlistment of volunteers, and the proclamation includes "people of African origin."

In Virginia, at the Rappahannock River, the weather changes from snow to rain storms and interferes with General Burnside's strategy to get the Army of the Potomac back across the river to regain Fredericksburg. As the temperature rises, the area becomes permeated with mud.

In Confederate general officer activity, Major William L. Cabell, who had served at Manassas as chief quartermaster and later in the Trans-Mississippi Department under General Van Dorn, is appointed brigadier general. Confederate Major George Blake Cosby is promoted to brigadier general. Cosby will be transferred to General Van Dorn's command and will lead a cavalry brigade. He later participates under General Joseph E. Johnston in Mississippi. At Vicksburg, Cosby is transferred to the Department of West Virginia and East Tennessee until the close of hostilities. General Cosby moves to California after the war. He commits suicide at Oakland—blamed on damage to his health from wounds sustained during the war—on 29 June 1909 at about the age of 89. Colonel Marcellus Augustus Stovall, formerly lieutenant colonel of the 3rd Georgia (battalion) and at present in the artillery section, is promoted to the rank of brigadier general effective this date. General Stovall will be assigned duty in Georgia and Tennessee, and toward the final months of the conflict, he will serve under General Joseph E. Johnston in the Carolinas. Confederate Brigadier General Joseph Wheeler is promoted to the rank of major general, effective this date. Also, Frank Crawford Armstrong, the stepson of General Persifor Frazer, is promoted to brigadier general to rank from this day. After the death of Armstrong's father, his mother remarried General Frazer.

January 21 (Wednesday)   In Mississippi, the Union fleet carrying McClernand's force from Napoleon arrives at Young's Point following a rough voyage that included a tremendous storm. The troops debark on the following day and prepare to take Vicksburg.

In Texas, the Confederate Navy, having recently scored successes at Galveston, again tries its luck. Gunboats of the Texas Marine fleet, including the *Uncle Ben,* a cotton-clad steamer, and the *Josiah Bell* engage two Union ships, the *Morning Light* and the *Fairy* (formerly *Velocity*) in the vicinity of Sabine Pass. Both Union vessels are captured.

In Missouri, Union and Confederate contingents skirmish at Columbia.

In Tennessee, a contingent of Confederate cavalry led by Lt. Colonel Hutchinson attacks Union lines at Murfreesboro. Casualty figures are unavailable.

In Virginia, Union Major General Fitz John Porter (West Point, 1845) is dismissed from the Army after a court-martial. He is charged with disloyalty and disobedience on the field to his superiors while facing the enemy. General Porter had served admirably in the Mexican War, the Peninsular Campaign of McClellan and during the Maryland campaign; however, like most officers under McClellan, General Pope, who had brought the charges against Porter, was immensely disliked. Pope's charges cost Porter his career; however, 16 years later, General Porter is exonerated of all charges. The chair of the board that returns his reputation is General John Schofield. When Schofield was a cadet at West Point, General Porter voted to have him expelled for disciplinary reasons. Schofield graduated West Point during 1853, while Porter graduated during 1845.

In Naval activity, Commodore Wilkes orders the USS *Santiago* and the *Cuyler* (Admiral Farragut's fleet) to search for the blockade runner *Oreto,* which had successfully run the blockade at Mobile. The *Cuyler* and another of Farragut's fleet, the USS *Oneida,* had also initiated pursuit. On 3 February, following only twelve days with Wilkes' squadron, the *Cuyler,* in need of repairs, is ordered by Wilkes to sail for Key West.

January 22 (Thursday)   In Mississippi, General Grant, commander of the Department of Tennessee, receives command of all forces in Arkansas "within reach of his orders."

In Virginia, the Army of the Potomac continues to be hindered by inclement weather, which forbids progress. The ongoing rains have created a quagmire, preventing easy movement of equipment and wagons. The anticipated crossing of the Rappahannock is again stalled by the mud.

January 23 (Friday)   In Arkansas, the Union abandons Arkansas Post, but reduces it prior to departing. In other activity, a Union scouting contingent departs Fayetteville on a mission to Van Buren. The operation is completed on 27 January.

In Tennessee, a group of Tennesseans loyal to the Union skirmishes with Confederate cavalry led by Colonel Folk at Fish Springs.

In Virginia, the elements continue to prevent General Burnside's Army of the Potomac from crossing the Rappahannock River to attempt to regain Fredericksburg. By this time, conditions are miserable and the entire command is more than ten miles from the closest Union camp. Yet another snowstorm hits, which inflicts the final obstacle and causes the operation to be aborted. The army will begin to move back to its positions at Fredericksburg on the opposite bank of the river at Stratton Heights. Meanwhile, on this day, General Burnside, in command of the army for only several months, issues orders that remove some of his generals from command, but the orders are subject to the approval of the president. Those officers include Joseph Hooker and William B. Franklin; however, the order is never carried out. Instead, within a short time, Burnside is replaced.

In Naval activity, on or about this day, Commodore Wilkes, upon entering the port at Havana, is informed that the CSS *Florida* or the *Oreta* had recently been in the port. On the same day, the USS *Oneida* (Admiral Farragut's fleet) is at the harbor. Wilkes and the *Oneida* both move to catch the Rebel ship.

January 24 (Saturday)   In Tennessee, at Woodbury, the Union 2nd Division, commanded by General John McCauley Palmer (General Crittenden's corps), skirmishes with a Confederate force composed of about seven regiments. The Union sustains two killed and one wounded. The Confederates sustain about 35 killed and 100 missing.

In Virginia, by this time, the near-paralyzed Army of the Potomac has completed its soggy march back to its original positions opposite Fredericksburg to terminate what becomes known as the "mud march," the failed offensive to retake Fredericksburg.

January 25 (Sunday) President Lincoln continues to seek the perfect general. He replaces General Burnside with General Joseph Hooker, nicknamed "Fighting Joe." Burnside had submitted his resignation and it was accepted. He retires to Providence, Rhode Island, but in March he is recalled to replace General Horatio G. Wright as commander of the Army of the Ohio. Other changes also occur, pursuant to General Order No. 20: "The President of the United States has directed: First, That Major General A. E. Burnside, at his own request, be relieved from the command of the Army of the Potomac. Second, That Major General E.V. Sumner, at his own request, be relieved from duty in the Army of the Potomac. Third, That Major General W.B. Franklin be relieved from duty in the Army of the Potomac. Fourth, That Major General J. Hooker be assigned to the command of the Army of the Potomac. II.-The officers relieved as above will report, in person to the Adjutant General of the Army."

General Hooker immediately begins to reform the Army of the Potomac. The grand divisions are replaced by corps. The individual corps are "designated by a badge, and the badges denote the divisions by the respective colors of red, white and blue." In the case of the 12th Corps, the 1st Division wears a red star and the 2nd Division a white star; however, because it has no 3rd Division, there is no blue star. The Army is reorganized into corps with the following commanders:

- 1st Corps, General J.F. Reynolds, 17,000 troops, divisions under Generals James S. Wadsworth, John C. Robinson and A. Doubleday.
- 2nd Corps, General D.N. Couch, 17,000 troops, divisions under Generals W.S. Hancock, J. Gibbon and W.H. French.
- 3rd Corps, General Daniel E. Sickles, 18,000 troops, divisions under Generals D.B. Birney, H.G. Berry and A.A. Whipple.
- 5th Corps, General G.G. Meade, 17,000 troops, divisions under Generals C. Griffin, George Sykes and A.A. Humphreys.
- 6th Corps, General John Sedgwick, 22,000 troops, divisions under Generals W.T.H. Brooks, A.P. Howe and J. Newton.
- 11th Corps, General O.O. Howard, 11,000 troops, divisions under Generals Charles Devens, A. Von Steinwehr and Carl Schurz.
- 12th Corps, General Henry W. Slocum, 17,000 troops, divisions under Generals A.S. Wlliams and J.W. Geary.

The three cavalry divisions, designated the "Eyes of the Army," are commanded by General George Stoneman, with Generals Alfred Pleasonton, J. Buford and W.W. Averill each receiving command of a division. The total Union force under Hooker, including infantry, cavalry and unattached units, numbers more than 120,000 troops.

In contrast, the Confederate Army of Northern Virginia, commanded by General Robert E. Lee, remains an army composed of two corps during the imminent campaign; these are commanded by Lt. Generals James Longstreet and Stonewall Jackson. Jackson's corps is composed of the following divisions: General A.P. Hill (11,800 troops), Robert E. Rodes (9,600 troops), Jubal A. Early (7,800 troops) and Ralph E. Colston (6,400 troops). Longstreet's corps is composed of the divisions of R.H. Anderson (9,500 troops) and Lafayette McLaws (8,500 troops).

In Tennessee, a Confederate contingent attacks a unit of the 10th Michigan Volunteer Regiment at Murfreesboro. Reinforcements arrive and the attack is repelled. Casualty figures are unavailable.

In Naval activity, in response to an urgent request from General Rosecrans, the USS *Lexington* and other warships head for the Cumberland River to bolster the ground forces under Rosecrans to neutralize Confederate raiders.

January 26 (Monday) **In Arkansas,** a Union contingent skirmishes with Confederates at Mulberry Springs.

In Florida, a contingent of the 32nd Union "Colored Troops" skirmishes with Confederates at Township. Casualty figures are unavailable.

In Virginia, a 21-man detachment of Union cavalry, while scouting in the vicinity of Morrisville, encounters Confederate infantry. A skirmish develops and the Union sustains one killed and one wounded. Confederate casualty figures, if any, are unavailable.

January 27 (Tuesday) **In Georgia,** a Union naval force — composed of the ironclad USS *Montauk*, several gunboats and a mortar schooner, commanded by Captain Worden — lambastes Confederate Fort McAllister.

In Louisiana, a detachment of the Louisiana cavalry commanded by Colonel J.M. Williams skirmishes with Confederates at Placquemine Bayou (Indian Village). Casualty figures are unavailable.

In Missouri, a contingent of the 68th Missouri Militia, led by Colonel J. Lindsay, attacks Confederate guerrilla positions in the vicinity of Bloomfield. The Union captures about 50 prisoners.

In Naval activity, the secretary of the Navy issues orders to Lt. Baldwin, commanding officer of the USS *Vanderbilt*, to initiate a search for the CSS *Alabama*. During the following month on 23 February, the *Vanderbilt* is attached to the West India Squadron by its commander, Rear Admiral Charles Wilkes.

General Joseph Hooker (Johnson, *Campfire and Battlefield: History of the Conflicts and Campaigns*, 1894).

January 28 (Wednesday) **In Missouri,** a Union scouting party composed of elements of the 1st Arkansas Cavalry and the 10th Illinois Cavalry initiate a scouting mission in the vicinity of Van Buren.

In Confederate general officer activity, Captain John D. Imboden, 1st Virginia Partisan Rangers (62nd Virginia Mounted Infantry), is promoted to brigadier general.

January 29 (Thursday) THE BATTLE OF BEAR RIVER Four companies of the 2nd California Cavalry and one company of the 3rd California Volunteer Regiment, commanded by Colonel Patrick Edward Connor, arrive in the vicinity of Bear River (Preston, Idaho) in the Cache Valley following a tedious march of nearly 120 miles through the snow from Fort Douglas, Utah. The vanguard of the force begins to ford the river, but the Shoshones under Chief Bear Hunter hold formidable positions in the heights and are prepared to meet the soldiers. The Indians effortlessly repel the first assault, a frontal attack that begins just after the first crack of dawn; however, Connor arrives with the main body and the attack plans are quickly modified. He spreads his troops out, dispatching some to the heights and others to cover the entrance to the ravine to sever an escape route. Meanwhile, the soldiers who had gained the high ground descend upon the Indians and a turkey shoot begins.

The unending ring of fire quickly cuts down many of the 300 warriors, but it also slays some women, children and older men. The Army suffers 20 dead and 46 wounded. The Indians sustain about 250 killed and some captured. The Utah Territory will be safe for settlers by fall

1863. The soldiers had been ordered from Fort Douglas to terminate the raids of Chief Bear Hunter that had been occurring throughout the winter of 1862–1863. Colonel Patrick E. Connor is promoted to brigadier general on the strength of the victory.

In Arizona Territory, one company of the 1st California Volunteers skirmishes with a detachment of Confederates at Pinos Altos.

In Louisiana, U.S. Grant arrives at Young's Point to assume personal command of the troops there. General McClernand takes exception to this action but Grant overlooks this insubordination, being more concerned for the good of the entire service. Grant also recognizes that McClernand was a Democratic U.S. Congressman when war erupted and relinquished his seat to participate in the war.

In Missouri, Brigadier General Thomas J. McKean assumes command of the District of Northern Missouri.

In Naval activity, the *Princess Royal* (built in Scotland) attempts to run the blockade and enter the port at Charleston; however, Union blockaders, including the USS *Quaker City* and the USS *Unadilla,* on patrol at the time, intercept the vessel and capture it. The vessel's cargo includes a steam engine, which the Union puts to good use in the USS *Kansas* (commissioned December 1863). In March, the Navy acquires the ship by purchase, and within a short time, it is transformed into a warship and becomes the USS *Princess Royal.*

Late January Severe winter storms keep Lee and Burnside apart at Fredericksburg, Virginia. Lee is extremely concerned with Southern positions in North Carolina and Union General Hooker's threatening position near Richmond.

January 30 (Friday)   In Georgia, Union warships, including the *Monitor, Montauk* and the steamers *Dawn, Nashville* and *Seneca* move against Fort McAllister on the Ogeechee River outside Savannah. The Confederate batteries sink the *Nashville.*

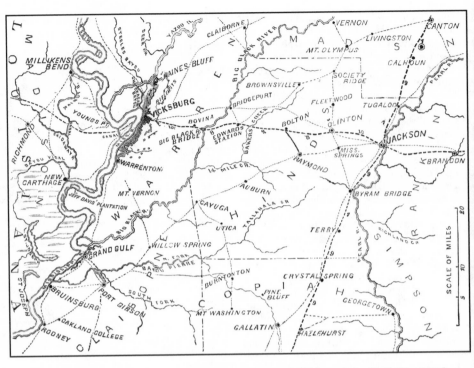

General Grant's Vicksburg campaign (*Harper's Pictoral History of the Civil War*, 1896).

General McClernand's corps move through bogs (*Harper's Pictoral History of the Civil War*, 1896).

In Mississippi, Union forces under General Grant initiate their Vicksburg campaign to secure the Mississippi River for the Union on the 24th of February.

In South Carolina, Confederates capture the USS *Isaac Smith* at Stono River. The vessel reaches a point just beyond Legareville when it is struck by Confederate batteries that fire from concealed positions along the shore. Lt. Conover had been aboard the vessel to initiate a reconnaissance mission, but the barrage disables the ship and Conover is forced to surrender. Eight men are killed and a large number are wounded. The *Isaac Smith* is renamed the CSS *Stono.* The Rebels, emboldened by this success, on the following day select a few of the smaller Union vessels that are blockading Charleston and attack them.

In Tennessee, a contingent of the 22nd Ohio Volunteers, led by Colonel Wood, skirmishes with Confederate guerrillas under Captain Dawson at Dyersburg (Trenton). The Union reports no casualties. The Confederates sustain some killed and wounded.

In Virginia, a Union force, attached to General Peck's command and led by General Michael Corcoran and Colonel Spear, engages Confederates under General Pryor at Cassville and Kelly's Store (or Deserted House), Suffolk. The

Union sustains 24 killed and 80 wounded. The Confederates suffer about 50 killed and wounded.

January 31 (Saturday)   In South Carolina, off Charleston during the early morning hours, the Confederate vessels *Palmetto State* and *Chicora,* both ironclads under the command of Flag Officer Ingraham, move out of Charleston Harbor and initiate an attack against the Southeast Blockading Squadron, composed of the vessels *Augusta, Keystone State, Housatonic, Memphis, Mercedita, Quaker City, Powhatan* and the *Canandaigua.* The last two vessels had departed for Port Royal to replenish their coal supplies. U.S. Marines stationed at secondary guns aboard the vessels participate in the wild battle that damages three of the Union vessels, the *Keystone State,* the *Mercedita* and the *Quaker City.* The *Mercedita* sustains casualties, primarily from explosions in the boiler room. Four men succumb and several others are injured. The *Mercedita* actually surrenders; however, the two Confederate ironclads move against the other vessels, permitting the damaged *Mercedita* to escape. It is sent to get repairs and does not re-enter service until the following April, when it is assigned to duty in the West Indies and in the Gulf of Mexico until decommissioned during October 1865. The *Quaker City,* having sustained savage damage, had been disabled and was close to surrendering, but other Union vessels rush to its aid, and the Confederate ships choose to return to Charleston, thereby saving the *Quaker City* from falling into Confederate hands.

The *Quaker City* afterward sails north to receive repairs, and on 9 March it seizes a schooner, the *Douro* of Wilmington, North Carolina. The *Memphis* tows the *Keystone State* to safety. The USS *Augusta*, following this action, is ordered to assist in the search for the CSS *Florida*. After a couple of weeks of searching, it moves to New York to receive repairs and remains out of service until May 1864. After returning to service, it escorts the monitor *Tecumseh* to Pensacola, then patrols between the U.S. and Panama until it sustains engine problems. The *Augusta* is towed to its home port and is placed out of service in January 1865. It is not recommissioned until April 1866. Afterward, it remains in service until sold during December 1888 and renamed the *Magnolia*.

The Confederates sustain no damage; however, the main purpose of the attack fails, as the Union continues to maintain its blockade at Charleston. Nevertheless, the Confederates claim victory. General Beauregard, Admiral D.N. Ingraham (commander of Naval forces in the area) and General Thomas Jordan (West Point, 1841), chief of staff, issue the following proclamation: "At the hour of five o'clock this morning the Confederate States' naval forces on this station attacked the United States blockading fleet off the harbor of the city of Charleston and sunk, dispersed or drove off and out of sight for the time, the entire hostile fleet." The proclamation further states that the blockade had been ended by a "superior Confederate force."

In Tennessee, a Union contingent composed of elements of the 4th Ohio Cavalry engages Confederates under Major General Wheeler at Rover. The Union reports no casualties. The Confederates sustain 12 killed, about 12 wounded and 300 captured. Meanwhile, a Union force led by General Jefferson C. Davis occupies Shelbyville. Also, a Union contingent of the 2nd and 3rd Tennessee Cavalry led by Colonel Stokes clashes with Confederates under Major Douglass at Middleton.

In Confederate general officer activity, Colonel William Smith (former state senator, former U.S. congressman and former governor of Virginia), 49th Virginia Regiment, is promoted to the rank of brigadier general, effective this date. He is promoted in August to major general.

February *In Confederate general officer activity,* Lt. Colonel Daniel Chevilette Govan, 2nd Arkansas Infantry, and Colonel Alfred E. Jackson are promoted to the rank of brigadier general. Jackson changes duties, relinquishing his job as paymaster at Knoxville to command an infantry brigade (Department of East Tennessee).

In Naval activity, the USS *Sangamon* is commissioned this month at Chester, Pennsylvania. It sees service along the James River; however, during the early part of 1864, the *Sangamon* is transferred to the Blockading Squadron of Charleston, but later that year returns to Virginia. After the war, the *Sangamon* is decommissioned, but during 1869 it is renamed the *Jason*.

February 1 (Sunday)   In Georgia, for the third time since 27 January 1863, Union warships, including the monitors *Montauk, Patapsco, Mahant* and *Passaic,* bombard Confederate-held Fort McAllister.

In Tennessee, Union troops commanded by General R. Johnson seize Franklin, defended by troops under General Nathan Bedford Forrest. Although the town is occupied by Union troops, calm does not return to the area for some time. The Yankees and Rebels will fight sporadically until the final bell, which occurs on the 30 November 1864. Confederate General Hood's command is devastated and though he begins to besiege Nashville, he is not strong enough to dominate. Another force commanded by General Joseph Jones Reynolds (West Point, 1843) reconnoiters in the vicinity of Auburn and Liberty.

In Confederate general officer activity, Brigadier General William Henry Carroll, following his appearance at an inquiry investigating charges against him, including "drunkenness, incompetency and neglect" by General Bragg, resigns from the Confederate service. General Carroll heads for Canada to join his family, which fled there when the Union seized Memphis. He dies in Montreal on 3 May 1868.

In Virginia, elements of the 1st and 5th Virginia Cavalry attack Confederate positions at Warrenton.

In Naval activity, the USS *Tacoma,* while on patrol off St. Petersburg, Florida, intercepts and seizes a blockade runner, the schooner *Margaret.*

February 2 (Monday)   In Arkansas, Union and Confederate forces clash at Vine Prairie along the White Oak River, and other fighting erupts near the mouth of the Mulberry River. The contingents again clash on the following day.

In Mississippi, the ram *Queen of the West,* commanded by General Alfred Ellet, defies Confederate guns to speed past Vicksburg, sustaining only slight damage. The vessel had been ordered to attack the CSS *City of Vicksburg,* but although it encounters and attacks the vessel by ramming it, the *Queen of the West* is struck by shells that ignite the protective cotton bales that buffer the machinery, forcing the ship to retire. En route to Natchez, General Alfred Ellet captures the Confederate vessels *A.W. Baker, Moro* and *Berwick Bay,* each laden with supplies. Subsequently, the *Queen of the West* again passes Vicksburg and prepares to test the batteries. The fallibility of the shore batteries allows further excursions by the U.S. Navy to quicken the fall of Vicksburg. The *City of Vicksburg,* although not sunk, sustains heavy damage. The engines are taken to Mobile, where they are to be transferred to another ship. Meanwhile, the *City of Vicksburg* is used by the Confederates at Vicksburg as a wharf boat. On 29 March the vessel drifts down the river and is destroyed by fire.

In Missouri, in the vicinity of Mingo Swamp, skirmishing occurs at various times between today and February 13.

In Naval activity, the USS *General Lyon* departs Cairo, Illinois, to join the Mississippi Squadron. It operates on the western rivers as a multi-function vessel, including a dispatch ship as well as a delivery vessel carrying stores and ordnance to the other ships in the squadron. After about two and one-half years on station, it returns to Mound City during February 1865. On 3 August, the *General Lyon* is decommissioned and later the same month is sold to become the merchant ship *Alabama.* The *Alabama* remains in service until 1 April 1867, when it is destroyed by fire at Grand View, Louisiana.

February 3 (Tuesday)   In Washington, D.C., the French extends to the Union government an offer to intervene and initiate mediation. The generous offer of France is politely but succinctly declined when Secretary of State Seward informs the French minister, Monsieur Mercier, that France's assistance is not necessary.

In Tennessee, Union troops at Fort Donelson (or Cumberland Iron Works), numbering only about 600, handily repulse a Confederate attack from the combined forces of Major General Joseph Wheeler and Brigadier General Nathan B. Forrest, which total about 4,500 troops, supported by about eight guns. The Confederates, during the afternoon, twice send parties under a flag of truce to demand surrender, but Colonel Harding ignores the ultimatum and ignores the shot and shell that has plastered the fort. At about 2000, the Rebels close and attack three sides of the fort, those not protected by the river, and then they begin to rally for a final thrust to seize the prize. Meanwhile, it is becoming more grim within the walls of the fort as the ammunition supply is nearly exhausted. At about this time, several Union gunboats, including the USS *Fair Play,* commanded by Captain Fitch, appear on the scene and their deadly power quickly evens the odds. The Navy launches bolts of thunderous fire against the Rebels and the effect is devastating. The assault is thwarted; the Confederates sustain severe

The ram USS *Queen of the West* engages the CSS *City of Vicksburg* (*Harper's Pictorial History of the Civil War*, 1896).

losses. The Union suffers approximately 16 dead, 60 wounded and 50 missing. Confederates suffer 140 dead, 400 wounded and 130 missing. Colonel Abner Harding is soon promoted to brigadier general for his brilliant defense at Donelson, but his vision has continued to deteriorate, and by June 1863 he is compelled to retire. The defiant refusal of Harding to capitulate and the victory for the Union over elite Confederate cavalry assures control of the Cumberland River for the Union.

The *Lexington* also participates in repelling the attack. Upon the arrival of the *Lexington* and five other warships, the tide had turned. The garrison had expended its ammunition, but the Navy had been able to quickly resupply the troops and the naval power soon after ensured the Rebels would not take the fort. The *Lexington* moves to support General Sherman in October, and afterward, during February 1864, it returns to the Mississippi.

In Missouri, the 12th Missouri Cavalry, led by Major Reeder, skirmishes with Confederate guerrillas at Mingo Swamp. The Union reports no casualties. The Confederates suffer nine killed and about 20 captured. Also, elements of the 5th Missouri Militia Cavalry clash with Confederates at Independence. Casualty figures are unavailable.

In Naval activity, the Passaic class monitor USS *Nantucket* is commissioned at about this time. The *Nantucket*, built at Boston, soon joins the South Atlantic Blockading Squadron.

February 4 (Wednesday) In Arkansas, Union cavalry (John W. Davidson's division) commanded by Colonel George Waring, while on a reconnaissance and foraging mission, launches a night attack against Confederate-held Batesville. The Rebels, commanded by General Marmaduke, are unable to withstand the charge led by Captain G.C. Rose (4th Missouri Cavalry). The Confederates evacuate Batesville by boarding ferry boats; many cannot get into the boats and swim to the opposite bank while others are captured. The Union occupies the town and on the following morning, the two sides exchange fire from the opposing

banks. General Davidson, at West Plains, Missouri, dispatches a battalion to bolster Waring and to cover the column's rear as it moves back into Missouri.

In Mississippi, at Lake Providence, General Grant confers with General McPherson. McPherson's command is working on a canal to permit water from the river to flow into the lake. During his stay, Grant realizes it is not practical to transport troops through enemy territory, but he directs that the project continue because he believed employment for the men was better than idleness.

In Naval activity, the USS *New Era*, operating in the vicinity of Island No. 10, Tennessee, intercepts and captures the Confederate steamer *W.A. Knapp*. The USS *Cricket*, on patrol in the vicinity of Memphis, Tennessee, confiscates cargoes of cotton from two Confederate vessels and delivers them to Cairo. It moves to White River Station, located between Memphis and the Arkansas River, to maintain a vigil through April 7 on Confederates attempting to cross the Mississippi. It also ensures that Confederate batteries are not erected along the banks of the river.

February 5 (Thursday) In Arkansas, skirmishing between Union and Confederate contingents erupts in Pope County. Also, a Union force departs Fayetteville on a scouting mission that proceeds to the Arkansas River and culminates on 12 February. During the mission, skirmishes erupt at Threlkeld's Ferry and in the vicinity of the town of Van Buren.

In Missouri, the 40th Missouri Enrolled Militia, commanded by Captain Ranney, skirmishes with Confederates while on a scouting mission in the vicinity of Bear Creek (Johnson County). The Union reports no casualties. The Confederates sustain seven killed.

In Virginia, Confederate cavalry attacks Union positions at Wigginton's Mills. The Union sustains one wounded.

In Naval activity, the USS *Lodona*, with the *Weehawken* in tow, arrives at Port Royal, South Carolina. The *Weehawken* had been commissioned the previous month.

February 6 (Friday) In Virginia, a Union contingent of the 5th New York Cavalry led by Captain Penfield clashes with Confederates at Middleburg. The Union captures about eight Confederates. A detachment composed of two companies of the 1st New York Cavalry, commanded by Captain Jones and Lieutenant Lafferty, comes under attack by Confederates at Milwood. The Union sustains one wounded. The Confederates suffer one killed and one captured.

In Naval activity, gunboats, including the ram USS *Lioness*, form a section of the Yazoo Pass

Expedition. The *Lioness* stays with the operation until 12 April, when it and several other rams begin to bolster General Alfred Ellet's ram fleet. The *Lioness* continues to operate in the region until the Confederate Navy is eliminated on the Tennessee River. Afterward, it moves to Mound City, where it remains until sold during 1865. The USS *Conestoga*, *Tyler*, and *Lexington*, while operating on the Tennessee River in Alabama through February 10, capture three Confederate ships and destroy six others.

February 7 (Saturday) In Virginia, one squadron of the 5th Pennsylvania Cavalry skirmishes with Confederates in the vicinity of Williamsburg. The Union sustains some killed and five missing or captured.

In Union Naval officer activity, Captain John A. Dahlgren, chief of the Ordnance Bureau, is promoted to the rank of rear admiral. In July he is assigned as commander of the South Atlantic Blockading Squadron. While the USS *Glide* is at Cairo, Illinois, receiving repairs, a fire erupts aboard the vessel and destroys it.

February 8 (Sunday) In Mississippi, tremendous water pressure causes the dam at the mouth of the canal which is being constructed across the peninsula by the Union to collapse. Owing to the disaster, the project is aborted. The focus moves to the construction of a channel that will lead to Lake Providence and forge a link with the forces of General Banks through the Tensas and Black Rivers into the Red River, then from there to the Atchafalaya River. This operation will permit the Union forces to avoid the batteries at Vicksburg and Port Hudson.

In Missouri, a contingent of the 5th Missouri Militia Cavalry again battles Confederates at Independence. The Union reports no casualties. The Confederates suffer eight killed and two captured.

In Tennessee, Union forces occupy Lebanon.

In Virginia, General Robert E. Lee states in a letter to his wife, Mary: "We are in a liquid state at present, up to our knees in mud and what is worse on short rations for men and beast … I am willing to starve myself, but cannot bear my men or horses to be pinched."

February 9 (Monday) In Virginia, Union cavalry commanded by Major Knox skirmishes with Confederates at Summerville. Casualty figures are unavailable.

In Confederate activity, Major General William Henry Talbot Walker (Georgia militia) is reappointed brigadier general in the Confederate Army. Walker, a West Point graduate and a seasoned veteran of the Mexican War, is shortly afterward promoted to major general. He is assigned a division in the command of General Joseph E. Johnston and participates during the defense of Vicksburg. At Chickamauga, he commands a reserve corps. General Walker had, during October 1861, resigned his original commission as brigadier general.

The Confederate Southwest Army, commanded by General E. Kirby Smith, is ex-

General McPherson's headquarters, Lake Providence, Mississippi (Mottelay, *The Soldier in Our Civil War*, 1886).

panded to include the Trans-Mississippi Department. Also, John Taylor Wood, a former U.S. Naval officer (resigned April 1861) is appointed colonel of cavalry in the Confederate service and aide to President Davis. Wood's mother, Ann Margaret Mackall Taylor, is the daughter of former President Zachary Taylor and the sister of Sarah Knox Taylor (first wife of Jefferson Davis). Wood had been commissioned a naval lieutenant in the Confederacy on 4 October 1861. Alfred Eugene Jackson, who served as quartermaster to General Zollicoffer until the latter's death and afterward became paymaster at Knoxville, is appointed brigadier general effective this day. He receives command of an infantry brigade attached to the Department of East Tennessee.

In Union general officer activity, Joseph Pannell Taylor, the brother of former President Zachary Taylor, is appointed brigadier general. A veteran of the War of 1812 and the Mexican War, Taylor had been appointed commissary general during September 1861. General Taylor continues in his capacity until his death on 29 June 1864. General Joseph Taylor's nephew is Confederate General Richard Taylor; his niece, Sarah Knox, had been the first wife of Confederate President Jefferson Davis.

February 10 (Tuesday) In Louisiana, a Union contingent, composed of elements of the 1st Kansas, 17th and 95th Illinois, the 16th Wisconsin and the 3rd Louisiana Cavalry, commanded by Captain Tucker, skirmishes with Confederates at Old River, Lake Providence. The Union sustains one killed and seven wounded. The Confederates sustain four killed, seven wounded and about 26 captured.

In Missouri, Union and Confederate contingents skirmish at Sarcoxie Prairie.

In Tennessee, a Union contingent of the 18th Missouri Volunteer Regiment skirmishes with Confederates at Bone Yard.

In Texas, a contingent of loyal Delaware and Shawnee Indians capture the Wachita Indian Agency.

In Virginia, a Union contingent skirmishes with Confederates at Gloucester Point. Specific units and casualty reports are unavailable.

In Naval activity, the USS *Lodona,* with the USS *E.W. Gardner* in tow, departs Port Royal, South Carolina, en route to Charleston.

February 11 (Wednesday) In Virginia, Union General Hooker's troops reach Hampton Roads. General Robert E. Lee directs Jeb Stuart to depart Fredericksburg and proceed with his cavalry to New Market to meet General William E. Jones (West Point, 1848) with instructions to "drive the enemy from Martinsburg if possible and destroy as much of the railroad as possible." Lee later informs Stuart of a large Union force that landed at Newport News on the 11th, and gives him authority to strike Union lines on the Potomac River if he thinks it necessary.

February 12 (Thursday) In Arkansas, a Union contingent led by Lt. Colonel Stuart on a scouting mission to the Arkansas River and Confederate contingents skirmish in the vicinity of Frog Bayou. About 100 troops cross the river near its mouth and attack a Confederate force commanded by C.A. Carroll. The Confederates are dispersed, permitting the advance to continue for another ten miles, where they reduce the Rebel encampment and overwhelm part of Carroll's force. Meanwhile, the Confederates attempt to ambush Stuart on his return to Fayetteville; however, the plan fails when the two sides engage about eight miles east of Van Buren. The Union seizes about 40 prisoners and many horses, mules and supplies. Union loss stands at one man drowned and one man captured.

In Union general officer activity, Captain Cyrus Hamlin (son of Vice President Hannibal Hamlin) is commissioned colonel of the 80th U.S. Colored Infantry Regiment (formerly 8th Corps d'Afrique). The regiment is not organized at Port Hudson, Louisiana, until the following September, and it does not receive its name until 4 April 1864.

In Confederate Naval activity, the CSS *Florida* seizes a clipper ship, the *Jacob Bell,* which is transporting a cargo that includes silk and tea, valued at about $1,500,000, giving the *Florida* the honor of the largest monetary seizure of a solitary vessel by the Confederate Navy. The merchant ship had been en route from Foo Chow, China, to New York when it was intercepted. After the cargo is seized, the *Jacob Bell* is set afire. On 8 May, the *Florida* arrives at Pernambuco, Brazil.

February 12–15 In Mississippi, the USS *Queen of the West,* accompanied by a small steamer, the *DeSoto,* sails to pass the Confederate positions at Vicksburg and if possible also run the Port Hudson batteries to attempt a link with Farragut's fleet, which is below Port Hud-

Ellis' Cliffs, Mississippi (*Harper's Pictorial History of the Civil War,* 1896).

The *Queen of the West* (*Harper's Pictorial History of the Civil War,* 1896).

son. During the evening of the 12th, both vessels anchor at the mouth of the Old River. The next morning, the *Queen of the West* ventures into the Atchafalaya, but the *DeSoto* remains in place. The troops aboard the ship then capture a train composed of eleven Confederate Army wagons and demolish several buildings on six separate sugar plantations. The *Queen of the West* then moves into the Red River, where it captures a Confederate steamer, the *Era,* at a point just above the mouth of the Black River. On the following morning, the ship moves another twenty miles to reach Fort Taylor, where, during an exchange, the *Queen of the West* becomes bogged down on the river. Rather than face capture, General Alfred Ellet (Marine brigade) and the crew abandon the *Queen of the West* on the 14th. Using cotton bales, they drift down river until they are picked up by the *DeSoto.* All seems well until the *DeSoto* begins to have problems with its rudder, causing yet another emergency. Losing little time, the crew jumps from the *DeSoto* to the captured *Era*, and after tossing the cargo overboard to give the vesssel more speed, the Yankees race toward the Mississippi River. Meanwhile, the Confederates have initiated pursuit. The *Era*, now a transplanted Rebel in the Union Navy, reaches the Mississippi on the morning of the 15th, and as it comes upon Ellis' Cliffs, the USS *Indianola*, which has also successfully passed the batteries at Vicksburg, is there to greet it. At about the same time, the Confederate warships arrive to pounce upon the *Era*, but they had not anticipated the presence of the *Indianola*. The situation is soon reversed and the Union vessels move toward the Rebel flotilla, prompting it to retire. The Confederates refloat the ram *Queen of the West*, which becomes the CSS *Queen of the West*.

February 13 (Friday)   In Washington, D.C., Commodore Charles Davis, chief of the Bureau of Navigation, is promoted to rear admiral effective this day. During the following year, Admiral Davis is appointed superintendent of the Naval Observatory, and in 1767 he is appointed commander of the South Atlantic Squadron.

In Tennessee, a detachment of Union cavalry clashes with Confederate cavalry at Bolivar. The Confederates sustain four killed and five wounded.

In Virginia, a detachment of the 12th Pennsylvania Cavalry led by Lieutenant Taylor is attacked by a contingent of Confederates at Smithfield. The Union sustains one killed and two wounded. The Confederates sustain four captured. The opposing forces actually clash twice, with the Confederates prevailing at first. However, the Union takes the second skirmish.

In Union activity, Major General John Pope resumes command of the Department of the Northwest. Also, Brigadier General Abram Sanders Piatt, injured badly at Fredericksburg the previous December, resigns his commission.

In Naval activity, the USS *New Era,* while on patrol duty in the vicinity of Island No. 10 in Tennessee, captures two blockade runners, the *Rowena* and the *White Cloud*. In other activity, the USS *Wamsutta* arrives back at Port Royal, South Carolina, following time out of service in New York for repairs.

The USS *Indianola* runs the Vicksburg batteries (*Harper's Pictoral History of the Civil War*, 1896).

February 14 (Saturday)   In Virginia, a Union force composed of elements of the 5th Michigan Cavalry is attacked by a Confederate contingent at Annandale. The Union sustains about 15 killed and wounded. Confederate casualty figures are unavailable. Meanwhile, a contingent of the 1st Michigan Cavalry skirmishes with a Confederate force at Brentsville. The Union sustains 15 wounded. Confederate casualty figures are unavailable.

Confederate General Robert E. Lee becomes aware that Union General Hooker's troops had reached Hampton Roads on the 11th. The Confederates have also learned from Union deserters that the naval vessels at Baltimore have been directed to depart from there to Aquia, from where they will strike either Tennessee or North Carolina. General Lee suspects North Carolina is the objective.

February 15 (Sunday)   In Arkansas, a Union contingent led by Captain Brown skirmishes with a detachment of Confederates at Arkadelphia. The Union sustains two killed and 12 wounded. The Confederates suffer 14 killed and 12 wounded.

In Tennessee, a Union detachment of the 2nd Minnesota Infantry, consisting of about 15 men, commanded by Sergeant Holmes, repulses a Confederate cavalry force of 125 at Nolensville. This action saves the Union wagon train which is under assault. In other activity, a Union contingent commanded by Colonel James Monroe, composed of elements of the 123rd Illinois Volunteer Regiment, bolstered by one company of the 5th Tennessee Cavalry, engages Confederates at Cainesville. The Union sustains three wounded. The Confederates suffer about 20 killed and six captured.

February 16 (Monday)   In West Virginia, a detachment of the 116th and 122nd Ohio Regiments, while guarding a forage train, are attacked by Confederates in the vicinity of Romney. The Confederates capture the train. The Union suffers 72 wounded and four captured. Robert E. Lee orders General Hood to move towards Hanover Junction. Pickett's division was sent to Richmond on the 14th, with orders to halt at Attlee's Station on the Central Railroad.

In Naval activity, the *Curlew* (formerly the *Florence*) is commissioned the USS *Curlew*. Acting Master G. Hentig receives command of the gunboat. On the following day, it sails from Cairo, Illinois, to join Rear Admiral David D. Porter's fleet, where it initiates patrol duty on the Mississippi River and its tributaries.

February 17 (Tuesday)   In Tennessee, the Union initiates several expeditions, including one that departs Lexington and others that operate out of the Memphis area. The force from Lexington encounters resistance at Clifton on the 18th. Confederate guerrillas, operating near Memphis, attack and burn the steamer USS *Hercules*.

In Arkansas, a Union contingent burns the town of Hopefield in an operation that lasts through the 19th.

February 18 (Wednesday)   In Virginia, General Robert E. Lee continues his plans for the defense of Richmond in the event of an attack by Union forces, which are building up, according to reports flowing into General Lee's headquarters. Lee informs Lt. General Longstreet that two of his divisions had been ordered to the James River to be in position to rush toward Richmond if necessary. Lee instructs Longstreet to join the men at the James. The weather in the region has not been favorable to either side, as the area has been hit with snow storms.

In Tennessee, elements of the 2nd Michigan and 3rd Ohio Cavalry skirmish with Confederates at Milton. Casualty figures are unavailable. In other activity, a contingent of the 3rd Michigan Cavalry attacks and captures Clifton, destroying the town in the process.

In Naval activity, the USS *Somerset*, while in the vicinity of New Inlet, St. George's Sound, detects a blockade runner, *Hortense,* en route from Havana, Cuba, to Mobile, Alabama. Commander A.F. Crosman, the commanding officer of the *Somerset*, dispatches the USS *Brockenborough* to intercept and capture the runner. After the ship is seized, the prize is taken to Key West and is condemned. In other activity, the *Wamsutta* moves to Doboy Sound to tow the *Fernandina* to a position where it blockades the entrance to the sound.

February 19 (Thursday)   In Arkansas, Union troops continue an attack on the town of Hopefield that began on the 17th.

In Virginia, the troops at Fredericksburg receive another severe storm, adding to the misery of the one which had started on the 17th. Neither side can be comfortable in the snow, sleet and rain, but the Union is better supplied. The Southerners remain in great need of clothing.

In Mississippi, Union cavalry on a reconnaissance mission, commanded by Colonel Wood, skirmishes with about 200 Confederate cavalrymen at Cold Water. The Confederates sustain nine killed and 15 wounded.

In Missouri, a contingent of the 9th Kansas Regiment skirmishes with Confederates at Spring River. Casualty figures are unavailable. Union scouting contingents operate in Barton and Jasper Counties through the 22nd.

In Naval activity, the USS *Genesee*, having been transferred to the West Gulf Blockading Squadron, departs for New Orleans and arrives there on 7 March. Upon arrival, it joins Admiral Farragut's expeditions on the Mississippi River that move beyond Port Hudson,

Louisiana, and participates in operations against Vicksburg.

February 20 (Friday) In the Dakota Territory, a skirmish erupts in the vicinity of Fort Halleck between forces of the post and Indians.

In Mississippi, Union troops attached to the 5th Illinois Cavalry (Grant's command) again engage with Rebels at Yazoo Pass. These skirmishes have been occurring daily since the 16th.

In Union activity, the 1st Maine Cavalry Regiment is transferred from Bayard's cavalry brigade (presently under command of General David Gregg). General George Bayard was slain at Fredericksburg, Virginia, in December.

February 21 (Saturday) In Mississippi, a contingent of the 2nd Iowa Cavalry clashes with Confederates at Prairie Station.

In Kentucky, a detachment of the 8th Kentucky Cavalry skirmishes with a contingent of Confederate guerrillas at Greenville. Casualty figures are unavailable.

In Naval activity, two Union gunboats, the USS *Dragon* and *Freeborn,* commanded by Lt. Commander Magaw, initiates a reconnaissance mission in the vicinity of Fort Lowrey on the Rappahannock River in Virginia. The gunboats exchange blows for about one hour. The Union sustains three wounded and the *Freeborn* incurs some damage. Confederate casualty figures are unavailable. In other activity, the CSS *Alabama* engages and destroys two vessels, the *Golden Eagle* and the *Olive Jane,* off the coast of Africa.

February 22 (Sunday) In Alabama, a Union Cavalry Brigade commanded by Colonel F.M. Cornyn reconnoiters in the vicinity of Tuscumbia. Some skirmishing occurs.

In Mississippi, the master plan to capture Vicksburg continues. Union vessels are active on the rivers and the plans for troop deployments are being completed.

In Naval activity, Commodore Wilkes, with the USS *Vanderbilt* and the USS *Oneida,* both in search of the CSS *Florida,* arrives in port at San Juan, Puerto Rico, but they have had no success since the cruise began on 23 January. From San Juan, they sail to St. Thomas. In other activity, the USS *Tahoma* seizes the yacht *Stonewall* off Pea Creek, Florida.

February 23 (Monday) In Kentucky, a Union contingent skirmishes with Confederates at Athens. Specific units are not reported and casualty figures are unavailable.

In Mississippi, General Burbridge's Division (13th Corps) engages Confederates under General Samuel W. Ferguson at Deer Creek. Casualty figures are unavailable.

In Confederate general officer activity, Brigadier General Edward Johnson is promoted to major general.

In Naval activity, the USS *Potomska,* on patrol in the vicinity of Sapelo Sound, encounters and seizes a blockade runner, the British schooner *Belle,* which is transporting coffee and salt to the Confederates. Afterward, the *Potomska* returns to St. Simond's Sound, and shortly thereafter the vessel moves to Port Royal for repairs before departing for Philadelphia in March for additional repairs. In other activity, the gunboat USS *Colonel Kinsman,* while sailing in Berwick Bay (Louisiana) during a reconnaissance mission, strikes a submerged log that tears its bottom. The crew is able to get the ship to shore at a point near Brashear City, but it continues to take on water and soon slips from the embankment into deep water and sinks. Five crew members die during the incident. The *Kinsman,* built in Pennsylvania at Elizabeth during 1854, had been seized at New Orleans in May 1862 and used by the U.S. Army as a gunboat until transferred to the U.S. Navy during early 1863.

February 24 (Tuesday) In Washington, D.C., the United States divides the Territory of New Mexico and forms the Arizona Territory.

In Naval activity, the USS *Indianola,* commanded by Lieutenant George Brown, is attacked by a Confederate fleet just above Grand Gulf on the Mississippi. The Confederate fleet consists of four vessels, including the CSS *Queen of the West,* which was raised by the Confederates, the ram *Webb* and two other steamships. The *Indianola,* ordinarily strong enough to destroy the other ships, is burdened with towing coal. The ship fights for more than one hour in darkness and is rammed seven times. The vessel afterward begins to sink. The crew throws the guns overboard and then runs the ship aground at Vicksburg before surrendering. The Union sustains one killed and one wounded. The Confederates suffer 35 killed. The *Indianola* had originally been built to defend Cincinnati from a Confederate attack. Rear Admiral David D. Porter orders his forces to build a raft in the form of an ironclad. Once it is completed, Porter lets the imposter drift down the river toward the *Indianola,* which the Confederates are working to salvage. When they spot the encroaching raft, which they believe to be a genuine ironclad, the Rebels hurriedly blow up the *Indianola.* Subsequent to the seizure of Vicksburg in July, the Union will initiate a prolonged project to salvage the vessel. The *Indianola* is refloated in January 1865, but the effort is in vain. The ship is unsalvageable. The Navy sells its hulk during November of 1865.

In other activity, the CSS *Florida,* the object of a U.S. squadron search since the previous January, arrives at Barbados to refuel and then departs. Also, the Union steamer *Hetty Gillmore* is captured by Confederates (General Breckinridge's command) at Woodbury, Tennessee.

February 25 (Wednesday) In Virginia, Confederate cavalry attached to General Jeb Stuart's command strikes Union cavalry of General Averell's brigade at Hartwood Church. The Confederates sustain two killed.

In Naval activity, Rear Admiral Charles Wilkes attaches the USS *Vanderbilt* to the West India Squadron and transfers his flag to the vessel. Wilkes' flagship, the *Wachusett,* has severe engine problems, and by the following month, the *Wachusett* returns to the United States for repairs. The *Vanderbilt* remains with the squadron until 13 June. As of this date, the only ships in the squadron that are seaworthy are the USS *Alabama, Octorara, Santiago de Cuba, Sonoma* and *Tioga.* Wilkes orders Lt. Baldwin of the *Vanderbilt* to board the *Peterhoff,* search for contraband and seize the vessel. The *Peterhoff* is captured and sailed to the United States.

February 26 (Thursday) In Virginia, Union cavalry (13th Pennsylvania and 1st New York) clashes with a contingent of Confederate cavalry on the Strasburg Road. The Confederates inflict heavy casualties; about 200 Union soldiers are killed or captured.

In Naval activity, the USS *Fort Henry* seizes the schooner *Anna* when it tries to penetrate a blockade on the Suwanee River to bring in a cargo from the Bahamas. The *Anna* is not known to have had any previous names; however, later reports indicate but do not verify that it had initially been named the *La Criala,* which had been seized off South Carolina by the USS *Bienville* and sold by the federal prize court in Philadelphia. In yet other reports, the *Anna* is said to have been named the *La Criolla* when captured and renamed the *Anna* after entering service in the Union Navy.

February 27 (Friday) In Georgia, Confederate guns at Fort McAllister damage the USS *Wissahickon;* however, courageous actions save the ship from sinking or blowing up.

In North Carolina, a detachment of the 3rd New York Cavalry, commanded by Captain Jacobs, clashes with Confederate infantry at New Bern. The Union sustains one wounded. The Confederates sustain three killed and about 48 captured.

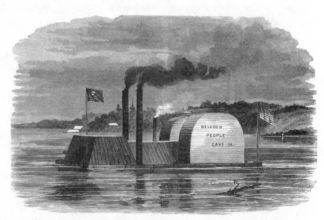

Admiral Porter's dummy ironclad (*Harper's Pictorial History of the Civil War,* 1896).

In Union general officer activity, Major General Schuyler Hamilton resigns his commission because of failing health. He had come down with malaria during the campaign (spring 1862) to seize Corinth. Due to his ongoing illness and regulations that forbid submitting a nomination to the Senate when a man is unable to serve, Hamilton resigns. His commission, received during September 1862, is scheduled to expire on 3 March unless confirmed by the Senate. At about this time, Union General John Cochrane (Army of the Potomac) resigns from the service, claiming ill health. Cochrane had been one of four generals (with W.T. Brooks, William B. Franklin and John Newton) who had claimed the ongoing campaign plan to take Richmond would fail. The opinions apparently aided in shortened or less prominent careers. Nevertheless, Cochrane, the following year, joins the political ticket of John Frémont as his vice president against Abraham Lincoln. Later, Cochrane and Frémont withdraw. Cochrane is in his mid-eighties when he succumbs during 1898.

In Confederate general officer activity, General Sterling Price is ordered to repair to the Trans-Mississippi Department.

February 28 (Saturday)   In Georgia, several Union vessels, including the *Dawn, Seneca* and *Montauk,* aware that the privateer *Rattlesnake* (formerly the CSS *Nashville* and *Thomas L. Wragg*) had been aground off Fort McAllister and under the protection of the fort's guns, advance from their positions at the mouth of the Ogeechee River to eliminate it. During the early morning hours, the fleet, under Captain Worden of the U.S. Navy, moves within range, and from there the USS *Montauk,* using its 12-inch and 15-inch guns, supported by fire from the heavy gunboats, knocks out the privateer *Nashville,* which sustains a fatal blow to the magazine. The *Rattlesnake,* following the explosion, is set ablaze and soon plummets to the bottom. The Confederate guns at Fort McAllister are too far away to fire upon the Union vessels.

In Mississippi, the Union decides to commence another expedition up the Yazoo River to destroy Confederate vessels in the area, which, according to intelligence reports, are greatly increasing in numbers. About 5,000 accompanying ground forces will be commanded by General L.F. Ross. The flotilla will encounter obstructions along the Tallahatchie River on 11 March. The mission is designed to take the contingent up the Yazoo Pass to a point from where they can strike Vicksburg, Mississippi, from the rear. This is the third time General Grant has attempted to get infantry behind Vicksburg. Subsequent to this mission, Ross is assigned to duty in Helena, Arkansas, until he resigns from the Army during July of this year.

In the Indian Territory (Oklahoma), a skirmish develops in the vicinity of Fort Gibson, recently reoccupied by Union troops. The post is renamed Fort Blunt in honor of General James Blunt.

In Missouri, a Union contingent under Adjutant Fred R. Poole arrives at the Castor River near Bloomfield, but the river is impassable due to a destroyed bridge. Nevertheless, up to this point, the Confederates at Bloomfield are not aware of the presence of the Union. Poole orders his force to cross by swimming and by about the break of dawn on 1 March, the town is encircled.

In Union general officer activity, General Ebenezer Dumont, out on sick leave since the previous December, resigns his commission; however, his resignation is not due to his health. He resigns to take a seat in the Congress, where he serves until 1867, at which time President Grant appoints him governor of the Idaho Territory. He dies in Indianapolis on 16 April 1871, prior to taking the oath of office.

In Confederate general officer activity, General Albert G. Blanchard (West Point, 1829) receives orders during February to report to General Kirby Smith's command at Alexandria, Louisiana, but he does not receive a command. His career is spent primarily in clerical and instruction activities. Brigadier General Edward Johnson is promoted to the rank of major general and serves with the Army of Northern Virginia in command of Stonewall Jackson's old division. Johnson, an 1838 graduate of West Point, had also fought during the Mexican War and against the Seminole Indians in Florida.

In Naval activity, the USS *New Era,* on patrol in the vicinity of Island No. 10 in Tennessee, intercepts and seizes a Confederate blockade runner, the *Curlew.* The commanding officer, Executive Officer William C. Hansford, is relived on 4 March by Acting Lt. Henry A. Glassford. In other activity, the USS *Wamsutta* is ordered to Sapelo Sound from DoBoy Sound, Georgia, where it relieves the USS *Potomska.* It remains on patrol there until late March. The monitor USS *Catskill* (Passaic class) is commissioned at about this time (late February). It is assigned to the South Atlantic Blockading Squadron.

March 1 (Sunday)   In Tennessee, Contingents of the 3rd and 4th Ohio Cavalry and 1st Tennessee Cavalry, commanded by General David Sloane Stanley, engage Confederate guerrillas under Colonel Duke at Bradyville, handily defeating them. The Union suffers one dead and six wounded. The Confederates sustain five dead, 25 wounded, and about 100 captured.

In Virginia, a Union contingent of the 1st Vermont Cavalry, commanded by Captains Ward and Huntcou, clash with a 50-man

Confederate guerrilla force at Aldie. Casualty figures are unavailable.

In Union activity, Major Frederick Tracy Dent (4th U.S. Infantry), the brother-in-law of General Grant, is at about this time ordered east from his post at San Francisco. After his arrival in New York, he is assigned to a military commission which tries prisoners. He remains there until the following year, when he is appointed aide-de-camp to General Grant with the rank of lieutenant colonel. Subsequently, he is promoted to brigadier general of volunteers, effective 5 April 1865, and at the same time he receives the brevet rank of brigadier general in the Regular Army. He retires from the army during December 1883, while he is colonel of the 3rd U.S. Artillery.

In Naval activity, at about this time (March), the U.S. Navy acquires a civilian steamer that is commissioned USS *James Thompson* in April. The ship's name is changed twice prior to 1864. In June it is renamed the USS *Manitou,* and sin November it becomes the USS *Fort Hindman.* During July, while known as the *Manitou,* it participates in the capture of the Confederate steamer CSS *Louisville* (later, USS *Ouachita.*).

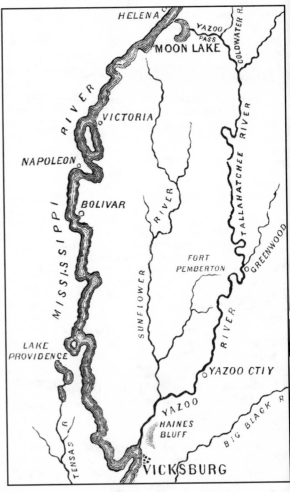

Yazoo Pass (*Harper's Pictoral History of the Civil War,* 1896).

In other activity, the ironclad river gunboat USS *Tuscumbia* is commissioned at about this time (March). The vessel is assigned duty in Tennessee and afterward in Mississippi, where it participates in the operations against Vicksburg and Grand Gulf.

March 1–2 In Missouri, a Union force led by Adjutant Fred R. Poole, which had reached the vicinity of Bloomfield on 28 February while scouting, by 1 March has the town surrounded. Poole launches a surprise attack that succeeds in seizing the town and twenty-one prisoners, including the Confederate provost marshal, R. Seckel, who is still in possession of his official documents. During the assault, one Confederate officer (recruiter) attempts to escape and he fires upon Poole, but the Confederate, Lt. J. D. Brazeau, is shot from his horse. After vanquishing the Rebels, Poole, prior to departing, also seizes some horses as well as the ammunition supplies and weapons. The Union sustains no casualties. Afterward, Poole initiates a forced march throughout the night that moves about 35 miles. On the following morning, he is informed of a Rebel camp about 15 miles distant. He gathers 20 of his finest horses and leads a contingent down the Arkansas River toward Chalk Hill. The detachment encounters three Confederates outside the Rebel camp and Poole calls for them to surrender, but they choose to flee. Firing commences and one Confederate is killed. The others are seized; however, the fire alerts the camp and the Rebels take quick flight and leave their weapons behind.

March 2 (Monday) In Washington, D.C., Congress approves an increase in the number of Union generals. The present number of 253 is increased to 358. The following day, Congress authorizes the secretary of the treasury to borrow an additional $900,000,000 on the credit of the U.S., and the secretary is also authorized to issue $50,000,000 in fractional currency (denominations less than one dollar). The loans are to run from 10 to 40 years.

In Tennessee, a Union force composed of elements of the 15th, 16th, 18th and 19th U.S. Infantry Regiments, commanded by Colonel Shepherd, engages Confederate cavalry at Eagleville. Casualty figures are unavailable. Another Union force, composed of elements of the 1st Tennessee Cavalry, led by Lt. Colonel Brownlow, battles Confederate cavalry at Petersburg. The Union reports no casualties. The Confederates sustain 12 wounded and about 20 captured.

In Virginia at Aldie, where a skirmish had occurred the previous day, a new fight erupts when a detachment of U.S. cavalry, led by Captain Schutze, encounters Confederate cavalry. The Union reports no casualties. The Confederates sustain about 30 captured.

March 3 (Tuesday) In Washington D.C., during the final days of the 37th Congress, which adjourns on the following day, Congress authorizes a draft by passing the Conscription Act (Enrollment Act). The legislation calls for

three years' service, and it is not well received by the civilian population. Nevertheless, the legislation is signed by President Lincoln. In other activity, the Idaho Territory (carved from Washington) is established by Congress. Also, President Lincoln is authorized by Congress to issue letters of marque and reprisal to privateers for three years.

In Georgia, Union vessels, commanded by Commander Drayton, move against Fort McAllister. The monitors *Passaic* (flagship), *Nahant* and *Patapsco*, supported by three mortar boats, proceed up the Ogeechee River to Genesis Point. Unable to advance farther due to obstacles, from there they bombard the Confederate stronghold. The warships maintain the bombardment until late in the afternoon and then retire. Meanwhile, the mortar boats pick up the pace and shell the fort until the following morning; however, the fort sustains no damage. The Confederate return fire causes no damage to the fleet. Drayton retires, aware that this fort will not easily capitulate. The *Passaic* and *Nahant* head for Port Royal for repairs. The USS *Dandelion* also participates in the action at Fort McAllister.

In Louisiana, a detachment of the 2nd California Cavalry clashes with Confederates at Owen's Valley. Casualty figures are unavailable.

In Missouri, a 100-man contingent of Confederate guerrillas (Missouri scouts) led by Major Thomas R. Livingston attacks the town of Granby, garrisoned by 25 troops of a battalion, commanded by Major E.B. Eno. The Confederates first seize two patrol guards who are captured "and probably killed," according to Eno's report. Two other troops, unarmed and outside the stockade giving aid to a family with sick members, are also killed. However, Livingston's raiders do not attack the stockade; rather they depart.

March 4 (Wednesday) In North Carolina, elements of the 3rd New York Cavalry, commanded by Captain Richardson, skirmish with Confederates at Skeet (Swan Quarter). The Union sustains three killed and 15 wounded. The Confederates suffer about 28 killed.

In Tennessee, the Confederates under Van Dorn clash with the Union at Thompson's Station (Spring Station) this day and the next. The Union, commanded by Colonel Coburn, had departed Franklin to reconnoiter the area at Springfield. At first contact, the Confederates, numbering well over 5,000 troops, feign retreat and prompt the Union to give chase. The ruse works and the Union, after being trapped in a gorge, finds itself with no escape, compelling the force to surrender. The Union participants, commanded by Colonel John Coburn, include the 2nd Michigan Cavalry, 9th Pennsylvania

Union ironclads *Patapsco, Passaic* and *Nahant,* on the Ogeechee River, bombard Fort McAllister, Georgia (Mottelay, *The Soldier in Our Civil War,* 1886).

Cavalry, the 4th Kentucky Cavalry, the 33rd and 85th Indiana Regiments, the 22nd Wisconsin, the 19th Michigan Regiment and 124th Ohio Volunteer Regiment, bolstered by artillery (18th Ohio Battery). The Confederates, commanded by Generals Van Dorn and Nathan B. Forrest, capture 1,306 Union soldiers. Union losses are 100 dead and 300 wounded. The Confederates lose 150 dead and 300 wounded.

In other activity, a Union force composed of elements of the 1st East Tennessee Cavalry, commanded by Majors Burkhart and Macy, clash with Confederate cavalry, led by Colonel Rogers, at Harpeth River (Chapel Hill). The Confederates sustain 12 killed and about 72 wounded.

In Union general officer activity, the appointment of Brigadier General Robert C. Buchanan (West Point, 1830) expires. It was enacted on November 29, 1862. Buchanan commanded troops at Second Manassas (Bull Run) under Pope, and participated at Sharpsburg (Antietam) and Fredericksburg, where his command suffered high casualties but served well. He subsequently assumes command of the defenses of Fort Delaware until he becomes colonel of the 1st Infantry. At the close of hostilities, he is breveted brigadier and major general of the U.S. Army. The appointment of Brigadier General Robert Cowdin also expires. He is relieved from duty at the end of the month.

With the adjournment of Congress on this day, another general, Isham N. Haynie, who saw duty at Fort Donelson and at Shiloh, where he was wounded, retires because his appointment is not reconfirmed. Also due to inaction by the U.S. Senate, General John M. Thayer's commission expires. Nonetheless, Thayer is reappointed to rank from 13 March and afterward confirmed by the Senate. General Thayer commands the 1st Division, XV Corps, during the Vicksburg Campaign. General Andrew Jackson Hamilton's commission expires due to non-action by the Senate; however, President Lincoln again appoints him as brigadier general effective 18 September. During 1865, Lincoln's successor, President Andrew Johnson, ratifies Hamilton's appointment as governor of Texas, a post he holds until 1866, when elections are held. Also, General John Franklin Farnsworth resigns his commission to take a seat in Congress today. Also, the nomination of

Brigadier General Wladimir Kryzanowski, appointed November 29, expires due to inaction by the Senate. However, he remains in the service. His brigade participates at the Battle of Chattanooga and afterward, it is attached to the 4th Division (XX Corps). On 2 March 1865, General Kryzanowski is breveted brigadier general of volunteers. He musters out of the army on 1 October 1865. In yet other activity, the commission of Brigadier General Orlando M. Poe expires due to inaction by the Senate. He reverts to his regular rank of captain. In 1864 he becomes chief engineer of the military Division of the Mississippi, and near the close of hostilities, he receives the brevet of brigadier general and afterward is promoted to colonel of engineers (1888). In yet other activity, the commission of Brigadier General Gustavus Adolphus Smith expires due to inaction by the Senate. He reverts to his prior rank of colonel with the 35th Illinois. It was recorded in F.B. Heitman's register that General Smith is dismissed from the service on 22 September 1863. Nonetheless, he is remustered as colonel of the 35th Regiment on 28 February 1865.

In Confederate general officer activity, Brigadier General Robert Augustus Toombs resigns his commission. Nevertheless, he later participates against the Union advance through Georgia. Subsequently, during 1865, Toombs leaves the United States to evade capture and imprisonment by the Union; however, he will return to Georgia about two years later, but he never applies for a pardon to regain his citizenship. He remains active in politics but does not hold any public office. He dies on 15 December 1885 at Washington, Georgia. Also, Confederate Colonel Robert B. Vance, 29th North Carolina Infantry, is promoted to the rank of brigadier general effective this date. General Vance, the brother of North Carolina Governor Zebulon Vance (elected 1862 and re-elected 1864), initially entered the Confederacy during 1861 when a command (Buncombe Life Guards) raised by him entered. The company became part of the 29th North Carolina Infantry, of which he became colonel.

March 5 (Thursday) In Mississippi, General William T. Sherman's troops return to Vicksburg after their successful raid on Meridian, which Confederates reoccupy.

In Confederate activity, John Yates Beall receives a special commission as master of the Confederate States Navy. He receives command of as expedition executed by what becomes known as the Volunteer Coast Guard or the Marine Coast Guard. The group receives no pay from the Confederacy. Compensation is to be received from the prizes taken. The expedition initiates its operation at Mathews County, the peninsula between the Piankatank River and Mobjack Bay in Virginia.

March 5-12 In Arkansas, the Union initiates an expedition commanded by Colonel Powell Clayton that originates at Helena and proceeds up the St. Francis and Little Rivers. The column is composed of 50 troops (24th Indiana Volun-

teers), 25 cavalry troops (3rd Iowa Volunteers), and one section of the 2nd Ohio Battery carrying 6-pounders. The steamer *Hamilton Belle* transports the force to a point near Madison, where the Memphis and Little Rock Railroad crosses the Saint Francis River without detection by the Confederates in the town, arriving there about dawn on the 6th.

As the troops debark, the Confederates observe the landing; however, there is no clash. The Confederates, about 75-strong, abandon Madison in great haste, essentially taking only their clothes along with them. Pursuit is immediately commenced. The Union captures 27 of the defenders and takes them back to the ship, along with the horses, weapons and equipment that is seized. Colonel Powell proceeds to the mouth of the Saint Francis River in search of a Confederate vessel, the steamer *Miller,* then moves about 25 miles up that river, where it encounters the *Miller;* but no action is taken because it had sunk. Consequently, Powell begins his return to Helena about 250 miles distant.

En route to Helena, Powell confiscates bales of cotton which are used to buffer the vessel against anticipated enemy fire. At Madison, the Confederates are waiting for Powell to attempt to pass, but Powell is aware of the ambush. At a point about two miles above Madison, Powell notices bales of cotton positioned in the heights above the river. He orders his artillery to commence fire and at the same time he spots a number of saddled but riderless horses. Powell lands his entire contingent, leaving about one-half to protect the vessel and to prepare to advance if necessary. The others attack.

A heated skirmish develops, but the Union presses the Confederates and the latter moves into the hills after sustaining four killed. Powell's force sustains one wounded, Lt. William E. Niblack (3rd Iowa Cavalry). He is hit in the shoulder with buckshot while leading a cavalry charge. Afterward, Powell arrives at Madison and encounters some resistance, but succeeds in scattering it with artillery fire. After removing the obstacles that block passage, the vessel resumes its voyage back to Helena, arriving there on the 12th.

March 5-13 In Missouri, the Union initiates an expedition into Jasper and Newton Counties. Captain D. Mefford departs Camp Salomon on the 5th with Companies A, C and D, 6th Kansas Cavalry, en route for Newtonia, where the column establishes night quarters. On the following morning, the column moves to the vicinity of Granby and a reconnaissance of the area near Shoal Creek is made. From there the column moves to Neosho, where it remains until Saturday, the 7th. On the 7th, Mefford continues in a northerly direction toward Savilla, an innocent appearing village of less than fifteen houses; however, the village homes are each occupied by Confederate sympathizers. Nevertheless, the Union encamps there for the night. Captain Mefford later notes in his report that during the night, he lost one of his valuable horses.

On the 8th, Mefford's detachment moves toward Diamond Grove and, discovering no enemy presence, advances to Turkey Creek and beyond to Sherwood in Jasper County. At the latter, signs of recent Confederate presence are detected, but no intelligence is received that assists the column. Mefford, however, remains in Sherwood until 0300 on the 9th, then resumes the advance. Shortly the Confederates announce their presence when a Rebel picket fires at the column, striking Sergeant Fountain in the face. Fire is immediately returned and the picket is wounded. Afterward, the column arrives at the abandoned camp, from which the guerrilla leader, Major Thomas Livingston, had hurriedly abandoned and vanished into the woods. Pursuit at that point ceases; the woods are too thick, preventing the cavalry from giving chase. Back at Turkey Creek, several Rebels are spotted and pursuit begins.

Meanwhile, Livingston's whole force, about one mile from the creek, suddenly launches an attack on the pursuers, which compels the vanguard to retire back to the main body. As the cavalry returns, Mefford regroups his force to the rear of a group of trees and thick brush, then orders his troops to dismount. As Livingston's guerrillas close to about ninety yards from his positions, Mefford orders his force to commence fire. A brief exchange occurs, but the guerrillas quickly retire. The Union sustains one man wounded in addition to the earlier wounding of Sgt. Fountain. Confederate casualties are unknown to Mefford.

Again the cavalry is unable to pursue due to the wooded terrain. Mefford heads for Neosho and remains there during the night and into the following day to get attention for his horses. On the following day, Wednesday the 11th, Mefford receives some welcome support. Captain A.C. Spillman, 3rd Indiana Regiment, provides 40 Indian scouts. Mefford then advances into the Indian Territory and makes camp at Crawford Seminary. On Thursday, Mefford resumes following the trail of the guerrillas and advances about an additional 35 miles; however, without success.

Mefford, low on supplies and his horses close to exhaustion, decides at about 1400 to return to Savilla and arrives there during the night. On the 13th, a small party of Company A had left camp without orders and while at a house where they intended to eat breakfast, they had been fired upon, disarmed and captured. One of the three had been wounded. A search found none of the enemy. The wounded man is taken by the Indians to Neosho, while Mefford leads his command back to camp, returning there at about 2100.

March 6 (Friday) In Arkansas, a skirmish erupts along the White River.

In South Carolina, at about this time, General David Hunter (Department of the South) authorizes the drafting of Negroes for garrison duty. A Union expedition is initiated at Helena and will continue through the 10th. The contingent advances to Big Creek and Lick Creek.

March 7 (Saturday) *In Confederate activity,* General E. Kirby Smith assumes command of all Confederates west of the Mississippi River.

March 8 (Sunday) **In North Carolina,** Union troops of the 43rd Massachusetts Regiment, commanded by Colonel Holbrook, engage Confederates along Trent Road and capture an unknown number of Confederate cavalrymen.

In Virginia, Confederates commanded by Captain John S. Mosby surprise and capture the headquarters of Union General Edwin Henry Stoughton (West Point, 1859). Stoughton and 35 soldiers are taken prisoner at the Fairfax County Court House, after Mosby's small command of 29 men elude thousands of Union troops by sneaking into the town and taking the sleeping general right from his quarters in one of the biggest swashbuckling capers of the war. Mosby rides out of town with 33 prisoners, including the general, and the Rebels also confiscate sixty horses. Stoughton loses his command and his generalship, which had lapsed four days prior to his capture due to inactivity by the Senate. He dies still a young man of 30 in New York City on Christmas Day, 1868. During the previous month, Confederates under General Jeb Stuart unsuccessfully attempted to seize the Union-held town of Gloucester Point, and on this day, a contingent led by General W.H.F. Lee is driven off.

March 9 (Monday) **In Tennessee,** a contingent of Union troops skirmishes with Confederate guerrillas at Bolivar. Specific units are not reported; however, it is reported that 18 Confederates are captured. Another contingent of Union troops attached to the 125th Ohio Volunteer Regiment skirmishes with Confederates in the vicinity of Franklin. Casualty figures are unavailable.

March 9–15 **In Missouri,** the Union initiates an expedition that moves from Bloomfield to Chalk Bluff, Arkansas, and other places, including Gum Blough, Kennett and Hornersville, Missouri. The column, led by Colonel John McNeil, is composed of 500 troops bolstered by two mountain howitzers and carries rations for two days, but no tents are taken on the mission. The column arrives at Chalk Bluff on the following day at about 0900. A spearhead of the force had arrived earlier and is skirmishing with the Confederates on the opposite bank of the river when McNeil's main body arrives. Meanwhile, Confederates are posted at the ferry boats, preventing Union passage.

McNeil brings up his artillery, which plasters the Confederate positions, and after about three hours of exchanging blows, the Confederates abandon the river bank positions. Meanwhile, about fifty of McNeil's troops volunteer to swim across the river and secure the ferry, which is taken back to the Union side. Shortly thereafter three companies are carried across the river and they immediately advance to clear the hills. The Union also sets fire to a large supply of corn. Af-

terward, the Union destroys a large but uncompleted ferry boat, and the buildings there are also torched. During the fighting the Union sustains two wounded, the blacksmith, William J. Dryden (Company E), and Private Cicero G. Davis (Company H).

The Union remains at the bluff until 0400 on the following day and then advances to Thompson's Fort in the vicinity of Gum Slough, arriving near the fort by about 1200. About thirty defenders are at the slough, but they are driven off. Afterward, the Union moves to Thompson's Fort (General M. Jeff Thompson, Missouri State Guard) and finds it abandoned. The Confederates, having been alerted to the Union advance, evacuated the fort prior to the arrival of McNeil's column. After receiving information that the Confederates had moved to positions on the Varney River, McNeil gives chase, sending a contingent under Lt. Poole out in advance to find and destroy the Confederate dugouts (canoes). Nevertheless, when Poole arrives at the place, about eight miles above Kennett, he discovers that the Rebels had departed on the previous night.

McNeil establishes his camp at Kennett and remains there for two days. During that time he captures more than 60 Confederates, including four officers. The Union also seizes some mules and 65 horses in addition to provisions and supplies. After resuming the mission, McNeil's column secures Holcombe, Ten-Mile, Buffalo, Horse, and Two-Mile Islands. The mission succeeds in driving Thompson and Colonel (later general) John B. Clark out of Arkansas. One of the horses picked up by McNeil is that of Jeff Thompson, and it is a mare about to give birth to a foal.

Colonel McNeil in his report notes that erroneous charges of killing innocent civilians and raping women were rapidly spreading, but he also reports that the women apparently did not believe the rumors and remained as the column passed various places, although the men had fled. He also reports that he administered the oath of loyalty to eighty people during the mission. One other note reported as follows: "The last that was heard of this doughty hero he [Jeff Thompson] was floating down the Saint Francis [River], the solitary tenant of a dug-out, quite drunk and very melancholy." The column arrives back at Bloomfield at 0900 on the 15th.

March 10 (Tuesday) **In Florida,** the USS *Norwich* and the USS *Uncas,* while operating on the St. John's River in the vicinity of Jacksonville, on escort duty with some transports, bombard Confederate positions. The shelling of the defensive positions succeeds and the operation proceeds. The landing force (1st South Carolina Regiment, Colored Troops) debarks and enters Jacksonville, where the contingent destroys parts of the city. The Union force withdraws from the vicinity of Jacksonville during the latter part of the month.

In Louisiana and Texas, Union General Andrew Jackson Smith (West Point, 1838), escorted by a Union fleet of 20 vessels, initiates an assault on Louisiana and Eastern Texas, de-

fended by Confederate General Kirby Smith. The journey down the Mississippi and Red Rivers is arduous, yet they capture Fort DeRussy (Louisiana) on 14 March.

In Tennessee, elements of the 6th and 7th Illinois Cavalry, commanded by Colonel (later general) Benjamin Henry Grierson, attack a Confederate encampment in the vicinity of Covington. The Confederates, numbering about 400 and led by Colonel Richardson, lose about 25 killed. Grierson initially received a commission as major during October 1861 and was promoted to colonel of the 6th Illinois Cavalry in April 1862. Also, the 4th Cavalry Brigade, commanded by Colonel Mundy, skirmishes with Confederates at Rutherford's Creek. An unknown number of Confederates is captured.

In Union general officer activity, Brigadier General Robert H. Milroy is promoted to major general, effective 29 November 1862. Brigadier General Francis Jay Herron and Brigadier General Richard James Oglesby are appointed major general to rank from the same day. General Oglesby is still recuperating from a severe wound sustained at Corinth during the previous year. He returns to duty the following month.

March 11 (Wednesday) **In Kentucky,** Union troops protecting a wagon train repel an attack by Confederate guerrillas at Paris.

In Mississippi, a Union fleet, composed of seven gunboats, two mortar boats and about twenty troop transports, having moved up the Cold Water and Tallahatchie Rivers, reaches a point about three miles north of Greenwood, where it encounters obstacles that impede passage. The Confederates have established a line of cotton bale breastworks which hold some guns that dominate the approach route from the Tallahatchie. The channel is further obstructed by a sunken steamer and log rafts. Union Lt. Commander Watson Smith repeatedly attempts to break through, but to no avail. Confederate-held Fort Pemberton (Fort Greenwood), an island at Greenwood, Mississippi, is unscathed by the effort. General Ross' men, numbering about 5,000, although on board, are unable to attack General Lloyd Tilghman's defenders. The Union force makes another attempt on the 13th.

In Union general officer activity, Lt. Colonel George Jerrison Stannard, colonel of the 4th Vermont (militia) at the opening of hostilities, is commissioned brigadier general. He was appointed lieutenant colonel of the 2nd Vermont during July 1861 and colonel of the 9th Vermont in July 1862.

In Naval activity, the U.S. Navy acquires the vessel *Anna* (*La Criolla*), which had been condemned by the prize court in Key West, Florida. The *Anna,* which becomes known as the *Annie,* retains its nickname throughout its service. It is assigned duty with the East Gulf Blockading Squadron. By 1 October, it is on duty at Boca Grande, Florida. The USS *Western World,* which left New York on the 16th, arrives at Newport News to join the North Atlantic Blockading Squadron; however, the ship has structural problems. By the latter part of the month, it is sent to Philadelphia to rectify the problems. On 1 April it initiates patrol duty in the area between Fortress Monroe and the Piankatank River. It continues to patrol off the Virginia coast and in Chesapeake Bay throughout the summer.

March 12 (Thursday) In Washington, D.C., the Senate rejects the earlier appointment of Brigadier General Horatio Wright to major general. On 24 March, Wright's commission is rejected. Nonetheless, he will be reappointed on 12 May 1864 and his appointment is confirmed by the Senate.

In Mississippi, General Ross's force, being transported by Lt. Commander Watson Smith's fleet, remains north of Greenwood, the location of Fort Pemberton. This day, the Union confines itself to establishing batteries and refrains from trying to push past the obstacles which continue to hold up progress.

In Union general officer activity, Lt. Colonel Henry Baxter is appointed brigadier general of volunteers. Baxter fought in the Peninsular Campaign and was wounded. At Fredericksburg, he was wounded more severely. In the Battle of Gettysburg, he commands a brigade in the I Corps, which suffers heavy casualties. On the previous day, March 11, General Cassius M. Clay, had resigned his commission of major general. Clay subsequently leaves the United States for Russia, remaining there until 1869. On the 13th, Union Colonel Thomas Ewing, Jr., is appointed brigadier general. He will see action against Confederate General Sterling Price in Missouri. Brigadier General Isaac Stevens, killed on 1 September 1862, is posthumously promoted to major general to rank from 18 July 1862. The Senate denies the commission of Major General Gouverneur Wright (appointed 18 July 1862). The commission is revoked on 24 May; however, he is reappointed major general in May of the following year.

In Naval activity, the USS *New Era,* operating in the vicinity of Island No. 10 in Tennessee, intercepts and seizes the Confederate steamer *Ruth,* which is caught while carrying "contraband and Confederate mail."

March 13 (Friday) THE ATTACK ON FORT PEMBERTON Union land batteries, recently established several miles north of Greenwood, Mississippi, commence firing at Rebel positions at Fort Pemberton in coordination with the fleet's bombardment. Lt. Commander Watson Smith and General Ross have determined the terrain is too unstable to handle a landing of the ground troops, and instead decide to maintain the bombardment throughout the day and into the following day. The Union believes that if the Rebel guns can be silenced, the transports can easily move up and debark the troops at the doorsteps of the fort. However, the formidable defenses under the command of Brigadier Gen-

eral Lloyd Tilghman withstand the assault and perplex the Union.

While retiring, the Union encounters the forces of General I.F. Quinby, which had been dispatched by General Grant, but the forces are believed insufficient to seize the Rebel positions. These Confederate batteries still prevent Union ships from passing Fort Pemberton, and they continue to do so throughout March, preventing the Union vessels from using this route to reach Vicksburg. The expedition is aborted.

In Louisiana, Union vessels converge at Prophet's Island to prepare to run the batteries at Port Hudson. General Nathaniel Banks initiates a diversionary action by dispatching about 20,000 troops to the rear of Port Hudson. Also, a baggage train attached to the forces of General Christopher Columbus Augur, en route to Port Hudson, crosses Montecino Bayou. On the following day, the vessels *Hartford,* with the *Albatross* tied to its side, remains at the point. It is trailed by the *Richmond* with the *Genesee, Monongahela, Kineo* and the *Mississippi,* along with the *Essex* and *Sachem.* The Confederates are prepared for the Union fleet and greet it with a trap. As the vessels approach, the Confederates create a huge bonfire that spreads across the water, and they follow that action with incessant fire that lasts for several hours. The *Hartford* (and the attached *Albatross*) run the gauntlet, but the others fail to pass. The *Richmond* takes a severe hit and retires toward Prophet's Island. The remainder of the fleet, except the *Mississippi,* also returns to Prophet's Island. The *Mississippi* runs aground and continues firing until it is no longer feasible. Captain Melancthon Smith then sets the ship afire. Smith and the crew escape by making it to the opposite shore. The *Kineo,* attached to the *Monongahela,* is about to make the pass when the *Monongahela* sustains damage to its rudder, which imperils both ships; however, the *Kineo* pulls the *Monongahela* out of harm's way. The land troops are directed to return to Baton Rouge after it is decided the force is not strong enough to take the city.

A contingent of the 160th New York Volunteer Regiment skirmishes with Confederates at Berwick City. Subsequent to this action, the USS *Kineo* continues with the fleet until August, when it sails north for repairs that keep it out of service until March 1864. At that time, it operates off the Texas coast and along the Mississippi until it is decommissioned during the closing days of the war (May 1865). After the war the *Kineo* is sold and becomes the merchant schooner *Lucy H. Gibson* (October 1866).

A baggage train attached to General Christopher Columbus Augur, en route to Port Hudson, crosses Montecino Bayou (Johnson, *Campfire and Battlefield: History of the Conflicts and Campaigns,* 1894).

In Union general officer activity, Colonel William Ward Orme is promoted to brigadier general. He is assigned duty with General Grant at Vicksburg. General Orme arrives to join Grant on 11 June but later contracts tuberculosis. Promotions effective 29 November 1862 include Brigadier General Benjamin Mayberry Prentiss, major general, Colonel John Dunlap Stevenson, brigadier general, Brigadier General John Alexander Logan, major general, and Brigadier General Cadwallader C. Washburn, major general. Washburn participates in the Vicksburg campaign. He resigns from the army on 25 May 1865, following the surrender of Robert E. Lee at Appomattox during April 1865. Colonel Robert Brown Potter is promoted to brigadier general. Potter receives command of a division which participates in the operations against Vicksburg, and it joins the Knoxville campaign. In 1864 he participates as part of the IX Corps during the Overland Campaign.

In South Carolina, Confederates attack a signal party led by Lt. Fenner at Spanish Wells. Nine Union troops are reported missing.

March 13–14 In North Carolina, Fort Anderson is struck during the night of the 13th–14th by a surprise attack, but the Rebels are foiled by Union vessels stationed on the Neuse River. The guns of the *Ceres, Hetzel, Hunchback* and *Shawsheen* force the Confederates to abort the attack and retire. The USS *Agassiz* participates in this action. Commander Alexander Murray, the senior naval officer on duty in the sounds of North Carolina, states: "The gallant part taken by that vessel was alike creditable to its commanding officer [Robert H. Travers] and serviceable in the repulse of the enemy." The *Agassiz* sustains damage and heads to Norfolk for repairs. Subsequent to being repaired, the *Agassiz* heads farther north to New Bedford, Massachusetts, where it sees duty for the remainder of the war. Subsequent to the close of hostilities, the *Agassiz* moves to Newport, Rhode Island, on 10 October 1865 for a short while, then heads for New York and resumes duty as a vessel of the Coast Survey.

March 14 (Saturday)   In Louisiana, Port Hudson is bombarded by Farragut's fleet. The USS *Mississippi,* attempting to pass Port Hudson, Louisiana, is disabled by Confederate batteries after it runs aground. The Union sets it afire to prevent capture; however, the *Hartford* passes safely. During this expedition, Admiral Farragut orders that the gunboats be tied to the sides of his steamers to protect them from Confederate guns and to increase their maneuverability. The ships are paired. The *Genesee* is fastened to the USS *Richmond.* The *Genesee* sustains severe damage, including having its rigging severed. The *Richmond* sustains damage to its steam line. Only the *Hartford* and the *Albatross* (tied together) are able to run past the Confederate batteries. The *Genesee,* subsequent to receiving repairs, resumes its patrol duty on the Mississippi, and it remains on station until the fall of Vicksburg on 4 July. During September, it is transferred to the Gulf to initiate blockade duty there.

In North Carolina, a Union force composed of about 450 troops of the 92nd New York Volunteer Regiment, commanded by Colonel Anderson, and Union gunboats attack New Bern. The Union sustains five wounded. The Confederates sustain about 15 killed and 30 wounded.

March 14–15   In California, during the night of the 14th, a Confederate conspiracy begins to unfold in San Francisco. Fourteen of a 15-man detachment board the schooner *J.C. Chapman,* earlier acquired by J.M. Greathouse in conjunction with another, named Harpending, the latter having in his possession a letter of marque from Confederate President Jefferson Davis. The Confederates on the ship are still aboard on the following day when the plan is foiled. The ship is in the process of embarking when it is seized. The authorities discover papers aboard the vessel that disclose a proclamation to the

Californians to "throw off the authority of the United States; a plan for the capture of the United States forts at San Francisco and particularly Alcatraz; a draft of an oath of fidelity to their cause, and an imprecation of vengeance on all who should prove false." Those captured are tried and convicted, then sentenced to ten years in prison and fined ten thousand dollars each. One of the men, Rubery, receives a pardon from President Lincoln in response to a request from an Englishman, John Bright. The others also win their releases subsequent to Lincoln's Amnesty Proclamation of 8 December 1863. The schooner is condemned and its cargo sold.

March 15 (Sunday)   In Rhode Island, Union General Ambrose Burnside, recently retired and residing in Providence, is recalled to service. He is to succeed General Horatio Wright and assume command of the Department of the Ohio. He will move with the Ninth Army Corps, taking it from Newport News to East Tennessee to bolster General Rosecrans. The army departs Virginia in May.

March 16 (Monday)   In Mississippi, Union General William T. Sherman's force, including Brigadier General David Stuart's 15th Corps, boards transports to carry the troops to Eagle Bend on the Mississippi. The flotilla comprises five gunboats and several transports. They debark, then march to Steele's Bayou, where they re-board other vessels. The protective gunboats advance too far into Black's Bayou and become cramped by fallen trees and other obstacles that restrain their maneuverability at about the same time that they encounter a 4,000-man Confederate force, including many sharp-

shooters. General Sherman's division finally speeds on foot to reach and rescue the stalled fleet. Admiral Porter (Union naval commander) is prepared to destroy his fleet rather than have it captured, but Sherman arrives in time to extricate it. Nevertheless, the Confederates forestall the demise of Vicksburg. The Union fleet quickly returns toward the safety of their lines, but the threat stays with the fleet as it returns. Not until the 25th, when it arrives at Hill's Plantation, does it appear that they have reached safety.

In Union general officer activity, Colonel William Hopkins Morris (West Point, 1851), 96th New York Heavy Artillery, is appointed brigadier general, effective 29 November 1862. He participates at Gettysburg and afterward in various actions in Virginia. Also, Colonel Joseph Andrew Jackson Lightburn is promoted to brigadier general of volunteers. He participates at the Battle of Chattanooga and in the Atlanta Campaign. Colonel Joseph Anthony Mower (11th Missouri Infantry), a veteran of the Mexican War, where he served as a private, and later was 2nd lieutenant of the 1st U.S. Infantry,

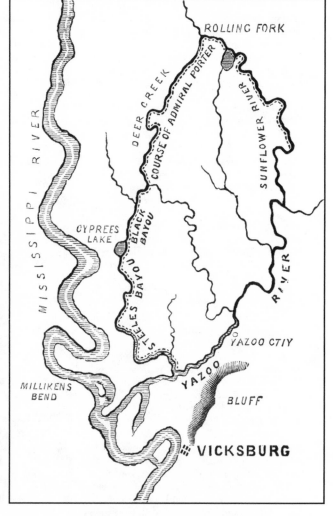

Left: The CSS *Mississippi,* still under construction, is burned to prevent its capture by a Union fleet near New Orleans (*Harper's Pictoral History of the Civil War,* 1896).*Right:* Admiral Farragut's fleet at Vicksburg (Mottelay, *The Soldier in Our Civil War,* 1886).

is promoted to brigadier general. Colonel Franklin Stillman Nickerson is promoted to brigadier general. He remains in Louisiana for the duration of the war. Brigadier General John McCauley Palmer is appointed major general to rank from 29 November 1862. Colonel Thomas Church Haskell Smith, on the staff of General John Pope, is promoted to brigadier general. He moves to Minnesota with Pope. Later this year Smith receives command of the District of Wisconsin. After the war, General Smith again moves with General Pope, who assumes command of the Department of Missouri. General Smith musters out of the service during 1866. He later loses his sources of income (1871) after the great fire in Chicago, where he raises livestock. Afterward, he becomes a paymaster in the army with the rank of major. He retires during 1883 and dies in California during April 1897. Also, Colonel Thomas W. Sweeny (52nd Illinois) is promoted to brigadier general to rank from 29 November 1862. He is assigned garrison duty at various places in Mississippi and Tennessee, but later he commands a division of the XVI Corps during the operations against Atlanta. Colonel Isaac Jones Wistar (71st Pennsylvania) is promoted to brigadier general effective 29 November 1862. General Wistar, having earlier sustained a wound that costs him some use of his right arm, had partial use of his left arm at Antietam. Subsequent to his promotion he continues to serve in Virginia and participates in minor skirmishes; however, during May 1864, he receives command of a brigade in the XVIII Corps, Army of the James, but by mid–May, he is relieved. Also, Brigadier General George Stoneman is promoted to major general.

March 17 (Tuesday) BATTLE OF KELLY'S FORD The 1st and 5th U.S. Regulars; 3rd, 4th, and 16th Pennsylvania; 1st Rhode Island, 6th Ohio and the 4th New York Cavalry (2nd Cavalry Division), commanded by General W.W. Averell (West Point, 1851), engage Confederates of Fitzhugh Lee's brigade in a skirmish at Kelly's Ford, Virginia. Averell had crossed the Rappahannock at Kelly's Ford about 27 miles above Fredericksburg en route to raid the country around Culpeper Court House. His force also includes two artillery brigades under Colonels John B. McIntosh and Duffie. About one mile from the ford, the contingent encounters Confederate cavalry (3rd, 4th and 5th Virginia Regiments), which attacks to turn the Union right; however, extremely deadly fire from the 6th New York Regiment scatters the attackers. Undaunted, the Rebels launch another assault to penetrate the right side of the line, but here, too, the Union holds firmly as Duffie's brigade propels forward and drives the Rebels back, inflicting severe casualties. The grueling skirmishing continues throughout the day, but by nightfall, General Averell pulls back and returns to the opposite bank of the river. The Union suffers nine dead and 35 wounded. The Confederates lose 11 dead and 88 wounded. Confederate Colonel Thomas L. Rosser is wounded during this action.

In Union general officer activity, Colonel James M. Shackelford (8th Kentucky Cavalry) is promoted to the rank of brigadier general, effective 2 January 1863. General James Barnet Fry is appointed provost marshal general. According to the U.S. War Department, Provost Marshal General Bureau, *Historical Report of the Acting Assisting Provost Marshal General of Ohio,* Provost Marshal General Collection, National Archives, the three provost marshals were "General [Colonel A E.] Parrott, April 29, 1863–February 15, 1864; General Joseph H. Porter [Potter], February 15, 1864–September 2, 1864; and Colonel James A. Wilcox, September 2, 1864–August 30, 1865."

Brigadier General Carl Schurz is promoted to major general. After the Battle of Gettysburg, he is assigned to the West with the XI Corps and the XII Corps. Brigadier General Julius Stahel is also promoted to major general. General Stahel had participated in the Shenandoah Valley under General Hooker, and at Second Manassas (Bull Run), he commanded a division in General Sigel's corps after General Robert C. Schenk had sustained a wound. Subsequent to

Close-quartered combat at Kelly's Ford between Union cavalry under General Averell and Confederate General Stuart (Mottelay, *The Soldier in Our Civil War,* 1886).

this promotion, he is assigned command of the cavalry forces along the defenses of the capital.

March 18 (Wednesday) In Louisiana, a contingent of the 1st Louisiana Cavalry led by Captain Perkins clashes with Confederate cavalry at Brashear City. The Confederates lose about 10 killed and 20 wounded. The two sides maintain a running fight, the Union initially winning a bout, then the Rebels prevailing during the second contest.

In Confederate activity, Lt. General Theophilus H. Holmes assumes command of the Department of Arkansas. Later he is sent to

Left: General Fitzhugh Lee. *Right:* General William W. Averell (Johnson, *Campfire and Battlefield: History of the Conflicts and Campaigns,* 1894).

North Carolina to organize reserves. After the war he resides in the vicinity of Fayetteville, Arkansas, on a farm. He dies there during June 1880.

March 19 (Thursday) **In Arkansas,** a skirmish between Union and Confederate forces erupts at Frog Bayou. The Union contingent, a reconnaissance detachment of nine men led by Captain Whiteford, encounters a force of 20 Confederates at Bill Young's in the vicinity of Frog Bayou, slightly less than twenty miles from the Arkansas River. The Confederates sustain 10 killed or mortally wounded and they lose most of their weapons and blankets. The Confederate commander, Captain Wright, is among the mortally wounded. Captain Whitehead and his detachment, which sustains no casualties, arrive back at Fayetteville during the night of the 22nd.

In Florida, a contingent drawn from the USS *Norwich* and the USS *Hale* uses a boat to move against and destroy a lighthouse in the vicinity of Jacksonville.

In Mississippi, a Union fleet, including the USS *Hartford*, bombards Grand Gulf. U.S. Marines aboard the *Hartford* participate.

In Ohio, a party of five Catholic nuns (Sisters of Mount St. Vincent), in response from a request from the Union military, departs for Nashville, Tennessee, to nurse sick and wounded soldiers. The nuns, Sisters Anthony, Benedicta, Constantina, Gabriella and Louise, accompanied by Father Tracy, will work at the hospital that had previously been a cotton mill on College Hill. Many of the wounded from the Battle of Stones River are taken there for treatment.

In Tennessee, a Union contingent skirmishes with Confederates at Duck River. Specific units are unreported and casualty figures are unavailable.

In Naval activity, the *Alona,* a British blockade runner captured in Florida in January, is commissioned at Philadelphia, Pennsylvania. Litigation regarding the actions of the *Alona* continues into the following year. Consequently, the U.S. Navy is not able to officially purchase the vessel until 28 March 1864. In the meantime, the *Alona* operates on the lower Mississippi River as a dispatch ship, operating primarily between New Orleans and Port Hudson, Louisiana. Upon the seizure of Vicksburg on the Fourth of July, 1863, and the capture of Port Hudson on 9 July, the *Alona* is released for other duty. The USS *Wissahickon* encounters and destroys the Confederate steamer *Georgiana* off Charleston. During the following month, on the 25th, the *Wissahickon* sails north to Philadelphia for repairs and remains there into the following month. After returning to its squadron, the *Wissahickon* resumes patrols and participates in several actions, including the operations against Savannah, Georgia. The vessel is decommissioned on 1 July 1865 and sold on 25 October. On 20 January 1866, it is renamed *Adele.*

March 19–23 **In Missouri,** a column, composed of 75 troops under Regimental Adjutant Fred R. Poole (2nd Missouri Cavalry, state militia) departs Bloomfield on a scouting mission in the area west of the St. Francis River. When the contingent advances to Williams' Crossing, Poole orders 25 of his troops under Lt. Donahoo to remain at the crossing to protect two ferry boats, one of which had been captured by Poole at Mingo, and the other seized at Punches' Crossing. Poole's contingent had also seized some canoes and they too are at Williams' Crossing, located less than one mile south of where the Mingo Creek converges with the St. Francis River. Poole leads the main body beyond the river on the 20th and moves to Poplar Bluff. The 50-man contingent moves out of the town (pro-Union) and camps near the bridge that spans the Blackwater River east of the town.

On the 21st, still unaware of the location of Marmaduke's forces and too far from any reinforcements, Poole selects Pocahontas as the next objective in an attempt to pick up a lead on the Confederates. The choice bears fruit. At about 1300, the detachment startles a Rebel picket, who takes flight back toward Pitman's Ferry and Doniphan Roads. Afterward three pickets are captured and two that escape are intercepted and killed. Meanwhile, Poole is informed by the captives that Marmaduke's forces are in the vicinity of Batesville. Poole records intelligence on the roads and foraging in the area and notes also that he has come across recent newspapers out of St. Louis that are not available in Bloomfield, proving that Marmaduke is in direct communication with the city. Poole returns to Bloomfield, arriving there on the 23rd.

March 20 (Friday) **In Tennessee,** about 1,400 Union troops, commanded by Colonel A.S. Hall, encounter and defeat a larger Confederate contingent under Brigadier General John Hunt Morgan and Major General Joseph Wheeler at Vaught's Hill in Milton. The skirmish lasts for several hours; Confederate General John Morgan becomes one of the wounded. Union casualties total seven killed and 48 wounded. Confederates have 63 killed and approximately 300 wounded. The 101st Ohio, 101st Indiana, and 80th and 123rd Illinois Regiments, supplemented by the 1st Tennessee Cavalry and the 9th Indiana Battery, participate.

In Union general officer activity, Major Thomas Gamble Pitcher (West Point, 1845) is commissioned brigadier general. General Pitcher's previous field duty was at the Battle of Cedar Mountain, where he sustained a serious wound while commanding a battalion (General Henry Prince's brigade, General Augur's Division). The wound keeps Pitcher out of service for several months. Subsequent to his promotion, General Pitcher becomes state provost marshal general, in Vermont and then in Indiana, for the federal government. He musters out of the volunteer service during 1866; however, he is immediately appointed colonel of the 44th U.S. Infantry. Afterward, he is appointed superintendent of the Military Academy at West

Point. He succumbs at Fort Bayard, New Mexico, on 21 October 1895. Brigadier General William W. Burns (West Point, 1847) resigns his commission to remain in an administrative position as major of commissary, a post he retains until his retirement in 1889.

In Naval activity, the USS *Brockenborough,* pursuant to orders of Lt. George E. Welch of the USS *Amanda,* transports the executive officer of the bark to the mouth of the Ocklocknee River to verify whether a blockade runner is taking on cargo. The voyage lasts three days as the ship maneuvers through St. George's Sound's marshy waters. The vessel approaches the suspected location and spots the ship, which is partially submerged. At the sight of the Union sloop, the Confederates abandon the ship and reach shore in boats. The runner *Onward* is not fully refloated until the following morning, but once it gets underway en route to deeper water, the ship again grounds after taking the wrong channel. While waiting for the tide to rise, a contingent of Confederate cavalry composed of about 40 troops, bolstered by about 150 infantry troops, appears. A clash erupts, but the Union manages to set the *Onward* afire before retiring in the *Brockenborough* and the launch. During the harrowing retreat, the Confederates continue to fire upon the Union vessels. One man is killed and eight others are wounded. Nonetheless, the Union returns to waters in the vicinity of St. Mark's, Florida, and once there, the USS *Hendrick Hudson* accepts the wounded. Meanwhile, the *Brockenborough* returns to St. George's Sound.

March 21 (Saturday) *In Union activity,* Union Major General Edwin Vose Sumner, who has served in the U.S. Army since 1819, dies of natural causes in New York at Syracuse while traveling to the Department of Missouri.

In Tennessee, the Union 3rd Tennessee Cavalry skirmishes with a contingent of Confederates at Salem Pike. Also, a skirmish breaks out at Cottage Grove, where Confederate guerrillas attack a Union garrison. The attack is repelled.

In Mississippi, the 2nd Division, 15th Corps, under General William T. Sherman, engages Confederates at Deer Creek. General David Stuart, who commands a brigade in General M.L. Smith's 2nd Division (Sherman's Corps), had been in command of the division since Smith was wounded in January. However, Congress neglects to renew his commission, compelling Sherman, once informed, to relieve him of command. Nothing in Stuart's record explains the action of Congress. Stuart resigns from the service in early April.

In Union general officer activity, Lt. Colonel Davis Tillson (West Point attendance, 1848–1851) is appointed brigadier general to rank from 29 November 1862. Tillson, compelled to leave West Point due to an accident, had initially served with the 2nd Maine Battery as a captain beginning in November 1861 and afterward as chief of artillery for several commanding officers. In January 1865, he is appointed commander of the District of Tennessee. He commands the Army of the Cumberland during the closing months of the war. He resigns from the army in December 1866.

March 22 (Sunday)   In Kentucky, a Confederate force (command of Colonel R.S. Cluke) attacks a contingent of the 10th Kentucky Cavalry under Captain Radcliff and captures Mt. Sterling. The Union, although forced to evacuate, will recapture the town the following day.

In Mississippi, at Deer Creek, Rebels pour fire upon Union vessels, including the *Carondelet* and the *Tug Ivy.*

In Missouri, a 50-man contingent of the 5th Missouri Militia Cavalry and an artillery company, commanded by Captain H.B. Johnson, skirmishes with Confederates under Quantrill at Blue Springs, in the vicinity of Independence. The guerrillas outnumber the Union and force the column to retire. The Union sustains nine killed, three wounded and six missing. Following his return to camp, the commanding officer, Colonel W.R. Penick, states in a letter to Major General Samuel R. Curtis: "The guerrillas, as usual, have scattered all over the county in twos, threes, & it will be impossible for United States soldiers to drive them out of this county unless the government can afford to send ten soldiers for one guerrilla. The only way to get them out is to destroy all subsistence in rocky and brushy parts of the country, and send off their wives and the children; also the wives and children of sympathizers who are aiding and abetting them."

In Arkansas, a contingent of 25 troops and 10 civilians departs Fayetteville to assist a contractor with his herd of stock. The detachment comes under a multi-sided attack by Confederates under Major McConnell near the mouth of the White River. Confederate strength is estimated at 200 and thought to be attached to Brook's regiment operating out of Clarksville. The diminutive detachment is mauled and sustains three killed and seven captured. In addition, the civilian section loses one killed, one wounded and eight captured. Confederate Major McConnell is shot from his horse while leading the charge and killed. Colonel H. Larue Harrison notes in his report to Major General Samuel Ryan Curtis: "If our cavalry could get horses, they would not be half liable to such disasters. At present all escorts have to be sent out dismounted." General Curtis is having personal difficulties with Missouri Governor Hamilton Gamble, which leads to Curtis being relieved by Lincoln in May. At that time Curtis is transferred to the Department of Kansas as commander.

In Naval activity, the USS *Tioga,* while operating in the vicinity of the Bahamas, seizes a blockade runner, the *Granite City.* Subsequently, the *Granite City* is acquired by the U.S. Navy on 16 April 1863. Acting Master Charles W. Lamson receives command. The ship arrives in New Orleans on 27 August.

March 23 (Monday)   In Mississippi, Union gunboats continue to bombard Confederate batteries south of Vicksburg, and on this day the batteries at Warrenton are the targets. The USS *Hartford* reports that no return fire is received. The *Hartford* anchors below the town.

In Union general officer activity, Brigadier General Thomas Welsh (commission of 1862, expired due to no action by the U.S. Senate) is recommissioned brigadier general. Welsh is assigned command of the IX Corps during the Vicksburg Campaign, but in August, he becomes ill and succumbs. Major George Crockett Strong, chief of staff to General Benjamin F. Banks, is promoted to brigadier general effective 29 November 1862. Also, Colonel Samuel Kosciusko (57th New York) is promoted to brigadier general. He participates at Chancellorsville and at Gettysburg.

March 24 (Tuesday)   In Kentucky, a Union contingent composed of elements of the 1st Kentucky and 2nd Tennessee Cavalry Regiments, the 18th and 22nd Michigan Volunteer Regiments and the 1st Indiana Battery, commanded by Colonel Clark, engages a Confederate force at Danville. Casualty figures are unavailable.

In Louisiana, a Union contingent composed of elements of the 165th and 177th New York Regiments, the 9th Connecticut, 14th and 24th Maine and the 6th Michigan Volunteer Regiments capture Ponchatoula. The Union sustains nine wounded. The Confederates suffer four killed and 12 wounded.

In Naval activity, the U.S. Navy acquires the stern wheel river steamer *Argosy,* and on the 29th, it is commissioned the USS *Argosy.* Command of the ship, built during 1862 in Monongahela, Pennsylvania, is given to Acting Master William N. Griswold. On 3 April it departs to hook up with other gunboats on the Ohio River. The gunboat squadron also operates on the Cumberland and Tennessee Rivers Under the command of Lt. Commander Le Roy Fitch. They operate in conjunction with Union land forces in Tennessee, and later the gunboats continue to provide support when the land forces move into Georgia.

March 24–April 1   In Missouri at Bloomfield, a contingent led by Major William H. Torrey, 1st Wisconsin Cavalry, departs on a scouting mission on the morning of the 24th. The column is composed of detachments of the 1st Wisconsin Cavalry and 2nd Missouri State Militia Cavalry, bolstered by one howitzer. At about 1600, the column arrives at Chalk Bluff to discover its advance pickets exchanging fire with about two companies of Confederates that are de-

ployed in the bluffs. Major Torrey sends a party to acquire tools to construct a raft and another to get a canoe, but the latter is unattainable. On the morning of the 25th, the raft is completed, and it carries 70 troops across the St. Francis River despite enemy fire. Torrey introduces his howitzer to the Confederates and its effective fire pushes them back, permitting the raft to safely reach the opposite bank. Some minor skirmishing develops and the Confederates sustain two fatal wounds; however, Torrey is able to acquire the location of Confederate Colonel Preston's camp, about one mile distant and manned by about 400 troops. Consequently, the Union recrosses the river.

On the 26th, 100 troops recross the river. An attempt is made to get the horses to swim across; however, the currents remain too strong and he horses balk at entering the river. Consequently, the operation stalls as the troops return to the opposite bank and await the construction of a modified bridge, which is completed the next day. On that day, the 28th, the Union resumes the mission. It proceeds to Scatterville, but the Confederate camp had been abandoned. Later the column encounters a contingent of the Rebels and the Union vanguard initiates a charge. A few Rebels are captured but most flee. The prisoners reveal that Colonel Preston had moved to Pocahontas about 20 miles distant. After establishing camp for the night, the Union resumes the march at 0200 on the 29th and encroaches the Rebel camp at about 0700, but again, Preston's contingent had moved in the direction of Jonesboro, Arkansas. The Union aborts the pursuit and returns to Bloomfield, arriving on 1 April.

March 25 (Wednesday)   In Mississippi, in the vicinity of Vicksburg, the crew of the USS *Hartford* hears the noise of heavy firing farther up the river. At 0610 it heads toward the sound of the guns, where Confederate batteries are exchanging blows with the USS *Lancaster* and the *Switzerland.* While passing Warrenton, the

The USS *Lancaster* and USS *Switzerland* run the Vicksburg batteries (*Harper's Pictorial History of the Civil War,* 1896).

Hartford bombards the batteries and the Confederates return fire with rifled field pieces. The *Switzerland* sustains eight hits to its boilers while passing the batteries, but remains operable. However, the *Lancaster* is sunk.

In Tennessee, a detachment of the 22nd Wisconsin and 19th Michigan is defeated by Confederate Cavalry under General Bedford Forrest at Brentwood. Forrest's force attacks the Nashville and Columbia Railroad and is able to burn the bridge and capture the force under Colonel Bloodgood. The Union suffers one dead, four wounded and 300 prisoners. The Confederates sustain one dead and five wounded. Another Union force, composed of about 600 troops commanded by General Green Clay Smith, arrives in time to strike the Rebels' rear and salvage some of the damage by recapturing much of the seized property. Smith's force pursues the Confederates toward Little Harpeth, where Rebels have a large force.

March 26 (Thursday)   In Mississippi, the Union force that had recently retired from Greenwood arrives at Young's Point. Also, General U.S. Grant arrives aboard the USS *Hartford* to discuss strategy with Admiral Farragut regarding the campaign to seize Vicksburg.

March 27 (Friday)   In New Mexico, a skirmish between Union troops and Indians erupts at Rio Bonita.

In Virginia, General Robert E. Lee responds to a letter from Lt. General James Longstreet and instructs him to continue with discretion the plan to gather provisions and forage in all invaded districts south of the James River. Longstreet, in Petersburg, is also told if he makes a surprise raid on Suffolk, the Confederates can secure it from the Union. Longstreet has 40,000 men under him and Lee feels that the Union can field no more against him.

In Naval activity, Admiral Farragut's Union squadron bombards Confederate batteries at Warrenton, located below Vicksburg; Marines aboard the vessels participate in the action.

March 28 (Saturday)   In Louisiana, a detachment of the U.S. 12th Connecticut and 160th New York Infantry, attached to the USS *Diana*, is captured by Confederates at Pattersonville. Also, a Union contingent attached to the 14th and 24th Maine Volunteers skirmishes with Confederates at Amite River.

In Missouri, Confederate guerrillas board the steamer *Sam Gaty* at Sibley rob the passengers, steal their clothes and capture about eighty Negroes, killing twenty of the latter. After confiscating or destroying various government stores, the guerrillas permit the vessel to resume its voyage.

In Ohio, Union General Brigadier General James Cooper, who saw action during the 1862 Shenandoah Valley campaign, dies while commanding the post at Camp Chase near Columbus.

In South Carolina, the 100th New York Volunteer Regiment commanded by Colonel Dandy occupies Cole's Island, South Carolina.

In Union general officer activity, Brigadier General James Shields resigns his commission. He had served as a division commander in the Shenandoah with General Frémont, but after the poor showing against Confederate Thomas "Stonewall" Jackson, Shields' activity does not appear in army records. General Shields, born in Ireland, had served in the U.S. Senate twice prior to the outbreak of the war, once representing Illinois and afterward Minnesota. He had also held the rank of brevet major general during the Mexican War. Subsequent to his military career, General Shields again serves in the Senate, representing Missouri when he was selected during 1879 to serve out an unexpired term.

In Naval activity, a Confederate battery commences fire on the transport USS *Diana* in the vicinity of Bayou Teche near Pattersonville, Louisiana. The *Diana* becomes disabled, drifts toward shore and is captured. The captain, Acting Master T.L. Patterson, and five crew members are killed; three others are wounded during the standoff that lasts about two hours. The *Diana* is taken into Confederate service. The USS *Stettin*, while on patrol off Charleston, encounters the *Aries*, a blockade runner built in England during 1861–1862. The runner is chased ashore at Bull's Bay, South Carolina. Afterward, it is acquired by the U.S. Navy (May 1863) and commissioned the USS *Aries* the next month. The *Aries* becomes a transport operating out of Port Royal. In August it becomes damaged during a storm and requires repairs that keep it out of service until November. Then it is assigned to the North Atlantic Blockading Squadron with patrol duty off North Carolina's coast.

Brigadier General James Shields (Mottelay, *The Soldier in Our Civil War,* **1886).**

March 29 (Sunday)   In Mississippi, General Grant dispatches General John A. McClernand with his Corps (4 divisions) to New Carthage via Richmond, Louisiana, to capture Grand Gulf, Mississippi. He is to be followed by the 15th and 17th Corps. The passages are in deplorable condition; the roads are flooded in many places. The troops improvise and fabricate boats from available material and confiscate others from bayous in the area, successfully reaching New Carthage on 6 April. Grant also directs Commodore Porter's fleet to pass the Vicksburg batteries (mid–April).

In Tennessee, a detachment of the 6th Illinois Cavalry is attacked by Confederates under Colonel Richardson at Somerville. The Union contingent (Colonel Loomis' command) loses about nine killed and 29 wounded.

In Virginia, a Confederate cavalry contingent attacks the Union lines at Williamsburg, striking the 5th Cavalry detachment (pickets). The Union sustains two killed, six wounded and three captured. Confederate casualty figures are unavailable.

In Naval activity, the USS *Wamsutta* is ordered to Wassaw Sound, Georgia, to relieve the USS *Marblehead*. By the beginning of March, it is back off Charleston and remains on duty there until mid–June, when it moves to Port Royal for repairs. Afterward it does a few short missions and sails north to Philadelphia, where it is decommissioned on 14 September 1863. During April 1864, it is recommissioned.

In Naval activity, the CSS *City of Vicksburg,* damaged in February while it was secured, has its machinery removed for use in another warship. Its hulk is used as a wharf boat; however, on this day it goes adrift and begins to float down the river. Nonetheless, it is destroyed by fire. The Confederates had acquired the side wheel steamer about 1862–1863 for use as a transport.

March 29–April 5   In Arkansas, the Union dispatches several scouting detachments, and other contingents are dispatched to acquire ammunition and supplies at Cassville and Springfield. The scouting missions include Carroll and Newton Counties. Two of the scouting contingents return to their base on Friday, the 27th. The contingent of the 1st Arkansas Cavalry succeeds in clearing the area of guerrillas and reports the Confederate casualties at 22 killed, including the leader, McFarland. The contingent operating in Carroll and Newton Counties reports 19 Confederate casualties.

March 30 (Monday)   In Arkansas, a skirmish erupts at Tahlequah (Indian Territory).

In Kentucky, a vicious skirmish occurs in the vicinity of Somerset (Dutton Hill). The struggle drags on furiously for approximately five hours, culminating with Union victory. Union casualties are 10 dead and 25 wounded. The Confederates lose 290 killed, wounded, or missing. This engagement includes participation by the Union 1st Kentucky Cavalry and the 7th Ohio Cavalry.

In Louisiana, a Union force composed of the 69th Indiana Volunteer Regiment and a detachment of the 2nd Illinois Cavalry commanded by General McClernand engages and defeats Confederates in a two-hour battle at Richmond (Roundaway Bayou). The Union occupies the town.

In Missouri, Union and Confederate contingents clash at "The Island" in Vernon County.

In North Carolina, Confederate General D.H. Hill issues a surrender ultimatum to General John G. Foster at Washington (Rodman's Point). Foster had recently departed New Bern, leaving General Palmer in charge, while he establishes positions in Washington to check a threat by Confederates under General D.H. Hill. General Foster rejects the demand and prepares to defend. Troops from Suffolk had also arrived at Washington village to support Foster. Meanwhile, the Confederates isolate the town and place obstacles in the Pamlico River to prevent Union warships from reinforcing and supporting the besieged defenders. The Confederates maintain the attacks until April 4.

In West Virginia, one company of the U.S. 13th West Virginia Cavalry, led by Captain Carter, engages a contingent of Confederates under Colonel Albert Jenkins at Point Pleasant, scoring a victory. The Union sustains one killed and three wounded while the Confederates suffer nearly 50 killed or wounded.

In Union general officer activity, Brigadier General John Newton is appointed major general of volunteers. He later participates at Chancellorsville and Gettysburg.

March 31 (Tuesday)   In Arkansas, a skirmish erupts at Clapper's Saw Mill. A Union contingent under Lt. Col. Richard H. White, 3rd Wisconsin Cavalry, departs camp near Carrollton and moves toward Crooked Creek, southeast of the camp. A Confederate picket is spotted on the opposite bank, but the Union sends a detachment which crosses below and maneuvers to the rear. As the picket retires, the party under Captain Horn waits in ambush and the picket detachment is seized without incident; however, one man bolts from his horse and vanishes in the woods. The Union pushes ahead, and at about 2200 the column approaches the Clapper residence in which the Confederates are convening a war council. Some activity occurs there due to an exchange of pistol fire, which is thought to have alerted the Confederate camp. Col. White moves directly against the encampment. Shortly afterward, White deploys his artillery and orders a cavalry charge. Suddenly, the Confederates become the recipients of the incoming artillery fire and hear galloping horses dashing through the darkness. Nevertheless, without too much contemplation, the Confederates react. The camp is hurriedly abandoned, leaving only one man, a casualty, for the Union to capture. The Union confiscates a large amount of arms and ammunition as well as some wagons, cattle and mules. White also initiates a night pursuit against an esti-

mated 400 Rebels under the command of Colonel Woodson, but the chase ends after an advance of about two miles.

In Mississippi, at Vicksburg, General Grant initiates the march from Milliken's Bend (twenty miles northwest of Vicksburg), then deploys his troops along the Mississippi above Grand Gulf, from where the assault against Vicksburg will begin. A Union fleet commanded by Admiral Farragut, including the *Albatross* and *Hartford,* makes a defiant pass through Confederate shore batteries without any vessels being destroyed.

In Missouri, a skirmish develops at Owensville.

In Union general officer activity, Brigadier General Louis (Ludwig) Blenker, on duty in Washington subsequent to the Battle of Cross Keys and the arrival of General Franz Sigel (August 1862), retires from the service. General Blenker succumbs on 31 October. Major General Oliver Otis Howard, promoted to major general on 29 November 1862, receives command of the XI Corps. He succeeds General Franz Sigel. General Howard participates at Chancellorsville and at Gettysburg, then is ordered to Chattanooga, Tennessee. Brigadier General George Archibald McCall, on sick leave since his parole the previous August, resigns his commission.

In Naval activity, the USS *Sumter* departs Hampton Roads with the submarine *Alligator* in tow en route to Charleston. Inclement weather on the following day jeopardizes the ships. The weather continues to worsen. On 2 April, the *Alligator* is cut loose and, once adrift, it sinks, terminating the career of the initial submarine of the U.S. Navy.

March 31–April 16   In North Carolina, a Confederate force launches an attack against the Union garrison at Washington. The Union holds; however, the Rebels initiate a siege. The USS *Seymour,* on 2 April, speeds to the aid of the garrison to deliver stores and ammunition to forestall disaster. The relief mission succeeds despite heavy fire from Confederate batteries. The Confederates, having failed to reduce the garrison, withdraw on 17 April.

April   In Mississippi, General Sherman, stopping on his way to Big Black River, finds a volume of the U.S. Constitution lying on the ground. On page one is the name Jefferson Davis. A house situated nearby is that of Joseph Davis, the Confederate president's brother. General Sherman stops momentarily to speak briefly with him, then continues the march.

In Union activity, the 5th Minnesota Volunteer Regiment, attached to the 16th Corps, is transferred to the 2nd Brigade, 3rd Division, 15th Army Corps, this month and will remain attached until December. In early May, the regiment deployed at Duckport, Louisiana, since the previous month will depart to join the Union Army at Vicksburg, Mississippi, to participate in the siege.

In Confederate activity, Hood's brigade, commanded by General Jerome B. Robertson and attached to General Hood's division, is transferred from the Army of Northern Virginia and will serve in North Carolina for a short while, returning to Virginia by the following month in time to make the move towards Gettysburg with General Robert E. Lee.

April 1 (Wednesday)   In Arkansas, skirmishes erupt at Chalk Bluff and at Clarendon.

In Mississippi, Union gunboats *Albatross,* *Hartford* and *Switzerland* engage Confederate batteries at Grand Gulf. Also, one company of the 2nd Missouri Militia Cavalry skirmishes with a Confederate contingent at Chalk Bluff. Casualty figures are unavailable.

In Virginia, the Confederate cause is suffering from many problems, not the least of which are shortages of food and lack of reinforcements along most fronts. According to a letter from Robert E. Lee to Confederate Secretary of War Seddon, a few days ago, rations for a good part of the Army of Northern Virginia consists of "18 ounces of flour, 4 ounces of bacon of indifferent quality, with occasional supplies of rice, sugar or molasses." Lee contends that the stringent rations have not demoralized his men, but that it is mandatory to increase their food if they are "to endure the hardships of the enduring campaign." On a typical day, details are sent out to procure lamb's quarters, poke sprouts, sassafras buds and wild onions. Some examples of prices for food in the South this date are butter, $3.00 per pound, ham, $1.45 a pound, and coffee, $4.50 a pound.

A contingent of Confederate cavalry led by Captain Mosley strikes Union positions and engages elements of the 1st Vermont and 5th New York Cavalry Regiments at Broad Run. The Union sustains two wounded. Confederate casualty figures are unavailable.

In Missouri, a Union scouting contingent operates in the vicinity of Linden and the White River through the 5th.

In Union activity, Major General Francis J. Herron succeeds Brigadier General John M. Schofield as commander of the Army of the Northwest.

In Naval activity, a fast merchant ship, the *Japan*—built in Scotland during 1862, acquired by the Confederacy during March 1863 and renamed the CSS *Georgia*—departs Greenock for the East Indies; however, the ship's crew of about fifty men had signed for a voyage to Singapore. The *Georgia* will link with the steamer *Alar* off France to receive arms and ammunition. The USS *Adolph Huger,* attached to the Potomac Flotilla, seizes a Confederate vessel carrying a full cargo of whiskey. The river gunboat USS *Champion* is commissioned at about this time (April). The U.S. Navy had acquired the *Champion No. 4* (built during 1859 at Cincinnati) during the previous March and converted into a tinclad gunboat. The *Champion* is assigned duty on the Mississippi River and its tributaries, where it remains for the duration.

During July 1865, the *Champion* is decommissioned and in November it is sold. The vessel operates commercially as the *Champion No. 4.*

April 1–June 10 The West India Squadron under Commodore Charles Wilkes initiates a cruise on 1 April. The squadron, dubbed the "Flying Squadron," covers the sea lanes in the vicinity of the West Indies, the Bahamas and Texas, but it still is not well prepared for the tough duty. The ships' conditions remain unsatisfactory and the squadron is also dubbed the "Creeping Squadron of Disabled Ships." Nonetheless, Wilkes, who gave the squadron the latter name, is pleased to announce that during the cruise, the squadron captures 13 steamers and 20 other vessels, each one being a blockade runner.

April 2 (Thursday) In Arkansas, a contingent of the 6th Kansas Cavalry, led by Major Ransom, skirmishes with Confederates in Jackson County. The Union reports no casualties. The estimated Confederate casualties are 17 killed. In addition, a contingent of the 5th Cavalry skirmishes with Confederates on Little Rock Road. Casualty figures are unavailable.

In North Carolina, the Union forces under General John G. Foster at Washington remain under siege by Confederates under General D.H. Hill. The Union still has not received any supplies or ammunition due to the Rebel siege. One Union vessel attempts to run the course to bring in supplies on the following day.

In Tennessee, the 3rd and 4th Ohio Cavalry Regiments commanded by Generals Charles Cruft and William B. Hazen skirmish with Confederates at Woodbury. The two sides also clash on the following day. The Union sustains one killed and eight wounded. The Confederates suffer about 50 killed and wounded and about 30 captured. In other activity, additional contingents of the Ohio 4th Cavalry and detachments of the 2nd Ohio Cavalry commanded by General David Stanley skirmishes with Confederates on the 2nd at Snow Hill, Tennessee. The Union sustains one killed and two wounded. The Confederates suffer about 50 killed and wounded and 60 captured.

In Virginia, at Richmond, the citizens begin to riot; however, the militia ends the turmoil.

In Naval activity, the USS *Tahoma* exchanges fire with a Confederate battery at Gadsden's Point, Florida. The USS *Queen City,* a ferryboat, after being acquired by the U.S. Navy and transformed into a side-wheel tinclad river gunboat, is commissioned art about this time (April). It is attached to the Mississippi Squadron and operates primarily on various rivers in Arkansas. The U.S. Navy acquires the *Silver Cloud* at about this time (April); it is commissioned the USS *Silver Cloud* the following month and assigned duty on the Tennessee River and other rivers in the region. As a tinclad river gunboat it is well suited for interrupting Confederate shipping. It participates in various operations, including the defense of Fort

Pillow when it is struck by forces under Confederate General Nathan Bedford Forrest and when the Union regains it. After the war it is decommissioned and then sold in August 1865. During the following year while in operation as a commercial ship, it strikes an obstacle near Buffalo Bayou, Texas, and sinks.

April 3 (Friday) In North Carolina, the gunboat USS *Ceres,* commanded by Captain McDiarmid, braves a heavy barrage of Confederate fire during the darkened hours of this evening to bring needed supplies to the command of General John G. Foster at Washington, which is under siege by Confederate General D.H. Hill. Other vessels, including the USS *Southfield,* continue to support the beleaguered garrison during the siege.

In Virginia, Confederate General Lee is ill. At first thought a severe cold, the diagnosis is "acute pericarditis." Lee is still confronted with deployment of his men across a front that stretches from the Atlantic to the Mississippi and which is facing tremendous opposition from the Union, especially around Chancellorsville.

In Arkansas, a Union scouting contingent departs Carrollton and proceeds toward the vicinity of Yellville. The mission continues until the 8th.

In Naval activity, Union gunboats, including the tinclad USS *Saint Clair,* engage Confederate batteries at Palmyra, Tennessee. The *Saint Clair* sustains damage that knocks it out of action; however, another warship moves in and tows it out of the range of the guns. After repairs the *Saint Clair* is assigned escort duty on the Mississippi River to protect supply transports. In September, it sails to Louisiana to provide support to ground forces, and it participates in the Red River Expedition. It is decommissioned during July 1865 and sold the following month. Afterward, it operates as a commercial vessel until about 1869.

April 4 (Saturday) In Arkansas, a contingent of the 1st Arkansas Cavalry, led by Captain Worthington, completes a scouting mission in Carroll County. During the operation, the Union sustains one wounded. The Confederates sustain some killed and wounded and about seven captured. Meanwhile, elements of the 3rd Iowa Cavalry skirmishes with Confederates at Madison. Casualty figures are unavailable.

In Mississippi, U.S. Grant, who has made four unsuccessful assaults on Vicksburg in the last few months, makes another. In a letter to Halleck, he states: "March the troops up the west side of the river and join Porter's fleet to be ferried across the river." The plan is successful and will lead to the eventual fall of Vicksburg.

In North Carolina, Union infantry attacks a Confederate Battery at Rodman's Point at Washington. The Union sustains five killed and wounded.

In Union general officer activity, Colonel William Harrow is promoted to brigadier general of volunteers, effective 29 November 1862. General Harrow will command a brigade at Gettysburg, but after General John Gibbon becomes wounded there, General Harrow assumes command of the 2nd Division, II Corps. Also, Colonel George D. Wagner is promoted to brigadier general to rank from 29 November 1862. He later participates at Murfreesboro. Also, Colonel George Washington Deitzler (1st Kansas Volunteer Infantry) is promoted to brigadier general effective the same date. General Deitzler afterward takes sick leave. He then resigns his commission on 27 August 1863. Nonetheless, during the following year, as a major general, Deitzler commands the Kansas militia against the Confederates under General Sterling Price. Colonel Edward Harland is commissioned brigadier general effective 29 November 1862. He is afterward assigned to command of various districts in North Carolina until the close of hostilities. He resigns from the service during June 1865.

Colonel James Winning McMillan (appointed colonel of the 21st Indiana during 1861) is named brigadier general effective 29 November 1862. He will command a brigade in the XIV Corps until May, and during the Red River expedition, he commands the 1st Division, Emory's XIV Corps. In July he moves to the Shenandoah Valley to serve under Major General Philip Sheridan. The next March, McMillan receives the brevet of major general of volunteers and afterward, during May 1865, he musters out of the army. General Sheridan had been promoted to major general to rank from 31 December 1862, the date of the Battle of Murfreesboro. James St. Clair Morton (West Point, 1851) is appointed brigadier general to rank from 29 November 1862. Major Adam J. Slemmer, not yet back in service subsequent to being wounded at Murfreesboro, is promoted to brigadier general effective the same date. Slemmer is unable to return to field service. He is assigned duty in Ohio as president of a board that examines sick and wounded troops. He receives the brevet of major general in the Regular Army during 1865 and remains in the service beyond the close of hostilities. While based as commander of Fort Laramie, Wyoming, he dies on 7 October 1868. He is later interred in Norristown, Pennsylvania.

Colonel Francis McGinnis (11th Indiana) is promoted to brigadier general to rank from 29 November 1862. McGinnis had participated in various actions with his regiment, including the operations against Fort Donelson and the Yazoo Expedition (Vicksburg operations). Nevertheless, General McGinnis does not gather a series of major accomplishments during his service, which includes command of a division in General Nathaniel Banks' Department of the Gulf and the Department of Mississippi. During the closing days of the war, he is based near the mouth of the White River in Arkansas with a command composed only of two companies of cavalry and an infantry regiment, bolstered by one artillery battery. He musters out of the army after the war; however, he does not receive any brevet ranks.

In Naval activity, the Union gunboat, USS *Lexington,* commanded by Lt. L. Fitch, U.S. Navy, enters the waters near Palmyra, Tennessee, and reduces the town with cannon fire.

April 5 (Sunday)   In Arkansas, a scouting contingent operates in the vicinity of Fayetteville.

In North Carolina, Union gunboats exchange blows with Confederate batteries for about two hours at Hill's Point.

In South Carolina, a Union squadron under Rear Admiral Du Pont at the mouth of the North Edisto River makes final preparations for an attack against Fort Sumter. About 4,000 troops, commanded by General Truman Seymour (Hunter's chief of staff), are at Folly Island in the vicinity of Lighthouse Inlet, positioned to move from there across Morris Island to attack the forts, once the fleet reduces the guns.

In Louisiana, a division of Major General Frederick Steele's 15th Corps initiates a five day expedition into Black Bayou.

In Union general officer activity, Captain John Haskell King, a veteran of the Mexican War, is promoted to brigadier general. His rank is effective as of 29 November 1862. At the eruption of the war, he had been in Texas. Despite the circumstances, he did not surrender; rather he led nine companies of regular troops out of Texas and safely arrived in New York. Afterward, he participated in various actions, including Corinth, Shiloh and at Murfreesboro. General King will lead a brigade of regulars at Chickamauga.

April 6 (Monday)   In Mississippi, Union General John A. McClernand's force, ferried by boats, reaches New Carthage. He brings artillery and one division. General U.S. Grant arrives on the 17th to confer with him.

In Tennessee, a Union cavalry force under General Robert B. Mitchell attacks a Confederate encampment at Green Hill. The Union sustains one wounded. The Confederates suffer five killed and 15 captured.

In Naval activity, in the vicinity of Charleston, South Carolina, Rear Admiral Du Pont arrives with an attack force near where the Union blockade vessels are presently maintaining the vigil of Charleston Harbor. Confederates seize the Union steamer USS *Fox* at Pass a L'Outre, Mississippi. The Union gunboats *Albatross, Hartford* and *Switzerland* initiate an expedition to Bayou Sara, Louisiana. In addition, the U.S. Navy acquires the stern wheel gunboat *Exchange,* which was built in Pennsylvania at Brownsville the previous year. During the following June, the USS *Exchange* joins the Mississippi Squadron. Acting Volunteer Lieutenant J.S. Kurd receives command.

April 7 (Tuesday)   In South Carolina, U.S. naval vessels initiate an attack against Forts Sumter, Moultrie, Beauregard and Putnam, all within the area encompassing Charleston Harbor. The fleet, commanded by Flag Officer Samuel Du Pont, is composed of nine ironclad vessels: the *Catskill* (Commander George W. Rodgers); *Keokuk* (Commander Alexander C. Rhind); *Montauk* (Commander John Worden); *Nahant* (Commander John Downes); *Nantucket* (Commander Donald McNeill Fairfax); *New Ironsides* (flagship; Commander Thomas Turner); *Passaic* (Captain Percival Drayton); *Patapsco* (Commander Daniel Ammen) and the *Weehawken* (Captain John Rodgers). These warships are bolstered by five gunboats, including the *Passaic.*

By about 0900, the ironclads, using the natural camouflage of a dense fog, are in position in the main channel about one mile from shore. By about noon the fog dissipates, giving the pilots clear view of the impending obstructions in their path. Pursuant to orders from Du Pont, the fleet advances, intent on holding its fire until all vessels pass through the gunfire of the batteries on Morris Island, unless new orders are passed on to "commence action." Otherwise, Morris Island is to remain unscathed until after the reduction of Sumter and Moultrie.

The signal to advance is given. The *Weehawken* incurs some problems when its grappling irons on a torpedo raft get tangled with its anchor cables. Following about one hour's toil,

Captain John Rogers, U.S. Navy (*Harper's Pictoral History of the Civil War,* 1896).

the problem is solved and the fleet resumes the attack. Surprisingly, the guns on Morris Island remain silent as the fleet passes, but the artillery at Fort Sumter provides a vociferous greeting, which is duplicated by the artillery on James and Sullivan Islands. The battle commences at about 1430 and the initial barrage is joined by the guns from Forts Beauregard and Putnam, seemingly with every shell arcing toward the *Weehawken.* Captain John Rodgers, aboard the *Weehawken,* orders retaliatory fire, but the 11-inch and 15-inch cannon cannot neutralize the superior firepower of the Confederates.

While the *Weekawken* is exchanging blows with the shore batteries, a torpedo, which causes no injuries, explodes near the besieged vessel. Rodgers extricates his ship from the heavy fire and the deadly entanglements in the channel and retires to the open sea, trailed by the remainder of the fleet. During the operation, the *Weehawken* had been hit more than fifty times. After being repaired, it is sent to operate off the Georgia coast.

Left: The USS *Weehawken* bombards Confederate-held Fort Sumter, South Carolina (Mottelay, *The Soldier in Our Civil War,* 1886). *Right:* The USS *Keokuk* sinks (*Harper's Pictoral History of the Civil War,* 1896).

All the while, the Confederates pour incessant fire upon the retreating vessels. The Union fleet fires about 139 shots at Fort Sumter and in return becomes the recipient of about 3,000 incoming shells, 515 of which strike the target, inflicting damage to the *Weekawken* (60), *Patapsco* (45), *New Ironsides* (65), *Keokuk* (90), *Montauk* (20), *Nantucket* (51), *Nahant* (80), *Passaic* (53), and *Catskill* (51).

The *Keokuk* sinks early on the following morning. However, other vessels, including the USS *Dandelion*, rescue the crew.

For the Confederate defenses, Fort Sumter is commanded by Colonel Alfred Rhett, with Lt. Colonel J.A. Yates in command of the parapet guns and Major Ormsby Blanding in charge of the casement batteries; the garrison is comprised of seven companies of the 1st South Carolina Artillery (Regulars), commanded by Captains D.G. Flemming, F.H. Harleston, J.C. King, J.C. Mitchel, J.R. MacBeth, C.W. Parker and W.H. Peronneau. Fort Moultrie is commanded by Colonel William Butler, supported by Major T.M. Baker and five companies of the 1st South Carolina Regiment (Regulars), commanded by Captains T. A. Huguenin, R. Press Smith, B.S. Burnett, C.H. Rivers and Lt. E.A. Erwin.

Battery Bee on Sullivan's Island is commanded by Lt. Colonel J.C. Simkins and three companies of the 1st South Carolina Regiment (Regulars), commanded by Captains Warren Adams, W. Tabourne and R. De Treville. Battery Beauregard is commanded by Captain J.A. Sitgreaves, 1st South Carolina Artillery (Regulars), and includes two companies of infantry under Captain J.H. Warley and Lt. W.E. Erwin from Fort Sumter and Fort Moultrie. Battery Wagner is commanded by Major C.K. Huger with two companies of the 1st South Carolina Artillery (Regulars). In addition, the Cumming's Point Battery is commanded by Lt. H. R. Lesesne; it is composed of a contingent of the 1st South Carolina Artillery (Regulars).

In Naval activity, the USS *Barataria,* formerly the CSS *Barataria* (captured at New Orleans during April 1862), a diminutive stern-wheel ironclad which had been transferred from the U.S. Army to Admiral Farragut's command on 1 January, encounters serious trouble at 0600 when it gets caught on an obstacle on Lake Maurepas near the mouth of the Amite River. The crew attempts to free the ship, but all the while Confederate guerrillas maintain fire against the stranded vessel. All efforts to refloat the ship fail. The struggle continues until about dusk. At that time, the crew sets the ship afire and abandons it, as does a company of the 6th Michigan Volunteer Regiment under Colonel Thomas S. Clark. The troops are able to escape capture by departing the area in boats.

The vessel *Emma Duncan,* constructed in Pennsylvania at Monongahela during 1860 and in use by the Union after purchase during March 1863 at Cairo, Illinois, had been used as a wooden gunboat. On this day, Admiral Porter recommends that the name be changed to the *Hastings.* Also, the *Passaic* sails to New York to receive repairs and returns to South Carolina in

late July. It then resumes patrols off Georgia and South Carolina until decommissioned during June 1865. In November 1876, it is recommissioned and remains in and out of service until September 1898.

April 8 (Wednesday) In Missouri, a Union force, commanded by Major Winslow and composed of elements of the 4th Iowa Cavalry and U.S. cavalry, engages Confederates in St. Francis County.

In South Carolina, the 3rd Rhode Island Artillery, aboard the gunboat USS *George Washington,* engages Confederates at Broad River. The *George Washington* is sunk.

April 9 (Thursday) In Arkansas, Union and Confederate skirmishes occur at White River.

In Mississippi, Union troops under General Gordon Granger, at New Carthage, make preliminary probes to locate new routes to accommodate artillery, cavalry and wagon trains for the upcoming assault against Vicksburg. The final conclusion is that pontoon bridges must be built. Four bridges are constructed, with the span of two exceeding six hundred feet. In total, over 2,000 feet of bridges are constructed by General McClernand's troops under the direct supervision of Lieutenant P.C. Haines' engineer corps. Grant later remarks about the endeavor: "The ingenuity of the Yankee soldier was equal to any emergency." In other activity, the 74th U.S. Colored Troops (2nd Louisiana), commanded by Colonel Daniels, advances into the vicinity of East Pascagoula on an expedition.

In Missouri, Union and Confederate units skirmish at Sedalia.

In North Carolina, a Union contingent composed of elements of the 3rd and 17th Massachusetts Regiments and the 1st Rhode Island Regiment, bolstered by the 3rd New York Artillery, commanded by Captain Pond, skirmishes with Confederates at Blount's Mills. The Union sustains 10 wounded.

In Union general officer activity, Colonel Halbert E. Paine is promoted to the rank of brigadier general. General Paine participates in the defense of Washington, D.C., against the raids of Confederate General Jubal Early. Subsequently, he is appointed commander of the District of Illinois. Colonel Hugh Thompson-Reid is promoted to brigadier general to rank from 13 March of this year. General Reid receives command of a brigade in Louisiana. Also, Lt. Colonel Hector Tyndale is promoted to brigadier general.

In Confederate naval activity, the merchant ship *Japan,* after being acquired by the Confederacy, on this day raises the Confederate flag and is commissioned the CSS *Georgia,* commanded by Commander W.L. Murray. The *Georgia* has been armed off France after a rendezvous with the vessel *Alar.* The *Georgia* is under orders to disrupt and destroy U.S. shipping. The ship crosses the Atlantic in search of prey at places including Brazil, Trinidad and off the coast of Africa. Afterward, it recrosses the

Atlantic to arrive at Cherbourg on 28 October. During the cruise, the *Georgia* seizes nine prizes. This CSS *Georgia* is separate from the CSS *Georgia* that is a floating battery built in Savannah during 1862. Articles about the CSS *Georgia* at times erroneously described the *Georgia* as the *Virginia.*

April 10 (Friday) In Kansas, an expedition force departs Humboldt and moves to Cottonwood.

In Kentucky, a Union contingent of cavalry, led by Lt. Rickertson, clashes with Confederates at Germantown. The Union reports no casualties. The Confederates sustain one killed and three wounded.

In Tennessee, U.S. troops, including the 40th Ohio and a detachment of Gordon Granger's cavalry, engage Confederates under General Van Dorn at Franklin and Harpeth River. The Confederate attack against Franklin is handily repelled. The Union force includes about 2,700 cavalrymen (General David S. Stanley's cavalry) and about 1,600 infantrymen under Generals Baird and Charles C. Gilbert, which face General Van Dorn's nine thousand troops. The Union suffers approximately 100 dead and wounded. The Confederates have 19 dead, 35 wounded and 83 missing. In other activity, a one-company detachment of the 5th Iowa Cavalry, led by Major Blondin, skirmishes with Confederates at Waverly. The Confederates lose 21 captured. Other action in Tennessee occurs at Antioch Station when a detachment of the 10th Michigan Cavalry skirmishes with Confederates. The Union sustains eight killed and 12 wounded. Confederate casualty figures are unavailable.

April 11 (Saturday) In Colorado, a skirmish erupts in the vicinity of Squirrel Creek when a contingent led by Lt. Colonel George L. Shoup surprises a small Confederate guerrilla camp. One guerrilla is killed and two others are captured; of those, one is wounded in the leg.

In the Indian Territory (Oklahoma), a skirmish erupts at Webber's Falls between a Union contingent and forces of Stand Watie. Another clash occurs here on the 25th.

In South Carolina, Union Admiral Du Pont, following the failed attack against the Confederate forts in Charleston Harbor, has concluded that the positions cannot be taken by naval power alone. Preparations are made for the fleet to return to Port Royal. On the following day the flotilla departs, but Du Pont directs the *New Ironsides* to remain in the area.

In Tennessee, a Union force commanded by Colonel Abel Streight initiates an expedition into Alabama and Georgia.

In Virginia, a contingent of the 5th Pennsylvania Cavalry battles elements of the Confederate 59th Virginia Infantry Regiment, commanded by Colonel Tabb, at Whittaker's Mills. The Union sustains five killed. The Confederates sustain two wounded and about 19 captured. Another skirmish erupts when Union and Confederate troops clash at Blackwater. Casualty figures are unavailable.

In Naval activity, the CSS *Diana*, commanded by Lieutenant Nettles (attached to Valverde Battery), engages Union forces at Bayou Teche and the Union is forced to withdraw. Lieutenant Nettles becomes severely ill. He is replaced on the 13th by Captain Semmes (artillery officer). Meanwhile, more Union reinforcements begin arriving in the region near Confederate-held Camp Bisland, and the clash continues throughout the day on Bayou Teche and at Camp Bisland. During the engagement, the *Diana* is struck by shells from a Union battery of Parrott guns. It sustains severe damage and casualties when a shell plows through its front plating before detonating in the engine room. Nonetheless, the *Diana* is able to pull out of range of the Union guns. By midnight (11th–12th), repairs are completed. On the morning of the 12th it advances to Franklin Louisiana to bolster a Confederate contingent. The Union, however, drives the Rebels. After covering the retreat and remaining on scene near a burning bridge until a contingent of Rebels under General Mouton are safely across, the crew sets the *Diana* on fire to prevent capture.

April 11–May 4   In Virginia, about 25,000 Union troops (Major General Peck's command) at Suffolk become jeopardized when Confederate James Longstreet initiates a siege of Peck's positions. The Confederates also establish gun emplacements that prevent the U.S. Navy from supporting Peck; however, Peck undertakes the task with his troops. On the 19th, Peck unleashes an amphibious landing that permits the Union to hit Fort Huger at the convergence of the forks of the Nansemond River. The landing at Hill's Point is successful and the fort is taken, which again opens the river to the navy. On 19 April, a strong force under Brigadier General Michael Corcoran departs Fort Dix for a drive against Confederate General Pickett's far right flank to dislodge his force and ease the stress still threatening Peck at Suffolk. The Confederates under Pickett are not vanquished; rather the assault is repelled. Nevertheless, Peck continues to hold his positions. On 29 April, General Longstreet receives modified orders from General Robert E. Lee, which instruct Longstreet to abort the siege and move to Richmond to bolster the forces at Fredericksburg. Meanwhile, the siege is phased out and by 4 May, the final elements of Longstreet's force of about 20,000 troops has completed crossing the Blackwater River and are en route to Richmond. The Union sustains 44 killed and 202 wounded. General Peck is severely injured during the struggle; however, he recuperates and then is transferred to North Carolina for a while until he is again transferred during early July 1864. The Confederates sustain about 500 killed and wounded and about 400 captured.

April 12 (Sunday)   In Louisiana, Union forces under General William Emory move toward Franklin, compelling Confederate Major General Richard Taylor to retire toward Fort Bisland (Irish Bend) near Pattersonville.

In Virginia, the combined forces of Jeb Stuart, Fitzhugh Lee and W.H.F. Lee successfully prevent Union cavalry from setting up on the south side of the Rappahannock, in the vicinity of Chancellorsville. In other activity, a reconnaissance infantry force, commanded by Lt. Colonel Tevis, initiates an expedition at Gloucester Point and encounters Confederate Cavalry under Colonel Godwin. The Confederates lose two captured. Also, the 9th New York Zouaves arrive at Suffolk. Later that same day, an altercation occurs when a party, including Brigadier General Michael Corcoran, attempts to pass a sentry who refuses to grant passage without the countersign to the password. Lt. Colonel Edgar Kimball moves to the sentry's side and also calls for a countersign. General Corcoran and Kimball exchange harsh words and Kimball informs Corcoran that he does not care who he is and without the countersign, the party is not passing. Corcoran draws his pistol and shoots Kimball. The shot strikes Kimball in the neck and severs an artery, which causes his death.

April 12–14   In Louisiana, Union troops of the 19th Corps, including the 25th Connecticut Infantry, skirmish with a contingent of Confederates under Major General Richard Taylor at Irish Bend and Fort Bisland. The Confederates retire toward New Iberia and from there to Vermilionville. Taylor is pressed to again move, and from the latter location he heads for Alexandria with the Union in hot pursuit. Sgt. Major William Edgar Simons becomes a recipient of the Medal of Honor for his extraordinary heroism during the campaign. In the vicinity of Bayou Teche, the Confederate ram *Queen of the West* is destroyed on Grand Lake by Union guns which fire from long range. The Confederate gunboats CSS *Diana* and CSS *Hart* are also destroyed.

In Virginia, a U.S. fleet, including the USS *Mount Washington*, bombards Confederate positions on the Nansemond River. Seaman Henry Thielberg, U.S. Navy, positions himself in the pilot house, giving information concerning enemy movements on shore, at great risk to his life. The *Mount Washington* is temporarily stranded during this six-hour bombardment and heavily pummeled by Confederate guns. The Union sustains 350 killed, wounded and missing. The Confederates sustain 400 wounded and 2,000 missing or captured. The number of Confederate deaths is unavailable.

April 13 (Monday)   In Louisiana, Union

Lt. Colonel Edgar Kimball (Mottelay, *The Soldier in Our Civil War*, 1886).

General Cuvier Grover's division lands several miles west of Franklin. On the previous day, General Grover had been with the gunboats on Grand Lake en route to secure the Confederate rear. Also, skirmishing occurs at Porter's Plantation and at McWilliams' Plantation at Indian Bend.

In North Carolina, the steamer USS *Escort*, carrying General Innis Palmer from New Bern with the 5th Rhode Island Regiment under Colonel McChesney and Lt. Hoffman, arrives at Washington to bring in supplies and ammunition to lift the siege.

The Battle of Indian Bend (Johnson, *Campfire and Battlefield: History of the Conflicts and Campaigns*, 1894).

In **Virginia,** General Stoneman is directed to initiate reconnaissance missions toward Bealton, Liberty, Warrenton, and Rappahannock Bridge. The Union encounters only slight opposition during these operations, permitting the troops to secure the fords of the Rapidan. Nasty weather begins to set in around the area, and the conditions prevent the Union from extending its movements. Also, the inclement weather causes General Hooker to modify his plans. He is compelled to suspend his advance to strike the rear of Lee's lines until the 27th.

In Union general officer activity, General Charles S. Hamilton had been in line to command James McPherson's XVII Corps, but Hamilton had made disparaging remarks about U.S. Grant, who raised vehement opposition to Hamilton's appointment. Hamilton this day offers his resignation and it is immediately accepted. In 1869, the first year of Grant's presidency (18th U.S. president), he appointed Hamilton as federal marshal in the city of Milwaukee.

In Naval activity, the USS *Annie* (*Anna*), commanded by Acting Ensign James S. Williams, seizes a blockade runner, the schooner *Mattie,* just as it attempts to enter the Crystal River in Florida. The prize is taken to Key West.

April 14 (Tuesday) **In North Carolina** at Washington, which is under siege, the steamer *Escort,* which had arrived with troops on the previous day, awaits nightfall and departs for New Bern carrying General John G. Foster, who is leaving to raise to raise a relief force to lift the siege. Before Foster can form the rescue force and return, the Confederates under D.H. Hill evacuate the area and return to Suffolk, Virginia. A Union force under General Innis Palmer gives pursuit and during the following month a heavy engagement erupts in the vicinity of Kinston.

In Virginia, Union gunboats, including the *Commodore Barney, West End, Stepping Stones* and *Mount Washington,* commanded by Lt. Cushing, U.S. Navy, engages Confederate batteries at West Branch and Nansemond in a contest that lasts about four hours. The Union sustains three killed and seven wounded. Confederate casualty figures are unavailable.

In Naval activity, the CSS *Grand Duke*—a side-wheel steamer built during 1859 in Jeffersonville, Indiana, and acquired by the Confederate Army during February 1863 and utilized as a transport, while on the Atchafalaya River in Louisiana accompanied by the CSS *Mary T.* and the ram *Queen of the West*—is intercepted by the USS *Arizona, Calhoun* and the *Estrella.* The *Grand Duke* comes under attack, but it is able to evade damage and outrun the pursuers. The Rebel vessels safely arrive at Fort Taylor. In other activity, the ironclad steamer CSS *Hart,* which had participated in the support of Camp Bisland on Bayou Teche, Louisiana (November 1862), at Berwick Bay (1 November 1862), and in other clashes, is intentionally sunk on this day to prevent capture by the Union. Camp Bis-

land is seized by forces of Major General Nathaniel P. Banks, bolstered by gunboats. Subsequently, the Rebels initiate action to refloat the *Hart*; however, on 28 July a report from the USS *Clifton* states that it had been partially refloated only to again be sunk at the approach of Union gunboats.

April 15 (Wednesday) **In Kentucky,** elements of the 39th Kentucky Mounted Infantry, led by Colonel Dills, skirmishes with Confederates at Pikeville. The Confederates sustain about 75 captured.

In Louisiana, Union contingents of the 2nd Illinois Cavalry skirmish with Confederates at Dunbar Plantation. The Union sustains one killed and two wounded. In other activity, Union forces attached to General Nathaniel Banks' command occupy Franklin.

In the Utah Territory, the 2nd California Cavalry, led by Colonel Evans, engages Indians at Spanish Fork Canyon. The Union sustains one killed and two wounded. The Indians lose about 30 killed and wounded.

In Union general officer activity, Colonel Thomas E. Ransom is promoted to brigadier general, effective 29 November 1862. Ransom had been wounded at Charleston, Missouri, at Fort Donelson, and at Shiloh. Subsequently, Ransom participates in the Red River campaign under General Banks. Colonel Joseph F. Knipe (46th Pennsylvania) is promoted to brigadier general to rank from 29 November 1862. General Knipe is later assigned duty in Memphis and charged with recruiting cavalry deserters. Subsequently he moves to Nashville, while it is under siege. General George H. Thomas places him in command of a cavalry division (General J.H. Wilson's Cavalry Corps). Also, Colonel Mortimer Dormer Leggett and Colonel Thomas Hewson Neill are promoted to brigadier general effective 29 November 1862.

April 16 (Thursday) **In Mississippi,** Admiral Porter's flagship, the USS *Benton,* and ten other vessels (six ironclads), defiantly pass 14 miles of Confederate batteries at Vicksburg. The Confederate artillery hits houses on the Louisiana side, illuminating the sky with fire. The U.S. gunboats return fire as they pass. The *Benton* is damaged and the *Henry Clay* destroyed; however, the rest of the flotilla makes the voyage successfully, positioning Union naval forces and other troops behind enemy lines. Other vessels in the Union fleet that participate: *Lafayette,*

which is towing the *Price* (a captured steamer), *Baron De Kalb* (formerly *Louisville*), *Mound City, Pittsburg, Carondelet, Forest Queen, Silver Wave,* and *Tuscumbia.* The *Forest Queen* sustains severe damage, but it is saved and towed down the river. In six days, Union transports attempt to pass the batteries as the fleet moves toward Grand Gulf.

In Minnesota, an 18-man contingent of the 7th Minnesota Volunteer Regiment engages Indians at Medalia. The Union sustains one killed and two wounded. Indian casualty figures are unavailable.

In Naval activity, the USS *Key West,* built in California, Pennsylvania (1862), is commissioned at Cairo, Illinois. It had been acquired by the U.S. Navy the previous month. Acting Master E.M. King receives command of the gunboat, a wooden stern-wheel steamer. The *Key West* departs this day to begin patrol duty on the Tennessee River in support of army operations in the region. Another task is to guard the Union positions in the Tennessee Valley against incursions by Confederate cavalry. In other activity, the *Naumkeag* (wooden stern-wheel steamboat) acquired by the U.S. Navy at Cairo, Illinois, is commissioned at Mound City, Illinois. Lt. Commander George Brown receives command.

April 17 (Friday) **In Alabama,** elements of the 10th Missouri and the 7th Kansas Cavalry Regiments, commanded by General Dodge, skirmish at Bear Creek, Cherokee Station and Lundy's Lane. The Union sustains one killed. Confederate casualty figures are unavailable.

In Louisiana, Union forces under General Cuvier Grover and William Dwight (4th Division, XIX Army Corps, Army of the Gulf) and Confederates led by General Richard Taylor clash at the Battle of Vermilion Bayou. General Banks had decided to pursue General Taylor following recent clashes at Fort Bisland and Irish

Battle of Vermilion Bayou (Johnson, *Campfire and Battlefield: History of the Conflicts and Campaigns,* 1894).

Bend. Confederate artillery compels the Union to pull back from a burning bridge; however, Union artillery counteracts the Confederate guns, and by nightfall, the Rebels continue to retire toward Opelousas. Rear Admiral Porter remains above Port Hudson with the USS *Hartford* and the USS *Albatross*.

In Missouri, a scouting contingent, composed of fifty men commanded by Captain Humphrey, departs Cassville and heads to the White River Country about 20 miles distant. Captain Humphrey dispatches 20 men to perform reconnaissance mission near Relleford's Mill. The diminutive squad gets attacked by a contingent of Rebels estimated at between 80 and 100 troops. The Union squad fights off the Confederates in a running battle; however, eight of the twenty become missing and three others are killed. The others find themselves in jeopardy after the four mile chase and they dismount and head for the woods. On the following day, Major David McKee, the commanding officer, reports the incident and adds: "I sent out re-enforcement of 66 men about 2 o'clock this morning [Saturday, the 18th]. Would it be convenient for you [Colonel Cloud] to send me a couple of companies of infantry! Our horses are run down, and it is impossible for me to keep up the telegraph patrol and forage, besides doing guard duty."

In Virginia, a contingent composed of the 99th and 130th New York Volunteers skirmish with Confederates at South Quay. The Union sustains two killed and three wounded. Confederate casualty figures are unavailable.

April 17–May 2 (Friday)   GRIERSON'S RAID
A total of 1,700 Union troops commanded by Colonel Benjamin H. Grierson depart La Grange, Tennessee, en route to raid Confederate territory as far away as Baton Rouge, Louisiana. On the following day, Colonel Grierson's cavalry passes through Ripley, Tennessee, en route to destroy Confederate communication lines while moving to Louisiana from Northern Tennessee. Grierson's command is composed of his regiment, the 6th Illinois Cavalry (Colonel Loomis), the 7th Illinois Cavalry (Colonel Edward Prince) and the 2nd Iowa Cavalry (Brigadier General Edward Hatch). The main body will head toward New Albany (east), while the 2nd Iowa moves southeast and crosses the Tallahatchie. One battalion of the 7th Illinois moves on the left flank of the column and crosses the Tallahatchie near New Albany. The main body spends the night near New Albany subsequent to repulsing an attack that had been sprung against the 2nd Iowa. The force encamps in the vicinity of Pontotoc at Wetherall's Plantation about eight miles from the town. The successful operation culminates at Baton Rouge, on May 2. This is a ruse to attract attention and drain some of the Southern forces away from bolstering Vicksburg. Grierson's men trek 800 miles, disrupting the Confederates and destroying two of their railroads.

April 18 (Saturday)   In Arkansas, the Union 1st Arkansas Regiment and the 1st Arkansas Cavalry, led by Colonel Harrison, skirmishes with Confederates at Fayetteville for more than five hours, but the Confederates fail to seize the town. The Union sustains four killed, 26 wounded, about 16 captured and 35 missing. The Confederates sustain 20 killed, about 50 wounded and 50 captured. The Union also seizes about 100 stands of arms.

In Mississippi, the 2nd Brigade, cavalry division and infantry and artillery (16th Corps), skirmish with Confederates at Hernando.

In Missouri, a Union scouting contingent departs Salem and operates in the area between Sinking Creek, Current River and Big Creek.

In Texas, the gunboats USS *Cayuga* and *New London* dispatch a small detachment in boats on a reconnaissance mission at Sabine Pass. The contingent clashes with Confederates. The Union sustains one killed, five wounded and five captured. Confederate casualty figures are unavailable.

In Virginia, Robert E. Lee instructs General William E. Jones (commanding officer, Shenandoah Valley) to keep General Jeb Stuart ap-

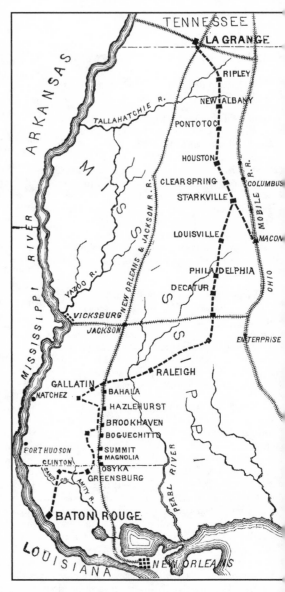

Left: General William Dwight in command at the bridge at Vermilion Bayou (Johnson, *Campfire and Battlefield: History of the Conflicts and Campaigns*, 1894). *Right:* The path of Grierson's Raid (*Harper's Pictorial History of the Civil War*, 1896).

prised of all Union movements around Culpeper Court House. A contingent of the 89th New York and 8th Connecticut Regiments skirmishes with Confederates at Battery Huger (Hill's Point). Casualties are not recorded. Also, at Richmond, the Confederate Congress passes legislation which authorizes the establishment of a volunteer navy. The act authorized that "any person or persons who produced to President Davis satisfactory evidence as to character, competency and means, were to be, under certain regulations, commissioned by the Confederate government, as regular officers of the volunteer navy, to procure and fit out vessels of over 100 tons burden for cruising against the enemy."

April 19 (Sunday) **In Mississippi,** elements of the 7th Illinois Cavalry skirmish with Confederates at New Albany. Casualty figures are unavailable. A contingent composed of units of the 2nd Brigade, cavalry division and infantry, bolstered by artillery from the 16th Corps, commanded by Colonel Bryant, skirmishes with Confederates at Coldwater. The Union sustains 10 killed and 20 wounded. The Confederates sustain 20 killed and 40 wounded.

In Missouri, a Union contingent initiates a two day scouting mission in the vicinity of Neosho.

In Naval activity, the USS *Arletta* departs for Beaufort, North Carolina, its final duty station. The *Arletta* remains in the region until 17 September 1865. At that time it sails north to Philadelphia, where it is decommissioned on 28 September. On 30 November 1865, it is sold. The USS *Western World,* accompanied by the USS *Commodore Morris,* runs escort for army transports which are taking forces attached to the Army of the Potomac up the York River to its junction with the Pamunkey River.

April 20 (Monday) **In Louisiana,** the USS *Estrella, Clifton, Arizona* and *Calhoun,* commanded by Lt. A.R. Cooke, attack and capture Bute LaRose. In related activity, Union General Banks's forces enter Opelousas. From here, Banks will proceed to Alexandria, which by then will have been captured by Admiral Porter.

In Missouri, an estimated 2,000 to 4,000 Confederate troops under Colonel John S. Marmaduke defeat a Union force of the 3rd Missouri Militia Cavalry commanded by Colonel Smart at Patterson. The Union is pushed from the town and retires to Pilot Knob. The initial Union report of the 21st lists 200 killed, wounded or missing; however, later estimates are 60 dead, wounded or missing. Confederate casualties are unavailable.

In Tennessee, a contingent of the 1st Brigade of Cavalry (Army of the Cumberland) occupies McMinnville.

In Naval activity, the USS *Lodana* (South Atlantic Blockading Squadron) intercepts and seizes a blockade runner, the *Minnie,* a British brigantine which was en route from Nassau, Bahamas, to South Carolina, but it is snagged in Bull's Bay, South Carolina. The prize is sent to Philadelphia. In other activity, the Confederates

destroy the CSS *Natchez* at about this time to prevent it from being captured by Admiral Porter's forces.

April 21 (Tuesday) **In Georgia,** one regiment of Colonel Benjamin Grierson's Union cavalry, commanded by General Edward Hatch, is sent to destroy the railroad between Columbus and Macon. A skirmish develops at Columbus. Hatch's force destroys the rails at Okalona and Tupelo, but it is unable to assault the town. They withdraw, moving toward the main column. The balance of Grierson's force continues destroying the Vicksburg and Meridian Railroad, and the New Orleans and Jackson Railroads. They arrive in Baton Rouge, Louisiana, on 2 May.

In Mississippi, a contingent of the 2nd Iowa Cavalry clashes with Confederates at Palo Alto. The two sides again clash on the following day.

In Missouri, a Union contingent departs Lake Spring and initiates an expedition to Chalk Bluff, Arkansas, that lasts through May 2.

In Virginia, elements of the 1st New York Cavalry and the 2nd Virginia Infantry Regiment, led by Lieutenants Powell and Wykoff, clash with Confederate Cavalry at Berryville. The Confederates lose eight men captured. Also, General Stoneman's cavalry initiates a reconnaissance mission in the vicinity of Kelly's Ford.

In Naval activity, the USS *Rachel Seaman,* while on patrol in the vicinity of Pass Cavallo, intercepts and seizes a schooner, the *Nymph.* This vessel is separate from the USS *Nymph,* a stern-wheel tinclad river gunboat acquired by the U.S. Navy during March 1864.

April 22 (Wednesday) **In Mississippi,** Union ships make another run past the Confederate batteries at Vicksburg. The transport *Tigress* is lost, but five other vessels (*Anglo-Saxon, Cheeseman, Empire City, Arizona* and *Moderator*) make it safely, giving Grant more than enough supplies and ships south of the city for him to finalize plans for the siege.

In Missouri, a Union contingent skirmishes with Confederates under Colonel John S. Marmakuke.

In Virginia, a contingent of the 3rd West Virginia Cavalry led by Major McGee skirmishes with Confederates at Strasburg Road. The Union sustains one killed and one wounded. The Confederates sustain about five killed, nine wounded and 25 captured.

In Confederate general officer activity, Brigadier Generals Daniel Smith Donelson and William Henry C. Whiting are appointed to the rank of major

general in the Confederacy, but apparently it is not known in Richmond that Donelson had succumbed of natural causes while in command of the Department of East Tennessee on April 17. Colonel Henry DeLamar Clayton is promoted brigadier general effective this day.

April 23 (Thursday) **In Missouri,** Union and Confederates clash in the vicinity of Independence.

In Virginia, the crew of the gunboat USS *Commodore Barney,* commanded by Lt. Cushing, U.S. Navy, engages a 40-man detachment of Confederate cavalry at Chuckatuck. The Union sustains one killed. The Confederates sustain two killed.

In Confederate activity, Lt. Colonel John Smith Preston is promoted to colonel. He had previously served on General Pierre Beauregard's staff at Charleston. At this time, Preston, about fifty-four years old, is the father-in-law of Brigadier General Wade Hampton. Colonel Preston attains the rank of brigadier general during June of the following year. His duties include command within the Confederate prison system.

April 24 (Friday) **In Alabama,** Union troops (2nd Division, 16th Corps) commanded by Brigadier General Greenville Dodge defeat a contingent of Confederates under Colonel Chalmers at Tuscumbia. Following the capture of the town, the forces of Dodge and those of Colonel A.D. Streight (Independent Provisional Brigade) move out in different directions. Dodge moves toward Northern Alabama, while Streight's command advances toward Atlanta, Georgia.

In Arkansas, a contingent of Union troops commanded by Colonel Phillips skirmishes with a Confederate unit at Weber Falls. Casualty figures are unavailable.

In Virginia, Union troops enter Port Royal, helping themselves to horses, mules and sup-

General Stoneman's cavalry on a reconnaissance mission in the vicinity of Kelly's Ford, Virginia (Mottelay, *The Soldier in Our Civil War,* 1886).

plies, and afterward, they return to Union lines without incident.

In West Virginia, a Confederate force led by Colonel George S. Patton attacks a Union outpost manned by the 5th West Virginia Cavalry, commanded by Colonel Latham, at Beverly.

In Missouri, elements of the 1st Missouri State Militia and the 24th Missouri Cavalry skirmish with Confederates at Mill (or Middle) Creek Bridge at White Water. The Confederates attack at night, but the forces under Captain Isaac D. Johnson repel the assault. The Union loses one killed and the Confederates sustain three killed and 12 wounded. The Rebels burn the bridge and retire, leaving the casualties on the field, but Union troops quickly extinguish the fire and preserve the bridge.

In Union general officer activity, Colonel Edward Augustus Wild (35th Massachusetts) is promoted to brigadier general. He begins to raise a force of Negro regiments, then participates with his brigade (Wild's African Brigade) in South Carolina prior to being sent north to Virginia, where he participates at Cold Harbor and other actions until the end of the war. General Wild's command is part of the force that occupies Richmond at war's end. He musters out of the service during January 1866.

In Naval activity, Captain William Radford is promoted to the rank of commodore. Radford receives command of the USS *New Ironsides* and participates as part of the ironclad division of Admiral David Porter's fleet that attacks Fort Fisher in late December 1864 and January 1865. The gunboat USS *Hastings* (formerly the *Emma Duncan*) comes under fire by Confederates in the vicinity of Green Bottom on the Tennessee River while it is reporting for its first duty as a gunboat. Nevertheless, the ship continues its voyage following its initial combat and afterward is assigned duty as a convoy ship for the army transports operating on the Tennessee River. In May, the *Hastings* pulls some short duty at the mouth of the Yazoo River; however, it quickly returns to the Tennessee in support of General William T. Sherman's forces. Also, the gunboat USS *Rotan,* attached to the North Atlantic Blockading Squadron the previous January, while on patrol with the USS *Western World* encounters suspicious vessels near Horn Harbor. The gunboats seize both vessels, the schooners *Martha Ann* and the *A. Carson.*

April 25 (Saturday)   In the Indian Territory, following a crossing of the Arkansas River the previous night, a Union Indian brigade under Colonel William A. Phillips, on the morning of the 25th, attacks the Confederate 1st Cherokee Mounted Rifles under Colonel (later general) Stand Watie at Webber's Falls. Watie's command is routed. The Confederate force sustains some fatalities, and many others are captured. On the Union side, one of the two fatalities is Doctor Gillpatrick, who is killed while he is providing medical help to one of the Confederates. The Cherokee legislature had planned a meeting for this day at Webber Falls; however,

the Cherokee politicians flee along with the men of the 1st Mounted Rifles.

In Tennessee, a Union Naval force, including General Alfred W. Ellet's Mississippi River ram fleet, the gunboat USS *Lexington* and the Ram *Monarch* clash with Confederate batteries at Little Rock Landing (Duck River Shoal). The Union, commanded by Lt. Commander Fitch, U.S. Navy, loses two killed and one wounded. The Confederates lose about 25 killed and wounded.

In West Virginia, elements of the 23rd Illinois and the 14th West Virginia Regiments skirmish with Confederates under General William Edmundson Jones. The Union sustains two killed and four wounded. Confederate casualty figures are unavailable.

In Union activity, Brigadier General Calvin E. Pratt resigns from the service.

April 26 (Sunday)   In Missouri, U.S. forces, including the 32nd Iowa, 1st Wisconsin Cavalry, and the 1st Missouri Light Artillery, commanded by General Vandever, engage and decisively defeat Confederates under Colonel John S. Marmaduke at Cape Girardeau. The Union strikes at night and the Confederates are stunned and routed. They retire toward Bloomfield, with a Union contingent in pursuit. Other forces at Columbus (Generals Vandever and McNeil) are notified of the flight, and requests are sent to have them "strike a blow through New Madrid to prevent or embarrass their escape." The Union suffers six dead and six wounded. The Confederates have 60 dead and 275 wounded or missing. Marmaduke's contingent also skirmishes with Union forces in the vicinity of Jackson on this day.

In Confederate general officer activity, Colonel Arthur M. Manigault is promoted to the rank of brigadier general.

April 27 (Monday)   In Missouri, Confederate Colonel John S. Marmaduke continues his raids in Missouri and on this day units under the combined forces of Generals Vandever and McNeil intercept the Rebels in the vicinity of White Water Bridge. A battle erupts at about 1000 and lasts until 0300 in the following day. The Rebels burn the bridge and retire. Marmaduke's raiders also skirmish with the Union in the vicinity of Jackson, where he had skirmished on the previous day.

In Virginia, Union General Hooker, who replaced General Burnside, moves his Army up to the Rappahannock River, crossing at Bank's Ford, and from there the force heads toward General Robert E. Lee's positions at Chancellorsville. Lee, aware of Hooker's movements, counters with a diversionary tactic the following day by moving west. This causes Hooker to modify his plan and forces him to become defensive.

In Tennessee, Union Cavalry led by Colonel Louis D. Watkins (promoted in March) skirmishes with Confederates at Franklin. The

Union captures some of the Confederate contingent.

In Union general officer activity, Colonel Edward Moody McCook is appointed brigadier general effective this day.

April 27–May 2   In Alabama, Union troops depart Tuscumbia to raid the area around Rome, Georgia. This force, commanded by Colonel A.D. Streight, encounters some furious action en route, including skirmishes at Day's Gap on the 30th, Warrior Creek on May 1, and at Blount's Farm near Rome on May 2. The Confederates surround the contingent outside of Rome and it is forced to capitulate. The contingent is composed of the 3rd Ohio, 51st and 73rd Indiana, 80th Illinois, mounted infantry and two companies of the 1st Alabama Cavalry. The Union sustains 12 killed, 69 wounded and 1,466 missing and captured.

April 28 (Tuesday)   In Alabama, a Union force of the 16th Corps, commanded by General Dodge, clashes with Confederates at Town Creek.

In Kentucky, a contingent of the 1st Kentucky Cavalry, led by Captain Alexander, skirmishes with Confederate pickets at Howe's Ford (Weaver's Store). Casualty figures are unavailable. The Union captures four Confederates.

In Mississippi, the 6th Illinois Cavalry skirmishes with Confederates at Union Church.

In North Carolina, a Union force (General Innis Newton Palmer's command) engages Confederates at Dover Road.

In Naval activity, the USS *Anna* (*Annie*), operating as part of the East Gulf Blockading Squadron, observes what appears to be a blockade runner, the British vessel *Dream.* The *Anna* commences fire; however, the *Dream* outruns the *Anna* and reaches the safety of the Spanish waters off Cuba.

April 28–29   In Mississippi, General Grant orders an assault on Grand Gulf (frontal positions at Vicksburg). Porter's fleet — including the gunboats *Benton, Carondelet, Lafayette, Baron De Kalb* (formerly *Louisville*), *Mound City, Pittsburg* and the *Tuscumbia*—fires continuously for over five hours. McClernand's force of 10,000 men cannot disembark, allowing the Confederates to hold and force Porter to withdraw. The Steamer *Cheeseman* receives heavy enemy fire but survives the ordeal. The Union suffers about 75 casualties. Grant now realizes that a frontal attack against Grand Gulf is futile and moves McClernand's force to the west bank of the Mississippi. It debarks under cover of darkness at Bruinsburg, without opposition, then marches to Port Gibson, where troops see nominal action the following day. The USS *Tuscumbia* becomes disabled during the attack after sustaining 81 hits from Confederate batteries. After repairs, in May the Tuscumbia rejoins the fleet in its operations against Vicksburg; however, afterward, it spends most of the rest of the war out of service. It is decommissioned during February 1865. In November

1865 it is sold. In other activity, Colonel Benjamin Grierson's cavalry reaches Bahala and Union Church; the rails at Bahala are destroyed.

In Virginia, Confederate General Thomas "Stonewall" Jackson withdraws from Port Royal to Fredericksburg. Lee requests Colonel John Critcher to move his 15th Virginia Regiment and join Jackson. General Lee also informs General Samuel Cooper (Confederate inspector general) of Hooker's movements. Lee, with no troops available except Stuart's brigades, requests additional forces to engage Hooker at Fredericksburg. Lee directs General Richard H. Anderson to protect the road from Chancellorsville down the river.

April 29 (Wednesday) In Missouri, Confederate Colonel John S. Marmaduke's raiders, on an expedition in Missouri since 30 April, again skirmish with Union forces on this day at the Castor River.

In Mississippi, Colonel Benjamin Grierson's cavalry destroys Confederate rails at Brookhaven. The Rebels lose many cars, bridges and tracks as well as the Confederate depots there. From Brookhaven, Grierson moves to Bogue Chitto and Summit, where the rails are also destroyed to further disrupt Confederate activity. Grierson's cavalry drives toward Liberty and encounters a Confederate force at the Oskya and Clinton Road, where one regiment of Confederates is posted at Wall's Bridge and another is deployed at Edward's Bridge. Grierson's cavalry engages and beats both contingents, enabling him to push the main body toward Greensburg, Louisiana. He also moves toward Osyka, where the Confederates have set a trap. Nevertheless, Grierson, anticipating the ambush, orders a charge which succeeds in getting his troops through the lines of the Rebel infantry before the nearby Confederate cavalry can outflank him. Nevertheless, the charge costs the Union some casualties, including Lt. Colonel Blackburn of the 7th Illinois.

In Virginia, elements of the 1st Corps, Army of the Potomac, engage Confederates at Fitzhugh's Crossing. Casualty figures are unavailable.

In West Virginia, a Union contingent of about 300 troops, composed of elements of the 106th New York Regiment and the 6th West Virginia and Virginia Militia, commanded by Captain Chamberlain, clashes with a Confederate force of more than 5,000 troops (General W.E. Jones' command) at Fairmount. The Confederates take the town, but the Union resists with vigor. The Union sustains one killed and six wounded. The Confederates sustain about 100 killed and wounded. The Confederate 25th Virginia Infantry (Early's brigade) has participated in the action in West Virginia this month as part of General W.E. Jones' force.

In Naval activity, the *Sunflower* is commissioned at Boston. Acting Master Edward Sice receives command of the screw gunboat, which is assigned to the East Gulf Blockading Squadron. It arrives on station at Key West, Florida, during mid–May to initiate patrol duty.

April 29–May 2 *In Naval activity,* the Mississippi Squadron, commanded by Admiral David D. Porter, attacks Confederate positions at Haines Bluff, Mississippi. Porter remains aboard his flagship, the *Blackhawk* (formerly *New Uncle Sam*), commanded by Commander K.R. Breese. The USS *Romeo* participates in this operation, which is actually a diversion. The fleet feigns an attack to compel the Confederates to defend, thereby preventing the Rebels from massing a force at Grand Gulf. Subsequently, the Romeo patrols along the White River and the Little Red River throughout the summer and fall during the operations against Vicksburg and after the city is seized. During October, the *Romeo* is transferred to the duty on the Tennessee River.

April 29–May 3 (Alabama) BATTLE OF DAY'S GAP (SAND MOUNTAIN) AND SURRENDER AT ROME Confederates under Nathan B. Forrest relentlessly pursue the Union forces of Colonel Streight. Without regard to exhaustion, sleeplessness and nasty weather, Forrest departs Courtland, Alabama, at 0100 on April 29, moving through the darkness along sloppy roads straight through until the break of dawn. At about 0800, Forrest finally calls a halt, but not for too long. The column pauses for only about one hour to give the animals a reprieve, and then he proceeds to Moulton.

In the meantime, Forrest's prey, the column under Union Colonel Abel Streight, continues its trek and reaches the vicinity of Sand Mountain at about dusk. The column stands at a gorge known as Day's Gap, which is the path to the crest of the mountain. While en route to the mountain, Streight's command had scooped up substantial amounts of provisions stored in wagons, and the horses and mules in their path are also confiscated. The Union troops remains unaware of the Confederate force that is closing upon them when they make camp at the base of the mountain.

At Streight's encampment in the gorge, all remains well at midnight (29th–30th), and still there is no knowledge that the Rebels are less than five miles from their position. Rebel scouts pinpoint the Union camp and report to Forrest, who gains a sense of relief knowing the Union is unsuspiciously at rest. He instructs his weary cavalry to momentarily pause to eat and grab some sleep in preparation for yet another grueling day and yet another bold attack; however, much of his column had not yet reached the main body and was still trekking through the darkness with cautious movement to preserve men and animals alike. The final

section does not arrive at the Confederate camp until about dawn on the 30th.

While most of Forrest's command gets some sleep, one contingent, the "Forty Scouts," commanded by Forrest's brother, Captain William Forrest, forgoes its rest upon orders from Forrest to nudge right up to the Union camp to investigate the situation there. From a point where the Union campfires are quite visible, Captain Forrest discerns that the Union is totally at rest. He decides his command is in no jeopardy, prompting him to direct his scouts to get some sleep, but to no avail. Unexpectedly, from the Union lines, at about dawn, an eerie and annoying boisterous ear-deafening echo of peculiar sounds erupts, as about 2,000 mules in nearly total unison begin to bellow.

In the slumbering Union camp, the troops had apparently become accustomed to the mule-calls, as the mules seemingly announce breakfast. Prior to dawn the entire column is awake if not yet alert and the ascent of the mountain begins with the wagons in the front. By about dawn, the tip of the column reaches the crest, but the primitive, obstacle-filled, slim and serpentine path is still crowded near the base and some of the command are not yet on the move. Nevertheless, the Confederates, also awake before dawn, initiate an attack against Streight's rear, to deliver the first announcement of their presence with cannon fire.

The unexpected cannon fire bursts in the vicinity of the camp and those still there bolt for the mountain path, abandoning their fires and breakfast utilities hurriedly in a dash to outrun the advancing vanguard, the scouts under Captain Forrest. Colonel Streight is informed that the rear of the column is under assault. At the same time, Streight, about two miles from the rear, hears the Confederate artillery; however, due to the terrain, he feels confident that any assault can be repelled. Streight also has some home country experience with the column, the two Union Alabama companies are familiar with the terrain and its passes. General Forrest, aware that a frontal assault would fail, maneuvers to cut of Streight by using another less

A night encampment (*Harper's Pictorial History of the Civil War,* 1896).

known pass. The opposing leaders each race to outsmart the other. Streight accelerates the move across the mountain, aware that Forrest has passed through the gap. Meanwhile the rear guard is closely tailed by Captain Forrest's scouts.

The confrontation becomes imminent either in a running battle or a standing battle. Streight chooses the latter. He establishes a line about two miles from the summit in an area speckled with hickory, oak and pine trees, which provide a formidable defensive position along a ridge that circles to his rear, while his right side is buffeted by a shear ravine and on his left the ground is a marshy run. The skirmish lines are drawn, and in the center of the line, Streight deploys two 12-pounders in concealed positions to the rear of some thick brush. Just as the preparations are completed and the troops are deployed in prone positions, Streight's rear guards come into view as they are rushing down the road, just barely ahead of the trailing Confederates, the latter not expecting a defensive firing line.

In quick time, the rear guard passes through a slim gap in the line left open for them, but once they enter the lines, an iron fence arises on either side of the road and the Confederates become recipients of a hurricane of fire. One of the first to fall is Captain Forrest, who receives a hit from a Minié ball that shatters his thigh bone. The Rebels work to regroup and calm their horses to retire and move out of range of the Union fire. Meanwhile, General Bedford Forrest arrives at the front, with only some of the regiments of Edmundson and Roddey, giving Forrest about one thousand troops at the summit.

With Edmundson's force dismounted, Colonel Roddey and other mounted troops cover the left and right of Forrest's line. Two guns attached to Morton's battery are brought to the front and immediately, they commence fire. At the same time, Edmundson's dismounted troops advance to a distance of about 100 yards from Streight's lines, and at that same time, two cavalry units, Roddey's and Julian's, dart out well in front of the dismounted force and enter exposed ground well within the killing field range of the Union fire. An avalanche of murderous shot and shell pours down on the cavalry and shreds the ranks mercilessly. The raging storm of fire incites pandemonium within the Rebel ranks and it is conspicuous. Colonel Streight snatches the advantage.

While the Confederate cavalry remains in a temporary state of disorder, leaving no time to regroup, Colonel Streight gives the order: "Charge!" At the signal, the Union plows forward and further disorients the Confederate cavalry and pushes it back in some disarray, but the thrust simultaneously leaves the dismounted troops of Edmundson in great peril. Lacking cavalry support and now the sole immediate recipient of relentless fire, Edmondson's regiment also faces isolation and capture. Edmundson reacts by ordering a disciplined withdrawal to preserve his regiment as well as escort troops and Forrest's scouts.

In the heat of the grueling exchange, the Confederates have also lost horses, causing a larger predicament, forcing the Rebels to leave two guns on the field, which causes General Forrest to react with rage, particularly toward the lieutenant in command of the artillery. Forrest refuses to consider the dead horses, the disabled carriages and the closing Union cavalry; rather, he is concerned only with losing his "pet cannon." Meanwhile, Forrest displays his discontent with the situation and informs his troops that all will be dismounted because men are "too scarce," and while continuing to ride among his troops with his saber drawn to enunciate his passion, he informs them that the "guns had to be retaken if every man died in the attempt." In addition, Forrest tells his troops that if the guns are not recovered, "they will never need their horses again."

With undaunted determination, Forrest aligns the force, and on the signal, the advance proceeds; however, the incoming fire falls far short of that which had only a short while ago rained down on them. Soon the reason becomes perfectly clear. Unknown to Forrest, Colonel Streight, once the Confederates had been thumped and their two pieces confiscated, the Union abandoned their lines and resumed the advance toward Blountville, accompanied by Forrest's pet artillery pieces. Afterward, the dismounted Confederates return to their horses, but in the meantime, Streight's column has a one hour lead. Nevertheless, the chase continues, as Forrest adamantly intends to eliminate Streight, but he refuses to let go of his two missing artillery pieces. Colonel Streight reports about thirty killed and wounded. General Forrest reports about "fifty or 75" killed or wounded. Lt. Colonel Sheets, 51st Indiana, is mortally wounded during the fighting. Confederate Captain William Forrest, despite his debilitating wound, recovers and later returns to the field.

The contest ends by about 1100; however, General Forrest resumes the chase and moves eastward. After advancing about six miles, the column encounters the 4th and 9th Tennessee Cavalry Regiments, which had been ordered earlier to initiate the flanking movement. As they join at the intersection, the Union had already moved beyond, eliminating any opportunity to cut Streight off.

Meanwhile, Forrest remains concerned that the Union might modify their path and move toward the Tennessee River to link with General Charles C. Dodge. Colonel Philip D. Roddey (4th Alabama Cavalry Regiment) and Lt. Colonel William R. Julian (Alabama cavalry battalion) are ordered to move to a position from which they can monitor General Dodge's command. Lt. Colonel Henry A. Edmundson (54th Virginia Infantry) is ordered to head toward Brooksville and Somerville, traveling on a parallel route to that being used by the Union column, but being in positions that stand between Streight and the river.

Forrest continues with the direct pursuit, assisted by the tracks left by the mules. About nine miles from Day's Gap, the mule tracks become conspicuously fresh and deeply imprinted in the sandy soil as the 4th Tennessee advances as vanguard. In a repeat performance, Colonel Streight, at the front of the column, becomes aware of the skirmishing at the rear of the column and once again decides that a standing battle outweighs a running battle. The Union halts progress and establishes a defensive line on a ridge dubbed Hog Mountain. At about one hour before dusk, the Confederates are on scene and another tenacious clash erupts. The Confederates press against Streight's right, but without progress. A new strike is launched against the left, and with the assistance of Forrest's two artillery pieces, captured earlier, and the two mountain howitzers, the surge against the left is repelled, but not effortlessly.

The slug-fest ensues until about 2200, with neither side relenting as the Union holds steadfastly and the Confederates mount charge after charge. The darkness favors neither side, and in such close-quartered fighting it is difficult to even convincingly discern who is friend and who is the enemy, but the inability to have a clear and unobstructed view does not limit the brutality of the contest. General Forrest, in the thick of the fighting, loses one horse killed under him and two others knocked out of the fight by wounds.

A change in the bitter stalemate occurs when Colonel Biffle's 9th Tennessee, using the darkness as a shield, maneuvers his way to the rear of the Union column from where he pounces upon the positions of those maintaining the mules. The sudden and unexpected blow finally forces Colonel Streight to relinquish ground. The Union immediately initiates a retreat and takes no time to recover the wounded or killed. Afterward, General Forrest once again has his two cannon. Colonel Streight later reports that, having exhausted the ammunition of the Confederate artillery pieces, he intentionally left them behind, but first he directed that they be "spiked and the carriages destroyed."

With the Union in fast retreat, the 9th Tennessee, now in the vanguard, remains close behind. Once again, Streight faces a decision, continue the running exchange or draw another defensive line. He chooses the latter. After arriving at a particular piece of ground upon which many pine trees stand, he deploys Colonel Gilbert Hathaway's 73rd Indiana on both sides of the road. Clouds that had been hovering have disappeared and the moonlight illuminates the terrain; however, the Union is deployed in concealed positions. In the meantime, the mules are moved farther up the line.

As the troops of the 73rd Regiment lie prone amid the trees, it appears as if a perfect ambush is about to unfold; however, as the vanguard approaches within range of the regiment, the horse of the man at the point suddenly halts in mid stride. The soldier takes it as a warning and moves back to the column to alert them of a possible ambush. General Forrest immediately takes steps to flush out the Union by calling for volunteers to draw fire. Three men volunteer. They are under orders to proceed with caution and at the first sign of the enemy or if the Union fires upon them, they are to withdraw. The ruse works, and just as the Union prepares to fire, the skilled horsemen draw close to the necks of their horses as they spin around and evade death or injury while exposing the ambush.

The positions of the Union are pointed out to Forrest by one of the volunteers and Forrest directs an artillery piece to commence fire from a distance of about two hundred yards. Soon another piece is brought forward and joins in the bombardment. The Union then resumes its retreat, but between 0200 and 0300 it is again compelled to draw a line to impede the progress of Forrest. After an exhausting night, Streight's column arrives at Blountville at 1000 on 1 May, completing an arduous combat-filled march of 43 miles in about twenty-eight hours.

By this time, Forrest concludes that Streight's column has extended well beyond his post at Tuscumbia, which forbids an attempt to get back there. Forrest also discerns that his most probable objective would be to reach Rome, Georgia, where the Union has an arsenal. He directs Edmundson and Anderson to protect the route to Guntersville and then orders his troops to dismount to get some rest, but by that time it is nearly time to awaken. Forrest gives the order to get some sleep at 0300 on 1 May, but beforehand, the troops are directed to give the animals care and to feed them. His order also stipulates that they are to sleep for only two hours.

Meanwhile, Colonel Streight acquires fresh ammunition, supplies and animals (impressed from the area) and the column moves out, with the supplies on pack mules and the wagons in flames, but yet again, the tenacious Rebels are on the attack. A cavalry clash occurs when the rear guard is stormed by a contingent, including the 4th Tennessee, led by Forrest. The powerful thrust quickly pushes the guard under Captain Smith from Blountsville and compels the troops to accelerate their pace to rejoin the column. In the wake, Forrest's troops have time to extinguish the fires and claim the supplies.

Shortly thereafter, Streight's column again comes under attack, but the rear guard effectively impedes progress while the Union moves toward the Black Warrior River. Under cover fire of a new line, the troops cross the unruly stream, and in the process two pack mules are lost. Two howitzers on the east bank support the crossing, which is completed about 1700, but the Confederates still show no signs of releasing the pressure to give Streight an opportunity to escape; however, Forrest does call for a new pause of about three hours.

Meanwhile, Colonel Streight continues his march, and at 0900 on 2 May, the rear guard of the column comes under attack at Black Creek Crossing in the vicinity of Gadsden. The Confederates maintain pressure, but the crossing is successful. Afterward the bridge is burned and there are no other known bridges within at least two miles, and without either a bridge or a boat, the river is known to be impassable, but General Forrest unexpectedly gets support from a young woman, Emma Sansom, who is aware of a point in the unruly current where she has

watched her family's cattle cross. Sansom asks General Forrest to have a horse saddled for her so she can take him to the ford, but the general looks down at Sansom from his horse and says: "There is no time for a horse. Get up here behind me."

With Sansom's hands wrapped around General Forrest, the two ride about two hundred yards, still remaining on the family property, to an obscure ford known only to members of her family. Once at the ford, Sansom is in front of the general and they are within sight of the Union. General Forrest quickly steps in front to get between her and the Union and says: "I am glad to have you for a pilot, but I am not going to make breastworks of you." All the while, Union artillery shells are passing over their heads. Before Sansom returns to her house, the general asks her name, but in a poignant moment, the general also asks her to give him a lock of her hair.

Sansom's presence of mind and her dedication to the Confederacy saves Forrest at least several hours and increases his chances of catching the evasive Union column. The personal encounter between her and the general picks up again back near the house. General Forrest makes a request as he speaks to Sansom, saying: "One of my bravest men has been killed, and he is laid out in the house. His name is Robert Turner. I want you to see that he is buried in some graveyard near here." With that, the Confederates depart in pursuit of Colonel Streight. Emma Sansom later related: "My sister and I sat up all night watching over the dead soldier, who had lost his life fighting for our rights, in which we were overpowered but never conquered. General Forrest and his men endeared themselves to us forever."

The cavalry crosses the ford with the riders carrying the ammunition for the caisson. In a more tedious operation, the guns and empty caissons are rolled to the edge of the creek, and through the use of a rope and double teams of horses at the opposite bank, the Rebels get their guns to the other side. Within a short time, the Confederates arrive at Gadsden and again stun the Union, which thought it had halted the Rebels after burning the Black Creek bridge. The Union pushes forward after destroying some ammunition supplies and provisions. Streight's command is over exhausted by this point, and it appears that survival depends on another all-night march. Meanwhile, the Confederates remain determined to intercept the column, but the Confederates are also beyond exhaustion.

The column moves toward Rome, Georgia, with Colonel Streight anticipating that he will reach it and cross before the Confederates intercept him. He further believes that once they are across the bridge, it can be destroyed to forestall Forrest. But by this point, some of the troops as well as the animals are no longer able to maintain the grueling pace. As the troops fall out of the column, they are seized by the trailing Rebels.

At about 1600, Streight's column pauses at Blount's plantation, about fifteen miles from

Gadsden. The desperate retreat is called to a halt to acquire forage for the animals; however, in anticipation of a new assault, a skirmish line is drawn. At the same time, the rear guard comes under assault by Forrest's force, quite smaller than when the saga began on 29 April. The Union prepares another ambush in an attempt to sufficiently punish the Confederates to terminate the chase, but the Confederates again are not fooled. Forrest avoids entering the trap. During the skirmishing, Colonel Gilbert Hathaway receives a mortal wound from the weapon of a sharpshooter, Private Joseph Martin, who picks him off. Within a few minutes, Hathaway expires. The death of Colonel Hathaway inflicts a fatal blow also on the entire body and leads to the termination of the chase.

The Confederates, having discovered the concealed positions of Streight, initiate a flanking movement, which compels Streight to retire without eliminating Forrest, and the troops become more demoralized due to the death of Hathaway. Meanwhile, Forrest continues to end the chase without getting snared in an ambush. He sends a rider, Colonel John H. Wisdom, to Rome, Georgia, to forewarn the citizens of the approach of the Union column. The messenger instructs them to burn the bridge to prevent a crossing by Streight. Meanwhile, Forrest pauses. His force has been greatly diminished and he chooses not to risk a dangerous night attack with a small command. A contingent continues the pursuit while the main body halts for the night.

At about the same time, Colonel Streight, unaware of the diminished size of his pursuing force and aware of the importance of gaining the bridge, dispatches two hundred troops under Captain Milton Russell with orders to gain and hold the bridge. The column does not rest for the night. It advances while Russell's contingent presses forward, and after arriving at the Chattanooga River, the unit crosses on a ferry. On 3 May, Russell arrives at Rome only to discover the bridge is held by Confederates (Home Guards) and it is barricaded. Meanwhile, when Streight's main body reaches the Chattanooga River, because no guards had been posted to protect the ferry, it was taken from the crossing to prevent its use by the column. Undaunted, though greatly fatigued, Streight refuses to quit. He marches the column several miles upstream to a bridge, but the arduous trek takes another high toll as more troops fall off in the darkness, overcome by exhaustion.

Slightly before dawn, the column crosses the bridge and then destroys it. At about 0900, the column reaches Lawrence and takes a short pause, and only extreme efforts cause the troops to resume the march. At about this same time, word arrives from Wisdom that the bridge is blocked. Making a desperate situation more grave, Colonel Streight is informed that a fresh Confederate contingent is also closing upon the column. Before Streight can even consider any options, he hears the action at the rear of the column. It is Forrest and the destroyed bridge at the Chattanooga River had not delayed his force.

At about 0900, a fully refreshed force under Forrest, standing at only about 600 operable men, initiates a skirmish, but avoids a direct attack. His forces maneuver into positions which encircle about one-half of the Union column. The rejuvenated Rebels have also fully regained their "Rebel Yell," and although numbering only 600, the resounding noise gives the impression that a huge force has the column surrounded. Streight confers with his officers and despite the miserable odds, they choose to fight.

The line is formed, and from prone positions, the Union soldiers are prepared to fire as the Confederates approach, but by this time, the troops begin to fall into a dead sleep on the firing line amid the ongoing charge and accompanying noise of battle. The troops had literally been too exhausted to keep their eyes open as the Confederates penetrate the camp. General Forrest sends in a messenger under a white flag and demands surrender. Colonel Steight meets with Forrest and asks for terms and receives the response: "Immediate surrender — your men to be treated as prisoners of war, the officers to retain their side arms and personal property."

Colonel Streight asks for time to confer with his officers and Forrest embellishes his strength, saying, "All right, but you will not require much time. I have a column of fresh troops at hand, now nearer Rome than you are. You cannot cross the river in your front. I have men enough right here to run over you." Although Forrest is exaggerating his strength, it is considered a fair tactic of war. Colonel Streight informs his officers of the proposal and it is decided against the objections of Colonel Streight to surrender. At the time of surrender, the Union still does not realize that Forrest's command had been cut by more than half.

The Confederates, having chased and fought Speight nearly constantly since the 30th over a distance of about 150 miles, remain concerned until they move troops into more commanding positions and actually see the Union men to lay down their arms. Of the original 2,000 troops that departed Nashville on 10 April, the beleaguered troops, numbering about 1,600, capitulate. Streight's force, although specially selected, did not include experienced cavalrymen; they are infantry transformed into cavalry. Their unfamiliarity with horses added to the difficulties during the campaign, particularly due to Forrest's command being composed of skilled cavalry. Forrest receives accolades from the Confederate government. The Congress of the Confederate States of America resolved that "the thanks of Congress are again due to General N.B. Forrest and the officers and men of his command for meritorious service on the field, and especially for the daring, skill, and perseverance exhibited in the pursuit and capture of the largely superior forces of the enemy near Rome, Georgia."

April 30 (Thursday)   In the Indian Territory (Oklahoma), Union and Confederate contingents skirmish in the vicinity of Fort Gibson.

In Missouri, Confederate Colonel John S. Marmaduke's force clashes with a Union contingent at Bloomfield.

In Mississippi, following the successful passage of Grand Gulf by the Union fleet, troops are landed at Bruinsburg for the march against Port Gibson.

In Virginia, General Robert E. Lee telegraphs Confederate President Davis, informing him of Stuart's favorable action in the vicinity of Germanna on the previous day. As Union forces cross the Rappahannock on the 29th, Stuart intercepts them in the vicinity of Madden's Ford north of the Rapidan and captures prisoners from the 5th, 11th, and 12th Union Corps. Lee then tells Davis: "If I had Longstreet's division, would feel safe." Lee is conspicuously concerned about Union General Meade's approach. In other action, the 3rd Virginia Cavalry under Confederate Colonel T.H. Owen and the 2nd North Carolina under Colonel W.H. Payne advance towards Tabernacle Church to reinforce General Richard H. Anderson. Confederate Major General McLaws departs Fredericksburg to join Richard H. Anderson's Division (1st Corps) on the Plank Road. Confederate General Jackson arrives the following day. Meanwhile, Union General Hooker establishes headquarters in the vicinity of Chancellorsville late in the day. Hooker dispatches cavalry units to cut the rail lines between General Lee's positions and Richmond. In the meantime, the divisions of Union Generals French and Hancock, having crossed the Rappahannock at the Banks and United States Fords respectively, are advancing toward Chancellorsville, followed by two divisions of Reynolds, commanded by Generals Doubleday and John C. Robinson and General Sickles' Third Corps.

General Brooks' division (John Sedgwick's Sixth Corps) has crossed below Fredericksburg and General Wadsworth's division (Reynolds' I Corps) has also forded the river about one mile farther down from Fredericksburg. General Solomon Meredith's brigade (two Indiana, one Michigan and three Wisconsin regiments), known as the Iron Brigade, is attached to Wadsworth's division. General Gibbon's division (Couch's corps) holds at Falmouth across from Fredericksburg and in a diversionary move to pull off a ruse, the divisions of Howe and Newton (Sedgwick's corps) initiate a march overland through the hills to create an illusion that a huge force nearby to threaten Lee. Nevertheless, Lee deduces the real intent of Hooker and calls for aid from Stonewall Jackson, by directing him to link up with General Richard H. Anderson's force at Tabernacle Church.

April 30–May 1   In Missouri, elements of the 3rd Missouri and 1st Iowa Cavalry, supported by the 2nd Missouri Militia and Battery E, 1st Missouri Light Artillery, clash at Chalk Bluff and St. Francis River. The Union sustains two killed and 11 wounded.

May 1 (Friday)   In Arkansas, a Union contingent of the 3rd Iowa Cavalry, commanded by Captain De Huff, skirmishes with Confederates at La Grange. The Confederates prevail. The Union loses about three killed, nine wounded and 30 missing or captured. Confederate forces under Colonel John S. Marmaduke cross into Arkansas after an expedition in Missouri which began on 30 April. The raiders, upon their arrival in Arkansas, clash with Union forces on the 1st and the 2nd.

In Kentucky, the 2nd Tennessee and 1st Kentucky Regiments and the 7th Ohio Cavalry, bolstered by the 45th Ohio and the 112th Illinois Mounted Rifle Regiments, commanded by General Carter, engage Confederates under Colonel Morrison at Monticello. The Union force of about 5,000 troops prevails. Casualty figures are unavailable.

In Louisiana, Colonel Benjamin Grierson's cavalry reaches Greensburg and heads for Clinton. The force crosses the Amite River after dusk and then drives down the Greenville Spring Road, encountering Confederates at Big Sandy Bridge about ten miles outside of Baton Rouge. Grierson's force overwhelms the contingent and captures forty Confederate cavalrymen, including their commanding officer, Colonel Stewart.

In Mississippi, the 7th Illinois Cavalry skirmishes with Confederates at Tickfaw River.

In Virginia, a two company detachment of General Stoneman's cavalry skirmishes a Confederate contingent at Louisa Court House. Meanwhile, a contingent of the 99th New York Volunteer Regiment commanded by Lt. Colonel Nixon battles a Confederate unit at South

General Stoneman's cavalry skirmishes with Confederates at Louisa Court House, Virginia (Mottelay, *The Soldier in Our Civil War*, 1886).

Quay Bridge. The Union loses about 41 killed and wounded. At Rapidan Station, General Averell's cavalry division, Army of the Potomac, clashes with a Confederate force. Casualty figures are unavailable.

In Naval activity, the USS *Western World*, on patrol with the USS *Crusader*, encounters two abandoned schooners at Milford Haven, Virginia. Both vessels are destroyed. The *Crusader* continues its patrols until the cessation of hostilities. It is decommissioned in Washington, D.C., in June 1865. The *Crusader* is sold the next month and renamed *Kalorama*. It remains in service as a commercial vessel until it is wrecked on 25 February 1876. At about this time (May), the stern-wheel tinclad river gunboat *Fawn* is commissioned the USS *Fanny*; the following month it is renamed *Fawn*. The *Fawn* is assigned duty on the western rivers and remains in the region until the final days patrolling on the Mississippi. It is decommissioned during June 1865 and sold in August, when its name is changed to the *Fanny Barker*. It remains operational until it is wrecked during March 1873. The single-turret ironclad USS *Neosho* is commissioned at about this time (May). It is assigned duty on the Mississippi River and its tributaries and remains in that region for the duration of the war.

The USS *Ticonderoga*, a sloop of war constructed at the New York Navy Yard in Brooklyn, is commissioned at about this time (May). Initially, it serves in the West Indies on patrol in search of Confederate raiders, and later on the same duty in the northwestern Atlantic from October 1863 to July 1864. It then is sent in search of a specific Rebel raider, the cruiser CSS *Florida*. In December 1864 while attached to the North Atlantic Blockading Squadron, it participates in the operations against Fort Fisher, North Carolina. In January 1865, while attached to the South Atlantic Blockading Squadron, it continues patrols until taken out of service during March 1864, prior to the close of hostilities; however, it is recommissioned during the following year, modified, and assigned duty off Europe. From there it is transferred to the Mediterranean as well as the African coast until 1869. Afterward, the *Ticonderoga* is assigned to various duties and is in and out of commission until finally decommissioned during September 1882. In August 1887 it is sold.

May 1–2 BATTLE OF PORT GIBSON Grant's Union forces (13th Corps, 3rd Division, 17th Corps) during the initial engagement to gain Vicksburg, engages Confederates under General John S. Bowen at Port Gibson (Magnolia Hills and Thompson Hill), Mississippi. The vanguard of the Thirteenth Army Corps encroaches a church about four miles from Port Gibson and less than 15 miles from Bruinsburg, where Grant earlier crossed the river. As the 14th Division arrives at about 0100 on 1 May, the Confederates awaiting the arrival greets the point troops with small arms fire, but soon after, Confederate artillery commences fire in an attempt to punish the troops that had reached a ravine.

The Union, anticipating a tenacious encounter, is prepared to meet the resistance. As the Union lines form for attack, artillery bellows in response to the Confederate thunderclap. The Union firepower is immediately effective, and following a short but ferocious exchange, the Rebel guns fall silent. Nonetheless, with darkness still dominating, the Union pulls back beyond range of the Confederate guns to await dawn before resuming the advance.

With the sun beginning to break, the Ninth Division is directed to the road on the left, with its 1st Brigade at the point. While maneuvering to hasten the advance, the brigade meets a determined Confederate line at about 0500 which ignites a huge exchange of fire that continues for about one arduous hour. Initially, the Rebels remain immovable; however, the powerful streams of incessant fire that rake their positions finally force the line to retire.

With the first obstacle eliminated, Grant's Ninth Division, composed of only two brigades, grinds forward and encounters new obstacles that obstruct progress and clearly point out that to launch a frontal attack would prove disastrous. Instead, Grant orders a maneuver designed to permit an assault against the Confederate right flank. The troops form, and in a swift movement, the Union races across a running brook and ascends a steep incline, their bayonets leading the way. The assault troops crash into the flank with a powerful blow that causes the Rebels to once again give ground. Three of their artillery pieces, which had earlier been pounding the Union during the predawn hours, are gained by the Union.

The troops on the high ground retire, taking a road on the right which passes the church and leads to positions where another Rebel battery had been deployed. A new confrontation is ignited. The Yankees continue to eliminate the opposition, but yet again the Confederates resist with enormous tenacity. The Confederates remain bold and defiant, unwilling to grant the Union passage to Port Gibson. Fatalities on both sides rise dramatically. Meanwhile, the Union, unwilling to be outdone by heroism in the field, mounts another assault that compels the Confederates to again surrender ground as they regroup at nearby hills, from where they will establish a new line, defended in the center along the Port Gibson Road, with other troops posted to the right and left.

General Grant suspends an immediate ground assault and initiates his attack with artillery that delivers riveting fire into the Rebel positions on the road. Under cover of the umbrella fire, the vanguard advances into the caul-

A Union column advances toward Port Gibson (***Harper's Pictorial History of the Civil War***, 1896).

dron as the Confederates raise fierce resistance and deliver waves of withering fire. Nonetheless, the Union remains undaunted, and despite the avalanche of fire, the line advances and plows into the Confederate positions, bolstered by continuing artillery fire. The pressure collapses the Confederates' stamina and again they are compelled to relinquish ground. In an attempt to halt the juggernaut, the Rebels form to strike the Union flank to release the pressure; however, the Union detects the strategy and reinforces the right wing, where it is thought the Confederates would strike.

Union reserves bolster the wing, and when the Confederates launch their powerful thrust, it is met with rigid resistance, but the Confederates still penetrate and gain ground. Ferocious fighting continues as the Union moves to evict the Rebels, but despite several hours of incessant fighting, the Rebels refuse all efforts to expel them. On the Union left, the Confederates hold formidable positions in the heights that overlook an impassable canebrake. To their flank, the Confederate positions are further protected by ravines, ensuring that the Union would be shredded by enfilade fire if a direct were launched. The Confederates continue to deliver punishing fire that accelerates the number of casualties.

Reinforcements are committed to the fight. The 1st Brigade, Third Division (17th Army Corps), speeds along the road leading to Grand Gulf, then upon arrival, the brigades form for attack and in unison a tremendously loud shout emerges from the brigade troops as they fix their bayonets and defiantly execute a daring charge, not at a particularly swift pace, as the troops first have to penetrate the cane.

The troops are literally on their hands and knees as they slash through the cane, but once the troops emerge, the charge resumes in earnest and without compassion. All Confederates to their front either surrender or are liquidated. After acquiring domination on the opposite side of the thicket, the Union concentrates on eliminating the defenders at the battery. Supported by Union artillery, the battery is seized and the guns are incorporated into the Union arsenal. Having sustained horrific losses, including about 150 killed, 300 wounded and 500 captured, the remaining defenders retire to Port Gibson, but as they quickly stream toward the town, they are trailed and harassed by more effective Union artillery fire and small arms fire from those in pursuit.

By the time the Confederates race back to Port Gibson, the sun has disappeared beyond the horizon, replaced by a brightly shining moon, which casts an aura of surreal tranquility over the field of death and destruction, now concealed by somber darkness except for the glowing sparkles of moonlight. In cadence with the night sky, pursuit is suspended, permitting the Confederates to complete their retreat without further interruption. The din of battle has been overtaken by stark silence. The exhausted troops of both sides reflect on the day's fury and get some rest for the next unfolding event.

At dawn on 2 May, the Union discovers that a second day of incessant battle is cancelled, at least for awhile. During the night, the Confederates had abandoned Port Gibson, which permits the Thirteenth Army Corps to enter the town without incident. The Union easily spots the direction in which the Rebels headed, as the bridge that spans Bayou Pierre is still burning when they take the town. Some Rebels attached to the rear guard had remained to observe the crossing, and while the engineers construct the bridge, the Rebels fire upon them, but the harassment does not seriously impede the project. The new floating bridge is completed by afternoon and the army initiates pursuit.

Several miles outside Port Gibson, while the Union moves along Raymond Road, it discovers a conspicuous and unusual supply of Confederate provisions, two huge piles of bacon,

weighing in at about 50,000 pounds, which are enthusiastically confiscated. Meanwhile, the advance continues to bridge that spans Pierre Bayou at the upper causeway. Confederate efforts to destroy it had failed, due in great part because of its size and composition (it is an iron suspension bridge) in addition to the lack of time. After some superficial repairs, the Union crosses and accelerates the pace of the chase.

Suddenly, as it encroaches a small town (known at the time as Willow Springs), the vanguard is met with a flurry of volleys from Confederate artillery. The unexpected resistance quickly jolts the column into a battle ready force. Almost immediately, a contingent charges toward the position, but despite the quick action, it had not been quick enough to seize the artillery.

In a flash, the Confederates vanish. Using a little additional caution, the advance resumes and the column reaches the Big Black River just as the sun begins to slip away. The Rebels, in the meantime, had prepared a welcoming committee; however, the Union is not caught by surprise and reacts with great speed. The Rebels are driven from their positions and forced to cross to the opposite bank. In an effort to impede Union pursuit, the Confederates attempt to destroy a pontoon bridge, but they are foiled immediately as Union sharpshooters provide a steady blanket of protective and pernicious fire.

While standing at the river, the Union remains only about eighteen miles from Vicksburg and about seven miles beyond Grand Gulf. Meanwhile, the Confederates abandon Grand Gulf, and prior to their departure, they detonate the magazine. Grand Gulf, due to the constant bombardment by Admiral David D. Porter's fleet, combined with General Grant's flanking movement, had become untenable. General Grant, escorted by only 15 troops, pushes to Grand Gulf,

where he re-establishes headquarters and orders the supply depot at Bruinsburg transferred in.

The Union suffers 130 dead and 718 wounded. Confederates suffer 1,150 killed or wounded and 500 missing. Confederate Brigadier General Edward D. Tracy arrives to assist with five Alabama Regiments; however, he is killed while leading his brigade when struck in the chest. He dies instantly. The Union attackers, although temporarily repulsed by the Rebels, receive reinforcements and handily rout the Confederates by sunset. The Rebels withdraw to Vicksburg. The Union will occupy Grand Gulf on the following day, then proceed eight miles to North Fork, closing the ring on the beleaguered city of Vicksburg.

Union Surgeon James L. Kiernan is badly wounded at this battle and considered dead. He is captured by the Confederates but successfully escapes through the swamp. Kiernan is appointed brigadier general in August 1863, but he resigns because of ill health the following February. After the war, General Kiernan is appointed to a consular post at Chinkiang, China, but yet again his health fails, compelling him to return to the United States. He resumes his former medical practice. He dies during November 1868 at the age of 32 years.

May 1–4 THE BATTLE OF CHANCELLORSVILLE General Joseph Hooker is preparing to launch an attack against the Confederates under General Robert E. Lee; however at about 1100, General Lee's forces are also set in motion. General Thomas J. "Stonewall" Jackson's force starts moving toward Chancellorsville, Virginia, by advancing on the left along Plank Road, while on the right, General McLaws' force advances along the turnpike heading for Chancellorsville. They are the same routes that the Union is preparing to use to strike Lee, insuring a staggering confrontation. On the Confed-

Left: Chancellorsville on 1 May 1863 (*Harper's Pictoral History of the Civil War*, 1896). *Right:* Confederate prisoners after the Battle of Chancellorsville (Mottelay, *The Soldier in Our Civil War*, 1886).

Left: **Forces massing near Chancellorsville on May 1, 1863.** *Right:* **Troops at Chancellorsville on May 2, 1863** (*Harper's Pictoral History of the Civil War*, 1896).

erate side, in General Lafayette McLaws' sector, cavalry rides at the point. Some Union troops, the divisions of Griffin and Humphreys, march along the Military Road on the left and head toward Banks' Ford without encountering any resistance, but things turn out differently when Slocum's corps, trailed by Howard's corps, advances along Plank Road, in coordination with the divisions of Sykes and Hancock, which are advancing along the turnpike.

In the meantime, contingents of Alfred Pleasonton's Cavalry encounter and engage Confederate units of McLaw's 11th Virginia Cavalry at a point about one mile beyond Chancellorsville. Initially, the Yankees drive the Rebel cavalry back; however, it is only temporary, as reinforcements attached to Robert Emmett Rodes' force and Richard H. Anderson's division rush forward and promptly drive Sykes's troops back to the positions of Hancock's division. Soon after, Hancock's command jumps over the retiring force and re-establishes control of the situation. They secure some high ground, giving the Union dominating positions upon a ridge just outside Chancellorsville.

All the while, General Slocum's troops are heavily involved on the Plank Road against General Thomas J. "Stonewall" Jackson. Slocum intends to shove Jackson back to permit his own force to link with General Sykes to galvanize their forces. However, instead, Jackson initiates a flanking movement that imperils the forces of both Slocum and Sykes. Jackson increases the pressure and closes to annihilate the two columns before they can be extricated by reinforcements, but Hooker is able to call a retreat in time to forestall disaster. The entire line pulls

back toward Chancellorsville with the Confederates hot on their heels. Nonetheless, the retreat is orderly and without excessive casualties. After dark the Union force, having been pushed back to its original positions, is compelled to take the defense and spends the night reinforcing the roads leading to Chancellorsville.

By morning on the 2nd, Union General Meade's forces guard the left, and this line extends from Scott's Dam along the Rappahannock to Elley's Ford Road. General Hancock's division holds the eastward terrain along the turnpike, and in reserve, the forces of Generals French and Berry are deployed near the Chancellorsville roads intersection. Meanwhile, the 3rd Division under Sickles and Slocum's 12th Corps are posted slightly south of Fairview to retain the security of the center. To the rear, Howard's corps defends the Union Army's right flank at the Orange Plank Road, and Reynolds' corps, bolstered by Humphrey's division, deploys upon the roads that stretch from the United States Ford to the Old Mine and the Elley's Ford roads.

The Confederates hold sturdy positions that stretch from the Old Mine Road to the Catherine Furness; the former guarded by Williams Carter Wickham's cavalry and Owens' cavalry. At the latter place, Fitzhugh Lee's cavalry and contingents of Stuart's cavalry hold the line. The territory extending between the previously mentioned forces holds the troops under Generals Richard H. Anderson and McLaws, stretching from the Chancellorsville Plank Road to and beyond the Old Turnpike Road, while the force of General Wilcox is deployed near Banks' Ford.

On 2 May, General Thomas Jackson's divisions jump off early and head toward the positions of Union General Birney in the vicinity of Catherine Furnace. His route is protected by cavalry of Fitzhugh Lee's unit, but General Stuart leads the contingent. The Union is able to observe the movement of Jackson's divisions, but inadvertently, it assumes that the Rebels are retiring to Richmond rather than advancing to attack. The road presents a bit of confusion; it takes a severe turn that points toward the Confederate capital. Reacting to the movement, General Sickles receives orders to launch an assault. At about 1500, his troops drill into the rear of Jackson's columns and hammer the line, dazing the troops and permitting Sickles' force to inflict casualties and capture large numbers of Rebels. With the quickly gained success, Sickles calls for more support to finish the job.

Two brigades, of Howard's and Slocum's corps arrive, as does a contingent of Pleasonton's cavalry. With these fresh troops, the attack is renewed and the Rebels begin to falter as the pressure begins to demoralize the lines. During this encounter, nearly the entire 23rd Georgia Regiment is scooped up as prisoners, but at about this time, the Confederates bounce back. Reinforcements, including artillery and infantry, which had been drawn from General R.H. Anderson's force, arrive to intercept Sickles and neutralize the Union's success. The new arrivals succeed in compelling Sickles' force, including General Washington Elliott's 3rd Division, to withdraw.

All the while, Confederate General Thomas J. Jackson continues his advance. Some units by this time are across the Orange Plank Road heading north toward the Old Turnpike Road. The force arrives at the turnpike at about 1700, and within an hour, the troops under Generals Rodes, Colston and A.P. Hill are deployed on and around the turnpike, prepared to bolt forward. Once the signal is given, the lines, in unison, sprint forward full throttle and pounce simultaneously upon the rear and flank of General Howard's lines. The crushing impact forces the far right positions held by Charles Devens at the Tally House to collapse under the strength of the overwhelming waves of Confederates. The Rebels had struck so swiftly that there had been no time for the Union to properly form a solid defense.

The onslaught creates a domino effect. Van Gilsa's brigade topples, followed by McLean's force as the division haphazardly falls back to the positions of General Schurz, who is attempting to hold the center. But here, too, the tents fold as the bulk of the force races toward the rear. Only the heroic actions of Schimmelfennig's brigade preserve the honor of the division. It holds untenable positions and stands firmly for some time before being forced to withdraw. The nearby division under Steiwehr also begins to fade into the rear, but one

brigade, Buschbeck's, refuses to budge and holds its positions at Dundall's Tavern against all odds. The overwhelming pressure eventually forces the brigade to fall back; however, its steadfastness remains intact until more Rebel reinforcements arrive and turn both flanks, making it quite necessary to pull back. This potent Rebel attack ignites panic that swiftly passes through many of the Union ranks, and in some cases, the troops are fleeing at top speed right past the recently abandoned headquarters of General Hooker. As the weary day wears on, the situation for the Yankees becomes grim.

By 1900, the XI Corps has lost its spine as it speeds to the rear. In the meantime, General Robert E. Lee is turning up the heat. He has ordered a general assault to be launched as soon as General A.P. Hill's force can be rushed to the front to replace the exhausted troops under Generals Rodes and Colston. In a short while, the Rebels are simultaneously plastering Slocum's corps, which is deployed south at Fairview, and Couch's command at the center. Meade's forces, which are holding to the northeast, are getting whacked by the combined forces of R.H. Anderson and McLaws. Despite the setbacks, General Hooker had some luck; he had earlier re-posted the Eleventh Corps artillery at the Plank Road, and he had brought up additional guns and posted them at Fairview. These decisions buy him some time. As the Confederates press forward, finally, these big guns, confiscated from the Third Corps, halt the Confederate tide.

The Union artillery commences firing and keeps a rapid pace that begins to mow down the approaching Confederates on the right. In concert, Meade's force is holding the attackers that are encroaching his line at bay, and the center, which is the key to whether the line holds, also maintains its discipline and withstands the attack.

Meanwhile, General Hooker had sent urgent requests for two divisions, Berry's and French's, and under the protection of Pleasonton's cavalry, both units arrive to add some muscle to the lines, just prior to the arrival of Jackson's Confederate forces at Fairview. The Yankees open up with a barrage of riveting fire that rakes the ranks of the advancing Confederates, but despite the severe casualties, Jackson's force continues the advance, ignoring the hurricane of fire. Pleasonton's cavalry, merely two regiments, is insufficient to launch a counter-charge against the

huge force. Such a charge would surely be a suicidal mission. Nonetheless, one officer, Major Peter Keenan, surprisingly requests permission to lead the Eighth Pennsylvania Cavalry against what appears to be unending hordes of Confederate troops. Equally startling, the order to attack is given, and to the rousing sounds of incessant cheers, the cavalry darts from the woods and charges directly toward the encroaching waves of attackers.

Confederate fire rings heavily upon the horsemen as they charge. Major Keenan is among the first to fall, slain by the fierce fire. Undaunted, these troops pound against the flanks, still receiving horrific fire that knocks out about fifty percent of the force in about ten minutes. The remaining cavalrymen continue the attack, and although it is of short duration, if measured by blood and guts, and what it accomplishes, these men have exemplified what is known as the ultimate sacrifice for their cause. In the meantime, Hooker is able to redeploy the horse artillery, regroup the remnants of the demoralized Eleventh Corps and reorganize the battered remnants of the forces of Generals Warren, Birney, Barlow, and Whipple.

With Jackson still on the attack and Hooker's forces having regained their discipline, the bloodbath continues, but the Yankees are back in a position from which they can return equally punishing fire. The ongoing fighting takes severe casualties on both sides, but the infusion of the Union artillery brings the advance to a halt. The Confederates now must await the arrival of fresh troops.

During the lull, General Jackson and his staff move out on a reconnaissance mission to gather information on the Union positions. His force had been issued orders that in his absence they were not to fire unless Union cavalry is spotted. Following the mission, Jackson and his entourage are inadvertently misidentified as Union cavalry as they re-approach their own lines. These Confederates unleash a series of volleys that jolt the party and either kill or wound most, but Jackson, although wounded, is able to gallop for the woods.

General A.P. Hill assumes command but becomes wounded and the command is again transferred. General Rodes succeeds temporarily, but he, too, sustains a wound, tossing the command again. It then reverts to General Jeb Stuart. Following these incidents, neither side takes aggressive action due in great part to the darkness that has settled over the area; however, some heated activity occurs at about midnight when troops under Union General Birney launch an attack along Plank Road. Birney's assault succeeds in capturing some Confederate troops and seizing some guns.

Prior to dawn on the 3rd, the opposing armies have completed their respective realignment of their positions. Union Generals Alpheus S. Williams and Hiram G. Berry hold responsibility for the center and far right, General Hancock is anchored along the crossroads (Mott Run and River Road) and the forces of Birney, French and Whipple stand at Fairview and on and around the Elley's Ford Road.

General Thomas "Stonewall" Jackson forces an attack on the right wing at Chancellorsville (Johnson, *Campfire and Battlefield: History of the Conflicts and Campaigns*, 1894).

In addition, the forces of Generals Howard and Meade are posted along the route that heads for Scotts Dam, while Reynolds' corps holds in the vicinity of Elley's (Ely's) Ford Road, beyond United States Ford. The Union has also concentrated artillery near the intersection, which has the road leading to Scotts Dam crossing Elley's Ford Road.

The Confederate forces of Colston, Hill and Rodes extend across the Plank Road. Hill's forces, including McGowan's South Carolina brigade, posted on the far left, stare down those of Berry and Williams (Union right and center), and those deployed on his right face off with Union General John Geary's force, which holds positions in the rear of Hazel Grove. Union artillery, unaware of the strategic location of Hazel Grove, had abandoned it on the previous night, giving the Confederates easy access. From the heights they are able to pound the rifle pits of the 125th Pennsylvania Regiment. The positions become untenable and Confederate artillery dominates. The Confederate troops under Generals R.H. Anderson and McLaws form their columns in positions that stretch between Catherine Furnace to a point near the Old Mine Road.

During the early morning hours of the 3rd, the Confederates again initiate the action. General Jeb Stuart orders an assault that jumps off with a blaze of fury, and in quick time, he secures a strategic ridge where Howard's XI Corps had been driven off the previous day. The Rebels speed artillery to the position and prepare to lay a massive thunderclap upon the Union lines of General Berry on the right and center and against General French's lines at Fairview. In conjunction with the gargantuan barrage, the Confederate infantry launches lightning-speed assaults that ignite ferocious fighting that gives no quarter to either side.

General Berry is mortally wounded while driving forward to stabilize the lines after Jackson plows through General Howard's XI Corps. Command of Berry's division (III Corps) is assumed by General Joseph W. Revere; however, rather than intercepting the charging Confederates, he chooses to withdraw to the rear to reform before attacking. During this furious encounter, Confederate General Paxton is killed by a Minié ball while at the head of his troops. Nevertheless, following the bloodbath, the Confederates gain the high ground and the Union guns there, giving the Rebels further advantage as they swivel the artillery pieces and hurriedly open fire on the Union with its own weapons. The bombardment compels the Union to withdraw further to their third line of defense, but the energized Confederates maintain full speed while they advance.

Meanwhile, Union reinforcements under General Meade arrive to neutralize the progress of the assault, forcing the Rebels to suspend their motion and fall back. All the while, Confederate Generals McLaws and R.H. Anderson continue to slam against the forces of Generals Hancock and Slocum, igniting more grueling slug-fests that chill spines on both sides. The desperate fight for survival hangs on a thread,

as neither side can gain the advantage, while both sides are butchering the other. And then suddenly more reinforcements arrive to bolster the Rebels on Anderson's left. Soon artillery is deployed and the stakes are raised. Under this new umbrella of cover fire, the Rebels reinitiate a charge. They bolt from their positions and overwhelm the defenders, inflicting casualties so heavy that ground must be surrendered. This key advance links the forces of R.H. Anderson with the far right positions of Stuart, spelling out more gloom for Hooker's command.

Once the link-up is in place, the entire Confederate line bursts forward and crashes through the center bastion of the Union lines, collapsing it at nearly every point. Only the forces of Geary and Hancock succeed in withstanding the pressure. The Rebels, having already punctured the right of the Union lines and pushed it back to Chancellorsville and Fairview, now press the forces in the center. General Hooker's calls for reinforcements have remained unanswered, and to add more complications, an irreverent Rebel cannon shot strikes the Chancellorsville House and knocks out one of the pillars. Hooker is injured by the falling timber and he is taken from the field. The command falls to General Darius Couch, but circumstances at this point have become especially perplexing, and the ongoing confusion makes it impossible for the moment to get any support.

In the meantime, the Confederates exhibit no empathy for the struggling Yankees, rather they increase the momentum and hammer the remaining forces of Hancock and Geary, who continue to forestall disaster despite their untenable positions. Geary's 2nd Division, XII Corps, remains steadfast, but eventually, both Hancock and Geary are also forced to fall back in order to attempt yet one more desperate line of defense; the point will be the Chancellorsville crossroads. All the while, the Confederates rack up more progress, and at an alarming rate, their concentrated fire eliminates many more Union defenders. By 1000, the Union is completely pushed out of Chancellorsville and on the brink of extinction.

Meanwhile, at Fredericksburg, General John Sedgwick receives orders to launch an offensive to gain the heights and the town, then speed to Chancellorsville in time to reinforce Hooker by dawn on the following day, Sunday, the 4th of May. With the orders in hand at 2300, Sedgwick orders his force to attack.

Fredericksburg is secured in the early morning hours, then General Gibbon's division moves from Falmouth and joins Sedgwick at Fredericksburg. With the chilling reminder of what had happened to the troops under Burnside in December 1862 at the heights in the rear of the town, Sedgwick is determined to not repeat history. With sheer determination, the attack is mounted against both the infamous "stone wall" and the equally obstinate Marye's Heights, steadfastly defended by General Early's troops, including the 21st North Carolina Regiment.

Initially, Rebel forces under Generals Barksdale and Harry T. Hays had forestalled the Yan-

kees, but this dogged attack that costs about 1,000 troops and culminates with gruesome hand-to-hand fighting for control of the crest terminates with the Yankees dominating the hill. Confederate reinforcements under Wilcox had been en route to aid Early, but they are unable to arrive in time. The battle had been costly to both sides, but essentially, the blue gains the advantage over the gray. General Early is compelled to surrender the terrain and retire southward, leaving the Plank Road to the Yankees, while his force moves out along the Telegraph Road. Immediately following the conquest of area, Sedgwick speeds toward Chancellorsville.

Back at Chancellorsville, the Confederates had concluded that an attack against the newly formed Union positions would prove too costly. The V-shaped line had by necessity been created subsequent to the main body being pushed back. It has been redrawn with the right nudging against the Rapidan River and the left leaning upon the Rappahannock River, two formidable natural obstacles, while the point stands at Bullock's, seemingly creating an insurmountable position defended by the fresh forces of Generals Meade and Reynolds, both of whom had not been pressed into action earlier, despite being desperately needed.

While pondering the plan of attack against the Union, General Lee is informed of the news regarding Early's setback at Fredericksburg at the hands of Union General Sedgwick's VI Corps. Lee reacts sharply and dispatches General McLaws and four brigades to intercept Sedgwick. Without delay, McLaws advances and establishes positions at Salem Church, about midway between Fredericksburg and Chancellorsville. The Confederates deploy artillery in the high ground while the ground forces spread out and wait to spring the trap. Soon after, a division under General William Brooks, the vanguard of the Union column, approaches the In the meantime, Confederate General Wilcox's brigade, which had not been able to assist Early, has arrived at Salem Church to add more support to McLaws' force.

Suddenly the Confederates commence firing, but the whirlwind does not deter the troops under Brooks, who continue to advance. The strategic hill holding the guns is secured by Bartlett's brigade and by now, the trailing division of General Newton is on scene and battling to knock out the opposition. The contest for the heights had been victorious for the Yankees, but it had also been extremely costly. Sedgwick is still able to hold firmly and resist a series of bold attacks by McLaws, but he is unable to withstand the pressure following the arrival of more reinforcements that strengthen both Generals Wilcox and Paul Semmes. This development leaves no good options for Sedgwick. He orders a pull-back.

Meanwhile, the Rebels maintain the attack and press the Yankees to retire nearly to their line of reserves. But, Sedgwick, having had few options at his former line, is still holding one trump card, the artillery under Colonel Tompkins. In a flash, as the situation is turning more grim, Tompkins' artillery unleashes a furious barrage that finally halts the impetuous charge, stopping the Confederates in their tracks. The thunderous sounds of the guns then become silent at about the same time as the sun slips behind the horizon, permitting both sides to gain some rest and tend their wounded.

During the night of the 3rd–4th, both sides modify their positions. The opposing commanders, Lee and Hooker, each take measures to ensure that they gain the advantage on the following day. Prior to dawn, reinforcements under Union General J.T. Owens depart Scott's Dam to bolster Sedgwick. Lee dispatches the remaining troops in R.H. Anderson's division to speed to the support of McLaws. Consequently, Lee has only the forces of Jackson's original command to restrain Hooker, but he has concluded that he must eliminate Sedgwick before assaulting Hooker. Hooker has concluded that a defensive posture is his only alternative. Following the complicated maneuvers, the stage is set on the following day for yet another massive conflagration between Sedgwick and McLaws.

Confederate General R.H. Anderson's three brigades arrive in the vicinity of Salem Heights at about noon on Sunday, the 4th, and find themselves on Sedgwick's left. Meanwhile, General Jubal Early works to coordinate the actions of his force and the new arrivals. Early had recaptured the heights at Fredericksburg during the firestorm of the previous night, and in the process, he had also compelled General Gibbon to move across the river. Howes' division had not been dislodged from its positions, which control the ground slightly beyond Marye's Hill and extending from there to Taylor's Hill. This day, the Confederates again attempt to nudge the force out, but effective artillery prevents this from occurring.

The main contest redevelops at 1800. The Rebels strike against the divisions of Newton and Brooks. Initially, the Yankees are able to withstand the incessant assaults, but eventually Sedgwick is compelled to retire from the line behind Salem Church. He pulls back to Banks Ford under a pitch black sky, so deep that the Confederates are unable to pursue. From Banks Ford, Sedgwick crosses the Rappahannock without incident and his force completes the operation prior to dawn on the following day, Monday, May 5.

At Chancellorsville, General Lee prepares to deliver the final blow against General Hooker. An attack is scheduled for the Tuesday, 6 May. His plans are foiled due to the unexpected actions of General Hooker, known by many as "Fighting Joe." During the night of May 5th–6th, following a meeting with his commanders, a decision is reached to retreat across the Rappahannock River. The withdrawal, undertaken during a terrible storm and an extremely moonless night, is completed without detection by the Confederates, but it is not remembered as a meritorious moment in the history of the Army of the Potomac. Hooker is not able to bring out his dead and wounded, nor is he able to extricate fourteen pieces of artillery, huge stacks of arms and a large supply of ammunition. Nevertheless, through the protection of

General Meade's corps, it is a disciplined withdrawal. Within three days, Hooker re-establishes his headquarters at Falmouth, and several days afterward, Stoneman's cavalry, which had been operating between Chancellorsville and Richmond, rejoins the command. The Union's 116th Pennsylvania Infantry had held the Confederates at bay while the army retreated.

Confederate General Stonewall Jackson is mortally wounded by his own men while returning to his lines after a night reconnaissance mission. Jackson is moved by ambulance on May 4 to Chandler's Plantation at Guinea Station, where he dies from pneumonia on the 10th. Stonewall Jackson's philosophy of war had been: "Always mystify, mislead and surprise the enemy if possible; and when you strike and overcome him, never give up the pursuit as long as your men have strength to follow; for an army routed, if hotly pursued, becomes panic stricken and can then be destroyed by half their number." His cousin, Colonel William Lowther "Mudwall" Jackson, who enlisted in the army as a private and rose to become colonel of the 31st Virginia Infantry, had served on Jackson's staff until just recently. "Mudwall" Jackson now commands the 19th Virginia Cavalry, which he formed. His regiment will participate with the Army of Northern Virginia (General Albert Gallatin Jenkins' command).

The Union suffers 1,512 dead, 9,518 wounded and 5,000 missing. Among the Union units, the heaviest casualties had been sustained by the corps of Generals Sickles (Third) and Sedgwick (Sixth). The Confederates sustain 1,581 dead, 8,700 wounded and 2,000 missing. Union Major General Hiram Gregory Berry is killed. Union Brigadier General Amiel Weeks Whipple (West Point, 1841), appointed major general this day, is struck with a fatal shot. He dies on the 7th. At the time he was shot, General Whipple was atop his horse authorizing the elimination of a Confederate sharpshooter who had his sights on nearby officers; however, the sharpshooter strikes before Whipple completes the order. Generals Charles Devens, Daniel E. Sickles and Gershom Mott are wounded. General Joseph B. Carr assumes temporary command of General Berry's division. Also, Colonel John Ramsay, 8th New Jersey Regiment, is wounded, but he recuperates in time to participate at Gettysburg. Colonel (later brigadier general) Patrick Henry Jones (154th New York) is captured and not exchanged until the following October.

On the Confederate side, Brigadier General Elisha Paxton is killed and General Ambrose P. Hill is wounded. Confederate Colonel Cullen A. Battle is not on the field with his regiment, the 3rd Alabama, as he has fallen from his horse; however, he and his regiment will reform as a portion of Stephen Ramseur's brigade. Colonel (later General) William Ruffin Cox, 2nd North Carolina Infantry (Ramseur's brigade), sustains three separate wounds during the fighting, but he declines to leave the field until he is totally drained and carried away. Cox remains incapacitated from these wounds until after the Confederate Pennsylvania Campaign (June–July

1863), but he doesn't again see field duty until the contests at the Wilderness and in Spotsylvania during spring of 1864. Colonel Nelson A. Miles displays admirable service in the field, with heroism above and beyond the call of duty. He becomes a recipient of the Medal of Honor; however, he does not receive it until 23 July 1892.

Lt. Colonel William H. Fitzhugh Payne, 2nd North Carolina Cavalry, and Brigadier General Micah Jenkins participate in this action for the Confederacy. Subsequent to the battle at Chancellorsville, Payne moves with General Jeb Stuart into Pennsylvania, but he is captured and imprisoned at Johnson Island. One Confederate General, John Robert Jones, removes himself from the field, describing his ailment as a problem with one of his legs. He will be relieved and cut from the rolls of the Confederate Army. Jones' brigade, a contingent of General Trimble's division, 2nd Corps, will be transferred to Brigadier General John Marshall Jones' (no relative) command. The divisions which suffer the highest casualties on the Confederate side are those of Generals A.P. Hill and R.E. Rodes. Rodes' actions at this battle propel him to a promotion as major general. Brigadier General Stephen D. Ramseur is wounded in the leg and his brigade (North Carolina Regiments) sustains a casualty rate of about 50 percent.

General Samuel McGowan (A.P. Hill's division) is wounded, and command of his brigade moves to Colonel Abner M. Perrin, 14th South Carolina Regiment. Confederate Brigadier General Robert F. Hoke sustains a serious wound at Marye's Heights. Brigadier General Edward A. Perry leads his Florida brigade during this action; he sustains no wounds, but subsequent to the battle, he is struck by a bad case of typhoid fever, which apparently keeps him from the field throughout the winter of 1863–64. Confederate Brigadier General Robert Emmett Rodes, for his actions at this battle, is promoted to major general.

May 2 (Saturday) In Alabama, the 51st and 73rd Indiana Regiments, the 80th Illinois Volunteers, supplemented by the 3rd Ohio Mounted Infantry and the 1st Alabama Cavalry (Colonel A.D. Streight's command), skirmish Confederates led by General Nathan Bedford Forrest at Blount's Farm. The Union sustains 12 killed and 69 wounded. Confederate casualty figures are unavailable.

In Louisiana, Colonel Benjamin Grierson's Union cavalry completes his raids into southern territory and arrives in Baton Rouge at about 1600, terminating an 800-mile march. The sixteen-day mission, in addition to destroying huge amounts of Confederate supplies and rail equipment, has also gained about 1,000 captured Confederates. Colonel Grierson's force sustains a total loss of twenty-seven men and twenty-five horses. This expedition has helped to further devastate Southern railroads and has captured enormous amounts of war supplies.

In Mississippi, Port Gibson (Thompson's Hill) is occupied by the Union, subsequent to its

Left: General Grierson's cavalry enters Baton Rouge (*Harper's Pictoral History of the Civil War,* 1896). *Right:* Confederates transporting cattle at Vicksburg (*Harper's Pictoral History of the Civil War,* 1896).

abandonment by the Confederates, who have moved across Bayou Pierre heading for Vicksburg. Union troops pursue, but the Rebels burn the bridges that span both forks of the bayou. The Union halts at Hawkinson's Ferry to await supplies and Sherman's Corps (see also, **May 1–2** BATTLE OF PORT GIBSON).

In Virginia, Union artillery commanded by General George W. Getty, supported by a gunboat, exchanges blows with Confederate artillery at the Nansemond River. The Union sustains about 41 killed and wounded. The Confederate casualty figures are unavailable. Also, Union General Charles Devens is wounded this day at Chancellorsville. General Nathaniel C. McLean assumes command of the battered command, but he fails to regroup the disorganized troops until they arrive at General Hooker's headquarters at the Chancellor house (see also, **May 1–4** BATTLE OF CHANCELLORSVILLE). Also, General Grant orders General Joseph B. Carr to move to General Benjamin Butler's headquarters (Army of the James). He receives command of a division of Negro troops. At the termination of the war he receives the rank of brevet major general.

In Confederate general officer activity, Colonel Douglas Hancock Cooper (1st Choctaw and Chickasaw Mounted Rifles) is promoted to brigadier general. General Cooper, who participated at Elkhorn Tavern (Pea Ridge) and at Newtonia, Missouri, later participates under General Sterling Price during his second invasion of Missouri. After the war, General Cooper represents the Chickasaw and Choctaw tribes and on their behalf prosecutes claims against the U.S. Government.

In Naval activity, the USS *Cricket* exchanges fire with a Confederate battery in the vicinity of Argyle Landing.

May 3 (Sunday) In Georgia, at Rome, Union Colonel Abel Streight surrenders his entire force of more than 1,600 troops to General Nathan Bedford Forrest (see also, **April 29–May 3** BATTLE OF DAY'S GAP [SAND MOUNTAIN] AND SURRENDER AT ROME). The citizens and Home Guards provide Forrest with a triumphant welcome when he enters the town. The people plan a huge celebration for 6 May.

In Mississippi, a contingent of the 7th Division, 17th Corps, skirmishes with Confederates at Haukinson's Ferry in Forty Mills. General Grant informs General Halleck by letter of the details regarding the operation at Port Gibson:

> We landed at Bruinsburg April 30th, moved immediately on Port Gibson, met the enemy, 11,000 strong, four miles south of Port Gibson, at two o'clock a.m., on the 1st inst., and engaged him all day, entirely routing him, with the loss of many killed, and about 500 prisoners, besides the wounded. Our loss is about 100 killed and 500 wounded. The enemy retreated towards Vicksburg, destroying the bridges over the two forks of the Bayou Pierre. These were rebuilt, and the pursuit has continued until the present time. Besides the heavy artillery at the place, four field-pieces were captured and some stores, and the enemy were driven to destroy many more. The country is the most broken and difficult to operate in I ever saw. Our victory has been most complete, and the enemy is thoroughly demoralized.

Governor Yates of Illinois had been visiting with General Grant at the time of the move to seize port Gibson. He sends word to the state capital: "We gained a glorious victory at Port Gibson, on the 1st instant. The enemy are in full retreat. Our forces are in close pursuit. The Illinois troops, as usual, behaved with the greatest gallantry." (See also, **May 1–2** BATTLE OF PORT GIBSON.)

After dark, the Union sends two barges laden with supplies (commissary and hospital stores) down river to pass the Vicksburg batteries; however, Confederate fire scores a fortuitous hit that ignites bales of cotton and hay. Consequently, the fires spread and the barges are destroyed. The respective crews (twenty men) and four passengers, each a newspaper correspondent, are left with no options. They surrender.

In other activity, General Banks informs Grant that his force of 15,000 men will not reach Port Hudson until the 10th. Grant modifies his plan to assault Port Hudson jointly with Generals Banks and McClernand by planning an attack from the rear of Vicksburg. In the Western Theater, Confederates holding at Grand Gulf, Mississippi, are forced to evacuate or face Grant's advance. Troops attached to Admiral Porter's fleet occupy the city.

In Missouri, a Union force initiates a scouting mission that operates in Bates and Casa Counties through the 11th.

In Virginia, Union Major General John Sedgwick's troops capture Marye's Heights above Fredericksburg as they attempt to reach Hooker at Chancellorsville. Lee, aware of the capture, rushes reinforcements in an attempt to regain the heights. In the fighting around Chancellorsville, Lee's command has initiated an attack against the Federals under Sedgwick in the vicinity of Salem Heights, to check further Union gains. During this tenacious skirmish, Captain Lewis A. Grant (later brigadier general) exhibits enormous gallantry against the enemy, a feat which earns him the Medal of Honor, which he will receive in thirty years (May 11, 1893).

During the fighting at Chancellorsville, Rebels under General Pender succeed in capturing nearly the entire staff of General William Hays (West Point, 1840), including the general himself, during the confusing morning of May 3. In addition, Union Lieutenant Edmund Kirby, a cousin of Confederate General Edmund Kirby Smith, is mortally wounded when a shell tears into his thigh. General Kirby dies on the day he is commissioned brigadier general, 28 May. General Kirby is he grandson of Major General Jacob Brown (commander in chief, U.S. Army, 1815–1828). Union Brigadier General Alfred Sully (West Point, 1841) participates in this battle and subsequently is ordered back to Indian Territory, where he achieved major accomplishments before the Civil War. Sully serves against the Sioux in the Dakotas and Minnesota.

A contingent of the 1st West Virginia Cavalry and the 5th New York Cavalry, led by Colonel De Forest, skirmishes with Confederate guerrillas under John S. Mosby at Warrenton Junction. The Union sustains one killed and 16 wounded. The Confederates lose 15 wounded and 23 captured.

In Union general officer activity, Brigadier General Thomas Henry Walton Wessells, earlier slightly wounded at Seven Pines and afterward transferred to North Carolina, is appointed commander of the District of the Albemarle.

May 4 (Monday)   In Ohio, in response to remarks made during the previous Congress by Clement L. Vallandigham, in which he attacked the Lincoln administration, renounced the war, and disparaged General Burnside, is on this day arrested. Vallandigham is seized at his home in Dayton and transported to Cincinnati. On 6 May, Vallandigham is tried by court-martial and convicted of aiding the enemy. Per Burnside's direction, he is to be incarcerated at Fort Warren at Boston. However, President Lincoln intervenes and instead, Vallandigham is turned over to the Confederates. Afterward he boards a blockade runner and succeeds in making his way to Canada. By the end of this month, Burnside, due to this incident, offers his resignation to the president on the 29th.

In Virginia, General Hooker orders his Union Army to withdraw across the Rappahannock River rather than initiate another assault on Confederate positions at Chancellorsville. The 6th Maine Infantry escapes capture at Brook's Ford. Lt. Charles Clark leads his men to safety. Union and Confederate troops also skirmish at Salem Heights. The 26th New Jersey Infantry and the Vermont brigade participate. Colonel Lewis Addison Grant leads a charge against the Confederate positions and his Vermonters capture three regimental flags. Colonel Grant becomes a recipient of the Medal of Honor for his actions during the struggle at Salem Heights; however, he does not receive it until thirty years after the battle. Meanwhile, he is promoted to brigadier general on 27 April 1864, and he receives the brevet of major general from the date of the battle. In other action, the siege at Suffolk ends. The Confederates are ordered to repair to Richmond. Meanwhile, the 12th Illinois Cavalry skirmishes with Confederates at Tunstall Station. The 5th New York Cavalry clashes with Confederates at Shannon Hill.

In Naval activity, the USS *Albatross* commences firing on Confederate Fort De Russy (Louisiana), Gordon's Landing on the Red River, but does not accomplish much except to sustain damage from the Confederate guns. Also, at the time of the attack, the CSS *Grand Duke* and the *Mary T.* are in the process of loading armaments. Afterward, the *Grand Duke* moves to Shreveport, Louisiana. The *Grand Duke* is destroyed by fire at Shreveport late in the year. The USS *Albatross* continues to patrol, primarily in Mobile Bay, until it goes out of service for repairs during June and remains

out of service until recommissioned in December 1864. It is decommissioned during August 1865 after the war and sold the following month. The USS *Cricket*, while on patrol, exchanges fire with a Confederate shore battery in the vicinity of Greenville, Mississippi.

May 5 (Tuesday)   In Georgia at Rome, the people are preparing a grand celebration in honor of General Bedford Forrest for his recent capture of the forces of Colonel Abel Streight. At the time, about 1,600 Union prisoners are under guard; however, news arrives during the night that causes the celebration to be cancelled. Forrest is informed that a new Union force is en route from Tuscumbia to Talladega, Alabama. Forrest orders his men to saddle their horses and soon the column races to Gadsden; however, on 7 May, Forrest is informed that the Union column under General Charles Dodge had not advanced east of Courtland and instead had retired toward Corinth, Mississippi.

In Louisiana, Union troops under Admiral Porter occupy Fort DeRussey on the Red River.

In North Carolina, the 3rd New York Cavalry captures a Company of Confederates at Pettie's Mills.

In Virginia, Lee states in a letter to Jefferson Davis: "I marched back yesterday [Guiney's] with Genl. [Richard H.] Anderson, and uniting with McLaws and Early in the afternoon, succeeded in driving General John Sedgwick across the river. We have reoccupied Fredericksburg and no enemy remains south of the Rappahannock in its vicinity."

In Kansas, a contingent departs Fort Scott and initiates a scouting mission that moves toward Sherwood, Missouri and operates until the 9th.

In Union general officer activity, General Francis L. Vinton (West Point, 1856) resigns. General Vinton sustains severe wounds at Fredericksburg while commanding a brigade in General Howe's division, which virtually ends his service on the field. Also, Brigadier General Thomas T. Crittenden resigns his commission.

In Naval activity, the USS *Tahoma*, operating off Gadsden's Point, Florida, seizes a schooner, the *Crazy Jane*, which is transporting a cargo of turpentine and cotton. The USS *Argosy* and other gunboats, including the *Champion, Covington, Queen City* and the *Silver Cloud*, initiate an expedition up the Tennessee River on a mission intended to destroy all craft encountered to prevent use by the Rebels. On the 11th, the *Argosy, Covington* and the *Queen City* advance beyond Cerro Gordo to Eastport, Tennessee; however, the *Queen City* and the *Champion* remain at Cerro Gordo. General Rosecrans, aware of the progress, considers Eastport as a regrouping point where naval guns can support his army in the event Confederate pressure forces him to withdraw. At this time the Union is anticipating a Confederate full-scale attack. Several days later, Confederate General Earl Van Dorn is killed and the attack does not commence.

May 6 (Wednesday)   In Mississippi, Sherman's troops reach Grand Gulf, and on the following day they move towards Vicksburg. Elements of the 10th Missouri Cavalry and the 7th Kansas Cavalry, commanded by Colonel Florence M. Cornyn, skirmish with Confederates under General Ruggles at Tupelo. The Union captures about 90 Confederates.

In Virginia, Lee plans to attack Hooker at Fredericksburg, but Hooker has withdrawn to safer positions. His force abandons Fredericksburg and redeploys on the north bank of the Rappahannock River. Confederate General Lee is still pressing for reinforcements from Longstreet to avoid being forced to evacuate. Lee requests cavalry to meet the threat of Union General George Stoneman (West Point, 1846), who has been reported in the vicinity of the James River.

In Naval activity, forces under Admiral David D. Porter occupy Alexandria, Mississippi. The CSS *Florida*, under Commander J.N. Naffitt, intercepts the merchant ship *Clarence* (also known as *Couquet*), which is transporting a cargo of coffee and is en route from Brazil to Baltimore. Initially, the Confederates intend to destroy the *Clarence*; however, they develop a plan to sail the ship into Hampton Roads under the guise of a merchant ship so they can sneak into the harbor and destroy merchant vessels moored there. The scheme also includes an attempt to seize a Union gunboat. The 20-man prize crew is commanded by Lt. C. W. Read. After boarding, the *Clarence* is armed with one gun.

In Union general officer activity, General Edward Ferrero's commission as brigadier general, having expired during the previous March, is reappointed this day. He becomes junior in rank to General R.B. Potter. General Potter, a major under Ferrero in the 51st New York Regiment, becomes Ferrero's division commander. General Ferrero participates in the Vicksburg campaign and afterward at Knoxville, Tennessee, prior to returning to the IX Corps in Virginia.

In Confederate general officer activity, Brigadier General William G.M. Davis resigns his commission. Afterward, he divides his residence between Wilmington, North Carolina, and Richmond, Virginia, while he switches careers and begins to operate a fleet of blockade runners. After the war he moves to Washington, D.C., and resumes his law practice. He dies in Alexandria, Virginia, during March 1898.

In Arkansas, a Union contingent initiates a scouting mission that operates through the 15th in the terrain between the White River and the Saint Francis River.

In the Indian Territory, a Union contingent departs the Creek Agency and initiates a scouting mission that moves to Jasper County, Missouri, and continues through the 19th. Skirmishes occur at Martin's House, Centre Creek and in the vicinity of Sherwood, which is destroyed.

May 7 (Thursday)   In Alabama, at Gadsden, General Forrest, while preparing to move against a Union column, is informed that the emergency has ended and that the column is retiring to Corinth (see also, May 5 [Tuesday] In Georgia). Forrest remains in Gadsden for the night at the home of R.B. Kyle. Kyle is surprised by his guest, because all the conversation he had heard about Forrest surrounded his sole focus on the war, but while visiting, Forrest spends most of his time with Kyle's young son of about two years old. Forrest keeps him on his lap and carries him around during the evening. On the following day, when Forrest departs en route to Guntersville, the boy is up in the saddle in front of Forrest, and he rides out of town for about three miles. Forrest then gives the boy a little kiss as he hands him back to his father and says: "My God, Kyle, this is worth living for!" Forrest receives orders to move to Athens, Alabama. Arriving at General Bragg's headquarters, Forrest is assigned command of the cavalry on the left wing of Bragg's army in place of General Van Dorn, who had been killed on this day in Tennessee. Forrest arrives at Spring Hill on 16 May.

In Virginia, Confederate cavalry, including Stuart's and Fitzhugh Lee's, move to thwart General George Stoneman on the Rappahannock. A Union reconnaissance force departs West Point for White House.

In Tennessee, Confederate Major General Earl Van Dorn is shot and killed at his headquarters in Spring Hill, Tennessee, by Dr. George Peters of Maury County, who believes the general to be having an affair with his wife.

In Union general officer activity, Colonel James Henry Van Alen, aide-de-camp to General Joseph Hooker, is promoted to brigadier general. He is assigned to command at Acquia Creek, Virginia, with his responsibility including the Richmond, Fredericksburg and Potomac Railroad in his sector; however, he resigns his commission in July.

May 8 (Friday)   In Mississippi, General Sherman's Corps arrives at Hawkinson's Ferry. Sherman's force has, for the past two days, pounded the Rebel batteries at Haines Bluff. Union gunboats, including the USS *Petrel*, and mortar schooners bombard Confederate batteries at Port Hudson.

In Naval activity, the CSS *Florida* arrives at Pernambuco, Brazil, as it continues to cruise and seize merchant ships. A Union squadron has been in pursuit since January, but without success. From here the *Florida* resumes its cruise, and on 16 July, it arrives at St. George's in Bermuda. In other activity, the blockade runner *Cherokee* (formerly *Thistle*), built in Renfrew, Scotland, in 1859, is seized by the USS *Canandaigua* off Charleston after its runs aground. The *Cherokee*, afterward, is acquired by the U.S. Navy and commissioned the USS *Cherokee* during April 1864. Before being officially acquired, the *Cherokee* is utilized during July to assist in the search for the CSS *Tacony*,

a Confederate raider. Subsequent to being commissioned, the *Cherokee* is assigned blockade duty off North Carolina's coast.

May 9 (Saturday)   In Louisiana, Union troops under General Nathaniel Banks arrive safely in Alexandria, culminating their quick-raids against the Confederates.

In Tennessee, the 2nd Indiana Cavalry, led by General Edward Moody McCook, while on a scouting mission in the vicinity of Stones River, captures eight Confederates.

In Missouri, Union and Confederate contingents skirmish in Stone County.

In Virginia, detachments of General Stoneman's cavalry begin to arrive at Falmouth to rejoin the main body of the Army of the Potomac under General Hooker. Other units of the cavalry, under Colonel Kilpatrick and Davis, are now at Gloucester Point. The cavalry under General George Stoneman numbers about 10,000. It was supposed to play a major part in the recent campaign with General Hooker, but it had not. Stoneman had been instead dispatched to destroy communications of the Confederates at several locations, but bad weather hindered the operation. Nevertheless, his missions included Rapidan Station, Louisa Court House, White House, Gordonsville and Hanover Junction; these raids damage or destroy much of the Virginia Central Railway, several canal bridges and part of the stone aqueduct that crosses the Rivanna River at Columbia. Two units, the 12th Illinois (Colonel Hasbrook Davis) and the 2nd New York (Judson Kilpatrick), score the most memorable raids. Davis seizes a train laden with Confederate troops and later paroles them. His unit also destroys much of the rails at Ashland, slightly north of Richmond, and it also severely damages the rails running into Hanover Court House. Kilpatrick's raids take him within two miles of the Southern capital and the people in Richmond become quite alarmed, especially when they learn that these insolent Yankees are destroying the Richmond and Fredericksburg Railway. Kilpatrick's unit also devastates the Confederate depots at Hungary Station before returning to Gloucester Point on the May 7.

In Confederate general officer activity, Colonel John Wilkins Whitfield, 27th Texas Regiment, is promoted to the rank of brigadier general. Whitfield continues to serve under General Joseph E. Johnston, and subsequently he receives command of a brigade in the Trans-Mississippi Department under General William Hicks Jackson.

May 10 (Sunday)   In Kentucky, a contingent of the 20th Michigan Infantry, led by Major Byron M. Cutcheon, attacks a Confederate-held home at Horseshoe Bend.

In Louisiana, elements of the 14th and 24th Maine Regiments, the 177th New York Volunteers, bolstered by the 21st New York Battery, skirmish with Confederates at Civique's Ferry. Casualty figures are not available.

In Virginia, Union Lt. Thomas W. Custer of the 6th Michigan Cavalry receives a Medal of Honor for his courageous actions at Namozine Church, capturing Confederate colors. Custer receives a second Medal of Honor for his actions on May 26, 1865 at Sayler's Creek. Confederate General Thomas "Stonewall" Jackson, mortally wounded on May 3, succumbs this day.

In Union general officer activity, Captain Charles Russell Lowell (3rd U.S. Cavalry, later 6th U.S. Cavalry) is commissioned colonel of the 2nd Massachusetts Cavalry, a regiment he raised.

May 11 (Monday)   In Arkansas, a Union contingent composed of elements of the 5th Kansas Cavalry and the 5th Illinois Cavalry, commanded by Colonel Powell Clayton, skirmishes with Confederates at Mount Vernon. Casualty figures are unavailable. In other activity, a skirmish also erupts at Taylor's Creek (or Crowley's Creek).

In Kentucky, Union troops commanded by Colonel R.T. Jacobs skirmish with Confederates (General John Hunt Morgan's command) at Horse Shoe Bend (Greasy Creek). The fighting lasts for about seven hours. The Union sustains 10 killed, 20 wounded and 40 missing. The Confederates suffer about 100 killed and wounded.

In Mississippi, a contingent of Union Cavalry occupies and devastates Crystal Springs and the rail facilities located there.

May 12 (Tuesday)   In Mississippi, Union troops (17th Corps), under Major General James McPherson, in a three-hour battle, defeat

General John A. Logan (Johnson, *Campfire and Battlefield: History of the Conflicts and Campaigns*, 1894).

a Confederate force composed of about 6,000 men commanded by General John Gregg at Raymond, placing Grant's army between Generals J. Johnston and John C. Pemberton, which essentially severs Confederate communications. General John A. Logan's division plays a pivotal part in the battle and sustains high casualties, but a bayonet attack forces the Rebels to retire from their positions at Farnden's Creek. The Union suffers 69 dead and 341 wounded. Confederates suffer 969 dead or wounded.

In Missouri, Union and Confederate contingents skirmish in the vicinity of Bloomfield.

In Tennessee, the 1st Western Tennessee Cavalry under Colonel Breckinridge attacks a Confederate contingent at Linden. The Union reports no casualties. The Confederates sustain three killed and 47 captured. Also, elements of the 13th and 15th Corps (General Grant's command) skirmish with Confederates at Fourteen Mile Creek. The Union sustains four killed, 24 wounded and five missing. Confederate casualties are unavailable.

May 13 (Wednesday)   In Kentucky, a Union force guarding a wagon train repels a Confederate attack at South Union.

In Louisiana, a Union contingent led by Colonel Davis skirmishes with a Confederate contingent composed of guerrillas and Indians at Ponchatoula. The Union captures 17 Indians.

In Mississippi, Confederate Joseph E. Johnston arrives at Jackson to take command of all troops in southern Mississippi. Union General McPherson arrives late in the day at Clinton and his force begins to destroy the rails. Afterward, General Sherman's force arrives and links with McPherson's force. Preparations are made to march on Jackson. General M.M. Crocker's division acts as vanguard for the advance. Also, Union gunboats commanded by Lt. J.G. Walker, U.S. Navy, capture Yazoo City. In other activity, a contingent of the 2nd Illinois Cavalry clashes with Confederates at Hall's Ferry. Casualty figures are unavailable.

In Missouri, A union contingent departs Newtonia and initiates a scouting mission that extends to French Point and Center Creek and lasts until the 18th.

May 14 (Thursday)   In Louisiana, General Banks departs Alexandria to assault Port Hudson, a strategic Confederate stronghold north of Baton Rouge.

In Mississippi, the Union forces (15th and 17th Corps) under Major Generals Sherman and McPherson engage and defeat Confederates under General J.E. Johnston at Jackson. The defending troops are under the immediate command of Confederate General W.H.T. Walker. Union forces under McClernand held in reserve are not used. The city falls to Union troops and the Rebels withdraw to the east. Later in the day, General Grant arrives. Soon after, Grant is informed that General Johnston had assumed supreme command and that General John C. Pemberton had been directed to depart Vicksburg to strike the Union's rear. Grant orders McPherson to return to Clinton, while the remaining forces will be directed to converge at a point near Bolton's Station and then move to Edward's Station. The Union sustains 40 dead and 240 wounded. Confederates suffer 450 killed or wounded. Grant and Sherman ride to the State House in Jackson to watch Union General M. Crocker advance with his troops (59th Indiana) and hoist the Stars and Stripes over the capital of Mississippi. Sherman's troops remain in Jackson, destroying all rails and manufacturing facilities, prior to pushing on to Edward's Station. Grant is moving closer to Vicksburg.

In the Indian Territory, a skirmish develops between Confederates and Union forces at Fort Gibson (Oklahoma).

In Union general officer activity, General Thomas Meagher, who organized the Irish Brigade, having been denied permission to recruit new men for the brigade, particularly sine its heavy losses from an impetuous charge at

Fredericksburg (December 1862), resigns his commission. Nonetheless, his resignation is not accepted and is officially cancelled on 23 December 1863. General Meagher joins with General Sherman for the remainder of the war. He again resigns on 15 May 1865, subsequent to the surrender of General Robert E. Lee at Appomattox. Later he serves for a time as acting governor of Montana. On 1 July 1867, while at Fort Benton, Montana, in a state of intoxication, he falls overboard from a steamboat and drowns.

May 15 (Friday)   In Arkansas, a skirmish erupts between Confederate troops and Union forces at Fort Smith.

In Virginia, Confederate troops assault Union lines at Clarksville, forcing Union General John Peck to retreat. The Confederates take prisoners, including Pvt. Joseph S. G. Sweatt of the 6th Massachusetts Infantry, who refuses to retreat, choosing to remain with the wounded. He receives the Medal of Honor for his gallantry.

In Louisiana, a Union force commanded by Colonel Davis engages and defeats a Confederate contingent at Camp Moore. Confederates capture a company of Union cavalry at Charlestown, but on the following day, Union cavalry led by Captain Vitt rescues the captives.

In Confederate general officer activity, former U.S. Army Captain John Marshall Jones who had after the outbreak of hostilities resigned his commission (captain, 7th U.S. Infantry) to join the Confederate service, is this day appointed brigadier general. Initially, Marshall, a graduate of West Point, class of 1841, was on the staff of Generals Early, Ewell and Magruder. General John Marshall Jones is assigned command of General John Robert Jones' brigade (Trimble's Division, 2nd Corps) after J.R. Jones removed himself from the field during the fighting at Chancellorsville because of what he described as a medical problem with one of his legs. Colonel James Alexander Walker, 13th Virginia Infantry, is promoted to

Left: General McPherson's command enters Clinton, Mississippi (Mottelay, *The Soldier in Our Civil War*, 1886). *Right:* General Marcellus Crocker leads a charge against Confederates at Jackson, Mississippi (*Harper's Pictoral History of the Civil War*, 1896).

Above: The XV Corps crosses the Big Black River en route to Vicksburg on the night of 16 May 1863 (Johnson, *Campfire and Battlefield: History of the Conflicts and Campaigns*, 1894). *Right: top* — General James McPherson at the cotton bridge built by his forces on the Big Black River; *bottom* — Union vessels navigating a bayou (*Harper's Pictorial History of the Civil War*, 1896).

the rank of brigadier general and assigned duty as a brigade commander in the 2nd Corps, Army of Northern Virginia.

May 16 (Saturday) BATTLE OF CHAMPION HILLS Union troops under U.S. Grant defeat Confederates under General Joseph Johnston at Champion Hills or Baker's Creek, Mississippi, during the campaign to seize Vicksburg, the very heart of the Southern rail supply. Union General McPherson engages two divisions and Union General Alvin Hovey skirmishes against another. Two Rebel batteries pound the Union forces as they attempt to engage a force under General John C. Pemberton. General McGinnis commits the 11th and 46th Indiana and the 29th Wisconsin Regiments to eliminate the batteries. Following a bayonet charge and a gruesome fight, the batteries are seized; however, Confederate reinforcements arrive and the Union is compelled to pull back.

In the meantime, the Union reverts to using its artillery to maintain the battle while the troops reform for another attack. Contingents of General Crocker's (previously General Quinby's) division arrive, and a new assault is ordered. General Thomas drives against General John C. Pemberton's left flank, increasing the pressure as his right flank remains heavily engaged. Thomas' thrust drills straight into the lines and pushes the line back, which temporarily cuts off the brigade under General Loring and causes total confusion in the ranks of General John Stevenson's lines. By about 1600, the Union assault compels the Confederates to retire toward Big Black River.

Union contingents of Generals Carr and Osterhaus (McPherson's Corps) give chase. Confederate General Lloyd Tilghman (West Point, 1836) is killed by a shell fired by the Chicago Mercantile Battery while fighting a rear-guard action. Also, Colonel (later general) Alpheus

Baker is seriously wounded, but he will return to the field. In the meantime, Sherman departs Jackson, reaching Bolton, a 20-mile march, on the following day, and from there he proceeds to Bridgeport on the Big Black River. The Union loses about 426 dead, 1,842 wounded and 189 missing. Confederates sustain 2,500 killed or wounded and 1,800 missing.

The Confederates destroy bridges across the river, but the Union rebuilds modified spans. One such bridge, built by General McPherson's command, is known as the Cotton Bridge. General Grant describes it: "Two heavy beams thirty-five feet in length were joined together by smaller beams ten feet in length, spiked two feet apart. This frame now turned over, cotton bales were rolled into it in two rows, and secured by stanchions at the side of each bale, and a beam crossing the top." The unusual bridge, its construction overseen by Major Hickenlooper (McPherson's chief engineer), was decked over with planks from demolished gin houses.

In Missouri, elements of the 7th Missouri Militia Cavalry skirmish with Confederates at Carthage. Casualty figures are unavailable.

In Ohio, Congressman C.L. Vallandigham, arrested on May 4 for activities regarded as treasonous and conspiring with the enemy, is found guilty by General R.B. Potter. Vallandigham had been making incendiary speeches. Initially he is sentenced to confinement until the end of the war, but President Lincoln instead transfers him to the Confederates. He is moved to an

area in which General Bragg is operating and from there he departs for Canada.

In Virginia, a detachment of the 1st New York Cavalry, led by Lt. Vermuillion, skirmishes with Confederates at Berry's Ferry. The Union reports no casualties. The Confederates sustain two killed, five wounded and 10 captured. Also, a Union contingent, composed of elements of West Virginia and Pennsylvania cavalry commanded by Captain Vitt, clashes with Confederates at Piedmont Station. The Union sustains two killed. The Confederates suffer two killed and about 40 captured. A contingent of the Union 5th Tennessee Cavalry attacks Confederates led by Lt. Colonel Thompson at Cripple Creek (Bradysville). The Union captures 18 Confederates.

May 17 (Sunday) **In Louisiana,** General Banks is deploying his troops at Port Hudson on the opposing bank of the Mississippi River.

In Mississippi, the Union's 13th Corps, commanded by Major General John A. McClernand, decisively defeats Confederates under Johnston at Big Black River Bridge, bringing U.S. Grant to the fringes of Vicksburg. General Lawler, operating on the right, moves his force along the river bank without detection by the Rebels and initiates a stunning attack that succeeds in seizing the ground and evicting the Rebels. However, not all of them escape. Lawler's force seizes about 1,000 prisoners. The Union also captures the seventeen guns posted there, and as the Rebels retire they burn the bridges, essentially preventing many of their own troops from reaching the west bank. While the Confederates head for Vicksburg, the Union begins to construct floating bridges to give the contingents of McClernand and McPherson easy access to the opposite banks. General Grant, in his memoir, lists Union casualties at 410 killed, 1,844 wounded and 187 missing. Confederates have over 3,000 killed or wounded and over 3,000 captured. Grant's figures might include other actions too. Other sources of casualties said to be official figures say the Union had 29 killed and 242 wounded, and Confederates had 600 killed and wounded and about 2,500 captured.

Grant's forces, in less than three weeks, march 200 miles, win four decisive battles and now control the high ground on the Yazoo River in the vicinity of Vicksburg. General Lawler is afterward assigned duty in Louisiana and Texas for the duration. He receives the brevet of major general during March 1865 and musters out of the service after the close of hostilities.

In Virginia, pickets of the 12th and 91st Ohio Volunteer Regiments and the 2nd West Virginia Cavalry, commanded by Captain Wilson, skir-

mish with Confederates at Fayetteville through the 19th. The Union sustains 17 killed, wounded and missing. Confederate casualty figures are unavailable.

May 18 (Monday)   In Mississippi, advance detachments of Grant's army are on the verge of striking the outside fortifications of Vicksburg. General Sherman's force has reached Bridge-port. This day Sherman's forces build a pontoon bridge and cross the river. His forces will take control of Walnut Hills near Chickasaw Bayou. Also, General John A. McClernand's force moves from Black River, using the main road leading to Vicksburg, and halts at Mount Albans on the Baldwin Ferry Road. McPherson will trail Sherman and operate on Sherman's left. In the meantime, Confederate General John C. Pemberton's defenders, concerned about being outflanked, leave their positions in front of Vicksburg and head for the town. By this day, Grant has isolated Vicksburg on land, while Porter's fleet controls the Mississippi River. Union troops attached to Porter occupy Haines Bluff on the Yazoo. The siege ends July 4, 1863. Confederate General William W. Loring's division had been cut off from Pemberton's main body on the 16th and thus avoids capture when the city falls. The 5th Minnesota Volunteer Regiment, within the past several days, has arrived from Duckport, Louisiana, to form in the rear of Vicksburg.

In Missouri, a 54-man detachment of the 2nd Kansas Artillery and the 1st Kansas (29th U.S. Colored Troops), commanded by Major Ward, skirmish with Confederate guerrillas led by Colonel Livingston at Sherwood. The Union sustains 17 killed, 18 wounded and four captured. Confederate casualty figures are unavailable. Also, the 170th New York

Volunteer Regiment inadvertently sustains casualties when a mixup causes one unit to fire upon another. The Regiment sustains three killed and four wounded. A Union contingent operating in the vicinity of Richfield (Clay County) skirmishes with a contingent of Confederates.

In Union general officer activity, General Nathaniel C. McLean, who recently assumed command of a disorganized force at Chancellorsville upon the wounding of General Devens, is transferred to Cincinnati to serve under General Ambrose Burnside. Shortly after his arrival, McLean is appointed provost marshal general of the Department of the Ohio.

In Naval activity, Confederate guerrillas attack the Union vessel *Crescent City,* which is transporting elements of the 3rd Iowa Volunteer Regiment. Casualty figures are unavailable. No damages are reported by the Union. In other activity, the USS *Linden* escorts a convoy of five army transports along the Mississippi, but a concealed Confederate battery on Island No. 82 commences fire. The battery is put out of action. Afterward, the Union troops debark and destroy Confederate structures in the area.

May 18–July 4   The Siege of Vicksburg Grant's 13th, 15th and 17th Corps and Admiral Porter's naval fleet participates. The Union launches a major assault on the 19th and another on the 22nd of May. Following these attacks, additional Union forces, including two divisions of the Ninth Corps and three divisions of the Sixteenth Corps, join the contest. In addition, Major General Herron's division (Department of the Missouri) further bolsters the force, and it is able to fill a gap at the far left of the Union line. After the Vicksburg campaign General Herron is transferred to Texas, where he commands the XII Corps at Brownsville and the Northern District of Louisiana. Subsequent to the close of hostilities, he leaves the service during June 1865.

May 19 (Tuesday)   In Mississippi, General Grant orders an assault on Confederate positions around Vicksburg. The Union gains

Left: Union and Confederate forces exchange hand grenades during the siege of Vicksburg (Mottelay, *The Soldier in Our Civil War*, 1886). *Right:* Vicksburg batteries (*Harper's Pictorial History of the Civil War*, 1896).

Left: Union and Confederate troops skirmish at Vicksburg (Mottelay, *The Soldier in Our Civil War,* 1886). *Right:* Union entrenchments during siege of Vicksburg (Johnson, *Campfire and Battlefield: History of the Conflicts and Campaigns,* 1894).

ground and secures safer positions against enemy guns. McClernand's corps occupies the high ground across Two Mile Creek and in a while, the 4th Ohio Cavalry secures Haines Bluff, the latter being hurriedly abandoned upon the approach of Grant's forces. At 1400, a general assault is ordered. Sherman drives forward and reaches the Rebel fortifications, while McPherson and McClernand gain ground, but not equal to that gained by Sherman's force. Sherman's troops, with Blair's division at the point, assault Fort Hill and engage Brigadier General Francis A. Shoup's Louisiana brigade. The Rebels raise an iron wall of fire that staggers the Union assault force when it reaches a point about thirty yards from the defenses, but they recover and defy the incessant fire, choosing to renew the charge across the ditch. Elements of the 13th U.S. Regulars, 83rd Indiana and the 127th Illinois Regiments climb to the crest. However, the Rebels again respond with even more devastating fire that seals off any further passage, forcing the Union to withdraw to more tenable positions. The Confederates hold while the Union regroups. During the next several days, Grant continues planning his next attack on the assumption that "Confederate morale had collapsed." He orders his main assault on the 22nd.

In Missouri, a contingent of Confederate guerrillas captures some men of the 25th Missouri Volunteer Regiment at Richmond. The Union loses two killed. Confederate casualty figures, if any, are unavailable.

In Virginia, a contingent of General Milroy's cavalry skirmishes with Confederates at Winchester. The Union reports no casualties. The Confederates suffer six killed and seven captured.

In Confederate general officer activity, Colonel John Wesley Frazer (West Point, 1849), commanding officer of the 28th Alabama Infantry Regiment, is promoted to the rank of brigadier general. Frazer receives a new com-

mand, composed of several regiments drawn from Georgia and North Carolina, augmented by one artillery battery. The force under Frazer will advance to Cumberland Gap to support the efforts to evict the Union troops from East Tennessee; however, the Union contingents of General Ambrose Burnside have other plans.

In Naval activity, the USS *Huntsville* seizes the blockade runner *Union* in the Gulf of Mexico. Also, the USS *Baron DeKalb,* operating on the Yazoo River during the Vicksburg campaign, discovers the CSS *Alonzo Child* along a channel of the river Haines Bluff and Snyder's Bluff. The ship, having been previously reduced to a barge, is abandoned; however, according to the commander of the *DeKalb,* he "found her there, abandoned and … much knocked to pieces." He also reported they found "guns, ammunition, tents, etc." along the riverbank in and about abandoned Rebel positions. The *Alonzo*

Child had been prepared as a fire ship to be sent downstream as an obstacle. Also, the Mississippi Squadron, commanded by Admiral David D. Porter, participates in the operations against Vicksburg during the siege that terminates on 4 July.

May 20 (Wednesday)   In Mississippi, General Ulysses S. Grant confers with Generals John A. McClernand, James B. McPherson and Sherman to synchronize an attack on Vicksburg at 10 A.M. on 22 May 1863. Orion P. Howe, a 14 year old drummer, is wounded but continues his trek to advise Sherman that Colonel Malmborg's 55th Illinois is in desperate need of ammunition.

In the Indian Territory, a Union contingent — commanded by Colonel Phillips and composed of elements of the 6th Kansas Cavalry and the 3rd Wisconsin Cavalry, in support of the 1st, 2nd and 3rd Kansas Indian Home Guards —

A Union battery during the siege of Vicksburg (Mottelay, *The Soldier in Our Civil War,* 1886).

engages Confederates at Fort Gibson (Oklahoma). The Union sustains 25 killed and 12 wounded. Confederate casualty figures are unavailable.

In Tennessee, Union General David S. Stanley's force attacks Confederates at Middleton. The Union seizes about 80 prisoners and confiscates about 200 horses and 600 stands of arms. The 4th Michigan, 7th Pennsylvania, 3rd and 4th Ohio Infantry Regiments, the 4th U.S. Cavalry and the 39th Indiana Mounted Infantry participate in this raid.

In Union general officer activity, Lt. Colonel Adelbert Ames (West Point, 1861) is promoted to the rank of brigadier general of volunteers. Ames, a recipient of the Medal of Honor, is the son-in-law of Union General Benjamin F. Butler.

In Naval activity, the USS *Linden,* working in conjunction with the USS *Forest Rose* in the vicinity of Quiver River, Mississippi, lowers a boat and its party captures two vessels, the *Dew Drop* and the *Emma Bett.* Both vessels are destroyed by fire.

May 21 (Thursday)   In Mississippi at Vicksburg, the Union continues to bring up supplies, deploy artillery and speed up communications in order to better prepare for a second attack, scheduled for the following day, against the Confederate stronghold.

In Missouri, Confederate guerrillas operate along the Santa Fe Road in the vicinity of Kansas City.

In Tennessee, a Union force commanded by General David S. Stanley, which includes elements of the 4th Michigan, 3rd Indiana, 7th Pennsylvania, the 3rd and 4th Ohio and the 4th U.S. Cavalry as well as the 39th Indian Mounted Rifles, attacks Confederates at Middleton. The Union reports eight wounded. The Confederates lose about 90 captured.

In West Virginia, the 2nd Virginia Infantry (later 5th West Virginia), which had been driven from Beverly on 24 April, returns there on this day and operates out of that place, primarily with scouting missions, until later ordered to Grafton to receive mounts.

In Virginia, Union Cavalry (8th Illinois Cavalry) under Lt. Colonel Glendenin initiates a raid into the area around and below Fredericksburg. The mission continues until the 28th and succeeds in capturing about 100 Confederates.

In Arkansas, a Union force departs from Cassville and initiates a mission that moves through northern Arkansas and crosses into Jasper and Newton Counties. Skirmishes erupt at Bentonville, Arkansas, on the 22nd and in the vicinity of Carthage, Missouri, on the 26th.

In Naval activity, the CSS *Mobile,* an ironclad gunboat on duty on the Yazoo River and vicinity, is destroyed by the Confederates to prevent capture by the Union squadron under Admiral David Porter that is closing against Vicksburg. In conjunction, the *Mobile,* a wooden steamer,

initially built in Philadelphia, was acquired by Confederate commander W.W. Hunter for a $5,000 lien during July 1861. In other activity, the ironclad USS *Galena,* on picket duty at Hampton Roads and Newport News since September of the previous year, arrives in Philadelphia for repairs. Having sustained serious damage to its armor at Drewry's Bluff and wear on its machinery, it receives an overhaul, including the stripping of its armor. It heads back to sea as a wooden hulled ship after being recommissioned on 15 February 1864. In other activity, the USS *Linden, Baron De Kalb, Choctaw, Forrest Rose* and the Petrel move up the Yazoo River to Yazoo City, Mississippi, on a mission to destroy several Confederate vessels.

May 22 (Friday)   In Mississippi, the assault on Vicksburg is launched as a three-pronged attack. The Union troops' assault is repulsed by deadly Confederate fire. However, to the surprise of Generals Sherman and Grant, it is reported that McClernand has broken through the Rebel lines and the Stars and Stripes fly over Vicksburg. This report by McClernand had been both premature and inaccurate. His forces had taken some earthworks outside the main lines, but his men are actually entrapped by the Rebels, with most of his force later being captured. They have not penetrated Vicksburg. Their breakthrough merely secures two distant outposts. The Union sustains about 3,000 casualties, while the Confederates sustain about 1,000. The siege will continue.

In North Carolina, a Union reconnaissance force, which includes contingents of the 58th Pennsylvania and the 5th, 25th, 27th and 46th Massachusetts Volunteer Regiments, skirmishes with Confederates at Gum Swamp. The Union reports one killed. The Confederates lose about 165 captured.

In the Indian Territory at Fort Gibson, Union and Confederates again skirmish.

In Tennessee, units of the 103rd Illinois Regiment and about one company of civilian Unionists skirmish with Confederates led by Captain Street at Middleton. The Confederates lose 11 captured.

May 23 (Saturday)   In Mississippi, General Grant concentrates on building up his forces and defenses to facilitate the operation to secure Vicksburg. Grant orders the construction of earthworks and forts, and he also directs the artillery and the fleet to maintain bombardments to camouflage the continuing effort to dig tunnels that lead to the Confederate lines. A Union contingent of Marines, cavalry and infantry engages and defeats Confederates at Beaver Dam Lake. Casualty figures are unavailable.

In Missouri, Union and Confederate contingents skirmish at Hartville. The Confederate 8th Missouri Cavalry Regiment under Colonel William K. Jeffers, in its initial engagement, sustains high casualties. The regiment continues to operate as part of General Marmaduke's brigade.

In North Carolina, Sgt. Andrew A. Bryant of the 46th Massachusetts Infantry holds a bridge at New Bern, repulsing a Confederate attack. Sgt. Bryant and his contingent of 16 men, by their actions, save the city from capture. In related activity, elements of the 58th Pennsylvania and the 46th Massachusetts Regiments are skirmishing at Batchelor's Creek.

In Louisiana, the Yankees are moving on Port Hudson as Banks' force, at Hickey's Landing, boards transports and crosses the muddy Mississippi to strike from the north. Meanwhile, the overflow of his force, which had been unable to board the vessels, moves overland to Simm's Point, from where it crosses the Atchafalaya River to a point across from Bayou Sarah. Other troops, under Generals C.C. Augur and Thomas W. Sherman, are closing against it from Baton Rouge to launch an attack from the east and south.

In Arkansas, a Union contingent departs Helena and initiates an expedition that extends to Napoleon and includes a skirmish with Confederates at Island No. 65 on the Mississippi River. The expedition concludes on the 26th.

In West Virginia, Brigadier General Averell receives command of the 4th Separate Brigade, which is composed of mounted infantry and cavalry. The 2nd Virginia Regiment (later 5th West Virginia) is part of the brigade.

In Union general officer activity, Colonel Gustavus A. DeRussy (West Point attendance, three years) is appointed brigadier general of volunteers. DeRussy had served admirably during the Peninsular Campaign and at Fredericksburg, where he directed the artillery on Burnside's left. Union Brigadier General Orris S. Ferry, who commanded a brigade in General James Shields' command during the Shenandoah Valley Campaign, is promoted to the rank of major general. Rufus Ingalls (West Point, 1843), having served as chief quartermaster of the Army of the Potomac under George McClellan, Ambrose Burnside, Joseph Hooker and George Meade, is appointed brigadier general effective this date. During June 1864, General Grant appoints him as chief quartermaster of all the U.S. armies engaged against Richmond. By war's end, General Ingalls achieves the brevet ranks, including major general.

In Confederate general officer activity, Major General Richard S. Ewell, subsequent to the demise of Lt. General Thomas J. "Stonewall" Jackson, is assigned command of the 2nd Corps with the rank of lieutenant general.

In Naval activity, Commodore Wilkes, commander of the East India Squadron, at St. Thomas, sends a dispatch to the secretary of the Navy informing him that the USS *Vanderbilt* had completed repairs to its engines, permitting Wilkes to sail to LaGuayra, Venezuela, in response to a request of 29 January from the secretary of state regarding presence of a U.S. warship, in the event it becomes necessary to protect the interests of U.S. citizens there. A large debt remained unpaid, and during the course of the cruise, Wilkes succeeds in receiving $150,000.

Also, the USS *Brockenborough* captures a sloop, the *Fashion*, which is carrying a cargo of cotton. Within a few days hurricane winds threaten the safety of the *Brockenborough* and the captured sloop. On the 27th, the prize is beached on St. George's Island and set on fire to ensure it is not salvaged by the Rebels. In other activity, the *Moose*, a stern-wheel steam gunboat built at Cincinnati during 1863 as the vessel *Florence Miller*, is acquired by the U.S. Navy and commissioned. Commander LeRoy Fitch receives command of the gunboat, which is assigned to the Mississippi Squadron. It departs 2 July to patrol the Ohio River from Louisville upriver during a period when the region is being invaded by Morgan's Raiders.

May 24 (Sunday)   In Mississippi, the Union is busily constructing fortifications at Vicksburg to offset any possible Confederate threat to lift the siege. The labor of constructing the trenches and batteries, according to General Grant, was "largely done by prisoners assisted by Negroes who came within our lines and were paid for their work." Grant intends his line to be as strong as the enemy's is against them. The Yankees are without siege guns, except for six 32 pounders. Admiral Porter subsequently appropriates a battery of large caliber guns, which allows the siege to continue.

In Union general officer activity, Major General John M. Shofield succeeds Major General Samuel R. Curtis as commander of the Department of the Missouri. Also, Lt. Colonel (later brigadier general) Americus Vespucius Rice is promoted to the rank of colonel (57th Ohio).

In Confederate general officer activity, Major General Ambrose P. Hill is promoted to the rank of lieutenant general, and he will be assigned command of the 3rd Corps.

In Naval activity, the USS *Kenwood* is commissioned at Cairo, Illinois. The stern-wheel steamer, assigned to the Mississippi Squadron, arrives on station on 1 June to begin patrols on the Arkansas River.

May 25 (Monday)   In Arkansas, elements of the 3rd Iowa and the 5th Kansas Cavalry skirmish with Confederates at Polk's Plantation in the vicinity of Helena.

In Kentucky, a Union contingent skirmishes with Confederates at Fishing Creek. Specific units are unreported.

In Louisiana, a contingent of the 41st Massachusetts Volunteer Regiment and other units commanded by Colonel Chickering skirmish with Confederates at Franklin.

In Mississippi, a contingent of the 3rd Illinois Cavalry commanded by Colonel McCrellis clashes with Confederates at Senatoria. The Confederates sustain six killed and three captured.

In Confederate general officer activity, Brigadier General John Stevens Bowen is ap-

pointed major general in the Confederate Army effective this day.

May 26 (Tuesday)   In Missouri, skirmishes erupt at Mountain Store and Bush Creek.

In Union general officer activity, Alexander Shaler, commissioned colonel after the Battle of Malvern Hill, is promoted to brigadier general. During the winter of 1863, General Shaler becomes commander of the prison on Johnson's Island; however, he does return to the Army of the Potomac and participates in the battle of the Wilderness during May 1864.

In Confederate general officer activity, Brigadier General Robert Ransom, Jr., is promoted to the rank of major general effective this date. Ransom had previously seen service in Virginia and North Carolina, but at this time he is assigned duty in Virginia, including participation in the Confederate cavalry raid into Washington, D.C. His health later fails, compelling him to resign his commission during the latter part of 1864. His brother, Matt Whitaker Ransom, also a Confederate general, will remain with the Army of Northern Virginia until the close of hostilities.

Major General Robert Ransom, Jr (Johnson, *Campfire and Battlefield: History of the Conflicts and Campaigns,* 1894).

In Naval activity, the USS *Ceres, Brinker* and *Shawsheen* initiate a mission on the Neuse River in North Carolina and seize a series of small-sized schooners and some boats. At the same time, they debark ground troops, while providing protection to permit the soldiers to establish positions. Once the soldiers anchor their positions, the gunboats withdraw.

May 27 (Wednesday)   In Alabama, a brigade of Union cavalry led by Colonel Connyn clashes with Confederates at Florence.

In Louisiana, the 47th U.S. Colored Troops skirmish with Confederates at Lake Providence. The Union sustains one killed and one wounded. Confederate casualty figures are unavailable.

In Tennessee, Confederate Brigadier General John Hunt Morgan, commanding a force of about 3,000 to 4,000 cavalry troops, departs Sparta en route for Kentucky.

In Mississippi, in the vicinity of Vicksburg, the Union gunboat *Cincinnati*, while attempting to eliminate a Confederate water battery, sustains a deadly shot from Fort Hill that causes an explosion in the magazine and costs 40 men killed and wounded, including those who succumb by drowning; the fleet sustains no other casualties. The ship goes down "with her colors being nailed to the mast." The Union is able to raise the *Cincinnati* for the second time in its career as a fighting ship, and it later returns to service on patrol duty, primarily on the Mississippi River. In February 1865 the *Cincinnati* is transferred to the area near the Mississippi Sound, where it operates in the sound and Mobile Bay until it is decommissioned in August 1865.

In Confederate general officer activity, Brigadier General William D. Pender is promoted to the rank of major general. Pender, who had commanded a brigade (A.P. Hill's division, Army of Northern Virginia) at various battles, including Seven Days' and Chancellorsville, since the previous June, had been wounded several times. He is assigned command of a division in the Army of Northern Virginia.

In Naval activity, the CSS *Chattahoochee,* a twin-screw steam gunboat in Confederate service since early 1863 subsequent to being built in Georgia for service in that state and the northern sector of Florida, sustains an explosion that causes heavy casualties, including fatalities. The next June, the ship is taken to Columbus, Georgia, to be repaired; however, by December it is destroyed to prevent capture by Union forces. Also, the USS *Western World* intercepts and seizes two sailboats at Stokes Creek, Virginia, which are carrying cash in both coins and currency. In addition, two prisoners are captured.

May 27–July 9   SIEGE OF PORT HUDSON A combined attack launched by the Union captures Port Hudson, Louisiana. Participants are U.S. Generals Godfrey Weitzel (West Point, 1855), Curvier Grover (West Point, 1850), H.E. Paine, Christopher Augur (West Point, 1843) and William Dwight (attended West Point), division of the 19th Corps, and General Banks, Army of the Gulf, assisted by the U.S. Navy under Admiral Farragut. The Confederates do not easily give ground. The forces of Grover, Paine and Weitzel initiate their attack at 1000, and following three earnest assaults finally break through on the left at about 1600 to drive the Rebels through the woods to the fortifications. In the meantime, the forces of General Thomas W. Sherman and Christopher Augur are not

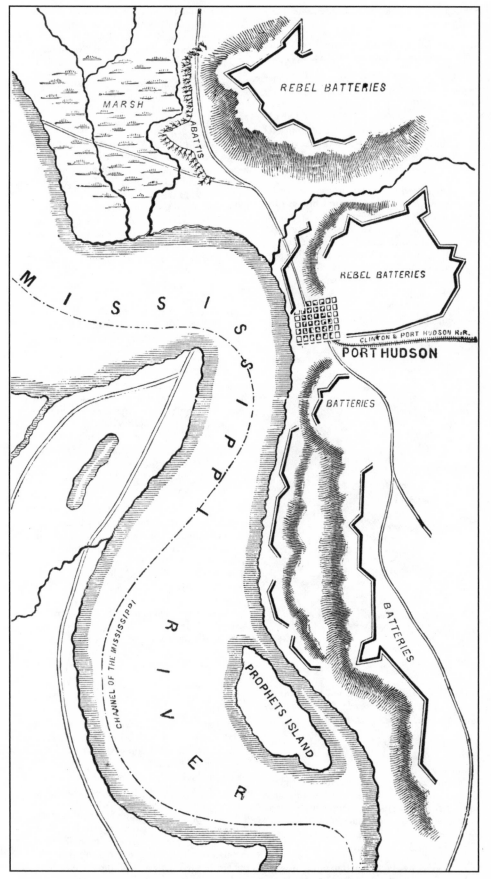

MARSH

ABATTIS

REBEL BATTERIES

REBEL BATTERIES

M I S S I S S I P P I

CLINTON & PORT HUDSON R.R.

PORT HUDSON

BATTERIES

CHANNEL OF THE MISSISSIPPI

R I V E R

PROPHETS ISLAND

BATTERIES

Port Hudson (*Harper's Pictoral History of the Civil War*, 1896).

formed for attack until about noon. Here, the Yankees make progress against the Confederate batteries; however, by dusk, the Rebels are able to compel the Yankees to withdraw.

At day's end, the Union holds an advantage on the left, but Port Hudson remains in Rebel hands and the Yankees sustain many casualties, including Colonels Clark (6th Michigan), Chapin (30th Massachusetts), Cowles (128th New York) and Paine (2nd Louisiana). General Neal Dow sustains a minor wound, and while recovering he is captured. General Dow is held initially at Mobile and afterward at Richmond. Nevertheless, the Confederates — anxious to gain the release of General William Henry Fitzhugh "Rooney" Lee (son of Robert E. Lee) — negotiate an exchange. Lee, captured during 1862 at Brandy Station, is exchanged during March 1864 for General Dow. Lee is promoted to major general the month following his exchange. General Dow, having suffered from poor health during his captivity, is compelled to resign from the service in November 1864. General Thomas Sherman suffers a serious wound which costs him one of his legs (amputated). He returns to duty, but not until March 1864. Afterward, he commands various districts in and around New Orleans. Near the close of hostilities, he receives the brevet of major general in the Regular Army and of volunteers. He resigns from the army with the rank of major general in 1870.

Meanwhile, the Union again launches a major assault on 11 June and yet another on the 14th, after the Confederate Commander, General Frank K. Gardner (West Point, 1843), refuses a surrender demand issued by General Banks. The attack has been planned as a simultaneous thrust by the three divisions of Generals Grover, Paine and Weitzel, but the Confederate obstacles make this impractical, prompting modification of the strategy.

Grover's and Weitzel's divisions strike the far left of the Confederate lines, while the right is struck by the forces of Augur and Dwight. Included are sharpshooters, who also carry 5-pound hand grenades, which are to be lobbed over the parapets. And the 24th Connecticut Regiment carries cotton bags to be tossed into the ditches to facilitate crossing the obstacle. The assault commences at dawn and the troops race through formidable Confederate fire to reach the parapets, only to be met by a wall of fire that bars passage. Repeatedly the Union moves forward only to be repulsed. The Union's attempt to implement the hand grenades also fails, and in fact many of them are retrieved by the Rebels and thrown back into the Union ranks to inflict many casualties. This day's contest terminates at about 1100, except for the fire of the supporting gunboats, which continues throughout the day.

The Union contingents under Generals Dwight, Grover, Paine and Weitzel do gain more advantageous ground, but at high cost, including about 700 casualties, the great majority of which are sustained by the division of General Paine, who himself loses his leg during this battle. Meanwhile, the Union continues to tunnel closer to the fortifications until the project finally nudges the tunnel precariously close to the works and essentially places capitulation within reach. And then, on the 7th of July, word reaches Port Hudson that Vicksburg has capitulated. At about midnight on the 7th, General F.K. Gardner dispatches a messenger under a flag of truce to the Union lines to inquire as to the truth of the report. General Banks informs Gardner that Vicksburg had indeed capitulated, and he includes a portion of the dispatch received from General Grant regarding its capture. Following receiving this information, General Gardner and his staff confer, and an agreement to surrender is reached.

The forty-five day siege ends officially on July 9. The Union suffers 500 dead and 2,500 wounded; the Confederates have 100 dead, 700 wounded and 6,408 taken prisoner. Union General E.P. Chapin is killed while leading an attack; within about four months he is posthumously promoted to brigadier general, effective the date of his death. Union General Thomas West Sherman (West Point, 1836) and Halbert E. Paine are both wounded and lose legs. Union Colonel Charles J. Paine, commander of the 2nd Louisiana Regiment, participates in this battle. Paine becomes brigadier general on 4 July 1864. General Frank K. Gardner, captured during the siege of Vicksburg, is later exchanged. He then serves in Mississippi under Major General Richard Taylor (later lieutenant general) until the closing days of the conflict. Confederate Brigadier General Francis A. Shoup is captured at Vicksburg. After his release, he is assigned duty with General Joseph E. Johnston and afterwards in the command of General John B. Hood, where he serves as chief of staff. After the war for a while he holds the chair of mathematics at the University of Mississippi, but in 1868, he becomes rector of St. Peter's Episcopal Parish in Oxford, Mississippi. Later he teaches mathematics and becomes chaplain at Sewanee (University of the South). He dies on 4 September 1896.

May 28 (Thursday)   In Missouri, a contingent of the 13th Illinois Cavalry, commanded by Major Lippert, engages Confederates at Bushy Creek on the Little Black River in a contest that lasts only about one-half hour. The Union sustains about 80 killed and wounded. Confederate casualty figures are unavailable.

In the Indian Territory, Union and Confederate contingents skirmish at Fort Gibson (Oklahoma) for the fifth time since 30 April.

May 29 (Friday)   In Washington, D.C., General Burnside (commander of the Department of Ohio), who this day offers his resignation, receives a response from President Lincoln: "Your despatch of to-day received. When I shall wish to supersede you I will let you know. All the cabinet regretted the necessity of arresting, for instance, Vallandigham, some perhaps doubting there was a real necessity for it; but, being done, all were for seeing you through with it." (See also, **May 4 [Monday] In Ohio.**)

In Kentucky, a skirmish erupts in the vicinity of Mill Springs.

In Mississippi, elements of the Union 17th Corps under General Major General Blair clash with Confederates at Mechanicsville. Casualty figures are unavailable.

In Virginia, a detachment of the 1st Vermont Cavalry skirmishes with Confederates at Thoroughfare Gap. The Union sustains one killed. The Confederates suffer two killed. Each side captures one solider.

May 30 (Saturday)   In Tennessee, a contingent of the 26th Ohio Regiment attacks a Confederate encampment at Carthage. The Yankees capture 22 Rebels.

In Virginia, a Union cavalry force, composed of contingents of the 1st Vermont, 5th New York and 7th Michigan Regiments, commanded by Lt. Colonel Preston, clashes with Confederate guerrillas under John Singleton Mosby at Greenwich. The Union prevails. Also, Union gunboats capture Tappahannock.

In Naval activity, the gunboat *Lafayette* is participating in operations on the Red River. In the log, the CSS *Doubloon* is mentioned as being trapped somewhere farther up the river, but no engagement occurs. The *Doubloon* is not again mentioned in any official records. The *Doubloon* had originally been built in Cincinnati during 1859 and seized by the Confederates in New Orleans in 1861. In other activity, the CSS *Dew Drop,* a side-wheel steamer built during 1858 and in use by the Confederate Army, encounters Union gunboats on the Sunflower River. The ship, en route to transport supplies to a Confederate force, is destroyed to prevent its capture. The vessel afterward is totally destroyed by Union troops under Lieutenant G.W. Brown.

May 31 (Sunday)   In Missouri, a Union contingent composed of elements of the 1st Missouri Enrolled Militia and the 9th Missouri Militia Cavalry skirmishes with Confederate guerrillas at Rochefort. The Union loses 10 killed. Confederate casualty figures are unavailable.

In Kentucky, a detachment of Union cavalry departs Somerset on a reconnaissance mission which takes them to Monticello.

In Naval activity, the gunboat USS *Alert* is destroyed in the vicinity of the Norfolk Navy Yard. The USS *Sunflower,* on patrol in the Marquesas Keys, encounters and seizes a blockade runner, the schooner *Echo,* which is transporting a cargo of cotton.

June 1 (Monday)   In South Carolina, a Union reconnaissance force led by Colonel Montgomery initiates a mission that moves up the Combahee River.

In Louisiana, Union cavalry under Colonel Grierson clashes with Confederates at Clinton. The Union sustains 21 killed and wounded. Confederate casualty figures are unavailable.

In Naval activity, on this day, Admiral Charles Wilkes is detached from the West India Squadron. He remains in Havana, Cuba, until the 30th, when he embarks aboard the USS *Roanoke* for the United States. In early 1864, Admiral Wilkes receives a court-martial and the court announces its decision on 24 April. Earlier this year the Roanoke had been transformed into a triple turret ironclad; however, it is not suited for combat on the ocean. It remains in service in Virginia, primarily on the James River. Subsequent to the war it remains in service with periods of inactivity until finally decommissioned in 1882. Also, at about this time (June), the USS *Peosta* is acquired by the U.S. Navy. It is commissioned during October after being transformed into a tinclad gunboat (Tinclad Gunboat No. 36). The *Peosta,* originally constructed as a river boat during 1857 at Cincinnati, Ohio, is assigned duty on the Tennessee River.

June 2 (Tuesday)   In Ohio, General Burnside moves his headquarters from Cincinnati to Lexington, Kentucky. He is to move into East Tennessee to protect it while General Rosecrans moves against the Confederates at Chattanooga; however, the Ninth Corps, which he had brought from Virginia, will soon be detached and sent to Vicksburg to bolster General Grant. The East Tennessee Campaign is postponed. Consequently Burnside will remain in Lexington for about two months to maintain the security of the communications around Lexington.

In Virginia, the Union pulls out of West Point. Also, Confederate Brigadier General Alexander P. Stewart is promoted to the rank of major general, effective this date. General Stewart is promoted the next June to lieutenant general.

In Union general officer activity, Union General Gillmore succeeds General David Hunter as

Admiral Du Pont's machine shop at Charleston Harbor, South Carolina (Mottelay, *The Soldier in Our Civil War,* 1886).

commander of the Department of the South. Gillmore proceeds to Hilton Head. Once there he is informed by Admiral Du Pont that the Confederates are about to launch an attack with the newly constructed ironclad CSS *Atlanta* (formerly a British blockade runner, the *Fingal*) to harass the blockading squadron. The Rebel vessel had on several occasions unsuccessfully attempted to break the blockade and make it to the sea. The *Atlanta* is commanded by Lt. W.A. Webb (formerly in the U.S. Navy).

In Confederate general officer activity, Brigadier General Alexander Peter Stewart is promoted to major general.

In Naval activity, the USS *Curlew,* while operating in support of Union ground forces, exchanges fire with Confederate troops on Arkansas terrain in the vicinity of Island No. 67 and Island No. 68 (Arkansas).

June 3 (Wednesday)   In Virginia, General Robert E. Lee marches from Fredericksburg, en route to Pennsylvania, with approximately 60,000 men. Lee keeps General A.P. Hill's 3rd Corps at Fredericksburg to guard the Rappahannock. The corps of Generals Richard S. Ewell and James Longstreet are sent to Culpeper to bolster J.E.B. Stuart, but Lee's maneuver goes undiscovered by the Union and in turn, General Hooker remains convinced the Lee's infantry had remained at Fredericksburg. James Longstreet and Richard Ewell both arrive at Culpeper by 8 June, one day prior to an attack that is launched by the Union. In other activity, Colonel Hugh Kilpatrick (promoted to brigadier general on June 14) and his cavalry unit returns to Falmouth to rejoin General Hooker.

General Benjamin Grierson (*Harper's Pictoral History of the Civil War*, 1896).

In Mississippi, a Union brigade from Major General Stephen A. Hurlbut's command arrives at Vicksburg. The force is dispatched to Mechanicsburg to reinforce a brigade under Major General Francis P. Blair, Jr., who had been sent there earlier.

In South Carolina, the reconnaissance force under Colonel Montgomery reaches Ashepoo. The town is destroyed.

In Union general officer activity, Colonel Benjamin Grierson is promoted to brigadier general effective this day. General Grierson subsequently commands a cavalry division and, for awhile, a cavalry corps. Nevertheless, he does not get raised to the rank of major general until 19 March 1866, effective 27 May 1865.

In Naval activity, in response to a request from Major General Benjamin Franklin Butler for ten of Admiral Porter's schooners to support the operations against Vicksburg, Admiral Porter departs Pensacola, Florida, with his entire flotilla. On 6 June, the ships cross the bar at Pass a l'Outre, but as they move into the river, it becomes obvious that they will need steamers from the Union Army to tow them upstream due to the currents.

June 4 (Thursday)   In Louisiana, a cavalry force under General Benjamin Grierson engages Confederates at Clinton. Casualty figures are unavailable.

In South Carolina, a skirmish develops at Bluffton. Specific units are not reported.

In Mississippi, Confederates attack Union lines at Mechanicsburg and Sartoria. Benjamin F. Hilliker, a musician attached to the 8th Wisconsin Infantry, puts down his drum, to replace it with a rifle to oppose the superior Confederate force. Enemy fire severely wounds Hilliker in the head. Laid down to die, he recovers and becomes a recipient of the Medal of Honor for his actions. The 5th Illinois Cavalry also participates.

In Tennessee, U.S. Troops, including the 4th, 6th & 7th Kentucky, 9th Pennsylvania and 2nd Michigan Cavalry, commanded by Colonel Baird, defeat Confederates led by General Forrest at Franklin. The Union loses 25 killed or wounded, the Confederates 200.

In Naval activity, the ram USS *Switzerland,* commanded by Lt. Colonel Ellet, bombards the town of Simmsport.

June 5 (Friday)   In South Carolina, the CSS *Stono,* formerly the USS *Isaac Smith* (captured on 30 January 1863), attempts to run the naval blockade at Charleston and is wrecked off Fort Moultrie.

In Virginia, there is heavy fighting between Union troops under General John Sedgwick and Confederates under General A.P. Hill at Franklin's Crossing near Fredericksburg. Although the majority of Lee's Army is gone, Hill is able to hold off the Union assault. In other activity, the 26th New Jersey and 5th Vermont Volunteer Regiments, the 15th and 50th New

York Engineers and the 6th Corps engages Confederates at Franklin Crossing. The Union sustains 25 killed and wounded. The Confederates sustain about 200 killed and wounded. The 2nd Division (6th Corps) commanded by General Albion P. Howe crosses the Rappahannock at Deep Run, initiating a reconnaissance mission.

June 6 (Saturday)   In Kansas, Confederate bushwackers under Gordon and Dick Yeager (also known as Ellsworth Wyatt) destroy Shawneetown. The Union sustains four killed.

In Tennessee, Confederates under Major General Joseph Wheeler attack a Union cavalry contingent, which includes the 8th Indiana Cavalry under Colonel Harrison, at Murfreesboro and Shelbyville. Casualty figures are unavailable.

In Virginia, Confederates attack a Union wagon train guarded by a detachment of the 67th Pennsylvania Volunteer Regiment at Berryville. The Union sustains one killed.

In Union general officer activity, Captain Stephen Weed, who commanded the V Corps artillery at Fredericksburg and Chancellorsville, is promoted to brigadier general.

In Virginia, Confederate cavalry under General Jeb Stuart is quartered at Brandy Station. In two days, they engage the Union cavalry in a deadly two-day battle.

In Confederate general officer activity, Colonel Edward A. O'Neal, 26th Alabama, is promoted to the rank of brigadier general, effective this date. However, his commission is not received and the promotion is later canceled by President Jefferson Davis. Nonetheless, O'Neal participates at Gettysburg, but later returns to Alabama with the 26th Alabama, where he is relieved of duty the following year. Later he is involved with arresting deserters in northern Alabama. After the war he resumes his law practice and is elected as governor of Alabama in 1882 and 1884. General O'Neal dies on 7 November 1890 at Florence.

In Naval activity, the USS *New Era,* aware of Confederate activity, moves to a point above Island No. 10 and spots its targets, nine Confederate boats and barges, which the Confederates had placed there in preparation for launching an attack against Island No. 10. The boats and barges are quickly destroyed. Following this action, the *New Era* spends its time in service for the duration in the upper Mississippi and along its tributaries until it is decommissioned in June 1865 and sold at auction the following month. The USS *Tahoma* on patrol in Tampa Bay encounters a blockade runner, the schooner *Statesman,* and seizes it.

The merchant ship *Clarence,* a prize of the Confederates, seized while it was en route to Baltimore, is now en route to Fortress Monroe, Virginia, to launch a surprise raid at Hampton Roads. The *Clarence* intercepts the bark *Windward* (also known as *Whistling Wind*) on the 6th. The *Clarence,* on the following day, seizes another vessel, the schooner *Alfred H. Partridge,*

Major General Alfred Pleasonton (*Harper's Pictoral History of the Civil War*, 1896).

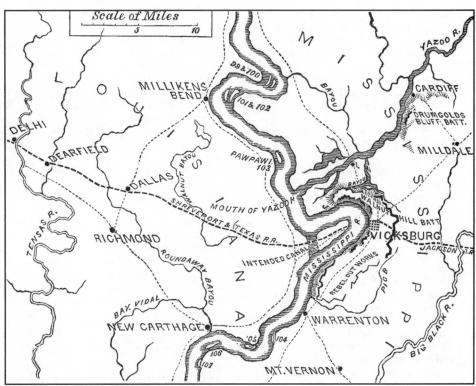

Milliken's Bend to New Carthage (*Harper's Pictoral History of the Civil War*, 1896).

Battle of Milliken's Bend (Mottelay, *The Soldier in Our Civil War*, 1886).

and on the 9th it captures the brig *Mary Alvina*. During this series of seizures, Lt. Read, commanding the *Clarence*, is informed by captives that merchant ships are prohibited from entering Hampton Roads. The intelligence foils his original scheme to launch the raid. Consequently, he aborts the plan. Nevertheless, the Rebels continue to seize merchant ships, including the *Tacony*, which is taken on 12 June.

June 7 (Sunday) French troops, which have been in Mexico since they landed at Vera Cruz during October 1861, move into Mexico City, intent on seizing total control of Mexico. The French will place Archduke Ferdinand Maximilian as emperor of Mexico. He entertains the offer to become emperor for about six months and then during April 1864 accepts it, with a contingency that France agrees to afford him military support for three years. Still, the U.S. is not in position to take action, as the ensuing struggle between North and South prevents intervention. Nevertheless, opposition in Mexico continues to resist the regime, and following the conclusion of the war in the United States, the time is found to act. The United States, which does not recognize the regime of Maximilian, demands on the authority of the Monroe Doctrine that France relinquish its hold on Mexico. The French Army, during March 1867, departs Mexico. The new emperor of Mexico is the youngest brother of Emperor Francis Joseph of Austria (Hapsburg). His wife, Carlotta, is the daughter of the king of Belgium.

In Louisiana, Confederates commanded by Major General Richard Taylor (General Edmund Kirby Smith's command) assault a Union force at Milliken's Bend. The Union contingent includes the 23rd Iowa Regiment, the 5th U.S. Colored Heavy Artillery, the 9th Louisiana Regiment, the 49th U.S. Colored Troops, the 11th Louisiana, the 51st U.S. Colored Troops and the 1st Mississippi Regiment under Brigadier General Dennis. U.S. gunboats, including the *Lexington* and the *Choctaw*, support the defenders. The contest is vicious with neither side granting any quarter. The assault, launched by troops including General Henry E. McCulloch's Texans, is repelled by the Union. The Confederates are compelled to retire by June 8. The Union sustains 154 killed, 223 wounded and 115 missing. The Confederates sustain 125 killed, 400 wounded and 200 missing. Confederate Generals Paul O. Hebert (West Point, 1840) and Henry E. McCulloch (1st Texas Mounted Riflemen) participate.

In Tennessee, Confederate guerrillas destroy the railroad bridge at Brentwood.

In Union general officer activity, Brigadier General Alfred Pleasonton is promoted to commander of the cavalry, succeeding General George Stoneman, who has fallen into disfavor with General Joseph Hooker. Pleasonton becomes major general later in the month.

June 8 (Monday) **In Virginia,** Confederate Generals Jubal Early and James Longstreet arrive at Culpeper.

In Mississippi, Union General Sooy Smith (West Point, 1853) arrives at Vicksburg with his troops. This division is directed to Haines Bluff to be joined several days later by a division under General Francis Herron.

In Tennessee, at Union headquarters in Franklin, two Union officers unexpectedly arrive with somber news, exclaiming that they are inspectors general of the Union Army and had been held up by Confederates while en route. These officers, Colonel Austin and Major Dunlap, are holding official papers from General Rosecrans. Following a short stay and after borrowing some money from the commanding officer, General Baird, the two men resume their trip, leaving for Nashville. Soon after, Baird suspects that he has been fooled and he dispatches a contingent to seize the two men, whom he now believes are spies. They are captured and General Rosecrans verifies that they are not Union officers. Shortly after the arrival of the telegram exposing the ruse, the two spies each receive a court-martial. On the following day, both men are hanged at 0900.

June 9 (Tuesday) BATTLE OF BEVERLY FORD AND BRANDY STATION General Hooker, unaware that General Robert E. Lee had dispatched the corps of Longstreet and Ewell to Culpeper to bolster Jeb Stuart, dispatches a force under General Alfred Pleasonton to Culpeper (Brandy Station) to strike Stuart's camps and to gather intelligence on the enemy's operations and movements. Hooker bolsters Alfred Pleasonton's force with two brigades (Generals Adelbert Ames and David A. Russell). The addition of the 3,000 infantry troops builds the column to just under 11,000 men. For the Union, it is somewhat of a measuring stick on the skills of the cavalry, which from the early days of the war had been much less skilled than the southern cavalry. Their opponent, Stuart, commands seasoned troops, many of whom have been riding horses since they were young boys.

The Union column forms an extended line along the railroad tracks along the Rappahannock, near Rappahannock Station, which stands

General William S. Smith (*Harper's Pictoral History of the Civil War*, 1896).

about ten miles from Culpeper and about five miles from Brandy Station, which is slightly south of Fleetwood Hill. The Union forms into two columns with the commands of Ames and John Buford crossing at Beverly Ford, while the forces of Colonel Alfred N. Duffie (1st Rhode Island Cavalry), Brigadier General David M. Gregg and Brigadier General David A. Russell cross at Kelly's Ford.

After crossing, the troops are to move to Brandy Station, with Duffie's force advancing to Stevensburg to maintain a vigil at the Fredericksburg Road, but afterward, it, too, is to move to Culpeper. The first clash of the morning occurs at the break of dawn when Brigadier General John Buford bolts across the river and engages Confederate pickets, the latter being pushed back to the Confederate main body posted near St. James' Church. Word of the incursion into Stuart's positions reaches him immediately and he dispatches contingents to deal with the threat. Brigadier General Beverly H. Robertson's brigade speeds to Kelly's Ford, while Colonel M.C. Butler (2nd Carolina) races to Brandy Station. Meanwhile, J.E.B. Stuart takes personal command of the main body near the church, the pivotal point that is attacked by General Buford.

Heavy fighting erupts at Brandy Station and the Confederates take a momentary setback when General W.H.F. Lee becomes wounded; however, command of the brigade is quickly assumed by Colonel John R. Chambliss. At about the same time, the conflagration begins to rapidly spread. Gregg accelerates his advance toward Brandy Station and sends word to Duffie to follow. The Confederates counter by dispatching artillery to meet Gregg's column, while also sending two regiments, attached to General William E. "Grumble" Jones, to Fleetwood Hill (Stuart's headquarters). In addition, the 2nd South Carolina and the 4th Virginia (Colonel William C. Wickham) rush to Stevensburg; however, the Rebels encounter two squadrons of the 6th Ohio attached to the forces that hold the town.

The Ohioans deliver tenacious fire and the Confederates return equally ferocious fire. The Confederates are stymied and driven back; however, two regiments arrive to bolster the staggered Rebel column, which then regroups and initiates a new attack. The powerful thrust, primarily by the South Carolinians, retakes Stevensburg. During the tenacious free-swinging slug-fest, Confederate Colonel Butler sustains a severe wound which costs him part of one leg, and Lt. Colonel Frank Hampton, the 2nd Regiment's second in command, is killed.

In the meantime, the column under General

A Union fleet attacks Grand Gulf (*Harper's Pictoral History of the Civil War*, 1896).

Gregg approaches Brandy Station and by then, the Confederates have artillery in place at Fleetwood Hill prepared to intercept the advance. Nonetheless, Gregg bellows the command "Attack!" And the Union initiates a charge which plows forward, and the troops ascend the hill to seize it and drive the Confederates back. Both regiments dispatched by Stuart are compelled to retire, but possession does not amount to permanent residency. The contest rages with each side delivering crushing blows against the other. As the fight continues and the casualties continue to mount, possession of the coveted elevation changes several times. Duffie's force, however, does not arrive to bolster Gregg, which causes the latter to pull back, leaving three guns behind, but two are disabled prior to withdrawing. During the menacing exchange of fire, most of the artillery men are killed and very few of Gregg's horses survive the enfilade fire.

Back at Buford's positions near the church, the Union continues to apply immense pressure, increasing the odds of vanquishing the Rebels, due in great part because Gregg's command had forced Stuart to reinforce Fleetwood Hill. While Buford is grinding forward, Gregg continues to outpace the pursuing Rebels, and before the Confederates can close, Gregg gets a welcome reprieve. The reserve cavalry of Buford arrives in time to halt the pursuit, and just behind that cavalry, Duffie's command arrives. The Confederates are halted, but Gregg continues and reports to General Alfred Pleasonton about the infantry that is advancing from Culpeper.

By this time, General Alfred Pleasonton is satisfied with the performance of his troops and has captured significant Confederate documents. Consequently, he concludes that his initial mission has been accomplished. General Pleasonton orders a withdrawal. During the trek back across the river, the Union cavalry carries a special sense of accomplishment, having met and equaled some of the Confederate's best cavalry. The contest boosts Union morale. The movement continues without incident. By dusk, the Rappahannock again separates the opposing force.

The battle, however, does not impede Gen-

A Union scouting party (10th New York Zouaves) discovers a Confederate battery at Messech's Point on the Potomac near the mouth of the Back River (Mottelay, *The Soldier in Our Civil War*, 1886).

eral Robert E. Lee's plans to invade Pennsylvania, nor his strategy regarding the valley. Lee has sent General John D. Imboden to Cumberland to destroy the rails there as well as a canal that extends to Martinsburg in northwestern Virginia (later West Virginia). On the following day, General Richard Ewell departs for Cedarville, which he reaches on 12 June.

Brigadier General William Edmondson Jones' cavalry had been responsible for guarding the rear and flank of Robert E. Lee's army as it moved toward Pennsylvania. The Union forces that engage the Confederates here include the 2nd, 3rd and 7th Wisconsin, the 2nd and 33rd Massachusetts, the 6th Maine, and the 88th and 104th New York Volunteer Regiments. The cavalry units include the 1st, 2nd, 5th and 6th U.S. Cavalry, the 2nd, 6th, 8th, 9th and 10th New York Cavalry Regiments, the 1st Maryland, 8th Illinois, 3rd Indiana, 1st New Jersey, the 1st, 6th and 17th Pennsylvania Cavalry Regiments and the 1st Maine and 3rd West Virginia Cavalry Regiments under the command of Generals David McMurtie Gregg and Napoleon Bonaparte Buford.

The Union sustains approximately 500 killed, wounded or missing, while inflicting approximately 700 casualties against the Confederates. Colonel B.F. Davis, 8th New York, is among the killed. Confederate Major Matthew C. Butler is severely wounded at Brandy Station, losing his right foot. Butler becomes a brigadier general on 1 September 1863 and a major general on 19 September 1864. Long after the conflict, General Matthew Butler becomes a major general of U.S. Volunteers, sporting the blue uniform of the Union in the war against Spain during 1898. Brigadier General William Henry Fitzhugh Lee (son of Robert E. Lee) is wounded during this action. While Lee is still recovering, he is captured by a Union contingent and kept until the next March. Also, the 2nd New York Cavalry (Colonel Henry E. Davies) sustains high casualties. It does not participate at Gettysburg because of being posted at Westminster, Maryland. During September,

Davies is promoted to brigadier general. He receives brigade command and afterward divisional command (cavalry) Army of the Potomac.

In Washington, D.C., two new departments are created, the Department of the Susquehanna, commanded by Major General Darius N. Couch, and the Department of the Monongahela, commanded by Major General W.T.H. Brooks. With these new departments, the number now stands at nineteen. The others are: Department of New England, Major General John Dix; Department of New Mexico, Brigadier General James H. Carleton; Departments of North Carolina and of Virginia, Major General J.G. Foster; Department of Kansas, Major General James G. Blunt; Department of Key West, Brigadier General J.M. Brannan; Department of Missouri, Major General John M. Schofield; Department of Washington, Brigadier General S. P. Heintzelman; Department of Western Virginia, Brigadier General B.F. Kelley; Department of the Cumberland, Major General W.S. Rosecrans; Department of the Gulf, Major General N.P. Banks; Department of the Northwest, Major General John Pope; Department of the Ohio, Major General A.E. Burnside; Department of the Pacific, Brigadier General George Wright; Department of the South, Brigadier General Q.A. Gillmore; Department of Tennessee, Major General U.S. Grant; and the Middle Department, Major General Robert C. Schenck.

In Kentucky, troops of the Union 2nd and 7th Ohio Cavalry, 112th Illinois Mounted Infantry, 1st Kentucky Cavalry and other contingents, commanded by Colonels Carter and Kantz, encounter and engage a contingent of Confederate cavalry led by General John Pegram at Monticello and Rocky Gap. The Union suffers four killed and 26 wounded. The Confederates sustain 20 dead and 80 wounded.

In Tennessee, a Union Cavalry division (General Thomas, Army of the Cumberland), commanded by General Robert B. Mitchell, is attacked by a Confederates under General Nathan Bedford Forrest at Triune. The Union sustains about 100 killed, wounded and captured. Confederate casualty figures are unavailable.

In Virginia, the 3rd New York Artillery at Fort Lyons clashes with Confederates.

In Naval activity, on or about this day, Rear Admiral Charles Wilkes receives orders from the secretary of the Navy directing him to release the USS *Vanderbilt* from his squadron. The Navy Department had not authorized Wilkes to attach the vessel; however, it was attached by

Wilkes the previous February. Wilkes is afterward severely censored and his action later leads to a court-martial for alleged "gross neglect of duty." Nonetheless, on this day, Wilkes sends a dispatch to the secretary of the Navy, explaining in detail his various actions, including his earlier cruise to Venezuela and accompanying reasons for taking the actions, but he receives no immediate reprimand or response of any kind.

June 10 (Wednesday) In Louisiana, a Union contingent skirmishes a Confederate unit at Lake Providence. Specific units are unreported.

In Virginia, Confederate General Richard Ewell departs Culpeper (Brandy Station), heading towards Winchester by way of Port Royal. His command is joined by General Micah Jenkins' force at Cedarville on the 12th.

In Union general officer activity, Union brigadier general William T.H. Brooks (West Point, 1841) is appointed major general, but the appointment will be revoked April 6, 1864. Brooks resigns from his commission of brigadier general of volunteers on July 14, 1864, due to poor health.

June 11 (Thursday) In Georgia, the Union reconnaissance force under Colonel Montgomery attacks and devastates the town of Darien. Also, Brigadier General William Vandever, during the Vicksburg campaign, is attached to the XVII Corps. On the 20th, he receives command of a brigade in General Francis Herron's division at Rome. On 2 August he becomes commander at Marietta, where he remains until November, when he is assigned court-martial duty.

In Kentucky, a Union force composed of elements of the 1st Tennessee Cavalry and the 14th Kentucky Cavalry come under attack by Confederates at Silver Creek, near Mt. Sterling.

In Louisiana, the Union forces under General Nathaniel Banks launch a second major assault against Port Hudson. The Union strikes at 0300 and reaches the parapets, but heavy fire forces a retreat. The Union sustains heavy casualties (see also, **May 27–July 9 SIEGE OF PORT HUDSON.** A contingent of the 14th New York Cavalry led by Major Mulvey is captured by Confederates under Colonel Logan during the engagement.

In Virginia, Union contingents of the 87th Pennsylvania and the 13th Pennsylvania Cavalry, bolstered by Battery L, 5th U.S. Cavalry, commanded by Colonel Shaw, skirmish with a Confederate cavalry force of about 400 troops at Middleton. The Confederates sustain eight killed, 42 wounded and 37 captured.

In Maryland, a Confederate cavalry contingent, composed of more than 200 troops, attacks a one-company contingent of the 6th Michigan Cavalry at Seneca. The Union sustains four killed and one wounded. The Confederates suffer two killed.

In Mississippi, General Grant's force at Vicksburg is augmented by the arrival of General F.J. Herron's division from the Department of the

Missouri. More reinforcements arrive in several days.

In Tennessee, Confederates under General Forrest clash with Union forces at Triune. Forrest's forces had also skirmished on the previous day and on the 4th at Franklin. His combined casualties for these incidents stand at about 100. The Union losses against General Nathan B. Forrest are about seventeen.

June 12 (Friday)   In Virginia, Confederate General Ewell, having departed Brandy Station on the 10th, arrives at Cedarville. He dispatches Confederates under General Rodes to attack the 1st Brigade (General Milroy's division) commanded by Colonel Andrew McReynolds at Berryville. The Union retreats to Winchester. Meanwhile, Ewell proceeds toward Martinsburg (West Virginia).

In Union general officer activity, Union Brigadier General Charles C. Dodge resigns his commission. He is stationed at Suffolk, Virginia, serving under Major General John Dix. Dodge had been promoted to brigadier general effective 29 November 1862; however, complications developed when a subordinate officer had received command of the cavalry at Suffolk and Dodge remained unwilling to serve under a subordinate. Union Colonel Robert S. Foster, who commands a regiment (13th Indiana) in Shields' division in the Shenandoah Valley, is appointed brigadier general. General Foster's command had also participated at Suffolk during spring 1863.

In Naval activity, the merchant ship *Clarence,* in the control of Confederates under Lt. C.W. Read, seizes the vessel *Tacony.* Lt. Read afterward seizes the schooners *M. Shindler* and *Kate Stewart.* Meanwhile, Read transfers his force from the *Clarence* to the captured *Tacony.* Afterward, the *Clarence* is burned. The *Clarence,* while operating as a Confederate ship, has seized six vessels since 6 June. Also, the USS *Lodona* in Charleston harbor exchanges blows with Confederate batteries on Morris Island and Folly Island through the 16th.

June 13 (Saturday)   In Virginia, the Confederates commanded by General Richard S. Ewell strike Union lines at Winchester, then pull away to occupy Berryville, where they will plan another assault against Winchester on the 15th. Ewell had departed Culpeper on the 10th to initiate the seventy-mile march, stopping at Port Royal to leave troops under General Rodes to facilitate the severing of Union communication lines with Berryville. Generals Jubal Early and Edward Johnson are accompanying Ewell. This expedition by Ewell has stretched the lines of General Lee an additional one hundred miles. In related activity, General Hooker, now informed that Ewell has ventured into the Shenandoah Valley, is convinced that Lee is definitely preparing to launch an attack into the North. Hooker begins to move north to defend Washington. The 3rd and 5th Corps remain to protect the fords, but the rest of the army marches north and moves through Bealeton,

Catlett's Station, Warrenton and Fairfax Court House en route to Manassas. Once General Hooker abandons his positions near Fredericksburg, the Confederates under A.P. Hill move from their positions and link up with Longstreet at Culpeper.

In Kentucky, the provost guard commanded by Captain Hare repulses an attack by Confederates at Wilson's Creek. The Confederates sustain four killed and five captured.

In Confederate general officer activity, Colonel Matt W. Ransom, the brother of Confederate brigadier general Robert Ransom, Jr., is promoted to the rank of brigadier general, effective this date. General Ransom will command a brigade in his brother's division (Army of Northern Virginia) fighting alongside Robert E. Lee until the close of hostilities. Colonel Alfred M. Scales of the 13th North Carolina Regiment is promoted brigadier general, also effective this date. Scales participates at Gettysburg and later action of the Army of Northern Virginia, but his health becomes poor toward the end of the conflict and he removes himself from the field.

In Naval activity, the gunboat USS *Marmora* is fired upon in the vicinity of Eunice, Alabama. The gunboat responds with a bombardment that destroys the town. In other activity, the *Reindeer* (a wooden stern-wheel gunboat, No. 35) is acquired by the U.S. Navy. It begins active service as the USS *Reindeer* in July as a member of the Mississippi Squadron; however, it is not yet commissioned. During July, the *Reindeer* is officially commissioned. In other activity, the USS *Sunflower,* on patrol off Tortugas, Florida, intercepts and seizes a schooner, the *Pushmatatta.* Also, the USS *Western World* sails northward to join the search for the Rebel raider Tacony; however, its cruise is short-lived. Its rudderhead is lost when it encounters a nasty storm; this forces it to move to Norfolk (17th) for repairs, which place it out of action for about one week.

June 13–15   In Virginia, a Confederate force of about 18,000 troops under General Ewell engages the Union force of General Milroy at Winchester. Milroy's force numbers only about 7,000 troops and includes the 2nd, 67th and 87th Pennsylvania, the 18th Connecticut, 12th West Virginia, 110th, 116th, 122nd and 123rd Ohio, the 3rd, 5th and 6th Maryland, the 12th and 13th Pennsylvania, the 1st New York and the 1st and 3rd West Virginia Cavalry. In addition, Milroy is bolstered by the Baltimore battery and one company of the 14th Massachusetts Heavy Artillery of the 2nd Division, 8th Corps. The Union sustains about 3,000 killed, wounded and missing. Milroy and between 200 and 300 of his cavalry troops escape capture. General Milroy's field command terminates with this action, but subsequently he is exonerated following an inquiry, and he sees some duty in Nashville under General George H. Thomas, but not field duty. He organizes militia regiments. The Confederates sustain about 700 killed wounded and missing. The Union

also loses more than 20 guns and about 3,000 stands of arms. (See also, **June 13, June 14 and June 15, in Virginia.**)

June 14 (Sunday)   In Louisiana, Union General Banks demands surrender from the troops holding Port Hudson, but the offer is declined, prompting the Confederates to brace for an attack. The Southerners, commanded by General Gardner, although outnumbered, are again able to repulse the Union attempt to take the town. (See also, **May 27–July 9 SIEGE OF PORT HUDSON.**)

In Mississippi, General Grant again receives reinforcements as Major General John G. Parke (West Point, 1849) arrives with two divisions of the Ninth Corps. With these new arrivals and the force under General C.C. Washburn, the Union force at Vicksburg now numbers about 70,000. Also, General Mower's brigade and General Alfred Washington Ellet's Mississippi Marine brigade attack a Confederate force attached to Major General William H.T. Walker's division (Joseph E. Johnston's command) at Richmond.

In South Carolina, the USS *Water Witch,* subsequent to receiving substantial repairs, returns to Port Royal.

In Virginia, scouts bring information to Union General Milroy that verifies the evacuation of Berryville by a brigade under Colonel McReynolds due to the approach of a large Rebel force. Milroy and his staff confer and decide that rather than get caught and surrounded by this superior numbered force, the town of Winchester would be abandoned. The operational guns that must be left behind are spiked and the column pulls out before dawn on the following day heading for the Potomac.

In Maryland, Confederates occupy Hagerstown.

In West Virginia, the Union sustains heavy casualties (missing in action) when a contingent of troops, including elements of the 106th New York and the 108th Ohio Volunteer Regiments and the West Virginia Battery (3rd Brigade, 2nd Division, 8th Corps), are attacked at Martinsburg. About 150 Union troops are captured.

In Union general officer activity, Colonel Hugh Judson Kilpatrick (2nd New York Cavalry) is promoted to the rank of brigadier general.

In Naval activity, the USS *Adela,* on its second day as a U.S. vessel, receives orders to join in the search for the CSS *Clarence.* At the time, the *Adela* is in the vicinity of New York en route to the southern states. The *Adela* continues its voyage toward Ocracoke Inlet, North Carolina; however, the crew halts numerous ships while en route to board them and examine their papers. No hostile vessels are encountered. Meanwhile, on the 12th, Lt. Charles William Read, Confederate States Navy, the commander of the *Clarence,* had captured a bark, the *Tacony,* and after determining that the *Tacony* has more speed than the *Clarence,* he switches his flag to the *Tacony* and destroys the *Clarence* on 18 June.

The USS *Lackawanna* seizes the blockade runner *Neptune* as it attempts to move into Mobile, Alabama. The prize, built in Scotland during 1861, is acquired in June by the U.S. Navy and commissioned the USS *Neptune* (renamed USS *Clyde* the following month). During September the USS *Clyde* sails for the Gulf of Mexico to patrol off the coast of Florida. It remains in the region until the close of hostilities, and it is decommissioned at Philadelphia during August 1865. It is then sold and renamed *Indian River*; however, its career as a commercial ship is terminated in early December 1865 when it is wrecked on the Indian River.

June 15 (Monday) **In Pennsylvania,** Confederate cavalry commanded by General Albert G. Jenkins enters and ravages Chambersburg.

In Virginia, Confederates under General Richard S. Ewell attack and defeat a Union force commanded by General Robert H. Milroy near Winchester, as it heads for the Potomac to avoid getting trapped by the Rebels. About four miles outside the town the column is thrashed by units under General Robert D. Johnston. This victory for the Southerners forces Union General Robert H. Milroy to retreat toward Harpers Ferry, in northwestern Virginia (later West Virginia). The Union has taken a severe thrashing from General Richard S. Ewell who has, in two attacks on the 13th and 15th, inflicted serious casualties on the Union. Union losses are approximately 3,000 or more killed, wounded, or captured, and the Confederates have 250 to 800 killed, wounded, or missing. General Robert H. Milroy loses all his artillery to the Rebels. A few hundred cavalrymen with Milroy are able to escape. General Milroy is subsequently relieved of command.

Meanwhile, General Robert E. Lee moves north toward Gettysburg, Pennsylvania. Also, elements of General Hooker's force arrive at Manassas. By the following day, the First, Sixth and Eleventh Corps arrive, soon to be joined by the Third Corps, which had remained behind near Fredericksburg. Later the Second, Fifth and Twelfth Corps move to Fairfax Court House as reserves, and the cavalry under General Pleasonton remains at Warrenton to protect the left flank of the Army of the Potomac. In other activity, Union troops under General Erasmus D. Keyes occupy New Kent Court House.

June 16 (Tuesday) The war approaches the northern states. Robert E. Lee is about to strike the Yankees at Gettysburg, Pennsylvania. Jeb Stuart's cavalry is spearheading General Longstreet's corps, pushing from Culpeper Court House, Virginia. In related activity, Confederates move against Harpers Ferry, West Virginia. Other Confederate cavalry units occupy Littlestown, Pennsylvania.

In Kentucky, a Union contingent commanded by Colonel De Courcey (including elements of the 10th and 14th Kentucky Cavalry and the 7th and 9th Michigan Cavalry, bolstered by the 15th Michigan Volunteer Regiment and the 11th Michigan Battery) skirmishes with Confederates at Triplett's Bridge. The Union sustains 15 killed and 30 wounded. The Confederates lose about 100 captured. Also, elements of the 15th Michigan Volunteer Regiment engage Confederates in Fleming County. Casualty figures are unavailable.

In New Mexico, one company of the 1st New Mexico Cavalry skirmishes with Confederates at Jornada Del Muerto.

June 17 (Wednesday) **In Indiana,** the Home Guards skirmish with Confederates at Orleans. The Confederates sustain three wounded and 12 captured.

In Mississippi, during the siege of Vicksburg, Union sharpshooters fire incessantly with great accuracy on Rebel positions, making it extremely difficult for the Confederate troops. Confederate Colonel Isham Warren Garrott, 20th Alabama Regiment, incensed at the severe casualties being inflicted upon his men, clasps a rifle to return fire personally, only to be shot through the heart. His death occurs without the knowledge that he has been promoted to brigadier general. Upon the death of Garrott, Lt. Colonel Edmund Pettus, also of the 20th Alabama, is promoted to the rank of colonel. General Garrott had raised the 20th Alabama during the initial days of the war and it was based in Mobile during 1861–1862, prior to being sent to Mississippi to support the defense of Port Hudson.

In Missouri, a contingent of the 9th Kansas Volunteers commanded by Captain Fletcher is attacked by Confederate guerrillas at Westport. The Union sustains 14 killed and six wounded. A contemporary source lists Union casualties as 10 killed and 17 wounded and missing.

In Virginia, Union troops commanded by General Kilpatrick (General Pleasanton's command) clash with Confederates under General Jeb Stuart at Aldie. The Union 2nd and 4th New York Cavalry, the 6th Ohio Cavalry, the 1st Massachusetts and 1st Maine Cavalry Regiments and the 1st Rhode Island Cavalry participate. The Union suffers approximately 24 killed, 41 wounded and 89 missing. The Confederates have 100 wounded and about 100 captured. Union Colonel Louis P. DiCesnola rallies the 4th Regiment to charge the Confederates, but he is injured and taken prisoner. This Union cavalry contingent, led by Kilpatrick, pursues the Rebels toward Ashby Gap and beyond to Upperville. Meanwhile, Confederates under Generals A.P. Hill and Longstreet are heading for Winchester.

In Confederate general officer activity, Confederate General Humphrey Marshall resigns his commission. He had also resigned the previous June, but was reinstated three days later. He enters law practice in Richmond and becomes a member of the 2nd Confederate Congress representing Kentucky. Following the resignation of Marshall, Confederate General John S. Williams becomes commander of the Department of East Tennessee.

In Naval activity, the Confederate ram *Atlanta,* supported by two gunboats, cruises down

Left: Citizens at Gettysburg, Pennsylvania, build fortifications in anticipation of a Confederate invasion by General Robert E. Lee's army. *Right:* Aldie, Virginia, is the scene of the victory of General Hugh Kilpatrick's cavalry (General Alfred Pleasonton's command) over Confederate General J.E.B. Stuart (Mottelay, *The Soldier in Our Civil War*, 1886).

the Wilmington River en route to attack the Union Blockading Squadron; however, Admiral Du Pont, in anticipation of its arrival, has made preparations to greet the Rebel ironclad. At about dawn, the vessels *Nahant* and *Weehawken* observe the *Atlanta* and soon after retire up the river with the *Atlanta* giving hot pursuit. The *Atlanta* commences firing, sending only one shot toward the Union vessels before deciding to halt and shut down the engines. Shortly thereafter, the *Weehawken* closes to a distance of about three hundred yards from the *Atlanta* and commences firing, inflicting immediate damage that knocks out the pilot house. The *Weehawken*, then, from a distance of only 100 yards, again delivers effective fire. The *Atlanta's* four-inch armor and dense oak planking is unable to withstand the barrage. Lt. Webb, in an apparent effort to prevent more of his men from injury or death, pulls down the ship's flag and hoists a white flag of surrender near Warsaw Sound, Georgia. The USS *Weehawken* captures more than 140 prisoners, including 21 officers. In addition, the Confederates sustain one killed and 17 wounded. The *Weehawken* and its crew become celebrities following this action. The *Weehawken* is also sent to Charleston following the capture of the Atlanta. In conjunction, the CSS *Isondiga*, a diminutive gunboat, accompanies the *Atlanta* but apparently escapes harm. Subsequently, the *Isondiga* is at Savannah when the Union threatens it. The *Isondiga* departs Savannah on 21 December to escape capture; however, shortly thereafter the crew destroys the *Isondiga* to prevent capture by the Union. The *Nahant*, subsequent to this action, supports the operations against Charleston of June through September 1863.

June 18 (Thursday)   **In Louisiana,** a 300-man contingent of Confederate cavalry commanded by Colonel William Phillips attacks a Union force (specific units unreported) at Placquemine.

In Mississippi, Union General McClernand has a letter published in a newspaper that congratulates his troops while complaining of troops from other commands. When Grant hears of it, he relieves McClernand of command and orders him to return to Springfield, Illinois. General McClernand's only military experience prior to being appointed a brigadier general during May 1861 had been three months' service as a private during the Blackhawk War (1832). He is succeeded as commander of the XIII Corps by Major General Edward O.C. Ord (West Point, 1839) during the latter part of this month.

In Pennsylvania, Confederates under General Richard S. Ewell enter Bedford. They expand their operations, with their troop count of nearly 100,000 marching with Lee toward Gettysburg. The Rebels occupy positions at Chambersburg, Shippensburg, Gettysburg and York, but Chambersburg is abandoned.

In Virginia, Union cavalry units occupy Middlesburg and Philomont.

In Naval activity, the USS *Tahoma*, operating off Anclote Keys, Florida, encounters and seizes a British blockade runner, the schooner *Harrietton*. On the same day, the *Tahoma* also encounters and destroys another blockade runner, the *Mary Jane*, in the vicinity of Clearwater. The USS *Winona* reacts to the occupation of Placquemine, Louisiana. It bombards Confederate positions and forces the Rebels to abandon the town. Afterward, the *Winona* moves to Donaldsonville to forewarn the garrison of the Rebels' approach. The *Winona* remains the area to support the garrison if necessary, and while maintaining a vigil, it bombards Confederate positions on more than one occasion during the next ten days. In other activity, the USS *Sebago* runs aground in Wassaw Sound and sustains damage. On 29 July it is sent north to receive repairs, then is recommissioned on 2 December 1863. Afterward it sails from New York for the Gulf of Mexico to join the West Gulf Blockading Squadron. Subsequently, it participates in the operations in Mobile Bay (August 1864). After the close of hostilities, the *Sebago* returns to New York, where it is decommissioned on 29 July 1865. It is sold on 19 January 1867.

June 19 (Friday)   **In Indiana,** a contingent of Indiana Home Guards, commanded by Major Glendenin, skirmish with Confederates near Leavenworth at Blue Island.

In Mississippi, the Union siege of Vicksburg continues. At present, the Union Army comprises the following units: General Sherman's corps is composed of the brigades of Frank Blair, Jr., Frederick Steele, J.M. Tuttle and J. McArthur; General James B. McPherson's corps is composed of the brigades of John A. Logan and M.M. Crocker (James B. McPherson's corps will be assigned to General E.O.C. Ord during the latter part of June); General James B. McPherson's corps comprises the brigades of Eugene A. Carr, P.J. Osterhaus, A.J. Smith and A.P. Hovey; General Washburn's force is composed of the brigades of Nathan Kimball, F.J. Herron, W.S. Smith and E.G. Lanman; and General John G. Parke's force comprises the brigades of J. Walsh and R.B. Potter.

In Virginia, Union cavalry contingents that had skirmished with General Richard S. Ewell's Confederate cavalry on the 17th at Aldie again engage there. The Union has been reinforced with the 10th New York and the 4th and 16th Pennsylvania cavalries. Jeb Stuart's cavalry is pursued for nearly ten miles in a running fight in the vicinity of Middleburg that continues for about eight hours. The Union forces commanded by Generals David M. Gregg and Hugh Kilpatrick sustain about 50 killed and

wounded. The Confederates suffer about 30 killed and wounded and 40 captured.

In Maryland, the Confederates abandon Boonesboro.

In West Virginia, the process of gaining admittance to the Union is completed. West Virginia is admitted as the 35th state.

In Naval activity, the *Tawah*, a wooden river steamer, is acquired by Rear Admiral David D. Porter at St. Louis. It is assigned to the Mississippi Squadron. Acting Master Alfred Phelps, Jr., receives command The *Tawah* remains at St. Louis until the next spring, when it initiates escort duty on the Tennessee River.

June 20 (Saturday)   **In Louisiana,** a Union contingent composed of the 6th and 7th Illinois Cavalry and the 2nd Rhode Island Cavalry, supported by the 52nd Massachusetts Volunteer Regiment and one detachment of artillery, engages and defeats a Confederate force at Jackson's Cross Roads. Also, a Union contingent of about 400 troops, composed of elements of the 5th Ohio and 2nd Illinois and the 1st Missouri Cavalry Regiments commanded by Major Henry, engages Confederates under General Chambers at Fernando, Mississippi. The Confederates, numbering about 2,000 troops, capture an unknown amount of Union troops.

A Union force — detachments of the 23rd Connecticut, 21st Indiana, 176th New York, and the 42nd and 47th Massachusetts Regiments — encounter and engage a Confederate force numbering about 2,000 troops at La Fourche (or Thibodeau) this day and the next. The Union suffers eight dead and 40 wounded; the Confederates lose 53 dead, 150 wounded and about 70 captured. (A contemporary source lists Union casualties as eight killed and 16 wounded, and Confederate casualties as 60 killed, 240 wounded and 70 captured.).

In Maryland, elements of General Stuart's Confederate cavalry occupy Frederick.

In Mississippi, a Union contingent composed of elements of the 9th Illinois Mounted Rifles, the 5th Ohio Cavalry and one detachment of

Mortar boats in action at Vicksburg (*Harper's Pictoral History of the Civil War*, 1896).

the 18th Missouri Regiment, commanded by Lt. Colonel Phillips, battles a Confederate force near Fernando, Mississippi. The Union sustains about seven killed and 28 wounded. The Confederates suffer about 35 killed and 100 wounded and captured.

In New Mexico, a detachment of the 1st New Mexico Cavalry skirmishes with Confederates at Warm Springs, Fort McRae. Casualty figures are unavailable.

In Pennsylvania, a contingent of the 1st New York Cavalry skirmishes with Confederates at Greencastle. About 20 Confederates are captured.

In the Indian Territory, elements of the 2nd Nebraska Cavalry engage Indians at the Pawnee Reservation. Casualty figures are unavailable.

June 21 (Sunday)   In Virginia, Union cavalry under General Alfred Pleasonton's command engage Confederate cavalry under General Richard S. Ewell at Upperville (Middleburg). The Union sustains 94 wounded. The Confederates sustain 20 killed, 100 wounded and 60 captured.

In West Virginia, a Union contingent skirmishes with Confederates at Low Creek. Specific units are unreported.

In Naval activity, the USS *Santiago de Cuba,* while operating in the Atlantic as part of a blockading squadron, seizes a blockade runner, the steamship *Victory.* In other activity, the USS *Velocity* (formerly blockade runner *Velocity*) is recaptured by the CSS *Bell* and the CSS *Uncle Ben.* The ram fleet under General Alfred Ellet seizes a ferryboat on the Mississippi River below Memphis; it had been in use carrying Confederate troops arriving from the west across the river.

June 22 (Monday)   In Pennsylvania, Confederate cavalry under General Richard S. Ewell arrives in the vicinity of Chambersburg in late day. His force has recently moved from the vicinity of Winchester, Virginia, and has passed through Shepherdstown and Hagerstown, Maryland, en route to Pennsylvania. Some diminutive Union garrisons in his path have retired. From Chambersburg, he moves to Kingston, near Harrisburg. Other Confederate cavalry units under General Early are simultaneously raiding such towns as Emmitsburg, Gettysburg and York to the consternation of the Pennsylvanians, who had not expected the war to reach them. Citizens from all points begin pouring into the area to fortify it from the intrusive Rebels.

In Mississippi, Grant receives information that Confederate General Joseph E. Johnston has been able to reach the rear of the Union lines at Vicksburg. This prompts General Grant to place General William T. Sherman in command of all Union troops between Haines Bluff and Big Black River, thus allowing Grant to continue the siege of Vicksburg to the west, while enabling him to glance east against possible attack from Johnston.

Detachments form three separate companies of the 4th Iowa Cavalry skirmish with Confederates at Hill's Plantation. The Union sustains four killed, 10 wounded and 28 missing. Confederate casualty figures are unavailable. Also, Union gunboats bombard Cypress Bend, Mississippi.

In Union general officer activity, Brigadier General Alfred Pleasonton is promoted to major general.

In Naval activity, the USS *Shawsheen* and the *Henry Brinker,* while on a reconnaissance mission on the Bay River, intercept and seize the schooner CSS *Henry Clay* on Spring Creek in North Carolina. Afterward, the Union warships dispatch a detachment in a small boat with orders to move to Dimbargon Creek. The detachment seizes its objective, a small unarmed schooner carrying a cargo of turpentine. In November 1863, the *Henry Brinker* returns to Hampton Roads for repairs and remains out of service until 9 April 1864, when it is assigned as a tender to the USS *Minnesota.*

June 23 (Tuesday)   In Louisiana, U.S. troops, including a detachment of the 114th, 176th New York, 23rd Connecticut, 42nd Massachusetts and the 21st Indiana, engage Confederates under Generals Thomas Green and Jean Mouton at Brashear City. The Confederates rout the Union troops. The Union sustains 46 dead, 40 wounded and about 300 missing. The Confederates suffer three dead and 18 wounded.

In Union general officer activity, Alexander S. Webb (West Point, 1855) is promoted to brigadier general. He had participated in the defense of Fort Pickens and had served as chief of artillery (Army of the Potomac, June '61 through April '62), and afterward was acting chief of staff in General Porter's V Corps. He participates at Gettysburg in command of four Pennsylvania regiments. Colonel Alfred Napoleon Alexander Duffie (1st Rhode Island Cavalry) is promoted to brigadier general. General Duffie was in the Second Manassas campaign and in various actions on the Rappahannock, including Kelly's Ford. Subsequent to the battles at Gettysburg (July 1863), he is transferred to the Department of West Virginia.

In Naval activity, the USS *Western World* and other gunboats, including the *Commodore Barney, Commodore Morris, Jesup, Morse* and *Smith Briggs,* form an escort flotilla to provide support for a landing force at White House, Virginia. The *Western World* carries about 300 cavalry troops during the week-long mission.

June 23–30   In Tennessee, Union General Rosecrans departs Murfreesboro with 60,000 men (14th, 20th and 21st Corps, Reserve and Cavalry Corps, Army of the Cumberland) to raid the Confederates at Tullahoma, including skirmishes at Hoovers Gap, Liberty Gap and Beech Grove. These victorious raids keep Confederate General Bragg's force from reaching Vicksburg with reinforcements. Union casualties are 85 dead and 462 wounded. The Confederates have about 1,634 dead, wounded or captured. Confederate General Bragg begins withdrawing toward Chattanooga.

June 24 (Wednesday)   In Louisiana, about five companies of the 9th Connecticut Volunteer Regiment skirmish with Confederates at Chakahoola. Casualty figures are unavailable.

In Tennessee, in General Rosecrans' Campaign, the 1st Cavalry Division, Army of the Cumberland, commanded by General Robert B. Mitchell, engages a Confederate force under Major General Joseph Wheeler at Middletown (Shelbyville Pike). The Union sustains six killed and 20 wounded. The Confederates sustain about 200 killed and wounded and more than 600 captured. Union Colonel Wilder leads a force, including elements of the 17th and 72nd Indiana, the 123rd and 98th Illinois Mounted Infantry and the 18th Indiana Battery, against Confederates commanded by General William Brimage Bate at Hoover Gap. The Union sustains about 61 killed and wounded. The Confederates sustain about 100 killed and wounded and 500 captured.

In Virginia, General Robert E. Lee's forces are heading north. This day, Confederate forces under Generals A.P. Hill and James Longstreet begin fording the Potomac at Williamsport and Shepherdstown. Both forces will converge on Hagerstown, Maryland, and march from there to Chambersburg, Pennsylvania, arriving on the 27th. Union General Joseph Hooker, acutely aware of the intentions of Lee, prepares to give pursuit. His forces begin to ford the Potomac on the 26th.

In Pennsylvania, the Union abandons Shippensburg. It is soon occupied by Confederate

General Joseph Hooker's tent at the Army of the Potomac headquarters (*Harper's Pictorial History of the Civil War,* 1896).

troops. Other Confederates occupy Mc-Connellsburg.

In Naval activity, the USS *Saratoga,* a sloop of war, which had been decommissioned in August 1861, is recommissioned. The *Saratoga* is dispatched to the Delaware Capes to patrol Delaware Bay and to protect shipping departing and entering the bay. In other activity, Lt. Charles William Read, Confederate States Navy, commander of the recently captured bark *Tacony,* after determining that a large number of Union warships are prowling the seas for his ship, he again transfers his flag to another cap-

tured vessel, the schooner *Archer.* The crew transfers during the night of the 24th-25th.

June 25 (Thursday)   In Mississippi, General Grant's forces are inching toward Confederate lines (Fort Hill) at Vicksburg, while simultaneously tunneling (work had commenced in late May) under Confederate lines. In turn, the Confederates are also tunneling to reach Union lines but they do not succeed. At precisely 1500, explosives are detonated, synchronized with artillery barrages as Grant explains that he intends to "blow the top of the hill off and make a crater where it stood." The effort fails to give the Union access to Vicksburg, although two Union regiments, concealed nearby, are able to quickly seize the crater and prevent the Rebels from taking possession. The Union detonates another such explosion on 1 July. The Confederate counterattack proves unsuccessful.

In Tennessee, elements of the 20th Corps under Colonel Wilder (Rosecrans' Campaign) skirmish with Confederates under Major General Patrick R. Cleburne at Beech Grove (Liberty Gap). Union Generals August Willich and Samuel P. Carter participate. Also, Colonel (later brevet major general) John Franklin Miller is wounded and placed out of action until May 1864.

In West Virginia, Confederate General Robert E. Lee orders his men to cross the

Potomac at Harpers Ferry to position his Army of Northern Virginia to invade Pennsylvania. The intention is to bring the war to the North. Lee reaches Chambersburg on the 27th.

In Union general officer activity, Colonel Walter Chiles Whitaker (6th Kentucky) is promoted to brigadier general.

In Confederate general officer activity, George Washington Custis Lee (oldest son of Robert E. Lee, West Point, 1854) is promoted to brigadier general. General Lee is apparently utilized by President Davis on various duties including missions, but his only field command occurs during the final month of the war while the Rebels attempt to hold Richmond.

In Naval activity, the USS *Santiago de Cuba,* while operating in the Atlantic Ocean as part of the blockading squadron, seizes a blockade runner, the steamship *Britannica.* In other activity, the *Howquah,* acquired by the Union in Boston on 17 June 1863, is immediately pressed into active service to aid in the search for the CSS *Tacony,* which is ravaging Union shipping. It departs Boston on 25 June en route to the Banks of Newfoundland with Acting Volunteer Lieutenant E.F. Devens as commander. Unknown to the crew of the *Howquah,* the *Tacony* had been abandoned and destroyed by Lt. Charles W. Read on the night of the 24th-25th after transferring to the captured schooner *Archer.* Nonetheless, the Confederate-held *Archer* is caught in the vicinity of Portland, Maine, within a few days. The *Howquah* returns to Boston on 3 July and afterward is transferred to the North Atlantic Blockading Squadron, where it will operate off North Carolina.

June 25–27   In Tennessee, the Union is still concentrating on pushing the Confederates under Bragg from Tennessee and simultaneously preventing his joining forces with the Rebels

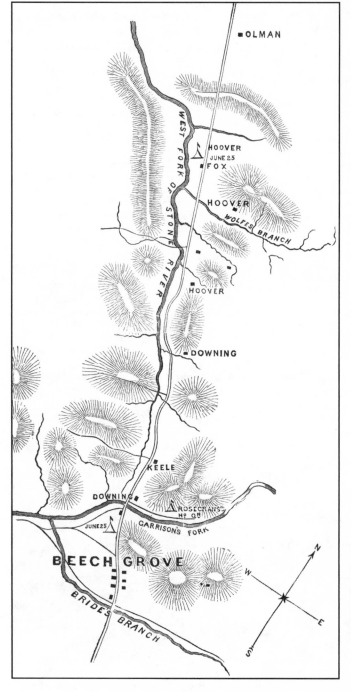

Left: Hoover Gap. *Right:* Mine explosion at Fort Hill (*Harper's Pictoral History of the Civil War,* 1896).

besieged at Vicksburg, Mississippi. Skirmishes develop in the vicinity of Liberty Gap, Shelbyville, and Guy's Gap. The Rebels take a pounding from the troops of the Army of the Cumberland and General Gordon Granger's support cavalry. General Bragg continues the withdrawal, but many of his men are taken prisoner. Union troops will occupy the town of Manchester on the 27th while Bragg moves towards Tullahoma. Union Colonel John F. Miller, commanding a brigade of Alexander McCook's XX Corps, is wounded at Liberty Gap. Miller will be promoted to brigadier general in April 1864. Confederate Colonel (later brigadier general) Richard M. Gano leads the Confederate Kentucky cavalry during the Tullahoma Campaign. Following this duty, he moves to the Trans-Mississippi Department, where he receives command of a cavalry brigade and some artillery based in the Indian Territory.

June 26 (Friday) **In Maryland,** Union troops move into Frederick and occupy it.

In Virginia, General Hooker's force begins to cross the Potomac at Edwards Ferry en route to Frederick City, Maryland, from where he will await the arrival of other forces before heading for Chambersburg, Pennsylvania, to attack the rear of General Lee's Army; however, complications develop between him and General Halleck, the latter being opposed to Hooker's plan of action. Also, elements of the 11th Pennsylvania Cavalry, bolstered by the 2nd Massachusetts and 12th Illinois Volunteer Regiments and commanded by Colonel Spear, engage Confederates at South Anna, near Hanover Court House. The Union sustains three killed and eight wounded. The Confederates lose about 111 captured. In other activity, elements of the 4th Corps, commanded by Major General Erasmus Keyes, engage Confederates at Baltimore Crossroads. Casualty figures are unavailable. Meanwhile, the Confederates under General Jeb Stuart who occupied McConnellsburg on the 24th abandon it.

In Union Naval officer activity, Rear Admiral A.H. Foote, recently selected to succeed Rear Admiral Du Pont, suddenly succumbs this date. Rear Admiral John A. Dahlgren is quickly delegated to replace Du Pont, who has been at odds with General Gillmore on the strategies regarding the capture of Charleston. Dahlgren arrives at Port Royal, South Carolina, early the following month.

June 26–27 **In** *Naval activity,* Confederates under Lt. Charles William Read, aboard the recently captured *Archer,* enter the harbor at Portland, Maine, without incident at about dusk. The Rebels remain inconspicuous in the harbor while they await the opportunity to strike their target, the revenue cutter *Caleb Cushing,* also anchored there. At about 0130 on the 27th, while the majority of the crew of the *Caleb Cushing* is asleep, the Rebels board and capture the ship with only minor resistance from the guards. Nevertheless, Read's raiders' success is short-lived. By 1130 on the 27th, the Rebels are

compelled to surrender to the *Forrest City,* a commandeered Boston Line steamer. The chase that began on the 14th of June being finally terminated, the USS *Adela* resumes its initial orders, to sail to join the East Gulf Blockading Squadron.

June 27 (Saturday) **In Kentucky,** the 39th Kentucky Volunteer Regiment skirmishes with Confederates at Beaver Creek. Casualty figures are unavailable.

In Tennessee, Union forces under General Joseph Jones Reynolds occupy Manchester.

In Virginia, one squadron of the 11th New York Cavalry, commanded by Major Remington, skirmishes a contingent of Confederate cavalry at Fairfax. The Union captures about 80 Confederates.

In Mississippi, Confederate General Martin E. Green, who was slightly wounded at Vicksburg on the 25th, is struck this day with a fatal blow to his head from a Union sharpshooter.

In Pennsylvania, a contingent of the Pennsylvania Militia skirmishes with Confederates at Walnut Bottom Road. The Union loses one wounded and 10 captured. In other activity, the Union abandons Carlisle. Within a short while, Confederates occupy it. A group of citizens of Carlisle under a white flag meet the Confederates to surrender he city. There was great apprehension once the cavalry at Carlisle Barracks cavalry school withdrew and moved to Harrisburg; however, the Union strategy had been to abandon the town to the Confederates to spare battle, which would have caused civilian casualties. All of Cumberland County is to be sacrificed without a fight, but the Union intends to intercept the Rebels at the bridges that span the Susquehanna River to prevent any Confederate attempt to move against Washington, D.C. Meanwhile, more than 10,000 Confederates congregate in and around Carlisle.

In Union activity, General Joseph Hooker, anxious to move against General Robert E. Lee, again requests permission from General Henry W. Halleck to take French's corps, which is at Harpers Ferry, West Virginia, with him to pursue Lee. General Hooker had recently dispatched General Slocum's force to Harpers Ferry. Halleck denies the request. Hooker explains to Halleck that lacking French's corps, he is too under-strength to move against Lee. He requests that he be relieved of command and his resignation is immediately accepted. Later in the day, Union General George Meade (West Point, 1835), the commanding officer of the Fifth Corps, is appointed to succeed Hooker as commander, Army of the Potomac. Meade is informed of his promotion on the following day. In a peculiar turn of events, once General Meade assumes command, he receives permission from General Halleck to utilize French's force at Harpers Ferry in any way that he chooses. Consequently, French is directed to abandon Harpers Ferry and establish positions at Frederick City, Maryland, from where he can guard the Baltimore and Ohio Railroad. Gen-

eral George Sykes succeeds General Meade as commander of the V Corps. Confederate troops continue to enter Pennsylvania, including Brigadier General Samuel McGowan's brigade (A.P. Hill's division). The 12th South Carolina Regiment arrives at Funkstown and deploys there for several days and then departs for Cashtown, Pennsylvania.

In Naval activity, the U.S. Navy acquires a screw steamer, the *United States,* built in New York the previous year. The *United States* is commissioned the USS *New Berne* on 15 August of this year and designated a supply ship. Acting Volunteer Lt. Thomas A. Harris receives command.

June 28 (Sunday) **In Louisiana,** the Union garrison at Donaldsonville repels a Confederate assault by troops commanded by Major General Richard Taylor. Union Major J.D. Bulle's besieged garrison holds off the assault with the assistance of U.S. naval fire power, including the USS *Princess Royal* and the *Winona.* Subsequent to this action, the *Winona* moves to support the campaign to seize Vicksburg. The Confederates sustain 39 killed, 112 wounded and 150 missing or captured. After this encounter, the *Princess Royal* patrols off the coast of Texas until summer of 1865, when it heads north; in August it is decommissioned and becomes a merchant ship, the *General Sherman.*

In Pennsylvania, Mechanicsburg surrenders to Confederate troops. Also, the 71st New York Militia and Miller's Philadelphia Artillery Battery skirmish with Confederates at Oyster Point. Casualty figures are unavailable. Other Pennsylvania troops (led by Colonel Frick) battle against Confederates at Wrightsville. At Carlisle, the Confederates raise their colors over Carlisle Barracks.

In Tennessee, a contingent of a Union division, commanded by General Robert B. Mitchell, engages a Confederate force at Rover. The Union sustains seven wounded. Confederate casualty figures are unavailable.

In West Virginia, General French, pursuant to orders of the previous day, abandons the Union positions at Harpers Ferry. About 7,000 of his troops move to Frederick, Maryland, while a force of about 4,000 men departs for Washington, D.C., bringing the Union property and supplies with them.

June 29 (Monday) **In Louisiana,** a skirmish between Union and Confederate units develops at Lake Providence. Specific units are unreported.

In Maryland, at Westminster, a Union 90-man detachment of the 1st Delaware Cavalry, led by Major Napoleon Knight, clashes with Confederates. The Union sustains two killed and seven wounded. The Confederates suffer three killed and 15 wounded. Also, in Baltimore, the citizens construct barricades.

In Pennsylvania, General George G. Meade's Union army is on the march. By day's end, the right wing will be deployed at New Windsor, while the left wing deploys at Emmitsburg.

Left: Citizens of Baltimore build barricades (Mottelay, *The Soldier in Our Civil War*, 1886). *Above:* Burning of a bridge over the Susquehanna at Columbia, Pennsylvania (*Harper's Pictoral History of the Civil War*, 1896).

Meade's left flank is guarded by General John Buford's cavalry, some of which is at Gettysburg, and the right flank is protected by General Hugh Kilpatrick's division at Hanover. At McConnellsburg, a contingent of the 1st New York Cavalry, commanded by Captain Jones, engages a Confederate cavalry contingent. The Union sustains one wounded. The Confederates suffer two killed and about 95 captured. Meanwhile, the Union occupies Hanover and York. The Confederates abandon Wrightsville. Another Pennsylvania town, Columbia, is placed under martial law. At Carlisle, occupied by the Confederates on the 27th, Confederate General Ewell receives orders to depart for Gettysburg. The citizens become elated as the Rebels move out, but unknown to the civilians, the Confederates will return on 1 July.

In Virginia, the Confederate cavalry of Jeb Stuart turns back a contingent of Union cavalry led by Major Knight at Winchester.

In Union general officer activity, Colonel George Armstrong Custer is promoted to the rank of brigadier general. On the following day, Custer assumes command of Brigadier General Joseph Copeland's Michigan regiments. About one week after the fighting at Gettysburg, General Copeland is appointed commander of the "depot for drafted men" located at Annapolis Junction. Also, Colonel Wesley Merritt (West Point, 1860) is promoted to brigadier general. He commands a brigade (General John Buford's division) at Gettysburg the following month and afterward serves with the Army of the Potomac. Captain Elon John Farnsworth (8th Illinois Regiment), a member of General Pleasonton's staff, is appointed brigadier general. Farnsworth is the nephew of General John Franklin Farnsworth. Also, Captain (later major general) Wesley Merritt (West Point, 1860) is appointed a brigadier general. At the time the war erupted, Captain Merritt held the rank of lieutenant in a company of dragoons in Utah, but he was ordered to return to the East. He became aide-de-camp to General Philip St. George Cooke and afterward to General George Stoneman, the latter having succeeded Cooke as

commander of cavalry, Army of the Potomac; however, he also commanded a reserve brigade during the Chancellorsville campaign.

June 30 (Tuesday) In Louisiana, the Mississippi Marine Brigade under General Alfred Ellet engages Confederates at Bayou Tensas.

In Pennsylvania, Stuart's cavalry again clashes with Union forces (3rd Division, Cavalry Corps, Army of the Potomac) at Hanover, outside Gettysburg. The Union troops commanded by General Hugh Judson Kilpatrick (West Point, 1861) mount a counter-attack, inflicting heavy casualties on the Confederates. Generals George Custer and Alfred Pleasonton participate in this action. The Union sustains 12 killed and 43 wounded. The Confederates suffer three killed and 15 wounded.

General Meade, recently appointed commander of the Army of the Potomac, sets his battle plans for the imminent engagement with the Confederates under Lee. He chooses to establish positions along the Big Pipe Creek slightly beyond Westminster Hills; his army units receive their movement instructions on the following morning. Meade stipulates the anticipated tenacity of the Confederates and he emphasizes the past heroism of the Union troops; however, he mandates firmness in the face of the enemy and issues specific instructions regarding the troops. He authorizes his corps' commanders "to order the instant death of any soldier who fails to do his duty at this hour." In other activity, a Union contingent under Colonel Roome composed of elements of the 22nd and 37th New York Militia and Lander's Battery skirmish with Confederates at Sporting Hill. The Confederates sustain 13 killed and 20 wounded.

In Maryland, Baltimore comes under martial law.

In Union activity, United States Marine Corps active duty strength stands at 3,000, including 2,931 enlisted men and 61 officers.

In Union general officer activity, Brigadier General Erastus B. Tyler, after having com-

manded a brigade at Fredericksburg and at Chancellorsville, is transferred to Baltimore, where he assumes a command with the defenses of Baltimore. His brigade's (Pennsylvania regiments) enlistments had expired. He remains in Baltimore for the duration. In March 1865, he receives the rank of brevet major general. In August 1865 he is mustered out of the service.

Summer In Arizona, hostilities with the Navajos continue to plague the U.S. Army. Due to the ongoing war with the Confederate States, it is prevented from executing a full fledged campaign against them. General Carleton dispatches a force under Kit Carson to eliminate the problem. The column, composed of U.S. Army regulars, New Mexico volunteers and allied Indians (Ute and Zuni), departs Fort

Major General Erastus Tyler (Mottelay, *The Soldier in Our Civil War*, 1886).

Union, New Mexico, en route to the Pueblo–Colorado River region. By autumn, the troops arrive and make headquarters at Fort Defiance (abandoned during 1861). The fort at this time is also known as Fort Canby. The arrival of the army in great strength leads to difficult times for the Indians. Throughout the winter months of 1863-1864, the Indians little by -little are compressed into nearly untenable positions in canyons while their food supply is severed. Army riflemen liquidate the livestock and either kill or seize the horses. Conditions for the Indians continue to deteriorate until finally, in spring of 1865, the Navajo are compelled to surrender. The alternative is starvation. The Navajo and a group of Mescalero Apaches are corralled at Fort Defiance until they are later forced to march to Fort Sumner. Thousands of captives make the journey the following winter. Meanwhile, the fort is again abandoned, giving some fugitive Navajos an easy target. They destroy the fort. Subsequently, a new treaty (Navajo Treaty of 1868) is agreed upon. Once again Fort Defiance rises as the Navajo return to their lands and the old fort becomes an Indian agency.

July In Utah, representatives of the Bannocks, Goshutes and Shoshones hold a conference with General Patrick Connor at Fort Bridger. An Indian superintendent, James D. Doty, attends the meeting, which results in an agreement. The Indians agree to vacate their lands in both Box Elder and Cache Counties. Many find new grounds near Fort Hall, Idaho. The Southern Paiutes come to terms with the Mormons and they settle in Utah, while the Navajos, who continue to resist the army campaign against them, wind up in San Juan County. At the conclusion of the Civil War, the Army still has not vanquished the Utes. Nonetheless, the Utes are unable to overcome the natural elements, and acute shortage of food during the winter of 1865–1866 inflicts horrendous injury to the tribe.

Samuel Wragg Ferguson (West Point, 1857), a staff officer with Confederate General Beauregard, is promoted to brigadier general. Fergu-

General Smith's headquarters, Carlisle, Pennsylvania, and the barracks destroyed by Confederates under Fitzhugh Lee (Mottelay, *The Soldier in Our Civil War*, 1886).

son receives command of a brigade that will become attached to the forces of Brigadier General William Hicks "Red" Jackson. Jackson's division participates at Vicksburg, the Meridian Expedition, the Atlanta Campaign and various other places in Georgia and the Carolinas until the conclusion of the conflict.

July 1 (Wednesday)   In Mississippi, General Grant's Army is preparing to launch a general assault against Vicksburg. The order was issued to "assault on the sixth of July." Also, a contingent of the 17th Corps skirmishes with Confederates at Black River on this day and the next.

In the Indian Territory (Oklahoma), a Union force composed of the 3rd Wisconsin, 6th and 9th Kansas and 2nd Colorado Cavalry Regiments, the 1st Kansas (79th U.S. Colored Troops) and 3rd Indian Home Guards, commanded by Colonel Williams, engages a Confederate force led by Colonel (later general) Watie at Cabin Creek. The Union sustains two killed and 15 wounded. The Confederates suffer 40 killed, unknown wounded and three captured. Colonel Watie, part Cherokee, had sided with the Confederates; however, most of the Cherokees support the Union.

In Pennsylvania, at Gettysburg the setting is fixed. Two confident armies prepare to dev-

astate the enemy, realizing only one may be victorious. Union cavalry sets the pace, seizing the hill and ridges to the north and west of Gettysburg, delaying the advance of the Confederates under Lt. General Ambrose P. Hill. Additional troops from the 1st and 11th Corps support the cavalry by midday. Confederates control the territory northeast of Culpsville, west through Gettysburg and south to Seminary Ridge and Little Round Top, setting the battle lines for the upcoming battle. General George G. Meade instructs General John Sedgwick to move his force (Sixth Corps) from the far right to Manchester to the rear of Big Pipe Creek. The First, Third and Eleventh Corps are directed to relocate from Marsh Creek (far left) to Gettysburg to join Buford's command, which had arrived there from Middleburg. Meade's center, composed of the Fifth Corps (Sykes) and Twelfth (Slocum), are to move to Two Taverns and Hanover. Also, General Hancock is directed to transfer his Second Corps to Taneytown, where Meade's headquarters will be.

General Lee, in an attempt to outmaneuver and out-think Meade, orders General Ewell to retire from Carlisle and redeploy at Gettysburg. He orders Generals Longstreet and Hill to move from Chambersburg and Fayetteville to the

Left: **Devil's Den at Gettysburg, Pennsylvania** (Johnson, *Campfire and Battlefield: History of the Conflicts and Campaigns,* 1894). *Right:* **Breastworks in the woods at Gettysburg** (*Harper's Pictorial History of the Civil War,* 1896).

same area as General Ewell. General Jeb Stuart is en route, but he encounters difficulty at Hanover (30th) and his progress is greatly hindered. The 12th South Carolina Regiment, part of Confederate Brigadier General Samuel's McGowan's brigade, General William D. Pender's division (A.P. Hill's corps) arrives with the vanguard of McGowan's force, led by Colonel Abner Perrin. It is one of the initial units to enter Gettysburg.

Confederate General Jeb Stuart's cavalry arrives at Carlisle. A contingent under General Fitzhugh Lee arrives on the outskirts of the town, but since other Confederates departed Carlisle on 29 June, Union forces had arrived. Nevertheless, the Confederates demand surrender of the town, but the ultimatum is ignored by General W. F. Smith. Meanwhile, an agreement is reached permitting the women and children to evacuate. Afterward, the Confederates reinitiate a bombardment. General Fitzhugh Lee later issues more ultimatums and they, too, are declined by General Smith. The town remains under Union control, but prior to departing the area at about midnight (1st–2nd), Lee orders the burning of Carlisle Barracks. A lumberyard is also set afire. Inadvertently, Stuart's daylong delay at Carlisle aids the Union, because General Robert E. Lee loses intelligence that would provide details on the Union strength and positioning at Gettysburg. Union casualties at Carlisle are light, but the bombardment does inflict damage to some buildings, including the courthouse on the town square.

In Tennessee, Union forces occupy Tullahoma.

In Virginia, elements of the 4th Corps, commanded by Major General Erasmus Darwin Keyes and General George Washington Getty, again skirmish with a Confederate force at Baltimore Crossroads. The 4th Corps had also engaged the enemy there on June 26. The Union sustains two killed and five wounded. Confederate casualty figures are unavailable. After additional duty (engineering) in Virginia, General Getty, during January 1864, is assigned as acting inspector general of the Army of the Potomac, then he commands a division of the VI Corps at the Wilderness.

In Confederate general officer activity, Colonel Henry Harrison Walker is promoted to the rank of brigadier general. Walker remains with the Army of Northern Virginia and participates in various battles, including Spotsylvania, where he sustains a wound, his second since entering the Confederacy.

In Naval activity, the USS *Western World* is ordered to initiate patrol on the Pamunkey River in Virginia. Later in the month it runs mail to blockade ships operating off North Carolina's coast. During the mission, it also carries 100 sailors to Beaufort, North Carolina, for duty with the blockading squadron ships operating in the sounds. At about this time (July), the U.S. Navy acquires the civilian vessel *Union,* a wooden side-wheeled steamship. It is transformed into a gunboat and commissioned the USS *Fort Jackson* during August 1863; however, it cannot immediately be placed into service due to problems with its boiler. Finally, during the

latter part of the year, it is assigned to the North Atlantic Blockading Squadron. Also at about this time (July), the ironclad monitor USS *Osage* is commissioned. It is assigned to the Mississippi Squadron and patrols primarily on the Mississippi River; later it conducts operations on the Black and Ouachita Rivers (February–March 1864) and the Red River (March–May 1864). In February 1865, it is transferred to the West Gulf Blockading Squadron to assist in the operations in Mobile Bay.

July 1–3 THE BATTLE OF GETTYSBURG General Robert E. Lee's forces engage an overwhelming Union force under General George G. Meade at Gettysburg, in a furious three-day battle fought gallantly on both sides. Seven corps are dispersed along Union lines in what is to be a defensive posture to deal with the threat posed by Lee. The Confederates press forward early to test the mettle of the lines. Slightly beyond Seminary Ridge in the vicinity of Willoughby's Run, a force under Confederate General Henry Heth, en route to Gettysburg, slams into the troops of General Buford, initiating a heated skirmish. Buford, convinced that forces under General John F. Reynolds would hear the ruckus and rush to his aide, raises rigid opposition to the larger attacking force, and for one hour holds well, giving only some ground.

Meanwhile, elements of the First Corps (James S. Wadsworth's division) arrive to bolster Buford. General John F. Reynolds, accompanying Wadsworth, directs Lysander Cutler's brigade to fan out on both sides of the Chambersburg Road and along the railroad cut. However, advancing troops of Jefferson Davis' North Carolina and Mississippi regiments foil the plan and force the Yankees to fall back. During this tenacious skirmish, the Rebels are able to seize one of the guns of Hall's battery. All the while, other Confederates under General James J.

Left: **Confederate General Robert E. Lee's headquarters at Gettysburg (***Harper's Pictoral History of the Civil War,* 1896). *Right:* **General George Gordon Meade (Mottelay,** *The Soldier in Our Civil War,* 1886).

Above: General John F. Reynolds (Mottelay, *The Soldier in Our Civil War*, 1886). *Right:* Little Round Top (*Harper's Pictoral History of the Civil War*, 1896).

Archer are advancing toward some heavy woods opposite Willoughby's Run. This pressure against the Yankees causes alarm, as the understrength defenders ponder pulling back, but the Union's Iron Brigade, bringing up the rear of James S. Wadsworth's force, arrives to neutralize the Confederate superiority.

General Solomon Meredith's Iron Brigade (James S. Wadsworth's division) initiates a flanking movement which stuns the Rebels and gives the Yankees possession of the high ground west of Willoughby's Run, and in the process about 800 Confederate troops, including General Archer himself, are captured. General Archer is held until exchanged during the summer of 1864. Colonel Birkett D. Fry assumes command of Archer's brigade. General John F. Reynolds, directly involved in this maneuver, is struck by a sharpshooter's bullet and succumbs. He is immediately replaced by General Abner Doubleday, who in turn is replaced later in the day upon the arrival of General Winfield S. Hancock. After assuming command, Doubleday directs Meredith to pull back across from Willoughby's Run and simultaneously, he orders reinforcements to speed to support Cutler's besieged troops. The operation succeeds. General Meade selects General John Newton to command the I Corps after Reynolds' death. Later, after the I Corps is disbanded, Newton moves to join General William T. Sherman. John Burns, a civilian older than 70 and a veteran of the War of 1812, left his house and fought with the Iron Brigade. Burns, the only civilian who engages in the battle, is wounded three times, but Union troops get him back to his house and he recuperates.

Meanwhile, as the reinforcements arrive, Cutler's troops initiate a charge and compel the Rebels to fall back, giving Cutler the opportunity to regain a lost gun and to seize two Mis-

sissippi regiments that are snagged at the deep cut of the railroad. The Union receives more muscle when at about 1100, two additional First Corps' divisions, under Generals John C. Robinson and Thomas A. Rowley, arrive at Gettysburg along with four batteries of artillery. General Robinson's division is held in reserve in the vicinity of Oak Knoll, but Rowley's three brigades launch an attack to solidify the extreme left of the Union line.

General Oliver O. Howard arrives at about noon with the 11th Corps. He dispatches two divisions, commanded by Generals Francis C. Barlow and Carl Schurz, to the ridge north of Gettysburg to bolster the 1st Corps, which is steadfastly holding its ground. To further augment the Union positions, Howard directs Steinwehr's division and several batteries of artillery to quickly deploy south of Gettysburg on Cemetery Hill in hopes of neutralizing an expected influx of more Confederate troops, under A.P. Hill, who are pouring out of the mountains near the Cashtown Road. During the intense fighting Schurz is temporarily knocked out of action by the "blow of a gun." During that time, General Schimmelfennig assumes temporary command of Schurz's division.

By about 1400, the Confederate reinforcements funneling from the mountains converge with Ewell's corps, which is advancing along the Harrisburg and Yorktown Roads, emboldening their determination and causing instant alarm within the Union lines of the 1st and 11th Corps. The Rebel surge greatly presses the rigidity of the lines. Following about two hours of incessant fighting, at about 1600, General Howard directs the Union to pull back and redeploy at Cemetery Ridge, but the pull back is not without cost as the Union is hotly pursued through Gettysburg. Confusion makes it worse for the Union as several thousand troops are captured.

Although the Rebels force the withdrawal, Congress later officially thanks Howard for selecting Cemetery Hill and Cemetery Ridge as the fall-back point.

During the heavy fighting, the 143rd Pennsylvania (First Corps) slowly give some ground; however, Sergeant Benjamin Crippen remains a lucrative target as he steadfastly waves the flag for the troops to rally around. Crippen is the last man to retire, but the Confederates slay him as he is waving his fist at them in defiance.

While the Confederates are forcing the withdrawal, General Hancock arrives to assume command due to the recent death of General Reynolds. Hancock is to hold things together until the arrival of General George Meade. Meanwhile, both Hancock and Howard move to restore the lines and repulse the relentless Confederate attacks. Soon the Union begins to regroup. Troops are directed to hold the right flank while other forces are ordered to move upon and hold Cemetery Ridge (Hill).

The ridge, strategically located south of the town, provides the Union with the time it needs to regroup and clearly presents a dilemma to the Confederates, who choose to halt the attack rather than chance sustaining high casualties. Nevertheless, the Confederates remain confident that they can use the pause to regroup and prepare to seize the advantage on the following day. General Meade fully anticipates that General Robert E. Lee will surely propel every available force against the haggard Union lines at first light on the 2nd.

While the Confederates seemingly prepare to deal the final blow at Gettysburg, the battered Union forces, still standing at only two corps, prepare to meet the imminent thrust, but to a man they are beleaguered, having completed long tedious marches to arrive at Gettysburg and being immediately compelled to fend off repeated attacks throughout the day. The Confederates are also suffering from the results of the incessant fighting, but their spirits remain high due to their interpretation of the results of the day's combat. Meanwhile, headquarters at Taneytown is closed as General Meade moves out for Gettysburg to be there to greet Robert E. Lee in the morning. Meade has ordered all troops to converge upon Gettysburg. Throughout the night the troops move to their designated positions, and the trains are dispatched to the rear and will stand at Westminster.

On the 2nd, by about 0700, the Union lines are formed at Gettysburg, prepared to again face the tenacious assaults of the Confederates. Still weary from the previous day's fighting, the Union is intent on raising defiant resistance, but its numbers remain well below the opposing Confederates. Surprisingly, Lee does not order an immediate attack; rather he continues mounting forces in preparation for the assault, inadvertently buying time for the beleaguered Yankees. Meanwhile, additional troops under General John Sedgwick (Sixth Corps) are en route; they had initiated a 32-mile march on the previous night. The Second and Fifth Corps reach the area and the remainder of the Third Corps also arrives to augment Meade's forces.

Opposite the town, the 11th Corps holds at the cemetery, and to its right at Culp's Hill stands the First Corps. Culp's Hill is linked to a ridge that stretches south and east; the Second Corps establishes positions on this ridge. The 12th Corps, which had arrived on the previous night, digs in along the Baltimore Turnpike and places its right near Rock Creek, a small stream. Cemetery Ridge stretches westward and southward, leaning toward Round Top, a pronounced strategic ridge; it is in this area, the continuation of Cemetery Ridge, where the 2nd and Third Corps deploy to establish lines to the left of the 11th Corps. Meanwhile, the Union 2nd Corps remains in reserve while awaiting the arrival of Sedgwick's 6th Corps. In addition, the 5th Corps (General George Sykes), upon the arrival of the 6th Corps (Sedgwick) at 1400, will deploy on the left, permitting the 6th Corps to be held in reserve.

In the meantime, the Confederates, suspending the launching of an assault, continue to deploy their forces. Two divisions of General James Longstreet, those of Generals John B. Hood and Lafayette McLaws, line up on the right opposite Cemetery Hill against the forces of Sickles and Hancock, which extend from Little Round Top to Ziegler's Grove. General A.P. Hill's forces hold the center facing Howard's Corps and General George J. Stannard's brigade from a point at Seminary Ridge to Culp's Hill. The Union forces are bolstered also by three other divisions, those of Generals Doubleday, Wadsworth and John C. Robinson. The far left of the Confederate lines are held by General Ewell's division, which stands in the area near Rock Creek. General Wadsworth's division at Culp's Hill is joined by Slocum's Corps. General Sykes' Fifth Corps, upon its arrival from Union Mills, deploys to the rear of the 12th Corps.

The Union lines remain under an eerie calm as no assault is yet launched, providing more time to prepare for the inevitable; however, the situation had drastically changed since the previous day and Lee fully understands that the Union is not easily going to falter. Lee methodically prepares for the attack rather than risk failure. Nevertheless, the Union reaps the prize as the troops get some well needed rest and the reinforcements are pouring into the area, evening the sides. Confederate Lt. General Longstreet later pays a price for assertions that his force should have mounted an attack on this day at the crack of dawn.

At 1630, the tranquility is shattered as the Confederate artillery sounds the attack. The Union left is belted by a furious infantry assault. The Rebels strike the position hard but are repelled. Longstreet assaults Sickles' and Sykes' positions at Peach Orchard and Wheatfield. Sickles' Third Corps is attacked at the orchard near Emmitsburg Road; the Yankees hold for awhile, but they are forced to give some ground. Sickles rallies his troops, but again, superior numbered Confederate forces compel Sickles (by this time himself wounded) to pull back. This attack places John B.

Hood's division, which includes Hood's Texas Brigade, between Sickles' left and Little Round Top. Sickles had been ordered to deploy at the Round Tops, but instead he deploys in the Peach orchard, creating the salient that Longstreet overruns. Union General Gouverneur K. Warren notes the absence of infantry on Little Round Top and persuades General George Sykes to fill the void with artillery and a couple of brigades to insure the holding of the ground. Warren, at this time also chief engineer of the Army of the Potomac, by his observation, essentially preserves the Union positions on Cemetery Ridge, terminating the threat of Confederate General John B. Hood, on the move from positions between Big and Little Round Top.

In the meantime, 2nd Corps troops dispatched by Hancock firm up Sickles' right. And then, at about 1700, Sykes' troops arrive to bolster his left, and fortuitously, Sykes' arrival ensures that the Union holds Little Round Top against the ferocious attack by General Hood. At about 1800, Samuel W. Crawford's division (5th Corps), composed of two brigades, both of which are reserves from Pennsylvania, mount a vicious attack, seemingly mimicking the Rebel yell as they advance with boisterous shouts. The tactics work flawlessly. They descend upon the Rebels and chase them down the dangerous rocky slopes of Little Round Top and well beyond, pushing the Rebels across the valley and across the next hill. The Confederates make it into the woods, but they lose about 300 captured during the skirmish. This attack by the Pennsylvanians forestalls any further damage to the left side of the line, but the Rebels surely had inflicted great damage. During the heavy fighting, General Weed's brigade is ordered into a breach at Little Round Top, and the vanguard (140th New York), with unloaded guns and no fixed bayonets, charges the Confederates. Weed sustains a fatal wound that passes through his arm and enters his chest.

General David B. Birney, having assumed command following the wounding of General

Left: General Hancock's force at Little Round Top, Gettysburg. *Right:* Sergeant Benjamin Crippen refuses to surrender the flag at Gettysburg (Johnson, *Campfire and Battlefield: History of the Conflicts and Campaigns,* 1894).

Left: John Burns' house. Burns, a civilian more than 70 years old, participated with the Iron Brigade at Gettysburg and sustained three wounds (Johnson, *Campfire and Battlefield: History of the Conflicts and Campaigns,* 1894). *Right:* Battle of Gettysburg landscape (*Harper's Pictoral History of the Civil War,* 1896).

Sickles, despite the rout at Little Round Top directs his forces to pull back and redeploy about one-half mile at their prior positions near the Emmitsburg Road at Cemetery Ridge, rather than risk needless casualties in the face of a superior force. Once at these new positions, the Union regroups.

While the Union left had been successfully defended, the right is only now coming under assault in a belated attack, one which had been expected much earlier in the day. Confederates under Ewell swoop in rapidly from the north, gaining some unoccupied trenches. Forces under Jubal Early strike fiercely against Cemetery Hill, but this assault is met with a cascade of artillery shells and a wall of fire that inflicts severe casualties upon the attacking troops, which are soon compelled to disengage. In concert with this attack, other troops under Confederate General Edward Johnson (2nd Corps), including a brigade under General John M. Jones, pound against Culp's Hill, which had been short on manpower due to the calls from General John W. Geary (2nd Division, XII Corps) to send reinforcements to other points of attack.

At the point of the assault, it is defended only by one brigade, that of General George S. Greene. The Yankees raise stiff opposition; however, the Confederates make progress and gain some ground on the right. Nonetheless, the major attacks are repulsed, with the Yankees holding firmly as darkness settles in on 2 July. Greene's force preserves the Union line of communication along the Baltimore Pike. Confederate General J.M. Jones sustains a severe wound during this attack.

During the night of the 2nd-3rd, General Lee still thinks that the troops under Ewell might gain Culp's Hill and the area at the Baltimore Road (Pike), but General Meade entertains other ideas. In the midst of darkness at about 0400 on the 3rd, Union artillery rivets the

positions on the Union right that had been gained by Ewell, disrupting the Confederate blueprint, which had been drawn to collapse the Union right and bring victory to Lee. The guns again fall silent on 3 July until after the noon hour.

General Meade correctly anticipates Robert E. Lee's intention on 3 July. Almost eighty pieces of Union artillery under General Henry J. Hunt lay silent as 140 Confederate cannon, the majority of which are posted on the hills occupied by Generals Hill and Longstreet, open up at about 1300. Seventy-five of the Confederate guns are under the command of Colonel (later General) Edward P. Alexander, who has read the same books as his Yankee adversaries on Cemetery Ridge, the latter receiving much of his concentrated fire. After an earth-shattering two-hour barrage, the Yankee artillery survives, and it still retains sufficient ammunition to begin mowing down the 15,000 (George Pickett's command) who exit the woods and move in cadence toward nearly invincible Union positions.

As the Confederates confidently advance closer, the march turns into a futile charge with the losses becoming grave. Some of Pickett's men reach the stone wall, only to be slain or captured. The famous charge of 47 regiments under Pickett is the turning point of the battle. The charge is remembered for its gallantry, but also for its horrendous casualties. The 28th North Carolina Regiment, attached to Isaac R. Trimble's division, loses nearly one-half of its troops to Union fire. The Confederates are badly beaten and the imminent threat to Pennsylvania is terminated by the end of the day's fighting on 3 July. Ironically, the commander for whom the charge is remembered does not actually participate in the attack.

The charge had been expected to succeed; however, the troops held in reserve, including the 12th South Carolina Regiment, remain in

place at the sunken road, once it becomes clear that Pickett's Charge had been shattered. Also, during the Confederate charge, four Pennsylvania regiments under General Alexander Webb sustain about 450 either killed or wounded. General Webb subsequently becomes a recipient of the Medal of Honor for his courageous actions during the engagement.

Major General George G. Meade (West Point, 1835) delivers Robert E. Lee (West Point, 1829) his worst defeat of the war, and the North is spared of any future invasion by the South. The field of battle is silent except for the scurrying of men trying to comfort the wounded. The smell of gunpowder still permeates the air, cloaking the bodies of fallen heroes from both sides. Some of the troops, such as the Confederate snipers who controlled Devil's Den, are not located until months after the battle. One Union unit of the 6th Pennsylvania assaults a Confederate log cabin around Devil's Den, capturing a whole squad.

The Union has 3,155 killed, 14,529 wounded and 5,365 missing. Confederates have 3,903 killed, 18,735 wounded and 5,425 missing.

Among Union officers, Major General John Fulton Reynolds (West Point, 1841) and Brigadier Generals Stephen H. Weed (West Point, 1854), Samuel K. Zook and Elon J. Farnsworth are killed. General Zook, while moving his command to replace General Barnes' troops on the line, had been hit in the stomach on the 2nd. He dies just after midnight (2nd-3rd). Colonel Kenner Garrard assumed command of Weed's brigade after he was slain on Little Round Top. Union Colonel Strong Vincent is killed while showing tremendous heroism at Little Round Top, and for his actions, he is posthumously appointed brigadier general effective the date of the battle. Colonel James C. Rice, while in temporary command of a brigade at Little Round Top, maintains discipline and his brigade contributes greatly to the

Left: Colonel Edward Cross (Mottelay, *The Soldier in Our Civil War*, 1886). *Above:* The wheatfield at Gettysburg where General Reynolds fell (*Harper's Pictoral History of the Civil War*, 1896).

Union's success there. He is promoted to brigadier general. Rice's brigade sustains about 350 casualties. Union General Daniel E. Sickles loses his right leg.

Winfield Scott Hancock is wounded in the thigh. General Andrew A. Humphreys assumes temporary command of Hancock's II Corps until Hancock returns to duty late in the year. General Solomon Meredith (Iron Brigade) is severely injured when his horse is shot from under him. Also, after this engagement, General Alexander Webb leads General Gibbon's division during the Rappahannock campaign, and he sustains a severe wound at Spotsylvania. General Schimmelfennig, subsequent to the contest at Gettysburg, requests a transfer from the XII Corps. He is assigned to South Carolina, but once again he is struck with illness (malaria) that prevents him from immediately departing for his new post. He arrives in Charleston in time to see its fall to the Union during February 1865.

Gabriel R. Paul (West Point, 1834) is wounded. A bullet passes through his temple and exits through his left eye, causing blindness, on the first day of the battle. John Gibbon is wounded and carried from the field. General Gibbon, after recuperating, receives easy duty as commanding officer of the Cleveland and Philadelphia draft depots for awhile; however, he returns to the field in tine to command a division under General Grant during 1864 (Overland Campaign). Union General James Barnes (West Point, 1829), whose division had taken and held Little Round Top, is also wounded. General Barnes is wounded at Gettysburg and afterward his field service is terminated. He serves during the remainder of the war in garrison duty and some prison duty. Union Colonel John Rutter Brooke (brigadier general, May 1864) is wounded. Union General Solomon Meredith, commander of the Iron Brigade, is wounded severely and knocked out of action until the following November. It is Meredith's brigade which initiates infantry action at the battle. In addition, Colonel Lucius Fairchild (later brigadier general) and Brigadier General Charles K. Graham are both wounded and captured. Fairchild sees no further action.

Union Brigadier General David A. Russell (West Point, 1845) participates. Union General Daniel Sickles acquired notoriety prior to the outbreak of war when in 1859 he shot and killed the son of Francis Scott Key (author of the "Star Spangled Banner") when he discovered the younger Key was having an affair with his wife. Sickles was acquitted at his trial. He lives until May 1914, but in the latter part of his life he loses his faculties. Also, Colonel Edward Cross (9th New Hampshire Infantry Regiment) is mortally wounded. Colonel John Ramsay is wounded on the 2nd while engaged in the Wheatfield. After recovering, Colonel Ramsay returns to duty and participates at the battles of the Wilderness, Spotsylvania and at Cold Harbor. On 5 June 1864, he receives command of the 2nd Brigade, 2nd Division (II Corps).

The 149th New York supported the stance that forestalled disaster at Culp's Hill, but its colonel, Henry A. Barnum, was absent due to wounds sustained at Malvern Hill. Nevertheless, the regiment performed admirably under the command of Lt. Colonel Charles B. Randall. Colonel Barnum returns to the field, after two operations, in time to participate at the Battle of Lookout Mountain. Also, following the fighting at Gettysburg, General Doubleday sees no more field action. He is transferred to

Left: Union positions at Gettysburg (*Harper's Pictoral History of the Civil War*, 1896). *Right:* Union artillery in action at Gettysburg (Johnson, *Campfire and Battlefield: History of the Conflicts and Campaigns*, 1894).

Washington, D.C. At the end of the conflict, Doubleday receives the brevet of major general. He becomes colonel of the 35th Infantry during 1867 and retires from the army in 1873. Afterward he pens *Reminiscences of Forts Sumter and Moultrie (1860–1861)*. Colonel John B. McIntosh is injured in September when his horse falls upon him. After recuperation (May 1864), he resumes command of his brigade and participates at the Battle of Winchester.

After the victory at Gettysburg, General Henry J. Hunt continues as chief of artillery until June of the following year, when General Grant places him in command of the siege operations at Petersburg. General Thomas Kane, having contracted pneumonia during May, participates in the battle. He is breveted major general during 1865 for his actions in the predawn hours of 3 July. Nevertheless, his health does not rebound. He is compelled to resign from the army during November 1863. He returns to Pennsylvania.

Among Confederate officers, Brigadier Generals Richard B. Garnett (West Point, 1841), William Barksdale, Paul J. Semmes, and Lewis A. Armistead (West Point attendance) are killed. Semmes succumbs in Martinsburg, West Virginia, on the 10th. Armistead receives a fatal blow; he succumbs on July 5 in a Union field hospital. Confederate Major General William D. Pender suffers a pernicious leg wound; he succumbs July 18 en route back to Staunton, Virginia, subsequent to the amputation of his leg. General Pender had been promoted on May 27. Colonel Benjamin G. Humphreys, 21st Mississippi Infantry, assumes command of Barksdale's brigade; Humphreys is promoted to the rank of brigadier general during August.

Confederate Generals William Smith, George Thomas "Tige" Anderson, Henry Heth (West Point, 1847), Wade Hampton, Alfred M. Scales, John Marshall Jones, Jerome B. Robertson, Eppa Hunton and Isaac R. Trimble (West Point, 1822) are wounded. Trimble loses one leg and is not released until February 1865. He returns to Baltimore, where he succumbs on 2 January 1888. General Birkett D. Fry (while leading General Archer's brigade) is wounded and captured). Brigadier General James J. Pettigrew assumes command of Heth's division after General Heth is taken out by a wound. General Scales recuperates and participates in the Virginia campaigns during 1864; however, toward the closing days of the war, he is again on sick leave and does not receive an official parole. Nonetheless, he applies for amnesty during 1866 and afterward he practices law. After serving in the North Carolina state legislature, he is elected to the U.S. Congress, serving from 1875 to 1884, followed by his election as governor during 1884, a post he holds for four years. He dies on 8 February 1892.

During Lee's retreat from Gettysburg, Confederate Colonel Collett Leventhorpe, 11th North Carolina, is also wounded, and soon after, he is captured while returning to Virginia. Leventhorpe is held prisoner for nearly one year. After his release, he will be appointed brigadier general. Another Confederate brigadier general,

James L. Kemper, is wounded and captured. After his release, Kemper is unable to resume duty in the field; however, later he is promoted to the rank of major general and assigned to command the Confederate reserve forces in Virginia. After the war he is elected governor of Virginia. He serves from 1874 until 1877. His death occurs on 7 April 1895 in Orange County, Virginia.

Confederate Generals Albert G. Jenkins and John B. Hood are wounded. Hood's wound separates him from his division and his original

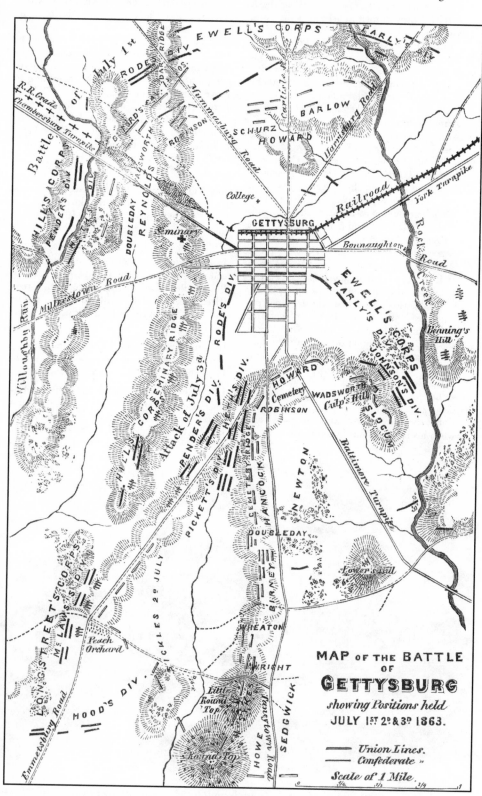

Battle of Gettysburg (*Harper's Pictoral History of the Civil War*, 1896).

unit, Hood's Texas Brigade. At Chickamauga, Hood again sustains a wound. Brigadier General Albert G. Jenkins essentially remains out of service until the fall. Also, General John Geary, subsequent to the action at Gettysburg, is transferred west, where he participates at Wauhatchie and at Chattanooga. Afterward, when the XI and XII Corps are merged to become XII Corps, Geary receives command of the 2nd Division and participates in Sherman's "March to the Sea." After Sherman takes Savannah, Georgia, General Geary is made its military governor.

Also, Captain William H. Forney (brother of Confederate General John Forney) is wounded and left on the field when his unit, the 10th Alabama, is forced to withdraw. Captain Forney will be kept prisoner for more than one year, and after exchange he becomes a brigadier general in William Mahone's division. Confederate Brigadier General Junius Daniel is personally unscathed; however, his brigade, heavily engaged during the first day of battle, sustains the heaviest amount of casualties of all the brigades in the Confederate 2nd Corps. General James J. Archer and a substantial number of his Tennessee brigade are seized by Federal troops. Jeb Stuart's tired troops arrive at Gettysburg on the 2nd, too late to be of any importance to the cause, and they are intercepted on the 3rd by General Custer's Michigan brigade, which prevents the Confederate cavalry under Stuart from participating in the main action. Custer's cavalry held steadfastly on the Union right flank, playing a pivotal role in securing the Union victory.

Lt. General Richard S. Ewell, although not wounded, is in bad health since the loss of his one leg the previous year. Nonetheless, he continues the grueling pace through Spotsylvania, when his ill health finally compels him to take some time off (temporary retirement). Colonel (later brigadier general) Clement Anselm Evans commands the 31st Georgia Infantry Regiment (General John Brown Gordon's division) during this action. Brigadier General Stephen D. Ramseur participates. His brigade engages the Union in General John C. Robinson's sector near Seminary Ridge on the first day of fighting. The attack is a success, and his troops press the Union troops as they retreat; however, the attack is halted and an anticipated attack on the following day, the 2nd, is postponed due to complications that occur while attempting to move into position. Confederate Colonel Jerome B. Robertson, after recovering from his wound (his second), will lead his Texas Brigade into Tennessee under the command of Lt. General James Longstreet. Sometime after the campaign in Knoxville, General Robertson is ordered to the Trans-Mississippi Department.

July 2 (Thursday) **In Tennessee,** Union soldiers from the 104th Illinois skirmish with a contingent of Confederates at Elk River, capturing the Rebel-held stockade and holding the bridge.

In Kentucky, Confederate cavalry under General Morgan crosses the Cumberland River at Burkesville (Marrowbone) en route to Green River. Morgan's Raid had been met by the 1st and 9th Kentucky Cavalry and the 24th Indiana Battery.

In Louisiana, the 2nd Rhode Island Cavalry skirmishes with Confederates at Springfield Landing. Casualty figures are unavailable.

In Virginia, a contingent of the 5th Pennsylvania Cavalry skirmishes with a Confederate unit at Bottom's Ridge. The Union sustains one killed. The Confederates lose 25 captured. Also, a Union force with elements of the 10th West Virginia Volunteer Regiment, one com-

pany of cavalry, and Battery G, West Virginia Artillery, led by Colonel Thomas M. Harris, repulses an attack launched by Confederates under General William Lowther Jackson at Beverly. Casualty figures are unavailable. Also, the Union evacuates Suffolk.

In Naval activity, a double-ended side-wheel steamer, the *Eutaw*, is commissioned the USS *Eutaw.* Lieutenant Commander H.C. Blake receives command. The *Eutaw* is assigned to the North Atlantic Blockading Squadron and placed on patrol duty along the James and Potomac Rivers, but it also patrols as far south as the southern tip of North Carolina. Near the mouth of the Piankatank River, the USS *Samuel Rotan* encounters and seizes the *Champion*, a schooner. Afterward, the *Rotan* resumes its normal patrol schedule and subsequently seizes some small craft. By October, the *Rotan* sails to Norfolk for repairs; it remains out of service until January 1864. Then it serves in the Chesapeake, and toward the latter part of the year, it supports General Grant's campaign against Petersburg and Richmond. The *Rotan* is decommissioned in New York on 10 June 1865 and is sold on 15 August.

July 3 (Friday) **In Alabama,** forces under General Rosecrans move into Bridgeport and Stevenson. A supply depot is established at Stevenson.

In Tennessee, Confederate General Bragg on this day arrives at Tullahoma. Rosecrans' force poses a threat to Bragg's rear, and the Union also is positioned to sever Bragg's primary supply line, the Western and Atlantic Railroad.

In Pennsylvania, Union troops, including the 6th U.S. Cavalry led by Major S.H. Starr, engage southern cavalry under Generals Beverly Holcombe Robertson and John Marshall Jones at Fairfield. Pvt. George C. Platt becomes the recipient of the Medal of Honor for gallantry at this action. During the heavy fighting at Get-

UNION GRAVES.

Left: Union graves after the Battle of Gettysburg (Mottelay, *The Soldier in Our Civil War*, 1886). *Right:* General George Meade's headquarters at Gettysburg (Johnson, *Campfire and Battlefield: History of the Conflicts and Campaigns*, 1894).

Left: The third day of the Battle of Gettysburg. *Right:* Pickett's Charge at Gettysburg (Johnson, *Campfire and Battlefield: History of the Conflicts and Campaigns*, 1894).

tysburg, Sgt. William Hincks and two other troopers jump a wall and overrun a contingent of the 14th Tennessee, seizing their flag, which boasted 12 battle honors.

In Kentucky, John Hunt Morgan raids Columbia. He is opposed by the 1st Kentucky and 2nd Ohio Cavalry and the 45th Ohio Mounted Volunteers. Casualty figures are unavailable.

July 3–4 SURRENDER OF VICKSBURG White flags arise at Confederate positions in Vicksburg. At about 0730, two Confederate officers, General John S. Bowen (West Point, 1853) and Colonel L.N. Montgomery approach Union lines in General Burbridge's sector requesting terms for the surrender of Vicksburg. The Confederates carry a letter from General John C. Pemberton. At 3:00 P.M., Grant—accompanied by Generals Ord, James B. McPherson, John A. Logan and A.J. Smith—meets with Confederates John C. Pemberton, John S. Bowen and L.M. Montgomery. Grant, standing under an oak tree about halfway between the positions of the opposing forces, meets with John Pemberton and the two shake hands. Confederate General Pemberton seeks terms, but they are rejected. Grant's ultimatum is unconditional surrender.

Differences are settled and surrender occurs the following day. Grant allows the Confederates to "sign paroles and [agree] not to fight again until exchanged and to permit officers to retain firearms and a mount." Initially, Pemberton, in response to the offer of surrender, requests that his command march out of the city with their colors and arms, and at that time, they will lay them down in the front of their lines while turning over possession of the city. The Union responds, saying that if they decide to march out and lay down their arms and then return within the works as prisoners, the Union will permit it. Pemberton agrees to the terms. The Confederates march out according to Union dictates while McPherson's corps stands by.

Surrender occurs at 10:00 A.M. on July 4.

Some Confederate units, including the brigade under General Winfield Scott Featherston (Loring's division), are not with the main body, and this turns into a good fortune. His force heads east and joins with General Joseph E. Johnston's force at Jackson, Mississippi. Subsequently, Featherston's brigade is attached to General Polk's command, also in Mississippi, and participates in the various battles still to be fought in the campaign in Atlanta and those in Tennessee. From there, the brigade moves to the Carolinas. Also, Brigadier General John D. Stevenson participates in this action as commander of a brigade in General Logan's division (XVII Corps).

Meanwhile, General William T. Sherman, aware of the imminent surrender of Vicksburg, leaves his positions at Haines Bluff to pursue Johnston, who has withdrawn upon the fall of Vicksburg toward Jackson. General Sherman's five divisions are bolstered by the remainder of the Thirteenth and Fifteenth Corps. General Johnston, with four divisions, is deeply entrenched at Jackson with the divisions of Generals Loring, Breckinridge, French and William H.T. Walker. Confederate Lieutenant General John C. Pemberton (born in Philadelphia, Pa. and a graduate of West Point, 1837) is captured.

Confederate Major Generals John Horace Forney (West Point, 1852), Carter L. Stevenson, Martin L. Smith (West Point, 1842), Franklin Gardner (West Point, 1843; commanding Port Hudson) and John Stevens Bowen are captured. General Bowen was wounded at Shiloh and fought against the Union at Port Gibson, but he contracts dysentery during the siege of Vicksburg and dies on 13 July. Major General John H. Forney, subsequent to his release, is transferred to the Trans-Mississippi Department and for awhile, he commands a division (General John G. Walker's), but he winds up without any command. After the close of hostilities, he takes up farming and civil engineering until his death in September 1903.

Confederate Brigadier Generals Seth M. Bar-

ton (West Point, 1849), William E. Baldwin, and Stephen D. Lee (West Point, 1854) are captured. Barton is later exchanged. He will then receive command of General Armistead's brigade in General George Pickett's division. General Stephen D. Lee, who had commanded General John C. Pemberton's artillery at Vicksburg, is also exchanged. He will command the cavalry in the Department of Mississippi, Alabama, East Louisiana and West Tennessee. On 9 July, General William Nelson Rector Beall (West Point, 1844) surrenders at Port Hudson. One Confederate officer, Lieutenant Colonel Hylan B. Lyon (West Point, 1856), commanding the 8th Kentucky, manages to lead his entire command away from the Union net. Lyon subsequently becomes brigadier general in the Confederate Army.

Confederate Brigadier General John C. Moore (West Point, 1849) is captured. Following his release, Moore is assigned duty in General Bragg's command and then is transferred to Mobile, Alabama, to help forestall the Union advance there. Confederate Colonel Alexander W. Reynolds (50th Virginia Infantry) is also captured at Vicksburg. After his parole, Reynolds is promoted to brigadier general and attached to General William Joseph Hardee's corps during the Atlanta campaign against Sherman. Another future Confederate colonel (later general), Charles M. Shelley, presently colonel of the 30th Alabama, is seized at the fall of Vicksburg. After exchange, Shelley participates with his regiment as part of the Army of Tennessee. He is in various actions in Tennessee and afterward in the Carolinas. Shelley is appointed brigadier general during September 1864.

Confederate Colonel Thomas Neville Waul, commanding the Texas Legion, is also captured. Following his release, he is appointed brigadier general and participates against Banks during the Red River Campaign and against General Steele when he advances overland to assist Banks during spring 1864. In addition, Confederate Colonel Thomas P. Dockery, 19th Arkansas Regiment, in command of a brigade in General John S. Bowen's division, is seized. After release Dockery is promoted to brigadier general in August. Beyond those mentioned above, most of the brigade of General John C. Vaughn surrenders to the Union. After his release, General Vaughn will be deployed in the Shenandoah Valley where he, along with a cavalry brigade, accompanies Jubal Early on a raid to the outskirts of the federal capital in 1864.

Brigadier General Alfred Cumming (West Point, 1849), attached to General Pemberton's command, is seized at the surrender. After being released, he will command a brigade in General Carter L. Stevenson's division (Army of Tennessee). General Carter L. Stevenson is also seized here. Subsequent to his release Stevenson is reassigned within the Army of Tennessee. Confederate Colonel (later brigadier general) Edward Higgins is again captured. He is released and promoted to brigadier general effective 29 October 1863.

Union Generals John B. Sanborn and John Eugene Smith participate at this battle. Subsequently, General Smith is in the Atlanta campaign and Sherman's "March to the Sea." Also, Confederate General John Adams, leading a Mississippi brigade, makes it to Mississippi. Colonel William Wirt Adams, the brother of John Adams, will be promoted to brigadier general (effective September 1863) for his gallant service leading Mississippi cavalry during the Vicksburg Campaign. Confederate Brigadier General Thomas H. Taylor is also captured during this action. Following his release, Taylor, provost marshal on the staff of General S.D. Lee at the time of his capture, after his exchange becomes post commander at Mobile. General John Crawford Vaughn, along with his entire brigade, is also captured.

General U.S. Grant receives the nickname "Unconditional Surrender Grant" after demanding and receiving the surrender of Vicksburg. The siege, which began on May 22, finally ends when well over 29,000 Confederate soldiers surrender to the Union Army, relinquishing both the city and control of the Mississippi River. This is the first day the Mississippi is free of Confederate forts and troops since the outbreak of the war. Confederate-held Port Hudson, Louisiana, surrenders on 8 July.

The USS *Ivy*, at times the flagship of Admiral David Porter during the campaign against Vicksburg, and a participant on the Red River (towing gunboats) after the capture of Vicksburg, becomes a dispatch boat, a towship and a detaining ship for Confederate prisoners. During 1864, the USS *Ivy* participates in the Red River Campaign as a primary ship in Porter's fleet when it encounters obstacles above the rapids at Alexandria, Louisiana. At the conclusion of the campaign, the *Ivy* is utilized to tend coal barges at Donaldsonville until it is decommissioned and afterward sold on 17 August 1865. The USS *Winona* also participates in the seizure of Vicksburg. Meanwhile, during this year, the U.S. Navy acquires a steam tug, the *Ivy*, purchased as a monitor and commissioned the USS *Monterey*. The steam tug *Monterey* is renamed the *Ivy* on 3 January 1891.

July 4 (Saturday) **In Arkansas,** a Union force composed of one division under Major General Prentiss clashes with Confederate forces of Generals Marmaduke, Price and Theophilus Holmes at Helena. The Confederates under Holmes include the troops under Generals Sterling Price, Marmaduke, L.M. Walker and James Fagan, the latter out of Little Rock. The combined force numbers more than 7,000 troops. The Union force at Helena numbers about 4,000, due to the recent departure of many units that moved to Vicksburg. Confederates under Marmaduke strike Rightor Hill and hit a wall of fire that forbids progress. Meanwhile, L.M. Walker, expected to bolster Marmaduke, finds his positions jeopardized and he fails to cover Marmaduke's left flank. On the Confederate right, Union fire originating on Graveyard Hill pounds Fagan's positions, preventing Fagan from jumping off on time to assault Hindman Hill.

In the meantime, Price assaults Graveyard Hill, but without success. Further attacks reach the Union on Graveyard Hill, but confusion among the Confederates continues to hinder their attack. At Hindman Hill, Fagan's force gains the rifle pits, but artillery fire from Helena batteries focuses on his positions and prevents further progress. Some of the troops under Price move toward Fort Curtis, but others advance to try to aid the forces of Fagan. At the rifle pits, Fagan retires. By 1000, the Confederates disengage and retreat. Union Major General Prentiss' division of the 16th Corps and the gunboat USS *Tyler* successfully repel the ferocious assaults, due in great part to the *Tyler* and the Helena batteries. The Union suffers about 57 dead, 146 wounded and 32 missing; Confederates count 173 dead, 687 wounded and 776 missing.

In Kentucky, Confederate cavalry under General Morgan encounters Union forces under Colonel Moore (25th Michigan Cavalry) at Green River Bridge (Tebb's Bend). The Rebels attack, but the Union repels the assault and inflicts severe casualties, particularly among the Confederate officers. The Union sustains six killed and 23 wounded. The Confederates sustain 50 killed and about 200 wounded. Following the skirmish, Morgan heads for Lebanon, defended by a contingent of about 400 troops commanded by Lt. Colonel Charles Hanson.

In Mississippi at Vicksburg, General Grant arrives at Stone House, within the Confederate lines. The Confederate Commander, Lt. General John C. Pemberton, capitulates. The surrender ceremony takes place at 1000. Confederates (enlisted) are permitted to retain their clothing, but no other property. Union losses during the siege number nearly 10,000 killed, wounded and missing, and the Confederate losses are similar (see also, **July 3–4 SURRENDER OF VICKSBURG**). Confederate General Pemberton is not released until May 1864, but at that time, he is not assigned to a new command. He resigns his commission; however, through the actions of President Jefferson Davis, Pemberton is appointed lieutenant colonel of artillery. After the war, General Pemberton, a

Philadelphian, resides in Virginia on a farm near Warrenton, but later he returns to Pennsylvania, where he succumbs on 13 July 1881 at Penllyn in Montgomery County. He is interred in Philadelphia.

Union troops (General William T. Sherman's command) engage the Confederates' Rear Guard at Bolton and Birdsong Ferry, Black River, through the next day. The Confederates lose about 2,000 captured.

In Pennsylvania, at Gettysburg, the two massive armies had clashed in furious combat in and around Gettysburg. Only one civilian is killed during the entire contest. A stray bullet enters a home, killing a young woman named Jennie Wade. The Confederate Army, decisively defeated, begins the long journey back to Virginia. The defeat weighs heavily on the broad shoulders of Robert E. Lee. Union General George Meade's exhausted, triumphant troops savor the victory as they tend to their own battered army. As the Confederates depart, using their wagons to cart the wounded and act as mobile hospitals, the Union ambulances are working tirelessly to prevent as much additional death as possible. Meade's forces do not pursue Lee, who arrives in Virginia on the 13th. Also, Union Brigadier General (Volunteers) Adelbert Ames, who had led a brigade in General Howard's XI Corps, receives the brevet rank of colonel, Regular Army. Following his leadership of a division during the attack against Fort Fisher, North Carolina, Ames will be breveted

Jennie Wade is the only woman killed at Gettysburg (Johnson, *Campfire and Battlefield: History of the Conflicts and Campaigns,* 1894).

major general, volunteers, and brigadier and major general, Regular Army.

In South Carolina, Rear Admiral John A. Dahlgren arrives at Port Royal to assume command of the Naval squadron that is blockading Charleston. He assumes command on 6 July.

In Tennessee, a skirmish develops at Smithsburg. Confederate Brigadier General John Robert Jones is captured and held initially on Johnson's Island and afterward at Fort Warren, Massachusetts. He is finally released on 24 July 1865. During his captivity, the Confederate government makes no move to gain his exchange, and the Confederate Senate does not confirm his commission of brigadier general. He engages in business and afterward becomes chancery of the circuit court, a post he retains until his death in Winchester, Virginia, on 1 April 1901.

In Virginia, Union troops of the 5th Michigan Cavalry repel an assault at Newby's Crossroads. In other activity, Union Major Charles Capehart's 1st West Virginia Cavalry charges down Monterey Mountain at midnight during a treacherous rainstorm in pursuit of a Rebel wagon train retreating from Gettysburg. The raid is successful and destroys many trains in addition to capturing prisoners. The 3rd Cavalry Division, Army of the Potomac, under General Hugh Kilpatrick, engages for two days Confederates under General Jeb Stuart at Monterrey Gap and Smithsburg, and the Union also captures a Confederate troop train. The Union sustains about 30 killed and wounded. The Confederates suffer about an equal number of casualties. In addition, the Union captures a large number of troops.

In Naval activity, Commander David Dixon Porter is promoted to the rank of rear admiral.

July 5 (Sunday)   In Kentucky, a Confederate cavalry force, composed of more than 3,000 troops under General Morgan, attacks a force of Union troops at Lebanon. The Union forestalls defeat for about seven hours, but the superior Confederate force compels surrender of the contingent of about 400 troops under Lt. Colonel Charles Hanson. From here, John Hunt Morgan sets out for Ohio.

In Mississippi, Union troops, including the 5th Minnesota Volunteer Regiment, subsequent to its participation at Vicksburg, move to Jackson. The 5th Minnesota will spend some time guarding the Black River Bridge and eventually moves to La Grange and Memphis, Tennessee, to protect the Memphis and Charleston Railroad (November 1863 to January 1864).

In Pennsylvania, a cavalry component of the Army of the Potomac engages a Confederate force at Fairfield. Casualty figures are unavailable.

July 6 (Monday)   In Kentucky, Confederates under General Morgan surprise a small contingent of four Union troops at Bardstown. The troops, attached to the U.S. 4th Cavalry, attempt to fight the huge force, but after their

ammunition is expended, they emerge from a barn and surrender. Later, Morgan's Raiders halt a Union passenger train at Shepherdsville on the Salt River and capture twenty Union troops.

In Maryland, a contingent of Union cavalry (20th Pennsylvania), led by Colonel John E. Wynkoop, captures about one company of Confederates at Hagerstown. Meanwhile, the 3rd Cavalry Division, Army of the Potomac, clashes with Confederate cavalry at Williamsport. Casualty figures are unavailable.

In Mississippi, the 6th Iowa and the 48th Illinois Volunteers skirmish with a Confederate contingent at Jones' Ford, Black River.

In North Carolina, a Union force composed of the 9th New Jersey, 17th, 23rd and 27th Massachusetts and the 81st and 158th New York Volunteers, commanded by General Charles Adam Heckman, engages Confederates at Quaker Bridge (Comfort). Heckman's force is bolstered by Belger's and Angel's artillery batteries. Casualty figures are unavailable.

In South Carolina, a Union naval squadron debarks a battalion of U.S. Marines to reinforce army troops on Morris Island in an attack against Fort Wagner; however, the Confederates repel the assault, preventing the Union from closing on Charleston.

In Tennessee, a Union contingent led by Major Brown and composed of elements of the 10th Kentucky and the 1st Ohio Cavalry Regiments, operating in the vicinity of Pound Gap, clashes with Confederates. The Union sustains one killed and 14 wounded. The Confederates sustain about 30 killed and wounded and more than 100 captured.

In Union Naval officer activity, Rear Admiral John A. Dahlgren assumes command of the South Atlantic Blockading Squadron. He succeeds Rear Admiral Du Pont.

July 7 (Tuesday)   In California, one company of the 1st Battery, California Mountaineers, engages Indians in a fight at Redwood Creek.

In Kentucky, Confederate General Morgan, en route to Ohio, passes through Lawrenceville and enters Brandenburg along the Ohio River. The town, renowned for its southern sympathies, helps the large force of more than 3,000 Rebels ford the river and enter Indiana. Two confiscated steamboats, the *McComb* and the *Alice Dean,* will begin to transport them on the following day. The USS *Moose* and the *Victory* are en route to neutralize the Confederate threat.

In Mississippi, a Confederate force of about eleven companies, led by Colonel Roddey, attack a one-company contingent of the 39th Iowa Volunteers at Convalescent Corral in the vicinity of Corinth. The Union suffers two wounded and about 21 captured. The Confederates sustain two killed. At Iuka, the 10th Missouri and the 7th Kansas Cavalry Regiments

skirmish with Confederates through the 9th. The Union sustains five killed and three wounded. Confederate casualty figures are unavailable.

In Maryland, a contingent of Union cavalry, including elements of the 6th U.S. Cavalry, commanded by Captain O. Chaflant, sustains nine killed and about 45 wounded while on a reconnaissance mission in the vicinity of Boonsborough. The two sides clash in this area until the 9th.

In West Virginia, the Potomac Home Brigade and the 1st Massachusetts Heavy Artillery skirmish with Confederates at Harpers Ferry bridge.

In the Indian Territory, the 9th Kansas Volunteers commanded by Lieutenants Brundley and Williams engage a war party of Ute Indians at Grand Pass, Fort Halleck (Wyoming) in the Indian Territory (Idaho Territory). The fight lasts for about one hour. The Union sustains one killed. The Indians suffer 21 killed and about 39 wounded.

July 8 (Wednesday)   In Indiana, across from Brandenburg, Kentucky, a small Union force, composed of one gun, attempts to thwart the crossing of the Ohio River by Confederate General Morgan's cavalry. The Confederates, aboard two steam boats, are not hindered by the Union. Rather, the unit is effortlessly overwhelmed and their Parrott gun is confiscated. The Rebels burn the Steamer *Alice Dean,* but only abandon the *McComb.* While Morgan's Raiders move through southern Indiana and Ohio, Lt. Commander Le Royo Fitch orders his ships to initiate pursuit. The USS *Naumkeag* joins the squadron on the following day. Morgan is intercepted on the 19th at Buffington Island. Subsequent to this mission, the *Naumkeag* resumes its normal patrol duties until it is decommissioned at Mound City, Illinois, on 11 August 1865. During the following month, it is renamed the *Montgomery,* and it operates as a commercial vessel until destroyed by fire at Erie, Pennsylvania, on 19 January 1867.

In Louisiana, Union forces, including General Banks' Army of the Gulf and naval forces under Admiral Farragut, overpower the Confederate garrison, commanded by General Frank Gardner, at Port Hudson. The Union has been tightening the vise around Port Hudson, despite being unable to force its capitulation, but with word of the surrender of Vicksburg, General Gardner and his commanders agree to surrender. Gardner had conferred with General N.R. Beall, Colonel Lyle and other officers prior to agreeing to surrender the stronghold. After a meeting with Union General Charles P. Stone, Colonel Henry W. Birge and Lt. Colonel R.B. Irwin, the official surrender takes place on the following day. The siege had begun on May 27. The Union suffers 500 dead and 2,500 wounded. The Confederates suffer 100 killed and 700 wounded. In addition, 445 officers and 6,408 enlisted men are captured.

The capture of Port Hudson essentially ends

Left: **Old Glory being saluted at Port Hudson** (*Harper's Pictorial History of the Civil War*, 1896). *Right:* General Kilpatrick's cavalry after repulsing Confederate cavalry under J.E.B. Stuart at Boonsboro on 8 July (Mottelay, *The Soldier in Our Civil War*, 1886).

the River War. Union control of the Mississippi River splits the Confederacy in half. General Beall, upon his release from prison during 1864, acts under a special agreement between the Confederate and Union governments to establish an office in New York City to work on behalf of Confederates being held in northern prison camps. With the authority of Washington, D.C., Beall is able to sell cotton and use the profits to procure blankets, clothing and other pertinent items to ease the hardship of the Rebel prisoners. This experiment lasts until early August 1864, when Beall is officially released by the Union.

In Maryland, Union cavalry under General Hugh Kilpatrick, in pursuit of Robert E. Lee, clashes with Jeb Stuart's cavalry at Hagerstown. The Union is forced to withdraw to Boonsboro after being repulsed by the Rebels, but at Boonsboro, Kilpatrick repels the Rebels.

In Confederate general officer activity, Colonel Gabriel C. Wharton, 45th Virginia, is promoted to the rank of brigadier general. General Wharton had been at Fort Donelson but escaped capture by fleeing with General Floyd. Afterward he served under Generals Loring and Samuel Jones in western Virginia. Subsequent to his promotion, General Wharton for a while is based in command of the Valley District, and later he is ordered to East Tennessee, where he serves through the winter of 1863–1864 under General Longstreet.

In Naval activity, the *Banker* (wooden merchant steamer) constructed at Cincinnati during 1863, is acquired by the U.S. Navy. It is commissioned the USS *Victory* on 8 July, although not officially purchased until 15 July. The *Victory*, transformed into a tinclad (lightly armored), is assigned to the Mississippi Squadron and afterward operates on the Cumberland, Ohio and Tennessee Rivers on reconnaissance missions.

July 9 (Thursday)   In Kentucky, Confederate General Morgan's entire force of cavalry completes its crossing of the Ohio River and

moves through Indiana en route to Ohio. Union forces under Colonel Frank Wolford, in pursuit, team up with the forces of Generals Edward H. Hobson and James Shackelford at Springfield. The combined force arrives at Brandenburg slightly after the successful crossing. By the latter part of the day, Morgan reaches Corydon, Indiana, where his force destroys the mill and some other property. Indiana Home Guards under Colonel Timberly offer resistance, but lack the power to halt Morgan. The Confederates seize about 200 Union prisoners. From there, the Confederates proceed to Greenville, Palmyra and Salem, the latter being the capital of Washington County, Indiana. At Salem, the Rebels capture about 350 Home Guards, destroy the Louisville and Chicago Railway Depot, and demolish three bridges. Morgan's Raiders will follow the rails of the Madison and Indiana Railroad traveling to Canton and beyond to Vienna. From Vienna, a contingent of his force moves to Old Vernon and another heads for Madison, Indiana. At

General John Hunt Morgan (Mottelay, *The Soldier in Our Civil War*, 1886).

Old Vernon, about 1,200 troops under Colonel Lowe (Barkham) refuses an ultimatum to surrender and engages the Rebels, but Morgan moves on to Versailles. General Hobson's force is composed of about 3,000 troops, including cavalry and artillery. In addition, General Judah, garrisoned in Southern Kentucky, had also received orders to give chase, but his contingent arrives in Louisville well after Morgan had made the crossing. Judah's force is dispatched in boats to intercept the marauding Rebels under Morgan. Also, the USS *Moose* and the *Victory* arrive at Brandenburg. The *Moose* encounters a band of the guerrillas at Twelve Mile Island on 11 July.

In Louisiana, the Union takes official control of Port Hudson, as General Nathaniel Banks accepts the surrender of General Frank Gardner.

In Mississippi, General William T. Sherman's force reaches the vicinity of Jackson. Also, a Union force under General U.S. Grant initiates a siege of Jackson. The 9th, 13th, 15th and a contingent of the 16th Corps participate. The campaign to take Jackson includes fighting at Rienzi, Bolton Depot, Canton and Clinton and continues through the 16th. The Union sustains about 100 killed, 800 wounded and 100 missing. The Confederates sustain about 71 killed, 504 wounded and 764 missing or captured.

July 10 (Friday)   In Arkansas, a Union contingent skirmishes with Confederates at Big Creek. Specific units and casualties are unreported.

In California, at Camp Independence, Captain Moses A. McLaughlin (previously the commander of Camp Babbitt) informs the chiefs and other members of the tribes that they will have to relocate to Fort Tejon, about 200 miles away from their lands. McLaughlin had taken steps to prevent trouble by inconspicuously encircling the Indians, who had assembled on the parade field at Camp Independence. The Indians had not anticipated the bad news. Nevertheless, on the following day, the march begins, with an escort of about seventy troops. Most of the women and children are compelled to walk because only a few wagons are provided. About 1,000 Indians began the trek, and of those, more than 100 never complete the march to Fort Tejon. Some manage to escape en route, but others perish. The Indians do not adapt to the treatment at Fort Tejon and many later make it back to their lands. By summer 1864, there are few if any Indians still at Fort Tejon. Consequently, Fort Tejon is abandoned.

In Kentucky, General Edward H. Hobson's force, composed of about 3,000 troops, completes its crossing of the Ohio River at Brandenburg, and reinitiates pursuit of Confederate General John Hunt Morgan. Morgan continues to raid the area as he travels, but the Union relentlessly chases the Rebel cavalry. Louisville is placed under martial law. The governors of Indiana and Ohio call out the population in an attempt to capture Morgan's force when it enters their states.

In Tennessee, the 4th Missouri Cavalry skirmishes with Confederates at Union City. Casualty figures are unavailable.

In Naval activity, the gunboats USS *Essex, Monongahela, New London* and *Tennessee* exchange fire with Confederates at Whitehall Point. The *Tennessee,* a wooden-hulled, sidewheel steamship, built during 1853 in Baltimore, was seized by Confederates at New Orleans during January 1862. It was recaptured by the Union in April of 1862 when the Union seized New Orleans, and was commissioned the USS *Tennessee* that May.

In Union general officer activity, Brigadier General Quincy Adams Gillmore is promoted to major general. As the commanding officer of the X Corps and the Department of the South, his main priority is the recapture of Fort Sumter, South Carolina, which the Confederates have held since April 1861. The USS *Allegheny Belle, Moose, Naumkeag, Reindeer, Springfield* and the *Victory* (Mississippi Squadron) initiate a mission to intercept the force under Confederate General John H. Morgan, which had crossed the Tennessee River on 8 July to initiate raids in Indiana. The mission continues through July 19.

July 10–September 6 SIEGE OF FORT WAGNER Union forces under General Quincy A. Gillmore have been preparing for the assault on Fort Wagner for some time. General Israel Vogdes has installed batteries on Folly Island, South Carolina, south of Lighthouse Inlet. From Folly Island, the artillery can neutralize the Rebel guns on the southern tip of Morris Island. In addition, the Union has successfully pulled off a ruse by sending out two forces. One under General Alfred Terry, composed of about 3,900 troops, had been brought up the Stono River to James Island. Another contingent, under Colonel Higginson (General Rufus Saxton's command), had departed Beaufort, South Carolina, and advanced up the Edisto River; the mission is to sever Rebel communications via the Charleston Savannah Railroad. The

Confederates, having taken the bait, drop their guard and concentrate on James Island and General Terry rather than Morris Island, setting the stage for the assault, which commences at 0400 on the 10th. Higginson's force encounters extremely heavy resistance and is unable to complete its mission.

U.S. troops under Major General Quincy Adams Gillmore and the U.S. fleet under Admiral John A. Dahlgren attack Fort Wagner. The naval guns of the vessels USS *Catskill* (flagship), *Weehawken, Montauk* and *Nahant* coordinate with the artillery on Folly Island to bombard the fort. Following the tumultuous two-hour bombardment, a force under General George C. Strong moves against the Confederate lines, initiating a fierce contest. Eventually the overwhelming Union pressure forces the Confederates to give some ground and pull back toward Fort Wagner. Relentlessly, the Union advances and encroaches within rifle shot range of the fort. All the while, the naval vessels nudge forward to provide support for the ground troops. The Confederates maintain return fire until about 1200, when Admiral Dahlgren disengages and pulls his vessels back. At about 1300, the Union warships reinitiate the bombardment and continue to pour fire upon the fort until 1800. As night approaches, both sides begin to prepare for the next episode in the saga that will determine the fate of the besieged fortress.

On the 11th, the Union launches a ground assault against the fort, but the troops within the walls establish an impenetrable wall of fire. The attacking brigades under General George C. Strong include his own and that of General Truman Seymour. The attack steps off confidently with the full power of the 3rd New Hampshire, 6th and 7th Connecticut, 9th Maine, 76th Pennsylvania and the 48th and 100th New York Regiments. Nevertheless, the attack force is less than equal to the defensive fire that compels the Union to retire as soon as it advances to the parapets. The hurricane of fire inflicts only slight casualties as the retreat comes off successfully.

While the siege continues, reinforcements from Virginia arrive to augment the fort's garrison. General Beauregard concludes that with his added strength, he could launch an assault to demoralize the Union. On the 16th, a Confederate force under General Johnson Hagwood strikes the positions of General Terry in an attempt to surprise the Yankees and capture the entire command; however, the Rebels, who jump off from Secessionville and gain some immediate success by driving back the pickets, receive an unexpected surprise. Union warships posted nearby join the fight and pound the Rebels. The gunboats, posted on both the Stono and Folly Rivers, pummel the Confederates and inflict about 200 casualties, forcing General Hagwood to retire. General Quincy A. Gillmore withdraws General Alfred Terry's force from James Island. The artillery, including twenty-nine Parrott guns and fourteen mortars, are implanted on Morris Island and positioned from where they can commence firing from dis-

tances ranging from 1,300 to 1,900 yards. Soon after this redeployment, the fort again is targeted with blistering bombardments in coordination with the strategy of Gillmore, who is laying the blueprint for a combined naval-ground assault to reduce the stronghold.

On 18 July in late morning, the warships and the Union artillery commence a thunderous bombardment. The flotilla of ironclads is composed of the USS *Montauk* (flagship), *New Ironsides, Catskill, Nantucket, Weehawken,* and *Patapsco.* Slightly to the rear stand the gunboats *John Paul Jones* (Commander Rhind), *Ottawa* (Lt. Commander Whiting), *Seneca* (Lt. Commander Gibson), *Chippewa* (Lt. Commander Harris) and *Wissahickon* (Lt. Commander Davis), each of which bombards the fort from their long distance positions. The defenders hold on as best they can, returning fire only at intervals during the incessant barrages which last throughout the day. At about dusk, the bombardment subsides while a drenching rainstorm saturates the area. Although the boisterous sounds of the cannons cease, the waterlogged Union ground troops are preparing to advance.

The signal to attack is sounded and two columns step off, tracking along the beach, moving directly toward the heavily defended fortress. The vanguard, led by General George

General Quincy Gillmore (Johnson, *Campfire and Battlefield: History of the Conflicts and Campaigns,* 1894).

Strong, is composed of the 3rd New Hampshire (Colonel John H. Jackson), 6th Connecticut, a contingent of the 7th Connecticut (Colonel John L. Chatfield), 9th Maine (Colonel William Emory), 48th New York (Colonel William Barton), 54th Colored Massachusetts (Colonel Robert G. Shaw), and the 76th Pennsylvania (Colonel D. C. Strawbridge). When the column reaches a point about one-half mile from the fort, the troops are ordered to march at double-quick.

In the meantime, the Confederates anxiously await the storm of blue uniforms that are sweeping forward. Soon the Rebel artillery unleashes a deadly barrage from positions within Forts Sumter and Battery Gregg as well as the guns at Fort Wagner. The Union maintains its pace, advancing even more closely until they come into the range of the riflemen. Still they plod forward, all the while being pummeled by every available weapon. Some have encroached so close that they become recipients of hand grenades.

Undaunted, Strong's troops doggedly brave the hurricane of fire and inch closer, but still the objective seems a world away. In an attempt to evade some of the incessant fire, Strong's troops try to maneuver through a ditch, which at this time has about four feet of water, making the operation more difficult. The first unit to ford the ditch, the 54th Massachusetts, reaches the parapets and ignites a donnybrook. The close-quartered fighting causes many severe wounds as the clashing steel and point-blank fire shreds the opposing units.

One sergeant, Carney, manages to drive the regimental colors into the parapet, but he sustains a severe wound in the process and the commanding officer, Colonel Shaw, receives a mortal blow. The Confederates continue to pummel the 54th and inflict a casualty rate of about 50 percent upon it, forcing the unit to withdraw from its untenable positions. Other units move up, but they too encounter the horrific fire and are unable to penetrate the parapets. General Strong orders the attacking regiments to retire. The effort has been costly, as General Strong has been mortally wounded from a shot that strikes his thigh. The other column under Colonel Putnam then takes the front and it too hammers against the Confederate lines. The 7th New Hampshire, 100th New York, 62nd Ohio and the 67th Ohio drive forward, igniting yet another unruly contest that lasts for about one-half hour. But still the fort holds. Colonel Green also sustains a fatal wound.

The day's fighting has taken a high toll on the Union officer corps. In addition to the loss of General George Crockett Strong, Colonel Putnam is killed and Colonel Chatfield is fatally wounded. General Strong dies 12 days after the battle. On the day following his death, 31 July, he is nominated and confirmed as major general of volunteers effective the day he sustained the wound, 18 July. Also, General Truman Seymour is wounded.

Undaunted by the inability to reduce the fort, General Gillmore makes preparations for yet another assault. Using the cover of darkness, Gillmore redeploys his artillery to more strategic positions and prepares to introduce the Rebels to a new Union ally, dubbed the "Swamp Angel," a formidable 8-inch 200-pound rifle Parrott gun that is poised to spring its power upon Fort Sumter. Nevertheless, the Confederates remain in control of their stronghold.

General Gillmore immediately prepares to re-strengthen his force for another attack, which will be scheduled for mid–August. Gillmore directs that the artillery be moved even closer to fort, and he instructs his commanders to reinforce the earthworks. On the 16th, during the evening, he orders that the Parrott guns commence a short barrage of seven shots to find the range. Of these, only four strike the main walls of Fort Sumter. On 17 August, the Union commences a gargantuan artillery attack, releasing the fury of its guns against Fort Sumter, Fort Moultrie and Battery Gregg, while the fleet commences an equally powerful barrage against Fort Wagner. The Confederate forts zealously return fire in a duel which lasts for several hours, but by then the guns at Fort Wagner are silenced and many of the guns at Battery Gregg also become inoperable. At Fort Sumter, the walls finally show signs of the terrible shellacking it has been sustaining.

A while later, Admiral Dahlgren transfers his flag to the *Passaic*, then it and the *Patapsco* move in close to Fort Sumter and proceed to bombard it from a distance of about 2,000 yards. Then these two vessels turn their guns toward Fort Wagner to interrupt the troops who are repairing damage. The Confederates; however, retain control of the forts at the end of the day, and they exhibit no signs of capitulating. During this day's fighting, Commander G.W. Rodgers (*Catskill*) is killed.

The Union maintains its stance and continues its daily bombardments of the Rebel strongholds until the 24th. On Thursday, the 20th, the fort's flag is severed by a shell at about noon, but soon after, the Rebels hoist another. The relentless bombardment has delivered about 2,500 hits upon Fort Sumter since it began four days ago. By Friday, the 21st, Fort Sumter's south wall is demolished and the north wall fares only slightly better. Again, the flag is shot from its staff, replaced and shot down again, giving the Union artillerymen a total of six hits on the Confederate standard.

The flag is again flying, but is placed atop the ruinous pile of rubble, the south wall. The Rebels receive no reprieve on Saturday as thunderous fire plows into the besieged strong point. According to Confederate reports, of 923 shots propelled toward the fort, 704 hit the target, and the Confederate flag is struck yet another four times. All the while, Fort Wagner also comes under continuous assault.

The besieged defenders wake up on Sunday to more horrific fire as the shells toll rather than the bells. The fleet turns its guns to the east and west in symphony with the artillery that is plugging its shells into the north and south, implanting an iron picket fence. Sumter's east wall comes tumbling down, removing some of the

protection. Devastating barrages then rip through the fort. One of the shells strikes inside the walls and injures Colonel Rhett, Lt. Boyelston and several other officers. Another slays Colonel Gaillard. On this day, while Rhett is calculating the number of shells (5,750) fired upon the fort and assessing the damage, he receives orders to hold the fort.

In the meantime, on the 22nd, Gillmore demands that Beauregard abandon Morris Island and Fort Sumter. In addition, Gillmore informs the Confederates that Charleston will be bombarded if the ultimatum is ignored. Beauregard buys some time by responding that the order is not signed, and he also complains about striking a city that contains civilians. Gillmore extends the time of the bombardment and explains to Beauregard that the civilians who had a desire to leave had done so months ago. Beauregard is informed through an official letter that Charleston would become a target on the 23rd. General Quincy A. Gillmore, receiving no response to this message, unleashes the "Swamp Angel" on the 23rd as scheduled. The giant gun propels 36 shells into the city, but the last one causes the gun to explode.

On September 5, the Union guns initiate another massive artillery bombardment of the Confederate positions. The incessant attack lasts for 42 hours. Afterward the Union readies for an attack to be launched on the following day. However, in the meantime, the Confederates, under cover of darkness during the night of the 6th-7th, evacuate Fort Wagner and Battery Gregg. The Union occupies Fort Wagner on the 7th and captures seventy-five troops; the others, using small boats at Cummings Point, safely escape.

On 7 September, following seizure of Fort Wagner, General Gillmore dispatches a message to General Halleck: "I have the honor to report that Fort Wagner and Battery Gregg are ours ... captured dispatches show that Fort Wagner was commanded by Colonel Keit, of South Carolina and garrisoned by 1,400 men and Battery Gregg by between 100 and 200 men ... the city and harbor of Charleston are now completely covered by our guns." With control of the harbor attained, Admiral Dahlgren's Blockading Squadron remains inside the bar, and with the seizure of Morris Island, Charleston's role as a safe port for blockade runners is terminated. The Union sustains 1,757 killed, wounded and missing or captured. The Confederates sustain 561 killed, wounded and missing.

July 11 (Saturday)   In Indiana, Confederate cavalry led by John Hunt Morgan attacks and devastates the Jefferson railroad depot and the bridge at Vienna.

In Maryland, a contingent of Union cavalry (Army of the Potomac) clashes with Confederate Cavalry at Hagerstown. Casualty figures are unavailable.

In Confederate general officer activity, Major General Daniel H. Hill is promoted to lieutenant general. He moves to the Army of Tennessee and serves under General Bragg in command of a corps; however, he is unable to build a working relationship with Bragg. Consequently, D. H. Hill is relieved and his promotion is not forwarded by President Davis to the Confederate Senate. He will, however, retain the rank of major general and see some service in Virginia and the Carolinas; the latter duty finds him in command under General J.E. Johnston.

In Naval activity, the USS *Anna* (*Annie*) intercepts a whaleboat, the *Alice,* and captures its six-man crew in the vicinity of Cotteral's Key, Florida. In other activity, the USS *Moose,* recently arrived at Brandenburg, Kentucky, due to the incursions by Morgan's Raiders, encounters a band of guerrillas at Twelve Mile Island. Of the force, about 1,500 strong, nearly fifty cross the Ohio River en route to join Morgan; however, thirty-nine of them are seized by the *Moose.* The rest either drown or make it back across the river.

July 12 (Sunday)   In Maryland, a Union contingent composed of infantry, cavalry and artillery occupy Funkstown and Hagerstown.

In Mississippi, Union forces occupy Natchez. Also, at the capital, Jackson, Confederates pummel the command of Brigadier General Jacob Lauman as he tries to maneuver his division into position as part of General Sherman's plan to reduce the city. One of Lauman's brigades sustains more than 50 percent casualties. General Edward O.C. Ord, displeased, claims Lauman had acted without orders and has him relieved of command. General Lauman is ordered to repair to Vicksburg to report to General Grant. Afterward, Grant directs Lauman to return to Iowa to await new orders. No orders arrive. Nonetheless, at the close of the war, Lauman receives the brevet rank of major general.

In Virginia, the U.S. 2nd Massachusetts Cavalry is involved in a skirmish with Confederates at Ashby's Gap. The Union loses two killed and eight wounded.

In Indiana, John Hunt's Confederate Cavalry attacks Vernon, defended by the Indiana Minutemen. Although the Union force stands at about 1,000 men, the Confederates prevail.

In Naval activity, the USS *Iroquois* seizes the

CSS *Kate* off the coast of the Carolinas. Some sources list the capture on 31 July; however, the U.S. Navy Historical Division places the seizure on this day. In other activity, at about this time, the USS *Osage* (single-turret ironclad river monitor) is commissioned at Carondelet, Missouri. It operates along the Mississippi River during 1863 and 1864 and participates in operations on the Black and Ouachita Rivers in Louisiana (February–March 1864). Subsequently, it is attached to the West Gulf Blockading during 1865 and participates in the action in Mobile Bay. On patrol near Smith's Island, North Carolina, the USS *Penobscot* compels a blockade runner, the *Kate,* to run ashore. Later the *Penobscot* is transferred to the Gulf of Mexico, where it patrols off the coast of Texas.

Union warships initiate an expedition that advances along three separate rivers, the Black, Red and Tensas, and lasts through the 20th. The Union during this operation seizes some vessels, including the steamers *Louisville* and *Elmira.* The USS *Curlew* participates in this mission. Detachments from the vessels also reduce a sawmill. In late December, the *Curlew* patrols along the Ohio and Tennessee Rivers until mid January, when it sails to Mound City, Illinois, for repairs.

July 13 (Monday)   In Mississippi, U.S. General Grant, with a great deal of respect for the defenders of Vicksburg, forbids his men from taunting or jeering the captured Confederates (their paroles completed) who march out of Vicksburg. The Union troops offer no victory cheers; however, much friendly discussion ensues between both sides as the Confederates file out of the city. Meanwhile, Union General Sherman begins to close in on Jackson and initiates an artillery bombardment. Sherman continues to pour in shells until the 17th, when he is notified Johnston has withdrawn during the night.

U.S. gunboats and troops under General Herron capture Yazoo City. They take 250 Confederates prisoner. Also, Confederate Major General John Stevens Bowen, severely ill with dysentery when captured at Vicksburg, succumbs at Raymond. Subsequently, during 1887, General Bowen's remains are removed and he is

reinterred at Vicksburg. The recently commissioned *Kenwood,* commanded by Acting Master John Swaney, participates in the campaign to seize Yazoo City. Afterward it moves to Baton Rouge, Louisiana, to serve with the Port Hudson Division.

In Tennessee, a Union contingent, including detachments of the 3rd Michigan, 3rd Iowa, 1st Tennessee and the 9th Illinois Cavalry Regiments, commanded by Colonel Edward Hatch, skirmishes with Confederates in the vicinity of Jackson. The Union sustains two killed and 20 wounded. The Confederates suffer 38 killed and 150 wounded.

In Indiana, Confederate General Morgan maintains his relentless raids and so far evades capture by Union forces trailing his cavalry. This day, he crosses from Indiana into Ohio by use of a bridge that spans the White Water River, and after crossing, he burns the bridge. Meanwhile, Union forces continue the hunt.

In Louisiana, a Union contingent (units of Generals Weitzel and Grover's divisions, 19th Corps), commanded by Colonel Dudley, clashes with Confederates at Donaldsonville. The Union sustains about 450 killed, wounded and missing. Confederate casualty figures are unavailable.

In New York, riots break out in New York City because of federal enrollment legislation (the draft law of March 3). Mobs begin ravaging the city. A colored orphan asylum is burned and in the rioting, colored people are hanged in the streets. The rioters do not stop short of looting. Federal troops, including Marines, are rushed in to quell the disturbance of the mob, which primarily consists of Irish workingmen. The riots are quieted by the 15th.

In Naval activity, a force (General Banks' command) transported by a Union fleet occupies Fort Powhatan, Virginia. Admiral Lee participates. Also, four Union gunboats under Captain Flusser bombard Williamston on the Roanoke River. The USS *Seymour* participates in this expedition. The *Seymour* continues its patrols with the North Atlantic Blockading Squadron off North Carolina and in support of

Left: Natchez Under the Hill (*Harper's Pictorial History of the Civil War,* 1896). *Right:* General Butler lands at Fort Powhatan on the James River in Virginia (Mottelay, *The Soldier in Our Civil War,* 1886).

General Grant's action in Virginia for the duration of the war. In other Naval activity, the USS *Baron DeKalb*, formerly the gunboat *St. Louis*, is destroyed when it hits a mine while engaged in operations along the Yazoo River. Also, the USS *Manitou* (formerly USS *James Thompson*, later USS *Fort Hindman*) and *Rattler*, operating on the Little Red River in Louisiana, seize a Confederate transport, the CSS *Louisville* (originally built in Indiana as a tinclad 720-ton side-wheel river gunboat). The *Louisville*, after modifications, is commissioned during January 1864 as USS *Ouachita*, an oversized but lightly armored gunboat that operates as part of the Mississippi Squadron. The *Ouachita* participates in the Red River Expedition (March–May 1864) and finishes out the war on patrol duty. Afterward it moves up the Red River to assume responsibility for the CSS *Missouri*, a Confederate ironclad. The *Ouachita* is decommissioned during June 1865. Later it becomes the merchant ship *Vicksburg* and operates until it is destroyed by fire during July 1869.

The USS *Antona* sails from New Orleans and heads down the Mississippi River. Early the next morning it collides with the gunboat USS *Sciota* and sustains no fatal damage; however, the *Sciota* sinks about eight miles above Quarantine. The *Antona* is able to resume its voyage on the 15th.

July 14 (Tuesday) In Maryland, Union forces (General Hugh Kilpatrick's command, Army of the Potomac), including Company A, 7th Michigan Cavalry, engage Confederates, including elements of Samuel McGowan's brigade (William D. Pender's division, Ambrose P. Hill's corps) at Falling Waters, capturing 1,500 men. The retreating Confederates are covered by the rear guard action afforded by General Heth as they move towards Darksville. The Union loses 29 dead and 36 wounded. Confederates suffer 125 killed or wounded and 1,500 captured.

In Ohio, Morgan's Raiders attack Lawrenceburg, defended by the 105th Indiana Minutemen.

In South Carolina, Union troops, including the 48th New York, battle Confederates around Fort Wagner.

In Tennessee, the vanguard of the 14th Corps skirmishes with Confederates under General Buckner at Elk River. The Union sustains 10 killed and 30 wounded. The Confederates sustain 60 killed, 24 wounded and about 100 missing or captured.

In Virginia, Confederates skirmish with a Union contingent of the 1st Connecticut Cavalry at Bolivar Heights. Also, Confederate Brigadier General James J. Pettigrew, in command of General Heth's division, is mortally wounded while acting as part of the rear-guard during the march back to Virginia following Lee's defeat at Gettysburg; he succumbs three days later in the vicinity of Bunker Hill.

In West Virginia, a Union contingent (2nd West Virginia Cavalry) clashes with Confederates at Shady Spring. Casualty figures are unavailable.

In Union general officer activity, Brigadier General James Henry Van Alen resigns his commission and returns to private life. While on a voyage returning to the U.S. from England, he dies at sea by either falling overboard or intentionally jumping from the deck of the *Umbria* during the pre-dawn hours on 22 July 1886.

In Naval activity, the USS *Antona* collides with the USS *Sciota* on the Mississippi River. The *Sciota* sustains damage and sinks, but it is afterward refloated. It returns to patrol off the coast of Texas.

July 15 (Wednesday) In Alabama, elements of the 3rd Ohio Cavalry and the 5th Tennessee Cavalry encounter and engage a Confederate force at Pulaski.

In the Indian Territory at Fort Gibson (Oklahoma), General Blunt, in anticipation of an advancing Confederate force moving against his position, moves out to intercept the Confederates under Brigadier General Douglas H. Cooper at Honey Springs before Cooper is reinforced by a separate brigade under Brigadier General William Cabell, which is on the march from Fort Smith, Arkansas. The Union column crosses the Arkansas River, and by about mid-

night on the 16th-17th, a column of several thousand troops is across the river and en route to the objective.

In Virginia, detachments of the 16th Pennsylvania and the 1st Maine Cavalry Regiments clash at Halltown. About 100 Confederates are captured.

In Naval activity, the USS *Santiago de Cuba*, while operating in the Atlantic as part of the blockading squadron, seizes a blockade runner, the *Lizzie*. Also, the U.S. Navy acquires a screw steamer, the *Fahkee*, which had been built during the previous year. The ship is commissioned the USS *Fahkee* on 24 September 1863. It is attached to the North Atlantic Blockading Squadron for the duration of the war with its primary function consisting of towing and transporting coal and freight to various posts and ships stretched along the East Coast from New York to North Carolina; however, it does at times serve on blockade duty.

July 16 (Thursday) In Louisiana, the river boat *Imperial*, which had departed St. Louis on 8 July, arrives in New Orleans. The arrival of the *Imperial* signals Union control of the Mississippi River after General Grant's victory at Vicksburg.

In Mississippi, at Jackson, General Sherman continues to bombard Confederate positions held by General Joseph E. Johnston. A train laden with ammunition for the Yankees arrives at the Union lines, giving Sherman the supplies he needs to launch an attack. However, Johnston evacuates during the night of the 16th-17th subsequent to torching the bridges that span the Pearl River. A skirmish does develop when Union forces encounter Confederate troops from South Carolina. The skirmish lasts for about one-half hour.

In South Carolina, Confederates attack Union positions (General Terry's brigade) at Secessionville. Casualty figures are unavailable.

In Virginia, Union cavalry (Army of the Potomac) chases retreating Confederates and clashes with Stuart at Martinsburg. Confederate General Fitzhugh Lee attacks, forcing the Union to retreat.

In West Virginia, a Union force — 1st, 4th and 16th Pennsylvania, the 1st Maine, and 10th New York Cavalry Regiments, commanded by General Gregg — engages Confederates at Shepherdstown. The Union sustains about 150 killed, wounded and missing. The Confederates sustain about 25 killed and 75 wounded.

In Naval activity, Japanese shore batteries commence a bombardment of the USS *Wyoming* while it is cruising in the Straits of Shimonoseki. Following the shelling, the Prince of Magato orders his ships to attack the U.S. warship; however, the crew, including its Marine detachment, returns fire, discouraging the Japanese from prolonging the encounter.

The CSS *Florida*, out to sea since the latter part of January, arrives at St. George's,

Union cavalry charges Confederates near Falling Waters, Maryland, on 14 July 1863 (Mottelay, *The Soldier in Our Civil War*, 1886).

Left: Union forces (Army of the Potomac) struggle with a wagon as they cross a stream on an improvised bridge (Mottelay, *The Soldier in Our Civil War*, 1886). *Right:* The riverboat *Imperial* arrives at New Orleans, signaling the opening of the Mississippi River (*Harper's Pictoral History of the Civil War*, 1896).

Bermuda. Up to this point, the *Florida* has seized and destroyed fourteen merchant ships and bonded three others. The ship departs on 25 July, and prior to arriving at Brest, France, on 23 August, it seizes two more prizes, the *F.B. Cutting*, which is afterward destroyed, and the *Avon*, which is bonded. In the Gulf of Mexico, the USS *Antona* captures a British blockade runner, the *Cecilia D.*, and sends the ship to New Orleans. The *Antona* then heads toward Galveston, arriving on the 18th to join the blockading forces there.

July 17 (Friday)   In Alabama, Union troops under Major General David S. Stanley occupy Huntsville.

In Mississippi, Union General Sherman occupies Jackson. He remains there until ordered back to Vicksburg, where he re-establishes his positions at Haines Bluff. His forces pursue the retreating Confederates for a while, but once they reach Brandon, the Union contingent halts and returns to its lines. General Stephen A. Hurlbut's forces (16th Corps) occupy Corinth.

In Virginia, General Meade's Army of the Potomac begins to cross the Potomac River at two points, Harpers Ferry and at Berlin. They reach Warrenton on the 25th. In Wytheville, a Union contingent composed of elements of the 34th Ohio and the 1st and 2nd West Virginia Cavalry Regiments skirmish with Confederates. The Union sustains 17 killed and 61 wounded. The Confederates suffer 75 killed and 125 missing or captured.

In the Indian Territory (Oklahoma), a strong Union force of about 3,000 troops skirmishes with Confederates under General Douglas H. Cooper at Honey Springs Depot during the early morning hours; by about 1500, the confrontation explodes into a major battle. The Confederate force is composed primarily of Indians, but the Union contingent also contains

Indians who are allied with the Union, and colored units are also participants. The Confederates' powder has become wet and during the confrontation a rain storm develops, creating more problems. The Union's initial attack is repulsed, but the Confederates' weapons frequently misfire due to the damaged ammunition. At about the same time, Blunt moves to turn Cooper's left flank. Blunt senses an auspicious opportunity and the strategy works. The Confederates initiate a retreat, raising tenacious resistance as they withdraw, and some of the rear-guard troops launch a counterattack. Nonetheless, the effort fails to break the Union momentum. The retreat continues, and with the rout, the Union eliminates the possibility of Fort Gibson coming under an attack, but the victory also gives the Union domination of the Indian Territory north of the Arkansas River. The Union forces that participate include the 2nd, 6th, and 9th Kansas Cavalry, 2nd and 3rd Kansas Batteries, and the 2nd and 3rd Kansas Home Indian Guards. The Union sustains 17 killed and 60 wounded. Confederates suffer 150 killed, 400 wounded and about 60 captured.

In Union general officer activity, Colonel John Converse Starkweather and Colonel William Denison Whipple are promoted to brigadier general. Whipple is appointed assistant adjutant general of the army and of the Department of the Cumberland in November. In December 1863, he becomes chief of staff to General George H. Thomas. He participates in the Chattanooga and Atlanta campaigns. He remains with General Thomas beyond the war and accompanies him to California. During 1870, upon the death of General Thomas, Whipple, assigned to the adjutant general's office, returns to Washington, D.C. After other duty, he retires during 1890.

July 18 (Saturday)   In Mississippi, a Union force engages Confederates at Canton. It in-

cludes the 76th Ohio, 25th and 31st Iowa, 3rd, 13th and 17th Missouri Regiments, the 2nd Wisconsin Cavalry, 5th Illinois Cavalry, 3rd and 4th Iowa Cavalry and one battery of artillery, commanded by Colonels Bussey and Wood. It is reported that the Union loses about 20 killed and wounded, but captures about 72 Confederates. In other activity, the *Hartford City* (separate from USS *Hartford*) — in Confederate service as a river steamer since it was confiscated by the Confederates at Vicksburg during May 1862 and used to tow rafts and other vessels — is thought to have been one of the ships with a group of vessels ordered destroyed. The order is received by Confederate Captain A.H. Forrest, who dispatches a contingent to destroy ships on the Tallahatchie and Yazoo Rivers to prevent capture by the Union.

In Ohio, Confederates under General John Morgan, feeling the pressure of the Union pursuit forces, attempt to escape by crossing the Ohio River near Pomeroy and re-enter Kentucky. The force reaches Buffington Island, Ohio, but nearby Union gunboats and other Union forces prevent escape.

In New Mexico, one company of the 1st New Mexico Cavalry skirmishes with Indians at Rio Hondo.

In Virginia, during an affair in Wytheville, Colonel William Henry Powell (2nd West Virginia Cavalry) is captured. Powell had initially entered the service as captain of a company in the regiment during November 1861. Colonel Powell is exchanged in February 1864. He is assigned to General Sheridan's cavalry. He participates in the Shenandoah operations, including the Battle of Winchester (October 1864). For his actions there, as commander of the 2nd Cavalry Division, he is promoted to brigadier general, effective on the date of the battle.

In North Carolina, Union Brigadier General Potter departs New Bern on a reconnaissance mission into the area around the Tar River and Rocky Mount through the 21st. His force includes the 3rd and 12th New York Cavalry Regiments and the 1st North Carolina Cavalry. The contingent sustains about 60 wounded.

In Confederate general officer activity, Colonel Francis Marion Cockrell, earlier captured at Vicksburg while commanding the Missouri brigade, is promoted to brigadier general.

In Naval activity, the Union gunboats *Jacob Bell, Resolute,* and *Teaser,* bolstered by the mortar boat *Don Smith* and augmented by ground troops, clash with Confederates at Yates Point on the Potomac. In other activity, the CSS *Battle,* a vessel used as an army transport after being declined as a gunboat, is intercepted and captured about 70 miles southeast of Mobile bar. The *Battle* is transporting a cargo of more than 600 bales of cotton. The Union arms the *Battle* with four 12-pounders and utilizes it to patrol the coast between Tampa and St. Marks and other operations in Florida. The Union ships also capture the CSS *William Bagley.*

July 18–26   In Ohio, the steamer USS *Moose* assists Union troops in the capture of Morgan's Raiders at Buffington Island (St. George's Creek). U.S. Brigadier General Shackelford accepts surrender of General Morgan and his raiders, at New Lisbon on the 26th. The Union has 33 killed, 97 wounded and 805 missing or captured. The Confederates suffer 795 killed or wounded and about 4,100 captured. Morgan is jailed, but he later escapes. Confederate General Adam Rankin Johnson and many in his command escape by swimming across the Ohio River. However, Colonel Basil Duke, the brother-in-law of Morgan, is also captured during this raid, and he is imprisoned for more than a year. Upon his release, Duke receives a command in East Tennessee and Kentucky. During September 1864 he is promoted to brigadier general.

July 19 (Sunday)   In Ohio, Union troops seize about 700 of Morgan's Raiders at Buffington, but General John H. Morgan is not among

the prisoners. General James Shackelford reinitiates the hunt. A huge amount of booty is confiscated by the Union. The Rebels had, in some cases, stuffed jewelry and other valuables in their ammunition boxes. In addition, many horses and mules are seized. Most of the Union currency is destroyed by the Rebels at the time of their capture. Sources of the time note that none of the recovered valuables are ever returned to the rightful owners. The USS *Moose* and the *Allegheny Belle* participate in the action and shell Confederate positions on Buffington Island. Detachments from the ships seize some abandoned artillery. Following this action, the *Moose* and the *Allegheny Bell* resume their patrols of the Cumberland, Ohio and Tennessee Rivers.

While Morgan remains on the loose, General James M. Shackelford still gives pursuit and chases the Rebels for an additional sixty miles as the Confederates head westward. The Union closes on them and soon a Confederate regiment under Johnson surrenders; however, the elusive Morgan and about 600 troops escape the net. On the morning of July 21, General James M. Shackelford once again resumes the chase.

In Virginia, General Robert E. Lee orders Longstreet to move through Front Royal to Culpeper Court House to meet the enemy threat at Chester and at Manassas Gap.

July 20 (Monday)   In Naval activity, the USS *Shawsheen,* operating on the Neuse River in North Carolina, encounters five separate Confederate vessels, the *Dolphin, Elizabeth, Helen Jane, James Brice* and *Sally.* All five vessels are captured. In other activity, the USS *Adolph Huger,* operating in the vicinity of Washington, D.C., seizes a small vessel with a two-man crew, which is carrying a cargo of liquor. Also, the USS *Antona* is ordered by Commodore Henry H. Bell to take a position at a point between Velasco, Texas, and the mouth of the Rio Grande River. The *Antona* arrives at its destination on the 24th.

July 21 (Tuesday)   In Virginia, Union troops, including the 8th New York, 3rd Indiana, 12th Illinois, and advance cavalry from the Army of the Potomac, engage Confederates at Chester Gap this day and the next. The Union suffers 35 dead and 102 wounded; the Confederates sustain 300 killed or wounded.

In Confederate general officer activity, James Patrick Major (West Point, 1856) is promoted to brigadier general. General Major had resigned from U.S. service on 21 March 1861, before the seizure of Fort Sumter. General Major is the son-in-law of Confederate General Thomas Green. He commands a cavalry brigade under General John A. Wharton during the closing days of the war and receives a parole on 11 June at Iberia, Louisiana. After the war he spends some time in France, then returns to the States, where he becomes a planter in Louisiana and Texas until his death at Austin, Texas, on 7 May 1877.

July 22 (Wednesday)   In New Mexico, one company of the New Mexico cavalry skirmishes with Confederates at Concha Springs.

In Virginia, Union General French is ordered by General Meade to speed to Manassas Gap to flank General Robert E. Lee's retreating army; however, effective action by Confederate rear guards under General Richard S. Ewell prevents the Union from launching an attack as intended. Confederate Lt. General James Longstreet arrives at Culpeper on the 24th.

In Union general officer activity, Brigadier General Leonard Fulton Ross resigns from the army to return to private life in Illinois.

In Naval activity, the vessel *Ion* (afterward *Grampus*), a side-wheel steamer, is purchased at Cincinnati by Rear Admiral David Dixon Porter. The *Grampus* remains unarmed except for "ten cutlasses and revolvers" and is based at Cincinnati as part of the Mississippi Squadron. After the war it moves from Cincinnati to Mound City, Illinois, where it is sold on 1 September 1868.

July 23 (Thursday)   In Virginia, the Third Corps, Army of the Potomac (Generals Francis Barretto Spinola and Major General French), engage Confederates under General Ambrose R. Wright at Wapping Heights (Manassas Gap). During the pursuit of Lee's army, General Francis B. Spinola is wounded.

In Union general officer activity, Colonel Kenner Garrard, the brother of Union General Theophilus Toulmin Garrard, is promoted to brigadier general. He commands a brigade during the actions along the Rappahannock and afterward, he moves to Washington to assume command of the cavalry bureau; however, by February 1863, he receives command of the 2nd Cavalry Division (Army of the Cumberland). He participates in the campaign against Atlanta and afterward, he returns to the infantry to command a division in the Army of the Tennessee during the Battle of Nashville.

In Confederate general officer activity, Colonel Lunsford L. Lomax, 11th Virginia Cavalry, is promoted to the rank of brigadier general. Lomax leads a brigade in Brigadier General Fitzhugh Lee's cavalry division. Also, Laurence (Lawrence) Simmons Baker (West Point, 1851), who resigned from the army during May 1861 and joined the 1st North Carolina Cavalry as lieutenant colonel (later colonel), is promoted to brigadier general. The regiment, attached to General Wade Hampton's brigade, had participated in the campaigns of the Army of Northern Virginia, including Gettysburg.

July 24 (Friday)   In Louisiana, Union forces occupy Brashear City.

The Tar River bridge in North Carolina, built by Union troops (Mottelay, *The Soldier in Our Civil War,* 1886).

In Ohio, Union troops led by Major Krouse attack a contingent of Confederate cavalry (guerrillas under John Hunt Morgan) at Washington.

In Virginia, Union troops, including the 2nd U.S. Artillery, hold their ground as other Union troops withdraw at Newby's Crossroads. Lt. Carle Woodruff's battery refuses to retreat, continuing its fire, which enables the Union to repel the attack. Confederate Lt. General Longstreet's troops arrive at Chester Gap. Longstreet is soon joined by General A.P. Hill and General Richard S. Ewell's corps. Union troops under Meade begin building their forces at Manassas Gap.

In Naval activity, the USS *Iroquois* seizes the CSS *Merrimac* off the coast of North Carolina near Wilmington. Some sources list the capture on 25 July; however, the U.S. Naval Historical Division lists the capture of the *Merrimac* on the 24th. In other activity, Acting Master Charles T. Chase, commanding officer of the USS *Antona,* goes ashore at Matamoros, Mexico, to mail a packet of dispatches to the U.S. consul. He boards a Mexican boat, the *Margarita,* to return to the *Antona;* however, a contingent of men on the Texas bank of the river opens fire upon the *Margarita* and demands that it return to the Texas shore. The boat moves to shore and Lt. Chase is captured by the force, which is composed of Confederate soldiers. Those aboard the *Antona* are unaware of Chase's capture until a passing British vessel informs the crew of his detainment. Lt. Chase is transported to Brownsville, Texas. Once the report of his capture is verified, the *Antona,* under the command of the executive officer, Acting Master Spiro V. Bennis, moves to Galveston, arriving there on the 27th.

July 24–28 In the Dakota Territory, elements of the 1st Minnesota Cavalry (Mounted Rangers) and the 6th, 7th and 10th Minnesota Volunteer Regiments bolstered by the 3rd Minnesota Battery engage in a fight with Sioux Indians at Big Mound. The force, commanded by General Henry Hastings Sibley, had moved from Fort Ridgely, Minnesota, in pursuit of the Santee Sioux, who participated in an uprising the previous August in the Minnesota River Valley. These Sioux had joined with another tribe, the Teton Sioux. At about 1300, a band of Sioux approach the lines of Sibley's scouts, who are near the main camp, and give the impression they are seeking only to talk, but shortly thereafter, a shot rings out and slays Josiah S. Weiser, surgeon of the mounted rangers. This is followed by the sudden appearance of many concealed Indians that commence firing on the scouts. Sibley's main force enters the fight and commits artillery to plow the ridges. The effective fire compels the Indians under Chief Inkpaduta to break from their positions in disarray. The cavalry gives chase, and a running fight continues until darkness. The army and the Sioux clash again on the 26th at Dead Buffalo Lake, but here, too, after the army is attacked, primarily on their left flank, the troops are able to drive off the Sioux. Two days later,

on the 28th, a large band of Sioux attempts to attack General Sibley's force near Stony Lake, but apparently fearing the column too strong, no major assault is launched. Instead the Sioux again retire.

July 25 (Saturday) *In Naval activity,* the Union gunboat USS *Iroquois* seizes the Confederate steamers CSS *Lizzie* in the vicinity of Wilmington, North Carolina. In other activity, the CCS *Alonzo Child,* captured on 19 May near Vicksburg, having received only minor repairs, is sent under tow by the USS *New National* to Cairo, Illinois, by Admiral Porter with a recommendation that it be transformed into a receiving ship. En route, the vessel *Sam Young,* which had run aground, is spotted in the vicinity of the White River. The *Sam Young* is transporting about 350 Confederate prisoners. The Rebels are transferred to the *Alonzo Child,* which carries them as far as Helena, Arkansas. The *New National* delivers the *Alonzo Child* to Cairo in early August. Subsequent to its participation at Vicksburg and Yazoo City, the *New National* resumes its patrol duty on the Mississippi and its tributaries until it is decommissioned during April 1865, at Mound City, Illinois, and returned to its original owner. Also, the USS *Reindeer,* in service since the previous July, is officially commissioned this day. It resumes its patrols on the Ohio River from Louisville, Kentucky, to Madison, Indiana, until transferred to the Cumberland River in November 1863.

July 26 (Sunday) In North Carolina, a Union force attached to District of North Carolina skirmishes with Confederates at Pattacassey Creek (Mount Tabor Church). The Union sustains three killed and 17 wounded.

In Ohio, Confederate cavalry under General John Morgan is captured by Union forces under General James Shackelford, following a hard chase that had begun in Kentucky the early part of July. Hunt, Colonel Chike, Captain Hines, and the other officers are imprisoned in the Ohio penitentiary due to the lack of a military prison. On November 28th, he and six other officers, including Captain Hines, escape by making their way through a sewer; the other officers' names are Burnett, Hookersmith, McGhee, Shelton and Taylor. It is reported that during his raids, Morgan's band destroyed more than thirty bridges and that his contingent had caused a total of about $10 million worth of damage. Morgan will again engage the Union, and in September 1864 near Greenville, Tennessee, he fights his final battle.

In the Dakota Territory, elements of the 1st Minnesota Cavalry, the 6th, 7th and 10th Minnesota Volunteers and the 3rd Minnesota Battery engage Sioux Indians in a battle at Dead Buffalo Lake (see also, **July 24–28 In the Dakota Territory**).

In Naval activity, Union gunboats and steamers bombard Smyrna, Florida. Florida has not been a priority for either side, but following the loss of Vicksburg, Mississippi, the South now

depends heavily on Florida for staples such as beef for the Army.

July 27 (Monday) In Missouri, a Union scouting contingent of the 2nd U.S. Infantry, out of the post at Cassville, encounters a contingent of about 20 Confederates about 25 miles southeast of there. A skirmish erupts and the Confederates lose one officer and four enlisted men killed and four others wounded. The Union sustains three missing. The Union confiscates some Confederate weapons.

July 28 (Tuesday) In the Dakota Territory, the 1st Minnesota Cavalry, the 6th, 7th and 10th Minnesota Volunteer Regiments and the 3rd Minnesota Battery engage Sioux Indians at Stony Lake (see also, **July 24–28 In the Dakota Territory**).

In Virginia, a detachment of the 6th Vermont Cavalry led by Lt. John W. Clark thwarts a Confederate assault on a train it is escorting to Warrenton.

In Tennessee, a Union contingent under Colonel Rowett skirmishes with Confederates led by Colonel Alexander W. Campbell at Lexington. Campbell is captured and not exchanged until February 1865. At the time of his capture, Campbell had been on a mission of Governor Isham Harris to oversee elections and to initiate recruiting in the western sector of the state.

In Missouri, a detachment of the 4th Missouri Militia Cavalry clashes with Confederates at the town of Marshall. Casualty figures are unavailable.

In Kentucky, a Union force commanded by Colonel William P. Sanders clashes with Confederates at Lexington and Richmond. Lexington is placed under martial law.

In Mississippi, a contingent of the 72nd Illinois Volunteer Regiment clashes with Confederates at St. Catherine's Creek. Also, a skirmish breaks out between Union and Confederate troops at Coldwater. Specific units and casualty figures are unavailable.

In Confederate general officer activity, Colonel Otho F. Strahl (4th Tennessee) is promoted to the rank of brigadier general. He is assigned to duty as a brigade commander in General Cheatham's division (General Leonidas Polk's corps). Also, Colonel James Deshler (West Point, 1854) is appointed brigadier general. He receives command of a brigade in the division of General Cleburne (Army of Tennessee) and commands it at Chickamauga.

July 29 (Wednesday) In Kentucky, a large force of Confederate cavalry led by General John Pegram attacks Union positions at Paris and ignites a battle that lasts for about two hours. Casualty figures are unavailable.

In Mississippi, a Union contingent of the 72nd Illinois Regiment commanded by Captain James skirmishes with Confederates at Natchez. The Union captures about 50 Confederates.

In Naval activity, the USS *Shawsheen,* operating in Rose Bay, North Carolina, seizes the CSS *Telegraph.*

July 30 (Thursday)   In the Dakota Territory, the 1st Minnesota Cavalry and the 3rd Minnesota Battery, 6th Minnesota Volunteer Regiment, engages Sioux Indians along the Missouri River.

In Kentucky, two squadrons of the 14th Kentucky Cavalry clash with a Confederate contingent led by Colonel Scott in Irvine, Estill County. The Union sustains four killed, five wounded and 10 captured. The Confederates sustain seven killed, 18 wounded and 75 captured.

In Missouri, the 1st and 4th Missouri Enrolled Militia commanded by Captain Cannon clash with Confederates led by Captain Blunt in Saline County. The Union sustains two killed and one wounded.

In Naval activity, the USS *Adela,* at New York for repairs, departs for duty at Key West, Florida. By about 28 August it is assigned duty off St. Andrew's Sound. By late September, the *Adela* moves to Tampa Bay to relieve the USS *Sagamore.*

July 31 (Friday)   In Kentucky, heavy fighting breaks out at Stanford. The Confederates capture the town, but Union cavalry regains it. Union General Burnside imposes martial law throughout Kentucky.

August 1 (Saturday)   In South Carolina, Union gunboats commence firing on Charleston as the siege continues. Confederate artillery still defiantly returns fire and succeeds in impeding Union progress. During this month the gunboat USS *Mahaska* joins the squadron after previous service in Virginia, since it was commissioned during May 1862. After being transferred, the *Mahaska* serves off Florida during February through August 1864, then, following repairs, it returns there for the duration and beyond. It is decommissioned in September 1868, sold in November and renamed *Jeannette.*

In Virginia, Union and Confederate cavalry units battle at Brandy Station, as General George Meade continues to pursue General Robert E. Lee. In addition, a contingent of Union cavalry clashes with elements of the 14th South Carolina Regiment in the vicinity of Culpeper Court House, but the pickets receive support from the regiment and the Union cavalry is compelled to disengage. Meanwhile, Lee, at Culpeper Court House, telegraphs Jefferson Davis requesting reinforcements be sent to Orange Court House to meet a possible Union attack. Also, the 1st Cavalry Division under General John Buford engages Confederates at Rappahannock Station. Buford's cavalry also clashes with Confederates at Kelly's Ford. Buford's forces, while engaged with the Confederate until the 3rd of August, sustain 16 killed and 134 wounded. Confederate Colonel Matthew Calbraith Butler (2nd South Carolina), later major general, sustains a wound

that costs him his right foot. Colonel Butler initially joined the Confederacy as a captain in Hampton's Legion.

In Union general officer activity, Major General John E. Wool retires from the U.S. Army after completing 50 years of service to his country.

August 2 (Sunday)   In West Virginia, the 153rd Ohio Regiment skirmishes with Confederates at Green Springs. The Union sustains one killed and five missing. The Confederates sustain five killed and 22 wounded.

In South Carolina, a four-company Union contingent of New York Volunteers, known as the "Lost Children," capture about 500 Confederates in the vicinity of Folly Island, Charleston Harbor, South Carolina.

August 3 (Monday)   In Louisiana, during skirmishing around Jackson, Union General William P. Benton is wounded while leading the 73rd, 74th and 78th U.S. Colored troops. The Union suffers two wounded, two killed and approximately 25 missing.

In Confederate general officer activity, Brigadier Generals Wade Hampton, Fitzhugh Lee (nephew of Robert E. Lee), and Stephen Dill Lee are promoted to the rank of major general. Stephen D. Lee, no relation to Robert E. Lee, is assigned command of the cavalry within the Department of the Mississippi, Alabama, West Tennessee and East Louisiana. Confederate Colonel Philip D. Roddey, 4th Alabama Cavalry, is promoted to the rank of brigadier general. Brigadier General Cadmus Marcellus Wilcox is promoted to the rank of major general. General Wilcox receives command of General Pender's division. Pender had died from a wound while on the retreat from Gettysburg.

August 4 (Tuesday)   In Virginia, Union cavalry pickets (General Buford's command) skirmish with Confederate cavalry at Rappahannock Station. The Union sustains one killed and two wounded.

In Union general officer activity, Colonel Maltby (succeeded Colonel John E. Smith, who was promoted to brigadier on 29 November 1862) is promoted to brigadier general of volunteers. He remains in the Vicksburg area for most of the war, primarily assigned to garrison duty. Subsequent to the close of hostilities, General Maltby receives command of a subdistrict in Mississippi, where he remains until he leaves the army during January 1866; however, following his service during the Vicksburg campaign, he does not appear to be con-

spicuous in the plans of his superiors and is left in the shadows of opportunity. He is appointed mayor of Vicksburg by General Edward Ord, but his term is abruptly terminated about three months later when he dies of yellow fever on 12 December 1867.

Colonel John Benjamin Sanborn is commissioned brigadier general. Sanborn, who was Minnesota's quartermaster general at the outbreak of the war, was commissioned colonel of the 4th Minnesota Regiment late in 1861. Later this year, he receives command of the district of Southwest Missouri, and he participates against Confederate General Sterling Price, who invades Missouri in 1864. Also, Charles Robert Woods (West Point, 1852), colonel of the 76th Ohio Regiment, is promoted to brigadier general. Woods' regiment had participated for a while in West Virginia (autumn 1861) and at Fort Donelson, Tennessee, and at Shiloh and Corinth. At the latter he commanded a brigade. In addition, he commanded a brigade (Sherman's IV Corps) during the operations against Vicksburg. General Woods is the younger brother of Union General William Burnham Woods.

In Naval activity, the U.S. Navy initiates an expedition up the James River. During the mission, which continues through the 7th, the USS *Commodore Barney* sustains damage when a torpedo (mine) explodes and damages its engine; however, the ship is towed and remains in service for the duration of the mission. The *Commodore Barney* continues to operate in Virginia until 1864, when it moves to North Carolina and participates in a mission in late April before returning to Virginia. Subsequently, on 5 May 1865, it is ordered to sail to the Washington Navy Yard, where it is decommissioned. The *Commodore Barney* is sold on 20 July 1865.

August 5 (Wednesday)   In Virginia, the Union gunboats USS *Commodore Barney* and *Cohasset* engage Confederate gunboats at Dutch

The USS *Commodore Barney* strikes a mine on the James River (Mottelay, *The Soldier in Our Civil War,* 1886).

Gap, James River. The Union sustains three killed.

In Union general officer activity, General William T. Sherman orders General John McArthur to move to the area near Atlanta to protect the communications from there to Chattanooga.

August 6 (Thursday)   In California, civilians create a disturbance in Visalia (Tulare County), but the chaos is quickly quashed by Union troops.

In Naval activity, the USS *Antona,* which had departed from the Galveston area on the 4th, encounters and seizes a blockade runner, the *Betsy,* about fifteen miles southeast of Corpus Christi, Texas. The *Betsy* is flying the British colors. Acting Master Lyman Wells, commanding the *Antona* in the absence of Lieutenant Chase (recently captured by the Confederates), sends the *Betsy* to New Orleans. Two days later, the *Antona,* while off the mouth of the Rio Grande River, is reunited with Lt. Chase, who is released by Confederate General Hamilton P. Bee. The *Antona* sustains damage while off Galveston on the 12th and is towed to New Orleans by the USS *Bermuda.*

August 7 (Friday)   In Mississippi, General Grant issues orders that dispatch the 13th Corps to General Banks at New Orleans. Grant previously sent about 4,000 men to Banks after the fall of Vicksburg. He also orders a brigade under General Thomas E. Ransom to Natchez. Other troop movements include returning the Ninth Corps to Kentucky and sending 5,000 Union reinforcements to General Schofield to assist him against General Sterling Price's raids in Missouri. General T.E. Ransom confiscates thousands of head of cattle and a fair share of supplies as his command heads for Natchez.

In Missouri, one company of the 24th Missouri Volunteer Regiment skirmishes with Confederates at New Madrid. The Union sustains one killed and one wounded.

In Virginia, a contingent of the 1st Connecticut Cavalry and the 6th Michigan Cavalry skirmishes with Confederates at Waterford.

August 8 (Saturday)   Confederate General Robert E. Lee, deeply saddened by the great loss at Gettysburg, writes his letter of resignation to Confederate President Davis: "The general remedy for the want of success in a military commander is his removal. For no matter what may be the ability of the officer, if he loses the confidence of his troops disaster must sooner or later ensue." General Lee also mentions his present ill health, but Davis denies the request.

In Union general officer activity, Brigadier General Gouverneur Kemble Warren is promoted to major general to rank from 3 May. Warren for a time commanded the II Corps well in the absence of General Winfield Scott Hancock who was wounded at Gettysburg, but sees his career sink into obscurity during the operations against Richmond (1865) while he commands the V Corps (Overland campaign).

Grant inexplicably informs General Sheridan to relieve Warren "at his discretion."

August 9 (Sunday)   In Tennessee, a cavalry force (Army of the Cumberland) engages Confederates at Sparta. The Union sustains six killed and 25 wounded. Confederate casualty figures are unavailable.

In Mississippi, a Union reconnaissance force, led by Major Warden, departs Natchez en route to Woodville.

In Confederate general officer activity, Colonel Eppa Hunton (98th Virginia) is promoted to brigadier general.

In Naval activity, the USS *Catskill,* operating near Fort Moultrie, at Charleston, South Carolina, spots a stranded vessel, the blockade runner *Prince Albert,* and destroys it.

August 10 (Monday)   In Maryland, Brigadier General (brevet) William C. Morris becomes commander of the Middle Military Department. He succeeds Major General Robert C. Schenck and retains the post until 31 August.

In South Carolina, a battalion of U.S. Marines, commanded by Major Jacob Zeilin, arrives to reinforce other Marines attached to the South Atlantic Squadron on Morris Island. The combined force provides artillery support for the forces ashore.

In Union general officer activity, Brigadier General Joseph Revere, due to actions at the Battle of Chancellorsville, had received a court-martial, and his sentence was dismissal from the service. However, President Lincoln arranges to permit Revere to resign from the army, effective this day. General Revere is the grandson of Paul Revere of the Revolutionary War.

In Confederate general officer activity, Colonel Thomas Pleasant Dockery (19th Arkansas), who initially entered Confederate service as colonel of the 5th Arkansas (state troops), is promoted to brigadier general. His regiment's actions included Wilson's Creek and Corinth. At Vicksburg, he commanded the 2nd Brigade (General John S. Bowen's division) until he was captured. Subsequent to his promotion, General Dockery receives command of a brigade composed of Arkansas regiments. He participates in the fighting at Jenkins Ferry and at Marks' Mills.

August 11 (Tuesday)   In South Carolina, the Confederate guns at the fortification in Charleston Harbor deliver punishing artillery barrages against Union positions, which impedes Union progress and a planned attack.

In Union general officer activity, Colonel Thomas Kilby Smith is promoted to brigadier general. Smith participates in the Red River Campaign in command of a combined infantry-cavalry force, but afterward poor health compels him to resign from the service. Nevertheless, on 13 March 1865, he receives the rank of brevet major general of volunteers. Colonel Robert Alexander Cameron (34th Indiana) is promoted to brigadier general effective this day. Toward the end of the war he receives the brevet

rank of major general. Also, Colonel Manning Ferguson Force (20th Ohio Volunteer Regiment) is promoted to the rank of brigadier general. General Force becomes a recipient of the Medal of Honor for his extraordinary actions at the Battle of Atlanta. His entire service in the field is under Generals Grant and William T. Sherman. Colonel Walter Quintin Gresham is promoted to brigadier general. He receives a brigade (XVII Corps) command at Natchez, Mississippi. Lt. Colonel John Aaron Rawlins is also promoted to brigadier general. Since his initial entrance into the service as an aide-de-camp, he has remained with Grant. On 3 March 1865, is made brigadier general chief of staff. Toward the end of hostilities, he is breveted major general in the volunteers and in the Regular Army. In conjunction, the relationship between Grant and Rawlins continues beyond the war. During 1869, President Grant appoints Rawlins Secretary of War. At that time he is suffering from tuberculosis, the disease which killed his first wife. General Rawlins dies on 6 September 1869. Also, Colonel Thomas Kilby Smith (54th Ohio) is promoted to brigadier general. Smith, who served on the staff of General Grant during the operations against Vicksburg, will be assigned Lt. General Banks' command, and he will participate in the Red River Expedition. The expedition is considered a failure and the officers engaged all sustain damage to their careers. Smith suffers no severe setbacks while his command, including infantry and cavalry charged with protecting the accompanying gunboats, returns from the expedition with about 800 able-bodied men out of his original force of 1,800. He is afterward assigned to pursue General Nathan Bedford Forrest, a mission that fails to capture the Rebel commander. Smith's health fails and he is relieved of any further service in the field. He receives the brevet of major general toward the close of hostilities on 13 March 1865. During 1866, General Smith is appointed consul at Panama, but he returns to the U.S. after a short tour there. He resides in Torresdale (present-day Philadelphia) and later relocates in New York, where he dies during December 1887.

August 12 (Wednesday)   In South Carolina, the Union begins another assault on Fort Sumter. The relentless array of shells continues to pound the fort, while a land and sea attack occurs on the 17th without success. The Confederate defenders receive thousands of incoming shells but suffer few casualties. The fort, its walls shattered, remains under Rebel control on 23 August.

August 13 (Thursday)   In Mississippi, elements of the 3rd, 4th, 9th and 11th Illinois Cavalry Regiments, the 3rd Michigan and 2nd Iowa Cavalry Regiments, bolstered further by the 9th Illinois Volunteer Regiment, engage Confederates at Granada. Casualty figures are not reported.

In Tennessee, a Union force under Lt. Colonel Phillips departs La Grange en route to Central Mississippi.

August 14 (Friday) In Arkansas, Union gunboats, including the *Cricket, Lexington* and *Marmora,* supported by troops of the 32nd Iowa Volunteer Regiment, move up the White River and clash with Confederates at West Point, White County. The Union sustains two killed and seven wounded. Confederate casualty figures are unavailable. Afterward, the *Cricket* advances up the Little Red River and encounters two Confederate States Army transport vessels, the *Kaskaskia* and the *Thomas Sugg.* Both are seized. The *Thomas Sugg,* known also as the *Sugg,* a wooden river steamboat, had been built in Cincinnati. The *Sugg* is afterward acquired (29 September 1863) by the U.S. Navy and commissioned the USS *Tensas.* While moving back toward the Mississippi, the *Cricket* is repeatedly under fire from Confederate ground troops, but their small arms are no serious threat. In November, the *Cricket* moves onto the Tennessee River, where it patrols to rid the area of Confederate guerrillas through December. Then it joins the Navy units at Red River Station.

In Tennessee, both Union and Confederate commanders are making preliminary plans for the campaign in Tennessee. Federal troops begin moving toward Chattanooga to strike General Bragg. Other Union troops also begin moving through the next week to various points to foil Bragg's railway lifeline to Chattanooga and Chickamauga.

In Ohio, Union General Thomas T. Welsh, who participated at such battles as Antietam (Sharpsburg), dies today of natural causes in Cincinnati.

August 15 (Saturday) In Arkansas, a skirmish develops between a contingent of Confederates and a Union force at Bentonville.

August 16 (Sunday) In Alabama, the Confederates evacuate Bridgeport.

In Tennessee, Union General Rosecrans' force begins to cross the Cumberland Mountains. He reaches the Tennessee River on the 26th and then establishes headquarters at Stephenson, while awaiting orders to reinitiate his advance.

In Kentucky, General Burnside, having closed the operations against General John H. Morgan, departs Camp Nelson en route for Lexington to surprise the Rebels there. The force moves out in three columns led by Generals Ambrose Burnside, George L. Hartsuff and Julius White, via the towns of London, Somerset and Jamestown, respectively.

In Naval activity, the USS *DeSoto,* while operating in the Gulf of Mexico, intercepts and captures the Confederate steamer *Alice Vivian,* which carries a cargo of cotton. The vessel is afterward acquired by the U.S. Navy and commissioned the USS *Alice Vivian.* Among the items captured on the vessel is the baggage of Confederate General James E. Slaughter, but Slaughter is not among the captured. In the Bahamas, the gunboat USS *Rhode Island* seizes the blockade runner *Cronstadt* in the vicinity of Abaco.

August 17 (Monday) In South Carolina, Union naval forces, including the USS *Lodona* and *Catskill* of the South Atlantic Blockading Squadron, bombard Morris Island and Fort Sumter. The Union establishes a siege against Charleston. During the exchange of fire, the *Catskill's* commanding officer, Captain George W. Rodgers, is killed. The *Catskill* remains on duty off Charleston for the duration of the war.

In Union general officer activity, Colonel Alvan Cullem Gillem is appointed as a brigadier general. General Gillem (West Point, 1851), a veteran of the Seminole Wars, had also served on the Texas frontier. During the previous year, he was quartermaster under General George H. Thomas and afterward was chief quartermaster under General Buell (Army of the Ohio), prior to becoming colonel of the Union 10th Tennessee Regiment. He also had been provost marshal at Nashville and adjutant general of Tennessee, the latter during June 1863. Also, Colonel James Clay Rice is promoted to brigadier general. He is assigned to command a brigade in General Lysander Cutler's division (I Corps). Afterward, when the corps is dissolved, General Rice returns to the V Corps and participates in the operations against Richmond while attached to General Wadsworth's division.

August 18 (Tuesday) In Arkansas, a Union contingent of engineers, commanded by Lt. Bross, skirmishes with Confederates led by Colonel Street at Pocahontas.

In New Mexico Territory, three companies of the 1st New York Cavalry skirmish with Confederates at Pueblo.

In North Carolina, elements of the 1st New York Mounted Rifles and the 11th Pennsylvania Cavalry Regiment repulse an attack by Confederate guerrillas at Pasquotank.

In Confederate general officer activity, at about this time, Brigadier General Roger A. Pryor resigns his commission; however, he remains with the Confederacy until the latter part of the following year, when he is captured while on a mission delivering messages between commands. Also, Major Henry Brevard Davidson (West Point, 1853) earlier captured at Island No. 10 and exchanged, is promoted to brigadier general. He will be assigned to duty in Major General Joseph Wheeler's cavalry in Georgia, where he leads a brigade. The following spring, he serves under Brigadier General Lunsford L. Lomax (West Point, 1856) during the Valley Campaign in Virginia.

In Naval activity, the USS *Lodona* bombards Fort Wagner in Charleston Harbor.

August 19 (Wednesday) In Confederate general officer activity, Colonel Henry Watkins Allen, 4th Louisiana Infantry Regiment, is promoted to brigadier general. Allen is seriously wounded this month during the fighting at Baton Rouge. During the final year of the conflict, Allen becomes governor of Louisiana. He had served in Texas during its war for independence from Mexico and had enlisted in the Confederate Army as a private.

August 20 (Thursday) In Kansas, Quantrill's Raiders prepare to strike Lawrence on the night of the 20th-21st, and at about dawn on the 21st, the attack commences when more than 400 guerrillas plunder the town and massacre about 150 men and boys. Others are wounded.

In Confederate general officer activity, Colonel Cullen Andrews Battle, 3rd Alabama Regiment, is appointed brigadier general effective this date. General Battle had participated in the fighting at Gettysburg as part of General Ramseur's brigade.

In Naval activity, the USS *Lodona,* which for several days has been attacking Confederate positions in the vicinity of Charleston Harbor, bombards Morris Island. The wooden steamer *Mary Sanford,* acquired by the U.S. Navy on 20 July 1863, is commissioned at the New York Navy Yard. Acting Master's Mate Alfred P. Hich receives command of the transport, which is assigned to the South Atlantic Blockading Squadron; however, later, it is transformed into a gunboat.

August 21 (Friday) In Kansas, Quantrill and his raiders attack and devastate Lawrence, killing and wounding civilians.

In Mississippi, elements of the 3rd and 4th Iowa Cavalry and the 5th Illinois Cavalry skirmish with Confederates at Coldwater. The Union sustains 10 wounded.

In South Carolina, Union Major General Quincy A. Gillmore issues Confederate-held Fort Sumter an ultimatum to surrender. The defenders reject it.

In Tennessee, Union forces under General Rosecrans reach the Tennessee River near their objective, Bragg's troops at Chattanooga. The Union begins crossing the river on 1 September. Meanwhile, Rosecrans' artillery bombards Chattanooga. This day, the Confederate positions come under attack for about seven hours.

In Naval activity, the USS *New Ironsides,* attached to the South Atlantic Blockading Squadron off Charleston, comes under an unsuccessful torpedo attack. During early October the Confederates again attempt to sink the *New Ironsides.* In other activity, the USS *Bainbridge* had sustained damage in a storm near Aspinwall, Colombia, in 1862 and afterward sailed to New York for repairs. On this day, while en route back to its squadron off South Carolina, it capsizes off Cape Hatteras, North Carolina. The crew, except for one man, is lost.

August 22 (Saturday) In North Carolina, Union troops from the USS *Shokokon* land near Wilmington and surprise a larger Confederate contingent, which takes flight. The Union captures a Confederate schooner in addition to many supplies.

In South Carolina, Union guns devastate Fort Sumter; however, the Confederates still refuse to surrender.

In Virginia, a Union reconnaissance force under Captain Gerry departs Martinsburg for Leetown.

August 23 (Sunday) *In Naval activity,* a Union frigate, the USS *Minnesota,* bombards Fort Fisher, North Carolina. In other activity, the CSS *Florida,* at Bermuda until 25 July, arrives at Brest, France. By this time, the *Florida* has been at sea since the latter part of January and has seized nineteen vessels. The ship remains in port until the following January and while in France, Captain Maffitt's health deteriorates to the point that he must relinquish command. He is succeeded by Commodore Joseph Barney, but he too becomes ill and is also relieved of command before the ship leaves port.

A Confederate contingent, commanded by Colonel John Taylor Wood, utilizing a group of boats, seizes two Union gunboats, the USS *Reliance* and *Satellite,* in the vicinity of the mouth of the Rappahannock. In early September, Union forces locate the two vessels. Colonel Wood had been appointed as an aide to President Davis in February and as a colonel of cavalry; however, he has also devoted time to small naval operations in Virginia. On 7 December, Colonel Wood is promoted to the rank of commander in the Confederate States Navy. The *Reliance* is sailed to Port Royal, Virginia; however, it is not taken into Confederate service. The vessel is destroyed to prevent it from being recaptured by General Kilpatrck's cavalry, which is on the advance in the region.

August 24 (Monday) **In Virginia,** the 2nd Massachusetts Cavalry, led by Colonel Charles Lowell, skirmishes with Confederate guerrillas under John Singleton Mosby at Coyle's Tavern in the vicinity of Fairfax Court House. The Union sustains two killed, four wounded and nine captured. Also, elements of the 3rd Division Cavalry Corps, Army of the Potomac, skirmish with Confederates in King George County. Casualty figures are unavailable.

In Arkansas, a contingent of Union Missouri cavalry led by Colonel Woodson attacks Pocahontas and captures about 50 Confederates.

August 25 (Tuesday) **In Missouri,** a contingent of the 5th Missouri Militia Cavalry skirmishes with Confederates at Waynesville. Casualty figures are unavailable.

In West Virginia, Union General William W. Averell leads his cavalry force on a mission from Hardy to Pocahontas County through the 30th.

In Arkansas, a large Union cavalry force commanded by General John W. Davidson approaches Brownsville. The Confederates evacuate the town in the two-day incident.

In Confederate general officer activity, Jeremy F. Gilmer (West Point, 1839) is promoted from colonel to major general. General Gilmer continues his duties as chief engineer of the Department of Northern Virginia and as chief of the engineer bureau of the Confederate war department. Later he supervises the defenses of

Charleston and Atlanta. After the war, he becomes president of a private company, a position he retains until his death during December 1883.

In Naval activity, the USS *Winona,* subsequent to duty at Vicksburg, arrives at Baltimore for repairs. It remains out of service until February 1864, when it departs for South Carolina to join the South Atlantic Blockading Squadron.

August 26 (Wednesday) **In Arkansas,** the 6th Missouri Militia, 3rd Wisconsin and 2nd Kansas Cavalry Regiments, bolstered by the 2nd Indiana Battery, engage Confederates at Perryville.

In South Carolina, the Union offensive against Charleston nears success as Battery Wagner falls. Also, a Union contingent under Major General Quincy A. Gillmore captures a group of Confederate pickets at Vinegar Hill.

In Virginia, Confederate Brigadier General John B. Floyd dies of natural causes. In other activity, the 2nd and 3rd West Virginia Cavalry and the 14th Pennsylvania Cavalry, augmented by the 3rd and 8th West Virginia Volunteer Regiments, under General William W. Averell, engage Confederates led by Major General Samuel Jones and Colonel George S. Patton at Rocky Gap (White Sulphur Springs). The Rebels under Colonel Patton and the Union force clash at the intersection of Anthony's Creek Road and the James River Pike, with the Confederates advancing along the former and the Union on the latter. The clash drains the ammunition of both sides as it rages throughout the day. The Union is the first to leave the field. The Union sustains 16 killed and 113 wounded. The Confederates suffer about 156 killed and wounded. The Confederates under Patton prevent the loss of the Union objective, the law books at Virginia State Law Library at Lewisburg.

August 27 (Thursday) **In Kansas,** Union Brigadier General George W. Deitzler, on leave at Lawrence due to illness, resigns his commission and accepts a position as major general, Kansas Militia. Deitzler concentrates his efforts against the invasion of Sterling Price, whose Confederates raid the state of Missouri.

In Mississippi, the 5th Heavy Artillery (U.S. Colored Troops) skirmish with Confederates at Vicksburg.

In Kentucky, the 39th Kentucky Volunteer Regiment skirmishes with Confederates at Clark's Neck.

In Arkansas, a contingent of cavalry (General Davidson's command) led by Colonel Glover clashes with Confederates at Bayou Meto.

In Alabama, a detachment of Colonel Wilder's cavalry clashes with Confederates at Hanover. No Union casualties are reported. The Confederates sustain three killed and one captured.

In Union general officer activity, Brigadier General George H. Thomas (volunteers) is promoted to brigadier general, Regular Army.

In Naval activity, the USS *Granite City* arrives in New Orleans from New York, but due to an epidemic of sickness aboard the warship, it is placed in quarantine until September. In other activity, the USS *Sunflower* captures the schooner *General Worth* in the Straits of Florida.

August 28 (Friday) *In Naval activity,* the USS *Saco* is launched at the Boston Navy Yard. On 11 July 1864, it is commissioned. Lt. Commander John G. Walker receives command of the gunboat. It joins the search for the Confederate raiders and blockade runners throughout the summer and the winter of 1864, but the ship is plagued with mechanical problems, poor performance and breakdowns of its boilers. It is decommissioned on 27 January 1865 while undergoing repairs and later recommissioned in June 1866. The *Saco* remains in active service until decommissioned in Norfolk, Virginia, on 17 December 1868. However, during July 1870, it is recommissioned yet again. After tours in Europe and the Far East, it is decommissioned the final time at Mare Island, California, on 13 July 1876 and sold on 20 November 1883.

August 29 (Saturday) **In South Carolina** at Charleston, the Confederates prepare to test the submarine CSS *Hunley.* Naval Lieutenant John A. Payne of the CSS *Chicora* had volunteered to assume command of the vessel. Other crew members who volunteer to serve are from the CSS *Palmetto State.* The new commander touches the wrong lever and causes the ship to dive while the hatches remain open. The ship sinks, but it is recovered and a new test run is scheduled for October.

In Tennessee, Union General Rosecrans' force begins to cross the Tennessee River to close against General Bragg. The operation is complete by September 4, pressing Bragg to begin to evacuate Chattanooga and Tullahoma. The Confederates under Bragg move to Lafayette, Georgia, on 7 September due to the pressure mounted by Rosecrans, who initiates his move through the gaps in Lookout Mountain.

In Virginia, a Union force composed of elements of the 1st New York Mounted Rifles and the 5th Pennsylvania Cavalry (General Isaac Wistar's command), led by Colonel Onderdonk and Lt. Colonel Lewis, skirmish with Confederate infantry and cavalry at Bottom's Bridge (Dry Creek). The Union sustains one killed and one wounded. The Confederates suffer four killed and five captured.

In Confederate general officer activity, William W. Kirkland, 21st North Carolina Infantry Regiment, is promoted to the rank of brigadier general. Also, Colonel Goode Bryan (West Point, 1834), a veteran of the Mexican War (1st Alabama Volunteers) and colonel of the 16th Georgia, is promoted to brigadier general. General Bryan had participated at Fredericksburg, Chancellorsville and Gettysburg.

August 30 (Sunday) **In Tennessee,** Union forces under General Ambrose Burnside, crossing the Cumberland Mountains, reach Montgomery. Another column led by General Julius

White joins him there. A cavalry contingent, led by Colonel Burt, moves out on a reconnaissance mission and discovers a Confederate force under General John Pegram holding positions at a gap in the vicinity of the Emory Iron Works, located in front of the Clinch River Valley. A larger force is dispatched to engage Pegram.

August 31 (Monday)   In Arkansas, Union cavalry (General John Davidson's division, Department of the Missouri) engages Confederates at Austin.

In Maryland, Major General Robert C. Schenck again becomes commander of the Middle Military Department. He succeeds General William Morris and retains the post until 28 September.

In Tennessee, Union forces under General Burnside advance to engage a Rebel force under General John Pegram at the Emory Iron Works, but the Rebels have evacuated the area, leaving the road to Knoxville wide open. One contingent under Colonel Foster speeds toward Kingston, a mere six miles away. Another contingent led by General James Shackelford gallops toward Loudon, which stands about twenty miles from Kingston. The Confederates destroy the bridge, which spans the Tennessee River at Loudon, prior to the arrival of the cavalry. Nonetheless, the Rebels are unable to forestall the Yankees' arrival. The Confederate commander in the area, General Simon B. Buckner, is stunned by the unexpected appearance of Burnside's command. Departing before dousing the campfires, Buckner moves out of Eastern Tennessee so quickly that the Confederates at Cumberland Gap are not informed, nor does he transmit any orders to them prior to the evacuation. Buckner's hurried flight eases the task of Burnside, whose force has just culminated a horrid two weeks, which included a 250-mile march across the mountains.

September   In Oregon, a contingent of the 1st Oregon Volunteer Cavalry led by Major Charles C. Drew establishes Fort Klamath in the Wood River Valley near present-day Klamath Falls. The fort was deemed necessary by the commander of the Department of the Pacific, General George Wright, to afford security for the Klamath Indian agency as well as settlers traveling westward toward Idaho and the Pacific Ocean. Nonetheless, the site for the fort proves to be of little value due to its distance from the routes traveled by the pioneers. During 1864, the garrison becomes involved with hostile Indians, and again during 1872 hostilities erupt (Modoc War) that involve the troops at Fort Klamath, but otherwise, the post is considered a dreary duty station. After the Modoc War, Fort Klamath troops participate in the Nez Perce War in 1877. The Oregon volunteers garrison the fort until 1867, when elements of the 1st U.S. Cavalry arrive to assume responsibility. The fort is scheduled for abandonment during 1886 and a presidential executive order to that effect is issued by President Grover Cleveland. The decision is not well re-

ceived by the citizens in the region. Their vivid memories of recent hostilities with the various Indian tribes prompt an unexpected response to Washington, which is inundated with urgent requests to countermand the order. The campaign succeeds and the life of the fort is extended until 1890, when all thoughts of new Indian uprisings have vanished in the state.

In the Dakota Territory, Union forces under General Alfred Sully defeat the Santee Sioux. The victory alleviates the problems in Iowa and will permit the governor to dissolve the Northern Border Brigade, which had been established during 1862 to protect the territory from Indians when the army was recalled after the outbreak of the Civil War. General Sully establishes a temporary fort, known as Fort Sully, along the Missouri River in the vicinity of present-day Pierre during his campaign against the Sioux. Temporary becomes several years, despite the poor conditions there. During 1866, the garrison with great enthusiasm abandons the fort for a more tenable location with better conditions for the health of the troops. The new site for the fort will remain on the Missouri River, but will be about twenty-five miles above the present fort.

September 1 (Tuesday)   In Arkansas, Union troops (General Samuel Rice's division, Department of Kansas) engage Confederates at Bayou Meto. Also, the Union 1st Arkansas Volunteers, 6th Missouri Militia, 2nd Kansas Cavalry and the 2nd Indiana Battery commanded by Colonel Cloud engage Confederates at Devil's Back Bone and Cotton Gap. The Union sustains four killed and 12 wounded. The Confederates sustain 25 killed and 40 wounded. In related activity, Union forces under General Blunt seize Fort Smith.

In South Carolina, the Stars and Bars still flies over Fort Sumter; however, some of its protective artillery is moved into Charleston to meet the approaching Union Army.

In Tennessee, Confederate General Bragg's defenders at Chattanooga are reinforced by additional troops in an attempt to thwart a Union assault on the city. General Rosecrans' Army of the Cumberland begins to cross the Tennessee River, heading for Chattanooga to seize the Confederate stronghold.

In Virginia, a contingent of the Ohio 6th Cavalry, commanded by Major Cryor, skirmishes with Confederates at Barbee's Cross Roads. The Union sustains two killed, four wounded and 24 captured.

In Confederate general officer activity, Colonel William Carter Wickham are promoted to the rank of brigadier general to rank from this day. Wickham serves under General Jubal Early in Virginia, but he leaves the army in January 1864 to enter the Confederate Congress. General Johnston is wounded at Spotsylvania during 1864, but he recuperates and participates in the raids launched against Washington by General Jubal Early and later in the defense of Richmond. Also, Colonel Matthew Calbraith But-

ler and Lt. Colonel Robert Daniel Johnston (23rd North Carolina, wounded earlier at Seven Pines), are promoted to brigadier general.

In Naval activity, the supply ship USS *New Berne* (formerly screw steamer *United States*) leaves New York en route to join the North Atlantic Blockading Squadron in Virginia. The *New Berne* is used primarily to deliver mail to the various ships in the squadron and transport supplies to the ships and stations. In 1864 it sees service in the Carolinas.

September 2 (Wednesday)   In Virginia, Union forces under General Kilpatrick destroy the Union vessels *Reliance* and *Satellite* at Port Conway. The vessels had been captured the previous month.

In Tennessee, Kingston falls to Union troops commanded by Colonel (brevet brigadier general) Robert G. Minty. Knoxville, Tennessee, also falls to the Union Army when a contingent of General Burnside's force, commanded by Colonel John Foster, enters the city; Burnside arrives on the 4th and receives a rousing welcome: U.S. flags, which had been concealed for a long time, are brought to the foreground, dusted off and plastered all over the town. Greetings included, "Welcome General Burnside. Welcome to East Tennessee!" "Bless the lord! The old flag's come back to East Tennessee!" In related activity, Confederate Brigadier General Jerome B. Robertson (Texas Brigade) participates in this action around Knoxville. Afterward Robertson's brigade is transferred to the Trans-Mississippi Department.

In Naval activity, the gunboat *Nipsic*, built at the Portsmouth Navy Yard during 1862, is commissioned. Lt. Commander George Bacon receives command. The *Nipsic* is assigned to the South Atlantic Blockading Squadron and arrives off Morris Island, South Carolina, on 5 November, 1863.

In Union general officer activity, John Grant Mitchell (later brevet major general) is appointed lieutenant colonel of the 113th Ohio Infantry. He initially entered service on 27 June 1861 and was commissioned lieutenant and adjutant of the 3rd Ohio Infantry on 30 July. He becomes colonel of the regiment the next May.

September 3 (Thursday)   In the Dakota Territory at White Stone Hill, Union contingents of the 2nd Nebraska, 6th Iowa and Company I, 7th Iowa Cavalry, commanded by General F. Sully, engage a force of Sioux Indians led by Chief Inkpaduta, which had only the previous month clashed unsuccessfully with army forces under General Henry Hastings Sibley. The Sioux and Blackfeet camp is discovered at about 1500 by a contingent of the 6th Iowa Cavalry. A runner is dispatched to the main body, while the cavalry establishes positions from which to launch an attack. General Alfred Sully arrives about one hour later as the Sioux, having discovered the army, attempts to hurriedly depart. A clash erupts and the Indians mount a counterattack, but the army prevails. The cavalry initiates pursuit until last light, and on the following morning, the chase begins anew. The skirmishing lasts for several days. On 5 September, a small contingent of fewer than 30 troops is attacked by a large war party. The unit attempts to return fire while retiring toward the main body, which is camped nearly fifteen miles away. The army loses about twenty troops killed and thirty wounded with some estimates at about 70–72 total casualties. The Indians lose about 300 killed and about the same number captured, with some estimates set at about 750 total casualties. The force under General Sully establishes winter quarters along the Missouri River.

In Naval activity, the USS *Shawsheen,* operating as part of the blockading squadron in North Carolina, is ordered to return north for repairs. After reaching Hampton Roads, the *Shawsheen* is ordered to report to Norfolk for a major overhaul, which includes some work being done at Baltimore. Afterward the *Shawsheen* operates out of Newport News and begins patrolling along the James and York Rivers and their tributaries. In addition, the *Shawsheen* participates in various operations in support of ground troops.

September 4 (Friday)   In Alabama, a bread shortage causes riots in Mobile.

In Tennessee, Union General Rosecrans has his army perched for an assault against Chattanooga, following the completion of the crossing of the Tennessee River with very little Confederate resistance. Meanwhile, Burnside's Union troops are safely entrenched in Knoxville, having secured it two days earlier. During the march, which encompassed fourteen grueling days, Burnside's endeavor has seized about 2,500 prisoners, several Confederate locomotives, eleven guns and a bountiful supply of arms and ammunition.

In Texas, General Banks and Admiral Farragut complete their strategy for an operation against Confederate-held Sabine Pass. The operation will be commanded by Brigadier General W.B. Franklin and Lieutenant Frederick Crocker (Navy); the flotilla departs New Orleans on the following day.

September 5 (Saturday)   In Louisiana, a Union force composed of 4,500 troops under General W.B. Franklin departs for Sabine Pass, Texas, transported by a naval force commanded by Lt. Crocker. Crocker's flagship, the gunboat *Clifton,* is supported by the vessels *Arizona* (Acting Master H. Tibbets), *Granite City* (Acting Master C. W. Lamson) and *Sachem* (Lt. Amos Johnson).

In Tennessee, General Burnside, informed that Cumberland Gap is garrisoned by a strong Confederate force, orders General James Shackelford to depart Knoxville to bolster a smaller force which had earlier been sent against the stronghold. In other activity, elements of the 100th Ohio Regiment engage Confederates under at Limestone Station, but the five companies suffer severely, losing 12 killed, 20 wounded and

240 missing. The Confederates sustain six killed and 10 wounded.

In West Virginia, a Union contingent composed of five companies of the 1st West Virginia Volunteers led by Major Stephens engages Confederates under Captain McNeil at Morefield.

In Naval activity, Union warships bombard Forts Wagner and Gregg in Charleston Harbor, South Carolina. The USS *Quaker City* seizes a schooner, the *Elsie,* off Charleston.

September 6 (Sunday)   In Arkansas, Confederate General Lucius M. Walker (West Point, 1850) is mortally wounded in a duel with General John S. Marmaduke at Little Rock. Walker succumbs on the following day.

In South Carolina, during the night of the 6th–7th, the Confederates abandon Fort Wagner and Battery Gregg under orders of General Pierre G.T. Beauregard. By this time, Beauregard discerns that his defenders are holding untenable positions in the event of the anticipated attack by the Union. Nonetheless, the remnant fortress, Fort Sumter, continues to hold and Charleston is still prepared to resist.

In Tennessee, Confederate General Braxton Bragg, realizing his precarious position, orders the evacuation of Chattanooga. The Confederates head toward Chickamauga.

In Virginia, Union cavalry led by General George Armstrong Custer skirmishes with Confederate cavalry under General Jeb Stuart at Brandywine Station. The Union sustains one wounded.

In Naval activity, the USS *Hunchback* departs North Carolina for Hampton Roads to receive repairs. The USS *Argosy* debarks a contingent at Bruinsburg, Mississippi, that is on a mission to destroy a ferry. The landing party encounters a contingent of mounted Confederates, but the Rebels, upon the approach of the Yankees, abandon the area. The Union contingent destroys the ferry and confiscates a "wagonload consisting of 250,000 waterproof percussion caps, 1 box containing 5,000 friction pruners … and a few other items."

September 7 (Monday) SIEGE OF CHARLESTON Fort Wagner comes under Union control. Troops under General Quincy A. Gillmore seize it and Battery Gregg. This siege of Charleston had begun on July 10, 1863. The Union had installed a huge piece of artillery, known by the troops as the "Swamp Angel," "Mud Lark" or the "Marsh Croaker." This enormously powerful weapon had been able to launch shells for a distance of five miles to strike Charleston. The gun, which had fired thirty-six shells before exploding, had been placed at a battery in the swamp commanded by Colonel E.W. Serrill, 1st New York Volunteers, and supported by Captain McKenna and Lieutenant Parsons. With the fall of Fort Wagner and Battery Gregg on Morris Island, the Union is able to move its artillery even closer to Charleston and dominate the harbor. Fort Wagner contains a bomb proof shelter that is capable of holding

about 1,800 troops; this protection greatly helped the Confederates keep their casualties down during the siege. After dark on this day, the *Weehawken,* a Union ironclad, moves up the channel between Fort Sumter and Cummings Point to reconnoiter and see if it is possible to clear the obstacles, but en route, the vessel becomes grounded in a precarious position. The Confederate batteries at Fort Sumter, Fort Moultrie and on Sullivan's Island each bombard the stranded warship, inflicting twenty-four hits upon it. Meanwhile, the *Weehawken,* which sustains three men wounded, returns fire and plasters Fort Moultrie and Fort Sumter. The bombardment pounds the Confederate positions, and at Fort Sumter, one shell strikes a magazine, which costs the Confederates sixteen casualties. While the *Weehawken* is attempting to trade fire with the ground batteries, other Union vessels, led by the *New Ironsides,* brave the horrific fire and successfully move in close to free the *Weehawken.* After being repaired the *Weehawken* rejoins the squadron in October.

The USS *Nantucket* also participates at this action. It continues to patrol as part of the South Atlantic Blockading Squadron until it is sent to Philadelphia during July 1865, where it is decommissioned. About ten years later it is recommissioned and for a short while renamed *Medusa.* Afterward, it is transferred to Portsmouth, New Hampshire, and spends time in and out of service between 1882 and 1884 prior to being sent to New York. About 1896, it sees duty with the North Carolina Naval Militia, and upon the outbreak of the Spanish American War, it serves actively at Charleston in support of the coast defenses. During November 1900, the *Nantucket* is sold for scrap.

In Arkansas, cavalry attached to General John W. Davidson's command skirmishes with Confederates at Ashley's Mills.

In Louisiana, a contingent of the 2nd Brigade, 2nd Division, 13th Corps, commanded by Major Montgomery, skirmishes with Confederates at the Atchafalaya River.

In Missouri, the 2nd Missouri Cavalry clashes with Confederates at Bear Skin Lake.

In Tennessee, General Rosecrans directs General Alexander McCook to move to Winston's Gap and from there cross Lookout Mountain to occupy Alpine on the east side of the mountain. General George H. Thomas is ordered to cross the mountain from two points, Stevens Gap and Cooper's Gap, and occupy McClemore's Cove in a valley between Lookout and Pigeon Mountains. General Thomas L. Crittenden is ordered to remain in Will's Valley, from where he can maintain a reconnaissance of the Rebels at Chattanooga.

In Texas, General William B. Franklin's force arrives in the vicinity of Sabine Pass. The troops aboard the vessels prepare to attack the Confederates on the following day.

In Union general officer activity, John Wesley Turner (West Point, 1855) is appointed brigadier general of volunteers to rank from this day. General Turner had served on the West coast and in Florida before the war. Afterward, he served in Kansas and as chief commissary for General Butler in New Orleans, prior to becoming chief of staff and chief of artillery under General Hunter.

September 8 (Tuesday) In Louisiana, a contingent of the 4th Wisconsin Cavalry skirmishes with Confederates at Baton Rouge.

In Tennessee, the Confederates abandon Chattanooga. General Dan H. Hill's corps, composed of the divisions of John C. Breckinridge and Patrick R. Cleburne, are the first to depart. The column pauses after a 22-mile march at Lafayette, located east of Pigeon Mountain, the latter standing between the column and McLemore's Cove, where Union General Thomas arrives on the 9th. General Hill, once at Lafayette, sends Cleburne toward Pigeon Mountain with instructions to deploy his force at three separate gaps: Catlett's in the north, Dug in the center and Blue Bird in the south.

Meanwhile, General Breckinridge is directed to remain at Lafayette with responsibility for protecting the wagon trains and the reserve artillery. Confederate Colonel (later brigadier general) James T. Holtzclaw participates in this action around Chattanooga, and he is actively engaged at Chickamauga. Also, a five-company contingent of the 100th Ohio Regiment, led by Lt. Colonel Hayes, engages a large Confederate contingent led by General Alfred E. Jackson at Telford (Battle of Limestone Station). The Union expends all of its ammunition and surrenders. More than 240 men are captured and sent to Richmond, where 87 of them die in captivity. By the end of the war, General Jackson loses everything. He is able to rent some land in Virginia and works the farm. President Andrew Johnson gives him a "special pardon" in appreciation of some kindnesses afforded Johnson's family during the war. Consequently, he regains his lost properties, allowing him to move back to Tennessee, where he dies during October 1889.

In Texas, the Union gunboats *Arizona, Granite City, Clifton* and *Sachem* move through the east-

ern channel at Sabine Pass. The gunboat *Granite City* escorts a Union division (General Weitzel). Initially the situation for the Union looks positive. The ships maneuver without incident, but once they encroach upon the defensive works, the Confederate artillery rips into the gunboats with devastating effect. The *Clifton* and the *Sachem* sustain horrific hits in their respective boiler rooms and the crews choke on their own steam as they get stranded. The *Arizona* is grounded but works itself free, and with the *Granite City,* re-crosses the bar. The *Clifton* and *Sachem* (built during 1844 and acquired by the U.S. Navy on 20 September 1861) hoist the white flag and surrender. The *Clifton* is taken into service by the Texas Marine Department. General Weitzel and the remaining units of his force retire to Brashear City, Louisiana, and from there they move back to New Orleans, reaching it on the 11th. The Confederates in this area accept the victory as a huge morale booster.

In Virginia, a contingent of the Union 70th Pennsylvania Cavalry repels an attack at Bath.

In Naval activity, the side-wheel steamer *Honduras,* constructed at New York during 1861, is acquired by the U.S. Navy and commissioned the USS *Honduras* at the New York Navy Yard. The vessel, commanded by Acting Lieutenant T. Stites, is utilized as a supply ship in the East Gulf Blockading Squadron. Shortly after being commissioned, it sails for Key West. It also delivers dispatches and mail; however, it at times performs blockade patrols.

September 8–9 In South Carolina, U.S. Marines and sailors attack Confederate-held Fort Sumter. At 2200, under cover of darkness, a contingent of about 400 troops launches the attack. The force, commanded by Lt. Commander T.H. Stevens, is composed of five contingents commanded by Lt. Commander E.P. Williams (USS *Patapsco*), and Lieutenants Higginson, Preston, and Remey and Ensign Craven. The Marine contingent is commanded by Captain

McCawley. The Union plans to surprise the Rebels at Sumter; however, the Confederates are expecting the visit. Once the units reach the ruins of the fort, Major Elliott gives the order to open fire. The Union troops are inundated with a hurricane of fire that compels them to head for their boats. The Rebels bombard the vessels, causing more complications. Nearly half of the attacking force is captured. The USS *Lodona* loses one boat and its crew is captured. Following this action, the *Lodona* sails north to Philadelphia for repairs and remains there until 11 November.

September 9 (Wednesday) In Arkansas, a Union contingent, including elements of the 2nd Kansas Cavalry and the 2nd Indiana Battery, commanded by Colonel Cloud, leads an attack against Confederates at Dardanelle. Casualty figures are unavailable.

In Tennessee, Cumberland Gap falls to the Union when cavalry commanded by General James M. Shackelford and other forces under Colonel De Courcey (infantry brigade) seize the town following a heated battle at Tazewell. The Union seizes about 2,000 prisoners and captures fourteen pieces of artillery. Confederate General John Wesley Frazer (West Point, 1849), aware Knoxville is falling to the Yankees, surrenders Cumberland Gap to General Burnside. The capitulation stuns the Confederacy. The actions of Frazer reverberate all the way to the halls of the Confederate Senate, which declines to sanction his recent promotion (May 1863) to brigadier general. Frazer's luck doesn't get any better as he, unlike many of the high ranking officers, is not released from Fort Warren, nor is he offered in exchange for Union officers until after the war. After his release, General Frazer resides on a plantation in Arkansas, but relocates to New York City, where he has a fatal accident on 31 March 1906.

General Burnside is at this time in poor

Left: **Union warships attack Confederate-held Sabine Pass.** *Right:* **Union troops occupy Cumberland Gap (***Harper's Pictoral History of the Civil War,*** 1896).**

health and has requested to be relieved of command; however, President Lincoln is not yet willing to accept his resignation. In other activity, troops under the command of Union General W.S. Rosecrans (Crittenden's Corps) occupy the city of Chattanooga as Confederates under Braxton Bragg evacuate it. This Union victory puts Federal troops in total control of another important railroad. Bragg's forces move out heading for Lafayette. His command, counting reinforcements from Mississippi, East Tennessee and Virginia, exceeds 66,000.

In Virginia, General Longstreet departs Virginia with over 10,000 men and ample artillery to reinforce General Bragg in Tennessee. Longstreet arrives on the 18th. Brigadier General Benjamin G. Humphreys' brigade is among those that move out with Longstreet.

In the Indian Territory, the 2nd Colorado Cavalry skirmishes with Confederates at Webber's Falls (Oklahoma).

In Confederate general officer activity, Brigadier General Howell Cobb is promoted to major general effective this day. He will command the District of Georgia for the duration. He dies in New York on 9 October 1868 while on a trip. He is the brother of Confederate General Thomas Reade Rootes Cobb.

September 10 (Thursday)   In Arkansas, Union troops under Major General Frederick Steele, including cavalry under General John Davidson, engage Confederates attached to General Price's command at Little Rock, and the Yankees capture the town. The Union 3rd Arkansas Cavalry, commanded by Colonel Abraham H. Ryan, enters Little Rock subsequent to evacuation by Confederates under General John Marmaduke, who retires toward Arkadelphia. General John W. Davidson's cavalrymen arrive at the arsenal and hoist the Stars and Stripes at the Tower Building. General Steele had been ordered to Arkansas to command all U.S. Forces in the state after the capture of Vicksburg. The U.S. Army deactivates the arsenal during 1890.

In Georgia, a contingent of Union cavalry (Army of the Cumberland) skirmishes with Confederates at Graysville. Casualty figures are unavailable.

In Tennessee, a scheduled attack by Confederates against Union General Negley's force in the McLemore's Cove near Dug Gap fails to materialize, purportedly due to Bragg's unfamiliarity with the conditions of the roads and of the obstacles at the gap.

In Kentucky, the 11th Kentucky Mounted Volunteer Regiment under Colonel Love skirmishes with Confederate guerrillas at Brimstone Creek. The Confederates sustain seven wounded and two captured.

In Confederate general officer activity, Colonel Abner Perrin, who has commanded Brigadier General Samuel McGowan's brigade in the latter's absence, is promoted to the rank of brigadier general effective this date. Perrin's

regiment, the 14th South Carolina, will be commanded by Colonel Joseph N. Brown.

In Naval activity, the USS *Western World,* desperately in need of repairs, is sent to the navy yard at Washington, D.C. It remains out of service until early February 1864.

September 11 (Friday)   General Henry W. Halleck sends Burnside a congratulatory letter following the victory at Cumberland Gap. The letter also instructs Burnside to hold the North Carolina mountains and the Holston River, while it is determined whether General William S. Rosecrans will move into Georgia or Alabama.

In Washington, D.C., President Lincoln declines the offer of resignation made by General Burnside, the latter being in command at Knoxville, Tennessee, at this time.

In Arkansas, a contingent of the 14th Kansas Cavalry skirmishes with Confederates at Waldron. Casualty figures are unreported.

In Georgia, the vanguard of the Union 21st Corps, led by General Van Cleve and Colonel Wilder, engages Confederates at Ringgold. The Union sustains eight killed and 19 wounded. The Confederates sustain three killed and 18 missing. Other contingents of the Army of the Cumberland skirmish with Confederates at Dug Alpine and Stevens Gap (Davis' Crossroads).

In Tennessee-Georgia (Chickamauga), for the second day in succession, the Confederates fail to launch an attack against General James S. Negley's division at McClemore's Cove. Bragg blames the failure on Major General Thomas Hindman. In related activity, elements of General Daniel Hill's signal corps and some of his scouts in the vicinity of Blue Bird Gap inform Hill that Union forces are maneuvering to the left and advancing up the cove. The information is forwarded to General Bragg. At this time, General Crittenden has two divisions (Van Cleve's and John McCauley Palmer's) at Ringgold, Georgia, about twenty miles distant from Chattanooga, and another of his divisions (Thomas Wood's) stands at Lee and Gordon's Mills, only ten miles from Chattanooga; however, the latter is essentially isolated without reinforcements until the following day. By 13 September, Crittenden has his entire corps at the mills.

In West Virginia, Union and Confederate contingents skirmish at Morefield. Specific units and casualty figures are unreported.

In Naval activity, the USS *Iron Age* (commissioned 25 June 1863), commanded by Lt. Comdr. E.E. Stone, after serving in New England, arrives this day at New Inlet in North Carolina to join the

blockading squadron. On its fifth day on duty, the *Iron Age* encounters a blockade runner moving out from Wilmington. The *Iron Age* compels it to reverse course with the *Iron Age* in pursuit. The blockade runner is forced to run aground in the vicinity of Fort Fisher.

The USS *Genesee* is directed to sail to the Gulf to initiate blockade duty there. On this day, the *Genesee* spots the blockade runner *Fanny,* which is attempting to enter Mobile. The *Genesee* and other vessels initiate pursuit. The *Fanny,* however, is run ashore and set afire to prevent capture. Later the *Genesee* participates in the attacks against Fort Morgan, and afterward, it is utilized as a store ship and as one of the vessels maneuvering in Mobile Bay to eliminate torpedoes (mines). It is decommissioned in July 1865.

September 12 (Saturday)   In Alabama, the USS *Genesee* and the gunboats *Calhoun* and *Jackson* engage Confederates at Grant's Pass, Mobile.

In Missouri, a one-company contingent of the 5th Missouri Militia Cavalry repels an attack launched by about 300 Confederate guerrillas in Texas County. The Union sustains three wounded. The estimated Confederate casualties are about 20 killed.

In Georgia, Union forces under General Edward M. McCook make camp at Alpine, about twenty miles from Lafayette, where the Confederate trains and reserve artillery of Bragg are under guard by General Daniel Hill and two divisions. Earlier in the day, Hill's pickets were driven back.

In Louisiana, Union artillery engages Confederates at Sterling's Plantation. The Union suffers three killed and three wounded. Confederate casualties are unavailable.

In Tennessee-Georgia (Chickamauga), General William S. Rosecrans, involved only in chasing the retreating General Braxton Bragg from Chattanooga, realizes that his own army is in trouble. Rosecrans attempts to bring his scattered troops together to avoid disaster at the hands of Bragg. However, Bragg's cunning plan goes astray the following day because of bad

Union troops depart Ringgold, Georgia, by rail for the front (Johnson, *Campfire and Battlefield: History of the Conflicts and Campaigns,* 1894).

communications, forcing him to wait apprehensively for reinforcements. On this day, General Bragg at 1800 dispatches the following order to General Leonidas Polk: "GENERAL: I inclose you a dispatch from General [John] Pegram. This presents you a fine opportunity of striking [Thomas L.] Crittenden in detail, and I hope you will avail yourself of it at daylight tomorrow. This division crushed, and the others are yours. We can then turn again on the force in the cove. Wheeler's cavalry will move on Wilder so as to cover your right. I shall be delighted to hear of your success." Afterward, another message from Bragg is received by Polk: "The enemy is approaching from the south—and it is highly important that your attack in the morning should be quick and decided. Let no time be lost."

Nonetheless, Polk receives intelligence that the forces to his front are well beyond one division and his strategy immediately turns toward taking defensive steps rather than launching an offensive. Meanwhile, General Crittenden crosses the river late on the night of the 12th and joins with General Thomas Wood at Lee and Gordon's Mills to consolidate his entire corps.

In Union general officer activity, Colonel Henry L. Eustis is promoted to brigadier general.

September 13 (Sunday)   In Georgia, near Chickamauga, a Union contingent, Wilder's Mounted Brigade, engages Confederates at Lett's Tan Yard. The Union sustains 50 killed and wounded. The Confederates suffer 10 killed and 40 wounded. At Lafayette, General Daniel Hill is informed during the morning by a messenger sent by General John A. Wharton about the Union encampment of the previous night at Alpine, about 20 miles distant. Shortly afterward, Union troops skirmish with his troops along the Alpine Road about two miles outside Lafayette. Meanwhile, General Alexander McCook orders his wagon trains to be moved to the crest of Lookout Mountain. McCook is also aware that reinforcements have arrived to bolster General Bragg.

At about midnight on the 13th–14th, McCook receives orders to break camp and speed to McLemore's Cove to support General George H. Thomas, which initiates a treacherous forced march across Lookout Mountain to forestall disaster at the cove. The overtired column treks through Lookout Valley and reaches Stevens Gap (Georgia) on the 17th. Confusion is interfering on both sides, but Bragg is more seriously affected, as he remains uncertain where the Union forces are, and he is unaware that McCook's force is departing. By this time General Rosecrans has concluded that Bragg had not been in retreat, which is the reason he begins to reel in his forces and reform at McLemore's Cove.

Confederate General Daniel Hill is informed that his corps is to assume responsibility for the trains and reserve artillery at Lafayette, in place of General Leonidas Polk, who is directed to attack General Thomas L. Crittenden's positions at Lee and Gordon's Mills. During the day and into the night, Crittenden crosses the Chickamauga River with his force to join with his division under Wood at the mills, increasing his strength, although he is unaware that the Confederates had a plan to assault his lines at Ringgold this day. Nevertheless, again the Confederates fail to launch an attack.

In Tennessee, a contingent of Missouri cavalry and one company of Kentucky infantry clashes with Confederates at Paris. The Confederates sustain about six killed, 21 wounded and more than 75 captured.

In Missouri, Union troops repel a Confederate attack at Salem.

In Virginia, Union General George G. Meade advances his troops across the Rapidan River and occupies Culpeper Court House, taking advantage of the Confederate decision to weaken the lines in Virginia by sending Longstreet's command to Tennessee. During the operation, the 1st, 2nd and 3rd Cavalry Divisions (Army of the Potomac) skirmish with Confederates. The Union sustains three killed and 40 wounded. The Confederates sustain 10 killed, 40 wounded and 75 missing.

In Naval activity, following participation in expeditions up the Red, Black Tensa (also Tensas) and Ouachita Rivers, where the USS *Rattler* and the *Manitou* had seized the *Louisville,* on this day, the *Rattler*'s crew is captured. The commanding officer and 16 crewmen are seized while attending church services at Rodney, Mississippi. Nonetheless, the ship itself is not taken. It continues to patrol in the same region for the next year.

September 14 (Monday)   In Georgia, General Bragg summons his four corps commanders (Simon B. Buckner, Daniel Hill, Leonidas Polk and William H.T. Walker) to his headquarters at Lafayette. Bragg tells his commanders that Union General Alexander McCook is at Alpine (although he departed for Stevens Gap), and that General Thomas L. Crittenden is at Lee and Gordon's Mills. Unaware that McCook had departed and that only Wood's division is at the mills, Bragg fails to take the offense out of fear that McCook might strike his rear. Bragg states: "There is not an infantry soldier of the enemy south of us." The remark is in response to that information forwarded to him by General Hill about the Union troop movements.

Union General Crittenden, having arrived at Lee and Gordon's Mills near Ringgold the previous day, moves back to Missionary Ridge, Tennessee with two divisions, but General Wood's division remains at the mills for the remainder of the day. Crittenden feels confident that as long as his forces hold the bridge, the Confederates could not maneuver to get to his rear where the road leads to Chattanooga. It is Wood's division at Ringgold that was the target of General Polk, pursuant to the orders of Bragg on the 12th. After Crittenden departs, Wood is again isolated.

In Louisiana, a 30-man contingent of the 2nd Missouri Volunteer Regiment engages and defeats a contingent of Confederates at the town of Vidalia. The Union sustains two killed and four wounded. The Confederates sustain six killed, 11 wounded and two captured.

In the Indian Territory, about 300 troops of

Left: Cavalry crossing the Rapidan River in Virginia. *Right:* Troops on the move at Culpeper Court House (Mottelay, *The Soldier in Our Civil War*, 1886).

the 1st Arkansas Volunteer Regiment skirmish with Confederates at Seneca Station, Buffalo Creek (Oklahoma). The Confederates sustain five wounded.

In Virginia, a contingent of cavalry (Army of the Potomac) engages Confederates at Rapidan Station. The Union sustains eight killed and 40 wounded. Confederate casualties are unavailable. In other activity, Union cavalry (General Alfred Pleasonton's command) skirmishes with Confederate Cavalry at Racoon Ford.

In Confederate general officer activity, Colonel Alexander Welch Reynolds (West Point, 1838) is appointed brigadier general. Reynolds was captured at Vicksburg and subsequently exchanged. He is assigned command of a brigade, which he will lead during various actions in Tennessee and in Georgia.

In Union general officer activity, General Herman Haupt, appointed brigadier general on 5 September 1862, resigns his commission. General Haupt has served as chief of construction and transportation (U.S. military railroad cars).

September 15 (Tuesday)   In Virginia, a detachment of the 1st New York Cavalry and the 12th Pennsylvania Cavalry commanded by Captains Jones and Bailey engage in a battle that lasts about two hours at Smithfield. The Confederates sustain two wounded and 10 captured.

In Union general officer activity, Colonel George Douglas Ramsay is appointed brigadier general and becomes chief of ordnance; however, Secretary of War Edwin Stanton has placed Captain George T. Balch in the department and through Stanton, Balch essentially takes over the bureau. Nonetheless, General Ramsay remains in service by special appointment and his experience is utilized as an inspector of arsenals. General Ramsay receives the brevet of major general toward the close of hostilities, on 13 March 1865, but his military career does not terminate. He continues as an inspector and other assignments until he retires in 1870.

In Confederate general officer activity, Colonel Joseph Robert Davis, a Mississippian and a nephew of Confederate President Jefferson Davis, is commissioned brigadier general. He participates in Gettysburg and in the defense of Richmond. He is seized at the end of the war and afterward paroled at Appomattox Court House during April 1865. After returning home, he resumes his law practice.

September 16 (Wednesday)   In Virginia, Union troops (specific units unreported) skirmish with Confederates at White Plains. Casualty figures are unavailable.

In Georgia, with General Bragg's failure to launch an attack, General Rosecrans has had sufficient time to realign his forces. His line stretches from General Thomas Wood's positions at Lee and Gordon's Mills to Stephens Gap, where General George H. Thomas, bolstered by McCook, holds the line, which extends east to southwest about eleven miles. The Confederates hold the gaps in Pigeon Mountain, and they dominate the fords leading to Lee and Gordon's Mills. Both sides will complete their maneuvering by the 17th, with both Rosecrans and Bragg attempting to turn the left flank of their opponent.

September 17 (Thursday)   In Missouri, Confederate guerrillas operating in the vicinity of Dover Landing capture the Union steamer USS *Marcella.*

In Georgia, General Burnside receives a dispatch (dated Sept. 14) from General Henry W. Halleck, reiterating an earlier message regarding reinforcing General Rosecrans when the latter encounters strong forces under General Bragg. The Union continues to move its forces into position. Rosecrans is convinced that Bragg will move to seize the Dry Valley and Rossville Roads, west and east of Missionary Ridge respectively. General Alexander McCook is sent to Pond Spring to relieve General George H. Thomas and Thomas is to move to Crawfish Springs to relieve two of General Thomas L. Crittenden's divisions. Once relieved, Crittenden's two divisions are to move to Lee and Gordon's Mills to bolster that of General Wood and protect his left and the road to Chattanooga. The strategy calls for prolonged marches, some straight through the night. By dusk, McCook is in place; however, it is near midnight on the 17th–18th when General Thomas L. Crittenden's forces reach their positions. Crittenden, however, does not arrive at General Rosecrans' headquarters (Widow Glen's) until about dawn on the 19th.

In other activity, troops under General Gordon Granger reconnoiter in the vicinity of Reed's Bridge at the Chickamauga River and encounter a Rebel force. One contingent under Colonel Robert G. Minty observes the area at Ringgold Road and Colonel Wilder stands at the route leading from Napier Gap. Sharp skirmishing occurs, but when faced with an assault against their rear, the Union pulls back. Another contingent of the Union force under General Alexander McCook advances toward Pond Spring, about seventeen miles south of Chattanooga, Tennessee.

In related activity, General Bragg at Lafayette, Georgia, issues an order to inspire his troops: "Having accomplished our object in driving back the enemy's flank movement, let us now turn on his main force and crush it in its fancied security. Your general will lead you. You have but to respond to assure us of a glorious triumph over an insolent foe."

In Union general officer activity, General Ormsby MacKnight Mitchel resigns from the service, but his resignation is declined. He is transferred from General Buell's command (Army of the Tennessee) to the Department of the South and is stationed at Hilton Head, South Carolina. He succumbs there during October due to yellow fever.

In Naval activity, the sloop USS *Adolph Huger,* attached to the Potomac Flotilla, seizes the sloop *Music.*

September 17–October 1   In Virginia, at Mathews County, the Confederates launch an expedition to raid Union shipping. The expedition force is composed of Master John Yates Beall, C.S. Navy, and seventeen volunteers, including Acting Master Edward McGuire, in the yawls *Swan* and *Black Raven* respectively. On their first day out, the sloop *Mary Anne* is captured off Raccoon Island, along with a few fishing scows. The Confederate raiders under Beall wear civilian clothes, and the success of their operation becomes a major problem for the Union. On the 18th, the raiders seize the schooner *Alliance* while it is en route to Port Royal. On the 19th, the *J.J. Houseman,* a schooner, is seized. And on the following day, the Rebels seize two additional schooners, the *Samuel Pearsall* and the *Alexandria.* Beall's raiders strip the vessels of their cargoes and only the *Alliance* is retained. The others are sent to sea as derelict. Union blockade warships recover the *J.J. Houseman* and the *Samuel Pearsall.* In addition, Beall takes 14 prisoners to Richmond. Later, while attempting to sail the *Alliance* up the Piankatank River, Beall runs it aground at Milford Haven, compelling him to burn the ship upon the approach of a Union warship.

The group becomes known as the Marine Coast Guard (or Volunteer Coast Guard). As they continue their harassing raids, the Union intensifies its efforts to dismantle the force. During October, a large force that includes naval vessels and ground troops initiates a manhunt across Mathews County. The force is commanded by General Isaac Wistar, who leads the 4th U.S. Colored Infantry and cavalry contingents. Wistar is bolstered by the USS *Commodore John Paul Jones,* the *Putnam* and the *Stepping Stones.* Four army gunboats join the hunt. Acting Master Edward McGuire, commander of the *Black Raven,* is seized during the dragnet, but Beall evades capture until the following month. On 14 November, the Union discovers one boat and its fourteen occupants. The boat is seized and of the 14 prisoners, one man is hanged; however, Beall and the remainder of his force still evade capture. On the following day, using information revealed by the prisoners, Beall and the others are captured. On written orders from Secretary of War Stanton, the prisoners are detained as "pirates or marauding robbers," not Confederate troops. Nevertheless, Beall is exchanged during 1864 and renews his partisan activity.

September 18 (Friday)   In Tennessee and Georgia, Confederate General Bragg positions his Army between Rosecrans' forces and Chattanooga, extending from Reed's Bridge to just opposite Gordon and Lee's Mill on the west bank of Chickamauga Creek. This is the prelude to the vicious battle of Chickamauga, Georgia, which will rage for the following two days. The corps of General W.H.T. Walker, composed of about 5,000 troops, at Alexander's Bridge, and General "Bushrod" Johnson's division of about 3,000 troops slightly north of Walker's position at Reed's Bridge, advance against the crossings south of their respective positions and drive General Wilder's mounted infantry back, opening a path for General Bragg's infantry. By day's end, Bragg's army is poised to launch a major attack. General Daniel Hill's command stands along the far left in the vicinity of Glass' Mills. Polk's force is at Lee and Gordon's Crossing, while Simon Buckner holds at Byram's Ford and John B. Hood stands at Telford's Ford. During the night of the 18th-19th, General Cheatham's division (Polk's corps) advances down the Chickamauga and crosses at Hunt's Ford at 0700.

In Tennessee, a contingent of the Union 83rd Illinois Regiment comes under attack by Confederate guerrillas at Fort Donelson, but the assault is repulsed.

In Confederate general officer activity, Colonel Edmund W. Pettus, who was captured at Vicksburg while leading his regiment, the 20th Alabama, is promoted to brigadier general. General Pettus had been colonel of the unit until the death of General Isham W. Garrott on 17 June. Pettus will also participate with General John B. Hood during the Tennessee campaign. General Pettus will be in the Carolinas toward the end of the hostilities, but afterward, he returns to Mississippi and resumes his law practice. In 1896 he is elected to the U.S. Senate, where he serves until his death on 27 July 1907 while at Hot Springs, North Carolina. Also, Colonel Thomas Neville Waul (Waul's Texas Legion), captured while leading his regiment at Vicksburg in July, is promoted to the rank of brigadier general, effective this date.

September 19 (Saturday)   In Virginia, Confederates and a contingent of Buford's cavalry clash at Rapidan Station. The Union sustains four killed and 19 wounded. Confederate casualties are unavailable. In other activity, elements of the 1st Cavalry Division, Army of the Potomac, initiate a reconnaissance mission near Raccoon Ford, where a skirmish had developed on 14 September.

In Union general officer activity, Colonel Henry Warner Birge is appointed brigadier general.

September 19–20   BATTLE OF CHICKAMAUGA The Union, in preparation for being attacked, is deployed on a line extending from Lee and Gordon's to a point beyond Kelly's farm. The immediate defending force, extending right to left, is composed of the divisions of Generals Wood, Van Cleve and Palmer (Thomas L. Crittenden's corps) followed by the divisions of Baird and Brannan (Thomas' corps). Two other divisions under Thomas have not yet arrived, those of Negley and Reynolds. Other Union forces (Alexander McCook's) are still en route, but McCook's point division (R.W. Johnson's) reaches Crawfish Springs, with the forces of Davis and Sheridan close behind.

General Thomas, at Kelly's Ford, is informed by General Daniel McCook (commander, reserve brigade) that the only Confederate force west of the Chickamauga, Georgia, was a thin brigade that crossed the river on the previous day at Reed's Bridge. McCook suggests that the brigade was isolated and subject to being captured because McCook's force burned the bridge to the rear to prevent escape. Afterward, Thomas orders General Brannan to lead two brigades toward Reed's Bridge and deploy a third brigade at Alexander's Bridge.

Shortly thereafter, Croxton's brigade (Brannan's division) arrives in the vicinity of Reed's Bridge and suddenly a tenacious skirmish develops when the column encounters cavalry under General Nathan Bedford Forrest. The Confeder-

Battle of Chickamauga (Johnson, *Campfire and Battlefield: History of the Conflicts and Campaigns*, 1894).

ates are pushed back toward two advancing infantry brigades under Ector and Wilson. The Confederate infantry assesses the situation, and immediately, in cadence with the roar of the "Rebel yell," the charge is initiated. The Union column is driven back by the infantry, which plows into and overruns Croxton's battery. Success for the Rebels is short-lived, however, as reinforcements, those of Baird and Brannan, drive forward and compel the Rebels to pull back.

The engagement heats up while the Union begins to realign. While Baird is reforming his lines, a fresh Confederate division under Liddell arrives, and it pounces upon the brigades of Generals Scribner and John H. King, igniting another ferocious fight in which the Confederate pressure causes the two brigades to hurriedly retire in haphazard fashion. The Confederate thrust overwhelms the defenders and captures Loomis' battery, commanded by Lt. Van Pelt, and the Rebels also capture Bush's Indiana battery.

The attack continues to make progress due to the pandemonium within the Union ranks as they continue to retire, but suddenly, Liddell's forces are confronted by fresh Union troops racing forward. The reorganized division under Brannan moves against Liddell's right, while another division under R.W. Johnson (McCook's corps) is closing against Liddell's other flank. In the meantime, General Bragg sends General Cheatham's command to reinforce Liddell, but he does not arrive in time to help. The Confederates under Liddell are able to extricate themselves, but at extremely high cost, and the recently captured guns are left behind. The arrival of Johnson's division is timely and prevents the Rebels from collapsing Rosecrans' left.

While the donnybrook continues, Cheatham advances with his force of about 7,000 troops, but he too encounters unexpected difficulty. In line with the defeat of Liddell, General Thomas forms a column that initiates an advance, and two other forces (Palmer's of Crittenden's corps and Reynolds' corps) push forward and halt

Cheatham's progress, then drive the Confederate division back.

As the day's fighting moves from morning into the afternoon, a gap exists in the Union lines that leaves a two-mile hole between Thomas' positions and Crittenden; however, the Confederates fail to launch a general advance and the opportunity to blow through the Union defenses to a point from which they can bolt against either flank is lost. While Cheatham is being pushed back, more Confederates arrive. General A.P. Stewart's division (Buckner's corps) drives into Palmer's division, while the former is maneuvering against Cheatham's flank. Palmer's divisions are compelled to pull back, while Stewart's Confederates maintain the advance and encounter yet another division, Van Cleve's, also of Crittenden's corps, which is en route to bolster General G.H. Thomas. The Confederates drive Van Cleve's forces back and still continue to advance.

At about 1430, a force under General John B. Hood plows against the Union right center and devastates the defensive line, which collapses, giving the Rebels control of the Chattanooga Road, and they seize a large number of artillery pieces. But yet again, the Union is unwilling to concede ground. Soon after the seizure of the road, the Rebels are forced to face a new threat.

Four new divisions, those of Generals Wood, Davis, Sheridan and Negley, are pushing against the Confederate positions with a powerful thrust that bursts the steadfastness of the Rebels and drives them back to positions east of the road. At 1500, Confederate General Daniel Hill is ordered report to Bragg at Tedford's Ford. He is directed also to dispatch Cleburne's division to the identical place. Bragg's orders direct Hill to send Breckinridge's division to relieve Hindman at Lee and Gordon's Mills. By about dusk, Cleburne reaches his new position on the far right.

During the same period the Confederates are in motion, Union General Thomas had also rearranged his positions, switching General Brannan from his left to the right. At the same time, Baird and R.W. Johnson are maneuvering somewhat to the rear to more tenable positions, when suddenly, Thomas' left comes under a severe assault by Cheatham and Cleburne. The Rebel surge encounters fierce resistance; however, the momentum stays with the Confederates and they seize several artillery pieces, two stands of colors, some caissons and about three hundred prisoners. The pressure continues to build and the Union positions on the left are compelled to retire. The Rebels, after penetrating, encounter breastworks, but General Daniel Hill brings up artillery, which completes the task. The breastworks are abandoned as the Union seeks more tenable positions. During the fighting at the breastworks, Confederate General Preston Smith is spotted and identified as a Rebel officer as he inadvertently rides in front of a detachment, which opens fire and kills him. With nightfall, the sounds of battle subside. The Union has lost some ground.

During the course of the grueling day, the Union had committed all but two of Rosecrans' brigades; however, the Confederates have yet to commit two of their brigades, Kershaw's and Humphreys,' which have not arrived at Chickamauga, and three divisions, those of Breckinridge, Hindman and Preston. General James Longstreet arrives at the Confederate positions about 2300. Prior to midnight, 19th-20th, General Bragg gathers some of his officers to change his tactics. He separates his force into two wings. Polk is in command of the right, composed of the corps of Generals Hill and Walker, bolstered by Cheatham's division, totaling just under 19,000 men, including about 3,500 cavalry troops. The left wing comes under the command of General Longstreet and is composed of the corps of Simon Buckner and John B. Hood, augmented by Hindman's division, bringing the strength of the wing to slightly under 23,000 men, including about 4,000 men of General Wheeler's cavalry. The conference terminates with Bragg's order directing both wings to commence their attacks at dawn on the 20th.

Despite the order to attack at daybreak, dawn arrives without incident, and many of the Confederate units are still unaware of the plan. Breckinridge's unit does not begin to move to its positions until after 0200 on the 20th and General Daniel Hill is not informed of the attack; a written order from Polk was distributed but never reached Hill. To add to the confusion, Hill and Polk speak prior to dawn, but Polk never mentions the attack. At about 0800, Bragg appears and he is disturbed that the attack had not commenced. During the tense conversation, Hill explains that he had not seen the order to attack. During the same conversation, Bragg states: "I found Polk after sunrise sitting down reading a newspaper at Alexander's Bridge, two miles from the line of battle, where he ought to have been fighting."

In the meantime, the Union lines are formed and they stretch in the vicinity of the Rossville (Chattanooga) and Dry Valley Roads, beginning about 400 yards east of the former with,

from left to right, the divisions of Baird's (Thomas' corps), R.W. Johnson's (McCook's corps), John M. Palmer's (Crittenden's corps) and Reynolds' (Thomas' corps), with each of the separate commands deployed behind breastworks composed of logs. Further right of Reynolds, Brannan's division, also of Thomas' corps, stands, followed by Negley (Thomas' corps); the latter's lines curve toward the rear. In addition, the divisions of Sheridan and Davis, both attached to McCook's corps, extend across the Chattanooga Road and lean toward Missionary Ridge. Meanwhile, General Rosecrans holds two of Crittenden's divisions (Thomas Wood's and Van Cleve's) in reserve. Rosecrans continues to maintain his headquarters at Widow Glenn's home. Cavalry (Colonel Robert Minty's) deploys southwest of Reynolds positions near Missionary Mills and General Wilder's cavalry deploys on the far right of the line.

At about the time of the Confederate movement by Breckinridge at 0930, the Confederates are formed in a line running north to south with General Hill's corps on the right, followed by Stewart's division, with General Hood's force held in reserve. The line continues with Bushrod Johnson followed by Hindman's force, the latter on the far left with Preston in reserve. As the attack begins, Bragg also places the divisions of Cheatham and William H.T. Walker, as well as Kershaw's brigade, in reserve. The Confederates plow into the right, but they encounter fierce resistance and the breastworks become an obstinate barrier, however, the Rebels continue to relentlessly pound against the line with enormous pressure, which prompts General Thomas to call for reinforcements.

Just after Cleburne's command advances, General Nathan B. Forrest orders General Armstrong's cavalry division to dismount and move to maintain support of Cleburne by remaining abreast of his line as it advances. Forrest, however, orders Pegram's division to remain in reserve. Meanwhile, the brigades of Adams and Stovall meet less resistance than Helm's brigade, which is the recipient of a whirlwind of fire that devastates his command as it plows into the left side of the breastworks. During the charge, Helm is slain. Colonel J.H. Lewis immediately assumes command of the battered brigade as it withdraws from the attack. During this period, General Daniel Hill approves of a suggestion of Breckinridge and directs Breckenridge to spin his force toward the left, from where he can gain positions to the rear of the breastworks.

The brigades execute a left oblique and drive beyond the Chattanooga Road to a point past the Cloud house, where the General Thomas had erected a field hospital in a cabin known as Snodgrass cabin or house, where a family of nine lives on Snodgrass Hill. Stovall's brigade plows forward and reaches positions to the rear of the flank of the breastworks, while Adams' brigade penetrates even further to gain positions to the rear of the breastworks. However, Union reinforcements begin to arrive, including James Wilson's command, and in time they

are able to stem the tide. During the brutal exchange of fire, General Daniel Adams sustains a debilitating wound and he is captured. Meanwhile, John Beatty's brigade (Negley's division), the first of the reinforcements to arrive to support Baird's imperiled command, encounters a far superior force and it too becomes endangered; however, fresh regiments (Palmer's reserve) and part of both Van Der Veer's and David S. Stanley's brigades arrive to neutralize the progress of the Confederate advance, preserve the line, and drive Breckinridge's two brigades back. The swift Union action rescues the rear and flanks of General Baird.

The Rebel forces banging against the breastworks include the divisions of Breckinridge and Cleburne, both attached to Hill's corps, and their efforts are followed by several brigades (Gist, Govan and Walthall). Rosecrans sends help to Thomas, but the reinforcements that rush to support Thomas leave a weak link along the right side of the line. The hole is noticed by General James Longstreet and he funnels through without much effort at about noon, but his attacking force avoids the breastworks entirely.

Meanwhile, action erupts in the vicinity of Widow Glen's house, which is near the only available water in the center of the battlefield. General Wilder's brigade, following a tenacious exchange, gains domination of the well, and as the troops pause to quench their thirst, they are amid many dead soldiers as well as horses who expired there while attempting to get a drink. While Cleburne and Breckinridge's commands are locked in mortal battle, General Polk's brigade is heavily engaged against the Union forces protected by the breastworks, and the Confederates are compelled to pull back.

Wood's brigade nearly reaches Poe's home when his column is struck by an avalanche of enfilade fire which inflicts heavy casualties. While Cleburne is in the middle of withdrawing his division, Union fire strikes and instantly kills Brigadier General Deshler while he is examining cartridge boxes, just prior to a scheduled assault. General Deshler's brigade is then taken over by Colonel R.Q. Mills. The fighting in this area continues until about 1030, but the two diminutive Confederate divisions are numerically outmatched by the four full strength Union divisions, augmented by the log breastworks. The Confederates withdraw under the pressure of the Union reinforcements that speed to assist Thomas, but the Rebels inflict sufficient punishment upon the Union that their retirement does not ignite pursuit.

Slightly after 1000, Rosecrans directs McCook to prepare to rush to Thomas' positions, and by 1030, Sheridan's division, accompanied by McCook, moves at a rapid pace en route to Thomas' lines. It is this movement that creates the hole in the line on the right. In contrast, by 100, General Stewart drives forward with three brigades under Bate, Brown and Clayton in synchronization with General Wood's command. The Rebel line pushes through a corn field and reaches a point about 300 yards beyond the Chattanooga Road, from where they drive into the breastworks and ignite yet another ferocious exchange. Nonetheless, the Union counters and catapults streams of artillery fire into the Rebel ranks, delivering an avalanche of pernicious fire into the front of the line and the flank, which forces the attacking force to withdraw; however, the assault inflicts severe punishment to the Union forces of both Reynolds and Brannan.

The Confederates are not content with partial success. While Reynolds and Brannan are subjected to heavy attacks, a new force is forming on the right. In addition, General Daniel Hill proposes that General Polk launch a second assault. After conferring with Polk, a fresh brigade under General J.K. Jackson moves to fill a gap that had been created where Helm's had been deployed prior to his death, but Jackson deploys too far to be of any genuine value, leaving the Union the opportunity to spend the remainder of the day propelling a combination of flank fire and crossfire from that general area.

General Gist duplicates the earlier attack of General Helm, but as his forces advance within the range of the defenders behind the breastworks, they again pour sheets of devastating fire. Gist evades death, but the attack force is repelled and withdraws. Meanwhile, General Liddell advances with only one brigade, Govan's, and the brigade seizes once again the Chattanooga Road. Liddell's column lurches forward to get behind the breastworks, when suddenly, he discovers his positions are untenable due to the unexpected arrival of a strong Union column that is encroaching his rear and his flank. Liddell quickly orders a retreat. The attacks of Gist and Liddell occur at about the same time General Stewart is on the offensive.

Back in Longstreet's zone, he initiates his attack at about noon with a force of eight brigades (Bushrod Johnson's original brigade, McNair's, Gregg's, Kershaw's, Law's, Humphreys,' Benning's and Felix Robertson's). After penetrating the Union lines, Longstreet, under orders to swivel to the right, instead pivots left to strike Crittenden's positions and those of McCook's corps. The bold maneuver ignites a donnybrook. Nevertheless, the raging brawl quickly sees the momentum moving to the Rebels, who pounce upon the defenders there. Two Union brigades of General Davis' command and General Sheridan's division are struck by fire from the flank and against their front, compelling Davis' brigades and Sheridan's division to retire from the field. Soon after Longstreet turns to his left, the Rebels push five of McCook's brigades off the field. Confederate General Daniel Hill afterward remarks: "I have never seen the Federal dead lie so thickly on the ground, save in front of the sunken wall at Fredericksburg" (December 1862). Union General Lytle is killed during this part of the day's fighting.

By this time, Rosecrans' entire army is jeopardized and the Confederates are poised to clearly and decisively terminate the battle; however, one major obstacle remains in their path: a stubborn Virginian, General George H. Thomas. The unshakable Thomas jumps on his horse to speed up reinforcements that are en

route, and soon after getting onto the saddle his spirits are lifted when he spots an approaching column, but to his great disappointment, the column is Confederate rather than one of Sheridan's command. Undaunted and still un-rattled, Thomas instantly accesses the situation and chooses his strategy without hesitation. To prepare against what is inevitably a powerful blow, he selects a pragmatic but formidable position from which to defend, a spur on Missionary Ridge (Tennessee), which runs east and west.

Thomas sends Brannan's division to the spur to initiate the redeployment, then adds two of Negley's brigades. General Wood's division (Thomas L. Crittenden's corps) deploys to the immediate left Brannan's positions. The diminutive force faces assault by a much stronger force under General James Longstreet. Nonetheless, Thomas, with a bit of luck in addition to his military instincts, has redeployed in near-invincible positions, and by 1500, reinforcements under General James B. Steedman (General Gordon Granger's corps) will arrive if he can forestall Longstreet until then.

Earlier in the day, at about 1100, General Gordon Granger discerns that Bragg is focusing on Thomas and he declares to Brevet Brigadier General J.R. Fullerton: "I am going to Thomas, orders or no orders!" And Fullerton replies, "And if you go, it may bring disaster to the army and you to a court-martial." Granger then replies: "There's nothing in our front now but ragtag, bobtail cavalry. Don't you see Bragg is piling his whole army on Thomas? I am going to his assistance."

The spur where Thomas is making his stand forms a right angle linked to a sturdy line of log breastworks that stand along the west side of the Rossville Road, while his left and right are naturally bolstered by an enclosed fortification and a shear slope. The fate of Rosecrans' entire army is essentially in the hands of Thomas and his small force. Most of the Union army is in retreat toward Chattanooga; however, Thomas ignores the order to withdraw and remains convinced that he can hold.

Meanwhile, at the Confederate lines, at about 1430, General Longstreet is getting a little nourishment. He and some of his staff are enjoying some sweet potatoes when a message arrives from General Bragg, directing him to meet Bragg in the rear positions. Longstreet confers with Bragg and requests reinforcement with which to hold the captured terrain, while he dispatches troops to intercept the retreating Union forces and works to sever the retreat path of Thomas, who is isolated at Missionary Ridge. Bragg, however, informs Longstreet that Polk's entire command is thoroughly exhausted, incapable of further combat and that no reinforcements are available. The response to Longstreet's request is peculiar because neither Cheatham's division nor a part of Liddell's command had been committed at any time during the day's fighting.

The short pause in the battle resumes as the Confederates prepare to liquidate Thomas' force on the spur with a two pronged assault to collapse the rear while grinding down the frontal

defenses. The attack force composed of six light brigades is formed, and they include those of Anderson, Deas, Gregg, Manigault, and Mc-Nair. Two other brigades, those of Humphreys and Kershaw, are nearby to the right of Anderson, and both are expected to support the attacks.

The advances begin at about 1530. The two sides exchange blows that include extremely close-quartered fighting that erupts into in savage beatings. The bayonet is a priority weapon; however, muskets and rifles double as clubs. No holds barred becomes the usual exchange during this barbarian duel in which each side intends to bludgeon the other either by shot and shell or by pulverization. After about one-half hour of brutal and uncivilized combat, a Union column approaches, but it is intercepted and halted. Nonetheless, Granger's corps instills some fear into Longstreet's force due to the possibility of a flank attack.

Confederate Major General Walker proposes a pull back to prevent an assault against the flank, but Longstreet sees that suggestion as a path to disaster which would lead to a definite attack. Meanwhile, Cheatham's division arrives on scene; however, the reinforcements are neutralized because of Granger's boldness and determination. Granger had moved on his own, lacking orders, to ensure Thomas did not remain alone, and he continues to advance straight toward the horrendous sounds of the guns and crashes into the Confederate lines. The Confederates meet the assault with equal tenacity. A column led by General Steed initiates a charge which ignites yet another close-quartered bloodbath with Granger's vanguard. The Confederates prevail, but the price is exorbitant. About 1,000 Confederates are either killed or wounded during the charge.

The struggle however, does not terminate. Longstreet directs General Preston's three brigades, those of Gracie, Kelly and Trigg, augmented by Robertson's brigade (Hood's division) in a direct frontal attack to gain the heights. More bloodshed is the instant result. The two sides blast one another with incessant fire during the waves of advances and retreats. Nevertheless, Thomas remains rigid, with no signs of relinquishing his positions. At about 1530, Polk sends word to Longstreet to assume command of the attacking forces on his right and to initiate yet another assault to dislodge Thomas.

By the time a regrouping maneuver is completed, the attack resumes at 1600. The batteries of General Cleburne are shoved to the front and positioned within several hundred yards of Thomas' breastworks. His infantry follows close behind and the thrust is strong enough to carry the works. General Cheatham's division encounters impenetrable resistance initially, when General J.K. Jackson storms the works; however, the brigades of George E. Maney and Marcus J. Wright rush to the front to interject the added weight that permits the breakthrough.

Meanwhile, Generals John C. Breckinridge and Walker encounter only slight opposition until they cross over the Chattanooga Road. At that point, they encounter a rear guard protecting the Union retreat. The Confederates head for nearby woods and encounter yet another force, but it is not Union; rather General Simon Buckner is on the advance, and at the instant Buckner is recognized, the roaring cheers exceed the sounds of the guns. By about 1630, General William Preston seizes the heights and captures about 1,000 Union troops and 4,500 stands of arms. Nevertheless, General Thomas still defiantly refuses to retreat. General Granger delivers orders directing Thomas to retire. He informs Granger that he will hold until darkness before abandoning his positions.

Just after 1700, General Thomas moves to the left side of his lines, while General Gordon Granger holds command at the center. By this time, the ammunition for the entire defending force is close to exhaustion, including the ammunition carried to the lines by Granger when he arrived. Still more that had been on the field in the cartridge boxes of the dead, both Union and Confederate, had been retrieved and expended. As time moves quickly by, the situation becomes more grave. Just prior to 1800, General Brannan arrives at Thomas' position and informs him: "The enemy are forming for another assault; we have not another round of ammunition. What shall we do?" Thomas immediately replies: "Fix bayonets and go for them."

The Confederates close while the Union remains in a prone position until the order, one word, is bellowed: "Forward." The Union troops bolt to their feet and advance with fixed bayonets to intercept the charge, and they succeed in driving the enemy back. One other Confederate attack is also launched, but Thomas' force holds. At dusk, Thomas conducts a disciplined retreat. Due to his actions at the battle and his refusal to relinquish his positions, General Thomas becomes known as "The Rock of Chickamauga."

General Bragg remains unaware of Longstreet's victory until the following day. In the meantime, the tireless General Nathan Bedford Forrest is in the saddle, and his cavalry observes the haphazard retreat of Rosecrans' army. Word of the Union confusion is rushed to Bragg; however, he takes no action. On the 21st, the Confederates do not initiate pursuit. Bragg's troops scour the battlefield for the dead to ensure they receive a proper burial, and they gather the captured supplies and weapons.

Rosecrans, however, is able to retire safely to Chattanooga, the original objective of his campaign, and the city is held. Confederate General Daniel Hill later relates his observations:

<ex>There was no more splendid fighting in '61, when the flower of the Southern youth was in the field, than was displayed in those bloody days of September, '63. But it seems to me that the elan of the Southern soldier was never seen after Chickamauga — that brilliant dash which had distinguished him was gone forever. He was too intelligent not to know that the cutting in two of Georgia meant death to all his hopes. He knew that Longstreet's absence was imperiling Lee's safety, and that what had to be done must be done quickly. The delay in striking was ex-

asperating to him; the failure to strike after the success was crushing to all his longings for an independent South. He fought stoutly to the last, but, after Chickamauga, with the sullenness of despair and without the enthusiasm of hope. That barren victory sealed the fate of the Southern Confederacy.

General Rosecrans' career suffers from the loss; however, his chief-of-staff, General James Garfield, is soon promoted to major general. Nevertheless, the promotion occurs after Garfield is elected to the House of Representatives, where he serves nine terms. Later he is elected the 20th president of the United States, only to be assassinated on 2 July 1881, about four months after his inauguration. General Alexander McCook and T.L. Crittenden also receive blame for the loss. McCook requests and receives an inquiry, which officially exonerates him; however, this is his final command in the field. Nonetheless, he receives the brevet rank of brigadier and major general in the U.S. Army at the close of the war. After the war, McCook becomes lieutenant colonel of the 26th Infantry during 1867. He retires during 1895 with the rank of major general.

During the battle, General Philip Sheridan loses approximately 1,500 men out of his force of 4,000 (Alexander McCook's XX Corps). The Union faces two terrible alternatives, surrender or starvation, unless Grant is capable of finding available troops and rushing them by all possible means to Chattanooga to keep Rosecrans' army from destruction. Brigadier General Micah Jenkins' brigade, the Palmetto Sharpshooters (South Carolina), arrives in the area from Virginia, but too late to join the battle. Nonetheless, the brigade, as part of General John Bell Hood's division, will participate at Chattanooga and at Knoxville before heading back to the Army of Northern Virginia.

The Union sustains 16,500 dead, wounded or missing out of a force of about 58,000. The Confederates sustain approximately 18,000 killed, wounded or missing out of a total force of about 66,000. The relentless combat takes a high toll on both sides and in one case, the brigade of Confederate General Archibald Gracie, more than six hundred casualties are sustained in about a two-hour period. Union General Horatio Van Cleve's division (XXI Corps) loses more than 960 men during the Confederate breakthrough. Consequently, he is delegated to command of Murfreesboro and sees no more field command; however, he receives the brevet of major general of volunteers. Van Cleve musters out of the army during August 1865. The XXI Corps is dissolved the following month. Also, Union General William H. Lytle is killed while leading a charge against the Confederates. General August Willich participates at this battle. Confederate Brigadier Generals Preston Smith and James Deshler (West Point, 1854) are killed. Smith is slain by a volley of fire when he accidentally rides into the vanguard of a Union detachment. General Alfred Jefferson Vaughan, Jr., assumes command of General Smith's brigade.

Union Major General Negley is accused of

poor performance and cowardice. He is cleared of all charges; however, his career had essentially terminated with the charges. He resigns from the army in January 1865 and returns to Pittsburgh. After the war, Negley is elected to the U.S. Congress (1868). In contrast, the actions of General James B. Steedman are noted as being "the most conspicuous act of personal courage recorded of any general officer on the Federal side." Nevertheless, despite being known as the "salvation of the Union forces left on the field," he does not advance in rank until April of the following year due to his Democratic sentiments.

Confederate General Benjamin Helm (West Point, 1851) is mortally wounded. Colonel Joseph H. Lewis succeeds Helm in command of the brigade known as the "Orphan Brigade"; Lewis is promoted to brigadier general later this month. Also, Confederate Brigadier General Evander McNair is wounded. Confederate Major General J.B. Hood (West Point, 1853) loses a leg. Brigadier General Evander McIvor Law succeeds John Bell Hood as commander of the division. Also, Brigadier General Daniel Weisiger Adams is wounded and captured. General Adams was wounded twice before, including losing an eye at Shiloh. General Adams will regain his health and be exchanged. Once freed, he receives a cavalry unit in Northern Alabama.

Confederate Generals John Gregg and Patrick Cleburne are also wounded at the battle. Confederate Colonel (later brigadier general) Joseph Benjamin Palmer, repeatedly wounded at Murfreesboro, is again wounded, and the injury keeps him from the field until just prior to the Atlanta Campaign. Confederate Colonel (later brigadier general) Clement Hoffman Stevens is wounded (for the second time) during this action.

Union Generals John C. Starkweather and Walter C. Whitaker are wounded. On the first day of battle, both Union General John M. Brannan (West Point, 1841) and John H. King's division of Thomas' XIV Corps take severe losses as they fall back, but on the 21st, although they had suffered staggering losses, they fight marvelously on Horseshoe Ridge, contributing greatly to saving the Union cause. Also, Brigadier General Deas' brigade, composed of the 19th, 22nd, 25th, 39th, and 50th Alabama Regiments, the 17th Alabama Battalion Sharpshooters and Dent's Alabama Artillery, participates in this battle. Confederate Brigadier General William W. Mackall, chief of staff to General Bragg, resigns from the Army (his request); however, the next year, he re-enters the Confederate service and will serve under General Joseph E. Johnston. General Whitaker recuperates from his wound and later participates at Franklin and Nashville, Tennessee, as a brigade commander in the IV Corps. He receives the brevet of major general of volunteers for his actions at Atlanta. He musters out of the army during August 1865, and then resumes his law practice.

September 20 (Sunday) **In Missouri,** a skirmish develops at Hornersville.

In Virginia, the brigade of Confederate Brigadier General Samuel McGowan (wounded at Chancellorsville) remains under the leadership of Brigadier General Abner Perrin, attached to General Cadmus M. Wilcox's division in A.P. Hill's 3rd Corps. The force, composed of South Carolina units, will participate in the fighting around Bristoe Station and Mine Run between October and December. General McGowan will recuperate from his wound sustained at Chancellorsville and return to the brigade the next February.

September 21 (Monday) In Washington, D.C., President Abraham Lincoln, in an attempt to bolster General William S. Rosecrans' position at Chattanooga, Tennessee, orders General Ambrose Burnside to leave Knoxville to reinforce the Union defenders at Chattanooga, but Confederate fire prevents his departure.

In Tennessee, Union forces, including elements of General John G. Foster's cavalry brigade and General Shackelford's cavalry division, clash with Confederates at Bristol. Many roving contingents of Rebels still operate in the area. Another large encounter occurs at Blue Springs when a force under General Sam Jones attempts to crash through Burnside's left flank.

In Virginia, a contingent of cavalry attached to the Army of the Potomac engages Confederates at White's Ford. Casualty figures are unavailable.

In Confederate general officer activity, Colonel Armistead L. Long (West Point, 1850) is appointed brigadier general to command artillery in the 2nd Corps, Army of Northern Virginia. General Long had been on Robert E. Lee's staff. He remains with the 2nd Corps for the duration.

September 22 (Tuesday) In Maryland, contingents of the 11th New York Cavalry engage Confederates at Rockville. The Union reports no casualties. The Confederates sustain 34 killed and wounded.

In Tennessee, Union General Rosecrans, recently a bold attacker, is now forced to fortify Chattanooga and hold there until reinforcements can be diverted from all available places to lift the siege. His defensive fortifications force the Confederates to abort their impending assault. In related activity, the 11th Corps and 12th Corps (Army of the Potomac) under Generals Oliver O. Howard and Henry W. Slocum, respectively, are separated from General Meade's force and ordered to move to bolster the Army of the Cumberland operating in the vicinity of Chattanooga. In other activity, elements of the 2nd Brigade, Foster's cavalry, including the 11th New York Cavalry, skirmishes with Confederate forces at Blountville. The Union sustains five dead and 22 wounded. Confederates suffer 15 dead and 50 wounded. Also, the 3rd Brigade, cavalry division, Army of the Ohio, clashes with Confederates at Carter's Station. Also, elements of the 8th Tennessee Volunteer Regiment skirmish with Confederates at Johnson's Depot.

In Virginia, Union contingents of the 1st Division, Buford's cavalry, skirmish with Confederates at Jack's Shop, Madison Court House. The Union sustains one killed and 20 wounded. Confederate casualties are unavailable.

September 23 (Wednesday) In Washington, D.C., President Lincoln, realizing General William Rosecrans' Army of the Cumberland is trapped in Chattanooga, confers with General Halleck and dispatches 20,000 men under General Joseph Hooker to reinforce the besieged city. Seventeen thousand men under General William T. Sherman are sent from Mississippi. Lincoln's order to reinforce Rosecrans at Chattanooga forces a contingent of Hooker's Army of the Potomac to move expeditiously by rail to extricate the Army of the Cumberland from disaster.

In Louisiana, a 14-man contingent of the 14th New York Cavalry is captured by Confederate guerrillas at Donaldsonville. Major General Henry Rootes Jackson (Georgia state militia), prior to turning his command over to the Confederacy, is appointed brigadier general in the Confederate Army. He will participate with General John B. Hood in Tennessee until his untimely capture during the Nashville campaign, while he was in command of a brigade in General Benjamin F. Cheatham's corps.

September 24 (Thursday) In Tennessee, the 3rd Brigade, cavalry division, Army of the Ohio, clashes with Confederates at Zollicoffer.

In Naval activity, the blockade runner *Elizabeth,* formerly the CSS *Atlanta,* a wooded steamer operating out of Wilmington, North Carolina, runs aground at Lockwood's Folly on the Cape Fear River about ten miles from Fort Caswell. The vessel is burned to prevent capture by the Union.

September 25 (Friday) In Virginia, the 1st Maryland Potomac Home Brigade of cavalry, commanded by Major Henry Cole, skirmishes with Confederate guerrillas at Upperville. The Confederates sustain one killed and nine captured.

In Louisiana, Union troops skirmish with Confederate guerrillas at Donaldsonville.

In Missouri, the 2nd Wisconsin Cavalry clashes with Confederates at Red Bone Church.

September 26 (Saturday) In Tennessee, a contingent of Cavalry (Army of the Ohio) engages Confederates at Calhoun (Haguewood Prairie). The Union sustains six killed, 20 killed and 40 missing. Confederate casualties are unavailable.

September 27 (Sunday) In South Carolina, the U.S. fleet initiates yet another naval bombardment of Confederate-held Fort Sumter.

Union General William T. Sherman recalls the division that had been sent to reinforce General Frederick Steele in Arkansas and diverts it to Memphis. Sherman departs Memphis to take personal charge of the rescue effort to relieve General Rosecrans, who is under siege at Chattanooga.

In Arkansas, contingents of the 1st Arkansas Regiment encounter and engage Confederates at Moffat's Station. The Union sustains two killed and two wounded. The Confederates sustain five killed and 20 wounded.

September 28 (Monday) In Maryland, Brigadier General Erastus B. Tyler is appointed as commander of the Middle Military Department. He succeeds Major General Robert C. Schenck and holds the post only until 10 October, when he is replaced by his predecessor, General Schenck.

In Tennessee, the Union situation in Chattanooga remains grave. General Braxton Bragg anticipates a Union withdrawal, but none is forthcoming, prompting the Confederates to put the beleaguered defenders under siege to cut them off and starve them if at all possible. Union reinforcements are being rushed to Rosecrans as quickly as possible. Confederate cavalry continues to harass the Union supply lines. General U.S. Grant arrives on 23 October to observe the dilemma personally. After Grant, General Hooker's troops arrive, followed soon after by General Sherman's contingent. In related activity, a Union contingent skirmishes with Confederates at McMinnville. Casualty figures are unavailable.

In Louisiana, a detachment of the 4th Wisconsin Cavalry, led by Lieutenant Earl, captures a contingent of Confederate guerrillas at Amite and Comite Rivers.

In Confederate general officer activity, Colonel Pierce Manning Young, an aggressive supporter of the southern cause who chose to re-

Union pickets are approached by Confederates disguised in cedar bushes (Mottelay, *The Soldier in Our Civil War*, 1886).

sign from West Point upon word of Georgia's secession in January 1861, is appointed brigadier general effective this date. General Young was with Hampton's cavalry through the Maryland campaign and will participate in the Carolinas under General Wade Hampton against General Sherman's forces. Also, Colonel James Byron Gordon, 1st North Carolina Infantry Regiment, is promoted to the rank of brigadier general. Prior to his promotion, Gordon was part of Hampton's Legion in General Stuart's cavalry corps, Army of Northern Virginia. General Gordon is assigned to command a North Carolina brigade, still in the Army of Northern Virginia. Also, Confederate colonel Thomas L. Rosser is promoted to the rank of brigadier general, effective this date. Rosser will be assigned command of the Laurel Brigade, succeeding General Beverly Robertson, who has been transferred out of General Stuart's command. General Robertson remains in South Carolina until the approach of General Sherman, when the Confederates abandon the region. After the war he moves to Washington, D.C., and engages in the insurance business. He dies in the capital at the age of 84 on 12 November 1910.

September 29 (Tuesday) In Louisiana, the 19th Iowa and 26th Indiana Regiments under the command of Colonel Leake and Major Montgomery engage Confederates under General Thomas Green at Sterling's Farm in the vicinity of Morganza. The Union sustains 14 killed, 40 wounded and 400 missing. Confederate casualties are unavailable.

In Naval activity, the CSS *Louisville*, captured on 13 July 1863, is renamed the *Ouachita*. On 18 January 1864, it is commissioned in the U.S. Navy.

September 30 (Wednesday) In Tennessee, elements of the 7th Kansas Cavalry and the 7th Illinois Cavalry, commanded by Colonel Rowett, skirmish with Confederate guerrillas at Swallow's Bluff. The Union sustains one killed and two wounded. The Confederates lose 120 captured.

In Confederate general officer activity, Colonel James Argyle Smith (West Point, 1853) is promoted to the rank of brigadier general, effective this date. He participates in the defense of Atlanta and is wounded during the campaign. Also, Colonel Joseph Horace Lewis (6th Kentucky Infantry) is promoted to brigadier general. He receives command of a brigade that participates in the defense of Atlanta. After the city is lost, General Lewis' brigade is attached to General Joseph Wheeler's cavalry corps. He later surrenders while part of the escort which attempts to get President Jefferson Davis to safety when Richmond is abandoned. He is pardoned at Washington, Georgia, on 9 May 1865.

In Naval activity, the USS *Iron Age* is commissioned. Also, the U.S. Navy acquires the *Governor Buckingham*. It is commissioned on 13 November. Acting Volunteer Lt. W.G. Saltonstall is appointed commander.

October 1 (Thursday) In Tennessee, the 21st Kentucky Regiment skirmishes with Confederates under Major General Joseph Wheeler at Anderson's Gap (Anderson's Crossroads). The Confederates capture a wagon train attached to General Rosecrans' command. The Union sustains 38 killed and wounded. Confederate casualties are unavailable.

In Naval activity, the U.S. Navy at about this time commissions the USS *Sassacus*, which was built at Kittery, Maine, as the initial 974-ton double-ender side-wheel steam gunboat. The *Sassacus* is not yet ready for service, but a few months later, after receiving repairs, it departs the Portsmouth Navy Yard for duty in the North Carolina sounds. Also, at about this time, the U.S. Navy acquires the screw steamship *Nereus*, which is still under construction at New York. The *Nereus* is commissioned during April 1864 and assigned to the North Atlantic Blockading Squadron, where it operates in the vicinity of Wilmington, North Carolina until August. After escorting a vessel to Panama, it returns to New York for repairs. The USS *Nereus* afterward participates in the failed attack during December to capture Fort Fisher. In May 1865, the *Nereus* is decommissioned; during July 1865, it is sold and renamed the *Somerset*.

October 2 (Friday) In Tennessee, Union and Confederate cavalry forces clash at Anderson's Crossroads. Union contingents — including the 1st Wisconsin, 2nd Indiana and 1st Tennessee Cavalry (Army of the Cumberland) under Brigadier General Daniel McCook — suffer 70 dead or wounded. Confederates have 200 killed or wounded and about 200 captured. Confederate General Bragg's forces are attempting to tighten the noose around Chattanooga; his cavalry has been operating above Chattanooga and had recently destroyed am immense wagon train in the Sequatchie Valley. In other activity, Union General Joseph Hooker advances toward the besieged city of Chattanooga. His troops are arriving and the long line continues for a couple of days until over 20,000 men begin bulging out of Bridgeport. These troops have traveled by rail from Virginia in a little over a week.

In Louisiana, a contingent of Union cavalry skirmishes with Confederate cavalry under Captain Squires at Franklin.

October 3 (Saturday) In Washington, D.C., President Lincoln proclaims the last Thursday in November as Thanksgiving Day.

In Tennessee, General Sherman's son Willie dies of typhoid fever in Memphis. Union Captain C.C. Smith, commanding 13th United States Regulars, affords the Sherman family a military funeral. Young Willie had believed himself to be a sergeant of the 13th. General Sherman remarks, "Child as he was, he had the enthusiasm, the pure love of truth, honor and love of country, which should animate all soldiers" (from a letter dated 10-4-63 from General Sherman to Captain C.C. Smith). Also, the

4th Tennessee Regiment led by Major Patterson engages Confederates at McMinnville. The Union sustains seven killed, 31 wounded and 350 missing. The Confederates suffer 23 killed and wounded. Also, elements of the 1st Brigade, 2nd Division, cavalry, and Wilder's Brigade, mounted infantry, clash with Confederates at Thompson Cove.

October 4 (Sunday) In Louisiana, a skirmish between Union and Confederate contingents occurs at Newtown. Specific units and casualty figures are unreported.

In Missouri, three companies of the 6th Missouri Cavalry (militia) engage Confederates at Neosho. The Union sustains one killed, 14 wounded and 43 missing. Confederate casualties are unavailable.

In Tennessee, General Sherman, en route to join General Rosecrans at Chattanooga, reaches Memphis. His force is composed of four divisions. The First Division is commanded by General Peter J. Osterhaus and includes the 1st Brigade, General Charles Woods, and 2nd Brigade, Colonel James A. Williamson. The Second Division, commanded by General Morgan L. Smith, comprises the 1st Brigade, General Giles A. Smith, and 2nd Brigade, General J.A. Williamson. The Third Division is commanded by General John E. Smith. It includes the 1st Brigade, 2nd Brigade, Colonel G.B. Baum, and the 3rd Brigade commanded by Colonel J.J. Alexander. General Hugh Ewing commands the Fourth Division, which includes the 1st Brigade, General John M. Corse, 2nd Brigade, Colonel Loomis, and 3rd Brigade, Colonel J.R. Cockrell.

In other activity, a Union contingent composed of elements of the 2nd Kentucky Cavalry and Wilder's Brigade of Mounted Infantry, commanded by Colonel Utley, skirmishes with Confederates under General Nathan Bedford Forrest along the Murfreesboro Road.

In Confederate general officer activity, Colonel Mark P. Lowrey, 32nd Mississippi Infantry Regiment, is promoted to the rank of brigadier general. General Lowrey is assigned command of a brigade in General Cleburne's division (General Joseph Hardee's corps).

October 5 (Monday) In Kentucky, elements of the 37th Kentucky Mounted Infantry, commanded by Captain Nun, comes under attack by Confederates led by Colonel John M. Hughes at Glasgow.

In Tennessee, Confederate cavalry continues attacks on Union lines around Chattanooga. One contingent assaults the Union at Stones River, capturing 44 men of the 19th Michigan. Also, a Union force (General Burnside's command) engages Confederates at Blue Springs. Casualty figures are unavailable. Meanwhile, the 5th Iowa Cavalry skirmishes with Confederates at Wartrace.

In West Virginia, a 16-man contingent of Union cavalry, led by Captain Bean, encounters Confederates while on a scouting mission in the vicinity of Harpers Ferry. A skirmish develops. The Union sustains one killed and three wounded. The Confederates under Brigadier General John D. Imboden lose 10 captured.

In Naval activity, in South Carolina, the Confederates at Fort Sumter dispatch the CSS *David,* a submarine that resembles a huge "iron cigar," to move against the USS *Weehawken,* but the attempt to sink it fails. The *Weehawken* spots the vessel at about 2000 and attempts to get it to halt, but instead, the vessel fires a torpedo. The *Weehawken* has slight damage and the explosion nearly sinks the *David,* but it recovers. During the same attack, the *New Ironsides* also sustains damage, but the ship remains on duty off Charleston until May 1864, when it sails to Philadelphia for major repairs.

October 6 (Tuesday) In Kansas, Union forces under General James Blunt are surprised by Confederate guerrillas under William Quantrill at Baxter Springs (Cherokee County). The guerrillas, dressed in Union garb, suddenly open fire while the band is preparing to play. The attack is actually a massacre, as there is no time to react and many in the detachment of the 14th Kansas Cavalry and the 83rd U.S. Colored troops are killed. Nevertheless, General Blunt and some of the troops escape harm. Other cavalrymen of the 3rd Wisconsin, led by Lt. James E. Pond, repel the assault and drive the guerrillas back. Lt. Pond singlehandedly leaves his position to use a howitzer to rout the attackers. The Union sustains 54 killed, 18 wounded and five missing. Confederate casualties are unavailable.

In Kentucky, the 37th Kentucky Mounted Infantry engages Confederates at Glasgow. The Union sustains three wounded and 100 missing. The Confederates sustain 13 wounded.

In Tennessee, Confederate cavalry under General Bragg engages Union cavalry led by Colonel Robert Mitchell at Shelbyville. Another clash occurs on the following day when Crook's cavalry skirmishes with Rebel cavalry at Farmington. The Confederates receive the short end of the skirmishes, buying more time for the besieged troops at Chattanooga. Also, elements of the 19th Michigan skirmish with Confederates at the stockade on Stones River. The Union sustains six wounded and 44 captured. Confederate casualties are unavailable.

October 7 (Wednesday) In Tennessee, Union and Confederate units clash heavily in the vicinity of Farmington. The Union 1st, 3rd and 4th Ohio Cavalry, the 2nd Kentucky Cavalry, Long's 2nd Cavalry Division and Wilder's Mounted Infantry participate. The Union sustains 15 killed and 60 wounded. The Confederates sustain 10 killed, 60 wounded and 240 missing.

October 8 (Thursday) In Missouri, a contingent of the 7th Missouri Cavalry clashes with Confederates at Warsaw. Casualty figures and specific units are unreported. Also, Confederates devastate the town of Carthage.

In Mississippi, about 5,000 Union cavalrymen (brigades of Colonels McCrellis and Phillips) encounter a Confederate cavalry force of about 4,000 troops, commanded by General S.D. Lee, at Salem. The Confederates sustain about 15 killed and wounded.

In West Virginia, a Confederate force composed of about 400 troops (62nd Virginia Mounted Infantry) under Brigadier General J.D. Imboden attacks and defeats a one-company contingent of cavalry under Captain Somers at Charlestown. The Union sustains 10 killed and 10 wounded. The Confederates capture four guns. Confederate casualty figures are unreported.

In Confederate general officer activity, Colonel Leroy A. Stafford is promoted to the rank of brigadier general. He is assigned to duty as commander, 2nd Louisiana Brigade, Army of Northern Virginia.

In Naval activity, following blockade duty in the South, the USS *Iroquois* arrives in Baltimore for repairs. Later, on 31 March 1864, the *Iroquois* is re-commissioned and C.R.P. Rodgers receives command. The *Iroquois* is ordered to duty in the North Atlantic, but after a short tour, it heads for the Mediterranean. In 1864 it participates in a wide search to snare a Rebel raider, the *Shenandoah,* and eventually, after circling around South America, it enters the Pacific and sails to Singapore, arriving in May 1865, just after the close of hostilities. The *Iroquois* arrives back in the United States at New York on 1 October 1865. On 6 October it is decommissioned. Subsequently, in January 1867, it is re-commissioned, and with some interruptions, it remains in service (including Marine Hospital Service) until 1904, when its name is changed to *Ionie.* Its name is removed from Navy lists during 1910.

October 9 (Friday) In Tennessee, elements of the 3rd Brigade, 2nd Cavalry Division, engage Confederates at Sugar Creek.

In Virginia, Confederate General John Imboden receives instructions from Robert E. Lee to advance with caution from his positions at Staunton through the valley to Strasburg to protect the Confederate rear. The Army of Northern Virginia is operating around Sperryville and Woodville.

October 10 (Saturday) In Louisiana, the Union 1st Brigade, 1st Division, 19th Corps, under General Weitzel engages a Confederate force at Vermilion Bayou. Estimated Confederate casualties are five wounded.

In Maryland, Major General Robert C. Schenck (for the third time) is appointed commander of the Middle Military Department. He succeeds Brigadier General

Erastus B. Tyler and holds the post until 5 December.

In Virginia, a contingent of the 1st Cavalry Division (General Meade's Army of the Potomac) commanded by General Buford engages Confederates at Rapidan. The Union suffers 20 wounded. Another skirmish occurs at Robertson's Run, James City, when elements of the 3rd Cavalry Division, Army of the Potomac, under General Kilpatrick encounter Confederates under General Jeb Stuart. The Union cavalry loses 10 killed and about 40 wounded.

In Mississippi, the 2nd Wisconsin Cavalry under General Edward Hatch engages a Confederate force at Ingham's Plantation. Estimated Union casualties are about 50 killed and wounded. Confederate casualties are unreported.

In Tennessee, a Confederate force under General Sam Jones encroaches Union lines at Blue Springs in an attempt to penetrate Burnside's left. The Union's Ninth Corps, supported by General James M. Shackelford's cavalry and a division commanded by General Orlando Bolivar Willcox, advances to intercept the Rebels. In coordination, another Union force, Colonel John W. Foster's cavalry, takes a circuitous route via the Rogersville Road to strike the Confederates in the rear. The Rebels get plastered at the front and pummeled at the rear, but they fight doggedly throughout the day, refusing to capitulate. The heavy fighting continues into the following day with equally grim consequences. Once darkness settles in on the 11th, the Rebels under Jones retire and move about ten miles, where they cross into Virginia. The Union suffers 100 dead, wounded or missing; the Confederates suffer 66 dead or wounded and 150 missing (prisoners).

In Union general officer activity, Major General Joseph J. Reynolds is appointed chief of staff to General George H. Thomas (Army of the Cumberland). In January 1864, General Reynolds receives command of the defenses of New Orleans and becomes commander of the XIX Corps during July 1864. Reynolds participates in the campaign to seize Mobile, Alabama, and afterward, he is commander of the Department of Arkansas.

General Banks' force crosses the Vermilion Bayou (Mottelay, *The Soldier in Our Civil War,* 1886).

October 11 (Sunday) In Tennessee, a Union train is attacked by Confederate cavalry about one-half mile outside the depot of Colliersville. The Rebels demand surrender of the depot and the train, but General William T. Sherman declines. The train is set afire, but Union reinforcements arrive, helping to drive off the Rebels. Sherman orders Colonel McCoy to get messages over the wires to both Memphis and Germantown, requesting Corse's division. Sherman holds off the Rebels until dark, when they are finally driven away. The Union sustains about 15 killed. The Confederates suffer about 30 wounded. The 66th Indiana Volunteers and the 13th U.S. Infantry participate. Sherman, who departed Memphis earlier in the day, is heading for Corinth, 330 miles away. Sherman continues his trip, but on the 22nd, receives orders from Grant to change plans and divert his force to Stephenson, Alabama, to offset a Confederate movement that might be against Nashville.

The 5th Indiana Cavalry under Colonels Felix Graham and Thomas H. Butler engages Confederates led by General John Stuart Williams (commander of East Tennessee) at Henderson's Mill in a heated battle that lasts about two hours. The Union strength stands at about 500 against the Confederate force of about 2,700. The Union suffers 11 wounded and eight missing or captured. The Confederates sustain 30 killed and wounded and 10 captured. There is much activity in Tennessee with the XXIII Corps, commanded by Major General George L. Hartsuff (West Point, 1852). His command has just skirmished heavily at Blue Springs and will fight viciously again on the 16th at Campbell's Station, where Confederates strike hard, attempting to crush the Union defenders. During November, General Hartsuff's wounds from earlier knock him out of service until March of 1865. Upon his return, he assumes a command at the Bermuda front during the ongoing siege of Petersburg. After the war, General Hartsuff, who had been breveted brigadier and major general in the Regular army, returns to his pre-war service and holds the rank of lieutenant colonel. In other activity, the 2nd Brigade, Cavalry Division, Army of the Ohio, clashes with Confederates at Rheatown. Casualty figures are unavailable.

In Virginia, the Union abandons Culpeper. General George G. Meade's forces torch the Rappahannock Station Bridge after re-crossing the river.

October 12 (Monday) In Virginia, General George G. Meade is informed that General Robert E. Lee has not moved beyond Culpeper. Nearly convinced that this would be the intended battlefield, Meade dispatches the 2nd, 5th and 6th Corps, bolstered by Buford's cavalry, to Brandy Station, while he directs the 3rd Corps to deploy at Freeman's Farm. In addition, Meade assigns Gregg's Cavalry to guard the routes at the Upper Rappahannock. Later it is discovered that Lee had moved from Culpeper to launch a flanking attack against Meade. Lee's forces have actually moved to Sulphur Springs

and his army, during the latter part of this day, crosses the Rappahannock River, which compels General Meade to withdraw further. However, Lee's Confederates are able to attack Meade's lines at Jefferson. Pvt. Michael Dougherty of the 13th Pennsylvania Cavalry receives the Medal of Honor for his heroic actions at this engagement. The Union thwarts several attacks from the Confederates. Pvt. Dougherty later is captured and sent to Andersonville; Dougherty keeps a daily diary of life in the prison. Both the Confederates and the Union are moving toward Alexandria.

Also, cavalry attached to the Army of the Potomac skirmishes with Confederates at Culpeper and Sulphur Springs. The Union sustains eight killed and 46 wounded. Confederate casualties are unavailable.

In Missouri, the Missouri Enrolled Militia, 1st Missouri Militia Battery and the 1st, 4th and 7th Missouri Militia Cavalry engage in a two-day skirmish with Confederates at Merrill's Crossing and Lamine Crossing.

October 13 (Tuesday) In Alabama, elements of the 1st Division, Cavalry Corps, Army of the Cumberland, skirmish with Confederates at Maysville.

In Mississippi, the 2nd Brigade, Cavalry Division, 16th Corps, led by General Edward Hatch clashes with Confederates at Wyatt. Other Union contingents, including cavalry and infantry (General James B. McPherson's command), skirmish with Confederates at Big Black River.

In Tennessee, U.S. Cavalry troops under General James M. Shackelford engage Confederates at Blountville. The Union suffers six wounded, the Confederates eight dead, 26 wounded.

In Virginia, a Union outpost (6th and 11th West Virginia Regiments) at Bull Town, defended by a detachment of the 6th and 11th West Virginia Volunteers, repulses a Confederate attack. The Confederates, led by Colonel (later General) William Lowther Jackson, sustain nine killed and more than 50 captured.

October 14 (Wednesday) In Virginia, a Confederate force commanded by A.P. Hill, Army of Northern Virginia, attacks the Army of the Potomac, commanded by General George G. Meade, while it is crossing Broad Run. The Union repulses the assault and deals a severe defeat to the Rebels. General Gouverneur K. Warren's 11th Corps is held in reserve behind a railroad embankment. This reserve force rushes to the aid of General Meade, assisting in the victory at Bristoe Station. The Union suffers 51 dead,

329 wounded; the Confederates suffer some 750 killed or wounded and 450 missing. Brigadier General Carnot Posey sustains a minor wound; however, he succumbs on 13 November from unexpected complications while at the home of his friend, Doctor Davis. Posey's brigade is attached to Richard H. Anderson's brigade (3rd Corps). Confederate Brigadier General William W. Kirkland is wounded. The Confederate 25th Virginia Infantry participates at this action (General W.E. Jones' brigade, Edward Johnson's division, Richard S. Ewell's corps). Asst. Surgeon Joseph K. Corson, 6th Pennsylvania Reserves, receives the Medal of Honor for his actions at this battle. In other activity, a contingent of the 2nd Cavalry Division (Army of the Potomac) commanded by Major Howe engages Confederates under Colonel W.L. Jackson at Salt Lick.

October 15 (Thursday) In South Carolina, at Charleston, the Confederate submarine CSS *H.L. Hunley,* previously sunk during a trial in August, is again plagued by problems and sinks, costing the lives of the crew and the inventor, Horace Lawson Hunley.

In Virginia, the New Jersey Brigade, 3rd Corps, skirmishes with Confederates at McLean's Ford (Liberty Mills). The Union sustains two killed and 25 wounded. The Confederates sustain 60 killed and wounded. In other activity, a Union contingent composed of elements of the 1st New York and 12th Pennsylvania Cavalry Regiments and the 116th Ohio Volunteer Regiment, commanded by Colonel Pierce, capture about 60 Confederates at Hedgeville. Meanwhile, a cavalry contingent under General John Buford, attached to the 2nd Corps, Army of the Potomac, captures about 60 Confederates at Blackburn Ford.

In Mississippi, contingents of the Union 15th and 17th Corps encounter and skirmish with Confederates at Brownsville, Canton and Clinton through the 18th. The Union reports no casualties. The Confederates sustain 200 killed and wounded. Also, General McPherson crosses

General James McPherson crosses the Big Black River in the vicinity of Messenger's Ferry, Mississippi (Mottelay, *The Soldier in Our Civil War,* 1886).

the Big Black River near Messenger's Ferry on the 15th. The Union, during this series of skirmishes, spends some time foraging at the headquarters of Confederate General John Whitfield.

In the Indian Territory, the 1st Indian Home Guards and the 2nd Indiana Battery skirmish with Confederates at Creek Agency (Oklahoma).

In Naval activity, the USS *Honduras,* while on blockade duty in the Gulf of Mexico, seizes a British blockade runner, the *Mail.*

October 16 (Friday)   In Washington, D.C., President Lincoln names Ulysses S. Grant (West Point, 1843) commander of the Army of the West. Grant replaces Rosecrans with General George H. Thomas for command at Chattanooga, Tennessee (Army of Cumberland). In related activity, Grant telegraphs Thomas: "Hold Chattanooga at all hazards." Thomas immediately responds: "We will hold the town 'till we starve."

In Missouri, the Union 18th Iowa engages a contingent of Confederates at Cross Timbers. The Union reports no casualties. The Confederates sustain two killed and eight wounded.

In Tennessee, Union troops of the 9th and 23rd Corps engage Confederates under Longstreet at Campbell's Station. Union casualties are approximately 40 killed and 340 wounded. The Confederates suffer over 550 killed or wounded.

In Naval activity, the *Willet Rowe* (wooden-hulled side-wheel steamer), which was built during 1863 and used by the U.S. Navy as a gunboat, is purchased by the U.S. Navy on this day. Within a short time, it is renamed the *Iris.*

October 16–17   In Naval activity, the USS *Adela* and the USS *Tahoma,* under orders from Rear Admiral Theodorus Bailey, commanding officer of the East Gulf Blockading Squadron,

encroach Tampa, Florida, on a mission to destroy two blockade runners on the Hillsboro River thought to be taking on cargoes of cotton. The Union vessels bomb Fort Brooke as a ruse to divert attention from the original intent, to destroy the blockade runners. Nonetheless, the guns at the fort do not return fire. Meanwhile, the Rebels prepare to defend the fort, and after dusk, a force is dispatched to a position northeast of the fort to intercept the anticipated ground force. The gunboats, after failing to draw fire from Fort Brooke, withdraw in late afternoon, but after dark a contingent of several officers and 100 troops arrives. Forty troops from the *Adela* and sixty from the *Tahoma* are lowered into boats that carry them ashore at the western bank of Old Tampa Bay, less than 15 miles from the blockade runners at the Hillsboro River. The ground force is being guided by a Floridian, James Henry Thompson, who is loyal to the Union; however, he is too ill to walk and has to be carried.

The column arrives within sight of the two targets, the steamer *Scottish Chief* and the *Kate Dale.* Both vessels are set afire, but two of the crew members are able to escape and reach Tampa to sound the alarm. In the meantime, the column begins the return march to the boats. Near the beach, the column encounters a Rebel scouting party and immediately attacks. Two of the Rebels are captured, but the others take flight. Afterward the column resumes the trek, but the troops soon discover that a new Rebel force, composed of infantry and cavalry, is concealed in the woods near the beach. Lookouts aboard the gunboats spot the column and boats are again lowered to retrieve the landing force. However, the Confederates intend to destroy the column. While the boats are rowing to shore, the Confederates open fire. The *Adela* in turn commences fire and bombards the woods. The Confederate fire succeeds in killing two and wounding ten others, one of whom receives a mortal wound, but the landing force reaches the ships. The Confederates capture one man. Subsequent to this action, the *Adela* moves to St. George's Sound and patrols there until spring of 1864.

October 17 (Saturday) In Washington, D.C., President Lincoln calls for the induction of an additional 300,000 men to assist in the war effort.

In Virginia, a contingent of Union Cavalry (1st Division, Cavalry Corps, Army of the Potomac) commanded by General John Buford engages Confederates at Rapidan.

In Missouri, a detachment of the 6th Missouri Militia Cavalry skirmishes with Confederates at Humansville.

In Confederate general officer activity, Brigadier General Sterling Alexander M. Wood resigns his commission and resumes his law practice in Alabama. He is elected to the state legislature, in which he also served prior to the war; this term is for 1882-1883. He dies in Tuscaloosa, Alabama, during January 1891.

October 18 (Sunday)   In Virginia, Union and Confederate troops skirmish at Berryville. The Union suffers two dead and four wounded. Confederates sustain five dead and 20 wounded.

In West Virginia, the 9th Maryland Volunteer Regiment led by Colonels Simpson and Wells engages Confederates (62nd Virginia Mounted Infantry) under General John Daniel Imboden at Charlestown. The Union seizes the town, only to lose it to the Confederates and then recapture it. The Union sustains 10 killed, 30 wounded and 379 captured. The Confederates sustain about 30 killed and wounded and 21 captured.

In Kentucky, General Ulysses S. Grant arrives at Louisville from New Orleans, where he had been convalescing after sustaining an injury when he had fallen off his horse. Grant issues a general order giving him command of the recently established Military Division of the Mississippi, comprising the departments of the Cumberland, Ohio and of the Tennessee. Grant clarifies his plan for the new division: "Headquarters will be in the field."

In Union general officer activity, General William Rosecrans is relieved of command and succeeded by General George H. Thomas (Army of the Cumberland). Also, General Ambrose Burnside assumes command of the Army of the Ohio (in December, he is succeeded by General John Gray Foster). Also, General William T. Sherman will assume command of the Army of the Tennessee. General Washington L. Elliott, whose 1st Cavalry Division participated in the relief of General Burnside, will participate under General Thomas during the campaign to eliminate the force of General John B. Hood.

October 19 (Monday)   In Virginia, in response to a communication from General Alexander Lawton, General Robert E. Lee explains his dilemma about supplies. He requests shoes, overcoats, blankets and other articles of clothing to continue operations against General George G. Meade. The Confederates under Jeb Stuart and W.H.F. Lee defeat a detachment of Hugh Kilpatrick's Union cavalry under General George A. Custer at Buckland Mills. The Union withdraws to Gainesville and Haymarket, where Union lines afford safety. The Union loses 20 dead, 60 wounded and 100 missing. The Confederates sustain 10 killed and 40 wounded.

October 20 (Tuesday)   In Arizona, Union troops, including the 8th U.S. Cavalry, skirmish with guerrillas at the Chiricahua Mountains.

Union forces under General McPherson forage at the abandoned headquarters of Confederate General John Whitfield (Mottelay, *The Soldier in Our Civil War,* 1886).

In Tennessee, the 45th Ohio Mounted Infantry, 1st, 11th and 12th Kentucky Cavalry and the 24th Indiana Battery skirmish with a contingent of Confederates at Philadelphia. In other activity, Confederates attached to General James Longstreet's force attack and defeat a Union force (1st Kentucky Cavalry) under Colonel Frank Wolford in the vicinity of Philadelphia. An engagement erupts on the 20th, and following the Confederate victory, the Union gives pursuit; the two sides again clash on the 22nd, with the Union prevailing at the latter contest. General Burnside has been pondering for some time the possibility of pulling in his forces to prevent larger enemy contingents from overwhelming them. He orders his overextended units to pull back and regroup on the north side of the river near Loudon. The Union sustains 20 killed, 80 wounded and 354 missing or captured. The Confederates suffer 15 killed, 82 wounded and 111 missing.

In Mississippi, a contingent of the cavalry (Army of the Tennessee), composed of about 500 troops led by Colonel George E. Spencer, engages a Confederate force of about 1,000 men led by General Samuel W. Ferguson (General W.H. Jackson's division) at Barton Station. The Union sustains 15 killed. In July, Spencer, chief of staff to Brigadier General Grenville M. Dodge, had requested command of the 1st Alabama Cavalry, which had no commander. He was promoted to colonel on 11 September and received command of the regiment.

In Union general officer activity, Colonel James Wilson (West Point, 1860) is promoted to brigadier general.

In Naval activity, the USS *Anna* (*Annie*), operating as part of the East Gulf Blockading Squadron, seizes a blockade runner, the *Martha Jane,* a British schooner. The *Martha Jane,* intercepted after it departed Baywood, Florida, is carrying a cargo of cotton. On the 30th, the *Annie* and another vessel intercept another British blockade runner, the *Meteor,* which is transporting goods from Havana when it attempts to penetrate the blockade and enter Bayport.

October 21 (Wednesday)   In Alabama, a Union force—1st Division, 15th Corps, Army of the Tennessee, commanded by General Peter J. Osterhaus—engages a Confederate force under General Stephen D. Lee at Cherokee Station. The Union sustains seven killed and 37 wounded. The Confederates sustain 40 dead or wounded.

In Louisiana, General William B. Franklin's Division engages and defeats a Confederate force at Opelousas. The Union occupies the town. Franklin had graduated from West Point in the same class as Ulysses S. Grant, 1843. Franklin commanded the VI Corps during the Peninsular Campaign and a division in the Maryland Campaign, but difficulties with General Burnside prompted his transfer to Louisiana.

In Naval activity, several ships, the USS *Iron Age,* USS *Nansemond* (side-wheeler steamer) and USS *Niphon* (screw steamer), on patrol off North Carolina, encounter and destroy a blockade runner, the *Venus,* which began to take on water. The vessel makes it to shore, but on the following day, the Confederates set it afire.

October 22 (Thursday)   In Tennessee, the 32nd Iowa Volunteer Regiment skirmishes with Confederates at New Madrid Bend.

In Virginia, a Union force composed of elements of the 2nd Pennsylvania and the 1st Maine Cavalry Regiments, commanded by Lt. Colonel Joseph P. Brinton, skirmishes with Confederate pickets at Beverly Ford and Rappahannock Crossing. The Union sustains six killed. Confederate casualties are unavailable.

October 23 (Friday)   In Tennessee, General U.S. Grant arrives in Chattanooga and is in a good position to observe firsthand the food and supply shortages of the Union Army there. General Joseph Hooker arrives a few days later to alleviate the situation. Meanwhile, General William T. Sherman is placed in command of the Army of the Tennessee. In other activity, a 30-man contingent of the 70th Indiana Volunteer Regiment, commanded by Lt. Campbell, while

guarding a Union supply train comes under attack by Confederates in the vicinity of Tullahoma. The attack is repelled.

October 24 (Saturday)   In Tennessee, a Union cavalry contingent attached to the Army of the Ohio skirmishes with Confederates at Sweetwater.

In Virginia, the 1st Division, Cavalry Corps, Army of the Potomac, skirmishes with Confederates at Bealeton and Rappahannock Bridge. Casualty figures are unavailable.

October 25 (Sunday)   In Arkansas, a Union force composed of about 500 troops of the 5th Kansas and 1st Indiana Cavalry Regiments, commanded by Colonel Clayton, defeats a Confederate force of about 2,500 troops led by General John S. Marmaduke, commander of Price's Cavalry, in a five-hour battle at Pine Bluff. The Union loses 11 killed and 27 wounded. The Confederates suffer 53 dead, 164 wounded and 33 captured.

In Tennessee, a Union contingent skirmishes this day and the next with Confederates at Colliersville. Specific units and casualties are unreported. Confederates attempt to blow up a supply train at the Cumberland Tunnel, which links Kentucky and Tennessee at Cumberland Gap.

October 26 (Monday)   In Alabama, Union General Hooker's force departs Bridgeport, still rushing to relieve the beleaguered defenders of Chattanooga. In other activity, the 1st Division, 15th Corps, under General Peter J. Osterhaus, skirmishes with Confederates at Cane Creek (Bear Creek or Tuscumbia). The Union sustains two killed and six wounded. The Confederates sustain 10 killed and 30 wounded.

In Tennessee, General Charles F. Smith moves 4,000 men from Chattanooga to seize Brown's Ferry. General John McCauley Palmer leads a division of the 14th Corps to hold at White-

Left: A Confederate signal station in the vicinity of Beverly Ford, Virginia. *Right:* Confederates attempt to blow up a supply train at Cumberland Tunnel (Mottelay, *The Soldier in Our Civil War,* 1886).

sides on the Tennessee River, activating a rear guard action to protect Hooker's rear as he approaches Chattanooga.

In Louisiana, another expedition gets underway as General Banks dispatches a force of about 3,500 troops, commanded by General Napoleon J.T. Dana, toward the Rio Grande. General Banks moves with the flotilla, which includes the gunboats *Monongahela, Owasco* and *Virginia.* The fleet is commanded by Captain James H. Strong. En route it encounters nasty weather and gets separated; however, following the storm, the force arrives off Brazos Santiago on 2 November.

In Mississippi, Union troops, including the 1st Alabama Cavalry under Colonel George Spencer, engage a Confederate force at Bay Springs (Vincent's Crossroads). The Union loses 14 dead; Confederate casualties are unavailable.

In South Carolina at Fort Sumter, determined Confederate defenders again repulse a Union attack.

In Union general officer activity, Colonel Stephen Miller of the 7th Minnesota is promoted to brigadier general. Miller, based in Mankato, has been engaged in suppressing the Sioux uprising. Following his election as governor of Minnesota, he resigns his commission on 18 January 1864.

In Naval activity, the USS *Hastings* arrives at Eastport, Tennessee, to bolster General William T. Sherman's army while it crosses the Tennessee River during the activity revolving around control of Chattanooga. In other activity, the USS *Sunflower* supports the USS *Beauregard* in the capture of the sloop *Last Trial.*

October 27 (Tuesday)   In Tennessee, Confederates under Longstreet unsuccessfully skirmish with Union forces at Brown's Ferry. This Union contingent of General Giles A. Smith is

composed of 1,200 troops specifically selected by Smith. They include detachments from the 5th, 6th and 23rd Kentucky, the 1st, 6th, 41st, 93rd and 124th Ohio, and the 26th Indiana Volunteers. His operation is bolstered by General Turchin's force, which has guided him across Moccasin Point to Brown's Ferry. In addition, three batteries of artillery (Major J. Mendenhall) protect the landing and the laying of a pontoon bridge. Another 1,800 troops under General William Babcock Hazen (commissioned during April 1863) are crossing about nine miles farther down the river; both units converge at the ferry. Meanwhile, Hazen's contingent, under the direct command of General C.F. Smith, has floated quietly down the Tennessee River. The troops are carried by sixty pontoon boats that pass directly under the noses of the Rebel pickets, which stretch for three miles along the river without being detected and seize the objective by surprise. After Brown's Ferry is seized, pontoon bridges are constructed across the river to allow the balance of Smith's force to cross and bring the entire force together, essentially eliminating the threat of starvation at Chattanooga. General Hooker arrives on the 28th, giving the Union control of the Tennessee River in the area.

In Naval activity, Union warships bombard Fort Sumter, South Carolina. In other activity, the USS *Granite City,* while on patrol off the coast of Texas, seizes a blockade runner, the schooner *Anita.*

October 28 (Wednesday)   In Arkansas, the 3rd Wisconsin Cavalry skirmishes with Confederates at Clarksville.

In Tennessee, Union General Howard's Corps arrives at Brown's Ferry and links with General William B. Hazen's command. The Confederates under General Lafayette McLaws, deployed at Signal Rock on Lookout Mountain, observe the influx of the Union troops, and during the night of the 28th–29th, Confederate artillery blasts the Union positions of General John W. Geary, which are to the rear of Brown's Ferry at Wauhatchie. Following the bombardment, the Rebels launch an assault against Geary. The Rebels under General James Longstreet, including the Palmetto Sharpshooters (South Carolina) and a brigade led by Brigadier General Micah Jenkins, encroach from three sides. The skirmish, ongoing about three hours, heavily presses the Yankees, but instead of retiring, they

launch a tenacious bayonet attack, which finally breaks up the onslaught and drives the enemy back. Meanwhile, General Hooker, hearing the sound of battle, dispatches General Carl Schurz to speed to Geary's aid, but soon after the division advances, it too is struck by McLaw's force, compelling it to defend itself. This conflagration is equally unruly, and again the Yankees are on the brink of disaster; however, another division under General Von Steinwehr is rushed to bolster Schurz. Both sides roll up high casualties as the close-quartered fighting in the darkness is intensified by the clashing of bayonets, particularly while the Union charges up a Confederate-held slope. The pressure forces the Rebels to relinquish the ground, and by about 0430 on the 29th, the Union holds the high ground.

Among the casualties is Captain Geary, the son of General Geary. In addition, General George S. Greene is wounded. General Greene's wound is in his face and his recuperation is long-term. He does not return to the field until 1865. (See also, **October 28–29 In Tennessee.** Also, elements of the 11th and 37th Kentucky and the 112th Illinois Volunteers skirmish with Confederates at Leiper's Ferry.)

In Union general officer activity, Major General Benjamin Mayberry Prentiss resigns from the service. His resignation is tied to his health and family circumstances, but it is thought that his real reason was because he believed he had been overlooked by the higher command.

In Naval activity, the USS *Alabama,* prepared for launch during 1819 but held in inactive service until after the eruption of the Civil War, is on this day renamed the USS *New Hampshire.* It is launched on 23 April 1864 for use as a depot vessel attached to the South Atlantic Blockading Squadron. It is officially commissioned on 13 May 1864. Commodore Henry K. Thatcher receives command. This *Alabama* is separate from the side-wheeled steamer USS *Alabama* commissioned in September 1861.

October 28–29   In Tennessee, Confederates attack the Union lines at Wauhatchie, commanded by Union General John W. Geary, to attempt to break the supply line into Chattanooga. This unusual night raid causes confusion on both sides, each suffering heavy casualties. Union General Otis Howard rushes his troops from Brown's Ferry to reinforce General Geary. Union supply mules left unattended stampede into Confederate lines, causing much disruption. The Union "Cracker Line" is open and will not be attacked again. The 2nd Division, XII Corps and the XI Corps, which are both involved, are afterward transferred to assist in the west. Union General George S. Greene is badly wounded in his face. He remains out of active service until 1865 and is mustered out during 1866. General Greene's son, Samuel Dana Greene, had been the executive officer aboard the USS *Monitor* during its engagement with the CSS *Virginia* (formerly *Merrimac*) during 1862.

Overall Union casualties are 75 killed and

General Hazen's brigade on the Tennessee River (*Harper's Pictoral History of the Civil War***, 1896).** *Right:*

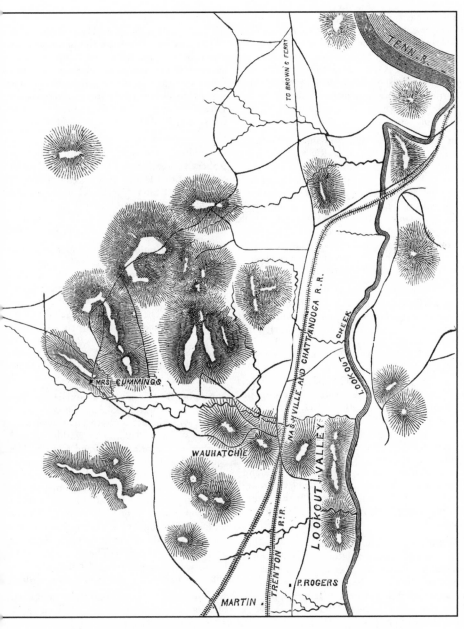

The Battle of Wauhatchie (*Harper's Pictoral History of the Civil War*, 1896).

339 wounded. The Rebels receive the worst of it, with 300 killed and 1,220 wounded. Two days later, with heavy fighting still ringing the entire area, Union Colonel Adin Underwood's brigade of the XI Corps sees intensified action as it attempts to break the siege of Chattanooga. On the 29th, fighting viciously to reopen the Tennessee River, Colonel Underwood receives a severe wound that will incapacitate him for life. General Grant opened this supply line on the 28th from Bridgeport, Alabama, to Chattanooga to relieve the drastic conditions. Captain Moses Veale, 109th Pennsylvania Infantry, is wounded and has his horse shot from under him four times, yet continues to fight. He receives the Medal of Honor for his gallantry during this action.

In a lighter moment, General Grant, accompanied by only a bugler, rides into the Union picket post to the call, "Turn out the guard for the commanding general." Grant quickly adds, "Never mind the guard." The soldiers return to their tents. Another cry rings out from the Confederate lines on the opposing bank. "Turn out the guard for the commanding general. Turn out the guard for the commanding general." The Confederates fall out, face north and render a salute to U.S. Grant, which he returns.

October 29 (Thursday)   In Alabama, again the Union clashes with Confederates at Cherokee Station. Contingents of the 1st Division, 15th Corps, engage the Confederates, but casualties are not recorded.

In South Carolina, the Confederates at Fort Sumter, still under siege, receive a day-long bombardment that delivers about several thousand rounds. The remnant fortification, which

resembles debris more than a fort, withstands the horrific firepower and continues to decline capitulation.

In the Indian Territory (Oklahoma), Confederate Colonel Watie, leading a contingent of about 500 to 800 troops, fords the Arkansas River and strikes Park Hill. During the raid, the residence (Rose Cottage) of Chief John Ross is destroyed by fire due to the chief's loyalty being with the Union. The raiders also discover some Union troops and civilians at the cottage. They are killed. Watie continues his raids until the following month before moving northeast toward the Illinois River. Tahlequah is also attacked during mid–December. Union forces in the meantime fail to intercept the guerrillas.

In Confederate general officer activity, Colonel Edward Higgins is promoted to brigadier general. General Higgins receives command of the harbor defenses, including the bay defenses at Mobile. Higgins, however, is not in command at the close of the war. By February 1865, he is living in Macon, Georgia, awaiting orders. No record of his capture or parole exists. Subsequent to the close of hostilities, he becomes involved in insurance and as an importer at Norfolk. In 1872 he moves to California to become an agent for the Pacific Mail Steamship Company. He dies in San Francisco in January 1875.

October 30 (Friday)   In South Carolina, the Confederates at Fort Sumter again come under bombardment by Federal guns, including land batteries and naval guns. Despite the Union pressure, the Rebels remain confident. Thomas Jordan, chief of staff at Charleston, sends a message to General R.S. Ripley, commander, 21st Military District at Charleston: "As a boat attack may be anticipated on Fort Sumter after the heavy bombardment which that work has been undergoing for some days, the commanding general directs that all the batteries bearing on it shall be held ready at night to sweep its exterior faces at a concerted signal from Major Elliott, or whensoever the approach of hostile boats shall be evident. Concert of action, however, is most desirable."

A message on the following day from General Beauregard to General S. Cooper details this day's activity: "Enemy's land batteries and three monitors kept up terrible bombardment on Sumter yesterday [30th], firing nearly 1,000 shots in twelve hours, wounding only one negro laborer. Major Elliott and garrison are in good spirits." Also on this day, Beauregard sends the following message to Ripley: "Bombardment of Sumter from enemy's land and naval batteries has been incessant, night and day, since yesterday's report. Casualties very few in Sumter. New Ironsides has not fired one shot since attack upon her by cigar torpedo-boat David."

In Union general officer activity, Lt. Colonel James H. Wilson, attached to General Grant's staff, is promoted to brigadier general of volunteers. Wilson is the sole member of Grant's staff to be promoted to troop command.

October 31 (Saturday) In New York, Union Brigadier General Louis Blenker dies of natural causes at his home. He had participated in Virginia at First Manassas (Bull Run) and Centreville, and his brigade also served with General Frémont against General Thomas "Stonewall" Jackson in the Shenandoah Valley before he was mustered out of the service during March 1863.

In South Carolina, at Charleston, General Beauregard continues to remain confident. Some reinforcements (Anderson's brigade) from Bragg had been declined because Beauregard believes the command was needed in Tennessee. Also, the chief of staff sends a message to Colonel Alfred Rhett: "All walls in Fort Sumter, the fall of which will endanger the lives of the garrison, must be thrown or blown down by powder. This, it is hoped, may be done at night without risk, after consultation with the engineer."

November The Minnesota 5th Volunteer Regiment, having completed duty in Mississippi, deploys in La Grange, Tennessee, to protect the Memphis and Charleston Railroad. The duty lasts until the latter part of January 1864.

In Confederate general officer activity, Jesse Johnson Finley, who entered the Confederate Army as a private in the 12th Florida Infantry, is promoted to the rank of brigadier general. Finley receives command of all Florida infantry regiments attached to the Army of Tennessee. Finley's command participates in the fighting at Chattanooga and during the Atlanta Campaign of 1864. Also, Brigadier General John S. Williams, commanding officer Department of East Tennessee, is relieved by his own request. Nevertheless, Williams maintains his service with the Confederacy and later commands a brigade in Major General Joseph Wheeler's corps.

November 1 (Sunday) In North Carolina, a contingent of Union troops skirmishes with Confederates at Washington. Casualty figures are unavailable.

In South Carolina, the Confederates initiate an operation to exchange various pieces of artillery from one fort to another and some pieces are sent out of Charleston to Secessionville. Also, General Pierre G.T. Beauregard says in a message to General S. Cooper (adjutant and inspector general, Richmond, Va.): "Bombardment of

Sumter has continued steadily since yesterday. Damage considerable, but not vital; 15 casualties, 13 of which due to fall of barrack walls. Ruins of fort will be defended to last extremity. Ironsides [Union ironclad] is still silent." Also, the transport USS *Mary Sanford,* transporting ordnance supplies, arrives at Morris Island. After arriving, it is transformed from a transport into a gunboat.

In Tennessee, General William T. Sherman's troops cross the Tennessee River at Eastport. Sherman, at the front, advances to Florence. General Grant issues orders to have General Grenville M. Dodge repair the rails leading from Decatur north to Nashville, adding mobility to Union supply movements. General Dodge completes this difficult task in just over a month. He is both a military and a civil engineer. Also, the 4th Indiana Cavalry clashes with Confederates at Fayetteville.

In West Virginia, General William W. Averell departs Beverly with his command, the Fourth Separate Brigade, composed of the 28th Ohio Volunteer Infantry (Colonel A. Moor), 10th West Virginia Cavalry (Colonel T. M. Harris), 2nd West Virginia Mounted Infantry (2nd Virginia, later 5th West Virginia; Lt. Colonel A. Scott), 3rd West Virginia Mounted Infantry (Lt. Colonel F.W. Thompson), 8th West Virginia Mounted Infantry (Colonel J.H. Oley), 14th Pennsylvania Cavalry (Colonel J.N. Schoonmaker), Gibson's Battalion (Captain J.V. Keeper), and Batteries B and G, 1st West Virginia Light Artillery (Captain T. Ewing). The column moves along the Staunton Pike and passes Camp Bartow and Greenbank before arriving at Huntersville on the 4th. En route, Confederate pickets are encountered and driven away.

In Union general officer activity, Brigadier General Lovell Harrison Rousseau at about this time (November) becomes commander of the military district of Nashville. He later commands the military district of Tennessee until he retires during November 1865 to take a seat in the U.S. Congress as a representative from Kentucky. President Andrew Johnson appoints Rousseau as a brigadier general (Regular Army) on

28 March 1867, and he receives the brevet of major general the same day. He is dispatched to Alaska to officially receive the purchase from Russia on behalf of the United States. Later he succeeds General Philip Sheridan as commander of the Department of Louisiana. He dies in the city of New Orleans on 7 January 1869. General Rousseau was the father-in-law of General Louis D. Watkins, who had predeceased Rousseau by about nine months.

November 2 (Monday) In Virginia, General Robert E. Lee informs Confederate General Sam Jones that he can spare no reinforcements because of Union General George Meade's threat to the Army of Northern Virginia. Nonetheless, General Jones heads for Tennessee to attempt the occupation of Knoxville.

In Texas, Union troops under General Nathaniel Banks arrive at Brazos Santiago from New Orleans. The troops, under the immediate command of General Napoleon J.T. Dana, encounter Confederate cavalry, and skirmishing develops. The Union drives back the Confederates. By the 4th, the Rebels have been shoved beyond Brownsville. On the 17th, the Union seizes Mustang Island. Also, this day, elements of the 13th Corps under Colonel Dwyer occupy Brazos Santiago.

November 3 (Tuesday) In Louisiana, Confederate cavalry led by General Thomas Green clashes with the 3rd and 4th Divisions led by Generals Cadwallader C. Washburn and Stephen G. Burbridge at Grand Coteau. The actions of Lt. William Marland, 2nd Independent Battery, Massachusetts Light Artillery, saves his command from capture, even though many of his support troops had already surrendered; he becomes a recipient of the Medal of Honor for his heroism under fire. During the ferocious contest, the 60th Indiana under Colonel Owens leads a tenacious assault. The Union loses 700 killed, wounded or missing. Confederates lose approximately 445 killed, wounded or missing.

In Tennessee, a Union contingent, composed of troops from several regiments and led by Lt.

Left: Union forces seize Brazos Santiago, Texas (*Harper's Pictorial History of the Civil War,* 1896). *Right:* 315) The 16th Indiana is on the attack at Battle of Grand Coteau, Louisiana (Mottelay, *The Soldier in Our Civil War,* 1886).

Colonel Shelby, skirmishes with Confederates at Centerville and Piney Factory. Union casualties are unavailable. Confederates sustain 15 killed. Also, a cavalry brigade (16th Corps) under General Edward Hatch engages in a two-day clash with Confederates at Colliersville, Lafayette and Moscow. The Union sustains six killed and 57 wounded. The Confederates suffer about 100 casualties.

November 4 (Wednesday)   In Tennessee, Grant decides to keep his troops at Chattanooga rather than reinforce Burnside at Knoxville. This decision works in Grant's favor, allowing the Union to lift the siege on Chattanooga on November 24. Grant postpones his offensive until Sherman's reinforcements arrive. Also, contingents of the 14th Michigan Mounted Cavalry, commanded by Colonel Fitzgibbon, engage a Confederate force composed of about 400 troops at Lawrenceburg. The Union sustains three wounded. The Confederates sustain about eight killed, seven wounded and 24 captured. Another skirmish develops at Metly's Ford, Little Tennessee River. Union cavalry (Army of the Ohio) under General William Sanders and Colonel Silas Adams attack Confederate positions there and capture about 40 troops. The Confederates also sustain about 40 wounded.

In Virginia, Confederate President Jefferson Davis diverts a portion of Bragg's force from Chattanooga to Knoxville, Tennessee. This contingent (Longstreet's, 15,000, and Wheeler's cavalry, 5,000) severely cuts Confederate strength at Chattanooga, allowing General Grant to make his bold move shortly thereafter.

In West Virginia, General William Averell's force, the 4th Separate Brigade, arrives at Huntersville at about 1200. Averell is informed that a Confederate force under Confederate Brigadier General Edward Jackson has a contingent of about 600 troops under Lt. Colonel F.W. Thompson deployed at Marlin's Bottom. Averell dispatches the 2nd and 8th West Virginia Mounted Infantry Regiments bolstered by some artillery to Marlin's Bottom, while simultaneously sending the 14th Pennsylvania and the 3rd West Virginia Cavalry toward Mill Point to set up an interception force to sever the escape route of Thompson, to prevent his force from reaching Lewisburg. However, by 0900, word arrives that Thompson had already retired toward Mill Point. At about midnight on the 4th–5th, Averell receives a message from Colonel Schoonmaker (14th Pennsylvania) informing him that Thompson's contingent had linked with General Edward Jackson and that his (Schoonmaker's) cavalry is under threat of attack.

In Confederate general officer activity, Brigadier General Dabney H. Maury is promoted to the rank of major general.

November 5 (Thursday)   In Tennessee, the Union 16th and 51st Illinois, 69th Ohio, 14th Michigan, 5th Tennessee Cavalry, and 7th Pennsylvania Cavalry engage the Confederates at Nashville, capturing 23 Rebel troops.

In Texas, Union troops (General Nathaniel Banks' command) occupy Brownsville, Texas, without incident.

In West Virginia, a Union contingent composed of detachments of the 14th Pennsylvania and the 3rd West Virginia Cavalry Regiments engage a Confederate force at Mill Point. During the previous night, Confederate Colonel Thompson had evaded the forces of General Averell at Marlin's Bottom and moved to join General Edward Jackson at Mill Point. In early morning, General Averell sends infantry and some artillery (Keeper's battery) to augment the cavalry. He dispatches Colonel Oley's 8th West Virginia Infantry to further bolster the Union forces at Mill Point. In the meantime, General Averell arrives at the front at about 0800, just as the Confederates are retiring. At this time, Averell stands slightly less than 35 miles from Lewisburg. He chooses not to initiate a full-scale pursuit, in an attempt lessen the pressure and simultaneously slow the pace of the Confederate march to Lewisburg. Averell estimates that his own column will arrive at Lewisburg during the early afternoon of the 7th. The Union strategy calls for the interception of the Confederates by sending three cavalry regiments to sever the route of retreat. Nonetheless, the Confederates outpace the cavalry and reach Droop Mountain, where they fortify their positions on the summit.

In Naval activity, the USS *Howquah*, USS *Nansemond* and the army transport *Fulton* seize a blockade runner, the *Margaret and Jessie*, which had previously run the blockade about fifteen times. The *Margaret and Jessie* was originally built in Scotland as an iron side-wheeled steamship called the *Douglas*, but it was acquired by the Confederates during November 1862, transformed into a blockade runner and renamed *Margaret and Jessie* sometime after its initial successful voyage. The prize is acquired later this month by the U.S. Navy and commissioned the USS *Gettysburg* during May 1864.

November 5–8   In Naval activity, the CSS *Ella and Annie*, a blockade runner stranded in Bermuda since the previous September due to damage inflicted by a hurricane, departs for North Carolina. It is accompanied by the steamer CSS *R.E. Lee*. The two Rebel ships travel as a pair until they reach a point off Carolina where they separate, with the *Ella and Annie* moving toward Wilmington. En route the vessel encounters a strong storm that impedes its progress, but the storm does not deter the blockading squadron from maintaining its vigil for blockade runners. On 8 November, the USS *Niphon* spots the *Ella and Annie* in the

The Confederates abandon Brownsville, Texas, just before it is occupied by Union forces (*Harper's Pictorial History of the Civil War*, 1896).

vicinity of New Inlet. A slight contest erupts when the blockade runner rams the *Niphon*, but to no avail. Acting Master Joseph B. Breck immediately orders the *Niphon's* guns fired, and an effective broadside brings the contest to a close. The devastating hit demolishes the *Ella and Annie's* hull. The ship is taken to Boston and its captain, Frank N. Bonneau, is afterward tried for piracy. A Boston court rules guilty, but the presiding officer countermands the ruling and suspends Bonneau's sentence, declaring that he, too, had been a flag officer, and under similar circumstances, he would have acted identically. The prize is afterward acquired by the U.S. Navy and commissioned (provisionally) the USS *Malvern* in Boston on 10 December. On 9 February 1864, it is officially commissioned.

November 6 (Friday)   BATTLE OF DROOP MOUNTAIN The Union 4th Separate Brigade under General William Averell launches an attack against Confederates under Generals John Echols, Albert G. Jenkins and Edward Jackson at Droop Mountain, West Virginia. The battle erupts when three infantry companies advance to draw fire and define the precise Confederate positions, but at the same time, a small cavalry contingent supported by infantry is sent to the right to maneuver from where the Confederate rear and flank could be struck. In addition, Averell initiates a diversionary movement by sending the 14th Cavalry and Keeper's artillery battalion toward the Confederate right. Meanwhile, as the main body forms for attack, the sounds of a Confederate band carries over the Union lines, conspicuously signaling the arrival of Rebel reinforcements. Nevertheless, Colonel A. Moor's 28th Ohio initiates its attack by moving nearly ten miles over the mountains and through the woods to gain positions to the Confederates' left. By about 1345, the sounds of gunfire near Moor's positions on the left and the other operations to the Confederate front inform Averell that the plan is unfolding on schedule. He orders the main attack. The 2nd, 3rd and 8th West Virginia Regiments (dismounted) advance. As they ascend, the broad line is joined by Moor's Ohioans. The Union artillery pounds the Confederate positions. By 1500, the Yankees claim the summit. The Confederates get a head start during the retreat, but the Union infantry and some artillerymen give chase while the dismounted cavalry troops wait for their horses to be brought to the summit. Afterward, Averell's entire brigade joins the pursuit. However, at dusk, the chase is terminated. Averell orders the halt and anticipates that a Union reinforcing column under General Duffie, en route from the Kanawha Valley, will intercept the retreating column on the 7th, thereby trapping Jackson between the forces. The Confederate units, totaling about 4,000 troops, include the 14th Virginia Cavalry, 22nd Virginia Infantry, Derrick's battalion, Edgar's battalion and Jackson's brigade. The Union suffer 31 dead and 94 wounded. The Confederates sustain 50 dead, 250 wounded and 100 missing.

The Confederate Army of Southwestern Virginia sustains devastating casualties and its effectiveness is almost destroyed. The 22nd Virginia, commanded by Colonel George S. Patton, is nearly annihilated. Nevertheless, General Lee, by spring of 1864, calls upon the Army of Southwestern Virginia to move to the Shenandoah to bolster the forces there. By then, the 22nd Virginia rebuilds its strength.

In Tennessee, a Confederate cavalry force composed of about 2,500 troops, commanded by General William E. Jones, launches a surprise assault against the Union garrison at Rogersville. General Jones had been assigned with the cavalry under Jeb Stuart, but he was relieved and assigned to the Department of Southwest Virginia and East Tennessee after some difficulties with Stuart during the Gettysburg Campaign. The Union force, commanded by Colonel (later general) Theophilus T. Garrard, including the 7th Ohio Cavalry, 2nd Tennessee Mounted Infantry and the 2nd Illinois Battery, is overwhelmed by the strength of the attack. The Rebels capture 750 troops, several guns and more than thirty wagons. This raid and others in the area convince the Union to pull in its forces and converge on Bull's Gap in order to multiply the force with which to meet the next heavy Confederate attack. At this time, General Ambrose Burnside's forces are scattered along the southern sides of the Holston and Tennessee Rivers, but soon Burnside will redeploy his forces on the north bank in the vicinity of Loudon.

In other activity, a Union contingent skirmishes with Confederates at Kincaels. Specific units and casualty figures are unavailable.

November 7 (Saturday)   In Virginia, Union troops attached to General George G. Meade's Army of the Potomac, including the 5th and 6th Maine, 49th Pennsylvania, 27th New York and the 121st New York, advance on Confederates at Rappahannock Station. Union persistence prevails, with the Confederates suffering 1,738 killed, wounded or captured. The 5th and 6th Cavalry under Union General Sedgwick perform masterfully against the Confederates. Late in the afternoon, brigades (6th Corps) of Colonel Emery Upton and General David A.

Russell storm the Confederate works and overwhelm the defenders, seizing about 1,500 prisoners. Union casualties total 370 dead or wounded. The flag of the 8th Louisiana Infantry (CSA) and seven other battle flags, along with four pieces of artillery, are lost to the Union. Under the direction of General Grant, the captured artillery and battle flags are taken to the capital by General David Russell. Subsequently, General Russell receives command of a division in the VI Corps.

Union troops — including the 1st U.S. Sharpshooters and the 40th New York, plus the 3rd and 5th Michigan, under General Birney — engage Confederates under Colonel Archibald C. Godwin at Kelly's Ford. The Union loses 70 dead or wounded; Confederates suffer five dead, 59 wounded and 295 missing. Major (later general) Archibald C. Godwin is captured in the vicinity of Rappahannock Bridge. He is afterward paroled. Following these skirmishes, General Lee heads for the Rapidan River, but the Union does not follow; the Union Army is equally exhausted as that of General Lee. Consequently, neither gains any advantage. In other action, the 3rd Cavalry Division, commanded by General Hugh Kilpatrick, engages Confederates at Stevensburg.

In West Virginia, troops from the 14th West Virginia Cavalry under General William Averell, on the day following the victory at Droop Mountain, begin to arrive at Lewisburg, and the contingent encounters General Alfred Napoleon A. Duffie. His force, composed of four regiments, had arrived from the Kanawha Valley. General Duffie, the son of a French count, had arrived in the United States during 1859. He resigned his commission in the French army and joined the service of the United States. Earlier this day, some of the main body of the Confederates had passed through the town en route to Dublin, where General John Echols is supposed to receive reinforcements promised by General Robert E. Lee.

In Naval activity, the USS *Anna* (*Annie*) participates in the capture of yet another British blockade runner, the *Paul*, which is the third British ship seized by the *Annie* since 20 October. One other escaped capture. The *Paul* is supposedly en route from Havana, Cuba, to Matamoros, Mexico; however, it is captured as it approaches the coast of Florida while transporting "diverse merchandise." The *Annie*, which has been operating with the USS *Sagamore*, begins to operate in conjunction with the USS *Tacoma* during February 1864. Afterward the *Annie* participates as a tender to numerous other blockade ships. The *Sagamore* continues duty as a patrol vessel until December, when it is

decommissioned for repairs; however, it does not return to active service. It is sold during June 1865 and afterward it is renamed the *Kaga no Kami* and operates as a Japanese merchant ship. In 1868 it becomes a Japanese warship, the *Yoshum.*

November 8 (Sunday)   In Arkansas, a contingent of the 3rd Wisconsin Cavalry engages Confederates at Clarksville. The Union sustains two killed. Confederate casualties are unavailable.

In Mississippi, Union cavalry clashes with a contingent of Confederates at Hudsonville. The Union casualties are light and a large number of Rebels are captured.

In Virginia, elements of the 1st Cavalry Division (Army of the Potomac) commanded by General John Buford engage Confederates at Muddy Run in the vicinity of Culpeper. The Union sustains four killed and 25 wounded. Confederate casualties are unavailable.

In West Virginia, General W.W. Averell initiates an advance toward Dublin, where it is suspected that Confederate General Echols is posted awaiting reinforcements. General Napoleon Duffie's force, which linked with Averell on the previous day, joins the pursuit. However, prior to reaching the objective, the column encounters a Confederate blockade. The Union is compelled to slice its way through to permit the march to resume. Meanwhile, General Duffie maintains that his force it overexhausted and unable to continue the march. Duffie's command has expended all of its rations except for one day. Averell, unwilling to keep Duffie's force, which claims it can only proceed at a rate of about ten miles per day, orders Duffie to retire to Meadow Bluff. Averell also directs the 28th Ohio, 10th West Virginia Cavalry and Keeper's battery to retire to Beverly. Moor's 28th Ohio takes many of the prisoners from Droop Mountain and some of the wounded along with him. The column arrives at Beverly on 12 November. Meanwhile, General Averell, with a diminished command, advances toward Callaghan's, arriving there on the following day.

Union cavalry advances past a blockhouse of the Nashville and Chattanooga Railroad (Mottelay, *The Soldier in Our Civil War*, 1886).

In Naval activity, the USS *Hastings* arrives at Paducah, Kentucky, to bolster the Union forces against a threat by Confederate cavalry. In December the *Hastings* sails to Cairo, Illinois, for repairs and remains out of service until April 1864. A Union naval force, including the *Moose, Fair Play, Springfield, Silver Lake,* and *Victory* engage and vanquish Confederate guerrillas who attempt to cross the Ohio River following their withdrawal from Harpeth Shoals.

November 9 (Monday) In Mississippi, a detachment of Union cavalry engages a contingent of Confederate guerrillas at Bayou Sara. The Union reports no casualties. Confederates sustain about 50 wounded and 40 captured.

In West Virginia, General Averell's column arrives at Callaghan's. Averell is informed that Confederate General John D. Imboden had arrived at Covington with a reinforcing column of between 900 and 1,500 men, and is en route to join General Echols at Union. Averell discounts the threat of Imboden and decides to dispatch only a contingent, composed of two squadrons of the 8th West Virginia Mounted Infantry, to scatter Imboden's command, while the main column resumes it march and heads for Monterey, then beyond to Hightown. The mounted infantry under Major Slack succeeds in driving Imboden's column out of the area, assuring an uninterrupted march for Averell. He arrives at Petersburg on the 13th, and after being resupplied with forage and rations, he proceeds to New Creek on the 17th.

In Naval activity, the blockade runner *Robert E. Lee,* formerly the merchant steamer *Giraffe* (built in Scotland), having broken through the naval blockade at least twenty times in the last year, finally gets snagged. The USS *James Adger* and the USS *Iron Age* intercept the vessel while it is trying to get to Wilmington, North Carolina. On duty off North Carolina, the *James Adger* also either seizes or participates in the seizure of more vessels, including the blockade runners *Ella, Kate* and the *Cornubia.* In December the *Adger* goes out of commission until June 1864. Meanwhile, the captured *Robert E. Lee* receives a new name, the USS *Fort Donelson.* After the war, the *Fort Donelson* is decommissioned and becomes known as the *Isabella,* then is later acquired by Chile and renamed *Concepcion.*

Also, the USS *Niphon* seizes the blockade runner steamship *Ella and Annie* off New Inlet, North Carolina. The *Ella and Annie* was initially the SS *William G. Hewes,* built in Wilmington, Delaware in 1860. It was seized by Louisiana in April 1861 and became the CSS *William G. Hewes.* In 1862, the vessel is transferred to civilian use to become a blockade runner, the *Ella and Annie.* When it is acquired by the U.S. Navy, it is commissioned the USS *Malvern.* It is sold at auction in October 1865 and reverts to its original name, the *William G. Hewes,* and operates until it is wrecked off Cuba on 20 February 1895. The commanding officer at the time of capture, Acting Master Francis N. Bonneau of the Confederate States Navy, is tried and convicted of piracy; however, the sentence is suspended and he receives parole in September 1864.

November 10 (Tuesday) In Tennessee, Union General U.S. Grant continues to work to lift the siege of Chattanooga. Meanwhile, General Ambrose Burnside, holding at Knoxville without benefit of reinforcements, continues to send dispatches stating that he can hold the city.

In Confederate general officer activity, Brigadier Generals William T. Martin and John Austin Wharton are promoted to the rank of major general. Martin will command a cavalry brigade during the struggle for Atlanta, and afterwards, he will be assigned command of the Department of Northwest Mississippi. Wharton will subsequently be assigned duty with Lt. General Richard Taylor, and following the Red River Campaign, he will be transferred to the Trans-Mississippi Department. Martin receives command of a division in General Joseph Wheeler's corps. Toward the closing days of the conflict, he becomes commander of the District of Northwest Mississippi. After the war, General Martin is president of the construction of the Natchez, Jackson and Columbia Railroad and serves twelve years in the Mississippi Senate. He dies on 16 March 1910 near Natchez, Mississippi.

In Naval activity, the USS *Howquah,* while operating off Wilmington, North Carolina, intercepts and seizes the CSS *Ella,* a side-wheel steamer operating as a Confederate picket ship. On the following day while on patrol, the *Howquah* pursues an unidentified vessel until it runs ashore, where it is destroyed by heavy seas.

November 11 (Wednesday) In Mississippi, the 58th U.S. Colored Regiment, commanded by Captain Hitchcock, engages Confederate guerrillas under John Singleton Mosby at Natchez. The Union sustains four killed and six wounded. The Confederates sustain four killed and eight wounded.

In Naval activity, the USS *Lodona,* having completed its repairs, departs Philadelphia en route to South Carolina to rejoin the South Atlantic Blockading Squadron.

November 12 (Thursday) In Arkansas, a two-company contingent of the 2nd Kansas Cavalry skirmishes with Confederates at Roseville.

November 13 (Friday) In California, at Trinity River, a contingent composed of two companies of the 1st Battalion, California Mountaineer Infantry, skirmishes with a contingent of Confederates. The Union sustains two wounded. Confederate casualties are unavailable.

In Georgia, a contingent of the 1st South Carolina Colored Troops Regiment, commanded by Lt. Colonel Oliver T. Beard, 48th New York Infantry, while operating along the Doboy River with the support of a Union gunboat, engages a contingent of Confederates. The Union repulses the attack.

In Tennessee, a one-company contingent of Union mounted infantry led by Captain Cutter skirmishes with Confederate guerrillas at Palmyra. The Union sustains two wounded. The Confederates sustain two killed, five wounded and one captured.

In West Virginia, a Union contingent skirmishes with Confederates at Mill Creek Valley.

November 14 (Saturday) In Alabama, Union General William T. Sherman, in his race to reach Grant at Chattanooga, approaches Bridgeport with 17,000 reinforcements.

In Tennessee, Confederate General James Longstreet, at Loudon awaiting completion of a bridge, dispatches a large body of cavalry toward Knoxville, held by Union General Ambrose Burnside. The contingents under Major General Joseph Wheeler and Brigadier General Nathan Bedford Forrest are instructed to secure the heights above Knoxville. However, the resistance raised by the Yankees when the Rebels arrive on the 19th is more than they expect. During the early morning hours, Longstreet's forces begin to cross the Tennessee River at Hough's Ferry (Huff's Ferry). A skirmish erupts. The Union 111th Ohio, 107th Illinois, 11th and 13th Kentucky, the 23rd Michigan and the 24th Michigan Battery under General Julius White (General Burnside's command, Department of the Ohio) clash with a group of Confederates under Major William P. Chapin at the ferry. The Union sustains 100 killed and wounded. Confederate casualties are unavailable. Union forces also clash with Confederates at Marysville and Rockford. At Marysville, the Union 11th Kentucky Cavalry sustains 100 killed and wounded. At Rockford, the Union 1st Kentucky Cavalry and the 45th Ohio Mounted Infantry sustain 25 wounded. Confederate casualties are unavailable.

General Burnside is planning to assault General Longstreet on the 15th; however, during the latter part of this day, orders arrive from General Grant instructing him to withdraw to Knoxville at a sluggish pace. The intent is to draw Longstreet toward Knoxville and prevent him from closing on Chattanooga.

In Naval activity, the USS *Wave* (originally *Argosy No. 2*) is acquired by the U.S. Navy. It is assigned duty in the western waters as a gunboat and on 6 May 1864 is seized by Confederates at Calcasieu Pass, Texas.

November 15 (Sunday) In Texas, Corpus Christi Pass falls to Union troops commanded by General Nathaniel Banks.

In Tennessee, Confederates under General James Longstreet drive a contingent of Union troops (Burnside's command) from their positions at the Holston River, forcing the Yankees to fall back to regroup at Bull's Station. In related activity, Union troops under General Robert B. Potter are at Lenoir Station with General Julius White's division (Twenty-third Corps) and a contingent of the Ninth Corps, which had been sped to the town from Kentucky. Longstreet's forces, expecting another easy victory, are bushwhacked by the steadfast defense and resistance. General White's troops advance and drive the Rebels back, ending the threat. Also, Union troops attached to the 111th Ohio Regiment clash with Confederates at Loudon Creek. The Union sustains four killed and 12 wounded. The Confederates sustain six killed and 10 wounded.

In Naval activity, the USS *Lodona,* en route from Philadelphia to Charleston Harbor encounters and captures a blockade runner, the *Arctic.* The prize is sailed to Washington, D.C., while the *Lodona* resumes its voyage. It arrives off Charleston on the 17th, and by 20 November it is on post in Sapelo Sound, Georgia.

In Naval activity, the USS *Reindeer* is ordered to shift its operations from the Ohio River near Louisville to the Cumberland River. Later, during April 1864, the *Reindeer,* at Mound City, Illinois, is again reassigned. It becomes a dispatch ship there until it is decommissioned on 7 August 1865. The *Reindeer* is sold on the 17th. On 5 October 1865, it is renamed *Mariner.* It continues to operate as a commercial vessel until it runs aground and is destroyed near Decatur, Alabama, on 9 May 1867.

November 16 (Monday)   In South Carolina, the USS *Lehigh,* although stranded in Charleston Harbor, is saved by Union volunteers, including men attached to the USS *Nahant.* Heavy fire from Confederate-held Fort Moultrie severely hampers the rescue. The *Nahant,* following this action, remains in the vicinity of Charleston for the duration of the war. It is decommissioned in August 1865 and sent to Philadelphia, where it remains inactive until the outbreak of the Spanish American War; then it is recommissioned during April 1898. It had been renamed the *Atlas* during June 1869, but by the end of summer it reverted to its original name. Following duty off New York to protect the coastal defenses during the war, it returns to Philadelphia, where it is sold for scrap in April 1904.

In Tennessee, Union forces, including elements of the 9th Corps and the 2nd Division, 23rd Corps, and General William P. Sanders' cavalry force (General Burnside's command), engage and defeat Confederates under General James Longstreet at Campbell Station. The Union has 60 dead and 340 wounded. Confederates have 570 killed or wounded and many others captured.

General Burnside is pulling back toward Knoxville during this confrontation. While General Hartranft, with a contingent of the Ninth Corps, engages Longstreet, Burnside's main body continues along the Loudon Road and reaches the defenses of Knoxville. In other action, Union troops, including the 17th Michigan, clash with Confederates at Lenoir Station.

In Confederate general officer activity, Colonels James H. Clanton and John Herbert Kelly are promoted to the rank of brigadier general, effective this day. Kelly and Clanton are assigned to Georgia and both participate in the Atlanta Campaign, the former serving in Major General Joseph Wheeler's cavalry corps. Also, Confederate Colonel John Tyler Morgan, 51st Alabama Partisan Rangers, is promoted to brigadier general effective this date. Morgan, having served at Chickamauga, will also serve in Georgia, raising resistance against General William T. Sherman's army as it drives from Atlanta toward Savannah (Sherman's March to the Sea). Also, Colonel Jesse Johnson Finley is appointed brigadier general to rank from this date. He receives command of the Florida regiments operating in Tennessee. Captain William Young Conn Humes, chief of artillery to General Joseph Wheeler, is promoted to brigadier general. He commands a division late in the war, but no records indicate a promotion to major general. Subsequent to the close of hostilities, General Humes resumes his law practice in Memphis. He dies in Huntsville, Alabama, in September 1882.

In Naval activity, the USS *Granite City,* operating off the coast of Texas, seizes the blockade runner *Amelia Ann.* On the following day, it seizes another, the bark *Teresita.* During this same period, the *Granite City* also supports two separate landings of Union ground troops that go ashore on the Texas coast.

November 16–17   In Virginia, a Union reconnaissance force is initiated by Colonel R.M. West, commanding officer at Williamsburg. The force, composed of six companies of the 1st New York Mounted Rifles, commanded by Colonel B.F. Onderdonk, and several companies of the 139th New York Regiment, commanded by Colonel Roberts, moves from Williamsburg toward Charles City Court House, located along the northern bank of the James River, slightly more than five miles beyond the Chickahominy River. The infantry serves as vanguard, followed by the cavalry, the latter not beginning its advance until about 2200. The path to the objective is impeded due to storm clouds and stark darkness; however, the cavalry column, despite two guides, advances blindly and the trek becomes more undesirable when the clouds open and deliver torrents of rain.

The elements cause more confusion and some of the officers to stray from the column to find themselves temporarily lost in the wilderness. Eventually the strays rejoin the column; however, the road seems to vanish in the darkness. By about 0300 on the 17th, further progress becomes impossible although the road has been found. The column halts with nowhere for the troops to find shelter and no piece of dry ground. The paralyzed cavalrymen remain in the saddle until dawn.

At first light the soaked cavalrymen resume the advance and soon catch up with the infantry, which has seized a few Confederate pickets near the Chickahominy. The cavalry accelerates the pace and crosses the river, which rises to their saddle bags, at Ford's Crossing. After reaching the west bank, a few sentinels, still asleep, are captured. The cavalry then races toward a hill that overlooks Charles City Court House. Once atop the hill, the Confederate camp becomes visible, and after finalizing the strategy, the command is issued, "Charge!" The cavalry, with Colonels R.M. West and Onderdonk at the point, descend to the sounds of a "Union Yell," catching the Confederates by total surprise while they are in the middle of an inspection, leaving little time for the Rebels to react to the horses that are galloping directly into their formation.

The cavalry crashes into the camp against minimum resistance, and within a short while the Confederates, still dressed in their best uniforms, find themselves prisoners. The charge had overwhelmed the Rebels within about fifteen minutes. About ninety men are seized, along with 150 stands of arms. Eight officers are among the prisoners. The cavalry also gains about fifty new horses. Subsequent to reducing the camp, Colonel West moves against Charles City Court House and encounters some resistance; however, the Union, which by now has seized all the momentum, surrounds the two primary buildings from where the resistance originates and seals the fate of those defenders. A white flag is soon spotted. The Confederate prisoners are from a contingent (commanded by J.A. Robinson) of the 42nd Virginia Regiment, a well known crack unit. The Union after-action report details the luck of catching the Confederates off guard and having Robinson absent ("away on his wedding tour") when the raid unfolded.

Following the victory, the column returns toward the Chickahominy and pauses for a short while, unconcerned about any pursuit. While en route back to Williamsburg, Colonel West dispatches a small contingent to the Diascon Bridge and the arrival is timely, as it comes upon a Confederate contingent in the process of destroying the bridge. On 14 December, Major General Benjamin Franklin Butler sends a report to General Isaac Wistar at Fortress Monroe which details the success of the mission and notes that a group of the captured enlisted men had taken the oath of allegiance to the Union. He notes that one of the captured soldiers had been a southern woman dressed in a man's attire. Captain Rogers, in charge of the contingent that had been captured, owned most of the captured horses as well as the equipment being used by the unit.

November 17 (Tuesday)   In California, the 1st California Battalion, Mountaineer Infantry, skirmishes with Confederates at Willow Creek.

In Tennessee, Confederate troops have Knoxville isolated. The unorthodox siege lasts until 4 December.

In Texas, troops attached to General Banks' command, led by General T.E.G. Ransom, having moved from Brownsville, encounter Confederates at Mustang Island and Aransas Pass. Following a skirmish, which costs the Confederates about 100 casualties, the Union occupies Aransas Pass. In addition, Corpus Christi at the southern tip of Mustang Island is occupied. The 13th and 14th Maine, 34th Iowa, and 8th Indiana Volunteers, Battery F, 1st Missouri Artillery, and the gunboat *Monongahela* participate at this action.

In Virginia, elements of the 1st New York Cavalry skirmish with Confederates at Mount Jackson. The Union sustains two killed and three wounded. The Confederates sustain about 27 missing.

In Union general officer activity, Colonel Isaac Fitzgerald Shepard (51st U.S. Colored Infantry, formerly of the 3rd Missouri) is promoted to brigadier general to rank from 27 October. Subsequently, at Vicksburg, he commands a brigade composed of three Negro regiments in the Negro division of General John P. Hawkins. In the meantime, the Senate takes no action on General Shepard's nomination and it expires in March 1864. He then leaves the service and returns to Missouri. Later he becomes adjutant general of Missouri on a few separate occasions, and he becomes a consul in Hankow and Swatow, China. Upon his return to the U.S., he lives in Massachusetts, were he succumbs on 25 August 1889.

November 17–December 4 SIEGE OF KNOXVILLE On November 17, the Confederates commence a bombardment that continues seemingly without pause until the midnight hour of the 28th–29th. Union General Burnside's force comes under attack by strong Rebel forces, and he attempts to hold out without massive reinforcements. The enduring Yankees come close to disaster, but General James Longstreet is forced to pull out on 4 December, ending the siege. Union General Milo S. Hascall (West Point, 1852) participates in this confrontation.

November 18 (Wednesday) In Kentucky, outside of Knoxville, Brigadier General William P. Sanders (commissioned the previous month), while engaged against Confederates under General James Longstreet, sustains a fatal wound on Kingston Road while he is dismounted. He dies on the following day.

In Louisiana, the 6th Missouri Cavalry skirmishes with a Confederate contingent at Carrion Crow Bayou. Casualty figures are unavailable.

In Tennessee, Lt. Samuel Benjamin is appointed to command Fort Sanders. He requests additional support by asking that the 79th Highlanders be assigned to garrison the post. Benjamin deploys the regiment's companies to their respective positions. Companies B, H and K deploy in the northwest bastion and the remainder of the regiment is scattered about in various locations on the north and west fronts.

In Confederate general officer activity, Colonel Alfred Jefferson Vaughan, Jr. (13th Tennessee Infantry Regiment), is promoted to the rank of brigadier general. General Vaughan had participated in various actions in the west under Generals Leonidas Polk, Albert Sydney Johnston, and Braxton Bragg. Subsequently, he serves in the same area under General Joseph Johnston.

November 19 (Thursday) In Pennsylvania, President Lincoln gives his Gettysburg Address while dedicating the military cemetery on the battlefield. Lincoln remarks, "The world will little note nor long remember what we say here today."

In Tennessee, elements of the 2nd Illinois Cavalry and a detachment of the 58th Illinois Infantry Regiment led by Colonel Moore skirmish with Confederates at Union City. The Confederates sustain 11 killed and 53 captured. In other activity, General William Price Sanders moves out of Knoxville to meet Confederate General Longstreet's vanguard, cavalry contingents of Generals Nathan B. Forrest and Joseph Wheeler. The Union is commanded on the field by General Sanders, while General John G. Parke remains at Knoxville. The battle is fast and furious with both sides giving no quarter for several hours while they clash in the vicinity of Kingston Road, one mile outside of Knoxville. The 3rd Michigan, 12th Kentucky, 45th Ohio, and the 112th Illinois hold the line preventing the Confederates from securing the heights outside Knoxville. During the fighting, General Sanders is struck with a mortal wound by a sniper's bullet; he succumbs on the following day.

In Texas, Union forces under General Cadwallader C. Washburn advance against Confederate-held Pass Cavallo and its strongpoint, Fort Esperanza, fortified by about 2,000 troops. This strategic pass dominates Matagorda Bay. The Union continues to lay siege until the 30th.

In Union general officer activity, Colonel Adin Ballou, who sustained a debilitating wound on 29 October, is promoted to brigadier general; however, his injury prevents any further service. He receives the brevet of major general of volunteers toward the close of the war and musters out of the service during August 1865. He becomes the surveyor of the port of Boston, where he dies on 24 January 1888.

November 20 (Friday) In Virginia, Confederate guerillas under Colonel John S. Mosby disguise themselves as Union troops and pull a surprise raid against Bealton Station. The Confederate plan is foiled and Mosby's men are driven off.

In Tennessee, Confederate Major Generals James Longstreet and Joseph Wheeler postpone their attack on Knoxville, anticipating further reinforcement. A small Union assault team from the 17th Michigan Infantry penetrates enemy lines at Knoxville and it destroys buildings that had been sheltering Rebel snipers. The structures are reduced to ashes by fire. In other activity, Union General William T. Sherman's force reaches Brown's Ferry at the Tennessee River; however, much of his command is still some distance out. Hugh Boyle Ewing's division, in a diversionary move, is at Trenton, in an attempt to deceive the South into thinking Lookout Mountain is under attack from the south. When the assault is mounted, Ewing's division takes high casualties. Ewing attended West Point but resigned on the day before graduation.

In Confederate general officer activity, Colonel George B. Hodge is promoted to brigadier general; however, the Confederate Senate declines approving the commission. He is promoted to that rank during August 1864, but again the Senate takes no action. Nevertheless, Hodge will command a cavalry brigade (Major General Joseph Wheeler's command).

November 21 (Saturday) In Tennessee, General Sherman prepares to strike against the Confederates from positions at the northern end of Missionary Ridge, but this day, while advancing to the area, only General John E. Smith is able to cross the river. The remaining units are forced to await repairs on the bridge and a change in the weather. The movement begins anew on the 24th.

In Naval activity, the steamer USS *Welcome* clashes with Confederate guerrillas at Waterproof, Louisiana. Also, the steamer USS *Black Hawk* comes under attack by Confederate batteries and guerrillas in the vicinity of Red River Landing on the Mississippi River. In other activity, the USS *Grand Gulf* (formerly the *Onward*), operating with the army transport *Fulton*, seizes a blockade runner, the *Banshee*, as the runner attempts to penetrate the blockade to enter Wilmington, North Carolina. The *Fulton*, a side wheel steamship, had been built in England during 1862, and until its capture had succeeded in running cargo between the West Indies and Wilmington. The prize is acquired

Bealton Station, Virginia (Mottelay, *The Soldier in Our Civil War*, 1886).

by the U.S. Navy and commissioned as the USS *Banshee* during June 1864. It serves as part of the North Atlantic Blockading Squadron. Subsequent to the ill-fated attack against Fort Fisher during December 1865, the *Banshee* transfers to the Potomac Flotilla. Following the war, the *Banshee* is sold in November 1865 and renamed the *T.L.* (or *J.L.*), but afterward, it is resold to the English and is renamed *Irene*. It remains a British merchant ship until the 1890s and possibly into the 20th century.

The USS *Grand Gulf*, built in New York during 1863 and named the *Onward*, had been acquired by the U.S. Navy and commissioned the *Grand Gulf* during September 1863. Later it participates in the massive search for the CSS *Tallahassee*, and during that cruise, it recovers the *Billow* (August 1864), which had been seized by the *Tallahassee*. In other activity, the *Emma Brown*, a side-wheel steamer constructed at Madison, Indiana, during 1863, is acquired by the U.S. Navy. The ship is renamed the *Gazelle* and assigned to the Mississippi Squadron. It is commissioned by February 1864. Acting Master Charles Thatcher receives command. It sails to the mouth of the Red River in time to join the expedition (12 March to 22 May) led by Admiral Porter.

November 22 (Sunday)   In Tennessee, pressure continues to build as the defenders under Burnside continue to see their supplies diminish, and up to this point no reinforcements have arrived to lift the siege. At Chattanooga, the Union continues to prepare for an attack. General George H. Thomas receives orders from General Grant to initiate a demonstration in view of the Confederate positions at Missionary Ridge.

November 23 (Monday) In Tennessee, Union General Ambrose Burnside at Knoxville telegraphs Grant to report he could hold out for ten or twelve days, but if not relieved, he would be forced to retreat or surrender to

Longstreet. Grant directs General William T. Sherman to depart Graysville to relieve Burnside. At this time, a contingent of Sherman's force, composed of the 15th Corps and one Division of the 16th Corps, commanded by General Francis Preston Blair, Jr., stands near a crossing site (Tennessee River) slightly below the South Chickamauga.

November 24 (Tuesday)   In South Carolina, the 33rd U.S. Colored Troops (1st South Carolina Regiment) skirmishes with Confederates at Barnwell's Island.

In Tennessee, the weather brightens up somewhat and Sherman gets two more divisions on the opposite bank, but one, that of General Peter Joseph Osterhaus, is stranded as again the bridge breaks. Despite the shortage of manpower, General Sherman requests permission to engage the enemy with his three divisions that have crossed and General Jefferson C. Davis' division of the Fourteenth Corps. Sherman receives an affirmative response; General Osterhaus is directed to have his division join with General Joseph Hooker, who will be assaulting Lookout Mountain as a diversion. Also, by about noon, Union engineers complete the laying of two spans (pontoon bridges) across the Tennessee and the South Chickamauga Rivers; the former stretches 1,400 feet and the latter 200 feet. Eight thousand troops are in place, but as the day continues, the remainder of Sherman's force also arrives. Sherman soon after determines that the positions are invulnerable. A contingent of cavalry under Colonel (later general) Eli Long moves out and successfully severs the railroad, eliminating another possible source of trouble. The Union forces of Grant now hold strategic positions. General George H. Thomas has about 25,000 troops and about 5,000 of these are crossing the river at a point about

six miles above Chattanooga, from where they will assault Missionary Ridge. The steamboat USS *Dunbar* (formerly Confederate) transports about 6,000 troops across the river by day's end.

In other activity, elements of the 1st Tennessee Regiment and the 9th Pennsylvania Cavalry skirmish with Confederates at Sparta. The Union reports no casualties. The Confederates sustain one killed and two wounded.

November 24–25   The Battle of Lookout Mountain and the Battle of Missionary Ridge U.S. Grant, in a bold, daring move, has driven across the mountains and now prepares to over-run enemy positions and force the Confederates to end their siege of Chattanooga, Tennessee. Grant selects Orchard Knob to establish his headquarters as he begins his offensive against Missionary Ridge on November 25.

At 0200 on the 24th, General Giles A. Smith moves out of North Chickamauga with a force of 1,500. A pontoon bridge is constructed to allow Sherman's force to cross the Tennessee River and prepare his assault against Missionary Ridge. Colonel (later general) William Grose's brigade seizes the bridges, crosses the creek and captures the pickets, securing a safe crossing for General Osterhaus' troops.

At about 1300, Sherman's forces, commanded by General Francis P. Blair, advance during a pesky rain. General Hugh Ewing's division operates on the right while General Morgan L. Smith's division holds the left. The center force is led by General John E. Smith. Soon a ferocious skirmish occurs and the Confederates hold tightly on the first ridge. The Union discovers a deep hollow that stands between them and the hill that contains a tunnel. It is decided to hold in place until the following morning.

Left: **Battle of Lookout Mountain (Johnson, *Campfire and Battlefield: History of the Conflicts and Campaigns*, 1894).** *Right:* **The crest of Lookout Mountain (*Harper's Pictoral History of the Civil War*, 1896).**

Left: Old Glory atop the summit of Lookout Mountain. *Right:* A Confederate battery on Lookout Mountain (*Harper's Pictoral History of the Civil War*, 1896).

In the meantime, the Confederates attempt to catch the Yankees off guard. During the afternoon, a rousing charge is offered against the lines of Sherman's troops, who remain focused on establishing defenses. Nonetheless, they react with a fervor that checks the assault and prompts the Confederates to discontinue the attack. By about dusk, the Rebels withdraw to their positions near the tunnel.

At Lookout Mountain, where a deep fog hovers above the imminent field of battle, Hooker's force is held up due to the lack of a bridge. While it is under construction, Hooker dispatches General John Geary to Lookout Creek. Once there, Geary's command is met and engaged by troops under Confederate General Bushrod Johnson, who commands a colossal line of earthworks that extends along the entire ridge and dominates the approach routes from either the Lookout or Chattanooga Valleys. Undaunted, Geary advances and reaches the right bank. By this time the bridge is complete and the forces of Generals William Grose and Thomas J. Wood move out to join him.

General Hooker also deploys a large amount of artillery to cover the anticipated assault. Once the advance is initiated, the Yankees encounter tenacious opposition. Meanwhile, the remainder of Hooker's force also crosses and joins the attack. By about 1300, the Confederates are driven back from the crest, but the dense fog paralyzes any further advance. Hooker decides to hold his positions rather than blindly shoot it out in the pea soup fog.

Early on the 25th, the Yankees are back on the attack. General Sherman's troops step off, utilizing his left and right wings under Generals Hugh Ewing and Morgan L. Smith respectively, to advance on the east and west of Missionary Ridge. Sherman's troops hit resistance

raised by Generals Benjamin F. Cheatham, Patrick Clebourne, States Rights Gist, William Joseph Hardee and Carter Stevenson. Meanwhile, Hooker also experiences difficulty in unfolding his diversionary assault against Lookout Mountain. The problem is duly noted by General George H. Thomas, who speeds from Orchard Knob, bringing with him the center of the Union force composed of the divisions of Generals Absalom Baird, Richard W. Johnson, Philip Sheridan and Thomas J. Wood.

Soon the Yankees receive the order to charge, and they unleash a powerful blow that places them at the foot of a strongly reinforced ridge and in the middle of a raging firestorm of fire and clashing steel. General Bragg's efforts to bolster the forces here are insufficient to halt the propelling Yankees. Grim and gruesome hand-to-hand fighting ensues. Finally the Rebels are compelled to seek higher ground, but the Yankees remain right on their heels. The two sides intermingle as they relentlessly club each other along the slopes.

The Rebels make flight for the crest and the Union troops are ordered to hold their positions. The order is considered unhealthy, as the Rebels crank up about fifty pieces of artillery that are scattered about the heights and pummel the Yankees where they hold. Rather than remain under incessant fire, the infantry quickly abandon their positions and charge toward the crest, ignoring the riveting fire and the order to remain in place.

The troops from General Sheridan's command are the first to hit the summit, but many others are close behind. Within a short while the entire mountain is immersed in combat, as the crest is swollen with tattered blue and gray uniforms. Heavy fighting ensues at more than five separate points on the mountain. The forces

of both Sheridan and Thomas continue to pound the Rebels until finally regiment after regiment becomes demoralized. The Yankees capitalize on the confusion within the Confederate ranks and seize huge numbers of troops. Relentlessly, the Union continues to hammer the weary Rebels. With their newly captured batteries, the Union pivots the guns and propels additional firepower against the Rebels as they attempt to retreat under a steel firestorm that rivets the slopes. Sheridan's forces give hot pursuit. The chase proves profitable, and the Yankees soon capture another eight guns at yet another strategic strongpoint. The Rebels also abandon a huge supply of arms and ammunition.

Back at Lookout Mountain, Hooker dispatches reconnaissance units to check out the remaining enemy strength on the crest. The Yankees discover that the Rebels had evacuated during the night. By dawn on the 25th, elements of the 8th Kentucky Regiment, without incident, hoist the Stars and Stripes at the highest most dominant part of the summit. Hooker, at about 1000, receives orders to pursue Bushrod Johnson as he attempts to get to Rossville. The chase is suspended when the troops reach Chattanooga Creek and discover that the Rebels have destroyed the bridge.

At about 1400, the main Union attack commences along a two-mile line when twenty-two pieces of artillery bellow the signal to advance against the formidable Confederate positions at Missionary Ridge. The Union's charge is met at some points by fierce fire and at others, uncharacteristically, the Confederates bolt from their positions and flee. The Union doggedly ascends the slopes and manages to plant the Stars and Stripes, followed shortly thereafter by a series of identical implants. Old Glory is sprouting up all along the summit.

In the meantime, General Grant is making his way to the top of the mountain, while General Bragg is abandoning his headquarters. The Union, now controlling this dominant height and the Confederate artillery upon it, pivots the guns and turns them upon the Rebels to inflict more severe punishment. The wall of fire shreds the log emplacements of the Rebels. In the meantime, another Union contingent, climbing the slopes to the right of this center assault, also gains the summit and prompts the Rebels to hurriedly descend the slopes. Hooker's troops maneuver into position and seize many of these Confederates. The fighting subsides by dusk, but the darkness of night also forbids the Union from mounting a pursuit.

While the main body is overcoming General Bragg's resistance on Missionary Ridge, Hooker's contingents are still engaged with the Rebels under Bushrod Johnson, who had fled from Lookout Mountain. General Joseph Osterhaus had sprinted ahead at Chattanooga Creek while a crossing was being built, and his column snags many Confederates outside of Rossville. The forces of Thomas J. Wood and James A. Williamson arrive soon and overwhelm the Rebels, compelling them to make flight hurriedly and leaving no time for them to take their supplies or wagons. The flight is not effortless. The Union relentlessly pursues the Rebels during their haphazard retreat.

Meanwhile, General Geary moves toward the valley west of Missionary Ridge, while General Joseph Osterhaus heads east and Charles Cruft moves straight up the center. Each are on a collision course with Rebels under Lt. General Alexander Peter Stewart (West Point, 1842), who had taken up residence in the defenses that General Thomas had constructed subsequent to the battle at Chickamauga. These Confederates take a severe beating as a thunderous charge is unleashed. The thrust of the Union is so powerful that the Confederates break in many directions in a desperate race to escape death or capture. Nonetheless, the Rebels are swept up in a whirlwind of action. Geary's forces scoop up large numbers and those who evade capture fall into the hands of either Joseph Osterhaus or

General Joseph Hooker attacks Confederate positions on Lookout Mountain (*Harper's Pictoral History of the Civil War*, 1896). 327) Lookout Mountain.

Charles Cruft during this incessant confrontation that lasts throughout the day and into the night.

Following the blistering defeat, General Bragg heads for Dalton, Georgia, by way of Ringgold. By dawn on the 26th, the Confederates have withdrawn from the front of Sherman's lines and the situation is stable, allowing part of General Thomas' force to be dispatched to Knoxville to support General Burnside's beleaguered forces.

This brilliant maneuver and victory by General Grant at Missionary Ridge secures the entire area for the Union and gives it control of the Mississippi River. The Yankees are now positioned for the next step, the march by General Sherman across Georgia to the sea, where he is to link with the U.S. Navy offshore, thus further splitting the Confederacy. The railroad, formerly held by the Confederates in Chattanooga, is also in the hands of the Union.

The Union participants include the 4th and 11th Corps, Army of the Cumberland, Major General George H. Thomas, 11th Corps, General Geary's Division of the 12th Corps, elements of General McPherson's XV Corps, Army of the Tennessee, Major General William T. Sherman. General Charles L. Matthies sustains a bullet wound in his head; however, he survives. By February 1864, he receives temporary command of the XV Corps at Cleveland, Tennessee. Nonetheless, by spring, his health deteriorates and he is relieved of field duty and assigned to Decatur, Alabama. Also, subsequent to this action, Major General Carl Schurz is relieved of field command and given command of a recruit depot in Nashville. Later in the year, he is attached to the staff of General Slocum during the campaign in the Carolinas. After the war he engages in the publishing industry and serves one term in the U.S. Senate.

The Union sustains 757 killed, 4,529 wounded and 330 missing. The Confederates suffer 361 killed, 2,181 wounded and 6,142 missing. These losses include those at Lookout Mountain on the 24th and Missionary Ridge on the 25th. Union Generals William Sherman, Philip Sheridan and Joe Hooker participate in this victory. Also, Sergeant Norman F. Potter, 149th New York Infantry, captures the battle flag of Bragg's army. Potter becomes a recipient of the Medal of Honor for his gallantry during this action. Also, Colonel Henry Barnum (149th New York), recently recovered from injuries, remains in the thick of the battle; he also receives the Medal of Honor (July 1889) because of his extraordinary heroism during the battle. Barnum's regiment captures one-half of the battle flags seized

during the engagement. General George H. Thompson designates Barnum with the task of transporting the captured flags to Washington, D.C. After its return to Georgia, the 149th Regiment participates in the campaign to seize Atlanta.

Union General Samuel Thomas Beatty participates, leading a brigade of General Thomas Woods' division, General Gordon Granger's IV Corps. The 19th, 22nd, 25th, 39th, and 50th Alabama Regiments, the 17th Alabama Battalion Sharpshooters and Dent's Alabama Artillery (Brigadier General Zachariah Cantey Deas' Brigade) captures 17 artillery pieces. Deas' brigade continues to fight as part of the Army of Tennessee; however, General Deas will take ill during the brigade's participation in the Carolinas the following spring, which impedes the Alabama Brigade. Nonetheless, it remains in the field until the close of hostilities in North Carolina. Also, Confederate Colonel Robert C. Tyler sustains a severe wound, which costs him one of his legs. Tyler continues to serve following his recovery and becomes a brigadier general in February.

November 25 (Wednesday)   In North Carolina, a Union force, including elements of the 12th New York Cavalry, 1st North Carolina Volunteers, and the 24th New York Battery, commanded by Captain Graham, attack a Confederate encampment at Greenville. It is reported that about 50 Confederates are captured and 100 guns are seized.

In Naval activity, the USS *Fort Hindman,* operating in the vicinity of Natchez Island, Mississippi, encounters and seizes the Confederate transport *Volunteer.* It is commissioned the USS *Volunteer,* after being acquired by the U.S. Navy in February 1864. The *Volunteer* had initially been constructed in Monongahela, Pennsylvania, as a stern-wheel river steamer for commercial use. In the service of the Union, the *Volunteer* performs patrol duty as a gunboat. It participates in the defense of Fort Pillow when attacked by Rebels under General Nathan Bedford Forrest the following April. It remains active until the close of hostilities. It is decommissioned during August 1865 and sold during November 1865, then renamed *Talisman,* when it initiates operations as a civilian vessel and remains in service until about 1872.

November 26 (Thursday)   In Louisiana, elements of the 31st Massachusetts Volunteer Regiment and the 4th Massachusetts Battery skirmish with Confederates at Bonfouca.

In North Carolina, a Union force, composed of about 400 troops (unit not specified), skirmishes with Confederate contingent at Warm Springs.

In Tennessee, General Sherman initiates pursuit of Bragg; his force departs by the Dalton Railroad at Chickamauga Station. Sherman orders General Howard to destroy the rails stretching between Dalton and Cleveland in an effort to sever Bragg's route to Knoxville. General Hooker heads for Ringgold, Georgia, where his force encounters strong resistance by a force under General Patrick Cleburne. In other activity, a cavalry contingent of the Army of the Tennessee skirmishes with Confederates at Kingston. Other Union troops attached to the Alabama and Tennessee Scouts, led by Captain Brixir, skirmish with Confederates at Bersheeba Springs. Fifteen Confederates are captured. Also, elements of the 1st Tennessee and the 9th Pennsylvania Cavalry Regiments, led by Lt. Colonel Brownlow, engage a Confederate force under Colonel John P. Murray at Sparta.

In Virginia, at dawn, General George G. Meade's Army of the Potomac moves toward the lower fords of the Rapidan. General Lee counters by moving his force to Spotsylvania Court House. At this time, Lee is deployed at Morton's Ford along the Rapidan. However, the fords at Ely's, Culpeper, Mine, Germanna and Jacob's Mills are unprotected, giving Meade an auspicious opportunity. General Richard S. Ewell's corps is posted from Morton's Ford to Orange Court House, while General A.P. Hill's Corps is positioned south of it and holding ground along the rails to a point near Charlottesville, but between the two forces a several mile gap exists.

In Naval activity, the USS *Antona,* under the command of Acting Master Alfred L.B. Zerega, seizes a blockade runner, the *Mary Ann.* The cargo, a shipment of cotton en route to Tampico, Mexico, is transferred to the *Bermuda.* The *Mary Lee,* which is taking on water and sinking, is destroyed.

November 26–28 In Virginia, Union troops, including the 90th Pennsylvania Infantry, Army of the Potomac, and 1st and 2nd Cavalry Divisions, skirmish at Bartlett's Mills, Mine Run, Locust Grove, Locust Run, New Hope and Robertson's Tavern. Both sides suffer about 100 dead and 400 wounded each. Union General Albion Parris Howe participates in this action, but following the fighting around Mine Run, he is transferred with command of the Union artillery depot, and he receives responsibility for the Office of the Inspector of Artillery in Washington, D.C. The move is apparently done at the request of either General Grant or General John Sedgwick to remove him from his infantry command. General Henry Prince participates at this engagement as part of General French's corps. Afterward, General Prince is assigned primarily to garrison duty in Alabama, South Carolina and Tennessee. Later he receives the brevet of brigadier general in the Regular Army. After the war he is assigned as deputy paymaster general with the rank of lieutenant colonel. He retires on 31 December 1879. He commits suicide in his hotel room on 19 August 1892 in London.

November 27 (Friday) In Georgia, General U.S. Grant, having successfully lifted the siege of Chattanooga, arrives at Ringgold (20 miles east of Chattanooga), taking note of the enemy's retreat and that most of their supplies have been left behind. Although the Rebels retreated, their cavalry remains in the hills around Ringgold.

General Hooker's command engages a force of General Cleburne's tenacious troops and sustains heavy casualties, but the Union continues pressing, finally driving Patrick Cleburne's command from the area. Northern forces capture more than 200 prisoners and three cannon. In other activity, Confederate General Claudius Wilson dies of fever at Ringgold. Wilson had only recently been informed of his promotion to brigadier general. His commission is awarded posthumously by the Confederate Senate during February 1864.

In Tennessee, the Union troops are safe in their positions and make Knoxville the next priority. They prepare to remove the siege against General Ambrose Burnside and to expel the Rebels from the area. In related activity, General Sherman directs General Howard to destroy the rails (Atlanta Railroad) from Graysville (Greysville) to the border with Georgia. Also, the 2nd Brigade, 2nd Cavalry Division, captures 200 Confederates at Cleveland. Skirmishes also occur at Pea Vine Creek. The divisions of Union Generals Richard W. Johnson (14th Corps), Joseph Osterhaus (15th Corps) and John Geary (12th Corps) participate.

In Virginia, General Lee informs Confederate President Davis by telegram of Union General Meade's movement toward Chancellorsville. Lee also informs Davis that he will counter with a move of his own intended to turn Meade's right flank. In other action, Confederate troops successfully repulse a Union attack at Raccoon Ford, forcing the Union to withdraw without progress. Meade's Army had begun to cross the Rapidan on the previous day, but complications had developed impeding the operation; General French's 3rd Corps is behind schedule and another snafu is that the pontoon bridges had been too short to span the river.

In Texas, elements of the Union 1st and 2nd Divisions, 13th Corps, under General C.C. Washburn, engage Confederates at Fort Esperanza. The Confederates self-destruct the fort and subsequently, the Union occupies it by the 30th. The Union sustains one killed and two wounded. The Confederates sustain one killed.

November 28 (Saturday) In Kentucky, the 6th Illinois Cavalry clashes with Confederate cavalry at Louisville.

In Tennessee, the Union halts its pursuit of General Bragg's forces. General Hooker and General John M. Palmer shortly return to Chattanooga. Sherman continues to push reconnaissance units toward the Hiawassee River. In other activity, General Burnside transfers his headquarters from Knoxville to Loudon, but when the danger of a

large Confederate attack passes, he moves back to Knoxville (31st). During his absence, Knoxville, under the supervision of Captain O.M. Poe, is being heavily fortified in anticipation of a huge enemy assault. Burnside had recently conferred with Asst. Secretary of War, Charles A. Dana and General James H. Wilson while they had been visiting with him at Knoxville. In conjunction, intelligence reports soon ascertain that about 12,000 infantry troops and 5,000 cavalry had been detached from Bragg for the express purpose of moving against Burnside.

In Virginia, General Robert E. Lee writes in a telegram to General Sam Cooper, the inspector general of Confederate States of America: "Union whole force is on road to Orange Court House [Virginia]. His progress was successfully resisted."

November 29 (Sunday) In Tennessee, Union troops under General Burnside defend Fort Sanders at Knoxville against a major Confederate assault by troops attached to General James Longstreet. At midnight 28th–29th, following the cessation of an artillery bombardment, which had begun on November 17th and continued incessantly, the Rebels launch an attack to seize the fort, which is just outside Knoxville at a strategic spot that dominates the Kingston Road. It is defended by the 29th Massachusetts and the 79th New York Regiments and by elements of the 20th Michigan and the 2nd and 20th Massachusetts Regiments. The Confederates attack with great vigor and attempt to scale the walls to overwhelm the defenders. Undaunted by the intense Union fire, the Confederate units, including contingents of the brigades of George T. Anderson, Goode Bryan and Benjamin G. Humphreys, charge the fort. And even more strength is gathered as Lafayette McLaws' division has committed two brigades, under Colonel William Phillips (Phillips' Legion) and Brigadier General William T. Wofford (Cobb's old brigade). Nonetheless, the effective fire of Colonel Ed-

Fort Sanders under attack by Confederates (Guernsey, *Harper's Pictoral History of the Civil War,* 1884).

ward Ferrero's guns, combined with the batteries of Captain Jacob Roemer and Lt. Samuel Benjamin, the Confederates are handily repelled. They are unable to scale the walls, nor are they able to crack the defiance of the defenders. The Union holds firmly but continues to rip into the Confederate ranks. Confederate Major General Lafayette McLaws is relieved of command for "failing to make proper preparations," but President Davis restores him to duty. Fort Sanders is called Fort Loudon by the Confederates.

The Confederate attack is plagued with problems and the defeat is severe enough for General Bragg that he also resigns his commission on the following day. The implanted colors of the 51st Georgia Infantry are captured by a contingent of the 79th New York Infantry, which promptly carries the flag into the fort. Sergeant Mahoney of the 29th Massachusetts duplicates the effort by capturing the flag of the 17th Mississippi Infantry. The Confederates sustain severe losses against the Union losses of about twenty. General Burnside offers and the Rebels accept an proposal to move upon the field between 1000 and 1700 to retrieve the wounded and dead. Following this defeat, Confederate General Longstreet concludes that he must terminate the siege of Knoxville. Longstreet pulls up and moves toward Virginia; however, his forces continue to harass the Union positions in Tennessee throughout the foreseeable future. Longstreet does not link up with General Lee in Virginia until the next spring.

November 30 (Monday) In Kentucky, a Union contingent of the 14th Kentucky Volunteer Regiment skirmishes with Confederates at Salyersville.

In Louisiana, Union and Confederate contingents clash at Vermilion Bayou.

In Tennessee, Confederate General Braxton Bragg resigns his commission in the Confederate Army.

In Texas, the Confederates defending Fort Esperanza at Pass Cavallo apparently conclude that their positions within the stronghold are no longer tenable. The troops detonate the powder magazine and evacuate the fort to prevent the Union forces of General Cadwallader C. Washburn from seizing the ammunition. The garrison escapes to the mainland. The Union, having gained control of the pass that overlooks Matagorda Bay, widens its activity. The gunboats *Estrella* and *Granite City* move inward along the peninsula. General Nathaniel Banks, satisfied that he has gained a strategic foothold in Texas, returns to New Orleans to make plans for the next step in seizing control of Texas. General Napoleon J.T. Dana remains behind to hold the Rio Grande River, while Banks lays plans to conquer Galveston and the Confederate stronghold at the mouth of the Brazos River. While Banks prepares for the next operation, he receives instructions from General Halleck that divert his attention from Galveston. Halleck states that a new mission will be launched to seize Texas by implementing a combined naval-

ground assault along the Red River, specifically against Shreveport, Louisiana, defended by the forces under Major General Richard Taylor. Shreveport lies on the line separating Louisiana from Texas. Halleck also tells Banks that he will receive reinforcements from General Grant's army to bolster the effort. At this time, in addition to the forces under Richard Taylor, General Sterling Price has his forces deployed at Monroe, Louisiana, and the lines stretch from there to Arkadelphia, Arkansas.

In Virginia, a rainstorm has been saturating the area where the Army of Northern Virginia and the Union Army of the Potomac are encamped, thus preventing skirmishing since the 28th, but now, both sides are preparing to take action. Union artillery blasts enemy positions but does not initiate an attack. When General John Sedgwick's artillery commences firing, there is no accompanying fire from the guns of General Gouverneur Kemble Warren, the latter having spotted Lee's strength and concluded that an attack would be fruitless. Subsequently, when General Meade is informed of the situation, he concurs with Warren's decision and the attack is canceled. On the following night, Meade retires to his old positions and there is no pursuit by the Confederates. The Confederate 25th Virginia Infantry participates in this action.

December 1 (Tuesday) In Tennessee, the Union 5th Minnesota Volunteer Regiment, attached to the 15th Army Corps, is transferred (this month) to the 2nd Brigade, 1st Division, 16th Army Corps. In November 1864, it again will be transferred and become attached to a detachment of the 2nd Brigade, 1st Division, Army of the Tennessee (Department of the Cumberland).

In Virginia, the Union at Mine Run begins preparations to withdraw from its positions, following General George Meade's decision of the previous day to cancel the imminent attack. During the operations along the Rappahannock and Mine Run, General Grant becomes impatient with the lack of aggressiveness of General Sykes. Consequently, before the end of the year, Sykes is relieved and transferred to the Department of Kansas, where he remains for the duration of the war. In 1866 he reverts to his regular rank of lieutenant colonel with the 5th Infantry. During 1868, he becomes colonel of the 20th Infantry. He succumbs at Fort Brown, Texas, on 8 February 1880.

In Mississippi, the 2nd Brigade of Cavalry (Stephen A. Hurlbut's 16th Corps, Army of the Tennessee), commanded by General Edward Hatch, clashes with Confederates at Ripley and Moscow Station (Wolf River Bridge). In addition, the cavalry force engages Confederates at Salisbury. The Union abandons the town on the 3rd. The Union sustains 175 casualties, including killed and wounded. The Confederates sustain fifteen killed and about forty wounded.

In Naval activity, the USS *Dawn* is transferred from the South Atlantic Blockading Squadron to the North Atlantic Blockading Squadron at about this time (December). The *Dawn* has just completed repairs that have kept it out of service for about five months. It departs from New York to join the squadron and initiate patrols on the James River and other waterways in Virginia. It is decommissioned during July 1865 and renamed *Eutaw.* As a merchant vessel it remains operational until it is wrecked during December 1889. Also, the U.S. Navy acquires the *Countess,* a side-wheeled river boat at about this time (December). It is renamed the *Elk* and transformed into a tinclad gunboat, the USS *Elk* (Tinclad No. 47) and commissioned during May 1863. The *Elk,* assigned to the West Gulf Blockading Squadron, operates in the Gulf of Mexico and along the lower Mississippi River for the duration of the war. It is sold in August 1865. Afterward, it is renamed the *Countess* and operates as a commercial vessel. During 1868, it sinks. In other activity, the steamer USS *Vicksburg,* acquired by the U.S. Navy the previous October, is commissioned at about this time (December). The *Vicksburg* was originally built in Mystic, Connecticut, for use as a commercial ship. Having been transformed into a warship, it is initially assigned to inspection service at New York Harbor and vicinity. Nevertheless, during February 1864, it is transferred

Positions of the armies of General George Meade and General Robert E. Lee at Mine Run on 1 December 1863 (Mottelay, *The Soldier in Our Civil War,* 1886).

to the North Atlantic Blockading Squadron. It is sent to Annapolis during July for a short period when the Confederates threaten the town. Afterward, it returns to blockade duty, and then it participates in the operations against Fort Fisher, North Carolina, in December 1864 and January 1865.

December 2 (Wednesday) Confederate President Jefferson Davis replaces General Braxton Bragg with Lt. General William J. Hardee as commander of the Confederate Army of Tennessee.

In Virginia, the Union Army withdraws across the Rapidan. General Meade begins to establish positions for the winter. Meanwhile, Confederates under General A.P. Hill advance eight miles along the Plank Road. Confederate Generals Early and Stuart advance to Germanna Ford, but the Union has already withdrawn, unknown to the Rebels.

In West Virginia, the U.S. 5th Indiana Cavalry dispatches Pvt. Louis Bruner behind Confederate lines at Walker's Ford to reach Union troops with instructions to prevent them from being captured; Bruner becomes a recipient of the Medal of Honor for his heroism during this dangerous mission. The Union 65th, 116th and 118th Indiana Regiments and the 21st Ohio Battery, as well as the 5th Indiana Cavalry and the 14th Illinois Cavalry, participate in this heated skirmish. The Union sustains nine killed and thirty-nine wounded. The Confederates suffer twenty-five killed and fifty wounded.

December 3 (Thursday) **In Tennessee,** Confederate Major General James Longstreet initiates his retreat from Knoxville toward Greeneville, where he will establish his winter quarters. Longstreet's withdrawal gives the Union forces control of Tennessee. Meanwhile, Union reinforcements are soon on their way from Chattanooga. After Knoxville is saved, Union General Sherman returns to his camp outside Chattanooga and later, from there, he moves to northern Alabama to establish winter quarters. In the meantime, General U.S. Grant prepares to vanquish the Confederates at Atlanta.

In Confederate general officer activity, Colonel Robert Vinkler Richardson is promoted to the rank of brigadier general, effective this date. Nonetheless, in February of the following year, his commission seems to have been pulled by the Confederate Senate. Richardson, however, maintains his service in the Confederacy leading his regiment under the command of General James R. Chalmers (District of Mississippi and East Louisiana). On 5 January 1870, while at a tavern in Clarkton, Missouri, he is fatally wounded, but his assassin in never identified.

In Naval activity, the USS *Adolph Huger,* attached to the Potomac Flotilla, seizes the schooner *F.U. Johnson,* which is transporting a cargo that includes liquor. In other activity, the USS *Kansas* is commissioned at about this time (December). The *Kansas,* built in Philadelphia, is assigned to the North Atlantic Blockading

Squadron. It will operate primarily off the coasts of North Carolina, but also in Virginia.

December 4 (Friday) **In Nebraska,** one company of the 7th Iowa Cavalry skirmishes with Confederates at Niobrara.

In Virginia, the Union army under Brigadier General George Meade, having withdrawn across the Rapidan, is now fortifying positions on his old lines along the Rappahannock. General Lee, on the opposite bank, is disappointed because the Union had not launched an attack. Lee had been extremely confident because the terrain his forces hold is more favorable to defense.

In Tennessee, Union Major General John G. Parke's command pursues General Longstreet's forces, which are en route from Knoxville to Rogersville by way of Rutledge. During the mission, Parke dispatches General James M. Shackelford's force to continue the pursuit. The Confederates reach Rogersville on the 9th; however, Longstreet reverses himself and moves back to take Bean's Station, where General Shackelford's cavalry deploys.

In Union general officer activity, Brigadier General Green Clay Smith, having been elected to Congress the previous month, resigns his commission. He resigns from Congress during 1866 to become governor of the Montana Territory. General Smith had also received the brevet of major general of volunteers for his service during the war.

In Confederate general officer activity, Confederate Brigadier General Nathan Bedford Forrest is promoted to the rank of major general.

December 5 (Saturday) **In Maryland,** Union Brigadier General Henry H. Lockwood is appointed commander of the Middle Military Department. He succeeds Major General Robert C. Schenck and holds the position until 22 March 1864.

In South Carolina, Georgetown is devastated by fire.

In Naval activity, the USS *Governor Buckingham* departs from Hampton Roads. It sails to join the South Atlantic Blockading Squadron off Wilmington, North Carolina.

In Union general officer activity, Major General Robert C. Schenck, who sustained a debilitating wound at Second Manassas (Bull Run), and presently, commander of the Middle Department, resigns from the service to take his seat once again in the U.S. Congress. In 1870, he loses his bid for re-election. However, President Ulysses S. Grant appoints him as minister to London. After his return to the United States, he dies on 23 March 1890.

December 6 (Sunday) **In South Carolina,** the USS *Weehawken* sinks accidentally off Morris Island near Charleston. Other vessels attempt rescue, but the ship is overloaded with ammunition. It takes on water through its ports and goes down. More than thirty officers and enlisted men aboard are lost. The *Weehawken*

had been part of the Union Blockading Squadron that stands off Charleston.

In Tennessee, a contingent of Union cavalry (Army of the Ohio) under General John G. Foster attacks a Confederate cavalry force at Clinch Mountain. Also, a Union cavalry reconnaissance force, led by Major Rufus Scott, initiates a mission in the vicinity of Madison Court House. The column encounters a small group of pickets at James City and quickly scatters them. Afterward, Scott proceeds to Thoroughfare Mountain and disables a signal station there, and then the column moves to the Robertson's River. Scott concludes that only some small Confederate scouting parties are operating on the Union side of the Rapidan. No Confederate forces are encountered at Madison Court House. In related activity, the Union notes that the cavalry of Confederate Major General Fitzhugh Lee is operating on the opposite bank of the Rapidan in the vicinity of Wickham's Mills.

In Naval activity, Union blockade ships, including the USS *Aries,* seize the steamer *Ceres* off Wilmington, North Carolina. In December, the *Aries* participates in salvaging a stranded blockade runner, the *Antonica,* which is then destroyed by the Union gunboats.

December 7 (Monday) **In Washington, D.C.,** President Lincoln suggests by proclamation that all loyal Americans observe a day of thanksgiving in view of the recent victories of the Union armies.

In Kentucky and Tennessee, the Union 13th Kentucky Cavalry skirmishes with Confederates at Creelsboro, Kentucky, and at Celina, Tennessee. Union casualties are unavailable. The Confederates sustain 15 killed.

In Mississippi, one company of the 4th Iowa Cavalry skirmishes with Confederates at Natchez.

In Massachusetts, the steamship *Chesapeake,* while off Cape Cod during a regular run between New York and Portland, Maine, is suddenly seized by fifteen Confederates led by John C. Braine. All had boarded the ship posing as passengers. During the struggle to seize the vessel, the second engineer is shot and killed and the first mate is wounded. Braine confronts Captain Willets with an order (letter of marque) from Captain John Parker (real name is V.G. Locke, a British citizen) of the CSS *Retribution,* the officer who ordered the seizure of the *Chesapeake.*

After gaining control of the ship, Braine sails to Grand Menan, an island off the coast of Maine, to rendezvous with Parker; however, the latter had already separated from the *Retribution* in Nassau and did not arrive to meet Braine. Afterward, the *Chesapeake* sails toward Shelburne, Nova Scotia, to refuel. En route the ship is intercepted in the Bay of Fundy by a pilot boat carrying Captain Parker. He assumes command of the vessel and uses the pilot boat to carry the crew and Captain Willets to St. John's, Nova Scotia.

In the meantime, a U.S. squadron had been dispatched to recapture the ship. One of the six pursuit vessels, the *Ella and Annie* (USS *Malvern*), discovers the ship in the vicinity of Halifax in Sambro Harbor on the 17th. The Confederates abscond and make it to shore, permitting the vessel to be regained with little effort, but the rescue had been too late to save the crew, except for the engineer, whom the Confederates coerced into their service. Nearby, a gunboat, the British schooner *Investigator*, becomes involved and its captain discovers one of the Confederates aboard his vessel. The *Chesapeake* is taken to Halifax, but the man who was seized is able to escape with help from southern sympathizers. Several other members of Parker's contingent are seized, but the authorities later release them on the basis that piracy is not a valid reason for extradition.

After an appeal, the case is heard by the Supreme Court, but it, too, through the ruling of Judge Ritchie, releases the Confederates (10 March 1864) on the claim that "that no proper requisition had been made for their extradition; that piracy was not an extraditable offence; that a magistrate had no jurisdiction over questions of piracy, and that the warrant was bad on its face." In the meantime, Braine and Parker had fled British jurisdiction during December 1863. They reappear on 29 September 1864 when Parker duplicates his escapade that seized the *Chesapeake*.

December 8 (Tuesday) In Washington, D.C., President Lincoln issues an amnesty proclamation offering full pardon to any and all Confederate soldiers willing to take an oath of loyalty to the Union. Exceptions are Union soldiers who resigned to join the South and all high-ranking Confederate officials.

In Arkansas, a contingent of Union cavalry skirmishes with Confederates at Princeton.

In Naval activity, a "screw, steam schooner-rigged tug" built in East Boston, Massachusetts, and launched as the *Vicksburg* during September 1863, is acquired by the U.S. Navy during October 1863 and on this day is commissioned the USS *Acacia*. Acting Master John D. Childs receives command.

In Virginia, Union General William W. Averell's raid into Southwest Virginia gathers 200 Confederate prisoners between this day and the 21st. The Union losses are six dead and five wounded. Averell's force includes the 2nd, 3rd, 4th and 8th West Virginia Mounted Infantry, the 14th Pennsylvania Battery, Dodson's Battery and Battery G, West Virginia Artillery. The force is also augmented by cavalry.

December 9 (Wednesday) In Tennessee, Union Major General J.G. Foster replaces General Ambrose Burnside as commander of the Union troops (Army of the Ohio) at Knoxville. General Burnside resigns, but it had been his decision.

In Virginia, General Robert E. Lee meets with President Jefferson Davis in Richmond, remaining there until the 21st. During these talks, Lee suggests that General Beauregard be sent "to

command the Western Armies." Nevertheless, Davis appoints General Joseph E. Johnston. Also at Richmond, Brigadier General Daniel Marsh Frost is removed from the Army roster. He apparently quit without officially giving notice earlier this year when his family was forced to leave their home near St. Louis by irate citizens opposed to Frost's service with the Confederates. After the war, Frost returns to Missouri from Canada.

In Naval activity, the recently commissioned USS *Acacia* is making preparations to join the South Atlantic Blockading Squadron when orders arrive for it to join in pursuit of the Confederates who seized the *Chesapeake* on the 7th and are en route to Canada. The *Acacia* departs by 1600 to give pursuit. Shortly thereafter, it discovers a severe problem. It begins to take on water at an alarming rate. The *Acacia* begins to sink, but makes its way back to Portland, Maine. Once there, with the quick action of the fire department, the *Acacia* is secured to a wharf and is saved from sinking in the harbor. After receiving repairs, the *Acacia* does arrive at Halifax, where it delivers witnesses to appear against the Confederates who had captured the *Chesapeake*. Following this duty, it resumes preparations to join the squadron and finally arrives at Morris Island, South Carolina, on 6 January 1864.

December 10 (Thursday) In Washington, D.C., President Lincoln states in a telegram to General Grant his pleasure at the victories at Chattanooga and Knoxville: "I wish to tender to you and all under your command, my more than thanks, my profoundest gratitude for the skill, courage, and perseverance with which you and they, over so great difficulties, have effected that great object. God bless you all. God bless you all."

In Tennessee, a brigade of Union cavalry (Union General James Shackelford's cavalry division, Army of the Ohio) led by Colonel William Emory B. Bond engages Confederates under General Longstreet at Morristown (Bean's Station) through the 14th. Colonel Israel Garrard's brigade participates. The Union sustains about 700 killed or wounded. The Confederates suffer 932 killed or wounded and 150 captured. This series of fights terminates the Knoxville campaign. The Confederates move to Russellville and establish their winter quarters. The following month, General Shackelford resigns from the army and returns to Kentucky to resumes his law practice.

In Confederate general officer activity, Brigadier General John C. Moore is assigned to command the Eastern and Western Districts of the Department of the Gulf; however, Moore resigns his commission in February.

December 11 (Friday) In South Carolina, the Union continues to relentlessly shell the Confederate defenders at Fort Sumter. Nonetheless, the incessant stream of in-coming shells does not humble the defiant defenders. The Stars and Bars continues to fly over the now crumbled walls of the fort.

December 12 (Saturday) In Washington, D.C., the authorities are informed by Union General Benjamin F. Butler that the Confederates in Richmond refuse to accept any additional supplies for the Union prisoners. Sentiment in the North is already at a high pitch because of the shoddy treatment given Union prisoners, and this compounds the anger.

In Arkansas, the 8th Missouri Cavalry Regiment skirmishes with Confederates at Duvall's Bluff. Casualty figures are unavailable.

In West Virginia, Union troops under General Eliakim P. Scammon repulse a Confederate attack led by General John Echols at Lewisburg. Also, the 12th Ohio Volunteer Regiment skirmishes with Confederates at Big Sewell and Meadow Bluff.

December 13 (Sunday) In Tennessee, General U.S. Grant issues an order regarding the seizure of property belonging to secessionists.

In Union Naval general officer activity, Captain Thomas Turner is promoted to the rank of commodore. In command of the frigate USS *New Ironsides*, Commodore Turner had participated in the attacks against the Confederate-held forts in Charleston Harbor on 7 August. During 1864, Commodore Turner is assigned to special duty in New York through 1865, followed by special assignment in Philadelphia during 1866–1867. He is promoted to rear admiral with command of the South Pacific Squadron on 27 May 1868.

December 14 (Monday) A Union contingent of General James Shackelford's cavalry division, Army of the Ohio, skirmishes with Confederates at Bean's Station in a contest that lasts about two hours (see also, **December 10 [Friday] In Tennessee**).

December 15 (Tuesday) In Virginia, elements of the 155th New York Cavalry Regiment skirmish with Confederates at Sangster's (Sandster's) Station. The Union sustains one wounded and four missing or captured.

In the Indian Territory (Oklahoma), Confederate raiders under Colonel Stand Watie raid Tahlequah. The mounted force runs wildly on the streets firing at will. No Union opposition is in the area; however, word is sent to Fort Gibson to summon Union troops.

In Confederate general officer activity, Colonel Joseph O. Shelby is promoted to the rank of brigadier general, effective this date. General Shelby had raised a cavalry company and serves primarily in the major campaigns west of the Mississippi, usually attached to the forces of General Sterling Price. He continues to operate in that region until the close of hostilities. After the war, he and some of his command bury their battle flag near the Rio Grande and cross into Mexico. He engages in some negotiations with both sides in the Mexican conflict, Maximilian and General Juarez; but nothing materializes as to taking sides. Following the ouster of Maximilian, General Shelby returns to Missouri. During 1893, President Grover Cleveland appoints him as U.S. marshal for the Western District. He dies while in that office on 13 February 1897.

December 16 (Wednesday) In Tennessee, a contingent of the Army of the Ohio skirmishes with Confederates at Blain's Cross Roads. Casualty figures are unavailable. Also, Union cavalry, under the command of General William Averell, successfully raids the Virginia and Tennessee Railroad and a Confederate supply base, destroying 4,000 barrels of flour and meat, 160,000 bushels of grain and an array of military supplies.

In Virginia, Confederate President Davis appoints General J.E. Johnston as permanent commander of the Army of Tennessee. Davis also puts General Leonidas Polk in command of the Army of Mississippi. Confederate Brigadier General Samuel B. Maxey (West Point, 1846) is assigned command of the Indian Territory.

In other activity, Union Major General of Volunteers John Buford dies of typhoid fever. He has had a successful career that carried him through the war with the Army of the Potomac. Buford made a gallant stand at Gettysburg by ordering one of his cavalry brigades (General William Gamble's) to dismount and stand against the onrushing forces of Confederate General Ambrose P. Hill, which bought needed time for other troops to regain discipline and order. During Buford's final days, he is presented with his commission as major general.

In Naval activity, the U.S. Navy acquires the wooden steamer *Maggie Baker.* The vessel is renamed the *Heliotrope,* commissioned at New York on 24 April 1864, and assigned to the North Atlantic Blockading Squadron. Once it arrives at Hampton Roads, the *Heliotrope* is utilized as a tug boat and an ordnance ship, but at times it is used on patrol along the James River. It remains in the region until January 1865, when it is transferred to the Potomac Flotilla.

December 17 (Thursday) In North Carolina, a contingent of the 58th Pennsylvania Regiment commanded by Captain Theodore Blakely captures about 34 Confederates after encountering a Confederate cavalry contingent at Washington.

In Mississippi, the Union Mississippi Marine Brigade skirmishes with Confederates at Port Gibson and Port Rodney through the 26th. The Union sustains two killed. Confederate casualties are unavailable.

In the Indian Territory, riders arrive at Fort Gibson to inform the commanding officer of the raids against Park Hill by Confederate guerrillas under Colonel Stand Watie. A contingent is dispatched to pursue the guerrillas. The detachment led by Captain Spillman moves toward Park Hill and Tahlequah; however, the contingent is only to locate the band and assess the strength before attempting to attack, and if necessary postpone the attack until reinforcements from Rhea's Mills can join with him. Spillman's column is composed of contingents of the 1st, 2nd and 3rd Regiments (Indian

Home Guards), totaling just under 300 troops. He is accompanied by one howitzer. The column hurriedly moves toward the Illinois River.

In Naval activity, the merchant ship *Chesapeake* (formerly the *Totten*) is recaptured by the USS *Ella and Annie* in Nova Scotia (see also, **December 7 [Monday] In Massachusetts**).

December 18 (Friday) In North Carolina, the 36th U.S. Colored Troops (2nd North Carolina) and the 5th U.S. Colored Troops Regiments engage Confederates at Indian Town. Casualty figures are unavailable.

In the Indian Territory, a contingent of the Union Indian Brigade, commanded by Colonel William A. Phillips, engages Confederate guerrillas under Quantrill at Fort Gibson.

In the Indian Territory, the 1st and 3rd Kansas Indian Home Guards, engage Confederates at Barren Fork or Sheldon's Place (Oklahoma). The Union, under Captain Alexander C. Spillman, is greatly outnumbered; however, Spillman pulls off a ruse that prompts the Confederates to attack. The Union artillery piece and the re-formed Union commence fire, and the Confederate Indians retire haphazardly. Colonel Stand Watie moves to establish winter quarters near Spavinaw Creek. Meanwhile, Spillman's victory terminates Watie's attacks north of the Arkansas River. Spilman's command sustains one killed, Captain Willits, and two men wounded. Some mules and two horses are also wounded. Confederate casualties total 25 killed and 25 wounded. Spillman's command numbered about 290 men, while the Confederate force had been between 500 and 600.

In Union general officer activity, Colonel Augustus Louis Chetlain (12th Illinois) is assigned to recruit Negros in Kentucky and Tennessee. He establishes headquarters in Memphis, Tennessee. In January 1865, General Chetlain is assigned command of the post at Memphis and the city's defenses. He is breveted major general on 18 June 1865.

December 19 (Saturday) In *Confederate general officer activity,* Colonel John Randolph Chambliss (W.P. 1853) is promoted to brigadier general effective this day.

December 20 (Sunday) In Tennessee, Confederate General Longstreet has not left the state, as thought by General Ambrose Burnside, but remains for the winter. General George H. Thomas is placed in command at Chattanooga while General Grant moves his headquarters to Nashville. In late December, Grant tours Chattanooga, Strawberry Plains and Lexington and other sites in both Tennessee and Kentucky, returning to his headquarters on January 13, 1864. People along the way for the most part are loyal to the Union and await his arrival with anticipation. Grant remarks: "The people expect the commanding general to be the oldest person in the party." Grant can dismount his horse inconspicuously as people approach Grant's medical director, because he looks much older than Grant's 41 years.

In Naval activity, the USS *Aries* and the USS *Governor Buckingham* join together off North Carolina and intercept and capture a blockade runner, the *Antonica,* after it runs ashore. The crew of the blockade runner attempts to escape by boats; however, naval guns fire warning shots and the crew men are discouraged from moving any farther. They surrender.

December 21 (Monday) In South Carolina, activity between the Union and Confederate forces is more or less in a state of suspension for the winter. Decisions have been made in Washington, D.C., regarding General Quincy A. Gillmore's command and the blockading squadron that is maintaining a steady vigil of Charleston Harbor. On the following day, Gillmore receives new orders giving him some options. He is informed that he can modify the fleet operations and initiate activity in other areas of the department as he and Admiral John A. Dahlgren deem necessary during the lull at Charleston. They decide to occupy the St. John's River and to move into Florida to establish military bases. The operations begin during the early part of February 1864. An effort to regain Florida as a loyal state is also getting underway, particularly because 1864 is an election year and President Lincoln concurs with some others that Florida could be gained by the Republicans. In early February, General Gillmore, commander of the Department of the South, receives authority to launch an expedition to gain Jacksonville.

In Confederate general officer activity, Colonel Lawrence Sullivan "Sul" Ross, 6th Texas Cavalry, is appointed to the rank of brigadier general in early January 1864, effective this date. Ross will command a Texas brigade composed of four dismounted Texas cavalry regiments, the 3rd, 6th, 9th and 27th. General Ross recently succeeded General John Wilkins Whitfield as brigade commander when Whitfield's health became poor. For a short while, beginning in late October, the brigade was under the command of Colonel Hinche P. Mabry (3rd Texas). General Ross will operate in the vicinity of the Yazoo River, then his brigade is ordered to Georgia to resist the Union forces under General William T. Sherman. During the upcoming campaign, the Texas brigade will participate in more than eighty clashes, the first of these occurring in the vicinity of Dallas, Georgia, in May 1864, followed by more action in Tennessee.

In Naval activity, the USS *Kansas* is commissioned in Philadelphia, where the gunboat had been built at the navy yard. Machinery taken from a prize, the steamer *Princess Royal,* is installed on the *Kansas.* Lt. Commander Pendleton G. Watmough receives command. It is assigned to the North Atlantic Blockading Squadron and departs for Hampton Roads soon after being commissioned, arriving at its destination on 30 December. Nevertheless, upon its arrival, mechanical trouble and a problem with its boiler cause a delay. It is sent to the Washington Navy Yard to get repairs. In March it

1863

December 22 (Tuesday) In Mississippi, General Alfred W. Ellet's Mississippi Marine Brigade skirmishes with Confederates at Fayette.

In Tennessee, Confederate cavalry attacks Union pickets commanded by Major White at Cleveland. The Union sustains one killed and six captured.

In Virginia, General Robert E. Lee is of course the commanding general of a great army, but he is no different from a private when it comes to Christmas and missing being with his family. Lee writes to his wife: "I hope you will all have a happy Xmas and that your hearts will expand in love and gratitude to your glorious Creator and Saviour for all his mercies and benefits.... I shall be with you in mind though absent in body."

Union General Michael Corcoran, the officer who replaced General Rufus King after Second Manassas (Bull Run) as a division commander in McDowell's III Corps, is killed near Fairfax Courthouse when his horse falls, while he is in the company of General Thomas Meagher. At the time, Corcoran's divisions in the area are in winter quarters.

December 23 (Wednesday) In Arkansas, the 2nd Missouri Cavalry skirmishes with Confederates at Jacksonport. Casualty figures are unavailable.

December 24 (Thursday) In Mississippi, the Union Mississippi Marine Brigade (Ellet's) engages a Confederate force at Rodney.

In North Carolina, Union warships, including the USS *Howquah* and the *Iron Age*, participate in a raid against a salt depot at Bear Inlet. The raid succeeds in destroying a huge supply of salt and the landing force destroys or dismantles the equipment used to manufacture the salt.

In Tennessee, Confederate guerrillas attack and kill a Union foraging party in Lincoln County.

In Naval activity, the USS *Antona*, operating in the vicinity of Velasco, Texas, encounters and seizes a vessel, *Exchange 10*, with cargo that includes liquor that had been loaded in Mexico at Vera Cruz, supposedly en route to New Orleans; however, the ship is far off course for New Orleans. The prize is taken to New Orleans while the *Antona* resumes its patrol. In other activity, the Union 7th Illinois Cavalry, commanded by Colonel Edward Prince, engages Confederate cavalry under Nathan Bedford Forrest for two days at Bolivar and at Summerville. The Union sustains three killed and eight wounded. Confederate casualties are unavailable.

The gunboat *Mary Sanford* (formerly a transport) participates in an expedition to Murrells Inlet, South Carolina, to search for and destroy a blockade runner and to scatter Confederates that have been engaging Union gunboats. Subsequent to the successful mission, the *Mary Sanford* is assigned duty off Charleston on 4 January 1864. It remains on station until autumn 1864, when it is reassigned to duty on the Big

Scatilla River. In other activity, the USS *Sunflower*, while on patrol in Tampa Bay, Florida, intercepts and seizes the blockade runner *Hancock*, which is carrying a cargo of borax and salt.

December 25 (Friday) In South Carolina, the USS *Marblehead* shells Confederate positions in the vicinity of Legareville on the Stono River. These Confederate fortifications on John's Island are also pummeled by Federal artillery, forcing the defenders to withdraw. The *Marblehead* sustains damages that require it to be sent north for repairs. Afterward it remains in the North and is used as a practice ship at the Naval Academy in Annapolis until September 1866. However, for a short time during late 1864, it is used on patrols. After its tour at Annapolis, the *Marblehead* is sent to the Caribbean, where it remains from the latter part of 1866 until about June 1868; it is sold in September 1868.

In Tennessee, the 117th Illinois Volunteer Regiment skirmishes with Confederates at Lafayette.

December 26 (Saturday) The Mississippi Marine Brigade (General Ellet's) engages Confederates at Port Gibson.

In Union general officer activity, Colonel (and chaplain, Methodist minister) William Anderson Pile is promoted to brigadier general. He is assigned command of a brigade composed of Negro troops in St. Louis at Benton Barracks. Subsequently, General Pile commands a brigade during the operations against Mobile. He is later breveted major general for his actions there. He musters out of the army in August and later becomes a U.S. congressman (1868), followed by being appointed governor of the New Mexico Territory by President Grant. And, following that appointment, he becomes "minister resident" to Venezuela. General Pile dies while residing in California on 7 July 1889.

December 27 (Sunday) In Mississippi, Confederates defending Drumgould's Bluff repel a U.S. naval attack. Confederate fire is so heavy that it forces the fleet to retire.

In Tennessee, a Union cavalry contingent (Army of the Tennessee) skirmishes with a Confederate force at Colliersville.

In Virginia, General Robert E. Lee, after hearing the fateful news of the death of his daughter-in-law Charlotte, states in a letter to his wife, Mary: "I grieve our lost darling as a father can only grieve for a daughter. My sorrow is heightened by the thought of the anguish her death will cause our dear son. What a glorious thought it is that it has joined her little cherubs and our angel Annie in heaven!"

December 28 (Monday) In South Carolina, a contingent of Marines and sailors attached to the steamer USS *Marblehead* debark at Stono to attack and seize a Confederate supply base.

In Tennessee, a detachment of the 2nd Missouri and 4th Ohio Cavalry, commanded by Colonel Bernard Laibold, is attacked while guarding a wagon train near Charlestown. The

Union suffers two dead and 15 wounded. The Confederates suffer eight killed, 39 wounded and 121 captured.

December 29 (Tuesday) In Tennessee, Union contingents continue to battle with Confederates. This day, a Union contingent composed of elements of the 1st Brigade, 2nd Division (23rd Corps), and the 1st Tennessee Cavalry, 1st Wisconsin Cavalry, the 2nd and 4th Indiana Infantry Regiments and the 24th Indiana Battery, commanded by Lt. Colonel Isham Young, clashes with Rebels led by General William T. Martin at Mossy Creek and Talbot's Station. Casualty figures are unavailable.

In Texas, a Union detachment of 100 men from the 13th Maine Infantry, supported by the gunboat USS *Sciota*, successfully evades capture and fights off an overwhelming Confederate force at Matagorda Bay on this day and the next.

December 30 (Wednesday) In Arkansas, the 2nd Kansas Cavalry skirmishes with Confederates at Waldron. The Union sustains two killed and six wounded. Confederate casualties are unavailable.

In Florida, a contingent composed of elements of the 10th Connecticut and the 24th Massachusetts Regiments skirmish with Confederates at St. Augustine when the Rebels launch an attack against a wagon train that the units are protecting. The attack is repelled. The Union sustains four killed. Confederate casualties are unavailable.

In North Carolina, a Union contingent, composed of elements of the 12th New York, 1st North Carolina and 23rd New York Battery and commanded by Colonel McChesney, engages a Confederate force led by Major Moore at Greenville. The Union sustains one killed and six wounded. The Confederates suffer six killed.

December 31 (Thursday) The year ends with optimism for the upcoming Union Army and pessimism for the struggling Confederates. The Union seems to keep its troops over-supplied and ammunition is always in abundance. The Confederate Army has been plagued by desertions, and food shortages in some camps are acute. Moreover, the Confederates cannot match the manpower of the northern states. For example, on this day, Union General Isaac F. Quinby (West Point, 1843) resigns due to faltering health and there is no great strain caused by his departure. General Quinby participated at Bull Run (colonel, 13th New York), and later at Champions' Hill and the preliminary assaults against Vicksburg. Also, General George D. Ramsay (West Point, 1820), in command of the arsenal at Washington, D.C., prepares to retire and will do so effective September 1864, yet the drain on Union manpower is non-existent.

In Naval activity, the USS *Granite City* and the USS *Sciota*, operating off Pass Cavallo, bombard Confederate cavalry positions. The guns scatter the force, which permits a reconnaissance contingent to land without resistance.

1864

In Nebraska, at about this time, the settlers (Germans who had relocated here) establish Fort Independence on the north side of the Platte River on Grand Island as a defense against the Indians. In addition, an establishment in the vicinity known as the O.K. Store is transformed into a fortification. Nevertheless, the forts do not come under assault. By the following year, the U.S. Army arrives and provides the settlers with a cannon to bolster the defenses.

January The Union threat against Richmond causes the Confederacy to transfer Union prisoners from Richmond to Andersonville. The compound, known as Camp Sumter, confines more than 45,000 prisoners. About 12,000 Union soldiers die while in detention at Andersonville, a small town in southwestern Georgia.

In Union general officer activity, General Jeremiah T. Boyle is relieved of command (Department of Kentucky) and ordered to Knoxville, Tennessee. General Boyle resigns and is replaced by Brigadier General Stephen G. Burbridge, also a Kentuckian. Burbridge fares well in aborting John Hunt Morgan's raids into Kentucky and is awarded the brevet of major general on 4 July 1864 for his actions. In other activity, General Joseph J. Reynolds (West Point, 1843) is assigned the post at New Orleans, where he is given responsibility for the city's defenses. Major General Reynolds assumes command of the XIX Corps during July and begins to organize the campaign to seize Mobile, prior to assuming command of the Department of Arkansas toward the latter part of the year.

In Confederate general officer activity, Colonel Randall Lee Gibson, 13th Louisiana Infantry Regiment, is promoted to the rank of brigadier general, effective this date. Gibson had been aide-de-camp to Governor Moore of Louisiana. Also, Colonel Nathaniel H. Harris, 19th Mississippi Regiment, is promoted to the rank of brigadier general. Harris is assigned to the 3rd Corps, General William Mahone's division, Army of Northern Virginia.

January 1 (Friday) **In Kentucky,** a Union detachment captures a Confederate scout, Colonel Hawkins, at Lick Creek.

In South Carolina, a Union contingent of Marines and sailors raid Murrells Inlet. The unit succeeds in sinking a Confederate schooner.

In Tennessee, some Union soldiers are discovered dead, having frozen to death on Island No. 10. At this time parts of the nation are caught in a deep freeze.

In Virginia, Confederate Major General William Smith, former governor of Virginia, is again inaugurated as governor. Smith has been wounded five times since joining the Confederacy as colonel of the 49th Virginia Regiment and has participated in such engagements as Antietam (Sharpsburg), Gettysburg, Seven Days' and Second Manassas (Bull Run). Also, a division under Confederate General Jubal Early advances down the valley and reaches the fringes of Winchester. At Bunker Hill, about ten miles from Martinsburg, a Confederate contingent skirmishes with Union pickets and drives the pickets back.

In Naval activity, the *Tom Sugg,* captured during the previous August by the USS *Cricket,* is commissioned the USS *Tensas.* It is assigned to the Mississippi Squadron and remains attached until it is decommissioned on 7 August 1865. On 17 August, it is sold at auction at Mound City, Illinois. Also, the USS *Metacomet,* a double-ender steam gunboat initially built in Brooklyn, is commissioned at about this time (January). It is assigned to the West Gulf Blockading Squadron.

January 1–4 **In Virginia,** a reconnaissance force (contingent of 2nd Brigade, 1st U.S. Cavalry) under Colonel John P. Taylor departs Bealeton en route to Front Royal. The column reaches Warrenton during the early afternoon of the 1st and pauses to confer with Lt. Colonel Kester (commander, 1st Brigade, 2nd Division). Taylor departs and advances along the Waterloo Pike toward the Hedgeman River and from there to Orleans. On 2 January, Lt. Myers arrives at Chester Gap and from there he moves to Front Royal at about dusk. A contingent is dispatched to investigate the fords of the Shenandoah, and during the course of the day (3rd), Taylor arrives at the fords. He is informed that 2,800 Confederate cavalrymen under Rosser and Imboden, bolstered by infantry under General Early, are deployed between New Market and Strasburg. On the 4th, Myers arrives at Warrenton and his contingent has 17 prisoners, including one officer, with the column. The contingent destroys a tannery and a distillery. Myers returns to Bealeton on the 4th.

The Union's 1st Maryland Cavalry, Potomac Home Brigade, engages with Confederates under Major John S. Mosby (43rd Virginia Cavalry Battalion) in and around London Heights and Rectortown through the 10th. The Union sustains 21 killed and wounded and 41 missing. The Confederates sustain four killed and wounded.

January 2 (Saturday) At about this time, Confederate Colonel Tyree H. Bell is given command of a cavalry brigade (General Nathan Bedford Forrest's command). Bell is promoted to brigadier general in February of the following year.

January 3 (Sunday) **In Virginia,** a contingent of the 16th Illinois Cavalry and the 22nd Ohio Battery, led by Major Charles H. Beers, engages a large Confederate force under General Sam Jones at Jonesville. The Confederates prevail. The Union suffers 12 killed, 48 wounded and 300 missing. The Confederates lose four dead and 12 wounded. Beers is among the captured. He is exchanged during August 1864.

In West Virginia, a Union force under Colonel Joseph Thoburn at Petersburg is under siege. General B.F. Kelley (commander, Department of West Virginia) at Cumberland, Maryland, reports that he cannot send reinforcements without jeopardizing his stores. Kelley's report also notes that Thoburn is deployed in good positions with his three regiments and a battery. The report also notes that Confederate General Early moved back to Middleton, Virginia, in anticipation of an attack by General Meade's army, which is moving against Front Royal. Also, Kelley, having discerned that General Robert E. Lee is preparing to move into the valleys, orders General William Averell to lead his cavalry to Winchester. Meanwhile, General Kelley prepares to prevent Lee from driving his forces from New Creek and Cumberland, Maryland. He also suggests that General Meade dispatch a strong cavalry force into the Luray Valley. The Confederates capture a wagon train that is returning to Thoburn, but it carries no supplies.

In South Carolina, the gunboat USS *Fahkee* clashes with Confederate batteries at Lockwood's Folly Inlet while it is attempting to examine a stranded blockade runner, the *Bendigo.* The *Fahkee* withstands the shore battery fire and in the meantime begins to shell the *Bendigo* to inflict more damage. The *Bendigo* is not totally destroyed; however, on the following day, other Union ships fire upon it and they terminate its days on the sea. The USS *Governor Buckingham* participates in this action. Also, on this day, the *Aries, Daylight, Governor Buckingham* and the USS *Minnesota* combine to intercept the blockade runner *Ranger,* which had just debarked passengers at Murrells Inlet. The *Ranger* is beached and the crew sets it on fire. Attempts to extinguish the fire by the Union seamen are prevented by Confederate sharpshooters along the banks. Following this action, the *Governor Buckingham* sails north to Norfolk for repairs. It returns to service off North Carolina during early July 1864.

January 4 (Monday) **In New Mexico,** Company B, 2nd California, composed of Apaches and civilians, engages in a fight with Navajo Indians at Fort Sumner. The Navajo sustain about 40 killed and 25 wounded.

In Maryland at Cumberland, General B.F. Kelley (commander, Department of West Virginia) sends a report to Brigadier General Cullum (chief of staff in Washington) indicating that he has not received any news from Colonel Thoburn at Petersburg, West Virginia. Kelley prepares for an attack against New Creek, but he is in need of reinforcements. On this day, Confederates drive back the Union pickets at New Creek (West Virginia).

In Virginia, a Union cavalry reconnaissance force (Army of the Potomac) led by Colonel John P. Taylor moves into the area near Front Royal.

In Naval activity, Admiral Farragut embarks from New York en route to take command of the East Gulf Squadron. Also, on or about this day, the CSS *Florida*, in port at Brest, France, since the previous August, receives a new commander, Lt. Charles Manigault Morris. He succeeds Commodore Joseph Barney, the successor of Captain Maffitt. Both Maffitt and Barney had become too ill while in France to command. The *Florida* does not depart until 12 February. The USS *Honduras* participates in a large operation in the vicinity of the mouth of the Caloosahatchie River, Florida, when a naval force debarks ground troops.

January 5 (Tuesday)   In Maryland, General B.F. Kelley reports to the chief of staff at Washington, Brigadier Cullum, that Cumberland is prepared to repel an attack by the forces of Lee and T.L. Rosser. Kelley also informs Washington that he is preparing to relieve Colonel Thoburn at Petersburg, West Virginia.

In Virginia, a detachment of Confederate cavalry attacks Union pickets at Eldorado, Culpeper County. Three Union troops are captured.

In West Virginia, at Petersburg, Confederates continue to threaten the command of Colonel Thoburn, but the Rebels continue to remain out of range of Thoburn's battery.

In Union general officer activity, Colonel Philippe Regis Denis de Trobriand, 55th New York, is appointed brigadier general. The 55th had been known as the Lafayette Guard. De Trobriand had participated at Gettysburg and the Peninsular campaigns. He will be breveted major general the day Robert E. Lee surrenders to U.S. Grant, 9 April 1865. In addition, Colonel John W. Fuller is promoted to brigadier general. Fuller will participate in both the Atlanta and Carolina campaigns. Colonel Christopher Columbus Andrews is appointed brigadier general (volunteers). Also, Colonel Cyrus Bussey is promoted to brigadier general. Later, on 13 March 1865, he receives the rank of brevet major general.

January 6 (Wednesday)   In West Virginia, Colonel Thoburn continues to hold at Petersburg while the Confederates remain in the vicinity but do not launch an attack against his 1st Virginia Regiment.

In Naval activity, the USS *Acacia* arrives at Morris Island, South Carolina, from Massachusetts to join the South Atlantic Blockading Squadron. The *Acacia* remains as part of the squadron for the duration of the war. Most of its time on duty is spent in the vicinity of Breach Inlet, located outside the Charleston bar.

January 7 (Thursday)   In Arkansas, the 11th Missouri Cavalry skirmishes with Confederates at Martin's Creek. The Union sustains one killed and one wounded. Confederate casualties are unavailable.

In Louisiana, Union forces occupy Madisonville.

In South Carolina, Union artillery under General Quincy A. Gillmore bombards Confederate-held Charleston.

In West Virginia, the Confederates, poised to strike the 1st Virginia Infantry Regiment at Petersburg, withdraw and move toward the Shenandoah Valley. Colonel Joseph Thoburn informs General Kelley at Cumberland, Maryland, that Rebel deserters have entered his lines and that the Confederate forces in the South Branch Valley Dispatch are the brigades of Fitzhugh Lee, Thomas L. Rosser and Henry H. Walker under the command of Lee. Thoburn also reports that the Confederates have not launched assaults against New Creek and Cumberland because they were unable to bring up the required artillery. Also, a Confederate contingent of about 50 troops under Major John S. Mosby (43rd Virginia Cavalry Battalion) attacks Union (3rd Pennsylvania Cavalry) positions at Warrenton about 0430. The Rebels pass through a gap in the picket lines without being detected to reach a position to strike the Union rear. The Union sustains eight wounded, including the commander, Captain Harry W. Gilmor, and 18 men (pickets) captured, along with about 43 horses. Some in Gilmor's command evaded capture and no shots had been fired. The Union captures three of Mosby's troops. The commander of the 3rd Cavalry, Major J.W. Walsh, dispatches a contingent to rescue the prisoners, but although the column of about 100 men are able to follow tracks in the snow, Mosby outruns the pursuers. The column returns to camp at about 1300.

In Naval activity, Union warships remain active off the coasts of North Carolina and Alabama against blockade runners. The *Dare,* a British steamer, is chased and runs aground at Wilmington, North Carolina. The USS *Aries* participates. In addition, the runner *John Scott* is destroyed off Mobile, Alabama. In other activity, the USS *Young America*, in Union service since its capture 24 April 1861, is officially acquired by the U.S. Navy from the prize court at Boston. The *Young America* is assigned on 9 April 1864 to the captured ram CSS *Atlanta* as its tow ship.

January 8 (Friday)   In West Virginia, a Union contingent (Colonel Joseph Thoburn's command) skirmishes with Confederates (General Fitzhugh Lee's command) in the vicinity of Petersburg. In other activity, a Union scouting contingent under Lt. Henry A. Myers arrives back at Romney and reports that the Confederates under General Fitzhugh Lee had been gone since the 6th. The Confederates had been spotted along the Wardensville and Moorefield Pike. Much of the nation remains in a deep freeze and Myers' contingent had observed Confederate soldiers frozen to death lying along the road.

In Arkansas, in Little Rock, the Union executes David O. Dodd as a spy. Dodd is remembered by the Confederacy as the "Boy Martyr," and a plaque still hangs in the Old Little Rock Arsenal, now the MacArthur Museum of Arkansas Military History.

January 9 (Saturday)   In Kentucky, elements of the 39th Kentucky Volunteer Regiment skirmish with Confederates at Turman's Ferry.

In Naval activity, Union gunboats exchange blows with Confederate batteries at Fort Morgan, Mobile Bay, Alabama. The contest lasts about two hours. Casualty figures are unavailable.

January 10 (Sunday)   In Tennessee, Union General William T. Sherman arrives at Memphis to gather his entire force, then he proceeds to Vicksburg, where he assembles 20,000 troops. Sherman prepares to move against Confederate General Leonidas Polk, based at Meridian, Mississippi.

In Kentucky, the 58th Illinois Regiment engages Confederates at Mayfield. The Union sustains one killed and one wounded. The Confederates suffer two killed.

In Virginia, a contingent of the 1st Maryland, Potomac Home Brigade, led by Major Henry A. Cole, skirmishes with Confederates led by Major John S. Mosby (43rd Virginia Cavalry Battalion) at Loudon Heights. The Rebels attempt to duplicate their recent effort against the 3rd Pennsylvania at Warrenton. Between 0200 and 0300, the Rebels squeeze through the picket lines to launch a surprise attack against the camp while most of the men are sleeping. After entering the lines, the vociferous "Rebel Yell" rings out and the troops at the point of attack react slowly and without tenacity; however Company A, the next target, is up and prepared due to the quick thinking of the commander, Captain George W.F. Vernon. The Yankees raise fierce resistance, buying time for the main body to bolt to get to their weapons. Consequently, John S. Mosby's guerrillas find themselves within a cauldron and they are unable to overrun the camp. Mosby's band sustains the loss of three officers and two privates killed and two other privates that sustain mortal wounds. Despite being routed, the Confederates are able to carry away their wounded. The Union sustains four enlisted men killed and 16 wounded, including Captain Vernon, who receives a head wound.

January 11 (Monday) **In Kentucky,** at Paducah, General George H. Thomas, aboard the steamer *Tarascon*, sends a message to General Henry Halleck at Washington, D.C.: "I shall start up the Tennessee today, and can assemble Schofield's corps by the end of this week, either at Clifton or Eastport. If I receive no further orders from you I will direct Schofield to proceed to Annapolis, Md., as expeditiously as possible. The information I get here confirms the report of Colonel Palmer that Hood has gone to Tuscaloosa [Alabama] and that Forrest is somewhere about Okolona [Mississippi]." Later the same day, Thomas reports: "Report this morning from Generals Wood and Granger inform me that the rebel General Lyon attacked the little garrison at Scottsborough, Ala., where he was handsomely repulsed three times, losing one colonel and 16 men killed, with a loss to our forces of six wounded and nine missing. Lyon is retreating in haste toward the Tennessee River, which I have requested the commanding officer (Captain Forrest) of the fleet at Bridgeport to have closely watched and patrolled, to prevent his escape across the river." Also, during this exchange of letters, General Thomas receives a message from Secretary of War Charles A. Dana that includes: "The following dispatch has been received at the War Department from Macon, Ga.: General Hood reports from Tupelo, January 6, 1864, that Thomas appeared to be moving up the Tennessee River until 9 o'clock A.M. on the 5th. Scouts report six gun-boats about and sixty transports had passed Savannah, going toward Eastport, loaded with troops and supplies."

In Naval activity, the USS *Aries* is among the warships that run the blockade runner *Ranger* ashore off Wilmington, North Carolina. The *Ranger* is seized and destroyed.

In Confederate general officer activity, Colonel Randall Lee Gibson (13th Louisiana Infantry) is promoted to brigadier general. He participates in the defense of Atlanta and afterward, he accompanies General John B. Hood during his invasion of Tennessee. Afterward, General Gibson joins the defenders at Spanish Fort outside Mobile.

January 12 (Tuesday) **In Kentucky,** a contingent of the 58th Illinois Regiment skirmishes with a Confederate contingent at Mayfield.

January 13 (Wednesday) **In Tennessee,** elements of Colonel (later brigadier general) Edward M. McCook's cavalry, led by Colonel James P. Brownlow (1st Tennessee Cavalry), engages Confederates at Mossy Creek. The Union sustains two officers and seven enlisted men killed and nine wounded. The Confederates sustain 14 killed and 47 captured. Also, Brigadier General William Tatum Wofford is transferred from Virginia to Georgia to assume command of the Department of North Georgia. He remains there for the duration and is paroled at Resaca in May 1865.

In Naval activity, the sloop of war USS *Saratoga*, on patrol duty off the Delaware Capes

since the previous June, is reassigned. The *Saratoga* is sent southward to join the South Atlantic Blockading Squadron off the Carolinas.

January 14 (Thursday) **In Tennessee,** a Union contingent composed of detachments of the 15th Pennsylvania and 10th Ohio Cavalry Regiments captures a Confederate wagon train at Crosby Creek (Terrisville) in East Tennessee, only to lose it and have to again seize it. During the contest, Confederate Brigadier General Robert B. Vance is captured by Sgt. Anderson of the 15th Pennsylvania Cavalry. Vance is detained at Fort Delaware until March of 1865, essentially too late to participate in the closing days of the war. Afterward General Vance serves six terms in the U.S. Congress, from 1875–1893. He is later appointed as assistant commissioner of patents in Washington, D.C., and from 1894 to 1896 serves in the North Carolina state legislature. He dies on 28 November 1899 in the vicinity of Asheville, North Carolina. Also, the 35th Iowa Volunteer Regiment skirmishes with Confederates at Middleton.

In Virginia, one company of the 9th Massachusetts repulses an attack by a Confederate force of about 200 troops at Bealeton. The Union suffers two wounded; the Confederates have three killed and 12 wounded.

In Naval activity, the USS *John L. Lockwood* arrives back at New Bern, North Carolina, following the completion of repairs at Norfolk, Virginia. It resumes patrols in the sounds and remains in the area until it is decommissioned at New Bern on 23 May 1865. Soon after its return, it seizes a blockade runner, the *Twilight*, at Elizabeth City. It is towed to Baltimore later in the month and from there it is moved to Washington, D.C., during July. The *John L. Lockwood* is sold on 15 September 1865 and renamed *Henry Smith* on 3 April 1866. On 30 June 1876, the U.S. Army purchases it and renames the ship *Chester A. Arthur* in honor of President Chester A. Arthur.

January 15 (Friday) **In Tennessee,** cavalry attached to General Sturgis' command drives Confederates from Dandridge.

January 16 (Saturday) **In Washington, D.C.,** Secretary of War Edwin M. Stanton receives a message from Major General Darius N. Couch regarding possible problems in Pennsylvania surrounding an inauguration: "It is reported that a mob will prevent Governor [Andrew G.] Curtin being inaugurated on the 19th instant. I think not. By invitation of the Legislature committee I shall be present."

In Ohio, the 27th U.S. Colored Regiment is organized at Camp Delaware. The regiment is ordered to repair to Annapolis, Maryland, where it is attached to the 1st Brigade, 4th Division, 9th Corps of the Army of the Potomac.

In Tennessee, contingents of the 4th Corps and one cavalry division of the Army of the Ohio come under a two-day attack by elements of Confederate Brigadier General Montgomery D. Corse's brigade at Dandridge. The Union, com-

manded by Colonel (later brigadier general) Edward M. McCook, sustains 150 wounded. Confederate casualties are unavailable. Corse's brigade (15th, 17th, 29th, 30th and 32nd Virginia Regiments) returns to the vicinity of Petersburg following this engagement, and afterwards it is dispatched to Kinston, North Carolina. Corse remains in North Carolina until spring, when he is ordered by General Robert E. Lee to return to Virginia with his force to support the defense of Richmond.

In Mississippi, Ellet's Mississippi Marine Brigade clashes with Confederates through the 18th at Grand Gulf.

January 17 (Sunday) **In Arkansas,** a detachment of the 3rd Arkansas Cavalry commanded by Captain David Hamilton skirmishes with Confederate Cavalry at Lewisburg. The Union sustains two killed and four wounded. The Confederates sustain six killed and six wounded.

In South Carolina, Union artillery under General Quincy A. Gillmore again bombards Confederate-held Charleston.

January 18 (Monday) **In Virginia,** Union pickets at Flint Hill repel a Confederate attack launched by a 15-man contingent.

In Tennessee, Confederate troops occupy New Market.

In Naval activity, Admiral Farragut concludes that he should use his squadron, which is off Mobile Harbor, to attack the Confederate positions in an effort to prevent them from completing the work on the ironclads that are being built. However, he is faced with the fact that no army troops are available because they are involved with the Red River Expedition; he impatiently waits for Washington to supply troops. Farragut has no ironclads and must operate with his wooden vessels. His requests for ironclads have thus far been unanswered, giving a reprieve to the Rebel forts, Gaines (Dauphin Island), Morgan (Mobile Point) and Powell (Tower Island). The support does not arrive until July.

At Mobile, Admiral Franklin Buchanan commands the diminutive Confederate fleet, composed of the vessels *Tennessee* (a ram), the gunboat *Morgan*, commanded by Commander George W. Harrison, the *Selma*, commanded by Lt. P.U. Murphy, and a few ironclads of light draught posted near the city of Mobile. In other activity, the USS *Ouachita* (formerly CSS *Louisville*) is commissioned. It remains in service for the duration and after the close of hostilities it operates as a commercial vessel, the *Vicksburg*. The USS *Stars and Stripes*, attached to the East Gulf Blockading Squadron since September 1862, seizes the blockade runner *Laura*. Afterward it continues its patrols off Florida for the rest of the war. It is decommissioned during June 1865 and sold the following August. It operates as a commercial ship under the original name and later as the *Metropolis* until January 1878, when it is wrecked along the North Carolina coast.

January 19 (Tuesday) In Washington, D.C., Congress authorizes the position of assistant secretary of war.

In Arkansas, a contingent of the 5th Kansas Cavalry commanded by Colonel Clayton attacks a Confederate cavalry force at Ivy Ford near Pine Bluff, Branchville.

In Texas, a Union force composed of a few hundred troops land in the vicinity of Smith's Landing under protective fire of Union gunboats, including the USS *Granite City*. Subsequent to this action, the *Granite City* remains on patrol in the region for several months, then is directed to move to Calcasieu Pass, Louisiana.

January 20 (Wednesday) In Tennessee, a contingent of the 20th Connecticut Regiment skirmishes with Confederates at Tracey (Tracy) City. The Union sustains two killed. Confederate casualties are unavailable.

In Mississippi, Battery E, 2nd Colored Light Artillery, engages a Confederate contingent at Island No. 76.

In Confederate general officer activity, Colonel Clement Hoffman Stevens is promoted to the rank of brigadier general, effective this date. Stevens is assigned command of a brigade which he will lead in the Atlanta Campaign as part of General William Henry Talbot Walker's division. General Stevens initially joined the Confederacy at the beginning of hostilities. He planned and constructed the battery on Morris Island in Charleston Harbor. Later, upon the demise of General Barnard Bee, he became colonel of the 24th South Carolina. He participated in various actions including, Secessionville and the defense of Vicksburg, followed by service at Chickamauga, where he sustained a wound. Also, Colonel Nathaniel Harrison Harris (19th Mississippi), who raised the "Warren Rifles" during 1861 as part of the regiment, is promoted to brigadier general. He receives command of a brigade in General Mahone's division (3rd Corps).

In Naval activity, the USS *Wateree* is commissioned at Philadelphia. Commander F.E. Murray receives command of the side-wheel gunboat, which is assigned to the Pacific Squadron. By serving in the Pacific Squadron, it does not participate in the naval actions of the Civil War. Its naval career is abruptly ended on 15 August 1868. While the *Wateree* is in port at Arica, Peru, the area sustains a severe earthquake, which also creates substantial tidal waves, one of which staggers the *Wateree* and disables its anchor chains, causing it to be tossed nearly "500 yards inland from the normal high water mark." The gunboat sustains severe damage and could not be salvaged. It is sold on 21 November 1868 and transformed into an inn.

January 21 (Thursday) In Georgia, a Union contingent composed of elements of the 28th Kentucky Mounted Infantry and the 4th Michigan Cavalry Regiments skirmishes with Confederates at Dalton.

January 22 (Friday) In Tennessee, a Union contingent skirmishes with Confederates at Armstrong Ferry.

In Virginia, Union forces clash with Confederates at Woodstock. The Rebels rout the Yankees, pushing them back.

January 23 (Saturday) In Arkansas, the 11th Missouri Cavalry encounters and engages Confederates at Rolling Prairie. The Union sustains 11 killed. Confederate casualties are unavailable.

In Mississippi, Confederate cavalry commanded by General William Wirt Adams springs a raid on Gelsertown.

In Tennessee, Union Cavalry launches a raid into Cocke County.

In Naval activity, the U.S. Navy acquires the *Cricket No. 4* (a wooden-hulled side-wheel steamer) and renames it the *Tallahatchie* on 26 January, and it is designated Tinclad Gunboat No. 46. During early February, it departs Cincinnati for Cairo, Illinois, and undergoes work to transform it into a lightly armored gunboat. Following completion of the work, the *Tallahatchie*, on 9 March, departs for the Gulf of Mexico. After arriving at New Orleans, it receives more modifications. Its bottom is layered with sheet copper to make it suitable for operations in salt water. Afterward, it sails to bolster Admiral David Porter's operations on the Red River, and afterward, it joins the West Gulf Blockading Squadron.

January 24 (Sunday) In Michigan, Union General Stephen G. Champlin dies from wounds he suffered at Seven Pines (Fair Oaks) during the battle of May 31–June 1, 1862. He returned to duty during Second Battle of Bull Run (Manassas), but his wounds had not healed, causing further complications. He was transferred to recruitment duty at Grand Rapids where, he remained until his death.

In Arkansas, detachments of the 2nd and 6th Kansas Cavalry Regiments, while on a scouting mission, skirmishes with Confederates commanded by Captain Williamson at Baker Springs. The Union sustains one killed and two wounded. The Confederates sustain six killed and two wounded.

In Tennessee, at Tazewell, the 34th Kentucky, 18th and 116th Indiana, the 11th Tennessee Cavalry and the 11th Michigan Battery skirmish with Confederates. Union casualties unlisted. The Confederates sustain 31 killed.

January 25 (Monday) In Washington, D.C., Congress thanks Cornelius Vanderbilt for his gracious gift of the steamer *Vanderbilt* to the Union cause. The vessel, worth approximately $800,000, has just completed a cruise around the world. This *Vanderbilt* is separate from the USS *Vanderbilt* (wooden side-wheel steamship) built in 1856 and commissioned during September 1862.

In Louisiana, a contingent of about 100 Union troops (specific units unreported) repulses a Confederate attack by a force numbering about 600 troops at Athens. The Union sustains about 20 killed, wounded and missing or captured. Confederate casualties are unavailable.

In Tennessee, a Union contingent under Colonel John K. Miller engages Confederates in the vicinity of Florence. The Confederates are repulsed. Union losses, according to General Grenville M. Dodge's report, are 15 killed and 25 wounded.

In Virginia, Union brigadier general Lawrence P. Graham leads an expedition into the area around Brandon Farms, along the James River. In other activity, Major George Tyler Burroughs, a Confederate guerrilla, attempts to escape from his captivity at Fort Monroe, but he fails and gets shot in the process.

In Mississippi, Union forces abandon Corinth.

January 26 (Tuesday) In Tennessee, the 5th Minnesota Volunteer Regiment departs La Grange en route for Vicksburg, Mississippi. The regiment arrives there on 3 February.

In Tennessee, Union troops under Colonel Miller engage a Confederate brigade in the vicinity of Florence. The Confederates are repelled and Miller's command seizes three prisoners. Also, a large cavalry force (General Grenville M. Dodge's command) had departed Athens on the previous day en route to Colbert Reserve to strike Confederates under General Philip D. Roddey. Meanwhile, Confederates strike Athens at 0400, but the diminutive defending force under Captain Hannon repulses the attack; however, about 20 men are killed.

January 27 (Wednesday) In Tennessee, Union General William Tecumseh Sherman directs General Sooy Smith to leave Memphis with his force of well over 5,000 to head for Meridian, Mississippi, on February 1. Smith does not leave until February 11. At Fair Garden (French Broad and Kelly's Ford), Union cavalry commanded by General Edward M. McCook (General Sturgis' cavalry division, Army of the Ohio) engages Confederates. The Union sustains 100 killed and wounded. The Confederates suffer 65 killed and 100 captured. In other activity, Confederate cavalry attacks Union pickets (13th Kentucky and 23rd Michigan Volunteer Regiments) under Colonel Chapin at Scott's Mills Roads. Initially, the Confederates prevail, but during a second fight, the Union vanquishes the Rebels. The Union sustains one killed. The Confederates suffer 12 captured.

In Kentucky, a Union contingent on a mission to the Cumberland River attacks a guerrilla contingent under Confederate Colonel Richardson. Two of the guerrillas are killed and the Union pursues the fleeing contingent for about 15 miles. Colonel Richardson (a guerrilla leader, separate from Brigadier General Robert V. Richardson) is captured late February or early March.

January 28 (Thursday) In Georgia, Union contingents, attached to the General Davis' Division, 14th Corps, Army of the Cumberland, encounter and skirmish with Confederates at

Tunnel Hill. The Union sustains two wounded. The Confederates suffer 32 wounded.

In Tennessee, a Union contingent led by Colonel Jesse Phillips pushes Confederate General Philip D. Roddey's forces across the Tennessee River to the south bank.

In Union general officer activity, General William Rosecrans is given command of the Department of Missouri. Prior to this appointment, Rosecrans held command at Chattanooga until relieved by General George H. Thomas on 18 August 1863. Rosecrans retains the post until 9 December 1864.

January 29 (Friday)   In Kentucky, a Union force under Major Johnson repels a Confederate attack at Scottsville.

In Arizona, a Union contingent commanded by Colonel Kit Carson engages Indians at Canyon de Chelly.

In Mississippi, a Union steamer carrying elements of the 21st Missouri Regiment, commanded by Colonel David Moore, clashes with Confederate guerrillas at Islands No. 70 and No. 71.

In North Carolina, a 300-man Union contingent, including elements of the 158th New York, 9th Vermont and Mix's Cavalry, commanded by Colonel Jourdan, launches a raid into Jones and Onslow Counties.

In West Virginia, Union troops commanded by Colonel Joseph Thoburn abandon Petersburg.

In Tennessee, a Union contingent (specific units unreported) skirmishes with Confederates at Cumberland Gap.

In West Virginia, a Confederate contingent attacks a Union wagon train at Medley (near Williamsport). The Union losses are 10 dead and 70 wounded; the Confederates lose 100 wounded. Union troops participating are the 1st and 14th West Virginia, 23rd Illinois, 2nd Maryland and the 4th West Virginia Cavalry. The Union force is commanded by Colonel J.W. Snyder.

January 30 (Saturday)   In Washington, D.C., Provost Marshal General James B. Fry gives a favorable report on the condition of the North. The report says the "states and counties are actively raising troops with the hope of conquering the Confederates before it would be necessary to submit to a general draft." The president is prodded to call for a draft of 500,000 troops beginning on 10 March "in all localities which had not filled their quotas by March 1st." The figure of 500,000 is to include the call on 17 October for 300,000 troops and all of the troops raised during the draft of the previous year.

January 31 (Sunday)   In North Carolina, the town of Warsaw is destroyed by fire.

In Tennessee, a Union contingent at Marysville initiates an expedition to Qualltown, North Carolina. The mission lasts until 7 February.

February   In Virginia, Hood's Texas Brigade returns to Virginia following its temporary service in Tennessee. Brigadier General John Gregg will succeed Brigadier General Jerome B. Robertson as commander of the Texas Brigade and will lead it during the fighting around Richmond.

In Confederate general officer activity, Brigadier General Charles W. Field, following duty in Richmond, Virginia, and full recovery form a serious wound sustained during August 1862 at 2nd Manassas, is promoted to major general. Field receives command of General John B. Hood's division (James Longstreet's corps) and will lead it for the duration as part of the Army of Northern Virginia. Hood is promoted this month to lieutenant general and will lead a corps under General Joseph E. Johnston. Also, Brigadier General Samuel McGowan, again in good health following a wound at Chancellorsville, returns to his command. McGowan's brigade will participate in battles at the Wilderness and Spotsylvania, Virginia, among others. Brigadier General Abner Perrin, temporary commander of McGowan's brigade, is transferred to a new command. He receives a brigade (Cadmus Wilcox's) in General Richard H. Anderson's division, 3rd Corps.

February 1 (Monday)   In Washington, D.C., President Lincoln calls for another surge of manpower. He orders a draft of 500,000 men to serve three years or to the end of the conflict.

In Arkansas, the 2nd Kansas Cavalry skirmishes with Confederates at Waldron.

In Tennessee, General William S. Smith is given command of General Sherman's cavalry. Sherman orders Smith to depart Memphis with his command of about 10,000 troops and advance to Meridian to join with him; however, the column does not depart Memphis until 11 February. Sherman moves out of Vicksburg en route to Meridian on 3 February.

In Virginia, a Union contingent — elements of the 21st Connecticut, 99th New York Regiments, the 20th New York Cavalry and the 3rd Pennsylvania Artillery, commanded by General Charles K. Graham and supported by crew men of the steamer USS *Minnesota*— engages Confederates at Smithfield. Confederate troops capture the transport USS *Smith Briggs.* The Union sustains 90 missing or captured. Confederate casualties are unavailable. General Graham had been captured at Gettysburg. He was exchanged during September 1863 and transferred to command the army gunboats in the Army of the James. During his service there, pursuant to orders from the secretary of war, he orders the burning of the house of the brother of the Confederate secretary of war. The order had been issued in response to troops under Jubal Early torching the home of the postmaster general, Montgomery Blair, in Maryland. General Graham receives the rank of brevet major general the following year. After leaving the service, he becomes chief engineer of the department of docks in New York.

In West Virginia, a company of Union infantry clashes with Confederates at New Creek Valley.

In North Carolina, Confederates under General Pickett hand the Union troops a defeat at Bachelor's Creek. The 132nd New York, 9th Vermont, 17th Massachusetts, 2nd North Carolina, 12th New York Cavalry and the 3rd New York Artillery participate. Additional skirmishes occur at Newport Barracks and New Bern. Action ends on the 4th. The Union suffers 16 dead, 50 wounded and 280 missing. The Confederates suffer five killed and 30 wounded.

In Mississippi, the Union executes an operation known as the Yazoo Expedition along the Yazoo River through the 8th. Participating units include the 11th Illinois, 47th U.S. Colored, 3rd U.S. Colored Cavalry, and warships of Rear Admiral Porter's Mississippi Squadron. The Union sustains 35 killed and 121 wounded. The Confederates sustain 35 killed and 90 wounded.

In Naval activity, the ironclad monitor USS *Ozark* is commissioned at about this time. It was originally built in Peoria, Illinois, for use as a river monitor. It is attached to the Mississippi Squadron for the duration. Its primary combat operation occurs during the Red River Expedition from March to May. After the war, it is decommissioned during July 1865 and sold in November 1865. Also, the *Tacony* (double-ender side-wheel gunboat) is commissioned the USS *Tacony* at about this time (February). It departs from Philadelphia en route to the Gulf of Mexico; however, while at sea it receives new orders and is directed to head for the North Carolina Sounds.

In Union general officer activity, John Parker Hawkins (West Point, 1852), commissioned brigadier general during 1863, subsequent to several months of sick leave, is assigned to Vicksburg with command of a Negro division. Previously, he had served primarily as chief of commissary in various commands. Toward the closing days of the war, he receives the brevet of major general of volunteers in the Regular Army. He retires with the rank of brigadier general on 22 December 1892.

February 2 (Tuesday)   In North Carolina, a Confederate contingent, composed of 13 officers and 222 men of the Confederate Marine Corps under Captain T.S. Wilson (General George Pickett's command), led by Commander John Taylor Wood, uses boats to approach and board the USS *Underwriter* off New Bern. The contingent seizes the ship and captures the crew (85 officers and men). The Union land batteries fire upon the ship, preventing it from being carried off. Consequently, Wood orders the vessel to be destroyed. The Confederates sustain five killed during the mission. In other activity, Union forces abandon Newport Barracks, North Carolina; 1st Lieutenants Jewett and J. Livingston, 9th Vermont Infantry, burn the approach bridges to slow the advancing Confederates. Jewett and Livingston each receive the Medal of Honor for their valor. Participants are the 132nd New York, 9th Vermont, 17th Massachusetts,

2nd North Carolina Volunteers, the 12th New York Cavalry, and the 3rd New York Artillery.

In Naval activity, the USS *Western World*, having completed repairs, is assigned duty with the Potomac Flotilla. It has a short tour due to the need for repairs. It returns to the navy yard in Washington D.C., on 1 April and remains out of service until early November 1864.

February 3 (Wednesday)   In West Virginia, Confederate guerrillas, operating along the Kanawha River, spot a Union vessel and pull a surprise raid. The Rebels capture General Eliakim P. Scammon, who is held until exchanged on 3 August 1864. Also, a Union contingent (specific units unreported) under Lt. Colonel F.W. Thompson skirmishes with Confederate cavalry at Patterson Creek and Springfield. The Union sustains two killed and 10 wounded. Confederate casualties are unavailable.

In Mississippi, a Union contingent composed of the 11th Illinois Volunteers and the 47th U.S. Colored Troops (8th Louisiana) Regiments, commanded by Colonel James H. Coates, skirmishes with Confederates at Liverpool Heights. The Union sustains five killed and 28 wounded. Confederate casualties are unavailable. Union gunboats, including the USS *Petrel II*, support the Union forces during the skirmish.

Sherman departs Vicksburg (Meridian Campaign) for Meridian with a force close to 20,000 men. Meridian is located at a strategic point about 100 miles east of Vicksburg, where the Jackson to Selma Railroad line intersects with the Mobile and Ohio Railroad. The Union departs in two columns. General Stephen A. Hurlbut's force moves by rail and McPherson takes an overland route. Hurlbut's 16th Corps includes the divisions of Generals Veatch and A.J. Smith, bolstered by one Infantry Brigade led by Colonel Chambers, one battalion of cavalry under Colonel E.F. Winslow and Captain J.P. Foster and seven artillery batteries. The 17th Corps, under General James B. McPherson, includes the divisions of Generals Crocker and Leggett; McPherson moves overland through Messenger's Ferry. General William Sooy Smith assembles the cavalry units, which exceed 5,000 men; Smith departs Memphis on the 11th to join Sherman at Meridian. The operation includes action at Champion Hills, Clinton, Decatur, Raymond and Chunky Station. Sherman's troops also take control of Lauderdale Springs, Marion and Meridian. During this mission, the Union sustains 56 killed, 138 wounded and 105 missing. The Confederates sustain 503 killed and wounded and 212 captured. The 5th Minnesota Volunteer Regiment participates.

In Confederate general officer activity, Brigadier General John Creed Moore resigns his commission. After the war Moore becomes a school teacher in Texas.

In Naval activity, a Union Naval force engages a Confederate force under General Ross at Sartartia, Mississippi.

February 4 (Thursday)   In Arkansas, the 3rd Missouri Cavalry clashes with Confederates at Hot Springs.

In Missouri, the 8th Missouri Cavalry skirmishes with Confederates at Rolling Prairie. Casualties are unreported.

In Mississippi, the Union 10th Missouri, 4th Iowa and 5th and 11th Illinois Cavalry Regiments, bolstered by Foster's Ohio battalion of cavalry and a detachment of the 17th Corps (General James B. McPherson's command), engage Confederate cavalry at Big Black River.

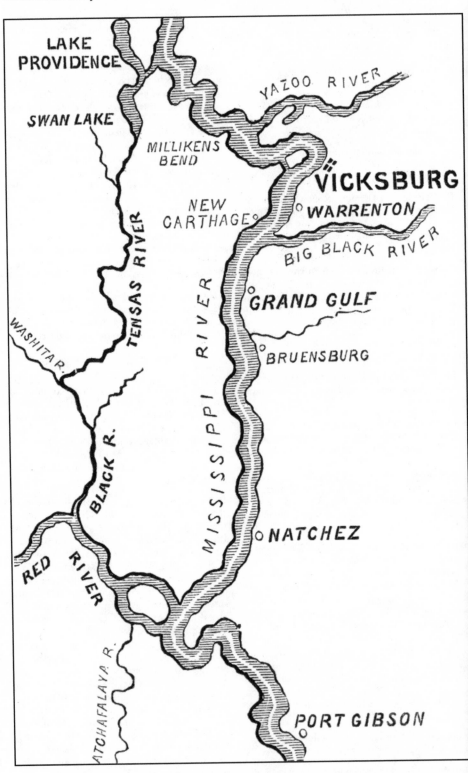

Lake Providence, Mississippi, to Port Gibson (*Harper's Pictoral History of the Civil War,* 1896).

In West Virginia, a Union force attached to the Department of West Virginia and a detachment of the 23rd Illinois Infantry Regiment commanded by Colonel James A. Mulligan engage Confederates under General Thomas L. Rosser at Moorefield.

In Confederate general officer activity, Colonel Allen Thomas, formerly 29th Louisiana Infantry Regiment, is promoted to the rank of brigadier general and assigned duty in the Department of Alabama and Mississippi, commanded by his brother-in-law, Major General Richard Taylor.

February 5 (Friday)   In Mississippi, Union troops (Sherman's command) reach Jackson. In related activity, Union cavalry and a contingent of the 17th Corps skirmishes with Confederates at Clinton and Jackson. The Union sustains about 25 killed and wounded.

In North Carolina, a Union contingent composed of a detachment of the 14th Illinois Cavalry, led by Major Davis, attacks a Confederate encampment at Qualltown. The Union sustains three killed. The Confederates sustain high casualties, and in addition, the Union captures 50 troops. In related activity, a Union reconnaissance force commanded by Colonel James Jourdan departs Newport, North Carolina, en route to the White River. The Union captures 28 Confederates.

In South Carolina, outside of Charleston, an expeditionary force, composed of twelve regiments, is organized. General Quincy A. Gillmore has selected General Truman Seymour to lead the operation, which will depart for Florida the next day. Seymour's force is composed of about 6,000 troops. Its first objective is Jacksonville, and from there the Union intends to expand its strength throughout the northeastern part of the state.

In Missouri, a contingent of the 2nd Missouri Cavalry, led by Captain Selby, attacks a Confederate guerrilla camp at Cape Girardeau. The Confederates sustain seven killed and eight captured.

In Virginia, where the Army of the Potomac has been inactive for most of the winter, preparations are complete for an attack against General Lee. General Benjamin F. Butler dispatches cavalry under General Isaac Wistar from New Kent Court House to strike against Richmond, thought to be lightly defended.

In Union general officer activity, William Badger Tibbits is appointed colonel (later brevet major general) of the 21st New York Regiment. Tibbits had earlier mustered out of the 2nd New York, a two-year regiment, in which he swerved as a major. He participates in the Battle of New Market.

February 6 (Saturday)   In Mississippi, after a short stay, Sherman departs Jackson for Meridian, where a Confederate force of nearly 20,000 men, commanded by General Leonidas Polk, is entrenched.

In South Carolina, a fleet (Rear Admiral John A. Dahlgren's command) composed of twenty steamers and eight schooners, supported by the gunboat USS *Norwich,* leaves Hilton Head for Jacksonville, Florida. The naval contingent is transporting General Truman Seymour's expeditionary force, which is taken along the St. John's River, from where it will debark to seize the objective. Subsequent to this duty, the *Norwich* returns to patrols around Florida and Georgia until the end of hostilities. On 30 June 1865, it is decommissioned in Philadelphia. During August 1865, it is sold at auction and is a commercial vessel until lost in February 1873.

In Tennessee, a detachment of Union cavalry skirmishes with Confederate troops near Bolivar. The Union loses one dead and three wounded; Confederates sustain 30 wounded. The Union occupies Bolivar.

In Virginia, contingents of the 2nd Corps engage Confederates at Morton's Ford. The Union sustains 10 killed and 201 wounded. The Confederates sustain 100 missing. In other activity, General Isaac Wistar's cavalry force reaches the Chickahominy Bridge at Bottom's Ridge, but he discovers that it is blockaded and soon returns to New Kent Court House.

In Naval activity, the USS *Adolph Huger,* attached to the Potomac Flotilla, encounters a small boat that moves to pass the warship without responding to signals. The boat, carrying only one man, is fired upon, and the man is wounded. The boat sinks and its cargo, whiskey, is thrown overboard by crewmembers of the *Adolph Huger.*

In Union general officer activity, Brigadier General James Gallant Spears, having vehemently complained about the Emancipation Proclamation, which he proclaimed unconstitutional due to "depriving him of his slaves," is arrested. Subsequent to an investigation, initiated by President Lincoln, he is dismissed from the army during August 1864.

February 7 (Sunday)   In Florida, the Union occupies Jacksonville, a base that is to be used to further disrupt the Southern supply lines. Twelve Union regiments debark against minimal resistance. The USS *Dandelion,* subsequent to participating in the operation against Jacksonville, is ordered north. It is decommissioned during July and sold the following month.

In Louisiana, the 2nd Mississippi, 64th U.S. Colored Troops, 7th Louisiana and the 30th Mississippi Volunteers and the 6th U.S. Colored Artillery skirmish with a contingent of Confederates led by Lt. Colonel McCaleb at Vidalia. Union casualties are unlisted. The Confederates sustain six killed, 10 wounded and eight captured.

In Virginia, General John Sedgwick, acting commander of the Army of the Potomac in the absence of General George G. Meade, orders General Hugh Kilpatrick's cavalry to cross the Rapidan River at Ely's Ford. He directs Merritt's cavalry to cross at Barnett's Ford. In addition,

Sedgwick has sent two divisions of the Union 2nd Corps across at Germanna Ford, but this raid, in coordination with troops under General Isaac Wistar, who had departed New Kent Court House, is uneventful as the attack against Richmond fizzles out. The cavalry battles Confederates at Barnett's Ford. The Union sustains 20 killed and wounded. Confederate casualties are unavailable.

February 8 (Monday)   In Florida, General Truman Seymour's force departs Jacksonville. The force moves in three columns commanded by Colonels William B. Barton (48th New York Volunteer Infantry), Joseph Roswell Hawley and John Y. Scammon. Barton's column advances along the main route, while Hawley and Scammon move on the left and right respectively. The target is Baldwin in the interior, but en route, after dusk, the Yankees come upon and surprise a Confederate camp. They capture several troops and seize four guns and a good supply of equipment. The columns reach Baldwin on the following day. Some units go as far as the area near Lake City, about fifty miles west of Jacksonville. Other units advance against Gainesville. The Confederates in Florida under Brigadier General Joseph Finegan, commander of the District of East Florida, which includes the part of Florida east of the Suwanee River, are under strength, as most of the Confederate troops are attached to armies based outside of the state. Finegan's force numbers fewer than 2,000 troops. He puts out urgent calls for reinforcements from General Pierre G.T. Beauregard, commander Department of South Carolina, Georgia and Florida; however, any attempt at dispatching reinforcements is impeded due to the lack of direct railroad routes to the affected area. Nonetheless, General Beauregard will send help. Troops from various locations will be transported by rail to South Carolina and from there they debark and move by highway to points in Florida, where they again board trains. Within one week, reinforcements begin to arrive to bolster Finegan. Reinforcements include General Alfred Colquitt's brigade and a force under Colonel George Harrison. Also, at about this time, John Jay, a representative of President Lincoln, arrives in Florida to gather supporters and seek their oaths of allegiance to the Union, a first step in establishing a state government that will remain loyal.

In Louisiana, the 4th Wisconsin Cavalry skirmishes with Confederates at Donaldsonville.

In Mississippi, Union movements to rid Confederates from the states of Arkansas, Mississippi, and Louisiana are underway. General Banks will lead the less than successful Red River Campaign, but the mission is put off until March when conditions on the river should improve. While Sherman makes for Meridian, the Union continues to retain strength at Vicksburg. Union General John P. Hawkins (West Point, 1852) will be stationed at Vicksburg for the duration, in command of a Negro division. In related activity, Union cavalry occupies Morton.

In Naval activity, the vessel *Wyalusing,* launched on 12 May 1863, is commissioned the USS *Wyalusing* at the Philadelphia Navy Yard. Lt. Commander Walter W. Queen receives command of the gunboat, which is assigned duty with the North Atlantic Blockading Squadron.

February 9 (Tuesday) In Arkansas, contingents of the 4th Arkansas, 11th Missouri and 1st Nebraska Cavalry Regiments skirmish with Confederates at Morgan's Mills (Spring River). The Union sustains one killed and four wounded. The Confederates sustain 65 killed and wounded.

In North Carolina, Union troops destroy approximately $700,000 worth of cotton at various facilities in Wilmington.

In Florida, Union forces under General Seymour arrive at Baldwin during the early morning hours and seize a three-inch rifled cannon, a few railroad cars and property estimated at $500,000 (1864 value). Later, a contingent advances to Barber's Place at the St. Mary's River while on a reconnaissance mission to ascertain the strength of the enemy in the region. Fighting breaks out there between elements of the 40th Massachusetts Mounted Infantry and Rebel cavalry. A skirmish also breaks out between Confederates and the 7th Vermont Volunteers at Point Washington. The Union contingent encounters a small force and a brief skirmish follows, with each side sustaining about seventeen casualties. Following this skirmish the Union advances to Sanderson, a small town about forty miles from Jacksonville, reaching it in late afternoon. The Yankees discover the town abandoned and decide to remain there for the night. It is determined that General Joseph Finegan, commanding the Confederate troops in this region of Florida, had abandoned the area and removed to Lake City. Colonel Guy V. Henry's force initiates pursuit, but is later recalled to Sanderson.

In Virginia, Union Colonel Abel D. Streight and slightly more than 100 other Union officers succeed in breaking out of Libby Prison in Richmond. Forty-eight of these are recaptured. Colonel Streight had been captured in the vicinity of Rome, Georgia, in 1863.

In Naval activity, the USS *Malvern* is officially commissioned at the Boston Navy Yard and attached to Admiral David D. Porter's North Atlantic Blockading Squadron, becoming Porter's flagship.

February 10 (Wednesday) *In Naval activity,* a contingent from the USS *Ancona* joins an expedition with a force from the USS *Princess Royal,* led by Lieutenant Charles E. McKay. The force moves by boats and destroys the iron-hulled steamer *Will o' the Wisp,* which is stranded at Galveston after running aground.

February 10–25 In Tennessee, Union cavalry under Generals W.S. Smith and Benjamin Grierson initiate the advance from Memphis to Mississippi. During this operation, the Union

sustains 43 killed and 207 wounded. The Confederates sustain 50 wounded and 300 captured. Participants include the 4th Missouri, 2nd New Jersey, 7th Indiana, 19th Pennsylvania, 2nd Iowa, 2nd, 3rd, 6th, 7th, and 9th Illinois, 3rd Tennessee, 4th U.S. and 5th Kentucky Cavalry, 72nd Indiana Mounted Infantry and some additional regiments.

February 11 (Thursday) In Florida, Union General Truman Seymour pens a message to General Quincy A. Gillmore implying that the information regarding loyalists in Florida had been greatly exaggerated and that there was no genuine interest among the Floridians to re-enter the Union. Seymour also deduces that he lacks sufficient transportation to launch an assault against Lake City. The tone of the message prompts Gillmore to speed from Hilton Head, South Carolina, to confer with Seymour. Meanwhile, Gillmore orders Seymour to establish positions at Baldwin.

In Tennessee, Union General W. Sooy Smith's cavalry (including General Benjamin Grierson's) departs Memphis to join Sherman at Meridian, Mississippi, and to assist in the struggle against the forces of Confederate Generals Leonidas Polk and Nathan Bedford Forrest. Smith's force is composed of three cavalry brigades under Colonel George Waring (4th Missouri), Lt. Colonel Hepburn (2nd Iowa) and Colonel Lafayette McCrellis (3rd Illinois), one brigade of infantry and a contingent of artillery. Smith crosses the Tallahatchie River and drives toward Okolona, Mississippi. The town is easily secured. From here, General Smith moves against West Point, while he dispatches Grierson's cavalry toward Columbus, Mississippi.

In West Virginia, Confederate guerrillas attack and capture a train (Baltimore and Ohio Railroad) in the vicinity of Harpers Ferry.

February 12 (Friday) In Arkansas, the 2nd Kansas Cavalry skirmishes with Confederates at Caddo Gap and Scott's Farm.

In Florida, the 40th Massachusetts Volunteer Regiment and the Independent Battalion, Massachusetts Cavalry, under Colonel Guy V. Henry, defeat a Confederate contingent, driving it from Lake City. The Union sustains three wounded. The Confederates sustain two killed.

In Mississippi, Sherman's Army encroaches Meridian. The Confederates there under General Leonidas Polk are withdrawing, heading for Alabama. In addition, a Union Regiment guarding a wagon train defeats a Confederate force and occupies Decatur. General Hurlbut's column makes camp for the night about four miles beyond the town, but one of his regiments is ordered to guard the crossroads at Decatur to assure the trailing column of James B. McPherson has uninterrupted passage. General Sherman eats dinner at a private residence and afterward grabs some sleep; however, he is soon rousted as gun fire erupts near the house. The Rebels arrive to disrupt the Union advance and surround Sherman. Meanwhile, the regiment at

the crossroads had departed for Hurlbut's camp. Sherman and others (clerks and orderlies) begin to defend themselves by gathering at a corn crib in the rear of the log cabin. Sherman also dispatches his aide, Major Audenreid, to get reinforcements. All the while, a running fight is underway in Decatur as Union wagons are flying by the house and the troops are exchanging fire. The rebels, however, fail to capture Sherman. Audenreid had caught up with Hurlbut's regiment and they race back in time to drive the Rebels from the town.

Also, a Union contingent composed of elements of the 20th, 29th, 31st, 45th and 124th Illinois Volunteers engage Confederates at Chunky Station. This Union Army has advanced about 150 miles in eleven days, meeting only minimal opposition from the 9,000 troops under the commands of Generals S.G. French, William W. Loring and Leonidas Polk, nor have the 4,000 cavalry troops under Generals William W. Adams (1st Mississippi), Samuel W. Ferguson and Stephen D. Lee provided any heavy opposition. In conjunction, Ferguson comes under consideration for promotion to major general during August; however, Major General Joseph Wheeler is opposed on the grounds that Ferguson's command is plagued with desertions and Wheeler believes Ferguson is an instigator.

In West Virginia, the 14th Kentucky Regiment engages Confederates at Rock House. The Union sustains 12 killed and four wounded. Confederate casualties are unavailable.

In Confederate general officer activity, Brigadier General Charles William Field is promoted to major general. After sustaining a serious wound at Second Manassas (Bull Run), General Field had been in command of the Bureau of Conscription in Richmond, Virginia. He is assigned command of a division (previously General John B. Hood's division). He remains with the Army of Northern Virginia for the duration and is later paroled at Appomattox.

In Naval activity, the CSS *Florida,* commanded by Lt. Charles Manigault Morris, having been in port at Brest, France, since the previous August, departs for the West Indies. The vessel, which had a successful run prior to arriving in France, finds no targets of value in the West Indies In July it encounters a Union vessel off the Delaware Capes.

February 13 (Saturday) In Mississippi, a contingent of Union cavalry (General William T. Sherman's command) engages Confederates at Tunnel Hill. Also, the 52nd U.S. Colored Troops and the 2nd Mississippi Regiment engage Confederates at Vicksburg.

February 14 (Sunday) In Arkansas, the U.S. 51st Colored Regiment, operating in the vicinity of Ross Landing, encounters and engages Confederates. The Union sustains 13 killed and seven wounded. Confederate casualties are unavailable.

In Florida, a 49-man contingent of the 40th Massachusetts Mounted Volunteer Regiment, led by Captain George E. Marshall (General Seymour's command), seizes Gainesville after penetrating a force of more than 100 Confederate infantrymen at about 0200. Shortly afterward the unit abandons the town, but not before successfully defending it against the attack by Confederates, including the 2nd Florida Cavalry led by J.J. Dickison. The Rebel cavalrymen lose about 40 men. The Union loses one wounded, two captured and one missing. The Confederate attackers had been totally unaware that the Union troops holding the town also held new repeating rifles.

In related activity, General Quincy A. Gillmore arrives at Jacksonville from Hilton Head, South Carolina, and meets with General Truman Seymour regarding Seymour's apparent queasiness toward an offensive. Subsequent to listening to Seymour, General Gillmore directs him to establish defensive positions at Jacksonville and Baldwin. Seymour is also directed to fortify Barber's Plantation; however, Seymour is ordered to advise Gillmore prior to initiating any offensive action, and he is await permission to execute the action. Gillmore appoints Seymour commander of the recently established District of Florida. On the following day, Gillmore departs for Hilton Head.

In Mississippi, General William T. Sherman's Army occupies Meridian, subsequent to its abandonment by the Confederates. The Union proceeds to devastate the town, destroying ammunition depots, store houses, buildings and railroads. Union General William S. Smith's troops have been stymied at the Ohio River by ice, which prevents them from reaching the city. Sherman's orders read: "The destruction of the railroads intersecting at Meridian is of great importance. Every tie and rail for many miles should be destroyed or injured and every bridge and culvert should be completely destroyed." General Stephen A. Hurlbut's force handles the task to the east and north. McPherson is directed to handle the area to the west and south.

General James McPherson and his chief engineers (*Harper's Pictoral History of the Civil War*, 1896).

The working parties are guarded by Winslow's cavalry. The operation gets underway on the 16th. The rails being destroyed are known as "Jeff Davis' neckties" and "Sherman's hairpins." Sherman also reduces buildings, including factories and stations, to prevent future use by the Confederates, but private homes remain unscathed.

In Virginia, a contingent of the 13th Pennsylvania Cavalry led by Major Larmer skirmishes with a contingent of Confederates at Brentsville. The Union sustains four killed and one wounded. Confederate casualties are unavailable.

In Louisiana, the 49th Colored Regiment, led by Captain Johnson and supported by the gunboat USS *Forest Rose*, battles for two days with Confederates at Waterproof. The Union sustains eight killed and 14 wounded. The Confederates sustain 15 killed. Afterward, the *Forest Rose* remains on patrol for the duration of the war. It is decommissioned and sold during August 1865. The *Forest Rose* is renamed *Anna White* and operates as a civilian vessel until February 1868, when it is destroyed by ice at St. Louis, Missouri.

February 15 (Monday) In Florida, Union General Gillmore departs for Hilton Head, South Carolina. The twelve regiments under General Truman Seymour remain; however, Gillmore instructs Seymour to remain in the area around Baldwin and refrain from moving into the interior of Florida. Nevertheless, General Seymour, who had recently expressed concern about an attack, apparently has a change of heart. Without awaiting approval from Gillmore, he prepares to launch an offensive on the 19th, subsequent to sending Gillmore a message on his plans.

February 16 (Tuesday) In Alabama, Union gunboats bombard Confederate positions at Grant's Pass.

In Mississippi at Meridian, Union troops begin to destroy the Confederate property and rails. The operation lasts for about five days and concludes with the destruction of about 120 miles of rails, more than sixty bridges, twenty locomotives, lumber mills, depots and anything within a radius of twenty miles that is even remotely connected with the railroads. In other activity, the 32nd Wisconsin Volunteer and one Indiana regiment skirmishes with Confederates at Lauderdale Springs.

February 17 (Wednesday) In Mississippi, a contingent of the 17th Corps skirmishes with Confederates at Marion.

In Confederate general officer activity, General James Patton Anderson is promoted to major general.

In Union general officer activity, General James H. Wilson is appointed as chief of the cavalry bureau, headquartered in Washington, D.C. Later, during the campaign to seize Richmond, General Grant assigns him as commander of a cavalry division (General Sheridan's command), but in October, Wilson is transferred to the west, where he becomes chief of cavalry in General Sherman's Military Division of the Mississippi. The new appointment essentially elevates Wilson to a position held by Sheridan in the east.

In Naval activity, a Confederate submarine, the *H.L. Hunley*, referred to at this time as a "fish torpedo boat," initiates submarine warfare by sinking a Federal ship, the *Housatonic*, in Charleston Harbor, South Carolina. The Confederate *Hunley* also sinks itself during the engagement. Late last year, another Confederate submarine, the *David*, had unsuccessfully attacked the USS *Weehawken*. In other activity, the USS *Tahoma* lands a contingent near St. Marks, Florida. The column, composed of two detachments, moves about seven miles from the landing point and succeeds in destroying the salt works there.

February 18 (Thursday) In Florida, despite instructions from General Gillmore (commander, Department of the South) not to enter the interior, General Seymour informs Gillmore that he is advancing to the Suwanee River. Once informed, Gillmore speeds his chief of staff to halt the march, but by the time General John W. Turner (chief of staff and artillery, Department of the South) arrives on the 20th, Seymour's force has already reached the river and is heavily engaged with the Confederates.

In Virginia, Union cavalry under General David McMurtie Gregg departs Warrenton en route to Middleburgh.

In Confederate general officer activity, Colonel William Raine Peck is promoted to the rank of brigadier general, effective this date. Also, Colonel Travis Hawthorn is promoted to brigadier general.

In Naval activity, the USS *Galena*, having recently completed its repairs and been recommissioned, departs Philadelphia for its new duty station in the Gulf of Mexico; however, the weather is less than fair. The *Galena* becomes stranded due to ice when it reaches New Castle, Delaware. More misfortune follows. It is towed out to open seas by an ice boat, but afterward, it begins taking on water and is forced to halt yet again at Norfolk. Consequently, its southern course is reversed and it returns to Baltimore for additional repairs. On 20 May, it arrives at Pensacola to join the West Gulf Blockading Squadron.

February 19 (Friday) In Alabama, Confederate General William E. Baldwin is killed when he falls from his horse in the vicinity of Dog River Factory. General Baldwin participated at Fort Donelson and again at Vicksburg; at both places he was captured and paroled.

In Arkansas, Union troops of the 4th Arkansas and 4th Missouri Cavalry, commanded by Captain William Castle, while guarding a forage train, repulse a Confederate attack at Batesville. The Union suffers three dead and four wounded. The Confederates sustain six dead and 10 wounded.

In Louisiana, at Grosse Tete Bayou, the 4th Wisconsin Cavalry encounters and skirmishes with a contingent of Confederates. The Union sustains two wounded. The Confederates sustain four killed and six wounded.

February 20 (Saturday) THE BATTLE OF OLUSTEE A Union force under General Truman Seymour departs Baldwin moving toward the Suwanee River in Florida. Some contact is made by the vanguard of the Union force, and Rebel cavalrymen who intercept the advance withdraw towards Olustee, where brigadier general Joseph Finegan has laid some primitive yet fairly elaborate traps to snare the Union and halt its progress. By utilizing some nasty terrain and deploying to gain the advantage, Finegan lays in wait with a blocking line of infantry. He is flanked by cavalry at a strategic point that affords his right with a lake known as Lake Pond and his left with treacherous swamps. The layout of the Confederate defenses forces the Union to essentially funnel through a slim pathway that leads through an otherwise tranquil forest lined with pine trees, which impedes progress for the three columns and the accompanying artillery.

During the early part of the afternoon the vanguard under Colonel Guy V. Henry makes contact with the intercepting force; however, the initial Confederate cavalry unit is unable to quickly herd the Union toward the main defenses about two miles away. Instead, the battle escalates and Finegan dispatches additional troops to bolster the first wave and hurry the process. Nonetheless, the Union also commits additional troops. By this time, the Rebels have received reinforcements and hold nearly equal strength with the Yankees. Colonel Guy Henry's cavalry and the 7th Connecticut Regiment is in the lead when the Confederates strike. Using the swamp and the heavy brush, five Georgia regiments sprint to the sounds of the guns at about the same time as the main body of Colonel Joseph R. Hawley's brigade, the 7th New Hampshire and the 8th U.S. Colored Troops.

Soon after, the forest is transformed into a fiery quagmire. Instead of pine needles falling from the trees, cold steel is viciously clashing and the only limbs dropping are those of the opposing sides except for some of the trees that are severed by artillery shells. Meanwhile, the Union, which has encountered less than stiff resistance since they arrived in Florida, appears poised for a grand victory, but in the process of seizing the momentum, while the 7th New Hampshire Regiment is being positioned, there is either a mixup or a wrong interpretation concerning an order and the situation immediately turns grim for General Seymour's force. Unexpectedly, the entire line of the 7th New Hamp-

shire loses its discipline and this catastrophe is followed by more problems. Some troops bolt toward the rear, while the remainder at the front lack cohesion.

The golden opportunity is not wasted by the Confederates. They sprint toward the U.S. 8th Colored Troops who hold the left portion of the line. Unknown to the Rebels, the 8th U.S. Colored Troops is a fresh unit, which again provides Finegan's troops an opportunity. Colonel Charles Fribley exerts enormous energy to retain calm among the regiment and simultaneously hold the line to forestall disaster. Initially, his efforts bear fruit, but the pressure of the advancing Confederates, mostly seasoned veterans, drives a crack in the lines and begins to push the Union back. Suddenly, Colonel Fribley sustains a mortal wound. Following his demise, the regiment is unable to hold. It folds and retreats hurriedly. The collapse had been caused by the attacks of Colquitt and Harrison on the right and left respectively.

The Confederates had sprung their attack and seemingly strike from every direction, pressing the Union to take desperate action. Rugged hand-to-hand combat has turned the forest floor into a blood-bath, but the ordeal is overwhelming for the Union, which is sustaining casualties at an alarming rate. Even the batteries of Captains Samuel Elder, L.L. Langdon and John Hamilton, stretched from the left to right, respectively, are unable to stem the tide.

The 47th, 48th and 115th New York Regiments (Colonel William Barton's Brigade) are committed to the field and their tenacity finally halts the progress of the attackers. The toll up to this point is extremely high on both sides, but neither antagonist is prepared to give quarter. The intensity of the fighting lessens in great part because the Confederates have nearly expended their supply of ammunition. Runners are dispatched to Olustee to get a new supply of ammo while troops move among the men who have fallen to search for any remaining ammunition.

At this time, the outcome of the battle is unpredictable, but as the afternoon progresses, the Confederates are re-supplied and General Joseph Finegan arrives on the field. He brings in the available reserves and still controls the terrain, giving the Union few options, considering they are nearly encircled with swamps and the pine field in their path is swarming with Rebels. The arrival of the fresh troops (the 1st Florida Battalion and Major A. Bonaud's Battalion) invigorates the Confederates. General Seymour's force again sustains a feverish attack. Relentlessly, the Rebels advance and pour constant fire upon the Yankees. Eventually, it becomes clear to Seymour that his force is no longer capable of withstanding the force of the assaults. He takes measures to save his command by rushing his reserve force (Colonel James Montgomery's Brigade) to plug the gap and afford cover fire while the retreat is executed.

Montgomery's 35th U.S. Colored Troops and the 54th Massachusetts Colored Infantry Regiment advance and deploy, but despite their steadfastness, the Rebels are restrained for only

a short while. Nonetheless, their stand permits Seymour to extricate his remaining forces from their precarious positions and begin the march that takes them back to Jacksonville. While the Union retreats, the withdrawal is covered by the 54th Massachusetts, the 7th Connecticut and U.S. Cavalry. The Union departs in great haste, which causes many of the wounded to be left on the field. In addition, the Confederates also gain much equipment. Despite the disorganized retirement, the pursuing Confederate cavalry are unable to intercept the main body, permitting most of Seymour's troops to reach Barber's Plantation before the night has passed. Colonel Caraway Smith, who had commanded the cavalry that gives chase, receives criticism for his failure to catch Seymour. The Union makes it back to Jacksonville by the 22nd. By the time the guns had subsided, both sides had become exhausted, which might explain why the Confederates did not initiate a full pursuit.

The 54th Massachusetts Regiment loses the majority of its top rank officers while forestalling the late-day assault. The Union suffers 193 dead, 1,175 wounded and 400 missing. The Confederates suffer 100 killed and 400 wounded. Participating were the 47th, 48th and 115th New York, 7th Connecticut, 7th New Hampshire, 40th Massachusetts Volunteers, 54th Massachusetts Colored Troops and the 8th U.S. Colored Troops (1st North Carolina Colored Troops). In addition, the force is bolstered by the 1st and 3rd U.S. Artillery and the 3rd Rhode Island Artillery. The Confederate units that participate are Brigadier General Alfred H. Colquitt's Brigade, composed of the 6th Florida Infantry Battalion, 6th, 19th, 23rd, and 28th Georgia Infantry, Chatham's Artillery (Georgia), and Gamble's (Leon, Light) Artillery (Florida); and Colonel George P. Harrison's Brigade, composed of the 1st Florida Infantry Battalion, 1st Georgia Regular Infantry, 32nd and 34th Georgia Infantry, Bonaud's Battalion (28th Georgia Artillery Battalion) reinforced by some additional Florida troops, Abell's Artillery (Florida unit) and Guerard's Battery (Georgia). In addition, the Confederate forces include Colonel Caraway Smith's cavalry brigade, composed of the 4th Georgia Cavalry, 2nd Florida Cavalry and the 5th Florida Cavalry Battalion.

This engagement is the only major battle fought in Florida. Afterward, General Seymour confines his activity to initiating raids throughout the area. On the Confederate side, a battalion of partisan raiders led by Colonel Theodore Washington Brevard participates at Olustee as a contingent of a Florida infantry regiment. Following the battle at Olustee, Brevard is appointed colonel of the regiment. Also, Confederate General William M. Gardner participates.

In Illinois, a contingent of U.S. Marines, commanded by 1st Lieutenant Richard S. Collum, arrives at Mound City to protect the ammunition depot there.

In Mississippi, inclement weather prevents General William S. Smith's forces from reaching Sherman at Meridian. Sherman, tired of waiting, evacuates Meridian and moves back to

Vicksburg. He accompanies General Stephen Hurlbut's column, which moves northerly through Marion and Muckalusha (Old Town) to Union. From there Sherman dispatches cavalry to Columbus. The main body departs Union for Hillsboro. McPherson moves along the main road and joins Sherman at Hillsboro on the 23rd. In related activity, a contingent of General William Sooy Smith's cavalry skirmishes with Confederates at Prairie Station.

February 21 (Sunday)   In Maryland, the town of Cumberland, held by a strong Union force, is raided at night by John Hanson McNeil's Confederate partisan rangers. The surprise raid is successful and the Rebels leave town with Union Generals George Crook and Benjamin F. Kelley as prisoners. The generals are taken to Richmond and exchanged there.

In Mississippi, detachments of General William S. Smith's cavalry skirmish with Confederates at West Point.

February 22 (Monday)   In Arkansas, General Alfred Ellet's Mississippi Marine Brigade engages Confederates at Luna Landing.

In South Carolina, the 85th Pennsylvania and the 4th New Hampshire Regiments, operating in the vicinity of Whitemarsh Island, skirmish with Confederates. The Union sustains four killed. The Confederates lose about 40 captured.

In Florida, following the defeat at Olustee, the Union forces under General Truman Seymour arrive back at Jacksonville. The Confederate victory eradicates any thoughts of a Union takeover of Florida as a loyal state in the Union as President Lincoln had hoped. The Union does succeed in interrupting the Confederates' task of getting Florida cattle to its troops in the other states, partly because they retain Jacksonville for the duration of the conflict.

In Tennessee, Union troops under General W.S. Smith, including the 9th Tennessee Cavalry, are defeated by Confederates at Mulberry Gap (Wyerman's Mills). The Union sustains 13 killed or wounded and 256 men captured. Smith had recently abandoned a planned attack against Columbus, Mississippi, thinking it too heavily defended by Confederates; however, it had only about 3,000 troops under Nathan Bedford Forrest. The Rebels, having attacked Smith, compel him to fight a running retreat, but once at Okolona, Mississippi (Ivy Farm or Ivy Hills), things take a bad turn and the Union gets thrashed. The 4th Missouri Cavalry participates. After dark, Smith retires toward Memphis. A Union counter-charge temporarily helps the fleeing Union soldiers, who arrive at Memphis on the night of the 25th-26th.

In other activity, a 24-man detachment from the 5th Tennessee Cavalry is captured and executed by a band of Confederate renegades (Champ Ferguson's command) in the vicinity of Johnson's Mills, White County. In other activity, two companies of the 34th Kentucky Infantry clash with Confederates in a close-quartered fight that lasts for about four hours at Powell's River Bridge. Also, a one-company contingent of the 91st Indiana Volunteers skirmishes with Confederates at Cumberland.

In Virginia, a contingent of the 2nd Massachusetts Cavalry encounters and engages Confederates under John S. Mosby at Dranesville. The Union sustains 10 killed, seven wounded and 57 captured. The Confederates sustain two killed and four wounded.

In Union general officer activity, Brigadier General John Milton Thayer is appointed commander of the District of the Frontier. He operates out of Fort Smith, Arkansas. He remains in Arkansas for the rest of the war and participates in support action of the Red River Expedition.

In Naval activity, the USS *Linden* attempts to give some aid to the transport *Ad. Hines,* which is in distress on the Arkansas River. However, the *Linden* hits an obstacle and sinks.

February 23 (Tuesday)   In Georgia, Brigadier General William D. Whipple, in the vicinity of Tunnel Hill, sends a message to General George H. Thomas that the force of General Cruft is making camp at Catoosa Creek and that he is closing on General Absalom Baird. He also reports that the Confederates seem to be abandoning Dalton. In addition, he reports that a contingent under Colonel Eli Long had engaged a Confederate contingent outside of Dalton and scattered them. Long also reports capturing 12 prisoners.

In Mississippi, General William T. Sherman's Army, at Hillsboro, heads for Canton. The columns cross the Pearl River at Edward's Ferry and at Ratcliffe Ferry. In other activity, the 5th Tennessee Cavalry engages Confederates at Calf Killer Creek on this day and on the 18th of March. The Union sustains eight killed and three wounded. The Confederates sustain 33 killed.

In Confederate general officer activity, Colonel Robert C. Tyler, still recuperating from the loss of his leg at Missionary Ridge the previous November, is promoted to the rank of brigadier general.

In Naval activity, the *Elfin,* a light-draft gunboat, is acquired by the U.S. Navy at Cincinnati and assigned to the Mississippi Squadron. Acting Master A.F. Thompson becomes commander.

February 24 (Wednesday)   In Georgia, General John M. Palmer receives a message from General George H. Thomas (Commander Army of the Cumberland). It directs General Palmer that if he seizes Dalton, all wagons are to be sent back to Thomas's headquarters to be loaded with provisions and supplies. At 1625, General

Whipple sends General Thomas a message: "Your message received. We have just gained possession of Tunnel Hill; small loss."

February 25 (Thursday)   In Alabama, a Union naval force approaches and bombards Fort Powell, which lies just below Mobile. During this period, the USS *Calhoun* acts as Admiral Farragut's flagship. It is decommissioned the following May. It is transferred to the U.S. Army during June and renamed the *General Sedgewick.* It remains in service until after the conclusion of the war. It is sold later in the year and operates as the *Calhoun.*

In Georgia, Union troops (4th and 14th Corps and Cavalry Corps) under General George H. Thomas and Confederate forces under General Joseph E. Johnston engage at Buzzard Roost, Tunnel Hill and Rocky Face Ridge through the 27th. The Union casualties are 17 dead and 272 wounded; Confederates have 20 dead, 120 wounded and several hundred captured.

February 26 (Friday)   In Washington, D.C., Congress re-authorizes the rank of lieutenant general of the Army. George Washington had held the rank, and General Winfield Scott had held the rank of brevet lieutenant general.

In Georgia, a contingent of the 4th Michigan Cavalry, led by Captain W.W. Van Antwerp, departs on a reconnaissance mission to investigate the Dalton Road to the front of the advancing columns (1st Division, Fourth Corps). The reconnaissance contingent, after advancing about four miles, skirmishes with Confederate pickets and drives them off, but due to firing to the rear, Captain Antwerp, out if concern of being cut off, heads for the woods, arrives at Varnell's Station, and afterward moves to Stone Church.

In Mississippi, General Sherman's Army reaches Canton. Skirmishes will develop.

In Confederate general officer activity, Colonel William Wirt Allen becomes a brigadier general effective this day.

February 27 (Saturday)   In Georgia, Captain W.W. Antwerp, 4th Michigan Cavalry,

Saving the Pearl River bridge (***Harper's Pictorial History of the Civil War,*** 1896).

which had investigated the Dalton Road to the front of the division on the previous day, on this day reconnoiters the Tunnel Hill Road. Shortly after beginning its advance, Antwerp's contingent encounters Confederate skirmishers and the Union is able to neutralize the Rebels. Meanwhile, General Cruft's columns pass. Afterward, Antwerp's command acts as rear guard.

In Mississippi, for two days the 3rd and 32nd Iowa engage Confederates at Canton. The Union suffers two dead and six wounded. Confederates suffer 18 dead or wounded.

In Naval activity, a landing party from the USS *Tahoma* destroys a Confederate salt works complex at Goose Creek, Florida. The contingent has a harrowing experience with Confederate cavalry, but it succeeds in evading discovery. The party also seizes 12 prisoners, including a Confederate infantry captain.

February 28 (Sunday)   In Mississippi, the 3rd U.S. Colored Cavalry and the 1st Mississippi Regiments skirmish with Confederates at Yazoo City.

In Kentucky, a contingent of the 7th Tennessee Cavalry engages Confederates at Dukedom.

In Naval activity, the USS *Penobscot,* while on patrol off the coast of Texas near Velasco, seizes a British blockade runner, the schooner *Lilly,* and its cargo of gunpowder. On the following day, the *Penobscot* intercepts two additional blockade runners, the *Stingray* and the *John Douglas,* both schooners.

February 28–March 4   In Virginia, Union troops commanded by General Hugh J. Kilpatrick, composed of more than 3,000 cavalrymen, set out to raid Richmond, but the Confederates have prior knowledge and make the necessary preparations to repulse the assault. When Kilpatrick moves out, General John Sedgwick's corps and cavalry under General George A. Custer initiate a diversionary raid to distract the troops at General Lee's lines. Meanwhile, Kilpatrick's force crosses the Rapidan at Ely's Ford and moves to Spotsylvania Court House. From there, Colonel Ulric Dahlgren, in command of 500 specially selected cavalrymen, moves out to the James River. Kilpatrick, leading the main body, drives toward Beaver Dam Station to destroy the Virginia Central Railroad. While there, some Confederate troops arrive from Richmond, but the skirmish is short-lived, as the Rebels retire. Colonel Dahlgren's force gets held up along its route, making the raid more difficult for the Union.

Following the minor skirmish, Kilpatrick moves freely and arrives at the entrance to Richmond on March 1. However, Dahlgren, who has reached the James River, sustains some ill-gotten assistance. Dahlgren acquires a guide at the River, but the man intentionally takes Dahlgren a full day's march out of the way. Consequently, the guide is hanged from a tree and the column speeds from Goochland Court House toward Richmond to join Kilpatrick. The troops under Dahlgren arrive at the steps of Richmond during the latter part of the night

of March 1. However, in the meantime, General Kilpatrick, having had no communication from Dahlgren, decides to move back down the peninsula. By now the Confederates in Richmond are well aware of the encroaching Yankees.

While Fitzpatrick and Dahlgren are both retiring, more confusion enters the picture. Dahlgren and about 100 of his men, on the night of the 2nd–3rd, become separated from the main body and they are ambushed by Confederates. Colonel Uric Dahlgren is slain and many others are captured. The survivors are able to rejoin Kilpatrick for the long march back. Dahlgren's body is recovered by Confederates, who discover documents in his possession calling for the burning of Richmond. Colonel Dahlgren was the son of Admiral John A. Dahlgren. The Union is forced to withdraw without consummating their orders to free Union prisoners held in Richmond. The Confederates pursue the retreating Union troops. The Union sustains 330 killed, wounded or missing. Confederates suffer 308 killed, wounded or missing.

February 29 (Monday)   In North Carolina, a Union contingent (specific units not reported) skirmishes with Confederates at New Bern.

In Virginia, a detachment of the 6th New York Cavalry led by Major Hall (part of Kilpatrick's Raid) skirmishes with Confederates at Taylorsville, South Anna River.

In Naval activity, Admiral David D. Porter initiates an expedition on the Black and Ouachita Rivers that lasts through March 5. Porter remains aboard the USS *Cricket* as his flagship. The squadron advances as far as Springfield Landing, Louisiana, but the mission is unexpectedly aborted after Porter is informed of a Confederate victory at Pleasant Hill. Porter turns back and returns to the Red River Station. The Confederates observe the difficulty the squadron experiences due to low water levels that impede the voyage back to the Mississippi. Confederate ground troops at various spots along the river banks repeatedly fire upon the ships, but no serious harm is inflicted.

March 1 (Tuesday)   In Virginia, General Custer's Cavalry, part of General Kilpatrick's Cavalry, engages Confederates at Stanardsville and Burton's Ford, Rapidan. The 1st, 2nd, 5th, and 6th Pennsylvania, the 1st New York and the 1st New Jersey Cavalry Regiments participate. The Union sustains 10 wounded. The Confederates lose 10 captured. Other contingents of Kilpatrick's cavalry capture about 60 Confederates along the Brooks Turnpike. And yet another contingent of Kilpatrick's cavalry clashes with Confederates at Atlee's, Bidnella Crossroads.

In Confederate general officer activity, Captain Richard L. Page, Confederate States Navy, a first cousin of Robert E. Lee, is appointed to the rank of brigadier general. After switching his uniform from that of the Confederate Navy he is assigned responsibility for the defenses of

Mobile Bay, Alabama. Colonel Claudius W. Sears is also promoted to the rank of brigadier general, effective this date. Sears had been with the 46th Mississippi at Vicksburg and was among those captured. Sears is assigned duty with General John B. Hood's command. Also, Colonel William Feimster Tucker, 41st Mississippi Regiment, is promoted to the rank of brigadier general, effective this day.

In Naval activity, at about this time (March), the USS *Massasoit* (double-ender steam gunboat) is commissioned. The *Massasoit,* however, remains at Boston until August, when it initiates patrol duty off the New England coast. In October it is assigned to the North Atlantic Blockading Squadron for a while before it is transferred to duty on the James River in Virginia. In April 1865 it is sent south to North Carolina for the duration. It is decommissioned during June 1865 and sold in October 1867. In other activity, the U.S. Navy acquires the vessel *Cricket,* a steamer, at about this time (March). It is transformed into a tinclad river gunboat, commissioned USS *Nymph* the following month, attached to the Mississippi Squadron, and assigned duty on the western rivers for the duration. It is decommissioned soon after the close of hostilities, in June 1865, and is sold the following month. The *Nymph* at that time reverts back to its original name, *Cricket,* and operates as a civilian vessel.

March 2 (Wednesday)   In Washington, D.C., President Lincoln shelves the intended "death penalty" for those troops imprisoned for desertion. Instead, the president issues an order sentencing them to "imprisonment during the war." They are to be detained at Dry Tortugas, Florida.

In Virginia, elements of General Hugh Kilpatrick's cavalry raid Walkertown.

In Naval activity, Union vessels attached to Admiral David D. Porter's squadron encounter Confederates at Harrisonburg, Louisiana. The USS *Hindman* sustains serious damage from Confederate shore batteries. James Duncan (a seaman) becomes a recipient of the Medal of Honor when he risks his life to get a burning cartridge, set afire from an incoming shell. He tosses it overboard. In other activity, a large Union flotilla, including the USS *Mound City* and more than fifteen other warships, joins General Sherman's Red River Expedition.

March 3 (Thursday)   In Tennessee, one company from the 3rd Tennessee Infantry engages a Confederate contingent at Panther Springs. The Confederates sustain 30 men wounded, but they capture 22 Union soldiers. The Union also loses two dead and eight wounded.

In Virginia, the 7th Michigan and the 1st Vermont Cavalry Regiments commanded by Colonel (later brevet brigadier general) Allyne C. Litchfield and Lt. Colonel Addison W. Preston repulse a Confederate attack upon their positions at Tunstall Station. On 3 June, during the fighting in and around Cold Harbor, Lt. Colonel Preston is killed.

March 4 (Friday) **In Mississippi,** Ellet's Mississippi Marine Brigade engages Confederates at Rodney.

March 5 (Saturday) **In Mississippi,** during the Yazoo River Campaign in the vicinity of Yazoo City, troops from the USS *Marmora* engage Confederate troops. Seaman Batlett Laffey, U.S. Navy, lands with a twelve-pound howitzer. Laffey, with the rest of the crew, repositions the gun despite heavy enemy fire and commences firing, successfully forcing the Confederates to withdraw. Laffey receives the Medal of Honor for his gallantry. In conjunction, the 3rd U.S. Colored Cavalry (1st Mississippi), 47th U.S. Colored Troops (8th Louisiana) and the 11th Illinois Volunteers participate. Following this action, the *Marmora* resumes its duty on the Little Red River and the White and Yazoo Rivers until it is decommissioned during July 1865. It is sold the following month.

In other activity, the 1st Mississippi Marine Brigade (General Alfred Ellet) clashes with Confederates at Coleman. Also, a contingent of the 3rd Tennessee Regiment skirmishes with Confederates at Panther Springs. The Union sustains two killed, eight wounded and ten captured. The Confederates sustain 30 wounded.

In Confederate general officer activity, Colonel Alpheus Baker (54th Alabama) is appointed brigadier general. Colonel Daniel Harris Reynolds, 1st Arkansas Mounted Rifles, is promoted to the rank of brigadier general effective this date. General Reynolds is assigned duty with Lt. General John B. Hood. He will participate in Georgia and in the Carolinas.

March 6 (Sunday) **In Arkansas,** the 14th Kentucky Cavalry skirmishes with Confederates at Flint Creek.

In Mississippi, at Vicksburg, General William T. Sherman directs General Andrew J. Smith to move to the mouth of the Red River to rendezvous with Admiral David Porter. Smith's force is drawn from the 1st and 3rd Divisions of the 16th Corps. Twenty transports carry the force, which is to participate in the operation to seize control of Texas.

In Confederate general officer activity, Colonel John Bullock Clark, Jr., is promoted brigadier general effective this day. He serves for the duration under General Marmaduke and General Shelby in the Trans-Mississippi Department. After the war he returns to his law practice. His father, John Bullock Clark, Sr., during the years 1861–1862, was a brigadier general in the Missouri State Guard.

In Naval activity, the USS *Memphis* comes under attack near Charleston on the North Edisto River by a Confederate submarine, the CSS *David*, but the *Memphis* survives serious damage because the torpedoes misfire. The *Memphis* continues its service in the South until the conclusion of the war and remains in active service until decommissioned during 1867. In 1869, the *Memphis* again becomes a merchant ship (*Mississippi*) until it is destroyed by fire on 13 May 1883 while at Seattle. In other activity,

the USS *Monticello* and the USS *Peterhoff* collide. The *Monticello*, which inadvertently slams in to the *Peterhoff*, escapes; however, the *Peterhoff* sinks.

March 7 (Monday) **In Alabama,** contingents of the Army of the Tennessee (General Grenville Dodge's command) skirmish with Confederates at Decatur. The Union captures the town.

In Naval activity, the steamer *Ben Gaylord* is acquired by the U.S. Navy at Cincinnati, Ohio. During the following month, it is commissioned the USS *Undine*. The *Undine* is assigned duty with the Mississippi Squadron.

March 8 (Tuesday) **In Virginia,** Union troops, including the 93rd New York Infantry under the command of Lt. Robert S. Robertson, engage Confederates at Corbin's Station. Robertson calls for the troops to regroup and initiates a countercharge that rejuvenates the Yankees, who then hold off the Confederates. Robertson becomes a recipient of the Medal of Honor for his courage during this engagement.

In Union general officer activity, Colonel Charles Jackson Paine resigns to take a position on General Butler's staff. In turn, through General Butler's efforts, Paine is promoted to brigadier general, to rank from 4 July 1864. Subsequently, he participates at Drewry's Bluff, New Market and the operations against Fort Fisher, North Carolina, followed by service with General William T. Sherman in North Carolina. He remains in the army beyond the close of hostilities and musters out of the service during 1866 with the brevet rank of major general.

In Naval activity, the USS *Conestoga* collides with the USS *General Price* (formerly CSS *General Price*) off Bondurant Point on the Red River. The *Conestoga* sinks. The *Conestoga*, prior to its being commissioned, had been renamed the *Sangamon* (9 September 1862); however, it is separate from the USS *Sangamon*. Also, the USS *General Price*, subsequent to this activity, participates in the Red River Expedition in April. Afterward it continues in service until decommissioned in July 1865. It is sold during October 1865.

March 9 (Wednesday) **In Washington, D.C.,** General Ulysses Simpson Grant is promoted to general in chief, commander of the Union Armies, replacing General Henry Halleck. This Union force at this time exceeds 500,000 men. Grant personally commands the Army of the Potomac and soon after, places General William T. Sherman in charge of the Western Armies. Lincoln personally presents Grant's commission. Part of Lincoln's statement to Grant reads: "As the country here intrusts you, so, under God, it will sustain you." General Grant, prior to initiating his Overland campaign against Richmond, makes changes in his force. The troops of the I Corps and III Corps, each severely depleted at Gettysburg, are merged into the II, V and VI Corps. Consequently, Grant also reduces the number of general officers, one of whom is General Francis

Barretto Spinola. General Spinola, once detached from the Army of the Potomac, returns to New York to initiate recruiting duty in New York City. Spinola is later accused of defrauding recruits. At a court-martial he is sentenced to be dismissed from the army. Nonetheless, at some point the sentence is apparently countermanded. His resignation is accepted on 8 June 1865. His reputation does not derail his resumption of a political career. He dies while beginning his third term in the U.S. Congress during 1891.

In Virginia, the 2nd U.S. Colored Regiment skirmishes with Confederates at Suffolk. The Union sustains eight killed and one wounded. The Confederates sustain 25 wounded. In other activity, a contingent of Confederate guerrillas captures about 40 Union cavalry troopers at Bristoe Station.

In Mississippi, Confederate guerrillas attack the Union steamer USS *Hillman* in the vicinity of Island No. 18.

In Union general officer activity, Brigadier General William Farrar Smith, having received accolades from General Grant as well as Generals Sherman and George H. Thomas for his "genius" in getting supplies and food to Chattanooga to prevent General Rosecrans' command from catastrophe due to the threat by General Braxton Bragg, is promoted to major general. He had also been noted for his heroic actions at Missionary Ridge. After his promotion, he is ordered north, where he receives command of the XVIII Corps, Army of the Potomac.

In Naval activity, the *Agawam*, a double-ended, side-wheel gunboat, is commissioned. Alexander C. Rhind receives command. Also, Union gunboats (Admiral David D. Porter's fleet), commanded by Lt. Commander Owen, accompanied by a contingent of troops led by Colonel E.D. Osband (in place of Colonel James H. Coates, 11th Illinois), move up the Yazoo River to launch an attack to seize Yazoo City, Mississippi. The Rebels repel the assault and the action concludes on April 22. Colonel Osband, commander of the 3rd U.S. Colored Regiment, had formerly been colonel of the 4th Illinois.

March 10 (Thursday) **In Louisiana,** at Bayou Teche, General William B. Franklin receives orders to move to support the assault against Alexandria, but the unit does not arrive there by the 17th. Franklin's force moves out on the 13th, but the final elements of his command do not arrive at Natchitoches until 3 April. Also, the 1st New York Veteran Cavalry skirmishes with Confederates at Cabletown.

In Virginia, General Grant confers with General George G. Meade, commander of the Army of the Potomac, at Brandy Station to prepare strategy for upcoming actions against the Confederacy. Meade suggests that General William T. Sherman be chosen to replace Grant as commander in the West and Grant concurs. General Meade is considered a general's general, a man who does his duty without regard for personal triumph. Another change made is the transfer of Major Frederick T. Dent (West Point, 1843) from his command in New York to Grant's staff. Major Dent is Grant's brother-in-law. Dent becomes brigadier general during April 1865.

March 11 (Friday) **In Florida,** Union forces led by Colonel William Barton occupy Pilatka.

In Louisiana, the forces of Union General A.J. Smith arrive from Vicksburg at the mouth of the Red River, where it converges with the Atchafalaya and Mississippi Rivers to join with the fleet of Admiral David D. Porter.

March 12 (Saturday) **In *Naval activity,*** the gunboat USS *Curlew,* subsequent to completing repairs, departs from Mound City, Illinois. It is transporting a team from the U.S. Coast Survey which will survey Grand Gulf, Mississippi. The mission concludes on 31 May.

March 12–May 29 **In Louisiana,** Admiral Porter, aboard his flagship *Blackhawk,* on March 12 divides his fleet into two squadrons. Porter leads one up the Atchafalaya River, while Lt. Commander S.L. Phelps advances up the Red River with the other. Porter's squadron is composed of nine vessels, the *Benton* (Lt. Commander J.A. Greer), *Carondelet* (Lt. Commander J.G. Mitchell), *Chillicothe* (Lt. S.P. Couthony), *Gazelle* (Master Charles Thatcher), *Lexington* (Lt. G.M. Bache), *Baron de Kalb* (formerly *Louisville*; Lt. Commander E.K. Owen), *Mound City* (Lt. A.R. Langthorne), *Ouachita* (Lt. Commander Byron Wilson) and the *Pittsburg* (Lt. W.R. Hoel). Phelps' Squadron comprises the vessels *Eastport* (Phelps), *Black Hawk* (Lt. Commander K.R. Breese), *Cricket* (Master H. Gorringe), *Essex* (Commander Robert Townsend), *Fort Hindman* (Lt. John Pearce), *Lafayette* (Lt. Commander J.P. Foster), *Neosho*

(Lt. Samuel Howard), *Osage* (Lt. Commander T.O. Selfridge) and the *Ozark* (Lt. G.W. Browne).

The USS *Fort Hindman* had initially been commissioned as the USS *James Thompson* and later the USS *Manitou.* The *Fort Hindman* participates in the Red River Expedition and afterward patrols the lower sector of the Mississippi River for the duration. In August 1865, it is decommissioned and becomes a merchant ship, renamed *James Thompson.* Also, the USS *Essex* completes its services when it is decommissioned during July 1865. Afterward, the *Essex* is sold and it is renamed, reverting back to its original name, *New Era.* The USS *Benton* returns to Louisiana during June 1865. After the war, it is decommissioned during July and sold in November. The USS *Pittsburg,* following this action, resumes its patrols until the war ends. It is decommissioned shortly after that and sold in November 1865.

March 13 (Sunday) **In Louisiana,** Admiral Porter's Fleet arrives at Simmesport, prompting the Confederates there to make their way to Fort DeRussy. The Union, under the command of General Andrew J. Smith, launches an attack to reduce the fort on the following day.

In Virginia, a Union force composed of elements of the 1st New York Mounted Rifles, 11th Pennsylvania Cavalry, the 6th, 27th and 45th

U.S. Colored Troops, bolstered by artillery and commanded by General Isaac Wistar, engages Confederates at Carrollton. The Confederates sustain about 20 killed and 70 wounded or captured.

In *Naval activity,* at about this time (March 1864), the U.S. Navy commissions the USS *Onondaga,* a twin-turret monitor. It operates as part of the James River Flotilla and participates in various actions against the Confederates during the summer and during December 1863 and January 1865. The *Onondaga* is decommissioned in June 1865 and then is returned to the firm that built it in Greenpoint, New York. After congressional approval, the ship is sold to France for service in the French Navy under the name *Onondaga.*

March 14 (Monday) **In Louisiana,** during the Red River Campaign, Union troops (under General Nathaniel Banks and Admiral David D. Porter) attack and capture Fort DeRussy. The Confederates are commanded by Major General Richard Taylor. The Union commander is General Andrew J. Smith. Union General Joseph A. Mower (previously

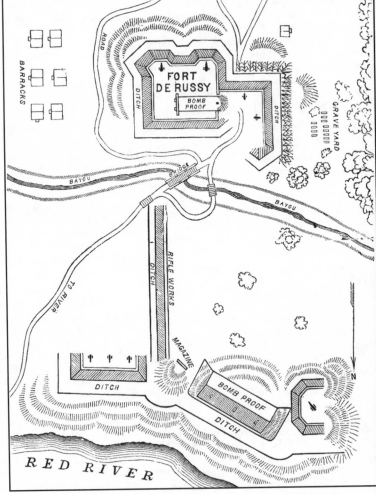

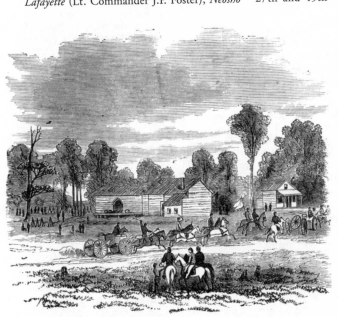

Left: **Brandy Station, Virginia** (Mottelay, *The Soldier in Our Civil War,* 1886). *Right:* **Plan of Fort DeRussy** (*Harper's Pictoral History of the Civil War,* 1896).

woundedand captured at the battle of Corinth) heads the assault column, which moves thirty miles and strikes the fort during the afternoon. A few gunboats reach the area subsequent to the capture of the fort. The Union suffers seven dead and 41 wounded. The Confederates lose five dead, four wounded and 260 taken prisoner. Following this seizure, the fleet moves against Alexandria.

In Tennessee, Union cavalry commanded by General Israel Garrard skirmishes with Confederates at Cheek's Crossroads.

March 15 (Tuesday)   In Washington, D.C., President Lincoln requests 200,000 additional troops for service in the navy and as reserves.

In Louisiana, Union troops being transported by Admiral David D. Porter's fleet arrive at Alexandria. Following some heated skirmishing during the latter part of this Tuesday night, advance troops enter the city. The remainder of the fleet arrives on the following day.

In Arkansas, contingents of the 8th Missouri Cavalry skirmish with Confederates at Clarendon. The Union suffers one killed and three wounded. Confederate casualties are unavailable.

March 16 (Wednesday)   In Louisiana, the main body of Admiral David D. Porter's fleet arrives at Alexandria to join those vessels already there. Union troops, including elements of the 5th Minnesota Volunteer Regiment assisted by U.S. gunboats, occupy the city.

In Tennessee, Union troops (specific units unreported) skirmish with Confederates at Fort Pillow.

In Virginia, Corporal Andrew Traynor, 1st Michigan Cavalry, and other Union prisoners overpower their captors at Mason's Hill and safely escape; Traynor becomes a recipient of the Medal of Honor for his heroism during the escape.

In Union general officer activity, Brigadier General Hugh Thompson Reid is relieved of command. His resignation is accepted on 4 April.

March 17 (Thursday)   In Tennessee at Nashville, Generals U.S. Grant and W.T. Sherman formulate attack plans against the Confederates positioned at Dalton, Georgia, commanded by General Joseph E. Johnston. In other activity, the 5th Tennessee Cavalry (formerly First Middle Tennessee Cavalry), led by Colonel William B. Stokes, encounters and battles a contingent of Confederate guerrillas commanded by Champ Ferguson, a partisan ranger at Manchester. No casualties are reported by the Union. The Confederates sustain 21 killed.

March 18 (Friday)   In Arkansas, the 7th Missouri Cavalry skirmishes with Confederates at Monticello.

In Tennessee, General Grant prepares to leave Nashville and travel to Washington, D.C., to assume command of all U.S. armies. General

Sherman succeeds Grant as commander of the Military Division of the Mississippi, which includes the departments of the Ohio, Arkansas, Cumberland and Tennessee. General William T. Sherman accompanies Grant as far as Cincinnati to confer on future assignments. Also, the 5th Tennessee Cavalry, commanded by Colonel William B. Stokes, attacks Confederate guerrillas led by Champ Ferguson at Calf Killer. The Confederates sustain eight killed.

March 19 (Saturday)   In Louisiana, General Charles P. Stone, General Banks' chief of staff, arrives at Alexandria. A division of cavalry under General Albert Lindley P. Lee accompanies him. General Lee makes it known that General Banks is now at Opelousas, about 65 miles from Alexandria.

March 20 (Sunday)   In Tennessee, elements of the 5th Tennessee Cavalry skirmishes with Confederates at Beersheba Springs.

March 21 (Monday)   In Louisiana, Union forces under General Joseph Mower, including a detachment of the 16th Corps and the 19th Corps' cavalry division, engage and defeat the Confederate contingent commanded by Major General Richard Taylor at Henderson Hills (Bayou Rapids or Rapides). The Union sustains one dead; the Confederates, eight dead and 250 captured. The 5th Minnesota Volunteer Regiment participates. In addition, the Union confiscates about 200 horses and several guns. Some of the Rebels following this skirmish encounter elements of General William B. Franklin's force, which is en route to Alexandria.

In Texas, the CSS *Clifton* (formerly USS *Clifton*), while trying to break through the naval blockade near Sabine Pass, runs aground. The crew disposes of the cotton cargo; however, they are unable to free the ship. It is burned to prevent capture.

March 22 (Tuesday)   In Maryland, at Baltimore, Union Major General Lew Wallace assumes com-

mand of the Middle Department, Eighth Corps. He succeeds Brigadier General Henry H. Lockwood and holds the post until 1 February 1865.

March 23 (Wednesday)   In Arkansas, Union troops (7th Corps), numbering about 7,000 under General Frederick Steele, depart Little Rock to reinforce General Nathaniel Prentiss Banks at Alexandria, Louisiana. Steele's force, including about 3,000 cavalry under General Eugene Asa Carr, has been operating in and

The Red River Campaign (*Harper's Pictorial History of the Civil War,* 1896).

around Little Rock since its capture during September of the previous year; however, the initial strength was about 12,000 troops. The corps had sustained battle casualties during the various skirmishes, but many others had become casualties due to sickness, particularly due to the swampy terrain the columns had to cross while moving from Helena to Little Rock during July 1863. General Steele moves to Arkadelphia, where he is to be joined by General John M. Thayer and about 5,000 troops from Fort Smith.

In Tennessee, Confederate General Forrest, whose force now stands at about 6,000 troops, captures Jackson.

March 24 (Thursday) **In Kentucky,** Confederate cavalry of General Nathan B. Forrest's command, under the direct command of Colonel William Duckworth and bolstered by artillery, launch the strike against Union City at 0430. The Rebel force of about 1,200 men surrounds the fort, recently erected by Colonel Isaac R. Hawkins, but his garrison of only by about 500 troops also lacks artillery. The defenders, however, do not easily capitulate. According to Captain John W. Beatty, 7th Tennessee Volunteer Cavalry, the defenders repulse four attacks before the garrison surrenders. At 1100, Forrest demands surrender and the officers, except one, choose to fight. Nevertheless, it is agreed that if the Confederates offer parole to the officers and allow them to keep their sidearms, they will surrender. Otherwise, the choice is to "fight to the last man." Hawkins surrenders, but unknown to his command, the terms are unconditional. Once informed of his action, he is cursed and those officers in his command vow never to serve under him again. Hawkins surrenders at about 1110. By noon, the Rebels set the barracks on fire.

During the march into Tennessee, some of the captives escape at Trenton. Captain Beatty and Captain P.K. Parsons escape at Humboldt on the 26th. About 450 men of the U.S. 7th Tennessee Cavalry are taken prisoner and marched toward Dresden, Tennessee. An engine had been sent to Hawkins' aid, but the Rebels had burned the railroad bridge over the Obion River at the Kentucky-Tennessee state line, forcing the engine to return to Columbus, Kentucky. Also, the Confederates seize Hickman. Forrest then proceeds to assault Paducah the following day.

In other activity, Union Major General William Henry French, who has lost much favor with General Meade since the campaign the previous November, is released from the Army of the Potomac; he will muster out of the service in May.

In Naval activity, the USS *Sunflower* seizes a blockade runner, the *Josephine,* in Sarasota Sound while the ship attempts to reach Havana from Tampa, Florida.

March 25 (Friday) **In Kentucky,** Union and Confederate troops engage at Fort Anderson in Paducah. The Confederates are led by Generals Nathan Bedford Forrest, Abraham Buford and Colonel Albert P. Thompson. Union forces are commanded by Colonel S.G. Hicks with the contingents of Colonel Cunningham (8th U.S. Colored Artillery), Major Barnes (16th Kentucky Cavalry) and Major Chapman (122nd Illinois Regiment), totaling about 650 troops. The Union is assisted by the USS *Peosta* and *Pawpaw.* Once informed of the approach of the huge Confederate force, Hicks reels in all the troops and he has them well prepared for the imminent assault, particularly due to the assistance of the nearby gunboats, commanded by Captain Skirk, U.S. Navy. Forrest issues an ultimatum, offering the Yankees an opportunity to surrender or face his overwhelming strength with "no quarter given." Hicks informs him that his government had instructed him to defend the fort and he would do just that. The Rebels seize the nearby buildings and launch two assaults, but neither succeeds. Just before midnight (25th-26th), the Confederates disengage and retire. The Union suffers 14 dead and 46 wounded. The Confederates sustain ten dead, including Colonel A.P. Thompson, who is killed by an explosion of a shell. The Confederates also suffer about 40 wounded and 30 captured. The USS *Peosta,* commissioned during October 1863, continues to operate on the Tennessee River for the duration of the war. It is decommissioned during August 1865 and soon after sold. After sailing as a merchant ship, the *Peosta,* while at Memphis, is destroyed by fire on Christmas Day 1870.

In Ohio, General William T. Sherman departs Cincinnati, returning to Nashville, and from there he leaves for Huntsville, Alabama, to confer with General James B. McPherson. Sherman and McPherson move to Chattanooga and Knoxville, checking the condition of the troops and conferring with Generals George Thomas and John Schofield. In other activity, Major Generals Alfred Pleasonton and John Newton are released from the Army of the Potomac due to reorganization. Pleasonton is assigned to the Department of Missouri, commanded by William S. Rosecrans. Newton is sent to the West, where he serves with General William T. Sherman. Afterward, General Newton is transferred to Florida to command the Department of West Florida for the duration of the war. In the meantime, his promotion to major general the previous March is cancelled on 18 April. Nevertheless, toward the close of hostilities, Newton is breveted major general in the volunteers and in the Regular Army. After the war, General Newton remains in the army. He is appointed chief of engineers on 56 March 1884 with the rank of brigadier general. He retires during 1886.

In Naval activity, the USS *Winona,* while operating on the Suwanee River, intercepts and destroys an unidentified Confederate steamer. Subsequently, the *Winona* participates in attacks against Confederate-held Forts Rosedon and Beaulieu, both in the vicinity of Savannah, Georgia. It finishes its duty on the Combahee River, also in Georgia. On 9 June 1865, it is decommissioned at Portsmouth, New Hampshire. From there it is moved to New York during the following November and sold on the 30th.

March 26 (Saturday) **In Kentucky,** Union cavalry under General William T. Sherman is sent against Nathan Bedford Forrest's cavalry at Paducah. The Confederates, aware that Union reinforcements are en route from Cairo, Illinois, withdraw, heading toward Fort Pillow, Tennessee, which is located along the Mississippi River about seventy miles above Memphis.

In Virginia, General U.S. Grant decides to establish his headquarters at Culpeper.

In Arkansas, Union and Confederate forces clash through March 30 at and in the vicinity of Longview and Mt. Elba. The 28th Wisconsin Regiment and the 5th Kansas and 7th Missouri Cavalry Regiments participate. The Union sustains four killed and 18 wounded. The Confederates suffer 12 killed, 35 wounded and about 300 captured.

March 27 (Sunday) **In Tennessee,** Confederate Colonel John M. Hughes surrenders his command, the 25th Tennessee Regiment, to Colonel William B. Stokes (Union 5th Tennessee Cavalry) at Sparta. It is reported that Colonel Hughes requests permission from Colonel Stokes to take the oath of allegiance to the Union. Also, the Confederate 25th Tennessee Regiment is soon re-established and rejoins the ongoing conflict by the following month.

March 28 (Monday) **In Arkansas,** the 2nd Kansas Cavalry skirmishes with Confederates at Danville. Also, the vanguard of the 7th Corps' cavalry skirmishes with Confederates at Arkadelphia.

In Illinois, troops from the 54th Illinois Volunteers, led by Colonel Grenville M. Mitchell, are attacked in Charleston by a mob of Copperheads (Southern sympathizers) who have been called to action in states under Union control. The Union suffers two dead and eight wounded. The Confederates sustain three dead, four wounded and twelve taken prisoner.

March 29 (Tuesday) **In Louisiana,** Confederate soldiers have been flowing into Major General Richard Taylor's encampment on the Red River, hoping to prevent advancement of Union troops under General Nathaniel Banks into Shreveport. The Union, meanwhile, is perplexed by the low tide on the river, which prevents the naval fleet from making its advance.

In Tennessee, the 6th Tennessee Cavalry engages Confederates at Bolivar. The Union sustains eight killed and 35 wounded. Confederate casualties are unavailable.

In Naval activity, the federal court in Springfield declares the vessel *Alonzo Child* as a legitimate prize. At this time, it is a receiving ship at Cairo, Illinois. On 29 March 1865, exactly one year later, the *Alonzo Child* is sold when the Mississippi Squadron is downsized.

March 30 (Wednesday) **In Arkansas,** a Union force, including the 7th Missouri and

General Banks' army crosses the Cane River on 31 March, en route to Shreveport (Johnson, *Campfire and Battlefield: History of the Conflicts and Campaigns*, 1894).

5th Kansas Cavalry and the 28th Wisconsin Volunteers, captures a large number of Confederates at Mount Elba.

In Louisiana, a Union contingent of the 118th Illinois Volunteer Regiment skirmishes with Confederates at Grosse Tete Bayou.

March 31 (Thursday) **In Louisiana,** a 600-man contingent of Union cavalry, attached to the 19th Corps and commanded by General Nathaniel Banks, clashes with a Confederate cavalry force numbering about 1,500 troops at Natchitoches. The Union reports no casualties. The Confederates sustain six killed and wounded and about 25 captured. Banks' force crosses the Cane River en route to Shreveport.

In Mississippi, the 3rd U.S. Colored Cavalry (1st Mississippi) engages Confederates at Roach's or Brook's Plantation in the vicinity of Snydersville. The Union loses 16 killed and three wounded. The Confederates suffer three killed and seven wounded.

April 1 (Friday) **In Florida,** skirmishing develops at Fort Gates.

In Arkansas, a Union force commanded by General Christopher Columbus Andrews clashes with Confederates under General Dandridge McRae at Augusta (Fitzhugh's Woods). The Union 3rd Minnesota Infantry Regiment and the 8th Missouri Cavalry participate. The Union sustains eight killed and 16 wounded. The Confederates sustain 15 killed and 45 wounded.

In Kentucky, Union troops under Colonel Stephen G. Hicks (40th Illinois Cavalry) repel the Confederate forces of General Nathan B. Forrest at the Ohio River near Paducah. Forrest withdraws, heading for Fort Pillow, Tennessee.

In Virginia, the Union 1st Connecticut Cavalry skirmishes with Confederates at the Rappahannock River.

In Naval activity, at about this time (April), the U.S. Navy acquires a 974-ton double-ender side-wheel steamer built at Boston. It is com-

missioned the USS *Mattabesett* and attached to the blockading vessels operating in the North Carolina sounds. In other activity, the USS *Iosco* is commissioned at about this time (April). It is assigned duty farther north than most warships brought into the U.S. Navy: in the Gulf of St. Lawrence, with responsibility for protecting U.S. shipping. As summer fades, it is reassigned and ordered to join the North Atlantic Blockading Squadron. Also, the USS *Mackinaw* is commissioned at about this time (April). The double-ender steam gunboat is assigned duty on the James River; however, during January 1865, it participates in the operations against Fort Fisher in North Carolina. Following that action it initiates patrols on the Cape Fear River until it is decommissioned during May 1865. It is recommissioned in January 1866; however, during the following May it is decommissioned and sold during October 1867. Also during April, the USS *Petrel* is captured and burned off Yazoo City, Mississippi.

April 2 (Saturday) **In Arkansas,** a Union contingent composed of the 13th Illinois and the 1st Iowa Cavalry Regiments (General Frederick Steele's Raid) clash with Confederates at Antoine. Also, other units under General Steele)—including the 20th Iowa, 9th Wisconsin, 50th Indiana and the 1st Missouri Cavalry led by General Samuel Rice—battle at Spoonville (Terre Noire Creek). The Union sustains 10 killed and 35 wounded. The Confederates suffer 100 killed and wounded. Advance troops of the 7th Corps under Steele clash with Confederates at Camden.

In Florida, a detachment of the 14th New York Cavalry led by Captain Schmidt engages a contingent of Confederate cavalry composed of about 50 troops, led by Major Randolph, at Pensacola. The fighting quickly turns to hand-to-hand combat. The Union sustains three wounded. The Confederates sustain about 10 killed and wounded and 11 captured.

In Louisiana, elements of the 14th New York Cavalry, the 2nd Louisiana, 2nd Illinois and 16th Missouri Cavalry Regiments, supported by the 5th U.S. Colored Artillery commanded by Albert Lindley Lee, engage Confederates at Crump's Hill (Piney Woods). The Union sustains 20 wounded. The Confederates sustain 10 killed, 25 wounded and some captured.

In Tennessee, a Union contingent of the 1st Wisconsin Cavalry skirmishes with Confederates at Cleveland.

In Naval activity, the tinclad river gunboat USS *Naiad* is commissioned at about this time (April). The *Naiad* had originally been built in

Pennsylvania at Freedom and held the name *Princess* until acquired by the U.S. Navy during March 1864. It is sent south and assigned duty in the western rivers, including operations around New Orleans. It is decommissioned during June 1865 and sold the following August, at which time it reverts to its original name, *Princess*. It remains in service as a commercial vessel until 1 June 1868, when it strikes an obstacle and sinks off Napoleon, Missouri.

April 3 (Sunday) **In Arkansas,** Union contingents (Steele's expedition)—including the 35th Iowa, 40th Iowa, 77th Ohio, 43rd Illinois Infantry Regiments and the 1st Missouri and 13th Illinois Cavalry Regiments—skirmish with Confederate units at Okolona. The Union sustains 16 killed and 74 wounded. The Confederates sustain 75 killed and wounded.

In Louisiana, the trailing contingents of General William B. Franklin's force encounter and engage Confederates, but following the skirmishing, the troops enter Natchitoches to join the main body. From there, General William B. Franklin, commanding General Banks' force, will depart for the vicinity of Loggy Bayou. Franklin's instructions direct him to seek out and engage the Confederates, but to avoid a major confrontation. The vanguard of the advancing column is General A.L. Lee's cavalry, which continually intercepts Confederate units as it advances. Then, on the 8th, the cavalry encounters the main body of Confederate General Thomas Green's cavalry at a point only several miles above Pleasant Hill. In conjunction, Colonel (later brigadier general) James E. Harrison, 15th Texas Infantry, participates with Green during this Louisiana campaign.

In Tennessee, General William T. Sherman sends General John M. Corse (Sherman's inspector general) on a mission to see General Nathaniel Banks. Corse carries a letter addressed to Banks requesting the return of two divisions that Sherman lent to Banks' Army of the Gulf for the Shreveport Campaign.

In Naval activity, the monitor USS *Saugus* is commissioned at about this time (April). It is attached to the North Atlantic Squadron.

April 4 (Monday) **In Louisiana,** General A.J. Smith's force arrives at Grand Ecore. Smith had been with Admiral Porter's fleet, but with the river too shallow to accommodate the large warships, the bulk of the troops reverted to taking an overland route. In other activity, the 35th Iowa and 5th Minnesota Infantry Regiments, the 2nd New York, 18th New York and 3rd Rhode Island Cavalry Regiments, led by Colonel (later brevet brigadier general) Oliver P. Gooding, encounter and engage Confederates at Campti. The Union suffers 10 killed and 18 wounded. The Confederates sustain three killed and 12 wounded.

In Arkansas, Union (General Frederick Steele's Raid) and Confederate units continue to clash at various points. From the 4th to the 6th, the 43rd Indiana, 29th and 36th Iowa, bolstered by the 1st Iowa Cavalry and Battery E, 2nd Missouri Light Artillery, skirmish with Rebel units at Elkin's Ford, Little River. The Union sustains 19 killed and 11 wounded. The Confederates sustain 18 killed and 30 wounded.

In Union general officer activity, Brigadier General William R. Montgomery (West Point, 1825), another of the older Federal leaders, is forced to retire from active service because of ill health, but his contribution to the Union cause is timely. General Montgomery, during the pressing first months of the conflict, had organized the New Jersey Volunteers, with whom he served as colonel from April 1862 through March 1863. Also, Brigadier General Theophilus Garrard resigns his commission. General William Reading Montgomery, while based in Memphis serving on a military commission, is compelled to resign from the army due to ill health. Brigadier General Andrew Porter, having been in active service but quite ill for some time, resigns his commission. Subsequently, he travels to Europe for his heath; he settles in France, where he dies on 3 January 1872.

Brigadier General Charles Pomeroy Stone, attached to General Banks' command in the Department of the Gulf, receives more grief from higher command. Despite having performed well at both Port Hudson and during the Red River Campaign, he is mustered out of the volunteer commission of brigadier general because of the actions of Secretary of War Edwin M. Stanton, but Stanton also causes him to lose his rank as colonel in the Regular Army. Essentially, he is again absent of a command. Consequently, he resigns on 13 September 1864. He becomes chief of staff of the Army of the Khedive (Egypt) and serves with distinction. Upon his death in New York City on 24 January 1887, he is interred at West Point.

April 5 (Tuesday)   In Arkansas, a contingent of troops, composed of 75 men drawn from the 2nd and 6th Kansas Cavalry, skirmish with Confederate guerrillas at Roseville. The Union sustains 19 killed and 11 wounded. The Confederates sustain 15 killed, 25 wounded and 11 captured. In other activity, another detachment of the 6th Kansas Cavalry encounters Confederate guerrillas. This unit, composed of only 26 troops, sustains heavy casualties when it attempts to beat off the Rebels at Stone's Farm. Eleven of the men, including the assistant surgeon Fairchild, are captured and summarily executed.

April 6 (Wednesday)   In Kentucky, Company I, 14th Kentucky Regiment, skirmishes with Confederates at Quicksand Creek. Union casualties not reported. The Confederates sustain 10 killed and seven wounded.

In Louisiana, the Red River Campaign inches along. Low water nearly paralyzes the Federal fleet as it crawls toward Shreveport. Simultaneously, General Nathaniel Banks' ground forces move precariously along a terrible road through Rebel-held terrain. A force of more than 15,000 Confederates now stand between the Union Army and Shreveport.

In Union general officer activity, Brigadier General Daniel Tyler (West Point, 1819) exceeds the mandatory retirement age of 65 and resigns from the army. General Tyler participated at First Manassas and Corinth. He is the uncle of Union General Robert O. Tyler.

In Naval activity, the vessel *Julia A. Hodges*—used by the Confederates for several purposes, including as a mail carrier, dispatch carrier and a flag of truce vessel—is seized by the gunboat USS *Estrella* in the vicinity of Indianola, Texas. The *Estrella* remains in the Gulf region beyond the close of hostilities and becomes the flagship of the Gulf Squadron. In summer of 1867, it is decommissioned; then it is sold during July 1867. It operates as a commercial vessel until 1870.

April 7 (Thursday)   In Louisiana, the Confederates prepare to attack the Union troops advancing against Shreveport. Confederate Major General Richard Taylor orders an all-out assault on Union lines at Sabine Crossroads on the 8th. This upcoming action will determine who will hold this part of Louisiana. In other activity, Union General Andrew J. Smith leaves Lt. Commander Phelps and General Thomas Kilby Smith with a force of about 2,000 troops at Grand Ecore. Smith takes the remainder of his force aboard ships of Admiral David D. Porter's Fleet and heads for Loggy Bayou, which stands directly opposite Springfield Landing. The flotilla, which includes the light-draught gunboats *Chillicothe, Cricket, Hindman, Lexington, Neosho* and the *Osage*, expects to reach its destination on the 10th, at about the same time General Nathaniel Banks' force is to arrive. The USS *Chillicothe*, subsequent to this action, remains in service on the lower Mississippi for the duration. It is sold during November 1865 and remains in service as a commercial vessel until destroyed by fire during September 1872.

In related activity, General A.P. Lee's cavalry, the vanguard of General W.B. Franklin's force, advances to the vicinity of Pleasant Hill and discovers the main body of Confederate General Thomas Green's cavalry. Colonel H. Robinson's brigade attacks the Rebel force and ignites a ferocious two-hour battle in the vicinity of Wilson's Farm. The Confederates are pushed back to St. Patrick's Bayou (Bayou de Paul), but it is heavily defended by artillery and infantry. Rather than attack with only his cavalry, Robinson halts activity for the night to await the ar-

rival of reinforcements. A brigade under Colonel William J. Landrum arrives on the following morning. Another skirmish develops at Plain's Store in the vicinity of Port Hudson. Also, a contingent of the 118th Illinois Regiment, the 3rd Illinois Cavalry and the 21st New York Battery clashes with Confederate cavalry. The Union sustains one killed and four wounded. Confederate casualties are unavailable, but six are captured.

In Oregon, the 1st Oregon Cavalry engages Confederates at Harney Lake Valley. Casualty figures are unavailable.

In Naval activity, the USS *Lexington,* accompanied by five other gunboats en route to Shreveport, passes over the falls to bolster General Nathaniel Prentiss Banks. Several days afterward, the hulk of the steamer *New Falls City* sinks in the vicinity of Springfield Landing, creating an obstacle that prevents the squadron from passing. Other complications develop shortly thereafter when the news of General Banks' defeat at Sabine Cross Roads arrives.

April 8 (Friday)   In Arkansas, Battery I, 2nd Missouri Light Artillery, commanded by Lt. Phillips, repels a Confederate attack upon its camp at Pembescott Bayou. The Union sustains four killed and seven wounded. Confederate Casualty figures are unavailable.

In Louisiana, Confederates attack a Union wagon train attached to General Alfred L. Lee in the vicinity of Mansfield. General Lee's cavalry is at this time participating in the fighting at Mansfield (Sabine Cross Roads).

Confederates attack General Alfred E. Lee's wagon train in the vicinity of Mansfield, Louisiana (Mottelay, *The Soldier in Our Civil War*, 1886).

In Tennessee, Union cavalry under General Benjamin Grierson, operating in the vicinity of Wolf River, destroys a bridge and skirmishes with Confederates. During the operation the Union sustains about eight killed and wounded. The Confederates lose two captured.

In Union general officer activity, Brigadier General Camille de Polignac, who had succeeded to divisional command upon the death of General Mouton at Sabine Cross Roads (April 8–9) is promoted to the rank of major general effective this date.

In Confederate general officer activity, Major General Richard Taylor is promoted to lieutenant general, effective this date.

April 8–9 Battle of Sabine Cross Roads (Mansfield) A Union force under Colonel George D. Robinson, supported by Colonel William J. Landrum's brigade, advances toward Sabine Cross Roads, Louisiana. During the afternoon, the column encounters the Confederates and a skirmish develops. The Confederates are unable to withstand the thrust and decide to pull back. The running battle lasts for about seven miles as the Rebels move into some dense woods. Unknown to the Union, the main body of General Richard Taylor's force, including General De Polignac's Texas brigade (Jean Mouton's division), is also in the woods. The Union and the Confederates slug it out, but at this point no major confrontation occurs.

Later in the afternoon, more reinforcements advance to join Robinson and Landrum, but still Taylor does not show his strength. With the addition of General Thomas E. Ransom's brigade the Union feels confident, but soon, the full thrust of the Confederate force burst from the woods, stinging the Union. The contingents of Generals Richard Taylor, Thomas Green, Jean Moulton and Kirby Smith intensify the fury by whacking the entire front lines of the Union, followed by tenacious penetration at the right and center. While the troops on the Union's left attempt to stiffen the lines, the Confederates seize the advantage and pummel the weakened left flank. The pressure collapses the left, and the blankets of fire that had enveloped the area had inadvertently killed most of the horses there. Consequently, some of the artillery is abandoned, giving the Rebels three guns (Nin's Battery).

In the meantime, the right and center are about to fold, but the defenders remain steadfast and hold the line just long enough for fresh troops to arrive. A brigade of Indianians under General Robert A. Cameron plugs the holes and the lines are rejuvenated. The battle becomes even more furious as the Union attempts to smash the Rebels back to oblivion. Nevertheless, the Confederates relentlessly punch their way forward, and despite the initial steadfast stand, the Union grudgingly gives ground to a tide of gray uniforms that begins to wildly sweep forward in unstoppable fashion. The Union pulls back, but slowly and with great discipline, heading toward their baggage trains.

Meanwhile, General Albert Lindley Lee's cavalry moves boldly to intercept the Confederate units that are driving toward the rear of the lines, but here, too, the overwhelming power of the Rebel attack is too strong to neutralize. Suddenly, as it becomes clear that the cavalry is unable to stem the tide, the Union lines begin to collapse. Rather than hang tightly and resist by offering a holding action to cover a withdrawal, the troops lose their fearlessness and race to the rear. The officers, including General Nathaniel Banks, are unable to maintain discipline. It becomes the equivalent of every man for himself.

The Confederates accelerate their speed and chase the fleeing Yankees, following them for a distance of nearly three miles. But here, they encounter the 1st Division, (Nineteenth Corps) led by General W.H. Emory. He had been ordered by General William Franklin to establish positions at Pleasant Grove. The 162nd New York Regiment, 3rd Brigade, commanded by Colonel William B. Kinsey, stretches out to intercept the imminent wave of sliding steel. Colonel Lewis Benedict holds the remainder of the 3rd Brigade on the far left beyond General William Dwight's 1st Brigade on the other side of the road. In addition, the 2nd Brigade under General James W. McMillan holds in reserve. This remains the final line of defense. If it folds, the fleet itself might perish. All the while, the Confederates continue their rapid-paced advance, tossing the opposition asunder.

The endless waves of Confederates smash into the New Yorkers and deliver a stunning blow that drives the unit back into the main body. The fighting quickly moves to close-quartered slashing and bashing that has bodies flying everywhere. Both sides claw feverishly to pound the final blow. The Rebels swing toward and then into the defenses of General Dwight, jeopardizing the Union line and making the situation more desperate. At this point, the reserves bolt to the front to retain the lines and bolster the defenses. Nevertheless, the Rebels pack even more ferociousness into their assault. Neither side is ready to relent. General William Emory's lines are boldly struck and some penetration is made here by the Confederates; however, the attack fails to turn the flank, and Emory's troops hold.

The bloody slug-fest continues for about one and one-half hours without reprieve. In a superlative effort to forestall catastrophe, the 162nd New York Regiment, which had earlier been shoved back from its positions, reaches for some inner strength and launches a counterattack. It is joined by the 173rd New York Regiment. Combined, these two regiments somehow raise the momentum to drive straight into the Rebel lines and bring the conflagration to an end. The Union, aware that its positions remain jeopardized, decides at about midnight that it would be prudent to retire to Pleasant Hills.

In the meantime, the Confederates are regrouping in the vicinity of Mansfield. The mighty charge of the Rebels is halted. Both sides have sustained enormous casualties. This massive show of force by the Confederates is unable to destroy General Banks' force, but it does suc-ceed in preventing the Union fleet from reaching Shreveport. In contrast, General W.H. Emory's division prevents the Confederates from totally devastating the Union force, including the warships in the area. The sounds of battle subside for the night, but they begin anew on the following day.

On the 9th, the Confederates, aware that the Union had retired, dispatch cavalry to intercept and attempt to finish the task of whipping Banks' forces. The Union front lines are manned by General W. Emory's troops, which had done an outstanding job on the previous day. The Confederates encounter the pickets slightly before 1300 and a hellish skirmish erupts, but the major confrontation occurs at about 1630 when the Rebels storm the right side of Emory's positions.

The Confederates confidently pound against the lines; this assault is soon joined by a full-scale assault against the entire line. Fresh troops from Arkansas, commanded by General Thomas J. Churchill, stiffen the punch as the Rebels drill forward against riveting fire, seemingly oblivious to the shot and shell that is falling in their midst. Forward, forward is the order of the day. The troops trudge step by step through a tunnel of whirlwind fire and many fall in the process, while others, badly wounded, still push ahead. However, the Yankees, which are sustaining equally horrid and punishing fire, maintain their perspective. Casualties continue to climb and behind this rigid Union line lay countless broken bodies. But the pride along the line remains indelible, ensuring only more grim results for both sides.

The combined forces of Generals John G. Walker, Camille de Polignac (succeeded Moulton), Thomas Green and Thomas J. Churchill press against the troops of Union brigades of McMillan, Dwight and Benedict. Slightly to the rear in reserve stands the force of General Andrew J. Smith. Another Union force, that of General Thomas E.G. Ransom, which still has not completely recovered from the chaos of the previous day, remains out of the fight; it is directed to move to Grand Ecore. The initial skirmishing had been like a simmering fuse, but now, as the Confederates suddenly bolt from the woods to lambast Banks' bastion, the rolling thunder and the clashing steel turns the battlefield into a crimson field of carnage.

General Lewis Benedict's brigade receives the brunt of this massive assault, but the 30th Maine and the 165th and 173rd New York firmly receive the juggernaut and return devastating fire, including artillery from a nearby knob that inflicts serious casualties upon the assault force. The endless stream of gray uniforms dashes straight ahead, the men pounding their way yard by yard. All the while, more shot and shell pummel the columns, but still the Rebels advance, ignoring the avalanche of fire. Close-quartered bloody fighting occurs and each side bludgeons the other, inflicting savage wounds. But the staunch resistance by the Union is unable to stem the tide. More Confederates pile on and Emory's right side, having lost great numbers, shows signs of collapse. Colonel Lewis

Benedict rushes to rally his troops to launch a counterattack, but he sustains a fatal wound before it jumps off.

The Confederates maintain the offensive and punch a hole on Emory's right. Attempts are made to close the hole and an excruciating battle ignites, but the pressure compels the Union to pull back at this point. Confidently, the Rebels pour through the gap, giving wild chase as Emory's force withdraws toward the positions of the 16th Corps, which is concealed just beyond the crest of a hill. Unexpectedly, the charging Rebels encounter the forces of General Andrew Jackson Smith, which are still held in reserve. Smith's command commences firing from every direction, with every available gun spreading riveting fire upon the charging Confederates. The walls of fire prove too formidable for the attackers.

The Confederates, who had been happily hunting the Yankees for two days, are now the hunted. The Union launches a potent counterattack that heavily whacks the Confederates as they retire. This violent raging skirmish escalates into a donnybrook as the Union infantry drives the Confederates back to the woods. During this final battle of the enduring day, the Confederates lose many to the casualty list and many more are captured before the hostilities end after dusk. The Union, which had previously lost some guns, recaptures six guns, including the four which had been abandoned by Benedict on the previous day.

The Union suffers 300 dead, 1,600 wounded and 2,100 missing. Confederates suffer 600 killed, 2,400 wounded and 500 missing. Confederate General Jean J.A. Mouton (West Point, 1850), leading his Louisiana brigade, initiates the battle at Sabine Cross Roads (Mansfield) and he is killed during the charge. Union General Lewis Benedict is mortally wounded. Union Brigadier General Thomas E.G. Ransom, leading a detachment of the XIII Corps, is gravely wounded (4th wound). Union Major General William B. Franklin is also wounded. Other Union officers include Colonel Vance (96th Ohio), Lt. Colonel Webb (77th Ohio), Captain Dickey, staff officer of General Ransom, and Colonel Robinson.

This victory for General Richard Taylor is a tremendous triumph for the Confederacy because it repulses the Union attempt to secure Louisiana. Taylor is not permitted to take advantage of the situation and requests being relieved of command. Taylor blames his superior, General Kirby Smith. However, for his actions, Taylor is promoted to lieutenant general and placed in command of the Department of Alabama and Mississippi. Confederate Major General John G. Walker will be assigned command of the District of Louisiana, succeeding Taylor, but later he is transferred to command a division in the District of Texas, Arizona and New Mexico. At the close of hostilities, he moves into Mexico without receiving a parole. Later, after his return to the U.S., he engages in various enterprises, including an appointment as consul general in Bogota, Colombia, and later as a special commissioner of the Pan-American Con-

vention to the South American Republics. He dies in Washington, D.C., on 20 July 1893. Also, Confederate Colonel Walter P. Lane (3rd Texas Cavalry) is seriously wounded. For his heroism he is promoted to brigadier general in March 1865.

Confederate Generals Price and James C. Tappan are present in this confrontation. Tappan's brigade, part of Churchill's division, is subsequently dispatched to assist against Union troops of General Frederick Steele, who are advancing from Little Rock to assist Banks in the Red River Campaign. Confederate Brigadier General Thomas Waul, among the captured at Vicksburg, also participates in this battle. The 28th Louisiana Infantry and the 4th Alabama Regiments under Colonel Henry Gray and General Evander McIvor Law, respectively, are also participants. Brigadier General William R. Scurry also takes part. Scurry's force is dispatched as part of the units that will intercept General Wilson's cavalry. The following July, General William Dwight is transferred to General Emory's XIX Corps, where he commands a division and participates in various actions in the Shenandoah Valley, including Cedar Creek, Fisher's Hill and Winchester. General Dwight becomes spotlighted not for his heroism; rather for his timetable for dining. He is accused of moving from the field of battle to eat his lunch out of the line of fire. Nonetheless, no formal action is taken. He resigns from the army during January 1865 and his name is not among those officers who receive brevet promotions at the conclusion of the war.

April 9 (Saturday) In Louisiana, Union forces, including the 5th Minnesota Volunteer Regiment, battle Confederates at Pleasant Hills (see also, **April 8–9 Battle of Sabine Cross Roads [Mansfield]**).

In Naval activity, a Confederate torpedo boat, the *Squib,* encroaches the USS *Minnesota* (Atlantic Blockading Squadron), which is anchored at Newport News and launches an attack. A torpedo detonates near the ship, but no damage or casualties occur.

April 10 (Sunday) In Louisiana, Confederate General Richard Taylor's victorious stand at Sabine Cross Roads and Pleasant Hills now assures control of this area for the Confederates, and they retain it for the duration of the war. The Union is stymied by these two defeats. Brigadier General St. John R. Liddell, who had transferred to Richard Taylor's command subsequent to the Confederates' loss of Corinth, participates in the Red River Campaign. Union reinforcements under Major General Frederick Steele never reach General Banks. They are halted by Confederates who force them to withdraw to Little Rock, Arkansas.

In other activity, General Banks prepares to continue to move against Shreveport, but he receives orders to retire to Grand Ecore. In the meantime, the Union fleet arrives this day at Springfield Landing following a difficult journey along a slim channel that contains many dangerous obstacles. Following the end of the

voyage that has extended more than one hundred miles, Admiral David D. Porter and General Thomas Kilby Smith, who had accompanied him, discover they can go no farther. A demolished, sunken ship blocks passage. Admiral Porter is informed of the retreat of Banks' Army and he is directed to immediately return to Grand Ecore.

In Virginia, Company K, 54th Pennsylvania Volunteer Regiment, skirmishes with Confederates at Little Cacapon. Casualty figures are unreported.

In Union general officer activity, Colonel John Franklin Miller is promoted to brigadier general to rank from January 5, 1864. At this time, he is still recuperating from a wound received the previous June. Nevertheless, he receives command of Nashville the next month. Also, Colonel Charles Garrison Harker is promoted to brigadier general for his heroic actions at the Battle of Chickamauga, effective the date of the battle.

In Naval activity, the steamer USS *General Hunter,* a transport vessel, is sunk by torpedoes in the St. John's River, Florida.

April 10–13 In Arkansas, the 3rd Division of Union General Steele's 7th Corps, en route to bolster General Banks' force, encounters stiff opposition raised by Confederates under General Sterling Price at Prairie D'Ann (D'Ane). The Union sustains about 100 casualties. The Confederates sustain about fifty. General Steele becomes aware of Nathaniel Banks' defeat at Sabine Cross Roads, Louisiana, and he finds that his own force is unable to make it to Shreveport. Consequently, Steele decides to move toward Camden, Arkansas. Confederates under General James Fleming Fagan launch several attacks against the columns as they move, but the Rebels are unable to turn the Union back. Nonetheless, soon after their arrival at Camden on the 15th, Steele becomes aware that large numbers of Confederate reinforcements under General E. Kirby Smith are converging on the area for a scheduled attack against Little Rock.

In Confederate general officer activity, Brigadier General James F. Fagan is promoted to major general effective 25 April 1864.

April 11 (Monday) In Louisiana, General Nathaniel Banks arrives at Grand Ecore from Sabine Cross Roads. The fleet is en route to Grand Ecore from Springfield Landing. It arrives this day at Conshattee (Conshutta) Chute and is met by a force of Confederates, led by General St. John R. Liddell and Colonel James E. Harrison. The combined strength is about 2,500 troops, and they are deployed on both sides of the Red River. The vessels sustain heavy fire; however, the ships are heavily padded with mattresses and items such as bales of hay, which contain the damage and keep the casualties to a minimum.

April 12 (Tuesday) Attack against Fort Pillow Confederates under General Nathan

Confederates massacre the garrison at Fort Pillow (Mottelay, *The Soldier in Our Civil War*, 1886).

Bedford Forrest assault Fort Pillow, Tennessee. The defending troops include the 11th U.S. Colored Troops (6th U.S. Colored Heavy Artillery and the 1st Alabama), Battery F, 2nd U.S. Colored Light Artillery, and Bradford's Battery of the 13th Tennessee Cavalry. The colored troops are commanded by Major L.F. Booth and the white troops are commanded by Major W.F. Bradford. During the early morning hours, the brigades of Bell and McCulloch (General Chalmers' division) storm the outside entrenchments and drive the pickets back. A sharp contest continues until about 0900, when the troops are ordered into the fort by Major Bradford, who now assumes command following the death of Major Booth.

At this point the Union is able to check the Confederate advance, due in great part to the support of the gunboat USS *New Era*, commanded by Captain Marshall, which propels shot after shot upon the Rebels deployed close to the river. By 1500, the fighting remains heated, but neither side is able to gain the advantage. The Confederates cease fire and send a party under a flag of truce to the fort to issue an ultimatum. The defenders have twenty minutes to respond.

While the Yankees ponder the question, the time lapses and the Confederates issue yet another ultimatum. Major Bradford, presenting himself as Major Booth so the Rebels will not know he had been killed, declines. Soon after, the Rebel bugles blow in cadence with a "Rebel yell" and the assault is reinitiated. Suddenly, from concealed positions, the Confederates bolt forward and the fort is taken. The Union defenders break in every direction, but to no avail. The Confederates pursue giving no-quarter, particularly to the colored troops. Subsequent to the capture of the fort, the commanding officer, Major Bradford, is among the prisoners forced to march to Jackson, Tennessee. Along the way, he is taken from the ranks and executed. The Confederates massacre most of the colored defenders attached to the 6th U.S. Colored Heavy Artillery and Battery F, 2nd Colored U.S. Light Artillery.

The Union suffers 350 killed, 60 wounded and 164 missing. The Confederates sustain 80 killed or wounded. Also, the Union 13th Tennessee Cavalry participates in this battle. Fort Pillow was previously ordered evacuated by Sherman, but General Stephen A. Hurlbut retained a small colored garrison to encourage blacks to enlist. Sherman, after the massacre, states: "Forrest's men acted like a set of barbarians, shooting down the helpless Negro garrison after the fort was in their possession."

In Colorado, a two-company contingent of the 1st Colorado Cavalry engages a band of Indians at Frémont's Orchard in Denver. The Union sustains two killed and four wounded.

In Naval activity, the U.S. 17th Corps, under General Banks and supported by Union gunboats, including the *Alice Vivian*, *Osage* and *Lexington*, attack Pleasant Hills (Blair's Landing), Louisiana. The *Alice Vivian* runs aground at about the same time the transport *Hastings* is approaching the bank to pause for repairs. Confederates posted nearby take this opportunity to commence firing. The Rebels having only four guns, but about 2,000 troops under General Thomas Green exchange shot and shell with the flotilla for about two hours. The heavy guns of the U.S. Navy force the Confederates to retire. Confederate General Thomas Green (brother-in-law of General James P. Major) is killed by fire from one of the Union gunboats. The vessels *Rob Roy* and *Emerald*, the latter equipped with 13-inch Rodman guns, also participate in the fighting. Confederate General William Steele assumes temporary command of Green's cavalry division until it is permanently taken by General John A. Wharton. After the war General Steele becomes a merchant in San Antonio, Texas. In 1873, he relocates to Austin and becomes the adjutant general of the state of Texas, a post he holds for six years. He dies in San Antonio on 12 January 1885. The Union loses seven wounded. Confederates lose 200 killed or wounded.

The *Hastings* is ordered to speed to Fort Pillow to support another gunboat, the *New Era*; however, the *Hastings* arrives too late. Nevertheless, it does arrive on the 14th. Subsequent to this incident, the *Hastings* begins to patrol the White River. It supports forces under General Frederick Steele in June 1864. It returns to Cairo during early January 1865 and is decommissioned on 7 July 1865. It is sold at Mound City on 17 August to become the merchant vessel *Dora*. The *Dora* remains in service until 1872 as a river freighter.

In other activity, after repairs (March–June 1862), the USS *South Carolina* joins the South Atlantic Blockading Squadron. On this day, while on patrol, the *South Carolina* seizes the blockade runner *Alliance* after it runs ashore.

Afterward it continues on blockade duty until March 1865, when it is placed out of service for modifications that change it into a store ship. It is recommissioned after the war during June 1865, and from that point it initiates duty as a supply transport that delivers stores to various ships in the Gulf of Mexico and in the Western Atlantic until decommissioned during August 1866. It is sold during October 1866 and renamed *Juniata*. Much later, during 1893, it is transformed into a barge. On 17 February 1902, while being towed, it sinks.

April 13 (Wednesday)   In Alabama, a contingent of the 9th Ohio Cavalry skirmishes with Confederates at Florence.

In Arkansas, Union troops from the 18th Iowa, 6th Kansas Cavalry, and the 2nd Indiana Battalion, attached to General Frederick Steele, engage Confederates at Moscow. The Union suffers five dead and 17 wounded. The Confederates sustain 30 dead or wounded. In other activity, the 56th U.S. Colored Troops (3rd Arkansas) skirmish with Confederates at Indian Bay.

In Kentucky, Confederate General Abraham Buford arrives at Columbus from Fort Pillow, Tennessee, and issues an ultimatum to the city, demanding surrender. The Union defenders reject the demands, but the Confederates hedge the bet and fail to launch an attack. Rather, they return to Fort Pillow to rejoin General Nathan Bedford Forrest. After being informed that a large Union force under General Samuel D. Sturgis is about to move against them, the Confederates depart for Mississippi. General Samuel Sturgis' force does not depart Bolivar, Tennessee, until 30 April, much too late to arrive in time to intercept Forrest. Also, skirmishes erupt for two days between Confederates and Kentucky volunteers at Half-Mount and Paintsville. The Union sustains four wounded. The Confederates sustain 25 killed and 25 wounded.

In Tennessee, a detachment of the 1st Wisconsin Cavalry clashes with Confederates at Cleveland.

In Naval activity, the USS *Rachael Seaman*, while on patrol on the Mermantau River, Louisiana, intercepts and captures a British blockade runner, the schooner *Maria Alfred*, which becomes its final prize. The *Rachael Seaman* returns to New York on 21 May and resumes duty as a supply ship for a short time prior to being decommissioned on 22 May 1865. It is sold at auction on 30 May. In other activity, the USS *William H. Brown* attempts to assist another warship, the *Chillicothe*, during the campaign on the Red River; however, the *William H. Brown* sustains hits by Confederate artillery. The vessel had been acquired by War Department during 1861 and transferred to the U.S. Navy during September 1862. It had been utilized primarily as a transports ship and a dispatch vessel. The *William H. Brown* is decommissioned in August 1865 and sold in November. It remains in service as a commercial vessel until about 1875.

April 14 (Thursday) In Arkansas, the 6th Kansas Cavalry (General Frederick Steele's Raid) clashes with Confederates at Dutch Mills. In addition, a contingent of the 7th Corps' vanguard (Steele's Raid) skirmishes with Confederates at Camden.

In Louisiana, Union vessels, which had recently been engaged against troops under the late General Thomas Green, begin to reach Grand Ecore, with the remainder of the fleet arriving there on the following day. This day some of the troops depart for Alexandria. The Confederate shore batteries keep pumping shells into the path of the departing ships. Many of the vessels remain in this area for several weeks. The low water level greatly impedes Union progress during this operation and the Confederates ensure that the vessels remain imperiled. During the voyage to Alexandria, the *Eastport* is sunk by a torpedo (mine) on the 15th. On the 26th, following failed efforts to refloat it, it is destroyed to prevent capture by the Confederates. According to the records of the Naval Historical Division, it is possible that the *Eastport* formerly had been the *C.E. Hillman*.

In Virginia, the 9th New Jersey, 23rd and 25th Massachusetts and the 118th New York Regiments engage Confederates at Smithfield (Cherry Grove). The Union contingents sustain five wounded. The Confederates suffer six wounded.

In Naval activity, Admiral David D. Porter arrives at Grand Ecore, Louisiana, and links with a part of his fleet earlier left there. Those vessels are still held up by the bar. Since Porter had left them, the river water levels had decreased, threatening the ships. Porter at the time comments: "Providence provided a man for the occasion." The fleet fortuitously has on hand Lt. Colonel Bailey, the acting engineer of the 19th Army Corps. Bailey moves expeditiously and oversees the construction of a chain of dams that stretch across the river at the falls that succeed in raising the water levels. The project saves the endangered vessels as they pass over the bar unharmed. Following the success of the mission, Admiral Porter is detached from the Mississippi Squadron and given command of the North Atlantic Blockading Squadron. As commander of the new squadron, Porter receives responsibility for the port of Wilmington and the Cape Fear River. In other activity, the USS *Victory* supports a Union force at Paducah, Kentucky, that repels a Confederate raid.

April 15 (Friday) In Arkansas, the 29th Iowa, 50th Indiana and 9th Wisconsin Volunteers (attached to General Frederick Steele's command) clash with Confederates at Liberty Post Office.

In Virginia, the 13th Pennsylvania Cavalry engages Confederate cavalry at Bristoe Station. The Union sustains one killed and two wounded. Confederate casualties are unavailable.

April 15–16 In Arkansas, Union troops under General Frederick Steele engage Confed-

erates in a heavy skirmish at Camden. This operation is in conjunction with the campaign of General Nathaniel Banks at Red River. Steele is attempting to complement Banks' advance to Alexandria by moving overland from Little Rock. This move by Steele's 7th Corps culminates without success, but he eventually returns his beleaguered force to Little Rock. Steele's force, unlike that of General Banks, has no naval support. During this skirmish, Confederate Colonel Richard M. Gano is wounded. Steele's troops again skirmish with Confederates at Camden on the 18th and on 24 April. Subsequently, Colonel Gano is appointed brigadier general by General Kirby Smith, but afterwards, it is officially given to him by President Davis, effective 17 March 1865. After the war, General Gano changes uniforms. He becomes a Protestant minister until his death in Dallas, Texas on 27 March 1913.

April 16 (Saturday) In Arkansas, the 2nd Arkansas Volunteers skirmish with Confederates at King's River.

In the Indian Territory, the 3rd Kansas Indian Home Guards engage Confederates at Scullyville (Oklahoma). Casualty figures are unavailable.

April 17 (Sunday) In Alabama, a contingent of the 25th Wisconsin Regiment exchanges blows with Confederates at Decatur. The Union sustains two wounded. Confederate casualties are unavailable.

In Virginia, with the realization that the Southerners are getting short on manpower, General U.S. Grant ceases all prisoner exchanges in hopes of shortening the war. This decision does work; however, Union prisoners suffer immensely due to shortages of food and supplies at Southern prisons. There are some exceptions to the rule. In one instance, the Union executes several Confederate spies and the Confederates announce they are about to execute several Union prisoners in retaliation. One particular Union prisoner is a personal friend of Abraham Lincoln and an officer in the New Jersey cavalry. The Union proclaims that General Robert E. Lee's son Rooney will be shot (William Henry Fitzhugh Lee is called Rooney to differentiate him and his cousin General Fitzhugh Lee) if the Confederates carry out their threat. A prisoner exchange is agreed upon. Subsequent to his exchange, Rooney Lee participates greatly near the end of the war with his cavalry and becomes second in command at Appomattox in April 1865.

April 17–20 In North Carolina, the Union positions at Plymouth, including several forts, come under siege by a large Confederate force commanded by Brigadier General Robert F. Hoke. The Rebels pound the Union defenders, which compels their commander, General Henry W. Wessells (West Point, 1833), to capitulate, despite the support of two steamers, the USS *Miami* and the *Southfield*. General Wessells is held prisoner for four months, then exchanged. Afterward he serves as commissary for

prisoners and other duty in New York. He receives the brevet of brigadier general in the Regular Army toward the close of hostilities. Subsequently, he becomes lieutenant colonel of the 18th U.S. Infantry. After some time on the western frontier and some recruiting duty, he retires during 1871. General Hoke's victory had been entirely unexpected by General U.S. Grant. General Wessells fought at Seven Pines as part of Major General Erasmus D. Keyes' corps, and he transferred to Plymouth, North Carolina, where he served for about one year. Union losses at Plymouth include Forts Gray, Wessells and Williams.

Union killed stands at 20 and the missing and wounded exceeds 1,500 men, with some estimates placing the loss at several thousand. The Confederates sustain losses in the area of 500 killed, wounded or missing. The 85th New York, 103rd Pennsylvania and the 16th Connecticut Regiments participate in this action with the support of the vessels *Miami* and *Southfield*. Also, General Hoke will be promoted to the rank of major general with an effective date of 20 April 1864. Hoke, subsequent to this action, moves to Virginia for awhile, but later he is transferred back to North Carolina (Fort Fisher).

April 18 (Monday) In Arkansas, Union General Frederick Steele's 7th Corps is involved in a vicious skirmish against Confederates at Poison Springs, a few miles outside of Camden. The Union force accompanying a supply train takes heavy casualties. Troops from two Confederate forts at Camden — Fort Southerland on Bradley Ferry Road and Fort Lookout on Van Buren Road (Ouachity County), constructed during the conflict — participate in this attack against the train. Both forts will later be utilized by the Union when Camden is occupied.

In North Carolina, Confederate forces commanded by General Robert Frederick Hoke encircle the Union-held town of Plymouth, North Carolina, and make final preparations to seize the objective. This ferocious battle ends in a Confederate victory on the 20th (see also, **April 17–20 In North Carolina**). In other activity, a boat transporting a spar torpedo and manned by Confederates unsuccessfully attempts to sink the USS *Wabash* off the Carolina Coast.

In South Carolina, the 54th Massachusetts Colored Troops skirmish with Confederates at Boyken's Mills.

In Confederate general officer activity, Brigadier General Samuel B. Maxey, commanding the Indian Territory, is promoted to the rank of major general by General Kirby Smith; however, the promotion is not approved by President Jefferson Davis. He serves for the duration. After the war, he resumes his law practice and then serves two terms in the U.S. Senate. He dies in Eureka Springs, Arkansas, in August 1895.

In Naval activity, the CSS *David,* a submarine, attacks the USS *Wabash,* but the *Wabash* escapes damage. It is thought that the *David* is among the vessels captured at Charleston dur-

The CSS *Albermarle* attacks the Union fleet at Plymouth, North Carolina. The USS *Southfield* sinks (*Harper's Pictoral History of the Civil War*, 1896).

ing 1865, but no documented evidence confirms the capture.

April 19 (Wednesday) In Kentucky, the 45th Kentucky Volunteers engage Confederates at Pound Gap.

In Louisiana, Union cavalry, including the 3rd Massachusetts (4th Brigade, Cavalry Division, 19th Corps), clashes with Confederates at Natchitoches this day and again on May 5. Sgt. Elliott captures one of the Rebel officers.

In Naval activity, the Confederate ram *Albemarle* attacks the U.S. fleet near Plymouth, North Carolina, sinking the USS *Southfield* and chasing three other U.S. warships out of the area. During the two-day engagement, the commanding officer, Lt. Commander Charles W. Flusser, of the USS *Miami* is killed.

April 20 (Wednesday) In Louisiana, the 63rd U.S. Colored Troops (9th Louisiana) skirmishes with Confederates at Waterproof.

In North Carolina, Confederates overrun Federal-held Plymouth. The Union shortly thereafter evacuates Washington, allowing it to fall into Confederate control. The Union has 20 dead, 80 wounded and 1,500 missing. Among the Confederates, 500 are killed, wounded or missing. This Confederate victory improves morale for the South, which had not had any strategic victories for quite a while. The Union, with the loss of Plymouth, also ceases to control several other fortifications in the vicinity.

In Union general officer activity, Brigadier General James B. Steadman is promoted to major general. Also, General William Ward Orme, who was with Grant outside of Vicksburg in June 1863, is forced to resign from the army due to ill health from tuberculosis, which he got while in Mississippi. For a while he had been on special duty, including inspecting prisons in various states and afterward command of the military post at Chicago until the disease had gone too far to allow him to continue in the army. President Lincoln intervenes and Orme is appointed as a supervising special agent in the Treasury Department.

April 21 (Thursday) In Arkansas, Union contingents of the 8th Missouri Cavalry clash with Confederates at Cotton Plate (Cotton Plant), Cache River. The Union sustains five killed and two wounded. Confederate casualties are unavailable.

In Louisiana, General Banks still marches toward Alexandria, Louisiana, following his miserably unsuccessful Shreveport expedition. The situation for the Union Naval vessels is still dangerous because of low water levels, but drastic actions are initiated to alleviate the crisis. In another action, the Union is involved in a brisk skirmish with the cavalry of General John A. Wharton who, is assigned to the area to lend his cavalry to the effort to finish Banks' Red River Campaign. The two forces clash at Natchitoches and the skirmish culminates with the Union troops retreating towards Cloutiersville. Confederate General Hamilton P. Bee is ordered to catch and cut off Banks at Cloutiersville, but Bee's battlefield experience is limited. He had spent most of his time as an administrative general, and the Union is able to drive his Confederates away. Banks' force finally reaches Alexandria beginning on the 24th. General Bee is given a command in Major General John A. Wharton's cavalry during early 1865.

In related activity, the USS *Eastport*, which had been recently sunk, is raised this day. Nevertheless, during the next several days it is only able to proceed about 21 miles; on the 26th, the vessel is intentionally destroyed with explosives to ensure the Confederates are unable to use it. The crew of the *Eastport* transfers to the USS *Fort Hindman*.

In Mississippi, the 2nd Wisconsin Cavalry skirmishes with Confederates at Red Bone.

In Union activity, General U.S. Grant, noting the importance of the port of New Bern, North Carolina, directs the commanders to continue to strengthen the fortifications there.

In Naval activity, the USS *Howquah* and the USS *Niphon* launch an attack against a Confederate salt works on Masonboro Sound. While the naval guns pound the positions, a landing force debarks and destroys the facility.

April 22 (Friday) In Louisiana, the force of General Nathaniel Banks departs Grand Ecore en route to Alexandria, where it arrives on the 26th. Also, a contingent composed of three companies of the 3rd Rhode Island Cavalry encounters and engages Confederates in the vicinity of Tunica Bend, Red River. The Union sustains two killed and 17 wounded. Confederate casualties are unavailable.

In Mississippi, the Confederates capture the USS *Petrel* on the Yazoo River while the vessel is bombarding Confederate batteries at Yazoo City. The Rebels remove the guns and stores, then burn the ship.

In Union general officer activity, General Joseph G. Totten, who graduated from West Point in 1805 while the United States was fighting the Barbary Coast Pirates, dies of natural causes. General Totten served with General Winfield Scott as chief engineer and was chief engineer of the Army at the time of his death. He was promoted to brigadier general, Regular Army, during 1863. Brigadier General John D. Stevenson, having been placed in command at Decatur, Alabama, and prior to that at Corinth during the Chickamauga and Chattanooga campaigns, resigns his commission this day. Nonetheless, during August 1864, he is recommissioned as brigadier general.

April 23 (Saturday) In Arkansas, the 5th Kansas Cavalry clashes with Confederates at Swan Lake.

In Georgia, a 64-man contingent of the 92nd Illinois Volunteers (pickets) led by Lt. Scoville skirmishes with Confederates at Nickajack Trace. The Union sustains five killed, nine wounded and about 22 captured. The Confederates execute 12 of the prisoners and another six succumb to their wounds.

In Confederate general officer activity, Brigadier General William Henry Fitzhugh Lee (middle son of Robert E. Lee), having recently been exchanged following his capture the previous year, is promoted to the rank of major general. After the war, General Lee returns to being a farmer. In 1887, following his service as a state senator, he is elected to Congress during 1887, where he serves until his death on 15 October 1891. James Chestnut, Jr., who has served as an aide to General Beauregard and at this time is a staff officer to President Jefferson Davis, is appointed brigadier general effective this day.

April 23–24 In Louisiana, heavy skirmishing continues between Confederates and the Union forces under General Nathaniel Banks. During the morning, the Union rear guard encounters and skirmishes with Rebels at Cloutersville (Cloutiersville). The contest lasts for several hours, but the Union is able to whip the Confederate contingent.

During the early morning hours, Union cavalry led by General Richard Arnold (West Point, 1850), bolstered by artillery, engages Confederate troops under General Hamilton Bee at Monett's Bluff on the Cane River. The battle lasts about three hours, and at its conclusion, the Union retains control of the bluff. The Union sustains about 350 killed and wounded. Colonel Lewis Benedict (3rd Brigade, XIX Corps) is killed. After Benedict's death, Colonel Francis Fessenden leads a charge in an attempt to rally the troops and he also becomes wounded. Fessenden, who was wounded at Shiloh, takes a severe hit which costs him one leg. He is promoted to brigadier general in May 1864. The Confederates sustain about 400 killed and wounded. The 5th Minnesota Volunteer Regiment participates at this action.

April 24 (Sunday)   In Arkansas, the 1st Nebraska Cavalry skirmishes with Confederates at Jacksonport.

In Naval activity, the USS *Wamsutta,* out of service since the previous September, is recommissioned at Philadelphia and again assigned to the South Atlantic Blockading Squadron.

April 25 (Monday)   In Arkansas, a Union contingent, including the 36th Iowa, 77th Ohio, 43rd Illinois Infantry Regiments and the 1st Indiana and 7th Missouri Cavalry, commanded by Colonel Francis M. Drake, clashes with Confederate forces at Mark's Mills. The Union is also bolstered by Battery E, 2nd Missouri Light Artillery. The Union sustains 100 killed, 250 wounded and about 100 missing. The Confederates capture a Union wagon train. The Confederates sustain 110 killed, 228 wounded and 40 missing. Confederate Brigadier General Thomas P. Dockery participates at this action.

In Tennessee, the 19th Michigan Cavalry (General Frederick Steele's command) skirmishes with Confederates at Watauga Bridge this day and the next. The Union sustains three killed and nine wounded. Confederate casualties are unavailable.

In Confederate general officer activity, Brigadier General James Fleming Fagan is promoted to major general.

April 26 (Tuesday)   In North Carolina, Washington is evacuated by Union troops under orders of General Grant. Grant is holding to the strategy that New Bern must be held.

In Arkansas, Union contingents, including the 33rd and 40th Iowa, 5th Kansas, 2nd and 4th Missouri Infantry Regiments and the 1st Iowa Cavalry, clash with Rebels at Moro Creek. The Union sustains five killed and fourteen wounded. Confederate casualties are unavailable.

In Louisiana, General Nathaniel Banks arrives at Alexandria. He is informed by General David Hunter (West Point, 1822) that orders that call for a speedy conclusion of the campaign have arrived from General Grant. The termination of the campaign is easier said than done, as the water levels have become dangerously low and the vessels are unable to progress below the rapids. However, Banks discovers a solution. Lt. Colonel Joseph Bailey (4th Wisconsin Volunteers), the acting chief engineer of the XIX Corps (General William B. Franklin), initiates the construction of a huge dam on the Red River which will provide the necessary water to permit passage. The project is completed on Sunday, 8 May. In other activity, the 14th New York and 6th Missouri Cavalry Regiments engage Confederates at Alexandria. Also, the Union gunboats *Cricket* and *Fort Hindman* engage Confederates at Red River. The 5th Minnesota Volunteer Regiment participates in the campaign against Alexandria.

In Union general officer activity, the results of a court-martial of Acting Rear Admiral Charles Wilkes that began during the early part of the year are announced. The court-martial was due in great part to a letter written by Wilkes and addressed to Gideon Welles in response to the secretary's comments about Wilkes in his annual report. Wilkes had been accused of various charges of gross negligence and insubordination. Wilkes offered testimony and evidence to prove he was innocent of all charges. Nevertheless, the court finds Wilkes guilty. The sentence includes a public reprimand, and Wilkes is suspended from active duty for a period of three years. However, President Lincoln intervenes and cuts the sentence down from three years to one year. At the termination of the suspension, Admiral Wilkes retires from the navy. Admiral Wilkes succumbs on 8 February 1877. He is interred in Oak Hill Cemetery in Washington; in August 1909 he is reinterred at Arlington National Cemetery. Also, Colonel Hiram Burnham (6th Maine) is promoted to brigadier general, effective this day.

In Naval activity, in Louisiana, the USS *Cricket,* Admiral Porter's flagship, barely escapes capture when it encounters a huge Confederate force supported by 18 artillery pieces. The battery pummels the *Cricket,* inflicting 38 hits, and the ground troops number about 1,200, but the attempt to board it fails. The *Cricket* escapes; however, the cost is high. About one-half of the crew is lost to the enemy fire. After passing beyond the range of the artillery, the *Cricket* makes it to the *Black Hawk* (Porter's regular flagship) and afterward, the *Cricket* departs for Cairo for repairs. Following repairs, the *Cricket* returns to the region in August 1864 and operates out of White River Station for the duration of the

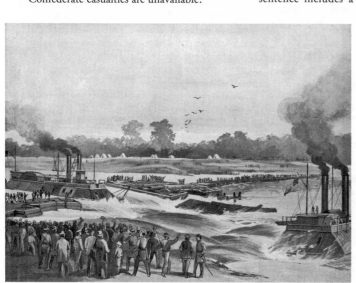

Left: **Bailey's dam on the Red River** (Johnson, *Campfire and Battlefield: History of the Conflicts and Campaigns,* 1894). *Right:* **Confederate ground troops attack Admiral Porter's fleet** (*Harper's Pictorial History of the Civil War,* 1896).

A Union camp at the battery in Annapolis (Mottelay, *The Soldier in Our Civil War*, 1886).

war. It is decommissioned on 30 June 1865 and sold the following month.

During the Union withdrawal following the defeat at Sabine Cross Roads, the USS *Juliet*, on more than one occasion, encounters Confederate resistance, including artillery and small arms. The *Juliet* sustains two killed and 14 wounded, along with heavy damage, but the crew works feverishly to make repairs to keep the gunboat from sinking and they prevail. The *Juliet* succeeds in passing the batteries. Afterward, the *Juliet* is sent to Cairo to receive repairs. It is placed out of commission until 6 September, and upon completion of the work it returns to the Mississippi Squadron, where it is utilized on patrols and as an escort vessel until it is decommissioned at Mound City on 30 June 1865. On 17 August, the *Juliet* is sold at auction and renamed the *Goldina*. On 31 December, it becomes stranded and is abandoned.

April 27 (Wednesday) In Virginia, General U.S. Grant orders General Ambrose Burnside (who has been reinstated) to move from Annapolis, Maryland, with the IX Corps at full strength to support General George G. Meade, who is about to advance from positions along the Rappahannock River to the James River toward the ultimate objective, Richmond. General Burnside reaches Centreville on the 30th.

April 28 (Thursday) In South Carolina, Confederate-held Fort Sumter is once again the recipient of a Union bombardment. The heavy shelling extends for days, with the Stars and Bars still holding defiantly in the murderous breeze.

In Missouri, the 1st Missouri Militia Cavalry skirmishes with Confederates at Offett's Knob. Casualty figures are unavailable.

In Naval activity, the USS *Granite City*, while on duty in the vicinity of Calcasieu Pass with the USS *Wave*, comes under fire from Confederate batteries and from ground troops as they attempt to receive refugees. The two gunboats exchange fire with the Rebels for about two hours; however, the Rebels prevail. Both ships

surrender. The *Granite City*, earlier a Confederate vessel, after being regained is transformed into a blockade runner, which it was prior to capture by the Union.

April 29 (Friday) In Arkansas, the 40th Iowa, 43rd Illinois, 6th Kansas Cavalry and the 3rd Illinois Battery, while operating in the vicinity of Princeton, encounter and engage a contingent of Confederates. Casualty figures are unavailable.

In Missouri, the 2nd Colorado Cavalry skirmishes with Confederates at Snia Hills. Casualty figures are unavailable.

In Virginia, Union troops (specific units unspecified) attack Confederate pickets on Ringgold Road.

In Confederate general officer activity, Major James Dearing (West Point, attendance 1858–1861) is promoted to brigadier general. General Dearing had commanded a battalion of artillery at Gettysburg. Subsequent to his promotion, he commands a brigade and participates in the defense of Petersburg.

April 30 (Saturday) In Arkansas, at Jenkin's Ferry, Union engineers begin construction of a dam on the Red River. They build a series of dams for Union vessels stranded in the low water to pass through on the way to Alexandria, Louisiana. This venture ends in a mere ten days, extraordinary for that day and age. There is brisk fighting in the vicinity of Jenkins Ferry, Saline River (near Leola, Grant County), between Steele's 7th Corps and Confederates who continue to push the Union back. The Rebels,

including a brigade under General Thomas P. Dockery, strike the Union's rear and are challenged by the 33rd Iowa, but the Union regiment is unable to withstand the superior numbers. The 39th Iowa and the 9th Wisconsin are also pushed back.

At about this time the 50th Indiana tries to hold the line, but it, too, is overmatched. Finally, the forces which had already crossed the Sabine move back to halt the tide. The Rebels are finally checked. Contingents under Generals S.A. Rice, Frederick (Friedrich) Salomon and John Milton Thayer and Colonels A.C. Barton and Adolph Engleman initiate charge after charge. The offensive action succeeds and the Confederates retire.

Following this contest, Steele is able to complete his retirement to Little Rock; he arrives there on June 2. The Confederate forces include those of Generals Thomas J. Churchill, Sterling Price, Kirby Smith and W.H.T. Walker. Casualties on both sides exceed 1,000 killed, wounded, or missing. Union General Samuel Rice is wounded in the ankle, but it becomes a mortal wound; he succumbs on 6 July. Confederate General William Read Scurry is also mortally wounded. Scurry declined to be removed from the field to receive medical attention and bleeds to death. Participants include the 77th Ohio, 4th, 18th, 29th, 33rd, 36th and 40th Iowa Regiments, the 79th U.S. Colored Troops (1st Kansas) and the 83rd U.S. Colored Troops (2nd Kansas), Battery A, 3rd Illinois, and 2nd Indiana Battery. In addition, the 1st Iowa, 2nd, 6th and 14th Kansas, the 1st and 2nd Missouri and the 13th Illinois Cavalry Regiments, 3rd Division of the 17th Corps, participate. Confederate Brigadier Generals Dandridge McRae, Mosby M. Parsons, James Camp Tappan and Thomas Neville Waul are among the leaders. General Waul continues in the field for the duration, and after the war, he returns to Texas and resumes his law practice in Galveston. Later, he retires on his farm in the vicinity of Greenville. He dies during July 1903 at the age of 91, but no relatives survive him. Parsons had recently been appointed major general

A Union fleet passes a dam on the way to Alexandria, Louisiana (*Harper's Pictorial History of the Civil War*, 1896).

by General Edmund Kirby Smith, but his promotion is never officially approved by President Jefferson Davis. General Waul had served in Louisiana, but subsequent to the battle at Sabine Cross Roads, he was transferred to Arkansas to support the effort against the Union forces there.

Confederate Brigadier General Thomas P. Dockery, owner of a plantation in Tennessee prior to the war, finds by the end of the conflict that he has lost everything. He becomes engaged in civil engineering. For some time after the war he resides in Houston, Texas. He dies in New York City on 27 February 1898. General Tappan, after this action, accompanies General Sterling Price into Missouri. After the war General Tappan returns to Arkansas and resumes his law practice. He dies at Helena in March 1906.

In Georgia, General William T. Sherman is directed by General Grant to launch an offensive to destroy the forces of Confederate General Joseph E. Johnston that are deployed in the vicinity of Dalton. Simultaneously, Grant will be initiating an offensive at Culpeper, Virginia, against Richmond. The Confederates under Johnston include the corps of Generals William J. Hardee, John B. Hood, Leonidas Polk and Joseph Wheeler, the latter commanding a corps of cavalry numbering about 10,000 troops. The combined force amounts to about 50,000 men. Sherman commences his operation in early May.

In Tennessee, Union General Samuel Sturgis departs Bolivar en route to the vicinity of Fort Pillow to destroy General Nathan B. Forrest's command, but the Confederates have already begun to abandon the area and are en route to Mississippi. Although Sturgis is unable to immediately catch Forrest, he receives intelligence during June that Forrest is attempting to raise an even larger force. Sturgis, upon learning of Forrest's intentions, again heads for Memphis to prepare to derail this new threat. The two sides clash during June at Guntown, Mississippi (Brice's Cross Roads).

In Confederate general officer activity, Colonel Richard Waterhouse is promoted to the rank of brigadier general effective this date. His commission is not quickly validated. President Jefferson Davis makes it effective 17 March 1865. General Waterhouse is assigned command of a brigade attached to Lt. General Edmund Kirby Smith. After the war he resides in St. Augustine, Florida, and becomes a land speculator. In March 1876, he falls down a set of stairs and sustains a dislocated shoulder, thought to be minor; however, two days later, on 22 March, he dies of pneumonia. Brigadier General Mosby Monroe Parsons is promoted to major general by General Kirby Smith; however, he is not officially appointed by President Davis. Nonetheless, he carries the rank and accompanies General Sterling Price in Missouri. After the close of hostilities, he enters Mexico. Upon his parole, General Parsons is listed as a major general.

May Confederate Colonel Stephen Elliott, Jr., is promoted to brigadier general. He will be assigned command of the brigade previously led by General Nathan George "Shanks" Evans, who was continually plagued with difficulties, particularly with regard to charges of disobeying orders and intoxication. Twice accused and twice tried, he is acquitted. Nevertheless, Evans had lost favor. His service record subsequent to the Vicksburg Campaign and some time in North Carolina seemingly remains inconspicuous. However, Evans (West Point, 1848) serves for the duration, and after the close of hostilities, he relocates in Alabama, where he succumbs several years later. Also, Confederate Colonel Birkett D. Fry, 11th Alabama Infantry, subsequent to his release from a Union prison where he has been since the fighting at Gettysburg (July 1863), is promoted to the rank of brigadier general. General Fry moves to Petersburg, Virginia, but shortly thereafter he commands a district that incorporates a part of southern Georgia and a sector of adjoining South Carolina. Colonel Martin Witherspoon Gary, commander of Hampton's Legion, is promoted to brigadier general. Samuel Jameson Gholson, who joined the Confederacy (Mississippi militia) shortly after the secession of Mississippi, is promoted to brigadier general in the Confederate Army. Confederate Colonel Edwin G. Lee, who re-entered the army the previous year following illness, is assigned command of Staunton, Virginia. However, during autumn of this year, his health again becomes poor. Lee, the son-in-law of General William Pendleton, in September 1864 is promoted to the rank of brigadier general. Confederate Colonels William Terry (4th Virginia Infantry) and William Richard Terry (24th Virginia Infantry) are promoted to the rank of brigadier general. Both William Terry (wounded three times) and William Richard (wounded seven times) serve with the Army of Northern Virginia.

General William T. Sherman lists his battle casualties for the month of May as 1,868 killed or missing and 7,486 wounded. He also lists the Confederate casualties during the Atlanta campaign during May as 8,638 killed, wounded, or missing.

May 1 (Sunday) In Georgia, General William T. Sherman initiates his campaign to find and destroy the Confederates under General Joseph E. Johnston. His force numbers just under 99,000 infantry troops and more than 250 pieces of artillery and includes the Army of the Cumberland (General George H. Thomas), Army of the Tennessee (General James McPherson) and the Army of the Ohio (General John Schofield). Sherman also has about 12,000 cavalry troops commanded by Generals Israel Garrard, Hugh Kilpatrick, Edward M. McCook and George Stoneman.

In Union general officer activity, Brigadier General John P. Hatch is appointed commander of the Department of the South. He succeeds Major General Quincy Adams Gillmore, whose corps is transferred to the Army of the James under the command of General Benjamin F. Butler.

In Naval activity, the 7th U.S. Colored Regiment engages Confederates at Jacksonville, Florida. The unit sustains one killed. Confederate casualties are unavailable. In other activity, at about this time (May 1864), the USS *Huntsville* initiates support activity for the Union troops operating in the vicinity of Tampa Bay. Many of the crew are struck by yellow fever. During July, the *Huntsville* is ordered to sail to New York, where it is temporarily decommissioned during August. In March it is recommissioned; however, it serves as a transport and sails to New Orleans and Panama. Afterward, it carries passengers between New York and Boston rather than return to the Gulf for blockade duty. In August 1865, it is again decommissioned. During November, the *Huntsville* again operates as a civilian vessel until it is lost to fire in December 1877.

The USS *Pontoosuc* is commissioned at about this time (May). It is a double-ender steam gunboat built in Portsmouth, Maine. Initially it is assigned blockade duty off the Atlantic coast. In December of this year and January 1865 it participates in the operations against Fort Fisher at Wilmington, North Carolina. Afterward, it runs patrols on the Cape Fear River until the end of hostilities. During June 1865, it sails north to Boston, where it is decommissioned the next month. In October of the following year, it is sold.

In Louisiana, elements of the 13th and 19th Corps' cavalry skirmishes with Confederates at Alexandria. Also, Union Cavalry attached to the 19th Corps engages Confederates at Hudnot's Plantation. Meanwhile, the 64th U.S. Colored Troops skirmish with Confederates at Ashwood Landing. Also, at Clinton, Union troops (specific units unreported) clash with Confederates.

In Virginia, General Benjamin Butler's force has been along the York River at Yorktown and Gloucester Point. The force is composed of the 18th Corps (W.F. Smith) and the 10th Corps (Q.A. Gillmore); the 18th Corps' commanding generals are W.T.H. Brooks and Godfrey Weitzel, two divisions of white troops, and Edward W. Hinks, commanding one division of colored troops. The X Corps' commanding generals are Alfred H. Terry, Adelbert Ames and John W. Turner. In addition, General August V. Kautz commands a division of cavalry, which is deployed in the vicinity of Norfolk and Portsmouth. The Union Army operating in the Shenandoah Valley and West Virginia is divided into two sections, one under General George Crook, composed of infantry and one division of cavalry led by General William Averell, and another led by General Franz Sigel. General George Crook moves out via the Kanawha River to operate against the East Tennessee and Virginia Railroad. General Franz Sigel moves out to strike Confederate strongholds in the Virginia valley. Sigel's force encounters Confederates on the 15th at New Market.

In Naval activity, the USS *General Putnam* and the USS *Shawsheen* cruise along the Pamunkey River in Virginia in support of Union ground troops who had earlier in the day seized West Point. After the mission, the ships return to Hampton Roads. In other activity, the USS *Mendota* is commissioned at about this time (May). It is a Sassacus class double-ender steam gunboat, which had been built in New York at Brooklyn. The *Mendota* is assigned to the James River Flotilla. During 1865, it is utilized as a shipping control vessel, initially in Hampton Roads and afterward the mouth of the Delaware River, where it finishes its service and is decommissioned in Philadelphia during May 1865. It is sold in 1867.

May 2 (Monday)   In Louisiana, elements of the 83rd Ohio and the 3rd Rhode Island, while on a foraging mission, encounter and skirmish with Confederates at Governor Moore's Plantation. The Union sustains two killed and 10 wounded. The 5th Minnesota Volunteer Regiment participates in this action. Confederate casualties are unavailable.

In Tennessee, the 7th Kansas Cavalry engages Confederates at Memphis.

In Georgia, Confederate General Joseph Johnston, who had assumed command of General Bragg's army subsequent to the loss at Missionary Ridge, is operating in Georgia and will face the advancing Army of Sherman. As of this date, General Joseph E. Johnston's force is composed of the corps of Joseph Hardee, Leonidas Polk and John B. Hood. The force numbers about 45,000 troops, including nearly 2,400 cavalry. Johnston's division commanders are Alexander P. Stewart, William Brimage Bate, Benjamin F. Cheatham, W.H.T. Walker, Littlepage Stevenson, Thomas C. Hindman and Patrick R. Cleburne. The cavalry is commanded by General Joseph Wheeler.

In Virginia, Union troops occupy West Point.

In Union general officer activity, Brigadier General Hector Tyndale is granted a leave of absence due to poor health. General Tyndale had commanded a brigade at Chattanooga, but during the winter he was in command at Shel-

mound, Tennessee. Tyndale was wounded twice at Antietam. He resigns his commission on 26 August 1864; however, toward the end of the war, he does receive the brevet of major general of volunteers.

In Confederate Naval activity, the CSS *Georgia* departs from France for Liverpool, England. The Confederates had planned to transfer their armaments to the CSS *Rappahannock,* but the transfer does not occur. The Rappahannock had suffered engine trouble and was held up at Calais, France. The *Rappahannock,* built in England during 1857 as the HMS *Victor,* purchased by a Confederate agent after going to sea during November 1863, essentially ends its short sea duty at Calais. The French prevent the vessel from leaving the country. After the war, the French transfer the ship to the U.S. government. Meanwhile, the *Georgia,* despite protests from the minister to Great Britain (Charles F. Adams), is sold on 1 June. On 11 August, the *Georgia* leaves England; however, on the 15th, while off Portugal, the frigate USS *Niagara* intercepts the *Georgia* and seizes it. The prize is sailed to Boston and condemned there. On 5 August 1865, the Georgia is listed as a U.S. merchant ship.

May 3 (Tuesday)   In Arkansas, Union forces commanded by General Frederick Steele arrive back at Little Rock after the dismal failure of the Shreveport expedition. At Baton Rouge, the 4th Wisconsin Cavalry skirmishes with Confederates. Casualty figures are unavailable. Also, the Union 2nd Arkansas Cavalry skirmishes with Confederates at Richland. The Union sustains 20 killed. Confederate casualties are unavailable.

In Georgia, Union cavalry attached to General Edward McCook's division engages Confederates at Red Clay. The Union sustains 10 killed and wounded. Confederate casualties are unavailable.

In Tennessee, a Union cavalry contingent (General Samuel Sturgis' command) numbering about 700 troopers engages a Confederate cav-

alry force under Nathan Bedford Forrest at Bolivar. The Union sustains about two killed and 10 wounded. Confederate casualty figures are unavailable.

In Colorado Territory, the 1st Colorado Cavalry clashes with Confederates at Cedar Bluffs.

In Louisiana, the Union transport *City Belle,* carrying elements of the 120th Ohio Volunteers and the 73rd U.S. Colored Troops, comes under attack by Confederates at Snaggy Point, Red River.

In Virginia, General George Meade begins a forced march across the Rapidan River with a force exceeding 100,000 men en route to capture Richmond and its 60,000 defenders under General Robert E. Lee. Union Generals Ambrose Burnside, Winfield S. Hancock, John Sedgwick and Gouverneur Warren are corps commanders. In what is to be a two-pronged assault to crush the Confederacy, while the Union is approaching Richmond, Grant orders Sherman to march on Atlanta, Georgia. General Sherman is expected to march to the sea to hook up with Union vessels at Savannah, Georgia. The march will be both arduous and triumphant. The Confederacy fights vehemently in an attempt to forestall Sherman's advance, but Sherman drives relentlessly without thought of turning back.

In Union general officer activity, Brigadier General Erasmus Darwin Keyes resigns his commission and relocates on the West Coast at San Francisco.

May 4 (Wednesday)   In Arizona, a contingent of the 5th California Cavalry and the 1st California Cavalry engage Confederates at Doubtful Canyon. The Union sustains one killed and six wounded. The Confederates sustain 10 killed and 20 wounded.

In Tennessee, U.S. General William T. Sherman, commanding 100,000 with 187 cannons, sets out from Chattanooga to engage Confederate General J.E. Johnston's 65,000 troops at

Left: Union troops on a foraging mission in Georgia (Mottelay, *The Soldier in Our Civil War,* 1886). *Right:* General Hancock's force crosses the Rapidan River (*Harper's Pictorial History of the Civil War,* 1896).

Atlanta, Georgia. Grant's directive to Sherman reads, in part: "Attack the Confederate Army in Georgia. Break it up and go into the interior of the enemy's country as far as you can, inflicting all the damage you can upon their war resources."

In Mississippi, the 3rd U.S. Colored Cavalry, 11th, 72nd and 76th Illinois Volunteers, 5th Illinois Cavalry and the 7th Ohio Battery participate in the Yazoo City Expedition.

In Virginia, General Robert E. Lee, informed of Union General Franz Sigel's 7,000-man force nearing Front Royal, directs General John C. Breckinridge to intercept the Yankees and prevent them from moving on Lee's left flank. Lee then advises Breckinridge to send Beauregard to Richmond, bringing with him all available troops in North Carolina. In the meantime, Union General George Meade's Army of the Potomac continues its march on Richmond by crossing the Rapidan River heading for the Wilderness with over 120,000 men led by Hancock, Sedgwick, Burnside and Warren. Also, General Benjamin Butler's Army of the James departs its positions around Yorktown and sails down the York River, passing Fortress Monroe and moving into the James River. On the following day, troops debark on the south side of the James, some at City Point and some at Fort Powelton, while the main body lands at Bermuda Hundred. Butler is under orders from Grant to make Richmond his target.

General August V. Kautz departs Suffolk to execute a series of raids. His cavalry force, attached to the 10th Corps, Army of the James, skirmishes at Jarrett's Station, Stoney Creek Station, Wall's Bridge, White's Bridge and City Point. During this expedition, his force—which includes the 5th and 11th Pennsylvania Cavalry, the 3rd New York Cavalry, the 1st D.C. Cavalry and the 8th New York Battery—sustains 10 killed, wounded or missing. Confederates sustain 20 wounded and 50 captured. Kautz's command will initiate another offensive on the 12th.

In Union general officer activity, General Willis A. Gorman is mustered out of the serv-

ice. He returns to Minnesota and practices law in St. Paul until he dies on 20 May 1876.

In Naval activity, the USS *Eutaw* supports ground operations along the James River in Virginia. It debarks ground forces below City Point. Its participation continues into the following day.

May 5 (Thursday) *In Naval activity,* Union-held New Bern, North Carolina, repels a Confederate assault. Several U.S. gunboats—including the USS *Ceres, Commodore Hull, Covington, Mattabesett, Miami, Sassacus, Seymour, Whitehead* and *Wyalusing*— clash with the Confederate *Albemarle* on the Roanoke River. The ironclad ram *Albemarle* holds its own against the eight Union vessels. During the action, the CSS *Bombshell* is captured. The USS *Sassacus* becomes damaged after ramming the *Albemarle,* but remains in service. It operates in the North Carolina waters and later in Virginia until September, when it is sent in for repairs. It does not return to duty until November 1864. Also, during the latter part of the month, a detachment from the *Mattabesett* launches a raid in an attempt to destroy the *Albemarle,* but the plan fails. The *Mattabesett* remains in service until it is decommissioned during May 1865. Following this action, the *Miami* moves north to operate in Virginia, primarily along the James River until it is decommissioned during May 1865.

At Dunn's Plantation on the Red River in Louisiana, the USS *Signal* is disabled by Confederate batteries. A white flag is flown. Nevertheless, the ship is destroyed to prevent capture. The 50th Ohio Regiment is with this flotilla, which also includes the gunboat steamer *Covington* and the transport *Warner.* The *Covington* is badly damaged and

after becoming disabled, it is destroyed to prevent capture. The *Covington* (Tinclad No. 25), initially a civilian steamer, had been acquired by the U.S. Navy during February 1863.

In Virginia, Union Major General Benjamin F. Butler's force of 40,000 lands at Bermuda Hundred, close to both Petersburg and Richmond. On the 6th, Butler dispatches troops to destroy the rails connecting the two cities to ease the campaign to take Richmond. The Confederates give staunch resistance and the endeavor fails. On the 7th, Butler makes another assault against the rails but is again repelled. Butler returns to Bermuda Hundred on the 10th. Also, a Union cavalry contingent (attached to General Ambrose Burnside's command) clashes with Confederates at Thoroughfare Gap. Casualty figures are unavailable. Meanwhile, the 3rd Cavalry Division, Army of the Potomac, engages Confederates at Craig's Meeting House. Also, the USS *Hunchback* tows the USS *Saugus* up the James River during the ongoing land battle in the area, and during the mission, the *Hunchback* selects Confederate targets and bombards the positions. The *Hunchback* remains in Virginia until March 1865 to support ground operations. It operates out of Deep Bottom on the James River.

May 5–6 THE BATTLE OF THE WILDERNESS The Union forces of General Gouverneur War-

Left: The USS *Sassacus* rams the CSS Albemarle (*Harper's Pictoral History of the Civil War,* 1896). *Right:* Confederates attack General Alfred E. Lee's wagon train in the vicinity of Mansfield, Louisiana (Mottelay, *The Soldier in Our Civil War,* 1886)

ren (5th Corps) encounter and skirmish viciously on the Orange Turnpike. The sounds of gunfire and clashing steel intensify with additional brutal combat ensuing between the Yankees under Hancock (2nd Corps) and Confederate General A.P. Hill's Corps at Plank Road. Hundreds of men on both sides are thrown into mortal combat, ending with no victors but enormous casualties. On 6 May, Confederates mount a major counter-attack while the Union is preparing to mount its own assault with a combined offensive by Generals Hancock, Warren and Sedgwick. The Rebels crash through Sedgwick's positions on the right flank.

The area becomes a blazing inferno as the guns bellow and propel streams of fire and create hovering clouds of choking smoke as the infantry, using fixed bayonets, charges. General Winfield S. Hancock reacts immediately. He

orders a charge to disrupt the Confederate momentum. Hancock's charge plows forward and the momentum carries the Yankees right through the lightly defended positions of General Hill. Meanwhile, General Sheridan is dis-

Brevet Major General Alexander Webb, Medal of Honor recipient.(Mottelay, *The Soldier in Our Civil War*, 1886).

Brigadier General James Samuel Wadsworth is killed at the Battle of the Wilderness on 6 May (*Harper's Pictoral History of the Civil War*, 1896).

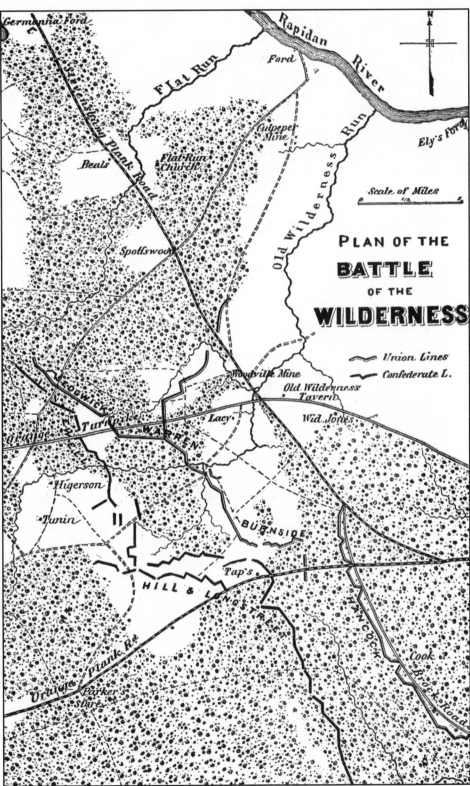

Battle of the Wilderness (Johnson, *Campfire and Battlefield: History of the Conflicts and Campaigns*, 1894).

Above: The 14th New York, in the Wilderness, awaits a Confederate attack. *Right:* General Grant talks with General Meade in the Wilderness (Motte-lay, *The Soldier in Our Civil War*, 1886).

patched to Hancock's left, and his force engages Rebels at Todd's Tavern and the junction of Brock Road and Furnace Road. Sheridan's attack also succeeds, and afterward, the Confederates mount a counterattack, but it fails to dislodge Sheridan's line. General Grant arrives at Todd's Tavern slightly before midnight.

At the Wilderness itself (6th), the Rebels are faltering, but reinforcements under General James Longstreet stream down the road with bugles blaring, flags flying and an incessant Rebel battle cry. These fresh troops arrive in time to serve the Rebel cause and succeed in driving the Union troops back, giving the Southerners control of the breastworks by 10 A.M. and an impression of sure victory, but the Union is not yet ready to concede. Instead, the troops along the battered line become galvanized and defiantly hold, despite a powerful assault. The Yankees forbid further penetration beyond the right flank. As the noon hour approaches, there still is desperate combat, but no victor emerges.

The Confederates launch yet another assault against the left flank of the Union lines and seriously threaten the entire Union position. A total collapse is anticipated by the Rebels, who smell victory in this densely wooded slaughterhouse. Both Union and Confederate artillery remain virtually silent, each side realizing the great possibility of deadly harm to friendly troops entangled in the thicket. Confederate General Longstreet, accompanied by Generals Micah Jenkins and Joseph Kershaw, move directly to the front to inspect the situation and close for the kill, but in an unusual turn of events, the nearly victorious Rebels become confused and commence firing on their own troops, including the generals.

The murderous woods, almost impassible, even by foot soldiers, do not hamper a sudden burst of fire from behind the brush. In a flash, Longstreet is wounded by friendly fire and Jenk-

ins is killed by the same volley, causing serious dismay for the Rebels, who finally regroup. There is simply not enough time. Only mere moments before his death, and shortly after a successful charge against General Hancock, while conversing with General Longstreet, General Jenkins remarks to Longstreet that he was now confident that the Union would be driven back across the Rapidan River before sunset. Longstreet, subsequent to the tragic loss, pens a worthy tribute to his fallen friend: "His beautiful spirit, through the mercy of god, rest in peace."

Meanwhile, the Yankees capitalize on this Confederate error by digging in deeply. The stunned Rebels prepare another assault but it is not to be. The Yankees move against the Rebels, and even the added support of Robert E. Lee is insufficient to prevent the Union advance. The charging Union troops burst ahead, implanting their colors conspicuously atop the Confederate fortifications. Union General Samuel S. Carroll's brigade ramrods through, driving the Rebels back and inflicting heavy casualties. The burdensome battle finally ends in stalemate. The two exhausted armies, unable to strike a final blow in the Wilderness, begin converging simultaneously on the vital position of Spotsylvania Court House, Virginia, the scene of the next bloody chapter in the struggle for Richmond, tiring the heart of the Confederacy and becoming a painful thorn in the spine of the Union.

The Confederates under Robert E. Lee are first to grasp positions at Spotsylvania, and these fortifications are immediately bolstered to prepare for the imminent Union assault by the forces of U.S. Grant. Confederates under General Jubal Early achieve some quick success during the contest, causing embarrassment to the Union. During one of many rampant con-

frontations, Early's men penetrate and capture approximately 600 Union prisoners, including Generals Alexander Shaler and Truman Seymour. General Shaler, previous to his capture, was in command of the Union prison at Johnson's Island in Sandusky Bay, Ohio, a place nearly forgotten, but almost as infamous as Andersonville. Shaler is later exchanged and ordered to New Orleans. He receives command of a division of the VII Corps as well as command of the White River District. He resigns from the service during August 1865.

Also, General Seymour is exchanged the following August. Afterward, he commands a division (VI Corps) in the Shenandoah Valley, and he also participates in the operations against Petersburg and Richmond. He receives the brevet of major general in the volunteers and in the Regular Army, and after the close of hostilities, he becomes major of the U.S. 5th Artillery, a command he retains until he retires during 1876. General Seymour relocates in Italy and dies in Florence during 1891.

Union casualties are 2,466 killed, 12,037 wounded and 3,383 captured or missing. Grant's force numbered approximately 102,000. Confederate casualties, including killed, wounded or missing, are 11,400 men. The Confederate force is about 61,000 strong. Union Major Generals James S. Wadsworth and Alexander Hays are mortally wounded. General Hays is posthumously breveted major general effective the date of his death. General Wadsworth, leading his command during a Confederate charge, is shot from his horse on the 6th. The bullet enters the back of his head and strikes him in the brain. He succumbs in a

Left: A defensive line during the Battle of the Wilderness (*Harper's Pictorial History of the Civil War*, 1896). *Right:* Columns on the move during the Battle of the Wilderness, 6 May 1864 (Mottelay, *The Soldier in Our Civil War*, 1886).

Confederate field hospital on 8 May. Also, Union Brigadier General Alexander S. Webb is seriously wounded and does not return to duty until January 1865, when he becomes chief of staff to General George Meade.

General Webb later receives the brevet of brigadier general In 1866, Webb is appointed lieutenant colonel of the 44th U.S. Infantry. Union Generals Carroll, George Washington Getty and W.F. Bartlett are also wounded, and Colonel Joseph Hayes is wounded (hit in the skull). General Thomas H. Neill assumes command of Getty's 2nd Division and leads it up to the early actions against Petersburg. Following a short time on staff at XVIII Corps, General Neill moves in September to serve with General Sheridan in the Shenandoah Valley. Confederate General Micah Jenkins is killed by his own troops' fire, close to where Stonewall Jackson was felled a year earlier. After Jenkins' death, Confederate Colonel John Bratton is appointed brigadier general. Confederate General LeRoy Augustus Stafford is mortally wounded while leading an attack; he succumbs several days later in Richmond, Virginia.

Confederate Brigadier General John Marshall Jones (West Point, 1841) is also killed while under the pressure of a Union counterattack. Confederate Generals John Pegram and James Longstreet are wounded in this battle. Longstreet's injuries keep him from the field until late autumn. Confederate Brigadier General Edward A. Perry also sustains a wound, his second. Perry apparently does not resume duty in the field, rather he is transferred to the Trans-Mississippi Department to work with the Alabama reserve troops. After the war he resumes his law practice. In conjunction, the Confederate Virginia 25th Regiment (Brigadier General W. E. Jones' brigade, Edward Johnson's division, Richard S. Ewell's corps) loses its regimental flag at this action to a contingent of the 5th Wisconsin Regiment; the colors are eventually returned, but not until 1905, when the War Department transfers the regimental colors to the Commonwealth of Virginia.

May 5–September 8 The Armies of the Cumberland, Ohio and Tennessee move the campaign into Northern Georgia and advance from Chattanooga, Tennessee, to Atlanta.

May 5–9 In Georgia, more than 65,000 of General Sherman's forces battle Confederates under General J.E. Johnston at Rocky Face Ridge. Skirmishes include those at Dug Creek Gap, where Sherman's force is commanded by General James B. McPherson. The Rebels repulse General McPherson's force and inflict heavy casualties on the Yankees at Buzzard's Roost, Mill Creek Gap and Tunnel Hill. General George H. Thomas occupies Tunnel Hill on the 7th.

The remainder of Sherman's force (35,000) marches 15 miles to Snake Creek Gap to destroy the railroad supply system that connects General Johnston with Atlanta. The Yankees force the Rebels at Snake Creek Gap to withdraw toward Resaca, but the Union, upon reaching the outskirts, determines that it is too heavily fortified. It then withdraws to its positions at Snake Creek Gap. By this time, Johnston realizes the Union is behind his lines, and he orders Dalton abandoned. Meanwhile, the two sides continue to ignite minor skirmishes until the night of the 11th.

May 6 (Friday) In Florida, Tampa is captured by Union forces supported by gunboats, including the USS *Honduras, Sunflower* and the *James L. Davis.* Fort Brooke also falls to the Union. The *Honduras* and other vessels had transported General Woodbury and his force to Tampa, and the *Honduras* contributes a contingent to the landing force. During the operation (4–7 May), the ships also capture the blockade runner *Neptune* on the 6th.

In Virginia, the Confederates continue to bolster their defenses and they prepare for additional offensive action, following the Battle of the Wilderness. Meanwhile, the Union stabilizes its defenses and prepares to continue the operations against Petersburg as it inches closer to Richmond. Also, elements of the 10th and 18th Corps clash with Confederates in the vicinity of Chester Station, along the route of the Richmond and Petersburg Railroad. The two sides skirmish here again on the following day. The Union sustains 48 killed and 256 wounded. The Confederates suffer 50 killed and 200 wounded.

In West Virginia, Union forces under General George Crook engage Confederates in the vicinity of Princeton. Casualty figures are unavailable.

In Union general officer activity, Major General William H. French resigns his commission. Due to his seniority, he becomes colonel of the 4th U.S. artillery.

In Confederate general officer activity, Colonel Stand Watie, 1st Cherokee Rifles, and Colonel John Bratton are appointed to the rank of brigadier general, effective this date.

In Naval activity, the USS *Commodore Jones* is destroyed on the James River at City Point, Virginia, by a Confederate torpedo ("electrically-fired mine"); the incident costs the Union 23 killed and nearly 50 wounded. The *Commodore Jones* had been built in New York the previous year and commissioned by the Navy during May 1863. During its short career, the *Commodore Jones* operated primarily on the rivers in Virginia; however, it did participate in the search for the CSS *Tacony* in June 1863. In other action, the USS *Granite City* and *Wave* are captured by Confederate forces in Calcasieu Pass, Texas. Originally the *Argosy No. 2,* it had been acquired by the U.S. Navy on 14 November 1863 at Monongahela, Pennsylvania, and transformed into the gunboat *Wave.* The Confederates use it as a transport vessel.

Also, the USS *Grand Gulf,* operating as part of the North Atlantic Blockading Squadron, seizes a blockade runner, the *Young Republic.* In early March 1865, the *Grand Gulf* moves into the Gulf of Mexico and remains on duty there for the duration of the war. Then it moves to

New Orleans, and in November 1865 at New York, the *Grand Gulf* is decommissioned. In the hands of civilian ownership, the *Grand Gulf* is renamed the *General Grant*. The vessel is destroyed by fire at New Orleans on 19 April 1869. In Portland, Maine, the USS *Agawam*, assigned to the North Atlantic Blockading Squadron, departs en route to Hampton Roads and arrives there on the 9th. Also, the USS *Wamsutta* arrives back in Port Royal, South Carolina, from Philadelphia. It is assigned duty off Georgetown, South Carolina.

The ironclad steam sloop CSS *Raleigh*, commissioned on 30 April, moves out of the Cape Fear River in North Carolina accompanied by two wooden gunboats, the CSS *Equator* and the *Yadkin*. The trio of Rebel warships soon encounters six Union ships attached to the blockading squadron and a battle ensues, but the results are not conclusive. However, on the following day, the Union blockaders, including the USS *Howquah, Kansas, Mount Vernon* and *Nansemond*, are again on scene. The ironclad *Raleigh* attempts to move back up the river; however, it strikes the Wilmington bar and becomes disabled. Nonetheless, the Confederates are able to salvage its iron plating.

This CSS *Raleigh* is separate from the small propeller-driven towing steamer *Raleigh*, which originally belonged to North Carolina and eventually moved to the Confederacy and operates in the coastal waters of Virginia and North Carolina. From May 1862 until April 1865, the *Raleigh*'s service is restricted to "flag of truce or patrol service." It is destroyed by the Confederates during the last days of the war. The *Yadkin*, a wooden propeller steamer, is commanded by Lieutenant Commander W.A. Kerr, Confederate States Navy, and it is also acts as flagship for Confederate Commodore W.F. Lynch.

May 7 (Saturday)   In Louisiana, contingents of the 16th Corps, including elements of the 5th Minnesota Volunteer Regiment, encounter and

skirmish with Confederates at Bayou La Mourie. The Union sustains 10 killed and 31 wounded. Confederate casualties are unavailable.

In Mississippi, a Union contingent, including elements of the 11th, 72nd, and 76th Illinois Volunteer Regiments and the 7th Ohio Battery, commanded by General John McArthur, skirmishes with a Confederate force at Benton. General John MacArthur at this time is in command at Vicksburg.

In Virginia, Union General Benjamin F. Butler's troops, ordered to move on Petersburg a few days earlier, are now less than 10 miles from their objective. Petersburg, considered the rear entrance to Richmond, protects its supply line and must be held at any cost. In related activity, Confederate General Pierre G.T. Beauregard's force reaches Petersburg. During the morning, five Union brigades advance to destroy the Richmond and Petersburg Railroad, but Beauregard's troops intercept and engage the Union advance. The Confederates, stretched from Walthall Junction to Chester Station, are initially pushed back by troops under General W.T. Brooks. Shortly thereafter, the Confederates regain their composure and drive the Yankees back, essentially ending the skirmish as both sides disengage.

In other activity, the 2nd Division Cavalry Corps, Army of the Potomac, under General Wesley Merritt, engages Confederate cavalry at Todd's Tavern. The Union sustains about 80 killed and wounded. Confederate casualty figures are unavailable.

In Georgia, General William T. Sherman's troops attack Confederate General Joseph E. Johnston's flank at Dalton, forcing the Confederates to withdraw from some of their positions. These Union attacks continue throughout May, but the Confederates manage to hold firmly at their near invincible positions in the Allatoona Mountains. In addition, elements of the 4th Corps and cavalry, Army of the Cumberland, commanded by Generals George H. Thomas and David S. Stanley, engage Confederates at Tunnel Hill.

In Union general officer activity, Colonel August V. Kautz is promoted to the rank of brigadier general. Kautz, who initially entered the army as a private during the Mexican War (1st Ohio Infantry), later entered West Point and graduated in the class of 1852. His service during this war, prior to this appointment, included command of a

cavalry brigade in the Army of the James (April 1864–March 1865). In March 1865, he assumes command of a division of Negro troops in the XXV Corps. After the war, Kautz, having received the brevets of major general in the volunteers and the U.S. Army, is attached as a lieutenant colonel with the 8th U.S. Infantry during 1866. He retires at the rank of brigadier general during 1891, following duty on the frontier at various posts.

In Naval action, the USS *Shawsheen*, which departed Hampton Roads on the previous day with Admiral S.P. Lee aboard, encounters difficulty along the James River, but Admiral Lee is no longer aboard. He had transferred his flag to the USS *Malvern*. The *Shawsheen* is repeatedly struck by Confederate fire from shore battery fire and small arms fire while it is engaged in dragging the river near Turkey Bend in the vicinity of Chaffin's Bluff. The crew of the *Shawsheen* is close to the river bank and unable to free themselves before the vessel becomes disabled. With no options, the colors are struck and the crew is taken ashore by Confederate boats; however, the ship is destroyed by fire, which causes the magazine to explode.

May 8 (Sunday)   In Virginia, Union troops, including the 95th Pennsylvania, clash with Confederates at Alsop's Farm. Private George N. Galloway is awarded the Medal of Honor for heroism during this action. In other activity, Union cavalry commanded by General Gouverneur Warren (5th Corps) skirmishes with Jeb Stuart's cavalry early in the day at Spotsylvania, but reinforcements rush to Stuart and force Warren to withdraw.

Troop movements are furious this day. Union General Sedgwick's 6th Corps bolsters Warren, while Confederate General Richard S. Ewell rushes to the aid of Confederate General Richard H. Anderson, who took command after General Longstreet was wounded at the Wilderness. Union General J.C. Robinson is wounded at Spotsylvania. Lieutenant Colonel Joseph Bailey, the officer responsible for the safe passage of the vessels, is heartily thanked by Congress, and he is further rewarded with a commission as brigadier general. In addition, Brigadier General John Cleveland Robinson, during the first day's fighting, is ordered to attack a Confederate position. He advances at the point of the brigade, but without first massing his force. Confederate fire strikes him in his left knee. The wound terminates his field duty due to the amputation of his leg. Subsequently, he receives the brevets of major general of volunteers and in the Regular Army. He retires during May 1869 and is placed on the army's retired list as a major general. General Robinson becomes blind about five years prior to his death. During that period, he belatedly becomes a recipient of the Medal of Honor for his heroism at Spotsylvania on 28 March 1894. He succumbs on 18 February 1897. Also, Brevet Brigadier General James Meech Warner is promoted to full rank brigadier general of volunteers to rank from this date. He resigns from the service during early January 1866.

Troops at Petersburg, Virginia (*Harper's Pictoral History of the Civil War*, 1896).

Left: Dug Gap, Georgia (*Harper's Pictoral History of the Civil War*, 1896). *Right:* General Grant's line (right center) awaits orders to attack (Mottelay, *The Soldier in Our Civil War*, 1886).

In other activity, Union troops occupy Fredericksburg. Also, a Union cavalry contingent (Army of West Virginia) skirmishes with Confederates at Jeffersonville (Abb's Valley).

In Georgia, a contingent attached to the 20th Corps Army of the Cumberland clashes with Confederates at Mill Creek Gap and Dug Gap.

May 8–21 BATTLE OF SPOTSYLVANIA Confederate General Robert E. Lee, expecting a Union move on Richmond, sets his defenses at Spotsylvania on Fredericksburg Road, Laurel Hill, New York River, Dug Gap, and Todd's Tavern in hopes of cutting off Grant's attack on Richmond. The anticipation of Lee is correct, and both armies fight fast and furious for five days with no decisive victory. On 11 May 1864, U.S. Grant writes to General Halleck, chief of staff: "I propose to fight it out, on this line, if it takes all summer."

May 9 (Monday) **In Louisiana,** above Alexandria, the dam under construction on the Red River nears completion, but on this day the current becomes unruly and two barges break loose and plow into the dam. Admiral Porter observes the accident. He mounts a horse and rides to the vessels upstream and directs the *Lexington* to hurriedly move. Lieutenant Bache guides it over the upper falls and straight into the opening in the dam. At full speed, the *Lexington* makes a successful run for a short while, but it has difficulty with some rocks. Nevertheless, soon it is back in calm waters. About 30,000 troops begin to cheer. The remainder of the fleet then gets underway and the vessels also pass. Consequently, the fleet is saved from being trapped.

In Georgia, in the vicinity of Dalton, the Confederates repulse several Union assaults, but pressure forces Rebel evacuation within a few days. The Yankees fail to dislodge the Rebels at Dug Gap. Meanwhile, a force under General James B. McPherson clashes with Confederates at Snake Creek Gap. The additional fighting

occurs at Varnell's Station between Confederates and the 2nd Indiana Cavalry (1st Division, Edward M. McCook's cavalry).

In Virginia, during the ongoing operation of General Kautz, the 11th Pennsylvania Cavalry and the 8th New York Battery clash with Confederates at Jarrett's Station, Weldon Railroad. In addition, the 3rd New York and 1st D.C. Cavalry Regiments, bolstered by the 8th New York Artillery Battery, engage Confederates at White's Bridge, Nottaway Creek. In yet other activity, the 6th Ohio and the 1st New Jersey Regiments (General Philip Sheridan's Raid) clash with Confederates at Childsbury. Also, General William Hopkins Morris is wounded during the fighting around Spotsylvania and the severity terminates his command in the field. Prior to the close of hostilities, he receives the brevet of major general.

Elements of the Union 10th and 18th Corps (General Charles A. Heckman's command) clash with Rebels for two days near Petersburg. Lt. Colonel John Croughton, 10th New Hampshire, leads his regiment forward and repulses a Rebel assault, pushing the Rebels back to Swift's Creek (Arrowhead Church) about three miles outside of Petersburg. The battle remains heated with both sides sustaining high casualties. The Union suffers 90 killed and 400 wounded. The Confederates sustain about 500 killed, wounded and missing. Also, on the 9th and 10th, a Union force composed of the 14th Pennsylvania, 1st, 2nd, and 3rd West Virginia Cavalry Regiments and the 34th Ohio Mounted Volunteers, commanded by General William Averell, engages Confederates under General William Jones at Cove Mountain (Wytheville, Grassy Lick). Finally, Union General Philip Sheridan's cavalry initiates an attack through Confederate lines in Virginia. The 1st and 2nd Cavalry Divisions, Army of the Potomac, participate.

In Naval activity, the USS *Agawam* arrives at Hampton Roads; however, by this time, the

forces under General Butler had lost their momentum and the element of surprise due to timidity with regard to launching an attack against the Rebel-held railroad and turnpike that links Petersburg with Richmond. The USS *Agawam* joins with other Union warships to maintain domination of the James River, particularly since the arrival of fresh Confederate reinforcements. The mission of controlling the James gives the naval forces a huge responsibility. If they fail, Banks' force, composed of about 30,000 troops at Bermuda Hundred, might perish. The James is full of torpedoes (mines) and there also is a threat from Confederate ironclads.

General John Sedgwick (Mottelay, *The Soldier in Our Civil War*, 1886).

Left: General John Sedgwick is killed during the Battle of Spotsylvania (Johnson, *Campfire and Battlefield: History of the Conflicts and Campaigns*, 1894). *Right:* A fireproof in the vicinity of where General John Sedgwick is killed (*Harper's Pictoral History of the Civil War*, 1896).

May 9–10 **BATTLE OF CLOYD'S MOUNTAIN** Heavy fighting develops around New River Bridge, Virginia. The Union participants, commanded by General Crook, include the 12th, 34th, and 36th Ohio. Union troops of the 3rd and 4th Pennsylvania Reserves, as well as contingents of West Virginia commands, are also engaged against Confederates under Brigadier General Albert G. Jenkins. Colonel Isaac Duval leads a charge against the Confederate positions. His regiment, the 9th West Virginia, drills through the defenses, but the cost is high. The regiment sustains a casualty rate of about 30 percent while it crashes through the line. Subsequent to the wounding of Jenkins, Colonel John McCausland, 36th Virginia, assumes command of his brigade, but still the Confederates are unable to forestall disaster. McCausland is compelled to retire, but his force brings at least 200 Union prisoners with him. McCausland will be promoted to the rank of brigadier general effective May 18, and he assumes permanent command of Jenkins' brigade.

The Union suffers approximately 126 killed and 585 wounded; the Confederates suffer nearly 600 killed and 300 missing. Confederate General Jenkins, in addition to being wounded, is captured. Union doctors operate on the wounds of General Jenkins but he succumbs on 21 May. General Jenkins had received a devastating wound at Gettysburg. Confederate General William Edmundson Jones participates in this battle. Jones is ordered to move his command into the valley to engage and defeat Union General Hunter, who is attacking through the valley. They clash at Piedmont in the early part of June. Union General Rutherford B. Hayes (later the 19th U.S. president) participates at Cloyd's Mountain.

May 9–11 **BATTLE OF SPOTSYLVANIA** Union General Philip Sheridan's cavalry initiates action against the Confederate positions in Virginia (Richmond Raid). Union cavalry under General George Custer engages the Confederates at Beaver Dam, where it recaptures 400 Union prisoners that are being moved to Richmond and Yellow Tavern. Sheri-

dan's cavalry also destroys the Squirrel Church Bridge near South Anna. Union troops then continue on toward Richmond. Confederate General Jeb Stuart (the son-in-law of Union General Philip St. George Cooke) is killed on the 11th during Sheridan's raid on Yellow Tavern. The death of Stuart is a devastating loss for the South. On the same day at Yellow Tavern, a successful charge led by Lt. John T. Rutherford of the 9th New York Cavalry gains 90 Confederate prisoners. The Confederates unsuccessfully attack Sheridan from the rear at Meadow Bridge and Sheridan extricates his troops on the 12th, beating the enemy back, then rejoining the Army of the Potomac as it moves toward Cold Harbor.

At Meadow Bridge, Confederate General James Byron Gordon is mortally wounded; he succumbs in Richmond on the 18th. Union Major General John Sedgwick, believing he is out of range, is killed on the 9th by a Confed-

Left: Spotsylvania (*Harper's Pictoral History of the Civil War*, 1896). *Right:* The V Corps hospital at the Battle of Spotsylvania (Mottelay, *The Soldier in Our Civil War*, 1886).

General Philip Sheridan (Johnson, *Campfire and Battlefield: History of the Conflicts and Campaigns*, 1894).

erate sharpshooter. General Horatio Wright succeeds General Sedgwick as commander of the 66th Corps. Also, Union Brigadier General James C. Rice is mortally wounded on the 10th when his thigh is shattered by a rifle shot. General William H. Morris (West Point, 1851) is severely wounded on the 9th. He is not able to return to the field. Subsequently, while living in New York, General Morris becomes a brigadier general in the National Guard and later he achieves the rank of brevet major general.

May 10 (Tuesday) In Arkansas, a Union contingent of the 6th Kansas Cavalry clashes with Confederates at Dardanelle. Casualty figures are unavailable.

In Confederate general officer activity, Colonel Thomas Moore Scott, 12th Louisiana Regiment, is promoted to the rank of brigadier general effective this date. Scott had participated at Vicksburg and will move to Tennessee with Lt. General John Bell Hood and participate at the devastating Battle of Franklin in November 1864.

In Virginia Union General Grant authorizes General Winfield S. Hancock to assault General Lee's positions at Spotsylvania with Gouverneur Warren and Wright's corps. Lee spots the isolated division of Francis C. Barlow and orders an attack to crumble the line, but Union troops repulse this attack. The two opposing forces each suffer great casualties. A second assault occurs, but again the Union holds its position. During late morning, General Gouverneur Warren reconnoiters his front, being repelled twice by Lee. The main assault commences at 4:00 P.M. with Colonel Emery Upton leading 12 regiments into intense battle, causing the Union to suffer heavy casualties and be forced back. Upton, with no desire to withdraw, is sent additional troops (W.S. Hancock, G. Warren, and Horatio Wright) for a final assault. The charge makes inroads but the ground cannot be held; the Union is forced to withdraw with their prisoners.

Grant, while on the battlefield, promotes Colonel Emory Upton to brigadier general.

There is no fighting on the 11th due to inclement weather at Spotsylvania. Union General Thomas G. Stevenson is instantly killed by a Rebel sharpshooter at this action. In addition, Union General Henry Baxter apparently sustains a wound. At the same time, his horse is killed. The 4th Division, Hancock's II Corps, commanded by General Gershom Mott, sustains devastating casualties at Spotsylvania. The division is accused of not providing sufficient support to General Emory Upton and it is transformed into a brigade in General Birney's division; however, later, General Mott receives command of the 3rd Division. General James Clay Rice, while commanding his brigade, sustains a wound that costs him one leg; however, he dies soon after the operation.

In Union general officer activity, Colonel Francis Fessenden is promoted to brigadier general; however, due to earlier injuries that cost him one leg, he has administrative duties in and around Washington, D.C. He is promoted to major general on 9 November 1865. Rather than accept the rank of lieutenant colonel when the U.S. Army is reorganized during 1866, he retires as a brigadier general and resumes his career as a lawyer.

In Naval activity, the USS *Mound City* hits some shallow water and runs aground along with the USS *Carondelet* near the winged dams on the Red River. Ground troops are able to free the *Mound City* after a strenuous effort. After the mission, it moves to Indianola and patrols in that area to help protect the town. After the war, the *Mound City* is decommissioned at Mound City, where it is sold on 9 November, 1865 In other activity, the side wheel gunboat USS *Pontoosuc*, constructed in Maine, is commissioned at Portland. Lieutenant Commander George A. Stevens receives command of the gunboat, which is assigned to the South Atlantic Blockading Squadron.

May 11 (Wednesday) In Virginia, Confederate cavalry under General Jeb Stuart engages Union troops under General Devens (Sheridan's Raid) at Yellow Tavern. The Rebels hold, but Sheridan mounts a forceful assault during late afternoon to bruise the Rebels considerably. The cavalry charges with guns blazing and swords swaying, forcing the Confederates to fall back. Confederate General Jeb Stuart is killed. General Stuart, the son-in-law of Confederate General Philip St. George Cooke, is also the brother-in-law of Confederate General John Rogers Cooke, his wife's brother. Major General Wade Hampton assumes command of Stuart's Brigade. On the following day, Confeder-

ate General James Byron Gordon is mortally wounded.

Sheridan's cavalry (1st Massachusetts Cavalry) skirmishes with Confederates at Ashland and captures about 30 Rebels. At Petersburg, Union (Butler's Army of the James) contingents advance toward Richmond, but Rebels intercept them and they are compelled to withdraw to Proctor's Creek.

In Georgia, Sherman issues orders directing a full-scale attack against Resaca to be commenced on the following morning.

May 12 (Thursday) In Georgia at Resaca, the Confederates under General Joseph Johnston evacuate Dalton and deploy outside Resaca to await the advancing Union troops under General Sherman. The Fourth Corps (General Howard) and some cavalry that remains at Buzzard's Roost do not participate; however, the remainder of Sherman's army launches the offensive at sunrise. McPherson's column marches directly behind General Hugh Kilpatrick's cavalry, which acts as vanguard. The sparks begin to fly when Confederate cavalry under General Joseph Wheeler strikes Kilpatrick at a point about two miles outside Resaca. A grueling contest erupts with both sides pouncing upon each other. During this encounter, the Union cavalry drives the Rebels back, but Kilpatrick receives a severe wound that debilitates him. Command is passed to Colonel Murray. At about this time, General James B. McPherson's troops move up and charge into the Confederate pickets, nudging them out after a ferocious struggle. McPherson gains valuable ground that includes a strategic ridge on his left and the Oostenaula River.

General James McPherson (Johnson, *Campfire and Battlefield: History of the Conflicts and Campaigns*, 1894).

In an effort to increase the pressure on the Rebels and gain even greater advantage against General Johnston, General George H. Thomas speeds to McPherson's left to bolster it, and General John Schofield deploys the 23rd Corps among a series of rolling hills along the Dalton-Resaca Road. Sherman continues to lay the foundation, but still, the full-scale thrust remains several days away. Sherman is informed that Confederate General Johnston had recently directed three of General John Hood's divisions to depart Dalton and that the remainder of Hood's army had joined them at Resaca. Consequently, General Howard's Fourth Corps dominates Dalton.

In Mississippi, the 11th, 72nd and 76th Illinois Volunteer Regiments under General John McArthur engage Confederates at Vaughn. Casualty figures are unavailable.

In the Indian Territory, the 1st Nebraska Battalion (cavalry) skirmishes with Confederates at Smith's Station.

In Virginia, Union forces (1st and 3rd Divisions, Cavalry Corps, Army of the Potomac) under General Sheridan repulse a Confederate attack at Meadow Bridge, Chickahominy River. Also, Union General August V. Kautz conducts a series of raids against Confederate positions. On the 17th, he launches raids against the Petersburg and Lynchburg Railroad. His force (cavalry of the Army of the James) sustains six killed and 28 wounded. Confederate casualties are unavailable.

In Union activity, Colonel John Harris, the sixth commandant of the United States Marine Corps, succumbs while in office. He will be succeeded by Major Zeilin the following month. In other activity, Colonel Joseph Hayes is pro-

moted to the rank of brigadier general, effective this day. Also, Brigadier General John Henry Hobart Ward, recognized by his peers as a heroic officer, is relieved of command pursuant to charges "for misbehavior and intoxication in the presence of the enemy at the Battle of the Wilderness." On 18 July, General Ward is honorably discharged. Attempts to reverse the dismissal fail to make progress. General Ward, after his release, works as a court clerk in New York. On 24 July 1903, Ward is struck by a train and killed while he is in Monroe, New York, where one of his daughters had been interred. Also, Colonel James Meech Warner, while forming his positions and inspecting the earthworks at Spotsylvania, suffers a neck wound from a ball; however, he survives and afterward participates under General Sheridan in the Shenandoah. In addition, Colonel Emory Upton, Colonel Simon Goodell Griffin (6th New York), Colonel John Rutter Brooke and Colonel Samuel Sprigg Carroll are promoted to brigadier general. Carroll was wounded on 5 May at the Wilderness and again on 13 May at Spotsylvania and is out of service until December of this year. He remains in active service beyond the close of hostilities and retires during June 1869 with the rank of major general. Brigadier General Horatio Gouverneur Wright, turned down as major general by the Senate during the previous year, is reappointed and the Senate confirms his commission.

In Naval activity, thirty-three Union vessels push through the new canal on the way to Alexandria, Louisiana, as they continue their retreat along the Red River. It takes the efforts of 3,000 men, including Maine regiments (lumberjacks), to complete this feat. In other activity, Lt. William Budd, commander of the USS *Somerset*, a converted ferryboat, having been informed of a Confederate scheme to capture the USS *Adela*, moves to foil the plot. He leads a contingent, composed of members of his crew and others from the schooner USS *James S. Chambers*, against the Confederates at Apalachicola, Florida, before they can launch their strike. The Union assault succeeds in scattering the Rebels just as they are embarking in boats to seize the *Adela*. The Yankees capture four men and confiscate six of the seven Rebel boats, along with a huge supply of equipment. Subsequent to this action, the *Adela* transfers to the West Pass of St. George Sound and in August to the East Pass of Apalachicola. During the following month, the *Adela* moves to St. Marks, Florida, and by November, it patrols again in St. George Sound.

May 12–13   In Virginia, General U.S. Grant orders Hancock's 6th Corps to assault the Con-

A New York ferryboat converted into a Union gunboat (Johnson, *Campfire and Battlefield: History of the Conflicts and Campaigns*, 1894).

federate Mule Shoe salient discovered on the 11th during a reconnaissance mission near Spotsylvania Court House. Two Union corps begin their assault under a dense fog, which hampers progress. At approximately 0430, Union troops charge through the woods moving toward the enemy positions. They gain some ground. Hand-to-hand combat, including the use of rifles as clubs, follows. The Union defeats the Rebels, gains control of their objective, and captures about 4,000 prisoners, including nearly the entire brigade of Confederate General George H. Steuart (General Edward Johnson's division). The scene of the battle is dubbed "The Bloody Angle." The Confederates counterattack and succeed in driving the Union under Hancock into a disciplined retreat. During the struggle, the brigade (21 regiments) under Colonel Oliver Edwards had held the point known as "Bloody Angle" for 24 hours of incessant combat. Subsequent to this battle and at Winchester, Colonel Edwards is breveted brigadier general. Edwards is offered the position of provost marshal general (Middle Military Division) by General Sheridan; however, he declines and prefers to remain in field command. Later he participates in the Petersburg campaign. General Edwards' brigade is in the forefront during the final attack and it is Edwards who accepts the surrender of Petersburg during April 1865.

General Robert E. Lee's forces continually assault Union lines, and they are repulsed in five separate attacks that inflict severe casualties. The Union positions hold firm. The gunpowder of the Confederates is wet, giving them serious problems. The fighting keeps up at a grueling pace until well after midnight (12th–13th), but on the 13th, the field of battle is relatively

Brigadier General J.H. Hobart Ward (Mottelay, *The Soldier in Our Civil War*, 1886).

Confederate Generals Edward Johnson and George H. Steuart are taken to the rear by Negro cavalry troops (Mottelay, *The Soldier in Our Civil War*, 1886).

quiet with no actual fighting except small skirmishes. Lee repositions his troops, fortifying the ground they still hold. Union Generals Gouverneur Warren and Horatio Gouverneur Wright are placed to the left of Union General Burnside's positions. The Union sustains 14,322 casualties between 8 May and 12 May.

The Confederates lose between 9,000 and 12,000 casualties in this battle for Spotsylvania, including 4,000 captured. Confederate Generals James Alexander Walker, Henry Harrison Walker (West Point, 1853) and Harry T. Hays are wounded. After recuperating, Hays is transferred to the Trans-Mississippi Department. Confederate Generals Junius Daniel and Abner M. Perrin are killed; Daniel is mortally wounded while attacking to recapture the Confederate positions on the Mule Shoe. General Perrin, prior to the battle, stated: "I shall come out of this fight a live major general or a dead brigadier." General Perrin sustains seven wounds as he falls from his horse. Colonel Bryan Grimes assumes command of Daniel's brigade and shortly thereafter, he is promoted to brigadier general. Colonel John Caldwell C. Sanders, 11th Alabama Infantry, succeeds Perrin. Confederate Generals George H. Steuart (West Point, 1848) and Edward Johnson are both captured. Steuart, subsequent to being released, will rejoin the army and command a brigade (Pickett's division) at Five Forks, Virginia, in early April of the following year. Johnson, subsequent to exchange, will serve in Tennessee, leading a division at Nashville in December. Confederate Colonel William Ruffin Cox, 2nd North Carolina, operating with his regiment as part of General Ramseur's brigade, exhibits such

valor on the field that he is promoted after the battle to commanding officer of the brigade, composed of the 2nd, 4th, 14th, and 30th North Carolina Regiments. The 1st and 3rd Regiments, which had evaded capture at the Mule Shoe salient with General George H. Steuart, are also attached to the brigade. Colonel Ruffin Cox is promoted to brigadier general effective May 31. Also, Confederate General John B. Gordon and Colonel (later brigadier general) Clement Anselm Evans participate at the fighting around Spotsylvania, Gordon in command of a division and Evans, a brigade. The Union captures nearly the entire 25th Virginia Regiment, which is attached to General W.E. Jones' brigade (General Edward Johnson's division). Nevertheless, the 25th will continue the struggle, participating as part of Colonel General William Terry's (4th Virginia Infantry) consolidated brigade, attached to General Gordon's division (General John C. Breckinridge's 2nd Corps).

In the meantime, fighting continues at Spotsylvania until May 21.

May 12–16 In Virginia, Union and Confederate troops engage in and around Drewry's Bluff (Fort Darling). Union General Sheridan's force, while moving swiftly to join General Benjamin Butler for a combined assault against Drewry's Bluff, is attacked by troops from Richmond. Sheridan avoids capture and defeat on the 13th by getting away from the Chickahominy River and continuing toward General Butler. Butler will cancel an attack against Drewry's Bluff on the 15th and Beauregard attacks the Union with strength on the 16th. The Union improvises and lays barbed wire to help hold the line. The Rebels assault continuously, but the Union repels five assaults before the right flank collapses under this enormous Confederate pressure.

Four hundred Union troops, including General Charles Adam Heckman (Heckman's brigade) are captured when the Rebels take advantage of the fog in the early morning hours and seize his command. The left flank and center of the Union line holds fast, saving the day for the Union. General Butler safely withdraws to Bermuda Hundred without pursuit by the Confederates. During the fighting, Colonel Thomas Ogden Osborn sustains a wound that costs him the use of his right arm. Skirmishes include Wierbottom Church, Proctor's Creek and Palmer's Creek. General Beauregard now has the Union troops under Butler bottled up at Bermuda Hundred. During the struggle at Drewry's Bluff, Confederate General Robert Ransom (West Point, 1850) relieves General

Seth M. Barton from command. Barton remains without a command until autumn, when he is assigned a brigade at Richmond. General Bate, during the war, is wounded three times and six of his horses are shot from under him, prior to his capture during the closing days of the hostilities. After the war, General Bate is elected governor of Tennessee during 1882 and as a U.S. Senator during 1886. He dies while in the Senate on 9 March 1905.

Colonel Young M. Moody, 43rd Alabama, sustains a severe wound, but he recovers and continues in command of the regiment (Gracie's brigade). Confederate General Montgomery D. Corse's brigade (15th, 17th, 29th, 30th and 32nd Virginia Regiments) participates at this engagement. And Confederate Brigadier General Henry A. Wise's command, including Wise's Legion, participates. Wise also spends time at Richmond as part of General Richard H. Anderson's corps. General Heckman is among officers transported to Charleston, and while there, he and the other Union captives are subject to the U.S. naval bombardments. Heckman is exchanged during September. Afterward, he assumes command of the 2nd Division, XVIII Corps.

May 13 (Friday) In Louisiana, U.S. vessels attempting to return safely to Alexandria successfully complete their mission with the aid of dams constructed through efforts of General Joseph Bailey. The ships have now traveled the rapids of the Red River, enabling them to reach the Mississippi River.

In South Carolina, Fort Sumter is again the recipient of a Union artillery bombardment, but again the defenders hold. The fort is a great symbol of defiance for the Southern cause and of the persistence and determination for the Union cause. At this late stage of the war, the strategic location of the fort is much less important than its great importance as a symbol.

In Tennessee, the 111th U.S. Colored Troops (3rd Alabama) clash with a Confederate force at Pulaski. Meanwhile, other Union troops (1st Division, Cavalry, Army of the Cumberland) engage Confederates at Tilton.

In Virginia, Confederates in the vicinity of Petersburg withdraw from their positions opposite Butler's force at Proctor's Creek and draw a new defensive line more to the rear and closer to Petersburg. The Union schedules an attack for the following day, but it is postponed until the 16th. Also, a continent of the 36th U.S. Colored Troops and a detachment of sailors of the Potomac Fleet skirmish with a Confederate contingent at Point Lookout. Casualty figures are unavailable.

May 13–15 BATTLE OF RESACA The Union Army under General William T. Sherman (110,000) advances and engages the Confederates (60,000) under General Joseph Eggleston Johnston at Resaca, Georgia. On the 14th, Sherman's force constructs a pontoon bridge that provides a launch pad from which Sweeny's division (16th Corps) will sprint to Calhoun, while cavalry under General Israel Garrard strikes against Rome in an effort to demolish the rails stretching between it and Kingston. Meanwhile, the Confederates are deployed behind Camp Creek, entrenched atop some high hills and within forts. The left, held by Leonidas Polk, is nudged along the Oostenaula River, while the center is controlled by General Joseph Hardee, whose lines extend to those of General John B. Hood protecting the far right. Hood's forces stretch around Resaca toward Connasauga to the northeast.

By afternoon, General James McPherson, trailed by General George H. Thomas, fords Camp Creek and plows into Polk's sector, compelling Polk to pull back and surrender the strategic ground to General James B. McPherson, who immediately deploys his artillery. All the while, Israel Garrard and Thomas W. Sweeny are striking their respective targets. Later, Thomas' force moves into Camp Creek Valley, where he is joined shortly thereafter by General John Schofield. The latter directs his troops to deploy on Thomas' left in the vicinity of Resaca.

In the meantime, General Joseph Johnston prepares to strike the Union by launching a strong assault on the following morning, but complications develop. He learns that Polk, who had been driven from his formidable positions, now holds untenable ground. Johnston resorts to improvisation and dispatches General W.H.T. Walker's division to Calhoun, where the Confederate base and the reserves are located. During the afternoon of the 14th, Union troops pound against the Rebels under Colonel Isaac W. Avery's 4th Georgia Cavalry and its supporting artillery at Tanner's Ferry (Lay's Ferry), near the mouth of Snake Creek at a bend in the river about two and one-half miles from Calhoun.

The Union constructs a pontoon bridge at the crossing, which permits Sherman to further tighten the noose around Resaca. Calls are sent out for aid from Walker's force and from General John Tyler Morgan's force, but by the time they arrive from Calhoun, Colonel Isaac Avery's force had been badly mauled and driven back.

At Calhoun, slightly more than five miles below Resaca, on the 15th, it is expected that the opponents would badly bloody each other in a

major skirmish, but the action here, which occurs during the morning, is confined to the infantry units, due mainly to the dense woods and the nasty terrain. The Union is quiet and the Confederates under Johnston think the foe had not crossed the river in strength.

During the morning of the 15th, a Confederate brigade advances, and to its surprise, the Yankees had indeed forded the Oostenaula River. The Union meets the attack with devastating fire and the Confederates retire. Just after 1300, the Union divisions of Butterfield, Geary and Alpheus S. Williams advance. The columns encounter the advancing troops of General Littlepage Stevenson (Hood's command). This collision quickly becomes gruesome. The Union drives doggedly and the Confederates raise heavy opposition, but the resistance lacks cohesion. The Rebels doggedly fight, but they are unable to hold the line. The Yankees push forward and the Rebels give ground. The Union seizes four guns which had been reluctantly abandoned. Throughout the day, the battering remains relentless. Finally, at dusk, the sounds of battle and the cries of anguish subside.

Both sides rack up heavy casualties, but the Confederates, with only about half the strength of the Union, can ill afford the losses. The Union's overpowering numbers defeat the Confederates; however, Confederate General Hood manages to successfully withdraw and avoid total disaster at the hands of Union General Joseph Hooker (Sherman's command). Confederate General Johnston continues to fall back toward the mountains. The retirement occurs during the night of the 15th-16th. Union Captain Thomas Box captures the flag of the Confederate 38th Alabama Infantry; he receives the Medal of Honor for his actions. The battle flag of the 35th Alabama Regiment is also captured.

General Sherman enters Resaca, Georgia (*Harper's Pictoral History of the Civil War*, 1896).

Although the Yankees are making progress, the Rebels still control the Western and Atlantic Railroad. The Union losses stand at about 600 killed and 2,147 wounded. The Confederate losses are 300 killed, 1,500 wounded and 1,000 missing. General August Willich is wounded in the shoulder during the fighting around Resaca, but he recovers and returns to service as commander at Covington and Newport Barracks, Kentucky, which are combined as one post in Cincinnati. Subsequent to the close of hostilities, General Willich receives the brevet of major general of volunteers to rank from 21 October 1865. He later returns to his native Germany to serve in its ongoing war with France, but his service is declined because of his age. He returns to America and settles in Ohio, where he dies on 22 January 1878.

May 14 (Saturday)   In Georgia, heavy skirmishing occurs in the vicinity of Resaca, between General William T. Sherman's troops and the Confederates under General Joseph E. Johnston. During the day, Confederate Brigadier General William F. Tucker is severely wounded. The wound terminates his service in

Left: The Battle of Resaca. *Right:* General Geary's forces charge up the mountain at Resaca (Mottelay, *The Soldier in Our Civil War*, 1886).

the field; however, he again serves during the final days of the conflict as commander of the District of Southern Mississippi and Louisiana. Afterward he resumes his law practice in Mississippi. He is assassinated in Okolona County, Mississippi, on 14 September 1881. The Union does not take Resaca, as Johnston holds his position. Union General Mahlon Manson is seriously wounded and resigns on 21 December 1864. In addition, Union General Thomas Ward, who assumes command of General Butterfield's Division at Resaca, is wounded, but he declines being removed from the fight.

In Louisiana, a large Union force departs Alexandria en route for Simmesport. The Union strength under Nathaniel Banks has been increased since the recent arrival of the force under General John A. McClernand, which had moved from Matagorda Bay. Meanwhile, General Fitz Henry Warren remains as commanding officer at Matagorda Bay.

In Virginia, Union General Emory Upton (Horatio Wright's corps) assaults Confederate lines in the vicinity of Spotsylvania, pushing the Rebels back. The Confederate troops mount a counterattack that impedes Grant's further progress. The Union secures the immediate area they hold, thus extending their line east of the courthouse while Lee maneuvers to confront the newly acquired Union positions. During the action, General Upton leads 12 regiments into the Confederate positions (Bloody Angle). General Robert E. Lee states in a telegram to Confederate General John C. Breckinridge: "If you can drive back the different expeditions threatening the valley, it would be desirable for you to join me with your whole force." In other activity, Union troops (attached to Army of West Virginia) occupies Rood's Hill.

In Union general officer activity, Brigadier General Andrew Jackson Smith is promoted to major general.

In Confederate general officer activity, Brigadier General John Brown Gordon is promoted to major general. General Gordon is with General Robert E. Lee during the final days at Richmond. During the retreat from its back door, Petersburg, Gordon commands about one-half of the infantry. After the war, he returns to Georgia and is three times elected to the U.S. Senate. He succumbs on 9 January 1904.

In Louisiana (Red River Campaign), the 3rd Division, 16th Corps and contingents of the 19th Corps' cavalry clash through the 16th with Confederates at Mansura (Avoyelle's Prairie, Morreausville or Marksville).

In Naval activity, Rear Admiral Samuel Phillips Lee (commanding officer, North Atlantic Blockading Squadron) switches his flag from the USS *Malvern* to the USS *Agawam.* Admiral Lee believes that being aboard the *Agawam,* he will be better positioned to personally examine the minesweeping operations on the James River.

May 15 (Sunday) BATTLE OF NEW MARKET This clash in Virginia had not been unexpected.

On 12 May, at VMI, the cadets receive notice at evening parade when the following is published to the troops: "HEADQUARTERS VALLEY DEPT, GENERAL ORDERS NO. I, STAUNTON VA.: The command will move tomorrow morning (13th) promptly at six o'clock, on turnpike leading to Harrisonburg. The following order of march will be observed: Wharton's Brigade; Echol's Brigade; Cadet Corps; Reserve Forces; Ambulance and Medical Wagons; Artillery; Trains. The Artillery will for the present be united and form a battalion under command of Major McLaughlin, &c., &c., &c. By command of Maj. Gen. BRECKENRIDGE. J. STODARD JOHNSTON, A. AG."

During the first day's march, the column arrives at Harrisonburg, and on the following day, it is at Lacy's Springs, about ten miles outside of New Market. The march had been trying, as many places on the roads had become obstacles due to abandoned equipment as well as carts and wagons. In addition, it became apparent the Union threat was imminent. Hordes of civilians were met as they abandoned the areas and flooded the valley pike to escape.

The column also received a series of reports, none of which contained encouraging news, from retreating Confederate soldiers who detailed the overwhelming odds that they had faced. Nonetheless, the VMI cadets, although not veterans in the field, continued the march unabashedly willing to share in the sacrifices of the experienced veterans that had gone before them. The column finds a small flicker of hope when it halts for the night on the eve of the battle near a church where some Union prisoners, most of whom were German, were being held. For many of the cadets, it was their first glance at a Union soldier. As dusk settles over the area, the rain which had plagued the advance also returns as the troops try to settle in for the night. Meanwhile, other reports arrive to inform the Confederates that Union General Franz Sigle's command had made camp less than ten miles away.

At about 0100, an officer arrives with orders. Soon after, the drums, saturated by the rain, begin a muffled, eerie beat that rouses the sleeping troops, and shortly thereafter, the camp is broken and the column, including the cadets under Colonel Ship, is again on the move in the darkness and along a mud-filled road. That latest order to march carries with it a stark, silent message, particularly for the untested cadets. Imminent battle and carnage will arrive with dawn, giving much sober thought to those en route to New Market. Meanwhile, the Union forces have undergone identical preparations and they, too, have been pummeled by the frequent rain storms; however, their recent successes have aroused a rim of optimism within the lines.

The column halts at a bend in the road, aware that Union lines are beyond the curve. The valley turnpike leads directly into New Market, a quaint village nestled among meadows and hills, about to burst into a cauldron. Suddenly the attack is commenced. Confederate artillery is being sped down the pike, while cavalry breaks into a gallop riding into a ring of Union fire as

it dashes toward a creek. Colonel George S. Patton leads his brigade briskly into the thick of the fight, moving from the valley pike with his left anchored across the meadow. They are met by resounding force from Union troops in the orchards. While Confederate sharpshooters maintain heavy fire, the artillery under McLaughlin deploys in the meadow and immediately pounds the Union positions. Meanwhile, the cadets' artillery targets a Union battery at the cemetery.

Suddenly two Confederate wings are in action. Wharton is on the left with the 62nd Virginia under Colonel Smith, 30th Virginia under Colonel Clark and Colonel Forsburg's 51st Virginia. The cadets and Edgar's battalion coordinates with Colonel George S. Patton, who commands the right wing, which includes the 22nd Virginia and Derrick's battalion. Patton's brigade lies prone for a while on the opposite side of the valley pike from the cadets. The cadets are ordered, "Battalion forward! Guide center." The cadets advance. Soon after, Patton's brigade is up and in motion charging the Union positions. The whirlwind of fire intensifies as Union artillery gets the range of the advancing Rebels.

As if in cadence with the troops of Patton's brigade who are rallying themselves with the Rebel yell as they charge forward, the cadets, having drawn up to their artillery, begin to descend the slope. They remain under heavy fire as they advance under a heavy rain. In the meantime, a Union battery at the cemetery is dislodged and driven back into some high ground. Colonel Patton's brigade continues to apply pressure, and it succeeds in driving the Union back into the town. However, Union reinforcements are bolstering the positions at the second line. Behind the lines slightly below the town, a large Union reserve force is deployed.

Meanwhile, Colonel Patton's brigade enters New Market, and during the complicated maneuver some confusion develops, and the Union detects the Confederates as they emerge on the pike. A cavalry force is prepared to initiate a charge to crush the brigade, but in the meantime, McLaughlin's artillery is brought up to neutralize the cavalry thrust. The cavalry charges and the Confederate guns spew round after round into their ranks, devastating the formation. Horses and riders alike are shot down and some riderless horses maintain their gallop, but pose little harm to the right wing. The cavalry is eliminated from the contest, leaving General Sigel at a disadvantage.

Wharton's left wing continues to dent the Union lines and break the infantry from its steadfast positions. In the process two Union artillery pieces are seized. The Union sustains heavy casualties as the troops brave the fire to find more tenable positions on the opposite side of the field. However, with a new line drawn, that deadly crossing faces the Confederates. The Union stands several hundred yards distant in well entrenched positions, anticipating that the Confederates will charge across the open field. Soon after, the order to advance is given and the rain-drenched Rebels, near exhaustion, soiled with mud and some shoeless, having lost them to the mud, advance into a thunderburst of shot and shell, with troops dropping at every yard. During the murderous advance, Colonel S. Ship, the commander of the cadets, is struck and he falls. Oblivious to the sheets of fire, a cry is heard: "Rally on Edgar's Battalion."

Nonetheless, the left wing is being devastated. The cadets, faced with imminent death if they remain in place, hear their captain, Henry Wise, shout: "We must charge or fly." The cadets attack toward a farmhouse and the defenders are dislodged. While the Union troops seek positions behind some buildings, the Confederates continue their forward progress. Union artillery attempts to stem the tide, but it is unable to get properly positioned, due in great part because the Confederates have shot the horses. The artillery troops abandon the guns. Meanwhile, the cadets, having had their initial baptism under fire, enter into hand-to-hand close quartered fighting. The cadets seize the battery and suddenly the VMI colors are waving back and forth in victory by a cadet standing on an artillery piece.

After the momentary burst of pride, the cadets, still under some Union fire, participate in the chase. The Union is in retreat moving hurriedly toward Mount Jackson. Artillery posted on Rude's Hill plasters the escape route while Confederate cavalry closes on the rear. The Union, however, safely gets across a bridge, which is then set afire to halt the pursuit. The Confederate victory is stunning and helps the sagging morale of the Confederacy, and is a morale booster even for Robert E. Lee. By evening, the exasperated Union force finds safety at Mount Jackson and the exhausted Confederates make camp. The pickets encamp on the opposite side of the river in the vicinity of Mount Airy, while the main body makes camp slightly below New Market.

Inside the town itself, a large number of Union prisoners, primarily German, are detained on a street within earshot of the spontaneous celebration that erupts. At the conclusion of the battle it was evident that the veterans had appreciated the conduct and performance of the cadets and they freely commended their actions and bravery under fire. In appreciation of the contribution of the cadets, they later march in parade in Richmond to the cheers of thousands.

The Union sustains Union 120 dead, 560 wounded and slightly less than 250 missing or captured. Confederates suffer 85 dead and 320 wounded. Union Sergeant James Burns, 1st West Virginia Infantry, rallies a few men who, at great risk, save the colors from being captured by the Confederates. Burns also retraces his steps, moving back about 100 yards through heavy enemy fire to rescue a fellow trooper who had become wounded. Burns receives the Medal of Honor for his valor. During the battle of New Market, 247 courageous "boy soldiers" of the Virginia Military Institute assist in the engagement against the Union. Ten of the cadets pay the ultimate price of war. The cadets had only participated in a support role, but they were in the thick of some of the fighting. Also, Confed-

erate Brigadier General John Echols participates in this battle. Since his promotion during April 1862, his service has been confined mainly in the western sector of Virginia and remains so for the duration. General Echols, subsequent to the close of hostilities, becomes involved in organizing the Chesapeake and Ohio Railway from the old Virginia Central Railroad. He practices his business operations in Staunton, Virginia, and Louisville, Kentucky. General Echols dies in Staunton on 24 May 1896. Also, General Gabriel Colvin Wharton participates.

In Georgia, a contingent of the Army of the Cumberland, the 2nd Cavalry Division, engages Rebels at Tanner's Bridge. The Union sustains two killed and 16 wounded. Confederate casualties are unavailable. Meanwhile, a contingent of the 16th Corps, Army of the Tennessee, engages Confederates at Ley's Ferry.

In Kansas, Union troops from the 3rd Wisconsin Cavalry engage and rout a larger Confederate force at Dry Wood, while successfully rescuing several Union prisoners.

In Louisiana, the 67th U.S. Colored Regiment engages Confederates at Mount Pleasant Landing. The unit sustains three killed and one wounded. Confederate casualties are unavailable.

In Virginia, Union General Benjamin Butler reports capture of the outer works at Drewry's Bluff (Fort Darling) and of his cavalry's success in severing Confederate rails and telegraph lines South of Richmond on the Danville Road.

In Naval activity, the USS *Kansas,* on patrol during the early morning hours, detects a blockade runner that is using the cover of darkness to break through the blockade; however, pursuit begins and the *Kansas* intercepts the British steamer *Shandy,* which is transporting turpentine, cotton and tobacco. On the 16th, the *Shandy,* under tow, arrives in the harbor at Beaufort, North Carolina.

May 16 (Monday)   In Georgia, elements of the 16th Corps, Army of the Tennessee, commanded by General James B. McPherson, engages Confederate General Dodge's command at Rome Crossroads. Meanwhile, Sherman's forces enter Resaca. Work parties immediately begin repairs on the damaged bridges and soon the troops begin to cross the Oostanaula River. Generals Edward M. McCook and George Stoneman lead their cavalry units in pursuit of the retreating Rebels. Generals George H. Thomas and McPherson cross at Resaca and Lay's Ferry respectively. General John Schofield's force crosses at two points, Fite's Ferry at the Connasauga River and McClure's Ferry at the Coosawattee River. Union General Jefferson C. Davis leads his division to Rome, but the remainder of Sherman's army, using several different routes, drives south. Rome and Kingston will fall to the Union.

In Kentucky, the 39th Kentucky Volunteer Regiment skirmishes with Confederates at Pond Creek, Pike County.

In Louisiana, the Union army under General Nathaniel Banks arrives at Simmesport. It de-

parts there on the 20th. Recently, General U.S. Grant had ordered that the Red River Campaign be terminated because General Sherman is in need of additional troops for his campaign across Georgia to the sea.

In Missouri, a two-company contingent of the 15th Kansas Cavalry skirmishes with Confederates at Clear Creek.

In Colorado, one company of the 1st Colored Cavalry, bolstered by McClain's Colorado Battery, engages Confederates at Smoky Hill. Casualty figures are unavailable.

In South Carolina, the 34th U.S. Colored Troops skirmish with Confederates at Ashepoo River.

In Virginia, U.S. Grant receives word Sherman has driven the Rebels out of Dalton, Georgia, and is pursuing them south. Union General Sheridan reports cutting roads and telegraph lines in all directions from Richmond. Grant telegraphs Halleck: "Constant rain for five days holding up operations. Need 24 hours of dryness. Roads are impassable." Also, the 3rd New York, 5th and 11th Pennsylvania and the 1st D.C. Cavalry Regiments (General August Kautz's Raid) attack Confederates at Belcher's Mills. Casualty figures are unavailable.

In Union general officer activity, General Charles Matthies, recently assigned to Decatur, Alabama, after being relieved of field duty due to poor health, resigns his commission on this day. He returns home to Burlington, Iowa, where he dies during October 1868. Also, Brigadier General John C. Starkweather is assigned command of Pulaski, Tennessee. Toward the latter part of the year, Starkweather requests duty with General Sheridan; however, his application is denied. He resigns his commission on 11 May 1865.

May 16–30   In Virginia, Union troops under General Benjamin F. Butler and Confederate troops commanded by General Pierre G.T. Beauregard clash in the vicinity of Bermuda Hundred. The 10th and 18th Corps, Army of the James, participate. Before dawn, while the Union readies the attack, it is suddenly and violently struck by a ferocious artillery barrage which is unleashed by General Beauregard, who had anticipated the imminent attack. Beauregard advances his main force, but he directs General William H.C. Whiting to hang back in positions to the rear of Butler's left. Meanwhile, Union General William F. Smith stretches out his XVIII Corps in a dangerously thin line and still leaves a gap between his right flank, defended by General Charles Heckman's brigade, and the James River. It is precisely here that the Rebels propel their first thrust and it is powerful. The Union line gets stunned and nearly overwhelmed. Other Union forces, namely the three regiments of General A. Ames, are standing in reserve to augment Smith. With quick reaction, Ames sends up the 112th New York and the 9th Maine to intercept the Rebels. They clash at the road that leads back to Bermuda Hundred. The persistence of these two regiments foils the Confederate plan to secure the road.

In the meantime, General Beauregard launches a frontal assault against General Smith's lines, but here, the troops under Generals William T. Brooks and Godfrey Weitzel stand rigidly and repel the attack. Undaunted, Beauregard again attempts to crack the right flank by hitting it with his full strength. Meanwhile, General Smith, aware that he lacks the manpower to hold against a full-scale assault, orders a retirement to more tenable positions from which to meet the threat. While Smith pulls back, General Quincy A. Gillmore, deployed on the left, modifies his lines to adapt to the movement. Later, General Benjamin Butler, after concluding that his positions are too poor to operate against Richmond, orders the entire force to withdraw to Bermuda Hundred.

May 17 (Tuesday)   In Alabama, a contingent of the 3rd Division, 15th Corps, Army of the Tennessee, engages Confederates at Madison Station. Casualty figures are unavailable.

In Georgia, the Union (Sherman's Army) advances to Adairsville and encounters General Joseph E. Johnston's rear guard forces, which had been posted to impede the advance. Infantry under General Benjamin F. Cheatham and cavalry under Major General Joseph Wheeler duel with General George H. Thomas's troops. The fighting includes action at Grave's House and Calhoun. The columns of Confederate Generals Hood and Polk move on the left and Hardee's force moves on the right. General George H. Thomas's Union force encounters General Benjamin Cheatham's division and Wheeler's cavalry, igniting skirmishing that lasts until dusk, when the Confederates disengage. Brigadier General Henry B. Davidson leads his cavalry brigade along with the cavalry of Generals John T. Morgan and Lawrence S. Ross in support of General Matthew D. Ector's brigade (Major General Samuel G. French's Division) In addition, resistance is encountered at Calhoun. Sherman is heading toward Kingston. Confederate Lt. General William Joseph Hardee arrives at Kingston on Sunday, the 18th, and the forces of both Generals Polk and Hood pause just outside of Cassville on the same day.

In Oregon at Camp Watson, a stockade fort is established near the Deschutes River in the vicinity of present-day Mitchell by a contingent of the First Oregon Volunteer Cavalry commanded by Lieutenant Stephan Watson. On May 17 1864, the camp is attacked by Indians and the command is massacred. It is re-garrisoned and remains operational until 1866.

In Virginia, Corporal Patrick Monaghan of Company F, 48th Pennsylvania Infantry, recaptures the colors of the 7th New York Infantry during skirmishing at Petersburg. Monaghan becomes the recipient of the Medal of Honor for his heroism above the call of duty.

May 18 (Wednesday)   In Georgia, Rome and Kingston are seized by the Union; they are captured by the 2nd Division, 14th Corps, Army of the Cumberland. The Union sustains 16 killed and 59 wounded. Confederate casualties are unavailable.

In Louisiana, the plagued campaign of General Nathaniel Banks is multiplying the problems of the North, as the Confederates do well in the East against General Benjamin F. Butler, who is about to be replaced. Today, Federals under General Joseph Mower cover the retreat of Banks' troops from Yellow Bayou. It was General Mower who led the initial assault into Fort DeRussy earlier in the campaign.

At Bayou De Galize (Calhoun Station), contingents of the 16th and 17th Corps and cavalry attached to the 19th Corps skirmish heavily with Confederates. The contest costs the Union 60 killed and 30 wounded. The Confederates sustain 500 killed and wounded. Confederate Brigadier General Dandridge McRae, who served during the Red River campaign, will resign his commission subsequent to the campaign and return to Arkansas.

In Oregon, the 1st Oregon Cavalry skirmishes with Confederates at Crooked River. Casualty figures are unavailable.

In Virginia, Union artillery bombards Lee's positions in conjunction with ground attacks. Union Generals Winfield S. Hancock and Horatio Wright unsuccessfully assault Lee's lines at Spotsylvania and are driven back after fierce fighting. News reaches Grant of Sigel's devastating defeat at New Market and of his retreat down the Shenandoah Valley. General Franz Sigel is relieved by General David Hunter (West Point, 1822). General Grant also gets the disheartening word that General Benjamin F. Butler has been pushed back from Drewry's Bluff; however, Butler's troops still control Petersburg Road. Grant is also notified of General Nathaniel Banks' defeat in Louisiana. General Banks is replaced by General Edward Canby. Banks' unsuccessful expedition comes to a close as his troops cross the Atchafalaya River, en route back to Union lines. In other activity, the USS *Agawam,* operating on the James River in support of General Butler's force, bombards Confederate positions in the vicinity of Hewlett's House on the high ground from where Confederates dominate Trent's Reach. In other activity, Brigadier General Isaac Jones Wistar, recently appointed as a brigade commander, is relieved by Colonel Griffin Stedman. At this time, General Wistar's name disappears from the *Official Records.* His resignation is accepted by the War Department on 15 September 1864.

In Confederate general officer activity, Major General Samuel Gibbs French is transferred from duty in Mississippi to the Army of Tennessee. He commands a division; however, he misses the contest at Nashville due to sustaining an eye infection, which causes him to be re-

General Sherman enters Kingston, Georgia (Mottelay, *The Soldier in Our Civil War,* 1886).

lieved. Upon his recovery, General French is ordered to Mobile, where he is captured when the city falls during April 1865. After receiving parole, he returns to his plantation in Mississippi, but later, he retires in Florida where he dies at the age of 92 on 20 April 1910. Also, Colonel John McCausland is promoted to brigadier general to rank from this day. Brigadier General Joseph B. Kershaw is promoted to the rank of major general. Subsequent to Kershaw's promotion, Colonel John D. Kennedy assumes command of his regiment, the 2nd South Carolina Infantry.

May 19 (Thursday)   In Arkansas, the 6th Kansas Cavalry clashes with Confederates at Fayetteville.

In Florida, the 17th Connecticut Volunteer Regiment skirmishes with Confederates at Saunders and Welaka.

In Georgia, General Sherman, moving swiftly in pursuit of General Johnston's army, intercepts the Confederates at Cassville. The Confederates, under John B. Hood, miscalculate and thwart their own offensive. General Hood is thrown back, forcing Johnston to retreat further. He retires toward the high ground at Allatoona. Confederates patrolling their positions around Kingston encounter a Union patrol reconnoitering the terrain. The Rebels surprise the patrol and capture the XV Corps' chief of artillery, Major Charles J. Stolbrand. He later escapes and reaches his lines October, where he will command more than 1,000 men and just under 50 guns during Sherman's "March to the Sea." President Lincoln appoints Stolbrand as a brigadier general during January 1865.

General Johnston later holds a war council, and at the conference, it is concluded that neither Hood nor Polk could hold the line against the Union strength; however, General William Joseph Hardee believes his force, although holding the weakest positions, can repel an attack and hold firmly. Nevertheless, Johnston sides with Polk and Hood and concludes that they must pull back and forego a fight.

In Virginia, Union troops under General Robert O. Tyler, with recently arrived reinforcements from Fredericksburg, while deployed to the right of Grant, withstand a Confederate attack at Spotsylvania by General Richard S. Ewell's corps. During this heavy fighting, Colonel Bryan Grimes' 4th North

Carolina Infantry executes some strategic moves that prevents General Ewell's corps from being overwhelmed. Union reinforcements are swiftly rushed to General Tyler's aid, with David B. Birney to his right and Samuel W. Crawford to his left, enabling the Union to quickly dispose of General Ewell's threat.

In Union general officer activity, Colonel Richard Delafield is promoted to brigadier general and becomes chief of engineers. In 1865 he receives the brevet rank of major general. General Delafield, about 63 years old at the time the war erupted does not see field duty. His expertise had been focused on the defenses of New York, including the harbor, Governors Island, the Narrows and Sandy Hook.

In Confederate general officer activity, Colonel Clement Anselm Evans is promoted to brigadier general. General Evans continues to serve with the Army of Northern Virginia and participates in the defense of Richmond during the closing days of the war. Afterward he returns to Georgia, and later he becomes a Methodist minister. After retiring during 1892, the lawyer turned minister becomes an author. He pens a 12-volume work, the *Confederate Military History,* published during 1899. General Evans dies in Atlanta on 2 July 1911. Also, Colonel Martin Witherspoon Gary (Hampton's Legion) is promoted to brigadier general. General Gary initially joined the legion as a captain during 1861. He receives three additional regiments to bolster his brigade, which is the final unit to depart Richmond. Gary is able to break out and avoid capture and participates in the attempt to get President Davis out of the Union net. Confederate Colonel Bryan Grimes (4th North Carolina) is promoted to brigadier general effective this date; he will be promoted to major general in February 1865. Grimes remains in the field and participates at Appomattox, where he leads one of the last assaults there during the Confederacy's final days.

May 20 (Friday)   In Georgia, General Joseph Johnston's retreating Army crosses the Etowa

Confederate forces under General Robert E. Lee in Virginia (Mottelay, *The Soldier in Our Civil War,* 1886).

River. The trailing unit is Colonel Isaac W. Avery's Cavalry; Avery is the last person to cross. While the Confederates are destroying the bridges to delay pursuit, the Union is close by and delivering heavy fire upon the columns. General Joseph Johnston officially reports that his force has sustained 445 killed and 2,943 wounded, totaling 3,388. At this time Johnston has received reinforcements, including the infantry divisions of Generals James Cantey, William W. Loring and Samuel G. French, increasing his force by about 12,000 troops and 7,400 cavalry troops under Generals W.T. Martin and William Hicks Jackson. Considering the casualties sustained and the infusion of reinforcements, Jackson's command now numbers about 61,000 troops.

In Louisiana, General Nathaniel Prentiss Banks is replaced by General E.R.S. Canby. Banks returns to New Orleans. The army, now under Canby, begins to depart Simmesport. The columns cross the Atchafalaya River by marching across a bank-to-bank string of attached transport steamers. The Union ground force reaches Morganzia Bend on the following day. There is some slight skirmishing at Mansura, which is near Marksville, and at Yellow Bayou. Admiral David D. Porter leads the fleet down the Red River and returns to the Mississippi River, where he remains until the summer, when he is relieved.

In Virginia, General U.S. Grant concludes that no apparent Confederate assault threatens Union positions at Spotsylvania. He orders part of his army to move on the left flank to attempt to get between General Robert E. Lee and Richmond, while leaving Generals Ambrose Burnside and Horatio G. Wright (West Point, 1841) at Spotsylvania to threaten an attack. General Hancock, spearheading Grant's flanking movement, reaches Milford by way of Bowling Green late on the 21st, and his force collides with a Confederate division led by General George Pickett, which is rushing to aid General Lee. The Union pushes Pickett's force aside and captures a few hundred men attached to General James L. Kemper's force. Union General Warren, following General Hancock, advances to Guiney's Station on the night of the 21st without incident.

In skirmishing at Petersburg, Confederate General William Stephen Walker (born in Pittsburgh, Pennsylvania) is wounded and captured. Walker's wound, although not fatal, does severely impede his future, as he loses a foot. After his release, Walker returns to command in North Carolina, where he remains for the duration. After the war, General Walker resides in Georgia, where he succumbs in Atlanta during June 1899. Also, the 5th New York Cavalry clashes

with Confederates at Downer's Bridge. In addition, the 1st Cavalry Division, Army of the Potomac, occupies Milford Station.

In Naval activity, the USS *Galena* arrives at Pensacola, Florida, to join the West Gulf Blockading Squadron. It is assigned duty at Mobile Bay. In other activity, the *B.N. Crary* is acquired by the U.S. Navy. The wooden-hulled steamer, constructed in Brooklyn this year, is renamed the USS *Wilderness* and commissioned on 20 July. It is assigned duty with the North Atlantic Blockading Squadron and used primarily as a supply vessel, but also as a transport and a dispatch ship.

May 21 (Saturday)   In Mississippi, the Union 4th Missouri Cavalry engages a contingent of Confederates at Mt. Pleasant. The Union sustains two killed and wounded. Confederate casualties are unavailable.

In Missouri, the 2nd Colorado Cavalry clashes with Confederates at Snia Hills.

In Virginia, General Robert E. Lee does not attack the Union troops that are flanking his lines at Spotsylvania, nor does he attempt to land a decisive blow against the Union remnants at Spotsylvania while General Grant withdraws from the field. Union troops under Ambrose Burnside and Horatio Wright can now move unchallenged toward Guiney's Station. The columns arrive there at Grant's headquarters on the 22nd.

In Confederate general officer activity, Brigadier General Bushrod Rust Johnson (West Point, 1840) is promoted to the rank of major general.

May 22 (Sunday)   In West Virginia, the Union 1st West Virginia Cavalry, commanded by Colonel Henry Capehart, skirmishes with Confederates at Greenbriar River.

May 23 (Monday)   In Georgia, General Sherman's force, after having seized Kingston, move out and cross the Etowah River to advance deeper into Georgia. The Union force is divided into three columns. General John Schofield (left) takes the Cassville Road to eventually line up on the left of General George H. Thomas (center) who moves toward Euharlee and Burnt Hickory. General James McPherson (right) crosses at the mouth of the Conasene Creek in the vicinity of Kingston and moves via Van Wert. General Sherman directs General Jefferson C. Davis to depart Rome and move directly for Dallas. Davis' column is to also move via Van Wert. During the latter part of the night, Confederate General Joseph Johnston dispatches a contingent of cavalry under Major General Joseph Wheeler to execute a reconnaissance mission to determine whether the Union had totally abandoned the Etowah River line. Wheeler's route takes his contingent through the terrain covered by General Hugh Kilpatrick's cavalry, but by using a circuitous route and crossing about three miles to the right, he evades contact. Consequently, the Confederates are able to overcome a small contingent that had

Top: Confederate prisoners take the oath of allegiance (Mottelay, *The Soldier in Our Civil War*, 1886). *Bottom:* Union troops cross the North Anna River. *Right:* Rifle pits, North Anna (*Harper's Pictoral History of the Civil War*, 1896).

been posted at Cassville to guard the supplies. The Rebels carry what they can, destroy what they can't transport and capture some troops. Following the raid, Wheeler returns to Johnston's headquarters and informs him that an attack against Dallas by Sherman is imminent.

In Louisiana, the 6th Missouri Cavalry engages Confederates at Old River.

In Florida, Confederates capture the steam tug *Columbine*, commanded by Lt. Commander Breese, at Horse Landing, St. Johns River. A contingent of the 35th U.S. Colored Troops is aboard. The Confederates capture 30, including soldiers and sailors.

In Virginia, the Union begins searching for Lee's positions at 5 A.M. with General Gouverneur Warren's corps in the lead, followed by Horatio Wright's corps, with both advancing toward Jericho Ford. The Union troops are compelled to wade through waist high water, under cover fire of sharp shooters. Pontoon bridges are constructed, allowing the main force to cross, and with Generals Samuel Wylie Crawford deployed on the left, Charles Griffin

(West Point, 1847) in the center and Lysander Cutler on the right, they are staring directly at Lee's entrenched troops. The Confederates react by charging boldly, driving Cutler back, but reinforcements from Horatio Wright arrive in time to deliver a heavy blow to A.P. Hill's corps. Initially, only Colonel Joseph N. Brown, leading one brigade of General Cadmus Wilcox's divi-

sion, stands against the Yankees, but reinforcements, the brigades of Alfred M. Scales, James B. Gordon and Edward L. Thomas, arrive, followed shortly thereafter by General Henry Heth's division. Nevertheless, when Union General William F. Bartlett's force moves up to cover Charles Griffin, who is pulling back, the void is filled and the Confederates are foiled. Approximately 500 Confederate prisoners are taken. Meanwhile, Hancock's corps arrives at

Battery on the North Anna (*Harper's Pictoral History of the Civil War*, 1896).

the North Anna River at Chesterfield Ford to discover the Fredericksburg railroad bridge is defended by Rebels attached to General McLaws' division (Longstreet's Corps, commanded by Richard A. Anderson). General Birney's division leads the way, bolstered by the artillery of Colonel Tidball. General Thomas W. Egan's Brigade synchronizes his assault with Colonel Byron Pierce's brigade, striking and permitting an attack from the left and right in such fashion as to compel an immediate Rebel retreat. Many Southerners are pushed to their death in the river below in this disorganized withdrawal. The Union captures a few hundred prisoners. Hancock's exhausted troops wait until morning before crossing the bridge unopposed. In the morning the Confederates abandon their positions on the southern bank of the North Anna River. Confederate Colonel Joseph N. Brown, who succeeded General Abner Perrin as commanding officer of the 14th South Carolina Regiment (McGowan's brigade) is captured during this action. Another Officer, Lt. Colonel Edward Croft, assumes command of the regiment. Also, General U.S. Grant is informed of the fall of Kingston to Sherman's troops.

May 23–26 In Virginia, the Union continues to press General Lee's Army of Northern Virginia. Skirmishing develops along the North Anna River at Jericho Mill and Hanover Junction. The V Corps crosses the North Anna at Jericho Mill on the 23rd and comes under attack by elements of General A.P. Hill. On the 24th, Union infantry engages Confederates in the vicinity of Oxford; however, the Union is able to make progress. In the meantime, General Lee, who is sick, is unable to launch an offensive. Grant orders the army to recross the river, chooses another crossing to evade Lee's positions, and resumes his offensive to seize Richmond. Other names for these skirmishes include Quarles Mill and Telegraph Road Bridge.

May 24 (Tuesday) In Georgia, Confederate General Joseph Hardee's force arrives at New Hope Church and joins with General Johnston. General John B. Hood arrives on the following day. General William T. Sherman's forces are closing fast. General Joseph Hooker will bolster the force upon his arrival on the 25th. In other activity, a Union wagon train, guarded by elements of the 50th Ohio and 14th Kentucky Volunteer Regiments, bolstered by the 2nd Kentucky Cavalry, commanded by Colonel Holman, is attacked by a Confederate force at Kingston.

In Mississippi, the 4th Missouri Cavalry skirmishes with Confederates at Holly Springs.

In Tennessee, the 15th U.S. Colored Troops clashes with Confederates at Nashville.

In Virginia, Union General Winfield S. Hancock's corps destroys as much as possible of the Fredericksburg Railroad, while General Horatio Wright's corps crosses the North Anna River at Jericho Ford, to the right of Gouverneur Warren, and proceeds to do much damage to the Virginia Central Railroad. Union General Ambrose Burnside doesn't fare as well. General Robert E. Lee, greatly fortified at Oxford, forces Burnside to improvise and cross closer to Jericho Ford. Union General Thomas L. Crittenden crosses at this point, meeting deadly fire from the guns of A.P. Hill, which inflicts heavy Union casualties, but Crittenden eventually joins Warren. The Union brigades, after checking, find Robert E. Lee's lines too strong to attack. In the meantime, reinforcements which have been desperately needed by Lee are rushing into camp. George Pickett's division arrives from Richmond. General Hoke (North Carolina) and General John C. Breckinridge's troops also arrive. During the engagement at the North Anna River, Lieutenant Colonel Michael C. Murphy, 170th New York Infantry, receives the Medal of Honor for heroism. The troops of Murphy's regiment, their ammunition exhausted, remain on the battlefield to assist in any way possible.

Left: Jericho Mill. ***Right:*** Quarles' Mill (*Harper's Pictoral History of the Civil War*, 1896).

The Battle of Jericho Ford on the North Anna River, Virginia (Mottelay, *The Soldier in Our Civil War*, 1886).

Also, the 10th U.S. Colored Regiment, 1st D.C. Cavalry, and Battery B, of Colored Artillery, engages Confederates at Wilson's Wharf. The Union sustains two killed and 24 wounded. The Confederates sustain 20 killed, about 100 wounded and one captured. At Wilson's Wharf, along the James River, Confederates attack Union positions. The USS *Young America* supports the Union in its repulse of the assault.

In Confederate general officer activity, Colonel Stephen Elliott, Jr., is promoted to brigadier general. He will be assigned command of the brigade previously led by General Nathan George "Shanks" Evans, who was continually plagued with difficulties, particularly with regard to charges of disobeying orders and intoxication. Twice accused and twice tried, Evans is acquitted. Nevertheless, Evans loses favor. His service record subsequent to the Vicksburg Campaign and some time in North Carolina remains inconspicuous. However, Evans (West Point, 1848) serves for the duration, and after the close of hostilities, he moves to Alabama, where he succumbs several years later.

Colonel Birkett Davenport Fry, a veteran of the Mexican War, who attended VMI and West Point, is appointed brigadier general. General Fry had commanded the 13th Alabama at Seven Pines and sustained a wound during the fighting. He led the regiment at Sharpsburg (Antietam) and Chancellorsville, becoming wounded during each of those contests. Following that duty, he participated at Gettysburg, where he sustained yet a fourth wound and was captured. Subsequent to his promotion, General Fry, toward the latter part of the war, receives command of a district in South Carolina and Georgia. After the war he lives in Cuba, but later returns to the States and engages in business in Alabama and Florida. He then moves to Richmond to become president of a cotton mill. He dies in Richmond on 21 January 1891.

In Naval activity, the transport USS *Boston* (on lease to the government since 1861, not an official navy vessel) is stranded on the Ashepoo

River, South Carolina, under heavy Confederate fire. However, the Union troops on board are rescued, making it to shore. Also, the USS *Curlew,* engaged in a mission with surveyors who are surveying Grand Gulf, Mississippi, encounters enemy fire at Grand Landing, Arkansas. The *Curlew* exchanges fire with a 12-gun battery and sustains some damage after being hit a few times. The *Curlew* returns to Mound City on 30 May. In other activity, the USS *Vindicator,* acquired by the U.S. government during 1863, utilized by the Union Army and then transferred to the U.S. Navy (1864), is commissioned this day. Lt. Commander Thomas O. Selfridge receives command of the vessel, which is transformed into a ram and assigned to the Mississippi Squadron.

May 25 (Wednesday)   In Georgia, at New Hope Church (Dallas), the Confederate corps of Generals Joseph Hardee, John B. Hood and Leonidas Polk hold the line, awaiting a Union attack. During the latter part of the day, the Union strikes, permitting itself only about one and one-half hours of daylight to seize the town. A heavy thrust is propelled upon Lt. General Alexander P. General Stewart's division, but the Rebels are up to the task and withstand two major assaults by the forces of General Hooker. The Union forces, because of the grim combat here, dub this tranquil church as "the Hell Hole." In other activity, the Union 1st and 11th Kentucky Cavalry skirmish with Confederates at Cassville Station. The Union sustains eight killed and 16 wounded. The Confederates suffer two killed and six wounded.

In Virginia, Union General David Hunter (Franz Sigel's successor) is ordered to move on Charlottesville and from there to Lynchburg to destroy the canal and rails. Upon fulfillment of his orders, he is to join the troops with General Grant. In the meantime, General Philip Sheridan makes it back to Grant's lines following his raid near Richmond. Also, General David Hunter has ordered the burning of the Virginia Military Institute at Lexington, in retaliation for the defeat of Sigel. On this day, General Grant informs General Henry Halleck of his intended move to capture Hanover Town, twenty miles outside of Richmond. Grant moves his supply base from Port Royal to White House. Union General W.F. Smith begins to prepare the rails in the vicinity of White House in order to better utilize the supply line.

In Naval activity, the transport USS *Boston,* while transporting the 34th U.S. Colored Reg-

iment and a contingent of cavalry on the Ashepoo River at a point a few miles above Bennett's Point, South Carolina, gets snagged on a sandbar. The Confederates at Fort Chapman become aware of the stranded vessel and initiate a bombardment that pummels the vessel with more than 70 hits. Other warships speed to its rescue. The crew and troops abandon the ship and set it on fire. Also, Union vessels unsuccessfully attempt to destroy the CSS *Albemarle* on the Roanoke River in North Carolina. The USS *Wyalusing* participates in this river action.

May 25–June 4   Battle of New Hope Church Union forces commanded by General Sherman, including those of Major General Thomas, Major General John Schofield and Major General James B. McPherson, engage the Confederate forces commanded by General Joseph Johnston and Generals Hood and Wheeler at New Hope Church, Dallas (Burned Church), Burned Hickory, Pumpkin Vine Creek, Pickett's Mill and Allatoona Hills, Georgia. Sherman's troops approach Dallas, advancing in five columns with Jefferson C. Davis and James B. McPherson on the right, Thomas in the center, supported by Schofield, held in reserve in the rear, and Joe Hooker's 20th Corps on the point. As the Yankees advance, they encounter Rebel resistance at Pumpkin Vine Creek at about noon, and as they drive the Rebel cavalry away, a bridge crossing the creek is set afire.

Hooker's command pursues the Rebels and encounters resistance at New Hope Church from Confederate infantry, commanded by Colonel Bush Jones. When the two sides collide, they ignite a vicious skirmish that lasts well into the night, causing heavy casualties to both sides. Jones' force is composed Major J.E. Austin's Louisiana Sharpshooters and the 32nd and 58th Alabama Regiments. While the deadly battle rages, both sides are hindered by a tremendous storm which pounds them relentlessly. In an effort to bolster Hooker, Sherman rushes more troops to the front; however, with William T. Ward's and Alpheus S. Williams' divisions traveling on separate roads, the reinforcements are not in position and ready until about 1700. The Rebels repel all assaults. Night falls and the contest halts without a victor, but the battle is reinitiated the following morning.

Union troops under Hooker are staring at a large force of Confederates on this battlefield, New Hope Church, notably dubbed "Hell Hole," the scene of vicious battle between Hooker and the Confederates under Johnston. General James B. McPherson, rushing from Dallas to aid Hooker, is assaulted by a strong Rebel force, but the Yankees drive them back; however, the Rebels tie McPherson up until 1 June. During the afternoon of the 26th, the Union launches an assault to turn General Johnston's right, but the Confederates retain the stamina to raise tenacious resistance. Colonel Isaac Avery's cavalry speeds to intercept the Yankees and plows directly into the advancing force, composed of two Union divisions. The weakened Confederate contingent forestalls disaster and holds until more reinforcements arrive. Colonel Isaac Avery, the final man to cross the Etowa River, is grievously wounded during this action. However, he remains in the saddle, supported by one of his troops, until his reinforcements arrive.

This grueling contest continues to rage around New Hope Church until 4 June with the Union forces of Generals James B. McPherson (right), Hooker (center), and Thomas and Schofield (both on left) opposing Generals Joseph Hardee (left), John B. Hood (center) and Leonidas Polk (right). The Union 4th Corps (General George H. Thomas), during the afternoon of 27 May, attacks to break the Confederate right held by Leonidas Polk, but by now, Patrick Cleburne's division has moved into position on Polk's right, giving the line extra strength. The Rebels—Hiram B. Granbury's brigade, Robert Lowry's brigade, two divisions of Daniel C. Govan's brigade, bolstered by General Joseph Wheeler's cavalry—repel the attack and inflict heavy casualties upon the Union.

Confederates under General William B. Bate jump off on the 28th. They launch a fierce assault against General James B. McPherson's lines at Dallas, but the Union repels the attack and inflicts heavy casualties on the Rebels. Following a slight pause, the skirmishing here begins anew on 1 June and continues until 4 June.

In the meantime, on 30 May, Generals Sherman, William F. Barry, John A. Logan and James McPherson while in conversation find themselves inadvertently within range of a Confederate sharpshooter. The Rebels fires a shot which strikes General Logan with a deadly blow to the chest, but his life is spared by a thick notebook in this pocket. By the 1st, Sherman is moving on Allatoona and securing wagon routes along the way. Sherman shifts the entire Union line to the left, and by 1 June, the operation is complete and the Union seizes the roads leading to Allatoona and Acworth.

Meanwhile, cavalry of Union General George Stoneman enters Allatoona from the eastern end of the pass, and other cavalry under General Kenner Garrard (West Point, 1851) enters through the rear from the west, each without incident, as the Confederates have abandoned it. Confederate General Joseph Johnston pulls out on the 4th, retreating towards Marietta and Kennesaw Mountain. Brigadier General Richard W. Johnson is wounded during this action. After recuperation, he is assigned as chief of cavalry, Military Division of the Mississippi. General Johnson later receives the brevet of major general in the volunteer service and in the Regular Army. He retires during 1867 with the rank of major general.

Confederate Brigadier General Alexander W. Reynolds is wounded during the fighting at New Hope Church. Afterward Reynolds is transferred to the region which covers the northern part of Alabama and the middle sector of Tennessee. After the war, General Reynolds travels to Egypt and becomes colonel in the army of the Kedive. He dies in Egypt in May 1876. General Lawrence S. Ross's Texas

brigade participates in this action; however, the attached regiments begin to take casualties that soon after gravely affect the strength of the brigade. Also, General Nathaniel C. McLean, who had raised the ire of the corps commander General Oliver O. Howard at Chancellorsville, again serves under him at this battle and yet again, his service falls short of Howard's expectations. McLean loses command of his brigade and he is transferred to Kentucky. He then serves for the duration in North Carolina under General John Schofield. McLean resigns his commission on 20 April 1865.

May 26 (Thursday)   In Washington, D.C., Congress authorizes the Territory of Montana. It is formed by an acquisition of land from the Territory of Idaho.

In Georgia, General William T. Sherman's troops fortify their positions at Dallas and New Hope.

In North Carolina, at Bachelor's Creek, a torpedo explodes, inflicting injuries upon the 132nd and 158th New York Regiments; the units lose 35 killed and 19 wounded.

In Missouri, the 2nd Wisconsin Cavalry skirmishes with Confederates at Lane's Prairie, Morris County.

In Virginia, the Army of the Potomac, in an effort to gain more tenable positions, begins to pull back to Hanover Town, reaching it on the 27th; however the Confederates under Robert E. Lee (Army of Northern Virginia) are there to provide a welcome. Union General Philip Sheridan moves out from the North Anna, heading for the Hanover Ferry. Sheridan's cavalry under General David Gregg (West Point, 1855) and Alfred T. Torbert (West Point, 1855), cross under cover of darkness. Torbert and Gregg had both been assigned command of a division by Sheridan during the previous month. Colonel William Penrose assumed command of Torbert's brigade upon his promotion to divisional command. A division under David A. Russell (West Point, 1845) follows. By morning of the 27th, Union lines are firmly established on the south side of the Pamunkey River. A skirmish does develop at Hanover Town, with the advance cavalry of Sheridan against a Confederate brigade commanded by Major Rufus Barringer. The Union manages to drive the Rebels away.

In Union general officer activity, Major General Richard James Oglesby resigns his commission. He is elected governor of Illinois the following November. He serves two more terms as governor and one term in the U.S. Senate. He dies during April 1899.

In Alabama, the 1st, 3rd and 4th Ohio Cavalry Regiments and the 2nd Cavalry Regiment skirmish with Confederates at Decatur (Courtland Road) and at Moulton. These clashes occur in and about these towns for three days. The Union sustains 48 killed and wounded. The Confederates sustain 60 killed and wounded.

In Naval activity, a five-man detachment from the USS *Wyalusing* rows along the Middle River to attempt to blow up the CSS *Albemarle*. The boat carries two 100-pound torpedoes (mines). The sailors land and concoct a stretcher to transport the torpedoes through a swamp located between the Middle and Roanoke Rivers. The detachment advances to a point near where the *Albemarle* is anchored and at that time, two of the sailors swim across the river and each man carries a towline that is attached to a torpedo. The torpedoes are then bound together. While the two men move to attach the devices to the Confederate ram, they are detected just as they get close to the ship. The plot is foiled; however, the five sailors escape harm and safely return to the *Wyalusing* within the next two days, but not as a unit. Two of the three are picked up by the *Commodore Hull* and taken to their ship. Each of the five sailors becomes a recipient of the Medal of Honor.

May 27 (Friday)   In California, Company K, 5th California Infantry Regiment, skirmishes with Confederates at the San Carlos River.

In Virginia, a unit of the 9th New York Cavalry scatters a Confederate force at Crumps Creek; subsequent to the skirmish, the contingent assaults another Confederate cavalry unit and also routs it, taking 27 prisoners in the process. Also, the Union Army of the Potomac arrives at Hanover Town from its positions at the North Anna River. The entire force crosses the Pamunkey River, but General Robert E. Lee's force has his focus on the Chickahominy, thwarting Grant's plans to close toward Richmond. By the following day, the Union changes its plan of march.

The cavalry corps of the 1st and 2nd Divisions (Army of the Potomac) under General Philip Sheridan clash for two days with Confederates at Hawes' Shop, Hanover Town and Salem Church. The Union sustains 25 killed, 119 wounded and 200 missing. The Confederates suffer about 475, including killed, wounded or missing.

In Naval activity, the USS *Kansas* while on patrol in the vicinity of New Inlet, North Carolina, spots a suspected blockade runner and moves to hail it; however, it runs. The Kansas pursues and continues the chase into the following day, but the unidentified ship evades capture. On the morning of the 28th, the *Kansas* experiences problems with its boiler. Consequently, another blockade runner gets a pass because the *Kansas* is unable to give chase. The ship, which had departed Wilmington, North Carolina, breaks through the blockade. The Kansas afterward is able to remain in service at New Inlet until it is ordered during August to sail to Philadelphia for repairs. In late September it returns to service.

May 28 (Saturday)   In Arkansas, the 57th U.S. Colored Troops skirmish with Confederates at Little Rock.

In Florida, the 7th U.S. Colored Troops skirmishes with Confederates at Jacksonville.

In **Georgia,** a Union contingent (General William T. Sherman's command) engages Confederates under General Richard H. Anderson (Longstreet's Corps, but Longstreet is recuperating) at Dallas.

In **Missouri,** a Union contingent of the 2nd Colorado Cavalry clashes with Confederates at Pleasant Hill.

In **Virginia,** with the greater part of the Union contingents safely across the Pamunkey River, they are one step closer to Richmond. Union General Ambrose Burnside remains on the north side to guard the army's wagon train, while General Philip Sheridan inches closer to Mechanicsville where his troops confront Confederate cavalry at Hawes' Shop. The Confederates withstand the assault by General David Gregg, but an additional charge by General George A. Custer's brigade wins the day for the Yankees, although both sides sustain heavy casualties (Custer's men had dismounted before charging). General U.S. Grant determines that General Robert E. Lee's Army of Northern Virginia is too well entrenched, and rather than move against Richmond, he moves his Army across Totopotomoy Creek (Salem Church) and beyond to Cold Harbor. Lee also speeds forces there and they arrive before the Yankees, as Lee once again correctly anticipates Grant's move.

In **Alabama,** the 1st, 3rd and 4th Ohio Cavalry, Army of the Cumberland, engages Confederates for two days at Moulton. Forty Confederates are captured.

May 29 (Sunday)   In Virginia, Union troops under General U.S. Grant continue to stretch their lines in search of Robert E. Lee's main force. Union General Horatio Wright's 6th Corps extends toward Hanover Court House and Winfield S. Hancock's 2nd Corps leans toward Totopotomoy Creek, while General Gouverneur Warren's 5th Corps advances to Shady Grove Church Road. Wright reaches his objective, but Hancock's corps halts at the Totopotomoy Creek. At Shady Grove Church Road, the Yankees under Warren encounter the full force of General Richard S. Ewell's corps. At the latter place, the Confederates attempt to turn Warren's flank by driving against the line from the Mechanicsville Road, but a brigade of reserves, led by Colonel Martin D. Hardin, moves there and covers the road.

The Confederates under General Robert E. Rodes strike the flank, but the Union rushes the remainder of the reserves, led by Colonel J.H. Kitching, into the action and the attack is repelled. General Ambrose Burnside's 9th Corps is kept in reserve, but his force is positioned from where the units can spring to support either the 2nd or 5th Corps. In the meantime, General Robert E. Lee's Army of Northern Virginia is fanning out toward Cold Harbor and preparing to intercept the Union advance. Robert E. Lee confers with General Pierre G.T. Beauregard at Atlee's Farm to discuss tactics against U.S. Grant. Lee informs Confederate President Davis: "If Grant advances tomorrow I will engage him with my present force."

In Naval activity, Admiral David D. Porter's Mississippi Squadron concludes its participation in the Red River Campaign, which was initiated on 12 March. Following this action, the USS *Blackhawk* patrols along the Mississippi River and its tributaries until 22 April 1865.

May 30 (Monday)   In Virginia, at Cold Harbor, General Winfield S. Hancock's corps spots the Rebels, who are firmly entrenched along the Totopotomoy. As the Union is tightening its line, Confederate General Jubal Early springs an assault against General Gouverneur Warren's positions at Huntley Corners, pushing the Union back. Hancock rushes reinforcements to Warren's left flank, buying time for Warren to repulse the assault. Meanwhile, General Grant's army is now about 10 miles from Richmond. Other Union troops are positioned on the outskirts of Petersburg, the rear door to Richmond.

In related activity, contingents of the 3rd Division's cavalry corps (Army of the Potomac) under General James H. Wilson engage Confederates at Ashland and Hanover. The Union sustains 26 killed and 130 wounded. Confederate casualties are unavailable. Another clash occurs at Old Church, where General Albert T. Torbert's cavalry engages a contingent of Confederates. The Union sustains 16 killed and 74 wounded. Confederate casualties are unavailable.

In Naval activity, the blockade runner Caledonia is captured by the USS *Massachusetts*.

May 30–June 12   BATTLE OF COLD HARBOR Union and Confederate forces clash at Cold Harbor, Virginia. The losses of leaders on both sides are high. Union General John R. Brooke is severely wounded on the 12th, ending his field service. Union General George Stannard, previously wounded at Gettysburg, is wounded again while leading a Division of the XVIII Corps. Union General Robert O. Tyler, a prominent figure who led the 1st Connecticut Heavy Artillery during the Peninsular campaign under McClellan (he lost one gun during the whole campaign), is wounded terribly, handicapping the rest of his life. Nevertheless, he recuperates sufficiently to remain in the army beyond the close of hostilities. During 1866, with the rank of lieutenant colonel, he is appointed deputy quartermaster general; however, he continues to attempt to improve his health by taking voyages abroad, but without success. He dies in Massachusetts at Boston on 1 December 1874. Confederate General James Henry Lane is also wounded, prompting Colonel John Decatur Barry to assume command of Lane's 28th North Carolina Regiment until he recuperates. Barry is appointed brigadier general. Nonethe-

Union cavalry attacks a Confederate battery near Richmond (Mottelay, *The Soldier in Our Civil War*, 1886).

less, General Barry is also wounded within a few days after his appointment, essentially ending his short career as a general. Barry's commission is invalidated and he is transferred to staff duty in North Carolina. McGowan's brigade, composed of South Carolina Regiments, participates in the fighting around Cold Harbor. Confederate Brigadier General James Barbour Terrill (brother of Union General William Rufus Terrill, killed at Perryville, 1862) is killed on the 30th in the vicinity of Bethesda Church and is buried there by Union soldiers. Terrill had recently been nominated to the rank of brigadier general to become effective May 31; the actual date of his promotion is June 1.

May 31 (Tuesday)   In Virginia, Union General Philip Sheridan's cavalry, following a tenacious clash that has given them control of Old Cold Harbor, prepares to withdraw from the positions in the face of an overpowering Confederate counter attack, but Sheridan receives orders to "hold the place at all hazards." Sheridan immediately countermands his directive to evacuate and prepares to defend his positions until reinforcements can be rushed in to hold off any Confederate onslaught. Two Confederate assaults are repulsed by Sheridan by turning captured Rebel guns on the attackers. Reinforcements, the 6th Corps under Horatio Wright, arrive on 1 June at 0900. Union General W.F. Smith's force, en route from White House, also arrives on the 1st, getting to Sheridan at about 1500, with an additional 12,500 reinforcements (10th and 18th Corps) attached to General Benjamin F. Butler's Army of the James. General William F. Smith's force is being transported by ships that carry the force down the James River to the York River and from there to the Pamunkey River.

In other activity, the Bucktail Regiment (42nd Pennsylvania Volunteer Regiment), initially commanded by General Thomas Kane, which has participated as part of the Army of the Potomac since the early part of the war, completes its service this day. The Bucktails had participated in most of the campaigns of the army from Seven Days' Battle through Gettysburg and Spotsylvania and at Bethesda. Men who choose not to re-enlist in the 190th Pennsylvania Regiment are mustered out of the service.

In Confederate general officer activity, General Richard Heron Anderson is promoted to lieutenant general effective this day. Lt. Colonel William Gaston Lewis is promoted to the rank of brigadier general. General Lewis had served at such battles as Gettysburg and for a time in the defense of Petersburg, but following his promotion he serves with a brigade in General Early's command. Major Robert Doak Lilley and Colonel John C.C. Sanders also are promoted to the rank of brigadier general. Sanders will command a brigade in General William Mahone's division (Army of Northern Virginia). Also, Colonel David A. Weisiger is promoted to the temporary rank of brigadier general, effective this date, and to permanent rank from July 30, 1864. And Colonel Zebulon York is promoted to the rank of brigadier general, effective this date. York, who has seen service with the 14th Louisiana in Virginia and Maryland prior to being transferred to Louisiana, is assigned again to Virginia, where he will lead a brigade.

In Union general officer activity, Colonel Americus V. Rice is promoted to the rank of brigadier general of volunteers. He participates as commander of the 3rd Brigade, 2nd Division, XV Corps, at Kennesaw Mountain the

next month. Colonel William Ruffin Cox (2nd North Carolina) is appointed brigadier general (temporary rank). He receives command of a brigade and in April 1865 is paroled at Appomattox. Afterward, he becomes a congressman (1880–1896) and later, secretary of the Senate (1893–1900). General Cox dies in Richmond on 26 December, 1919. In yet other activity, Lt. Colonel William Gaston Lewis, initially major of the 33rd North Carolina and later with the 43rd North Carolina Regiment, is promoted to brigadier general. He participates at Petersburg and with General Jubal Early in the Shenandoah Valley.

Also, Colonel Thomas Fentress Toon (20th North Carolina), a participant at various actions, including Seven Pines, Seven Days' Battle, South Mountain and Fredericksburg, the latter during December 1862, is promoted to brigadier general. Afterward, he commands a brigade under General Early during his raids around the capital. General Toon promoted after General R.D. Johnston, who was wounded at Spotsylvania, reverts back to his rank of colonel upon the return of Johnston to active service.

June 1 (Wednesday) **In Virginia** at Cold Harbor, Union spotters notice Confederate R.H. Anderson's troops moving around General Gouverneur Warren's positions. Warren uses a flanking movement and attacks in force, while General Horatio Wright strikes the Rebels directly at their front. Bad maneuvering on the part of Warren complicates matters, allowing the Confederates time to fortify their positions. The Confederates unsuccessfully assault Warren three times before 1800, when Wright and Smith commence their attack, which gains ground and captures more than 700 prisoners. The Rebels regroup and assault Union lines at Cold Harbor several times during the night, but each assault is repulsed.

In Tennessee, General Samuel D. Sturgis, pursuant to orders issued by Sherman, departs Memphis in a column of about 7,000 men that advances toward Mississippi to intercept Confederate troops under General Nathan B. Forrest. General Forrest is simultaneously departing Tupelo, Mississippi, to destroy the rails between Nashville and Chattanooga, Tennessee. Forrest's force consists of approximately 3,500 men and their mission is to destroy Sherman's supply line. Forrest successfully reaches Russellville, Alabama, but withdraws shortly thereafter, to avoid the stalking forces of Sturgis. The two opposing forces clash feverishly at

Brice's Crossroads on June 9. Stoneman's contingent of Sherman's army defeats Confederates at Allatoona Pass, Georgia, and captures the railroad. Meanwhile, General Sherman keeps pressing forward, driving relentlessly toward the sea.

In Union general officer activity, Major General Don Carlos Buell, awaiting orders for more than one year, resigns his commission. Afterward, General Grant recommends that Buell be recommissioned, but no action is taken.

In Confederate general officer activity, Major Rufus Barringer is appointed brigadier general. He will receive command of a brigade under W.H. Lee's division. Lee remains with the brigade throughout the war and in the defense of Richmond. In his first marriage Barringer was the brother-in-law of both General Daniel Harvey Hill and Thomas "Stonewall" Jackson, as each had married one of the six Morrison sisters, daughters of Doctor R.H. Morrison. Also, Colonel Adam Rankin "Stovepipe" Johnson is promoted to the rank of brigadier general effective this date. Colonel James Conner, who initially entered service in the Confederacy as a captain in Hampton's Legion, is appointed brigadier general. In the 1850s Conner had served as U.S. district attorney.

In Naval activity, the USS *Exchange,* while operating on the Yazoo River, engages a Confederate battery at Columbia, Arkansas. The contest continues for about forty-five minutes, and during the intense duel, the *Exchange* sustains 35 hits, eight of which penetrate its hull. The Union casualties total one man killed. The commanding officer, Lt. J.S. Kurd, sustains a wound. The *Exchange,* however, survives and continues in service for the duration of the war. Afterward, it transports and at times tows various armaments and ammunition to Jefferson Barracks, Louisiana. It is decommissioned at

Lieutenant General Richard H. Anderson (Johnson, *Campfire and Battlefield: History of the Conflicts and Campaigns,* 1894).

Allatoona Pass looking north (Johnson, *Campfire and Battlefield: History of the Conflicts and Campaigns,* 1894).

Mound City, Illinois, on 6 August 1865 and is sold on the 17th. In other activity, the USS *James Adger*, after duty off North Carolina and undergoing repairs since the previous December, returns to the South Atlantic Squadron at about this time (June). It resumes blockade duty off Charleston and other areas in the sector for the duration of the war. During April 1865, it is assigned duty in the Caribbean and operates there from August 1865 until February 1866. In May 1866, it is decommissioned in New York City; it is sold during October of the same year. Afterward it operates as a commercial vessel under the name *James Adger* until 1878.

June 2 (Thursday)   In Virginia (Cold Harbor), Union troops under General Grant prepare to assault the Confederates at Cold Harbor, but the late arrival of reinforcements causes postponement until the following morning. Union General Ambrose Burnside's corps is to be held in reserve at Bethesda Church, while the corps of Gouverneur Warren, W.F. Smith, Winfield S. Hancock and Horatio Wright position their lines for the imminent battle. The Union perimeter is taunted with multiple lightning-fast hit and run tactics, but the Union handily repulses all such attacks, particularly because of the determined efforts of General Joseph Jackson Bartlett's 2nd Brigade. The Confederates do succeed in capturing several hundred prisoners during these raids, while the Union is being pushed through the swamps. This action forces General Warren to take a defensive stance. Confederate General George Pierce Doles is killed by Union fire while checking his fortifications in the vicinity of Bethesda Church, prior to the upcoming battle at Cold Harbor. Colonel Philip Cook succeeds Doles as commander of the brigade.

Confederate Brigadier General William W. Kirkland is wounded (third time) at Gaines' Mill (Cold Harbor). Kirkland recuperates and is able to rejoin the Army in the field during the following August, when he receives command of a brigade in General Robert F. Hoke's division. Later in the year Kirkland moves to North Carolina to support the defense of Fort Fisher. Confederate Colonel William MacRae, 15th North Carolina, is promoted to brigadier general subsequent to the wounding of Kirkland, effective June 22 on a temporary basis. His rank is made permanent in late 1864.

In Confederate general officer activity, Captain Samuel Barron, Sr., is appointed captain in the Confederate Provisional Navy, effective May 13, 1863. Barron has been the flag officer, commanding Confederate Naval officer, in Europe since the previous year.

In Naval activity, three armed boats from the USS *Sunflower* move ashore in Tampa Bay and destroy a Confederate salt works.

June 3 (Friday)   In Virginia at the Battle of Cold Harbor, Confederate positions of General Robert E. Lee extend from New Cold Harbor to the Totopotomoy Creek, opposing the Union force, which is spread from Bethesda through Old Cold Harbor and beyond to the Chickahominy River. General U.S. Grant orders the Union attack to commence at 0430, with Generals Francis Barlow and John Gibbon spearheading the assault. Barlow attempts to penetrate swampland while facing heavy Rebel gunfire. The Union is able to gain some expensive ground, capturing a few hundred Rebels and several pieces of artillery, which are promptly turned against the Rebels. General Gibbon also experiences a difficult time, yet his troops advance close to the enemy lines and hold their positions.

Union Generals Ambrose Burnside and Gouverneur Warren subsequently move forward, unifying the lines. During the assault, Colonel James P. McMahon, commanding a regiment in Brigadier General John Gibbon's command, reaches the Rebel parapets and drills his colors into the ground, but immediately thereafter, he is struck by a mortal wound. Colonels Orlando H. Morris and Peter A. Porter also are killed and General Robert O. Tyler is among the wounded. In addition, Colonel Preston of the 1st Vermont Cavalry is killed. Major William Wells assumes command of the regiment.

All hostilities cease at about 0730, but the Union sustains severe casualties. Grant fortifies his positions, attempting to neutralize Lee's strength. U.S. Grant would accept full blame for the great loss of life sustained by the Union assault troops and even states the assault was a bad decision on his part. Grant and Lee now communicate on the removal of casualties from the field. Agreeable terms are not reached for three days, and by this time, only two of the wounded remain alive.

Grant, unable to unseat the Rebels holding Cold Harbor, turns his attention and full fury toward Petersburg. He moves south of the James River to prepare the siege of Petersburg, which will last until April 3, 1865. Shortly after the battle, Grant redeploys his forces. The 9th Corps holding the right is withdrawn and redeployed between the 5th an 18th Corps, essentially placing the 5th Corps on the right. And on 6 June, the 5th Corps is pulled back and placed in positions to the rear of the center, placing once again the 9th Corps on the right.

On the 7th, the 2nd Corps is deployed on the left side of the line and directed to extend to the Chickahominy, while Grant also directs the 5th Corps to move to the flank and stretch its line to Dispatch Station on the York River. Skirmishes continue in and around Cold Harbor until the 12th of June and include battles at Gaines Mill, Salem Church, and Hawes' Shop.

Union losses amount to just under 2,000 dead, 10,500 wounded, and approximately 2,450 missing. The Confederates lose 1,700 killed, wounded, or missing. The losses on both sides are extremely high, but Richmond gets another reprieve. The defiant Rebels have forestalled the inevitable again and will continue to do so for a long time. Union General Gilman Marston participated in this action as part of General W.F. Smith's XVIII Corps. Subsequent to this engagement, General Marston is assigned duty in eastern Virginia, where he serves until he musters out of the army on 20 April 1865.

The Confederates, commanded by Robert E. Lee, including Robert Hoke, John C. Breckinridge, Joseph Finegan, Richard H. Anderson and Jubal Early, inflict over 7,000 casualties upon the Union on the 3rd of June alone. Union General Marston Gilman participates at this battle, commanding a brigade of W.F. Smith's XVIII Corps. Confederate Colonel William F. Perry subsequently commands Brigadier General Evander McIvor Law's brigade. Law requests relief from the command after suffering from wounds in this campaign. Subsequent to recuperating, General Law assumes command of a cavalry force under General Joseph Johnston during the final campaigns in the Carolinas. He becomes involved in the newspaper business until he reaches his 80th birthday. He dies on 31 October 1920, about two years after the termination of World War I.

Colonel William Perry, who joined the 44th Alabama as a private and rose to be its commanding officer, is appointed brigadier general during February 1865. Perry, a former college president, will later surrender at Appomattox with Lee and after the war will return to teaching after a short stint at farming. General Law, upon recuperation, transfers to the Carolinas and serves with General Joseph Johnston, and General William F. Perry assumes command of Law's Brigade. Also, Confederate Brigadier General William Ruffin Cox's Brigade (North Carolina regiments) participates. Following the fighting at Cold Harbor, Cox departs and joins with General Jubal Early to afford relief to the Rebels at Lynchburg, Virginia.

In Arkansas, a detachment of the 3rd Missouri Cavalry skirmishes with Confederates at Searcy. Casualty figures are unavailable.

In Louisiana, Confederate Naval forces at Red River surrender to the United States Fleet.

In South Carolina, the USS *Water Witch*, while operating in Ossabaw Sound in the waters between Georgia's mainland and Ossabaw Island, is raided by a Confederate force under Lt. Thomas P. Pelot, Confederate States Navy. The Rebels approach the *Water Witch* by boat and board the vessel. Following a struggle, the ship is gained by the Confederates. Two of the Union crew men are killed and 12 others are wounded. Afterward, it is taken to White Bluff, Georgia, from where it is to leave for Savannah as a Confederate ship, the CSS *Water Witch*. However, it never departs White Bluff due to Union pressure during mid–December.

In West Virginia, a skirmish between the Union and Confederate troops at Panther Gap and Buffalo Gap, through the 6th, leaves 25 Union soldiers dead or wounded. The Confederate forces also have 25 dead or wounded.

In Naval activity, the U.S. Navy acquires a screw tug, the *Fred Wheeler*. The ship is one of six similar vessels acquired at Philadelphia this day. The U.S. Navy purchases these vessels in an effort to create a stronger line of protection for its warships and army transports, a move necessitated due to the Confederates' ability to inflict destruction by surprise, such as the attacks by the CSS *Virginia* (formerly *Merrimack*) and the CSS *Hunley* at Hampton Roads (March 1862) and the sinking of the *Housatonic* (February 1864). The *Fred Wheeler* is named *Picket Boat No. 1* and command is given to Acting Ensign Nathaniel R. Davis. The other vessels purchased this day become Picket Boat No. 2 through Picket Boat No. 6. Nonetheless, confusion emerges when the vessels join the North Atlantic Blockading Squadron because it already has six vessels with similar names, Picket Launch No. 1 through Picket Launch No. 6. The problem is remedied by changing the names of the new arrivals to the first six letters of the Greek alphabet: *Alpha, Beta, Gamma, Delta, Epsilon* and *Zeta*. Davis' *Alpha* (also called Tug No. 1), after arriving to join the squadron, initiates its operations on the James River during November 1864. It continues in service until the surrender of Robert E. Lee and afterward returns to Washington, where it is sold during October 1865 and reverts back to its original name, *Fred Wheeler*.

The USS *Wamsutta*, operating in the vicinity of Georgetown, South Carolina, encounters and pursues a British steamer, the blockade runner *Rose*. It runs aground and is set afire.

June 4 (Saturday)   In Georgia, General William T. Sherman, although well fortified at Allatoona, attempts to outflank General Joseph E. Johnston. General Johnston, sensing his bad positioning, withdraws toward the mountains in the vicinity of Marietta. The Union (2nd Division Cavalry, Army of West Virginia) drives toward Acworth to seize the railroad there.

In Louisiana, the 5th Minnesota Volunteer Regiment, following duty in the Red River Campaign, has since begun its return to Memphis, Tennessee. The regiment will participate in the battle against Confederates at Lake Chicot, Arkansas, on the 6th.

In Naval activity, the USS *Fort Jackson*, while operating off Wilmington, North Carolina, seizes the blockade runner *Thistle*. The *Thistle*, a 636-ton (burden) iron side-wheel steamship, is acquired by the U.S. Navy in July and transformed into a warship. It is commissioned the USS *Dumbarton* during August. Afterward, it participates in the search for the CSS *Tallahassie*; however, the Rebel warship evades contact. Afterward, the *Dumbarton* returns to its blockade duty off Wilmington. During February 1865, the *Dumbarton* moves to the James River. After the war it is decommissioned at Washington, D.C. During November 1865 the *Dumbarton* moves to New York, where it is sold in October 1867 and later switched to British registry under the name *City of Quebec*. The vessel sinks during late April or early May 1870 after colliding with another vessel off Canada. Also, the USS Fort *Jackson*, following the seizure of the *Thistle*, later participates in the operations against Fort Fisher, North Carolina.

June 5 (Sunday)   In Virginia, Union General David Hunter's force, moving toward Piedmont, near Staunton, is engaged by Confederates commanded by Brigadier General William E. Jones. The Union fights vehemently, driving the Confederates back in disarray, which allows the Yankees to capitalize and seize many prisoners. Meanwhile, Confederate Brigadier General John McCausland leads his brigade toward Lynchburg, and at this time his command is the sole cohesive force standing between the advancing Union and the city of Lynchburg.

Union losses are 130 killed and 650 wounded. Confederates lose 460 killed, 1,450 wounded and 1,060 missing or captured. Confederate General William E. Jones (West Point, 1848) is killed when a Minié ball strikes him as he is leading his troops. Apparently, Brigadier General George Maney receives temporary command of the brigade; however, he is relieved of it during the latter part of August. The 54th Pennsylvania Infantry participates in the engagement. Union General Julius Stahel, who was born in Hungary, becomes a recipient of the Medal of Honor for his heroism at this battle, but he does not receive it until 1893. Confederate Colonel Bradley T. Johnson, following the death of General W.E. Jones, is appointed brigadier general in June. General Johnson will hold direct command of the Rebels who later burn the town of Chambersburg, Pennsylvania, for failure to pay the ransom on July 30, 1864.

Following this encounter, General Hunter moves toward Staunton, Virginia, arriving there on the 8th to join up with Generals George Crook and William Averell. General Stahel is assigned court-martial duty and he remains in that capacity until he resigns during February 1865.

June 6 (Monday)   In Virginia, Union General David Hunter's troops occupy Staunton with no Confederate opposition. Hunter soon moves from Staunton in an attempt to capture Lynchburg. In other activity, at Cold Harbor, General Grant orders General Philip Sheridan and two cavalry divisions to prepare for a mission designed to demolish the Virginia Central Railroad.

In West Virginia, a brigade of the 2nd Division, Army of West Virginia, commanded by General Rutherford B. Hayes, engages Confederates at Buffalo Gap. Also, the 22nd Pennsylvania Cavalry clashes with Confederates at Greenland Gap Road in the vicinity of Moorefield.

In Georgia, General Sherman's forces take Acworth. The Confederates, reacting to the Union progress, evacuate their positions at Hope Church and move to the mountains.

In Arkansas, elements of the 16th Corps encounter and engage Confederates at Lake Chicot (Old River Lake), Dutch Bayou, Columbia and Fish Bayou. The Union sustains 40 killed and 70 wounded. The Confederates suffer 100 killed and wounded. The 5th Minnesota Volunteer Regiment participates in this action.

In Naval activity, the Confederate blockade runner *Donegal* is seized by the USS *Metacomet* off Mobile. The *Metacomet* had been commissioned during January 1864 and immediately transferred to the West Gulf Blockading Squadron, which patrols the seas in and around Mobile. Later, the *Metacomet* participates in the action that causes the blockade runner *Ivanhoe* to run aground in early July, and it also participates in the Battle of Mobile Bay during August.

June 7 (Tuesday)   In Mississippi, the vanguard of General Samuel Sturgis' cavalry, en route to Guntown, clashes with Confederate cavalry at Ripley.

In Virginia, General U.S. Grant dispatches General Philip Sheridan with two divisions to join General David Hunter to assist him in destroying the Virginia Central Railroad and the James River Canal. Hunter is instructed to return with Sheridan to Grant's lines after the mission is completed. Sheridan's force crosses the Pamunkey River at New Castle Ferry, making camp at Dunkirk and Aylett's, near the Mattapony. Sheridan's cavalry has wagons and artillery attached to the column for added support. In other activity, General Grant directs General John Joseph Abercrombie (West Point, 1822), commander at White House, to uproot the rails of the York River Railroad and prepare to transport them by ships to City Point. Subsequently, Abercrombie is ordered to send all organized arriving troops to General Benjamin F. Butler at Cold Harbor.

General David Hunter (Mottelay, *The Soldier in Our Civil War*, 1886).

In Union general officer activity, Brigadier General Grenville M. Dodge is promoted to the rank of major general. Dodge had fought at Pea Ridge, Arkansas (March 1862), and was wounded there; he had three horses shot from under him while leading his brigade. During his activity with General Sherman, Dodge is wounded in the Atlanta campaign. Also, Brigadier General John Gibbon is promoted to major general. In January 1865, Gibbon receives command of the XXIV Corps, which is established at about the time he assumes command. Also, Colonel Patrick Henry Jones receives command of a brigade in the XX Corps. He remains in command for the duration of the war. On 11 April 1865, he is appointed brigadier general, effective 6 December 1863. General Jones musters out of the army on 17 June 1865. In yet other activity, Colonel Byron Root Pierce is promoted to brigadier general.

June 8 (Wednesday)   In Georgia, Union General Frank P. Blair, Jr., arrives at Acworth to augment Sherman's force. General Blair's contingent includes Colonel Eli Long's cavalry brigade and two divisions of the 17th Corps. These new arrivals are immediately attached to General James McPherson's force.

In Virginia, General David Hunter arrives at Staunton and links with Generals George Crook and William Averell. The combined force moves from Staunton to Lynchburg. However, Lynchburg, having been reinforced by General John McCausland's brigade and arrivals from Jubal Early's force, is considered too strongly defended to attack, and it is noted that trains continually arrive at Lynchburg, bringing in additional reinforcements. The Union force returns to Staunton by marching through the Alpine area of West Virginia. In conjunction, Confederate Brigadier General William Ruffin Cox's brigade participates (General Early's command) and later moves to join the campaigns in Maryland. From there, Cox leads his North Carolinians into the Shenandoah Valley. Despite being wounded more than ten times since joining the Confederacy, Cox maintains his determination and defiance. His brigade will be with General Robert E. Lee at Appomattox when hostilities cease.

June 9 (Thursday)   In Georgia, Sherman's forces move from Acworth to strike Big Shanty, which is situated midway between Acworth and Kennesaw. Much of the ground lying between Acworth and Marietta is mountainous, and it includes three dominant crests on Kennesaw (East), Lost Mountain (southwest) and Pine Mountain located between the other two; the Confederates have established formidable defenses and they have created a well organized series of signal stations. Atop Kennesaw Mountain, the dominant position of the region, the Confederates have deployed artillery to further bolster the area around Marietta and to provide protection to the nine infantry divisions and the Georgia militia. The militia, called out by Governor Joseph E. Brown, is placed under the command of General Gustavus W. Smith.

Meanwhile, General Sherman's army closes in three columns, George H. Thomas against Kennesaw and Pine Mountain, John Schofield against Lost Mountain and James McPherson toward Marietta.

General William Joseph Hardee is deployed at Lost Mountain on the Confederate far left, while Leonidas Polk guards the center and John B. Hood holds the right along the Acworth and Marietta Road. Sherman's force continues to nudge up against the Rebels' until the 14th. Georgia is receiving an enormous amount of inclement weather; it has been raining sine the beginning of the month.

In Kentucky, Union cavalry (Kentucky Division) skirmishes with Confederates at Mount Sterling. The Union sustains 35 killed and 150 wounded. The Confederates suffer 50 killed, 200 wounded and 250 captured.

In Maryland, at Point of Rocks, elements of the 2nd U.S. Colored Cavalry encounter and engage Confederates. The unit sustains two killed. Confederate casualties are unavailable.

In Mississippi, Confederate General Nathan B. Forrest extends his force of 3,500 men along the railroad in the vicinity of Guntown and Booneville. At dawn on the following day, Confederates under Forrest and the Union forces under Samuel D. Sturgis (West Point, 1846) clash at Brice's Crossroads.

In Tennessee, the 7th Tennessee Cavalry skirmishes with Confederates at Lafayette.

In Virginia, at Petersburg, Union troops under General Benjamin Butler launch an attack, but fail to capture the city.

In Union general officer activity, Major Jacob W. Zeilin is appointed seventh commandant of the United States Marine Corps, succeeding Colonel John Harris, who died the previous month. In other activity, Nelson Miles (61st New York), appointed colonel 31 May 1862, is promoted to brigadier general.

In Naval activity, the USS *New Berne* and the *Dacotah* intercept a blockade runner, the *Pevensey* and initiates pursuit. The Rebel *Pevensey* runs aground in the vicinity of Beaufort, North Carolina. Within a short while it explodes. The ship had been transporting a cargo that included weapons, food, including bacon, and uniforms that were to be delivered to General Lee in Virginia. Thomas Harding, captain of the forecastle aboard the *Dacotah*, becomes a recipient of the Medal of Honor for his actions during this engagement. In other naval activity, the USS *Wamsutta* comes under fire from Confederate batteries at Winjah Bay, South Carolina, while it is executing a recon-

Lost Mountain, Georgia (*Harper's Pictoral History of the Civil War*, 1896).

naissance mission at Confederate Island. It returns to Charleston on the 14th.

June 10 (Friday)   BATTLE OF BRICES CROSSROADS Union General Samuel D. Sturgis' troops, which had departed Memphis on June 1 in search of Forrest, catch the Confederates at Guntown, Mississippi (Brice's Crossroads). General Samuel Sturgis' command is bolstered by Benjamin Grierson's cavalry and a portion of General Andrew Jackson Smith's division, the latter having arrived from the Red River after that campaign. This day, Grierson's cavalry, leading the advance, encounters and engages a strong Confederate contingent and drives it back, but the ferocious battle still causes Grierson to call for reinforcements. General Samuel Sturgis' troops, at a point about six miles to the rear, rush to the front to assist, but the march is costly, as the heat of the day takes a toll on the men. Nevertheless, they plow into the Confederates, giving more punch to the attack.

All the while, the Confederate flanks remain unscathed, giving the Rebels a golden opportunity to pummel the Union. Artillery, well deployed on the ridges, commences firing, causing the Union lines to falter. Confederate pressure then cracks the whole line, compelling the Union to retreat. The Southern force, less than half the size of the Union force, hammers the Yankees, which include Benjamin H. Grierson's cavalry, the 114th, 120th Illinois and the 55th and 59th Colored Troops. The Union in disarray speeds toward Ripley, abandoning its entire complement of wagons, which are stranded directly under the Rebel artillery. The Union holds at Ripley and successfully forestalls further disaster. From here, the Union again makes the trek to Memphis.

The Union sustains 223 dead, 394 wounded and 1,625 missing. The Confederates suffer 131 dead and 475 wounded. The disorganized Union withdrawal, which began as a disciplined retreat, turns into a chaotic nightmare. In its attempt to retreat, the Union loses nearly all supplies and artillery, surrendering them to the terrain and the river bottom. Sherman, upon learning of the defeat at Brices Crossroads, orders his commander at Memphis to "make a force up and go out and follow Forrest if it costs 10,000 lives and breaks the treasury." In early July, General A.J. Smith, at Memphis, sets out to again attack Forrest.

In Alabama, the 106th Ohio Volunteers skirmish with Confederate guerrillas at Cane Creek. Casualty figures are unavailable.

In Georgia, General Sherman's Army continues its advance toward Confederate-held Kennesaw Mountain, hoping to overrun outposts in the area north of Marietta. Sherman, in order to protect his supply line, moves south and southwest of Marietta. Bad weather has been impeding his operations. General Sherman's forces, including the recently arrived reinforcements of General Blair with two Divisions of the 17th Corps, move to Big Shanty. The 9,000 reinforcements under Blair bring Sherman's force to a strength of about 100,000 troops.

In Kentucky, the 168th Ohio (100 day regiment) and the 171st Ohio Regiment engage the Confederates under John Hunt Morgan at Cynthiana and Kellar's Bridge, Licking River. The Union suffers 21 killed, 71 wounded and 980 captured. General Hobson is among the captured. He is permitted to go to Cincinnati in an effort to get exchanged for some of Morgan's troops held by the Union. Toward the close of the war, Hobson commands the Department of Kentucky. He musters out of the service during August 1865. Also, Kentucky militiamen and civilians, under Colonel George Monroe, repulse an attack by Confederates led by Lt. Colonel Pryor (Morgan's Raiders) at Fort Boone in Frankfort. Meanwhile, the 4th Kentucky Cavalry clashes with Confederates at Lexington. Other Union troops (specific units unreported) skirmish with Confederates at Princeton.

In Mississippi, the 2nd New Jersey Cavalry engages Confederates at Corinth. Casualty figures are unavailable.

In Virginia, elements of the 10th Corps and August Kautz's Cavalry engage Confederates at Petersburg. The Union sustains 20 killed and 67 wounded. Confederate casualties are unavailable. Other Union troops attached to the 3rd Division, Cavalry, Army of the Potomac, skirmish with Confederates at Old Church, and the two antagonists again clash on the following day.

In Union general officer activity, Lt. Colonel William Henry Seward, Jr., is promoted to colonel (later brigadier general) of the New York 9th Heavy Artillery (formerly the 138th New York Regiment). Seward, the son of the secretary of state, had initially been appointed as lieutenant colonel of the regiment during August 1861.

In Confederate general officer activity, Colonel John Smith Preston is promoted to brigadier general. He sees no field command; rather he remains in command of the bureau of conscription in Richmond, a post he has held since 30 July 1863. After the war, he travels to England and remains there until 1868. Upon his return,

General Preston remains a steadfast advocate of the rights of a state to secede from the Union, and he holds the position for the remainder of his life. He dies on 1 May 1881 in Columbia, South Carolina.

In Naval activity, the *Huntress*— a stern-wheel steamer acquired by the U.S. Navy in May 1864 and later commissioned the USS *Huntress*— on this day arrives to join the 8th District, Mississippi Squadron. Acting Master J.S. Dennis has been appointed commanding officer. The ship is assigned patrol duty on the Mississippi in the area between Memphis, Tennessee, and Columbus, Kentucky. Subsequently, it is decommissioned on 10 August 1865 and sold on 17 August. It becomes a commercial vessel; however, it is lost off Alexandria, Louisiana, on 30 December 1865 after becoming grounded.

June 11 (Saturday)   In Georgia, the Union forces under General Sherman complete repairs on the Etowah River Bridge and finish repairing the rails, easing the strain on his advancing army as trains once again roll straight up to the skirmish lines.

In Kentucky, Union General Stephen G. Burbridge's force attacks Morgan's raiders at Cynthiana. Union forces suffer 150 killed or wounded; the Confederates sustain 300 killed or wounded and 400 captured.

In Mississippi, the 3rd and 4th Iowa, 2nd New Jersey and 4th Missouri Cavalry Regiments engage Confederates at Ripley. Casualty figures are unavailable.

In Virginia, the 1st and 2nd Division, Cavalry Corps, Army of the Potomac, engage Confederates at Trevilian Station and other places, including Louisa, for two days. The Confederates, under Generals Fitzhugh Lee and Wade Hampton, had been dispatched by General Robert E. Lee to halt the progress of Sheridan's cavalry. At Trevilian Station, Union General Custer strikes the Rebels from the rear, allowing Sheridan to seize Trevilian Station and capture over 500 prisoners, which are subsequently sent to City Point. Other Confederate casualties are unavailable. The Union sustains 85 killed, 490 wounded and 160 missing. (See also, **June 12 In Virginia.**) Other cavalry under General David Hunter is engaged by Confederates under General Jubal Early in the vicinity of Lexington.

In Union general officer activity, Colonel Selden Connor is promoted to brigadier general. General Connor originally joined the army as a private during May 1861. He participated at Big Bethel with the 1st Vermont Infantry, which mustered out on 15 August. On 22 August 1862 he was appointed lieutenant colonel of the 7th Maine. Later,

on 11 January, he became colonel of the 19th Maine.

June 12 (Sunday)   In Louisiana, Union cavalry attached to the Army of the Cumberland engages Confederates at McAfee's Crossroads.

In Missouri, the 1st Missouri Militia Cavalry skirmishes with Confederates at Kingsville.

In Virginia, Union cavalry, including the 6th Pennsylvania Cavalry under General Philip Sheridan, battles the Confederates again at Trevilian Station, as Sheridan persists in driving the Confederates from the Shenandoah Valley. Sheridan's troops continue to destroy the rails as they move back to White House, arriving there on the 21st. Meanwhile, General Grant is redeploying his army at the south bank of the James River. On this day, Union General W.F. Smith is instructed to move his troops by night to White House, where boats await to transfer them to City Point. Smith's trains and artillery follow by land. Colonel James Wilson's cavalry, trailed by General Warren's force, which had secured the crossings of the Chickahominy at Long Bridge, also move back to the James. General Winfield S. Hancock's corps moves out behind Warren and heads for Wilcox Landing on the left bank of the James.

June 13 (Monday)   In Tennessee, General Samuel Sturgis' battered troops finally arrive back in Memphis. They are weary and beaten, far from victorious. Forrest enjoyed one of his finest hours at Sturgis' expense. General Sturgis' service terminates following his return to Memphis; however, he is breveted brigadier and major general during March 1865 and subsequently, during August 1865, he musters out of the volunteers and reverts to his rank of lieutenant colonel in the 6th U.S. Cavalry. In 1867 he becomes colonel of the 7th U.S. Cavalry, of which General Custer becomes lieutenant colonel. General Sturgis retires in 1886 after a long career on the western frontier.

In Virginia, General Grant, after failing to take Cold Harbor in 10 days of bitter fighting, begins to shift his Army towards Petersburg. Also,

The Confederate cavalry charge at Trevilian Station, Virginia (Johnson, *Campfire and Battlefield: History of the Conflicts and Campaigns*, 1894).

General Robert E. Lee is informed of the Union's retirement to the James River. The Confederates pursue, but only for a short while. Lee then retires to Richmond. At this time, Grant's Army has arrived at the James River in the vicinity of Harrison's Landing. In other activity, skirmishing between Confederates and cavalry units of General James H. Wilson and General Samuel W. Crawford occurs at White Oak Swamp Bridge, Charles City Crossroads. The Union sustains 50 killed and 250 wounded. Confederate casualties are unavailable.

In West Virginia, the 6th West Virginia Cavalry clashes with Confederates at White Post. Casualty figures are unavailable.

June 14 (Tuesday) In Georgia, Confederate Generals Leonidas Polk, William J. Hardee and Joseph E. Johnston continue to examine the terrain and each command maintains scouting patrols to gather intelligence on Union positions in the vicinity of Pine Mountain at Marietta. Union General George H. Thomas orders a contingent of his artillery to commence firing at the exposed gathering of Confederates, but is unaware that one of the groups is composed of the top generals. The effective fire scatters the Rebels; however, General Polk returns to the scene and Knapp's Battery again commences firing; one of the shells kills Lieutenant General Polk (West Point, 1827). General William Loring assumes temporary command of Polk's corps, and his division is given to General Winfield S. Featherston until the arrival of General S.D. Lee, who assumes permanent command of the center army.

Sherman's army, which has been steadily advancing, arrives at positions that encroach the Confederate stronghold at Kennesaw. Union contingents engage Confederate pickets and force them to pull back. General Howard's corps advances to positions between Pine Mountain and the Rebel fortifications to the east. Soon after, General Joseph Hooker's troops deploy on Howard's right. This activity is not without incident; the Confederates pour a steady ring of fire upon the Yankees as they maneuver for positions. Although the thunderous fire continues incessantly, both sides receive a reprieve from the weather when finally, the rains, ongoing for nearly two weeks without pause, come to a temporary halt.

In Missouri, elements of the 1st Missouri Cavalry skirmish at Lexington, Lafayette County. The Union sustains eight killed and one wounded. Confederate casualties are unavailable.

In Virginia, General U.S. Grant's force begins building a pontoon bridge to cross the James River to initiate the siege of Petersburg. Grant moves by steamer to confer with General Benjamin F. Butler at Bermuda Hundred. In other activity, the vanguard of the Army of West Virginia encounters and engages Confederates at Buchanan in the vicinity of Lexington.

In Union general officer activity, Brigadier General James Madison Tuttle resigns his commission.

In Confederate general officer activity, Colonel Hylan B. Lyon is promoted to the rank of brigadier general, effective this date.

June 15 (Wednesday) In Georgia, General William T. Sherman's confident troops continue their advance toward Marietta. Sherman learns that General Joseph E. Johnston has evacuated the positions on Pine Mountain and collected his forces along a strong series of defenses that stretch along the hills that link Lost Mountain and Kennesaw Mountain. The Union seizes the advantage and occupies Pine Mountain. Union General James McPherson's command begins skirmishing with the troops on the outer perimeter positions of Johnston, but the weather conditions are too terrible for any genuine type of action to commence, causing Sherman to postpone his main assault until June 27. Nonetheless, the two sides continue skirmishing through the 16th and into the 17th.

In Tennessee, the 55th U.S. Colored Troops (1st Alabama) skirmishes with Confederates in Moscow.

In Virginia, cavalry under General James H. Wilson encounters and engages Confederates at Samaria Church and Malvern Hill. The Union sustains 25 killed and three wounded. The Confederates sustain 100 killed and wounded. In other action, the Union 3rd Division, 10th Corps, Army of the James, engages Confederates at Baylor's Farm.

Fierce fighting occurs in and around Petersburg, including Baylor's Farm on the 15th, Wathal and Weirbottom on the 16th. The Confederates repulse the Union forces and prevent them from cutting off Richmond's supplies. U.S. Grant puts the city under siege. The Union has 1,298 killed, 7,474 wounded and 1,814 missing. Confederate casualties are unavailable; however, they are heavy. Union Generals W.F. Smith, Winfield Scott Hancock and George Meade participate in these actions.

In Naval activity, the Mississippi Squadron engages Confederate shore artillery at Ratliff's Landing, Louisiana. The recently commissioned (April 1864) USS *Winnebago*, a 1300-ton Milwaukee class twin-turret ironclad river monitor, participates. After this action, the *Winnebago* is attached to the West Gulf Blockading Squadron. In other activity, the USS *Lexington*, while operating in the vicinity of Beaulah Landing, Mississippi, captures the Confederate steamers *Mattie, M. Walt* and *R.E. Hill.* Both vessels are carrying cargoes of cotton.

In other activity, the USS *New Hampshire* leaves Portsmouth, New Hampshire, for Port Royal, South Carolina. It arrives there on 29 July, relieves the USS *Vermont,* and remains at that station until its return to Norfolk, Virginia, on 8 June 1866. Afterward, the *New Hampshire* remains at Norfolk as a receiving ship until May 1876, when it returns to Port Royal. It is renamed the *Granite State* on 30 November 1904 to permit the name New Hampshire to be given to a new battleship. The *Granite State* sinks in the Hudson River on 23 May 1921.

June 16 (Thursday) In Virginia, Union General Winfield S. Hancock requires relief because of a wound suffered at the battle of Gettysburg; he is temporarily replaced by General George G. Meade. Confederate reinforcements under Robert F. Hoke arrive to assist General Beauregard, who informs Robert E. Lee that his force had repelled two Union attacks at Bermuda Hundred. Beauregard also reports the capture of eleven Union officers. In other activity, by noon this day, Grant's entire army has crossed to the south side of the James, having forded it at Douthard's, several miles below Harrison's Landing. The pontoon bridge constructed at a site selected by General Godfrey Weitzel is 2,000 feet long, the distance between the two banks; at this point on the river, the water is 13 fathoms deep. Also, Brevet Major General John Ramsay (Ramsey), 2nd Brigade, 2nd Division, II Corps, is seriously wounded during skirmishing in front of Petersburg. Subsequent to recovering from his third wound, he receives command of the 1st Brigade, 1st Division, II Corps. He remains with the brigade until the surrender of General Lee at Appomattox during April of 1865. Afterward, he receives temporary command of the 2nd Division, II Corps. On 17 July 1865, he is mustered out of the service.

On the following day (17th), Beauregard assaults Union lines to recapture lost territory. Also, Union troops under General David Hunter (Army of West Virginia) skirmish Confederates at Otter Creek in the vicinity of Liberty. The Union sustains three killed and 15 wounded. Confederate casualties are unavailable. In yet other activity, the 2nd Division, 10th Corps, Army of the James, engages Confederates at Weirbottom Creek. Also, the 1st Division, 10th Corps, Army of the James, skirmishes with Confederates at Walthal, and the 36th U.S. Colored Troops clashes with Confederates at Pierson's Farm.

June 17 (Friday) In Georgia, the Union forces of General Sherman continue to press the Confederates, compelling them to abandon Lost Mountain and close ranks at Kennesaw Mountain. From the latter place, General John B. Hood holds the right and guards Marietta, while General William Hardee, on the left, strings his lines to extend behind Nose Creek to secure the rails between there and the Chattahoochee River. Still the Union nudges along, trying to further tighten the noose. Skirmishes are occurring in this area.

In Virginia, General Robert E. Lee orders General Ambrose Hill to move from Riddell's Shop to the Petersburg Turnpike. Confederate General Joseph Kershaw is also summoned to Petersburg. During one of the many skirmishes in the vicinity of Petersburg, Union Major James St. Clair Morton is killed. Major Morton, an 1851 graduate of West Point, served as brigadier general from April 1863 and served with Generals Buell and Thomas as chief engineer. He was mustered out of the volunteers at about the time of the Battle of Chickamauga and reverted to his rank of major in the Regular U.S. Army.

In conjunction, Major Morton is posthumously promoted to brevet brigadier general, U.S. Army. He is interred at Laurel Hill Cemetery in Philadelphia.

Two Union divisions led by Generals George Crook and Jeremiah Sullivan, bolstered by cavalry under Generals William Averell and Alfred Napoleon Duffie, skirmish heavily for two days with Confederates at Lynchburg. The Union sustains 100 killed, 500 wounded and 100 missing. The Confederates suffer 200 killed and wounded.

June 18 (Saturday) In Virginia, General Robert E. Lee states in a telegram to Confederate General Jubal Early: "If circumstances authorize, carry out the original plan or move upon Petersburg without delay." Union troops, under General David Hunter, having been pinned down by General Early's Confederate artillery at Lynchburg, avoid disaster when a charge by the 54th Pennsylvania Infantry forces the Confederates to withdraw. Hunter, his ammunition nearly exhausted, retires to Harpers Ferry, West Virginia.

In Union general officer activity, Colonel Joshua Lawrence Chamberlain, 20th Maine, is promoted on the spot to brigadier general by U.S. Grant for his gallantry at Petersburg (Chamberlain had been wounded six times during this campaign and thought mortally wounded by Grant on the day of his promotion). Chamberlain was a recipient of the Medal of Honor for bravery at Petersburg. Chamberlain is elected governor of Maine in autumn 1866 and re-elected three times. He succumbs in Portland, Maine, on 24 February 1914.

In Confederate general officer activity, Colonel William L. Brandon is promoted brigadier general effective this day. However, Brandon, lacking one leg due to a wound sustained in 1862 at Malvern Hill, will not return to the field. Instead he heads for Mississippi and takes command of the conscription services there.

June 19 (Sunday) THE BATTLE BETWEEN THE USS *KEARSARGE* AND THE CSS *ALABAMA* The Confederate privateer *Alabama,* commanded by Captain Raphael Semmes, is in port at Cherbourg, France, for repairs when the USS *Kearsarge,* commanded by Captain John A. Winslow, nears the harbor. The *Alabama* moves out to challenge the Union vessel but the *Kearsarge,* equipped with more accurate weaponry, is able to outfight and destroy the *Alabama* after a battle which lasts about one hour. The *Alabama* is a grand catch for the Union because the Confederate vessel had taken about 60 prizes with a value of some six million dollars. The *Alabama* had been thought of as a British pirate ship because it had been constructed in England and permitted to get to the high seas against a treaty and because the majority of its crew had been British seamen. The British had built the CSS *Alabama,* the CSS *Florida* and the CSS *Shenandoah* and all swept the high seas to devastate Union commercial vessels, but only the *Florida* ever entered a Confederate port city.

In Georgia, Union and Confederate forces clash at Pine Knob during the fighting at Kennesaw Mountain. Specific units are unreported.

June 20 (Monday) In Georgia, Confederate General Joseph Johnston withdraws further to a well-fortified position at Kennesaw Mountain, with Sherman's troops in close pursuit. Confederate engineers place lines of entrenchments with a complete array of cannon and riflemen to repulse the approaching Yankees. General William Hardee's force is deployed toward the south at Lost Mountain, with the contingents of Generals Benjamin Cheatham, Patrick Cleburne, William B. Bate and Walker aligned from left to right. The center is held by William Loring's corps with the divisions of Samuel G. French, Edward C. Walthall and Winfield S. Featherston linked from left to right. And General John B. Hood's corps stands to the right, stretched between the railroad and the Marietta Road, but it is di-

rected to redeploy to the left to bolster General Cheatham's division. Union General Sherman expands his line, stretching it toward the Chattahoochee River.

Also, cavalry under Confederate Major General Joseph Wheeler clashes with the Union cavalry of General Kenner Garrard. The Rebels repel Garrard, but both sides sustain casualties. The Union loses 50 killed and 100 captured. The Confederates suffer 15 killed and 50 wounded. Meanwhile, Union cavalry (Army of the Cumberland) clashes with Confederates at Powder Springs and Lattmore's Mills, Noonday Creek.

In Virginia, a Union brigade under General Abercrombie (Sheridan's command) engages Confederates at White House. Casualty figures are unavailable. In other activity, the 2nd Division, Cavalry, Army of West Virginia, engages Confederates at Liberty. Also, General U.S. Grant's forces continue to besiege Petersburg, but the defenders in and around the town hold out and continue to engage in close-quartered skirmishing. A major confrontation occurs on 30 July.

June 21 (Tuesday) In Arkansas, the 27th Wisconsin Regiment skirmishes with Confederates at Pine Bluff.

In Virginia, Union General William Averell's cavalry battles Confederates at Salem. The Union sustains six killed and 10 wounded. The Confederates sustain 10 killed and wounded. Another clash occurs at Buford's Gap, where the 23rd Ohio Regiment sustains 15 killed. Confederate casualties are unavailable. Also, elements of the 1st and 2nd Divisions, Cavalry Corps, Army of the Potomac, clash with Confederates at White House Landing.

In Naval activity, a clash occurs between Union and Confederate naval forces on the James River in the vicinity of Dutch Gap and Trent's Reach. The USS *Canonicus* participates in this action. The *Canonicus,* a monitor was built at Boston and commissioned during April 1864. Following this action, the *Canonicus* re-

Left: The battle between the USS *Kearsarge* and the CSS *Alabama* (Johnson, ***Campfire and Battlefield: History of the Conflicts and Campaigns,*** 1894).***Middle:*** Captain John A. Winslow, commander of the USS *Kearsarge.* ***Right:*** Captain Raphael Semmes (***Harper's Pictorial History of the Civil War,*** 1896).

The James River below Dutch Gap (Johnson, *Campfire and Battlefield: History of the Conflicts and Campaigns*, 1894).

sumes its patrol duty. It remains primarily off Charleston for the duration until it is decommissioned in June 1865. It is known as the *Scylla* between June and August 1869. Afterward it is recommissioned as *Canonicus* and remains in service until 1877. Also, the CSS *Virginia II* (built at Richmond), commanded by Commander Robert B. Pegram, enters active service on this day as the flagship of Commodore J. K. Mitchell, Confederate States Navy. In other activity, the USS *Saugus* participates in an engagement with Confederate warships and batteries at Trent's Reach, Virginia. Subsequent to this action, it remains in the region, but later in the year, it participates against Fort Fisher, North Carolina (December 1864 and January 1865). Following the operations in North Carolina, it returns to the James River, where it serves on patrol until April, when it is ordered to the Washington Navy Yard to serve as a temporary holding ship for Confederate sympathizers accused of assassinating President Lincoln. After the war, the *Saugus* is decommissioned during June and remains inactive until recommissioned in April 1869. The same year it is renamed *Centaur*, but about two months later, it reverts to its original name. It is assigned patrol duty during the greater part of 1872 through 1877 and is sold in May 1891.

June 22 (Wednesday) In Arkansas, three companies of the 12th Iowa Regiment, supported by the gunboat *Lexington*, battles Confederates at White River. The Union sustains two killed and four wounded. The Confederates sustain two killed and three wounded. Afterward the *Lexington* resumes patrol duty and at times acts as an escort ship until the war ends. It is decommissioned at Mound City, Illinois, on 2 July, and during the following month, on the 17th, it is sold at auction.

In Georgia, Union General Sherman dispatches a force to assault General Joseph E. Johnston's flank. Confederate General John Bell Hood's 11,000 men are diverted to deal with this Union

threat, hitting the Union furiously southwest of Marietta at Kulp's Farm (House) to no avail. The gallant Rebel assault, executed by the divisions of Generals Thomas C. Hindman and Carter L. Stevenson, fails to move Sherman back, except for a temporary setback. The Union forces of Hooker stand close to the Confederate defenses and General John Schofield is moving up to deploy on his right. And at about this time, without warning, the Confederates are closing. The divisions of Generals John Geary, Milo Hascall and Alpheus Williams are ordered to move up and meet the threat, but before they can complete their maneuvers, the Confederates initiate a charge. Simultaneously, Geary's right and Williams' center are struck with horrific attacks, while the forces of Carter L. Stevenson pounce upon Hascall, threatening the entire line.

The endless fury forces the Union to give some ground, and they pull back to marshy terrain, but the Confederates have severed the two forces, causing some additional concern. Nevertheless, the Yankees hold and regroup and then answer the attack with a volcanic thrust that pours fire upon the Rebels. The combined power of the rifle guns of the Woodbury and Winegar batteries and the artillery of the 13th New York Artillery, stops General Hood's force in its tracks. The Yankees' fire continues and the Rebels are compelled, following severe casualties, to retire to their defenses. Sherman, impatient for the victory and disgusted with the elements (impassable roads), concludes that a major assault with diversionary moves against Kennesaw Mountain and Johnston's left flank may crumble the whole Southern Army. Sherman initiates his plan at 8:00 a.m. on the 27th. Also, a Union contingent engages Confederates at Culp's House as part of the Kennesaw Mountain battle.

In Virginia (GENERAL JAMES WILSON'S RAID), a Union force composed of General August Kautz's cavalry (Army of the James) and the 3rd Division, Army of the Potomac, clashes with Confederate troops at Weldon Railroad, Stoney Creek and Ream's Station. On the 29th, a vicious struggle erupts.

In Union general officer activity, Colonel Elliott Warren Rice (7th Iowa) is promoted to brigadier general. He participates in the Atlanta campaign and Sherman's "March to the Sea." After the fall of Savannah, he participates as a brigade commander (General Corse's division, General Logan's XV Corps) during the campaign in the Carolinas. He receives the brevet

of major general of volunteers during the closing days of the war and musters out of the service during August 1865.

In Confederate general officer activity, Colonel William MacRae (15th North Carolina) is promoted to brigadier general.

June 23 (Thursday) In Virginia, a major battle develops on the Weldon Railroad. The Confederates devastate the Yankees, who sustain 5,000 killed, wounded or missing. The Confederates lose approximately 500 men. Sgt. James Drury of the 4th Vermont Infantry manages to save his regimental colors, although almost the entire regiment is killed or captured. Drury is afterward awarded the Congressional Medal of Honor for his courage in the face of the enemy. In other activity, elements of the 3rd Division Cavalry, Army of the Potomac, skirmish with Confederates at Nottaway Court House (General James Wilson's raid). Also, the 1st and 2nd Division (Albert Torbert's and David Gregg's cavalry), Army of the Potomac, and the 28th U.S. Colored Troops clash with Confederates at Jones' Bridge.

In Confederate general officer activity, Major General Stephen Dill Lee (West Point, 1854) is promoted to the rank of lieutenant general. General Lee assumes command of General John B. Hood's corps (Army of Tennessee), which he commands until the surrender of General Joseph E. Johnston in North Carolina. After the war, General Lee takes up farming in Mississippi, and later he is elected to the state Senate and he becomes the first president of Mississippi State College. He dies in Vicksburg on 28 May 1908. Also, Major General Alexander Peter Stewart is promoted to lieutenant general. He receives command of General Polk's corps and leads it until the surrender of General Johnston at Greensboro, North Carolina, in May 1865.

In Naval activity, the USS *Henry Brinker*, inactive at Newport News, is dispatched to White House, Virginia, to lend support to Union ground forces. The *Henry Brinker* moves up the Pamunkey River and for a short while provides support fire to the ground forces. Afterward, it returns to Yorktown. On 1 July, the *Henry Brinker* moves to Hampton Roads to receive repairs, but it does not again leave port on military patrol. The *Henry Brinker* is decommissioned at Hampton Roads on 29 June 1865 and is sold the following month on the 20th.

June 24 (Friday) In Arkansas, a skirmish develops between the Union and Confederate forces at Baker's Springs. The Union loses a man. The Confederates lose six killed and three wounded.

In Georgia, outside of Marietta, General William T. Sherman orders an attack against the Confederate forces of General Joseph E. Johnston at Kennesaw Mountain; it is scheduled for June 27.

In Virginia, Union troops of the 1st Maine Cavalry clash with Confederates at St. Mary's

Church. Colonel Charles H. Smith becomes a recipient of the Medal of Honor for his heroic action during this engagement. The 1st and 2nd Cavalry Divisions, Army of the Potomac, also participate in this action. At Staunton Bridge, the 3rd Division, Cavalry Corps, Army of the Potomac, and General August Kautz's cavalry (Army of the James) clash with Confederates as part of General James Wilson's raid.

In Tennessee, Union troops skirmish with Confederates at Lafayette, Macon County.

In Union general officer activity, Colonel Louis D. Watkins receives the brevet of brigadier general. He participates in the Tennessee campaign (November–December 1864), and following the battle of Nashville, he is involved with pursuit of the Confederates under General John B. Hood. Nonetheless, toward the latter part of January 1865, his brigade is dissolved. In April, he receives command of the post at Louisville. He is promoted to brigadier general, full rank, on 25 September 1865. During 1866, he reverts to the rank of lieutenant colonel of the 20th Infantry Regiment, initially in Richmond, Virginia, and later in Baton Rouge, Louisiana. He dies in New Orleans on 29 March 1868.

In Naval activity, the USS *Queen City* sustains damage during an exchange with Confederate batteries at Clarendon, Arkansas. After becoming dead in the water the gunboat is compelled to surrender. Meanwhile, a nearby warship, the USS *Tyler,* closes to assist the *Queen City;* however, the Confederates destroy it to prevent the *Tyler* from recapturing it. The *Tyler* resumes its normal patrol duties and remains active for the duration of the war. Shortly afterward, it is decommissioned, and it is sold during August 1865.

June 25 (Saturday)   In Georgia, at Kennesaw Mountain, clashes occur between General Sherman's forces and Confederate General Carter L. Stevenson. The two sides have been skirmishing, but Sherman is preparing to commence a full-scale attack on the 27th.

In Louisiana, the 64th U.S. Colored Troops skirmish with Confederates at Point Pleasant.

In Arkansas, Union forces, including the 126th Illinois, 11th Missouri, 9th Iowa, 3rd Michigan Cavalry and Battery D, 2nd Missouri Artillery, engage Confederate troops at Clarendon, St. Charles River, through the 29th. The Union suffers 200 wounded, the Confederates, 200 wounded and 200 missing.

In Virginia, General Robert E. Lee writes to General Wade Hampton: "For want of cavalry, our railroad communications south have been cut." General Lee also requests reinforcements, including John R. Chambliss' brigade, for Petersburg.

In Union general officer activity, Union Colonel Edward Stuyvesant Bragg (no relation to Braxton Bragg), 6th Wisconsin (a contingent of the "Iron Brigade"), is appointed brigadier general from this date. Bragg participates in all

battles of the Army of the Potomac from Second Manassas (Bull Run) through the surrender at Appomattox except at Gettysburg, which he misses because of ill health.

June 27 (Monday)   THE BATTLE OF KENNESAW MOUNTAIN General Sherman's artillery commences a bombardment of Confederate General Joseph E. Johnston's positions on Kennesaw Mountain, Georgia, to signal the imminent attack that will advance from positions stretching along the entire Union line. This mammoth bombardment is followed by a massive assault on two fronts, with more than 5,000 men braving thick woods and swampy ground under intense enemy fire. Once they sprint beyond these obstacles, the troops face granite resistance by the persistent Rebels. The deadly sharpshooting of the Confederates halts the Yankees at Pigeon Hill, far short of the initial objectives. The Union attackers are also the recipients of many boulders, which are heaved upon them by Rebels who are holding the higher ground.

The other Union attack force fares no better. Five heroic brigades of Union infantry gallantly charge two elite divisions of General Johnston. The respective commanders, General Patrick Cleburne and Benjamin Cheatham, have their troops hold a rigid stance while initiating a withering fire that mows the attackers down at will. Some of the assault troops reach the actual defenses, engaging in brutal hand-to-hand fighting, only to be thrown back. General James McPherson's force battles William Loring's corps, while General George H. Thomas's corps strikes against General William Hardee's corps. During the grueling duel between James B. McPherson and William Loring, other Confederates, Thomas M. Scott's brigade, a contingent of Winfield S. Featherston's division, takes the brunt of a heavy attack. At one point, many Union troops bolt ahead and drive directly into

the rifle pits of General William Quarles, but most are killed or captured.

At another point, the Union hammers against Samuel French's division and inflicts heavy casualties upon General Francis M. Cockrell's Missouri brigade. General Benjamin Cheatham's lines also come under severe attack, but at the conclusion of the struggle, the Confederates hold their lines, and to their immediate front lay an enormous amount of dead Union troops. The raging battle finally terminates at 1130. General Johnston repulses Sherman. By accident, Sherman seizes a road that places him closer to the Chattahoochee River, from where he continues his flanking movements. Both sides call this battlefield "Dead Angle."

The Union loses 3,000 killed, wounded, or missing; the Confederates lose about 800 (27th). These two armies have been clashing since the 9th. Other skirmishes include Pine Mountain, Pine Knob, Golgotha and Kulp's House. Union Brigadier General Charles Harker (West Point, 1858) is mortally wounded while leading a division against Johnston's entrenched defenses. Harker has already seen four horses shot from under him in other battles, but this time he does not escape injury. Union General Daniel McCook is mortally wounded as he reaches the Confederate defenses. General McCook dies on 17 July. As mentioned previously, Confederate Lieutenant General Leonidas Polk was killed on Pine Mountain while scouting Union positions on the 14th. Confederate Brigadier General Eugene Polk, nephew of Lt. General Leonidas Polk, is gravely wounded (his fourth wound of the war) and compelled to retire from active service. After the war, General Polk lives a relatively private life at his residence outside Columbia, South Carolina, until his death on 1 December 1892. Two of General Polk's sons serve in the Spanish American War (1898) and another son, who lives in Pennsylvania, becomes a U.S. Congress-

Left: **General Charles G. Harker.** *Right:* **General William T. Sherman** (*Harper's Pictoral History of the Civil War,* 1896).

General Duffie's cavalry, the rear guard, engages Confederates near the Hunter house, Charleston, West Virginia, during retreat of elements of the 1st Division, Army of West Virginia (Mottelay, *The Soldier in Our Civil War*, 1886).

man. Also, Confederate Major General Thomas Hindman sustains a serious wound that terminates his service in the field due to temporary problems with his eyesight. He moves to Mexico after the war, but during 1868, he returns to Arkansas to practice law. General Hindman is assassinated at his home in Helena on 28 September 1868, but the assassin is never apprehended.

Union General Americus V. Rice is wounded during this action. He is out of active service due to his wounds until June 1865. For the period June 9 to June 30, the Union lists casualties as 1,370 killed, 6,500 wounded and 800 missing. The Confederates sustain 1,100 killed and wounded and 3,500 missing.

In Virginia, Confederate General Jubal Early prepares to leave Virginia and launch raids on Union lines guarding Washington, D.C. His force reaches Shepherdstown, Maryland, on July 5, after his army crosses the Potomac. Union General David Hunter, withdrawing from Lynchburg, leaves the area unprotected and in essence opens a route to Washington for Early.

In Charlestown, West Virginia, the 1st Division, Army of West Virginia, engages Confederates at Charlestown. Cavalry under General Duffie acts as rear guard.

In Union general officer activity, General Henry Lawrence Eustis (West Point 1842) resigns his commission. His reason is unclear. One reason stated was poor health, but according to a telegram of 12 June from C.A. Dana, assistant secretary of war, to Edwin M. Stanton: "General Eustis is relieved … and ordered up to Washington. He is to be informed that if he does not resign, charges of neglect of duty and general inefficiency will be preferred against him. He is said to eat opium."

In Naval activity, the vessel *Carroll*, built during 1863 and 1864, had been acquired by the U.S. Navy while it was still under construction und commissioned as the USS *Proteus* in March. On this day the *Proteus*, while operating off Florida, encounters and seizes the blockade runner *Jupiter*. In other activity, the USS *Nipsic* encounters and captures a blockade run-

ner, the schooner *Julia*, as it attempts to enter Charleston Harbor. During most of its active service with the South Atlantic Blockading Squadron, the *Nipsic* is farther south, off Brazil and in the West Indies. It remains in active service until 1873. It is recommissioned in 1879 and remains in service until 1892, when it sails to Puget Sound Navy Yard, where it is utilized as a prison and as a receiving ship until sold during 1913. As a merchant vessel, in 1919 it is renamed the *Pinola*.

June 28 (Tuesday) In Virginia, General Robert E. Lee writes to Confederate Secretary of War Seddon: "Enemy strengthening positions at Petersburg…. His cavalry repulsed at Staunton Bridge on the 25th retired in direction of Christianville." In other activity, General James Wilson's raid continues to unfold as his force skirmishes with Confederates at Stoney Creek.

In Confederate general officer activity, Colonel Bradley Tyler Johnson, commanding officer of the 1st Confederate Maryland Infantry Regiment, is promoted to the rank of brigadier general.

June 29 (Wednesday) In Georgia, at Kennesaw Mountain, a truce is agreed upon to permit the Union to bury its deceased troops. The recent loss suffered at Kennesaw Mountain by General Sherman reaffirms his belief that flanking movements far outweigh the frontal attacks against entrenchments. He revises his strategy and soon, he will reinitiate flanking assaults to speed the demise of General Joseph E. Johnston's army. By July 3, Johnston's army will pull back from Kennesaw Mountain and move toward the Chattahoochee River.

In Virginia, Union Capt. Edward W. Whitaker of the 1st Connecticut Cavalry (Wilson's raid) leads a single troop through an entire Confederate division at Ream's Station. About one-half of the escort is lost, but the important dispatches get through to General George G. Meade. Confederate General Robert E. Lee, in

Left: General Wilson's cavalry forages in the Shenandoah Valley (Mottelay, *The Soldier in Our Civil War*, 1886). *Right:* A view of Kennesaw Mountain from Little Kennesaw (*Harper's Pictoral History of the Civil War*, 1896).

a telegram to Seddon, states: "Hampton reports he attacked Wilson's cavalry driving them beyond Sappony Church and at daylight this morning routed them when they hit Ream's Station…. They were confronted by a portion of Mahone's division in front and their left flank by General Fitzhugh Lee's cavalry." Union General August V. Kautz (West Point, 1852) participates at this battle. During the bitter skirmishing at Ream's Station, which has seen both sides jousting since the 22nd, much valor and impetuous recklessness has been exhibited. One example is the 2nd North Carolina Volunteers, who dismount and charge the Union riflemen's positions under the leadership of Colonel William Roberts (later brigadier general).

In Union general officer activity, Amos Beebe Eaton (West Point, 1826), a classmate of Confederate General Albert Sydney Johnson, is appointed commissary general of the U.S. Army with the rank of brigadier general. Eaton had been a veteran of the Seminole War (1837–1841) and of the Mexican War. At the outbreak of this war, he was on the West Coast (Department of the Pacific) as chief of commissariat, and after the outbreak of the war, he was transferred to New York, where he served as deputy commissary. He serves beyond the conclusion of the war into 1874, when he retires due to a mandatory retirement law (passed 17 July 1862) after serving more than forty-five years in the army.

June 30 (Thursday)   In Washington, D.C., it is recorded that the active duty strength of the U.S. Marine Corps stands at sixty-four officers and 3,075 enlisted men, totaling 3,139.

In Georgia, a Union force composed of elements of the 4th and 6th Kentucky Cavalry clashes with Confederates at LaFayette.

In the Indian Territory (Dakota), a force under Union General Alfred Sully rendezvous with a column of troops from Minnesota (dispatched by General John Pope) at the mouth of

Burdache Creek on the upper Missouri River. The combined force under Sully advances to intercept and engage the Sioux. By September 7, Fort Rice is established at the mouth of the Cannonball River, and from there the army will advance toward the Little Missouri River, about 200 miles distant.

In Naval activity, the USS *Curlew,* while on patrol on the Mississippi River, engages Confederate land forces at a point between Natchez and Vicksburg, Mississippi. The steamer USS *Hunchback* and the monitor *Saugus,* led by Commanders Nichols and Calhoun, clash with Confederate batteries at Four Mills Creek. In other activity, Rear Admiral Samuel Lee transfers his flag back to the *Malvern* from the *Agawam.* He moves back to Hampton Roads; however, the *Agawam* remains in position on the James River.

July   In North Dakota, at this time the U.S. Army is engaged against the Sioux (Sully Campaign). General Alfred Sully directs the construction of Fort Rice to support the effort. The fort is established by a contingent of the 30th Wisconsin Infantry commanded by Colonel Daniel J. Dills and it is named in honor of Brigadier General James C. Rice, a hero at Gettysburg who succumbed on 10 May 1864 at Spotsylvania after having his thigh crushed by a shell and not recovering from the operation. Fort Rice is modified and bolstered in 1868, but it remains at its original location outside present-day Fort Rice across from the mouth of Long Lake Creek on a dominant position along the right side of the Missouri River. The fort remains operational until November 1878; it is abandoned in conjunction with the establishment of Fort Yates. Meanwhile, its garrison maintains a watch over the region. It handles duties in line with protecting the pioneers moving west from Minnesota toward Montana, as well as maintaining a vigilant watch on the river traffic flowing along the Missouri. The final complement departs Fort Rice on 6 February 1879; the property comes under the jurisdiction of the Department of the Interior during 1884.

In Virginia, Union and Confederate forces continue to engage in the vicinity of Petersburg. These contests include skirmshes at Deep Bottom (21st, 27th and 28th), New Market (July 27–28) and Malvern Hill (1st). On the 30th, contingents of Union regiments detonate mines at Petersburg. The 2nd, 5th, 9th, 10th and 18th Corps participate. Union casualties are 898 killed, 4,000 wounded and 3,110 missing.

July 1 (Friday)   *In Union general officer activity,* General Irvin McDowell,

Major General Israel B. Richardson (Johnson, *Campfire and Battlefield: History of the Conflicts and Campaigns,* 1894).

who has been in near obscurity following the Second Battle of Bull Run (Manassas), is appointed commander of the Department of the Pacific.

In Confederate general officer activity, General John King Jackson at about this time is appointed commander of the District of Florida; he later participates with General Hardee in the defense of Savannah against General Sherman, and afterward, he is in the Carolinas during the final months of the conflict as commander of supply depots. After the war General Jackson resumes his law practice in Augusta, Georgia; however, he is struck by pneumonia while on a trip to Milledgeville. He dies on 27 February 1866.

At about this time, Confederate Brigadier General John King Jackson prepares to assume command of the District of Florida. General Jackson had begun his service in the Confederacy with the 5th Georgia Infantry at Pensacola during the early days of the war. He will also participate in Georgia and in the Carolinas prior to the close of hostilities. After the war, General Jackson resumes his career as an attorney; however, he succumbs the following year on 27 February.

In Naval activity, Union warships operating off Mobile force the blockade runner *Ivanhoe* to run ashore. In other activity, the USS *Agawam* and the *Mendota* bombard Confederate positions at Four Mile Creek, where the Confederates had turned five guns against the *Hunchback* and the monitor *Saugus* on the pre-

Entrenchments on Kennesaw Mountain (Johnson, *Campfire and Battlefield: History of the Conflicts and Campaigns,* 1894).

vious day. Lt. George Dewey assumes temporary command of the *Agawam* during early July, but by 13 August, Lt. Alexander Rhind is back in command. Lt. George Dewey later becomes the hero at Manila Bay as Admiral Dewey, when the Spanish armada is thrashed during the Spanish American War (1898). In other activity, The U.S. Navy receives the USS *General Sherman* (tinclad river gunboat), built during 1864 at Chattanooga, Tennessee, for the War Department. It is commissioned this month and assigned duty on the upper Tennessee River. In June 1865, the *General Sherman* is returned to the War Department.

July 2 (Saturday)   In Georgia, Confederate General Joseph E. Johnston, having concluded that General Sherman is in the process of turning his left to isolate Johnston's force from Atlanta, orders a withdrawal. The Confederates abandon their fortifications on Kennesaw Mountain. Essentially, the Confederates are backing up to their next round of preset defenses at the Chattahoochee River, which guards the route to Atlanta. Sherman directs General George H. Thomas to advance along the main road to Marietta, while the remainder of the force heads for Nickajack Creek. Sherman plans to simultaneously strike Johnston's rear and flanks.

In Arkansas, the U.S. 64th Colored Regiment skirmishes with Confederates at Pine Bluff. The Union sustains six killed. Confederate casualties are unavailable.

In Mississippi, the 3rd Iowa Cavalry skirmishes with Confederates at Saulsbury.

In South Carolina, units of the Department of the South clash with Confederates at Fort Johnson, James Island. The Union sustains 19 killed, 97 wounded and 135 missing. Confederate casualties are unavailable.

In Maryland, the Confederates commanded by Major General Jubal Early initiate raids in Maryland as his cavalry moves toward Washington, D.C.

In Georgia, the Union Army of the Cumberland arrives at Marietta; Sherman is traveling with it.

In Union general officer activity, Colonel Martin Davis Hardin (12th Pennsylvania Reserve Volunteer Regiment) is promoted to brigadier general. General Hardin had been wounded twice at Second Manassas (Bull Run) and more recently, during December, while checking his picket line near Cattlet's Station, Virginia. He is ambushed along the Orange and Alexandria Railroad. The Confederate guerrillas strike him in the left arm (it is afterward amputated). He is wounded yet again during the advance by General Grant against Richmond. After the war, having received the brevet of brigadier general (regular army), he becomes major of the 43rd Infantry Regiment during 1866. In 1870 at age 35, he retires with the rank of brigadier general.

In Naval activity, the USS *Kickapoo* (double turret ironclad river monitor) is commissioned at about this time (July). It is assigned to the West Gulf Blockading Squadron and serves on patrol duty in Louisiana in the vicinity of the mouth of the Red River until it is transferred to duty in Mobile Bay, where it participates in the operations to reduce Mobile during the closing months of the war.

July 2–5   In Georgia, skirmishing develops in the vicinity of Vining Station (Smyrna and Nickajack Creek), between Confederates under General Joseph Johnston and Yankees under General Sherman. Confederate General Alfred Jefferson Vaughan, Jr., who has had eight horses shot from under him without suffering any injuries, is finally struck with misfortune when a Union shell severs his leg. After the war, General Vaughan engages in farming in Mississippi until he relocates to Memphis during 1872. He succumbs in Indianapolis, Indiana, in October 1899. During the battle, the Union suffers 60 killed and 310 wounded. The Confederates sustain 100 killed or wounded. Again, the Union loses men, but more are available. The Confederates can ill afford to continue losing troops.

In Washington, D.C., Union Brigadier General Martin D. Hardin (West Point, 1859), who saw action at 2nd Manassas and Gettysburg, is among the Union commanders waiting at the outskirts of Washington for the approach of Jubal Early. The U.S. has kept the defenses around Washington sound since the embarrassment suffered during the early days of the war at Bull Run (1st Manassas). Colonel James M. Warner, of the 11th Vermont, is also at the gates of Washington. Following the efforts to repel Early's raids, Warner is appointed brevet brigadier general, and then the regiment moves to assist Sheridan from Cedar Creek to Petersburg.

July 3 (Sunday)   In Missouri, the 9th Missouri Militia Cavalry clashes with Confederates at Platte City.

In South Carolina, a contingent of soldiers and Marines (accompanied by two light howitzers) skirmish with a Confederate force at the Dawho River in White Point.

In Virginia, the 10th West Virginia Regiment and the 1st New York Cavalry skirmish with Confederates at Leetown. The Union sustains three killed. The Confederate casualties are unavailable. In addition, Confederates attack the outposts of the 153rd at North Mountain.

In West Virginia, the 153rd Ohio National Guard battles Confederates at Hammack's Mills, North River. The Union sustains three killed and seven wounded.

In Mississippi, the Union 1st Division, 17th Corps, departs Vicksburg, initiating an expedition toward Jackson that continues through the 9th. The Union sustains 150 wounded. The Confederates sustain 200 wounded.

In Georgia, the battle casualties of the Union forces of General William T. Sherman spanning the period 6/1 through this day are as follows. Army of the Cumberland: Howard's Fourth Corps, 602 killed or missing and 1,542 wounded, totaling 2,144 casualties; Palmer's Fourteenth Corps, 353 killed or missing and

Left: Old Glory atop the Confederate Military College, Marietta, Georgia (Mottelay, *The Soldier in Our Civil War*, 1886). *Right:* A Union signal station along the Chattahoochee River within sight of Atlanta (*Harper's Pictoral History of the Civil War*, 1896).

1,466 wounded, totaling 1,819 casualties; Hooker's Twentieth Corps, 322 killed or missing and 1,246 wounded, totaling 1,568 casualties. Army of the Tennessee: John A. Logan's Fifteenth Corps, 179 killed or missing and 687 wounded, totaling 866 casualties; Grenville Mellen Dodge's Sixteenth Corps, 52 killed or missing and 157 wounded, totaling 209 casualties; Francis P. Blair's Seventeenth Corps, 47 killed or missing and 212 wounded, totaling 259 casualties. Army of the Ohio: Schofield's Twenty-Third Corps, 105 killed or missing and 362 wounded, totaling 467 casualties. Cavalry: 130 killed or missing and 68 wounded, totaling 198 casualties.

For the Confederates, totals are as follows. William Joseph Hardee's Corps, 200 killed or missing and 1,433 wounded, totaling 1,633 casualties. John Bell Hood's Corps, 140 killed or missing and 1,121 wounded, totaling 1,261 casualties. William Wing Loring's Corps (Polk's Corps until his death), 128 killed or missing and 926 wounded, totaling 3,948 casualties.

In Naval activity, the USS *Governor Buckingham,* having completed its repairs, sails back to North Carolina to rejoin the South Atlantic Blockading Squadron.

July 4 (Monday)   In Arkansas, the 3rd Arkansas Cavalry, led by Captain David Hamilton, skirmishes with Confederates at Searcy.

In Mississippi, at Vicksburg, the 48th U.S. Colored Regiment (10th Louisiana) skirmishes with a contingent of Confederates. The Union sustains one killed and seven wounded. Confederate casualties are unavailable. Meanwhile, the 2nd Wisconsin Cavalry skirmishes with Confederates at Clinton. Also, the 52nd U.S. Colored Troops and the Mississippi Marine Brigade (General Alfred Ellett's brigade) engage Confederate forces at Coleman's Plantation, in the vicinity of Port Gibson, for two days. The Union suffers six killed and 18 wounded. Confederate casualties are unavailable.

In Georgia, General Sherman's army advances toward Confederate positions at Smyrna Church and seizes the Confederate line of rifle pits that had been erected along the main road and in the vicinity of the Nickajack and Rottenwood Creeks. Confederate General Joseph E. Johnston, unwilling to get turned by Sherman, directs his force to move back to the Chattahoochee River. However, Sherman still intends to trap Johnston. Sherman dispatches General John Schofield and some cavalry to pursue the Rebels, who are retiring. Schofield advances along the Sandtown Road and crosses the river at Powell's Ferry, while General Kenner Garrard drives to Roswell. In addition, other Union forces move to Campbellton.

In Maryland, the 1st Maryland Potomac Home Brigade clashes with Confederates at Point of Rocks.

In Missouri, the 9th Missouri Militia Cavalry clashes with Confederates in Clay County.

In Virginia, additional skirmishes develop between the Union and Confederate forces, between the 4th and 7th of July, at Bolivar Heights. Also, Union forces under General Franz Sigel, acting as a reserve division, skirmish with Confederates through the 7th at Bolivar and Maryland Heights. The Union sustains 20 killed and wounded. Confederate casualties are unavailable.

In Union general officer activity, Charles J. Paine, who resigned his commission as colonel during March of this year to take a position on General Benjamin F. Butler's staff, is promoted to brigadier general effective this date. General Paine participates at Drewry's Bluff and at New Market, Virginia, and subsequently he participates in the attacks against Fort Fisher, North Carolina, during December 1864 and January 1865.

Also, Brigadier General Stephen G. Burbridge receives the brevet of major general due in great part to his successful repulse of Confederate General John H. Morgan's invasion of Kentucky. General Burbridge had succeeded General Boyle as commander of the Department of Kentucky in early 1864. General Burbridge is relieved of command during January 1865. Also, Brigadier General Alvin Hovey is breveted major general. He had commanded a division in the XXIII Corps until the previous June, when the corps was disbanded. He retains the post until 1865, when he is appointed as minister to Peru (1865–1870); afterward he is elected to Congress (1886). Later he becomes governor of Indiana. General Hovey is a distant cousin of Union general Charles Edward Hovey.

July 5 (Tuesday)   In Tennessee, Union troops commanded by General Andrew Jackson Smith (West Point, 1838) depart La Grange en route to Tupelo, Mississippi. The column returns on 18 July. Smith had previously been ordered to organize a troop to destroy General Nathan B. Forrest. General A.J. Smith's forces, combined with General Joseph Mower's command, amount to approximately 24,000 men, and their column extends a distance of approximately 15 miles.

In Maryland, the Union 1st Maryland Cavalry, Potomac Home Brigade, sustains two killed and six wounded while skirmishing with Confederates at Hagerstown. Confederate casualties are unavailable. The Confederates occupy Hagerstown.

In Union general officer activity, Major General John J. Peck, on duty in North Carolina, is appointed commander of the Canadian frontier (Department of the East). Peck resigns his commission on 24 August 1865. Brigadier General Montgomery C. Meigs, quartermaster general, is breveted major general, U.S. Army. General Meigs remains in the service beyond the close of hostilities until he retires during 1882. Also, Union General Andrew Jackson Smith departs La Grange, Tennessee, en route to Mississippi. His force is composed of three divisions of the 16th Corps, one brigade of U.S. colored troops and General Benjamin Grierson's cavalry. During the mission, which lasts through the 18th, the Union sustains 85 killed and 567 wounded. The Confederates suffer 110 killed and 600 wounded.

In South Carolina, U.S. Major General John G. Foster's troops (Department of the South) engage the Confederates at John's Island through the 7th. The Union sustains 16 killed and 82 wounded; the Confederates sustain 20 killed and 80 wounded.

In Naval activity, a Union landing party boards the blockade runner *Ivanhoe,* which was intentionally run aground on 1 July in the vicinity of Mobile. The contingent sets the stranded vessel afire to prevent further use by the Confederates.

July 6 (Wednesday)   In Missouri, the Union 2nd Colorado Cavalry skirmishes with Confederates at Little Blue. The Union sustains eight killed and one wounded.

In Virginia, the 2nd Massachusetts Cavalry Regiment skirmishes with Confederates at Mount Zion Church.

In Maryland, the 8th Illinois Cavalry, bolstered by Alexander's Baltimore Artillery Battery, clashes with Confederates at Hagar's Mountain and Middletown.

In Georgia, the Army of the Tennessee, under William T. Sherman, in addition to the Army of the Ohio and the Army of the Cumberland (also under his command), engages the Confederates through July 10 at the Chattahoochee River. The Union has 80 killed, 450 wounded and 200 missing. Confederate casualties are not available.

In Union general officer activity, General Samuel Rice dies of injuries suffered on 30 April

Confederates pillage at Hagerstown, Maryland (*Harper's Pictorial History of the Civil War,* 1896).

1864 at Jenkins Ferry. His wound had been in the ankle, but surgery brings complications which kill him.

In Confederate general officer activity, Brigadier General Edward C. Walthall is promoted to the rank of major general, effective this date. Walthall had commanded a brigade in Tennessee, including the battles at Chickamauga and Chattanooga during the previous autumn. At Chattanooga, Walthall sustained a minor wound. Subsequent to his promotion, he continues to serve in Georgia as part of General John B. Hood's force.

July 7 (Thursday) **In Georgia,** the Union forces of Sherman are heavily involved in the Atlanta campaign. General Oliver O. Howard dispatches a reconnaissance team to probe the Rebel positions. The Rebels manage to capture Union Colonel (later brigadier general) Francis T. Sherman on Howard's staff (IV Corps). Sherman is exchanged during October and afterward assigned to General Sheridan's staff in Virginia (Shenandoah Valley) and designated inspector general.

In Maryland, the 8th Illinois Cavalry, Potomac Home Brigade and Alexander's Baltimore Battery engage Confederates at Solomon's Gap and Frederick City. The Union sustains five killed and 20 wounded.

In Mississippi, at Clinton, the 11th Illinois and 2nd Wisconsin Cavalry Regiments, supported by a battery of the 2nd Illinois Artillery, engage a Confederate force. Another Union force composed of about 2,000 troops under General Elias S. Dennis clashes with Confederates on Canton Road. In addition, the 2nd Iowa Cavalry skirmishes with Confederates at Ripley.

In Tennessee, Union General Andrew Jackson Smith, commanding a force of about 12,000 troops, moves from the vicinity of Memphis to attack General Forrest, expected to be at Tupelo, Mississippi.

In Confederate general officer activity, General Alexander P. Stewart assumes command of the late General Lucius E. Polk's corps. In addition, Colonel John Carpenter Carter (38th Tennessee) is appointed brigadier general, effective this day. Carter initially joined the Confederacy as a captain of the regiment and afterward participated at Shiloh and Perryville, followed by the regiment's participation at Murfreesboro and Chickamauga. Brigadier General Henry D. Clayton is promoted to major general effective this day. Clayton will assume command of Lt. General Alexander Stewart's division upon the latter's succession to Polk's corps. General James T. Holtzclaw will receive command of Clayton's brigade and lead it during the Kentucky Campaign of General John Bell Hood.

In Naval activity, the U.S. Navy acquires the vessel *Pontiac* (wooden, double-ended, side-wheel gunboat) when it arrives at the Philadelphia Navy Yard. It is commissioned on the same day and assigned to the South Atlantic Blockading Squadron. Lt. Commander John H. Russell receives command.

July 8 (Friday) The USS *Sonoma,* while on patrol duty as part of the South Atlantic Blockading Squadron, intercepts the blockade runner *Ida* after it leaves Sapelo Sound, Georgia.

July 9 (Saturday) **In Georgia,** Union General Lovell H. Rousseau (Sherman's command) departs Decatur to begin destroying Confederate rails between Georgia and Alabama. His force, composed of the 5th Iowa, 8th Ohio, 2nd Kentucky and the 4th Tennessee Cavalry, wrecks the railroad at Opelika and along a 20 mile route before changing direction and heading north, where they will rejoin Sherman on the 22nd at Marietta. General Rousseau reports to Sherman on the 23rd that losses for the entire operation are several killed and 30 wounded. The Confederates sustain 95 killed

and wounded. General Sherman continues his advance toward Atlanta. Union General Kenner Garrard's cavalry is at Roswell, where they cross the Chattahoochee River, while General John Schofield crosses at Soap's Creek and quickly captures the sparse Rebel contingent on guard. The Union fortifies its positions and places pontoon bridges across the river to enhance its advantage. Confederate General Joseph E. Johnston abandons his position along the Chattahoochee, after first burning all bridges, both pontoon and railroad, then he moves closer to his next line of defenses outside of Atlanta. This line stretches from the Chattahoochee River to Peach Tree Creek. Sherman now believes Johnston has made a big mistake by allowing the Union to control both banks of the river above Johnston.

In Maryland, Union forces under General Lew Wallace unsuccessfully repulse the Confederate advance on Washington at Monocacy (Monocacy Bridge). The Union suffers heavy casualties and General Jubal Early's troops continue toward Washington, D.C. A small, mostly green contingent of the 10th Vermont stalls Early's advance, but only temporarily. Confederate Brigadier General Clement A. Evans is wounded. Colonel William H. Seward, Jr., sustains a wound to the arm; however, he is also injured when his horse falls, and he sustains a broken leg. General John B. Gordon's division, to which Evans is attached, had moved from Spotsylvania to join with the survivors of General Edward Johnson's division, most of which had been captured at Spotsylvania. Evans had been promoted to brigadier general in May. In other activity, a contingent of Confederate cavalry raids New Windsor.

In Naval activity, the USS *Gettysburg* on patrol duty off the coast of the Carolinas seizes a blockade runner, the *Little Ada.*

July 10 (Sunday) **In Arkansas,** a 20-man scout detachment the 10th Illinois Cavalry Vol-

Left: Confederate cavalry at New Windsor, Maryland. *Right:* The XVI Army Corps fords the Chattahoochee River in the vicinity of Roswell's Ferry (Mottelay, *The Soldier in Our Civil War,* 1886).

unteer Regiment skirmishes with Confederates at Little Rock. The Confederates sustain four killed and wounded and one captured.

In Georgia, Union forces under General Sherman continue to bolster their positions at both Roswell and Soap's Creek as part of the Atlanta campaign.

In Virginia, General Robert E. Lee writes to Jefferson Davis regarding Early's campaign on the Potomac: "I have the honour to send you a New York Herald of the 8th concerning some items of interest. You will see the people in the U.S. are mystified about our forces."

In Naval activity, the CSS *Florida* seizes the vessel *Electric Spark,* a mail carrier, while it is en route to New Orleans from New York. The vessel is seized about thirty miles from the Delaware Capes. The Confederates transfer the crew and passengers to a British vessel that is nearby. The *Electric Spark* is destroyed. Following the capture, the *Florida* continues its cruise and later seizes additional vessels, the *Harriet Stevens, Golconda, Margaret Y. Davis* and the *Mondamin,* prior to sailing to the island of Teneriffe, west of the archipelago between the islands of Grand Canary and Gomera. Afterward, the *Florida* sails back toward Brazil, arriving in early October 1864. In Sapelo Sound, Georgia, the USS *Lodona* intercepts a blockade runner, the sloop *Hope.* The *Lodona* remains on patrol in the region until 20 April 1865, when it heads north to Philadelphia. On 11 May 1865, it is decommissioned and sold at auction the following month.

July 11 (Monday)   In Washington, D.C., Confederate troops under General Jubal Early slip into the capital city; however, no fighting occurs. The Rebels withdraw. Early skirmishes with the Union at Fort Stevens the following day, then withdraws across the Potomac. Union reinforcements under Horatio G. Wright and the 19th Corps under William H. Emory arrive in the district.

In Virginia, General Robert E. Lee advises Confederate General Early in the Shenandoah Valley of Union General Hunter's moving from Charleston, West Virginia, with his command to meet Early. He also mentions, "I hope you get the northern papers, as they will keep you advised of their preparations to oppose you."

In Maryland, a contingent of U.S. Marines, commanded by 1st Lieutenant James Forney, and sailors, each based at the Naval Yard in Philadelphia, reopen the Washington-Baltimore Railroad at Havre de Grace, about thirty miles north of Baltimore.

In Alabama and Georgia, Union General Lovell H. Rousseau leads raids through the 22nd. The 8th Indiana, 5th Iowa, 9th Ohio, 2nd Kentucky and 4th Tennessee Cavalry Regiments, bolstered by Battery E, 1st Michigan Artillery, participate.

In Mississippi, a Union contingent composed of the 8th Wisconsin, 5th Minnesota and 11th Missouri Volunteers, augmented by the 2nd Iowa Cavalry, occupies Pontotoc.

July 12 (Tuesday)   In Washington, D.C., the Confederates under General Jubal Early press Fort Stevens with running skirmishes throughout the day. Early's force had previously penetrated Washington D.C., but without executing a genuine assault. He and his Confederates pull out after nightfall, having been repulsed by the combined forces of the 6th Corps, the 22nd Corps and U.S. Marines. Early's losses amount to some 500 killed or wounded and the Union defenders sustain 54 dead and 314 wounded. Union Colonel Joseph A. Haskin (West Point, 1839), in command of artillery, does a magnificent job repelling this assault.

In Arkansas, one company of the 3rd Arkansas Cavalry, led by Captain Gill, skirmishes with Confederates at Petit Jean, Arkansas River.

In Georgia, U.S. troops of the 19th Michigan Infantry skirmish with a Georgia Regiment at Peach Tree. Union Captain Baldwin captures two Confederate officers. Also on this day, General Robert E. Lee states in a letter to Jefferson Davis: "It is a bad time to release the commander of an army [Joseph Johnston] situated as that of Tennessee. We may lose Atlanta and the army too."

In Virginia, the 2nd Division, David Gregg's cav-

alry, skirmish with Confederates at Lee's Mills in the vicinity of Ream's Station. The Union sustains three killed and 13 wounded. The Confederates suffer 25 killed and wounded.

In Naval activity, the USS *Penobscot,* while on patrol near Galveston, Texas, intercepts and captures a blockade runner, the schooner *James Wilson.* Its cargo includes coffee, liquor and medicine.

July 13 (Wednesday)   In Georgia, General Sherman sends a report to General Henry Halleck: "Have three places at which to cross the Chattahoochie in our possession and only await the return of General (George) Stoneman from his trip down river to cross the army in force and move on Atlanta."

In Mississippi, Union General Andrew Jackson Smith, ordered to chase and intercept Nathan B. Forrest's troops, moves within striking distance of Tupelo. Forrest's Confederates assault a Union column, only to be thrown back. The column reaches Harrisonburg by evening.

In Virginia, a force of about 15,000 Union troops under General Horatio Wright chases Early's Raiders toward Leesburg.

July 14 (Thursday)   In Alabama, the 8th Indiana and the 5th Iowa Cavalry Regiments skirmish with Confederates under General James H. Clanton at Ten Islands, Coosa River (Jackson's Ford) as part of Rousseau's Raid.

In Arkansas, a contingent of the 4th Arkansas Cavalry engages Confederates at Farr's Mills. The Union sustains one killed and seven wounded. The Confederates sustain four killed and six wounded.

Left: **Confederates under General Jubal Early cross the Potomac River.** *Right:* **Rousseau's Raid into Alabama and Georgia** (*Harper's Pictoral History of the Civil War,* 1896).

In **Mississippi,** Union troops fortify their positions at Tupelo. General A.J. Smith's defenders, recently recalled from Louisiana, throw back numerous assaults by Forrest's Confederates, dealing them heavy losses and forcing them to withdraw. Skirmishes occur between the two forces on the 15th as the Union withdraws. Spoiled provisions and dwindling ammunition force the Union to leave both Northern and Southern wounded in pulling back to La Grange, Tennessee. Neither side achieves absolute victory, but the Confederates under Nathan B. Forrest suffer severe losses. General Andrew Jackson Smith's command makes it back to Tennessee to participate in the battle of Nashville against Confederate General John Bell Hood. Brigadier General Hylan B. Lyon's brigade, composed of four regiments of Kentucky Confederate cavalry, is attached to Nathan B. Forrest's force during this campaign.

In **Missouri,** the 14th Kansas Cavalry skirmishes for two days with Confederates at Ozark. The Union sustains two killed and one wounded. Confederate casualties are unavailable.

In Naval activity, the USS *Eutaw* bombards Confederate positions at Malvern Hill, Virginia. It duplicates the attack on the 17th. During the following July, it tows the monitor USS *Tecumseh* to Pensacola, Florida. In August it resumes patrol duty on the James River until the war terminates. The *Eutaw* is decommissioned on 8 May 1865 and sold on 15 October 1867.

July 15 (Friday)   In Alabama, the 8th Indiana and 5th Iowa Cavalry regiments engage Confederates at Stone's Ferry.

In **Mississippi,** the forces of General A.J. Smith and General Nathan B. Forrest again clash, as cavalry from the opposing sides hammer each other in the vicinity of Old Town Creek. The 1st and 3rd Cavalry Divisions, 16th Corps, and one brigade of colored troops under General Joseph Mower overwhelm the Confederate contingent. Following this skirmish, Forrest withdraws and Smith returns to Memphis to prepare for yet another operation to victimize the forces under Forrest. The 5th Minnesota Volunteer Regiment participates.

In Union general officer activity, Brigadier General William Sooy Smith, suffering from poor health, resigns his commission. General Smith engages in engineering and is credited with the construction of the world's first all-steel bridge at Glasgow, Missouri, over the Missouri River. He also becomes involved with the construction of the original tall buildings in Chicago beginning about 1890. General Smith dies at age 86 in March 1916. Brigadier General John B. Turchin—dubbed the "Russian Thunderbolt" due to his tenacity at Chickamauga while leading a brigade in J.J. Reynolds' division of the XIV Corps—is compelled to take sick leave. On 4 October, he resigns from the army due to poor health. General Turchin, during 1873, establishes a Polish settlement in Radon, Illinois; however, later he becomes mentally ill. He dies on 19 June 1901.

In Naval activity, Confederate batteries near Malvern Hill fire upon Union ships. During the night, the USS *Wilderness* moves down the James River to pick up casualties and carry them to a hospital at Norfolk.

July 16 (Saturday)   In Maryland and Virginia, the Confederate cavalry under General Jubal Early, having terminated the raids against the Washington defenses, moves back toward the Shenandoah Valley.

In **Georgia,** the Union maintains its strategy to envelop Atlanta. Meanwhile, the Confederate government is preparing to change commanders in Georgia, replacing Joseph E. Johnston with John B. Hood.

In **Mississippi,** the 72nd and 76th Illinois, the 53rd Colored and the 2nd Wisconsin Cavalry engage Confederates at Grand Gulf, Port Gibson. Casualties for the two-day skirmish are unavailable.

In **Tennessee,** Union General A.J. Smith's force continues to withdraw to La Grange. The Confederates have lost massive amounts of men and do not initiate any major assaults against the retreating Yankees. Smith, on the other hand, cannot deliver a decisive blow, but he manages to keep Sherman's rail lines safe for the time being. Sherman, in August, again orders A.J. Smith's force to chase Forrest. General Forrest's force will ride again in September, raiding Tennessee, but the Union negates his contribution. These later raids will not alter the Southern cause in any way.

July 17 (Sunday)   In Georgia, General Sherman's force is closing in on Atlanta from three directions, while Confederate General John Bell Hood's Army of Tennessee is preparing to attack the approaching Union Army. Sherman's army is now crossing the Chattahoochee River between Powers Ferry and Roswell.

In **Missouri,** the 2nd Colorado Cavalry engages Confederates at Fredericksburg.

In **Virginia,** a Union force (Army of West Virginia) and contingents of the 6th Corps, commanded by General George Crook, engage Confederates for two days at Snicker's Gap and Island Ford. The Union sustains 30 killed, 181 wounded and 100 missing. Confederate casualties are unavailable.

In Union general officer activity, General Daniel McCook, who had been promoted on the previous day, dies at the home of his brother George at Steubenville, Ohio, where he had been taken after being wounded at Kennesaw Mountain on 27 June. Also on this day, General James Clifford Veatch is granted sick leave. He is commander of the 4th Division, XVI Corps, Army of the Tennessee River. He returns to duty during September; however, General Howard orders him to remain at Memphis. He lingers there without a command until February 1865, when he is assigned to the Department of the Gulf. He commands a division of the XIII Corps during the operations against Mobile. He receives the brevet of major general to-

ward the close of hostilities for his performance at Mobile. Afterward, he commands a district in West Louisiana. He musters out of the army during August 1865 and later becomes adjutant general of Indiana 1869, followed by employment as a U.S. collector of internal revenue. He dies at Rockport, Indiana, on 22 December 1895.

In Confederate general officer activity, President Jefferson Davis replaces General Joseph E. Johnston with General John B. Hood as commander of the Army of Tennessee. Hood is promoted to full rank general effective the following day. General Johnston receives a telegram from President Davis informing him of the command change. This decision by President Davis is not well received by those in the Confederate Army or those at home, as Johnston is a highly respected leader. When word of the action reaches Sherman, he gives his hearty approval. At this point, Davis is totally unsatisfied with Johnston's lack of fighting spirit. General Johnston will be without command until General Robert E. Lee reinstates him with a battle command during February 1865 to help impede Sherman's northern advance through the Carolinas. General Sherman, aware that General John Schofield had been a classmate of Hood at West Point, inquires to the characteristics of the new commander who would oppose them. Schofield responds by telling Sherman that Hood is "bold to rashness." Schofield implies that the change could be interpreted as "fight." General Hood receives about 50,600 troops when he assumes command of the remaining forces of Johnston.

July 18 (Monday)   In Georgia, General William T. Sherman's force is advancing with General George H. Thomas toward Buckhead to form a line of battle facing Peach Tree Creek, with John Schofield along his left flank and James B. McPherson between Decatur and Stone Mountain. McPherson makes a sharp turn toward Atlanta and begins destroying Confederate rails as he advances. General Nathan Kimball participates in the action. Subsequently, he commands a division in the IV Corps. He also participates in the battles of Franklin and at Nashville. He remains in service and receives the brevet rank of major general during the closing months of the war. In other activity, Sherman is notified by a spy about the Confederate change of command at Atlanta. General John B. Hood, who had only been informed of his new position at 2300 on the 17th, prepares for a confrontation with Sherman and schedules it for the 20th. Meanwhile, Brigadier General William W. Mackall refuses to serve with General Hood and requests for the second time to be relieved. His request is granted and his service in the Confederacy is terminated. Subsequently, General Mackall returns to his farms in Fairfax County, Virginia. He succumbs at one of his farms, Langley, on 12 August 1891.

Also, the 9th Ohio and 4th Tennessee Cavalry (Rousseau's Raid) skirmishes with Confederates at Auburn. The 8th Indiana, 5th Iowa and 4th Tennessee Cavalry Regiments skirmish with Confederates along the Montgomery and West Point Railroad. The Union sustains about 200 killed wounded and missing. The Confederates sustain about 100 killed.

In Virginia, the Union cavalry of Alfred N. Duffie skirmishes with Confederates at Ashby's Gap. The Union sustains 200 killed and wounded. Confederate casualties are not unavailable.

July 19 (Tuesday)   In Georgia, General John B. Hood prepares to take action against the advancing Union forces. The Union force, moving confidently, detects a gap in their lines between General George H. Thomas and General John Schofield. Sherman orders two divisions of General Oliver O. Howard to fill that void. McPherson is moving to the Georgia Railroad between Stone Mountain and Decatur. Thomas, operating on the right, is crossing Peach Tree Creek. General Schofield is positioned between McPherson and Thomas. Sherman is aware that the Confederates, placed with Atlanta at their backs, will choose the time and place for the imminent battle.

In Virginia, the 21st New York Cavalry skirmish with Confederates at Ashby's Gap. Also, Union troops, including General William W. Averell's Cavalry, engage Confederates at Darksville and Winchester (Stephenson's Depot and Carter's Farm) through the next day. The Union suffers 27 dead and 175 wounded; Confederates have 300 wounded and 200 captured.

In Union general officer activity, Major General William Farrar Smith is relieved of command of the XVI Corps. Nonetheless, he receives the brevet of major general in the Regular Army at the close of hostilities. General Smith resigns from the volunteers during 1865. He does not resign his commission in the regulars as major of engineers until 1867. He later succumbs on 28 February 1903.

July 20 (Wednesday)   ATLANTA CAMPAIGN Confederates in Georgia under General John B. Hood launch a bold but unsuccessful assault against General Thomas' right, which had just begun to relax during the noon hour. The full brunt of the assault is felt by General Hooker's 20th Corps, General Richard Johnson's division of the Fourteenth Corps and General John Newton's Fourth Corps, soon after they cross Peach Tree Creek, which lies directly north of Atlanta. The Confederates, scheduled to attack at 1300, delay the jump-off and initiate the assault at 1600. Nevertheless, the Confederates startle the Union, which is not expecting a major assault. General A.P. Stewart's Corps pounces upon General Joseph Hooker's corps, Johnston's division (14th Corps) and Newton's Division (4th Corps), none of which are on alert. The battle rages with the Rebels penetrating the Union lines and compelling both sides to resort to close-quartered hand-to-hand combat. General George H. Thomas is positioned in the rear, which enables him to quickly deploy artillery that is able to achieve high success

against a large contingent of Rebels who are massing in the vicinity of Newton's left flank.

The Union by this time finally pushes the Rebels back. Union Generals John Newton (West Point, 1842) and Richard W. Johnson (West Point, 1849) suffer only light casualties because they are supported by defensive positions, but General Hooker's men engage the enemy in wide open spaces, which costs him about 1,500 casualties. The Confederates set the pace and now German Sherman is aware of what to expect next. He takes precautions to forestall any disasters for the Union. General Hood prepares for yet another attack and sets its commencement for the 22nd.

The Confederates leave approximately 400 dead on the field and Hooker estimates that the Confederates suffer about 4,000 wounded, although most return to their own lines. After the close of hostilities, the Union closes ranks and advances to completed entrenchments and stands in a position to peer into the houses of Atlanta. However, all is not to be easy for the Yankees. Confederate Colonel Jeremy F. Gilmer has provided strengthened fortifications outside Atlanta. Union General Walter Q. Gresham is seriously wounded when a shell shatters his knee, ending his military career. Confederate Brigadier General Clement H. Stevens is mortally wounded. He dies on 25 August from his wounds.

In Virginia, Union troops, including the 14th West Virginia Infantry, clashes with Confederates at Carter's Farm. Private John Shanes advances in front of the attacking troops to capture a Confederate cannon; Shanes receives the Medal of Honor for his gallantry under fire. Confederate General Lawrence "Sul" Ross' Texas Brigade participates in this action. The beleaguered Texans have been in the thick of the fighting since the clash at New Hope Church during the latter part of the previous May. The boldness of the 3rd, 6th, 9th and 27th Texas Regiments has cost them extremely high casualties.

In Confederate general officer activity, Colonel Thomas Benton Smith, 20th Tennessee Infantry Regiment, is promoted to brigadier general. General Smith's actions include those at Mill Springs, Shiloh, Murfreesboro, Baton Rouge and the Atlanta Campaign. Subsequent to his promotion, he participates at the Battle of Nashville.

July 21 (Thursday)   In Georgia, the Confederates at Atlanta under General John B. Hood take precautions for the imminent assault expected to be commenced by Gen-

eral Sherman, while tending their wounded from the skirmish at Peach Tree Creek on the day before. Union surgeons are working diligently on the wounded at their positions outside Atlanta. Union Colonel Tom Reynolds, wounded badly on the 20th, while listening to the doctors discussing whether to amputate his leg, unhesitatingly quips, "I beg you to spare my leg as it is very valuable, being an imported leg." The surgeons, aware that Reynolds is of Irish birth, take his well-timed humor and save his leg, trusting his vitality. Also, Colonel Henry A. Barnum is wounded for a third time. Nevertheless, Colonel Barnum is able to participate in Sherman's "March to the Sea."

In Kentucky, a contingent of Union troops skirmishes with Confederates at Henderson. Specific units and casualties are unreported.

In Virginia, the 1st Division, 10th Corps, Army of the James, engages Confederates at Deep Bottom.

July 22 (Friday)   THE BATTLE OF ATLANTA The Union Army, positioned outside Atlanta, Georgia, under General William T. Sherman, is attacked by Confederates under General John B. Hood. General James McPherson's troops, having secured a position at Leggett's Hill on the night of the 21st, from their positions are able to spot an active Confederate foundry, which is to be a priority after taking Atlanta. General Mortimer Leggett's division had secured and defended the hill dubbed Leggett's Hill. James B. McPherson's Fifteenth Corps is deployed along the Augusta Railroad, supported by General Francis P. Blair's Seventeenth Corps to the left. General John Schofield is on the right, followed by the corps of Generals Joseph Hooker, Oliver O. Howard and John McCauley Palmer, deployed on the far right, each with strong reserves in addition to their trains, which are kept out of harm's way.

The Army of the Tennessee for the most part

General Henry Barnum's headquarters in Atlanta (Mottelay, *The Soldier in Our Civil War*, 1886).

Left: The Battle of Atlanta on July 22. *Right:* General James McPherson's death during the fight for Atlanta (Johnson, *Campfire and Battlefield: History of the Conflicts and Campaigns*, 1894).

is solely involved with repulsing the Confederates under Hood, by direction of General Sherman. The battle rages along a seven-mile front, stretching from Howard's House to the positions of Union General Giles A. Smith, who is deployed about one mile on the other side of the Augusta Railroad. General James B. McPherson is at the Howard House discussing battle plans with Sherman, and during the discussion, shots are heard around Decatur, which causes alarm. McPherson jumps to his horse and informs Sherman he will send a dispatch back with information, but as he gallops to his command, a volley of Confederate fire slays him. McPherson's horse returns from the woods riderless and full of blood.

The Confederate offensive, with participation by Generals Alexander P. Stewart (West Point, 1842), William J. Hardee, G.W. Smith and Joseph Wheeler, is met with rigid resistance at Legget's Hill, but another segment of the assault makes progress at the railroad, where it overruns Union positions and captures the guns, quickly turning them against the Union. The Confederates also break the line between General Charles Woods and John Schofield near

the Howard House and the railroad. General Schofield rushes 20 guns to a higher position and pours fire right over the heads of Woods' troops, devastating the Confederates and allowing Wood's force to advance. The Union finally regains the ground lost and the Rebels are driven back into Atlanta itself after a long and gruesome day. Simultaneously, the division that the Confederates had pushed back at the railroad is rejuvenated by the personal leadership of General John Logan, who leads his men to a successful recapture of this previously lost terrain. The Union recaptures most of the guns that had earlier been seized by the Rebels. However, two of Captain de Gress' favorite six-pounders are dragged into Atlanta with the retreating troops. Captain de Gress has had all his horses shot by the Confederates and only a few of his men remain operable once the guns are back in Union hands. In addition, Colonel Charles C. Walcutt had been ordered to retreat with is 46th Ohio Regiment; however, he disregards the order and continues to hold the ground. Walcutt's refusal to retire had preserved General Blair's XVII Corps from probable destruction.

The Confederate assault is totally repulsed by day's end (1600) and the siege of Atlanta begins, with both time and superior forces on the side of General Sherman. Union General James B. McPherson is killed during his attempt to rejoin his command, but an important document taken by Confederates who frisk his body is recovered later in the day when the Union searches Confederate prisoners. McPherson, a close friend of General Sherman, is laid on a door ripped from its hinges for use as a bier. The stout-hearted Sherman is overcome with grief when he sees McPherson's corpse. General McPherson had plans to get married and had requested leave to travel to Baltimore for his wedding; however, Sherman, convinced McPherson was indispensable, did not grant him leave. General John A. Logan assumes temporary command of McPherson's Army of the Tennessee, but General Sherman, giving preference to West Point officers, gives the command of McPherson's XV Corps to General O.O. Howard. The change of command does not sit well with General Logan or General Hooker.

General Hooker requests that he be relieved of command and Sherman has him relieved. It

Left: Fuller's division rallies after being forced back by Rebels in the Battle of Atlanta (Johnson, *Campfire and Battlefield: History of the Conflicts and Campaigns*, 1894). *Right:* A battered house near Atlanta (Mottelay, *The Soldier in Our Civil War*, 1886).

terminates Hooker's field command. Nevertheless, he remains in the army beyond the close of hostilities and retires during 1868 with the rank of major general. General David S. Stanley replaces General Oliver O. Howard as commander of the 4th Corps. Confederate General William Henry Talbot Walker is also killed in this battle, while attacking in support of General William Hardee.

Confederate General Samuel Benton is mortally wounded (twice wounded, a shell fragment to the heart and a foot wound) and dies within the week. Benton had only received command of a brigade (General Edward C. Walthall's brigade) on or about 6 July. Benton's commission as brigadier general arrives subsequent to his death and is effective 26 July 1864. Some reports indicate that General Benton succumbs on July 28 while participating in an attack at Ezra's Church; however, other records clearly indicate that Benton's brigade is under the command of General William Felix Brantley on that date. Brantley is appointed brigadier general effective 26 July 1864. General Brantley will participate at various battles in Tennessee, and he serves until the close of hostilities under General Joseph E. Johnston in North Carolina.

Meanwhile, the Union holds the field and General John Logan states to Sherman in his report that the Union loss is 3,521 total casualties; Confederates, at least 10,000 casualties. He adds, "We captured 18 stands of colors and 5,000 stands of arms. The attack was made against our lines seven times and was seven times repulsed." Union Chaplain Milton L. Haney, 55th Illinois Infantry, receives the Medal of Honor for his gallantry during this action. Private Charles F. Sancrainte singlehandedly captures the colors of the 5th Texas Regiment and he, too, becomes a recipient of the Medal of Honor. Union Brigadier General Manning Ferguson Force successfully assaults an enemy position and holds out, although wounded,

until help arrives. General Force's wound to his face appears mortal but he survives. Nonetheless, his face remains disfigured for the remainder of his life. He too becomes a recipient of the Medal of Honor; it is not presented to him until 1892. Meanwhile, he returns to service the following October and participates in Sherman's "March to the Sea" and the Carolina campaign. He is breveted major general.

General John M. Palmer, who participates in this action, requests to be relieved of command the following month because he is disgruntled about rank. General Sherman does relieve him. Later, Palmer receives command of the Department of Kentucky. After the war, General Palmer is elected governor of Illinois (1868). In addition, Brigadier General Thomas Sweeny participates at this action in command of a division of the XIV Corps. Subsequently, he is arrested on charges pressed by General Grenville M. Dodge. He is acquitted after a prolonged court-martial but does not receive a new command. In December 1865, General Sweeny is dismissed from the Regular Army due to unauthorized leave, but he bounces back and is restored to duty on 8 November 1866. During the same period, he had become involved in a movement (Fenian movement) to invade Canada to gain the freedom of Ireland from England. For this involvement, Sweeny is placed under arrest by the U.S. government, but he is afterward released. Despite his actions, he is placed on the army's retirement list with the rank of brigadier general on 11 May 1870.

In Georgia, the 2nd Brigade, 4th Division, 16th Corps, engages Confederates at Decatur during the fighting in and around Atlanta. Confederate General William H.T. Walker is killed during the battle. In addition, Colonel (later brigadier general) John Sprague becomes a recipient of the Medal of Honor for his heroism above and beyond the call of duty in saving the Union trains at Decatur; however, the medal is not presented until years later.

In Louisiana, the 6th U.S. Colored Troops Heavy Artillery (2nd Mississippi) skirmishes with Confederates at Vidalia. In other activity, in accordance with orders from General Richard S. Canby, General Franklin Stillman Nickerson is relieved of command (Louisiana, Department of the Gulf). Nickerson is directed to repair to the adjutant general in Washington, D.C. for assignment; however, General Nickerson's name vanishes from the *Official Records,* which indicates either that no orders arrived prior to the end of the war or that he was engaged in administrative duty in the capital.

July 23   In *Union general officer activity,* Brigadier General Peter Joseph Osterhaus is promoted to major general. General Osterhaus had been promoted over the objections of General William T. Sherman. Nonetheless, Osterhaus serves with Sheridan during the campaign in Georgia. During the campaign in the Carolinas, General Osterhaus temporarily commands General Logan's XV Corps. After the war he moves back and forth between Europe and the

United States, while serving in France as consul. Later he becomes consul in Germany. During 1905, pursuant to an Act of Congress on 27 March, his name is placed on the U.S. Army list of retired officers as a brigadier general.

In Naval activity, the USS *Tahoma,* attached to the East Gulf Blockading Squadron and in New York for repairs, is decommissioned. It is recommissioned subsequent to completing its repairs on 13 April 1865, following the surrender of General Robert E. Lee to General Ulysses S. Grant at Appomattox. It returns to service until it is again decommissioned at Boston on 27 July 1865. It is commissioned once again in autumn and attached to the Gulf Squadron, where it serves on patrol until August 1867 when it is decommissioned for the final time on the 27th. It is sold in October.

July 23–24   Battle of Kernstown (Second) Contingents of the Army of West Virginia under General George Crook skirmish with Confederates led by General Early at Kernstown (23rd) and Winchester (24th), Virginia, igniting heavy fighting. At Kernstown, acting on information that General Jubal Early had terminated his raids against Washington and moved to Strasburg, General Grant shuffles some of his forces. General Wright's corps is ordered back to the area around the capital and General William Emory's division receives similar orders. The intent of the orders is to position both forces from where they can be shifted back to City Point. However, once General Early learns of Wright's return to Washington, he decides to attack Crook's forces at Kernstown, and he sets the date for the 24th. Crook's force includes the commands of Generals Hunter and Franz Sigel as well as William Averell's cavalry. Meanwhile, General Crook remains unaware on the night of the 23rd–24th that an attack is imminent.

On the morning of the 24th, the Confederates launch the attack. General Early sends Stephen Ramseur's command toward Bartonsville to evade the right flank of Crook, while other forces advance along the Valley Pike. In the meantime, Ransom's cavalry moves in two columns. One advances along the road leading from Front Royal to Winchester, while the other moves on the left on a route west of Winchester, with both under orders to converge at Winchester. The cavalry's mission is to sever the Union's escape route. General Ramseur's health is beginning to fail. He is compelled to retire the following autumn.

The force of Union Colonel James A. Mulligan is encamped in the heights at this time and he has two artillery pieces to support the Union cavalry that is being thrown back toward Kernstown. Mulligan also commits his force in support of the cavalry and his contingent is bolstered by more than 1,000 troops under Colonel Rutherford B. Hayes. As the Union advances, a Confederate force (Echols' division) commanded by Brigadier General Wharton, under the overall command of General John C. Breckinridge, suddenly emerges from the rear of a hill and advances toward Hayes' command from the

General Joseph Wheeler (Mottelay, *The Soldier in Our Civil War,* 1886).

east, enabling the Rebels to plow into Hayes' left flank with a powerful thrust that quickly causes problems for the Union. Discipline is rapidly lost as the ranks become disoriented, and shortly thereafter the entire line collapses.

In a desperate effort, Hayes moves to rally his force in the vicinity of Pritchard Hill, while the forces of Colonel Mulligan attempt to halt the Rebel surge from their positions near the base of the hill. During the donnybrook, a contingent of Hayes' command, the 13th West Virginia Infantry Regiment, gets snagged in a nearby orchard by a superior force. While the West Virginians raise tenacious resistance, the Confederates continue to pour fire upon them, making their positions nearly untenable, but the unit is able to extricate itself and join the main body.

In the meantime, the remainder of the Confederate force arrives to ensure a rout. The Union retreats through Winchester with the Confederates in pursuit, but the Confederate cavalry is not involved with the chase, pursuant to orders of General Early. Consequently, the Union is able to preserve the majority of its artillery and its wagons. Nevertheless, the Confederates seize between 200 and 300 prisoners and among them is Colonel Mulligan, who is mortally wounded. No pursuit occurs on the 25th due to exhaustion of the infantry; however, the cavalry does resume the chase. The Union makes it across the Potomac into Maryland Heights and at Harpers Ferry. The Union sustains 1,200 killed and wounded. The Confederates sustain 600 killed and wounded.

July 24 (Sunday) In Georgia, General William T. Sherman telegraphs General Henry Halleck and recommends that General Oliver Howard be placed in command of the Army of the Tennessee to replace General James McPherson, who was killed on the 22nd. General David S. Stanley is appointed to replace General Howard as commander of the IV Corps. General Howard had been named commander of the Army of the Cumberland. Both appointments are ratified by the president. General John Logan retains command of his Fifteenth Corps.

In Mississippi, the 6th Michigan Artillery skirmishes with Confederates at Carrolton Landing, Carolina Bend.

In Virginia, General Jubal Early's force, following the victory on the 24th at Kernstown (see also, **July 23–24 BATTLE OF KERNSTOWN [SECOND]**), orders the infantry to rest. Nevertheless, Rebel cavalry does resume the chase this day and the next. The Union is had been pushed beyond Winchester and is making its way into Maryland and Harpers Ferry, West Virginia. General George Crook (West Point, 1852) continues his retreat, but the Union is able to repulse the pursuing units in the vicinity of the Potomac River near Williamsport, Maryland.

July 25 (Monday) In Arkansas, Union troops, including the 3rd Missouri Cavalry, skirmish with Confederates commanded by Brigadier General George M. Holt (Arkansas Militia) at Benton. General Holt is chased and killed during this action by Union Pvt. George W. Lucas, Company C, 3rd Cavalry. Lucas becomes a recipient of the Medal of the Honor for his actions.

In Alabama, the 18th Michigan and 32nd Wisconsin Volunteers skirmish with Confederates at Courtland.

In Naval activity, the USS *Undine,* while operating on the Tennessee River off Clifton, Tennessee, strikes an obstacle and sinks, but only partially. The crew is able to get the guns ashore and deployed from where they can defend against a Confederate assault. Later, on 1 August, the crew, with help from the USS *Little Champion,* succeeds in refloating the *Undine.*

July 26 (Tuesday) In Arkansas, the 15th Illinois Cavalry and the 56th (3rd Arkansas) and 60th (1st Iowa) U.S. Colored Troops, bolstered by Company E, 2nd U.S. Colored Artillery, skirmish with Confederates at Wallace's Ferry. The Union sustains 16 killed and 32 wounded. Confederate suffers 150 killed and wounded. Also, the 11th Missouri Cavalry skirmishes with Confederates at Des Arc.

In Florida, the 75th Ohio Mounted Infantry clashes with Confederates at St. Mary's Trestle.

In Georgia, Union General George Stoneman's force, bolstered by General Kenner Garrard's cavalry division (Army of the Cumberland), leads an expedition toward Macon. The campaign succeeds in capturing more than 2,000 Confederates by the 31st. Also, Union General Edward McCook leads his force — which includes the 1st Wisconsin, 5th and 8th Iowa, 2nd and 8th Indiana, 1st and 4th Tennessee and the 4th Kentucky Cavalry Regiments — to Lovejoy Station through the 31st.

In Confederate general officer activity, Colonels Robert Houston Anderson and Felix H. Robertson (son of Confederate Brigadier General Jerome P. Robertson) are appointed brigadier generals. Anderson will command a cavalry brigade in Wheeler's cavalry corps and Robertson, also under Wheeler, will command the artillery. General Anderson (West Point, 1857) became a lieutenant of artillery during September 1861. Later, in January 1863, he became colonel of the 5th Georgia Cavalry. Also, Colonel George Doherty Johnston, 25th Alabama Regiment, is promoted to brigadier general. He had initially entered Confederate service as a 2nd lieutenant in the 4th Alabama. Jacob H. Sharp, 44th Mississippi Regiment, is also promoted to brigadier general. Sharp will succeed General William F. Tucker, who had sustained severe wounds at Resaca on May 14. In addition, Colonel Samuel Benton, mortally wounded on the 22nd of July, is promoted to brigadier general to rank from this day, but he succumbs on the 28th, before he receives his commission. Colonel William Felix Brantley is appointed brigadier general. He will assume command of General Samuel Benton's brigade, the latter having been mortally wounded on July 22 at Atlanta, Georgia.

July 27 (Wednesday) In Georgia, outside of Atlanta, Sherman begins to redeploy his forces. General Oliver O. Howard's 4th Corps is to move to strike the Macon Railroad, with part of his force, Stoneman's Cavalry, on the move to hit the rails farther down at Jonesboro, but this initial plan is modified, incorporating Stoneman's Cavalry into the Macon raid.

In Virginia, a Union force — including the 1st Cavalry Division, Army of the James, and the 2nd Corps and 1st and 2nd Cavalry Divisions, Army of the Potomac — is in a two-day engagement with Confederates, including Brigadier General Samuel McGowan's South Carolina Brigade (Ambrose P. Hill's corps), at Deep Bottom, New Market and Malvern Hill.

In Arkansas, a contingent of the 6th Kansas Cavalry, composed of 200 troops led by Captain David Mefford, comes under attack when a Confederate force commanded by General Richard M. Gano, estimated at about 1,500 troops, assaults the Union outpost at Mazzard Prairie, Fort Smith. The Union suffers 12 killed, 17 wounded and 152 captured. The Confederates sustain 12 killed and 20 wounded.

In Florida, the 35th U.S. Colored Troops (1st North Carolina) clash with Confederates at Whiteside, Black Creek.

In Union general officer activity, Brigadier General James Bowen (appointed on October 11, 1862) resigns his commission. General Bowen, born in the early 1800s, saw only administrative service because of his age, but he is breveted major general for "meritorious service" during March 1865, when such Union promotions become prevalent.

In Naval activity, the USS *Wilderness,* while supporting a large contingent of troops crossing two pontoon bridges that span the James River, is motionless in the river at a point between the two bridges, but it is within sight of two other gunboats, the *Agawam* and *Mendota,* both of which are exchanging fire with Confederate positions at Four Mile Creek.

July 28 (Thursday) BATTLE OF EZRA'S CHURCH Confederate General John B. Hood detects the movement of contingents of General Sherman's Army of the Tennessee as they move toward the Macon Railroad in Atlanta, Georgia. Hood initiates another attack against Sherman's lines at Atlanta and nearby at Ezra's Church. At Ezra Church some of the heavy fighting occurs at Dead Brook. The Union right flank, guarded by General John Logan's Fifteenth Corps, holds firm against six separate attacks between 1130 and 1500, with dreadful casualties sustained by the Rebels during each attack. The Union displays extraordinary courage, and if the line had surrendered a few yards, they would have been driven from their positions. During the evening, several more attacks are launched, again with tremendous losses being inflicted on the Rebels. Union Brigadier Generals Charles R. Woods (West Point, 1852), William Harrow and Morgan L. Smith receive credit for holding off incessant Confederate assaults. The timely release of reinforcements dispatched from the commands of Major Generals Francis P. Blair and Grenville Dodge also greatly aid the Union cause against the Confederates under General Hood. Union Major General John Logan states in his report to General Sherman: "The division of General Harrow captured five battle flags. There were between 1,500 and 2,000 muskets left on the field. There were 106 prisoners exclusive of 73 wounded and sent to our [Union] hospitals. 565 rebels have and about 200 are supposed to be unburied. A large amount of enemy wounded has been carried off during the night as the enemy did not withdraw until nearly daylight. The enemy loss could not have been less than six or seven thousand men." General Logan, in his report, puts Union losses at 50 killed, 449 wounded and 73 missing.

Confederate Brigadier General George D. Johnston is seriously wounded. His leg injury causes him to remain on crutches during General John B. Hood's invasion of Tennessee. There is no documentation on General Johnston being paroled at the end of the conflict. Nonetheless, after the war, he becomes commandant of cadets at the University of Tennessee. Afterward, he becomes superintendent of South Carolina Military Academy and serves in the Alabama Senate. He dies in Tuscaloosa on 8 December 1910. Confederate General Alpheus Baker is also wounded. Union General Oliver O. Howard, commander of Army of the Tennessee, adds to his report: "I never saw better conduct in battle. General John Logan [Fifteenth Corps], though ill and much worn out, was indefatigable and the success of the day is as much attributable to him as to any one man."

In Arkansas, the 11th Missouri Cavalry skirmishes with Confederates at West Point.

In Georgia, Union General Edward McCook's cavalry strikes Confederates at Campbellton. Meanwhile, General Kenner Garrard's cavalry (Stoneman's Raid) clashes with Confederates at Flatshoals.

Ezra's Church (*Harper's Pictoral History of the Civil War,* **1896**).

In Louisiana, a contingent of the 19th Corps clashes with Confederates at Atchafalaya River.

In the Indian Territory (Dakota Territory), a Union force, composed of the 8th Minnesota Mounted Infantry, 6th and 7th Iowa and Dakota and Breckett's cavalry, led by General Alfred Sully, engages Indians at Tah-Kah-o-Kuty Mountain (Killdeer Mountain). Initially, attempts are made to speak with the various chiefs; however, their combined strength, which ranges between 5,000 and 6,000 braves, provides the Indians with great confidence. Subsequent to the failed talks, Sully's force of about 2,000 troops, bolstered by formidable artillery, launches an attack against the well-entrenched Indians who dominate the thick woods and ravines as well as the heights. Fierce fighting erupts, but the artillery weighs in heavily and disrupts the fighting spirit of the braves. The Sioux disengage and take flight with the army in pursuit. The fast-running battle continues into the following day, but the Sioux are unable to match the fire power of the army. Casualty figures are unavailable.

In Naval activity, the USS *Ascutney,* a wooden-hulled, side-wheel gunboat launched in early April 1863 at Newburyport, Massachusetts, is commissioned this day at the New York Navy Yard. The navy had acquired the vessel during June 1863. Lieutenant Commander William Mitchell receives command of the ship.

July 29 (Friday) **In Georgia,** Union troops attached to the Army of the Cumberland clash for two days with Confederates at Lovejoy Station during McCook's Raid. Union Brigadier General Edward M. McCook is dispatched to destroy the Macon Railroad south of Atlanta to further squeeze the Confederates. General McCook, commanding a cavalry division, Army of the Cumberland, is able to sever the lines at Lovejoy Station, but the damage is temporary. The Confederates are operating on home ground and quickly repair the damaged rails, but the Yankees, who must return to the main body, lose nearly one thousand men captured during the march. General McCook, a cousin to Union Generals Alexander, Robert and Daniel McCook, himself escapes capture and subsequently participates at Selma, Alabama, against Nathan B. Forrest. Subsequently, McCook participates with General James Wilson during raids into Alabama and Georgia.

In Arkansas, Union forces clash through the 31st with Confederates at Fort Smith. Specific units and casualty figures are unreported.

In Maryland, Confederate General Jubal Early and his

seasoned troops continue to raid Union lines in West Virginia and Maryland. At Clear Springs, Maryland, the 12th and 14th Pennsylvania Cavalry Regiments engage Confederates. The Union reports no casualties. The Confederates sustain 17 killed and wounded.

In Confederate general officer activity, Colonel Thomas Benton Smith, 20th Tennessee Regiment, is promoted to the rank of brigadier general.

In Union general officer activity, General William T. Sherman responds to a telegram on the 28th from General James A. Hardie (inspector general) requesting that Sherman nominate eight colonels for promotion to brigadier general. His answer is prompted by of the promotion of Brigadier Generals Alan P. Hovey and Peter J. Osterhaus to the rank of major general. Sherman had sent a frosty dispatch to General Hardie complaining about the promotions of the two rear-guard generals: "If the rear be the post of honor, then we had better all change front on Washington." To his amazement, Sherman receives a direct response from President Lincoln, explaining his great feelings for the men in Sherman's command. Sherman quickly nominates Colonel William Grose (later brevet major general), 36th Indiana; Colonel Charles C. Walcutt, 46th Ohio; James W. Ripley, 104th Ohio; Luther P. Bradley, 51st Illinois; John W. Sprague, 63rd Ohio; Joseph A. Cooper, 6th East Tennessee; John T. Croxton, 4th Kentucky; and William W. Belknap, 15th Iowa. All nominees' promotions are approved by President Lincoln.

In Naval activity, the *Mingoe,* a side-wheel gunboat, is commissioned at Philadelphia. Under the command of Commander J.B. Creighton, the *Mingoe* joins the South Atlantic Squadron on 13 August to begin duty as a blockade ship. The *Mingoe* supports General Sherman's advance along the James River during February 1865. After the war, the *Mingoe* sails north to Philadelphia. Later, on 3 October 1867, while at League Island, it is sold.

July 30 (Saturday) BATTLE OF PETERSBURG In Virginia, General Grant and General George G. Meade have both consented on June 25 to an idea from Colonel Henry Pleasants' Pennsylvania Volunteers, a regiment composed mostly of coal miners from Pennsylvania, to tunnel well below the surface and set a massive explosive charge directly under Confederate lines. The expected damage and confusion would set up a Union attack intended to capture the works, if successful. Grant states in his memoir that the plan would at least keep the soldiers busy. Completion of the tunnel occurred on 23 July, but Grant sets the date of detonation for today.

Anxiety is great around Petersburg, with rumors of a possible explosion of the entire town as if it were sitting atop an active volcano. Grant anticipates that when the explosion occurs, disorganization will cause supreme confusion and allow the Union assault troops to capitalize and charge in an orderly, disciplined fashion to seize the objective. The obvious does not always

Left: Troops of the Union 48th Pennsylvania prepare explosives in a tunnel in front of Petersburg (Mottelay, *The Soldier in Our Civil War*, 1886). *Right:* The explosion at the Crater (Petersburg) (*Harper's Pictoral History of the Civil War*, 1896).

emerge in the implementation of plans. The detonation is delayed, but by approximately 0500, the attack is commenced when Brigadier General Robert B. Potter's 48th Pennsylvanians ignite the charges. The devastating shock and force of the explosion creates a massive crater that extends 100 feet in length and reaches a depth of 20 feet. Simultaneously, more than 100 cannon, supported by 50 mortars, roar, shattering the silence of the early morning hours and causing the Rebels to scatter in any direction to avoid the fright of the explosion and the stark terror of the incoming shells.

The unexpected attack inflicts high casualties upon the Rebels, including massive casualties in Colonel William H. Wallace's 18th South Carolina, which had four companies blown up in the explosion. The Union IX Corps (under General Ambrose Burnside) advances blindly through the smoky field, struggling furiously to climb from their own defenses without the aid of ladders, finally taking positions in the crater. The men in the crater find themselves with no leader, as both General James H. Ledlie and Edward Ferrero (born in Italy) are far back in the rear in a bombproof position.

The assault force is a colored division just recently organized with Ferrero as commander. With no general officer to issue orders or control discipline, the operation becomes a disaster. The Confederates bring in artillery and reinforcements, which prompts a quick reaction after their prior disarray. A gallant counterattack led by Confederate Captain Victor Jean Baptiste Girardey helps to turn the tide. Girardey is thereafter promoted to brigadier general, effective July 30, for his courageous actions on the field at Petersburg. Confederate Generals William Mahone and David A. Weisiger the latter being wounded, also contribute greatly to the success of the day's action.

Reinforcements sent by General Lee take the advantage and seize the day. The Union assault is expensive, costing more than 4,000 casualties (more than 1,900 missing or captured after being stuck in their own crater), due directly to the mismanagement of the two generals in charge of the operation. The Confederates sustain about 1,200 casualties.

General Grant, aware that the bulk of Lee's Army is still north of the James River, orders General Meade to deploy cavalry to intercept General Jubal Early. When things begin to go wrong, the pattern usually continues, and because of a communications gap (a break in the Union cable laid across the Chesapeake), Gen-

eral Sheridan is unaware that General Wright has not pursued Early.

The Confederates hold Petersburg and the Union must continue its siege indefinitely. During the Rebel counter-attack, Union General William Bartlett is seriously wounded when a bullet shatters his leg. He is captured and exchanged. The Rebel counter-attack succeeds in capturing a total of 73 Union officers and 855 enlisted men in the crater, according to General Robert E. Lee. The defiant Rebel piece of real estate will not falter until the final days of the conflict. Confederate General William Mahone is soon promoted to the rank of major general for his gallantry at the crater. Also, Confederate Brigadier General Stephen Elliott, Jr., is severely wounded at this action and he is compelled to spend a long time recuperating; however, he will regain his health and join General Joseph E. Johnston's command in North Carolina. Also, General Ferrero receives the brevet rank of major general the following December. He remains involved with the Petersburg campaign, but later he is transferred to Bermuda Hundred, where he serves for the remaining days of the war.

Elsewhere in Virginia, a Union force, Colonel J. Mansfield Davies' cavalry brigade, 2nd Cavalry Division, Army of the Potomac, battles a contingent of Confederates at Lee's Mills. The Union sustains two killed and 11 wounded. Confederate casualties are unavailable.

In Georgia, a contingent of cavalry, Army of the Cumberland, under General George Stoneman conducts raids at Macon. In addition, General Edward McCook's cavalry (Army of the Cumberland) continues its raids and clashes with Confederates at Newnan. A large number of Confederates are captured.

In Kentucky, one company of the 12th Ohio Cavalry skirmishes with Confederates at Lebanon. No Union casualties are reported. The Confederates sustain six killed.

General Edward Ferrero (Mottelay, *The Soldier in Our Civil War*, 1886).

In Pennsylvania, a contingent of Confederate cavalry, led by Brigadier General Bradley T. Johnson, upon orders from his commander, Brigadier General John McCausland, makes its way into Pennsylvania and sets fire to the town of Chambersburg, leaving hundreds of families homeless. General Jubal Early initially ordered the mission into Chambersburg. From there, the cavalry advances to McConnellsburg until Union cavalry commanded by General Benjamin Kelley is dispatched to intercept the Rebels. Kelley's cavalry encounters and defeats the Rebels and forces them to withdraw into Virginia.

In Union general officer activity, Colonel Charles C. Walcutt (46th Ohio Regiment) and Colonel John Wilson Sprague are promoted to the rank of brigadier general. General Walcutt will receive command of a brigade in General Logan's XV Corps, and he will participate at Missionary Ridge the following November. Subsequently, Walcutt will command a division for the remainder of the war. He remains in the army until January 1866. General Sprague participates in Sherman's March to the Sea and afterward is with Sherman during the campaign in the Carolinas. On 13 March 1865, Sprague receives the brevet rank of major general. Also, Colonel William Grose is appointed brigadier general, effective this date. Colonel James William Reilly (104th Ohio) is promoted to brigadier general. He participates in the Atlanta campaign and afterward departs Georgia with General George H. Thomas en route back to Tennessee.

July 31 (Sunday) In Georgia, General George Stoneman is captured while on a mission to attempt to rescue the Union prisoners at Andersonville. He is exchanged the following October. Afterward, he serves in North Carolina, East Tennessee and in the southwestern sector of Virginia. He receives the brevet of major general in the U.S. Army toward the end of the war; however, he remains in the army beyond the close of hostilities. During 1866, he becomes colonel of the 21st U.S. Infantry and receives command of the Department of Ari-

General George Stoneman (Mottelay, ***The Soldier in Our Civil War,*** 1886).

zona until he retires during 1871 due to a disability.

In Virginia, Confederate troops under Jubal Early are pursued by elements of Union General Wright's command, but due to a mixup in Union communications, Early finds himself without his tail. He changes course from Strasburg and returns to Winchester, where he engages a smaller force of Union troops under the command of General George Crook. Crook's troops are thoroughly routed and forced to retire from Winchester. During the course of fighting in and around Winchester this month, Confederate Brigadier General Robert D. Lilley is wounded several times and loses an arm; however, his captors leave him in Winchester, giving him an opportunity to recuperate and rejoin the service. He had commanded a brigade. After recovering, Lilley will participate in the final defenses in Virginia at Richmond.

July 31–August 1 In Georgia, Union Generals Edward M. McCook and George Stoneman are on a mission to destroy the Confederate Macon Railroad at Lovejoy Station and then rescue the Union captives prisoners at Andersonville prison. General Edward McCook's cavalry utilizes pontoon bridges to cross the Chattahoochee River at Campbellton and once across the column advances to Lovejoy Station, but there is no rendezvous with Stoneman. General McCook discovers and burns five hundred Confederate wagons that are attached to the Confederates at Atlanta. He also kills approximately eight hundred mules and captures 422 prisoners, including 72 officers; however his good fortune does not last. There is still no contact with Stoneman, who has disregarded his original orders and gone directly to Macon, instead of hitting the railroad. While Stoneman is being captured on the 31st at Sunshine Church by a contingent of Major General Joseph Wheeler's cavalry, led by General A. Iverson, General McCook finds his command completely surrounded by Confederate cavalry and Infantry. McCook releases his prisoners and has to fight viciously to avoid total disaster.

The Union loses approximately 600 men killed or captured at Newnan before McCook cuts his way out of the trap and reaches the safety of Turner's Ferry. General Stoneman, meanwhile, is in serious jeopardy after bypassing Lovejoy Station. His command succeeds in crossing the Ocmulgee River at Covington and moves down river to Clinton, where he hits the Confederate railroad stretching from Macon to Griswold Station at Savannah. There they destroy seventeen locomotives and more than 100 railroad cars before torching a bridge across the Oconee River. Afterward, Stoneman regroups his command outside of Macon. His cavalry commences shelling the town, but his command cannot cross the bridge, which compels him to return to Clinton, to the jubilation of the Confederates who surround his force.

General Stoneman, thinking the Confederates are much stronger in numbers than his force, dispatches Colonels Silas Adams and Horace Capron to fight their way back to Atlanta, while Stoneman remains with 700 men to hold off the enemy. Colonel Horace Capron returns with his command intact, but Colonel Adams' force is met by fierce opposition, and they return to camp in dribs and drabs. Stoneman is detained until exchange during late September (1864) at Rough and Ready. General Sherman is quite distressed with the loss of his cavalry. Consequently, he is forced to change his strategy regarding the destruction of the rails below Atlanta, by utilizing infantry instead of cavalry.

August In South Dakota, a contingent of the 30th Wisconsin Cavalry, commanded by Major John Clooney, establishes Fort Wadsworth, named in honor of General James S. Wadsworth, who had a fatal wound to his brain fighting in the Wilderness, Virginia, on 6 May 1864. In August 1876, the fort is renamed Fort Sisseton. The fort is constructed at a place known as Coteau des Prairies, thought to be a

Chambersburg, Pennsylvania, is burned by Confederates (***Harper's Pictoral History of the Civil War,*** 1896).

strategic location from which the U.S. Army could maintain presence along the routes used by the many wagons moving across the northern frontier toward the gold strikes in Idaho and Montana, while simultaneously protecting the settlers east of the James River from harm by unfriendly Indians in the region. Fort Sisseton is named for the Sisseton Sioux. It is abandoned during June 1889.

In Virginia, Union forces continue to clash with Confederates at the trenches in front of Petersburg.

August 1 (Monday) In Maryland, Union troops attached to Brigadier General B.F. Kelley engage Confederates at Plock's Mills, Cumberland.

In Missouri, the 5th Missouri Militia Cavalry clashes with Confederates at Rolla. Casualty figures are unavailable.

In Virginia, General Grant differs with General Henry Halleck in his opinion on the qualifications of General Philip Sheridan. Halleck thinks Sheridan is too young for the job in the Shenandoah Valley and Grant wants him more than anyone else. In a letter to Halleck, Grant states, "Unless General Hunter is in the field in person, I want Sheridan put in command of all troops in the field, with instructions to put himself south of the enemy [Jubal Early] and follow him to the death."

In other activity, elements of the 2nd, 5th, 9th and 18th Corps skirmish with Confederates in the vicinity of Petersburg. The Union sustains 87 killed and 484 wounded. Confederate casualties are unavailable.

In Union general officer activity, Brigadier General Gershom Mott, earlier wounded at Second Manassas and at Chancellorsville, receives the rank of brevet major general in recognition of his actions at the Battle of the Crater (Petersburg). On 1 December, he is promoted to full rank major general effective 26 May 1865. He leaves the army during 1868 after declining an assignment as a colonel. Also, Colonel Powell Clayton, 95th Kansas Cavalry, is appointed brigadier general. He serves afterward in Arkansas and Missouri and participates at Wilson's Creek. In December 1863, he receives command of a post at Pine Bluff, Arkansas. After the war he is elected as the "first carpetbag governor" of Arkansas. Colonel James Meech Warner (11th Vermont) is breveted brigadier general of volunteers.

In Naval activity, the recently commissioned gunboat USS *Ascutney* receives orders to depart from New York to join in the search for the steamer *Electric Spark,* captured by the CSS *Florida.* The ship is thought to be in the vicinity of the French Islands in the Gulf of St. Lawrence. While en route, the *Ascutney,* on the 4th, develops undisclosed problems that prevent it from completing the mission. Secretary of the Navy Gideon Welles issues new orders that direct the *Ascutney* to sail to Washington, D.C., and from there the ship is assigned to the North Atlantic Blockading Squadron. The *As-*

cutney arrives at Beaufort, North Carolina, on 21 August. In other activity, the U.S. Navy at about this time (August) acquires the side-wheel steamship *Eolus.* It is commissioned and dispatched to join the search for the CSS *Tallahassee.* Afterward, it joins the North Atlantic Blockading Squadron. It captures the blockade runner *Hope* in October 1864, and it participates in the capture of the *Lady Sterling* in January 1865. Subsequent to its operations against Fort Fisher, North Carolina, in January 1865, the *Ascutney* remains in service until decommissioned and sold in August 1865.

August 2 (Tuesday) In Arkansas, the 2nd and 3rd Militia and the 1st and 6th Missouri Cavalry engage Confederates at Osceola.

In Maryland, a contingent of the 153rd Ohio Volunteers and Confederates skirmish at Green Springs Depot in the vicinity of Old Town. The Union sustains one killed, five wounded and 90 missing. The Confederates sustain five killed and two wounded.

In Tennessee, Brigadier General Thomas E. Ransom receives command of a division in the XVI Corps. When General Grenville Dodge is wounded, Ransom assumes command of the corps.

In Confederate general officer activity, Colonel William Miller is promoted to the rank of brigadier general. Miller had fought at Murfreesboro, Tennessee, and sustained a severe wound that temporarily forced him from the field. Subsequently, he was assigned to his present station in Florida commanding the reserve forces. At the close of hostilities, General Miller is in command of the District of Florida.

August 3 (Wednesday) In Missouri, Union troops commanded by Colonel Burris clash with Confederates at Elk Chute.

In Virginia, General Grant arrives in Monocacy. He reorganizes General David Hunter's disillusioned troops that are encamped there. Grant instructs General Hunter to move his troops by rail toward Halltown (four miles from Harpers Ferry) in the Shenandoah Valley. Orders from Washington, which are constantly changing, thoroughly confuse Hunter's tactics against Early. Hunter's cavalry and wagons advance toward the objective. After further conferences with Grant, Hunter requests to be relieved, for what he considers to be for the good of the Union cause. General Philip Sheridan is summoned to Monocacy to initiate Grant's plan to move against the Confederates in the Shenandoah. Sheridan's force now totals about 30,000 men, including 8,000 cavalry troops. Confederates under General Jubal Early are of equal pro-

portion, but General Robert E. Lee dispatches reinforcements to Early because of the vast importance of the Shenandoah to the supply requirements of the Confederate forces.

In Naval activity, the U.S. naval fleet under Admiral David Farragut prepares for the siege of Mobile, Alabama. The fleet opens fire on Confederate-held Fort Gaines. Farragut's armada consists of 20 vessels.

August 4 (Thursday) In Alabama, Union forces under General Gordon Granger land at Dauphin Island. It had been scheduled for them to coordinate with Admiral Farragut's fleet and assault Fort Gaines, Alabama, but the fleet does not arrive. Granger awaits further orders.

In South Carolina, the Union and Confederates initiate a prisoner exchange with fifty Union officers being exchanged for fifty Confederate officers.

In Tennessee, a Union force under General Andrew Jackson Smith again departs Memphis, in search of Confederate General Nathan B. Forrest. While Smith is on the hunt, Forrest evades contact and makes his way to Memphis to pull a surprise raid on the 18th.

In Virginia, a Union contingent (specific units unreported) clashes with Confederates at New Creek. Casualty figures are unavailable.

In Union general officer activity, Colonel Charles R. Woods (West Point, 1852) who participated in the Union victory at Fort Donelson, Tennessee, is appointed brigadier general. General Woods commands the 1st Brigade of the XV Corps during Sherman's "March to the Sea." One of the officers in his brigade is his brother, William Woods, who himself is promoted to brigadier general at the conclusion of the conflict.

In Confederate general officer activity, Colonel Bryan M. Thomas (West Point, 1858), attached to Brigadier General James H. Clanton's command, is promoted to the rank of brigadier general, effective this date. Thomas is assigned duty in the Department of the Gulf as a brigade

A laundry establishment in the Army of the Shenandoah (Mottelay, *The Soldier in Our Civil War,* 1886).

commander (Alabama troops). Also, Brigadier General John Calvin Brown is promoted to major general.

August 5 (Friday) THE BATTLE OF MOBILE BAY At the mouth of Mobile Bay, Alabama, the call to battle is signaled to the Union fleet at 0500. By about 0630, every vessel briskly hoists the Stars and Stripes atop the peak and the three mastheads. Shortly thereafter, the *Tecumseh* commences fire, propelling two shots toward the Confederates, and by 0655 the fleet advances. Within ten minutes, the Confederates

Brigadier General Griffin A. Stedman (Johnson, *Campfire and Battlefield: History of the Conflicts and Campaigns*, 1894).

return fire, catapulting rounds toward the USS *Brooklyn*. At about the same time, the Confederate fleet under Admiral Franklin Buchanan sails from its positions to the rear of Fort Morgan and establishes a defensive line across the channel to intercept the attacking armada.

Meanwhile, the U.S. fleet, led by the 21-gun *Hartford* (flagship of Farragut), commanded by Captain Percival Drayton, enters Mobile Bay. The trailing warships include the *Richmond* (Captain Thornton A. Jenkins, 20 guns), *Brooklyn* (Captain James Alden, 24 guns), *Metacomet* (Lt. Cmdr. James E. Jouett, six guns), *Lackawanna* (Capt. John B. Marchand, eight guns), *Chickasaw* (Lt. Cmdr. George H. Perkins, four guns), *Galena* (Lt. Cmdr. Clark H. Wells, 10 guns), and the *Tecumseh* (Cmdr. Thomas T. Craven, two guns). Once within range, they bombard Confederate-held Forts Gaines, Morgan, and Powell.

The Confederate ram *Tennessee*, commanded by Commander J.D. Johnston, becomes the focus of the *Tecumseh*, which only moments ago was apprehensive about moving within the restrained area of the buoy. However, Commander Craven, aboard the *Tecumseh*, orders his ship to head directly for the *Tennessee*. And then suddenly a torpedo strikes and detonates, delivering a fatal blow to the *Tecumseh*. Craven instructs the pilot, John Collins, to go first with the other survivors, but Craven plummets to the bottom with his ship.

In the meantime, the other Union vessels continue the fight and pour incessant fire into the forts and the Confederate fleet. Farragut, expressing his concern for the *Tecumseh* during the heated duel, directs a rescue team to search for the survivors of the ill-fated vessel. Of the crew, which had numbered more than 100, twenty-one are saved, including the pilot. An ensign, H.C. Nields, braves the fire and uses a small boat to execute the rescue, but nearly becomes a casualty himself as the *Hartford* mistakes the tiny boat for a possible disguised

torpedo. Only at the last second is Nields recognized. The gunner is promptly stopped from unleashing some 100-pound shells upon the boat.

The Confederate batteries continue to pound the fleet. A thunderous barrage hammers the *Brooklyn*. As it attempts to back up, a collision with the USS *Richmond*, which has lost its engines, nearly occurs; however, an accident is avoided thanks to change in the tide that permits the *Brooklyn* to turn around.

The *Hartford* continues its advance, but the narrowness of the channel restricts its maneuverability and gives the CSS *Tennessee* an advantage. While the Rebel warship pours fire at the *Hartford*, return fire can only originate from the guns on the bow. As the *Hartford* attempts to pass, the *Tennessee* moves to ram the wooden warship, but speed saves a disaster and no collision occurs.

The *Tennessee* initiates pursuit, but as the *Hartford* breaks away, the *Tennessee* goes after the other approaching wooden ships. The USS *Brooklyn*, in the lead, receives a two-shot barrage from the Rebels, but in return the *Tennessee* receives a hefty broadside. Following this, the *Tennessee* moves against the approaching *Richmond*, but it, too, propels a mighty broadside which stuns the *Tennessee*. In cadence with the broadside, the riflemen aboard the *Richmond* effectively pour fire through the ports, seemingly catching the Rebel gunners by surprise. Nevertheless, the *Tennessee* maintains its pace and moves against the *Lackawanna*.

A nearby participant, Captain Strong, aboard the *Monongahela*, spots the impending collision and attempts to intercept the *Tennessee*. Strong attempts to rush ahead and strike the *Tennessee* at a right angle; however, having the *Kennebec* in tow hinders the maneuver and the *Tennessee* is struck only with a slight blow by the *Kennebec*, permitting the *Tennessee* to continue the fight. It pours shells into the *Kennebec* and inflicts casualties, then speeds ahead and encounters the *Ossipee*, which plows into but doesn't halt the *Tennessee*. Afterward, the *Tennessee* attempts to give a broadside to the inoperable

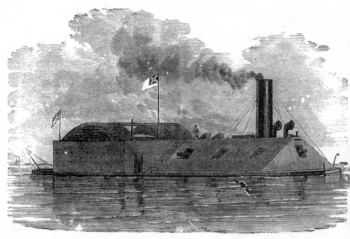

Left: The USS *Hartford* engages the CSS *Tennessee*. *Right:* The CSS *Baltic* on patrol in defense of Mobile (Mottelay, *The Soldier in Our Civil War*, 1886).

Oneida, but its guns misfire. Nonetheless, once it passes the cripple, another attempt to destroy it is made. The guns of the *Tennessee* plaster the stern and inflict injury and damage; Captain Mullany sustains the loss of an arm. The *Galena* is tied to the *Oneida* and sustains seven hits, and one man is killed prior to its entering the bay. Using all of its power, the *Galena* manages to get itself and the *Oneida* out of the range of the guns at the forts.

Another approaching vessel, the feisty ironclad *Winnebago*, maneuvers to intercept the *Tennessee* and save the *Oneida*. Despite the punishing exchange, the crew of the *Oneida* bolts to the rails and begins to give rousing cheers as the *Winnebago* moves up; its commander, Thomas H. Stevens is their former commander. The *Tennessee* then moves to positions behind Fort Morgan. All the while, the other vessels continue to pummel each other.

The *Hartford* is still pursued by smaller ironclads. One, the *Gaines*, receives a barrage that knocks it out of commission. Shortly thereafter, the *Gaines* is destroyed by its crew just off Fort Morgan. Other Confederate vessels are pursued by the *Metacomet* in an effort to destroy them before they can escape to Mobile. The tenacious exchange remains relentless in its fury. The Confederate vessel CSS *Selma* (formerly CSS *Florida*) pulls down its colors after being chased by the *Metacomet* for about one hour. The *Selma* terminates its career in the Confederate Navy; however, it is immediately brought into Union service as the USS *Selma*.

The CSS *Morgan* retires behind Fort Morgan and from there bolts to temporary safety at Mobile; the *Gaines* is torched. But still the *Tennessee* runs free. It closes on the *Hartford*, which is anchored about four miles from Mobile. The Rebel ram encroaches the *Hartford* while the crew is eating breakfast. The alarm sounds and the mess is cleared, while the decks are manned for imminent action. The Union vessels coordinate their activity. The *Lackawanna*, *Monongahela* and *Ossipee* advance to run it down, while the *Hartford* moves into action on its own. Quickly, the *Monongahela* commences fire, which inflicts damage, and this is followed by an effective broadside as the *Tennessee* passes the *Monongahela*. Soon after, the *Tennessee* is again struck, this time by the guns of the *Lackawanna*. These shots damage the port, forcing the vessel to list and be inadvertently swung around just in time for the *Hartford* to close as if it were a ram.

The two vessels collide, but only nominal damage is inflicted. However, the guns still rock the Confederate vessel. As the two ships separate, the *Hartford*, from a distance of about ten feet, unleashes yet another riveting broadside. Again, the obstinate Rebel vessel sustains no substantive damage. In turn, the *Hartford* escapes serious harm because when the *Tennessee* attempts to initiate another volley, the guns' primers fail to operate.

All the while, other Union vessels circle like steel sharks to finish victimizing the Rebel warship that seems to have nine lives. The *Hartford* maneuvers to make another run against it, but

in the meantime, the *Lackawanna* crashes into it at a point near to where Admiral Farragut is positioned. He escapes harm, but the vessel becomes disabled and sustains damage below the water line. At about the same time, the monitors begin raking the *Tennessee* with shot and shell, pummeling the cripple and destroying its steering apparatus, jamming its guns and creating further havoc by severing the smokestack. Choking smoke permeates the paralyzed ship, essentially sealing the fate of the iron warrior. The proud *Tennessee* attempts to escape and heads back, but relentlessly the Union gives chase.

The *Hartford* maneuvers for position to ram while the vessels *Chickasaw*, *Manhattan* and *Winnebago* continue to propel fire upon the *Tennessee*. Still, the defiant Rebels maintain their feistiness and pride by refusing to capitulate. Admiral Buchanan continues to oversee the battle plan and personally sets the sights on the guns, but suddenly the captain gets struck by an iron sliver which breaks his leg. At about this time, the Confederates realize further resistance is futile. The Confederate colors are struck, but the Union is unsure of the reason, for it has already once shot the flag from the mast and the ship continued to fight. Union fire continues to rain upon the *Tennessee*. Finally, Captain Johnston ascends to the top of the vessel and displays a white flag to terminate the battle that had lasted little more than one hour.

The USS *Chickasaw* places the *Tennessee* under tow and drops its anchor near the flagship *Hartford*, then moves forward to reduce Fort Powell. Fortuitously for the Union, the fort had been constructed to hold off an attack of this type from only the front, giving the *Chickasaw* an easy objective. The Rebels evacuate the fort and blow up the fortifications. The fleet will move against the remaining forts on the following day. During this engagement, Admiral Farragut coins the phrase "Damn the torpedoes, full steam ahead." In addition, Farragut notes in a letter regarding the battle: "Notwithstanding the loss of life, particularly to this ship [*Hartford*], and the terrible disaster to the *Tecumseh,* the result of the fight was a glorious victory, and I have reason to feel proud of the officers, seamen, and marines of the squadron under my command."

The USS *Tecumseh* is lost. Mobile falls to the Union on August 23. Participating vessels also include the *Manhattan* (Cmdr. J.W.A. Nicholson, two guns), *Winnebago* (Cmdr. Thomas H. Stevens, four guns) *Octorara* (Lt. Cmdr. Charles H. Greene, six guns), *Port Royal* (Lt. Cmdr. Bancroft Gherardi, six guns), *Seminole* (Cmdr. Edward Donaldson, eight guns) *Monongahela* (Cmdr. James H. Strong, eight guns), *Kennebec* (Lt. Cmdr. William P. McCann, five guns), *Ossipee* (Cmdr. William E. Leroy), *Itasca* (Lt. Cmdr. George Brown, five guns) and the *Oneida* (Cmdr. J.R.M. Mullany, nine guns).

The CSS *Selma*, captured by the USS *Metacomet*, continues serving in the war as the USS *Selma*. It remains in Mobile Bay until January 1865, when it is transferred to New Orleans until it is decommissioned during July 1865.

After being decommissioned the ship retains its name, the *Selma*, and operates as a merchant ship until 24 June 1868, when it founders near the mouth of the Brazos River in Texas. The *Metacomet* returns to patrol duty, primarily searching for mines in Mobile Bay. It is later, during August 1865, decommissioned in Philadelphia, Pennsylvania.

Another Confederate vessel, the ram *Baltic*, had been part of the defending force of the harbor, but by 1863, it had deteriorated. By July of this year, its armor had been stripped and it was dismantled. During May 1865, U.S. forces seize its hulk on the Tombigbee River in Alabama. Subsequent to capture, during December 1865, the hulk is sold.

The *Ossipee*, commissioned during November 1862 at Portsmouth, New Hampshire, remains in the Gulf of Mexico for the duration of the war. In 1866 it is sent to the Pacific, where it remains on duty from 1866 to 1872, and from there, the *Ossipee* moves to the Atlantic, where it serves until 1884. Subsequently, it operates in the waters off Asia until 1887, then in the Atlantic and West Indies until decommissioned during November 1889. The USS *Conemaugh* had participated in the operations to seal the entrances to Mobile Bay. Following its service in the Gulf, it returns to duty off the Carolinas, where it remains active until November 1865. It is decommissioned during July 1867. The USS *Chickasaw*, a 1300-ton Milwaukee class twin turret ironclad river monitor commissioned in May 1864, operates in the region for the remainder of the war and participates against Rebel-held Mobile during spring 1865. Afterward it moves to New Orleans, where it is decommissioned. From June to August 1869, it is renamed the *Samson*. Later, the ship becomes a railroad ferry under the name *Gouldsboro* until 1944. The steam sloop CSS *Nashville* is at Mobile but is not yet completed and does not participate. The vessel is later seized (May 1865) by the Union at Nanna Hubba, Alabama.

The ironclad CSS *Tennessee* becomes the USS *Tennessee*. An older Union vessel with the same name — a wooden-hulled side-wheel steamship built in New York during 1853 — is renamed the USS *Mobile* in September 1864. The ironclad *Tennessee*, after entering Union service, is assigned duty in the Gulf of Mexico. The USS *Mobile* continues its duty in the West Gulf Squadron; however, by early 1865, the need for repairs causes the ship to be decommissioned. By the latter part of March 1865, the USS *Mobile* is sold and enters the commercial shipping service under the name *Republic*. It is lost during a hurricane off Savannah on 25 October 1865. Also, the USS *Kennebec*, subsequent to this action, moves to patrol off the coast of Texas. It is decommissioned during August 1865 and sold the following November.

In Missouri, the 8th Missouri Militia Cavalry clashes with Confederates at Cowskin through the 7th.

In Georgia, the 2nd Cavalry Division, Army of the Cumberland, engages Confederates at Decatur.

In Louisiana, the 11th New York Cavalry engages Confederates at Donaldsville. The Union loses 60 missing. Confederate casualties are unavailable. Also, a Union contingent, composed of units of the Armies of the Cumberland, Ohio, and Tennessee, engage in a two-day skirmish with Confederates at Utoy Creek.

In Virginia, the 1st U.S. Colored Cavalry clashes with Confederates at Cabin Point. In other activity, Colonel Griffin A. Stedman is mortally wounded during skirmishing in the vicinity of Petersburg. His appointment as brigadier general, through he recommendation of General Edward O.C. Ord, arrives after his death.

In Union general officer activity, Colonel Joseph Abel Haskin is promoted to brigadier general effective this date. Subsequently, during March 1865, he is breveted brigadier general in the regular army. Following the close of hostilities, he becomes lieutenant colonel of the 1st Artillery. He retires during 1870.

In Confederate general officer activity, Major Archibald C. Godwin is promoted to the rank of brigadier general. Also, Philip Cook, a lawyer who joined the 4th Georgia as a private during 1861 and rose to colonel of the regiment after the Battle of Antietam, is named brigadier general.

August 6 (Saturday)   In Louisiana, elements of the 4th Wisconsin Cavalry and the 11th and 14th Rhode Island Heavy Artillery engage a Confederate force at Plaquemine (Indian City Village). The Union sustains two killed. Confederate casualties are unavailable.

In Naval activity, a contingent of 26 Marines led by Capt. Charles Heywood and attached to the USS *Hartford* and *Richmond,* debark and occupy Fort Powell in Mobile, Alabama. In related activity, the USS *Chickasaw* bombards Fort Gaines, another of the Confederate strong points in Mobile Bay. In December the *Hartford* returns to New York for repairs and remains out of service until July 1865. At that time the war is over and the *Hartford* is designated as the flagship of the recently organized Asiatic Squadron. It remains in that capacity until August 1868, when it is recommissioned in New York. Later, during October 1872, it is recommissioned and reassigned to the Asiatic Squadron until October 1875. It remains in service at various stations until 14 January 1887, when it is decommissioned at Mare Island, California, and used in sea-training. However, on 2 October 1899, the *Hartford* is yet again recommissioned and assigned duty on the East Coast as a training ship for midshipmen until 12 October 1912, when it is transferred to Charleston, South Carolina. At Charleston, the *Hartford* is used as a station ship until decommissioned on 20 August 1926. Even after active service in the Civil War and World War I, the *Hartford* still does not fade away. On 18 October 1938, it is transferred to Washington, D.C., where it remains throughout World War II. On 19 October 1945, the *Hartford* is towed from D.C. to the Norfolk Navy Yard and designated

a "relic." Subsequently, on 20 November 1956, three years after the end of the Korean War (by armistice), the *Hartford* sinks while in its berth. Some of the relics from the warship are preserved at the National Navy Memorial Museum in Washington (D.C.) Navy Yard.

August 7 (Sunday)   In Virginia, General Philip Sheridan is given command of the 6th and 19th Corps, the West Virginia Infantry and Cavalry under Generals Crook and William Averell, as well as two cavalry divisions led by Albert Torbert, providing him with a force of about 40,000 troops to check the activity of the Confederates Jubal A. Early and Fitzhugh Lee, who are operating in the Shenandoah Valley.

In West Virginia, Union troops under General William Averell, including the 14th Pennsylvania, 8th Ohio, 1st and 3rd West Virginia and the 1st New York Cavalry, inflict heavy losses on the Confederate troops under General Jubal Early at Moorefield. Union troops suffer nine killed and 22 wounded. Confederates suffer 100 killed or wounded and 400 missing.

In Alabama, Confederate Fort Gaines falls to the Union, but the defenders at Fort Morgan refuse to capitulate.

In Mississippi, fighting breaks out between Union and Confederates along the Tallahatchie River. Also, Union forces of the 16th Corps and Confederate contingents clash at various points along the Tallahatchie River through the 14th, including Abbeville, Oxford and Hurricane Creek. General John Hatch's cavalry and General Joseph Mower's force of the 16th Corps participate. The 5th Minnesota Volunteer Infantry Regiment also participates in this action. No casualties are reported.

August 8 (Monday)   In the Dakota Territory, a Union force composed of elements of the 8th Minnesota Volunteers, the 2nd Minnesota, 6th and 7th Iowa, Brackett's artillery battery and the 1st Battalion, Dakota Cavalry, engage Confederates at Two Hills, Badlands, at the Little Missouri River. Casualty figures are unavailable.

In Naval activity, the USS *General Burnside* is commissioned at Bridgeport, Alabama. The vessel, constructed during 1861 at Wilmington, Delaware, was purchased by the War Department during 1863 and afterward chartered by the U.S. Navy. Acting Volunteer Lt. H.A. Glassford receives command of the *General Burnside,* which becomes the flagship of the upper Tennessee River Fleet (Mississippi Squadron) on 15 October 1864. From its base at Bridgeport, the General Burnside patrols along the river in the region stretching between Whitesburg, Decatur, and Chattanooga.

In Union general officer activity, Colonel James Deering Fessenden is promoted to brigadier general, effective this day. General Fessenden will command a brigade (General Williams' division, XIX Corps) at the battle of Cedar Creek, and following that action he is assigned garrison duty at Winchester, Virginia,

for the duration of the war. John Dunlap Stevenson, who resigned his commission as brigadier general the previous August, is recommissioned to rank from his original date (13 March 1863). He is assigned command of Harpers Ferry, West Virginia. General Stevenson remains in that command for the duration; however, for a short time during February 1865, he temporarily commands the Department of West Virginia. He receives the brevet of major general of volunteers toward the close of hostilities and remains in the service beyond the war. During 1866, he becomes colonel of the 30th U.S. Infantry. Subsequently, he receives the brevet of brigadier general in the U.S. Army during 1867. Nevertheless, he retires on 31 December 1870.

In Naval activity, the USS *General Thomas,* a light wooden gunboat built at Chattanooga, Tennessee, for the War Department earlier this year, is commissioned at Bridgeport, Alabama. Acting Master Gilbert Morton receives command of the ship, which is assigned duty with the Mississippi Squadron.

August 9 (Tuesday)   In Virginia, General Philip Sheridan's Union cavalry prepares to drive General Jubal Early's raiders out of the Shenandoah Valley. It is Sheridan's hope to intercept them at Winchester. Various skirmishes occur throughout the following month until the two opposing forces clash in a major confrontation at Winchester on 19 September. In other activity, an explosion occurs at an ammunition sector at City Point, costing the Union 70 killed and 130 wounded.

In Naval activity, the USS *Pontoosuc* departs New York in search of the CSS *Tallahassee,* which has been ravaging Union shipping. Nonetheless, its search is in vain. It returns to New York on 30 August and is assigned escort duty. Late in the year, it returns to its original squadron in time to participate in the attack against Fort Fisher, North Carolina, and the new attacks during January 1865. The *Pontoosuc* later participates in the campaign to reduce Wilmington, North Carolina. It sails north after the close of hostilities and is decommissioned at Boston on 5 July 1865. It is sold on 3 October 1866.

August 10 (Wednesday)   In Georgia, General William T. Sherman's command receives several Parrott thirty-pound cannon. Immediately, the Union puts them into use and catapults shells into Atlanta.

In Virginia, Union troops occupy Millwood. Also, the 1st Cavalry Division, bolstered by one reserve brigade (Army of the Potomac) skirmishes with Confederates for two days along Berryville Pike, Sulphur Springs and White Post. Union casualties are 34 killed, 90 wounded and 200 missing. Confederate casualties are unavailable.

In Confederate general officer activity, Brigadier General Lunsford L. Lomax (West Point, 1856) is appointed major general. He will command Lt. General Jubal Early's cavalry.

In Naval activity, the transport steamer USS *Empress* and two other vessels, the *Prairie Bird* (formerly *Mary Miller*) and the *Romeo,* while operating on the Mississippi River in the vicinity of Gaines Landing, Arkansas, exchange fire with a Confederate battery. The *Prairie Bird* is able to tow the disabled *Empress* out of harm's way, but all of the ships (attached to Mississippi Squadron) sustain damage. The *Empress* sustains six killed, including Captain John Molloy, and 12 wounded. The *Prairie Bird,* initially a civilian vessel, had been converted into a tinclad river gunboat after it was acquired by the U.S. Navy in December 1862. The *Romeo,* following this duty, continues to patrol in the region between Natchez and Vicksburg in Mississippi and at the mouth of the Arkansas River. In May 1865, it moves to Cairo and from there to Mound City. The *Romeo* is decommissioned at Mound City on 30 June 1865. During the following month it is sold to Nathaniel Williams.

August 11 (Thursday)   In Arkansas, the 2nd and 6th Kansas Cavalry Regiments clash with Confederates at Van Buren.

In Mississippi, Union cavalry attached to the 16th Corps clashes with Confederates at Abbeyville and Oxford.

In Virginia, General Robert E. Lee orders Confederate General Wade Hampton to move his cavalry to Culpeper to reinforce General Richard H. Anderson. Hampton is to assume command of all cavalry in the region. Lee rescinds his order and directs Hampton on the 14th: "Halt your command and return towards Richmond.... Gregg's cavalry [Union] is crossing at deep bottom."

August 12 (Friday)   In Virginia, General Grant directs General Winfield S. Hancock to move to the north side of the James River to duplicate an effort that took place during the previous month. Hancock, leading his own corps and the Tenth Corps (General David Birney) and David Gregg's cavalry, embarks aboard transports from City Point and they arrive the

The Battle of Cedar Creek (Mottelay, *The Soldier in Our Civil War,* 1886).

following morning at Deep Bottom, held by troops under General Robert S. Foster. Grant is speculating that Lee will be convinced that the flotilla is returning to Washington, D.C.

In Mississippi, elements of the 16th Corps (cavalry and infantry) clash with Confederates at Abbeville and Oxford, Mississippi.

In the Dakota Territory, a contingent of the 7th Iowa Cavalry skirmishes with Confederates at Little Blue.

In Union general officer activity, Major General Winfield Scott Hancock (volunteers) is promoted to brigadier general in the Regular Army. Brigadier General Joseph Anthony Mower is promoted to major general.

In Confederate general officer activity, Brigadier General William Smith is promoted to major general, effective this date. However, General Smith, former governor of Virginia, is re-elected to the office later this year.

In Naval activity, the USS *Pontiac* arrives at Port Royal, South Carolina, and joins the South Atlantic Blockading Squadron. It is assigned blockade duty off Charleston. In other activity, the USS *Yantic* is commissioned in Philadelphia. Command of the gunboat is given to Lt. Commander Thomas C. Harris. On the day following its commission it sails in company with the USS *Aster* and the *Moccasin* to join the search for the CSS *Tallahassee,* a Confederate raider. The *Yantic* returns to Philadelphia about one week later. Subsequent to receiving repairs, it again sails north and arrives in Massachusetts on 13 September, where it receives new orders to resume patrols in an area stretching from New York to Hampton Roads, Virginia. It also sails to Halifax, Nova Scotia, arriving there on 1 November, but without results, as the *Tallahassee* had departed the area prior to its arrival. Subsequently, the *Yantic* is attached to the North Atlantic Blockading Squadron.

August 13 (Saturday)   In Virginia, John S. Mosby's raiders attack a Union contingent of the 144th and 149th Ohio Volunteer Regiments while they guard a supply train at Berryville. The Rebels escape with 75 wagons, 500 horses, 200 head of cattle and a contingent of Confederates that had been held prisoner by the Union.

In Union general officer activity, the division under General Lysander Cutler, following the Battle of the Wilderness, is not full strength and stands at slightly more than 1,300, down from about 3,700. In addition, Cutler's health, due to former wounds and exposure, is poor. He requests

relief at Petersburg and it occurs during the following September. He is breveted major general on 19 August 1864 and resigns from the service during June 1865.

In Naval activity, while the Union is driving across the James River, Confederate warships, including the CSS *Richmond* and the CSS *Virginia II,* attack Union positions at Dug Gap to draw attention away from Confederate troop movements. The *Richmond,* an ironclad ram built at Norfolk and launched during May 1864, is attached to the James River Squadron. In related activity, the USS *Agawam,* at about 1500, comes under fire from three Confederate batteries along the James. The *Agawam* returns fire in a battle that lasts more than four hours. The *Agawam* expends its ammunition and is forced to retire. Three crew members are killed and four others are wounded.

August 13–14   In Virginia, U.S. Grant diverts troops under General Winfield S. Hancock from Petersburg to the north side of the James River to prevent General Robert E. Lee from rushing reinforcements to assist General Jubal Early. Union General George G. Meade continues to concentrate his efforts on the siege of Petersburg. There is heavy skirmishing near Petersburg, but the Confederates hold the ground against the attacks by Generals Gershom Mott and Francis Barlow at Bailey's Creek.

August 14 (Sunday)   In Virginia, Union and Confederates clash at Strawberry Plains, as the Union 6th and 10th Corps and Gregg's cavalry pound against General Robert E. Lee's forces through the 18th. The Union sustains 400 killed, 1,755 wounded and 1,400 missing. The Confederate casualties are listed as 1,000 wounded.

In Georgia, the 2nd Missouri Volunteer Regiment and the 14th U.S. Colored Regiment engage Confederates at Dalton through the 16th. Casualties are not reported.

In Mississippi, a Union contingent including Cavalry and Infantry skirmishes with Confederates at Hurricane Creek.

In Union general officer activity, General Ambrose Burnside is relieved of command (IX Corps). No new orders arrive for him. Consequently, General Burnside resigns from the service on 15 April 1865. The IX Corps receives several commanders during the remainder of the war. Brigadier General Orlando B. Willcox commands for two days, 13–14 August 1864, and is replaced by Major General John G. Parke from 14 August to 1 September 1864. Willcox then succeeds Parke on 1 September until 10 September, then Parke resumes command and holds it until 30 December 1864. Willcox commands again until 12 January, when Parke again succeeds Willcox. On 24 January, Willcox retains command until the 2 February, when Parke yet again resumes command. On 22 February, 1865, General Robert Potter succeeds Parke; however, on 1 March, General Parke succeeds Potter. Parke retains command until 7

June, when he is relieved by General Willcox. On 26 June, Parke becomes the final commander of the IX Corps, which is disbanded on 27 July 1865.

In Naval activity, the Mississippi Squadron, commanded by Rear Admiral Lee, is disbanded. The fleet had been commanded by Admiral Porter until earlier this summer, when was been relieved temporarily by Captain Pennock prior to the arrival of Rear Admiral S.P. Lee.

August 15 (Monday)   In Georgia, Confederate General John B. Hood's cavalry continues harassing General Sherman's lines in the vicinity of Atlanta. Major General Joseph Wheeler's force is also quite active, and it continues to inflict damage to Sherman's rail lines, although no serious Union casualties occur. During Wheeler's operation, one of his brigades, led by Brigadier General John S. Williams, becomes separated from the main body. It is transferred to Virginia.

In Louisiana, General U.S. Grant is concerned that Confederates under Kirby Smith (Trans-Mississippi Department) might evade General Frederick Steele and move toward Sherman in Georgia. On his orders, an expeditionary force departs New Orleans this day en route to Mobile to intercept Kirby Smith's forces.

In Virginia, Union forces under Sheridan engage and defeat the Confederates at Crooked Run (Front Royal), capturing many soldiers and their regimental colors. The 1st and 2nd Brigade, 1st Cavalry Division, Army of the Potomac, and the 45th New York Cavalry are among the participants. At Fisher Hill, near Strasburg, elements of the Union 6th and 8th Corps, bolstered by the 1st Cavalry, Army of the Potomac, skirmish with Confederates. The Union sustains 30 wounded. Confederate casualties are unreported.

In Union activity, Brigadier General Daniel P. Woodbury (West Point, 1836) dies of yellow fever. General Woodbury supervised at Fredericksburg placement of the pontoon bridges the Union needed to ford the Potomac.

In Confederate general officer activity, Colonel George Washington Gordon (11th Tennessee) is promoted to brigadier general. General Gordon had participated in various actions, including Murfreesboro, Chickamauga, Chattanooga and the Atlanta campaign. Also, Colonel William Hugh Young (9th Texas Infantry) is promoted to brigadier general. He had sustained multiple wounds while with his regiment at Murfreesboro, Vicksburg and Chickamauga. At Kennesaw Mountain he sustained his fourth and fifth wounds.

In Naval activity, the USS *Niagara,* out of service from June 1862, recommissioned in October 1863, and finally back to sea during June 1864, is operating in European waters on this day when it encounters and captures the CSS *Georgia,* a Confederate raider. The *Niagara* remains in European waters for the duration of the war. In March 1865, it blocks the ironclad CSS *Stonewall* at Ferrol, Spain; however, the *Niagara* fails to make an attempt to engage the Confederate ship. After the war, the *Niagara* returns to the U.S. during the summer of 1865 and moves into the Boston Navy Yard, where it remains for about twenty years before being sold for scrap during May 1886. In other activity, the USS *Isonomia,* acquired by the U.S. Navy earlier this year, is commissioned on or about this day. It is assigned duty off North Carolina, but is ordered to Key West in September. After arriving at its station it is assigned patrol duty off the Florida coast and in the Bahamas. In July 1865 it is decommissioned and sold, then renamed the *City of Providence.* During 1867, it is again sold to a foreign buyer.

August 16 (Tuesday)   In Kansas, a Union force composed of detachments of the 7th Iowa and U.S. cavalry skirmish with Confederates at Smoky Hill Crossing.

In Virginia, Union troops, including the 39th Illinois Infantry, skirmish with Confederates at Deep Run. Pvt. Henry M. Hardenberg becomes the recipient of a Medal of Honor for his valor during this skirmish. Confederate General Victor Jean B. Girardey is killed while leading his brigade against Union forces at Darbytown

Road in the vicinity of Fussell's Mill. Also, Confederate General John Randolf Chambliss (West Point, 1853) is killed while skirmishing with Union cavalry under General David Gregg along the Charles City Road. Wesley Merritt's cavalry engages Confederates under Generals Lunsford L. Lomax (West Point, 1856) and William C. Wickham at Crooked Run. The Union sustains 13 killed and 58 wounded. The Confederates sustain 30 killed, 150 wounded and 102 missing; a contemporary source lists about 300 Confederates captured.

August 17 (Wednesday)   In Florida, the 75th Ohio Mounted Infantry skirmishes with Confederates at Gainesville. The Union sustains 16 killed, 30 wounded and 102 missing. Confederate casualties are unavailable.

In Tennessee, the 6th Ohio Heavy Artillery skirmishes with Confederates at Cleveland. Also, General A.J. Smith, having departed Memphis on August 4, reaches the Tallahatchie River, but his force has been unable to discover the positions of Confederate General Nathan B. Forrest. Smith returns to Memphis.

In Virginia, the New Jersey Cavalry Brigade, 6th Corps, and General James Wilson's cavalry engage Confederates at Winchester. The Union does not list any casualties. The Confederates sustain 50 wounded and 250 missing.

August 18 (Thursday)   In Alabama, a Union contingent composed of the 2nd Cavalry Division, Army of the Cumberland, and the 1st U.S. Colored Artillery engages a Confederate force at Decatur.

In Georgia, Union cavalry attached to the Army of the Cumberland clashes with Confederates at Fairburn. Also, Union General Hugh J. Kilpatrick's cavalry initiates raids through the 22nd against the Atlanta Railroad. The Union sustains about 350–400 casualties. Confederate casualties are unavailable; however about 1,000 Rebels are captured.

In Tennessee, while General Andrew J. Smith is in Tennessee attempting to locate General Nathan B. Forrest's forces, contingents of Forrest's command raid Memphis. The Confeder-

Left: **The CSS *Georgia*** (Johnson, *Campfire and Battlefield: History of the Conflicts and Campaigns,* 1894). *Right:* Confederates under Nathan Bedford Forrest raid Irving prison in Tennessee (*Harper's Pictoral History of the Civil War,* 1896).

ates expect to seize Generals Ralph P. Buckland, Stephen A. Hurlbut and Cadwallader C. Washburn, but none of the targeted officers are in Memphis. Nonetheless, the Rebels do seize some officers and capture about three hundred other troops. In addition, Forrest attempts to attack the Irving prison to rescue Confederates held there, but the operation fails. Forrest returns to Mississippi and remains inactive until late September.

General Stephen Hurlbut, subsequent to this action, is assigned as commander of the Department of the Gulf. While there, Hurlbut becomes involved in some practices that are in his self-interest. His action provokes the president. A commission formed to investigate recommends that Hurlbut be placed under arrest and tried on charges of corruption. General Edward Canby orders that the recommendation be carried out; however, the incident fades away without action. On 20 June 1865, Hurlbut musters out of the service. Despite his reputation, Hurlbut later becomes minister to Colombia (by President Grant) and minister to Peru (by President Garfield). He is also elected to two terms in Congress, beginning in 1872. He dies in Peru at Lima on 27 March 1882.

In Union general officer activity, Colonel Eli Long (4th Ohio Cavalry) is promoted to brigadier general. In November he is sent to Nashville to assume command of General Kenner Garrard's cavalry division.

August 18–21   In Virginia, skirmishes develop around Petersburg. Union forces (V Corps and contingents of the II and IX Corps) under General Gouverneur Warren are in the process of moving from the Petersburg entrenchments to the Weldon Railroad. Warren's advance, which begins at about dawn on the 18th, drives the Confederates back and reaches the railroad at Globe Tavern. Simultaneously, General Winfield S. Hancock is operating at Deep Bottom, located north of the James River. During the afternoon, Major General Henry Heth's unit clashes with Confederate General Ayres' division. The Yankees under Heth succeed in pushing the Ayres' force back, compelling it to retire toward Globe Tavern. The skirmishes continue throughout the day, then resume on the 19.

On the morning of the 19th, Confederate Major General William Mahone, who had been diverted from his positions north of the James River, joins the battle, attacks the positions of General Crawford, and turns his right flank. However, fresh Union reinforcements arrive to augment Warren's force and he is able to launch a potent counterattack during the afternoon which neutralizes Mahone's five infantry brigades and regains the greater part of the ground that had earlier been relinquished. By about dusk, General Warren begins to regroup his force; he establishes a defensive line in the vicinity of Globe Tavern and the Glick House. On the 20th, Warren's lines are further strengthened and extended to link with the primary Union positions along the Jerusalem Plank Road. The Union lines by dusk on the

20th are well fortified and able to withstand pressure.

On the morning of the 21st, Confederate General Ambrose P. Hill fails to discover any vulnerable point in the Union lines. In contrast, General Grant's strategy has further severed the rail supply system of the Confederates at Petersburg, who until now have relied on the rails to transport their supplies from Wilmington, North Carolina. Confederate trains are now compelled halt at Stony Creek Station and transfer the stores to wagons that have to advance about thirty miles along the Boydton Plank Road to reach the defenders at Petersburg. Clashes also occur along the Union-held Weldon Railroad and Six Mile House. Both Union and Confederate losses are severe. The Union has 212 killed, 1,155 wounded and 3,176 missing. Confederates have 4,000 killed, wounded or missing. Petersburg holds on against overwhelming odds. Pvt. Richard Smith, 95th New York Infantry, captures two officers and 20 enlisted men from General Johnson Hagwood's brigade as they attempt escape at Weldon Railroad.

On the 21st, Confederate General John C. Calhoun Sanders is severely wounded in both legs and dies. Confederate General Thomas L. Clingman is grievously wounded but recovers to rejoin his command just prior to the surrender of the Confederates at Greensboro, North Carolina, at the end of hostilities. After the war, General Clingman practices law and engages in exploration of the Allegheny Mountain range. Also, during the initial attacks against Petersburg, Colonel Thomas W. Egan, 40th New York, sustains a wound close to his spine. He is slightly paralyzed and out of action; however, he returns to action in about two months, after the slight paralysis in his legs ends. These battles in Dinwiddie County are known by numerous names, including Battle of Globe Tavern, Second Battle of Weldon Railroad, Yellow Tavern, Yellow House and Blick's Station.

August 19 (Friday)   In Arkansas, a contingent (Company B) of the U.S. 83rd Illinois Mounted Infantry is attacked by a band of Rebel renegades at Pine Bluff. The Union sustains about eight killed, but the Union Force under Colonel R. Clayton repulses the attack.

In Georgia, a detachment of cavalry (General Hugh Kilpatrick's raid) skirmishes with Confederates at Red Oak. The opposing sides again clash on the following day.

In Tennessee, a one-company contingent of the 115th Ohio Volunteer Regiment skirmishes with Confederates at Blockhouse No. 4 on the N&C Railroad.

In Virginia, Confederates attack the Union lines of General Gouverneur Warren outside of Petersburg in the vicinity of the Danville Road. Initially the Union holds, but the Confederates fold the flank, and once it turns, the Rebels strike Warren's left, creating chaos. The Rebels capture huge numbers of prisoners. Union reinforcements, led by Generals Orlando B. Will-

cox and Julius White, arrive and the lines are rebuilt. The Rebels are halted. A detachment of the 5th Michigan Cavalry is captured by John Singleton Mosby's irregulars at Snicker's Gap Pike. These Union prisoners and wounded are killed by their captors. Union Brigadier General Joseph Hayes is among the captured on this day. He is seized near the Weldon Railroad and held until exchanged about six month later. All officers of the 14th U.S. Volunteers are wounded, compelling Sgt. Ovila Cayer to assume command of the regiment. In other activity, a contingent of General William Averell's cavalry clashes with Confederates under General Jubal Early at Martinsburg.

August 19–20   In Georgia, a Union force (General Hugh Kilpatrick's Raid) composed of elements of the 2nd Cavalry Division, Army of the Cumberland, commanded by Colonel Robert G. Minty, clashes with Confederates under Brigadier General Samuel W. Ferguson at Jonesboro. The Union occupies and devastates the town. The Union sustains slightly more than 300 killed, wounded and missing. The Confederates suffer about 1,000 casualties. Confederate Brigadier General Jesse Johnson Finley is wounded severely at this battle. He is no longer able to serve in the field. After the war, General Finley serves three terms, each contested, in the U.S. Congress. Later, due to a technicality, he is denied a seat in the U.S. Senate. He remains in Florida and dies there at Lake City on 6 November 1904.

August 20 (Saturday)   In Georgia, General Hugh Kilpatrick's raid continues. Union cavalry (2nd Cavalry Division, Army of the Cumberland) led by Colonel Robert Minty clashes with Confederates at Lovejoy Station.

In Virginia, General Grant dispatches General Gouverneur Warren with a large force (5th Corps) against the Confederates at Weldon Station. Union troops, ordered to cross the James

General Hugh Judson Kilpatrick (*Harper's Pictoral History of the Civil War***, 1896).**

River and hold Lee at Richmond, are recalled to fill the void after a division had been sent from Petersburg to reinforce Warren at Weldon Station. Heavy fighting ensues, with the Yankees gaining and holding ground against several Confederate attacks. Union Generals David Gregg and Winfield S. Hancock advance further and destroy the rails and damage additional Southern supply lines. By the 21st, the Yankees destroy the rails up to three miles beyond Ream's Station.

In West Virginia, General Philip Sheridan establishes camp at Harpers Ferry, which is less than 50 miles from Gettysburg, Pennsylvania.

August 21 (Sunday) **In Arkansas,** a contingent of the 11th Cavalry clashes with Confederates at Duvall's Bluff.

In Kentucky, a large contingent of Confederates, led by Brigadier General Adam R. (Stovepipe) Johnson, attacks Union positions in the vicinity of Grubb's Crossroads. During the assault, General Johnson is accidentally fired upon and struck in the face. The accident costs him the sight in both eyes. After the termination of hostilities he returns to Texas and lives a long life in the Lone Star State. General Johnson, nearly ninety years of age, succumbs during 1922, about three years after the conclusion of World War I.

In Tennessee, contingents of the 8th Iowa, 108th and 113th Illinois, 39th, 40th and 41st Wisconsin, 61st U.S. Colored and the 3rd and 4th Iowa Cavalry Regiments, bolstered by Battery G, 1st Missouri Light Artillery, engage Confederate Cavalry at Memphis. The Union sustains 30 killed and 100 wounded. The Confederates suffer 100 killed and wounded.

In Virginia, the Union 6th Corps and the cavalry forces of Generals Wesley Merritt and James Wilson skirmish with Confederates at Berryville, Summit Point and Flowing Springs. The Union sustains 600 killed and wounded. The Confederates sustain 400 killed and wounded. Also, Private George W. Reed captures the 24th North Carolina Volunteers' flag (CSA). Reed becomes the recipient of the Medal of Honor for his action above and beyond the call of duty.

In Mississippi, the Union 4th Iowa, 5th Minnesota, 11th and 21st Missouri Infantry Regiments and the 3rd Iowa and the 12th Missouri Cavalry Regiments skirmish for two days with Confederates at College (Oxford Hill). No Union casualties are reported. The Confederates sustain 15 killed.

August 22 (Monday) **In Kentucky,** a Confederate contingent clashes with a Union force at Canton. Specific units and casualty figures are unreported.

In Tennessee, Union and Confederate contingents skirmish at Rogersville. Specific units and casualty figures are unavailable.

In Confederate general officer activity, Congressman Lucius J. Gartrell, formerly colonel of the 7th Georgia Infantry Regiment, had re-entered the Army and is promoted to the rank of brigadier general effective this date. Gartrell organizes four regiments of Georgia troops and afterward heads for South Carolina to bolster the defenses against General William T. Sherman.

In Alabama, U.S. troops and naval forces attack Fort Morgan. The fort surrenders after heated Union pressure on August 23. The USS *Galena* participates in this action. Afterward the *Galena* departs the region for Key West, Florida, to join the East Gulf Blockading Squadron.

In Union general officer activity, Joseph K. Barnes is appointed brigadier general and simultaneously is appointed surgeon general. He succeeds General William Alexander Hammond as surgeon general. Also, Lt. Colonel James Hughes Stokes resigns from the service; however, on the same day, he is remustered into the service as a captain and as assistant adjutant general. On 22 July 1865, he is promoted to brigadier general of volunteers, one month before he resigns from the service. Subsequently, General Stokes' eyesight continues to deteriorate and eventually he becomes blind. Later he relocates from Chicago to New York, where he dies on 27 December 1890.

In Confederate general officer activity, Colonel John Dunovant, 5th South Carolina Infantry, is promoted by President Jefferson Davis to brigadier general. Dunovant had been cashiered out of the service during June 1862 while he was based on John's Island as colonel of the 1st South Carolina; however, later, Governor Pickens appoints him colonel of the 5th South Carolina, and his subsequent action causes President Davis to reinstate him with a commission of brigadier general.

In Naval activity, off Natchez, Mississippi, a Union squadron, including the USS *Vindicator,* repels a Confederate contingent that attempts to cross the Mississippi River.

August 23 (Tuesday) **In Alabama,** the Union has tightly squeezed the Southern naval cause by seizing Fort Morgan, and it simultaneously terminates the blockade runners using the port. Confederate Brigadier General Richard L. Page (Annapolis midshipman class of 1824), in command of the outer defenses of Mobile, had resisted tenaciously, but this day he is forced to capitulate. He is held at Fort Delaware on an island near Salem, New Jersey, until 24 July 1865. After being paroled, he re-

turns to Virginia and becomes superintendent of schools in the city of Norfolk. Subsequent to retirement, he dies in Blue Ridge Summit, Pennsylvania, on 9 August 1901. The other two posts, Fort Powell and Fort Gaines, had been secured during early this month. In December, Admiral David Farragut departs for the North, leaving the squadron under the command of Commodore James S. Palmer, who remains in command until the following February, when Rear Admiral H.K. Thatcher arrives to assume command. Upon his relief, Palmer becomes commander of the Western Gulf Blockading Squadron.

In Mississippi, Union and Confederate troops engage at Abbeville. The 10th Missouri, 14th Iowa, 5th and 7th Minnesota and the 8th Wisconsin Volunteers participate. The Union sustains 20 wounded. The Confederates suffer 15 killed.

August 24 (Wednesday) **In Arkansas,** skirmishing erupts in various parts of the state. Clashes occur at Fort Smith, Ashley Station, Hay's Station and Long Prairie. At Fort Smith, the 11th U.S. Colored Regiment engages the Rebels. The Union sustains one killed and 13 wounded. Confederate casualties are unavailable. At Ashley Station and Hay's Station, the 9th Iowa and 8th and 11th Missouri Cavalry Regiments participate. The Union sustains five killed and 41 wounded. The Confederates sustain 60 wounded.

In Georgia, during General Sherman's operations around Atlanta, General Joseph Lightburn is severely wounded. He sustains a bullet wound in the head; however, he does survive. Subsequent to his recuperation, he is reassigned and given duty in his home state, West Virginia, and some duty in Maryland. After the war Lightburn musters out of the service. Later, during 1867, he becomes a Baptist minister.

A U.S. gunboat off Mobile in pursuit of a blockade runner during the night (Mottelay, *The Soldier in Our Civil War*, 1886).

In Virginia, the 10th Corps, Army of the James, engages Confederate troops at Bermuda Hundred through the next day. The Union suffers 31 wounded; Confederates have 61 missing. Also, a detachment of the 8th Corps, Army of West Virginia, engages the Confederates at Halltown through the 27th. The Union suffers 39 killed and 178 wounded; the Confederates suffer 138 killed or wounded.

In Confederate general officer activity, Colonel Walter Husted Stevens (West Point, 1848), the brother-in-law of Confederate General Louis Hebert, is promoted to brigadier general. General Stevens initially entered the Confederate service during 1861 and participated at First Manassas (Bull Run) as an engineer officer attached to General Beauregard. Later he was appointed chief engineer of the Army of Northern Virginia with the rank of colonel.

In Naval activity, the gunboat USS *Fahkee* engages a blockade runner in the vicinity of Wilmington, North Carolina, but the Rebel vessel is not destroyed or captured. In January 1865 the *Fahkee* participates in the operation against Fort Fisher by delivering cargo to the fleet. Later, during April 1865, it is transferred to the Southern Atlantic Squadron. It operates out of Port Royal and provides supplies and provisions to the fleet at Charleston and the blockade ships off the Carolinas, and for a while it accompanies the squadron in a cruise off Cuba. During June 1865, the *Fahkee* sails for Philadelphia and arrives there on the 19th to be decommissioned on the 28th. The *Fahkee* is sold on 10 August 1865. In other activity, the USS *Gettysburg* seizes a blockade runner, the *Lilian.*

August 25 (Thursday)   In Arkansas, a contingent of cavalry (Army of the Gulf) engages Confederates at Conee Creek, Clinton.

In Georgia, General William T. Sherman takes action to secure the Macon Railroad. He directs the 20th Corps to deploy at the Chattahootchie River to guard it, while infantry contingents prepare to strike the West Point Railroad.

In Virginia, Union troops under Generals Winfield S. Hancock and David Gregg and Confederate forces commanded by Jubal Early engage in a bitter contest at Ream's Station. The Confederates initially overrun the Union position, capturing five of guns, but the Union strikes back. General John Gibbon's division assaults to recapture the position, but the Rebels repel the attempt. Meanwhile, General Nelson Miles' division picks up the slack and makes up for the lackadaisical performance by Gibbon's troops. General Miles rallies his troops and a contingent of the 61st New York and the 1st New York Artillery counterattacks and recaptures the terrain; Captain George F. McKnight's (12th New York Independent Battery) guns are regained. Lacking reinforcements, General Winfield S. Hancock retires from Ream's Station. Union troops also retain control of Weldon Railroad for the duration of the war. The Union suffers 127 killed, 546 wounded and over

1,750 missing. The Confederates have 1,500 killed or wounded.

In other activity, the combined force of Merritt's and Wilson's cavalry skirmishes heavily at Smithfield and Shepherdstown (Kearneysville). The Union sustains 20 killed, 61 wounded and 100 missing. The Confederates suffer 300 killed and wounded. Confederate Colonel (later brigadier general) William Paul Roberts, in command of a brigade, participates in this action.

In Naval activity, the gunboat *Ascutney* is patrolling the outer sector of the blockade vessels near Wilmington when it encounters the CSS *Tallahassee* at 0430. A lookout observes the ship as it approaches Wilmington following a cruise that had caused a high amount of destruction while the ship was at sea for less than three weeks. Pursuit begins once the Rebel ship is detected; however, the *Ascutney* lacks the power to intercept the *Tallahassee,* which speeds into the darkness and evades an encounter. The *Ascutney* also encounters mechanical problems with the engine. Subsequent to this incident, the war career of the *Ascutney* essentially ends. It is towed to Washington, D.C. and decommissioned on 22 September 1864 to undergo extensive repairs; it is out of service beyond the close of hostilities; however, in October 1865, the *Ascutney* is recommissioned.

In other activity, Acting Rear Admiral S.P. Lee, the commanding officer of the North Atlantic Blockading Squadron, informs the Secretary of the Navy Gideon Welles that the services of the USS *Wilderness* are needed to increase the effectiveness of the blockade of Wilmington, North Carolina. On 1 September, a report of Lee's squadron lists the *Wilderness* as "supply steam; ordered to fit out as gunboat and join [the] blockade." The *Wilderness,* by the latter part of October, is fitted out with four 24-pounders.

August 26 (Friday)   In Georgia, Union troops under Sherman operating in the vicinity of Atlanta raid the West Point Railroad. On the following day, the rails stretching between East Point and Fairburn are torn out to sever the route and prevent any supplies or reinforcements from arriving.

In Arkansas, the 9th Kansas and 3rd Wisconsin Cavalry Regiments clash with Confederates at Bull Bayou.

In Virginia, elements of the 1st and 2nd Divisions, 8th Corps, Army of West Virginia, engages Confederates at Halltown.

In Union general officer activity, Union Brigadier General Hector Tyndale resigns from the army because of failing health. General Tyndale fought at Cedar Mountain and Second Manassas, and he served at Antietam as commander of the XII Corps, where he was twice wounded. In the campaign at Chattanooga, three different horses were shot from under him while he was commanding a brigade of the XI Corps.

August 27 (Saturday)   In Georgia, General William T. Sherman pulls a diversionary tactic

at Atlanta, dispatching troops around Hood's Confederate lines. Hood mistakenly accepts this Union move as a withdrawal, which causes temporary excitement in Atlanta, but the maneuver successfully severs the railroad and supply routes to the Confederate-held city. Sherman begins to tighten his noose around Atlanta, the beleaguered Confederate stronghold.

In Kentucky, a contingent of the 108th U.S. Colored Troops skirmishes with Confederates at Owensboro.

In Mississippi, the 14th Iowa, 10th Missouri Cavalry and the 11th U.S. Colored Artillery skirmish for two days with Confederates at Holly Springs. The Union sustains one killed and two wounded. Confederate casualties are unavailable.

August 28 (Monday)   In Virginia, General William T. Sheridan's Union cavalry, including the 1st U.S. Cavalry, continues its relentless pursuit of General Jubal Early's raiders, striking again with fury at Smithfield. The Union suffers 10 killed and 90 wounded; the Confederates have some 200 dead or wounded. During Early's raid, one of his commanders, Brigadier General John C. Vaughn, had been wounded in a skirmish in the vicinity of Martinsburg, West Virginia, and subsequent to his recovery he is transferred to East Tennessee.

In Missouri, Company E, 4th Missouri Militia Cavalry, skirmishes with Confederates in Howard County.

In the Indian Territory (Nevada Territory), the 7th Iowa Cavalry Regiment engages Indians at Fort Cottonwood.

In Confederate general officer activity, Colonel Walter Husted Stevens, on duty in Richmond, is promoted to the rank of brigadier general. Stevens (West Point, 1848) continues to work on strengthening the defenses of Richmond.

In Naval activity, Rear Admiral David D. Porter, the recently appointed commanding officer of the North Atlantic Blockading Squadron, directs the *Wilderness* to report to the Eastern Bar on the Cape Fear River to initiate duty as blockader.

August 29 (Monday)   In Kentucky, the 117th U.S. Colored Troops Regiment skirmishes with Confederates at Ghent.

In Virginia, a Union force composed of the 1st Division, Cavalry Corps, and the 3rd Division, 6th Corps, Army of the Potomac, under General Merritt, clashes with Confederate infantry and cavalry at Smithfield. Meanwhile, another Union contingent, led by Captain Blazer, battles Confederates at Wormley's Gap. The 2nd Cavalry Division, Army of the Potomac engages Confederates for two days at Arthur's Swamp.

August 30 (Tuesday)   In Georgia, Union troops skirmish with Confederates at Flint River. Union Captain L.G. Estes leads a bold charge over a burning bridge to assault the Confederate positions.

In Union general officer activity, Brigadier General James Gallant Spears is dismissed from the army after having complained in February that the Emancipation Proclamation deprived him of his slaves. Also, General George Crook assumes command of the Department of West Virginia, replacing Major General David Hunter. Soon after assuming command, in October, Crook is promoted to major general.

August 31 (Wednesday)   In Georgia, Union forces under General John Schofield arrive at Rough and Ready. Meanwhile, General O.O. Howard moves to within two miles of Jonesboro and General Thomas stands between both forces as General William T. Sherman further tightens the noose around Atlanta.

In Tennessee, the Union 115th Ohio Regiment skirmishes with Confederates at Blockhouse No. 5 on the Nashville and Chattanooga Railroad. The Union sustains three killed. The Confederates suffer 25 wounded.

August 31–September 1   BATTLE OF JONESBORO Union troops from General William T. Sherman's command at Atlanta, including the 15th, 16th and 17th Divisions, 14th Corps, and Brigadier General Jefferson C. Davis' cavalry, engage Confederates from General William Hardee's Army of Tennessee, at Jonesboro, Georgia. General Hardee attacks, but his strength is insufficient to dislodge the Yankees. In turn, the Union, after repulsing the assault, successfully slices the rail lines that have been feeding John B. Hood's troops in Atlanta. By seizing the Macon and Western Railroad, Sherman has eliminated the last of the railroads that connect Atlanta with the remainder of the South. After dusk on September 1, Union General Jefferson C. Davis and his 14th Corps shut down the northern front of Jonesboro and link with General Howard's force by stretching out toward the railroad. Meanwhile, General David S. Stanley's IV Corps, trailed by Schofield, advances toward Jonesboro. In contrast, General William Hardee evades further trouble by abandoning Jonesboro and moving to Lovejoy's Station.

The Union loss is 1,149 killed or wounded; the Confederates lose 2,000 killed, wounded, or missing. Confederate Brigadier Generals James P. Anderson and Alfred Cumming (West Point, 1849) are wounded. Cumming will not participate in any further actions. Union Sgt. Patrick Irwin, 14th Michigan, accepts the surrender of Confederate General Daniel C. Govan. General Govan is exchanged and later joins General Joseph E. Johnston in the Carolinas. Confederate Brigadier General Jesse J. Finley sees no additional field action after this battle because of old wounds suffered during the campaigns around Chattanooga and Atlanta, where he commanded Florida infantry regiments. Confederate Colonel Joseph B. Palmer, 18th Tennessee Regiment, receives his fifth wound. He recovers and will participate in the battle of Franklin, Tennessee; later he transfers to the Carolinas. Confederate General John Carpenter Carter participates, and for a while,

he commands General Cheatham's division. Also, Union brigadier general Absalom Baird becomes the recipient of the Medal of Honor for his heroism while leading a charge.

September   In South Dakota, a contingent of Dakota cavalry commanded by Captain Nelson Minor establishes Fort Thompson (also known as the Crow Creek Agency), named for Colonel Clark W. Thompson, the superintendent of Indian Affairs in St. Paul, Minnesota. The fort is constructed at a point near the left side of the Missouri River and the mouth of Soldier Creek. The garrison abandons the post during June 1867 and redeploys at Fort Sully.

In Virginia, the Union forces under General Grant continue to battle Confederates at Petersburg through October 30. The Union sustains 170 killed, 822 wounded and 812 missing. Confederates report 1,000 missing.

September 1 (Thursday)   In Georgia, the Confederates evacuate Atlanta. Confederate troops in the vicinity of Jonesboro also withdraw to join General John B. Hood's main force. The Texas Brigade, led by Brigadier General Lawrence S. Ross and greatly decreased in strength following severe combat with the cavalry of Union Generals Edward McCook and Hugh Kilpatrick, will move with General Hood to Tennessee and act as rear guard. Confederate General Hood directs that all public property be destroyed and the city of Atlanta evacuated. Although the city is abandoned and Union troops occupy it on the following day, General Sherman does not arrive in the city until the 8th.

German Sherman's conquest of a prize jewel of the Confederacy is a rejuvenating achievement for the North, as the ongoing duel between Robert E. Lee and U.S. Grant has not yet reaped similar results; the Rebels defiantly hold at Petersburg and Richmond. Nevertheless, the loss of Atlanta raises spirits in the North and diminishes optimism in the South. The casualty reports for the Union during the Georgia Campaign are: killed 4,423; wounded, 22,822; and missing 4,442; totaling 31,687. Confederate casualties during the Georgia campaign: killed 3,044; wounded 18,692; missing, unreported. However, General Sherman reports the capture of 12,983 Confederates.

In Union general officer activity, Brigadier General Mortimer Leggett receives the brevet of major general. Leggett's division is participating in the Atlanta Campaign. Subsequently, Leggett participates in Sherman's March to the Sea, in command of the 3rd Division (XVII Corps). Colonel Giles Alexander Smith (8th Missouri Infantry) is promoted to brigadier general. He participates in the March to the Sea and the Carolinas campaign. After the war he is promoted to major general of volunteers, and during the following year, he resigns from the service.

In Naval activity, the CSS *Stag,* a steel paddle steamer built in England at Liverpool and acquired by the Confederacy, had departed England during August of this year. On or about

this day, it departs Nassau for the Carolinas. In other activity, the monitor USS *Mahopac* is commissioned at about this time (September). It is assigned to duty on the James River, but by the latter part of the year, it moves to North Carolina. The USS *Maumee* is also commissioned at about this time. It is immediately ordered to join the search for the CSS *Tallahassee,* a Confederate raider. Subsequent to this two-month mission, it participates in the operations against Fort Fisher at Wilmington, North Carolina, during December 1864 and January 1865, prior to moving to the Cape Fear River and the James River to patrol for the duration. After the war is terminated, it is decommissioned during June 1865. In December 1869, the *Maumee* is sold. In other activity, the USS *Tallapoosa* is commissioned at about this time (September). Its initial orders direct it to join the search for the Confederate raider *Tallahassee;* however, the *Tallapoosa* encounters nasty weather and sustains damage that sends it to Boston for repairs. Next it embarks to join the East Gulf Blockading Squadron. It remains in the region well beyond the close of hostilities until made inactive during 1867. In 1869, it is recommissioned and utilized as a dispatch ship and then at Annapolis as a training vessel, prior to some service as a transport. It sinks off Vineyard Haven, Massachusetts, in August 1874 after colliding with the schooner *James S. Lowell.* Nonetheless, it is refloated and recommissioned during January 1886 and assigned to the South Atlantic Squadron the following July. It is sold at Montevideo, Uruguay, during March 1892.

September 1–8   In Tennessee, Union General Lovell H. Rousseau's cavalry — supported by the 1st and 4th Tennessee, 2nd Michigan, 1st Wisconsin, 8th Iowa, 2nd and 8th Indiana and the 6th Kentucky Regiments — give chase to Confederates under Major General Joseph Wheeler in Tennessee. During the eight-day mission, the Union inflicts casualties upon the Rebels, totaling 300 killed, wounded and missing. Brigadier General Joseph H. Lewis' brigade (Orphan Brigade) is transformed into a mounted unit and attached to Major General Joseph Wheeler's cavalry. At this action, the Union sustains 10 killed and 30 wounded.

September 2 (Friday)   In Georgia, Atlanta falls to the Union forces of General William T. Sherman, ending the northern Georgia campaign. The Confederates, under the command of General John B. Hood, evacuate Atlanta, as General Henry W. Slocum's XX Corps (Sherman's command) occupies the city. Sherman burns part of Atlanta before initiating his March to the Sea, destroying rails and farms along the way. Sherman telegraphs Washington: "Atlanta is ours and fairly won." Sherman calmly enters the city on the 6th. He spreads his troops from Decatur through Atlanta for many miles to the right of the city. The Stars and Stripes once again fly over Atlanta. Also, the 9th Ohio Cavalry encounters and engages Confederates along the railroad at Big Shanty.

Left: A Confederate jail in Decatur, Georgia, where Union prisoners are confined. *Right:* Citizens of Atlanta seek passes to the north and south at the provost marshal's headquarters in accordance with General Sherman's directive for the residents to evacuate (Mottelay, *The Soldier in Our Civil War*, 1886).

In other activity, the Union 4th Corps (Army of the Cumberland) and 23rd Corps (Army of the Ohio) skirmshes through the 6th with Confederate units at Lovejoy's Station. Union Brigadier General Thomas J. Wood, despite having sustained a shattered leg on the first day of the clash, remains in the field and continues to direct and rally his troops.

In Tennessee, Union troops attached to the Army of the Cumberland — including cavalry attached to the 14th Corps — and the 15th, 16th and 17th Corps, Army of the Cumberland, skirmish heatedly with a contingent of Confederates in the vicinity of Franklin. Confederate Brigadier General John Herbert Kelly, commanding a division of Major General Joseph Wheeler's cavalry, is mortally wounded during the contest.

In Arkansas and Missouri, Union forces, including the 5th Minnesota Volunteer Infantry Regiment, initiate a forced march through Arkansas and Missouri to join the forces in pursuit of Confederate General Sterling Price's command. Major General James F. Fagan accompanies Price on this mission into Missouri.

In Confederate general officer activity, during the Atlanta Campaign, Confederate Brigadier General Matthew Duncan Ector had lost one leg by amputation due to wounds. Colonel William Hugh Young assumes command of Ector's brigade, and he is promoted to brigadier general effective August 15, 1864. Young was also wounded twice (his fourth and fifth wounds) at Kennesaw Mountain, but he maintains command.

September 3 (Saturday)   In Tennessee, the 100th U.S. Colored Troops skirmish Confederates at Murfreesboro.

In Virginia, on the 3rd and 4th, General Sheridan's cavalry again clashes with Confederates led by Major General McCausland (General Jubal Early's command) at Berryville. Also,

Confederate General Richard Anderson's troops, en route to Richmond, are halted by Union troops and forced to withdraw to Winchester. Confederate General Benjamin Grubb Humphreys (later governor of Mississippi) is wounded as the Rebels withdraw to Richmond.

In Union general officer activity, Colonel Thomas Wilberforce Egan (40th New York), subsequent to recuperating from a severe debilitating wound, is promoted to brigadier general. By this time, the 40th has sustained heavy casualties; however, after the contest at Chancellorsville, fresh recruits of the 87th New York and veterans from the 37th, 38th, 55th and 101st New York Regiments bring the 40th back up in strength.

September 4 (Sunday)   In Tennessee, Union troops, including the 9th and 13th Tennessee and the 10th Michigan Cavalry Regiments, under General Alvan C. Gillem (West Point, 1851), close in on the notorious General John Hunt Morgan and his raiders. The Union stalkers catch the Confederates off guard at Greenville, capturing many of them. General Morgan is killed just outside the house in which he had slept for the night, while he attempts escape.

In Virginia, elements of the 3rd Cavalry Division (Army of the Potomac) under General George Crook engage Confederates led by General Joseph B. Kershaw at Darksville.

September 5 (Monday)   In Virginia, Confederate General Jubal Early is still moving south, with Philip Sheridan on his heels.

In South Carolina, Union shelling of Fort Sumter ceases.

In Tennessee, Union Cavalry (Rousseau's pursuit) engages Confederates under Major General Joseph Wheeler at Campbellville.

September 6 (Tuesday)   In Arkansas, a skirmish develops between a contingent of the 9th

Iowa Cavalry and Confederates at Searcy. The Union sustains two killed and six wounded. Confederate casualties are unavailable.

September 7 (Wednesday)   In Georgia, General William T. Sherman issues an order directing all civilians to leave Atlanta. The citizens are livid.

In Virginia, forces of General Philip Sheridan skirmish with Confederates under General Jubal Early near Winchester. Confederates launch an artillery bombardment against a signal tower assigned to the 4th U.S. Colored Troops at Dutch Gap. Casualty figures are unavailable.

In Tennessee, a contingent of the 9th Pennsylvania Cavalry skirmishes with Confederates at Readyville.

September 8 (Thursday)   In New Jersey, General George McClellan pens a letter to the Honorable Horatio Seymour (governor of New York) in which he accepts the nomination as the Democratic Party candidate for president: "Believing that the views here expressed are those of the convention, and the people you represent, I accept the nomination. I realize the weight of the responsibility to be borne should the people ratify your choice. Conscious of my own weakness, I can only seek fervently the guidance of the Ruler of the Universe, and, relying on His all powerful aid, do my best to restore Union and peace to a suffering people, and to establish and guard their liberties and rights. Very respectfully, GEO. B. MCCLELLAN."

September 8–9   *In Naval activity,* a Union flotilla — including the USS *Rodolph*, *Stockdale* and *Tritonia*, along with an army transport — initiate a mission to reduce a Confederate saltworks of large capacity located along the Bon Secour River at Salt House Point, Alabama. Two of the vessels reach the objective prior to noon; however, the works is a massive operation that takes time to dismantle and destroy. At about mid-afternoon on the following day, the detachment returns to the ships and the flotilla withdraws. Admiral David Farragut reports: "There were 55 furnaces, in which were manufactured nearly 2,000 bushels of salt per day, and their destruction must necessarily inconvenience the rebels."

September 9 (Friday)   In Arkansas, the Union steamer *J.D. Perry* comes under attack by about 100 Confederates in the vicinity of Clarendon. Brigadier General Christopher C. Andrews, commander 2nd Division, Seventh Corps, sends a report to Major General Steele informing him of the attack and of his need for fresh troops. Andrews states that he is concerned that he lacks sufficient strength to do the duties assigned to him. He has only eight companies of the 11th Missouri and eight companies of the 12th Michigan.

September 10 (Saturday)   In Virginia, the 99th Pennsylvania, 20th Indiana and the 2nd U.S. Sharpshooters, commanded by General De Trobriand, seize Fort Hell in the vicinity of Jerusalem Plank Road. The Union suffers 20 wounded; 90 Confederates are taken prisoner. Grant states in a letter to Sherman: "So soon as your men are rested, it is desirable that another campaign be commenced." General Grant suggests moving General Edward Canby against Savannah and for Sherman to hit Augusta.

In Naval activity, the USS *Santiago de Cuba*, while operating in the Atlantic as part of the blockading squadron, seizes the steamer *Advance*. In early November it seizes another blockade runner, the steamer *Lucy*. The *Advance*, initially named *Lord Clyde*, a side-wheel steamer built in Scotland during 1862 and purchased by North Carolina, is acquired by the U.S. Navy and commissioned the USS *Advance*. Prior to capture, the *Advance* (also known as *A.D. Vance*) had run the blockade successfully about twenty times. Later, during June 1865, the *Advance* is decommissioned and renamed the *Frolic*. The USS *Santiago de Cuba* continues in service for the duration. It participates in the operations against Fort Fisher, North Carolina (December 1864 and January 1865), and following the conclusion of hostilities, it is decommissioned in June 1865. In September it is sold at auction and initiates service as a commercial vessel until 1886, when it is turned into a barge and renamed *Marion*. It remains in service until 1889.

September 11 (Sunday)   In Virginia at Fort Hell (Fort Sedgwick) in the vicinity of Petersburg, the Union and Confederates exchange fire this day and the next.

September 12 (Monday)   In Virginia, the Union maintains its pressure against the Rebels in Richmond and against their rear door at Petersburg. Meanwhile, the Union and Confederates continue to taunt each other in the vicinity of Winchester. On the Petersburg front, Colonel Joshua Blackwood Howell (formerly brigadier general, Pennsylvania militia) is severely injured when his horse falls while he is in

the saddle. Two days later, while at X Corps headquarters outside Petersburg, he dies from his injuries. The following spring he receives a posthumous promotion to brigadier general to rank from this day.

The X Corps had been attached to the Department of the South until directed to move north to join the Army of the James at Petersburg. Lt. Colonel Richard Henry Jackson, assigned as commander of the 2nd Division at Petersburg (General Weitzel's XXV Corps), commands the division until the close of hostilities. He is finally promoted to brigadier general during May of 1865.

In Union general officer activity, Colonel Alexander Brydie Dyer is promoted to the rank of brigadier general in the Regular Army. General Dyer, who invented and patented the "Dyer" shell, donates it to the government. He receives the brevet rank of major general. He remains with the ordnance department after the war, but his health begins to fail during 1869. General Dyer, a Virginian who remained loyal to the Union, is considered one of the top three southerners who accomplished distinguished careers in the Union Army, the other two being General Winfield Scott and George H. Thomas.

September 13 (Tuesday)   In Arkansas, two companies of the Union 1st Indiana Cavalry skirmish with Confederates at Pine Bluff.

In Virginia, Union soldiers on a reconnaissance mission near Berryville skirmish with Confederates. The Union captures the colors of the 8th South Carolina Infantry during the battle at Lock's Ford. Torbert's cavalry captures 181 troops. The Union sustains two killed and 18 wounded. Also, a Union reconnaissance force under General George W. Getty (Sheridan's command) initiates a mission that leads them to the Opequon River.

In Union general officer activity, Colonel Joseph Roswell Hawley, 7th Connecticut Infantry, is appointed brigadier general of volunteers. He participates in various actions, including the Port Royal expedition and the expedition against Fernandina, Florida (January 1863). Subsequently, he participates in the campaign to gain Fort Fisher, North Carolina. Toward the end of the war, he receives command of a district in Connecticut. He receives the brevet of major general after the war and musters out of the service in 1866.

In Union general officer activity, General John Henry Martindale, attached to the XVIII Corps since the previous spring, subsequent to being the military governor of the capital, resigns his commission on this day due to ill health. He had led a division at Cold Harbor as well as Bermuda Hundred and at Petersburg before his health compelled him to resign. Also, Colonel William H. Seward, Jr., is promoted to brigadier general. Subsequent to recuperating from injuries sustained at Monocacy, he is assigned to the Department of West Virginia. He remains in the department until he resigns from the service on 1 June 1865.

September 14 (Wednesday)   In Virginia, during the Richmond campaign, the forces at Fort Crawford near Weldon Railroad have a quiet day until about 1700, when Confederate artillery bombards the railroad. Union guns return fire.

September 15 (Thursday)   In Georgia, Confederates, having lost Atlanta, concentrate on harassing the Union supply lines.

In Virginia, the situation around Winchester and Petersburg remains quiet. General Grant prepares to meet with General Sheridan to discuss strategy to neutralize the Confederate tactics with regard to bolstering their defenses at Petersburg.

In Confederate general officer activity, Colonel Basil Wilson Duke is promoted to brigadier general.

In Naval activity, the USS *Tallahatchie*, acting on intelligence regarding a blockade runner, positions a picket boat near the mouth of the Blind River. As expected, subsequent to dusk, the vessel is spotted and ordered to surrender. The crew tosses the ledger book overboard; however, it is recovered.

September 16 (Friday)   In West Virginia, General U.S. Grant confers with General Sheridan at Charles Town, 10 miles south of Harpers Ferry. The two men are aware of Early's dispatch of Richard Anderson's troops to reinforce Petersburg and plan for another offensive to defeat Early.

In Virginia, the 1st D.C. Cavalry and the 13th Pennsylvania Cavalry encounter and engage Confederates at Sycamore Church. The Union suffers 400 killed, wounded and missing. The Confederates sustain 50 killed and wounded.

In the Indian Territory, the 2nd Kansas Cavalry and the 79th U.S. Colored Regiment battle Confederates at Fort Gibson (Oklahoma) in the Indian Territory through the 18th. The Union sustains 38 killed and 48 missing. Confederate casualties are unreported.

September 17 (Saturday)   In Virginia, the cavalry commands of Generals August Kautz and David Gregg encounter and skirmish with Confederates at Belcher's Mills. The Union sustains 25 wounded. Confederate casualties are unreported. Also, the 1st D.C. Cavalry and the 13th Pennsylvania Cavalry (Generals David Gregg and August Kautz) skirmish with Confederates led by General Wade Hampton at Sycamore Church. The Union sustains about 110 killed, wounded and missing. The Confederates suffer about 90 killed, wounded and missing. In other activity, the 13th and 16th New York Cavalry Divisions clash with Confederates at Fairfax Station.

In Missouri, one company of the 3rd Missouri Militia Cavalry battles Confederates at Doniphan and Black River through September 20.

In Confederate general officer activity, Colonel Charles Miller Shelley is promoted to brigadier general.

In Naval activity, the USS *Tallahatchie* confiscates Confederate supplies and cotton bales near the mouth of the Amite River. The *Tallahatchie* is decommissioned at Mobile, Alabama, on 21 July. It is sold at auction on 12 August and renamed *Coosa*; it serves a commercial vessel until it is lost by fire at Licking River, Kentucky, on 7 July 1869.

September 18 (Sunday)   In the Nevada Territory, the 7th Iowa Cavalry engages Confederates at Fort Cottonwood.

In Virginia, Union General Philip Sheridan makes preparations to assault the now-weakened forces of Confederate General Jubal Early at Winchester. Early's forces are deployed on the west bank of Opequon Creek about four miles outside Winchester. Sheridan's force is posted about twelve miles away at Berryville. The fighting rages in this area for several days. This day, a contingent of General Early's force initiates a reconnaissance mission toward Martinsburg. Elements of the Union 2nd Cavalry Division, Army of West Virginia, skirmish with Confederates at Martinsburg.

September 19 (Monday)   In Virginia, Union troops attached to General Philip Sheridan, including the 38th Massachusetts Infantry, clash with General Jubal Early's force at Belle Grove, Opequon Creek (see also, **September 19–22 BATTLE OF WINCHESTER [OPEQUON]**).

In the Indian Territory, the 2nd, 6th and 14th Kansas Cavalry Regiments, supported by the 1st and 2nd Kansas Indian Home Guards, engage a Confederate force at Cabin Creek.

In Confederate general officer activity, Brigadier General Matthew Calbraith Butler is promoted to major general.

In Naval activity, the USS *Michigan,* built during 1842 and commissioned in September 1844, spends its active service during the war on the Great Lakes with responsibility for guarding against a Confederate attack originating in Canada. On this day, Confederates led by John Yates Beall, posing as passengers, board the steamer *Philo Parsons* and seize the vessel. After gaining control of the ship, it is used to move against another steamer, the *Island Queen.* Beall's plan, concocted earlier in Canada, includes seizing the sole U.S. warship on the Great Lakes, the *Michigan;* however, the commanding officer of the *Michigan* has advance knowledge of the plot, which also includes raiding Johnson's Island on Lake Erie off Sandusky, Ohio. Beall aborts the operation to seize the *Michigan.* He and his cohorts sail to Canada and destroy the *Philo Parsons.* Beall had earlier destroyed the *Island Queen.*

His operation is the final attempt by the Confederacy to launch an attack on the Great Lakes. Although Beall escapes capture by the Union, he is later seized at Niagara Falls and transported to Fort Lafayette, New York. From there he is transported to Fort Columbus on Governor's Island, where he is tried and convicted on charges including being a spy. He is convicted by the military tribunal and hanged

on 24 February 1865. After the war the *Michigan* continues in service on the Great Lakes. During 1905, it is renamed the USS *Wolverine.* Decommissioned in May 1912, the *Wolverine* is transferred to the Pennsylvania Naval Militia to be used as a training vessel. Finally, the *Wolverine* is sold for scrap, terminating the long career of the U.S. Navy's first iron-hulled warship.

September 19–22   BATTLE OF WINCHESTER (OPEQUON) Union General Sheridan assaults Confederates under General Jubal Early during the morning of September 19 at Winchester (Opequon Creek), Virginia. The 6th Corps and the Kanawha Infantry cross the creek and encroach the lines of Fitzhugh Lee, while Wilson's cavalry attacks the positions and secures the positions, inflicting heavy casualties and forcing the Rebels to retreat to Fisher's Hill, leaving their casualties behind. Meanwhile, Sheridan awaits the arrival of Emory's 19th Corps. This pause permits Early to speed from Bunker Hill to intercept the assaulting forces. Sheridan deploys his troops along a line that will launch them against Winchester from the north and from the east, while Early's troops on the left command the high ground west of the town. The Confederates defending Winchester number about 8,300 infantrymen and 3,000 cavalry troops, bolstered by three artillery battalions, but these are dwarfed by Sheridan's force, which numbers 25,000 infantrymen and 10,000 cavalry troops. Nevertheless, the Confederates equal the Union's stamina and unleash a furious round of blows that maintain the ground, despite the odds.

The two sides continue to pound each other for about three hours, but neither gains the advantage. Finally, at about 1600, General Sheridan orders a full-scale assault. The combined cavalry of Averell and Merritt burst forth and overwhelm those on the fortified hill. During the attacks, Colonel Charles Lovell performs heroically while leading his cavalry brigade. Simultaneously, the infantry barges through the lines and drives the Confederates back into Winchester. While the Union sprints through this gap in the center, another cavalry contingent under General Wilson makes progress on the right and penetrates deeply, forcing the Confederates to make a hurried withdrawal through the city with Union troops running up their heels.

By dusk, the fighting subsides, but the Confederates pay a heavy toll. Darkness prevents further pursuit. In one particular action, Col. James M. Schoonmaker, 14th Pennsylvania Cavalry, charges the enemy's left flank, causing the Confederates to flee. This gallant charge helps to change the tide of battle. Early moves his force about thirty miles to Fisher's Hill before he calls a halt. Sheridan continues in pursuit and keeps his command in full stride, skirmishing fiercely until the 22nd at Fisher's Hill. Sheridan's momentum forces the Confederates to withdraw south toward New Market and Jackson. Colonel John B. McIntosh is gravely wounded during the fighting and the doctors amputate his right leg. For his actions, McIn-

tosh receives the brevet rank of brigadier general in the Regular Army. At the close of hostilities, he receives the brevet rank of major general in the Volunteers and the Regular Army. Despite his handicap, General McIntosh remains in the service. During 1866 he becomes colonel of the 42nd Infantry. Later he retires with the rank of brigadier general.

Union Colonel George Beal also participates at this battle and becomes brigadier general in November 1864.

Union casualties total 693 dead, 4,033 wounded and 623 missing. The Confederates sustain 3,250 killed or wounded and 3,600 captured. Union Brigadier General David A. Russell (West Point, 1845) is killed while leading a charge. Upon his death, General Emory Upton assumes command of Russell's division, and in the course of action, he sustains a wound. Upton remains in the field, directing his command from a stretcher, which is being carried around in the midst of the ongoing battle. Subsequent to his recovery, General Upton joins General James Wilson (1865) and participates as commander of the 4th Division during Wilson's cavalry raids in Alabama and Georgia.

Confederate Brigadier General Archibald C. Godwin, 57th North Carolina Infantry, and Confederate Major General Robert Emmett Rodes are also killed. Brigadier General John Pegram will succeed Rodes and lead his division, but he does not attain the rank of major general. Also, Confederate General Zebulon York (born in Maine) is wounded and loses one arm. Confederate General Robert Daniel Johnston, 23rd North Carolina, participates in this battle. Afterwards, Johnston will defend Petersburg, but during March of 1865, he again transfers, moving to the Carolinas to establish a line at the Roanoke River to intercept deserters. He resumes his law practice after the war. General Johnston dies in Winchester, Virginia, on 1 February 1919.

Also, Colonel George S. Patton, 22nd Virginia, is shot in the leg and afterward captured. The wound proves fatal. He dies at the age of 31 while in Union hands on 26 September. Colonel Patton had refused to let the doctors amputate his leg. He is interred in Winchester at the Stonewall Cemetery. He is interred in the same grave as his brother, Colonel W. Tazwell Patton, 7th Virginia, who died at age 29 in Pickett's Charge at Gettysburg in July 1863. A marker states: "Here asleep in one grave, the Patton brothers." The tombstone has a more profound epitaph, which reads: "In Christ alone, perfectly content." Colonel Patton, although often a brigade commander, had not officially been commissioned a brigadier general. He had married Susan Thornton Glassell, and subsequent to his death, she moved to California with her four children, including George S. Patton II. Once in California, the family resides with her brother, Andrew Glassell. George Smith Patton II, the father of George S. Patton III, does not serve in the military.

September 20 (Tuesday)   In Georgia at Atlanta, General Sherman's force still faces some problems because Confederates operating behind the lines continue to strike supply trains.

In Louisiana, the 2nd New York Veteran Cavalry engages Confederates at Alabama Bayou. In New York, General Nathaniel James Jackson receives orders to repair south to join with General William T. Sherman. Upon his arrival, Jackson is attached to the 1st Division (XX Corps), and he accompanies the command on the March to the Sea. Subsequently, General Jackson, temporary commander of the 1st Division, is relieved when General A.S. Williams resumes command. Jackson receives the brevet of major general and musters out of the army on 24 August 1865.

In Confederate general officer activity, General Goode Bryan (West Point, 1834), who served in the Seven Days' Battles, Richmond, Chancellorsville, Gettysburg and Chickamauga, resigns his commission. Lieutenant General Simon Buckner (West Point, 1844) is appointed lieutenant general and chief of staff to General Kirby Smith in the Trans-Mississippi Department. He remains in that department until the close of hostilities. After the war, Buckner, a Kentuckian, moves to New Orleans, where he stays for several years. General Simon Buckner had the dubious honor of watching Generals Floyd and Pillow depart Fort Donelson, leaving him to surrender the fort to the Union. Also, Colonel Patrick M. Moore is promoted to the rank of brigadier general effective this date. General Moore had been in administrative type positions, including a stint with court-martial cases since sustaining a wound at 1st Manassas; however, toward the latter part of the conflict, he is assigned a brigade in General

The monitor USS *Tunxis* (Mottelay, *The Soldier in Our Civil War*, 1886).

Richard S. Ewell's command at Richmond. Also, Confederate colonel William H. Wallace, 18th South Carolina Regiment, is promoted to the rank of brigadier general. Wallace's regiment had been severely stung at Petersburg the previous August when a large part of the unit was wiped out from an explosion and falling earth and debris. General Goode Bryan, plagued by ill health, renders his resignation from the service. He returns to Georgia, where he remains semi-retired. He dies on 16 August 1885 in Augusta.

September 21 (Wednesday) In Virginia, a contingent of the 3rd Division, Cavalry Corps, Army of the Potomac, engages Confederates at Front Royal Pike.

In Naval activity, a severe fire breaks out on the USS *Montauk* in the ammunition storage area. Fireman 1st Class John Roundtry, U.S. Navy, above and beyond the call of duty, puts out the fire in the magazine chamber and saves the ship; he receives the Medal of Honor for his heroism. In other activity, the USS *Tunxis*, a light-draft monitor, commissioned on 12 July, departs the Philadelphia Navy Yard on its initial voyage, but soon after leaving the dock, the ship begins to take on water, forcing the cruise to be aborted. The *Tunxis* returns to the yard and by the following month, it is decommissioned. Work begins anew to make the vessel seaworthy, but the work is not completed until more than a year after the war. On 12 July, 1866, the second anniversary of its initial commission, the *Tunxis* is prepared for sea duty; however, the design proves less than expected. Consequently, the *Tunxis* is taken to the League Island Navy Yard, where it remains. On 15 June 1869, its name is changed to *Hydra*. And by the following month, it undergoes another name change to become the *Ostego*. Nonetheless, the ship with three separate names never serves a tour of duty.

September 22 (Thursday) In Virginia, Confederate General Jubal Early is at Fisher's Hill (Woodstock) while his troops continue to recuperate and regain their composure since the recent defeat at Winchester. However, Sheridan's force arrives this day and yet another ferocious skirmish occurs, despite the fact that the Confederates are not yet ready for heavy fighting. Fisher's Hill is a strategic piece of terrain that dominates the slim Strasburg Valley between the Shenandoah River and North Mountain. Sheridan, seemingly aware of Early's

situation, immediately launches an assault, but he also dispatches General Alfred Torbert with two cavalry divisions to strike against the Confederates' rear at New Market, about twenty miles from the targeted hill. Sheridan's frontal assault initially makes little progress, but Sheridan changes strategy. He orders cavalry to divert attention by striking Early's right to conceal an infantry attack against North Mountain.

The ground troops burst through and gain the Confederate left, which causes additional complications for Early, who is still concerned about his rear. In the meantime, Sheridan orders a full assault that jumps off and shatters Early's front lines, creating total chaos among the Confederate ranks. While Early is being bludgeoned, General Torbert is experiencing heavy and effective opposition at Milford by a small but determined contingent of Confederate cavalry under Colonel Munford. Essentially it is Munford and his command that preserves Early's force by preventing Torbert from driving through the rear to join with Sheridan's main body. Following the deep penetration by the Yankees, Early is compelled to retreat. He pulls out and heads toward the Blue Ridge Mountains; however, his force has now been sliced in half.

The Union gives pursuit, but only to Staunton. From there, Sheridan moves back to the vicinity of Strasburg and deploys at Cedar Creek. In conjunction, General Jubal Early will be sent additional reinforcements to bring his battered force back to fighting strength. General Robert E. Lee will dispatch about 600 cavalry troops and one division of infantry, commanded by General Joseph B. Kershaw. Kershaw traces Sheridan's route and re-establishes Confederate positions at Fisher's Hill, inviting another visit by Sheridan. The 6th Corps, 1st and 2nd Cavalry Divisions, Army of the Potomac, 8th Corps, Army of West Virginia, and the 1st and 2nd Divisions, 19th Corps, participate in this action. The Union sustains about 600 killed and wounded. The Confederates suffer about 400 killed and wounded and more than 1,000 captured.

September 23 (Friday) In Alabama, Confederates under General Nathan B. Forrest strike hard against the Union forces at Athens. The 106th, 110th and 114th U.S. Colored Troops and the 3rd Tennessee Cavalry, plus the 18th Michigan, participate. The Union sustains 950 missing. Confederates sustain five killed and 25 wounded.

General Simon Buckner (Mottelay, *The Soldier in Our Civil War*, 1886).

In Missouri, the 3rd Missouri Militia Cavalry engages Confederates at Rockport. The Union sustains 10 killed. Confederate casualties are unreported. Also, one battalion of the 1st Missouri Militia Cavalry skirmishes with Confederates at Blackwater.

In Virginia, General Robert E. Lee, in a telegram to Confederate General Richard Anderson at Orange Court House, states: "Early has again met with a reverse, falling back to New Market.... Send Kershaw's division with battalion of artillery to report to him at once."

In Confederate general officer activity, Colonel Edwin Gray Lee is commissioned brigadier general to rank from 20 September. Lee entered service during 1861 and resigned in December due to poor health, then re-entered the service during December 1863. In November, General Lee receives a six-month leave of absence due to a relapse regarding his health. Meanwhile, the Confederate Senate declines confirming his appointment on 24 February 1865. Nonetheless, his name continues to remain on the army's roll. Toward end of the war, General Lee and his wife board a blockade runner and flee to Canada. The Lees subsequently return to Virginia, but General Lee's sickness (lung disease) cuts his life short. He dies at Sulphur Springs, Virginia, on 24 August 1870 at the age of 34.

September 24 (Saturday) **In Missouri,** the 9th Missouri Cavalry (Militia) battles Confederates at Fayette. The Union sustains three killed and five wounded. The Confederates suffer six killed and 30 wounded.

In Tennessee, a Union force of infantry and cavalry clashes with Confederates at Bull's Gap.

In Virginia, Confederate General Jubal Early has pulled back toward New Market after successive losses around Winchester inflicted by General Philip Sheridan. The Union cavalry does not pursue Early's retreating army, but the

General Sterling Price (Johnson, *Campfire and Battlefield: History of the Conflicts and Campaigns,* 1894).

area is now controlled by the Union. General Grant is ecstatic over Sheridan's spectacular victory and orders a 100-gun salute. The beleaguered Confederate defenders at Petersburg become the recipients of Grant's jubilation. The guns used to celebrate are aimed directly at Petersburg. In other activity, the 1st Cavalry Division, Cavalry Corps, Army of the Potomac, clashes with Confederates at Luray. Pvt. Philip Baybutt, 2nd Massachusetts Cavalry, receives the Medal of Honor for his heroism.

In Union general officer activity, Colonel Isaac Hardin Duval is promoted to the rank of brigadier general, effective this day. He continues to serve with General Crook's command for the duration. Later he receives the brevet rank of major general. After the war he holds several elective offices, including the U.S. Congress (1869–1871). Also, Colonel John Edwards (18th Iowa Infantry), commander at Fort Smith, Arkansas, is promoted to the rank of brigadier general. Prior to his tour at Fort Smith, Edwards had served under General John M. Schofield (Army of the Southwest) at Springfield; earlier he was a lieutenant colonel on the staff of the governor of Iowa, Samuel J. Kirkwood. General Edwards serves at Fort Smith for the duration of the war, and during the closing days, he receives the brevet rank of major general. After the war he is appointed to the post of assessor of internal revenue at Fort Smith. In 1870 he is elected to Congress by defeating the incumbent Thomas Boles (a former Confederate officer). Nevertheless, he serves only until 9 February 1872. Boles contests the election and prevails.

September 24–28 **In Missouri,** Confederate General Sterling Price invades the state, and his contingent is engaged by the forces of General Andrew J. Smith, which includes Missouri militia cavalry, Kansas militia and cavalry of the Army of the Border. The Union sustains slightly less than 200 casualties. The Confederates suffer slightly more than 300 casualties and nearly 2,000 captured. Confederate Brigadier General John D. Imboden, although not captured during this campaign, is forced to depart the field, as he is brought down from typhoid-fever. Nonetheless, Imboden provides his remaining energy to the cause by serving in the military prison system at Aiken, South Carolina. He resumes his law practice after the war.

September 25 (Sunday) **In Alabama,** Confederate troops under General Nathan B. Forrest seize the Union garrison at Sulphur Branch, Trestle, which is garrisoned by the 111th U.S. Colored Troops (3rd Alabama) and the 9th Indiana Cavalry.

In Georgia, General William T. Sherman informs Washington that Confederates attached to General John B. Hood's force have maneuvered behind his lines, causing Sherman to order two divisions to counter these Rebels. One division is diverted to Rome, Georgia, and the other moves to Chattanooga. In other activity, General Hood, having expressed dissatisfaction with General William Hardee and forwarded a request to President Davis to have him removed, receives a response. President Davis arrives at Palmetto and confers with General Hood. During Davis' visit, some of the troops proclaim, "Give us General Johnston" to let Davis know there is great dissatisfaction with his earlier decision to replace Joe Johnston with Hood. At the conclusion of the conference, General Hardee is transferred out of Hood's command and sent to command the troops in South Carolina and Florida. Hardee succeeds Confederate Major General Samuel Jones, commanding officer, Department of South Carolina, Georgia and Florida; however, Jones remains commander of the Department of South Georgia and Florida until the close of hostilities.

In Kentucky, the 118th U.S. Colored Troops clash with Confederates at Hendersonville.

In Tennessee, the 13th U.S. Colored Troops skirmish with Confederates at Johnsonville.

In Naval activity, the USS *Howquah* assists in the destruction of the Confederate blockade runner *Lynx* off Wilmington, North Carolina. Rebel shore batteries keep up an intense bombardment in addition to the guns of the *Lynx* that pound against the flotilla, which also includes the USS *Niphon* and the *Governor Buckingham.* Nevertheless, the Union vessels succeed in the attack. The *Lynx,* laden with a cargo of cotton, is set ablaze during the engagement and the fire continues to spread as the vessel crashes ashore.

September 26 (Monday) **In Arkansas,** the 14th Kansas Cavalry skirmishes with Confederates at Vache Grass.

In Tennessee, the 111th U.S. Colored Troops (3rd Alabama) clashes with Confederates at Richland.

In Virginia, the 1st Cavalry Division, Army of the Potomac, and 2nd Cavalry Division, Army of West Virginia (General William Averell's command), repulses a Confederate attack at Brown's Gap.

In Kentucky, Union General Nathaniel C. McLean leads a reconnaissance force on a two-day journey from Prestonburg to Saltville.

September 26–28 **BATTLE OF PILOT KNOB** Fort Davidson, a small post established by the Union in the vicinity of Pilot Knob, Missouri, comes under assault by General Sterling Price. The fort is an earthwork post formed in the shape of a hexagon (six-sided). The garrison is composed of more than 1,000 troops bolstered by eleven pieces of artillery; however, the Confederates number about 12,000 troops.

During the latter part of the 26th, the Union pickets are compelled to withdraw to the fort, but the commander, General Thomas Ewing, despite the odds, is unwilling to capitulate. Meanwhile, Price establishes night positions and prepares to take the fort on the following day. Price is aware that many of his troops are fresh and some others have no arms, but he remains confident that the overwhelming numbers will offset any disadvantages; however, he is unaware that Ewing's command has artillery.

On the morning of the 27th, the Union is pressured quickly and two regiments pull back and regroup near Pilot Knob and Shepherd Mountain. The Confederates maintain pressure and the Union contingent at Pilot Knob sustains severe punishment; however, the regiment at the mountain makes it to the fort. The Confederates begin to pick up momentum and confidence as they close fast. The Confederates plow forward, giving chase to the retreating Union forces, but unexpectedly, as they encroach the fort, they are met with withering streams of fire. Most are cut down before they can reach the fort. Those Rebels that do reach the fort receive no reprieve. The Union rivets the area to the front of the fort to inflict more punishment upon the attack force, including grenades that are thrown from the fort's walls, and from the artillery as well as small arms.

The Confederates are repulsed, but General Price remains determined to reduce the post. Once again, Price establishes night positions and finalizes his strategy to seize the fort on the following day. Meanwhile, General Ewing assesses the situation and concludes that the garrison's supply of ammunition is insufficient to withstand another full-scale day-long attack. He decides to abandon the post prior to dawn on the 28th. While the main body evacuates the fort, a rear guard remains behind to destroy the supplies and ammunition that is left behind. The magazine is detonated about 0330, more than one hour after the garrison departs. The Union column makes it without incident to Rolla following a long march.

The Union garrison at Fort Davidson includes the 5th Minnesota Volunteer Regiment, the 47th and 50th Missouri Volunteer Regiments, the 14th Iowa, the 2nd and 3rd Missouri Cavalry and the 2nd Missouri Light Artillery. The Union sustains 184 killed, wounded or missing. The Confederates sustain about 1,500 killed or wounded. General Thomas Ewing, Jr., is the brother of Union Generals Charles and Hugh Ewing. The Ewing brothers are also brothers-in-law of General William Tecumseh Sherman.

September 27 (Tuesday) **In Arkansas,** Union cavalry and mounted infantry contingents under General Jacob Ammen clash with Confederates at Carter's Station, Watauga River.

In Florida, Union forces, including elements of the 82nd U.S. Colored Troops, 7th Vermont Volunteers and the 2nd Maine Cavalry, seize Mariana.

In Missouri, three companies of the 39th Missouri Infantry are massacred by General Sterling Price's Confederate troops at Centralia. The Union suffers 122 killed and two wounded. Meanwhile, some Union troops on furlough are massacred at the North Missouri Railroad.

In the Indian Territory (Dakota), a contingent of the 6th Iowa Cavalry engages Indians at Fort Rice (North Dakota).

In Tennessee, Union cavalry (General Lovell Rousseau's command) repels an attack by Confederates under General Forrest at Pulaski.

In Virginia, General U.S. Grant states in a letter to General Sherman: "I have directed all recruits and new troops from the western states to be sent to Nashville to receive their further orders from you." Also, the 2nd Cavalry Division, Army of West Virginia, engage Confederates at Weyer's Cave.

September 28 (Wednesday) **In Arkansas,** the 3rd Wisconsin Cavalry skirmishes with Confederates at Clarkesville.

In Virginia, the 3rd Division, 9th Corps, clashes with Confederates at Fort Sedgwick, Jerusalem Plank Road. Also, the 3rd Division, Cavalry Corps, Army of the Potomac, led by General Alfred Torbert, engages Confederates at Waynesboro.

In Naval activity, the *Nyack,* a wooden-hulled screw gunboat, is commissioned. It is assigned to the North Atlantic Blockading Squadron. Lt. Commander L. Howard Newman receives command. The *Nyack* participates in the attack against Fort Fisher (December 1864) and later against Fort Anderson (February 1865). Following the war, during 1866, it is transferred to the Pacific Squadron, where it remains in service until 1871. It is decommissioned on 15 March 1871 and sold during November 1883.

September 28–30 **In Virginia,** the Union 18th Corps, under General Edward Otho C. Ord, assaults and captures Fort Harrison near Richmond, but the offensive to capture the Confederate-held Fort Gillmore fails. The fighting includes clashes in New Market Heights (Chapin's Farm and Laurel Hill). The following day, Confederates mount an offensive to drive the Union from their positions. The Confederates, commanded by General Richard Anderson, pay dearly. George I. Stannard's Union force holds firmly, but Stannard becomes a casualty. General Lee transfers eight brigades from Petersburg but the attempt to recapture Fort Harrison fails. Union General Ord is gravely wounded during this unsuccessful attempt to capture Fort Gillmore. He is unable to return to duty until January 1865.

Both sides suffer excessive casualties. The Union loses 400 dead and 2,029 wounded. Confederates losses are 2,000 killed or wounded. Private Barns, the 38th U.S. Colored Troops, is the recipient of the Medal of Honor for his heroism at Chapin's Farm, Virginia. Sgt. Lester Archer of the 96th New York Infantry plants the Stars and Stripes over the captured fort. Union General Hiram Burnham is killed during the assault on Fort Harrison. Union General George J. Stannard, who was among those captured at Harpers Ferry in September 1862, is seriously wounded and loses his arm, which ends his field duty. He is promoted to major general in October and serves in New England for the duration.

September 29 (Thursday) **In Georgia,** General William T. Sherman orders General George Thomas to move against Nashville, Tennessee, by way of Chattanooga. James D. Morgan's division will accompany him. Sherman prepares to move on Milledgeville and then to Savannah, Georgia.

In Tennessee, the Union 2nd Tennessee Mounted Infantry battles Confederates at Centreville. The Union sustains 10 killed and 25 wounded. Confederate casualties are unreported.

In Missouri, the Union 14th Iowa and 2nd Missouri Cavalry (Militia), bolstered by Battery H, 2nd Missouri Light Artillery, led by General Ewing, skirmish with Confederates (General Price's invasion) at Leesburg and Harrison this day and the next. No casualties are reported.

In Naval activity, the CSS *Richmond* participates in the attack against Fort Harrison through October 1. In other activity, the steamship *Roanoke* (Havana line) departs Havana; however, unknown to the crew, some of the passengers are Confederates under Captain Parker and his cohort, John C. Braine. Both Parker and Braine were responsible for the seizure of the steamship *Chesapeake* during December 1863. After dusk, the Confederates overwhelm the ship's officers and seize control of the vessel. One of the crew members, the carpenter, attempts to resist and he is slain. Another man, the 2nd engineer, is wounded. The Confederates sail to Bermuda, and en route, Braine snatches $21,000 from the ship's safe. The *Roanoke* arrives in Bermuda and Braine holds the ship outside the harbor, but still he is able to get more fuel. Afterward, the *Roanoke*

Entrenchments and fortifications at Pilot Knob, Missouri (Johnson, *Campfire and Battlefield: History of the Conflicts and Campaigns,* 1894).

sails off and soon encounters a British brigantine, the *Mathilde*, and arrangements are made to transfer the crew and passengers. Subsequent to transferring the captives, Braine destroys the *Roanoke* by fire and then the Confederates head for shore in Bermuda, where they are detained by British authorities. Nonetheless, they are held only a short time before being released.

After the close of hostilities, John Braine returns to the United States and arrives in New York, expecting to remain free due to the amnesty proclamation of President Johnson, who becomes president upon the assassination of President Lincoln during the closing days of the war. Braine is held on charges of piracy and murder, but then is released by the U.S. government.

September 30 (Friday) In Virginia, the 1st Division, V Corps, and the 2nd Division, 9th Corps, under General Gouverneur Warren, engage Confederates at Preble's Farm, Poplar Springs Church. The fighting continues into the following day. The Union sustains 141 killed and 788 wounded. The Confederates sustain about 900 killed and wounded and about 1,750 captured. Also, the 2nd Cavalry Division (Gregg's Cavalry), Army of the Potomac, engages Confederates at Arthur's Swamp. The Union sustains about 60 wounded and 100 missing. Confederate casualty figures are unavailable.

In Union general officer activity, Brigadier General Fitz Henry Warren, commander at Brownsville, Texas, suffering from poor health, is ordered east. On 24 August 1865, he is breveted major general of volunteers, and on the same day, he musters out of the army.

September 30–October 1 In Virginia, two more days of bloody skirmishing occur as Confederates under General Ambrose P. Hill desperately attempt to drive the oncoming Union troops back while holding on to Petersburg. Union losses are 141 dead, 788 wounded and 1,756 missing. The Confederates lose 800 wounded and 100 missing. Petersburg remains in Confederate control.

October In Iowa, Confederate troops disguised as Union soldiers move into Davis County from Missouri. Iowa militia (Southern Border Brigade) intercepts the Rebels and drives them off. At the conclusion of the conflict during 1865, the Southern Border Brigade is dissolved. In addition to the militia forces, Iowa had been pressed to volunteer one regiment for the war. Initially, it was thought to be a difficult task due to the size of the territory; however, in relationship to its size Iowa supplied more than its share of troops to the cause, about 76,000 men. And of these, about 13,000 give the ultimate sacrifice for their country and twenty-seven become recipients of the Medal of Honor.

October 1 (Saturday) In Alabama, a detachment of the 12th and 13th Indiana Cavalry Regiments under General Napoleon B. Buford reject a Confederate demand to surrender at Huntsville. The Union afterward repels the attack. At Athens, the 73rd Indiana Volunteer Regiment, led by Lt. Colonel Slade, repels a two-day attack against its garrison by Confederates under General Nathan B. Forrest.

In Georgia, Confederate cavalry under General Hood skirmishes Sherman's lines at Salt Springs, in the vicinity of Atlanta. Sherman receives valuable information on enemy troop movements from Sgt. Joseph S. Keen, 13th Michigan Infantry. A contingent of Union cavalry, Army of the Cumberland, under General Hugh Kilpatrick, skirmishes with Confederates at Sweetwater, Nose's Creek and Powder Springs through October 3.

In Kentucky, the 30th and 45th Kentucky Regiments, bolstered by two companies of the 40th Kentucky Volunteers, clash with Confederates at Clinch Mountain. Also, other elements of the 40th Kentucky and the 13th Kentucky Regiment led by General Hobson skirmish with Confederates under Colonel True at Laurel Gap.

In Missouri, the Enrolled Missouri Militia skirmishes with Confederates at Franklin.

In Virginia, Union General James G. Spear's cavalry brigade and General Alfred H. Terry's brigade, 10th Corps, Army of the James, initiates a reconnaissance mission at Charles City Crossroads. Also, Union forces occupy Port Republic.

In Union general officer activity, Colonel Thomas Alfred Smyth (1st Delaware) is promoted to brigadier general. General Smyth participates in various actions in Virginia, including Deep Bottom and Hatcher's Run, and during the drive against Appomattox, he commands a division. Confederate General John Dunovant is mortally wounded at Vaughn Road during a cavalry charge against Union lines. Sergeant James Clancy, 1st New Jersey Cavalry, shoots Dunovant. He had been promoted to brigadier general the previous month. Also, the 3rd Division, 2nd Corps, Army of the Potomac, engages through the 5th against Confederates at Yellow Tavern and Weldon Railroad.

In Naval activity, the Marines aboard the USS *Wabash* receive recognition for saving the ship after it grounded off the Virginia coast at Frying Pan Shoals. The USS *Monadnock*, one of two twin-turret monitors constructed at the Boston Navy Yard, is commissioned at about this time (October). It is assigned duty at Norfolk, Virginia. After a short tour there it heads south to participate in the operations to reduce Fort Fisher at Wilmington, North Carolina. During April 1865, it is back in Virginia, but shortly thereafter it embarks for Cuba. Following time out of service for repairs, it departs for the West Coast, and after rounding South America and moving through the Straits of Magellan, it arrives at San Francisco during June 1866, but its career terminates there. It is decommissioned at Mare Island soon after its arrival. In other activity, the *Stromboli*, an armored torpedo vessel, is completed at about this time (October) in Mystic, Connecticut. During the following month it is renamed *Spuyten Duyvil*. By early December, it is on duty at Hampton Roads as the USS *Spuyten Duyvil* on the James River.

Left: A contingent of the Union's V Corps attacks a Confederate fort at Poplar Springs Church, Virginia (Mottelay, *The Soldier in Our Civil War*, 1886). *Right:* Saltville, Virginia (*Harper's Pictoral History of the Civil War*, 1896).

October 2 (Sunday)   In Virginia, Confederates under General John C. Breckinridge repulse a Union attack at Saltville. The 11th and 13th Kentucky Cavalry, the 12th Ohio, 11th Michigan, 5th and 6th U.S. Colored Cavalry, and the 26th, 30th, 35th, 37th, 39th, 40th and 45th Kentucky Mounted Infantry participate. The Union retreats after sustaining heavy casualties. The Union loses 54 killed, 190 wounded and 104 missing. The Confederates suffer 18 killed, 71 wounded and 21 missing. At Waynesboro, Union cavalry attached to Generals George A. Custer and Wesley Merritt skirmish with Confederate contingents. The Union sustains 50 killed and wounded. Confederate casualties are unreported. Also, a contingent composed of elements of the 1st Kentucky Cavalry, supported by the 3rd Kentucky Mounted Infantry and led by Major Keene, clash with Confederates at Gladesville Pound Gap.

October 3 (Monday)   In Georgia, General Sherman's lines remain under attack by General John B. Hood. On the following day, Sherman relocates his headquarters at Kennesaw Mountain to obtain strategic positioning for his offensive against Hood.

October 4 (Tuesday)   In Tennessee, the 7th Indiana Cavalry clashes with Confederates in the vicinity of Memphis.

In Union general officer activity, Colonel Ferdinand Van Derveer, mustered out of the army the previous summer at the end of the regiment's (35th Ohio) enlistment, re-enters the service and is commissioned a brigadier general. He does not get reassigned to General William T. Sherman; rather, he is ordered to Alabama, where he commands a brigade in the VI Corps in the Huntsville area. In conjunction with the reorganization of the army, he resigns on 7 June 1865. He returns to Ohio to resume his law practice.

In Naval activity, the CSS *Florida*, commanded by Lt. Charles Manigault Morris, arrives back at Brazil following its departure from the Delaware Capes in July. During that time, the *Florida* has captured the merchant ships *B.F. Hoxie, Cairaissanne, David Lapsley, Estelle, George Latimer, Southern Rights, Greenland, William C. Clark, Windward* and *Zelinda.* After

entering the port at Bahia, Captain Morris spots a Union vessel, the USS *Washusett*, a steam corvette commanded by Captain Napoleon Collins. Morris, assuming he is protected due to the neutral port, gives the crew liberty, with some remaining aboard on watches; however, the Union warship has plans to seize the Confederate vessel on the night of the 6th-7th.

October 5 (Wednesday)   In Georgia, Union troops, under General John M. Corse, skirmish with the Confederate troops commanded by General French (Hood's command) at Allatoona. The Union troops suffer 142 killed, 352 wounded and 212 missing. The Confederates have 231 killed, 500 wounded and 411 missing. Confederate Brigadier General William Hugh Young, who was wounded at Murfreesboro, Vicksburg, Chickamauga and during the Atlanta Campaign, is again severely wounded (his left foot nearly shot off) and captured at Allatoona. He is taken to Johnson's Island, Ohio, and not released until July 1865. Afterward General Young practices law and becomes involved in real estate. He dies in San Antonio on 28 November 1901.

In Louisiana, units including the 23rd Wisconsin, 1st Louisiana Cavalry and the 2nd and 4th Massachusetts Batteries skirmish Confederates at Jackson. The Union sustains four killed and 10 wounded. Confederate casualties are unreported. Also, the 2nd Wisconsin and the 3rd U.S. Colored Cavalry skirmishes with Confederates at Fort Adams.

In Missouri, Confederate troops occupy Herman.

October 6 (Thursday)   In Alabama, the 60th Illinois Volunteer Regiment and the 3rd and 6th Tennessee Cavalry engage Confederates at Florence.

In Mississippi, a Union contingent (units unspecified) clashes with Confederates at Woodville. The Union captures about 56 Rebels. Also, Union cavalry captures a 47-man contingent of Confederates at Clinton.

In Missouri, the Union 1st, 7th and 9th Missouri Militia Cavalry skirmishes with Confederates under General Sterling Price at Price's Place, Osage River, Cole County.

In Virginia, the 8th Ohio Cavalry skirmishes with Confederates at North Shenandoah.

In Naval activity, at the port of Bahia, most of the crew of the CSS *Florida* is on liberty, giving the men a break after a long series of cruises. Confederate Lt. Charles Manigault Morris, the commander, was unconcerned about the presence of a Union warship, the USS *Wachusett*, because of both ships being in a neutral port. During the night (6th-7th), while about one-half of the crew and the captain are in town, the Union executes a plan to seize the ship, manned by about eighty men, including officers commanded by Lt. Thomas Parker.

At 0300 on the 7th, without warning, the USS *Wachusett*, commanded by Captain Napoleon Morris, rams the *Florida* in synchronization with small arms fire and two accompanying point-blank range shots from its cannon, stunning the relaxed crew. The watch party on deck returns fire, but only from their muskets and pistols. The Union demands surrender, but there is chaos aboard the *Florida*. Some men jump overboard to attempt to swim to shore; however, marksmen aboard the *Wachusett* fire at them in the dark. Nine of the Confederates are killed either by drowning or Union fire.

The lightning quick operation gives Lt. Porter no chance to defend the ship. It is surrendered. The *Wachusett*, unwilling to await word from the Brazilian authorities or afford Porter time to contact his captain, tows the *Florida* out to sea, ignoring fire from a Brazilian ship and the fort at Bahia. The *Florida* is taken to Hampton Roads. Brazil protests strongly and demands that the vessel and its crew members be immediately returned.

The U.S. has no grounds on which to object and agrees to the demand, but before the ship is en route, it is accidentally rammed ("accidentally" is questioned by the Confederates) by a Union Army transport. The vessel is then moored at an isolated location around Newport News.

Afterward, an engineer and two other troops go aboard the vessel. On 27 November, the ship suddenly sinks. The Confederates believe the

Left: **Allatoona, Georgia, the scene of the battle of 5 August 1864 (Mottelay,** *The Soldier in Our Civil War*, **1886).** *Right:* **Bahia, Brazil (***Harper's Pictoral History of the Civil War*, **1896).**

engineer had opened the ship's water cocks, and the belief is bolstered by U.S. Admiral Porter, commander at Hampton Roads at the time, who noted in his *Naval History of the Civil War*: "It is tolerably well apparent that the engineer in charge of the ship [*Florida*] opened the water-cocks in her hull and purposely left her to go to the bottom."

Brazil's demand that the ship and Confederate crew be returned is not met. Those men are detained at several places — Fort Warren, Point Lookout and Washington, D.C. — where they remain as prisoners until 1 February 1865. At the time of their release, they are compelled to sign an agreement that they will depart the United States within ten days. The crew is released in Boston, Massachusetts, but they are not given any funds for travel and all are without money. Nevertheless, they somehow get transportation aboard a vessel (or vessels) that carry them to Europe.

October 6–9   In Virginia, Union General Philip Sheridan begins to move his troops down the Shenandoah with Confederates under General Jubal Early close behind. Sheridan's force is pushing the livestock in front of the column and destroying the forage and food supplies within reach to prevent use by the Rebels. As the Rebels begin to encroach the Union column, Sheridan maneuvers his force to positions from which he can swing right into Early's column. The two sides clash in vicious combat on 9 October at Fisher's Hill.

October 7 (Friday)   In Missouri, a Union force composed of Missouri militia cavalry, infantry and artillery units skirmish with Confederates at Moreau Bottom in the vicinity of Jefferson City.

In Virginia, Union cavalry commanded by General George Armstrong Custer repels a Confederate charge in the vicinity of Petersburg at New Market Road. Although the Rebels are driven back, the Union is unable to penetrate and conquer the defiant defenders of Petersburg. Also, the 10th Corps and cavalry, Army of the James, under General Butler, engages Confederates at Darbytown Road in the vicinity of New Market Heights. Confederate General John Gregg (Hood's Texas Brigade) is killed while leading his men in an attack at Charles City Road and New Market Road during the struggle to keep the Union from Richmond. General Gregg, assigned to Hood's command during the battle of Chickamauga, was severely wounded during that action. General Gregg exemplified courage and leadership while commanding his Texas Brigade. The brigade is temporarily placed under the command of Colonel C.M. Winkler and Colonel F.S. Bass; however, it is later taken over by Colonel Robert M. Powell, the latter leading the brigade until it surrenders with Robert E. Lee at Appomattox.

In Naval activity, the USS *Mohican*, having been out of service since the previous April, is recommissioned and assigned to the North Atlantic Blockading Squadron. It departs Philadelphia and initiates patrol duty off Wilm-

ington, North Carolina. In December 1864, the *Mohawk* participates in the attack against Fort Fisher, North Carolina (24–25 December). It also participates in the second and successful attack during January 1865.

October 7–11   In Missouri, Confederate General Sterling Price continues to execute raids. His force strikes various places, including Jefferson City, Booneville and the town of California. Union units, including the 5th Minnesota, the 1st, 4th, 5th, 6th and 7th Missouri Militia Cavalry, the 15th Missouri Cavalry and the 17th Illinois Cavalry, participate in the effort to intercept and defeat Price. Battery H, 2nd Missouri Light Artillery also takes part. Casualties are unreported. Confederate Major General Mosby M. Parsons accompanies General Price during this activity in Missouri.

October 8 (Saturday)   In Virginia, a reconnaissance force, composed of elements of the 5th and 9th Corps under Generals Samuel Crawford and John G. Parke, sustain about 50 casualties in the vicinity of the Boydton Plank Road.

In Naval activity, the CSS *Shenandoah*, formerly a British merchant ship, the *Sea King* sails eastward from London. The *Sea King* had been purchased by Captain Bulloch, an English merchant, to replace the CSS *Alabama*, which had been destroyed by the USS *Kearsarge* on 19 June. At the same time Bulloch purchased the *King*, he also acquired the *Laurel*, and on this day the *Laurel* leaves Liverpool. The two unarmed vessels rendezvous on the 18th, and two days later, in the vicinity of Madeira, the *Laurel* transfers the armaments to the *Shenandoah*, now commanded by Captain James Iredell Waddell. It receives four 8-inch smooth bore guns, two 32-pounder rifles and two 12-pounders. Although eighty men sign up to sail aboard the vessel from London supposedly to the East Indies, only twenty-three of the crew agree to sail under the Confederate colors. Initially, the crew, including nineteen commissioned and warrant officers, totals only forty-two men. After being armed, the *Shenandoah* sails toward Australia, and while en route, it intercepts and captures the barks *Alina*, *Godfrey*, *Edward*, and the *Delphine*. In addition, the schooners *Charter Oak* and *Lizzie M. Stacey* were also seized, along with a brigantine, the *Susan*. Each of the vessels is burned soon after capture and the crews are taken captive. The steamer *Kate Prince* and the bark *Adelaide* are also captured. The *Kate Prince* is ransomed and carries the prisoners to safety. The *Adelaide* is bonded. The *Shenandoah* arrives at Melbourne, Australia, on 25 January 1865 and remains there until 8 February.

October 9 (Sunday)   In Virginia, General Philip Sheridan continues his mission of driving the Confederates from the Shenandoah. He directs cavalry under General George Custer, Major General Wesley Merritt, and General Alfred Torbert to attack jointly. The Union cavalry strikes in the vicinity of Strasburg (Tom's Brook) and Woodstock (Fisher's Hill). The

Union suffers about 60 casualties, including fewer than 10 killed. The Confederates are pushed back about 25 miles and sustain heavy casualties. Many Rebels are taken prisoner. Sheridan renews his march down the valley the following day, but General U.S. Grant directs him to change direction and dash towards the James River Canal and the Virginia Central Railroad in hopes of capitalizing on the weakened condition of the Confederates. Bad communications from Washington again confuse things and Sheridan is not given proper orders; however, Grant clears up the confusion.

The 2nd U.S. Cavalry captures the flag of the 32nd Battalion, Virginia Cavalry, at Woodstock. Confederate General Thomas Lafayette Rosser is in command of General Early's cavalry there. He attended West Point but dropped out a few weeks prior to his graduation. General Rosser will be engaged again by the Yankees at Winchester (Cedar Creek) on the 19th.

In Missouri, a Union force composed of units of the 1st, 4th, 5th, 6th and 7th Missouri Militia Cavalry, the 15th Missouri and 17th Illinois Cavalry Regiments, bolstered by Battery H, 2nd Missouri Light Artillery, engage a Confederate force through the 11th at Booneville. Also, other Union elements of the 4th and 7th Missouri Cavalry, supported by Batteries H and L, 2nd Missouri Artillery, clash with Confederate General Price's forces at California.

In Naval activity, the USS *Key West* and the *Undine*, along with the transports *Aurora*, *City of Pekin*, and the *Kenton* leave Clifton, Tennessee, and head for Eastport, Tennessee, in an operation to prevent the cavalry of General Bedford Forrest from moving across the Tennessee River. The Union also intends to establish an outpost at Eastport to intercept an expected advance by Confederate General John B. Hood.

October 10 (Monday)   In Mississippi, Union troops, including the 113th Illinois Infantry and the 61st U.S. Colored Troops, skirmish with a contingent of Confederates at Eastport.

In Tennessee, the 40th U.S. Colored Troops clash with Confederates at South Tunnel.

In Naval activity, the USS *Montgomery* seizes the *Bat*, a vessel in the service of the Confederacy, but sailing under British registry. The ship had been built earlier this year in England and is seized during its first voyage as it attempts to arrive at Wilmington, North Carolina. In November the *Bat* is acquired by the U.S. Navy and commissioned as the gunboat USS *Bat*, then directed to serve both in the Atlantic and on the Potomac River for the duration of the war. It is decommissioned in May 1865. The *Bat* is sold and afterward operated as a commercial vessel under the name *Teazer*. In 1872, the vessel operates again under British registry as the *Miramichi* until it is scrapped during 1902.

At Eastport, Tennessee, the USS *Key West* and the *Undine* arrive with several transports which had been under escort since departing Clifton,

Tennessee. A Confederate 6-gun battery deployed at Eastport and a 3-gun battery in the vicinity of Chickasaw commence firing and inflict damage to two of the transports. In addition, the *Key West* sustains damage from two rifle shots. The unexpected fire from concealed positions compels the Union vessels to retire to a point out of range of the Rebel guns.

October 11 (Tuesday) **In Tennessee,** the garrison force at Union-held Fort Donelson repels a Confederate attack. The 4th U.S. Colored Heavy Artillery participates. The Union sustains four killed and nine wounded. The Confederates sustain three killed and 23 wounded.

In Georgia, a Union force (Garrard's cavalry), Army of the Potomac, skirmishes with Confederates at Narrows.

In Virginia, the 13th Pennsylvania Cavalry engages Confederates at Stony Creek Station. The Union captures 14 Confederates.

October 12 (Wednesday) **In Virginia,** Union cavalry contingents led by Generals William Emory and George Crook operate in and around Strasburg. The Union sustains 30 killed, 144 wounded and 40 missing. Confederate casualties are unavailable.

In Georgia, a Union force under Colonel Weaver at Resaca repels a Confederate attack led by General John B. Hood.

October 13 (Thursday) **In Georgia,** the 44th U.S. Colored Regiment, led by Colonel Lewis Johnson, engages Confederate troops at Dalton. The Union has 400 missing. General John B. Hood's force, in addition to capturing many prisoners here, destroys the rails between Resaca and Tunnel Hill. At Buzzard's Roost Gap, Union troops, including the 115th Illinois Infantry, repulse General Hood's cavalry. Also, a Union contingent skirmishes with Confederates at Tilton. Specific units and casualty figures are unavailable.

In Virginia, Union cavalry engages a contingent of Confederates in a brisk skirmish near Cedar Creek. Confederate General James (General Joseph B. Kershaw's command) is wounded and loses a leg. General Conner had been severely wounded in the leg during the Seven Days' Battles early in the war. After the war, General Conner resumes his law practice and later becomes attorney general of South Carolina. Also, the 1st and 2nd Divisions, 19th Corps, and the 1st and 2nd Divisions, Army of West Virginia, under General George Crook, clash with Confederates at Strasburg.

October 14 (Friday) **In Georgia,** the 1st and 2nd Divisions, 10th Corps and Cavalry, Army of the James, under General Alfred H. Terry, engage Confederates at Darbytown. The Union sustains about 400 killed and wounded. The Confederates sustain about 200 killed and wounded.

October 15 (Saturday) **In Georgia,** Confederates under General Hood arrive at Cross Plains, less than ten miles south of LaFayette.

From here they move toward Decatur, Alabama, arriving on the 25th. Meanwhile, General Sherman dispatches General George H. Thomas and two divisions to Chattanooga, Tennessee. General Sherman and the remainder of the army head for Gaylesville, arriving there on the 21st. A contingent of Sherman's force clashes with Confederates at Snake Creek Gap.

In Missouri, Confederate cavalry under Sterling Price attacks and captures Glasgow. About 400 troops of the defending Union force are also seized. General Sterling Price enjoys much success during this stage of his raid into Missouri. The 43rd Missouri Volunteers, a contingent of the 17th Illinois, the 9th Missouri Militia, the 13th Missouri Cavalry and the 62nd U.S. Colored Troops participate in this action. Also, the 1st and 7th Missouri Militia Cavalry is attacked and defeated by a Confederate force at Sedalia.

In Virginia, Union General Philip Sheridan departs his headquarters for Washington, stopping at Front Royal while en route. The following day, Sheridan is informed by General Horatio Wright that a Confederate dispatch has been captured and that General James Longstreet has ordered General Jubal Early to prepare to move and crush Sheridan as soon as Longstreet arrives. Based on this information, Sheridan dispatches ample cavalry to bolster General Horatio Wright in the valley. In conjunction, by this time, General Longstreet has recovered from a wound sustained during the previous May at the Wilderness.

In Naval activity, the USS *Mary Sanford,* accompanied by the *Braziliera,* while operating on the Big Scatilla River and its tributaries, frees a group of slaves at a plantation on White Oak Creek, Georgia. Subsequent to the close of hostilities, the *Mary Sanford* sails north and is decommissioned in Philadelphia on 21 June 1865. Shortly thereafter, on 13 July, it is sold at auction and from that point operates as a commercial vessel until 1871.

October 16 (Sunday) **In Washington, D.C.,** President Lincoln confers with Generals Grant and Sheridan at Washington to discuss further strategy to eliminate the Confederate forces in the Shenandoah Valley.

In Georgia, the 1st Division, 15th Corps (General Sherman's command), captures a group of Confederates at Ship's Gap, Taylor's Ridge.

October 17 (Monday) **In Virginia,** a contingent of Union Connecticut cavalry (General Sheridan's command) repulses a Confederate attack at Cedar Run.

October 18 (Tuesday) **In Florida,** the 19th Iowa Volunteer Regiment and the 2nd Maine and 1st Florida Cavalry Regiments engage Confederates at Pierce's Point, Blackwater. In other activity, Union Major General David Bell Birney dies in Philadelphia of natural causes. General Birney participated at Fair Oaks, Fredericksburg, Chancellorsville and Gettysburg. He was selected by General Grant to command the

X Corps for the Overland Campaign during the latter part of July.

October 18–19 **BATTLE OF WINCHESTER (CEDAR CREEK, SHERIDAN'S RIDE)** In Virginia, Confederate General Jubal Early sends contingents of his force under darkened skies and heavy fog with instructions to advance to the rear of Sheridan's left flank, which they accomplish without incident late on the 18th. General Horatio G. Wright is in command while Sheridan is in Washington. The lines stretch along the left bank of the creek. The Union's left is held by the 8th Corps under General Crook, the center by William Emory's 9th Corps, and General James B. Ricketts' 6th Corps defends the right. The left flank is protected by Averell's cavalry led by General W.H. Powell (2nd Cavalry Division), and the right flank is guarded by the cavalry of Generals George Custer and Wesley Merritt. The Confederates, aware of the superior Union forces, prepare to spring a surprise.

Slightly after midnight (18th–19th), the Rebels initiate a feint against the right held by Ricketts, while simultaneously, another column advances southeasterly, following the Manassas Gap Railroad from Strasburg to sneak behind the Union's left flank. Yet another column establishes jump-off positions to the rear of the Union picket line, from where the direct assault will be launched. Prior to dawn the plan is executed. The Rebels swiftly strike, permitting no time for the Union to set up and react. The first column bolts from its positions and plows into General Crook's positions, snaps the trap and seizes the pickets. Meanwhile, the Rebel force under Early emerges from its positions in the hills west of Cedar Creek to stun the defenders holding Crook's right. The attack devastates the lines and deflates the discipline of the troops. The Union defenders make a rapid retreat, leaving eighteen cannon behind. The Confederates seize approximately 1,000 Federals who are snagged during in the startling Rebel maneuver before they can escape.

In the meantime, the right flank of Sheridan holds without flinching under the leadership of General George W. Getty (West Point, 1840), who pulls back toward Winchester to make his stand. The Confederates have the momentum from their surprise assault, but General Sheridan, who arrives back at Winchester, will make the decisive difference. In the meantime, the 6th Corps holds the line and checks the Confederates. General Horatio Wright orders a general retreat to insure that he can regroup the command. Eventually the Union draws a new line that stretches between Middletown and Newtown. By about 1000, the regiments have been reunited and Wright is able to maintain some control. Sheridan, who had returned from Washington to Winchester on the previous night, hears the roaring sounds of the gunfire.

During this morning of the 19th, Sheridan takes the precaution of deploying enough troops to defend Winchester and then speeds toward the front. As he advances, many of his troops holding the line to the south flee in panic.

Sheridan reacts by fanning out his cavalry to cut off any deserters or stragglers, while he begins a tremendous gallop to the sounds of the gunfire, stopping along the way to remind the retreating Union soldiers they are heading in the wrong direction. Surprisingly, the presence of Sheridan calms their fears, and an about face is quickly put into place. Soldiers in blue who had run scared get the opportunity to regain credibility. As Sheridan continues his race to the front lines, he continues to inspire those with him. At the front, Generals Custer and Getty are fighting furiously without giving ground. General Sheridan reinforces his positions to brace for another assault, and the 19th Corps of Emory, which had been pummeled the first time with severe losses, repulses the assault of General Early, inflicting heavy losses. The Rebels retire toward Fisher's Hill. General Early begins to take a defensive stance instead of launching another assault, but Sheridan, with a rejuvenated and confident command, takes the initiative and sends out his cavalry to thrash the Rebels.

The Union cavalry assaults from different directions and the battle becomes extremely bitter, with both sides exhausting their energy. However, the Confederate left flank collapses and the Union capitalizes on this by applying more pressure, which forces the remainder of the Confederate line to give way to the cavalry, which by this time has fully enveloped the rear of the Confederate positions. The cavalry quickly seizes about 25 pieces of artillery and the troopers regain all territory lost to the Rebels during the beginning of the contest.

This spectacular comeback victory for the Union cavalry and Sheridan seals the fate of the Confederates in the Shenandoah Valley. The remainder of General Jubal Early's force is sent to Richmond with the exception of a small contingent of cavalry and about one division of Confederate infantry. Union General Rutherford B. Hayes, who later succeeds General Grant as president of the United States, participates.

The Union loses 588 killed, 3,516 wounded and 1,891 missing. The Confederates sustain 3,000 killed and wounded and about 1,200 missing. The contest at Winchester on this day and its aftermath become known as "Sheridan's Ride." One of the cavalry units participating for the Union was that commanded by General George A. Custer. In addition, Colonel Stephen Thomas (8th Vermont), while in command of a brigade, performs above and beyond the call of duty. He becomes a recipient of the Medal of Honor; however, he receives it belatedly during 1892. Also, the 116th New York Infantry takes part.

Union Brigadier General Daniel D. Bidwell (General Horatio G. Wright's VI Corps) is mortally wounded. Union General Charles R. Lowell is wounded at the beginning of the skirmish but will not consent to leave the battlefield. As the day progresses, Colonel Lowell leads a counterattack and is mortally wounded. He dies on the following day. Through the efforts of General Sheridan, Colonel Lovell is promoted to brigadier general on the day of his death. Union

Major General James B. Ricketts is shot in the chest and although the wound is serious and disabling, he returns to duty two days before the surrender of Robert E. Lee at Appomattox in April 1865. Union Brigadier General Cuvier Grover is also wounded. General Grover, while in command of Savannah at the end of the war, is breveted major general. Also, Union Brigadier General Joseph E. Hamblin (Wright's VI Corps) is wounded. Union Colonel J. Howard Kitching is mortally wounded. Union Colonels Ranald Slidell Mackenzie and William H. Penrose are also wounded. Mackenzie is the general who, during the Plains Wars with the Indians, avenges the massacre of Custer at the Little Big Horn in 1876. Colonel Mackenzie (promoted the previous July to colonel of the 2nd Connecticut), wounded six times, is again promoted after he recuperates. He is appointed brigadier general and assigned to the Petersburg area, where he continues to serve with General Sheridan. At the close of hostilities, Mackenzie is breveted brigadier general in the Regular Army and major general in the Volunteers. He retires from the army as a brigadier general during 1884, and during his post–Civil War service he receives a seventh wound. The wounds contribute to his deteriorating health and eventually, he loses his mind. He dies on 19 January 1889 and is interred at West Point.

Confederate Major General Stephen Dodson Ramseur is mortally wounded (hit in both lungs) and captured. Ramseur is carried to General Sheridan's headquarters (Belle Grove) in the vicinity of Meadow Mills, where he dies the following day. Brigadier General Bryan Grimes assumes command of Ramseur's division. Confederate Major (later general) James Monroe Goggin (West Point, attendance, class of 1842) commands a brigade after General James Conner (Connor) is seriously wounded on the 13th at Cedar Creek and compelled to terminate his service in the field due to the amputation of one leg. Confederate Brigadier General Cullen A. Battle receives a crippling wound and is prevented from further field duty.

October 19 (Wednesday) **In Missouri,** the Union 5th, 11th, 15th and 16th Kansas Cavalry Regiments and the 3rd Wisconsin Cavalry Regiment, led by General James G. Blunt, engage Confederates under General Sterling Price at Lexington. The Confederates prevail and occupy Lexington.

In Vermont, a Confederate contingent of about 20 to 25 men enters St. Albans dressed in civilian clothes and posing as regular citizens, but after scrutinizing the location of the banks and locating a place to leave their horses, the Rebels begin to terrorize the town. They rob three banks and confiscate horses, while shooting up the town before returning to Canada with more than $20,000. The Rebels are later held for trial in Canada, but they are freed. The banks that had been robbed are subsequently reimbursed by Canada for their losses. The Rebels make it back to the South and the stolen money is delivered to the Confederate government. Lt. Young is appointed major general on 30 De-

cember 1864. He moves to the South and serves under General Wade Hampton against the forces of General William T. Sherman in the Carolinas.

In Union General officer activity, Colonel Rutherford B. Hayes is promoted to brigadier general. In March 1865, he receives the brevet rank of major general. After the war Hayes serves as a member of Congress, governor of Ohio and, in 1876, president of the United States (successor to President Ulysses S. Grant). Also, Colonel Alfred Gibbs is promoted to brigadier general. Subsequent to the promotion, General Gibbs is primarily involved against the Army of Northern Virginia until its surrender during April 1865. Subsequent to the close of hostilities he receives the rank of brevet major general of volunteers and the Regular Army. The following year he becomes colonel of the 7th Cavalry. While at Fort Leavenworth, Kansas, he dies on 26 December 1868.

In Naval activity, the *Sea King*, built in Scotland and launched during October 1863 as a civilian steamer, after being acquired by the Confederacy, embarks under the pretense of a civilian voyage to India. It later has a rendezvous off Madeira with a Confederate vessel that is transporting officers, crew members and armaments. The *Sea King* is commissioned the CSS *Shenandoah* on this day under command of Lieutenant (later commander) James Iredell Waddell. From the date of its commission through the latter part of January 1865, while operating in the Atlantic and the Indian Oceans, the *Shenandoah* seizes nine prizes (merchant ships). By late January, the *Shenandoah* arrives in Australia at Melbourne.

October 20 (Thursday) **In Tennessee,** Union cavalry and a contingent of the 19th Corps engages Confederates at Little River.

In Kansas, Union forces clash with Confederates at Fort Leavenworth through 26 October. Specific units and casualty figures are unavailable.

October 21 (Friday) **In Kentucky,** the 5th U.S. Colored Troops skirmishes with Confederates at Harrodsburg.

In Missouri, Union forces under General Samuel Curtis and Confederate cavalry led by General Sterling Price clash in the vicinity of Independence and Little Blue. The Confederates under Price fare well, pushing the Union back towards Westport, where they clash again on the 23rd. Participants are the 2nd Colorado, 3rd Wisconsin, 5th, 11th, 15th and 16th Kansas Cavalry, the 1st Brigade, Kansas Militia, 2nd and 5th Missouri Militia and two battalions of the 2nd Missouri Artillery.

In Union general officer activity, Brigadier General George Crook is promoted to major general, effective this day. Also, Colonel William Badger Tibbits is breveted brigadier general. Subsequently, he commands a brigade of cavalry (Middle Military Division) under General Sheridan in the Shenandoah. Later, during March 1865, he receives the brevet of major general of volunteers, and after the close of hostilities he is promoted to full rank brigadier general of volunteers during October 1865. He musters out of the army the following year.

In Naval activity, the USS *Fort Jackson,* while on patrol off Wilmington, North Carolina, intercepts and seizes the blockade runner *Wando.* The *Wando,* originally built in Scotland and named *Let Her Rip,* is acquired in November by the U.S. Navy. In December it is commissioned the gunboat USS *Wando* and assigned to the South Atlantic Blockading Squadron. It patrols off South Carolina for the duration of the war. After being decommissioned it is sold in August. It operates as a commercial vessel until it sinks during 1872.

October 22 (Saturday)   In Arkansas, the 53rd U.S. Colored Troops skirmishes with Confederates at White River.

In Missouri, a Union force — elements of the 2nd Colorado, 5th, 7th, 11th, 15th, and 16th Kansas Cavalry, some Kansas militia, the 1st, 2nd, 4th, 6th, 7th, 8th, and 9th Missouri Militia Cavalry, the 13th Missouri Cavalry and the 3rd Iowa and 17th Illinois Cavalry (General Alfred Pleasonton's command) — clashes with Confederates (General Price's Invasion) led by Major General James F. Fagan at Independence. The Union casualties are unreported. The Confederates sustain about 40 killed and 100 wounded. These antagonists again clash on October 26.

In Virginia, Confederate gunboats under Commodore John K. Mitchell, including his flagship the CSS *Virginia II,* bombard Union batteries along the James River. In related activity, the CSS *Richmond,* near Chaffin's Bluff, comes under fire from a Union battery. In South Carolina, the USS *Wamsutta* and other blockade ships give chase when a blockade runner, the *Flora,* is spotted in the vicinity of Fort Moultrie. The *Flora* is run aground.

October 23 (Sunday)   In Arkansas, the 3rd Missouri Cavalry skirmishes with Confederates at Princeton.

In Mississippi, the 1st Iowa and the 9th Kansas Cavalry engage Confederates at Hurricane Creek. The Union sustains one killed and two wounded.

In Missouri, General Sterling Price's cavalry attacks Union lines at Westport (Big Blue). The larger Union force under General Samuel Curtis finally scores a success against Price and repels the attackers led by General Joseph O. Shelby by mounting a countercharge. Union forces succeed in ridding the area of Confederates, and the Union also gains control of Missouri. The Union seizes about 1,000 Confederates. General Price makes his way to Texas following these raids and his force travels with him; however, Major General James Fagan does not accompany them. He is paroled on 20 June 1865 and afterward becomes a planter and then

becomes involved in politics. In 1875, he is appointed U.S. marshal by President Grant. He dies in Little Rock, Arkansas, on 1 September 1893. Confederate General William L. Cabell (West Point, 1850), who commanded a cavalry brigade under Price, has also been captured during this campaign. He will be released during August 1865. The Union victory could have been disastrous. Two of the Union generals, John McNeil and Egbert Brown, ordered to attack with their respective commands, fail to do as ordered. Although General Alfred Pleasonton relieves both, each receives a new command and no charges are filed. During January 1865, General Brown, having earlier lost one arm at Springfield, Missouri, assumes command of the Department of Rolla, a post he retains for the duration. General McNeil receives command of the district of Central Missouri. He leaves the service with the brevet of major general on 12 April 1865.

October 24 (Monday)   In Missouri, a contingent of Kansas cavalry clashes with Confederates at Cold Water Grove at Osage.

In Virginia, Confederate General James Jay Archer succumbs in Richmond. He had been captured during 1863 at Gettysburg and exchanged the previous summer.

October 25 (Tuesday)   BATTLE OF MINE CREEK In Kansas, Union troops under Generals James G. Blunt, Samuel R. Curtis and Alfred Pleasonton arrive near the encampment of Confederates under Sterling Price at Kansas City. The Confederates are defeated and Price is compelled to retire across the Missouri River. Confederate Brigadier General John S. Marmaduke (West Point, 1857) is captured while

Colonel William N. Jeffers (Mottelay, *The Soldier in Our Civil War,* 1886).

using his cavalry to fight a rear action, covering the retreat of General Price against troops commanded by General A. Gillem at Mine Creek, a branch of the Maria des Cygnes in the vicinity of Osage, Kansas. He is captured by Pvt. James Dunlavy, Company D, 3rd Iowa Cavalry. Marmaduke is promoted to major general the following March while he is still interned by the Union. Colonel William Jeffers, 8th Missouri Confederate Cavalry Regiment, is also captured. He is transported to Johnson's Island in Ohio. Subsequent to being paroled, Jeffers returns to Missouri.

In Virginia, on or about this date, Union General Alfred Napoleon Duffie is captured in the vicinity of Bunker Hill and the Confederates do not parole him until February 1865. Subsequent to parole, General Duffie is assigned to the Department of Missouri. He musters out of the service during August 1865. General Grant had remained incensed because Duffie failed to take precautions that would have prevented his capture. Later, General Duffie, a Frenchman, is appointed U.S. consul to Spain. He remains in that capacity until his death due to tuberculosis on 8 November 1868.

In Washington, Seattle celebrates the arrival of Western Union telegraph lines, which places the city in communication with the east. News from the East had until now taken weeks to arrive, but by the following day, Seattle is informed of the news as it happens by way of Morse Code.

October 26 (Wednesday)   In Alabama, Confederate General John B. Hood's force arrives in the vicinity of Decatur, but anticipating the arrival of reinforcements under General Nathan B. Forest, he hesitates rather than attacking the Union lines. Meanwhile, General Sherman anticipates General Hood's presence, but he concludes that General George H. Thomas can handle the situation. Sherman prepares for his advance to the sea. Union troops, including the 18th Michigan, 102nd Ohio, and the 14th U.S. Colored Troops, engage and repel Confederates at Decatur. The Union suffers 10 dead, 45 wounded and 100 missing. The Confederates suffer 100 dead and 300 wounded.

In Florida, units of the Union 19th Iowa Volunteers and the 2nd Maine Cavalry skirmish with Confederates at Milton Blackwater.

In Kansas, General Alfred Pleasonton's cavalry and General Samuel R. Curtis' cavalry combine to defeat General Price's Confederates at Mine Creek (Maria Des Cygnes) and Little Osage River. The Union seizes about 1,500 Confederates.

October 27 (Thursday)   In Virginia, Union troops from Gregg's Cavalry, the 19th Massachusetts and the 7th Michigan Infantry battle Confederates at Hatcher's Run, South Side Railroad. General Hancock's II Corps flanks the Confederate works near Armstrong's Mill. The Union suffers over 1,700 casualties and the Confederates about 1,000 casualties. This battle also includes Boydton Plank Road. Captain Andrew

Left: General Hancock's II Corps' troops flank the Confederate works near Armstrong's Mill on Hatcher's Run, Virginia (Mottelay, *The Soldier in Our Civil War*, 1886). *Right:* Confederate fortifications at Hatcher's Run, Virginia (*Harper's Pictoral History of the Civil War*, 1896).

H. Embler leads a victorious charge with the 59th New York Regiment and one other regiment that drives the Rebels back toward the Burgess House. The bold advance gains the hill's summit for the Union. Embler becomes a recipient of the Medal of Honor for his valor. General Thomas W. Egan performs meritoriously, and for his actions under fire, in November he is breveted major general.

In Confederate general officer activity, Colonel Gilbert M. Sorrel is promoted to the rank of brigadier general. He is assigned duty as a brigade commander in Georgia under General William Mahone. Also, Brigadier General Milo S. Hascall resigns his commission. During the previous month, Hascall received praise from General John Schofield (Commander Army of the Ohio), and he recommended Hascall for promotion to major general in recognition of his actions during the Atlanta campaign. Nonetheless, no action is taken.

October 27–28   In Virginia, the 10th and 18th Corps, bolstered by General Kautz's cavalry, skirmishes with Confederates at Fair Oaks, outside of Richmond. The Union sustains 120 killed, 783 wounded and 400 missing. The

Confederates sustain 60 killed, 311 wounded and 80 missing.

In Naval activity, U.S. Navy Lt. William B. Cushing and a combined detachment of Marines and sailors (13 officers and men) from the North Atlantic Blockading Squadron move up the Roanoke River and successfully pass the Confederate pickets and the USS *Southfield,* the latter having been sunk there earlier, and approach the *Albemarle* without detection. Lt. Cushing attaches the mine to the Rebel ironclad while under fire and succeeds in destroying the vessel while it remains at the wharf. The Union assault boat *Pickett No. 1* is also destroyed, but not until its torpedo (mine) strikes the target. The USS *Shamrock,* commissioned in June and assigned duty off North Carolina, acts as "mother ship" to *Picket No. 1.* The Confederates demand surrender of the men in the boat, but the men ignore the ultimatum. Only Cushing and one other man, Acting Master's Mate Woodman, attached to the *Commodore Hull,* escape; however, Cushing reports that he was unable to get Woodman (who had been wounded) to shore. The others are either killed or captured. Cushing evades capture by enter-

ing a swamp. He notes in his report after arriving back on the *Valley City* on the night of the 28th that the destruction of the *Albemarle* at Plymouth was confirmed.

October 28 (Friday)   In Alabama, the USS *General Thomas* exchanges fire with Confederate batteries attached to Confederate General John B. Hood. The *General Thomas* sustains some damage and afterward moves to Stones River and commences fire upon the Confederate positions there. The Confederates sustain round after round of effective fire and are compelled to abandon their positions.

In Arkansas, the 1st Arkansas Cavalry skirmishes with Confederates at Fayetteville.

In Missouri, Union cavalry under General Samuel Curtis clashes with General Sterling Price's cavalry at Newtonia. General Price is still on the retreat after his raid into Missouri.

In Tennessee, a contingent of General Alvan C. Gillem's cavalry encounters and defeats the Confederates at Morristown in East Tennessee. The Union suffers light casualties.

In Virginia, Confederate troops under General Henry Heth attack Union positions in the vicinity of Boydton Plank Road (Petersburg), and the attack succeeds in forcing the Union line to pull back. A skirmish also develops on the Williamsburg Road. The Confederates prevail and capture about 400 Union troops.

In Union general officer activity, Brigadier General George Jerrison Stannard receives the brevet rank of major general of volunteers. Since he sustained a wound at Fort Harrison that cost him one of his arms (his third wound), General Stannard has been attached to the Department of the East assigned to duty along the border of Vermont. He retires from the army during 1867.

In Naval activity, the USS *Eolus,* USS *Aries* and the USS *Calypso,* while operating off Wilmington, North Carolina, capture the English-built blockade runner *Lady Sterling,* an 835-ton

Destruction of the CSS *Albermarle* (*Harper's Pictoral History of the Civil War,* 1896).

side-wheel gunboat. The ship is acquired by the U.S. Navy, transformed into a gunboat and commissioned during April 1865, initially as the USS *Lady Sterling*. In June 1865, it is renamed the USS *Hornet*. In October 1865, after the war is over, the *Hornet* sails to Cuba to retrieve the ironclad CSS *Stonewall*. The *Hornet* is decommissioned in December 1865. During 1869, the ship is sold and becomes the merchant ship *Hornet* until 1872, when it enters service with the Spanish and is renamed the *Marco Aurelia*. The USS *Aries*, following this seizure, continues to patrol off North Carolina, and it participates in the operations against Fort Fisher at Wilmington during December 1864 and January 1865.

October 29 (Saturday)   In Tennessee, Union cavalry (General Alvan C. Gillem's command) engages Confederates at Morristown. The Union sustains about eight killed and 42 wounded. The Confederates sustain more than 200 casualties and about 200 captured.

In West Virginia, the 8th Ohio Cavalry clashes with a contingent of Confederates at Beverly. The Union sustains eight killed, 25 wounded and 13 missing. The Confederates suffer 17 killed, 27 killed and 92 missing.

In Union general officer activity, General Thomas Edward Greenfield Ransom, who has been in command of the XVII Corps and involved with driving the Confederates out of North Georgia and into Alabama, dies of complications of an old wound while he is with the corps during its return to Georgia.

In Naval activity, a squadron of gunboats, including the USS *Wyalusing*, moves up the Roanoke River to Plymouth, North Carolina; however, a Confederate-placed obstacle prevents passage at a point just short of the town. The squadron, after halting, chooses to take a circuitous route rather than abort the mission. They swing back and take the Middle River and to a point above Plymouth, from where they move into the Roanoke River and head downstream to reach Plymouth the next day. The gunboats encounter heavy fire from Confederate batteries; however, the naval fire proves to be more formidable, as it pummels the batteries and Confederate rifle pits. The overwhelming fire power drives the Rebels from their positions and opens the way for a landing force to debark and seize Fort Williams. The Union seizes some prisoners, and it continues to support the operation to seize Plymouth.

October 30 (Sunday)   In Arkansas, the Union 7th Iowa and the 11th Missouri Cavalry engage Confederates in the vicinity of Brownsville.

In Alabama, Union cavalry (General Kenner Garrard's cavalry division), Army of the Cumberland, clashes with Confederates at Ladija, Terrapin Creek.

In Tennessee, Union General George H. Thomas continues to maintain garrisons in the area around Chattanooga, Bridgeport, Decatur,

General George H. Thomas (Mottelay, *The Soldier in Our Civil War*, 1886).

and Florence. Thomas' total strength, including James H. Wilson's 10,000 cavalry at Nashville, stands at about 45,000. Reinforcements bring the strength of his command to about 75,000 men available for the defense of Tennessee. Confederate General John B. Hood arrived in the vicinity of Decatur on the 29th, but he does not attack the Union lines. On the 30th, Hood makes camp opposite the Union force at Florence. General U.S. Grant meets with General Sherman the following day to discuss the destruction of Hood's army before a Confederate campaign can be initiated.

In Naval activity, the USS *Undine* escorts the transport Anna from Johnsonville, Tennessee, to Sandy Island. While on the return to Johnsonville, the *Undine*'s commander, Acting Master Bryant responds to artillery reports from the river below. The *Undine* moves toward the sounds of the guns, and as it approaches Paris Landing, the *Undine* is ambushed. It is joined by the *Cheeseman* and *Venus*. The two transports and the *Undine* exchange fire for several hours, but by that time, the *Undine* expends its ammunition supply and the two transports are disabled by the Confederate guns. In addition, the *Undine*'s engine is disabled, leaving few options. Bryant is compelled to lower the colors. The Confederates seize the three vessels. Subsequently, Acting Master Bryant is exonerated of any wrongdoing by an inquiry board.

October 31 (Monday)   Nevada is admitted to the Union, becoming the 36th state.

In Naval activity, Union gunboats, including the *Belle*, *Commodore Hull*, *Shamrock* (flag ship), *Tacony* and *Whitehead*, attack and capture Plymouth, North Carolina. Afterward, the Union refloats the CSS *Albemarle*, which had been sunk by Union forces the previous October. During April 1865, the *Albemarle* is taken to Norfolk where it remains until sold during October 1867. Afterward, the USS *Tacony* partici-

pates in the attacks against Fort Fisher, North Carolina, during December 1864 and January 1865, then it continues on patrol for the duration. It remains in active service until it is decommissioned in August 1867.

A U.S. sailor assigned to the attack force, Henry Brutsche, lands and spikes a 9-inch Confederate gun while under heavy enemy fire, greatly aiding the success of the mission at tremendous risk to his life. This act of heroism makes Brutsche a recipient of the Medal of Honor. The *Shamrock* remains on patrol in the sounds until it is decommissioned for a short while during August 1865. In October of the same year, it is recommissioned and serves in European waters until August 1868, when it is again decommissioned and sold. The *Commodore Hull* sustains severe damage during the engagement; however, it is able to continue in service for the duration. The *Commodore Hull* is decommissioned during June 1865 and shortly thereafter sold to become the merchant ship *Waccamaw*. The USS *Belle*, built this year in Philadelphia and acquired by the U.S. Navy in June, following this activity moves to the North Carolina sounds to serve as a tugboat, dispatch vessel and spar-torpedo boat. After the war it is sold during July 1865 and afterward, using the same name, *Belle*, it remains in commercial service until 1891. Also, the USS *Whitehead*, initially commissioned during November 1861, remains in service for the duration of the war and is decommissioned during June 1865 and sold the following August. At that time it is renamed the *Nevada*. It operates as a commercial vessel until it is lost by fire during September 1872 at New London, Connecticut.

The USS *Kansas*, while operating off Old Inlet, North Carolina, spots a blockade runner, the steamer *Annie*; however, it outruns the *Kansas*. Nevertheless, two other blockaders, the USS *Niphon* and the *Wilderness*, snare the *Annie* after it evades the *Kansas*. At about 1905, the *Wilderness* spots the *Annie* off New Inlet, North Carolina, as it attempts to cross the bar. At about the same time, it is detected by the *Niphon*. At 1945, the blockade runner, a British vessel, is seized, along with its cargo of 540 bales of cotton and thirty tons of pressed tobacco. It is also transporting 14 casks containing turpentine. While the *Wilderness* takes possession of the *Annie*, the *Niphon* takes the crew and passengers aboard.

The Confederates at nearby Fort Fisher commence firing while the crew is being transferred. The *Wilderness* sustains a hit that inflicts damage when one shell passes through its hurricane deck and a water tank before exploding on the port gangway. The port wheel is damaged, but it receives repairs after arriving at Beaufort, North Carolina. In conjunction, the USS *Niphon*, commissioned during April 1863, is placed out of service for repairs. However, before re-entering active service the war begins to wind down and the *Niphon* remains decommissioned. It is sold during April 1865. Also, following this activity, the USS *Tacony* participates in the seizure of Plymouth, North Carolina, and in the operations against Fort Fisher, North

Carolina. The *Tacony* remains in active service until October 1867, when it is decommissioned. Afterward, during August 1868, it is sold.

November 1 (Tuesday) **In Virginia,** General Grant's Union forces and General Lee's Confederates are settling in for the winter at Petersburg. The Union had attempted to make additional progress in the latter part of October, but the Confederates held their positions, causing Grant to cancel plans to seize the South Side Railroad. Richmond remains safe for the winter, except for minor skirmishes that develop.

In Tennessee, the Union 10th Missouri Cavalry encounters and skirmishes with Confederates at Union Station through 4 November. The Union sustains two killed, two wounded and two missing. Confederate casualties are unavailable.

In Louisiana, the 6th U.S. Colored Cavalry Regiment battles Confederates at Black River. Casualty figures are unreported.

In Confederate general officer activity, Lt. Colonel William H. Fitzhugh Payne is promoted to the rank of brigadier general. He serves as a brigade commander under General Thomas T. Munford, 2nd Virginia Cavalry (Munford is appointed brigadier general in November 1864). Munford will command Fitzhugh Lee's division at several battles, including Five Forks and Sayler's Creek, before Appomattox. Brigadier General Thomas L. Rosser is promoted to the rank of major general, effective this date. Colonel Jerome Bonaparte Robertson (5th Texas Infantry) is also promoted to brigadier general. He participates at various actions, including Seven Days,' Second Manassas (Bull Run) and Gettysburg, and sustains wounds at Manassas and Gettysburg. Afterward, he is transferred to the West, where he serves under General Longstreet at Chickamauga and during the Knoxville campaign, prior to his transfer to Texas, where he commands the Texas reserve corps. After the war, General Roberston practices medicine and later becomes involved in building railroads until his death during January 1891.

In Naval activity, the U.S. Navy acquires the *Dictator,* a single-turret monitor at about this time (November). The *Dictator,* built in New York, is commissioned during November 1864; however, it is decommissioned the following September and left out of service until recommissioned in July 1869. Afterward it is mostly out of service due to problems and is sold for scrap during September 1883. Also, the U.S. Navy acquires the *Hibiscus* at about this time (November). The *Hibiscus* is a screw steamship built in Connecticut at Fairhaven earlier this year. It is commissioned shortly after being purchased. It is assigned to the East Gulf Blockading Squadron for patrol duty off the coast of western Florida until the conclusion of hostilities. It returns to New York during August 1865, where it is decommissioned; it is sold in October 1866. Afterward it operates as the civilian vessel *Francis Wright* and later as the *Hibiscus*

until lost at sea on 1 May 1873. Also, the gunboat USS *Shawmut,* received by the U.S. Navy on 16 October 1864, is commissioned in New York at the navy yard. Lt. Commander George U. Morris receives command of the gunboat. It embarks from New York on the 3rd en route to join the search for Confederate raider *Tallahassee* (renamed *Olustee*); however, no contact is made. It returns to Portsmouth on 20 November. The following January, it departs for North Carolina to join the North Atlantic Blockading Squadron.

November 2 (Wednesday) **In Georgia,** the Union XV Corps, commanded by General P.J. Osterhaus, and the XVII Corps (General Ransom, recently deceased), have accomplished its mission of pushing John B. Hood's Army from the area. General Sherman sets plans for his March to the Sea to reach Savannah. He leaves General George H. Thomas to deal with General Hood in Tennessee. Union General Schofield will arrive to assist Thomas.

In Naval activity, the USS *Key West* and the USS *Tawah* recapture the transport *Venus* at Johnsonville, Tennessee, where it had been seized on 30 October. However, the *Undine,* also captured with the *Venus,* is able to escape and reach positions covered by Confederate guns on Reynoldsburg Island. Nevertheless, the Confederates destroy the *Venus* on 4 November to prevent the Union from recapturing it.

November 3 (Thursday) **In Arkansas,** a one-company contingent of the 46th Missouri Volunteer Regiment skirmishes with Confederates at Vera Cruz.

November 4 (Friday) **In Tennessee,** Confederates under General Nathan B. Forrest move out of Reynoldsburg Island and head towards Johnsonville to evade the closing Union troops. The 11th Tennessee Cavalry, 43rd Wisconsin Volunteer Regiment and the 12th U.S. Colored Troops Regiment engage Confederates for two days at Johnsonville. Casualty figures are unavailable. The USS *Moose* participates in this action. It shells a Confederate contingent of about forty cavalrymen at a crossing of the Memphis and Clarksville Railroads in the vicinity of Johnsonville.

In Confederate general officer activity, Colonel Peter Burwell Starke, 28th Mississippi Cavalry, is promoted to the rank of brigadier general. Starke is assigned to duty in General Forrest's command and will participate in the Tennessee campaign with Lt. General John B. Hood. Toward the close of the war, he is transferred to Mississippi, where he serves under General Chalmers. After the war, General Starke serves a term as sheriff of Bolivar County, Mississippi.

In Naval activity, Confederate shore batteries exchange fire with the USS *Elfin, Key West* and *Tawah* on the Tennessee River in a clash that continues for about three hours. The Union concludes that the ships cannot be saved. Consequently, all three vessels are set afire to prevent capture. In other activity, a squadron composed

of six gunboats, including the USS *Victory,* participates at Johnsonville, Tennessee, in an action that repulses a cavalry raid executed by General Nathan Bedford Forrest. The USS *Victory* remains with the Mississippi Squadron until the close of hostilities. Later, on 30 June 1865, it is decommissioned at Mound City, Illinois, and on 17 August sold at auction. During the following year, it is renamed the *Lizzie Tate;* on 22 November 1867, it becomes a barge.

November 5 (Saturday) **In Virginia,** Union and Confederates clash at Fort Sedgwick (also known as Fort Hell). The Union 2nd Corps participates, sustaining five killed and 10 wounded. The Confederates sustain 15 killed and 35 wounded.

In Tennessee, a contingent of the 3rd North Carolina Mounted Infantry engages a Confederate force for two days at Big Pigeon River.

In Union general officer activity, Brigadier General James Nagle, who had served with Winfield Scott during the Mexican War, musters out of the service and returns to his home in Pottsville, Pennsylvania. During his Civil War service, Nagle had participated at Groveton, Virginia, against Rufus King in August 1862, in addition to duty at Sharpsburg (Antietam), Maryland, and at Fredericksburg, Virginia, where he commanded six regiments against the granite-like positions of Robert E. Lee's Confederates.

November 6 (Sunday) **In Arkansas and Missouri,** Confederate General Sterling Price's cavalry, in full retreat, crosses out of Missouri into Arkansas. After entering Arkansas, the Confederates skirmish with Union troops at Cane Hill. Union General Andrew J. Smith, commanding two divisions of the XVI Corps, assisting General Rosecrans' campaign to drive Price out of Missouri, is no longer needed there. General Smith is under orders to lead his command of 8,000 to 10,000 troops to Nashville to support General George H. Thomas. The 5th Minnesota Volunteer Regiment departs for Nashville on or about November 24 and will participate in the battle for Nashville.

In Virginia, General Grant has been in communication with General Sherman concerning the decision whether to march on Savannah or to concentrate on the destruction of General Hood's force. General Grant agreed with Sherman on 2 November that General Thomas has sufficient forces to deal with Hood. Grant sends the following message to Thomas: "I do not see that you can withdraw from where you are to follow Hood, without giving up all we have gained in territory I say, then, go as you propose." General Sherman informs Grant on the 6th: "I am ready to march as soon as the election is over, appointing November 10th as the day for starting."

In Virginia, Confederate President Jefferson Davis appoints Colonel Lucius B. Northrop to the rank of brigadier general, effective this date, but the nomination for promotion is not sent to the Confederate Senate, apparently because his efforts in providing food for the troops and the Union prisoners has not impressed the Confederate government.

In Naval activity, the USS *Adela,* while on duty in St. George's Sound (middle entrance), seizes a blockade runner, the schooner *Badger,* which is carrying a cargo of cotton from St. Marks to Havana. Subsequent to this capture, the *Adela* moves to New York for repairs. In March 1865 it is assigned duty with the Potomac Flotilla to support the defenses of the water approaches to the capital during the trying days following the assassination of President Lincoln. In August 1865, the Potomac Flotilla is disbanded. The *Adela* heads north to New York; however, the records of the date it is decommissioned has been lost. Nonetheless, the *Adela* is sold in New York at an auction on 30 November 1865.

November 7 (Monday)   In Alabama, at Selma, General Richard Taylor receives a message from General Beauregard which states that due to the "enemy's contemplated movement into Georgia, it would be prudent to start again manufacture of powder at Selma. Correspond with Colonel [Josiah] Gorgas on the subject."

In Confederate general officer activity, Brigadier General Samuel Reid Anderson, who resigned during 1862 due to poor health, is recommissioned brigadier general to rank from this day by President Davis. Anderson, who is in his late 50s, is placed in command of the bureau of conscription for the state of Tennessee, however his headquarters are established in Selma, Alabama.

President Abraham Lincoln (Mottelay, *The Soldier in Our Civil War,* 1886).

In Union activity, the 18th Army Corps is abolished. It will be reorganized as the 18th Corps during February 1865.

In Naval activity, the USS *Pontiac,* commanded by Lt. Commander Stephen B. Luce, engages Confederates (Battery Marshall) on Sullivan's Island. During the engagement, the *Pontiac* sustains some damage to the forecastle. Six crew members are injured.

November 8 (Tuesday)   President Abraham Lincoln is re-elected. His vice president is Andrew Johnson.

November 9 (Wednesday)   In Alabama, elements of the 5th Cavalry Division, Army of the Cumberland, engage Confederates at Shoal Creek. The Union sustains five killed and 10 wounded. The Confederates suffer about 50 killed, wounded and missing.

In Georgia, a contingent of the 2nd Division, 20th Corps, skirmishes with Confederates at Atlanta. The Union suffers five killed and 10 wounded. The Confederates sustain 20 killed or wounded.

In Confederate general officer activity, Brigadier General Williams Carter Wickham resigns his commission. Shortly thereafter, on 9 November, General Wickham takes his seat in the Confederate Congress. He remains in that capacity until the close of the war. He becomes involved with the railroad industry after the war, and he serves in the Virginia Senate. He dies on 23 July 1888 in Richmond.

November 10 (Thursday)   In Georgia, Union General W.T. Sherman's army departs Kingston, heading toward Atlanta to set his course for Savannah. In other activity, Union forces under General John M. Corse, while in Rome, destroy all Confederate military supplies discovered in the town and facilities that could by used for military purposes.

In Union general officer activity, Colonel Edmund J. Davis, who crossed the Mexican border during the initial stages of the war to recruit what became known as the 1st Texas Cavalry, is appointed brigadier general. After the war, General Davis becomes governor of the state (1869). Also, Colonel Thomas John Lucas (16th Indiana) is named brigadier general. Prior to his appointment, Lucas had participated at Ball's Bluff, the Battle of Richmond, Kentucky, and in the Vicksburg campaign. Following Vicksburg, Colonel Lucas participated in the Red River campaign, and during that same time period, he sustained three wounds. He participates in the campaign against Mobile and sees service in Florida and south Georgia. He receives the brevet of major general of volunteers in March 1865. At the conclusion of hostilities, he commands a cavalry brigade at Vicksburg. He musters out of the army in 1866. In other activity, Colonel James Richard Slack is promoted to brigadier general. On 13 March 1865, he receives the brevet of major general of volunteers. He remains in the service beyond the close of hostilities and leaves the army in early 1866.

In Confederate general officer activity, Colonel Josiah Gorgas (West Point, 1841), a Pennsylvanian, is appointed brigadier general, effective this date, for his contribution as the chief of ordnance, CSA, which has greatly aided the cause by coordinating the supply of guns and ammunition throughout the various campaigns. General Gorgas, appointed chief of ordnance in 1861, has no field command, but he has been totally committed to maintaining a flow of supplies and ammunition to troops in the field. In addition, he had been responsible in great part for success against the naval blockade. He purchased five blockade runners to support the cause by getting foreign materials to the Confederacy. After the war, General Gorgas becomes superintendent of the Brierfield Iron Works in Alabama, but later, he becomes chancellor of the University of the South in Sewanee, Tennessee. He retires and dies in Tuscaloosa, Alabama, during May 1883.

In Naval activity, the USS *Western World* is assigned to the North Atlantic Blockading Squadron with patrol duty along the coast of Virginia between Lawn's Creek and the Nansemond River.

November 11 (Friday)   In Georgia, Union troops under General John M. Corse, en route to join forces with those at Atlanta, depart Rome.

In Confederate general officer activity, William M. Browne is appointed brigadier general in the Confederacy; however, the Senate does not confirm the appointment. In February 1865, the Senate rejects Browne's nomination. General Browne had served on the staff of President Jefferson Davis. From 17 February 1862 to 18 March 1862, he acted as secretary of state. He also participated in the defense of Savannah as a brigade commander against the advance of General William T. Sherman. During April 1864, Browne was appointed commandant of conscripts for the state of Georgia.

In Naval activity, the USS *Lancaster,* attached to the Pacific Squadron, undertakes a clandestine mission. A contingent using boats intercepts a passenger ship, the steamer *Salvador,* off the Bay of Panama to foil a Confederate plot. A band of Confederates is seized while they are preparing to take control of the *Salvador* to use it as a Confederate raider against U.S. ships transporting gold from California. After the war, the *Lancaster* is decommissioned on 8 March 1867; however, later it is recommissioned, and except for some periods of being decommissioned, it remains in active service until 1915. This *Lancaster* is separate from the ram USS *Lancaster.*

In other activity, the USS *Tulip,* originally built for the Chinese and named *Chi Kiang,* was acquired by the U.S. Navy during 1863. On this day, it experiences problems with a boiler, but the captain ignores the problem as he attempts to speed to the Anacostia naval base on the Potomac. The cruise is cut short abruptly when the troubled starboard boiler explodes while the gunboat is off Ragged Point, Virginia. Consequently, the *Tulip* sinks.

November 12 (Saturday) **In Georgia,** General William T. Sherman reaches Cartersville, where he receives a dispatch from General Thomas that states: "I have no fears that Beauregard can do us any harm now…. If he attempts to follow you, I will follow him as far as possible. If he does not follow you, I will organize my troops and believe I have men enough to ruin him unless he gets out of the way very rapidly." This communication is the last between the two men, as the Confederates cut the lines between Cartersville and Nashville.

In Virginia, a Union contingent of the 1st West Virginia Cavalry skirmishes with Confederates at Nineveh. Private James F. Adams captures the flag of the 14th Virginia Cavalry (CSA). Sgt. Levi Shoemaker captures the flag of the 22nd Virginia Cavalry (CSA). Both soldiers receive the Medal of Honor for their heroism above and beyond the call of duty.

In Virginia, cavalry units under Generals George A. Custer, Wesley Merritt and William H. Powell battle Confederates under General Lunsford L. Lomax at Cedar Springs and at Newtown. The Union sustains 84 wounded and 100 missing. The Confederate casualties are reported as 150 captured.

November 13 (Sunday) **In Tennessee,** the 8th, 9th and 13th Tennessee Cavalry Regiments, bolstered by some artillery, engage Confederate forces at Bull's Gap, Morristown. The Union loses 36 wounded and 200 missing. Confederate casualties are unavailable.

November 14 (Monday) **In Georgia,** Union troops destroy Confederate railroad house in Atlanta and machine shops in the vicinity of the city.

In Tennessee, Union reinforcements (4th and 23rd Corps and General James H. Wilson's cavalry) under General John M. Schofield arrive in Pulaski. Schofield takes command of 35,000 Union troops in the city and maintains a vigil on General John B. Hood, but he attempts to avoid battle.

Union troops destroy machine shops in Atlanta (Mottelay, *The Soldier in Our Civil War*, 1886).

In Virginia, General Egan becomes wounded during a minor operation and it disables him; however, upon his return to duty, he receives the rank of brevet major general to rank from 27 October 1864 "for gallant and distinguished service at the battle of Boydton Plank Road." General Egan serves for the duration of the war. He resigns from the army during 1866. He dies in obscurity alone in a charity hospital in New York on 24 February 1887. He is interred in the National Cemetery in Brooklyn.

In Arkansas, the 54th U.S. Colored Troops (2nd Arkansas) and the 3rd Kansas Indian Home Guards battle Confederates at Cow Creek through 28 November.

In Union general officer activity, General George McClellan resigns from the service, effective from November 8.

November 15 (Tuesday) **In Louisiana,** Union cavalry forces under General Albert Lindley Lee move from Baton Rouge to Clinton and Liberty Creek. Problems for Lee develop with General Edward Canby, successor to General Banks, that lead to Lee being sent to Washington, only to be returned to his command in New Orleans. Nevertheless, on 2 April, Canby confines Lee to New Orleans "until further orders." On 4 May, Lee's resignation is accepted.

In Georgia, General William T. Sherman separates his army into two contingents. The left wing, commanded by General Henry W. Slocum, is composed of the 14th Corps and the 20th Corps, commanded by Generals Jefferson C. Davis and A.S. Williams, respectively, and the right wing, commanded by General Oliver O. Howard and composed of the 15th Corps and the 17th Corps, commanded by Generals Joseph Osterhaus and F.P. Blair. The 14th Corps is composed of three divisions commanded by Generals W. P. Carlin, J.D. Morgan and A. Baird. The 20th Corps includes the divisions of Generals N.J. Jackson, J.W. Geary and W.T. Ward. The 15th Corps contains the four divisions of Generals C.R. Woods, W.B. Hazen, J.E. Smith and J.M. Corse. The 17th Corps is composed of the divisions of Generals Joseph A. Mower, Mortimer D. Leggett and G.A. Smith. The cavalry components are one division led by General Hugh Kilpatrick and two brigades, commanded by Colonels E.H. Murray and S.D. Atkins. The Army as a whole numbers more than 62,000 troops, including 55,329 infantry, 5,063 cavalry and 1,812 artillery. Sherman's force is augmented by 64 cannon (four guns per battery), about 2,500 wagons drawn by six mules each, and about 600 ambulances, each drawn by two horses. General Oliver

O. Howard, leading the right wing, advances with the cavalry along the Jonesboro Road, while General Slocum, with the left wing, moves by rail along the Georgia Railroad from Decatur to Madisonville.

On the following day, General Sherman departs Atlanta with the 14th Corps and the rear guard of the 14th Corps.

In Confederate general officer activity, Colonel Joseph B. Palmer is promoted to brigadier general effective this date.

November 16 (Wednesday) **In Georgia,** General William T. Sherman departs Atlanta for Savannah. The force destroys Confederate rails and sources of supply as it advances. When the column reaches Covington, General Jefferson C. Davis' 14th Corps pivots to the right and moves toward Milledgeville. General Henry Slocum's XX Corps heads for Madison. Sherman's troops skirmish with a Confederate force under Major General Joseph Wheeler at Lovejoy's Station and Bear Creek Station. The Union captures approximately 50 Confederates. Sherman's Bummers (50 men to a party) are assigned details to gather supplies for his quick-marching army. They start out each day on foot and return at night with food and stock, almost never on foot. As Sherman's command steps out along the Decatur Road, Sherman and other officers look about over the ruins of their past battles. Sherman remarks about the conspicuous spot where General James McPherson was slain at a bloody battle of July 22. The Union departs with Atlanta haloed by the ominous smoke hovering over the burning, destroyed city. As the Union troops get into the distance, the day is brilliantly illuminated by the sun, and Atlanta becomes a campaign of the past. Union bands begin picking up the pace, and in an enthusiastic spontaneous outcry, the men commence singing a rousing rendition of "Glory Glory Hallelujah" as their horses make an oblique left towards Savannah. One enlisted man yells to Sherman: "Uncle Billy, I guess Grant is waiting for us at Richmond."

In Confederate general officer activity, Colonel Dudley McIver Dubose is promoted to brigadier general. He is attached to the forces under General Ewell and remains with him for the duration.

November 17 (Thursday) **In Alabama,** the 2nd Iowa Cavalry clashes with Confederates at Aberdeen and Butler Creek.

In Georgia, Confederate General William J. Hardee assumes command of all Confederate troops in the state. Meanwhile, General Sherman's command, its first night out of Lithonia, stands in front of Stone Mountain, where his men spend a great deal of time diligently wrecking the rails and placing them over huge bonfires to insure permanent destruction.

In Virginia, the 209th Pennsylvania skirmishes with a Confederate contingent at Chester Station, Bermuda Hundred. The Union sustains 10 wounded and 120 missing. The Confederate casualties are reported as 10 wounded.

In Union general officer activity, Brigadier General Godfrey Weitzel is promoted to full rank major general.

November 18 (Friday) **In Virginia,** a contingent of the 91st Ohio Volunteer Regiment engages Confederates at Myerstown. The Union sustains 60 killed and wounded. The Confederates suffer 10 killed and wounded.

November 19 (Saturday) **In Louisiana,** the 11th Wisconsin Volunteer Regiment and the 93rd U.S. Colored Troops clash with Confederates at Bayou La Fouche (Ash Bayou).

In Union general officer activity, Brigadier General Julius White, commander of the 1st Division (IX Corps), upon General Burnside's departure from the army during the previous August, had become ill soon after taking command and saw no field duty. His resignation is accepted by the War Department this day. Nevertheless, despite his resignation and apparently due to the respect he gained from higher command, he receives the brevet of major general of volunteers.

November 20–21 **In Georgia,** General William T. Sherman's army continues to advance toward Savannah. On this day, skirmishes erupt at Macon and Griswoldville. The Union continues to punish the Rebel forces, which include regulars and reserves. At Macon, General Hugh Kilpatrick's force against the Confederates includes the 10th Ohio Cavalry, 9th Pennsylvania Cavalry, 92nd Illinois Mounted Infantry and the 10th Wisconsin Battery.

November 21 (Monday) **In Alabama,** Confederate General John B. Hood departs Florence en route to Tennessee. His force exceeds 35,000 men. The Confederates encounter Union forces under General John Schofield at Mt. Pleasant on the 23rd.

In Georgia, Union cavalry under General Oliver O. Howard clashes with Confederates under Major General Joseph Wheeler at Gordon.

In Louisiana, the 4th Wisconsin Cavalry, bolstered by the 1st Wisconsin Battery, engages Confederates at Jackson and Liberty.

In Tennessee, Union General John Schofield, who had previously sent his trains to the rear, now moves his troops back to Columbia, and from there to Franklin to await reinforcements from General George H. Thomas who will enable him to confront the approaching force of General Hood. Nevertheless, Thomas decides not to reinforce Schofield. In other activity, Union cavalry led by General John P. Hatch battles Confederates at Campbellville, Lynnville and Lawrenceburg. The Union sustains 75 killed and wounded. The Confederate casualties are reported as 50 killed and wounded.

In Virginia, Union cavalry commanded by General Alfred Torbert engages Confederates at Rood's Hill. The Union sustains 18 killed and 52 wounded. Confederate casualties are unreported. In other activity, Confederate Brigadier General John Henry Winder (West Point, 1820), provost marshal in Richmond, also receives responsibility as commissary general for prisoners detained at all prison camps east of the Mississippi River.

In Naval activity, the USS *Iosco,* while on patrol off Wilmington, North Carolina, intercepts the blockade runner *Sybil.*

November 22 (Tuesday) **In Georgia,** General Sherman's army (left wing under Henry Slocum, right wing under O. O. Howard and Cavalry under Kilpatrick) nears Savannah. The troops occupy Milledgeville and destroy all military facilities, including factories. The local politicians at Milledgeville had hastily abandoned the legislature as the Yankees approached, leaving legislation unfinished. The Confederates attempt to stymie the Union advance, but to no avail. In other activity, General Charles C. Walcutt's brigade, 1st Division, 15th Corps, and the 1st Brigade, 3rd Cavalry Division, Army of the Tennessee, clash with Confederates at Griswoldville. The Union sustains 10 killed and 52 wounded. The Confederates sustain 50 killed, 200 wounded and 400 captured.

In Mississippi, the 3rd U.S. Colored Cavalry (1st Mississippi) skirmishes with Confederates at Rolling Fork.

In Tennessee, Confederate General John B. Hood's force advances toward Columbia to attempt to split the Union Forces between Columbia and Pulaski. In addition, Confederate troops occupy Lawrenceburg.

In Virginia, a Union force composed of elements of the 1st and 3rd Divisions (Cavalry Corps), Army of the Potomac, and the 2nd Cavalry Division, Army of West Virginia, engage Confederates at Rood's Hill. The Union sustains 18 killed and 52 wounded.

November 23 (Wednesday) **In Georgia,** at Milledgeville, the prison is set afire by the Union.

In Tennessee, Confederate units under General John B. Hood occupy Pulaski.

November 24 (Thursday) **In Tennessee,** Union forces under General John Schofield arrive at Columbia to reinforce the Union lines. Schofield's appearance enables the Union to repel a Confederate assault by General Nathan B. Forrest's cavalry. At Campbellville and Lynnville, the 5th Cavalry Division, Military Division of the Missouri, battles Confederates. Colonel Horace Capron's Brigade, 1st Cavalry Division, and the 4th and 23rd Corps (General Thomas' Army), engage Confederates at Columbia, Duck Run. The Confederates prevail and occupy Columbia by the 28th. Estimated Union casualties stand at about 800 killed, wounded and missing. The estimated Confederate casualties stand at about 600 killed, wounded and missing.

In Georgia, General William T. Sherman departs Milledgeville. General Oliver O. Howard's right wing moves parallel with the Central Railroad, and it destroys the tracks as it advances. Meanwhile, General Henry Slocum's left wing drives down the Louisville Dirt Road. General Hugh Kilpatrick's cavalry diverts and attempts to rescue some Union prisoners. Also, the vanguard (1st Alabama Cavalry) of the Army of the Tennessee engages Confederates at Ball's Ferry, Oconee River, on this day and the next.

Left: Union troops hoist Old Glory atop the capitol in Milledgeville, Georgia. *Above:* The prison at Milledgeville burns (Mottelay, *The Soldier in Our Civil War,* 1886).

Union troops destroy the railroad roundhouse in Atlanta (Mottelay, *The Soldier in Our Civil War*, 1886).

In Texas, the 1st California Cavalry clashes with Confederates at Bent's Old Fork.

In Virginia, food supplies for the Southerners have not improved, but the Union Army remains well supplied. The Union Army of the Potomac receives 59,000 pounds of turkey from the North and General Sheridan's troops receive 35,000 pounds of turkey for Thanksgiving.

In Union general officer activity, Brigadier General Charles Robert Woods, due to his actions at Chickamauga, had earlier received the brevet of colonel in the Regular Army. On this day he is breveted major general of volunteers. Subsequently, toward the close of hostilities, he receives the brevet rank of major general in the Regular Army. He remains in the army beyond the end of the war, and during July 1866, he becomes lieutenant colonel of the 33rd U.S. Infantry. He retires during 1872 due to ill health while holding the rank of colonel with the 2nd U.S. Infantry.

In Naval activity, the USS *Galena* arrives at Philadelphia from Key West to receive repairs. It is decommissioned on 24 November, but recommissioned on 29 March 1865, following completion of repairs on 29 November 1864. The *Galena,* assigned to the North, leaves Philadelphia and arrives at Newport News, Virginia, on 2 April.

November 25 (Friday)   In Georgia, Union and Confederate troops skirmish at Sandersville. When the smoke clears, each suffers approximately 100 casualties; however, the Union holds the town.

In Kansas, a one-company contingent of the 1st Colorado Cavalry clashes with Confederates at Pawnee Force.

In New Mexico, the 1st New Mexico Cavalry skirmishes with Confederates at St. Vrain's Old Fort.

In New York, Southern sympathizers unsuccessfully attempt to disrupt the city of New York. They set fire to fifteen hotels, and additional fires are set at various buildings to cause panic. The plot fails and the fires are quickly extinguished.

November 26 (Saturday)   In Tennessee, Union troops at Columbia are by this time well

fortified, and they are preparing to withstand a major assault by Confederate General John B. Hood's Army of the Tennessee.

In Georgia, the 3rd Brigade, 1st Division, XX Corps (General Slocum), engages Confederates at Saundersville (Buffalo Creek). The Union, which gains the town, sustains about 100 missing or captured. The Confederates also sustain about 100 missing or captured. No other casualties are reported. In other activity, General Hugh Kilpatrick's Union cavalry (8th Indiana and 2nd Kentucky) battles Confederates at Sylvan Grove.

In Alabama, the 101st U.S. Colored Troops skirmish with Confederates at Madison Station.

In Confederate general officer activity, Confederate brigadier general Ambrose Ransom Wright is promoted to the rank of major general. Following his promotion, Wright is transferred from Virginia to Georgia, where he serves for the duration. After the war he resumes his law practice and later is elected to the U.S. Congress; however, he succumbs on 21 December 1872 at Augusta prior to taking his seat.

In Naval activity, the *Napa,* a light draft monitor, is launched at Wilmington, Delaware. However, it is not completed and transformed into a torpedo ship until after the surrender of General Robert E. Lee at Appomattox (April 1865) on 4 May 1865. The *Napa* does not get commissioned. It is sold during 1875.

November 26–29   In Georgia, Union cavalry (General Kilpatrick's command) and Confederate forces under Major General Joseph Wheeler exchange blows at several locations, including Browne's (Brown's) Crossroads, Sylvan Grove and Waynesboro. Other skirmishes include Thomas' Station and Reynolds Plantation. Meanwhile, the Confederates under General William Hardee at Savannah attempt to fortify their positions to meet the imminent Union threat.

In Naval activity, at about this time, the sidewheel steamer *Colonel Lamb* penetrates the blockade and successfully arrives in Wilmington, North Carolina, from England, where it was built. During the following month, it again evades the blockading squadron and sails to the Gulf of Mexico; however, the ship is not suited for operations at the southern stronghold at Galveston. It returns to England without contributing anything substantial to the Confederate cause. The *Colonel Lamb* afterward is thought to have been sold to owners in Greece, who rename the vessel the *Bouboulina.* It is destroyed by an explosion while at Liverpool, England, taking on a cargo of munitions in 1866 or 1867.

November 27 (Sunday)   In Mississippi, Union cavalry, bolstered by some artillery, commanded by General Napoleon J. Dana, skirmishes with Confederates led by Colonel Osband at Big Black River Bridge (Central Railroad). The Union devastates the bridge. The Union warships *Vindicator* and *Prairie Bird* support the ground troops while they destroy a line of tracks stretching about thirty miles. General Dana later states the following about the gunboats: "The assistance of the vessels of the Sixth Division Mississippi Squadron rendered the expedition a complete success." The USS *Vindicator* remains with the Mississippi Squadron until the close of hostilities. On 29 November 1865, it is sold at auction at Mound City, Illinois. On 27 February, it is renamed the *New Orleans.*

In Virginia, Roger Atkinson Pryor (formerly Confederate general) is captured while in service as a cavalry courier delivering communications. He is detained as a prisoner until just prior to the end of hostilities. General Pryor, a Virginian, relocates in New York City and becomes involved with the *New York Daily News.* Later, he resumes his law practice. On 20 July 1915, the *New York Times* wishes General Pryor a happy birthday, his 87th. He was born on 19 July 1828. The greeting mentions how General Pryor related his capture and how General Grant and Secretary of War Stanton wanted him to be hanged, but President Lincoln saved him from execution. The article also notes that General Pryor needs glasses only for reading and that his hearing is also fine.

November 27–29 1864   In Georgia, Union forces (3rd Cavalry Division, Military Division of the Mississippi) skirmishes with Confederates at Buckhead Creek (also Thompson's Station, Reynolds Plantation and Brown's Crossroads). Confederate General Felix Huston Robertson is wounded on the 29th, terminating his service in the field. Robertson's appointment to brigadier general, as well as his earlier promotions from major upward, are not confirmed by the Confederate Senate. His rank of brigadier general is declined by the Senate on 22 February 1865. After the war he returns to Texas and studies law. At the time of his death on 22 February 1928, he is the dean of the bar in Waco.

November 28 (Monday)   In South Carolina, a Marine battalion, commanded by 1st Lieutenant George G. Stoddard, sailors and Union Army troops attack Confederate positions along the Charleston-Savannah Rail Line at Boyd's Neck, South Carolina, but the assault fails to dislodge the Confederates, who thwart the effort.

In Tennessee, Confederate cavalry seizes Shelbyville.

In West Virginia, Confederate cavalry units led by Major General Thomas Lafayette Rosser attack and overwhelm the Garrison at Fort Kelly, New Creek. About 700 Union troops are captured. The Confederates sustain about five killed and four missing.

In Virginia, Confederate artillery batteries lambaste Union positions at Fort Brady and Dutch Gap.

In Naval activity, the USS *John Adams* captures the Confederate *Beatrice* off Sullivan's Island, South Carolina, near Charleston. The *Beatrice* is set afire after its supplies are confiscated. The *John Adams* was originally built during 1799. It was on a cruise in the Pacific at the opening of the Civil War. It left Siam on 6 July 1861 and arrived back in New York on 11 January 1862. The king of Siam gave the captain two letters for the president of the United States and a gift, two elephant tusks. After returning to the U.S. the *John Adams* for a while acted as a training ship at the U.S. Naval Academy in Newport, Rhode Island, but during 1863 it was transferred to the South Atlantic Blockading Squadron. The *John Adams* remains in the region for the duration. After the war it is decommissioned during September 1865 and sold in October 1867. In other activity, the USS *Adolph Huger* seizes the sloop *James Landry*. Afterward, the ship continues to serve as part of the Potomac Flotilla until the close of hostilities. Subsequently, on 17 June 1865, the *Adolph Huger* is decommissioned. It is sold at auction at the Washington Navy Yard on 20 July 1865.

In Naval activity, the gunboat *Tallahoma* (wooden-hulled, sidewheel, double-ended) is launched in New York. Nonetheless, it is not completed until 1867 and is unable to go into service during the war. It is sold on 29 August 1868 and renamed the *Mary M. Roberts* on 10 November 1868. It is transformed into a barge on 21 December 1870.

November 29 (Tuesday)   In Colorado, a promise of peace given to the Indians by Major E.W. Wynkoop is broken, and more than 600 Colorado state militiamen under Colonel J.M. Chivington attack the reservation in the vicinity of Fort Lyon (Sand Creek), devastating the tribe, comprising at that time mostly women and children. Chief White Antelope is killed, but Chief Black Kettle escapes. Chief Black Kettle had raised both a white flag and the American flag, but the soldiers fire relentlessly.

In Tennessee, Union General John Schofield, now aware of Hood's plans to attack, moves his Army from Columbia to Franklin to join his cavalry. A skirmish develops and the Union prevails. In other action, Union troops commanded by Major John W. Steele repulse a Confederate attack led by Major General Benjamin F. Cheatham on a wagon train carrying ammunition at Spring Hill (Mount Carmel).

In Confederate general officer activity, Colonel Robert Bullock, who joined the Confederacy as captain of the 7th Florida Infantry, is promoted to brigadier general. He participates at Chickamauga and during the Atlanta campaign. Later, while on the retreat from Nashville, General Bullock sustains a severe wound. Subsequent to the close of hostilities, he returns to Florida and resumes his law practice.

November 30   BATTLE OF FRANKLIN   Union General John Schofield's force, which exceeds 30,000 men, successfully evades a Confederate entrapment maneuver and reaches Franklin, Tennessee, unscathed, while passing close to Confederate lines without detection. For a reason never to be known, the Confederates (either Hood or Cheatham) made a capital mistake in not intercepting General Schofield. General Hood is close behind the column of Schofield, but his force arrives at Franklin just after Schofield's arrival. General George D. Wagner, in command of a division of the IV Corps, acts as rear guard to cover the retirement of General Schofield. This is to be one more bloody day in a continuous string of battles that ravages the men of both sides. The Confederates mount continual attacks to annihilate the Union at Franklin, but none succeed. The losses incurred by the Rebels are staggering. The Union repulses all assaults and inflicts massive losses on the enemy. One Confederate brigade, that of General Charles M. Shelley, loses more than 400 killed and wounded. Nevertheless, although General Shelley's horse is killed and his uniform has several bullet holes, he is unscathed. After the war Shelley he serves in the U.S. Congress for four terms. He dies in Birmingham, Alabama, on 20 January 1907.

After a day filled with fury while opposing infantry and cavalry claw at each other, the battlefield becomes blanketed with casualties, primarily Rebels. Their bold attacks cost them six generals. Confederate General John Adams (West Point, 1846) is seriously wounded, but he refuses to quit. Instead he leads a charge against Union positions, and while attempting to jump a barricade, he is hit with multiple shots and killed. Colonel (later brigadier general) Robert Lowry assumes command of John Adams' brigade. Also, General Patrick Cleburne (born in Ireland on March 17, 1828) is killed. Brigadier General James Argyle Smith assumes command of Cleburne's division. Brigadier General States Rights Gist is felled as he approaches Union breastworks. Brigadier Generals Hiram Bronson Granbury, 7th Texas, and Otho French Strahl are killed. Brigadier General John Carpenter Carter is mortally wounded and dies within two weeks, on 10 December.

Brigadier General Thomas H. Ruger participates in this action as a divisional commander (XXIII Corps), and his heroism in the field earns him the brevet of major general of volunteers. Afterward, General Ruger finishes out the war by participating in the Carolinas with General William T. Sherman. After the war, General Ruger becomes colonel of the 33rd U.S. Infantry and then superintendent of West Point. He retires during 1895 with the rank of major general.

Confederate Generals Francis M. Cockrell and Arthur M. Manigault are wounded; the latter sustains a head wound and is compelled to terminate his service. He becomes a planter in South Carolina and is also elected as the state's adjutant and inspector general, a post he holds until his death on 17 August 1886. General Cockrell recuperates and participates at Mobile,

where he is captured. He resumes his law practice after the war, and in 1874 he is elected to the U.S. Senate, where he serves for thirty consecutive years. He dies on 13 December 1915. Confederate General William A. Quarles is wounded and captured; he does not gain his release until May 1865. Afterward he returns to his law practice. In 1875, he is elected to the Tennessee Senate. Confederate General Felix H. Robertson (attended West Point, 1857–1861) is wounded on the 29th at Buckhead Creek near Augusta, Georgia; this injury terminates his service in the field; however, he will be among those representing the Confederates later at Macon, Georgia. Brigadier General John Calvin Brown is wounded and incapacitated. He finally returns to duty during early April 1865, when he joins the forces in North Carolina just prior to the surrender. Brown is released during May of 1865. He returns to Tennessee and later becomes governor of the state.

Brigadier General Thomas Moore Scott sustains a severe wound that terminates his service in the field. General Scott does not receive an official parole and there is no documentation regarding his capture. He returns to his farm in the vicinity of Homer, Louisiana, where he resides until his death in New Orleans on 21 April 1876. In addition, General George Washington Gordon is wounded and captured. After his release from Fort Warren, Massachusetts, he returns home and begins to study law. Afterward, he opens a practice in Memphis. He is elected to Congress in 1906 and re-elected to two additional terms, making him the final Confederate general to be a member of Congress. He dies while in office on 9 August 1911.

The severe losses suffered by General John Bell Hood prompt him to call off the fight for the night and in so doing, he allows the Union forces of John Schofield to begin a withdrawal toward Nashville, pursuant to orders of General George H. Thomas. General Grant is amazed that Thomas chose not to reinforce Schofield in order to finish the Rebels under Hood right there at Franklin. Two of General Hood's divisions, those of Generals H.D. Clayton and Carter L. Stevenson, are spared high casualties because they had been deployed on the opposite side of the Duck River to divert Schofield, while the remainder of the army executed a flanking movement. The Union withdrawal also pays dividends for the Confederates, who can safely move against Nashville without harm.

Union Generals David Stanley and Luther Bradley are wounded. General Stanley, during the intense fighting, rallies his force by sprinting to the front of one of his brigades, reforming the lines and leading a successful attack. He becomes a recipient of the Medal of Honor for his heroism in the face of the enemy. General Stanley remains in camp near Nashville for the duration. He receives the brevet of major general, U.S. Army, and on 28 July 1866 is commissioned colonel of the 22nd Infantry. He returns to the Indian Territory, where he served prior to the outbreak of the war. He retires with the rank of brigadier general while in command of the Department of Texas during 1884.

General John Schofield (Johnson, *Campfire and Battlefield: History of the Conflicts and Campaigns*, 1894).

There is a connection between the family of General Stanley and that of Confederate Colonel George S. Patton. After the war, General Stanley's daughter, impressionist artist Anna, married one of his aides, Lt. Willard A. Holbrook (later, the first chief of cavalry, U.S. Army). Their son Lt. Willard A. Holbrook, Jr. (later brigadier general, 11th Armored Division in World War II) married Helen Hoyle Herr, daughter of (later) Major General John K. Herr, who became the last chief of cavalry before the tanks of armor replaced the horse. Joanne Stanley Holbrook, eldest daughter of Helen and Willard, Jr., and great-granddaughter of Union General Stanley, later married Captain (later major general) George S. Patton, great-grandson of Confederate George S. Patton, nearly ninety years after the American Civil War. General David S. Stanley, following his retirement from active duty, becomes the governor of the Soldiers' Home in Washington, D.C. He dies there during 1902.

Also, General James William Reilly participates at this battle. His command (temporarily command of a division) claims that it captures 22 battle flags. Also during the vicious skirmish, Corporal Newton Hall, 104th Ohio Infantry, captures a flag of Alexander P. Stewart's corps. The 2nd Mississippi Infantry flag and the 16th Alabama Artillery flag are also captured. Newly selected Colonel Ellison Capers, 24th South Carolina Infantry, assumes command of General Gist's brigade after the death of Gist. Capers is promoted to brigadier general; however, it does not become official until March of 1865.

Union troops under Colonel P.H. Jones destroy a Georgia Central Railroad bridge on the Ogeechee River (Mottelay, *The Soldier in Our Civil War*, 1886).

Also, Confederate General James A. Smith (West Point, 1853) assumes command of Patrick Cleburne's division. Confederate Brigadier General Mark P. Lowrey participates in this battle in command of a brigade.

Union losses at Franklin are 189 killed, 1,033 wounded and 1,104 captured or missing. Confederate losses are 1,750 killed, 3,800 in hospital and 702 prisoners.

November 30 (Wednesday) In Georgia, Union forces under Colonel P.H. Jones destroy the Georgia Central Railroad Bridge that spans the Ogeechee River.

In South Carolina, Union troops attempt to destroy the railroad tracks between Savannah, Georgia and Charleston. Confederate troops intercept and repel a Union assault at Honey Hill (Grahamsville), Broad River. Troops from the 25th Ohio, 56th and 155th New York Volunteers and the 26th, 32nd, 35th and 102nd U.S. Colored Troops participate.

In Virginia, Union pickets of the 20th Colored Troops Regiment skirmish with Confederate contingents at Bermuda Hundred through 4 December.

In Union general officer activity, Brigadier General John A. McClernand resigns his commission. McClernand, after the Vicksburg campaign and some time in Illinois, had been in Louisiana and Texas as commander of the XIII Corps. Also, Colonel Henry Goddard Thomas is appointed brigadier general and assigned to the Army of the James, where he commands a brigade. He receives the brevet of brigadier general in the Regular Army and major general of volunteers. He musters out of the volunteers during January 1866 and reverts to the rank of captain. During 1876, he is promoted to major of the 4th U.S. Infantry, followed by duty in the

paymaster's department, from where he retires and appears on the army's retirement list on 23 January 1897. Also, Colonel George Lafayette Beal (10th Maine) is appointed brigadier general. He receives the rank of brevet major general on 15 March 1865. In other activity, General Benjamin F. Butler resigns his commission.

In Confederate general officer activity, Colonel Benjamin Jefferson Hill, a lawyer, is promoted to the rank of brigadier general. General Hill had been provost marshal, Army of Tennessee, until the previous August. In conjunction, General Hill initially entered service as colonel of the 5th Regiment (Provisional Army of Tennessee), later the 35th Tennessee, at the outbreak of hostilities.

December In Virginia, Union forces (Army of the Potomac) skirmish with Confederates in the trenches in front of Petersburg throughout the month.

In Naval activity, the USS *Casco*, a light draft monitor launched in Boston in May, is commissioned. It had been determined that there is a flaw in the design. Consequently, it is finished as a torpedo vessel, but it lacks an armored gun turret. The *Casco* is assigned to the duty along the James River, but later it is transferred to the Potomac. Nonetheless, its career terminates with the conclusion of the war. It is decommissioned during June 1865. In June 1869, it is renamed *Hero*, but it does not get reactivated and is scrapped in 1875.

December 1 (Thursday) In Georgia, the 5th Kentucky and the 8th Indiana Cavalry Regiments (General Sherman's command) clash with Confederates at Miller Grove.

In Tennessee, Union reinforcements under Schofield, who withdrew from Franklin on orders of Thomas, arrive at Nashville to bolster

General George H. Thomas. General John B. Hood's force is in pursuit, but his numbers are too slim to besiege the Yankees. Hood confines his activity to the outskirts of Nashville. At this time, Thomas' force numbers about 6,000 infantry and artillery, augmented by about 3,000 cavalry. Thomas is also bolstered by about 9,000 troops under General Andrew J. Smith and another 5,000 troops are expected to arrive by mid–December, with the latter forces to be placed under the command of General Charles Cruft.

In Mississippi, the Union 2nd Wisconsin Cavalry battles Confederates in the vicinity of Yazoo City. The Union suffers five killed, nine wounded and 25 missing. Confederate casualties are unlisted.

In Tennessee, skirmishes continue through 14 December outside Nashville between the forces of General George H. Thomas and the Confederates under John B. Hood.

In Virginia, Union cavalry under General David Gregg skirmishes with Confederates at Stony Creek Station, Weldon Railroad. The Union sustains 40 wounded. Confederate casualties are reported as 175 captured.

In Union general officer activity, General Thomas L. Crittenden resigns his commission at about this time. In 1866 he is appointed treasurer of Kentucky and later, President Andrew Johnson appoints him as colonel in the Regular Army, where he serves until 1881.

December 2 (Friday)   In Tennessee, Major General George H. Thomas receives orders from General Grant that direct him to arm his quartermaster employees and citizens to prepare to meet the Confederate threat against Nashville. Grant repeats this order on the 5th, 8th and 11th. Grant soon becomes quite impatient with Thomas, but Thomas is concerned with the bleak weather conditions, include ice and frigid temperatures, which eliminates any genuine advantage. Grant, on the other hand, is concerned that General John B. Hood will find a way to mobilize during this time and escape the clutches of the Yankees by moving north to positions beyond the Cumberland River. If this happens, Grant will be forced to divert troops from the east to meet this threat.

Communications continue between Grant and Thomas, but Thomas does not move until the 15th.

A Union contingent composed of elements of the 115th Ohio, the 44th U.S. Colored Regiment and two companies of the 14th U.S. Colored Regiment, commanded by Colonel Lewis Johnson, engages Confederates at Blockhouse No. 2, Mill Creek, Chattanooga, on this day and the next. Union casualties are reported as 12 killed, 46 wounded and 57 missing. Confederate casualties are unavailable.

In Georgia, the 3rd Kentucky and the 5th Ohio Cavalry, the vanguard of General Sherman's army, skirmishes with Confederates at Rocky Creek Church.

In Mississippi, the 2nd New York Cavalry skirmishes with Confederates at Yazoo City Road. The Union seizes 23 Confederates.

In Virginia, operating around Petersburg, the Union commences an artillery barrage. Casualties include Confederate General Archibald Gracie (West Point, 1854; born in New York) who is struck and killed by a shell that explodes near where he is positioned. Colonel Young M. Moody, 43rd Alabama Regiment, succeeds him as brigade commander. Moody is promoted to the rank of brigadier general the following March.

December 3 (Saturday)   In Georgia, General Sherman continues his advance to the sea. His column reaches Millen. The Union comes upon a Confederate prison there. Millen Junction is destroyed. A contingent of his force skirmishes at Thomas Station. On the following day, Sherman pushes to Savannah, while General Braxton Bragg is joining Confederate General Wade Hampton at Augusta.

In Union activity, the 24th Army Corps is established. It is composed of infantrymen of the 10th and 18th Corps, Army of the James, commanded by General Edward O.C. Ord. Also, the 25th Corps (Colored) is established and is composed of troops of the Department of Virginia and North Carolina. Major General Godfrey Weitzel becomes commanding officer.

In Naval activity, the USS *Fair Play* exchanges fire with a

Confederate battery at Bell's Mill in the vicinity of Nashville, Tennessee. On the following day the *Fair Play* seizes two Confederate steamers. It remains in service for the duration of the war and is decommissioned during August 1865; afterward it is renamed the *Cotile*. The USS *Moose* engages Confederate batteries at Belle Hills, Tennessee, on this day and the next. The *Moose* puts the guns out of action, and it recaptures several transports before returning to Nashville.

December 4 (Sunday)   In Georgia, a contingent of the 15th Corps, on a foraging mission, skirmish with Confederates at Statesboro. Also, the 3rd Division Cavalry, Army Military Department of the Mississippi under General Kilpatrick, engages Confederates at Waynesboro and Briar Creek.

In South Carolina, the 25th Ohio Volunteers skirmish with Confederates at the Coosa River.

In Tennessee, a heated clash occurs between Union and Confederate contingents in the vicinity of Murfreesboro at Blockhouse No. 7, Overall's Creek. The Union troops under General Robert H. Milroy sustain 44 killed and wounded. The Confederates led by General William B. Bate sustain about 100 killed and wounded.

In Virginia, the 3rd Pennsylvania Cavalry (pickets) come under attack by Confederates at Jerusalem Plank Road.

In Confederate general officer activity, Colonel James M. Goggin is promoted to the rank of brigadier general, effective this date.

In Naval activity, the USS *R.R. Cuyler* participates in the capture of the blockade runner *Armstrong*. Subsequently, the *R.R. Cuyler* participates (January 1865) in the capture of Fort Fisher, North Carolina. During July 1865, the *Cuyler* is decommissioned and after some service as a merchant ship, it is acquired during 1866 by the Republic of Colombia and renamed the *El Rayo*. While in the service of Colombia, the *El Rayo* is lost in a storm on 12 September 1867 at Cartagena.

The *Monocacy*, a side-wheel gunboat, is

Left: Confederate prison at Millen, Georgia. *Right:* Interior view of the Confederate prison at Millen (*Harper's Pictorial History of the Civil War*, 1896).

launched at Baltimore; however, the gunboat does not see service during the war. It is completed during the latter part of 1865 and begins active service during 1866 after being attached to the Asiatic Squadron. The *Monocacy* remains in active service as part of the squadron beyond the Spanish American War until 1903, when it disappears from the list of Navy ships after being sold on 22 June. In conjunction, the *Monocacy*, due to the prolonged tour, picks up the nickname "Jinricksha of the Navy." In other activity, the USS *Gettysburg*, while on patrol, intercepts and seizes a blockade runner, the *Armstrong*. Subsequent to this action, the *Gettysburg* participates in the attacks against Fort Fisher, North Carolina.

December 5 (Monday)   In Tennessee, Union troops (General Robert H. Milroy's command) again come under attack at Blockhouse No. 7, but the Confederates also strike Blockhouse No. 6 at Overall's Creek near Murfreesboro. Confederates continue to strike Union positions in the vicinity of Nashville through the 8th. Union forces under General L.H. Rousseau, including the 33rd New Jersey Infantry, engage Confederate cavalry under Nathan B. Forrest at Murfreesboro (Cedars), Tennessee. Union casualties are 30 dead and 175 wounded. Confederates have 197 missing.

In Naval activity, the USS *Mahopac* engages a Confederate Battery at Howlett's Farm, Virginia. Subsequent to this action, it sails to North Carolina to participate in the operations against Fort Fisher. In mid–January, it returns to the James River. After the war it is decommissioned at Washington, D.C. It is recommissioned in June 1869 and soon reverts back to its original name. It spends time in and out of commission during 1877–1895 before becoming inactive at Philadelphia. It is sold during 1902.

December 6 (Tuesday)   In Tennessee, General George H. Thomas receives a message from General Grant regarding the situation at Nashville, which is encircled by Confederates. The order states: "Attack at once and wait no longer for a remnant of your cavalry." Nonetheless, General Thomas remains reluctant to follow the orders, because the inclement weather continues and there is a shortage of horses. General Thomas holds off his offensive until December 15.

In South Carolina, 1st Lieutenant George C. Stoddard's Marine battalion again links with Union Army troops for an attack. The Union force, supported by Commodore Preble's naval force, strikes positions at Tullifinney (Tulifing) Crossroads and Derang's (Deveaux) Neck (see also, **December 6–10 In South Carolina**). Also, the USS *Neosho* receives heavy fire from Confederate batteries at Bell's Mills on the Cumberland River (Tennessee).

In Virginia, a contingent composed of 50 troops of the 21st New York Cavalry encounter and skirmish with Confederates at White Post. The Union sustains 30 wounded. Confederate casualties are unreported.

In Naval activity, the USS *Sunflower*, while on patrol off St. George's Sound, Florida, intercepts and captures a blockade runner, the Pickwick.

December 6–10   In South Carolina, a Union force under General Edward E. Potter — composed of elements of the 26th, 33rd, 34th and 102nd U.S. Colored Troops, the 54th and 55th Massachusetts Colored Troops, the 56th and 155th New York, 25th and 107th Ohio Volunteers and the 3rd Rhode Island Artillery — engages Confederates in the vicinity of Deveaux's Neck, Tuliffiney River, Mason's Ridge and Gregory's Farm. The Union receives assistance from the navy, which has gunboats in the area to provide naval support fire. The Union suffers 39 killed and approximately 390 wounded plus 200 captured. The Confederates sustain approximately 400 killed or wounded.

December 7 (Wednesday)   In Georgia, the 21st New York Cavalry occupies Gregory's Plantation and McKay's Point. In other activity, the 9th Michigan and the 9th Ohio Cavalry, acting as rear guard to the left wing of Sherman's force, engages Confederates at Ebenezer Creek, Cypress Swamp.

In Tennessee, a Union contingent attached to General Robert H. Milroy's command attacks Confederates positions at Murfreesboro along the Wilkinson Pike. The Union sustains 205 killed and wounded. The Confederates lose 208 captured. Confederate casualty figures are unavailable. Elements of the right wing of the Army of the Military Division of the Mississippi, the 15th and 17th Corps under General Potter, engage Confederates led by Captain Thompson at Eden Station on the Ogeechee River through the 9th. Casualties are not reported. The action includes skirmishes at Jenk's Ridge and Poole's Station.

In Virginia, the Union initiates the Weldon Railroad Expedition, commanded by General Gouverneur K. Warren. The 5th Corps, 3rd Division (2nd Corps) and the 2nd Division of the Cavalry Corps set out to wreak havoc through the 11th on Confederates operating in the area. The Union sustains 100 wounded. The Confederate casualties are unreported.

In Naval activity, Admiral David D. Porter and General Benjamin Franklin Butler work on strategy to find the correct plan to seize Wilmington, North Carolina, and its formidable strong point, Fort Fisher, to finally eliminate it and terminate the port operations. Meanwhile, as the Confederates continue to attempt to outsmart the blockaders, another runner, the *Stormy Petrel*, is spotted by the USS *Kansas*. The *Stormy Petrel* attempts to flee, but it is run ashore by the *Kansas*. The Rebels, however, after grounding the ship, abandon it. Within a few days strong winds rip through the area and victimize the stranded *Stormy Petrel*, which is destroyed by the elements.

December 8 (Thursday)   In Georgia, General William T. Sherman reaches Poole's Station about eight miles outside of Savannah.

In Virginia, a Union force composed of about 6,000 troops, commanded by General Benjamin F. Butler, heads toward Fortress Monroe, where it joins a naval fleet under Admiral David D. Porter in an attempt to capture Confederate Fort Fisher, near Wilmington, North Carolina. In other activity, General Grant states in another dispatch to General George H. Thomas: "Now is one of the finest opportunities ever presented of destroying one of the three armies [Hood's Army of Tennessee]. If destroyed, he never can replace it. Use the means at your command and you can do this and cause a rejoicing that will resound from one end of the land to the other." In other activity, the 2nd Cavalry Division, Army of the Potomac, led by General Gouverneur K. Warren, skirmishes with Confederates attached to General Wade Hampton's command at Bellefield and Hicksford.

The 1st Division, 2nd Corps, the 3rd and 13th Pennsylvania Cavalry Regiments and the 6th Ohio Cavalry engage Confederates at Hatcher's Run. The Union sustains 125 killed and wounded. Confederate casualties are unavailable for the two-day skirmish. Also, the 1st and 3rd Cavalry Divisions, Army of the Potomac, under Generals George A. Custer and Wesley Merritt, ride against Confederate positions in and around Gordonsville through the 28th.

In Confederate general officer activity, Colonel James P. Simms is promoted to the rank of brigadier general.

In Naval activity, the USS *Cherokee*, while on patrol off the North Carolina coast, intercepts and seizes the steamship *Emma Henry*. Subsequent to this action, the *Cherokee* participates in the actions against Fort Fisher, North Carolina, at Wilmington during December 1864 and January 1865. It remains in the vicinity until February 1865, when it is sent to patrol in the area between Florida and Cuba. Later, after the war, the *Cherokee* is decommissioned in June 1865 and sold the following August. Subsequently, in 1868, it is acquired by the government of Chile and renamed the *Ancud*. As a merchant ship, the *Ancud* is wrecked at Chiloe, Chile, on 25 August 1889.

December 9 (Friday)   In Georgia, elements of the Union 14th Corps, commanded by General John Hatch, acting as left wing of the Army Military Division of the Mississippi, are defeated by Confederates under General Lucius Jeremiah Gartrell at Cuyler's Plantation, Monteith Swamp. Casualty figures are unavailable. Gartrell had earlier been colonel of the 7th Georgia Infantry, but upon his election to the Confederate Congress, he resigned his commission during January 1862. In August of this year he was appointed brigadier general. Subsequently, Gartrell raised four regiments of Georgia reserve troops.

In North Carolina, the Union 3rd North Carolina Volunteer Regiment initiates an expedition into the western sector of the state. The mission continues until January 14, 1865. Union

Colonel Jones Frankle leads units of the 27th Massachusetts, 9th New Jersey Volunteers, a contingent of North Carolina cavalry and the 3rd New York Artillery on an expedition into the region around Hamilton through the 12th.

In Tennessee, at Nashville, inclement weather continues to stall General George H. Thomas' offensive against Lt. General John B. Hood.

In Union activity, General George D. Wagner is relieved of duty. Wagner had requested relief due to what is thought to be the declining health of his wife. He returns to Indianapolis to await new orders; however, none are forthcoming. He musters out of the army on 24 August 1865.

In Union general officer activity, General William Rosecrans is relieved as commander of the Department of Missouri, a post he held since January 18. General Rosecrans returns to Cincinnati to await new orders, but none arrive.

In Naval activity, while engaged in operations on the Roanoke River in North Carolina, the USS *Bazely* strikes a torpedo (mine) in the vicinity of Rainbow Bluff and sinks. The tugboat had been acquired by the U.S. Navy during the previous June. Prior to being assigned to North Carolina, the *Bazely* operated along the James River for a time; however, it arrived in the South in time to participate in the capture of Plymouth, North Carolina, on 31 October. The double-ender side-wheel gunboat USS *Ostego,* commissioned during spring of this year, also hits mines during the operations on the Roanoke and sinks. The USS *Wyalusing* participates in this action. It and the other gunboats move farther up the river, but the two ships that had sunk still remain partially above the water and their guns are operable. As the operation against Rainbow Bluff continues the squadron encounters strong defenses and the waters are permeated with torpedoes, compelling the gunboats to halt the mission. The *Wyalusing* returns to Plymouth on 28 Decem-

ber. In other activity, the U.S. Navy acquires the screw tug *America,* which had been built this year in Philadelphia. The tug is commissioned the USS *Periwinkle* in early January 1865. Acting Master Henry C. Macy receives command of the ship, which is assigned to the Potomac Squadron. The Periwinkle, transformed into a gunboat, arrives on station on 15 January.

December 10 (Saturday)   In Georgia, General W.T. Sherman's force, which exceeds 60,000 troops, arrives in the vicinity of Savannah. Sherman prepares to initiate a siege of the city. The 14th Corps, under General Jefferson C. Davis, deploys on the left and nudges against the Ogeechee River, while the 20th Corps under General Henry Slocum establishes positions next to the 14th Corps. From there, the 17th and 15th Corps extend farther to cover the right. The cavalry is moved to the south bank of the river and directed to open communications with the fleet, which is standing by in Ossabaw Sound. In the meantime, Confederate General William J. Hardee takes appropriate defensive measures in hopes of repelling the assault.

In North Carolina, a Union force composed of the 27th Massachusetts, 9th New Jersey Volunteers, North Carolina Cavalry and the 3rd New York Artillery, led by Colonel Jones Frankle, engages Confederates at Forster's Bridge and Spring Green Church. The Confederates lose 35 captured.

In Naval activity, the CSS *Ida,* a side-wheel steamer utilized as a transport and as a tow ship, while operating in Georgia on the Savannah River, is captured by Union forces and destroyed by fire.

December 11 (Sunday)   In Georgia, Union troops, General William B. Hazen's division (15th Corps), prepare to assault Fort McAllister. Located on the outskirts of Savannah, the stronghold is defended by about 250 troops under Major George W. Anderson. The 2nd Division under General Hazen is the unit that Sherman had earlier commanded at Shiloh and Vicksburg.

December 12 (Monday)   In Kentucky, Confederates under Brigadier General Hylan B. Lyon capture Hopkinsville. Also, the 1st Cavalry Division under General Edward McCook skirmishes with Confederate rear guard troops of General Lyon at Elkton.

In North Carolina, the Union force under Colonel Jones Frankle skirmishes with Confederates at Butler's Bridge.

In Virginia, Union General George Stoneman's cavalry, having left Knoxville, Tennessee, on the previous day, initiate skirmishes with Confederates at Abingdon, Glade Springs, Marion and Saltville. The mission lasts until the 21st.

In Naval activity, a Confederate naval squadron, including the transport CSS *Resolute* and the *Macon* and *Sampson,* attempts to destroy the Charleston and Savannah railway bridge on the Savannah River and encounters heavy resistance originating at a Union battery. The *Resolute* sustains some damage from two hits; however, soon after, it collides with the two gunboats and that disables it. The *Sampson* and the *Macon* are able to retire; however, the *Resolute* runs aground on Argyle Island. Later in the day, a contingent attached to General William T. Sherman's force, led by Colonel W. Hawly, U.S. Army, seizes the *Resolute.* Subsequently, it is taken into Union service. The transport CSS *Resolute* is separate from the cottonclad ram CSS *Resolute.*

In other activity, the owl class CSS *Stag,* at Wilmington, North Carolina, is transferred to the Confederate Department of the Navy. Confederate Lieutenant Richard H. Gayle relieves British Captain J.M. Burroughs. This CSS *Stag* is separate from another vessel with the identical name; the latter had been renamed *Kate Gregg* in October. The sizes of the two vessels are also quite different; the *Stag* (*Kate Gregg*) has a capacity to carry 1,200 bales of cotton, while the new ship can transport 850 bales of cotton.

December 13 (Tuesday)   In Georgia, Union troops under General William B. Hazen attack and capture Fort McAllister, held by troops

Left: General Foster, aboard the USS *Nemaha* on the Ogeechee River on Dec. 14, greets General William T. Sherman. *Right:* General Sherman's troops make contact with Admiral Dahlgren, who is on the Ogeechee River off Fort McAllister, Georgia, linking Sherman's ground forces and the U.S. Navy (Mottelay, *The Soldier in Our Civil War,* 1886).

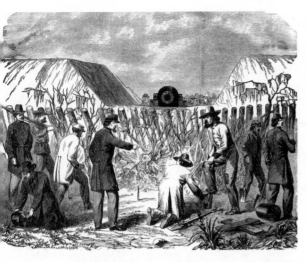

Left: At Fort McAllister, Georgia, Confederate prisoners dig up mines (Mottelay, *The Soldier in Our Civil War*, 1886). *Right:* Fort McAllister is captured by General Sherman's forces (*Harper's Pictoral History of the Civil War*, 1896).

under Confederate Major George W. Anderson. The capture of the fort opens communications between the Union fleet offshore and Sherman's land forces. The Union has 24 killed and 110 wounded. Confederates sustain about 14 killed, 21 wounded and 211 captured.

In Tennessee, the 8th, 9th and 13th Tennessee Cavalry Regiments under General Stephen Burbridge (General George Stoneman's Raid) clash with Confederates at Kingsport. The Union sustains about 150 killed, wounded and captured. The Confederates suffer about 34 killed and wounded and 100 captured.

In Union general officer activity, Colonel Cyrus Hamlin is appointed brigadier general. During the closing days of the war, he is breveted major general. He remains in New Orleans after the conflict, but on 28 August 1867, he dies of yellow fever.

December 14 (Wednesday) **In Washington, D.C.,** President Lincoln countermands an order given by Union Major General John Adams Dix to pursue any invaders from Canada across the border and if necessary, seize them on Canadian soil. General Dix, prior to the outbreak of the conflict, while secretary of the treasury, impetuously sent a telegram to the Treasury Department in New Orleans: "If anyone attempts to haul down the American flag, shoot him on the spot."

In Tennessee at Nashville, Union General George H. Thomas, confident the weather will clear, sends word to General Grant that his offensive will commence on the 15th. In other activity, General George Stoneman's cavalry clashes with a Confederate force and defeats it at Bristol (Mount Airy), capturing about 300 Confederate troops. At Memphis, the Union 4th Iowa Cavalry clashes with Confederates. The Union suffers three killed and six wounded. Confederate casualties are unavailable.

In Union general officer activity, Colonel William Gamble receives the brevet rank of brigadier general. In May 1864, Gamble was re-

lieved of duty with the Army of the Potomac and transferred to command of the cavalry division (Department of Washington), where he remains for the duration. He leaves the service during August 1865, but only temporarily. On 25 September 1865 he re-enters active service with the full rank of brigadier general. He musters out of the service during March 1866, but shortly thereafter he again enters active service as major of the 8th Cavalry. He is transferred to California; however, en route he is struck by cholera. He succumbs at Virgin Bay, Nicaragua, on 20 December 1866.

December 15 (Thursday) **In Tennessee,** a Union contingent led by General Rousseau engages and defeats a Confederate force at Murfreesboro.

In Virginia, a contingent of Union cavalry (General George Stoneman's Raid) captures Abingdon and seizes about twenty Rebels in the process. Casualty figures are unavailable. Other cavalry under Stoneman defeats a Confederate force at Glade Springs.

In Union general officer activity, Major General George Webb Morell, lacking any type of

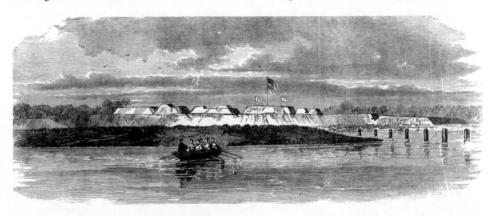

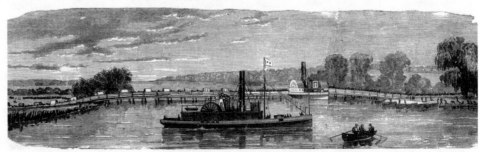

Top: A view of Fort McAllister, Georgia, from the Ogeechee River (Mottelay, *The Soldier in Our Civil War*, 1886). *Bottom:*King's Bridge, Georgia, was destroyed by the Confederates and reconstructed by General Sherman's troops within 36 hours (Mottelay, *The Soldier in Our Civil War*, 1886).

field command since Antietam, resigns his commission.

In Georgia, Union forces (General William T. Sherman's command) engage Confederates under General William J. Hardee at Savannah through the 21st. The Union sustains about 400 killed and wounded. The Confederates sustain about 600 killed and wounded and 1,000 captured.

In Naval activity, the USS *Moose,* operating out of Nashville, Tennessee, engages a Confederate battery and a detachment from the ship seizes the guns. Two days later, on the 17th, the *Moose* joins the USS *Neosho* to form an escort for Union transports, but the appearance of a huge Confederate force compels the mission to be aborted. In conjunction, the *Neosho* is decommissioned during July 1865. In June 1869, it is renamed *Vixen,* and in August it is again renamed to become the *Osceola.* The vessel is sold during 1873.

December 15–16 Battle of Nashville U.S. Troops numbering about 50,000 under General George H. Thomas, including the 4th Corps, 1st and 3rd Division, 16th Corps, 23rd Corps and General James H. Wilson's cavalry, engage and defeat the Confederates under General Hood numbering about 40,000 outside Nashville, Tennessee, at Overton's Hills (Princeton). General James B. Steedman commands a provisional detachment, composed of about 11 regiments. The battle is heated and lasts all day, with each side once again giving their best during the nine hour conflagration. Union cavalry is forced to improvise for want of horses, but undeterred, they advance on foot, joining in the rout. The Rebels withdraw with the horseless cavalry in chase. After calling up their mounts, a pursuit is begun, and they engage the entrenched Rebels a few miles back and succeed in driving them out again. Union General John McArthur's 1st Division, XVI Corps, forces the collapse of Hood's left flank, allowing the Union advance.

During the fighting, the 13th Mississippi Infantry's battle flag is captured. Darkness silences the guns and clashing steel, but only for the night. The Union fares well on the first day of fighting, and at first light on the 16th, the Yankees jump off to finish General Hood's beleaguered force, which had sustained severe losses on the 15th. General Hood beats the Yankees to Franklin and remains way out in front of the pursuers. The Confederates cross the Duck River and burn all bridges, including the railroad bridge, which brings an abrupt end to the chase. The previous bout with consistent bad weather made the river unconquerable without the use of bridges, enabling General Hood's escape. The Confederate Army of General Hood is now essentially beaten, unable to regroup for major action.

Pvt. William May of the 32nd Iowa Infantry captures the flag of Bonanchad's Confederate battery. He becomes a recipient of the Medal of Honor for his heroism. The Union suffers 400 killed and 1,740 wounded. Major General Darius N. Couch escapes injury; however, his horse is shot from under him during the fighting. Colonel Charles C. Doolittle commands the 1st Brigade (General Cox's 3rd Division. Also, General Steedman continues service beyond the close of hostilities until he resigns during 1866.

The Confederates sustain about 15,000 killed, wounded and missing. About 2,000 Confederates are captured. Hood's Army of Tennessee retreats and reaches Tupelo, Mississippi, on 10 January 1865. Confederate Brigadier General William Hicks Jackson's cavalry is attached to General Hood's command during this campaign in Tennessee. Jackson, in February, will receive command of the entire complement of cavalry in General Nathan B. Forrest's force.

Confederate General Claudius Sears sustains a near-fatal injury when his horse is killed. The accident costs Sears one of his legs. He is captured within several days after this action in the vicinity of Pulaski, Tennessee. This terminates Sears' service in the Confederacy; he is not released until the latter part of June 1865. Subsequently, he becomes the chair of mathematics at the University of Mississippi, serving in that capacity from 1865 to 1889. He dies in

In related activity, Confederate General Samuel G. French (West Point 1843) of Woodbury, New Jersey, has been in command of a division, but a nasty eye infection renders him nearly blind and incapacitates him until the last part of the conflict. Nevertheless, General French will participate in the defense of Mobile, Alabama, until it capitulates during April 1865. Confederate General Edward Johnson (West Point, 1838) is captured; when he is released in July 1865, the war is over. He returns to Virginia and becomes a farmer until his death during March 1873. Confederate Brigadier General Thomas Benton Smith is wounded and captured along with most of his command at Nashville. General Smith undergoes severe treatment while being escorted to the rear. Union Colonel William Linn McMillen (95th Ohio) strikes Smith multiple times with his sword, and when he arrives at the field hospital, doctors report that Smith's brain is visible and he is expected to die. However, he lives for about 47 more years. In 1876, he is admitted to the state asylum at Nashville, where he dies during May 1923. Confederate Generals George Washington Gordon (wounded) and Henry "Rootes" Jackson are also captured. The Confederates are losing too many leaders and there are but few replacements. Confederate Brigadier General Mark P. Lowrey participates in this battle in command of a brigade in General James A. Smith's division (Smith had assumed command of General Patrick Cleburne's Division upon the latter's demise at Franklin). The Army of Tennessee retires from the area and moves toward the Carolinas. Major General Edward C. Walthall's force accompanies the remnants of the army away from Nashville and later moves to the Carolinas. A brigade under Brigadier General Joseph Benjamin Palmer participates as part of the rear guard.

After the conclusion of the victory over General John B. Hood, General Grant and the political leaders in D.C. acknowledge that after all, General Thomas' instincts had been correct and he did in fact know when the proper time to strike Hood would arrive. Thomas receives much praise for the victory; however, although he intends to give his army some rest, orders will instruct him to keep his army moving. The 4th Corps (General Thomas J. Wood) will head for Huntsville, Alabama. The forces of Generals John Schofield (23rd Corps), Andrew J. Smith (three divisions, Army of Tennessee) and James H. Wilson (cavalry) will be transferred to the vicinity of Eastport, Mississippi. After reaching his destination, Schofield will again move, heading for the East Coast to operate in North Carolina.

General Washington L. Elliott, commander of a division of the IV Corps, subsequent to this action, is transferred to take command of the Department of Kansas. He serves for the duration. Before he eaves the service during March 1866, he receives the brevet rank of major general in the volunteers and the Regular Army. General Kenner Garrard's division (XVI Corps) participates in the battle and is recognized for meritorious service in the field; he receives the rank of brevet major general of volunteers. In March he is breveted in the Regular Army. In addition, Colonel James Isham Gilbert participates at this engagement. While leading his brigade, he is rewarded for his "distinguished services" by being promoted to brigadier general the following February. Also, General McArthur's actions during this battle cause him to receive the brevet rank of major general. Afterward he moves to Selma, Alabama, where he remains until he musters out of the service during the summer of 1865.

December 16 (Friday) **In Tennessee,** Union troops, including the 41st Ohio Infantry, skirmish with Confederates at Brentwood Hills. Union General Joseph F. Knipe, commanding a large cavalry force (Division of James H. Wilson), receives orders from General Thomas to pursue the retreating Rebels under Hood, who are withdrawing from Nashville. Knipe's command captures more than 6,000 Confederates and eight battle flags during the chase. However, at the close of hostilities, General Knipe does not receive any brevet promotions. He musters out of the army and becomes the postmaster in Harrisburg, Pennsylvania, during 1866.

While General Hood retreats, Confederate General Edward C. Walthall attempts to impede the pursuing Yankees with his command. The Yankees do not succeed in capturing Walthall, who makes it back with his stragglers of the once proud and defiant Army of Tennessee to join the battered remnants of the Confederates who are operating on borrowed time in the Carolinas. The Confederates remain determined and defiant, but their resources in both manpower and supplies are rapidly diminishing.

In Kentucky, elements of the 2nd and 3rd Brigades, General Edward McCook's 1st Cavalry

Division (General George Stoneman's Raid), engage Confederates at Hopkinsville.

In Virginia, the 8th, 9th and 13th Tennessee Cavalry Regiments engage Confederates at Marion and Wytheville. Union casualties are unreported. Confederates sustain about 20 killed, 20 wounded and 309 captured.

In Naval activity, the Confederate schooner *G.O. Bigelow* is seized by the USS *New Berne* and the USS *Mount Vernon* at Bear Inlet, North Carolina. The ship is destroyed. The *New Berne's* primary duties revolve around delivering supplies and mail, but on occasion it does participate in patrol duty. Following the close of hostilities, the *New Berne* continues on active duty as a supply ship until it is decommissioned on 29 March 1868, when it is transferred to the War Department (1 December 1868). Also, the USS *Marietta,* a light draft single-turret ironclad built at Pittsburgh, Pennsylvania, and launched earlier this month, is completed. However, it is not acquired by the U.S. Navy until 25 April 1866. The *Marietta* does not get commissioned; rather it remains inactive at Mound City, Illinois. On 15 June 1869, it is renamed the *Circe,* but only for about a month. In August, it reverts to its original name. The *Marietta* is sold on 12 April 1873.

December 17 (Saturday) In Georgia, Union General Sherman issues an ultimatum to Confederate General Hardee demanding the surrender of Savannah. General William Hardee, acutely aware of Robert E. Lee's inability to send reinforcements, still refuses Sherman's demand. He notifies Sherman of his intent to refuse surrender on the 18th. Hardee's troops number about 10,000; however they have insufficient food to withstand a siege. Confederate Generals H.W. Mercer, H.R. Jackson, W.R. Boggs, and J.F. Gilmer are also in Savannah with Hardee. General Boggs, during the closing months of the war, is with General Kirby Smith as his chief of staff. After the close of hostilities, General Boggs returns to Georgia, but he later relocates in St. Louis and engages in civil engineering. Later still he becomes a teacher at Virginia Polytechnic Institute. He dies on 11 September 1911.

In Tennessee, the Union forces of General H. Thomas gain on the retreating forces of General John B. Hood. The 6th Cavalry Division (General Thomas' command) intercepts Hood's Army of Tennessee at Franklin and the 5th and 7th Cavalry Divisions clash with Hood's Army at Hollow Tree Gap. The Union seizes about 1750 Confederates at Franklin. The Minnesota 5th Volunteer Infantry Regiment participates in this action and with the pursuit of Hood's army. At Harpeth River, the 4th U.S. Cavalry engages Confederates and captures supplies and many prisoners. General James H. Wilson, after the seizure of Franklin with its many wounded Confederates, finishes the war with additional strokes of great success, including the defeat of Nathan B. Forrest at Selma, Alabama, during early April 1865.

In Florida, elements of the 82nd U.S. Colored Troops skirmish with Confederates at Mitchell's Creek.

In Virginia, the 13th and 16th New York and the 8th Illinois Cavalry initiate a reconnaissance mission to Blue Ridge.

In Alabama, the 82nd and 97th U.S. Colored Troops engage Confederates through the 19th at Pine Barren Creek. The Union sustains nine killed, 53 wounded and 11 missing. Confederate casualties are unavailable. The casualty figures include fighting on the previous day at Mitchell's Creek, Florida.

December 18 (Sunday) In Mississippi, a Union force attached to the 3rd Corps led by General Gordon Granger engages Confederates at Franklin Creek.

In Virginia, General George Stoneman's raid continues. Union cavalry (Army of the Ohio) under General Alvan C. Gillem engages and defeats Confederates at Marion. The Union captures about 200 Rebels. Also, Union Generals Wesley Merritt and William Powell lead an expedition from Winchester in search of Confederate forces. The mission costs the Union about 50 killed and wounded. Confederate casualty figures are unavailable.

In Tennessee, Union cavalry attached to General Thomas' army skirmishes with Confederates at Rutherford Creek.

In Naval activity, a U.S. naval fleet, commanded by Rear Admiral David D. Porter, transports General Benjamin Butler's assault force toward Wilmington, North Carolina. The objective is Fort Fisher, located on a peninsula north of the Cape Fear River and east of the city.

December 19 (Monday) In Georgia, the CSS *Water Witch*—formerly the USS *Water Witch,* captured on 3 June and at White Bluffs, Georgia, awaiting orders to depart for Savannah—is destroyed by the Confederates to prevent capture by the Union.

In Virginia, Brevet Brigadier General Thomas Maley Harris (received brevet in conjunction with the Battle of Winchester), receives orders to move to the Petersburg area with his division. Harris' command is attached to the Army of the James, and it participates in the campaign to reduce Richmond. General Harris is selected for the commission that tries the conspirators involved with the assassination of President Lincoln. After having received the brevet rank of major general, he leaves the service during 1866.

December 20 (Tuesday) In Tennessee, Confederate General John B. Hood's Army of Tennessee skir-

mishes briefly with its Union pursuers at Columbia.

In Georgia, the Confederate forces at Savannah evacuate the city. The Rebels depart but they leave large amounts of artillery and supplies behind while they head north to South Carolina. A contingent under Colonel Henry Barnum (149th New York) is the first Union unit to enter the abandoned city. In other activity, Fort Jackson, on the outskirts of Savannah and held by the Rebels since its seizure during January of 1861, is abandoned, as is Fort Thunderbolt and other batteries. The Confederates scuttle all vessels except the CSS *Savannah,* which remains to bombard the fort's new inhabitants, the 28th Pennsylvania and 29th Ohio Regiments. On the following day, as the Union hoists Old Glory, the Rebels aboard the CSS *Savannah* open fire to no avail. Return fire damages the vessel and compels it to retire. The crew destroys the *Savannah* later in the day. The ship had been built in Savannah and commissioned in the Confederate service during June 1863. Its entire tour of duty revolved around the defense of the city. Some Confederate vessels, including the transport CSS *General Lee,* are seized by the Union.

In Virginia, elements of General George A. Custer's cavalry come under attack at their camp by Confederates led by General Rosser at Lacey's Springs (Lacy's Springs). The Union sustains two killed, 22 wounded and 40 captured. Confederate casualties are unavailable. Union General George Stoneman's cavalry, which had departed Tennessee, reaches Saltville and destroys the Confederate saltworks in that area. At Madison Court House, a brigade of Michigan cavalry, 1st Cavalry Division, Army of the Potomac, led by General Peter Stagg (breveted but never acquires full rank), skirmishes with a force of Confederates.

In North Carolina, Union gunboats bombard Confederate positions this day and the next at Poplar Point along the Roanoke River.

December 21 (Wednesday) In Georgia at Savannah, the Confederates destroy the navy yard while they are evacuating the city. Vessels, including the CSS *Georgia,* an ironclad floating battery built in Savannah during 1862, are de-

Confederates destroy the navy yard at Savannah (Mottelay, *The Soldier in Our Civil War,* 1886).

 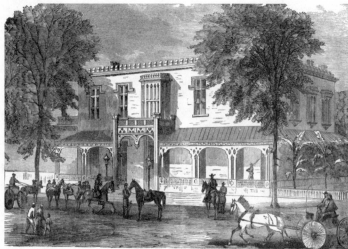

Left: General Sherman's army enters Savannah, Georgia. *Right:* General Sherman's headquarters in Savannah (*Harper's Pictoral History of the Civil War*, 1896).

stroyed to prevent capture by the Union. Another vessel, the CSS *Sampson*, is sailed to Augusta, where it remains until the war is ended.

In Virginia, Union General George Stoneman's cavalry begins its return trip to Tennessee following a successful campaign against the Confederates in this state. In Stanardsville, a brigade of Union cavalry led by General William B. Tibbits engages Confederates.

In Naval activity, the *Abeona,* a stern-wheel steamer built during 1831 at Pittsburgh, Pennsylvania, is acquired at Cincinnati by the U.S. Navy. It sails to Mound City, Illinois, where it is transformed into a tinclad gunboat. The ship is commissioned the USS *Abeona* at Mound City on 10 April 1865, one day after the capitulation of General Robert E. Lee at Appomattox, Virginia. Acting Master Samuel Hall, U.S. Navy, receives command of the ship. Nevertheless, the military career of the *Abeona* lasts only

until the final Confederate units surrender. The *Abeona* is decommissioned on 4 August at Mound City. One week later, on the 11th, it is sold. The *Abeona* is destroyed by fire at Cincinnati on 7 March 1872.

December 22 (Thursday)   In Georgia, this day culminates General William T. Sherman's March to the Sea. The army begins to enter Savannah unopposed. The Confederate troops evacuated the city on 21 December. A flotilla of ships offshore awaits Sherman, as promised by Quartermaster General Montgomery C. Meigs (West Point, 1836), prior to Sherman's departure from Atlanta. Sherman now prepares to push north toward the James River and Richmond. General Grant makes it clear Sherman devised the

plan for his March from Atlanta to the sea: "It was clearly Sherman, and to him also belongs the credit of its brilliant execution." Union General Henry Birge will assume command of the city of Savannah after the surrender. General Birge will be breveted major general on 25 February 1865. He participated in the ill-fated Red River campaign. Also, Brigadier General John Eugene Smith participates in the March to the Sea and continues with General Sherman through the Carolinas. He receives the brevet of major general of volunteers toward war's end and remains in the service beyond the close of hostilities. In late 1865 he commands the Dis-

Above: Citizens of Savannah receive passes from General John Geary (Mottelay, *The Soldier in Our Civil War*, 1886). *Right:* Fort Thunderbolt in Savannah (*Harper's Pictoral History of the Civil War*, 1896).

trict of Western Tennessee. He resigns from the volunteer service during April 1866, but the following July, he becomes colonel of the 27th U.S. Infantry. Later, he receives the brevets of brigadier and major general in the Regular Army (1867) and he continues to serve on the western frontiers at various posts until he retires on 19 May 1881.

Meanwhile, General Sherman reports his losses for the campaign from Atlanta to Savannah: 103 killed, 424 wounded, 278 missing and 530 captured. General Sherman's devastation of the Confederate forces in Georgia is a severe blow to the Confederate cause.

In Confederate general officer activity, Colonel John D. Kennedy, 2nd South Carolina, is promoted to the rank of brigadier general. Kennedy had assumed command of the 2nd South Carolina Regiment after the promotion of Joseph Kershaw to major general the previous May. Toward war's end he receives the rank of brevet major general. Subsequently, during 1885, President Grover Cleveland appoints Kennedy as consul general at Shanghai, China. He dies from a stroke in Camden, South Carolina, on 14 April 1865. Colonel James E. Harrison, 15th Texas Infantry, is promoted to the rank of brigadier general, effective this month. Harrison is the brother of Confederate colonel (later brigadier general) Thomas Harrison. The services of James Harrison have been primarily under Generals T. Green and Richard Taylor, who opposed the Union in Louisiana.

December 23 (Friday) In North Carolina, the forces of General Benjamin F. Butler and Admiral David D. Porter arrive at Wilmington and immediately prepare to assault Confederate-held Fort Fisher, commanded by General William Henry C. Whiting, at the mouth of the Cape Fear River. U.S. Marines serving the South Atlantic Squadron manning secondary guns, participate in the bombardment of Fort Fisher. Later, under cover of darkness, the U.S. powder boat *Louisiana,* towed by the USS *Wilderness,* is taken close to Fort Fisher. Commander A.C. Rhind and Lt. Roswell H. Lamson are aboard the *Louisiana.* A fire is set in the shaft and a fuse is set. Neither the Louisiana nor the launch that returns from the *Louisiana* to the *Wilderness* is spotted by the Confederates. Nonetheless, the *Louisiana* is pushed off course by some winds and an undertow. The Union fleet anticipates an explosion, but it does not occur until about 0020 on the 24th, and due to the winds, no damage is inflicted upon the fort.

In Tennessee, Union cavalry (General George H. Thomas' command) skirmishes with Confederates at Buford's Station and Lynnville.

In Virginia, the 1st Cavalry Division, Army of the Potomac, and the 2nd Cavalry Division, Army of West Virginia, engages Confederates at Jack's Shop in the vicinity of Gordonsville.

In Naval activity, the USS *Acacia,* is engaged in carrying provisions from the vicinity of Charleston to Georgetown, South Carolina, to be delivered to the USS *Canandaigua,* a screw

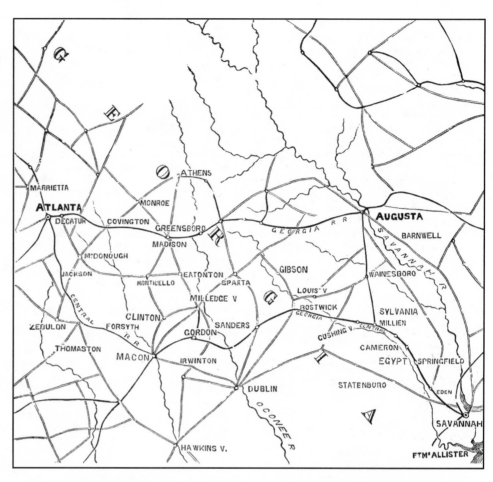

General Sherman's March to the Sea (*Harper's Pictoral History of the Civil War,* 1896).

sloop. One of the ship's lookouts spots two white smokestacks at Cape Romain. The *Acacia* modifies its course and closes upon shore to discover a side-wheel steamer. It flies no colors but activity is accelerating, as men on deck are abandoning the ship. After some warning shots, the *Acacia* lowers boats and sends a contingent to stranded steamer, which quickly hoists a white flag to halt any further fire. As the boats from the *Acacia* move toward the blockade runner, the boats from the latter continue to take on crew members who are heading for Alligator Creek. The boarding party seizes the grounded ship, but no crew members are aboard. The vessel turns out to be the *Julia,* built in Scotland during 1863 to run blockades. After taking possession of the *Julia,* the crew of the *Acacia* works throughout the night to refloat the vessel, and on the following morning, their efforts succeed. The *Julia* is sailed to Key West, Florida, and from there to Washington, D.C. Afterward the *Acacia* remains with the South Atlantic Squadron until the close of hostilities. On 24 April 1865, it sails to Philadelphia, where it is decommissioned on 12 May

The powder boat *Louisiana* (*Harper's Pictoral History of the Civil War,* 1896).

1865. Afterward, the *Acacia* is sold at auction in the navy yard. On 13 October 1865, it is renamed the *Wabash* and serves as a merchantman until 1881. In other activity, the USS *Kate*, initially the *Kate B. Porter*, built in Belle Vernon, Pennsylvania, during 1864, is acquired by the U.S. Navy at Cincinnati. After being transformed into a tinclad gunboat, it is commissioned the USS *Kate* at Mound City, Illinois. Acting Volunteer Lt. W.R. Wells receives command and is assigned to patrol duty on the Mississippi. On 28 April, subsequent to the surrender of General Robert E. Lee to General Ulysses Grant at Appomattox, the *Kate* is ordered to the Tennessee River to intercept Confederate President Jefferson Davis, who is attempting to flee to escape capture. After the mission, it returns to the Mississippi, where it remains until the following year. It is decommissioned at Mound City on 25 March 1866 and sold before the month ends. On 12 April 1866, it is renamed *James J.J. Trover*.

December 24 (Saturday)   In Tennessee, the 1st Wisconsin Cavalry skirmishes with Confederates at Elizabeth. At Richlands Creek, Union troops clash with Confederates. Corporal Collins, 1st U.S. Tennessee Cavalry, captures the colors of Chalmer's division. Collins becomes the recipient of the Medal of Honor for his heroism at this action. Meanwhile, the 12th U.S. Colored Troops skirmishes with a Confederate contingent at Murfreesboro.

In Virginia, the 8th Tennessee Cavalry (General George Stoneman's raid) clashes with Confederates at Moccasin Gap.

In Confederate general officer activity, James E. Harrison of the 15th Texas Infantry is appointed brigadier general effective this date.

December 24–25   In North Carolina, at dawn on Christmas Eve, the Union fleet arrives off Wilmington and the gunboats initiate a bombardment of Fort Fisher. The tumultuous thunderclap relentlessly pounds Fort Fisher, but the defenders scurry to bombproofs to avoid injuries. Sheets of fire are incessantly catapulted into the Confederate positions. Nevertheless, the plan of attack goes awry when the transports run late. They finally arrive, but too late to strike. During the day's action, the USS *Yantic* experiences an accident when its 100-ponder rifled gun explodes. The division officer and the gun captain are mortally wounded. Four other crewmen receive fatal wounds. Commander Harris pulls his ship out of the line, but soon after checking the damage, he returns to the firing line. On the following day, it participates in the landing of the attack force. On Christmas morning, the naval guns resume their fire and rattle the earth, but still, the Rebels, about 700-strong, under General William H.C. Whiting (West Point, 1845), withstand the iron storm, due in great part to the bombproofs, which have saved many casualties.

Meanwhile, under the umbrella fire of the fleet, General Butler's ground forces debark in the vicinity of Flag Pond Battery. During the landing, the USS *Minnesota*, from a point about one mile from the Confederate position, catapults round after round to bolster the assault force, which numbers about 2,000 ground troops. Once the beachhead is established, contingents advance and the vanguard reaches positions near the fortress; however, the progress of the fleet is negated and in vain due to Butler's decision that the fort is too strong to be taken by his force. General Butler aborts the attacks after deciding to retire. Admiral Porter staunchly opposes aborting the attack and remains confident that the fort can be reduced. Subsequent to the failed assault, Porter refuses to relent. He requests of General Grant that another attack be launched under a new commander of the ground forces. Grant concurs, and during the following month, the fleet returns with another army.

Lt. Aeneas Armstrong of the Confederate States Navy later describes the scene within the fort: "The whole of the interior of the fort, which consists of sand, merlons, etc., was as one 11-inch shell bursting. You can not inspect the works and walk on nothing but iron." Lt. Commander Harris of USS *Yantic* subsequently notes: "At 1400, on the 25th, the troops landed amidst deafening and encouraging cheers from the men-of-war and from the troops still aboard the transports, cheers which were echoed by the fleet by a fire that elicited but a feeble response from the fort." He adds: "To the surprise and mortification of all, [General Nathaniel Banks] recalled the troops; and the landing operation ceased."

The new attack occurs on 13 January 1865, when Admiral Porter returns with about sixty ships and a force of about 10,000 troops, composed of 2,000 Marines and sailors along with the main body, 8,000 soldiers under the command of Major General Alfred Terry. Also, the USS *Chippewa* participates in the operation against Fort Fisher now and again during January 1865. Afterward, it moves to the James River in Virginia. It is decommissioned during June 1865.

December 25 (Sunday)   In Mississippi, the 7th Indiana Cavalry skirmishes with Confederates at Verona.

In North Carolina, Union troops under General Adelbert Ames debark from the USS *Santiago* and land near Fort Fisher under cover of the naval guns of Porter's North Atlantic Squadron. The troops seize a small garrison, Flag Pond Battery (or Pond Hill Battery) and capture about 65 prisoners. These captives inform General Butler that many Confederate reinforcements have arrived to halt the Union takeover attempt. This information provokes Butler to withdraw, causing Flag Officer Porter to plead with Butler to remain. Additional ammunition is on the way and Porter's fleet could give cover fire so assault troops could reach within 20 foot of the fort. Butler declines, boards his troops (except General Curtis' brigade), and returns to Fortress Monroe. Porter, as expected, becomes infuriated and writes the Navy Department requesting more troops and a different commander in order to capture the Confederate fort. Grant asks Porter to hold. Later, Grant sends the same troops, commanded by General Alfred H. Terry, during January 1865.

In Tennessee, Confederate General John B. Hood's army encounters the Union at Richland Creek and Devil's Gap. After these skirmishes, the Confederates finally cross the Tennessee River on the 26th. Other skirmishes occur at Pulaski, Lamb's Ferry, Anthony's Hill and Sugar Creek.

December 26 (Monday)   In Tennessee, Union forces, including the 5th Minnesota Volunteer Regiment, continue the pursuit of General John B. Hood's force. The Rebels cross the Tennessee River. Following this duty, the 5th Minnesota departs on the 28th for Eastport, Mississippi, where it will remain deployed until February 1865.

December 27 (Tuesday)   In Georgia at about this time (late December), the CSS *Beauregard*, in the Confederate service since 1861 as a transport and utility vessel, is captured in the vicinity of Savannah.

In Virginia, General Grant orders General Sherman, in Georgia, to march north toward Richmond.

December 27–28   In Alabama, a Union force (General James B. Steedman's provisional division) clashes with Confederates at Decatur. The Union is bolstered by the USS *General Burnside* and the *General Thomas*. Their guns aid the land forces in forcing the Rebels to abandon Decatur. Subsequent to this action, the *General Burnside* resumes patrol duty until 1 June 1865, at which time it is transferred back to the War Department at Bridgeport, Alabama. It returns to Bridgeport on the 30th.

December 28 (Wednesday)   In Mississippi, the Union again inflicts a severe loss upon the Confederates, this time at Egypt Station. The Union force, General James B. Steedman's provisional division, includes the 7th Indiana, 4th and 11th Illinois Cavalry, 4th and 10th Missouri, 2nd Wisconsin, 2nd New Jersey, 1st Mississippi and 3rd U.S. Colored Troops. The Union suffers 23 killed, 88 wounded. The Confederate casualty figures are unavailable; however, about 500 are captured. Confederate General Samuel I. Gholson, attached to General Nathan B. Forrest's corps, is wounded. He loses one arm. After the war General Gholson, a lawyer, serves twice in the Mississippi Legislature. Before the war, he had served three terms in the legislature and two terms in the U.S. Congress. He succumbs at his residence in Aberdeen, Mississippi, in October 1883.

December 29 (Thursday)   In Alabama, the 15th Pennsylvania and a contingent of the 2nd Tennessee and the 10th, 12th and 13th Indiana Cavalry Regiments engage Confederates at Pond Spring.

December 30 (Friday)   *In Confederate general officer activity,* Brigadier General Pierce Manning Butler Young is promoted to the rank of major general (temporarily), effective this date. General Young is assigned duty in North Carolina to bolster the resistance against General William T. Sherman. After the war Young serves five terms (1868–1875) in the U.S. Congress. He dies in New York City on 6 July 1896.

In Naval activity, the USS *Anna* (*Annie*) departs Key West, Florida, en route to Charlotte Harbor, Florida, for blockade duty; however, the ship never reaches its destination. It is thought to have been lost to an explosion. No trace of the crew is discovered; however, the sunken hull is found about two weeks after it

departed Key West. Also, the *Lenapee*, a double-ended side-wheel gunboat, is commissioned. Lt. Commander Samuel Magaw receives command and is assigned to the North Atlantic Blockading Squadron. It arrives at Beaufort, North Carolina, on 23 January 1865 and begins patrols as well as some reconnaissance missions.

The USS *Rattler* (Tinclad No. 1) is hit by strong winds while it is on patrol near Grand Gulf, Mississippi. Its anchor cable becomes partially dislodged and the gale pushes it ashore, where it hits an obstacle and sinks. The crew is able to salvage most of its armaments and the

ship's supplies; however, the vessel is not refloated. Later, Confederates board the abandoned ship and set it afire.

December 31 (Saturday)   In Virginia, a contingent of Union troops (pickets) come under attack by Confederates at Forts Howard and Wadsworth. The Union sustains two killed, three wounded and 35 captured. The Confederate casualty figures are unavailable. In other activity, Brigadier General Alfred Ellett (Ellett's Marine Brigade) resigns his commission to return to civilian life as a civil engineer.

1865

In Kansas, Fort Dodge, thought to be named for Major General Grenville M. Dodge, is established in Ford County near Dodge City. The U.S. Army uses this base as a supply depot and as a pivotal fort to deal with the Plains Indians. About two years after its founding, the army constructs a road stretching nearly 100 miles from Fort Dodge to Camp Supply (subsequently Fort Supply) in Oklahoma. The route becomes an imperative task to support the forces of General Philip Sheridan and the outposts established farther west during the campaign of 1868.

Also, Fort Hays is established in the western sector of Kansas outside of present-day Hays (Ellis County). The garrison is responsible for guarding the military routes in the region. Later it will also be directed to ensure the safety of the crews laying the tracks for the Union Pacific Railroad; however, it is also considered to be a primary supply depot for the other army posts scattered about the region.

In Kansas and Texas, following the close of the Civil War in April, life on the frontier again begins to change. And with the arrival of the railroads new opportunities begin to emerge. One of these new enterprises is prodded by a merchant in Kansas who is convinced that with the emergence of the Iron Horse on the Plains, the cattle in Texas could be driven overland to Kansas and from there distributed around the nation. This concept introduced by Joseph McCoy is well received by the ranchers in Texas. Soon after, the cattle drives would bring the Texas longhorns and cowboys into Abilene. The route becomes known as the Chisholm Tail, named after Jesse Chisholm.

In Oklahoma, U.S. troops under Colonel Kit Carson establish Fort Nichols, a temporary post along the Santa Fe Trail outside of the town of Wheeless (Cimarron County) in present-day Black Mesa State Park. The fort is named in honor of brevet Major General William A. Nichols (West Point, 1838), who had served during the Mexican-American War and the Civil War.

January 1 (Sunday)   In Virginia, Confederate Major General William Smith, a governor of the state prior to the war, is again inaugurated governor. He remains in office until the close of hostilities. Afterward he returns to his estate, known as Monterosa, and resumes farming. He dies at his residence near Warrenton at the age of 90, during May 1887.

In Naval activity, the Union sloop *San Jacinto* is wrecked at the Bahama Banks near New Providence in the Bahamas. In other activity, the CSS *Texas* is launched at Richmond at about this time (January). Nevertheless, when the Union seizes Richmond in April, the *Texas*, an ironclad ram, is not yet completed. It is seized by the Union and in October is sold. Also, the light draft monitor USS *Chimo,* at about this time (January), is commissioned. In April, after being modified as a spar torpedo vessel, it moves from Boston to Hampton Roads, Virginia. By the latter part of the month, it sails to Point Lookout, North Carolina, where it remains only until May 1865; then it is ordered to move to the Washington Navy Yard. It is decommissioned in June. During June 1869, the *Chimo* is renamed *Orion,* but in August it is renamed the *Piscataqua.* Nonetheless, it remains inactive until sold during 1874.

The USS *Spirea,* acquired by the U.S. Navy in December, is commissioned at about this time (January). It is assigned as a gunboat with the East Gulf Blockading Squadron and initiates patrols along the rivers in northwestern Florida. After the war it is decommissioned

in New York during August 1865. In August 1866 it is sold. After being renamed *Sappho,* it operates as a civilian ship until lost off Cape Hatteras, North Carolina, on 14 December 1867.

January 2 (Monday)   In Virginia, General U.S. Grant shows concern about the possibility of General John B. Hood re-establishing his force by gathering the stragglers from the Army of Tennessee. He instructs General Sherman to take precautions to protect Savannah while continuing his operations. Sherman, in Georgia, responds to Grant and informs him that the Seventeenth Corps will be sent to Port Royal by transporting them aboard Admiral Dahlgren's

Dutch Gap Canal (*Harper's Pictorial History of the Civil War,* 1896).

boats. He also states that he is about to march inland toward Richmond.

In South Carolina, Confederates fire upon Union pickets at Hardeeville.

In Georgia, a contingent of Confederate artillery bombards Union positions at Dutch Gap Canal.

In Mississippi, the 4th and 11th Illinois Cavalry Regiments and the 3rd U.S. Colored Cavalry skirmish with Confederates at Franklin.

In Alabama, a Union contingent, composed of elements of the 15th Pennsylvania, 2nd Tennessee, and the 10th, 12th and 13th Indiana Cavalry Regiments, clashes for two days with Confederates under General John B. Hood at Nauvoo. Hood's supply and pontoon train are seized and destroyed on the 2nd. On the following day, the Union force under Colonel William J. Palmer attacks Confederates (4th Alabama) under Colonel Alfred A. Russell at Thorn Hill. The Union sustains one killed and two wounded. The Confederates suffer three killed, two wounded and 95 captured.

January 3 (Tuesday)   In Georgia, General William Sherman dispatches a contingent of his force to Beaufort, South Carolina.

In South Carolina, the guns at Fort Putnam bombard Charleston.

In Virginia, Union artillery and Confederate batteries exchange fire at Howlett Batteries.

January 4 (Wednesday)   In Virginia, Union artillery bombards the Richmond and Petersburg Railroad.

In Naval activity, the USS *San Jacinto* becomes stranded on a reef off the Bahamas. The USS *Honduras* works to transfer equipment and ordnance from the immobilized ship.

January 5 (Thursday)   In Kentucky, the 6th U.S. Colored Troops Regiment clashes with Confederates at Smithfield. *In Union general officer activity,* the War Department accepts the resignation of Brigadier General William Henry Powell. Several days later, he presents a farewell address to his command. At the close of hostilities, he receives the brevet rank of major general of volunteers.

January 6 (Friday)   In Virginia, the second major offensive against Confederate Fort Fisher commences with the departure of approximately 80,000 men under General Alfred H. Terry from Bermuda Hundred. The fleet arrives at Beaufort, North Carolina, on the 8th.

In Confederate general officer activity, Colonel Richard Lee Turberville Beale is promoted to brigadier general effective this date. General Beale has been involved in the Confederate cavalry since his appointment to the 9th Virginia (known as Lee's Light Horse) as first lieutenant, with participation in nearly every campaign of the Army of Northern Virginia. Beale will return to Virginia after the war, and later, during 1878, he will be elected to Congress for the second time; he had previously served in the House of Representatives for one term prior to the war (1846–1848). Colonel Tyree H. Bell, commanding a company of cavalry (Forrest's command), receives command of a brigade prior to the end of this month. In late March, Colonel Bell is promoted to the rank of brigadier general. As the Confederates continue to make command changes, General William H. Jackson (West Point, 1856), who commanded General Leonidas Polk's cavalry during the Meridian campaign and subsequently the cavalry of the Army of Mississippi, will assume command of all Tennessee cavalry units under Nathan B. Forrest for the remainder of the conflict until Forrest capitulates at Selma. General Jackson assumes this command

during February. The Texas brigade of Brigadier General Lawrence Sul (Sullivan) Ross remains with General Forrest, but the ranks of Forrest's forces have been badly battered by non-stop action since spring. Now the unit is also plagued by desertions.

January 7 (Saturday)   In the Indian Territory (Colorado), a one-company contingent of the 7th Iowa Cavalry clashes with Indians at Julesburg, Indian Territory. Casualty figures are unavailable.

January 8 (Sunday)   In Arkansas, the 79th U.S. Colored Troops skirmish with Confederates at Ivy Ford.

In North Carolina, Union General Alfred H. Terry arrives at Beaufort. His force will depart on the 4th en route to assault Fort Fisher, the dominant strong point guarding Wilmington.

In Alabama, the 101st U.S. Colored Troops Regiment skirmishes with Confederates at Scottsboro.

In Union general officer activity, at about this time, Union General Edward Otho C. Ord, wounded severely last September at Fort Harrison, now succeeds General Butler as commander of the Department of Virginia and North Carolina. General Butler had received orders from General Grant to leave for home and await orders. No further orders arrive for him. Butler, after receiving instructions from Grant the previous November, resigned from the service on 30 November 1864. Butler is elected to Congress as a Republican during 1866 and serves for ten years. Meanwhile, Major General Ord is promoted to brigadier general of the Regular Army on 26 July 1866. He remains in the army and retires during 1881 with the rank of major general. Subsequently, while on a voyage from New York to Vera Cruz, Mexico, he is stricken with yellow fever. He dies in Ha-

Left: Union pickets skirmish with Confederate cavalry in the vicinity of Beaufort, South Carolina. *Right:* General Gillmore's artillery at Fort Putnam bombards Charleston, South Carolina (Mottelay, *The Soldier in Our Civil War,* 1886).

General Edward O.C. Ord (Johnson, *Campfire and Battlefield: History of the Conflicts and Campaigns*, 1894).

vana, Cuba, on 22 July 1883. His remains are returned to the United States and he is interred at Arlington National Cemetery.

January 9 (Monday)   In Mississippi, a contingent of the 17th Iowa at Eastport moves out to Iuka and returns the same day after a 16-mile march. In other activity, the Confederate Army of Tennessee arrives at Tupelo. Confederate General John B. Hood is relieved of duty and the fragments of his army are transferred to other units. Hood's beleaguered troops suffered through a disastrous Nashville campaign. Also, Confederate Brigadier General Peter B. Starke is ordered to Mississippi to serve with General James R. Chalmers. After the war, Chalmers, a native Virginian, resides in Mississippi and serves in Congress several times, while also losing elections for Congress several times. He retires during 1888 and moves to Memphis, where he practices law until he dies during 1898.

In Naval activity, the USS *Wyalusing* intercepts and seizes a schooner, the *Triumph,* which is transporting a cargo of salt at the mouth of the Perquimans River. Afterward, it remains on patrol in the Cape Hatteras region and in Albemarle Sound until May. That same month on the 20th, it arrives in New York and is decommissioned on 10 June 1865. From there it is transferred to New York, where it is sold on 15 October 1867.

January 10 (Tuesday)   In Alabama, a contingent of Confederate General John B. Hood's force attacks Union positions at Scottsboro.

In Virginia, a scouting contingent, composed of units of the 1st New York and 1st Virginia Cavalry Regiments, operates along the Winchester Pike and advances toward Berry's Ferry.

In Kentucky, Colonel Oscar H. LaGrange's brigade clashes with Confederates under General Hylan B. Lyon at Greensburgh. After the war, Lyon heads for Mexico, but he returns to Kentucky during 1866 and takes up farming. He succumbs during April 1907.

In Naval activity, Union Admiral David D. Porter and General Alfred H. Terry finalize plans for a joint attack on Fort Fisher, North Carolina. Bad weather continues to stall the attack.

January 11 (Wednesday)   In West Virginia, Confederate troops commanded by General Thomas Rosser skirmish with Union forces at Beverly. Union troops lose five killed, 20 wounded and 583 missing. Confederate casualties are unavailable.

In Virginia, General Robert E. Lee states in a telegram to Confederate Secretary of War James A. Seddon: "There is nothing within reach of this army to be impressed. The country is swept clear. Our only reliance is upon the railroads. We have but two days supplies." Lee's headquarters are in the vicinity of Petersburg.

In Confederate general officer activity, Colonel Thomas Harrison, the brother of Confederate General James E. Harrison, is promoted to brigadier general effective this day.

January 12 (Thursday)   In South Carolina, the ironclad ram CSS *Columbia,* built in Charleston the previous year, inadvertently strikes one of the sunken wrecks designed to halt Union progress at Charleston. The *Columbia* sustains fatal damage and sinks off Fort Moultrie. Subsequent to seizing the city, the Union raises the *Columbia* and tows it north to Norfolk during May 1865. Later, in October 1867, the hulk is sold.

In Union general officer activity, Colonel John G. Mitchell is promoted to brigadier general. General Mitchell had participated at Chickamauga, commanding one of General James B. Steedman's divisions. At the Battle of Kennesaw Mountain, Mitchell commanded a brigade in General Jefferson C. Davis' division of the XIV Corps. The closing days of the conflict will place Mitchell in the heat of battle in North Carolina. He is at that time promoted to brevet major general, during March of 1865. Also, Brigadier General John Geary receives the rank of brevet major general. General Geary remains in the army until 1866 and afterward is elected governor of Pennsylvania. He fulfills two terms and about two and one-half weeks after leaving office, he dies suddenly on 8

February 1873. In yet other activity, Colonel John Morrison Oliver is appointed brigadier general. After the war, General Oliver commands at Louisville and then Little Rock, prior to his departure from the army on August 24, 1865.

Also, Colonel Benjamin Franklin Potts is promoted to brigadier general. He receives the brevet rank of major general effective 13 March. After the war, Potts fails to gain a colonelcy in the Regular Army. Consequently, he resigns from the service and resumes his law practice. In 1870, he is appointed governor of the Montana Territory by President Grant, a post he retains until the succeeding president, Chester Arthur, removes him from office. In yet other activity, Colonel James Sidney Robinson is appointed brigadier general, following his brevet of brigadier during the previous December. He participates in the campaign of Sherman in the Carolinas. After the war he becomes a U.S. Congressman (1881–1885) and then secretary of Ohio (1885–1889).

In Naval activity, the *Ajax,* built in Scotland for the Confederacy, departs from the *Clyde* en route for Nassau. Secretary of War Mallory had ordered the Ajax and another vessel, the *Hercules,* during the previous year. The two ships were designed as towboats to deceive Federal spies. The two vessels were smaller than another two vessels ordered, the *Adventure* and *Enterprise.* The *Ajax* apparently makes it to Madeira, but the situation of the Confederates at the time in the United States prompts the *Ajax* to remain outside the country. A later report notes that it returns to Ireland. The same report notes that none of the other three vessels (*Hercules, Adventure* and *Enterprise*) arrive to serve the Confederacy.

January 13 (Friday)   In North Carolina, during the attack against Fort Fisher, the USS *Buckingham,* stationed off Half Moon Battery, supports the troops which are debarking from transports. Subsequent to the reduction of the fort, the *Governor Buckingham* remains on station near Half Moon Battery. While there it fires upon various Confederate positions as they attempt to regroup. On the 17th, a large Con-

The Union invasion force lands in the vicinity of Fort Fisher, North Carolina (*Harper's Pictoral History of the Civil War,* 1896).

Above: A Union fleet bombards Fort Fisher (*Harper's Pictorial History of the Civil War,* 1896). *Right:* The Union's final attack against Fort Fisher, North Carolina (Mottelay, *The Soldier in Our Civil War,* 1886).

federate force is detected along the beach. The *Governor Buckingham* initiates a bombardment that drives the Rebels from their positions in conjunction with a force that advances toward them. The Union gains some prisoners. During the following month, the *Governor Buckingham* returns to Virginia for additional repairs; however, it is decommissioned on 27 March 1865 and sold at auction in July.

In Naval activity, the USS *Pontiac,* operating off Charleston, is ordered to Savannah to support the advance of General William T. Sherman's left wing, which is advancing across the Savannah River at Sister's Ferry, Georgia. General Sherman's northward advance is placing more pressure on the defenders at Charleston.

January 13–15   BATTLE OF FORT FISHER A U.S. naval assault (about sixty vessels) combined with a land attack by forces under General Alfred H. Terry prove to be too much for Confederate-held Fort Fisher, North Carolina. The fleet includes the *Advance, Aries, Cherokee, Colorado, Fort Jackson, Gettysburg, Huron, Iosco, Kansas, Keystone State, Minnesota, Mohican, Mahopac, Monadnock, Nereus, New Ironsides, Pontoosuc, Rhode Island, Santiago de Cuba, Sassacus, Governor Buckingham, Ticonderoga* and *Wabash.*

During the early morning hours of the 15th, the naval guns blast the Rebel fort and the bombardment continues until 0900. The *New Ironsides* leads three monitors to positions within 1,000 yards from the fort, which is already permeated with iron and debris from the previous attack (December 1864) and commences fire, sending a steady stream of shells into the Rebel positions. In the meantime, the *Kansas* and other wooden warships form into a battle line and open fire in unison against Flag Pond Battery and the woods in the area. After about one-half hour of incessant fire, the wooden gunboats lower boats to send detachments to support the landing force, which moves ashore at terrain which is out of range of the Confederate guns. Afterward, the *Kansas* maneuvers into positions

alongside of the main body, which is saturating Fort Fisher with round after round. The fort continues to sustain incoming fire for the following two days. In the meantime, during the landing, some confusion occurs with regard to overall command of the naval and Marine forces. It is cleared up when Lt. Commander Kidder Breese, U.S. Navy, displays a letter from the admiral and he assumes command of the troops, although some naval officers outrank him. The ships' troops are organized into three divisions under the commands of Lt. Commanders Charles H. Cushman, James Parker and Thomas O. Selfridge.

While the Army strikes by land, the naval force and the Marines face a more arduous task because they lack proper weapons and carry only revolvers while they brave heavy fire as they trudge along the beach. This Confederate fortress had held firmly against an earlier attack during December 1864; however, the three-day-bombardment and the combination of the army, commanded by General Ames attacking by land, and the Marines and seamen, commanded by K.R. Breeze (U.S. Navy) by sea, overwhelm the Confederate defenders. The victory becomes apparent at 2200, when the fleet becomes illuminated. Suddenly cheers ring out on land and sea as if in unison when the fleet lights the lamps of victory. Although there are no cheers from the vanquished under General Whiting, they had not lost their will to fight.

The cessation of the fighting is due mainly to the Rebels running out of ammunition and because reinforcements under General Robert Hoke do not arrive. Hoke's division had been a short distance away, a mere two miles, but the naval guns had kept the division at bay. The Confederates that are able make it to the inside of the fort and from there they escape.

Union losses are 184 killed and 749 wounded. Confederates lose 400 killed or wounded and 2,083 captured. Union Brigadier General Newton M. Curtis, wounded four

times, is the first man to pass through the gates of Fort Fisher. Confederate General William H.C. Whiting is badly wounded and captured. Whiting succumbs due to complications from his wounds on 10 March 1865.

A tremendous explosion occurs aboard the USS *Ticonderoga* when gun number two explodes while firing upon the Confederate positions. Coxswain William Shipman, in an effort to reorganize his men in spite of the death and destruction on the deck, yells to the other gunners: "Go ahead boys; this is only the fortunes of war." The Confederate artillery that had withstood the Union since the first attack in 1864 was commanded by General Louis Hebert (West Point, 1845). After the war, Hebert becomes editor of a newspaper and is a teacher in private schools (Iberville and St. Martin Parishes) until his death during January 1901.

Union Colonel Galusha Pennypacker participates in great measure at this battle, rendering extraordinary gallantry in the field, according to General Alfred H. Terry, who gives credit for victory to Pennypacker. He is severely wounded during the assault and remains hospitalized for nearly one year. Colonel Pennypacker, no stranger to danger, was previously wounded four times during the ongoing siege of Petersburg. He will be breveted brigadier general to rank from February 1865, and he receives the brevet of major general effective March 13. Major General Pennypacker will be twenty-one years old on 1 June 1865.

Also, 400 Marines attached to Admiral David Farragut's squadron participate in the attack to seize the fort. John Griffiths (USS *Santiago de Cuba*) is one of six sailors who are among the first troops to land. He receives the Medal of Honor for his actions of this day. Also, Commodore (rear admiral) William Radford, commander of the ironclad USS *New Ironsides,* subsequently, during 1866, is appointed commandant of the Washington Navy Yard, and in

1869 he is appointed as commander of the European Squadron.

Also, Commodore Henry K. Thatcher, commander of the USS *Colorado*, subsequent to the seizure of Fort Fisher, is appointed commander of the Western Gulf Squadron. Commodore Thatcher cooperates with General Canby in a determined effort to reduce Mobile. The USS *New Ironsides*, following the operations at Fort Fisher, sails to Hampton Roads and supports Union activity there until it is decommissioned during April 1865. During the following year, the *New Ironsides*, while moored in Philadelphia, is destroyed when an accidental fire breaks out on 16 December.

The *Sassacus* continues to operate in the North Carolina waters and Virginia until it is decommissioned during May 1865. The *Wabash*, initially commissioned during 1856, is decommissioned during February 1865; however, it is recommissioned during 1871. In 1876 it becomes a receiving ship at the Boston Navy Yard until sold during 1912. Also, the USS *Advance*, after the capture of the fort, remains in the region only until March. At that time it moves to New York and is put out of commission until June, when it is recommissioned and renamed the *Frolic* and assigned to the European Squadron. Subsequently, it serves in various places, including South America, until it is decommissioned during October 1877. The USS *Frolic* is sold for use as a merchant ship in 1883.

Also, the USS *Kansas*, subsequent to this action, remains in North Carolina until late February, when it is ordered to sail north to support the actions against Richmond. It operates on the James River in support of army operations that are slowly nudging toward the Rebel capital against heavy resistance, including at Petersburg, the rear door to Richmond, which has been forestalling disaster since the previous summer. The USS *Aries* is ordered to sail to Boston, where it is decommissioned during June 1865 and sold in early August. Afterward it serves as a commercial vessel until 1908.

In addition, the USS *Fort Jackson*, following this activity, is transferred from the North Atlantic Blockading Squadron to the West Gulf Blockading Squadron. It is assigned patrol duty off the coast of Texas until the conclusion of hostilities in the state. It is decommissioned and sold in August 1865. It operates as a civilian vessel, the *North America*, until 1879. Another ship, the USS *Gettysburg*, following the action at Fort Fisher, changes roles. It becomes a transport for

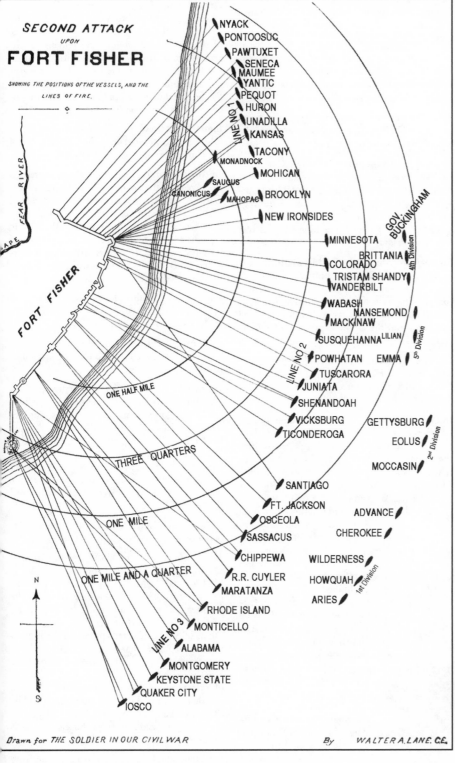

The Union attack against Fort Fisher, North Carolina, on 13 January 1865 (Mottelay, *The Soldier in Our Civil War*, 1886).

General Alfred Terry (Mottelay, *The Soldier in Our Civil War*, 1886).

the remainder of the war. It is decommissioned during June 1865. Nonetheless, in December 1866 it is recommissioned and remains in service until the following March. After another year of inactivity, it is again recommissioned, followed by periods of active and inactive service until decommissioned for the final time at Genoa, Italy, where it is sold during May 1879.

The USS *Huron,* after this action, is dispatched to the Gulf of Mexico, where it joins other warships on patrol in search of Confederate officials attempting to escape capture. After war's end, the *Huron* is ordered to move to the South America station. It is decommissioned in October 1868 and sold during June 1869; it becomes a merchant ship, the *D.H. Bills.* Also, the USS *Iosco* resumes patrols on the North Carolina sounds and participates in various missions, including an expedition on the Roanoke River during May. Afterward, it sails north, where it is decommissioned in New York during July 1865 and afterward used as a coal hulk in the New York Navy Yard. The *Keystone State,* after participating at Fort Fisher, remains in service only a couple of months. It is decommissioned during March 1865 and sold in September. (See appendix for a complete list of ships participating in the attack.)

January 14 (Saturday)   In Alabama, Union Colonel William J. Palmer, 15th Pennsylvania Cavalry, and a force of fewer than 200 men attack and defeat a superior Confederate force at Red Hill. The Union takes 100 prisoners, suffering no casualties themselves.

In Arkansas, Union troops, including the 2nd Kansas Cavalry, some Iowa cavalry and the 3rd Wisconsin Cavalry, skirmish with the Confederates at Dardanelle. First Sergeant William Ellis (3rd Wisconsin) becomes a recipient of the Medal of Honor for his heroism during this action. Although wounded four times, Ellis remains on the firing line.

In South Carolina, a contingent of the 17th Corps, Army of the Tennessee, under General John Hatch, engages Confederates through the 16th at Pocotaligo. The Rebels are led by General Lafayette McLaws. The Union sustains 25 wounded. Confederate casualty figures are unavailable. After the war, Hatch becomes a major with the 4th U.S. Cavalry. He retires during 1881 with the rank of colonel and the brevet rank of brigadier general in the Regular Army and major general of volunteers.

In Naval activity, the USS *Patapsco,* while clearing obstacles in Charleston Harbor, South Carolina, strikes a mine and sinks. Many of the crewmen are lost.

In Confederate general officer activity, Colonel Thomas Harrison (8th Texas Cavalry, known also as "Terry's Texas Rangers") is promoted to brigadier general.

In Union general officer activity, Major General John Gibbon becomes commander of the 24th Corps, Army of the James.

January 15 (Sunday)   In North Carolina, this sign appeared after the assault on Fort Fisher: "Wanted: flag bearer for the 97th Pennsylvania Volunteer Regiment! This day our regimental flag received 107 bullet holes and one cannister shot while approaching Confederate held Fort Fisher."

January 16 (Monday)   In Mississippi, a division of the XVI Corps, bolstered by the 1st Cavalry Division, led by General John T. Croxton, departs Eastport on a reconnaissance mission which takes the force to Corinth. During the operation, the Union captures 35 Confederates.

In Virginia, recently captured Forts Campbell and Caswell are reduced by the Confederates. Meanwhile, the Confederates evacuate Fort Smithville and Reeve's Point.

In North Carolina, Confederate General Braxton Bragg, literally pinned down outside Fort Fisher by General Alfred H. Terry's troops since the initial siege, receives word from President Jefferson Davis to attempt to recapture the fort. Also, an accidental explosion occurs in Fort Fisher when a large amount of ammunition detonates and causes death and destruction to both Union troops and Southern prisoners of war. The cause of the explosion remains unknown, but the Union and Confederates each lose about 200 killed.

In other activity, Confederates evacuate Fort Caswell on the Cape Fear River. The Rebels also destroy their defenses on Smith's Island and other fortifications prior to abandoning the area and heading for Wilmington. Also, General William T. Sherman initiates his campaign through the Carolinas. He relocates his headquarters from Savannah Georgia, to Beaufort, South Carolina, within a few days.

In Union general officer activity, Brigadier General Alfred Howe Terry is promoted to major general. He remains in the army beyond the close of hostilities, and during 1776, when the 7th Cavalry under General Custer is decimated, Terry is commander of the Department of Dakota. He advances to major general, U.S. Army, during 1886 and later, during 1888, he retires. Also, Brigadier General George H. Thomas is promoted to major general, Regular Army, to rank from 15 December 1864, the date of the Battle of Nashville. He remains in the army beyond the close of hostilities. During 1869, at his request, General Thomas is appointed commander of the Department of the Pacific. He dies in his headquarters in San Francisco on 28 March 1870.

January 17 (Tuesday)   The Department of the Ohio is incorporated into the Department of the Cumberland.

In Naval activity, the USS *Mohican* is ordered to move from the vicinity of Fort Fisher, North Carolina, to deliver dispatches for General William T. Sherman to Rear Admiral John Dahlgren's South Atlantic Blockading Squadron. It remains with the squadron and initiates patrol duty off Ossabaw, South Carolina, on 3 February and remains on station until ordered north on 24 February.

January 18 (Wednesday)   In Kentucky, a contingent of Tennessee Union cavalry skirmishes with Confederates at Columbia.

In North Carolina, General Charles Jackson Paine departs Fort Fisher on a reconnaissance mission to Wilmington.

January 19 (Thursday)   In North Carolina, a Union force composed of elements of the 24th and 25th Corps, Army of the James, engages Confederates at Half Moon Battery and Sugar Loaf Hill. The Union, supported by the USS *Wilderness,* occupies Smithville. The *Wilderness* remains near the mouth of the Cape Fear River into the following month, then returns to the James River. It operates there primarily until the close of hostilities.

In Louisiana, Confederates attack a Union dispatch boat at Fort St. Philip.

In Naval activity, the USS *Malvern* (Admiral David Porter's flagship), commanded by Lt. Cushing and the Maratanza, intercept and capture (19th–20th) two blockade runners, the steamers *Charlotte* and the *Stag* (Lt. R.H. Gayle), in the vicinity of New Inlet, North Carolina. In Admiral Porter's report on the following day, he relates that his ships exchanged signals with the *Stag* and *Charlotte*: "I had the blockade runners' lights lit last night, and was obliging enough to answer their signals, whether right or wrong we don't know." The *Stag* was taken to New York. Later this year, it enters commercial service as the *Zenobia.* It is again sold during 1867.

January 20 (Friday)   In Kansas, fighting erupts between Union soldiers and Indians near Fort Larned.

Pocotaligo Depot, South Carolina (Mottelay, *The Soldier in Our Civil War,* 1886).

In Confederate general officer activity, Colonel William McComb (14th Tennessee Infantry), born a Pennsylvanian, is promoted to brigadier general. General McComb has served with the Army of Northern Virginia and will be with Lee at Appomattox. General McComb suffered two separate wounds during his service at Sharpsburg (Antietam) and Chancellorsville. Later, he is paroled at Appomattox Court House. Afterward he engages in farming until he dies on his plantation in the vicinity of Gordonsville, Virginia, on 21 July 1918.

In Naval activity, the CSS *Granite City,* a blockade runner, departs from Velasco, Texas, using a fog as cover to evade the blockade ships. It succeeds in breaking out, but on the following day, the *Granite City* is detected by a Union blockade ship, the Penguin, which gives chase. The Rebels run the *Granite City* aground, which causes it to break apart. In other activity, the USS *Maratanza* participates in the seiure of two Rebel steamers, the *Stag* and the *Charlotte.* In conjunction, the *Maratanza* had participated in the attacks against Fort Fisher (December 1864 and January 1865). After this seizure, it also participates in the assault against Fort Anderson at Wilmington, North Carolina.

January 21 (Saturday) *In Union general officer activity,* Colonel Stephen Thomas (8th Vermont) is mustered out of the volunteer service. However, on 21 April, he is appointed brigadier general of volunteers, to rank from 1 February 1865. He becomes lieutenant governor of Vermont during 1867 and serves into 1868.

January 23 (Monday) *In Union general officer activity,* Brigadier General James Hewett Ledlie, having been severely criticized for his actions during the previous year at Petersburg (Crater), resigns from the army.

In Confederate activity, Confederate Lt. General Richard Taylor today assumes command of the Army of Tennessee, replacing General John B. Hood. In May 1865, General Hood surrenders at Natchez. He succumbs from yellow fever on 30 August 1879.

In Naval activity, the USS *Suwanee,* a doubleended iron-hulled gunboat, is commissioned. Commander Paul Shirley receives command. The *Suwannee* leaves Philadelphia on 17 February initially patrols along the Atlantic coast, then sails to the West Coast during July and joins the Pacific Squadron on the 30th. It joins the search for the USS *Shenandoah.* It is lost in Shadwell Passage, Queen Charlotte Sound, British Columbia, on 9 July 1868. In other activity, the USS *Heliotrope* is transferred to the Potomac Flotilla. It participates in operations along the Rappahannock River against Fredericksburg, Virginia, during early March.

January 24 (Tuesday) **In Virginia,** a contingent of U.S. colored troops, supported by artillery, clashes with a Confederate naval squadron commanded by Lt. Dunnington off Fort Brady (Fort Burnham or Bogg's Mills). The Union reports no casualties. The Confederates suffer five killed and 14 wounded.

In Naval activity, Confederate warships, including the CSS *Fredericksburg, Drewry, Nansemond, Richmond* and the *Virginia II,* bolstered by the torpedo boats *Scorpion, Hornet* and *Wasp,* attempt to pass Union obstructions to attack Union positions on the James River. The *Drewry,* a gunboat attached to Confederate Flag Officer F. Forrest's squadron, is struck by Union fire by the 1st Connecticut Artillery while the vessel is engaged in helping to refloat the CSS *Richmond* at Trent's Reach on the James River. The *Drewry* sustains one hit and survives, but a second shot launched by a 100-pounder rifle strikes its magazine, which explodes. At the time of the explosion only two of the crew remains aboard. The rest had reached shore prior to the ship's demise. The *Fredericksburg,* an ironclad ram, and the *Richmond* survive the Union fire, but in early April, the Rebels destroy both to prevent capture by the Union. The *Scorpion,* acquired by the Confederacy during 1864, sustains heavy damage from the explosion of the *Drewry*'s magazine. The crew abandons the *Scorpion* and the ship is afterward taken by the Union. Also, the *Virginia* sustains heavy damage, but survives. Later, when Richmond is abandoned, the *Virginia* is destroyed to prevent capture.

The USS *Spuyten Duyvil* participates in the engagement at Treat's Reach. Afterward it resumes normal duty on the James. It is utilized to eliminate obstructions on the river to create clear and unobstructed passage for President Lincoln when he moves to Richmond via the James after the surrender of the Confederates. Afterward, it is decommissioned when it arrives in New York. It is sold during 1880.

January 25 (Wednesday) **In Kentucky,** the 5th U.S. Colored Cavalry clashes with Confederates at Simpsonville.

In South Carolina, elements of the 15th and 17th Corps (General William T. Sherman's command) skirmish with Confederates at the Combahee River.

In Virginia, the 1st U.S. Colored Cavalry Regiment skirmishes with Confederates at Powhatan. Also, clashes occur between General Sherman's advancing army and Confederates units in the vicinity of the Combahee River, Rivers Bridge, Salkehatchie and Lawtonville through February 9. The Union sustains about 138 killed and wounded. Confederate casualty figures are unavailable.

January 27 (Friday) **In Arkansas,** Private James H. Robinson, Company B, 3rd Michigan Cavalry, singlehandedly holds off a contingent of seven Confederates led by Cpt. W.C. Stephenson at Brownsville. Stephenson is killed, but the remainder of the Confederates withdraw. Private Robinson becomes a recipient of the Medal of Honor.

In Virginia, a Union contingent skirmishes with Confederates at Chunky River. Specific units and casualty figures are unreported.

In Union general officer activity, Colonel Charles Camp Doolittle is promoted to the rank

of brigadier general. He commands at Nashville for a time before being transferred to the northeastern district of Louisiana. Later he is breveted major general of volunteers. He resigns from the service on 30 November 1865.

January 28 (Saturday) *In Confederate general officer activity,* Colonel George Gibbs Dibrell, 8th (also known as 13th) Tennessee Cavalry, is promoted to brigadier general effective 26 July 1864. General Dibrell is designated responsibility for the Confederate archives when the Confederate government abandons Richmond during the closing days of the war. At Washington, Georgia, he is paroled on 9 May 1865. Afterward, he becomes involved in various careers, including becoming a merchant and a financier, but he also gets elected to Congress and serves ten years (1874–1884). Subsequently, General Dibrell becomes involved in the coal mining industry and becomes president of the Southwestern Pacific Railroad. He retires in Sparta, Tennessee, where he dies on 9 May 1888.

In Naval activity, the CSS *Saint Patrick,* a small, semi-submersible torpedo boat under the command of the Confederate Army, attacks the USS *Octorara* in Mobile Bay. The *Octorara* escapes damage because the torpedo misfires. The *Octorara* returns fire; however, the *St. Patrick* sustains no damage and successfully returns to Mobile.

January 29–February 11 **In North Carolina,** the Union 2nd North Carolina Regiment initiates an expedition into the western sector of the state.

January 30 (Monday) **In South Carolina,** a Union force led by General Oliver Otis Howard engages a Confederate force at White's Point.

January 31 (Tuesday) **In Virginia,** three Confederate peace commissioners, Alexander H. Stephens, vice president of the Confederacy, John A. Campbell, Confederate assistant secretary of war, and R.M.T. Hunter arrive at General Grant's headquarters outside Petersburg. Grant is directed to detain them until President Lincoln or his representative reaches City Point. The Confederates are quartered as guests on the steamer *Mary Martin* and are permitted to move about at will. Grant does not discuss their mission, choosing not to recognize them as representatives of a government. In other activity, General Robert E. Lee, due to an act by President Jefferson Davis issued on 23 January 1865, assumes command of all Confederate forces.

February The 5th Minnesota Volunteer Infantry Regiment, deployed at Eastport, Mississippi, departs this month for new duty in New Orleans, Louisiana. The Regiment will participate in the battle to secure Mobile, Alabama.

In Confederate general officer activity, Colonel Alexander W. Campbell, 33rd Tennessee Regiment, who was recently released from a Union prison, will receive a cavalry command under Confederate General William H. Jackson (Nathan B. Forrest's corps). General Jackson, although not having reached the rank of major general, does command a division. Colonel Campbell will be promoted to brigadier general the next month. Major General Wade Hampton is promoted to the rank of lieutenant general. Hampton had been involved in the fighting around Petersburg; however, early last January, he was transferred to North Carolina to support the defense of Fort Fisher. Also, Major General Nathan Bedford Forrest is again promoted. He becomes a lieutenant general effective February 28.

February 1 (Wednesday) In Maryland, Brigadier General (Brevet) William C. Morris is appointed commander of the Middle Military Department. He succeeds Major General Lewis Wallace and retains the post until 19 April 1865.

In South Carolina, General William T. Sherman divides his army in half, with one part on the advance to Augusta, while the other half initiates a diversionary move toward Charleston with intent of causing some confusion among the Confederates. At this time, General Sherman's army consists of 58,928 infantrymen, 4,448 cavalry and 1,718 artillerymen. Sherman's force also contains 68 artillery pieces, 2,500 supply wagons and hundreds of ambulances. Sherman establishes his headquarters at Hickory Hill Post Office, South Carolina. Sherman establishes quarters on the following night at Duck Branch Post Office, South Carolina.

February 2 (Thursday) In Virginia, General U.S. Grant receives a dispatch from Washington, directing him to send the Confederate peace commissioners to Hampton Roads to meet with President Lincoln. The president informs the commissioners that there will be no negotiations unless they recognize that the Union must be forever preserved and slavery must be abolished. In other activity, Sherman's Army continues to move through the Carolinas against the remnants of the battered Confederates, who maintain as much pressure as they can to forestall the Yankees' progress. The XVII Corps, like the other contingents of Sherman's army, find their advances meeting resistance. While attempting to cross the Salkehatchie River, Confederate guns open up against the troops and Colonel Wager Swayne is wounded. Colonel Swayne will be promoted to brevet brigadier general effective 5 February. On 13 March, he is promoted to full rank. However, his wound is severe and his leg is amputated. Nonetheless, General Swayne remains in the service beyond the close of hostilities. On 1 May 1866, he is promoted to major general of volunteers, to rank from 20 June 1865. Subsequently, he becomes colonel of the 45th U.S. Infantry, and during 1867, he is breveted brigadier general and major general in the Regular Army. He retires during 1870.

February 3 (Friday) In South Carolina, the Union 15th and 17th Corps (General Sherman's command) engage Confederates at the River's Bridge in Salkehatchie and at Hickory Hill, Owen's Crossroads, Lowtonville, Duck Creek and Whipley Swamp through the 9th. The Union sustains about 80 casualties, including killed and wounded. Confederate casualty figures are unavailable. Confederates burn all bridges across the channels of the Salkehatchie River to impede Sherman's advance.

In Virginia, peace talks aboard a ship off Hampton Roads among President Lincoln, Confederate Vice President Alexander Stephens and the other peace commissioners are unsuccessful. President Lincoln denies the request by the South for autonomy.

In Union general officer activity, Brigadier General David McMurtie Gregg resigns his commission from the regular army and the volunteers.

February 4 (Saturday) In Virginia, Confederate President Jefferson Davis appoints Major General John C. Breckinridge as secretary of war. It is a classic tale of too little too late. The Confederacy is plagued by lack of proper food and supplies and has lost its ports. The ranks of general officers have been dwindling, as well as those of the rank and file troops, while the Union is on the move, counting major successes with their cavalry and infantry. The South has lost its ports except for Wilmington, North Carolina, and it is being squeezed on all fronts.

In Confederate general officer activity, Colonel Robert Lowry is promoted to brigadier general effective this date. Lowry initially entered the Confederate service during 1861 when he joined the "Rankin Grays," but soon he became major of the 6th Mississippi. After sustaining two wounds at Shiloh, he was raised to colonel of the regiment.

In Naval activity, the USS *Wamsutta* and the *Potomska* encounter a blockade runner off Charleston, South Carolina, but the ship is destroyed before the Union can seize it. The *Wamsutta* is ordered to St. Simon's Island, Georgia, in late April. It remains on station there until May, when it sails north to Portsmouth, New Hampshire, where it is decommissioned on 29 June 1865. It is sold at auction on 20 July.

February 5 (Sunday) In South Carolina, General William T. Sherman, while at Buford's Bridge, issues orders to march on the railroad at Midway. In the meantime, contingents under Sherman devastate the town of Barnwell.

In Florida, a contingent of the 17th Connecticut Volunteer Regiment skirmishes with Confederates at Dunn's Lake in Volusia County.

February 5–7 In Virginia, Union troops defeat the Confederates at Dabney's Run and Hatcher's Run. The 5th Corps, 1st Division of the 6th Corps, the 210th Pennsylvania Infantry and General David Gregg's cavalry participate. The Union sustains 232 killed, 1,062 wounded and 186 missing. Confederates sustain 1,200 killed or wounded. Confederate General John Pegram (West Point, 1854) is killed at Dabney's Run on the 6th. Confederate General Gilbert M. Sorrel is badly wounded in the leg at Hatcher's Run, but he recovers. After the close of hostilities, General Sorrel becomes a businessman in Savannah, Georgia, and later becomes involved with a steamship company. He dies in the vicinity of Roanoke, Virginia, during August 1901.

February 6 (Monday) In Virginia, during the ongoing fighting at Hatcher's Run, General Henry E. Davies is wounded. Nevertheless, he returns to service and continues with his cavalry command for the duration. In January 1866, he resigns from the service. He returns to his law practice and later writes a biography on General Philip Sheridan.

February 7 (Tuesday) In South Carolina, General William T. Sherman continues to advance. The Union encounters resistance from Confederates under Major General Joseph Wheeler at Blackville. Nonetheless, Sherman, with the 15th Corps, reaches the railroad station at Midway. General Oliver O. Howard tells him that control of the South Carolina railroad was achieved by a group of foragers. The generals anticipate a battle, but it never materializes. The Confederates once again retreat, burning bridges as they depart. Sherman's men destroy the railroad, choking the already deteriorating southern supply lines. Also, Union cavalry under General Hugh Kilpatrick skirmishes with Confederates led by Major General Joseph Wheeler at Williston, Aiken and Blackville through the 14th.

In Texas, a contingent attached to the USS *Bienville* is sent into Galveston Bay after dusk, and the boat party succeeds in seizing two schooners, each carrying a cargo of cotton. The *Bienville* remains in the region for a while, but

Union troops entering Blackville, South Carolina (*Harper's Pictorial History of the Civil War*, 1896).

shortly after the war, it is decommissioned on 15 August 1865. Nearly two years later it is sold. The *Bienville* remains in commercial service until it is lost to fire at Watling Island in the Bahamas in August 1872.

In Union general officer activity, Brigadier General Henry Dwight Terry's resignation is accepted by the War Department. General Terry had been ordered (with his division of the VI Corps) to Sandusky, Ohio, during 1864, where he assumed command of a prison on Johnson's Island. He was relieved during May 1864 and his name vanished from the official records, indicating he had no command. After separating from the service, he returns to Washington and resumes his law practice.

In Confederate general officer activity, General John Henry Winder (West Point, 1820) dies of natural causes at Florence, South Carolina. Brigadier General Gideon J. Pillow, subsequent to the death of Winder (February 1865), assumes the duties of commissary general of prisoners. Subsequent to returning home after the war, General Pillow is compelled to file for bankruptcy; however, he is able to resume his law practice at Memphis in partnership with Isham G. Harris, former governor of Tennessee. He dies in the vicinity of Helena, Arkansas, on 8 October 1878.

February 8 (Wednesday) In South Carolina, General Sherman's force leaves much destruction behind as it moves toward Columbia. Also, General Grant orders Sheridan to move through the Shenandoah and "strike the canal at or about Lynchburg."

In the Indian Territory, a Union contingent composed of elements of the 11th Ohio and 7th Iowa Cavalry Regiments engage Indians at Mud Springs.

In Union general officer activity, Major General Julius Stahel, out of field command and on court-martial duty since just after the battle at Piedmont (5 June 1864), resigns his commission. He serves in China and Japan in the consular service, and upon his return to the United States he becomes involved with an insurance company. General Stahel dies in New York on 4 December 1912.

In Naval activity, the CSS *Shenandoah,* in port in Australia since the previous month, departs. By the latter part of June, it is operating in the Okhotsk Sea, the Bering Sea and the Arctic Ocean, and from 28 June through 28 June, nearly 30 ships are seized.

February 9 (Thursday) In South Carolina, a contingent of the 17th Army Corps, Army of the Tennessee, engages Confederates at Binnaker's Bridge at the South Edisto River.

In the Indian Territory, the 11th Ohio and 7th Iowa Cavalry Regiments clash with Indians at Rush Creek. Casualty figures are unavailable.

In Union general officer activity, Colonel James Isham Gilbert is promoted to brigadier general of volunteers. Afterward he leads the 2nd Brigade (3rd Division, XVI Corps) as part of the right wing during the campaign against Mobile. He receives the brevet rank of major general toward the close of the war. He resigns from the army during August 1865. In other activity, Union General Quincy Adams Gillmore again assumes command of the Department of the South. Gillmore had earlier (July 1864) been sidelined and severely injured when he and his horse fell during the fighting against General Jubal Early in the vicinity of Washington, D.C.

In Naval activity, the USS *Sonoma,* while providing support for General William T. Sherman's northern advance from Savannah, engages Confederate batteries. After the war the *Sonoma,* sails north to New York, where it is decommissioned in June of this year and sold in October 1867.

February 10 (Friday) In South Carolina,

Union forces of General Gillmore engage Confederates on James Island (Mottelay, *The Soldier in Our Civil War,* 1886).

U.S. troops under General Alexander Schimmelfennig (Major General Quincy Adams Gillmore's command) assault James Island. The Union sustains 20 killed and 70 wounded. The Confederates sustain 200 killed and 70 wounded.

In Union general officer activity, Major General Samuel R. Curtis replaces Major General John Pope as commander of the Northwest. General Pope becomes commanding officer of the Military Division of the Missouri, which includes the Departments of Missouri, Arkansas and Kansas. He remains in the service after the war. He retires in 1882 with the rank of major general. Also, Brigadier General John Benjamin Sanborn receives the brevet of major general of volunteers. He continues in command of the District of Southwest Missouri, and after the war he is charged with leading a campaign against various hostile Indian tribes. The cam-

Left: General Sherman's column crosses a pontoon bridge on the South Edisto River (Mottelay, *The Soldier in Our Civil War,* 1886). *Right:* A Union column and wagons cross the South Edisto River (*Harper's Pictorial History of the Civil War,* 1896).

paign culminates with treaties; however, they prove to be of no value. Afterward, he contributes to arbitrating differences between the Five Civilized Tribes, then retires to practice law in St. Paul, Minnesota. He also serves in the legislature, including the state Senate, from 1891 to 1893. He dies on 16 May 1904.

In Naval activity, Lt. Commander Cushing initiates a reconnaissance mission up the Cape Fear River in North Carolina. Also, the USS *Kenwood,* at Baton Rouge, is ordered to Natchez (4th River District) to support the efforts to reduce Confederate forces operating west of the Mississippi River. On 28 May, it is ordered to New Orleans to be used as a transport for officers. It is decommissioned at Mound City, Illinois, on 7 August of this year. The *Kenwood* is sold on 17 August and becomes the *Cumberland.* As the *Cumberland,* it operates as a merchant ship until it is destroyed by an explosion at Shawneetown, Illinois, on 14 August 1869.

February 11 (Saturday)   In North Carolina, the 2nd Division and the 1st Brigade, 1st Division, XXIV Corps, bolstered by the 3rd Division, XXV Corps, Army of the James, commanded by General Alfred H. Terry, engages Confederates at Sugar Loaf Battery, Federal Point. The Union sustains 14 killed and 114 wounded. The Confederates suffer about 100 killed and 65 captured. In related activity, the USS *Vicksburg* bombards Half Moon Battery, one of the Confederate posts near Fort Fisher. Subsequent to this action, the *Vicksburg* is ordered north to the James River to support the operations against Petersburg and Richmond. The *Vicksburg* remains active during the final push to secure Richmond, and shortly after the war, during April 1865, it is decommissioned. It is sold in July. Afterward, it operates as a commercial vessel until about 1868.

In South Carolina, General Sherman advances on Orangeburg. General Giles A. Smith's force

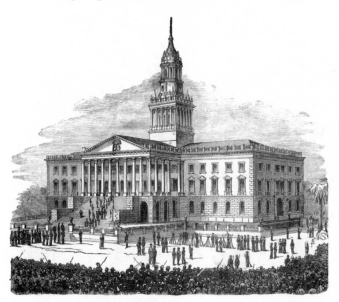

New State House in Columbia, South Carolina (Mottelay, *The Soldier in Our Civil War,* 1886).

is halted at a destroyed bridge on the Edisto River. Meanwhile, General Francis P. Blair crosses the Edisto River about four miles downstream. The Union occupies the town, destroys the railroad and severs communications between Southern troops at Charleston and those at Columbia. Confederate troops engage the 3rd Cavalry in a heated skirmish at Aiken. The Confederates sustain 240 killed and about 100 missing. In related activity, the Confederates evacuate Branchville.

February 12 (Sunday)   In South Carolina, Union forces under General Sherman occupy Branchville.

February 13 (Monday)   In South Carolina, one of General Sherman's aides, Colonel J.C. Audenried, captures a Rebel officer and learns through questioning that Columbia is protected by nothing except General Wade Hampton's cavalry. General Beauregard had departed for Charleston, believing it is the primary objective of Sherman.

February 14 (Tuesday)   In South Carolina, General Sherman advances on Columbia. His advance force occupies the unfinished Confederate fort on the outskirts of the town. Union General Charles R. Woods' troops repel a Confederate cavalry charge and afterward initiate pursuit of the retreating Rebels, who head for the woods. In related activity, a skirmish develops when the 3rd Cavalry Division (Sherman's Army) encounters Confederates at Gunter's Bridge.

February 15 (Wednesday)   In South Carolina, elements of the 15th Corps under General John Logan engage Confederates at Congaree Creek. Between this day and the 17th, forces under General William T. Sherman encroach and enter Columbia.

In Confederate general officer activity, General Wade Hampton is promoted to the rank of lieutenant general. He is one of three men to receive that rank during the struggle, the other two being Richard Taylor and Nathan B. Forrest. Colonel Thomas Muldrup Logan, who had been with General Hampton when he arrived in South Carolina, is promoted to brigadier general effective this date. Brigadier General Bryan Grimes is promoted to the rank of major general. General Grimes is ambushed and assassinated on 14 August 1880 by William Parker. Also, Confederate Colonel Isaac M. St. John is promoted to the rank of brigadier general, effective this date. General St. John is assigned duty as commissary general. Later, he is paroled at Thomasville, Georgia. He engages in civil

engineering until his death at White Sulphur Springs, West Virginia, during April 1880. Colonel William H. Forney, who was captured in 1863 at Gettysburg, is appointed brigadier general. Forney's brigade is attached to Major General William Mahone's division in the 2nd Corps, Army of Northern Virginia, until the surrender of Robert E. Lee at Appomattox.

February 16 (Thursday)   In South Carolina, General Sherman issues General Order 26 at Columbia: "General [Oliver Otis] Howard will occupy Columbia, destroy the public buildings, railroad property, manufacturing and machine shops; but will spare libraries, asylums, and private dwellings." In other activity, Governor Milledge Bonham, a former general, having fulfilled his term as governor of South Carolina, is again commissioned brigadier general and will lead a cavalry force under General Joseph E. Johnston in the Carolinas.

In Florida, the 2nd U.S. Colored Troops Regiment skirmishes with Confederates at Cedar Keys.

In Naval activity, the USS *Agawam,* following a prolonged absence from service while undergoing repairs, returns to duty. It arrives at Pamlico Sound, North Carolina, on the 18th and patrols in the waters off North Carolina until the close of hostilities. It remains in active service until it is decommissioned during March 1867. It is sold in October 1867.

In Union general officer activity, General Gabriel Rene Paul, blinded at Gettysburg, is placed on the retired list. He had attempted after some recovery to handle administrative tasks, but his blindness was too much of a handicap. General Paul lives in the capital until his death during May 1886.

In Naval activity, the USS *Minnesota,* which had participated in the capture of Fort Fisher, North Carolina, is decommissioned. During 1867, it is recommissioned and remains in service until 1868. In 1875 it again is recommissioned and used as a training ship. In October 1895 the *Minnesota* is acquired by loan by the Massachusetts Naval Militia, where it remains active until August 1901, when it is sold to the Thomas Butler Company of Boston. It had originally been commissioned on 21 May 1857.

February 17 (Friday)   In North Carolina, Admiral David D. Porter's naval force closes on Fort Anderson. The gunboats *Lenapee, Montauk, Pawtuxet, Pequot* and *Unadilla* bombard the fort. Meanwhile, Brigadier General Schofield is closing with his force of about 8,000 troops. On the following day, the gunboats advance closer to the objective and fire from close range. The USS *Yantic* participates. Afterward it resumes its blockade duty. It remains on active duty until 1898, at times with duty as a training ship on the Great Lakes. During July 1919, it is taken from the list of active navy ships and scheduled to be sold, but the name is removed from that list to once again become a training ship for the U.S. Naval Reserve. It is commissioned on 15 May 1921, redesignated the

General Sherman's army enters Columbia, South Carolina (*Harper's Pictorial History of the Civil War*, **1896**).

Columbia is on fire as Union troops enter the city (*Harper's Pictorial History of the Civil War*, 1896).

IX-32, and operates out of Cleveland, Ohio, until 1926, when it is again loaned to Michigan. Unexpectedly, it sinks at the dock in Detroit on 22 October 1929, due to the deterioration of its structure. The USS *Unadilla*, initially commissioned in September 1861, remains in service only until May 1865. However, during December 1866, it is recommissioned and assigned to the Far East Squadron. In November 1869 it is renamed *Dang Wee*, but its commercial career lasts only until the following year, when it is lost off Hong Kong.

In South Carolina, Confederate troops under General Wade Hampton evacuate Columbia as Sherman's army approaches the city. The Union troops (15th Corps) cross into Columbia by way of a pontoon bridge and occupy the town. Many troops march in and out on the Camden and Winnsboro Roads. The 17th Corps (General Francis Blair) bypasses the city, heading directly toward Winnsboro Road. Columbia is on fire as the Yankees enter. Both Hampton and Sherman disclaim any part in starting the flames. General Sherman cooperates with the town's citizens by allowing his Union soldiers to aid in extinguishing the flames. General Sherman is informed that Confederate General Joseph Johnston has been reinstated to command all troops in North and South Carolina. The remnants of John B. Hood's army are commanded by General Pierre Beauregard.

In other activity, excited Union soldiers who had been prisoners of war in Columbia present General Sherman with a copy of a song they had been singing during their captivity. The title is "Sherman's March to the Sea," written by a Union prisoner. The men sang it to help their morale. A portion of the third stanza goes like this:

> Then cheer upon cheer for bold Sherman
> Went up from each valley and glen
> And the bugles echoed the music
> That came from the lips of his men
> When Sherman marched down to the sea

In Virginia, Union troops repel a Confederate attack at Bermuda Hundred.

February 18 (Saturday)   In Kentucky, the 12th U.S. Colored Troops skirmishes with Confederates at Fort Jones.

In North Carolina, Admiral David D. Porter's fleet, including his flagship, the *Malvern*, moves along the Cape Fear River and reduces Fort Anderson. After dusk, the Confederates abandon the fort. Admiral Porter, during the year following the close of hostilities, is appointed as superintendent of the U.S. Naval Academy at Annapolis.

In South Carolina, Fort Sumter, held by the Confederates since 1861, surrenders and the Confederates evacuate Charleston. The U.S. fleet and Union troops combine to take control of the fort. At this time of evacuation, Charleston is commanded by Confederate General Lafayette McLaws due to the absence of General William Hardee, who is ill. The Rebels depart the city and head for Greensboro to link with Generals Beauregard and Wade Hampton. The Union also gains Fort Moultrie and Castle Pinckney. The Confederates self-destruct vessels in the harbor, including the Richmond class ironclad

rams CSS *Chicora* and CSS *Palmetto*, and the CSS *Charleston*. The *Charleston* had not entered the Confederate service until early 1864 and was unofficially known as the "Ladies Gunboat."

James Island is also evacuated. The CSS *Peedee*, a wooden gunboat in Confederate service since about April 1864, is destroyed by the Confederates in conjunction with the abandonment. The *Peedee* at the time is on the Pee Dee River more than 100 miles from Georgetown. Also, the CSS *Midge*, a torpedo boat built in Charleston during 1864, is captured. The *Midge* is taken to New York and placed on display at the navy yard until May 1877, when it is sold. And yet another vessel, the not yet completed CSS *David* (known as *David the Larger* and separate from the torpedo boat thought to have been captured art the same time), is seized and sent to Washington, D.C. *David the Larger* had been constructed in Charleston during 1864–1865. Also, the USS *Catskill*, during the final

Citizens of Charleston take an oath of allegiance to the Union (Mottelay, *The Soldier in Our Civil War*, 1886).

Left: Hulls intentionally sunk by Confederates prevent passage of Union warships into southern harbors (Mottelay, *The Soldier in Our Civil War*, 1886). *Right:* Winnsboro, South Carolina (*Harper's Pictoral History of the Civil War*, 1896)

operations against Charleston on the 17th–18th, seizes two blockade runners, the *Celt* and the *Deer.* The vessels attempt to escape, but both run aground and are destroyed by the *Catskill.* The *Catskill* remains at Charleston until July, when it sails north to Philadelphia to be decommissioned. The *Catskill* is for a short while renamed *Goliath* (June through August). Later it is reactivated and assigned duty along the East Coast. It is deactivated in 1877. During the Spanish American War, it is recommissioned and assigned patrol duty off the coast of New England. It remains active until decommissioned during September 1898. The *Catskill* is sold during 1901.

In Virginia, a contingent of the 14th Pennsylvania Cavalry skirmishes with Confederates at Ashby's Gap. The Union sustains six killed, 19 wounded and 64 missing. Also, the Confederate Senate rejects the earlier appointment of Colonel William M. Browne as brigadier general (11 November 1864).

In Union general officer activity, Colonel Galusha Pennypacker is promoted to brigadier general to rank from this day. Major General Gordon Granger becomes commanding officer of the 13th Corps, which is reorganized. Also, Major General Andrew J. Smith is appointed commanding general of the 16th Corps, which is also reorganized.

In Confederate general officer activity, Colonel Reuben L. Walker, chief of artillery, 3rd Corps, is promoted to the rank of brigadier general, effective this date. Walker had been chief of artillery for General Ambrose P. Hill. During the war, General Walker had participated in more than sixty actions. When the war is over he returns to his farm; however, during 1872, he moves from Virginia to Selma, Alabama, for a couple of years, where he works as an engineer for a railroad. He returns to Virginia during 1876 and becomes superintendent of the Richmond and Allegheny Railroad. Subsequently he

moves to Texas to superintend the construction of the state capitol in Austin, then returns to Virginia during 1888. He dies on his farm in Fluvanna County on 7 June 1890.

In other activity, Confederate Admiral Raphael Semmes (promoted February 10, 1865) assumes command of the James River Blockading Squadron. Also, Colonel William Raine Peck (9th Louisiana) is promoted to brigadier general. General Peck is paroled at Vicksburg on 6 June 1865. A conspicuous figure at about 6 feet, 6 inches tall, Peck, since his enlistment during June 1861, had consistently been on the fields of battle. Despite being a lucrative target, he never sustained even a minor wound during the war. After being paroled he returns to his plantation, known as the "Mountain," where he dies on 22 January 1871.

In Naval activity, the USS *Penobscot,* while on patrol at Aransas Pass, seizes two blockade runners, the *Louisa* and the *Mary Agnes,* both schooners. On the following day, a boat from the *Penobscot* boards the vessels and destroys both of them. These are the final seizures by the *Penobscot* for the duration of the war. It is decommissioned on 31 July at New York and sold on 19 October 1869.

February 18–22   In North Carolina, the Union defeats Confederate troops at Fort Anderson, Town Creek and Wilmington. The 23rd and 24th Corps and Admiral David D. Porter's gunboats participate. The Union suffers 40 dead and 204 wounded. The Confederates lose 70 killed, 400 wounded and 375 missing. At about this time, the CSS *Yadkin* is destroyed by Confederates to prevent capture.

February 19 (Sunday)   In South Carolina, Lt. Colonel Bennett, in command at Charleston, places the city under martial law.

In Naval activity, the USS *Pinola* seizes a Confederate private schooner, the *Anna Dale,* in Pass Cavallo, Texas.

February 20 (Monday)   In Florida, a contingent of Union troops skirmishes with Confederates at Fort Myers. Specific units and casualty figures are unavailable.

In South Carolina, General Sherman's army departs Columbia for Winnsboro and from there it advances to Fayetteville, North Carolina. Once again, Sherman sends a diversionary force towards Charlotte to fool Beauregard and cause confusion.

In North Carolina, Wilmington, the last of the Confederate-held ports, falls into Union hands. Union troops under General John Schofield land at Smithville, crossing the waterway with pontoon bridges south of the city, then the troops converge with another force hitting the town from the North side. Also, the 3rd Division, 23rd Corps, Army of the Ohio, clashes with Confederates at Town Creek. Forces of Generals Alfred H. Terry, Charles J. Paine and Adelbert Ames participate. At Wilmington, the Confederates destroy some vessels, including the wooden steamer gunboat CSS *Equator,* to prevent capture by the Union. In related activity, a boat attached to the USS *Shawmut* is blown up when it strikes a mine off Fort Anderson, while engaged in a mine clearing operation. The *Shawmut* has been participating in the operations against Wilmington since the 18th. The next month, the vessel is sent north to Hampton Roads, where it patrols in the area from White House, Virginia, to the mouth of the York River. Subsequent to General Robert E. Lee's surrender at Appomattox (April 1865), the *Shawmut* sails to New York, where it is decommissioned on 17 April; however, it is recommissioned on 15 June and sent to waters off Brazil to protect American interests there. On 26 December 1866, it again is decommissioned, but only for about six months. On 12 August 1867, the *Shawmut* joins the North Atlantic Squadron and afterward moves in and out of active service until 1877. It is sold that year on 27 September.

February 21 (Tuesday) **In Maryland,** a contingent of about 65 Confederate "Partisan Rangers" eludes a force of about 10,000 Union troops at Cumberland and succeeds in capturing Generals George Crook and Benjamin F. Kelley by snatching them right out of their private rooms in the Revere House. Both generals are transported to Richmond, Virginia, and later exchanged. Crook later marries Mary Daily (Dailey), the daughter of the proprietor of the Revere House. Crook's future brother-in-law is a member of the partisans that captures him and General Kelley. Kelley resigns from the army on 1 June 1865.

In Confederate general officer activity, Colonel William P. Roberts, initially a member of the 19th North Carolina Volunteers (subsequently the 2nd North Carolina Volunteers), is promoted to the rank of brigadier general, effective this date. Also, Colonel William Flank Perry is promoted to brigadier general. He returns to Alabama after the war, but he does not resume his law practice. He becomes a planter for about two years prior to moving to Kentucky to become a teacher. General Perry had no formal education; he taught himself. He dies on 18 December 1901 while a professor teaching English and philosophy at Ogden College.

February 22 (Wednesday) **In Arkansas,** the 13th Illinois Cavalry skirmishes with Confederates at Douglass Landing at Pine Bluff.

In North Carolina, at Wilmington, the Union forces fire a national salute in honor of the birthday of George Washington. Also, the 2nd and 3rd Divisions, 23rd Corps, Army of the Ohio, and a contingent of the 24th Corps, Army of the James, participate in the capture of Wilmington, an operation that had begun on the 20th.

In Naval activity, the USS *Lenapee,* which participates in the capture of Fort Anderson and the city of Wilmington, remains on the Cape Fear River with only two other warships to clear obstacles and to defend Wilmington. The *Lenapee* remains on duty until decommissioned on 17 October 1867. Subsequently, on 26 August 1868, the *Lenapee* is sold at Portsmouth, New Hampshire.

In Union general officer activity, Brigadier General Thomas John Wood is promoted to major general effective 27 January 1864. He remains in the army beyond the close of hostilities and retires after service in Mississippi during 1868.

February 23 (Thursday) **In North Carolina,** Confederates capture the garrisons at Athens and Sweetwater.

In South Carolina, Union troops from a U.S. naval fleet occupy Georgetown, subsequent to the Confederates abandoning it. The occupation force is composed of six companies of U.S. Marines, commanded by 1st Lieutenant George C. Stoddard.

In Confederate general officer activity, Colonel William Paul Roberts is promoted to

brigadier general. He is assigned command of a brigade in General W.H.F. Lee's division.

February 23–March 7 An army-naval force initiates an expedition to the mouth of the St. Mark's River (Florida). Union ground forces during the mission debark and destroy various Confederate installations. The USS *Honduras* participates in this expedition and afterward, remains on duty until July 1865, when it is ordered to sail north. The Honduras is decommissioned at New York on 5 August 1865 and sold on 5 September. It retains its name and remains in service until 1870.

February 24 (Friday) *In Union general officer activity,* Brigadier General William Thomas Ward receives the brevet of major general of volunteers to rank from this day. General Ward, in command of the 3rd Division since General Daniel Butterfield became ill during the Atlanta campaign, resigns from the army on 24 August 1865.

February 25 (Saturday) **In North Carolina,** the CSS *Chickamauga,* in Confederate service since 1864, is destroyed on the Cape Fear River in the vicinity of Wilmington to prevent capture. The *Chickamauga,* initially built in England, is a running screw steamer that was a blockade runner, the *Edith,* prior to its service with the Confederacy.

In Naval activity, the *Yucca* is acquired by the U.S. Navy. On 3 April 1865, just days before the surrender of General Robert E. Lee at Appomattox, it is commissioned; however, it sees no combat duty. After serving primarily in the Gulf of Mexico, it sails to Portsmouth, New Hampshire, where it is sold on 26 August 1868.

In Union general officer activity, Brigadier General Henry W. Birge is breveted major general. He remains in the service until October 1865.

February 26 (Sunday) **In Louisiana,** at Morganza, the commanding officer, Brigadier General Daniel Ullman, is ordered to repair to Cairo, Illinois, to await orders. After arriving at Cairo, he sees no further service. He receives the brevet of major general and musters out of the army during August 1865.

In South Carolina, a contingent of Union mounted troops, led by Captain Duncan, skirmishes with Confederate cavalry commanded by General Matthew C. Butler at Mount Clio. Also, the 15th Corps advances against Confederate positions at Lynch Creek.

In Tennessee, the 16th U.S. Colored Troops skirmishes with Confederates at Chattanooga.

In Naval activity, a naval squadron, including the USS *General Thomas,* crosses Elk River Shoals and initiates a bombardment of Confederate positions (General Roddey's command). The encampment is reduced. In addition, the Union flotilla debarks a landing force, which destroys a Confederate communication station at Lamb's Ferry, Alabama, and the troops confiscate supplies. The ships return to Bridge-

port, Alabama, on 4 March. The *General Thomas* resumes patrols in a sector between Bridgeport and Decatur until it is transferred to the War Department on 3 June 1865.

February 27 (Monday) **In Arkansas,** General John M. Thayer is relieved at Fort Smith. He receives command of the post at Saint Charles. Thayer's force is composed of one Kansas regiment and one battery. Thayer receives the rank of brevet major general at the conclusion of the war, and on 19 July 1865, he offers his resignation to the War Department. It is accepted. Subsequently, President U.S. Grant appoints Thayer as governor of the Wyoming Territory.

In North Carolina, General Hugh Kilpatrick's Union cavalry skirmishes with Generals Wade Hampton and Joseph Wheeler's Confederate cavalry in the vicinity of Lancaster, keeping the Confederates thinking that Charlotte is the next objective of General Sherman.

In Virginia, General Philip Sheridan departs Winchester with 10,000 cavalry troops to rid the Shenandoah of the Rebels under General Jubal Early.

In Naval activity, Rear Admiral John A. Dahlgren arrives at Georgetown, South Carolina, recently occupied by the Union. In other activity, the USS *Proteus,* while operating off Florida, seizes the steamer *Ruby.* The next month it participates in the expedition to St. Marks, Florida, prior to its voyage to New York that same month to be decommissioned. After the war the *Proteus* is sold (July 1865) and again named the *Carroll.* As a merchant ship, the *Car-*

Rear Admiral John Dahlgren (Mottelay, *The Soldier in Our Civil War*, 1886).

roll remains in service until it is scrapped during 1894. Also, the USS *Arizona* is destroyed by fire about forty miles below New Orleans.

February 28 (Tuesday) *In Union general officer activity,* Colonel Green Berry Raum, who was severely wounded at Missionary Ridge and out of action from then until February 1864, had received the brevet rank of brigadier general on 19 September 1864. On this day, he is promoted to full rank brigadier general, effective 15 February. Also, Brigadier General Gustavus Smith, who reverted to the rank of colonel on 4 March 1863 due to inaction by the Senate, is remustered into the service as colonel of the 35th Illinois. He has still not completely recuperated from serious wounds sustained at Pea Ridge (Elkhorn Tavern). Nonetheless, he is back in the field and will participate on guard duty with his regiment to protect the Nashville and Chattanooga Railroad. At the close of hostilities, Smith is breveted brigadier general of volunteers. He musters out of the service on 14 December 1865. President Grant appoints his friend General Smith as internal revenue collector for the District of New Mexico in 1869. He dies in Santa Fe on 11 December 1885.

In Naval activity, Flag Officer Samuel Barron, Sr., in command of Confederate officers in Europe, resigns his commission. Barron had been in command of the naval forces at Forts Hatteras and Clark during 1861. Also, Colonel Tyree Bell (12th Tennessee) is commissioned brigadier general. General Bell had participated at the Battle of Richmond, Kentucky, and during January 1864, he receives command of a brigade. Subsequent to the close of hostilities, Bell relocates in California. He dies on 1 September 1902 at New Orleans after having traveled to Tennessee for a Confederate reunion.

March 1865   At about this time, a Confederate vessel transporting Confederate General Camille Prince de Polignac (born in France) runs the Union naval blockade and makes its way towards France. De Polignac is on a mission to attempt to persuade France (Napoleon III) to enter the war on the Southern side. However, the war comes to a conclusion before de Polignac reaches his destination. In the absence of de Polignac, Brigadier General Allen Thomas (brother in law of General Richard Taylor) assumes command of his division. General Polignac, in Spain when the war concludes, returns to France and begins intensive studies of mathematics; however, he joins the French Army during the Franco–Prussian War and commands a division. Afterward, he resumes his mathematics studies. General de Polignac, the last surviving Confederate major general, dies in Paris on 15 November 1913. General Allen Thomas engages in various activities after the war, including being a planter in Louisiana. He also serves as U.S. consul and minister to Venezuela. He resides in Florida and then moves to a plantation in Mississippi during 1897; he dies there on 3 December of that year.

In other activity, the United States informs Canada that it is going to void, effective March

1866, the Canadian Reciprocity Treaty that was consummated in 1854. U.S. leaders believe the Canadians have taken advantage of the war in the United States to reap great profits from the fishing rights along the East Coast of the U.S.

In Union general officer activity, Brigadier General Benjamin Alvord is relieved of duty as commander of the Department of Oregon. He travels back to the East. Alvord resigns his volunteer commission during August and soon after, during September, he becomes Army paymaster in New York City and later paymaster general, U.S. Army (1872). He retires as brigadier general during 1876.

In Naval activity, the gunboat USS *Pontiac* seizes the CSS *Amazon,* formerly an ironclad, which is transporting a cargo of cotton. This is the final seizure by the *Pontiac.* After the war, it sails from Charleston to New York and is decommissioned in New York on 21 June 1865. The *Pontiac* is sold on 15 October 1867 and renamed the *Larkspur.*

March 1 (Wednesday)   *In Confederate general officer activity,* Colonel Alexander William Campbell is promoted to brigadier general. General Campbell remains with General Forrest's corps until its defeat and surrender at Selma during early April. Also, Colonel Ellison Capers (24th South Carolina), who succeeded to brigade command following the death of General States Rights Gist at the Battle of Franklin, is promoted to brigadier general. After the war, General Capers becomes an Episcopal minister. He is ordained a bishop during 1894. Upon his death in April 1909, he is interred at the Trinity Churchyard in Columbia, South Carolina. A monument is erected with the following inscription: "He rendered unto Caesar the things that are Caesar's and unto God the things that are God's."

In Naval activity, the USS *Harvest Moon* (flagship of Rear Admiral Dahlgren) is destroyed by a Confederate torpedo (mine) in the vicinity of Georgetown, South Carolina. One of its crewmen is lost. The side-wheeled steamship had been built during 1862 at Portland, Maine, and was acquired by the U.S. Navy during 1863. Commissioned in February 1864, it was assigned to the South Atlantic Blockading Squadron.

In Virginia, the 3rd Brigade, 3rd Cavalry Division, Army of the Potomac, under General Henry Capehart, clashes with Confederates led by General Thomas L. Rosser as part of Sheridan's Raid. In Petersburg, General U.S. Grant instructs his forces to "keep a keen eye on the anticipated breakout of Lee's besieged army." Confederate President Jefferson Davis and General Robert E. Lee acknowledge the necessity of breaking away and joining Johnston in an attempt to crush Sherman. General Lee, aware that Petersburg and Richmond can no longer hold out against overpowering forces, is attempting to pull off a major miracle. Meanwhile, General Sherman's army continues its march through the Carolinas, with its strength

standing at 51,598 infantrymen, 44,001 cavalry and 1,677 artillerymen.

In other activity, Union cavalry (Sheridan's Raid) under General Thomas C. Devin attack and capture Staunton. Devin receives his official commission several days later, on March 13.

In Naval activity, the USS *Trefoil,* a wooden-hulled screw steamer, is commissioned at Boston. The ship had been constructed during 1864 and acquired by the U.S. Navy on 4 February 1865. Acting Master Charles C. Wells receives command of the ship, which is assigned to the West Gulf Blockading Squadron.

In Union general officer activity, Brigadier General Thomas Hewson Neill, at about this time (March), is breveted major general in the volunteers and brigadier general in the Regular Army. Neill had been on the staff of General Sheridan, but apparently only until the end of the previous year. Subsequent to the close of hostilities, General Neill remains in the service. In 1866 he reverts to his permanent rank of major and serves in the infantry until 1870, when he is transferred to a cavalry unit. Afterward, he is appointed commandant of West Point. Following his service at the military academy, he is appointed colonel of the U.S. 8th Cavalry and assigned duty on the Texas frontier. He retires during 1883.

March 2 (Thursday)   Robert E. Lee requests negotiations with President Abraham Lincoln. His request is turned down.

In Louisiana, the 4th Wisconsin Cavalry engages Confederates at Clinton.

In South Carolina, the vanguard of the 17th Corps (General Sherman's command) attacks Cheraw and captures it by the following day.

In Virginia (Sheridan's Raid), General Philip Sheridan's troops (General Custer's cavalry) enter the town of Chesterfield and clash with a contingent of General Matthew C. Butler's cavalry. The Confederates are compelled to retreat. Other troops under Sheridan clash with Confederates under Major General Jubal Early at Waynesboro. The Rebels sustain heavy casualties and abandon most of their supplies, leaving the wagons behind as they retire. General Gabriel Wharton's command is scattered by the Union thrust. Custer finishes off Early's command, which had scored many successes until overmatched by General Philip Sheridan in September at Winchester. Confederate Brigadier General Gabriel Wharton's brigade also disperses. Wharton will be paroled at Lynchburg during June. General Sheridan orders General Custer and General Thomas C. Devin to accompany him to Petersburg. A small contingent under General George H. Chapman, however, remains in the valley with some artillery and a small brigade. General Chapman resigns his commission on 7 January 1866. Afterward, he becomes a judge in Indiana, and later he is elected to the state Senate.

In Union general officer activity, Colonel John Henry Ketcham (150th New York), having been

Left: The final meeting of the Confederate cabinet (Johnson, *Campfire and Battlefield: History of the Conflicts and Campaigns,* 1894). *Right:* Union forces (Sherman's XVII Corps) drive Confederates out of Cheraw, South Carolina (Mottelay, *The Soldier in Our Civil War,* 1886).

elected to Congress, resigns his commission. Although Ketcham had not commanded more than one regiment through the various campaigns, while in Congress, he receives the brevet of major general of volunteers on 13 March. He receives the full rank of brigadier general on 23 October 1865. Afterward, Ketchum is re-elected to Congress at least seventeen times over the span of about forty years. He suffered one defeat, and on another occasion, he declined accepting the nomination. General Ketcham dies while in office as a New York Congressman on 4 November 1906.

March 3 (Friday) In South Carolina, General Sherman, still on the march toward Cheraw from Chesterfield, stops to ask a Negro if any guerrillas are on the route. The man replies: "Oh; no master, dey is gone two days ago; you could have played cards on der coat-tails, dey was in such a hurry." The Union then occupies the town, which is abandoned by General William Hardee's forces. General Wade Hampton moves his cavalry toward Charlotte, and later, he joins with Hardee on the 11th at Fayetteville, North Carolina. In other activity, a contingent of Union mounted infantry (General Sherman's command) skirmishes with Confederates at Florence.

In Naval activity, the stern-wheel steamer *Mist,* constructed at Pittsburgh, Pennsylvania, during 1864 and acquired by the U.S. Navy on 24 December 1864, is commissioned at Mound City, Illinois, after being transformed into a tinclad gunboat. Acting Master W.E.H. Fontress receives command. It is assigned duty to the 8th District, Mississippi Squadron, and during the final months of the war, it patrols the river

to protect steamers and to guard the various towns and villages from Confederate raiders. After the war, the *Mist* is decommissioned on 4 August 1865. It is sold at auction at Mound City, Illinois, on 17 September 1865. As a commercial vessel, the *Mist* remains in service until 1874.

March 4 (Saturday) In Washington, D.C., Abraham Lincoln is inaugurated to his second term as president of the United States. Andrew Johnson is his vice president.

In Confederate general officer activity, General William Wirt Allen is appointed major general by President Jefferson C. Davis. The Confederate Senate is unable to act upon the promotion, which coincidentally is the final appointment to major general by Jefferson Davis. Consequently, upon his parole in North Carolina, Allen retains the rank of brigadier. He subsequently returns to private life and at one point becomes a U.S. marshal during the first administration of Grover Cleveland (1885–1889).

March 5 (Sunday) In Virginia (Sheridan's Raid), Union cavalry (General Sheridan's command) defeats a remnant contingent of General Jubal Early's force around Staunton and in the vicinity of Charlottesville. Confederate General Early escapes and makes it to Mexico, where he remains for several years, but most of his force is by now captured by Union cavalry. Meanwhile, General Philip Sheridan continues his advance toward Lynchburg in an attempt to hook up with the advancing forces of General William T. Sherman near Danville, but bad weather and swollen streams force Sheridan to change plans. Instead, he heads toward White House to join with the forces of General Ulysses S. Grant at Petersburg. While Sheridan advances, his troops destroy the rails that lead to Richmond and Lynchburg.

In Florida, Confederate-held St. Mark's, Florida, is attacked by the USS *Magnolia* and *Hendrick Hudson* this day and the next. During this action, the U.S. Army troops handle the navy's guns. The *Hendrick Hudson* then resumes patrols. It is decommissioned during August 1865 and sold the following month. It remains active until November 1867, when it is wrecked off Havana, Cuba, on the 13th.

In Union general officer activity, Brigadier General Charles Croft receives the brevet rank of major general. After the war, on 24 August, General Croft musters out of the army.

In Naval activity, the USS *Western World* arrives on the Rappahannock River to provide naval support to the ground forces operating near Fredericksburg. Subsequently, it moves to Maryland to patrol with the Potomac Flotilla and afterward operates in Mobjack Bay (Virginia) until April. Later it sails to the Washington Navy Yard, where it is decommissioned on 26 May and sold at auction on 24 June.

March 6 (Monday) In Louisiana, the 4th Wisconsin Cavalry skirmishes with Confederates at Olive Branch. The Union sustains three killed and two wounded.

In South Carolina, General William T. Sherman's army departs Cheraw by crossing the Pee Dee River and heading directly to Fayetteville, North Carolina, to attack Generals Wade Hampton and William Hardee.

In Virginia, a contingent of Union cavalry led by Colonel Thompson (Sheridan's Raid) clashes with Confederates commanded by General Thomas L. Rosser at North Fork in the Shenandoah. The Confederates are driven away.

In Florida, the 2nd and 99th U.S. Colored Troops, bolstered by other units, battle Confederates under General Samuel Jones at Natural Bridge (Tallahassee). The Rebels hold steadfastly, preventing the Union from seizing St.

Marks, located south of Tallahassee along the coast. General Jones had recently been relieved of command at the Department of Western Virginia and assigned to the Department of South Carolina, Georgia and Florida. Tallahassee will remain in Confederate hands until the beginning of May. After returning home, General Jones engages in farming and later works for the War Department. He dies at Bedford Springs, Virginia, on 31 July 1887.

March 7 (Tuesday)   In North Carolina, Union cavalry commanded by General Hugh Kilpatrick engages Confederates at Rockingham.

March 8 (Wednesday)   In North Carolina, General William T. Sherman, while in Laurel Hill, sends two identical messages by separate couriers to Union forces at Wilmington: "We are marching for Fayetteville, Will be there Saturday, Sunday and Monday, and will then march for Goldsboro." In other activity, a Union contingent under General John Schofield clashes with Confederates in the vicinity of Kinston.

March 8–10   In North Carolina, Confederates led by Colonel Upham (General Braxton Bragg's command) attack Union forces under General Jacob D. Cox at Wilcox's Bridge. The Union receives reinforcements, forcing Bragg to break off and retire toward Kinston. The Union suffers 80 dead, 421 wounded and 600 missing. The Confederates sustain about 1,500 killed, wounded or missing. The 1st and 2nd Divisions of the District of Beaufort and the 1st Division, 23rd Corps, Army of the Ohio, participate.

March 9 (Thursday)   In Union general officer activity, Brigadier General Christopher Columbus Andrews is breveted major general of volunteers. Andrews remains in the service until January of the following year.

March 10 (Friday)   In North Carolina, a contingent of Confederate General Wade Hampton's cavalry raids General Kilpatrick's quarters in the vicinity of Fayetteville at the stroke of dawn. Kilpatrick's men escape through

a swamp, but the Confederates capture enormous numbers of horses and free many Confederate prisoners. The Union regroups and countercharges. The attack succeeds and drives the Rebels back, which will permit Kilpatrick's troops to occupy Fayetteville. Other units of Kilpatrick's cavalry, led by General John Schofield, clash with Confederates under General Bragg at Monroe Crossroads (Kinston). The Union sustains about 1,000 killed, wounded and missing. The Confederates sustain about 1,200 killed and wounded and 400 captured. General Kilpatrick, known for embellishing his exploits and at times using eloquent fiction, does not drink or play cards; however, his reputation with the ladies is well known. Kilpatrick is known to have barely escaped capture during the raid because he was with a Southern woman. Had he waited to completely put on his uniform, he would have most probably been captured. In other activity, Union General Sheridan reaches Columbia while en route to White House.

March 11 (Saturday)   In Arkansas, the Union 3rd Wisconsin Cavalry skirmishes with Confederates at Clear Lake.

In North Carolina, General Henry Slocum arrives at Fayetteville with General Jefferson C. Davis' 14th Corps. The Confederate cavalry under General Wade Hampton and William J. Hardee had avoided capture by burning the bridge they had crossed to escape. Major General Matthew C. Butler also participates in this action. General Slocum remains in the army beyond the close of hostilities and resigns on 28 September 1865.

March 12 (Sunday)   In North Carolina, troops under General Sherman at Fayetteville become ecstatic as an approaching vessel turns out to be a U.S. warship. The earlier messages sent by Sherman had reached Wilmington, and the vessel that arrives with General Alfred Terry is laden with supplies. The USS *Maratanza*, two other gunboats and the *Eolus* make the rendezvous at Fayetteville, and with the link-up, communication is established between Sherman and the fleet. The *Maratanza*, subsequent to the close of hostilities, is detached from its station on the Cape Fear River during June 1865 and sent north, where it is decommissioned at the Portsmouth Navy Yard on 21 June. Later, during 1868, the *Maratanza* is sold.

After Fayetteville is in Union hands, Sherman states in a letter to Grant: "If I can now add Goldsboro without too much cost, I will be in a position to aid you materially in the spring campaign." In another letter on the same day to Secretary of War Stanton, Sherman states:

"My army is as united and cheerful as ever and as full of confidence in itself and its leaders."

In Naval activity, the USS *Quaker City,* while on patrol in the Gulf of Mexico, overtakes and seizes the schooner *R. H. Vermilyea.*

March 13 (Monday)   In Virginia, Confederate President Jefferson Davis signs a bill which grants freedom to any slave enlisting in the Confederate Army. Confederate General Patrick R. Cleburne, killed at Franklin, Tennessee, on 30 November 1864, greatly supported this action.

In North Carolina, the advance units of the 14th and 17th Corps engage Confederates at Silver Run, Fayetteville. Also, General Sherman's army crosses the Cape Fear River and continues its march toward Goldsboro to capture the city and vanquish Confederate General Joseph E. Johnston's 32,000 defenders.

In Union general officer activity, Brigadier General William Birney is breveted major general. Brigadier General John Ramsay (Ramsey) receives the rank of brevet major general. He was breveted brigadier general on 2 December 1864. He participates during the siege of Petersburg. After the war he is mustered out of the service on 17 July 1865. Brigadier General Marcena R. Patrick, who has been provost marshal general of all armies under Grant, is promoted to brevet major general. Brigadier General (Volunteers) John J. Abercrombie is breveted brigadier general in the Regular Army. He retires form the Army during June of this year. Brigadier General Joseph K. Barnes (surgeon general), Colonel Morgan Henry Chrysler, who entered service with the 30th New York Regiment as a private during 1861, and Brigadier General James Deering Fessenden receive the brevet rank of major general. Fessenden remains in the U.S. Army until 1866, when he resigns in conjunction with the army's reorganization. Like his brother, General Francis Fessenden, James returns to his career as an attorney. Kenner Garrard, brevet major general of volunteers, receives the brevet rank of brigadier and major general in the Regular Army. General Garrard resigns his commission on 9 November 1866.

Also, Brigadier General John Gibbon receives the rank of brevet major general. General Gibbon remains in the army beyond the close of hostilities. On 10 July 1885, he is appointed brigadier general in the U.S. Army. He retires during 1891. General Quincy Adams Gillmore receives the brevet rank of brigadier and major general in the regular service. After the war, General Gillmore resigns his volunteer commission but remains in the regular service as major of engineers. He becomes a lieutenant colonel during 1874, and during 1883 he is promoted to colonel. Brigadier General John Franklin Miller is breveted major general. He remains in command at Nashville until he leaves the service on 25 September 1865. General Miller turns down a colonelcy in the U.S. Army and returns to California. Subsequently, he is elected (by the state legislature) to the U.S. Senate in 1880, and while in office, he dies during March 1886.

Heavy fighting between Union and Confederate troops at Kinston, North Carolina (Mottelay, *The Soldier in Our Civil War,* 1886).

Major General (volunteers) Joseph Anthony Mower is breveted major general in the Regular Army. After the reorganization of the U.S. Army during 1866, General Mower assumes command of the 39th Regiment (colored troops). Later, during 1869, he transfers to the 25th Infantry Regiment. Afterward, while commanding officer at New Orleans in the Department of Louisiana, General Mower dies on 6 January 1870. Also, Brigadier General Marsena Rudolph Patrick (provost marshal general) receives the brevet of major general of volunteers. Subsequent to the defeat of the Confederates, General Patrick receives command at Richmond.

Brigadier General Galusha Pennypacker receives the brevet of major general of volunteers, effective this date. General Pennypacker also receives the brevet rank of major general in the Regular Army during 1867. Upon the reorganization of the army in 1866, he becomes colonel of the 34th Infantry, which he commands until he retires during 1883. In yet other activity, Brigadier General Edward Elmer Potter receives the brevet rank of major general. He resigns from the service on 24 July, 1865. Colonel Francis Trowbridge Sherman receives the brevet of brigadier general.

Also, Brigadier General John Wesley Turner receives the brevet of brigadier general and major general of the Regular Army. He remains in the army beyond the close of hostilities and in June 1865 receives command of the District of Henrico, which includes Richmond, Virginia, and retains the post until April 1866. Afterward, he musters out of the volunteers and reverts to the rank of colonel. He serves as depot commissary at St. Louis for about five years prior to retiring during 1871. Also, Major General Horatio Gouverneur Wright is breveted major general in the Regular Army. Subsequent to mustering out of the volunteers, he reverts to his rank of lieutenant colonel of engineers, and during 1879, he is promoted to brigadier general and raised to chief engineer of the army. After retirement about 1884, he remains in Washington, D.C., where he dies on 2 July 1899.

In Naval activity, the ram CSS *Neuse* is destroyed by the Confederates to prevent capture by the Union.

March 14 (Tuesday) *In Confederate general officer activity,* General Mark Perrin Lowrey, who commanded troops in the corps of Generals William J. Hardee and John B. Hood during the conflict and participated in such battles as Nashville and Franklin, resigns his commission this day.

In North Carolina, Union forces occupy Kinston.

March 15 (Wednesday)   In North Carolina, Union General Hugh Kilpatrick's cavalry engages the Confederate rear guards at Taylor's Hole Creek. Confederate Colonel Albert Rhett, the former commander of Fort Sumter, is captured by Kilpatrick's force. Rhett expresses disgust at having been captured without a fight.

Sherman's force is advancing toward Goldsboro. He dispatches his left wing toward Raleigh as a diversion to confuse the Rebels and keep them from gaining a proper perspective on his movements. General Joseph Johnston, concerned about Raleigh, raises a force at Smithfield, and General William Hardee heads from Fayetteville to Raleigh to meet the threat.

In Virginia, the 2nd Brigade, 3rd Division, Army of the Potomac (General Philip Sheridan's force) reaches Ashland, where it is struck hard by a Confederate force, but the Union repulses the attack and continues the journey, crossing the South and North Anna Rivers. The column arrives at White House on the 19th. Also, the 5th U.S. Cavalry, led by General Thomas C. Devin, clashes with Confederates at the South Anna River. Devin's force destroys the bridge at the river.

In Naval activity, the USS *Periwinkle* and the USS *Morse,* attached to the Potomac Flotilla, on or about this day arrive at the Rappahannock and Piankatank Rivers to establish a blockade to defend a fleet of "oyster schooners" which have been imperiled by a Confederate force. In addition to protecting the fishermen, the gunboats also engage in clearing mines, and their presence disrupts Confederate runners carrying contraband flowing between lower Maryland and Virginia. In conjunction, the *Periwinkle* remains with the Potomac Flotilla until June 1865, when it is ordered to Norfolk. Afterward, it operates out of the navy yard until 1867, when it is placed in ordinary. However, during 1870, it returns to service and participates in an expedition to the Arctic for scientific purposes (Hall Scientific Expedition). Following the duty in the Arctic, the *Periwinkle* reports to the Washington Navy Yard on 9 June 1871 for repairs. Renamed the *Polaris,* during July 1872 the vessel again sails to the Arctic, commanded by Captain Charles F. Hall. It departs from New York during July falls short of its objective, the North Pole, but reaches farther north than any other ship. While sailing back to the U.S. in October 1872, the *Polaris* gets trapped in a wall of ice that carries the ship aimlessly for a short distance and then crushes it. The crew, however, escapes death and is rescued.

March 16 (Thursday)   In Virginia, General U.S. Grant writes to General William T. Sherman: "I deemed the capture of Wilmington the greatest importance. Butler came near losing that prize to us. But Terry and Schofield [Army of the Ohio] have since retrieved his blunders."

In North Carolina, Confederate troops under General William Hardee (Joseph E. Johnston's command) encounter Sherman's army while en route to Raleigh. Union troops under General Nathaniel J. Jackson (XX Corps) are bolstered by the commands of Generals Ward and Kilpatrick at Averasboro (Smith's Farm). A fierce exchange is ignited. The Confederates fight hard but are pushed back. General William B. Taliaferro's troops hold well for several hours, but the Union pressure forces the Rebels to fall back to the next line. With the support of General Lafayette McLaws, the line is also held there. Nonetheless, the flank is extremely weak and the continuing pressure compels the Rebels to withdraw during the night and move to Smithfield. The Union sustains 77 killed and 477 wounded. The Confederates suffer 108 killed, 540 wounded and many captured, including about 217 men from Colonel Rhett's brigade. General Hardee withdraws on the 17th. Subsequent to this battle, Union General Joseph A. Mower resumes permanent command of the XX Corps and General Nathaniel Jackson is relieved of his temporary command of the 1st Division. He is replaced by General A.S. Williams. Jackson receives an honorable discharge during August 1865.

In Georgia, Union forces under General William T. Sherman capture Columbus. Union Major General John G. Mitchell participates.

In Naval activity, the USS *Quaker City* seizes the vessel *Telemico* in the Gulf of Mexico. In other activity, a Union flotilla, including the USS *Heliotrope,* initiates a two-day mission to Maddox Creek. A detachment aboard boats from the *Heliotrope* succeeds in seizing three schooners and a large cache of supplies. Subsequent to this activity, the *Heliotrope* continues to patrol along the Potomac until ordered north during April. It arrives in New York on the 20th. It is decommissioned during June 1865 and sold on 17 June to the Department of the Treasury, which assigns it to the Lighthouse Service.

March 17 (Friday)   In Tennessee, Union General Wilson departs Nashville with a cavalry force of about 15,000 troopers to raid Alabama.

In Confederate general officer activity, Colonel William P. Hardeman, 4th Texas Cavalry, is appointed brigadier general, effective this date. It is a little late for Hardeman to contribute much to the crumbling Confederacy as a general, but he had fought with valor at such places as Valverde, New Mexico, when Confederates under General Sibley were beaten by General Edward R.S. Canby, and he distinguished himself during the strong Confederate campaign against General Banks on the Red River. Also, Colonel Henry Gray, who joined the Confederacy as a private and rose to colonel of the 28th Louisiana Infantry, is promoted to brigadier general. At this time he is a member of the Confederate Congress as a representative of the northern portion of Louisiana. In other activity, Colonel Walter Paye Lane is promoted to brigadier general. General Lane returns to Texas and becomes a merchant after the war.

In Naval activity, the USS *Wandank* encounters a strong Rebel force in the vicinity of Maddox Creek (Virginia). Heavy fire from the howitzers on board ship forces the Rebels to withdraw. Confederate fire severely damages the *Wandank.* At one point, the artillery fire is so heavy it cuts the oars in half and severs the barrel off a musket. Boatswains Mate Patrick Mullen becomes the recipient of the Medal of Honor for his heroic actions during this battle.

Mullen receives a second award for bravery on 1 May 1865. Also, the USS *Hunchback*, operating along the James River, is ordered to return to North Carolina. It returns to its patrol duty in the sounds and various other places, including the Chowan River, but only for a short duration. On 1 April, it is ordered north, where it is decommissioned on 12 June and afterward sold. The *Hunchback* is operated as a ferry boat (New York and Brooklyn Ferry Company) in New York, and it is renamed the General Grant during 1866. In other activity, the USS *Quaker City* captures the vessel *George Burkhart*. On the following day, while off Brazos Santiago, Texas, it accepts the surrender of the vessel *Cora*, a Confederate steamer. After the termination of the war, the *Quaker City* is decommissioned at the Philadelphia Navy Yard on 18 May 1865. It is sold at auction on 20 June.

March 18 (Saturday) In North Carolina, General Sherman's army arrives to a point within five miles of Bentonville and slightly more than 20 miles from Goldsboro. The weather remains terrible and the roads continue to present major problems. General Joseph E. Johnston, convinced that Sherman's lines are spread too thin and unable to form quickly enough to react, plans to spring an attack. He is massing a force at Bentonville. Confederate reinforcements are also en route. General Roswell S. Ripley's force had been directed to join Johnston, and it arrives and participates in the contest. After the war, General Ripley travels to England; however, his business venture does not succeed. He returns to the U.S. and resides in Charleston. Later, during March 1887, he succumbs while in New York City. In other activity, the Confederate Congress convenes for the final time. One of its last acts has been to induct slaves into the Confederate Army, and by this service they are automatically to receive their freedom.

In Alabama, the 109th U.S. Colored Troops skirmishes with Confederates at Boyd's Station.

In Confederate general officer activity, Brigadier General Thomas James Churchill is appointed major general, effective this date. Subsequently, he becomes state treasurer (1874–1880) of Arkansas, and he is elected governor of the state during 1880. He succumbs in Little Rock on 14 May 1905. In addition, Brigadier General John S. Marmaduke is promoted to the rank of major general effective 17 March. Marmaduke is the last Confederate officer promoted to the rank of major general; however, it is of small value, as Marmaduke remains in prison since his capture during the previous year. Subsequent to his release from Fort Warren, General Marmaduke returns to Mississippi and engages in the insurance business. In 1884 he is elected governor. He dies in office prior to the expiration of his term, on 28 December 1887.

March 19 (Sunday) In Virginia, Union General Philip Sheridan reaches his supply base at White House, and he remains in this area until the 24, when he jumps off en route for the James River.

In Naval activity, the USS *Massachusetts* strikes a mine in Charleston Harbor, but it fails to detonate. The *Massachusetts* is able to remain in service for the duration. It is decommissioned in New York in September 1865. It is sold and renamed the *Crescent City* in October 1867 and afterward operates as a civilian vessel until 1892.

March 19–21 BATTLE OF BENTONVILLE A Union force — composed of the 14th and 20th Corps, the left wing, and the 15th and 17th Corps, the right wing, bolstered by General Hugh Kilpatrick's cavalry — engages and defeats a Confederate force under General Joseph E. Johnston at Bentonville, North Carolina. General Wade Hampton's cavalry engages elements of the 14th Corps under General Jefferson C. Davis at a point about eight miles outside of Bentonville. Davis is compelled to fall back, but in the meantime General Henry Slocum's force moves up and takes the offensive. The skirmish becomes a slugfest, as the determined Rebels refuse to slack off and the confident troops of Sherman are unwilling to give ground. Both sides batter each other throughout the day. The fighting subsides as darkness overtakes the area. During the tranquility of the night, General Sherman speeds reinforcements to the front. Generals Howard, Logan and Hugh Kilpatrick each send forces from Sherman's left wing. Simultaneously, Sherman directs the 15th Corps at Goldsboro to drive down to strike Johnston's flank.

On the 20th Sherman remains on the field, and he concludes that Johnston intends to retain his dominant positions to buy time to execute a disciplined retirement to Smithfield. By noon on the 21st, Sherman presses for the advantage, and soon after, General Joseph Mower's troops find a hole. From their positions on Sherman's far right, Mower's boys maneuver swiftly to gain positions in Johnston's rear. They are met there by General Joseph Wheeler's cavalry and by infantry under General Robert Lowry (Benjamin Cheatham's division). All the while, General Oliver O. Howard remains unaware of Mower's situation. Suddenly, after he hears the ruckus, he directs General Francis Blair to advance his 17th Corps to the right. Following this, he orders General John Logan to move forward and strike Bragg's front. In the meantime, General Sherman steps in to drastically change the strategy. Fearful of losing men unnecessarily in the swamps, he cancels Logan's attack and waits for what he believes is imperative to the Rebels: that Johnston retreat to regroup his entire army. Sherman calculates that Johnston will reform on more open ground in the vicinity of Neuse.

General Alfred H. Terry's force is advancing toward the identical spot.

As suspected, the Confederates retire during the night of the 21st. Sherman reinitiates his advance on the 22nd. The Rebel forces number about 15,000, but the cavalry of Generals Matthew C. Butler and Joseph Wheeler do not arrive in time, and another 2,000 troops under General Benjamin F. Cheatham fail to make it in time. The Union suffers 191 dead, 1,168 wounded and 287 missing. The Confederates have 267 dead, 1,200 wounded and 1,625 missing. Union Corporal George Clute, 14th Michigan Infantry Regiment, captures the flag of the 40th North Carolina. Clute becomes a recipient of the Medal of Honor for his heroism during this battle. Confederate Brigadier General Daniel Harris Reynolds is wounded and loses one leg. He is paroled at Charlottesville, Virginia, during the latter part of May 1865. Subsequently, he returns to his law practice in Arkansas and serves one term in the state legislature. Cheatham loses a bid for the U.S. Congress during 1872, but afterward, he becomes the superintendent of prisons in Nashville, Tennessee. He also becomes postmaster of Nashville, a position he holds until his death on 5 September 1886.

Confederate General Robert Lowry, who assumed command of a brigade subsequent to the death of General John Adams, participates in this battle, and he continues to serve with Johnston until the conclusion of hostilities. He is pardoned in May. Following service in the state Senate, he is elected governor of Mississippi. Confederate Brigadier General Stephen Elliott, Jr., is also wounded, which follows a severe wound that he had sustained the previous July at Petersburg. This new wound essentially terminates his service. The wounds take a high toll on Elliott, and by 1866, they hasten his demise. He succumbs during February 1866, while a member of the South Carolina state legislature. Confederate Brigadier General Jacob H. Sharp participates at this action and it seems to be his last appearance in the field. There is no record of him receiving a parole at Greensboro. After

General Schofield's forces pass the Confederate works at Wilmington as they advance to Goldsboro, North Carolina (Mottelay, *The Soldier in Our Civil War*, 1886).

the war he resumes his law practice. Later he acquires the *Columbus Independent*, a Mississippi newspaper, and he becomes president of the Mississippi Press Association. Also, he serves in the state legislature from 1886 to 1890 and for a while, is speaker of the house. He dies at Columbus, Mississippi, in September 1907.

Confederate General Lawrence S. Baker participates at Bentonville. General Baker had been severely wounded several times prior to this skirmish and is not in the best of health due to these earlier wounds. Confederate General Alpheus Baker also participates in this battle, and his force captures a large Union contingent. Subsequent to the surrender, General Baker returns to Alabama and resumes his law practice. Confederate Major General Daniel H. Hill participates in this action in command of a division.

Union Colonel (later brigadier general, May 1865) Robert F. Catterson participates. He began his career as an enlisted man and fought at Kernstown and Vicksburg, and with Sherman on the March to the Sea. Union General John G. Mitchell also participates, as does Confederate Brigadier General Joseph Benjamin Palmer.

March 20 (Monday)   In North Carolina, General Sherman continues to advance, destroying Confederate war supplies and facilities as the columns move.

In Union activity, the 19th Corps is disbanded. Its last major participation in the field was at Cedar Creek (Middleton), Virginia, the previous October.

In Confederate activity, Brigadier General Joseph Finegan, in Virginia since May of the previous year, returns with his brigade to Florida. After the war Finegan serves in the Florida legislature (1865–1866) and then becomes a cotton broker operating out of Savannah, Georgia. Later he retires and returns to Florida, where he succumbs on 29 October 1885.

March 20–April 6   In Tennessee, General George Stoneman's raiders (Union cavalry) depart Jonesborough en route to North Carolina. Stoneman's cavalry skirmishes at various places, including the towns of Boone and Snow Hill. Stoneman destroys the rails as he advances and continues to rip up the rails as far Lynchburg. General Stoneman subsequently turns south to get behind Johnston at nearly the same time General Sherman is negotiating surrender terms with Johnston.

March 21 (Tuesday)   In North Carolina, Union troops under General John Schofield (General Sherman's command) occupy Goldsboro.

In Virginia, the 12th Pennsylvania Cavalry skirmishes with Confederates at Hamilton.

March 22 (Wednesday)   In North Carolina, General William T. Sherman, following the action against General Joseph E. Johnston at Averasboro and Bentonville, reinitiates his march

and arrives at Goldsboro on the following day. (See also, **March 19–21 BATTLE OF BENTONVILLE**).

In Naval activity, the *Florence Miller* (sternwheel river steamer), acquired by the U.S. and converted into a gunboat, is commissioned the USS *Oriole*. It had earlier, while still the *Florence Miller*, been assigned by the navy to the Mississippi Squadron during early February. On this day, the *Oriole* embarks from Mound City, Illinois, to join the squadron. Upon arrival it prepares to patrol the Mississippi on a stretch between Natchez and Vicksburg. After the war, the *Oriole* is decommissioned on 4 July 1865 at Mound City, and on 17 August is sold.

March 22–April 24   In Tennessee, Union General James H. Wilson begins his expedition from Tennessee into Alabama, with a mission for his cavalry to destroy the Southern railroads and the munitions depot at Selma. There are also actions at Elyton, Chickasaw and Montevallo, Alabama, and Macon, Georgia. General Wilson's command engages and defeats Nathan B. Forrest's force at Selma on 2 April before his cavalry swings eastward to strike the remnants of the Confederates still roaming the region. The Union suffers 63 dead, 345 wounded and 63 missing. The Confederates suffer 22 dead, 38 wounded and 6,766 prisoners. A contemporary source lists the Union casualties at 99 killed, 598 wounded and 28 missing, and Confederate casualties at 1,200 killed and wounded and 6,820 captured. In addition, the Confederates lose 288 guns.

March 23 (Thursday)   In North Carolina, General William T. Sherman's army occupies Goldsboro, culminating an extraordinary march of 425 miles in 50 days. Union General Schofield's troops, previously sent to Wilmington, are there to meet him.

In South Carolina, a Union contingent skirmishes with Confederates at Sumterville. Specific units and casualty figures are unreported.

In Virginia, General Charles A. Heckman is relieved of command by order of General U.S. Grant. Heckman's performance during the operations to seize Fort Harrison were deemed poor by his corps commander, General O.C. Ord. In an after-battle report, Ord does not place Heckman on the list of those who were "conspicuous for their gallantry." General Heckman resigns his commission on 25 March. During his civilian life, for a while, Heckman ventures into business as a contractor, but later he becomes a dispatcher for the Jersey Central Railroad. He succumbs in Germantown (Philadelphia), Pennsylvania, on 14 January 1896 and is interred in Easton, Pennsylvania.

In Naval activity, the side-wheel steamer *Gamage*, acquired by the U.S. Navy at Cincinnati on 22 December 1864, is commissioned at Mound City, Illinois, as the gunboat USS *Gamage*. Acting Master William Neil receives command. The *Gamage* is assigned to the 5th Division, Mississippi Squadron. It arrives at

Natchez, Mississippi, on 2 April, just prior to the surrender of General Lee to General Grant at Appomattox, Virginia. Subsequent to Lee's surrender, on 1 June, the *Gamage* joins a flotilla composed of eight steamers charged with receiving surrendered Confederate vessels and their crews. The force is commanded by Lt. Commander W.E. Fitzhugh. The *Ida May*, an army steamer, accompanies the force. Major General F.J. Herron, accompanied by his staff, is aboard the *Ida May*, which takes the ironclad CSS *Missouri* and the *Cotton*. The *Gamage* afterward remains at Alexandria, Louisiana, to support General Herron until the latter part of June. Later, the *Gamage* arrives at Mound City, Illinois, where it is decommissioned on 29 July 1869. It is sold on 17 August 1865. On 4 October 1865, as a merchant ship, it is renamed *Southern Belle*. It remains operational until it is destroyed by fire at Placquemine, Louisiana, on 11 October 1876.

March 24 (Friday)   In the Arizona Territory, the 1st New Mexican Cavalry engages Confederates at Red Rock. Casualty figures are unavailable.

In North Carolina, General William T. Sherman realizes there is no Confederate force strong enough to prevent him from joining Grant in Virginia, unless Robert E. Lee escapes the clutches of Grant at Petersburg, allowing him to join with General Joseph E. Johnston. Grant, at present, has Lee pinned at Richmond while Sherman's men are overpowering and successfully whipping Johnston at will. Numerous consecutive defeats and setbacks cause the morale of Johnston's men to suffer. Grant, in retrospect, states: "The men of both Lee's and Johnston's armies were like their brethren of the North as brave as men can be; but no man is so brave that he may not meet such defeats and disasters as to discourage him and dampen his ardor for any cause, no matter how just he deems it." Also, a Union force (General Alfred Terry's provisional brigade) skirmishes with Confederates at Coxe's Bridge.

In Naval activity, the USS *Niagara* and the *Sacramento* encounter the CSS *Stonewall*, a recently acquired ironclad ram, at Ferrol, Spain. When the *Stonewall* departs port on this day, it is not attacked. The two Union wooden warships discern that the *Stonewall* is too powerful. The *Stonewall*, built in France at Bordeaux, had been embargoed by the French during February 1864 and was initially sold to Denmark, but the Danes declined to accept it. Consequently, the builder sold it to the Confederacy. While en route to the States, the *Stonewall* had encountered a storm that forced it to enter the harbor in Spain. The *Stonewall*, after the tranquil encounter with the *Sacramento* and *Niagara*, arrives at Cuba, but by then (May) the war was over. The *Stonewall* is then handed over to the Spanish, who in turn deliver it to the U.S. government during July 1865. In 1867, while at the navy yard in Washington, D.C., it is sold to Japan and renamed *Kotetsu*; after 1871 it is renamed *Azuma*. In conjunction, the ironclad ram *Stonewall* is separate from the cottonclad ram CSS *Stonewall*, lost during April 1862 at New Orleans. In other activity, the USS *Trefoil* arrives at Mobile Bay and initiates duty as a dispatch boat operating between the bay and Pensacola. It remains in the area until July, when it returns north and is decommissioned on 30 August in Boston. On 28 May 1867, it is sold at auction.

March 24–25   In Alabama, Union general Edward R.S. Canby's forces arrive in the vicinity of Mobile. On the following day they unsuccessfully assault the major Confederate defensive fortification protecting the city (Spanish Fort). Mobile holds firm until April 9, when the city finally falls to Union troops. Brigadier General Randall L. Gibson's force participates in the defense of Mobile. After the war he returns to Louisiana and later becomes a congressman and a U.S. senator. General Gibson dies while in the Senate at Hot Springs, Arkansas, on 15 December 1892. Confederate Brigadier General Martin Luther Smith, who had devoted much time to the defenses of Mobile, returns to Georgia after the war; however, he succumbs prematurely in July 1866.

In Virginia, General Robert E. Lee unsuccessfully attempts to break through the Union lines near Fort Stedman (vicinity of Petersburg). Lee directs Confederate General John Brown Gordon to lead the attack in an attempt to permit a breakout between Fort Stedman and Battery No. 10. Gordon achieves some success, capturing the battery and fort. This is followed by the seizing of Batteries 11 and 12 and directing them toward Union Lines at City Point. Union General John G. Parke assumes command during the absence of General George G. Meade and dispatches Generals John F. Hartranft and Orlando B. Willcox to drive the Rebels back.

The Union pushes at a feverish pace and recaptures a couple of batteries, surrounding the Rebels in the fort and compelling them to surrender. The Union suffers 68 killed, 337 wounded and 63 missing. The Confederates sustain about 800 killed and wounded, 209 missing and 834 captured. Following the victory, the Union occupies the fort, which is located at the immediate front of Petersburg. The 1st Connecticut Artillery and other units of the 1st and 3rd Divisions, 9th Corps, Army of the Potomac, participate.

Union Captain Joseph F. Carter, 3rd Maryland Infantry, captures the Confederate 51st Virginia Infantry flag during the siege. Carter becomes a Medal of Honor recipient. During one of the Confederate movements, General Philip Cook, leading a contingent of Rebels against Fort Stedman, is wounded during what can be considered the last strategic assault mounted by the Confederates in these closing days of the conflict. Cook will later be captured while recuperating in Petersburg. Confederate Generals William Terry and Thomas F. Toon (seventh wound since joining the Confederacy, June 1861) are also wounded during this action. General Toon had reverted back to his rank of colonel upon returning to duty during the pre-

vious August. After the war he returns to North Carolina, where he dies during February 1902.

Brigadier General William Ruffin Cox leads his brigade as part of General John Brown Gordon's corps in the unsuccessful attempt to displace the Union forces. Cox's brigade stands out during the retreat, as most of the Confederate units are badly disorganized. Nevertheless, the North Carolinians proceed with discipline, and enthusiasm seems to permeate the ranks. It is told that General Robert E. Lee, while trying to reorganize the retreating units, is startled by a contingent that is marching in cadence, prompting him to remark: "What troops are those?" After being told they were from Cox's Brigade, he responds: "God bless gallant old North Carolina."

General John G. Parke remains in the army subsequent to the close of hostilities. He receives the brevet of major general in the Regular Army. Later, he becomes colonel of engineers, and during 1887, he becomes superintendent of the United States Military Academy at West Point, a post he holds until he retires during 1879. Also, Brigadier General Orlando B. Willcox musters out of the army during January 1866; however, the following July, he re-enters the service as colonel of the 29th U.S. Infantry. In 1869 he transfers to the 12th Infantry and remains in San Francisco until he assumes command of the Department of Arizona, a post he retains until 1882. He retires during 1887 with the rank of brigadier general.

March 25 (Saturday)   In Alabama, Union Major General Edward R.S. Canby, who fought against the Confederates under General Henry Hopkins Sibley in New Mexico, encroaches Mobile. General Andrew Jackson Smith commands the XX Corps during the operation against Vicksburg. Naval forces under Admiral David Farragut are also closing on Mobile. Confederate General Matt D. Ector (previously Colonel, 14th Texas Cavalry) participates at Mobile during these final days of the war. Ector suffered the loss of a leg earlier in the war, from wounds sustained during the Atlanta campaign. Union troops under General Frederick Steele (Canby's command) are closing on Bluff Springs (Pine Barren) during their trek toward Mobile, and Steel's column skirmishes with a Confederate force of about 800 troops led by General James Holt Clanton. The Union prevails. About 265 Rebels are captured. In addition, General Clanton is wounded during the fighting. He will be paroled at Mobile shortly after the close of hostilities (May). Also, Major General Frederick Steele, after the war, is transferred to Texas. He does not muster out of the volunteers until 1867; however, in Texas, he is ranked at colonel of the 20th U.S. Infantry. During 1866, Steele is moved to the West Coast, where he commands the Department of Columbia. Later, during 1868, while driving a carriage, he falls from it and dies from the injuries on 12 January.

March 25–27   In Virginia, elements of the 2nd and 6th Corps, Army of the Potomac, clash heavily with Confederates at Petersburg. The

Union sustains about 103 killed and 864 wounded. The Confederates suffer 834 killed, wounded and missing. In addition, about 2,800 Confederates are captured. On the 25th, Confederate Brigadier General Philip Cook sustains his third wound in the war, while leading his brigade against Fort Stedman. While recuperating in the hospital in Petersburg, he is seized on 2 April when the town falls to the Union. After being paroled during the latter part of July 1865, he returns to Georgia and resumes his law practice at Americus. Subsequently, he is elected to the U.S. Congress and serves from 1873 to 1883. Afterward, during 1890, he becomes secretary of the state of Georgia, a post he holds until his death on 21 May 1894 while he is in Atlanta.

Also, Confederate General William Terry participates in the attack against Fort Stedman. After the war he resumes his law practice at Wytheville, Virginia, and then serves in the U.S. Congress (1871–1873 and 1875–1877). On 5 September 1888, he drowns while attempting to cross Reed Creek near his home.

March 26 (Sunday)   In Virginia, Union General Sheridan's cavalry arrives in the vicinity of Petersburg to assist Grant's assault on the city.

In Union general officer activity, Brigadier General William P. Benton receives the brevet rank of major general. Also, at about this time, General Jefferson Columbus Davis receives the brevet rank of major general. After the war he becomes colonel of the U.S. 22nd Infantry Regiment. He is transferred to Alaska and participates against the Modoc Indians responsible for the murder of General Edward R.S. Canby (11 April 1873).

March 26–April 8   Siege of Spanish Fort Union ground troops (Canby's command) assisted by naval vessels place Spanish Fort, Alabama, under siege in an effort to strangle the Rebel hold on Mobile. The flotilla is composed of the *Octorara* (Captain W.W. Low) and the ironclads *Kickapoo* (Captain M.P. Jones), *Osage* (Captain William M. Gamble), *Milwaukee* (Captain James H. Gillis), *Winnebago* (Captain W.A. Kirkland) and the *Chickasaw* (Captain George H. Perkins). The Rebels hold the Yankees off until finally forced to evacuate on 8 April, when the overpowering force of the Union assault troops makes the Rebel position untenable. Confederate General Randall L. Gibson, who saw service with the 13th Louisiana Infantry at Shiloh, defends the fort, which falls on the 9th. In conjunction, the 5th Minnesota Volunteer Regiment participates in this action.

March 27 (Monday)   In Alabama, Union General Canby arrives in the vicinity of Spanish Fort and Fort Blakely at Mobile.

In North Carolina, Major General Alfred Terry, U.S. Army, commanding officer of the 10th Corps, reorganizes all Union troops in North Carolina, except those attached to the 2nd, 9th and 23rd Corps and General William T. Sherman's army.

March 27–28 In Virginia, General William T. Sherman arrives at Fort Monroe, then proceeds to City Point to confer with General Grant and President Lincoln on the steamer *River Queen*. The discussion with the president centers around how to prevent further loss of life by offering good surrender terms to the Confederacy. On the 28th, General Sherman asks Lincoln if he is ready for the end of the war and what should be done with the Confederate armies and political leaders. Lincoln said all he wanted was to defeat the opposing armies and to get the men back to their homes and work. Sherman departs the *River Queen* at about noon, bidding goodbye to Lincoln. He returns to Goldsboro, never to see the president again. General Sherman later states: "Of all the men I ever met, he seemed to possess more of the elements of greatness, combined with goodness, than any other."

March 28 (Tuesday) *In Confederate general officer activity,* Colonel Theodore Washington Brevard is appointed brigadier general by President Davis, effective on 26 March. It is Davis' final general officer appointment.

In Naval activity, the USS *Milwaukee*, an ironclad river monitor commissioned during August 1864 at Carondelet, Missouri, is destroyed when it strikes a mine while operating on the Blakeley River against Confederates in the vicinity of Fort Blakeley and Spanish Fort near Mobile. The USS *Kickapoo*, also operating in the area, initiates a rescue operation to save crew members. On the following day, the *Kickapoo* is again engaged in rescuing crew members when another vessel strikes a Confederate mine.

March 29 (Wednesday) In Virginia, Union troops (Army of the Potomac), including Generals Gouverneur K. Warren's V Corps and Charles Griffin's 1st Division, engage Confederates led by General Bushrod Johnson at Gravelly Run. The Union suffers 55 dead and 306 wounded. The Confederates sustain 135 dead, 400 wounded and 100 missing. In other activity, Union Colonel Alfred L. Pearson, 155th Pennsylvania Infantry, leads a countercharge against attacking Confederates at Lewis Farm. The brigade successfully recaptures lost ground. Meanwhile, General U.S. Grant detains troops at Petersburg, while he begins his move to the southwest in an attempt to finish off Lee's beleaguered forces. General Philip Sheridan is ordered to move to Five Forks and position himself there as a direct threat to Robert E. Lee's right line. Meanwhile, the 21st Pennsylvania Cavalry clashes with Confederates in the vicinity of Dinwiddie.

Also, at about this time, Confederate Major General Lunsford L. Lomax is assigned responsibility for the Valley District; however, within a short while, his division surrenders at Greensboro, North Carolina. After the war he engages in farming, and in 1885, he becomes president of the Virginia Polytechnic Institute.

In Naval activity, the USS *Osage*, while operating on the Blakeley River against the Confederates at Fort Blakely and Spanish Fort in the vicinity of Mobile, strikes a mine and sinks. The USS *Kickapoo*, which is nearby, initiates a rescue operation to pick up survivors of the *Osage*. Following the operation against Mobile, the *Kickapoo* moves to New Orleans and remains there until it is decommissioned in July. Subsequently, during 1869, it is twice renamed the *Cyclops* and then the *Kewaydin*. It is sold in 1874.

March 30 (Thursday) In North Carolina, General William T. Sherman arrives at Goldsboro. He prepares for what he expects to be the last major battle against the Confederates under General Joseph E. Johnston. Sherman's Army is divided into three parts, with Major General Oliver O. Howard commanding the Army of the Tennessee (right wing), the Army of Georgia, commanded by General H.W. Slocum (left wing), and the Army of the Ohio commanded by General J.M. Schofield (center). They are bolstered by Hugh Kilpatrick's cavalry.

In Virginia, the Confederates continue to cling to the fragile hold at Petersburg. The weather remains horrific and the Union is stymied, unable to make a strong advance. Lee's forces are spread especially thin and their arms are sparse. The Confederates are holding a line of breastworks that extends about 35 miles from left to right. Despite his disadvantage, Lee completely understands that Grant is postured to penetrate his right. With some daring moves, he draws troops from the commands of Generals G.W. Gordon, Bushrod Johnson, George Pickett and Cadmus Wilcox to bolster the right side. Meanwhile, the fortifications in front of Petersburg are manned only by 5,000 troops with the task of holding a nine-mile line. The cavalry under General Fitzhugh Lee moves under cover of darkness and deploys in and about some swampy ground to the immediate front of the stalled forces of Union Generals Humphreys and Warren. In addition to the dreariness of the pitch-dark night, the area is struck by another rain storm which continues throughout the night and into the following day. The roads become flooded and the streams swollen.

In Confederate general officer activity, Brigadier General Daniel Ruggles is assigned to the post of commissary general of prisoners. Subsequent to the close of hostilities, General Ruggles returns to Fredericksburg, Virginia, where he resides for the remainder of his life, except for a period of about four years in Texas, where he manages a ranch. He dies in Fredericksburg at the age of 88 on 1 June 1897.

In Naval activity, the USS *Somerset*, on duty with the USS *Sunflower*, attacks and destroys a Confederate saltworks on St. Joseph's Bayou, Florida. After the war, the *Somerset*, in need of repairs, is towed to New York. It is sold at auction on 12 July 1865, and during the following year it begins to operate as a ferry boat in New York. It remains in service until 1914.

March 31 (Friday) In Alabama, the 4th Cavalry Division, commanded by General James Wilson (Wilson's Raid), battles Confederates at Montevallo and Six Mile Creek.

In Virginia, Confederates under General Ambrose P. Hill attack the Union at Boydtown and White Oak Roads. The Union counterattacks and drives the Confederates back. Union forces sustain 177 killed, 1,134 wounded and 556 missing. Confederates sustain 1,000 wounded and 235 missing. In a separate action, Sergeant William H. Sickle, 7th Wisconsin Infantry, and one other man capture nine Confederates plus a stand of Confederate colors at Gravelly Run. Sickle becomes a recipient of the Medal of Honor for his actions above and beyond the call of duty. Another skirmish between Union troops of the 1st New Jersey Cavalry and Confederates occurs at Chamberlain's Creek. The Union repels the attack.

General Grant who has been waiting to launch a major assault to demolish Robert E. Lee's army, is still constrained by inclement weather. Also, the 1st, 2nd and 3rd Divisions, Cavalry Corps, Army of the Potomac, clash with Confederates at Dinwiddie Courthouse. Confederate General William Richard Terry sustains his seventh wound at Dinwiddie Courthouse. After the war he serves eight years in the Virginia Senate, and from 1886 to 1893 he serves as superintendent of the penitentiary. He succumbs on 28 March 1897 at Chesterfield Courthouse, Virginia.

Late March Union Brigadier General (Volunteers) Benjamin Alvord, commander of the District of Oregon since April 1862, is relieved of command and ordered back East. Alvord re-

General Sheridan's forces seize Five Forks, Virginia (Johnson, *Campfire and Battlefield: History of the Conflicts and Campaigns,* 1894).

signs his volunteer commission during August and becomes paymaster at New York City. In 1876 he becomes brigadier general, U.S. Army. In other activity, at about this time, Brigadier General Innis Newton Palmer receives the brevets of brigadier general in the Regular Army and major general of volunteers. He remains in the army beyond the war's end, and during 1868 he is appointed colonel of the 2nd Cavalry. His duty stations are primarily in Nebraska and Wyoming. In 1876, he takes ill and remains out of service until 1879. On 29 March 1879, General Palmer retires. He dies in Chevy Chase, Maryland, on 9 September 1900.

March 31–April 1 In Virginia, General Philip H. Sheridan's cavalry advances to Five Forks to aid the Union troops already there, including the 157th Pennsylvania Infantry. A formidable contingent of men under Confederate General George Pickett forces the Yankees to withdraw to Dinwiddie Courthouse. The Yankees hold, but Sheridan withdraws to await reinforcements from the 2nd and 5th Corps (Andrew A. Humphrey's and G.K. Warren's). Nonetheless, Sheridan afterward criticizes Warren for his actions, terminating further success for the remainder of Warren's career. However, years later (1879), Warren is cleared of and wrongdoing.

Sheridan's men next repel a joint assault by Pickett's cavalry and two divisions of infantry. Lt. Ferris of the 30th Massachusetts Infantry thwarts an attack by a contingent of Colonel John S. Mosby's Cavalry at Berryville. Sheridan, after the Union success at Dinwiddie, captures Five Forks and over 5,000 Confederate prisoners. Confederate Brigadier General George Hume "Maryland" Steuart participates at this action and later at Appomattox. After the war, he returns to Maryland and engages in farming until his death on 22 November 1903.

Confederate Brigadier General William Richard Terry (unrelated to Confederate Brigadier General William Terry) is wounded at Dinwiddie Courthouse; this is the seventh wound sustained by Terry during the conflict. Confederate Brigadier Generals Eppa Hunton and Montgomery D. Corse play decisive roles in trying to hold off the inevitable disaster at Five Forks, but because of the great odds, the Rebels are unable to stem the tide. Generals Eppa Hunton and Montgomery Dent Corse manage to avoid capture, but they fall into the Union net at Sayler's Creek on the sixth. General Hunton, subsequent to his release from Fort Warren, Massachusetts, returns to Virginia to resume his law practice. Afterward, he elected to Congress and serves 1873 to 1881. He serves in the U.S. Senate from 1892 to 1895. He dies in Richmond on 11 October 1908. Also, Confederate Brigadier General William Paul Roberts is captured at Five Forks. Brigadier General John McCausland escapes with some remnants of his brigade and arrives at Lynchburg. Later he is paroled at Charleston, West Virginia; however, his old hometown is staunchly loyal to the Union and he is unable to adjust. He leaves the country, and after spending time in Mexico and

Europe, he acquires a farm in West Virginia, where he resides until his death on 22 January 1927.

Meanwhile, Confederate General George Pickett receives blame for the loss and finds himself during the closing days of the war in trouble with General Robert E. Lee. After the debacle at Sayler's Creek on the 6th, General Pickett is relieved of active command, but he continues to serve until the surrender at Appomattox. After the war he becomes an insurance agent in Norfolk, Virginia, where he succumbs on 30 July 1875. In addition, Major General Thomas L. Rosser breaks through the Union lines and escapes with his brigade; however, he is later seized and paroled one month after the close of hostilities. General Rosser, who began his military career at West Point and served with the Confederates, again changes uniforms during 1898 when he is appointed a brigadier general of volunteers in the U.S. Army.

Also, Confederate Brigadier General Samuel McGowan's brigade (initially Maxcy Gregg's brigade), composed of South Carolina Regiments, participates in this action. One of McGowan's regiments, the 14th South Carolina, had sustained the deaths of about twenty officers and more than 525 enlisted men during the conflict. The unit had sustained more deaths from illness and disease than by fire in the field, losing about sixty percent to disease. Confederate Brigadier General William P. Roberts leads his command at this action, but the Union forces plow through his lines. Roberts is among those paroled at Appomattox. After the conflict, General McGowan is elected to Congress; however, he is prevented from taking his seat. Later he becomes a member of the South Carolina Supreme Court, a post he holds until 1873. He dies on 9 August 1897 at his residence in Abbeyville.

March 31–April 9 Siege of Fort Blakely Although most of the attention concerning the war is centered on the East and specifically the entrapment of General Robert E. Lee with his Army of Northern Virginia, there is heavy skirmishing around Mobile, where the siege of Fort Blakely is ongoing. The Confederates are finally overtaken on 9 April. Union General William A. Pile and his 1st Brigade of John Harkins' Negro division participate admirably in the successful capture of the fort. Additional Confederate strongholds collapse under Union pressure and Mobile comes into Union hands with Old Glory flying over the city on 12 April, four years to the day that Confederate guns opened up against Fort Sumter, South Carolina, the action which initiated the war. The Union troops capture many Confederates when they seize Fort Blakely. On April 8, another contingent of General Edward Canby's command had seized Spanish Fort, which had been under siege for a couple of weeks.

April 1865 Confederate Brigadier General Edmund Winston Pettus, initially with the 20th Alabama Regiment, had served in the Carolinas at the end of the hostilities. He heads back for Mississippi and returns to his profession as an

attorney, but towards the end of the century, he is elected to the U.S. Senate (1896) and during 1902, he is re-elected. General Pettus, at the time of his demise at about age 76 during 1907, is the final Confederate general to hold a seat in the Senate. Pettus' brother, John J. Pettus, had been the governor of Mississippi during the hostilities. Also, Confederate Major General Sterling Price is not captured. After being driven from Missouri by the Union, Price proceeds to Texas. Upon the termination of the conflict, he moves into Mexico with many of his men and establishes headquarters at a place named Carlota in Vera Cruz; however, the time spent there is less than romantic due to the climate, lack of proper medical attention and frequent guerrilla attacks. By 1867, the Mexican oasis is abandoned. Price returns to Missouri. General Mosby M. Parsons, one of the officers who had gone into Mexico with Price, never returns, but the precise reasons for his demise are unknown. Missouri had not seceded from the Union; however many Missourians like Price fought for the Confederacy and the Confederate flag carried two extra stars, one for Missouri and the other for Kentucky, which also remained loyal to the Union. Major General Sterling Price succumbs in St. Louis during September 1867.

Confederate Major General James Fagan, who accompanied Price on the raids into Missouri, had not traveled to Texas. He is paroled during June of this year. Fagan returns to Arkansas and is appointed a U.S. marshal by President U.S. Grant during 1875.

In New Mexico, Fort Selden is established near the Rio Grande River in the vicinity of Leasburg, north of Las Cruces. Leasburg soon becomes off limits to the troops due in part to its lawlessness and its apparent abundance of saloons and ladies of the night. The fort is constructed by volunteers from Albuquerque, but by the following year, elements of the 3rd U.S. Cavalry deploy here. The 8th Cavalry succeeds the 3rd Cavalry during 1870. Subsequently, elements of the 9th and 10th Colored Cavalries garrison the fort during the period 1876–1888 with some interruption, and the U.S. 4th Cavalry arrives during 1883. Meanwhile, the fort's initial infantry contingent is the 125th Colored Infantry Regiment (1866), and it is replaced by the 38th U.S. Colored Infantry during 1867–1869. Other units that garrison the fort at various times between 1870 and 1888 are contingents of the 10th, 13th and 15th U.S. Infantry Regiments. The fort is deactivated during 1891 due in great part to the growing responsibility of Fort Bliss in El Paso, Texas. However, most troops at Fort Selden had departed during 1888.

April 1 (Saturday) In Alabama, Union General Edward Canby's troops skirmish briskly with a contingent of Confederates at Blakely. Also, a contingent of General James Wilson's cavalry, composed of elements of the 2nd Brigade, 1st Division, Cavalry Corps, Military Division of the Mississippi led by General McCook, clashes with Confederates this day at Centreville. Meanwhile, other units of General

Canby's cavalry (Wilson's Raid) battle Confederates at Mount Pleasant. Also, the 2nd and 4th Cavalry Divisions, Military Division of the Mississippi (Wilson's Raid) engage Confederates led by General Nathan B. Forrest at Bogler's Creek and Plantersville (Ebenezer Church and Maplesville). And yet other contingents of Wilson's Cavalry (1st Brigade 1st Division, Cavalry Corps, Military Division of the Mississippi led by General Edward McCook) exchange blows with Confederates at Trion.

In Virginia, the Confederates are bracing for the worst. Richmond is under the command of General Walter Husted Stevens (West Point, 1848), but there are not enough men or supplies to hold off the overpowering Union forces that are closing fast. Petersburg, the rear entrance to Richmond, is still under severe stress and about to collapse under the Union pressure. Stevens will be among the last of the troops to evacuate the capital. After the close of hostilities, General Stevens travels to Mexico and accepts a position as superintendent and engineer of the imperial railroad. The railroad, a design of Maximilian, is to run between Vera Cruz and Mexico City. Nevertheless, afterward, the French abandon Mexico. General Stevens dies in Mexico City during November 1867.

In North Carolina, Union Cavalry (Stoneman's Raid) skirmishes with Confederates in the mountains in the vicinity of Boone.

In Union activity, General Sherman's army stands at 74,105 infantry, 4,781 cavalry and 2,264 artillerymen. This number is increased by 10 April to reach 88,948 men.

In Union general officer activity, Brigadier General Wesley Merritt is promoted to the full

rank of major general of volunteers. After the war, General Merritt becomes lieutenant colonel, 9th Cavalry, followed by colonel of the 6th Cavalry during 1876. He is promoted to the rank of major general in 1895. General Merritt also serves actively during the Spanish-American War and participates as commander of the First Philippine expedition. Subsequent to his death during 1900, he is interred at West Point. Also, Colonel James Alexander Williamson is promoted to brigadier general. He had received the brevet of major general of volunteers the previous month. He resigns from the army during November 1865.

In Naval activity, the USS *Rodolph*, a tinclad river gunboat built during 1863, acquired by the U.S. Navy during December of that year, and commissioned during May 1864, is involved with the operation on the Blakely River to salvage the USS *Milwaukee*, a monitor which had been sunk on 28 March. While towing a barge, the *Rodolph* strikes a mine and sinks.

April 2 (Sunday)   **In Alabama,** Union troops (Wilson's Raid) commanded by General Wilson, including the 4th Iowa Cavalry, capture Selma, along with huge quantities of Confederate supplies. Over 2,500 prisoners are taken by Wilson's cavalry, including the commands of Generals Abraham Buford (West Point, 1841) and General Frank C. Armstrong. General Armstrong, following the close of hostilities, works in Texas with the Overland Mail Service. He is Indian inspector in 1885–1889, then is named commissioner of Indian affairs (1893–1895). He dies at Bar Harbor, Maine, on 8 September 1809. Also, Union General Eli Long sustains his fifth wound of the war in the fighting at Selma. After the war, Long is given command of the military district of New Jersey, and he receives the brevets of rank up to major general of volunteers and of the Regular Army. He resigns from the army with the rank of major general; however, during 1875, his rank is reduced to brigadier general.

The flag of the 12th Mississippi Cavalry is also captured. Confederates attempt to stem the tide, but after heavy fighting, Montgomery, Tuscaloosa and West Point also fall to the Union. General James H. Wilson seizes Selma after finally defeating General Nathan B. Forrest's cavalry. Generals Forrest and Philip D. Roddey are among the Rebels who swim to safety across the Alabama River, escaping the Union net. After the war, Nathan B. Forrest returns to Tennessee and reinitiates his private business interests, but his previous success is not attained. It is reported that Forrest also joins a new secret society, the Ku Klux Klan. The society was apparently formed for several reasons, including disdain for the new ar-

rivals in Tennessee known as Carpetbaggers, an equal dislike for Union troops and Republicans, which most native citizens of Tennessee regarded as radicals, and last but not least, the new citizens known as "freedmen." Forrest, despite becoming a leader of the group, subsequently finds the organization too violent and he terminates the Ku Klux Klan. Nevertheless, the group survives and its violent acts become more horrid. Forrest is remembered by some as the founder of the Klan, but history seems to neglect the fact that he too turned against the Klan and disbanded it. The Ku Klux Klan will continue to exist and will fuel the fires of racism and bigotry with its primary targets, "colored" people, followed by Catholics and those whites who attempt to give aid to the former slaves. General Forrest dies on 29 October 1877 at Memphis, Tennessee.

The 2nd Brigade, 1st Cavalry Division, Military Division of the Mississippi, skirmishes with Confederates at Scottsville. Also, Confederate General Abraham Buford, who had accompanied Forrest since Vicksburg, returns to his farm in Kentucky. He serves one term in the Kentucky legislature, but he suffers continually from financial setbacks. He loses his property in the process. During 1884, while in Danville, Indiana, he leaves a note requesting burial back in Kentucky at Lexington, where his wife and son are buried, then he commits suicide.

In Virginia, at Petersburg, the Confederate defenders, proud and defiant almost to the bitter end, fall to the Union after a long bloody siege

General Nathan B. Forrest (Johnson, *Campfire and Battlefield: History of the Conflicts and Campaigns*, 1894).

Union troops overcome fierce resistance and capture Fort Gregg at Petersburg, Virginia (Johnson, *Campfire and Battlefield: History of the Conflicts and Campaigns*, 1894).

initiated during May 1864. The initial Union penetration of the defensive lines is made by General George Washington Getty's division. Brevet Brigadier General James Meech Warner (11th Vermont) is reported to be the first mounted man to enter the works. During the night of the 2nd-3rd, Robert E. Lee evacuates the city, and prior to dawn on the 3rd, he is about 16 miles away. The Union is unaware of the massive pullout. Lee intends to join General Joseph E. Johnston, leaving the town to the forces of General Grant. Confederate Lt. General Ambrose P. Hill (West Point, 1847) is killed during this action. Confederate-held Forts Gregg and Whitworth outside Petersburg also fall to Union troops, following repeated attacks by the division of General Robert S. Foster and John W. Turner against ferocious resistance of Confederates under Major General Cadmus M. Wilcox (West Point, 1846), whose efforts permit Lt. General James Longstreet time to move out and position his command from where it can provide cover fire for the general retreat. General Foster is breveted major general during September 1865 and resigns in 1866. General Wilcox, after the war, resides in Washington, D.C., and later, during 1886, President Grover Cleveland appoints him chief of the railroad division of the Land Office, a post he holds until his death on 2 December 1890. At his funeral, four of his pallbearers are former Confederate general officers and four others are former general officers of the U.S. Army.

Private Richard Mangam, 148th New York Regiment, captures the colors of the 8th Mississippi Infantry; he becomes a recipient of the Medal of Honor. In addition, 20 Union artillerymen volunteer to assist an infantry assault at Petersburg. These men from the 1st Rhode Island Light Artillery turn the captured Confederate guns on the Confederates, greatly assisting the capture of the city. General Sheridan speeds from Five Forks to assist in the battle. The Confederates fall back to Sutherland Station, while being aggressively pursued by Union generals Nelson Miles and Philip Sheridan. The Rebels are soundly defeated by the Union. During the heated fighting, Brigadier General Robert Brown Potter sustains a serious wound. Potter, having been breveted major general of volunteers in August 1864, is promoted to full rank on 29 September 1865. He resigns from the army the following January.

In other activity, Confederate President Davis receives information from Robert E. Lee (delivered by a guide) concerning the movements of Lee's battered Army of Northern Virginia. The guide is to aid Davis in reaching the retreating force as they head for Amelia Court House. Confederate General Basil Duke's brigade will escort Davis from Richmond. General Martin W. Gary subsequently escapes from Appomattox to support the flight of Jefferson Davis and his cabinet. Lee orders General Richard S. Ewell to make his way to Amelia Court House and informs him that General George Washington Gordon is to remain at Scott's Shop until the arrival of General Richard S. Ewell. Once Ewell arrives, Gordon is to pro-

ceed to Amelia Court House. Meanwhile, General William Mahone attempts to hold the bridge at Goode's Ferry until Gordon is sure Ewell does not require its use. General Mahone, when assured that Ewell no longer requires the bridge, is under orders to destroy the span to prevent its use by the Union. Also, Confederate General Philip Cook is captured near Petersburg. Also, General G.W. Getty, after the war, receives command of the 38th Infantry during 1866. In 1871, he transfers to the 3rd Artillery. And afterward he commands the artillery school at Fort Monroe. He retires during 1883. General Lewis Addison Grant is wounded during the fighting at Petersburg. He declines a commission in the regular army and returns to Vermont; however, later he relocates in Chicago and from there moves to Des Moines, Iowa. He moves yet again and finally settles in Minneapolis. In 1890 he becomes assistant secretary of war.

In Union general officer activity, Brigadier General Charles Griffin is promoted to major general. Subsequently, during 1866, General Griffin becomes colonel of the 35th Infantry Regiment. He assumes command of the District of Texas. However, during the following year, an epidemic of yellow fever breaks out in Galveston and Griffin chooses to remain in the city. He contracts the disease and dies on 15 September 1867. Also, Brigadier General Simon Goodell Griffin is breveted major general. He musters out of the service during August 1865.

April 2–6   In Virginia, Yankees chase the Confederates and surround and capture Lt. General Richard S. Ewell's corps at Sayler's Creek. The Union, including the 6th Corps and General Philip Sheridan's cavalry, suffer 166 dead and 1,014 wounded. The Confederates have 1,000 killed, 1,800 wounded and 6,000 captured. The 2nd Ohio Cavalry also participates. This devastating defeat for the Confederates leads to General Robert E. Lee's surrender at Appomattox in the next few days. The Union troops, which include General George A. Custer's cavalry, capture a large number of Lee's general officers, making it too difficult to continue the struggle. Captured at Sayler's Creek are Confederate Generals Seth Maxwell Barton (West Point, 1849), Theodore W. Brevard, Montgomery D. Corse (his eyesight begins to fail and toward the latter part of his life he becomes completely blind), Thomas Fenwick Drayton (West Point, 1828), Dudley McIver Dubose, Richard S. Ewell, James Monroe Goggin, Joseph B. Kershaw, George Washington Custis Lee (son of Robert E. Lee, West Point, 1854) and James P. Simms. General G.W.C. Lee is granted special consideration due to the poor health of his mother and he escapes captivity at Fort Warren by receiving parole shortly after his imprisonment. After the close of hostilities, he becomes involved with Washington College (later Washington and Lee University), and upon the death of his father, Robert E. Lee, William succeeds him as president. General James P. Simms returns to Georgia and resumes

General George Armstrong Custer (Mottelay, *The Soldier in Our Civil War,* 1886).

his law practice in Covington, where he also serves in the state legislature during 1865–1866 and later during 1877. He remains in Covington until his death in May 1887. General Ewell, subsequent to his release from Fort Warren, returns to Tennessee, where he resides on a farm in the vicinity of Spring Hill until he dies on 25 January 1872. He is interred in Nashville. Most of Confederate General Richard H. Anderson's command is captured, but he escapes. He is relieved of duty the day prior to Lee's surrender. Major General Bushrod Rust Johnson also escapes; however, during the struggle, his division had been devastated. He is paroled at Appomattox.

Fort Sedgwick on Jerusalem Plank Road falls to the Union. Sergeant Charles Ilgenfritz, amid a wall of fire, grabs the flag of the 207th Pennsylvania Regiment from the color bearer as he falls after being hit by seven shots. Undaunted by the withering fire, Ilgenfritz advances and plants the colors on the fort. He becomes a recipient of the Medal of Honor for his extraordinary bravery in the face of the enemy. General Andrew A. Humphreys (West Point, 1831) is breveted major general in the Regular Army for his actions at Sayler's Creek. On 8 August 1866 he is appointed brigadier general in the U.S. Army. He retires during 1879, terminating more than fifty years of service. He dies on 27 December 1883.

April 3 (Monday)   In Alabama, a Union force composed of elements of the 1st Brigade, 1st Cavalry Division, Military Division of the Mississippi, clashes with Confederates at Northport.

In Georgia, a contingent of the 147th Illinois Infantry skirmishes with Confederate troops at Oostanaula. Cpl. Wesley J. Powers swims the river under heavy fire and captures a ferry boat in which the Union troops cross the river. Powers becomes a recipient of the Medal of Honor for his valor.

Also, at about this time (April), Union forces encounter and destroy the CSS *Muscogee* (also known as CSS *Jackson*) by fire on the Chattahoochee River. The *Muscogee*, an ironclad ram, was built in Columbus. Work began during the latter part of 1862, but it was not launched until December 1864.

In North Carolina, a contingent of Union troops (Stoneman's Raid) attacks and captures Salem.

In Virginia at Richmond and Petersburg, as dawn emerges, there is no activity behind the Confederate lines. Once the early morning mist dissipates, it becomes clear that General Robert E. Lee has abandoned his positions. Soon after the discovery, Union troops led by Generals U.S. Grant and George G. Meade enter and occupy Petersburg. The Confederates had evacuated the city on April 2. The Confederates valiantly attempted to repel the Yankees' march on Petersburg; however, after nearly one year, the quest fails. The Yankees equaled the zest of their Southern counterparts, and the greatly outnumbered Confederates finally relinquished their hold on Petersburg. Brevet Brigadier General Oliver Edwards accepts the surrender of Petersburg.

Union troops commanded by Major General Godfrey Weitzel also occupy Richmond, the capital of the Confederacy, taking many thousands of Confederates as prisoners. As at Petersburg, throngs of Confederates escape. General Martin W. Gary leads his command, "Hampton's Legion," and the last of the regimented troops from Richmond prior to Union takeover. General Walter Husted Stevens heads for Appomattox. General Godfrey Weitzel telegraphs Grant at 0815, informing him of Union control of Richmond. General Weitzel arrives in Richmond to find two separate parts of the city on fire. The consensus is the retreating Rebels preferred to torch the city rather than leave it to the Union. Union troops are immediately ordered to extinguish the flames.

In other activity, the 15th Pennsylvania Cavalry (General Stoneman's Raid) seizes Wytheville.

In Union general officer activity, General Joseph Hayes assumes command of the 1st Brigade of General Romeyn B. Ayres' 2nd Division (V Corps). Ayers had been breveted brigadier and major general toward the latter part of the war. He is appointed in 1866 as lieutenant colonel of the 29th Infantry.

In Naval activity, the CSS *Fredericksburg,* built at Richmond the previous year, is destroyed by the Confederates in conjunction with the evacuation of Richmond to prevent its capture by the Union. The CSS *Nasemond,* a twin-screw gunboat built at Norfolk and commissioned just prior to the city being taken by the Union, is also sunk to prevent its capture. The CSS *Patrick Henry,* used as a school ship since the fall of Norfolk and from October 1863 as the Confederate States Naval Academy, is destroyed to prevent capture, as is the CSS *Virginia II.* The Union later raises the *Virginia.* Yet another vessel, the CSS *Hampton,* built at Norfolk during 1862, is destroyed to prevent its capture. The *Hampton* had participated in various battles, including Dutch Gap (August 1864).

April 4 (Tuesday)   In Alabama, a Union force (General James Wilson's Raid) composed of elements of the 1st Brigade, 1st Cavalry Division, Military Division of the Mississippi, led by General John T. Croxton, clashes with Confederates at Tuscaloosa.

In Virginia, President Abraham Lincoln arrives in Richmond aboard the USS *Malvern,* Admiral David D. Porter's flagship, and to the jubilation of the thousands of Union soldiers there, he makes his rounds and passes along his heartfelt thanks for their endurance. Lincoln remains in Richmond, where he confers with a Confederate representative on the grounds for peace, which primarily depend on the South's reaffirming allegiance to the Federal Union. The *Malvern* remains in service until it is decommissioned on 24 October in New York. Afterward, it is sold to its initial owner and it reverts to its original name, the *William G. Hewes.* The *Hewes* is lost in a storm off the coast of Cuba during February 1895, when it crashes into the Colorado Reef off Cuba.

In other activity, the Union continues to tighten the net on the Army of Northern Virginia, with General Philip Sheridan closing with his cavalry and General George G. Meade driving from the east to entrap the remnant forces of Robert E. Lee. At this time, General Robert E. Lee is at Amelia Court House, located about 34 miles west of Richmond. Much to Lee's dismay, supplies that were supposed to have been previously sent there did not arrive. Accidentally the supplies had been sent to Richmond, compelling Lee to send out foraging parties for food to feed the Army. While the Confederates attempt to discover sources of food and supplies, General Sheridan, riding with about 15,000 Cavalry troops, closes on General Lee.

With the presumption that the war is essentially over, several Union officers lighten their vigilance and retire early for the night. The following morning (5th), Union General Andrew A. Humphreys visits the headquarters of the 2nd Division, II Corps, at 0630 and discovers that everyone is asleep. The commander, General William Hays, is instantaneously relieved of command, a mere three days before Lee's surrender at Appomattox. Also, the Confederates destroy the CSS *Raleigh,* a vessel that has acted under a "flag of truce" since May 1862.

In Naval activity, the sloop of war *Saratoga,* originally commissioned during January 1843 under Commander Josiah Tatnall, is this day separated from the South Atlantic Blockading Squadron. It heads north, and on the 28th, it once again is decommissioned. This vessel, the third in a long line of USS *Saratoga*s, sees some service during 1869 and 1871. On 1 May 1875, it is used as a gunnery ship at the U.S. Naval Academy at Annapolis before spending another year in ordinary starting during May 1876. On 19 May 1877, the *Saratoga* is decommissioned for the last time; however, it still has not finished its tour of about thirty-four years. It becomes a training ship for instructing navy apprentices and remains in that capacity until decommissioned for the final time on 8 October 1888.

Following its long career in the U.S. Navy, the *Saratoga* finds itself back in service when the state of Pennsylvania borrows it during 1890 and retains it until 1907, utilizing the old war horse as a "state marine school ship" based in Philadelphia. The *Saratoga* is sold to a commercial company, Thomas Butler and Co. of Boston, on 14 August 1907.

In other activity, the USS *Ibex,* built during 1863 in Ohio and initially named the *Ohio Valley,* is commissioned at Mound City, Illinois. Lt. Commander R.L. May receives command. The tinclad side-wheel gunboat is assigned to the Mississippi Squadron and operates out of Memphis. The ship's military career is short-lived. It is decommissioned on 5 August 1865 and sold that same month. As a merchant ship, it is renamed *Harry Dean* and remains in service until it is destroyed by an explosion at Gallipolis, Ohio, on 3 January 1868.

April 5 (Wednesday)   In Virginia, Union troops under General George Crook encounter and engage Confederates at Amelia Springs (Jetersville). The Union suffers 20 killed and 96 wounded. Confederate casualties are not available. Union troops, including the 2nd New York Cavalry, capture at least two Confederate battle flags. A contingent of the 1st and 8th Pennsylvania Cavalry Regiments skirmishes with Confederates at Paine's Crossroads, and the troops repel a surprise attack at Farmville. The 59th New York Veteran Infantry also participates at this skirmish. The Union holds the bridge, forcing the Confederates to withdraw. There is much confusion within the ranks of the Confederates as they attempt to converge on Amelia Springs. Generals William Mahone and George Pickett both take the wrong road, which forces them to waste valuable time in reaching Jetersville. Confederate General Richard Anderson is informed of their misfortune, to ensure his command does not make the same mistake. As the Confederates continue their flight, the Union keeps pressing and works to cut them off before they break out to join forces with General Joseph E. Johnston. This tactical mistake by Mahone and Pickett sets the stage for the doom at Appomattox. After the war, General Mahone establishes the Norfolk and Western Railroad and is elected to the U.S. Senate (1880). He dies in Washington on 8 October 1895.

Meanwhile, General Robert E. Lee departs

Amelia Court House during the night of the 5th–6th, but General Sheridan's cavalry maintains pursuit. Contingents of Generals George A. Custer and Philip Sheridan each engage Confederates in a series of running battles this day and on the following day as the Rebels continue to attempt to escape.

In Union general officer activity, General Eleazer Arthuru Paine, awaiting orders since September of 1864, resigns from the army. He returns to Monmouth, Illinois, and resumes his law practice. Later in life, while living with one of his daughters in Jersey City, New Jersey, he dies of pneumonia on 16 December 1882.

April 6 (Thursday)   In Texas, Confederate Major General John A. Wharton, subsequent to a disagreement with Colonel George A. Baylor, 2nd Texas Cavalry, is shot and killed by Baylor at a hotel in Houston.

In Virginia, General Grant's forces continue the pursuit of the Confederates who evacuated Richmond and Petersburg and are attempting to regroup under General Lee at Danville. A detachment of the 24th Corps engages the Confederates at High Bridge, near the Appomattox River. The Confederates capture a large number of Union troops. Confederate Brigadier General James Martin Green, one of the defenders at Petersburg, had been inflicted by ill-health prior to the fall of Petersburg and is not in the net, as he had transferred to command the District of North Carolina.

In another skirmish, Union troops, including the 86th New York, meet the Confederates at Amelia Springs. Lt. William H. Newman becomes a recipient of the Medal of Honor for his bravery while capturing a Confederate flag during this skirmish. In yet another action, Private Morgan D. Lane, U.S. Signal Corps, becomes a recipient of the Medal of Honor for his actions at Jetersville, where he captures the flag of the Confederate gunboat *Nansemond.*

General George Armstrong Custer is credited with preserving Amelia County official records by placing a Union guard at the courthouse with orders that "all records be preserved." During the Rebel withdrawal at High Bridge, Confederate General James Dearing is involved in a shootout with Union Colonel Theodore Read. Read is killed and Dearing receives a fatal blow, dying several days later.

A Union force composed of contingents of Sheridan's Cavalry, including Cavalry Corps, 2nd and 6th Corps, Army of the Potomac, engages Confederates at Sayler's Creek (Hunter's Farm, Dentonville). The Union sustains 166 killed and 1,014 wounded. The Confederates suffer about 1,000 killed and wounded and about 6,000 captured. Confederate Major General Richard Heron Anderson's force is scattered, but he manages to escape the net. Afterward, lacking a command, he receives permission on 8 April to return to his home in South Carolina. The Union also captures 16 guns.

April 7 (Friday)   In Virginia, although the war is nearly over, it is difficult to distinguish between the gallantry of the two sides. Unques-

tionably, the Confederates have been thoroughly thrashed by a most powerful and confident Union force under General U.S. Grant, but the Confederates, although badly beaten and exhausted, as well as being deprived of supplies and food, maintain their pride. The remnants of the Army of Northern Virginia are scattered all over and are dropping out of the ranks in great numbers, but fighting goes on, as if there is still a chance for a miracle. Heavy sporadic skirmishing develops in the vicinity of Farmville, and when the smoke clears, Confederate General William Gaston Lewis (wounded) is among the many captured Rebels. Union General Thomas A. Smyth is struck by a Confederate sharpshooter's bullet, dropping him from the skirmish line, mortally wounded. General Smyth, who dies of his wounds on the 9th, is the last Union general to be slain during the conflict.

As the closing days and hours of the war approach, Union forces under Grant are in excellent position, while the South is virtually split into pieces, presenting a situation that gives Grant the opportunity to request Robert E. Lee's surrender. Colonels Francis Washburn and Theodore Read had delayed General Lee on the previous day, while General Humphreys engages Lee at Farmville and Union cavalry converges on Prince Edward Courthouse to join General Charles Griffin's division (V Corps). General Horatio Wright's corps drives west of Farmville supported by Crook's cavalry. In symphony with the other Union movements, General Sheridan's cavalry is racing to intercept the retreating Army of Lee at Appomattox Courthouse. Custer's cavalry, attached to Sheridan's command, gallops to a position southwest of the courthouse at Appomattox, arriving at their objective on the 8th and proceeding to capture the Rebel trains. His men succeed in seizing four trains, but the Confederates manage to escape with three.

General Grant, aware of the Rebels' impossible circumstances, writes to General Lee: "It is my duty to shift from myself the responsibility of any further effusion of blood by asking of you the surrender of that portion of the Confederate Army known as the Army of Northern Virginia." General Lee responds the same day: "Though not entertaining your opinion on the hopelessness of further resistance, I reciprocate your desire to avoid useless effusion of blood and therefore before considering your proposition, ask the terms you will offer on condition of its surrender." Although Lee maintains communication with Grant, he maintains his quick-paced retreat.

In related activity, a Union cavalry force attached to the Army of the Potomac, XXIV Corps, and one division of the XXV Corps engage Confederates at Appomattox Court House (Clover Hill). The Confederates sustain about 500 killed and wounded. In related activity, General Robert E. Lee directs General Henry A. Wise to assume command of a division. Nevertheless, General Wise is not officially promoted to major general. After the surrender at Appomattox, he resumes his law practice in Rich-

mond, but he never seeks amnesty. He succumbs in Richmond on 12 September 1876.

April 8 (Saturday)   In Alabama, Confederate-held Spanish Fort and Fort Alexandria surrender (see also, **March 26–April 8 SIEGE OF SPANISH FORT**).

In Virginia, General Grant responds to General Lee's letter of the 7th: "Peace being my great desire, there is but one condition I would insist upon, mainly: that the men and officers surrendered shall be disqualified for taking up arms against the government of the United States until properly exchanged." Also, during the heavy skirmishes in the vicinity of Appomattox Court House, prior to General Lee's surrender to General Grant, Chief Bugler Charles Schorn of Company M, 1st West Virginia Cavalry, becomes a recipient of the Medal of Honor for his valor and bravery in capturing the battle flag of the Sumter Flying Artillery (CSA). Union Pvt. Bernard Shields, 2nd West Virginia Cavalry, captures the flag of the Washington Artillery (CSA) at Appomattox Court House and receives the Medal of Honor for bravery. Also, General George A. Custer continues to remain extremely busy with cutting off the Rebels' supplies.

In South Carolina, General Alexander Schimmelfennig, having been appointed commander of Charleston subsequent to its fall the previous February, again is struck by illness (tuberculosis). He is granted a 30-day sick leave. His type of tuberculosis is particularly pernicious and he does not recover. General Schimmelfennig dies on 5 September 1865.

April 8–9   In Virginia, Union and Confederate troops skirmish prior to the surrender in the vicinity of Appomattox Court House. Lt. Morton A. Read, 8th New York Cavalry, captures the flag of the 1st Texas Infantry (CSA). The Union losses are 200 killed or wounded. Confederates lose 500 killed. Confederate Brigadier General William Ruffin Cox, leading his North Carolina regiments (Cox's Brigade), and additional troops had led the final charge of the Confederates during the last-ditch effort to forestall disaster at Appomattox, but despite their steadfastness, while covering the retreat, the brigade is able only to temporarily stall the Union thrust. Nonetheless, the Union forces facing the rear action brigade realize the Rebels will not easily fold. The Yankees, nevertheless, are equal to the task and finally capture the command.

April 9 (Sunday)   In Alabama, a vicious battle erupts when Union troops, including the 119th Illinois, assault Confederate positions at Fort Blakely. Lt. Charles M. Rockefeller of the 178th New York Infantry, solely on his own, ventures through intense enemy fire to ascertain information necessary to capture the Rebel fort. Prior to Rockefeller's endeavor, a contingent of 25 men attempted to accomplish the same task but were turned back by heavy fire that inflicted heavy casualties. Rockefeller's courageous action leads to another assault against the fort which causes the surrender of the Rebels. He leads a small detachment and manages to capture 300 of the Rebels before they make their escape. The Confederate-held fort falls to the Union, and Confederate Generals St. John R. Liddell and Bryan M. Thomas (West Point, 1858) are among the captured. On 2 February 1870, General Lidell becomes involved in an altercation with Charles Jones (former lieutenant colonel, 17th Louisiana) and his two sons while on a Black River steamboat. General Liddell is killed.

In South Carolina, Union troops, including the 107th Ohio Infantry, skirmish at Dingle's Mill.

In Virginia, at Appomattox, General Robert E. Lee surrenders to General Ulysses S. Grant. After accepting the surrender of Lee, Grant allows nearly 29,000 Confederates to keep their horses. Grant, in an obvious way, forbids all Union troops from firing victory salutes or raising cheers as the defeated yet proud Southerners march home. The meeting between Grant and Lee at the home of Wilmer McLean in Appomattox Court House is the last time these two men meet as adversaries. The surrender is signed as follows: "We the undersigned prisoners of war belonging to the Army of Northern Virginia, having been this day surrendered by General Robert E. Lee (CSA), commanding said army, to Lieut Genl U.S. Grant, commanding armies of the United States, do hereby give our solemn parole of honor that we will not hereafter serve in the armies of the Confederate States or in any military capacity whatever, against the United States of America or render aid to the enemies of the latter until properly exchanged, in such manner as shall be mutually approved by the respective authorities done at Appomattox Court House, Virginia this 9th day of April, 1865." This document is signed by the following: "R.E. LEE GENL; W.H. TAYLOR LT COL AAG; CHARLES S. VENABLE, LT COL & AAG; CHARLES MARSHALL LT COL & AAG; H.E. PEYTON, LT COL & A & INSPT GENL; GILES B. COOKE, MAJ & AA & IG; AND H.E. YOUNG MAJ AAG, JUDGE ADV."

Major General John Gibbon is one of the commissioners appointed to accept the surrender of the Confederate forces. Following the conclusion of the war, Gibbon is appointed colonel of the 36th U.S. Infantry and afterward, the 7th U.S. Infantry. In 1876 he arrives to secure the survivors of General Custer's force at Little Big Horn. He is promoted to brigadier general, Regular Army, on 10 July 1885.

Confederate Generals Charles William Field (West Point, 1849), George Washington Custis Lee (son of Robert E. Lee), William H.F. Lee (son of Robert E. Lee), Young Marshall Moody (recently appointed brigadier), William Nelson Pendleton (West Point, 1830), Nathaniel Harrison Harris, Fitzhugh Lee (West Point, 1856 and nephew of Robert E. Lee), General William Ruffin Cox (wounded more than ten times during the war), James H. Lane, Henry Lewis Benning and Edward Lloyd Thomas are among those captured and paroled at Appomattox.

Also, Confederate General Edward Porter Alexander (West Point, 1857), who was wounded while fighting in defense of Petersburg, is at Appomattox for the final days. The command of General William R. Peck surrenders at Appomattox, but the general himself is not there. He will be paroled later at Vicksburg. The nephew of Confederate President Davis, General Joseph Robert Davis, who fought at Gettysburg and Petersburg, is also paroled at Appomattox. Brigadier General Walter H. Stevens is also paroled. In conjunction, General John Cabell Breckinridge, the recently appointed Confederate secretary of war, departs for England following the surrender of the Confederates, and he remains there for about three years. Afterward, he returns to the United States and settles in Kentucky to restart his law practice.

General Charles W. Field, subsequent to his parole, returns home and for a while engages in business, but afterward, he joins the Egyptian Army. After returning to the States, General Field serves as doorkeeper of the U.S. House of Representatives and engages in civil engineering. He is appointed superintendent of the Hot Springs Reservation in Arkansas. He succumbs on 9 April 1892. Another general officer, General James Alexander Walker, in divisional command at the time of surrender, returns to his home accompanied by two army mules. General Walker uses the mules to plant a crop of corn on his farm in Pulaski County, Virginia; however, he does not rely on his farm for a livelihood; rather, he resumes his law practice. In addition he enters politics, serving in the House of Delegates and later serving as lieutenant governor of the state (1871). He serves in the U.S. Congress from 1895 until 1899. General Walker dies in Wytheville, Virginia, in October 1901.

Confederate Brigadier General Raleigh E. Colston, who saw service in Virginia, following the close of hostilities relocates to North Carolina and accepts a commission as colonel in the Egyptian Army; however, he returns to the States during 1879. While in the Egyptian service, he sustains debilitating wounds. After his savings are expended, he spends the remainder of his life in a state of poverty. From 1894 to 1896, he resides in the Confederate Soldiers' Home in Richmond, where he succumbs on 29 July 1896. Lt. General James Longstreet after the war enters politics as a Republican. General Grant, his old foe, turns into a close friend. After Grant becomes president, he appoints Longstreet as U.S. minister to Turkey.

Brigadier Generals William MacRae and William Henry Wallace also surrender at Appomattox. General MacRae, having lost everything during the war, finds employment as superintendent of a number of southern railroads; however, his health continues to worsen. He dies at Augusta, Georgia, on 11 February 1882. General Wallace returns to his plantation in South Carolina and resumes his law practice. He also serves three terms in the state legislature. Subsequently, he becomes a circuit judge, a post he retains until retirement during 1893.

General Wallace dies in Union, South Carolina, on 21 March 1901.

Major General Fitzhugh Lee, the nephew of Robert E. Lee, returns to private life as a farmer, but later he is elected governor of Virginia. In 1893 he unsuccessfully runs for the U.S. Senate. President Grover Cleveland appoints him consul-general at Havana. At the outbreak of the Spanish-American War, Lee re-enters the U.S. Service as a major general of volunteers during 1901 with the rank of brigadier general in the Regular Army. He dies in Washington, D.C., on 28 April 1905. He is interred at Richmond, Virginia, in the Hollywood Cemetery.

The United States Marine Corps, during the Civil War, sustains a total of 551 casualties: these include those killed in battle, those dying of their wounds and those who had been lost at sea or succumbed to disease; the figure also includes those wounded during the conflict.

April 10 (Monday) **In Alabama,** the 2nd Brigade, 1st Cavalry Division, Military Division of the Mississippi, engage Confederates at Lowndesville.

In South Carolina, a Union force attached to the Department of the South clashes with Confederates at Sumterville.

In Virginia, General William T. Sherman's army advances toward Smithfield rather than Richmond, where he is better positioned to challenge and destroy General Joseph Johnston's 35,000 Confederates. At this time, Confederate Brigadier General Henry H. Walker and the troops at Danville are directed to move out for North Carolina to join with General Joseph E. Johnston to bolster his army. In other activity, Confederate General Henry Harrison Walker, at Danville, is ordered by President Davis to abandon the place and join with General Joseph E. Johnston in North Carolina. Nevertheless, he is paroled at Richmond on 7 May. Subsequently, he resides in New Jersey and becomes an investment broker. He succumbs at Morrisville during March 1912.

In Naval activity, the USS *Kansas* is ordered to move to a position off Cape Henry to cut off the escape route of Confederate sympathizers. The Union is aware of an alleged scheme for Southern sympathizers to seize ships in the bay. Shortly after this final duty, the *Kansas* sails to Philadelphia, where it is decommissioned on 4 May 1865. Nonetheless, its inactivity is short-lived. The *Kansas* is recommissioned on 28 July, just prior to embarking on a four-year cruise in the South Atlantic on 5 August 1865. It arrives back in the United States on 15 September 1869 and within one week is again decommissioned. Nonetheless, its retirement lasts only one year. On 26 September 1870, the *Kansas* is recommissioned, and on 13 October it departs Hampton Roads on a surveying mission with two other ships, the *Mayflower* and the *Tehuantepec*. It returns during the following year after accomplishing a number of objectives, including determining that the Isthmus of Tehuantepec (southern Mexico) is suitable for the construction of a canal and that one can be constructed due to obstacles "in the way of the canal route are of the most ordinary nature." The voyage had been costly. While in the tropics an epidemic of fever had struck the crew. The *Kansas* remains in active service until 1875. On 21 October of that year, it arrives at Portsmouth, New Hampshire, from Pensacola, Florida. On 10 August, it is decommissioned. It is sold on 27 September 1883.

April 11 (Tuesday) In Alabama, Union troops occupy Confederate-held Forts Huger and Tracy in Mobile Bay. The siege of Mobile ends with heavy costs sustained by both sides, but the Confederates, under the command of Major General Dabney H. Maury (West Point, 1846), capitulate. Confederate Generals Francis M. Cockrell and J.T. Holtzclaw are captured. Cockrell, subsequent to his release, returns to Missouri. He will serve in the U.S. Senate from 1874 until 1904. Holtzclaw is paroled during May 1865 at Meridian, Mississippi. He dies in Montgomery, Alabama, on 19 July 1893. In other activity, Union troops, including the 1st Louisiana Cavalry, skirmish with Confederates at Mt. Pleasant. Private August Dooley Company B, 1st Louisiana Cavalry, receives the Medal of Honor for his bravery during this action.

In Virginia, Confederate General Joseph E. Johnston evacuates Smithfield, avoiding a major confrontation with General William T. Sherman's prowling army. There is sporadic skirmishing in the area. Also, elements of the 8th (also known as 13th) Tennessee Cavalry, apparently unaware that General Lee had capitulated, continue to move, and on the following day, the regiment confirms the surrender. Nonetheless, it advances to Greensboro, North Carolina, but holds out until early May before capitulating. A brigade under Brigadier General John C. Vaughn, after Lee's surrender, moves from East Tennessee to North Carolina to hook up with General Johnston. Also, at about this time, General Henry Jackson Hunt, having received the brevet rank of major general (volunteers) for his actions at Gettysburg, receives the same rank in the Regular service at about this time. Afterward, he reverts to his permanent rank, lieutenant colonel, 3rd Artillery. Later he becomes colonel of the 5th Artillery. He retires during 1883. Major General Andrew Jackson Smith (XX Corps) remains in the army beyond the close of hostilities. During the following year, he becomes colonel of the 7th U.S. Cavalry. President Grant appoints Smith as postmaster at St. Louis during 1869. He accepts the appointment and resigns his commission. Subsequently, during a period of turbulence, while he is the auditor of the city of St. Louis (1877), strikes break out and Smith leads a brigade of Missouri militia to quell the strikers. On 22 January 1889, Smith is recommissioned in the army, and on the identical day, he is appointed colonel of cavalry. He dies on 30 January 1897.

April 12 (Wednesday) In Alabama, a Union fleet, including the *Octorara* and several ironclads commanded by Commodore James Palmer, moves up the Blakely River to a spot where it breaks off from the Tensaw River and sails from there to a point about one mile outside the city of Mobile. In addition, the forces under General Granger, numbering about 8,000, cross the bay and prepare to attack the city. The attack becomes unnecessary, as Mobile surrenders. It is brought under Union control and Confederate General Samuel G. French surrenders along with General Dabney H. Maury, the commandant of Mobile. After the war, French lives in Florida until his demise during 1910. General Maury founds the Southern Historical Society and later pens *Recollections of a Virginian* (1894). The 5th Minnesota Volunteer Regiment participates in the action to gain Mobile.

In Virginia, General William T. Sherman receives word from Grant of Robert E. Lee's surrender at Appomattox on the 9th. In other activity, General James H. Wilson's cavalry captures Montgomery, Alabama. General Wilson is accomplishing spectacular results during the latter part of this war and is in the process of spanning out to sever the escape routes of Confederates attempting to make a break. His command will arrive at Macon, Georgia, on 20 April. General Wilson (West Point, 1860) is promoted to the rank of major general of volunteers the following June, effective 4 May 1865, and he is breveted major general in the Regular U.S. Army. Later, during 1866, he is appointed colonel of the 35th U.S. Infantry but is assigned duty with the Corps of Engineers. He retires during 1870, but not permanently. At the outbreak of the Spanish-American War, Wilson suspends his law practice and re-enters the army as major general of volunteers. He actively serves in Cuba and Puerto Rico. And, during the Boxer Rebellion, he again serves in China. Finally during 1901, through congressional action, he is placed on the army's retirement list as brigadier general. He succumbs during 1925 on 23 February.

In North Carolina, General George Stoneman's cavalry captures the city of Salisbury (Grant's Creek), and he accepts the surrender of the Confederate troops garrisoned there. Confederate Brigadier General Bradley T. Johnson, transferred to Salisbury during the last months of the war to command the stockade, is among the captured. Subsequent to his parole, General Johnson practices law in Richmond, Virginia. With the capture of Salisbury, General Stoneman's troops acquire about 7,000 bales of cotton and a fully stocked arsenal.

In Confederate general officer activity, General James Green Martin, at the close of hostilities, commands the District of Western North Carolina after becoming ill at Petersburg. Following his termination of service, he becomes a lawyer and practices in Asheville, North Carolina, until his death on 4 October 1878.

April 13 (Thursday) In Alabama, Union Major John F. Weston, 4th Cavalry, leads a contingent of troops toward Wetumpka and successfully captures a number of Confederate supply steamboats. In other activity, the 5th Minnesota Regiment departs Mobile for Montgomery from where the regiment will muster out of the service during September. The 5th Minnesota had mustered in the service during 1862. Also, the 3rd Division, XIII Corps, Army of the West Mississippi, engages Confederates at Whistler's Station.

In North Carolina, Union General William T. Sherman enters Raleigh and promptly dispatches sufficient troops to Asheville, Salisbury and Charlotte. In the interim, Confederate General Joseph E. Johnston dispatches General Wade Hampton to Sherman requesting surrender negotiations. Sherman agrees to meet with Johnston on the 17th.

April 14 (Friday) In Alabama, the USS *Ada Laura, Itasca, Rose* and *Sciota* are destroyed by Confederate torpedoes (mines) at Mobile Bay.

In South Carolina, Union General Robert Anderson, the commanding officer at the time the Confederates bombarded and captured Fort Sumter four years earlier, receives the honor of being at Fort Sumter for the official raising of Old Glory. The fort had been recaptured during February 1865, subsequent to Confederate takeover during April 1861. This ceremony occurs four years to the day that the flag had been removed by the Confederates.

In Virginia, sporadic skirmishes continue to occur. Confederate General William Fitzhugh Payne is captured in the vicinity of Warrenton. He is released on 29 May 1865. Afterward, he returns to his home and resumes his law practice. He serves one term in the Virginia House of Delegates (1879), then relocates in Washington, D.C., where he becomes counsel to the Southern Railway. He succumbs in the capital on 29 March 1904.

In Naval activity, the USS *Sciota*, operating in Mobile Bay since the previous January, strikes a mine and sinks. It is raised and refloated, then sent to New York, where it is decommissioned and sold during October 1865. Afterward, it operates as a commercial ship, then is sold to Chile for use as a warship.

April 14–15 In Washington, D.C., President Lincoln is assassinated by a Southern sympathizer, John Wilkes Booth. President Lincoln, mortally wounded April 14 while attending a play at Ford's Theater in Washington, D.C., dies the following morning, on April 15. Lincoln and His wife, Mary Todd Lincoln, were watching a play called *Our American Cousin*. Secretary of State William Seward, confined to his bed at home because of injuries suffered in an accident, is accosted by Booth's co-conspirator and stabbed, however; Seward is saved by the quick actions of his son and a nurse who drive off the attacker. General Grant was not in attendance, although he was invited to spend the evening with President Lincoln. Grant had departed Washington to visit his children attending school in Burlington, New Jersey, and he is informed of the tragedy while in Philadelphia awaiting a ferry to take him across the Delaware River to New Jersey. Grant is requested to return to Washington immediately and he does so.

There is grave concern throughout Washington because of the attacks, and precautions must be taken to insure that the conspiracy is thwarted before additional panic begins to plague the country. President Abraham Lincoln is the first president of the United States to be assassinated. Ground forces and Union warships initiate a search for the assassins. The USS *Thomas Freeborn* participates.

April 15 (Saturday)   In Washington, D.C., within a few hours after the death of President Abraham Lincoln, Andrew Johnson, the vice president, is sworn in as the 17th president of the United States at 11 a.m. U.S. Marines, commanded by Captain Frank Monroe and attached to the Navy Yard in Washington, D.C., are assigned responsibility for guarding those accused of assassinating the president.

April 16 (Easter Sunday)   The tragedy of Lincoln's untimely death is felt deeply by people on both sides of the conflict. Confederate General John Wesley Frazer, one of 15 Confederate generals being held at Fort Warren (Massachusetts), sends regrets of Lincoln's death to General Grant. In other activity, General Sherman's response to Confederate General Johnston arrives at Johnston's headquarters. An agreement to meet on terms of surrender has been reached. Sherman will meet with Johnston on the following day.

In Georgia, elements of the 4th Iowa Cavalry, led by General Emory Upton (Wilson's Raid), skirmish with Confederates at Columbus. The Union captures the colors of Austin's battery. About 1,200 Confederates are seized. General Upton receives the brevet of major general in the volunteer service and the Regular Army. He remains in the service beyond the close of hostilities and becomes captain of the 5th U.S. Artillery. He becomes lieutenant colonel of the 25th Infantry during 1866. In addition, Upton becomes commandant of cadets (1870–1875) at the United States Military Academy at West Point. During 1880, he receives command of the Presidio in San Francisco. He apparently continues to suffer from an ailment thought to be migraine headaches, which compel him to frequently take leaves. On 15 March 1881, while at the Presidio, he commits suicide by shooting himself.

Around Culloden, the 17th Indiana Mounted engages Worrill's Grays. Pvt. John Davis captures the Rebel regimental flag. Also, Confederate Brigadier General Robert Charles Tyler is killed during fighting at Fort Tyler while he leads his diminutive command against Major General James Wilson's cavalry brigade. Although the earthwork was constructed beside the bridge during 1863, the name Fort Tyler actually came to be on the day of the battle. Tyler had been recuperating from wounds and was still on crutches near West Point when he was informed of the Union presence. Tyler gathers Georgia militia and convalescents to bolster troops from Tennessee and Georgia, but the determined defense is insufficient to overcome the odds against a brigade which included the 2nd and 4th Indiana, 1st Wisconsin and 7th Kentucky regiments with dismounted supported by the 18th Indiana Battery. The Rebels refuse to surrender. Many of the killed and seriously wounded are shot in the head. Approximate Confederate losses stand at eighteen killed and 28 wounded and about 200 captured.

In Oregon, the 1st Oregon Cavalry skirmishes with Confederates at South Fork, John Day's River.

April 17 (Monday)   In Washington D.C., Mary Surratt is arrested for her involvement in the assassination of President Lincoln. After a military trial, which begins on May 9 and lasts to the end of June, she receives the death penalty, "to die by hanging on July 7th," along with three other co-conspirators, Lewis Paine (who attempted assassination of Secretary of State Seward), George Atzerodt and David Herold. Doctor Samuel Mudd (who aided the wounded Booth), Samuel Arnold and Michael O'Laughlin receive life sentences for their part in the assassination, and Edward Spangler, a stagehand at the theater, another conspirator, receives a six year sentence.

Mary Jenkins Surratt is the first woman executed by the U.S. government. She had married John Surratt and they owned a tavern in Surrattsville, Maryland, but during 1864, about two years after the death of her husband, Mary leased the tavern and moved to a house she owned on High Street in Washington, D.C. The tavern also served as a safe house for Confederates during the war. John, one of Mary's three children, operated during the war as a secret agent for the Confederacy.

In North Carolina, Sherman arrives by train at Durham's Station to discuss surrender terms with General Joseph E. Johnston. The talks are held in a farmhouse owned by the Bennett (Bennitt) family. Sherman, while speaking with Johnston, reveals the dispatch concerning Lincoln's assassination, causing Johnston immediate discomfort. Johnston condemns the action and hopes Sherman will not blame the Confederate Army. Sherman states that he "did not blame Lee or Confederate officers, but would not say as much for Jeff Davis." The talks end for the day, but they meet again on the following day.

In Virginia, a Union force led by General Winfield S. Hancock accepts the surrender of Confederate partisans under John Singleton Mosby at Berryville.

April 18 (Tuesday)   In North Carolina, a letter addressed to U.S. Grant or Major General Halleck is written by General Sherman, following a second day of discussions with General Johnston. It states: "I enclose herewith a copy of an agreement made this day between General Joseph E. Johnston and myself, which, if approved by the President of the United States, will produce peace from the Potomac to the Rio Grande." Many of the Confederates under Johnston had anticipated the surrender, and rather than wait for the formalities, large numbers of the troops had on their own started to head back to their homes. General Pierre Beauregard, second in command to Johnston, returns to Louisiana following the surrender.

In South Carolina, a Union contingent (Department of the South) engages Confederates at Bradford's Springs (Boykin's Mills).

April 19 (Wednesday)   President Lincoln's body lies in state in Washington this day, then moves to Baltimore (21st); Philadelphia (23rd); and New York (24th).

In Maryland, Major General Lewis Wallace is appointed again as commander of the Middle Military Department. He succeeds Brevet Brigadier General William C. Morris and holds the post until 29 June 1865. General Wallace is the last of the commanders of the department.

In North Carolina, Lt. Colonel Charles Betts and his contingent of the 15th Pennsylvania Cavalry, consisting of 75 men, capture a battalion of Confederate cavalry at Greensboro. Also, General George Stoneman's cavalry engages Confederates under Brigadier General John Porter McCown (West Point, 1840) in the vicinity of Morgantown on the Catawba River. McCown is down to a small force of about 300 men and a solitary piece of artillery, certainly no genuine threat to the advancing division of cavalry under General Alvan C. Gillem. Other units of Stoneman's cavalry clash with Rebels at Dallas.

McCown had been more or less placed in the closet of the Confederacy in March 1862, following a trial that found him guilty of disobeying orders given by General Braxton Bragg. After the war General McCown becomes a teacher in Tennessee; however, later he acquires a farm in Arkansas. He dies in Little Rock on 22 January 1879.

In South Carolina, a contingent of Union troops attached to the Department of the South clashes with Confederates at Swift Creek.

In Tennessee, a Union contingent deployed along the Hatchie River initiates operations in the vicinity of Brownsville.

In Naval activity, the Union transport steamer USS *Mary* is sunk by a torpedo (mine) off Mobile, Alabama.

April 20 (Thursday)   In Georgia, Confederate Major General Howell Cobb dispatches Brigadier General Felix H. Robertson to discuss surrender terms with Union General James H. Wilson, a friend while they both attended West Point. Also, Macon capitulates to the Union, culminating Wilson's mission. Wilson's forces (17th Indiana Mounted Infantry) also encounter Confederates at Tobosofkee. Major General (state militia) Gustavus W. Smith (West Point, 1842) is among the Confederate prisoners; he surrenders with his Georgia militia. After the war, Smith becomes superintendent of an ironworks company at Chattanooga and later is insurance commissioner of Tennessee. He dies during June 1896.

In Union general officer activity, Brigadier General James William Reilly resigns from the army.

April 21 (Friday)   In North Carolina, President Johnson rejects General Sherman's "Memorandum" or "Basis of Agreement" with General Joseph E. Johnston. Union Secretary of War Stanton instructs General Grant to inform General Sherman to renew hostilities in a letter dated this day. Sherman receives word on the 25th. Nevertheless, Sherman accepts the surrender of Johnston on the 26th at Durham's Station.

In Union general officer activity, Colonel Robert Kingston Scott is promoted to brigadier general of volunteers to rank from 12 January. In December 1865, he receives the brevet of major general. Later, during 1868, he is elected governor of South Carolina.

April 22 (Saturday)   In Alabama, a contingent of Union General James Wilson's cavalry (1st Brigade, 1st Cavalry Division, Military Division of the Mississippi) occupies Talladega.

In Union general activity, General Henry Halleck resumes command of the Military Division of the James. Also, General Nathaniel P. Banks again assumes command of the Department of the Gulf.

In Naval activity, the USS *Blackhawk,* engaged in patrolling along the Mississippi River, is accidentally destroyed by fire at a point several miles from Cairo, Illinois. In 1867, the *Blackhawk* is raised and sold at St. Louis during April.

April 23 (Sunday)   In Alabama, Union cavalry (Wilson's Raid) of the 1st Brigade, 1st Cavalry Division, Military Division of the Mississippi, seizes Mumford's Station at Blue Mount.

In North Carolina, Union General Alvan Cullem Gillem (Stoneman's Raid) engages a Confederate force at Suwano Gap. General Gillem receives the brevet rank of major general, U.S. Army. During the following year he becomes colonel of the 28th Infantry Regiment. Subsequently, during January 1868, he is appointed commander of the Fourth Military District, which includes Arkansas and Mississippi. Afterward he is transferred to the West Coast, and he participates against the Modoc Indians in retaliation for the assassination of General Edward Canby on 11 April 1873. During the campaign, General Gillem is ill; however, he leads the force despite his illness. He is compelled to take sick leave during January 1875. He dies while at Soldiers' Rest Home at Nashville, Tennessee, on 2 December 1875.

April 24 (Monday)   In North Carolina, General William T. Sherman notifies Johnston that the truce will end 48 hours after he receives the message, as agreed upon earlier. Another letter from Sherman to Johnston on the same day is a demand for surrender based on the same terms as those afforded Lee at Appomattox. General Grant had secretly met with Sherman concerning surrender terms.

In Naval activity, the USS *Manhattan* and the *Lafayette* engage the CSS *Webb* on the Mississippi River near New Orleans. On the previous day, the *Webb* ran through the blockade at the mouth of the Red River, but the escape was not complete. The Union warship immediately gave chase. The *Webb* is run ashore and the crew sets it afire. The USS *Quaker City* participates in this action, then sails north. It is decommissioned at Philadelphia on 18 May. On 20 June 1865, the *Quaker City* is sold at auction. It retains American registry until resold to owners in Europe during 1869.

The USS *Manhattan* is also decommissioned at New Orleans, Louisiana, during August 1865 and is renamed *Neptune.* Afterward, it is moved to Key West and from there to Philadelphia, where it remains out of service until November 1873, when it is recommissioned and returns to service at several stations in the U.S. until 1888. It moves to Philadelphia to be decommissioned and in 1902 is sold for scrap. In other activity, the USS *Argosy,* on patrol on the Mississippi River, encounters the CSS *Webb,* a steam ram which emerges from the mouth of the Red River. The *Webb* passes the *Argosy;* however, its identity is discovered and word is transmitted to other vessels down river. The *Webb,* aware that escape is fruitless, runs aground. The commanding officer, Lieutenant Charles W. Read, Confederate States Navy, orders the ship to be set afire and directs the crew to scatter. Following this incident, the *Argosy* remains on duty until it is decommissioned at Mound City, Illinois, on 11 August 1865. Soon after, on 17 August, it is sold at auction. The *Argosy* operates as a civilian vessel until destroyed by fire at Cincinnati on 7 March 1872.

April 24–27   Pursuant to orders, Lt. Doherty of the 16th New York Cavalry embarks from Washington, D.C., aboard the *John S. Ide* in search of John Wilkes Booth, president Lincoln's assassin, who is thought to be somewhere between the Potomac and James Rivers. Doherty leads a 25-man contingent and two detectives on this mission. On the evening of the 25th, the detachment arrives near Bowling Green, Virginia, and by about midnight, the detachment surrounds a home of Mrs. Goldman in Bowling Green.

After receiving information on the whereabouts of their targets, they and a Rebel captive taken at the Goldman house, Captain Jett, returned to a house about ten miles outside of Bowling Green. Once there, during the early morning hours of the 26th, the Garrett house is surrounded. Afterward, as reported by Lt. Edward P. Doherty, Mr. Garrett initially tells Doherty that the assailants had departed on the previous night and fled into the woods. Meanwhile, Garrett's son arrives and tells his father to tell Doherty where the men are. Doherty seizes the senior Garrett by the collar and pulls him out of the door and down the steps. Doherty "put my revolver to his head and told him to tell me at once where the two assassins were; he replied, in the barn." His force surrounds the barn, but Booth refuses to surrender. Two detectives with Doherty urge him to set the barn on fire, but he declines and decides to await dawn.

Booth continues to resist surrendering, and he states that he intends to use his ammunition against the cavalry detachment. Meanwhile, the other man with Booth, David Herold, surrenders, and at about the same time, one of the detectives, Conger, sets the barn on fire. Shortly thereafter, Booth is shot by Sergeant Boston Corbett (16th New York Cavalry). Booth dies about two hours later. Afterward, the detachment, with Booth's corps in a wagon, arrives at Port Royal about 0900 on the 26th. Lt. Doherty also has detained Captain Jett, the two Garretts and Herold. On the evening of the 26th, the detachment re-boards the vessel *John S. Ide* at Belle Plain and returns to Washington.

In the meantime, Captain Jett, while under guard of the detectives, escapes. On 27 April at 0300, subsequent to arriving back in Washington, Lt. Doherty transfers David Herold, the two Garretts and the body of John Wilkes Booth to Colonel L.C. Baker. Doherty notes in his report: "For nearly sixty hours hardly an eye was closed or a horse dismounted until the errand was accomplished."

April 26 (Wednesday)   In North Carolina, General John Schofield, in the absence of General Sherman, paroles 36,817 Confederate prisoners of war, held at Greensboro. Also, General James H. Wilson paroles 52,453 in Georgia and Florida, for a total of 89,270 men. U.S. troops, Army of the Tennessee, Georgia and Ohio, under Major General William T. Sherman, accept the surrender of more than 29,000

Wharf at Belle Plain (Johnson, *Campfire and Battlefield: History of the Conflicts and Campaigns,* **1894).**

(29,924) Confederate soldiers commanded by General Joseph Johnston at Bennett's House near Durham's Station. Confederate Generals Henry B. Davidson, Robert H. Anderson, Matthew C. Butler, Samuel Cooper, Henry D. Clayton, James Cantey, Alfred H. Colquitt, Daniel C. Govan, Johnson Hagood, W.J. Hardee, William W. Kirkland, Lafayette McLaws, Joseph B. Palmer, Stephen D. Lee and Brigadier General Winfield Scott Featherston surrender with Johnston at Greensboro. Records indicate that Brigadier General George E. Maney is paroled at Greensboro during May; however, there are no reports of his activity after August 1864. Subsequent to the close of hostilities, Maney becomes president of the Tennessee and Pacific Railroad and serves in various diplomatic posts in South America. He dies unexpectedly while in Washington, D.C., on 9 February 1901.

Confederate General Lawrence Baker (West Point, 1851), who was participating in the final months of the war in spite of severe injuries, is also captured in North Carolina. Confederate General William B. Bate surrendered during the fighting in the vicinity of Greensboro. Upon his release, Bate returns to Tennessee and becomes its governor. Subsequently, he again returns to the U.S. Senate, where he had served prior to the war. At the time of the surrender, Brigadier General George D. Johnston is en route to hook up with Lt. General Richard Taylor and is not snagged in the capitulation. However, after the war, he returns to Alabama. Also, Confederate Major General Carter L. Stevenson is seized and paroled early the following May. Lt. General Alexander P. Stewart is paroled at Goldsboro the next month. Brigadier General John C. Vaughn is paroled during early May. General Henry H. Walker, who had recently arrived in the North Carolina from Virginia, will be paroled at Richmond in early May. Confederate Major General Edward Cary Walthall is also paroled at Greensboro (May). General Govan, subsequent to being paroled, returns to his plantation in Arkansas. In 1894, President Grover Cleveland appoints him Indian agent for the state of Washington. He dies in Memphis while residing with one of his children on 12 March 1911.

In other activity, Union troops have been tracking Lincoln's assassin, John Wilkes Booth. They locate Booth and a co-assailant at a farm in the vicinity of Bowling Green, Virginia. The soldiers demand the two men to come from their hiding place, but Booth refuses and the barn is torched to give Booth some added incentive. Gunfire occurs at the same time and Booth is felled, mortally wounded (see also, **April 24–27**). His body is returned to Washington and taken aboard the USS *Montauk*, where the corpse is examined. The *Montauk* also is used to detain some of Booth's co-conspirators.

In other activity, a severe fire erupts in Mobile. John Cooper, U.S. Navy, receives the Medal of Honor for his actions during this crisis.

In Naval activity, the USS *Mohawk* is decommissioned at Boston, Massachusetts. It is recommissioned on 18 August 1866 and assigned to the Pacific Squadron. It remains on active duty until 25 June 1872, when it is decommissioned at Mare Island, California. Later, during the latter part of the year, it sinks while moored.

April 27 (Thursday)   In Virginia, Confederate General Samuel Cooper, who had surrendered on the previous day, had been the adjutant and inspector general. He receives great accolades for his meticulous recordkeeping and overseeing the safety of the Confederate war records, including the removal of such records from Richmond to a place of safety where they could be held and turned over to the federal government. General Cooper attempts to return to his home in the vicinity of Alexandria, Virginia, shortly after the war, only to discover that his property had been transformed into a federal fort. Undaunted, he moves into a nearby house and attempts to become a farmer. Things go rather badly for him and financially he is wiped out. Several former Confederate officers, including Robert E. Lee, attempt to come to his aid, but about one year after they contribute approximately $300 to the desperate Cooper, he succumbs (1876). He is buried in Christ Church Cemetery in Alexandria, just across the Potomac from the capital.

April 28 (Friday)   In North Carolina, General William T. Sherman summons all of his commanders to the governor's mansion in Raleigh. Generals John Schofield, Alfred Terry and Hugh Kilpatrick are ordered to march toward Richmond to await Sherman's arrival.

General Kilpatrick received the brevet of major general of the U.S. Army during the previous month. He is promoted to major general of volunteers during June 1865. Nonetheless, during the latter part of the year, General Kilpatrick resigns both of his commissions to undertake a diplomatic career. He is appointed as minister to Chile. He dies in Santiago on 4 December 1881. Also, General John Schofield is sent to France at the close of hostilities to negotiate with the French to get their forces out of Mexico. In other activity, Confederate Admiral Raphael Semmes is paroled at Greensboro.

April 30 (Saturday)   *In Naval activity,* the USS *Moose* spots a Confederate force as it moves to cross the Cumberland River at Eddyville, Indiana. The Confederates scatter. Subsequent to this activity, the *Moose* returns to duty on the Ohio River until early July, when it is ordered to move to Mound City, Illinois. It is decommissioned prior to being sold at auction on 17 August. On 9 October, it is renamed the *Little Rock,* under which it operates as a commercial vessel until destroyed by fire at Clarendon, Arkansas, on 23 December 1867.

In Virginia, Brigadier General Patrick Theodore Moore apparently did not accompany General Ewell during the retreat from Richmond and no documentation exists regarding his capture at Sayler's Creek. He is paroled this

day at Manchester. General Moore, having lost everything during the course of the war, establishes an insurance agency in Richmond, where he dies on 19 February 1883.

May   In South Dakota, a contingent of the 6th Iowa Cavalry, led by Captain Daniel F. Eicher, establishes Fort Dakota. It is part of a larger operation by General Alfred Sully, who has directed that a series of military posts be strung along the frontier from Minnesota to the Missouri River in order to provide security for the pioneers and settlers traveling through Sioux territory. The fort remains active until June 1869.

In Confederate general officer activity, Major General Joseph Wheeler is captured in Georgia. He is transported to Fort Delaware and released during June. Brigadier General Winfield Scott Featherston is paroled this month. His brigade had culminated its fighting during the closing days of the hostilities. General Featherston returns home to resume his law practice. In addition, he serves several terms in the Mississippi state legislature. In 1882 he becomes a judge. Featherston dies at Holly Springs on 28 May 1891. Brigadier General Harry T. Hays is promoted to major general by General E. Kirby Smith, not the Confederate Congress, which has been terminated. Upon his parole by the Union, he is referred to as major general. In 1866, Hays becomes sheriff of Orleans Parish, but he is removed from office by General Sheridan. Afterward, he practices law until his death during August 1876.

May 1 (Monday)   In Kentucky, the remaining command of General John Hunt Morgan surrenders to General Edward H. Hobson at Mt. Sterling. In other activity, at about this time, Major General Gouverneur Warren becomes commanding officer, Department of the Mississippi, succeeding General Napoleon Jackson T. Dana. Warren had encountered some difficulty with Grant and Sheridan that affected his career. His remaining time in the army, after the war, is confined to the engineer corps. He finally reaches the rank of lieutenant colonel during 1879 after he is cleared of any wrongdoing at Five Forks outside of Petersburg during the closing days of the war; however, the inquiry does fault him for his "manner of relief."

In North Carolina, General William T. Sherman receives reports from General James F. Wilson regarding his expedition from Eastport, Mississippi, 30 days prior. Wilson marched 50 miles in 30 days, capturing 6,300 Confederates, 23 colors and 156 guns. Wilson defeated Forrest's cavalry and destroyed every railroad and factory in northern Alabama and Georgia. Thirteen thousand, five hundred men and horses reach Macon, Georgia. Also, Confederate Major General Carter Littlepage Stevenson is paroled at Greensboro. Subsequently, he engages in civil engineering until he dies in Caroline County, Virginia, in August 1888.

In Union general officer activity, Colonel Thomas Ogden Osborn receives the brevet rank of brigadier general and major general of volunteers. On 1 May 1865, he is promoted to full rank brigadier general. General Osborn musters out of the army at the close of hostilities. He has lost the use of his right arm, but this disability does not inhibit him from again practicing law in Chicago. In 1874, he is appointed minister to Argentina, a post he retains until 1885. Nonetheless, he remains in South America until 1890. He dies while visiting Washington, D.C., on 27 March 1904. He had a law practice in the capital when the war broke out.

Colonel Joseph Haydn Potter is appointed brigadier general of volunteers and receives the brevet of major general in the Regular Army. He remains in the service beyond the close of hostilities and serves primarily on the Western frontier posts until he retires with the rank of brigadier general during 1887.

In Confederate general officer activity, Brigadier Generals Joseph Benjamin Palmer and James Argyle Smith are paroled at Greensboro, North Carolina. Palmer leads his command back to Tennessee, then resumes his law practice. He succumbs on 4 November 1890 in Murfreesboro, where he had served as mayor prior to the war. General Smith moves to Mississippi and engages in farming and later becomes superintendent of public education of the state. He dies at Jackson during December 1901. Also, Major General Edward Cary Walthall is paroled at Greensboro. After returning to his home in Mississippi, he resumes his law practice. He serves in the U.S. Senate from 1885 until his death in the capital on 21 April 1898. Brigadier General Benjamin Grierson remains in the service beyond the close of hostilities, but he is not raised in rank (major general) until 19 March 1866, effective this day. On 30 April 1866, he musters out of the army; however, in conjunction with the reorganization of the U.S. Army, he is appointed colonel of the 10th Cavalry during July 1866. He receives the brevets of brigadier and major general in the Regular Army in 1877. He retires at the rank of full rank brigadier general during April 1890. Subsequently, on 1 September 1911, he succumbs at his summer residence at Omena, Michigan. General Alfred Holt Colquitt is also paroled at Greensboro. After the close of hostilities, Colquitt serves two terms as governor of Georgia and later is elected to the U.S. Senate (1882).

In Naval activity, the monitor USS *Camanche* is commissioned in San Francisco at about this time (May). The monitor had been built as a prefab vessel and its parts had been transported from Jersey City to the West Coast; however, the *Acquila,* which transported the parts, sank at San Francisco during 1863. Nevertheless, the parts were salvaged. The *Camanche* remains the sole monitor on the West Coast until the USS *Monadnock* arrives there during 1866. The USS *Camanche* is sold in 1899. Also, the light draft monitor USS *Napa,* constructed at Wilmington, Delaware, is acquired by the U.S. Navy this month. The *Napa* had been transformed into a torpedo ship during its construction period; however, with the war essentially over except

for some units in the west, it does not participate. In addition, the *Napa* does not get commissioned. It remains inactive at League Island in Philadelphia. In 1869 it is renamed the *Nemesis,* but still it is not assigned active service, and within about two months it reverts back to *Napa.* It is scrapped during 1875.

May 2 (Tuesday) In Washington, D.C., President Andrew Johnson sets a reward of $100,000 for the capture of Confederate President Jefferson Davis. Davis and his party are attempting to make it to safety by passing through South Carolina to the Gulf Coast and then on to Texas. The Confederates have still not officially ended the struggle and there is discontent between President Davis and his cabinet on exactly what course to follow, especially since they are specifically tagged with conspiracy in the murder of President Lincoln.

In North Carolina, Confederate Major General William Booth Taliaferro, who had served during the final part of the war in Georgia, Florida and South Carolina, is paroled at Greensboro. Taliaferro had been promoted to brigadier general during 1862, and although paroled as a major general, there is no official documentation available to validate the promotion. After the war he becomes a member of the state legislature (1874–1879) and later a judge of the Gloucester County Court (1891–1897). He dies on his estate (Dunham Massie) during February 1898.

In South Carolina at Abbeville, President Jefferson Davis and his cabinet convene their final meeting. Attending are Davis; Judah P. Benjamin (secretary of state); John C. Breckinridge (secretary of war); Samuel R. Mallory (secretary of the Navy) and John H. Reagan (postmaster general). The cabinet also meets with several Confederate generals — George Gibbs Dibrell, Basil W. Duke, Samuel Wragg Ferguson, Braxton Bragg and John Crawford Vaughn — to conduct a council of war. It is concluded that to continue the war would be fruitless. Consequently, it is decided that the Confederate government is to be disbanded.

General Ferguson settles in Mississippi after the war and becomes a lawyer. He succumbs in Jackson on 3 February 1917. General Vaughn is paroled on the 9th at Washington, Georgia. He lives in Tennessee and Georgia after the war and serves one term in the Tennessee Senate. He dies during September 1875. In other activity, Confederate Brigadier General William Tatum Wofford is paroled at Resaca, Georgia. Subsequent to the close of hostilities, General Wofford is elected to the U.S. Congress; however, he is prevented from taking his seat. He dies in the vicinity of Cass Station, Georgia, during May 1884.

In Naval activity, the *Mohongo,* built in New Jersey at Jersey City, is commissioned the USS *Mohongo* at about this time (May), too late to participate in the war. It is assigned to the Pacific Squadron and embarks for the West Coast during the latter part of this month. During May of the following year, it is based at

Callao, Peru, during a period of turbulence due to an ongoing war between Peru and Spain. The gunboat *Mohongo* does not participate in the conflict; rather it is in the area to protect American interests in Peru. In August 1866, it sails northward to join the North Atlantic Blockading Squadron. During 1867, it departs for Hawaii on a dual mission, one of which is diplomatic and the other, a surveying operation. For a while during 1868, it operates off the coast of Mexico until it is decommissioned that same year. The *Mohongo* is sold in November 1870 and at that time begins its career as a merchant ship.

May 3 (Wednesday) In Georgia, the Confederate Cabinet begins to break up. Judah Benjamin, President Davis' secretary of state, resigns, leaves the party traveling with Davis and heads for Texas. Davis arrives in Georgia from South Carolina.

In Illinois, the train carrying the remains of President Abraham Lincoln arrives at its final destination, Springfield.

In Confederate general officer activity, General Laurence (Lawrence) Simmons Baker is paroled at Raleigh, North Carolina, at about this time. After his return to his home in North Carolina he becomes a farmer, but later he is a railroad station agent at Suffolk, Virginia, until his death in April 1907.

May 4 (Thursday) In Alabama, General Edward Canby accepts the surrender of Confederate Lt. General Richard Taylor, ending organized Southern resistance east of the Mississippi River. The surrender occurs at Citronelle. Taylor is the senior Confederate officer still in action east of the Mississippi. With the surrender of Taylor's forces, it is clear that the Confederates cannot sustain battle for any length of time. Confederate Secretary of State Judah P. Benjamin is in the process of escaping the country by attempting to make it alone and falling away from Davis' group, which is still in flight. After the war Taylor pens *Destruction and Reconstruction* on his war experiences. It is published by D. Appleton and Company just prior to his death in New York City on 12 April 1879.

Also, General Franklin Gardner, serving under General Taylor since his exchange during August 1864, retires as a planter in Louisiana near present-day Lafayette. He dies there on 29 April 1873. Franklin, a native of New York, had sided with the Confederates; however, his father, Colonel Charles Gardner, a veteran of the War of 1812, and his brother were both supporters of the Union.

In Mississippi, the Texas Brigade (Brigadier General Lawrence "Sul" Ross), temporarily commanded by Colonel Dudley W. Jones (9th Texas), surrenders at Jackson; however, Ross is in Texas on leave. By the time he arrived back in Texas, he had lost everything and finds himself in dire straits. Nevertheless, he rebounds after engaging in farming. During 1881 he is elected to the state Senate and is re-elected in 1883. Later, during 1887, he is elected to his first of two terms as governor of Texas. Afterward, he becomes president of the Agriculture and Mechanical College of Texas, located at College Station. He dies holding that office on 3 January 1898.

In North Carolina, the Confederate 8th (also known as 13th) Tennessee Cavalry surrenders to the 4th Iowa Cavalry at Washington. Confederate Brigadier General George Gibbs Dibrell, who had earlier led a cavalry regiment, had been promoted during the early part of this year and transferred to Richmond. He is in charge of the government archives when the government abandons the city to flee southward. Dibrell will be seized and paroled this month. Also, Major General Franz Sigel resigns his commission.

In Naval activity, the CSS *Morgan,* initially the U.S. revenue cutter *Morgan,* seized by the Confederates during 1861, is surrendered to the Union pursuant to orders by Commodore E. Ferrand, the commanding officer of Confederate naval forces in Alabama. It served as a flagship for Flag Officer G.N. Hollins during 1861, after being transformed into a partially armored gunboat. The CSS *Morgan* had also been known as the *Admiral.* It participated in the Battle of Mobile Bay in August 1864. It is sold in December of this year.

May 5 (Friday) In Alabama, by about this time, Commodore Henry K. Thatcher is winding up his participation in the reduction of Mobile and targets along the Gulf Coast. By late May, Confederate resistance is totally terminated in the region. Commodore Thatcher (acting rear admiral) remains in the region until early 1866, when he is ordered to sail north. Subsequently, on 25 July 1866, Commodore Thatcher is promoted to the rank of rear admiral and given command of the North Pacific Squadron, a position he retains during 1867–1868.

May 6 (Saturday) In Washington, D.C., the United States government begins to prepare for the trial of the conspirators in the death of Abraham Lincoln. Secretary of War Edwin Stanton chooses and appoints the commission-ers delegated to conduct the trial proceedings. Two of the appointees are Generals David Hunter and Lew Wallace (later author of *Ben Hur*). Hunter, having received the brevets of brigadier and major general in the Regular Army, retires during 1866 as colonel of cavalry. In other activity, General Edward L. Molineaux (General Quincy Adams Gillmore's command) assumes command of Augusta, Georgia. Confederate Brigadier General Zebulon York is paroled in North Carolina. He had lost everything during the course of the war; however, later he operates the York House at Natchez, Mississippi, until his death on 5 August 1900. Brigadier General James H. Wilson is promoted to major general of volunteers, effective this date. Brigadier General Green Berry Raum resigns his commission.

May 9 (Tuesday) In Washington, D.C., President Andrew Johnson declares a "Peace Proclamation."

In Confederate general officer activity, General Daniel Weisiger Adams, the brother of General William Wirt Adams, is paroled at Meridian, Mississippi. Daniel moves to New Orleans to reinitiate his law practice. William, who served with General Nathan B. Forrest, resides in Vicksburg after the war and later at Jackson. Daniel succumbs during 1871 and William dies in 1888. Both are buried in Jackson. Also, Confederate Brigadier General David A. Weisiger is paroled at Appomattox, Virginia. He becomes a cashier at a bank in Petersburg, Virginia, and afterward engages in business in Richmond, where he dies during February 1899. Major General Arnold Elzey is paroled at Washington, Georgia. He retires to his farm in Anne Arundel County and later dies in Baltimore on 21 February 1865. Brigadier General Marcellus Augustus Stovall is paroled. He returns to Augusta, Georgia, and becomes a cotton broker, but he also becomes involved in manufacturing fertilizers with the Georgia Chemical Works. General Stovall succumbs on 4 August 1895.

May 10 (Wednesday) In Kentucky, Confederate guerrilla leader William Clark Quantrill dies while on a mission of plunder in the vicinity of Taylorsville. Quantrill was one of the most notorious of the Confederate raiders. Many of the western outlaws rode with Quantrill, including Jesse James.

In Georgia, a Union contingent led by Lt. Colonel Pritchard and composed of elements of the 1st Wisconsin and 4th Michigan Cavalry Regiments captures Confederate President Jefferson Davis in Irwinsville. He is jailed for trial. Confederate General Joseph H. Lewis is among the Rebel leaders who surrender with Davis. Davis is freed when President Andrew Johnson grants amnesty to all Southerners during 1868.

In Florida, eight thousand Confederate soldiers, commanded by General Sam Jones, surrender in Tallahassee to Union troops under General Edward McCook (General James Wilson's cavalry). Tallahassee is the final state capital of the Confederacy (east of the Mississippi River) to come under Union control. General McCook receives the brevets of brigadier general in the Regular Army and major general in the volunteers at the close of hostilities. He musters out of the army during 1866. Afterward he is named minister to Hawaii, and during 1869, he is appointed governor of the Colorado Territory.

In Mississippi, Confederate General George B. Hodge is paroled today at Meridian. General Hodge graduated from the U.S. Naval Academy during 1845 and served in the U.S. Navy. He participated in various campaigns during the war as a member of General John C. Breckinridge's staff, prior to commanding a brigade under General Joseph Wheeler. He returns to his law practice.

In Naval activity, the Confederate naval forces in the vicinity of Mobile surrender to Commodore (acting rear admiral) Henry K. Thatcher. The surrender eliminates the majority of remaining resistance in the Gulf Coast region. Only Sabine Pass and Galveston, in Texas, remain as Confederate strongholds.

May 11 (Thursday) In Arkansas, Confederate General M. J. (Jeff) Thompson surrenders all Confederate forces under him at Chalk Bluff. In other activity, Lewis Baldwin Parsons is commissioned brigadier general. General Parsons, an 1840 Yale graduate who did further studies at Harvard to gain a law degree, initially served as a volunteer aide to Frank Blair (brigadier general, 1862) during 1861. Afterward, he served as assistant quartermaster with the rank of captain. He saw no field command; rather his entire focus was on transportation, including movements by water and by rail. He remains in the service beyond the close of hostilities and musters out on 30 April 1866. On the same day, he is breveted major general of volunteers. Also, Brigadier General Jeremiah Cutler's resignation is accepted by the War Department. He does not receive the brevet of major general, although during the conflict he had at times served in divisional command.

May 12 (Friday) In Texas, Union soldiers occupy Palmetto Ranch on the Rio Grande. They skirmish with Confederates the following day in the last active battle of the Civil War.

In Naval activity, the USS *Shamrock* intercepts and seizes the CSS *Halifax* on the Roanoke River. Later, on or about 25 June, the USS *Ceres* tows the *Halifax* to Norfolk and from there it is taken to Philadelphia; however, there are no further references to the *Halifax* in the U.S. Navy's records. Also, the *Ceres* is decommis-

Caissons and horses on the field following a battle (Mottelay, *The Soldier in Our Civil War,* 1886).

sioned at New York during July 1865. It is sold in October.

May 13 (Saturday)   In Texas, the 62nd U.S. Colored Troops, 34th Indiana Volunteers and the Union 2nd Texas Cavalry, led by Colonel Barrett, engage a Confederate force under General James Edwin Slaughter at Palmetto Ranch. The Confederates prevail. The Union sustains about 70 casualties including killed, wounded and captured. General Slaughter's brigade is attached to Major General John George Walker's division. Walker, after the war, travels to Mexico. General Slaughter also moves into Mexico and remains there for a few years prior to his return to the U.S. in Mobile. He engages in civil engineering and later relocates in New Orleans. He dies while in Mexico City on 1 January 1901.

In Union general officer activity, Brigadier General Franklin Stillman Nickerson, essentially inactive since the previous July, resigns from the army. He moves to Boston and practices law there until 1905, then retires. He dies in 1917 while residing with his son. Also, Brigadier General Max Weber resigns his commission. He is later appointed as American consul at Nantes, France, and afterward, he becomes tax assessor in New York City. By appointment by President Grant, he becomes collector of internal revenue in New York. He dies on 15 June 1901.

In Confederate general officer activity, Brigadier General Hugh Weedon Mercer, who participated in the field until the Battle of Jonesboro when ill health prevented him from further field command, is paroled at Macon, Georgia. He engages in the banking industry in Savannah, but later relocates in Baltimore. As his health continues to fail, he sails to Germany and dies there on 9 June 1877.

May 15 (Monday)   In Illinois, Brigadier General Halbert E. Paine (brevet major general), commander of the District of Illinois, resigns his commission. Shortly thereafter, Paine is elected to the U.S. Congress. Following three terms as a Congressman, Paine accepts an appointment as assistant secretary of the interior under his former law partner, Secretary of the Interior (1877–1891) Carl Schurz, a former brigadier general.

May 16 (Tuesday) The USS *Seymour* is decommissioned at Washington, D.C. Afterward, on 20 June 1865, it is transferred to the Light House Board, where it serves under the name *Tulip* until June 1882, when it is sold and renamed *Magnolia*. It is sold to a foreign owner in 1888.

May 17 (Wednesday) The Military Division of West Mississippi is disbanded. Also, the Department of Key West is terminated. General Canby receives command of the Department of the Gulf, which is composed of the states of Alabama, Louisiana, Mississippi and Florida, and includes Key West. He replaces General Nathaniel P. Banks. In conjunction, General Banks musters out of the service dur-

ing August 1865 and is returned to Congress, where he serves six terms. He also serves in the Massachusetts Senate (one term) and as a U.S. marshal. Subsequent to retirement, he succumbs on 1 September 1894. In other activity, General Philip Sheridan is relieved of command of the Military Middle Division; he receives command of area west of the Mississippi River. Also, Confederate General Philip Dale Roddey is paroled. Subsequent to the close of hostilities, Roddey becomes a businessman in New York. He dies in London on 20 July 1897.

May 18 (Thursday) General William Woods Averell resigns his commission. He receives the brevets of brigadier general and major general in the Regular Army. After the war, Averell for a while becomes consul general to Canada (1866–1869). He becomes wealthy from several inventions, the most well known being asphalt pavement. He dies at Bath, New York, during February 1900.

May 19 (Friday)   *In Union general officer activity,* General John A. Logan receives command of the Army of the Tennessee. He succeeds General Oliver O. Howard. Also, Brevet Brigadier General Oliver Edwards is promoted to full rank brigadier general of volunteers. General Edwards for a while takes a position in manufacturing and later becomes the mayor of Warsaw, Massachusetts (three terms). In other activity, Brevet Brigadier General James W. Forsyth is promoted to full rank brigadier general of volunteers. He remains with Sheridan in the post-war period in the Division of Missouri. Later, he serves with the 1st Cavalry (1878), and during 1886, he receives command of the 7th Cavalry (formerly General Custer's Regiment at Little Big Horn) and commands it at the Battle of Wounded Knee (December 1890). He is promoted to brigadier general in 1894 and becomes a major general in 1897. He retires two days after his promotion on 13 May 1897. Also, Brevet Brigadier General Joseph E. Hamblin is appointed full rank brigadier general effective this day. He had been breveted major general in the latter part of the war. Also, Lt. Colonel Richard Henry Jackson, acting commander of the 2nd Division (XXV Corps), is promoted to brigadier general. He also receives the brevet of major general of volunteers and the brevet of brigadier general in the Regular Army. He musters out of the service during February 1866 and reverts to his regular rank of captain of the 4th Artillery. He dies at Fort McPherson at Atlanta, Georgia, on 28 November 1892. At the time he holds the rank of lieutenant colonel. Colonel William Wells (1st Vermont Cavalry) is promoted to full rank brigadier general. General

Wells had initially joined the 1st Vermont Cavalry as a private during 1861. He assumed command of the regiment on 3 June 1864 at Salem Church.

In Confederate general officer activity, Brigadier General Marcus Joseph Wright, commander of the District of North Mississippi and West Tennessee at the close of hostilities, is paroled at Grenada, Mississippi. He returns to Tennessee and resumes his law practice in Memphis. General Wright later contributes to the compilation of the government publication *The War of the Rebellion: Official Records of the Union and Confederate Armies.* He remains involved with the massive project until his retirement during 1917. He dies in his 92nd year in Washington, D.C., on 27 December 1922.

May 21 (Sunday) The USS *Morse* is decommissioned. The *Morse* had served with the James River Flotilla during 1864 and afterward with the Potomac Flotilla. It is sold on 20 July 1865, and on 12 December as a commercial vessel, it becomes the *Lincoln* and remains in service until 1885. In other activity, Lt. Colonel Charles Hale Morgan is promoted to brigadier general of volunteers. He remains in the army beyond the close of hostilities. On 15 January 1866, he musters out of volunteer service, and with his regular rank of captain, he is assigned to the 4th Artillery. Subsequently, while based in California, he dies in San Francisco on 20 December 1875.

May 22 (Monday)   In Virginia, Union troops arrive at Fort Monroe with their prisoner, Jefferson Davis. Davis is held at Fort Monroe until October 22, and at that time he is transferred to Carroll Hall, where he remains until his subsequent pardon. There is much controversy between Sherman and Washington over the surrender terms afforded Johnston and Jefferson Davis' route toward safety. Sherman responds on May 22 to the allegations when he appears before the Committee on the Conduct of the War, in Washington, D.C., to testify about the question of Johnston's surrender and Jefferson Davis' alleged escape through Golds-

General Kirby Smith's army voluntarily disperses at Shreveport, Louisiana (Mottelay, *The Soldier in Our Civil War,* 1886).

The Union parade in Washington, D.C (Johnson, *Campfire and Battlefield: History of the Conflicts and Campaigns*, 1894).

boro, North Carolina, with a supposed thirteen million dollars in gold. Sherman expresses outrage at General Henry Halleck's handling of the affair and of Halleck's insinuations concerning Sherman's conduct. The amount Davis had with him when captured was approximately ten thousand dollars.

May 23 (Tuesday) **In Washington D.C.,** the victorious Union Army marches through the city. General Sherman observes the parade from the reviewing stand with President and Mrs. Johnson as General George Meade's Army of the Potomac marches in review. Sherman's troops march in parade on the following day. Meade's troops continue to pass the grandstand for more than six hours. General Meade is finally promoted to major general on 8 August 1865. He remains in the service after the war and is based in Philadelphia at the military Division of the Atlantic headquarters when he succumbs on 6 November 1872.

General William B. Hazen is assigned command of the 15th Army Corps. He succeeds General John A. Logan, who is to command the Army of the Tennessee. Hazen, appointed major general the previous month, and having received the brevets of brigadier and major general in the Regular Army, becomes colonel of the 38th Infantry during July 1866 and afterward serves with the 6th Infantry (1869). He succumbs on 16 January 1887.

May 24 (Wednesday) **In Washington D.C.,** the parade of the victorious army continues from the previous day. General William T. Sherman, at precisely 1000, marches down Pennsylvania Avenue in review with his army. Sherman later remarks: "The column was compact and the glittering muskets looked like a solid mass of steel, moving with the regularity of a pendulum. The sight was simply magnificent. Sixty-five thousand men of the Army of the West, marched in precision, past the White House. The national flag, our Stars and Stripes was flying from nearly every building in the capital during the parade."

In Naval activity, the USS *Gazelle* picks up Confederate Generals Simon Buckner and Sterling Price at the mouth of the Red River and carries them to Baton Rouge, Louisiana, to have a conference with General Edward Canby regarding surrender of their forces. Subsequent to this mission, the *Gazelle* arrives at Mound City on 25 June. On 7 July, it is decommissioned, and on 17 August is sold.

May 25 (Thursday) **In Texas,** the Confederate stronghold at Sabine Pass surrenders to Union forces, leaving only one more obstacle, the Confederates at Galveston.

In Confederate general officer activity, General James Holt Clanton, wounded in March at Bluff Spring, Florida, is paroled at Mobile, Alabama. General Clanton, during an altercation with a former Union officer in Knoxville, is killed on 27 February 1871. Also, Brigadier General Thomas Hart Taylor, post commander at Mobile, after his parole, becomes a businessman at Mobile and later, during 1870, he returns to Kentucky. He becomes a deputy U.S. marshal for about five years and then is chief of police in Louisville. He dies during April 1901.

May 26 (Friday) **In Texas** at Galveston, U.S. Major General Edward R. Canby (West Point, 1839) accepts the surrender of Confederate General Edmund Kirby Smith (West Point, 1845) and 20,000 prisoners. This surrender basically ends Southern organized resistance. Some Southern contingents refuse to capitulate and continue their raids. One such officer is General Joseph O. Shelby, whose troops operate from within Mexico and for some time attempt to become involved with the struggling parties in that country, but when Emperor Maximilian is overthrown, Shelby returns across the Rio Grande for the final time and remains in the United States.

Brigadier General Hamilton P. Bee is among the captured at Galveston. He is released in late June as a major general; however, no records validate any promotion. Lt. General Simon Buckner, chief of staff to General Kirby Smith, becomes governor of Kentucky in 1887. Buckner succumbs during 1914 at the age of 91. General Henry H. Sibley, who lacks a command as the war ends, departs the United States and joins the Egyptian Army during 1869. He remains in the service for several years before returning to the United States. After his return, General Sibley's health continues to worsen. He dies at Fredericksburg, Virginia, on 23 August 1886. In other activity, Union Major General Darius N. Couch resigns his commission.

May 27 (Saturday) Jubilation is short-lived for many released Union prisoners and other passengers aboard the *Sultana*, which sustains an explosion, a not unusual occurrence aboard steamships, as it travels along the Mississippi River returning soldiers who had been released from Southern prisons. More than 1,500 people are lost.

In Naval activity, the USS *Nina*, an iron screw steamer, is launched at Chester, Pennsylvania, too late to participate in the war. In January 1866, it enters active service at the Washington Navy Yard to serve as a yard tug. The *Nina* remains active until its tragic loss on 6 February 1910, when it departs Norfolk en route to Boston and encounters a storm off Virginia, where it is last seen. The crew at the time of its disappearance had been one officer and thirty crewmen.

May 29 (Monday) The USS *Hetzel*, attached to the North Atlantic Blockading Squadron but out of service since the previous November while undergoing repairs, returns to North Carolina from Hampton Roads. It remains on duty there until October 1865 when it sails north. In late October, the *Hetzel* is returned to the U.S. Coast Survey.

May 31 (Wednesday) *In Union general officer activity,* Colonel Henry A. Barnum, 149th New York Regiment, is promoted to full rank brigadier general. Also, Colonel Robert Francis Catterson is appointed brigadier general. Catterson initially joined the army during April 1861 as an enlisted man. He was promoted to first sergeant during June 1861 and commissioned as an officer (1st lieutenant) the next month. By March 1862 he rose to the rank of captain, and from there he rose to colonel of the 9th Indiana. General Catterson had been a doctor prior to the outbreak of war, but he does not return to the profession. For a while he leads the Arkansas Negro militia and serves as a U.S. marshal. In addition, he serves as mayor of Little Rock (1872–1874). During his later years he suffers a debilitating stroke and dies during March 1914 in a veterans' hospital in San Antonio, Texas. Also, Colonel William Burnham Woods (76th Ohio) is promoted to brigadier general. General Woods joined the regiment commanded by his younger brother General Charles Robert Woods as lieutenant colonel during February 1862 and was raised to colonel upon his brother's promotion to brigadier general during August of the previous year. In addition, he receives the brevet of major general of volunteers; however, there is no documentation to verify that he ever commanded a division at any time during the war. After mustering out of the army he settles in Alabama, and during 1869, Woods, a lawyer, is appointed as circuit judge by President Grant. His district encompasses Georgia and the Gulf States. He resides in Atlanta until he is appointed as a Supreme Court justice by President Hayes during 1880. He succumbs in Washington on 14 May 1887.

June Brigadier General Stand Watie, commander of the 1st Cherokee Mounted Rifles, surrenders. Watie, three-quarters Cherokee Indian, returns to his plantation and engages in other enterprises. Although the majority of the Cherokee remained loyal to the Union, Watie had led the others for the Confederate cause. Watie, having learned English as a child at a mission school in the Indian Territory, had also been involved with a publication of the Cherokee newspaper prior to the outbreak of war. He succumbs at his home at Honey Creek, Oklahoma, on 9 September 1871 at about age 65. Also, Confederate General John Selden Roane is paroled at Shreveport, Louisiana.

June 1 (Thursday) The Twentieth Corps is disbanded.

In Confederate general officer activity, General Gabriel Colvin Wharton is paroled at Lynchburg, Virginia. Subsequently, he resides at Radford, Virginia, and later serves several terms in the state senate. He dies in Radford during May 1906.

In Naval activity, the USS *Howquah*— on duty at Key West and on patrol in Saint George's Sound since the fall of Fort Fisher, North Carolina, in January — is ordered to sail north. It arrives at Philadelphia on 22 June and soon after, on 10 August 1865, it is sold. Also, at about this time (June), the USS *C.P. Williams* departs from the South Atlantic Blockading Squadron and sails north to be decommissioned. In August it is sold and afterward renamed *Sarah Purves.* The USS *Winooski* (double-ender gunboat) is commissioned at about this time (June). It is decommissioned during 1867 and sold in August of that year.

In Union general officer activity, Brigadier General William Vandever, attached as a brigade commander under General Jefferson C. Davis during the Carolinas campaign, receives the brevet of major general of volunteers at about this time (June). He musters out of the army during August and resumes his law practice; however, in 1873 he is appointed U.S. Indian inspector, a post he retains until 1877. Vandever, a congressman (Iowa) prior to the war, is re-elected to Congress as a California representative during 1886; he serves until he retires during 1891.

June 3 (Saturday) General George Armstrong Custer receives command of the Department of Missouri, which includes the states of Kansas and Missouri.

In Naval activity, the USS *Sunflower* is decommissioned in Philadelphia and on 10 August is sold at auction.

June 5 (Monday) The USS *Galena*, having completed service on the James River, departs the area for Portsmouth, New Hampshire. On 17 June it is decommissioned. Subsequently, during 9 April 1869, it is recommissioned; however, after departing for Hampton Roads, it is again placed out of service and later, during

1870, it is condemned. It is "broken up" during 1872 while at Norfolk.

June 8 (Thursday) Confederate Major General Joseph Wheeler is released from Fort Delaware. He will be elected to Congress and serve for sixteen years beginning in 1881. Wheeler also will serve as a major general of volunteers in the U.S. Army during the Spanish-American War (1898). He retires on 10 September 1900 at the rank of brigadier general in the Regular Army. General Wheeler dies in Brooklyn in January 1906.

June 9 (Friday) The USS *Young America* is decommissioned at the Norfolk Navy Yard. During the following July, the *Young America* is sold at auction and purchased by the Camden and Amboy Railroad Company. Also, the USS *Wyandotte* is decommissioned at about this time (June). In August it is sold and, using the same name, enters service as a commercial ship. The *Wyandotte* is wrecked off Duxbury, Massachusetts, on 26 January 1866.

June 10 (Saturday) The USS *Wilderness* is decommissioned. At Boston on 5 September it is acquired by the U.S. Treasury Department. It departs for Baltimore on the 17th to begin its service as a revenue cutter in Florida. It remains in service until directed to sail to New York on 2 September 1872. Later, on 11 June, it is renamed the *John A. Dix* and assigned duty at New Orleans and afterward other duty stations. It remains in active service until it is placed out of commission on 7 April 1891 and sold during the following month at Algiers, Louisiana.

June 11 (Sunday) Confederate General John Selden Roane is paroled at Shreveport, Louisiana. He retires to his residence at Pine Bluff, Arkansas, where he succumbs on 8 April 1865.

June 21 (Wednesday) Brigadier General James Harrison Wilson is promoted to major general to rank from 6 May 1865. He also receives the brevet of major general in the Regular Army. During 1866, be is appointed lieutenant colonel of the 35th Infantry Regiment;

General James Wilson (*Harper's Pictorial History of the Civil War*, 1896).

however, his assignments remain within the corps of engineers. He retires during 1870. Nevertheless, during the Spanish-American War (1898), General Wilson reenters the service as a major general and participates at Puerto Rico and Cuba. Afterward, he participates in China during the Boxer Rebellion. He again retires during 1901 as a brigadier general. He succumbs on 23 February 1925.

June 22–28 *In Naval activity,* although hostilities have ended, the CSS *Shenandoah* remains at sea since its departure from Australia in February. While cruising in the waters of the Okhotsk Sea, Bering Sea, and the Arctic Ocean, Captain James Iredell Waddell and his crew ravage the whalers during this short time span, capturing or destroying twenty ships and ransoming four others. Four vessels required ransoming because of the high amount of captives that needed to be delivered to shore. The whalers, having no means to defend against a powerful warship, are snagged sometimes in pairs or larger groups, including one bonanza of eight vessels taken at one time on the 28th. The initial prizes include the *Abigail, Casey, Edward, Euphrates, Hector, Jireh Swift, Sophia, Thornton, Susan, William Thompson* and the *Milo,* with the latter vessel used to transport the captives to San Francisco. Others include the *Brunswick, Congress 2nd, Covington, Favorite, Hillman, James Murray, Martha 2nd, Nassau, Nile* and the *Waverly.* Since it first departed London during October of the previous year, the *Shenandoah* has seized a total of thirty-eight ships, all of which are destroyed except for four, which are ransomed to assure safe passage for the captives. Captain Waddell had been informed of the negotiations between General Lee and General Grant regarding surrender; however, the same packet also had informed Waddell that the Confederate seat of government had been moved to Danville and that President Jefferson Davis had made it clear that the war was to continue. Nevertheless, on 2 August, the *Shenandoah,* while sailing toward California from the Straits, encounters a British vessel, the bark *Baracouta.* At that time, Waddell learns of the surrender of Confederate President Davis and the end of the war.

June 27 (Tuesday) *In Virginia,* a diminutive wooden gunboat, recently captured at Edwards Ferry, North Carolina, arrives at Hampton Roads. It is thought the vessel is the CSS *Fisher* or the not yet completed *Alexander Oldham,* a side-wheeler which is "documented for commercial service" on 27 September 1865.

In Union general officer activity, Colonel William Henry Penrose is promoted to full rank brigadier general of volunteers. He remains in the army beyond the close of hostilities and after he musters out of the volunteer service. Nevertheless, he is confined to the rank of captain for seventeen years before rising to the rank of major during 1883, followed by promotion to lieutenant colonel in 1883. Later, during 1893, Penrose becomes colonel of the 20th Infantry. Colonel Penrose transfers to the 20th Infantry during 1894 and remains with the regiment until he retires in 1896.

June 28 (Wednesday)   The U.S. Army disbands the Second, Fifth and Sixth Army Corps.

June 29 (Thursday)   Confederate Brigadier General John Wilkins Whitfield is paroled at Columbus, Texas. Afterward, he resides in Lavaca County. He dies near Hallettsville during October 1879.

June 30 (Friday)   At this time, the active duty of the United States Marine Corps stands at 3,860, including eighty-seven officers and 3,773 enlisted men. In other activity, Confederate Brigadier General Lucius B. Northrop (West Point, 1831), relieved of duty during the previous January, is seized by the Union and imprisoned with charges of attempting to starve Union prisoners. Northrup, the former commissary general of the Confederacy, is set free in October 1865. Northrup's responsibility seemed to fall short of the Confederate government's expectations, but throughout much of the conflict, the Confederate Army was plagued by massive food shortages and the means to deliver what was available to the far-flung forces.

July 1 (Saturday)   The USS *R.R. Cuyler* is decommissioned at New York. On 15 August, it is sold at auction. During the following year, it is resold to the Republic of Colombia and renamed the *El Rayo*. Also, the USS *Monticello* is decommissioned at about this time (July). It is sold in November and afterward operates as a merchant vessel until it sinks off Newfoundland during April 1872.

July 3 (Monday)   Brevet Major General John Grant Mitchell resigns from the army. He returns to his home in Ohio. Also, Brigadier General Adolph von Steinwehr resigns from the army. Steinwehr, a divisional commander, had been demoted to a brigade command after the campaign at Chickamauga when the XI and XII Corps were merged into the XX Corps (1864); however, he apparently chose to decline the command, which would have placed him in a subordinate position to a junior ranking officer, General John W. Geary, the division commander of his brigade.

July 11 (Tuesday)   Robert E. Lee is elected president of Washington College, in Lexington, Virginia (later named Washington and Lee University). He will be succeeded upon his demise (1870) by his son George Washington Custis Lee.

July 20 (Thursday)   The army abolishes the Thirteenth and Sixteenth Army Corps. Also, Brevet Brigadier General Francis Trowbridge Sherman, at this time provost marshal general (Military District of the Gulf), is promoted to full rank brigadier general. He remains in the service at New Orleans until February 1866.

July 22 (Saturday)   *In Naval activity,* the USS *Corwin* moves in to assist the USS *Quinnebaug,* which becomes grounded off Beaufort, North Carolina. The *Corwin* is returned to the Coast Survey, Treasury Department.

July 25 (Tuesday)   Emerson Opdyke, having received the brevet of major general of volunteers following the Battle of Franklin, is finally promoted to brigadier general of volunteers. After he leaves the service he moves to New York. On 22 April 1884, while in the process of cleaning a revolver, he accidentally shoots himself in the stomach. He dies within several days.

July 27 (Thursday)   The Army abolishes the Ninth Army Corps.

In Naval activity, the USS *Antona,* which has been operating off the coast of Texas and in the Gulf of Mexico, departs Pensacola, Florida, for New York. It is decommissioned on 12 August and afterward, on 30 November 1865, sold at auction. On 5 January 1867, it is renamed *Carlotta* and operates out of New York until 1874, when it is destroyed by fire.

August 1 (Tuesday)   The Army disbands the Fourth, Seventh, Eighth, Tenth, Fourteenth, Fifteenth, Seventeenth, Twenty-third and Twenty-fourth Corps. Nearly 801,000 troops will muster out of the Army during the period April 29 through November 15, 1865.

August 2 (Wednesday)   *In Union general officer activity,* Brigadier General Mortimer D. Leggett is promoted to major general, full rank. On 21 September he separates from the service and resumes his law practice in Zanesville, Ohio. Later he is appointed commissioner of patents by President Ulysses S. Grant.

In Naval activity, Captain James Iredell Waddell of the CSS *Shenandoah,* while about fourteen days out of California, is informed by the British aboard the bark *Baracouta* that President Davis had been captured and the Confederates had surrendered to end the war. Captain Waddell, upon receiving the news, disarms his ship and closes its ports, giving it the appearance of a merchant ship. Rather than proceed to the United States, he sails the *Shenandoah* into the harbor at Liverpool on 6 November and hands the vessel over to British Captain Paynter, the commander of the HMS *Donegal.* In conjunction, Captain Waddell pens a letter to the British authorities recommending that the ship be included with other Confederate property being turned over to the U.S. government. However, John Adams, minister to England, objects to Waddell's actions after the close of hostilities and refers to them as "piracy." Nonetheless, the British authorities reject the accusation due to lack of evidence. On 8 November, Captain Paynter holds a roll call aboard the *Shenandoah* and after he determines that none of the crew are British citizens, he releases them. After acquiring the *Shenandoah,* the U.S. government sells it to Sultan of Zanzibar, and while in the service of the sultan, the ship sinks in the Indian Ocean during 1879.

August 3 (Thursday)   The USS *Cimarron,* attached to the South Atlantic Blockading Squadron, departs South Carolina and sails north. It is decommissioned on 17 August at the Philadelphia Navy Yard. On 6 September, the *Cimarron* is sold.

August 9 (Wednesday)   The USS *Alfred Robb* is decommissioned at Mound City, Illinois. Soon after, on 9 August, it is sold at auction and renamed the *Robb.* It continues to operate until 1873.

August 11 (Friday)   The USS *Oneida* is decommissioned at New York. In May 1867, it is recommissioned and assigned to the Asiatic Squadron. While in the Far East, it departs from Yokohama, Japan, on 24 January 1870. At about 1830, the *City of Bombay* (British Peninsula and Oriental steamer) strikes it in the vicinity of Saratoga Spit. The *Oneida's* starboard quarter severs after impact and it is left to itself. The *City of Bombay* fails to give any type of assistance; rather it continues on its journey. The *Oneida* goes down within fifteen minutes after being struck. Japanese fishermen in two separate boats attempt to rescue the crew. Sixty-one men are saved, while 121 are lost.

August 13 (Sunday)   Brigadier General William Grose is breveted major general effective this day. In January 1866 he resigns from the service.

August 14 (Monday)   General Solomon Meredith, badly wounded at Gettysburg, receives the brevet of major general of volunteers. Since his recovery from the wound during November 1864, his duty had been switched from command of various posts, including Cairo, Illinois, and Paducah, Kentucky, where he succeeds General Paine. He remains at Paducah until the termination of hostilities. He retires from the army during 1869. In conjunction General Meredith had been one of the many native southerners who remained loyal to the Union. He was born in Guilford Court House, North Carolina, during May 1810, but later moved to Indiana. Three of General Meredith's sons joined the Union Army during the war and only one survived.

August 24 (Thursday)   Brigadier General Sullivan Amory Meredith, posted at St. Louis since early 1864, musters out of the service. Also, Brigadier General Byron Root Pierce musters out of the army. General Pierce, wounded five times during the war, had been breveted major general of volunteers just after his participation at Sayler's Creek. Also, Brigadier General William Thomas Ward, wounded twice at Resaca, Georgia, resigns from the army. General Ward had participated in the Atlanta campaign, the March to the Sea, and the final campaign in the Carolinas. He returns to Kentucky and resumes his law practice.

September   **In South Dakota,** as a part of a general directive by General Alfred Sully, another military post, Fort James, is established by a contingent of the 6th Iowa Cavalry commanded by Captain Benjamin King. Fort James becomes another link in the security chain of forts lying in the Sioux territory between Minnesota and the Missouri River. Fort James is located along the James River near Fire Steel Creek in the vicinity of present-day Rockport. The garrison remains active on the frontier until it is abandoned during October 1866. General Sully, toward the close of hostilities, received the brevet of major general of volunteers. During December of this year, following his resignation from the volunteers, reverts to his regular rank of major in the U.S. Army, but soon he is promoted to lieutenant colonel. During December 1875, he becomes colonel of the 21st U.S. Infantry Regiment. He succumbs at his final duty station, Fort Vancouver, Washington, on 27 April 1879.

September 20 (Wednesday) Captain James N. Moore reports that in excess of 12,000 graves have been marked for Union prisoners who died while incarcerated at Andersonville, Georgia.

October 19 (Thursday) *In Naval activity,* the USS *Ascutney,* out of service for repairs since the summer of the previous year, is recommissioned. It operates out of the Washington Navy Yard and carries cargo and passengers along the Atlantic coast from New York to Virginia Capes and in the Chesapeake Bay region until it is again decommissioned on 1 August 1868 and sold on the 28th. Records beyond that date do not disclose any further activity. The civilian owner, John Roach, was in engaged in shipbuilding and is thought to have disassembled the *Ascutney* for material for other vessels.

October 25 (Wednesday) General Nelson A. Miles is promoted to major general of volunteers. He had sustained four wounds during the war, and prior to the end of hostilities, he received the brevet of major general of volunteers. During July 1866, he becomes colonel of the 40th U.S. Infantry (Colored troops). Later, he marries a niece of General William T. Sherman. He remains in the army and during 1880, he is promoted to brigadier general, followed by his rise to major general during 1890. In 1895, he also becomes general-in-chief of the U.S. Army. Later, during 1901, President McKinley promotes him to lieutenant general. General Miles retires during 1903. He dies on 15 May 1925.

November 10 (Friday) **In Washington, D.C.,** Confederate Captain Henry Wirz, the commandant of Andersonville Prison (Georgia), is hanged subsequent to being found guilty by a military tribunal for alleged inhumane treatment of Union prisoners and of "murder in violations of the laws of war." Public outrage in the North contributes to the sentence. Major General Lew Wallace presided as president of the court-martial board that tried Wirz. Brevet Brigadier General Norton P. Chipman was the army prosecutor against Wirz. Chipman had been breveted brigadier general on 13 March.

November 11 (Saturday) The Medal of Honor is presented this day to Mary E. Walker, a civilian, for her courage at the Battle of Bull Run, July 21 1861, her duty at the Patent Office Hospital during October 1861, her courage at Chattanooga, Tennessee, following the Battle of Chickamauga during September 1863, her devotion to others as a prisoner of war from 10 April 1864 through 12 August 1864 at Richmond, Virginia, and for her actions during the Battle of Atlanta in September 1864. In 1916, the Board of Medal Awards rules her medal unwarranted along with 910 other recipients. On 10 June 1977, the Secretary of the Army Clifford L. Alexander, Jr., reinstates her medal as presented originally by President Andrew Johnson in 1865.

November 15 (Wednesday) The United States Army is reorganized and will consist of five Grand Divisions commanded by Major Generals George G. Meade, William T. Sherman, Philip Sheridan, George H. Thomas and Henry Halleck. The Army will be split into nineteen departments commanded by Generals Joseph Hooker, Winfield S. Hancock, Christopher Augur, Edward O.C. Ord, George Stoneman, John M. Palmer, John Pope, Alfred Terry, John Schofield, Daniel Sickles, James B. Steedman, John G. Foster, Thomas J. Wood, Charles R. Woods, Edward Canby, Horatio G. Wright, Joseph J. Reynolds, Frederick Steele and Irvin McDowell. General Hancock dies at Governors Island while in command of the Department of the East on 9 February 1886. General McDowell dies on 4 May 1885 while in command of the Department of the Pacific.

Also, General Shofield serves as secretary of war during 1868 under President Johnson; however, upon the promotion of General Sheridan to lieutenant general, Schofield is promoted to major general and appointed as successor to Sheridan. Afterward, he is appointed superintendent of West Point (1876–1881). Upon the death of General Sheridan (1888), General Schofield succeeds him as commander of the U.S. Army. During February 1895, he is promoted to lieutenant general. Shortly thereafter, during September, he retires on his 64th birthday, 29 September 1895, about eleven years prior to his death in Florida on 4 March 1906. Also, upon the reorganization of the army, General Sherman is promoted to lieutenant general. Later, when General Grant is inaugurated president (1869), Sherman becomes full general and commander-in-chief of the U.S. Amy. He retires during February 1884.

November 20 (Monday) Colonel Joel A. Dewey is promoted to the rank of brigadier gen-

A Confederate officer and his wife, posing with a trooper well after the war (Seniram collection).

eral of volunteers. Dewey was appointed colonel of the 11th Colored Infantry during April 1865.

Winter 1865–1866 **In Utah,** the Ute Indians experience great deprivations — lack of food combined with exposure to the weather during a harsh winter — and begin to raid Mormon settlements. The clashes initially are confined to the theft of livestock and horses, but the Indians, led by Black Hawk, soon fond themselves amid a full-scale war (Black Hawk War). The forces of Black Hawk begin to swell as Utes on the reservation leave to join with the raiders. Shortly thereafter Black Hawk finds more support as Paiute and Navaho warriors fight by his side. The conflict continues until 1867, when Black Hawk sues for peace, but some others continue the struggle, with the final raids occurring during 1870.

December 18 (Monday) Secretary of State Seward announces the official end of slavery in the United States in conjunction with the ratification of the 13th Amendment to the Constitution.

1866

January 8 (Monday)   The U.S. Army abolishes the XXV Corps.

May 29 (Tuesday)   Lieutenant General Winfield Scott dies at West Point. General Scott is buried on the grounds of the academy. General Scott had an extraordinary career as a soldier and patriot, of which the Civil War was only a minor part. He was originally appointed to the military by President Thomas Jefferson. He participated at the famous battle of Lundy's Lane and was triumphant at the gates of Mexico City during the Mexican War. General Scott, born in 1786, is known to have said at the time of the Civil War: "I have served my country under the flag of the Union for more than 50 years and I will defend that flag with my sword, even if my native state [Virginia] assails it."

President U.S. Grant, while terminally ill and writing his memoirs, would state: "To maintain peace in the future, it is necessary to be prepared for war. There can scarcely be a possible chance of a conflict, such as the last one occurring among our own people again; but growing as we are, in population, wealth and military power we may become the envy of nations, which led us in all these particulars a few years ago; and unless we are prepared for it, we may be in danger of a combined movement being someday made to crush us out."

Appendices

Appendix I

Total Casualties

The Union Army lost 138,154 men killed in battle and 221,374 killed from other causes, including Southern prisons and disease, for a total of 359,528 men. Wounded in action totaled 280,040.

Confederate Army records were not as accurate but provide these figures: 94,000 were killed in battle, 70,000 died from other causes, and 30,000 died in Northern prisons.

Appendix II

Roster of Union Generals

The listing contains highest rank attained and year of graduation at West Point; the number immediately following the year of graduation is the personal cadet number. An asterisk denotes death circumstances during the war.

Abercrombie, John Joseph (West Point, 1822, No. 322). Brigadier General, USA, Brevet, 3-13-65.

Allen, Robert (West Point, 1836, No. 874). Maj. Gen. USA, Brevet, 3-13-65.

Alvord, Benjamin (West Point, 1833, No. 728). Brigadier General, USA, Brevet, 4-9-65.

Ames, Adelbert (West Point, 1861, No. 1892). Major General, USA, Brevet, 3-16-65.

Ammen, Jacob (West Point, 1831, No. 640). Brigadier General, Volunteers, Full Rank, 7-16-62.

Anderson, Robert (West Point, 1825, No. 406). Major General, USA, Brevet, 3-13-1865.

Andrews, Christopher Columbus. Major General, Volunteers, Brevet, 2-3-65.

Andrews, George Leonard (West Point, 1851, No.

1494). Major General, Volunteers, Brevet, 3-26-65.

Arnold, Lewis Golding (West Point, 1837, No. 900). Brigadier General, USA, Brevet, 3-13-65.

Arnold, Richard (West Point, 1850, No. 1462). Brigadier General, Volunteers, Brevet, 1-24-62.

Asboth, Alexander Sandor. Major General, Volunteers, Brevet, 3-13-65.

Augur, Christopher Columbus (West Point, 1843, No. 1182). Brigadier General, USA, Brevet, 3-13-65.

Averell, William Woods (West Point, 1855, No. 1702). Major General, USA, Brevet, 3-13-65.

Ayres, Romeyn Beck (West Point, 1847, No. 1352). Brevet, Major General, USA, end of war.

Bailey, Joseph. Major General, Volunteers, Brevet, 3-13-65.

Baird, Absalom (West Point, 1849, No. 1415). Brevet Major General, Volunteers, March 1865.

Baker, Edward Dickinson (*Balls Bluff, Oct. 21, 1861). Major General, Volunteers, Full Rank, 9-21-61.

Baker, LaFayette Curry. Brigadier General, Volunteers, Full Rank, 4-26-65.

Banks, Nathaniel Prentiss. Major General, Volunteers, Full Rank, 5-16-61.

Barlow, Francis Channing. Major General, Volunteers, Full Rank, 5-25-65.

Barnard, John Gross (West Point, 1833, No. 708). Major General, USA, Brevet, 3-13-65.

Barnes, James (West Point, 1829, No. 545). Major General, Volunteers, Brevet, 3-13-65.

Barnes, Joseph K. Major General, USA, Brevet, 3-13-65.

Barnum, Henry Alanson. Major General, Volunteers, Brevet, 3-13-65.

Barry, William Farquhar (West Point, 1838, No. 957). Major General, USA, Brevet, 3-13-65.

Bartlett, Joseph Jackson. Brigadier General, Volunteers, Brevet, 2-1-64.

Bartlett, William Francis. Major General, Volunteers, Brevet, 3-13-65.

Baxter, Henry. Major General, Volunteers, Brevet, 4-1-65.

Bayard, George Dashiell (*Fredericksburg, Dec. 13, 1862) (West Point, 1856, No. 1721). Brigadier General, Volunteers, Full Rank, 4-28-62.

Beal, George LaFayette. Major General, Volunteers, Brevet, 3-13-65.

Beatty, John. Brigadier General, Volunteers, Full Rank, 11-29-62.

Beatty, Samuel. Major General, Volunteers, Brevet, 3-13-65.

Belknap, William Worth. Major General, Volunteers, Brevet, 3-13-65.

Benham, Henry Washington (West Point, 1837, No. 891). Major General, USA and Volunteers, Brevet, 3-26-65.

Benton, William Plummer. Brigadier General, Volunteers, Brevet, 3-26-65.

Berry, Hiram Gregory (*Chancellorsville, 5-3-63). Major General, Volunteers, Brevet, 11-29-62.

Bidwell, Daniel Davidson (*Cedar Creek, 10-18-64). Brigadier General, Volunteers, Brevet, 11-29-62.

Birge, Henry Warner. Major General, Volunteers, Brevet, 2-25-65.

Birney, David Bell (*natural causes, 10-18-64). Major General, Volunteers, Full Rank, 5-20-63.

Birney, William. Major General, Volunteers, Brevet, 3-13-65.

Blair, Francis Preston. Major General, Volunteers, Full Rank, 11-29-62.

Blenker, Louis (*natural causes, 10-31-63). Brigadier General, Volunteers, Full Rank, 8-9-61.

Blunt, James Gillpatrick. Major General, Volunteers, Full Rank, 3-16-63.

Bohlen, Henry (*Freeman's Ford, 8-22-62). Brigadier General, Volunteers, Full Rank 4-28-62.

Bowen, James. Major General, Volunteers, Brevet, 3-13-65.

Boyle, Jeremiah Tilford. Brigadier General, Volunteers, Full Rank, November 1861.

Bradley, Luther Prentice. Brigadier General, Volunteers, Brevet, 7-30-64 (Brevet Brigadier General, USA, 1867).

Bragg, Edward Stuyvesant. Brigadier General, Volunteers, Full Rank, 6-25-64.

Brannan, John Milton (West Point, 1841, No. 1081). Major General, USA, Full Rank, 3-13-65.

Brayman, Mason. Major General, Volunteers, Brevet, 3-13-65.

Briggs, Henry Shaw. Brigadier General, Volunteers, Full Rank, 7-17-62.

Brisbin, James Sanks. Major General, Volunteers, Brevet, 3-13-65.

Brooke, John Rutter. Major General, Volunteers, Brevet, August 1864.

Brooks, William Thomas Harbaugh (West Point,

1841, No. 1104). Major General, Volunteers, Full Rank, 6-10-63.

Brown, Egbert Benson. Brigadier General, Volunteers, Full Rank, 6-10-63.

Buchanan, Robert Christie (West Point, 1830, No. 617). Major General, USA, Brevet, 3-13-65.

Buckingham, Catharinus Putnam (West Point, 1829, No. 546). Brigadier General, Volunteers, Full Rank, 7-16-62.

Buckland, Ralph Pomeroy. Major General, Volunteers, Brevet, 3-13-65.

Buel, Don Carlos (West Point, 1841, No. 1090). Major General, Volunteers, Full Rank, 3-22-62.

Buford, John, Jr. (*December 16, 1863, natural causes) (West Point, 1848, No. 1384). Major General, Volunteers, Full Rank, December 1863.

Buford, Napoleon Bonaparte (West Point, 1827, No. 475). Major General, Volunteers, Brevet, 3-13-65.

Burbridge, Stephen Gano. Major General, Volunteers, Brevet, 7-14-64.

Burnham, Hiram (*Chaffin's Bluff, 9-29-64). Brigadier General, Volunteers, Full Rank, April 1864.

Burns, William Wallace (West Point, 1847, No. 1358). Brigadier General, Volunteers, Full Rank, 9-28-61 (resigns commission during the war and receives his staff rank of major for the duration).

Burnside, Ambrose Everett (West Point, 1847, No. 1348). Major General, Volunteers, Full Rank, 3-18-62.

Bussey, Cyrus. Major General, Volunteers, Brevet, 3-13-65.

Busteed, Richard. Brigadier General, Volunteers, Full Rank, 8-7-62.

Butler, Benjamin Franklin. Major General, Volunteers, Full Rank, 5-16-61.

Butterfield, Daniel. Major General, USA, Brevet, 3-13-65.

Cadwalader, George. Major General, Volunteers, Full Rank, 4-25-62.

Caldwell, John Curtis. Brigadier General, Volunteers, Brevet, 4-28-62.

Cameron, Robert Alexander. Major General, Volunteers, Brevet, 3-13-65.

Campbell, Charles Thomas. Brigadier General, Volunteers, Full Rank, 11-29-62.

Campbell, William Bowen. Brigadier General, Volunteers, Full Rank, 6-30-62.

Canby, Edward Richard Sprigg (West Point, 1839, No. 1015). Major General, Volunteers, Full Rank, 5-7-64.

Carleton, James Henry. Major General, USA, Brevet, 3-13-65.

Carlin, William Passmore (West Point, 1850, No. 1469). Major General, USA, Brevet, 3-13-65.

Carr, Eugene Asa (West Point, 1850, No. 1468). Major General, USA, Brevet, 3-13-65 (receives the Medal of Honor at Elkhorn Tavern 3-8-1862). General Carr had been called "War Eagle" by the Indians.

Carr, Joseph Bradford. Major General, Volunteers, Brevet, 3-13-65.

Carrington, Henry Beebee. Brigadier General, Volunteers, 1862, Breveted Brigadier General, USA, at end of war.

Carroll, Samuel Sprigg (West Point, 1856, No. 1754). Major General, USA, Brevet, 3-13-65.

Carter, Samuel Powhatan (Annapolis, 1846). Major General, Volunteers, Brevet, 3-13-65.

Casey, Silas (West Point, 1826, No. 467). Major General, Volunteers, Brevet, 5-31-65.

Catterson, Robert Francis. Brigadier General, Volunteers, Full Rank, 5-31-65.

Chamberlain, Joshua Lawrence. Major General, Volunteers, Brevet 3-29-65 (receives Medal of Honor at Gettysburg, July 1863).

Chambers, Alexander (West Point, 1853, No. 1621). Brigadier General, Volunteers, Full Rank, 8-11-63.

Champlin, Stephen Gardner (*January 24, 1864 from wounds originally suffered at Seven Pines, Spring 1862). Brigadier General, Volunteer, Full Rank, 11-29-62.

Chapin, Edward Payson (*5-27-63, Port Hudson). Brigadier General, Volunteers, Full Rank, posthumously from date of death.

Chapman, George Henry. Major General, Volunteers, Brevet, 3-13-65.

Chetlain, Augustus Louis. Major General, Volunteers, Brevet. 6-18-65.

Chrysler, Morgan Henry. Major General, Volunteers, Brevet, 3-13-65.

Clark, William Thomas. Major General, Volunteers, Brevet, 3-13-65.

Clay, Cassius Marcellus. Major General, Volunteers, Full Rank, 4-11-62.

Clayton, Powell. Brigadier General, Volunteers, Full Rank, 8-1-64.

Cluseret, Gustave Paul. Brigadier General, Volunteers, Full Rank, 10-14-62.

Cochrane, John. Brigadier General, Volunteers, Full Rank, 7-17-62.

Connor, Patrick Edward. Major General, Volunteers, Brevet, 3-30-65.

Connor, Selden. Brigadier General, Full Rank, Volunteers, 7-11-64.

Cook, John. Major General, Volunteers, Brevet, 8-24-65.

Cooke, Philip St. George (West Point, 1827, No. 492). Major General, USA Brevet, 3-13-65.

Cooper, James (*3-28-63, natural causes). Brigadier General, Volunteers, Full Rank, 5-17-61.

Cooper, Joseph Alexander. Major General, Volunteers, Brevet, 3-13-65.

Copeland, Joseph Tarr. Major General, Volunteers, Full Rank, 11-29-62.

Corcoran, Michael (*December 22, 1863, by accident). Brigadier General, Volunteers, Full Rank, 7-21-61.

Corse, John Murray (West Point, attendance 1853–1855). Major General, Volunteers, Brevet, 10-5-64.

Couch, Darius Nash (West Point, 1846, No. 1284). Major General, Volunteers, Full Rank, 7-4-62.

Cowdin, Robert. Brigadier General, Volunteers, Full Rank, 9-26-62.

Cox, Jacob Dolson. Major General, Volunteers, Full Rank 10-6-62.

Craig, James. Brigadier General, Volunteers, Full Rank, 3-21-62.

Crawford, Samuel Wylie. Major General, USA, Brevet, 3-16-65.

Crittenden, Thomas Leonidas. Major General, Volunteers, Full Rank, 7-17-62.

Crittenden, Thomas Turpin. Brigadier General, Volunteers, Full Rank, 4-28-62.

Crocker, Marcellus Monroe (*8-26-65, natural causes) (West Point, attendance 1847–1849). Brigadier General, Volunteers, Full Rank, 11-29-62.

Crook, George (West Point, 1852, No. 1573). Major General, USA, Brevet, 3-13-65.

Croxton, John Thomas. Major General, Volunteers, Brevet, April 1865.

Cruft, Charles. Major General, Volunteers, Brevet, 3-5-65.

Cullum, George Washington (West Point, 1833, No. 709). Major General, USA, Brevet, March 1865.

Curtis, Newton Martin. Major General, Volunteers, Brevet, 3-13-65.

Curtis, Samuel Ryan (West Point, 1831, No. 655). Major General, Volunteers, Full Rank, 11-21-62.

Custer, George Armstrong (West Point, 1861, No. 1966). Major General, USA, Brevet, 3-13-65.

Cutler, Lysander. Major General, Volunteer, Brevet, 8-19-64.

Dana, Napoleon Tecumseh (West Point, 1842, No. 1139). Major General, Volunteers, Full Rank, 11-29-62.

Davidson, John Wynn (West Point, 1845, No. 1257). Major General, Volunteers, Brevet, 3-13-65.

Davies, Henry Eugene. Major General, Volunteers, Full Rank, 11-29-1862.

Davies, Thomas Alfred (West Point, 1829, No. 565). Major General, Volunteers, Brevet, July 1865.

Davis, Edmund Jackson. Brigadier General, Volunteers, Full Rank, 11-10-64.

Davis, Jefferson Columbus. Major General, USA, Brevet, 3-13-65.

Deitzler, George Washington. Brigadier General, Volunteer, Full Rank, 5-29-62.

Delafield, Richard (West Point, 1818, No. 180). Major General, USA, Brevet, 3-13-65.

Dennis, Elias Smith. Major General, Volunteers, Brevet, March, 1865.

Dent, Frederick Tracy (West Point, 1843, No. 1199). Brigadier General, Volunteers, Full Rank, April 5, 1865.

Denver, James William. Brigadier General, Volunteers, Full Rank, 8-14-1861.

DeRussy, Lewis Gustavus (West Point, attendance 1836–1838). Major General, USA, Brevet, end of war.

de Trobriand, Philippe Regis. Major General, Volunteers, Brevet, 4-9-1865.

Devens, Charles, Jr. Major General, Volunteers (1863, subsequent to battle of Chancellorsville).

Devin, Thomas Casimer. Major General, Volunteers, Brevet, 3-13-65.

Dewey, Joel Allen. Brigadier General, Full Rank, Volunteers, 11-20-65 (Last appt. during Civil War).

Dix, John Adams. Major General, Volunteers, Full Rank, 5-16-1861.

Dodge, Charles Cleveland. Brigadier General, USA, Full Rank, November 29, 1862.

Dodge, Grenville Mellen. Major General, USA, Full Rank, 6-7-64.

Doolittle, Charles Camp. Major General, Volunteers, Brevet, June 1865.

Doubleday, Abner (West Point, 1842, No. 1134). Major General, USA, Brevet, 3-13-65.

Dow, Neal. Brigadier General, Volunteers, Full Rank, 4-28-62.

Duffie, Alfred Napoleon Alexander. Brigadier General, USA, Full Rank, 6-23-63.

Dumont, Ebenezer. Brigadier General, Volunteers, Full Rank, 9-3-61.

Duryee, Abram. Major General, Volunteers, Brevet, 3-13-65 (previously resigned commission as brigadier general during 1863).

Duval, Isaac Hardin. Major General, Volunteers, Brevet, 3-13-65.

Dwight, William, Jr. (West Point, attendance 1849–1853). Brigadier General, USA, Full Rank, November 29, 1862.

Dyer, Alexander Brydie (West Point, 1837, No. 896). Major General, USA, Brevet, 3-13-65.

Eaton, Amos Beebe (West Point, 1826, No. 464). Major General, USA, Brevet, 3-13-65.

Edwards, John. Brigadier General, Volunteers, Full Rank, 9-24-64.

Edwards, Oliver. Major General, Volunteers, Full Rank, 5-19-65.

Egan, Thomas Wilberforce. Major General, USA, Brevet, 10-27-64.

Ellet, Alfred Washington. Brigadier General, Volunteers, Full Rank, 11-1-62.

Elliott, Washington LaFayette (West Point, attendance 1841–1844). Brigadier General, USA, and Volunteers, Brevet, close of hostilities.

Emory, William Hemsley (West Point, 1831, No. 642). Major General, USA, Brevet, 3-13-65, Full Rank, September 1865.

Estey, George Peabody. Brigadier General, USA, Full Rank, after close of war.

Eustis, Henry Lawrence (West Point, 1842, No. 1111). Brigadier General, USA, Full Rank, Sept. 12, 1863 (resigns during 1864).

Ewing, Charles. Brigadier General, Volunteers, Full Rank, 3-8-65.

Ewing, Hugh Boyle (West Point, attendance 1844–1848). Major General, Volunteers, Brevet (after close of hostilities).

Ewing, Thomas, Jr. Major General, Volunteers, Brevet (resigns February 1865).

Fairchild, Lucius. Brigadier General, Volunteers, Full Rank, 10-19-63 (resigns November 1863).

Farnsworth, Elon John (*Gettysburg, July 1863). Brigadier General, Volunteers, Full Rank, 6-29-63.

Farnsworth, John Franklin. Brigadier General, Volunteers, Full Rank, November 29, 1862 (resigns during March 1863).

Ferrero, Edward. Major General, Volunteers, Brevet, December 1864.

Ferry, Orris Sanford. Major General, Volunteers, Brevet, May 23, 1865.

Fessenden, Francis. Major General, USA, Brevet, 3-13-65.

Fessenden, James Deering. Major General, Volunteers, Brevet, 3-13-65.

Fisk, Clinton Bowen. Major General, Volunteers, Brevet, 3-13-65.

Force, Manning Ferguson. Major General, Volunteers, Brevet, 3-13-65 (receives the Medal of Honor during Atlanta campaign, presented during 1892).

Forsyth, James William (West Point, 1856, No. 1738). Brigadier General, Volunteers, Brevet, Full Rank, subsequent to close of hostilities.

Foster, John Gray (West Point, 1846, No. 1275). Major General, USA, Brevet, 3-13-65.

Foster, Robert Sanford. Major General, Volunteers, Brevet, end of war.

Franklin, William Buell (West Point, 1843, No. 1167). Brigadier General, Volunteers, Full Rank, May 1861.

Frémont, John Charles. Major General, USA, Full Rank, May 14, 1861.

French, William Henry (West Point, 1837, No.

912). Major General, Volunteers, Full Rank, November 29, 1862.

Fry, James Barnett (West Point, 1847, No. 1344). Major General, Brevet, USA, 3-13-65.

Fry, Speed Smith. Brigadier General, Volunteers, Full Rank, March 21, 1862.

Fuller, John Wallace. Major General, Volunteers, Brevet, 3-13-65.

Gamble, William. Brigadier General, Volunteers, Full Rank, September 25, 1865.

Garfield, James Abram. Major General, Volunteers, Full Rank, 9-19-63 (Chicamauga). Later elected president of U.S. and assassinated, dying 19 September 1881.

Garrard, Kenner (West Point, 1851, No. 1501). Major General, USA, Brevet, 3-13-65.

Garrard, Theophilus Toulmin. Brigadier General, Volunteers, Full Rank, 11-29-62.

Geary, John White. Major General, Volunteers, Brevet, 1-12-65.

Getty, George Washington (West Point, 1840, No. 1031). Major General, USA, Brevet, 3-13-65.

Gibbon, John (West Point, 1847, No. 1350). Major General, USA, Brevet, 3-13-65.

Gibbs, Alfred (West Point, 1846, No. 1315). Major General USA, Brevet, 3-13-65.

Gilbert, Charles Champion (West Point, 1846, No. 1292). Brigadier General, Volunteers, Full Rank, September 1862.

Gilbert, James Isham. Major General, Volunteers, Brevet (end of war).

Gillem, Alvan Cullem (West Point, 1851, No. 1504). Major General, USA, Brevet, April 1865.

Gillmore, Quincy Adams (West Point, 1849, No. 1407). Major General, USA, Brevet, 3-13-65.

Gordon, George Henry (West Point, 1846, No. 1314). Major General, Volunteers, Brevet, April 1865.

Gorman, Willis Arnold. Brigadier General, Volunteers, Full Rank, 9-17-61.

Graham, Charles Kinnaird. Major General, Volunteers, Brevet, 3-13-65.

Graham, Lawrence Pike. Brigadier General, Volunteers, Brevet, August 1865.

Granger, Gordon (West Point, 1845, No. 1265). Major General, USA, Brevet, 3-13-65.

Granger, Robert Seaman (West Point, 1838, No. 968). Brigadier General, USA, Brevet, 3-13-65.

Grant, Lewis Addison. Major General, USA, Brevet, 10-19-64 (Medal of Honor Chancellorsville, May 1863).

Grant, Ulysses Simpson Grant (West Point, 1843, No. 1187). Lieutenant General, March 2, 1864, and later 18th president of the U.S.

Greene, George Sears (West Point, 1823 No. 327). Major General, Volunteers, Brevet (close of war).

Gregg, David McMurtrie (West Point, 1855, No. 1864). Major General, Volunteers, August 1864.

Gresham, Walter Quintan. Major General, Volunteers, Brevet, 3-13-65.

Grierson, Benjamin Henry. Major General, USA, Brevet, March 1867.

Griffin, Charles (West Point, 1847, No. 1353). Major General, USA, Brevet (end of war).

Griffin, Simon Goodell. Major General, Volunteers, Brevet, 4-2-65.

Grose, William. Major General, Volunteers, Brevet, August 1865.

Grover, Cuvier (West Point, 1850, No. 1453). Major General, USA, Brevet (end of war).

Hackleman, Pleasant Adam (*Shiloh, April 1862). Brigadier General, Volunteers, Full Rank, 4-28-62.

Halleck, Henry Wager (West Point, 1839, No. 988). Major General, USA, Full Rank, 8-19-61.

Hamblin, Joseph Eldridge. Major General, Volunteers, Brevet, April 1865.

Hamilton, Andrew Jackson. Brigadier General, Volunteers, Full Rank, 11-14-62.

Hamilton, Charles Smith (West Point, 1843, No. 1192). Major General, Volunteers, Full Rank, 9-18-62.

Hamilton, Schuyler (West Point, 1841, No. 1082). Major General, Volunteers, Full Rank, 9-17-62.

Hamlin, Cyrus. Major General, Volunteers, Brevet, 3-13-65.

Hammond, William Alexander. Brigadier General, USA, Full Rank, 4-25-62.

Hancock, Winfield Scott (West Point, 1844, No. 1223). Major General, USA, Full Rank, July 1866.

Hardie, James Allen (West Point, 1843, No. 1177). Major General, USA, Brevet, March 1865.

Hardin, Martin Davis (West Point, 1859, No. 1835). Brigadier General, USA, Brevet, 3-13-65.

Harding, Abner Clark. Brigadier General, Volunteers, Full Rank, 3-13-65.

Harker, Charles Garrison (*Kennesaw Mountain, June 1864) (West Point, 1858, No. 1813). Brigadier General, Volunteers, Full Rank, July 20, 1863.

Harland, Edward. Brigadier General, Volunteers, Full Rank, 11-29-62.

Harney, William Selby. Brigadier General, USA, Brevet, 3-13-65.

Harris, Thomas Maley. Major General, Volunteers, Brevet (end of hostilities).

Harrow, William. Major General, Volunteers, Full Rank, 11-29-62.

Hartranft, John Frederick. Brigadier General, Volunteers, Brevet, March 1865.

Hartsuff, George Lucas (West Point, 1852, No. 1554). Major General, USA, Brevet, March 1865.

Hascall, Milo Smith (West Point, 1852, No. 1549). Brigadier General, Volunteers, Full Rank, 4-25-62.

Haskin, Joseph Abel (West Point, 1839, No. 995). Brigadier General, USA, Brevet, March 1865.

Hatch, Edward. Brigadier General, Volunteers, Brevet, 3-13-1865.

Hatch, John Porter (West Point, 1845, No. 1247). Brigadier General, Volunteers, Brevet, March 1865 (Medal of Honor South Mountain, September 1862).

Haupt, Herman (West Point, 1835, No. 816). Brigadier General, Volunteers, Full Rank, 9-5-62.

Hawkins, John Parker (West Point, 1852, No. 1575). Major General, USA, Brevet, 3-13-65.

Hawley, Joseph Roswell. Major General, Volunteers, Brevet (after close of hostilities).

Hayes, Joseph. Major General, Volunteers, Brevet, 3-13-65.

Hayes, Rutherford Birchard. Brigadier General, Volunteers, Brevet, 10-19-64, later the 19th president of the U.S.

Haynie, Isham Nicholas. Brigadier General, Volunteers, Full Rank, 11-29-62.

Hays, Alexander (*Wilderness, May 1864). Major General, Volunteers, Brevet, 5-5-64 (posthumously).

Hays, William (West Point, 1840, No. 1034). Brigadier General, Volunteers, Full Rank, 12-27-62.

Hazen, William Babcock (West Point, 1855, No. 1704). Major General, USA, Brevet, 3-13-65.

Heckman, Charles Adam. Brigadier General, Volunteers, Full Rank, 11-29-62.

Heintzelman, Samuel Peter (West Point, 1826, No. 445). Major General, USA, Brevet (end of war).

Herron, Francis Jay. Major General, Volunteers, Full Rank, 11-29-62 (Medal of Honor, Pea Ridge, March 1862).

Hincks, Edward Winslow. Major General, Volunteers, Brevet, 3-13-65.

Hitchcock, Ethan Allen (West Point, 1817, No. 177). Major General, Volunteers, Full Rank, February 1862.

Hobson, Edward Henry. Brigadier General, Volunteers, Full Rank, 11-29-62.

Holt, Joseph. Brigadier General, USA, Brevet, 3-13-65.

Hooker, Joseph (West Point, 1837, No. 919). Major General, USA, Brevet, 3-13-65.

Hovey, Alvin Peterson. Major General, Volunteers, Brevet, 7-4-64.

Hovey, Charles Edward. Major General, Volunteers, Brevet, 3-13-65.

Howard, Oliver Otis (West Point, 1854, No. 1634). Major General, USA, Brevet, 3-13-65 (Medal of Honor, Fair Oaks, Va., June 1862).

Howe, Albion Parris (West Point, 1841, No. 1066). Brigadier General, USA, Brevet, 3-13-65.

Howell, Joshua Blackwood (*9-14-64, accident with horse on 12th). Brigadier General, Volunteers, Full Rank, September 1864.

Humphreys, Andrew Atkinson (West Point, 1831, No. 641). Major General, USA, Brevet (end of war).

Hunt, Henry Jackson (West Point, 1839, No. 1004). Major General, USA, Brevet, 3-13-65.

Hunt, Lewis Cass (West Point, 1847, No. 1363). Brigadier General, USA, Brevet, 3-13-65.

Hunter, David (West Point, 1822, No. 310). Major General, USA, Brevet, 3-13-65.

Hurlbut, Stephen Augustus. Major General, Volunteers, Full Rank, 7-17-62.

Ingalls, Rufus (West Point, 1843, No. 1198). Major General, USA, Brevet, 3-13-65.

Jackson, Conrad Feger (*Fredericksburg, December 1862). Brigadier General, Volunteers, Full Rank, July 17, 1862.

Jackson, James Streshly (*Perryville, October, 1862). Brigadier General, Volunteers, Full Rank, July 1862.

Jackson, Nathaniel James. Major General, Volunteers, Brevet, 3-13-65.

Jackson, Richard Henry. Brigadier General, Volunteers, Brevet (end of war).

Jameson, Charles Davis (*November 6, 1862, natural causes). Brigadier General, Volunteers, Full Rank, 9-3-61.

Johnson, Andrew. Brigadier General, Volunteers, Full Rank, March 4, 1862. Later 17th president of the U.S., taking office after the death of President Lincoln.

Johnson, Richard W. (West Point, 1849, No. 1436). Major General, USA, Brevet, 3-13-65.

Jones, Patrick Henry. Brigadier General, Volunteers, Full Rank, 12-6-64.

Judah, Henry Moses (West Point, 1843, No. 101). Brigadier General, Volunteers, Full Rank, 3-21-62.

Kane, Thomas Leiper. Major General, Volunteers, Brevet, 3-13-65.

Kautz, August Valentine (West Point, 1852, No. 1570). Major General, USA, Brevet, 3-13-65.

Kearny, Philip (*September 1, 1862, Chantilly, 2nd Bull Run). Major General, Full Rank, Volunteers, 7-4-62.

Keim, William High (*May 1862, natural causes). Brigadier General, Volunteers, Full Rank, 12-20-61.

Kelley, Benjamin Franklin. Major General, Volunteers, Brevet, 3-13-65.

Kenly, John Reese. Major General, Volunteers, Brevet, 3-13-65.

Ketchum, John Henry. Major General, Volunteers, Brevet, 3-13-65.

Ketchum, William Scott (West Point, 1834, No. 781). Major General, USA, Brevet, 3-13-65.

Keyes, Erasmus Darwin (West Point, 1832, No. 671). Major General, Volunteers, Full Rank, Spring 1862.

Kiernan, James Lawlor. Brigadier General, Volunteers, Full Rank, August 1, 1863.

Kilpatrick, Hugh Judson (West Point, 1861, No. 1904). Major General, USA, Brevet, 3-13-65.

Kimball, Nathan. Major General, Volunteers, Brevet, February 1865.

King, John Haskell. Major General, USA, Brevet, 3-13-65.

King, Rufus (West Point, 1833, No. 710). Brigadier General, Volunteers, Full Rank, 5-17-61.

Kirby, Edward (*May 28, 1863, from wounds suffered May 3 at Chancellorsville) (West Point, 1861, No. 1897). Brigadier General, Volunteers, Full Rank, 5-28-63.

Kirk, Edmund Needles (*July 21, 1863, from wounds suffered at Murfreesboro 12-31-62). Brigadier General, Volunteers, Full Rank, 11-29-62.

Knipe, Joseph Farmer. Brigadier General, Volunteers, Full Rank, 11-29-62.

Krzyzanowski, Wiadimir. Brigadier General, Volunteers, Full Rank, 11-29-62.

Lander, Frederick West (*March 2, 1862, Camp Paw Paw, natural causes). Brigadier General, Volunteers, Full Rank, 5-17-61.

Lauman, Jacob Gartner. Major General, Volunteers, Brevet, 3-13-65.

Lawler, Michael Kelly. Major General, Volunteers, Brevet, 3-13-65.

Ledlie, James Hewett. Brigadier General, Volunteers, Full Rank, 12-24-62.

Lee, Albert Lindley. Brigadier General, Volunteers, Full Rank, 11-29-62.

Leggett, Mortimer Dormer. Major General, Volunteers, Full Rank, August 2lt, 1865.

Lightburn, Joseph Andrew Jackson. Brigadier General, Volunteers, Full Rank, March 1863.

Lockwood, Henry Hayes (West Point, 1836, No. 863). Brigadier General, Volunteers, Full Rank, 8-8-61.

Logan, John Alexander. Major General, Volunteers, Full Rank, 11-29-62.

Long, Eli. Major General, USA, Brevet, 3-13-65.

Lowell, Charles Russell (*Cedar Creek, October 19, 1864). Brigadier General, Volunteers, Full Rank, 10-19-64.

Lucas, Thomas John. Major General, Volunteers, Brevet, 3-26-65.

Lyon, Nathaniel (*Wilson's Creek, Missouri, August 10, 1861) (West Point, 1841, No. 1069). Brigadier General, Volunteers, Full Rank, 5-17-61.

Lytle, William Haines (*Chickamauga, September 20, 1863). Brigadier General, Volunteers, Full Rank, 11-29-62.

MacArthur, John. Major General, Volunteers, Brevet, 12-15-64.

MacKenzie, Ranald Slidell (West Point, 1862, No. 1967). Major General, Volunteers, Brevet, March 1865.

Maltby, Jasper Adalmorn. Brigadier General, Volunteers, Full Rank, 8-4-63.

Mansfield, Joseph King (*Sharpsburg, September 18, 1862, from wounds suffered the previous day) (West Point, 1822, No. 287). Major General, Volunteers, Full Rank, July, 18, 1862.

Manson, Mahlon Dickerson. Brigadier General, Volunteers, Full Rank, March 24, 1862.

Marcy, Randolf Barnes (West Point, 1832, No. 690). Brigadier General, USA, September, 28, 1861 (expires by law during 1863, but during 1878, appointed to rank as Brigadier General, Inspector General, USA).

Marston, Gilman. Brigadier General, Volunteers, Full Rank, 11-29-62.

Martindale, John Henry (West Point, 1835, No. 788). Major General, Volunteers, Brevet, 3-13-65.

Mason, John Sanford (West Point, 1847, No. 1339). Brigadier General, USA, Brevet, 3-13-65.

Matthies, Charles Leopold. Brigadier General, Volunteers, Full Rank, 11-29-62.

Meade, George Gordon (West Point, 1835, No. 804). Major General, USA, Full Rank, 8-18-64.

Meagher, Thomas Francis. Brigadier General, Volunteers, Full Rank, 2-3-62.

McCall, George Archibald (West Point, 1822, No. 311). Brigadier General, Volunteers, Full Rank, 5-17-61.

McClellan, George Brinton (West Point, 1846, No. 1273). Major General, USA, Full Rank, 5-14-61.

McClernand, John Alexander. Major General, Volunteers, Full Rank, 3-21-62.

McCook, Alexander McDowell (West Point, 1852, No. 1565). Major General, USA, Brevet, 3-13-65.

McCook, Daniel, Jr. (*July 17, 1864, from wounds suffered at Kennesaw Mountain, June 1864). Brigadier General, Volunteers, Full Rank, 7-16-64.

McCook, Edward Moody. Major General, Volunteers, Brevet, 3-13-65.

McCook, Robert Latimer (*August 6, 1862, from wounds suffered on August 5, vic. Winchester, Tenn.). Brigadier General, Volunteers, Full Rank, 3-21-62.

McDowell, Irvin (West Point, 1838, No. 963). Major General, USA, Brevet, 3-13-65.

McGinnis, George Francis. Brigadier General, Volunteers, Full Rank, 11-29-62.

McIntosh, John Baille. Major General, USA, Brevet (close of hostilities).

McKean, Thomas Jefferson (West Point, 1831, No. 647). Brigadier General, November 21, 1861.

McKinstry, Justus (West Point, 1838, No. 980). Brigadier General, Volunteers, Full Rank, September 1861.

McLean, Nathaniel Collins. Brigadier General, Volunteers, Full Rank, 11-29-62.

McMillan, James Winning. Major General, Volunteers, Brevet, March 1865.

McNeil, John. Major General, Volunteers, Brevet, 4-12-65.

McPherson, James Birdseye (*Atlanta, July 22, 1864) (West Point, 1853, No. 1579). Major General, Volunteers, Full Rank, 11-8-62.

Meigs, Montgomery Cunningham (West Point, 1836, No. 846). Major General, USA, Brevet, 7-5-64.

Meredith, Solomon. Major General, Volunteers, Brevet, 8-14-65.

Meredith, Sullivan Amory. Brigadier General, Volunteers, Full Rank, 11-29-62.

Merritt, Wesley (West Point, 1860, No. 1868). Major General, USA, Brevet, 3-13-65.

Miles, Nelson Appleton. Major General, Volunteers, Brevet, August 1864 (Brev. Maj. Genl., USA, during 1867). (Medal of Honor, while Colonel, 61st N.Y. Infantry, Chancellorsville).

Miller, John Franklin. Major General, Volunteers, Brevet, 3-13-65.

Miller, Stephen. Brigadier General, Volunteers, Full Rank, 10-26-63.

Milroy, Robert Huston. Major General, Volunteers, Full Rank, 11-29-62.

Mitchel, Ormsby McKnight (*October 30, 1862, natural causes) (West Point, 1829, No. 555). Major General, Volunteers, Full Rank, 4-11-62.

Mitchell, John Grant. Major General, Volunteers, Brevet, 3-13-65.

Mitchell, Robert Byington. Brigadier General, Volunteers, Full Rank, 4-8-62.

Montgomery, William Reading (West Point, 1825, No. 419). Brigadier General, Volunteers, Full Rank, 5-17-61.

Morell, George Webb (West Point, 1835, No. 786). Major General, Volunteers, Full Rank, 7-4-62.

Morgan, Charles Hale (West Point, 1857, No. 1711). Brigadier General, USA, Brevet, 3-13-65 (Full Rank Brigadier General, Volunteers, May 1865).

Morgan, Edwin Denison. Major General, Volunteers, Full Rank, 9-28-61.

Morgan, George Washington (West Point, attendance 1842–1844). Brigadier General, Volunteers, Full Rank, 11-12-61.

Morgan, James Dada. Major General, Volunteers, Brevet, 3-19-65.

Morris, William Hopkins (West Point, 1851, No. 1520). Major General, Volunteers, Brevet, 3-13-65.

Morton, James St. Clair (*Petersburg, 6-17-64), (West Point, 1851, No. 1495). Brigadier General, Brevet, USA, posthumously.

Mott, Gershom. Major General, Volunteers, Full Rank, 5-26-65.

Mower, Joseph Anthony. Major General, USA, Brevet, 3-13-65.

Nagle, James. Brigadier General, Full Rank, 9-10-62.

Naglee, Henry Morris (West Point, 1835, No. 808). Brigadier General, Volunteers, Full Rank, February 1862.

Negley, James Scott. Brigadier General, Volunteers, Full Rank, 10-1-61.

Neill, Thomas Hewson (West Point, 1847, No. 1357). Major General, Volunteers, Brevet, March 1865.

Nelson, William. Major General, Full Rank, Volunteers, 7-17-62.

Newton, John (West Point, 1842, No. 1112). Major General, USA, Brevet, 3-13-65.

Nickerson, Frank Stillman. Brigadier General, Volunteers, Full Rank, 11-29-62.

Oglesby, Richard James. Major General, Volunteers, Full Rank, 11-29-62.

Oliver, John Morrison. Major General, Volunteers, Brevet (close of hostilities).

Opdycke, Emerson. Major General, Volunteers, Brevet, 11-30-64.

Ord, Edward Otho Cresap (West Point, 1839, No. 1002). Major General, Volunteers, Full Rank, 5-3-62.

Orme, William Ward. Brigadier General, Volunteers, Full Rank, 11-29-62.

Osborn, Thomas Ogden. Major General, Volunteers, Brevet, 4-2-65.

Osterhaus, Peter Joseph. Major General, Volunteers, Full Rank, 7-23-64.

Owen, Joshua Thomas. Brigadier General, Volunteers, Full Rank, 11-29-62.

Paine, Charles Jackson. Major General, Volunteers, Brevet, January 1865.

Paine, Eleazer Arthur (West Point, 1839, No. 1009). Brigadier General, Volunteers, Full Rank, 9-3-61.

Paine, Halbert Eleazer. Major General, Volunteers, Brevet (end of war).

Palmer, Innis Newton (West Point, 1846, No. 1309). Major General, Volunteers, Brevet, 3-13-65.

Palmer, John McCauley. Major General, Volunteers, Full Rank, 11-29-62.

Parke, John Grubb (West Point, 1849, No. 1408). Major General, Volunteers, Full Rank, July 1862.

Parsons, Lewis Baldwin. Major General, Volunteers, Brevet, 4-30-66.

Patrick, Marsena Rudolph (West Point, 1835, No. 833). Major General, Volunteers, Brevet, 3-13-65.

Patterson, Francis Engle (*Fairfax, Va., 11-22-62, alleged accidental discharge of personal weapon). Brigadier General, Volunteers, Full Rank, 4-11-62.

Paul, Gabriel Rene (West Point, 1834, No. 767). Brigadier General, USA, Brevet, February 1865.

Peck, John James (West Point, 1843, No. 1174). Major General, Volunteers, Full Rank, 7-4-62.

Pennypacker, Galusha. Major General, USA, Brevet, 3-2-67.

Penrose, William Henry. Brigadier General, Volunteers, Full Rank, June 1865.

Phelps, John Smith. Brigadier General, Volunteers, Full Rank, 7-19-62.

Phelps, John Wolcott (West Point, 1836, No. 865). Brigadier General, Volunteers, Full Rank, 5-17-61.

Piatt, Abram Sanders. Brigadier General, Volunteers, Full Rank, April, 1862.

Pierce, Byron Root. Major General, Volunteers, Brevet (end of war).

Pile, William Anderson. Major General, Volunteers, Brevet, April 65.

Pitcher, Thomas Gamble (West Point, 1845, No. 1270). Brigadier General, Volunteers, Full Rank, 11-29-62.

Pleasonton, Alfred (West Point, 1844, No. 1212). Major General, USA, Brevet, March 65.

Plummer, Joseph Bennett (West Point, 1841, No. 1080). Brigadier General, Volunteers, Full Rank, 10-22-61.

Poe, Orlando Metcalfe (West Point, 1856, No. 1716). Brigadier General, USA, Brevet, 3-13-65.

Pope, John (West Point, 1842, No. 1127). Major General, Volunteers, Brevet, end of war.

Porter, Andrew. Brigadier General, Volunteers, Full Rank, 5-17-61.

Porter, Fitz John (West Point, 1845, No. 1238). Major General, Volunteers, Full Rank, July 1862.

Potter, Edward Elmer. Major General, Volunteers, Brevet, 3-13-65.

Potter, Joseph Hayden (West Point, 1843, No. 1188). Brigadier General, USA, Brevet, 3-1-65.

Potter, Robert Brown. Major General, Volunteers, Brevet, 9-29-65.

Potts, Benjamin Franklin Major General, Volunteers, Brevet, 3-13-65.

Powell, William Henry. Major General, Volunteers, Brevet, 3-13-65.

Pratt, Calvin Edward. Brigadier General, Volunteers, Full Rank, 9-10-62.

Prentiss, Benjamin Mayberry. Major General, Volunteers, Full Rank, 11-29-62.

Prince, Henry (West Point, 1835, No. 815). Brigadier General, USA, Brevet, 3-13-65.

Quinby, Isaac Ferdinand (West Point, 1843, No. 1172). Brigadier General, Volunteers, Full Rank, 3-17-62.

Ramsay, George Douglas (West Point, 1820, No. 257). Major General, USA, Brevet, 3-13-65.

Ransom, Thomas Edward Greenfield (*10-29-64, sickness and complications from old wounds). Major General, Volunteers, Brevet, 9-1-64.

Raum, Green Berry. Brigadier General, Volunteers, Full Rank, 2-15-64.

Rawlins, John Aaron. Major General, USA, Brevet, 4-9-65.

Read, Theodore. Brigadier General, Volunteers, Brevet, 9-29-64.

Reid, Hugh Thompson. Brigadier General, Volunteers, Full Rank, 3-13-63.

Reilly, James William. Brigadier General, Volunteers, Full Rank, 7-30-64.

Reno, Jesse Lee (*Fox's Gap, South Mountain, 9-14-62) (West Point, 1846, No. 1279). Major General, Volunteers, Full Rank, 7-18-62.

Revere, Joseph Warren. Brigadier General, Volunteers, Full Rank, 10-25-62.

Reynolds, John Fulton (*Gettysburg, July 1863) (West Point, 1841, No. 1084). Major General, Volunteers, Full Rank, 11-29-62.

Reynolds, Joseph Jones (West Point, 1843, No. 1176). Major General, Volunteers, Full Rank, 11-29-62.

Rice, Americus Vespucius. Brigadier General, Volunteers, Full Rank, 5-31-65.

Rice, Elliott Warren. Major General, Volunteers, Brevet, 3-13-65.

Rice, James Clay (*Spotsylvania, 5-10-64). Brigadier General, Volunteers, Full Rank, 8-17-63.

Rice, Samuel Allen (*7-6-64 from wounds suffered at Jenkins Ferry, 4-30-64). Brigadier General, Full Rank, 8-4-63.

Richardson, Israel Bush (*mortally wounded at Sharpsburg, dies 11-3-62). (West Point, 1841, No. 1096). Major General, Volunteers, Full Rank, 7-4-62.

Ricketts, James Brewerton (West Point, 1839, No. 1001). Major General, USA, Brevet, 3-13-65.

Ripley, James Wolfe (West Point, 1814, No. 102). Major General, USA, Brevet, 3-13-65.

Roberts, Benjamin Stone (West Point, 1835, No. 838). Major General, Volunteers, Brevet, 3-13-65.

Robinson, James Sidney. Brigadier General, Volunteers, Full Rank, January 1865.

Robinson, John Cleveland (West Point, attendance 1835–1836). Brigadier General, USA, Brevet, 3-13-65 (Medal of Honor, Spotsylvania, May 1864).

Rodman, Isaac Peace (*9-30-62 from wounds suffered 9-17-62 at Antietam). Brigadier General, Volunteers, Full Rank, 4-28-62.

Rosecrans, William Stark (West Point, 1842, No. 1115). Major General, Volunteers, Full Rank, 3-21-62.

Ross, Leonard Fulton. Brigadier General, Volunteers, Full Rank, April 1862.

Rousseau, Lovell Harrison. Major General, USA, Brevet, 3-28-67.

Rowley, Thomas Algeo. Brigadier General, Volunteers, Full Rank, 11-29-62.

Rucker, Daniel Henry. Major General, USA, Brevet, 3-13-65.

Ruger, Thomas Howard (West Point, 1854, No. 1633). Major General, Volunteers, Brevet, 11-30-64.

Russell, David Allen (*Winchester, Va. 9-19-64) (West Point, 1845, No. 1268). Major General, USA, Brevet, 9-19-64.

Salomon, Friedrich (Frederick). Major General, Volunteers, Brevet, 3-13-65.

Sanborn, John Benjamin. Major General, Volunteers, Brevet, 2-10-65.

Sanders, William Price (*Knoxville, 11-18-63, mortally wounded, dies following day) (West Point, 1856, No. 1751). Brigadier General, Volunteers, Full Rank.

Saxton, Rufus, Jr. (West Point, 1849, No. 1424). Major General, Volunteers, Brevet, 1-12-65 (Medal of Honor Harper's Ferry, May 1862).

Scammon, Eliakim Parker (West Point, 1837, No. 899). Brigadier General, Volunteers, Full Rank, 10-15-62.

Schenck, Robert Cumming. Major General, Volunteers, Full Rank, 8-30-62.

Schimmelfennig, Alexander (*September 5, 1865, natural causes). Brigadier General, Volunteers, Full Rank, 11-29-62.

Schoepf, Albin Francisco. Brigadier General, Volunteers, Full Rank, 9-30-61.

Schofield, John McAllister (West Point, 1853, No. 1585). Major General, USA, Brevet, 3-13-65 (Full Rank, USA during 1868).

Schurtz, Carl Major General, Volunteers, Full Rank, March 1863.

Scott, Robert Kingston. Major General, Volunteers, Brevet, December 1865.

Scott, Winfield. Lieutenant General (rank to date from 1847). USA, Brevet.

Sedgwick, John (*May 9, 1864, Spotsylvania) (West Point, 1837, No. 914). Major General, Volunteers, Full Rank, 7-4-62.

Seward, William Henry, Jr. Brigadier General, Volunteers, Full Rank, 9-13-64.

Seymour, Truman (West Point, 1846, No. 1290). Major General, USA, Brevet, 3-13-65.

Shackelford, James Murrell. Brigadier General, Volunteers, Full Rank, 1-2-63.

Shaler, Alexander. Major General, Volunteers, Brevet (after end of war) (Medal of Honor, Fredericksburg, Marye's Heights, May 3, 1863).

Shephard, Isaac Fitzgerald. Brigadier General, Volunteers, Full Rank, 10-27-63.

Shepley, George Foster. Brigadier General, Volunteers, Full Rank, 7-18-62.

Sheridan, Phillip Henry (West Point, 1853, No. 1612). Major General, USA, Full Rank, 11-8-64 (Full Rank, General, USA, June 1888).

Sherman, Francis Trowbridge. Brigadier General, Volunteers, Full Rank, 7-21-65.

Sherman, Thomas West (West Point, 1836, No. 859). Major General, USA, Brevet, 3-13-65.

Sherman, William Tecumseh (West Point, 1840, No. 1022). Major General, USA, Full Rank, 8-12-64 (later, Full General of the Army, succeeding Grant as Commander in Chief of Army 1869).

Shields, James. Brigadier General, Volunteers, Full Rank, 8-19-61.

Sibley, Henry Hasting. Major General, Volunteers, Brevet, 11-29-65.

Sickles, Daniel Edgar. Major General, Volunteers, Full Rank, 11-29-62, and subsequently Breveted, USA, after close of hostilities (Medal of Honor, Gettysburg, 1863).

Sigel, Franz. Major General, Volunteers, Full Rank, March 1862.

Sill, Joshua Woodrow (*Murfreesboro, Tenn., 12-31-62). Brigadier General, Full Rank, 7-16-62.

Slack, James Richard. Major General, Volunteers, Brevet, 3-13-65.

Slemmer, Adam Jacoby (West Point, 1850, No. 1461). Brigadier General, USA, Brevet, 3-13-65.

Slocum, Henry Warner (West Point, 1852, No. 1542). Major General, Volunteers, Full Rank, 7-4-62.

Slough, John Potts. Brigadier General, Volunteers, Full Rank, 8-25-62.

Smith, Andrew Jackson (West Point, 1838, No. 976). Major General, USA, Brevet, 3-13-65.

Smith, Charles Ferguson (West Point, 1825, No. 410). Major General, Volunteers, Full Rank, March 1862.

Smith, Giles Alexander. Major General, Volunteers, Full Rank, 11-24-65.

Smith, Green Clay. Brigadier General, Volunteers, 6-11-62. Brevet Major General, end of war.

Smith, Gustavus Adolphus. Brigadier General, Volunteers, Full Rank, 9-19-62.

Smith, John Eugene. Major General, USA, Brevet, 3-2-67.

Smith, Morgan Lewis. Brigadier General, Volunteers, Full Rank, 7-16-62.

Smith, Thomas Church Haskell. Brigadier General, Volunteers, Full Rank, 3-13-63.

Smith, Thomas Kilby. Major General, Volunteers, Brevet, 3-13-65.

Smith, William Farrar (West Point, 1845, No. 1234). Major General, USA, Brevet, 3-13-65.

Smith, William Sooy (West Point, 1853, No. 1584). Brigadier General, Volunteers, Full Rank, 4-15-62.

Smyth, Thomas Alfred (*Farmville, Va., mortally wounded, April 7, 1865, succumbs two days later). Major General, Volunteers, Brevet, 4-7-65, posthumously. Smyth is the final Union general killed during the war.

Spears, James Gallant. Brigadier General, Volunteers, Full Rank, 3-5-62.

Spinola, Francis Barretto. Brigadier General, Volunteers, Full Rank, 10-2-62.

Sprague, John Wilson. Major General, Volunteers, Brevet, 3-13-65 (Medal of Honor, Decatur, Georgia, July, 1864).

Stahel, Julius. Major General, Volunteers, Full Rank, March 1863 (Medal of Honor, Piedmont, Va., June 1864).

Stanley, David Sloan (West Point, 1852, No. 1544). Major General, USA, Brevet, 3-13-65 (Medal of Honor, Franklin, Tenn., November 1864).

Stannard, George Jerrison. Major General, Volunteers, Brevet, 10-28-64.

Starkweather, John Converse. Brigadier General, Volunteers, Full Rank, 7-17-63.

Steedman, James Blair. Major General, Volunteers, Full Rank, April 1864.

Steele, Frederick (West Point, 1843, No. 1196). Major General, Volunteers, Full Rank, 11-29-62.

Stevens, Isaac Ingalls (*Chantilly, Va., 9-1-62) (West Point, 1839, No. 986). Major General, Volunteers, Full Rank, 7-18-62.

Stevenson, John Dunlap. Major General, Volunteers, Brevet, 3-13-65.

Stevenson, Thomas Greely (*Richmond Campaign, May 10, 1864). Brigadier General, Volunteers, Full Rank, 3-14-63.

Stokes, James Hughes (West Point, 1835, No. 802). Brigadier General, Volunteers, Full Rank, July 1865.

Stolbrand, Charles John. Brigadier General, Volunteers, Full Rank, 2-18-65.

Stone, Charles Pomroy (West Point, 1845, No. 1237). Brigadier General, Volunteers, Full Rank, 5-17-61.

Stoneman, George, Jr. (West Point, 1846, No. 1304). Major General, USA, Brevet, 3-13-65.

Stoughton, Edwin Henry (West Point, 1859, No. 1841). Brigadier General, Volunteers, Full Rank, 11-5-62.

Strong, George Crockett (*Mortally wounded, 7-18-63, Fort Wagner, succumbs, 7-30-63) (West Point, 1857, No. 1764). Major General, Volunteers, Full Rank, 7-18-63.

Strong, William Kerley. Brigadier General, Volunteers, Full Rank, 9-28-61.

Stuart, David. Brigadier General, Volunteers, Full Rank, 11-29-62.

Stumbaugh, Frederick Shearer. Brigadier General, Volunteers, Full Rank, 11-29-62.

Sturgis, Samuel Davis (West Point, 1846, No. 1303) Major General, USA, Brevet, 3-13-65.

Sullivan, Jeremiah Cutler. Brigadier General, Volunteers, Full Rank, 4-28-62.

Sully, Alfred (West Point, 1841, No. 1092). Major General, Volunteers, Brevet, March 1865.

Sumner, Edwin Vose (*Syracuse, N.Y., 3-21-63, natural causes). Major General, Volunteers, Full Rank, May 5th, 1862.

Swayne, Wager. Major General, USA, Brevet, 3-2-67.

Sweeny, Thomas Williams. Brigadier General, Volunteers, Full Rank, 11-29-62.

Sykes, George (West Point, 1842, No. 1149). Major General, Volunteers, Full Rank, 11-29-62.

Taylor, George William (*9-1-62 from wounds suffered June 1862, vic. of Bull Run). Brigadier General, Full Rank, Volunteers, 5-9-62.

Taylor, Joseph Pannell (*6-29-64, natural causes). Brigadier General, USA, Full Rank, 2-9-63 (brother of President Zachary Taylor).

Taylor, Nelson. Brigadier General, Volunteers, Full Rank, 9-7-62.

Terrill, William Rufus (*Perryville, October 1862) (West Point, 1853, No. 1594). Brigadier General, Volunteers, Full Rank, 9-9-62.

Terry, Alfred Howe. Major General, Volunteers, Full Rank, January 65.

Terry, Henry Dwight. Brigadier General, Volunteers, Full Rank, 7-17-62.

Thayer, John Milton. Major General, Volunteers, Brevet, 3-13-65.

Thomas, George Henry (West Point, 1840, No. 1028). Major General, USA, Full Rank, December 15, 1864.

Thomas, Henry Goddard. Major General, Volunteers, Brevet, 3-13-65.

Thomas, Lorenzo (West Point, 1823, No. 342). Major General, USA, Brevet, 3-13-65.

Thomas, Stephen. Brigadier General, Volunteers, Full Rank, 2-1-65 (Medal of Honor, Cedar Creek, October 19, 1864).

Thruston, Charles Mynn (West Point, 1814, No. 105). Brigadier General, Volunteers, Full Rank, 9-7-61.

Tibbits, William Badger. Major General, Volunteers, Brevet, 3-13-65 (Full Rank Brigadier, October, 1865).

Tilison, Davis (West Point, attendance 1849–1851). Brigadier General, Volunteer, Full Rank, 11-29-62.

Todd, John Blair Smith (West Point, 1837, No. 929). Brigadier General, Volunteers, Full Rank, 9-19-61.

Torbert, Alfred Thomas A. (West Point, 1855, No. 1697). Major General, USA, Brevet, 3-13-65.

Totten, Joseph Gilbert (*natural causes, 4-22-64) (West Point, 1805, No. 10). Major General, USA, Breveted, Posthumously 4-22-64.

Tower, Zealous Bates (West Point, 1841, No. 1059). Brigadier General, USA, Brevet, 3-13-65.

Thrchin, John Basil. Brigadier General, Volunteers, Full Rank, 7-17-62.

Turner, John Wesley (West Point, 1855, No. 1690). Major General, USA, Brevet, 3-13-65.

Tuttle, James Madison. Brigadier General, Volunteers, Full Rank, 6-1-62.

Tyler, Daniel (West Point, 1819, No. 216). Brigadier General, Volunteers, Full Rank, 3-13-62.

Tyler, Erastus Barnard. Major General, Volunteers, Brevet, 3-13-65.

Tyler, Robert Ogden (West Point, 1853, No. 1600). Major General, USA, Brevet, 3-13-65.

Tyndale, Hector. Major General, Volunteers, Brevet, 3-13-65.

Ullman, Daniel. Major General, Volunteers, Brevet, 3-13-65.

Underwood, Adin Ballou. Major General, Volunteers, Brevet, 8-13-65.

Upton, Emory (West Point, 1861, No. 1895). Major General, USA, Brevet 3-13-65.

Van Alen, James Henry. Brigadier General, Volunteers, Full Rank, 4-15-62.

Van Cleve, Horatio Phillips (West Point, 1831, No. 652). Major General, Volunteers, Brevet, 3-13-65.

Van Derveer, Ferdinand. Brigadier General, Volunteers, Full Rank, 10-4-64.

Vandever, William. Major General, Volunteers, Brevet, 6-7-65.

Van Vliet, Stewart (West Point, 1840, No. 1025). Major General, USA, Brevet, 3-13-65.

Van Wyck, Charles Henry. Brigadier General, Volunteers, Full Rank, 9-27-65.

Veatch, James Clifford. Major General, Volunteers, Brevet, 3-26-65.

Viele, Egbert Louis (West Point, 1847, No. 1360). Brigadier General, Volunteers, Full Rank, 8-17-61.

Vincent, Strong (*July 2, 1863, mortally wounded at Gettysburg, dies on the 7th). Brigadier General, Volunteers, Full Rank 7-3-63.

Vinton, Francis Laurens (West Point, 1856, No. 1720). Brigadier General, Volunteers, Full Rank, 9-19-62.

Vogdes, Israel (West Point, 1837, No. 901). Brigadier General, Volunteers, Full Rank 1862, Breveted, USA, April 1865.

Von Steinwehr, Adolph Wilhelm A.F. Brigadier General, Volunteers, Full Rank, October, 1861.

Wade, Melancthon Smith. Brigadier General, Volunteers, Full Rank, 10-1-61.

Wadsworth, James Samuel (*Wilderness, mortally wounded on 5-6-64, dies 5-8-64). Major General, Volunteers, Brevet, 5-6-64.

Wagner, George Day. Brigadier General, Volunteers, Full Rank, 11-29-62.

Walcutt, Charles Carroll. Major General, Volunteers, Brevet, 3-13-65.

Wallace, Lewis. Major General, Volunteers, Full Rank, 3-21-62 (author of the novel *Ben Hur*).

Wallace, William Harvey Lamb (*Shiloh, April 1862, mortally wounded, dies on the 10th). Brigadier General, Volunteers, Full Rank, 3-21-62.

Ward, John Henry. Brigadier General, Volunteers, Full Rank, 10-4-62.

Ward, William Thomas. Major General, Volunteers, Brevet, 2-24-65.

Warner, James Meech (West Point, 1860, No. 1886). Brigadier General, USA, Brevet, May, 1865.

Warren, Fitz Henry. Major General, Volunteers, Brevet, 8-24-65.

Warren, Gouverneur Kemble (West Point, 1850, No. 1451). Major General, Volunteers, Full Rank, 5-3-62.

Washburn, Cadwallader Colden. Major General, Volunteers, Full Rank, 11-29-62.

Watkins, Louis Douglass. Brigadier General, Volunteers, Brevet, 6-24-64 (Full Rank, September, 1865).

Webb, Alexander Stewart (West Point, 1855, No. 1689). Major General, USA, Brevet, 3-13-65 (Medal of Honor, Gettysburg, July 1863).

Weber, Max. Brigadier General, Volunteers, Full Rank, 4-28-62.

Webster, Joseph Dana. Major General, Volunteers, Brevet, 3-13-65.

Weed, Stephen Hinsdale (*Gettysburg, July 1863) (West Point, 1854, No. 1657). Brigadier General, Full Rank, 6-6-63.

Weitzel, Godfrey (West Point, 1855, No. 1678). Major General, Volunteers, Full Rank, November 1864 (Brevet, USA, at end of war).

Wells, William. Major General, Volunteers, 3-13-65 (Full Rank Brigadier, May 1865).

Welsh, Thomas (*August 14, 1863, natural causes). Brigadier General, Volunteers, Full Rank, 3-13-63.

Wessells, Henry Walton (West Point, 1833, No. 735). Brigadier General, USA, Brevet, 3-13-65.

West, Joseph Rodman. Major General, Volunteers, Brevet, 1-4-66.

Wheaton, Frank. Major General, USA, Brevet, 3-13-65 (son-in-Law of Confederate General Samuel Cooper).

Whipple, Amiel Weeks (*mortally wounded 5-4-63, Chancellorsville, dies on the 7th) (West Point, 1841, No. 1063). Major General, USA, Brevet, 5-7-63.

Whipple, William Dennison (West Point, 1851, No. 1524). Major General, USA, Brevet (close of hostilities).

Whitaker, Walter Chiles. Major General, Volunteers, Brevet, 3-13-65.

White, Julius. Major General, Volunteers, Brevet, 3-13-65 (retired due to poor health, late 1864).

Wild, Edward Augustus. Brigadier General, Volunteers, Full Rank, 4-24-63.

Willcox, Orlando Bolivar (West Point, 1847, No. 1338). Major General, USA, Brevet, 3-13-65 (Medal of Honor, as Colonel 1st Michigan Infantry, 1st Bull Run, June 1861).

Williams, Alpheus Starkey. Major General, Volunteers, Brevet (after close of hostilities).

Williams, David Henry. Brigadier General Volunteers, Full Rank, 11-29-62.

Williams, Nelson Grosvenor (West Point, attendance 1839–1840). Brigadier General, Volunteers, Full Rank, 11-29-62.

Williams, Seth (West Point, 1842, No. 1133). Major General, USA, Brevet, 3-13-65.

Williams, Thomas (*Baton Rouge, 8-5-62) (West Point, 1837, No. 902). Brigadier General, Volunteers, Full Rank, 9-28-61.

Williamson, James Alexander. Major General, Volunteers, Brevet, 3-13-65.

Willich, August. Major General, Volunteers, Brevet, 10-21-65.

Wilson, James Harrison (West Point, 1860, No. 1852). Major General, USA, Brevet (after close of hostilities).

Wistar, Isaac Jones. Brigadier General, Volunteers, Full Rank, 11-29-62.

Wood, Thomas John (West Point, 1845, No. 1235). Major General, Volunteers, Full Rank, January, 1865.

Woodbury, Daniel Phineas (*8-15-64, natural causes) (West Point, 1836). Major General, USA, Brevet, 8-15-64.

Woods, Charles Robert (West Point, 1852, No. 1555). Major General, USA, Brevet, 3-13-65.

Woods, William Burnham. Brigadier General, Volunteers, Full Rank, May 65.

Wool, John Ellis. Major General, USA, Full Rank, 5-16-62.

Wright, George (*shipwreck off California coast, July 1865) (West Point, 1822, No. 309). Brigadier General, Volunteers, Full Rank, 9-28-61.

Wright, Horatio Gouverneur (West Point, 1841, No. 1060). Major General, USA, Brevet, 3-13-65.

Zook, Samuel Kosciuszko (*Gettysburg, July 1863). Brigadier General, Volunteers, Full Rank, 11-29-62.

Appendix III

Prominent Union Brigadier Generals Who Received the Rank Only by Brevet

The number of Union officers to achieve this rank is well over 1,000; therefore, the names chosen have either graduated or attended West Point. The year of graduation is listed and the number following is the official cadet number.

Abbot, Henry L. (West Point, 1854, No. 1632).
Alexander, Barton S. (West Point, 1842, No. 1117).
Amory, Thomas J.C. (West Point, 1851, No. 1523).
Babbitt, Edwin B. (West Point, 1826, No. 456).
Babcock, Orville E. (West Point, 1861, No. 1890).
Bache, Hartman (West Point, 1818, No. 198).
Bankhead, Henry C. (West Point, 1850, No. 1484).
Barnes, Charles (West Point, attendance).
Barriger, John W. (West Point, 1856, No. 1723).
Bartlett, William C. (West Point, 1862, No. 1986).
Batchelder, Richard N. (West Point, attendance).
Beckwith, Amos (West Point, 1850, No. 1470).
Beckwith, Edward G. (West Point, 1842, No. 1123).
Bell, George (West Point, 1853, No. 1592).
Bell, John H. (West Point, attendance).
Biggs, Herman (West Point, 1856, No. 1745).
Bomford, James V. (West Point, 1832, No. 695).
Bonneville, Benjamin L.E. (West Point, 1815, No. 155).
Breck, Samuel, Jr. (West Point, 1855, No. 1683).
Brewerton, Henry (West Point, 1819, No. 207).
Brice, Benjamin W. (West Point, 1829, No. 580).
Brooks, Horace (West Point, 1835, No. 794).
Brown, Harvey (West Point, 1818, No. 185).
Burbank, Sidney (West Point, 1829, No. 557).
Cady, Abemarle (West Point, 1829, No. 564).
Callender, Franklin (West Point, 1839, No. 993).
Clarke, Henry F. (West Point, 1843, No. 1178).
Clary, Robert E. (West Point, 1828, No. 520).
Clitz, Henry B. (West Point, 1845, No. 1266).
Cole, George W. (West Point, attendance).
Comstock, Cyrus B. (West Point, 1855, No. 1677).
Conrad, Joseph Speed (West Point, 1857, No. 1791).
Cram, Thomas J. (West Point, 1826, No. 432).
Crosman, George H. (West Point, 1823, No. 355).
Cross, Osborn (West Point, 1825, No. 417).
Dandy, George B. (West Point, attendance).
Davis, Nelson H. (West Point, 1846, No. 1320).
Dawson, Samuel K. (West Point, 1839, No. 1007).
Day, Hannibal (West Point, 1823, No. 348).
De Russy, Rene E. (West Point, 1812, No. 89).
Deveraux, Arthur F. (West Point, attendance).
DeWitt, David P. (West Point, 1836, No. 855).
Dimick, Justin (West Point, 1819, No. 213).
Donaldson, James L. (West Point, 1836, No. 856).
Duane, James C. (West Point, 1848, No. 1371).
Dutton, Arthur H. (West Point, 1861, No. 1935).
Dye, William McE. (West Point, 1853, No. 1610).
Eastman, Seth (West Point, 1829, No. 562).
Easton, Langdon (West Point, 1838, No. 962).
Easton, Joseph H. (West Point, 1835, No. 828).
Erskine, Albert R. (West Point, attendance).
Fitzhugh, Charles L. (West Point, attendance).
Frink, Henry A. (West Point, attendance).
Fry, Cary H. (West Point, 1834, No. 769).
Fyffe, Edward P. (West Point, attendance).
Gates, Willia (West Point, 1806, No. 11).
Gibson, Horatio G. (West Point, 1847, No. 1347).
Gooding, Oliver P. (West Point, 1858, No. 1821).
Graham, William M. (West Point, 1817, No. 164).
Greene, Oliver D. (West Point, 1854, No. 1656).
Grier, William N. (West Point, 1835, No. 839).
Hagner, Peter V. (West Point, 1836, No. 866).
Haines, Thomas J. (West Point, 1849, No. 866).
Hall, Cyrus (West Point, 1842, No. 1148).
Harris, Benjamin F. (West Point, attendance).

Harris, Charles L. (West Point, attendance).
Hayman, Samuel B. (West Point, 1842, No. 1161).
Henry, Guy V. (West Point, 1861, No. 1914).
Hill, Bennett H. (West Point, 1837, No. 911).
Hoffman, William (West Point, 1829, No. 558).
Holibird, Samuel B. (West Point, 1849, No. 1437).
Ihrie, George P. (West Point, attendance).
Johns, Thomas D. (West Point, 1848, No. 1400).
Jones, William P. (West Point, 1840, No. 1020).
Kelton, John C. (West Point, 1851, No. 1519).
Kingsbury, Charles P. (West Point, 1840, No. 1018).
Lee, William R. (West Point, attendance).
Leech, William A. (West Point, attendance).
Leslie, Thomas J. (West Point, 1815, No. 147).
Loomis, Gustavus (West Point, 1811, No. 62).
Lowe, William W. (West Point, 1853, No. 1608).
Markoe, John, Jr. (West Point, attendance).
Marshall, Elisha C. (West Point, 1850, No. 1474).
Maynadier, Henry E. (West Point, 1850, No. 1510).
Maynadier, William (West Point, 1827, No. 472).
McAlester, Miles D. (West Point, 1856, No. 1713).
McKeever, Chauncey (West Point, 1849, No. 1420).
McKibbon, David B. (West Point, attendance).
Merchant, Charles S. (West Point, 1814, No. 92).
Merrill, Lewis (West Point, 1855, No. 1696).
Michie, Peter S. (West Point, 1863, No. 1996).
Michier, Nathaniel, Jr. (West Point, 1848, No. 1375).
Miller, Morris S. (West Point, 1834, No. 763).
Mizner, John K. (West Point, 1856, No. 1743).
Moore, Tredwell, (West Point, 1847, No. 1356).
Morgan, Michael R. (West Point, 1854, No. 1646).
Morris, William W. (West Point, 1820, No. 261).
Murray, Edward (West Point, 1841, No. 1099).
Myer, Albert J. (West Point, attendance).
Myers, Frederick (West Point, 1846, No. 1315).
Myers, George R. (West Point, attendance).
Myers, William (West Point, 1852, No. 1567).
Nichols, William A. (West Point, 1838, No. 959).
Oakes, James (West Point, 1846, No. 1305).
Palfrey, John C. (West Point, 1857, No. 1760).
Patterson, Robert E. (West Point, 1851, No. 1522).
Pease, William R. (West Point, 1855, No. 1707).
Pelouze, Louis H. (West Point, 1853, No. 1595).
Perry, Alexander J. (West Point, 1851, No. 1506).
Porter, Horace (West Point, 1860, No. 1849).
Prime, Frederick E. (West Point, 1850, No. 1450).
Randol, Alanson M. (West Point, 1843, No. 1171).
Ratliff, Robert W. (West Point, attendance).
Raynolds, William F. (West Point, 1843, No. 1171).
Reese, Chauncey B. (West Point, 1859, No. 1828).
Reeve, Isaac V.D. (West Point, 1835, No. 830).
Reno, Marcus A. (West Point, 1857, No. 1779).
Roberts, Joseph (West Point, 1835, No. 793).
Rodman, Thomas J. (West Point, 1841, No. 1065).
Ruff, Charles F. (West Point, 1838, No. 984).
Sacket, Delos B. (West Point, 1845, No. 1268).
Sawtelle, Charles C. (West Point, 1854, No. 1854).
Schiver, Edmund (West Point, 1833, No. 723).
Seawell, Washington (West Point, 1825, No. 411).
Shepherd, Oliver L. (West Point, 1840, No. 1049).
Shiras, Alexander E. (West Point, 1833, No. 726).
Sibley, Caleb C. (West Point, 1829, No. 568).
Sidell, William H. (West Point, 1833, No. 712).
Simpson, Marcus D.L. (West Point, 1846, No. 1293).
Small, Michael P. (West Point, 1855, No. 1687).
Smith, Benjamin F. (West Point, 1853, No. 1617).
Smith, Joseph R. (West Point, 1823, No. 347).
Sweitzer, Nelson B. (West Point, 1853, No. 1602).
Swords, Thomas, Jr. (West Point, 1829, No. 563).

Thayer, Sylvanus (West Point, 1808, No. 33).
Thom, George (West Point, 1839, No. 992).
Thornton, William Anderson (West Point, 1825, No. 403).
Tidball, John C. (West Point, 1848, No. 1379).
Totten, James (West Point, 1841, No. 1083).
Townsend, Edward D. (West Point, 1839, No. 906).
Van Buren, Daniel T. (West Point, 1847, No. 1336).
Vinton, David H. (West Point, 1822, No. 299).
Wallen, Henry D. (West Point, 1840, No. 1050).
Warner, Edward R. (West Point, 1857, No. 1780).
West, George W. (West Point, attendance).
Whistler, Joseph N.C. (West Point, 1846, No. 1318).
Whitely, Robert H.K. (West Point, 1830, No. 599).
Wildrick, Abram C. (West Point, 1857, No. 1773).
Wilson, Thomas, (West Point, 1853, No. 1607).
Woodruff, Israel C. (West Point, 1836, No. 871).

Appendix IV

Roster of Confederate Generals

The listing contains highest rank attained and year of graduation at West Point. The number following the year of graduation is the personal cadet number. An asterisk indicates circumstances of death.

Adams, Daniel Weisiger. Brigadier General, May 23, 1862.
Adams, John (*Franklin, Tenn., November 1864) (West Point, 1846, No. 1296). Brigadier General, December 29, 1862.
Adams, William Wirt. Brigadier General, September 25, 1863.
Alexander, Edward Porter (West Point, 1857, No. 1762). Brigadier General, September 26, 1864.
Allen, Henry Watkins. Brigadier General, August 19, 1863.
Allen, William Wirt. Major General, March 4, 1865.
Anderson, George Burgwin (*Antietam, mortally wounded, 9-17-62, succumbs 10-16-62) (West Point, 1852, No. 1545). Brigadier General, June 9, 1862.
Anderson, George Thomas. Brigadier General, November 1, 1862.
Anderson, James Patton. Major General, February 17, 1864.
Anderson, Joseph Reid (West Point, 1836, No. 845). Brigadier General, September 3, 1861.
Anderson, Richard Herron (West Point, 1842, No. 1150). Lieutenant General, May 31, 1864.
Anderson, Robert Houstoun (West Point, 1857, No. 1794). Brigadier General.
Anderson, Samuel Read. Brigadier General, July 9, 1861.
Archer, James Jay (*Natural causes, 10-24-64). Brigadier General, June 3, 1862.
Armistead, Lewis Addison (*Gettysburg, July 2, 1863, mortally wounded. Dies on the 5th). Brigadier General, April 1, 1862.
Armstrong, Frank Crawford. Brigadier General, January 20, 1863.

Ashby, Turner (*Harrisonburg, 6-6-62). Brigadier General, May 23, 1862.

Baker, Alpheus. Brigadier General, March 5, 1864.

Baker, Lawrence Simmons (West Point, 1851, No. 1535). Brigadier General, July 23, 1863.

Baldwin, William Edwin (*Killed in a horse fall in Alabama, 2-19-64). Brigadier General, September 19, 1862.

Barksdale, William (*Gettysburg, wounded 7-2-63, dies on the 3rd). Brigadier General, August 12, 1862.

Barringer, Rufus. Brigadier General, June 1, 1864.

Barry, John Decatur. Brigadier General, August 3, 1864.

Barton, Seth Maxwell (West Point, 1849, No. 1434). Brigadier General, March 11, 1862.

Bate, William Brimage. Major General, February 23, 1864.

Battle, Cullen A. Brigadier General, August 20, 1863.

Beale, Richard Lee Turberville. Brigadier General, January 6, 1865.

Beall, William Nelson R. (West Point, 1848, No. 1398). Brigadier General, April 11, 1862.

Beauregard, Pierre Gustave Toutant (West Point, 1838, No. 942). Full General, July 21, 1861.

Bee, Barnard Elliott (*1st Bull Run, June 21, dies on the following day) (West Point, 1845, No. 1263). Brigadier General, June 17, 1861.

Bee, Hamilton Prioleau. Brigadier General, March 4, 1862.

Bell, Tyree Harris. Brigadier General, February 28, 1865.

Benning, Henry Lewis. Brigadier General, January 17, 1863.

Benton, Samuel (*Ezra Church, wounded 7-22-64, dies on the 28th). Brigadier General (special appointment), July 26, 1864.

Blanchard, Albert Gallatin (West Point, 1829, No. 566). Brigadier General, September 21, 1861.

Boggs, William Robertson (West Point, 1853, No. 1582). Brigadier General, November 4, 1862.

Bonham, Milledge Luke. Brigadier General, April 23, 1861.

Bowen, John Stevens (*7-13-63, natural causes) (West Point, 1853, No. 1591). Major General, May 25, 1863.

Bragg, Braxton (West Point, 1837, No. 895). Full General, April 6, 1862.

Branch, Lawrence O'Bryan (*Antietam, September 1862). Brigadier General, November 16, 1861.

Brandon, William Lindsay. Brigadier General, June 18, 1864.

Brantley, William Felix. Brigadier General, July 26, 1864.

Bratton, John. Brigadier General, May 6, 1864.

Breckinridge, John Cabell. Major General, April 14, 1862 (February 1865, appointed Confederate secretary of war).

Brevard, Theodore Washington. Brigadier General, March 22, 1865.

Brown, John Calvin. Major General, August 4, 1864.

Brown, Goode (West Point, 1834, No. 774). Brigadier General, August 29, 1863.

Browne, William Montague. Brigadier General, November 11, 1864.

Buckner, Simon Bolivar (West Point, 1844, No. 1216). Lieutenant General, September 20, 1864.

Buford, Abraham. (West Point, 1841, No. 1109). Brigadier General, September 2, 1862.

Bullock, Robert. Brigadier General, November 29, 1864.

Butler, Matthew Calbraith. Major General, September 19, 1864 (during the Spanish American War, 1898, Butler serves as Major General, USA).

Cabell, William (West Point, 1850, No. 1482). Brigadier General, January 20, 1863.

Campbell, Alexander William. Brigadier General, March 1, 1865.

Cantey, James. Brigadier General, January 8, 1863.

Capers, Ellison. Brigadier General, March 1, 1865.

Carroll, William Henry. Brigadier General, October 26, 1861.

Carter, John Carpenter (*Franklin, Tenn., wounded 11-30-64, dies 12-10-64). Brigadier General, July 7, 1864.

Chalmers, James Ronald. Brigadier General, February 13, 1862.

Chambliss, John Randolf (*Vicinity James River at Charles City Road, 8-16-64) (West Point, 1853, No. 1609). Brigadier General, December 19, 1863.

Cheatham, Benjamin Franklin. Major General, March 10, 1862.

Chestnut, James, Jr. Brigadier General, April 23, 1864.

Chilton, Robert Hall (West Point, 1837, No. 938). Brigadier General, October 20, 1862.

Churchill, Thomas James, Jr. Major General, mid-March 1865).

Clanton, James Holt. Brigadier General, November 16, 1863.

Clark, Charles. Brigadier General, May 23, 1861.

Clark, John Bullock. Brigadier General (March 6 1864).

Clayton, Henry Delamar. Major General, July 7, 1864.

Cleburne, Patrick Ronayne (*Franklin, Tenn., November 1864). Major General, December 13, 1862.

Clingman, Thomas Lanier. Brigadier General, May 17, 1862.

Cobb, Howell. Major General, September 9, 1863.

Cobb, Thomas R. Rootes (*Fredericksburg, 12-13-62). Brigadier General, November 1, 1862.

Cocke, Philip St. George (*12-26-61, suicide) (West Point, 1832, No. 667). Brigadier General, October 21, 1861.

Cockrell, Francis Marion. Brigadier General, July 18, 1863.

Colquitt, Alfred Holt. Brigadier General, September 1, 1862.

Colston, Raleigh Edward. Brigadier General, December 24, 1861.

Conner, James. Brigadier General, June 1, 1864.

Cook, Philip. Brigadier General, August 5, 1864.

Cooke, John Rogers. Brigadier General, November 1, 1862 (son of Major General Philip St. Cooke, USA, and brother-in-law of Jeb Stuart).

Cooper, Douglas Hancock. Brigadier General, May 2, 1863.

Cooper, Samuel (West Point, 1815, No. 156). Regular General, May 16, 1861.

Corse, Montgomery Dent. Brigadier General, November 1, 1862.

Cosby, George Blake (West Point, 1852, No. 1552). Brigadier General, January 20, 1863.

Cox, William Ruffin. Brigadier General, May 31, 1864.

Crittenden, George Bibb (West Point, 1832, No. 687). Major General, November 9, 1861 (brother-in-law of Major General Thomas L. Crittenden, USA).

Cumming, Alfred (West Point, 1849, No. 1441). Brigadier General, October 29, 1862.

Daniel, Junius (*mortally wounded, Spotsylvania, 5-12-64, dies on the 13th) (West Point, 1851, No. 1526). Brigadier General, September 1, 1862.

Davidson, Henry Brevard. Brigadier General, August 18, 1863.

Davis, Joseph Robert. Brigadier General, September 15, 1862 (nephew of Confederate President Jefferson Davis).

Davis, William George Mackey. Brigadier General, November 4, 1862.

Dearing, James (*High Bridge, Virginia, 4-6-65) (West Point, attendance 1858–1861). Brigadier General, April 29, 1864.

Deas, Zachariah Cantey. Brigadier General, December 13, 1862.

De Lagnel, Julius Adolph. Brigadier General, April 15, 1862.

De Polignac, Camille Armand J. Major General, April 8, 1864 (dies on 11-15-1913, last surviving Major General of the Confederacy).

Deshler, James (*Chickamauga, 9-20-63) (West Point, 1854, No. 1637). Brigadier General, July 28, 1863.

Dibrell, George Gibbs. Brigadier General, July 26, 1864.

Dockery, Thomas Pleasant. Brigadier General, August 10, 1863.

Doles, George Pierce (*Bethesda Church, 6-2-64). Brigadier General, November 1, 1862.

Donelson, Daniel Smith (*4-17-63, natural causes) (West Point, 1825, No. 396). Major General, January 17, 1863 (nephew of Andrew Jackson).

Drayton, Thomas Fenwick (West Point, 1828, No. 535). Brigadier General, September 25, 1861.

DuBose, Dudley McIver. Brigadier General, November 16, 1864 (son-in-law of Confederate General Robert Toombs).

Duke, Basil Wilson. Brigadier General, September 15, 1864 (brother-in-law of Confederate General John Hunt Morgan).

Duncan, Johnson Kelly (*12-18-62, vic. Knoxville, natural causes) (West Point, 1849, No. 1411). Brigadier General, January 7, 1862.

Dunovant, John (*Vaughn Road, vic. James River, Va., 10-1-64). Brigadier General, August 22, 1864.

Early, Jubal Anderson (West Point, 1837, No. 908). Lieutenant General, May 31, 1864.

Echols, John. Brigadier General, April 16, 1862.

Ector, Matthew Duncan. Brigadier General, August 23, 1862.

Elliott, Stephen (*February 1866, from a combination of ill health and past battle wounds). Brigadier General, May 24, 1864.

Elzey, Arnold (West Point, 1837, No. 923). Major General, December 4, 1862.

Evans, Clement Anselm. Brigadier General, May 19, 1864.

Evans, Nathan George (West Point, 1848, No. 1404). Brigadier General, October 21, 1861.

Ewell, Richard Stoddert (West Point, 1840, No. 1029). Lieutenant General, May 23, 1863.

Fagan, James Fleming. Major General, April 25, 1864.

Featherston, Winfield Scott. Brigadier General, March 4, 1862.

Ferguson, Samuel Wragg (West Point, 1857, No. 1778). Brigadier General, July 23, 1863.

Field, Charles William (West Point, 1849, No. 1433). Major General, February 12, 1864.

Finegan, Joseph. Brigadier General, April 5, 1862.

Finley, Jesse Johnson. Brigadier General, November 16, 1863.

Floyd, John Buchanan (*8-26-63, from natural causes, vic. Abingdon, Va.) (had been secretary of war, USA, 1857–1860). Brigadier General, May 23, 1861.

Forney, John Horace (West Point, 1852, No. 1557). Major General, October 27, 1862.

Forney, William Henry. Brigadier General, February 15, 1865.

Forrest, Nathan Bedford. Lieutenant General, February 28, 1865 (General Forrest is one of only three civilians who attain the rank of lieutentant general in the Confederacy).

Frazer, John Wesley (West Point, 1849, No. 1440). Brigadier General, May 19, 1863.

French, Samuel Gibbs (West Point, 1843, No. 1180). Major General, August 31, 1862.

Frost, Daniel Marsh (West Point, 1844, No. 1209). Brigadier General, March 1862.

Fry, Birkett Davenport (West Point, attendance, class of 1846 but does not graduate). Brigadier General, May 24, 1864.

Gano, Richard Montgomery. Brigadier General, March 17, 1865.

Gardner, Franklin, born in New York (West Point, 1843, No. 1183). Major General, December 13, 1862 (his family sides with the Union).

Gardner, William Montgomery (West Point, 1846, No. 1326). Brigadier General, November 14, 1861.

Garland, Samuel Jr. (*South Mountain, 9-14-62). Brigadier General, May 23, 1862.

Garnett, Richard Brooke (*Gettysburg, 7-3-63) (West Point, 1841, No. 1087). Brigadier General, November 14, 1861.

Garnett, Robert Selden (*Rich Mountain, 7-13-61) (West Point, 1841, No. 1085). Brigadier General, June 6, 1861 (cousin of Richard B. Garnett).

Garrott, Isham Warren (*Vicksburg, 6-17-63). Brigadier General, May 28, 1863.

Gartrell, Lucius Jeremiah. Brigadier General, August 22, 1864.

Gary, Martin Witherspoon. Brigadier General, May 19, 1864.

Gatlin, Richard Caswell (West Point, 1832, No. 696). Brigadier General, July 8, 1861.

Gholson, Samuel Jameson. Brigadier General, May 6, 1864.

Gibson, Randall Lee. Brigadier General, January 11, 1864.

Gilmer, Jeremy Francis (West Point, 1839, No. 989). Major General, August 25, 1863.

Girardey, Victor Jean B. (*Petersburg, 8-16-64). Brigadier General, July 30, 1864.

Gist, States Rights (*Franklin, Tenn., 11-30-64). Brigadier General, March 20, 1862.

Gladden, Adley Hogan (*Shiloh, wounded April 6, dies on the 12th). Brigadier General, September 30, 1861.

Godwin, Archibald Campbell (*Opequon, 9-19-64). Brigadier General, August 5, 1864.

Goggin, James Monroe (West Point, attendance). Brigadier General, September 4, 1864.

Gordon, B. Franklin. Brigadier General, May 16, 1865 (Trans Mississippi). Unconfirmed by President Davis.

Gordon, George Washington. Brigadier General, August 15, 1864.

Gordon, James Byron (*Mortally wounded, 5-12-64, vic. Yellow Tavern, dies on the 18th). Brigadier General, September 28, 1863.

Gordon, John Brown. Major General, May 14, 1864.

Gorgas, Josiah (West Point, 1841, No. 1064). Brigadier General, November 10, 1864.

Govan, Daniel Chevilette. Brigadier General, 1863.

Gracie, Archibald, Jr. (West Point, 1854, No. 1644) (*Petersburg, 12-2-64). Brigadier General, November 4, 1862 (born in New York, his family remains with the Union).

Granbury, Hiram Bronson (*Franklin, Tenn., 11-30-64). Brigadier General, February 29, 1864.

Gray, Henry. Brigadier General, March 17, 1865.

Grayson, John Breckinridge (*10-21-61, natural causes). (West Point, 1826, No. 450) Brigadier General.

Green, Martin Edin (*Vicksburg, 6-27-63). Brigadier General, July 21, 1862.

Green, Thomas (*Blairs Landing, La., 4-12-64). Brigadier General, May 20, 1863.

Greer, Elkanah Brackin. Brigadier General, October 8, 1862.

Gregg, John (*Richmond vic., 10-7-64). Brigadier General, August 29, 1862.

Gregg, Maxcy (*Mortally wounded at Fredericksburg, 12-13-62, dies on the 15th). Brigadier General, December 14, 1861.

Griffith, Richard (*Savage Station, 6-29-62). Brigadier General, November 1861.

Grimes, Bryan. Major General, February 15, 1865.

Hagood, Johnson. Brigadier General, July 21, 1862.

Hampton, Wade. Lieutenant General, February 14, 1865 (General Hampton is one of three men who attain the rank of lieutenant general in the Confederacy with no military experience prior to the conflict).

Hanson, Roger Weightman (*mortally wounded at Murfreesboro, 1-2-63, dies two days later). Brigadier General, December 13, 1862.

Hardee, William Joseph (West Point, 1838, No. 966). Lieutenant General, October 10, 1862.

Hardeman, William Polk. Brigadier General, March 17, 1865.

Harris, Nathaniel Harrison. Brigadier General, December 1864.

Harrison, James Edward. Brigadier General, December 22, 1864 (brother of Confederate General Thomas Harrison).

Harrison, Thomas. Brigadier General, January 14, 1865. (*5-31-62 Fair Oaks Station).

Hatton, Robert Hopkins. Brigadier General, May 23, 1862.

Hawes, James Morrison (West Point, 1845, No. 1259). Brigadier General, March 5, 1862.

Hawthorne, Alexander Travis. Brigadier General, February 18, 1864.

Hays, Harry Thompson. Major General, May 1865.

Hebert, Louis (West Point, 1845, No. 1233). Brigadier General, May 26, 1862.

Helm, Benjamin Hardin (*mortally wounded at Chickamauga, 9-20-63, dies on the 21st) (West Point, 1851, No. 1502). Brigadier General, March 14, 1862 (related to President Lincoln by marriage).

Herbert, Paul Octave (West Point, 1840, No. 1017). Brigadier General, August 17, 1861.

Heth, Henry (West Point, 1847, No. 1368). Major General, October 10, 1862.

Higgins, Edward. Brigadier General, October 29, 1863.

Hill, Ambrose Powell (*Petersburg, 4-2-65) (West Point, 1847, No. 1345). Lieutenant General, May 24, 1863.

Hill, Benjamin Jefferson. Brigadier General, November 30, 1864.

Hill, Daniel Harvey (West Point, 1842, No. 1138). Lieutenant General, July 11, 1863.

Hindman, Thomas Carmichael. Major General, April 14, 1862.

Hodge, George Baird (Annapolis, 1845). Brigadier General, November 20, 1863.

Hogg, Joseph Lewis (*dies 5-16-62, natural causes). Brigadier General, February 14, 1862.

Hoke, Robert Frederick. Major General, April 20, 1864.

Holmes, Theophilus Hunter (West Point, 1829, No. 584). Lieutenant General, October, 1862.

Holtzclaw, James Thadeus. Brigadier General, July 7, 1864.

Hood, John Bell (West Point, 1853, No. 1622). Full General, July 18, 1864.

Huger, Benjamin (West Point, 1825, No. 399). Major General, October 7, 1861.

Humes, William Young C. Brigadier General, November 16, 1863.

Humphreys, Benjamin Grubb (West Point, attendance 1825–1826). Brigadier General, August 12, 1863.

Hunton, Eppa. Brigadier General, August 9, 1863.

Imboden, John Daniel. Brigadier General, January 28, 1863.

Iverson, Alfred. Brigadier General, November 1, 1862.

Jackman, Sidney D. Brigadier General, May 16, 1865 (unconfirmed by President Davis).

Jackson, Alfred Eugene. Brigadier General, February 9, 1863.

Jackson, Henry Rootes. Brigadier General, June 4, 1861.

Jackson, John King. Brigadier General, Early 1862.

Jackson, Thomas Jonathan "Stonewall" (*Chancellorsville, wounded mortally, 5-2-63, dies on the 10 May) (West Point, 1846, No. 1288). Lieutenant General, October 10, 1862.

Jackson, William Hicks (West Point, 1856, No. 1748). Brigadier General, December 29, 1862.

Jackson, William Lowther. Brigadier General, December 19, 1864 (cousin of Confederate General Stonewall Jackson).

Jenkins, Albert Gallatin (*mortally wounded at Cloyd's Mountain, 5-9-64, dies on 5-21-64). Brigadier General, August 5, 1862.

Jenkins, Micah (*Wilderness, 5-6-64). Brigadier General, July 22, 1862.

Johnson, Adam Rankin. Brigadier General, June 1st, 1864.

Johnson, Bradley Tyler. Brigadier General, June 28, 1864.

Johnson, Bushrod Rust (West Point, 1840, No. 1039). Major General, May 21, 1864.

Johnson, Edward (West Point, 1838, No. 972). Major General, February 28, 1863.

Johnston, Albert Sidney (*Shiloh, 4-6-62) (West Point, 1826, No. 436). Full General, May 30, 1861.

Johnston, George Doherty. Brigadier General, July 26, 1864.

Johnston, Joseph Eggleston (West Point, 1829, No. 553). Full General, July 4, 1861.

Johnston, Robert Daniel. Brigadier General, September 1, 1863.

Jones, David Rumple (*1-15-63, natural causes) (West Point, 1846, No. 1312). Major General, March 10, 1862.

Jones, John Marshall (*Wilderness, 5-2-64) (West Point, 1841, No. 1097). Brigadier General, May 15, 1863.

Jones, John Roberts. Brigadier General, June 23, 1862.

Jones, Samuel, Jr. (West Point, 1841, No. 1077). Major General, March 1862.

Jones, William Edmondson (*Piedmont, Va., 6-5-64) (West Point, 1848, No. 1378). Brigadier General, September 19, 1862.

Jordan, Thomas (West Point, 1840, No. 157). Brigadier General, April 14, 1862.

Kelly, John Herbert (*Franklin, Tenn., Mortally wounded on 9-2-64, succumbing within a few days) (West Point, attendance 1857–1860). Brigadier General, November 16, 1863.

Kemper, James Lawson. Major General, September 19, 1864.

Kennedy, John Doby. Brigadier General, December 22, 1864.

Kershaw, Joseph Brevard. Major General, May 18, 1864.

Kirkland, William Whedbee (West Point, attendance) (USMC, 1855–1860). Brigadier General, August 29, 1863.

Lane, James Henry. Brigadier General, November 1, 1862.

Lane, Walter Paye. Brigadier General, March 17, 1865.

Law, Evander Mcllvor. Brigadier General, October 1862.

Lawton, Alexander Robert (West Point, 1839, No. 998). Brigadier General, April 13, 1861.

Leadbetter, Danville (West Point, 1836, No. 844). Brigadier General, February 27, 1862.

Lee, Edwin Gray. Brigadier General, September 20, 1864.

Lee, Fitzhugh (West Point, 1856, No. 1755). Major General, August 3, 1863 (nephew of Robert E. Lee; participates in the Spanish-American War during 1898 as a major general, USA).

Lee, George Washington Custis (West Point, 1854, No. 1631). Major General, October 20, 1864 (son of Robert E. Lee).

Lee, Robert Edward (West Point, 1829, No. 542). Full General, June 14, 1861 (January 1865, commander-in-chief all Confederate armies). General Robert E. Lee is the son of Revolutionary War General Henry "Light Horse Harry" Lee.

Lee, Stephen Dill (West Point, 1854, No. 1647). Lieutenant General, June 23, 1864.

Lee, William Henry Fitzhugh. Major General, April 23, 1864 (Son of Robert E. Lee).

Leventhorpe, Coliett. Brigadier General, February 1865.

Lewis, Levin M. Brigadier General, May 16, 1865 (unconfirmed by President Davis).

Lewis, Joseph Horace. Brigadier General, September 30, 1863.

Lewis, William Gaston. Brigadier General, May 31, 1864.

Liddell, St. John Richardson (West Point, attendance, 1833) Brigadier General, July 1862.

Lilley, Robert D. Brigadier General, May 31, 1864.

Little, Lewis Henry (*Iuka, Miss., 9-19-62). Brigadier General, April 16, 1862.

Logan, Thomas Muldrup. Brigadier General, February 15, 1865.

Lomax, Lunsford Lindsay (West Point, 1856, No. 1731). Major General, August 10, 1864.

Long, Armistead Lindsay (West Point, 1850, No. 1466). Brigadier General, Artillery, September 21, 1863.

Longstreet, James (West Point, 1842, No. 1164). Lieutenant General, October 9, 1862.

Loring, William Wing. Major General, February 1862.

Lovell, Mansfield (West Point, 1842, No. 1119). Major General, October 7, 1861.

Lowrey, Mark Perrin. Brigadier General, October 4, 1863.

Lowry, Robert. Brigadier General, February 4, 1865.

Lyon, Hylan Benton (West Point, 1856, No. 1729). Brigadier General, June 14, 1864.

McCausland, John. Brigadier General, May 18, 1864 (General McCausland dies on 1-22-1927).

McComb, William. Brigadier General, January 20, 1865.

McCown, John Porter (West Point, 1840, No. 1026). Major General, March 10, 1862.

McCulloch, Ben (*Pea Ridge, 3-7-62) Brigadier General, May 11, 1861 (brother of Confederate General Henry E. McCulloch).

McCulloch, Henry Eustace. Brigadier General, March 14, 1862.

McGowan, Samuel. Brigadier General, January 17, 1863.

McIntosh, James McQueen (*Pea Ridge, 3-7-62) (West Point, 1849, No. 1449). Brigadier General, January 24, 1862 (brother of Union General John B. McIntosh).

Mackall, William Whann (West Point, 1837, No. 898). Brigadier General, February 27, 1862.

McLaws, Lafayette (West Point, 1842, No. 1158). Major General, May 23, 1862.

Maclay, Robert P. Brigadier General, April 30, 1864 (unconfirmed by President Davis).

McNair, Evander. Brigadier General, November 4, 1862.

McRae, Dandridge. Brigadier General, November 5, 1862.

MacRae, William. Brigadier General, November 4, 1864.

Magruder, John Bankhead (West Point, 1830, No. 601). Major General, October 7, 1861.

Mahone, William. Major General, July 30, 1864.

Major, James Patrick (West Point, 1856, No. 1733). Brigadier General, July 21, 1863.

Maney, George Earl. Brigadier General, April 16, 1862.

Manigault, Arthur Middleton. Brigadier General, April 26, 1863.

Marmaduke, John Sappington (West Point, 1857, No. 1789). Major General, March 17, 1865.

Marshall, Humphrey (West Point, 1832, No. 703). Brigadier General, October 30, 1861.

Martin, James Green (West Point, 1840, No. 1030). Brigadier General, May 15, 1862.

Martin, William Thompson. Major General, November 10, 1863.

Maury, Dabney Herndon (West Point, 1846, No. 1308). Major General, November 4, 1862.

Maxey, Samuel Bell (West Point, 1846, No. 1329). Brigadier General, March 4, 1862.

Mercer, Hugh Weedon (West Point, 1828, No. 510). Brigadier General, October 29, 1861 (grandson of Revolutionary War General Hugh Mercer).

Miller, William. Brigadier General, August 2, 1864.

Moody, Young Marshall. Brigadier General, March 4, 1865.

Moore, John Creed (West Point, 1849, No. 1423). Brigadier General, May 26, 1862.

Moore, Patrick Theodore. Brigadier General, September 20, 1864.

Morgan, John Hunt (*Greenville, N.C., 9-4-64). Brigadier General, December 11, 1862.

Morgan, John Tyler. Brigadier General, 1863.

Mouton, Jean Jacques A.A. (*Mansfield, La., Red River campaign, 4-8-64) (West Point, 1850, No. 1487). Brigadier General, April 16, 1862.

Nelson, Allison (10-7-62, natural causes). Brigadier General, September 12, 1862.

Nicholls, Francis Redding T. (West Point, 1855, No. 1688). Brigadier General, October 14, 1862.

Northrop, Lucius Ballinger (West Point, 1831, No. 650). Brigadier General, November 26, 1864.

O'Neal, Edward Asbury. Brigadier General, June 6, 1863.

Page, Richard Lucian. Brigadier General, March 1, 1864 (first cousin of Robert E. Lee).

Palmer, Joseph Benjamin. Brigadier General, November 15, 1864.

Parsons, Mosby Monroe. Brigadier General, November 5, 1862.

Paxton, Elisha Franklin (*Chancellorsville, 5-3-63). Brigadier General, November 1, 1862.

Payne, William Henry Fitzhugh. Brigadier General, November 1, 1864.

Peck, William Raine. Brigadier General, February 18, 1865.

Pegram, John (*Hatcher's Run, Va., 2-6-65) (West Point, 1854, No. 1640). Brigadier General, November 7, 1862.

Pemberton, John Clifford (West Point, 1837, No. 917). Lieutenant General, October 10, 1862.

Pender, William Dorsey (*Gettysburg, mortally wounded 7-2-63, dies 7-18-63) (West Point, 1854, No. 1649). Major General, May 27, 1863.

Pendleton, William Nelson (West Point, 1830, No. 591). Brigadier General, March 26, 1862.

Perrin, Abner Monroe (*Spotsylvania, 5-12-64). Brigadier General, September 10, 1863.

Perry, Edward Aylesworth. Brigadier General, August 28, 1862.

Perry, William Flank. Brigadier General, February 21, 1865.

Pettigrew, James Johnston (*Falling Waters, Md., mortally wounded, 7-14-63, dies on 7-17.) Brigadier General, February 26, 1862.

Pettus, Edmund Winston. Brigadier General, September 18, 1863.

Pickett, George Edward (West Point, 1846, No. 1330). Major General, October 10, 1862.

Pike, Albert. Brigadier General, August 15, 1861.

Pillow, Gideon Johnson. Brigadier General, July 9, 1861.

Polk, Leonidas (*Marietta, Georgia, 6-14-64) (West Point, 1827, No. 477). Lieutenant General, October 10, 1862.

Polk, Lucius Eugene. Brigadier General, December 13, 1862.

Posey, Carnot (*Bristoe Station, wounded 10-14-63, dies 11-13-63). Brigadier General, November 1, 1862.

Preston, John Smith. Brigadier General, June 10,

1864 (father-in-law of General Wade Hampton).

Preston, William. Brigadier General, April 14, 1862 (brother-in-law of Confederate General Albert Sidney Johnston).

Price, Sterling. Major General, March 6, 1862.

Pryor, Roger Atkinson. Brigadier General, April 16, 1862.

Quarles, William Andrew. Brigadier General, August 25, 1863.

Rains, Gabriel James (West Point, 1827, No. 482). Brigadier General, September 23, 1861.

Rains, James Edwards (*Stone's River, 12-31-62). Brigadier General, November 4, 1862.

Ramseur, Stephen Dodson (*Cedar Creek 10-19-64) (West Point, 1860, No. 1860). Major General, June 1, 1864.

Randolf, George Wythe. Brigadier General, February 12, 1862.

Ransom, Matt Whitaker. Brigadier General, June 13, 1863.

Ransom, Robert, Jr. (West Point, 1850, No. 1467). Major General, May 26, 1863.

Reynolds, Alexander Welch (West Point, 1838, No. 975). Brigadier General, September 14, 1863.

Reynolds, Daniel Harris. Brigadier General, March 5, 1864.

Richardson, Robert Vinkler. Brigadier General, December 1863.

Ripley, Roswell Sabin (West Point, 1843, No. 1173). Brigadier General, August 15, 1861.

Roane, John Selden. Brigadier General, 1862.

Roberts, William Paul. Brigadier General, February 21st, 1865.

Robertson, Beverly Holcombe (West Point, 1849, No. 1431). Brigadier General, June 9, 1862.

Robertson, Felix Huston (West Point, attendance 1857–1861). Brigadier General, July 26, 1864. (Son of Confederate General Jerome Robinson; the last surviving general officer of the Confederacy, d. April 20, 1928).

Robertson, Jerome Bonaparte. Brigadier General, November 1, 1862.

Roddey, Philip Dale. Brigadier General, August 3, 1863.

Rodes, Robert Emmett (*Winchester, 9-19-64). Major General, May 2, 1863.

Ross, Lawrence Sullivan. Brigadier General, December 21, 1863.

Rosser, Thomas LaFayette (West Point, attendance 1856–1861 as Cadet but does not graduate). Major General, November 1, 1864 (General Rosser participates in the Spanish American War during 1898 as a Brigadier General, USA).

Ruggles, Daniel (West Point, 1833, No. 740). Brigadier General, August 9, 1861.

Rust, Albert. Brigadier General, March 4, 1862.

St. John, Isaac Munroe. Brigadier General, February 16, 1865.

Sanders, John Caldwell C. (*Weldon Railroad 8-21-64). Brigadier General, May 31, 1864.

Scales, Alfred Moore. Brigadier General, June 1863.

Scott, Thomas Moore. Brigadier General, May 10, 1864.

Scurry, William Read (*Jenkins Ferry, Ark., 4-30-64). Brigadier General, September 12, 1862.

Sears, Claudius Wistar (West Point, 1841, No. 1089). Brigadier General, March 1, 1864.

Semmes, Paul Jones (*Gettysburg, wounded 7-2-63, dies on 7-10-63). Brigadier General, March 11, 1862.

Sharp, Jacob Hunter. Brigadier General, July 26, 1864.

Shelby, Joseph Orville. Brigadier General, December 15, 1863.

Shelley, Charles Miller. Brigadier General, September 17, 1864.

Shoup, Francis Asbury. (West Point, 1855, No. 1691) Brigadier General, September 12, 1862.

Sibley, Henry Hopkins (West Point, 1838, No. 971). Brigadier General, June 17, 1861.

Simms, James Phillip. Brigadier General, December 1864.

Slack, William Yarnel (*Pea Ridge, Wounded 3-7-62, dies 21 March). Brigadier General, April 12, 1862, posthumously.

Slaughter, James Edwin. Brigadier General, March 8, 1862.

Smith, Edmund Kirby (West Point, 1845, No. 1255). Full Rank General, Provisional Army, February 19, 1864.

Smith, Gustavus Woodson (West Point, 1842, No. 1118). Major General, September 19, 1861.

Smith, James Argyle (West Point, 1853, No. 1623). Brigadier General, September 30, 1863.

Smith, Martin Luther (West Point, 1842, No. 1126). Major General, November 4, 1862.

Smith, Preston (*Chickamauga, 9-19-63). Brigadier General, October 27, 1862.

Smith, Thomas Benton. Brigadier General, July 29, 1864.

Smith, William. Major General, August 12, 1863.

Smith, William Duncan (*10-4-62, natural causes, vic. Charleston). Brigadier General, March 7, 1862.

Sorrel, Gilbert Moxley. Brigadier General, October 27, 1864.

Stafford, Leroy Augustus (*Wilderness, wounded 5-5-64, dies on 5-8-64). Brigadier General, October 8, 1863.

Starke, Peter Burwell. Brigadier General, November 4, 1864.

Starke, William Edwin (*Antietam, 9-17-62). Brigadier General, August 6, 1862.

Steele, William (West Point, 1840, No. 1047). Brigadier General, September 12, 1862.

Sterling, A.M.W. Brigadier General, January 1862.

Steuart, George Hume, Jr. (West Point, 1848, No. 1405). Brigadier General, March 6, 1862.

Stevens, Clement Hoffman (*Peach Tree Creek, Ga., wounded, 7-20-64, dies on 7-25-64). Brigadier General, January 20, 1864.

Stevens, Walter Husted (West Point, 1848, No. 1372). Brigadier General, August 28, 1864.

Stevenson, Carter Littlepage (West Point, 1838, No. 982). Major General, October 10, 1862.

Stewart, Alexander Peter (West Point, 1842, No. 1122). Lieutenant General, June 23, 1864.

Stovall, Marcellus Augustus (West Point, attendance 1836). Brigadier General, early 1863.

Strahl, Otho French (*Franklin, Tenn., 11-30-64). Brigadier General, July 28, 1863.

Stuart, James Ewell Brown "Jeb" (*mortally wounded at Yellow Tavern, Va., 5-11-64, dies on the following day) (West Point, 1854, No. 1643). Major General, July 25, 1862.

Taliaferro, William Booth. Brigadier General, March 4, 1862.

Tappan, James C. Brigadier General, November 5, 1862.

Taylor, Richard. Lieutenant General, April 8, 1864 (son of President Zachary Taylor; one of only three civilians who attain the rank of lieutenant general in the Confederacy).

Taylor, Thomas Hart. Brigadier General, November 4, 1862.

Terrell, Alexander W. Brigadier General, May 16, 1865 (unconfirmed by President Davis).

Terrill, James Barbour (*Bethesda Church, Va., 5-30-64). Brigadier General, May 31, 1864.

Terry, William. Brigadier General, May 19, 1864.

Terry, William Richard. Brigadier General, May 31, 1864.

Thomas, Allen. Brigadier General, February 4, 1864 (brother-in-law of Confederate General Richard Taylor).

Thomas, Bryan Morel (West Point, 1858, No. 1819). Brigadier General, August 4, 1864.

Thomas, Edward Lloyd. Brigadier General, November 1, 1862.

Tilghman, Lloyd (*Champion's Hill, Miss., 5-16-63) (West Point, 1836, No. 887). Brigadier General, October 18, 1861.

Toombs, Robert Augustus. Brigadier General, July 19, 1861.

Toon, Thomas Fentress. Brigadier General, May 31, 1864.

Tracy, Edward Dorr (*Port Gibson, Miss., 5-1-63). Brigadier General, August 16, 1862.

Trapier, James H. (West Point, 1838, No. 943). Brigadier General, October 21, 1861.

Trimble, Isaac R. (West Point, 1822, No. 302). Major General, January 17, 1863.

Tucker, William F. Brigadier General, March 1, 1864.

Twiggs, David Emanuel (*Augusta, Ga., natural causes, July 15, 1862). Major General, May 22, 1861.

Tyler, Robert Charles (*West Point, Ga., Ft. Tyler, 4-16-65). Brigadier General, February 23, 1864.

Vance, Robert Brank. Brigadier General, March 4, 1863.

Van Dorn, Earl (*Spring Hill, Tenn., 5-7-63, assassinated) (West Point, 1842, No. 1162). Major General, September 19, 1861.

Vaughan, Alfred Jefferson. Brigadier General, November 18, 1863.

Vaughn, John Crawford. Brigadier General, September 22, 1862.

Villepique, John Bordenave (*11-9-62, natural causes) (West Point, 1854, No. 1652). Brigadier General, March 13, 1862.

Walker, Henry Harrison (West Point, 1853, No. 1619). Brigadier General, July 1, 1863.

Walker, James Alexander. Brigadier General, May 15, 1863.

Walker, John George. Major General, November 8, 1862.

Walker, Leroy Pope. Brigadier General, September 17, 1861.

Walker, Lucius Marshall (*Little Rock, Ark., mortally wounded in a duel with Confederate General Marmaduke on September 6, 1863; succumbs on the 7th.) (West Point, 1850, No. 1464). Brigadier General, early 1862.

Walker, Reuben Lindsay. Brigadier General, Artillery, February 18, 1865.

Walker, William Henry Talbot (*Atlanta, 7-22-64) (West Point, 1837, No. 936). Major General, May 23, 1863.

Walker, William Stephen. Brigadier General, October 30, 1862.

Wallace, William Henry. Brigadier General, September 20, 1864.

Walthall, Edward Cary. Major General, July 6, 1864.

Waterhouse, Richard. Brigadier General, March 17, 1865.

Watie, Stand. Brigadier General, May 6, 1864.

Waul, Thomas Neville. Brigadier General, September 18, 1863.

Wayne, Henry Constantine (West Point, 1838, No. 954). Brigadier General, December 16, 1861.

Weisiger, David Addison. Brigadier General, July 30, 1864.

Wharton, Gabriel C. Brigadier General, July 8, 1863.

Wharton, John Austin (*4-6-65, killed during a confrontation with another Confederate officer). Major General, November 10, 1863.

Wheeler, Joseph, Jr. (West Point, 1859, No. 1843). Major General, January 20, 1863 (serves during the Spanish American War in 1898 as a Major General, USA).

Whitfield, John Wilkins. Brigadier General, May 9, 1863.

Whiting, William Henry Chase (*Dies 3-10-65 from wounds suffered while defending Fort Fisher, N.C.) (West Point, 1845, No. 1231). Major General, April 22, 1863.

Wickam, Williams Carter. Brigadier General, September 1, 1863.

Wigfall, Louis Trezevant. Brigadier General, October 1861.

Wilcox, Cadmus Marcellus (West Point, 1846, No. 1325). Major General, August 3, 1863.

Williams, John Stuart. Brigadier General, April 16, 1862.

Wilson, Claudius Charles (*11-27-63, Ringgold, Ga., natural causes). Brigadier General, November 16, 1863.

Winder, Charles Sidney (*Cedar Mountain, Va., 8-9-62) (West Point, 1850, No. 1471). Brigadier General, March 1st, 1862.

Winder, John Henry (*2-7-65, natural causes) (West Point, 1820, No. 242). Brigadier General, June 21st, 1861.

Wise, Henry Alexander. Brigadier General, June 5, 1861 (brother-in-law of Union Major General George Gordon Meade).

Withers, Jones Mitchell (West Point, 1835, No. 829). Major General, April 6, 1862.

Wofford, William Tatum. Brigadier General, January 17, 1863.

Wood, Sterling Alexander Martin. Brigadier General, January 7, 1862.

Wright, Ambrose Ransom. Major General, November 26, 1864.

Wright, Marcus Joseph. Brigadier General, December 13, 1862.

York, Zebulon. Brigadier General, May 31, 1864.

Young, Pierce Manning Butler (West Point, attendance resigns just prior to graduation, class of 1861). Major General, December 1864.

Young, William Hugh. Brigadier General, August 15, 1864.

Zollicoffer, Felix Kirk (*1-19-1862, Mill Springs or Fishing Creek, Kentucky). Brigadier General, July 9, 1861.

Appendix V

Prominent Union Naval Officers

If available, birthplace is listed in parentheses. This is sometimes followed by date of appointment as midshipman. Noted are some of the ships assigned, including those commanded by the individual. On occasion, certain engagements are listed which might not be covered in the primary text.

Alden, James, Commodore (Maine). Midshipman 4-1-1828; Assigned to USS *John Adams*, Mediterranean Squadron, 1832–33; Commanded USS *South Carolina*, early part of 1861 and USS *Richmond* against Forts St. Philip and Jackson; Commanded USS *Brooklyn* against Forts Morgan and Gaines and against Fort Fisher; Commissioned Commodore, 7-25-1866.

Almy, John J., Captain (Rhode Island). Midshipman, 2-2-1829; Assigned Pacific Squadron, 1834, Brazil Squadron, 1835–36, Mediterranean Squadron, 1840, and USS *Ohio*, Home Squadron, 1846, including participation at Vera Cruz and Tuspan; Assigned USS *Ohio*, 1847–50, Pacific Squadron; Command USS *South Carolina*, South Atlantic Squadron, 1862, USS *Connecticut*, 1863–64.

Ammen, Daniel, Captain (Ohio). Midshipman, 7-7-1836; Commanded USS *Seneca*, South Atlantic Squadron, 1861–62, including battles at Port Royal and Tybee Ferry; Commanded USS *Patapsco*, 1863, and USS *Mohican*, North Atlantic Squadron, 1864–65.

Armstrong, James F., Captain (New Jersey). Midshipman, 3-7-1832; Commanded USS *Sumter*, 1861, USS *State of Georgia*, North Atlantic Squadron, 1862–63; Commanded USS *San Jacinto*, Eastern Gulf Squadron, 1864, and Commandant of the Pensacola Navy Yard, 1865–68.

Arnold, H.N.T., Commander. USS *Mystic*, South Atlantic Sq., 1862–63; USS *Mercedita*, North Atlantic Sq., 1863–64; USS *Chickopee*, Atlantic Sq., 1865–66.

Badger, Oscar C., Commander. USS *Anacostia*, Potomac Flotilla, 1861–62; USS *Patapsco* (against Confederate Forts Wagner and Gregg, July and August, 1863); Fleet captain of South Atlantic Squadron when wounded grievously on September 1, 1863.

Bailey, Theodorus, Rear Admiral (New York). Midshipman 1-1-1818; Served aboard USS *Vincennes*, Pacific Squadron, 1834–36; USS *Constitution*, East India Squadron 1843; Commanded USS *Lexington* during Mexican War (1846–48); USS *St. Mary's*, 1856–57, and USS *Colorado*, Western Gulf Blockading Squadron, 1861–62 (second in command to Admiral Farragut at New Orleans); late 1862, while suffering from poor health, Commodore Bailey requests active participation and receives command of Eastern Gulf Blockading

Squadron against blockade runners; Commissioned Rear Admiral, July 25, 1866.

Baker, Francis H., Commander. USS *Huron*, South Atlantic Sq., 1863–64; USS *Vicksburg*, 1864–65.

Balch, George B., Captain (Tennessee). Midshipman, 12-30-1837; Attached to the USS *Sabine*, 1860, and involved with the rescue of nearly 400 Marines who were sinking with the transport *Governor* (November 1861); Commanded the USS *Pocahontas*, South Atlantic Squadron, 1861–62, including the taking of Tybee Island (December 1861); USS *Pawnee*, South Atlantic Squadron, 1863–65, including engagement with enemy fire on July 16, 1863, that caused the Pawnee to be struck by enemy fire 46 times. General Terry congratulated Balch and advised him that "the Pawnee had saved his command."

Baldwin, Augustus, Captain (New Jersey). Midshipman, 2-2-1829; Commanded USS *Wyandotte*, Potomac Flotilla, 1861; USS *Vermont*, South Atlantic Squadron, 1862.

Baldwin, Charles H., Captain (New York). Midshipman, 4-24-1839; Commanded USS *Clifton*, 1861–62; USS *Vanderbilt*, 1863–64.

Barrett, Edward, Commander. USS *Massasoit*, 1863–64; USS *Catskill*, 1864–65.

Beaumont, John C., Commander. USS *Sebago*, South Atlantic Sq., 1862–63; USS *Mackinaw*, North Atlantic Sq., 1864–65.

Belknap, George E., Commander. Commanded a launch boat at Canton, China (November 1856); USS *St. Louis*, reinforcing Ft. Pickens, April 1861; USS *Seneca*, North Atlantic Sq., 1864; USS *Canonicus*, December 1864–January 1865.

Bell, Charles H., Rear Admiral (New York). Midshipman, 1-18-1812; Attached to Commodore Decatur's Squadron, 1813 and Spring of 1814; Attached to Commodore Chauncey's Squadron (Lake Ontario) during remainder of 1814 through the war's (1812) end; transferred to Decatur's Squadron in the Mediterranean Squadron, 1815; Commanded USS *Constellation*, Mediterranean Squadron, 1856–58, Commanded Pacific Squadron, 1862–64; Commissioned Rear Admiral, 7-25-1866.

Benham, A.E.K., Commander. USS *Penobscot*, Western Gulf Sq., 1863–65.

Berrien, John M., Commodore (Georgia). Midshipman, 3-1-1825; Assigned USS *Constellation*, West Indies Squadron, 1827; USS *Guerriere*, Pacific Squadron, 1829, and USS *Vincennes*, 1830; Commanded USS *John Adams*, 1861; Assigned ordnance duty, Pittsburgh, 1862–64; Commissioned Commodore, 1-2-1863.

Bissell, Simon B. (Vermont). Midshipman, 11-6-1824; Assigned USS *Vincennes*, Pacific Squadron, 1826–29, USS *United States*, Mediterranean Squadron, 1833–34; Assigned Home Squadron during Mexican War and present during siege of Vera Cruz; Commanded USS *Cyane*, Pacific Squadron, 1861–62; Commissioned Commodore, 10-10-1866.

Blake, Homer C., Commander. USS *Hatteras*, 1862–63 (engages Confederate vessel *Alabama* and is sunk within ten minutes; crew is rescued by Rebels and later released); USS *Utah*, North Atlantic Sq., 1863–65.

Boggs, Charles S., Commodore (New Jersey). Midshipman 11-1-1826; Assigned USS *Warren*, Mediterranean Squadron, 1829–32, USS

Saratoga, 1846–47, commanding boat expedition that destroys USS *Truxton* after its surrender to Mexicans; Commanded USS *Varuna*, 1862 (only vessel lost by Farragut during assaults against Forts St. Philip and Jackson, April 1862); Commissioned Commodore, 7-25-1866.

Bowers, Edward C., Captain (Connecticut). Midshipman, 2-2-1829; Commanded receiving ship *Vandalia*, 1864–65.

Bradford, Joseph M., Commander. USS *Nipsic*, South Atlantic Sq., 1863; Appointed Fleet Captain, South Atlantic Squadron, November 1863–June 25, 1865.

Braine, Daniel L., Commander. USS *Monticello*, North Atlantic Sq., 1861–62, including capture of Rebel Forts Clarke and Hatteras (October 5, 1861); Commanded USS *Monticello*, *Vicksburg* and *Pequot* during 1862–64 and saw much activity, including numerous skirmishes with Rebel Forts Caswell and Fisher.

Brasher, Thomas M., Captain (New York). Midshipman 6-6-1831; Commanded USS *Bainbridge*, 1861.

Breese, K. Randolph, Commander. USS *Blackhawk*, 1862 (against Arkansas Post and Vicksburg); Assigned with Admiral Porter during entire war.

Breese, S. Livingston, Commander. USS *Ottawa*, South Atlantic Sq., 1863–64.

Breeze, Samuel L. (New York). Rear Admiral, Midshipman 9-10-1810; Present at battle of Vera Cruz, 1847; Commissioned Rear Admiral, July 16, 1862.

Brown, George, Commander. USS *Indianola*, Mississippi Sq., 1863, including action against Rebel rams *William H. Webb* and *Queen of West* and the steamers *Dr. Batey* and *Grand Era* at Upper Palmyra Island, Mississippi River (the *Indianola* is forced to surrender and Brown is severely wounded).

Bryson, Andrew, Captain (New York). Midshipman 12-21-1837; Commanded USS *Chippewa*, 1862–63, USS Lehigh, South Atlantic Squadron, 1863 (present at destruction of Fort Macon and at all major engagements of the ironclads in vicinity of Charleston (September 22, 1863, to April 4, 1864), where he is slightly injured, Commanded USS *Essex*, Mississippi Squadron, 1864–65.

Caldwell, Charles H.B., Captain (Massachusetts). Midshipman, 2-27-1838; Assigned USS *Vandalia*, Pacific Squadron, 1858–59, including engagement with cannibals at Wega, a Fejee Island (defeats cannibals and burns the town, 10-11-58); Commanded USS *Itasca*, Western Gulf Squadron, 1862, USS *Essex*, Mississippi Squadron, 1862–63, USS *Glaucus*, 1863–64, and steamer USS *R.R. Cyler*, 1864–65.

Carr, Overton, Captain (District of Columbia). Midshipman 3-1-1827; Commanded USS *Quaker City*, South Atlantic Squadron, 1861.

Carter, John C., Commodore (Virginia). Midshipman, 3-1-1825; Assigned USS *Lexington*, 1827, USS *Delaware*, Mediterranean Squadron, 1829–30, and USS *Macedonian*, West Indian Squadron, 1840; Commanded USS *Michigan* (steamer) on the Lakes, 1861–64; Commissioned Commodore, 7-16-62.

Carter, Samuel P., Commander. Appointed Midshipman, 2-14-1840; Reports to secretary of war during July 1861 and subsequently appointed Brigadier General (Union), during

September 1861; Carter's command repulses Confederate General Zollicoffer in Kentucky and continues through various campaigns, receiving cavalry division during July of 1863; At conclusion of hostilities, reassigned to Navy and commanded USS *Monocacy*, 1867–69.

Case, Augustus L. Commodore (New York). Midshipman, 4-1-1828; Assigned USS *Nelson*, Brazil Squadron, 1830–32; USS *St. Louis*, West Indies Squadron, 1833; Participates at siege of Vera Cruz and Tobasco during Mexican War; USS *Vincennes*, Pacific Squadron, 1848–51; Commanded USS *Minnesota*, 1861–62; USS *Iroquois*, North Atlantic Squadron, 1863; Commissioned Commodore December 8, 1867.

Chandler, Ralph, Commander. USS *Huntsville*, 1863–64; USS *Maumee*, North Atlantic Sq., 1864–65.

Clary, Albert G., Captain (Massachusetts). Midshipman, 5-8-1832; Commanded USS *Anacostia*, Potomac Flotilla, 1861, including engagements at Acquia Creek and Port Royal; USS *Mt. Vernon*, North Atlantic Squadron, 1862, USS *Tioga*, West India Squadron, 1863, USS *Dacotah*, 1864, and USS *Seminole*, 1864–65.

Clitz, John M.B., Captain (New York). Midshipman, 8-12-1837; Attached to USS *Decatur*, Pacific Squadron, 1858–59, USS *Iroquois*, 1861; Commanded USS *Penobscot*, North Atlantic Squadron, 1863, and the USS *Juniata* (1863), East Gulf Squadron; Commanded USS *Osceola*, 1864–65 and is present at both assaults against Fort Fisher.

Colhoun, Edmund R., Captain (Pennsylvania). Midshipman 4-1-1829; Commanded USS *Hunchback*, 1861–62; USS *Ladona*, 1863; USS *Weehawken*, 1863; USS *Saugas*, 1864–65.

Collins, Napoleon, Captain (Pennsylvania). Midshipman, 1-12-1834; Commanded gunboat USS *Unadilla*, South Atlantic Squadron, 1861–62, operating off coast of South Carolina, Florida and Georgia; USS *Octorara*, West Indies Squadron, 1863, and USS *Wachusett*, West India Squadron, 1863–64 (captures Confederate vessel *Florida* in vic. of Bahia, Brazil, 10-7-1864).

Colvocoresses, George M., Captain (born in Greece). Midshipman, 2-21-1832; Commanded store ship supply, 1861–63; USS *Saratoga*, 1864; USS *St. Mary's*, 1865–66.

Cooper, George H., Captain (New York). Midshipman, 8-14-1837; Commanded USS *Massachusetts*, 1862, USS *Mercedita*, 1863, USS *Sangamon* (temporary, seven weeks), USS *Sonoma*, 1863–64, USS *Glaucus*, 1864–65.

Corbin, Thomas G. (Virginia). Midshipman, 5-15-1838; Commandant of Annapolis, 1863; Commanded USS *Augusta*, 1864–65, Fleet Captain, West India Squadron, 1865–66.

Crabbe, Thomas, Rear Admiral (Maryland). Appointed Midshipman 11-15-1809; Commanded USS *Vandalia*, West India Squadron, 1837; Squadron off coast of Africa, 1855–57; Commissioned Rear Admiral, 7-25-1866.

Craven, Thomas T., Rear Admiral (District of Columbia). Midshipman, 1822; Assigned USS *Peacock*, Pacific Squadron, 1827; Commanded USS *Brooklyn* during attacks against Forts St. Philip and Jackson and subsequent battles along Mississippi River up to capitulation of Vicksburg; USS *Niagara*, 1864–65; Commissioned Rear Admiral, 10-10-1866.

Creighton, Johnston B., Captain (Rhode Island). Midshipman, 2-10-1838; Commanded USS *Ottawa*, South Atlantic Squadron, 1862; USS *Mahaska*, 1863–64; USS *Mingo*, 1864–65.

Crosby, Peirce, Captain (Pennsylvania). Midshipman, 1-5-1838; Commanded USS *Pinola*, Western Gulf Squadron, 1862; USS *Sangamon*, 1863; USS *Florida*, North Atlantic Squadron, 1863–64; USS *Metacomet*, Western Gulf Squadron, 1864–65 (plans and constructs torpedo dragnets on the Blakely River and occupies Forts Tracy and Huger after evacuation by Rebels).

Dahlgren, John A. (Philadelphia, Pa.). Rear Admiral, Midshipman, 2-1-1826; Assigned USS *Macedonian*, Brazil Squadron, 1827–29; Commissioned as Captain and Commandant of the Washington Navy Yard, July 16, 1862, by President Lincoln for his loyalty (many of the officers including the commandant of the Navy Yard left the service for the South); Promoted to Rear Admiral, February 7, 1863.

Dana, William H., Commander. USS *Cayuga*, 1863–64; USS *Winona*, South Atlantic Sq., 1864–65.

Davenport, Henry K., Captain (Georgia). Midshipman, 2-19-1838; Participates against Chinese Forts, Canton River, China (November 1856); Commanded USS *Hetzel*, 1862–64 (defeats entire Rebel naval force February 10, 1862 with assistance of five gunboats); Commanded USS *Lancaster*, 1864–66; Captures seven pirates on board USS *Salvador* in vicinity of Panama (November 10, 1864).

Davis, Charles H. (Massachusetts). Rear Admiral, Midshipman, 8-12-1823; Assigned to USS *United States*, Pacific Squadron, 1827–28; Appointed Flag Officer, Mississippi Flotilla, on May 9, 1862; Commissioned Rear Admiral, 2-7-1863.

Davis, John Lee, Commander. USS *Vixen*, South Atlantic Sq., 1862; USS *Wissahickon*, South Atlantic Sq., 1862–63; USS *Montauk*, South Atlantic Sq., 1863–64; USS *Sassacus*, North Atlantic Sq., 1864–65.

De Camp, John, Commodore (New Jersey). Midshipman, 10-1-1827; Assigned USS *Vandalia*, Brazil Squadron, 1829–30, USS *Constellation*, West India Squadron, 1837, USS *Peacock*, 1840, USS *Boston*, 1845–46, Brazil Squadron; Commanded USS *Relief* (store ship), 1861; Commanded USS *Iroquois*, 1861–62, including assaults against Forts St. Philip and Jackson, the seizure of New Orleans and capitulation of Vicksburg; USS *Wabash*, South Atlantic Squadron, 1863–64; Commissioned Commodore, September 28, 1866.

De Krafft, J.C.P., Commander. USS *Conemaugh*, West Gulf Sq., 1864–66.

Donaldson, Edward, Captain (Maryland). Midshipman, 7-31-1835; Commanded USS *Keystone State*, 1863–64.

Drake, Andrew J., Commander. USS *Sassacus*, 1865–66.

Emmons, George F., Commodore (Vermont). Midshipman, 4-1-1828; Assigned USS *Brandywine*, Mediterranean Squadron, 1831–33; Commanded USS *Hatteras*, Western Gulf Squadron, 1862 (seizes approximately 20 prizes, including Rebel ram *Webb*); USS *Lackawanna*, Western Gulf Squadron, 1864–65 (including defense of New Orleans against Rebels); Commissioned Commodore, 9-20-1868.

English, Earl, Commander. USS *Somerset*, 1862; USS *Sagamore*, 1863 (captures and destroys New Smyrna, Florida, 7-28-63); USS *Pontiac*, 1864; USS *Wyalusing*, North Atlantic Squadron, 1864–65.

Erben, Henry, Commander. USS *Panola*, Western Gulf Squadron, 1864–65.

Fairfax, Donald McNeil, Captain (Virginia). Midshipman, 8-12-1837; Commanded USS *Cayuga*, Western Gulf Squadron, June 1862– February 1863; attached to South Atlantic Gulf Squadron with Admirals Dahlgren and Dupont, 1863; stationed at Annapolis, 1864–65.

Farragut, David Glascoe, Admiral (East Tennessee). Midshipman, 12-17-1810; Vice Admiral, 12-21-64; Admiral, 7-25-1866. (Wounded only once during his career, at Bay of Valparaiso on 3-28-1814, while serving on the USS *Essex*.)

Febiger, John C., Captain (Pennsylvania). Midshipman, 9-14-1838; Commanded USS *Katahdin*, 1862–63, USS *Mattabesset*, 1864–65.

Fillebrown, T. Scott, Commander. USS *Chenango*, 1863; USS *Passaic* (May 1864); USS *Montauk* (July 1864); USS *Sonoma*, 1864–65.

Frailey, James M., Captain (Maryland). Midshipman, 3-1-1828; Commanded store ship USS *Release*, 1860–61; USS *Quaker City*, South Atlantic Squadron, 1862–64, USS *Tuscarora*, North Atlantic Squadron, 1864–65; Commissioned Captain, 2-6-1866.

Franklin, Samuel R., Commander. USS *Aroostook*, James River Flotilla, 1862, and same vessel, West Gulf Sq., 1863; Special duty with Rear Admiral Thatcher, 1865.

Gamble, William M., Commander. USS *Pocahontas*, Western Gulf Sq., 1863, and South Atlantic Sq., 1864.

Gherardi, Bancroft, Commander. USS *Chocura*, West Gulf Sq.; USS *Port Royal*, 1865, including Battle of Mobile Bay.

Gibson, Alexander, Captain (Virginia). Midshipman, 4-4-1822; Commanded store shop supply, North Atlantic Squadron, 1861–62; Store ship, *Potomac*, Western Gulf Squadron, 1864–65.

Gibson, William, Commander. USS *Yankee*, Potomac Flotilla, 1862; USS *Seneca*, South Atlantic Sq., 1864; USS *Mahaska*, 1865.

Gillis, James H., Commander. USS *Milwaukee*, Western Gulf Sq., 1864–65, including engagement at Spanish Fort, 3-28-65, when vessel is sunk.

Gillis, John P., Commodore (Delaware). Midshipman, 12-12-1825; Assigned to Pacific Squadron, 1827–29, USS *Congress*, Mediterranean Squadron, 1843, and back to Pacific Squadron 1846; Assigned *Plymouth*, East Indies Squadron, 1853–54; Commanded USS *Monticello*, 1861, USS *Ossipee*, Western Gulf Squadron, 1863–64; Commissioned Commodore, 9-28-1866.

Glasson, John J., Commodore (New York). Midshipman, 2-21-1823; Assigned USS *North Carolina*, Mediterranean Squadron, 1827, USS *Warren*, 1829, USS *Falmouth*, Pacific Squadron, 1840, USS *Spitfire*, Home Squadron, 1847, and USS *Falcon*, 1848; Commissioned Commodore, September 28, 1866.

Glendy, William M. (Virginia). Midshipman, 1-1-1818; Assigned USS *Boston*, Brazil Squadron, 1827–29; Commanded USS *Saratoga*, 1861–62; Commissioned Commodore, 7-16-1862.

Glisson, Oliver S., Commodore (Ohio). Midshipman 11-1-1826; Assigned USS *Delaware*, Mediterranean Squadron, 1832–35; Commanded USS *Mount Vernon*, 1861, USS *Iroquois*, Western Gulf Blockading Squadron, 1862, USS *Mohican*, 1863–64, and USS *Santiago de Cuba*, 1864–65; Commissioned Commodore, 7-25-1866.

Godon, Sylvanus W. (Pennsylvania). Rear Admiral, Midshipman, 3-1-1819; Commanded USS *Mohican*, Pacific Squadron, 1860; Promoted to Commodore, January 2, 1863; Commanded USS *Susquehanna* and 4th Division of Porter's Squadron against Fort Fisher, December 1864 and January 1865; Commissioned Rear Admiral, 7-25-1866.

Goldsborough, John R., Commodore (District of Columbia). Midshipman, 11-6-1824; Assigned to USS *North Carolina*, Mediterranean Squadron, 1829, USS *Ontario*, Brazil Squadron, 1834, and various other vessels through 1836; Commanded USS *Union*, 1861, USS *Florida*, South Atlantic Squadron, 1862, USS *Colorado*, Western Gulf Squadron, 1863; Commissioned Commodore, April 13, 1867.

Goldsborough, Louis M., Rear Admiral (Washington, D.C.). Midshipman, 6-18-1812, assigned to USS *Porpoise*, Mediterranean Squadron, 1827–29; Commissioned Rear Admiral, July 16, 1862.

Grafton, Edward C., Commander. USS *Genessee*, Western Gulf Sq., 1864–65.

Green, Charles, Commodore (Connecticut). Midshipman, 5-1-1826; Assigned receiving ship *Boston*, 1827, USS *Peacock*, West India Squadron, 1830–32, and USS *Brandywine*, Pacific Squadron, 1837; Commanded USS *Jamestown*, 1861; receiving ship *Boston*, 1864–65; Commissioned Commodore, 9-28-1866.

Green, Joseph F., Commodore (Maine). Midshipman, 11-1-1827; Assigned USS *Vandalia*, Brazil Squadron, 1830; Commanded USS *Canandaigua*, South Atlantic Squadron, 1862–64; Commissioned Commodore, 7-24-1867.

Greene, Theodore P., Commodore (Vermont). Midshipman, 11-1-1826; Assigned USS *Vincennes*, Pacific Squadron, 1834–36; Commanded USS *Richmond*, Pacific Squadron, Western Gulf Squadron, 1865; Commissioned Commodore July 24, 1867.

Greer, James A., Commander. Assigned Mississippi Sq., 1863–64 and Commanded USS *Benton*, plus a division of Admiral Porter's squadron.

Guest, John, Captain (Missouri). Midshipman, 12-16-1837; Commanded USS *Owasko*, 1862, USS *Lehigh*, South Atlantic Squadron, 1863, and the USS *Owasko*, North Atlantic Squadron, 1864–65.

Handy, Robert, Commodore (Rhode Island). Midshipman, 2-1-1826; Assigned USS *Adams*, West India Squadron, 1827, USS *Hudson*, Brazil Squadron, 1829–30, and USS *Vincennes*, Pacific Squadron, 1832–35; Pacific Squadron, 1862–65; Commissioned Commodore, September 28, 1866.

Harmony, David B., Commander. USS *Sebego*, West Gulf Sq., 1864–65.

Harrell, A. Davis, Captain (Virginia). Midshipman, 1-4-1834; Commanded USS *Thomas Freeborn*, 1861; USS *Chicopee*, 1864–65; USS *Kearsarge*, European Squadron, 1865–66.

Harris, Thomas C., Commander. USS *Chippewa*, South Atlantic Sq., 1863–64; USS *Yantic*, North Atlantic Sq., 1864–65.

Harwood, Andrew H., Rear Admiral (Pennsylvania). Midshipman, 1-21-1818; Assigned to USS *Constitution*, Mediterranean Squadron, 1827; Served with Mediterranean Squadron and with special assignments until promoted to chief of bureau of ordnance in 1861; Commissioned Rear Admiral, 1869.

Harrison, Napoleon B., Captain (Virginia). Midshipman, 2-26-1838; Served in California during Mexican War and participates with expedition that rescues General Kearny's troops; Commanded USS *Cayuga*, 1862, USS *Mahaska* on the James River, assisting General McClellan prior to Richmond and the retreat to Harrison's Landing; USS *Minnesota*, North Atlantic Squadron, 1862–63; dispatched to the South Atlantic Squadron, 1863–65; Commandant of Naval Academy, 1868–69.

Haxton, Milton, Commander. USS *Kineo*, 1863; USS *Maratanza*, 1864; USS *Mercedita*, 1864–65.

Henry, Edmund W., Commander. USS *Owasko*, Western Gulf Sq., 1864.

Hitchcock, Robert B., Commodore (Connecticut). Midshipman, 1-1-1825; Assigned USS *Shark*, West Indies Squadron, 1827, and USS *Delaware*, Mediterranean Squadron, 1829–31; Commanded frigate USS *Merrimack*, Pacific Squadron, 1858–60, USS *Susquehanna*, Western Gulf Squadron, 1862–63 (senior officer of blockading squadron at Mobile); Commissioned Commodore, July 16, 1862.

Hoff, Henry K., Rear Admiral (Pennsylvania). Midshipman, 10-28-1823; Assigned USS *Constitution*, Mediterranean Squadron, 1827; Commanded USS *Lancaster*, Pacific Squadron 1861–62, North Atlantic Squadron, 1868–69; Commissioned Rear Admiral, April 13, 1867.

Hopkins, William E., Commander. USS *Saginaw*, Pacific Sq., 1863–65.

Howell, John C., Captain (Pennsylvania). Midshipman, 6-9-1836; Commanded USS *Tahamo*, Eastern Gulf Squadron, 1862–63, USS *Nereus*, 1864–65 (participates against Fort Fisher, December 1864 and January 1865).

Hughes, Aaron K., Captain (New York). Midshipman, 10-20-1838; Commanded USS *Mohawk*, 1862–63; USS *Cimarron*, 63–64; Assigned to ordnance duty, Mound City, Illinois, 1864–66.

Hunt, Timothy A., Commodore (Connecticut). Midshipman, 2-1-1825; Assigned USS *Vincennes*, Pacific Squadron, 1827, USS *Warren*, Mediterranean Squadron, 1829, and reassigned to USS *Vincennes*, 1830; Commanded USS *Electra*, 1847–48, USS *Narragansett*, Pacific Squadron, 1860–61; Commissioned Commodore, 1-2-1863.

Hunter, Charles, Captain (Rhode Island). Midshipman, 4-25-1831; Commanded USS *Montgomery*, 1861–62.

Jeffers, William N., Commander. USS *Underwriter*, North Atlantic Sq., 1861; USS *Monitor*, 1862 (capture of Sewell's Point and Fort Darling, May, 1862); Ordnance duty, Philadelphia, 1863, and Washington, D.C., 1864.

Jenkins, Thornton A., Commodore (Virginia). Midshipman, 11-1-1828; Assigned USS *Natchez*, West Indies Squadron, 1830–31; Commanded USS *Wachusett* during early and mid–1862 along James River; USS *Oneida*, fall of 1863, sees action with Farragut's Squadron against Port Hudson, La., March through May 1863; Commanded USS *Richmond* at surrender of Port Hudson and against the Rebels at Mobile Bay, August 1864; Commissioned Commodore, 7-25-1866.

Johnson, Philip C., Jr., Commander. USS *Tennessee*, 1861–63.

Jouett, James E., Commander. Leads contingent of Marines and Sailors (attached to USS *Santee*) in a successful assault against the Rebel vessel *Royal Yacht* (Galveston Bay, November 7, 1861), destroying the Rebel schooner; Commanded USS *Cuyler*, 1863; USS *Metacomet*, 1863–64.

Kitty, Augustus H., Commodore (Maryland). Midshipman, 7-4-1821; Assigned USS *Constellation*, West Indies Squadron, 1827, and USS *Hudson*, Brazil Squadron, 1829; Commanded one of vessels attached to Foote's Mississippi Flotilla during 1861–62 (loses an arm during one engagement); USS *Roanoke*, North Atlantic Squadron, 1864–65; Commissioned Commodore, 7-25-1866.

Lanier, Edmund, Captain (Virginia). Midshipman, 7-9-1831; Commanded USS *Alabama*, 1861; receiving ship *Boston*, 1862–64; receiving ship *Baltimore*, 1864–65.

Lanman, Joseph, Rear Admiral (Connecticut). Midshipman 1-1-1825, assigned to USS *Macedonian*, Brazil Squadron, 1827; Commissioned Commodore, 8-29-1862; Commanded 2nd Division of Porter's Squadron against Fort Fisher, December 1864 and January 1865; Commissioned Rear Admiral, December 8, 1867.

Lardner, James L., Rear Admiral (Pennsylvania). Midshipman, 7-28-1820; Assigned Pacific Squadron, 1827–30, Mediterranean Squadron 1834–35; Commanded USS *Date* off the African coast, 1853; Eastern Gulf Blockading Squadron, 1862, West India Squadron, 1864; Commissioned Rear Admiral, 7-25-1866.

Law, Richard L., Commander. USS *Tacony*, North Atlantic Sq., USS *Clifton*, 1862–63.

Lee, Samuel Phillips, Commodore (Virginia). Midshipman, 11-22-1825; Assigned to USS *Java*, Mediterranean Squadron, 1828–32; Commanded USS *Oneida*, 1861; North Atlantic Blockading Squadron with rank of Acting Rear Admiral, Summer 1864, transferred to Command, Mississippi Squadron, with responsibility of keeping the Cumberland River open; Commissioned Commodore, 7-25-1866.

Le Roy, William E., Captain (New York). Midshipman, 1-11-1832; Commanded USS *Mystic*, 1861, USS *Keystone State*, 1862–63, USS *Oneida*, 1864, and USS *Ossipee*, 1864–65, including Battle at Mobile Bay, August 1864, where Captain Le Roy accepts surrender of Rebel ram *Tennessee* from Confederate Captain Johnson.

Lewis, Robert F.R., Commander. USS *Itasca*, 1862–63.

Lockwood, Samuel, Commodore (Connecticut). Midshipman, 6-12-1820; Assigned USS *Warren*, Mediterranean Squadron, 1828, and USS *Shark*, West India Squadron, 1832–34; Commanded USS *Daylight*, North Atlantic Squadron, 1861; Commissioned Commodore, July 16, 1862.

Low, William W., Commander. USS *Octorara*, 1863–65.

Lowry, Reigart B., Commander. USS *Freeborn*, 1861; USS *Sciotta*, West Gulf Sq., 1862–63; USS *Sabine*, 1864–65.

Luce, Stephen B., Commander. USS *Nantucket*, South Atlantic Sq., 1863–65.

Lynch, Dominic, Captain (New York). Midshipman, 2-2-1829; Commanded USS *St. Lawrence*, 1863–65.

Macomb, William H., Captain (Michigan). Midshipman, 4-10-1834; Assigned USS *Portsmouth*, East India Squadron, 1856–58 (participated against Barrier Forts, Canton, China, with USS *Levant* during November 1856); Commanded USS *Pulaski*, Brazil Squadron, 1860–61, USS *Genessee*, 1862–63, participating in heavy fighting along Mississippi River during April, May and June, 1863; USS *Shamrock*, 1864–65, including participation at capture of Plymouth, N.C., October 1864.

Madigan, John, Commander. USS *Vincennes*, West Gulf Sq., 1862–63; USS *Patapsco*, 1864–65; USS *Paul Jones*, 1865–66.

Magaw, Samuel, Commander. USS *Thomas Freeborn*, Potomac Flotilla, 1862–63; USS *Commodore Read*, Potomac Flotilla, 1863–64. USS *Lenapee*, North Atlantic Sq., 1865.

Mann, Matthias C., Captain (Florida). Midshipman, 1-3-1832; Commanded USS *St. Louis*, 1862–63.

Marchand, John B., Commodore (Pennsylvania). Midshipman, 5-1-1828; Assigned USS *Ontario*, Mediterranean Squadron, 1830–32; Commanded USS *Van Buren*, August 1841–August 1842, operating from canoes against Seminoles in Florida Everglades; Wounded by enemy fire during an excursion up the Stono River, March 16, 1862 (USS *James Adger*); Commanded USS *Lackawanna*, Western Gulf Blockading Squadron 1863–64; Commissioned Commodore, 7-25-1866.

Mayo, William K., Commander. USS *Kanawha*, West Gulf Sq., 1863–64; USS *Nahant*, South Atlantic Sq., 1864–65.

McCann, William P., Commander. USS *Kennebec*, 1863–64, including assault against Fort Morgan, July 3, 1864.

McCauley, Edward Y., Commander. USS *Fort Henry*, East Gulf Sq., 1862–63; USS *Tioga*, East Gulf Sq., 1863–64 and Mississippi Sq., 1864–65.

McDougal, David D., Commodore (Ohio). Midshipman, 4-1-1828; Assigned USS *Brandywine*, Mediterranean Squadron, 1832–35 and USS *Natchez*, West India Squadron 1837–39; Assigned USS *Mississippi* during siege of Vera Cruz; Commanded USS *Wyoming*, Asiatic Squadron, 1861–64 (his vessel engaged six batteries and three warships at Simonsaki, Japan, on July 16, 1863, losing 11 killed or wounded, while sinking one enemy vessel and destroying another; Commanded USS *Powhatan*, South Pacific Squadron, 1868–69; Commissioned Commodore, 1869.

McKinstry, James P., Commodore (New York). Midshipman, 2-1-1826; Assigned USS *Warren*, Mediterranean Squadron, 1829–30; USS *Concord*, West Indies Squadron, 1837, USS *Dolphin*, Brazil Squadron, 1840, USS *Falmouth*, Home Squadron, 1843, and USS *Michigan*, 1845–46; Commanded USS *Dakota*, 1861, USS *Monongahela*, Western Gulf Squadron, 1862,

including assaults against Port Hudson and Vicksburg; wounded during these operations, causing termination of active service; Commissioned Commodore, 7-25-1866.

Meade, Richard W., Captain (born in Spain). Midshipman, 4-1-1826; Commanded a receiving ship, New York, 1861–64; USS *San Jacinto*, Eastern Gulf Squadron, 1864–66.

Meade, Richard W., Commander. USS *Chocura*, Western Gulf Sq., 1864–66.

Middleton, Edward, Commodore (South Carolina). Midshipman, 7-1-1828; Assigned USS *Dolphin*, Pacific Squadron, 1829–30, USS *Vandalia*, West Indies Squadron, 1832–34, and assigned at Washington and Oregon Territories during winter of 1865–66 against hostile Indians; Commanded USS *St. Mary's*, Pacific Squadron, 1861–65; Commissioned Commodore, 11-26-1868.

Montgomery, John B., Rear Admiral (New Jersey). Midshipman, 6-4-1812; Commanded USS *Portsmouth*, Pacific Squadron, 1845–48; Commanded Pacific Squadron, 1860–61; Commissioned Rear Admiral, 7-25-1866.

Morris, George, Commander. Temporarily in command of USS *Cumberland*, 1862 (sunk while engaged in combat with the Rebel ironclad *Virginia* [*Merrimack*], 3-8-1862); USS *Port Royal*, North Atlantic Squadron, 1862 (wounded at Fort Darling); USS *Shawmut*, West Gulf Sq., 1864–65.

Mullany, J.R. Madison, Captain (New York). Midshipman, 1-7-1832; Commanded USS *Wyandotte*, April–May 1861, including supporting sailors and Marines during defense of Fort Pickens, Florida; Commanded USS *Bienville* in North Atlantic and Western Gulf Squadrons, April 1862 through August 1864; USS *Oneida* during engagements at Fort Gaines and Morgan, and a confrontation at Mobile Bay during August 1864, in which he loses his left arm during a confrontation with Rebel vessel *Tennessee*.

Murray, Alexander, Captain (Pennsylvania). Midshipman, 8-22-1835; Commanded USS *Louisiana*, South Atlantic Squadron, 1861–62; Participates against repulse of enemy vessel Yorktown off Newport News (September 1861); Commanded various naval forces at such engagements as Kinston and New Bern, North Carolina (1862) and a successful expedition along the York and Panucky Rivers, reaching almost to Richmond and destroying 23 Rebel vessels as they progressed (May 1862).

Nichols, Edward T., Captain (Georgia). Midshipman, 12-14-1836; Commanded USS *Winona*, West Gulf Squadron, 1861–62, USS *Alabama*, West India Squadron, 1863, and the USS *Mendota*, 1864–65.

Nicholson, J.W.A., Captain (Massachusetts). Midshipman, 2-10-1838; Commanded USS *Isaac Smith*, South Atlantic Squadron, 1861–62, Assigned to ordnance duty in New York during 1863, then reassigned to the South Atlantic Squadron during 1864; Commanded the USS *Manhattan*, participating with the ironclad at Mobile Bay (August 5, 1864); closes hostilities in command of the USS *Mohongo*, Pacific Squadron, 1865–66.

Nicholson, Somerville, Commander. USS *State of Georgia*, North Atlantic Sq., 1864; USS *Galatea*, West India Sq., 1865.

Owen, Elias K., Commander. Assigned Mississippi Sq., 1862–64, and commanded USS *Louisville* and a division of Admiral Porter's Squadron.

Parker, Foxhall A. (New York). Midshipman, 3-11-39; Commanded USS *Mahaska*, 1863, In command of naval battery on Morris Island during bombardment of Fort Sumter (August 17–23); Commanded Potomac Flotilla, 1864–65, and in one incident, leads a contingent of Marines and sailors who drive inland and chase Rebels out of Matthews Court House, Va.

Parrott, Enoch G., Captain (New Hampshire). Midshipman, 10-10-1831; Participated with expedition that destroys Norfolk Navy Yard, April 1861; Commanded USS *Augusta*, 1861–63, USS *Canonicus*, North Atlantic Squadron, 1864–65, including engagement on James River between Union naval vessels and Howlett's Battery; Commanded USS *Monadnock*, late 1864–65, including assault against Fort Fisher.

Patterson, Thomas, Captain (Louisiana). Midshipman, 4-5-1836; Commanded steam gunboat USS *Chocura*, North Atlantic Squadron, 1862, USS *James Adger*, North Atlantic Squadron, 1863–65.

Pattison, Thomas, Commander. USS *Philadelphia*, Potomac Flotilla, 1861; USS *Sumter*, South Atlantic Sq., 1862; Commandant, Naval Station, Memphis, Tennessee, 1863–66.

Paulding, Hiram, Rear Admiral (New York). Midshipman, 9-1-1811; Commanded USS *Shark*, West Indies Squadron, 1834–36; Commissioned Rear Admiral, 7-16-1862.

Pendergrast, Austin, Commander. Temporarily in command of USS *Congress* during engagement with Confederate vessel *Virginia* (*Merrimack*) after senior officer Lt. Joseph Smith is killed; USS *Water Witch*, South Atlantic Sq., 1862–64.

Pennock, Alexander M. (Virginia). Commodore, Midshipman, 4-1-1828; Assigned USS *Guerriere*, Pacific Squadron, 1829–30, receiving ship *Norfolk*, 1833, USS *Natchez*, Brazil Squadron, 1834; Assigned Fleet Captain, Mississippi Squadron, 1862–64; Commissioned Commodore, 5-6-68.

Perry, Roger, Captain (Maryland). Midshipman, 7-1-1828; Assigned USS *United States*, 1848–49, Mediterranean Squadron; receiving ship *Baltimore*, 1850–51; Commanded USS *Fredonia*, Pacific Squadron, 1863–64.

Phelps, Thomas S., Commander. USS *Saugas*, North Atlantic Squadron, 1864–65.

Pickering, Charles W., Captain (New Hampshire). Midshipman, 5-1-1822; Commanded USS *Kearsarge*, 1862–63; USS *Housatonic*, 1863–64; USS *Vanderbilt*, 1864–66.

Poor, Charles H., Rear Admiral (Massachusetts). Midshipman 3-1-1823, assigned to USS *John Adams*, West Indies Squadron, 1827, Commissioned Commodore, January 2, 1863; In command of USS *Saranac*, Pacific Squadron, 1863–65 and compelled authorities at Rio La Hatchie to raise and salute the American flag, which had been insulted; Commissioned Rear Admiral, 9-20-1868.

Porter, David D., Vice Admiral (Pennsylvania). Midshipman, February 2, 1829, attached to USS *Constellation*, 1830; Promoted to Rear Admiral, 7-4-1863; Vice Admiral, 7-25-1866.

Potter, Edward E., Commander. USS *Mahopac*, North Atlantic Sq., 1864–65.

Powell, Levin M., Rear Admiral (Virginia). Midshipman 3-1-1817; Assigned Mediterranean Squadron, 1829 (USS *Porpoise*) and 1830 (USS *Java*); West India Squadron, 1836–37; Commanded USS *John Adams* off Coast of Africa, 1849–50, USS *Potomac*, Blockading Squadron, 1861; Commissioned Rear Admiral, 1869.

Preble, George H., Captain (Maine). Midshipman, 10-10-1835; Commanded USS *Katahdin*, Western Gulf Squadron, 1862, USS *Oneida*, Western Gulf Squadron, 1862, USS *St. Louis*, 1863–65, including engagements at Honeyhill and Deveraux's Neck, South Carolina, December 6, 7, and 9, 1864.

Price, Cicero, Commodore (Kentucky). Midshipman, 2-1-1826; Assigned USS *Macedonian*, Brazil Squadron, 1827, USS *Falmouth*, West India Squadron, 1829, and USS *Erie*, 1830; Commanded USS *Constellation*, Mediterranean Squadron, 1856, USS *Hunts ville*, 1861, USS *Jamestown*, East India Squadron, 1862–65, Commissioned Commodore, 9-28-1866.

Purviance, Hugh Y., Commodore (Maryland). Midshipman, 11-3-1818; Assigned USS *North Carolina*, Mediterranean Squadron, 1827, USS *Falmouth*, West Indies Squadron, 1829–30; Commanded USS *St. Lawrence*, 1861; Commissioned Commodore, 7-16-1862.

Quackenbush, S.P., Commander. USS *Delaware*, 1861–62; USS *Unadilla*, South Atlantic Sq., 1863; USS *Pequot*, North Atlantic Sq., 1864–65.

Queen, Walter W., Commander. USS *Wyalusing*, 1863–64.

Radford, William, Rear Admiral (Virginia). Midshipman 3-1-1825; Attached to Mediterranean Squadron, USS *Erie*, 1827–28; Promoted to Commodore, September 14, 1855; Promoted to Rear Admiral, April 24, 1863, and commanded the ironclad USS *New Ironsides* against Fort Fisher in December 1864 and January 1865.

Ramsay, Francis M., Commander. USS *Choctaw* and division of Mississippi Squadron, 1863–64.

Ransom, George M., Commander. USS *Narragansett*, Pacific Sq., 1860–61; USS *Kineo*, Western Gulf Sq., 1862–63; USS *Grand Gulf*, North Atlantic Sq., 1864; USS *Muscoota*, North Atlantic Sq., 1864–65.

Renshaw, Richard T., Captain (Pennsylvania). Midshipman, 2-26-1838; Commanded USS *Louisiana*, 1861–64 (captures Roanoke Island, February 8, 1862); USS *Massasoit*, North Atlantic Squadron, 1864–65.

Reynolds, William, Captain (Pennsylvania). Midshipman, 11-17-1831; Commanded USS *Vermont*, South Atlantic Squadron, 1862–64; Commanded USS *New Hampshire*, South Atlantic Squadron, 1864–66.

Rhind, Alexander C., Commander. USS *Crusader*, 1862; USS *Seneca*, 1862; USS *Keokuk*, 1862–63, including 4-17-63, when the vessel is struck by 90 enemy shots in the vicinity of Charleston, causing the ship to sink the following day (South Atlantic Sq.); USS *Paul Jones*, 1863; USS *Wabash*, 1863 (South Atlantic Sq.); USS *Louisiana* (self-destroyed at Fort Fisher, December 1864); USS *Agawan*, 1864–65.

Rodgers, C.R.P., Captain (New York). Midshipman, 10-5-1833; Commandant of Annapolis, 1859–61; Commanded USS *Wabash*, South Atlantic Squadron, 1861–62, including battle at Port Royal, November 1861, and at Fort Pulaski during January 1862; Commanded a division of gunboats to St. Augustine, Fernandina and along the St. Mary's River (March 1862); Assigned as Fleet Captain, Atlantic Blockading Squadron, 1863, and Commanded USS *Iroquois* during 1864–65.

Rodgers, John, Commodore (Maryland). Midshipman, 4-18-1828; Assigned to USS *Constellation*, Mediterranean Squadron, 1829–32; Commanded USS *John Hancock* during 1853–56 touring North Pacific and China Seas on exploring expedition; Supervises construction of Benton type ironclads: Commanded USS *Galena*, North Atlantic Blockade Squadron, 1862; During assault against Fort Darling (May 15, 1862), the *Galena* takes heavy casualties, losing two-thirds of its crew; Commanded USS *Weehawken* against Confederate vessel *Atlanta* (June 17, 1863) at Warsound, Ga., defeating the Rebel ship after a 15 minute battle; Commissioned Commodore, June 17, 1863.

Roe, Francis A., Commander. USS *Katahdin*, West Gulf Sq., 1862–63; USS *Sassacus*, 1862–63; USS *Michigan*, 1864–66.

Ronckendorff, William, Captain (Pennsylvania). Midshipman, 2-17-1832; Commanded USS *Water Witch*, 1861, USS *San Jacinto*, North Atlantic Squadron, 1862, and the Eastern Gulf Squadron, 1863; USS *Powhatan* (flagship), West India Squadron, 1863–64, and subsequently assigned to New York for special duty in 1865.

Rowan, Stephen C., Rear Admiral (Ireland). Midshipman, February 15, 1826, assigned to USS *Vincennes* Pacific Squadron; Commanded Pawnee at Acquia Creek, May 1861 (first action of war); Promoted to Commodore, July 16, 1862; Commissioned Rear Admiral, 7-25-1866.

Russell, John H., Commander. USS *Kennebec*, 1862–63; USS *Cyane*, Pacific Sq., 1864–65.

Sands, Benjamin E. Commodore (Maryland). Midshipman, 4-1-1828; Attached to USS *Vandalia*, Brazil Squadron, 1830–32, and USS *St. Louis*, West India Squadron, 1833–34; Commanded USS *Dakota*, 1863, USS *Fort Jackson*, North Atlantic Blockading Squadron, 1864–65; Commissioned Commodore, 7-25-1866.

Sands, Joshua R., Rear Admiral (New York). Midshipman, 6-18-1812; Assigned USS *Vandalia*, Brazil Squadron, 1829–30; Commanded USS *Susquehanna*, Mediterranean Squadron, 1857–58; Commanded Brazil Squadron, 1860; Commissioned Admiral, 7-25-1866.

Sartori, Louis C., Captain (New Jersey). Midshipman, 2-22-1829; Commanded USS *Flag*, 1861, Commanded receiving ship *Boston*, 1862, and USS *Portsmouth*, Western Gulf Squadron, 1863–65.

Schenck, James F., Commodore (Ohio). Midshipman, 3-1-1825; Assigned USS *Hornet*, West Indies Squadron, 1829, USS *Brandywine*, 1830, and USS *John Adams*, Mediterranean Squadron, 1833–34; Assigned USS *Congress*, Pacific Squadron, 1846–47 (chief military aide to Commodore Stockton during Mexican War); Participated at capture of Los Angeles, Santa Barbara and San Pedro, Guaymas and Mazatlan (Mexican War); Commanded USS *Saginaw*, East India Squadron, 1860–61 (on June 30, 1861, hostile fire was received by the USS *Congress* offshore at Quin Hone, China.

Naval guns responded and the fort was silenced); Commanded USS *St. Lawrence*, 1862, and USS *Powhatan*, 1864–65, including action against Fort Fisher, North Carolina; Commissioned Commodore, 7-2-1863.

Scott, Gustavus H., Commodore (Virginia). Midshipman, 8-1-1828; Assigned USS *Guerriere*, Pacific Squadron, 1829–31, USS *Vandalia*, West Indies Squadron, 1835–36; Commanded USS *Maratanza*, North Atlantic Squadron, 1862–63, USS *DeSoto*, 1864, and USS *Canandaigua*, 1865; Commissioned Commodore, 1869.

Semmes, Alexander A., Commander. Commanded a 23 man contingent of sailors and Marines against a force of approximately 100 Russian American Indians at Puget Sound (November 1856); USS *Wamsutta*, South Atlantic Sq., 1862–63; USS *Tahoma*, East Gulf Sq., 1863–64; USS *Lehigh*, 1865.

Shaw, T. Darrah, Commodore (Pennsylvania). Midshipman, 5-28-1820; Assigned USS *Macedonian*, Brazil Squadron, 1827, and USS *Lexington*, 1833–34; Commanded USS *Montgomery*, Western Gulf Squadron, 1860–61; Commissioned Commodore, 7-16-1862.

Shirk, James W., Commander. USS *Tuscumbia* and division of Mississippi Sq., 1863–64.

Shirley, Paul, Commander. USS *Cyane*, Pacific Sq., 1863–64; USS *Suwanee*, Pacific Sq., 1865–67.

Shubrick, William B., Rear Admiral (South Carolina). Midshipman, 6-20-1806, and assigned command (lieutenant) of an American gunboat during June 1813 against a British frigate at Hampton Roads; Commissioned Rear Admiral, July 16, 1862.

Shufeldt, Robert W., Commander. USS *Proteus*, 1863–65, East India Sq.; USS *Hartford*, 1865–66.

Simpson, Edward, Commander. Commandant Naval Academy, 1862–63; USS *Passaic*, South Atlantic Sq., 1863–64; USS *Isonomia*, East Gulf Sq., 1864; Fleet Captain, West Gulf Sq., 1865.

Skerrett, Joseph S., Commander. USS *Aroostook*, Western Gulf Sq., 1863–65.

Smith, Joseph, Rear Admiral (Massachusetts). Midshipman 1-16-1809, serves with distinction at Battle of Lake Champlain, September 1814, and against pirates during 1815. Commissioned Rear Admiral, 7-16-1862.

Smith, Melancthon, Commodore (New York). Midshipman, 3-1-1826; Assigned USS *Dolphin*, 1827–29 (Pacific Squadron), USS *Poinsett* during the Florida War, and with the USS *Fairfield*, Mediterranean Squadron, 1841–43; Commanded USS *Mississippi*, 1862, and defeats the Confederate ram *Manassas* during attacks against Forts St. Philip and Jackson; Commanded USS *Onondaga*, North Atlantic Blockade Squadron, 1864, and USS *Wabash* late 1864–65 against Fort Fisher; Commissioned Commodore, 7-25-1866.

Smith, William, Commodore (Kentucky). Midshipman, 3-4-1823; Assigned USS *John Adams*, West Indies Squadron, 1827; Commanded USS *Wachusett*, James River Flotilla, 1862; Commissioned Commodore, 7-16-1862.

Spicer, William F., Commander. USS *Cambridge*, North Atlantic Sq. 1864–65.

Spoils, James H., Captain (North Carolina). Midshipman, 8-2-1837; Commanded USS *Magnolia*, East Gulf Squadron, 1862, USS *South Carolina*, South Atlantic Squadron, 1863–64, and in command of the USS *Powhatan*, 1864–65, including participation at both assaults against Fort Fisher and in February 1865 against Fort Anderson.

Stanly, Fabius, Captain (North Carolina). Midshipman, 10-20-1831; Commanded USS *Narragansett*, 1862–63, ordnance assignment, Mississippi Squadron, 1864, and Commanded USS *State of Georgia*, 1864–65.

Steedman, Charles, Commodore (South Carolina). Midshipman, 4-1-1828; Assigned USS *Grampus*, West Indies Squadron, 1834–35, USS *Constitution*, Mediterranean Squadron, 1836–38 and USS Macedonian, West Indies Squadron, 1840; Commanded USS *Dolphin*, 1859–60, USS *Bienville* at Battle of Port Royal, S.C., November 1861, and Commanded the *Paul Jones* and additional gunboats against Fort McAllister (Ogeechee River) August 1862, plus other engagements, including assisting troops under General Bannon who are fighting along the St. John's River, Florida; Commanded the USS *Ticonderoga* against Fort Fisher; Commisssioned Commodore, 7-25-1866.

Stembel, Roger N., Captain (Maryland). Midshipman, 3-27-1832; Assigned to Mississippi Flotilla, August 1861–May 1862, participating at such places as Lucas Bend, September 1861, Belmont, November 1861, Fort Henry, Island No. 10, and Fort Pillow, where he was wounded during action with Rebel rams (May 1862).

Stevens, Thomas H., Captain (Connecticut). Midshipman, 10-14-1836; Commanded USS *Maratanza*, North Atlantic Squadron, 1862 (Battle of West Point, May 1862); Commanded gunboats moving up Pamunkey River toward White House in advance of McClellan's Army; Capture of Rebel gunboat *Teazer*; Commanded USS *Sonoma*, West India Squadron, later in 1862; USS *Patapsco*, 1863–64, command of USS *Oneida*, 1864–65, and USS *Winnebago* (Battle of Mobile Bay, August 5, 1864, including capture of Rebel fleet, Fort Powell and Fort Gaines).

Stone, Edward E., Commander. USS *Iron Age*, 1864.

Stribling, Cornelius K., Rear Admiral (South Carolina). Midshipman 6-18-1812; Assigned to USS *Macedonian* under Commodore Decatur during 1815 against Algerian pirates; Served off the coast of Cuba during 1823 against pirates; Commissioned Rear Admiral, 7-25-1866.

Stringham, Silas H., Rear Admiral (New York). Midshipman, 6-19-1810, Attached to USS *President*, 1811–12; Commanded N.A.B. Squadron, 1861, operating between Virginia and Florida, blockading Southern ports; In command of Naval forces which assisted in capture of Forts Clark and Hatteras, 1861; Commissioned Rear Admiral, 7-16-1862.

Strong, James H. Rear Admiral (New York). Midshipman, February 2, 1829; Commissioned Commander, April 24, 1861; Commanded USS *Mohawk*, South Atlantic Squadron, 1861; Commanded USS *Flag*, South Atlantic Squadron, 1862; Commanded USS *Monongahela*, Western Gulf Squadron, 1863–65, including participation at Aransas Pass, November 1863, and at Mobile Bay, August 1864; Commissioned Captain, August 5, 1865.

Taylor, Alfred, Commodore (Virginia). Midshipman, January 1, 1825; Assigned USS *North Carolina*, Mediterranean Squadron, 1826–29, USS *Vincennes*, Pacific Squadron, 1830–32; Commanded USS *Saratoga*, 1861; Stationed navy yard, Boston, 1862–65; Commanded flagship USS *Susquehanna*, Brazil Squadron, 1866; Commissioned Commodore, September 27, 1866.

Taylor, Bushrod B., Commander. USS *Kanawha*, Western Gulf Sq., 1863–65.

Taylor, William Rogers, Commodore (Rhode Island). Midshipman April 1, 1828; Assigned to USS *St. Louis*, Pacific Squadron 1829–32; Commanded USS *Housatonic*, South Atlantic Blockading Squadron, 1862–63; Participated with Admiral Dahlgren against Rebel held Morris Island; Participated against Forts Sumter and Wagner (USS *Catskill*, July 10, and USS *Montauk* July 18, 1863); USS *Juniata*, North Atlantic Squadron, 1864–65; Commissioned Commodore, July 25, 1866.

Temple, William G., Commander. USS *Pontoosuck*, North Atlantic Squadron, 1864–65.

Thatcher, Henry K., Rear Admiral (Maine). Midshipman, March 4, 1823; Assigned to Pacific Squadron, 1827; Assigned Mediterranean Squadron, 1834–35, and after special service is reassigned to Mediterranean Squadron, 1840; Commanded USS *Constellation*, Mediterranean Squadron 1862–63; USS *Colorado* (steam frigate) N.A.B. Squadron, 1864–65; this tour includes assault against Fort Fisher, N.C., 12-64 and 1-65; January 1865, Commanded Western Gulf Squadron and assisted General Canby with the taking of Mobile (seized on 12 April); Admiral (acting) Thatcher also accepts the surrender of Confederate Naval forces which had been operating in the waters around Alabama; Commissioned Rear Admiral, July 25, 1866.

Thompson, Edward R., Commodore (Pennsylvania). Midshipman, 12-1-1826; Assigned USS *Ontario*, Mediterranean Squadron, 1830–32; Assigned USS *John Adams*, East India Squadron, 1840, Assigned ordnance duty, Philadelphia, 1858–60; Commanded USS *Seminole*, 1861; Commissioned Commodore, September 28, 1866.

Thompson, Egbert, Captain (New York). Midshipman, 3-13-1837; Commanded USS *Pittsburg*, 1861–62, stationed in Philadelphia, 1863–64 and commanded USS *Commodore McDonough*, 1864–65.

Thornton, James S., Commander. USS *Winona*, 1863, and subsequently becomes executive officer attached to USS *Kearsarge*.

Totten, Benjamin J., Commodore (West Indies). Midshipman, 3-4-1823; Assigned USS *Dolphin*, 1830–34; Assigned USS *Shark*, Mediterranean Squadron, 1837, and USS *Decatur*, 1845; Commanded USS *Vincennes*, 1858–60; USS *Brandywine*, North Atlantic Squadron, 1861–62; Commissioned Commodore, July 16, 1862.

Trenchard, Stephen D., Captain (New York). Appointed Midshipman, 10-23-1834; Commanded steamer USS *Rhode Island*, 1861–65.

Truxton, William T., Commander. USS *Dale*, South Atlantic Sq., 1862; USS *Chocura*, North Atlantic Sq., 1863; USS *Tacony*, 1863–65.

Turner, Thomas, Rear Admiral (Virginia). Midshipman 4-21-1825 and assigned to USS *Con-*

stellation, Mediterranean Squadron, 1827; Commanded USS *New Ironsides* against Confederate Forts Moultrie, Sumter and Beauregard at Charleston, 4-7-1863; Commissioned Rear Admiral, 5-27-1868.

Upshur, John H., Commander. USS *Flambeau*, South Atlantic Sq., 1862–63; USS *Minnesota* (flagship), North Atlantic Sq., 1863–64; followed by USS *Advance*.

Walke, Henry, Commodore (Virginia). Midshipman, 2-1-1827; Assigned USS *Delaware*, Mediterranean Squadron, 1828–31; Commanded USS *Carondolet* at Battle of Belmont, November 1861, and assaults against Forts Henry and Donelson (February 1862); Continues to command *Carondolet* against Island No. 10, Fort Pillow, battle of Memphis and Yazoo River expedition; Commanded USS *Sacramento*, 1864–65; Commissioned Commodore, 7-25-1866.

Walker, John G., Commander. USS *Baron De Kalb*, Mississippi Squadron, 1862–63; Commanded naval battery in 15th Army Corps at siege of Vicksburg; USS *Saco*, North Atlantic Sq., 1864–65; USS *Shawmut*, 1865–66.

Weaver, Aaron W., Commander. USS *Winona*, West Gulf Sq., 1862–64; USS *Chippewa*, North Atlantic Sq., 1864; USS *Mahopac* (both major assaults against Fort Fisher).

Wells, Clarke H., Commander. USS *Vandalia*, South Atlantic Sq., 1861–62; USS *Galena*, West Gulf Sq., 1864–65.

Werden, Reed, Captain (Pennsylvania). Midshipman, January 9, 1834; Commanded USS *Stars and Stripes*, North Atlantic Squadron, 1861, and USS *Conemaugh*, South Atlantic Squadron, 1862–63; Assigned as Fleet Captain, East Gulf Blockading Squadron, 1864–65.

Whiting, William D., Commander. USS *Wyandotte*, Potomac Flotilla, 1862; USS *Ottawa*, 1863; school ship *Savannah*, 1864–65.

Wilkes, Charles, Rear Admiral (New York). Midshipman, 1-1-1818; As captain aboard USS *San Jacinto* (1861–62), captured Confederate ministers Mason and Slidell, who were aboard HMS *Trent* (mail carrier); West Indies Squadron, 1863, against blockade runners; Commissioned Rear Admiral, July 25, 1866.

Williamson, James C., Captain (New Jersey). Midshipman, 1-7-1832; Commanded the troops that land at Fort Pickens, Florida, 1861, Commanded the USS *Penguin*, East Gulf Squadron, 1862–63, and the USS *Flag*, South Atlantic Squadron, 1864–65.

Wilson, Henry, Commander. USS *Owasco*, Western Gulf Sq., 1862–63.

Winslow, John A., Commodore (North Carolina). Midshipman, 2-1-1827; Attached to USS *Falmouth*, West India Squadron, 1829–31; Commanded USS *Kearsarge*, 1863–64, defeating Confederate vessel *Alabama* on June 10, 1864 (France), this famous sea battle was the only confrontation on the high seas during the entire war; Commissioned Commodore, 6-19-1864.

Woolsey, Melancton B., Captain (New York). Midshipman, December 24, 1832; Commanded USS *Ellen*, South Atlantic Squadron, 1862; USS *Princess Royal*, Western Gulf Squadron, including successful defense of Donaldsonville and Fort Butler against several thousand Rebel troops (June 28, 1863).

Worden, John L., Commodore (New York). Midshipman, 1-12-1835; Assigned USS *Erie*, Brazil Squadron, 1836–37; Commanded USS *Monitor* against Confederate vessel CSS *Virginia* (*Merrimack*), March 1862 (injured during confrontation by a hostile shell fragment); USS *Montauk*, engaged Rebels at Fort McAllister (January 27 and February 1, 1863) and defeated the Rebel privateer *Nashville* on 2-28-1863; Commissioned Commodore, May 27, 1868.

Wyman, Robert H. (New Hampshire). Midshipman, 3-11-1837; Commanded Potomac Flotilla, 1862, USS *Sonoma* 1862–63 and subsequently assigned special duty in Washington.

Young, Jonathan, Commander. USS *Pembina*, 1863; Ordnance duty, New York Navy Yard, 1864; USS *Cimarron*, South Atlantic Sq., July 1864 to February 1865.

Appendix VI

Prominent Naval Actions

Includes naval actions and the Union vessels that participated, including the commander of the ship. Confederate fleets were often fragmented or did not participate in these actions. Information is spotty at best so is not included here.

North Atlantic Blockading Squadron

CAPTURE OF HATTERAS INLET, AUGUST 28, 1861

1. Steam frigate *Minnesota* (flagship), Silas H. Stringham, flag officer; Captain, J.G. Van Brunt.
2. Steam frigate *Wabash*, Captain Samuel Mercer.
3. Steam sloop *Pawnee*, Commander S.C. Rowan.
4. Steamer *Monticello*, Commander John P. Gillis.
5. Revenue cutter *Harriet Lane*, Captain John Faunce.
6. Chartered steamer *Adelaide*, Commander, Henry S. Stellwagen.
7. Chartered steamer *George Peabody*, Lieutenant R.B. Lowry.
8. Tug *Fanny*, Lieutenant Pierce Crosby.

CAPTURE OF ROANOKE ISLAND, FEBRUARY 8, 1862

1. Steamer *Valley City*; flag officer, L.M. Goldsborough; lieutenant commanding, J.C. Chaplin.
2. Steamer *Stars and Stripes*; Lieutenant Reed Werden.
3. Steamer *Louisiana*; Lieutenant A. Murray.
4. Steamer *Hetzel*; Lieutenant H.K. Davenport.

5. Steamer *Underwriter*; Lieutenant William N. Jeffers.
6. Steamer *Delaware*; Commander S.C. Rowan (commanding flotilla).
7. Steamer *Commodore Perry*; Lt. Commander Charles W. Flusser.
8. Steamer *Commodore Barney*; Lieutenant R.S. Renshaw.
9. Steamer *Hunchback*; Acting Lieutenant Edmund R. Colhoun.
10. Steamer *Southfield*; Acting Lieutenant Charles F.W. Behm.
11. Steamer *Morse*; Acting Master Peter Hayes.
12. Steamer *Whitehead*; Acting Master Charles A. French.
13. Steamer *Lockwood*; Acting Master G.W. Graves.
14. Steamer *Henry Brinker*; Acting Master I.E. Giddings.
15. Steamer *J.N. Seymour*; Acting Master Francis S. Wells.
16. Steamer *Ceres*; Acting Master John McDiarmid.
17. Steamer *General Putnam*; Acting Master William S. Hotchkiss.
18. Steamer *Shawsheen*; Acting Master Thomas J. Woodward.

CAPTURE OF FORT FISHER, JANUARY 15, 1865

1. *Malvern* (4th Rate) Flagship; Rear Admiral David D. Porter; Lieutenant Commander, K.R. Breeze, Fleet Captain.
2. *Colorado* (1st Rate) Flagship; Commodore Henry K. Thatcher.
3. *Minnesota* (1st Rate) Flagship; Commodore Joseph Lanman.
4. *Powhatan* (1st Rate); Commodore James F. Schenck.
5. *Susquehanna* (1st Rate); Commodore S.W. Godon.
6. *New Ironsides* (1st Rate); Commodore William Radford.
7. *Santiago De Cuba* (2nd Rate); Captain O.S. Glisson.
8. *Wabash* (1st Rate); Captain Melancton Smith.
9. *Vanderbilt* (2nd Rate); Captain Charles W. Pickering.
10. *Juniata* (2nd Rate); Captain William R. Taylor.
11. *Fort Jackson* (2nd Rate); Captain B.F. Sands.
12. *Shenandoah* (2nd Rate); Captain Daniel B. Ridgely.
13. *Ticonderoga* (2nd Rate); Captain Charles Steedman.
14. *Brooklyn* (2nd Rate); Captain James Alden.
15. *Tuscarora* (3rd Rate); Commander James M. Frailey.
16. *Monadnock* (3rd Rate); Commander E.G. Parrott.
17. *Rhode Island* (2nd Rate); Commander Stephen D. Trenchard.
18. *Chicopee* (3rd Rate); Commander A.D. Harrell.
19. *Nereus* (3rd Rate); Commander J.C. Howell.
20. *Mohican* (3rd Rate); Commander Daniel Ammen.
21. *Keystone State* (3rd Rate); Commander Henry Rolando.
22. *Mendota* (3rd Rate); Commander Edward T. Nichols.
23. *Iosco* (3rd Rate); Commander John Guest.

24. *Osceola* (3rd Rate); Commander John M.B. Clitz.
25. *Pawtuxet* (3rd Rate); Commander James H. Spoils.
26. *Mackinaw* (3rd Rate); Commander J.C. Beaumont.
27. *Saugus* (4th Rate); Commander Edmund R. Colhoun.
28. *Quaker City* (2nd Rate); Commander W.F. Spicer.
29. *Pontoosuc* (3rd Rate); Lieutenant Commander William G. Temple.
30. *Advance* (4th Rate); Lt. Commander J.H. Upshur.
31. *Yantic* (4th Rate); Lt. Commander T.C. Harris.
32. *Sassacus* (3rd Rate); Lt. Commander John L. Davis.
33. *Tacony* (3rd Rate); Lt. Commander W.T Truxtun.
34. *Kansas* (4th Rate); Lt. Commander P.G. Watmough.
35. *Maratanza* (3rd Rate); Lt. Commander George W. Young.
36. *Maumee* (4th Rate); Lt. Commander Ralph Chandler.
37. *Pequot* (4th Rate); Lt. Commander Daniel L. Braine.
38. *Nyack* (4th Rate); Lt. Commander L.H. Newman.
39. *Canonicus* (3rd Rate); Lt. Commander George E. Belknap.
40. *Chippewa* (4th Rate); Lt. Commander A.W. Weaver.
41. *Unadilla* (4th Rate); Lt. Commander Frank M. Ramsay.
42. *Mahopac* (4th Rate); Lt. Commander E.E. Potter.
43. *Huron* (4th Rate); Lt. Commander Thomas 0. Self ridge.
44. *Seneca* (4th Rate); Lt. Commander Montgomery Sicard.
45. *Monticello* (4th Rate); Lieutenant W. B. Cushing.
46. *Gettysburg* (4th Rate); Lieutenant R.H. Lamson.
47. *Alabama* (3rd Rate); Acting Lieutenant A.R. Langthorne.
48. *Montgomery* (3rd Rate); Acting Lieutenant T.C. Dunn.
49. *Governor Buckingham* (3rd Rate); Acting Lieutenant John MacDearmid.
50. *Cherokee* (4th Rate); Acting Lieutenant William E. Dennison.
51. *Howquah* (4th Rate); Acting Lieutenant J.W. Balch.
52. *Emma* (4th Rate); Acting Lieutenant J.M. Williams.
53. *Tristam Shandy* (4th Rate); Acting Lieutenant F.M. Green.
54. *Mount Vernon* (4th Rate); Acting Lieutenant James Frathen.
55. *Brittania* (4th Rate); Acting Lieutenant Samuel Huse.
56. *Ceres* (4th Rate); Acting Master, H.H. Foster.
57. *Little Ada* (4th Rate); Acting Master, S.P. Crafts.
58. *Wilderness* (4th Rate); Acting Master, H. Arey.
59. *Nansemond* (4th Rate); Acting Master, James H. Porter.
60. *Moccasin* (4th Rate); Acting Ensign James Brown.

South Atlantic Blockading Squadron

BATTLE OF PORT ROYAL, NOVEMBER 7, 1861.

1. Steam frigate *Wabash* (flagship); Flag Officer Samuel Dupont; Fleet Captain Charles H. Davis.
2. Steam sloop *Susquehanna*; Captain J.L. Lardner.
3. Steam sloop *Mohican*; Commander S.W. Godon.
4. Sloop *Vandalia*; Commander F.S. Haggarty.
5. Steamer *Seminole*; Commander John P. Gillis.
6. Steamer *Augusta*; Commander E.G. Parrott.
7. Steamer *Bienville*; Commander Charles Steedman.
8. Steam gunboat *Unadilla*; Lieutenant N. Collins.
9. Steam gunboat *Ottawa*; Lieutenant Thomas H. Stevens.
10. Steam gunboat *Seneca*; Lieutenant Daniel Ammen.
11. Steam sloop *Pawnee*; Captain Percival Drayton.
12. Steam gunboat *Pembina*; Lieutenant John P. Bankhead.
13. Steam gunboat *Isaac Smith*; Lieutenant J.W.A. Nicholson.
14. Steam gunboat *Penguin*; Lieutenant Thomas A. Budd.

West Gulf Blockading Squadron

BOMBARDMENT OF CONFEDERATE FORTS JACKSON, ST. PHILIP AND SEIZURE OF NEW ORLEANS, LOUISIANA, APRIL 1862.

1. Steam sloop *Hartford*; Flag Officer David G. Farragut; Fleet Captain Henry H. Bell.
2. Steam frigate *Colorado*; Captain Theodorus Bailey.
3. Steam sloop *Pensacola*; Captain Henry W. Morris.
4. Steam sloop *Brooklyn*; Captain Thomas T. Craven.
5. Sloop *Portsmouth*; Commander Samuel Swartwout.
6. Steam sloop *Oneida*; Commander S. Philips Lee.
7. Steam sloop *Mississippi*; Captain Melancton Smith.
8. Steam sloop *Varuna*; Commander Charles S. Boggs.
9. Steam sloop *Iroquois*; Commander John de Camp.
10. Steam sloop *Richmond*; Commander James Alden.
11. Steamer *Sciota*; Lieutenant Edward Donaldson.
12. Steamer *Katahdin*; Lieutenant George H. Preble.
13. Steamer *Winona*; Lieutenant E.T. Nichols.
14. Steamer *Itasca*; Lieutenant C.H.B. Caldwell.
15. Steamer *Cayuga*; Lieutenant Napoleon B. Harrison.
16. Steamer *Pinola*; Lieutenant Peirce Crosby.

17. Steamer *Wissahickon*; Lieutenant A.N. Smith.
18. Steamer *Kineo*; Lieutenant George M. Ransom.
19. Steamer *Kennebec*; Lieutenant John H. Russell.
20. Steamer *Harriet Lane*; Commander D.D. Porter (Commanding Mortar Flotilla); Lieutenant Commanding, J.M. Wainwright.
21. Steamer *Westfield*; Commander William B. Renshaw.
22. Steamer *Miami*; Lt. Commander A.D. Harrell.
23. Steamer *J.P. Jackson*; Lieutenant Selim A. Woodworth.
24. Mortar schooner *Norfolk Packet*; Lieutenant Watson Smith.
25. Mortar schooner *T.A. Ward*; Lieutenant Walter W. Queen.
26. Mortar schooner *Horace Bealls*; Lieutenant Commander K.R. Breese.
27. Steamer *Clifton*; Acting Lieutenant C.H. Baldwin.
28. Bark *Houghton*; Acting Master, Newell Graham.
29. Mortar schooner *Henry Janes*; Acting Master, Lewis W. Pennington.
30. Mortar schooner *William Bacon*; Acting Master, William P. Rogen.
31. Mortar schooner *Sea Foam*; Acting Master, Henry E. Williams.
32. Mortar schooner *Para*; Acting Master, E.G. Furber.
33. Mortar schooner *George Mangham*, Acting Master, John Collins.
34. Mortar schooner *Sara Bruen*; Acting Master, Abraham Christian.
35. Mortar schooner *Racer*; Acting Master, Alvin Phinney.
36. Mortar schooner *O.H. Lee*; Acting Master, Washington Godfrey.
37. Mortar schooner *Dan Smith*.
38. Mortar schooner *Adolph Hugel*.
39. Mortar schooner *Maria J. Carlton*; Acting Master, Charles E. Jack.
40. Mortar schooner *Sydney C. Jones*; Acting Master, James D. Graham.
41. Mortar schooner *Sophronia*; Acting Master, Lyman Bartholomew.
42. Mortar schooner *Matthew Vassar*; Acting Master, Hugh H. Savage.
43. Mortar schooner *C.P. Williams*; Acting Master, A.R. Langthon.
44. Mortar schooner *J. Griffith*; Acting Master, Henry Brown.
45. Mortar schooner *Orvetta*; Acting Master, Francis E. Blanchard.
46. Mortar schooner *Arletta*; Acting Master, Thomas E. Smith.
47. Coast survey steamer *Sachem*.

BATTLE OF MOBILE BAY, AUGUST 5, 1864.

1. Steam sloop *Hartford* (flagship); Rear Admiral David G. Farragut; Fleet Captain Percival Drayton.
2. Steam sloop *Lackawanna*; Captain J.B. Marchand.
3. Steam sloop *Brooklyn*; Captain James Alden.
4. Steam sloop *Richmond*; Captain Thornton A. Jenkins.
5. Monitor *Tecumseh*; Commander T. Augustus Craven.

6. Steam sloop *Monongahela*; Commander James H. Strong.
7. Steam sloop *Ossipee*; Commander William E. LeRoy.
8. Steam sloop *Oneida*; Commander J.R. Madison Mullany.
9. Steam sloop *Seminole*; Commander Edward Donaldson.
10. Ironclad *Winnebago*; Commander Thomas H. Stevens.
11. Monitor *Manhattan*; Commander J.W.A. Nicholson.
12. Steamer *Galena*; Lt. Commander Clark H. Welles.
13. Steamer *Conemaugh*; Lt. Commander J.C.P. De Krafft.
14. Steamer *Port Royal*; Lt. Commanders Bancroft, Gherardi and Thomas C. Bowen.
15. Steamer *Metacomet*; Lt. Commander James E. Jouett.
16. Steamer *Octorara*; Lt. Commander Charles Greene.
17. Steamer *Kennebec*; Lt. Commander William P. McCann.
18. Steamer *Sebago*; Lt. Commander William E. Fitzhugh.
19. Steamer *Pinola*; Lt. Commander Oscar F. Stanton.
20. Steamer *Itasca*; Lt. Commander George Brown.
21. Monitor *Chickasaw*; Lt. Commander George H. Perkins.
22. Steamer *J.P. Jackson*; Acting Lieutenant S.W. Pennington.
23. Steamer *Cowslip*; Acting Lieutenant Charles G. Arthur.
24. Steamer *Stockdale*; Acting Lieutenant Thomas Edwards.
25. Steamer *Buckthorn*; Acting Lieutenant Washington Godfrey.
26. Steamer *Genessee*; Acting Master, George E. Nelson.
27. Steamer *Glasgow*; Acting Master, Richard J. Hoffner.
28. Steamer *Estrella*; Acting Master, G.P. Pomeroy.
29. Steamer *Narcissus*; Acting Ensign William G. Jones.
30. Steamer *Pembina*; Lt. Commander J.G. Maxwell.

Mississippi Squadron

CAPTURE OF FORT HENRY, FEBRUARY 6, 1862.

1. Gunboat *Cincinnati*; Flag Officer A.H. Foote.
2. Gunboat *Conestoga*; Lieutenant S.L. Phelps.
3. Gunboat *Essex*; Commander William D. Porter.
4. Gunboat *Lexington*; Lieutenant James W. Shirk.
5. Gunboat *Tyler*; Lieutenant William Gwin.
6. Gunboat *St. Louis*; Lieutenant Leonard Paulding.
7. Gunboat *Carondelet*; Commander Walke.

CAPTURE OF MEMPHIS, TENNESSEE, JUNE 6, 1862.

1. Ironclad *Benton*; Flag Officer Charles H. Davis.

2. Ironclad *Louisville*; Commander Benjamin M. Dove.
3. Ironclad *Carondelet*; Commander Henry Walke.
4. Ironclad *Cairo*; Lieutenant N.C. Bryant.
5. Ironclad *St. Louis*; Lieutenant Wilson McGunnegle.

PASSAGE OF VICKSBURG BATTERIES, APRIL 6, 1863.

1. Ironclad *Benton*; Rear Admiral David D. Porter.
2. Ironclad *Lafayette*; Captain Henry Walke.
3. Ironclad *Louisville*; Lt. Commander E.K. Owen.
4. Ironclad *Ibscumbia*; Lt. Commander James W. Shirk.
5. Ironclad *Mound City*; Lieutenant Byron Wilson.
6. Ironclad *Pittsburg*; Acting Lieutenants W.R. Hoel and J.C. Bentley.
7. *Henry Clay* (destroyed).
8. Steamer *Price* (captured earlier from Rebels).
9. *Forrest Queen*.
10. *Silver Queen*.
11. *Carondelet*.

CONFRONTATION WITH REBEL BATTERIES AT GRAND GULF, MISSISSIPPI, APRIL 29, 1863.

1. Ironclad steamer *Benton*; Lt. Commander James A. Greer.
2. Ironclad steamer *Lafayette*; Lt. Commander James P. Foster.
3. Ironclad steamer *Louisville*; Lt. Commander Elias K. Owen.
4. Ironclad steamer *Tuscumbia*; Lt. Commander James W. Shirk.
5. Ironclad steamer *Mound City*; Acting Lieutenant A.R. Langthorn.
6. Ironclad steamer *Pittsburg*; Acting Lieutenant W.R. Hoel.
7. Ironclad steamer *Carondelet*; Lt. Commander J.C. Mitchell.

RED RIVER EXPEDITION, MARCH AND APRIL, 1864.

1. Steamer *Black Hawk* (flagship); Rear Admiral D.D. Porter.
2. Ironclad steamer *Essex*; Commander Robert Townsend.
3. Ironclad steamer *Eastport*; Lt. Commander S.L. Phelps.
4. Ironclad steamer *LaFayette*; Lt. Commander James P. Foster.
5. Ironclad steamer *Benton*; Lt. Commander James A. Greer.
6. Ironclad steamer *Louisville*; Lt. Commander Elias K. Owen.
7. Ironclad steamer *Carondelet*; Lt. Commander J.C. Mitchell.
8. Ironclad steamer *Choctaw*; Lt. Commander Francis M. Ramsay.
9. Ironclad steamer *Osage*; Lt. Commander T.O. Selfridge.
10. Steamer *Ouichita*; Lt. Commander Byron Wilson.
11. Ironclad steamer *Lexington*; Lieutenant George M. Bache.

12. Ironclad steamer *Chillicothe*; Acting Lieutenant J.P. Couthouy.
13. Ironclad steamer *Pittsburg*; Acting Lieutenant W.R. Hoel.
14. Ironclad steamer *Mound City*; Acting Lieutenant A.R. Langthorn.
15. Ironclad steamer *Neosho*; Acting Lieutenant Samuel Howard.
16. Steamer *Fort Hindman*; Acting Lieutenant John Pearce.
17. Steamer *Cricket*; Acting Master Henry H. Gorringe.

Appendix VII

Medal of Honor Recipients, 1863–1865

An asterisk indicates the award was given posthumously.

Adams, James F. Private, 1st West Virginia Cavalry, November 12, 1864 (Nineveh, Virginia).

Adams, John G.B. 2nd Lieutenant, 19th Massachusetts Infantry, December 13, 1862 (Fredericksburg, Virginia).

Aheam, Michael. Paymaster's Steward, U.S. Navy, June 19, 1864 (off the coast of France).

Alber, Frederick. Private, 17th Michigan Infantry, May 12, 1864 (Spotsylvania, Virginia).

Albert, Christian. Private, 47th Ohio Infantry, May 22, 1863 (Vicksburg).

Allen, Abner P. Corporal, 39th Illinois Infantry, April 2, 1865 (Petersburg).

Allen, James. Private, 16th New York Infantry, September 14, 1862 (South Mountain, Maryland).

Allen, Nathaniel M. Corporal, 1st Massachusetts Infantry, July 2, 1863 (Gettysburg).

Ames, Adelbert. First Lieutenant, 5th U.S. Artillery, July 21, 1861 (Bull Run).

Ammerman, Robert W. Private, 148th Pennsylvania, May 12, 1864 (Spotsylvania).

Anderson, Bruce. Private, 142nd New York Infantry, January 15, 1865 (Fort Fisher, N.C.).

Anderson, Charles W. Private, 1st New York (Lincoln) Cavalry, March 2, 1865 (Waynesboro, Va.).

Anderson, Everett W. Sergeant, 15th Pennsylvania Cavalry, January 14, 1864 (Crosby's Creek, Tennessee).

Anderson, Frederick C. Private, 18th Massachusetts Infantry, August 21, 1864 (Weldon Railroad, Va.).

Anderson, Marion T. Captain, 51st Indiana Infantry, December 16, 1864 (Nashville, Tennessee).

Anderson, Peter. Private, 31st Wisconsin Infantry, March 19, 1865 (Bentonville, N.C.).

Anderson, Robert. Quartermaster, U.S. Navy (gallantry on various occasions, including service on the USS *Keokuk* during assault against Charleston).

Anderson, Thomas. Corporal, 1st West Virginia Cavalry, April 8, 1865 (Appomattox Station, Virginia).

Angling, John. Cabin Boy, U.S. Navy (born in

1850), December 24, 1864, and January 22, 1865 (Fort Fisher and Wilmington, N.C.).

Apple, Andrew O. Corporal, 12th West Virginia Infantry, April 2, 1865 (Petersburg, Va.).

Appleton, William H. 1st Lieutenant, 4th U.S. Colored Troops, June 15, 1864 (Petersburg, Va.). Second Award: September 29, 1864 (New Market Heights, Va.).

Archer, James W. 1st Lieutenant, 59th Indiana Infantry, October 4, 1862 (Corinth, Mississippi).

Archer, Lester. Sergeant, 96th New York Infantry, September 29, 1864 (Fort Harrison, Va).

Archinal, William. Corporal, 30th Ohio Infantry, May 22, 1863 (Vicksburg).

Armstrong, Clinton L. Private, 83rd Indiana Infantry, May 22, 1863 (Vicksburg).

Arnold, Abraham K. Captain, 5th U.S. Cavalry, May 10, 1864 (Davenport Bridge, Virginia).

Arther, Matthew. Signal Quartermaster, U.S. Navy, February 6 and 14, 1862, plus other actions (Fort Donelson aboard USS Carondelet).

Asten, Charles. Quarter Gunner, U.S. Navy, May 5, 1864, Red River (aboard USS Signal).

Atkinson, Thomas E. Yeoman, U.S. Navy, August 5, 1864 (Mobile Bay and other actions).

Avery, James. Seaman, U.S. Navy, August 5, 1864 (Mobile Bay aboard USS Metacomet).

Avery, William B. Lieutenant, U.S. Army, 1st New York Marine Artillery, June 5, 1862 (Tranter's Creek, N.C.).

Ayers, David. Sergeant, 57th Ohio Infantry, May 22, 1863 (Vicksburg).

Ayers, John G.K. Private, 8th Missouri Infantry, May 22, 1863 (Vicksburg).

Babcock, William J. Sergeant, 2nd Rhode Island Infantry, April 2, 1865 (Petersburg).

Bacon, Elijah W. Private, 14th Connecticut Infantry, July 3, 1863 (Gettysburg).

Baird, Absalom. Brigadier General, U.S. Volunteers, September 1, 1864 (Jonesboro, Ga.).

Baker, Charles. Quarter Gunner, U.S. Navy, August 5, 1864 (Mobile Bay).

Baldwin, Charles. Coal Heaver, U.S. Navy, May 25, 1864.

Baldwin, Frank D. Captain, 19th Michigan Infantry (1st Lieutenant, 5th U.S. Infantry), July 12, 1864 (Peach Tree, Ga.) Second award, November 8, 1874 (McClellans Creek, Texas).

Ballen, Frederick. Private, 47th Ohio Infantry, May 3, 1863 (Vicksburg).

Banks, George L. Sergeant, 15th Indiana Infantry, November 25, 1863 (Missionary Ridge, Tenn.).

Barber, James A. Corporal, 1st Rhode Island Light Artillery, April 2, 1865 (Petersburg).

Barker, Nathaniel C. Sergeant, 11th New Hampshire Infantry, May 12, 1864 (Spotsylvania).

Barnes, William H. Private, 38th U.S. Colored Troops, September 29, 1864 (Chapins Farm, Va.).

Barnum, Henry A. Colonel, 149th New York Infantry, November 23, 1863 (Chattanooga, Tenn.).

Barnum, James. Boatswains Mate, U.S. Navy (assaults against Fort Fisher, December 1864 and January 1865, aboard USS New Ironsides).

Barrell, Charles L. 1st Lieutenant, 102nd U.S. Colored Troops, April 1865 (vicinity Camden, S.C.).

Barrick, Jesse T. Corporal, 3rd Minnesota Infantry, May 26–June 2, 1863 (vicinity Duck River, Tennessee).

Barringer, William H. Private, 4th West Virginia Infantry, May 22, 1863 (Vicksburg).

Barry, Augustus. Sergeant Major, 16th U.S. Infantry (medal issued February 28, 1870). Place and date undetermined other than 1863–1865.

Barter, Gurdon H. Landsman, U.S. Navy, February 15, 1865 (aboard USS Minnesota during assault against Fort Fisher).

Barton, Thomas. Seaman, U.S. Navy, October 3, 1862 (aboard USS Hunchback, assault against Franklin, Tenn.).

Bass, David L. Seaman, U.S. Navy, January 1865 (USS Minnesota, assault against Fort Fisher).

Batchelder, Richard N. Lieutenant Colonel, 2nd Corps, October 13–15, 1863 (vicinity Catlett and Fairfax Stations, Virginia).

Bates, Delavan. Colonel, 30th U.S. Colored Troops, July 30, 1864 (Cemetery Hill, Va.)

Bates, Norman F. Sergeant, 4th Iowa Cavalry, April 16, 1865 (Columbus, Ga.).

Baybutt, Philip. Private, 2nd Massachusetts Cavalry, September 24, 1864 (Luray, Va.).

Bazaar, Philip. Ordinary Seaman, U.S. Navy, January 15, 1865 (assault against Fort Fisher).

Beatty, Alexander M. Captain of Company F, 3rd Infantry, June 5, 1864 (Cold Harbor, Va.).

Beaty, Powhatan. First Sergeant, 5th U.S. Colored Troops, September 29, 1864 (Chapin's Farm, Va.).

Beaufort, Jean J. Corporal, 2nd Louisiana Infantry, May 20, 1863 (Port Hudson, La.).

Beaumont, Eugene B. Major, Cavalry Corps, Army of the Mississippi, December 17, 1864 (Harpeth River, Tennessee) and April 2, 1865 (Selma, Alabama).

Bebb, Edward J. Private, 4th Iowa Cavalry, April 16, 1865 (Columbus, Ga.).

Beckwith, Wallace A. Private, 21st Connecticut Infantry, December 13, 1862 (Fredericksburg).

Beddows, Richard Private, 34th New York Battery, May 18, 1864 (Spotsylvania).

Beebe, William S. 1st Lieutenant, Ordnance Department, U.S. Army, April 23, 1864 (Cane River Crossing, La.).

Beech, John P. Sergeant, 4th New Jersey Infantry, May 12, 1864 (Spotsylvania Court House, Va.).

Begley, Terrence. Sergeant, 7th New York Heavy Artillery, June 3, 1864 (Cold Harbor, Va.).

Belcher, Thomas. Private, 9th Maine Infantry, September 29, 1864 (Chapin's Farm, Va.).

Bell, George. Captain (of the Afterguard), U.S. Navy, November 7, 1861 (Galveston Bay).

Bell, James B. Sergeant, 11th Ohio Infantry, November 25, 1863 (Missionary Ridge, Tennessee).

Benedict, George G. 2nd Lieutenant, 12th Vermont Infantry, July 3, 1863 (Gettysburg).

Benjamin, John F. Corporal, 2nd New York Cavalry, April 6, 1865 (Sailors Creek, Va.).

Benjamin, Samuel N. 2nd Lieutenant, 2nd U.S. Artillery, July 18, 1861, through May 1864 (various actions, Bull Run through Spotsylvania).

Bennett, Orren. Private, 141st Pennsylvania Infantry, April 6, 1865 (Sailors Creek, Va.).

Bennett, Orson W. 1st Lieutenant, 102nd U.S. Colored Troops, November 30, 1864 (Honey Hill, S.C.).

Bensinger, William (2nd man to receive the Medal of Honor) Private, 21st Ohio Infantry, April 1862 (Big Shanty, Ga.).

Benyaurd, William H.H. 1st Lieutenant, Engineers, April 1st 1865 (Five Forks, Va.).

Betham, Asa. Coxswain, U.S. Navy, December

24, 1864, and January 22, 1865, aboard USS Pontoosuc (assault against Fort Fisher and Wilmington, N.C.).

Betts, Charles M. Lieutenant Colonel, 15th Pennsylvania Cavalry, April 19, 1865 (Greensboro, N.C.).

Beyer, Hillary. 2nd Lieutenant, 90th Pennsylvania Infantry, September 17, 1862 (Antietam, Md.).

Bibber, Charles J. Gunner's Mate, U.S. Navy, December 23, 1864 (aboard USS Agawam, Fort Fisher, N.C.).

Bickford, Henry H. Corporal, 8th New York Cavalry, March 2, 1865 (Waynesboro, Va.).

Bickford, John F. Captain of the Top, U.S. Navy, June 19, 1864, aboard the USS Kearsarge vic. France).

Bickford, Matthew. Corporal, 8th Missouri Infantry, May 22, 1863 (Vicksburg).

Bieger, Charles. Private, 4th Missouri Cavalry, February 22, 1864 (Ivy Farm, Mississippi).

Binder, Richard. Sergeant. U.S. Marine Corps, December 1864, and January 1865 (on board USS Ticonderoga, assault against Fort Fisher, N.C.).

Bingham, Henry H. Captain, 140th Pennsylvania Infantry, May 6, 1864 (Wilderness, Va.).

Birdsall, Horatio L. Sergeant, 3rd Iowa Cavalry, April 16, 1865 (Columbus, Ga.).

Bishop, Francis A. Private, 57th Pennsylvania Infantry, May 12, 1864 (Spotsylvania).

Black, John C. Lieutenant Colonel, 37th Illinois Infantry, December 7, 1862 (Prairie Grove, Ark.).

Black, William P. Captain, Company K, 37th Illinois Infantry, March 7, 1862 (Pea Ridge, Ark.).

Blackmar, Wilmon W. Lieutenant, 1st West Virginia Cavalry, April 1, 1865 (Five Forks, Va.).

Blackwood, William R.D. Surgeon, 48th Pennsylvania Infantry, April 2, 1865 (Petersburg, Va.).

Blagheen, William. Ship's Cook, U.S. Navy, August 5, 1864 (on board USS Brooklyn during assault against Fort Morgan, Mobile Bay).

Blair, Robert M. Boatswain's Mate, U.S. Navy, December 24, 1864, and January 22, 1865 (on board USS Pontoosuc during assault on Fort Fisher, N.C.).

Blake, Robert (escaped slave). U.S. Navy, December 25, 1863 (on board USS Marblehead vic. Legareville, Stono River).

Blasdel, Thomas A. Private, 83rd Indiana Infantry, May 22, 1863 (Vicksburg).

Blickensderfer, Milton. Corporal, 126th Ohio Infantry, April 3, 1865 (Petersburg, Va.).

Bliss, George N. Captain, 1st Rhode Island Cavalry, September 28, 1864 (Waynesboro, Va.).

Bliss, Zenas R. Colonel, 7th Rhode Island Infantry, December 13, 1862 (Fredericksburg, Va.).

Blodgett, Wells H. 1st Lieutenant, 37th Illinois Infantry, September 30, 1862 (Newtonia, Mo.).

Blucher, Charles. Corporal, 188th Pennsylvania Infantry, September 29, 1864 (Fort Harrison, Va.).

Blunt, John W. 1st Lieutenant, 6th New York Cavalry, October 19, 1864 (Cedar Creek, Va.).

Boehm, Peter M. 2nd Lieutenant, 15th New York Cavalry, March 31, 1865 (Dinwiddie Court House, Va.).

Bois, Frank. Quartermaster, U.S. Navy, May 27, 1863 (aboard USS Cincinnati, Vicksburg).

Bond, William. Boatswain's Mate, U.S. Navy, June 19, 1864 (on board USS *Kearsarge*, vic. of France).

Bonebrake, Henry G. Lieutenant, 17th Pennsylvania Cavalry, April 1, 1865 (Five Forks, Va.).

Bonnaffon, Sylvester, Jr. 1st Lieutenant, 99th Pennsylvania Infantry, October 27, 1864 (Boydon Plank Road).

Boody, Robert. Sergeant, 40th New York Infantry, May 5, 1862 (Williamsburg, Va.).

Boon, Hugh P. Captain, 1st West Virginia Cavalry, April 6, 1865 (Sailors Creek, Va.).

Boquet, Nicholas. Private, 1st Iowa, August 10, 1861 (Wilson's Creek, Mo.).

Boss, Orlando. Corporal, 25th Massachusetts, June 3, 1864 (Cold Harbor, Va.).

Bourke, John G. Private, 15th Pennsylvania Cavalry, December 31, 1862–January 2, 1863 (Stones River, Tennessee).

Bourne, Thomas. Seaman, U.S. Navy, April 24, 1862 (on board USS *Varuna*, assault against Forts Jackson and St. Philip).

Boury, Richard. Sergeant, 1st West Virginia Cavalry, March 5, 1865 (Charlottesville, Va.).

Boutwell, John W. Private, 18th New Hampshire Infantry, April 2, 1865 (Petersburg, Va.).

Bowen, Chester B. Corporal, 19th New York Cavalry (1st New York Dragoons), September 19, 1864 (Winchester, Va.).

Bowen, Emmer. Private, 127th Illinois, May 22, 1863 (Vicksburg).

Bowman, Edward R. Quartermaster, U.S. Navy, January 13–15, 1865 (on board USS *Ticonderoga*, assault against Fort Fisher, N.C.).

Box, Thomas J. Captain, 27th Indiana Infantry, May 14, 1864 (Resaca, Ga.).

Boynton, Henry V. Lieutenant Colonel, 35th Ohio Infantry, November 25, 1863 (Missionary Ridge, Tennessee).

Bradley, Amos Landsman. U.S. Navy, April 24, 1862 (on board USS *Varuna*, assault against Forts Jackson and St. Philip and Confederate vessel *Morgan*).

Bradley, Charles. Boatswain's Mate, U.S. Navy (various actions aboard USS *Louisville*).

Bradley, Thomas W. Sergeant, 124th New York Infantry, May 3, 1863 (Chancellorsville, Va.).

Brady, James. Private, 10th New Hampshire Infantry, September 29, 1864 (Chapin's Farm, Va.).

Brandle, Joseph E. Private, 17th Michigan Infantry, November 16, 1863 (Lenoir, Tenn.).

Brannigan, Felix. Private, 74th New York Infantry, May 2, 1863 (Chancellorsville, Va.).

Brant, William. Lieutenant, 1st New Jersey Veteran Battalion, April 3, 1865 (Petersburg, Va.).

Bras, Edgar A. Sergeant, 8th Iowa Infantry, April 8, 1865 (Spanish Fort, Alabama).

Brazell, John. Quartermaster, U.S. Navy, August 5, 1864 (aboard USS *Richmond*, Mobile Bay).

Breen, John. Boatswain's Mate, U.S. Navy, October 3, 1862 (on board USS *Commodore Perry*)

Brennan, Christopher. Seaman, U.S. Navy, April 24–25, 1862 (on board USS *Mississippi* against Forts Jackson and St. Philip, La.).

Brest, Lewis F. Private, 57th Pennsylvania Infantry, April 6, 1865 (Sailors Creek, Va.).

Brewer, William J. Private, 2nd New York Cavalry, April 4, 1865 (vic. Appomattox, Va.).

Breyer, Charles. Sergeant, 90th Pennsylvania Infantry, August 23, 1862 (Rappahannock Station, Va.).

Briggs, Elijah A. Corporal, 2nd Connecticut Heavy Artillery, April 3, 1865 (Petersburg).

Bringle, Andrew. Corporal, 10th New York Cavalry, April 6, 1865 (Sailors Creek, Va.).

Brinn, Andrew. Seaman, U.S. Navy, March 14, 1863 (on board USS *Mississippi*, Port Hudson, La.).

Bronner, August F. Private, 1st New York Artillery June 30, 1862 (Malvern Hill, Va.).

Bronson, James H. 1st Sergeant, 5th U.S. Colored Troops, September 29, 1864 (Chapin's Farm, Va.).

Brosnan, John. Sergeant, 164th New York Infantry, June 17, 1864 (Petersburg, Va.).

Brouse, Charles W. Captain, 100th Indiana Infantry, November 25, 1863 (Missionary Ridge, Tenn.).

Brown, Charles. Sergeant, 50th Pennsylvania Infantry, August 19, 1864 (Weldon Station, Va.).

Brown, Edward, Jr. Corporal, 62nd New York Infantry, May 3–4, 1863 (Fredericksburg and Salem Heights, Va.).

Brown, Henri Le Fevre. Sergeant, 72nd New York Infantry, May 6, 1864 (Wilderness, Va.).

Brown, James. Quartermaster, U.S. Navy, May 4, 1863 (on board USS *Albatross* against Fort De Russy, Red River).

Brown, Jeremiah Z. Captain, 148th Pennsylvania Infantry, October 27, 1864 (Petersburg, Va.).

Brown, John. Captain of the Forecastle, U.S. Navy, August 5, 1864 (on board USS *Brooklyn*, Mobile Bay).

Brown, John H. 1st Sergeant, 47th Ohio Infantry, May 19, 1863 (Vicksburg, Miss.).

Brown, John Harties. Captain, 12th Kentucky Infantry, November 30, 1864 (Franklin, Tenn.).

Brown, Morris, Jr. *Captain, 126th New York Infantry, July 3, 1863 (Gettysburg, Pa.).

Brown, Robert. U.S. Navy, Captain of the Top, August 5, 1864 (Mobile Bay).

Brown, Robert B. Private, 15th Ohio Infantry, November 25, 1863 (Missionary Ridge, Tenn.).

Brown, Uriah. Private, 30th Ohio Infantry, May 22, 1863 (Vicksburg, Miss.)

Brown, William H. Landsman, U.S. Navy, August 5, 1864 (on board USS *Brooklyn* against Fort Morgan and Confederate vessels, Mobile Bay).

Brown, Wilson. Landsman, U.S. Navy, August 5, 1864 (on board USS *Hartford*, Mobile Bay).

Brown, Wilson W. Private, 21st Ohio Infantry, April 1862 (Big Shanty, Ga.).

Brownell, Francis E. Private, 11th New York Infantry, May 24, 1861 (Alexandria, Va., first Civil War deed to merit Medal of Honor).

Brownell, William P. Coxswain, U.S. Navy, May 2, 1863, and May 22, 1863 (Great Gulf Bay and Vicksburg, Mississippi, respectively).

Bruner, Louis J. Private, 5th Indiana Cavalry, December 2, 1863 (Walker's Ford, Tenn.).

Brush, George W. Lieutenant, 34th U.S. Colored Troops, May 24, 1864 (Ashepoo River, S.C.).

Bruton (Braton), Christopher C. Captain, 22nd New York Cavalry, March 2, 1865 (Waynesboro, Va.).

Brutsche, Henry. Landsman, U.S. Navy, October 31, 1864 (on board USS *Tacony* against Plymouth, N.C.).

Bryant, Andrew S. Sergeant, 46th Massachusetts Infantry, May 23, 1863 (New Bern, N.C.).

Buchanan, George A. *September 29, 1864 (Chapin's Farm, Va.).

Buck, F. Clarence. Corporal, 21st Connecticut

Infantry, September 29, 1864 (Chapin's Farm, Va.).

Buck, James. Quartermaster, U.S. Navy, April 24–25, 1862 (on board USS *Brooklyn* assault against Forts Jackson and St. Philip).

Buckingham, David E. 1st Lieutenant, 4th Delaware Infantry, February 5, 1865 (Rowantry Creek, Va.).

Buckles, Abram J. Sergeant, 19th Indiana Infantry, May 5, 1864 (Wilderness, Va.).

Buckley, Denis. Private, 136th New York Infantry, July 20, 1864 (Peach Tree Creek, Ga.).

Buckley, John C. Sergeant, 4th West Virginia Infantry, May 22, 1863 (Vicksburg).

Bucklyn, John K. 1st Lieutenant, 1st Rhode Island Light Artillery, May 3, 1863 (Chancellorsville, Va.).

Buffington, John E. Sergeant, 6th Maryland Infantry, April 2, 1865 (Petersburg, Va.).

Buffum, Robert. Private, 21st Ohio Infantry, April 1862 (Big Shanty, Ga.).

Buhrman, Henry G. Private, 54th Ohio Infantry, May 22, 1863 (Vicksburg).

Bumgarner, William. Sergeant, 4th West Virginia Infantry, April 2, 1864 (Petersburg, Va.).

Burbank, James H. Sergeant, 4th Rhode Island Infantry, October 3, 1862 (Franklin, Va., Blackwater).

Burger, Joseph. Private, 2nd Minnesota Infantry, February 15, 1863 (Nolensville, Tenn.).

Burk, E. Michael. Private, 125th New York Infantry, May 12, 1864 (Spotsylvania, Va.).

Burk, Thomas. Sergeant, 97th New York Infantry, May 6, 1864 (Wilderness, Va.).

Burke, Daniel W. Sergeant, 2nd U.S. Infantry, September 20, 1862 (Shepherdstown Ford, Va.).

Burke, Thomas. Private, 5th New York Cavalry, June 30, 1863 (Hanover Court House, Va.).

Burns, James M. Sergeant, 1st West Virginia Infantry, May 15, 1864 (New Market, Va.).

Burns, John M. Seaman, U.S. Navy, August 5, 1864 (on board USS *Lackawanna*, Mobile Bay).

Burritt, William W. Private, 113th Illinois Infantry, April 27, 1863 (Vicksburg, Miss.).

Burton, Albert. Seaman, U.S. Navy, January 15, 1865 (on board USS *Wabash*, assault against Fort Fisher, N.C.).

Butterfield, Daniel. Brigadier General, June 27, 1862 (Gaines Mill, Va.).

Butterfield, Frank G. 1st Lieutenant, 6th Vermont Infantry, May 4, 1863 (Salem Heights, Va.).

Butts, George. Gunner's Mate, U.S. Navy May 5, 1864 (on board USS *Signal*, Red River campaign).

Byrnes, James. Boatswain's Mate, U.S. Navy (gallantry while serving aboard USS *Louisville*), citation, April 3, 1863.

Cadwallader, Abel G. Corporal, 1st Maryland Infantry, February 6, 1865 (Dabney's Mill and Hatcher's Run, Va.).

Cadwell, Luman L. Sergeant, 2nd New York Veteran Cavalry, September 20, 1864 (Alabama Bayou, La.).

Caldwell, Daniel. Sergeant, 13th Pennsylvania Cavalry, February 6, 1865 (Dabney's Mill and Hatcher's Run, Va.).

Calkin, Ivers 5. 1st Sergeant, 2nd New York Cavalry, April 6, 1865 (Sailors Creek, Va.).

Callahan, John H. Private, 122nd Illinois Infantry, April 9, 1865 (Fort Blakely, Alabama).

Camp, Canton N. Private, 18th New Hampshire Infantry, April 2, 1865 (Petersburg, Va.).

Campbell, James A. Private, 2nd New York Cavalry, April 5, 1865 (Amelia Court House, Va.).

Campbell, William. Boatswain's Mate, U.S. Navy, December 24-25, 1864, and January 15, 1865 (on board USS *Ticonderoga*, assault against Fort Fisher, N.C.).

Campbell, William. Private, 30th Ohio Infantry, May 22, 1863 (Vicksburg, Miss.).

Capehart, Charles E. Major, 1st West Virginia Cavalry, July 4, 1863 (Monterey Mountain, Pa.).

Capehart, Henry. Colonel, 1st West Virginia Cavalry, May 22, 1864 (Greenbrier River, West Va.).

Capron, Horace Jr. Sergeant, 8th Illinois Cavalry, June 1862 (Chickahominy and Ashland, Va.).

Carey, Hugh Sergeant, 82nd New York Infantry, July 2, 1863 (Gettysburg, Pa.).

Carey, James L. Sergeant, 10th New York Cavalry, April 9, 1865 (Appomattox Court House, Va.).

Carlisle, Casper R. Private, Independent Pennsylvania Light Artillery, July 2, 1863 (Gettysburg, Pa.).

Carman, Warren. Private, 1st New York (Lincoln) Cavalry, March 2, 1865 (Vicksburg, Miss.).

Carmin, Isaac H. Corporal, 48th Ohio Infantry, May 22, 1863 (Vicksburg, Miss.).

Carney, William H. Sergeant, 54th Massachusetts Colored Infantry, July 18, 1863 (Fort Wagner, S.C.).

Carr, Eugene A. Colonel, 3rd Illinois Cavalry, March 7, 1862 (Pea Ridge, Arkansas).

Carr, Franklin. Corporal, 124th Ohio Infantry, December 16, 1864 (Nashville, Tenn.).

Carr, William M. Master at Arms, U.S. Navy, August 5, 1864 (on board USS *Richmond*, Mobile Bay).

Carson, William J. Musician, 15th U.S. Infantry, September 19, 1863 (Chickamauga, Ga.).

Cart, Jacob. Private, 7th Pennsylvania Reserve Corps, December 13, 1862 (Fredericksburg, Va.).

Carter, John J. 2nd Lieutenant, 33rd New York Infantry, September 17, 1862 (Antietam).

Carter, Joseph F. Captain, 3rd Maryland Infantry, March 25, 1865 (Fort Stedman).

Caruana, Orlando. E. Private, 51st New York Infantry, March 14, 1862 (New Bern, N.C., South Mountain).

Casey, David. Private, 25th Massachusetts Infantry, June 3, 1864 (Cold Harbor, Va.).

Casey, Henry. Private, 20th Ohio Infantry, April 22, 1863 (Vicksburg, Miss.).

Cassidy, Michael Landsman. U.S. Navy, August 5, 1864 (aboard USS *Lackawanna*, Mobile Bay).

Catlin, Isaac S. Colonel, 109th New York Infantry, July 30, 1864 (Petersburg, Va.).

Cayer, Ovila. Sergeant, 14th U.S. Volunteers, August 19, 1864 (Weldon Railroad, Va.).

Chamberlain, Joshua L. Colonel, 20th Maine Infantry, July 2, 1863 (Gettysburg, Pa.).

Chamberlain, Orville. 2nd Lieutenant, 74th Indiana Infantry, September 20, 1863 (Chickamauga, Ga.).

Chambers, Joseph B. Private, 100th Pennsylvania Infantry, March 25, 1865 (Petersburg, Va.).

Chandler, Henry F. Sergeant, 59th Massachusetts Infantry, June 17, 1864 (Petersburg, Va.).

Chandler, James B. Coxswain, U.S. Navy, August 5, 1864 (on board USS *Richmond*, Mobile Bay).

Chandler, Stephen E. Quartermaster Sergeant, 24th New York Cavalry, April 5, 1865 (Amelia Springs, Va.).

Chapin, Alaric B. Private, 142nd New York Infantry, January 15, 1865 (Fort Fisher, N.C.).

Chapman, John. Private, 1st Maine Heavy Artillery, April 6, 1865 (Sailors Creek, Va.).

Chaput, Louis G. Landsman, U.S. Navy, August 5, 1864 (on board USS *Lackawanna*, Mobile Bay).

Chase, John F. Private, 5th Battery, Maine Light Artillery, May 3, 1863 (Chancellorsville, Va.).

Child, Benjamin H. Corporal, 1st Rhode Island Artillery, September 17, 1862 (Antietam).

Chisman, William W. Private, 83rd Indiana Infantry, May 22, 1863 (Vicksburg, Miss.).

Christiancy, James. 1st Lieutenant, 9th Michigan Cavalry, May 28, 1864 (Hawes Shops, Va.).

Churchill, Samuel J. Corporal, 2nd Illinois Light Artillery, December 15, 1864 (Nashville, Tenn.).

Cilley, Clinton A. Captain, 2nd Minnesota Infantry, September 20, 1863 (Chickamauga, Ga.).

Clancy, James. Sergeant, 1st New Jersey Cavalry, October 1, 1864 (Vaughn Road, Va.).

Clapp, Albert A. 1st Sergeant, 2nd Ohio Cavalry, April 6, 1865 (Sailors Creek, Va.).

Clark, Charles A. Lieutenant, 6th Maine Infantry, May 4, 1863 (Brooks Ford, Va.).

Clark, Harrison. Corporal, 125th New York Infantry, July 2, 1863 (Gettysburg, Pa.).

Clark, James G. Private, 88th Pennsylvania Infantry, June 18, 1864 (Petersburg, Va.).

Clark, John W. 1st Lieutenant, 6th Vermont Infantry, July 28, 1863 (vic. Warrenton, Va.).

Clark, William A. Corporal, 2nd Minnesota Infantry, February 15, 1863 (Nolensville, Tenn.).

Clarke, Dayton P. Captain, 2nd Vermont Infantry, May 12, 1864 (Spotsylvania, Va.).

Clausen, Charles H. 1st Lieutenant, 61st Pennsylvania Infantry, May 12, 1864 (Spotsylvania, Va.).

Clay, Cecil. Captain, 58th Pennsylvania Infantry, September 29, 1864 (Fort Harrison, Va.).

Cleveland, Charles F. Private, 26th New York Infantry, September 17, 1862 (Antietam).

Clifford, Robert. Master at Arms, U.S.Navy, August 22, 1863 (on board USS *Shokokon*, vic, New Topsail Inlet, Wilmington, N.C.).

Clopp, John E. Private, 71st Pennsylvania Infantry, July 3, 1863 (Gettysburg, Pa.).

Clute, George W. Corporal, 14th Michigan Infantry, March 19, 1865 (Bentonville, N.C.).

Coates, Jefferson. Sergeant, 7th Wisconsin Infantry, July 1, 1863 (Gettysburg, Pa.).

Cockley, David L. 1st Lieutenant, 10th Ohio Cavalry, December 4, 1864 (Waynesboro, Ga.).

Coey, James. Major, 147th New York Infantry, February 6, 1865 (Hatcher's Run, Va.).

Coffey, Robert J. Sergeant, 4th Vermont Infantry, May 4, 1863 (Banks Ford, Va.).

Cohn, Abraham. Sergeant Major, 6th New Hampshire Infantry, May 6, 1864 (Wilderness, Va.).

Colbert, Patrick. Coxswain, U.S. Navy, October 31, 1864 (on board USS *Commodore Hull* at Plymouth, N.C.).

Colby, Carlos W. Sergeant, 97th Illinois Infantry, May 22, 1863 (Vicksburg, Miss.).

Cole, Gabriel. Corporal, 5th Michigan Cavalry, September 19, 1864 (Winchester Va.).

Collins, Harrison. Corporal, 1st Tennessee Cavalry, December 24, 1864 (Richland Creek, Tenn.).

Collins, Thomas D. Sergeant, 143rd New York, Infantry, May 15, 1864 (Resaca, Ga.).

Collis, Charles H.T. Colonel, 114th Pennsylvania Infantry, December 13, 1862 (Fredericksburg, Va.).

Colwell, Oliver. 1st Lieutenant, 95th Ohio Infantry, December 16, 1864 (Nashville, Tenn.).

Compson, Hartwell B. Major, 8th New York Cavalry, March 2, 1865 (Waynesboro, Va.).

Conaway, John W. Private, 83rd Indiana Infantry, May 22, 1863 (Vicksburg, Miss.).

Conboy, Martin. Sergeant, 37th New York Infantry, May 5, 1862 (Williamsburg, Va.).

Congdon, James (service rendered under name of James Madison) Sergeant, 8th New York Cavalry (also listed here as James Madison).

Conlan, Dennis. Seaman, U.S. Navy, December 23, 1864 (on board USS *Agawam* against Fort Fisher, N.C.).

Connell, Trustrim. Corporal, 138th Pennsylvania Infantry, April 6, 1865 (Sailors Creek, Va.).

Conner, Richard. Private, 6th New Jersey Infantry, August 30, 1862 (Bull Run, Va.).

Connor, Thomas. Ordinary Seaman, U.S. Navy, January 15, 1865 (on board USS *Minnesota* against Fort Fisher, N.C.).

Connor, William C. Boatswain's Mate, U.S. Navy, September 25, 1864 (on board USS *Howquah*, vic. Wilmington, N.C., against Confederate vessel *Lynx*).

Connors, James. Private, 43rd New York Infantry, September 22, 1864 (Fisher's Hill, Va.).

Cook, John Bugler (15 years old). Battery B, 4th U.S. Artillery, September 17, 1862 (Antietam).

Cook, John H. Sergeant, 119th Illinois Infantry, April 9, 1864 (Pleasant Hill, La.).

Cooke, Walter H. Captain, 4th Pennsylvania Infantry, Militia July 21, 1861 (Bull Run, Va.).

Cooper, John. Coxswain, U.S. Navy, August 5, 1864 (on board USS *Brooklyn*, Mobile Bay). Second award: April 26, 1865 (Mobile).

Copp, Charles D. 2nd Lieutenant, 9th New Hampshire Infantry, December 13, 1862 (Fredericksburg, Va.).

Corcoran, John. Private, 1st Rhode Island Light Artillery, April 2, 1865 (Petersburg, Va.).

Corcoran, Thomas E. Landsman, U.S. Navy, May 1863 (on board the ill-fated USS *Cincinnati* at Vicksburg).

Corliss, George W. Captain, 5th Connecticut Infantry, August 9, 1862 (Cedar Mountain, Va.).

Corliss, Stephen P. 1st Lieutenant, 4th New York Heavy Artillery, April 2, 1865 (South Side Railroad Railroad, Va.).

Corson, Joseph K. Assistant Surgeon, 6th Pennsylvania Reserves (35th Pennsylvania Volunteers), October 14, 1863 (vic. Bristoe Station, Va.).

Cosgriff, Richard H. Private, 4th Iowa Cavalry, April 16, 1865 (Columbus, Ga.).

Cosgrove, Thomas. Private, 40th Massachusetts Infantry, May 15, 1864 (Drury's Bluff, Va.).

Cotton, Peter. Ordinary Seaman, U.S. Navy, December 23-27, 1862 (on board the USS *Baron de Kalb* during expedition along Yazoo River).

Coughlin, John. Lieutenant Colonel, 10th New Hampshire Infantry, May 9, 1864 (Swift's Creek, Va.).

Cox, Robert M. Corporal, 55th Illinois Infantry, May 22, 1863 (Vicksburg, Miss.).

Coyne, John N. Sergeant, 70th New York Infantry, May 5, 1862 (Williamsburg, Va.).

Cranston, William W. Private, 66th Ohio Infantry, May 2, 1863 (Chancellorsville, Va.).

Crawford, Alexander. Fireman, U.S. Navy, May 25, 1864 (on board USS *Wyalusing* in action against CSS *Albemarle* on Roanoke River).

Creed, John. Private, 23rd Illinois Infantry, September 22, 1864 (Fisher's Hill, Va.).

Cripps, Thomas. Quartermaster, U.S. Navy, August 5, 1864 (on board USS *Richmond*, Mobile Bay).

Crocker, Henry M. Captain, 2nd Massachusetts Cavalry, October 19, 1864 (Cedar Creek, Va.).

Crocker, Ulric L. Private, 6th Michigan Cavalry, October 19, 1864 (Cedar Creek, Va.).

Croft, James E. Private, 12th Battery, Wisconsin Light Artillery, October 5, 1864 (Allatoona, Ga.).

Cronin, Cornelius. Chief Quartermaster, U.S. Navy, August 5, 1864 (on board USS *Richmond*, Mobile Bay).

Crosier, William H.H. Sergeant, 149th New York Infantry, July 20, 1864 (Peach Tree Creek, Ga.).

Cross, James E. Corporal, 12th New York Infantry, July 18, 1861 (Blackburn's Ford, Va,).

Crowley, Michael Private, 22nd New York Cavalry, March 2, 1865 (Waynesboro, Va.).

Cullen, Thomas Corporal, 82nd New York Infantry, October 14, 1863 (Bristoe Station, Va.).

Cummings, Amos J. Sergeant Major, 26th New Jersey Infantry, May 4, 1863 (Salem Heights, Va.).

Cumpston, James M. Private, 91st Ohio Infantry, August through November 1864 (Shenandoah Valley campaign).

Cunningham, Francis M. 1st Sergeant, 1st West Va. Cavalry, April 6, 1865 (Sailors Creek, Va.).

Cunningham James S. Private, 8th Missouri Infantry, May 22, 1863 (Vicksburg, Miss.).

Curran, Richard. Assistant Surgeon, 33rd New York Infantry, September 17, 1862 (Antietam).

Curtis, John C. Sergeant Major, 9th Connecticut Infantry, August 5, 1862 (Baton Rouge, La.).

Curtis, Josiah M. 2nd Lieutenant, 12th West Virginia Infantry, April 2, 1865 (Petersburg, Va.).

Curtis, Newton Martin. Brigadier General, U.S. Volunteers, January 15, 1865 (Fort Fisher, N.C.).

Custer, Thomas W. 2nd Lieutenant, 6th Michigan Cavalry, April 2, 1865 (Namozine Church, Va.). Second award: April 1865 (Sailors Creek, Va.).

Cutcheon, Byron M. Major, 20th Michigan Infantry, May 10, 1863 (Horseshoe Bend, Ky.).

Culls, James M. Captain, 11th U.S. Infantry (Wilderness and Spotsylvania campaigns, spring 1864).

Darrough, John S. Sergeant, 113th Illinois Infantry, October 10, 1864 (Eastport, Miss,).

Davidsizer, John A. Sergeant, 1st Pennsylvania Cavalry, April 5, 1865 (Paine's Crossroads, Va.).

Davidson, Andrew. Assistant Surgeon, 47th Ohio Infantry, May 3, 1863 (Vicksburg, Miss.).

Davidson, Andrew. 1st Lieutenant, 30th U.S. Colored Troops, July 30, 1864 (Petersburg, Va.).

Davis, Charles C. Major, 7th Pennsylvania Cavalry, June 27, 1863 (Shelbyville, Tenn.).

Davis, Freeman. Sergeant, 80th Ohio Infantry, November 25, 1863 (Missionary Ridge, Tenn.).

Davis, George E. 1st Lieutenant, 10th Vermont Infantry, July 9, 1864 (Monacy, Md.).

Davis, Harry. Private, 46th Ohio Infantry, July 28, 1864 (Atlanta, Ga.).

Davis, John. Quarter Gunner, U.S. Navy, February 10, 1862 (on board USS *Valley City*, vic. Elizabeth City, N.C.).

Davis, John. Private, 17th Indiana Mounted Infantry, April 1865 (Culloden, Ga.).

Davis, Joseph. Corporal, 104th Ohio Infantry, November 30, 1864 (Franklin, Tenn.).

Davis, Martin K. Sergeant, 116th Illinois Infantry, May 22, 1863 (Vicksburg, Miss.).

Davis, Samuel W. Ordinary Seaman, U.S. Navy, August 5, 1864 (on board USS *Brooklyn*, Mobile Bay).

Davis, Thomas. Private, 2nd New York Heavy Artillery, April 6, 1865 (Sailors Creek, Va.).

Day, Charles. Private, 210th Pennsylvania Infantry, February 6, 1865 (Hatcher's Run, Va.).

Day, David F. Private, 57th Ohio Infantry, May 22, 1863 (Vicksburg).

Deakin, Charles. Boatswain's Mate, U.S. Navy, August 5, 1864 (on board USS *Richmond*, Mobile Bay).

Deane, John M. Major, 29th Massachusetts Infantry, March 25, 1865 (Fort Stedman, Va.).

De Castro, Joseph H. Corporal, 19th Massachusetts Infantry, July 3, 1863 (Gettysburg, Pa.).

DeLacey, Patrick. 1st Sergeant, 143rd Pennsylvania Infantry, May 6, 1864 (Wilderness, Va.).

Deland, Frederick N. Private, 40th Massachusetts Infantry, May 27, 1863 (Port Hudson, La.).

Delaney, John C. Sergeant, 107th Pennsylvania Infantry, February 6, 1864 (Danby's Mills, Va., Hatcher's Run).

De Lavie, Hiram H. Sergeant, 11th Pennsylvania Infantry, April 1, 1865 (Five Forks, Va.).

Dempster, John. Coxswain, U.S. Navy, December 24–25, 1864, and January 13-15, 1865 (on board USS *New Ironsides* against Fort Fisher, N.C.).

Denig, J. Henry. Sergeant, U.S. Marine Corps, August 5, 1864 (on board USS *Brooklyn*, Mobile Bay).

Denning, Lorenzo. Landsman, U.S. Navy, October 27, 1864 (on board picket boat against Confederate ram *Albemarle*).

Dennis, Richard. Boatswain's Mate, U.S. Navy, August 5, 1864 (on board USS *Brooklyn*, Mobile Bay).

Densmore, William. Chief Boatswain's Mate, August 5, 1864 (on board USS *Richmond*, Mobile Bay).

De Puy, Charles H. 1st Sergeant, 1st Michigan Sharpshooters, July 30, 1864 (Petersburg, Va,).

De Witt, Richard W. Corporal, 47th Ohio Infantry, May 22, 1863 (Vicksburg, Miss.).

Di Cesnola, Louis P. Colonel, 4th New York Cavalry, June 17, 1863 (Aldie, Va.).

Dickey, William D. Captain, 15th New York Heavy Artillery, June 17, 1864 (Petersburg, Va.).

Dickie, David. Sergeant, 97th Illinois Infantry, May 22, 1863 (Vicksburg, Mississippi).

Diggins, Bartholomew. Ordinary Seaman, U.S. Navy, August 5, 1864 (on board USS *Hartford*, Mobile Bay).

Dilger, Hubert. Captain, 1st Ohio Light Artillery, May 2, 1863 (Chancellorsville, Va.).

Dillon, Michael A. Private, 2nd New Hampshire Infantry, May 5, 1862 (Williamsburg, Va.).

Ditzenback, John. Quartermaster, U.S. Navy, December 6, 1864 (on board the monitor USS *Neosho*, vic. Bells Mills, Cumberland River).

Dockum, Warren C. Private, 121st New York Infantry, April 6, 1865 (Sailors Creek, Va.).

Dodd, Robert F. Private, 27th Michigan Infantry, July 30, 1864 (Petersburg, Va.).

Dodds, Edward E. Sergeant, 21st New York Cavalry, July 19, 1864 (Ashby's Gap, Va.).

Dolloff, Charles W. Corporal, 1st Vermont Infantry, April 2, 1865 (Petersburg, Va.).

Donaldson, John. Sergeant, 4th Pennsylvania Cavalry, April 9, 1865 (Appomattox Court House, Va.).

Donnelly, John. Ordinary Seaman, U.S. Navy, August 5, 1864 (on board USS *Metacomet*, Mobile Bay).

Donoghue, Timothy. Private, 69th New York Infantry, December 13, 1862 (Fredericksburg, Va.).

Doody, Patrick. Corporal, 164th New York Infantry, June 7, 1864 (Cold Harbor Va.).

Doolen, William. U.S. Navy, Coal Heaver, August 5, 1864 (on board USS *Richmond*, Mobile Bay).

Dore, George H. Sergeant, 126th New York Infantry, July 3, 1863 (Gettysburg, Pa.).

Dorley, August. Private, 1st Louisiana Cavalry, April 11, 1865 (Mount Pleasant, Alabama).

Dorman, John. Seaman, U.S. Navy (for gallantry on board USS *Carondelet* during various actions).

Dorsey, Daniel A. Corporal, 33rd Ohio Infantry, April 1862 (Big Shanty, Georgia).

Dorsey, Decatur. Sergeant, 39th U.S. Colored Troops, July 30, 1864 (Petersburg, Va.).

Dougall, Allan H. 1st Lieutenant, 88th Indiana Infantry, March 19, 1865 (Bentonville, N.C.).

Dougherty, Michael. Private, 13th Pennsylvania Cavalry, October 12, 1863 (Jefferson, Va.).

Dougherty, Patrick. Landsman, U.S. Navy (gallantry on board USS *Lackawanna*, including actions at Mobile Bay, August 1864).

Dow, George P. Sergeant, 7th New Hampshire Infantry, October 1864 (Richmond vicinity).

Dow, Henry. Boatswain's Mate, U.S. Navy, May 27, 1863 (on board USS *Cincinnati* at Vicksburg).

Downey, William. Private, 4th Massachusetts Cavalry, May 24, 1864 (Ashepoo River, S.C.).

Downs, Henry W. Sergeant, 8th Vermont Infantry, September 19, 1864 (Winchester, Virginia).

Drake, James M. 2nd Lieutenant, 9th New Jersey Infantry, May 6, 1864 (Bermuda Hundred, Va.).

Drury, James. Sergeant, 4th Vermont Infantry, June 23, 1864 (Weldon Railroad, Va.).

Duffey, John. Private, 4th Massachusetts Cavalry, May 24, 1864 (Ashepoo River, South Carolina).

Duncan, Adam. Boatswain's Mate, August 5, 1864 (on board USS *Richmond*, Mobile Bay).

Duncan, James K.L. Ordinary Seaman, U.S. Navy, March 2, 1864 (on board USS *Fort Hindman*, vic. Harrisonburg).

Dunlavy, James. Private, 3rd Iowa Cavalry, October 25, 1864 (Osage, Kansas).

Dunn, William. Quartermaster, U.S. Navy, December 1864 and January 1865 (on board USS *Monadnock* against Fort Fisher, N.C.).

Dunne, James. Corporal, Chicago Mercantile Battery, Illinois Light Artillery, May 22, 1863 (Vicksburg, Miss.).

Dunphy, Richard D. Coal Heaver, U.S. Navy, August 5, 1864 (on board USS *Hartford*, Mobile Bay).

Du Pont, Henry A. Captain, 5th U.S. Artillery, October 19, 1864 (Cedar Creek, Va.).

Durham, James R. 2nd Lieutenant, 12th West Virginia Infantry, June 14, 1863 (Winchester, Virginia).

Durham, John S. Sergeant, 1st Wisconsin Infantry, October 8, 1862 (Perryville, Ky.).

Eckes, John N. Private, 47th Ohio Infantry, May 22, 1863 (Vicksburg, Miss.).

Eddy, Samuel E. Private, 37th Massachusetts Infantry, April 6, 1865 (Sailors Creek, Va.).

Edgerton, Nathan H. Lieutenant, 6th U.S. Colored Troops, September 29, 1864 (Chapins Farm, Va.).

Edwards, David. Private, 146th New York Infantry, April 1st 1865 (Five Forks, Va.).

Edwards, John. Captain of the Top, U.S. Navy, August 5, 1864 (on board USS *Lackawanna* against Confederate Fort Morgan, Mobile Bay).

Elliott, Alexander. Sergeant, 1st Pennsylvania Cavalry, April 5, 1865 (Paines Crossroads, Va.).

Elliott, Russell C. Sergeant, 3rd Massachusetts Cavalry, April 19, 1864 (Natchitoches, La.).

Ellis, Horace. Private, 7th Wisconsin Infantry, August 21, 1864 (Weldon Railroad, Va.).

Ellis, William. 1st Sergeant, 3rd Wisconsin Cavalry, January 14, 1865 (Dardanelles, Ark.).

Ellsworth, Thomas F. Captain, 55th Massachusetts, November 30, 1864 (Honey Hill, S.C.).

Elson, James M. Sergeant, 9th Iowa Infantry, May 22, 1863 (Vicksburg).

Embler, Andrew H. Captain, 59th New York Infantry, October 27, 1864 (Boydton Plank Road, Va.).

Enderlin, Richard. Musician, 73rd Ohio Infantry, July 1–3, 1863 (Gettysburg, Pa.).

Engle, James E. Sergeant, 97th Pennsylvania Infantry, May 18, 1864 (Bermuda Hundred, Va.).

English, Edmund. 1st Sergeant, 2nd New Jersey Infantry, May 6, 1864 (Wilderness, Va.).

English, Thomas. Signal Quartermaster, U.S. Navy, December 24–25, 1864, to January 13–15, 1865 (on board USS *New Ironsides* against Fort Fisher, N.C.).

Ennis, Charles D. Private, 1st Rhode Island Light Artillery, April 2, 1865 (Petersburg, Va.).

Erickson, John P. Captain of the Forecastle, U.S. Navy, December 24, 1864, and February 22, 1865 (on board USS *Pontoosuc*, Fort Fisher, N.C., and Wilmington, N.C.).

Estes, Lewellyn G. Captain and Assistant Adjutant General, Volunteers, August 30, 1864 (Flint River, Ga.).

Evans, Coron D. Private, 3rd Indiana Cavalry, April 6, 1865 (Sailors Creek, Va.).

Evans, Ira H. Captain, 116th U.S. Colored Troops, April 2, 1865 (Hatchers Run, Va.).

Evans, James R. Private, 62nd New York Infantry, May 5, 1864 (Wilderness, Va.).

Evans, Thomas. Private, 54th Pennsylvania Infantry, June 5, 1864 (Piedmont, Va.).

Everson, Adelbert. Private, 185th New York Infantry, April 1, 1865 (Five Forks, Va.).

Ewing, John C. Private, 211th Pennsylvania Infantry, April 2, 1865 (Petersburg, Va.).

Falconer, John A. Corporal, 17th Michigan Infantry, November 20, 1863 (Fort Sanders, Knoxville, Tenn.).

Fall, Charles S. Sergeant, 26th Michigan Infantry, May 12, 1864 (Spotsylvania Court House, Va.).

Fallon, Thomas T. Private, 37th New York Infantry, May 5, 1862 (Williamsburg, Va.); May 30–31, 1862 (Fair Oaks, Va.); and June 14–15, 1864 (Big Shanty, Ga.).

Falls, Benjamin F. *Color Sergeant, 19th Massachusetts Infantry, July 3, 1863 (Gettysburg, Pa.).

Fanning, Nicholas Private, 4th Iowa Cavalry, April 2, 1865 (Selma, Alabama).

Farley, William. Boatswain's Mate, U.S. Navy, December 25, 1863 (on board USS *Marblehead*, vic. Stone River, Legareville).

Farnsworth, Herbert E. Sergeant Major, 10th New York Cavalry, June 11, 1864 (Trevilian Station, Va.).

Farquhar, John M. Sergeant Major, 89th Illinois Infantry, December 31, 1862 (Murfreesboro, Tenn.).

Farrell, Edward. Quartermaster, U.S. Navy, April 24, 1862 (on board USS *Owasco* against Forts Jackson and St. Philip).

Fasnacht, Charles H. Sergeant, 99th Pennsylvania Infantry, May 12, 1864 (Spotsylvania, Va.).

Fassett, John B. Captain, 23rd Pennsylvania Infantry, July 2, 1863 (Gettysburg, Pa.).

Fernald, Albert E. 1st Lieutenant, 20th Maine Infantry, April 1, 1865 (Five Forks, Va.).

Ferrell, John H. Pilot, U.S. Navy, December 6, 1864 (on board monitor USS *Neosho*, vic. Bells Mills, Cumberland River, Nashville).

Ferrier, Daniel T. Sergeant, 2nd Indiana Cavalry, May 9, 1864 (Varnella Station, Ga.).

Ferris, Eugene W. 1st Lieutenant, 30th Massachusetts Infantry, April 1, 1865 (Berryville, Va.).

Fesq, Frank. Private, 40th New Jersey Infantry, April 2, 1865 (Petersburg).

Finkenbiner, Henry S. Private, 107th Ohio Infantry, April 9, 1865 (Dingles Mill, S.C.).

Fisher, John H. 1st Lieutenant, 55th Illinois, May 22, 1863 (Vicksburg, Miss.).

Fisher, Joseph. Corporal, 61st Pennsylvania Infantry, April 2, 1865 (Petersburg, Va.).

Fitzpatrick, Thomas. Coxswain, U.S. Navy, August 5, 1864 (on board USS *Hartford*, Mobile Bay).

Flanagan, Augustin. Sergeant, 55th Pennsylvania Infantry, September 29, 1864 (Chapins Farm, Va.).

Flannigan, James. Private, 2nd Minnesota Infantry, February 15, 1863 (Nolensville, Tenn.).

Fleetwood, Christian A. Sergeant Major. 4th U.S. Colored Troops, September 29, 1864 (Chapins Farm, Va.).

Flood, Thomas. Ranked as Boy, U.S. Navy, April 24–25, 1862 (on board USS *Pensacola* against Forts St. Philip and Jackson).

Flynn, Christopher. Corporal, 14th Connecticut Infantry, July 3, 1863 (Gettysburg, Pa.).

Flynn, James E. Sergeant, 6th Missouri Infantry, May 22, 1863 (Vicksburg, Miss.).

Follett, Joseph L. Sergeant, 1st Missouri Light Artillery, March 3, 1862 (New Madrid, Mo.) and December 31, 1862 (Stones River, Tenn.).

Force, Manning F. Brigadier General, U.S. Volunteers, July 22, 1864 (Atlanta, Ga.).

Ford, George W. 1st Lieutenant, 88th New York Infantry, April 6, 1865 (Sailors Creek, Va.).

Forman, Alexander A. Corporal, 7th Michigan Infantry, May 31, 1862 (Fair Oaks, Va.).

Fout, Frederick W. 2nd Lieutenant, 15th Battery, Indiana Light Artillery, September 15, 1862 (vic. Harper's Ferry, West Virginia).

Fox, Henry. Sergeant, 106th Illinois Infantry, December 23, 1862 (Jackson, Tenn.).

Fox, Henry M. Sergeant, 5th Michigan Cavalry, September 19, 1864 (Winchester, Va.).

Fox, Nicholas. Private, 28th Connecticut Infantry, June 14, 1863 (Port Hudson, La).

Fox, William R. Private, 95th Pennsylvania Infantry, April 2, 1865 Petersburg, Va.).

Foy, Charles H. Signal Quartermaster, U.S. Navy, January 13–15, 1865 (on board the USS *Rhode Island* against Fort Fisher, N.C.).

Franks, William J. Seaman, U.S. Navy, March 5, 1864 (on board USS *Marmora*, vic. Yazoo City, Miss.).

Frantz, Joseph. Private, 83rd Indiana Infantry, May 22, 1863 (Vicksburg, Miss.).

Fraser (Frazier), William W. Private, 97th Illinois Infantry, May 22, 1863 (Vicksburg, Miss.).

Freeman, Archibald. Private, 124th New York Infantry, May 12, 1864 (Spotsylvania, Va.).

Freeman, Henry B. 1st Lieutenant, 18th U.S. Infantry, December 31, 1862 (Murfreesboro, Tenn.).

Freeman, Martin. Pilot, U.S. Navy, August 5, 1864 (on board USS *Hartford*, Mobile Bay).

Freeman, William H. Private, 169th New York Infantry, January 15, 1865 (Fort Fisher, N.C.).

French, Samuel S. Private, 7th Michigan Infantry, May 31, 1862 (Fair Oaks, Va.).

Frey, Franz. Corporal, 37th Ohio Infantry, May 22, 1863 (Vicksburg).

Frick, Jacob G. Colonel, 129th Pennsylvania Infantry, December 13, 1862 (Fredericksburg, Va.) and May 3, 1863 (Chancellorsville, Va.).

Frisbee, John B. Gunner's Mate, April 24, 1862 (on board USS *Pinola* during assaults against Forts Jackson and St. Philip and seizure of New Orleans).

Frizzell (Frazell), Henry F. Private, 6th Missouri Infantry, May 22, 1863 (Vicksburg, Miss.).

Fry, Isaac N. Sergeant, U.S. Marine Corps, January 13–15, 1865 (on board USS *Ticonderoga* against Fort Fisher, N.C.).

Fuger, Frederick. Sergeant, 4th U.S. Artillery, July 3, 1863 (Gettysburg, Pa.).

Funk, West. Major, 121st Pennsylvania Infantry, April 9, 1865 (Appomattox Courthouse, Va.).

Furman, Chester S. Corporal, 6th Pennsylvania Reserves July 2, 1863 (Gettysburg, Pa.).

Furness, Frank. Captain, 6th Pennsylvania Cavalry, June 12, 1864 (Trevilian Station, Va.).

Gage, Richard J. Private, 104th Illinois Infantry, July 2, 1863 (Elk River, Tenn.).

Galloway, George N. Private, 95th Pennsylvania Infantry, May 8, 1864 (Alsop's Farm, Va.).

Galloway, John. Commissary Sergeant, 8th Pennsylvania Cavalry, April 7, 1865 (Farmville, Va.).

Gardiner, James. Private, 36th U.S. Colored Troops, September 29, 1864 (Chapins Farm, Va.).

Gardner, Charles N. Private, 32nd Massachusetts Infantry, April 1, 1865 (Five Forks, Va.).

Gardner, Robert J. Sergeant, 34th Massachusetts Infantry, April 2, 1865 (Petersburg, Va.).

Gardner, William. Seaman, U.S. Navy, August 5, 1864 (on board USS *Galena*, Mobile Bay).

Garrett, William. Sergeant, 41st Ohio Infantry, December 16, 1864 (Nashville, Tenn.).

Garrison, James R. Coal Heaver, U.S. Navy, August 5, 1864 (on board USS *Hartford*, Mobile Bay).

Garvin, William. Captain of the Forecastle, U.S. Navy, December 23, 1864 (on board USS *Agawam* against Fort Fisher, N.C.).

Gasson, Richard. *Sergeant, 47th New York Infantry, September 29, 1864 (Chapins Farm, Va.).

Gaunt, John C. Private, 104th Ohio Infantry, November 30, 1864 (Franklin, Tenn.).

Gause, Isaac. Corporal, 2nd Ohio Cavalry, September 13, 1864 (Berryville, Va.).

Gaylord, Levi B. Sergeant, 29th Massachusetts Infantry, March 25, 1865 (Fort Stedman, Va.).

George, Daniel G. Ordinary Seaman, U.S. Navy, October 27, 1864 (on board U.S. Picket Boat No. 1 against CSS Albermarle).

Gere, Thomas P. 1st Lieutenant, 5th Minnesota Infantry, December 16, 1864 (Nashville, Tenn.).

Geschwind, Nicholas. Captain, 116th Illinois Infantry, May 22, 1863 (Vicksburg, Miss.).

Gibbs, Wesley. Sergeant, 2nd Connecticut Heavy Artillery, April 2, 1865 (Petersburg, Va.).

Gifford, Benjamin. Private, 121st New York Infantry, April 6, 1865 (Sailors Creek, Va.).

Gifford, David L. Private, 4th Massachusetts Cavalry, May 24 (Ashepoo River, S.C.).

Gile, Frank S. Landsman, U.S. Navy, November 16, 1863 (on board USS Lehigh, vic. Charleston, S.C.).

Gillespie, George L. 1st Lieutenant, Corps of Engineers, U.S. Volunteers, May 31, 1864 (Bethesda Church, Va.).

Gilligan, Edward L. 1st Sergeant, 88th Pennsylvania Infantry, July 1, 1863 (Gettysburg, Pa.).

Gillmore, John C. Major, 16th New York Infantry, May 3, 1863 (Salem Heights, Va.).

Ginley, Patrick. Private, 1st New York Light Artillery, August 25, 1864 (Reams Station, Va.

Gion, Joseph. Private, 74th New York Infantry, May 2, 1863 (Chancellorsville, Va.).

Godley, Leonidas M. 1st Sergeant, 22nd Iowa Infantry, May 22, 1863 (Vicksburg, Miss.).

Goettel, Philip. Private, 149th New York Infantry, November 27, 1863 (Ringgold, Ga.).

Goheen, Charles A. 1st Sergeant, 8th New York Cavalry, March 2, 1865 (Waynesboro, Va.).

Goldsbery, Andrew E. Private, 127th Illinois Infantry, May 22, 1863 (Vicksburg, Miss.).

Goodall, Francis H. 1st Sergeant, 11th New Hampshire Infantry, December 13, 1862 (Fredericksburg, Va.).

Goodman, William E. 1st Lieutenant, 147th Pennsylvania Infantry, May 3, 1863 (Chancellorsville, Va.).

Goodrich, Edwin. 1st Lieutenant, 9th New York, November 1864 (Cedar Creek, Va.).

Gould, Charles G. Captain, 5th Vermont Infantry, April 2, 1865 (Petersburg, Va.).

Gould, Newton. Private, 113th Illinois Infantry, May 22, 1863 (Vicksburg, Miss.).

Gouraud, George E. Captain, Aide-de-camp, U.S. Volunteers, November 30, 1864 (Honey Hill, S.C).

Grace, Peter. Sergeant, 83rd Pennsylvania Infantry, May 5, 1864 (Wilderness, Va.).

Graham, Robert. Landsman, U.S. Navy, October 31, 1864 (on board USS Tacony, assault against Plymouth, N.C.).

Graham, Thomas N. 2nd Lieutenant, 15th Indiana Infantry, November 25, 1863 (Missionary Ridge, Tenn.).

Grant, Gabriel. Surgeon, U.S. Volunteers, June 1, 1862 (Fair Oaks, Va.).

Grant, Lewis A. Colonel, 5th Vermont Infantry, May 3, 1864 (Salem Heights, Va.).

Graul, William. Corporal. 188th Pennsylvania Infantry, September 29, 1864 (Fort Harrison, Va.).

Gray, John. Private, 5th Ohio Infantry, June 9, 1862 (Port Republic, Va.).

Gray, Robert A. Sergeant, 21st Connecticut Infantry, May 16, 1864 (Drury's Bluff, Va.).

Grebe, M.R. William. Captain, 4th Missouri Cavalry, August 31, 1864 (Jonesboro, Ga.).

Green, George. Corporal, 11th Ohio Infantry, November 25, 1863 (Missionary Ridge, Tenn.).

Greenawalt, Abraham. Private, 104th Ohio Infantry, November 30, 1864 (Franklin, Tenn.).

Greene, John. Captain of the Forecastle, U.S. Navy, April 24–25, 1862 (on board USS Varuna, assault against Forts St. Philip and Jackson.).

Greene, Oliver D. Major and Assistant Adjutant General, U.S. Army, September 17, 1862 (Antietam, Md.).

Gregg, Joseph. Private, 133rd Ohio Infantry, June 16, 1864 (vic. Richmond and Petersburg Railroad, Va.).

Greig, Theodore W. 2nd Lieutenant, 61st New York Infantry, September 17, 1862 (Antietam, Md.).

Gresser, Ignatz. Corporal, 128th Pennsylvania Infantry, September 17, 1862 (Antietam, Md.).

Gribben, James H. Lieutenant 2nd New York Cavalry, April 6, 1865 (Sailors Creek, Va.).

Griffiths, John. Captain of the Forecastle, U.S. Navy, January 15, 1865 (on board USS Santiago de Cuba, assault against Fort Fisher, N.C.).

Grimshaw, Samuel. Private, 52nd Ohio Infantry, August 6, 1864 (Atlanta, Ga.).

Grindlay, James G. Colonel, 146th New York Infantry, April 1, 1865 (Five Forks, Va.).

Griswold, Luke M. Ordinary Seaman, U.S. Navy, December 30, 1862 (on board USS Rhode Island, vic. Cape Hatteras during rescue operations with USS Monitor).

Grueb, George. Private, 158th New York Infantry, September 29, 1864 (Chapins Farm, Va.).

Guerin, Fitz W. Private, 1st Missouri Light Artillery, April 28–29, 1863 (Grand Gulf, Miss.).

Guinn, Thomas. Private, 47th Ohio Infantry, May 22, 1863 (Vicksburg, Mississippi).

Gwynne, Nathaniel. Private, 13th Ohio Cavalry, July 30, 1864 (Petersburg, Va.).

Hack, John. Private, 47th Ohio Infantry, May 3, 1863 (Vicksburg, Miss.).

Hack, Lester G. Sergeant, 5th Vermont Infantry, April 2, 1865 (Petersburg, Va.).

Hadley, Cornelius M. Sergeant, 9th Michigan Cavalry, November 20, 1863 (Knoxville, Tenn.).

Hadley, Osgood. Corporal, 6th New Hampshire Veteran Infantry, September 30, 1864 (Pegram House, Va.).

Haffee, Edmund. Quartermaster, U.S. Navy, December 1864 and January 1865 (on board USS New Ironsides during assault against Fort Fisher, N.C.).

Hagerty, Asel. Private, 61st New York Infantry, April 6, 1865 (Sailors Creek, Va.).

Haight, John H. Sergeant, 72nd New York Infantry, May 5, 1862 (Williamsburg, Va.).

Haight, Sidney. Corporal, 1st Michigan Sharpshooters, July 30, 1864 (Petersburg, Va.).

Haley, James. Captain of the Forecastle, U.S. Navy, June 19, 1864 (on board USS Kearsarge, vic. France).

Hall, Francis B. Chaplain, 16th New York Infantry, May 3, 1863 (Salem Heights, Va.).

Hall, Henry. S. 2nd Lieutenant, Company G, 27th New York Infantry, and Captain, Company F, 121st New York Infantry, June 27, 1862 (Gaines Mills, Va.) and November 7, 1863 (Rappahannock Station, Va.).

Hall, Newton H. Corporal, 104th Ohio Infantry, November 30, 1864 (Franklin, Tenn.).

Hallock, Nathan M. Private, 124th New York Infantry, June 15, 1863 (Bristoe Station, Va.).

Halstead, William. Coxswain, U.S. Navy, August 5, 1864 (on board USS Brooklyn, in Mobile Bay).

Ham, Mark G. Carpenter's Mate, U.S. Navy, June 19, 1864 (on board the USS Kearsarge, vic. Cherbourg, France).

Hamilton, Hugh. Coxswain, U.S. Navy, August 5, 1864 (on board USS Richmond, Mobile Bay).

Hamilton, Richard. Coal Heaver, U.S. Navy, October 27, 1864 (on board U.S. Picket Boat No. 1 against CSS Albemarle).

Hamilton, Thomas W. Quartermaster, U.S. Navy, May 27, 1863 (on board USS Cincinnati, vic. Vicksburg).

Hammel, Henry A. Sergeant, 1st Missouri Light Artillery, April 28–29, 1863 (Grand Gulf, Miss.).

Hand, Alexander. Quartermaster, U.S. Navy, July 9, 1862 (on board USS Ceres, vic. Hamilton, Roanoke River).

Haney, Milton L. Chaplain, 55th Illinois Infantry, July 22, 1864 (Atlanta, Ga.).

Hanford, Edward R. Private, 2nd U.S. Cavalry, October 9, 1864 (Woodstock, Va.).

Hanks, Joseph. Private, 37th Ohio Infantry, May 22, 1863 (Vicksburg).

Hanna, Marcus A. Sergeant, 50th Massachusetts Infantry, July 4, 1863 (Port Hudson, La.).

Hanna, Milton Corporal, 2nd Minnesota Infantry, February 15, 1863 (Nolensville, Tenn.).

Hanscom, Moses C. Corporal, 19th Maine Infantry, October 14, 1863 (Bristoe Station, Va.).

Hapeman, Douglas. Lieutenant Colonel, 104th Illinois Infantry, July 20, 1864 (Peach Tree Creek, Ga.).

Harbourne, John H. Private, 29th Massachusetts Infantry, June 17, 1864 (Petersburg, Va.).

Harcourt, Thomas. Ordinary Seaman, U.S. Navy, January 15, 1865 (on board USS Minnesota against Fort Fisher, N.C.).

Hardenbergh Henry M. *Private, 39th Illinois Infantry, August 16, 1864 (killed at Petersburg, Va., August 28, 1864).

Harding, Thomas. Captain of the Forecastle, U.S. Navy, June 9, 1864 (on board USS Dacotah during engagement and destruction of CSS Pevensey, vic. Beaufort, N.C.).

Haring, Abram P. 1st Lieutenant, 132nd New York Infantry, February 1, 1864 (Bachelors Creek, N.C.).

Harley, Bernard. Ordinary Seaman, U.S. Navy, October 27, 1864 (on board U.S. Picket Boat No. 1).

Harmon, Amzi D. Corporal, 211th Pennsylvania Infantry, April 2, 1865 (Petersburg, Va.).

Harrington, Daniel. Landsman, U.S. Navy (citation issued April 3, 1863), award due to actions while a crewman of USS Pocahontas.

Harrington, Ephraim W. Sergeant, 2nd Vermont Infantry, May 3, 1863 (Fredericksburg, Va.).

Harris, George W. Private, 148th Pennsylvania Infantry, May 12, 1864 (Spotsylvania).

Harris, James H. Sergeant, 38th U.S. Colored Troops, September 29, 1864 (New Market, Va.).

Harris, John. Captain of the Forecastle, U.S. Navy, August 5, 1864 (on board USS Metacomet, Mobile Bay).

Harris, Moses. 1st Lieutenant, 1st U.S. Cavalry, August 28, 1864 (Smithfield, Va.).

Harris, Sampson. Private, 30th Ohio Infantry, May 22, 1863 (Vicksburg).

Harrison, George H. Seaman, U.S. Navy, June 19, 1864 (on board USS *Kearsarge*, vic. France).

Hart, John W. Sergeant, 6th Pennsylvania Reserves, July 2, 1863 (Gettysburg, Pa.).

Hart, William E. Private, 8th New York Cavalry, for conspicuous gallantry during Shenandoah Campaign, 1864 through 1865 (including capture of Rebel guerrilla Harry Gilmore).

Hartranft, John F. Colonel, 4th Pennsylvania Militia, July 21, 1861 (Bull Run, Va.).

Harvey, Harry. Corporal, 22nd New York Cavalry, March 2, 1865 (Waynesboro, Va.).

Haskell, Frank W. Sergeant Major, 3rd Maine Infantry, June 1, 1862 (Fair Oaks, Va.).

Haskell, Marcus M. Sergeant, 35th Massachusetts Infantry, September 17, 1862 (Antietam).

Hastings, Smith H. Captain, 5th Michigan Cavalry, July 24, 1863 (Newby's Crossroads, Va.).

Hatch, John P. Brigadier General, U.S. Volunteers, September 14, 1862 (South Mountain).

Hathaway, Edward W. Seaman, U.S. Navy, June 28, 1862 (on board USS *Sciota*, vic. Vicksburg).

Havron, John H. Sergeant, 1st Rhode Island Light Artillery, April 2, 1865 (Petersburg, Va.).

Hawkins, Charles. Seaman, U.S. Navy, December 23, 1864 (on board USS *Agawam*, vic. Fort Fisher).

Hawkins, Gardner. 1st Lieutenant, 3rd Vermont Infantry, April 2, 1865 (Petersburg).

Hawkins, Martin J. Corporal, 33rd Ohio Infantry, April 1862 (Big Shanty, Georgia).

Hawkins, Thomas R. Sergeant Major, 6th U.S. Colored Troops, September 29, 1864 (Chapins Farm, Va.).

Hawthorne, Harris S. Corporal, 121st New York Infantry, April 6, 1865 (Sailors Creek, Va.).

Hayden, Joseph B. Quartermaster, U.S. Navy, January 13–15, 1865 (on board USS *Ticonderoga* against Fort Fisher, N.C.).

Hayes, John. Coxswain, U.S. Navy, June 19, 1864 (on board USS *Kearsarge*, vic. Cherbourg, France).

Hayes, Thomas. Coxswain, U.S. Navy, August 5, 1864 (on board USS *Richmond*, Mobile Bay).

Haynes, Asbury F. Corporal, 17th Maine Infantry, April 6, 1865 (Sailors Creek, Va.).

Hays, John H. Private, 4th Iowa Cavalry, April 16, 1865 (Columbus, Ga.).

Healey, George W. Private, 5th Iowa Cavalry, July 29, 1864 (Newnan, Ga.).

Hedges, Joseph. 1st Lieutenant, 4th U.S. Cavalry, December 17, 1864 (vic. Harpeth River, Tenn.).

Heermance, William L. Captain, 6th New York Cavalry, April 30, 1863 (Chancellorsville, Va.).

Heller, Henry. Sergeant, 66th Ohio Infantry, May 2, 1863 (Chancellorsville, Va.).

Helms, David H. Private, 83rd Indiana May 22, 1863 (Vicksburg).

Henry, Guy V. Colonel, 40th Massachusetts, June 1, 1864 (Cold Harbor, Va.).

Henry, James. Sergeant, 113th Illinois Infantry, May 22, 1863 (Vicksburg).

Henry, William W. Colonel, 10th Vermont Infantry, October 19, 1864 (Cedar Creek, Va.).

Herington, Pitt B. Private, 11th Iowa Infantry, June 15, 1864 (Kennesaw Mtn., Ga.).

Herron, Francis J. Lieutenant Colonel, 9th Iowa Infantry, May 7, 1862 (Pea Ridge, Ark.).

Hesseltine, Francis S. Colonel, 13th Maine Infantry, December 29–30, 1863 (Matagorda Bay, Texas).

Hibson, Joseph C. Private, 48th New York Infantry, July 13 and July 18, 1863 (Fort Wagner, S.C.).

Hickey, Dennis W. Sergeant, 2nd New York Cavalry, June 29, 1864 (Stony Creek Bridge, Va.).

Hickman, John. Second Class Fireman, U.S. Navy, March 14, 1863 (on board USS *Richmond* during assault against Port Hudson).

Hickok, Nathan E. Corporal, 8th Connecticut Infantry, September 29, 1864 (Chapins Farm, Va.).

Higby, Charles. Private, 1st Pennsylvania Cavalry, March 29–April 9, 1865 (Appomattox Campaign).

Higgins, Thomas J. Sergeant, 99th Illinois Infantry, May 22, 1863 (Vicksburg).

Highland, Patrick. Corporal, 23rd Illinois Infantry, April 2, 1865 (Petersburg).

Hill, Edward. Captain, 16th Michigan Infantry, June 1, 1864 (Cold Harbor, Va.).

Hill, Henry. Corporal, 50th Pennsylvania Infantry, May 6, 1864 (Wilderness, Va.).

Hill, James. 1st Lieutenant, 21st Iowa Infantry, May 16, 1863 (Champion Hills, Miss.).

Hill, James. Sergeant, 14th New York Heavy Artillery, July 30, 1864 (Petersburg, Va.).

Hilliker, Benjamin F. Musician, 8th Wisconsin Infantry, June 4, 1863 (Mechanicsburg, Miss.).

Hills, William G. Private, 9th New York Cavalry, September 26, 1864 (North Fork, Va.).

Hilton, Alfred B. Sergeant, 4th U.S. Colored Troops, September 29, 1864 (Chapins Farm, Va.).

Hincks, William B. Sergeant Major, 14th Connecticut Infantry, July 3, 1863 (Gettysburg, Pa.).

Hinnegan, William. Second Class Fireman, U.S. Navy, December 23, 1864 (on board USS *Agawam*, vic. Fort Fisher, N.C.).

Hodges, Addison J. Private, 47th Ohio Infantry, May 3, 1863 (Vicksburg).

Hoffman, Henry. Corporal, 2nd Ohio Cavalry, April 6, 1865 (Sailors Creek, Va.).

Hoffman, Thomas W. Captain, 208th Pennsylvania, April 2, 1865 (Petersburg, Va.).

Hogan, Franklin. Corporal, 45th Pennsylvania Infantry, July 30, 1864 (Petersburg, Va.).

Hogarty, William P. Private, 23rd New York Infantry, September 17, 1862 (Antietam).

Holcomb, Daniel I. Private, 41st Ohio Infantry, December 16, 1864 (Brentwood Hills, Tenn.).

Holehouse, James (John). Private, 7th Massachusetts Infantry, May 3, 1863 (Marye's Heights, Va.).

Holland, Lemuel F. Corporal, 104th Illinois Infantry, July 2, 1863 (Elk River, Tenn.).

Holland, Milton M. Sergeant Major, 5th U.S. Colored Troops, September 29, 1864 (Chapins Farm, Va.).

Hollat, George. Third Class Boy, U.S. Navy, April 24, 1862 (on board USS *Varuna* during attack against Forts St. Philip and Jackson).

Holmes, Lovilo N. 1st Sergeant, 2nd Minnesota Infantry, February 15, 1863 (Nolensville, Tenn.).

Holmes, William T. Private, 3rd Indiana Cavalry, April 6, 1865 (Sailors Creek, Va.).

Holton, Charles M. 1st Sergeant, 7th Michigan Cavalry, July 14, 1863 (Failing Waters, Va.).

Holton, Edward A. 1st Sergeant, 6th Vermont Infantry, April 16, 1862 (Lees Mills, Va.).

Homan, Conrad. Color Sergeant, 29th Massachusetts Infantry, July 30, 1864 (vic. Petersburg, Va.).

Hooker, George W. 1st Lieutenant, 4th Vermont Infantry, September 14, 1862 (South Mountain, Md.).

Hooper, William B. Corporal, 1st New Jersey Cavalry, March 31, 1865 (Chamberlains Creek, Md.).

Hopkins, Charles F. Corporal, 1st New Jersey Infantry, June 27, 1862 (Gaines Mills, Va.).

Horan, Thomas. Sergeant, 72nd New York Infantry, July 2, 1863 (Gettysburg, Pa.).

Horne, Samuel B. Captain, 11th Connecticut Infantry, September 29, 1864 (Fort Harrison, Va.).

Horsfall, William H. Drummer, 1st Kentucky Infantry, May 21, 1862 (Corinth, Miss.).

Horton, James. Gunner's Mate, U.S. Navy, September 21, 1864 (on board USS *Montauk*, fire in ammunition room).

Horton, Lewis A. Seaman, U.S. Navy, December 30, 1862 (on board USS *Rhode Island*, vic. Cape Hatteras).

Hottenstine, Solomon J. Private, 107th Pennsylvania Infantry, August 19, 1864 (Vic. Petersburg and Norfolk Railroad, Va.).

Hough, Ira. Private, 8th Indiana Infantry, October 19, 1864 (Cedar Creek, Va.).

Houghton, Charles H. Captain, 14th New York Artillery, July 30, 1864 (Petersburg, Va.).

Houghton, Edward C. Ordinary Seaman, U.S. Navy, October 27, 1864 (on board U.S. Picket Boat No. 1, action against CSS *Albemarle*).

Houghton, George L. Private, 104th Illinois Infantry, July 2, 1863 (Elk River, Tenn.).

Houlton, William. Commissary Sergeant, 1st West Virginia Cavalry, April 6, 1865 (Sailors Creek, Va.).

Howard, Henderson C. Corporal, 11th Pennsylvania Reserves, June 30, 1862 (Glendale, Va.).

Howard, Hiram R. Private, 11th Ohio Infantry, November 25, 1863 (Missionary Ridge, Tenn.).

Howard, James. Sergeant, 158th New York Infantry (Battery Gregg, vic. Petersburg, Va.).

Howard, Martin. Landsman, U.S. Navy, October 31, 1864 (on board USS *Tacony* during assault against Plymouth, N.C.).

Howard, Oliver O. Brigadier General, U.S. Volunteers, June 1, 1862 (Fair Oaks, Va.).

Howard, Peter. Boatswain's Mate, U.S. Navy, March 14, 1863 (on board USS *Mississippi*, vic. Port Hudson).

Howard, Squire E. 1st Sergeant, 8th Vermont Infantry, January 14, 1863 (Bayou Teche, La.).

Howe, Orion P. Musician, 55th Illinois Infantry, May 19, 1863 (Vicksburg).

Howe, William H. Sergeant, 29th Massachusetts Infantry, March 25, 1863 (Fort Stedman, Va.).

Hubbell, William S. Captain, 21st Connecticut Infantry, September 30, 1864 (Fort Harrison, Va.).

Hudson, Aaron R. Private, 17th Indiana Mounted Infantry, April 1865 (Culloden, Ga.).

Hudson, Michael. Sergeant, U.S. Marine Corps, August 5, 1864 (on board USS *Brooklyn*, Mobile Bay).

Hughes, Oliver. Corporal, 12th Kentucky Infantry, June 24, 1864 (Weldon Railroad, Va.).

Hughey, John. Corporal, 2nd Ohio Cavalry, April 6, 1865 (Sailors Creek, Va.).

Huidekoper, Henry S. Lieutenant Colonel, 150th

Pennsylvania Infantry, July 1, 1863 (Gettysburg, Pa.).

Hunt, Louis T. Private, 6th Missouri Infantry, May 22, 1863 (Vicksburg).

Hunter, Charles A. Sergeant, 34th Massachusetts Infantry, April 2, 1865 (Petersburg, Va.).

Hunterson, John C. Private, 3rd Pennsylvania Cavalry, June 5, 1862 (Peninsular campaign vic. Williamsburg).

Huskey, Michael. Fireman, U.S. Navy, March 1863 (on board USS *Carondelet*).

Hyatt, Theodore. 1st Sergeant, 127th Illinois Infantry, May 22, 1863 (Vicksburg).

Hyde, Thomas W. Major, 7th Maine Infantry, September 17, 1862 (Antietam).

Hyland, John. Seaman, U.S. Navy, May 5, 1864 (on board USS *Signal*, Red River Campaign).

Hymer, Samuel. Captain, 115th Illinois Infantry, October 13, 1864 (Buzzard's Roost Gap, Ga.).

Ilgenfritz, Charles H. Sergeant, 207th Pennsylvania Infantry, April 2, 1865 (Fort Sedgwick, Va., Petersburg vic.).

Immel, Lorenzo D. Corporal, 2nd U.S. Artillery, August 10, 1861 (Wilson's Creek, Mo.).

Ingalls, Lewis J. Private, 8th Vermont Infantry (Boutte Station, La.).

Inscho, Leonidas H. Corporal, 12th Ohio Infantry, September 14, 1862 (South Mountain, Md.).

Irlam, Joseph. Seaman, U.S. Navy, August 5, 1864 (on board USS *Brooklyn* at Mobile Bay).

Irsch, Francis. Captain, 45th New York Infantry, July 1, 1863 (Gettysburg, Pa.).

Irving, John. Coxswain, U.S. Navy, August 5, 1864 (on board USS *Brooklyn*, Mobile Bay).

Irving, Thomas. Coxswain, U.S. Navy, November 16, 1863 (on board USS *Lehigh*, vic. Charleston Harbor, S.C.).

Irwin, Nicholas. Seaman, U.S. Navy, August 5, 1864 (on board USS *Brooklyn* at Mobile Bay).

Irwin, Patrick. 1st Sergeant, 14th Michigan Infantry, September 1, 1864 (Jonesboro, Ga.).

Jackson, Frederick R. 1st Sergeant, 7th Connecticut Infantry, June 16, 1862 (James Island, S.C.).

Jacobson, Eugene P. Sergeant Major, 74th New York Infantry, May 2, 1863 (Chancellorsville, Va.).

James, Isaac. Private, 110th Ohio Infantry, April 2, 1865 (Petersburg).

James, John H. Captain of the Top, U.S. Navy, August 5, 1864 (on board USS *Richmond*, Mobile Bay).

James, Miles. Corporal, 36th U.S. Colored Troops, September 30, 1864 (Chapins Farm, Va.).

Jamieson, Walter. 1st Sergeant, 139th New York Infantry, July 30, 1864 (Petersburg), and September 29, 1864 (Ft. Harrison, Va.).

Jardine, James. Sergeant, 54th Ohio Infantry, May 22, 1863 (Vicksburg).

Jellison, Benjamin H. Sergeant, 19th Massachusetts Infantry, July 3, 1863 (Gettysburg, Pa.).

Jenkins, Thomas. Seaman, U.S. Navy, May 27, 1863 (on board USS *Cincinnati*, vic. Vicksburg).

Jennings, James T. Private, 56th Pennsylvania, August 20, 1864 (Weldon Railroad Station, Va.).

Jewett, Erastus W. 1st Lieutenant, 9th Vermont Infantry, February 2, 1864 (Newport Barracks, N.C.).

John, William. Private, 37th Ohio Infantry, May 22, 1863 (Vicksburg).

Johndro, Franklin. Private, 118th New York Infantry, September 30, 1864 (Chapins Farm, Va.).

Johns (Jones), Elisha. Corporal, 113th Illinois Infantry, May 22, 1863 (Vicksburg).

Johns, Henry T. Private, 49th Massachusetts Infantry, May 27, 1863 (Port Hudson, La.).

Johnson, Andrew. Private, 116th Illinois Infantry, May 22, 1863 (Vicksburg).

Johnson, Follett. Corporal, 60th New York Infantry, May 27, 1864 (New Hope Church, Ga.).

Johnson, Henry. Seaman, U.S. Navy, August 5, 1864 (on board USS *Metacomet* at Mobile Bay).

Johnson, John. Private, 2nd Wisconsin Infantry, December 13, 1862 (Fredericksburg, Va.).

Johnson, Joseph E. 1st Lieutenant, 58th Pennsylvania Infantry, September 29, 1864 (Fort Harrison, Va.).

Johnson, Ruel M. Major, 100th Indiana Infantry, November 25, 1863 (Chattanooga, Tenn.).

Johnson, Samuel. Private, 9th Pennsylvania Reserves, September 17, 1862 (Antietam).

Johnson, Wallace W. Sergeant, 6th Pennsylvania, July 2, 1863 (Gettysburg, Pa.).

Johnston, David. Private, 8th Missouri Infantry, May 22, 1863 (Vicksburg).

Johnston, William P. Landsman, U.S. Navy, March 2, 1864 (on board USS *Fort Hindman*, vic. Harrisonburg, La.).

Johnston, Willie. Musician, 3rd Vermont Infantry, date of issue, September 16, 1863; place and date of action unknown.

Jones, Andrew. Chief Boatswain's Mate, U.S. Navy, August 5, 1864 (on board ironclad USS *Chickasaw*, Mobile Bay).

Jones, David. Private, 54th Ohio Infantry, May 22, 1863 (Vicksburg).

Jones, John. Landsman, U.S. Navy, December 30, 1862 (on board USS *Rhode Island*, vic. Cape Hatteras).

Jones, John E. Quartermaster, U.S. Navy, August 5, 1864 (on board USS *Oneida*, vic. Mobile Bay).

Jones, Thomas. Coxswain, U.S. Navy, December 1864 and January 1865 (on board USS *Ticonderoga* against Fort Fisher, N.C.).

Jones, William. Captain of the Top, U.S. Navy, August 5, 1864 (on board USS *Richmond*, Mobile Bay).

Jones, William. 1st Sergeant, 73rd New York Infantry, May 12, 1864 (Spotsylvania, Va.).

Jordan, Absalom. Corporal, 3rd Indiana Cavalry, April 6, 1865 (Sailors Creek, Va.).

Jordan, Robert. Coxswain, U.S. Navy, April 14, 1863 (on board USS *Mount Washington* at Nansemond River and the USS *Minnesota*).

Jordan, Thomas. Quartermaster, U.S. Navy, August 5, 1864 (on board USS *Galena*, Mobile Bay).

Josselyn, Simeon T. 1st Lieutenant, 13th Illinois Infantry, November 25, 1863 (Missionary Ridge, Tenn.).

Judge, Francis W. 1st Sergeant, 79th New York Infantry, November 29, 1863 (Fort Sanders, Knoxville).

Kaiser, John. Sergeant, 2nd U.S. Artillery, June 27, 1862 (Richmond).

Kaltenbach, Luther. Corporal, 12th Iowa Infantry, December 16, 1864 (Nashville).

Kane, John. Corporal, 100th New York Infantry, April 2, 1865 (Petersburg).

Kane, Thomas. Captain, U.S. Navy, January 15, 1865 (on board USS *Nereus* at Fort Fisher, N.C.).

Kappesser, Peter. Private, 149th New York Infantry, November 24, 1863 (Lookout Mountain, Tenn).

Karpeles, Leopold. Sergeant, 57th Massachusetts Infantry, May 6, 1864 (Wilderness, Va.).

Kauss (Kautz), August. Corporal, 15th New York Heavy Artillery, April 1, 1865 (Five Forks, Va.).

Keele, Joseph. Sergeant Major, 182nd New York Infantry, May 23, 1864 (North Ana River).

Keen, Joseph S. Sergeant, 13th Michigan Infantry, October 1, 1864 (vic. Chattahoochee River, Ga.).

Keene, Joseph. Private, 26th New York Infantry, December 13, 1862 (Fredericksburg).

Kelley, Andrew J. Private, 17th Michigan Infantry, November 20, 1863 (Knoxville, Tenn).

Kelley, George V. Captain, 104th Ohio Infantry, November 30, 1864 (Franklin, Tenn.).

Kelley, John. Second Class Fireman, U.S. Navy, July 9, 1862 (on board USS *Ceres*, vic. Hamilton, Roanoke River).

Kelley, Leverett M. Sergeant, 36th Illinois Infantry, November 25, 1863 (Missionary Ridge, Tenn.).

Kelly, Alexander. 1st Sergeant, 6th U.S. Colored Troops, September 29, 1864 (Chapins Farm, Va.).

Kelly, Daniel. Sergeant, 8th New York Cavalry, March 2, 1865 (Waynesboro, Va.).

Kelly, Thomas. Private, 6th New York Cavalry, August 16, 1864 (Front Royal, Va.).

Kemp, Joseph. 1st Sergeant, 5th Michigan Infantry, May 6, 1864 (Wilderness, Va.).

Kendall, William W. 1st Sergeant, 49th Indiana Infantry, May 17, 1863 (Black River Bridge, Miss.).

Kendrick, Thomas. Coxswain's Mate, U.S. Navy, August 5, 1864 (on board USS *Oneida*, Mobile Bay).

Kenna, Barnett. Quartermaster, U.S. Navy, August 5, 1864 (on board USS *Brooklyn*, Mobile Bay).

Kennedy, John. Private, 2nd U.S. Artillery, June 11, 1864 (Trevilian Station, Va.).

Kenyon, Charles. Fireman, U.S. Navy, May 15, 1862 (on board USS *Galena*, Drewry's Bluff).

Kenyon, John S. Sergeant, 3rd New York Cavalry, May 15, 1862 (Trenton, N.C.).

Kenyon, Samuel P. Private, 24th New York Cavalry, April 6, 1865 (Sailors Creek, Va.).

Keough, John. Corporal, 67th Pennsylvania Infantry, April 6, 1865 (Sailors Creek, Va.).

Kephart, James. Private, 13th U.S. Infantry, May 19, 1863 (Vicksburg).

Kerr, Thomas R. Captain, 14th Pennsylvania Cavalry, August 7, 1864 (Moorefield, W. Va.).

Kiggins, John. Sergeant, 149th New York Infantry, November 24, 1863 (Lookout Mountain, Tenn).

Kimball, Joseph. Private, 2nd West Virginia Cavalry, April 6, 1865 (Sailors Creek, Va.).

Kindig, John M. Corporal, 63rd Pennsylvania Infantry, May 12, 1864 (Spotsylvania).

King, Horatio C. Major and Quartermaster, U.S. Volunteers, March 31, 1865 (Dinwiddie Courthouse, Va.).

King, Robert H. Landsman, U.S. Navy, October 27, 1864 (on board Picket Boat No. 1 against Confederate vessel *Albemarle*).

King, Rufus Jr. 1st Lieutenant, 4th U.S. Artillery, June 30, 1862 (White Oak Swamp Bridge, Va.).

Kinnaird, Samuel W. Landsman, U.S. Navy, August 5, 1864 (on board USS *Lackawanna*, Mobile Bay).

Kinsey, John. Corporal, 45th Pennsylvania Infantry, May 18, 1864 (Spotsylvania).

Kirby, Dennis T. Major, 8th Missouri Infantry, May 22, 1863 (Vicksburg).

Kirk, Jonathan C. Captain, 20th Indiana Infantry, May 23, 1864 (North Anna River).

Kline, Harry. Private, 40th New York Infantry, April 6, 1865 (Sailors Creek, Va.).

Kloth, Charles H. Private, Chicago Mercantile Battery, Illinois Light Artillery, May 22, 1863 (Vicksburg).

Knight, Charles H. Corporal, 9th New Hampshire Infantry, July 30, 1864 (Petersburg).

Knight, William J. Private, 21st Ohio Infantry, April 1862 (Big Shanty, Ga.).

Knowles, Abiather J. Private, 2nd Maine Infantry, July 21, 1861 (Bull Run, Va.).

Knox, Edward M. 2nd Lieutenant, 15th New York Battery, July 2, 1863 (Gettysburg).

Koogle, Jacob. 1st Lieutenant, 7th Maryland Infantry, April 1, 1865 (Five Forks, Va.).

Kountz, John S. Musician, 37th Ohio Infantry, November 25, 1863 (Missionary Ridge, Tenn.).

Kramer, Theodore L. Private, 188th Pennsylvania Infantry, September 29, 1864 (Chapins Farm).

Kretsinger, George. Private, Chicago Mercantile Battery, Illinois Light Artillery, May 22, 1863 (Vicksburg).

Kuder, Andrew. 2nd Lieutenant, 8th New York Cavalry, March 2, 1865 (Waynesboro, Va.).

Kuder, Jeremiah. Lieutenant, 74th Indiana Infantry, September 1, 1864 (Jonesboro, Ga.).

Labill, Joseph S. Private, 6th Missouri Infantry, May 22, 1863 (Vicksburg).

Ladd, George. Private, 22nd New York Cavalry, March 2, 1865 (Waynesboro, Va.).

Lafferty, John. U.S. Navy, Fireman, May 25, 1864 (on board USS *Wyalusing* on Roanoke River against CSS *Albemarle*).

Laffey, Bartlett. U.S. Navy, Seaman, March 5, 1864 (on board USS *Marmora*, vic. Yazoo City, Miss.).

Laing, William. Sergeant, 158th New York Infantry, September 29, 1864 (Chapins Farm).

Lakin, Daniel. U.S. Navy, Seaman, October 3, 1862 (on board USS *Commodore Perry*, vic. Franklin, Va.).

Landis, James P. Chief Bugler, 1st Pennsylvania Cavalry, April 5, 1865 (Paines Crossroads, Va.).

Lane, Morgan D. Private, Signal Corps, U.S. Army, April 6, 1865 (Jetersville, Va.).

Lanfare, Aaron S. 1st Lieutenant, 1st Connecticut Cavalry, April 6, 1865 (Sailors Creek, Va.).

Langbein, J.C. Julius. Musician, 9th New York Infantry, April 19, 1862 (Camden, N.C.).

Lann, John S. U.S. Navy, Landsman, Citation issued June 22, 1865 (gallantry aboard USS *Magnolia*, St. Mary's, Florida).

Larimer, Smith. Corporal, 2nd Ohio Cavalry, April 6, 1865 (Sailors Creek).

Larrabee, James W. Corporal, 55th Illinois Infantry, May 22, 1863 (Vicksburg).

Lawson, Gaines. 1st Sergeant, 4th East Tennessee Infantry, October 3, 1863 (Minnville, Tenn.).

Lawson, John. U.S. Navy, Landsman, August 5, 1864 (on board USS *Hartford*).

Lawton, Henry W. Captain, 30th Indiana Infantry, August 3, 1864 (Atlanta, Ga.).

Lear, Nicholas. Quartermaster, U.S. Navy, December 1864, and January 1865 (on board USS *New Ironsides* against Fort Fisher, N.C.).

Lee, James H. Seaman, U.S. Navy, June 19, 1864 (on board USS *Kearsarge*).

Leland, George W. Gunner's Mate, U.S. Navy, November 16, 1863 (on board USS *Lehigh*, Charleston Harbor).

Leon, Pierre. Captain of the Forecastle, U.S. Navy, December 23–27, 1862 (on board USS *Baron de Kalb*, Yazoo River Expedition).

Leonard, Edwin. Sergeant, 37th Massachusetts Infantry, June 18, 1864 (Petersburg).

Leonard, William E. Private, 85th Pennsylvania Infantry, April 16, 1864 (Deep Bottom, Va.).

Leslie, Frank. Private, 4th New York Cavalry, August 15, 1864 (Front Royal Va.).

Levy, Benjamin. Private, 1st New York Infantry, June 30, 1862 (Glendale, Va.).

Lewis, DeWitt C. Captain, 97th Pennsylvania Infantry, June 16, 1862 (Secessionville, S.C.).

Lewis, Henry. Corporal, 47th Ohio Infantry, May 3, 1863 (Vicksburg).

Lewis, Samuel E. Corporal, 1st Rhode Island Light Artillery, April 2, 1865 (Petersburg).

Libaire, Adolphe. Captain, 9th New York Infantry, September 17, 1862 (Antietam).

Lilley, John. Private, 205th Pennsylvania Infantry, April 2, 1865 (Petersburg).

Little, Henry F.W. Sergeant, 7th New Hampshire Infantry, September 1864 (Vic. Richmond).

Littlefield, George H. Corporal, 1st Maine Veteran Infantry, March 25, 1865 (Fort Fisher, Va.).

Livingston, Josiah O. 1st Lieutenant and Adjutant, 9th Vermont Infantry, February 2, 1864 (Newport Barracks, N.C.).

Lloyd, Benjamin. U.S. Navy, Coal Heaver, May 25, 1864 (on board USS *Wyalusing*, Roanoke River).

Lloyd, John W. Coxswain, U.S. Navy, May 25, 1864 (USS *Wyalusing* on Roanoke River).

Locke, Lewis. Private, 1st New Jersey Cavalry, April 5, 1865 (Paines Crossroads, Va.).

Logan, Hugh. *Captain of the Afterguard, U.S. Navy (on board USS *Rhode Island*, December 30, 1862, Mobile Bay).

Lonergan, John. Captain, 13th Vermont Infantry, July 2, 1863 (Gettysburg).

Longshore, William H. Private, 30th Ohio Infantry, May 22, 1863 (Vicksburg).

Lonsway, Joseph. Private, 20th New York Cavalry, October 16, 1864 (Murfrees Station, Va.).

Lord, William. Musician, 40th Massachusetts Infantry, May 16, 1864 (Drury's Bluff, Va.).

Lorish, Andrew J. Commissary Sergeant, 19th New York Cavalry (1st New York Dragoons), September 19, 1864 (Winchester, Va.).

Love, George M. Colonel, 116th New York Infantry, October 19, 1864 (Cedar Creek).

Lovering, George M. 1st Sergeant, 4th Massachusetts Infantry, June 14, 1863 (Port Hudson, La.).

Lower, Cyrus B. Private, 13th Pennsylvania Reserves, May 7, 1864 (Wilderness, Va.).

Lower, Robert A. Private, 55th Illinois Infantry, May 22, 1863 (Vicksburg).

Loyd, George Private, 122nd Ohio Infantry, April 2, 1865 (Petersburg).

Lucas, George W. Private, 3rd Missouri Cavalry, July 25, 1864 (Benton, Ark.).

Luce, Moses A. Sergeant, 4th Michigan Infantry, May 10, 1864 (Laurel Hill, Va.).

Ludgate, William. Captain, 59th New York Veteran Infantry, April 7, 1865 (Farmville, Va.).

Ludwig, Carl. Private, 34th New York Battery June 18, 1864 (Petersburg).

Lunt, Aiphonso M. Sergeant, 38th Massachusetts, September 19, 1864 (Winchester, Va., Opequan Creek).

Lutes, Franklin W. Corporal, 111th New York Infantry, March 31, 1865 (Petersburg).

Luther, James H. Private, 7th Massachusetts Infantry, May 3, 1863 (Fredericksburg, Va.).

Luty, Gotlieb. Corporal, 74th New York Infantry, May 3, 1863 (Chancellorsville).

Lyman, Joel H. Quartermaster Sergeant, 9th New York Cavalry, September 19, 1864 (Winchester, Va.).

Lyon, Frederick A. Corporal, 1st Vermont Cavalry, October 19, 1984 (Cedar Creek, Va.).

Lyons, Thomas. Seaman, U.S. Navy, April 24, 1862 (on board USS *Pensacola* against Forts St. Philip and Jackson).

MacArthur, Arthur, Jr. 1st Lieutenant (father of Douglas MacArthur), 24th Wisconsin Infantry, November 25, 1863 (Missionary Ridge, Tenn.).

Machon, James. Boy, U.S. Navy, August 5, 1864 (on board USS *Brooklyn*, Mobile Bay).

Mack, Alexander. Captain of the Top, U.S. Navy, August 5, 1864 (on board USS *Brooklyn*, Mobile Bay).

Mack, John. Seaman, U.S. Navy, March 5–6, 1865 (on board USS *Hendrick Hudson* against enemy at St. Marks, Fla.).

Mackie, John F. Corporal, U.S. Marine Corps, May 15, 1862 (on board USS *Galena* during assault against Fort Darling, Drewry's Bluff).

Madden, Michael. Private, 42nd New York Infantry, September 3, 1861 (Mason's Island, Md.).

Madden, William. Coal Heaver, U.S. Navy, August 5, 1864 (aboard USS *Brooklyn* at Fort Morgan).

Madison, James. Sergeant, 8th New York Cavalry, March 2, 1865 (Waynesboro, Va.).

Magee, William. Drummer, 33rd New Jersey Infantry, December 5, 1864 (Murfreesboro, Tenn.).

Mahoney, Jeremiah. Sergeant, 29th Massachusetts, November 29, 1863 (Fort Sanders, Knoxville).

Mandy, Harry J. 1st Sergeant, 4th New York Cavalry, August 15, 1864 (Front Royal, Va.).

Mangam, Richard C. Private, 148th New York Infantry, April 2, 1865 (Hatcher's Run, Va.).

Manning, Joseph S. Private, 29th Massachusetts Infantry, November 29, 1863 (Knoxville, Fort Sanders).

Marland, William. 1st Lieutenant, 2nd Independent Battery, Massachusetts Light Artillery, November 3, 1863 (Grand Coteau, La.).

Marquette, Charles. Sergeant, 93rd Pennsylvania Infantry, April 2, 1865 (Petersburg).

Marsh, Albert. Sergeant, 64th New York Infantry, May 12, 1864 (Spotsylvania).

Marsh, Charles H. Private, 1st Connecticut Cavalry, July 31, 1864 (Back Creek Valley, Va.).

Marsh, George. Sergeant, 104th Illinois Infantry, July 2, 1863 (Elk River, Tenn.).

Martin, Edward S. Quartermaster, U.S. Navy, August 5, 1864 (on board USS *Galena*, Mobile Bay).

Martin, George (see Schwenk, Martin; he served under that name).

Martin, James. Sergeant, U.S. Marine Corps, August 5, 1864 (on board USS *Richmond*, Mobile Bay).

Martin, Sylvester H. Lieutenant, 88th Pennsylvania, August 19, 1864 (Weldon Station, Va.).

Martin, William. Boatswain's Mate, U.S. Navy, December 27, 1862 (on board USS *Benton*, Haines Bluff, Yazoo River).

Martin, William. Seaman, U.S. Navy, April 24, 1862 (on board USS *Varuna*).

Mason, Elihu. Sergeant, 21st Ohio Infantry, April 1862 (Big Shanty, Ga.).

Mathews, William H. *1st Sergeant, 2nd Maryland Veteran Infantry, July 30, 1864 (Petersburg).

Matthews, John C. Corporal, 61st Pennsylvania Infantry, April 2, 1865 (Petersburg).

Matthews, Milton. Private, 61st Pennsylvania, April 2, 1865 (Petersburg).

Mattingly, Henry B. Private, 10th Kentucky Infantry, September 1, 1864 (Jonesboro, Ga.).

Mattocks, Charles P. Major, 17th Maine Infantry, April 6, 1865 (Sailors Creek, Va.).

Maxham, Lowell M. Corporal, 7th Massachusetts Infantry, May 3, 1863 (Fredericksburg, Va.).

May, William. Private, 32nd Iowa Infantry, December 16, 1864 (Nashville).

Mayberry, John B. Private, 1st Delaware Infantry, July 3, 1863 (Gettysburg).

Mayes, William B. Private, 11th Iowa Infantry, June 15, 1864 (Kennesaw Mountain).

Maynard, George H. Private, 13th Massachusetts Infantry, December 13, 1862 (Fredericksburg).

McAdams, Peter. Corporal, 98th Pennsylvania Infantry, May 3, 1863 (Salem Heights, Va.).

McAlwee, Benjamin F. Sergeant, 3rd Maryland Infantry, July 30, 1864 (Petersburg, Va.).

McAnallly, Charles. Lieutenant, 69th Pennsylvania Infantry, May 12, 1864 (Spotsylvania).

McCammon, William W. 1st Lieutenant, 24th Mississippi Infantry, October 3, 1862 (Corinth, Miss.).

McCarren, Bernard. Private, 1st Delaware Infantry, July 3, 1863 (Gettysburg).

McCauslin, Joseph. Private, 12th West Virginia Infantry, April 2, 1865 (Petersburg).

McCleary, Charles H. 1st Lieutenant, 72nd Ohio Infantry, December 16, 1864 (Nashville).

McClelland, James M. Private, 30th Ohio Infantry, May 22, 1863 (Vicksburg).

McClelland, Matthew. First Class Fireman, U.S. Navy, March 14, 1863 (on board USS *Richmond*, Port Hudson, La.).

McConnell, Samuel. Captain, 119th Illinois Infantry, April 9, 1865 (Fort Blakely, Alabama).

McCormick, Michael. Boatswain's Mate, U.S. Navy, May 5, 1864 (on board USS *Signal*, Red River campaign).

McCornack, Andrew. Private, 127th Illinois Infantry, May 22, 1863 (Vicksburg).

McCullock, Adam. Seaman, U.S. Navy, August 5, 1864 (on board USS *Lackawanna*, Mobile Bay).

McDonald, George E. Private, 1st Connecticut Heavy Artillery, March 25, 1865 (Fort Stedman, Va.).

McDonald, John. Boatswain's Mate, U.S. Navy, December 23–27, 1862 (on board USS *Baron de Kalb*, Yazoo River Expedition).

McDonald, John Wade. Private, 20th Illinois Infantry, April 6, 1862 (Pittsburg Landing, Tenn.).

McElhinny, Samuel O. Private, 2nd West Virginia Cavalry, April 6, 1865 (Sailors Creek, Va.).

McEnroe, Patrick H. Sergeant, 6th New York Cavalry, Septmember 19, 1864 (Winchester, Va.).

McFall, Daniel. Sergeant, 17th Michigan Infantry, May 12, 1864 (Spotsylvania).

McFarland, John. Captain of the Forecastle, U.S. Navy, August 5, 1864 (on board USS *Hartford*, Mobile Bay).

McGinn, Edward. Private, 54th Ohio Infantry, May 22, 1863 (Vicksburg).

McGonagle, Wilson. Private, 30th Ohio Infantry, May 22, 1863 (Vicksburg).

McGonnigle, Andrew J. Captain and Assistant Quartermaster, U.S. Volunteers, October 19, 1864 (Cedar Creek, Va.).

McGough, Owen. Corporal, 5th U.S. Artillery, July 21, 1861 (Bull Run).

McGowan, John. Quartermaster, U.S. Navy, April 24, 1862 (against Confederate vessel *Morgan* and on board the USS *Varuna* during assaults against Forts Jackson and St. Philip).

McGraw, Thomas. Sergeant, 23rd Illinois Infantry, April 2, 1865 (Petersburg, Va.).

McGuire, Patrick. Private, Chicago Mercantile Battery, Illinois Light Artillery, May 22, 1863 (Vicksburg).

McHale, Alexander U. Corporal, 26th Michigan Infantry, May 12, 1864 (Spotsylvania).

McHugh, Martin. Seaman, U.S. Navy, May 27, 1863 (on board USS *Cincinnati*, Vicksburg).

McIntosh, James. Captain of the Top, U.S. Navy (on board USS *Richmond*, Mobile Bay).

McKay, Charles W. 154th New York Infantry, May 8, 1864 (Dug Gap, Ga.).

McKee, George, Color Sergeant, 89th New York Infantry, April 2, 1865 (Petersburg).

McKeen, Nineveh S. 1st Lieutenant, 21st Illinois Infantry, December 30, 1862 (Stones River, Tenn.).

McKeever, Michael. Private, 5th Pennsylvania Cavalry, January 19, 1863 (Burnt Ordinary, Va.).

McKnight, William. Coxswain, U.S. Navy, April 24, 1862 (on board USS *Varuna*, action against Confederate vessel Morgan).

McKown, Nathaniel A. Sergeant, 58th Pennsylvania Infantry, September 29, 1864 (Chapins Farm).

McLeod, James. Captain of the Foretop, U.S. Navy, April 24–25, 1862 (on board USS *Pensacola* against Forts Jackson and St. Philip).

McMahon, Martin T. Captain, U.S. Volunteers, June 30, 1862 (White Oak Swamp, Va.).

McMillen, Francis M. Sergeant, 110th Ohio Infantry, April 2, 1865 (Petersburg).

McVeane, John P. *Corporal, 49th New York Infantry, May 4, 1863 (Fredericksburg Heights, Va.).

McWhorter, Walter F. Commissary Sergeant, 3rd West Virginia Cavalry, April 6, 1865 (Sailors Creek, Va.).

McWilliams, George W. Landsman, U.S. Navy, December 24, 1864, through February 1865 (on board USS *Pontoosuc*, including assault against Fort Fisher).

Meach, George E. Farrier Company I, 6th New York Cavalry, September 19, 1864 (Winchester, Va.).

Meagher, Thomas. 1st Sergeant, 158th New York Infantry, September 29, 1864 (Chapins Farm, Va.).

Mears, George W. Sergeant, 6th Pennsylvania Reserves, July 2, 1863 (Gettysburg, Pa.).

Melville, Charles. Ordinary Seaman, U.S. Navy, August 5, 1864 (on board USS *Hartford*, Mobile Bay).

Menter, John W. Sergeant, 5th Michigan Infantry, April 6, 1865 (Sailors Creek, Va.).

Merriam, Henry C. Lieutenant Colonel, 73rd U.S. Colored Troops, April 9, 1865 (Fort Blakely, Ala.).

Merrifield, James K. Corporal, 88th Illinois Infantry, November 30, 1864 (Franklin, Tenn.).

Merrill, Augustus. Captain, 1st Maine Veteran Infantry, April 2, 1865 (Petersburg).

Merrill, George. Private, 142nd New York Infantry, January 15, 1865 (Fort Fisher).

Merritt, John G. Sergeant, 1st Minnesota Infantry, July 21, 1861 (Bull Run).

Meyer, Henry C. Captain, 24th New York Cavalry, June 17, 1864 (Petersburg).

Mifflin, James. Engineer's Cook, U.S. Navy, August 5, 1864 (on board USS *Brooklyn*, Mobile Bay).

Miles, Nelson A. Colonel, 61st New York Infantry (later General), May 2–3, 1863 (Chancellorsville).

Miller, Andrew. Sergeant, U.S. Marine Corps, August 5, 1864 (on board USS *Richmond*, Mobile Bay).

Miller, Frank. Private, 2nd New York Cavalry, April 6, 1865 (Sailors Creek, Va.).

Miller, Henry A. Captain, 8th Illinois Infantry, April 9, 1865 (Sailors Creek, Va.).

Miller, Jacob C. Private, 113th Illinois Infantry, May 22, 1863 (Vicksburg).

Miller, James. Quartermaster, U.S. Navy, December 25, 1863 (on board gunboat USS *Marblehead*, vic. Legareville, Stono River).

Miller, James P. Private, 4th Iowa Cavalry, April 2, 1865 (Selma, Ala.).

Miller, John. Corporal, 8th Ohio Infantry, July 3, 1863 (Gettysburg).

Miller, John. Private, 8th New York Cavalry, March 2, 1865 (Waynesboro, Va.).

Miller, William E. Captain, 3rd Pennsylvania Cavalry, July 3, 1863 (Gettysburg).

Milliken, Daniel. Quartermaster, U.S. Navy, December 24–25 and January 13–15, 1865 (on board USS *New Ironsides*, Fort Fisher).

Mills, Charles. Seaman, U.S. Navy, January 15, 1865 (on board USS *Minnesota*, Fort Fisher).

Mills, Frank W. Sergeant, 1st New York Mounted Rifles, September 4, 1862 (Sandy Cross Roads, N.C.).

Mindil, George W. Captain, 61st Pennsylvania Infantry, May 5, 1862 (Williamsburg, Va.).

Mitchell, Alexander H. 1st Lieutenant, 105th Pennsylvania, May 12, 1864 (Spotsylvania).

Mitchell, Theodore. Private, 61st Pennsylvania Infantry, April 2, 1865 (Petersburg).

Moffitt, John H. Corporal, 16th New York Infantry, June 27, 1862 (Gaines Mill, Va.).

Molbone, Archibald. Sergeant, 1st Rhode Island Light Artillery, April 2, 1865 (Petersburg).

Molloy, Hugh. Ordinary Seaman, U.S. Navy, March 2, 1864 (on board USS *Fort Hindman*, Harrisonburg, La.).

Monaghan, Patrick. Corporal, 48th Pennsylvania Infantry, June 17, 1864 (Petersburg).

Montgomery, Robert. Captain of the Afterguard, U.S. Navy, December 23, 1864 (on board USS *Agawam* against Fort Fisher).

Moore, Charles. Landsman, U.S. Navy, December 25, 1863 (on board USS *Marblehead*, Stono River).

Moore, Charles. Seaman, U.S. Navy, June 19, 1864 (on board USS *Kearsarge*, vic. France).

Moore, Daniel B. Corporal, 11th Wisconsin Infantry, April 9, 1865 (Fort Blakely, Ala.).

Moore, George. Seaman, U.S. Navy, December 30, 1862 (on board USS *Rhode Island*, vic. Cape Hatteras).

Moore, George G. Private, 11th West Va. Infantry, September 22, 1864 (Fisher's Hill, Va.).

Moore, Wilbur F. Private, 117th Illinois Infantry, December 16, 1864 (Nashville, Tenn.).

Moore, William. Boatswain's Mate, December 27, 1862 (on board USS *Benton*, Haines Bluff, Yazoo River).

Morey, Delano. Private, 82nd Ohio Infantry, May 8, 1862 (McDowell, Va.).

Morford, Jerome. Private, 55th Illinois Infantry, May 22, 1863 (Vicksburg).

Morgan, James H. Captain of the Top, U.S. Navy, August 5, 1864 (on board USS *Richmond*, Mobile Bay).

Morgan, Lewis. Private, 4th Ohio Infantry, May 12, 1864 (Spotsylvania).

Morgan, Richard H. Corporal, 4th Iowa Cavalry, April 16, 1865 (Columbus, Ga.).

Morrill, Walter G. Captain, 20th Maine Infantry, November 7, 1863 (Rappahannock Station, Va.).

Morris, William. Sergeant, 1st New York (Lincoln) Cavalry, April 6, 1865 (Sailors Creek, Va.).

Morrison, Francis. Private, 85th Pennsylvania Infantry, June 17, 1864 (Bermuda Hundred).

Morrison, John G. Coxswain, U.S. Navy, July 15, 1862 (on board USS *Carondelet* against Rebel vessel *Arkansas* on the Yazoo River).

Morse, Benjamin. Private, 3rd Michigan Infantry, May 12, 1864 (Spotsylvania).

Morse, Charles E. Sergeant, 62nd New York Infantry, May 5, 1864 (Wilderness, Va.).

Morton, Charles W. Boatswain's Mate, U.S. Navy, December 23-27, 1863 (on board USS *Benton*, Yazoo River Expedition).

Mostoller, John W. Private, 54th Pennsylvania Infantry, June 18, 1864 (Lynchburg, Va.).

Mulholland, St. Clair A. Major, 116th Pennsylvania Infantry, May 4-5, 1863 (Chancellorsville).

Mullen, Patrick. Boatswain's Mate, U.S. Navy, March 17, 1865 (on board USS *Wyandank*, Mattox Creek); second award: May 1, 1865, during a rescue operation while serving on the USS *Don*.

Mundell, Walter L. Corporal, 5th Michigan Infantry, April 6, 1865 (Sailor Creek).

Munsell, Harvey M. Sergeant, 99th Pennsylvania Infantry, July 1-3, 1863 (Gettsyburg).

Murphy, Charles J. 1st Lieutenant, 38th New York Infantry, July 21, 1861 (Bull Run).

Murphy, Daniel J. Sergeant, 19th Massachusetts Infantry, October 27, 1864 (Hatcher's Run, Va.).

Murphy, Dennis J.F. Sergeant, 14th Wisconsin Infantry, October 3, 1862 (Corinth, Miss.).

Murphy, James T. Private, 1st Connecticut Artillery, March 25, 1865 (Petersburg).

Murphy, John P. Private, 5th Ohio Infantry, September 17, 1862 (Antietam).

Murphy, Michael C. Lieutenant Colonel, 170th New York Infantry, May 24, 1864 (North Anna River).

Murphy, Patrick. Boatswain's Mate, U.S. Navy, August 5, 1864 (on board USS *Metacomet*, Mobile Bay).

Murphy, Robinson B. Musician, 127th Illinois Infantry, July 28, 1864 (Atlanta).

Murphy, Thomas. Corporal, 158th New York Infantry, September 30, 1864 (Chapins Farm, Va.).

Murphy, Thomas C. Corporal, 31st Illinois Infantry, May 22, 1863 (Vicksburg).

Murphy, Thomas J. 1st Sergeant, 146th New York Infantry, April 1, 1865 (Five Forks, Va.).

Myers, George S. Private, 101st Ohio Infantry, September 19, 1863 (Chickamauga, Ga.).

Myers, William H. Private, 1st Maryland Cavalry, April 9, 1865 (Appomattox Courthouse, Va.).

Nash, Henry H. Corporal, 47th Ohio Infantry, May 3, 1863 (Vicksburg).

Naylor, David. Landsman, U.S. Navy, August 5, 1864 (on board USS *Oneida*, Mobile Bay).

Neahr, Zachariah C. Private, 142nd New York Infantry, January 16, 1865 (Fort Fisher, N.C.).

Neil, John. Quarter Gunner, U.S. Navy, December 23, 1864 (on board USS *Agawam*, Fort Fisher, N.C.).

Neville, Edwin M. Captain, 1st Connecticut Cavalry, April 6, 1865 (Sailors Creek, Va.).

Newland, William. Ordinary Seaman, U.S. Navy, August 5, 1864 (on board USS *Oneida*, Mobile Bay).

Newman, Marcellus J. Private, 111th Illinois Infantry, May 14, 1864 (Resaca, Ga.).

Newman, William H. Lieutenant, 86th New York Infantry, April 6, 1865 (Amelia Springs, Va.).

Nibbe, John N. Quartermaster, U.S. Navy, April 22, 1864 (aboard USS *Peterel* on the Yazoo River).

Nichols, Henry C. Captain, 73rd U.S. Colored Troops, April 9, 1865 (Fort Blakely, Ala.).

Nichols, William. Quartermaster, U.S. Navy, August 5, 1864 (on board USS *Brooklyn*, Mobile Bay).

Niven, Robert. 2nd Lieutenant, 8th New York Cavalry, March 2, 1865 (Waynesboro, Va.).

Noble, Daniel. Landsman, U.S. Navy, August 5, 1864 (on board USS *Metacomet*, Mobile Bay).

Nolan, John J. Sergeant, 8th New Hampshire Infantry, October 27, 1862 (Georgia Landing, La.).

Noll, Conrad. Sergeant, 20th Michigan Infantry, May 12, 1864 (Spotsylvania).

North, Jasper N. Private, 4th West Virginia Infantry, May 22, 1863 (Vicksburg).

Norton, Elliott M. 2nd Lieutenant, 6th Michigan Cavalry, April 6, 1865 (Sailors Creek, Va.).

Norton, John R. Lieutenant, 1st New York (Lincoln) Cavalry, April 6, 1865 (Sailors Creek, Va.).

Norton, Llewellyn P. Sergeant, 10th New York Cavalry, April 6, 1865 (Sailors Creek, Va.).

Noyes, William W. Private, 2nd Vermont Infantry, May 12, 1864 (Spotsylvania).

Nugent, Christopher. Sergeant, U.S. Marine Corps, June 15, 1863 (on board USS *Fort Henry*, Crystal River, Florida).

Nutting, Lee. Captain, 61st New York Infantry, May 8, 1864 (Todd's Tavern, Va.).

O'Beirne, James R. Captain, 37th New York Infantry, May 31–July 1, 1862 (Fair Oaks, Va.).

O'Brien, Henry D. Corporal, 1st Minnesota Infantry, July 3, 1863 (Gettysburg).

O'Brien, Oliver. Coxswain, U.S. Navy, November 28, 1864 (on board USS *John Adams*, Sullivan's Island Channel, action against Rebel vessel Beatrice).

O'Brien, Peter. Private, 1st New York (Lincoln) Cavalry, March 2, 1865 (Waynesboro).

O'Connell, Thomas. Coal Heaver, U.S. Navy, August 5, 1864 (on board USS *Hartford*, Mobile Bay).

O'Connor, Albert. Sergeant, 7th Wisconsin Infantry, March 31–April 1, 1865 (Gravely Run, Va.).

O'Connor, Timothy. Private, 1st U.S. Cavalry, date and place unknown. Medal awarded January 5, 1865.

O'Dea, John. Private, 8th Missouri Infantry, May 22, 1863 (Vicksburg).

O'Donnell, Menomen. 1st Lieutenant, 11th Missouri Infantry, May 22, 1863 (Vicksburg) and Fort DeRussey, La., March 14, 1864.

O'Donoghue, Timothy. Seaman, U.S. Navy, May 5, 1864 (on board USS *Signal*, Red River Campaign).

Oliver, Charles. Sergeant, 100th Pennsylvania Infantry, March 25, 1865 (Petersburg).

Oliver, Paul A. Captain, 12th New York Infantry, May 15, 1864 (Resaca, Georgia).

O'Neill, Stephen Corporal, 7th U.S. Infantry, May 1, 1863 (Chancellorsllle).

Opel, John N. Private, 7th Indiana Infantry, May 5, 1864 (Wilderness, Va.).

Orbansky, David. Private, 58th Ohio Infantry, April 1862 (Shiloh, Tenn., and Vicksburg during 1863).

Orr, Charles A. Private, 187th New York Infantry, October 27, 1864 (Hatcher's Run, Va.).

Orr, Robert L. Major 61st Pennsylvania Infantry, April 2, 1865 (Petersburg).

Ortega, John. Seaman U.S. Navy, award due to gallantry on various occasions while attached to USS *Saratoga*. Citation awarded December 31, 1864.

Orth, Jacob C. Corporal, 28th Pennsylvania Infantry, September 17, 1862 (Antietam).

Osborne, William H. Private, 29th Massachusetts Infantry, July 1, 1862 (Malvern Hill, Va.).

Oss, Albert. Private, 11th New Jersey Infantry, May 3, 1863 (Chancellorsville, Va.).

Overturf, Jacob H. Private, 83rd Indiana Infantry, May 22, 1863 (Vicksburg).

Oviatt, Miles M. Corporal, U.S. Marine Corps, August 5, 1864 (on board USS *Brooklyn*, Mobile Bay).

Packard, Loron F. Private, 5th New York Cavalry, November 27, 1863 (Raccoon Ford, Va.).

Palmer, George H. Musician, 1st Illinois Cavalry, September 20, 1861 (Lexington, Mo.).

Palmer, John C. Corporal, 21st Connecticut Infantry, December 13, 1862 (Fredericksburg).

Palmer, William J. Colonel, 15th Pennsylvania Cavalry, January 14, 1865 (Red Hill, Ala.).

Parker, Thomas. Corporal, 2nd Rhode Island Infantry, April 2, 1865 (Petersburg).

Parker, William. Captain of the Afterguard, U.S. Navy, April 24-25, 1862 (on board USS *Cayuga* during action against Forts St. Philip and Jackson).

Parks, George. Captain of the Forecastle, U.S. Navy, August 5, 1864 (on board USS *Richmond*, Mobile Bay).

Parks, Henry Jeremiah. Private, 9th New York Cavalry, October 19, 1864 (Cedar Creek, Va.).

Parks, James W. Corporal, 11th Missouri Infantry, December 16, 1864 (Nashville).

Parrott, Jacob. Private, 33rd Ohio Infantry (1st man to receive the Medal of Honor, one of the 19 of 22 men, including two civilians, who penetrated nearly 200 miles south into enemy territory and captured a railroad train at Big Shanty, Georgia, in April 1862).

Parsons, Joel. Private, 4th West Virginia Infantry, May 22, 1863 (Vicksburg).

Patterson, John H. 1st Lieutenant, 11th U.S. Infantry, May 5, 1864 (Wilderness, Va.).

Patterson, John T. Principal Musician, 122nd Ohio Infantry, June 14, 1863 (Winchester, Va.).

Paul, William H. Private, 90th Pennsylvania Infantry, September 17, 1862 (Antietam).

Pay, Byron E. Private, 2nd Minnesota Infantry, February 15, 1863 (Nolensville, Tenn.).

Payne, Irvin C. Corporal, 2nd New York Cavalry, April 6, 1865 (Sailors Creek, Va.).

Payne, Thomas H.L. 1st Lieutenant, 37th Illinois Infantry, April 9, 1865 (Fort Blakely, Ala.).

Pearsall, Platt. Corporal, 30th Ohio Infantry, May 22, 1863 (Vicksburg).

Pearson, Alfred L. Colonel, 155th Pennsylvania Infantry, March 29, 1865 (Lewis Farm, Va.).

Pease, Joachim. Seaman, U.S. Navy, June 19, 1864 (on board USS Kearsarge, vic. Cherbourg, France).

Peck, Cassius. Private, 1st U.S. Sharpshooters, September 19, 1862 (Blackburn's Ford, Va.).

Peck, Oscar E. Second Class Boy, U.S. Navy, April 24, 1862 (on board USS Varuna during an attack on Forts Jackson and St. Philip).

Rebmann, George F. Sergeant, 119th Illinois Infantry, April 9, 1865 (Blakely, Ala.).

Reddick, William H. Corporal, 33rd Ohio Infantry, April 1862 (Big Shanty, Georgia).

Reed, Axel H. Sergeant, 2nd Minnesota Infantry, September 19, 1863 (Chicamauga, Ga.).

Reed, Charles W. Bugler, 9th Independent Battery, Massachusetts Light Artillery, July 2, 1863 (Gettysburg).

Reed, George W. Private, 11th Pennsylvania Infantry, August 21, 1864 (Weldon Railroad, Va.).

Reed, William. Private, 8th Missouri Infantry, May 22, 1863 (Vicksburg).

Reeder, Charles A. Private, 12th West Virginia Infantry, April 2, 1865 (Petersburg).

Regan, Jeremiah, Quartermaster, U.S. Navy, May 15, 1862 (on board USS Galena, Drewry's Bluff, Va.).

Reid, Robert. Private, 48th Pennsylvania Infantry, June 17, 1864 (Petersburg).

Reigle, Daniel P. Corporal, 87th Pennsylvania Infantry, October 19, 1864 (Cedar Creek, Va.).

Reisinger, J. Monroe. Corporal, 150th Pennsylvania Infantry, July 1, 1863 (Gettysburg).

Renninger, Louis. Corporal, 37th Ohio, May 22, 1863 (Vicksburg).

Reynolds, George. Private, 9th New York Cavalry, September 19, 1864 (Winchester, Va.).

Rhodes, Julius D. Private, 5th New York Cavalry, August 28, 1862 (Bull Run, Va.)

Rhodes, Sylvester D. Sergeant, 61st Pennsylvania Infantry, September 22, 1864 (Fisher's Hill, Va.).

Rice, Charles. Coal Heaver, U.S. Navy (on board USS Agawam), December 23, 1864 (Fort Fisher).

Rice, Edmund. Major, 19th Massachusetts Infantry, July 3, 1863 (Gettysburg).

Rich, Carlos H. First Sergeant, 4th Vermont Infantry, May 5, 1864 (Wilderness, Va.).

Richards, Louis. Quartermaster, U.S. Navy, 24-25 August 1862 (New Orleans).

Richardson, William R. Private, 2nd Ohio Cavalry, April 6, 18665 (Sailors Creek, Va.).

Richey, William E. Corporal, 15th Ohio Infantry, September 19, 1863 (Chickamauga, Ga.).

Richmond, James. Private, 8th Ohio Infantry, July 3, 1863 (Gettysburg).

Ricksecker, John H. Private, 104th Ohio Infantry, November 30, 1864 (Franklin, Tenn.).

Riddell, Rudolph. Lieutenant, 61st New York Infantry, April 6, 1865 (Sailors Creek, Va.).

Riley, Thomas. Private, 1st Louisiana Cavalry, April 4, 1865 (Fort Blakely, Ala.).

Ringold, Edward. Coxswain, U.S. Navy, October 22, 1862 (on board USS Wabash, Pocotaligo, S.C.).

Ripley, William Y.W. Lieutenant Colonel, 1st U.S. Sharpshooters July 1, 1862 (Malvern Hill, Va.).

Roantree, James S. Sergeant, U.S. Marine Corps, August 5, 1864 (on board USS Oneida, Mobile Bay).

Robbins, Augustus J. 2nd Lieutenant, 2nd Vermont Infantry, May 12, 1864 (Spotsylvania).

Roberts, James. Seaman, U.S. Navy, December 23, 1864 (on board USS Agawam, vic. Fort Fisher, N.C.).

Roberts, Otis O. Sergeant, 6th Maine Infantry, November 7, 1863 (Rappahannock Station, Va.).

Robertson, Robert S. 1st Lieutenant, 93rd New York Infantry, May 8, 1864 (Corbin's Bridge, Va.).

Robertson, Samuel. Private, 33rd Ohio Infantry, April 1862 (Big Shanty, Ga.).

Robie, George F. Sergeant, 7th New Hampshire Infantry, September 1864 (vic. Richmond, Va.).

Robinson, Alexander. Boatswain's Mate, September 25, 1864 (on board USS Howquah in action against Rebel blockade runner Lynx, vic. Wilmington, N.C.).

Robinson, Charles. Boatswain's Mate, U.S. Navy, December 23-27, 1862 (on board USS Baron de Kalb, Yazoo River Expedition).

Robinson, Elbridge. Private, 122nd Ohio Infantry, June 14, 1863 (Winchester, Va.).

Robinson, James H. Private, 3rd Michigan Cavalry, January 27, 1865 (Brownsville, Ark.).

Robinson, John C. Brigadier General, U.S. Volunteers, May 8, 1864 (Laurel Hill, Va.).

Robinson, John H. Private, 19th Massachusetts Infantry, July 3, 1863 (Gettysburg).

Robinson, Thomas. Private, 81st Pennsylvania Infantry, May 12, 1864 (Spotsylvania).

Rock, Frederick. Private, 37th Ohio Infantry, May 22, 1863 (Vicksburg).

Rockefeller, Charles M. Lieutenant, 178th New York Infantry, April 9, 1865 (Fort Blakely, Ala.).

Rodenbough, Theophilus F. Captain, 2nd U.S. Cavalry, June 11, 1864 (Trevilian Station, Va.).

Rohm, Ferdinand. Chief Bugler, 16th Pennsylvania Cavalry, August 25, 1864 (Ream's Station, Va.).

Rood, Oliver P. Private, 20th Indiana Infantry, July 3, 1863 (Gettysburg).

Roosevelt, George W. 1st Sergeant, 26th Pennsylvania Infantry, August 30, 1862 (Bull Run, Va.).

Ross, Marion A. Sergeant Major, 2nd Ohio Infantry, April 1862 (Big Shanty, Ga.).

Rossbach, Valentine. Sergeant, 34th New York Battery, May 12, 1864 (Spotsylvania).

Rought, Stephen. Sergeant, 141st Pennsylvania Infantry, May 6, 1864 (Wilderness, Va.).

Rounds, Lewis A. Private, 8th Ohio Infantry, May 12, 1864 (Spotsylvania).

Rountry, John. 1st Class Fireman, U.S. Navy, September 21, 1864 (for gallantry on board USS Montauk).

Roush, J. Levi. Corporal, 6th Pennsylvania Reserves, July 2, 1863 (Gettysburg).

Rowand, Archibald H., Jr. Private, 1st West Virginia Cavalry (einter of 1864-1865 for gallantry while involved with hazardous duty for U.S. Grant).

Rowe, Henry W. Private, 11th New Hampshire Infantry, June 17, 1864 (Petersburg).

Rundle, Charles W. Private, 116th Illinois Infantry, May 22, 1863 (Vicksburg).

Rush, John. 1st Class Fireman, U.S. Navy, March 14, 1863 (on board USS Richmond, Port Hudson, La.).

Russell, Charles L. Corporal, 93rd New York Infantry, May 12, 1864 (Spotsylvania).

Russell, Milton. Captain, 51st Indiana Infantry, December 29, 1862 (Stones River, Murfreesboro, Tenn).

Rutherford, John T. 1st Lieutenant, 9th New York Cavalry, May 11, 1864 (Yellow Tavern, Va.).

Rutter, James M. Sergeant, 143rd Pennsylvania Infantry, July 1, 1863 (Gettysburg).

Ryan, Peter J. Private, 11th Indiana Infantry, September 19, 1864 (Winchester, Va.).

Sacriste, Louis J. 1st Lieutenant, 116th Pennsylvania Infantry, May 3, 1863 (Chancellorsville).

Sagelhurst, John C. Sergeant, 1st New Jersey Cavalry, February 6, 1865 (Hatcher's Run, Va.).

Sancrainte, Charles F. Private, 15th Michigan Infantry, July 22, 1864 (Atlanta, Ga.).

Sanderson, Aaron. Landsman, U.S. Navy, March 17, 1865 (on board USS Wyandank, vic. Mattox Creek).

Sands, William. 1st Sergeant, 88th Pennsylvania Infantry, February 6-7, 1865 (Dabney's Mills, Va.).

Sanford, Jacob. Private, 55th Illinois Infantry, May 22, 1863 (Vicksburg).

Sargent, Jackson. Sergeant, 5th Vermont Infantry, April 2, 1865 (Petersburg).

Sartwell, Henry. Sergeant, 123rd New York Infantry, May 3, 1863 (Chancellorsville).

Saunders, James. Quartermaster, U.S. Navy, June 19, 1864 (on board USS Kearsarge, vic. Cherbourg, France).

Savacool, Edwin F. *Captain, 1st New York (Lincoln) Cavalry, April 6, 1865 (Sailors Creek).

Savage, Auzella. Ordinary Seaman, U.S. Navy, January 15, 1865 (on board USS Santiago de Cuba against Fort Fisher, N.C.).

Saxton, Rufus. Brigadier General, U.S. Volunteers, May 26-30, 1862 (Harpers Ferry, West Va.).

Scanlan, Patrick. Private, 4th Massachusetts Cavalry, May 24, 1864 (Ashepoo River, S.C.).

Scheibner, Martin E. Private, 90th Pennsylvania Infantry, November 27, 1863 (Mine Run, Va.).

Schenck, Benjamin W. Private, 116th Illinois Infantry, May 22, 1863 (Vicksburg).

Schiller, John. Private, 158th New York Infantry, September 29, 1864 (Chapin's Farm, Va.).

Schlachter, Philipp. Private, 73rd New York Infantry, May 12, 1864 (Spotsylvania).

Schmal, George W. Blacksmith. 24th New York Cavalry, April 5, 1865 (Paines Crossroads).

Schmauch, Andrew. Private, 30th Ohio Infantry, May 22, 1863 (Vicksburg).

Schmidt, Conrad. First Sergeant, 2nd U.S. Cavalry, September 19, 1864 (Winchester, Va.).

Schmidt, William. Private, 37th Ohio Infantry,

November 25, 1863 (Missionary Ridge, Tenn.).

Schneider, George. Sergeant, 3rd Maryland Veteran Infantry, July 30, 1864 (Petersburg, Va.).

Schnell, Christian. Corporal, 37th Ohio Infantry, May 22, 1863 (Vicksburg).

Schofield, John M. Major, 1st Missouri Infantry, August 10, 1861 (Wilson's Creek, Mo.).

Schoonmaker, James M. Colonel, 14th Pennsylvania Cavalry, September 19, 1864 (Winchester, Va.).

Schorn, Charles. Chief Bugler, 1st West Virginia Cavalry, April 8, 1865 (Appomattox, Va.).

Schubert, Martin. Private, 26th New York Infantry, December 13, 1862 (Fredericksburg, Va.).

Schutt, George. Coxswain, U.S. Navy, March 5-6, 1865 (on board USS *Hendrick Hudson*, St. Marks, Fla.).

Schwan, Theodore. 1st Lieutenant, 10th U.S. Infantry, October 1, 1864 (Peebles Farm, Va.).

Schwenk, Martin. Sergeant, 6th U.S. Cavalry, July 1863 (Millerstown, Pa.).

Scofield, David H. Quartermaster Sergeant, 5th New York, U.S. Cavalry, October 19, 1864 (Cedar Creek, Va.).

Scott, Alexander. Corporal, 10th Vermont Infantry, July 9, 1864 (Monocacy, Md.).

Scott, John M. Sergeant, 21st Ohio, April 1862 (Big Shantry, Ga.).

Scott, John Wallace. Captain, 157th Pennsylvania Infantry, April 1, 1865 (Five Forks, Va.).

Scott, Julian A. Drummer, 3rd Vermont Infantry, April 16, 1862 (Lees Mills, Va.).

Seaman, Elisha B. Private, 66th Ohio Infantry, May 2, 1863 (Chancellorsville).

Seanor, James. Master at Arms, U.S. Navy, August 5, 1864 (on board USS *Chickasaw*, Mobile Bay).

Sears, Cyrus. 1st Lieutenant, 11th Artillery, Ohio Light Battery, September 19, 1862 (Iuka, Miss.).

Seaver, Thomas O. Colonel, 3rd Vermont Infantry, May 10, 1864 (Spotsylvania).

Seitzinger, James M. Private, 116th Pennsylvania Infantry, June 3, 1864 (Cold Harbor, Va.).

Sellers, Alfred J. Major, 90th Pennsylvania Infantry, July 1, 1863 (Gettysburg).

Seston, Charles H. *Sergeant, 11th Indiana Infantry, September 19, 1864 (Winchester, Va.).

Seward, Griffin. Wagoner, 8th U.S. Cavalry, October 20, 1863 (Chiricahua Mountains, Ariz.).

Seward, Richard E. Paymaster's Steward, U.S. Navy, November 23, 1863 (on board USS *Commodore*, Ship Island Sound, La.).

Sewell, William J. Colonel, 5th New Jersey Infantry, May 3, 1863 (Chancellorsville).

Shafter, William R. 1st Lieutenant, 7th Michigan Infantry, May 31, 1862 (Fair Oaks, Va.).

Shahan, Emisire. Corporal, 1st West Virginia Cavalry, April 6, 1865 (Sailors Creek, Va.).

Shaler, Alexander. Colonel, 65th New York Infantry, May 3, 1863 (Mare's Heights, Va.).

Shambaugh, Charles. Corporal, 11th Pennsylvania Reserves, June 30, 1862 (Charles City Crossroads, Va.).

Shanes, John. Private, 14th West Virginia Infantry, July 20, 1864 (Carter's Farm, Va.).

Shapland, John. Private, 104th Illinois Infantry, July 2, 1863 (Elk River, Tenn.).

Sharp, Hendrick. Seaman, U.S. Navy, August 5, 1864 (on board USS *Richmond*, Mobile Bay).

Shea, Joseph H. Private, 92nd New York Infantry, September 29, 1864 (Chapins Farm, Va.).

Shellenberger, John S. Corporal, 85th Pennsylvania Infantry, August 16, 1864 (Deep Run, Va.).

Shepard, Irwin. Corporal, 17th Michigan Infantry, November 20, 1863 (Knoxville).

Shepard, Louis C. Ordinary Seaman, U.S. Navy, January 15, 1865 (on board USS *Wabash*, Fort Fisher, N.C.).

Shepherd, William. Private, 3rd Indiana Cavalry, April 6, 1865 (Sailors Creek, Va.).

Sheridan, James. Quartermaster, U.S. Navy, August 5, 1864 (on board USS *Oneida*, Mobile Bay).

Sherman, Marshall. Private, 1st Minnesota Infantry, July 3, 1863 (Gettysburg).

Shiel (Shields), John. Corporal, 90th Pennsylvania Infantry, December 13, 1862 (Fredericksburg, Va.).

Shields, Bernard. Private, 2nd West Virginia Cavalry, April 8, 1865 (Appomattox, Va.).

Shilling, John. 1st Sergeant, 3rd Delaware Infantry, August 21, 1864 (Weldon Railroad, Va.).

Shipley, Robert F. Sergeant, 140th New York Infantry, April 1, 1865 (Five Forks, Va.).

Shipman, William. Coxswain, U.S. Navy, January 15, 1865 (on board USS *Ticonderoga*, Fort Fisher, N.C.).

Shivers, John. Private, U.S. Marine Corps, January 15, 1865 (on board USS *Minnesota* during the assault against Fort Fisher, N.C.).

Shoemaker, Levi. Sergeant, 1st West Virginia Cavalry, November 12, 1864 (Nineveh, Va., captured flag of 22nd Virginia Confederate Cavalry).

Shopp, George J. Private, 191st Pennsylvania Infantry, April 1, 1865 (Five Forks, Va.).

Shubert, Frank. Sergeant, 43rd New York Infantry, April 2, 1865 (Petersburg).

Shutes, Henry. Captain of the Forecastle, U.S. Navy, April 24-25, 1862, during battle against New Orleans, and February 27, 1863, against Fort McAllister (on board USS *Wissahickon*).

Sickles, Daniel E. Major General, U.S. Volunteers, July 2, 1863 (Gettysburg).

Sickles, William H. Sergeant, 7th Wisconsin Infantry, March 31, 1865 (Gravely Run, Va.).

Sidman, George E. Private, 16th Michigan Infantry, June 27, 1862 (Gaines Mills, Va.).

Simkins, Lebbeus. Coxswain, U.S. Navy, August 5, 1864 (on board USS *Richmond*, Mobile Bay).

Simmons, John. Private, 2nd New York Heavy Artillery, April 6, 1865 (Sailors Creek, Va.).

Simmons, William T. Lieutenant, 11th Missouri Infantry, December 16, 1864 (Nashville).

Simonds, William Edgar. Sergeant Major, 25th Connecticut Infantry, April 14, 1863 (Irish Bend, La.).

Simons, Charles J. Sergeant, 9th New Hampshire Infantry, July 30, 1864 (Petersburg).

Sivel, Henry (see William H. Matthews, his true name).

Skellie, Ebenezer. Corporal, 112th New York Infantry, September 29, 1864 (Chapins Farm, Va.).

Sladen, Joseph A. Private, 33rd Massachusetts Infantry, May 14, 1864 (Resaca, Ga.).

Slagle, Oscar. Private, 104th Illinois Infantry, July 2, 1863 (Elk River, Tenn.).

Slavens, Samuel. Private, 33rd Ohio Infantry, April 1862 (Big Shanty, Ga.).

Sloan, Andrew J. Private, 12th Iowa Infantry, December 16, 1864 (Nashville).

Slusher, Henry C. Private, 22nd Pennsylvania Cavalry, September 11, 1863 (Vic. Moorefield, West Va.).

Smalley, Reuben. Private, 83rd Indiana Infantry, May 22, 1863 (Vicksburg).

Smalley, Reuben S. Private, 104th Illinois Infantry, July 2, 1863 (Elk River, Tenn.).

Smith, Alonzo. Sergeant, 7th Michigan Infantry, October 27, 1864 (Hatcher's Run, Va.).

Smith, Charles H. Colonel, 1st Maine Cavalry, June 24, 1864 (St. Mary's Church, Va.).

Smith, Charles H. *Coxswain, U.S. Navy, December 30, 1862 (on board USS *Rhode Island*, Mobile Bay).

Smith, David L. Sergeant, 1st New York Light Artillery, April 6, 1862 (Warwick Court House, Va.).

Smith, Edwin. Ordinary Seaman, U.S. Navy, October 3, 1862 (on board USS *Whitehead*, vic. Franklin, Va.).

Smith, Francis M. 1st Lieutenant and Adjutant, 1st Maryland Infantry, February 6, 1865 (Dabney Mills, Va.).

Smith, Henry I. 1st Lieutenant, 7th Iowa Infantry, March 15, 1865 (Black River, N.C.).

Smith, James (Ovid). Private, 2nd Ohio Infantry, April 1862 (Big Shanty, Georgia).

Smith, James. Captain of the Forecastle, U.S. Navy, August 5, 1864 (on board USS *Richmond*, Mobile Bay).

Smith, John. Captain of the Forecastle, U.S. Navy, August 5, 1864 (on board USS *Lackawanna*, Mobile Bay).

Smith, John. Second Captain of the Top, U.S. Navy, August 5, 1864 (on board USS *Richmond*, Mobile Bay).

Smith, Joseph S. Lieutenant Colonel and Commissary of Subsistence, U.S. 2nd Army Corps, October 27, 1864 (Hatchers Run, Va.).

Smith, Oloff. Coxswain, U.S. Navy, August 5, 1864 (on board USS *Richmond*, Mobile Bay).

Smith, Otis W. Private, 95th Ohio Infantry, December 16, 1864 (Nashville).

Smith, Richard. Private, 95th New York Infantry, August 21, 1864 (Weldon Railroad, Va.).

Smith, S. Rodman. Captain, 4th Delaware Infantry, February 5, 1865 (Rowanty Creek, Va.).

Smith, Thaddeus S. Corporal, 6th Pennsylvania Reserve Infantry, July 2, 1863 (Gettysburg).

Smith, Thomas. Seaman, U.S. Navy, March 5-6, 1865 (on board USS *Magnolia*, St. Marks, Fla.).

Smith, Walter B. Ordinary Seaman, U.S. Navy, August 5, 1864 (on board USS *Richmond*, Mobile Bay).

Smith, Willard M. Corporal, U.S. Marine Corps, August 5, 1864 (on board USS *Brooklyn*, Mobile Bay).

Smith, William. Quartermaster, U.S. Navy, June 19, 1864 (on board USS *Kearsarge*, vic. France).

Smith, Wilson. Corporal, 3rd New York Light Artillery, September 6, 1862 (Washington, N.C.).

Snedden, James. Musician, 54th Pennsylvania Infantry, June 5, 1864 (Piedmont, Va.).

Southard, David. Sergeant, 1st New Jersey Cavalry, April 6, 1865 (Sailors Creek, Va.).

Sova, Joseph E. Saddler, 8th New York Cavalry, March 29–April 9, 1865 (Appomattox Campaign).

Sowers, Michael. Private, 4th Pennsylvania Cavalry, December 1, 1864 (Stony Creek Station, Va.).

Spalding, Edward B. Sergeant, 52nd Illinois Infantry, April 6, 1862 (Pittsburg Landing, Tenn.).

Sperry, William J. Major, 6th Vermont Infantry, April 2, 1865 (Petersburg).

Spillane, Timothy. Private, 16th Pennsylvania Cavalry, February 5-7, 1865 (Hatchers Run, Va.).

Sprague, Benona. Corporal, 116th Illinois Infantry, May 22, 1863 (Vicksburg).

Sprague, John W. Colonel, 63rd Ohio Infantry, July 22, 1862 (Decatur, Ga.).

Sprowle, David. Orderly Sergeant, U.S. Marine Corps, August 5, 1864 (on board USS *Richmond*, Mobile Bay).

Spurling, Andrew B. Lieutenant Colonel, 2nd Maine Cavalry, March 23, 1865 (Evergreen, Ala.).

Stacey, Charles. Private, 55th Ohio Infantry, July 2, 1863 (Gettysburg).

Stahel, Julius. Major General, U.S. Volunteers, June 5, 1864 (Piedmont, Va.).

Stanley, David S. Major General, U.S. Volunteers, November 30, 1864 (Franklin, Tenn.).

Stanley, William A. Shell Man, U.S. Navy, August 5, 1864 (on board USS *Hartford*, Mobile Bay).

Starkins, John H. Sergeant, 34th New York Battery, November 16, 1863 (Campbell Station, Tenn.).

Steele, John W. Major and Aide-de-camp, U.S. Volunteers, November 29, 1864 (Spring Hill, Tenn.).

Steinmetz, William G. Private, 83rd Indiana Infantry, May 22, 1863 (Vicksburg).

Stephens, William G. Private, Chicago Mercantile Battery, Illinois Light Artillery, May 22, 1863 (Vicksburg).

Sterling, James E. Coal Heaver, U.S. Navy, August 5, 1864 (on board USS *Brooklyn*, Mobile Bay).

Sterling, John T. Private, 11th Indiana Infantry, September 19, 1864 (Winchester, Va.).

Stevens, Daniel D. Quartermaster, U.S. Navy, January 13, 1865 (on board USS *Canonicus*, vic. Fort Fisher, N.C.).

Stevens, Hazard. Captain and Assistant Adjutant General, U.S. Volunteers, April 19, 1863 (Fort Huger, Va.).

Stewart, George W. 1st Sergeant, 1st New Jersey Cavalry, April 5, 1865 (Paines Crossroads, Va.).

Stewart, Joseph. Private, 1st Maryland Infantry, April 1, 1865 (Five Forks, Va.).

Stickels, Joseph. Sergeant, 83rd Ohio Infantry, April 9, 1865 (Fort Blakely, Ala.).

Stockman, George H. 1st Lieutenant, 6th Missouri Infantry, May 22, 1863 (Vicksburg).

Stoddard, James. Seaman, U.S. Navy, March 5, 1864 (attached to USS *Marmora*, vic. Yazoo City, Miss.).

Stokes, George. Private, 122nd Illinois Infantry, December 16, 1864 (Nashville).

Stolz, Frank. Private, 83rd Indiana Infantry, May 22, 1863 (Vicksburg).

Storey, John H.R. Sergeant, 109th Pennsylvania Infantry, May 28, 1864 (Dallas, Ga.).

Stout, Richard. Landsman, U.S. Navy, January 30, 1863 (on board USS *Isaac Smith*, Stono River).

Strahan, Robert. Captain of the Top, U.S. Navy, June 19, 1864 (on board USS *Kearsarge*, vic. France).

Strausbaugh, Bernard A. 1st Sergeant, 3rd Maryland Infantry, June 17, 1864 (Petersburg).

Streile, Christian. Private, 1st New Jersey Cavalry, April 5, 1865 (Paines Crossroads, Va.).

Strong, James N. Sergeant, 49th Massachusetts Infantry, May 27, 1863 (Port Hudson, La.).

Sturgeon, James K. Private, 46th Ohio Infantry, June 15, 1864 (Kennesaw Mountain, Ga.).

Sullivan, James. Ordinary Seaman, U.S. Navy, December 2, 1864 (on board USS *Agawam* against Fort Fisher, N.C.).

Sullivan, John. Seaman, U.S. Navy, June 23-25, 1864 (on board USS *Monticello*, vic. Wilmington, N.C.).

Sullivan, Timothy. *Coxswain*, U.S. Navy, various actions of the USS *Louisville*, citation issued April 3, 1863.

Summers, James C. Private, 4th West Virginia Infantry, May 22, 1863 (Vicksburg).

Summers, Robert. Chief Quartermaster, U.S. Navy, January 13-15, 1865 (on board USS *Ticonderoga* against Fort Fisher, N.C.).

Surles, William H. Private, 2nd Ohio Infantry, October 8, 1862 (Perryville, Ky.)

Swan, Charles A. Private, 4th Iowa Cavalry, April 2, 1865 (Selma, Alabama).

Swanson, John. Seaman, U.S. Navy, January 15, 1865 (on board USS *Santiago de Cuba* against Fort Fisher, N.C.).

Swap, Jacob E. Private, 83rd Pennsylvania Infantry, May 5, 1864 (Wilderness, Va.).

Swatton, Edward. Seaman, U.S. Navy, January 15, 1865 (on board USS *Santiago de Cuba*, during assault against Fort Fisher, N.C.).

Swayne, Wager. Lieutenant Colonel, 43rd Ohio Infantry, October 4, 1862 (Corinth, Miss.).

Swearer, Benjamin. Seaman, U.S. Navy, August 29, 1861 (on board USS *Pawnee*, vic. Fort Clark, off Baltimore Inlet).

Sweatt, Joseph S.G. Private, 6th Massachusetts Infantry, May 15, 1863 (Carrsville, Va.).

Sweeney, James. Private, 1st Vermont Cavalry, October 19, 1864 (Cedar Creek, Va.).

Swegheimer, Jacob. Private, 54th Ohio Infantry, May 22, 1863 (Vicksburg).

Swift, Frederic W. Lieutenant Colonel, 17th Michigan Infantry, November 16, 1863 (Lenoir Station, Tenn.).

Swift, Harlan J. 2nd Lieutenant, 2nd New York Militia Regiment, July 30, 1864 (Petersburg).

Sype, Peter. Private, 47th Ohio Infantry, May 3, 1863 (Vicksburg).

Tabor, William L.S. Private, 15th New Hampshire Infantry, July 1863 (Siege of Port Hudson, La.).

Taggart, Charles A. Private, 37th Massachusetts Infantry, April 6, 1865 (Sailors Creek, Va.).

Talbott, William. Captain of the Forecastle, U.S. Navy, January 10-11, 1863 (on board USS *Louisville* during the capture of Arkansas Post).

Tallentine, James. *Quarter Gunner, U.S. Navy, October 31, 1864 (on board USS *Tacony* during capture of Plymouth, N.C.).

Tanner, Charles B. 2nd Lieutenant, 1st Delaware Infantry, September 17, 1862 (Antietam, Md.).

Taylor, Anthony. 1st Lieutenant, 15th Pennsylvania Cavalry, September 20, 1863 (Chickamauga, Ga.).

Taylor, Forrester L. Captain, 23rd New Jersey Infantry, May 3, 1863 (Chancellorsville).

Taylor, George. Armorer, U.S. Navy, August 5, 1864 (on board USS *Lackawanna*, Mobile Bay).

Taylor, Henry H. Sergeant, 45th Illinois Infantry, June 25, 1863 (Vicksburg).

Taylor, John. Seaman, U.S. Navy, September 9th 1865 (due to actions while serving on board a picket boat, vic. New York Navy Yard).

Taylor, Joseph. Private, 7th Rhode Island Infantry, August 18, 1864 (Weldon Railroad, Va.).

Taylor, Richard. Private, 18th Indiana Infantry, October 19, 1864 (Cedar Creek, Va.).

Taylor, Thomas. Coxswain, U.S. Navy, August 5, 1864 (on board USS *Metacomet*, Mobile Bay).

Taylor, William. Sergeant, Company H, and simultaneously, 2nd Lieutenant, Company M, 1st Maryland Infantry, May 23, 1862 (Front Royal, Va.).

Taylor, William G. Captain of the Forecastle, U.S. Navy, December 24-25, 1864 (on board USS *Ticonderoga*, vic. Fort Fisher, N.C.).

Terry, John D. Sergeant, 23rd Massachusetts Infantry, March 14, 1862 (New Bern, N.C.).

Thackrah, Benjamin. Private, 115th New York Infantry, April 1, 1864 (Fort Gates, Fla.).

Thatcher, Charles M. Private, 1st Michigan Sharpshooters, July 30, 1864 (Petersburg).

Thaxter, Sidney W. Major, 1st Maine Cavalry, October 27, 1864 (Hatchers Run, Va.).

Thielberg, Henry. Seaman, U.S. Navy, April 14, 1863 (on board USS *Mount Washington*, Nansemond River).

Thomas, Hampton S. Major, 1st Pennsylvania Veteran Cavalry, April 5, 1865 (Amelia Springs, Va.).

Thomas, Stephen. Colonel, 8th Vermont Infantry, October 19, 1864 (Cedar Creek, Va.).

Thompkins, George W. Corporal, 124th New York Infantry, March 25, 1865 (Petersburg).

Thompson, Allen. Private, 4th New York Heavy Artillery, April 1, 1865 (White Oak Road, Va.).

Thompson, Charles A. Sergeant, 17th Michigan Infantry, May 12, 1864 (Spotsylvania).

Thompson, Freeman C. Corporal, 116th Ohio Infantry, April 2, 1865 (Petersburg).

Thompson, Henry A. Private, U.S. Marine Corps, January 15, 1865 (on board USS *Minnesota* against Fort Fisher, N.C.).

Thompson, James. Private, 4th New York Heavy Artillery, April 1, 1865 (White Oak Road, Va.).

Thompson, James B. Sergeant, 1st Pennsylvania Rifles July 3, 1863 (Gettysburg).

Thompson, J. (James) Harry. Surgeon, U.S. Volunteers, March 14, 1862 (New Bern, N.C.).

Thompson, John. Corporal, 1st Maryland Infantry, February 6, 1865 (Hatchers Run, Va.).

Thompson, Thomas. Sergeant, 66th Ohio Infantry, May 2, 1863 (Chancellorsville, Va.).

Thompson, William. Signal Quartermaster, U.S. Navy, November 7, 1861 (on board USS *Mohican* in action against Forts Beauregard and Walker).

Thompson, William P. Sergeant, 20th Indiana Infantry, May 6, 1864 (Wilderness, Va.).

Thomson, Clifford. 1st Lieutenant, 1st New York Cavalry, May 2, 1863 (Chancellorsville).

Thorn, Walter. 2nd Lieutenant, 116th U.S. Colored Troops, January 1, 1865 (Dutch Gap Canal, Va.).

Tibbets, Andrew W. Private, 3rd Iowa Cavalry, April 16, 1865 (Columbus, Ga.).

Tilton, William. Sergeant, 7th New Hampshire Infantry, awarded for services (gallantry) rendered during the Richmond Campaign of 1864.

Tinkham, Eugene M. Corporal, 148th New York Infantry, June 3, 1864 (Cold Harbor, Va.).

Titus, Charles. Sergeant, 1st New Jersey Cavalry, April 6, 1865 (Sailors Creek, Va.).

Toban, James W. Sergeant, 9th Michigan Cavalry, February 11, 1865 (Aiken, S.C.).

Tobie, Edward P. Sergeant Major, 1st Maine Cavalry, March 29–April 9, 1865 (Appomattox Campaign, Va.).

Tobin, John M. 1st Lieutenant and Adjutant, 9th Massachusetts Infantry, July 1, 1862 (Malvern Hill, Va.).

Todd, Samuel. Quartermaster, U.S. Navy, August 5, 1864 (on board USS *Brooklyn*, Mobile Bay).

Toffey, John J. 1st Lieutenant, 33rd New Jersey Infantry, November 23, 1863 (Chattanooga, Tenn.).

Tomlin, Andrew J. Corporal, U.S. Marine Corps, January 15, 1865 (on board USS *Wabash* against Fort Fisher, N.C.).

Tompkins, Aaron B. Sergeant, 1st New Jersey Cavalry, April 5, 1865 (Sailors Creek, Va.).

Tompkins, Charles H. 1st Lieutenant, 2nd U.S. Cavalry, June 1, 1861 (Fairfax, Va.).

Toohey, Thomas. Sergeant, 24th Wisconsin Infantry, November 30, 1864 (Franklin, Tenn.).

Toomer, William. Sergeant, 127th Illinois Infantry, May 22, 1863 (Vicksburg).

Torgler, Ernst. Sergeant, 37th Ohio Infantry, July 28, 1864 (Ezra Chapel, Ga.).

Tozier, Andrew J. Sergeant, 20th Maine Infantry, July 2, 1863 (Gettysburg).

Tracy, Amasa A. Lieutenant Colonel, 2nd Vermont Infantry, October 19, 1864 (Cedar Creek, Va.).

Tracy, Benjamin F. Colonel, 109th New York Infantry, May 6, 1864 (Wilderness, Va.).

Tracy, Charles H. Sergeant, 37th Massachusetts Infantry, May 12, 1864 (Spotsylvania).

Tracy, William G. 2nd Lieutenant, 122nd New York Infantry, May 2, 1863 (Chancellorsville).

Traynor, Andrew. Corporal, 1st Michigan Cavalry, March 16, 1864 (Masons Hill, Va.).

Treat, Howell B. Sergeant, 52nd Ohio Infantry, May 11, 1864 (Buzzard's Roost, Va.).

Tremain, Henry E. Major and Aide-de-camp, U.S. Volunteers, May 15, 1864 (Resaca, Ga.).

Tribe, John. Private, 5th New York Cavalry, August 25, 1862 (Waterloo Bridge, Va.).

Tripp, Othniel. Chief Boatswain's Mate, U.S. Navy, January 15, 1865 (on board USS *Seneca* against Fort Fisher, N.C.).

Trogden, Howell G. Private, 8th Missouri Infantry, May 22, 1863 (Vicksburg).

Truell, Edwin M. Private, 12th Wisconsin Infantry, July 21, 1864 (Atlanta, Ga.).

Truett, Alexander H. Coxswain, U.S. Navy, August 5, 1864 (on board USS *Richmond*, Mobile Bay).

Tucker, Allen. Sergeant, 10th Connecticut Infantry, April 2, 1865 (Petersburg).

Tucker, Jacob R. Corporal, 4th Maryland Infantry, April 1st 1865 (Petersburg).

Theedale, John. Private, 15th Pennsylvania Cavalry, December 31, 1862–January 1, 1863 (Stone River, Murfreesboro, Tenn.).

Thrombly, Voltaire P. Corporal, 2nd Iowa Infantry, February 15, 1862 (Fort Donelson, Tenn.).

Tyrrell, George William. Corporal, 5th Ohio Infantry, May 14, 1864 (Resaca, Ga.).

Uhrl, George. Sergeant, 5th U.S. Artillery, June 30, 1862 (White Oak Swamp Bridge, Va.).

Urell, M. Emmett. Private, 82nd New York Infantry, October 14, 1863 (Bristoe Station, Va.).

Vale, John. Private, 2nd Minnesota Infantry, February 15, 1863 (Nolensville, Tenn.).

Vance, Wilson. Private, 21st Ohio Infantry, December 31, 1862 (Stone River Murfreesboro, Tenn.).

Vanderslice, John M. Private, 8th Pennsylvania Cavalry, February 6, 1865 (Hatchers Run, Va.).

Van Matre, Joseph. Private, 116th Ohio Infantry, April 2, 1865 (Petersburg, Va.).

Vantine, Joseph E. 1st Class Fireman, U.S. Navy, March 14, 1863 (on board USS *Richmond*, vic. Port Hudson, La.).

Van Winkle, Edward (Edwin). Corporal, 148th New York Infantry, September 29, 1864 (Chapins Farm, Va.).

Vaughn, Pinkerton R. Sergeant, U.S. Marine Corps, March 14, 1863 (on board USS *Mississippi*, vic. Port Hudson, La.).

Veal, Charles. Private, 4th U.S. Colored Troops, September 29, 1864 (Chapins Farm, Va.).

Veal, Moses. Captain, 109th Pennsylvania Infantry, October 28, 1863 (Wauhatchie, Tenn.).

Veazey, Wheelock G. Colonel, 16th Vermont Infantry, July 3, 1863 (Gettysburg).

Vernay, James D. 2nd Lieutenant 11th Illinois Infantry, April 22, 1863 (Vicksburg).

Verney, James W. Chief Quartermaster, U.S. Navy, December 24, 1864, and February 22, 1865 (on board USS *Pontoosuc* against Fort Fisher and Wilmington, N.C.).

Vifquain, Victor. Lieutenant Colonel, 97th Illinois Infantry, April 9, 1865 (Fort Blakely, Ala.).

Von Vegesack, Ernest. Major and Aide-de-camp, U.S. Volunteers, June 27, 1862 (Gaines Mills, Va.).

Wageman, John H. Private, 60th Ohio Infantry, June 17, 1864 (Petersburg).

Wagg, Maurice. Coxswain, U.S. Navy, December 31, 1862 (on board USS *Rhode Island*, vic. Cape Hatteras).

Wagner, John W. Corporal, 8th Missouri Infantry, May 22, 1863 (Vicksburg).

Wainwright, John. 1st Lieutenant, 97th Pennsylvania, January 15, 1865 (Fort Fisher).

Walker, James C. Private, 31st Ohio Infantry, November 25, 1863 (Missionary Ridge, Tenn.).

Walker, Mary E., M.D. Dr. Walker's award for various contributions during the war was rescinded by the Board of Medal Awards by an act of June 3, 1916, along with 910 other recipients as unwarranted. On June 10, 1977, Army Secretary Clifford L Alexander, Jr. approved the recommendation by the Army Board for correction and restored the official citation as signed by President Andrew Johnson on November 11, 1865.

Wall, Jerry. Private, 126th New York Infantry, July 3, 1863 (Gettysburg).

Waller, Francis A. Corporal, 6th Wisconsin Infantry, July 1, 1863 (Gettysburg).

Walling, William H. Captain, 142nd New York Infantry, December 25, 1864 (Fort Fisher, N.C.).

Walsh, John. Corporal, 5th New York Cavalry, October 19, 1864 (Cedar Creek, Va.).

Walton, George W. Private, 97th Pennsylvania Infantry, August 29, 1864 (Petersburg).

Wambsgan, Martin. Private, 90th New York Infantry, October 19, 1864 (Cedar Creek, Va.).

Ward, James. Quarter Gunner, U.S. Navy, August 5, 1864 (on board USS *Lackawanna*, Mobile Bay).

Ward, Nelson W. Private, 11th Pennsylvania Cavalry, June 25, 1864 (Staunton River Bridge, Va.).

Ward, Thomas J. Private, 116th Illinois Infantry, May 22, 1863 (Vicksburg).

Ward, William H. Captain, 47th Ohio Infantry, May 3, 1863 (Vicksburg).

Warden, John. Corporal, 55th Illinois Infantry, May 22, 1863 (Vicksburg).

Warfel, Henry C. Private, 1st Pennsylvania Cavalry, April 5, 1865 (Paines Crossroads, Va.).

Warren, David. Coxswain U.S. Navy, June 23-25, 1864 (on board USS *Monticello*, vic. Wilmington, N.C.).

Warren, Francis E. Corporal, 49th Massachusetts Infantry, May 27, 1863 (Port Hudson, La.).

Webb, Alexander S. Brigadier General, U.S. Volunteers, July 3, 1863 (Gettysburg).

Webb, James. Private, 5th New York Infantry, August 30, 1862 (Bull Run, Va.).

Webber, Alason P. Musician, 86th Illinois Infantry, June 27, 1864 (Kennesaw Mountain, Ga.).

Webster, Henry S. Landsman, U.S. Navy, January 15, 1865 (on board USS *Susquehanna* against Fort Fisher).

Weeks, Charles H. Captain of the Foretop, U.S. Navy, September 21, 1864 (on board USS *Montauk*).

Weeks, John H. Private, 152nd New York Infantry, May 12, 1864 (Spotsylvania).

Weir, Henry C. Captain and Assistant Adjutant General, U.S. Volunteers, June 24, 1864 (St. Mary's Church, Va.).

Welch, George W. Private, 11th Missouri Infantry, December 16, 1864 (Nashville).

Welch, Richard. Corporal, 37th Massachusetts Infantry, April 2, 1865 (Petersburg).

Welch, Stephen. Sergeant, 154th New York Infantry, May 8, 1864 (Dug Gap, Ga.).

Wells, Henry S. *September 29, 1864 (Chapins Farm).

Wells, Thomas M. Chief Bugler, 6th New York Cavalry, October 19, 1864 (Cedar Creek, Va.).

Wells, William. Major, 1st Vermont Cavalry, July 3, 1863 (Gettysburg).

Wells, William. Quartermaster, U.S. Navy, August 5, 1864 (on board USS *Richmond*, Mobile Bay).

Welsh, Edward. Private, 54th Ohio Infantry, May 22, 1863 (Vicksburg).

Welsh, James. Private, 4th Rhode Island Infantry, July 30, 1864 (Petersburg).

Westerhold, William. Sergeant, 52nd New York Infantry, May 12, 1864 (Spotsylvania).

Weston, John F. Major, 4th Kentucky Cavalry, April 13, 1865 (vicinity Wetumpka, Ala.).

Wheaton, Loyd. Lieutenant Colonel, 8th Illinois Infantry, April 9, 1865 (Fort Blakely, Ala.).

Wheeler, Daniel D. 1st Lieutenant, 4th Vermont Infantry, May 3, 1863 (Salem Heights, Va.).

Wheeler, Henry W. Private, 2nd Maine Infantry, July 21, 1861 (Bull Run, Va.).

Wherry, William M. 1st Lieutenant, 3rd U.S. Reserve, Missouri Infantry, August 10, 1861 (Wilson's Creek, Mo.).

Whitaker, Edward W. Captain, 1st Connecticut Cavalry, June 29, 1864 (Reams Station, Va.).

White, Adam. Corporal, 11th West Virginia Infantry, April 2, 1865 (Hatchers Run, Va.).

White, J. Henry. Private, 90th Pennsylvania Infantry, August 23, 1862 (Rappahannock Station, Va.).

White, Joseph. Captain of the Gun, U.S. Navy,

December 24-25, 1864, and January 13-15, 1865 (on board USS *New Ironsides* against Fort Fisher, N.C.).

White, Patrick H. Captain, Chicago Mercantile Battery, Illinois Light Artillery, May 22, 1863 (Vicksburg).

Whitehead, John M. Chaplain, 15th Indiana Infantry, December 31, 1862 (Murfreesboro, Stones River, Tenn.).

Whitfield, Daniel. Quartermaster, U.S. Navy, August 5, 1864 (on board USS *Lackawanna*, Mobile Bay).

Whitman, Frank M. Private, 35th Massachusetts Infantry, September 17, 1862 (Antietam, Md.).

Whitmore, John. Private, 119th Illinois Infantry, April 9, 1865 (Fort Blakely, Ala.).

Whitney, William G. Sergeant, 11th Michigan Infantry, September 20, 1863 (Chickamauga, Ga.).

Whittier, Edward N. 1st Lieutenant, 5th Battery, Maine Light Artillery, September 22, 1864 (Fisher's Hill, Va.).

Widick, Andrew J. Private, 116th Illinois Infantry, May 22, 1863 (Vicksburg).

Wilcox, Franklin L. Ordinary Seaman, U.S. Navy, January 15, 1865 (on board USS *Minnesota* against Fort Fisher).

Wilcox, William H. Sergeant, 9th New Hampshire Infantry, May 12, 1864 (Spotsylvania).

Wiley, James. Sergeant, 59th New York Infantry, July 3, 1863 (Gettysburg).

Wilhelm, George Captain, 56th Ohio Infantry, May 16, 1863 (Champion Hill or Baker's Creek, Miss.).

Wilkes, Henry. Landsman, U.S. Navy, October 27, 1864 (on board U.S. Picket Boat No. 1 in action against Confederate vessel *Albemarle*).

Wilkes, Perry. Pilot, U.S. Navy, May 5, 1864 (on board USS *Signal* during Red River Campaign).

Wilkins, Leander A. Sergeant, 9th New Hampshire Infantry, July 30, 1864 (Petersburg).

Willcox, Orlando B. Colonel, 1st Michigan Infantry, July 21, 1861 (Bull Run, Va.).

Williams, Anthony. Sailmaker's Mate, U.S. Navy, December 24, 1864, and February 22, 1865 (on board USS *Pontoosuc* against Fort Fisher and Wilmington, N.C.).

Williams, Augustus. Seaman, U.S. Navy, January 15, 1865 (on board USS *Santiago de Cuba* against Fort Fisher, N.C.).

Williams, Elwood N. Private, 28th Illinois Infantry, April 6, 1862 (Shiloh, Tenn.).

Williams, George C. Quartermaster Sergeant, 1st Battalion, 14th U.S. Infantry, June 27, 1862 (Gaines Mills, Va.).

Williams, John. Boatswain's Mate, U.S. Navy, November 7, 1861 (on board USS *Mohican* against Forts Beauregard and Walker).

Williams, John. Captain of the Maintop, U.S. Navy, June 26, 1861 (on board USS *Pawnee*, vicinity Mathias Point, Va.).

Williams, John. Seaman, U.S. Navy, October 3, 1862 (on board USS *Commodore Perry*, vic. Franklin, Va. against Rebel positions along Blackwater River.).

Williams, Le Roy. Sergeant, 8th New York Heavy Artillery, June 3, 1864 (Cold Harbor, Va.).

Williams, Peter. Seaman, March 9, 1862 (on board USS *Monitor*, vic. Hampton Roads, Va.).

Williams, Robert. Signal Quartermaster, December 23-27, 1862 (on board USS *Benton*, Yazoo River Expedition, including Drumgould's Bluff, on the 27th.).

Williams, William. Landsman, U.S. Navy, November 16, 1863 (on board USS *Lehigh*, vic. Charleston Harbor.).

Williams, William H. Private, 82nd Ohio Infantry, July 20, 1864 (Peach Tree Creek, Ga.).

Williamson, James A. Colonel, 4th Iowa Infantry, December 29, 1862 (Chickasaw Bayou, Miss.).

Willis, Richard. Coxswain, U.S. Navy, December 24-25 1864, and January 13-15, 1865 (on board USS *New Ironsides*, Fort Fisher, N.C.).

Williston, Edward B. 1st Lieutenant, 2nd U.S. Artillery, June 12, 1864 (Trevilian Station, Va.).

Wilson, Charles E. Sergeant, 1st New Jersey Cavalry, April 6, 1865 (Sailors Creek, Va.).

Wilson, Christopher. W. Private, 73rd New York Infantry, May 12, 1864 (Spotsylvania).

Wilson, Francis A. Corporal, 95th Pennsylvania Infantry, April 2, 1865 (Petersburg).

Wilson, John. Sergeant, 1st New Jersey Cavalry, March 31, 1865 (Chamberlain's Creek, Va.).

Wilson, John A. Private, 21st Ohio Infantry, April 1862 (Big Shanty, Ga.).

Wilson, John M. 1st Lieutenant, U.S. Engineers, August 6, 1862 (Malvern Hill, Va.).

Winegar, William W. Lieutenant, 19th New York Cavalry (1st New York Dragoons), April 1, 1865 (Five Forks, Va.).

Wisner, Lewis S. 1st Lieutenant, 124th New York Infantry, May 12, 1864 (Spotsylvania).

Withington, William H. Captain, 1st Michigan Infantry, July 21, 1861 (Bull Run).

Wollam, John. Private, 33rd Ohio Infantry, April 1862 (Big Shanty, Georgia).

Wood, H. Clay. 1st Lieutenant, 11th U.S. Infantry, August 10, 1861 (Wilson's Creek, Va.).

Wood, Mark. Private, 21st Ohio Infantry, April 1862 (Big Shanty, Ga.).

Wood, Richard H. 97th Illinois Infantry, May 22, 1863 (Vicksburg).

Wood, Robert B. Coxswain, U.S. Navy, April 14, 1863 (attached to USS *Minnesota*, but temporarily serving on USS *Mount Washington*, vic. Nansemond River).

Woodbury, Eri D. Sergeant, 1st Vermont Cavalry, October 19, 1864 (Cedar Creek).

Woodruff, Alonzo. Sergeant, 1st U.S. Sharpshooters, October 27, 1864 (Hatchers Run, Va.).

Woodruff, Carle A. 1st Lieutenant, 2nd U.S. Artillery, July 24, 1863 (Newby's Crossroads, Va.).

Woods, Daniel A. Private, 1st Virginia Cavalry, April 6, 1865 (Sailors Creek, Va.).

Woods, Samuel. Seaman, U.S. Navy, April 14, 1863 (on board USS *Mount Washington*, vic. Nansemond River).

Woodward, Evan M. 1st Lieutenant and Adjutant, 2nd Pennsylvania Reserve Infantry, December 13, 1862 (Fredericksburg).

Woon, John. Boatswain's Mate, U.S. Navy, April 29, 1863 (on board USS *Pittsburg*, vic. Mississippi River, Grand Gulf).

Woram, Charles B. Seaman, U.S. Navy, August 5, 1864 (on board USS *Oneida*, Mobile Bay).

Wortick (Wertick), Joseph. Private, 8th Missouri Infantry, May 22, 1863 (Vicksburg).

Wray, William J. Sergeant, 1st Veteran Reserve Corps, July 12, 1864 (Fort Stevens, D.C.).

Wright, Albert D. Captain, 43rd U.S. Colored Troops, July 30, 1864 (Petersburg).

Wright, Edward. Quartermaster, U.S. Navy, April 24-25, 1862 (on board USS *Cayuga* against Forts Jackson and St. Philip).

Wright, Robert. Private, 14th U.S. Infantry, October 1, 1864 (Chapel House Farm, Va.).

Wright, Samuel. Corporal, 2nd Minnesota Infantry, February 15, 1863 (Nolensville, Tenn.).

Wright, Samuel C. Private, 29th Massachusetts Infantry, September 17, 1862 (Antietam, Md.).

Wright, William. U.S. Navy, Yeoman June 23-25, 1864 (on board USS *Monticello*, vic. Wilmington, N.C.).

Yeager, Jacob F. Private, 101st Ohio Infantry, May 11, 1864 (Buzzard's Roost, Ga.).

Young, Andrew J. Sergeant, 1st Pennsylvania Cavalry, April 5, 1865 (Paines Crossroads, Va.).

Young, Benjamin F. Corporal, 1st Michigan Sharpshooters June 17, 1864 (Petersburg).

Young, Calvary M. Sergeant, 3rd Iowa Cavalry, October 25, 1864 (Osage, Kansas).

Young, Edward B. Coxswain, U.S. Navy, August 5, 1864 (Mobile Bay, on board USS *Galena*).

Young, Horatio N. Seaman, U.S. Navy, November 16, 1863 (on board USS *Lehigh*, Charleston Harbor).

Young, James M. Private, 72nd New York Infantry, May 6, 1864 (Wilderness, Va.).

Young, William. Boatswain's Mate, April 24-25, 1862 (on board USS *Cayuga* against Forts Jackson and St. Philip).

Younker, John L. Private, 12th U.S. Infantry, August 9, 1862 (Cedar Mountain Va.).

Bibliography

Abbott, John S.C. *Lives of the Presidents*. B. B. Russell, 1870.

____, William Garnett, W.W. Birdsall, and Fletcher Johnson. *Beacon Lights of American History*. Philadelphia: Crescent, 1896.

Abraham Lincoln: Complete Works. Edited by John G. Nicolay and John Hay, Volume Two. Century Company, 1920.

An Alphabetical List of the Battles of the War of the Rebellion. Compiled from Official Records of the Adjutant General and the Surgeon-General, U.S.A. Revised by Newton A. Strait. J. H. Soule, 1878.

American Military History (Diary of the U.S. Army colonial times through the 1980s). Revised. Washington, D.C.: Government Printing Office, 1969.

Anderson, Charles C. *Fighting By Southern Federals*. Neale, 1912.

Andrews, E. Benjamin. *History of the United States*. New York: Scribner's, 1905.

Annual Report of the American Historical Society, Volume II. 1916.

Baker, Samuel T. *Fort Sumter and Its Defenders*. Charles Wells Moulton, 1891.

Bancroft, Frederick. *The Life of William H. Seward*. Harper and Brothers, 1900.

Barton, George. *Angels of the Battlefield*. Catholic Art Publishing, 1897.

Batchellor, Albert Stillman. *Military Annals of New Hampshire*. Rumford Press, 1898.

Bates, Samuel P. *History of Pennsylvania Volunteers (1861–65)*, Volume 5. B. Singerly, State Printer. 1871.

Battine, Cecil. *The Crisis of the Confederacy*. Longmans, Green, 1905.

Battle, J.H., W.H. Perrin, and G.C. Kniffin. *Kentucky: A History of the State*. N.P. Hardin, 1885.

Battlefields of the South: Bull Run to Fredericksburg. New York: John Bradburn, 1864.

Battles and Leaders of the Civil War. Four Volumes. Century Company, 1888.

Bevier, R.S. *History of the First and Second Missouri Confederate Brigades (1861–1865)*. Bryan Brand, 1879.

Biographical Register of the Officers and Graduates of the U.S. Military Academy. 2 Volumes. Houghton Mifflin, 1891.

Biography of Lt. Colonel Julius P. Garesche, Assistant Adjutant General, U.S. Army. J. Lippincott, 1887.

Bosson, Charles P. *History of the Forty-second Massachusetts Regiment: Infantry, 1862–1864*. Mills, Knight and Co., 1886.

Boyd, James P. *The Life of William T. Sherman*. Publishers Union, 1891.

Boynton, H.V. *Sherman's Historical Raid*. Wilstach, Baldwin and Co., 1875

Brackett, Albert B. *History of the United States Cavalry*. Harper and Brothers, 1885,

Brockett, L.P., and Mary C. Vaughan. *Woman's Work in the Civil War*. Philadelphia, Chicago and Cincinnati: Zeigler, McCurdy and Co.; and Boston: R.H. Cochran, 1867.

Brown, Henry Clinton. *Handbook of Dates*. A. Lovell and Co., 1883.

Brown, John Howard (ed.). *Lamb's Biographical Dictionary of the United States*. James H. Lamb Co., 1900

Burr, Fearing, and George Lincoln. *The Town of Hingham in the Late Civil War*. Published by the town, 1876.

Butler, Benjamin Franklin. *Autobiography and Personal Reminisces of Major General Benjamin F. Butler*. A.M. Thayer and Co., 1892.

Carnahan, J. Worth. *Excerpts from Manual of the Civil War and Key to the Grand Army of the Republic and Kindred Societies*. Washington, D.C.: 1897. Reprinted as *Authentic Civil War Battle Sites*. E.S. "Rocky" LeGaye, ed. Western Heritage Press, 1978.

Casey, Powell A.; *Encyclopedia of Forts, Posts, Named Camps, and Other Military Installations in Louisiana*. Baton Rouge, La.: Claitor's.

The Century Illustrated, Vol. 38 (May–October 1889).

Chadwick, French Ensor. *The American Nation: A History*. Volume 19. Harper and Brothers, 1906.

Clark, Charles M. *The History of the Thirty-Ninth Regiment Illinois Volunteer Veteran Infantry in the War of the Rebellion, 1861–1865*. Veterans Association of the Regiment, 1880.

Cooke, John Esten. *Life of Gen. Robert E. Lee*. D. Appleton and Co., 1871.

Coffin, Charles Carleton. *The Boys of '61: Or, Four Years of Fighting*. Estes and Lauriat, 1881.

____. *Drum-Beat of the Nation: The First Period of the War the Rebellion from Its Outbreak to the Close of 1862*. New York and London: Harper and Brothers, 1887.

____. *Marching to Victory*. Harper and Brothers, 1916.

Collum, Richard S. *History of the United States Marine Corps*. L.R. Mammersly, 1890 and 1903.

Confederate Military History, Vols. 1–7, 11, and 12. Confederate Publishing Company, Atlanta. 1899

Cox, James. *My Native Land*. St. Louis: Blair, 1895.

Crawford, Samuel Wylie. *The Genesis of the Civil War*. Charles L. Webster and Co., 1887.

Davenport, Charles Benedict. *Naval Officers: Their Heredity and Development*. Carnegie Institution of Washington, 1919.

Davis, Washington. *Campfire Chats of the Civil War*. Lewis Publishing Co., 1888.

Defense of Commodore Charles Wilkes. Washington, McGill and Witherow, 1864.

Denison, Frederick. *Sabres and Spurs: First Rhode Island Cavalry in the Civil War*. First Rhode Island Veterans Association, 1876.

Drake, Edwin. L. *Chronological Summary of the Battles and Engagements of the Western Armies of the Confederate States*. 1879.

Dwight, Theodore. *Critical Sketches of Some of the Federal and Confederate Commanders*. Military Historical Society. Houghton, Mifflin and Co., 1895.

Dyer, Frederick H. *A Compendium of the War of the Rebellion Compiled and Arranged from Official Records of the Federal and Confederate Armies, Reports of he Adjutant Generals of the Several States, the Army Registers, and Other Reliable Documents and Sources*. Des Moines, Iowa: Dyer Publishing, 1908.

Early, Jubal A. *A Memoir of the Last Year of the War for Independence in the Confederate States of America*. New Orleans, 1867.

Elias, Edith L. *Abraham Lincoln*. London: George G. Harrap and Co., 1916.

Ellsworth, Harry A. *One Hundred Eighty Landings of U.S. Marines, 1800–1934*. Washington, D.C.: Historical Section, United States Marine Corps.

Emerson, Edwin, Jr. *A History of the Nineteenth Century, Year by Year*. P.F. Collier and Son, 1901.

Encyclopedia of Virginia Biography. Vol. 3. Lewis Historical Publishing Co., 1915.

Fast, Richard Ellsworth. *The History and Government of West Virginia*. Acme Publishing Co., 1901.

Faust, Albert Bernhardt. *The German Element in the United States*. Vol. 1. Houghton Mifflin Co., 1909.

Fitch, Michael Hendrick. *The Chattanooga Campaign*. Wisconsin History Commission, 1911.

Floyd, David Bittle. *History of the Seventy-fifth Regiment of Indiana Infantry Volunteers, 1862–1865*. Lutheran Publication Society, 1893.

Forney, John W. *Winfield Scott Hancock's Life and Career*. J.P. McCauley and Co., 1880.

Fout, Frederick W. *The Dark Days of the Civil War*. F.A. Wagenfuehr, 1904.

Frost, Jennett Blakeslee. *The Rebellion in the United States: Or, The War of 1861*. Vol. 2. Hartford, 1863.

Garrett, William Robertson. *The History of North America, Volume 14: The Civil War from a Southern Standpoint*. Philadelphia: George Barrie and Sons, 1905.

General Orders of the War Department: 1861, 1862, 1863, Vols. 1 and 2. Derby and Miller, 1864.

Goldsborough, W.W. *The Maryland Line in the Confederate Army*. Published under authority of the Board of Governors, Association of Maryland Line, 1900.

Gordon, George H. *Brook Farm to Cedar Mountain*. Houghton Mifflin, 1885.

_____. *History of the Campaign of the Army of Virginia, Under John Pope, from Cedar Mountain to Alexandria*. Houghton, Osgood and Co., 1880

Gordon, John B. *Reminiscences of the Civil War*. Charles Scribner's Sons, 1903.

Gould, John M. *History of the First, Tenth, and Twentieth-ninth Maine Regiment*. Stephen Berry, 1871.

Grant, Ulysses S. *Personal Memoirs of U.S. Grant*. 2 vols. Charles L. Webster and Co., New York, 1886.

Hale, Will T., and Dixon L. Merritt. *A History of Tennessee and Tennesseans*, Volume 6, 1913.

Hamersly, Lewis R. *Naval Operations During the Rebellion of 1861–65*. Publication date unknown.

_____. *The Records of Living Officers of the United States Navy and Marine Corps*. J. B. Lippincott and Co., 1870.

Hancock's Diary: A History of the Second Tennessee Confederate Cavalry. Brandon Printing Co., 1887.

Hannaford, E. *A History of the Campaigns and Associations in the Field of the Sixth Regiment Ohio Volunteer Infantry*. Self-published, 1868.

Hannings, Bud. *Forts of the United States*. McFarland and Co., 2006.

_____. *Portrait of the Stars and Stripes*. Glenside, Pa.: Seniram, 1989.

Harper's Pictoral History of the Civil War. 2 vols. Copyright 1884.

Hart, Bushnell Albert. *American History Told by Contemporaries: Vol. 4, Welding of the Nation 1845–1903*. McMillan Company, 1918.

Hawthorne, Julian. *The History of the United States, 1492–1910*. New York: P.F. Collier, 1910.

Head, Thomas. *History of the 16th Tennessee Regiment*. Cumberland Presbyterian Publishing House, 1885.

Headley, J.T. *Farragut and Our Naval Commanders, 1861–1865*. New York: E.B. Treat; Chicago, R.C. Treat, 1880.

Heitman, Francis B. *Historical Register of the U.S. Army*, Vol. 2. 1903.

Henty, G.A. *With Lee in Virginia*. A.L. Burt, no date.

Hicken, Victor. "Illinois Camps, Posts, and Prisons." *Illinois Civil War Sketches*, No. 9. Published by Illinois State Historical Library for the Civil War Centennial Commission of Illinois.

Hill, Luther B. *A History of the State of Oklahoma*. Lewis Publishing Co., 1910.

Hinsdale, Mary L. *A History of the President's Cabinet*. Ann Arbor, Mich.: George Wahr, 1911.

Historical Register and Dictionary of the United States Army: From Its Organization, September 29, 1789 to March 2, 1903. Government Printing Office, 1903.

History of the Michigan Organizations at Chickamauga, Chattanooga and Missionary Ridge. Authorized by the Legislature. Robert Smith, 1899.

History of New Mexico. Vol. 1. Pacific States Publishing Co., 1907.

History of the 125th Pennsylvania Regiment, 1862–1863. J. B. Lippincott, 1906.

History of the Third Pennsylvania Cavalry, 1861–1865. Third Pennsylvania Cavalry Association. Franklin Printing Co., 1905.

History of the Twenty-third Pennsylvania Volunteer Infantry (Birney's Zouaves). Survivors Association, 23rd Pennsylvania Infantry, 1903.

Hittell, Theodore H. *History of California*. Vol. 4. N.J. Stone and Co., 1898.

Hoppin, James Mason. *Life of Andrew Hull Foote*. New York: Harper and Brothers, 1874.

Hosmer, James Kendall. *The American Civil War*. Harper and Brothers, 1913.

Houck, L. *A Missouri History*. Chicago: Donnelley and Son, 1908.

Howe, Daniel Wait. *Civil War Times, 1861–1865*. Bowen Merrill Co., 1902.

Howells, William D. *Sketch of the Life and Character of Rutherford B. Hayes*. Hurd and Houghton, 1876.

Ingersoll, L.D. *History of the War Department of the United States*. Francis B. Mohun, 1879.

Johnson, H.A. *The Sword of Honor*. Blanchard Press, publication date unknown.

Johnson, Rossiter. *Campfire and Battlefield: History of Conflicts and Campaigns*, New York: John Williams, 1894.

_____. *A Short History of the War of Secession (1861–1865)*. Houghton, Mifflin and Co., 1889.

Jones, Samuel. *The Siege of Charleston*. Neale, 1911.

Journal of the Congress of the Confederate States of America, 1861–1865. Vol. 1. Government Printing office, 1904.

Kellogg, Sanford C. The Shenandoah Valley and Virginia, 1861–1865. Neale, 1903.

Knight, Lucian Lamar. *Georgia's Landmarks, Memorials and Legends*. Vol. 2. Byrd Printing Co. (State Printers), 1914.

Lang, Theodore F. *Loyal West Virginia from 1861 to 1865*. Deutsch Publishing Company 1895.

Lanman, Charles. *The Red Book of Michigan*. E.B. Smith Co., 1871.

Larke, Julian K. *General Grant and His Campaigns*. J.C. Derby and N. C. Miller, 1864.

Lee, Captain Robert E. (Gen. Robert E. Lee's son). *Recollections and Letters of General Robert E. Lee*. Doubleday Page and Co., 1904.

Lee, Robert E. (General). *Wartime Papers of Robert E. Lee*. Copyright, Commonwealth of Virginia, 1941.

Lewis, Virgil A. *History of West Virginia*. Hubbard Brothers, 1889.

List of Field Officers, Regiments and Battalions in the Confederate States Army. J.W. Burke Co., 1912.

Livermore, William Roscoe. *Story of the Civil War*. G.P. Putnam's Sons, 1933.

Lossing, Benson J. *A History of the Civil War*. Copyrighted 1895 by Charles P. Johnson. Reprinted 1912 by the War Memorial Association, New York, 1912.

_____. *The Pictorial Field Book of the Civil War*. 3 vols. T. Belknap, 1874.

Mabie, Hamilton Wright. *A New History of the United States*. Philadelphia and Chicago: International Publishing Co., 1898.

Mackenzie, Robert. *America: A History*. Edinburgh and New York: T. Nelson and Sons, Paternoster Row, 1882.

Maine Bugle. Maine Association. 1897.

Massachusetts in the Army and Navy During the War of 1861–65. 2 vols. Wright and Potter, State Printers, 1895.

McCabe, James D., Jr. *Life and Campaigns of General Robert E. Lee*. 1867.

McClellan, George B. *The Life, Campaigns and Public Services of General McClellan*. T.B. Peterson and Brothers, 1864.

_____. *McClellan's Own Story: The War for the Union*. Charles L. Webster and Co, 1887.

McGroarty, John Steven. *Los Angeles from the Mountains to the Sea*. American Historical Society. 1921.

Meade, George. *The Life and Letters of George Gordon Meade*. Charles Scribner's Sons, 1913.

Men of West Virginia. Biographical Publishing Company, 1903.

Miller, William M., and John H. Johnston. *Chronology of the United States Marine Corps, 1775–1934*. 1970.

Minnesota in the Civil and Indian Wars, 1861–1865. Pioneer Press Club, 1891.

Missouri Historical Review. Vol. 1. State Historical Society, 1906.

Moore, Frank. *The Rebellion Record*. Multiple volumes including 7. D. Van Nostrand, 1844.

Morris, Charles. *Heroes of the Army in America*. J.B. Lippincott, 1919.

Moses, John. *Illinois Historical and Statistical*, Vol. 2. Fergus Printing Co., 1892.

Mottelay, Paul Fleury, and Thomas Campbell-Copeland, eds. *The Soldier in Our Civil War*. G.W. Carleton & Company, 1886.

Muzzey, David Saville, and John A. Krout; *American History for Colleges*. Boston: Ginn and Company, 1933.

Official Records of the Union and Confederate Navies in the War of the Rebellion. Multiple volumes, including 21 and 25. Government Printing Office, 1912.

Orton, Richard H. *Records of California Men in the War of the Rebellion*. Office of State Printing, 1890.

Phisterer, Frederick. *New York in the War of the Rebellion*. Weed, Parsons and Co., 1890.

_____. *Statistical Record of the Armies of the United States*. Charles Scribner's Sons, 1883.

Photographic History of the Civil War. 10 Vols. Review of Reviews Co., 1911.

Piatt, Don. *General George H. Thomas: A Critical Biography*. Robert Clarke, 1893.

Pierson, John S. *A Complete History of the Great Rebellion of the U.S., 1861–1865*. Quaker City Publishing House, 1875.

Pittenger, William. *The Great Locomotive Chase*. Jones and Stanley, 1887.

Pond, George E. *The Shenandoah Valley in 1864*. Charles Scribner's Sons. 1888

Porter, David D. *Incidents and Anecdotes of the Civil War*. D. Appleton and Co., 1885.

_____. *Memoir of Commodore David D. Porter*. J. Munsell, 1875.

_____. *The Naval History of the Civil War*. Sherman Publishing Co., 1886.

Porter, Robert P. *Life of William McKinley*. W.G. Hamilton, 1896.

Price, William T. *Historical Sketches of Pochahontas County, West Virginia*. Price Brothers, 1901.

Publications of the American Jewish Historical Society. No. 17, 1909.

Reed, Major D.W. *The Battle of Shiloh*. Government Printing Office, 1903.

Reid, Whitelaw. *Ohio in the War: Her Statesmen, Her Generals, and Soldiers*. 2 vols. Moore, Wilstach and Baldwin, 1868.

Report of the Secretary of the Navy. December 1865. Government Printing Office, 1865.

Reports of the Operations of the Army of Northern Virginia. 2 vols. M. Smith, Public Printers, 1864.

Reynolds, Cuyler. *Genealogical and Family History of Southern New York*. Lewis Historical Publishing Co., 1914.

Rhodes, Charles D. *History of the Cavalry of the Army of the Potomac*. Hudson-Kimberly, 1900.

Rhodes, James Ford. *History of the United States: From the Compromise of 1850 to the McKinley-Bryan Campaign of 1896*. New York and London: Harper and Brothers, 1899.

Riley, Elihu S. *Stonewall Jackson*. Annapolis, Md.: Elihu S. Riley, 1920.

Robinson, Charles. *The Kansas Conflict*. Harper and Brothers, 1892.

Rodenbough, Theophilus Francis, and William L. Haskin, eds. *Army of the United States: Historical Sketches of Staff and Line with Portraits of Generals-in-Chief*, New York: Maynard, Merrill and Co., 1896.

Ropes, John Codman. *The Army Under Pope*. Charles Scribner's Sons, 1881.

_____. *The Story of the Civil War*. 1894.

Roscoe, Theodore. *This is Your Navy*. Navy Institute Press, 1950.

Sarlento, F.L. *Life of Pauline Cushman*. Keystone, 1890.

Scharf, J. Thomas. *History of the Confederate States Navy*. Rogers and Sherwood, 1887.

Shambaugh, Benjamin F. *The Journal of History and Politics*. Vol. 15. State Historical Society of Iowa, 1917.

Shaw, William H. *History of Essex and Hudson Counties, New Jersey*. Vol. 1. Everts and Peck, 1884.

Shenandoah Valley Pioneers and their Descendants. T.K. Cartmell, 1909.

Sherman, William T. *Personal Memoirs of General W.T. Sherman*. Charles L. Webster Co., 1891.

Shoemaker, Henry W. *The Last of the War Governors*. Altoona Tribune Publishing Co., 1916.

Sketches of War History, 1861–1865, Vol. 2., Military Order of the Loyal Legion of the United States. Robert Clarke and Co., 1888.

Smith, George Gillman. *The Story of Georgia and the Georgia People*. Atlanta: Franklin Printing and Publishing, 1900.

Smith, Thomas West. *The Story of a Regiment: 11th New York Cavalry*. Veterans Association of the Regiment, Publication date unknown.

Smith, Z.F. *The History of Kentucky*. Courier-Journal Job Printing Company, 1892.

Soley, James Russell. *The Navy in the Civil War*. Sampson Low, Marston and Co., 1898.

Southern History of the War: The First Year of the War. Charles B. Richardson, 1862.

Sparks, Edwin Erle. *The United States*. New York and London: G.P. Putnam's Sons, 1904.

Spencer, J.A. *Complete History of the United States of America*. Completed by Benson J. Lossing. Philadelphia: William T. Amies, 1878.

_____; *History of the United States*. Continued to 1891 by Benson J. Lossing and continued to 1896 By John Hastings. Albany, N.Y.: James B. Lyon, New York.

Sprunt, James. *Chronicles of the Cape Fear River*. Edwards and Broughton, 1916.

Stevens, Hazard. *The Life of Isaac Ingalls Stevens*. 2 vols. Houghton, Mifflin and Co., 1900.

Stone, Edwin W. *Rhode Island in the Rebellion*. George H. Whitney, 1854.

The Story of One Regiment: 11th Maine. New York: Regimental Association, 1896.

Stribling, Robert M. *Gettysburg Campaign and Campaign of 1864–1865 in Virginia*. Franklin Press, 1905.

Sweetser, M.F. *King's Handbook of the United States*. Buffalo, N.Y.: Moses King Corp., 1891.

Swinton, William. *Campaigns of the Army of the Potomac 1861–1865*. Charles B. Richardson, 1866.

Taylor, Frank H. *Philadelphia in the Civil War*. City of Philadelphia, 1913.

Tenney, W.J. *The Military and Naval History of the Rebellion in the United States*. D. Appleton and Co., 1865.

Thwaites, Reuben Gold. *Collections of the State Historical Society of Wisconsin*. Vol. 14. Madison Democrat Printing Co., State Printer, 1898.

Todd, William. *The Seventy-ninth Highlanders in the War of the Rebellion*. Press of Brandow, Barton and Co., 1886.

Twitchell, Ralph Emerson. *The Leading Facts of New Mexican History*. Vol. III. Torch Press, 1917.

Van Horn, Thomas B. *History of the Army of the Cumberland*. Robert Clarke and Co., 1875.

Waitt, Robert W., Jr. *Confederate Military Hospitals in Richmond*. Richmond, Va.: Richmond Civil War Centennial Committee, 1964.

Walcott, Charles F. *History of the Twenty-first Regiment, Massachusetts Volunteers*. Houghton, Mifflin and Co., 1882.

Walker, Francis A. *General Hancock*. D. Appleton, 1894.

_____. *History of the Second Army Corps, Army of the Potomac*. Charles Scribner's Sons, 1891.

The War of the Rebellion, Official Records of the Union and Confederate Armies. Multiple volumes, including 45. 1894.

Warner, Ezra J. Generals in Blue. Louisiana State University Press, 1964.

_____. *Generals in Gray*. Louisiana State University Press, 1959.

Weaver, Joseph H.; *Cumberland, 1787–1987: A Bicentennial History*. Fort Cumberland, Md.: Precision Printing Co., 1987.

Whitney, Henry C. *Lincoln: The President*, Vol. 2 of *A Life of Lincoln*, 1908.

Wilson, Leonard. *Makers of America*, Vol. 2. B.F. Johnson, 1916.

Winslow, W.H. *Cruising and Blockading*. J.R. Weldin and Co., 1895.

Wise, Barton H. *The Life of Henry A. Wise*. McMillan, 1899.

Wise, Jennings Cropper. *The Long Arm of Lee*. 2 vols. J.P. Bell Co., 1915.

Wise, John S. *Battle of New Market*, 1882.

Wood, Clement. *A Complete History of the United States*. Cleveland and New York: World Publishing Co., 1936, 1941.

Woodbury, Augustus. *Major General Ambrose E. Burnside and the Ninth Army Corps*. Sidney S. Rider and Brother, 1867.

Wyeth, John Allan. *Life of Lieutenant General Nathan Bedford Forrest*. Harper and Brothers, 1908.

Index

Numerical entries, in three parts, precede the alphabetical listing

Union Federal Units

Union State Units

Alphabetical Entries